P9-EMH-381

COLLECTOR'S
mart magazine

Price Guide to
LIMITED EDITION COLLECTIBLES

Published by

700 E. State Street • Iola, WI 54990-0001
Telephone: 715/445-2214

Please call or write for our free catalog.
Our toll-free number to place an order or obtain a free catalog is 800-258-0929
or please use our regular business telephone 715-445-2214
for editorial comment and further information.

Library of Congress Catalog Number: 95-77317
ISBN: 0-87341-468-3
Printed in the United States of America

Cover Photograph Credits:

Front cover: Dreams to Gather plate courtesy of The Bradford Exchange, Niles, Ill.; *Snow White* figurine courtesy of the Walt Disney Classics Collection, Los Angeles, Calif.; *Starship Enterprise* ornament courtesy of Brent Frankenhoff, Iola, Wis., and Hallmark, St. Louis, Mo.; *Angel Locks* doll courtesy of Lee Middleton Original Dolls, Belpre, Ohio; *Caprice Carousel Horse* crystal figurine courtesy of Iris Arc, Santa Barbara, Calif.

Back cover: Gray Wolf stein by Bud Kemper courtesy of Anheuser-Busch, St. Louis, Mo.; *Gate House* cottage courtesy of Department 56, Eden Prairie, Minn.

Table of Contents

How to Use This Price Guide

Information used in this price guide was obtained from various manufacturers, publishers, producers, retailers and other secondary market sources.

Because secondary market prices can vary from region to region—and even within a given locale—values listed in this price guide are just that: *guides* to help collectors, insurance agents, appraisers and others determine the "going" or "asking" price. These values reflect the most often asked-for or sold-for prices. This guide is not published to determine exact pricing information on collectibles and should not be taken as such.

YR	NAME	LIMIT	ISSUE	TREND
① **SCHMID**			③	
② **LOWELL DAVIS**			**L. DAVIS FARM SET**	
85	MAIN HOUSE	CL	42.50	125.00
④	⑤	⑥	⑦	⑧

How to Read the Price Guide

① Manufacturer or Publisher

② Artist

③ Series

④ Year of Production or Publication

⑤ Name of Piece

⑥ Edition Size or Status of Piece

⑦ Issue price

⑧ Quote price at time of this publication

These abbreviations will be used to indicate edition size or status of a piece:

CL = Closed

FD = Firing Days
(limited to a certain number of firing days)

OP = Open

RT = Retired

SO = Sold Out

ST = Set
(two or more items issued together with one price)

SU = Suspended

TL = Time Limited

UD = Undisclosed

YR = Year of issue
(limited to calendar year of issue)

DS = Discontinued

* = Unknown

Collectibles are listed alphabetically by category (Bells, Cottages, Dolls, etc.); alphabetically by company (Anri, Cybis, etc.); chronologically by year of issue; and alphabetically by title within each issue year.

Note: Price ranges may reflect various demands in the market from one geographic location to another; the condition of the collectible; specific markings found on the piece; and/or changes that occurred while the piece was in production.

Introduction

Welcome to the second edition of the *Price Guide to Limited Edition Collectibles*. We've taken the information from our first edition, studied it, added to it, and updated it to create an incredible resource of nearly 50,000 prices that cover the broad spectrum of limited edition collectibles.

Our goal for the *Price Guide to Limited Edition Collectibles* is a simple one: to provide a price guide covering thousands of secondary market values running the gamut of limited edition collectibles—bells, cottages, dolls, figurines, ornaments, plates, prints and steins. The term "secondary market" may be confusing to collectors, but simply put, it is the market for collectibles after they have left the original, primary point of retail sales. It exists because a buyer is searching for an item no longer available through regular retail distribution channels.

To arrive at what we consider a fair trend price—or the average price at which a collectible is currently trading hands—we employ a panel of limited edition collectibles experts as well as comb secondary market newsletters and auction results; work with secondary market dealers and exchange specialists; monitor the manufacturers of limited edition collectibles; and listen to our readers, many of whom know so much about their collectible of choice that they've become experts, too.

In most cases, our price information is an average value, but in some instances we offer price ranges. These ranges may reflect various demands in the market from one geographic location to another; the condition of the collectible; specific markings found on the piece; and/or changes that occurred while the piece was in production.

Collectors should keep in mind this book is simply a *guide* to be used in conjunction with every other bit of information you may be able to obtain to determine a realistic value for your collectible. In the end it's the collectors who actually purchase collectibles on the secondary market who determine the values of those collectibles.

We've divided this book into categories that make it easy for you to find the information relevant to the items you collect: bells, cottages, dolls, figurines, ornaments, plates, prints and steins.

Items within the listings are arranged alphabetically first by company name, then by series name, and then by the artist's last name. They are further organized chronologically by the year in which the collectible was issued, then alphabetically by the title of the piece. Folios at the top of each page mark each section and make flipping through the book quick and easy. Two indexes at the back of the book help you locate items for which you may not have the necessary information.

Our staff could have never completed this book without the help of our panel of secondary market specialists. Within their respective fields, these experts have provided us with prices and trends; filled in missing information; and prepared overviews of the various categories.

Dean Genth, owner of four Hallmark stores and highly regarded in many areas of collectibles, has compiled and provided updates for our "Figurines" section. He is the author of "Figurine Finesse," a column devoted to figurines published in every issue of *Collector's mart* magazine.

Meredith deGood, who owns and operates The Baggage Car, a secondary market brokerage dealing exclusively with ornaments, is recognized by many as the most proficient expert in the area of Hallmark Keepsake Ornaments. Her information on Hallmark serves as a basis for our "Ornaments" category.

The bulk of the "Prints" section was updated by Jay Brown, owner of Gallery One. Brown deals in limited edition prints by the industry's leading artists, especially those associated with Mill Pond Press and The Greenwich Workshop.

Both the "Cottages" and "Steins" portions were cultivated under the auspices of Ken Armke Sr., who operates Opa's House Inc. (OHI), a firm specializing in the import and production of collectible steins. OHI also operates a comprehensive secondary market exchange that deals in both steins and cottages.

Our "Plates" section received special focus this year. We worked with secondary market plate specialists, including Ross and Ruth Ernst of Collectors Plates, to make sure our information was the most accurate possible.

Others who deserve thanks for helping us with this book include: Matt Rothman, owner and operator of Lighthouse Trading Co., which specializes in retired and secondary market lighthouses; Sissy Thomas, a Byers' Choice aficionado; Don Newton of Willow Glen, whose expertise includes prints by Thomas Kinkade, Dennis Patrick Lewan and Jack Terry, and figurines by Shelia's Collectibles, Cat's Meow and JP Editions; Kay Laubaugh, a David Winter enthusiast; and many others who wrote or called with information and suggestions.

Even with all the information we've gleaned through our market experts and by studying auction reports and exchange service publications, we still strive for more accurate prices. That's where you can help. If you have information you feel will benefit this book, please send it our way so we may update our records. Send information to:

Mary Sieber, 700 E. State St., Iola, WI 54990-0001.

We hope you find our second edition useful and wish you many happy days of collecting.

Bells

Bells—one of the very oldest forms of art—harken back centuries to ancient civilizations long gone. They are steeped in mystery, surrounded by legends of special powers ranging from thwarting demons to invoking curses and lifting spells.

In general, bells were most often used as a signal, marking significant points of ritual, calling to worship, tolling the hours, announcing events, rejoicing, warning and mourning. Their power was at one time extremely significant to many religions. Bells have also been treasured as patriotic symbols and war trophies.

Most cultures today have turned these once utilitarian objects into works of art with respect to shape, materials and ornamentation. Created of porcelain, wood, metal, china, crystal and other materials, the melodious chimers are a double joy for those who collect them because they are both lovely to hear and see.

The hobby of collecting limited edition bells rocketed to its zenith in the 1970s, especially during the United States' Bicentennial when a multitude of special bells were produced to commemorate the historic occasion. Unfortunately, the bell market became saturated, and as a result the hobby settled into a quieter pastime.

Today, many special Bicentennial bells, as well as Lladro_ porcelain, Waterford crystal bells and Jan Hagara Christmas bells, which are no longer produced, remain popular and do well on the secondary market. Bells produced by Pairpoint still rank high on collectors' lists as well.

Today's popular bell manufacturers include Fenton Art Glass, Goebel Inc., Enesco Corp., Fort Inc., Seymour Mann and Roman Inc., among others.

BELLS

ANRI

YR	NAME	LIMIT	ISSUE	TREND
J. FERRANDIZ		**ANRI WOODEN CHRISTMAS BELLS**		
76	CHRISTMAS	YR	6.00	52.00
77	CHRISTMAS	YR	7.00	42.00
78	CHRISTMAS	YR	10.00	42.00
79	CHRISTMAS	YR	13.00	30.00
80	CHRISTMAS KING, THE	YR	17.50	18.00
81	LIGHTING THE WAY	YR	18.50	20.00
82	CARING	YR	18.50	19.00
83	BEHOLD	YR	18.50	19.00
85	NATURE'S DREAM	YR	18.50	20.00
J. FERRANDIZ		**JUAN FERRANDIZ MUSICAL CHRISTMAS BELLS**		
76	CHRISTMAS	YR	25.00	82.00
77	CHRISTMAS	YR	25.00	82.00
78	CHRISTMAS	YR	35.00	77.00
79	CHRISTMAS	YR	47.50	62.00
80	LITTLE DRUMMER BOY	YR	60.00	65.00
81	GOOD SHEPHERD BOY, THE	YR	63.00	65.00
82	SPREADING THE WORD	YR	63.00	65.00
83	COMPANIONS	YR	63.00	65.00
84	WITH LOVE	YR	55.00	57.00

ARTAFFECTS

YR	NAME	LIMIT	ISSUE	TREND
R. SAUBER		**BELLS**		
87	MOTHERHOOD BELL	*	25.00	26.00
87	NEWBORN BELL	*	25.00	26.00
87	SWEET SIXTEEN BELL	*	25.00	26.00
87	WEDDING BELL, THE (GOLD)	*	25.00	26.00
87	WEDDING BELL, THE (SILVER)	*	25.00	26.00
87	WEDDING BELL, THE (WHITE)	*	25.00	26.00
R. SAUBER		**BRIDE BELLES FIGURINE BELLS**		
88	CAROLINE	*	27.50	28.00
88	ELIZABETH	*	27.50	28.00
88	EMILY	*	27.50	28.00
88	GROOM	*	27.50	28.00
88	JACQUELINE	*	27.50	28.00
88	LAURA	*	27.50	28.00
88	MEREDITH	*	27.50	28.00
88	REBECCA	*	27.50	28.00
88	SARAH	*	27.50	28.00
G. PERILLO		**INDIAN BRAVE ANNUAL BELL**		
89	CHRISTMAS POW-WOW	YR	24.50	33.00
90	INDIAN BRAVE	YR	24.50	25.00
91	INDIAN BRAVE	YR	24.50	25.00
G. PERILLO		**INDIAN PRINCESS ANNUAL BELL**		
89	LITTLE PRINCESS, THE	YR	24.50	31.00
90	INDIAN PRINCESS	YR	24.50	25.00

ARTISTS OF THE WORLD

Price ranges may reflect various demands in the market from one geographic region to another; condition of piece; specific markings found on piece; and/or changes in production of piece.

YR	NAME	LIMIT	ISSUE	TREND
T. DEGRAZIA		**DEGRAZIA BELLS**		
80	FESTIVAL OF LIGHTS	5000	40.00	90.00
80	LOS NINOS	7500	40.00	90.00

BING & GRONDAHL

YR	NAME	LIMIT	ISSUE	TREND
E. JENSEN		**ANNUAL CHRISTMAS BELL**		
83	CHRISTMAS IN THE OLD TOWN	YR	45.00	46.00
84	CHRISTMAS LETTER, THE	YR	45.00	46.00
85	CHRISTMAS EVE AT THE FARMHOUSE	YR	45.00	46.00
86	SILENT NIGHT, HOLY NIGHT	YR	45.00	46.00
87	SNOWMAN'S CHRISTMAS EVE, THE	YR	47.50	48.00
88	OLD POET'S CHRISTMAS, THE	YR	49.50	50.00
89	CHRISTMAS ANCHORAGE	YR	52.00	53.00
90	CHANGING OF THE GUARDS	YR	55.00	56.00
91	COPENHAGEN STOCK EXCHANGE AT XMAS, THE	YR	59.50	60.00
J. STEENSEN		**ANNUAL CHRISTMAS BELL**		
92	CHRISTMAS AT THE RECTORY	YR	62.50	63.00
93	FATHER CHRISTMAS IN COPENHAGEN	YR	62.50	63.00
H. THELANDER		**ANNUAL CHRISTMAS BELL**		
80	CHRISTMAS IN THE WOODS	YR	39.50	40.00
81	CHRISTMAS PEACE	YR	42.50	43.00
82	CHRISTMAS TREE, THE	YR	45.00	46.00
J. WOODSON		**CHRISTMAS IN AMERICA BELL**		
88	CHRISTMAS EVE IN WILLIAMSBURG	YR	27.50	105.00
89	CHRISTMAS EVE AT THE WHITE HOUSE	YR	29.00	77.00
90	CHRISTMAS EVE AT THE CAPITOL	YR	30.00	31.00
91	INDEPENDENCE HALL	YR	35.00	36.00
92	CHRISTMAS IN SAN FRANCISCO	YR	37.50	38.00
93	COMING HOME FOR CHRISTMAS	YR	37.50	38.00

YR	NAME	LIMIT	ISSUE	TREND
	C.U.I./CAROLINA COLLECTION			
	J. HARRIS			**STERLING CLASSIC**
91	BARN OWL	RT	100.00	103.00
91	CAMBERWELL BEAUTY	RT	100.00	103.00
91	CLOUDED YELLOW	RT	100.00	103.00
91	KINGFISHER	RT	100.00	103.00
91	LARGE BLUE	RT	100.00	100.00
91	MOUSE	RT	100.00	100.00
91	PEACOCK	RT	100.00	100.00
91	SMALL TORTOISESHELL	RT	100.00	100.00
91	SWALLOWTAIL	RT	100.00	100.00
	CROWN & ROSE			
	J. BERGDAHL			**12 DAYS OF CHRISTMAS**
82	FIVE GOLDEN RINGS	7500	75.00	80.00
83	SIX GEESE A' LAYING	7500	75.00	80.00
84	SEVEN SWANS A' SWIMMING	7500	78.00	80.00
	M. DINKEL			**12 DAYS OF CHRISTMAS**
78	PARTRIDGE IN A PEAR TREE	7500	50.00	300.00
79	TWO TURTLE DOVES	7500	55.00	80.00
80	THREE FRENCH HENS	7500	60.00	85.000
	J. SPOUSE			**12 DAYS OF CHRISTMAS**
81	FOUR CALLING BIRDS	7500	70.00	80.00
	DANBURY MINT			
	N. ROCKWELL			**THE NORMAN ROCKWELL COMMEMORATIVE BELL**
79	TRIPLE SELF-PORTRAIT	*	29.50	35.00
	N. ROCKWELL			**THE WONDERFUL WORLD OF NORMAN ROCKWELL**
79	BABY-SITTER	*	27.50	30.00
79	BACK TO SCHOOL	*	27.50	30.00
79	BATTER UP	*	27.50	30.00
79	FRIEND IN NEED	*	27.50	30.00
79	GRAMPS AT THE REINS	*	27.50	30.00
79	GRANDPA'S GIRL	*	27.50	30.00
79	LEAPFROG	*	27.50	30.00
79	PUPPY IN THE POCKET	*	27.50	30.00
	N. ROCKWELL			**VARIOUS**
75	DOCTOR AND DOLL	*	27.50	55.00
76	DISCOVERY, THE	*	27.50	45.00
76	FREEDOM FROM WANT	*	27.50	45.00
76	GRANDPA SNOWMAN	*	27.50	45.00
76	NO SWIMMING	*	27.50	45.00
76	SAYING GRACE	*	27.50	45.00
77	KNUCKLES DOWN	*	27.50	40.00
77	PUPPY LOVE	*	27.50	40.00
77	REMEDY, THE	*	27.50	40.00
77	RUNAWAY, THE	*	27.50	40.00
77	SANTA'S MAIL	*	27.50	40.00
77	TOM SAWYER	*	27.50	40.00
	DAVE GROSSMAN CREATIONS			
	ROCKWELL INSPIRED			**NORMAN ROCKWELL COLLECTION**
75	FACES OF CHRISTMAS NRB-75	RT	12.50	37.00
76	BEN FRANKLIN (BICENTENNIAL)	RT	12.50	27.00
76	DRUM FOR TOMMY NRB-76	RT	12.00	32.00
80	LEAPFROG NRB-90	RT	50.00	58.00
	ENESCO			
	Price ranges may reflect various demands in the market from one geographic region to another; condition of piece; specific markings found on piece; and/or changes in production of piece.			
	P. HILLMAN			**CHERISHED TEDDIES CHRISTMAS**
92	ANGEL BEAR	*	20.00	65.00
*				**FROM BARBIE WITH LOVE**
96	HERE COMES THE BRIDE FI BELL 174734	YR	40.00	40.00
96	SWIRLED BELL W/HEART HANDLE 162272	*	12.50	12.50
	KINKA			**KINKA BELLS**
89	EASTER..FILLED W/HOPE & BLESSINGS 116610	OP	22.50	23.00
89	YOUR LOVE IS SPECIAL TO ME 116580	OP	22.50	23.00
90	CHRISTMAS IS A TIME OF LOVE 119962	YR	25.00	25.00
91	LIFE IS ONE JOYOUS STEP/ANOTHER 121320	YR	22.50	23.00
91	MAY THE GLOW OF GOD'S LOVE 120596	YR	22.50	23.00
	M. ATTWELL			**MEMORIES OF YESTERDAY**
90	HERE COMES BRIDE/GOD BLESS HER 523100	OP	25.00	26.00
	S. BUTCHER			**PRECIOUS MOMENTS ANNUAL BELLS**
80	LET THE HEAVENS REJOICE E-5622	YR	17.00	210.00
82	I'LL PLAY MY DRUM FOR HIM E-2358	YR	17.00	60.00
83	SURROUNDED WITH JOY E-0522	YR	18.00	55.00
84	WISHING YOU A MERRY CHRISTMAS E-5393	YR	19.00	50.00
85	GOD SENT HIS LOVE 15873	YR	19.00	40.00
85	WISHING YOU A COZY CHRISTMAS 102318	YR	20.00	40.00
86	LOVE IS THE BEST GIFT OF ALL 109835	YR	22.50	35.00
88	OH HOLY NIGHT 522821	YR	25.00	40.00
88	TIME TO WISH/MERRY CHRISTMAS 115304	YR	25.00	40.00
89	ONCE UPON A HOLY NIGHT 523828	YR	25.00	35.00
90	MAY YOUR CHRISTMAS BE MERRY 524182	YR	25.00	35.00
92	BUT THE GREATEST OF THESE/LOVE 527726	YR	25.00	30.00

YR	NAME	LIMIT	ISSUE	TREND
	S. BUTCHER	**PRECIOUS MOMENTS COLLECTION**		
92	WISHING YOU/SWEETEST CHRISTMAS 530174	YR	25.00	32.00
	S. BUTCHER	**PRECIOUS MOMENTS VARIOUS BELLS**		
80	GOD UNDERSTANDS E-5211	RT	17.00	55.00
80	JESUS IS BORN E-5623	SU	17.00	45.00
80	JESUS LOVES ME E-5208	SU	17.00	53.00
80	JESUS LOVES ME E-5209	SU	15.00	50.00
80	PRAYER CHANGES THINGS E-5210	SU	18.00	47.00
80	WE HAVE SEEN HIS STAR E-5620	SU	17.00	45.00
81	LORD BLESS YOU AND KEEP YOU, THE E-7175	SU	17.00	40.00
81	LORD BLESS YOU AND KEEP YOU, THE E-7176	SU	17.00	48.00
81	MOTHER SEW DEAR E-7181	SU	17.00	43.00
81	PURR-FECT GRANDMA, THE E-7183	SU	17.00	45.00
82	LORD BLESS YOU AND KEEP YOU, THE E-7179	SU	22.50	43.00

FENTON ART GLASS

YR	NAME	LIMIT	ISSUE	TREND
	D. JOHNSON	**BIRDS OF WINTER ED. I**		
87	BELL 7668BC 6 1/2"	4500	29.50	30.00
	D. JOHNSON	**BIRDS OF WINTER ED. II**		
88	BELL 7667BD 6 1/2"	4500	29.50	30.00
	D. JOHNSON	**BIRDS OF WINTER ED. III**		
89	BELL 7667BL 6 1/2"	4500	29.50	30.00
	D. JOHNSON	**BIRDS OF WINTER ED. IV**		
90	BELL 7667NB 6 1/2"	4500	29.50	30.00
	F. BURTON	**CHRISTMAS AT HOME ED. I**		
90	BELL 7668HD 6 1/2"	3500	39.00	39.00
	F. BURTON	**CHRISTMAS AT HOME ED. II**		
90	BELL 7668HJ 6 1/2"	3500	35.00	35.00
	F. BURTON	**CHRISTMAS AT HOME ED. III**		
92	BELL 7668HQ 6 1/2"	3500	39.00	39.00
	F. BURTON	**CHRISTMAS AT HOME ED. IV**		
93	BELL 7668HT	3500	39.50	40.00
	M. DICKINSON	**CHRISTMAS CLASSICS ED. I**		
78	BELL 7466CV	*	25.00	25.00
	K. CUNNINGHAM	**CHRISTMAS CLASSICS ED. II**		
79	BELL 7466NC	*	30.00	30.00
	D. JOHNSON	**CHRISTMAS CLASSICS ED. III**		
80	BELL 7466GH 6 1/2"	*	32.50	33.00
	D. JOHNSON	**CHRISTMAS CLASSICS ED. IV**		
81	BELL 7466AC 6 1/2"	*	35.00	35.00
	R. SPINDLER	**CHRISTMAS CLASSICS ED. V**		
82	BELL 7466OC 6 1/2"	*	35.00	35.00
	D. JOHNSON	**CHRISTMAS FANTASY ED. I**		
83	BELL 7667AI 6 1/2"	7500	35.00	35.00
	D. JOHNSON	**CHRISTMAS FANTASY ED. II**		
84	BELL 7667GE 6 1/2"	7500	37.50	38.00
	D. JOHNSON	**CHRISTMAS FANTASY ED. III**		
85	BELL 7667WP 6 1/2"	7500	37.50	38.00
	L. EVERSON	**CHRISTMAS FANTASY ED. IV**		
87	BELL 7667CV 6 1/2"	CL	37.50	38.00
	L. PIPER	**CHRISTMAS LIMITED EDITIONS**		
86	BELL, 6" 7667XS	5000	35.00	35.00
	M. REYNOLDS	**CHRISTMAS LIMITED EDITIONS**		
92	BELL, 6 1/2" 7463ZW WINTER ON TWILIGHT B	2500	29.50	30.00
93	BELL, 6 1/2" 7463SD MANGER SCENE ON RUBY	2500	39.50	40.00
93	BELL, 6 1/2" 7463TV REINDEER ON BLUE	2500	30.00	30.00
93	BELL, 6 1/2" 7465GQ FLORAL ON GRN/MUSICA	2500	39.50	40.00
94	BELL 7463VG 6 1/2" MAGNOLIA ON GOLD	1000	35.00	35.00
94	BELL 7463VP 6 1/2" ANGEL ON IVORY	1000	39.00	40.00
94	BELL, 6 1/2" 7465VK PARTIDGE ON RUBY-MTN	1000	48.50	49.00
95	BELL 2967TH 6 1/2": BOW & HOLLY ON IVORY	900	39.50	40.00
95	BELL 7463TP 6 1/2" CHICKADEE ON GOLD	900	39.50	40.00
95	BELL 7667TQ 5 1/2" ICED POINSETTIA ON RU	900	45.00	45.00
95	EGG 5145TQ 3 1/2" ICED POINSETTIA ON RUB	900	39.50	40.00
96	BELL , 6 1/2" 2967AC	2000	39.50	39.50
96	BELL, 6 1/2" 6662CH HOLLY BERRIES ON GOL	1500	39.50	39.50
96	BELL, 6 1/2" 7668QP PARTRIDGE ON SPRUCE	1500	35.00	35.00
96	BELL, 6" 5144AV	2000	39.50	39.50
	R. SPINDLER	**CHRISTMAS LIMITED EDITIONS**		
96	BELL, 6 1/2" 7768QV MOONLIT ON RUBY	1500	45.00	45.00
96	BELL, 6 1/2" 9463N7 NATIVITY SCENE	1500	49.00	49.00
	F. BURTON	**CHRISTMAS STAR "OUR HOME IS BLESSED"**		
95	BELL 7668VT 6 1/2"	2500	45.00	45.00
	F. BURTON	**CHRISTMAS STAR "SILENT NIGHT"**		
94	BELL 7463VS 6"	2500	45.00	45.00
	F. BURTON	**CHRISTMAS STAR ED. III**		
96	BELL 7463SN 6 1/2"	2500	48.00	48.00
	*	**CONNOISSEUR COLLECTION**		
83	CRAFTSMEN BELL 9660WI	3500	25.00	25.00
84	BELL 9163UR	3500	25.00	25.00
	D. BARBOUR	**CONNOISSEUR COLLECTION**		
86	BELL 7666SB	2500	60.00	60.00
	L. EVERSON	**CONNOISSEUR COLLECTION**		
83	BELL 7562UF	2000	50.00	50.00
85	BELL 7666EB 6 1/2"	2500	55.00	55.00

YR	NAME	LIMIT	ISSUE	TREND
88	BELL 7666ZW 7"	4000	45.00	45.00
89	BELL 9667KT 7"	3500	50.00	50.00
M. REYNOLDS			**CONNOISSEUR COLLECTION**	
91	BELL 6761UZ 7"	2000	50.00	50.00
F. BURTON			**DESIGNER BELLS**	
96	BELL 4568EB 6 1/2"	2500	60.00	60.00
K. PLAUCHE			**DESIGNER BELLS**	
96	BELL 7667HW 5 1/2"	2500	50.00	50.00
M. REYNOLDS			**DESIGNER BELLS**	
96	BELL 4564IN 6"	2500	60.00	60.00
96	VANITY SET 7199WB 4 PC	1500	250.00	250.00
R. SPINDLER			**DESIGNER BELLS**	
96	BELL 7562PP 7"	2500	55.00	55.00
*			**HISTORICAL COLLECTION**	
89	BELL 3645XC	*	17.50	17.50
90	BELL 8265BX 6"	*	16.50	17.00
91	BELL 9065DT 5 1/2"	*	25.00	25.00
91	BELL 9560BO 6 3/4" TEMPLBELLS	*	17.50	17.50
92	BELL 3567XV 6"	*	19.50	20.00
92	BELL 9667GF 7"	*	29.00	29.00
93	BELL 3645RV 5 1/2"	OP	17.50	18.00
94	BELL 9667SS 7"	OP	25.00	25.00
94	BELL 9667ST 7"	*	35.00	35.00
94	BELL 9667ST 7" AURORA	OP	25.00	25.00
95	BELL 9667JE 7"	OP	35.00	35.00
M. REYNOLDS			**MARY GREGORY**	
93	BELL 7463RQ 6" RUBY	CL	49.00	49.00
94	BELL 7463RY 6" RUBY	CL	49.00	49.00
95	BELL 7463RG 6 1/2"	CL	49.00	49.00
M. REYNOLDS			**VALENTINE'S DAY**	
92	BELL 7668XB 6"	CL	35.00	35.00

GOEBEL INC.

Price ranges may reflect various demands in the market from one geographic region to another; condition of piece; specific markings found on piece; and/or changes in production of piece.

YR	NAME	LIMIT	ISSUE	TREND
*			**M.I. HUMMEL**	
96	CHRISTMAS SONG	OP	65.00	65.00
M.I. HUMMEL			**M.I. HUMMEL ANNIVERSARY BELL**	
85	ANNIVERSARY BELL HUM-730	CL	*	500.00-1000.00
M.I. HUMMEL			**M.I. HUMMEL ANNUAL BELLS**	
78	LET'S SING HUM-700	CL	50.00	45.00
79	FAREWELL HUM-701	CL	70.00	50.00
80	THOUGHTFUL HUM-702	CL	85.00	55.00
81	IN TUNE HUM-703	CL	85.00	105.00
82	SHE LOVES ME HUM-704	CL	85.00	70.00
83	KNIT ONE HUM-705	CL	90.00	70.00
84	MOUNTAINEER HUM-706	CL	90.00	65.00
85	SWEET SONG HUM-707	CL	90.00	80.00
86	SING ALONG HUM-708	CL	100.00	90.00
87	WITH LOVING GREETINGS HUM-709	CL	110.00	150.00
88	BUSY STUDENT HUM-710	CL	120.00	100.00
89	LATEST NEWS HUM-711	CL	135.00	145.00
90	WHAT'S NEW? HUM-712	CL	140.00	175.00
91	FAVORITE PET HUM-713	CL	150.00	175.00
92	WHISTLER'S DUET HUM-714	CL	160.00	150.00
93	CELESTIAL MUSICIAN HUM-779	CL	50.00	55.00
95	FESTIVAL HARMONY W/FLUTE	CL	55.00	55.00
M.I. HUMMEL			**M.I. HUMMEL CHRISTMAS BELLS**	
89	CHRISTMAS BELL HUM-775	CL	35.00	60.00-70.00
90	CHRISTMAS BELL HUM-776	CL	37.50	60.00-70.00
91	CHRISTMAS BELL HUM-778	45	39.50	60.00-70.00
92	CHRISTMAS BELL HUM-778	CL	45.00	60.00-70.00
93	CHRISTMAS BELL HUM-780	CL	50.00	50.00-60.00
94	CHRISTMAS BELL HUM-781	OP	55.00	55.00

GORHAM

Price ranges may reflect various demands in the market from one geographic region to another; condition of piece; specific markings found on piece; and/or changes in production of piece.

YR	NAME	LIMIT	ISSUE	TREND
CURRIER & IVES			**CURRIER & IVES MINI BELLS**	
76	CHRISTMAS SLEIGH RIDE	YR	9.95	38.00
77	AMERICAN HOMESTEAD	YR	9.95	27.00
78	YULE LOGS	YR	12.95	21.00
79	SLEIGH RIDE	YR	14.95	20.00
80	CHRISTMAS IN THE COUNTRY	YR	14.95	21.00
81	CHRISTMAS TREE	YR	14.95	18.00
82	CHRISTMAS VISITATION	YR	16.50	18.00
83	WINTER WONDERLAND	YR	16.50	18.00
84	HITCHING UP	YR	16.50	18.00
85	SKATERS' HOLIDAY	YR	17.50	18.00
86	CENTRAL PARK IN WINTER	YR	17.50	18.00
87	EARLY WINTER	YR	19.00	20.00
N. ROCKWELL			**MINI BELLS**	
81	TINY TIM	YR	19.75	20.00
82	PLANNING CHRISTMAS VISIT	YR	20.00	20.00
N. ROCKWELL			**VARIOUS**	
75	SANTA'S HELPERS	YR	19.50	32.00

YR	NAME	LIMIT	ISSUE	TREND
75	SWEET SONG SO YOUNG	YR	19.50	52.00
75	TAVERN SIGN PAINTER	YR	19.50	32.00
76	FLOWERS IN TENDER BLOOM	YR	19.50	42.00
76	SNOW SCULPTURE	YR	19.50	48.00
77	CHILLING CHORE (CHRISTMAS)	YR	19.50	36.00
77	FONDLY DO WE REMEMBER	YR	19.50	58.00
78	GAILY SHARING VINTAGE TIMES	YR	22.50	23.00
78	GAY BLADES (CHRISTMAS)	YR	22.50	23.00
79	A BOY MEETS HIS DOG (CHRISTMAS)	YR	24.50	32.00
79	BEGUILING BUTTERCUP	YR	24.50	27.00
80	CHILLY RECEPTION (CHRISTMAS)	YR	27.50	28.00
80	FLYING HIGH	YR	27.50	28.00
81	SKI SKILLS (CHRISTMAS)	YR	27.50	28.00
81	SWEET SERENADE	YR	27.50	28.00
82	COAL SEASON'S COMING	YR	29.50	30.00
82	YOUNG MANS FANCY	YR	29.50	30.00
83	CHRISTMAS MEDLEY	YR	29.50	30.00
83	MILKMAID, THE	YR	29.50	30.00
84	MARRIAGE LICENSE	OP	32.50	33.00
84	TINY TIM	YR	29.50	30.00
84	YARN SPINNER	5000	32.50	33.00
84	YOUNG LOVE	YR	29.50	30.00
85	YULETIDE REFLECTIONS	5000	32.50	33.00
86	HOME FOR THE HOLIDAYS	5000	32.50	33.00
86	ON TOP OF THE WORLD	5000	32.50	33.00
87	ARTIST, THE	5000	32.50	33.00
87	MERRY CHRISTMAS GRANDMA	5000	32.50	33.00
88	HOMECOMING, THE	15000	37.50	38.00

HALLMARK GALLERIES

YR	NAME	LIMIT	ISSUE	TREND
R. CHAD			**DICKENS CAROLER BELL**	
90	MR. ASHBOURNE 1ST ED. 2175QX505-6	YR	21.75	38.00
91	MRS. BEAUMONT 2175QX503-9	YR	21.75	38.00
92	LORD CHADWICK 3RD EDITION 2175QX455-4	YR	21.75	38.00
93	LADY DAPHNE 4TH ED. 2175QX550-5	YR	21.75	33.00

HAMILTON GIFTS

YR	NAME	LIMIT	ISSUE	TREND
M. HUMPHREY				**BELLS**
92	HOLLIES 996095	OP	22.50	23.00
92	SARAH 999385	OP	22.50	23.00
92	SUSANNA 999377	OP	22.50	23.00

HAMPSHIRE PEWTER CO.

YR	NAME	LIMIT	ISSUE	TREND
*			**TWELVE DAYS OF CHRISTMAS**	
93	PARTRIDGE IN A PEAR TREE	500	65.00	70.00
94	TWO TURTLEDOVES	500	65.00	70.00

JAN HAGARA COLLECTABLES

YR	NAME	LIMIT	ISSUE	TREND
J. HAGARA			**VICTORIAN CHILDREN**	
86	BETSY	TL	25.00	75.00
86	JENNY	TL	25.00	75.00
86	JILL	YR	35.00	100.00
86	JIMMY	TL	25.00	75.00
86	JODY	TL	25.00	75.00
86	LISA	TL	25.00	75.00
86	LYDIA	TL	25.00	75.00
87	HOLLY	YR	35.00	40.00
88	MARIE	YR	35.00	35.00

KAISER

YR	NAME	LIMIT	ISSUE	TREND
K. BAUER			**KAISER CHRISTMAS BELLS**	
80	SLEIGH RIDE AT CHRISTMAS	15000	60.00	65.00
81	SNOWMAN	15000	60.00	65.00
N. PETER			**KAISER CHRISTMAS BELLS**	
79	ESKIMO CHRISTMAS	15000	60.00	65.00
T. SCHOENER			**KAISER CHRISTMAS BELLS**	
78	NATIVITY, THE	15000	60.00	65.00
K. BAUER			**KAISER TREE ORNAMENT BELLS**	
79	CAROLERS, THE	YR	27.50	45.00
80	HOLIDAY SNOWMAN	YR	30.00	45.00
81	CHRISTMAS AT HOME	YR	30.00	45.00
82	CHRISTMAS IN THE CITY	YR	30.00	45.00

KIRK STIEFF

YR	NAME	LIMIT	ISSUE	TREND
*				**BELL**
92	SANTA'S WORKSHOP CHRISTMAS BELL	3000	40.00	40.00
K. STIEFF			**CHRISTMAS BELLS**	
90	SILVER BELLS	YR	29.00	29.00
91	HERALD ANGEL	YR	29.00	29.00
*			**MUSICAL BELLS**	
92	ANNUAL BELL 1992	YR	30.00	30.00
K. STIEFF			**MUSICAL BELLS**	
77	ANNUAL BELL 1977	CL	17.95	80.00
78	ANNUAL BELL 1978	CL	17.95	75.00
79	ANNUAL BELL 1979	CL	17.95	55.00
80	ANNUAL BELL 1980	CL	19.95	55.00
81	ANNUAL BELL 1981	CL	19.95	70.00
82	ANNUAL BELL 1982	CL	19.95	80.00

YR	NAME	LIMIT	ISSUE	TREND
83	ANNUAL BELL 1983	CL	19.95	55.00
84	ANNUAL BELL 1984	CL	19.95	45.00
85	ANNUAL BELL 1985	CL	19.95	45.00
86	ANNUAL BELL 1986	CL	19.95	45.00
87	ANNUAL BELL 1987	CL	19.95	35.00
88	ANNUAL BELL 1988	CL	22.50	40.00
89	ANNUAL BELL 1989	CL	25.00	28.00
90	ANNUAL BELL 1990	CL	27.00	28.00
91	ANNUAL BELL 1991	CL	28.00	30.00

D. BACORN — **NUTCRACKER SUITE MUSICAL BELL**

YR	NAME	LIMIT	ISSUE	TREND
86	NUTCRACKER	OP	29.95	30.00
87	CLARA	OP	29.95	30.00

LANCE CORP.

P.W. BASTON — **HUDSON PEWTER BICENTENNIAL BELLS**

YR	NAME	LIMIT	ISSUE	TREND
74	BENJAMIN FRANKLIN	CL	*	90.00
74	GEORGE WASHINGTON	CL	*	90.00
74	JAMES MADISON	CL	*	90.00
74	JOHN ADAMS	CL	*	90.00
74	THOMAS JEFFERSON	CL	*	90.00

LENOX CHINA/CRYSTAL COLLECTION

* — **ANNUAL CRYSTAL CHRISTMAS BELLS**

YR	NAME	LIMIT	ISSUE	TREND
81	PARTRIDGE IN A PEAR TREE	15000	55.00	56.00
82	HOLY FAMILY	15000	55.00	56.00
83	THREE WISE MEN	15000	55.00	56.00
84	DOVE	15000	57.00	58.00
85	SANTA CLAUS	15000	57.00	58.00
86	DASHING THROUGH THE SNOW	15000	64.00	65.00
87	HERALDING ANGEL	15000	76.00	77.00
91	CELESTIAL HARPIST	15000	75.00	80.00

* — **BIRD BELLS**

YR	NAME	LIMIT	ISSUE	TREND
91	BLUEBIRD	OP	57.00	28.00
91	CHICKADEE	OP	57.00	58.00
91	HUMMINGBIRD	OP	57.00	58.00
92	ROBIN BELL	OP	57.00	58.00

* — **CAROUSEL BELL**

YR	NAME	LIMIT	ISSUE	TREND
92	CAROUSEL HORSE	OP	45.00	47.00

* — **SONGS OF CHRISTMAS**

YR	NAME	LIMIT	ISSUE	TREND
91	WE WISH YOU A MERRY CHRISTMAS	YR	49.00	50.00
92	DECK THE HALLS	YR	53.00	55.00

LINCOLN MINT BELLS

N. ROCKWELL — **LINCOLN BELLS**

YR	NAME	LIMIT	ISSUE	TREND
75	DOWNHILL DARING	*	25.00	70.00

LLADRO

Price ranges may reflect various demands in the market from one geographic region to another; condition of piece; specific markings found on piece; and/or changes in production of piece.

YR	NAME	LIMIT	ISSUE	TREND
*	CHRISTMAS BELLS 1987,88	*	*	250.00
*	CHRISTMAS BELLS 89, 90, 91 L-5525, 5616	*	*	250.00
94	1994 ETERNAL LOVE BELL	RT	95.00	110.00

* — **ANNUAL CHRISTMAS BELLS**

YR	NAME	LIMIT	ISSUE	TREND
87	CHRISTMAS BELL L5458M	YR	29.50	117.00-130.00
88	CHRISTMAS BELL L5525M	YR	32.50	40.00
89	CHRISTMAS BELL L5616M	YR	32.50	52.00-195.00
90	CHRISTMAS BELL L5641M	YR	35.00	60.00
91	CHRISTMAS BELL L5803M	YR	37.50	50.00

* — **LLADRO CHRISTMAS BELL**

YR	NAME	LIMIT	ISSUE	TREND
92	CHRISTMAS BELL L5913M	YR	37.50	45.00

MUSEUM COLLECTIONS INC.

N. ROCKWELL — **COLLECTORS BELLS**

YR	NAME	LIMIT	ISSUE	TREND
82	25TH ANNIVERSARY	OP	45.00	48.00
82	50TH ANNIVERSARY	OP	45.00	48.00
82	FOR A GOOD BOY	OP	45.00	48.00
82	WEDDING/ANNIVERSARY	OP	45.00	48.00

PICKARD

* — **CHRISTMAS CAROL BELL SERIES**

YR	NAME	LIMIT	ISSUE	TREND
77	FIRST NOEL, THE	3000	75.00	78.00
78	O LITTLE TOWN OF BETHLEHEM	3000	75.00	78.00
79	SILENT NIGHT	3000	80.00	83.00
80	HARK! THE HERALD ANGELS SING	3000	80.00	83.00

RECO INTERNATIONAL

J. MCCLELLAND — **JOYOUS MOMENTS**

YR	NAME	LIMIT	ISSUE	TREND
80	I LOVE YOU	5000	25.00	26.00
81	SEA ECHOES	5000	25.00	26.00
82	TALK TO ME	5000	25.00	26.00

S. KUCK — **SPECIAL OCCASIONS**

YR	NAME	LIMIT	ISSUE	TREND
89	WEDDING, THE	OP	15.00	17.00

C. MICARELLI — **SPECIAL OCCASIONS-WEDDING**

YR	NAME	LIMIT	ISSUE	TREND
91	FROM THIS DAY FORWARD	OP	15.00	17.00
91	TO HAVE AND TO HOLD	OP	15.00	17.00

S. KUCK — **THE RECO BELL COLLECTION**

YR	NAME	LIMIT	ISSUE	TREND
88	CHARITY	OP	15.00	17.00

YR	NAME	LIMIT	ISSUE	TREND
88	GRACE	OP	15.00	17.00
88	PEACE	OP	15.00	17.00

REED & BARTON

NOEL MUSICAL BELLS

YR	NAME	LIMIT	ISSUE	TREND
*				
80	1980 BELL	YR	20.00	53.00
81	1981 BELL	YR	22.50	48.00
82	1982 BELL	YR	22.50	38.00
83	1983 BELL	YR	22.50	48.00
84	1984 BELL	YR	22.50	51.00
85	1985 BELL	YR	25.00	41.00
86	1986 BELL	YR	25.00	36.00
87	1987 BELL	YR	25.00	35.00
88	1988 BELL	YR	25.00	28.00
89	1989 BELL	YR	25.00	28.00
90	1990 BELL	YR	27.50	28.00
91	1991 BELL	YR	30.00	31.00
92	1992 BELL	YR	30.00	31.00

YULETIDE BELLS

YR	NAME	LIMIT	ISSUE	TREND
*				
81	YULETIDE HOLIDAY	YR	14.00	15.00
82	LITTLE SHEPHERD	YR	14.00	15.00
83	PERFECT ANGEL	YR	15.00	16.00
84	DRUMMER BOY	YR	15.00	16.00
85	CAROLER	YR	16.50	18.00
86	NIGHT BEFORE CHRISTMAS	YR	16.50	17.00
87	JOLLY ST. NICK	YR	16.50	18.00
88	CHRISTMAS MORNING	YR	16.50	18.00
89	BELL RINGER, THE	YR	16.50	18.00
90	WREATH BEARER, THE	YR	18.50	18.00
91	A SPECIAL GIFT	YR	22.50	23.00
92	MY SPECIAL FRIEND	YR	22.50	23.00

RIVER SHORE

N. ROCKWELL — **NORMAN ROCKWELL SINGLE ISSUES**

YR	NAME	LIMIT	ISSUE	TREND
81	GRANDPA'S GUARDIAN	7000	45.00	47.00
81	LOOKING OUT TO SEA	7000	45.00	100.00
81	SPRING FLOWERS	347	175.00	180.00

N. ROCKWELL — **ROCKWELL CHILDREN SERIES I**

YR	NAME	LIMIT	ISSUE	TREND
77	FIRST DAY OF SCHOOL	7500	30.00	80.00
77	FLOWERS FOR MOTHER	7500	30.00	65.00
77	FOOTBALL HERO	7500	30.00	80.00
77	SCHOOL PLAY	7500	30.00	80.00

N. ROCKWELL — **ROCKWELL CHILDREN SERIES II**

YR	NAME	LIMIT	ISSUE	TREND
78	DRESSING UP	15000	35.00	53.00
78	FIVE CENTS A GLASS	15000	35.00	42.00
78	FUTURE ALL AMERICAN	15000	35.00	55.00
78	GARDEN GIRL	15000	35.00	42.00

ROMAN INC.

E. SIMONETTI — **ANNUAL FONTANINI CHRISTMAS CRYSTAL BELLS**

YR	NAME	LIMIT	ISSUE	TREND
91	1991 BELL	YR	30.00	30.00
92	1992 BELL	YR	30.00	30.00

I. SPENCER — **ANNUAL NATIVITY BELLS**

YR	NAME	LIMIT	ISSUE	TREND
90	NATIVITY	YR	15.00	16.00
91	FLIGHT INTO EGYPT	YR	15.00	16.00
92	GLORIA IN EXCELSIS DEO	YR	15.00	16.00
93	THREE KINGS OF ORIENT	YR	15.00	16.00

F. HOOK — **FRANCES HOOK BELLS**

YR	NAME	LIMIT	ISSUE	TREND
85	BEACH BUDDIES	15000	25.00	30.00
86	SOUNDS OF THE SEA	15000	25.00	30.00
87	BEAR HUG	15000	25.00	30.00

R. FERRUZZI — **THE MASTERPIECE COLLECTION**

YR	NAME	LIMIT	ISSUE	TREND
82	MADONNA OF THE STREETS	OP	25.00	26.00

F. LIPPE — **THE MASTERPIECE COLLECTION**

YR	NAME	LIMIT	ISSUE	TREND
79	ADORATION	OP	20.00	22.00

P. MIGNARD — **THE MASTERPIECE COLLECTION**

YR	NAME	LIMIT	ISSUE	TREND
80	MADONNA WITH GRAPES	OP	25.00	26.00

G. NOTTI — **THE MASTERPIECE COLLECTION**

YR	NAME	LIMIT	ISSUE	TREND
81	HOLY FAMILY, THE	OP	25.00	26.00

ROYAL COPENHAGEN

S. VESTERGAARD — **CHRISTMAS**

YR	NAME	LIMIT	ISSUE	TREND
92	QUEEN'S CARRIAGE, THE	YR	69.50	70.00
93	CHRISTMAS GUESTS	YR	69.50	70.00

SAMSONS STUDIOS

S. BUTCHER — **MCCOONS COUNTY**

YR	NAME	LIMIT	ISSUE	TREND
*	"5 O'CLOCK MAN" WITH POLKA DOT TIE	RT	15.00	50.00
*	"CHOW TIME" COWBOY	RT	15.00	70.00
*	"GET UP" WOMAN WITH CURLERS	RT	15.00	125.00
*	BREAK TIME	RT	15.00	50.00
*	DINNER TIME	RT	15.00	50.00
*	LUNCH TIME	RT	15.00	50.00

SANDSTONE CREATIONS

T. DEGRAZIA — **A FANTASY EDITION**

YR	NAME	LIMIT	ISSUE	TREND
*	PARTY TIME	7500	40.00	40.00
*	WEE THREE	7500	40.00	40.00

YR	NAME	LIMIT	ISSUE	TREND
80	LITTLE PRAYER	7500	40.00	40.00
81	FLOWER VENDOR	7500	40.00	40.00

SCHMID

Price ranges may reflect various demands in the market from one geographic region to another; condition of piece; specific markings found on piece; and/or changes in production of piece.

YR	NAME	LIMIT	ISSUE	TREND
L. DAVIS				**DAVIS BELLS**
91	BLOSSOM	OP	75.00	400.00-650.00
91	CARUSO	OP	75.00	250.00
91	KATE	OP	75.00	575.00
91	OLE BLUE & LEAD	OP	75.00	275.00
91	WILBUR	OP	75.00	285.00
91	WILLY	OP	75.00	300.00
*				**DISNEY ANNUALS**
85	SNOW BIZ	10000	16.50	17.00
86	TREE FOR TWO	10000	16.50	17.00
87	MERRY MOUSE MEDLEY	10000	17.50	18.00
88	WARM WINTER RIDE	10000	19.50	20.00
89	MERRY MICKEY CLAUS	10000	23.00	23.00
90	HOLLY JOLLY CHRISTMAS	10000	26.50	27.00
91	MICKEY & MINNIE'S ROCKIN' CHRISTMAS	10000	26.50	27.00
L. DAVIS				**LOWELL DAVIS MINI BELL**
92	NEW DAY	YR	10.00	10.00
M.I. HUMMEL				**M.I. HUMMEL CHRISTMAS BELLS**
72	ANGEL WITH FLUTE	YR	20.00	80.00
73	NATIVITY	YR	15.00	82.00
74	GUARDIAN ANGEL, THE	YR	17.50	47.00
75	CHRISTMAS CHILD, THE	YR	22.50	47.00
76	SACRED JOURNEY	YR	22.50	26.00
77	HERALD ANGEL	YR	22.50	52.00
78	HEAVENLY TRIO	YR	27.50	42.00
79	STARLIGHT ANGEL	YR	38.00	47.00
80	PARADE INTO TOYLAND	YR	45.00	58.00
81	A TIME TO REMEMBER	YR	45.00	55.00
82	ANGELIC PROCESSION	YR	45.00	52.00
83	ANGELIC MESSENGER	YR	45.00	58.00
84	A GIFT FROM HEAVEN	YR	45.00	75.00
85	HEAVENLY LIGHT	YR	45.00	80.00
86	TELL THE HEAVENS	YR	45.00	47.00
87	ANGELIC GIFTS	YR	47.50	48.00
88	CHEERFUL CHERUBS	YR	52.50	53.00
89	ANGELIC MUSICIAN	YR	53.00	53.00
90	ANGEL'S LIGHT	YR	53.00	53.00
91	MESSAGE FROM ABOVE	1500	58.00	58.00
92	SWEET BLESSINGS	5000	65.00	65.00
M.I. HUMMEL				**M.I. HUMMEL MOTHER'S DAY BELLS**
76	DEVOTION FOR MOTHERS	YR	22.50	57.00
77	MOONLIGHT RETURN	YR	22.50	47.00
78	AFTERNOON STROLL	YR	27.50	47.00
79	CHERUB'S GIFT	YR	38.00	47.00
80	MOTHER'S LITTLE HELPER	YR	45.00	47.00
81	PLAYTIME	YR	45.00	47.00
82	FLOWER BASKET, THE	YR	45.00	47.00
83	SPRING BOUQUET	YR	45.00	47.00
84	A JOY TO SHARE	YR	45.00	47.00
C. SCHULZ				**PEANUTS ANNUAL BELLS**
79	A SPECIAL LETTER	10000	15.00	30.00
80	WAITING FOR SANTA	10000	15.00	28.00
81	MISSION FOR MOM	10000	17.50	25.00
82	PERFECT PERFORMANCE	10000	18.50	20.00
83	PEANUTS IN CONCERT	10000	12.50	15.00
84	SNOOPY & THE BEAGLE SCOUTS	10000	12.50	15.00
C. SCHULZ				**PEANUTS CHRISTMAS BELLS**
75	WOODSTOCK, SANTA CLAUS	YR	10.00	25.00
76	WOODSTOCK'S CHRISTMAS	YR	10.00	25.00
77	DECK THE DOGHOUSE	YR	10.00	20.00
78	FILLING THE STOCKING	YR	13.00	15.00
C. SCHULZ				**PEANUTS MOTHER'S DAY BELLS**
73	MOM?	YR	5.00	15.00
74	SNOOPY/WOODSTOCK/PARADE	YR	5.00	15.00
76	LINUS AND SNOOPY	YR	10.00	15.00
77	DEAR MOM	YR	10.00	15.00
78	THOUGHTS THAT COUNT	YR	13.00	15.00
C. SCHULZ				**PEANUTS SPECIAL EDITION BELL**
76	BICENTENNIAL	YR	10.00	20.00
L. DAVIS				**RFD BELL**
79	BLOSSOM	RT	65.00	360.00
79	CARUSO	RT	65.00	350.00
79	KATE	RT	65.00	460.00
79	OLE BLUE & LEAD	RT	65.00	255.00
79	WILBUR	RT	65.00	360.00
80	WILLY	RT	65.00	395.00

STUDIOS OF HARRY SMITH

YR	NAME	LIMIT	ISSUE	TREND
H. SMITH				**CHRISTMAS TREE ORNAMENTS**
95	CANTERBURY BELL	150	195.00	195.00

YR	NAME	LIMIT	ISSUE	TREND
TOWLE SILVERSMITHS				
*		**SILVERPLATED CHRISTMAS BALL BELL**		
79	1979 BALL BELL	10000	14.50	15.00
80	1980 BALL BELL	10000	20.00	20.00
81	1981 BALL BELL	10000	20.00	20.00
82	1982 BALL BELL	5000	24.00	24.00
83	1983 BALL BELL	3500	25.00	25.00
84	1984 BALL BELL	4000	20.00	20.00
85	1985 BALL BELL	4500	25.00	25.00
86	1986 BALL BELL	2500	32.00	32.00
*		**SILVERPLATED CHRISTMAS BELL**		
80	1980 SILVERPLATED BELL	10000	17.50	18.00
81	1981 SILVERPLATED BELL	5000	20.00	20.00
82	1982 SILVERPLATED BELL	5000	24.00	24.00
83	1983 SILVERPLATED BELL	3500	24.00	24.00
84	1984 SILVERPLATED BELL	5000	20.00	20.00
85	1985 SILVERPLATED BELL	4500	30.00	30.00
86	1986 SILVERPLATED BELL	4500	30.00	30.00
87	1987 SILVERPLATED BELL	4500	30.00	30.00
88	1988 SILVERPLATED BELL	2500	32.00	32.00
89	1989 SILVERPLATED BELL	4500	34.00	34.00
91	1991 SILVERPLATED BELL	*	20.00	20.00
*		**SILVERPLATED CHRISTMAS MUSICAL BELL**		
81	1981 MUSICAL BELL	20000	27.50	28.00
82	1982 MUSICAL BELL	10000	27.50	28.00
83	1983 MUSICAL BELL	2500	27.50	28.00
84	1984 MUSICAL BELL	4500	25.00	25.00
85	1985 MUSICAL BELL	4000	30.00	30.00
86	1986 MUSICAL BELL	4000	32.00	32.00
87	1987 MUSICAL BELL	4000	32.00	32.00
88	1988 MUSICAL BELL	3500	34.00	34.00
89	1989 MUSICAL BELL	4000	35.00	35.00
90	1990 MUSICAL BELL	*	27.50	28.00
91	1991 MUSICAL BELL	*	27.50	28.00
WATERFORD WEDGWOOD USA				
*				**NEW YEAR BELLS**
79	PENGUINS	YR	40.00	40.00
80	POLAR BEARS	YR	50.00	50.00
81	MOOSE	YR	55.00	55.00
82	FUR SEALS	YR	60.00	60.00
83	IBEX	YR	64.00	64.00
84	PUFFIN	YR	64.00	64.00
85	ERMINE	YR	64.00	64.00

Cottages

Ken Armke

One of the most popular limited edition collectibles today is the miniature architectural structure, more commonly referred to as the "cottage." The giants in the industry—Department 56, David Winter and Lilliput Lane—still rank among collectors as their favorite cottage lines.

The genre has expanded in the last few years to include lighthouses, which have taken a considerable jump in popularity among collectors. The lighthouse companies casting the brightest beacon today include Harbour Lights, Forma Vitrum and Spencer Collin Lighthouses.

Whether composed of traditional cottages or recent lighthouses, or a combination of both, many individual collections harbor items of substantial value in today's secondary marketplace.

When *The Grange*, a relatively new David Winter creation, was retired by John Hine Studios in 1989 due to production problems, the impact was astounding. Within a single month of its retirement, the cottage doubled in value, then tripled, then climbed to more than seven times its retail issue price.

Among many examples from the Department 56 line, *Norman Church* could be bought for as little as $40 prior to its retirement in 1987. In today's secondary market, it is seldom offered for under $3,000.

It's no wonder, then, that the collectibles secondary market offers an investment lure; there are lots of collectors out there searching for *The Grange* or *Norman Church* at a ground-floor price.

The question: Are opportunities such as these still available today?

The answer: Possibly.

Be aware, though, that the collectibles secondary market is much more akin to, say, the commodities market than it is to a state lottery. A lottery winning is generally due totally to luck. Secondary market success, on the other hand, generally demands that luck be accompanied by a great deal of knowledge and information.

How does one gain knowledge and information? In all the customary ways, such as gleaning the information provided by this publication, and through the experience of buying and collecting for pleasure rather than for potential profit.

KEN ARMKE SR., president of Opa's Haus Inc. (OHI), initiated one of the first comprehensive secondary market exchanges covering architectural miniatures. His company has since become a primary source for cottages available on the secondary market.

COTTAGES

YR	NAME	LIMIT	ISSUE	TREND
	AMAZEE GIFTS			
	S. MEYERS	**CENTURY CLASSICS CENTURY LIGHTS**		
95	ADMIRALTY HEAD, WA	3995	66.00	66.00
95	BARNEGAT, NJ	10000	58.00	58.00
95	BOSTON HARBOR, MA	3475	58.00	58.00
95	BUFFALO, NY	3475	54.00	54.00
95	BURROWS ISLAND, WA	2995	66.00	66.00
95	CAPE BLANCO, OR	RT	58.00	58.00
95	CAPE HATTERAS, NC	10000	58.00	58.00
95	CHARLOTTE-GENESEE, NY	3475	40.00	40.00
95	COQUILLE RIVER, OR	2995	66.00	66.00
95	DIAMOND HEAD, HI	10000	54.00	54.00
95	FORT GRATIOT, MI	3475	58.00	58.00
95	GREAT POINT, MA	2475	58.00	58.00
95	HILTON HEAD, SC	10000	54.00	54.00
95	HOLLAND, MI	4975	66.00	66.00
95	MARBLEHEAD, OH	7500	54.00	54.00
95	MONTAUK POINT, NY	3475	54.00	54.00
95	NEW POINT, MA	RT	40.00	40.00
95	NORTH HEAD, WA	2995	58.00	58.00
95	OLD POINT LOMA, CA	4550	66.00	66.00
95	PLYMOUTH, MA	3475	58.00	58.00
95	PONCE DE LEON, FL	3475	54.00	54.00
95	SAND POINT, MI	3475	66.00	66.00
95	TYBEE ISLAND, GA	3475	58.00	58.00
95	UMPQUA, OR	2995	58.00	58.00
96	ASSATEAGUE, VA	4975	62.00	62.00
96	BLOCK ISLAND, RI	4896	86.00	86.00
96	CAPE MAY, NJ	4995	58.00	58.00
96	CHICAGO HARBOR, IL	4250	66.00	66.00
96	EAST QUODDY HEAD, CANADA	2475	58.00	58.00
96	JUPITER INLET, FL	7500	58.00	58.00
96	LORAIN LIGHT, OH	0105	66.00	66.00
96	NAUSET BEACH, MA	4995	56.00	56.00
96	OCRACOKE ISLAND LIGHT, NC	3975	54.00	54.00
96	PORT IRABEL, TX	3975	58.00	58.00
96	ROSE ISLAND, RI	4111	68.00	68.00
96	SANDY HOOK, NJ	4995	58.00	58.00
96	SPLIT ROCK, MN	4449	66.00	66.00
96	ST. AUGUSTINE, FL	10000	62.00	62.00
96	ST. GEORGE REEF, CA	4500	62.00	62.00
96	ST. SIMMONS, GA	3975	58.00	58.00
96	WEST QUODDY HEAD, ME	4995	66.00	66.00
96	YAQUIRA HEAD, OR	4500	60.00	60.00
	S. MEYERS	**CENTURY CLASSICS CENTURYVILLE**		
94	CATHEDRAL	RT	70.00	70.00
94	CENTURYVILLE B&O	3250	56.00	56.00
94	CRANES EYE POINT	RT	50.00	55.00
94	FOGGY POINT	RT	50.00	50.00
94	GOTHIC CHURCH	3436	60.00	60.00
94	MR. JOHN JOHNSON	2960	50.00	50.00
94	MR. LYLE E. WILSON	2960	50.00	50.00
94	MS. HILDA GRANT	RT	50.00	55.00
94	MS. MARY THOMPSON	2342	50.00	50.00
94	RICHARD AND JAN SMITH	2960	50.00	50.00
94	SCHOOLHOUSE	RT	56.00	56.00
94	VILLAGE CHURCH	3250	60.00	60.00
95	BED & BREAKFAST	1975	56.00	56.00
95	FIRE STATION	1975	60.00	60.00
95	LAWRENCE KEITH	1975	64.00	64.00
95	MRS. MARY WILLIAM	1975	60.00	60.00
95	SHIP ISLAND MISS	RT	48.00	48.00
95	SWEET SHOPPE	1975	56.00	56.00
	S. MEYERS	**CENTURY CLASSICS EVERGREEN VILLAGE**		
94	CANDYMAKER'S	2475	36.00	36.00
94	CARPENTER'S	2475	36.00	36.00
94	COBBLER'S	2475	36.00	36.00
94	COTTAGE POINT	RT	36.00	36.00
94	EVERGREEN CHURCH	RT	50.00	50.00
94	TRAIN CONDUCTOR'S	2475	36.00	36.00
	ASHTON-DRAKE GALLERIES			
	K. B.-HIPPENSTEEL	**CUDDLE CHUMS**		
96	JEFFREY	*	60.00	60.00
	BAND CREATIONS			
	*	**AMERICA'S COVERED BRIDGES**		
95	BRIDGE AT THE GREEN	OP	30.00	30.00
	*** RICHARDS/PENFIELD**	**AMERICA'S COVERED BRIDGES**		
95	BILLIE CREEK, PARKE COUNTY, IN	OP	29.95	30.00
95	BRIDGE AT THE FREEN, BENNINGTON COUNTY,	OP	29.95	30.00
95	BUNKER HILL, CATAWBA COUNTY, NC	OP	29.95	30.00
95	BURFORDVILLE, CAPE GIRADEAI COUNTY, MO	OP	29.95	40.00
95	CEDAR CREEK, OZAUKEE COUNTY, WI	OP	29.95	30.00

YR	NAME	LIMIT	ISSUE	TREND
95	CHISELVILLE, BENNINGTON COUNTY, VT	OP	29.95	30.00
95	ELDER'S MILL, OCONEE COUNTY, GA	OP	29.95	30.00
95	ELIZABETHTON, CARTER COUNTY, TN	OP	29.95	30.00
95	FALLASBURG, KENT COUNTY, MI	OP	29.95	30.00
95	GILLILAND, ETOWAH COUNTY, AL	OP	29.95	30.00
95	HUMPBACK, ALLEGHENY COUNTY, VA	OP	29.95	30.00
95	KNOX , CHESTER COUNTY, PA	OP	29.95	30.00
95	NARROWS, PARKE COUNTY, IN	OP	29.95	30.00
95	OLD BLENHEIM, SCHOHARIE COUNTY, NY	OP	29.95	30.00
95	PHILIPPI, BARBOUR COUNTY, WV	OP	29.95	40.00
95	ROBERTS, PREBLE COUNTY, OH	OP	29.95	40.00
95	ROBYVILLE, PENOBSCOT COUNTY, ME	OP	29.95	30.00
95	ROSEMAN, MADISON COUNTY, IA	OP	29.95	30.00
95	SHIMENAK, LINN COUNTY, OR	OP	29.95	30.00
95	THOMPSON MILL, SHELLY COUNTY, IL	OP	29.95	30.00
95	WAWONA, MARIPOSA COUNTY, CA	OP	29.95	30.00
95	ZUMBROTA, GOODHUE COUNTY, MN	OP	29.95	30.00
*** RICHARDS/PENFIELD**	**AMERICA'S FARMLAND COLL.- AMERICA'S COUNTRY BARNS**			
96	PENNSYLVANIA DUTCH BARN	OP	29.95	30.00
*** RICHARDS/PENFIELD**	**AMERICA'S FARMLAND COLL.- AMERICA'S COVERED BRIDGES**			
96	BRIDGTON COVERED BRIDGE, INDIANA	OP	29.95	30.00
96	KNOEBEL'S GROVE AMUSEMENT PARK, PENNSYLV	OP	29.95	30.00
96	OLINS COVERED BRIDGE, OHIO	OP	29.95	30.00
*** RICHARDS/PENFIELD**		**BEST FRIENDS - RIVER SONG**		
95	BRICK HOUSE	OP	19.95	20.00
95	CHURCH	OP	19.95	20.00
95	GINGERBREAD HOUSE	OP	19.95	20.00
95	STUCCO HOUSE	OP	19.95	20.00
95	WOOD HOUSE	OP	19.95	20.00

BRANDYWINE WOODCRAFTS

YR	NAME	LIMIT	ISSUE	TREND
M. WHITING				**ACCESSORIES**
94	ELM TREE W/BENCHES	OP	16.00	16.00
94	LAMP W/BARBER POLE	OP	10.50	11.00
M. WHITING				**COUNTRY LANE I**
95	BERRY FARM	OP	30.00	30.00
95	COUNTRY SCHOOL	OP	30.00	30.00
95	DAIRY FARM	OP	30.00	30.00
95	FARM HOUSE	OP	30.00	30.00
95	GENERAL STORE, THE	OP	30.00	30.00
95	SCHOOL	OP	30.00	30.00
M. WHITING				**COUNTRY LANE II**
95	ANTIQUES & CRAFTS	OP	30.00	30.00
95	BASKETMAKER	OP	30.00	30.00
95	COUNTRY CHURCH	OP	30.00	30.00
95	FISHING LODGE	OP	30.00	30.00
95	HERB FARM	OP	30.00	30.00
95	OLDE MILL	OP	30.00	30.00
95	SPINNERS & WEAVERS	OP	30.00	30.00
M. WHITING				**COUNTRY LANE III**
96	COUNTRY CLUB	OP	30.00	30.00
96	COUNTY AIRFIELD	OP	30.00	30.00
96	OLD ORCHARD	OP	30.00	30.00
96	POST OFFICE	OP	30.00	30.00
96	STATE FAIR	OP	30.00	30.00
96	VOLUNTEER FIREHOUSE	OP	30.00	30.00
M. WHITING				**CUSTOM COLLECTION**
94	SMITHFIELD CLERK'S OFFICE	OP	9.00	9.00
M. WHITING				**HOMETOWN VI**
93	COUNTRY CHURCH	RT	24.00	30.00
93	DINER	RT	24.00	30.00
93	GENERAL STORE	RT	24.00	30.00
93	PUBLIC SCHOOL	RT	24.00	30.00
93	TRAIN STATION	RT	24.00	30.00
M. WHITING				**HOMETOWN VII**
93	CANDY SHOP	OP	24.00	24.00
93	DRESS SHOP	OP	24.00	24.00
93	FLOWER SHOP	OP	24.00	24.00
93	PET SHOP	OP	24.00	24.00
93	POST OFFICE	OP	24.00	24.00
93	QUILT SHOP	OP	24.00	24.00
M. WHITING				**HOMETOWN VIII**
94	BARBER SHOP	OP	28.00	28.00
94	COUNTRY DOCTOR	OP	28.00	28.00
94	COUNTRY STORE	OP	28.00	28.00
94	FIRE COMPANY	OP	28.00	28.00
94	SEWING SHOP	OP	26.00	26.00
M. WHITING				**HOMETOWN IX**
94	BED & BREAKFAST	OP	29.00	29.00
94	CAFE/DELI	OP	29.00	29.00
94	HOMETOWN BANK	OP	29.00	29.00
94	HOMETOWN GAZETTE	OP	29.00	29.00
94	TEDDYS & TOYS	OP	29.00	29.00
M. WHITING				**HOMETOWN X**
95	BRICK CHURCH	OP	29.00	29.00
95	DOLL SHOPPE, THE	OP	29.00	29.00
95	GENERAL HOSPITAL	OP	29.00	29.00

O'Donovan's Castle *is an impressive issue created by David Winter for John Hine Studios.*

Blossom Cottage *is represenative of the romantic English cottages sculpted by David Winter.*

Pudding Cottage *by David Winter was issued in 1991 by John Hine Studios.*

Collectors purchasing David Winter's Birthstone Wishing Well *were given a choice of gemstones to signify the month in which they were born.*

Hogmanay *was created by David Winter for John Hine Studios.*

Cherry Hill School *was sculpted by Moe Wideman as part of the "American Collection" for John Hine Studios.*

YR	NAME	LIMIT	ISSUE	TREND
95	GIFT BOX, THE	OP	29.00	29.00
95	POLICE STATION	OP	29.00	29.00
M. WHITING				**HOMETOWN XI**
95	ANTIQUES	YR	29.00	29.00
95	CHURCH II	YR	29.00	29.00
95	GROCER	YR	29.00	29.00
95	PHARMACY	YR	29.00	29.00
95	SCHOOL II	YR	29.00	29.00
M. WHITING				**HOMETOWN XII**
96	BRIDAL & DRESS SHOPPE	YR	29.00	29.00
96	COUNTRY LANE SIGN	YR	20.00	20.00
96	FIVE & DIME	YR	29.00	29.00
96	HOMETOWN SIGN	YR	22.00	22.00
96	HOMETOWN THEATER	YR	29.00	29.00
96	POST OFFICE	YR	29.00	29.00
96	TRAVEL AGENCY	YR	29.00	29.00
M. WHITING				**NORTH POLE COLLECTION**
93	CANDY CANE FACTORY	OP	24.00	24.00
93	ELF CLUB	OP	24.00	24.00
93	TEDDY BEAR FACTORY	OP	24.00	24.00
93	TOWN CHRISTMAS TREE	OP	20.00	25.00
94	POST OFFICE	OP	25.00	25.00
94	TOWN HALL	OP	25.00	30.00
M. WHITING				**TREASURED TIMES**
94	HALLOWEEN HOUSE	750	32.00	32.00
94	HAPPY BIRTHDAY HOUSE	750	32.00	32.00
94	MOTHER'S DAY HOUSE	750	32.00	32.00
94	NEW BABY BOY HOUSE	750	32.00	32.00
94	NEW BABY GIRL HOUSE	750	32.00	32.00
94	VALENTINE'S DAY HOUSE	750	32.00	32.00
M. WHITING				**WILLIAMSBURG COLLECTION**
93	CAMPBELL'S TAVERN	OP	28.00	28.00
93	KINGS ARM TAVERN	OP	25.00	25.00
M. WHITING				**YORKTOWN COLLECTION**
93	DIGGES HOUSE	OP	22.00	27.00

CAVANAGH GROUP

YR	NAME	LIMIT	ISSUE	TREND
*				**COCA-COLA BRAND TOWN SQUARE COLLECTION**
92	CANDLER'S DRUG	RT	39.99	100.00
92	DEE'S BOARDING HOUSE	RT	39.99	400.00
92	DICK'S LUNCHEONETTE	RT	39.99	75.00
92	GILBERT'S GROCERY	RT	39.99	150.00
92	HOWARD OIL	RT	39.99	150.00
92	TRAIN DEPOT	RT	39.99	250.00
93	CITY HALL	RT	39.99	50.00
93	JACOB'S PHARMACY	5000	25.00	300.00
93	MOONEY'S ANTIQUE BARN	RT	39.99	50.00
93	ROUTE 93 COVERED BRIDGE	OP	19.99	20.00
93	T. TAYLOR'S EMPORIUM	RT	39.99	50.00
93	TICK TOCK DINER, THE	OP	39.99	40.00
94	FLYING "A" SERIES STATION	OP	39.99	40.00
94	MCMAHON'S GENERAL STORE	OP	39.99	40.00
94	PLAZA DRUGS	OP	39.99	40.00
94	STATION #14 FIREHOUSE	OP	39.99	40.00
94	STRAND THEATRE	OP	39.99	40.00
94	TOWN GAZEBO	OP	19.99	20.00
95	COCA-COLA BOTTLING WORKS	RT	40.00	40.00
95	GRIST MILL	RT	40.00	40.00
95	JENNY'S SWEET SHOP	OP	39.99	40.00
95	JENNY'S SWEET SHOPPE	RT	40.00	40.00
95	LIGHTHOUSE POINT SNACK BAR	OP	39.99	40.00
95	LIGHTHOUSE POINT SNACK BAR	OP	40.00	40.00
96	CHANDLER'S SKI RESORT	OP	40.00	40.00
96	CLARA'S CHRISTMAS SHOP	OP	40.00	40.00
96	COOPER'S TREE FARM	OP	20.00	20.00
96	SCOTTER'S DRIVE-IN	OP	40.00	40.00
96	TOWN BARBER SHOP	OP	40.00	40.00

CREATIVE CRAFTSMEN

YR	NAME	LIMIT	ISSUE	TREND
M. FENLEY				**VINTAGE VILLAGE**
95	OLD WINDMILL, THE	500	96.00	96.00
95	PRAIRIE CHURCH	500	145.00	145.00
96	BILLY'S LITTLE COTTAGE	300	50.00	50.00

DEPARTMENT 56

Price ranges may reflect various demands in the market from one geographic region to another; condition of piece; specific markings found on piece; and/or changes in production of piece.

YR	NAME	LIMIT	ISSUE	TREND
*				**ALPINE VILLAGE**
86	ALPINE VILLAGE 6540-4 (SET OF 5)	OP	150.00	185.00
86	APOTEHEKE 6540-4	OP	37.00	37.00
86	BESSOR BIERKELLER 6540-4	OP	37.00	37.00
86	E. STAUBR BAECKER 6540-4	OP	37.00	37.00
86	GASTHOF EISL 6540-4	OP	37.00	37.00
86	MILCH-KASE 6540-4	OP	37.00	37.00
87	ALPINE CHURCH 6541-2	RT	32.00	234.00-325.00
87	JOSEF ENGEL FARMHOUSE 5952-8	RT	33.00	1073.00-1170.00

YR	NAME	LIMIT	ISSUE	TREND
88	GRIST MILL 5953-6	OP	42.00	45.00
88	GRIST MILL 5953-6	OP	45.00	45.00
90	BAHNOF 5615-4	RT	42.00	60.00
91	ST. NIKOLAUS KIRCHE 5617-0	OP	37.50	38.00
92	GATE HOUSE 5530-1, SELECT OPEN HOUSE	RT	22.50	40.00
92	KUKUCK UHREN 5618-9, ALPINE SHOPS	OP	37.50	38.00
92	METTERNICHE WURST 5618-9, ALPINE SHOPS	OP	37.50	38.00
93	CLIMB EVERY MOUNTAIN 5613-8, (SET OF 4)	OP	27.50	28.00
93	SPORT LADEN 5612-0	OP	50.00	50.00
94	BAKERY & CHOCOLATE SHOP 5614-6	OP	37.50	38.00
94	POLKA FEST 5607-3, (SET OF 3)	OP	30.00	30.00
95	ALPEN HORN PLAYER AT ALPINE SIGN 5618-2	OP	20.00	20.00
95	CAMM HAUS 5617-1	OP	*	*
*				**BACHMAN'S**
87	HOME TOWN BOARDING HOUSE 670-0	SU	34.00	275.00
87	HOME TOWN CHURCH 671-8	SU	40.00	300.00
88	HOME TOWN DRUGSTORE 672-6	SU	40.00	675.00
*		**CHARLES DICKENS SIGNATURE**		
95	GRAPES INN, THE 5753-4	OP	120.00	120.00
*			**CHRISTMAS IN THE CITY**	
87	BAKERY 6512-9	RT	37.50	91.00-124.00
87	CATHEDRAL, THE 5962-5	RT	60.00	330.00
87	CHRISTMAS IN THE CITY 6512-9 (SET OF 3)	RT	112.00	450.00
87	CHRISTMAS IN THE CITY SIGN 5960-9	RT	6.00	11.00
87	PALACE THEATRE 5963-3	RT	45.00	1008.00-1040.00
87	SUTTON PLACE BROWNSTONES 5961-7	RT	80.00	710.00
87	TOWER RESTAURANT 6512-9	RT	37.50	228.00-260.00
87	TOY SHOP & PET STORE 6512-9	RT	37.50	182.00-325.00
87	VEHICLES 5964-1, (SET OF 3)	OP	22.00	22.00
88	CHOCOLATE SHOPPE, THE 5968-4	RT	40.00	130.00
88	CITY HALL 5969-2	RT	65.00	165.00
88	HANK'S MARKET 5970-6	RT	40.00	78.00-100.00
88	VARIETY STORE 5972-2	RT	45.00	150.00-208.00
89	5607 PARK AVENUE TOWNHOUSE 5977-3	RT	48.00	91.00-104.00
89	5607 PARK AVENUE TOWNHOUSE 5977-3	RT	48.00	70.00
89	5609 PARK AVENUE TOWNHOUSE 5978-1	RT	48.00	85.00-100.00
89	5609 PARK AVENUE TOWNHOUSE 5978-1	RT	48.00	70.00
89	BOULEVARD 5516-6	RT	25.00	40.00
89	DOROTHY'S DRESS SHOP 5974-9	RT	70.00	358.00-384.00
89	MAILBOX/FIRE HYDRANT 5517-4, RD, WH & BL	RT	6.00	15.00
89	RITZ HOTEL 5973-0	RT	55.00	55.00
89	TOWN SQUARE GAZEBO 5513-1	OP	19.00	19.00
89	UTILITIES SET 5512-3	OP	12.50	13.00
89	WROUGHT IRON FENCE EXTENSION SET 5515-8	OP	12.00	12.00
89	WROUGHT IRON GATE W/FENCE 5514-0	OP	15.00	15.00
90	'TIS THE SEASON 5539-5	RT	12.95	12.00
90	BUSY SIDEWALKS 5535-2, (SET OF 4)	RT	28.00	35.00
90	DOCTOR'S OFFICE, THE 5544-1	RT	60.00	105.00-125.00
90	MAILBOX/FIRE HYDRANT 5517-4, RED & GREEN	OP	6.00	6.00
90	RED BRICK FIRE STATION 5536-0	RT	55.00	60.00
90	REST YE MERRY GENTLEMEN 5540-9	OP	12.95	13.00
90	SUBWAY ENTRANCE 5541-7	OP	15.00	15.00
90	WONG'S IN CHINATOWN 5537-9	RT	55.00	65.00-85.00
91	"LITTLE ITALY" RISTORANTE 5538-7	RT	52.00	60.00
91	ALL SAINTS CORNER CHURCH 5542-5	OP	105.00	105.00
91	ARTS ACADEMY 5543-3	RT	45.00	60.00
91	DOCTOR'S OFFICE 5544-1	RT	60.00	65.00-104.00
91	HOLLYDALE'S DEPARTMENT STORE 5534-4	OP	85.00	85.00
91	ST. MARK'S CHURCH 5549-2	RT	120.00	1750.00
92	CATHEDRAL CHURCH OF ST. MARKS 5549-2	3024	120.00	2800.00-6000.00
92	CITY CLOCKWORKS 5531-0, UPTOWN SHOPPE	OP	56.00	56.00
92	HABERBASHERY 5531-0, UPTOWN SHOPPE	OP	40.00	40.00
92	MUSIC EMPORIUM 5531-0, UPTOWN SHOPPE	OP	54.00	54.00
93	POTTERS TEA SELLER 5880-7	OP	45.00	45.00
93	SPRING STREET COFFEE HOUSE	OP	45.00	45.00
94	CHAMBER ORCHESTRA 5884-0, (SET OF 4)	OP	*	*
94	CITY BROKERAGE HOUSE 5881-5	OP	48.00	48.00
94	FIRST METROPOLITAN BANK 5882-3	OP	60.00	60.00
94	HERITAGE MUSEUM OF ART 5883-1	OP	96.00	96.00
94	HOLIDAY FIELD TRIP 5885-8, (SET OF 3)	RT	*	*
95	BRIGHTON SCHOOL 5887-6	OP	*	*
95	BROWN STONES ON THE SQ. 5887-7 (SET OF 2	OP	*	*
95	CHOIR BOYS ALL IN A ROW 5889-2	OP	20.00	20.00
95	HOLY NAME CHURCH 5887-5	OP	96.00	96.00
95	IVY TERRACE APARTMENTS 5887-4	OP	60.00	60.00
95	KEY TO THE CITY AT CHRISTMAS CITY SIGN 5	OP	20.00	20.00
95	ONE MAN BAND & DANCING DOG 5889-1 (SET O	OP	17.50	18.00
95	VILLAGE EXPRESS VAN-CANADA OM216	OP	45.00	45.00
95	YES, VIRIGINA 5889-0, (SET OF 2)	OP	12.50	13.00
*				**DICKENS' VILLAGE**
84	ABEL BEESLEY BUTCHER 6515-3	RT	25.00	91.00-143.00
84	BEAN AND SON SMITHY SHOP 6515-3	RT	25.00	208.00-280.00
84	CANDLE SHOP 6515-3	RT	25.00	215.00-280.00
84	CROWNTREE INN 6515-3	RT	25.00	300.00
84	GOLDEN SWAN BAKER 6515-3	RT	25.00	195.00-215
84	GREEN GROCER 6515-3	RT	25.00	185.00
84	JONES & CO. BRUSH/BASKET SHOP 6515-3	RT	25.00	228.00-384.00
84	ORIGINAL SHOPS, THE 6515-3 (SET OF 7)	RT	175.00	1105.00-1560.00

YR	NAME	LIMIT	ISSUE	TREND
85	DICKENS' COTTAGES 6518-8 (SET OF 3)	RT	75.00	1235.00-1365.00
85	DICKENS' VILLAGE CHURCH (DARK CARAMEL) 6	RT	35.00	140.00
85	DICKENS' VILLAGE CHURCH (GREEN) 6516-1	RT	35.00	460.00
85	DICKENS' VILLAGE CHURCH (LT. CREAM) 6516	RT	35.00	440.00
85	DICKENS' VILLAGE CHURCH (TAN/FLESH) 6516	RT	35.00	200.00
85	DICKENS' VILLAGE MILL 6519-6	RT	35.00	4875.00-5200.00
85	STONE COTTAGE (SPLIT PEA GREEN) 6518-8	RT	25.00	400.00
85	STONE COTTAGE (TAN) 6518-8	RT	25.00	660.00
85	STONE COTTAGE (TAN/GREEN) 6518-8	RT	25.00	420.00
85	THATCHED COTTAGE 6518-8	RT	25.00	195.00-210.00
85	TUDOR COTTAGE 6518-8	RT	25.00	488.00-535.00
85	VILLAGE CHURCH (CREAM-YELLOW) 6516-1	RT	35.00	285.00
86	BLYTHE POND MILL HOUSE 6508-0	RT	37.00	286.00-325.00
86	BY THE POND MILL HOUSE 6508-0	RT	37.00	130.00-163.00
86	CHADBURY STATION & TRAIN 6528-5	RT	65.00	370.00
86	CHRISTMAS/COTTAGES 6500-5 (SET OF 3)	OP	75.00	90.00
86	COTTAGE OF BOB CRATCHIT & TINY TIM 6500-	RT	30.00	45.00
86	COTTAGE TOY SHOP 6507-2	RT	27.00	325.00-371.00
86	DICKENS' LANE SHOPS 6507-2 (SET OF 3)	RT	80.00	748.00
86	FEZZIWIG'S WAREHOUSE 6500-5	RT	30.00	30.00
86	NORMAN CHURCH 6502-1	3500	40.00	3850.00
86	SCROOGE & MARLEY COUNTING HOUSE	RT	30.00	30.00
86	THOMAS KERSEY COFFEE HOUSE 6507-2	RT	27.00	182.00-299.00
86	TUTTLE'S PUB 6507-2	RT	27.00	260.00-312.00
87	BARLEY BREE FARMHOUSE & BARN 5900-5 (SET	RT	60.00	468.00-572.00
87	BRICK ABBEY 6549-8	RT	33.00	423.00-442.00
87	CHESTERTON MANOR HOUSE 6568-4	RT	45.00	1430.00-1820.00
87	CJESTERTON MANOR	RT	45.00	1540.00
87	DICKENS' VILLAGE SIGN 6569-2	RT	6.00	15.00
87	DOVER COACH/ORIGINAL 6590-0	RT	18.00	85.00
87	KENILWORTH CASTLE 5916-1	RT	70.00	585.00-611.00
87	NEW ENGLAND VILLAGE SIGN 6532-3	RT	6.00	12.00
87	OLD CURIOSITY SHOP 5905-6	OP	40.00	40.00
87	OLD CURIOUSITY SHOP, THE 5905-6	OP	32.00	38.00
87	OX SLED/BLUE 5901-1	RT	20.00	117.00-156.00
87	OX SLED/TAN 5901-1	RT	20.00	270.00
88	BOOTER AND COBBLER 5924-2	RT	32.00	163.00-189.00
88	C. FLETCHER PUBLIC HOUSE 5904-8	12500	35.00	683.00-715.00
88	C.F. PUBLIC HOUSE 5904-8	RT	35.00	520.00
88	COBBLESTONE SHOPS 5924-2 (SET OF 3)	RT	95.00	377.00-403.00
88	COUNTING HOUSE & SILAS THIMBLRTON BARRIS	RT	32.00	75.00
88	GEORGE WEETON WATCHMAKER 5926-9	RT	32.50	40.00
88	IVY GLEN CHURCH 5927-7	RT	35.00	72.00-78.00
88	MERCHANT SHOPS 5926-9 (SET OF 5)	RT	150.00	234.00-254.00
88	MERMAID FISH SHOPPE 5926-9	RT	32.50	52.00-65.00
88	NIC(K)OLAS NICKLEBY COTTAGE 5925-0	RT	36.00	90.00
88	NICHOLAS NICKLEBY	RT	36.00	98.00
88	NICHOLAS NICKLEBY 5925-0 (SET OF 2)	RT	72.00	189.00-202.00
88	NICHOLAS NICKLEBY CHARACTER 5929-3, SET	RT	20.00	34.00-39.00
88	T. WELLS FRUIT & SPICE SHOP 5924-2	RT	32.00	117.00-156.00
88	WACKFORD SQUEERS BOARDING SCHOOL 5925-0	RT	36.00	91.00-124.00
88	WALPOLE TAILORS 5926-9	RT	32.50	40.00
88	WHITE HORSE BAKERY 5926-9	RT	32.50	45.00
88	WOOL SHOP, THE 5924-2	RT	32.00	182.00-227.00
89	BETSEY TROTWOOD'S COTTAGE 5550-6	RT	42.00	70.00
89	CHRISTMAS MORNING 5588-3 (SET OF 3)	OP	18.00	18.00
89	COBLES POLICE STATION 5583-2	RT	37.50	137.00
89	DAVID COPPERFIELD 5550-6 (SET OF 3)	RT	125.00	163.00-267.00
89	FLAT OF EBENEZER SCROOGE, THE 5587-5	OP	37.50	38.00
89	KINGS ROAD CAB 5581-6	OP	30.00	30.00
89	KNOTTINGHILL CHURCH 5582-4	RT	52.00	104.00
89	MR. WICKFIELD SOLITITOR 5550-6	RT	42.00	85.00
89	PEGGOTTY'S SEASIDE COTTAGE (TAN) 5550-6	RT	42.00	110.00
89	PEGGOTTY'S SEASIDE COTTAGE(GREEN) 5550-6	RT	42.00	45.00
89	ROYAL COACH 5578-6	RT	55.00	60.00
89	THEATRE ROYAL 5584-0	RT	45.00	65.00-78.00
89	TOWN SQUARE GAZEBO 5513-1	OP	19.00	19.00
89	VICTORIA STATION 5574-3	OP	110.00	110.00
90	BISHOPS OAST HOUSE 5567-0	RT	45.00	65.00
90	FLYING SCOT TRAIN, THE 5573-5 (SET OF 4	OP	50.00	50.00
90	HOLIDAY TRAVELERS 5571-9, (SET OF 3"	OP	25.00	25.00
90	KINGS ROAD 5568-9 (SET OF 2)	OP	72.00	75.00
90	TUTBURY PRINTER 5568-9	OP	40.00	40.00
90	VICTORIA STATION TRAIN PLATFORM 5575-1	OP	22.00	22.00
91	ASHBURY INN 5555-7	RT	60.00	60.00
91	BROWNLOW'S HOUSE 5553-0	RT	37.50	60.00
91	FAGIN'S HIDE-A-WAY 5552-2	RT	72.00	72.00
91	MAYLIE'S COTTAGE 5553-0	RT	37.50	45.00
91	NEPHEW FRED'S FLAT 5557-3	RT	36.00	91.00-104.00
91	OLIVER TWIST 5553-0 (SET OF 2)	RT	75.00	117.00-143.00
92	BLUEBIRD SEED AND BULB 5642-1	OP	48.00	48.00
92	CROWN & CRICKET INN 5750-9	RT	100.00	130.00-169.00
92	HEMBLETON PEWTERER 5800-9	RT	72.00	75.00
92	KING'S ROAD POST OFFICE 5801-7	OP	45.00	45.00
92	LIONHEAD BRIDGE 5864-5	OP	22.00	22.00
92	OLD MICHAEL CHURCH 5562-0	OP	46.00	46.00
92	YANKEE JUD BELL CASTING 5643-0	RT	44.00	44.00
93	A. BIELER FARM 5648-0 SET OF 2	OP	92.00	92.00
93	BOARDING & LODGING SCHOOL 5819-2 #18	RT	48.00	140.00

YR	NAME	LIMIT	ISSUE	TREND
93	BRINGING FLEECES TO MILL, 5819-0 (SET OF	OP	35.00	35.00
93	BUMPSTEAD NYE CLOAKS & TREACLE 5808-4	OP	37.50	38.00
93	C. BRADFORD WHEELWRIGHT & SON 5818-1, (S	OP	24.00	24.00
93	DASHING THRU THE SNOW 5820-3	OP	32.50	33.00
93	GREAT DENTON MILL 5812-2	OP	50.00	50.00
93	KINGFORD BREW HOUSE 5811-4	OP	45.00	45.00
93	LOMAS LIMITED MOLLASSES & TREACLE 5808-4	OP	37.50	38.00
93	PIED BULL INN, THE 5751-7	RT	100.00	130.00
93	PUMP LANE SHOPPES 5808-4 SET OF 3	OP	112.00	112.00
93	VISIONS OF CHRISTMAS PAST 5817-3, (SET O	OP	27.50	28.00
93	W.M. WHEATCAKES & PUDDINGS 5808-4	OP	37.50	38.00
94	BOARDING & LODGING SCHOOL 5810-6 #43	OP	48.00	48.00
94	BOARDING & LODGING SCHOOL 5809-2	YR	48.00	225.00-275.00
94	BOARDING & LODGING SCHOOL 5810-6	OP	48.00	72.00
94	CHELSEA MARKET CURIOUSITY 5827-0, (SET O	OP	27.50	28.00
94	CHELSEA MARKET MISTLETOE 5826-2, (SET OF	OP	25.00	25.00
94	CHRISTMAS CAROL HOLIDAY TRIMMING SET 583	OP	65.00	65.00
94	DEDLOCK ARMS 5752-5	RT	100.00	120.00
94	GIGGELSWICK MUTTON & HAM 5822-0	OP	48.00	48.00
94	HATHER HARNESS 5823-8	OP	48.00	48.00
94	PEACEFUL GLOW ON CHRISTMAS EVE 5830-8, (	OP	30.00	30.00
94	PORTOBELLO COTTAGES 5824-6, (SET OF 3)	OP	120.00	120.00
94	PORTOBELLO RD, PEDDLER, SET OF THREE	OP	27.50	28.00
94	POSTERN/10TH ANNIVERSARY PC 9871-0	RT	17.50	18.00
94	VICTORIAN WROUGHT IRON FENCE & GATE 5252	OP	15.00	15.00
94	WHITTLEBOURNE CHURCH	OP	85.00	85.00
94	WHITTLESBOURNE CHURCH 5821-1	OP	85.00	85.00
94	WINTER SLEIGHRIDE 5825-4	OP	18.00	18.00
95	BLENHAM STREET BANK 5833-0	OP	60.00	60.00
95	BRICKSTON ROAD WATCHMEN 5839-0, (SET OF	OP	25.00	25.00
95	CHELSEA MARKET HAT, MUNGER & CART 5839-2	OP	*	*
95	DURSLEY MANOR 5832-9	OP	50.00	50.00
95	J.D. NICHOLS TOY SHOP 5832-8	OP	48.00	48.00
95	MALTINGS, THE 5833-5	OP	50.00	50.00
95	PARTRIDGE/PEAR TREE, 12 DAYS OF CHRISTMA	OP	35.00	35.00
95	SIR JOHN FALLSTAFF INN	RT	100.00	120.00
95	START A HOLIDAY TRADITION DV STARTER SET	OP	85.00	85.00
95	TALLY HO 5839-1, (SET OF 5)	OP	25.00	25.00
95	TWO TURTLE DOVES-12 DAYS OF CHRISTMAS 58	OP	32.50	33.00
95	VILLAGE DUDDEN CROSS CHURCH, THE 5834-3	OP	45.00	45.00
95	WRENBURY SHOPS 5833-1, (SET OF 3)	OP	100.00	100.00
*	**DICKENS' VILLAGE LIMITED EDITION**			
89	GREEN GATE 5586-7	RT	65.00	286.00-312.00
89	RUTH MARION 5585-9	RT	65.00	390.00-475.00
*	**DICKENS' VILLAGE PROOF**			
89	GREEN GATE 5586-7	RT	65.00	240.00
89	RUTH MARION 5589-9	RT	65.00	330.00
*	**DICKENS' VILLAGE/WRENBURY SHOP**			
95	CHOP SHOP, THE	OP	35.00	35.00
95	PEA PUDDLEWICK SPECTACLE SHOP	OP	35.00	35.00
95	WRENBURY BAKER	OP	35.00	35.00
*	**HERITAGE VILLAGE COLLECTION**			
90	TOWN CRIER & CHIMNEY SWEEP 5569-7, (SET	OP	15.00	15.00
91	BRINGING HOME THE YULE LOG 5558-1, (SET	OP	28.00	28.00
91	HOLIDAY COACH 5561-1	OP	70.00	70.00
91	POULTRY MARKET 5559-0, (SET OF 3)	RT	32.00	32.00
92	CHURCHYARD GATE & FENCE 5806-8, (SET OF	OP	15.00	15.00
92	CHURCHYARD GATE & FENCE 5807-6, (SET OF	OP	16.00	16.00
*	**HERITAGE VILLAGE COLLECTION ACCESSORIES**			
84	CAROLERS 6526-9 (SET OF 3)	RT	10.00	25.00
85	VILLAGE TRAIN 6527-7 (SET OF 3) BRIGHTON	RT	12.50	390.00
86	CHRISTMAS CAROL FIGS. 6501-3 (SET OF 3)	RT	12.50	104.00
86	COVERED WOODEN BRIDGE 6531-5	RT	10.00	35.00
86	LIGHTED TREE W/CHILDREN & LADDER 6510-2	RT	35.00	280.00
86	NEW ENGLAND WINTER SET 6532-3 (SET OF 5)	RT	18.00	35.00
86	SLEIGHRIDE 6511-0	RT	19.50	40.00
87	BLACKSMITH 5934-0 (SET OF 3)	RT	20.00	72.00
87	CITY PEOPLE 5965-0 (SET OF 5)	RT	27.50	52.00-65.00
87	DOVER COACH 6590-0	RT	18.00	50.00
87	FARM PEOPLE & ANIMALS 5901-3 (SET OF 5)	RT	24.00	80.00
87	MAPLE SUGARING SHED 6589-7 (SET OF 3)	RT	19.00	230.00
87	OX SLED 5951-1	RT	20.00	120.00
87	SHOPKEEPERS 5966-8 (SET OF 4)	RT	15.00	30.00
87	SILO & HAY SHED, 5950-1 (SET OF 2)	RT	18.00	150.00
87	SILO AND HAY SHED 5901-1	RT	18.00	169.00-189.00
87	SKATING POND 6545-5	RT	24.00	78.00-85.00
87	STONE BRIDGE 6546-3	RT	12.00	78.00-91.00
87	VILLAGE WELL & HOLY CROSS 6547-1 (SET OF	RT	13.00	124.00-143.00
88	CHILDE POND & SKATERS 5903-0 (SET OF 4)	RT	30.00	85.00-104.00
88	CITY BUS & MILK TRUCK 5983-8 (SET OF 2)	RT	15.00	20.00
88	CITY NEWSSTAND 5971-4 (SET OF 4)	RT	25.00	39.00-65.00
88	FEZZIWIG AND FRIENDS 5928-5 (SET OF 3)	RT	12.50	78.00-117.00
88	NICHOLAS NICKLEBY 5929-3 (SET OF 4)	RT	20.00	39.99-46.00
88	ONE HOUSE OPEN SLEIGH 5982-0	RT	20.00	25.00
88	SALVATION ARMY BAND 5985-4 (SET OF 6)	RT	24.00	59.00
88	VILLAGE HARVEST PEOPLE 5941-2 (SET OF 4)	RT	27.50	30.00
88	VILLAGE TRAIN TRESTLE 5981-1	RT	17.00	72.00-98.00
88	WOODCUTTER AND SON 5986 (SET OF 2)	RT	10.00	39.00-52.00

Convent in the Woods *by Lilliput Lane received "Best Collectible" at the 16th International Collectible Exposition in South Bend, Indiana.*

Ship Inn *was created by the artists of Lilliput Lane.*

Pussy Willow *was exclusive to members of the Lilliput Lane Collector's Club.*

The Old Vicarage at Christmas *is one of the few Lilliput Lane cottages to be designed with snow.*

Honeysuckle Cottage, *introduced in 1992, was the Lilliput Lane 10th anniversary special.*

Home Sweet Home *is the creation of artist Ray Day. The piece is produced by Lilliput Lane.*

YR	NAME	LIMIT	ISSUE	TREND
89	CENTRAL PARK CARRIAGE 5979-0	OP	30.00	30.00
89	CONSTABLES 5579-4 (SET OF 3)	RT	17.50	39.00-59.00
89	FARM ANIMALS 5945-5 (SET OF 4)	RT	15.00	35.00
89	HERITAGE VILLAGE SIGN W/SNOWMAN 5572-7	RT	10.00	10.00
89	ORGAN GRINDER 5957-9 (SET OF 3)	RT	21.00	29.00-52.00
89	RIVER STREET ICE HOUSE CART 5959-5	RT	20.00	45.00
90	CAROLERS ON THE DOORSTEP 5570-0, (SET OF	OP	25.00	30.00
91	COME INTO THE INN 5560-3, (SET OF 3)	RT	22.00	20.00
92	CHURCH YARD 5563-8	RT	15.00	55.00
92	GATE HOUSE 5530-1	RT	22.50	46.00-59.00
92	GATE HOUSE 5530-1	RT	22.50	40.00
*	**LITTLE TOWN OF BETHLEHEM**			
87	LITTLE TOWN/BETHLEHEM 5975-7 (SET OF 12)	OP	150.00	150.00
*	**MEADOWLAND**			
79	ASPEN TREES 5052-6	RT	16.00	32.00
79	COUNTRYSIDE CHURCH 5051-8	RT	25.00	100.00
79	SHEEP 5053-4	RT	12.00	24.00
79	THATCHED COTTAGE 5050-0	RT	30.00	250.00-275.00
*	**NEW ENGLAND VILLAGE**			
86	APOTHECARY SHOP 6530-7	RT	25.00	85.00
86	BRICK TOWN HALL 6530-7	RT	25.00	160.00
86	GENERAL STORE 6530-7	RT	25.00	358.00-423.00
86	JACOB ADAMS FARMHOUSE & BARN 6538-2	RT	65.00	585.00-644.00
86	LIVERY STABLE & BOOT SHOP 6530-7	RT	25.00	125.00
86	NATHANIEL BINGHAM FABRICS 6530-7	RT	25.00	155.00
86	NEW ENGLAND 6530-7 (ORIGINAL SET OF 7)	RT	170.00	950.00
86	RED SCHOOLHOUSE 6530-7	RT	25.00	270.00
86	STEEPLE CHURCH 6530-7	RT	25.00	117.00-169.00
86	STEEPLE CHURCH 6539-0	RT	30.00	80.00
87	CRAGGY COVE LIGHTHOUSE 5930-7	RT	45.00	52.00-85.00
87	SMYTHE WOOLEN MILL 6543-1	RT	42.00	975.00-1268.00
87	TIMBER KNOLL LOG CABIN 6544-7	RT	38.00	124.00-163.00
87	VILLAGE EXPRESS ELECTRIC TRAIN/BLACK 599	RT	90.00	265.00
87	WESTON TRAIN STATION 5931-5	RT	42.00	195.00-260.00
88	ADA'S BED & BOARDING HOUSE 2ND 5940-4	RT	36.00	143.00-163.00
88	ADA'S BED & BOARDING HOUSE 3R 5940-4	RT	36.00	120.00
88	ADA'S BED & BOARDING HOUSE 5940-4 (1)	RT	36.00	275.00
88	ANNE SHAW TOYS 5939-0	RT	27.00	150.00
88	BEN'S BARBERSHOP 5939-0	RT	27.00	111.00-117.00
88	CHERRY LANE SHOPS 5939-0 (SET OF 3)	RT	80.00	228.00-312.00
88	OLD NORTH CHURCH 5932-3	OP	45.00	85.00-104.00
88	OTIS HAYES BUTCHER SHOP 5939-0	RT	27.00	85.00-98.00
88	RED COVERED BRIDGE 5987-0	RT	17.00	20.00
88	VILLAGE EXPRESS ELECTRIC TRAIN SET 5980-	OP	100.00	100.00
89	BERKSHIRE HOUSE (ORIG BLUE) 5942-0	RT	40.00	165.00
89	BERKSHIRE HOUSE/TEAL 5942-0	RT	40.00	130.00-156.00
89	HV PROMOTIONAL EARTHENWARE SIGN 9953-8	RT	5.00	20.00
89	JANNES MULLET AMISH BARN 5944-7	RT	48.00	98.00-104.00
89	JANNES MULLET AMISH FARM HOUSE 5943-9	RT	32.00	91.00-130.00
89	MIALBOX/FIRE HYDRANT 5517-4 RED,WH & BL	RT	6.00	15.00
90	AMISH FAMILY 5948-0, (SET OF 3)	RT	20.00	25.00
90	AMISH FAMILY 5948-0, SET OF 3 W/MOUSTACH	RT	20.00	50.00
90	CAPTAIN'S COTTAGE 5947-1	OP	42.00	42.00
90	ICHABOD CRAIN'S COTTAGE 5954-4	RT	32.00	35.00
90	MAILBOX & FIRE HYDRANT, RED & GREEN 5517	RT	6.00	6.00
90	SHINGLE CREEK HOUSE 5946-3	RT	40.00	52.00-85.00
90	SLEEPY HOLLOW CHURCH 5955-2	RT	36.00	45.00
90	SLEEPY HOLLOW SCHOOL 5954-4	RT	32.00	90.00
90	SLEEPY HOLLOW SCHOOL 5954-4 (SET OF 3)	RT	96.00	180.00
90	VAN TASSEL MANO 5954-4	RT	32.00	45.00
91	MCGREBE-CUTTERS & SLEIGHS 5640-5	RT	48.00	78.00
92	BLUEBIRD SEED & BULB 5642-1	OP	48.00	48.00
92	STONEY BROOK TOWN HALL 5644-8	RT	42.00	50.00
92	YANKEE JUD BELL CASTING	RT	44.00	44.00
93	A. BIELER BARN 5648-9	OP	50.00	50.00
93	A. BIELER FARMHOUSE 5648-9	OP	42.00	42.00
93	BLUE STAR ICE CO. 5647-2	OP	45.00	45.00
94	ARLINGTON FALLS CHURCH 5651-0	OP	40.00	40.00
94	CAPE KEAG FISH CANNERY 5652-9	OP	48.00	48.00
94	OLD MAN & THE SEA, THE 5655-3 (SET OF 3)	OP	25.00	25.00
94	OVER THE RIVER & THROUGH THE WOODS 5654-	OP	35.00	35.00
94	PIGEONHEAD LIGHTHOUSE 5653-7	OP	50.00	50.00
94	TWO RIVERS BRIDGE 5656-1	OP	35.00	35.00
95	CHOWDER HOUSE 5657-1	OP	*	*
95	FARM ANIMALS 5658-8, (SET OF 8)	OP	32.50	33.00
95	FRESH PAINT FOR THE N.E. SIGN 5659-2	OP	20.00	20.00
95	HARVEST PUMPKIN WAGON 5659-1	OP	45.00	45.00
95	LOBSTER TRAPPER 5658-9, (SET OF 4)	OP	35.00	35.00
95	LUMBERJACKS 5659-0, (SET OF 2)	OP	30.00	30.00
95	PERCE BOAT WORKS 5657-3	OP	*	*
95	WOODBRIDGE POST OFFICE 5657-2	OP	40.00	40.00
*	**NORTH POLE COLLECTION**			
90	ELK BUNKHOUSE 4601-4	OP	40.00	40.00
90	NORTH POLE 5601-4 (SET OF 2)	OP	70.00	75.00
90	REINDEER BARN 5601-4	OP	40.00	40.00
90	SANTA'S WORKSHOP 5600-6	RT	72.00	455.00-507.00
90	TRIMMING THE NORTH POLE 5608-1	RT	10.00	25.00
91	NEENEE'S DOLLS & TOYS 5620-0	RT	37.50	78.00

YR	NAME	LIMIT	ISSUE	TREND
91	NORTH POLE SHOPS 5621-9 (SET OF 2)	RT	75.00	75.00
91	ORLEY'S BELL & HARNESS SUPPLY 5621-9	RT	37.50	50.00
91	RIMPY'S BAKERY 5621-9	RT	37.50	45.00
91	TASSY'S MITTENS/HASSEL'S WOOLIES 5622-7	RT	50.00	98.00
92	ELFIE'S SLEDS & SKATES 5625-1	OP	48.00	48.00
92	OBBIE'S BOOKS & LETRINKA'S CANDY 5624-3	OP	70.00	70.00
92	POST OFFICE 5623-5	OP	45.00	45.00
93	NORTH POLE CHAPEL 5626-0	OP	45.00	45.00
93	NORTH POLE EXPRESS DEPOT 5627-8	OP	48.00	48.00
93	NORTH POLE GATE 5632-4	OP	32.50	33.00
93	SANTA'S LOOKOUT TOWER 5629-4	OP	45.00	45.00
93	SANTA'S LOOKOUT TOWER 5629-4	OP	45.00	45.00
93	SANTA'S WOODWORKS 5628-6	OP	42.00	42.00
93	SING A SONG FOR SANTA 5631-6, (SET OF 3)	OP	28.00	28.00
93	WOODSMAN ELVES 5630-8, (SET OF 3)	RT	30.00	40.00
94	BEARD BARBER SHOP 5634-0	OP	27.50	28.00
94	DOLLS & SANTA'S BEAR WORKS 5635-9, (SET	OP	96.00	96.00
94	ELFIN SNOW CONE WORKS 5633-2	OP	40.00	40.00
94	LAST MINUTE DELIVERY	OP	*	*
94	SNOW CONE ELVES 5637-5, (SET OF 4)	OP	30.00	30.00
95	BUSY ELF SCULPS THE N. POLE SIGN 5636-6	OP	20.00	20.00
95	CHARTING SANTA'S COURSE 5636-4, (SET OF	OP	25.00	25.00
95	ELFIN FORGE & ASSEMBLY SHOP 5638-4	OP	65.00	65.00
95	ELVES' TRADE SCHOOL 5638-7	OP	*	*
95	I'LL NEED MORE TOYS 5636-5, (SET OF 2)	OP	25.00	25.00
95	SANTA'S ROOMING HOUSE 5638-6	OP	*	*
95	TIN SOLDER SHOP 5638-3	OP	42.00	42.00
95	WEATHER & TIME OBSERVATORY 5638-5	OP	50.00	50.00
*	**ORIGINAL SNOW VILLAGE COLLECTION**			
76	COUNTRY CHURCH 5004-7	RT	18.00	475.00
76	GABLED COTTAGE 5002-1	RT	20.00	475.00
76	INN, THE- 5003-9	RT	20.00	488.00
76	MOUNTAIN LODGE 5001-3	RT	20.00	618.00
76	SMALL CHALET 5006-2	RT	15.00	633.00
76	STEEPLED CHURCH 5005-4	RT	25.00	813.00
77	MANSION 5008-8	RT	30.00	650.00-715.00
77	STONE CHURCH, 10 IN. 5009-6	RT	35.00	1300.00
77	VICTORIAN HOUSE 5007-0	RT	30.00	488.00
78	CAPE COD 5013-8	RT	20.00	449.00-455.00
78	GENERAL STORE 5012-0	RT	25.00	514.00
78	HOMESTEAD 5011-2	RT	30.00	195.00-338.00
78	NANTUCKET 5014-6	RT	25.00	293.00-338.00
78	SKATING RINK & DUCK POND 5015-3 (SET)	RT	16.00	715.00
78	SMALL DOUBLE TREES 5016-1	RT	13.50	46.00-65.00
79	ADOBE HOUSE 5066-6	RT	18.00	2000.00
79	BROWNSTONE 5056-7	RT	36.00	660.00-925.00
79	COUNTRYSIDE CHURCH 5058-3	RT	27.50	384.00
79	GIANT TREES 5065-8	RT	20.00	260.00
79	KNOB HILL 5055-9	RT	30.00	488.00-553.00
79	LOG CABIN 5057-5	RT	22.00	618.00
79	MISSION CHURCH 5062-5	RT	30.00	950.00
79	MOBILE HOME 5063-3	RT	18.00	1625.00
79	SCHOOL HOUSE 5060-9	RT	30.00	442.00-455.00
79	STONE CHURCH, 8.5 IN. 5059-1	RT	22.00	1073.00
79	TUDOR HOUSE	RT	25.00	488.00-494.00
79	VICTORIAN 5054-2	RT	30.00	325.00-371.00
80	CATHEDRAL CHURCH 5067-4	RT	36.00	2990.00
80	COLONIAL FARM HOUSE 5070-9	RT	30.00	312.00
80	STONE MILL HOUSE 5068-2	RT	30.00	618.00-780.00
80	TOWN CHURCH 5071-7	RT	33.00	260.00-293.00
80	TRAIN STATION WITH 3 CARS 5085-6	RT	100.00	325.00-390.00
81	BAKERY 5077-6	RT	30.00	78.00-345.00
81	BARN 5074-1	RT	32.00	455.00-559.00
81	CORNER STORE 5076-8	RT	30.00	254.00-286.00
81	ENGLISH CHURCH 5078-4	RT	30.00	375.00
81	ENGLISH COTTAGE 5073-3	RT	25.00	423.00
81	LARGE SINGLE TREE 5080-6	RT	17.00	52.00-65.00
81	WOODEN CLAPBOARD 5072-5	RT	32.00	293.00
82	BANK 5024-5	RT	32.00	637.00
82	CARRIAGE HOUSE 5021-0	RT	28.00	358.00-364.00
82	CENTENNIAL HOUSE 5020-2	RT	32.00	442.00-455.00
82	FLOWER SHOP 5082-2	RT	25.00	488.00-553.00
82	GABLED HOUSE 5081-4	RT	30.00	429.00
82	NEW STONE CHURCH 5083-0	RT	32.00	390.00-429.00
82	PIONEER CHURCH 5022-9	RT	30.00	345.00-442.00
82	SKATING POND 5017-2	RT	25.00	390.00
82	STREET CAR 5019-9	RT	16.00	520.00
82	SWISS CHALET 5023-7	RT	28.00	715.00
83	CHATEAU 5084-9	RT	35.00	585.00
83	ENGLISH TUDOR 5033-4	RT	30.00	384.00-423.00
83	FIRE STATION 5032-6	RT	32.00	650.00-676.00
83	GINGERBREAD HOUSE 5025-3	RT	24.00	572.00
83	GOTHIC CHURCH 5028-8	RT	36.00	351.00
83	GOVERNOR'S MANSION 5003-2	RT	32.00	390.00
83	GROCERY 5001-6	RT	35.00	325.00-390.00
83	PARSONAGE 5029-6	RT	35.00	390.00-416.00
83	TOWN HALL 5000-8	RT	32.00	260.00
83	TURN OF THE CENTURY 5004-0	RT	36.00	260.00
83	VICTORIAN COTTAGE 5002-4	RT	35.00	443.00

YR	NAME	LIMIT	ISSUE	TREND
83	VILLAGE CHURCH 5026-1	RT	30.00	160.00-200.00
83	WOODEN CHURCH 5031-8	RT	30.00	520.00
84	BAYPORT 5015-6	RT	30.00	228.00
84	CONGREGATIONAL CHURCH 5034-2	RT	28.00	475.00-510.00
84	DELTA HOUSE 5012-1	RT	32.00	280.00-449.00
84	GALENA HOUSE 5009-1	RT	32.00	228.00
84	HAVERSHAM HOUSE 5008-3	RT	37.00	221.00-260.00
84	MAIN STREET HOUSE 5005-9	RT	27.00	250.00
84	NEW SCHOOL HOUSE 5037-7	RT	35.00	241.00-260.00
84	PARISH CHURCH 5039-3	RT	32.00	345.00
84	RIVER ROAD HOUSE 5010-5	RT	36.00	98.00-286.00
84	STRATFORD HOUSE 5007-5	RT	28.00	293.00
84	SUMMIT HOUSE 5036-9	RT	28.00	501.00
84	TRINITY CHURCH 5035-0	RT	32.00	358.00
85	CHURCH OF THE OPEN DOOR 5048-2	RT	34.00	117.00-241.00
85	DEPOT AND TRAIN WITH TWO TRAINS 5051-2	RT	65.00	124.00-143.00
85	DUPLEX 5050-4	RT	35.00	124.00
85	PLANTATION HOUSE 5047-4-6	RT	37.00	98.00
85	RIDGEWOOD 5052-0	RT	35.00	176.00-189.00
85	SPRUCE PLACE 50499-0	RT	33.00	260.00
85	STUCCO BUNGALOW 2045-8	RT	30.00	416.00-455.00
85	WILLIAMSBURG HOUSE 5046-6	RT	37.00	91.00-98.00
86	2101 MAPLE 5043-1	RT	32.00	416.00
86	ALL SAINTS CHURCH 5070-9	OP	38.00	60.00-90.00
86	APOTHECARY 5076-8	RT	34.00	228.00-293.00
86	BAKERY 5077-6	RT	35.00	78.00-345.00
86	BEACON HILL HOUSE 5065-2	RT	31.00	234.00-260.00
86	CARRIAGE HOUSE 5071-7	RT	29.00	124.00-130.00
86	HIGHLAND PARK HOUSE 5063-6	RT	35.00	124.00-228.00
86	LINCOLN PARK DUPLEX 5060-1	RT	33.00	160.00
86	MICKEY'S DINER 5078-4	RT	22.00	546.00-553.00
86	PACIFIC HEIGHTS HOUSE 5066-0	RT	33.00	110.00-156.00
86	RAMSEY HILL HOUSE 5067-9	RT	36.00	137.00-234.00
86	SAINT JAMES CHURCH 5068-7	RT	37.00	215.00-221.00
86	SONOMA HOUSE 5062-8	RT	33.00	156.00-260.00
86	TOY SHOP 5073-3	RT	36.00	98.00-260.00
86	TWIN PEAKS 5042-3	RT	32.00	325.00
86	WAVERLY PLACE 5041-5	RT	35.00	300.00
87	CATHEDRAL CHURCH 5019-9	RT	50.00	137.00-195.00
87	CUMBERLAND HOUSE 5024-5	RT	42.00	44.00
87	FARM HOUSE 5089-0	RT	40.00	91.00-163.00
87	FIRE STATION NO. 2 5091-1	RT	40.00	195.00-254.00
87	JEFFERSON SCHOOL 5082-2	OP	36.00	208.00
87	LIGHTHOUSE 5030-0	RT	36.00	550.00-600.00
87	RED BARN 5081-4	RT	38.00	104.00-150.00
87	SNOW VILLAGE FACTORY 5013-0	RT	45.00	130.00-280.00
87	SNOW VILLAGE RESORT LODGE 5092-0	RT	55.00	130.00-195.00
87	SPRINGFIELD HOUSE 5027-0	RT	40.00	72.00-111.00
87	ST. ANTHONY HOTEL & POST OFFICE 5006-7	RT	40.00	163.00-195.00
88	COBBLESTONE ANTIQUE SHOP 5123-3	RT	36.00	65.00-117.00
88	CORNER CAFE 5124-1	RT	37.00	163.00-263.00
88	HOME SWEET HOME/HOUSE & WINDMILL 5126-8	RT	60.00	104.00-117.00
88	KENWOOD HOUSE 5054-7	RT	50.00	130.00-260.00
88	MAPLE RIDGE INN 5121-7	RT	55.00	85.00-98.00
88	PALOS VERDES 5141-1	RT	37.50	65.00-98.00
88	REDEEMER CHURCH 5127-6	RT	42.00	65.00-91.00
88	SERVICE STATION 5128-4	RT	37.50	358.00-514.00
88	SINGLE CAR GARAGE 5125-0	RT	22.00	169.00
88	STONEHURST HOUSE 5140-3	OP	37.50	46.00-72.00
88	VILLAGE MARKET 5044-0	RT	39.00	85.00-111.00
88	VILLAGE STATION AND TRAIN 5122-5	RT	65.00	104.00-130.00
89	COLONIAL CHURCH 5119-5	RT	60.00	65.00-104.00
89	COURTHOUSE 5144-6	RT	65.00	228.00-254.00
89	DOCTOR'S HOUSE 5143-8	RT	56.00	182.00-195.00
89	J. YOUNG'S GRANARY 5149-7	RT	45.00	98.00-208.00
89	JINGLE BELLE HOUSEBOAT 5114-4	RT	42.00	104.00-111.00
89	NORTH CREEK COTTAGE 5120-9	RT	45.00	72.00-91.00
89	PARAMOUNT THEATER 5142-0	RT	42.00	195.00
89	PINEWOOD LOG CABIN 5150-0	RT	37.50	38.00
89	VILLAGE WARMING HOUSE 5145-4	RT	42.00	65.00-78.00
90	56 FLAVORS ICE CREAM PARLOR 5151-9	RT	42.00	104.00-130.00
90	MAINSTREET HARDWARE STORE 5153-5	RT	42.00	91.00-228.00
90	MORNINGSIDE HOUSE 5152-7	RT	45.00	46.00-65.00
90	PRAIRIE HOUSE 5156-0	RT	42.00	91.00-98.00
90	QUEEN ANNE VICTORIAN 5157-8	OP	48.00	48.00
90	SPANISH MISSION CHURCH 5155-1	RT	42.00	65.00-98.00
90	VILLAGE REALTY 5154-3	RT	42.00	65.00-78.00
91	CHRISTMAS SHOP, THE 5097-0	OP	37.50	38.00
91	DOUBLE BUNGALOW 5407-0	RT	45.00	59.00-78.00
91	FINKLEA'S FINERY: COSTUME SHOP 5405-4	RT	45.00	59.00-85.00
91	GOTHIC FARMHOUSE 5404-6	OP	48.00	48.00
91	HONEYMOONER MOTEL 5401-1	RT	42.00	78.00-104.00
91	JACK'S CORNER BARBER SHOP 5406-2	RT	42.00	137.00-143.00
91	OAK GROVE TUDOR 5400-3	RT	42.00	52.00-72.00
91	SOUTHERN COLONIAL 5403-8	RT	48.00	98.00-111.00
91	VILLAGE GREENHOUSE 5402-0	RT	35.00	35.00
92	AL'S TV SHOP	RT	40.00	40.00
92	CRAFTSMAN COTTAGE	RT	55.00	55.00
92	GRANDMA'S HOUSE 5420-8	OP	42.00	42.00

YR	NAME	LIMIT	ISSUE	TREND
92	HARTFORD HOUSE	RT	55.00	55.00
92	POST OFFICE 5422-4	OP	35.00	35.00
92	ST. LUKE'S CHURCH 5421-6	RT	45.00	59.00-98.00
92	VILLAGE POST OFFICE	RT	35.00	38.00
92	VILLAGE VET & PET SHOP	RT	32.00	32.00
93	DAIRY BARN 5446-1	OP	55.00	55.00
93	DINAH'S DRIVE-IN 5447-0	OP	45.00	45.00
93	HUNTING LODGE 5445-3	OP	50.00	50.00
93	MOUNT OLIVET CHURCH 5442-9	OP	65.00	65.00
93	NANTUCKET RENOVATION 5441-0	YR	55.00	65.00-72.00
93	SNOWY HILLS HOSPITAL 5448-8	OP	48.00	48.00
93	VILLAGE PUBLIC LIBRARY 5443-7	OP	55.00	55.00
93	WOODBURY HOUSE 5444-7	OP	45.00	45.00
94	FISHERMAN'S NOOK BASS CABIN 5461-5	OP	*	*
94	FISHERMAN'S NOOK CABINS (SET/2) 5461-5	OP	50.00	50.00
94	FISHERMAN'S NOOK RESORT 5460-7	OP	75.00	75.00
94	FISHERMAN'S NOOK TROUT CABIN 5461-5	OP	*	*
94	ORIGINAL SNOW VILLAGE STARTER SET, THE	OP	49.99	50.00
*	**ORIGINAL SNOW VILLAGE COLLECTION ACCESSORIES**			
79	CAROLERS 5064-1	RT	12.00	117.00-143.00
80	CERAMIC CAR 5069-0	RT	5.00	46.00-65.00
81	CERAMIC SLEIGH 5079-2	RT	5.00	52.00-72.00
82	SNOWMAN WITH BROOM 5018-0	RT	3.00	21.00
83	MONKS-A-CAROLING 6459-9	RT	6.00	65.00-91.00
84	MONKS-A-CAROLING 5040-7	RT	6.00	39.00-52.00
84	SCOTTIE WITH TREE 5038-5	RT	3.00	115.00
85	FAMILY MOM/KIDS, GOOSE/GIRL 5057-1	RT	11.00	34.00-46.00
85	SANTA/MAILBOX 5059-8	RT	11.00	34.00-52.00
85	SINGING NUNS 5053-9	RT	6.00	75.00
85	SNOW KIDS SLED & SKIS 5056-3	RT	11.00	46.00
86	GIRL/SNOWMAN BOY 5095-4	RT	11.00	59.00
86	KIDS AROUND THE TREE 5094-6	RT	15.00	34.00-46.00
86	SHOPPING GIRLS WITH PACKAGES 5096-2	RT	11.00	34.00-39.00
87	3 NUNS WITH SONGBOOKS	RT	6.00	98.00-130.00
87	CAROLING FAMILY 5105-5 (SET OF 3)	RT	25.00	26.00-39.00
87	CHILDREN IN BAND 5104-7	RT	15.00	26.00-33.00
87	CHRISTMAS CHILDREN 5107-1 (SET OF 4)	RT	20.00	26.00-29.00
87	FOR SALE SIGN 5108-0	RT	3.50	15.00-21.00
87	PRAYING MONKS 5103-9	RT	6.00	52.00-65.00
87	SNOW KIDS 5113-6 (SET OF 4)	RT	20.00	34.00-65.00
88	APPLE GIRL/NEWSPAPER BOY 5129-2	RT	11.00	21.00-26.00
88	HAYRIDE 5117-9	RT	30.00	65.00-91.00
88	SCHOOL BUS/SNOW PLOW 5137-3 (SET OF 2)	RT	16.00	85.00
88	SCHOOL CHILDREN 5118-7 (SET OF 3)	RT	15.00	21.00-29.00
88	SISAL TREE LOT 8183-3	RT	45.00	72.00-91.00
88	WATER TOWER 5133-0	RT	20.00	195.00
88	WOODSMAN AND BOY 5130-6 (SET OF 2)	RT	13.00	34.00
88	WOODY STATION WAGON 5136-5	RT	6.50	23.00-34.00
89	CALLING ALL CARS 5174-8 (SET OF 2)	CL	15.00	34.00
89	KIDS TREE HOUSE 5168-3	CL	25.00	65.00-78.00
89	MAILBOX 5179-9	RT	3.50	21.00-46.00
89	SKATE FASTER MOM 5170-5	CL	13.00	46.00
89	SPECIAL DELIVERY 5148-9 (SET OF 2)	RT	16.00	65.00-78.00
89	STATUE OF MARK TWAIN 5173-0	CL	15.00	39.00-46.00
89	THROUGH THE WOODS 5172-1 (SET OF 2)	CL	18.00	23.00-34.00
*	**VILLAGE CCP MINIATURES**			
86	CHURCH 6564-1	CL	22.50	100.00-125.00
86	ESTATE 6564-1	CL	22.50	100.00-300.00
86	VICTORIAN MINIATURES 6563-3 (SET OF 5)	CL	65.00	*
86	VICTORIAN MINIATURES 6564-1 (SET OF 2)	CL	45.00	300.00
86	WILLIAMSBURG HOUSE, BLUE 6566-8	CL	10.00	60.00
86	WILLIAMSBURG HOUSE, BROWN BRICK 6566-8	CL	10.00	40.00
86	WILLIAMSBURG HOUSE, BROWN CLPBD 6566-8	CL	10.00	40.00
86	WILLIAMSBURG HOUSE, RED 6566-8	CL	10.00	60.00
86	WILLIAMSBURG HOUSE, WHITE 6566-8	CL	10.00	40.00
86	WILLIAMSBURG SNOWHOUSE 6566-8 (SET OF 6)	CL	60.00	500.00
87	ABEL BEESLEY BUTCHER 6558-7	CL	12.00	39.00
87	BARLEY BREE FARMHOUSE 6562-5	CL	15.00	52.00
87	BEAN AND SON SMITHY SHOP 6558-7	CL	12.00	39.00
87	BLYTHE POND MILL HOUSE 6560-9	CL	16.00	36.00-45.00
87	BRICK ABBEY 6562-5	CL	15.00	65.00-169.00
87	CANDLE SHOP 6558-7	CL	12.00	46.00
87	CHESTERTON MANOR HOUSE 6562-5	CL	15.00	143.00
87	CHRISTMAS CAROL 6561-7 (SET OF 3)	CL	30.00	189.00
87	COTTAGE OF BOB CRATCHIT/TINY TIM 6561-7	CL	10.00	26.00
87	COTTAGE TOY SHOP 6591-9	CL	10.00	46.00
87	CROWNTREE INN 6558-7	CL	12.00	39.00
87	DICKENS VILLAGE CHURCH 6560-9	CL	16.00	32.00-49.00
87	DICKENS' CHADBURY STATION & TRAIN 6592-7	CL	27.50	59.00
87	DICKENS' COTTAGES 6559-5 (SET OF 3)	CL	30.00	175.00
87	DICKENS' LANE SHOPS 6591-9 (SET OF 3)	CL	30.00	117.00-189.00
87	DICKENS' VILLAGE 6558-7 (SET OF 7)	CL	72.00	312.00-345.00
87	DICKENS' VILLAGE 6560-9 (SET OF 3)	CL	48.00	*
87	DICKENS' VILLAGE 6562-5 (SET OF 4)	CL	60.00	*
87	FEZZIWIG'S WAREHOUSE 6561-7	CL	10.00	46.00-65.00
87	GOLDEN SWAN BAKER 6558-7	CL	12.00	40.00-46.00
87	GREEN GROCER 6558-7	CL	12.00	39.00
87	JONES & CO BRUSH & BASKET SHOP 6558-7	CL	12.00	40.00
87	LITTLE TOWN/BETHLEHEM 5976-5 (SET OF 12)	CL	85.00	293.00-325.00

Ruth Marion Scotch Woolens *was limited to 17,500 pieces and is part of Department 56's Dickens' Village.*

Ada's Bed and Boarding House, *from Department 56's New England Village, was issued in several colors before it was retired in 1991.*

New England Village's Timber Knoll Log Cabin *was closed by Department 56 in 1990.*

Cobles Police Station *was not embraced by Department 56 collectors who chose to believe that no crime existed in their miniature town. The piece was issued in 1990 and retired in 1991.*

Otis Hayes Butcher Shop, *a 1988 addition to New England Village, is from the "Cherry Lane Shops" set of three produced by Department 56.*

Apothecary Shop *was issued with the original seven in Department 56's New England Village set.*

YR	NAME	LIMIT	ISSUE	TREND
87	NORMAN CHURCH 6560-9	CL	16.00	163.00-182.00
87	OLD CURIOSITY SHOP, THE 6562-5	CL	15.00	59.00
87	SCROOGE & MARLEY'S COUNTINGHOUSE 6561-7	CL	10.00	46.00
87	STONE COTTAGE 6559-5	CL	10.00	169.00
87	THATCHED COTTAGE 6559-5	CL	10.00	98.00-169.00
87	THOMAS KERSEY COFFEE HOUSE 6591-9	CL	10.00	59.00
87	TUDOR COTTAGE 6559-5	CL	10.00	100.00-150.00
87	TUTTLE'S PUB 6591-9	CL	10.00	39.00
88	APOTHECARY SHOP 5935-8	CL	10.50	21.00
88	BRICK TOWN HALL 5935-8	CL	10.50	254.00-260.00
88	CRAGGY COVE LIGHTHOUSE 5937-4	CL	14.50	124.00
88	DICKENS' KENILWORTH CASTLE 6565-0	CL	30.00	137.00-182.00
88	GENERAL STORE 5935-8	CL	10.50	46.00-59.00
88	JACOB ADAMS BARN 5937-4	CL	14.50	46.00
88	JACOB ADAMS FARMHOUSE 5937-4	CL	14.50	42.00-50.00
88	LIVERY STABLE & BOOT SHOP 5935-8	CL	10.50	34.00
88	MAPLE SUGARING SHED 5937-4	CL	14.50	32.00-48.00
88	NATHANIEL BINGHAM FABRICS 5935-8	CL	10.50	59.00
88	NEW ENGLAND VILLAGE 5935-8 (SET OF 7)	CL	72.00	275.00-300.00
88	NEW ENGLAND VILLAGE 5937-4 (SET OF 6)	CL	85.00	*
88	RED SCHOOLHOUSE 5935-8	CL	10.50	98.00
88	SMYTHE WOLLEN MILL 5937-4	CL	14.50	189.00
88	STEEPLE CHURCH 5935-8	CL	10.50	40.00-120.00
88	TIMBER KNOLL LOG CABIN 5937-4	CL	14.50	30.00-42.00

DIFFERENT DRUMMER STUDIOS

*		**COLLECTOR'S CLUB MEMBERSHIP**		
95	BOSTON COMMUNITY CHURCH	*	*	*
95	FRANKFORT METHODIST CHURCH	*	*	*
95	VINCENNES CATHEDRAL	*	*	*
96	GINGERBREAD HOUSE	OP	*	*
M. NENNI			**DOOR COUNTY**	
95	AL JOHNSON'S RESTAURANT	OP	12.50	13.00
95	CUPOLA HOUSE	OP	12.50	13.00
95	GILL'S ROCK	OP	12.50	13.00
95	ICE CREAM FACTORY	OP	12.50	13.00
M. NENNI			**HISTORIC HOME SERIES V**	
95	CULBERTSON MANSION OF NEW ALBANY, IN	OP	12.50	13.00
95	ELLER HOUSE OF FISHERS, IN	OP	12.50	13.00
95	PINK LADY OF LOUISVILLE, KY	OP	12.50	13.00
*			**HISTORIC HOME SERIES VI**	
96	CRAIG HOUSE	OP	12.50	12.50
96	MY OLD KENTUCKY HOME	OP	12.50	12.50
*			**HISTORIC LIGHTHOUSE**	
96	ASSATEAQUE LIGHTHOUSE	OP	12.50	13.00
96	GRAND HAVEN LIGHTHOUSE	OP	12.50	13.00
96	HOLLAND LIGHTHOUSE	OP	12.50	12.50
96	MACKINAC POINT LIGHTHOUSE	OP	12.50	13.00
96	MISSION POINT LIGHTHOUSE	OP	12.50	12.50
96	ROUND ISLAND LIGHTHOUSE	OP	12.50	13.00
*			**MACKINAC ISLAND**	
96	CHIPPEWA HOTEL	OP	12.50	13.00
96	WINDERMERE HOTEL	OP	12.50	12.50
M. NENNI			**MACKINAC ISLAND**	
95	BAY VIEW BED-BREAKFAST	OP	12.50	13.00
95	INN ON MACKINAC	OP	12.50	13.00
M. NENNI			**MAPLE STREET**	
95	DR. HUTCHING'S OFFICE OF MADISON, IN	OP	12.50	13.00
95	HOB NOB RESTAURANT OF NASHVILLE, IN	OP	12.50	13.00
95	MOTHER OF SORROWS CHURCH OF PENINSULA, O	OP	12.50	13.00
95	WOODSTOCK OPERA HOUSE OF WOODSTOCK, IL	OP	12.50	13.00
*			**SANTA TOWN**	
96	MRS. CLAUS CONFECTIONARY	OP	13.50	13.50
96	SNOW FACTORY	OP	13.50	13.50
M. NENNI			**SANTA TOWN**	
95	ANGEL SHOP	OP	13.50	14.00
95	REINDEER STABLE	OP	13.50	14.00
95	SANTA'S HOUSE	OP	13.50	14.00
95	SANTA'S WORKSHOP	OP	13.50	14.00
95	SLEIGH SHED	OP	13.50	14.00

ENESCO

Price ranges may reflect various demands in the market from one geographic region to another; condition of piece; specific markings found on piece; and/or changes in production of piece.

S. BUTCHER			**PRECIOUS MOMENTS**	
88	THERE'S A CHRISTIAN WELCOME HERE 523011	OP	45.00	80.00
S. BUTCHER		**PRECIOUS MOMENTS SUGAR TOWN**		
92	'94 SUGAR TOWN HOUSE COLL. SET 531773	OP	189.00	200.00
92	LIGHTED CHAPEL 529621	OP	85.00	90.00

FORMA VITRUM

B. JOB				
95	CONFECTIONER'S COTTAGE	RT	*	*
B. JOB			**COASTAL CLASSICS**	
95	BAYSIDE BEACON	OP	65.00	65.00
96	CAPE HOPE	OP	100.00	100.00
96	COZY COTTAGE	OP	70.00	70.00

YR	NAME	LIMIT	ISSUE	TREND
	B. JOB			**COASTAL HERITAGE**
95	CAPE NEDDICK ME	OP	140.00	140.00
95	MARBLEHEAD, OH	YR	75.00	75.00
95	NORTH HEAD, WA	YR	100.00	100.00
95	OLD POINT LOMA, CA	YR	100.00	100.00
95	PORTLAND HEAD, ME	YR	140.00	140.00
95	SANDY HOOK, NJ	3759	140.00	140.00
95	ST. SIMONS, GA	YR	120.00	120.00
96	CAPE HATTERAS, NC	3867	120.00	120.00
96	FIRE ISLAND, NY	2996	150.00	150.00
96	NEW LONDON, CT	2996	145.00	145.00
96	PEGGY'S COVE, NS	2500	75.00	75.00
96	PIGEON POINT, CA	2996	125.00	125.00
96	SPLIT ROCK, MN	2996	130.00	130.00
96	ST. AUGUSTINE, FL	2996	130.00	130.00
	B. JOB			**VITREVILLE**
95	BROOKVIEW BED & BREAKFAST	1250	295.00	700.00
95	FIRE STATION	OP	100.00	100.00
95	MAYOR'S MANOR MUSICAL	OP	95.00	95.00
95	MILLER'S MILL	OP	115.00	115.00
96	KRAMER BUILDING	OP	100.00	100.00

GENESIS DESIGNS

YR	NAME	LIMIT	ISSUE	TREND
	M. MORRIS			**BETHLEHEM VILLAGE**
92	BETHLEHEM STABLE	*	72.00	72.00
92	MARKETPLACE	*	66.00	66.00
92	PEASANT HOUSE	*	46.00	46.00
	M. MORRIS			**CASCADES**
93	ALMOST PARADISE - CENTRAL	*	46.50	47.00
	M. MORRIS			**CENTRAL OREGON**
93	MT. BACHELOR SKIER	*	26.00	26.00
	M. MORRIS			**COLUMBIA RIVER**
93	MULTNOMAH FALLS LODGE - 1925	*	58.00	58.00
	M. MORRIS			**JESUS' WORLD**
92	EMPLY TOMB	*	72.00	72.00
	M. MORRIS			**NORTHWEST**
94	TIMBERLINE LODGE - 1938	*	68.00	68.00
94	WINTER TIMBERLING LODGE - 1938	*	68.00	68.00
95	CRATER LAKE LODGE	3000	74.00	74.00
96	OLD FAITHFUL INN - YELLOWSTONE	3000	90.00	90.00
	M. MORRIS			**OREGON COAST**
94	HECETA HEAD LIGHTHOUSE	RT	60.00	60.00
94	LIGHTKEEPER'S COTTAGE	*	60.00	60.00
95	COQUILLE RIVER LIGHTHOUSE	3000	60.00	60.00
96	TILLAMOOK ROCK LIGHTHOUSE	3000	70.00	70.00
96	YAQUINA BAY LIGHTHOUSE	3000	60.00	60.00
	M. MORRIS			**PATRIARCHS, THE**
92	NOAH'S ARK	*	46.50	47.00
93	ABRAHAM AT THE OAKS	*	60.00	60.00
	M. MORRIS			**WILDLIFE**
95	REX NANOOK	OP	78.00	78.00

GOEBEL INC.

Price ranges may reflect various demands in the market from one geographic region to another; condition of piece; specific markings found on piece; and/or changes in production of piece.

YR	NAME	LIMIT	ISSUE	TREND
	M.I. HUMMEL			**BAVARIAN VILLAGE COLLECTION**
96	ANGEL'S DUET	*	50.00	50.00
96	BENCH & PINE TREE, THE/SET	*	25.00	25.00
96	CHRISTMAS MAIL	*	50.00	50.00
96	COMPANY'S COMING	*	50.00	50.00
96	SLED & PINE TREE, THE/SET	*	25.00	25.00
96	VILLAGE BAKERY, THE	*	50.00	50.00
96	VILLAGE BRIDGE, THE	*	25.00	25.00
96	WINTER'S COMFORT	*	50.00	50.00
96	WISHING WELL, THE	*	25.00	25.00

HADLEY COMPANIES

YR	NAME	LIMIT	ISSUE	TREND
	T. REDLIN			**HOMESTEAD COLLECTION**
95	COMFORTS OF HOME	45 DAYS	90.00	90.00
96	EVENING WITH FRIENDS	45 DAYS	90.00	90.00

HARBOUR LIGHTS

YR	NAME	LIMIT	ISSUE	TREND
95	SELKIRK, NY	9500	75.00	75.00
	*			**GREAT COAST REGION**
95	BILOXI, MS 149	5500	60.00	60.00
95	BOLIVAR, TX 146	5500	70.00	70.00
95	NEW CANAL, LA 148	5500	65.00	65.00
95	PENSACOLA, FL 150	9000	80.00	80.00
95	PORT ISABEL, TX 147	5500	65.00	65.00
	*			**GREAT LAKES REGION**
91	FORT NIAGARA, NY 113	RT	60.00	63.00
91	SAND ISLAND, WS 112	5500	60.00	64.00
92	BUFFALO, NY 122	RT	60.00	62.00
92	CANA ISLAND, WI 119	RT	60.00	66.00
92	GROSSE POINT, NY	5500	60.00	62.00
92	MARBLEHEAD, OH 121	RT	50.00	110.00
92	MICHIGAN CITY, IN 123	5500	60.00	62.00

YR	NAME	LIMIT	ISSUE	TREND
92	OLD MACKINAC POINT, MI 118	RT	65.00	125.00
92	SPLIT ROCK, MI 124	RT	60.00	1500.00
92	SPLIT ROCK, MN 124	RT	60.00	120.00
94	HOLLAND (BIG RED), MI 142	RT	60.00	155.00
95	ROUND ISLAND, MI 153	9500	66.00	85.00
95	TAWAS PT., MI 152	5500	75.00	75.00
95	WIND POINT, WS 154	9500	78.00	78.00
*	**GREAT LIGHTHOUSES OF THE WORLD**			
94	CAPE HATTERAS, NC 401	OP	50.00	50.00
*	**HARBOUR LIGHTS COLLECTOR'S SOCIETY**			
95	POINT FERMIN, CA 501	YR	80.00	80.00
*	**NORTHEAST REGION**			
91	BOSTON HARBOR, MA 117	RT	60.00	135.00
91	CASTLE HILL, RI 116	5500	60.00	60.00
91	GREAT CAPTAIN'S ISLAND, CT 114	RT	60.00	66.00
91	SANDY HOOK, NJ 104	RT	60.00	180.00
91	WEST QUODDY HEAD, ME 103	RT	60.00	140.00
92	MINOT'S LEDGE, MA 131	RT	60.00	60.00
92	NAUSET, MA 126	RT	66.00	150.00
92	NEW LONDON LEDGE, CT 129	RT	66.00	155.00
92	PORTLAND BREAKWATER, ME 130	RT	60.00	60.00
92	PORTLAND HEAD, ME 125	RT	66.00	275.00
92	SOUTHEAST BLOCK ISLAND, RI 128	RT	71.00	185.00
92	WHALEBACK, NH 127	5500	60.00	60.00
93	BARNEGAT, NJ 139	RT	60.00	150.00
94	CAPE NEDDICK (NUBBLE), ME 141	RT	66.00	165.00
94	MONTAUK, NY 143	RT	85.00	190.00
95	BRANT POINT, MA 162	9500	*	*
95	HIGHLAND, MA 161	9500	*	*
*	**SOUTHEAST REGION**			
91	CAPE HATTERAS, NC 102 W/ HOUSE	RT	60.00	3900.00
92	CAPE HATTERAS, NC 102R	RT	60.00	675.00
93	HILTON HEAD, SC 136	RT	60.00	185.00
93	KEY WEST, FL 134	RT	60.00	120.00
93	OCRACOKE, NC 135	RT	60.00	62.00
93	PONCE DE LEON, FL 132	RT	60.00	160.00
93	ST. AUGUSTINE, FL 138	RT	71.00	145.00
93	ST. SIMMONS, GA 137	RT	66.00	160.00
93	TYBEE, GA 133	RT	60.00	135.00
94	ASSATEAGUE, VA 145- MOLD ONE	RT	69.00	575.00
94	ASSATEAGUE, VA 145- MOLD TWO	RT	69.00	75.00
95	JUPITER, FL 151	9500	77.00	77.00
*	**SPECIAL EDITIONS**			
95	CHRISTMAS 1995 - BIG BAY POINT, MI 700	5000	75.00	125.00
95	LEGACY LIGHT 601	OP	65.00	65.00
*	**STAMP SERIES**			
95	FIVE PIECE MATCHED NUMBERED SET 400	OP	275.00	275.00
95	MARBLEHEAD, OH 413	OP	50.00	50.00
95	SPECTACLE REEF, MI 410	OP	60.00	60.00
95	SPLIT ROCK, MN 412	OP	60.00	60.00
95	ST. JOSEPH, MI 411	OP	60.00	60.00
95	THIRTY MILE POINT, NY 414	OP	62.00	62.00
*	**WESTERN REGION**			
91	ADMIRALITY HEAD, WA 101 MISSPELLED	RT	60.00	125.00
91	ADMIRALTY HEAD, WA 101	RT	60.00	125.00
91	BURROWS ISLAND, OR 108 MISSPELLED	RT	60.00	670.00
91	BURROWS ISLAND, WA 108	RT	60.00	155.00
91	CAPE BLANCO, OR 109	5500	60.00	60.00
91	COQUILLE RIVER, OR 111	RT	60.00	2400.00
91	NORTH HEAD, WA 106	5500	60.00	60.00
91	OLD POINT LOMA, CA 105	RT	60.00	145.00
91	ST. GEORGE'S REEF, CA 115	5500	60.00	60.00
91	UMPQUA RIVER, OR 107	5500	60.00	60.00
91	YAQUINA HEAD, WA 110	5500	60.00	62.00
94	DIAMOND HEAD, HI 140	RT	60.00	145.00
94	HECETA HEAD, OR 144	5500	60.00	72.00
95	PT. ARENA, CA 156	9500	60.00	80.00

HAWTHORNE

YR	NAME	LIMIT	ISSUE	TREND
*	**ANNE OF GREEN GABLES**			
*	GREEN GABLES W/ANNE 79151	*	49.95	50.00
*	**BEACONS OF FREEDOM/ILLUMINATED**			
95	PORTLAND HEAD LIGHTHOUSE 79181	*	39.90	40.00
95	WEST QUODDY HEAD LIGHTHOUSE 79182	*	39.90	40.00
K./H. LEVAN	**CHESTNUT HILL STATION**			
93	CHESTNUT HILL DEPOT 78253	CL	29.90	30.00
93	PARKSIDE CAFE 78252	CL	29.90	30.00
93	WISHING WELL COTTAGE 78251	CL	29.90	30.00
94	BICYCLE SHOP 78254	CL	29.90	30.00
*	**CHRISTMAS IN BEDFORD FALLS/ILLUMINATED**			
*	BAILY BROS. BUILDING & LOAN 79392	*	39.90	40.00
95	OLD GRANVILLE PLACE, THE 79391	*	39.90	40.00
*	**CLASSIC BALLPARKS**			
95	WRIGLEY FIELD-ERNIE BANKS 78461	*	99.95	100.00
*	**COLONIAL CHRISTMAS/ILLUMINATED**			
*	BRUTON PARISH CHURCH, THE 79463	*	39.90	40.00
95	MARGARET HUNTER'S SHOP 79462	*	39.90	40.00

YR	NAME	LIMIT	ISSUE	TREND
95	MARKET SQUARE TAVERN/FREE SIGN 79461	*	39.90	40.00
K./H. LEVAN	**CONCORD: HOMETOWN OF AMERICA LITERATURE**			
91	HAWTHORNE'S WAYSIDE RETREAT 78221	CL	39.90	40.00
92	EMERSON'S OLD MANSE 78222	CL	39.90	40.00
93	ALCOTT'S ORCHARD HOUSE 78223	CL	39.90	40.00
*	**CONNIE LAYTON'S VICTORIANA**			
95	MAY COTTAGE 78971	*	29.95	30.00
*	**CURRIER & IVES SUMMER**			
95	AMERICAN HOMESTEAD SUMMER 78731	*	29.90	30.00
95	HOME ON THE MISSISSIPPI 78732	*	29.90	30.00
*	**CURRIER & IVES: THE ART OF AMERICA**			
94	AMERICAN HOMESTEAD WINTER 78281	*	29.90	30.00
95	A COLD MORNING 78288	*	29.90	30.00
95	EARLY WINTER 78286	*	29.90	30.00
95	FEEDING THE CHICKENS 78283	*	29.90	30.00
95	OLD GRIST MILL, THE 78284	*	29.90	30.00
95	SNOW STORM 78282	*	29.90	30.00
95	WINTER EVENING 78285	*	29.90	30.00
95	WINTER MOONLIGHT 78287	*	29.90	30.00
K./H. LEVAN	**GONE WITH THE WIND**			
92	TARA...SCARLETT'S PRIDE 78171	CL	39.90	40.00
92	TWELEVE OAKS...THE ROMANCE 78172	CL	39.90	40.00
93	AGAINST HER WILL 78174	CL	42.90	43.00
93	MESSAGE FOR CAPT. BUTLER 78175	CL	42.90	43.00
93	RHETT'S RETURN 78173	CL	39.90	40.00
93	TARA 79421	CL	39.90	40.00
94	ALONE 78178	CL	45.90	46.00
94	ATLANTA CHURCH 79423	CL	39.90	40.00
94	HOPE FOR A NEW TOMORROW 78176	CL	42.90	43.00
94	I HAVE DONE ENOUGH 78180	CL	45.90	46.00
94	KENNEDY STORE 79424	*	39.90	40.00
94	RED HORSE SALOON 79425	*	39.90	40.00
94	SWEPT AWAY 78177	CL	45.90	46.00
94	TAKE ME TO TARA 78179	CL	45.90	46.00
94	TWELVE OAKS 79422	*	39.90	40.00
95	ASHLEY'S SAFE 78183	CL	45.90	46.00
95	BUTLER'S MANSION 79426	*	39.90	40.00
95	DIGNITY AND RESPECT 78182	CL	45.90	46.00
95	REVENGE ON SHANTY TOWN 78181	*	45.90	46.00
*	**GONE WITH THE WIND ACCESSORIES**			
95	BARBEQUE, THE 91253	*	24.90	25.00
95	BUTLERS, THE 91255	*	24.90	25.00
95	HELPING THE WOUNDED 91250	*	24.90	25.00
95	O'HARAS, THE 91252	*	24.90	25.00
95	RHETT & SCARLETT 91254	*	24.90	25.00
95	SCARLETT & ASHLEY 91251	*	24.90	25.00
*	**GONE WITH THE WIND MINIATURES**			
*	ASHLEY'S SAFE/TRAIN STATION	*	30.00	30.00
*	MESSAGE FOR CAPT. BUTLER/HOPE 78663	*	30.00	30.00
*	REVENGE/DIGNITY & RESPECT 78666	*	30.00	30.00
*	RHETT'S RETURN/AGAINST HER WILL 78662	*	30.00	30.00
*	SPRINGHOUSE/CARRIAGE HOUSE 78668	*	30.00	30.00
*	SWEPT AWAY/ALONE 78664	*	30.00	30.00
*	TAKE ME TO TARA/DONE ENOUGH 78665	*	30.00	30.00
*	TARA MILL/STABLE 78669	*	30.00	30.00
95	SCARLETT'S PRIDE/ROMANCE 78661	*	29.95	30.00
K./H. LEVAN	**GONE WITH THE WIND SPECIAL EDITIONS**			
94	BURNING OF ATLANTA 78185	10000	79.95	80.00
95	BUTLER MANSION, THE 78186	10000	80.00	80.00
*	**HAWTHORNE MINIATURE NATIVITY**			
95	NATIVITY 91010	*	39.90	40.00
95	PALM TREES 91018	*	24.90	25.00
95	SITTING CAMELS, BLESSED BEASTS/MARY'S DO	*	24.90	25.00
95	STABLE KEEPER & STANDING CAMEL 91016	*	24.90	25.00
*	**HELEN STEINER RICE ACCESSORIES**			
95	BOY W/LANTERN 91301	*	19.90	20.00
95	GIRL SNOWANGEL 91302	*	19.90	20.00
95	LAMPS 91303	*	19.90	20.00
*	**HELEN STEINER RICE: WINDOWS OF GOLD**			
94	INSPIRATION POINT LIGHTHOUSE 79541	*	34.90	35.00
94	PEACE ON FAITH 79542	*	39.90	40.00
94	WINTERS WARMTH 79543	*	39.90	40.00
*	**HERSHEY, PA: AN AMERICAN DREAM COME TRUE**			
95	BIRTHPLACE OF MILTON HERSHEY 78951	CL	29.90	30.00
95	DERRY CHURCH SCHOOL 78952	*	29.90	30.00
*	**HOMETOWN AMERICA**			
92	EVERGREEN COTTAGE 83601	*	34.95	35.00
93	EVERGREEN VALLEY SCHOOL 83602	CL	34.95	35.00
93	VILLAGE BAKERY, THE 83603	CL	37.95	38.00
94	EVERGREEN GENERAL STORE 83606	*	39.95	40.00
94	EVERGREEN VALLEY CHURCH 83605	*	38.00	38.00
94	WOODCUTTER'S REST 83604	*	38.00	38.00
95	WAITING FOR SANTA 83607	*	40.00	40.00
*	**HUMMEL ACCESSORIES**			
95	LARGE TREE/SLED 91312	*	24.90	25.00
95	SMALL TREE/BENCH 91313	*	24.90	25.00
95	VILLAGE BRIDGE 91310	*	24.90	24.90

YR	NAME	LIMIT	ISSUE	TREND
95	WISHING WELL 91311	*	24.90	25.00
*		**HUMMEL'S BAVARIAN CHRISTMAS**		
*	ALL ABOARD 79287	*	49.90	50.00
*	LITTLE BOOTMAKER 79288	*	49.90	50.00
*	OFF FOR THE HOLIDAYS 79286	*	49.90	50.00
94	ANGEL'S DUET 79281	*	49.90	50.00
94	BAKERY, THE 79282	*	49.90	50.00
95	COMPANY'S COMING 79283	*	49.90	50.00
95	POST OFFICE 79285	*	49.90	50.00
95	WINTER'S COMFORT 79284	*	49.90	50.00
K./H. LEVAN		**INSIDE GONE WITH THE WIND**		
*	WILKES LIBRARY 78582	*	39.90	40.00
94	PRIDE AND PASSION 78581	*	39.90	40.00
*		**KINKADE'S HOME FOR THE HOLIDAYS**		
*	MOONLIT VILLAGE CHURCH 78022	*	30.00	30.00
*	VICTORIAN CHRISTMAS 78021	*	29.95	30.00
*		**KINKADE'S LAMPLIGHT VILLAGE**		
96	KINKADE'S COTTAGE 78321	*	29.95	30.00
*		**LAS VEGAS**		
*	FLAMINGO, THE 79091	*	49.95	50.00
*	HARRAH'S 79092	*	50.00	50.00
R. BROUILETTE		**LOST VICTORIANS OF OLD SAN FRANCISCO**		
91	GRANDE DAME OF NOB HILL 78111	CL	34.90	35.00
92	EMPRESS OF RUSSIAN HILL 78112	CL	34.90	35.00
93	PRINCESS OF PACIFIC HEIGHTS 78113	CL	34.90	35.00
*		**MARTY BELL'S MARTHA'S VINEYARD**		
*	SUMMERLAND 79891	*	39.95	40.00
*		**MAYBERRY**		
94	COURTHOUSE, THE 79721	*	39.90	40.00
94	FLOYD'S BARBER SHOP 79722	*	39.90	40.00
94	MAYBERRY METHODIST CHURCH 79725	*	39.90	40.00
94	POST OFFICE 79726	*	39.90	40.00
94	TAYLOR HOME, THE 79724	*	39.90	40.00
94	WALLY'S FILLING STATION 79723	*	39.90	40.00
*		**MAYBERRY ACCESSORIES**		
95	ANDY & BARNEY 91350	*	21.90	22.00
95	AUNT BEE & OPIE 91351	*	21.90	22.00
95	PATROL CAR & GAS PUMPS 91352	*	21.90	22.00
*		**MCMEMORIES**		
95	MCDONALD'S RESTAURANT 31901	*	39.95	40.00
*		**NORTH POLE ACCESSORIES**		
94	GETTING READY FOR CHRISTMAS 91203	*	23.90	24.00
94	LETTERS FOR SANTA SET 91202	*	23.90	24.00
94	SANTA'S HELPER'S SET 91200	CL	23.90	24.00
94	SWEET DELIGHTS SET 91201	*	23.90	24.00
95	COOKIES FOR KIDDIES 91204	*	23.90	24.00
G. HOOVER		**P.O. #1, NORTH POLE**		
94	SANTA'S POST OFFICE 79102	*	39.90	40.00
94	SANTA'S TOY SHOPPE W/SIGN 79101	*	39.90	40.00
95	SANTA'S CANDY SHOP 79103	*	39.90	40.00
95	SANTA'S GIFT WRAP CENTRAL 79104	CL	39.90	40.00
K./H. LEVAN		**PEACEABLE KINGDOM**		
93	SQUIRE BOONE'S HOMESTEAD 78561	*	34.90	35.00
94	WHITE HOUSE INN 48562	*	34.90	35.00
*		**PEPPERCRICKET GROVE**		
*	BUDZEN'S ROADSIDE FOOD STORE 78784	*	49.90	50.00
95	EVENING SLED RIDE 78783	*	49.90	50.00
95	PEPPERCRICKET FARM 78781	*	49.90	50.00
95	VIRGINIA'S NEST 78782	*	49.90	50.00
*		**ROCKWELL'S FOUR FREEDOMS/ILLUMINATED**		
*	DOCTOR'S COUNTRY HOME 79947	*	39.90	40.00
*	FREEDOM FROM WANT: THE FARMHOUSE 79944	*	39.90	40.00
*	FREEDOM IS KNOWLEDGE: THE LIBRARY 79945	*	39.90	40.00
*	SCHOOL, THE 79946	*	39.90	40.00
94	FREEDOM FROM FEAR: THE ROCKWELL HOMESTEA	*	39.90	40.00
94	FREEDOM OF WORSHIP: ARLINGTON CHURCH 799	*	39.90	40.00
95	FREEDOM OF SPEECH: TOWN HALL 79943	*	39.90	40.00
*		**ROCKWELL'S HEART OF STOCKBRIDGE/ILLUMINATED**		
95	BELL TOWER 79235	*	39.90	40.00
95	CHURCH ON THE GREEN 79234	*	39.90	40.00
95	FIREHOUSE 79233	*	39.90	40.00
95	ROCKWELL'S HOME 79231	*	39.90	40.00
95	ROCKWELL'S STUDIO 79232	*	39.90	40.00
*		**ROCKWELL'S HOME FOR THE HOLIDAYS**		
92	BRINGING HOME THE TREE 78122	CL	34.90	35.00
92	BRINGING HOME THE TREE 82292	CL	34.90	35.00
92	CAROLERS IN THE CHURCHYARD 78123	*	37.90	38.00
92	CAROLERS IN THE CHURCHYARD 82293	CL	37.90	38.00
92	CHRISTMAS EVE AT THE STUDIO 78121	CL	34.90	35.00
92	CHRISTMAS EVE AT THE STUDIO 82291	CL	34.95	35.00
93	A ROOM AT THE INN 78127	*	39.90	40.00
93	A ROOM AT THE INN 82297	*	39.90	40.00
93	LETTERS TO SANTA 78128	*	39.90	40.00
93	LETTERS TO SANTA 82298	*	39.90	40.00
93	OVER THE RIVER 78125	CL	37.90	38.00
93	OVER THE RIVER 82295	CL	37.90	38.00

Weston Train Station *was out for a full year before Department 56 finally issued a train. The piece was retired in 1989.*

Guilford Lodge *from the "Gatehouse Collection" was produced in a limited edition of 400 by Patrick Gates for J.P. Editions.*

School Days is *from the "American Landmarks" collection by Lilliput Lane.*

Jacob Adams Farmhouse & Barn *are from the Dickens' Village produced by Department 56.*

YR	NAME	LIMIT	ISSUE	TREND
93	SCHOOL'S OUT 78126	CL	39.90	40.00
93	SCHOOL'S OUT 82296	CL	37.90	38.00
93	THREE-DAY PASS 78124	*	37.90	38.00
93	THREE-DAY PASS 82294	*	37.90	38.00
94	A GOLDEN MEMORY 78131	CL	41.90	42.00
94	A WHITE CHRISTMAS 78129	CL	41.90	42.00
94	A WHITE CHRISTMAS 82299	CL	41.90	42.00
94	LATE FOR THE DANCE 78130	*	41.90	42.00
94	LATE FOR THE DANCE 82300	*	41.90	42.00
95	A GOLDEN MEMORY 82301	CL	41.90	42.00
95	READY & WAITING 82302	CL	41.90	42.00
95	READY & WRITING 78132	CL	41.90	42.00
*	**ROCKWELL'S HOMETOWN COLLECTION**			
*	BELL TOWER, THE 82283	CL	36.95	37.00
90	ROCKWELL'S RESIDENCE 82281	CL	34.95	35.00
91	CHURCH ON THE GREEN, THE 82285	CL	39.95	40.00
91	FIRE HOUSE, THE 82284	CL	36.95	37.00
91	GREY STONE CHURCH 82282	CL	34.95	35.00
92	BERKSHIRE PLAYHOUSE 82288	CL	43.00	43.00
92	CITIZEN'S HALL 82287	CL	42.95	43.00
92	MISSION HOUSE, THE 82289	CL	43.00	43.00
92	OLD CORNER HOUSE, THE 82290	CL	43.00	43.00
92	TOWNE HALL 82286	CL	40.00	40.00
93	PARSONAGE COTTAGE 82207	CL	43.00	43.00
93	PLAIN SCHOOL 82206	CL	43.00	43.00
93	TRAIN STATION 82208	CL	43.00	43.00
94	OLD RECTORY 82209	CL	43.00	43.00
*	**ROCKWELL'S MAIN STREET**			
93	ANTIQUE SHOP 79843	*	29.90	30.00
93	BANK, THE 79845	*	29.90	30.00
93	COUNTRY STORE, THE 79842	*	29.90	30.00
93	LIBRARY, THE 79846	*	29.90	30.00
93	RED LION INN, THE 79847	*	29.90	30.00
93	ROCKWELL'S STUDIO 79841	*	29.90	30.00
93	STOCKBRIDGE SIGN 79840	CL	10.00	10.00
93	TOWN OFFICES, THE 79844	*	29.90	30.00
*	**ROCKWELL'S NEIGHBORHOOD**			
94	FIDO'S NEW HOME 78482	*	29.90	30.00
94	LEMONADE STAND, THE 78481	*	29.90	30.00
94	SIDEWALK SPEEDSTER 78483	*	29.90	30.00
*	**ROCKWELL'S SEASONS IN STOCKBRIDGE**			
*	COUNTRY STORE/ROCKWELL STUDIO 78823	*	30.00	30.00
*	FIREHOUSE/OLD CORNER HOUSE 78822	*	30.00	30.00
95	ROCKWELL RESIDENCE/ANTIQUE SHOP 78821	*	29.95	30.00
*	**SPRINGTIME ON MAIN STREET**			
93	ROCKWELL'S STUDIO 78381	*	29.95	30.00
K./H. LEVAN	**STONEFIELD VALLEY**			
92	CHURCH IN THE GLEN 78444	CL	37.90	38.00
92	MEADOWBROOK SCHOOL 78442	CL	34.90	35.00
92	SPRINGBRIDGE COTTAGE 78441	CL	34.90	35.00
92	WEAVER'S COTTAGE 78443	CL	37.90	38.00
93	FERRYMAN'S COTTAGE 78447	CL	39.90	40.00
93	HILLSIDE COTTAGE 78446	CL	39.90	40.00
93	PARSON'S COTTAGE 78445	CL	37.90	38.00
93	VALLEY VIEW FARM 78448	CL	39.90	40.00
K./H. LEVAN	**STROLLING THROUGH COLONIAL AMERICA**			
91	EASTBROOK CHURCH 78004	CL	37.90	38.00
91	HIGGIN'S GRIST MILL 78003	CL	37.90	38.00
91	JEFFERSON'S ORDINAIRE 78001	CL	34.90	35.00
91	MILLRACE STORE 78002	CL	34.90	35.00
92	CAPT. LEE'S GRAMMAR SCHOOL 78006	CL	39.90	40.00
92	COURTHOUSE ON THE GREEN 78005	CL	37.90	38.00
92	EVERETT'S JOINER SHOP 78008	CL	39.90	40.00
92	VILLAGE SMITHY, THE 78007	CL	39.90	40.00
K./H. LEVAN	**SUNSET COVE**			
94	WATERCOLOR COTTAGE 78051	*	34.90	35.00
95	ARTISTS DELIGHT 78052	*	34.90	35.00
K./H. LEVAN	**TARA: THE ONLY THING WORTH FIGHTING FOR**			
93	A DREAM REMEMBERED 78621	*	29.90	30.00
94	CARRIAGE HOUSE 78623	*	29.90	30.00
94	KITCHEN AND GATEWAY 78624	CL	29.90	30.00
94	MILL, THE 78625	*	29.90	30.00
94	SPRINGHOUSE AND HIDEAWAY 78622	CL	29.90	30.00
95	STABLE, THE 78626	*	29.90	30.00
*	**THATCHER'S CROSSING**			
93	CHAPEL CROSSING 78763	CL	29.90	30.00
93	MIDSUMMER'S COTTAGE 78762	CL	29.90	30.00
93	ROSE ARBOUR COTTAGE 78761	CL	29.90	30.00
94	WOODCUTTER'S COTTAGE 78764	CL	29.90	30.00
*	**THOMAS KINKADE'S CANDLELIGHT COTTAGES**			
92	OLDE PORTERFIELD TEA ROOM 78151	*	24.90	24.90
93	CHANDLER'S COTTAGE 78152	*	24.90	24.90
93	MERRITT'S COTTAGE 78154	*	27.90	28.00
93	SWANBROOKE COTTAGE 78153	*	24.90	25.00
94	CANDLELIT COTTAGE 78157	*	29.90	30.00
94	SEASIDE COTTAGE 78155	*	27.90	28.00
94	SWEETHEART COTTAGE 78156	*	29.90	30.00

YR	NAME	LIMIT	ISSUE	TREND
95	CEDAR NOOK COTTAGE 78158	*	29.90	30.00
*	**THOMAS KINKADE'S CANDLELIGHT COTTAGES/ILLUMINATED**			
93	CHANDLER'S COTTAGE 79002	CL	29.90	30.00
93	OLD PORTERFIELD TEA ROOM 79001	CL	29.90	30.00
*	**THOMAS KINKADE'S CHRISTMAS MEMORIES**			
95	HOME BEFORE CHRISTMAS 78876	*	34.90	35.00
95	HOME TO GRANDMA'S 78872	*	34.90	35.00
95	HOMESPUN HOLIDAY 78875	*	34.90	35.00
95	OLD PORTERFIELD GIFT & SHOPPE 78871	*	34.90	35.00
95	SILENT NIGHT 78873	*	34.90	35.00
95	STONEHEARTH HUTCH 78877	*	34.90	35.00
95	WARMTH OF HOME 78874	*	34.90	35.00
*	**THOMAS KINKADE'S ENCHANTED CHRISTMAS**			
*	COTTAGE BY THE SEA 78876	*	29.90	30.00
*	SWEETHEARTS COTTAGE 78885	*	29.90	30.00
95	HEATHER'S HUTCH 78884	*	29.90	30.00
95	JULIANNE'S COTTAGE 78882	*	29.90	30.00
95	MCKENNA'S COTTAGE 78881	*	29.90	30.00
95	MILLER'S COTTAGE 78883	*	29.90	30.00
*	**THOMAS KINKADE'S LAMPLIGHT LANE**			
95	KINKADE'S COTTAGE 79051	*	49.90	50.00
*	**THOMAS KINKADE'S ST. NICHOLAS CIRCLE/ILLUMINATED**			
93	TOWN HALL 79681	*	39.90	40.00
94	EVERGREEN APOTHECARY 79687	CL	39.90	40.00
94	FIREHOUSE, THE 79686	CL	39.90	40.00
94	HOLLY HOUSE INN 79688	CL	39.90	40.00
94	KRINGLE BROS. 79684	CL	39.90	40.00
94	MRS. C'S BAKERY 79685	CL	39.90	40.00
94	NOEL CHAPEL 79682	*	39.90	40.00
94	S.C. TOYMAKER 79683	*	39.90	40.00
K./H. LEVAN	**VICTORIA GROVE**			
92	LILAC COTTAGE 78331	CL	34.90	35.00
92	ROSE HAVEN 78332	CL	34.90	35.00
93	CHERRY BLOSSOM 78333	CL	34.90	35.00
*	**VILLAGE ACCESSORIES**			
94	BRINGING HOME THE TREE SET 91000	*	21.90	22.00
94	CHRISTMAS SHOPPING SET 91002	*	21.90	22.00
94	DECORATING THE TREE SET 91006	*	21.90	22.00
94	GREETINGS & GAMES SET 91001	*	21.90	22.00
94	NORMAN ROCKWELL & TRIO OF CAROLLERS 9100	*	21.90	22.00
94	OLD FASHIONED STREET LIGHTS SET 91700	*	21.90	22.00
94	ROARING ROADSTERS SET 91500	*	21.90	22.00
94	SHOPKEEPER & TRAVELERS SET	*	21.90	22.00
94	SKATING POND, THE 91007	*	23.90	24.00
94	SLIPPING & SLIDING SET	*	21.90	22.00
94	SNOW COVERED EVERGREENS SET 91600	*	21.90	22.00
94	WILLAGE VEHICLES SET 91502	*	21.90	22.00
94	WINTAGE V-8S SET 91502	*	21.90	22.00
95	AUTUMN TREES 91022	*	29.90	30.00
95	BACKYARD BARBEQUE 91019	*	21.90	22.00
95	COUNTRY FARMSTAND 91020	*	29.90	30.00
95	EARLY MORNING DELIVERY 91013	*	21.90	22.00
95	FIRE DRILL 91025	*	23.90	24.00
95	HOLIDAY MAIL 91011	*	21.90	22.00
95	LAST DAY OF SCHOOL BEFORE CHRISTMAS 9101	*	21.90	22.00
95	LAUNDRY DAY 91024	*	21.90	22.00
95	OUT FOR A STROLL 91015	*	21.90	22.00
95	PICKING OUT A PUMPKIN 91021	*	39.90	40.00
95	REFRESHMENTS 91014	*	21.90	22.00
95	SIDEWALK SELLERS 91009	*	21.90	22.00
95	SNOWMAN & TREE SET 91008	*	21.90	22.00
95	SUMMER TREES 91023	*	21.90	22.00
96	VILLAGE CLOCK 91701	*	21.90	21.90
*	**WIZARD OF OZ**			
95	JOURNEY BEGINS, THE 78891	*	149.50	150.00
*	**WYSOCKI SMALL TOWN CHRISTMAS**			
95	YE VERY OLDE FRUITCAKE SHOPPE 79121	*	39.95	40.00

JAN'S ORIGINALS

YR	NAME	LIMIT	ISSUE	TREND
J. BENSON	**BATESBURG, SOUTH CAROLINA SERIES**			
94	1ST BAPTIST CHURCH	500	48.00	48.00
J. BENSON	**CHARLESTON, SOUTH CAROLINA SERIES**			
92	CITADEL BARRACKS, THE	1000	50.00	50.00
92	ST. PHILIPS CHURCH	1000	48.00	60.00
93	MIDDLETON PLANTATION	1000	50.00	50.00
93	RAINBOW ROW	*	65.00	65.00
94	CHARLESTON HORSE CARR. CO.	1000	20.00	20.00
94	DOCK STREET THEATRE	1000	48.00	48.00
94	GAZEBO AT THE BATTERY	1000	20.00	20.00
94	PINEAPPLE FOUNTAIN	1000	20.00	20.00
95	CHARLESTON OLD FIREHOUSE	1000	50.00	50.00
95	CITADEL CHAPEL, THE	1000	52.00	52.00
95	PORGY & BESS CATFISH ROW	1000	50.00	50.00
J. BENSON	**GEORGIA OR SOUTH CAROLINA SERIES**			
93	COLLEGE OF CHARLESTON	1000	50.00	50.00
93	NO. 2 MEETING ST. INN	1000	48.00	48.00
93	PINK HOUSE, THE	1000	42.00	42.00

YR	NAME	LIMIT	ISSUE	TREND
93	ST. MICHAEL'S CHURCH	1000	48.00	48.00
94	HOUSE OF CHARLESTON	1000	48.00	48.00
94	MARKET HALL	1000	48.00	48.00
94	MORRIS ISLAND LIGHTHOUSE	1000	46.00	46.00
94	RUTLEDGE HOUSE, THE	1000	48.00	48.00
J. BENSON				**GEORGIA SERIES**
92	SWAN HOUSE, THE	1000	52.00	60.00
94	WREN'S NEST, THE	1000	52.00	52.00
95	LI'L CUMBERLAND LIGHTHOUSE	1000	48.00	48.00
J. BENSON				**LEESVILLE, SOUTH CAROLINA SERIES**
94	UNITED METHODIST CHURCH	500	48.00	48.00
J. BENSON				**LEESVILLE/BATESBURG, SOUTH CAROLINA SERIES**
95	PRESBYTERIAN CHURCH	500	48.00	48.00
J. BENSON				**SOUTH CAROLINA SERIES**
94	L. B. HAYNES CHAPEL	500	48.00	48.00
94	ST. JOHN'S UNITED METHODIST CHURCH	500	48.00	48.00

JEFFREY SCOTT CO.

YR	NAME	LIMIT	ISSUE	TREND
*				**LIGHTHOUSE POINT**
94	ADMIRALTY HEAD	15000	50.00	55.00
94	BOSTON HARBOR	15000	40.00	44.00
94	CAPE HATTERAS	15000	40.00	50.00
94	CHICAGO HARBOR	15000	40.00	46.00
94	KEY WEST	15000	45.00	47.00
94	OLD MACKINAC POINT	15000	45.00	49.00
94	POINT VICENTE	15000	40.00	44.00
94	PORTLAND BREAKWATER	15000	40.00	40.00
94	SPLIT ROCK	15000	45.00	49.00
94	ST. AUGUSTINE	15000	50.00	52.00
94	ST. SIMONS	15000	50.00	55.00
94	WEST QUODDY HEAD	15000	45.00	48.00

JOHN HINE STUDIOS LTD.

Price ranges may reflect various demands in the market from one geographic region to another; condition of piece; specific markings found on piece; and/or changes in production of piece.

YR	NAME	LIMIT	ISSUE	TREND
M. WIDEMAN				**AMERICAN COLLECTION**
89	BAND STAND	OP	90.00	100.00
89	BARBER SHOP	OP	40.00	44.00
89	BLOCKHOUSE, THE	RT	25.00	35.00
89	CAJUN COTTAGE	OP	50.00	70.00
89	CALIFORNIA WINERY	OP	180.00	230.00
89	CHERRY HILL SCHOOL	RT	45.00	70.00
89	COLONIAL WELLHOUSE	RT	15.00	30.00-35.00
89	DOG HOUSE	OP	10.00	30.00
89	FORTY-NINER CABIN	OP	50.00	70.00
89	GARCONNIERE	RT	25.00	40.00-45.00
89	GINGERBREAD HOUSE, THE	RT	60.00	75.00
89	HACIENDA	OP	51.00	56.00
89	HAUNTED HOUSE	OP	100.00	110.00
89	HAWAIIAN GRASS HUT	OP	45.00	50.00
89	KING WILLIAM TAVERN	RT	99.00	160.00-175.00
89	KISSING BRIDGE, THE	RT	50.00	56.00-60.00
89	LOG CABIN, THE	RT	45.00	56.00-60.00
89	MAPLE SUGAR SHACK, THE	OP	50.00	56.00-60.00
89	MISSION, THE	OP	99.00	110.00
89	NEW ENGLAND CHURCH, THE	RT	79.00	96.00
89	NEW ENGLAND LIGHTHOUSE	RT	99.00	125.00
89	OCTAGONAL HOUSE	OP	40.00	55.00
89	OLD MILL, THE	OP	100.00	115.00
89	OPERA HOUSE, THE	RT	89.00	100.00
89	OUT HOUSE, THE	RT	15.00	24.00
89	OXBOW SALOON	OP	90.00	125.00
89	PACIFIC LIGHTHOUSE, THE	RT	89.00	105.00
89	PLANTATION HOUSE	RT	119.00	160.00-175.00
89	PRAIRIE FORGE	OP	65.00	90.00
89	RAILHEAD INN	OP	250.00	295.00
89	RIVER BELL, THE	OP	99.00	110.00
89	SEASIDE COTTAGE	OP	225.00	275.00
89	SIERRA MINE	OP	120.00	150.00
89	SOD HOUSE	OP	40.00	55.00
89	STAR COTTAGE	OP	30.00	45.00
89	SWEETHEART COTTAGE	OP	45.00	70.00
89	TOBACCONIST	OP	45.00	48.00
89	TOWN HALL	RT	129.00	125.00
89	TREE HOUSE	OP	45.00	50.00
89	WISTERIA	RT	15.00	28.00
91	CHURCH IN THE DALE	RT	130.00	144.00
91	DESERT STORM TENT	RT	75.00	75.00
91	FIRE STATION	OP	160.00	176.00
91	JOE'S SERVICE STATION	OP	90.00	100.00
91	MILK HOUSE	OP	20.00	22.00
91	MO AT WORK	RT	35.00	35.00
91	MOE'S DINER	RT	100.00	300.00
91	PAUL REVERE'S HOUSE	RT	90.00	90.00
92	GRAIN ELEVATOR	OP	110.00	110.00
92	NEWSSTAND	OP	30.00	30.00
92	TELEPHONE BOOTH	OP	16.00	16.00
92	TOPPER'S DRIVE-IN	OP	120.00	120.00

YR	NAME	LIMIT	ISSUE	TREND
92	VILLAGE MERCANTILE	OP	60.00	60.00
	D. WINTER			**ANNUAL CHRISTMAS PIECES**
87	EBENEZER SCROOGE'S COUNTING HOUSE	RT	97.00	100.00-440.00
88	CHRISTMAS IN SCOTLAND & HOGMANAY	RT	100.00	89.00-225.00
88	HOGMANAY (CHRISTMAS IN SCOTLAND...)	RT	100.00	90.00-110.00
89	A CHRISTMAS CAROL	RT	135.00	99.00-250.00
90	MR. FEZZIWIG'S EMPORIUM	RT	135.00	75.00-220.00
91	FRED'S HOME	RT	145.00	75.00-175.00
92	SCROOGE'S SCHOOL	RT	160.00	110.00-240.00
93	OLD JOE'S BEETLING SHOP	RT	175.00	165.00-245.00
94	SCROOGE FAMILY HOME, THE	RT	175.00	175.00-275.00
94	SCROOGE FAMILY HOME, THE (PREM. ED.)	RT	230.00	250.00-300.00
94	UP ON THE HOUSE TOP (STAFF GIFT)	RT	*	185.00
95	MISS BELLE'S COTTAGE	OP	185.00	185.00
95	MISS BELLE'S COTTAGE (PREM. ED.)	2200	235.00	235.00-285.00
	D. WINTER			**BRITISH TRADITIONS**
90	BLOSSOM COTTAGE (MAY)	RT	59.00	50.00
90	BOAT HOUSE, THE (MARCH)	RT	37.50	50.00-65.00
90	BULL & BUSH, THE (DECEMBER)	RT	37.50	40.00
90	BURN'S READING ROOM (JANUARY)	RT	31.00	40.00
90	GROUSE MOOR LODGE (AUGUST)	RT	48.00	50.00
90	GUY FAWKES (NOVEMBER)	RT	31.00	50.00
90	HARVEST BARN (OCTOBER)	RT	31.00	45.00-50.00
90	KNIGHT'S CASTLE (JUNE)	RT	59.00	70.00-85.00
90	PUDDING COTTAGE (APRIL)	RT	78.00	60.00-110.00
90	ST. ANNE'S WELL (JULY)	RT	48.00	50.00-70.00
90	STAFFORDSHIRE VICARAGE (SEPTEMBER)	RT	48.00	50.00-70.00
90	STONECUTTERS COTTAGE (FEBRUARY)	RT	48.00	50.00
*				**BUGABOOS**
89	ARNOLD	CL	45.00	45.00
89	BERYL	CL	45.00	45.00
89	EDNA	CL	45.00	45.00
89	ENID	CL	45.00	45.00
89	GERALD	CL	45.00	45.00
89	LIZZIE	CL	45.00	45.00
89	OSCAR	CL	45.00	45.00
89	WESLEY	CL	45.00	45.00
89	WILBUR	CL	45.00	45.00
	D. WINTER			**CAMEOS COLLECTION**
92	BARLEY MALT KILN	RT	12.50	15.00
92	BROOKLET BRIDGE	RT	12.50	15.00
92	DIORAMA-BRIGHT	RT	30.00	33.00-52.00
92	DIORAMA-LIGHT	RT	52.00	59.00
92	GREENWOOD WAGON	RT	12.50	15.00
92	LYCH GATE	RT	12.50	15.00
92	MARKET DAY	RT	12.50	15.00
92	ONE MAN JAIL	RT	12.50	15.00
92	PENNY WISHING WELL	RT	12.50	15.00
92	POTTING SHED, THE	RT	12.50	15.00
92	POULTRY ARK	RT	12.50	15.00
92	PRIVY, THE	RT	12.50	15.00
92	SADDLE STEPS	RT	12.50	15.00
92	WELSH PIG PEN	RT	12.50	15.00
	D. WINTER			**CASTLE COLLECTION**
93	CASTLE COTTAGE OF WARWICK, THE-CARNIVAL	4000	160.00	330.00-415.00
93	GUARDIAN GATE, THE	OP	150.00	150.00-170.00
94	GUARDIAN CASTLE	8490	275.00	395.00-715.00
94	GUARDIAN CASTLE (PREM. ED.)	1500	350.00	400.00-825.00
94	GUARDIAN GATE, THE (PREM. ED.)	RT	199.00	199.00
94	KINGMAKER'S CASTLE, THE	7150	225.00	195.00-250.00
94	KINGMAKER'S CASTLE, THE (CARNIVAL EVENT)	2750	395.00	295.00-375.00
95	BISHOPSGATE	OP	175.00	175.00
95	BISHOPSGATE (PREM. ED.)	3500	225.00	225.00
95	CASTLE TOWER OF WINDSOR (CARNIVAL)	RT	435.00	395.00-435.00
95	CASTLE WALL, THE	OP	65.00	65.00
95	GUINEVERE'S CASTLE	2200	350.00	350.00
95	GUINEVERE'S CASTLE	4300	299.00	299.00
	D. WINTER			**CELEBRATION COTTAGES COLLECTION**
94	CELEBRATION CHAPEL	OP	75.00	75.00-87.00
94	CELEBRATON CHAPEL (PREM. ED.)	3500	150.00	150.00-210.00
94	SPRING HOLLOW	OP	65.00	65.00-76.00
94	SPRING HOLLOW (PREM. ED.)	3500	125.00	125.00-165.00
94	SWEETHEART HAVEN	OP	60.00	60.00-72.00
94	SWEETHEART HAVEN (PREM. ED.)	3500	115.00	115.00-145.00
95	MOTHER'S COTTAGE	OP	65.00	65.00
95	MOTHER'S COTTAGE (PREM. ED.)	3500	89.50	90.00
95	STORK COTTAGE/BOY	OP	65.00	65.00
95	STORK COTTAGE/GIRL	OP	65.00	65.00
	D. WINTER			**CENTRE OF THE VILLAGE**
80	LITTLE MARKET	RT	28.90	33.00-62.00
80	MARKET STREET	OP	48.80	55.00-99.00
80	ROSE COTTAGE	OP	28.90	55.00-77.00
80	WINE MERCHANT, THE	RT	28.90	39.00-66.00
80	WINE MERCHANT, THE (OLD STYLE)	RT	28.90	295.00
82	IVY COTTAGE	RT	22.00	39.00-66.00
82	VILLAGE SHOP, THE	OP	22.00	22.00-35.00
83	BAKEHOUSE, THE	OP	31.40	50.00-60.00
83	GREEN DRAGON INN, THE	OP	31.40	60.00

YR	NAME	LIMIT	ISSUE	TREND
84	CHAPEL, THE	RT	48.80	69.00-99.00
84	PARSONAGE, THE	OP	390.00	410.00-560.00
84	SPINNER'S COTTAGE	RT	28.90	33.00-109.00
85	COOPER'S COTTAGE, THE	RT	57.90	59.00-66.00
D. WINTER				**CHARITY EVENT**
88	JIM'LL FIXIT (WINTERS HILL)	250	350.00	2800.00-3500.00
90	CARTWRIGHTS COTTAGE	RT	45.00	33.00-125.00
D. WINTER				**COLLECTORS GUILD EXCLUSIVE**
87	QUEEN ELIZABETH SLEPT HERE	RT	183.00	290.00-475.00
87	ROBIN HOOD'S HIDEAWAY	RT	54.00	250.00-440.00
87	VILLAGE SCENE, THE	RT	*	165.00-295.00
88	BLACK BESS INN	RT	60.00	110.00-285.00
88	PAVILION, THE	RT	52.00	99.00-264.00
89	COAL SHED, THE	RT	112.00	110.00-325.00
89	HOME GUARD	RT	105.00	110.00-245.00
90	COBBLER, THE	RT	40.00	33.00-99.00
90	PLUCKED DUCKS, THE	RT	*	49.00-110.00
90	POTTERY, THE	RT	40.00	33.00-85.00
91	PERSHORE MILL	RT	*	49.00-88.00
91	TOMFOOL'S COTTAGE	RT	100.00	83.00-137.00
91	WILL O' THE WISP	RT	120.00	110.00-160.00
92	BEEKEEPER'S, THE	RT	65.00	75.00-143.00
92	CANDLEMAKER'S, THE	RT	65.00	75.00-110.00
92	IRISH WATER MILL	RT	*	49.00-77.00
92	PATRICK'S WATER MILL	RT	*	95.00-176.00
93	ON THE RIVERBANK	RT	*	49.00-55.00
93	SWAM UPPING COTTAGE	RT	69.00	59.00-120.00
93	THAMESIDE	RT	79.00	69.00-132.00
94	15 LAWNSIDE ROAD	RT	*	39.00
94	ASHE COTTAGE	RT	62.00	49.00
94	WHILEAWAY COTTAGE	RT	70.00	55.00
95	BUTTERCUP COTTAGE	OP	60.00	60.00
95	FLOWER SHOP, THE	OP	150.00	150.00
95	FRIENDSHIP COTTAGE	RT	45.00	45.00
95	GARDENER'S COTTAGE	OP	*	65.00
96	MODEL DIARY, THE	OP	*	*
96	PLOUGH FARMSTEAD	OP	125.00	125.00
96	PUNCH STABLES	OP	150.00	150.00
D. WINTER				**CURRENT PIECES**
91	CASTLE IN THE AIR	OP	675.00	710.00
91	INGLENOOK COTTAGE	OP	60.00	75.00
91	MOONLIGHT HAVEN	OP	120.00	155.00
91	WEAVER'S LODGINGS, THE	OP	65.00	75.00
D. WINTER				**DAVID WINTER RETIRED PIECES**
80	COACHING INN, THE	RT	165.00	3200.00-3800.00
80	DOVE COTTAGE	RT	60.00	1295.00
80	FORGE, THE	RT	60.00	1395.00
80	LITTLE FORGE	RT	27.00	1500.00
80	LITTLE MILL	RT	40.00	1150.00-1200.00
80	LITTLE MILL-REMOLDED	RT	40.00	1500.00
80	MILL HOUSE	RT	50.00	1100.00-2800.00
80	MILL HOUSE-REMOLDED '83	RT	50.00	1750.00
80	QUAYSIDE	RT	52.00	1695.00-1980.00
80	THREE DUCKS INN	RT	60.00	1700.00-1950.00
81	CASTLE KEEP	RT	30.00	900.00-1200.00
81	CHINCHESTER CROSS	RT	50.00	3200.00-3995.00
81	CORNISH COTTAGE	RT	30.00	795.00-1400.00
81	DOUBLE OAST	RT	60.00	3995.00
81	OLD CURIOSITY SHOP, THE	RT	40.00	1750.00
81	PROVENCAL ONE (FRENCH MKT.)	RT	*	*
81	PROVENCAL TINY A (FRENCH MKT.)	RT	*	1250.00
81	PROVENCAL TINY B (FRENCH MKT.)	RT	*	1250.00
81	PROVENCAL TWO (FRENCH MKT.)	RT	*	*
81	ST. PAUL'S CATHEDRAL	RT	40.00	1300.00-2000.00
81	TYTHE BARN	RT	39.30	1320.00-2100.00
82	BLACKSMITH'S COTTAGE	RT	22.00	395.00-440.00
82	CORNISH TIN MINE	RT	22.00	50.00-88.00
82	FAIRYTALE CASTLE	RT	115.40	198.00-330.00
82	HAYBARN, THE	RT	22.00	260.00-350.00
82	HOUSE ON TOP, THE	RT	92.30	275.00-300.00
82	MINER'S COTTAGE	RT	22.00	199.00-440.00
82	MOORLAND COTTAGE	RT	22.00	150.00-300.00
82	SABRINA'S COTTAGE	RT	30.00	2000.00-2350.00
82	WM. SHAKESPEARE'S BIRTHPLACE (LARGE)	RT	60.00	1295.00-1750.00
83	ALMS HOUS, THE	RT	59.90	250.00-440.00
83	COTTON MILL, THE	RT	41.30	440.00-880.00
83	HAYBARN, THE	RT	22.00	270.00-350.00
83	WOODCUTTER'S COTTAGE	RT	87.00	275.00-355.00
84	HOUSE OF THE MASTER MASON	RT	74.80	193.00-275.00
85	HERMIT'S HUMBLE HOME	RT	87.00	210.00-325.00
85	SUFFOLK HOUSE	RT	48.80	66.00-105.00
88	CROFTER'S COTTAGE	RT	51.00	49.00-94.00
91	PRINTERS AND THE BOOKBINDERS, THE (BOOKE	RT	120.00	95.00-165.00
92	AUDREY'S TEA ROOM	RT	90.00	55.00-225.00
92	AUDREY'S TEA SHOP	RT	90.00	100.00-330.00
95	WELCOME HOME COTTAGE	RT	99.00	99.00
95	WELCOME HOME COTTAGE-MILITARY	RT	99.00	99.00

Department 56's Smythe Woolen Mill, *from the New England Village, was issued in 1987 and is limited to 7,500 pieces.*

Berkshire House *was added to the Department 56 New England Village line in 1989.*

Nathaniel Bingham Fabrics, *also referred to as the Post Office because the mail came into and went out of the shop, was a 1986 New England Village issue from Department 56.*

Harbour Lights added Jupiter, FL *to its "Southeast Region" series in 1995. The edition was limited to 9,500.*

Department 56 issued the General Store *with their original set of seven New England Village pieces.*

The Brick Town Hall *was an original issue packaged with the set of seven starter New England Village pieces manufacturerd by Department 56.*

YR	NAME	LIMIT	ISSUE	TREND
D. WINTER				**DISNEYANA**
92	CINDERELLA CASTLE	500	250.00	250.00
93	SLEEPING BEAUTY CASTLE	500	250.00	250.00
94	EURO DISNEY CASTLE	500	250.00	250.00
D. WINTER		**ENGLISH VILLAGE COLLECTION**		
94	CAT & PIPE, THE	OP	53.00	53.00
94	CHANDLERY, THE	OP	53.00	53.00
94	CHURCH AND VESTRY, THE	OP	57.00	57.00
94	CONSTABULARY, THE	OP	60.00	60.00
94	CRYSTAL COTTAGE	OP	53.00	53.00
94	ENGINE HOUSE, THE (BRN. DR. GEN. VISION)	OP	55.00	55.00
94	ENGINE HOUSE, THE (RD. DR. DISNEY EXCLUS	OP	55.00	55.00
94	GLEBE COTTAGE	OP	53.00	53.00
94	HALL, THE	OP	55.00	55.00
94	ONE ACRE COTTAGE	OP	55.00	55.00
94	POST OFFICE, THE	OP	53.00	53.00
94	QUACK'S COTTAGE	OP	57.00	57.00
94	RECTORY, THE	OP	55.00	55.00
94	SEMINARY, THE	OP	57.00	57.00
94	SMITHY, THE	OP	50.00	50.00
94	TANNERY, THE	OP	50.00	50.00
J. KING				**FATHER CHRISTMAS**
88	FALLING	OP	70.00	70.00
88	FEET	OP	70.00	70.00
88	STANDING	OP	70.00	70.00
D. WINTER		**GARDEN COTTAGES OF ENGLAND**		
95	SPENCER HALL GARDENS	4300	395.00	395.00
95	SPENCER HALL GARDENS (PREM. ED.)	2200	495.00	495.00
95	WILLOW GARDENS	4300	250.00	250.00
95	WILLOW GARDENS (PREM. ED.)	2200	299.00	299.00
M. COOPER				**GREAT BRITISH PUBS**
89	BELL, THE	RT	79.50	85.00-350.00
89	BLACK SWAN	RT	79.50	85.00-350.00
89	BLUE BELL	RT	57.50	58.00
89	COACH & HORSES	RT	79.50	80.00
89	CROWN INN, THE	RT	79.50	80.00
89	DICKENS INN	RT	100.00	100.00
89	DIRTY DUCK	RT	25.00	25.00
89	EAGLE, THE	RT	35.00	35.00
89	FALKLAND ARMS	RT	25.00	25.00
89	FALSTAFF, THE	RT	35.00	35.00
89	FEATHERS, THE	RT	200.00	200.00
89	GEORGE & PILGRIMS	RT	25.00	25.00
89	GEORGE SOMERSET	RT	100.00	100.00
89	GEORGE, THE	RT	57.50	58.00
89	GREEN MAN, THE	RT	*	80.00
89	GRENADIER	RT	25.00	25.00
89	HAWKESHEAD	RT	25.00	900.00
89	JAMAICA INN	RT	39.50	40.00
89	KING'S ARMS	RT	28.00	28.00
89	LION, THE	RT	57.50	58.00
89	LYGON ARMS	RT	35.00	35.00
89	MONTAGUE ARMS	RT	57.50	58.00
89	OLD BRIDGE HOUSE	RT	37.50	38.00
89	OLD BULL INN	RT	87.50	88.00
89	PLOUGH, THE	RT	28.00	28.00
89	SHERLOCK HOLMES	RT	100.00	100.00
89	SMITH'S ARMS	RT	28.00	28.00
89	SUFFOLK BULL	RT	35.00	35.00
89	SWAN, THE	RT	35.00	35.00
89	WHEATSHEAF	RT	35.00	35.00
89	WHITE HORSE	RT	39.50	40.00
89	WHITE TOWER	RT	35.00	35.00
89	YE GRAPES	RT	87.50	88.00
89	YE OLD SPOTTED HORSE	RT	79.50	80.00
D. WINTER				**HEART OF ENGLAND**
85	APOTHOCARY SHOP, THE	RT	24.10	39.00-50.00
85	BLACKFRIARS GRANGE	RT	24.10	35.00
85	CRAFTSMAN COTTAGES	RT	24.10	40.00
85	HOGS HEAD TAVERN, THE	RT	24.10	50.00
85	MEADOWBANK COTTAGES	RT	24.10	40.00-55.00
85	SCHOOLHOUSE, THE	RT	24.10	45.00
85	SHIREHALL	RT	24.10	28.00-50.00
85	ST. GEORGE'S CHURCH	RT	24.10	45.00-55.00
85	VICARAGE, THE	RT	24.10	45.00
85	YEOMAN'S FARMHOUSE	RT	24.10	33.00-40.00
88	WINDMILL, THE	RT	37.50	44.00-50.00
D. WINTER				**IN THE COUNTRY**
82	BROOKSIDE HAMLET	RT	74.80	59.00-165.00
82	DROVER'S COTTAGE	OP	22.00	35.00-55.00
83	BOTHY, THE	OP	31.40	44.00-60.00
83	FISHERMAN'S WHARF	OP	31.40	60.00-77.00
83	PILGRAM'S REST	RT	48.80	55.00-66.00
84	SNOW COTTAGE	RT	74.80	69.00-149.00
84	TOLLKEEPER'S COTTAGE	RT	87.00	66.00-165.00
86	THERE WAS A CROOKED HOUSE	OP	96.90	110.00-165.00
87	JOHN BENBOW'S FARMHOUSE	RT	78.00	55.00-100.00

YR	NAME	LIMIT	ISSUE	TREND
D. WINTER				**IRISH COLLECTION**
92	FOGARTYS	RT	75.00	69.00-105.00
92	IRISH ROUND TOWER	OP	65.00	70.00
92	MURPHYS	OP	100.00	110.00
92	O'DONOVAN'S CASTLE	OP	145.00	170.00-193.00
92	ONLY A SPAN APART	OP	80.00	69.00
92	SECRET SHEBEEN	RT	70.00	60.00-77.00
C. LAWRENCE				**MUSHROOMS**
89	COBBLERS, THE	2500	265.00	265.00-375.00
89	CONSTABLES, THE	2500	200.00	200.00
89	ELDERS OF MUSHROOM, THE	2500	175.00	175.00-225.00
89	GIFT SHOP, THE	2500	350.00	420.00-525.00
89	MINISTRY, THE	2500	185.00	185.00-300.00
89	MUSH HOSPITAL FOR MALINGERERS, THE	2500	250.00	250.00-400.00
89	PRINCESS PALACE, THE	750	600.00	730.00-950.00
89	ROYAL BANK OF MUSHLAND	2500	235.00	235.00-350.00
D. WINTER				**PORRIDGE POT ALLEY COLLECTION**
95	COB'S BAKERY	OP	125.00	125.00
95	COB'S BAKERY (PREM. ED.)	OP	165.00	165.00
95	PORRIDGE POT ARCH	OP	50.00	50.00
95	SWEET DREAMS	OP	79.00	79.00
95	SWEET DREAMS (PREM. ED.)	OP	99.00	99.00
95	TARTAN TEAHOUSE	OP	99.00	99.00
95	TARTAN TEAHOUSE (PREM. ED.)	OP	129.00	129.00
D. WINTER				**SCOTTISH COLLECTION**
82	OLD DISTRILLERY, THE	RT	312.20	250.00-523.00
89	GATEKEEPER'S	OP	65.00	55.00-85.00
89	GATEKEEPERS COLOURWAY	1000	*	275.00-385.00
89	GILLIE'S COTTAGE	OP	65.00	85.00
89	HOUSE ON THE LOCH, THE	RT	65.00	69.00
89	MACBETH'S CASTLE	OP	200.00	220.00-260.00
89	OLD DISTILLERY (RE-RELEASED)	RT	450.00	750.00-800.00
89	SCOTTISH CROFTER (REMOLDED)	OP	42.00	54.00
89	SCOTTISH CROFTERS	OP	42.00	65.00
D. WINTER				**SEASIDE BOARDWALK**
95	BARNACLE THEATRE	OP	175.00	175.00
95	DOCK ASSEMBLY	OP	*	*
95	FISHERMAN'S SHANTY	OP	110.00	110.00
95	HARBOUR MASTER'S WATCH-HOUSE	OP	125.00	125.00
95	JOLLY ROGER TAVERN	OP	199.00	199.00
95	LODGINGS & SEA BATHING	OP	165.00	165.00
95	WATERFRONT MARKET	OP	125.00	125.00
D. WINTER				**SPECIAL EVENTS**
88	WINTERSHILL (JIM'LL FIX-IT)	250	375.00	2850.00-3500.00
92	BIRTHSTONE WISHING WELL	RT	40.00	40.00
92	MAD BARON FOURTHRITE'S FOLLY	18854	275.00	154.00-285.00
93	ARCHES THRICE	RT	150.00	165.00-285.00
93	HORATIO PERNICKETY'S AMOROUS INTENT	9990	350.00	225.00-350.00
93	PLUM COTTAGE	4500	50.00	198.00-250.00
94	BIRTHDAY COTTTAGE (ARCHES THWONCE)	RT	55.00	49.00
94	QUINDENE MANOR	3000	695.00	633.00-825.00
94	QUINDENE MANOR-PREM. ED.	1500	850.00	850.00-1100.00
94	WINTER ARCH	RT	25.00	39.00
94	WISHING FALLS COTTAGE	RT	65.00	59.00
95	GRUMBLEWEED'S POTTING SHED	OP	99.00	130.00
95	NEWTOWN MILLHOUSE	4500	195.00	195.00
95	WHISPERS COTTAGE	OP	99.00	65.00
D. WINTER				**THE LANDOWNERS**
81	TUDOR MANOR HOUSE	RT	48.80	50.00-145.00
81	TUDOR MANOR HOUSE (OLD STYLE)	RT	48.80	750.00
82	DOWER HOUSE, THE	RT	22.00	40.00-55.00
84	CASTLE GATE	RT	154.90	165.00-299.00
85	SQUIRES HALL	RT	92.30	66.00-165.00
86	FALSTAFF'S MANOR	RT	242.00	330.00-410.00
88	GRANGE, THE	RT	120.00	895.00-1075.00
D. WINTER				**THE MIDLANDS**
88	BOTTLE KILN	RT	78.00	73.00-110.00
88	COAL MINER'S ROW	OP	90.00	55.00-120.00
88	DERBYSHIRE COTTON MILL	RT	65.00	69.00
88	GUNSMITHS	OP	78.00	100.00
88	LACEMAKER'S	OP	120.00	132.00-165.00
88	LOCK KEEPERS COTTAGE	OP	65.00	44.00-110.00
D. WINTER				**THE NEW SHERWOOD FOREST COLLECTION**
95	DIORAMA	OP	100.00	10.00
95	FRIAR TUCK'S SANCTUM	OP	45.00	45.00
95	KING RICHARD'S BOWER	OP	45.00	45.00
95	LITTLE JOHN'S RIVERLOFT	OP	45.00	45.00
95	LOXLEY CASTLE	OP	150.00	150.00
95	MAID MARIAN'S RETREAT	OP	49.50	45.00-50.00
95	MUCH'S MILL	OP	45.00	45.00
95	WILL SCARLETT'S DEN	OP	49.50	45.00-50.00
D. WINTER				**THE REGIONS**
81	SINGLE OAST	RT	22.00	39.00-76.00
81	STRATFORD HOUSE	OP	74.80	55.00-130.00
81	TRIPLE OAST	RT	59.90	99.00-135.00
81	TRIPLE OAST (OLD STYLE)	RT	59.90	150.00-250.00
82	COTSWOLD COTTAGE	RT	22.00	35.00-88.00

YR	NAME	LIMIT	ISSUE	TREND
82	COTSWOLD VILLAGE	RT	59.90	59.00-125.00
82	SUSSEX COTTAGE	OP	22.00	50.00
83	HERTFORD COURT (ERIC)	RT	87.00	75.00-193.00
85	KENT COTTAGE	OP	48.80	55.00-65.00
D. WINTER				**THE SHIRES COLLECTION**
93	BERKSHIRE MILKING BYRE	RT	38.00	29.00-35.00
93	BUCKINGHAMSHIRE BULL PEN	RT	38.00	29.00-35.00
93	CHESHIRE KENNELS	RT	36.00	28.00-35.00
93	DERBYSHIRE DOVECOTE	RT	36.00	28.00-35.00
93	GLOUCESTERSHIRE GREENHOUSE	RT	40.00	31.00-35.00
93	HAMPSHIRE HUTCHES	RT	34.00	27.00-35.00
93	LANCASHIRE DONKEY SHED	RT	38.00	29.00-35.00
93	OXFORDSHIRE GOAT YARD	RT	32.00	26.00-35.00
93	SHROPSHIRE PIG SHELTER	RT	32.00	25.00-35.00
93	STAFFORDSHIRE STABLES	RT	36.00	28.00-35.00
93	WILTSHIRE WATERWHEEL	RT	34.00	35.00
93	YORKSHIRE SHEEPFOLD	RT	38.00	29.00-35.00
J. HERBERT				**THE SHOEMAKER'S DREAM**
91	BABY BOOTY (BLUE)	OP	45.00	45.00
91	BABY BOOTY (PINK)	OP	45.00	45.00
91	CASTLE BOOT	OP	55.00	55.00
91	CHAPEL, THE	OP	55.00	55.00
91	CLOCKTOWER BOOT, THE	OP	60.00	60.00
91	CROOKED BOOT, THE	OP	35.00	35.00
91	GATE LODGE, THE	OP	65.00	65.00
91	JESTER BOOT, THE	OP	29.00	29.00
91	RIVER SHOE COTTAGE	OP	55.00	55.00
91	ROSIE'S COTTAGE	OP	40.00	40.00
91	SHOEMAKER'S PALACE	OP	50.00	50.00
91	TAVERN BOOT	OP	55.00	55.00
91	WATERMILL BOOT	OP	60.00	60.00
91	WINDMILL BOOT	OP	65.00	65.00
92	CHRISTMAS BOOT	OP	55.00	55.00
92	CLOWN BOOT	OP	45.00	45.00
92	GOLF SHOE, THE	OP	35.00	35.00
92	SPORTS SHOE, THE	OP	35.00	35.00
92	UPSIDE DOWN BOOT	OP	45.00	45.00
92	WISHING WELL SHOE	OP	32.00	32.00
D. WINTER				**THE VILLAGE COLLECTION**
81	VILLAGE, THE	OP	362.00	580.00
81	VILLAGE, THE (OLD STYLE)	OP	362.00	1500.00
D. WINTER				**THE WINTERVILLE COLLECTION**
94	CLOCKHOUSE, THE	OP	165.00	165.00-187.00
94	CLOCKHOUSE, THE (PREM. ED.)	OP	215.00	215.00-275.00
94	TOYMAKER, THE	OP	135.00	135.00-143.00
94	TOYMAKER, THE (PREM. ED.)	OP	175.00	175.00-220.00
95	ST. STEPHEN'S	5750	150.00	150.00
95	ST. STEPHEN'S (PREM. ED.)	1750	195.00	195.00
95	YE MERRY GENTLEMEN'S LODGINGS	5750	125.00	125.00
95	YE MERRY GENTLEMEN'S LODGINGS (PREM. ED.	1750	170.00	170.00
D. WINTER				**TINY SERIES**
80	ANN HATHAWAY'S COTTAGE	RT	*	495.00-1250.00
80	COTSWOLD FARMHOUSE	RT	*	595.00
80	CROWN INN	RT	*	595.00
80	ST. NICHOLAS' CHURCH	RT	*	595.00
80	SULGRAVE MANOR	RT	*	595.00-1100.00
80	WM. SHAKESPEARE'S BIRTHPLACE	RT	*	495.00
D. WINTER				**WELSH COLLECTION**
93	A BIT OF NONSENSE	OP	52.00	50.00
93	PEN-Y-CRAIG	OP	88.00	90.00-109.00
93	TYDDYN SIRIOL	RT	88.00	69.00-90.00
93	Y DDRAIGG GOCH	RT	88.00	69.00-109.00
D. WINTER				**WEST COUNTRY**
86	DEVONCOMBE	RT	73.00	55.00-79.00
86	SMUGGLER'S CREEK	OP	390.00	330.00-520.00
86	TAMAR COTTAGE	OP	45.30	75.00
87	DEVON CREAMERY	OP	62.90	110.00
87	ORCHARD COTTAGE	RT	91.30	72.00-125.00
88	CORNISH ENGINE HOUSE	OP	120.00	110.00-168.00
88	CORNISH HARBOUR	OP	120.00	155.00

JP EDITIONS

YR	NAME	LIMIT	ISSUE	TREND
*				**ASPECT OF WINDSOR**
92	NORMAN GATE	100	270.00	2000.00
93	MARBECK'S	100	330.00	1500.00
93	SALISBURY TOWER	100	300.00	1500.00
94	CURFEW TOWER	100	315.00	1500.00
P. GATES				**CASTLES OF ENGLAND**
92	HEVER CASTLE	250	350.00	900.00
92	SCOTNEY CASTLE	250	350.00	1100.00
P. GATES				**CASTLES OF GREAT BRITAIN**
94	GRAIGIEVAR CASTLE	400	390.00	410.00
P. GATES				**CASTLES OF WALES**
94	CALDICOT CASTLE	400	380.00	400.00
94	CASTELL COCH	400	420.00	550.00
P. GATES				**GATE HOUSE COLLECTION**
93	GUILDFORD LODGE	400	420.00	440.00

YR	NAME	LIMIT	ISSUE	TREND
*				**GATES OF WARWICK**
92	EAST GATE	100	210.00	2000.00
92	NORTH GATE	100	280.00	2000.00
92	SOUTH GATE	100	295.00	2000.00
93	WEST GATE	100	350.00	2100.00
P. GATES				**GREAT ENGLISH HOMES**
94	GAINSBOROUGH HALL	450	420.00	500.00
P. GATES				**UNIVERSITY BUILDINGS**
92	RADCLIFFE CAMERA	250	295.00	875.00
93	GATE OF HONOUR	250	295.00	600.00

LILLIPUT LANE LTD.

Price ranges may reflect various demands in the market from one geographic region to another; condition of piece; specific markings found on piece; and/or changes in production of piece.

YR	NAME	LIMIT	ISSUE	TREND
91	GARDNER'S COTTAGE	RT	120.00	200.00
*				**A YEAR IN AN ENGLISH GARDEN**
95	SPRING GLORY	OP	120.00	85.00
95	SUMMER IMPRESSIONS	OP	120.00	85.00
D. TATE				**AMERICAN COLLECTION**
84	ADOBE CHURCH	RT	22.50	390.00-650.00
84	ADOBE VILLAGE	RT	60.00	1950.00
84	CAPE COD	RT	22.50	650.00
84	COUNTRY CHURCH	RT	95.00	65.00-124.00
84	COVERED BRIDGE	RT	22.50	2000.00
84	FORGE BARN	RT	22.50	650.00
84	GENERAL STORE	RT	22.50	650.00-750.00
84	GRIST MILL	RT	22.50	500.00
84	LIGHTHOUSE	RT	22.50	975.00
84	LOG CABIN	RT	22.50	910.00
84	MIDWEST BARN	RT	22.50	189.00-377.00
84	SAN FRANCISCO HOUSE	RT	22.50	878.00-910.00
84	WALLACE STATION	RT	22.50	910.00
R. DAY				**AMERICAN LANDMARK SERIES**
89	COUNTRYSIDE BARN	RT	75.00	78.00-104.00
89	FALLS MILL	RT	130.00	124.00-156.00
89	MAIL POUCH BARN	RT	75.00	98.00-273.00
90	COUNTRY CHURCH	RT	82.50	65.00-124.00
90	COVERED MEMORIES	RT	110.00	130.00-169.00
90	GREAT POINT LIGHT	OP	50.00	45.00
90	HOMETOWN DEPOT	RT	68.00	65.00-117.00
90	PEPSI COLA BARN	RT	87.00	169.00-189.00
90	PIONEER BARN	RT	30.00	39.00-117.00
90	RIVERSIDE CHAPEL	RT	82.50	98.00-130.00
90	ROADSIDE COOLERS	RT	75.00	98.00-111.00
90	SIGN OF THE TIMES	OP	33.70	35.00
91	FIRE HOUSE 1	OP	100.00	85.00
91	RAMBLING ROSE	RT	60.00	60.00
91	SCHOOL DAYS	OP	75.00	60.00
91	VICTORIANA	RT	295.00	312.00-358.00
92	16.9 CENTS PER GALLON	OP	150.00	150.00
92	GOLD MINERS' CLAIM	OP	110.00	110.00
92	HOME SWEET HOME	OP	120.00	95.00
92	SMALL TOWN LIBRARY	RT	130.00	130.00
92	WINNIE'S PLACE	RT	395.00	442.00-512.00
*				**ANNIVERSARY SPECIAL**
92	HONEYSUCKLE COTTAGE 1992	RT	195.00	85.00-137.00
93	COTMAN COTTAGE	RT	220.00	195.00-260.00
94	WATERMEADOWS	RT	189.00	124.00
95	GERTRUDE'S GARDEN	RT	192.00	192.00
96	CRUCK END	OP	130.00	130.00
*				**BLAISE HAMLET CLASSICS**
93	CIRCULAR COTTAGE	RT	95.00	117.00
93	DIAL COTTAGE	RT	95.00	100.00
93	DIAMOND COTTAGE	RT	95.00	98.00-130.00
93	DOUBLE COTTAGE	RT	95.00	100.00
93	JASMINE COTTAGE	RT	95.00	100.00
93	OAK COTTAGE	RT	95.00	100.00
93	ROSE COTTAGE	RT	95.00	100.00
93	SWEET BRIAR COTTAGE	RT	95.00	100.00
93	VINE COTTAGE	RT	95.00	100.00
D. TATE				**BLAISE HAMLET COLLECTION**
89	CIRCULAR COTTAGE	RT	110.00	135.00
89	DIAMOND COTTAGE	RT	110.00	135.00
89	OAK COTTAGE	RT	110.00	135.00
90	DIAL COTTAGE	RT	110.00	135.00
90	SWEET BRIAR COTTAGE	RT	110.00	135.00
90	VINE COTTAGE	RT	110.00	128.00
91	DOUBLE COTTAGE	OP	200.00	200.00
91	JASMINE COTTAGE	RT	140.00	140.00
91	ROSE COTTAGE	RT	140.00	124.00-254.00
*				**CHRISTMAS**
92	CRANBERRY COTTAGE	OP	46.50	47.00
92	HOLLYTREE HOUSE	OP	46.50	47.00
D. TATE				**CHRISTMAS**
88	DEER PARK HALL	RT	120.00	130.00-150.00
89	ST. NICHOLAS CHURCH	RT	130.00	111.00-130.00
90	YULETIDE INN	RT	145.00	130.00-150.00

YR	NAME	LIMIT	ISSUE	TREND
91	OLD VICARAGE AT CHRISTMAS, THE	RT	180.00	130.00-143.00
92	CHESTNUT COTTAGE	OP	46.50	47.00
*			**CHRISTMAS LODGE**	
92	HIGHLAND LODGE	RT	180.00	195.00-221.00
93	EAMONT LODGE	RT	185.00	195.00-221.00
94	SNOWDON LODGE	RT	175.00	200.00
95	KERRY LODGE	RT	160.00	160.00
*			**CHRISTMAS SPECIAL**	
96	ST. STEPHEN'S CHRUCH/1ST SERIES	OP	100.00	100.00
D. SIMPSON		**COUNTRYSIDE SCENE PLAQUES**		
89	BOTTLE KILN	RT	49.50	50.00
89	CORNISH TIN MINE	RT	49.50	50.00
89	COUNTRY INN	RT	49.50	50.00
89	CUMBRIAN FARMHOUSE	RT	49.50	50.00
89	LIGHTHOUSE	RT	49.50	50.00
89	NORFOLK WINDMILL	RT	49.50	50.00
89	OASTHOUSE	RT	49.50	50.00
89	OLD SMITTY	RT	49.50	50.00
89	PARISH CHURCH	RT	49.50	50.00
89	POST OFFICE	RT	49.50	50.00
89	VILLAGE SCHOOL	RT	49.50	50.00
89	WATERMILL	RT	49.50	50.00
D. TATE			**DUTCH COLLECTION**	
91	AAN DE AMSTEL	OP	79.00	60.00
91	BEGIJNHOF	OP	55.00	35.00
91	BLOEMENMARKT	OP	79.00	60.00
91	DE BRANDERIJ	OP	72.50	55.00
91	DE DIAMANTAIR	OP	79.00	60.00
91	DE PEPERMOLEN	OP	55.00	35.00
91	DE WOLHANDELAAR	OP	72.50	55.00
91	DE ZIJDEWEVER	OP	79.00	60.00
91	REMBRANT VAN RIJN	OP	120.00	85.00
91	ROZENGRACHT	OP	72.50	50.00
*			**ENGLISH COTTAGES**	
86	GULLIVER	RT	65.00	845.00
87	CLOCKMAKERS COTTAGE	RT	40.00	254.00-260.00
87	STREET SCENE #1	RT	40.00	350.00
87	STREET SCENE #10	RT	45.00	290.00
87	STREET SCENE #2	RT	45.00	350.00
87	STREET SCENE #3	RT	45.00	350.00
87	STREET SCENE #4	RT	45.00	290.00
87	STREET SCENE #5	RT	40.00	290.00
87	STREET SCENE #6	RT	40.00	290.00
87	STREET SCENE #7	RT	40.00	290.00
87	STREET SCENE #8	RT	40.00	290.00
87	STREET SCENE #9	RT	45.00	290.00
92	DERWENT-LE-DALE	OP	75.00	55.00
92	WHEYSIDE COTTAGE	OP	46.50	35.00
94	LEONORA'S SECRET	RT	350.00	455.00-624.00
95	CHERRY BLOSSOM	*	128.00	95.00
95	CHIPPING COOMBE	RT	525.00	525.00
95	DUCKDOWN COTTAGE	*	95.00	70.00
95	PIPIT TELL	*	64.00	50.00
95	RUSTLINGS, THE	*	128.00	95.00
96	BLUE BOAR	OP	85.00	85.00
96	CRADLE COTTAGE	OP	100.00	100.00
96	FUCHSIA COTTAGE	OP	30.00	30.00
96	GOSSIP GATE	OP	170.00	170.00
96	HONEY POT COTTAGE	OP	60.00	60.00
96	LITTLE LUPINS	OP	40.00	40.00
96	LOXDALE COTTAGE	OP	35.00	35.00
96	RAILWAY COTTAGE	OP	60.00	60.00
96	REFLECTIONS OF JADE	3950	350.00	350.00
96	ROSEMARY COTTAGE	OP	70.00	70.00
96	ST. JOHN THE BAPTIST	OP	75.00	75.00
M. ADKINSON			**ENGLISH COTTAGES**	
87	FOUR SEASONS	OP	70.00	59.00-98.00
87	SADDLERS INN	RT	50.00	52.00-72.00
87	SECRET GARDEN	RT	145.00	195.00-293.00
D. HALL			**ENGLISH COTTAGES**	
86	COBBLERS COTTAGE	RT	42.00	39.00-72.00
C. HANNENBERGER			**ENGLISH COTTAGES**	
88	SHIP INN	RT	210.00	215.00-468.00
T. RAINE			**ENGLISH COTTAGES**	
86	TUDOR COURT	RT	260.00	273.00-293.00
87	BEACON HEIGHTS	RT	125.00	130.00-165.00
87	GABLES, THE	RT	145.00	117.00-169.00
D. TATE			**ENGLISH COTTAGES**	
*	BURNSIDE COTTAGE	RT	30.00	585.00
82	ACORN COTTAGE	RT	40.00	39.00-78.00
82	APRIL COTTAGE	RT	*	39.00-72.00
82	BRIDGE HOUSE	RT	15.95	34.00-91.00
82	DALE HOUSE (MINI)	RT	25.00	1300.00
82	DRAPERS	RT	15.95	325.00
82	HONEYSUCKLE	RT	45.00	85.00-137.00
82	LAKESIDE HOUSE	RT	40.00	910.00-1105.00
82	OAK LODGE	RT	40.00	72.00-117.00

There are three versions of the Steeple Church *(New England Village). The first was issued by Department 56 in 1986.*

Ben's Barber Shop *was issued along with* Otis Hayes Butcher Shop *and* Anne Shaw Toys *in a set designed for the New England Village produced by Department 56.*

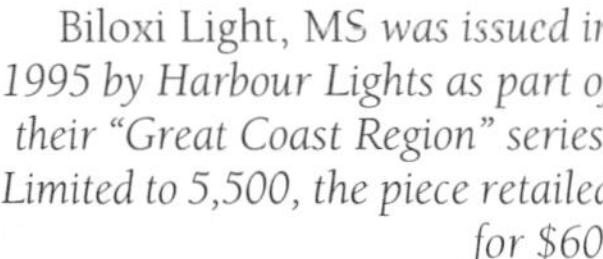

Biloxi Light, MS *was issued in 1995 by Harbour Lights as part of their "Great Coast Region" series. Limited to 5,500, the piece retailed for $60.*

The Counting House & Silas Thimbleton Barrister *(Dickens' Village) was only issued from 1988-90. Department 56 retired the piece after only two years.*

YR	NAME	LIMIT	ISSUE	TREND
82	OLD MINE	RT	15.95	2500.00
82	STONE COTTAGE	RT	40.00	325.00-350.00
82	SUSSEX MILL	RT	25.00	585.00
83	ANNE HATHAWAY'S	RT	40.00	52.00-85.00
83	CASTLE STREET	RT	130.00	442.00
83	COACH HOUSE (MINI)	RT	100.00	1170.00-1300.00
83	COOPERS	RT	15.00	358.00-390.00
83	HOLLY COTTAGE	RT	42.50	39.00-65.00
83	MILLERS	RT	15.00	169.00-195.00
83	MINERS COTTAGE	RT	15.00	488.00-650.00
83	OLD POST OFFICE, THE	RT	35.00	715.00-975.00
83	RED LION INN	RT	125.00	423.00-455.00
83	THATCHERS REST	RT	185.00	208.00-234.00
83	TOLL HOUSE	RT	15.00	85.00-170.00
83	TROUTBECK FARM	RT	125.00	358.00-390.00
83	TUCK SHOP	RT	35.00	1105.00-1300.00
83	WARWICK HALL	RT	185.00	2080.00-5525.00
83	WILLIAM SHAKESPEARE	RT	130.00	98.00-124.00
83	WOODCUTTERS	RT	15.00	124.00-182.00
84	CLIBURN SCHOOL	RT	22.50	7150.00
84	DALE FARM	RT	30.00	1170.00-1300.00
84	DOVE COTTAGE	RT	35.00	59.00-98.00
84	TINTAGEL	RT	39.50	124.00-228.00
85	BERMUDA COTTAGE	RT	29.00	325.00
85	BRONTE PARSONAGE	RT	72.00	156.00
85	BURNS COTTAGE	RT	35.00	90.00-130.00
85	CLARE COTTAGE	RT	30.00	34.00-65.00
85	FISHERMANS COTTAGE	RT	30.00	65.00-78.00
85	KENTISH OAST HOUSE	RT	55.00	59.00-78.00
85	MORETON MANOR	RT	55.00	65.00-78.00
85	OLD CURIOSITY SHOP, THE	RT	62.50	90.00-120.00
85	OSTLERS KEEP	RT	55.00	72.00-111.00
85	SAWYER GILL	RT	30.00	46.00-65.00
85	ST. MARY'S	RT	40.00	104.00-117.00
85	WATERMILL	RT	40.00	52.00-104.00
86	BAY VIEW	RT	39.50	65.00-85.00
86	DALE HEAD	RT	75.00	78.00-104.00
86	FARRIERS	RT	40.00	52.00-98.00
86	SCROLL ON THE WALL	RT	55.00	130.00-165.00
86	SEVEN DWARF'S COTTAGE	RT	*	1073.00-1300.00
86	SPRING BANK	RT	42.00	65.00-85.00
86	THREE FEATHERS	RT	115.00	143.00-176.00
87	CLOVER COTTAGE	RT	27.50	26.00-46.00
87	HOLME DYKE	RT	50.00	65.00-78.00
87	INGLEWOOD	RT	27.50	34.00-39.00
87	IZAAK WALTON'S COTTAGE	RT	75.00	59.00-117.00
87	KEEPERS LODGE	RT	75.00	72.00-156.00
87	MAGPIE COTTAGE	RT	70.00	59.00-65.00
87	RIVERVIEW	RT	27.50	34.00
87	RYDAL VIEW	RT	220.00	234.00-260.00
87	STONEYBECK	RT	45.00	52.00-91.00
87	SUMMER HAZE	OP	90.00	111.00
87	TANNER'S COTTAGE	RT	27.50	39.00-78.00
87	WEALDEN HOUSE	RT	125.00	130.00-156.00
88	BREDON HOUSE	RT	145.00	124.00-150.00
88	BROOKBANK	RT	58.00	46.00-72.00
88	CROWN INN	RT	120.00	117.00-163.00
88	PARGETTER'S RETREAT	RT	75.00	59.00-111.00
88	RISING SUN	RT	58.00	59.00-91.00
88	ROYAL OAK INN	RT	145.00	195.00-228.00
88	SAXON COTTAGE	RT	245.00	182.00-241.00
88	SMALLEST INN	RT	42.50	59.00-91.00
88	ST. MARK'S CHURCH	RT	75.00	111.00-130.00
88	SWAN INN	RT	120.00	124.00-143.00
88	SWIFT HOLLOW	RT	75.00	72.00-98.00
89	ANNE HATHAWAY'S COTTAGE	OP	130.00	130.00
89	ASH NOOK	RT	47.50	65.00
89	BEEHIVE COTTAGE	RT	72.50	65.00-124.00
89	BRIARY, THE	RT	47.50	65.00-85.00
89	BUTTERWICK	RT	52.50	39.00-65.00
89	CHILTERN MILL	RT	87.50	78.00-163.00
89	CHINE COT	RT	36.00	39.00
89	FIVEWAYS	RT	42.50	39.00
89	GREENSTED CHURCH	RT	72.50	90.00
89	HELMERE	RT	65.00	59.00-78.00
89	MAYFLOWER HOUSE	RT	87.50	182.00-260.00
89	ST. LAWRENCE CHURCH	OP	110.00	85.00
89	ST. PETER'S COVE	RT	1375.00	1268.00-1625.00
89	TANGLEWOOD LODGE	RT	97.00	117.00-130.00
89	TITMOUSE COTTAGE	RT	92.50	98.00-130.00
89	VICTORIA COTTAGE	RT	52.50	52.00-85.00
89	WIGHT COTTAGE	RT	52.50	65.00
89	WILLIAM SHAKESPEARE'S	OP	130.00	98.00
90	BRAMBLE COTTAGE	RT	55.00	70.00
90	BUTTERCUP COTTAGE	RT	40.00	46.00-72.00
90	CHERRY COTTAGE	RT	33.50	39.00
90	CONVENT IN THE WOODS	OP	175.00	195.00
90	KING'S ARMS, THE	OP	450.00	488.00-520.00
90	MRS. PINKERTON'S POST OFFICE	OP	72.50	70.00

YR	NAME	LIMIT	ISSUE	TREND
90	OLDE YORK TOLL	RT	82.50	117.00-195.00
90	OTTER REACH	OP	33.50	30.00
90	PERIWINKLE COTTAGE	OP	165.00	170.00
90	ROBIN'S GATE	RT	33.50	39.00
90	ROWAN LODGE	RT	50.00	65.00-137.00
90	RUNSWICK HOUSE	OP	62.50	55.00
90	STRAWBERRY COTTAGE	OP	36.00	35.00
90	SULGRAVE MANOR	RT	120.00	137.00
91	ANNE OF CLEVES	OP	250.00	250.00
91	ARMADA HOUSE	OP	175.00	130.00
91	BRIDGE HOUSE 1991	OP	25.00	20.00
91	CHATSWORTH VIEW	RT	250.00	390.00
91	DAISY COTTAGE	OP	37.50	30.00
91	DOVETAILS	RT	90.00	104.00
91	FARTHING LODGE	OP	37.50	30.00
91	FLOWER SELLERS, THE	RT	110.00	110.00
91	HOPCROFT COTTAGE	RT	120.00	124.00
91	JOHN BARLEYCORN COTTAGE	RT	130.00	150.00
91	LACE LANE	OP	90.00	70.00
91	LAPWORTH LOCK	RT	82.50	98.00
91	MICKLEGATE ANTIQUES	OP	90.00	80.00
91	MOONLIGHT COVE	RT	82.50	83.00
91	OLD SHOP AT BIGNOR	RT	215.00	220.00
91	PARADISE LODGE	RT	130.00	143.00
91	PEAR TREE HOUSE	RT	82.50	98.00
91	PRIEST'S HOUSE, THE	RT	180.00	293.00
91	PRIMROSE HILL	RT	46.50	47.00
91	SAXHAM ST. EDMUNDS	RT	1550.00	1365.00-1560.00
91	TILLERS GREEN	RT	60.00	60.00
91	VILLAGE SCHOOL	OP	120.00	120.00
91	WELLINGTON LODGE	RT	55.00	55.00
91	WITHAM DELPH	RT	110.00	120.00
92	BOW COTTAGE	RT	128.00	135.00
92	CHOCOLATE HOUSE, THE	OP	130.00	90.00
92	DERWENT-LE-DALE	OP	75.00	75.00
92	FINCHINGFIELDS	RT	90.00	90.00
92	GRANNY SMITHS	OP	60.00	45.00
92	GRANTCHESTER MEADOWS	OP	275.00	275.00
92	HIGH GHYLL FARM	OP	360.00	360.00
92	HONEYSUCKLE COTTAGE (10TH ANNIVERSARY)	YR	195.00	130.00-175.00
92	NUTSHELL, THE	RT	75.00	75.00
92	OAKWOOD SMITHY	OP	450.00	300.00
92	PIXIE HOUSE	RT	55.00	55.00
92	PUFFIN ROW	OP	127.50	95.00
92	RUSTIC ROOF HOUSE	OP	110.00	80.00
92	WEDDING BELLS	OP	75.00	50.00
*		**ENGLISH TEA ROOM COLLECTION**		
95	BARGATE COTTAGE TEA ROOM	OP	160.00	120.00
95	GRANDMA BATTY'S TEA ROOM	OP	120.00	90.00
D. TATE		**FRAMED ENGLISH PLAQUES**		
90	ASHDOWN HALL	RT	59.50	60.00
90	BATTLEVIEW	RT	59.50	60.00
90	CAT SLIDE COTTAGE	RT	59.50	60.00
90	COOMBE COT	RT	59.50	60.00
90	FELL VIEW	RT	59.50	60.00
90	FLINT FIELDS	RT	59.50	60.00
90	HUNTINGTON HOUSE	RT	59.50	60.00
90	JUBILEE LODGE	RT	59.50	60.00
90	STOWSIDE	RT	59.50	60.00
90	TREVAN COVE	RT	59.50	60.00
D. TATE		**FRAMED IRISH PLAQUES**		
90	BALLYTEAG HOUSE	RT	59.50	60.00
90	CROCKUNA CROFT	RT	59.50	60.00
90	PEARSES COTTAGES	RT	59.50	60.00
90	SHANNONS BANK	RT	59.50	60.00
D. TATE		**FRAMED SCOTTISH PLAQUES**		
90	BARRA BLACK HOUSE	RT	59.50	60.00
90	FIFE NESS	RT	59.50	60.00
90	KYLE POINT	RT	59.50	60.00
90	PRESTON OAT MILL	RT	59.50	60.00
D. TATE		**FRENCH COLLECTION**		
91	L'AUBERGE D'ARMORIQUE	OP	220.00	170.00
91	LA BERGERIE DU PERIGORD	OP	230.00	170.00
91	LA CABANE DYE GARDIAN	OP	55.00	45.00
91	LA CHAUMIERE DU VERGER	OP	120.00	95.00
91	LA MASELLE DE NADAILLAC	OP	130.00	95.00
91	LA PORTE SCHOENENBERG	OP	75.00	60.00
91	LE MANOIR DE CHAMPFLEURI	OP	265.00	215.00
91	LE MAS DU VIGNERON	OP	120.00	85.00
91	LE PETITE MONTMARTRE	OP	130.00	95.00
91	LOCMARIA	OP	65.00	50.00
D. TATE		**GERMAN COLLECTION**		
87	DAS GEBIRGSKIRCHLEIN	OP	120.00	120.00
87	HAUS IM RHEINLAND	OP	220.00	215.00
87	JAGHUTTE	OP	82.50	85.00
87	MEERSBURGER WEINSTUBE	OP	82.50	70.00
87	MOSELHAUS	OP	140.00	150.00
87	NURNBERGER BURGERHAUS	OP	140.00	150.00

YR	NAME	LIMIT	ISSUE	TREND
87	SCHWARZWALDHAUS	OP	140.00	120.00
88	DAS RATHAUS	OP	140.00	150.00
88	DER FAMILIENSCHREIN	RT	52.50	90.00
88	DIE KLEINEBACKEREI	RT	68.00	80.00
92	ALTE SCHMIEDE	OP	175.00	120.00
92	DER BUCHERWURM	OP	140.00	100.00
92	ROSENGARTENHAUS	OP	120.00	90.00
92	STRANDVOGTHAUS	OP	120.00	90.00
D. TATE				**IRISH COTTAGES**
87	DONEGAL COTTAGE	RT	29.00	34.00-98.00
89	BALLYKERNE CROFT	RT	75.00	78.00-124.00
89	HEGARTY'S HOME	RT	68.00	110.00
89	KENNEDY HOMESTEAD	OP	33.50	30.00
89	KILMORE QUAY	RT	68.00	117.00-130.00
89	LIMERICK HOUSE	RT	110.00	104.00-195.00
89	MAGILLIGANS	OP	33.50	30.00
89	O'LACEY'S STORE	OP	68.00	60.00
89	PAT COHEN'S BAR	RT	110.00	130.00
89	QUIET COTTAGE	RT	72.50	130.00
89	ST. COLUMBIA'S SCHOOL	OP	47.50	40.00
89	ST. KEVIN'S SCHOOL	OP	55.00	60.00
89	ST. PATRICK'S CHURCH	RT	185.00	254.00
89	THOOR BALLYLEE	RT	105.00	120.00
D. SIMPSON				**LAKELAND BRIDGE PLAQUES**
89	AIRA FORCE	RT	35.00	35.00
89	ASHNESS BRIDGE	RT	35.00	35.00
89	BIRKS BRIDGE	RT	35.00	35.00
89	BRIDGE HOUSE	RT	35.00	34.00-91.00
89	HARTSOP PACKHORSE	RT	35.00	35.00
89	STOCKLEY BRIDGE	RT	35.00	35.00
*				**LAKELAND CHRISTMAS**
95	LANGDALE COTTAGE	*	48.00	48.00
95	PATTERDALE COTTAGE	OP	48.00	35.00
95	RYDAL COTTAGE	OP	44.75	35.00
96	ALL SAINTS WATERMILLOCK	OP	50.00	50.00
96	BORROWDALE SCHOOL	OP	35.00	35.00
96	MILLBECK COTTAGE	OP	35.00	35.00
*				**LILLIPUT LANE COLLECTORS CLUB**
95	PORLOCK DOWN	RT	135.00	135.00
95	THIMBLE COTTAGE	RT	*	*
96	MEADOWSWEET COTTAGE	OP	110.00	110.00
D. TATE				**LILLIPUT LANE COLLECTORS CLUB**
86	CRENDON MANOR	RT	285.00	1008.00-1105.00
86	PACKHORSE BRIDGE	RT	*	358.00-780.00
87	LITTLE LOST DOG	RT	*	715.00
87	YEW TREE FARM	RT	160.00	182.00-260.00
88	WISHING WELL	RT	*	91.00-104.00
89	WENLOCK RISE	RT	175.00	189.00-208.00
90	BRIDLE WAY	RT	100.00	111.00-150.00
90	COZY CORNER	RT	*	34.00-52.00
90	DOVECOT, THE	RT	50.00	65.00-98.00
90	LAVENDER COTTAGE	RT	50.00	52.00-59.00
91	GARDENERS COTTAGE	RT	120.00	111.00-130.00
91	PUDDLEBROOK	RT	*	34.00-46.00
91	WREN COTTAGE	RT	13.95	78.00
92	FORGET-ME-NOT	RT	130.00	111.00-169.00
92	PUSSY WILLOW	RT	*	34.00-52.00
D. SIMPSON				**LONDON PLAQUES**
89	BIG BEN	RT	39.50	40.00
89	BUCKINGHAM PALACE	RT	39.50	40.00
89	PICCADILLY CIRCUS	RT	39.50	40.00
89	TOWER BRIDGE	RT	39.50	40.00
89	TOWER OF LONDON	RT	39.50	40.00
89	TRAFALGAR SQUARE	RT	39.50	40.00
D. TATE				**SCOTTISH COTTAGES**
82	CROFT, THE (WITHOUT SHEEP)	RT	29.00	1225.00-1300.00
84	CROFT, THE (RENOVATED)	RT	36.00	52.00-195.00
85	PRESTON MILL	RT	45.00	72.00-156.00
87	EAST NEUK	RT	29.00	34.00-98.00
87	PRESTON MILL (RENOVATED)	OP	62.50	72.50
89	BLAIR ATHOLL	RT	275.00	292.00-423.00
89	CARRICK HOUSE	OP	47.50	35.00
89	CLAYPOTTS CASTLE	OP	72.50	70.00
89	CRAIGIEVAR CASTLE	RT	185.00	215.00-375.00
89	CULLODEN COTTAGE	OP	36.00	35.00
89	INVERLOCHIE HAME	OP	47.50	40.00
89	JOHN KNOX HOUSE	RT	68.00	150.00-163.00
89	KENMORE COTTAGE	OP	87.00	85.00-100.00
89	STOCKWELL TENEMENT	OP	62.50	70.00
90	CAWDOR CASTLE	RT	295.00	450.00-660.00
90	ELLEAN DONAN	OP	145.00	195.00
90	FISHERMANS BOTHY	OP	36.00	35.00
90	GLENLOCHIE LODGE	RT	110.00	91.00-156.00
90	HEBRIDEAN HAME	RT	55.00	59.00-78.00
90	KINLOCHNESS	OP	79.00	111.00
90	KIRKBRAE COTTAGE	RT	55.00	85.00-90.00
92	CULROSS HOUSE	OP	90.00	70.00
92	DUART CASTLE	RT	450.00	630.00-715.00

Kenilworth Castle *(Dickens' Village) was available for $40 to collectors who were purchasing $100 worth of Department 56 merchandise.*

Anne Shaw Toys *was issued with the "Cherry Lane Shops" for Department 56's New England Village.*

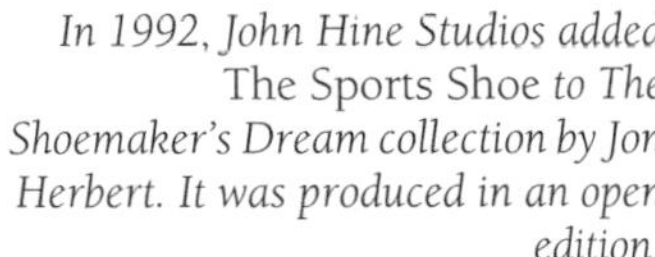

In 1992, John Hine Studios added The Sports Shoe *to The Shoemaker's Dream collection by Jon Herbert. It was produced in an open edition.*

C. Fletcher Public House *(Dickens' Village) was the fourth limited edition to be produced by Department 56.*

YR	NAME	LIMIT	ISSUE	TREND
92	ERISKAY CROFT	OP	50.00	40.00
92	MAIR HAVEN	OP	46.50	35.00
A. YARRINGTON			**SCOTTISH COTTAGES**	
85	7 ST. ANDREWS SQUARE	RT	15.95	130.00-169.00
D. TATE			**SPECIAL EVENT COLLECTION**	
89	COMMEMORATIVE MEDALLION-1989 SOUTH BEND	CL	*	105.00
90	ROWAN LODGE 1990-SOUTH BEND	RT	50.00	390.00-585.00
91	GAMEKEEPERS COTTAGE-1991 SOUTH BEND	RT	75.00	390.00-501.00
92	ASHBERRY COTTAGE-1992 SOUTH BEND	RT	*	325.00-455.00
*			**STUDLEY ROYAL COLLECTION**	
95	FOUNTAIN'S ABBEY	3500	395.00	395.00
D. TATE			**UNFRAMED PLAQUES**	
89	LARGE LOWER BROCKHAMPTON	RT	120.00	120.00
89	LARGE SOMERSET SPRINGTIME	RT	130.00	130.00
89	MEDIUM COBBLE COMBE COTTAGE	RT	68.00	68.00
89	MEDIUM WISHING WELL	RT	75.00	75.00
89	SMALL STONEY WALL LEA	RT	47.50	48.00
89	SMALL WOODSIDE FARM	RT	47.50	48.00
*			**VILLAGE SHOP COLLECTION**	
96	BAKER'S SHOP VAN	OP	16.00	16.00
96	CHINA SHOP VAN	OP	16.00	16.00
D. TATE			**VILLAGE SHOP COLLECTION**	
92	GREENGROCERS, THE	OP	120.00	80.00
*			**WELSH COLLECTION**	
92	ST. GOVAN'S CHAPEL	OP	75.00	75.00
D. TATE			**WELSH COLLECTION**	
84	HERMITAGE	RT	30.00	234.00-299.00
86	BRECON BACH	RT	42.00	52.00-72.00
87	RENOVATED HERMITAGE	RT	42.50	50.00-60.00
91	BRO DAWEL	OP	37.50	30.00
91	TUDOR MERCHANT	OP	90.00	70.00
91	UGLY HOUSE	OP	55.00	50.00

MICHAEL'S LTD.

YR	NAME	LIMIT	ISSUE	TREND
B. BAKER			**DEJA VU COLLECTION**	
93	AMERICAN CLASSIC	500	99.00	110.00
93	JAMES RIVER PLANTATION	500	108.00	120.00
94	HILL TOP MANSION	1200	100.00	110.00
94	PAINTED LADIES	1200	125.00	135.00
94	WHITE POINT	700	97.00	105.00

MIDWEST OF CANNON FALLS

YR	NAME	LIMIT	ISSUE	TREND
*			**COTTONTAIL LANE COLLECTION**	
92	CONFECTIONARY SHOP/LIGHTED 06335-5	RT	43.00	43.00
92	FLOWER SHOP/LIGHTED 06333-9	RT	43.00	43.00
92	SPRINGTIME COTTAGE/LIGHTED	RT	43.00	43.00
92	VICTORIAN HOUSE/LIGHTED 06332-1	OP	43.00	43.00
93	BAKER/LIGHTED 01396-0	OP	43.00	43.00
93	CHURCH/LIGHTED 01385-4	RT	42.00	42.00
93	COTTONTAIL INN/LIGHTED 01394-6	OP	43.00	43.00
93	PAINTING STUDIO/LIGHTED 01395-5	RT	43.00	43.00
93	ROSE COTTAGE/LIGHTED 01386-1	RT	43.00	43.00
93	SCHOOLHOUSE/LIGHTED 01378-6	OP	43.00	43.00
94	BED & BREAKFAST/LIGHTED 00337-4	OP	43.00	43.00
94	CHAPEL/LIGHTED 00331-2	RT	43.00	43.00
94	GENERAL STORE/LIGHTED 00340-4	OP	43.00	43.00
94	PORCELAIN LIGHTED GARDEN VALLEY CHAPEL	3000	43.00	275.00
94	TRAIN STATION/LIGHTED 00330-5	OP	43.00	43.00
95	BOUTIQUE & BEAUTY SHOP/LIGHTED 12301-0	OP	45.00	45.00
95	CAFE/LIGHTED 12303-4	OP	45.00	45.00
95	PORCELAIN LIGHTED ROSEBUD MANOR	3500	45.00	45.00
95	ROSEBUD MANOR/LIGHTED 12304-1	RT	45.00	45.00
95	TOWN HALL/LIGHTED 12300-3	OP	45.00	45.00
96	BANDSHELL/LIGHTED 15753-4	OP	50.00	50.00
96	BUNGALOW/LIGHTED 15752-7	OP	45.00	45.00
96	CATHEDRAL/LIGHTED 12302-7	OP	47.00	47.00
96	FIRE STATION W/FIGURINES/LIGHTED 15830-2	CL	90.00	90.00
96	TOWN GARDEN SHOPPE/LIGHTED 12751-0	OP	45.00	45.00
*			**CREEPY HOLLOW COLLECTION**	
92	DR. FRANKENSTEIN'S HOUSE/LIGHTED 01621-3	RT	40.00	40.00
92	DRACULA'S CASTLE/LIGHTED 01627-5	RT	40.00	40.00
92	MUMMY'S MORTUARY/LIGHTED 01641-1	RT	40.00	40.00
92	WITCHES COVE/LIGHTED 01665-7	RT	40.00	40.00
93	BLOOD BANK/LIGHTED 08548-6	OP	40.00	40.00
93	HAUNTED HOTEL/LIGHTED 08549-3	OP	40.00	40.00
93	SHOPPE OF HORROS/LIGHTED 08550-9	RT	40.00	40.00
94	CAULDRON CAFE/LIGHTED 10649-5	OP	40.00	40.00
94	MEDICASL GHOUL SCHOOL/LIGHTED 10651-8	OP	40.00	40.00
94	PHANTOM'S OPERA/LIGHTED 10650-1	OP	40.00	40.00
95	BEWITCHING BELFRY/LIGHTED 13355-2	OP	50.00	50.00
95	FUNERAL PARLOR 13356-9	OP	50.00	50.00
95	SKELETON CINEMA/LIGHTED 13354-5	CL	50.00	50.00
96	CASTLE/LIGHTED 16959-9	CL	50.00	50.00
96	GYPSY WAGON/LIGHTED 16663-5	OP	45.00	45.00
96	JACK-O-LANT-INN 16665-9	OP	45.00	45.00
96	SCHOOL HOUSE/LIGHTED 1662-8	OP	45.00	45.00

YR	NAME	LIMIT	ISSUE	TREND

PACIFIC RIM

YR	NAME	LIMIT	ISSUE	TREND
P. SEBERN				**BRISTOL TOWNSHIP**
90	BEDFORD MANOR	OP	30.00	30.00
90	BLACK SWAN MILLINERY	OP	30.00	30.00
90	BRISTOL BOOKS	OP	35.00	35.00
90	COVENTRY HOUSE	RT	30.00	30.00
90	GEO. STRAITH GROCER	OP	25.00	25.00
90	HIGH GATE MILL	OP	40.00	40.00
90	IRON HORSE LIVERY	RT	30.00	35.00
90	MAPS & CHARTS	OP	25.00	25.00
90	QUEEN'S ROAD CHURCH	OP	40.00	40.00
90	SILVERSMITH	OP	30.00	30.00
90	SOUTHWICK CHURCH	OP	30.00	30.00
90	TRINITY CHURCH	RT	30.00	35.00
90	VIOLIN SHOP	OP	30.00	30.00
90	WEXFORD MANOR	OP	25.00	25.00
91	BRIDGESTONE CHURCH	RT	30.00	35.00
91	ELMSTONE HOUSE	RT	30.00	35.00
91	FLOWER SHOP	OP	30.00	30.00
91	HARDWICKE HOUSE	RT	30.00	35.00
91	KILBY COTTAGE	RT	30.00	35.00
91	PEGGLESWORTH INN	RT	40.00	40.00
93	CHESTERFIELD HOUSE	OP	30.00	30.00
93	FOXDOWN MANOR	OP	30.00	30.00
94	SHOTWICK INN & SURGERY	OP	35.00	35.00
94	SURREY ROAD CHURCH	OP	40.00	40.00
95	KING'S GATE SCHOOL	OP	30.00	30.00
P. SEBERN				**BRISTOL WATERFRONT**
92	ADMIRALTY SHIPPING	OP	30.00	30.00
92	AVON FISH CO.	OP	30.00	30.00
92	CHANDLER	OP	30.00	30.00
92	CUSTOMS HOUSE	OP	40.00	40.00
92	HAWKE EXPORTS	OP	40.00	40.00
92	QUARTER DECK INN	OP	40.00	40.00
92	REGENT WAREHOUSE	OP	40.00	40.00
93	BRISTOL POINT LIGHTHOUSE	OP	45.00	45.00
93	LOWER QUAY CHAPEL	OP	40.00	40.00
93	RUSTY KNIGHT INN	OP	35.00	35.00
94	BRISTOL TATTLER	OP	40.00	40.00
94	PORTSHEAD LIGHTHOUSE	OP	30.00	30.00
95	BRISTOL CHANNEL LIGHTHOUSE	OP	30.00	30.00

SHELIA'S COLLECTIBLES

YR	NAME	LIMIT	ISSUE	TREND
S. THOMPSON				**ACCESSORIES**
94	AMISH QUILT LINE	1500	18.00	35.00
94	FORMAL GARDEN	1500	18.00	30.00
94	SUNRISE AT 80 MEETING	1500	18.00	30.00
94	VICTORIAN ARBOR	1500	18.00	35.00
95	FLOWER GARDEN	OP	13.00	13.00
95	REAL ESTATE SIGN	OP	12.00	12.00
95	WISTERIA ARBOR	OP	12.00	12.00
96	AUTUMN TREE	OP	14.00	14.00
96	BARBER GAZEBO	OP	13.00	13.00
96	GRAZING COWS	OP	12.00	12.00
96	SAILBOAT	OP	12.00	12.00
96	SPRING TREE	OP	14.00	14.00
96	SUMMERTIME PICKET FENCE	OP	12.00	12.00
96	TROPICAL PALM TREE	OP	14.00	14.00
S. THOMPSON				**AMERICAN BARNS**
94	PENNSYLVANIA DUTCH BARN	OP	18.00	18.00
94	ROCK CITY BARN	OP	18.00	18.00
95	CASEY BARN	OP	19.00	19.00
95	MAIL POUCH BARN	OP	19.00	19.00
S. THOMPSON				**AMERICAN GOTHIC**
93	GOTHIC REVIVAL COTTAGE	2500	20.00	20.00
93	MELE HOUSE	2500	20.00	20.00
93	PERKINS HOUSE	2500	20.00	20.00
93	ROSE ARBOR	2500	14.00	15.00
93	ROSELAND COTTAGE	2500	20.00	20.00
S. THOMPSON				**AMISH VILLAGE**
93	AMISH BARN	OP	17.00	17.00
93	AMISH BUGGY	OP	12.00	12.00
93	AMISH HOME	OP	17.00	17.00
93	AMISH SCHOOL	OP	15.00	15.00
93	COVERED BRIDGE	OP	16.00	16.00
S. THOMPSON				**ARTIST CHOICE**
95	BANTA HOUSE	RT	24.00	24.00
95	GREENMAN HOUSE	RT	24.00	24.00
95	RILEY-CUTLER	RT	24.00	24.00
95	WELLER HOUSE	RT	24.00	24.00
S. THOMPSON				**ATLANTA**
95	FOX THEATRE	OP	19.00	19.00
95	HAMMONDS HOUSE	OP	18.00	18.00
95	SWAN HOUSE	OP	18.00	18.00
95	TULLIE SMITH	OP	18.00	18.00
95	VICTORIAN PLAYHOUSE	OP	17.00	17.00
95	WREN'S NEST	OP	19.00	19.00

YR	NAME	LIMIT	ISSUE	TREND
S. THOMPSON				**CHARLESTON**
93	ASHE HOUSE	OP	16.00	16.00
93	CITADEL	OP	16.00	16.00
93	CITY HALL	1300	15.00	50.00
93	COLLEGE OF CHARLESTON	OP	16.00	16.00
93	DRAYTON HOUSE	OP	18.00	18.00
93	JOHN RUTLEDGE HOME	OP	16.00	16.00
93	SINGLE SIDE PORCH	OP	16.00	16.00
95	BOONE HALL PLANTATION	OP	18.00	18.00
95	MAGNOLIA PARLOR HOUSE	OP	19.00	19.00
95	O'DONNELLS FOLLY	OP	18.00	18.00
S. THOMPSON				**CHARLESTON BATTERY**
96	22 S. BATTERY	OP	19.00	19.00
96	24 S. BATTERY	OP	19.00	19.00
96	26 S. BATTERY	OP	19.00	19.00
96	28 S. BATTERY	OP	19.00	19.00
S. THOMPSON				**CHARLESTON CHURCHES & PUBLIC BUILDINGS**
96	HUGENOT CHURCH	OP	19.00	19.00
S. THOMPSON				**CHARLESTON HOUSE II**
96	SOTTILE HOUSE	OP	19.00	19.00
S. THOMPSON				**COLLECTIBLE ACCESSORIES**
93	APPLE TREE	RT	12.00	12.00
93	DOGWOOD TREE	RT	12.00	12.00
S. THOMPSON				**COLLECTORS SOCIETY**
93	ANNE PEACOCK HOUSE	*	16.00	16.00
93	SUSAN B. ANTHONY	*	*	70.00
94	IVY GREEN	*	*	*
94	SEASVIEW COTTAGE	*	17.00	17.00
S. THOMPSON				**GALVESTON**
95	BEISSNER HOUSE	OP	19.00	19.00
95	DANCING PAVILLION	OP	19.00	19.00
95	FRENKEL HOME	OP	19.00	19.00
95	REYMERSHOFFER	OP	19.00	19.00
S. THOMPSON				**GHOST HOUSE SERIES**
94	INSIDE-OUTSIDE HOUSE	RT	18.00	18.00
94	PIRATE'S HOUSE	RT	18.00	18.00
95	GAFFOS HOUSE	OP	19.00	19.00
95	RED CASTLE	OP	19.00	19.00
S. THOMPSON				**GONE WITH THE WIND**
95	AUNT PITTY POT'S	OP	24.00	24.00
95	GENERAL STORE	OP	24.00	24.00
95	LOEW'S GRAND	RT	24.00	24.00
95	TARA	OP	24.00	24.00
95	TWELVE OAKS	OP	24.00	24.00
96	SILHOUETTE	OP	16.00	16.00
S. THOMPSON				**INVENTOR SERIES**
93	FORD MOTOR COMPANY	OP	17.00	17.00
93	MENLO PARK LABORATORY	OP	16.00	16.00
93	NOAH WEBSTER HOUSE	OP	15.00	15.00
93	WRIGHT CYCLE SHOP	OP	17.00	17.00
S. THOMPSON				**JAZZY NEW ORLEANS**
94	BEAUREGARD KEYS	OP	18.00	18.00
94	GALLIER HOUSE	OP	18.00	18.00
94	LABRANCHE BUILD	OP	18.00	18.00
94	LEPRETRE HOUSE	OP	18.00	18.00
S. THOMPSON				**KEY WEST**
95	ARTIST HOUSE	OP	19.00	19.00
95	EYEBROW HOUSE	OP	18.00	18.00
95	HEMINGWAY HOUSE	OP	19.00	19.00
95	ILLINGSWORTH	OP	19.00	19.00
95	SHOTGUN HOUSE	OP	17.00	17.00
95	SHOTGUN SISTER	OP	17.00	17.00
95	SOUTHERNMOST	OP	18.00	18.00
S. THOMPSON				**LADIES BY THE SEA**
96	ABBEY II	OP	19.00	19.00
96	CENTENNIAL COTTAGE	OP	19.00	19.00
96	HALL COTTAGE	OP	19.00	19.00
96	HEART BLOSSOM	OP	19.00	19.00
S. THOMPSON				**LIGHTHOUSES**
93	ASSATEAGUE ISLAND LIGHT	OP	17.00	17.00
93	CHARLESTON LIGHT	OP	15.00	15.00
93	NEW LONDON LEDGE LIGHT	OP	17.00	17.00
93	ROUND ISLAND LIGHT	OP	17.00	17.00
93	THOMAS POINT LIGHT	OP	17.00	17.00
95	CAPE HATTERAS LIGHT	OP	18.00	18.00
S. THOMPSON				**MACKINAC**
96	AMBERG COTTAGE	OP	19.00	19.00
96	ANNE COTTAGE	OP	19.00	19.00
96	REARICK COTTAGE	OP	19.00	19.00
96	WINDERMERE HOTEL	OP	19.00	19.00
S. THOMPSON				**MAIL ORDER VICTORIANS**
94	BREHAUT HOUSE	3300	24.00	24.00
94	GOELLER HOUSE	3300	24.00	24.00
94	HENDERSON HOUSE	3300	24.00	24.00
94	TROTMAN HOUSE	3300	24.00	24.00

YR	NAME	LIMIT	ISSUE	TREND
S. THOMPSON				**MARTHA'S VINEYARD**
93	ALICE'S WONDERLAND	OP	16.00	16.00
93	CAMPGROUND COTTAGE	OP	16.00	16.00
93	GINGERBREAD COTTAGE	RT	16.00	16.00
93	WOOD VALENTINE	OP	16.00	16.00
95	BLUE COTTAGE	OP	18.00	18.00
95	TRAILS END	OP	18.00	18.00
95	WHITE COTTAGE	OP	18.00	18.00
S. THOMPSON				**OLD FASHIONED CHRISTMAS**
94	CONWAY SCENIC RAILROAD STATION	OP	18.00	18.00
94	DWIGHT HOUSE	OP	18.00	18.00
94	GENERAL MERCHANDISE	OP	18.00	18.00
94	OLD FIRST CHURCH	OP	18.00	18.00
95	CHRISTMAS INN	OP	19.00	19.00
95	TOWN SQUARE TREE	OP	18.00	18.00
S. THOMPSON				**PAINTED LADIES III**
93	GREEN STOCKTON	OP	16.00	16.00
93	LINDA LEE	OP	16.00	16.00
93	PINK STOCKTON	OP	16.00	16.00
93	TAN STOCKTON	OP	16.00	16.00
95	STEINER COTTAGE	OP	18.00	18.00
96	CREAM STOCKTON	OP	19.00	19.00
S. THOMPSON				**PANORAMIC LIGHTS**
96	JEFFRY HOOK	OP	19.00	19.00
96	NEW CANAL LIGHT	OP	19.00	19.00
96	QUADDY HEAD	OP	19.00	19.00
96	SPLIT ROCK LIGHTHOUSE	OP	19.00	19.00
S. THOMPSON				**PLANTATIONS**
95	FARLEY	RT	18.00	18.00
95	LONGWOOD	OP	19.00	19.00
95	MERRY SHERWOOD	OP	18.00	18.0
95	SAN FRANCISCO	OP	19.00	19.00
S. THOMPSON				**RAINBOW ROW**
93	AURORA RAINBOW ROW	OP	13.00	13.00
93	BLUE RAINBOW ROW	OP	13.00	13.00
93	CREAM RAINBOW ROW	OP	13.00	13.00
93	GRAY RAINBOW ROW	OP	13.00	13.00
93	GREEN RAINBOW ROW	OP	13.00	13.00
93	LAVENDER RAINBOW ROW	OP	13.00	13.00
93	OFF-WHITE RAINBOW ROW	OP	13.00	13.00
93	PINK RAINBOW ROW	OP	13.00	13.00
93	YELLOW RAINBOW ROW	OP	13.00	13.00
S. THOMPSON				**SAN FRANCISCO**
95	BRANDYWINE	OP	19.00	19.00
95	ECLECTIC BLUE	OP	19.00	19.00
95	EDWARDIAN GREEN	OP	19.00	19.00
95	QUEEN ROSE	OP	19.00	19.00
S. THOMPSON				**SAVANNAH**
93	CHESTNUT HOUSE	OP	18.00	18.00
93	OWENS THOMAS HOUSE	OP	16.00	16.00
96	ASENDORF HOUSE	OP	19.00	19.00
S. THOMPSON				**SHOW PIECE**
95	BALDWIN HOUSE	RT	20.00	20.00
96	WINNIE WATSON	OP	*	*
S. THOMPSON				**SOUTH CAROLINA LADIES**
96	CINNAMON HILL	OP	19.00	19.00
96	DAVIS-JOHNSEY	OP	19.00	19.00
96	INMAN HOUSE	OP	19.00	19.00
96	MONTGOMERY HOUSE	OP	19.00	19.00
S. THOMPSON				**VICTORIAN SPRINGTIME**
93	HEFFRON HOUSE	RT	17.00	17.00
93	JACOBSEN HOUSE	RT	17.00	17.00
93	RALSTON HOUSE	RT	17.00	17.00
93	SESSIONS HOUSE	RT	17.00	17.00
95	DRAGON HOUSE	OP	19.00	19.00
95	E.B. HALL	OP	19.00	19.00
95	GIBNEY HOME	OP	19.00	19.00
95	RAY HOME	OP	19.00	19.00
95	VICTORIA	OP	19.00	19.00
96	CLARK HOUSE	OP	19.00	19.00
96	GOODWILL	OP	19.00	19.00
96	QUEEN ANNE	OP	19.00	19.00
96	SHEPARD HOUSE	OP	19.00	19.00
96	URFER HOUSE	OP	19.00	19.00
S. THOMPSON				**WEST COAST LIGHTHOUSES**
95	EAST BROTHER LIGHTHOUSE	OP	19.00	19.00
95	MUKILTEO LIGHT	OP	18.00	18.00
95	PAINT FERMIN	OP	18.00	18.00
95	YAQUINA LIGHT	OP	18.00	18.00
S. THOMPSON				**WILLIAMSBURG**
95	CAPTIOL	OP	18.00	18.00
95	RALEIGH TAVERN	OP	18.00	18.00

SJS DESIGNS

YR	NAME	LIMIT	ISSUE	TREND
S. STENTIFORD				**IVY ROSE COLLECTION**
93	IVY POINT LIGHTHOUSE	2000	27.00	32.00
93	MELMACKER'S LOBSTER POT CAFE	2000	27.00	32.00

This festive and whimsical Christmas Boot *was the inspiration of Jon Herbert. The line of Boot Houses is produced by John Hine Studios.*

Audrey's Tea Room *was only issued for a limited time due to the mold being broken in a highway accident. The piece was created by David Winter for John Hine Studios.*

Clown Boot *makes an impressive residence for those tiny enough to enjoy it. This piece by Jon Herbert also makes an equally impressive collectible (John Hine Studios).*

The "Great Coast Region" series from Harbour Lights added Pensacola, FL *in 1995. The edition was limited to 9,500 pieces.*

YR	NAME	LIMIT	ISSUE	TREND
93	PERIWINKLE COTTAGE, THE	2000	27.00	32.00
93	SEAFLOWER INN, THE	2000	32.00	38.00
93	VALERIE ELIZABETH'S BEACH HOUSE	2000	25.00	30.00
94	ANTIQUES BARN	2000	28.00	33.00
94	AUNTIE GEN'S	2000	27.00	32.00
94	DARRELL'S COTTAGE	2000	27.00	32.00
94	DOROTHEA'S HOUSE	2000	29.00	34.00
94	FARMER'S MARKET, T HE	2000	27.00	33.00
94	GOG'S ANIMAL BARN	2000	30.00	35.00
94	INA'S FARMHOUSE	2000	30.00	35.00
94	LINDA IRENE'S	2000	28.00	33.00
94	MARY ELLEN'S	2000	27.00	32.00
94	MISS MARGARET'S	2000	29.00	34.00
94	POLICE STATION	2000	24.00	29.00
94	SUNFLOWER COTTAGE, THE	2000	25.00	30.00
94	TOWN PHARMACY	2000	28.00	33.00

SPENCER COLLIN LIGHTHOUSES

C. COLLIN

YR	NAME	LIMIT	ISSUE	TREND
84	PORTSMOUTH LIGHTHOUSE	CL	18.00	18.00
93	ANNISQUAM HARBOR LIGHTHOUSE	2000	46.00	46.00
93	CAPE MAY LIGHTHOUSE	OP	79.00	79.00
93	FORT GRATIOT LIGHTHOUSE	2000	52.00	52.00
93	JUPITER INLET LIGHTHOUSE	2000	84.00	84.00
93	MARSHALL POINT LIGHTHOUSE	2000	46.00	46.00
93	NEW LONDON LEDGE LIGHTHOUSE	2000	120.00	120.00
93	PEGGY'S POINT LIGHTHOUSE	OP	38.00	38.00
93	PONCE INLET LIGHTHOUSE	2000	86.00	86.00
93	SAND ISLAND LIGHTHOUSE	OP	66.00	66.00
93	SPLIT ROCK LIGHTHOUSE	OP	110.00	110.00
93	ST. SIMONS ISLAND LIGHTHOUSE	2000	116.00	116.00
94	POINT ISABEL LIGHTHOUSE	2000	52.00	52.00

C. COLLIN — **ADMIRAL'S LIGHTS--FLAG QUARTER SERIES**

YR	NAME	LIMIT	ISSUE	TREND
94	ALKI POINT LIGHTHOUSE	3000	70.00	70.00
94	DIAMOND HEAD LIGHTHOUSE	3000	124.00	124.00
94	HOSPITAL POINT LIGHTHOUSE	3000	68.00	68.00
94	YERBA BUENA LIGHTHOUSE	3000	90.00	90.00

C. COLLIN — **COMMEMORATIVE STAMP SERIES**

YR	NAME	LIMIT	ISSUE	TREND
89	CAPE HATTERAS LIGHTHOUSE	RT	70.00	70.00

C. COLLIN — **TRADEMARK SERIES**

YR	NAME	LIMIT	ISSUE	TREND
94	10TH ANNIVERSARY LIGHTHOUSE	CL	100.00	100.00

WB STUDIOS

R. KAY — **LIGHTED SNOWHOUSE**

YR	NAME	LIMIT	ISSUE	TREND
93	ESTATE HOUSE	1000	900.00	1000.00

J. TAYLOR — **LIGHTED SNOWHOUSE**

YR	NAME	LIMIT	ISSUE	TREND
92	GREENHOUSE W/WALKWAY	2000	490.00	525.00
94	RAMBLING ROSE	500	660.00	700.00

Dolls

Betty Hodges

Doll collecting has exploded in the collectibles arena, ranking second in popularity among hobbyists in the United States. There are more dolls available today than ever before. They abound in the marketplace in such a variety of genre that one can scarcely ignore them.

As with all buying, your own personal tastes play an important role in collecting. There are unknown factors behind every doll purchase. Why one appeals to you and another does not goes back to some dim reference point. Sometimes there is a special feeling connected with a certain doll, and before you know it, you've acquired it!

Childhood dolls are often the start of a collection. Collectors will go out of their way to acquire a doll they fondly remember from their early years. But no matter how you start collecting, the doll industry continues to proliferate, allowing you to add new creations to your collection at any given time.

No one can guess which dolls produced today will increase in value tomorrow. Through the years, some contemporary dolls have become quite valuable while others have not. The dolls of the early 1900s remain very desirable.

Despite the era in which they grew up, many collectors feel their childhood dolls are as sacrosanct as the ones made decades earlier. These dolls are quite different from their older cousins but still have the same allure.

Limited edition dolls are a new factor in the equation. Putting a production limit on the number of dolls made adds to their desirability. The doll that catches your eye may not be available for very long. This initial limit on the supply can increase the demand for the doll, oftentimes making the doll more valuable over the years.

Today's dolls have myriad diverse characteristics. The collector's desire to add more dolls to his or her collection grows increasingly, and makers fall over themselves to produce them.

There are two definite audiences for dolls produced today—children and adults. The number of dolls bought and kept by adults is unprecedented in the doll world. These dolls are genuine collectibles, which will be cherished. They retain their beauty indefinitely.

Keep accurate records when you acquire your dolls; include the producer's name and the exact outfit the doll is wearing. Take pictures of each doll. Should you ever decide to sell your collection, these details will be essential.

Your personal taste is the key to your collection. Do you know which dolls will become valuable? Probably not, but this should not reduce the enjoyment you get from this hobby.

BETTY HODGES has 25 years of experience in the doll market. A consultant to doll artists, she has supervised dealer booths in international toy and trade markets and edits a doll manufacturer's newsletter.

DOLLS & PLUSH

ANNALEE MOBILITEE

YR	NAME	LIMIT	ISSUE	TREND
91	10 IN. ANNALEE COLLECTOR DOLL	588	149.95	300.00
91	10 IN. AVIATOR FROG (WWI)	2110	19.95	275.00
91	10 IN. BEAR IN NIGHTSHIRT	2774	32.95	75.00
91	10 IN. BEAR IN VELOUR SANTA SUIT	3711	32.95	75.00
91	10 IN. BEAR W/SNOWBALL, KNIT HAT	3121	29.95	75.00
91	10 IN. BLACK CAT	6267	21.95	100.00
91	10 IN. BOB CRATCHET & 5 IN. TINY TIM	639	99.95	300.00
91	10 IN. BRIDE BEAR	2977	39.95	75.00
91	10 IN. CHRISTMAS ELF	16567	15.95	40.00
91	10 IN. CHRISTOPHER COLUMBUS	1132	119.50	400.00
91	10 IN. CONDUCTOR DOLL (MUSIC)	383	129.50	130.00
91	10 IN. COUNTRY BOY BUNNY	1844	42.95	125.00
91	10 IN. COUNTRY GIRL BUNNY	2044	34.95	90.00
91	10 IN. DOE	6541	20.95	75.00
91	10 IN. EASTER PARADE BOY BUNNY	4195	37.95	90.00
91	10 IN. EASTER PARADE GIRL BUNNY	5101	38.95	100.00
91	10 IN. GINGERBREAD BOY	10453	22.45	23.00
91	10 IN. GIRL W/BASKET	3592	37.95	100.00
91	10 IN. GROOM BEAR	2745	39.95	75.00
91	10 IN. HOBO CLOWN	2368	25.45	26.00
91	10 IN. HUSKIE W/5 IN. PUPPY	2860	54.95	150.00
91	10 IN. IN.TINSEL IN. THE ELF	17070	20.45	50.00
91	10 IN. INDIAN MAN	2719	32.95	65.00
91	10 IN. INDIAN WOMAN	2779	32.95	75.00
91	10 IN. JACOB MARLEY	598	89.95	175.00
91	10 IN. KITTEN ON SLED	3810	35.95	90.00
91	10 IN. KITTEN W/KNIT MITTENS	4124	33.95	75.00
91	10 IN. MAN SKATER	4881	45.95	125.00
91	10 IN. MARTHA CRATCHET W/PLUM	2136	59.95	175.00
91	10 IN. MUSIC CONDUCTOR DOLL	*	139.50	375.00
91	10 IN. NATIVITY ANGEL	2112	59.95	150.00
91	10 IN. NATIVITY SET	658	149.95	150.00
91	10 IN. PILGRIM MAN W/BASKET	2374	44.95	75.00
91	10 IN. PILGRIM WOMAN W/TURKEY	2502	44.95	75.00
91	10 IN. REINDEER W/CAP & BELL	10300	22.45	75.00
91	10 IN. SANTA FEEDING REINDEER	2618	79.95	200.00
91	10 IN. SANTA ON ROCKING HORSE	2398	49.95	150.00
91	10 IN. SANTA PIG	2685	31.95	75.00
91	10 IN. SANTA PLAYING W/TRAIN	1525	49.95	250.00
91	10 IN. SANTA W/REINDEER GOLFING	2462	79.95	150.00
91	10 IN. SCROOGE	592	89.95	200.00
91	10 IN. SHEPHERD BOY & LAMB	591	89.95	90.00
91	10 IN. SKATING BUNNY	6027	43.95	150.00
91	10 IN. SNOWY OWL	3163	25.95	50.00
91	10 IN. SPRING ELF	4060	15.95	35.00
91	10 IN. SUMMER SANTA	1926	59.95	225.00
91	10 IN. THE SPIRIT OF '76	1080	175.00	500.00
91	10 IN. TWO WISE MEN W/BRASS	476	109.95	110.00
91	10 IN. VICTORY SKI DOLL	1192	49.50	400.00
91	10 IN. WISE MAN W/CAMEL	650	109.95	400.00
91	10 IN. WOMAN SKATER	4975	45.95	125.00
91	12 IN. BASKET COUPLE	2028	96.95	200.00
91	12 IN. BAT	3113	29.95	50.00
91	12 IN. CHRISTMAS SWAN	674	63.95	225.00
91	12 IN. DRUMMER BOY	3298	39.95	75.00
91	12 IN. EASTER DUCK W/WATERING	1407	49.95	250.00
91	12 IN. PILGRIM BOY MOUSE	1980	42.95	43.00
91	12 IN. PILGRIM GIRL MOUSE	1978	42.95	43.00
91	12 IN. PJ KID W/BLONDE HAIR	2726	29.95	50.00
91	12 IN. PJ KID W/BROWN HAIR	2307	29.95	50.00
91	12 IN. SANTA DUCK	1187	53.45	250.00
91	12 IN. SANTA W/POT BELLED STOVE	5887	59.95	100.00
91	12 IN. SANTA'S HELPER PAINTING	5274	35.95	75.00
91	12 IN. SANTA'S POSTMAN	6980	35.95	50.00
91	12 IN. SCARECROW	2330	40.95	100.00
91	12 IN. SPIDER	5194	32.95	125.00
91	12 IN. SPRING SWAN	615	49.95	225.00
91	12 IN. TREE TOP ANGEL	2589	42.45	125.00
91	12 IN. TUCKERED COUPLE	2574	89.95	90.00
91	12 IN. VELOUR MRS. SANTA	3677	49.95	100.00
91	12 IN. VELOUR SANTA W/TOYBAG	3517	49.95	75.00
91	15 IN. HOBO CLOWN	1295	47.95	150.00
91	18 IN. ANGLE W/INSTRUMENT	1009	55.45	225.00
91	18 IN. BUNNY KID W/BUNNY	2859	49.95	75.00
91	18 IN. CHET SANTA	4511	46.95	125.00
91	18 IN. CHOIR BOY	3120	57.95	175.00
91	18 IN. CHOIR GIRL	2188	57.95	175.00
91	18 IN. DAY-AFTER-CHRISTMAS SANTA	2263	79.45	200.00
91	18 IN. EASTER PARADE BOY BUNNY	2056	62.45	125.00
91	18 IN. EASTER PARADE GIRL BUNNY	2254	62.45	125.00
91	18 IN. GINGERBREAD BOY	3966	50.95	65.00
91	18 IN. MRS. SANTA W/PRESENTS	5497	49.95	100.00
91	18 IN. MRS. SANTA W/TRAY	5143	49.95	125.00
91	18 IN. MRS. SANTA W/TRAY	*	49.95	50.00

YR	NAME	LIMIT	ISSUE	TREND
91	18 IN. NAUGHTY KID	547	74.95	100.00
91	18 IN. PJ KID	1307	39.45	100.00
91	18 IN. PJ KID HANGING STOCKING	1396	46.95	100.00
91	18 IN. PJ KID IN 2 FT. STOCKING	RT	61.95	100.00
91	18 IN. PUMPKIN COSTUME KID	1317	74.45	115.00
91	18 IN. REINDEER W/CHRISTMAS	4053	52.95	150.00
91	18 IN. SANTA W/CARDHOLDER	8056	59.95	125.00
91	18 IN. SANTA W/GIFT LIST	6334	43.95	80.00
91	18 IN. SANTA W/STOCKING	4466	47.95	90.00
91	18 IN. SNOWMAN W/BROOM	4218	43.45	150.00
91	18 IN. SNOWY OWL	965	65.95	175.00
91	18 IN. THORNY THE GHOST	1270	51.95	150.00
91	18 IN. TRICK OR TREAT BUNNY KID	625	49.95	90.00
91	18 IN. WITCH	2033	63.95	150.00
91	22 IN. CHRISTMAS STOCKING	4993	18.45	55.00
91	22 IN. RED CHRISTMAS ELF	3679	34.95	75.00
91	3 IN. WATER BABY IN POND LILY	3720	14.95	175.00
91	30 IN. MR. & MRS. TUCKERED	644	291.45	600.00
91	30 IN. MRS. SANTA W/CARDHOLDER	1483	119.95	150.00
91	30 IN. SANTA W/LIGHTED TREE	509	189.95	200.00
91	30 IN. VELOUR MRS. SANTA W/MUFF	755	160.45	200.00
91	30 IN. VELOUR SANTA W/PIPE & BAG	1221	160.45	200.00
91	36 IN. REINDEER (ANIMATED)	134	339.95	875.00
91	36 IN. REINDEER W/CARDHOLDER	879	148.45	300.00
91	5 IN. ANGEL	9844	22.95	50.00
91	5 IN. BABY SWAN	3168	13.95	50.00
91	5 IN. CHRISTMAS DRAGON	4125	23.95	75.00
91	5 IN. DUCK ON FLEXIBLE FLYER	3822	25.95	50.00
91	5 IN. EASTER PARADE BOY DUCK	4261	21.95	85.00
91	5 IN. EASTER PARADE GIRL DUCK	5105	23.95	85.00
91	5 IN. ELF (WORKSHOP)	16359	13.45	25.00
91	5 IN. FAWN	13027	14.45	25.00
91	5 IN. FLUFFY YELLOW CHICK	6979	15.95	50.00
91	5 IN. LAMB	4302	15.95	45.00
91	5 IN. LEPRECHAUN	6384	15.95	35.00
91	5 IN. SAILOR DUCK	2241	21.95	75.00
91	5 IN. SPRING LAMB	6709	16.95	45.00
91	5 IN. TRIM-A-TREE ELF	10108	12.95	25.00
91	5 IN. WINTER DUCK IN INNER TUBE	2.992	23.95	75.00
91	7 IN. ANGEL ON SLED W/CLOUD	2313	29.95	50.00
91	7 IN. ANGEL W/MUSICAL INSTRUMENT	5879	19.95	50.00
91	7 IN. ARTIST BUNNY W/BRUSH	5346	20.95	90.00
91	7 IN. BAKER MOUSE	6895	25.95	150.00
91	7 IN. BEN FRANKLIN MOUSE	5029	29.95	150.00
91	7 IN. BUNNY KID	3827	23.45	65.00
91	7 IN. CAROLLER BOY	510	22.95	50.00
91	7 IN. CAROLLER BOY MOUSE W/MUSIC	7281	15.45	50.00
91	7 IN. CAROLLER GIRL	5134	22.95	75.00
91	7 IN. CHRISTMAS GNOME	15503	17.95	35.00
91	7 IN. COUNTRY BOY BUNNY	3199	28.95	75.00
91	7 IN. COUNTRY BOY BUNNY	4421	20.45	75.00
91	7 IN. COUNTRY GIRL BUNNY	3805	20.45	100.00
91	7 IN. DISNEY COLLECTION	300	80.00	300.00
91	7 IN. DRAGON KID	1116	31.95	175.00
91	7 IN. DUMMMER BOY	7031	22.45	75.00
91	7 IN. EARTH DAY MOUSE	5863	299.95	150.00
91	7 IN. EASTER PARADE BOY	7043	20.95	50.00
91	7 IN. EASTER PARADE DRESS-UP BOY	*	27.45	28.00
91	7 IN. EASTER PARADE GIRL	9120	18.95	50.00
91	7 IN. FLYING ANGEL W/MISTLETOE	6003	18.95	50.00
91	7 IN. GHOST KID W/PUMPKIN	1982	24.45	75.00
91	7 IN. GNOME W/MUSHROOM	5007	29.95	80.00
91	7 IN. INDIAN BOY	3371	29.95	60.00
91	7 IN. INDIAN GIRL	2777	22.95	60.00
91	7 IN. LOGO KID	26516	19.50	125.00
91	7 IN. MOUSE IN BOX	5526	19.95	40.00
91	7 IN. MOUSE IN SANTA'S HAT	9742	17.95	50.00
91	7 IN. MOUSE W/CANDY CANE	5206	17.95	50.00
91	7 IN. MOUSE W/CHRISTMAS STOCKING	6543	17.95	50.00
91	7 IN. MOUSE W/MAILBAG	14546	25.95	55.00
91	7 IN. MOUSE W/PRESENTS	8075	17.95	50.00
91	7 IN. MOUSE W/SNOWBALL	6805	17.95	40.00
91	7 IN. MOUSE W/TENNIS RACQUET	5674	21.95	40.00
91	7 IN. MR. TUCKERED MOUSE	12413	19.95	40.00
91	7 IN. MRS. SANTA HANGING MERRY	11769	27.95	65.00
91	7 IN. MRS. SANTA W/PRESENTS	8060	26.45	75.00
91	7 IN. MRS. TUCKERED MOUSE	13266	19.95	40.00
91	7 IN. PILGRIM KIDS W/BASKET	2672	53.95	125.00
91	7 IN. PILGRIM MICE SET W/BASKET	2721	42.45	75.00
91	7 IN. PUMPKIN KID	3517	27.45	50.00
91	7 IN. RITZ SNOWMAN	10309	26.95	60.00
91	7 IN. SANTA BRINGING HOME	8604	27.95	70.00
91	7 IN. SANTA IN TUB W/RUBBER	5373	33.95	250.00
91	7 IN. SANTA W/GIFTLIST & TOY BAG	8886	22.45	50.00
91	7 IN. SANTA W/MAILBAG & LETTERS	12156	27.95	50.00
91	7 IN. SANTA W/SLEIGH	3407	39.95	90.00
91	7 IN. SECRETARY MOUSE	6394	29.95	100.00
91	7 IN. SHERIFF MOUSE (D.S)	1191	49.50	200.00
91	7 IN. SKELETON COSTUME KID	2596	24.45	55.00

YR	NAME	LIMIT	ISSUE	TREND
91	7 IN. SLEDDING MOUSE	5950	20.95	50.00
91	7 IN. SNOWMAN W/PIPE	7401	23.95	75.00
91	7 IN. SWEETHEART BOY MOUSE	7865	19.95	50.00
91	7 IN. SWEETHEART GIRL MOUSE	7865	18.95	50.00
91	7 IN. TRICK OR TREAT BUNNY KID	2187	25.95	100.00
91	7 IN. TWO IN A TENT MICE	*	34.95	80.00
91	7 IN. VELOUR MRS. SANTA W/COAT	5808	27.45	50.00
91	7 IN. VELOUR SANTA W/COAT & PIPE	*	27.45	50.00
91	7 IN. VIDEO MOUSE	4978	25.95	150.00
91	7 IN. WAITER MOUSE	4573	25.95	150.00
91	7 IN. WITCH KID	3311	27.45	100.00
91	7 IN. WORKSHOP MOUSE	12536	21.95	100.00
91	7 IN. WORKSHOP SANTA	3872	26.95	75.00
91	DESERT MOUSE HEAD PIN	9141	7.95	35.00
91	LARGE PUMPKIN	1872	48.95	125.00
91	LARGE TURKEY	1132	57.95	95.00
91	RED CROSS NURSE MOUSE HEAD	8572	7.95	25.00
91	SANTA W/PRESENTS	7863	22.95	50.00
91	SMALL TURKEY	2586	34.95	75.00
91	SMALL TURKEY W/7 IN. INDIAN GIRL	1658	57.45	95.00
92	10 IN. ANNALEE BASEBALL PLAYER	5760	29.95	250.00
92	10 IN. ANNALEE PITCHER	1283	35.95	36.00
92	10 IN. BEAR IN NIGHTSHIRT	3434	33.95	75.00
92	10 IN. BEAR IN VELOUR SANTA SUIT	3938	32.95	75.00
92	10 IN. BEAR W/SNOWBALL, KNIT HAT	3826	29.95	75.00
92	10 IN. BLACK CAT	4101	25.95	100.00
92	10 IN. CHRISTMAS ELF	18130	15.95	40.00
92	10 IN. CHRISTMAS EVE BOB	1681	69.95	70.00
92	10 IN. CHRISTMAS EVE SCROOGE	1722	59.95	199.00
92	10 IN. COUNTRY BOY BUNNY	2395	34.95	85.00
92	10 IN. COUNTRY GIRL BUNNY	2577	34.95	90.00
92	10 IN. DOE	2096	20.95	70.00
92	10 IN. EASTER PARADE BOY BUNNY	3902	38.95	90.00
92	10 IN. EASTER PARADE GIRL BUNNY	4832	38.95	90.00
92	10 IN. FATHER TIME	1796	54.95	100.00
92	10 IN. FISHING SANTA IN BOAT	1582	99.95	175.00
92	10 IN. FROG IN BOAT	3231	31.95	32.00
92	10 IN. GINGERBREAD BOY	7361	22.45	23.00
92	10 IN. IN.TINSEL IN. THE ELF	9967	20.45	50.00
92	10 IN. INDIAN MAN	1834	34.45	65.00
92	10 IN. INDIAN WOMAN	1816	32.95	75.00
92	10 IN. JACOB MARLEY	672	89.95	175.00
92	10 IN. KITTEN W/KNIT MITTENS	4004	33.95	75.00
92	10 IN. MAN SKATER	2688	45.95	125.00
92	10 IN. MARTHA CRATCHET W/PLUM	784	59.95	200.00
92	10 IN. MRS. BEAR IN NIGHTSHIRT	4661	38.95	100.00
92	10 IN. PILGRIM MAN W/BASKET	1803	44.95	75.00
92	10 IN. PILGRIM WOMAN W/TURKEY	1904	44.95	75.00
92	10 IN. REINDEER W/CAP & BELL	10650	22.95	75.00
92	10 IN. SANTA AT WORKBENCH	2209	69.95	150.00
92	10 IN. SAVING SANTA	1605	59.95	150.00
92	10 IN. SKATING BUNNY	4005	43.95	115.00
92	10 IN. SNOW QUEEN	4390	38.95	90.00
92	10 IN. SNOWY OWL	2634	25.95	50.00
92	10 IN. TENNIS SANTA	2115	49.95	150.00
92	10 IN. UNCLE SAM FOLK HERO	1034	87.50	88.00
92	10 IN. WOMAN SKATER	2754	45.95	125.00
92	12 IN .BASKET COUPLE	1	600.00	600.00
92	12 IN .BAT	2107	31.95	32.00
92	12 IN. CHEF SANTA	3353	44.95	90.00
92	12 IN. DRUMMER BOY	3316	39.95	75.00
92	12 IN. MRS. SANTA W/POINSETTA	3463	49.95	100.00
92	12 IN. PILGRIM BOY MOUSE	1449	42.95	43.00
92	12 IN. PILGRIM GIRL MOUSE	1474	42.95	43.00
92	12 IN. PJ BOY	7526	29.95	75.00
92	12 IN. PJ GIRL	7903	29.95	75.00
92	12 IN. SANTA W/POT BELLY STOVE	1818	61.95	100.00
92	12 IN. SANTA'S PAINTING HELPER	2737	38.95	75.00
92	12 IN. SANTA'S POSTMAN	3650	39.95	50.00
92	12 IN. SCARECROW	1873	41.95	100.00
92	12 IN. SNOWMAN	5457	41.95	75.00
92	12 IN. SPIDER	3461	38.95	100.00
92	12 IN. TALL NORTH POLE W/SNOW	2511	8.95	9.00
92	12 IN. TUCKERED COUPLE	1827	89.95	90.00
92	12 IN. VELOUR MRS. SANTA	2160	49.95	75.00
92	12 IN. VELOUR SANTA W/TOYBAG	2284	49.95	75.00
92	18 IN. BUNNY KID W/BUNNY	2117	49.95	75.00
92	18 IN. CHEF SANTA	5314	47.95	100.00
92	18 IN. COUNTRY BOY BUNNY	1501	54.95	135.00
92	18 IN. EASTER PARADE BOY BUNNY	1695	65.45	100.00
92	18 IN. EASTER PARADE GIRL BUNNY	1918	65.45	100.00
92	18 IN. GINGERBREAD BOY	2969	50.95	50.95
92	18 IN. GIRL BUNNY W/FLOWERS	1501	54.95	125.00
92	18 IN. MRS. SANTA W/POINSETTA	6790	53.95	125.00
92	18 IN. MRS. SANTA W/PRESENTS	4314	52.95	125.00
92	18 IN. REINDEER W/CHRISTMAS	3441	52.95	150.00
92	18 IN. REINDEER W/NORTH POLE	2755	63.95	160.00
92	18 IN. SANTA W/BANNER	6871	52.95	125.00
92	18 IN. SANTA W/CARDHOLDER	4260	59.95	100.00

YR	NAME	LIMIT	ISSUE	TREND
92	18 IN. SANTA W/GIFT LIST	4447	45.95	110.00
92	18 IN. SANTA W/STOCKING	3859	49.95	75.00
92	18 IN. SANTA W/TRAY	3955	52.95	125.00
92	18 IN. SNOWMAN W/BROOM	4405	46.95	100.00
92	18 IN. SNOWY OWL	740	65.95	175.00
92	18 IN. WITCH	1369	63.95	150.00
92	18 IN. WITCH W/STAND	2760	65.95	125.00
92	22 IN. CHRISTMAS STOCKING	6128	18.45	55.00
92	22 IN. RED CHRISTMAS ELF	4066	34.95	75.00
92	30 IN. MRS. SANTA W/CARDHOLDER	1380	119.95	150.00
92	30 IN. OUTDOOR SANTA	1724	99.95	150.00
92	30 IN. SANTA W/BANNER	1654	119.95	120.00
92	30 IN. SANTA W/NORTH POLE	1674	109.95	995.00
92	30 IN. VELOUR MRS. SANTA W/MUFF	576	160.45	200.00
92	30 IN. VELOUR SANTA W/PIPE & BAG	548	160.45	200.00
92	32 IN. STOCKING W/REMOVEABLE 10 IN.	2052	27.95	75.00
92	36 IN. REINDEER W/CARDHOLDER	1219	148.45	300.00
92	5 IN. CHRISTMAS DRAGON	3132	23.95	75.00
92	5 IN. CHRISTMAS LAMB	10104	19.95	65.00
92	5 IN. DUCK ON FLEXIBLE FLYER	3124	25.95	65.00
92	5 IN. EASTER PARADE BOY DUCK	3370	21.95	75.00
92	5 IN. EASTER PARADE GIRL DUCK	4468	23.95	75.00
92	5 IN. ELF (WORKSHOP)	13825	13.45	25.00
92	5 IN. EQUESTRIENNE W/10 IN. HORSE	1063	74.95	150.00
92	5 IN. FAWN	10939	14.45	25.00
92	5 IN. FLUFFY YELLOW CHICK	4342	17.95	50.00
92	5 IN. LEPRECHAUN	4705	15.95	35.00
92	5 IN. RAINCOAT DUCK	5397	26.95	65.00
92	5 IN. SPRING LAMB	5053	17.95	45.00
92	5 IN. TRIM-A-TREE ELF	11985	12.95	25.00
92	7 IN. ANGEL ON MOON	2885	39.95	70.00
92	7 IN. ANGEL W/MUSICAL INSTRUMENT	6347	19.95	50.00
92	7 IN. ARTIST BUNNY W/BRUSH	4493	20.95	55.00
92	7 IN. BABY NEW YEAR	6254	26.95	50.00
92	7 IN. BALLERINA KID	4553	27.95	65.00
92	7 IN. BALLERINA ON MUSIC BOX	2718	41.95	90.00
92	7 IN. BEACH KID W/BOAT	3817	29.95	65.00
92	7 IN. BIRTHDAY GIRL MOUSE	*	23.95	24.00
92	7 IN. BIRTHDAY MOUSE	9592	23.95	75.00
92	7 IN. BRIDE BUNNY	5929	22.95	60.00
92	7 IN. BUNNY IN SLEEPER-GREEN	6338	19.95	70.00
92	7 IN. BUNNY IN SLEEPER-YELLOW	6338	19.95	70.00
92	7 IN. CAROLLER BOY	4606	22.95	50.00
92	7 IN. CAROLLER GIRL	4913	22.95	75.00
92	7 IN. CAROLLER MOUSE W/BIG HAT	18789	19.95	50.00
92	7 IN. CHAMPAIGN MOUSE IN GLASS	9553	25.95	65.00
92	7 IN. CHEF SANTA	11297	28.95	60.00
92	7 IN. CHRISTMAS GNOME	9102	18.95	35.00
92	7 IN. COUNTRY BOY BUNNY	3993	20.45	75.00
92	7 IN. COUNTRY GIRL BUNNY	3937	20.45	80.00
92	7 IN. DESERT STORM MOUSE	3114	29.95	90.00
92	7 IN. DEVIL KID	6076	23.95	60.00
92	7 IN. DISNEY COLLECTION	300	59.95	400.00
92	7 IN. DRACULA KID	5637	25.95	26.00
92	7 IN. DRUMMER BOY	7297	22.45	75.00
92	7 IN. EASTER PARADE BOY BUNNY	6668	20.95	50.00
92	7 IN. EASTER PARADE GIRL BUNNY	9314	20.95	50.00
92	7 IN. FISHING MOUSE	6145	31.95	50.00
92	7 IN. FLYING ANGEL W/MISTLETOE	6457	18.95	50.00
92	7 IN. GNOME W/MUSHROOM	1691	35.95	75.00
92	7 IN. GOLFER MOUSE	7435	26.95	75.00
92	7 IN. GREEN THUMB MOUSE	5995	25.95	75.00
92	7 IN. GROOM BUNNY	5578	22.95	55.00
92	7 IN. INDIAN BOY	2315	29.95	60.00
92	7 IN. INDIAN GIRL	2297	22.95	60.00
92	7 IN. KID W/KITE	3850	29.95	65.00
92	7 IN. LADY BUG KID	4970	29.95	75.00
92	7 IN. LOGO KID	17524	24.95	75.00
92	7 IN. MOUSE IN BOX	4994	19.95	40.00
92	7 IN. MOUSE IN CORNUCOPIA	7833	22.95	40.00
92	7 IN. MOUSE IN SANTA'S HAT	10941	17.95	50.00
92	7 IN. MOUSE ON CHEESE	14923	25.95	60.00
92	7 IN. MOUSE W/MAILBAG	8000	25.95	55.00
92	7 IN. MOUSE W/NORTH POLE	10089	21.95	50.00
92	7 IN. MOUSE W/PRESENTS	*	17.95	50.00
92	7 IN. MOUSE W/SNOWBALL	7095	17.95	40.00
92	7 IN. MOUSE W/TENNIS RACQUET	4110	21.95	40.00
92	7 IN. MR. TUCKERED MOUSE	7533	19.95	40.00
92	7 IN. MRS. SANTA CANDLEHOLDER	9595	25.95	65.00
92	7 IN. MRS. SANTA HANGING MERRY	6411	27.95	65.00
92	7 IN. MRS. SANTA W/POINSETTA	11484	29.95	75.00
92	7 IN. MRS. SANTA W/PRESENTS	7124	27.95	65.00
92	7 IN. MRS. TUCKERED MOUSE	8321	19.95	40.00
92	7 IN. PILGRIM KID W/BASKET	2303	53.95	125.00
92	7 IN. PILGRIM MICE SET W/BASKET	2364	42.45	75.00
92	7 IN. PIRATE KID	5412	23.95	50.00
92	7 IN. PUMPKIN KID	3619	27.45	50.00
92	7 IN. RED CROSS NURSE MOUSE	*	29.95	75.00
92	7 IN. RITZ SNOWMAN	6037	26.95	60.00

YR	NAME	LIMIT	ISSUE	TREND
92	7 IN. SANTA BRINGING HOME	5921	27.95	70.00
92	7 IN. SANTA CARDHOLDER	9831	25.95	65.00
92	7 IN. SANTA IN CHIMNEY	8119	33.95	85.00
92	7 IN. SANTA ON 18 IN. MOON	4157	46.95	100.00
92	7 IN. SANTA SKUNK	6753	27.95	75.00
92	7 IN. SANTA W/GIFT LIST & TOY BAG	7815	23.95	50.00
92	7 IN. SANTA W/MAILBAG & LETTERS	7493	27.95	50.00
92	7 IN. SANTA W/PRESENTS	6594	23.95	50.00
92	7 IN. SCARECROW KID	4595	27.95	50.00
92	7 IN. SHERIFF MOUSE (D.S.)	283	49.50	150.00
92	7 IN. SKATEBOARD KID	3894	29.95	75.00
92	7 IN. SLEDDING MOUSE	6247	20.95	50.00
92	7 IN. SNOWMAN W/PIPE	7779	23.95	55.00
92	7 IN. SPRING CHICKEN W/BOAT	2753	34.95	35.00
92	7 IN. SPRING SKUNK	1590	22.95	55.00
92	7 IN. SWEETHEART BOY MOUSE	5723	19.95	50.00
92	7 IN. SWEETHEART GIRL MOUSE	6522	18.95	50.00
92	7 IN. TWO IN A TENT MICE	2910	34.95	80.00
92	7 IN. VELOUR MRS. SANTA W/COAT	5289	27.45	50.00
92	7 IN. VELOUR SANTA W/COAT & PIPE	5140	27.45	50.00
92	7 IN. WITCH KID	3592	27.95	100.00
92	7 IN. WORKSHOP MOUSE	6618	21.95	100.00
92	DESERT MOUSE HEAD PIN	991	8.95	35.00
92	LARGE FLOWER	2526	18.95	19.00
92	LARGE PUMPKIN	2469	48.95	125.00
92	MINI SANTA WREATH	2140	23.95	65.00
92	NURSE MOUSE HEAD PIN	1615	8.95	9.00
92	PINK FLOWER PICK	6611	5.95	20.00
92	RED CROSS NURSE MOUSE HEAD	*	8.95	25.00
92	SAILOR KID W/BOAT	*	*	900.00
92	SUN HEAD FLORAL PLANTER PICK	5419	5.95	20.00
92	SUN MAGNET	7133	6.45	15.00
92	SUN PIN	6395	5.95	25.00
92	YELLOW FLOWER PICK	6165	5.95	20.00
92	5 IN. ANGEL	7967	22.95	50.00
95	3 IN. MUSICAL BALLOONINGKIDS	OP	55.95	56.00
95	10 IN. BOSTON BRUINS HOCKEY PLAYER	OP	47.50	48.00
95	10 IN. CANADIAN MOUNTIE	OP	74.95	75.00
95	10 IN. CANADIAN MOUNTINE W/HORSE	OP	129.50	130.00
95	10 IN. COLLECTOR, MR. NASHVILLE SANTA	OP	44.95	45.00
95	10 IN. COLLECTOR, MR. SANTA W/WEE HELPER	OP	74.95	75.00
95	10 IN. COLLECTOR, MRS. NASHVILLE SANTA	OP	44.95	45.00
95	10 IN. DOE	OP	22.50	23.00
95	10 IN. EASTER PARADE BOY BUNNY	OP	40.95	41.00
95	10 IN. EASTER PARADE GIRL BUNNY	OP	40.95	41.00
95	10 IN. FROG ON LILY PAD	OP	23.95	24.00
95	10 IN. GREEN CHRISTMAS ELF	OP	17.50	18.00
95	10 IN. INDIAN MAN	OP	42.95	43.00
95	10 IN. INDIAN WOMAN	OP	42.95	43.00
95	10 IN. KITTEN W/ORNAMENT	OP	35.95	36.00
95	10 IN. LARGE FLOWER W/FACE	OP	20.95	21.00
95	10 IN. OLD WORLD CAROLLER MAN	OP	28.95	29.00
95	10 IN. OLD WORLD CAROLLER WOMAN	OP	28.95	29.00
95	10 IN. RED CHRISTMAS ELF	OP	17.50	18.00
95	10 IN. RED TREETOP ANGEL	OP	37.95	38.00
95	10 IN. REDCOAT W/CANNON	1000	79.95	80.00
95	10 IN. REINDEER	OP	23.95	24.00
95	10 IN. REINDEER W/7 IN. SANTA	OP	47.50	48.00
95	10 IN. REINDEER W/CAP & BELL	OP	24.95	25.00
95	10 IN. SKATING PENGUIN	OP	35.95	36.00
95	10 IN. TREE TOP ANGEL	OP	35.95	36.00
95	10 IN. VALENTINE GIRL BEAR	OP	35.95	36.00
95	10 IN. WHITE CHRISTMAS ELF	OP	17.50	18.00
95	10 IN. WHITE ST. NICHOLAS	OP	44.95	45.00
95	10 IN. WINDOW SHOPPER OSTRICH	OP	38.95	39.00
95	10 IN. WINTER ELF	OP	17.95	18.00
95	12 IN. BOY PILGRIM W/BASKET	OP	46.95	47.00
95	12 IN. CACTUS SET	OP	17.95	18.00
95	12 IN. CAROUSEL HORSE	OP	59.95	60.00
95	12 IN. CHEF SANTA	OP	46.95	47.00
95	12 IN. DRUMMER BOY	OP	39.95	40.00
95	12 IN. GIRL CAT KID	OP	36.95	37.00
95	12 IN. GIRL PILGRIM W/PIE	OP	46.95	47.00
95	12 IN. GIRL SCARECROW	OP	48.95	49.00
95	12 IN. MR. INDOOR SANTA W/TREE TOIP STAR	OP	49.95	50.00
95	12 IN. MRS. INDOOR SANTA W/GARLAND	OP	44.95	45.00
95	12 IN. MRS. SANTA CARDHOLDER	OP	43.50	44.00
95	12 IN. NORTH POLE	OP	9.95	10.00
95	12 IN. OLD WORLD ST. NICHOLAS	OP	54.95	55.00
95	12 IN. ROSE & IVY ARBOR	OP	49.95	50.00
95	12 IN. SANTA IN CHIMNEY	OP	71.95	72.00
95	14 IN. LARGE USABLE PUMPKIN W/REMOVABLE	OP	49.95	50.00
95	17 IN. TEE-PEE	OP	37.95	38.00
95	18 IN. CHEF SANTA	OP	51.95	52.00
95	18 IN. COUNTRY BOY BUNNY W/APPLE	OP	67.50	68.00
95	18 IN. COUNTRY GIRL BUNNY W/APPLE	OP	67.50	68.00
95	18 IN. EASTER PARADE BOY BUNNY	OP	67.50	68.00
95	18 IN. EASTER PARADE GIRL BUNNY	OP	67.50	68.00
95	18 IN. INDOOR SANTA W/LIGHTS	OP	63.50	64.00

YR	NAME	LIMIT	ISSUE	TREND
95	18 IN. MR. FUR SANTA ON STAND	OP	46.95	47.00
95	18 IN. MR. INDOOR SANTA W/TREE TOP STAR	OP	59.95	60.00
95	18 IN. MR. OLD WORLD SANTA	OP	52.95	53.00
95	18 IN. MRS. INDOOR SANTA W/GARLAND	OP	54.95	55.00
95	18 IN. MRS. OLD WORLD SANTA	OP	50.95	51.00
95	18 IN. MRS. OUTDOOR SANTA	OP	50.95	51.00
95	18 IN. MRS. SANTA CARDHOLDER	OP	53.95	54.00
95	18 IN. MUSICAL SANTA W/GIFT LIST	OP	61.95	62.00
95	18 IN. OLD WORLD REINDEER W/BELLS	OP	61.95	62.00
95	18 IN. PJ KID IN 2' STOCKING	OP	61.95	62.00
95	18 IN. REINDEER W/18 IN. SANTA	OP	89.95	90.00
95	18 IN. REINDEER W/CHRISTMAS SADDLEBAGS	OP	55.95	56.00
95	18 IN. SANTA ON TOBOGGAN	OP	73.50	74.00
95	18 IN. SANTA W/CARDHOLDER SACK	OP	59.95	60.00
95	18 IN. SANTA W/GIFT LIST & TOYBAG	OP	49.95	50.00
95	18 IN. SNOWMAN W/BROOM	OP	51.50	52.00
95	18 IN. WITCH W/STAND	OP	69.95	70.00
95	2 IN. PUMPKIN W/FACE	OP	6.95	7.00
95	2 IN. RED TOMATOES SET OF THREE	OP	12.95	13.00
95	22 IN. CHRISTMAS STOCKING	OP	19.50	19.50
95	22 IN. GREEN CHRISTMAS ELF	OP	35.95	36.00
95	22 IN. RED CHRISTMAS ELF	OP	35.95	36.00
95	3 IN. BABY JESUS IN MANGER	OP	17.95	18.00
95	3 IN. CHRISTMAS MORN' ITSIE VIGNETTE	OP	67.50	68.00
95	3 IN. SPRING PIXI PICK	OP	11.50	12.00
95	3 IN. SUN PIN	OP	5.95	6.00
95	3 IN. SWEETHEART ITSIE BOY MOUSE	OP	19.95	20.00
95	3 IN. SWEETHEART ITSIE GIRL MOUSE	OP	14.95	15.00
95	3 IN. WITCH W/18 IN. HALLOWEEN MOON	OP	44.95	45.00
95	3 IN. WITCH W/BROOM	OP	17.95	18.00
95	30 IN. COUNTRY BOY BUNNY W/APPLES	OP	124.95	125.00
95	30 IN. MR. OLD WORLD SANTA	OP	124.95	125.00
95	30 IN. MRS. OLD WORLD SANTA	OP	125.00	125.00
95	30 IN. MRS. SANTA W/CARDHOLDER APRON	OP	119.95	120.00
95	30 IN. OUTDOOR SANTA W/TOY BAG	OP	137.95	138.00
95	30 IN. SANTA W/CARDHOLDER SACK	OP	119.95	120.00
95	30 IN. SANTA W/NORTH POLE	OP	137.95	138.00
95	30 IN. SNOWMAN	OP	119.95	120.00
95	30 IN. WITCH KID	OP	149.95	150.00
95	36 IN. REINDEER W/CARDHOLDER SADDLEBAGS	OP	154.50	155.00
95	5 IN. ANGEL W.MISTLETOE	OP	16.50	17.00
95	5 IN. ANGEL W/18 IN. CHRISTMAS MOON	OP	44.95	45.00
95	5 IN. BABY JESUS IN MANGER W/HAY	OP	27.50	28.00
95	5 IN. BLACK CHRISTMAS LAMB	OP	20.50	21.00
95	5 IN. BOUDOIR BABY W/BLANKET	OP	19.95	20.00
95	5 IN. CACTUS SET 5 IN.	OP	17.95	18.00
95	5 IN. EASTER PARADE BOY DUCK	OP	23.50	24.00
95	5 IN. EASTER PARADE GIRL DUCK	OP	25.50	26.00
95	5 IN. ELK WORKSHOP	OP	14.50	15.00
95	5 IN. FAWN	OP	15.50	16.00
95	5 IN. GOLD FALL ELF W/LEAF	OP	14.95	15.00
95	5 IN. GREEN CHRISTMAS ELF	OP	14.50	15.00
95	5 IN. GREEN SPRING ELF	OP	14.50	15.00
95	5 IN. HALLOWEEN ELF/BLACK	OP	15.50	16.00
95	5 IN. HALLOWEEN ELF/ORANGE	OP	15.50	16.00
95	5 IN. LEPRECHAUN W/POT 'O GOLD	OP	19.95	20.00
95	5 IN. OLD WORLD CAROLLER BOY	OP	20.50	21.00
95	5 IN. OLD WORLD CAROLLER GIRL	OP	20.50	21.00
95	5 IN. OLD WORLD SANTA W/9 IN. WREATH	OP	33.95	34.00
95	5 IN. ORANGE FALL ELF W/LEAF	OP	14.95	15.00
95	5 IN. PIXIE PICCOLO PLAYER	OP	29.95	30.00
95	5 IN. RED CHRISTMAS ELF	OP	14.50	15.00
95	5 IN. SAILOR DUCK	OP	25.50	26.00
95	5 IN. WHITE CHRISTMAS ELF	OP	14.50	15.00
95	5 IN. WHITE CHRISTMAS LAMB	OP	20.50	21.00
95	5 IN. WINTER ELF	OP	14.50	15.00
95	5 IN. YELLOW SPRING ELF	OP	14.50	15.00
95	7 IN. ANGEL MOUSE	OP	23.50	24.00
95	7 IN. ANGEL W/HARP	OP	26.95	27.00
95	7 IN. ANGEL W/MUSICAL INSTRUMENT	OP	21.50	22.00
95	7 IN. ANGEL/BLACK HAIR	OP	24.50	25.00
95	7 IN. ANGEL/BLONDE HAIR	OP	24.50	25.00
95	7 IN. ANGEL/BROWN HAIR	OP	24.50	25.00
95	7 IN. ARTIST BUNNY W/BRUSH & PALETTE	OP	22.50	23.00
95	7 IN. BABY BUNNY W/BABY BOTTLE	OP	20.50	21.00
95	7 IN. BICYCLIST BOY MOUSE	OP	25.95	26.00
95	7 IN. BIRTHDAY GIRL MOUSE	OP	24.50	25.00
95	7 IN. BRIDE MOUSE	OP	23.50	24.00
95	7 IN. CALIFORNIA MUDSLIDE MOUSE	OP	29.95	30.00
95	7 IN. CAROLLER MOUSE W/BIG HAT & TREE	OP	21.50	22.00
95	7 IN. CHAMPAGNE MOUSE IN GLASS	OP	27.50	28.00
95	7 IN. CHEF MOUSE	OP	27.50	28.00
95	7 IN. CHEF SANTA	OP	30.50	31.00
95	7 IN. CHOIR BOY	OP	27.50	28.00
95	7 IN. CHOIR BOY W/BLACK EYE	OP	27.50	28.00
95	7 IN. CHOIR GIRL	OP	27.50	28.00
95	7 IN. CHRISTMAS PARTY GIRL MOUSE	OP	18.95	19.00
95	7 IN. COUNTRY BOY BUNNY W/APPLE	OP	21.95	22.00
95	7 IN. COUNTRY GIRL BUNNY W/APPLE	OP	21.95	22.00

Molly has learned not to put all her chicks in one basket. Her producer is Roman.

"Hush My Baby" sings the chubby-cheeked Suzy *created by artist Bette Ball. Suzy is from the "Victoria Ashlea Originals" collection by Goebel.*

Seventh in Yolanda's Picture-Perfect Babies collection, Jessica *by Yolanda Bello was issued by The Edwin M. Knowles China Co. in 1989.*

Here comes the bride. Jennifer *is produced by the Ashton-Drake Galleries.*

Lee Middleton pays tribute to the season of joy with her 1991 Christmas Angel.

YR	NAME	LIMIT	ISSUE	TREND
95	7 IN. DRUMMER BOY	OP	24.50	25.00
95	7 IN. EASTER BUNNY KID W/BASKET	OP	22.50	23.00
95	7 IN. FLYING ANGEL	OP	21.95	22.00
95	7 IN. GARDEN CLUB MOUSE	OP	22.50	23.00
95	7 IN. GHOST MOUSE	OP	27.50	28.00
95	7 IN. GIRL BUILDING A SNOWMAN	OP	24.95	25.00
95	7 IN. GRADUATION BOY MOUSE	OP	24.50	25.00
95	7 IN. GRADUATION GIRL MOUSE	OP	24.50	25.00
95	7 IN. GROOM MOUSE	OP	23.50	24.00
95	7 IN. GYPSY GIRL KID	OP	31.95	32.00
95	7 IN. HABITAT MOUSE	OP	30.50	31.00
95	7 IN. HERSHEY KID	OP	38.50	39.00
95	7 IN. HOCKEY KID	OP	30.95	31.00
95	7 IN. HOLLY GIRL MOUSE	OP	18.95	19.00
95	7 IN. HOUSEWIFE MOUSE	OP	25.95	26.00
95	7 IN. INDIAN BOY KID	OP	29.95	30.00
95	7 IN. INDIAN BOY KID W/SPEAR	OP	29.95	30.00
95	7 IN. INDIAN GIRL KID W/BEADS	OP	29.95	30.00
95	7 IN. JOSEPH CHILD	OP	28.95	29.00
95	7 IN. LARGE CABBAGE	OP	17.95	18.00
95	7 IN. LOGO KID/DOLL SOCIETY	OP	29.95	30.00
95	7 IN. MARBLES KID	OP	27.50	28.00
95	7 IN. MARY CHILD W/DOLL	OP	28.95	29.00
95	7 IN. MOTORCYCLE MOUSE IN.MIKEY THE BIK	OP	30.95	31.00
95	7 IN. MOUSE IN CORNUCOPIA	OP	25.50	26.00
95	7 IN. MOUSE IN SANTA'S HAT	OP	18.95	19.00
95	7 IN. MOUSE KID	OP	22.50	23.00
95	7 IN. MOUSE W/SNOWBALL	OP	18.95	19.00
95	7 IN. MR. & MRS. INDOOR SANTA W/TREE	OP	69.95	70.00
95	7 IN. MR. OLD WORLD SANTA	OP	28.95	29.00
95	7 IN. MRS. SANTA W/FUR-TRIMMED	OP	23.95	24.95
95	7 IN. MRS. SANTA W/PRESENTS	OP	30.95	31.00
95	7 IN. NASHVILLE BOY	OP	31.50	32.00
95	7 IN. NASHVILLE GIRL	OP	29.95	30.00
95	7 IN. NAUGHT ANGEL W/BLACK EYE	OP	25.95	26.00
95	7 IN. PILGRIM BOY HUGGING FAWN	OP	42.95	43.00
95	7 IN. PILGRIM GIRL W/PIE	OP	27.95	28.00
95	7 IN. PILGRIM MICE SET W/BASKET	OP	47.95	48.00
95	7 IN. PJ KID ON ROCKING HORSE	OP	29.95	30.00
95	7 IN. SANTA	OP	20.50	21.00
95	7 IN. SANTA HUGGING REINDEER	OP	47.50	48.00
95	7 IN. SANTA MOUSE IN CHIMNEY	OP	34.95	35.00
95	7 IN. SANTA SKIING	OP	29.95	30.00
95	7 IN. SANTA W/LIGHTS	OP	31.95	32.00
95	7 IN. SANTA W/NORTH POLE	OP	35.95	36.00
95	7 IN. SANTA W/PRESENTS	OP	27.95	28.00
95	7 IN. SANTA W/SLEIGH	OP	39.95	40.00
95	7 IN. SANTA W/SNOWSHOES & TREE	OP	29.95	30.00
95	7 IN. SANTA, INDOOR	OP	19.95	20.00
95	7 IN. SHEPHERD CHILD W/LAMB	OP	39.95	40.00
95	7 IN. SMALL CHRISTMAS DOVE	OP	27.50	28.00
95	7 IN. SNOWMAN ON TOBOGGAN	OP	30.95	31.00
95	7 IN. SNOWMAN W/PIPE	OP	26.50	27.00
95	7 IN. SNOWWOMAN/MRS. RITZ	OP	27.50	28.00
95	7 IN. SOUTH AMERICAN GIRL	YR	31.95	32.00
95	7 IN. ST. PATRICK;S DAY MOUSE	OP	26.95	27.00
95	7 IN. SWEETHEART BOY MOUSE	OP	20.95	21.00
95	7 IN. SWEETHEART GIRL MOUSE	OP	20.95	21.00
95	7 IN. SWISS ALPS BOY	YR	31.95	32.00
95	7 IN. TREE TOP STAR W/3 IN. ANGEL	OP	21.50	22.00
95	7 IN. TREETOP MOUSE IN CHIMNEY	OP	34.95	35.00
95	7 IN. VALENTINE GIRL KID W/CARD	OP	26.95	27.00
95	7 IN. WHITE MOUSE IN SLIPPER	OP	26.50	27.00
95	7 IN. WHITE MOUSE ON TOBOGGAN W/PRESENT	OP	30.95	31.00
95	7 IN. WHITE SKATING MOUSE	OP	26.50	27.00
95	7 IN. WITCH MOUSE	OP	27.50	28.00
95	7 IN. WIZARD MOUSE	OP	29.50	30.00
95	8 IN. BOY TURKEY	OP	35.50	36.00
95	8 IN. EAR OF CORN	OP	12.95	13.00
95	8 IN. EASTER PARADE BOY BUNNY	OP	27.95	28.00
95	8 IN. EASTER PARADE GIRL BUNNY	OP	27.95	28.00
95	8 IN. GIRL TURKEY	OP	35.50	36.00
95	LARGE PEA PODS & CARROTS SET OF THREE	OP	15.95	16.00
95	TREE SKIRT, 4' DIAMETER	OP	29.95	30.00
95	WYNKEN, BLYNKEN & NOD	OP	62.50	63.00
96	10 IN. BABY CAKES BEAR	OP	38.00	38.00
96	10 IN. CANDY BASKET ELVES	OP	42.00	42.00
96	10 IN. CAROLLING BOY BEAR	OP	42.00	42.00
96	10 IN. CAROLLING GIRL BEAR	OP	42.00	42.00
96	10 IN. CAROLLING REINDEER	OP	25.00	25.00
96	10 IN. COUNTRY BOY BEAR	OP	44.00	44.00
96	10 IN. COUNTRY BUMPKIN SCARECROW	OP	38.00	38.00
96	10 IN. COUTNRY GIRL BEAR	OP	42.00	42.00
96	10 IN. DOE	OP	22.50	22.50
96	10 IN. EASTER PARADE BOY BEAR	OP	42.00	42.00
96	10 IN. EASTER PARADE GIRL BEAR	OP	42.00	42.00
96	10 IN. FLYING WITCH	OP	38.00	38.00
96	10 IN. GHOST OF CHRISTMAS FUTURE	OP	29.50	30.00
96	10 IN. GHOST OF CHRISTMAS PAST	OP	39.50	39.50

YR	NAME	LIMIT	ISSUE	TREND
96	10 IN. GHOST OF CHRISTMAS PRESENT	OP	56.00	56.00
96	10 IN. GREEN CHRISTMAS ELF	OP	17.50	17.50
96	10 IN. HOOK, LINE AND SANTA	OP	45.00	45.00
96	10 IN. INDIAN MAN	OP	43.00	43.00
96	10 IN. INDIAN WOMAN	OP	43.00	43.00
96	10 IN. JESTER & FRIEND	OP	34.00	34.00
96	10 IN. JOSEPH	OP	37.50	37.50
96	10 IN. LEAPIN' FROG	OP	18.00	18.00
96	10 IN. LOVER BOY BEAR	OP	40.00	40.00
96	10 IN. MARY HOLDING BABY JESUS	OP	39.50	39.50
96	10 IN. MR. FARMER	OP	35.00	35.00
96	10 IN. MR. SCROOGE	OP	37.50	37.50
96	10 IN. MRS. FARMER	OP	35.00	35.00
96	10 IN. OLD TYME CAROLLING MAN	OP	39.00	39.00
96	10 IN. OLD TYME CAROLLING WOMAN	OP	39.00	39.00
96	10 IN. OLD WORLD TREE TOP ANGEL	OP	47.00	47.00
96	10 IN. PILGRAM WOMAN	OP	40.00	40.00
96	10 IN. PILGRIM MAN	OP	45.00	45.00
96	10 IN. PUMPKIN PATCH ELF	OP	24.00	24.00
96	10 IN. PUPPIED FOR CHRISTMAS SANTA	OP	79.50	80.00
96	10 IN. RED CHRISTMAS ELF	OP	17.50	17.50
96	10 IN. REINDEER	OP	24.00	24.00
96	10 IN. TREE TOP ANGEL	OP	40.50	40.50
96	10 IN. TRICK OR TREAT ELF	OP	21.00	21.00
96	10 IN. WANDERING ST. NICHOLAS	OP	49.00	49.00
96	10 IN. WINTER ELF	OP	18.00	18.00
96	10 IN. WISE MAN BEARING MYRRH	OP	44.00	44.00
96	10 IN. WISEMAN BEARING FRANKINCENSE	OP	44.00	44.00
96	10 IN. WISEMAN BEARING GOLD	OP	44.00	44.00
96	10 IN. WOMAN GOLFER	OP	44.00	44.00
96	10 IN. WOMAN TENNIS PLAYER	OP	44.00	44.00
96	10 IN. WOODLAND SANTA & REINDEER	OP	66.00	66.00
96	12 IN. BROWN HORSE	OP	35.50	36.00
96	12 IN. CAROLLING MRS. SANTA	OP	46.00	46.00
96	12 IN. CAROLLING SANTA	OP	56.00	56.00
96	12 IN. CAROUSEL HORSE	OP	*	*
96	12 IN. CAROUSEL HORSE #2	OP	68.00	68.00
96	12 IN. CHRISTMAS EVE MRS. SANTA	OP	59.50	60.00
96	12 IN. CHRISTMAS EVE SANTA	OP	59.50	60.00
96	12 IN. DRUMMER BOY	OP	44.50	44.50
96	12 IN. MOTHER DUCK	OP	49.50	50.00
96	12 IN. NORTH POLE	OP	10.50	11.00
96	12 IN. OLDE WORLD ST. NICHOLAS	OP	62.50	63.00
96	12 IN. ROSE & iVY ARBOR	OP	50.00	50.00
96	12 IN. STREET LAMP	OP	14.00	14.00
96	12 IN. TOMMY TURKEY	OP	76.00	76.00
96	12 IN. WORKSHOP SANTA	OP	54.00	54.00
96	15 IN. HAUNTED TREE	OP	45.00	45.00
96	17 IN. TEE-PEE	OP	38.00	38.00
96	18 IN. BEARRY CHRISTMAS STOCKING	OP	77.50	77.50
96	18 IN. BOUNTRY GIRL BUNNY	OP	67.50	68.00
96	18 IN. CHEF SANTA	OP	61.00	61.00
96	18 IN. COUNTRY BOY BUNNY	OP	67.50	68.00
96	18 IN. EASTER PARADE BOY BUNNY	OP	67.50	68.00
96	18 IN. EASTER PARADE GIRL BUNNY	OP	37.50	37.50
96	18 IN. MR. FUR SANTA ON STAND	OP	50.00	50.00
96	18 IN. MRS. OUTDOOR SANTA	OP	53.00	53.00
96	18 IN. MRS. SANTA HANGING CRANBERRRIED &	OP	59.50	60.00
96	18 IN. MUSICAL CAROLLING SANTA	OP	58.00	58.00
96	18 IN. OLD WORLD MRS. SANTA HUGGING LAMB	OP	84.00	84.00
96	18 IN. OLD WORLD SANTA	OP	76.00	76.00
96	18 IN. PUTTING ON THE RITZ SNOWMAN	OP	64.50	65.00
96	18 IN. REINDEER W/18 IN. VELOUR SANTA	OP	104.00	104.00
96	18 IN. REINDEER W/CHRISTMAS SADDLEBAGS	OP	59.50	60.00
96	18 IN. SANTA W/GIFT LIST & TOYBAG	OP	54.00	54.00
96	18 IN. SNOWMAN W/BROOM	OP	55.00	55.00
96	18 IN. SUNFLOWER	OP	23.50	23.50
96	18 IN. TUCKERED MRS. SANTA & PJ KID	OP	95.00	95.00
96	18 IN. TUCKERED SANTA & PJ KID	OP	92.00	92.00
96	18 IN. WITCHY BREW	OP	82.50	82.50
96	2 IN. PUMPKIN W/FACE	OP	7.00	7.00
96	2 IN. RED TOMATOES SET OF THREE	OP	13.50	13.50
96	22 IN. CHRISTMAS STOCKING	OP	19.50	19.50
96	22 IN. GREEN CHRISTMAS ELF	OP	39.50	39.50
96	22 IN. RED CHRISTMAS ELF	OP	39.50	39.50
96	24 IN. COUNTRY CATTAIL	OP	26.00	26.00
96	25 IN. SUNFLOWER	OP	26.00	26.00
96	3 IN. CANOEING INDIAN KIDS	OP	40.00	40.00
96	3 IN. BIRTHDAY MOUSE	OP	21.00	21.00
96	3 IN. BRIDE MOUSE	OP	24.00	24.00
96	3 IN. BUTTERFLY PICK	OP	15.00	15.00
96	3 IN. CAROLLING BOY	OP	18.00	18.00
96	3 IN. CAROLLING GIRL	OP	18.00	18.00
96	3 IN. COMPUTER MOUSE	OP	21.50	21.50
96	3 IN. EASTER BUNNY	OP	19.50	19.50
96	3 IN. FROGGIE	OP	13.50	13.50
96	3 IN. GHOST MOUSE	OP	20.00	20.00
96	3 IN. GROOM MOUSE	OP	22.00	22.00
96	3 IN. HERSHEY BOY MOUSE	OP	23.00	23.00

YR	NAME	LIMIT	ISSUE	TREND
96	3 IN. HERSHEY GIRL MOUSE	OP	23.00	23.00
96	3 IN. HIKER MOUSE	OP	25.00	25.00
96	3 IN. INDIAN BOY ITSIE SERIES	OP	20.00	20.00
96	3 IN. INDIAN GIRL	OP	20.00	20.00
96	3 IN. LADYBUG PICK	OP	15.00	15.00
96	3 IN. MAILMAN MOUSE	OP	22.00	22.00
96	3 IN. MATCHBOX MICE	OP	34.00	34.00
96	3 IN. MUSICAL BALLOONING BEARS	OP	60.00	60.00
96	3 IN. NURSE MOUSE	OP	21.50	21.50
96	3 IN. PILGRIM BOY	OP	22.00	22.00
96	3 IN. PILGRIM GIRL ITSIE SERIES	OP	22.00	22.00
96	3 IN. SLEIGH RIDE SANTA	OP	23.50	23.50
96	3 IN. TEACHER MOUSE	OP	20.00	20.00
96	3 IN. WITCH W/18 IN. HALLOWEEN MOON	OP	45.00	45.00
96	3 IN. WITCH W/BROOM	OP	19.00	19.00
96	3 IN. WIZARD MOUSE	OP	24.00	24.00
96	3 IN. YELLOW DUCKING	OP	21.00	21.00
96	30 IN. CHRIASTMS ELF/RED	OP	67.00	67.00
96	30 IN. DECK THE HALLS SANTA	OP	169.50	170.00
96	30 IN. MRS. SANTA W/CARDHOLDER APRON	OP	126.00	126.00
96	30 IN. OLD WORLD MRS. SANTA	OP	152.00	152.00
96	30 IN. OLD WORLD SANTA	OP	160.00	160.00
96	30 IN. SHOPPING MRS. SANTA	OP	156.50	157.00
96	30 IN. SKELETON KID	OP	123.00	123.00
96	30 IN. SUNDAY MORNING SANTA	OP	125.00	125.00
96	36 IN. OLD WORLD REINDEER	OP	146.00	146.00
96	4 IN. ANGEL W/MISTLETOE	OP	18.00	18.00
96	4 IN. PUPPY PRESENT	OP	19.00	19.00
96	4 IN. STREET LAMP	OP	8.00	8.00
96	5 IN. ANGEL CENTERPIECE	OP	31.00	31.00
96	5 IN. BLACK CHRISTMAS LAMB	OP	17.50	17.50
96	5 IN. BLANKET BABY BOY	OP	20.00	20.00
96	5 IN. BLANKET BABY GIRL	OP	20.00	20.00
96	5 IN. ELF CENTERPIECE	OP	27.00	27.00
96	5 IN. ELF WORKSHOP	OP	*	*
96	5 IN. FAWN	OP	16.50	16.50
96	5 IN. GREEN CHRISTMAS ELF	OP	15.00	15.00
96	5 IN. HALLOWEEN ELF/BLACK	OP	15.00	15.00
96	5 IN. HALLOWEEN ELF/ORANGE	OP	15.00	15.00
96	5 IN. HOLLY BERRY ANGEL	OP	22.00	22.00
96	5 IN. LEPRECHAUN W/POT 'O GOLD	OP	22.00	22.00
96	5 IN. OLD WORLD SANTA W/9 IN. WREATH	OP	34.00	34.00
96	5 IN. PIXIE PICCOLO PLAYER	OP	30.00	30.00
96	5 IN. RED CHRISTMAS ELF	OP	15.00	15.00
96	5 IN. SAILOR DUCK	OP	27.50	28.00
96	5 IN. TEE-PEE	OP	20.00	20.00
96	5 IN. WHITE CHRISTMAS LAMB	OP	17.50	17.50
96	5 IN. WINTER ELF	OP	15.00	15.00
96	5 IN. WOOLY LAMB	OP	17.00	17.00
96	5 IN. YELLOW DUCK	OP	22.00	22.00
96	7 IN. ANGEL MOUSE	OP	23.50	23.50
96	7 IN. ANGEL W/HARP	OP	27.00	27.00
96	7 IN. ANGEL W/MUSICAL INSTRUMENT	OP	21.50	21.50
96	7 IN. ANGEL/BLONDE HAIR	OP	24.50	24.50
96	7 IN. BAKER KID	OP	31.00	31.00
96	7 IN. BANANA KID	OP	27.50	28.00
96	7 IN. BICYCLIST BOY MOUSE	OP	28.00	28.00
96	7 IN. CAROLLER MOUSE W/BIG HAT & TREE	OP	24.00	24.00
96	7 IN. CAROLLING SNOWMAN	OP	29.50	30.00
96	7 IN. CHEF MOUSE	OP	27.50	28.00
96	7 IN. CHEF SANTA	OP	30.00	30.00
96	7 IN. CHRISTMAS PARTY GIRL MOUSE	OP	19.50	19.50
96	7 IN. COUNTRY BOY BUNNY	OP	24.50	24.50
96	7 IN. COUNTRY GIRL BUNNY	OP	23.00	23.00
96	7 IN. COUNTRY GIRL MOUSE	OP	26.00	26.00
96	7 IN. DRUMMER BOY	OP	29.00	29.00
96	7 IN. EASTER BUNNY KID W/BASKET	OP	24.50	24.50
96	7 IN. LETTER TO SANTA MOUSE	OP	23.00	23.00
96	7 IN. MAKING FRIENDS SNOWMAN	OP	28.00	28.00
96	7 IN. MOONBEAM SANTA MOBILE	OP	46.00	46.00
96	7 IN. MOUSE KID	OP	26.00	26.00
96	7 IN. MOUSE W/SNOWBALL	OP	19.50	19.50
96	7 IN. MR. & MRS. SANTA EXCHANGING GIFTS	OP	57.00	57.00
96	7 IN. NAUGHTY ANGEL W/BLACK EYE	OP	28.00	28.00
96	7 IN. NEW YEAR'S MOUSE	OP	20.00	20.00
96	7 IN. OLD WORLD MRS. SANTA	OP	32.00	32.00
96	7 IN. OLD WORLD SANTA	OP	40.00	40.00
96	7 IN. PILGRIM BOY MOUSE	OP	26.00	26.00
96	7 IN. PILGRIM GIRL MOUSE	OP	24.00	24.00
96	7 IN. PJ KID ON ROCKING HORSE	OP	30.00	30.00
96	7 IN. POWDER PUFF BABY	OP	21.00	21.00
96	7 IN. SAINT PATRICK'S DAY KID	OP	31.00	31.00
96	7 IN. SANTA	OP	22.00	22.00
96	7 IN. SANTA CENTERPIECE	OP	35.00	35.00
96	7 IN. SANTA HUGGING REINDEER	OP	51.00	51.00
96	7 IN. SANTA MOUSE IN CHIMNEY	OP	36.50	37.00
96	7 IN. SANTA SKIING	OP	30.00	30.00
96	7 IN. SHOPPING MRS. SANTA	OP	36.50	37.00
96	7 IN. SHOPPING SANTA	OP	36.50	36.50

YR	NAME	LIMIT	ISSUE	TREND
96	7 IN. SLEIGH RIDE SANTA COUPLE	OP	84.00	84.00
96	7 IN. SNOWBALL FIGHT KID	OP	30.50	30.50
96	7 IN. SNOWBALL W/PIPE	OP	30.00	30.00
96	7 IN. SPIDER KID	OP	27.50	28.00
96	7 IN. SWEETHEART BOY	OP	32.50	33.00
96	7 IN. SWEETHEART BOY MOUSE	OP	21.00	21.00
96	7 IN. SWEETHEART GIRL MOUSE	OP	*	*
96	7 IN. TRIM TIME SANTA	OP	33.00	33.00
96	7 IN. TUCKERED BOY MOUSE	OP	22.50	22.50
96	7 IN. TUCKERED GIRL MOUSE	OP	22.50	22.50
96	7 IN. VALENTINE GIRL KID W/CARD	OP	27.50	27.50
96	7 IN. WHITE SKATING MOUSE	OP	28.50	28.50
96	7 IN. WITCH KID	OP	32.00	32.00
96	7 IN. WITCH MOUSE	OP	28.00	28.00
96	8 IN. CORN STALK	OP	12.00	12.00
96	8 IN. EAR OF CORN	OP	13.00	13.00
96	8 IN. FLOWERING LILY PAD	OP	10.00	10.00
96	CACTUS SET 12 IN.	OP	6.00	6.00
96	CACTUS SET 5 IN.	OP	23.50	23.50
96	CRECHE FOR NATIVITY	OP	40.00	40.00
96	LARGE PEA PODS & CARROTS SET OF THREE	OP	23.00	23.00
96	SCROOGE'S BED	OP	44.00	44.00
96	TREE SKIRT 4' DIAMETER	OP	33.00	33.00
96	WYNKEN, BLYNKEN & NOD	OP	67.50	68.00
A. THORNDIKE				
50	10 IN. BOY & GIRL SKIERS	*	15.00	1250.00
50	10 IN. FROGMAN (GIRL DIVER)	*	9.95	3800.00
50	10 IN. GIRL GOLFER	*	*	475.00
50	20 IN. BOY & GIRL CALYPSO DANCERS	*	*	800.00
50	9 IN. CHOIR BOY	*	*	400.00
53	GIRL WATER SKIER	*	10.00	200.00
54	10 IN. COUNTRY GIRL	*	8.95	1000.00
54	10 IN. ELF	*	*	275.00
54	10 IN. SAKS FIFTH AVE. SKIER	50	9.95	1500.00
54	26 IN. BEAN NOSE SANTA	*	19.95	950.00
54	5 IN. SNO BUNNY (KID)	*	*	300.00
54	5 IN. SNO-BUNNY CHILD	*	2.95	350.00
54	8 IN. BOY SKIER	*	*	550.00
55	10 IN. BOY SWIMMER	*	*	550.00
55	7 IN. BOY SKIER	*	*	1250.00
56	10 IN. BABY ANGEL	*	5.50	550.00
56	10 IN. FISHING GIRL	*	*	425.00
56	10 IN. WATER SKIER GIRL	*	9.95	800.00
56	12 IN. SANTA WITH BEAN NOSE	*	20.00	1000.00
56	7 IN. BABY ANGEL WITH FEATHER HAIR	*	3.95	325.00
57	10 IN. BOY & GIRL IN BOAT	*	17.50	900.00
57	10 IN. BOY BUILDING BOAT	*	*	925.00
57	10 IN. BOY SKIER	*	16.00	800.00
57	10 IN. BOY SQUARE DANCER	*	9.95	800.00
57	10 IN. BOY WITH STRAW HAT	*	*	500.00
57	10 IN. CASUALTY SKI GROUP	*	35.00	3100.00
57	10 IN. CASUALTY TOBOGGAN GROUP	*	35.00	900.00
57	10 IN. EASTER HOLIDAY DOLL	*	10.00	800.00
57	10 IN. FOURTH OF JULY DOLL	*	10.00	1600.00
57	10 IN. GIRL SKIER	*	*	1000.00
57	10 IN. GIRL SQUARE DANCER	*	9.95	475.00
57	10 IN. HOLLY ELF	*	*	500.00
57	10 IN. MR. HOLLY ELF	*	*	1600.00
57	10 IN. SKIER	*	15.00	1500.00
57	10 IN. SKIER WITH LEG IN CAST	*	35.00	1950.00
57	10 IN. THANKSGIVING DOLL	*	*	600.00
57	10 IN. VALENTINE DOLL	*	10.00	900.00
57	9 IN. ELF WITH MUSICAL INSTRUMENT	*	3.50	550.00
58	10 IN. SPRING DOLL	*	10.00	3500.00
59	10 IN. ARCHITECT	*	*	700.00
59	10 IN. BOY & GIRL IN FISHING BOAT	*	17.00	1000.00
59	10 IN. BOY & GIRL ON BIKE	*	*	2000.00
59	10 IN. BOY GOLFER	*	10.00	475.00
59	10 IN. BOY SKIER	*	*	800.00
59	10 IN. BOY SQUARE DANCER	*	10.00	475.00
59	10 IN. DENTIST	*	10.00	600.00
59	10 IN. ELF WITH INSTRUMENT	*	3.50	400.00
59	10 IN. FOOTBALL PLAYER	*	10.00	600.00
59	10 IN. GIRL SKIER	*	*	825.00
59	10 IN. GIRL SQUARE DANCER	*	10.00	475.00
59	10 IN. GIRL SWIMMER	*	*	550.00
59	10 IN. GREEN WOODSPRITE	*	6.95	350.00
59	10 IN. TEXAS OIL MAN	*	16.00	1550.00
59	7 IN. GIRL SKIER	*	*	675.00
59	7 IN. SANTA WITH FUR TRIM SUIT	*	2.95	225.00
60	10 IN. BATHING GIRL	*	3.95	300.00
60	10 IN. GIRL SKI DOLL	*	*	450.00
60	10 IN. GIRL SKIER	*	*	400.00
60	12 IN. BIG ANGEL ON CLOUD	*	9.95	350.00
60	33 IN. BOY & GIRL ON TANDEM BIKE	*	*	3500.00
60	5 IN. ELF	*	*	200.00
60	7 IN. BABY ANGEL	*	*	300.00
60	7 IN. BABY ANGEL W/BLUE WINGS	*	*	300.00
60	7 IN. BABY ANGEL WITH STAR ON LEG	*	*	300.00

YR	NAME	LIMIT	ISSUE	TREND
60	7 IN. BABY IN STOCKING	*	*	275.00
60	7 IN. BABY WITH BOW	*	1.50	125.00
60	7 IN. BABY WITH PINK BOW	*	*	450.00
60	7 IN. MR. AND MRS. TUCKERED	*	*	500.00
62	10 IN. SKEEPLE (BOY)	*	9.00	425.00
62	5 IN. ELF W/FEATHER HAIR	*	9.00	300.00
63	10 IN. CHRISTMAS ELF W/TINSEL	*	*	250.00
63	10 IN. ELF SKIER	*	*	350.00
63	10 IN. GIRL WATERSKIER	*	7.50	450.00
63	10 IN. WHITE WOODSPRITE	*	*	325.00
63	10 IN. YELLOW WOODSPRITE	*	*	275.00
63	18 IN. FRIAR	*	*	400.00
63	18 IN. FRIAR BOTTLE COVER	*	3.00	350.00
63	22 IN. BELLHOP (RED)	*	*	700.00
63	24 IN. WOODSPRITE	*	5.45	125.00
63	5 IN. BABY	*	*	300.00
63	5 IN. BABY WITH ANGEL HALO	*	2.00	300.00
63	5 IN. BABY WITH SANTA HAT	*	2.50	175.00
63	5 IN. CHRISTMAS ELF	*	3.00	200.00
63	7 IN. BABY ANGEL ON CLOUD	*	2.45	300.00
63	7 IN. SATURDAY NIGHT BABY	*	2.95	350.00
64	10 IN. GENDARME	*	4.00	450.00
64	10 IN. IMP SKIER	*	4.00	350.00
64	10 IN. MONK (GREEN)	*	3.00	275.00
64	10 IN. MONK WITH CAP	*	3.00	275.00
64	12 IN. GEORGE & SHEILA-BRIDE/GROOM MOUSE	*	12.95	600.00
64	18 IN. P.J. BOY & GIRL	*	7.00	525.00
64	18 IN. WOODSPRITE	*	6.00	325.00
64	22 IN. WOODSPRITE	*	5.95	325.00
64	7 IN. ANGEL IN A BLANKET	*	2.45	350.00
64	7 IN. BRIDE & GROOM MICE	*	2.75	750.00
64	7 IN. CHRISTMAS MOUSE	*	3.95	450.00
64	7 IN. SAT. NITE ANGEL W/BLANKET	*	2.95	250.00
65	10 IN. BACK TO SCHOOL, BOY & GIRL	*	19.90	525.00
65	10 IN. FISHING BOY	*	7.95	300.00
65	10 IN. FISHING GIRL	*	9.95	400.00
65	10 IN. MONK WITH CHRISTMAS TREE PLANTING	*	3.00	450.00
65	10 IN. REINDEER	*	4.95	400.00
65	12 IN. NIPSY-TIPSY HARE	*	7.50	700.00
65	12 IN. SANTA	*	5.00	125.00
65	18 IN. SANTA	*	9.00	150.00
65	26 IN. MRS. SANTA WITH APRON	*	14.95	1000.00
65	5 IN. GREEN GNOME	*	*	125.00
65	7 IN. DRESDEN CHINA BABIES, 2	*	*	525.00
65	7 IN. DUMB BUNNY	*	3.95	400.00
65	7 IN. EEK, PEEK, SQUEEK MOUSE	*	3.95	500.00
65	7 IN. LAWYER MOUSE	*	6.95	425.00
65	7 IN. MR. AND MRS. SANTA	*	5.95	525.00
66	10 IN. BOY GO-GO DANCER	*	10.00	350.00
66	10 IN. CENTRAL GAS CO. ELF	*	*	350.00
66	10 IN. GO-GO BOY & GIRL	*	3.95	460.00
66	29 IN. MR. OUTDOOR SANTA	*	17.00	350.00
66	5 IN. NEW HAMPTON SCHOOL BABY	300	*	200.00
66	7 IN. ANGEL, WHITE WINGS	*	*	225.00
66	7 IN. MOUSE WITH CANDLE	*	*	225.00
66	7 IN. YUM YUM BUNNY	*	3.95	525.00
67	10 IN. ELF WITH ROUND BOX	*	2.50	350.00
67	10 IN. ELF WITH SKIS	48	3.00	650.00
67	10 IN. MONK	*	*	200.00
67	10 IN. SURFER BOY	*	4.95	300.00
67	10 IN. SURFER BOY	*	9.95	400.00
67	10 IN. SURFER GIRL	*	9.95	590.00
67	10 IN. WORKSHOP ELF	*	*	175.00
67	12 IN. FANCY NANCY CAT CHRISTMAS	*	6.95	700.00
67	12 IN. GNOME W/PJ SUIT	*	*	425.00
67	12 IN. LAURA MAY CAT	*	6.95	850.00
67	12 IN. YUM YUM BUNNY	*	9.95	800.00
67	18 IN. MONK W/PLANT	*	7.50	400.00
67	18 IN. NUN	296	8.00	525.00
67	36 IN. CHRISTMAS CAT	*	12.00	350.00
67	7 IN. CONDUCTOR MOUSE	*	3.95	300.00
67	7 IN. GARDEN CLUB BABY	*	2.95	350.00
67	7 IN. GNOME W/PJ SUIT	*	2.50	380.00
67	7 IN. MIGUEL THE MOUSE	*	3.95	400.00
67	7 IN. MR. SANTA MOUSE	*	3.95	300.00
67	7 IN. MRS. HOLLY MOUSE	*	3.95	365.00
67	7 IN. SANTA MOUSE	*	2.00	250.00
67	7 IN. SANTA WITH TOY BAG	*	3.95	275.00
68	10 IN. BOY WITH BEACHBALL	*	5.95	375.00
68	12 IN. ICE PACK CAT	*	6.95	500.00
68	12 IN. TESSIE TAR CAT	*	6.95	450.00
68	18 IN. MR. INDOOR SANTA	*	7.50	225.00
68	18 IN. MRS. INDOOR SANTA	*	7.50	250.00
68	29 IN. MR. SANTA WITH VEST & SACK	*	16.00	500.00
68	36 IN. RED NOSED REINDEER	*	*	300.00
68	5 IN. BABY ANGEL ON CLOUD	*	2.95	300.00
68	5 IN. BABY IN SANTA CAP	*	2.00	150.00
68	5 IN. BABY IN SANTA HAT	*	3.00	225.00
68	6 IN. MYRTLE TURTLE	*	3.95	700.00

YR	NAME	LIMIT	ISSUE	TREND
68	7 IN. BABY I'M READING	*	*	375.00
68	7 IN. BABY VAIN JANE	*	2.50	300.00
68	7 IN. FAT FANNY	*	5.95	375.00
68	7 IN. FAT FANNY	*	6.00	375.00
68	7 IN. MR. & MRS. SANTA TUCKERED	*	3.00	200.00
68	7 IN. MR. HOLLY MOUSE	*	3.95	250.00
68	7 IN. NIGHTSHIRT BOY MOUSE	*	3.95	200.00
69	10 IN. BRIDE & GROOM FROGS COURTIN'	*	7.95	550.00
69	10 IN. NUN ON SKIS	1551	4.50	300.00
69	10 IN. REINDEER WITH RED NOSE	*	4.95	350.00
69	10 IN. WHITE ELF WITH PRESENTS	*	*	180.00
69	12 IN. NIGHTSHIRT MOUSE	*	*	525.00
69	18 IN. SANTA KID	*	7.45	250.00
69	22 IN. GIRL GO-GO DANCER	*	10.00	300.00
69	25 IN. COUNTRY BOY	70	7.00	500.00
69	25 IN. COUNTRY GIRL (PAIR)	69	7.00	*
69	4 IN. PIG-BUBBLE TIME W/CHAMPAGNE GLASS	*	4.95	275.00
69	42 IN. FROG	30	29.95	700.00
69	7 IN. BUNNY W/OVERSIZED CARROT	*	4.95	400.00
69	7 IN. CHRISTMAS BABY ON 3 HOT BOXES	*	3.00	400.00
70	10 IN. CASUALTY ELF	991	2.25	600.00
70	10 IN. CHOIR BOY	3517	4.50	150.00
70	10 IN. CHOIR GIRL	7245	5.00	225.00
70	10 IN. CLOWN	2362	4.00	125.00
70	10 IN. ELF SKIER	597	*	200.00
70	10 IN. MONK WITH SKIS	406	4.00	350.00
70	10 IN. REINDEER WITH HAT	144	5.00	175.00
70	10 IN. XMAS MUSHROOM-7 IN. SANTA & DEER	*	11.00	600.00
70	14 IN. SPRING MUSHROOM	*	*	450.00
70	18 IN. BUNNY W/BUTTERFLY	258	10.95	500.00
70	18 IN. CLOWN	542	5.00	250.00
70	18 IN. GIRL BUNNY WITH EGG	1727	15.95	150.00
70	18 IN. PATCHWORK KID	496	7.50	250.00
70	29 IN. GIRL BUNNY	*	22.00	250.00
70	7 IN. ARCHITECT MOUSE	2051	3.95	375.00
70	7 IN. ARCHITECT MOUSE	205	3.95	350.00
70	7 IN. BLUE MONKEY	293	*	250.00
70	7 IN. BOXING MOUSE	321	3.95	400.00
70	7 IN. BUNNY W/BUTTERFLY	1264	4.95	150.00
70	7 IN. CARPENTER MOUSE	307	3.95	300.00
70	7 IN. MONKEY	293	4.95	525.00
70	7 IN. NIGHTSHIRT GIRL MOUSE	*	3.95	175.00
70	7 IN. PLUMBER MOUSE	196	3.95	350.00
70	7 IN. PROFESSOR MOUSE	248	3.95	225.00
70	7 IN. SANTA WITH 10 IN. XMAS MUSHROOM	*	7.00	125.00
70	7 IN. SHERIFF MOUSE	11	3.95	625.00
70	7 IN. TREASURE BABY	*	3.95	200.00
70	7 IN. YELLOW BUNNY	*	3.95	300.00
71	10 IN. BRIDE & GROOM FROGS ON BIKE	13	17.50	625.00
71	10 IN. CHOIR BOY	904	3.95	175.00
71	10 IN. CHOIR GIRL	925	3.95	250.00
71	10 IN. CLOWN	708	2.00	305.00
71	10 IN. ELF SKIER	*	*	270.00
71	10 IN. FROG W/INSTRUMENT	233	3.95	200.00
71	10 IN. NUN ON SKIS	617	4.00	300.00
71	10 IN. RED NOSED REINDEER	1588	4.95	225.00
71	18 IN. CHOIR GIRL	424	7.95	400.00
71	18 IN. FROG W/BASS VIOLA	224	11.95	1350.00
71	18 IN. MRS. SANTA WITH CARDHOLDER	1563	8.00	200.00
71	18 IN. PETER BUNNY	219	10.95	425.00
71	18 IN. SANTA FUR KID	1191	7.95	400.00
71	29 IN. SNOWMAN WITH BROOM	1075	19.95	200.00
71	30 IN. WHITE BUNNY WITH CARROT	172	*	165.00
71	36 IN. REINDEER WITH TWO 18 IN. GNOMES	624	38.00	700.00
71	5 IN. GNOME WITH CANDLE	*	3.00	300.00
71	7 IN. ANGEL WITH PAPER WINGS	608	3.00	325.00
71	7 IN. ARTIST MOUSE	422	3.95	175.00
71	7 IN. BABY BUNTING IN BASKET	195	3.95	350.00
71	7 IN. BASEBALL MOUSE	553	4.00	150.00
71	7 IN. CHEF MOUSE	*	*	75.00
71	7 IN. MOUSE WITH INNER TUBE	267	4.00	200.00
71	7 IN. MR. & MRS. SANTA WITH BASKET	3403	5.95	150.00
71	7 IN. SKI MOUSE	1326	3.95	175.00
71	7 IN. SNOWMAN	1917	3.95	275.00
71	7 IN. THREE GNOMES W/LARGE CANDLE	80	11.95	700.00
71	7 IN. YELLOW KITTEN	103	4.50	575.00
72	10 IN. DONKEY	861	5.95	425.00
72	10 IN. ROBIN HOOD ELF	*	2.50	175.00
72	12 IN. CAT WITH MOUSE	*	13.00	450.00
72	16 IN. ELEPHANT	230	12.95	810.00
72	18 IN. LEPRECHAUN	1372	*	200.00
72	18 IN. MR. SANTA WITH SACK	850	*	150.00
72	29 IN. EASTER PARADE MOM BUNNY	508	35.00	250.00
72	29 IN. SANTA WITH CARDHOLDER SACK	686	24.95	150.00
72	30 IN. BOY BUNNY	237	25.00	225.00
72	30 IN. ELECTION DONKEY	120	23.95	350.00
72	30 IN. GIRL BUNNY	223	25.00	225.00
72	36 IN. ELECTION ELEPHANT	113	*	550.00
72	7 IN. BALLERINA BUNNY	4700	4.00	100.00

YR	NAME	LIMIT	ISSUE	TREND
72	7 IN. BAR-BE-QUE MOUSE	907	3.95	225.00
72	7 IN. BUNNY (WITH BANDANA)	1615	3.95	150.00
72	7 IN. CHRISTMAS MOUSE	2793	3.95	425.00
72	7 IN. DIAPER MOUSE, IT'S A BOY	2293	4.50	175.00
72	7 IN. DIAPER MOUSE, IT'S A GIRL	2293	4.50	225.00
72	7 IN. GIRL GOLFER MOUSE	*	3.95	100.00
72	7 IN. HOUSEWIFE MOUSE	1768	3.95	250.00
72	7 IN. MR. & MRS. TUCKERED	1187	6.50	375.00
72	7 IN. MRS. SANTA WITH APRON AND CAP	8867	5.50	50.00
72	7 IN. PREGNANT MOUSE	820	5.50	100.00
72	7 IN. SANTA WITH MUSHROOM	540	*	275.00
72	7 IN. YACHTSMAN MOUSE	1130	3.95	250.00
73	12 IN. GIRL NIGHTSHIRT MONKEY	*	7.50	300.00
73	12 IN. NIGHTSHIRT MOUSE	122	7.50	350.00
73	18 IN. MRS. SANTA	3700	7.00	150.00
73	18 IN. MRS. SANTA WITH CARDHOLDER	3900	14.95	150.00
73	7 IN. BUNNY ON BOX	795	5.50	125.00
73	7 IN. CHRISTMAS PANDA	1094	8.95	350.00
73	7 IN. FIREMAN MOUSE	557	4.50	200.00
73	7 IN. FOOTBALL MOUSE	944	4.50	150.00
73	7 IN. GOLFER MOUSE	*	5.00	55.00
73	7 IN. MR. & MRS. SANTA-WICKER LOVESEAT	3973	10.95	250.00
73	7 IN. PAINTER MOUSE	*	4.50	275.00
73	7 IN. SANTA MAILMAN	3276	5.00	200.00
73	7 IN. SKIING MOUSE	2774	4.00	175.00
73	7 IN. WAITER MOUSE	*	4.00	250.00
73	7 IN. WHITE BUNNY	1600	5.50	125.00
74	10 IN. LAD & LASS	453	*	300.00
74	10 IN. WILLIE WOG GOIN' FISHING	*	5.50	200.00
74	12 IN. RETIRED GRANDMA MOUSE	1135	13.50	300.00
74	12 IN. RETIRED GRANDPA MOUSE (PAIR)	1103	13.50	*
74	22 IN. WORKSHOP ELF	1404	10.45	125.00
74	22 IN. WORKSHOP ELF WITH APRON	1404	10.95	882.00
74	29 IN. MRS. SANTA WITH CARDHOLDER	*	28.95	200.00
74	7 IN. ARTIST MOUSE	397	5.50	110.00
74	7 IN. BLACK SANTA	1157	5.50	225.00
74	7 IN. CARPENTER MOUSE	551	5.50	275.00
74	7 IN. COWBOY MOUSE	394	5.50	150.00
74	7 IN. DOCTOR MOUSE	720	5.50	200.00
74	7 IN. HOCKEY MOUSE	687	7.95	200.00
74	7 IN. HUNTER MOUSE W/BIRD	690	5.50	300.00
74	7 IN. HUNTER MOUSE WITH 10 IN. DEER	1282	11.50	175.00
74	7 IN. PAINTER MOUSE	*	4.00	175.00
74	7 IN. PREGNANT MOUSE	820	*	200.00
74	7 IN. SANTA IN SKI BOB	704	4.95	450.00
74	7 IN. SEAMSTRESS MOUSE	387	4.00	175.00
74	7 IN. SECRETARY MOUSE	364	4.00	150.00
74	7 IN. VACATION MOUSE	*	*	175.00
75	10 IN. CAROLER BOY	*	*	275.00
75	10 IN. LAD & LASS	162	12.00	249.00
75	10 IN. LAD ON BICYCLE	453	6.00	300.00
75	10 IN. LASS	558	6.00	300.00
75	10 IN. RED NOSED REINDEER	4854	*	100.00
75	18 IN. HORSE	221	17.00	200.00
75	18 IN. LAD	206	11.95	175.00
75	18 IN. LAD & LASS ON BIKE	206	24.00	275.00
75	18 IN. LASS	224	11.95	95.00
75	18 IN. MRS. SANTA WITH PLUM PUDDING	*	12.00	300.00
75	25 IN. LASS WITH BASKET OF FLOWERS	92	28.95	450.00
75	5 IN. BABY DUCK	1333	4.00	135.00
75	7 IN. BEAUTICIAN MOUSE	1349	4.00	300.00
75	7 IN. BICYCLIST MOUSE	1561	5.50	125.00
75	7 IN. BOUQUET GIRL MOUSE	*	3.95	300.00
75	7 IN. CHRISTMAS MOUSE IN SANTA'S MITTEN	3959	5.95	150.00
75	7 IN. FISHERMAN MOUSE	1343	5.50	200.00
75	7 IN. GOIN' FISHIN' MOUSE	4507	5.95	125.00
75	7 IN. HOUSEWIFE MOUSE	1632	5.50	250.00
75	7 IN. PREGNANT MOUSE	879	5.50	150.00
75	7 IN. RETIRED GRANDPA MOUSE	793	5.50	95.00
75	7 IN. SKI MOUSE	5219	5.50	200.00
75	7 IN. TWO IN TENT MICE	914	*	85.00
76	10 IN. BOY IN TIRE SWING	358	6.95	340.00
76	10 IN. CLOWN	2285	5.50	100.00
76	10 IN. COUNTRY GIRL IN TIRE SWING	357	*	200.00
76	10 IN. DONKEY	1202	5.95	175.00
76	10 IN. DRUMMER BOY	*	6.00	200.00
76	10 IN. ELEPHANT	1223	5.95	225.00
76	10 IN. GIRL IN TIRE SWING	357	6.95	225.00
76	10 IN. LASS W/PLANTER BASKET	313	6.95	200.00
76	10 IN. SCARECROW	2341	5.95	120.00
76	10 IN. SCARECROW	2341	6.00	200.00
76	10 IN. UNCLE SAM	1095	5.95	510.00
76	10 IN. VOTE DONKEY	1202	5.95	225.00
76	12 IN. COLONIAL BOY & GIRL MOUSE	*	26.90	900.00
76	12 IN. COLONIAL BOY MOUSE	838	13.50	400.00
76	12 IN. COLONIAL GIRL MOUSE	691	13.50	350.00
76	12 IN. GIRL MOUSE WITH PLUM PUDDING	1482	13.50	400.00
76	15 IN. ROOSTER	485	13.50	1050.00
76	18 IN. CHOIR BOY	*	*	500.00

YR	NAME	LIMIT	ISSUE	TREND
76	18 IN. CLOWN	916	13.50	200.00
76	18 IN. DRUMMER BOY	402	13.50	400.00
76	18 IN. EASTER PARADE BOY BUNNY	791	13.50	300.00
76	18 IN. ELEPHANT	285	16.95	500.00
76	18 IN. GIRL BUNNY WITH EGG	789	13.50	375.00
76	18 IN. SCARECROW	916	13.50	250.00
76	18 IN. UNCLE SAM	245	17.00	480.00
76	18 IN. VOTE 76 DONKEY	285	16.95	300.00
76	18 IN. YANKEE DOODLE DANDY	153	*	925.00
76	25 IN. YANKEE DOODLE DANDY/30 IN. HORSE	41	77.50	1600.00
76	30 IN. CLOWN	466	30.00	650.00
76	36 IN. ELECTION DONKEY	119	*	650.00
76	36 IN. HORSE	27	48.00	500.00
76	42 IN. SCARECROW	134	62.00	375.00
76	7 IN. BIRTHDAY GIRL MOUSE	732	5.50	250.00
76	7 IN. CARD PLAYING GIRL MOUSE	2878	5.95	175.00
76	7 IN. COLONIAL BOY MOUSE	5457	*	200.00
76	7 IN. COLONIAL GIRL MOUSE	5457	5.50	225.00
76	7 IN. GARDENER MOUSE	1255	5.50	225.00
76	7 IN. MISTLETOE ANGEL	17540	6.00	80.00
76	7 IN. MR. HOLLY MOUSE	2774	5.50	125.00
76	7 IN. MRS. HOLLY MOUSE	3078	5.50	125.00
76	7 IN. NURSE MOUSE	5164	5.95	250.00
76	8 IN. ELECTION ELEPHANT	1223	*	175.00
76	8 IN. ROOSTER	1094	5.50	250.00
76	8 IN. WHITE DUCK	3265	4.95	225.00
77	10 IN. CLOWN	4784	6.00	125.00
77	10 IN. SCARECROW	4879	5.95	225.00
77	15 IN. PURPLE ROOSTER	548	5.48	450.00
77	18 IN. CLOWN	2343	13.50	475.00
77	18 IN. EASTER PARADE BOY BUNNY	1567	13.50	150.00
77	18 IN. SCARECROW	*	13.50	175.00
77	18 IN. WHITE ELF	2600	*	150.00
77	22 IN. JACK FROST ELF	2600	11.95	400.00
77	29 IN. EASTER PARADE POP BUNNY	477	35.00	250.00
77	29 IN. MECHANICAL SEE-SAW BUNNY	*	300.00	900.00
77	29 IN. MRS. SANTA MOUSE	571	49.95	825.00
77	29 IN. MRS. SANTA MOUSE WITH MUFF	571	49.95	800.00
77	29 IN. POP BUNNY WITH BASKET	*	11.50	400.00
77	7 IN. BASEBALL MOUSE	1634	6.00	100.00
77	7 IN. BEAUTICIAN MOUSE	1521	5.50	250.00
77	7 IN. BINGO MOUSE	1221	6.00	150.00
77	7 IN. BUNNY W/EGG	2442	5.95	125.00
77	7 IN. BUNNY WITH BUTTERFLY	2721	6.00	125.00
77	7 IN. DIET TIME MOUSE	1478	6.00	200.00
77	7 IN. GROOM MOUSE	1211	6.95	50.00
77	7 IN. HOBO MOUSE	1004	5.95	250.00
77	7 IN. MR. NIGHTSHIRT MOUSE	309	49.95	650.00
77	7 IN. SWEETHEART MOUSE	3323	5.50	100.00
77	7 IN. VACATIONER MOUSE	1040	6.00	175.00
77	8 IN. DRUMMER BOY	6522	6.00	100.00
77	8 IN. ROOSTER	1642	6.00	360.00
78	10 IN. BOY PILGRIM	3465	7.00	325.00
78	10 IN. CLOWN	4020	6.50	175.00
78	10 IN. SNOWMAN	9701	6.95	175.00
78	12 IN. CHRISTMAS GNOME	10140	*	125.00
78	12 IN. GNOME	10140	9.50	175.00
78	18 IN. CANDY GIRL	1333	14.95	375.00
78	18 IN. CLOWN	4000	13.95	225.00
78	18 IN. REINDEER	*	18.00	125.00
78	18 IN. REINDEER	5134	9.00	125.00
78	18 IN. SNOWMAN	3971	79.95	250.00
78	29 IN. CAROLER MOUSE	658	50.00	750.00
78	29 IN. E.P. MOM & POP BUNNIES (PAIR)	529	36.95	400.00
78	36 IN. REINDEER WITH SADDLEBAGS	594	58.00	175.00
78	7 IN. AIRPLANE PILOT MOUSE	2308	6.95	400.00
78	7 IN. ARTIST BUNNY	4217	7.50	250.00
78	7 IN. BUNNIES WITH BASKET	2253	*	150.00
78	7 IN. C.B. MOUSE	2396	6.95	75.00
78	7 IN. DOCTOR MOUSE	2028	6.95	100.00
78	7 IN. DOCTOR MOUSE	816	6.95	75.00
78	7 IN. FIREMAN MOUSE	*	6.95	200.00
78	7 IN. GARDENER MOUSE	*	7.00	75.00
78	7 IN. GIRL GOLFER MOUSE	2215	6.95	100.00
78	7 IN. GROOM MOUSE	*	14.50	125.00
78	7 IN. GROOM MOUSE	2952	9.50	85.00
78	7 IN. NIGHTSHIRT MOUSE	6444	7.95	75.00
78	7 IN. POLICEMAN MOUSE	RT	7.00	150.00
78	7 IN. SANTA WITH DEER AND TREE	5813	18.50	400.00
78	7 IN. SKATEBOARD MOUSE	3733	7.95	300.00
78	7 IN. TEACHER MOUSE	2249	5.50	100.00
78	7 IN. TREE TOP ANGEL WITH WREATH	8613	6.50	100.00
79	10 IN. BOY FROG	5642	8.50	125.00
79	10 IN. SNOWMAN	12888	7.95	100.00
79	12 IN. MRS. SANTA MOUSE	7210	*	125.00
79	12 IN. NIGHTSHIRT MOUSE WITH CANDLE	5739	16.00	225.00
79	12 IN. SANTA MOUSE	*	*	125.00
79	14 IN. FATHER PIG	1500	18.95	150.00
79	14 IN. MOM PIG	1807	18.95	150.00

YR	NAME	LIMIT	ISSUE	TREND
79	18 IN. ARTIST BUNNY	1064	15.95	275.00
79	18 IN. GIRL FROG	2338	18.95	225.00
79	18 IN. GNOME	9048	16.95	210.00
79	18 IN. MR. SANTA WITH CARDHOLDER	*	*	75.00
79	29 IN. E.P. MOM BUNNY	662	42.95	200.00
79	29 IN. GNOME	1762	47.95	400.00
79	29 IN. MOTORIZED MR. & MRS. SANTA	136	400.00	1600.00
79	29 IN. SNOWMAN	917	42.95	400.00
79	7 IN. BOY GOLFER MOUSE	2743	7.95	100.00
79	7 IN. C.B. MOUSE	1039	7.95	100.00
79	7 IN. C.B. SANTA	2206	7.95	75.00
79	7 IN. CARPENTER MOUSE	2024	6.95	175.00
79	7 IN. CHIMNEY SWEEP MOUSE	6331	7.95	275.00
79	7 IN. FIREMAN MOUSE	1773	6.95	200.00
79	7 IN. FISHING MOUSE	3053	7.95	150.00
79	7 IN. GARDENER MOUSE	1939	7.95	375.00
79	7 IN. GIRL GOLFER MOUSE	2316	7.95	90.00
79	7 IN. MRS. SANTA MOUSE WITH HOLLY	*	7.95	50.00
79	7 IN. PREGNANT MOUSE	1856	7.95	225.00
79	7 IN. QUILTING MOUSE	213	*	375.00
79	7 IN. SANTA MOUSE	12649	7.95	100.00
79	7 IN. SANTA WITH MISTLETOE	*	7.95	50.00
79	7 IN. SKATEBOARD MOUSE	1821	6.00	300.00
79	7 IN. SWIMMER MOUSE	3640	9.50	225.00
80	10 IN. BOY FROG	4185	9.50	125.00
80	10 IN. BOY ON RAFT	1087	28.95	300.00
80	10 IN. BRIDE FROG	1653	14.95	150.00
80	10 IN. CLOWN	8136	12.50	75.00
80	10 IN. GIRL FROG	421	9.50	125.00
80	10 IN. GROOM FROG	1611	14.95	150.00
80	10 IN. SANTA FROG	7631	9.95	125.00
80	18 IN. BOY FROG	1285	23.00	150.00
80	18 IN. C.G. BUNNY W/BASKET	3964	19.95	150.00
80	18 IN. CLOWN	3192	24.95	125.00
80	18 IN. CLOWN WITH BALLOON	3192	24.95	100.00
80	18 IN. SANTA FROG	2126	25.00	145.00
80	18 IN. SANTA FROG	2126	25.00	225.00
80	4 FT. CLOWN	224	150.00	900.00
80	4 IN. PIG	1615	8.50	100.00
80	42 IN. CLOWN WITH STAND	224	84.95	710.00
80	42 IN. FROG	202	89.95	500.00
80	42 IN. SANTA FROG	206	100.00	700.00
80	7 IN. BABY IN BASSINETTE	*	*	125.00
80	7 IN. BACKPACKER MOUSE	1008	9.95	375.00
80	7 IN. BALLERINA BUNNY	*	8.95	175.00
80	7 IN. BOY DISCO MOUSE	363	9.50	150.00
80	7 IN. BRIDE & GROOM MICE	2418	9.50	175.00
80	7 IN. CARD PLAYING GIRL MOUSE	1826	9.50	125.00
80	7 IN. DISCO BOY MOUSE	363	9.50	150.00
80	7 IN. DISCO GIRL MOUSE	*	9.50	325.00
80	7 IN. FISHING MOUSE	*	7.50	150.00
80	7 IN. GIRL DISCO MOUSE	915	9.50	150.00
80	7 IN. GNOME	13238	9.50	150.00
80	7 IN. GREENTHUMB MOUSE	1869	9.50	60.00
80	7 IN. MOUSE WITH CHIMNEY	4452	*	75.00
80	7 IN. PILOT MOUSE	2011	9.95	100.00
80	7 IN. SANTA WITH STOCKING	17665	9.95	75.00
80	7 IN. SKATING MOUSE	3369	10.95	100.00
80	7 IN. VOLLEYBALL MOUSE	915	9.50	75.00
81	10 IN. BALLOONING SANTA	1737	39.95	325.00
81	10 IN. BOY ON RAFT	*	*	200.00
81	10 IN. BRIDE FROG	1239	14.95	150.00
81	10 IN. CLOWN	6479	9.95	125.00
81	10 IN. CLOWN	6479	12.95	100.00
81	10 IN. ELF ON BUTTERFLY	1625	24.95	300.00
81	10 IN. GROOM FROG	2061	14.95	150.00
81	10 IN. JACK FROST WITH SNOWFLAKE	5950	31.95	175.00
81	12 IN. BOY MONKEY WITH TRAPEZE	1800	23.95	300.00
81	12 IN. GIRL MONKEY WITH TRAPEZE	857	23.95	200.00
81	12 IN. SANTA MONKEY	1800	24.00	250.00
81	12 IN. WITCH MOUSE ON BROOM	1049	34.95	160.00
81	14 IN. DRAGON WITH BUSHBOY	1257	28.95	650.00
81	18 IN. BOY ON SLED	*	12.50	200.00
81	18 IN. BUTTERFLY WITH 10 IN. ELF	2517	27.95	525.00
81	18 IN. CAT W/7 IN. MOUSE & MISTLETOE	10999	46.95	140.00
81	18 IN. CAT W/MOUSE & MISTLETOE	18995	46.95	150.00
81	18 IN. CLOWN	2742	24.95	200.00
81	18 IN. COUNTRY BOY BUNNY WITH CARROT	1998	23.95	275.00
81	18 IN. ESCORT FOX	*	28.50	350.00
81	18 IN. FOXY LADY	*	28.50	350.00
81	18 IN. GIRL FROG	666	24.00	225.00
81	18 IN. MONK W/JUG	494	*	290.00
81	29 IN. DRAGON WITH BUSHBOY	76	69.95	1050.00
81	29 IN. DRAGON WITH BUSHBOY	75	63.95	1050.00
81	3 IN. PIG	3435	7.95	100.00
81	4 IN. PIG	3194	7.95	100.00
81	5 IN. MINIATURE REINDEER	9080	11.50	120.00
81	7 IN. AIRPLANE PILOT MOUSE	1910	9.95	325.00
81	7 IN. BACKPACKER MOUSE	1008	9.95	100.00

YR	NAME	LIMIT	ISSUE	TREND
81	7 IN. BASEBALL MOUSE	2380	*	100.00
81	7 IN. CARD PLAYING GIRL MOUSE	863	9.95	125.00
81	7 IN. COUNTRY BUNNIES	7940	*	185.00
81	7 IN. CROSS-COUNTRY SKI SANTA	5180	10.95	100.00
81	7 IN. ESCORT FOX	*	12.50	250.00
81	7 IN. FOXY LADY	*	12.50	250.00
81	7 IN. I'M LATE BUNNY	*	*	500.00
81	7 IN. ICESKATER MOUSE	1429	9.95	150.00
81	7 IN. JOGGER MOUSE	1783	9.95	65.00
81	7 IN. MONKEY WITH BANANA TRAPEZE	3075	*	125.00
81	7 IN. NAUGHTY ANGEL	12359	10.95	90.00
81	7 IN. NURSE MOUSE	3222	11.95	50.00
81	7 IN. SANTA MONKEY	4606	10.00	200.00
81	7 IN. SANTA WITH MISTLETOE	*	10.50	40.00
81	7 IN. SANTA WITH POT BELLY	*	11.95	75.00
81	7 IN. WITCH MOUSE ON BROOM WITH MOON	1585+	24.95	200.00
81	7 IN. WOODCHOPPER MOUSE	2121	11.00	75.00
81	8 IN. BOY BBQ PIG	4072	10.50	200.00
81	8 IN. BOY BBQ PIG	1159	11.95	100.00
81	8 IN. GIRL BBQ BUNNY	2596	9.95	250.00
81	8 IN. GIRL BBQ PIG (PAIR)	3854	10.50	*
82	10 IN. ELF ON BUTTERFLY	882	*	275.00
82	10 IN. JACK FROST WITH SNOWFLAKE	2289	13.50	250.00
82	10 IN. MONK	6968	12.95	130.00
82	12 IN. BOY SKUNK	935	27.95	225.00
82	12 IN. DUCK WITH KERCHIEF	5861	26.95	125.00
82	12 IN. GIRL SKUNK	936	27.95	225.00
82	12 IN. NIGHTSHIRT MOUSE	2319	25.95	125.00
82	12 IN. PILGRIM BOY MOUSE	2151	27.95	175.00
82	12 IN. PILGRIM GIRL MOUSE	2017	27.95	175.00
82	12 IN. SKUNK WITH SNOWBALL	1304	*	225.00
82	18 IN. GIRL P.J. KID	5389	25.50	125.00
82	18 IN. SANTA FOX	1499	29.95	575.00
82	22 IN. CHRISTMAS GIRAFFE WITH ELF	448	44.00	500.00
82	22 IN. SUN	838	*	200.00
82	4 FT. BOY BUNNY	186	190.00	450.00
82	5 IN. DRAGON WITH BUSHBOY	1066	17.95	475.00
82	5 IN. MRS. SANTA WITH GIFT BOX	7566	10.95	75.00
82	5 IN. SANTA WITH DEER	3072	20.00	235.00
82	7 IN. ANGEL WITH TEARDROP	3092	12.95	200.00
82	7 IN. BALLERINA BUNNY	4179	9.95	100.00
82	7 IN. BRIDE MOUSE	3681	10.95	50.00
82	7 IN. CHEERLEADER MOUSE	3441	10.95	150.00
82	7 IN. COWBOY MOUSE	3776	28.95	325.00
82	7 IN. EASTER PARADE BOY BUNNY	RT	11.95	50.00
82	7 IN. FOOTBALL MOUSE	2164	10.50	200.00
82	7 IN. GIRL TENNIS MOUSE	2443	10.95	135.00
82	7 IN. GRADUATE BOY MOUSE	4971	12.00	100.00
82	7 IN. GRADUATE GIRL MOUSE	3563	10.95	85.00
82	7 IN. GROOM MOUSE	3406	10.95	50.00
82	7 IN. I'M A 10 BABY	2159	12.95	125.00
82	7 IN. MOUSE WITH STRAWBERRY	*	11.95	75.00
82	7 IN. MRS. A.M. MOUSE	2184	11.95	80.00
82	7 IN. SANTA FOX	3726	12.95	250.00
82	7 IN. SANTA FOX W/BAG	3622	12.95	400.00
82	7 IN. SANTA WREATH CENTERPIECE	1150	*	150.00
82	7 IN. SWEETHEART MOUSE	4110	11.00	75.00
82	7 IN. WINDSURFER MOUSE	4114	13.95	250.00
82	7 IN. WITCH MOUSE ON BROOM	2798	12.95	75.00
82	7 IN. WOODCHOPPER MOUSE	1910	11.95	385.00
82	8 IN. BALLERINA PIG	1058	12.95	250.00
82	8 IN. BOY BBQ PIG	1044	11.95	55.00
83	10 IN. BALLOONING ELVES	7395	59.95	200.00
83	10 IN. WORKSHOP ELF	*	*	75.00
83	12 IN. BRIDE MOUSE	854	31.95	200.00
83	12 IN. GROOM MOUSE	826	31.95	200.00
83	16 IN. MONK WITH JUG	*	27.95	200.00
83	18 IN. FAWN	1444	32.95	225.00
83	18 IN. FAWN	*	33.00	200.00
83	18 IN. GINGERBREAD MAN	5027	28.95	250.00
83	18 IN. SCARECROW	2300	28.95	150.00
83	18 IN. SCARECROW	3896	32.95	200.00
83	18 IN. SCARECROW	3150	32.95	175.00
83	22 IN. SUN	*	*	75.00
83	24 IN. STORK WITH BABY	858	36.95	175.00
83	29 IN. EASTER PARADE GIRL BUNNY	*	71.95	200.00
83	5 IN. BUNNY ON MUSIC BOX	*	29.95	375.00
83	5 IN. COUNTRY GIRL BUNNY	5163	*	200.00
83	5 IN. DRAGON WITH WINGS & BABY	199	22.50	900.00
83	5 IN. DRAGON WITH WINGS & BABY	199	22.50	300.00
83	5 IN. E.P. BOY DUCK	5133	*	50.00
83	5 IN. E.P. GIRL DUCK	5577	*	50.00
83	5 IN. FLOPPY-EAR BOY BUNNY WITH BASKET	*	11.50	55.00
83	5 IN. SWEETHEART DUCK	1530	*	40.00
83	7 IN. COUNTRY BOY BUNNY WITH BUTTERFLY	*	12.50	100.00
83	7 IN. COWBOY MOUSE	1794	12.95	150.00
83	7 IN. COWGIRL MOUSE	1517	12.95	150.00
83	7 IN. E.P. BOY BUNNY	*	12.50	50.00
83	7 IN. E.P. GIRL BUNNY	RT	12.50	50.00

YR	NAME	LIMIT	ISSUE	TREND
83	7 IN. EQUESTRIAN MOUSE	*	12.95	200.00
83	7 IN. FISHING BOY	*	12.95	125.00
83	7 IN. QUILTING MOUSE	2786	11.95	75.00
83	7 IN. SNOWMAN	15980	12.95	75.00
83	7 IN. WINDSURFER MOUSE	2352	13.95	125.00
83	7.IN. CHEERLEADER MOUSE	2025	11.95	200.00
84	10 IN. AEROBIC DANCER	4875	17.95	150.00
84	10 IN. AEROBIC DANCER	4785	*	75.00
84	10 IN. CLOWN	6383	13.95	95.00
84	10 IN. DOWNHILL SKIER	3535	31.95	75.00
84	10 IN. GINGERBREAD MAN	4615	15.95	200.00
84	10 IN. SCARECROW	3008	15.95	125.00
84	12 IN. DEVIL MOUSE	1118	29.95	145.00
84	16 IN. MONK WITH JUG	1767	34.95	200.00
84	18 IN. AEROBIC DANCER	622	35.95	370.00
84	18 IN. BOB CRATCHET	1819	49.95	250.00
84	18 IN. BOY ON SLED	2205	29.95	150.00
84	18 IN. CANDY BOY	1350	29.95	300.00
84	18 IN. CANDY GIRL	1333	29.95	125.00
84	18 IN. CLOWN	*	32.95	150.00
84	18 IN. COUNTRY GIRL BUNNY WITH BASKET	1481	31.95	300.00
84	18 IN. FAWN WITH WREATH	1444	32.95	385.00
84	18 IN. GIRL ON SLED	2328	29.95	150.00
84	18 IN. MARTHA CRATCHET	1751	35.95	350.00
84	18 IN. MONK WITH JUG	1821	34.95	295.00
84	30 IN. CLOWN	381	165.00	325.00
84	30 IN. CLOWN	387	69.95	400.00
84	30 IN. MONK	432	78.50	300.00
84	30 IN. SNOWGIRL	685	79.50	475.00
84	30 IN. SNOWGIRL AND BOY	685	79.95	475.00
84	30 IN. SNOWMAN	956	79.50	475.00
84	32 IN. MONK WITH GARLAND	416	78.50	600.00
84	4 IN. SNOWMAN	*	169.95	350.00
84	5 IN. COUNTRY BUNNIES WITH BASKET	1110	*	150.00
84	5 IN. DUCK IN SANTA HAT	2371	12.95	75.00
84	5 IN. FLOPPY EAR GIRL BUNNY	2594	11.50	75.00
84	5 IN. GIRL BUNNY	2594	11.50	200.00
84	5 IN. PILOT DUCKLING	4396	14.95	150.00
84	7 IN. ANGEL MOUSE	2093	14.95	150.00
84	7 IN. ANGEL ON STAR	772	32.95	480.00
84	7 IN. BASEBALL KID	2079	13.00	200.00
84	7 IN. BOWLING MOUSE	1472	13.95	75.00
84	7 IN. BOY WITH FIRECRACKER	1893	19.95	410.00
84	7 IN. COUNTRY BUNNIES WITH BASKET	2345	25.95	75.00
84	7 IN. COUNTRY GIRL WITH BASKET	715	16.95	250.00
84	7 IN. CUPID IN HEART	2445	32.95	150.00
84	7 IN. CUPID KID	6808	14.95	150.00
84	7 IN. DEVIL MOUSE	3571	13.95	100.00
84	7 IN. DEVIL MOUSE	3571	12.95	3571.00
84	7 IN. E.P. BOY BUNNY	5989	12.95	35.00
84	7 IN. HOCKEYPLAYER MOUSE	1525	5.50	200.00
84	7 IN. JOGGER KID	*	17.95	85.00
84	7 IN. MOUSE WITH STRAWBERRY	1776	11.95	75.00
84	7 IN. MOUSE WITH WREATH	*	12.95	55.00
84	7 IN. MRS. RETIRED MOUSE	1356	13.95	95.00
84	7 IN. NAUGHTY ANGEL	4528	14.95	75.00
84	7 IN. NIGHTSHIRT MOUSE	*	11.95	150.00
84	7 IN. SANTA ON A MOON	*	*	150.00
84	7 IN. TEACHER MOUSE	3150	13.95	75.00
84	7 IN. TEACHER MOUSE	3023	13.95	225.00
84	7 IN. TEACHER MOUSE, GIRL	5064	13.95	200.00
84	7 IN. TWO BUNNIES WITH BUSHEL BASKET	2339	25.95	75.00
84	7 IN. VALENTINE BUNNY	5602	13.95	125.00
84	8 IN. MONK WITH JUG	3502	17.95	95.00
84	JOHNNY APPLESEED, #627	1500	80.00	900.00
84	ROBIN HOOD	1500	80.00	825.00
85	10 IN. BRIDE	318	*	125.00
85	10 IN. CROSS COUNTRY SKIER	1150	*	75.00
85	10 IN. GROOM	264	*	125.00
85	10 IN. PANDA WITH TOY BAG	1904	20.00	100.00
85	10 IN. PENGUIN, #178	3000	30.00	230.00
85	10 IN. REINDEER WITH BELL	6398	13.95	55.00
85	10 IN. SCARECROW	2930	15.95	325.00
85	12 IN. DUCK WITH RAINCOAT	*	*	275.00
85	12 IN. INDIAN BOY MOUSE	*	34.50	100.00
85	12 IN. JAZZ CAT	2622	*	250.00
85	12 IN. KID W/SLED	4707	31.50	115.00
85	12 IN. NAUGHTY ANGEL	1393	36.95	125.00
85	15 IN. JAZZ CAT	2622	31.95	250.00
85	18 IN. CHRISTMAS PANDA	2207	43.95	100.00
85	18 IN. CLOWN	2275	36.95	200.00
85	18 IN. CLOWN WITH BALLOON	1485	36.95	150.00
85	18 IN. COUNTRY BOY BUNNY W/WATERING CAN	2355	46.95	*
85	18 IN. VALENTINE CAT WITH HEART	2129	34.95	225.00
85	7 IN. BASEBALL KID	1221	16.95	425.00
85	7 IN. BASEBALL KID	1225	*	75.00
85	7 IN. BIRTHDAY GIRL	1017	18.95	75.00
85	7 IN. BOY BUNNY WITH CARROT	3273	14.95	55.00
85	7 IN. BOY GOLFER MOUSE	2099	14.95	75.00

YR	NAME	LIMIT	ISSUE	TREND
85	7 IN. BRIDE & GROOM MICE	2963	13.95	170.00
85	7 IN. DRESSUP BOY	1174	18.95	210.00
85	7 IN. DRESSUP GIRL	1536	18.95	210.00
85	7 IN. GET-WELL MOUSE	1425	14.95	75.00
85	7 IN. GIRL TENNIS MOUSE	1947	14.95	75.00
85	7 IN. GRADUATE GIRL MOUSE	2884	13.95	100.00
85	7 IN. GRADUATION MOUSE	1999	14.00	75.00
85	7 IN. HAPPY BIRTHDAY BOY	937	19.00	100.00
85	7 IN. HIKER MOUSE	1781	13.95	275.00
85	7 IN. HOCKEY PLAYER KID	1578	18.95	415.00
85	7 IN. JOGGER KID	654	17.95	85.00
85	7 IN. KID WITH KITE	1084	17.95	310.00
85	7 IN. LOGO KID	3562	*	250.00
85	7 IN. VALENTINE BUNNY	5602	13.95	125.00
85	8 IN. ELEPHANT-REPUBLICAN	*	4.95	225.00
85	ANNIE OAKLEY, #185	1500	95.00	700.00
85	CHRISTMAS TREE SKIRT	1332	24.95	110.00
86	10 IN. CHRISTMAS PANDA W/TOYBAG	4397	18.95	150.00
86	10 IN. CLOWN	3897	15.50	75.00
86	10 IN. KITTEN W/YARN & BASKET	3917	27.95	125.00
86	10 IN. UNICORN, #268	3000	36.50	365.00
86	12 IN. NAUGHTY ANGEL WITH SLINGSHOT	*	36.95	225.00
86	18 IN. C.B. BUNNY W/WHEELBARROW	1224	46.95	75.00
86	18 IN. C.G. BUNNY W/FLOWERS	1205	41.50	75.00
86	18 IN. MRS. VICTORIAN SANTA	2000	*	200.00
86	18 IN. VALENTINE CAT	*	*	125.00
86	30 IN. BOY BUNNY WITH WHEELBARROW	252	119.50	200.00
86	5 IN. DUCK WITH RAINCOAT	5029	*	200.00
86	7 IN. BALLERINA MOUSE	*	*	200.00
86	7 IN. BIRTHDAY GIRL MOUSE	3724	14.95	125.00
86	7 IN. BOATING MOUSE	2320	16.95	55.00
86	7 IN. BOY BUNNY WITH CARROT	2949	15.50	95.00
86	7 IN. BUNNY WITH EGG	2233	16.95	55.00
86	7 IN. CUPID IN HOT AIR BALLOON	391	54.95	175.00
86	7 IN. INDIAN GIRL MOUSE WITH PAPOOSE	6992	24.95	115.00
86	7 IN. LOGO KID	6271	*	175.00
86	7 IN. MOUSE WITH WHEELBORROW	2037	16.95	75.00
86	7 IN. SKIING KID	8057	18.45	75.00
86	7 IN. SWEETHEART MOUSE	6271	12.95	100.00
86	7 IN. TENNIS MOUSE	1947	15.95	75.00
86	7 IN. TENNIS MOUSE	1947	15.95	100.00
86	7 IN. VALENTINE BUNNY	*	14.50	125.00
86	7 IN. VICTORIAN SANTA W/SLEIGH & DEER	6820	44.00	200.00
86	7 IN. WITCH MOUSE IN PUMPKIN BALLOON	868	77.95	275.00
86	BALLOONING CLOWN	2700	16.95	110.00
86	LARGE PUMPKIN WITH 7 IN. WITCH M.	668	77.95	250.00
86	MARK TWAIN, #467	2500	119.50	520.00
87	10 IN. BRIDE & GROOM CAT	727	*	200.00
87	10 IN. CLOWN	*	17.95	55.00
87	10 IN. COLLECTOR SANTA TRIMMING TREE	*	130.00	250.00
87	10 IN. GROOM CAT (PAIR)	762	35.95	*
87	10 IN. HUCK FINN, #690	1200	102.95	700.00
87	12 IN. DUCK ON SLED	300	*	500.00
87	18 IN. BOTTLECOVER MONK	718	29.95	105.00
87	18 IN. MR. VICTORIAN SANTA	2150	57.50	200.00
87	18 IN. VICTORIAN COUNTRY BOY BUNNY	1394	49.95	350.00
87	18 IN. VICTORIAN COUNTRY GIRL BUNNY-PAIR	1492	49.95	*
87	18 IN. WORKSHOP SANTA	980	*	460.00
87	24 IN. CHRISTMAS GOOSE WITH BASKET	*	54.95	150.00
87	3 IN. BABY WITCH	*	13.95	55.00
87	3 IN. BRIDE & GROOM	1250	38.95	135.00
87	3 IN. CUPID IN HEART BALLOON	1715	38.95	175.00
87	30 IN. MR. VICTORIAN SANTA	450	150.00	350.00
87	30 IN. MRS. VICTORIAN SANTA	425	150.00	350.00
87	5 IN. MONK	*	13.95	50.00
87	7 IN. BABY MOUSE	2500	13.95	80.00
87	7 IN. BABY W/BLANKET & SWEATER	7836	21.95	60.00
87	7 IN. BARBEQUE MOUSE	1798	17.95	385.00
87	7 IN. BICYCLIST BOY MOUSE	1507	19.95	175.00
87	7 IN. BOY GRADUATE	2034	*	80.00
87	7 IN. BRIDE MOUSE	1801	14.50	55.00
87	7 IN. GIRL GRADUATE	2438	19.95	80.00
87	7 IN. GRADUATION BOY MOUSE	*	19.95	85.00
87	7 IN. GROOM MOUSE	1800	14.50	55.00
87	7 IN. INDIAN BOY	*	19.95	60.00
87	7 IN. KANGAROO	3000	37.50	470.00
87	7 IN. LOGO KID	11000	*	150.00
87	7 IN. VICTORIAN MR. & MRS. SANTA	*	23.95	500.00
87	BEN FRANKLIN, #1776	2500	119.50	525.00
87	CARROT	2503	9.95	300.00
88	10 IN. EASTER PARADE BOY PIG	3005	24.50	180.00
88	10 IN. EASTER PARADE GIRL PIG (PAIR)	3400	24.50	*
88	10 IN. STORK W/3 IN. BABY	500	49.95	145.00
88	18 IN. COUNTRY MOM BUNNY W/BABY	1800	68.95	140.00
88	30 IN. VICTORIAN MRS. SANTA WITH TRAY	*	119.95	360.00
88	5 IN. OWL	3000	37.50	295.00
88	7 IN. BUNNIES ON MUSIC BOX MAYPOLE	5602	13.95	75.00
88	7 IN. BUNNY WITH SLED	3050	21.95	45.00
88	7 IN. LOGO KID	*	*	100.00

YR	NAME	LIMIT	ISSUE	TREND
88	SHERLOCK HOLMES, #391	2500	119.50	520.00
89	10 IN. MERLIN	3565	69.95	300.00
89	12 IN. TRICK OR TREAT MOUSE	*	39.95	225.00
89	7 IN. BUSINESS MAN MOUSE	5085	21.95	150.00
89	7 IN. KNITTING MOUSE	5115	19.95	150.00
89	7 IN. LOGO KID	*	*	*
89	7 IN. POLAR BEAR CUB	3000	37.50	310.00
89	7 IN. SWEETHEART MOUSE	*	16.95	35.00
89	7 IN. TACKEY TOURIST MOUSE	5116	*	100.00
89	ABRAHAM LINCOLN	2500	119.50	480.00
90	18 IN. STRAWBERRY BUNNY	2365	59.95	200.00
90	30 IN. CLOWN WITH STAND	530	99.95	150.00
90	30 IN. STRAWBERRY BUNNY	582	135.95	300.00
90	7 IN. ARTIST MOUSE	7285	*	90.00
90	7 IN. CHICKEN, CURRENT ITEM	3000	37.50	290.00
90	7 IN. LOGO KID,	*	*	*
90	7 IN. MAUI MOUSE	7220	*	100.00
90	7 IN. SAILOR MOUSE	6838	23.95	100.00
90	BETSY ROSS	2500	119.50	425.00
91	7 IN. DESERT STORM MOURSE	37475	29.95	90.00
91	7 IN. RED CROSS NURSE MOUSE	8305	29.95	75.00
93	10 IN. ANGEL BEAR	OP	32.95	33.00
93	10 IN. BEAR IN NIGHTSHIRT W/CANDLE	OP	33.95	34.00
93	10 IN. CATCHER	OP	38.50	39.00
93	10 IN. CHRISTA MCAULIFFE/SKATER	OP	35.95	36.00
93	10 IN. CHRISTMAS ELF	OP	15.95	16.00
93	10 IN. CHRISTMAS EVE BOB CRATCHET	OP	69.95	70.00
93	10 IN. CHRISTMAS EVE SCROOGE	OP	59.95	60.00
93	10 IN. COUNTRY BOY BUNNY W/VEG.	OP	34.95	35.00
93	10 IN. COUNTRY GIRL BUNNY W. VEG.	OP	34.95	35.00
93	10 IN. DOCTOR BEAR	YR	35.95	600.00
93	10 IN. DOE	OP	20.95	21.00
93	10 IN. EASTER PARADE BOY BUNNY	5139	38.95	39.00
93	10 IN. EASTER PARADE GIRL BUNNY	6590	38.95	39.00
93	10 IN. FARMER W/ROOSTER	1	1000.00	1000.00
93	10 IN. FATHER TIME	OP	54.95	55.00
93	10 IN. FROG IN BOAT	OP	35.95	36.00
93	10 IN. GARDENING SUMMER SANTA	OP	69.95	550.00
93	10 IN. GINGERBREAD BOY	OP	22.45	23.00
93	10 IN. HEADLESS HORSEMAN W/PUMPKIN/HORSE	OP	56.95	825.00
93	10 IN. KITTEN W/ORNAMENT	OP	33.95	34.00
93	10 IN. MRS. BEAR IN NIGHTSHIRT W/CANDLE	OP	38.95	39.00
93	10 IN. MRS. SKATING SANTA	OP	49.95	700.00
93	10 IN. PONY EXPRESS RIDER	OP	97.50	1800.00
93	10 IN. SANTA W/FIREPLACE AND 3 IN. CHILD	OP	89.95	500.00
93	10 IN. SANTA W/TOBOGGAN	OP	59.95	375.00
93	10 IN. SANTA'S HELPER BEAR	OP	33.95	34.00
93	10 IN. SKATING PENQUIN	OP	34.95	525.00
93	10 IN. SKATING SANTA	OP	49.95	500.00
93	10 IN. SNOW QUEEN TREE TOPPER	OP	29.95	30.00
93	10 IN. SNOWY OWL	OP	25.95	26.00
93	10 IN. ST. NICK TREE TOP	OP	29.95	30.00
93	10 IN. TOBOGGAN SANTA	OP	59.95	375.00
93	10 IN. WINTER ELF	OP	16.95	17.00
93	12 IN. BOY PILGRIM W/BASKET	OP	44.95	45.00
93	12 IN. CHEF SANTA	OP	44.95	45.00
93	12 IN. DRUMMER BOY	OP	39.95	40.00
93	12 IN. GIRL PILGRIM W/PIE	OP	44.95	45.00
93	12 IN. INDIAN BOY	OP	35.95	36.00
93	12 IN. MRS. SANTA W/POINSETTA	OP	49.95	50.00
93	12 IN. PJ BOY	OP	29.95	30.00
93	12 IN. PJ GIRL	OP	29.95	30.00
93	12 IN. SANTA IN CHIMNEY	OP	69.95	70.00
93	12 IN. SANTA'S POSTMAN W/CDHLDR MAILBAG	OP	40.95	41.00
93	12 IN. SCARECROW	OP	41.95	42.00
93	12 IN. SNOWMAN	OP	41.95	42.00
93	12 IN. TUCKERED COUPLE	OP	89.95	90.00
93	14 IN. GRAPEVINE WREATH W/7 IN. E.P.GIRL	OP	31.95	32.00
93	14 IN. LG. USABLE PUMPKIN W/TOP	OP	49.95	50.00
93	14 IN. WREATH W/10 IN. WINTER ELF	OP	25.95	26.00
93	18 IN. CHEF SANTA	OP	47.95	48.00
93	18 IN. COUNTRY BOY BUNNY W/VEG.	OP	54.95	55.00
93	18 IN. COUNTRY GIRL BUNNY W/VEG.	OP	54.95	55.00
93	18 IN. EASTER PARADE BOY BUNN	OP	65.45	66.00
93	18 IN. EASTER PARADE GIRL BUNNY	OP	65.45	66.00
93	18 IN. MAN SKATER (BRN. HAIR)	OP	44.95	45.00
93	18 IN. MRS. OUTDOOR SANTA	OP	49.95	50.00
93	18 IN. MRS. SANTA W/POINSETTA	OP	53.95	54.00
93	18 IN. REINDEER W/CHRISTMAS SADDLEBAGS	OP	52.95	53.00
93	18 IN. SANTA IN SLEIGH	OP	74.95	75.00
93	18 IN. SANTA ON TOBOGGAN	OP	69.95	70.00
93	18 IN. SANTA W/BANNER	OP	52.95	53.00
93	18 IN. SANTA W/GIFT LIST & TOYBAG	OP	45.95	46.00
93	18 IN. SANTA W/LIGHTS	5441	54.95	55.00
93	18 IN. SNOWMAN W/BROOM	OP	47.95	48.00
93	18 IN. VICTORIAN MRS. SANTA	OP	64.95	65.00
93	18 IN. VICTORIAN SANTA	OP	64.95	65.00
93	18 IN. WITCH W/STAND	OP	65.95	66.00
93	18 IN. WOMAN SKATER (BLONDE)	OP	44.95	45.00

YR	NAME	LIMIT	ISSUE	TREND
93	22 IN. CHRISTMAS ELF	OP	34.95	35.00
93	22 IN. CHRISTMAS STOCKING	OP	18.45	19.00
93	3 IN. BABY JESUS IN MANGER/BLONDE	OP	16.95	17.00
93	3 IN. FISHING SANTA IN BOAT	OP	24.95	25.00
93	3 IN. SANTA PIN IN CARD	OP	16.95	17.00
93	30 IN. MRS. SANTA W/CARDHOLDER	OP	119.95	120.00
93	30 IN. SANTA W/NORTH POLE	OP	129.95	130.00
93	30 IN. WITCH KID	OP	149.95	150.00
93	36 IN. REINDEER W/CDHLDR SADDLEBAGS	OP	148.45	149.00
93	5 IN. BABY JESUS IN MANGER W/BABY	OP	25.95	26.00
93	5 IN. BLACK CHRISTMAS LAMB	OP	19.95	20.00
93	5 IN. CHRISTMAS LAMB WHITE FLEECE	OP	19.95	20.00
93	5 IN. DUCK ON FLEXIBLE FLYER SLED	2923	25.95	26.00
93	5 IN. EASTER PARADE BOY DUCK	OP	21.95	22.00
93	5 IN. EASTER PARADE GIRL DUCK	OP	23.95	24.00
93	5 IN. ELF	OP	13.45	14.00
93	5 IN. FAWN	OP	14.95	15.00
93	5 IN. LEPRECHAUN W/POT 'O GOLD	8775	15.95	16.00
93	5 IN. RAINCOAT DUCK	OP	22.45	23.00
93	5 IN. TRIM-A-TREE ELF	OP	12.95	13.00
93	7 IN. ANGEL (BLACK HAIR)	OP	22.95	23.00
93	7 IN. ANGEL (BLONDE HAIR)	OP	22.95	23.00
93	7 IN. ANGEL (BROWN HAIR)	OP	22.95	23.00
93	7 IN. ANGEL MOUSE	OP	21.95	22.00
93	7 IN. ANGEL W/MUSICAL INSTRUMENT	OP	19.95	20.00
93	7 IN. ARAB BOY	YR	35.95	36.00
93	7 IN. ARTIST BUNNY W/BRUSH & PALETTE	OP	20.95	21.00
93	7 IN. BABY NEW YEAR (BLONDE)	4127	26.95	27.00
93	7 IN. BALLERINA KID (BLONDE)	OP	27.95	27.95
93	7 IN. BALLERINA ON MUSIC BOX	OP	41.95	42.00
93	7 IN. BAR MITZVAH BOY	YR	27.95	27.95
93	7 IN. BASEBALL MOUSE	6291	25.95	525.00
93	7 IN. BASKETBALL BOY	YR	25.95	550.00
93	7 IN. BEDTIME KID	YR	25.95	450.00
93	7 IN. BIRTHDAY GIRL MOUSE	OP	23.95	24.00
93	7 IN. BIRTHDAY MOUSE	5550	23.95	24.00
93	7 IN. BOY BUILDING SNOWMAN	OP	21.95	450.00
93	7 IN. BOY BUNNY W/ VEGETABLE	5200	20.45	21.00
93	7 IN. BRIDE BUNNY	4529	22.95	23.00
93	7 IN. BUNNY IN SLIPPER/GREEN	2550	19.95	20.00
93	7 IN. BUNNY IN SLIPPER/YELLOW	OP	19.95	20.00
93	7 IN. BUTTERFLY KID	OP	27.95	27.95
93	7 IN. CAROLLER MOUSE W/BIG HAT & TREE	OP	19.95	20.00
93	7 IN. CHAMPAGNE MOUSE	6985	25.95	26.00
93	7 IN. CHEF SANTA	OP	28.95	29.00
93	7 IN. CHOIR BOY	OP	25.95	26.00
93	7 IN. CHOIR GIRL	OP	25.95	26.00
93	7 IN. CHRISTMAS GNOME	OP	18.95	19.00
93	7 IN. COUNTRY GIRL BUNNY W/VEG.	5621	20.45	21.00
93	7 IN. DEVIL KID	OP	23.95	24.00
93	7 IN. DRACULA KID	OP	25.95	26.00
93	7 IN. DRUMMER BOY	OP	22.45	23.00
93	7 IN. EASTER PARADE BOY BUNNY	OP	20.95	21.00
93	7 IN. EASTER PARADE GIRL BUNNY	OP	20.95	21.00
93	7 IN. FACTORY IN THE WOODS MOUSE	8226	29.95	550.00
93	7 IN. FIREMAN MOUSE	YR	25.95	425.00
93	7 IN. FISHING BOY	YR	29.95	500.00
93	7 IN. FLYING ANGEL W/MISTLETOE	OP	18.95	19.00
93	7 IN. GHOST MOUSE	7803	25.95	26.00
93	7 IN. GIRL EATING TURKEY	OP	38.95	525.00
93	7 IN. GROOM BUNNY	3887	22.95	23.00
93	7 IN. HOT SHOT BUSINESSMAN KID	YR	36.95	600.00
93	7 IN. INDIAN BOY (BLACK HAIR)	OP	29.95	30.00
93	7 IN. INDIAN GIRL (BLK. PONY TAILS)	OP	22.95	23.00
93	7 IN. JUMP ROPE GIRL	YR	25.95	500.00
93	7 IN. LADY BUG KID	OP	29.95	30.00
93	7 IN. LOGO KID (DOLL SOCIETY)	OP	27.50	28.00
93	7 IN. MOUSE IN CORNUCOPIA	OP	23.95	24.00
93	7 IN. MOUSE IN SANTA'S HAT	OP	17.95	18.00
93	7 IN. MOUSE ON CHEESE	OP	26.95	27.00
93	7 IN. MOUSE W/MAILBAG & LETTERS	OP	25.95	26.00
93	7 IN. MOUSE W/NORTH POLE	OP	21.95	22.00
93	7 IN. MOUSE W/SNOWBALL	OP	17.95	18.00
93	7 IN. MR. TUCKERED MOUSE	7059	19.95	20.00
93	7 IN. MRS. SANTA CANDLEHOLDER	OP	25.95	26.00
93	7 IN. MRS. SANTA HANGING IN.MERRY XMAS	OP	27.95	28.00
93	7 IN. MRS. SANTA W/POINSETTIA	OP	29.95	30.00
93	7 IN. MRS. SANTA W/PRESENTS	OP	27.95	28.00
93	7 IN. MRS. TUCKERED MOUSE	OP	19.95	20.00
93	7 IN. PILGRIM BOY HUGGING FAWN	OP	40.95	41.00
93	7 IN. PILGRIM GIRL W/PIE	OP	25.95	26.00
93	7 IN. PILGRIM MICE SET W/BASKET	OP	46.95	47.00
93	7 IN. PINK FLOWER KID	OP	25.95	26.00
93	7 IN. PIRATE KID	OP	23.95	24.00
93	7 IN. RITZ SNOWMAN	RT	26.95	27.00
93	7 IN. SANTA BRINGING HOME CHRISTMAS TREE	OP	27.95	27.95
93	7 IN. SANTA CANDLEHOLDER	OP	25.95	26.00
93	7 IN. SANTA IN CHIMNEY	OP	34.95	35.00
93	7 IN. SANTA SKIING	OP	27.95	27.95

YR	NAME	LIMIT	ISSUE	TREND
93	7 IN. SANTA SKUNK	OP	27.95	28.00
93	7 IN. SANTA W/DOVE	1	1250.00	1250.00
93	7 IN. SANTA W/LIGHTS	OP	29.95	30.00
93	7 IN. SANTA W/MAILBAG & LETTERS	OP	27.95	27.95
93	7 IN. SANTA W/PRESENTS	6996	23.95	24.00
93	7 IN. SANTA W/SLEIGH	OP	39.95	40.00
93	7 IN. SCARECROW KID	OP	27.95	28.00
93	7 IN. SNOWMAN (MRS. RITZ)	OP	25.95	26.00
93	7 IN. SNOWMAN ON TOBOGGAN	RT	29.95	30.00
93	7 IN. SNOWMAN W/PIPE	OP	23.95	24.00
93	7 IN. SPRING CHICKEN W/BOAT	OP	34.95	35.00
93	7 IN. SPRING ROOSTER	OP	34.95	35.00
93	7 IN. SPRING SKUNK	OP	22.95	23.00
93	7 IN. ST. PATRICK'S DAY MOUSE	OP	25.95	26.00
93	7 IN. SWEETHEART BOY MOUSE	OP	19.95	20.00
93	7 IN. SWEETHEART GIRL MOUSE	OP	18.95	19.00
93	7 IN. VICTORIAN MRS. SANTA	OP	29.95	30.00
93	7 IN. VICTORIAN SANTA	OP	29.95	30.00
93	7 IN. VICTORIAN SANTA IN SLEIGH	OP	49.95	500.00
93	7 IN. WHITE MOUSE IN SLIPPER	RT	24.95	25.00
93	7 IN. WHITE MOUSE ON TOBOGGAN	OP	29.95	30.00
93	7 IN. WHITE MOUSE W/PRESENT	OP	21.95	22.00
93	7 IN. WHITE SKATING MOUSE	OP	24.95	25.00
93	7 IN. WITCH MOUSE	OP	25.95	26.00
93	7 IN. WIZARD MOUSE	OP	27.95	28.00
93	7 IN. YELLOW FLOWER KID	OP	25.95	26.00
93	7 IN.FLOWER KID/YELLOW	OP	27.95	27.95
93	8 IN. BOY TURKEY	OP	34.95	35.00
93	8 IN. GIRL TURKEY	OP	34.95	35.00
93	BLUE FLOWER PICK	OP	7.95	8.00
93	CHRISTMAS CHICKEN	OP	34.95	35.00
93	LARGE FLOWER W/FACE	OP	20.95	250.00
93	SANTA NAPKIN RINGS SET OF 4	OP	39.95	40.00
93	SM. CHRISTMAS DOVE	OP	25.95	375.00
93	SUN PIN	OP	5.95	6.00
94	10 IN. ANGEL BEAR	3377	34.50	35.00
94	10 IN. BALLERINA BEAR	1	1100.00	1100.00
94	10 IN. BASKETBALL PLAYER, BLACK	2012	31.95	32.00
94	10 IN. BASKETBALL PLAYER, WHITE	3699	31.95	32.00
94	10 IN. BOSTON BRUINS HKY PLAYER	OP	47.50	48.00
94	10 IN. CATCHER	3440	38.50	39.00
94	10 IN. CTY. GIRL BEAR	1	925.00	925.00
94	10 IN. DOE	4319	21.95	22.00
94	10 IN. EASTER PARADE BOY BUNNY	4527	39.95	40.00
94	10 IN. EASTER PARADE GIRL BUNNY	5550	39.95	40.00
94	10 IN. EASTER PARADE SHOPPER OSTRICH	2368	33.50	450.00
94	10 IN. GINGERBREAD BOY	5182	23.50	24.00
94	10 IN. GREEN CHRISTMAS ELF	6719	16.95	17.00
94	10 IN. HEADLESS HORSEMAN W/PUMPKIN	1593	56.95	57.00
94	10 IN. HOBO CLOWN	6826	30.95	31.00
94	10 IN. KITTEN W/ORNAMENT	RT	34.95	35.00
94	10 IN. LG. FLOWER W/FACE	1807	20.95	21.00
94	10 IN. MRS. SANTA IN.LAST M IN. MENDING	5751	47.95	650.00
94	10 IN. OLD WORLD CAROLLER MAN	5549	27.95	27.95
94	10 IN. OLD WORLD CAROLLER WOMAN	5595	27.95	27.95
94	10 IN. OLD WORLD SANTA W/SKIS	4331	49.95	50.00
94	10 IN. OLD WORLD SKATERS ON MUSIC BOX	1660	119.95	120.00
94	10 IN. RED CHRISTMAS ELF	9079	16.95	17.00
94	10 IN. RED COAT	1000	79.95	80.00
94	10 IN. REINDEER W/CAP & BELL	10319	23.95	24.00
94	10 IN. SKATING PENQUIN	RT	34.95	35.00
94	10 IN. SOCCER PLAYER	5751	34.95	35.00
94	10 IN. TREE TOP ANGEL	3794	29.95	30.00
94	10 IN. WHITE CHRISTMAS ELF	RT	16.95	17.00
94	10 IN. WHITE ST. NICHOLAS	5560	43.95	44.00
94	10 IN. WINDOW SHOPPER OSTRICH	RT	37.95	38.00
94	10 IN. WINTER ELF	8504	17.50	18.00
94	12 IN. BOY PILGRIM W/BASKET	2132	45.95	46.00
94	12 IN. CHEF SANTA	1519	45.95	46.00
94	12 IN. DEVIL KID	2610	39.95	40.00
94	12 IN. DRUMMER BOY	3792	39.95	40.00
94	12 IN. GIRL CAT KID	3176	35.95	36.00
94	12 IN. GIRL PILGRIM W/PIE	2140	45.95	46.00
94	12 IN. GIRL SCARECROW	3978	47.95	48.00
94	12 IN. IN.50S STYLE IN. BEAN NOSE SANTA	OP	119.50	120.00
94	12 IN. MRS. SANTA CARDHOLDER	4443	39.95	40.00
94	12 IN. N. POLE W.POLE W/RD. RIBBON WRAP	1561	9.50	10.00
94	12 IN. SANTA IN CHIMNEY	668	69.95	70.00
94	14 IN. GRAPEVINE WREATH W/GIRL BUNNY	2505	34.95	35.00
94	14 IN. LG. USABLE PUMPKIN W/TOP	2486	49.95	50.00
94	17 IN. TEE-PEE	1838	37.95	38.00
94	18 IN. CHEF SANTA	2888	49.95	50.00
94	18 IN. COUNTRY BOY BUNNY W/HOE	1260	56.95	57.00
94	18 IN. COUNTRY GIRL BUNNY W/BASKET	1549	56.95	57.00
94	18 IN. EASTER PARADE BOY BUNNY	2019	65.50	66.00
94	18 IN. EASTER PARADE GIRL BUNNY	2299	65.50	66.00
94	18 IN. INDOOR SANTA W/LIGHTS	3785	56.95	57.00
94	18 IN. MR. FUR SANTA ON STAND	4546	45.95	46.00
94	18 IN. MR. OLD WORLD SANTA	OP	51.95	52.00

YR	NAME	LIMIT	ISSUE	TREND
94	18 IN. MRS. OLD WORLD SANTA	5278	49.95	50.00
94	18 IN. MRS. OUTDOOR SANTA	3614	49.95	50.00
94	18 IN. MRS. SANTA CARDHOLDER	4312	52.95	53.00
94	18 IN. MRS. SANTA W/POINSETTIA	2992	55.95	56.00
94	18 IN. MUSICAL MRS. SANTA	1498	59.95	60.00
94	18 IN. MUSICAL SANTA/GIFT LIST	1316	59.95	60.00
94	18 IN. OLD WORLD REINDEER W/BELLS	5201	59.95	60.00
94	18 IN. PJ KID W/2 XMAS STOCKINGS	2428	59.95	60.00
94	18 IN. REINDEER W/CHRISTMAS SADDLEBAGS	3235	54.95	55.00
94	18 IN. SANTA IN SLEIGH	1140	77.95	78.00
94	18 IN. SANTA ON TOBAGGAN	1499	69.95	70.00
94	18 IN. SANTA W/CDHLDR SACK	4899	54.95	55.00
94	18 IN. SNOWMAN W/BROOM	4092	49.95	50.00
94	18 IN. WITCH	1823	67.95	68.00
94	22 IN. CHRISTMAS ELF, BLACK HAIR	3606	34.95	35.00
94	22 IN. CHRISTMAS STOCKING	6796	18.95	19.00
94	24 IN. TURKEY	1116	99.95	100.00
94	3 IN. BABY JESUS IN MANGER	RT	17.50	18.00
94	3 IN. FISHING SANTA IN BOAT	3048	24.95	25.00
94	3 IN. SPRING PIXI PICK CHIL	3557	10.95	11.00
94	3 IN. SUN PICK PAINTED SUN FACE	1883	5.95	6.00
94	3 IN. SUN PIN	7346	5.95	6.00
94	30 IN. CTY. GIRL BUNNY W/BASKET	722	119.95	120.00
94	30 IN. MR. OLD WORLD SANTA	1453	124.95	125.00
94	30 IN. MRS. OLD WORLD SANTA	1410	124.95	125.00
94	30 IN. MRS. SANTA W/CDHLDR SKIRT	1141	119.95	120.00
94	30 IN. OUTDOOR SANTA W/TOY BAG	1019	125.95	126.00
94	30 IN. SANTA W/CDHOLDR SACK	1148	119.95	120.00
94	30 IN. SANTA W/N.POLE SUIT	643	131.95	131.95
94	30 IN. SNOWMAN	1782	119.95	120.00
94	30 IN. WITCH KID	722	149.95	150.00
94	36 IN. REINDEER W/CDHLDR SADDLEBAGS	902	154.50	155.00
94	5 IN. BABY JESUS IN MANGER	1726	26.95	27.00
94	5 IN. BLACK CHRISTMAS LAMB	4713	19.95	20.00
94	5 IN. CHRISTMAS LAMB/WHITE	6024	19.95	20.00
94	5 IN. DUCK/FLEXIBLE FLYER SLED	3186	26.95	27.00
94	5 IN. EASTER PARADE BOY DUCK	3678	22.95	23.00
94	5 IN. EASTER PARADE GIRL DUCK	4697	24.95	25.00
94	5 IN. ELF (WORKSHOP)	9416	13.95	14.00
94	5 IN. FAWN	8700	14.95	15.00
94	5 IN. GOLD FALL ELF	6153	14.50	15.00
94	5 IN. GREEN CHRISTMAS ELF	8834	13.95	14.00
94	5 IN. GREEN SPRING ELF	3261	13.95	14.00
94	5 IN. HALLOWEEN ELF, BLACK	4624	14.95	15.00
94	5 IN. HALLOWEEN ELF, ORANGE	4544	14.95	15.00
94	5 IN. LEPRECHAUN W/POT 'O GOLD	7410	17.95	18.00
94	5 IN. OLD WORLD CAROLLER BOY	7611	19.95	20.00
94	5 IN. OLD WORLD CAROLLER GIRL	7817	19.95	20.00
94	5 IN. OLD WORLD SANTA W/9 IN. WREATH	2330	32.95	33.00
94	5 IN. ORANGE FALL ELF	6280	14.50	15.00
94	5 IN. RAINCOAT DUCK	2410	27.95	28.00
94	5 IN. RED CHRISTMAS ELF	11911	13.95	14.00
94	5 IN. SPRING ELF W/6 IN. WREATH	1704	17.95	18.00
94	5 IN. WHITE CHRISTMAS ELF	RT	13.95	14.00
94	5 IN. WINTER ELF	10769	13.95	14.00
94	5 IN. YELLOW SPRING ELF	3932	13.95	14.00
94	7 IN. ANGEL MOUSE	10343	22.95	23.00
94	7 IN. ANGEL W/MUSCIAL INSTRUMENT	4302	20.95	21.00
94	7 IN. ANGEL, BLACK HAIR	2877	23.95	24.00
94	7 IN. ANGEL, BLONDE HAIR	4584	23.95	24.00
94	7 IN. ANGEL, BROWN HAIR	3362	23.95	24.00
94	7 IN. ARTIST BUNNY W/BRUSH/PALETTE	4303	21.95	22.00
94	7 IN. AUCTION TIMES MOUSE	5962	29.95	30.00
94	7 IN. BABY BUNNY W/BOTTLE	6588	19.95	20.00
94	7 IN. BIRTHDAY GIRL MOUSE	3777	23.95	24.00
94	7 IN. BRIDE MOUSE	4674	22.95	400.00
94	7 IN. BUTTERFLY KID, BLK BODY	2226	28.95	29.00
94	7 IN. CANDY KISS KID	1	2250.00	2250.00
94	7 IN. CHAMPAGNE MOUSE	6360	26.95	27.00
94	7 IN. CHEERLEADER GIRL	4568	26.95	650.00
94	7 IN. CHEF SANTA	5618	29.95	30.00
94	7 IN. CHOIR BOY	2873	26.95	27.00
94	7 IN. CHOIR BOY W/BLACK EYE	2912	26.95	27.00
94	7 IN. CHOIR GIRL, BLONDE HAIR	3424	26.95	27.00
94	7 IN. CHRISTA MCAULIFFE SNOWBD KID	OP	39.95	40.00
94	7 IN. CLOWN MOUSE	1	1050.00	1050.00
94	7 IN. COCKTAIL MOUSE	1	1100.00	1100.00
94	7 IN. COUNTRY BOY BUNNY W/HOE	4842	21.50	22.00
94	7 IN. COUNTRY GIRL BUNNY W/BASKET	6083	21.50	22.00
94	7 IN. DRACULA KID, BLACK HAIR	2126	26.95	27.00
94	7 IN. DRUMMER BOY	6817	23.95	24.00
94	7 IN. EASTER PARADE BOY BUNNY	9937	21.95	22.00
94	7 IN. EASTER PARAGE GIRL BUNNY	13186	21.95	22.00
94	7 IN. FLYING ANGEL	7237	19.95	20.00
94	7 IN. FOOTBALL MOUSE	5998	29.95	30.00
94	7 IN. GHOST MOUSE	4698	26.95	27.00
94	7 IN. GIRL BLDG A SNOWMAN	13459	23.95	24.00
94	7 IN. GIRL W/TEDDY BEAR	4712	26.95	27.00
94	7 IN. GRADUATION BOY MOUSE	3769	22.95	23.00

YR	NAME	LIMIT	ISSUE	TREND
94	7 IN. GROOM MOUSE	OP	22.95	23.00
94	7 IN. HABITAT MOUSE	5011	29.95	30.00
94	7 IN. HERSHEY KID	9698	37.50	38.00
94	7 IN. HOT SHOT BUSINESS GIRL	OP	*	700.00
94	7 IN. INDIAN BOY, BLACK HAIR	2848	30.95	31.00
94	7 IN. INDIAN GIRL, BLACK PONY TAILS	2892	22.95	23.00
94	7 IN. JAIL HOUSE MOUSE	3309	25.95	26.00
94	7 IN. LARGE CABBAGE	778	14.95	15.00
94	7 IN. LOGO KID (DOLL SOCIETY)	OP	27.50	28.00
94	7 IN. MISSISSIPPI LEVEE MOUSE	3012	29.95	30.00
94	7 IN. MOUSE IN CORNUCOPIA	6467	24.95	25.00
94	7 IN. MOUSE IN SANTA'S HAT	11641	18.50	19.00
94	7 IN. MOUSE W/SNOWBALL	8745	18.50	19.00
94	7 IN. MR. OLD WORLD SANTA	9620	27.95	28.00
94	7 IN. MRS. OLD WORLD SANTA	9439	27.95	28.00
94	7 IN. MRS. SANTA CARDHOLDER	4443	39.95	40.00
94	7 IN. MRS. SANTA W/FUR-TRIM	8848	22.50	23.00
94	7 IN. MRS. SANTA W/POINSETTA	5397	30.95	31.00
94	7 IN. MRS. SANTA W/PRESENTS	5923	28.95	29.00
94	7 IN. NAUGHTY ANGEL	8380	22.95	23.00
94	7 IN. PILGRIM BOY HUGGING FAWN	2004	41.95	42.00
94	7 IN. PILGRIM GIRL W/PIE BLONDE HAIR	2984	26.95	27.00
94	7 IN. PILGRIM MICE SET W/BSKT	2873	46.95	47.00
94	7 IN. POLICEMAN MOUSE	4788	27.95	28.00
94	7 IN. RITZ SNOWMAN	4903	27.95	28.00
94	7 IN. SANTA IN CHIMNEY	3255	35.95	36.00
94	7 IN. SANTA W/DOVE	1	1250.00	1250.00
94	7 IN. SANTA W/LIGHTS	4678	30.75	31.00
94	7 IN. SANTA W/PRESENTS	5586	24.95	25.00
94	7 IN. SANTA W/RD. FUR TRIM SUIT	8922	19.95	20.00
94	7 IN. SANTA W/SLEIGH	3301	39.95	40.00
94	7 IN. SANTA W/SNOWSHOES & TREE	8582	28.95	29.00
94	7 IN. SANTA W/TREE & SLED	8865	28.95	29.00
94	7 IN. SCOTTISH LAD	3995	29.95	675.00
94	7 IN. SMALL CHRISTMAS DOVE	RT	26.95	27.00
94	7 IN. SNOWMAN (MRS. RITZ)	5344	26.95	27.00
94	7 IN. SNOWMAN W/PIPE	6170	25.95	26.00
94	7 IN. ST. PATRICK'S DAY MOUSE	4746	26.95	27.00
94	7 IN. SWEETHEART BOY MOUSE	4424	19.95	20.00
94	7 IN. THANKSGIVING BOY	1881	39.95	650.00
94	7 IN. VALENTINE GIRL KID W/CARD	6220	24.95	750.00
94	7 IN. VICTORIAN SANTA IN SLEIGH	1179	49.95	50.00
94	7 IN. WHITE MOUSE IN SLIPPER	5838	25.95	26.00
94	7 IN. WHITE MOUSE ON TOBOGGAN	RT	29.95	30.00
94	7 IN. WHITE MOUSE W/PRESENT	8170	22.95	23.00
94	7 IN. WHITE SKATING MOUSE	11452	25.95	26.00
94	7 IN. WITCH MOUSE	5336	26.95	27.00
94	7 IN. WIZARD MOUSE	3892	28.95	29.00
94	7 IN. YELLOW FLOWER KID	OP	28.95	29.00
94	7 IN. YELLOW FLOWER KID, BLONDE	2303	26.95	27.00
94	7 IN.MARBLES KID/RED TANK TOP	OP	27.50	28.00
94	8 IN. BOY TURKEY	2852	34.95	35.00
94	8 IN. EAR OF CORN	1342	9.95	10.00
94	8 IN. GIRL TURKEY	2174	34.95	35.00
94	SET OF 3 LG. PEA PDS & CARROTS	1377	14.95	15.00
94	SET OF 3 RD. TOMATOES 2 IN.	805	9.95	10.00
94	SMALL PEA PODS & CARROTTS (3)	1342	12.50	13.00
94	TREE SKIRT 4' DIAMETER	2269	24.95	25.00
94	TREE TOP STAR W/ 3 IN. ANGEL	6424	20.95	300.00

ANRI

*

DISNEY DOLLS

YR	NAME	LIMIT	ISSUE	TREND
89	MICKEY MOUSE, 14 IN.	2500	850.00	895.00
89	MINNIE MOUSE, 14 IN.	2500	850.00	895.00
89	PINOCCHIO, 14 IN.	2500	850.00	895.00
90	DAISY DUCK, 14 IN.	2500	895.00	895.00
90	DONALD DUCK, 14 IN.	2500	895.00	895.00

J. FERRANDIZ

FERRANDIZ DOLLS

YR	NAME	LIMIT	ISSUE	TREND
89	GABRIEL, 14 IN.	1000	550.00	575.00
89	MARIA, 14 IN.	1000	550.00	575.00
90	MARGARITE, 14 IN.	CL	575.00	725.00
90	PHILIPE, 14 IN.	CL	575.00	675.00
91	CARMEN, 14 IN.	1000	730.00	730.00
91	FERNANDO, 14 IN.	1000	730.00	730.00
91	JUANITA, 7 IN.	1500	300.00	300.00
91	MIGUEL, 7 IN.	1500	300.00	300.00

S. KAY

SARAH KAY DOLLS

YR	NAME	LIMIT	ISSUE	TREND
88	BRIDE AND GROOM MATCHING SETS	*	1300.00	1350.00
88	BRIDE TO LOVE AND TO CHERISH	750	750.00	775.00
88	CHARLOTTE (BLUE)	1000	550.00	575.00
88	EMILY, 14 IN.	750	500.00	500.00
88	GROOM WITH THIS RING DOLL	750	550.00	575.00
88	JENNIFER, 14 IN.	750	500.00	500.00
88	KATHERINE, 14 IN.	750	500.00	500.00
88	MARTHA, 14 IN.	750	500.00	500.00
88	RACHAEL, 14 IN.	750	500.00	500.00
88	REBECCA, 14 IN.	750	500.00	500.00
88	VICTORIA, 14 IN.	750	500.00	500.00
89	ELEANOR (FLORAL)	1000	550.00	575.00

YR	NAME	LIMIT	ISSUE	TREND
89	ELIZABETH (PATCHWORK)	1000	550.00	575.00
89	HELEN (BROWN)	1000	550.00	575.00
89	HENRY	1000	550.00	575.00
89	MARY (RED)	1000	550.00	575.00
90	CHRISTINA, 14 IN.	1000	575.00	725.00
90	FAITH, 14IN.	CL	575.00	675.00
90	POLLY, 14 IN.	CL	575.00	675.00
90	SOPHIE, 14 IN.	CL	575.00	650.00
91	ANNIE, 7 IN.	1500	300.00	300.00
91	JANINE, 14 IN.	1500	750.00	750.00
91	JESSICA, 7 IN.	1500	300.00	300.00
91	JULIE, 7 IN.	1500	300.00	300.00
91	MICHELLE, 7 IN.	1500	300.00	300.00
91	PATRICIA, 14 IN.	1500	730.00	730.00
91	PEGGY, 7 IN.	1500	300.00	300.00
91	SUSAN, 7 IN.	1500	300.00	300.00

ARTAFFECTS

YR	NAME	LIMIT	ISSUE	TREND
G. PERILLO			**ART DOLL COLLECTION**	
86	MORNING STAR, 17 1/2 IN.	1000	250.00	250.00
88	SUNFLOWER, 12 IN.	2500	175.00	175.00
90	LITTLE DOVE, 12 IN.	5000	175.00	175.00
90	STRAIGHT ARROW, 12 IN.	5000	175.00	175.00
G. PERILLO			**CHILDREN OF THE PLAINS**	
92	BRAVE AND FREE	OP	111.00	111.00
93	BIRD SONG	OP	111.00	111.00
93	GENTLE SHEPHERD	OP	111.00	111.00
93	SONG OF SIOUX	OP	111.00	111.00
94	CACTUS FLOWER	OP	111.00	111.00
94	LITTLE FRIEND	OP	111.00	111.00
94	PATHFINDER	OP	111.00	111.00
94	PRINCESS OF THE SUN	OP	111.00	111.00
*			**COUNTRY MUSICIANS COLLECTION**	
94	DANNY	OP	118.00	118.00
*			**RUFFLES AND RHYMES DOLL COLLECTION**	
93	LITTLE BO PEEP (15 IN.)	OP	89.00	89.00
94	LITTLE BO PEEP	OP	107.00	107.00
G. PERILLO			**SINGLE ISSUE**	
94	LITTLE BREEZE	OP	114.00	114.00

ASHTON-DRAKE GALLERIES

YR	NAME	LIMIT	ISSUE	TREND
Y. BELLO			**1993 SPECIAL EDITION TOUR**	
93	MIQUEL	CL	70.00	75.00
93	ROSA	CL	70.00	75.00
J. SINGER			**A CHILD'S GARDEN OF VERSES**	
91	LAND OF NOD, THE	CL	79.00	80.00
93	MY SHIP & I	CL	85.00	85.00
93	MY TOY SOLDIERS	CL	80.00	80.00
93	PICTURE BOOKS IN WINTER	CL	85.00	85.00
K. B.-HIPPENSTEEL			**A SENSE OF DISCOVERY**	
93	SWEETIE	CL	60.00	65.00
Y. BELLO			**AMERICA THE BEAUTIFUL**	
96	BILLY	*	50.00	50.00
96	BOBBY	*	50.00	50.00
J. IBAROLLE			**AMISH INSPIRATIONS**	
96	ANNA	YR	74.95	75.00
96	SETH	YR	74.95	75.00
D. EFFNER			**AS CUTE AS CAN BE**	
93	SUGAR PLUM	*	50.00	55.00
J. GOOD-KRUGER			**BABY TALK**	
94	BYE, BYE!	*	49.95	55.00
T. TOMESCU			**BARELY YOURS**	
96	CLEAN AS A WHISTLE	YR	75.00	75.00
96	GOOD AS GOLD	YR	75.00	75.00
96	PRETTY AS A PICTURE	YR	75.00	75.00
G. RADEMANN			**BEAUTIFUL DREAMERS**	
92	KATRINA	CL	89.00	125.00
92	NICOLETTE	CL	89.95	90.00
93	BRIGITTE	CL	94.00	94.00
93	GABRIELLE	CL	94.00	94.00
93	ISABELLA	CL	94.00	94.00
J. SINGER			**BOYS WILL BE BOYS**	
93	FIRE'S OUT	CL	70.00	75.00
*			**CALENDAR BABIES**	
95	APRIL SHOWERS	*	25.00	25.00
95	BACK TO SCHOOL	*	25.00	25.00
95	HAPPY HAUNTING	*	25.00	25.00
95	JOLLY SANTA	*	25.00	25.00
95	JUNE BRIDE	*	25.00	25.00
95	LEPRECHAUN	*	24.95	25.00
95	MAY FLOWERS	*	25.00	25.00
95	SUN & FUN	*	25.00	25.00
95	THANKSGIVING TURKEY	*	25.00	25.00
95	UNCLE SAM	*	25.00	25.00
M. TRETTER			**CAUGHT IN THE ACT**	
92	STEVIE, CATCH ME IF YOU CAN	CL	49.95	90.00
93	KELLY, DON'T I LOOK PRETTY?	CL	50.00	65.00

YR	NAME	LIMIT	ISSUE	TREND
	K. B.-HIPPENSTEEL			**CHILDREN OF CHRISTMAS**
94	MY LITTLE BALLERINA	*	59.95	65.00
	M. SEVERINO			**CHILDREN OF THE SUN**
93	DESERT STAR	*	70.00	75.00
93	LITTLE FLOWER	*	70.00	75.00
	Y. BELLO			**CHRISTMAS MEMORIES**
94	JOSHUA	*	59.95	65.00
	E. WILLIAMS			**CLASSIC BRIDES OF THE CENTURY**
93	KATHLEEN, THE 1930S BRIDE	CL	150.00	150.00
	K. B.-HIPPENSTEEL			**DAYS OF THE WEEK**
96	FRIDAY	YR	50.00	50.00
96	SATURDAY	YR	50.00	50.00
96	SUNDAY	YR	50.00	50.00
96	THURSDAY	YR	50.00	50.00
96	TUESDAY	YR	49.95	50.00
96	WEDNESDAY	YR	50.00	50.00
	B. DEVAL			**DEVAL MADONNA**
96	MADONNA & CHILD	*	100.00	100.00
	D. EFFNER			**DIANNA EFFNER'S MOTHER GOOSE**
90	MARY, MARY, QUITE CONTRARY	CL	78.00	190.00
91	LITTLE GIRL WITH THE CURL, THE- (GOOD)	CL	79.00	115.00
91	LITTLE GIRL WITH THE CURL, THE- (HORRID)	CL	79.00	175.00
93	CURLY LOCKS	*	90.00	90.00
93	SNIPS & SNAILS	CL	85.00	125.00
93	SUGAR & SPICE	CL	90.00	130.00
	P. COFFER			**DOWN THE GARDEN PATH**
91	ANGELICA	CL	85.00	85.00
91	ROSEMARY	CL	79.00	80.00
93	AMANDA BY THE SHORE	CL	90.00	90.00
	L. DI LEO			**ELVIS: LIFETIME OF A LEGEND**
92	'68 COMEBACK	CL	99.95	100.00
	G. RADEMANN			**EUROPEAN FAIRYTALES**
96	SNOW WHITE	YR	79.95	80.00
	M. TRETTER			**FAMILY TIES**
96	HAPPILY EVER AFTER	YR	00.00	90.00
96	KISS AND MAKE IT BETTER	YR	89.95	90.00
	L. DI LEO			**FATHER'S TOUCH**
93	2 A.M. FEEDING	CL	100.00	105.00
	T. MENZENBACH			**FROM THE HEART**
92	CAROLIN	CL	79.95	110.00
92	ERIK	CL	79.95	130.00
	P. TUMMINIS			**FROM THIS DAY FORWARD**
96	BETH	YR	90.00	90.00
96	BETTY WHITE	YR	89.95	90.00
96	LISA	YR	90.00	90.00
	*			**GARDEN OF INSPIRATIONS**
96	GARDEN PRAYER	YR	75.00	75.00
96	HEART'S BOUQUET	YR	75.00	75.00
	M. ODOM			**GENE**
96	MONACO	YR	70.00	70.00
96	RED VENUS	YR	69.95	70.00
	S. BABIN			**GINGHAM & BOWS**
96	MALLORY	*	69.95	70.00
	C. HANFORD			**GONE WITH THE WIND**
96	SCARLETT	*	89.95	90.00
	K. B.-HIPPENSTEEL			**GROWING YOUNG MINDS**
91	ALEX	CL	79.00	89.00
	S. GUSTAFSON			**GUSTAFSON'S FAIRY TALES**
93	GOLDILOCKS AND THE THREE BEARS	CL	135.00	135.00
	K. B.-HIPPENSTEEL			**HAPPINESS IS...**
91	PATRICIA (MY FIRST TOOTH)	CL	69.00	135.00
92	CRYSTAL (FEEDING MYSELF)	CL	69.95	105.00
93	BRITTANY (BLOWING KISSES)	CL	70.00	105.00
93	JOY (MY FIRST CHRISTMAS)	CL	70.00	105.00
	K. B.-HIPPENSTEEL			**HAPPY THOUGHTS**
94	BUBBLE UP WITH JOY	*	59.95	65.00
	C. MCCLURE			**HEAVENLY INSPIRATIONS**
92	EVERY CLOUD HAS A SILVER LINING	CL	59.95	60.00
93	WISH UPON A STAR	CL	59.95	80.00
	J. LUNDY			**HERITAGE OF AMERICAN QUILTING**
96	ABIGAIL	YR	79.95	80.00
96	LOUISA	YR	84.95	85.00
96	RUTH ANNE	YR	85.00	85.00
	D. EFFNER			**HEROINES FROM THE FAIRY TALE FORESTS**
93	CINDERELLA	CL	80.00	225.00
	H. HUNT			**HOLY HUNT'S BONNET BABIES**
91	GRANDMA'S LITTLE GIRL (MISSY)	CL	69.00	70.00
91	MISSY (GRANDMA'S LITTLE GIRL)	CL	69.00	69.00
92	SUSIE (SOMEBODY LOVES ME)	CL	69.00	100.00
	K. B.-HIPPENSTEEL			**HOW LITTLE WAS I?**
96	BRITTANY	YR	60.00	60.00
96	CLAIRE	YR	60.00	60.00
	K. B.-HIPPENSTEEL			**I WANT MOMMY**
93	TOMMY (MOMMY I'M SORRY)	*	60.00	80.00

The first edition Legend of the Poinsettia *from 1992 was inspired by the Mexican tale of the miracle of the poinsettia. Wendy Lawton created this 14-inch porcelain doll that was distributed in a limited edition of 750 by the Lawton Doll Co.*

Blonde-haired and blue-eyed, Margot *is an all-American beauty. Produced by Goebel, she plays the tune "Playmates."*

The dramatic dark hair and intense eyes of Holly *are sure to steal the hearts of collectors. She is second in the "Gifts of the Garden" series by Gorham.*

Terry, *by doll designer Bette Ball, is music to the hearts of collectors. She plays the tune "Fly Me to the Moon." Produced by Goebel.*

YR	NAME	LIMIT	ISSUE	TREND
	K. B.-HIPPENSTEEL			**I WANT MOMMY**
93	TIMMY (MOMMY I'M SLEEPY)	CL	60.00	175.00
	K. B.-HIPPENSTEEL			**I'M JUST LITTLE**
96	I'M A LITTLE ANGEL	YR	49.95	50.00
96	I'M A LITTLE DEVIL	YR	50.00	50.00
	K. B.-HIPPENSTEEL			**INTERNATIONAL FESTIVAL OF TOYS AND TOTS**
89	CHEN, A LITTLE BOY FROM CHINA	CL	78.00	145.00
	F. WICK			**INTERNATIONAL SPIRIT OF CHRISTMAS**
89	AMERICAN SANTA	CL	125.00	125.00
	K. B.-HIPPENSTEEL			**JOYS OF SUMMER**
93	LITTLE SQUIRT	*	50.00	55.00
93	TICKLES	*	50.00	55.00
	B. BAMBINA			**JUST LIKE ME**
96	AMBER	YR	59.95	60.00
96	CARMEN	YR	60.00	60.00
96	TIFFANY	YR	60.00	60.00
	Y. BELLO			**KEEPSAKE VINYL COLLECTION**
96	CHRISTY	*	40.00	40.00
	C. LAYTON			**KEEPSAKES OF THE HEART**
96	CAMEO	*	*	*
	W. HANSON			**LASTING TRADITIONS**
93	SOMETHING OLD	CL	70.00	75.00
	G. RADEMANN			**LITTLE BITS**
93	LIL BIT OF LOVE	CL	40.00	42.00
93	LIL BIT OF SUNSHINE	CL	40.00	42.00
	M. SEVERINO			**LITTLE HANDFULS**
93	ABBY	*	40.00	45.00
93	JOSIE	*	40.00	45.00
93	RICKY	*	40.00	45.00
	J. IBAROLLE			**LITTLE HOUSE ON THE PRAIRIE**
92	LAURA	CL	79.95	130.00
93	ALMANZO	CL	85.00	90.00
93	MARY INGALLS	CL	80.00	130.00
93	NELLIE OLSON	CL	85.00	105.00
94	MA INGALLS	*	85.00	90.00
96	BABY GRACE	YR	85.00	85.00
	W. LAWTON			**LITTLE WOMEN**
94	AMY	TL	59.95	65.00
94	BETH	TL	59.95	65.00
94	MEG	TL	59.95	65.00
96	MARMIE	TL	59.95	60.00
	L. DI LEO			**LOOK AT ME**
93	ROSE MARIE	CL	50.00	55.00
	T. MENZENBACH			**LOTS OF LOVE**
93	HANNAH NEEDS A HUG	CL	50.00	55.00
93	KAITLYN	CL	50.00	55.00
	*			**MAGIC MOMENTS**
96	HAPPY ANNIVERSARY	*	50.00	50.00
96	HAPPY BIRTHDAY	*	40.00	40.00
	Y. BELLO			**MAGICAL MOMENTS OF SUMMER**
96	DANA	*	60.00	60.00
96	ZOE	*	60.00	60.00
	M. TRETTER			**MAINSTREET SATURDAY MORNING**
96	BETTY	YR	69.95	70.00
96	DONNY	YR	70.00	70.00
	J. LICERTZ			**MCMEMORIES 40TH ANNIVERSARY ICONS COLLECTION**
96	SPEEDEE	*	60.00	60.00
	D. EFFNER			**MCMEMORIES MCDONALDS & ME COLLECTION**
96	YOU DESERVE A BREAK TODAY	*	59.95	60.00
	*			**MEMORIES OF YESTERDAY**
96	BEAUTY IS IN THE EYE OF THE BEHOLDER	YR	60.00	60.00
	M. ATTWELL			**MEMORIES OF YESTERDAY/LITTLE WORDS OF WISDOM**
94	A FRIEND IN NEED IS A FRIEND INDEED	CL	59.95	65.00
94	TOMORROW IS ANOTHER DAY	TL	59.95	65.00
	T. TOMESCU			**MESSAGES OF HOPE**
86	GOOD SHEPHERD	YR	129.95	130.00
86	I STAND AT THE DOOR	YR	130.00	130.00
	Y. BELLO			**MOMENTS TO REMEMBER**
91	JUSTIN	CL	75.00	80.00
92	JILL	CL	80.00	115.00
93	BRANDON (RING BEARER)	CL	80.00	85.00
93	SUZANNE (FLOWER GIRL)	CL	80.00	85.00
	M. HOLSTAD			**MOMMY, CAN I KEEP IT?**
96	BELINDA'S NEW KITTY	*	50.00	50.00
	J. GOODYEAR			**MY CLOSEST FRIENDS**
92	BOO BEAR (EVIE)	CL	79.00	185.00
92	ME/BLANKIE (STEFFIE)	CL	79.00	130.00
92	MY SECRET PAL (ROBBIE)	CL	85.00	90.00
	J. GOOD-KRUGER			**OH HOLY NIGHT**
95	ANGEL	YR	60.00	60.00
95	BLUE KING, THE	YR	60.00	60.00
95	KNEELING KING, THE	YR	60.00	60.00
95	PURPLE KING, THE	YR	60.00	60.00
95	SHEPHERD WITH LAMB	YR	60.00	60.00
95	SHEPHERD WITH PIPES	YR	60.00	60.00

YR	NAME	LIMIT	ISSUE	TREND
Y. BELLO		**ONLY AT GRANDMA & GRANDPA'S COLLECTION**		
96	TEDDY MAKES THREE	*	99.95	100.00
J. GOOD-KRUGER		**PATCHWORK OF LOVE**		
96	FAMILY PRIDE	*	60.00	60.00
96	FONDEST MEMORIES	*	59.95	60.00
96	HARD WORK PAYS-OFF	*	60.00	60.00
96	LOVE ONE ANOTHER	*	60.00	60.00
96	SIMPLICITY IS BEST	*	60.00	60.00
96	WARMTH OF HEARTH	*	60.00	60.00
J. GOODYEAR		**PEEK-A-BOO**		
93	WHERE'S JAMIE?	CL	70.00	75.00
Y. BELLO		**PETTING ZOO**		
96	ANDY	YR	59.95	60.00
96	CORY W/BUNNY	*	60.00	60.00
96	KENDRA	YR	60.00	60.00
96	MADDIE W/CHICK	*	60.00	60.00
Y. BELLO		**PICTURE PERFECT BABIES**		
87	SARAH 14 IN.	CL	58.00	140.00
88	AMANDA 12 IN.	CL	63.00	160.00
89	JESSICA	CL	63.00	160.00
91	EMILY	CL	63.00	115.00
A. BROWN		**POTPOURRI BABIES**		
96	BUBBLE TROUBLE	*	50.00	50.00
*		**ROCKWELL CHRISTMAS**		
93	MERRY CHRISTMAS GRANDMA	CL	60.00	63.00
J. KOVACIK		**SECRET GARDEN**		
86	COLIN	YR	70.00	70.00
86	DICKON	YR	70.00	70.00
86	MARTHA	YR	70.00	70.00
C. MCCLURE		**SIBLINGS THROUGH TIME**		
96	ALEXANDRA	YR	70.00	70.00
96	GRACIE	YR	60.00	60.00
T. TOMESCU		**SNOW BABIES**		
96	FOLLOW THE LEADER	YR	75.00	75.00
96	SLIP SLIDIN'	*	75.00	75.00
96	SNOW BABY EXPRESS	YR	75.00	75.00
K. B.-HIPPENSTEEL		**SOMEONE TO WATCH OVER ME**		
94	ANGEL LULLABY	*	24.95	30.00
94	ANGEL NIGHT-NIGHT	*	24.95	30.00
95	LULLABY ANGEL	YR	25.00	25.00
95	NIGHT-NIGHT ANGEL	YR	24.95	25.00
96	SLEEPYHEAD ANGEL	YR	25.00	25.00
96	STARDUST ANGEL	YR	25.00	25.00
96	TUCK-ME-IN ANGEL	YR	25.00	25.00
M. TRETTER		**SOOO BIG**		
93	JIMMY	CL	60.00	65.00
L. TIERNEY		**TENDER MOMENTS**		
96	TENDER CARE	YR	50.00	50.00
96	TENDER HEART	YR	50.00	50.00
96	TENDER LOVE	YR	49.95	50.00
E. SHELTON		**THE LEGENDS OF BASEBALL**		
96	TY COBB	YR	79.95	80.00
S. KREY		**TOGETHER FOREVER**		
94	COURTNEY	TL	59.95	65.00
94	KIM	TL	59.95	65.00
94	KIRSTEN	TL	59.95	65.00
K. B.-HIPPENSTEEL		**TUMBLING TOTS**		
93	ROLY POLY POLLY	CL	70.00	75.00
K. B.-HIPPENSTEEL		**TWO MUCH TO HANDLE**		
93	JULIE (FLOWERS FOR MOMMY)	CL	60.00	65.00
93	KEVIN (CLEAN HANDS)	CL	60.00	65.00
K. B.-HIPPENSTEEL		**VICTORIAN DREAMERS**		
96	ROCK-A-BYE/GOOD NIGHT	YR	50.00	50.00
96	VICTORIAN STORYTIME	YR	50.00	50.00
C. LAYTON		**VICTORIAN LACE**		
93	ALICIA	CL	80.00	150.00
C. MCCLURE		**VICTORIAN NURSERY HEIRLOOM**		
94	VICTORIAN LULLABY	TL	79.95	80.00
96	VICTORIAN BUNNY BUGGY	YR	140.00	140.00
96	VICTORIAN HIGHCHAIR	YR	129.95	130.00
96	VICTORIAN PLAYTIME	YR	140.00	140.00
S. SHERWOOD		**WINTERFEST**		
91	BRIAN	CL	89.00	125.00
92	MICHELLE	CL	89.95	160.00
93	BRADLEY	CL	90.00	90.00
M. TRETTER		**WISHFUL THINKING**		
93	DANNY (PET SHOP)	CL	80.00	85.00
*** AKERS/GIRARDI**		**YEAR BOOK MEMORIES**		
93	GOING STEADY (PATTY JO)	CL	90.00	90.00
93	PROM QUEEN (BETTY JEAN)	CL	92.00	92.00
Y. BELLO		**YOLANDA'S HEAVEN SCENT BABIES**		
93	CHERRY BLOSSOM	TL	55.00	60.00
93	DAISY ANNE	CL	50.00	55.00
93	LILY	TL	55.00	60.00
93	MEAGAN ROSE	CL	50.00	55.00

YR	NAME	LIMIT	ISSUE	TREND
93	MORNING GLORY	TL	50.00	55.00
93	SWEET CARNATION	TL	55.00	60.00
	Y. BELLO			**YOLANDA'S LULLABY BABIES**
91	CHRISTY (ROCK-A-BYE)	CL	69.00	130.00
92	JOEY (TWINKLE, TWINKLE)	CL	69.00	75.00
93	AMY (BRAHMS LULLABY)	CL	75.00	80.00
93	EDDIE (TEDDY BEAR LULLABY)	CL	75.00	75.00
93	JACOB (SILENT NIGHT)	CL	75.00	80.00
	Y. BELLO			**YOLANDA'S PICTURE PERFECT BABIES**
85	JASON	CL	48.00	750.00
86	HEATHER	CL	48.00	285.00
87	JENNIFER	CL	58.00	315.00
87	MATTHEW	CL	58.00	245.00
90	LISA	CL	63.00	130.00
90	MICHAEL	CL	63.00	155.00
91	DANIELLE	CL	69.00	135.00
	Y. BELLO			**YOLANDA'S PLAYTIME BABIES**
93	LINDSEY	CL	60.00	63.00
93	SHAWNA	CL	60.00	63.00
93	TODD	CL	60.00	63.00
	Y. BELLO			**YOLANDA'S PRECIOUS PLAYMATES**
92	DAVID	CL	69.95	120.00
93	PAUL	CL	70.00	135.00
	J.W. SMITH			**YOUNG LOVE**
93	FIRST KISS	CL	120.00	125.00
	M. STAUBER			**YOUR HEART'S DESIRE**
91	JULIA	CL	99.00	130.00

ATTIC BABIES

M. MASCHINO

YR	NAME	LIMIT	ISSUE	TREND
87	BESSIE JO	RT	33.00	38.00
87	BETH SUE	RT	30.00	35.00
87	COUNTRY CLYDE	RT	30.00	35.00
87	DIRTY HARRY	RT	30.00	35.00
87	RAGGEDY SANTY	RT	75.00	205.00
88	BUNNIFER	RT	40.00	45.00
88	RAGGEDY SANTY	RT	90.00	95.00
89	ANNIE FANNIE	RT	45.00	50.00
89	COTTON PICKIN' NINNY	RT	50.00	95.00
90	DUCKIE DINKLE	RT	97.00	100.00
92	CANDY APPLEBEE	RT	16.00	20.00
92	CHRISTOPHER COLUMBUS	RT	80.00	85.00
87	HAROLD	RT	30.00	35.00
87	JACOB	RT	30.00	35.00
87	JENNY LOU	RT	37.00	40.00
87	MAGGIE MAE	RT	30.00	33.00
87	MISS PATTY PAT	RT	30.00	100.00
87	MUSLIN BUNNY	RT	10.00	15.00
87	MUSLIN TEDDY	RT	10.00	15.00
87	RACHEL	RT	30.00	35.00
87	RAGGEDY KITTY	RT	30.00	35.00
87	ROSE ANN	RT	40.00	45.00
87	SALLY FRANCIS	RT	40.00	65.00
87	SARA	RT	40.00	90.00
87	TODDY SUE	RT	30.00	90.00
88	FESTER CHESTER	RT	40.00	45.00
88	HANNAH LOU	RT	40.00	45.00
88	LAZY DAISY	RT	40.00	45.00
88	LAZY LIZA JANE	RT	48.00	53.00
88	LITTLE DOVE	RT	40.00	45.00
88	MOLLY BEA	RT	40.00	85.00
88	MOOSEY MATILDA	RT	40.00	85.00
88	NAUGHTY NELLIE	RT	33.00	90.00
88	RAGGEDY SAM	RT	60.00	120.00
88	ROTTEN WILBER	RT	37.00	145.00
88	RUFUS	RT	36.00	85.00
88	SILLY WILLIE	RT	40.00	80.00
88	SPRING SANTA	RT	50.00	55.00
88	SWEET WILLIAM	RT	40.00	155.00
88	WACKY JACKIE	RT	40.00	45.00
89	HEAVENLY HEATHER	RT	60.00	65.00
89	HEFFY CHEFFY	RT	77.00	80.00
89	JOLLY JIM	RT	32.00	35.00
89	MS. WADDLES	RT	50.00	55.00
89	OLD TYME SANTY	RT	80.00	85.00
89	PRISSY MISSY	RT	33.00	35.00
89	RAMMY SAMMY	RT	45.00	50.00
89	SKITTY KITTY	RT	45.00	145.00
89	WOOD DOLL-MEDIUM	RT	33.00	38.00
89	WOOD DOLL-SMALL	RT	25.00	30.00
90	FRANNIE FARKLE	RT	130.00	135.00
90	FRIZZY LIZZY	RT	97.00	100.00
90	HAPPY HUCK	RT	50.00	55.00
90	IVAN IVIE	RT	130.00	135.00
90	LAMPSIE DIVIE IVIE	RT	130.00	135.00
90	PHYLBERT FARKLE	RT	130.00	230.00
90	SALIE OLLIE OTIS	RT	130.00	135.00
90	YASNKEE DOODLE DEBBIE	RT	100.00	155.00

YR	NAME	LIMIT	ISSUE	TREND
90	ZITTY ZELDA	RT	90.00	180.00
91	MAIZIE MAE	RT	30.00	35.00
91	MANDI MAE	RT	30.00	35.00
91	MEMSIE MAE	RT	30.00	35.00
91	MR. RAGGEDY CLAUS	RT	70.00	125.00
91	MRS. RAGGEDY CLAUS	RT	70.00	125.00
91	PIPPY PAT	RT	50.00	55.00
91	WINKIE BINKIE	RT	55.00	60.00
92	OLD ST. NICK	RT	96.00	135.00
92	PUMPKIN PATTY	RT	80.00	85.00
92	SCARY LARRY SCARECROW	RT	80.00	85.00
92	TEENY WEENY ANGEL	RT	10.00	15.00
92	WITCHY WANDA	RT	80.00	85.00
93	HAPPY PAPPY CLAUS	RT	75.00	80.00
93	ITY BITTY SANTA	RT	7.00	9.00
93	JAMMY MAMMY CLAUS	RT	70.00	75.00
93	MERRY OLE FARLEY FAGAN DOOBERRY	RT	133.00	135.00
93	MR. SNO MO SNO	RT	53.00	55.00
93	OLD ST. KNICKERBOCKER	RT	80.00	85.00
94	NATTIE FAE TUCKER	RT	65.00	70.00
M. MASCHINO		**ATTIC BABIES COLLECTORS CLUB**		
92	BURTIE BUZBEE, SNL	RT	40.00	45.00
93	ISSIE B. RUEBOTTOM, SNL	RT	35.00	40.00
94	SUNFLOWER FLOSSIE, SNL	RT	42.00	47.00
M. MASCHINO			**BAGGIE COLLECTION**	
91	AMERICANA BAGGIE BEAR	RT	20.00	25.00
91	AMERICANA BAGGIE GIRL	RT	20.00	25.00
91	AMERICANA BAGGIE RABBIT	RT	20.00	25.00
91	AMERICANA BAGGIE SANTA	RT	20.00	25.00
91	CHRISTMAS BAGGIE BEAR	RT	20.00	25.00
91	CHRISTMAS BAGGIE GIRL	RT	20.00	25.00
91	CHRISTMAS BAGGIE RABBIT	RT	20.00	25.00
91	CHRISTMAS BAGGIE SANTA	RT	20.00	25.00
91	COUNTRY BAGGIE BEAR	RT	20.00	25.00
91	COUNTRY BAGGIE GIRL	RT	20.00	25.00
91	COUNTRY BAGGIE RABBIT	RT	20.00	25.00
M. MASCHINO				**FIRST EDITION**
90	RAGGEDY OLE CHRIS CRINGLE	RT	190.00	265.00
92	AMERICANA RAGGEDY SANTA	RT	87.00	90.00
M. MASCHINO				**SECOND EDITION**
90	RAGGEDY OLE CHRIS CRINGLE	RT	190.00	195.00
92	AMERICANA RAGGEDY SANTA	RT	90.00	95.00
M. MASCHINO				**TOUR BABIES**
93	TOUR BABY 1993	RT	20.00	25.00
94	TOUR BABY 1994	RT	25.00	25.00
M. MASCHINO			**VALENTINE COLLECTION**	
93	VALENTINE BEAR-BOY	RT	40.00	45.00
93	VALENTINE BEAR-GIRL	RT	40.00	45.00
94	HERWIN HEAPS O HUGS	RT	40.00	45.00
94	LOTTIE LOTS-A-LOVE	RT	40.00	45.00

AVONLEA TRADITIONS INC.

YR	NAME	LIMIT	ISSUE	TREND
*			**ANNE OF GREEN GABLES**	
89	ARRIVING AT THE STATION	OP	260.00	260.00
90	DIANA BARRY	OP	260.00	260.00
90	PUFFED SLEEVES	OP	260.00	260.00
90	SCHOOL DAYS	OP	260.00	260.00

DEPARTMENT 56

Price ranges may reflect various demands in the market from one geographic region to another; condition of piece; specific markings found on piece; and/or changes in production of piece.

YR	NAME	LIMIT	ISSUE	TREND
*		**HERITAGE VILLAGE DOLL COLLECTION**		
87	CHRISTMAS CAROL DOLLS 1000-6 (SET OF 4)	250	1500.00	1500.00
87	CHRISTMAS CAROL DOLLS 5907-2 (SET OF 4)	OP	250.00	250.00
88	CHRISTMAS CAROL DOLLS 1001-4 (SET OF 4)	350	800.00	800.00
88	MR. & MRS. FEZZIWIG 5594-8 (SET OF 2)	OP	172.00	172.00
*			**SNOWBABIES DOLLS**	
88	ALISON & DUNCAN 7730-5	RT	200.00	750.00

DIANNA EFFNER PORCELAIN DOLLS

YR	NAME	LIMIT	ISSUE	TREND
E. CHEN				
94	BENJAMIN	25	325.00	350.00
94	HEATHER	25	350.00	375.00
D. EFFNER				
93	BEDTIME JENNY	50	375.00	400.00
93	BIRTHDAY JENNY	50	375.00	400.00
93	DOLLY	50	95.00	110.00
93	EVERYDAY JENNY	CL	375.00	400.00
93	TINY (BOY OR GIRL)	50	250.00	275.00
94	KAYLA	50	450.00	475.00
L. WILSON				
93	SHEN	50	475.00	500.00

DOLLS BY JERRI

YR	NAME	LIMIT	ISSUE	TREND
J. MCCLOUD				**DOLLS BY JERRI**
*	BOY	1000	350.00	395.00
*	DENISE	1000	380.00	550.00

YR	NAME	LIMIT	ISSUE	TREND
*	GINA	1000	350.00	475.00
*	GOLDILOCKS	1000	370.00	525.00
*	JAMIE	800	380.00	450.00
*	LAURA	1000	350.00	465.00
*	LITTLE BO PEEP	1000	340.00	425.00
*	LITTLE MISS MUFFET	1000	340.00	425.00
*	MEGAN	750	420.00	550.00
*	MEREDITH	750	430.00	600.00
*	UNCLE REMUS	500	290.00	450.00
82	BABY DAVID	538	290.00	2000.00
84	CLARA	1000	320.00	1500.00
84	EMILY	1000	330.00	1200.00
85	BRIDE	1000	350.00	400.00
85	CANDY	1000	340.00	2000.00
85	MISS NANNY	1000	160.00	300.00
85	SCOTTY	1000	340.00	2000.00
85	UNCLE JOE	1000	160.00	300.00
86	ALFALFA	1000	350.00	350.00
86	ALLISON	1000	350.00	500.00
86	AMBER	1000	350.00	875.00
86	ANNABELLE	300	600.00	600.00
86	ASHLEY	1000	350.00	450.00
86	AUDREY	300	550.00	550.00
86	BRIDGETTE	300	500.00	500.00
86	CANE	1000	350.00	1200.00
86	CHARLOTTE	1000	330.00	450.00
86	CLOWN-DAVID, 3 YEARS OLD	1000	340.00	450.00
86	DANIELLE	1000	350.00	450.00
86	DAVID, 2 YEARS OLD	1000	330.00	550.00
86	DAVID-MAGICIAN	1000	350.00	500.00
86	ELIZABETH	1000	340.00	340.00
86	FOOL, THE	1000	350.00	350.00
86	HELENJEAN	1000	350.00	500.00
86	JACQUELINE	300	500.00	500.00
86	JOY	1000	350.00	350.00
86	LUCIANNA	300	500.00	500.00
86	MARY BETH	1000	350.00	350.00
86	NOBODY	1000	350.00	550.00
86	PRINCESS AND THE UNICORN	1000	370.00	370.00
86	SAMANTHA	1000	350.00	500.00
86	SOMEBODY	1000	350.00	550.00
86	TAMMY	1000	350.00	900.00
86	YVONNE	300	500.00	500.00
88	HOLLY	1000	350.00	825.00
89	GOOSE GIRL, GUILD	CL	300.00	850.00
89	LAURA LEE	1000	370.00	550.00

DYNASTY DOLL

YR	NAME	LIMIT	ISSUE	TREND
G. HOYT			**ANNA COLLECTION**	
92	COMMUNION GIRL	RT	125.00	130.00
*			**ANNUAL**	
89	AMBER	RT	90.00	95.00
90	MARCELLA	RT	90.00	95.00
91	BUTTERFLY PRINCESS	RT	110.00	115.00
93	ARIEL	RT	120.00	125.00
H. TERTSAKIAN			**ANNUAL**	
93	ANNUAL BRIDE	RT	190.00	195.00
94	ANNUAL BRIDE	*	200.00	205.00
K. HENDERSON			**BALLERINA SERIES**	
93	TINA BALLERINA	RT	175.00	180.00
L. PO NAN			**BALLERINA SERIES**	
91	MASHA-NUTCRACKER	RT	190.00	195.00
*			**CHRISTMAS**	
87	MERRIE	RT	60.00	65.00
88	NOEL	RT	80.00	85.00
90	FAITH	RT	110.00	115.00
91	JOY	RT	125.00	130.00
93	GENEVIEVE	RT	164.00	169.00
94	GLORIA '94	5000	170.00	175.00
R. LEE			**CLOWNS**	
94	BOO-BOO	5000	95.00	100.00
94	DANDY	5000	95.00	100.00
94	MUNCHIE	5000	95.00	100.00
94	PRISSY	5000	95.00	100.00
94	REGINALD	5000	95.00	100.00
*			**DYNASTY COLLECTION**	
91	LANA	OP	85.00	90.00
93	AMANDA	3000	195.00	200.00
93	ANGELA	1500	195.00	200.00
93	NICOLE	RT	135.00	140.00
93	PATRICIA	OP	160.00	165.00
93	SHANNON	1500	195.00	200.00
94	AMY	1500	175.00	180.00
94	CHRISTINA	3500	200.00	205.00
94	LAURELYN	2000	180.00	185.00
94	REBECCA	1500	175.00	180.00
M. COHEN			**DYNASTY COLLECTION**	
93	KADYROSE	OP	145.00	150.00

YR	NAME	LIMIT	ISSUE	TREND
93	KATY	RT	135.00	140.00
93	TAMI	7500	190.00	195.00
93	TORY	7500	190.00	195.00
K. HENDERSON			**DYNASTY COLLECTION**	
93	JULIE	RT	175.00	180.00
G. HOYT			**DYNASTY COLLECTION**	
93	CARLEY	OP	120.00	125.00
94	AMELIA	1500	170.00	185.00
S. KELSEY			**DYNASTY COLLECTION**	
94	GABRIELLE	1500	180.00	185.00
94	KELSEY	1500	225.00	230.00
G. TEPPER			**DYNASTY COLLECTION**	
93	HEATHER	RT	160.00	165.00
93	JULIET	RT	160.00	165.00
H. TERTSAKIAN			**DYNASTY COLLECTION**	
93	ANTOINETTE	5000	190.00	195.00
93	CATHERINE	5000	190.00	195.00
93	MEGAN	3500	150.00	155.00
*			**INDIAN COLLECTION**	
92	POCAHONTAS	RT	95.00	110.00
93	SITTING CLOUD	OP	100.00	105.00
94	CHIEF EAGLE'S WING	3500	165.00	170.00
94	SPRING WINDS AND LITTLE WOLF	3500	120.00	125.00
U. BRAUSER			**UTA BRAUSER'S CITY KIDS**	
93	JAMAAL	5000	220.00	225.00
93	KADEEM	3500	195.00	200.00
93	MIRAMBI	5000	190.00	195.00
93	RICKIA	3500	170.00	175.00
93	TISHA	3500	170.00	175.00
H. TERTSAKIAN			**VICTORIANS**	
94	BEVERLY	1500	195.00	200.00
94	DANIELLE	2500	195.00	200.00
94	MARGARET	1500	195.00	200.00
94	WINIFRED	1500	195.00	200.00

EDNA HIBEL STUDIOS

YR	NAME	LIMIT	ISSUE	TREND
E. HIBEL			**CHILD'S FANTASY**	
85	JENNY'S LADY JENNIFER	CL	395.00	1300.00
M. HOLCOMBE			**CHILD'S FANTASY**	
87	WENDY'S LADY GWENOLYN	CL	495.00	900.00
88	SAMI'S LADY SAMANTHA	CL	495.00	630.00
E. HIBEL			**GRANDMA'S ATTIC**	
87	ALICE	CL	129.00	380.00
88	MARTHA	CL	139.00	400.00
M. HOLCOMBE			**GRANDMA'S ATTIC**	
89	MELANIE	CL	139.00	180.00
89	SASSEE'S LADY SMITH	CL	495.00	640.00
91	KATIE	CL	139.00	150.00
E. HIBEL			**WAX DOLL COLLECTION**	
86	WAX DOLL	12	2500.00	3400.00

EDWIN M. KNOWLES

YR	NAME	LIMIT	ISSUE	TREND
J. GOOD-KRUGER			**AMISH BLESSINGS**	
90	REBECCAH	TL	68.00	68.00
91	ADAM	CL	75.00	75.00
91	RACHEL	CL	69.00	69.00
91	RACHEL AT PRAYER	TL	69.00	69.00
92	ELI	YR	79.95	80.00
92	RUTH	YR	75.00	75.00
K. B.-HIPPENSTEEL			**BABY BOOK TREASURES**	
90	ELIZABETH'S HOMECOMING	CL	58.00	80.00
91	CATHERINE'S CHRISTENING	TL	58.00	58.00
91	CHRISTOPHER'S FIRST SMILE	TL	63.00	63.00
K. B.-HIPPENSTEEL			**BORN TO BE FAMOUS**	
90	FLORENCE NIGHTINGALE	TL	87.00	87.00
90	LITTLE SHERLOCK	CL	87.00	110.00
91	LITTLE DAVEY CROCKETT	CL	92.00	92.00
92	LITTLE CHRISTOPHER COLUMBUS	YR	95.00	95.00
Y. BELLO			**CHILDREN OF MOTHER GOOSE**	
87	LITTLE BO PEEP	CL	58.00	250.00
87	MARY HAD A LITTLE LAMB	CL	58.00	250.00
88	LITTLE JACK HORNER	CL	63.00	150.00
89	MISS MUFFET	CL	63.00	85.00
C. MCCLURE			**CINDY'S PLAYHOUSE PETS**	
88	MEAGAN	TL	87.00	175.00
89	RYAN	TL	83.00	83.00
89	SHELLY	TL	87.00	87.00
91	SAMANTHA	TL	89.00	89.00
D. EFFNER			**HEROINES FROM THE FAIRY TALE FORESTS**	
88	LITTLE RED RIDING HOOD	CL	68.00	175.00
89	GOLDILOCKS	CL	68.00	80.00
90	SNOW WHITE	TL	73.00	73.00
91	RAPUNZEL	TL	79.00	79.00
92	CINDERELLA	CL	79.00	79.00
K. B.-HIPPENSTEEL			**INTERNATIONAL FESTIVAL OF TOYS AND TOTS**	
88	CHEN, A LITTLE BOY OF CHINA	CL	78.00	250.00

YR	NAME	LIMIT	ISSUE	TREND
89	NATASHA	CL	78.00	100.00
90	MOLLY	TL	83.00	83.00
91	HANS	TL	83.00	83.00
	FANGEL INSPIRED	**MAUDE FANGEL'S COVER BABIES**		
90	BENJAMIN'S BALL	TL	73.00	73.00
90	PEEK-A-BOO PETER	TL	73.00	73.00
	J. GOODYEAR	**MY CLOSEST FRIEND**		
91	BOO BEAR 'N ME	TL	78.00	78.00
91	ME AND MY BLANKIE	TL	79.00	79.00
	STEVENS/ SIEGEL	**PARADE OF AMERICAN FASHION**		
87	GLAMOUR OF THE GIBSON GIRL, THE	CL	77.00	210.00
87	SOUTHERN BELLE, THE	CL	77.00	185.00
90	VICTORIAN LADY	TL	82.00	82.00
91	ROMANTIC LADY	TL	85.00	85.00
	S. KREY	**POLLY'S TEA PARTY**		
90	POLLY	TL	78.00	78.00
91	LIZZIE	TL	79.00	79.00
92	ANNIE	TL	83.00	83.00
	M. TRETTER	**THE LITTLEST CLOWNS**		
91	BUBBLES	TL	65.00	65.00
91	SMOOCH	CL	69.00	69.00
91	SPARKLES	TL	63.00	63.00
92	DAISY	TL	69.95	70.00
	M. OLDENBURG	**YESTERDAY'S DREAMS**		
90	ANDY	TL	68.00	68.00
91	JANEY	TL	69.00	69.00
	Y. BELLO	**YOLANDA'S PICTURE-PERFECT BABIES**		
85	JASON	CL	48.00	1200.00
86	HEATHER	CL	48.00	450.00
87	JENNIFER	CL	58.00	425.00
88	AMANDA	CL	63.00	165.00
88	MATTHEW	CL	58.00	280.00
89	JESSICA	TL	63.00	63.00
89	SARAH	CL	58.00	105.00
90	LISA	TL	63.00	63.00
90	MICHAEL	TL	63.00	175.00
91	DANIELLE	TL	69.00	69.00
91	EMILY	TL	63.00	63.00

ELKE'S ORIGINALS

YR	NAME	LIMIT	ISSUE	TREND
	E. HUTCHENS	**ELKE HUTCHENS**		
89	ANNABELLE	250	575.00	1550.00
90	AUBRA	250	575.00	950.00
90	AURORA	250	595.00	950.00
90	KRICKET	500	575.00	525.00
90	LITTLE LIEBCHEN	250	475.00	1000.00
90	VICTORIA	500	645.00	650.00
91	ALICIA	250	595.00	625.00
91	BELINDA	400	595.00	825.00
91	BRAELYN	400	595.00	1500.00
91	BRIANNA	400	595.00	1000.00
92	BETHANY	400	595.00	825.00
92	CECILIA	435	635.00	775.00
92	CHARLES	435	635.00	550.00
92	CHERIE	435	635.00	925.00
92	CLARISSA	435	635.00	850.00
93	DAPHNE	435	675.00	625.00
93	DEIDRE	435	675.00	625.00
93	DESIRE	435	675.00	625.00

ENESCO

Price ranges may reflect various demands in the market from one geographic region to another; condition of piece; specific markings found on piece; and/or changes in production of piece.

YR	NAME	LIMIT	ISSUE	TREND
	S. BUTCHER	**JACK-IN-THE BOXES**		
90	AUTUMN'S PRAISE 408751	YR	200.00	205.00
90	SUMMER'S JOY 408743	YR	200.00	205.00
90	VOICE OF SPRING 408735	YR	200.00	205.00
90	WINTER'S SONG 408778	YR	200.00	205.00
91	MAY YOU/OLD FASHIONED CHRISTMAS 417777	YR	200.00	200.00
91	YOU HAVE TOUCHED SO MANY HEARTS 422282	YR	175.00	175.00
	KINKA	**KINKA LIMITED EDITION DOLL**		
91	WISHING YOU CLOUDLESS SKIES 408573	2500	120.00	120.00
	M. ATTWELL	**MEMORIES OF YESTERDAY**		
90	HILARY JACK-IN-THE-BOX 376027	3750	175.00	175.00
90	HILARY, 11 IN. 376019	2500	100.00	100.00
	S. BUTCHER	**PRECIOUS MOMENTS DOLLS**		
81	DEBBIE, 18 IN. E-6214G	SU	150.00	240.00
81	MIKEY, 18 IN. E-6214B	SU	150.00	230.00
82	CUBBY, 18 IN. E-7267B	5000	200.00	545.00
82	TAMMY, 18 IN. E-7267G	5000	300.00	545.00
83	KATIE LYNNE, 16 IN. E-0539	SU	165.00	190.00
83	MOTHER SEW DEAR, 18 IN. E-2850	RT	350.00	250.00
84	AARON, 12 IN. 12424	SU	135.00	155.00
84	KRISTY, 12 IN. E-2851	SU	150.00	190.00
84	MOTHER SEW DEAR, 16 IN. E-2850	RT	350.00	380.00
84	TIMMY, 12 IN. E-5397	OP	125.00	180.00
85	BETHANY, 12 IN. 12432	SU	135.00	155.00

YR	NAME	LIMIT	ISSUE	TREND
85	BONG BONG, 13 IN. 100455	12000	150.00	255.00
85	P.D., 7 IN. 12475	SU	50.00	80.00
85	TRISH, 7 IN. 12483	SU	50.00	55.00
86	CANDY, 13 IN. 100463	12000	150.00	355.00
86	CONNIE, 12 IN. 102253	7500	160.00	245.00
87	ANGIE, THE ANGEL OF MERCY 12491	12500	160.00	255.00
90	AUTUMN'S PRAISE 408808	YR	150.00	155.00
90	SUMMER'S JOY 408794	YR	150.00	155.00
90	VOICE OF SPRING, THE- 408786	YR	150.00	155.00
90	WINTER'S SONG 408816	YR	150.00	155.00
91	EYES OF THE LORD ARE UPON YOU, THE 42957	SU	65.00	70.00
91	EYES OF THE LORD ARE UPON YOU, THE 42958	SU	65.00	70.00
91	MAY YOU/OLD FASHIONED CHRISTMAS 417785	YR	150.00	155.00
91	YOU HAVE TOUCHED SO MANY HEARTS 427527	YR	90.00	95.00
	FENTON ART GLASS			
	M. REYNOLDS			**VALENTINE'S DAY**
95	DOLL 5228YB 7 IN.	2500	49.00	49.00
96	DOLL 5228WB &' W/MUSICAL WD. BASE	2500	55.00	55.00
	FITZ & FLOYD			
	M. COLLINS			**BLOOMERS FLOPPY FOLKS**
92	BLOOMER	OP	50.00	55.00
92	PEONY	OP	50.00	55.00
	V. BALCOU			**CHRISTMAS FLOPPY FOLKS**
93	SANTA CLAUS	OP	65.00	70.00
93	SANTA'S HELPER	OP	65.00	70.00
93	SANTA'S REINDEER	OP	65.00	70.00
	R. HAVINS			**DINOSAUR FLOPPY FOLKS**
94	JUNOR SAURUS	OP	55.00	60.00
94	MAMA SAURUS	OP	55.00	60.00
94	PAPA SAURUS	OP	55.00	60.00
	R. HAVINS			**HALLOWEEN HOEDOWN FLOPPY FOLKS**
92	DRAC-IN-THE BOX	RT	60.00	65.00
92	HALLOWEEN KAT	OP	50.00	55.00
92	HAZEL WITCH	OP	50.00	55.00
92	PUMPKIN PATCH	OP	50.00	55.00
92	WANDA WITCH	OP	50.00	55.00
	R. HAVINS			**WONDERLAND FLOPPY FOLKS**
93	CHESHIRE CAT, THE	3000	60.00	65.00
93	MAD HATTER, THE	3000	60.00	65.00
93	WHITE RABBIT, THE	3000	60.00	65.00
	GANZ			
	C. THAMMAVONGSA			**COWTOWN/CHRISTMAS COLLECTION**
94	BUFFALO BILL CODY	OP	20.00	20.00
94	OLD MOODONALD	OP	20.00	20.00
94	SANTA COWS	OP	25.00	25.00
*				**LITTLE CHEESERS/PICNIC COLLECTION**
92	SWEET CICELY	OP	85.00	90.00
	GEORGETOWN COLLECTION INC.			
	L. MASON			**AMERICAN DIARY DOLLS**
90	JENNIE COOPER	100-DAY	129.25	129.00
91	BRIDGET QUINN	100-DAY	129.25	129.00
91	CHRISTINA MEROVINA	100-DAY	129.25	129.00
91	MANY STARS	100-DAY	129.25	129.00
92	RACHEL WILLIAMS	100-DAY	129.25	129.00
92	TULU	100-DAY	129.25	129.00
93	SARAH TURNER	100-DAY	130.00	135.00
	T. DEHETRE			**BABY KISSES**
92	MICHELLE	100-DAY	118.60	119.00
	C. THEROUX			**CHILDREN OF THE GREAT SPIRIT**
93	BUFFALO CHILD	100-DAY	140.00	145.00
93	WINTER BABY	100-DAY	160.00	165.00
94	GOLDEN FLOWER	100-DAY	130.00	135.00
	B. DEVAL			**FAERIE PRINCESS**
89	FAERIE PRINCESS	CL	248.00	250.00
	S. SKILLE			**FARAWAY FRIENDS**
93	KRISTIN	100-DAY	140.00	145.00
94	DARA	100-DAY	140.00	145.00
	L. MASON			**GEORGETOWN COLLECTION**
93	QUICK FOX	100-DAY	138.95	139.00
	J. GALPERIN			**HEARTS IN SONG**
92	GRACE	100-DAY	149.60	150.00
93	MICHAEL	100-DAY	150.00	155.00
	V. WALKER			**KINDERGARTEN KIDS**
92	NIKKI	100-DAY	129.60	130.00
	T. DEHETRE			**LET'S PLAY**
92	EENTSY WEENTSY WILLIE	100-DAY	118.60	119.00
92	PEEK-A-B00 BECKIE	100-DAY	118.60	119.00
	L. MASON			**LINDA'S LITTLE LADIES**
93	SHANNON'S HOLIDAY	100-DAY	169.95	170.00
	B. DEVAL			**LITTLE LOVES**
88	EMMA	CL	139.20	139.00
89	KATIE	CL	139.20	139.00
89	MEGAN	CL	138.00	165.00

YR	NAME	LIMIT	ISSUE	TREND
90	LAURA	CL	139.20	139.00
P. THOMPSON				**MISS ASHLEY**
89	MISS ASHLEY	CL	228.00	230.00
T. DEHETRE				**NURSERY BABIES**
90	BABY BUNTING	CL	118.20	155.00
90	PATTY CAKE	CL	118.20	118.00
91	DIDDLE, DIDDLE	CL	118.20	118.00
91	LITTLE GIRL	100-DAY	118.20	118.00
91	ROCK-A-BYE BABY	100-DAY	118.20	118.00
91	THIS LITTLE PIGGY	100-DAY	118.20	118.00
A. TIMMERMAN				**PORTRAITS OF PERFECTION**
93	APPLE DUMPLING	CL	149.60	150.00
93	PEACHES & CREAM	100-DAY	149.60	150.00
93	SWEET STRAWBERRY	100-DAY	149.60	150.00
94	BLACKBERRY BLOSSOM	100-DAY	149.60	150.00
B. DEVAL				**RUSSIAN FAIRY TALES DOLLS**
93	VASILISA	100-DAY	190.00	195.00
B. DEVAL				**SMALL WONDERS**
90	COREY	100-DAY	97.60	98.00
91	ABBEY	CL	97.60	98.00
92	SARAH	100-DAY	97.60	98.00
L. MASON				**SUGAR & SPICE**
91	LITTLE SWEETHEART	100-DAY	118.25	118.00
91	RED HOT PEPPER	100-DAY	118.25	118.00
92	LITTLE SUNSHINE	100-DAY	141.10	141.00
P. COFFER				**TANSIE**
88	TANSIE	CL	81.00	85.00
L. MASON				**VICTORIAN INNOCENCE**
94	ANNABELLE	CL	130.00	135.00

GOEBEL INC.

Price ranges may reflect various demands in the market from one geographic region to another; condition of piece; specific markings found on piece; and/or changes in production of piece.

YR	NAME	LIMIT	ISSUE	TREND
B. BALL				
93	ANGEL SWEETIE	1000	50.00	50.00
93	BILLIE BUMPS	500	150.00	150.00
93	CORY	1000	135.00	135.00
93	DOLLY DINGLE	1000	115.00	115.00
96	BROTHER MURPHY	2000	125.00	125.00
96	BROTHER MURPHY	2000	125.00	125.00
K. KENNEDY				
96	BIRTHDAY BABIES	2500	80.00	80.00
96	BIRTHDAY BABIES	2500	30.00	30.00
96	COLLECTIBLE CATS	2000	39.00	39.00
96	COLLECTIBLE CATS	2000	39.50	39.50
96	HOLIDAY BABIES	1000	80.00	80.00
96	HOLIDAY BABIES	1000	30.00	30.00
B. BALL				**80TH ANNIVERSARY ISSUE**
93	DAISY DUMPLING	500	124.50	125.00
93	DIMPLES DUMPLING	500	150.00	150.00
93	DOLLY DINGLE	500	155.00	155.00
93	SNUGGLES SNOOKS	1500	65.00	65.00
93	TICKLEY TINGLE	500	129.00	129.00
B. BALL				**AMERICANA SERIES**
93	CLARA	1000	235.00	235.00
93	RITA	500	475.00	475.00
93	ROSEMARIE	1000	220.00	220.00
B. BALL				**ANNUAL TREE TOP ANGEL**
93	TREETOP ANGEL-6TH	1000	69.50	70.00
B. BALL				**BEST DRESSED TODDLER**
93	BUFFY	1000	245.00	245.00
93	JOSEPHINE	1000	159.75	159.75
K. KENNEDY				**BIRTHSTONE DOLLS**
94	APRIL/DIAMOND	2500	29.50	30.00
94	AUGUST/PERIDOT	2500	29.50	30.00
94	DECEMBER/ZIRCON	2500	29.50	30.00
94	FEBRUARY/AMETHYST	2500	29.50	30.00
94	JANUARY/GARNET	2500	29.50	30.00
94	JULY/RUBY	2500	29.50	30.00
94	JUNE/LIGHT AMETHYST	2500	29.50	30.00
94	MARCH/AQUAMARINE	2500	29.50	30.00
94	MAY/EMERALD	2500	29.50	30.00
94	NOVEMBER/TOPAZ	2500	29.50	30.00
94	OCTOBER/ROSE STONE	2500	29.50	30.00
94	SEPTEMBER/SAPPHIRE	2500	29.50	30.00
B. BALL				**BOB TIMBERLAKE COLLECTIBLE DOLLS**
96	ABBY LIZ/ MUSICAL	2000	195.00	195.00
B. BALL/TIMBERLAKE				**BOB TIMBERLAKE COLLECTIBLE DOLLS**
96	ABBY LIZ	2000	195.00	195.00
96	ANN	2000	195.00	195.00
96	ANN	2000	195.00	195.00
96	CARTER	2000	195.00	195.00
96	CARTER	2000	195.00	195.00
96	KATE	2000	195.00	195.00
96	KATE	2000	195.00	195.00

YR	NAME	LIMIT	ISSUE	TREND
K. KENNEDY			**CHERUBS COLLECTION**	
94	CHEERY CHERUB	500	169.50	169.50
B. BALL/TIMBERLAKE			**CINDY GUYER ROMANCE DOLLS**	
96	MACKENZIE	1000	225.00	225.00
B. BALL			**DOLLY DINGLE DOLLS**	
94	DOLLY DINGLE'S TRIP AROUND THE WORLD	500	129.00	129.00
96	MELVIS BUMPS	1000	99.00	99.00
B. BALL			**FOUR SEASONS**	
94	BARBARA	500	299.25	299.25
B. BALL			**HOLIDAY DOLLS**	
94	CANDY CORN	2000	89.00	89.00
94	SANTA CLAWS	500	145.00	145.00
B. BALL			**INVITATION TO A PARTY**	
94	VANESSA	1000	124.50	125.00
M.I. HUMMEL			**M.I. HUMMEL DOLLS**	
*	ANDERL 1718	CL	*	150.00
*	BABY 1101 A-H	CL	*	150.00
*	BABY 1102 A-H	CL	*	150.00
*	BERTL 1503	CL	*	150.00-250.00
*	BERTL 1603	CL	*	150.00-200.00
*	BERTL 1703	CL	*	150.00-200.00
*	BRIEFTRAGER 1720	CL	*	150.00-200.00
*	CHRISTL 1715	CL	*	150.00
*	FELIX 1608	CL	*	150.00-200.00
*	FELIX 1708	CL	*	150.00-200.00
*	FRANZL 1812	CL	*	150.00
*	GANSELIESL 1717	CL	*	150.00-200.00
*	GRETEL 1501	CL	*	150.00-250.00
*	GRETEL 1601	CL	*	150.00-200.00
*	GRETEL 1701	CL	*	150.00-200.00
*	HANSEL 1504	CL	*	150.00-250.00
*	HANSEL 1604	CL	*	150.00-200.00
*	HANSEL 1704	CL	*	150.00-200.00
*	JACKAL 1714	CL	*	150.00
*	JACKAL 1806	CL	*	125.00
*	KONDITOR 1723	CL	*	150.00-200.00
*	MARIANDL 1713	CL	*	150.00
*	MARIANDL 1805	CL	*	125.00
*	MAX 1506	CL	*	150.00-250.00
*	MAX 1606	CL	*	150.00-200.00
*	MAX 1706	CL	*	150.00-200.00
*	MIRZL 1811	CL	*	150.00
*	NACHWACHTER 1719	CL	*	150.00-200.00
*	PETERLE 1710	CL	*	150.00
*	PETERLE 1810	CL	*	150.00
*	PUPPENMETTERCHEN 1725	CL	*	150.00-200.00
*	RADI-BUB 1724	CL	*	150.00-200.00
*	ROSL 1709	CL	*	150.00
*	ROSL 1801	CL	*	125.00
*	ROSL 1809	CL	*	150.00
*	RUDI 1802	CL	*	125.00
*	SCHORSCHL 1716	CL	*	150.00
*	SCHUSTERBUB	CL	*	150.00-200.00
*	SEPPL 1502	CL	*	150.00-250.00
*	SEPPL 1602	CL	*	150.00-200.00
*	SEPPL 1702	CL	*	150.00-200.00
*	SEPPL 1804	CL	*	125.00
*	SKIHASERL 1722	CL	*	150.00-200.00
*	STRICKLIESL 1505	CL	*	150.00-250.00
*	STRICKLIESL 1605	CL	*	150.00-200.00
*	STRICKLIESL 1705	CL	*	150.00-200.00
*	VRONI 1803	CL	*	125.00
*	WANDERBUB 1507	CL	*	150.00-250.00
*	WANDERBUB 1607	CL	*	150.00-200.00
*	WANDERBUB 1707	CL	*	150.00-200.00
64	CHIMNEY SWEEP 1908	CL	55.00	115.00
64	FOR FATHER 1917	CL	55.00	95.00
64	GOOSE GIRL 1914	CL	55.00	85.00
64	GRETEL 1901	CL	55.00	130.00
64	HANSEL 1902	CL	55.00	115.00
64	LITTLE KNITTER 1905	CL	55.00	80.00
64	LOST STOCKING 1926	CL	55.00	80.00
64	MERRY WANDERER 1906	CL	55.00	90.00
64	MERRY WANDERER 1925	CL	55.00	115.00
64	ON SECRET PATH 1928	CL	55.00	85.00
64	ROSA-BLUE BABY 1904/B	CL	45.00	85.00
64	ROSA-PINK BABY 1904/P	CL	45.00	80.00
64	SCHOOL BOY 1910	CL	55.00	85.00
64	SCHOOL GIRL 1909	CL	55.00	80.00
64	VISITING AN INVALID 1927	CL	55.00	80.00
M.I. HUMMEL		**M.I. HUMMEL PORCELAIN DOLLS**		
84	BIRTHDAY SERENADE/BOY	CL	225.00	250.00-300.00
84	BIRTHDAY SERENADE/GIRL	CL	225.00	250.00-300.00
84	ON HOLIDAY	CL	225.00	250.00-300.00
84	POSTMAN	CL	225.00	250.00-300.00
85	CARNIVAL	CL	225.00	250.00-300.00
85	EASTER GREETINGS	CL	225.00	250.00-300.00
85	LOST SHEEP	CL	225.00	250.00-300.00

YR	NAME	LIMIT	ISSUE	TREND
85	SIGNS OF SPRING	CL	225.00	250.00-300.00
B. BALL				**MUSEUM COLLECTION**
94	MASAKO	500	145.00	145.00
B. BALL				**NANA'S DARLINGS**
94	COLLEEN	1000	195.00	195.00
94	MONIQUE	1000	195.00	195.00
B. BALL				**PARTY TIME**
93	SCARLETT	1000	259.50	259.50
B. BALL				**PERFECT PETS**
93	BOBBI SOCKS	1000	119.25	120.00
93	LIL' HONEYSUCKLE	500	124.50	125.00
93	PENNY PUSS	1000	200.00	200.00
93	SNOWFLAKE	250	129.00	129.00
93	WHISPURR	1000	150.00	150.00
94	CATSANOVA	500	129.00	129.00
K. KENNEDY				**RED HEADS**
93	GINGER MUFFIN	500	220.00	220.00
94	CARROT TOP	500	129.00	129.00
94	SHARON & DARREN O'HAIR	500	99.00	99.00
K. KENNEDY				**SITTING PRETTY**
94	SOMMER	500	139.50	140.00
B. BALL				**STERLING SERIES**
93	TAYLOR	1000	215.00	215.00
K. KENNEDY				**STOLEN KISSES**
93	KISSES	500	225.00	225.00
B. BALL				**SWEET ROMANTICS**
94	DEIDRE	500	179.50	179.50
K. KENNEDY				**TINY TOT CLOWNS**
94	BETH	2000	45.00	45.00
94	JULIE	2000	45.00	45.00
94	KAYLEE	2000	45.00	45.00
94	LESLIE	2000	45.00	45.00
94	NADINE	2000	45.00	45.00
94	SHANNON	2000	45.00	45.00
B. BALL				**U.S. HISTORICAL**
96	MARY	2000	185.00	185.00
K. KENNEDY				**VICTORIA ASHLEA BIRTHSTONE DOLLS**
90	APRIL BIRTHSTONE DOLL-912253	CL	25.00	25.00
90	AUGUST BIRTHSTONE DOLL-912257	CL	25.00	25.00
90	DECEMBER BIRTHSTONE DOLL-912261	CL	25.00	25.00
90	FEBRUARY BIRTHSTONE DOLL-912251	CL	25.00	25.00
90	JANUARY BIRTHSTONE DOLL-912250	CL	25.00	25.00
90	JULY BIRTHSTONE DOLL-912256	CL	25.00	25.00
90	JUNE BIRTHSTONE DOLL-912255	CL	25.00	25.00
90	MARCH BIRTHSTONE DOLL-912252	CL	25.00	25.00
90	MAY BIRTHSTONE DOLL-912254	CL	25.00	25.00
90	NOVEMBER BIRTHSTONE DOLL-912260	CL	25.00	25.00
90	OCTOBER BIRTHSTONE DOLL-912259	CL	25.00	25.00
90	SEPTEMBER BIRTHSTONE DOLL-912258	CL	25.00	25.00
93	APRIL DIAMOND-912397	2500	29.50	30.00
93	AUGUST PERIDOT-912401	2500	29.50	30.00
93	DECEMBER ZIRCON-912405	2500	29.50	30.00
93	FEBRUARY AMETHYST-912395	2500	29.50	30.00
93	JANUARY GARNET-912394	2500	29.50	30.00
93	JULY RUBY-912400	2500	29.50	30.00
93	JUNE LT. AMETHYST-912399	2500	29.50	30.00
93	MARCH AQUAMARINE-912396	2500	29.50	30.00
93	MAY EMERALD-912398	2500	29.50	30.00
93	NOVEMBER TOPAZ-912404	2500	29.50	30.00
93	OCTOBER ROSESTONE-912403	2500	29.50	30.00
93	SEPTEMBER SAPPHIRE-912402	2500	29.50	30.00
95	APRIL DIAMOND-912474	2500	29.50	30.00
95	AUGUST PERIDOT-912478	2500	29.50	30.00
95	DECEMBER ZIRCON-912482	2500	29.50	30.00
95	FEBRUARY AMETHYST-912472	2500	29.50	30.00
95	JANUARY GARNET-912471	2500	29.50	30.00
95	JULY RUBY-912477	2500	29.50	30.00
95	JUNE LT. AMETHYST-912476	2500	29.50	30.00
95	MARCH AQUAMARINE-912473	2500	29.50	30.00
95	MAY EMERALD-912475	2500	29.50	30.00
95	NOVEMBER TOPAZ-912481	2500	29.50	30.00
95	OCTOBER ROSESTONE-912480	2500	29.50	30.00
95	SEPTEMBER SAPPHIRE-912479	2500	29.50	30.00
B. BALL				**VICTORIA ASHLEA ORIGINALS**
*	CHARITY-912244	CL	70.00	70.00
82	CHARLEEN-912094	CL	65.00	65.00
82	CLOWN JOLLY-912181	CL	70.00	75.00
82	HOLLY-901233	CL	160.00	200.00
82	MARIE-901231	CL	95.00	100.00
82	TRUDY-901232	CL	100.00	100.00
83	DEBORAH-901107	CL	220.00	400.00
84	AMELIA-933006	CL	100.00	100.00
84	BARBARA-901108	CL	57.00	110.00
84	CLAUDE-901032	CL	110.00	225.00
84	CLAUDETTE-901033	CL	110.00	225.00
84	CLOWN-901136	CL	90.00	120.00
84	DIANA-901119	CL	55.00	135.00

Heather *has eyes shining bright with anticipation of her Sunday stroll. The doll, by designer Bette Ball, plays the tune "Let Me Be Your Teddy Bear."*

Sarah *by Yolanda Bello was fifth in the Yolanda's Picture-Perfect Babies collection by The Edwin M. Knowles China Co. Issued in 1989,* Sarah *is currently valued at $105.*

Among the "Parade of American Fashion," The Romantic Lady *dazzles collectors with the grace and beauty of a Southern belle. Produced by Ashton-Drake Galleries.*

Good things come in threes! Sheldon, Dacy *and* Brianna *are the work of artist Jan Hagara.*

YR	NAME	LIMIT	ISSUE	TREND
84	HENRI-901035	CL	100.00	205.00
84	HENRIETTA-901036	CL	100.00	200.00
84	JAMIE-912061	CL	65.00	100.00
84	JEANNIE-901062	CL	200.00	550.00
84	LAURA-901106	CL	300.00	575.00
84	SABINA-901155	CL	75.00	*
84	SHEILA-912060	CL	75.00	135.00
84	STEPHANIE-933012	CL	115.00	115.00
84	TOBIE-912023	CL	30.00	30.00
84	VICTORIA-901068	CL	200.00	1500.00
85	ADELE-901172	CL	145.00	275.00
85	CHAUNCEY-912085	CL	75.00	110.00
85	CLAIRE-901158	CL	115.00	160.00
85	CLOWN CASEY-912078	CL	40.00	40.00
85	CLOWN CHRISTIE-912084	CL	60.00	90.00
85	CLOWN JODY-912079	CL	100.00	150.00
85	DOROTHY-901157	CL	130.00	275.00
85	GARNET-901183	CL	160.00	295.00
85	LYNN-912144	CL	90.00	135.00
85	MARY-912126	CL	60.00	90.00
85	MICHELLE-912066	CL	100.00	225.00
85	MILLIE-912135	CL	70.00	125.00
85	PHYLLIS-912067	CL	60.00	60.00
85	ROSALIND-912087	CL	145.00	225.00
85	ROXANNE-901174	CL	155.00	275.00
86	ASHLEY-912147	CL	125.00	125.00
86	BABY BROCK BEIGE DRESS-912103	CL	60.00	60.00
86	BABY COURTNEY-912124	CL	120.00	120.00
86	BABY LAUREN PINK-912086	CL	120.00	120.00
86	CAT/KITTY CHEERFUL GR DR-901179	2500	60.00	60.00
86	CLOWN CALYPSO-912104	CL	70.00	70.00
86	CLOWN CAT CADWALADER-912132	CL	55.00	55.00
86	CLOWN CHRISTABEL-912095	CL	100.00	150.00
86	CLOWN CLARABELLA-912096	CL	80.00	80.00
86	CLOWN CLARISSA-912123	CL	75.00	110.00
86	CLOWN CYD-912093	CL	70.00	70.00
86	CLOWN KITTEN CLEO-912133	CL	50.00	50.00
86	CLOWN LOLLIPOP-912127	CL	125.00	225.00
86	GINA-901176	CL	300.00	300.00
86	GIRL FROG FREDA-912105	CL	20.00	20.00
86	GOOGLEY GERMAN ASTRID-912109	CL	60.00	60.00
86	PATTY ACRTIC FLOWER PRINT-901185	CL	140.00	140.00
86	PEPPER RUST DR/APPR-901184	CL	125.00	200.00
87	ALICE-901212	CL	95.00	135.00
87	AMANDA POUTY-901209	CL	150.00	215.00
87	BABY DOLL-912184	CL	75.00	75.00
87	BABY LINDSAY-912190	CL	80.00	80.00
87	BONNIE POUTY-901207	CL	100.00	100.00
87	BRIDE ALLISON-901218	CL	180.00	180.00
87	CAROLINE-912191	CL	80.00	80.00
87	CATANOVA-901227	CL	75.00	75.00
87	CATLIN-901228	CL	260.00	260.00
87	CHRISTINE-912168	CL	75.00	75.00
87	CLEMENTINE-901226	CL	75.00	75.00
87	CLOWN CHAMPAGNE-912180	CL	95.00	95.00
87	DOMINIQUE-901219	CL	170.00	225.00
87	DOREEN-912198	CL	75.00	75.00
87	JACQUELINE-912192	CL	80.00	80.00
87	JESSICA-912195	CL	120.00	135.00
87	JOY-912155	CL	50.00	50.00
87	JULIA-912174	CL	80.00	80.00
87	KITTLE CAT-912167	CL	55.00	55.00
87	KITTY CUDDLES-901201	CL	65.00	65.00
87	LILLIAN-901199	CL	85.00	100.00
87	MEGAN-912148	CL	70.00	70.00
87	MICHELLE-901222	CL	90.00	90.00
87	NICOLE-901225	CL	575.00	575.00
87	NOEL-912170	CL	125.00	125.00
87	SARAH-901220	CL	350.00	350.00
87	SOPHIA-912173	CL	40.00	40.00
87	SUZANNE-901201	CL	85.00	100.00
87	TASHA-901221	CL	115.00	130.00
87	TIFFANY POUTY-901211	CL	120.00	160.00
88	AMANDA-912246	CL	180.00	180.00
88	ANGELICA-912204	CL	150.00	150.00
88	ANNE-912213	CL	130.00	150.00
88	APRIL-901239	CL	225.00	225.00
88	ASHLEY-901235	CL	110.00	110.00
88	BABY DARYL-912200	CL	85.00	85.00
88	BABY JENNIFER-912210	CL	75.00	75.00
88	BABY KATIE-912222	CL	70.00	70.00
88	BERNICE-901245	CL	90.00	90.00
88	BETTY DOLL-912220	CL	90.00	90.00
88	BRANDON-901234	CL	90.00	90.00
88	BRITTANY-912207	CL	130.00	145.00
88	CAMPBELL KID/BOY-758701	CL	13.80	14.00
88	CAMPBELL KID/GIRL-758700	CL	13.80	14.00
88	CAT MAUDE-901247	CL	85.00	85.00
88	CATHERINE-901242	CL	240.00	240.00

YR	NAME	LIMIT	ISSUE	TREND
88	CHRISTINA-901229	CL	350.00	400.00
88	CLOWN COTTON CANDY-912199	CL	67.00	67.00
88	CRYSTAL-912226	CL	75.00	75.00
88	DIANA-912218	CL	270.00	270.00
88	ELIZABETH-901214	CL	90.00	90.00
88	ELLEN-901246	CL	100.00	100.00
88	ERIN-901241	CL	170.00	170.00
88	HEATHER-912247	CL	135.00	150.00
88	JENNIFER-901248	CL	150.00	150.00
88	JENNIFER-912221	CL	80.00	80.00
88	JESSE-912231	CL	110.00	115.00
88	KAREN-912205	CL	200.00	250.00
88	LAURA-912225	CL	135.00	135.00
88	LAUREN-912212	CL	110.00	110.00
88	MARITTA SPANISH-912224	CL	140.00	140.00
88	MELISSA-901230	CL	110.00	115.00
88	MELISSA-912208	CL	125.00	125.00
88	PAULETTE-901244	CL	90.00	90.00
88	POLLY-912206	CL	100.00	125.00
88	RENAE-912245	CL	120.00	120.00
88	SARAH W/PILLOW-912219	CL	105.00	105.00
88	STEPHANIE-912238	CL	200.00	200.00
88	SUSAN-901242	CL	100.00	100.00
88	WHITNEY BLK-912232	CL	62.50	65.00
89	ALEXA-912214	CL	195.00	195.00
89	ALEXANDRIA-912273	CL	275.00	275.00
89	ASHLEA-901250	CL	550.00	550.00
89	DIANA BRIDE-912277	CL	180.00	180.00
89	HOLLY-901254	CL	180.00	180.00
89	HOPE BABY W/PILLOW-912292	CL	110.00	110.00
89	JINGLES-912271	CL	60.00	60.00
89	LICORICE-912290	CL	75.00	75.00
89	LINDSEY-901263	CL	100.00	100.00
89	LISA-912275	CL	160.00	160.00
89	LONI-912276	CL	125.00	130.00
89	MARGOT-912269	CL	110.00	110.00
89	MARIA-912265	CL	90.00	90.00
89	MEGAN-901260	CL	120.00	120.00
89	MERRY-912249	CL	200.00	200.00
89	MISSY-912283	CL	100.00	120.00
89	NANCY-912266	CL	110.00	110.00
89	SARA-912279	CL	175.00	175.00
89	SIGRID-912282	CL	145.00	145.00
89	SUZANNE-912286	CL	120.00	120.00
89	SUZY-912295	CL	110.00	110.00
89	TAMMY-912264	CL	110.00	110.00
89	TERRY-912281	CL	125.00	135.00
89	VALERIE-901255	CL	175.00	175.00
89	VANESSA-912272	CL	110.00	110.00
90	AMY-901262	CL	110.00	110.00
90	ANNABELLE-912278	CL	200.00	200.00
90	BETTINA-912310	CL	100.00	110.00
90	EMILY-912303	CL	150.00	150.00
90	FLUFFER-912293	CL	135.00	140.00
90	HEATHER-912322	CL	150.00	150.00
90	HEIDI-901266	2000	150.00	150.00
90	HELGA-912337	CL	325.00	325.00
90	JILLIAN-912323	CL	150.00	150.00
90	JUSTINE-901256	CL	200.00	200.00
90	KELLY-912331	CL	95.00	95.00
90	KIMBERLY-912341	1000	140.00	150.00
90	MATTHEW-901251	CL	100.00	100.00
90	MRS. KATZ-912301	CL	140.00	150.00
90	PAMELA-912302	CL	95.00	95.00
90	PAULA-912316	CL	100.00	100.00
90	PRISCILLA-912300	CL	185.00	190.00
90	REBECCA-901258	CL	250.00	250.00
90	ROBIN-912321	CL	160.00	165.00
90	SAMANTHA-912314	CL	185.00	190.00
90	SHEENA-912338	CL	115.00	115.00
90	STEPHANIE-912312	CL	150.00	150.00
90	SUSIE-912328	CL	115.00	120.00
90	TRACIE-912315	CL	125.00	125.00
92	ALICIA-912388	500	135.00	140.00
92	ALLISON-912358	CL	160.00	170.00
92	ANGELICA-912339	1000	145.00	150.00
92	ASHLEY-911004	CL	99.00	110.00
92	BETSY-912390	500	150.00	150.00
92	CINDY-912384	1000	185.00	195.00
92	HILARY-912353	1000	130.00	130.00
92	HILARY-912353	CL	130.00	140.00
92	HOLLY BELLE-912380	500	125.00	125.00
92	KELLI-912361	1000	160.00	170.00
92	MARJORIE-912357	CL	135.00	140.00
92	TAMIKA-912382	500	185.00	190.00
92	TRUDIE-912391	500	135.00	140.00
93	AMANDA-912409	2000	40.00	45.00
93	JESSICA-912410	2000	40.00	45.00
93	KATIE-912412	2000	40.00	45.00

YR	NAME	LIMIT	ISSUE	TREND
93	LAUREN-912413	2000	40.00	45.00
93	NICOLE-912411	2000	40.00	45.00
93	SARAH-912408	2000	40.00	45.00
K. KENNEDY		**VICTORIA ASHLEA ORIGINALS**		
88	GOLDILOCKS-912234	CL	65.00	65.00
88	MOLLY-912211	CL	75.00	75.00
88	MORGAN-912239	CL	75.00	75.00
88	SANDY-901240	CL	115.00	115.00
88	SNOW WHITE-912235	CL	65.00	65.00
89	CANDACE-912288	CL	70.00	70.00
89	CLAUDIA-901257	CL	225.00	225.00
89	GINNY-912287	CL	140.00	140.00
89	JIMMY W/PILLOW-912291	CL	165.00	165.00
89	JOY-912290	CL	110.00	110.00
89	KRISTIN-912285	CL	90.00	95.00
89	MARISSA-901252	CL	225.00	225.00
89	MELANIE-912284	CL	135.00	135.00
89	PINKY CLOWN-912268	CL	70.00	75.00
90	ALICE-912296	CL	65.00	65.00
90	AMIE-912313	CL	150.00	150.00
90	ANGELA-912324	CL	130.00	135.00
90	ANNETTE-912333	CL	85.00	85.00
90	BARYSHNICAT-912298	CL	25.00	25.00
90	BRANDY-912304	CL	150.00	150.00
90	CAROLYN-901261	CL	200.00	200.00
90	DEBRA-912319	CL	120.00	120.00
90	GIGI-912306	CL	150.00	150.00
90	HELENE-901249	CL	160.00	160.00
90	JACQUELINE-912329	CL	136.00	142.00
90	JOANNE-912307	CL	165.00	165.00
90	JULIA-912334	CL	85.00	85.00
90	MARSHMALLOW-912294	CL	75.00	75.00
90	MELINDA-912309	CL	70.00	70.00
90	MONICA-912336	CL	100.00	110.00
90	MONIQUE-912335	CL	85.00	85.00
90	PENNY-912325	CL	130.00	130.00
90	SHERI-912305	CL	115.00	115.00
90	TASHA-912299	CL	25.00	25.00
90	TIFFANY-912326	CL	180.00	180.00
92	BRITTANY-912365	CL	140.00	150.00
92	CAROL-912387	1000	140.00	145.00
92	CASSANDRA-912355	1000	165.00	170.00
92	DENISE-912345	CL	145.00	155.00
92	DOTTIE-912393	1000	160.00	165.00
92	IRIS-912389	500	165.00	170.00
92	JENNY-912374	CL	150.00	155.00
92	KRIS-912345	CL	160.00	165.00
92	LAUREN-912363	1000	190.00	200.00
92	MARGARET-912354	1000	150.00	155.00
92	MICHELLE-912381	CL	175.00	180.00
92	NOELLE-912360	1000	165.00	175.00
92	SHERISE-912383	CL	145.00	150.00
92	SUSAN-912346	1000	325.00	325.00
92	TONI-912367	CL	120.00	125.00
92	TULIP-912385	500	145.00	150.00
92	WENDY-912330	1000	125.00	135.00
93	BETH-912430	2000	45.00	50.00
93	JULIE-912435	2000	45.00	50.00
93	KAYLEE-912433	2000	45.00	50.00
93	LESLIE-912432	2000	45.00	50.00
93	NADINE-912431	2000	45.00	50.00
93	SHANNON-912434	2000	45.00	50.00
K. KENNEDY	**VICTORIA ASHLEA ORIGINALS TINY TOT CLOWNS**			
94	DANIELLE	2000	45.00	50.00
94	LINDSEY	2000	45.00	50.00
94	LISA	2000	45.00	50.00
94	MARIE	2000	45.00	50.00
94	MEGAN	2000	45.00	50.00
94	STACY	2000	45.00	50.00
K. KENNEDY	**VICTORIA ASHLEA ORIGINALS TINY TOT SCHOOL GIRLS**			
94	ANDREA-12456	2000	47.50	50.00
94	CHRISTIN-912450	2000	47.50	50.00
94	MONIQUE-912455	2000	47.50	50.00
94	PATRICIA-912453	2000	47.50	50.00
94	SHAWAN-912449	2000	47.50	50.00
94	SUSAN-12457	2000	47.50	50.00

GOOD-KRUGER DOLLS

YR	NAME	LIMIT	ISSUE	TREND
J. GOOD-KRUGER			**LIMITED EDITION**	
90	ALICE	RT	250.00	275.00
90	ANNIE-ROSE	RT	219.00	475.00
90	CHRISTMAS COOKIE	RT	199.00	200.00
90	COZY	RT	179.00	275.00-380.00
90	DAYDREAM	RT	199.00	375.00
90	SUE-LYNN	RT	240.00	305.00
91	JOHNNY-LYNN	RT	240.00	505.00
91	MOPPETT	RT	179.00	280.00
91	TEACHERS PET	RT	199.00	255.00

YR	NAME	LIMIT	ISSUE	TREND
91	VICTORIAN CHRISTMAS	RT	219.00	280.00
92	ANNE	RT	240.00	505.00
J. GOOD-KRUGER		**LIMITED EDITION/PORCELAIN**		
92	JEEPERS CREEPERS	RT	725.00	805.00

GORHAM

Price ranges may reflect various demands in the market from one geographic region to another; condition of piece; specific markings found on piece; and/or changes in production of piece.

YR	NAME	LIMIT	ISSUE	TREND
B. PORT		**BEVERLY PORT DESIGNER COLLECTION**		
87	CHRISTOPHER PAUL BEARKIN, 10 IN.	CL	95.00	525.00
87	KRISTOBEAR KRINGLE, 17 IN.	CL	200.00	475.00
87	MOLLY MELINDA BEARKIN, 10 IN.	CL	95.00	325.00
87	SILVER BELL, 17 IN.	CL	175.00	775.00
87	TEDWARD JONATHAN BEARKIN, 10 IN.	CL	95.00	325.00
87	TEDWINA KIMELINA BEARKIN, 10 IN.	CL	95.00	325.00
88	AMAZING CALLIOPE MERRIWEATHER, THE 17 IN	CL	275.00	1175.00
88	BAERY MAB, 9 1/2 IN.	CL	110.00	325.00
88	HOLLYBEARY KRINGLE, 15 IN.	CL	350.00	475.00
88	MISS EMILY, 18 IN.	CL	350.00	625.00
88	T.R., 28 1/2 IN.	CL	400.00	575.00
88	THEODORE B. BEAR, 14 IN.	CL	175.00	525.00
M. SIRKO		**BONNET BABIES**		
93	CHELSEA'S BONNET	CL	95.00	100.00
B. GERARDI		**BONNETS & BOWS**		
88	ALICIA	CL	385.00	800.00-1000.00
88	ALLESSANDRA	CL	195.00	375.00-525.00
88	ANNEMARIE	CL	195.00	450.00
88	BELINDA	CL	195.00	450.00
88	BETHANY	CL	385.00	1250.00-1475.00
88	BETTINA	CL	285.00	475.00-550.00
88	ELLIE	CL	285.00	475.00-550.00
88	FRANCIE	CL	625.00	875.00-975.00
88	JESSE	CL	525.00	795.00-850.00
88	LISETTE	CL	285.00	475.00-550.00
D. VALENZA		**BRIDE DOLLS**		
93	SUSANNAH'S WEDDING DAY	9500	295.00	295.00
C. SHAFER		**CAROUSEL DOLLS**		
93	RIBBONS AND ROSES	CL	119.00	120.00
L. DI LEO		**CELEBRATIONS OF CHILDHOOD**		
92	HAPPY BIRTHDAY AMY	CL	160.00	160.00
D. VALENZA		**CHILDHOOD MEMORIES**		
91	AMANDA	CL	98.00	155.00
91	JENNIFER	CL	98.00	155.00
91	JESSICA-ANNE'S PLAYTIME	CL	98.00	155.00
91	KIMBERLY	CL	98.00	155.00
S. STONE AIKEN		**CHILDREN OF CHRISTMAS**		
89	CLARA, 16 IN.	CL	325.00	675.00
90	NATALIE, 16 IN.	1500	350.00	455.00
91	EMILY, 16 IN.	1500	375.00	480.00
92	VIRGINIA	1500	375.00	425.00
S. STONE AIKEN		**CHRISTMAS TRADITIONS**		
93	TRIMMING THE TREE	2500	295.00	300.00
S. STONE AIKEN		**CHRISTMAS TREASURES**		
93	CHRISSY	CL	150.00	150.00
S. STONE AIKEN		**DAYDREAMER DOLLS**		
92	HEATHER'S DAYDREAM	CL	119.00	120.00
R./L. SCHRUBBE		**DAYS OF THE WEEK**		
92	FRIDAY'S CHILD	CL	98.00	100.00
92	MONDAY'S CHILD	CL	98.00	100.00
92	SATURDAY'S CHILD	CL	98.00	100.00
92	SUNDAY'S CHILD	CL	98.00	100.00
92	THURSDAY'S CHILD	CL	98.00	100.00
92	TUESDAY'S CHILD	CL	98.00	100.00
92	WEDNESDAY'S CHILD	CL	98.00	100.00
J. PILALLIS		**DOLLIE AND ME**		
91	DOLLIE'S FIRST STEPS	CL	160.00	160.00
*** GORHAM**		**DOLLS OF THE MONTH**		
91	MISS APRIL	CL	79.00	130.00
91	MISS AUGUST	CL	79.00	130.00
91	MISS DECEMBER	CL	79.00	130.00
91	MISS FEBRUARY	CL	79.00	130.00
91	MISS JANUARY	CL	79.00	130.00
91	MISS JULY	CL	79.00	130.00
91	MISS JUNE	CL	79.00	130.00
91	MISS MARCH	CL	79.00	130.00
91	MISS MAY	CL	79.00	130.00
91	MISS NOVEMBER	CL	79.00	130.00
91	MISS OCTOBER	CL	79.00	130.00
91	MISS SEPTEMBER	CL	79.00	130.00
*** YOUNG/GERARDI**		**GIFT OF DREAMS**		
91	CHRISTINA (CHRISTMAS)	CL	695.00	695.00
91	ELIZABETH	CL	495.00	495.00
91	KATHERINE	CL	495.00	495.00
91	MELISSA	CL	495.00	495.00
91	SAMANTHA	CL	495.00	495.00

YR	NAME	LIMIT	ISSUE	TREND
	S. STONE AIKEN			**GIFTS OF THE GARDEN**
91	ALISA	CL	125.00	205.00
91	DEBORAH	CL	125.00	205.00
91	HOLLY (CHRISTMAS)	CL	150.00	205.00
91	IRENE	CL	125.00	205.00
91	JOELLE (CHRISTMAS)	CL	150.00	205.00
91	LAUREN	CL	125.00	205.00
91	MARIA	CL	125.00	205.00
91	PRISCILLA	CL	125.00	205.00
91	VALERIE	CL	125.00	205.00
	*** AIKEN/MATTHEWS**			**GORHAM BABY DOLL COLLECTION**
87	CHRISTENING DAY	CL	245.00	300.00
87	LESLIE	CL	245.00	330.00
87	MATTHEW	CL	245.00	290.00
	*			**GORHAM DOLLS**
82	BABY IN WHITE DRESS, 18 IN.	CL	250.00	350.00-400.00
82	M. ANTON, 12 IN.	CL	125.00	150.00-200.00
82	MLLE. MARSELLA, 12 IN.	CL	125.00	275.00-300.00
82	MLLE. YVONNE, 12 IN.	CL	125.00	375.00-450.00
	S. STONE AIKEN			**GORHAM DOLLS**
81	ALEXANDRIA, 18 IN.	CL	250.00	550.00-600.00
81	CECILE, 16 IN.	CL	200.00	700.00-950.00
81	CHRISTINA, 16 IN.	CL	200.00	425.00-475.00
81	CHRISTOPHER, 19 IN.	CL	250.00	725.00-975.00
81	DANIELLE, 14 IN.	CL	150.00	300.00-380.00
81	ELENA, 14 IN.	CL	150.00	650.00-750.00
81	JILLIAN, 16 IN.	CL	200.00	375.00-475.00
81	MELINDA, 14 IN.	CL	150.00	300.00-380.00
81	ROSEMOND, 18 IN.	CL	250.00	655.00-755.00
81	STEPHANIE, 18 IN.	CL	250.00	1625.00-2125.00
82	BABY IN APRICOT DRESS, 16 IN.	CL	175.00	325.00-380.00
82	BABY IN BLUE DRESS, 12 IN.	CL	150.00	350.00-380.00
82	BENJAMIN, 18 IN.	CL	200.00	550.00-605.00
82	CORRINE, 21 IN.	CL	250.00	375.00-625.00
82	CORRINE, 21 IN.	CL	250.00	400.00-600.00
82	ELLICE, 18 IN.	CL	200.00	550.00-625.00
82	JEREMY, 23 IN.	CL	300.00	750.00-825.00
82	KRISTIN, 23 IN.	CL	300.00	550.00-725.00
82	MELANIE, 23 IN.	CL	300.00	625.00-725.00
82	MLLE. JEANETTE, 12 IN.	CL	125.00	175.00-225.00
82	MLLE. LUCILLE, 12 IN.	CL	125.00	275.00-475.00
82	MLLE. MONIQUE, 12 IN.	CL	125.00	250.00-305.00
83	JENNIFER, 19 IN. BRIDAL DOLL	CL	325.00	725.00-825.00
85	ALEXANDER, 19 IN.	CL	275.00	375.00-525.00
85	AMELIA, 19 IN.	CL	275.00	350.00-425.00
85	GABRIELLE, 19 IN.	CL	225.00	350.00-475.00
85	LINDA, 19 IN.	CL	275.00	400.00-480.00
85	NANETTE, 19 IN.	CL	275.00	325.00-425.00
85	ODETTE, 19 IN.	CL	250.00	450.00-480.00
86	ALISSA	CL	245.00	325.00-375.00
86	EMILY, 14 IN.	CL	175.00	350.00-450.00
86	FLEUR, 19 IN.	CL	300.00	375.00-525.00
86	JESSICA	CL	195.00	275.00-375.00
86	JULIA, 16 IN.	CL	225.00	350.00-450.00
86	LAUREN, 14 IN.	CL	175.00	375.00-475.00
86	MEREDITH	CL	295.00	350.00-425.00
87	JULIET	CL	325.00	375.00-475.00
	*			**HOLLY HOBBIE**
83	BLUE GIRL, 14 IN.	CL	80.00	325.00
83	BLUE GIRL, 18 IN.	CL	115.00	395.00
83	CHRISTMAS MORNING, 14 IN.	CL	80.00	275.00
83	HEATHER, 14 IN.	CL	80.00	275.00
83	LITTLE AMY, 14 IN.	CL	80.00	275.00
83	ROBBIE, 14 IN.	CL	80.00	275.00
83	SUNDAY'S BEST, 18 IN.	CL	115.00	350.00
83	SWEET VALENTINE, 16 IN.	CL	100.00	350.00
83	YESTERDAY'S MEMORIES, 18 IN.	CL	125.00	450.00
	*			**HOLLY HOBBIE CHILDHOOD MEMORIES**
85	BEST FRIENDS	CL	45.00	125.00
85	CHRISTMAS WISHES	CL	45.00	125.00
85	FIRST DAY OF SCHOOL	CL	45.00	125.00
85	MOTHER'S HELPER	CL	45.00	125.00
	*			**HOLLY HOBBIE FOR ALL SEASONS**
84	FALL HOLLY, 12 IN.	CL	42.50	200.00
84	SPRING HOLLY, 12 IN.	CL	42.50	200.00
84	SUMMER HOLLY, 12 IN.	CL	42.50	200.00
84	WINTER HOLLY, 12 IN.	CL	42.50	200.00
	R. TONNER			**IMAGINARY PEOPLE**
93	MELINDA, THE TOOTH FAIRY	2900	95.00	100.00
	R. TONNER			**INTERNATIONAL BABIES**
93	NATALIA'S MATRIOSHKA	CL	95.00	100.00
	B. GERARDI			**JOYFUL YEARS**
89	KATRINA	CL	295.00	380.00
89	WILLIAM	CL	295.00	380.00
	KEZI			**KEZI DOLL FOR ALL SEASONS**
85	ADRIENNE, 16 IN.	CL	135.00	500.00
85	AMBER, 16 IN.	CL	135.00	500.00

YR	NAME	LIMIT	ISSUE	TREND
85	ARIEL, 16 IN.	CL	135.00	500.00
85	AUBREY, 16 IN.	CL	135.00	500.00
KEZI				**KEZI GOLDEN GIFTS**
84	CHARITY, 16 IN.	CL	85.00	185.00
84	FAITH, 18 IN.	CL	95.00	210.00
84	FELICITY, 18 IN.	CL	95.00	200.00
84	GRACE, 16 IN.	CL	85.00	175.00
84	HOPE, 16 IN.	CL	85.00	210.00
84	MERRIE, 16 IN.	CL	85.00	185.00
84	PATIENCE, 18 IN.	CL	95.00	175.00
84	PRUDENCE, 18 IN.	CL	85.00	175.00
R./L. SCHRUBBE				**KIDS WITH STUFFED TOYS**
93	TARA AND TEDDY	OP	119.00	119.00
S. STONE AIKEN				**LEGENDARY HEROINES**
91	GUINEVERE	1500	245.00	245.00
91	JANE EYRE	1500	245.00	245.00
91	JULIET	1500	245.00	245.00
91	LARA	1500	245.00	245.00
S. STONE AIKEN				**LES BELLES BEBES COLLECTION**
91	CHERIE	CL	375.00	475.00
91	DESIREE	1500	375.00	445.00
93	CAMILLE	1500	375.00	425.00
S. STONE AIKEN				**LIMITED EDITION DOLLS**
82	ALLISON, 19 IN.	CL	300.00	4250.00
83	ASHLEY, 19 IN.	CL	350.00	800.00-1200.00
84	HOLLY (CHRISTMAS), 19 IN.	CL	300.00	825.00
84	NICOLE, 19 IN.	CL	350.00	600.00-1000.00
85	JOY (CHRISTMAS), 19 IN.	CL	350.00	625.00
85	LYDIA, 19 IN.	CL	550.00	900.00-1800.00
86	NOEL (CHRISTMAS), 19 IN.	CL	400.00	600.00-800.00
87	JACQUELINE, 19 IN.	CL	500.00	550.00-875.00
87	MERRIE (CHRISTMAS), 19 IN.	CL	500.00	600.00-800.00
88	ANDREW, 19 IN.	CL	475.00	600.00-875.00
88	CHRISTA (CHRISTMAS), 19 IN.	CL	550.00	900.00-1500.00
90	AMEY (10TH ANNIVERSARY EDITION)	CL	650.00	700.00-1150.00
S. STONE AIKEN				**LIMITED EDITION SISTER SET**
88	KATELIN/KATHLEEN SET	CL	550.00	750.00-1000.00
S. STONE AIKEN				**LITTLE WOMEN**
83	AMY, 16 IN.	CL	225.00	575.00
83	BETH, 16 IN.	CL	225.00	575.00
83	JO, 19 IN.	CL	275.00	675.00
83	MEG, 19 IN.	CL	275.00	695.00
L. DI LEO				**LITTLEST ANGEL DOLLS**
92	MERRIEL	CL	49.50	50.00
R. TONNER				**NATURE'S BOUNTY**
93	JAMIE'S FRUITFUL HARVEST	CL	95.00	100.00
L. GORDON				**PILLOW BABY DOLLS**
93	ON THE MOVE	CL	39.00	40.00
93	SITTING PRETTY	CL	39.00	40.00
93	TICKLING TOES	CL	39.00	40.00
R. TONNER				**PORTRAIT PERFECT VICTORIAN DOLLS**
93	PRETTY IN PEACH	2900	119.00	120.00
S. STONE AIKEN				**PRECIOUS AS PEARLS**
86	COLETTE	CL	400.00	1275.00-1500.00
87	CHARLOTTE	CL	425.00	425.00-825.00
88	CHLOE	CL	525.00	525.00-925.00
89	CASSANDRA	CL	525.00	525.00-1250.00
R. SCHRUBBE				**PUPPY LOVE DOLLS**
92	KATIE AND KYLE	CL	119.00	120.00
B. GERARDI				**SMALL WONDERS**
88	MADELINE	CL	365.00	370.00
88	MARGUERITE	CL	425.00	430.00
88	PATINA	CL	265.00	265.00
S. STONE AIKEN				**SOUTHERN BELLES**
85	AMANDA, 19 IN.	CL	300.00	950.00
86	VERONICA, 19 IN.	CL	325.00	750.00
87	RACHEL, 19 IN.	CL	375.00	825.00
88	CASSIE, 19 IN.	CL	500.00	675.00
E. WORRELL				**SPECIAL MOMENTS**
91	BABY'S FIRST CHRISTMAS	CL	135.00	135.00-300.00
92	BABY'S CHRISTENING	OP	135.00	135.00
92	BABY'S FIRST BIRTHDAY	OP	135.00	135.00
92	BABY'S FIRST STEPS	CL	135.00	175.00
R. SCHRUBBE				**SPORTING KIDS**
93	UP AT BAT	CL	49.50	50.00
M. MURPHY				**TENDER HEARTS**
93	SAYING GRACE	CL	119.00	120.00
S. NAPPO				**THE FRIENDSHIP DOLLS**
91	ANGELA-THE ITALIAN TRAVELER	CL	98.00	98.00
L. O'CONNOR				**THE FRIENDSHIP DOLLS**
91	MEAGAN-THE IRISH TRAVELER	CL	98.00	98.00
P. SEAMAN				**THE FRIENDSHIP DOLLS**
91	PEGGY-THE AMERICAN TRAVELER	CL	98.00	98.00
S. UEKI				**THE FRIENDSHIP DOLLS**
91	KINUKO-THE JAPANESE TRAVELER	CL	98.00	98.00

YR NAME	LIMIT	ISSUE	TREND
E. WOODHOUSE	**THE VICTORIAN COLLECTION**		
92 VICTORIA'S JUBILEE	YR	295.00	295.00
L. DI LEO	**TIMES TO TREASURE**		
90 STORYTIME	CL	195.00	200.00
91 BEDTIME	CL	195.00	200.00
93 CRADLETIME	OP	195.00	195.00
93 PLAYTIME	CL	195.00	200.00
L. DILEO	**TIMES TO TREASURE**		
92 BEDTIME	OP	195.00	195.00
92 STORYTIME	OP	195.00	195.00
P. VALENTINE	**VALENTINE LADIES**		
87 ANABELLA	CL	145.00	395.00
87 ELIZABETH	CL	145.00	450.00
87 JANE	CL	145.00	350.00
87 LEE ANN	CL	145.00	325.00
87 MARIANNA	CL	160.00	400.00
87 PATRICE	CL	145.00	325.00
87 REBECCA	CL	145.00	325.00
87 ROSANNE	CL	145.00	325.00
87 SYLVIA	CL	160.00	350.00
88 FELICIA	CL	225.00	400.00
88 JUDITH ANNE	CL	195.00	325.00
88 MARIA THERESA	CL	225.00	275.00
88 PRISCILLA	CL	195.00	325.00
89 JULIANNA	CL	225.00	275.00
89 ROSE	CL	225.00	275.00
B. GERARDI	**VICTORIAN CAMEO COLLECTION**		
90 VICTORIA	1500	375.00	375.00
91 ALEXANDRA	CL	375.00	375.00
S. STONE AIKEN	**VICTORIAN CHILDREN**		
92 SARA'S TEA TIME	1000	495.00	550.00
93 CATCHING BUTTERFLIES	1000	495.00	495.00
J. PILLALIS	**VICTORIAN FLOWER GIRLS**		
93 ROSE	CL	95.00	100.00

GUND INC.

YR NAME	LIMIT	ISSUE	TREND
A	**MOHAIR COLLECTION**		
96 MAJOR BEARKIN	700	250.00	250.00
R. SWEDLIN-RAIFFE	**SIGNATURE COLLECTION**		
95 BEARNARD	350	180.00	180.00
95 BLACKBEARD	350	300.00	300.00
95 DUNBEARY	350	300.00	300.00
95 GULLIVER	250	400.00	400.00
95 O'BEARIGAN	450	140.00	140.00
95 PEANUT BUTTER	400	180.00	180.00
96 BEARBUSHKA	500	200.00	200.00
96 HUGH MONGUS	310	400.00	400.00
96 LITTLE BEAR BLUE	450	250.00	250.00
96 PAWTHORNE	540	150.00	150.00
96 SOMETHING'S BRUIN	425	350.00	350.00

H & G STUDIOS

YR NAME	LIMIT	ISSUE	TREND
B. BURKE	**BIRTHDAY PARTY**		
90 SUZIE	500	695.00	695.00
B. BURKE	**BRENDA BURKE DOLLS**		
89 ADELAINE	25	1795.00	3600.00
89 ALEXANDRA	125	995.00	2000.00
89 ALICIA	125	895.00	1800.00
89 AMANDA	25	1995.00	6000.00
89 ANGELICA	50	1495.00	3000.00
89 ARABELLE	500	695.00	1400.00
89 BEATRICE	85	2395.00	2395.00
89 BETHANY	45	2995.00	2995.00
89 BRITTANY	75	2695.00	2695.00
90 BELINDA	12	3695.00	3695.00
91 CHARLOTTE	20	2395.00	2395.00
91 CLARISSA	15	3595.00	3595.00
91 SLEIGH RIDE	20	3695.00	3695.00
91 TENDER LOVE	25	3295.00	3295.00
92 DOROTHEA	500	395.00	400.00
93 GIOVANNA	1	7800.00	7800.00
93 MELISSA	1	7750.00	7750.00
B. BURKE	**CHILDHOOD MEMORIES**		
89 EARLY DAYS	95	2595.00	2595.00
91 PLAYTIME	35	2795.00	2795.00
B. BURKE	**DANCING THROUGH THE AGES**		
90 MINUET	95	2495.00	2495.00
B. BURKE	**THE FOUR SEASONS**		
90 SPRING	125	1995.00	1995.00

HALLMARK GALLERIES

YR NAME	LIMIT	ISSUE	TREND
E. HIBEL	**GRANDMA'S ATTIC**		
89 MELANIE	CL	139.00	180.00
91 KATIE	CL	139.00	150.00
M. ENGELBREIT	**MARY ENGELBREIT'S FRIENDSHIP GARDEN**		
93 JOSEPHINE 6000QHG5003 PORCELAIN DOLL	12500	60.00	60.00
93 LOUISA 6500QHG5002 PORCELAIN DOLL	12500	65.00	70.00

YR	NAME	LIMIT	ISSUE	TREND
93	MARGARET 6000QHG5001 PORCELAIN DOLL	12500	60.00	60.00
	J. GREENE	**VICTORIAN MEMORIES**		
92	ABIGAIL 1QHG1019	4500	125.00	130.00
92	ABNER 1QHG1018	4500	110.00	110.00
92	ALICE 1QHG1020	4500	125.00	130.00
92	EMMA/2500QHG1016 MINIATURE DOLL	9500	25.00	30.00
92	KATHERINE 1QHG1017	1200	150.00	150.00
92	OLIVIA 1QHG1021	4500	125.00	130.00
93	BABY DOLL BEATRICE 2000QHG1029	RT	20.00	25.00
93	HANNAH 1QHG1030	2500	130.00	130.00

HAMILTON COLLECTION

YR	NAME	LIMIT	ISSUE	TREND
	B. VAN BOXEL	**A CHILD'S MENAGERIE**		
93	BECKY	OP	69.00	70.00
93	CARRIE	OP	69.00	70.00
94	MANDY	OP	69.00	70.00
	A. WILLIAMS	**ABBIE WILLIAMS DOLL COLLECTION**		
92	MOLLY	CL	155.00	205.00
	*	**ANNUAL CONNOISSEUR DOLL**		
92	LARA	7450	295.00	300.00
	B. PARKER	**BABY PORTRAIT DOLLS**		
91	MELISSA	CL	135.00	180.00
92	BETHANY	OP	135.00	140.00
92	JENNA	CL	135.00	200.00
93	MINDY	OP	135.00	140.00
	C. HEATH ORANGE	**BELLES OF THE COUNTRYSIDE**		
92	ERIN	OP	135.00	140.00
92	ROSE	OP	135.00	140.00
93	LORNA	OP	135.00	140.00
94	GWYN	OP	135.00	140.00
	C. MARSCHNER	**BEST BUDDIES**		
94	JODIE	OP	69.00	70.00
	*	**BOEHM DOLLS**		
94	ELENA	OP	155.00	160.00
	*** BOEHM**	**BRIDAL ELEGANCE**		
94	CAMILLE	OP	195.00	200.00
	*	**BRIDE DOLLS**		
91	PORTRAIT OF INNOCENCE	OP	195.00	200.00
92	PORTRAIT OF LOVELINESS	OP	195.00	200.00
	P. RYAN BROOKS	**BROOKS WOODEN DOLLS**		
93	ARE YOU THE EASTER BUNNY?	15000	135.00	140.00
93	WAITING FOR SANTA	15000	135.00	140.00
94	BE MY VALENTINE	OP	135.00	140.00
	C. MATHER	**CATHERINE MATHER DOLLS**		
93	JUSTINE	15000	155.00	160.00
	C. WOODIE	**CENTRAL PARK SKATERS**		
91	CENTRAL PARK SKATERS	OP	245.00	250.00
	*	**CHILDREN TO CHERISH**		
91	A GIFT OF BEAUTY	OP	135.00	140.00
91	A GIFT OF INNOCENCE	YR	135.00	140.00
	C.M. ROLFE	**CINDY MARSCHNER ROLFE DOLLS**		
93	JULIE	OP	95.00	100.00
93	KAYLA	OP	95.00	100.00
93	SHANNON	OP	95.00	100.00
94	JANEY	OP	95.00	100.00
	C.W. DEREK	**CONNIE WALSER DEREK BABY DOLLS**		
90	JESSICA	CL	155.00	250.00
91	AMANDA	OP	155.00	160.00
91	ANDREW	OP	155.00	155.00
91	SARA	CL	155.00	185.00
92	SAMANTHA	OP	155.00	160.00
	C.W. DEREK	**CONNIE WALSER DEREK BABY DOLLS II**		
92	BETH	OP	95.00	100.00
92	STEPHANIE	OP	95.00	100.00
	C.W. DEREK	**CONNIE WALSER DEREK DOLLS**		
92	BABY JESSICA	OP	75.00	80.00
93	BABY SARA	OP	75.00	80.00
	M. SNYDER	**DADDY'S LITTLE GIRL**		
92	LINDSAY	OP	95.00	100.00
93	CASSIE	OP	95.00	100.00
93	DANA	OP	95.00	100.00
	C.W. DEREK	**DEREK TODDLERS**		
94	JESSIE	OP	79.00	80.00
	A. BERWICK	**DOLLS BY AUTUMN BERWICK**		
93	LAURA	OP	135.00	140.00
	K. MCKEE	**DOLLS BY KAY MCKEE**		
92	ROBIN	OP	135.00	140.00
92	SHY VIOLET	CL	135.00	205.00
93	KATIE DID IT!	OP	135.00	140.00
93	RYAN	OP	135.00	140.00
	A. ELEKFY	**DOLLS OF AMERICA'S COLONIAL HERITAGE**		
86	KATRINA	OP	55.00	60.00
86	NICOLE	OP	55.00	60.00
87	COLLEEN	OP	55.00	60.00
87	MARIA	OP	55.00	60.00

YR	NAME	LIMIT	ISSUE	TREND
87	PRISCILLA	OP	55.00	60.00
88	GRETCHEN	OP	55.00	60.00
E. CAMPBELL			**ELAINE CAMPBELL DOLLS**	
94	EMMA	OP	95.00	100.00
*			**FIRST RECITAL**	
93	HILLARY	OP	135.00	140.00
94	OLIVIA	OP	135.00	140.00
H. KISH			**HELEN KISH II DOLLS**	
92	VANESSA	OP	135.00	140.00
H. KISH			**HELEN KISH III DOLLS**	
94	JORDAN	OP	95.00	100.00
U. LEPP			**HOLIDAY CAROLLERS**	
92	JOY	OP	155.00	160.00
93	NOEL	OP	155.00	160.00
*			**I LOVE LUCY/PORCELAIN**	
90	LUCY	CL	95.00	225.00
91	RICKY	CL	95.00	280.00
92	QUEEN OF THE GYPSIES	CL	95.00	165.00
92	VITAMEATAVEGAMIN	CL	95.00	125.00
*			**I LOVE LUCY/VINYL**	
88	ETHEL	CL	40.00	185.00
88	FRED	CL	40.00	140.00
90	LUCY	CL	40.00	140.00
91	RICKY	CL	40.00	160.00
92	QUEEN OF THE GYPSIES	OP	40.00	45.00
92	VITAMEATAVEGAMIN	OP	40.00	45.00
L. COBABE			**I'M SO PROUD DOLL COLLECTION**	
92	CHRISTINA	OP	95.00	100.00
93	JILL	OP	95.00	100.00
94	SHELLY	OP	95.00	100.00
94	TAMMY	OP	95.00	100.00
C. WOODIE			**INTERNATIONAL CHILDREN**	
91	ANASTASIA	OP	49.50	50.00
91	ANGELINA	OP	49.50	50.00
91	MIKO	CL	49.50	55.00
92	LIAN	OP	49.50	50.00
92	LISA	OP	49.50	50.00
92	MONIQUE	OP	49.50	50.00
J. ZIDJUNAS			**JANE ZIDJUNAS PARTY DOLLS**	
91	KELLY	OP	135.00	140.00
92	KATIE	OP	135.00	140.00
93	MEREDITH	OP	135.00	140.00
J. ZIDJUNAS			**JANE ZIDJUNAS TODDLER DOLLS**	
91	JENNIFER	OP	135.00	135.00
91	MEGAN	OP	135.00	160.00
92	AMY	OP	135.00	140.00
92	KIMBERLY	OP	135.00	140.00
J. WILSON			**JEANNE WILSON DOLLS**	
94	PRISCILLA	OP	155.00	160.00
C. JOHNSTON			**JOHNSTON COWGIRLS**	
94	SAVANNAH	OP	79.00	80.00
*			**JOIN THE PARADE**	
92	BETSY	OP	49.50	50.00
94	PEGGY	OP	55.00	60.00
94	SANDY	OP	55.00	60.00
J. GROBBEN			**JOKE GROBBEN DOLLS**	
92	HEATHER	OP	69.00	70.00
93	BRIANNA	OP	69.00	70.00
93	KATHLEEN	OP	69.00	70.00
94	BRIDGET	OP	69.00	70.00
H. KISH			**JUST LIKE MOM**	
91	ASHLEY	CL	135.00	230.00
92	ELIZABETH	OP	135.00	140.00
92	HANNAH	OP	135.00	140.00
93	MARGARET	OP	135.00	140.00
K. MCKEE			**KAY MCKEE KLOWNS**	
93	DREAMER, THE	15000	155.00	160.00
S. KUCK			**KUCK FAIRY**	
94	TOOTH FAIRY	OP	135.00	140.00
L. COBABE			**LAURA COBABE DOLLS**	
92	AMBER	OP	195.00	200.00
92	BROOKE	OP	195.00	200.00
L. COBABE			**LAURA COBABE DOLLS II**	
93	KRISTEN	OP	75.00	80.00
L. COBABE			**LAURA COBABE TALL DOLLS**	
94	CASSANDRA	OP	195.00	200.00
94	TAYLOR	OP	195.00	200.00
S./J. HOFFMANN			**LITTLE RASCALS**	
92	SPANKY	OP	75.00	80.00
93	ALFALFA	OP	75.00	80.00
94	BUCKWHEAT	OP	75.00	80.00
94	DARLA	OP	75.00	80.00
94	STYMIE	OP	75.00	80.00
J. ESTEBAN			**LITTLEST MEMBERS OF THE WEDDING**	
93	MATTHEW & MELANIE	OP	195.00	200.00

YR	NAME	LIMIT	ISSUE	TREND
	*	**MAUD HUMPHREY BOGART DOLLS**		
92	PLAYING BRIDESMAID	CL	195.00	230.00
	B. PARKER	**PARKER-LEVI TODDLERS**		
92	COURTNEY	OP	135.00	140.00
92	MELODY	OP	135.00	140.00
	P. PARKINS	**PARKINS PORTRAITS**		
93	KELSEY	OP	79.00	80.00
93	LAUREN	OP	79.00	80.00
94	CASSIDY	OP	79.00	80.00
94	MORGAN	OP	79.00	80.00
	P. PARKER	**PARKINS TREASURES**		
93	CHARLOTTE	OP	55.00	60.00
93	CYNTHIA	OP	55.00	60.00
	P. PARKINS	**PARKINS TREASURES**		
92	DOROTHY	CL	55.00	60.00
92	TIFFANY	CL	55.00	60.00
	P. PARKINS	**PHYLLIS PARKINS DOLLS**		
92	SWAN PRINCESS	9850	195.00	200.00
	J. ESTEBAN	**PICNIC IN THE PARK**		
91	REBECCA	OP	155.00	160.00
92	EMILY	OP	155.00	160.00
92	VICTORIA	OP	155.00	160.00
93	BENJAMIN	OP	155.00	160.00
	*	**PROUD INDIAN NATION**		
92	NAVAJO LITTLE ONE	CL	95.00	180.00
93	AUTUMN TREAT	OP	95.00	100.00
93	DRESSED UP FOR THE POW WOW	OP	95.00	100.00
94	OUT WITH MAMA'S FLOCK	OP	95.00	100.00
	*	**RUSSIAN CZARRA DOLLS**		
91	ALEXANDRA	CL	295.00	350.00
	S. KUCK	**SANDRA KUCK DOLLS**		
93	A KISS GOODNIGHT	OP	79.00	80.00
94	TEACHING TEDDY	OP	79.00	80.00
	C.W. DEREK	**SANTA'S LITTLE HELPER**		
92	NICHOLAS	OP	155.00	160.00
93	HOPE	OP	155.00	160.00
	T. MURAKAMI	**SONGS OF THE SEASONS HAKATA DOLL COLLECTION**		
85	AUTUMN SONG MAIDEN	9800	75.00	80.00
85	SPRING SONG MAIDEN	9800	75.00	80.00
85	SUMMER SONG MAIDEN	9800	75.00	80.00
85	WINTER SONG MAIDEN	9800	75.00	80.00
	E. DAUB	**STAR TREK DOLL COLLECTION**		
88	CAPTAIN KIRK	CL	75.00	125.00
88	MR. SPOCK	CL	75.00	155.00
89	DR. MCCOY	CL	75.00	125.00
89	SCOTTY	CL	75.00	125.00
90	CHEKOV	CL	75.00	125.00
90	SULU	CL	75.00	125.00
91	UHURA	CL	75.00	125.00
	L. DI LEO	**STORYBOOK DOLLS**		
91	ALICE IN WONDERLAND	OP	75.00	80.00
	*	**THE ANTIQUE DOLL COLLECTION**		
89	NICOLE	CL	195.00	195.00
90	COLETTE	OP	195.00	195.00
91	KATRINA	OP	195.00	195.00
91	LISETTE	OP	195.00	230.00
	B.P. GUTMANN	**THE BESSIE PEASE GUTMANN DOLL COLLECTION**		
89	HE WON'T BITE	CL	135.00	135.00
89	LOVE IS BLIND	CL	135.00	165.00
91	FIRST DANCING LESSON	OP	195.00	200.00
91	GOOD MORNING	OP	195.00	200.00
91	LOVE AT FIRST SIGHT	OP	195.00	200.00
91	VIRGINIA	OP	135.00	135.00
	M.H. BOGART	**THE MAUD HUMPHREY BOGART DOLL COLLECTION**		
89	PLAYING BRIDE	CL	135.00	155.00
90	FIRST LESSON, THE	CL	135.00	150.00
90	FIRST PARTY	CL	135.00	140.00
91	LITTLE CAPTIVE	OP	135.00	140.00
91	SEAMSTRESS	CL	135.00	150.00
92	KITTY'S BATH	OP	135.00	140.00
	*	**THE ROYAL BEAUTY DOLLS**		
91	CHEN MAI	OP	195.00	200.00
	V. TURNER	**THROUGH THE EYES OF VIRGINIA TURNER**		
92	DANIELLE	OP	95.00	100.00
92	MICHELLE	CL	95.00	130.00
93	WENDY	OP	95.00	100.00
94	DAWN	OP	95.00	100.00
	D. SCHURIG	**TODDLER DAYS DOLL COLLECTION**		
92	ERICA	OP	95.00	100.00
93	DARLENE	OP	95.00	100.00
94	KAREN	OP	95.00	100.00
	V. TURNER	**TREASURED TODDLERS**		
92	WHITNEY	OP	95.00	100.00
93	NATALIE	OP	95.00	100.00

YR	NAME	LIMIT	ISSUE	TREND
C.W. DEREK				**VICTORIAN TREASURES**
92	KATHERINE	OP	155.00	160.00
93	MADELINE	OP	155.00	160.00
*				**WOODEN DOLLS**
91	GRETCHEN	9850	225.00	280.00
91	HEIDI	9850	225.00	225.00
D. SCHURIG				**YEAR ROUND FUN**
92	ALLISON	OP	95.00	100.00
93	CHRISTY	OP	95.00	100.00
93	PAULA	OP	95.00	100.00
94	KAYLIE	OP	95.00	100.00
D. ZOLAN				**ZOLAN DOLLS**
91	A CHRISTMAS PRAYER	CL	95.00	255.00
92	QUIET TIME	OP	95.00	100.00
92	RAINY DAY PALS	OP	95.00	100.00
92	WINTER ANGEL	OP	95.00	100.00
93	FOR YOU	OP	95.00	100.00
93	THINKER, THE	OP	95.00	100.00
*				**ZOLAN DOUBLE DOLLS**
93	FIRST KISS	OP	135.00	140.00

HAMILTON GIFTS

YR	NAME	LIMIT	ISSUE	TREND
M. HUMPHREY				**MAUD HUMPHREY BOGART PORCELAIN DOLLS**
91	MY FIRST PARTY H5686	OP	135.00	135.00
91	PLAYING BRIDE H5618	OP	135.00	135.00
91	SARAH H5617	OP	37.00	37.00
91	SUSANNA H5648	OP	37.00	37.00

J.S. PERRY ORIGINALS

YR	NAME	LIMIT	ISSUE	TREND
J. ZOOK				
94	CHRISTMAS NOELLE	500	224.00	246.00

JAN HAGARA COLLECTABLES

YR	NAME	LIMIT	ISSUE	TREND
J. HAGARA				
95	ADDIE WITH PRINCESS 23 IN.	85	2000.00	2000.00
95	JOSEPH BLUE 12 IN.	150	250.00	250.00
95	JOSEPH PINK 12 IN.	150	250.00	250.00
95	JUNE 12 IN.	300	250.00	250.00
95	KELTON 8 IN.	300	300.00	300.00
95	MAY 12 IN.	300	250.00	250.00
J. HAGARA				**PHILLIPS COUSINS**
95	DEBRA 15 IN.	250	425.00	425.00
J. HAGARA				**VICTORIAN CHILDREN**
*	ADRIANNE	*	*	198.00
*	AMANDA	*	*	250.00
*	AMY	*	*	125.00
*	ANN MARIE	*	*	420.00
*	ASHLEY	*	*	125.00
*	BONNIE	*	*	450.00
*	CLARA	*	*	475.00
*	CRISTINA	*	*	100.00
*	DACY	*	*	490.00
*	JESSICA	*	*	650.00
*	JIMMY	*	*	200.00
*	JODY	*	*	450.00
*	MATTIE	*	*	400.00
*	MEG	*	*	195.00
*	MICHAEL	*	*	650.00
*	PAIGE	*	*	1200.00
*	SHARICE	*	*	200.00
*	SHELDON	*	*	490.00
*	SHELLEY	*	*	450.00
*	TINA	*	*	420.00
*	TRACY	*	*	135.00

JAN MCLEAN ORIGINALS

YR	NAME	LIMIT	ISSUE	TREND
J. MCLEAN				**FLOWERS OF THE HEART COLLECTION**
90	PANSY	100	2200.00	2700.00
90	POPPY	100	2200.00	2800.00
91	MARIGOLD	100	2400.00	2700.00
91	PRIMROSE	100	2500.00	2900.00
J. MCLEAN				**JAN MCLEAN ORIGINALS**
90	PHOEBE I	25	2700.00	3600.00
91	LUCREZIA	15	6000.00	6000.00
91	LUCREZIA	15	6000.00	6000.00

JOHANNES ZOOK ORIGINALS

YR	NAME	LIMIT	ISSUE	TREND
J. ZOOK				
93	ADRIANNE	500	198.00	240.00
93	ALYSSA	500	204.00	286.00
93	ANGEL GABRIEL	1000	250.00	303.00
93	BREANNA	500	190.00	230.00
93	BROOKE	1000	170.00	206.00
93	CALVIN CLOWN	500	198.00	240.00
93	CANDY CANE	*	164.00	198.00
93	CHRISTMAS CAROL	500	226.00	273.00
93	CLAIRE	1000	194.00	235.00
93	CODY	1000	194.00	235.00

YR	NAME	LIMIT	ISSUE	TREND
93	COLLETTE	500	198.00	240.00
93	DEANNE	100	170.00	206.00
93	DENISE	250	198.00	240.00
93	DIANNA	100	170.00	206.00
93	FRANCESCA	250	220.00	266.00
93	JASMINE	250	252.00	305.00
93	JOEY	500	198.00	240.00
93	KANIKA	1000	220.00	266.00
93	LITTLE MISS MUFFET	500	188.00	227.00
93	MARISSA	1000	170.00	206.00
93	MEREDITH	500	216.00	261.00
93	MONIKA	500	198.00	240.00
93	ROCKY	500	172.00	208.00
93	ROXANNE	500	172.00	208.00
93	SISSY	500	272.00	329.00
93	TOOTH FAIRY	500	198.00	240.00
93	VALERIE	500	240.00	290.00
94	ANALISSA	350	210.00	231.00
94	ANNETTE	100	230.00	253.00
94	ANNIE	25	148.00	163.00
94	ATHENA	500	198.00	218.00
94	BABY ELF	250	198.00	218.00
94	CHERRY	100	114.00	125.00
94	COOKIE	350	170.00	187.00
94	CORY	350	170.00	187.00
94	COWBOY	25	172.00	189.00
94	CYNTHIA	100	194.00	213.00
94	DANIEL BOONE	500	250.00	275.00
94	DANIELLE	500	188.00	207.00
94	EMMY	500	220.00	242.00
94	GOOD NIGHT KISS	500	158.00	174.00
94	GWEN	125	198.00	218.00
94	KAREEM	500	198.00	218.00
94	KATRINA	500	198.00	218.00
94	KAYLA	1000	198.00	218.00
94	LITTLE FEATHER	100	280.00	308.00
94	MELINDA	1000	190.00	209.00
94	MERCEDES	1000	218.00	240.00
94	NURSE BETTE	500	184.00	202.00
94	POLLYANNA	500	198.00	218.00
94	SHARON	1000	190.00	209.00
94	SHAYNA	1000	190.00	209.00
94	SHELLY	100	198.00	218.00
94	SOPHIE	500	198.00	218.00
94	STARR	25	150.00	165.00
94	TRISHA	500	198.00	218.00
95	ANGIE	RT	190.00	190.00
95	BETHANY	RT	210.00	210.00
95	BRENT	RT	230.00	230.00
95	CAROLYN	RT	210.00	210.00
95	CELESTE	RT	230.00	230.00
95	CHRISTINA	RT	398.00	398.00
95	CHRISTMAS TWINS/SET	RT	430.00	430.00
95	DESIREE	RT	198.00	198.00
95	GIANNA	RT	250.00	250.00
95	JAKE	RT	230.00	230.00
95	JARED	RT	198.00	198.00
95	KORTINEE ROSE	RT	218.00	218.00
95	LESLIE	RT	198.00	198.00
95	LIL DEVIL	RT	200.00	200.00
95	LIZZY	RT	198.00	198.00
95	MARY JO	RT	190.00	190.00
95	MYCELLE	RT	170.00	170.00
95	NANCY MAY	RT	190.00	190.00
95	NATALIE & NATHAN/SET	RT	398.00	398.00
95	NICHOLETTE	RT	210.00	210.00
95	PAIGE	RT	210.00	210.00
95	PAMELA SUE	RT	210.00	210.00
95	PENNY	RT	240.00	240.00
95	PRESTON	RT	290.00	290.00
95	SCARECROW	RT	290.00	290.00
95	SIERRA	RT	210.00	210.00
95	SNOW BONNY	RT	198.00	198.00
95	TREVOR	RT	180.00	180.00
96	ARIEL	RT	212.00	212.00
96	AUSTIN	RT	394.00	394.00
96	BRANDON & BREA/SET	RT	374.00	374.00
96	BRENNAN	RT	190.00	190.00
96	CHRIS	RT	198.00	198.00
96	CHRISTMAS BELLE	RT	308.00	308.00
96	CORJASHON	RT	190.00	190.00
96	DOTTIE	RT	198.00	198.00
96	GINA	RT	220.00	220.00
96	HALEY	500	234.00	234.00
96	JAMAL	250	216.00	216.00
96	JANEA	500	224.00	224.00
96	JUAN	500	190.00	190.00
96	KATY	500	198.00	198.00
96	KEIKO	500	190.00	190.00

YR	NAME	LIMIT	ISSUE	TREND
96	KEITH	250	212.00	212.00
96	KELSEY	1000	270.00	270.00
96	KEVIN	1000	246.00	246.00
96	LABRETT	500	212.00	212.00
96	LEXUS	150	346.00	346.00
96	LINDA	250	202.00	202.00
96	MAGGIE	250	214.00	214.00
96	MARIKO	500	212.00	212.00
96	PHOENIX	1000	256.00	256.00
96	SCOTTIE	500	170.00	170.00
96	SHASTIN	500	212.00	212.00
96	TOMMY	500	206.00	206.00
J. ZOOK				**AMISH SERIES**
93	JACOB	500	158.00	191.00
94	GRACE	500	220.00	242.00
95	RUTH	RT	190.00	190.00
96	DAVID	RT	164.00	164.00
J. ZOOK				**CAREER SERIES**
94	FIREMAN GREG	250	224.00	224.00
95	POLICEMAN GABE	RT	230.00	230.00
96	TEACHER LADY	500	284.00	284.00
J. ZOOK				**CHILDREN OF THE NATION**
94	AMERICA	500	188.00	207.00
95	NANOOK OF THE NORTH	RT	220.00	220.00
96	PIA	1000	210.00	210.00
J. ZOOK				**EXCLUSIVE FOR IDEX**
96	ANNABETH	50	198.00	198.00
J. ZOOK				**EXCLUSIVE FOR SHOW**
95	CHERISH	RT	165.00	165.00
95	KATARINA	RT	230.00	230.00
J. ZOOK				**EXCLUSIVE FOR STORE**
95	BABY DARLING	RT	199.00	199.00
95	BABY DEAR	RT	199.00	199.00
95	BABY PRECIOUS	RT	199.00	199.00
95	SCARLETT	RT	199.00	199.00
J. ZOOK				**EXCLUSIVE FOR TOY FAIR**
95	ROSEMARY	RT	240.00	240.00
96	CHANTEL	250	270.00	270.00
J. ZOOK				**FLOWER**
95	SUNFLOWER	RT	220.00	220.00
96	PANSY	1000	274.00	271.00
J. ZOOK				**HALLOWEEN SERIES**
93	TOMMY TURTLE	150	300.00	363.00
94	DONIE DINOSAUR	150	250.00	275.00
94	HERBIE HOLSTEIN	150	250.00	275.00
J. ZOOK				**STORYBOOK LINE**
93	LITTLE RED RIDING HOOD	1000	244.00	295.00
94	GOLDILOCKS & BABY BEAR	350	254.00	279.00
95	CINDERELLA	RT	270.00	270.00
96	HEIDI	1000	254.00	254.00

KAISER

*

YR	NAME	LIMIT	ISSUE	TREND
90	AMANDA, 17 IN.	1000	74.00	82.00
90	AMY, 19 IN.	1000	98.00	106.00
90	ANN, 24 IN.	1000	128.00	138.00
90	ASHLEY, 19 IN.	1000	98.00	106.00
90	ELIZABETH, 19 IN.	1000	98.00	106.00
90	HEATHER, 22 IN.	1000	116.00	126.00
90	JENNIFER, 22 IN.	1000	116.00	126.00
90	JESSICA, 22 IN.	1000	116.00	126.00
90	JILL, 24 IN.	1000	128.00	138.00
90	KELLY, 19 IN.	1000	98.00	106.00
90	KRISTY, 24 IN.	1000	128.00	138.00
90	LAURA, 24 IN.	1000	128.00	138.00
90	NEWBORN/CHRISTENING DRESS, 17 IN.	1000	74.00	82.00
90	NICOLE, 17 IN.	1000	74.00	82.00
90	SARAH, 22 IN.	1000	116.00	126.00
90	SUSAN, 17 IN.	1000	74.00	82.00

KURT S. ADLER/SANTA'S WORLD

YR	NAME	LIMIT	ISSUE	TREND
J. MOSTROM				**ROYAL HERITAGE COLLECTION**
93	ANASTASIA J5746	3000	125.00	125.00
93	GOOD KING WENCESLAS W2928	2000	130.00	130.00
93	MEDIEVAL KING OF CHRISTMAS W2981	RT	390.00	400.00
94	NICHOLAS ON SKATES J5750	3000	120.00	120.00
94	SASHA ON SKATES J5749	3000	130.00	130.00
J. MOSTROM				**SMALL WONDERS**
95	AMERICA-HOLLIE BLUE W3162	OP	30.00	30.00
95	AMERICA-TEXAS TYLER W3162	OP	30.00	30.00
95	IRELAND-CATHLEEN W3082	OP	28.00	28.00
95	IRELAND-MICHAEL W3082	OP	28.00	28.00
95	KWANZA-MUFARO W3161	OP	28.00	28.00
95	KWANZA-SHANI W3161	OP	28.00	28.00
J. MOSTROM				**WHEN I GROW UP**
95	DR. BROWN W3079	OP	27.00	27.00
95	FREDDY THE FIREMAN W3163	OP	28.00	28.00

YR	NAME	LIMIT	ISSUE	TREND
95	MELISSA THE TEACHER W3081	OP	28.00	28.00
95	NURSE NANCY W3079	OP	27.00	27.00
95	SCOTT THE GOLFER W3080	OP	28.00	28.00

L.L. KNICKERBOCKER CO. INC.

YR	NAME	LIMIT	ISSUE	TREND
	M. COSTA			
92	DIANA/BLOWING DANDELIONS C11246	1500	117.00	117.00
	A. JACKSON			
93	ALYSSA/GIRL ON SWING C1974	2500	158.00	158.00
*			**ANNETTE FUNICELLO BEARS**	
95	MARY LOU	5000	26.00	26.00
95	SILVER LINING	5000	29.00	29.00
	L. APPLEBERRY		**ANNETTE FUNICELLO BEARS**	
96	EMMY	2500	49.50	50.00
96	PEACH FUZZ	2500	29.00	29.00
	C. BLACK		**ANNETTE FUNICELLO BEARS**	
95	GRAPE SUZETTE	2500	34.95	35.00
95	TIZZIE TEA CUP	3000	45.00	45.00
96	CHUBS	1500	59.00	59.00
96	SHELLY	2500	39.00	39.00
96	STRAWBERRY JAM	2500	39.00	39.00
	G. BUTTITTA		**ANNETTE FUNICELLO BEARS**	
95	CELESTE	YR	119.00	119.00
96	MITZI	500	49.00	49.00
96	PRECIOUS & BAILEY	2500	46.00	46.00
96	VIRGINIA	1500	49.00	49.00
	K. CLARKE		**ANNETTE FUNICELLO BEARS**	
95	DOLLY	2500	49.00	49.00
95	RUDY	3000	24.95	25.00
95	SHARON	2500	47.00	47.00
96	BAD HAIR BEAR	3000	39.00	39.00
96	KAREN	1500	46.25	47.00
96	NIKKI	2500	49.50	50.00
	L. DEMERIT		**ANNETTE FUNICELLO BEARS**	
96	FAITH	YR	119.00	119.00
	J. HAUGHEY		**ANNETTE FUNICELLO BEARS**	
96	CHERYL ANN	2500	59.00	59.00
96	JILL ANGEL	20000	19.95	20.00
	L. HENRY		**ANNETTE FUNICELLO BEARS**	
96	CONTRARY MARY	1500	49.00	49.00
	B. KING		**ANNETTE FUNICELLO BEARS**	
95	3RD ANNIVERARY	3000	44.00	44.00
95	CARMELLA	2500	46.00	46.00
95	GABRIELLE	20000	39.00	39.00
95	ROSIE	5000	34.95	35.00
96	4TH ANNIVERSARY	400	44.00	44.00
96	ANGEL HEART	2000	59.00	59.00
96	BAMBINA	20000	29.00	29.00
	E. KISLINGBURY		**ANNETTE FUNICELLO BEARS**	
96	SAILOR SAM	1500	49.00	49.00
96	WINDY	2500	39.00	39.00
	C. ORLANDO		**ANNETTE FUNICELLO BEARS**	
95	JOEY & JOANNE	1500	50.00	50.00
	H. STODDARD		**ANNETTE FUNICELLO BEARS**	
96	PEACHES & CREAM	2500	59.00	59.00
	S. SWENSON		**ANNETTE FUNICELLO BEARS**	
96	OZZIE	2000	44.00	44.00
*				**ANNIVERSARY**
95	75TH ANNIVERSARY HOUSE	YR	125.00	125.00
95	BLUE BERRY	YR	49.95	50.00
95	CINNAMON	YR	36.95	37.00
95	JOY	YR	39.95	40.00
95	MERRY	YR	49.95	50.00
95	NUTMEG	YR	59.95	60.00
95	PIPPI	YR	36.95	37.00
95	ROSIE	YR	29.95	30.00
95	SHAGGY	YR	24.95	25.00
95	SQUEAKY	YR	29.95	30.00
	C. ORLANDO			**BEACH PARTY**
94	DEDE C15004	10000	29.00	29.00
*				**BEAN BAG**
94	HOLLYWOOD STAR C12880	5000	29.75	30.00
	A. FUNICELLO			**BEAN BAG**
93	CLEMENTINE C4735	2500	26.00	26.00
	C. ORLANDO			**BEARS BUDDIES**
94	PUPPY LUV C15006	2500	46.25	47.00
	J. HAUGHEY			**BEARS ON PARADE**
*	CLOWN #2 C9658	5000	79.50	80.00
*	LITTLE MAJORETTE C9659	YR	39.50	40.00
*	POM POM GIRL C9657	5000	59.50	60.00
92	MARINE C11513	604	47.50	48.00
92	NAVY C11512	604	47.50	48.00
93	ARMY C4756	2500	47.50	48.00
94	AIR FORCE C8146	2500	52.00	52.00
	B. MCCONNELL			**BEARS ON PARADE**
*	APRIL C9661-765	YR	49.50	50.00

Elegantly attired, Madame Du Pompadour *is a majestic beauty. She was created by doll artist Eda Mann and produced by Seymour Mann Inc.*

Cherubic in every way, Merriel *was Gorham's 1992 Christmas Angel.*

Rock a bye baby! Lullaby, *by one of today's most versatile artists, is the second issue in Sandra Kuck's "Precious Memories of Motherhood" collection. Produced by Reco.*

Allison *was the first limited edition doll in the Gorham Doll collection. Dated 1982 and numbered by hand in gold, the edition was limited to 1,000 dolls. The original price of $350 has been eclipsed by the current value of $4,700 - $4,900.*

YR	NAME	LIMIT	ISSUE	TREND
*	AUGUST C9661-769	YR	49.50	50.00
*	DECEMBER C9661-773	YR	49.50	50.00
*	FEBRUARY C9661-763	YR	49.50	50.00
*	JANUARY C9661-762	YR	49.50	50.00
*	JULY C9661-768	YR	49.50	50.00
*	JUNE C9661-767	YR	49.50	50.00
*	LITTLE LADY/LIAC C9673	YR	79.50	80.00
*	MARCH C9661-764	YR	49.50	50.00
*	MAY C9661-766	YR	49.50	49.50
*	NOVEMBER C9661-772	YR	49.50	50.00
*	OCTOBER C9661-771	YR	49.50	50.00
*	SEPTEMBER C9661-770	YR	49.50	50.00
M. NICOLE				**BEST FRIENDS**
92	ERIN/GIRL W/BUNNY C9635	2500	178.50	179.00
92	GEORGIA/GIRL W/KITTEN C9637	2500	179.00	179.00
92	HILLARY/GIRL W/DUCKS C9636	2500	178.50	179.00
J. MOWRY				**CHILDREN OF THE WORLD**
94	TOMIKA/ESKIMO C13710	2500	198.50	200.00
95	BONNIE JEAN C15218	2500	124.00	124.00
J. ARNETT				**CHRISTMAS**
94	FATHER CHRISTMAS '94 C13427	1000	313.00	313.00
C. BELLSMITH				**CHRISTMAS**
94	BRYANNA C14515	7500	149.25	150.00
R. SCHMIDT				**CHRISTMAS**
92	BRYANNA/GREEN VELVET C11240	1000	183.00	183.00
D. STEWART				**CHRISTMAS**
93	HOLLY/BEAN BAG/MUSIC C2086	2500	114.00	114.00
C./L. WAUGH				**CHRISTMAS**
94	KRIS-XMAS C8329	2500	89.00	89.00
B. MCCONNELL				**CIRCUS**
93	TRIXI-ELELPHANT C4755	2500	69.50	70.00
V. DEFILIPPO				**CLASSICAL BEAUTIES**
93	JULIA C11395	2500	169.00	169.00
93	PRISCILLIA/DRESSED IN PEACH C11385	2500	146.50	147.00
95	NATALIE C14829	2500	154.00	154.00
P. PARKINS				**CLASSICS**
93	ALESIA/BLACK BRIDE USA C11384	250	590.00	590.00
C. ROBINSON				**CLASSICS**
95	LAUREN C15216	500	436.00	436.00
*				**COFFEE CLUB**
94	HOLLYWOOD STAR C15002	OP	21.95	22.00
C. ROBINSON				**COLLECTIBLES**
95	MORGAN C15904	1500	155.00	155.00
D. STEWART				**COLLECTIBLES**
94	BUNNY LOVE C10941	2500	45.50	46.00
94	BUNNY LOVE CHRISTMAS C14642	2500	54.00	54.00
94	TUSH/CRAWLING BABY C10944	2500	76.50	77.00
95	BUNNY LOVE 1995 C15893	8000	41.00	41.00
95	SOME BUNNY LOVES YOU C15226	2500	45.00	45.00
G. LANGFORD				**COUNTRY**
94	COWBOY GLEN C8147	2500	127.00	127.00
M. NICOLE				**COUNTRY GIRL**
92	SARAH/DRESSED IN BLUE C9639	2500	159.00	159.00
92	SARITA/DRESSED IN PURPLE C9638	2500	159.00	159.00
A. FUNICELLO				**CUTE & CUDDLY**
93	TAMMY C12199	2000	39.50	40.00
G. LANGFORD				**CUTE & CUDDLY**
94	NOELLE C8188	2500	39.50	40.00
C./L. WAUGH				**CUTE & CUDDLY**
94	KASEY C8150	2500	69.00	69.00
C. BELLSMITH				**DEAR TO MY HEART**
92	OZEANNA/GERMAN ORIGIN C10414	2500	120.00	120.00
M. NICOLE				**DEAR TO MY HEART**
92	BRETA/DRESSED IN PEACH C9633	2500	115.00	115.00
92	GERRI/DRESSED IN MINT GRN. C9634	2500	115.00	115.00
92	TAMMY/DRESSED IN MAUVE C9632	2500	115.00	115.00
*				**ELEGANCE**
94	JOHNNY C12882	1500	108.50	109.00
B. MCCONNELL				**ELEGANCE**
*	CYNTHIA C9686	2500	149.50	150.00
J. OPENSHAW				**FAIRY TALE**
94	ALICE IN WONDERLAND C13706	5000	149.50	150.00
B. STOEHR				**FAIRY TALE**
93	SNOW WHITE C11397	5000	177.50	178.00
B. MCCONNELL				**FAMILY HELPERS**
*	JOSIE/MAMA IN KITCHEN C9687	2500	149.50	150.00
C./L. WAUGH				**FLAVORTIE**
94	CAROL C12881	1500	74.50	75.00
V. DEFILIPPO				**FOUR SEASON**
93	AMBER/FALL C11380	2500	188.00	188.00
B. MCCONNELL				**FOUR SEASONS**
*	DAISY C9694	2500	109.50	110.00
C. ROBINSON				**FOUR SEASONS**
94	SUZANNE 13882	1500	95.00	95.00

YR	NAME	LIMIT	ISSUE	TREND
	D. STEWART	**FOUR SEASONS SMALL WONDERS**		
94	SMALL WONDERS C12860	4000	56.00	56.00
95	WINTER WONDER C15224	4000	61.00	61.00
	B. FINLINSON	**GREETING CARDS**		
95	EASTER C15753	YR	25.00	25.00
95	VALENTINE C15225	YR	25.00	25.00
	D. STEWART	**GREETING CARDS**		
93	CHRISTMAS '93 C6483	YR	25.00	25.00
93	MOTHER'S DAY '93/DRESSED IN PINK C11945	20000	25.00	25.00
94	ALL OCCASION '94 C10943	YR	25.00	25.00
94	CHRISTMAS '94 C14645	YR	28.50	29.00
94	VALENTINE '94 C10942	YR	25.00	25.00
95	MOTHER'S DAY '95 C15754	YR	25.00	25.00
	M. YOKEE	**GREETING CARDS**		
94	LIANA C12862	2500	150.00	150.00
*		**HARLEQUIN**		
94	HARLEY C12886	1500	98.50	99.00
	B. MCCONNELL	**HARLEQUIN**		
*	HARLEGUIN C9692	2500	99.50	100.00
*	HARLEQUIN C9691	2500	139.50	140.00
	*** STEWART/GRIFFITH**	**HAT BOX**		
93	VIRGINIA MARIE/BRIDE C11902	3000	135.00	135.00
*		**HERMANN FACTORY**		
*	FATER C9683	1000	229.50	230.00
	D. CRYSTAL	**I CAN DREAM**		
94	PLAYING MOMMY C13714	YR	47.00	47.00
	V. DEFILIPPO	**INJURED**		
92	CHELSEA/HURT LEG C11250	5000	91.50	92.00
92	DOTTIE/CHICKEN POX C11252	5000	89.00	89.00
93	MACIE/HOSPITAL GOWN C11381	5000	87.50	88.00
93	SAVANNAH/SNIFFLES C11907	5000	92.50	96.00
	M. NICOLE	**INJURED**		
92	MCKENSIE/WOUNDED FINGER C9631	5000	88.00	88.00
	B. STOEHR	**JESSICA'S BEST FRIENDS**		
94	ANGELICA XMAS C14644	5000	228.00	228.00
94	ANGELICA/LAVENDER DRESS C13201	5000	199.50	200.00
	C. BELLSMITH	**LARGE TRUNK**		
92	TRICIA/TRAVEL THEME C10405	2500	277.00	277.00
	B. MACKIE	**LEGENDARY BEAUTIES**		
95	SPRING	10000	299.50	300.00
96	AUTUMN	10000	300.00	300.00
*		**MARIE OSMOND FINE PORCELAIN**		
95	A CHILD'S SONG	1995	25.00	25.00
95	COLLECTOR CARD	10000	12.00	12.00
95	OLIVE MAY	20000	180.00	180.00
95	STORYBOOK CASSETTE	1995	17.00	17.00
	C. BELLSMITH	**MARIE OSMOND FINE PORCELAIN**		
95	GOLDILOCKS	1994	48.00	48.00
95	PRINCESS AND THE PEA	1995	50.00	50.00
96	BEAUTY AND THE BEAST	1996	49.00	49.00
96	THUMBELINA	1995	49.00	48.00
	D. CRYSTAL	**MARIE OSMOND FINE PORCELAIN**		
96	PLAYING DOCTOR	1996	*	*
	V. DE FILLPPO	**MARIE OSMOND FINE PORCELAIN**		
95	NATALIE	2500	154.00	154.00
	B. FILINSON	**MARIE OSMOND FINE PORCELAIN**		
95	BIRTHDAY	1995	25.00	25.00
95	CONNIE	3000	43.50	44.00
95	EASTER	1995	25.00	25.00
95	VALENTINE '95	1995	25.00	25.00
96	AMANDA	3000	45.00	45.00
96	AMY KATHLYN	5000	213.00	213.00
96	BRUHILDA	5000	45.00	45.00
96	HANNAH	300	55.00	55.00
96	KAREN	2500	*	*
96	LYDIA	3000	*	*
96	VALENTINE	1996	25.00	25.00
	L. HATCH	**MARIE OSMOND FINE PORCELAIN**		
96	CINDERELLA	5000	15.00	*
	L. HENRY	**MARIE OSMOND FINE PORCELAIN**		
95	BLOSSOM BUNNY	5000	117.50	118.00
95	KELLY	5000	79.00	79.00
95	KRISTI	5000	117.00	117.00
95	SANTA BUNNY	5000	156.00	156.00
96	ALEXANDRA	1500	168.00	168.00
96	FUZZY BABY & HARIET	5000	*	*
96	JULIENNE RABBIT	5000	124.00	124.00
96	QUEEN BEE	7500	91.00	91.00
96	TATIANA	1500	*	*
	J. MOWRY	**MARIE OSMOND FINE PORCELAIN**		
95	BONNIE JEAN	2500	124.00	124.00
95	SPRING	5000	219.00	219.00
95	USHA	2500	142.00	142.00
96	RAPUNZEL	5000	170.00	170.00
96	SUNFLOWER	3000	39.00	39.00

YR	NAME	LIMIT	ISSUE	TREND
M. OSMOND		**MARIE OSMOND FINE PORCELAIN**		
96	DAISY	7500	249.00	249.00
96	DARLA	30	140.00	140.00
96	DENISE	1996	*	*
96	GEORGETTE	2500	170.00	170.00
96	I LOVE YOU BEARY MUCH	20000	193.00	193.00
96	MARTA	5000	98.00	98.00
96	MOTHER'S DAY GREETING CARD	50000	*	*
96	NIKKI	3000	42.00	42.00
96	WENDY	3000	*	*
C. ROBINSON		**MARIE OSMOND FINE PORCELAIN**		
95	GRANDMA KIT	500	456.00	456.00
95	LAUREN	500	436.00	436.00
95	MORGAN	1500	155.00	155.00
95	SOPHIA	2500	140.00	140.00
96	AUDREY	500	496.00	496.00
96	BABY RENEE	5000	200.00	200.00
96	MISTY ROSE	5000	46.00	46.00
96	MORGAN 1996	1500	156.00	156.00
96	ROSA LEIGH	1500	155.00	155.00
*** SCHMIDT/BELLSMITH**		**MARIE OSMOND FINE PORCELAIN**		
95	BRYANNA '95	3500	179.00	179.00
C. SHAFER		**MARIE OSMOND FINE PORCELAIN**		
96	CISSY	2500	136.00	136.00
96	FAITH	2500	150.00	150.00
96	SHELBY	5000	*	*
*** SHAFER/TURNER**		**MARIE OSMOND FINE PORCELAIN**		
95	GENNE	2500	342.00	342.00
D. STEWART		**MARIE OSMOND FINE PORCELAIN**		
95	BUNNY LOVE '95	8000	11.00	11.00
95	CHRISTMAS '95	1995	225.00	25.00
95	FALLIN LEAVER	4000	58.00	58.00
95	FIRST KISS	2500	137.00	137.00
95	MILLY	3000	55.00	55.00
95	MOTHER'S DAY '95	1995	25.00	25.00
95	POINSETTA	3000	41.00	41.00
95	SOME BUNNY LOVES U	2500	45.00	45.00
95	SUMMERY DAYS	4000	63.00	63.00
95	WINTER WONDER	4000	61.00	61.00
96	BUNNY LOVE CHERUB	5000	45.00	45.00
96	TEA CUP TREASURES	3000	60.00	60.00
B. STOCKER		**MARIE OSMOND FINE PORCELAIN**		
95	TREE TOP ANGEL	2500	186.00	186.00
B. STOEHR		**MARIE OSMOND FINE PORCELAIN**		
95	ASHEY	5000	195.50	196.00
95	BABY BEVERLY	5000	178.00	178.00
95	JINGLES & BELLE	15000	93.00	93.00
95	MOLLY	5000	134.50	135.00
95	POLLY PUMPKIN	3000	47.00	47.00
95	WATCH CASE DOLL	1995	66.50	67.00
96	ANGELICA'S	5000	180.00	180.00
96	BABY MARIE	5000	*	*
96	BABY MARIE - VINY;	2500	198.00	198.00
96	HANSEL & GRETY;	5000	206.00	206.00
96	MINDY	2000	234.00	234.00
96	MIRACLE ROSIE & RAGS	15000	121.00	121.00
96	STEPHEN	5000	235.00	235.00
96	STITCHIN STACY	5000	113.00	113.00
M. YOKEE		**MARIE OSMOND FINE PORCELAIN**		
96	CHRISSY	5000	175.00	175.00
96	KIM	5000	163.00	163.00
C. BELLSMITH			**MIRACLE CHILDREN**	
92	FRENDA/NEEDLEPOINT C10409	YR	91.50	92.00
92	GINA/HALLOWEEN CAT C10411	YR	88.00	88.00
93	FAITH/FLYING A KITE C1988	YR	76.50	77.00
94	BECKY/DADDY'S GIRL/BASEBALL C12857	YR	76.00	76.00
94	CAITLIN & BENTLY/GIRL W/DOG C12856	YR	79.00	79.00
S. BLACKALL			**MIRACLE CHILDREN**	
92	MARILYN/PLAYING DRESS-UP C11251	YR	83.50	84.00
93	AARON/GROOM C11364	YR	75.50	76.00
93	CODY/PLAYING PIRATE C11379	YR	80.00	80.00
L. HENRY			**MIRACLE CHILDREN**	
94	CELESTE/DRESSED LIKE AN ANGEL C14641	YR	82.00	82.00
L./B. HENRY/FINLINSON			**MIRACLE CHILDREN**	
94	TRACI/DEAF-SIGNING C13113	20000	82.00	82.00
M. NICOLE			**MIRACLE CHILDREN**	
92	BETTY/BAKING A CAKE C10413	YR	69.50	70.00
92	COURTNIE/CLOWN BABY C9627	YR	69.50	70.00
92	DANIELLE/LITTLE BALLERINA C9626	YR	69.50	70.00
92	LINDA/NO WINDOWS C10412	YR	74.00	74.00
92	PIERRE/LITTLE PICASSO C9629	YR	69.50	70.00
92	SHANNON/LITTLE NURSE C9628	YR	69.50	70.00
92	SHAWN/BORN TO SHOP C9630	YR	69.50	70.00
D. STEWART			**MIRACLE CHILDREN**	
93	ANNIE/GIRL ON BIKE C11911	YR	74.50	75.00
93	FLORA/WEDDING THEME C11910	YR	79.50	80.00

YR	NAME	LIMIT	ISSUE	TREND
93	MEKEL/PICNIC W/TEDDY C11909	YR	84.75	85.00
94	MOTHER'S DAY '94 C12863	YR	25.00	25.00
94	TINA/GIRL PLAYING C13711	YR	116.50	116.50
	D. STEWART			**MOTHER CHILD**
94	VIRGINIA & JORDAN C13735	3000	179.00	179.00
	S. & R. FOSKEY			**MUSICAL**
94	JOLLY C12883	2500	53.50	54.00
	M. NICOLE			**MUSICAL**
92	EMILY/MUSICAL SEWING C9640	2500	110.00	110.00
*				**NEW GENERATION**
95	BUZZ	2500	29.75	30.00
96	ANGELIQUE	5000	69.00	69.00
96	BAMBOO	2500	59.00	59.00
96	GULLIVER	5000	24.95	25.00
96	NICK	2500	75.00	75.00
*				**NOSTALGIC**
94	THORNEY C12887	2500	69.50	70.00
	K. CLARKE			**NOSTALGIC**
94	LITTLE JOE 13877	3000	49.00	49.00
	S. FOSKEY			**NOSTALGIC**
*	BERNIE C9676	2500	59.50	60.00
*	BROWNIE C9678	2500	129.50	130.00
*	MOLLIE C9677	2500	69.50	70.00
	A. FUNICELLO			**NOSTALGIC**
94	DAPPER DAN C8194	1500	72.00	72.00
	J. HAUGHEY			**NOSTALGIC**
94	HEINZ 13878	2500	100.00	100.00
	D. STEWART			**PETITE AMOUR**
93	GOLDIE/GIRL W/BEAR C11905	3000	48.50	49.00
94	ANITA C12858	3000	41.00	41.00
94	CHRISTMAS DARLINGS '94 C13428	4000	152.00	152.00
	B. STOEHR			**PETITE AMOUR**
94	GRETL C13200	3000	51.00	51.00
	C. BELLSMITH			**PICTURE DAY**
93	CAMILLE/DRESSED IN PINK C10406	2500	216.00	216.00
93	CAROLINE/DRESSED IN RED VELVET C10407	2500	220.00	220.00
	L. HENRY			**PICTURE DAY**
94	LITTLE RED RIDING HOOD C12861	5000	199.50	200.00
*				**POP UP BOOKS**
96	CHRISTOPHER COLUMBUS	5000	29.95	30.00
*				**RAGGEDY ANN & ANDY**
96	RAGGEDY ANN & ANDY 12 IN. PORCELAIN	2500	79.95	80.00
96	RAGGEDY ANN & ANDY 6 IN. RAG	2500	29.95	30.00
	C./L. WAUGH			**RUSSIAN**
*	ARTYOM/BABY C9681	5000	39.50	40.00
*	MIKHAIL/BROTHER C9679	5000	69.50	70.00
*	POLINA/SISTER C9680	5000	69.50	70.00
94	DMITRI C8281	2500	43.50	44.00
	J. MITCHELL			**SCRAPBOOK**
*	BALLERINA C9695	2500	145.00	145.00
*	LET IN SNOW SNOWMAN C9698	5000	89.50	90.00
*	LET IT SNOW ANNETTE C9697	5000	145.00	145.00
*	MASQUERADE C9696	5000	145.00	145.00
*	SADDLING UP C9700	5000	79.50	80.00
*	WESTERN ROUND UP C9699	5000	145.00	145.00
	D. STEWART			**SMALL TRUNK**
93	VANESSA C11386	2500	198.00	198.00
	J. HOLLENBRANDS			**SOMEWHERE IN TIME**
94	ELEANOR C14755	2500	212.00	212.00
*				**SPECIAL**
94	PEANUT BUTTER C15724	800	69.50	70.00
	K. CLARKE			**SPECIAL**
94	MARION C15005	1500	46.25	47.00
	A. FUNICELLO			**SPECIAL**
93	NO NO NANNETTE C4736	2500	62.00	62.00
	J. HAUGHEY			**SPECIAL**
94	TAPESTRY BEAR PURSE 13881	1500	57.00	57.00
	B. KING			**SPECIAL**
94	GUARDIAN ANGEL BEAR C14282	10000	29.25	30.00
94	I LOVE YOU 14143	10000	40.00	40.00
	B. MCCONNELL			**SPECIAL**
*	ANETTE MOUSKEBEAR C9674	7500	79.50	80.00
*	BOBBY MOUSKEBEAR C9675	7500	79.50	80.00
*	HUGO W/JUNGLE BELLS C9690	2500	149.00	149.00
*	SKIPPER C9689	2500	149.00	149.00
94	NO NO NANETTE C4736	2500	62.00	62.00
	J. MITCHELL			**SPECIAL**
94	MIKEY C8214	1000	71.00	71.00
	C./L. WAUGH			**SPECIAL**
94	MEL C12885	2500	66.50	67.00
	C. BELLSMITH			**STORY BOOK**
93	JULIETTE/MAGIC FERRIS WHEEL C10404	2500	121.50	122.00
94	LITTLE BO PEEP C13708	YR	49.50	50.00
94	LITTLE RED RIDING HOOD C13199	YR	48.00	48.00

YR	NAME	LIMIT	ISSUE	TREND
*				**SWEATER**
94	JESSICA C9685	2500	39.50	40.00
94	JOSHUA 13879	2500	41.00	41.00
	A. FUNICELLO			**SWEATER**
92	GINNY C11515	604	39.50	40.00
	G. LANGFORD			**SWEATER**
93	LITTLE NICK-X-MAS C4728	5000	54.50	55.00
	B. MCCONNELL			**SWEATER**
*	JESSICA/BABY C9685	2500	39.50	40.00
*	UNCLE TEDDY C9684	2500	129.50	130.00
92	JESSICA C9685	2500	39.50	40.00
	D. STEWART			**SWEET DREAMS**
93	OLIVIA/BABY ON PILLOW C11904	2500	93.00	93.00
94	SWEET DREAMS BABY/ON MOON C12859	2500	89.50	90.00
	G. LANGFORD			**SWEET PRESERVES**
94	SWEET GINA C8324	2500	138.50	139.00
	B. MCCONNELL			**SWEET PRESERVES**
*	FLORA C9693	2500	119.50	120.00
*				**T-SHIRT**
94	AF T-SHIRT A22433	*	21.75	22.00
*				**TEDDY BEAR PICNIC/HERMANN FACTORY**
*	MUSICAL C9682	1000	299.50	299.50
	V. DEFILIPPO			**TODDLER**
92	JESSICA/1ST BIRTHDAY C10415	2500	249.00	249.00
92	RACHAEL/MARIE'S DAUGHTER C11254	2500	219.00	219.00
93	JESSICA/CHRISTMAS C6508	5000	249.00	500.00
	J. HOLLEBRANDS			**TODDLER**
93	DEBBIE/DONNY'S DAUGHTER C11244	2500	262.00	262.00
	B. STOEHR			**TODDLER**
95	ASHLEY C15217	2500	195.50	196.00
	A. JACKSON			**TWIN**
93	NATHAN/BOY IN AQUA C11382	2000	104.00	104.00
93	NICOLE/GIRL IN AQUA C11383	2000	137.00	137.00
	M. NICOLE			**TWIN**
92	ANDY & SON/COUNTRY C9641	2500	190.00	190.00
	D. STEWART			**TWIN**
93	JENNY & JASON/CABBAGE PATCH C11430	5000	172.50	172.50
	B. STOEHR			**TWINS**
94	MOPSY C13202	5000	104.00	104.00
94	RAGS C13202	5000	104.00	104.00
	C.-L. WAUGH			**VALENTINE**
92	CANDI C11511	604	75.00	75.00
	B. MCCONNELL			**VARSITY**
*	SWEATER GIRL C9688	2500	79.00	79.00
	L. HENRY			**VELVETEEN RABBIT**
92	VELVET/WHITE PLUSH FUR C11245	5000	121.50	122.00
93	ROBBIE RABBIT C11363	5000	149.50	150.00
94	HARELOOM BUNNY C10940	5000	125.50	124.00
94	ROSEMARIE RABBIT/BRIDE W/MASK C13198	20000	149.50	150.00
95	BLOSSOM BUNNY C15739	5000	117.75	118.00

LADIE & FRIENDS

YR	NAME	LIMIT	ISSUE	TREND
	B.K. WISBER			**LIZZIE HIGH SOCIETY MEMBERS ONLY**
93	AUDREY HIGH 1301	CL	59.00	60.00
93	BECKY HIGH 1330	CL	96.00	100.00
94	CHLOE VALENTINE	OP	79.00	79.00
	B.K. WISBER			**THE CHRISTMAS CONCERT**
90	CLAIRE VALENTINE 1262	OP	56.00	56.00
92	JUDITH HIGH 1292	OP	70.00	70.00
93	JAMES VALENTINE 1310	OP	60.00	60.00
93	STEPHANIE BOWMAN 1309	OP	74.00	74.00
	B.K. WISBER			**THE CHRISTMAS PAGEANT**
85	IN.EARTH IN. ANGEL 1122	CL	30.00	110.00
85	IN.NOEL IN. ANGEL 1ST EDITION 1126	CL	30.00	110.00
85	IN.ONE IN. ANGEL 1121	CL	30.00	110.00
85	IN.PEACE IN. ANGEL 1ST EDITION 1120	CL	30.00	110.00
85	CHRISTMAS WOOLY LAMB 1133	CL	11.00	40.00
85	JOSEPH & DONKEY 1119	OP	30.00	30.00
85	MARY & BABY JESUS 1118	OP	30.00	30.00
85	WISEMAN #1 1123	OP	30.00	30.00
85	WISEMAN #2 1124	OP	30.00	30.00
85	WISEMAN #3 1125	OP	30.00	30.00
85	WOODEN CRECHE 1132	OP	28.00	30.00
86	SHEPHERD 1193	OP	32.00	32.00
89	IN.NOEL IN. ANGEL 2ND EDITION 1126	OP	48.00	48.00
89	IN.PEACE IN. ANGEL 2ND EDITION 1120	OP	48.00	48.00
	B.K. WISBER			**THE FAMILY & FRIENDS OF LIZZIE HIGH**
85	AMANDA HIGH 1ST EDITION 1111	CL	30.00	100.00
85	BENJAMIN BOWMAN 1129	CL	30.00	100.00
85	BENJAMIN BOWMAN/SANTA 1134	OP	30.00	30.00
85	CHRISTIAN BOWMAN 1110	CL	30.00	100.00
85	CORA HIGH 1115	CL	30.00	100.00
85	ELIZABETH SWEETLAND 1ST EDITION 1109	CL	30.00	100.00
85	EMMA HIGH 1103	CL	30.00	100.00
85	ESTHER DUNN 1ST EDITION 1127	CL	45.00	45.00

YR	NAME	LIMIT	ISSUE	TREND
85	FLOSSIE HIGH 1ST EDITION 1128	CL	45.00	130.00
85	HANNAH BROWN 1131	CL	45.00	130.00
85	IDA VALENTINE 1116	CL	30.00	100.00
85	KATRINA VALENTINE 1135	CL	30.00	100.00
85	LIZZE HIGH 1100	OP	30.00	30.00
85	LOUELLA VALENTINE 1112	CL	30.00	100.00
85	LUTHER BOWMAN 1ST EDITION 1108	CL	30.00	100.00
85	MARTIN BOWMAN 1117	CL	30.00	60.00
85	MARY VALENTINE 1105	CL	30.00	100.00
85	NETTIE BROWN 1ST EDITION 1102	CL	30.00	100.00
85	NETTIE BROWN/CHRISTMAS 1114	CL	30.00	100.00
85	PETER VALENTINE 1113	CL	30.00	90.00
85	REBECCA BOWMAN 1ST EDITION 1104	CL	30.00	100.00
85	RUSSELL DUNN 1107	CL	30.00	100.00
85	SABRINA VALENTINE 1ST EDITION 1101	CL	30.00	100.00
85	WENDEL BOWMAN 1ST EDITION 1106	CL	30.00	100.00
86	ALICE VALENTINE 1148	CL	32.00	100.00
86	ANDREW BROWN 1157	CL	45.00	130.00
86	ANNIE BOWMAN 1ST EDITION 1150	CL	32.00	100.00
86	CARRIE HIGH 1ST EDITION 1190	CL	45.00	100.00
86	CASSIE YOCUM 1ST EDITION 1179	CL	36.00	100.00
86	CHRISTOPHER HIGH 1182	CL	34.00	40.00
86	DAVID YOCUM 1195	OP	33.00	33.00
86	DELIA VALENTINE 1153	CL	32.00	100.00
86	DORA HIGH 1ST EDITION 1152	CL	30.00	100.00
86	EDWARD BOWMAN 1ST EDITION 1158	CL	45.00	130.00
86	EMILY BOWMAN 1ST EDITION 1185	CL	34.00	100.00
86	GRACE VALENTINE 1ST EDITION 1146	CL	32.00	100.00
86	JENNY VALENTINE 1181	CL	34.00	110.00
86	JEREMY BOWMAN 1192	CL	36.00	45.00
86	JILLIAN BOWMAN 1180	CL	34.00	110.00
86	JULIET VALENTINE 1ST EDITION 1147	CL	32.00	100.00
86	KARL VALENTINE 1ST EDITION 1161	CL	30.00	100.00
86	KATIE BOWMAN 1178	CL	36.00	80.00
86	LITTLE GHOSTS 1197	OP	15.00	15.00
86	MADALEINE VALENTINE 1ST EDITION 1187	CL	34.00	90.00
86	MAGGIE HIGH 1160	CL	30.00	100.00
86	MARIE VALENTINE 1ST EDITION 1184	CL	33.00	100.00
86	MARISA VALENTINE 1194A	OP	33.00	33.00
86	MARISA VALENTINE W/BROTHER PETEY 1194	OP	45.00	45.00
86	MARLAND VALENTINE 1183	CL	33.00	100.00
86	MARTHA HIGH 1151	CL	32.00	100.00
86	MATTHEW YOCUM 1186	CL	33.00	100.00
86	MOLLY YOCUM 1ST EDITION 1189	CL	34.00	100.00
86	RACHEL BOWMAN 1ST EDITION 1188	CL	34.00	100.00
86	SADIE VALENTINE 1163	OP	45.00	45.00
86	SALLY BOWMAN 1155	CL	32.00	110.00
86	SARA VALENTINE 1154	CL	32.00	55.00
86	SOPHIE VALENTINE 1164	CL	45.00	130.00
86	SUSANNA BOWMAN 1149	CL	45.00	130.00
86	THOMAS BOWMAN 1159	CL	30.00	100.00
86	TILLIE BROWN 1156	CL	32.00	100.00
86	WILLIAM VALENTINE 1191	CL	36.00	80.00
86	WILLIE BOWMAN 1162	CL	30.00	40.00
87	ABIGAIL BOWMAN 1199	CL	40.00	90.00
87	ADDIE HIGH 1202	OP	37.00	37.00
87	AMY BOWMAN 1201	CL	37.00	80.00
87	BRIDGET BOWMAN 1222	CL	40.00	90.00
87	CAT ON CHAIR 1217	CL	16.00	40.00
87	CHARLES BOWMAN 1ST EDITION 1221	CL	34.00	100.00
87	FLOWER GIRL, THE 1204	OP	17.00	17.00
87	GRETCHEN HIGH 1216	CL	40.00	45.00
87	IMOGENE BOWMAN 1206	CL	37.00	40.00
87	JOHANNA VALENTINE 1198	CL	37.00	100.00
87	KATIE AND BARNEY 1219	OP	38.00	38.00
87	LAURA VALENTINE 1223	CL	36.00	40.00
87	LITTLE WITCH 1225	OP	17.00	17.00
87	MARGARET BOWMAN 1213	OP	35.00	35.00
87	MELANIE BOWMAN 1ST EDITION 1220	CL	36.00	130.00
87	NAOMI VALENTINE 1200	CL	40.00	90.00
87	OLIVIA HIGH 1205	OP	37.00	37.00
87	PATSY BOWMAN 1214	OP	50.00	50.00
87	PENELOPE HIGH 1208	CL	40.00	400.00
87	PRISCILLA HIGH 1226	OP	56.00	56.00
87	RAMONA BROWN 1215	CL	40.00	50.00
87	REBECCA'S MOTHER 1207	OP	37.00	37.00
87	SANTA CLAUS/SITTING 1224	CL	50.00	60.00
87	WEDDING, THE BRIDE 1203	OP	37.00	37.00
87	WEDDING, THE GROOM 1203A	OP	34.00	34.00
88	ALLISON BOWMAN 1229	OP	56.00	56.00
88	BESS HIGH 1241	OP	45.00	45.00
88	BETSY VALENTINE 1245	OP	42.00	42.00
88	DAPHNE BOWMAN 1235	CL	38.00	40.00
88	EUNICE HIGH 1240	CL	56.00	60.00
88	HATTIE BOWMAN 1239	OP	40.00	40.00
88	JACOB HIGH 1230	CL	44.00	50.00
88	JANIE VALENTINE 1231	OP	37.00	37.00
88	KINCH BOWMAN 1237	OP	47.00	47.00
88	MARY ELLEN VALENTINE 1236	OP	40.00	40.00

YR	NAME	LIMIT	ISSUE	TREND
88	MEGAN VALENTINE 1227	CL	44.00	95.00
88	NETTIE BROWN 2ND EDITION 1102	OP	36.00	36.00
88	PHOEBE HIGH 1246	CL	48.00	60.00
88	RUTH ANNE BOWMAN 1232	CL	44.00	50.00
88	SABRINA VALENTINE 2ND EDITION 1101	OP	40.00	40.00
88	SAMANTHA BOWMAN 1238	OP	47.00	47.00
89	AMELIA HIGH 1248	OP	45.00	45.00
89	CARRIE HIGH 2ND EDITION 1190	OP	46.00	46.00
89	EMMY LOU VALENTINE 1251	OP	45.00	45.00
89	FLOSSIE HIGH 2ND EDITION 1128	OP	54.00	54.00
89	JASON HIGH 1254A	OP	20.00	20.00
89	JASON HIGH W/MOTHER 1254	OP	58.00	58.00
89	JESSICA HIGH 1253A	OP	20.00	20.00
89	JESSICA HIGH W/MOTHER 1253	OP	58.00	58.00
89	JOHANN BOWMAN 1250	OP	40.00	40.00
89	LUCY BOWMAN 1255	OP	45.00	45.00
89	MADALEINE VALENTINE 2ND EDITION 1187	OP	37.00	37.00
89	MIRIAM HIGH 1256	OP	46.00	46.00
89	MOLLY YOCUM 2ND EDITION 1189	OP	39.00	39.00
89	MRS. CLAUS 1258	OP	42.00	42.00
89	PEGGY BOWMAN 1252	OP	58.00	58.00
89	RACHEL BOWMAN 2ND EDITION 1188	OP	34.00	34.00
89	REBECCA BOWMAN 2ND EDITION 1104	OP	56.00	56.00
89	SANTA W/TUB 1257	OP	58.00	58.00
89	VANESSA HIGH 1247	OP	45.00	45.00
89	VICTORIA BOWMAN 1249	OP	40.00	40.00
90	ALBERT VALENTINE 1260	OP	42.00	42.00
90	AMANDA HIGH 2ND EDITION 1111	OP	54.00	54.00
90	EMILY BOWMAN 2ND EDITION 1185	OP	48.00	48.00
90	GRACE VALENTINE 2ND EDITION 1146	OP	48.00	48.00
90	JULIET VALENTINE 2ND EDITION 1147	OP	48.00	48.00
90	MARLENE VALENTINE 1259	OP	48.00	48.00
90	NANCY BOWMAN 1261	OP	48.00	48.00
91	ANNABELLE BOWMAN 1267	OP	68.00	68.00
91	BARBARA HELEN 1274	OP	58.00	58.00
91	CYNTHIA HIGH 1127A	OP	60.00	60.00
91	DEPARTMENT STORE SANTA, THE 1270	OP	76.00	76.00
91	ELIZABETH SWEETLAND 2ND EDITION 1109	OP	56.00	56.00
91	ESTHER DUNN 2ND EDITION 1127	OP	60.00	60.00
91	MICHAEL BOWMAN 1268	OP	52.00	52.00
91	SANTA'S HELPER 1271	OP	52.00	52.00
91	TRUDY VALENTINE 1269	OP	64.00	64.00
92	ASHLEY BOWMAN 1304	OP	48.00	48.00
92	CAROL ANNE BOWMAN 1282	CL	70.00	70.00
92	CASSIE YOCUM 2ND EDITION 1179	OP	80.00	80.00
92	CHARLES BOWMAN 2ND EDITION 1221	OP	46.00	46.00
92	DORA HIGH 2ND EDITION 1152	CL	48.00	50.00
92	EDWIN BOWMAN 1281	CL	70.00	70.00
92	FRANCIS BOWMAN 1305	OP	48.00	48.00
92	JOANIE VALENTINE 1295	OP	48.00	48.00
92	JOSEPH VALENTINE 1283	OP	62.00	62.00
92	MARIE VALENTINE 2ND EDITION 1184	OP	68.00	68.00
92	MELANIE BOWMAN 2ND EDITION 1220	OP	46.00	46.00
92	NATALIE VALENTINE 1284	OP	62.00	62.00
92	TIMOTHY BOWMAN 1294	OP	56.00	56.00
92	WENDEL BOWMAN 2ND EDITON 1106	OP	60.00	60.00
92	WENDY BOWMAN 1293	OP	78.00	78.00
93	ANNIE BOWMAN 2ND EDITION 1150	OP	68.00	68.00
93	CHRISTMAS TREE W/CATS 1293A	OP	42.00	42.00
93	JUSTINE VALENTINE 1302	OP	84.00	84.00
93	LUTHER BOWMAN 2ND EDITION 1108	OP	60.00	60.00
93	MOMMY 1312	OP	48.00	48.00
93	PEARL BOWMAN 1303	OP	56.00	56.00
93	PENNY VALENTINE 1308	OP	60.00	60.00
93	SANTA CLAUS 1311	OP	48.00	48.00
94	BONNIE VALENTINE 1323	OP	35.00	35.00
94	CHRISTINE BOWMAN 1332	OP	62.00	62.00
94	EDWARD BOWMAN 2ND EDITION 1158	OP	76.00	76.00
94	ELSIE BOWMAN 1325	OP	64.00	64.00
94	GILBERT HIGH 1335	OP	65.00	65.00
94	GWENDOLYN HIGH 1342	OP	56.00	56.00
94	JAMIE BOWMAN 1324	OP	35.00	35.00
94	JOSIE VALENTINE 1322	OP	76.00	76.00
94	KARL VALENTINE 2ND EDITION 1161	OP	54.00	54.00
94	MARISA VALENTINE 1333	OP	58.00	58.00
94	MINNIE VALENTINE 1336	OP	64.00	64.00
94	PRUDENCE VALENTINE 1331	CL	180.00	180.00
94	SHIRLEY BOWMAN 1334	OP	63.00	63.00
B.K. WISBER	**THE FAMILY & FRIENDS OF LIZZIE HIGH/LIMITED ED.**			
92	KATHRYN BOWMAN 1285	CL	140.00	300.00
B.K. WISBER	**THE GRUMMELS OF LOG HOLLOW**			
86	AUNT GERTIE GRUMMEL 1171	CL	34.00	85.00
86	AUNT HILDA GRUMMEL 1174	CL	34.00	85.00
86	AUNT POLLY GRUMMEL 1169	CL	34.00	85.00
86	COUSIN LOTTIE GRUMMEL 1170	CL	36.00	85.00
86	COUSIN MIRANDA GRUMMEL 1165	CL	47.00	85.00
86	GRANDMA GRUMMEL 1173	CL	45.00	85.00
86	GRANDPA GRUMMEL 1176	CL	36.00	120.00
86	LITTLE ONES-GRUMMELS, THE- BOY/GIRL 1196	CL	15.00	25.00

YR	NAME	LIMIT	ISSUE	TREND
86	MA GRUMMEL 1167	CL	36.00	85.00
86	PA GRUMMEL 1172	CL	34.00	85.00
86	SISTER NORA GRUMMEL 1177	CL	34.00	85.00
86	TEDDY BEAR BED 1168	CL	15.00	85.00
86	UNCLE HOLLIS GRUMMEL 1166	CL	34.00	85.00
86	WASHLINE 1175	CL	15.00	85.00
B.K. WISBER				**THE LITTLE ONES**
85	BLACK BOY 1ST EDITION 1130	CL	15.00	55.00
85	BLACK GIRL 1ST EDITION 1130	CL	15.00	55.00
85	WHITE BOY 1ST EDITION 1130	CL	15.00	55.00
85	WHITE GIRL 1ST EDITION 1130	CL	15.00	55.00
89	BLACK BOY 2ND EDITION 1130I	CL	20.00	25.00
89	BLACK GIRL/COUNTRY 2ND EDITION 1130G	CL	20.00	25.00
89	BLACK GIRL/PASTELS 2ND EDITION 1130E	CL	20.00	25.00
89	WHITE BOY 2ND EDITION 1130H	CL	20.00	25.00
89	WHITE GIRL/COUNTRY 2ND EDITION 1130F	CL	20.00	25.00
89	WHITE GIRL/PASTELS 2ND EDITION 1130D	CL	20.00	25.00
92	LITTLE ONE BOY W/EASTER FLOWERS 1306	OP	30.00	30.00
92	LITTLE ONE CLOWN 1290	OP	32.00	32.00
92	LITTLE ONE GIRL W/EASTER FLOWERS 1296	OP	34.00	34.00
92	LITTLE ONE READING 1286	OP	36.00	36.00
92	LITTLE ONE W/APPLES 1277	OP	26.00	26.00
92	LITTLE ONE W/BEACH BUCKET 1275	OP	26.00	26.00
92	LITTLE ONE W/BIRTHDAY GIFT 1279	OP	26.00	26.00
92	LITTLE ONE W/CHRISTMAS LIGHTS 1287	OP	34.00	34.00
92	LITTLE ONE W/EASTER EGGS 1276	OP	26.00	26.00
92	LITTLE ONE W/KITTEN & MILK 1280	OP	32.00	32.00
92	LITTLE ONE W/KITTEN & YARN 1278	OP	34.00	34.00
92	LITTLE ONE W/SLED 1289	OP	30.00	30.00
92	LITTLE ONE W/SNOWMAN 1288	OP	36.00	36.00
92	LITTLE ONE W/VALENTINE 1291	OP	30.00	30.00
93	LITTLE ONE 4TH OF JULY BOY 1307	OP	28.00	28.00
93	LITTLE ONE 4TH OF JULY GIRL 1298	OP	30.00	30.00
93	LITTLE ONE BALLERINA 1321	OP	40.00	40.00
93	LITTLE ONE BUNNY 1297	OP	36.00	36.00
93	LITTLE ONE PICNICKING 1320	OP	34.00	34.00
93	LITTLE ONE W/MOP 1300	OP	36.00	36.00
93	LITTLE ONE W/SPINNING WHEEL 1299	OP	36.00	36.00
93	LITTLE ONE W/VIOLIN 1319	OP	28.00	28.00
94	LITTLE ONE BOY DYEING EGGS 1327	OP	30.00	30.00
94	LITTLE ONE BOY W/PUMPKIN 1341	OP	29.00	29.00
94	LITTLE ONE GIRL DYEING EGGS 1326	OP	30.00	30.00
94	LITTLE ONE GIRL W/WAGON 1340	OP	42.00	42.00
94	LITTLE ONE NURSE 1328	OP	40.00	40.00
94	LITTLE ONE TEACHER 1329	OP	38.00	38.00
94	LITTLE ONE W/LAUNDRY BASKET 1338	OP	38.00	38.00
94	LITTLE ONE W/PUPPY IN TUB 1339	OP	43.00	43.00
B.K. WISBER				**THE LITTLE ONES AT CHRISTMAS**
90	LITTLE ONE W/BASKET OF GREENS 1263	OP	22.00	22.00
90	LITTLE ONE W/COOKIE 1264	OP	22.00	22.00
90	LITTLE ONE W/GIFT 1266	OP	22.00	22.00
90	LITTLE ONE W/TREE GARLAND 1265	OP	22.00	22.00
91	BLACK BOY W/SANTA PHOTO 1273A	OP	24.00	24.00
91	BLACK GIRL W/SANTA PHOTO 1272A	OP	24.00	24.00
91	WHITE BOY W/SANTA PHOTO 1273	OP	24.00	24.00
91	WHITE GIRL W/SANTA PHOTO 1272	OP	24.00	24.00
93	BOY PEEKING 1314	OP	22.00	22.00
93	BOY PEEKING W/TREE 1313	OP	60.00	60.00
93	GIRL PEEKING 1316	OP	22.00	22.00
93	GIRL PEEKING W/TREE 1315	OP	60.00	60.00
93	LITTLE ONE W/BAKING TABLE 1317	OP	38.00	38.00
93	LITTLE ONE W/NOTE FOR SANTA 1318	OP	36.00	36.00
94	LITTLE ONE W/GREENS ON TABLE 1337	OP	46.00	46.00
B.K. WISBER				**THE PAWTUCKETS OF SWEET BRIAR LANE**
86	AUNT LILLIAN PAWTUCKET 1ST EDITION 1141	CL	32.00	115.00
86	AUNT MINNIE PAWTUCKET 1ST EDITION 1136	CL	45.00	115.00
86	BROTHER NOAH PAWTUCKET 1140	CL	32.00	115.00
86	COUSIN CLARA PAWTUCKET 1ST EDITION 1144	CL	32.00	115.00
86	GRAMMY PAWTUCKET 1ST EDITION 1137	CL	32.00	115.00
86	LITTLE ONE BUNNIES, THE/BOY 1ST ED. 1145	CL	15.00	25.00
86	LITTLE ONE BUNNIES, THE/GIRL 1ST ED. 114	CL	15.00	55.00
86	MAMA PAWTUCKET 1ST EDITION 1142	CL	34.00	115.00
86	PAPPY PAWTUCKET 1143	CL	32.00	115.00
86	SISTER FLORA PAWTUCKET 1139	CL	32.00	115.00
86	UNCLE HARLEY PAWTUCKET 1ST EDITION 1138	CL	32.00	115.00
87	AUNT MABEL PAWTUCKET 212	CL	45.00	135.00
87	BUNNY BED 1218	CL	16.00	115.00
87	COUSIN ALBERTA PAWTUCKET 1210	CL	36.00	115.00
87	COUSIN ISABEL PAWTUCKET 1209	CL	36.00	115.00
87	SISTER CLEMMIE PAWTUCKET 1211	CL	34.00	115.00
88	COUSIN JED PAWTUCKET 1234	CL	34.00	115.00
88	COUSIN WINNIE PAWTUCKET 1233	CL	49.00	115.00
93	AUNT MINNIE PAWTUCKET 2ND EDITION 1136	OP	72.00	72.00
93	FLOSSIE PAWTUCKET 1136A	OP	33.00	33.00
94	AUNT LILLIAN PAWTUCKET 2ND EDITION 1141	OP	58.00	58.00
94	GRAMMY PAWTUCKET 2ND EDITION 1137	OP	68.00	68.00
94	LITTLE ONE BUNNIES, THE/BOY 2ND ED. 1145	OP	33.00	33.00
94	LITTLE ONE BUNNIES, THE/GIRL 2ND ED. 114	OP	33.00	33.00

The second limited edition Gorham doll, Ashley, *by S. Stone Aiken, was limited to 2,500 in 1983. Her value has soared to $800 - $1,200, a significant increase over the original retail of $350.*

Based on the classic orchestral tale by Prokofiev, Peter and the Wolf *was issued in 1992 by the Lawton Doll Co. as the first edition in their Childhood Classics II collection. Limited to 750 dolls, it retailed at $495.*

The Lawton Doll Co. issued three 1992 dolls in their Childhood Classics II collection. Dressed in a tattered suit and carrying a Rowe Pottery bowl, this third edition Oliver Twist *by Wendy Lawton was limited to 750.*

The Childhood Classics II collection from the Lawton Doll Co. offered this Tom Sawyer *doll in 1993. The edition size was 500.*

YR	NAME	LIMIT	ISSUE	TREND
94	MAMA PAWTUCKET 2ND EDITION 1142	OP	86.00	86.00
94	PAWTUCKET BUNNY HUTCH 1141A	OP	38.00	38.00
94	UNCLE HARLEY PAWTUCKET 2ND EDITION 1138	OP	74.00	74.00
	B.K. WISBER			**THE THANKSGIVING PLAY**
88	INDIAN SQUAW 1244	OP	36.00	36.00
88	PILGRIM BOY 1242	OP	40.00	40.00
88	PILGRIM GIRL 1243	OP	48.00	48.00

LAWTON'S

Price ranges may reflect various demands in the market from one geographic region to another; condition of piece; specific markings found on piece; and/or changes in production of piece.

YR	NAME	LIMIT	ISSUE	TREND
	W. LAWTON			**CENTERPIECES**
92	LOTTA ON STAGE	CL	*	N/A
93	LITTLE COLONEL II	CL	*	N/A
95	ALICE CENTERPIECE	CL	*	N/A
	W. LAWTON			**CHERISHED CUSTOMS**
90	BLESSING, THE/MEXICO	CL	395.00	950.00
90	GIRL'S DAY/JAPAN	CL	395.00	500.00
90	HIGH TEA/GREAT BRITIAN	CL	395.00	500.00
90	MIDSOMMAR/SWEDEN	CL	395.00	395.00
91	FROLIC/AMISH	CL	395.00	395.00
91	NDEKO/ZAIRE	CL	395.00	650.00
92	CARNIVAL/BRAZIL	CL	425.00	425.00
92	CRADLEBOARD/NAVAJO	CL	425.00	425.00
92	PASCHA/UKRAINE	CL	495.00	495.00
93	NALAUQATAQ/ESKIMO	CL	395.00	395.00
93	TOPENG KLANA/JAVA	CL	495.00	495.00
94	KWANZAA/AFRICA	CL	425.00	425.00
95	PIPING THE HAGGIS	CL	495.00	495.00
	W. LAWTON			**CHILDHOOD CLASSICS**
83	ALICE IN WONDERLAND	CL	225.00	2500.00-3000.00
84	HEIDI	CL	325.00	750.00
85	HANS BRINKER	CL	325.00	900.00-1800.00
86	ANNE OF GREEN GABLES	CL	325.00	2000.00-2500.00
86	LAURA INGALLS	CL	325.00	400.00-700.00
86	POLLYANNA	CL	325.00	1000.00-1600.00
87	JUST DAVID	CL	325.00	700.00-1100.00
87	MARY LENNOX	CL	325.00	500.00-600.00
87	POLLY PEPPER	CL	325.00	450.00-600.00
88	LITTLE EVA	CL	350.00	750.00
88	REBECCA OF SUNNYBROOK FARM	CL	350.00	500.00-600.00
88	TOPSY	CL	350.00	750.00-1000.00
89	HONEY BUNCH	CL	350.00	500.00-800.00
89	LITTLE PRINCESS	CL	395.00	500.00-800.00
90	MARY FRANCES	CL	350.00	350.00
90	POOR LITTLE MATCH GIRL	CL	350.00	550.00
91	BOBBSEY TWINS, THE/FLOSSIE	CL	365.00	600.00
91	BOBBSEY TWINS, THE/FREDDIE	CL	365.00	600.00
91	HIAWATHA	CL	395.00	525.00
91	LITTLE BLACK SAMBO	CL	395.00	700.00
	W. LAWTON			**CHILDHOOD CLASSICS II**
92	MARIGOLD GARDEN	CL	450.00	450.00
92	OLIVER TWIST	CL	450.00	450.00
92	PETER AND THE WOLF	CL	495.00	500.00
93	TOM SAWYER	CL	395.00	395.00
93	VELVETEEN RABBIT, THE	CL	395.00	395.00
94	GIRL OF THE LIMBERLOST	CL	425.00	425.00
95	LITTLE LORD FAUNTLEROY	CL	450.00	450.00
96	PHOEBE PREBLE AND HITTY	500	595.00	595.00
	W. LAWTON			**CHRISTMAS DOLL**
88	CHRISTMAS JOY	CL	325.00	625.00-1200.00
89	NOEL	CL	325.00	325.00-750.00
90	CHRISTMAS ANGEL	CL	325.00	325.00
91	YULETIDE CAROLE	CL	395.00	395.00
96	BIRDS' CHRISTMAS CAROL, THE	500	450.00	450.00
	W. LAWTON			**CHRISTMAS LEGENDS**
92	LEGEND OF THE POINSETTIA, THE	CL	395.00	395.00
93	LITTLE DRUMMER BOY, THE	CL	595.00	595.00
94	SANTA LUCIA	CL	425.00	425.00
95	NUTCRACKER, THE	CL	595.00	595.00
	W. LAWTON			**CLASSIC LITERATURE**
96	SCARLET LETTER, THE	250	1495.00	1495.00
	W. LAWTON			**CLASSIC PLAYTHINGS**
93	PATRICIA AND HER PATSY	CL	595.00	600.00
94	KATIE AND HER KEWPIE	CL	595.00	595.00
95	BESSIE AND HER BYE LO BABY	CL	595.00	595.00
96	KATHERINE AND HER KATHE KRUSE DOLL	750	795.00	795.00
	W. LAWTON			**CLASSIC PLAYTHINGS II**
96	HENRIETTE AND HER HILDA	350	1395.00	1395.00
	W. LAWTON			**EARLY AMERICAN PORTRAIT**
94	ABIGAIL AND JANE AUGUSTA	CL	995.00	995.00
95	CARRIE AND SOPHIA GRACE	CL	1250.00	1250.00
	W. LAWTON			**FABRIC OF AMERICA**
96	ZUDIE'S COVERLET	350	895.00	895.00
	W. LAWTON			**FOLKTALES AND FAIRY STORIES**
92	LITTLE EMPEROR'S NIGHTINGALE, THE	CL	425.00	500.00

YR	NAME	LIMIT	ISSUE	TREND
92	LITTLE RED RIDING HOOD	CL	450.00	450.00
92	SWAN PRINCESS	CL	495.00	495.00
92	WILLIAM TELL, THE YOUNGER	CL	395.00	395.00
93	GOLDILOCKS AND BABY BEAR	CL	595.00	595.00
93	SNOW WHITE	CL	395.00	395.00
94	LITTLE GRETEL	CL	395.00	400.00
95	RAPUNZEL	CL	450.00	450.00
W. LAWTON			**FUN WITH DICK AND JANE**	
96	DICK	750	495.00	495.00
96	JANE	750	495.00	495.00
W. LAWTON			**GENTLE PURSUITS**	
94	EMILY AND HER DIARY	CL	795.00	795.00
95	EUGENIA'S LITERARY SALON	CL	795.00	795.00
W. LAWTON			**GRAND TOUR**	
94	SPRINGTIME IN PARIS	CL	895.00	895.00
95	AFRICAN SAFARI	CL	995.00	995.00
W. LAWTON			**GUILD DOLLS**	
89	BAA BAA BLACK SHEEP	CL	395.00	700.00
90	LAVENDER BLUE	CL	395.00	425.00
91	TO MARKET, TO MARKET	CL	495.00	395.00
92	LITTLE BOY BLUE	CL	395.00	395.00
93	LAWTON LOGO DOLL	CL	350.00	525.00
94	WEE HANDFUL	CL	250.00	250.00
95	UNIQUELY YOURS	CL	395.00	500.00
96	TEDDY AND ME	500	450.00	450.00
W. LAWTON			**LITTLE WOMEN**	
88	AMY	CL	395.00	395.00
88	BETH	CL	395.00	395.00
88	JO	CL	395.00	395.00
88	MEG	CL	395.00	395.00
W. LAWTON			**MEMORIES & MELODIES**	
93	APPLE BLOSSOM TIME	CL	295.00	295.00
93	IN THE GOOD OL' SUMMERTIME	CL	295.00	295.00
93	LYDA ROSE	CL	295.00	295.00
93	SCARLET RIBBONS	CL	295.00	295.00
94	LET ME CALL YOU SWEETHEART	CL	295.00	295.00
95	EASTER PARADE	CL	295.00	295.00
W. LAWTON			**NEWCOMER COLLECTION**	
87	ELLIN ELIZABETH, EYES CLOSED	CL	325.00	1000.00
87	ELLIN ELIZABETH, EYES OPEN	CL	335.00	1200.00
W. LAWTON			**ONE-OF-A-KIND**	
89	AMELIA	CL	1400.00	1100.00
90	GOLDILOCKS AND BABY BEAR	CL	*	N/A
91	FELICITY MINDS THE QUINTS	CL	*	N/A
92	LITTLE MISS MUFFET	CL	3900.00	3900.00
93	CURLY LOCKS, CURLY LOCKS	CL	5700.00	5700.00
93	JACK AND THE BEANSTALK	CL	2500.00	2500.00
94	SARA CREWE ARRIVES AT MISS MINCHIN'S	CL	11000.00	11000.00
95	ERRANDS FOR GRANDMOTHER	CL	4600.00	4600.00
W. LAWTON			**PLAYTHINGS PAST**	
89	EDWARD AND DOBBIN	CL	395.00	475.00-600.00
89	ELIZABETH AND BABY	CL	395.00	400.00-675.00
89	VICTORIA AND TEDDY	CL	395.00	400.00
W. LAWTON			**POETRY COLLECTION**	
94	AT AUNTY'S HOUSE	CL	795.00	800.00
95	LUCY GRAY	CL	795.00	800.00
W. LAWTON			**SEASONS**	
88	AMBER AUTUMN	CL	325.00	400.00-525.00
89	SUMMER ROSE	CL	325.00	375.00-500.00
90	CRYSTAL WINTER	CL	325.00	325.00
91	SPRING BLOSSOM	CL	325.00	350.00
W. LAWTON			**SMALL WONDERS**	
93	JAFRY	CL	150.00	150.00
93	JAMILLA	CL	150.00	150.00
93	MEGHAN	CL	150.00	150.00
93	MICHAEL	CL	150.00	150.00
W. LAWTON			**SPECIAL EDITION**	
88	MARCELLA AND RAGGEDY ANN	CL	395.00	1025.00
93	FLORA MCFLIMSEY	CL	895.00	895.00
94	MARY CHILTON	CL	395.00	750.00
95	THROUGH THE LOOKING GLASS	CL	495.00	495.00
W. LAWTON			**SPECIAL OCCASION**	
88	NANTHY	CL	325.00	550.00
89	FIRST DAY OF SCHOOL	CL	325.00	550.00
90	1ST BIRTHDAY	CL	295.00	375.00
W. LAWTON			**STORE EXCLUSIVE**	
89	MAIN STREET, USA	CL	350.00	350.00
90	GARDEN SONG MARTA	CL	395.00	395.00
90	LIBERTY SQUARE	CL	350.00	350.00
90	LITTLE COLONEL	CL	395.00	395.00
91	TISH	CL	395.00	395.00
92	KAREN	CL	395.00	395.00
93	A GOOFY LITTLE KID	CL	395.00	395.00
93	BRITA/TEA PARTY	CL	395.00	395.00
93	KELLYN	CL	395.00	395.00
94	KITTY	CL	425.00	425.00

YR	NAME	LIMIT	ISSUE	TREND
94	MELISSA AND HER MICKEY	CL	495.00	495.00
94	MORGAN	CL	425.00	425.00
95	CHRISTOPHER ROBIN & WINNIE THE POOH	CL	495.00	495.00
95	JOSEPHINE	CL	*	N/A
W. LAWTON				**SUGAR 'N' SPICE**
86	JASON	CL	250.00	850.00-1600.00
86	JESSICA	CL	250.00	850.00-1600.00
86	KERSTEN	CL	250.00	600.00-825.00
86	KIMBERLY	CL	250.00	600.00-825.00
87	GINGER	CL	275.00	400.00-575.00
87	MARIE	CL	275.00	395.00-550.00
W. LAWTON				**THE CHILDREN'S HOUR**
91	EDITH WITH GOLDEN HAIR	CL	395.00	395.00
91	GRAVE ALICE	CL	395.00	395.00
91	LAUGHING ALLEGRA	CL	395.00	395.00
W. LAWTON				**TIMELESS BALLADS**
87	ANNABEL LEE	CL	495.00	600.00-725.00
87	HIGHLAND MARY	CL	495.00	600.00-900.00
87	YOUNG CHARLOTTE	CL	495.00	850.00
88	SHE WALKS IN BEAUTY	CL	550.00	700.00
W. LAWTON				**TREASURED TALES**
94	DREAMER, THE	CL	395.00	395.00
W. LAWTON				**TRIBUTE TO JUNE AMOS GRAMMER**
96	JUNE AMOS AND MARY ANNE	200	1395.00	1395.00
96	JUNE AMOS AND MARY ANNE (AUTOGRAPHED BK	125	1495.00	1495.00
W. LAWTON				**WEE BITS**
88	WEE BIT O' HEAVEN	CL	295.00	350.00-600.00
88	WEE BIT O' SUNSHINE	CL	295.00	350.00-600.00
88	WEE BIT O' WOE	CL	295.00	350.00-600.00
89	WEE BIT O' BLISS	CL	295.00	360.00
89	WEE BIT O' WONDER	CL	295.00	350.00-400.00

LENOX CHINA/CRYSTAL COLLECTION

YR	NAME	LIMIT	ISSUE	TREND
*				**BOLSHOI NUTCRACKER DOLLS**
91	CLARA	OP	195.00	195.00
*				**BONNET BABY DOLLS**
92	EASTER BONNET	OP	95.00	95.00
*				**CHILDREN OF THE WORLD**
89	HANNAH/THE LITTLE DUTCH MAIDEN	OP	119.00	119.00
90	HEATHER/LITTLE HIGHLANDER	OP	119.00	119.00
90	SCOTTISH/ LASS	OP	119.00	119.00
91	AMMA/AFRICAN GIRL	OP	119.00	119.00
91	SAKURA/JAPANESE GIRL	OP	119.00	119.00
92	GRETCHEN/GERMAN DOLL	OP	119.00	120.00
*				**CHILDREN WITH TOYS DOLLS**
91	TEA FOR TEDDY	OP	136.00	136.00
J. GRAMMER				**CHINA DOLLS - CLOTH BODIES**
85	AMY, 14 IN.	CL	250.00	995.00
85	ANNABELLE, 14 IN.	CL	250.00	995.00
85	ELIZABETH, 14 IN.	CL	250.00	995.00
85	JENNIFER, 14 IN.	CL	250.00	995.00
85	MIRANDA, 14 IN	CL	250.00	995.00
85	SARAH, 14 IN.	CL	250.00	995.00
*				**COUNTRY DECOR DOLLS**
91	MOLLY	OP	150.00	150.00
P. THOMPSON				**ELLIS ISLAND DOLLS**
91	MEGAN	CL	150.00	150.00
91	STEFAN	CL	150.00	150.00
92	ANGELINA	CL	150.00	150.00
92	ANNA	CL	152.00	152.00
92	CATHERINE	CL	152.00	152.00
*				**FIRST COLLECTOR DOLL**
92	LAUREN	OP	152.00	152.00
*				**INSPIRATIONAL DOLL**
92	BLESSED ARE THE PEACEMAKERS	OP	119.00	120.00
J. GRAMMER				**INTERNATIONAL BABY DOLL**
92	NATALIA/RUSSIAN BABY	OP	119.00	120.00
J. GRAMMER				**LENOX CHINA DOLLS**
84	ABIGAIL, 20 IN.	CL	425.00	2000.00
84	AMANDA, 16 IN.	CL	385.00	1700.00
84	JESSICA, 20 IN.	CL	450.00	1900.00
84	MAGGIE, 16 IN.	CL	375.00	1700.00
84	MARYANNE, 20 IN.	CL	425.00	2000.00
84	MELISSA, 16 IN.	CL	450.00	3100.00
84	REBECCA, 16 IN.	CL	375.00	1700.00
84	SAMANTHA, 16 IN.	CL	500.00	2800.00
*				**LENOX VICTORIAN DOLLS**
89	VICTORIAN BRIDE, THE	OP	295.00	295.00
90	CHRISTMAS DOLL, ELIZABETH	OP	195.00	195.00
91	VICTORIAN CHRISTENING DOLL	OP	295.00	295.00
92	LADY AT GALA	OP	295.00	300.00
*				**LITTLE WOMEN**
92	AMY, THE INSPIRING ARTIST	OP	152.00	152.00
*				**MUSICAL BABY DOLLS**
91	PATRICK'S LULLABYE	OP	95.00	95.00

YR	NAME	LIMIT	ISSUE	TREND
*				**NUTCRACKER DOLL**
92	SUGARPLUM	OP	195.00	200.00
93	NUTCRACKER	OP	195.00	200.00
*				**PRIMA BALLERINA COLLECTION**
92	ODETTE/QUEEN OF THE SWANS	CL	195.00	200.00
93	SLEEPING BEAUTY	OP	195.00	195.00
A. LESTER				**SIBLING DOLLS**
91	SKATING LESSON	OP	195.00	195.00

LINDA SUTTON ORIGINAL DOLLS

YR	NAME	LIMIT	ISSUE	TREND
L. SUTTON				**L.L. SUTTON ORIGINAL PORCELAIN DOLLS**
94	FALL BROOKE	5	1550.00	1600.00
94	SOPHIE	50	695.00	715.00
94	SPRING BROOKE	5	1550.00	1600.00
94	SUMMER BROOKE	5	1550.00	1600.00
94	WINTER BROOKE	20	1550.00	1575.00

MATTEL

YR	NAME	LIMIT	ISSUE	TREND
*				
*	PARISIENNE	*	*	110.00
90	HAPPY BIRTHDAY BARBIE	*	*	39.00
91	BIRTHDAY SURPRISE BARBIE	*	*	39.00
B. MACKIE				
*	SILK AND FLAMES BARBIE	*	*	195.00
*				**35TH ANNIVERSARY DOLL**
94	BLONDE BARBIE	RT	39.99	40.00
94	BRUNETTE BARBIE	RT	39.95	80.00
94	GIFT PACK BARBIE	RT	79.97	150.00
B. MACKIE				**BOB MACKIE BARBIE DOLL**
90	GOLD BARBIE 5405	RT	144.00	800.00
91	PLATINUM BARBIE 2703	RT	153.00	800.00
91	STARLIGHT SPLENDOR BARBIE 2704	RT	135.00	800.00
92	EMPRESS BRIDE BARBIE 4247	RT	232.00	850.00
92	NEPTUNE FANTASY BARBIE 4248	RT	160.00	850.00
93	MASQUERADE	RT	*	450.00
94	QUEEN OF HEARTS	RT	175.00	225.00
C. SPENCER				**GOLDEN JUBILEE**
94	GOLDEN JUBILEE	RT	325.00	1000.00
*				**HOLIDAY BARBIES**
88	HOLIDAY BARBIE	RT	24.99	700.00
89	HOLIDAY BARBIE	RT	34.99	250.00
90	HOLIDAY BARBIE	RT	*	200.00
91	HOLIDAY BARBIE	RT	*	190.00
92	HOLIDAY BARBIE	RT	*	150.00
93	HOLIDAY BARBIE	RT	*	140.00
94	HOLIDAY BARBIE	RT	44.95	175.00
95	HOLIDAY BARBIE	OP	44.95	45.00
*				**NOSTALGIC PORCELAIN BARBIE DOLL**
89	WEDDING DAY BARBIE 2641	RT	198.00	600.00
90	SOLO IN THE SPOTLIGHT 7613	RT	198.00	300.00
90	SOPHISTICATED LADY 5313	RT	198.00	240.00
*				**THE WINTER PRINCESS COLLECTION**
93	WINTER PRINCESS	RT	59.95	550.00
94	EVERGREEN PRINCESS	RT	59.95	150.00
94	EVERGREEN PRINCESS (RED HAIR)	RT	59.95	550.00
95	PEPPERMINT PRINCESS	RT	59.95	65.00

MIDDLETON DOLL CO.

YR	NAME	LIMIT	ISSUE	TREND
L. MIDDLETON				
94	HERSHEY KISSES	OP	99.50	100.00
95	ANGEL KISSES BELLY DANCER	1000	119.00	119.00
95	BELOVED-HAPPY BIRTHDAY/BLUE	1000	220.00	220.00
95	BELOVED-HAPPY BIRTHDAY/PINK	1000	220.00	220.00
95	BETH FLAPPER	1000	119.00	119.00
95	BETHIE BOWS	1000	150.00	150.00
95	BETHIE BUTTONS	1000	150.00	150.00
95	BLOSSOM/PORCELAIN	250	500.00	500.00
95	BRIDE	1000	250.00	250.00
95	CHRISTMAS ANGEL 1995	3000	190.00	190.00
95	ECHO LITTLE EAGLE	500	180.00	180.00
95	ELISE- 1860 FASHION	200	1790.00	1790.00
95	FIRST BORN MY BABY BOY	1500	160.00	160.00
95	FIRST MOMENTS LULLABY TIME	1000	180.00	180.00
95	GORDON/GROWING UP	1000	220.00	220.00
95	GRACE/GROWING UP	1000	220.00	220.00
95	HERSHEY KISSES/GOLD	OP	99.50	100.00
95	HERSHEY KISSES/SILVER	OP	99.50	100.00
95	JOEY/NEWBORN	1000	190.00	190.00
95	JOHANNA/NEWBORN	2000	190.00	190.00
95	LITTLE ANGEL BALLERINA	1000	119.00	119.00
95	LITTLE BLESSING BLESSED EVENT	1500	190.00	190.00
95	LITTLE BLESSING PRETTY IN PINK	1500	190.00	190.00
95	LITTLE BLESSING/AWAKE BOY	1000	180.00	180.00
95	LITTLE BLESSING/AWAKE GIRL	1500	180.00	180.00
95	LITTLE BLESSING/SLEEPING BOY	1000	180.00	180.00
95	LITTLE BLESSING/SLEEPING GIRL	1000	180.00	180.00
95	LITTLE LOVE VIOLEK	1500	160.00	160.00

YR	NAME	LIMIT	ISSUE	TREND
95	LITTLE LOVE VIOLETS	1500	160.00	160.00
95	POLLY ESTHER HERSHEY COUNTRY	OP	130.00	130.00
95	POLLY ESTHER SOCK HOP	1000	119.00	119.00
95	PORCELAIN TENDERNESS BABY CLOWN	250	590.00	590.00
95	TENDERNESS FRENCH BE BE	1500	220.00	220.00
96	BELOVED - GOOD FRIENDS	1500	180.00	180.00
96	BUBBA CHUBBS/BUBBA THE CHUBBS-KIS	1000	196.00	196.00
96	ECHO ALL DRESSED UP	500	180.00	180.00
96	FIRST BORN SO SNUGGLY	1000	160.00	160.00
96	FIRST MOMENTS/CHRISTENING	1000	238.00	238.00
96	GRACE FRESH AS A DAISY	300	176.00	176.00
96	HERSHEY KISSES/GREEN	OP	99.50	100.00
96	HERSHEY KISSES/RED	OP	99.50	100.00
96	JOEY GO BYE BYE	1000	190.00	190.00
96	LITTLE BLESSING CUDDLE UP	1000	180.00	180.00
96	LITTLE LOVE SUCH A GOOD BOY	1000	160.00	160.00
96	MOLLY ROSE - GOOD FRIENDS	1500	180.00	180.00
96	YOUNG LADY BRIDE IN WHITE SATIN	1000	250.00	250.00
L. MIDDLETON				**BIRTHDAY BABIES**
92	FALL	RT	170.00	170.00
92	SPRING	3000	170.00	170.00
92	SUMMER	RT	160.00	160.00
92	WINTER	RT	180.00	180.00
L. MIDDLETON				**CHRISTMAS ANGEL COLLECTION**
87	CHRISTMAS ANGEL 1987	RT	130.00	430.00
88	CHRISTMAS ANGEL 1988	RT	130.00	205.00
89	CHRISTMAS ANGEL 1989	RT	150.00	160.00
90	CHRISTMAS ANGEL 1990	RT	150.00	160.00
91	CHRISTMAS ANGEL 1991	RT	180.00	190.00
92	CHRISTMAS ANGEL - 1992	5000	190.00	190.00
93	CHRISTMAS ANGEL - 1993/GIRL	4000	190.00	190.00
93	CHRISTMAS ANGEL - 1993/SET	RT	390.00	500.00
94	CHRISTMAS ANGEL - 1994	5000	190.00	190.00
L MIDDLETON				**FIRST COLLECTIBLES**
90	DAY DREAMER (AWAKE)	RT	42.00	42.00
90	SWEETEST LITTLE DREAMER (ASLEEP)	RT	40.00	40.00
91	DAY DREAMER SUNSHINE	RT	49.00	49.00
91	TEENIE	RT	59.00	59.00
L. MIDDLETON				**FIRST MOMENTS SERIES**
84	FIRST MOMENTS (SLEEPING)	RT	69.00	150.00
86	FIRST MOMENTS (BLUE EYES)	RT	120.00	150.00
86	FIRST MOMENTS (BROWN EYES)	RT	120.00	150.00
87	FIRST MOMENTS BOY	RT	130.00	160.00
87	FIRST MOMENTS CHRISTENING (ASLEEP)	RT	160.00	180.00
87	FIRST MOMENTS CHRISTENING (AWAKE)	RT	160.00	180.00
90	FIRST MOMENTS SWEETNESS	OP	180.00	180.00
92	FIRST MOMENTS AWAKE (BLUE)	RT	170.00	170.00
92	FIRST MOMENTS AWAKE (PINK)	RT	170.00	170.00
93	FIRST MOMENTS HEIRLOOM	OP	190.00	190.00
L. MIDDLETON				**LIMITED EDITION PORCELAIN**
88	BABY GRACE	RT	500.00	500.00
88	CHERISH, FIRST EDITION	RT	350.00	500.00
88	DEVAN	RT	500.00	500.00
88	DEVAN II	100	500.00	500.00
88	JOHANNA	RT	500.00	500.00
88	MY LEE	RT	500.00	525.00
88	MY LEE II	100	500.00	500.00
88	SINCERITY, FIRST EDITION	RT	330.00	500.00
91	MOLLY ROSE	RT	500.00	500.00
L. MIDDLETON				**LIMITED EDITION VINYL**
81	LITTLE ANGEL-KINGDOM (HAND-PAINTED)	RT	40.00	300.00
85	LITTLE ANGEL-KING II (HAND-PAINTED)	RT	40.00	200.00
89	ANGEL FANCY	RT	120.00	130.00
90	ANGEL LOCKS	RT	140.00	150.00
90	BABY GRACE	RT	190.00	210.00
90	DEAR ONE (SUNDAY BEST)	RT	140.00	140.00
90	FIRST MOMENTS (TWIN BOY)	RT	180.00	180.00
90	FIRST MOMENTS (TWIN GIRL)	RT	180.00	180.00
90	FOREVER CHERISH	RT	170.00	180.00
90	MISSY (BUTTERCUP)	5000	160.00	170.00
90	SINCERITY (APPLES & SPICE)	RT	250.00	250.00
90	SINCERITY (PEACHES & CREAM)	RT	250.00	250.00
91	BUBBA BATBOY	RT	190.00	190.00
91	DEVAN DELIGHTFUL	RT	170.00	170.00
91	GRACIE MAE	5000	250.00	250.00
91	MY LEE CANDY CANE	RT	170.00	170.00
92	COTTONTOP CHERISH	RT	180.00	180.00
92	GRACIE MAE/BLONDE HAIR	OP	250.00	250.00
92	GRACIE MAE/BROWN HAIR	RT	250.00	250.00
92	JOHANNA	RT	190.00	190.00
92	MOLLY ROSE	5000	196.00	196.00
92	SERENITY BERRIES & BOWS	RT	250.00	250.00
92	SINCERITY PETALS & PLUMS	RT	250.00	250.00
93	AMANDA SPRINGTIME	2000	180.00	180.00
94	BRIDE, THE	200	1390.00	1425.00
L. MIDDLETON				**LITTLEST BALLET COMPANY**
88	APRIL (DRESSED IN PINK)	7500	100.00	110.00
88	JEANNIE (DRESSED IN WHITE)	7500	100.00	110.00

YR	NAME	LIMIT	ISSUE	TREND
88	LISA (BLACK LEOTARDS)	7500	100.00	110.00
88	MELANIE (DRESSED IN BLUE)	7500	100.00	110.00
89	APRIL (IN LEOTARD)	7500	100.00	110.00
89	JEANNIE (IN LEOTARD)	7500	100.00	110.00
89	MELANIE (IN LEOTARD)	7500	100.00	110.00
L. MIDDLETON		**PORCELAIN BEARS & BUNNY**		
93	BABY BUSTER	RT	230.00	230.00
93	BUSTER BEAR	RT	250.00	250.00
93	BYE BABY BUNTING	OP	270.00	270.00
L. MIDDLETON		**PORCELAIN COLLECTOR**		
92	BELOVED & BE'BE'	RT	590.00	590.00
92	SENCERITY II - COUNTRY FAIR	RT	500.00	500.00
93	CHERISH - LILAC & LACE	RT	500.00	500.00
L. MIDDLETON		**PORCELAIN LIMITED EDITION**		
94	BLOSSOM	250	500.00	550.00
94	TENDERNESS PETITE PIERROT	250	500.00	550.00
L. MIDDLETON		**TOWN & COUNTRY**		
94	ANGEL KISSES COUNTRY BOY	OP	118.00	120.00
94	ANGEL KISSES COUNTRY GIRL	OP	118.00	120.00
94	ANGEL KISSES GIRL	OP	98.00	100.00
94	ANGEL KISSES TOWN BOY	OP	118.00	120.00
94	ANGEL KISSES TOWN GIRL	OP	118.00	120.00
94	BELOVED HAPPY BIRTHDAY BLUE	1000	220.00	230.00
94	BELOVED HAPPY BIRTHDAY PINK	1000	220.00	230.00
94	BRIDE (RUBY SLIPPER)	1000	250.00	260.00
94	FIRST MOMENTS SWEETNESS (NEWBORN)	OP	180.00	180.00
94	JOEY (NEWBORN)	1000	180.00	190.00
94	JOHANNA (NEWBORN)	2000	180.00	190.00
94	LITTLE ANGEL COUNTRY BOY	OP	118.00	120.00
94	LITTLE ANGEL COUNTRY GIRL	OP	118.00	120.00
94	LITTLE ANGEL TOWN BOY	OP	118.00	120.00
94	LITTLE ANGEL TOWN GIRL	OP	118.00	120.00
L. MIDDLETON		**VINYL COLLECTORS SERIES**		
85	ANGEL FACE	RT	90.00	150.00
86	BUBBA CHUBBS	RT	100.00	175.00
86	DEAR ONE-FIRST EDITION	RT	90.00	145.00
86	LITTLE ANGEL-THIRD EDITION	RT	90.00	110.00
87	AMANDA-FIRST EDITION	RT	140.00	160.00
87	MISSY	RT	100.00	120.00
88	BUBBA CHUBBS RAILROADER	RT	140.00	155.00
88	CHERISH	RT	160.00	190.00
88	SINCERITY-LIMITED FIRST EDITION	RT	160.00	190.00
89	DEVAN	RT	170.00	170.00
89	MY LEE	RT	170.00	170.00
89	SINCERITY-SCHOOLGIRL	RT	180.00	190.00
92	BETH	OP	160.00	160.00
92	LITTLE ANGEL/BOY	OP	130.00	130.00
92	LITTLE ANGEL/GIRL	OP	130.00	130.00
92	POLLY ESTHER	OP	160.00	160.00
93	ECHO	OP	180.00	180.00
94	ANGEL KISSES BOY	OP	98.00	100.00
L. MIDDLETON		**WISE PENNY COLLECTION**		
93	ASHLEY/BLONDE HAIR	RT	120.00	120.00
93	ASHLEY/BROWN HAIR	RT	120.00	120.00
93	BABY DEVAN	RT	140.00	140.00
93	GORDON	RT	140.00	140.00
93	GRACE	RT	140.00	140.00
93	JENNIFER/PEACH DRESS	RT	140.00	140.00
93	JENNIFER/PRINT DRESS	RT	140.00	140.00
93	MERRY	RT	140.00	140.00
93	MOLLY JO	RT	140.00	140.00

MIDWEST OF CANNON FALLS

YR	NAME	LIMIT	ISSUE	TREND
S. HALE		**FOLK ART GALLERY COLLECTION**		
94	BEWITCHING BELINDA 11425-4	OP	40.00	40.00
94	GARDENING GIRL 11426-1	OP	45.00	45.00
94	HEARTFELT ANGEL 11422-3	OP	37.00	37.00
94	HEARTFELT ANGEL 11423-0	OP	20.00	20.00
94	SANTA GONE FISHING 12029-3	OP	65.00	65.00
94	SANTA OF CHRISTMAS PAST 12057-6	OP	130.00	130.00
94	SITTING SANTA 11424-7	OP	30.00	30.00

NABER KIDS

YR	NAME	LIMIT	ISSUE	TREND
H. NABER				
95	AL	RT	360.00	500.00
95	ALMA	1001	128.00	150.00
95	ANGEL	SO	128.00	300.00
95	BABY B. JOHN	DS	99.00	175.00
95	BABY B. RACHEL	DS	99.00	175.00
95	BABY B. SANDY	DS	99.00	175.00
95	BILL	1001	128.00	150.00
95	BONNI B	1001	128.00	150.00
95	CHARI	SO	1500.00	1800.00
95	CRYSTEL	OP	1500.00	1800.00
95	DANNY	1001	128.00	150.00
95	EMMA	1001	128.00	150.00
95	FORGET-ME-NOT	1001	128.00	150.00
95	GILBERT	1001	128.00	150.00

YR	NAME	LIMIT	ISSUE	TREND
95	GRETCHEN	1001	128.00	150.00
95	JAMES THE BUTLER	1001	79.00	150.00
95	KOOKY	SO	128.00	250.00
95	LESLI MARIE	1001	128.00	150.00
95	LOUI	1001	128.00	150.00
95	MELVIN	1001	128.00	150.00
95	MYSTIK	1001	128.00	150.00
95	POLLI	1001	128.00	150.00
95	THERESA	1001	128.00	150.00
95	TOBI	1001	128.00	150.00
95	WOLFGANG	1001	128.00	150.00
96	DAVID	1001	100.00	150.00
96	JOHN	1001	150.00	150.00
96	LACEY	1001	150.00	150.00
96	LIBBI	1001	150.00	150.00
96	MARGI	1001	100.00	150.00
96	MIMI	1001	150.00	150.00
96	MO	1001	150.00	150.00
96	MONTI	1001	150.00	150.00
96	PAT	1001	150.00	150.00
96	RACHEL	1001	150.00	150.00
96	SANDY	1001	150.00	150.00
96	STEVI	1001	150.00	150.00
96	TED	*	150.00	150.00
96	TRACY	1001	150.00	150.00

H. NABER — **NABER KIDS CLUB ONLY**

YR	NAME	LIMIT	ISSUE	TREND
95	BABY B. BEE	*	99.00	175.00

H. NABER — **NABER KIDS EXCLUSIVE**

YR	NAME	LIMIT	ISSUE	TREND
96	JONI	1001	150.00	150.00

NAHRGANG COLLECTION

J. NAHRGANG — **PORCELAIN DOLL SERIES**

YR	NAME	LIMIT	ISSUE	TREND
89	PALMER	250	270.00	270.00
90	ALICIA	250	330.00	330.00
90	GRANT (TAKE ME OUT TO THE BALL GAME)	500	390.00	390.00
90	KARISSA	500	350.00	395.00
90	KARMAN (GYPSY)	250	350.00	395.00
90	KASEY	250	450.00	450.00
90	KELSEY	250	350.00	350.00
90	MAGGIE	500	295.00	295.00
91	ANNA MARIE	250	390.00	390.00
91	AUBRY	250	390.00	390.00
91	CARSON	250	350.00	350.00
91	ERIN	250	295.00	295.00
91	HOLLY	175	295.00	295.00
91	LAURA	250	450.00	450.00
91	MCKINSEY	250	350.00	350.00
91	RAE	250	350.00	390.00
91	SOPHIE	250	450.00	450.00
92	ALEXIS	250	390.00	390.00
92	ANNIE SULLIVAN	25	895.00	895.00
92	BROOKE	250	390.00	390.00
92	DOLLY MADISON	100	395.00	395.00
92	FLORENCE NIGHTINGALE	100	395.00	395.00
92	HARRIET TUBMAN	100	395.00	395.00
92	KATIE	250	295.00	295.00
92	MOLLY PITCHER	100	395.00	395.00
92	POCAHONTAS	100	395.00	395.00
92	TAYLOR	250	395.00	395.00

J. NAHRGANG — **VINYL DOLL SERIES**

YR	NAME	LIMIT	ISSUE	TREND
90	KARMAN (GYPSY)	2000	190.00	190.00
91	ALEXIS	500	250.00	250.00
91	ANGELA	500	190.00	190.00
91	ANN MARIE	500	225.00	225.00
91	AUBRY	2000	225.00	225.00
91	BEATRIX	500	250.00	250.00
91	BROOKE	500	250.00	250.00
91	CHELSEA	250	190.00	190.00
91	LAURA	1000	250.00	250.00
91	MOLLY	500	190.00	190.00
91	POLLY	250	225.00	225.00
91	VANESSA	250	250.00	250.00
92	DOLLY MADISON	500	199.00	199.00
92	FLORENCE NIGHTINGALE	500	199.00	199.00
92	HARRIET TUBMAN	500	199.00	199.00
92	MOLLY PITCHER	500	199.00	199.00
92	POCAHONTAS	500	199.00	199.00

ORIGINAL APPALACHIAN ARTWORKS

X. ROBERTS — **CABBAGE PATCH KIDS**

YR	NAME	LIMIT	ISSUE	TREND
82	AMY	CL	125.00	600.00
82	BILLIE	CL	125.00	550.00
82	BOBBIE	CL	125.00	550.00
82	DOROTHY	CL	125.00	550.00
82	GILDA	CL	125.00	2000.00
82	MARILYN	CL	125.00	550.00
82	OTIS	CL	125.00	550.00
82	REBECCA	CL	125.00	550.00

YR	NAME	LIMIT	ISSUE	TREND
82	SYBIL	CL	125.00	550.00
82	TYLER	2500	125.00	2750.00
83	ANDRE/MADEIRA	CL	250.00	1250.00
84	DADDY'S DARLINS'-KITTEN	CL	300.00	460.00
84	DADDY'S DARLINS'-PRINCESS	CL	300.00	460.00
84	DADDY'S DARLINS'-PUN'KIN	CL	300.00	460.00
84	DADDY'S DARLINS'-TOOTSIE	CL	300.00	460.00
88	TIGER'S EYE-VALENTINE'S DAY	CL	150.00	300.00
89	TIGER'S EYE-MOTHER'S DAY	CL	150.00	250.00
90	JOY	500	250.00	575.00
93	HAPPILY EVER AFTER BRIDE	CL	230.00	340.00
93	HAPPILY EVER AFTER GROOM	CL	230.00	340.00
93	LITTLE PEOPLE/GIRL 27 IN.	CL	325.00	800.00
93	PREEMIE	CL	175.00	285.00
93	UNICOI BALLERINA	200	200.00	310.00
93	UNICOI KIDS	1500	195.00	325.00
94	LITTLE PEOPLE/BOY 27 IN.	CL	325.00	425.00
94	MTN. LAUREL BABY SIDNEY & LANIER	100	390.00	490.00
94	MTN. LAUREL EASTER	200	225.00	325.00
94	MTN. LAUREL IRISH BOYS	100	210.00	310.00
94	MTN. LAUREL IRISH GIRLS	200	210.00	310.00
94	MTN. LAUREL KIDS	CL	195.00	310.00
94	MTN. LAUREL MYSTERIOUS BARRY	CL	225.00	325.00
94	MTN. LAUREL NORMAN JEAN	CL	225.00	225.00
94	NEWBORN FORM MOBILE PATCH	CL	198.00	300.00
X. ROBERTS		**CABBAGE PATCH KIDS CIRCUS PARADE**		
87	BIG TOP CLOWN-BABY CAKES	2000	180.00	475.00
89	HAPPY HOBO-BASHFUL BILLY	1000	180.00	330.00
91	MITZI	1000	220.00	220.00
X. ROBERTS		**CABBAGE PATCH KIDS CONV.**		
94	MTN. LAUREL JUSTIN	200	225.00	325.00
X. ROBERTS		**CABBAGE PATCH KIDS INTERNATIONAL**		
83	AMERICAN INDIAN	CL	150.00	1300.00
83	ORIENTAL	CL	150.00	1350.00
X. ROBERTS		**CHRISTMAS COLLECTION**		
79	X CHRISTMAS PAIR	CL	300.00	3500.00
80	NICHOLAS/NOEL	CL	400.00	3000.00
82	BABY RUDY/CHRISTY NICOLE	CL	400.00	2000.00
83	HOLLY/BERRY	CL	400.00	1300.00
84	CAROLE/CHRIS	CL	400.00	975.00
85	BABY SANDY/CLAUDE	CL	400.00	600.00
86	HILLARY/NIGEL	CL	400.00	400.00
87	KATRINA/MISHA	CL	500.00	500.00
88	KELLY/KANE	CL	500.00	500.00
89	JOY	CL	250.00	600.00
90	KRYSTINA	CL	250.00	250.00
91	NICK	CL	275.00	275.00
92	CHRISTY CLAUS	CL	285.00	285.00
93	RUDOLPH	CL	275.00	275.00
94	NATALIE	500	275.00	275.00
X. ROBERTS		**COLLECTORS CLUB EDITIONS**		
87	BABY OTIS	CL	250.00	550.00
89	ANNA RUBY	CL	250.00	425.00
90	LEE ANN	CL	250.00	400.00
91	RICHARD RUSSELL	CL	250.00	425.00
92	BABY DODD	CL	250.00	350.00
93	PATTI W/CABBAGE BUD BOUTONNIER	CL	280.00	300.00
X. ROBERTS		**CONVENTION BABY**		
89	ASHLEY	CL	150.00	600.00
90	BRADLEY	CL	175.00	425.00
91	CAROLINE	CL	200.00	400.00
92	DUKE	CL	225.00	350.00
93	ELLEN	CL	225.00	310.00
94	JUSTIN	CL	238.50	238.50
X. ROBERTS		**HAPPILY EVER AFTER**		
93	BRIDE	CL	230.00	275.00
93	GROOM	CL	230.00	275.00
X. ROBERTS		**LITTLE PEOPLE**		
78	IN.A IN. BLUE	CL	150.00	4000.00
78	IN.B IN. RED	CL	125.00	3200.00-5000.00
78	IN.C IN. BURGUNDY	CL	100.00	2700.00
78	IN.E IN. BRONZE	CL	125.00	875.00
78	HELEN, BLUE	CL	150.00	6000.00
79	IN.D IN. PURPLE	CL	100.00	2300.00
80	IN.U IN. UNSIGNED	CL	125.00	400.00
80	CELEBRITY	CL	200.00	600.00
80	GRAND EDITION	CL	1000.00	1000.00
80	NOEL	2500	200.00	700.00
80	SP, PREEMIE	CL	100.00	550.00
81	IN.PR II IN. PREEMIE	CL	130.00	250.00
81	NEW IN.EARS IN.	CL	125.00	200.00
81	STANDING EDITION	CL	300.00	350.00
82	IN.U IN. UNSIGNED	CL	125.00	450.00
82	BABY RUDY	1000	200.00	850.00
82	CHRISTY NICOLE	1000	200.00	800.00
82	PE, NEW 'EARS PREEMIE	CL	140.00	375.00
84	DADDY'S DARLINS' SET OF FOUR	CL	1600.00	2250.00
93	LITTLE PEOPLE EDITION/STANDING 27 IN.	CL	300.00	450.00

YR	NAME	LIMIT	ISSUE	TREND
93	UNICOI EDITION	CL	210.00	280.00
X. ROBERTS				**PORCELAIN FRIENDS**
94	ANGELICA	CL	160.00	260.00
94	KAREN LEE	CL	150.00	250.00
94	KASSIS LOU	CL	150.00	250.00
94	KATIE LYN	CL	150.00	250.00

ORIGINALS BY BEVERLY STOEHR

YR	NAME	LIMIT	ISSUE	TREND
B. STOEHR				**BABY SERIES**
94	AMANDA	10	1000.00	1100.00
94	KATIE BABY	10	400.00	425.00
B. STOEHR				**CHILDREN OF MEMORIES**
94	BARBARA	50	495.00	525.00
94	JUDY	10	595.00	625.00
94	SARA	50	495.00	525.00

PEGGY MULHOLLAND INC.

YR	NAME	LIMIT	ISSUE	TREND
B. GERARDI				**CHRISTINA DOLL COLLECTION**
93	CHRISTINA	500	499.00	499.00
93	EMILY	500	499.00	499.00
93	MICHAEL	500	499.00	499.00
93	ROSE	500	499.00	499.00
93	SARAH	500	499.00	499.00
B. GERARDI				**SWEETMMM'S**
93	LILI	RT	130.00	140.00
93	LIZABETH	RT	130.00	140.00
93	MARGARET	RT	130.00	140.00
93	MISSY	RT	130.00	140.00
93	PETER	RT	130.00	140.00
93	ROSEBUD	RT	130.00	140.00
93	SAMANTHA	RT	130.00	140.00
93	TIFFANY	RT	130.00	140.00
94	ANGEL	2-YR	130.00	130.00
94	PRINCESS ORIANA	500	150.00	150.00
95	BUTTONS	1000	159.00	159.00
95	GEORGETTE	1000	159.00	159.00
95	PJ	OP	159.00	159.00
95	THEODORE	1000	159.00	159.00
B. GERARDI				**SWEETMMM'S FIRST PARTY**
94	SUZY	500	150.00	150.00
B. GERARDI				**SWEETMMM'S FIRST VIOLIN LESSON**
95	DOROTHY	1000	179.00	179.00
B. GERARDI				**SWEETMMM'S ROCK A BYE BABY**
94	BABY BLUE EYES	500	150.00	150.00
94	BABY BROWN EYES	500	150.00	150.00

PRINCETON GALLERY

YR	NAME	LIMIT	ISSUE	TREND
*				**BEST FRIENDS DOLLS**
91	SHARING SECRETS	OP	78.00	78.00
*				**CHILDHOOD SONGS DOLLS**
91	IT'S RAINING, IT'S POURING	OP	78.00	78.00
*				**DRESS UP DOLLS**
91	GRANDMA'S ATTIC	OP	95.00	95.00
*				**FABRIQUE SANTA**
91	CHRISTMAS DREAM	OP	76.00	76.00
*				**IMAGINARY PEOPLE**
92	MELINDA, TOOTH FIARY	OP	95.00	95.00
*				**LITTLE LADIES OF VICTORIAN ENGLAND**
90	VICTORIA ANNE	OP	59.00	59.00
91	ABIGAIL	OP	59.00	59.00
91	VALERIE	OP	58.50	59.00
92	CAROLINE	OP	58.50	59.00
92	HEATHER	OP	58.50	59.00
93	BEVERLY	OP	58.50	59.00
*				**ROCK-N-ROLL DOLLS**
93	YELLOW DOT BIKINI	OP	95.00	95.00
M. SIRKO				**ROCK-N-ROLL DOLLS**
91	CINDY AT THE HOP	OP	95.00	95.00
92	CHANTILLY LACE	OP	95.00	95.00
*				**SANTA DOLL**
91	CHECKING HIS LIST	OP	119.00	119.00
M. SIRKO				**TERRIBLE TWOS DOLLS**
91	ONE MAN BAND	OP	95.00	95.00

RECO INTERNATIONAL

YR	NAME	LIMIT	ISSUE	TREND
S. KUCK				**CHILDHOOD DOLL COLLECTION**
94	A KISS GOODNIGHT	OP	79.00	85.00
94	TEACHING TEDDY HIS PRAYERS	OP	79.00	85.00
95	READING WITH TEDDY	OP	79.00	79.00
J. MCCLELLAND				**CHILDREN'S CIRCUS DOLL COLLECTION**
91	JOHNNY THE STRONGMAN	YR	83.00	83.00
91	KATIE THE TIGHTROPE WALKER	YR	78.00	78.00
91	TOMMY THE CLOWN	YR	78.00	78.00
92	MAGGIE THE ANIMAL TRAINER	YR	83.00	83.00
S. KUCK				**PRECIOUS MEMORIES OF MOTHERHOOD**
90	LOVING STEPS	RT	125.00	175.00

YR	NAME	LIMIT	ISSUE	TREND
90	LULLABY	YR	125.00	125.00
92	EXPECTANT MOMENTS	RT	149.00	149.00
93	BEDTIME	RT	149.00	149.00
*		**TENDER MOMENTS DOLLS**		
90	KATHY	OP	40.00	47.00
90	KELLI	OP	73.00	73.00
90	KIM	OP	40.00	43.00
90	KRISTI	OP	47.00	50.00
91	CANDI	OP	106.00	106.00
91	CARRIE	OP	30.00	30.00
91	CASEY	OP	80.00	80.00
91	CHRISTINE	OP	85.00	85.00
91	CONNIE	OP	80.00	80.00
91	CORINNE	OP	79.00	79.00
91	KERRI	OP	64.00	64.00
91	TANYA	OP	45.00	45.00
91	TINA	OP	73.00	73.00
91	TONI	OP	47.00	47.00

RHODES STUDIO

YR	NAME	LIMIT	ISSUE	TREND
ROCKWELL INSPIRED		**A NORMAN ROCKWELL CHRISTMAS**		
90	SCOTTY PLAYS SANTA	CL	48.00	48.00
91	SCOTTY GETS HIS TREE	CL	59.00	59.00

ROMAN INC.

YR	NAME	LIMIT	ISSUE	TREND
E. WILLIAMS		**A CHRISTMAS DREAM**		
90	CAROLE	5000	125.00	125.00
90	CHELSEA	5000	125.00	125.00
E. WILLIAMS		**ABBIE WILLIAMS COLLECTION**		
91	MOLLY	5000	155.00	155.00
E. WILLIAMS		**CLASSIC BRIDES OF THE CENTURY**		
90	FLORA, THE 1900'S BRIDE	CL	145.00	145.00
91	JENNIFER, THE 1980'S BRIDE	CL	149.00	149.00
92	CATHLEEN, THE 1990'S BRIDE	TL	149.95	150.00
93	KATHLEEN - THE 1930'S BRIDE	YR	149.00	149.00
E. WILLIAMS		**ELLEN WILLIAMS DOLLS**		
89	NOELLE	5000	125.00	125.00
89	REBECCA	7500	195.00	195.00
*		**TYROLEAN TREASURES: SOFT BODY, HUMAN HAIR**		
90	ANDREW	2000	575.00	575.00
90	ELLAN	2000	575.00	575.00
90	ERIKA	2000	575.00	575.00
90	MARISA	2000	575.00	575.00
90	MATTHEW	2000	575.00	575.00
90	SARAH	2000	575.00	575.00
*		**TYROLEAN TREASURES: WOOD BODY, MOVEABLE JOINT**		
90	ANN	2000	650.00	650.00
90	DAVID	2000	650.00	650.00
90	KARIN	2000	650.00	650.00
90	LISA	2000	650.00	650.00
90	MELISSA	2000	650.00	650.00
90	MONICA	2000	650.00	650.00
90	NADIA	2000	650.00	650.00
90	SUSIE	2000	650.00	650.00
90	TINA	2000	650.00	650.00
90	VERENA	2000	650.00	650.00

SALLY-LYNNE DOLLS

YR	NAME	LIMIT	ISSUE	TREND
S. BEATTY		**FRENCH REPLICAS**		
85	ANNABELLE, 30 IN.	CL	950.00	2900.00
85	CANDICE, 30 IN.	100	950.00	2200.00
85	CHARLES, 30 IN.	100	1050.00	2200.00
85	VICTORIA, 30 IN.	100	1050.00	2900.00
86	VICTORIA AT CHRISTMAS, 30 IN.	CL	2500.00	4100.00

SAMSONS STUDIOS

YR	NAME	LIMIT	ISSUE	TREND
S. BUTCHER		**PRECIOUS MOMENTS SOFT SCULPTURE DOLLS**		
85	DONNY 4566	*	24.00	60.00
85	HEATHER 4562	*	24.00	60.00
85	PEGGY 4565	*	24.00	60.00
85	RUTHIE 4570 ORIGINAL	*	24.00	70.00
86	GWEN 1845	*	24.00	75.00
86	KATIE 5605	*	24.00	65.00
86	SNOWFLAKE 5379	*	34.00	80.00
86	TERRIE 5488	*	24.00	75.00

SANDY DOLLS INC.

YR	NAME	LIMIT	ISSUE	TREND
G. DY		**COLLECTOR ANGELS**		
95	CELESTE	CL	175.00	175.00
95	TIFFANY	CL	195.00	195.00
S. DY		**SANDRA**		
94	SANDRA AUTUMN	1500	50.00	60.00
94	SANDRA WINTER	1500	60.00	65.00
S. DY		**SANDY CLOWNS**		
94	JESTER	1000	75.00	80.00
94	JUJU	1000	60.00	65.00
R. TEJADA		**SWEET SPIRIT BABY**		
96	LITTLE BLOSSOM--CHEROKEE IN FRONT	1500	65.00	65.00

YR	NAME	LIMIT	ISSUE	TREND
R. TEJADA				**TRADITIONS**
94	GENTLE DOVE--WISHRAM WEDDING CEREMONY	3500	100.00	110.00
94	GREY OWL--HUNKPAPA SIOUX CHIEF	3500	250.00	275.00
94	MEADOW FLOWER--CHEROKEE PRINCESS	3500	85.00	95.00
94	SPRING WATER W/LITTLE SCOUT	3500	115.00	125.00
94	WAR CLOUD--OGLALA SIOUX CHIEF	3500	115.00	125.00
95	BRIGHT SKY--APACHE PUBERTY	3500	100.00	100.00
95	HUNTING WOLF--CROW WARRIOR	3500	100.00	100.00
95	LADY REBECCA, POWHATAN PRINCESS POCAHONT	3500	160.00	160.00
95	MOUNTAIN SHADOW--YAKIMA PRINCESS	3500	100.00	100.00
95	POCAHONTAS--POWHATAN PRINCESS	3500	85.00	85.00
95	PRINCESS BLUEBIRD	1000	295.00	295.00
96	WHITE MOON--BLACKFOOT NATION	3500	75.00	75.00
R. TEJADA			**WARRIOR & PRINCESS**	
94	FALLING SNOW--NEZ PERCE PRINCESS	5000	37.50	40.00
94	LAUGHING BROOK--COMANCHE PRINCESS	5000	37.50	40.00
94	ROARING RIVER--MOHAWK WARRIOR	5000	37.50	40.00
94	SHINING CLOUD--COMANCHE PRINCESS	5000	37.50	40.00
94	SOARING HAWK--COMANCHE WARRIOR	5000	37.50	40.00
94	SWIFT ELK--IROQUOIS WARRIOR	5000	37.50	40.00
94	WHITE EAGLE--APACHE WARRIOR	5000	37.50	40.00
95	BEAR'S TRACK--FOX WARRIOR	5000	37.50	38.00
95	GROWLING BEAR	5000	37.50	38.00
95	HOWLING DOG--CHEYENNE WARRIOR	5000	37.50	38.00
95	LITTLE OTTER--HUPA PRINCESS	5000	37.50	38.00
95	POCAHONTAS--POWHATAN PRINCESS	5000	37.50	38.00
95	SWAYING REED--OJIBWA PRINCESS	5000	37.50	38.00
96	LEAPING WATER--APACHE PRINCESS	5000	37.50	38.00

SARAH'S ATTIC

YR	NAME	LIMIT	ISSUE	TREND
S. SCHULTZ				
*	OPIE CLOTH DOLL	500	90.00	200.00
*	POLLY CLOTH DOLL	500	90.00	200.00
S. SCHUTLZ				
*	PEACE ANGEL CLOTH DOLL	500	50.00	200.00
S. SCHULTZ		**BEARY ADORABLES COLLECTION**		
91	CHRISTMAS BETTY BEAR	1000	160.00	160.00
S. SCHULTZ		**HEIRLOOMS FROM THE ATTIC**		
86	AMIE AMISH DOLL	CL	40.00	40.00
86	BETSY BOO DOLL	CL	40.00	40.00
86	BILLY BEAR	CL	80.00	80.00
86	BROWNIE BEAR	CL	36.00	36.00
86	BUFFY BEAR	CL	80.00	80.00
86	CHARITY WHITE ANGEL	CL	34.00	34.00
86	CUPCAKE DOLL	CL	32.00	32.00
86	HOLLY BLACK ANGEL	RT	34.00	180.00
86	HOPE BLACK ANGEL	CL	34.00	34.00
86	JENNIE WHITE ANGEL DOLL	CL	52.00	52.00
86	JENNIE WHITE DOLL	CL	44.00	44.00
86	JUDITH ANN BLACK DOLL	CL	34.00	34.00
86	KATIE DOLL	CL	32.00	32.00
86	LOUISA MAY BLACK COTH DOLL	CL	120.00	120.00
86	MAGGIE CLOTH DOLL	CL	32.00	32.00
86	MAGGIE CLOTH DOLL	CL	70.00	125.00
86	MATT CLOTH DOLL	CL	32.00	32.00
86	MATT CLOTH DOLL	CL	70.00	125.00
86	NELLIE DOLL	CL	32.00	32.00
86	PETER DOLL	CL	140.00	140.00
86	PRISCILLA DOLL	CL	140.00	310.00
86	SADIE BLACK DOLL	CL	70.00	120.00
86	SPIKE DOLL	CL	32.00	32.00
86	TILLIE DOLL	CL	32.00	32.00
86	TRAPP THE CAT	CL	36.00	36.00
86	TWINKIE DOLL	CL	32.00	32.00
86	WHIMPY DOLL	CL	32.00	32.00
86	WILLIE DOLL	CL	32.00	32.00
87	BENJI BEAR	CL	25.00	25.00
87	LEROY BLACK RAG DOLL	CL	54.00	54.00
87	LUCY BLACK RAG DOLL	CL	54.00	54.00
87	MOLLY SMALL 5 PIECE DOLL	CL	36.00	36.00
87	PATCHES WHITE RAG DOLL	CL	54.00	54.00
87	POLLY WHITE RAG DOLL	CL	54.00	54.00
87	ROXIE RABBIT	CL	32.00	32.00
87	SUNSHINE 5 PIECE DOLL	CL	79.00	79.00
87	TESS RAG DOLL	CL	140.00	140.00
87	TILLIE RAG DOLL	CL	32.00	32.00
87	WILLIE RAG DOLL	CL	32.00	32.00
88	ALBERT	CL	20.00	20.00
88	ASHLEE	CL	20.00	20.00
88	COUNTRY GIRL	CL	26.00	26.00
88	DAISY	CL	20.00	20.00
88	DAVID	CL	20.00	20.00
88	LILY BLACK DOLL	CL	90.00	90.00
88	MAYBELLE CLOTH BUNNY	CL	46.00	46.00
88	MELVILLE CLOTH BUNNY	CL	46.00	46.00
88	MICHAEL 5 PIECE DOLL	CL	44.00	44.00
88	MRS. CLAUS 5 PIECE DOLL	RT	120.00	120.00
88	SANTA 5 PIECE DOLL	RT	120.00	120.00

YR	NAME	LIMIT	ISSUE	TREND
88	SMILEY CLOWN	CL	126.00	126.00
88	VICTORIAN BOY	CL	24.00	24.00
88	VICTORIAN GIRL	CL	24.00	24.00
89	BECKY	RT	120.00	120.00
89	BEVERLY JANE BLACK DRESS	RT	160.00	160.00
89	BEVERLY JANE-RED DRESS	RT	160.00	160.00
89	BEVERLY JANE-SUNDAY'S BEST	RT	160.00	160.00
89	BOBBY	RT	120.00	120.00
89	FREEDOM CLOWN	RT	150.00	150.00
89	GLORY ANGEL	CL	50.00	225.00
89	GREEN BEVERLY JANE	RT	160.00	160.00
89	HARMONY CLOWN	RT	150.00	150.00
89	HOLLY ANGEL	CL	50.00	225.00
89	HOPE ANGEL	CL	50.00	225.00
89	JOY ANGEL	CL	50.00	225.00
89	LIBERTY ANGEL	CL	50.00	225.00
89	MEGAN DOLL	CL	70.00	70.00
89	NOEL-CHRISTMAS CLOWN	RT	120.00	120.00
89	PEACE ANGEL	CL	50.00	225.00
89	SCOTT DOLL	RT	70.00	100.00
89	SPIRIT OF AMERICA SANTA	RT	150.00	210.00
89	VICTOR	CL	120.00	120.00
89	VICTORIA	RT	120.00	120.00
90	AMERICANA BEAR	CL	160.00	160.00
90	AMERICANA HICKORY	RT	150.00	160.00
90	AMERICANA SASSAFRAS	RT	150.00	160.00
90	BEACHTIME HICKORY	RT	140.00	165.00
90	BEACHTIME SASSAFRAS	RT	140.00	165.00
90	BETTY BEAR SUNDAY	CL	160.00	160.00
90	BETTY BEAR-CHRISTMAS	CL	160.00	160.00
90	PLAYTIME HICKORY	RT	140.00	165.00
90	PLAYTIME SASSAFRAS	RT	140.00	165.00
90	SCHOOL DAYS HICKORY	RT	140.00	160.00
90	SCHOOL DAYS SASSAFRAS	RT	140.00	160.00
90	SUNDAY'S BEST HICKORY	RT	150.00	200.00
90	SUNDAY'S BEST SASSAFRAS	RT	150.00	165.00
90	SWEET DREAMS HICKORY	RT	140.00	165.00
90	SWEET DREAMS SASSAFRAS	RT	140.00	200.00
90	TEDDY BEAR SUNDAY	CL	160.00	160.00
90	TEDDY SCHOOL BEAR	CL	160.00	160.00
91	ALL CLOTH ADORA ANGEL	RT	90.00	190.00
91	ALL CLOTH ENOS ANGEL	RT	90.00	190.00
91	ALL CLOTH MUFFIN BLACK DOLL	CL	90.00	90.00
91	ALL CLOTH OPIE WHITE DOLL	CL	90.00	90.00
91	ALL CLOTH POLLY WHITE DOLL	CL	90.00	90.00
91	ALL CLOTH PUFFIN BLACK DOLL	CL	90.00	90.00
91	CHRISTMAS HICKORY	RT	150.00	160.00
91	CHRISTMAS SASSAFRAS	RT	150.00	160.00
91	CHRISTMAS TEDDY BEAR	CL	160.00	160.00
91	ENOS	RT	90.00	190.00
91	SPRINGTIME HICKORY	RT	150.00	175.00
91	SPRINGTIME SASSAFRAS	RT	150.00	200.00
92	ANGELLE GUARDIAN ANGEL	CL	170.00	170.00
92	COUNTRY EDIE	RT	170.00	170.00
92	COUNTRY EMILY	RT	250.00	250.00
92	COUNTRY EMMA	RT	160.00	160.00
92	COUNTRY HILARY	RT	200.00	200.00
92	HARPSTER W/BANJO	CL	250.00	250.00
92	KIAH GUARDIAN ANGEL	RT	170.00	170.00
92	PEACE ON EARTH SANTA	RT	175.00	325.00
92	PLAYTIME EDIE	RT	170.00	170.00
92	PLAYTIME EMMA	RT	160.00	160.00
92	SPRINGTIME BETTY BEAR	CL	160.00	160.00
92	SPRINGTIME TEDDY BEAR	CL	160.00	160.00
92	VICTORIAN EDIE	RT	170.00	170.00
92	VICTORIAN EMILY	RT	250.00	250.00
92	VICTORIAN HILARY	RT	200.00	200.00
92	WHOOPIE	CL	200.00	200.00
92	WOOSTER	CL	160.00	160.00
93	GRANNY QUILTING LADY	CL	130.00	130.00
93	JACK BOY	500	130.00	130.00
93	LILLA QUILTING LADY	CL	130.00	130.00
93	MILLIE QUILTING LADY	CL	130.00	130.00
93	SALLY BOOBA	500	130.00	130.00
94	STAR BLACK DOLL	500	120.00	120.00
94	TILLIE/CLOWN	1000	120.00	120.00
94	TWINKLE/WHITE ANGEL	500	120.00	120.00
94	WILLIE/CLOWN	1000	120.00	120.00
95	BABY DOLL/4341	RT	300.00	300.00
95	LABOR OF LOVE/4338	150	300.00	300.00
95	LABOR OF LOVE/4339	150	300.00	300.00
95	OLIVIA/4340	150	300.00	300.00
95	TILLIE/4337	RT	300.00	300.00
95	WILLIE/4336	150	300.00	300.00

S. SCHULTZ — LITTLE CHARMERS COLLECTION

YR	NAME	LIMIT	ISSUE	TREND
89	RED BEVERLY JANE	RT	160.00	160.00
89	SUNDAY'S BEST-BEVERLY JANE	RT	160.00	160.00
91	VICTORIAN EMMA	RT	160.00	160.00

YR	NAME	LIMIT	ISSUE	TREND
S. SCHULTZ		**SNUGGABLE HUGGABLES**		
96	AMERICANA POSIE/1900	100	130.00	130.00
96	HALLOWEEN POSIE/1902	100	130.00	130.00
96	POPPER W/JUMPSUIT/1904	100	90.00	90.00
96	POPPER W/PINAFORE/1903	100	90.00	90.00
96	SPRING POSIE/1901	100	130.00	130.00
S. SCHULTZ		**SPIRIT OF CHRISTMAS COLLECTION**		
89	FATHER CHRISTMAS DOLL	500	150.00	150.00

SCHMID

Price ranges may reflect various demands in the market from one geographic region to another; condition of piece; specific markings found on piece; and/or changes in production of piece.

YR	NAME	LIMIT	ISSUE	TREND
J. AMOS GRAMMER		**JUNE AMOS GRAMMER**		
80	LEIGH ANN	1000	195.00	210.00
88	ROSAMUND	750	225.00	225.00
89	KATIE	1000	180.00	180.00
89	VANESSA	1000	180.00	210.00
90	JESTER LOVE	1000	195.00	210.00
90	LAUREN	1000	279.00	280.00
90	MEGAN	750	380.00	380.00
91	HEATHER	1000	210.00	210.00
91	LAUREN	1000	280.00	280.00
91	MITSUKO	1000	210.00	210.00

SEYMOUR MANN

YR	NAME	LIMIT	ISSUE	TREND
J. WHITE		**CHRISTMAS COLLECTION**		
90	CUPID CPD-6	OP	13.50	14.00
90	DOLL TREE TOPPER OM-124	RT	85.00	85.00
90	HAT W/STREAMERS OM-118	RT	20.00	20.00
90	HEARTFACE OM-119	RT	12.00	12.00
90	LACE BALL OM-120	RT	10.00	10.00
90	TASSEL OM-118	RT	7.50	8.00
91	ELVES W/MALL CJ-454	OP	30.00	30.00
91	FLAT SANTA CJ-115	OP	7.50	8.00
91	SANTAS, SET OF 8 CJ-12	OP	60.00	60.00
P. APRILE		**CONNOISSEUR DOLL COLLECTION**		
92	BRIDE & FLOWER GRIL PAC-6	5000	800.00	800.00
92	OLIVIA PAC-12	5000	300.00	300.00
92	VIOLETTA PAC-18	5000	185.00	185.00
P. KOLESAR		**CONNOISSEUR DOLL COLLECTION**		
92	LITTLE TURTLE INDIAN PK-110	5000	150.00	150.00
92	REVAN ESKIMO PK-106	5000	130.00	130.00
E. MANN		**CONNOISSEUR DOLL COLLECTION**		
84	MISS DEBUTANTE DEBI	CL	75.00	200.00
85	CHRISTMAS CHEER-124	RT	40.00	110.00
85	WENDY-C120	CL	45.00	160.00
86	CAMELOT FAIRY-C84	RT	75.00	235.00
87	ALICIA-YK-4215	CL	90.00	90.00
87	AUDRINA-YK200	CL	85.00	150.00
87	CYNTHIA DOM-211	RT	85.00	85.00
87	DAWN-C185	RT	75.00	190.00
87	LINDA-C190	RT	60.00	125.00
87	MARCY-YK122	RT	55.00	110.00
87	NIRMALA YK-210	RT	50.00	65.00
87	RAPUNZEL-C158	RT	95.00	190.00
87	SABRINA-C208	RT	65.00	100.00
87	SAILORETTE-DOM217	RT	70.00	160.00
87	VIVIAN C-201P	RT	80.00	80.00
88	ASHLEY-C-278	CL	80.00	80.00
88	BRITTANY-TK-5	RT	120.00	120.00
88	CISSIE-DOM263	RT	65.00	140.00
88	CRYING COURTNEY PS75	RT	115.00	115.00
88	CYNTHIA-DOM-211	RT	85.00	85.00
88	DOLL OLIVER FH-392	RT	100.00	100.00
88	EMILY YK-243V	RT	70.00	70.00
88	FRANCES-C-233	CL	80.00	140.00
88	GISELLE ON GOOSE-FH176	RT	105.00	230.00
88	JESSICA-DOM-267	RT	90.00	90.00
88	JOANNE CRY BABY PS-50	RT	100.00	100.00
88	JOLIE-C231	RT	65.00	160.00
88	JULIE-C245A	RT	65.00	170.00
88	JULIETTE BRIDE MUSICAL C246L TM	RT	150.00	150.00
88	KIRSTEN-PS-40G	RT	70.00	70.00
88	LIONEL-FH206B	RT	50.00	125.00
88	LUCINDA-DOM-293	RT	90.00	90.00
88	MICHELLE & MARCEL-YK176	RT	70.00	160.00
88	PAULINE YK-230	RT	90.00	90.00
88	SABRINA C208	RT	65.00	100.00
88	SISTER AGNES C250	RT	75.00	75.00
88	SISTER IGNATIUS NOTRE DAME FH184	RT	75.00	75.00
88	SISTER TERESA FH187	RT	80.00	80.00
88	TRACY-C-3006	RT	95.00	160.00
88	VIVIAN-C201P	RT	80.00	80.00
89	AMBER-DOM-281A	CL	85.00	85.00
89	BETTY-PS27G	CL	65.00	130.00
89	BRETT-PS27B	RT	65.00	130.00
89	BRITTANY-TK-4	RT	150.00	150.00
89	CRYING COURTNEY PS-75	RT	115.00	115.00

YR	NAME	LIMIT	ISSUE	TREND
89	DAPHNE ECRU-C3025	CL	120.00	120.00
89	DAPHNE ECRU/MINT GREEN C3025	RT	85.00	85.00
89	ELISABETH OM-32	RT	120.00	120.00
89	ELIZABETH-C-246P	RT	150.00	210.00
89	EMILY-PS-48	RT	110.00	110.00
89	FRANCES-C233	RT	80.00	130.00
89	HAPPY BIRTHDAY-C3012	RT	80.00	130.00
89	HEIDI-260	RT	50.00	100.00
89	JAQUELINE-DOLL-254M	RT	85.00	85.00
89	JOANNE CRY BABY PS-50	RT	100.00	100.00
89	KAYOKO-PS24	RT	75.00	180.00
89	KIRSTEN PS-40G	RT	70.00	70.00
89	LING-LING-PS-87G	RT	90.00	90.00
89	LIZ-YK-269	RT	70.00	110.00
89	LUCINDA DOM-293	RT	90.00	90.00
89	MAI-LING-PS-79	RT	100.00	100.00
89	MARCEY YK-4005	RT	90.00	90.00
89	MARGARET-245	RT	100.00	160.00
89	MAUREEN-PS-84	RT	90.00	90.00
89	MEIMEI-PS22	RT	75.00	230.00
89	MELISSA-LL-794	RT	95.00	95.00
89	MISS KIM-PS25	RT	75.00	180.00
89	PATRICIA/PATRICK-215GBB	RT	105.00	140.00
89	PAULA PS-56	RT	75.00	75.00
89	PAULINE BONAPARTE OM-68	RT	120.00	120.00
89	RAMONA PS-31B	RT	80.00	80.00
89	REBECCA PS-34V	RT	45.00	45.00
89	ROSIE-290M	RT	55.00	90.00
89	SISTER MARY-C-249	RT	75.00	130.00
89	SUNNY PS-59V	RT	71.00	75.00
89	SUZIE-PS-32	RT	80.00	80.00
89	TATIANA PINK BALLERINA OM-60	RT	120.00	120.00
89	TERRI-PS-104	RT	85.00	85.00
89	WENDY-PS-51	RT	105.00	105.00
90	ANABELLE-C-3080	2500	85.00	85.00
90	ANGEL-DOM-335	2500	105.00	105.00
90	ANGELA-C-3084	2500	105.00	105.00
90	ANGELA-C-3084M	2500	115.00	115.00
90	ANITA-FH-277G	2500	65.00	65.00
90	ASHLEY-FH-325	2500	75.00	75.00
90	AUDREY-YK-4089	3500	125.00	125.00
90	BABY BETTY-YK-4087	3500	125.00	125.00
90	BABY JATE-WB-19	CL	85.00	85.00
90	BABY NELLY-PS-163	CL	95.00	95.00
90	BABY SUNSHINE-C-3055	CL	90.00	90.00
90	BETH-YK-4099A/B	2500	125.00	125.00
90	BETTINA-TR-4	2500	125.00	125.00
90	BEVERLY-DOLL-335	2500	110.00	110.00
90	BILLIE-YK-4056V	CL	65.00	65.00
90	CAITLIN YK-4051V	CL	90.00	90.00
90	CAITLIN-DOLL-11PH	RT	60.00	60.00
90	CAROLE-YK-4085W	RT	125.00	125.00
90	CHARLENE-YK-4112	RT	90.00	90.00
90	CHIN FA-C-3061	RT	95.00	95.00
90	CHINOOK-WB-24	RT	85.00	85.00
90	CHRISTIE WB-2	RT	75.00	75.00
90	DAISY-EP-6	RT	90.00	90.00
90	DAPHNE ECRU-C-3025	RT	85.00	85.00
90	DIANE-FH-275	RT	90.00	90.00
90	DIANNA-TK-31	RT	175.00	175.00
90	DOMINO-C-3050	RT	145.00	145.00
90	DOROTHY-TR-10	RT	135.00	135.00
90	DORRI-DOLL-16PH	RT	85.00	85.00
90	EILEEN-FH-367	RT	100.00	100.00
90	FELICIA-TR-9	RT	115.00	115.00
90	FRANCESCA-C-3021	RT	100.00	190.00
90	GERRI YK-4094	RT	95.00	95.00
90	GINNY-YK-4119	RT	100.00	100.00
90	HOPE YK-4118	RT	90.00	90.00
90	HYACINTH-DOLL-15PH	RT	85.00	85.00
90	INDIAN DOLL FH-296	RT	60.00	60.00
90	INDIAN DOLL-FH-295	CL	60.00	60.00
90	JANETTE-DOLL-385	RT	85.00	85.00
90	JILLIAN DOLL-41PH	RT	90.00	90.00
90	JOANNE-TR-12	RT	175.00	175.00
90	JULIE-WB-35	RT	70.00	70.00
90	KAREN-PS-198	RT	150.00	150.00
90	KATE-C-3060	RT	95.00	95.00
90	KATHY W/BEAR TE1	RT	70.00	70.00
90	KIKI-EP-4	RT	100.00	100.00
90	LAURA DOLL-25PH	RT	55.00	55.00
90	LAUREN-SP-300	RT	85.00	85.00
90	LAVENDER BLUE-YK-4024	RT	95.00	140.00
90	LIEN WHA-YK-4092	RT	100.00	100.00
90	LING-LING DOLL	RT	50.00	50.00
90	LISA BEIGE ACCORDION PLEAT YK-4093	RT	125.00	125.00
90	LISA-C-3053	CL	100.00	100.00
90	LISA-FH-379	RT	100.00	100.00
90	LISA-YK-4093	CL	125.00	135.00

YR	NAME	LIMIT	ISSUE	TREND
90	LIZA C-3053	RT	100.00	100.00
90	LOLA-SP-79	RT	105.00	105.00
90	LORETTA-FH-321	RT	90.00	90.00
90	LORI WB-72BM	RT	75.00	75.00
90	MADAME DU POMPADOUR-C-3088	RT	250.00	250.00
90	MAGGIE-PS-151P	RT	90.00	90.00
90	MAGGIE-WB-51	RT	105.00	105.00
90	MARIA-YK-4116	RT	85.00	85.00
90	MELANIE-YK-4115	RT	80.00	80.00
90	MELISSA-DOLL-390	RT	75.00	75.00
90	MERRY WIDOW-C-3040	RT	145.00	145.00
90	MERRY WIDOW-C-3040M	RT	140.00	140.00
90	NANOOK-WB-23	RT	75.00	75.00
90	NATASHA-PS-102	RT	100.00	100.00
90	ODESSA-FH-362	RT	65.00	65.00
90	PING-LING DOLL 363RV	RT	50.00	50.00
90	POLLY DOLL-22PH	RT	90.00	90.00
90	PRINCESS RED FEATHER PS-189	RT	90.00	90.00
90	PRINCESS-FH-268B	RT	75.00	75.00
90	PRISCILLA-WB-50	RT	105.00	105.00
90	SABRINA-C3050	RT	105.00	105.00
90	SALLY-WB-20	RT	95.00	95.00
90	SHIRLEY-WB-37	RT	65.00	65.00
90	SISTER MARY-WB-15	RT	70.00	70.00
90	SOPHIE-OM-1	RT	65.00	65.00
90	STACY-TR-5	RT	105.00	105.00
90	SUE CHUEN C-3061G	RT	95.00	95.00
90	SUNNY-FH-331	RT	70.00	70.00
90	SUSAN DOLL 364MC	RT	75.00	75.00
90	TANIA-DOLL376-P	RT	65.00	65.00
90	TINA-DOLL-371	RT	85.00	85.00
90	TINA-WB-32	RT	65.00	65.00
90	TNIA-DOLL-371	CL	85.00	85.00
90	TOMMY-C-3064	RT	75.00	75.00
90	WENDY-TE-3	RT	75.00	75.00
90	WILMA-PS-174	RT	75.00	75.00
90	YEN YEN-YK-4091	RT	05.00	95.00
91	ABBY C3145	CL	100.00	100.00
91	ABIGAIL-EP-3	RT	100.00	100.00
91	ABIGAL-WB-72WM	CL	75.00	75.00
91	ALEXIS-EP32	CL	220.00	220.00
91	ALICIA YK-4215	3500	90.00	90.00
91	AMANDA OM-182	2500	260.00	260.00
91	AMANDA TOAST-OM-182	CL	260.00	260.00
91	AMELIA-TR-47	CL	105.00	115.00
91	AMY-C-3147	CL	135.00	145.00
91	ANN TR-52	2500	135.00	135.00
91	ANNETTE TR-59	2500	130.00	130.00
91	ANNIE YK-4214	CL	145.00	145.00
91	ANTOINETTE FH-452	2600	100.00	100.00
91	ANTONINETTE-FH-452	CL	100.00	100.00
91	ARABELLA-C-3163	CL	135.00	145.00
91	ARIEL-EP-33	CL	175.00	175.00
91	AUDREY-FH-455	2500	125.00	125.00
91	AURORA-OM-181	2500	260.00	260.00
91	AZURE-AM-15	2500	175.00	175.00
91	BABBY ELLIE ECRU MUSICAL 402E	2500	27.50	28.00
91	BABY BETH-DOLL-406P	2500	27.50	28.00
91	BABY BONNIE W/WALKER MUSIC DOLL-409	2500	40.00	40.00
91	BABY BONNIE-SP-341	CL	55.00	55.00
91	BABY BRENT-EP-15	RT	85.00	85.00
91	BABY CARRIE-DOLL-402P	2500	27.50	28.00
91	BABY ELLIE17	2500	65.00	65.00
91	BABY GLORIA BLACK BABY-PS-289	CL	75.00	75.00
91	BABY JOHN-PS-498	CL	85.00	85.00
91	BABY LINDA-DOLL-406E	2500	27.50	28.00
91	BABY SUE-DOLL-402B	2500	27.50	28.00
91	BELINDA C-3164	RT	150.00	150.00
91	BERNETTA-EP-40	CL	115.00	125.00
91	BETSY-AM-6	RT	105.00	105.00
91	BETTINA YK-4144	3500	105.00	105.00
91	BLAINE-TR-61	CL	115.00	115.00
91	BLYTHE-CH-15V	CL	135.00	135.00
91	BO-PEEP W/LAMB-C-3128	CL	105.00	105.00
91	BRIDGET-SP-379	2500	105.00	105.00
91	BROOKE-FH-461	2500	115.00	115.00
91	BRYNA-AM-100B	2500	70.00	70.00
91	CAMELLIA FH-457	2500	100.00	100.00
91	CAROLINE LL-838	2500	110.00	110.00
91	CAROLINE LL-905	2500	110.00	110.00
91	CHERYL TR-49	2500	120.00	120.00
91	CHIN CHIN YK-4211	CL	85.00	85.00
91	CHRISTINA-PS-261	RT	115.00	115.00
91	CINDY LOU FH-264	RT	85.00	85.00
91	CINDY LOU-FH-464	2500	85.00	85.00
91	CISSY EP-56	RT	95.00	95.00
91	CLARE-DOLL 465	RT	100.00	100.00
91	CLAUDINE C-3146	RT	95.00	95.00
91	COLETTE-WB-7	RT	65.00	65.00

YR	NAME	LIMIT	ISSUE	TREND
91	COLLEEN YK-4163	RT	120.00	120.00
91	COOKIE GU-6	RT	110.00	110.00
91	COURTNEY-LL-859	RT	150.00	150.00
91	CREOLE-AM-17	RT	160.00	160.00
91	CRYSTAL YK-4237	RT	125.00	125.00
91	DANIELLE-AM-5	RT	125.00	125.00
91	DARCY EP-47	RT	110.00	110.00
91	DARCY FH-451	RT	105.00	105.00
91	DARLA C-3122	RT	110.00	110.00
91	DARLENE DOLL-444	RT	75.00	75.00
91	DAWN C-3135	RT	130.00	130.00
91	DENISE-LL-852	RT	105.00	105.00
91	DEPHINE-SP-308	RT	135.00	135.00
91	DESIREE LL-898	RT	120.00	120.00
91	DUANANE-SP-366	RT	85.00	85.00
91	DULCIE-YK-4131V	RT	100.00	100.00
91	DWAYNE C-3123	RT	120.00	120.00
91	EDIE YK-4177	RT	115.00	115.00
91	ELISABETH & LISA C-3095	RT	195.00	195.00
91	ELISE-PS-259	RT	105.00	105.00
91	ELIZABETH AM-32	RT	105.00	105.00
91	EMMALINE OM-191	RT	300.00	300.00
91	EMMALINE OM-197	RT	300.00	300.00
91	EMMY-C-3099	RT	125.00	125.00
91	ERIN-DOLL-4PH	RT	60.00	60.00
91	EVALINA C-3124	RT	135.00	135.00
91	FIFI AM-100F	RT	70.00	70.00
91	FLEURETTE PS-286	RT	75.00	75.00
91	FLORA TR-46	RT	125.00	125.00
91	FRANCESCA-AM-14	RT	175.00	175.00
91	GEORGIA YK-4143	RT	150.00	150.00
91	GEORGIA-YK-4131	CL	100.00	100.00
91	GIGI-C-3107	RT	135.00	135.00
91	GINGER LL-907	RT	115.00	115.00
91	GLORIA AM-100G	RT	70.00	70.00
91	GLORIA YK-4166	RT	105.00	105.00
91	GRETCHEN DOLL-446	RT	45.00	45.00
91	GRETEL DOLL-434	RT	60.00	60.00
91	HANSEL & GRETEL DOLL-448V	RT	60.00	60.00
91	HELENE AM-29	RT	150.00	150.00
91	HOLLY CH-6	RT	100.00	100.00
91	HONEY BUNNY-WB-9	RT	70.00	70.00
91	HONEY FH-401	RT	100.00	100.00
91	HOPE FH-434	RT	90.00	90.00
91	INDIRA-AM-4	RT	125.00	125.00
91	IRIS TR-58	RT	120.00	120.00
91	IVY PS-307	RT	75.00	75.00
91	JANE-PS-243L	RT	115.00	115.00
91	JANICE OM-194	RT	300.00	300.00
91	JESSICA-FH-423	RT	95.00	95.00
91	JOY-EP-23V	RT	130.00	130.00
91	JOYCE AM-100J	RT	35.00	35.00
91	JULIA-C-3102	RT	135.00	135.00
91	JULIETTE OM-192	RT	300.00	300.00
91	KAREN-EP-24	RT	115.00	115.00
91	KARMELA EP-57	RT	120.00	120.00
91	KELLY-AM-8	RT	125.00	125.00
91	KERRY-FH-396	RT	100.00	100.00
91	KIM AM-100K	RT	70.00	70.00
91	KINESHA SP-402	RT	110.00	110.00
91	KRISTI-FH-402	RT	100.00	100.00
91	KYLA YK-4137	RT	95.00	95.00
91	LAURA-WB-110P	RT	85.00	85.00
91	LEIGH DOLL-457	RT	95.00	95.00
91	LEILA-AM-2	RT	125.00	125.00
91	LENORE LL-911	RT	105.00	105.00
91	LENORE YK-4218	RT	135.00	135.00
91	LENORE-YK-4218	3500	135.00	135.00
91	LIBBY-EP-18	RT	85.00	85.00
91	LILA FH-404	RT	100.00	100.00
91	LILA-AM-10	RT	125.00	125.00
91	LINDSEY C-3127	RT	135.00	135.00
91	LINETTA C-3166	RT	135.00	135.00
91	LISA AM-100L	RT	70.00	70.00
91	LITTLE BOY BLUE C-3159	RT	100.00	100.00
91	LIZ C-3150	RT	100.00	100.00
91	LIZA YK-4226	RT	35.00	35.00
91	LOLA-SP-363	RT	90.00	90.00
91	LONI-FH-448	2500	100.00	100.00
91	LORI EP-52	RT	95.00	95.00
91	LORI FH-446	RT	100.00	100.00
91	LOUISE LL-908	RT	105.00	105.00
91	LUCY-LL-853	RT	80.00	80.00
91	MADELEINE-C-3106	RT	95.00	95.00
91	MARCY TR-55	RT	135.00	135.00
91	MARIEL C-3119	RT	125.00	125.00
91	MAUDE AM-100M	RT	70.00	70.00
91	MELISSA CH-3	RT	110.00	110.00
91	MELISSA LL-901	RT	135.00	135.00

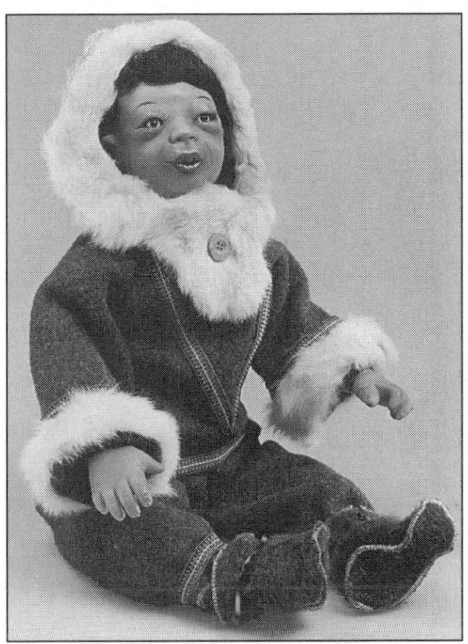

The popularity of ethnic dolls is on the rise. Enco *is by Seymour Mann.*

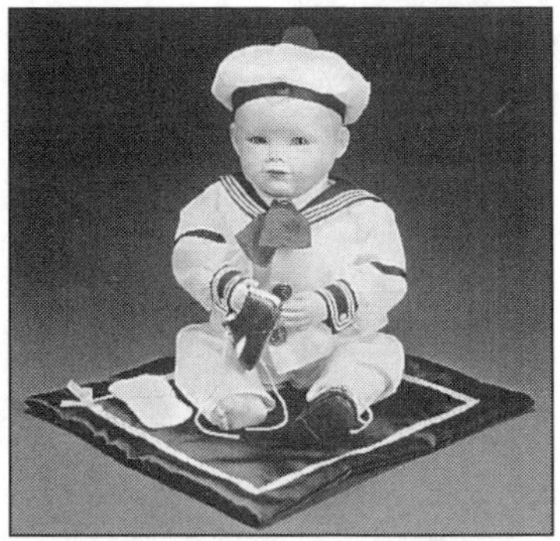

Perhaps no one knows children quite the way Yolanda Bello does. Matthew *is the fourth issue in her series of "Yolanda's Picture-Perfect Babies." Produced by Ashton-Drake Galleries.*

Chelsea *wears an outfit befitting little Red Riding Hood. She is produced by Roman.*

Watch your step, little one! Loving Steps *is the first issue in Sandra Kuck's "Precious Memories of Motherhood" collection. The doll is produced by Reco.*

YR	NAME	LIMIT	ISSUE	TREND
91	MELISSA-AM-9	RT	120.00	120.00
91	MEREDITH FH-391-P	RT	95.00	95.00
91	MERYL FH-463	RT	95.00	95.00
91	MICHAEL W/SCHOOL BOOKS FH-439B	RT	95.00	95.00
91	MICHELLE EP36	RT	95.00	95.00
91	MICHELLE W/SCHOOL BOOKS FH-439G	RT	95.00	95.00
91	MIRANDA-DOLL-9PH	RT	75.00	75.00
91	MISSY DOLL-464	RT	70.00	70.00
91	MISSY PS-258	RT	90.00	90.00
91	MON YUN W/PARASOL TR-33	RT	115.00	115.00
91	NANCY W/RABBIT EP-31	RT	165.00	165.00
91	NANCY WB-73	RT	65.00	65.00
91	NELLIE-EP-1B	RT	75.00	75.00
91	NICOLE-AM-12	RT	135.00	135.00
91	NOELLE PS-239V	RT	95.00	95.00
91	PATTI DOLL-440	RT	65.00	65.00
91	PATTY-YK-4221	RT	125.00	125.00
91	PEPPER PS-277	RT	130.00	130.00
91	PIA-PS-246L	RT	115.00	115.00
91	PRINCESS SUMMER WINDS FH-427	RT	120.00	120.00
91	PRINCESS SUMMER WINDS-FH-424	2500	120.00	120.00
91	PRISSY WHITE/BLUE-C-3140	RT	100.00	100.00
91	RAPUNZEL C-3157	RT	150.00	150.00
91	RED WING AM-30	RT	165.00	165.00
91	ROBIN AM-22	RT	120.00	120.00
91	ROSALIND-C-3090	RT	150.00	150.00
91	SAMANTHA GU-3	RT	100.00	100.00
91	SANDRA-DOLL-6PHE	RT	65.00	65.00
91	SCARLETT FH-399	RT	100.00	100.00
91	SCARLETT FH-436	RT	135.00	135.00
91	SHAKA SP-401	RT	110.00	110.00
91	SHAKA-SP-401	2500	110.00	110.00
91	SHARON BLUE-EP-34	RT	120.00	120.00
91	SHARON C-3237	2500	95.00	95.00
91	SHARON-EP-34	CL	120.00	120.00
91	SHAU CHEN GU-2	RT	85.00	85.00
91	SHELLEY CH-1	RT	110.00	110.00
91	SOPHIE TR-53	RT	135.00	135.00
91	STACY DOLL-6PH	RT	65.00	65.00
91	STEPHANIE FH-467	RT	95.00	95.00
91	STEPHANIE PINK & WHITE-OM-196	RT	300.00	300.00
91	STEPHANIE-AM-11	RT	105.00	105.00
91	SUMMER AM-33	RT	200.00	200.00
91	SYBIL BEIGE-C-3131	RT	135.00	135.00
91	SYBIL PINK-12PHMC	RT	75.00	75.00
91	SYBIL-C-3131	CL	135.00	135.00
91	SYBIL-DOLL-12PHMC	RT	75.00	75.00
91	TAMARA OM-187	RT	135.00	135.00
91	TERRI TR-62	RT	75.00	75.00
91	TESSA AM-19	RT	135.00	135.00
91	TESSA-AM-1	CL	135.00	135.00
91	TINA-AM-16	RT	130.00	130.00
91	VANESSA AM-34	RT	90.00	90.00
91	VICKI-C-3101	RT	200.00	200.00
91	VIOLET EP-41	RT	135.00	135.00
91	VIOLET OM-186	RT	270.00	270.00
91	VIOLET-OM-186	2500	270.00	270.00
91	VIRGINIA SP-359	YR	120.00	120.00
91	WAH-CHING/ORIENTAL TODDLER-YK-4175	RT	110.00	110.00
92	ALICE JNC-4013	OP	90.00	90.00
92	AMY-OM-06	2500	150.00	150.00
92	BETH-OM-05	CL	135.00	135.00
92	BETTE-OM-01	2500	115.00	115.00
92	CHARLOTTE-FH-484	2500	115.00	115.00
92	CHELSEA-IND-397	OP	85.00	85.00
92	CORDELIA OM-009	RT	250.00	250.00
92	CORDELIA OM-09	RT	250.00	250.00
92	CORDELIA-OM-09	2500	250.00	250.00
92	DEBBIE-JNC-4006	RT	90.00	90.00
92	DEIDRE FH-473	RT	115.00	115.00
92	DEIDRE-YK-4083	CL	95.00	95.00
92	DONA FH-494	RT	100.00	100.00
92	EUGENIE OM-225	RT	300.00	300.00
92	GISELLE OM-02	RT	90.00	90.00
92	JAN OM-012	RT	135.00	135.00
92	JANET FH-496	RT	120.00	120.00
92	JET FH-478	RT	115.00	115.00
92	JET-FH-495	2500	115.00	115.00
92	JODIE-FH-495	2500	115.00	115.00
92	JODY FH-495	RT	115.00	115.00
92	JULIETTE OM-08	2500	175.00	175.00
92	LAURA OM-010	RT	250.00	250.00
92	LAURIE JNC-4004	RT	90.00	90.00
92	LYDIA-OM-226	RT	250.00	250.00
92	MAGGIE FH-505	RT	125.00	125.00
92	MELISSA OM-03	RT	135.00	135.00
92	NANCY JNC-4001	RT	90.00	90.00
92	SALLY FH-492	RT	105.00	105.00
92	SAPPHIRES-OM-223	2500	250.00	250.00

YR	NAME	LIMIT	ISSUE	TREND
92	SAPPHITED OM-223	RT	250.00	250.00
92	SARA ANN FH-474	RT	115.00	115.00
92	SCARLETT FH-471	RT	120.00	120.00
92	SONJA FH-486	RT	125.00	125.00
92	SUE JNC-4003	RT	90.00	90.00
92	TIFFANY OM-014	RT	150.00	150.00
92	TIFFANY-OM-041	2500	150.00	150.00
92	TRINA OM-011	RT	165.00	165.00
92	VIOLETTE FH-503	RT	120.00	120.00
92	YVETTE OM-015	RT	150.00	150.00
93	ADRIENNE-C-3162	CL	135.00	135.00
93	ANTONIA-OM-227	RT	350.00	350.00
93	ARLENE SP-421	CL	100.00	100.00
93	BLAINE-C-3167	CL	100.00	100.00
93	CAMILLE-OM-230	2500	250.00	250.00
93	CINNAMON JNC-4014	RT	90.00	90.00
93	CLARE FH-497	RT	100.00	100.00
93	CLOTHILDE FH-469	RT	125.00	125.00
93	DONNA DOLL-447	RT	85.00	85.00
93	ELLEN YK-4223	RT	150.00	150.00
93	GENA OM-229	RT	250.00	250.00
93	HAPPY FH-479	RT	105.00	105.00
93	HEDY FH-449	RT	95.00	95.00
93	IRIS FH-483	RT	95.00	95.00
93	JAN DRESS UP OM-12	RT	135.00	135.00
93	JAN-OM-12	2500	135.00	135.00
93	JILLIAN SP-428	RT	165.00	165.00
93	JULIETTE OM-8	RT	175.00	175.00
93	KENDRA FH-481	RT	115.00	115.00
93	KIT SP-426	RT	55.00	55.00
93	LINDA SP-435	RT	95.00	95.00
93	LYNN FH-498	RT	120.00	120.00
93	MARIAH LL-909	RT	135.00	135.00
93	NINA YK-4232	RT	135.00	135.00
93	OONA TR-57	RT	135.00	135.00
93	REBECCA C-3177	RT	135.00	135.00
93	SARETTA-SP-423	2500	100.00	100.00
93	SHAKA TR-45	RT	100.00	100.00
93	SUZIE SP-422	RT	164.00	170.00
94	ABBY-YK-4533	3500	135.00	135.00
94	ADAK-PS-412	2500	150.00	150.00
94	ALICE-GU-32	2500	150.00	150.00
94	ALICE-IND-508	2500	115.00	115.00
94	ALLY-FH-556	2500	115.00	115.00
94	ALYSSA-C-3201	RT	110.00	110.00
94	ALYSSA-PP-1	2500	275.00	275.00
94	AMY-OC-43M	2500	115.00	115.00
94	ANGEL-LL-956	2500	90.00	90.00
94	ANGEL-SP-460	2500	140.00	140.00
94	ANGELICA-FH-219F	2500	85.00	85.00
94	ANGELICA-FH-291S	2500	85.00	85.00
94	ANGELICA-FH-291WG	2500	85.00	85.00
94	ANGELO-OC-57	2500	135.00	135.00
94	ANTONIA-OM-42	2500	150.00	150.00
94	ARILENE-LL-940	2500	90.00	90.00
94	ATANAK-PS-414	2500	150.00	150.00
94	BABY BELLE-C-3193	2500	150.00	150.00
94	BABY SCARLETT-C-3194	2500	115.00	115.00
94	BLAIR YK-4532	3500	150.00	150.00
94	BLAIR-YK-4532	3500	150.00	150.00
94	BOBBI NM-30	2500	135.00	135.00
94	BRANDY YK-4537	3500	165.00	165.00
94	BRONWYN IND-517	2500	140.00	140.00
94	CACTUS FLOWER INDIAN LL-944	2500	105.00	105.00
94	CALLIE TR-76	2500	140.00	140.00
94	CALLIE-TR-76	2500	140.00	140.00
94	CALYPSO-LL-942	2500	150.00	150.00
94	CARMEN-PS-408	2500	150.00	150.00
94	CASEY-C-3197	2500	140.00	140.00
94	CATHY GU-41	RT	140.00	140.00
94	CHRIS FH-561	2500	85.00	85.00
94	CHRISSIE FH-562	2500	85.00	85.00
94	CINDY OC-58	2500	140.00	140.00
94	CLARA IND-516	2500	140.00	140.00
94	CLARA IND-524	2500	150.00	150.00
94	CLARA-IND-518	2500	140.00	140.00
94	CLAUDETTE-TR-81	2500	150.00	150.00
94	COPPER-YK-4546C	3500	150.00	150.00
94	CORA-FH-565	2500	140.00	140.00
94	CORY-FH-564	2500	115.00	115.00
94	DALLAS-PS-403	2500	150.00	150.00
94	DARYL-LL-947	RT	150.00	150.00
94	DEE-LL-948	2500	110.00	110.00
94	DELILAH-C-3195	2500	150.00	150.00
94	FAITH-IND-522	2500	135.00	135.00
94	FAITH-OC-60	2500	115.00	115.00
94	FLORA-FH-583	2500	115.00	115.00
94	FLORETTE-INC-519	2500	140.00	140.00
94	GARDINER-PS-405	2500	150.00	150.00

YR	NAME	LIMIT	ISSUE	TREND
94	GEORGIA IND-510	2500	220.00	220.00
94	GEORGIA SP-456	2500	115.00	115.00
94	HATTY/MATTY-IND-514	2500	165.00	165.00
94	HEATHER-YK-4531	3500	165.00	165.00
94	HONEY-LL-945	2500	150.00	150.00
94	HYACINTH-LL-941	2500	90.00	90.00
94	INDIAN-IND-520	2500	115.00	115.00
94	IVY-C-3203	RT	85.00	85.00
94	JACQUELINE-C-3202	RT	150.00	150.00
94	JAN-FH-584R	2500	115.00	115.00
94	JANIS-FH-584B	2500	115.00	115.00
94	JENNY-OC-36M	2500	115.00	115.00
94	JILLIAN-C-3196	2500	150.00	150.00
94	JO-YK-4539	3500	150.00	150.00
94	JORDAN-SP-455	2500	150.00	150.00
94	KATE-OC-55	2500	150.00	150.00
94	KATIE-IND-511	2500	110.00	110.00
94	KELLY-YK-4536	3500	150.00	150.00
94	KEVIN YK-4543	3500	140.00	140.00
94	KEVIN-MS-25	2500	150.00	150.00
94	KIT-YK-4547	3500	115.00	115.00
94	KITTEN-IND-512	2500	110.00	110.00
94	LADY CAROLINE-LL-938	2500	120.00	120.00
94	LADY CAROLINE-LL-939	2500	120.00	120.00
94	LAUGHING WATERS-PS-410	2500	150.00	150.00
94	LAUREN-SP-458	2500	125.00	125.00
94	LINDSAY-SP-462	2500	150.00	150.00
94	LITTLE RED RIDING HOOD-FH-557	RT	140.00	140.00
94	LORETTA SP-457	2500	140.00	140.00
94	LUCINDA-PS-406	2500	150.00	150.00
94	MAGNOLIA FH-558	2500	150.00	150.00
94	MAIDEN-PS-409	2500	150.00	150.00
94	MANDY YK-4548	3500	115.00	115.00
94	MARGARET-C-3204	2500	150.00	150.00
94	MARIA GU-35	2500	115.00	115.00
94	MARY ANN-TR-79	2500	125.00	125.00
94	MARY JO-FH-552	RT	150.00	150.00
94	MARY LOU FH-565	2500	135.00	135.00
94	MARY-OC-56	2500	135.00	135.00
94	MEGAN C-3192	2500	150.00	150.00
94	MISS DEBUTANTE DEBI	RT	75.00	190.00
94	MISS ELIZABETH SP-459	2500	150.00	150.00
94	MISSY-FH-567	2500	140.00	140.00
94	MORNING DEW INDIAN PS-404	2500	150.00	150.00
94	MUSICAL DOLL-OC-45M	2500	140.00	140.00
94	NATALIE PP-2	2500	275.00	275.00
94	NIKKI SP-461	2500	150.00	150.00
94	NIKKI-PS-401	2500	150.00	150.00
94	NOEL-MS-27	2500	150.00	150.00
94	NOELLE-C-3199	2500	195.00	195.00
94	NOELLE-MS-28	2500	150.00	150.00
94	ODETTA IND-521	2500	140.00	140.00
94	ORIANA-IND-515	2500	140.00	140.00
94	PAIGE GU-33	2500	150.00	150.00
94	PAMELA-LL-949	RT	115.00	115.00
94	PANAMA OM-43	2500	195.00	195.00
94	PATTY-GU-34	2500	115.00	115.00
94	PAYSON YK-4541	3500	135.00	135.00
94	PAYTON-PS-407	2500	150.00	150.00
94	PEARL IND-523	2500	275.00	275.00
94	PEGEEN-C-3205	RT	150.00	150.00
94	PEGGY TR-75	2500	185.00	185.00
94	PETULA-C-3191	2500	140.00	140.00
94	PRINCESS FOXFIRD PS-411	2500	150.00	150.00
94	PRINCESS MOONRISE-YK-4542	3500	140.00	140.00
94	PRINCESS SNOW FLOWER PS-402	2500	150.00	150.00
94	PRISCILLA-YK-4538	3500	135.00	135.00
94	REBECCA C-3177	2500	135.00	135.00
94	REGINA-OM-41	2500	150.00	150.00
94	RITA FH-553	2500	115.00	115.00
94	ROBBY-NM-29	2500	135.00	135.00
94	SARETTA SP-423	2500	100.00	100.00
94	SHAKA-TR-45	2500	100.00	100.00
94	SISTER SUZIE-IND-509	2500	95.00	95.00
94	SOUTHERN BELLE FH-570	2500	140.00	140.00
94	SPARKLE-OM-40	2500	150.00	150.00
94	STEPHIE OC-41M	2500	115.00	115.00
94	SUE SWEL TR-73	2500	110.00	110.00
94	SUGAR PLUM FAIRY OM-39	2500	150.00	150.00
94	SUSIE SP-422	2500	164.00	165.00
94	SUZANNE LL-943	2500	105.00	105.00
94	SUZIE-GU-38	2500	135.00	135.00
94	SUZIE-SP-422	2500	164.00	165.00
94	TAFFEY TR-80	2500	150.00	150.00
94	TALLULAH-OM-44	2500	275.00	275.00
94	TERESA C-3198	RT	110.00	110.00
94	TIFFANY OC-44M	2500	140.00	140.00
94	TIPPI LL-946	RT	110.00	110.00
94	TODD YK-4540	3500	45.00	45.00

YR	NAME	LIMIT	ISSUE	TREND
94	TOPAZ TR-74	RT	195.00	195.00
94	TRIXIE TR-77	2500	110.00	110.00
94	VIRGINIA-TR-78	2500	195.00	195.00
94	WENDY MS-26	2500	150.00	150.00
95	BRENDA DOLL 551	2500	60.00	60.00
95	BRIANNA GU-300B	2500	30.00	30.00
95	BRIE C-3230	2500	30.00	30.00
95	BRIE CD-16310C	2500	30.00	30.00
95	BRIE OM-89W	2500	125.00	125.00
95	BRITT OC077	2500	40.00	40.00
95	BRITTANY DOLL 558	2500	35.00	35.00
95	BRUGUNDY ANGEL FH-291D	2500	75.00	75.00
95	BRYNA DOLL 555	2500	35.00	35.00
95	BUNNY TR-97	2500	85.00	85.00
95	CAITLIN LL-997	2500	115.00	115.00
95	CANDICE TR-94	RT	135.00	135.00
95	CARMEL TR-93	2500	125.00	125.00
95	CAROLOTTA OM-80	2500	175.00	175.00
95	CARRIE C-3231	2500	30.00	30.00
95	CATHERINE RDK-231	2500	30.00	30.00
95	CECILY DOLL 552	RT	60.00	60.00
95	CELENE FH-618	2500	120.00	120.00
95	CELESTINE LL-982	2500	100.00	100.00
95	CHELSEA DOLL 560	2500	35.00	35.00
95	CHERRY FH-616	2500	100.00	100.00
95	CHRISTMAS KITTEN IND-530	2500	100.00	100.00
95	CIANCY GU-54	2500	80.00	80.00
95	CODY FH-629	2500	120.00	120.00
95	CYNTHIA GU-300C	2500	30.00	30.00
95	DANIELLE MER-808	2500	65.00	65.00
95	DANIELLE PS-432	2500	100.00	100.00
95	DARCY FH-636	2500	80.00	80.00
95	DARCY LL-986	2500	110.00	110.00
95	DARLA LL-988	2500	100.00	100.00
95	DENISE LL-994	2500	105.00	105.00
95	DIANA RDK-221A	2500	35.00	35.00
95	DIANE PS-444	2500	110.00	110.00
95	DINAH OC-79	2500	40.00	40.00
95	DONNA GU-300D	2500	30.00	30.00
95	DULCIE FH-622	2500	110.00	110.00
95	ELAINE CD-02210	2500	50.00	50.00
95	ELEANOR C16669	2500	35.00	35.00
95	ELIZABETH DOLL 553	2500	35.00	35.00
95	ELLIE FH-621	2500	125.00	125.00
95	EMMA DOLL 559	2500	35.00	35.00
95	EMMA GU-300E	2500	30.00	30.00
95	EMMY IND-533	2500	85.00	85.00
95	ERIN RDK-223	2500	30.00	30.00
95	FAWN C-3228	2500	55.00	55.00
95	FELICIA TR-9	2500	30.00	30.00
95	FLEUR C16415	2500	30.00	30.00
95	GEORGIA IND-528	2500	125.00	125.00
95	GINNIE FH-619	2500	110.00	110.00
95	GOLD ANGEL FH-511G	2500	85.00	85.00
95	GREEN ANGEL FH-511C	2500	85.00	85.00
95	GRETCHEN FH-620	2500	120.00	120.00
95	GUARDIAN ANGEL OM-91	2500	200.00	200.00
95	GUARDIAN ANGEL TR-98	2500	85.00	85.00
95	HAPPY RDK-238	2500	25.00	25.00
95	HEATHER LL-991	2500	115.00	115.00
95	HEATHER PS-436	2500	115.00	115.00
95	HOLLY CD-16526	2500	30.00	30.00
95	HYACINTH C-3227	2500	130.00	130.00
95	IRENE GU-56	2500	85.00	85.00
95	IRINA RDK-237	2500	35.00	35.00
95	IVANA RDK-233	2500	35.00	35.00
95	JAMAICA LL-989	2500	75.00	75.00
95	JENNIFER PS-446	2500	145.00	145.00
95	JENNY CD-16673B	2500	35.00	35.00
95	JERRI PS-434	2500	100.00	100.00
95	JESSICA RDK-225	2500	30.00	30.00
95	JEWEL TR-100	2500	110.00	110.00
95	JOELLA CD-16779	2500	35.00	35.00
95	JOY CS-1450A	2500	35.00	35.00
95	JOY TR-99	2500	85.00	85.00
95	JULIA C-3234	2500	100.00	100.00
95	JULIA RDK-222	2500	35.00	35.00
95	JUNE CD-2212	2500	50.00	50.00
95	KARYN RDK-224	2500	35.00	35.00
95	KELSEY DOLL 561	2500	35.00	35.00
95	KIMMIE CS-15816	2500	30.00	30.00
95	KITTY IND-527	2500	40.00	40.00
95	LENORE FH-617	2500	120.00	120.00
95	LENORE RDK-229	2500	50.00	50.00
95	LESLIE LL-983	2500	105.00	105.00
95	LESLIE MER-809	2500	65.00	65.00
95	LILA GU-55	2500	55.00	55.00
95	LILI CD-16888	2500	30.00	30.00
95	LILY FH-630	RT	120.00	120.00

YR	NAME	LIMIT	ISSUE	TREND
95	LINDSAY PS-442	2500	175.00	175.00
95	LISETTE LL-993	2500	105.00	105.00
95	LITTLE BOBBY RDK-235	2500	25.00	25.00
95	LITTLE LISA OM-86	RT	125.00	125.00
95	LITTLE LORI RDK-228	2500	20.00	20.00
95	LITTLE LOU RDK-227	2500	20.00	20.00
95	LITTLE MARY RDK-234	2500	25.00	25.00
95	LITTLE PATTY PS-429	2500	50.00	50.00
95	LUCIE MER-607	2500	65.00	65.00
95	LYNN LL-995	2500	105.00	105.00
95	MAE PS-431	2500	70.00	70.00
95	MAGGIE IND-532	2500	80.00	80.00
95	MARIA PS-437	2500	125.00	125.00
95	MARIELLE PS-443	2500	175.00	175.00
95	MARTINA RDK-232	2500	35.00	35.00
95	MARY ANN FH-633	2500	110.00	110.00
95	MARY ELIZABETH OC-51	2500	50.00	50.00
95	MAXINE C-3225	RT	125.00	125.00
95	MC KENZIE LL-987	2500	100.00	100.00
95	MEGAN RDK-220	2500	30.00	30.00
95	MEREDITH MER-806	2500	65.00	65.00
95	MERRI MER-810	2500	65.00	65.00
95	MINDI PS-441	2500	125.00	125.00
95	MINDY LL-990	2500	75.00	75.00
95	MIRANDA C16456B	2500	30.00	30.00
95	MIRANDA TR-91	2500	135.00	135.00
95	MONICA TR-95	2500	135.00	135.00
95	NANCY FH-615	2500	100.00	100.00
95	NATASHA TR-90	RT	125.00	125.00
95	NORMAN C-3226	2500	135.00	135.00
95	OUR FIRST SKATES RDK-226/BG	2500	50.00	50.00
95	PAIGE IND-529	2500	80.00	80.00
95	PAN PAN GU-52	2500	60.00	60.00
95	PATTY C-3220	2500	60.00	60.00
95	PAULETTE PS-430	2500	80.00	80.00
95	PAULINE PS-440	2500	65.00	65.00
95	PEACHES IND-531	2500	80.00	80.00
95	RAINIE LL-984	2500	125.00	125.00
95	ROBIN C-3236	2500	60.00	60.00
95	RUSTY CS-1450B	2500	35.00	35.00
95	SARAH C-3214	RT	110.00	110.00
95	SASHA GU-57	2500	75.00	75.00
95	SHIMMERING CAROLINE LL-992	2500	115.00	115.00
95	SLEEPING BEAUTY OM-88	2500	115.00	115.00
95	SOPHIA PS-445	2500	125.00	125.00
95	SOUTHERN BELLE BRIDE FH-637	2500	160.00	160.00
95	STACY FH-634	2500	110.00	110.00
95	STACY OC-75	2500	40.00	40.00
95	SUZANNE DOLL 554	2500	35.00	35.00
95	SUZIE OC-80	2500	50.00	50.00
95	SWEET PEA LL-981	2500	90.00	90.00
95	SYLVIE CD-16634B	2500	35.00	35.00
95	TABITHA C-3233	2500	50.00	50.00
95	TERRI OM-78	2500	150.00	150.00
95	TINA OM-79	2500	150.00	150.00
95	TOBEY C-3232	2500	50.00	50.00
95	WEL LIN GU-44	2500	70.00	70.00
95	WENDY FH-626	2500	200.00	200.00
95	WINNIE LL-965	2500	75.00	75.00
95	WINTER WONDERLAND RDK-301	2500	35.00	35.00
95	WOODLAND SPRITE OM-90	2500	100.00	100.00
95	YELENA RDK-236	2500	35.00	35.00
H. PAYNE		**CONNOISSEUR DOLL COLLECTION**		
92	LITTLE MATCH GIRL HP-205	5000	150.00	150.00
92	POLLY HP-208	5000	120.00	120.00
M. SEVERINO		**CONNOISSEUR DOLL COLLECTION**		
92	MEGAN MS-12	5000	125.00	125.00
P. APRILE		**SIGNATURE DOLL SERIES**		
91	PAULETTE-PAC-2	5000	250.00	250.00
91	PAULETTE-PAC-4	5000	250.00	250.00
92	ALEXANDRIA-PAC-19	5000	300.00	300.00
92	CASSANDRA-PAC-8	CL	450.00	450.00
92	CASSIE FLOWER GIRL-PAC-9	CL	175.00	175.00
92	CELINE-PAC-11	5000	165.00	165.00
92	CLARISSA-PAC-3	5000	165.00	165.00
92	CYNTHIA-PAC-10	RT	165.00	165.00
92	EUGENIE BRIDE-PAC-1	5000	165.00	165.00
92	EVENING STAR-PAC-5	RT	500.00	500.00
92	MELANIE PAC-14	RT	300.00	300.00
92	NADIA PAC-18	RT	175.00	175.00
92	PAVOLVA PAC-17	RT	145.00	145.00
92	VANESSA PAC-15	RT	300.00	300.00
92	VIOLETTA PAC-16	RT	165.00	165.00
95	AMELIA PAC-28	5000	130.00	130.00
95	BRIE PPA-26	5000	180.00	180.00
95	IMAN PPA-24	5000	110.00	110.00
S. BILOTTO		**SIGNATURE DOLL SERIES**		
91	PRECIOUS BABY-SB-100	5000	250.00	250.00

YR	NAME	LIMIT	ISSUE	TREND
91	PRECIOUS PARTY TIME-SB-102	5000	250.00	250.00
91	PRECIOUS SPRING TIME-SB-104	CL	250.00	250.00
	M.A. BYERLY		**SIGNATURE DOLL SERIES**	
91	DOZY ELF WITH FEATHERBED-MAB-100	RT	110.00	110.00
91	DUBY ELF WITH FEATHERBED-MAB-103	RT	110.00	110.00
91	DUDLEY ELF WITH FEATHERBED-MAB-101	RT	110.00	110.00
91	DUFFY ELF WITH FEATHERBED-MAB-102	RT	110.00	110.00
	E. DALI		**SIGNATURE DOLL SERIES**	
95	CARA DALI-1	5000	400.00	400.00
95	PATRICIA DALI-3	5000	280.00	280.00
95	STACY DALI-2	5000	360.00	360.00
	K. FITZPATRICK		**SIGNATURE DOLL SERIES**	
95	AMANDA KSFA-1	5000	175.00	175.00
95	HAPPY JFC-100	5000	120.00	120.00
	J. GRAMMER		**SIGNATURE DOLL SERIES**	
94	SIS JAG-110	RT	110.00	110.00
94	TEX-JAG-114	5000	110.00	110.00
94	TRACY JAG-111	5000	150.00	150.00
94	TREVOR-JAG-112	5000	115.00	115.00
	H. KAHL-HYLAND		**SIGNATURE DOLL SERIES**	
93	GRACE-HKH-2	5000	250.00	250.00
93	HELENE-HKH-1	5000	250.00	250.00
93	REILLY-HKH-3	5000	260.00	260.00
95	AMY ROSE HKHF-200	5000	125.00	125.00
95	BRAD HKH-15	5000	85.00	85.00
95	LAUREL HKH-17R	5000	110.00	110.00
95	LAUREN HKH-202	5000	150.00	150.00
95	LUCY HKH-14	RT	105.00	105.00
95	NATASHA HKH-17P	5000	110.00	110.00
95	NIKKI HKHF-20	5000	125.00	125.00
95	SUZIE HKH-16	5000	100.00	100.00
	P. KOLESAR		**SIGNATURE DOLL SERIES**	
91	BRIDGETTE-PK-104	RT	120.00	120.00
91	CLAIR ANN-PK-252	5000	100.00	100.00
91	ENOC-PK-100	5000	100.00	100.00
91	SHUN LEE-PK-102	CL	120.00	120.00
91	SPARKLE-PK-250	5000	100.00	100.00
91	SUSAN MARIE-PK-103	RT	120.00	120.00
91	SWEET PEA-PK-251	CL	100.00	100.00
92	IN.LITTLE TURTLE IN. INDIAN-PK-110	RT	150.00	150.00
92	BABY CAKES CRUMBS-PK-CRUMBS	5000	17.50	18.00
92	BABY CAKES CRUMBS-PK-CRUMBS/B	5000	17.50	18.00
92	BABY CAKES CRUMBS/BLACK-PK-CRUMBS/B	5000	17.50	18.00
92	RAVEN ESKIMO-PK-106	RT	130.00	130.00
	G. MCNEIL		**SIGNATURE DOLL SERIES**	
95	ELEANORE GMNA-100	5000	225.00	225.00
95	HOLLY GMN-202	5000	150.00	150.00
	H. PAYNE		**SIGNATURE DOLL SERIES**	
92	CREOLE BLACK-HP-202	RT	250.00	250.00
92	DARLA-HP-204	5000	250.00	250.00
92	DULCIE-HP-200	RT	250.00	250.00
92	DUSTIN-HP-201	RT	250.00	250.00
92	POLLY-HP-206	5000	120.00	120.00
92	SPANKY-HP-25	RT	250.00	250.00
	P. PHILLIPS		**SIGNATURE DOLL SERIES**	
95	ADAK PPA-21	5000	110.00	110.00
95	ALAIN PPA-19	2500	100.00	100.00
95	CASEY PPA-23	5000	85.00	85.00
95	LATISHA PPA-25	5000	110.00	110.00
95	LENA PPA-20	5000	120.00	120.00
95	SHAO LING PPA-22	5000	110.00	110.00
	L. RANDOLPH		**SIGNATURE DOLL SERIES**	
95	GINNY LR-2	5000	360.00	360.00
95	LENORE LRC-100	500	140.00	140.00
95	MEREDITH LR-3	5000	375.00	375.00
95	TAMMY LR-4	5000	325.00	325.00
95	TIFFANY LR-1	5000	370.00	370.00
	M. SEVERINO		**SIGNATURE DOLL SERIES**	
91	ALICE-MS-7	RT	120.00	120.00
91	AMBER-MS-1	RT	95.00	95.00
91	BECKY-MS-2	RT	95.00	95.00
91	BIANCA-PK-101	RT	120.00	120.00
91	DADDY'S LITTLE DARLING-MS-8	RT	165.00	165.00
91	MIKEY-MS-3	RT	95.00	95.00
91	MOMMY'S RAYS OF SUNSHINE-MS-9	5000	165.00	165.00
91	STEPHIE-MS-6	RT	125.00	125.00
91	SU LIN-MS-5	RT	105.00	105.00
91	YAWNING KATE-MS-4	RT	105.00	105.00
92	ABIGAIL-MS-11	RT	125.00	125.00
92	ADORA-MS-14	5000	300.00	300.00
92	CODYY MS-19	RT	120.00	120.00
92	KATE-MS-15	RT	190.00	190.00
92	REBECCA BEIGE BONNET MS-17B	5000	175.00	175.00
92	REBECCA-MS-17B	5000	175.00	175.00
92	RUBY-MS-18	5000	135.00	135.00
92	SALLY-MS-25	RT	110.00	110.00
92	STACY-MS-24	RT	110.00	110.00

YR	NAME	LIMIT	ISSUE	TREND
92	VICTORIA W/ BLANKET-MS-10	RT	110.00	110.00
93	BONNETT BABY-MS-17W	5000	175.00	175.00

SPORTS IMPRESSIONS

*

PORCELAIN DOLLS

YR	NAME	LIMIT	ISSUE	TREND
90	DON MATTINGLY	1990	150.00	150.00
90	MICKEY MANTLE	1956	150.00	150.00

SUSAN WAKEEN DOLL CO. INC.

S. WAKEEN — **THE LITTLEST BALLET CO.**

YR	NAME	LIMIT	ISSUE	TREND
85	CYNTHIA	375	198.00	350.00
85	JEANNE	375	198.00	800.00
85	JENNIFER	250	750.00	750.00
85	PATTY	375	198.00	450.00
87	ELIZABETH	250	425.00	1000.00
87	MARIE ANN	50	100.00	1000.00

THE COLLECTABLES

D. EFFNER

YR	NAME	LIMIT	ISSUE	TREND
89	WELCOME HOME	1000	330.00	680.00
90	LIZBETH ANN	1000	420.00	425.00

P. PARKINS

YR	NAME	LIMIT	ISSUE	TREND
86	TATIANA	CL	270.00	680.00
87	STORYTIME BY SARAH JANE	CL	330.00	530.00
87	TASHA	CL	290.00	530.00
89	MICHELLE	250	270.00	455.00
90	BASSINET BABY	2000	130.00	430.00
90	DANIELLE	1000	400.00	480.00
90	IN YOUR EASTER BONNET	1000	350.00	355.00
91	ADRIANNA	CL	1350.00	1355.00
91	BETHANY	CL	450.00	455.00
91	KELSIE	500	320.00	325.00
91	LAUREN	300	490.00	495.00
91	NATASHA	CL	510.00	515.00
91	YVETTE	300	580.00	585.00
92	ANGEL ON MY SHOULDER (LILLIANNE W/CECE)	500	530.00	535.00
92	KARLIE	500	380.00	380.00
92	KARLIE	500	380.00	385.00
92	MARISSA	300	350.00	350.00
92	MARISSA	300	350.00	355.00
92	MARTY	250	190.00	195.00
92	MATIA	250	190.00	195.00
92	MISSY	OP	59.00	60.00
92	MOLLY	450	350.00	355.00
92	SHELLEY	300	450.00	450.00
92	SHELLEY	300	450.00	455.00
93	AMBER	500	330.00	335.00
93	HALEY	500	330.00	335.00
93	LITTLE DUMPLING (BLACK)	500	190.00	195.00
93	LITTLE DUMPLING (WHITE)	500	190.00	195.00
93	MAGGIE	500	330.00	335.00
93	MOLLY	450	350.00	400.00
94	AFTERNOON DELIGHT	500	410.00	415.00
94	AMBER HISPANIC	500	345.00	345.00
94	MADISON	250	350.00	355.00
94	MADISON SAILOR	250	370.00	375.00
94	MORGAN	250	395.00	395.00
94	MORGAN CHRISTMAS	500	390.00	410.00
94	MORGAN IN RED	250	395.00	395.00
94	SUGAR PLUM FAIRY	500	250.00	255.00
95	A MOTHER'S LOVE	450	770.00	770.00
95	ALEXUS	150	550.00	570.00
95	BRIANNA	SO	590.00	625.00
95	CHRISTINE	350	390.00	390.00
95	MY LITTLE ANGEL BOY	SO	450.00	450.00
95	MY LITTLE ANGEL GIRL	SO	450.00	450.00

P. PARKINS — **ANGELS SERIES**

YR	NAME	LIMIT	ISSUE	TREND
93	ANGEL ON MY SHOULDER	CL	530.00	535.00
93	MY GUARDIAN ANGEL	500	590.00	595.00
94	GUARDING THE WAY	RT	950.00	955.00

P. PARKINS — **BUTTERFLY BABIES**

YR	NAME	LIMIT	ISSUE	TREND
89	BELINDA	CL	270.00	380.00
90	WILLOW	CL	240.00	380.00
92	LATICIA	CL	320.00	325.00

D. EFFNER — **CHERISHED MEMORIES**

YR	NAME	LIMIT	ISSUE	TREND
88	TEA TIME	CL	380.00	455.00

P. PARKINS — **CHERISHED MEMORIES**

YR	NAME	LIMIT	ISSUE	TREND
86	AMY AND ANDREW	CL	220.00	330.00
88	BRITTANY	CL	240.00	305.00
88	HEATHER	CL	280.00	325.00
88	JENNIFER	CL	380.00	550.00
88	LEIGH ANN AND LELAND	CL	250.00	275.00
89	GENERATIONS	CL	480.00	505.00
89	TWINKLES	CL	170.00	280.00
90	CASSANDRA	CL	500.00	555.00

P. PARKINS — **COLLECTOR'S CLUB**

YR	NAME	LIMIT	ISSUE	TREND
91	MANDY	CL	360.00	365.00
92	KALLIE	CL	410.00	415.00

YR	NAME	LIMIT	ISSUE	TREND
92	MOMMY AND ME	CL	810.00	815.00
93	KRYSTAL	*	380.00	590.00
94	KRYSTAL	YR	385.00	385.00
	P. PARKINS		**ENCHANTED CHILDREN**	
90	KARA	CL	550.00	555.00
90	KATLIN	CL	550.00	555.00
90	KRISTIN	400	550.00	655.00
90	TIFFY	500	370.00	505.00
	P. PARKINS		**FAIRY**	
88	TABATHA	1500	370.00	425.00
	P. PARKINS		**LIMITED EDITION VINYL DOLLS**	
92	ANNIE	2500	190.00	190.00
92	BRENDA (BLUE DRESS)	2500	180.00	180.00
92	BRENDA (CHRISTMAS)	250	240.00	240.00
92	BRENDA (SPRING)	250	240.00	240.00
92	BRENT	2500	190.00	190.00
92	JENNY AND JEREMY (PUPPY LOVE)	2500	180.00	180.00
92	JESSICA	2500	190.00	190.00
	D. EFFNER		**MOTHER'S LITTLE TREASURES**	
85	1ST EDITION	CL	380.00	705.00
90	2ND EDITION	CL	440.00	600.00
	P. PARKINS		**SMALL ANGELS SERIES**	
94	EARTH ANGEL	500	195.00	200.00
	P. PARKINS		**TINY TREASURES**	
91	HOLLY	1000	150.00	150.00
91	LITTLE GIRL	1000	140.00	140.00
91	TODDLER BOY	1000	130.00	130.00
91	TODDLER GIRL	1000	130.00	130.00
91	VICTORIAN BOY	1000	150.00	150.00
91	VICTORIAN GIRL	1000	150.00	150.00
92	NICOLAUS	500	160.00	160.00
92	NICOLE	500	180.00	180.00
92	TOMMIE	1000	160.00	160.00
92	TORI	1000	170.00	170.00
	D. EFFNER		**YESTERDAY'S CHILD**	
82	CLEO	CL	180.00	255.00
82	COLUMBINE	CL	180.00	255.00
82	JASON AND JESSICA	CL	150.00	305.00
83	CHAD AND CHARITY	CL	190.00	195.00
83	NOEL	CL	190.00	245.00
84	KEVIN AND KARISSA	CL	190.00	275.00
84	REBECCA	CL	250.00	275.00
86	ASHLEY	CL	220.00	280.00
86	TODD AND TIFFANY	CL	220.00	255.00

TIMELESS CREATIONS

YR	NAME	LIMIT	ISSUE	TREND
	A. HIMSTEDT		**BAREFOOT CHILDREN**	
87	BASTIAN	CL	329.00	850.00
87	BECKUS	CL	329.00	1175.00
87	ELLEN	CL	329.00	825.00
87	FATOU	CL	329.00	975.00
87	FATOU (CORNROLL)	CL	329.00	650.00
87	KATHE	CL	329.00	825.00
87	LISA	CL	329.00	825.00
87	PAULA	CL	329.00	825.00
	A. HIMSTEDT		**BLESSED ARE THE CHILDREN**	
88	FRIEDERIKE	CL	499.00	1400.00
88	KASIMIR	CL	499.00	1450.00
88	MAKIMURA	CL	499.00	900.00
88	MALIN	CL	499.00	1400.00
88	MICHIKO	CL	499.00	1050.00
	A. HIMSTEDT		**FACES OF FRIENDSHIP**	
91	LILIANE/NETHERLANDS	2-YR	598.00	575.00
91	NEBLINA/SWITZERLAND	2-YR	598.00	525.00
91	SHIREEM/BALI	2-YR	598.00	450.00
	A. HIMSTEDT		**FIENE AND THE BAREFOOT BABIES**	
90	ANNCHEN/GERMAN BABY GIRL	2-YR	498.00	575.00
90	FIENE/BLEGIAN GIRL	2-YR	598.00	700.00
90	MO/AMERICAN BABY BOY	2-YR	498.00	500.00
90	TAKI/JAPANESE BABY GIRL	2-YR	498.00	750.00
	A. HIMSTEDT		**HEARTLAND**	
88	TIMI	CL	329.00	400.00
88	TONI	CL	329.00	400.00
	A. HIMSTEDT		**IMAGES OF CHILDHOOD**	
93	KIMA/GREENLAND	2-YR	599.00	599.00
93	LONA/CALIFORNIA	2-YR	599.00	599.00
93	TARA/GERMANY	2-YR	599.00	599.00
	A. HIMSTEDT		**REFLECTION OF YOUTH**	
89	ADRIENNE/FRANCE	CL	558.00	750.00
89	AYOKA/AFRICA	CL	558.00	1025.00
89	JANKA/HUNGRY	CL	558.00	800.00
89	KAI/GERMAN	CL	558.00	650.00
	A. HIMSTEDT		**SUMMER DREAMS**	
92	ENZO	2-YR	599.00	599.00
92	JULE	2-YR	599.00	535.00
92	PEMBA	2-YR	599.00	599.00
92	SANGA	2-YR	599.00	625.00

YR	NAME	LIMIT	ISSUE	TREND
	TUJAYS ARTIST DOLLS			
	MIKO			
86	HENRY VIII	10	650.00	800.00
87	ANNE BOLEYN	10	550.00	700.00
87	KATHERINE OF ARAGON	10	550.00	750.00
	BOSWORTH/ MIKO			
86	ANINA	20	595.00	925.00
87	AMANDA	20	595.00	950.00
87	ASHLEY	20	525.00	925.00
87	KATHERINE	20	675.00	1000.00
87	SOPHIE	20	475.00	875.00
88	ALTHEA	7	595.00	1000.00
88	ELIZABETH	25	395.00	595.00
88	MELISSA	25	325.00	350.00
88	SARAH	25	395.00	475.00
89	ALETA	20	575.00	825.00
89	CHARLOTTE	20	675.00	950.00
89	ESTELLE	20	575.00	850.00
89	HENRIETTA	20	575.00	800.00
90	GEORGETTE	100	475.00	740.00
90	LUCILLE	20	695.00	950.00
91	ABIGAIL	100	750.00	*
91	GENEVIEVE	10	975.00	*
91	JENNIFER	100	615.00	*
91	NATALIE	100	525.00	*
91	PHYLLIS	100	595.00	*
91	REBECCA	100	615.00	*
91	STEPHANIE	20	990.00	*
	VICTORIAN TRADITION			
	K. GLEASON			**CLASSICS COLLECTION**
93	OLIVER TWIST	50	795.00	795.00
	K. GLEASON			**LAND OF FAERYE TALES & NURSERY RHYMES**
93	RED RIDING HOOD	50	795.00	795.00
95	MISS MUFFET	50	795.00	795.00
	K. GLEASON			**LIFE IS FUN!**
94	2ND CHILDHOOD	20	995.00	995.00
95	MISS AMERICA	50	795.00	795.00
	K. GLEASON			**NORTHERN REALM OF FAERYE**
94	BUTTONWILLOW	20	795.00	795.00
94	PTARMINI	20	795.00	795.00
94	SPRUCE	20	795.00	795.00
	K. GLEASON			**PEOPLE OF THE COVENANT**
94	NOAHS WIFE	50	795.00	795.00
	K. GLEASON			**THE ALASKANS**
94	LADY DIVINE	75	795.00	795.00
	W.S. GEORGE			
	P. RYAN BROOKS			**MY FAIR LADY**
91	ELIZA AT ASCOT	CL	125.00	150.00
	M. RODERICK			**ROMANTIC FLOWER MAIDENS**
88	ROSE, WHO IS LOVE	CL	87.00	135.00
89	DAISY	CL	87.00	87.00
90	LILY	TL	92.00	160.00
90	VIOLET	TL	92.00	92.00
	R. AKERS/ S. GIRARDI			**STEPPING OUT**
91	MILLIE	TL	99.00	99.00
	P. RYAN BROOKS			**THE KING & I**
91	SHALL WE DANCE?	CL	175.00	175.00
	R. AKERS/ S. GIRARDI			**YEAR BOOK MEMORIES**
91	PEGGY SUE	TL	87.00	87.00

Figurines

Dean Genth

"Secondary market" is often a confusing term for novice collectors. Secondary market is not an outlet for "seconds" or "rejects." It is, however, the market for collectibles after they have left the original, primary point of retail sales.

The primary market for collectibles is represented by the many authorized dealers that retail the various lines of collectibles. Secondary market transactions are represented by sales between individual collectors as well as dealers who may or may not be involved with primary retail selling.

Collectors often wonder how the prices are determined for figurines on the secondary market. In our free market society, the answer is quite simple—supply and demand. It is the buyer/collector who really determines the secondary market price.

Price guides and books that list secondary market prices generally track selling prices from a geographical cross-section of dealers, swap and sell event results, as well as auction results. Oftentimes these collectibles price guides list current market prices as well as other pertinent information regarding each figurine or item.

Selling items on the secondary market can be easily accomplished if the price requested is fair and the choice of dispersal is to the owner's liking. Once the selling price is determined, the seller must decide upon which method of selling will be employed. The seller can choose to sell directly to other collectors by advertising in the local classifieds or in one of the many collectibles publications such as *Collector's mart* magazine.

Other collectors often choose to dispose of an entire collection quickly by selling to a reputable or well-known secondary market dealer. Many secondary market dealers are experts in certain areas of collectibles and are prepared to buy large collections for their inventories.

Sometimes collectors opt to have their large collections auctioned to the highest bidders. This method assures that dispersal will be quick and almost effortless on the part of the seller. Auction prices can vary widely from time to time and locale to locale. The prices, when averaged from several auctions, usually represent what is considered to be "fair market value."

A replacement value quotation on the secondary market represents the price a buyer can expect to pay for a figurine or other collectible if that purchase must be made fairly soon. Sometimes certain items are not readily available on the secondary market, thus driving up the price of the item.

Collectors must also determine whether they will sell to a dealer at wholesale price levels or attempt to advertise with the possibility of achieving closer to retail prices. Time availability and financial resources are considerations when undertaking the task of selling to other collectors at near-retail prices on the secondary market.

Always remember that secondary markets exist because a buyer is searching for an item no longer available through regular retail distribution channels. Many reputable secondary market dealers are in business to assist you with both selling and buying figurines.

Dealer and appraiser DEAN A. GENTH is a secondary market expert on Precious Moments, Swarovski Silver Crystal and M.I. Hummel. He serves as special consultant for **The No. 1 Price Guide to M.I. Hummel** ***and owns Miller's Hallmark and Gift Gallery in Eaton, Xenia and Cincinnati, Ohio.***

FIGURINES

YR	NAME	LIMIT	ISSUE	TREND
ADRIAN TARON & SONS				
S. ROSAS				**HOLIDAY**
96	HERR SCHNEEMANN	20000	40.00	20.00
96	KRISS KRINGLE	20000	40.00	40.00
S. ROSAS		**STEINBACH NUTCRACKER SUITE**		
95	TCHIAKOVSKY'S "CLARA"	10000	220.00	220.00
96	SUGAR PLUM FAIRY	10000	230.00	230.00
S. ROSAS				**WISEMEN**
95	MELCHIOR "WISEMAN"	10000	220.00	220.00
96	BALTHASAR	10000	230.00	230.00
AMERICAN ARTISTS				
F. STONE				
*	TRIPLE CROWN BOWL	*	395.00	395.00
*	TRIPLE CROWN VASE/SIGNED	*	250.00	250.00
*	TRIPLE CROWN VASE/UNSIGNED	*	195.00	195.00
F. STONE			**FRED STONE FIGURINES**	
85	BLACK STALLION, THE (PORCELAIN)	*	125.00	200.00
85	BLACK STALLION, THE (BRONZE)	*	150.00	160.00
86	ARABIAN MARE & FOAL	*	150.00	185.00
86	TRANQUILITY	*	175.00	225.00
87	REARING BLACK STALLION (BRONZE)	*	175.00	185.00
87	REARING BLACK STALLION (PORCELAIN)	*	150.00	160.00
AMERICAST INC.				
K. WINDRIX			**THE COMMANDERS**	
94	GEORGE A. CUSTER	500	195.00	200.00
94	JAMES LONGSTREET	500	195.00	200.00
94	JOSHUA L. CHAMBERLAIN	500	195.00	200.00
94	ROBERT E. LEE	5000	195.00	200.00
94	ULYSSES S. GRANT	5000	195.00	200.00
95	"STONEWALL" JACKSON	500	195.00	200.00
95	J.E.B. STUART	500	195.00	200.00
95	WILLIAM T. SHERMAN	500	195.00	200.00
ANHEUSER-BUSCH INC.				
95	HORSEPLAY F1	7500	65.00	65.00
96	BUDWEISER FROGS	OP	30.00	30.00
M. URDAHL				
96	SOMETHING'S BREWING	7500	65.00	65.00
*			**COLLECTIBLE FIGURINES**	
94	BUDDIES N4575	7500	65.00	65.00
ANNA-PERENNA				
P. BUCKLEY MOSS				
95	PARTRIDGE IN A PEAR TREE	OP	27.50	28.00
ANRI				
J. FERRANDIZ				
95	HOMEWARD BOUND 3"	OP	155.00	155.00
95	HOMEWARD BOUND 6"	OP	410.00	410.00
95	TENDER CARE 3"	OP	125.00	125.00
95	TENDER CARE 6"	OP	275.00	275.00
U. BERNARDI			**BERNARDI REFLECTIONS**	
94	MASTER CARVER, 4 IN.	500	350.00	355.00
94	MASTER CARVER, 6 IN.	250	600.00	605.00
W. & C. HALLETT			**CELESTIAL MESSENGERS**	
95	ANGEL OF CHARITY	250	375.00	375.00
96	ANGEL OF FAITH	250	375.00	375.00
96	ANGEL OF HOPE	250	375.00	375.00
L. GAITHER				**CHRISTMAS EVE**
95	GETTING READY	500	450.00	450.00
95	HITCHING PRANCER	500	450.00	450.00
S. KAY			**CHRISTMAS FIRSTS**	
94	SARAH KAY'S FIRST CHRISTMAS, 4 IN.	500	350.00	355.00
94	SARAH KAY'S FIRST CHRISTMAS, 6 IN.	250	600.00	605.00
*				**CLUB ANRI**
88	MAESTRO MICKEY, 4 1/2 IN.	CL	170.00	205.00
89	DAPPER DONALD, 4 IN.	5000	199.00	199.00
89	DIVA MINNIE, 4 1/2 IN.	CL	190.00	195.00
90	DAPPER DONALD, 4 IN.	CL	199.00	200.00
91	DAISY DUCK, 4 1/2 IN.	TL	250.00	255.00
J. FERRANDIZ				**CLUB ANRI**
83	WELCOME, 4 IN.	CL	110.00	400.00
84	MY FRIEND, 4 IN.	CL	110.00	405.00
85	HARVEST TIME, 4 IN.	CL	125.00	280.00
86	CELEBRATION MARCH, 5 IN.	CL	165.00	260.00
86	HARVEST'S HELPER, 4 IN.	CL	135.00	255.00
87	WILL YOU BE MINE, 4 IN.	CL	135.00	240.00
88	FOREVER YOURS, 4 IN.	CL	170.00	255.00
89	TWENTY YEARS OF LOVE, 4 IN.	CL	190.00	195.00
89	YOU ARE MY SUNSHINE, 4 IN.	YR	220.00	220.00
91	WITH ALL MY HEART, 4 IN.	*	250.00	255.00

YR	NAME	LIMIT	ISSUE	TREND
92	YOU ARE MY ALL, 4 IN.	*	260.00	265.00
S. KAY				**CLUB ANRI**
84	APPLE OF MY EYE, 4 1/2 IN.	CL	135.00	390.00
85	DAD'S HELPER, 4 1/2 IN.	CL	135.00	260.00
86	MAKE A WISH, 4 IN.	CL	165.00	280.00
86	ROMANTIC NOTIONS, 4 IN.	CL	135.00	240.00
87	A YOUNG MAN'S FANCY, 4 IN.	CL	135.00	215.00
88	I'VE GOT A SECRET, 4 IN.	CL	170.00	210.00
89	A LITTLE BASHFUL, 4 IN.	YR	220.00	220.00
89	I'LL NEVER TELL, 4 IN.	CL	190.00	195.00
90	A LITTLE BASHFUL, 4 IN.	YR	220.00	225.00
91	KISS ME, 4 IN.	*	250.00	255.00
92	MY PRESENT FOR YOU, 4 IN.	*	270.00	265.00
*				**COLLECTORS SOCIETY**
95	ANRI ARTIST TREE HOUSE	*	695.00	695.00
J. FERRANDIZ				**COLLECTORS SOCIETY**
95	SEALED WITH A KISS	*	275.00	275.00
96	ON CLOUD NINE	*	275.00	275.00
S. HALLETT				**COLLECTORS SOCIETY**
95	ON MY OWN 4"	*	175.00	175.00
S. KAY				**COLLECTORS SOCIETY**
96	SWEET TOOTH 4"	*	199.50	199.50
*				**DISNEY WOODCARVINGS**
87	DONALD DUCK, 4 IN.	CL	150.00	200.00
87	GOOFY, 4 IN.	CL	150.00	200.00
87	MICKEY AND MINNIE, 6 IN. (MATCHING NUM.)	CL	625.00	1660.00
87	MICKEY MOUSE, 4 IN.	CL	150.00	215.00
87	MINNIE MOUSE, 4 IN.	CL	150.00	215.00
87	PINOCCHIO, 4 IN.	CL	150.00	200.00
88	DONALD DUCK, 1 3/4 IN.	CL	80.00	105.00
88	DONALD DUCK, 4 IN.	CL	180.00	200.00
88	DONALD DUCK, 6 IN.	CL	350.00	705.00
88	GOOFY, 1 3/4 IN.	CL	80.00	105.00
88	GOOFY, 4 IN.	CL	180.00	200.00
88	GOOFY, 6 IN.	CL	350.00	705.00
88	MICKEY MOUSE, 1 3/4 IN.	CL	80.00	105.00
88	MICKEY MOUSE, 4 IN.	CL	180.00	200.00
88	MICKEY SORCERER'S APPRENTICE, 2 IN.	CL	80.00	105.00
88	MICKEY SORCERER'S APPRENTICE, 4 IN.	CL	180.00	200.00
88	MICKEY SORCERER'S APPRENTICE, 6 IN.	CL	350.00	505.00
88	PINOCCHIO, 1 3/4 IN.	CL	80.00	145.00
88	PINOCCHIO, 4 IN.	CL	180.00	200.00
88	PLUTO, 1 3/4 IN.	CL	80.00	105.00
88	PLUTO, 4 IN.	CL	180.00	200.00
89	DAISY, 4 IN.	CL	190.00	205.00
89	DONALD, 4 IN.	CL	190.00	205.00
89	GOOFY, 4 IN.	CL	190.00	210.00
89	MICKEY & MINNIE, 6 IN. (SET)	CL	700.00	705.00
89	MICKEY AND MINNIE, 20 IN. (MATCHED SET)	CL	7000.00	7100.00
89	MICKEY, 10 IN.	CL	700.00	755.00
89	MICKEY, 20 IN.	CL	3500.00	3505.00
89	MICKEY, 4 IN.	CL	190.00	210.00
89	MINI DAISY, 2 IN.	CL	85.00	105.00
89	MINI DONALD, 2 IN.	CL	85.00	105.00
89	MINI GOOFY, 2 IN.	CL	85.00	105.00
89	MINI MICKEY, 2 IN.	CL	85.00	105.00
89	MINI MINNIE, 2 IN.	CL	85.00	105.00
89	MINI PLUTO, 2 IN.	CL	85.00	105.00
89	MINNIE, 10 IN.	CL	700.00	755.00
89	MINNIE, 20 IN.	CL	3500.00	3505.00
89	MINNIE, 4 IN.	CL	190.00	210.00
89	PINOCCHIO, 10 IN.	CL	700.00	705.00
89	PINOCCHIO, 2 IN.	CL	85.00	105.00
89	PINOCCHIO, 20 IN.	CL	3500.00	3505.00
89	PINOCCHIO, 4 IN.	CL	190.00	200.00
89	PINOCCHIO, 6 IN.	CL	350.00	355.00
89	PLUTO, 4 IN.	CL	190.00	210.00
89	PLUTO, 6 IN.	CL	350.00	355.00
90	CHEF GOOFY, 2 1/2 IN.	CL	125.00	130.00
90	CHEF GOOFY, 5 IN.	CL	265.00	270.00
90	DONALD AND DAISY, 6 IN. (MATCHED SET)	CL	700.00	755.00
90	MICKEY MOUSE, 2 IN.	CL	100.00	105.00
90	MICKEY MOUSE, 4 IN.	CL	199.00	210.00
90	MICKEY SKATING, 4 IN.	CL	250.00	355.00
90	MINNIE MOUSE, 2 IN.	CL	100.00	105.00
90	MINNIE MOUSE, 4 IN.	CL	199.00	210.00
90	MINNIE SKATING, 4 IN.	CL	250.00	355.00
91	BELL BOY DONALD, 4 IN.	CL	250.00	255.00
91	BELL BOY DONALD, 6 IN.	CL	400.00	405.00
91	MICKEY SKATING, 2 IN.	*	120.00	120.00
91	MICKEY SKATING, 2 IN.	CL	120.00	165.00
91	MICKEY SKATING, 4 IN.	*	250.00	250.00
91	MINNIE SKATING, 2 IN.	CL	120.00	125.00
91	MINNIE SKATING, 2 IN.	*	120.00	120.00
91	MINNIE SKATING, 4 IN.	CL	250.00	355.00
J. FERRANDIZ				**FERRANDIZ BOY & GIRL**
76	COWBOY, 6 IN.	CL	75.00	555.00
76	HARVEST GIRL, 6 IN.	CL	75.00	605.00

YR	NAME	LIMIT	ISSUE	TREND
77	LEADING THE WAY, 6 IN.	CL	100.00	340.00
77	TRACKER, 6 IN.	CL	100.00	255.00
78	BASKET OF JOY, 6 IN.	CL	140.00	405.00
78	PEACE PIPE, 6 IN.	CL	140.00	390.00
79	FIRST BLOSSOM, 6 IN.	CL	135.00	365.00
79	HAPPY STRUMMER, 6 IN.	CL	160.00	280.00
80	FRIENDS, 6 IN.	CL	200.00	330.00
80	MELODY FOR TWO, 6 IN.	CL	200.00	280.00
81	MERRY MELODY, 6 IN.	CL	210.00	330.00
81	TINY SOUNDS, 6 IN.	CL	210.00	330.00
82	GUIDING LIGHT, 6 IN.	CL	225.00	305.00
82	TO MARKET, 6 IN.	CL	220.00	240.00
83	ADMIRATION, 6 IN.	CL	220.00	260.00
83	BEWILDERED, 6 IN.	CL	196.00	250.00
84	FRIENDLY FACES, 3 IN.	CL	93.00	100.00
84	FRIENDLY FACES, 6 IN.	CL	210.00	265.00
84	WANDERER'S RETURN, 3 IN.	CL	93.00	120.00
84	WANDERER'S RETURN, 6 IN.	CL	196.00	235.00
85	PEACEFUL FRIENDS, 3 IN.	CL	120.00	125.00
85	PEACEFUL FRIENDS, 6 IN.	CL	250.00	280.00
85	TENDER LOVE, 3 IN.	CL	100.00	115.00
85	TENDER LOVE, 6 IN.	CL	225.00	240.00
86	GOLDEN SHEAVES, 3 IN.	CL	125.00	130.00
86	GOLDEN SHEAVES, 6 IN.	CL	245.00	250.00
86	SEASON'S BOUNTY, 3 IN.	CL	125.00	130.00
86	SEASON'S BOUNTY, 6 IN.	CL	245.00	250.00
87	DEAR SWEETHEART, 3 IN.	CL	130.00	135.00
87	DEAR SWEETHEART, 6 IN.	CL	250.00	255.00
87	FOR MY SWEETHEART, 3 IN.	CL	130.00	135.00
87	FOR MY SWEETHEART, 6 IN.	CL	250.00	255.00
88	EXTRA, EXTRA!, 6 IN.	CL	320.00	325.00
88	SUNNY SKIES, 3 IN.	CL	145.00	150.00
88	SUNNY SKIES, 6 IN.	CL	320.00	325.00
89	BAKER BOY, 3 IN.	CL	170.00	175.00
89	BAKER BOY, 6 IN.	CL	340.00	345.00
89	PASTRY GIRL, 3 IN.	CL	170.00	175.00
89	PASTRY GIRL, 6 IN.	CL	340.00	345.00
89	SWISS BOY, 3 IN.	CL	180.00	185.00
89	SWISS BOY, 3 IN.	CL	180.00	185.00
89	SWISS BOY, 6 IN.	CL	380.00	385.00
89	SWISS GIRL, 3 IN.	CL	200.00	205.00
89	SWISS GIRL, 6 IN.	CL	470.00	475.00
90	ALPINE FRIEND, 3 IN.	CL	225.00	300.00
90	ALPINE FRIEND, 6 IN.	1500	450.00	450.00
90	ALPINE MUSIC, 3 IN.	CL	225.00	230.00
90	ALPINE MUSIC, 6 IN.	1500	450.00	515.00
91	CATALONIAN BOY, 3 IN.	CL	227.50	230.00
91	CATALONIAN BOY, 6 IN.	CL	500.00	505.00
91	CATALONIAN GIRL, 3 IN.	CL	227.50	230.00
91	CATALONIAN GIRL, 6 IN.	CL	500.00	505.00
92	MADONNA WITH CHILD ,3 INCHES	1000	190.00	195.00
92	MADONNA WITH CHILD, 6 INCHES	1000	370.00	375.00
92	MAY I, TOO?, 3 INCHES	1000	230.00	235.00
92	MAY I, TOO?, 6 INCHES	1000	440.00	445.00
92	PASCAL LAMB, 3 INCHES	1000	210.00	215.00
92	PASCAL LAMB, 6 INCHES	1000	460.00	465.00
92	WASTE NOT, WANT NOT, 3 INCHES	1000	190.00	195.00
92	WASTE NOT, WANT NOT, 6 INCHES	1000	430.00	435.00
J. FERRANDIZ		**FERRANDIZ MATCHING NUMBER WOODCARVINGS**		
88	BON APPETIT, 3 IN. (SET)	*	*	*
88	BON APPETIT, 6 IN. (SET)	*	*	*
88	DEAR SWEETHEART, 3 IN.	CL	285.00	395.00
88	EXTRA, EXTRA!, 3 IN.	CL	315.00	320.00
88	EXTRA, EXTRA!, 6 IN.	CL	665.00	670.00
88	PICNIC FOR TWO, 3 IN.	CL	390.00	395.00
88	PICNIC FOR TWO, 6 IN.	CL	845.00	850.00
88	SUNNY SKIES, 3 IN. (SET)	*	*	*
88	SUNNY SKIES, 6 IN. (SET)	*	*	*
89	BAKER/PASTRY, 3 IN.	CL	340.00	345.00
89	BAKER/PASTRY, 6 IN.	CL	680.00	685.00
89	DEAR SWEETHEART, 3 IN.	100	525.00	900.00
89	DEAR SWEETHEART, 6 IN. (SET)	*	*	*
90	ALPINE MUSIC/FRIEND, 3 IN.	CL	450.00	455.00
90	ALPINE MUSIC/FRIEND, 6 IN.	CL	900.00	905.00
91	CATALONIAN BOY/GIRL, 3 IN.	CL	455.00	460.00
91	CATALONIAN BOY/GIRL, 6 IN.	CL	1000.00	950.00
J. FERRANDIZ		**FERRANDIZ MESSAGE COLLECTION**		
89	GOD'S MIRACLE, 4 1/2 IN.	CL	300.00	305.00
89	GOD'S PRECIOUS GIFT, 4 1/2 IN.	CL	300.00	305.00
89	HE GUIDES US, 4 1/2 IN.	CL	300.00	305.00
89	HE IS THE LIGHT, 4 1/2 IN.	CL	300.00	305.00
89	HE IS THE LIGHT, 9 IN.	CL	600.00	605.00
89	HEAVEN SENT, 4 1/2 IN.	CL	300.00	305.00
89	LIGHT FROM WITHIN, 4 1/2 IN.	CL	300.00	305.00
89	LOVE KNOWS NO BOUNDS, 4 1/2 IN.	CL	300.00	305.00
89	LOVE SO POWERFUL, 4 1/2 IN.	CL	300.00	305.00
90	CHRISTMAS CARILLON, 4 1/2 IN.	CL	299.00	300.00
90	COUNT YOUR BLESSINGS, 4 1/2 IN.	CL	300.00	305.00
90	GOD'S CREATION, 4 1/2 IN.	CL	300.00	315.00

YR	NAME	LIMIT	ISSUE	TREND
J. FERRANDIZ		**FERRANDIZ MINI NATIVITY SET**		
84	INFANT, 1 1/2 IN. (SET)	CL	*	*
84	JOSEPH, 1 1/2 IN. (SET)	CL	*	*
84	LEADING THE WAY, 1 1/2 IN. (SET)	CL	*	*
84	MARY, 1 1/2 IN.	CL	300.00	545.00
84	OX DONKEY, 1 1/2 IN. (SET)	CL	*	*
84	SHEEP KNEELING, 1 1/2 IN. (SET)	CL	*	*
84	SHEEP STANDING, 1 1/2 IN. (SET)	CL	*	*
85	BABY CAMEL, 1 1/2 IN.	CL	45.00	55.00
85	CAMEL GUIDE, 1 1/2 IN.	CL	45.00	55.00
85	CAMEL, 1 1/2 IN.	CL	45.00	55.00
85	HARMONY, 1 1/2 IN.	CL	45.00	55.00
85	REST, 1 1/2 IN.	CL	45.00	55.00
85	REVERENCE, 1 1/2 IN.	CL	45.00	55.00
85	SMALL TALK, 1 1/2 IN.	CL	45.00	55.00
85	THANKSGIVING, 1 1/2 IN.	CL	45.00	55.00
86	ANGEL, 1 1/2 IN.	CL	45.00	55.00
86	BALTHASAR, 1 1/2 IN.	CL	45.00	55.00
86	CASPAR, 1 1/2 IN.	CL	45.00	55.00
86	FREE RIDE & MINI LAMB, 1 1/2 IN.	CL	45.00	55.00
86	HIKER, THE-1 1/2 IN.	CL	45.00	55.00
86	MELCHIOR, 1 1/2 IN.	CL	45.00	55.00
86	STAR STRUCK, 1 1/2 IN.	CL	45.00	55.00
86	STRAY, THE-1 1/2 IN.	CL	45.00	55.00
86	WEARY TRAVELLER, 1 1/2 IN.	CL	45.00	55.00
88	DEVOTION, 1 1/2 IN.	CL	53.00	55.00
88	JOLLY GIFT, 1 1/2 IN.	CL	53.00	55.00
88	LONG JOURNEY, 1 1/2 IN.	CL	53.00	55.00
88	SWEET DREAMS, 1 1/2 IN.	CL	53.00	55.00
88	SWEET INSPIRATION, 1 1/2 IN.	CL	53.00	55.00
J. FERRANDIZ		**FERRANDIZ SHEPHERDS OF THE YEAR**		
77	FRIENDSHIPS, 3 IN.	YR	53.50	335.00
77	FRIENDSHIPS, 6 IN.	YR	110.00	590.00
78	SPREADING THE WORD, 3 IN.	YR	115.00	265.00
78	SPREADING THE WORD, 6 IN.	CL	270.50	440.00
79	DRUMMER BOY, 3 IN.	YR	80.00	170.00
79	DRUMMER BOY, 6 IN.	YR	220.00	430.00
80	FREEDOM BOUND, 3 IN.	YR	90.00	155.00
80	FREEDOM BOUND, 6 IN.	YR	225.00	315.00
81	JOLLY PIPER, 6 IN.	2250	225.00	405.00
82	COMPANIONS, 6 IN.	2250	220.00	305.00
83	GOOD SAMARITAN, 6 IN.	2250	220.00	315.00
84	DEVOTION, 3 IN.	CL	82.50	105.00
84	DEVOTION, 6 IN.	CL	180.00	230.00
J. FERRANDIZ		**FERRANDIZ WOODCARVINGS**		
69	ANGEL SUGAR HEART, 6 IN.	CL	25.00	2525.00
69	GOOD SHEPHERD, THE-3 IN.	CL	12.50	120.00
69	GOOD SHEPHERD, THE-6 IN.	CL	25.00	245.00
69	HEAVENLY GARDENER, 6 IN.	CL	25.00	2025.00
69	HEAVENLY QUINTET, 6 IN.	CL	25.00	2025.00
69	LOVE LETTER, 3 IN.	CL	12.50	155.00
69	LOVE LETTER, 6 IN.	CL	25.00	255.00
69	LOVE'S MESSENGER, 6 IN.	CL	25.00	2025.00
69	QUINTET, THE 3 IN.	CL	12.50	145.00
69	QUINTET, THE 6 IN.	CL	25.00	325.00
69	SUGAR HEART, 3 IN.	CL	12.50	455.00
69	SUGAR HEART, 6 IN.	CL	25.00	530.00
69	TALKING TO THE ANIMALS, 3 IN.	CL	12.50	135.00
69	TALKING TO THE ANIMALS, 6 IN.	CL	45.00	55.00
70	ARTIST, 3 IN.	CL	30.00	115.00
70	ARTIST, 6 IN.	CL	25.00	355.00
70	DUET, 3 IN.	CL	36.00	175.00
70	DUET, 6 IN.	CL	*	365.00
71	GOOD SHEPHERD, THE-10 IN.	CL	90.00	95.00
71	QUINTET,THE- 10 IN.	CL	100.00	605.00
71	TALKING TO THE ANIMALS, 10 IN.	CL	90.00	300.00
73	GIRL IN THE EGG, 3 IN.	CL	30.00	135.00
73	GIRL IN THE EGG, 6 IN.	CL	60.00	275.00
73	GIRL WITH DOVE, 3 IN.	CL	30.00	115.00
73	GIRL WITH DOVE, 6 IN.	CL	50.00	230.00
73	HAPPY WANDERER, 10 IN.	CL	120.00	500.00
73	NATURE GIRL, 3 IN.	CL	30.00	35.00
73	NATURE GIRL, 6 IN.	CL	60.00	275.00
73	SPRING ARRIVALS, 3 IN.	OP	30.00	160.00
73	SPRING ARRIVALS, 6 IN.	OP	50.00	350.00
73	SWEEPER, 3 IN.	CL	35.00	135.00
73	SWEEPER, 6 IN.	CL	75.00	430.00
73	TRUMPETER, 3 IN.	CL	69.00	115.00
73	TRUMPETER, 6 IN.	CL	120.00	250.00
74	BOUQUET, THE 3 IN.	CL	35.00	180.00
74	BOUQUET, THE 6 IN.	CL	75.00	330.00
74	FLIGHT INTO EGYPT, 3 IN.	CL	35.00	135.00
74	FLIGHT INTO EGYPT, 6 IN.	CL	70.00	500.00
74	GREETINGS, 3 IN.	CL	30.00	305.00
74	GREETINGS, 6 IN.	CL	55.00	480.00
74	HAPPY WANDERER, 3 IN.	CL	40.00	105.00
74	HAPPY WANDERER, 6 IN.	CL	70.00	200.00

YR	NAME	LIMIT	ISSUE	TREND
74	HELPING HANDS, 3 IN.	CL	30.00	355.00
74	HELPING HANDS, 6 IN.	CL	55.00	710.00
74	LITTLE MOTHER 3 IN.	CL	136.00	220.00
74	LITTLE MOTHER, 6 IN.	CL	85.00	290.00
74	NEW FRIENDS, 3 IN.	CL	30.00	280.00
74	NEW FRIENDS, 6 IN.	CL	55.00	310.00
74	ROMEO, 3 IN.	CL	50.00	230.00
74	ROMEO, 6 IN.	CL	85.00	380.00
74	SPRING OUTING, 3 IN.	CL	30.00	630.00
74	SPRING OUTING, 6 IN.	CL	55.00	910.00
74	TENDER MOMENTS, 3 IN.	CL	30.00	380.00
74	TENDER MOMENTS, 6 IN.	CL	55.00	580.00
75	CHERUB, 2 IN.	CL	32.00	95.00
75	CHERUB, 4 IN.	CL	32.00	280.00
75	COURTING, 3 IN.	CL	70.00	240.00
75	COURTING, 6 IN.	CL	150.00	455.00
75	GIFT, THE 3 IN.	CL	40.00	120.00
75	GIFT, THE6 IN.	CL	70.00	185.00
75	GOING HOME, 3 IN.	CL	40.00	110.00
75	GOING HOME, 6 IN.	CL	70.00	240.00
75	HOLY FAMILY, 3 IN.	CL	75.00	250.00
75	HOLY FAMILY, 6 IN.	CL	200.00	670.00
75	INSPECTOR, 3 IN.	CL	40.00	230.00
75	INSPECTOR, 6 IN.	CL	80.00	380.00
75	LOVE GIFT, 3 IN.	CL	40.00	125.00
75	LOVE GIFT, 6 IN.	CL	70.00	185.00
75	MOTHER & CHILD, 3 IN.	CL	45.00	105.00
75	MOTHER & CHILD, 6 IN.	CL	90.00	190.00
75	SUMMERTIME, 3 IN.	CL	35.00	45.00
75	SUMMERTIME, 6 IN.	CL	70.00	265.00
75	WANDERLUST, 6 IN.	CL	70.00	455.00
76	CATCH A FALLING STAR, 3 IN.	CL	35.00	155.00
76	CATCH A FALLING STAR, 6 IN.	CL	75.00	255.00
76	COWBOY, 3 IN.	CL	35.00	155.00
76	FLOWER GIRL, 3 IN.	CL	40.00	45.00
76	FLOWER GIRL, 6 IN.	CL	90.00	310.00
76	GARDENER, 3 IN.	CL	32.00	115.00
76	GARDENER, 6 IN.	CL	65.00	110.00
76	GIRL W/ROOSTER, 3 IN.	CL	32.50	180.00
76	GIRL W/ROOSTER, 6 IN.	CL	60.00	280.00
76	LETTER, THE 3 IN.	CL	40.00	45.00
76	LETTER, THE 6 IN.	CL	90.00	600.00
76	SHARING, 3 IN.	CL	32.50	135.00
76	SHARING, 6 IN.	CL	75.00	180.00
76	WANDERLUST, 3 IN.	CL	32.50	130.00
77	BLESSING, THE 3 IN.	CL	45.00	155.00
77	BLESSING, THE 6 IN.	CL	125.00	255.00
77	HURDY GURDY, 3 IN.	CL	53.00	155.00
77	HURDY GURDY, 6 IN.	CL	112.00	395.00
77	JOURNEY, 3 IN.	CL	67.50	180.00
77	JOURNEY, 6 IN.	CL	120.00	405.00
77	LEADING THE WAY, 3 IN.	CL	62.50	125.00
77	NIGHT NIGHT, 3 IN.	CL	45.00	125.00
77	NIGHT NIGHT, 6 IN.	CL	67.50	185.00
77	POOR BOY, 3 IN.	CL	50.00	100.00
77	POOR BOY, 6 IN.	CL	125.00	200.00
77	PROUD MOTHER, 3 IN.	CL	52.50	155.00
77	PROUD MOTHER, 6 IN.	CL	130.00	355.00
77	RIDING THRU THE RAIN, 10 IN.	OP	400.00	1010.00
77	RIDING THRU THE RAIN, 5 IN.	OP	145.00	400.00
77	TRACKER, 3 IN.	CL	70.00	165.00
78	BASKET OF JOY, 3 IN.	CL	65.00	125.00
78	HARVEST GIRL, 3 IN.	CL	75.00	130.00
78	SPREADING THE WORD, 3 IN.	CL	115.00	195.00
78	SPREADING THE WORD, 6 IN.	CL	270.00	500.00
78	SPRING DANCE, 12 IN.	CL	950.00	1775.00
78	SPRING DANCE, 24 IN.	CL	47.50	6250.00
79	FIRST BLOSSOM, 3 IN.	CL	70.00	95.00
79	HAPPY STRUMMER, 3 IN.	CL	75.00	110.00
79	HE'S MY BROTHER, 3 IN.	CL	70.00	135.00
79	HE'S MY BROTHER, 6 IN.	CL	155.00	245.00
79	HIGH RIDING, 3 IN.	CL	145.00	205.00
79	HIGH RIDING, 6 IN.	CL	340.00	480.00
79	PEACE PIPE, 3 IN.	CL	85.00	120.00
79	STITCH IN TIME, 3 IN.	CL	75.00	130.00
79	STITCH IN TIME, 6 IN.	CL	150.00	240.00
80	DRUMMER BOY, 3 IN.	CL	130.00	205.00
80	DRUMMER BOY, 6 IN.	CL	300.00	405.00
80	SPRING ARRIVALS, 10 IN.	OP	435.00	670.00
80	SPRING ARRIVALS, 20 IN.	250	2000.00	3375.00
80	TRUMPETER, 10 IN.	CL	500.00	510.00
80	UMPAPA, 4 IN.	CL	125.00	145.00
81	JOLLY PIPER, 3 IN.	CL	100.00	125.00
81	MERRY MELODY, 3 IN.	CL	90.00	120.00
81	MUSICAL BASKET, 3 IN.	CL	90.00	120.00
81	MUSICAL BASKET, 6 IN.	CL	200.00	230.00
81	STEPPING OUT, 3 IN.	CL	95.00	115.00
81	STEPPING OUT, 6 IN.	CL	220.00	250.00
81	SWEET ARRIVAL (BLUE), 3 IN.	CL	105.00	120.00

YR	NAME	LIMIT	ISSUE	TREND
81	SWEET ARRIVAL (BLUE), 6 IN.	CL	225.00	265.00
81	SWEET ARRIVAL (PINK), 3 IN.	CL	105.00	110.00
81	SWEET ARRIVAL (PINK), 6 IN.	CL	225.00	230.00
81	SWEET DREAMS, 3 IN.	CL	100.00	145.00
81	TINY SOUNDS, 3 IN.	CL	90.00	110.00
82	BAGPIPE, 3 IN.	CL	80.00	100.00
82	BAGPIPE, 6 IN.	CL	175.00	195.00
82	BUNDLE OF JOY, 3 IN.	CL	100.00	305.00
82	BUNDLE OF JOY, 6 IN.	CL	225.00	325.00
82	CHAMPION, THE 3 IN.	CL	98.00	120.00
82	CHAMPION, THE 6 IN.	CL	220.00	260.00
82	CIRCUS SERENADE, 3 IN.	CL	100.00	165.00
82	CIRCUS SERENADE, 6 IN.	CL	220.00	225.00
82	CLARINET, 3 IN.	CL	80.00	105.00
82	CLARINET, 6 IN.	CL	175.00	205.00
82	COMPANIONS, 3 IN.	CL	95.00	120.00
82	ENCORE, 3 IN.	CL	100.00	120.00
82	ENCORE, 6 IN.	CL	225.00	240.00
82	FLUTE, 3 IN.	CL	80.00	100.00
82	FLUTE, 6 IN.	CL	175.00	195.00
82	GOOD LIFE, THE 3 IN.	CL	100.00	205.00
82	GOOD LIFE, THE 6 IN.	CL	225.00	265.00
82	GUIDING LIGHT, 3 IN.	CL	100.00	125.00
82	GUITAR, 3 IN.	CL	80.00	100.00
82	GUITAR, 6 IN.	CL	175.00	195.00
82	HARMONICA, 3 IN.	CL	80.00	100.00
82	HARMONICA, 6 IN.	CL	175.00	195.00
82	HITCHHIKER, 3 IN.	CL	98.00	100.00
82	HITCHHIKER, 6 IN.	CL	125.00	230.00
82	LIGHTING THE WAY, 3 IN.	CL	105.00	125.00
82	LIGHTING THE WAY, 6 IN.	CL	225.00	265.00
82	PLAY IT AGAIN, 3 IN.	CL	100.00	120.00
82	PLAY IT AGAIN, 6 IN.	CL	250.00	260.00
82	STAR BRIGHT, 3 IN.	CL	110.00	130.00
82	STAR BRIGHT, 6 IN.	CL	250.00	265.00
82	SURPRISE, 3 IN.	CL	100.00	155.00
82	SURPRISE, 6 IN.	CL	225.00	330.00
82	SWEET DREAMS, 6 IN.	CL	225.00	335.00
82	SWEET MELODY, 3 IN.	CL	80.00	100.00
82	SWEET MELODY, 6 IN.	CL	198.00	210.00
82	TO MARKET, 3 IN.	CL	95.00	120.00
82	VIOLIN, 3 IN.	CL	80.00	100.00
82	VIOLIN, 6 IN.	CL	175.00	200.00
83	COWBOY, 20 IN.	CL	2100.00	2125.00
83	EDELWEISS, 3 IN.	OP	95.00	185.00
83	EDELWEISS, 6 IN.	OP	220.00	430.00
83	GOLDEN BLOSSOM, 10 IN	OP	500.00	755.00
83	GOLDEN BLOSSOM, 20 IN	OP	3300.00	5160.00
83	GOLDEN BLOSSOM, 3 IN.	OP	95.00	145.00
83	GOLDEN BLOSSOM, 6 IN.	OP	220.00	340.00
83	LOVE MESSAGE, 3 IN.	CL	105.00	155.00
83	LOVE MESSAGE, 6 IN.	CL	240.00	370.00
83	PEACE PIPE, 10 IN.	CL	460.00	505.00
84	BIRD'S EYE VIEW, 3 IN.	CL	88.00	130.00
84	BIRD'S EYE VIEW, 6 IN.	CL	216.00	705.00
84	COWBOY, 10 IN.	CL	370.00	505.00
84	HIGH HOPES, 3 IN.	CL	81.00	95.00
84	HIGH HOPES, 6 IN.	CL	170.00	265.00
84	PEACE PIPE, 20 IN.	CL	2200.00	3475.00
84	SHIPMATES, 3 IN.	CL	81.00	120.00
84	SHIPMATES, 6 IN.	CL	170.00	250.00
84	TRUMPETER, 20 IN.	CL	2350.00	3000.00
85	BUTTERFLY BOY, 3 IN.	CL	95.00	145.00
85	BUTTERFLY BOY, 6 IN.	CL	220.00	325.00
86	A MUSICAL RIDE, 4 IN.	RT	165.00	240.00
86	A MUSICAL RIDE, 8 IN.	RT	395.00	560.00
86	EDELWEISS, 10 IN.	OP	500.00	755.00
86	EDELWEISS, 20 IN.	250	3300.00	4365.00
86	GOD'S LITTLE HELPER, 2 IN.	CL	170.00	260.00
86	GOD'S LITTLE HELPER, 4 IN.	CL	425.00	555.00
86	GOLDEN BLOSSOM, 40 IN.	CL	8300.00	13000.00
86	SWISS BOY, 3 IN.	CL	122.00	160.00
86	SWISS BOY, 6 IN.	CL	245.00	325.00
86	SWISS GIRL, 3 IN.	CL	122.00	125.00
86	SWISS GIRL, 6 IN.	CL	245.00	305.00
87	AMONG FRIENDS, 3 IN.	CL	125.00	150.00
87	AMONG FRIENDS, 6 IN.	CL	245.00	295.00
87	BLACK FOREST BOY, 3 IN.	CL	125.00	150.00
87	BLACK FOREST BOY, 6 IN.	CL	250.00	300.00
87	BLACK FOREST GIRL, 3 IN.	CL	125.00	150.00
87	BLACK FOREST GIRL, 6 IN.	CL	250.00	305.00
87	HEAVENLY CONCERT, 2 IN.	CL	200.00	205.00
87	HEAVENLY CONCERT, 4 IN.	CL	450.00	555.00
87	NATURE'S WONDER, 3 IN.	CL	125.00	150.00
87	NATURE'S WONDER, 6 IN.	CL	245.00	290.00
87	SERENITY, 3 IN.	CL	125.00	150.00
87	SERENITY, 6 IN.	CL	245.00	295.00
88	ABRACADABRA, 3 IN.	CL	145.00	175.00
88	ABRACADABRA, 6 IN.	CL	315.00	355.00

YR	NAME	LIMIT	ISSUE	TREND
88	BON APPETIT, 3 IN.	500	175.00	200.00
88	BON APPETIT, 6 IN.	500	395.00	440.00
88	PEACE MAKER, 3 IN.	CL	180.00	200.00
88	PEACE MAKER, 6 IN.	CL	360.00	405.00
88	PICNIC FOR TWO, 3 IN.	CL	190.00	210.00
88	PICNIC FOR TWO, 6 IN.	CL	425.00	475.00
88	WINTER MEMORIES, 3 IN.	CL	180.00	200.00
88	WINTER MEMORIES, 6 IN.	CL	398.00	445.00
89	MEXICAN BOY, 3 IN.	CL	170.00	180.00
89	MEXICAN BOY, 6 IN.	CL	340.00	355.00
89	MEXICAN GIRL, 3 IN.	CL	170.00	180.00
89	MEXICAN GIRL, 6 IN.	CL	340.00	355.00
93	CHRISTMAS TIME, 5 IN.	750	360.00	375.00
93	HOLIDAY GREETINGS, 3 IN.	1000	200.00	205.00
93	HOLIDAY GREETINGS, 6 IN.	1000	450.00	455.00
93	LOTS OF GIFTS, 3 IN.	1000	200.00	205.00
93	LOTS OF GIFTS, 6 IN.	1000	450.00	455.00
93	SANTA AND TEDDY, 5 IN.	750	360.00	375.00
94	DONKEY DRIVER, 3 IN.	OP	160.00	165.00
94	DONKEY DRIVER, 6 IN.	OP	360.00	365.00
94	DONKEY, 3 IN.	OP	200.00	205.00
94	DONKEY, 6 IN.	OP	450.00	455.00
94	SANTA RESTING ON BAG, 5 IN.	OP	400.00	405.00
W. & C. HALLETT			**HEAVENLY ANGELS**	
95	ANGEL OF KINDNESS - NATURAL	250	225.00	225.00
95	ANGEL OF KINDNESS - PAINTED	250	350.00	350.00
95	ANGEL OF LOVE - PAINTED	250	350.00	350.00
95	ANGEL OF MERCY - NATURAL	250	225.00	225.00
95	ANGEL OF MERCY - PAINTED	250	350.00	350.00
95	ANGEL OF PEACE - NATURAL	250	225.00	225.00
95	ANGEL OF PEACE - PAINTED	250	350.00	350.00
96	ANGEL OF LOVE - NATURAL	250	225.00	225.00
J. FERRANDIZ			**LIMITED EDITION COUPLES**	
85	FIRST KISS, 8 IN.	CL	590.00	955.00
85	SPRINGTIME STROLL, 8 IN.	CL	590.00	955.00
86	A TENDER TOUCH, 8 IN.	CL	590.00	855.00
00	MY HEART IS YOURS, 8 IN.	CL	590.00	855.00
87	HEART TO HEART, 8 IN.	CL	590.00	855.00
88	A LOVING HAND, 8 IN.	CL	795.00	855.00
*			**MICKEY MOUSE THROUGH THE AGES**	
90	STEAM BOAT WILLIE, 4 IN.	CL	295.00	305.00
91	MAD DOG, THE-4 IN.	CL	500.00	605.00
U. BERNARDI			**REFLECTIONS**	
95	LEARNING THE SKILLS 4"	500	275.00	275.00
95	LEARNING THE SKILLS 6"	250	550.00	550.00
95	PLANNING THE TOUR 4"	500	250.00	250.00
95	PLANNING THE TOUR 6"	250	450.00	450.00
S. KAY			**SARAH KAY 10TH ANNIVERSARY**	
93	CHRISTMAS BASKET, 4 IN.	1000	310.00	295.00
93	CHRISTMAS BASKET, 6 IN.	1000	600.00	585.00
93	INNOCENCE, 4 IN.	1000	345.00	320.00
93	INNOCENCE, 6 IN.	1000	630.00	635.00
93	JOY TO THE WORLD, 4 IN.	1000	310.00	295.00
93	JOY TO THE WORLD, 6 IN.	1000	600.00	585.00
93	MR. SANTA, 4 IN.	750	375.00	395.00
93	MR. SANTA, 6 IN.	750	695.00	735.00
93	MRS. SANTA, 4 IN.	750	375.00	395.00
93	MRS. SANTA, 6 IN.	750	695.00	735.00
93	MY FAVORITE DOLL, 4 IN.	1000	315.00	320.00
93	MY FAVORITE DOLL, 6 IN.	1000	630.00	635.00
S. KAY			**SARAH KAY FIGURINES**	
83	BEDTIME, 1 1/2 IN.	CL	45.00	115.00
83	BEDTIME, 4 IN.	CL	95.00	235.00
83	BEDTIME, 6 IN.	CL	195.00	440.00
83	FEEDING THE CHICKENS, 1 1/2 IN.	CL	45.00	115.00
83	FEEDING THE CHICKENS, 4 IN.	CL	95.00	250.00
83	FEEDING THE CHICKENS, 6 IN.	CL	195.00	450.00
83	FROM THE GARDEN, 1 1/2 IN.	CL	45.00	115.00
83	FROM THE GARDEN, 4 IN.	CL	95.00	240.00
83	FROM THE GARDEN, 6 IN.	CL	195.00	475.00
83	HELPING MOTHER, 1 1/2 IN.	CL	45.00	115.00
83	HELPING MOTHER, 4 IN.	CL	95.00	305.00
83	HELPING MOTHER, 6 IN.	CL	210.00	500.00
83	MORNING CHORES, 1 1/2 IN.	CL	45.00	115.00
83	MORNING CHORES, 4 IN.	CL	95.00	305.00
83	MORNING CHORES, 6 IN.	CL	210.00	505.00
83	PLAYTIME, 1 1/2 IN.	CL	45.00	115.00
83	PLAYTIME, 4 IN.	CL	95.00	250.00
83	PLAYTIME, 6 IN.	CL	195.00	450.00
83	SWEEPING, 1 1/2 IN.	CL	45.00	115.00
83	SWEEPING, 4 IN.	CL	95.00	235.00
83	SWEEPING, 6 IN.	CL	195.00	450.00
83	WAITING FOR MOTHER, 1 1/2 IN.	CL	45.00	115.00
83	WAITING FOR MOTHER, 11 IN.	CL	495.00	800.00
83	WAITING FOR MOTHER, 4 IN.	CL	95.00	235.00
83	WAITING FOR MOTHER, 6 IN.	CL	195.00	450.00
83	WAKE UP KISS, 6 IN.	CL	210.00	555.00
84	DAYDREAMING, 1 1/2 IN.	CL	45.00	130.00

Equine artist Fred Stone, typically known for his limited edition prints, aptly captures the care a young mother takes of her young foal. Arabian Mare & Foal is produced by American Artists.

From the tip of his arrow to the fringe on his moccasins, the detailed Resolute makes a bold statement. The mixed media figure was created by C.A. Pardell and produced by Legends.

The emotion and action captured by artist C.A. Pardell makes The Final Charge a true work of art. The piece is produced by Legends.

The Cornetist by Ed Rohn was Roman Inc.'s first issue in the Jam Session collection, which debuted in 1985. Limited to 7,500 pieces, the original cost of the piece was $145.

Displaying extensive detailing, Michael Boyett's Flat Out for Red River Station pewter sculpture, produced by the Lance Corp., is limited to 2,500.

Look into this wolf's eyes and you'll understand that he means no harm. Forest Spirit was crafted by artist Kitty Cantrell and produced by Legends.

YR	NAME	LIMIT	ISSUE	TREND
84	DAYDREAMING, 4 IN.	CL	95.00	240.00
84	DAYDREAMING, 6 IN.	CL	195.00	450.00
84	FINDING R WAY, 1 1/2 IN.	CL	45.00	140.00
84	FINDING R WAY, 4 IN.	CL	95.00	250.00
84	FINDING R WAY, 6 IN.	CL	210.00	500.00
84	FLOWERS FOR YOU, 1 1/2 IN.	CL	45.00	130.00
84	FLOWERS FOR YOU, 4 IN.	CL	95.00	250.00
84	FLOWERS FOR YOU, 6 IN.	CL	195.00	450.00
84	OFF TO SCHOOL, 1 1/2 IN.	CL	45.00	130.00
84	OFF TO SCHOOL, 11 IN.	750	*	880.00
84	OFF TO SCHOOL, 20 IN.	100	*	4150.00
84	OFF TO SCHOOL, 4 IN.	4000	95.00	240.00
84	OFF TO SCHOOL, 6 IN.	4000	195.00	450.00
84	SPECIAL DELIVERY, 1 1/2 IN.	CL	45.00	130.00
84	SPECIAL DELIVERY, 4 IN.	CL	95.00	195.00
84	SPECIAL DELIVERY, 6 IN.	CL	195.00	335.00
84	TAG ALONG, 1 1/2 IN.	CL	45.00	135.00
84	TAG ALONG, 4 IN.	CL	95.00	230.00
84	TAG ALONG, 6 IN.	CL	195.00	295.00
84	WAKE UP KISS, 1 1/2 IN.	CL	45.00	555.00
84	WAKE UP KISS, 4 IN.	CL	95.00	190.00
84	WATCHFUL EYE, 1 1/2 IN.	CL	45.00	130.00
84	WATCHFUL EYE, 4 IN.	CL	95.00	240.00
84	WATCHFUL EYE, 6 IN.	CL	195.00	450.00
85	'TIS THE SEASON, 4 IN.	CL	95.00	255.00
85	'TIS THE SEASON, 6 IN.	CL	210.00	430.00
85	'TIS THE SEASON, 6 IN.	CL	210.00	430.00
85	A SPECIAL DAY, 4 IN.	CL	95.00	195.00
85	A SPECIAL DAY, 6 IN.	CL	195.00	330.00
85	AFTERNOON TEA, 11 IN.	CL	*	775.00
85	AFTERNOON TEA, 20 IN.	CL	*	3525.00
85	AFTERNOON TEA, 4 IN.	CL	95.00	190.00
85	AFTERNOON TEA, 6 IN.	CL	195.00	350.00
85	EVERY GOOD BOY DESERVES FAVOR	4000	95.00	185.00
85	GIDDYAP!, 4 IN.	CL	95.00	250.00
85	GIDDYAP!, 6 IN.	CL	195.00	330.00
85	NIGHTIE NIGHT, 4 IN.	CL	95.00	190.00
85	NIGHTIE NIGHT, 6 IN.	CL	195.00	330.00
85	YULTIDE CHEER, 4 IN.	CL	95.00	250.00
85	YULTIDE CHEER, 6 IN.	CL	210.00	440.00
86	ALWAYS BY MY SIDE, 1 1/2 IN.	CL	45.00	100.00
86	ALWAYS BY MY SIDE, 4 IN.	CL	95.00	200.00
86	ALWAYS BY MY SIDE, 6 IN.	CL	195.00	380.00
86	BUNNY HUG, 1 1/2 IN.	CL	45.00	90.00
86	BUNNY HUG, 4 IN.	CL	95.00	175.00
86	BUNNY HUG, 6 IN.	CL	210.00	400.00
86	FINISHING TOUCH, 1 1/2 IN.	CL	45.00	90.00
86	FINISHING TOUCH, 4 IN.	CL	95.00	175.00
86	FINISHING TOUCH, 6 IN.	CL	195.00	315.00
86	GOOD AS NEW, 1 1/2 IN.	CL	45.00	95.00
86	GOOD AS NEW, 4 IN.	4000	95.00	290.00
86	GOOD AS NEW, 6 IN.	4000	195.00	500.00
86	OUR PUPPY, 1 1/2 IN.	CL	45.00	95.00
86	OUR PUPPY, 4 IN.	CL	95.00	190.00
86	OUR PUPPY, 6 IN.	CL	210.00	360.00
86	SWEET TREAT, 1 1/2 IN.	CL	45.00	90.00
86	SWEET TREAT, 4 IN.	CL	95.00	175.00
86	SWEET TREAT, 6 IN.	CL	195.00	315.00
86	TO LOVE AND CHERISH, 1 1/2 IN.	CL	45.00	90.00
86	TO LOVE AND CHERISH, 11 IN.	CL	*	670.00
86	TO LOVE AND CHERISH, 20 IN.	CL	*	3625.00
86	TO LOVE AND CHERISH, 4 IN.	CL	95.00	175.00
86	TO LOVE AND CHERISH, 6 IN.	CL	195.00	315.00
86	WITH THIS RING, 1 1/2 IN.	CL	45.00	90.00
86	WITH THIS RING, 11 IN.	CL	*	670.00
86	WITH THIS RING, 20 IN.	CL	*	3625.00
86	WITH THIS RING, 4 IN.	CL	95.00	175.00
86	WITH THIS RING, 6 IN.	CL	195.00	315.00
87	A LOVING SPOONFUL, 1 1/2 IN.	CL	49.50	95.00
87	A LOVING SPOONFUL, 4 IN.	4000	150.00	295.00
87	A LOVING SPOONFUL, 6 IN.	4000	295.00	545.00
87	ALL ABOARD, 1 1/2 IN.	CL	49.50	95.00
87	ALL ABOARD, 4 IN.	CL	130.00	190.00
87	ALL ABOARD, 6 IN.	CL	265.00	360.00
87	ALL MINE, 1 1/2 IN.	CL	49.50	100.00
87	ALL MINE, 4 IN.	CL	130.00	230.00
87	ALL MINE, 6 IN.	CL	245.00	470.00
87	CUDDLES, 1 1/2 IN.	CL	49.50	100.00
87	CUDDLES, 4 IN.	CL	130.00	230.00
87	CUDDLES, 6 IN.	CL	245.00	470.00
87	LET'S PLAY, 1 1/2 IN.	CL	49.50	95.00
87	LET'S PLAY, 4 IN.	CL	130.00	190.00
87	LET'S PLAY, 6 IN.	CL	265.00	360.00
87	LITTLE NANNY, 1 1/2 IN.	CL	49.50	95.00
87	LITTLE NANNY, 4 IN.	CL	150.00	205.00
87	LITTLE NANNY, 6 IN.	CL	295.00	405.00
87	MY LITTLE BROTHER, 1 1/2 IN.	CL	70.00	95.00
87	MY LITTLE BROTHER, 4 IN.	CL	195.00	230.00
87	MY LITTLE BROTHER, 6 IN.	CL	375.00	455.00

YR	NAME	LIMIT	ISSUE	TREND
88	GINGER SNAP, 1 1/2 IN.	CL	70.00	95.00
88	GINGER SNAP, 4 IN.	CL	150.00	190.00
88	GINGER SNAP, 6 IN.	CL	300.00	360.00
88	HIDDEN TREASURES, 1 1/2 IN.	CL	70.00	95.00
88	HIDDEN TREASURES, 4 IN.	CL	150.00	190.00
88	HIDDEN TREASURES, 6 IN.	CL	300.00	360.00
88	NEW HOME, 1 1/2 IN.	CL	70.00	95.00
88	NEW HOME, 4 IN.	CL	185.00	245.00
88	NEW HOME, 6 IN.	CL	365.00	515.00
88	PENNY FOR YOUR THOUGHTS, 1 1/2 IN.	CL	70.00	95.00
88	PENNY FOR YOUR THOUGHTS, 4 IN.	2000	185.00	215.00
88	PENNY FOR YOUR THOUGHTS, 6 IN.	CL	365.00	460.00
88	PURRFECT DAY, 1 1/2 IN.	CL	70.00	95.00
88	PURRFECT DAY, 4 IN.	CL	184.00	220.00
88	PURRFECT DAY, 6 IN.	CL	265.00	460.00
89	CHERISH, 1 1/2 IN.	CL	80.00	100.00
89	CHERISH, 4 IN.	2000	199.00	295.00
89	CHERISH, 6 IN.	2000	398.00	565.00
89	FIRST SCHOOL DAY, 1 1/2 IN.	CL	85.00	100.00
89	FIRST SCHOOL DAY, 4 IN.	2000	290.00	355.00
89	FIRST SCHOOL DAY, 6 IN.	2000	550.00	640.00
89	FISHERBOY, 1 1/2 IN.	CL	85.00	100.00
89	FISHERBOY, 4 IN.	2000	220.00	245.00
89	FISHERBOY, 6 IN.	CL	440.00	480.00
89	GARDEN PARTY, 1 1/2 IN.	CL	85.00	100.00
89	GARDEN PARTY, 4 IN.	2000	220.00	245.00
89	GARDEN PARTY, 6 IN.	CL	440.00	480.00
89	HOUSE CALL, 1 1/2 IN.	CL	85.00	100.00
89	HOUSE CALL, 4 IN.	CL	190.00	200.00
89	HOUSE CALL, 6 IN.	CL	390.00	395.00
89	TAKE ME ALONG, 1 1/2 IN.	CL	85.00	100.00
89	TAKE ME ALONG, 4 IN.	2000	220.00	290.00
89	TAKE ME ALONG, 6 IN.	1000	440.00	530.00
89	YEARLY CHECK-UP, 1 1/2 IN.	CL	85.00	100.00
89	YEARLY CHECK-UP, 4 IN.	CL	190.00	200.00
89	YEARLY CHECK-UP, 6 IN.	CL	390.00	395.00
90	BATTER UP, 1 1/2 IN.	CL	90.00	100.00
90	BATTER UP, 4 IN.	2000	220.00	270.00
90	BATTER UP, 6 IN.	2000	440.00	510.00
90	HOLIDAY CHEER, 1 1/2 IN.	CL	90.00	100.00
90	HOLIDAY CHEER, 4 IN.	2000	225.00	310.00
90	HOLIDAY CHEER, 6 IN.	1000	450.00	615.00
90	SEASONS GREETINGS, 1 1/2 IN.	CL	90.00	100.00
90	SEASONS GREETINGS, 4 IN.	2000	225.00	310.00
90	SEASONS GREETINGS, 6 IN.	1000	450.00	615.00
90	SHOOTIN' HOOPS, 1 1/2 IN.	CL	90.00	100.00
90	SHOOTIN' HOOPS, 4 IN.	2000	220.00	230.00
90	SHOOTIN' HOOPS, 6 IN.	2000	440.00	455.00
90	SPRING FEVER, 1 1/2 IN.	CL	90.00	100.00
90	SPRING FEVER, 4 IN.	2000	225.00	310.00
90	SPRING FEVER, 6 IN.	2000	450.00	615.00
90	TENDER LOVING CARE, 1 1/2 IN.	CL	90.00	100.00
90	TENDER LOVING CARE, 4 IN.	CL	220.00	245.00
90	TENDER LOVING CARE, 6 IN.	CL	440.00	480.00
91	DRESS UP, 1 1/2 IN.	3750	110.00	115.00
91	DRESS UP, 4 IN.	2000	270.00	275.00
91	DRESS UP, 6 IN.	2000	550.00	540.00
91	FIGURE EIGHT, 1 1/2 IN.	3750	110.00	115.00
91	FIGURE EIGHT, 4 IN.	2000	270.00	370.00
91	FIGURE EIGHT, 6 IN.	2000	550.00	665.00
91	FORE!!, 1 1/2 IN.	3750	110.00	120.00
91	FORE!!, 4 IN.	2000	270.00	330.00
91	FORE!!, 6 IN.	2000	550.00	585.00
91	SEASON'S JOY, 1 1/2 IN.	3750	110.00	120.00
91	SEASON'S JOY, 4 IN.	2000	270.00	310.00
91	SEASON'S JOY, 6 IN.	1000	550.00	625.00
91	TOUCH DOWN, 1 1/2 IN.	3750	110.00	115.00
91	TOUCH DOWN, 4 IN.	2000	270.00	275.00
91	TOUCH DOWN, 6 IN.	2000	550.00	540.00
91	WINTER SURPRISE, 1 1/2 IN.	3750	110.00	115.00
91	WINTER SURPRISE, 4 IN.	2000	270.00	275.00
91	WINTER SURPRISE, 6 IN.	1000	550.00	540.00
92	FREE SKATING, 1 1/2 IN.	3750	110.00	115.00
92	FREE SKATING, 4 IN.	1000	310.00	315.00
92	FREE SKATING, 6 IN.	1000	590.00	595.00
92	MERRY CHRISTMAS, 1 1/2 IN.	3750	110.00	115.00
92	MERRY CHRISTMAS, 4 IN.	1000	350.00	355.00
92	MERRY CHRISTMAS, 6 IN.	1000	580.00	585.00
92	RAINDROPS, 1 1/2 IN.	3750	110.00	115.00
92	RAINDROPS, 4 IN.	1000	350.00	355.00
92	RAINDROPS, 6 IN.	1000	640.00	645.00
92	TULIPS FOR MOTHER, 1 1/2 IN.	3750	110.00	115.00
92	TULIPS FOR MOTHER, 4 IN.	1000	310.00	315.00
92	TULIPS FOR MOTHER, 6 IN.	1000	590.00	595.00
92	WINTER CHEER, 4 IN.	2000	300.00	305.00
92	WINTER CHEER, 6 IN.	1000	580.00	585.00
94	BUBBLES & BOWS, 4 IN.	1000	300.00	305.00
94	BUBBLES & BOWS, 6 IN.	1000	600.00	605.00
94	CHRISTMAS WONDER, 4 IN.	1000	370.00	375.00

YR	NAME	LIMIT	ISSUE	TREND
94	CHRISTMAS WONDER, 6 IN.	1000	700.00	705.00
94	CLOWNING AROUND, 4 IN.	1000	300.00	305.00
94	CLOWNING AROUND, 6 IN.	1000	550.00	555.00
94	JOLLY PAIR, 4 IN.	1000	350.00	355.00
94	JOLLY PAIR, 6 IN.	1000	650.00	655.00
94	LITTLE CHIMNEY SWEEP, 4 IN.	1000	300.00	305.00
94	LITTLE CHIMNEY SWEEP, 6 IN.	1000	600.00	605.00
S. KAY			**SARAH KAY MINI SANTAS**	
91	JOLLY SANTA, 1 1/2 IN.	CL	110.00	115.00
91	JOLLY ST. NICK, 1 1/2 IN.	CL	110.00	115.00
91	KRIS KRINGLE, 1 1/2 IN.	CL	110.00	115.00
91	SARAH KAY SANTA, 1 1/2 IN.	CL	110.00	115.00
S. KAY			**SARAH KAY SANTAS**	
88	JOLLY SANTA, 12 IN.	CL	1300.00	1305.00
88	JOLLY SANTA, 4 IN.	CL	235.00	325.00
88	JOLLY SANTA, 6 IN.	CL	480.00	605.00
88	JOLLY ST. NICK, 4 IN.	CL	199.00	425.00
88	JOLLY ST. NICK, 6 IN.	CL	398.00	855.00
89	SANTA, 4 IN.	CL	235.00	355.00
89	SANTA, 6 IN.	CL	480.00	485.00
89	SARAH KAY SANTA, 4 IN.	750	275.00	275.00
89	SARAH KAY SANTA, 6 IN.	750	550.00	550.00
90	KRIS KRINGLE SANTA, 4 IN.	CL	275.00	355.00
90	KRIS KRINGLE SANTA, 6 IN.	CL	550.00	555.00
91	A FRIEND TO ALL, 4 IN.	750	300.00	305.00
91	A FRIEND TO ALL, 6 IN.	750	590.00	595.00
92	FATHER CHRISTMAS, 4 IN.	750	350.00	355.00
92	FATHER CHRISTMAS, 6 IN.	750	590.00	595.00
95	CHECKING IT TWICE 4"	500	250.00	25.00
95	CHECKING IT TWICE 6"	250	395.00	395.00
96	WORKSHOP SANTA 4"	500	295.00	295.00
96	WORKSHOP SANTA 6"	250	495.00	495.00
S. KAY			**SARAH KAY'S FIRST CHRISTMAS**	
95	FIRST XMAS STOCKING 4"	500	250.00	250.00
95	FIRST XMAS STOCKING 6"	250	395.00	395.00
96	ALL I WANT FOR CHRISTMAS 4"	500	325.00	325.00
96	ALL I WANT FOR CHRISTMAS 6"	250	550.00	550.00
S. KAY			**SCHOOL DAYS**	
95	I KNOW, I KNOW 4"	500	250.00	250.00
95	I KNOW, I KNOW 6"	250	395.00	395.00
96	HEAD OF THE CLASS 4"	500	295.00	295.00
96	HEAD OF THE CLASS 6"	250	495.00	495.00
S. KAY			**TRIBUTE TO MOTHER**	
95	MOM'S JOY 5"	RT	297.50	297.50
96	SWEETS FOR MY SWEET 4"	250	399.00	399.00

ARDLEIGH-ELLIOTT

YR	NAME	LIMIT	ISSUE	TREND
L. LIU			**BASKET BOUQUETS**	
96	MAGNOLIAS MUSIC BOX	*	29.95	30.00
96	PANSIES MUSIC BOX	*	29.95	30.00
96	ROSES "MY FAVORITY THINGS" MUSIC BOX	OP	29.95	30.00
*			**THE WONDERFUL WIZARD OF OZ**	
96	WE'RE OFF TO SEE THE WIZARD MUSIC BOX	OP	39.95	40.00

ARMANI

Price ranges may reflect various demands in the market from one geographic region to another; condition of piece; specific markings found on piece; and/or changes in production of piece.

YR	NAME	LIMIT	ISSUE	TREND
G. ARMANI			**CAN-CAN DANCERS**	
89	TWO CAN-CAN DANCERS 516C	1000	820.00	975.00
G. ARMANI			**CAPODIMONTE**	
95	YOUNG HEARTS	1500	850.00	850.00
G. ARMANI			**DISNEYANA COLLECTION**	
*	CINDERELLA 783C	RT	500.00	3000.00
G. ARMANI			**FIGURINE OF THE YEAR**	
96	LADY JANE	YR	200.00	200.00
G. ARMANI			**FLORENTINE GARDENS**	
96	EBONY	5000	*	*
G. ARMANI			**FOUR SEASONS**	
90	LADY ON SEASHORE (SUMMER) 540C	OP	440.00	440.00
90	LADY WITH BICYCLE (SPRING) 539C	OP	550.00	550.00
90	LADY WITH ICE SKATES (WINTER) 542C	OP	400.00	400.00
90	LADY WITH UMBRELLA (FALL) 541C	OP	475.00	475.00
G. ARMANI			**G. ARMANI SOCIETY MEMBERS ONLY FIGURINES**	
90	AWAKENING	CL	137.50	1000.00
90	MY FINE FEATHERED FRIENDS	CL	175.00	275.00-358.00
91	EVE 590T	RT	250.00	1320.00
91	PEACE & HARMONY 824C	7500	300.00	300.00
91	RUFFLES 745E	YR	139.00	400.00
92	ASCENT 866C	YR	195.00	265.00
92	BOY WITH DOG 409S	YR	200.00	300.00
92	LADY WITH BASKET OF FLOWERS 961C	YR	250.00	250.00
95	IRIS	RT	250.00	250.00
95	MELODY	RT	250.00	250.00
95	SCARLETT	RT	200.00	200.00
96	ALLEGRA	YR	250.00	250.00
96	ARIANNA	YR	125.00	125.00
96	ROSE	YR	125.00	125.00

YR	NAME	LIMIT	ISSUE	TREND
G. ARMANI				**GALLERIA COLLECTION**
95	GRACE	1000	465.00	465.00
95	JOY	1000	465.00	465.00
96	EROS	1500	*	*
G. ARMANI				**GARDEN SERIES**
91	LADY WITH CORNUCOPIE 870C	10000	600.00	600.00
91	LADY WITH HARP 874C	10000	500.00	500.00
91	LADY WITH PEACOCK 871C	10000	585.00	585.00
91	LADY WITH VIOLIN 872C	10000	560.00	560.00
G. ARMANI				**GOLDEN AGE**
96	FRAGRANCE	3000	500.00	500.00
96	PROMENADE	3000	600.00	600.00
96	SOIREE	3000	600.00	600.00
96	SPRING MORNING	3000	600.00	600.00
G. ARMANI				**MASTERWORKS**
96	AURORA	1500	3500.00	3500.00
G. ARMANI				**MOONLIGHT MASQUERADE**
90	HARLEQUIN LADY 740C	7500	450.00	450.00
90	LADY CLOWN WITH CANE 742C	7500	390.00	390.00
90	LADY CLOWN WITH DOLL 743	7500	410.00	410.00
90	LADY PIERROT 741C	7500	390.00	500.OO
90	QUEEN OF HEARTS 744	7500	450.00	450.00
G. ARMANI				**MY FAIR LADIES**
87	LADY WITH PEACOCK 385C	RT	440.00	2000.00-3510.00
88	FLAMENCO DANCER 389C	RT	400.00	450.00
88	LADY WITH BOOK 384C	RT	300.00	400.00
88	LADY WITH FAN 387C	RT	300.00	370.00
88	LADY WITH GREAT DANE 429C	RT	375.00	465.00
88	LADY WITH MIRROR 386C	RT	430.00	500.00-990.00
88	LADY WITH MUFF 388C	RT	250.00	320.00
88	MOTHER AND CHILD 405C	RT	410.00	500.00
89	LADY WITH PARROT 616C	RT	460.00	460.00
95	AT EASE	5000	650.00	650.00
95	ISADORA	5000	920.00	920.00
96	GEORGIA	5000	*	*
96	GRACE	5000	*	*
96	IN LOVE	5000	*	*
96	LARA	5000	*	*
G. ARMANI				**PEARLS OF THE ORIENT**
89	CHU CHU SAN 612C	10000	500.00	500.00
89	LOTUS BLOSOM 613C	10000	450.00	450.00
89	MADAME BUTTERFFLY 610C	10000	450.00	450.00
89	TURNADOT 611C	10000	475.00	475.00
G. ARMANI				**PREMIERE BALLERINAS**
88	BALLERINA 508C	7500	620.00	550.00-715.00
88	BALLERINA 517C	10000	325.00	340.00
88	BALLERINA GROUP 515C	7500	620.00	775.00-1008.00
88	BALLERINA GROUP IN FLIGHT 518C	7500	810.00	900.00-1170.00
88	BALLERINA IN FLIGHT 503C	10000	420.00	500.00-650.00
88	BALLERINA WITH DRAPE 504C	10000	450.00	550.00-748.00
G. ARMANI				**RELIGIOUS**
87	CHOIR BOYS 900	5000	350.00	660.00
88	CRUCIFIX 1158C	RT	190.00	990.00-1320.00
90	CRUCIFIX PLAQUE 711C	15000	265.00	265.00
91	CRUCIFIX 790C	15000	180.00	180.00
G. ARMANI				**RELIGIOUS WORKS**
95	ASSUMPTION, THE	5000	650.00	650.00
95	MOSES	2500	350.00	350.00
96	CRUCIFIXION, THE	5000	*	*
96	HOLY FAMILY	5000	*	*
G. ARMANI				**RENAISSANCE**
92	ABUNDANCE 870C	5000	600.00	600.00
92	DAWN 874C	5000	500.00	500.00
92	TWILIGHT 872C	5000	560.00	560.00
92	VANITY 871C	5000	585.00	585.00
G. ARMANI				**SPECIAL EVENTS**
95	PERFECT LOVE	3000	1200.00	1200.00
96	1996 MOTHER'S DAY PLAQUE	YR	150.00	150.00
96	TENDERNESS	5000	*	*
96	TOMORROW'S DREAMS	5000	*	*
G. ARMANI				**SPECIAL TIMES**
82	CARD PLAYERS-CHEATERS 3280	OP	400.00	850.00
82	GIRL WITH CHICKS 5122	RT	95.00	495.00
82	GIRL WITH SHEEP DOG 5117	OP	100.00	180.00
82	KISSING KIDS 5138	OP	125.00	225.00
82	SLEDDING 5111	OP	115.00	200.00
82	SOCCER BOY 5199	OP	75.00	150.00
91	COUPLE IN CAR 862C	5000	1000.00	1000.00
91	LADY WITH CAR 861C	3000	900.00	900.00
G. ARMANI				**VIA VENETO**
95	ALESSANDRA	5000	355.00	355.00
95	MARINA	5000	450.00	450.00
95	NICOLE	5000	500.00	500.00
95	VALENTINA	5000	400.00	400.00
G. ARMANI				**WEDDING**
84	WEDDING 5132	OP	175.00	225.00

YR	NAME	LIMIT	ISSUE	TREND
89	BRIDE AND GROOM 475P	OP	280.00	295.00
89	WEDDING 407C	OP	535.00	575.00
90	JUST MARRIED 827C	5000	950.00	950.00
91	WEDDING COUPLE 813C	7500	400.00	400.00
91	WEDDING COUPLE 814C	7500	600.00	600.00
91	WEDDING COUPLE 815C	7500	500.00	500.00
G. ARMANI				**WILDLIFE**
82	SNOW BIRD 5548	OP	100.00	185.00
83	EAGLE BIRD OF PREY 3213	OP	210.00	430.00
83	ROYAL EAGLE WITH BABIES 3553	OP	215.00	405.00
88	BIRD OF PARADISE 454S	5000	475.00	505.00
88	PEACOCK 455S	5000	600.00	680.00
88	PEACOCK 458S	5000	630.00	705.00
90	BIRD OF PARADISE 718S	5000	550.00	580.00
90	SOARING EAGLES 970S	5000	620.00	705.00
90	THREE DOVES 996S	5000	670.00	655.00
95	ELEGANCE IN NATURE	3000	1000.00	1000.00
95	RUNNING FREE	3000	850.00	850.00
96	COMPANIONS	3000	*	*
96	FEED US!	1500	*	*
96	LONE WOLF	3000	550.00	550.00
96	MIDNIGHT	3000	600.00	600.00
96	NIGHT VIGIL	3000	*	*
96	NOCTURNE	1500	1000.00	1000.00
96	PROUD WATCH	1500	*	*
96	SILENT WATCH	1500	*	*
96	VANTAGE POINT	3000	*	*
96	WILD HEARTS	3000	*	*
96	WISDOM	3000	*	*
G. ARMANI				**ZODIAC COLLECTION**
96	AQUARIUS	5000	*	*
96	GEMINI	5000	*	*
96	VIRGO	5000	*	*

ARMSTRONG'S

YR	NAME	LIMIT	ISSUE	TREND
R. LEE/ R. SKELTON				**ARMSTRONG'S**
84	CAPTAIN FREDDIE	7500	85.00	150.00
84	FREDDIE THE TORCHBEARER	7500	110.00	190.00
A. D'ESTREHAN				**CERAMIC PLAQUE**
85	FLAMBOROUGH HEAD	500	195.00	195.00
85	FLAMBOROUGH HEAD (ARTIST'S PROOF)	50	295.00	295.00
L. DE WINNE				**CERAMIC PLAQUE**
88	KATRINA	500	195.00	195.00
M. PAREDES				**CERAMIC PLAQUE**
85	MOTHER'S PRIDE	400	195.00	195.00
85	MOTHER'S PRIDE (ARTIST'S PROOF)	50	295.00	295.00
85	STAMP COLLECTOR, THE	400	195.00	195.00
85	STAMP COLLECTOR, THE- (ARTIST'S PROOF)	50	295.00	295.00
W. LANTZ				**HAPPY ART**
82	WOODY'S TRIPLE SELF-PORTRAIT	5000	95.00	300.00
*	**PRO AUTOGRAPHED CERAMIC BASEBALL CARD PLAQUE**			
85	BRETT, GARVEY, JACKSON, ROSE, SEAVER,	1000	149.75	150.00
*	**PRO CLASSIC CERAMIC BASEBALL CARD PLAQUES**			
85	GEORGE BRETT, 2 1/2 X 3 1/2 IN.	OP	9.95	10.00
85	PETE ROSE, 2 1/2 X 3 1/2 IN.	OP	9.95	10.00
85	REGGIE JACKSON, 2 1/2 X 3 1/2 IN.	OP	9.95	10.00
85	STEVE GARVEY, 2 1/2 X 3 1/2 IN.	OP	9.95	10.00
85	TOM SEAVER, 2 1/2 X 3 1/2 IN.	OP	9.95	10.00
R. SKELTON				**THE RED SKELTON COLLECTION**
81	CLEM KADIDDLEHOPPER	7500	75.00	75.00
81	FREDDIE IN THE BATHTUB	7500	80.00	80.00
81	FREDDIE IN THE GREEN	7500	80.00	80.00
81	FREDDIE THE FREELOADER	7500	70.00	70.00
81	JR. THE MEAN WIDDLE KID	7500	75.00	150.00
81	SAN FERNANDO RED	7500	75.00	150.00
81	SHERIFF DEADEYE	7500	75.00	75.00

ARTAFFECTS

YR	NAME	LIMIT	ISSUE	TREND
G. PERILLO				**CHILD LIFE**
83	SIESTA	2500	65.00	75.00
83	SWEET DREAMS	1500	65.00	*
A. TOBEY				**CHRISTIAN COLLECTION**
87	BRING TO ME THE CHILDREN	OP	65.00	100.00
88	HEALER, THE	OP	65.00	65.00
*				**HEAVENLY BLESSINGS**
85	BEDDY BYE	OP	15.00	19.00
85	BUBBLES	OP	15.00	19.00
85	DAY DREAMS	OP	15.00	19.00
85	FIRST STEP	OP	15.00	19.00
85	HAPPY BIRTHDAY	OP	15.00	19.00
85	HEAVEN SCENT	OP	15.00	19.00
85	JUST UP	OP	15.00	19.00
85	LISTEN!	OP	15.00	19.00
85	RACE YOU!	OP	15.00	19.00
85	SEE!	OP	15.00	19.00
85	SO SOFT	OP	15.00	19.00
85	YUM, YUM!	OP	15.00	19.00

YR	NAME	LIMIT	ISSUE	TREND
G. PERILLO			**MUSICAL FIGURINES**	
89	A BOY'S PRAYER	*	45.00	65.00
89	A GIRL'S PRAYER	*	45.00	65.00
R. SAUBER			**MUSICAL FIGURINES**	
84	WEDDING, THE	OP	65.00	70.00
86	ANNIVERSARY, THE	OP	65.00	70.00
87	FATHERHOOD	OP	65.00	70.00
87	HOME SWEET HOME	OP	65.00	70.00
87	MOTHERHOOD	OP	65.00	70.00
87	NEWBORN	OP	65.00	70.00
87	SWEET SIXTEEN	OP	65.00	70.00
G. PERILLO			**PERILLO COLLECTOR CLUB PIECE**	
83	APACHE BRAVE	*	50.00	98.00
G. PERILLO			**PRIDE OF AMERICA'S INDIANS**	
88	BRAVE AND FREE	10-DAY	50.00	125.00
89	DARK EYED FRIENDS	10-DAY	45.00	75.00
89	KINDRED SPIRITS	10-DAY	45.00	50.00
89	LOYAL ALLIANCE	10-DAY	45.00	75.00
89	NOBLE COMPANIONS	10-DAY	45.00	50.00
89	PEACEFUL COMRADES	10-DAY	45.00	50.00
89	SMALL & WISE	10-DAY	45.00	50.00
89	WINTER SCOUTS	10-DAY	45.00	50.00
MAGO			**REFLECTIONS OF YOUTH**	
88	JULIA	*	29.50	70.00
89	JESSICA	14-DAY	29.50	60.00
89	SEBASTIAN	14-DAY	29.50	40.00
G. PERILLO			**SAGEBRUSH KIDS**	
85	BLUE BIRD	OP	19.50	25.00
85	BOOTS	OP	19.50	25.00
85	DRESSING UP	OP	19.50	25.00
85	FAVORITE KACHINA	OP	19.50	25.00
85	HAIL TO THE CHIEF	OP	19.50	25.00
85	MESSAGE OF JOY	OP	19.50	25.00
85	OUCH!	CL	19.50	25.00
85	ROOM FOR TWO?	OP	19.50	25.00
85	STAY AWHILE	OP	19.50	25.00
85	TAKE ONE	CL	19.50	25.00
86	COUNTRY MUSIC	OP	19.50	25.00
86	DEPUTIES	OP	19.50	25.00
86	FINISHING TOUCHES	OP	19.50	25.00
86	HIDING PLACE, THE	OP	19.50	25.00
86	LONG WAIT, THE	OP	19.50	25.00
86	PRACTICE MAKES PERFECT	OP	19.50	25.00
86	PRAIRIE PLAYERS	OP	19.50	25.00
86	WESTWARD HO!	OP	19.50	25.00
87	JUST PICKED	OP	19.50	25.00
87	MY PAPOOSE	OP	19.50	25.00
87	PLAYING HOUSE	OP	19.50	25.00
87	ROW, ROW	OP	19.50	25.00
87	SMALL TALK	OP	19.50	25.00
87	WAGON TRAIN	OP	19.50	25.00
89	HARMONY	OP	37.50	38.00
89	MELODY	OP	37.50	38.00
89	SANTA'S LULLABY	OP	45.00	45.00
90	EASTER OFFERING	OP	27.50	28.00
90	HOW DO I LOVE THEE?	OP	37.50	38.00
90	JUST MARRIED	OP	45.00	45.00
91	BABY BRONC	OP	27.50	28.00
91	HEAVENLY PROTECTOR	OP	75.00	75.00
91	JUST BAKED	OP	27.50	28.00
91	LITTLE WARRIORS	OP	27.50	28.00
91	LOVIN' SPOONFUL	OP	27.50	28.00
91	OUT OF THE RAIN (UMBRELLA GIRL)	OP	95.00	95.00
91	SAFE AND DRY (UMBRELLA BOY)	OP	95.00	95.00
91	TEDDY TOO?	OP	27.50	28.00
91	TOY TOTEM	OP	27.50	28.00
G. PERILLO			**SAGEBRUSH KIDS BANKS**	
90	BUCKAROO BANK	OP	39.50	40.00
90	PERILLO'S PIGGY BANK	OP	39.50	40.00
90	WAMPUM WIG-WAM BANK	OP	39.50	40.00
G. PERILLO			**SAGEBRUSH KIDS CHRISTMAS CARAVAN**	
87	COMPLETE SET	OP	165.00	255.00
87	GOLD, FRANKINCENSE & PRESENTS	OP	35.00	35.00
87	LEADING THE WAY	OP	90.00	120.00
87	SINGING PRAISES	OP	45.00	50.00
87	SLEEPY SENTINELS	OP	45.00	50.00
G. PERILLO			**SAGEBRUSH KIDS NATIVITY**	
86	4 PIECE SET	OP	50.00	65.00
86	BACKDROP DOVE	OP	17.50	22.00
86	BACKDROP POTTERY	OP	17.50	22.00
86	CHRIST CHILD	OP	12.50	14.00
86	COW	OP	12.00	14.00
86	DONKEY	OP	12.00	14.00
86	GOAT	OP	8.00	10.00
86	JOSEPH	OP	17.50	19.50
86	KING WITH CORN	OP	17.50	23.00
86	KING WITH JEWELRY	OP	17.50	23.00

YR	NAME	LIMIT	ISSUE	TREND
86	KING WITH POTTERY	OP	17.50	23.00
86	LAMB	OP	6.00	8.00
86	MARY	OP	17.50	19.50
86	SHEPHERD KNEELING	OP	17.50	23.00
86	SHEPHERD WITH LAMB	OP	17.50	23.00
86	TEE PEE	OP	17.50	23.00
89	BUFFALO	OP	17.50	18.00
89	CACTUS	OP	24.50	25.00
89	PIG	OP	15.00	16.00
89	RACCOON	OP	12.50	13.00
G. PERILLO		**SAGEBRUSH KIDS WEDDING PARTY**		
90	BRIDE	OP	24.50	25.00
90	CHIEF	OP	24.50	25.00
90	DONKEY	OP	22.50	23.00
90	FLOWER GIRL	OP	22.50	23.00
90	GROOM	OP	24.50	25.00
90	RING BEARER	OP	22.50	23.00
90	WEDDING BACKDROP	OP	27.50	28.00
90	WEDDING PARTY OF 7	OP	165.00	165.00
G. PERILLO		**SAGEBRUSH KIDS-FLIGHT INTO EGYPT**		
90	MARY W/BABY, JOSEPH & DONKEY (3 PC SET)	OP	65.00	65.00
G. PERILLO		**SAGEBRUSH KIDS-SPECIAL ISSUE**		
91	ONE NATION UNDER GOD	5000	195.00	195.00
C. ROEDA			**SIMPLE WONDERS**	
91	BABY JESUS	*	35.00	35.00
91	BABY JESUS (BLACK)	*	35.00	35.00
91	BRIDE	*	55.00	55.00
91	FOREVER FRIENDS	*	39.50	40.00
91	GROOM	*	45.00	45.00
91	I LOVE EWE	*	37.50	38.00
91	JOSEPH	*	45.00	45.00
91	JOSEPH (BLACK)	*	45.00	45.00
91	LIGHTING THE WAY	*	39.50	40.00
91	LITTLEST ANGEL, THE	*	29.50	30.00
91	LITTLEST ANGEL, THE (BLACK)	*	29.50	30.00
91	MADE WITH LOVE	*	49.50	50.00
91	MARY	*	40.00	40.00
91	MARY (BLACK)	*	40.00	40.00
91	MOMMY'S BEST	*	49.50	50.00
91	OFF TO SCHOOL	*	49.50	50.00
91	PLAYING HOOKEY	*	49.50	50.00
91	SHEEP DOG	*	15.00	16.00
91	SONG OF JOY	*	39.50	40.00
91	STAR LIGHT STAR BRIGHT	*	35.00	35.00
92	A PERFECT FIT	*	45.00	45.00
92	CATCH THE SPIRIT (WISECHILD)	*	35.00	35.00
92	FALLEN ANGEL	*	35.00	35.00
92	FOLLOWING THE STAR (WISECHILD)	*	45.00	45.00
92	LIL' DUMPLIN	*	25.00	25.00
92	LIL' DUMPLIN (BLACK)	*	25.00	25.00
92	LITTLE BIG SHOT	*	35.00	35.00
92	POCKETFUL OF LOVE	*	35.00	35.00
92	POCKETFUL OF LOVE (BLACK)	*	35.00	35.00
92	RAINBOW PATROL	*	39.50	40.00
92	TEN PENNY SERENADE	*	45.00	45.00
92	TEN PENNY SERENADE (BLACK)	*	45.00	45.00
92	THIS TOO SHALL PASS	*	35.00	35.00
92	THREE BEARS, THE	*	45.00	45.00
92	TRICK OR TREAT	*	39.50	40.00
92	WITH OPEN ARMS (WISECHILD)	*	39.50	40.00
G. PERILLO				**SINGLE ISSUE**
84	BABYSITTER MUSICAL FIGURE	2500	65.00	90.00
G. PERILLO				**SPECIAL ISSUE**
82	PEACEABLE KINGDOM, THE	950	750.00	800.00
84	APACHE BOY BUST	CL	40.00	75.00
84	APACHE GIRL BUST	*	40.00	75.00
84	PAPOOSE	325	500.00	525.00
85	LOVERS	CL	70.00	125.00
G. PERILLO				**THE CHIEFTANS**
83	CRAZY HORSE	5000	65.00	200.00
83	GERONIMO	5000	65.00	135.00
83	JOSEPH	5000	65.00	250.00
83	RED CLOUD	5000	65.00	275.00
83	SITTING BULL	5000	65.00	500.00
G. PERILLO			**THE GREAT CHIEFTAINS**	
91	CHIEF JOSEPH	5000	195.00	195.00
91	COCHISE	5000	195.00	195.00
91	CRAZY HORSE (CLUB PIECE)	*	195.00	195.00
91	GERONIMO	5000	195.00	195.00
91	RED CLOUD	5000	195.00	195.00
91	SITTING BULL	5000	195.00	195.00
G. PERILLO			**THE LITTLE INDIANS**	
82	BLUE SPRUCE	10000	50.00	75.00
82	TENDER LOVE	10000	65.00	39.00
82	WHITE RABBIT	10000	50.00	39.00
G. PERILLO			**THE PRINCESSES**	
84	LILY OF THE MOHAWKS	1500	65.00	155.00

YR	NAME	LIMIT	ISSUE	TREND
84	MINNEHAHA	1500	65.00	42.00
84	POCAHONTAS	1500	65.00	60.00
84	SACAJAWEA	1500	65.00	125.00
	G. PERILLO		**THE PROFESSIONALS**	
80	BALLERINA'S DILEMMA	10000	65.00	75.00
80	BIG LEAGUER, THE	10000	65.00	150.00
81	QUARTERBACK, THE	10000	65.00	91.00
82	MAJOR LEAGUER	10000	65.00	98.00
82	RODEO JOE	10000	65.00	39.00
83	HOCKEY PLAYER	10000	65.00	125.00
	G. PERILLO		**THE STORYBOOK COLLECTION**	
80	LITTLE RED RIDINGHOOD	10000	65.00	90.00
81	CINDERELLA	10000	65.00	90.00
82	GOLDILOCKS & THE THREE BEARS	10000	80.00	110.00
82	HANSEL & GRETEL	10000	80.00	100.00
	G. PERILLO		**THE TRIBAL PONIES**	
84	ARAPAHO	1500	65.00	200.00
84	COMANCHE	1500	65.00	200.00
84	CROW	1500	65.00	200.00
	G. PERILLO		**THE WAR PONY**	
83	APACHE WAR PONY	495	150.00	200.00
83	NEZ PERCE PONY	495	150.00	200.00
83	SIOUX WAR PONY	495	150.00	200.00
	G. PERILLO		**WILDLIFE FIGURINES**	
91	BALD EAGLE	OP	65.00	65.00
91	BIGHORN SHEEP	OP	75.00	75.00
91	BUFFALO	OP	75.00	75.00
91	MOUNTAIN LION	OP	75.00	75.00
91	MUSTANG	OP	85.00	85.00
91	POLAR BEAR	OP	65.00	65.00
91	TIMBER WOLF	OP	85.00	85.00
91	WHITE-TAILED DEER	OP	95.00	95.00

ARTISTS OF THE WORLD

Price ranges may reflect various demands in the market from one geographic region to another; condition of piece; specific markings found on piece; and/or changes in production of piece.

YR	NAME	LIMIT	ISSUE	TREND
	T. DEGRAZIA			
93	FLOWERS FOR MOTHER	*	145.00	150.00
93	LITTLE MEDICINE MAN	*	175.00	185.00
93	MOTHER SILENTLY PRAYS	3500	345.00	380.00
93	SADDLE UP	5000	195.00	215.00
94	BEARING GIFT	*	145.00	150.00
94	FESTIVE FLOWERS	*	145.00	150.00
94	FIESTA FLOWERS	3500	197.50	210.00
94	LOVING MOTHER	3500	165.00	175.00
94	PEDRO	*	145.00	150.00
94	RIO GRANDE DANCER	*	97.50	100.00
94	SAGUARO DANCE	2500	495.00	510.00
94	SPRING BLOSSOMS	5000	170.00	180.00
	T. DEGRAZIA		**ANNUAL CHRISTMAS**	
93	FIESTA ANGELS	YR	295.00	315.00
94	LITTLEST ANGEL	YR	165.00	175.00
	T. DEGRAZIA		**DEGRAZIA FIGURINES**	
84	DISPLAY PLAQUE	CL	45.00	95.00
84	FLOWER BOY	OP	65.00	110.00
84	FLOWER GIRL	OP	65.00	110.00
84	MY FIRST HORSE	OP	65.00	110.00
84	SUNFLOWER BOY	CL	65.00	300.00
84	WHITE DOVE	OP	45.00	80.00
84	WONDERING	CL	85.00	135.00-175.00
85	JESUS	OP	25.00	55.00
85	JOSEPH	OP	55.00	90.00
85	LITTLE MADONNA	OP	80.00	125.00
85	MARY	OP	55.00	80.00
85	NATIVITY SET (3 PIECES)	OP	135.00	195.00
85	PIMA DRUMMER BOY	CL	65.00	110.00
86	BLUE BOY, THE	OP	79.00	95.00
86	FESTIVAL LIGHTS	OP	75.00	95.00
86	MERRY LITTLE INDIAN	12500	175.00	245.00
87	LOVE ME	OP	95.00	110.00
87	WEE THREE	CL	180.00	195.00
88	BEAUTIFUL BURDEN	CL	175.00	185.00-200.00
88	CHRISTMAS PRAYER ANGEL	CL	70.00	80.00
88	FLOWER BOY PLAQUE	CL	80.00	80.00
88	LOS NINOS	5000	595.00	645.00
88	MERRILY, MERRILY, MERRILY	CL	95.00	110.00-150.00
89	LOS NINOS	48	695.00	695.00
89	MY BEAUTIFUL ROCKING HORSE	OP	225.00	245.00
89	MY FIRST ARROW	OP	95.00	110.00
89	TWO LITTLE LAMBS	OP	70.00	80.00
90	ALONE	OP	395.00	475.00
90	BIGGEST DRUM	YR	110.00	125.00
90	CRUCIFIXION	YR	295.00	295.00
90	DESERT HARVEST	5000	135.00	145.00
90	EL BURRITO	OP	60.00	75.00
90	NAVAJO BOY	YR	110.00	125.00
90	SUNFLOWER GIRL	OP	95.00	95.00

YR	NAME	LIMIT	ISSUE	TREND
95	APACHE MOTHER	3500	195.00	195.00
95	BETHLEHEM BOUND	1995	195.00	195.00
95	FLORAL HARVEST	*	185.00	185.00
95	LITTLE FARM BOY	*	165.00	165.00
95	LITTLE HELPER	3500	185.00	185.00
95	LITTLE HOPI GIRL	*	110.00	110.00
95	LITTLE NAVAJO MUSIC MAN	950	175.00	175.00
95	MY BLUE BALLOON	*	115.00	115.00
95	PIMA INDIAN DRUMMER BOY/NATIVITY	*	135.00	135.00
95	WEDDING PARTY	*	175.00	175.00
95	WEDDING PARTY CHILDREN	*	75.00	75.00
	R. OLSZEWSKI	**DEGRAZIA: GOEBEL MINIATURES**		
85	FLOWER BOY 502-P	SU	85.00	165.00
85	FLOWER GIRL 501-P	SU	85.00	165.00
85	MY FIRST HORSE 503-P	SU	85.00	155.00
85	SUNFLOWER BOY 551-P	SU	93.00	145.00
85	WHITE DOVE 504-P	SU	80.00	135.00
85	WONDERING 505-P	SU	93.00	150.00
86	FESTIVAL OF LIGHTS 507-P	SU	85.00	225.00
86	LITTLE MADONNA 552-P	SU	93.00	200.00
86	PIMA DRUMMER BOY 506-P	SU	85.00	250.00
87	MERRY LITTLE INDIAN 508-P	CL	95.00	295.00
88	ADOBE DISPLAY 948-D	SU	45.00	85.00
89	BEAUTIFUL BURDEN 554-P	SU	110.00	175.00
90	ADOBE HACIENDA DISPLAY (LARGE) 958-D	SU	85.00	150.00
90	CHAPEL DISPLAY 971-D	SU	95.00	115.00
91	MY BEAUTIFUL ROCKING HORSE 555-P	SU	110.00	185.00
	T. DEGRAZIA			**NATIVITY**
93	BALTHASAR	*	135.00	145.00
93	EL TORO	*	95.00	99.00
93	GUSPAR	*	135.00	145.00
93	MELCHIOR	*	135.00	145.00
	T. DEGRAZIA			**VILLAGE COLLECTION**
93	LET'S COMPROMISE	*	65.00	75.00
93	PEACE PIPE	*	65.00	75.00
93	THREE FEATHERS	*	65.00	75.00
93	WATER WAGON	*	295.00	325.00

AVONLEA TRADITIONS INC.

YR	NAME	LIMIT	ISSUE	TREND
	*			**ANNE OF GREEN GABLES**
90	ARRIVING AT THE STATION	OP	50.00	50.00
94	A SOLEMN VOW AND PROMISE	OP	120.00	120.00
94	CARROTS! CARROTS!	OP	95.00	95.00
94	PERCHED ON THE WOODPILE	OP	120.00	120.00

BAND CREATIONS

YR	NAME	LIMIT	ISSUE	TREND
	*			**ANGELS OF THE MONTH**
95	APRIL ANGEL	OP	10.00	10.00
95	AUGUST ANGEL	OP	10.00	10.00
95	DECEMBER ANGEL	OP	10.00	10.00
95	FEBRUARY ANGEL	OP	10.00	10.00
95	JANUARY ANGEL	OP	10.00	10.00
95	JULY ANGEL	OP	10.00	10.00
95	JUNE ANGEL	OP	10.00	10.00
95	MARCH ANGEL	OP	10.00	10.00
95	MAY ANGEL	OP	10.00	10.00
95	NOVEMBER ANGEL	OP	10.00	10.00
95	OCTOBER ANGEL	OP	10.00	10.00
95	SEPTEMBER ANGEL	OP	10.00	10.00
	*** RICHARDS/PENFIELD**	**BEST FRIENDS - A STAR IS BORN**		
95	BASEBALL BOY	OP	6.00	6.00
95	BASEBALL GIRL	OP	6.00	6.00
95	BASKETBALL BOY	OP	6.00	6.00
95	BASKETBALL GIRL	OP	6.00	6.00
95	CHEERLEADER GIRL	OP	6.00	6.00
95	FOOTBALL BOY	OP	6.00	6.00
95	GOLFER BOY	OP	6.00	6.00
95	GOLFER GIRL	OP	6.00	6.00
95	HOCKEY BOY	OP	6.00	6.00
95	SOCCER BOY	OP	6.00	6.00
95	SOCCER GIRL	OP	6.00	6.00
95	SWIMMER BOY	OP	6.00	6.00
95	SWIMMER GIRL	OP	6.00	6.00
96	BIKER BOY	OP	6.00	6.00
96	BIKER GIRL	OP	6.00	6.00
96	FISHER BOY	OP	6.00	6.00
96	FISHER GIRL	OP	6.00	6.00
96	SKIER BOY	OP	6.00	6.00
96	SKIER GIRL	OP	6.00	6.00
96	TENNIS BOY	OP	6.00	6.00
96	TENNIS GIRL	OP	6.00	6.00
	*** RICHARDS/PENFIELD**	**BEST FRIENDS - ANGEL WISHES**		
94	ANNIVERSARY	OP	12.00	12.00
94	BEST WISHES	OP	12.00	12.00
94	BRIDE AND GROOM	OP	12.00	12.00
94	CONGRATULATIONS	OP	12.00	12.00
94	CREATE A WISH	OP	12.00	12.00
94	GET WELL	OP	12.00	12.00

YR	NAME	LIMIT	ISSUE	TREND
94	GOOD LUCK	OP	12.00	12.00
94	HAPPY BIRTHDAY	OP	12.00	12.00
94	INSPIRATIONAL	OP	12.00	12.00
94	NEW BABY	OP	12.00	12.00
*	**RICHARDS/PENFIELD**	**BEST FRIENDS - CELEBRATE AROUND THE WORLD**		
96	AROUND THE WORLD TREE	OP	19.50	19.50
96	BRITISH TREE	OP	19.50	19.50
96	ENGLAND SANTA	OP	12.00	12.00
96	GERMANY TREE	OP	19.50	19.50
96	MEXICO SANTA	OP	12.00	12.00
96	NORWAY SANTA	OP	12.00	12.00
96	RUSSIA SANTA	OP	12.00	12.00
96	SCANDINAVIAN TREE	OP	19.50	19.50
96	UNITED STATES TREE	OP	19.50	20.00
96	UNITED STATES/BLACK SANTA	OP	12.00	12.00
96	UNITED STATES/WHITE SANTA	OP	12.00	12.00
*	**RICHARDS/PENFIELD**	**BEST FRIENDS - CHRISTMAS PAGEANT**		
96	ANGEL-PEACE/JPY	OP	6.00	6.00
96	BENCH	OP	4.00	4.00
96	BOY W/STAR	OP	6.00	6.00
96	CHRISTMAS PAGEANT/10 PC SET	OP	60.00	60.00
96	DONKEY	OP	4.00	4.00
96	GIRL W/TREE	OP	6.00	6.00
96	JOSEPH	OP	6.00	6.00
96	MARY AND BABY JESUS	OP	6.00	6.00
96	SHEEP	OP	4.00	4.00
96	SIGN	OP	4.00	4.00
96	STAGE	OP	14.00	14.00
*	**RICHARDS/PENFIELD**	**BEST FRIENDS - HAPPY HEARTS**		
96	A GUIDING STAR	OP	35.00	35.00
96	ANGELS IN THE SNOW	OP	35.00	35.00
96	BEST FRIENDS	OP	35.00	35.00
96	JUST MARRIED	OP	35.00	35.00
96	MAKING NEW FRIENDS	OP	35.00	35.00
96	THANKSGIVING FRIENDS	OP	35.00	35.00
*	**RICHARDS/PENFIELD**	**BEST FRIENDS - HEAVENLY HELPERS**		
96	CHILDCARE	OP	12.00	12.00
96	EMERGENCY MEDICAL TEAM	OP	12.00	12.00
96	FIREMAN	OP	12.00	12.00
96	NURSE	OP	12.00	12.00
96	POLICEMAN	OP	12.00	12.00
96	TEACHER	OP	12.00	12.00
96	VOLUNTEER	OP	12.00	12.00
*	**RICHARDS/PENFIELD**	**BEST FRIENDS - O JOYFUL NIGHT NATIVITY**		
94	ANGEL ON STABLE/WALL	OP	16.00	16.00
94	CAMEL AND DONKEY/SET OF 2	OP	8.00	8.00
94	HOLY FAMILY (JOSEPH, MARY & JESUS)	OP	16.00	16.00
94	SHEPHERD BOY	OP	8.00	8.00
94	THREE KINGS/SET OF THREE	OP	24.00	22.00
95	CAMEL STANDING	OP	6.00	6.00
95	SHEPHERD W/SHEEP/SET OF 7	OP	8.00	8.00
*	**RICHARDS/PENFIELD**	**BEST FRIENDS - RAINBOW OF FRIENDS**		
96	RAINBOW OF FRIENDS	OP	24.00	24.00
96	RAINBOW OF FRIENDS MUSIC BOX	OP	17.50	18.00
*	**RICHARDS/PENFIELD**	**BEST FRIENDS - RIVER SONG**		
93	CAROLERS/SET OF 5	OP	30.00	30.00
94	THREE CAROLERS/ASSORTED	OP	22.00	22.00
95	DOUBLE ANGELS	OP	8.00	8.00
95	SKATERS SITTING/SET OF 2	OP	12.00	12.00
95	SKATERS STANDING/SET OF 2	OP	12.00	12.00
95	SNOWBALL FIGHT/SET OF 3	OP	15.00	15.00
95	SNOWMEN/SET OF 3	OP	12.95	13.00
*	**RICHARDS/PENFIELD**	**BEST FRIENDS - WINTER WONDERLAND**		
94	3 ASSORTED WHITE TREES & 3 PRESENTS	OP	18.00	18.00
94	ACCESSORIES: RABBITS. TEDDIES, PRESENTS/	OP	4.00	4.00
94	MR. SANTA	OP	9.00	9.00
94	MRS. SANTA	OP	9.00	9.00
94	REINDEER/SET OF 2/STANDING & SITTING	OP	10.00	10.00
*	**RICHARDS/PENFIELD**	**BEST FRIENDS-FIRST FRIENDS BEGIN AT CHILDHOOD**		
93	A WAGON FULL OF FUN/2 PC SET	OP	15.00	15.00
93	CASTLES IN THE SAND/4 PC SET	OP	16.00	16.00
93	CHECKING IT TWICE/2 PC SET	OP	15.00	15.00
93	DAD'S BEST PAL	OP	15.00	15.00
93	FEATHERED FRIENDS	OP	13.00	13.00
93	FISHING FRIENDS	OP	18.00	18.00
93	GRANDMA'S FAVORITE	OP	15.00	15.00
93	MY "BEARY" BEST FRIEND	OP	12.00	12.00
93	MY BEST FRIEND/2 PC SET	OP	24.00	24.00
93	OH SO PRETTY	OP	14.00	15.00
93	PURR-FIT FRIENDS	OP	12.00	12.00
93	QUIET TIME	OP	15.00	15.00
93	RAINBOW OF FRIENDS	OP	24.00	24.00
93	SANTA'S FIRST VISIT	OP	15.00	15.00
93	SANTA'S SURPRISE	OP	14.00	15.00
93	SHARING IS CARING	OP	12.00	12.00
*	**RICHARDS/PENFIELD**	**BEST FRIENDS-NOAH'S ARK**		
95	ANIMALS/SET OF 10	OP	20.00	20.00

YR	NAME	LIMIT	ISSUE	TREND
95	NOAH'S ART & RAFT	OP	42.00	42.00
*			**O JOYFUL NIGHT NATIVITY**	
95	ANGEL ON WALL	OP	16.00	16.00
95	CAMEL/DONKEY	OP	4.00	4.00
95	HOLY FAMILY	OP	16.00	16.00
95	SHEPHERD	OP	8.00	8.00
95	THREE KINGS	OP	8.00	8.00

BILL VERNON STUDIOS

YR	NAME	LIMIT	ISSUE	TREND
B. VERNON				**EVOLUTION**
95	CLOUD DANCER	OP	65.00	65.00
95	FINAL FLIGHT	OP	130.00	130.00
95	MYSTIC SPIRIT	OP	50.00	50.00
95	NIGHT SPIRIT	OP	125.00	125.00
95	PRAIRIE THUNDER	OP	110.00	110.00
95	RESTLESS SOULS	OP	50.00	50.00
95	THREE BEARS	OP	95.00	95.00
95	THREE WOLF	OP	60.00	60.00
95	TRANSFORMATION, THE	OP	195.00	195.00
95	TREE KEEPER	OP	50.00	50.00
95	WATER WALTZ	5000	80.00	80.00
95	WHITE FEATHER	OP	90.00	90.00
95	WIND RUNNER	OP	40.00	40.00

BOEHM STUDIOS

YR	NAME	LIMIT	ISSUE	TREND
83	GREAT EGRET	YR	1200.00	2400.00
*			**ANIMAL SCULPTURES**	
52	HUNTER	250	600.00	1375.00
57	POLO PLAYER	100	850.00	4600.00
69	ADIOS	130	1500.00	1850.00
71	BOBCATS	200	1600.00	1950.00
71	FOXES	200	1800.00	2350.00
71	RACCOONS	200	1600.00	2100.00
72	RED SQUIRRELS	100	2600.00	2750.00
73	NYALA ANTELOPE	100	4700.00	6500.00
75	GIANT PANDA	100	3800.00	6850.00
75	PUMA	60	5700.00	6500.00
76	AMERICAN MUSTANGS	75	3700.00	5500.00
76	OTTER	75	1100.00	1500.00
77	AFRICAN ELEPHANT	50	9500.00	14600.00
78	BLACK RHINOCEROS	50	9500.00	9900.00
78	CAMEL & CALF	50	3500.00	3650.00
78	GORILLA	50	3800.00	4500.00
78	SNOW LEOPARD	75	3500.00	4600.00
78	THOROUGHBRED W/JOCKEY	25	2600.00	2750.00
79	BENGEL TIGER 500-13	12	25000.00	26525.00
79	FALLOW DEER	30	7500.00	7500.00
79	HUNTER CHASE	20	4000.00	4050.00
79	YOUNG & FREE FAWNS	160	1875.00	2050.00
80	ARABIAN ORYX, PAIR 50015	60	3800.00	4130.00
80	ASIAN LION	100	1500.00	1600.00
80	CHEETAH	100	2700.00	2900.00
81	APPALOOSA HORSE 40193	75	975.00	1050.00
81	JAGUAR 50020	100	2900.00	3300.00
81	POLAR BEAR W/CUBS 40188	65	1800.00	1860.00
82	BUFFALO 50022	100	1625.00	1625.00
82	GREATER KUDU 50023	75	7500.00	7500.00
82	POLO PLAYS ON PINTO 55005	50	3500.00	3500.00
83	ARABIAN STALLION/PRANCING 55007	200	1500.00	1560.00
83	ARABIAN STALLION/REARING 55006	200	1500.00	1560.00
84	WHITE-TAILED BUCK 50026	200	1375.00	1650.00
85	ELEPHANT/WHITE BISQUE 200-44B	200	495.00	570.00
*			**BIRD SCULPTURES**	
51	WOOD THRUSH	2	375.00	*
52	MALLARDS, PAIR	500	650.00	1700.00
53	BOB WHITE QUAIL, PAIR	750	400.00	2450.00
54	GOLDEN PHEASANT, BISQUE	7	200.00	11350.00
54	GOLDEN PHEASANT, DECORATED	7	350.00	19200.00
54	RINGED-NECKED PHEASANTS, PAIR	500	650.00	1800.00
54	WOODCOCK	500	300.00	2050.00
55	CARDINALS, PAIR	500	550.00	3600.00
56	BLACK-TAILED BANTAMS, PAIR	57	350.00	4750.00
56	CEDAR WAXWINGS, PAIR	100	600.00	7800.00
56	GOLDEN-CROWNED KINGLETS	500	400.00	2300.00
56	SONG SPARROWS, PAIR	50	2000.00	38400.00
57	AMERICAN EAGLE, LARGE	31	225.00	11150.00
57	AMERICAN EAGLE, SMALL	76	225.00	9150.00
57	CALIFORNIA QUAIL, PAIR	500	400.00	2700.00
57	CAROLINA WRENS	100	750.00	5350.00
57	CERULEAN WARBLERS	100	800.00	4900.00
57	DOWNY WOODPECKERS	500	450.00	1750.00
57	MEADOWLARK	750	350.00	3175.00
57	RED-WINGED BLACKBIRDS, PAIR	100	700.00	5575.00
58	AMERICAN REDSTARTS	500	350.00	2000.00
58	BLACK-THROATED BLUE WARBLER	500	400.00	1775.00
58	MOURNING DOVES	500	550.00	1475.00
58	NONPAREIL BUNTINGS	750	250.00	1150.00
59	EASTERN BLUEBIRDS, PAIR	100	1800.00	12200.00
60	RUFFLED GROUSE, PAIR	250	950.00	5075.00

YR	NAME	LIMIT	ISSUE	TREND
61	GOLDFINCHES	500	400.00	1800.00
61	MOCKINGBIRDS, PAIR	500	650.00	3950.00
61	SUGARBIRDS	100	2500.00	14900.00
62	BLUE JAYS, PAIR	250	2000.00	12250.00
62	LESSER PRAIRIE CHICKENS, PAIR	300	1200.00	2350.00
62	PTARMIGAN, PAIR	350	800.00	3450.00
63	MEARN'S QUAIL, PAIR	350	950.00	3600.00
63	MOUNTAIN BLUEBIRDS	300	1900.00	5475.00
63	TOWHEE	500	350.00	2400.00
64	BOBOLINK	500	550.00	1500.00
64	KILLDEER, PAIR	300	1750.00	5100.00
64	ROBIN (DAFFODILS)	500	600.00	5625.00
65	CATBIRD	500	900.00	2075.00
65	FLEDGLING GREAT HORNED OWL	750	350.00	1550.00
65	PARULA WARBLERS	400	1500.00	3350.00
65	TUFTED TITMICE	500	600.00	2000.00
65	VARIED BUNTINGS	300	2200.00	4900.00
66	GREEN JAYS, PAIR	400	1850.00	4100.00
66	RUFOUS HUMMINGBIRDS	500	850.00	2350.00
66	WOOD THRUSHES, PAIR	400	4200.00	8200.00
67	BLUE GROSBEAK	750	1050.00	1500.00
67	CRESTED FLYCATCHER	500	1650.00	3000.00
67	FLEDGLING CANADA WARBLER	750	550.00	2200.00
67	IVORY-BILLED WOODPECKERS 474	4	*	*
67	NORTHERN WATER THRUSH	500	800.00	1400.00
68	COMMON TERN	500	1400.00	6000.00
68	KESTRALS, PAIR	460	2300.00	3150.00
68	MERGANSERS, PAIR	440	2200.00	2975.00
68	ROADRUNNER	500	2600.00	3650.00
69	BLACK-HEADED GROSBEAK	675	1250.00	1500.00
69	VERDINS	575	1150.00	1525.00
69	WESTERN BLUEBIRDS	300	5500.00	7000.00
69	YOUNG AMERICAN EAGLE	850	700.00	1500.00
70	ORCHARD ORIOLES	550	1750.00	2300.00
70	OVEN-BIRD	450	1400.00	1775.00
70	SLATE-COLORED JUNCO	500	1600.00	2200.00
71	FLICKER	250	2400.00	2750.00
71	LITTLE OWL	350	700.00	1375.00
71	MUTE SWANS, LIFE-SIZE, PAIR	3	*	*
71	MUTE SWANS, PAIR	400	4000.00	7800.00
71	NUTHATCH	350	650.00	1100.00
71	WESTERN MEADOWLARK	350	1425.00	1725.00
71	WINTER ROBIN	225	1150.00	1400.00
72	BARN OWL	350	3600.00	5375.00
72	BLACK GROUSE	175	2800.00	3025.00
72	BROWN PELICAN	100	10500.00	14350.00
72	CACTUS WREN	225	3000.00	3400.00
72	EUROPEAN GOLDFINCH	250	1150.00	1350.00
72	GOLDCREST	500	650.00	1200.00
72	SNOW BUNTINGS	350	2400.00	2675.00
72	TREE CREEPERS	200	3200.00	3200.00
72	YELLOW-BELLIED SAPSUCKER	250	2700.00	3150.00
73	BLACKBIRDS, PAIR	75	5400.00	6300.00
73	BLUE TITS	300	3000.00	3200.00
73	BROWN THRASHER	260	1850.00	1925.00
73	EVERGLADES KITES	50	5800.00	7325.00
73	GREEN WOODPECKERS	50	4200.00	4800.00
73	HORNED LARKS	200	3800.00	4400.00
73	LAPWING	100	2600.00	2975.00
73	LAZULI BUNTINGS	250	1800.00	2450.00
73	LONG TAIL TITS	200	2600.00	2900.00
73	PEREGRINE FALCON	350	4400.00	5450.00
73	SCREECH OWL	500	850.00	1475.00
73	YELLOWHAMMERS	350	3300.00	4175.00
73	YOUNG AMERICAN EAGLE, INAUGURAL	100	1500.00	2100.00
74	CHAFFINCH	125	2000.00	2500.00
74	CRESTED TIT	400	1150.00	1300.00
74	HOODED WARBLER	100	2400.00	3000.00
74	LARK SPARROW	150	2100.00	2325.00
74	MYRTLE WARBLERS	210	1850.00	2075.00
74	PURPLE MARTINS	50	6700.00	9100.00
74	RUBY-THROATED HUMMINGBIRD	200	1900.00	2800.00
74	SONG THRUSHES	100	2800.00	3575.00
74	STONECHATS	150	2200.00	2550.00
74	SWALLOWS	125	3400.00	4300.00
74	VARIED THRUSH	300	2500.00	3100.00
74	YELLOW-BELLIED BLACKBIRD	75	3200.00	3600.00
74	YELLOW-BILLIED CUCKOO	150	2800.00	3025.00
75	EASTERN KINGBIRD	100	3500.00	4200.00
75	PEKIN ROBINS	100	7000.00	9675.00
75	RED-BILLED BLUE MAGPIE	100	4600.00	6225.00
75	YOUNG AND SPIRITED, 1976	1121	950.00	1600.00
76	BLACK-THROATED BLUE WARBLER	200	900.00	1150.00
76	CHICKADEES 400-61	400	1450.00	1540.00
76	EAGLE OF FREEDOM I	15	35000.00	51350.00
76	EAGLE OF FREEDOM II 400-70	200	7200.00	7360.00
76	KINGFISHERS	200	1900.00	2200.00
76	RIVOLI'S HUMMINGBIRD	350	950.00	1530.00
77	CAPE MAY WARBLER	400	825.00	950.00

YR	NAME	LIMIT	ISSUE	TREND
77	CARDINALS	200	3500.00	4000.00
77	EASTERN BLUEBIRD 400-51	300	2300.00	2620.00
77	FLEDGLING BROWN THRASHERS	400	500.00	655.00
77	ROBIN (NEST)	350	1650.00	2050.00
77	RUFFED GROUSE/PAIR 400-65	100	4400.00	4480.00
77	SCARLET TANAGER	4	1800.00	4250.00
77	SCISSOR-TAILED FLYCATCHER	100	3200.00	3600.00
78	CANADA GEESE, PAIR	100	4200.00	4200.00
78	MOCKINGBIRDS	*	2200.00	3000.00
78	SISKENS 100-25	250	2100.00	2400.00
79	AVOCET	175	1200.00	1300.00
79	CALLIOPE HUMMINGBIRD 40104	200	900.00	1100.00
79	COSTA'S HUMMINGBIRD 40103	200	1050.00	1190.00
79	DOWNY WOODPECKER 40116	300	950.00	975.00
79	GREY WAGTAIL	150	1050.00	1375.00
79	LEAST TURN	350	1275.00	3025.00
79	PRINCE RUDOLPH'S BLUE BIRD OF PARADISE 4	10	35000.00	37150.00
79	RACQUET-TAIL HUMMINGBIRD 40105	310	1500.00	1960.00
79	RED-BREASTED NUTHATCH 40118	200	800.00	920.00
79	SCOPS OWL	300	975.00	1400.00
80	AMERICAN AVOCET 40134	300	1400.00	1650.00
80	AMERICAN REDSTART 40138	225	850.00	1075.00
80	AMERICAN WILD TURKEY 40154	75	1800.00	2010.00
80	AMERICAN WILD TURKEY/LIFE SIZE 40115	25	15000.00	16930.00
80	ARCTIC TERN	350	1400.00	2850.00
80	ARCTIC TERN 40135	350	1400.00	2050.00
80	BROWN PELICAN 40161	90	2800.00	2850.00
80	CEDAR WAXWING 40117	325	950.00	1030.00
80	CRIMSON TOPAZ HUMMINGBIRD 40113	310	1400.00	1625.00
80	KIRTLAND'S WARBLE 40169	130	750.00	885.00
80	PHEASANT 40133	100	2100.00	2170.00
80	SCREECH OWL	350	2100.00	3100.00
80	YELLOW WARBLER 40137	200	950.00	1060.00
81	AMERICAN BALD EAGLE 40185	655	1200.00	1325.00
81	BLUE JAY W/WILD RASPBERRIES 40190	350	1950.00	2400.00
81	BOREAL OWL 40172	200	1750.00	1870.00
81	LEAST SANDPIPERS 40136	350	2100.00	2525.00
81	MOCKINGBIRD'S NEST W/BLUEBONNET 10033	55	1300.00	1360.00
81	MOURNING DOVE 40189	300	2200.00	2320.00
81	NORTHERN ORIOLE 40194	100	1750.00	1875.00
81	OSPREY 10031	25	17000.00	21060.00
81	OSPREY 10037	100	4350.00	4700.00
81	PEREGRINE FALCON W/YOUNG 40171	105	1850.00	2010.00
81	ROBIN'S NEST W/WILD ROSE 10030	90	1300.00	1375.00
81	ROSE-BREASTED GROSBEAK 10032	165	1850.00	1875.00
81	WOOD DUCKS 40192	90	3400.00	3550.00
82	AMERICAN EAGLE/COMMEMORATIVE 40215	250	950.00	1125.00
82	AMERICAN EAGLE/SYMBOL OF FREEDOM 40200	35	16500.00	18550.00
82	BLACK-EARED BUSHFIT/FEMALE 10038	100	975.00	1040.00
82	BLACK-EARED BUSHFIT/MALE 10039	100	975.00	1040.00
82	BLUE JAY W/MORNING GLORIES 40218	300	975.00	1175.00
82	BLUE THROATED HUMMINGBIRD 10040	300	1100.00	1430.00
82	GREAT WHITE EGRET 40214	50	11500.00	15050.00
82	GREEN JAYS/PAIR 40198	65	3900.00	3900.00
82	KILLDEER 40213	125	1075.00	1085.00
82	MUTE SWANS/PAIR 40219	115	5800.00	6345.00
82	ROADRUNNER 40199	150	2100.00	2315.00
82	WREN 1036	50	1700.00	1940.00
82	YELLOW-SHAFTED FLICKER 40220	175	1450.00	1490.00
83	ANNA'S HUMMINGBIRD 10048	300	1100.00	1935.00
83	CATBIRD 40246	111	1250.00	1250.00
83	DOVE OF PEACE 40236	709	750.00	1475.00
83	DOVES W/CHERRY BLOSSOMS/PR 10049	150	7500.00	10575.00
83	EGRET/NATIONAL AUDUBON SOCIETY 40221	1029	1200.00	1575.00
83	FORSTER'S TERN/CRESTING 40224	300	1850.00	2070.00
83	FORSTER'S TERN/ON THE WIND 40223	300	1850.00	2070.00
83	GOLDEN EAGLE 10046	25	32000.00	36075.00
83	GOLDFINCH 40245	136	1200.00	1200.00
83	ROYAL TERNS 10047	75	4300.00	49.00
83	TOWHEE 40244	75	975.00	1040.00
84	LONG-EARED OWL 10052	12	6000.00	6250.00
84	MAGNOLIA WARBLER 40258	246	1100.00	1100.00
84	PELICAN 40259	93	1200.00	1230.00
84	PILEATED WOODPECKERS 40250	50	2900.00	2915.00
84	WHOOPING CRANE	647	1800.00	2000.00
85	CONDOR 10057	2	75000.00	75000.00
85	PARULA WARBLERS 40270	100	2450.00	2460.00
85	RACQUET-TAILED HUMMINGBIRD 10053	350	2100.00	2475.00
85	SCARLET TANDER 40267	125	2100.00	2120.00
85	SOARING EAGLE/BISQUE 40276B	304	950.00	955.00
85	SOARING EAGLE/GILED 40276G	35	5000.00	5280.00
85	TRUMPETER SWAN	500	1500.00	1600.00
86	GANNET 40287	30	4300.00	4275.00
86	SANDHILL CRANE 40286	205	1650.00	1660.00
87	CALLIOPE HUMMINGBIRD 40319	500	575.00	585.00
87	FLAMINGO W/YOUNG 40316	225	1500.00	1520.00
*				
				FIGURINES
77	BEVERLY SILLS	100	950.00	1000.00
77	JEROME HINES	12	825.00	1000.00

YR	NAME	LIMIT	ISSUE	TREND
86	AMANDA W/PARASOL 10269	27	750.00	750.00
86	ARIA 67003	100	875.00	875.00
86	AURORA 67001	100	875.00	875.00
86	CELESTE 6702	100	875.00	875.00
86	DEVINA 67000	100	875.00	875.00
86	JO/SKATING 10267	26	750.00	750.00
86	MATTINA 67004	100	875.00	875.00
86	MEG W/BASKET 10268	26	625.00	625.00
*			**FLORAL SCULPTURES**	
71	DAISIES	350	600.00	1025.00
71	SWAN CENTERPIECE	135	1950.00	2925.00
71	SWEET VIBURNUM	35	650.00	1375.00
72	CHRYSANTHEMUMS	350	1100.00	2000.00
73	DOGWOOD	250	625.00	1025.00
73	STEPTOCALYX POEPPIGII	50	3400.00	4450.00
74	DEBUTANTE CAMELIA	500	625.00	850.00
74	DOUBLE PEONY	275	575.00	975.00
74	GENTIANS	350	425.00	725.00
74	WATERLILY	350	400.00	700.00
75	EMMETT BARNES CAMELLIA	425	550.00	760.00
75	MAGNOLIA GRANDIFLORA	750	650.00	1500.00
76	ORCHID CACTUS	100	650.00	1025.00
76	QUEEN OF THE NIGHT CACTUS	125	650.00	850.00
76	ROSE, SUPREME PEACE	250	850.00	1725.00
76	ROSE, SUPREME YELLOW	250	850.00	1725.00
76	SWAN LAKE CAMELLIA	750	825.00	1775.00
78	DOUBLE CLEMATIS CENTERPIECE	150	1500.00	1775.00
78	EDWARD BOEHM CAMELLIA 300-23	500	850.00	950.00
78	HELEN BOEHM CAMELLIA	500	600.00	1100.00
78	HELEN BOEHM DAYLILY	175	975.00	1125.00
78	HELEN BOEHM IRIS	175	975.00	1175.00
78	PINK LOTUS 300-21	175	975.00	1050.00
78	RHODODENDRON CENTERPIECE	350	1150.00	1875.00
78	ROSE, BLUE MOON	500	650.00	900.00
78	ROSE, PASCALI	500	950.00	1500.00
78	ROSE, TROPICANA	500	475.00	1060.00
78	SPANISH IRIS	500	600.00	750.00
78	WATSONII MAGNOLIA	250	575.00	675.00
79	CACTUS DAHLIA	300	800.00	960.00
79	GRAND FLORAL CENTERPIECE	15	7500.00	8700.00
79	HONEYSUCKLE	200	900.00	1050.00
80	BEGONIA/PINK 30041	500	1250.00	1465.00
80	BLUEBONNETS 30050	160	650.00	765.00
80	CAPRICE IRIS/PINK 30049	235	650.00	720.00
80	MAGNOLIA GRANDIFLORA 300-47	350	1650.00	1930.00
80	MISS INDIANA IRIS/BLUE 30049	235	650.00	705.00
80	ORCHID/PINK 30036	175	725.00	775.00
80	ORCHID/YELLOW 30037	130	725.00	775.00
80	PARROT TULIPS 30042	300	850.00	975.00
80	ROSE, ALEC'S RED	500	1050.00	1375.00
80	ROSE/ELIZABETH OF GLAMIS 30046	500	1650.00	1965.00
80	ROSE/PEACH 30038	350	1800.00	2060.00
80	TREE PEONY 30043	325	1400.00	1480.00
81	DOGWOOD 30045	510	875.00	950.00
81	JULIA HAMITER CAMELLIA 30061	300	675.00	740.00
81	NANCY REAGAN CAMELLIA 30076	600	650.00	825.00
81	POINSETTIA 30055	200	1100.00	1225.00
81	POPPIES 30058	325	1150.00	1260.00
81	RHODODENDRON 30064	275	825.00	825.00
81	ROSE GRACE DE MONACO 30071	350	1650.00	1935.00
81	ROSE/ANNENBERG 30051	200	1450.00	1490.00
81	ROSE/GRANDPA DICKSON 30069	225	1200.00	1425.00
81	ROSE/JUST JOEY 30052	240	1050.00	1050.00
81	ROSE/LADY HELEN 30070	325	1350.00	1515.00
81	ROSE/NANCY REAGAN 35027	1200	800.00	900.00
81	ROSE/PRINCE CHARLES & LADY DIANA CENTERP	100	4800.00	6325.00
81	ROSE/PRINCE CHARLES & LADY DIANA FLORAL	600	750.00	845.00
81	ROSE/TROPICANA IN CONCH SHELL 30060	150	1100.00	1100.00
81	ROSE/YELLOW IN SHELL 30059	300	1100.00	1150.00
82	DOUBLE PEONY 30078	110	1525.00	1630.00
82	MAGNOLIA CENTERPIECE 30101	15	6800.00	6975.00
82	MARIGOLDS 30072	150	1275.00	1275.00
82	PONTIFF IRIS 30097	200	3000.00	3825.00
82	ROSE/JEHAN SADAT 30080	200	875.00	1025.00
82	ROSE/MOUNTBATTEN 30094	50	1525.00	1660.00
82	ROSE/PASCALI 30093	250	1500.00	1700.00
82	ROSE/PRINCESS MARGARET 30095	350	950.00	1165.00
82	ROSE/QUEEN ELIZABETH 30091	350	1450.00	1780.00
82	ROSE/ROYAL BLESSING 30099	500	1350.00	1710.00
82	ROYAL BOUQUET 30092	125	1500.00	1680.00
82	SCABIOUS W/JAPONICA 30090	50	1550.00	1570.00
82	TIGER LILLIES/ORANGE 30077	350	1225.00	1265.00
82	TULIPS 30089	180	1050.00	1085.00
83	CHRYSANTHEMUM 30105	75	1250.00	1460.00
83	EMPRESS CAMELLIA/WHITE 30109	350	1025.00	1045.00
83	ROSE/YANKEE DOODLE 30108	450	650.00	695.00
83	SPRING CENTERPIECE 30110	100	1125.00	1190.00
84	LADY'S SLIPPER ORCHID 30112	76	575.00	575.00
84	MARY HEATLEY BEGONIA 30111	200	1100.00	1120.00

YR	NAME	LIMIT	ISSUE	TREND
84	ORCHID CENTERPIECE/ASSORTED 30016	150	2600.00	2645.00
84	ORCHID CENTERPIECE/PINK 30115	350	2100.00	2485.00
84	ORCHID, CYMBIDIUM 30114	160	575.00	620.00
84	ORCHID, ODONTOGLOSSUM 30113	100	575.00	605.00
85	CHRYSANTHEMUM PETAL CAMELLIA 30125	500	575.00	595.00
85	EMMETT BARNES CAMELLIA 30120	275	625.00	630.00
85	KAMA PUA HIBISCUS/ORANGE 30128	122	1600.00	1610.00
85	PEONIES/WHITE 30118	100	1650.00	1650.00
85	RHODODENDRON/PINK, YELLOW 30122	125	1850.00	1885.00
85	ROSE/DUET 30130	200	1525.00	1540.00
85	ROSE/HELEN BOEHM 30121	360	1475.00	1480.00
85	SEMINOLE HIBISCUS/PINK 30129	100	1800.00	1810.00
86	CHERRIES JUBILEE CAMELLIA 10388	250	625.00	625.00
86	GLOBE OF LIGHT PEONY 10372	125	475.00	500.00
86	ICARIAN PEONY CENTERPIECE 30119	33	2800.00	2860.00
86	ROSE CENTERPIECE/YELLOW 10370	25	5500.00	5620.00

BOYDS COLLECTION

G. LOWENTHAL — THE BEARSTONE COLLECTION

YR	NAME	LIMIT	ISSUE	TREND
93	ARTHUR WITH GREEN SCARF	RT	10.50	95.00
93	ARTHUR WITH RED SCARF	RT	14.20	55.00
93	BAILEY BEAR WITH SUITCASE 2000 REVISED	OP	14.20	55.00
93	BAILEY IN THE ORCHARD	OP	14.20	60.00
93	BAILY BEAR WITH SUITCASE 2000	RT	14.20	150.00
93	BYRON & CHEDDA WITH CATMINT	RT	14.20	60.00
93	CHRISTIAN BY THE SEA	OP	14.20	55.00
93	DAPHNE HARE & MAISY EWE	TL	14.20	50.00
93	FATHER CHRISBEAR AND SON	RT	15.00	200.00
93	GRENVILLE AND NEVILLE THE SIGN	OP	15.75	35.00
93	GRENVILLE WITH GREEN SCARF	RT	10.50	200.00
93	GRENVILLE WITH RED SCARF	TL	10.50	70.00
93	MORIARTY	RT	13.75	30.00
93	NEVILLE THE BEDTIME BEAR	OP	14.20	45.00
93	SIMONE DE BEARVOIRE AND HER MOM	OP	14.20	60.00
93	VICTORIA THE LADY	OP	18.40	45.00
93	WILSON WITH LOVE SONNET	OP	12.60	150.00
94	AGATHA AND SHELLY SCAREDY CAT	OP	16.25	45.00
94	BAILEY & EMILY FOREVER FRIENDS	OP	34.00	60.00
94	BAILEY & WIXIE TO HAVE AND TO HOLD	OP	15.75	55.00
94	BAILEY AT THE BEACH	RT	15.75	55.00
94	BAILEY'S BIRTHDAY	OP	15.95	55.00
94	BESSIE THE SANTA COW	OP	15.75	45.00
94	CELESTE THE ANGEL RABBIT	OP	16.25	55.00
94	CHARLOTTE & BEBE	TL	15.75	50.00
94	CLARA THE NURSE	OP	16.25	100.00
94	CLARENCE ANGEL BEAR	RT	12.60	40.00
94	COOKIE THE SANTA CAT	TL	15.25	40.00
94	DAPHNE THE READER HARE	OP	14.20	50.00
94	EDMOND & BAILEY GATHERING HOLLY	OP	24.25	50.00
94	ELGIN THE ELF BEAR	OP	14.20	45.00
94	ELLIOT & SNOWBEARY	OP	15.25	40.00
94	ELLIOT AND THE TREE	OP	16.25	60.00
94	GRENVILLE AND BEATRICE, BEST FRIENDS	OP	26.25	75.00
94	GRENVILLE THE GRADUATE	OP	16.25	35.00
94	GRENVILLE THE SANTA BEAR	OP	14.20	150.00
94	HOMER ON THE PLATE	OP	15.75	45.00
94	JULIETTE ANGEL BEAR	RT	12.60	40.00
94	JUSTINA AND M. HARRISON	OP	26.25	45.00
94	KNUTE & THE GRIDIRON	OP	16.25	45.00
94	KRINGLE & BAILEY WITH LIST	OP	14.20	35.00
94	SEBASTIAN'S PRAYER	OP	16.25	50.00
94	SHERLOCK & WATSON IN DISGUISE	OP	15.75	45.00
94	TED AND TEDDY	OP	15.75	40.00
94	WILSON AT THE BEACH	OP	15.75	50.00
94	WILSON THE PERFESSER	OP	16.25	40.00
95	AMELIA'S ENTERPRISE	OP	16.25	30.00
95	ANGELICA THE GUARDIAN	OP	18.50	30.00
95	BAILEY THE BAKER WITH SWEETIE PIE	OP	12.60	35.00
95	BAILEY THE CHEERLEADER	OP	16.25	25.00
95	BAILEY THE HONEYBEAR	OP	16.25	35.00
95	BALDWIN AS THE CHILD	OP	15.00	15.00
95	COOKIE CATBERG	OP	18.75	30.00
95	DAPHNE & ELOISE WOMEN'S WORK	OP	18.00	35.00
95	EMMA THE WITCHY BEAR	OP	17.50	18.00
95	GRENVILLE & KNUTE FOOTBALL BUDDIES	OP	20.00	30.00
95	GRENVILLE THE STORYTELLER	YR	49.00	68.00
95	HOPALONG THE DEPUTY	OP	14.20	30.00
95	LEFTY ON THE MOUNT	OP	15.00	45.00
95	MISS BRUIN & BAILEY THE LESSON	OP	16.25	35.00
95	NEVILLE AS JOSEPH	OP	15.00	15.00
95	OTIS TAXTIME	OP	16.25	35.00
95	OTIS THE FISHERMAN	OP	15.75	16.00
95	SIMONE & BAILEY HELPING HANDS	OP	26.00	26.00
95	STAGE, THE	OP	34.50	35.00
95	THERESA AS MARY	OP	15.00	15.00
95	UNION JACK LOVE LETTERS	OP	19.00	30.00
95	WILSON THE WONDERFUL WIZARD OF WUZ	OP	15.25	25.00
96	ARKBUILDER, 2278 NOAH & CO.	YR	61.00	61.00

YR	NAME	LIMIT	ISSUE	TREND
G. LOWENTHAL		**THE FOLKSTONE COLLECTION**		
94	ANGEL OF FREEDOM	OP	16.75	17.00
94	ANGEL OF LOVE	OP	16.75	17.00
94	ANGEL OF PEACE	OP	16.75	17.00
94	BEATRICE/BIRTHDAY ANGEL	OP	20.00	20.00
94	CHILLY & SON WITH DOVE	OP	17.75	22.00
94	ELMER/COW ON HAYSTACKS	OP	19.00	20.00
94	FLORENCE KITCHEN ANGEL	OP	20.00	20.00
94	IDA & BESSIE/THE GARDENERS	OP	19.00	19.00
94	JILL-LANGUAGE OF LOVE	OP	19.00	19.00
94	JINGLE MOOSE 2830	OP	18.00	18.00
94	JINGLES & SON WITH WREATH	OP	18.00	18.00
94	LIZZIE/SHOPPING ANGEL	OP	20.00	20.00
94	MINERVA/BASEBALL ANGEL	OP	20.00	20.00
94	MYRTLE/BELIEVE	OP	20.00	20.00
94	NICHOLAI WITH TREE	OP	18.00	23.00
94	NICHOLAS WITH BOOK	OP	18.00	18.00
94	NICK ON ICE	RT	50.00	55.00
94	NICK ON ICE	OP	33.00	33.00
94	NIKKI WITH CANDLE	OP	18.00	23.00
94	OCEANA OCENA ANGEL	OP	17.00	17.00
94	PETE THE WHOPPER	OP	19.00	19.00
94	RUFUS/HOE DOWN	OP	19.00	19.00
94	SANTA'S CHALLENGE	OP	33.00	33.00
94	SANTA'S CHALLENGE	RT	50.00	55.00
94	SANTA'S FLIGHT PLAN	OP	33.00	33.00
94	SANTA'S FLIGHT PLAN	RT	50.00	50.00
94	WINDY WITH BOOK	OP	18.00	23.00
95	ABIGAIL PEACEABLE KINGDOM	OP	18.95	19.00
95	BEATRICE THE GIFTGIVER	OP	17.95	18.00
95	ERMEST HEMMINGMOOSE THE HUNTER	OP	17.95	18.00
95	ESMERALDA THE WONDERFUL WITCH	OP	17.95	18.00
95	ICABOD MOOSELMAN THE PILGRIM	OP	18.00	18.00
95	JEAN CLAUDE & JACQUES THE SKIERS	OP	17.00	17.00
95	NA-NICK OF THE NORTH	OP	18.00	18.00
95	NORTHBOUND WILLIE	OP	17.00	17.00
95	PRUDENCE MOOSELMAID THE PILGRIM	OP	18.00	18.00
95	SERAPHINA WITH JACOB AND RACHEL	OP	20.00	20.00
95	SIEGFRIED AND EGON THE SIGN	OP	19.00	19.00
95	SLIKNICK THE CHIMNEY SWEEP	OP	18.00	18.00
G. LOWENTHAL	**YESTERDAY'S CHILD/THE DOLLSTONE COLLECTION**			
96	TEA FOR FOUR..3507 SARA & HEATHER	YR	46.00	46.00
BRIERCROFT				
B. FARLOW		**INTERNATIONAL GIFTGIVERS**		
95	CZECHOSLOVAKIAN	5000	*	60.00
95	IRISH FATHER CHRISTMAS	5000	*	60.00
95	NORWEGIAN NISSE	5000	*	60.00
96	CHRISTKINDEL-AUSTRIA	5000	*	60.00
96	DANISH JULEMAND	5000	*	60.00
96	SAMICHLOUS-SWITZERLAND	5000	*	60.00
B. FARLOW		**INTERNATIONAL SANTAS**		
93	AMERICAN '40S BABY BOOMER	5000	26.50	45.00
93	ITALIAN BABBO NATALIE	5000	26.50	45.00
93	SANTA'S PUP	5000	5.00	9.00
93	SWEDISH TOMTEN & YULEBOCK	5000	26.50	45.00
94	AMERICAN '40S BABY BOOMER-BLACK	5000	26.50	45.00
94	BANJO SANTA (W/ORNAMENT)	5000	16.00	30.00
94	BELGIAN ST. NICHOLAS (W/ORNAMENT)	5000	6.00	10.00
94	DUTCH SINTER KLAAS	5000	26.50	45.00
94	DUTCH SINTER KLAAS (W/ORNAMENT)	5000	6.00	10.00
94	FRENCH PERE NOEL (W/ORNAMENT)	5000	6.00	10.00
94	MARIACHI SANTA	5000	26.50	45.00
94	POLISH GIFT GIVER	5000	26.50	45.00
94	POLISH GIFT GIVER (W/ORNAMENT)	5000	6.00	10.00
94	RUSSIAN RATHER CHRISTMAS (W/ORNAMENT)	5000	6.00	10.00
94	SPANISH GIFT GIVER	5000	26.50	45.00
94	SPANISH GIFT GIVER (W/ORNAMENT)	5000	6.00	10.00
94	SPOTTED PUP (W/ORNAMENT)	5000	6.00	10.00
94	U.S. '40S BABY BOOMER (W/ORNAMENT)	5000	6.00	10.00
94	U.S. '40S BABY BOOMER-BLACK (W/ORNAMENT)	5000	6.00	10.00
B. FARLOW				**MALE ANGELS**
94	ANGEL AT THE TOMB	5000	25.00	39.00
94	COMMANDER ANGEL	5000	25.00	39.00
94	GABRIEL ANGEL	5000	25.00	39.00
B. FARLOW				**NATIVITY**
93	INNKEEPER	5000	23.50	37.00
93	INNKEEPER'S WIFE	5000	23.50	37.00
94	EWE & NURSING LAMB	5000	12.50	24.00
94	EWE & SLEEPING LAMB	5000	12.50	24.00
94	GROUP OF SHEEP	5000	23.50	36.00
94	NATIVITY ANGEL	5000	26.50	45.00
94	SHEPHERD BOY WITH LAMB	5000	15.00	28.00
94	THRESHING FLOOR ANGEL	5000	25.00	39.00
B. FARLOW				**SMALL NISSE**
95	BALD SANTA	5000	*	47.00
96	CAKE LADY	5000	*	20.00
96	COFFEEBREAK LADY	5000	*	20.00

The Trombonist *was the second in Roman Inc.'s Ed Rohn's Jam Session collection. With a gold-plated brass trombone, the piece was limited to 7,500. The 1985 retail price was $185.*

Perhaps the beauty and grace of a ballerina can only be equaled by a porcelain figure depicting the craft. Ballet Shoes *is from Royal Doulton.*

Where's Muvver? The Long and Short of It, Got to Get Home for the Holiday *and* Just Watchin' Over You *are retired items from the Memories of Yesterday Collection from Enesco Corp.*

The elegantly attired Henley *is from the "British Sporting Heritage" series produced by Royal Doulton.*

YR	NAME	LIMIT	ISSUE	TREND
96	COFFEEBREAK MAN	5000	*	20.00
96	DANCING LADY	5000	*	20.00
96	LUKE'S GOSPEL NATIVITY/SMALL 5 PCS	5000	*	150.00
96	READING MAN	5000	*	20.00
96	VICTORIAN SANTA	5000	*	47.00

BYERS' CHOICE LTD.

Price ranges may reflect various demands in the market from one geographic region to another; condition of piece; specific markings found on piece; and/or changes in production of piece.

YR	NAME	LIMIT	ISSUE	TREND
J. BYERS				**CAROLERS**
82	VICTORIAN ADULT CAROLER (1ST VERSION)	CL	32.00	350.00
82	VICTORIAN CHILD CAROLER (1ST VERSION)	CL	32.00	375.00
83	VICTORIAN ADULT CAROLER (2ND VERSION)	OP	35.00	48.00
83	VICTORIAN CHILD CAROLER (2ND VERSION)	CL	33.00	350.00
86	SINGING DOGS	OP	13.00	13.00
86	TRADITIONAL GRANDPARENTS	OP	35.00	45.00
88	CHILDREN WITH SKATES	OP	40.00	46.00
88	SINGING CATS	OP	13.50	15.00
88	VICTORIAN GRANDPARENT CAROLERS	OP	40.00	48.00
91	ADULT SKATERS	CL	50.00	100.00
91	TODDLER ON SLED W/DOG	CL	30.00	100.00-175.00
92	CHILDREN SKATERS	OP	50.00	50.00
92	LIL' DICKENS-SHOVEL	CL	17.00	35.00
92	LIL' DICKENS-SLED	OP	17.00	17.00
92	LIL' DICKENS-SNOWBALL (LG)	CL	17.00	35.00
J. BYERS				**CHILDREN OF THE WORLD**
92	DUTCH BOY	CL	50.00	175.00-300.00
92	DUTCH GIRL	CL	50.00	175.00-300.00
93	BAVARIAN BOY	CL	50.00	175.00-216.00
94	IRISH GIRL	CL	50.00	132.00-174.00
J. BYERS				**COUNTRY CHRISTMAS STORE EXCLUSIVE**
88	TOYMAKER	600	59.00	875.00
J. BYERS				**CRIES OF LONDON**
91	LADY WITH APPLES	CL	80.00	850.00-1200.00
92	CRY OF LONDON-BAKER	CL	62.00	125.00-200.00
93	CHESTNUT ROASTER	CL	64.00	149.00-325.00
94	FLOWER VENDOR	CL	64.00	95.00-200.00
95	DOLLMAKER	CL	64.00	64.00
95	GIRL HOLDING DOLL	CL	48.00	48.00
J. BYERS				**DICKENS SERIES**
83	SCROOGE (1ST EDITION)	CL	36.00	1200.00-1500.00
84	MRS. CRATCHET (1ST EDITION)	CL	38.00	600.00-1000.00
84	SCROOGE (2ND EDITION)	OP	38.00	50.00
85	MR. FEZZIWIG (1ST EDITION)	CL	43.00	450.00-750.00
85	MRS. CRATCHIT (2ND EDITION)	OP	39.00	50.00
85	MRS. FEZZIWIG (1ST EDITION)	CL	43.00	600.00-750.00
86	MARLEY'S GHOST (1ST EDITION)	CL	40.00	300.00-450.00
86	MR. FEZZIWIG (2ND EDITION)	CL	43.00	350.00-600.00
86	MRS. FEZZIWIG (2ND EDITION)	CL	43.00	500.00
87	MARLEY'S GHOST (2ND EDITION)	CL	42.00	200.00-325.00
87	SPIRIT OF CHRISTMAS PAST (1ST EDITION)	CL	42.00	300.00-400.00
88	SPIRIT OF CHRISTMAS PAST (2ND EDITION)	CL	46.00	325.00
88	SPIRIT OF CHRISTMAS PRESENT (1ST ED.)	CL	44.00	300.00-400.00
89	SPIRIT OF CHRISTMAS FUTURE (1ST EDITION)	CL	46.00	300.00
89	SPIRIT OF CHRISTMAS PRESENT (2ND ED.)	CL	48.00	250.00-350.00
90	BOB CRATCHET & TINY TIM	CL	84.00	200.00-250.00
90	SPIRIT OF CHRISTMAS FUTURE (2ND EDITION)	CL	48.00	250.00-375.00
91	BOB CRATCHIT & TINY TIM (2ND EDITION)	OP	86.00	86.00
91	HAPPY SCROOGE (1ST EDITION)	CL	50.00	200.00-275.00
92	HAPPY SCROOGE (2ND EDITION)	CL	50.00	225.00
J. BYERS				**DISPLAY FIGURES**
81	DISPLAY LADY	*	*	2000.00
81	DISPLAY MAN	*	*	2000.00
82	DISPLAY DRUMMER BOY (1ST VERSION)	CL	96.00	1000.00
82	DISPLAY SANTA	CL	96.00	600.00
83	DISPLAY CAROLERS	CL	200.00	500.00
84	DISPLAY WORKING SANTA	CL	260.00	500.00
85	DISPLAY CHILDREN	CL	140.00	1200.00-1400.00
85	DISPLAY DRUMMER BOY (2ND VERSION)	CL	160.00	500.00
85	DISPLAY OLD WORLD SANTA	CL	260.00	500.00
86	DISPLAY ADULTS	CL	170.00	250.00
87	DISPLAY MECHANICAL BOY W/DRUM	CL	*	500.00-900.00
87	DISPLAY MECHANICAL GIRL W/BELL	CL	*	500.00-720.00
90	DISPLAY SANTA-BAYBERRY	CL	250.00	450.00
90	DISPLAY SANTA-RED	CL	250.00	400.00-475.00
J. BYERS				**MUSICIANS**
83	VIOLIN PLAYER MAN	CL	38.00	800.00
85	HORN PLAYER	CL	38.00	750.00
85	HORN PLAYER, CHUBBY FACE	CL	37.00	900.00
86	VICTORIAN GIRL WITH VIOLIN	CL	39.00	300.00-400.00
89	MUSICIAN WITH CLARINET	CL	44.00	450.00-600.00
90	MUSICIAN WITH MANDOLIN	CL	46.00	180.00-275.00
91	BOY WITH MANDOLIN	1000	48.00	175.00-270.00
91	MUSICIAN WITH ACCORDIAN	CL	48.00	200.00-275.00
92	MUSICIAN WITH FRENCH HORN	CL	52.00	83.00-225.00
J. BYERS				**NATIVITY**
87	ANGEL-GREAT STAR (BLONDE)	CL	40.00	150.00-290.00

YR	NAME	LIMIT	ISSUE	TREND
87	ANGEL-GREAT STAR (BRUNETTE)	CL	40.00	120.00-250.00
87	ANGEL-GREAT STAR (RED HEAD)	CL	40.00	175.00-275.00
87	BLACK ANGEL	CL	36.00	205.00-285.00
88	SHEPHERDS	CL	37.00	84.00-150.00
89	KING BALTHASAR	CL	40.00	225.00-375.00
89	KING GASPER	CL	40.00	100.00-150.00
89	KING MELCHIOR	CL	40.00	100.00-150.00
90	HOLY FAMILY	CL	90.00	300.00
J. BYERS				**NUTCRACKER**
93	MARIE 1ST ED.	CL	52.00	120.00-200.00
94	FRITZ 1ST ED.	CL	56.00	83.00-180.00
94	MARIE 2ND ED.	OP	53.00	53.00
95	FRITZ 2ND ED.	OP	57.00	57.00
95	LOUISE PLAYING PIANO 1ST ED.	CL	82.00	82.00
J. BYERS				**SALVATION ARMY**
92	WOMAN W/KETTLE 2ND ED.	OP	64.00	64.00
93	WOMAN W/TAMBOURINE	CL	58.00	58.00
94	MAN W/CORONET	OP	54.00	54.00
95	GIRL W/WAR CRY	OP	55.00	55.00
J. BYERS				**SANTAS**
78	OLD WORLD SANTA	CL	33.00	569.00-635.00
78	VELVET SANTA	CL	*	300.00
82	SANTA IN SLEIGH (1ST VERSION)	CL	46.00	800.00
83	WORKING SANTA	CL	38.00	84.00-175.00
84	MRS. CLAUS	CL	38.00	150.00-350.00
84	SANTA IN SLEIGH (2ND VERSION)	CL	70.00	700.00
84	VIOLIN PLAYER MAN (1ST & 2ND VERSION)	CL	38.00	1500.00
86	MRS. CLAUS ON ROCKER	CL	73.00	600.00-650.00
86	VICTORIAN SANTA	CL	39.00	250.00-350.00
87	VELVET MRS. CLAUS	OP	44.00	44.00
88	KNECHT RUPRECHT	CL	38.00	150.00-200.00
88	SAINT NICHOLAS	OP	44.00	48.00-225.00
89	RUSSIAN SANTA	CL	85.00	341.00-600.00
90	WEIHNACHTSMANN	CL	56.00	200.00
91	FATHER CHRISTMAS	CL	48.00	84.00-150.00
92	MRS. CLAUS (2ND EDITION)	CL	50.00	84.00-150.00
92	WORKING SANTA (2ND EDITION)	OP	52.00	55.00-140.00
93	SKATING SANTA	CL	60.00	78.00-125.00
94	VELVET SANTA W/STOCKING	OP	47.00	50.00
J. BYERS				**SNOW GOOSE EXCLUSIVE**
88	MAN WITH GOOSE	600	60.00	350.00
J. BYERS				**SPECIAL CHARACTERS**
81	THANKSGIVING LADY (CLAY HANDS)	CL	*	2000.00
81	THANKSGIVING MAN (CLAY HANDS)	CL	*	2000.00
82	CHOIR CHILDREN, BOY AND GIRL	CL	32.00	400.00-915.00
82	CONDUCTOR	CL	32.00	95.00-180.00
82	DRUMMER BOY	CL	34.00	150.00-192.00
82	EASTER BOY	CL	32.00	450.00-550.00
82	EASTER GIRL	CL	32.00	450.00-550.00
82	ICABOD	CL	33.00	1165.00
82	LEPRECHAUNS	CL	34.00	1250.00-2050.00
82	VALENTINE BOY	CL	32.00	450.00
82	VALENTINE GIRL	CL	32.00	450.00
83	BOY ON ROCKING HORSE	300	85.00	2700.00
83	VICTORIAN CHILD	OP	33.00	48.00
84	CHIMNEY SWEEP	CL	36.00	1200.00-1500.00
85	PAJAMA CHILDREN	CL	35.00	200.00-380.00
87	BOY ON SLED	CL	50.00	294.00-400.00
87	CAROLER WITH LAMP	CL	40.00	150.00-265.00
87	MOTHER'S DAY	225	94.00	265.00-450.00
88	ANGEL TREE TOP	100	*	275.00-375.00
88	MOTHER HOLDING BABY	CL	40.00	100.00-250.00
88	MOTHER'S DAY (DAUGHTER)	CL	125.00	450.00
88	MOTHER'S DAY (SON)	CL	125.00	500.00
89	GIRL WITH HOOP	CL	44.00	138.00-186.00
89	MOTHER'S DAY (WITH CARRIAGE)	3000	75.00	375.00-480.00
89	NEWSBOY WITH BIKE	CL	78.00	150.00-275.00
90	GIRL ON ROCKING HORSE	CL	70.00	100.00
90	PARSON	CL	44.00	60.00-200.00
90	POSTMAN	CL	45.00	94.00-200.00
91	BOY WITH TREE	CL	49.00	108.00-150.00
91	CHIMNEY SWEEP (CHILD)	OP	50.00	88.00-150.00
92	SALVATION ARMY-WOMAN WITH KETTLE 1ST	CL	64.00	175.00
92	TEACHER	CL	48.00	88.00-150.00
92	VICTORIAN MOTHER WITH TODDLER	CL	60.00	150.00-225.00
93	LAMPLIGHTER	OP	48.00	48.00
93	SCHOOL KIDS	CL	48.00	72.00-125.00
94	BOY W/GOOSE	CL	50.00	50.00
94	SANDIWCH BOARD MAN W/WHITE BOARD	OP	52.00	52.00
94	SANDWICH BOARD MAN W/RED BOARD	CL	52.00	52.00-122.00
95	COUPLE IN SLEIGH	CL	110.00	110.00
95	SHOPPER.WOMAN	CL	56.00	56.00
95	SHOPPER/MAN	CL	56.00	56.00
J. BYERS		**STACY'S GIFTS & COLLECTIBLES EXCLUSIVES**		
87	SANTA IN ROCKING CHAIR WITH BOY	100	130.00	550.00
87	SANTA IN ROCKING CHAIR WITH GIRL	100	130.00	450.00
J. BYERS		**WAYSIDE COUNTRY STORE EXCLUSIVES**		
86	COLONIAL LAMPLIGHTER	600	46.00	800.00-1000.00

YR	NAME	LIMIT	ISSUE	TREND
87	COLONIAL WATCHMAN	600	49.00	690.00
88	COLONIAL LADY	600	49.00	550.00
J. BYERS		**WOODSTOCK INN EXCLUSIVES**		
87	SKIER BOY	200	40.00	300.00
87	SKIER GIRL	200	40.00	300.00
88	SUGARIN KIDS	*	41.00	300.00
88	WOODSTOCK LADY	*	41.00	355.00
88	WOODSTOCK MAN	*	41.00	355.00

CAIRN STUDIO LTD.

Price ranges may reflect various demands in the market from one geographic region to another; condition of piece; specific markings found on piece; and/or changes in production of piece.

YR	NAME	LIMIT	ISSUE	TREND
*	WW II SOLDIER 328	*	*	450.00
T. CLARK			**ACORN COLLECTION**	
81	EL & EM 151	RT	5.00	30.00
81	EL KIM 152	RT	6.00	30.00
81	ELF 162	RT	7.00	30.00
81	ELK 154	RT	7.00	30.00
81	ELLA 153	RT	7.00	35.00
81	ELMER 155	RT	6.00	35.00
81	ELVA 157	RT	8.50	30.00
81	ELWOOD 156	RT	8.50	35.00
T. CLARK		**COLLECTOR SOCIETY ARTWORK SERIES**		
83	RORIE 48	RT	35.00	500.00
84	ERNEST 1030	RT	35.00	260.00
85	KILMER 1126	RT	55.00	300.00
87	HITCH 2018	RT	47.50	275.00
T. CLARK				**ESKIMOS**
81	KANUK 165	RT	28.50	165.00
81	KEEGLOO 158	RT	32.50	375.00
81	KLONDIKE 166	RT	30.50	180.00
T. CLARK			**GNOMES & WOODSPIRITS**	
78	AMANDA 108	RT	35.00	4000.00
78	BESSIE 107	RT	35.00	4000.00
78	CALLIE 51	RT	27.50	5000.00
78	ETHAN 106	RT	35.00	2100.00
78	HAMP 105	RT	35.00	2100.00
78	HAP 101	RT	35.00	1000.00
78	IVY 114	RT	35.00	3000.00
78	OBIE 104	RT	40.00	1600.00
78	PHINEAS 103	RT	35.00	1350.00
78	REUBEN 102	RT	42.50	850.00
78	SILAS 109	RT	35.00	4000.00
78	VANYA 42	RT	35.00	5000.00
79	ABNER 10	RT	35.00	750.00
79	DAISY & ERIC 116	RT	37.50	800.00
79	HUGH ROBERT 7	RT	45.00	1200.00
79	IRVIN 9	RT	35.00	860.00-1325.00
79	LUM 18	RT	35.00	1400.00
79	MODE 8	RT	35.00	1025.00
79	MOM 4	RT	35.00	140.00
79	NAOMI 19	RT	35.00	2100.00
79	OAKIE 3	RT	40.00	400.00
79	ROSCOE 6	RT	35.00	3000.00
79	SIMEON 2	RT	35.00	1385.00
79	STUMPY 5	RT	35.00	24.00
79	WIZARD 110	RT	37.50	960.00
79	XEROX 50	RT	15.00	8000.00
80	AHAB 120	RT	32.50	550.00
80	ARNOLD 124	RT	19.00	550.00
80	CALEB 129	RT	22.00	225.00
80	CHALMERS 15	RT	27.50	265.00
80	CHASE I 14	RT	27.50	400.00
80	CHASE II 128	RT	35.00	600.00
80	DEWEY 13	RT	25.00	650.00
80	DUSTY 122	RT	35.00	3600.00
80	FETZER 112	RT	25.00	750.00
80	GERBER 127	RT	29.50	525.00
80	IGOR 23	RT	31.00	375.00
80	JASON 113	RT	19.50	385.00-840.00
80	JEREMIAH 119	RT	29.50	550.00
80	KATIE 125	RT	42.50	1200.00
80	LUCKY 115	RT	17.50	450.00
80	MARTIN 111	RT	27.50	425.00
80	MCMAN 21	RT	27.50	775.00
80	MCNEIL 11	RT	25.00	210.00
80	MEG 12	RT	25.00	165.00
80	NORTON 16	RT	32.50	400.00
80	O.J. 130	RT	27.50	200.00
80	OLIN 17	RT	25.00	1300.00
80	PATRICK 117	RT	19.00	800.00
80	POPS 22	RT	28.50	210.00
80	ROCKY 132	RT	32.50	260.00
80	SEAN 131	RT	27.50	275.00
80	SHAW 126	RT	22.50	450.00
80	SHELLY 123	RT	19.00	725.00
80	STARR 133	RT	32.50	550.00

YR	NAME	LIMIT	ISSUE	TREND
80	WINK 24	RT	25.00	325.00
81	BABY JESUS 37	RT	10.00	125.00
81	BART 134	RT	27.50	285.00
81	BICK 188	RT	35.00	1150.00
81	CAL 142	RT	45.00	1425.00
81	CARDINAL 26	RT	19.00	*
81	DAFFY 140	RT	35.00	250.00
81	GNOME CROSSING SIGN 984	RT	39.00	150.00
81	HANS 139	RT	35.00	250.00
81	HOWDY 138	RT	35.00	235.00
81	JACKSON 149	RT	25.00	300.00
81	LENNON 135	RT	35.00	2000.00
81	LIEF 159	RT	31.00	225.00
81	PALMER 25	RT	35.00	300.00
81	PATCH 146	RT	32.50	200.00
81	RUMPKIN 160	RT	27.50	180.00
81	SANDY 93	RT	31.00	130.00
81	SECRET 190	RT	29.50	325.00
81	SOL 163	RT	35.00	200.00
81	SUNNY 150	RT	35.00	600.00
81	SWIFTY 96	RT	16.50	150.00
81	TEX 41	RT	27.50	1950.00
82	BANBURY 30	RT	25.00	215.00
82	BOOTS 31	RT	35.00	60.00-240.00
82	EGGBERT 194	RT	31.00	150.00
82	LUCKY II 198	RT	25.00	475.00
82	MICHAEL 195	RT	27.50	245.00
82	MRS. WINK 32	RT	27.50	35.00-120.00
82	NEMO 193	RT	28.50	160.00
82	TOM CLARK CREATIONS SIGN 994	RT	*	50.00
83	ABEDNEGO 1014	RT	35.00	120.00
83	BLARNEY 1004	RT	32.50	90.00
83	BUZZY 68	RT	15.00	60.00
83	CHEESE 189	RT	25.00	230.00
83	CHEF 98	RT	13.00	50.00
83	CINDY 92	RT	35.00	225.00
83	CURTIS 94	RT	45.00	90.00
83	FRANKLIN 28	RT	65.00	200.00
83	GARLENA 97	RT	13.00	60.00
83	GUS 89	RT	26.50	140.00
83	HAZEL WITCH 1003	RT	45.00	175.00
83	HEATHER & JAN 77	RT	47.50	200.00
83	HYKE 27	RT	90.00	250.00
83	JUAN 70	RT	35.50	150.00
83	JULIE 85	RT	26.50	100.00
83	KERNEL 75	RT	50.00	140.00
83	MARTHA & JAY 73	RT	65.00	150.00
83	MESHACH 1013	RT	35.00	75.00
83	NICK O' TIME 1010	RT	31.00	325.00
83	PAPA & PRINCESS 69	RT	45.00	125.00
83	PARSLEY, SAGE, THYME 1001	RT	110.00	200.00
83	PLENTY 33	RT	32.50	115.00
83	SATURDAY 90	RT	25.00	70.00
83	SHADRACH 1012	RT	35.00	75.00
83	SKIPPER 1005	RT	37.50	110.00
83	SMOKEY 95	RT	40.00	90.00
83	SOUTH BEND 43	RT	19.00	110.00
83	SPUD 34	RT	27.50	75.00
83	STU 71	RT	40.00	65.00
83	TEDDY 81	RT	25.00	*
83	WILBUR 1006	RT	33.50	90.00
83	WINK TOO 88	RT	27.50	75.00
83	WIZ, THE- 87	RT	35.00	85.00
83	WOODY & CHANE 1015	RT	65.00	150.00
84	7-UP 1070	RT	500.00	1800.00
84	ACE OF SPADES 1035	RT	25.00	87.00
84	ANAHEIM 1025	RT	22.00	81.00
84	BEN 1069	RT	47.50	*
84	BONNIE 1051	RT	25.00	*
84	BUBBLES 1062	RT	15.00	40.00
84	BUTCH, WICK & BISCUIT 1056	RT	70.00	175.00
84	C.D. 1050	RT	32.50	*
84	CLAMENTINE 1064	RT	29.50	75.00
84	COLETTE 1028	RT	22.00	45.00
84	D.G. 1031	RT	33.00	210.00
84	DOUG 1045	RT	25.00	*
84	EENIE 1021	RT	27.50	65.00
84	ELIZABETH 1017	RT	25.00	45.00
84	FATHER TIME 1008	RT	33.50	80.00
84	GATOR 1032	RT	25.00	185.00
84	GEORGIA 1044	RT	31.00	95.00
84	GNOME OF ZURICH 1007	RT	33.50	125.00
84	GOODFOOT 1063	RT	29.50	125.00
84	HAL 1072	RT	40.00	*
84	HAPPY 1061	RT	35.00	*
84	HENSON 1059	RT	32.50	65.00
84	HOGAN 1033	RT	35.00	60.00
84	HOMER 1058	RT	32.50	*
84	JACK B. NIMBLE 1055	RT	29.50	75.00

YR	NAME	LIMIT	ISSUE	TREND
84	JACK OF DIAMONDS 1038	RT	25.00	65.00
84	JACKIE B. QUICK 1065	RT	32.50	75.00
84	JOHNNY 1052	RT	25.00	*
84	KEN 1026	RT	45.00	110.00
84	KING OF CLUBS 1036	RT	25.00	65.00
84	LANCE 1042	RT	27.50	75.00
84	MABEL 1016	RT	67.50	175.00
84	MADRE 1068	RT	19.50	*
84	MCEVER 1067	RT	28.50	60.00
84	MEENIE 1022	RT	27.50	65.00
84	MELCHIOR 1060	RT	40.00	*
84	MINIE 1023	RT	25.00	50.00
84	MOE 1024	RT	25.00	60.00
84	MOM TOO 1020	RT	40.00	60.00
84	MUGMON 1011	RT	24.50	*
84	N.O. EVELS, THE 1053	RT	70.00	*
84	NEWT 1043	RT	27.50	60.00
84	NOEL 1066	RT	55.00	125.00
84	O'NEAL 1019	RT	25.00	45.00
84	PADRE 80	RT	19.00	*
84	PAWLEY 1047	RT	31.00	*
84	PEANUT 1041	RT	27.50	60.00
84	QUEEN OF HEARTS 1037	RT	25.00	65.00
84	SANTA III 1054	RT	75.00	210.00
84	SHAKESPEARE 1039	RT	72.50	200.00
84	SHEN 1040	RT	60.00	130.00
84	SHORTY 1046	RT	32.50	*
84	SORGHUM OF GLADE VALLEY 1057	RT	35.00	85.00
84	THISTLE 1029	RT	80.00	100.00
84	TIM & RANDY 1009	RT	40.00	100.00
84	TOPSIE-TURVIE 1034	RT	37.50	140.00
84	VALENTINE (VAL) 1018	RT	30.00	*
84	WINKIN, BLINKIN & NOD 1071	RT	65.00	150.00
84	YULE 1048	RT	55.00	140.00
85	JINGLE "E" 1124	RT	15.00	27.00
85	JINGLE "G" 1122	RT	15.00	27.00
85	JINGLE "I" 1120	RT	15.00	22.00
85	JINGLE "J" 1119	RT	15.00	27.00
85	JINGLE "L" 1123	RT	15.00	27.00
85	JINGLE "N" 1121	RT	15.00	27.00
85	LILIBET 1079	RT	17.50	35.00-120.00
85	MERRILL & LYNCH 1117	RT	60.00	140.00
86	ALPHA 2014	RT	79.00	*
86	BUTTON 1092	RT	29.50	*
86	CHIP 1094	RT	37.50	*
86	HOLDER 1105	RT	37.50	*
86	JULIUS 1097	RT	40.00	*
86	MOORE OR LES 1093	RT	65.00	140.00
86	PAR 1096	RT	45.00	*
86	RACHEL 1088	RT	65.00	*
86	SAMMY 1098	RT	35.00	*
86	UNCLE WHIT 1083	RT	65.00	*
87	'TWAS THE NIGHT 1130	RT	700.00	*
87	CASPAR 1150	RT	45.00	*
87	ED 2022	RT	*	140.00
87	TELLY 1189	RT	*	300.00
88	BALTHAZAR 5012	RT	35.00	*
88	BROTHER, SIS & DAD 1181	RT	100.00	*
88	EUREKA 1115	RT	70.00	*
88	PEDRO 1158	RT	35.00	*
89	ROSEMARY 1002	RT	65.00	165.00
T. CLARK				**MINIATURES**
83	BIRDIE 78	RT	*	100.00
83	EDDIE 83	RT	15.00	45.00
83	FREDDY 79	RT	17.50	100.00
83	JEFF 74	RT	17.00	50.00
83	JENNIE 84	RT	17.00	125.00
83	JOSHUA 82	RT	25.00	100.00
83	POKEY 86	RT	19.00	65.00
T. CLARK				**MOUNTAINEERS**
81	APPLE ANNIE 169	RT	47.50	310.00
81	JEREMIAH SALLIE 168	RT	65.00	420.00
81	NELLIE 164	RT	55.00	700.00
82	ENOCH 186	RT	80.00	175.00
82	MATTIE 184	RT	67.50	300.00
82	NATH 185	RT	65.00	400.00
T. CLARK				**NATIVITY**
81	INNKEEPER 171	RT	37.50	150.00
81	JOSEPH I 36	RT	35.00	200.00
81	MARY I 35	RT	35.00	175.00
82	ANGEL 196	RT	35.00	120.00
82	SHEPHERD 197	RT	37.50	85.00
83	HERDSMAN 72	RT	32.50	120.00
T. CLARK				**SEA CAPTAINS & SAILORS**
81	ABRAHAM 173	RT	65.00	225.00
81	ABRAHAM LAMP 174	RT	80.00	280.00
81	JOCK 172	RT	40.00	175.00
82	PYRATE 181	RT	75.00	780.00
82	SVEN 180	RT	55.00	280.00

YR	NAME	LIMIT	ISSUE	TREND
T. CLARK				**SPECIAL CHARACTERS**
80	SANTA I 121	RT	55.00	330.00
81	HATTIE 137	RT	55.00	250.00
81	LAWRENCE 136	RT	55.00	140.00
81	SLEUTH 179	RT	65.00	500.00
81	ST. FRANCIS 167	RT	50.00	150.00
81	ST. NICK 141	RT	40.00	600.00
82	BELLE KRINGLE 199	RT	55.00	250.00
82	DANIEL BOONE 182	RT	75.00	700.00
82	DANIEL BOONE LAMP 192	RT	85.00	1000.00
83	SANTA II 76	RT	55.00	200.00
T. CLARK				**SPECIAL COMMISSION**
78	RUBENSTEIN 39	RT	*	5000.00
80	HARRIS 118	RT	45.00	1200.00
81	ADAM 300	RT	*	210.00
81	FROSTY 304	RT	*	150.00
81	NEY 143	RT	35.00	125.00
81	OLLIE 303	RT	*	140.00
81	SMILEY 301	RT	*	120.00
81	STUCK 302	RT	*	125.00
82	GORDY 40	RT	*	750.00
83	BO SCHEMBECHLER 45	RT	57.50	220.00
83	COTTON 46	RT	*	220.00
83	D.C. 99	RT	*	100.00
83	HAMLET 47	RT	57.50	135.00
83	PA PAW 49	RT	*	600.00
83	WEST VIRGINIA MOUNTAINEER 91	RT	59.00	330.00
T. CLARK				**SPECIAL PROMOTIONAL**
82	UNCLE SAM 83	RT	80.00	250.00
T. CLARK				**THE WIND IN THE WILLOWS**
82	BADGER 177	RT	40.00	140.00
82	MOLE 176	RT	32.50	90.00
82	RATTY 175	RT	31.00	100.00
82	TOAD I 147	RT	50.00	550.00
82	TOAD II 148	RT	35.00	130.00
T. CLARK				**TRUE BUILDERS OF AMERICA**
83	DR. GREY 321	RT	120.00	3800.00
83	MISS MARY 320	RT	*	900.00
83	NEWSPAPER BOY 325	RT	120.00	625.00
84	AVIATOR 326	RT	150.00	450.00
84	PARSON PATTERSON 324	RT	150.00	340.00
84	RAILROAD CONDUCTOR 322	RT	120.00	285.00
87	BLACKSMITH 332	RT	150.00	320.00
T. CLARK				**WESTERN**
83	COWBOY 306	RT	60.00	140.00
83	INDIAN 307	RT	60.00	150.00
CAST ART				
*** HAYNES/HACKETT**				**CUDDL'SOMES**
95	CUBBY	RT	17.00	17.00
95	DRESS UP	RT	17.00	17.00
95	ROOSEVELT	RT	29.00	29.00
95	SUNDANCE	RT	29.00	29.00
K. HAYNES				**DREAMSICLES**
93	BY THE SILVERY MOON	RT	100.00	175.00
93	FINISHING TOUCHES, THE	RT	85.00	100.00
93	FLYING LESSON, THE	RT	80.00	250.00
93	TEETER TOTS	RT	100.00	250.00
94	HOLIDAY ON ICE	OP	85.00	95.00
94	RECITAL, THE	RT	135.00	150.00
K. HAYNES				**DREAMSICLES COLLECTORS CLUB**
93	A STAR IS BORN	RT	30.00	30.00
93	DAYDREAM BELIEVER	RT	29.95	35.00
94	JOIN THE FUN	RT	*	*
94	MAKIN' A LIST	RT	47.95	50.00
K. HAYNES				**DREAMSICLES/ANIMALS**
91	BUNNY HOP	RT	19.50	20.00
91	CARNATION	RT	16.00	16.00
91	DAIRY DELIGHT	RT	28.00	28.00
91	DIMPLES	RT	6.00	6.00
91	GATHERING FLOWERS	RT	18.00	18.00
91	HAMBONE	RT	10.00	10.00
91	HAMLET	RT	10.00	10.00
91	HEY DIDDLE DIDDLE	RT	16.00	16.00
91	HONEY BUN	RT	6.00	6.00
91	PIGLET	RT	10.00	10.00
91	PIGMALION	RT	6.00	6.00
91	PIGTAILS	RT	6.00	6.00
91	SOAP BOX BUNNY	RT	15.00	15.00
91	SWEET CREAM	RT	29.00	29.00
91	TINY BUNNY	RT	7.00	7.00
91	TRICK OR TREAT	RT	11.00	11.00
92	HELGA	RT	8.00	8.00
92	SARGE	RT	8.00	8.00
92	SIR HAREOLD	RT	39.00	39.00
93	PAL JOEY	RT	13.50	14.00
94	HENNIETTA	RT	28.00	28.00

YR	NAME	LIMIT	ISSUE	TREND
K. HAYNES		**DREAMSICLES/CALENDAR COLLECTION**		
94	AMONG FRIENDS	RT	24.00	24.00
94	AUTUMN LEAVES	RT	24.00	24.00
94	HOLIDAY MAGIC	RT	24.00	24.00
94	LOVE IN BLOOM	RT	24.00	24.00
94	NATURE'S BOUNTY	RT	24.00	24.00
94	NOW GIVE THANKS	RT	24.00	24.00
94	POOL PALS	RT	24.00	24.00
94	RIDE LIKE THE WIND	RT	24.00	24.00
94	SCHOOL DAYS	RT	24.00	24.00
94	SPECIAL DELIVERY	RT	24.00	24.00
94	SPRINGTIME FROLIC	RT	24.00	24.00
94	WINTER WONDERLAND	RT	24.00	24.00
K. HAYNES			**DREAMSICLES/CHERUBS**	
91	BABY LOVE	RT	7.00	7.00
91	CHERUB & CHILD	RT	15.00	15.00
91	FOREVER YOURS	RT	44.00	44.00
91	HEAVENLY DREAMER	RT	10.50	11.00
91	MISCHIEF MAKER	RT	10.00	10.00
91	SITTING PRETTY	RT	9.50	10.00
91	WILDLFLOWER	RT	10.00	10.00
92	1995 ICE COMMEMORATIVE, THE	RT	34.95	150.00
92	A CHILD'S PRAYER	RT	7.00	7.00
92	BEST PALS	RT	15.00	30.00
92	BLUEBIRD ON MY SHOULDER	RT	19.00	19.00
92	BUNDLE OF JOY	RT	7.00	7.00
92	CAROLER-CENTER SCROLL	RT	19.00	19.00
92	CAROLER-LEFT SCROLL	RT	19.00	19.00
92	CAROLER-RIGHT SCROLL	RT	19.00	19.00
92	CHERUB FOR ALL SEASONS	RT	23.00	23.00
92	DANCE BALLERINA DANCE	RT	37.00	37.00
92	DREAM A LITTLE DREAM	RT	7.00	7.00
92	LIFE IS GOOD	RT	10.00	10.00
92	LITTLE DARLIN	RT	7.00	7.00
92	LITTLEST ANGEL	RT	7.00	7.00
93	FOREVER FRIENDS	RT	15.00	30.00
93	LITTLE DICKENS	RT	24.00	24.00
93	LONG FELLOW	RT	24.00	24.00
93	ME AND MY SHADOW	RT	19.00	19.00
93	MISS MORNINGSTAR	RT	25.00	25.00
93	SWEET DREAMS	RT	29.00	29.00
94	CUDDLE BLANKET	RT	6.50	7.00
94	EAGER TO PLEASE	RT	6.50	7.00
94	HE'S LOOKING AT YOU	RT	25.00	25.00
94	I CAN READ	RT	6.50	7.00
94	SIDE BY SIDE	RT	31.50	32.00
94	SUCKING MY THUMB	RT	6.50	7.00
94	SURPRISE GIFT	RT	6.50	7.00
94	UP ALL NIGHT	RT	6.50	7.00
K. HAYNES			**DREAMSICLES/CHRISTMAS**	
91	CHERUB & CHILD	RT	14.00	15.00
91	FOREVER YOURS	RT	44.00	44.00
91	HEAVENLY DREAMER	OP	10.50	11.00
91	MISCHIEF MAKER	OP	10.00	10.00
91	SANTA BUNNY	RT	32.00	32.00
91	SITTING PRETTY	OP	9.50	10.00
91	STANA'S ELF	RT	19.00	19.00
91	WILDFLOWER	OP	10.00	10.00
92	A CHILD'S PRAYER	RT	7.00	7.00
92	BABY LOVE	RT	7.00	7.00
92	BLUEBIRD ON MY SHOULDER	RT	19.00	19.00
92	BUNDLE OF JOY	RT	7.00	7.00
92	CAROLER-CENTER SCROLL	RT	19.00	19.00
92	CAROLER-LEFT SCROLL	RT	19.00	19.00
92	CAROLER-RIGHT SCROLL	RT	19.00	19.00
92	DREAM A LITTLE DREAM	RT	7.00	7.00
92	LIFE IS GOOD	OP	10.00	10.00
92	LITTLE DARLIN'	RT	7.00	7.00
92	LITTLEST ANGEL	RT	7.00	7.00
93	LITTLE DICKENS	RT	24.00	24.00
93	LONG FELLOW	RT	24.00	24.00
93	ME AND MY SHADOW	OP	19.00	19.00
93	MISS MORNINGSTAR	OP	25.00	25.00
93	SWEET DREAMS	RT	29.00	29.00
94	HERE'S LOOKING AT YOU	RT	25.00	25.00
94	SIDE BY SIDE	RT	31.50	32.00

CAT'S MEOW

YR	NAME	LIMIT	ISSUE	TREND
F. JONES		**19TH CENTURY MASTER BUILDERS**		
93	ALEXANDER JACKSON DAVIS	OP	*	*
93	ANDREW JACKSON DOWNING	OP	*	*
93	HENRY HOBSON RICHARDSON	OP	*	*
93	SAMUEL SLOAN	OP	*	*
93	SET	OP	41.20	42.00
F. JONES				**ACCESSORIES**
83	FALL TREE	RT	4.00	7.00
83	PINE TREE	RT	4.00	7.00
83	SUMMER TREE	RT	4.00	7.00

YR	NAME	LIMIT	ISSUE	TREND
83	XMAS PINE TREE	RT	4.00	7.00
83	XMAS PINE TREE W/RED BOWS	RT	3.00	100.00
84	5 IN. HEDGE	RT	3.00	25.00
84	5 IN. PICKET FENCE	RT	3.00	3.00
84	8 IN. HEDGE	RT	3.25	25.00
84	8 IN. PICKET FENCE	RT	3.25	25.00
84	BANDSTAND	RT	6.50	7.00
84	DAIRY WAGON	RT	4.00	10.00
84	GAS LIGHT	OP	3.25	3.25
84	HORSE & CARRIAGE	RT	4.00	10.00
84	HORSE & SLEIGH	RT	4.00	4.00
84	LILAC BUSHES	RT	3.00	25.00
85	CHICKENS	RT	3.25	6.00
85	COWS	RT	4.00	10.00
85	DUCKS	RT	3.25	6.00
85	F.J. REAL ESTATE SIGN	RT	3.00	6.00
85	FLOWER POTS	OP	3.00	3.00
85	MAIN ST. SIGN	OP	3.25	3.25
85	TELEPHONE BOOTH	OP	3.00	3.00
85	U.S. FLAG	OP	3.25	3.25
86	5 IN. IRON FENCE	RT	3.00	45.00
86	8 IN. IRON FENCE	RT	3.25	25.00
86	CAROLERS	RT	4.00	10.00
86	CHERRY TREE	RT	4.00	5.00
86	ICE WAGON	RT	4.00	10.00
86	IRON GATE	RT	3.00	35.00
86	MAIL WAGON	OP	4.00	4.00
86	POPLAR TREE	RT	4.00	5.00
86	SKIPJACKS	OP	6.50	7.00
86	STREET CLOCK	OP	3.25	3.25
86	WISHING WELL	RT	3.25	6.00
86	WOODEN GATE	RT	3.00	3.00
87	CABLE CAR	RT	4.00	10.00
87	F.J. EXPRESS	RT	4.00	4.00
87	LIBERTY ST. SIGN	RT	3.25	6.00
87	RAILROAD SIGN	RT	3.00	3.00
87	WINDMILL	RT	3.25	3.25
88	ADA BELLE	OP	4.00	4.00
88	BUTCH & T.J.	RT	4.00	4.00
88	CHARLIE & CO	RT	4.00	4.00
88	COLONIAL BREAD WAGON	OP	4.00	4.00
89	CLOTHESLINE	OP	4.00	4.00
89	HARRY'S HOTDOGS	OP	4.00	4.00
89	MARKET ST. SIGN	RT	3.25	5.00
89	NANNY	RT	4.00	4.00
89	PASSENGER TRAIN CAR	OP	4.00	4.00
89	PONY EXPRESS RIDER	OP	4.00	4.00
89	PUMPKIN WAGON	OP	3.25	3.25
89	QUAKER OATS TRAIN CAR	OP	4.00	4.00
89	ROSE TRELLIS	OP	3.25	3.25
89	RUDY & ALDINE	OP	4.00	4.00
89	SNOWMEN	OP	4.00	4.00
89	TAD & TONY	OP	4.00	4.00
89	TOURING CAR	RT	4.00	5.00
89	WELLS FARGO WAGON	RT	4.00	10.00
90	1909 FRANKLIN LIMOUSINE	OP	4.00	4.00
90	1913 PEERLESS TOURING CAR	OP	4.00	4.00
90	1914 FIRE PUMPER	OP	4.00	4.00
90	5 IN. WROUGHT IRON FENCE	OP	3.00	3.00
90	AMISH BUGGY	OP	4.00	4.00
90	BLUE SPRUCE	OP	4.00	4.00
90	BUS STOP	OP	4.00	4.00
90	CHRISTMAS TREE LOT	OP	4.00	4.00
90	EUGENE	OP	4.00	4.00
90	GERSTENSLAGER BUGGY	OP	4.00	4.00
90	LITTLE RED CABOOSE	OP	4.00	4.00
90	POPCORN WAGON	OP	4.00	4.00
90	RED MAPLE TREE	OP	4.00	4.00
90	SANTA & REINDEER	OP	4.00	4.00
90	SCHOOL BUS	OP	4.00	4.00
90	TULIP TREE	OP	4.00	4.00
90	VETERINARY WAGON	OP	4.00	4.00
90	VICTORIAN OUTHOUSE	OP	4.00	4.00
90	WATKINS WAGON	OP	4.00	4.00
90	XMAS SPRUCE	OP	4.00	4.00
91	AMISH GARDEN	OP	4.00	4.00
91	BARNYARD	OP	4.00	4.00
91	CHESSIE HOPPER CAR	OP	4.00	4.00
91	CONCERT IN THE PARK	OP	4.00	4.00
91	JACK THE POSTMAN	OP	3.25	3.25
91	MARBLE GAME	OP	4.00	4.00
91	MARTIN HOUSE	OP	3.25	3.25
91	ON VACATION	OP	4.00	4.00
91	POPCORN WAGON	OP	4.00	4.00
91	SCAREY HARRY (SCARECROW)	OP	4.00	4.00
91	SKI PARTY	OP	4.00	4.00
91	USMC WAR MEMORIAL	OP	6.50	7.00
91	VILLAGE ENTRANCE SIGN	OP	6.50	7.00
92	DELIVERY TRUCK	OP	3.98	4.00

YR	NAME	LIMIT	ISSUE	TREND
92	FORSYTHIA BUSH	OP	3.98	4.00
92	GASOLINE TRUCK	OP	3.98	4.00
92	MR. SOFTEE TRUCK	OP	3.98	4.00
92	NUTCRACKER BILLBOARD	OP	3.98	4.00
92	POLICE CAR	OP	3.98	4.00
92	SCHOOL CROSSING	OP	3.98	4.00
92	SILO	OP	3.98	4.00
92	SPRINGHOUSE	OP	3.25	3.25
93	CANNONBALL EXPRESS	OP	7.95	8.00
93	CHIPPEWA LAKE BILLBOARD	OP	7.95	8.00
93	GARDEN HOUSE	OP	6.50	7.00
93	GETTING DIRECTIONS	OP	7.95	8.00
93	GRAPE ARBOR	OP	7.95	8.00
93	JENNIE & GEORGE'S WEDDING	OP	7.95	8.00
93	JOHNNY APPLESEED STATUE	OP	7.95	8.00
93	LITTLE MARINE	OP	7.95	8.00
93	MARKET WAGON	OP	7.95	8.00
93	RUSTIC FENCE	OP	7.95	8.00
F. JONES				**AMERICAN BARNS**
92	BANK BARN	OP	8.50	9.00
92	CRIB BARN	OP	8.50	9.00
92	OHIO BARN	OP	8.50	9.00
92	VERMONT BARN	OP	8.50	9.00
F. JONES				**CHIPPEWA LAKE AMUSEMENT PARK**
93	BALLROOM	OP	4.50	5.00
93	BATH HOUSE	OP	4.50	5.00
93	MIDWAY	OP	4.50	5.00
93	PAVILION	OP	4.50	5.00
F. JONES				**CHRISTMAS IN NEW ENGLAND**
89	HUNTER HOUSE	RT	8.00	45.00
89	OLD SOUTH MEETING HOUSE, THE	RT	8.00	45.00
89	SHELDON'S TAVERN	RT	8.00	45.00
89	VERMONT COUNTRY STORE, THE	RT	8.00	45.00
F. JONES				**COLLECTOR CLUB GIFT-HOUSES**
89	BETSY ROSS HOUSE	CL	*	150.00
90	AMELIA EARHART	CL	*	75.00
91	LIMBERLOST CABIN	CL	*	*
92	ABIGAIL ADAMS BIRTHPLACE	YR	*	*
F. JONES				**COLLECTOR CLUB PIECES-AMERICAN SONGWRITERS**
91	ANNA WARNER HOUSE	CL	9.25	10.00
91	BENJAMIN R. HANBY HOUSE	CL	9.25	10.00
91	OSCAR HAMMERSTEIN HOUSE	CL	9.25	10.00
91	STEPHEN FOSTER HOUSE	CL	9.25	10.00
F. JONES				**COLLECTOR CLUB PIECES-FAMOUS AUTHORS**
89	HARRIET BEECHER STOWE	CL	8.75	85.00
89	HERMAN MELVILLE'S ARROWHEAD	CL	8.75	85.00
89	LONGFELLOW HOUSE	CL	8.75	85.00
89	ORCHARD HOUSE	CL	8.75	85.00
F. JONES				**COLLECTOR CLUB PIECES-GREAT INVENTORS**
90	FORD MOTOR CO.	CL	9.25	30.00
90	SETH THOMAS CLOCK CO.	CL	9.25	30.00
90	THOMAS EDISON	CL	9.25	30.00
90	WRIGHT CYCLE CO.	CL	9.25	30.00
F. JONES				**COLLECTOR CLUB PIECES-SIGNERS OF THE DECLARATION**
92	GEORGE CLYMER HOME	YR	9.75	10.00
92	JOHN WITHERSPOON HOME	YR	9.75	10.00
92	JOSIAH BARTLETT HOME	YR	9.75	10.00
92	STEPHEN HOPKINS HOME	YR	9.75	10.00
F. JONES				**COLONIAL VIRGINIA CHRISTMAS**
90	DULANEY HOUSE	RT	8.00	25.00
90	RISING SUN TAVERN	RT	8.00	25.00
90	SHIRLEY PLANTATION	RT	8.00	25.00
90	ST. JOHN'S CHURCH	RT	8.00	25.00
F. JONES				**FALL**
86	GOLDEN LAMB BUTTERY	RT	8.00	16.00
86	GRIMM'S FARMHOUSE	RT	8.00	16.00
86	MAIL POUCH BARN	RT	8.00	16.00
86	VOLLANT MILLS	RT	8.00	16.00
F. JONES				**HAGERSTOWN**
88	J. HAGER HOUSE	OP	8.00	8.00
88	MILLER HOUSE	OP	8.00	8.00
88	WOMAN'S CLUB	OP	8.00	8.00
88	YULE CUPBOARD, THE	OP	8.00	8.00
F. JONES				**HOMETOWN CHRISTMAS**
92	AUGUST IMGARD HOUSE	RT	8.50	9.00
92	HOWEY HOUSE	RT	8.50	9.00
92	OVERHOLT HOUSE	RT	8.50	9.00
92	SET	RT	34.00	34.00
92	WAYNE CO. COURTHOUSE	RT	8.50	9.00
F. JONES				**LIBERTY STREET**
88	COUNTY COURTHOUSE	OP	8.00	8.00
88	GRAF PRINTING CO	OP	8.00	8.00
88	WILTON RAILWAY DEPOT	OP	8.00	8.00
88	Z. JONES BASKETMAKER	OP	8.00	8.00
F. JONES				**LIGHTHOUSE**
90	ADMIRALITY HEAD	OP	8.00	8.00
90	CAPE HATTERAS LIGHTHOUSE	OP	8.00	8.00

YR	NAME	LIMIT	ISSUE	TREND
90	SANDY HOOK LIGHTHOUSE	OP	8.00	8.00
90	SPLIT ROCK LIGHTHOUSE	OP	8.00	8.00
F. JONES				**MAIN STREET**
87	FRANKLIN LIBRARY	RT	8.00	8.00
87	GARDEN THEATRE	RT	8.00	8.00
87	HISTORICAL MUSEUM	RT	8.00	8.00
87	TELEGRAPH/POST OFFICE	RT	8.00	8.00
F. JONES				**MAINE CHRISTMAS**
87	CAPPY'S CHOWDER HOUSE	RT	7.75	125.00
87	CAPTAIN'S HOUSE	RT	7.75	125.00
87	DAMARISCOTTA CHURCH	RT	7.75	125.00
87	PORTLAND HEAD LIGHTHOUSE	RT	7.75	125.00
F. JONES				**MARKET STREET**
89	SCHUMACHER MILLS	OP	8.00	8.00
89	SEVILLE HARDWARE STORE	OP	8.00	8.00
89	WEST INDIA GOODS STORE	OP	8.00	8.00
89	YANKEE CANDLE COMPANY	OP	8.00	8.00
F. JONES				**MISCELLANEOUS**
85	PENCIL HOLDER	CL	3.95	210.00
85	RECIPE HOLDER	CL	3.95	210.00
F. JONES				**NANTUCKET**
87	JARED COFFIN HOUSE	RT	8.00	8.00
87	MARIA MITCHELL HOUSE	RT	8.00	8.00
87	NANTUCKET ATHENIUM	RT	8.00	8.00
87	UNITARIAN CHURCH	RT	8.00	8.00
F. JONES				**NANTUCKET CHRISTMAS**
84	CHRISTMAS SHOP	RT	6.50	7.00
84	POWELL HOUSE	RT	6.50	7.00
84	SHAW HOUSE	RT	6.50	7.00
84	WINTROP HOUSE	RT	6.50	7.00
F. JONES				**NAUTICAL**
87	H & E SHIPS CHANDLERY	RT	8.00	8.00
87	LORAIN LIGHTHOUSE	RT	8.00	8.00
87	MONHEGAN BOAT LANDING	RT	8.00	8.00
87	YACHT CLUB	RT	8.00	8.00
F. JONES				**OHIO AMISH**
91	ADA MAE'S QUILT BARN	OP	8.00	8.00
91	BROWN SCHOOL	OP	8.00	8.00
91	ELI'S HARNESS SHOP	OP	8.00	8.00
91	JONAS TROYER HOME	OP	8.00	8.00
F. JONES				**OHIO WESTERN RESERVE CHRISTMAS**
85	BELLEVUE HOUSE	RT	7.00	175.00
85	GATES MILLS CHURCH	RT	7.00	175.00
85	OLMSTEAD HOUSE	RT	7.00	175.00
85	WESTERN RESERVE ACCADEMY	RT	7.00	175.00
F. JONES				**PAINTED LADIES**
88	ANDREWS HOTEL	OP	8.00	8.00
88	LADY AMANDA	OP	8.00	8.00
88	LADY ELIZABETH	OP	8.00	8.00
88	LADY IRIS	OP	8.00	8.00
F. JONES				**PHILADELPHIA CHRISTMAS**
88	ELFRETH'S ALLEY	RT	7.75	65.00
88	GRAFF HOUSE	RT	7.75	65.00
88	HEAD HOUSE, THE	RT	7.75	65.00
88	HILL-PHYSICK-KEITH HOUSE	RT	7.75	65.00
F. JONES				**ROCKY MOUNTAIN CHRISTMAS**
91	FIRST PRESBYTERIAN CHURCH	RT	8.20	14.00
91	TABOR HOUSE	RT	8.20	14.00
91	WESTERN HOTEL	RT	8.20	14.00
91	WHELLER-STALLARD HOUSE	RT	8.20	14.00
F. JONES				**ROSCOE VILLAGE**
86	CANAL COMPANY	RT	8.00	16.00
86	JACKSON TWP. HALL	RT	8.00	16.00
86	OLD WAREHOUSE REST.	RT	8.00	16.00
86	ROSCOE GENERAL STORE	RT	8.00	16.00
F. JONES				**SAVANNAH CHRISTMAS**
86	J.J. DALE ROW HOUSE	RT	7.25	8.00
86	LAFAYETTE SQUARE HOUSE	RT	7.25	32.00
86	LIBERTY INN	RT	7.25	8.00
86	SIMON MIRAULT COTTAGE	RT	7.25	32.00
F. JONES				**SERIES I**
83	ANTIQUE SHOP	RT	8.00	45.00
83	APOTHECARY	RT	8.00	45.00
83	BARBERSHOP	RT	8.00	45.00
83	BOOK STORE	RT	8.00	45.00
83	FEDERAL HOUSE	RT	8.00	45.00
83	FLORIST SHOP	RT	8.00	45.00
83	GARRISON HOUSE	RT	8.00	45.00
83	INN	RT	8.00	45.00
83	SCHOOL	RT	8.00	45.00
83	SWEETSHOP	RT	8.00	45.00
83	TOY SHOP	RT	8.00	45.00
83	VICTORIAN HOUSE	RT	8.00	45.00
F. JONES				**SERIES II**
84	ATTORNEY/BANK	RT	8.00	30.00
84	BROCKE HOUSE	RT	8.00	30.00

YR	NAME	LIMIT	ISSUE	TREND
84	CHURCH	RT	8.00	30.00
84	EATON HOUSE	RT	8.00	30.00
84	GRANDINERE HOUSE	RT	8.00	30.00
84	MILLINERY/QUILT	RT	8.00	30.00
84	MUSIC SHOP	RT	8.00	30.00
84	S & T CLOTHIERS	RT	8.00	30.00
84	TOBACCONIST/SHOEMAKER	RT	8.00	30.00
84	TOWN HALL	RT	8.00	30.00
F. JONES				**SERIES III**
85	ALLEN-COE HOUSE	RT	8.00	20.00
85	CONNECTICUT AVE. FIREHOUSE	RT	8.00	20.00
85	DRY GOODS STORE	RT	8.00	20.00
85	EDINBURGH TIMES	RT	8.00	20.00
85	FINE JEWELERS	RT	8.00	20.00
85	HOBART-HARLEY HOUSE	RT	8.00	20.00
85	KALORAMA GUEST HOUSE	RT	8.00	20.00
85	MAIN ST. CARRIAGE SHOP	RT	8.00	20.00
85	OPERA HOUSE	RT	8.00	20.00
85	RISTORANTE	RT	8.00	20.00
F. JONES				**SERIES IV**
86	BENNINGTON-HULL HOUSE	RT	8.00	16.00
86	CHAGRIN FALLS POPCORN SHOP	RT	8.00	16.00
86	CHEPACHET UNION CHURCH	RT	8.00	16.00
86	JOHN BELVILLE HOUSE	RT	8.00	16.00
86	JONES BROS. TEA CO.	RT	8.00	16.00
86	LITTLE HOUSE GIFTABLES, THE	RT	8.00	16.00
86	O'MALLEYS LIVERY STABLE	RT	8.00	16.00
86	VANDENBERG HOUSE	RT	8.00	16.00
86	WESTBROOK HOUSE	RT	8.00	16.00
F. JONES				**SERIES V**
87	AMISH OAK/DIXIE SHOE	RT	8.00	8.00
87	ARCHITECT/TAILOR	RT	8.00	8.00
87	CONGRUITY TAVERN	RT	8.00	8.00
87	CREOLE HOUSE	RT	8.00	8.00
87	DENTIST/PHYSICIAN	RT	8.00	8.00
87	M. WASHINGTON HOUSE	RT	8.00	8.00
87	MARKETHOUSE	RT	8.00	8.00
87	MURRAY HOTEL	RT	8.00	8.00
87	POLICE DEPARTMENT	RT	8.00	8.00
87	SOUTHPORT BANK	RT	8.00	8.00
F. JONES				**SERIES VI**
88	BURTON LANCASTER HOUSE	OP	8.00	8.00
88	CITY HOSPITAL	OP	8.00	8.00
88	FIRST BAPTIST CHURCH	OP	8.00	8.00
88	FISH/MEAT MARKET	OP	8.00	8.00
88	LINCOLN SCHOOL	OP	8.00	8.00
88	NEW MASTERS GALLERY	OP	8.00	8.00
88	OHLIGER HOUSE	OP	8.00	8.00
88	PRUYN HOUSE	OP	8.00	8.00
88	STIFFENBODY FUNERAL HOME	OP	8.00	8.00
88	WILLIAMS & SONS	OP	8.00	8.00
F. JONES				**SERIES VII**
89	BLACK CAT ANTIQUES	OP	8.00	8.00
89	HAIRDRESSING PARLOR	OP	8.00	8.00
89	HANDCRAFTED TOYS	OP	8.00	8.00
89	JUSTICE OF THE PEACE	OP	8.00	8.00
89	OCTAGONAL SCHOOL	OP	8.00	8.00
89	OLD FRANKLIN BOOK SHOP	OP	8.00	8.00
89	THORPE HOUSE BED & BREAKFAST	OP	8.00	8.00
89	VILLAGE TINSMITH	OP	8.00	8.00
89	WILLIAMS APOTHECARY	OP	8.00	8.00
89	WINKLER BAKERY	OP	8.00	8.00
F. JONES				**SERIES VIII**
90	F.J. REALTY COMPANY	OP	8.00	8.00
90	GLOBE CORNER BOOKSTORE	OP	8.00	8.00
90	HABERDASHERS	OP	8.00	8.00
90	MEDINA FIRE DEPARTMENT	OP	8.00	8.00
90	NELL'S STEMS & STITCHES	OP	8.00	8.00
90	NOAH'S ARK VETERINARY	OP	8.00	8.00
90	PICCADILLI PIPE & TOBACCO	OP	8.00	8.00
90	PURITAN HOUSE	OP	8.00	8.00
90	VICTORIA'S PARLOUR	OP	8.00	8.00
90	WALLDORFF FURNITURE	OP	8.00	8.00
F. JONES				**SERIES IX**
91	ALL SAINTS CHAPEL	OP	8.00	8.00
91	AMERICAN RED CROSS	OP	8.00	8.00
91	CENTRAL CITY OPERA HOUSE	OP	8.00	8.00
91	CITY HALL	OP	8.00	8.00
91	CPA/LAW OFFICE	OP	8.00	8.00
91	GOV. SNYDER MANSION	OP	8.00	8.00
91	JEWELER/OPTOMETRIST	OP	8.00	8.00
91	OSBAHR'S UPHOLSTERY	OP	8.00	8.00
91	SPANKY'S HARDWARE CO	OP	8.00	8.00
91	TREBLE CLEF, THE	OP	8.00	8.00
F. JONES				**SERIES X**
92	CITY NEWS	OP	8.50	9.00
92	FUDGE KITCHEN	OP	8.50	9.00
92	GRAND HAVEN	OP	8.50	9.00

YR	NAME	LIMIT	ISSUE	TREND
92	HENYAN'S ATHLETIC SHOP	OP	8.50	9.00
92	LEPPERT'S 5 & 10 CENT	OP	8.50	9.00
92	MADELINE'S DRESS SHOP	OP	8.50	9.00
92	OWL AND THE PUSSYCAT	OP	8.50	9.00
92	PICKLES PUB	OP	8.50	9.00
92	PURE GAS STATION	OP	8.50	9.00
92	UNITED CHURCH OF ACWORTH	OP	8.50	9.00
F. JONES				**SERIES XI**
93	BARBERSHOP/GALLERY	OP	4.50	5.00
93	HADDONFIELD BANK	OP	4.50	5.00
93	IMMANUEL CHURCH	OP	4.50	5.00
93	JOHANN SINGER BOOTS & SHOES	OP	4.50	5.00
93	PET SHOP/GIFT SHOP	OP	4.50	5.00
93	POLICE-TROOP C	OP	4.50	5.00
93	SHRIMPLIN & JONES PRODUCE	OP	4.50	5.00
93	STONES RESTAURANT	OP	4.50	5.00
93	U.S. ARMED FORCES	OP	4.50	5.00
93	U.S. POST OFFICE	OP	4.50	5.00
F. JONES				**ST. CHARLES CHRISTMAS**
93	LEWIS & CLARK CENTER	OP	4.50	5.00
93	NEWBILL-MCELHINEY HOUSE	OP	4.50	5.00
93	ST. PETER'S CATHOLIC CHURCH	OP	4.50	5.00
93	STONE ROW	OP	4.50	5.00
F. JONES				**TRADESMAN**
88	BUCKEYE CANDY & TOBACCO	OP	8.00	8.00
88	C.O. WHEEL COMPANY	OP	8.00	8.00
88	HERMANNHOF WINERY	OP	8.00	8.00
88	JENNEY GRIST MILL	OP	8.00	8.00
F. JONES				**WASHINGTON D.C.**
91	NATIONAL ARCHIVES	OP	8.00	8.00
91	U.S. CAPITOL	OP	8.00	8.00
91	U.S. SUPREME COURT	OP	8.00	8.00
91	WHITE HOUSE	OP	8.00	8.00
F. JONES				**WILD WEST**
89	DRINK 'EM UP SALOON	OP	8.00	8.00
89	F.C. ZIMMERMAN'S GUN SHOP	OP	8.00	8.00
89	MARSHAL'S OFFICE	OP	8.00	8.00
89	WELLS FARGO & CO.	OP	8.00	8.00
F. JONES				**WILLIAMSBURG CHRISTMAS**
83	CHRISTMAS CHURCH	RT	6.00	6.00
83	FEDERAL HOUSE	RT	6.00	6.00
83	GARRISON HOUSE	RT	6.00	6.00
83	GEORGIAN HOUSE	RT	6.00	6.00

CAVANAGH GROUP

YR	NAME	LIMIT	ISSUE	TREND
*				**AMERICAN LIFE**
95	ELAINE	2500	100.00	100.00
95	GIRL ON SWING	2500	100.00	100.00
96	GONE FISHING	OP	60.00	60.00
N. ROCKWELL				**AMERICAN LIFE**
95	BOY AT WELL	5000	60.00	60.00
95	BOY FISHING	5000	60.00	60.00
96	A REFRESHING BREAK	OP	60.00	60.00
S. STEARMAN				**AMERICAN LIFE**
95	HOMECOMING, THE	2500	125.00	125.00
*				**COCA-COLA BRAND HERITAGE COLLECTION**
94	EIGHT POLAR BEARS ON WOOD	10000	150.00	160.00
94	SANTA AT HIS DESK	OP	45.00	45.00
94	SANTA AT THE LAMPPOST	OP	50.00	50.00
94	SINGLE POLAR BEAR ON ICE	OP	40.00	40.00
96	HOLLYWOOD SNOWGLOBE	OP	50.00	50.00
96	SANTA W/POLAR BEAR SNOWGLOBE	OP	50.00	50.00
96	SAY UNCLE SNOWGLOBE	OP	50.00	50.00
SUNDBLOM				**COCA-COLA BRAND HERITAGE COLLECTION**
94	EIGHT POLAR BEARS ON WOOD	10000	135.00	145.00
94	SANTA AT HIS DESK	5000	70.00	75.00
94	SANTA AT THE FIREPLACE	5000	70.00	75.00
94	TWO POLAR BEARS ON ICE	OP	30.00	30.00
*				**COCA-COLA BRAND HERITAGE COLLECTION MUSICALS**
94	CALENDAR GIRL 1916	OP	60.00	60.00
94	HILDA CLARK 1901	OP	60.00	60.00
94	HILDA CLARK 1903	OP	60.00	60.00
94	SANTA'S SODA SHOP	OP	50.00	50.00
SUNDBLOM				**COCA-COLA BRAND HERITAGE COLLECTION MUSICALS**
93	DEAR SANTA, PLEASE PAUSE HERE	OP	50.00	50.00
94	SANTA AT HIS DESK	5000	95.00	100.00
94	SANTA AT THE FIREPLACE	5000	95.00	100.00
94	TWO POLAR BEARS ON ICE	OP	45.00	45.00
95	SSHHH!	OP	35.00	55.00
*				**COCA-COLA BRAND NORTH POLE BOTTLING WORKS**
95	ALL IN A DAYS WORK	OP	25.00	25.00
95	AN ELF'S FAVORITE CHORE	OP	30.00	30.00
95	CHECKING HIS LIST	OP	30.00	30.00
95	FILLING OPERATIONS	OP	45.00	45.00
95	FRONT OFFICE	OP	50.00	50.00
95	KITCHEN CORNER	OP	55.00	55.00
95	KITCHEN CORNER, THE	OP	55.00	55.00

YR	NAME	LIMIT	ISSUE	TREND
95	MAINTENANCE MISCHIEF	OP	25.00	25.00
95	MAKING THE SECRET SYRUP	OP	30.00	30.00
95	PIPE MAINTENANCE	OP	20.00	20.00
95	QUALITY CONTROL	OP	30.00	30.00
95	RESTOCKING THE VENDING MACHINE	OP	30.00	30.00
95	SANTA AT HIS DESK	OP	30.00	30.00
95	SANTA'S OFFICE	OP	50.00	50.00
95	TAKING A BREAK	OP	20.00	20.00
95	TOP SECRET	OP	30.00	30.00
95	VAULT, THE	OP	25.00	25.00
96	A STROKE OF GENIUS	OP	25.00	25.00
96	AN ARTIST'S TOUCH	OP	25.00	25.00
96	ART DEPARTMENT	OP	50.00	50.00
96	BIG AMBITIONS	OP	25.00	25.00
96	DELIVERY FOR MRS. CLAUS	OP	25.00	25.00
96	ELF IN TRAINING	OP	25.00	25.00
96	OOPS!	OP	25.00	25.00
96	ORDER DEPARTMENT	OP	55.00	55.00
96	PRECIOUS CARGO	OP	25.00	25.00
96	SHIPPING DEPARTMENT	OP	55.00	55.00
96	SPECIAL DELIVERY	OP	25.00	25.00
*		**COCA-COLA BRAND TOWN SQUARE COLLECTION**		
92	AFTER SAKTING	CL	8.00	10.00
92	BRINGING IT HOME	CL	8.00	10.00
92	COCA-COLA AD CAR	CL	9.00	10.00
92	COCA-COLA DELIVERY TRUCK	CL	15.00	18.00
92	DELIVERY MAN	CL	8.00	10.00
92	GIL THE GROCER	CL	8.00	10.00
92	HORSE-DRAWN WAGON	CL	12.00	15.00
92	THIRSTY THE SNOWMAN	CL	9.00	11.00
*		**THE COCA-COLA POLAR BEAR COLLECTION**		
95	ALWAYS	OP	30.00	30.00
95	ALWAYS/MUSICAL	OP	50.00	50.00
96	COCA-COLA STAND	OP	45.00	45.00
96	COOL BREAK	OP	40.00	40.00
96	DECORATING THE TREE	OP	45.00	45.00
96	PLAYING WITH DAD	OP	40.00	40.00
96	REFRESHING TREAT	OP	45.00	45.00
*		**THE COCA-COLA POLAR BEAR CUBS**		
96	A CHRISTMAS WISH	OP	10.00	10.00
96	BALANCING ACT	OP	16.00	16.00
96	BEAR CUB CLUB, THE	OP	20.00	20.00
96	ENJOY	OP	12.00	12.00
96	GOOD FRIENDS ALWAYS STICK TOGETHER	OP	16.00	16.00
96	I'M NOT SLEEPY...REALLY	OP	10.00	10.00
96	IT'S MY TURN TO HIDE	OP	12.00	12.00
96	LOOK WHAT I CAN DO	OP	12.00	12.00
96	PATIENCE IS A VIRTUE	OP	16.00	16.00
96	RIDE'EM COWBOY	OP	20.00	20.00
96	SNOWDAY ADVENTURES	OP	12.00	12.00
96	SWEET DREAMS	OP	12.00	12.00
96	THANKS FOR THE LIFT	OP	20.00	20.00
96	THERE'S NOTHING LIKE A FRIEND	OP	16.00	16.00
96	TO GRANDMOTHER'S HOUSE WE GO	OP	12.00	12.00
96	WHO SAYS GIRLS CAN'T THROW	OP	16.00	16.00
*	**SUNDBLOM**	**THE COCA-COLA SANTA**		
95	BUSY MAN'S PAUSE	OP	80.00	80.00
95	FOR ME	OP	40.00	40.00
95	HOSPITALITY	5000	35.00	35.00
95	THEY REMEMBERED ME	5000	50.00	50.00

CHUST COUNTRY

YR	NAME	LIMIT	ISSUE	TREND
	T. NEIFFER	**PIGEON CREEK COLLECTIBLES**		
96	GRAMPY & ME	OP	160.00	160.00
96	OLD FAITHFUL AND OLD GLORY	OP	140.00	140.00

CONSTANCE COLLECTION

YR	NAME	LIMIT	ISSUE	TREND
	C. GUERRA	**ANNUAL SANTA CLAUS BY CONSTANCE**		
91	TEDDY CLAUS	YR	90.00	90.00
92	REACH FOR THE STARS SANTA	YR	90.00	90.00
	C. GUERRA	**FRIENDS & FAMILY COLLECTION**		
92	A MOMENT W/MARGO	2500	55.00	55.00
92	ANNETTE & CHRISTIAN	2500	48.00	48.00
92	BUTTERCUPS	2500	35.00	35.00
92	CHELSEA'S EASTER	2500	37.00	37.00
92	CHRISTOPHER	2500	37.00	37.00
92	COVERED WITH LOVE	2500	59.90	60.00
92	ELIZABETH AND PHILLIP	2500	55.00	55.00
92	FIRST LOVE	2500	57.00	57.00
92	FOREVER FRIENDS	2500	51.00	51.00
92	GRANDPOPS ANGEL	2500	51.00	51.00
92	LITTLE SIS	2500	48.00	48.00
92	LOVES TENDER TOUCH	2500	33.00	33.00
92	MICHELLI BELLE	2500	31.00	31.00
92	MISSY	2500	31.00	31.00
92	MOTHER'S DAY BOUQUET	2500	42.00	42.00
92	ONE ON ONE FATHER/SON	2500	55.00	55.00
92	PARTY PAMMY	2500	31.00	31.00

YR	NAME	LIMIT	ISSUE	TREND
92	PILLOW TALK	2500	42.00	42.00
92	PITZ AND SARA	2500	48.00	48.00
92	RACHEL'S BLUE BIRD	2500	42.00	42.00
92	SPECIAL SISTERS	2500	51.00	51.00
92	TIMEOUT TO LOVE	2500	37.00	37.00
92	TOGETHERNESS	2500	49.00	49.00
C. GUERRA				**HEAVEN SENT**
92	ALLELUIA	2500	45.00	45.00
92	CHRISTENING DAY	2500	55.00	55.00
92	ENDURING FAITH	2500	55.00	55.00
92	LOVE IS PATIENT	2500	49.00	49.00
C. GUERRA				**KITTY KAT KLUB**
90	KASSANDRA KITTY	1500	30.00	30.00
90	KATRINA	1500	30.00	30.00
90	KLARA KITTY	1500	30.00	30.00
90	KLARENCE KITTY	1500	30.00	30.00
90	KLAUDIUS KITTY	1500	30.00	30.00
90	KOCKEY KITTY	1500	30.00	30.00
90	KONRAD KITTY	1500	30.00	30.00
90	KOQUETTE KITTY	1500	30.00	30.00
C. GUERRA				**SANTA CLAUS BY CONSTANCE**
86	JOLLY ST. NICK	4000	72.00	72.00
86	VICTORIAN SANTA	4000	90.00	90.00
86	VICTORIAN SANTA WITH BEAR	4000	80.00	80.00
87	ANIMAL SANTA	4000	78.00	78.00
88	AMERICAN TRADITIONAL SANTA	4000	90.00	90.00
88	MIDNIGHT VISIT	4000	112.00	112.00
88	SAINT NICHOLAS OF MYRA	4000	90.00	90.00
88	SANTAS DELIVERY	4000	90.00	90.00
89	COBBLESTONE SANTA	4000	112.00	112.00
89	KITTY CHRISTMAS	4000	112.00	112.00
89	SANTA WITH BOY	1000	90.00	90.00
89	SANTA WITH DEER	4000	112.00	112.00
89	SANTA WITH GIRL	1000	90.00	90.00
89	SANTA WITH LAMB	4000	112.00	112.00
89	SANTAS SLEIGH	1000	190.00	190.00
89	SIBERIAN SANTA	1000	190.00	190.00
89	THOMAS NAST SANTA	4000	112.00	112.00
90	CANDY CANE SANTA	1000	124.00	124.00
90	ELF SANTA	1000	298.00	298.00
90	HUNT SANTA	1000	158.00	158.00
90	KITTY CLAUS	1000	78.00	78.00
90	ROCKINGHORSE SANTA	1000	124.00	124.00
91	FIRST CHRISTMAS	1000	79.00	79.00
91	FIRST FROST	1000	250.00	250.00
91	HEAVENLY BLESSING	1000	79.00	79.00
91	LITTLE BOY'S SANTA	1000	95.00	95.00
91	SANTA'S DANCE	1000	95.00	95.00
91	SANTA'S DAY OFF	1000	90.00	90.00
91	SANTA'S GIRL	1000	95.00	95.00
92	HUSH! HUSH! SANTA	2500	59.90	60.00
92	PEACE ON EARTH	2500	64.00	64.00
92	TEST RUN SANTA	2500	79.00	79.00
92	TOUCH UP SANTA	2500	64.00	64.00
C. GUERRA				**SEASONAL SANTA**
92	BASES LOADED	2500	90.00	90.00
92	FISHING DAY FUN	2500	90.00	90.00
92	FRESH POWDER FUN	2500	72.00	72.00
92	LOST BALL SANTA	2500	90.00	90.00
92	SPRING SERENITY	2500	112.00	112.00
C. GUERRA				**TENDER TOTS**
92	BABY BUNS	2500	31.00	31.00
92	BABY'S BLOCKS	2500	37.00	37.00
92	BABY'S FIRST ABC'S	2500	37.00	37.00
92	FIRST CRAWL	2500	37.00	37.00
92	FIRST DAY HOME (BOY)	2500	35.00	35.00
92	FIRST DAY HOME (GIRL)	2500	35.00	35.00
92	FIRST WORDS	2500	37.00	37.00
92	NIGHT-NIGHT	2500	31.00	31.00
92	PLAYMATES	2500	33.00	33.00
92	SUGARPLUM DARLINGS	2500	37.00	37.00
92	TOYLAND	2500	37.00	37.00
C. GUERRA				**THE BRIAR PATCH**
90	BARBARA BUNNY	1500	30.00	30.00
90	BARTHOLEMUE BUNNY	1500	30.00	30.00
90	BENEDICT BUNNY	1500	30.00	30.00
90	BERNARD BUNNY	1500	30.00	30.00
90	BERNICE BUNNY	1500	30.00	30.00
90	BERTRUM BUNNY	1500	30.00	30.00
90	BETSEY BUNNY	1500	30.00	30.00
90	BIRTHA BUNNY	1500	30.00	30.00
90	BLOSSUM BUNNY	1500	30.00	30.00
90	BONNIE BUNNY	1500	30.00	30.00
90	BRAIDA BUNNY	1500	30.00	30.00
90	BROTHERLY BUNNY	1500	30.00	30.00
90	BROWNIE BUNNY	1500	30.00	30.00
90	BUSTER BUNNY	1500	30.00	30.00
92	BUNNY'S BASKET	2500	21.90	22.00

YR	NAME	LIMIT	ISSUE	TREND
92	GRANDFATHER BUN	2500	21.90	22.00
92	GRANDMOTHER BUNNY	2500	21.90	22.00
92	LOVE BUN	2500	21.90	22.00
92	MOTHER WITH TWINS	2500	21.90	22.00
92	NEW MAMMA BUNNY	2500	21.90	22.00
92	NUMBER ONE BUN	2500	21.90	22.00
92	PAPPA BUNNY	2500	21.90	22.00
92	PONDERING BUN	2500	21.90	22.00
92	PROUD PAPPA BUNNY	2500	21.90	22.00
92	WOODLAND BUNNY	2500	31.50	32.00
C. GUERRA			**THE GOLDEN AMERICANS**	
91	ANDRES AND SAM	1500	37.00	37.00
91	BELINDA	1500	31.00	31.00
91	BLESSED WITH LOVE	1500	55.00	55.00
91	DADDY'S DARLING	1500	48.00	48.00
91	EFFIE AND COMPANY	1500	31.00	31.00
91	EMMA AND NICKIE	1500	37.00	37.00
91	ENDLESS LOVE	1500	48.00	48.00
91	FELICIA & FLUFF	1500	37.00	37.00
91	FROZEN FRIENDS	1500	42.00	42.00
91	GILBERT	1500	31.00	31.00
91	GLORYA	1500	75.00	75.00
91	GRANDMAS LOVE	1500	65.00	65.00
91	HANNAH AND KITTY	1500	42.00	42.00
91	INTO THE LIGHT	1500	31.00	31.00
91	LEARNING TO BRAID	1500	42.00	42.00
91	LETTIE THE DOLLMAKER	1500	48.00	48.00
91	MISSING YOU	1500	37.00	37.00
91	NEW PUPS	1500	31.00	31.00
91	PARTY TIME PALS	1500	55.00	55.00
91	PENNY PINCHER	1500	48.00	48.00
91	PLAY TIME	1500	31.00	31.00
91	PRAYING PALS	1500	31.00	31.00
91	PREACHER MAN	1500	31.00	31.00
91	PUDDLES	1500	37.00	37.00
91	PUPPY LOVE	1500	37.00	37.00
91	RUBY RAE AND TOM-TOM	1500	37.00	37.00
91	SCHOOL DAZE	1500	31.00	31.00
91	SUNDAY MORNING	1500	75.00	75.00
91	SWEET ASSURANCE	1500	48.00	48.00
91	SWEET DREAMS	1500	37.00	37.00
92	ANNELLE	2500	37.00	37.00
92	BALLA RENA	2500	31.00	31.00
92	BESTEST FRIENDS	2500	31.00	31.00
92	BUNNY LOVE	2500	31.00	31.00
92	CHRIS MISS	2500	31.00	31.00
92	CHURCH LADY ELLIE	2500	37.00	37.00
92	CHURCH LADY ETHEL	2500	37.00	37.00
92	CHURCH LADY PEARLE	2500	37.00	37.00
92	DUTCHIE	2500	31.00	31.00
92	FIRST POSITION	2500	31.00	31.00
92	FREE KICK DICK	2500	31.00	31.00
92	JOY BOY	2500	31.00	31.00
92	LITTLE CHASE	2500	31.00	31.00
92	LITTLE MAGIC	2500	31.00	31.00
92	LOVING EWE	2500	31.00	31.00
92	LOVING EWE TOO!	2500	33.00	33.00
92	MANDAS NABBIT	2500	31.00	31.00
92	P.S. I LOVE YOU	2500	42.00	42.00
92	PREPIE GREGORY	2500	37.00	37.00
92	PREPIE WINTHROP	2500	31.00	31.00
92	PRIMA DONA	2500	31.00	31.00
92	PUPPY LOVING	2500	37.00	37.00
92	QUARTERBACK JACK	2500	31.00	31.00
92	SCHOOL GIRL SAL	2500	31.00	31.00
92	SCHOOL GIRL SUE	2500	31.00	31.00
92	THERE YOU ARE!	2500	48.00	48.00
92	TOO MUCH HOMEWORK	2500	48.00	48.00
92	VALENTINE OF MINE	2500	31.00	31.00
92	VICTORY	2500	31.00	31.00
C. GUERRA			**VICTORIANA COLLECTION**	
91	FRITZ	1500	37.00	37.00
91	JULIA	1500	37.00	37.00
91	PENELOPE	1500	37.00	37.00
91	ROSIE	1500	37.00	37.00
91	VICTORIA	1500	37.00	37.00

COUNTRY ARTISTS

YR	NAME	LIMIT	ISSUE	TREND
93	FREEDOM OF THE SEAS	RT	325.00	325.00
D. IVEY				
94	LORD OF THE SKIES	RT	795.00	795.00
94	SPIRIT OF FREEDOM	1500	750.00	750.00
95	GRACEFUL FLIGHT	950	695.00	695.00
95	VISIONS OF DAWN	250	2700.00	2700.00
B. PRICE				
94	GUARDIAN OF THE HERD	RT	695.00	695.00
94	SUMMER DREAMS	RT	395.00	395.00
96	BROKEN DREAMS	850	375.00	375.00

YR	NAME	LIMIT	ISSUE	TREND
96	CHALLENGE, THE	850	325.00	325.00
96	EVER PATIENT	850	375.00	375.00
96	FAMILY ADVENTURE	850	375.00	375.00
96	RESTFUL DAYS	850	750.00	750.00
R. SEFTON				
94	COMING HOME	RT	395.00	395.00
95	STALLIONS OF THE CAMARQUE	950	795.00	795.00
96	A TRIAL OF STRENGTH	850	750.00	750.00
96	SPIRIT OF THE PLAINS	850	850.00	850.00
K. SHERWIN				
94	LAST FURROW, THE	RT	395.00	395.00
95	WINTER HOLT	1500	750.00	750.00
96	AFTER THE STORM	850	450.00	450.00
96	FIRST LIGHT	850	450.00	450.00
96	SPRING OF LIFE	850	295.00	295.00
S. LANGFORD			**BALD EAGLE COLLECTION**	
95	BALD EAGLE LANDING	OP	127.50	135.00
95	BALD EAGLE SOARING	OP	62.50	74.00
95	HIDDEN SANCTUARY	2500	289.00	289.00
95	SPIRIT OF FREEDOM	1500	750.00	765.00
D. IVEY			**BIG CAT COLLECTION**	
95	CHEETAH	OP	198.00	205.00
95	COUGAR	OP	182.50	195.00
95	LEOPARD	OP	198.00	205.00
95	SNOW LEOPARD	OP	189.00	200.00
95	TIGER	OP	215.00	220.00
K. SHERWIN			**GRAYWOLF COLLECTION**	
92	DAWN CHORUS	OP	375.00	400.00
92	FIRST ICE OF WINTER	RT	450.00	475.00
92	HIGH GROUND	OP	225.00	250.00
92	LARGE HOWLING WOLF	OP	150.00	165.00
92	MEDIUM HOWLING WOLF	OP	95.00	105.00
92	MOTHER & CUB	OP	175.00	195.00
92	RUNNING FREE	OP	175.00	195.00
92	SMALL HOWLING WOLF	OP	49.00	55.00
92	WOLF CUBS	OP	135.00	145.00
92	WOLF KISS	OP	250.00	275.00
92	WOLF PAIR	OP	225.00	250.00
95	UNTAMED WILDERNESS	3500	450.00	450.00
B. PRICE			**PENGUIN COLLECTION**	
95	MINIATURE PENGUIN	OP	24.95	28.00
95	MOTHER & CHICKS	OP	110.00	120.00
95	PENGUIN CHICK SLIDING	OP	52.50	55.00
95	PENGUIN CHICKS KISSING	OP	57.50	62.00
95	PENGUIN CHICKS--GROUP	OP	74.50	80.00
95	PENGUIN FAMILY	OP	169.00	180.00

CREART

YR	NAME	LIMIT	ISSUE	TREND
F. CONTRERAS			**AFRICAN WILDLIFE**	
93	CAPE BUFFALO	1500	418.00	418.00
94	NUMA LION'S HEAD	2500	418.00	418.00
E. MARTINEZ			**AFRICAN WILDLIFE**	
94	GRUMBLER CAPE BUFFALO	1500	498.00	498.00
V. PEREZ			**AFRICAN WILDLIFE**	
93	TRAVIESO	1500	198.00	198.00
F. CONTRERAS			**AMERICAN WILDLIFE**	
93	AMERICAN SYMBOL EAGLE	1500	246.00	246.00
93	RED FOX, THE	1500	199.00	199.00
93	WILD AMERICAN BISON	1500	338.00	338.00
C. ESTEVEZ			**AMERICAN WILDLIFE**	
94	CATAMOUNTAIN	2500	118.00	118.00
94	OUT OF THE DEN PUMA	1500	130.00	130.00
94	PUFFINS	1500	258.00	258.00
E. MARTINEZ			**AMERICAN WILDLIFE**	
93	BUENOS DIAS JACK RABBIT	1500	218.00	218.00
93	HOWLING COYOTE	1500	199.00	199.00
94	FREEDOM EAGLE	1500	500.00	500.00
B. NELSON			**AMERICAN WILDLIFE**	
94	AMBUSHING PUMA	1950	150.00	150.00
94	BRIEFLY REST PUMAS	1950	250.00	250.00
94	RED-TAILED HAWK	1950	130.00	130.00
V. PEREZ			**AMERICAN WILDLIFE**	
93	SCENT OF HONEY BEAR	1500	398.00	398.00
93	WHITE BLIZZARD WOLF	1500	275.00	275.00
94	OVER THE TOP PUMA	1500	398.00	398.00
94	SINGING TO THE MOON I WOLF	1500	398.00	398.00
94	SINGING TO THE MOON II WOLF	1500	358.00	358.00
J. ROBISON			**BIRDS OF PREY**	
94	GYRFALCON	450	1300.00	1300.00
94	VIGILANT EAGLE	650	780.00	780.00
F. CONTRERAS			**NATURE'S CARE**	
93	DOE & FAWNS	2500	99.00	99.00
93	EAGLE & EAGLET	2500	99.00	99.00
93	GORILLA & BABY	2500	99.00	99.00
93	LIONESS & CUBS	2500	99.00	99.00
93	WOLF & PUPS	2500	99.00	99.00

Precious Moments figures always offer inspiration of some sort. Thank You Lord for Everything *reminds us to appreciate what we have.*

I'll Never Stop Loving You *proclaims this little porcelain bisque figure artist by Sam Butcher, creator of the Precious Moments line produced by Enesco Corp.*

Even with all these beautiful Christmas decorations, You Are My Favorite Star. *The Precious Moments figure was created by Sam Butcher for Enesco Corp.*

15 Happy Years Together, What a Tweet! *is the Enesco Precious Moments 15th anniversary commemorative figurine.*

Lord Help Us Keep Our Act Together *implore these youngsters created by Precious Moments artist Sam Butcher and produced by Enesco Corp.*

May Only Good Things Come Your Way *is from Enesco's Precious Moments collection by Sam Butcher.*

YR	NAME	LIMIT	ISSUE	TREND
	C. ESTEVEZ			**NATURE'S CARE**
93	OTTERS	2500	99.00	99.00
	E. MARTINEZ			**NATURE'S CARE**
93	JACK RABBIT & YOUNG	2500	99.00	99.00
	V. PEREZ			**NATURE'S CARE**
93	GRIZZLY & CUBS	2500	99.00	99.00
93	PENGUIN AND CHICKS	2500	99.00	99.00

CRYSTAL WORLD

YR	NAME	LIMIT	ISSUE	TREND
	N. MULARGIA			**ANIMAL FRIENDS COLLECTION**
86	MINI BUTTERFLY	CL	15.00	18.00
86	MINI DACHSHUND	CL	15.00	18.00
86	MINI FROG MUSHROOM	CL	15.00	18.00
86	MINI KOALA	CL	15.00	18.00
86	MINI MOUSE	CL	15.00	18.00
86	MINI RABBIT	CL	15.00	18.00
86	MINI SWAN	OP	15.00	15.00
93	PIG	CL	50.00	50.00
94	OWLS	OP	53.00	53.00
95	WILBUR IN LOVE	OP	90.00	90.00
	R. NAKAI			**ANIMAL FRIENDS COLLECTION**
83	ALLIGATOR	CL	46.00	55.00
83	LARGE MOUSE	CL	36.00	42.00
83	LARGE PIG	CL	50.00	60.00
83	LARGE RABBIT	CL	50.00	60.00
83	LARGE TURTLE	CL	56.00	65.00
83	MEDIUM MOUSE	CL	28.00	33.00
83	MEDIUM PIG	CL	32.00	38.00
83	MEDIUM TURTLE	CL	38.00	45.00
83	MOUSE STANDING	CL	34.00	41.00
83	SMALL ELEPHANT	CL	40.00	48.00
83	SMALL MOUSE	CL	20.00	24.00
83	SMALL PIG	CL	22.00	26.00
83	SMALL RABBIT	CL	28.00	35.00
83	SMALL TURTLE	CL	28.00	35.00
84	BEAVER	CL	30.00	36.00
84	BUTTERFLY	CL	50.00	60.00
84	DACHSHUND	CL	28.00	33.00
84	DOG	CL	28.00	33.00
84	EXTRA LARGE PEACOCK	CL	420.00	500.00
84	LARGE HIPPO	CL	50.00	60.00
84	LARGE KANGAROO	CL	50.00	60.00
84	LARGE KOALA BEAR	CL	69.00	85.00
84	LARGE PEACOCK	CL	147.00	177.00
84	MINI TURTLE	CL	18.00	22.00
84	PEACOCK	CL	50.00	60.00
84	PENGUIN	CL	34.00	41.00
84	POODLE	CL	30.00	36.00
84	PORCUPINE	CL	42.00	50.00
84	RACOON	CL	69.00	84.00
84	SMALL HIPPO	CL	30.00	35.00
84	SMALL KANGAROO	CL	34.00	40.00
84	SMALL KOALA	CL	28.00	32.00
84	SMALL PEACOCK	CL	37.00	44.00
85	LARGE ELEPHANT	CL	54.00	65.00
85	LARGE LION	CL	60.00	72.00
85	RACOON	CL	50.00	60.00
85	SMALL LION	CL	36.00	43.00
85	SQUIRREL	CL	30.00	36.00
86	UNICORN	CL	110.00	132.00
87	LARGE CIRCUS PUPPY	CL	50.00	60.00
87	LARGE PANDA	CL	45.00	54.00
87	LARGE PLAYFUL PUP	CL	85.00	102.00
87	LARGE POODLE	CL	64.00	76.00
87	LARGE RABBIT W/CARROT	CL	55.00	66.00
87	LARGE SNOWBUNNY	CL	45.00	54.00
87	MOTHER KOALA AND CUB	CL	55.00	64.00
87	PENGUIN ON CUBE	CL	30.00	36.00
87	POSING PENGUIN	CL	85.00	102.00
87	RHINOCEROS	CL	55.00	66.00
87	SMALL CIRCUS PUPPY	CL	28.00	33.00
87	SMALL PANDA	OP	58.00	58.00
87	SMALL PLAYFUL PUP	CL	32.00	32.00
87	SMALL POODLE	CL	35.00	42.00
87	SMALL RABBIT W/CARROT	CL	32.00	36.00
87	SMALL RACOON	CL	30.00	36.00
87	SMALL SNOWBUNNY	CL	25.00	30.00
87	WALRUS	CL	70.00	84.00
89	MINI RAINBOW DOG	CL	25.00	30.00
89	MINI RAINBOW OWL	CL	25.00	30.00
89	MINI RAINBOW PENGUIN	CL	25.00	30.00
89	MINI RAINBOW SQUIRREL	CL	25.00	30.00
91	SPIKE	CL	50.00	60.00
91	SPOT	CL	50.00	60.00
93	TURTLE	CL	65.00	65.00
94	CHEESE MOUSE	OP	53.00	53.00
94	SEAL	CL	46.00	46.00
95	TEA TIME	OP	50.00	50.00

YR NAME	LIMIT	ISSUE	TREND
T. SUZUKI	**ANIMAL FRIENDS COLLECTION**		
90 BABY DINOSAUR	CL	50.00	60.00
90 BARNEY DOG	CL	32.00	38.00
90 BETSY BUNNY	CL	32.00	38.00
90 CLARA COW	CL	32.00	38.00
90 GEORGIE GIRAFFE	CL	32.00	38.00
90 HENRY HIPPO	CL	32.00	38.00
90 JUMBO ELEPHANT	OP	32.00	32.00
90 MIKEY MONKEY	CL	32.00	38.00
90 PUPPY LOVE	CL	45.00	54.00
92 TRUMPETING ELEPHANT	CL	50.00	50.00
93 PLAYFUL SEAL	OP	42.00	42.00
93 PUPPY-GRAM	OP	70.00	70.00
94 MOZART	OP	48.00	48.00
94 PLAYFUL PUP	OP	53.00	53.00
94 SWEETIE	OP	28.00	28.00
94 WILBUR THE PIG	OP	48.00	48.00
95 FIDO THE DOG	OP	27.00	27.00
95 FIRSKY FIDO	CL	27.00	27.00
95 LING LING	OP	53.00	53.00
95 PERCY PIGLET	OP	19.00	19.00
N. MULARGIA	**BIRD COLLECTION**		
86 BIRD BATH	CL	54.00	65.00
R. NAKAI	**BIRD COLLECTION**		
83 LARGE OWL	CL	44.00	54.00
83 MEDIUM OWL	CL	50.00	60.00
83 MINI OWL	CL	20.00	25.00
83 SMALL OWL	CL	22.00	26.00
84 BIRD FAMILY	CL	22.00	26.00
84 LOVE BIRDS	CL	44.00	54.00
85 EXTRA LARGE PARROT	CL	300.00	360.00
85 SMALL PARROT	CL	100.00	120.00
87 LARGE PARROT	CL	130.00	160.00
I. NAKAMURA	**BIRD COLLECTION**		
93 SONGBIRDS	OP	95.00	95.00
T. SUZUKI	**BIRD COLLECTION**		
90 OLLIE OWL	CL	32.00	37.00
90 SMALL WISE OWL	CL	40.00	48.00
90 TREE TOP OWLS	CL	96.00	105.00
90 WISE OWLS	CL	55.00	65.00
91 PARROT COUPLE	CL	90.00	108.00
N. MULARGIA	**BY THE BEAUTIFUL SEA COLLECTION**		
87 PALM TREE	CL	160.00	190.00
93 HARBOR LIGHTHOUSE	OP	75.00	75.00
R. NAKAI	**BY THE BEAUTIFUL SEA COLLECTION**		
83 LARGE CRAB	CL	20.00	24.00
83 LARGE OYSTER	CL	30.00	36.00
83 MINI OYSTER	CL	12.00	15.00
83 SMALL CRAB	CL	28.00	33.00
83 SMALL OYSTER	CL	18.00	22.00
84 FISH	CL	36.00	43.00
88 DANCING DOLPHIN	CL	130.00	156.00
88 ISLAND PARADISE	CL	90.00	108.00
88 LARGE LIGHTHOUSE	CL	150.00	180.00
88 SMALL DOLPHIN	CL	55.00	65.00
88 SMALL ISLAND PARADISE	CL	50.00	60.00
88 SMALL LIGHTHOUSE	OP	80.00	80.00
91 BEAVER	CL	47.00	47.00
91 PENGUIN ON CUBE	CL	40.00	40.00
92 TROPICAL FISH	CL	95.00	95.00
92 TUXEDO PENGUIN	CL	75.00	75.00
93 EXTRA LARGE OYSTER W/PEARL	CL	75.00	75.00
93 SAILBOAT	OP	100.00	100.00
94 SEAL	CL	47.00	47.00
96 FREDDY FROG	OP	30.00	30.00
96 FRIEDA FROG	OP	37.00	37.00
96 PELICAN	OP	65.00	65.00
96 PENGUIN ON CUBE	OP	48.00	48.00
T. SUZUKI	**BY THE BEAUTIFUL SEA COLLECTION**		
88 HATCHING SEA TURTLE	OP	45.00	45.00
92 BABY SEAL	OP	21.00	21.00
92 CUTE CRAB	OP	27.00	27.00
92 PLAYFUL DOLPHINS	CL	60.00	60.00
92 SEASIDE PELICAN	CL	55.00	55.00
92 WHALES, THE	CL	60.00	72.00
93 PLAYFUL SEAL	OP	45.00	45.00
94 OSCAR OTTER	OP	105.00	105.00
N. MULARGIA	**BY THE LAKE COLLECTION**		
86 LOVE SWANS	OP	83.00	83.00
96 LARGE LOVE SWANS	OP	252.00	252.00
R. NAKAI	**BY THE LAKE COLLECTION**		
83 LARGE FROG	CL	30.00	36.00
83 MINI FROG	CL	14.00	17.00
83 SMALL FROG	CL	26.00	32.00
83 SMALL SWAN	CL	28.00	34.00
84 DUCK	CL	30.00	36.00
84 FROG & MUSHROOM	CL	46.00	55.00

YR	NAME	LIMIT	ISSUE	TREND
85	BUTTERFLY CATERPILLAR	CL	40.00	48.00
85	BUTTERFLY ON DAISY	CL	30.00	36.00
87	KING SWAN	CL	110.00	132.00
87	LARGE SWAN	CL	100.00	100.00
87	MEDIUM SWAN	OP	63.00	63.00
87	MINI SWAN	OP	28.00	28.00
87	SMALL SWAM	OP	32.00	32.00
87	SMALL SWAN	OP	47.00	47.00
90	DUCK FAMILY	CL	70.00	84.00
T. SUZUKI		**BY THE LAKE COLLECTION**		
90	SWAN FAMILY	CL	70.00	84.00
A. KATO		**CASTLES AND LEGENDS**		
91	MAJESTIC CASTLE	OP	390.00	390.00
N. MULARGIA		**CASTLES AND LEGENDS**		
90	I LOVE YOU UNICORN	CL	58.00	70.00
90	PEGASUS	CL	50.00	60.00
90	RAINBOW UNICORN	OP	50.00	50.00
90	UNICORN	CL	38.00	45.00
92	MINI FANTASY CASTLE	OP	40.00	40.00
95	LARGE FANTASY COACH	OP	368.00	368.00
95	MEDIUM FANTASY COACH	OP	158.00	158.00
95	MINI MOUSE CASTLE	OP	52.00	52.00
95	SMALL FANTASY COACH	OP	100.00	100.00
95	SMALL MOUSE COACH	OP	95.00	95.00
R. NAKAI		**CASTLES AND LEGENDS**		
87	ICE CASTLE	CL	150.00	180.00
87	RAINBOW CASTLE	OP	150.00	150.00
88	IMPERIAL CASTLE	OP	320.00	320.00
88	MYSTIC CASTLE	OP	90.00	90.00
88	SMALL ICE CASTLE	CL	90.00	108.00
89	DRAGON BABY	CL	80.00	96.00
89	MAGIC FAIRY	CL	40.00	48.00
89	MINI RAINBOW CASTLE	OP	60.00	60.00
89	STAR FAIRY	CL	65.00	78.00
89	STARLIGHT CASTLE	CL	155.00	185.00
89	UNICORN & FRIEND	CL	100.00	120.00
91	CASTLE IN THE SKY	CL	150.00	180.00
92	SMALL FANTASY CASTLE	OP	85.00	85.00
93	LARGE FANTASY CASTLE	OP	230.00	230.00
93	MEDIUM FANTASY CASTLE	OP	130.00	130.00
94	CASTLE RAINBOW RAINBOW MT. BS.	OP	1575.00	1575.00
94	CASTLE ROYALE/CLEAR MOUNTAIN BS.	OP	130.00	130.00
95	TREASURE CASTLE	OP	63.00	63.00
96	EMERALD CASTLE	OP	105.00	105.00
N. MULARGIA		**CLOWN COLLECTION**		
92	BABY CLOWN	CL	30.00	36.00
92	FLOWER CLOWN	CL	70.00	84.00
96	BO-BO THE CLOWN	OP	53.00	53.00
R. NAKAI		**CLOWN COLLECTION**		
85	ACROBATIC CLOWN	CL	50.00	60.00
85	BASEBALL CLOWN	CL	54.00	64.00
85	CLOWN ON UNICYCLE	CL	54.00	64.00
85	GOLF CLOWN	CL	54.00	65.00
85	JUGGLER	CL	54.00	65.00
85	LARGE CLOWN	CL	42.00	50.00
85	LARGE JACK IN THE BOX	CL	64.00	77.00
85	SMALL CLOWN	CL	30.00	36.00
85	SMALL JACK IN THE BOX	CL	24.00	29.00
85	TENNIS CLOWN	CL	54.00	65.00
N. MULARGIA		**DECORATIVE ITEM COLLECTION**		
94	SAN FRANCISCO DOME PAPERWEIGHT	CL	75.00	75.00
96	FABULOUS FIFTIES JUKEBOX	OP	79.00	79.00
R. NAKAI		**DECORATIVE ITEM COLLECTION**		
87	MED. EMPIRE STATE BLDG.	OP	290.00	290.00
87	MED. STATUE OF LIBERTY	OP	175.00	175.00
87	SMALL STATUE OF LIBERTY	OP	65.00	65.00
87	STATUE OF LIBERTY, THE	OP	365.00	365.00
88	NATIVITY PAPERWEIGHT	CL	100.00	120.00
90	LIBERTY ISLAND	OP	95.00	95.00
90	MANHATTAN ISLAND	OP	275.00	275.00
91	POLAR BEAR PAPERWEIGHT	OP	98.00	98.00
91	WORLD TRADE CENTER	CL	168.00	168.00
92	HEART CLOCK PAPERWEIGHT	CL	100.00	100.00
92	MANHATTAN REFLECTIONS	OP	95.00	95.00
92	NIAGARA FALLS PAPERWEIGHT	OP	85.00	85.00
92	SMALL TWIN TOWERS	OP	137.00	137.00
93	DIAMOND 100MM	OP	525.00	525.00
93	DIAMOND 50MM	OP	70.00	70.00
93	DIAMOND 75MM	OP	285.00	285.00
93	MANATEE PAPERWEIGHT	OP	125.00	125.00
93	SMALL MANHATTAN ISLAND	OP	105.00	105.00
94	NY SKYLINE CLOCK PAPERWEIGHT	CL	158.00	158.00
94	WASHINGTON DC SKYLINE CLOCK PAPERWEIGHT	CL	158.00	158.00
94	WASHINGTON DX CITYSCAPE PAPERWEIGHT	OP	105.00	105.00
94	WASHINGTON VIETNAM MEMORIAL PAPERWEIGHT	CL	105.00	105.00
95	BOSTON "CITYSCAPE" PAPERWEIGHT	OP	105.00	105.00
95	MED. BOSTON SKYLINE PAPERWEIGHT	OP	80.00	80.00
95	MED. CHICAGO SKYLINE CLOCK PAPERWEIGHT	CL	158.00	158.00

YR	NAME	LIMIT	ISSUE	TREND
95	MED. PHILADELPHIA SKYLINE PAPERWEIGHT	OP	80.00	80.00
95	PHILADELPHIA CITYSCAPE PAPERWEIGHT	OP	105.00	105.00
95	SAN FRANCISCO SKYLINE CLOCK PAPERWEIGHT	CL	158.00	158.00
96	CRYSTAL EGG AND STAND	OP	83.00	83.00
96	DIAMOND 40MM	OP	48.00	48.00
	I. NAKAMURA	**DECORATIVE ITEM COLLECTION**		
89	CHICAGO SKYLINE PAPERWEIGHT	OP	150.00	150.00
89	SAN FRANCISCO SKYLINE PAPERWEIGHT	OP	150.00	150.00
89	WASHINGTON SKYLINE PAPERWEIGHT	OP	150.00	150.00
90	BASEBALL PAPERWEIGHT	CL	170.00	195.00
90	FISHING PAPERWEIGHT	CL	170.00	195.00
90	GOLFING PAPERWEIGHT	CL	170.00	195.00
90	TENNIS PAPERWEIGHT	CL	170.00	190.00
91	DALLAS SKYLINE PAPERWEIGHT	OP	180.00	180.00
93	SMALL SAN FRANCISCO SKYLINE PAPERWEIGHT	OP	45.00	45.00
	G. VEITH	**DECORATIVE ITEM COLLECTION**		
88	NY SKYLINE PAPERWEIGHT	OP	100.00	100.00
88	SMALL EMPIRE STATE BLDG.	OP	120.00	120.00
92	SMALL NY PAPERWEIGHT	OP	45.00	45.00
94	MED. NY SKYLINE PAPERWEIGHT	OP	80.00	80.00
94	MED. SAN FRANCISCO SKYLINE PAPERWEIGHT	OP	80.00	80.00
94	MED. WASH. DC SKYLINE PAPERWEIGHT	OP	80.00	80.00
94	NY "CITYSCAPE" PAPERWEIGHT	OP	105.00	105.00
94	NY DOME PAPERWEIGHT	CL	75.00	75.00
94	SAN FRANCISCO CITYSCAPE PAPERWEIGHT	OP	105.00	105.00
94	WASHINGTON DC DOME PAPERWEIGHT	CL	75.00	75.00
	R. NAKAI	**FRUIT COLLECTION**		
85	LARGE APPLE	OP	44.00	44.00
85	MEDIUM APPLE	OP	30.00	30.00
85	PEAR	CL	30.00	36.00
85	SMALL APPLE	OP	15.00	15.00
85	STRAWBERRIES	CL	28.00	33.00
87	MINI APPLE	OP	15.00	15.00
91	LARGE PINEAPPLE	CL	42.00	50.00
91	MEDIUM PINEAPPLE	CL	27.00	33.00
91	SMALL PINEAPPLE	CL	16.00	19.00
93	MEDIUM APPLE W/RED HEART	OP	37.00	37.00
93	SMALL APPLE W/RED HEART	OP	21.00	21.00
96	PINEAPPLE	OP	53.00	53.00
	N. MULARGIA	**HOLIDAY TREASURE COLLECTION**		
86	NATIVITY	OP	150.00	150.00
	R. NAKAI	**HOLIDAY TREASURE COLLECTION**		
85	LARGE ANGEL	CL	30.00	30.00
85	LARGE CHRISTMAS TREE	OP	126.00	126.00
85	MINI ANGEL	CL	16.00	19.00
85	MINI CHRISTMAS TREE	CL	10.00	12.00
85	SMALL CHRISTMAS TREE	OP	50.00	50.00
87	LARGE RAINBOW CHRISTMAS TREE	CL	40.00	40.00
87	SMALL RAINBOW CHRISTMAS TREE	CL	25.00	25.00
90	TRUMPETING ANGEL	CL	60.00	72.00
94	CATHEDRAL W/RAINBOW BASE	OP	104.00	104.00
94	COUNTRY CHURCH	OP	53.00	53.00
94	COUNTRY CHURCH W/RAINBOW BASE	OP	63.00	63.00
94	EXTRA LARGE CHRISTMAS TREE	OP	315.00	315.00
94	MINI ANGEL	CL	25.00	25.00
94	SNOWMAN	CL	38.00	45.00
95	HAPPY BIRTHDAY CAKE	OP	63.00	63.00
95	LARGE ANGEL	OP	53.00	53.00
96	FROSTY	OP	41.00	41.00
	T. SUZUKI	**HOLIDAY TREASURE COLLECTION**		
91	HOLY ANGEL BLOWING A TRUMPET	OP	38.00	38.00
91	HOLY ANGEL HOLDING A CANDLE	OP	38.00	38.00
91	HOLY ANGEL PLAYING A HARP	OP	38.00	38.00
91	SMALL NATIVITY	OP	85.00	85.00
	A. KATO	**KITTY LAND COLLECTION**		
92	SEE SAW PALS	OP	40.00	40.00
	C. KIDO	**KITTY LAND COLLECTION**		
92	KITTEN IN BASKET	OP	35.00	35.00
	R. NAKAI	**KITTY LAND COLLECTION**		
84	CAT	CL	36.00	42.00
87	LARGE CAT W/BALL	CL	70.00	84.00
87	SMALL CAT W/BALL	CL	32.00	38.00
89	RAINBOW MINI CAT	CL	25.00	30.00
90	MOONLIGHT CATS	CL	100.00	120.00
91	ROCKABYE KITTY	OP	80.00	80.00
	T. SUZUKI	**KITTY LAND COLLECTION**		
90	CAT N MOUSE	CL	45.00	45.00
90	CURIOUS CAT, THE	OP	45.00	45.00
91	CALAMITY KITTY	OP	60.00	60.00
91	HELLO BIRDIE	OP	65.00	65.00
91	KITTY W/HEART	OP	27.00	27.00
91	LARGE CURIOUS CAT	OP	90.00	90.00
91	LITTY W/BUTTERFLY	OP	60.00	60.00
91	PEEKABOO KITTIES	OP	65.00	65.00
91	STROLLING KITTIES	CL	65.00	72.00
92	COUNTRY CAT	OP	60.00	60.00
92	PLAYFUL KITTY	OP	32.00	32.00

YR	NAME	LIMIT	ISSUE	TREND
93	KITTY KARE	OP	70.00	70.00
93	LARGE PLAYFUL KITTY	CL	50.00	50.00
93	PINKY	CL	50.00	50.00
95	MOONLIGHT KITTIES	OP	83.00	83.00
N. MULARGIA		**LIMITED EDITION COLLECTION**		
86	CRUCIFIX	CL	300.00	360.00
92	SANTA MARIA	CL	1000.00	1200.00
93	RIVERBOAT	350	570.00	600.00
93	VICTORIAN HOUSE	CL	190.00	190.00
96	MERRY-GO-AROUND	750	280.00	280.00
R. NAKAI		**LIMITED EDITION COLLECTION**		
85	EXTRA LG. EMPIRE STATE BLDG.	CL	1000.00	1200.00
87	LG. EMPIRE STATE BLDG.	2000	650.00	650.00
89	DREAM CASTLE	500	9000.00	9000.00
89	GRAND CASTLE	CL	2500.00	2500.00
91	ELLIS ISLAND	CL	450.00	540.00
92	WHITE HOUSE, THE	CL	3000.00	3600.00
93	ENCHANTED CASTLE	750	800.00	850.00
94	INDEPENDENCE HALL	750	370.00	370.00
96	EMPIRE STATE BLDG., THE	475	1315.00	1315.00
T. SUZUKI		**LIMITED EDITION COLLECTION**		
86	AIRPLANE	CL	400.00	480.00
86	EIFFEL TOWER, THE	2000	1000.00	1000.00
87	LG. US CAPITOL BLDG.	CL	1000.00	1200.00
87	TAJ MAHAL	2000	2000.00	2000.00
88	SMALL EIFFEL TOWER	2000	500.00	500.00
89	SPACE SHUTTLE LAUNCH	CL	900.00	1080.00
90	TOWER BRIDGE	CL	600.00	720.00
91	CRUISE SHIP	1000	2000.00	2000.00
93	COUNTRY GRISTMILL	1250	340.00	340.00
95	CLASSIC MOTORCYCLE	950	420.00	520.00
G. VEITH		**LIMITED EDITION COLLECTION**		
87	MANHATTANSCAPE	CL	1000.00	1200.00
A. KATO		**NEW YORK COLLECTION**		
92	LARGE CONTEMP. EMPIRE STATE BLDG.	CL	475.00	475.00
N. MULARGIA		**NEW YORK COLLECTION**		
87	SMALL STATUE OF LIBERTY	OP	50.00	50.00
89	LIBERTY ISLAND	OP	75.00	75.00
93	HOLIDAY EMPIRE STATE BLDG.	OP	205.00	205.00
93	SMALL MANHATTAN ISLAND	OP	105.00	105.00
R. NAKAI		**NEW YORK COLLECTION**		
85	STATUE OF LIBERTY, THE	OP	250.00	250.00
87	MED. EMPIRE STATE BLDG.	OP	250.00	250.00
87	MED. STATUE OF LIBERTY	OP	120.00	120.00
87	SMALL EMPIRE STATE BLDG.	OP	120.00	120.00
90	MANHATTAN ISLAND	OP	240.00	240.00
91	MINI EMPIRE STATE BLDG.	OP	60.00	60.00
91	WORLD TRADE CENTER BLDG.	OP	170.00	170.00
92	MED. CONTEMP. EMPIRE STATE BLDG.	OP	170.00	170.00
92	MINI EMPIRE STATE BLDG. W/WINDOWS	OP	74.00	74.00
92	MINI STATUE OF LIBERTY	OP	50.00	50.00
92	SMALL CONTEMP. EMPIRE ST. BLDG. MV	CL	95.00	95.00
92	SMALL CONTEMP. EMPIRE STATE BLDG.	CL	95.00	95.00
92	SMALL TWIN TOWERS	OP	130.00	130.00
93	SMALL RAINBOW CONTEMP. EMPIRE	OP	95.00	95.00
95	CHRYSLEY BLDG.	OP	275.00	275.00
N. MULARGIA		**RELIGIOUS MOMENT COLLECTION**		
87	CROSS ON MOUNTAIN	CL	30.00	36.00
87	CRUCIFIX	CL	50.00	60.00
87	CRUCIFIX ON MOUNTAIN	CL	40.00	48.00
87	SMALL CROSS	CL	40.00	48.00
88	LARGE CROSS ON MOUNTAIN	CL	85.00	100.00
92	CROSS W/ROSE	CL	30.00	30.00
95	CROSS	OP	32.00	32.00
R. NAKAI		**RELIGIOUS MOMENT COLLECTION**		
87	FACE OF CHRIST	CL	35.00	42.00
87	STAR OF DAVID	CL	40.00	48.00
I. NAKAMURA		**RELIGIOUS MOMENT COLLECTION**		
92	PEACE ON EARTH	CL	95.00	95.00
T. SUZUKI		**RELIGIOUS MOMENT COLLECTION**		
87	CHURCH	CL	40.00	40.00
N. MULARGIA		**SPRING PARADE COLLECTION**		
89	WEDDING COUPLE	OP	75.00	75.00
92	CANDLEHOLDER	CL	125.00	125.00
92	HALF DZ. FLOWER ARRANGEMENT	CL	20.00	20.00
92	HAPPY HEART	CL	25.00	25.00
92	LONG STEM ROSE	OP	35.00	35.00
92	LOVING HEARTS	OP	35.00	35.00
92	MINI WEDDING COUPLE	OP	30.00	30.00
92	WATERFRONT VILLAGE	OP	190.00	190.00
94	RAINBOW ROSE	OP	82.00	82.00
95	DESERT CACTUS	OP	48.00	48.00
95	MEDIUM WEDDING COUPLE	OP	63.00	63.00
96	AMERICAN BEAUTY ROSE	OP	53.00	53.00
R. NAKAI		**SPRING PARADE COLLECTION**		
85	FLOWER BASKET	CL	50.00	60.00
85	WEDDING COUPLE	OP	38.00	38.00

YR	NAME	LIMIT	ISSUE	TREND
87	RED ROSE	OP	35.00	35.00
87	WHITE ROSE	CL	35.00	42.00
89	LARGE WINDMILL	CL	160.00	190.00
89	SMALL WINDMILL	CL	90.00	108.00
89	SPRING CHICK	OP	50.00	50.00
90	CROCUS	CL	45.00	54.00
91	MINI WINDMILL	CL	63.00	75.00
91	RAINBOW MINI BUTTERFLY	OP	27.00	27.00
94	ENCHANTED ROSE, THE	OP	126.00	126.00
94	LONG STEM ROSE IN VASE	OP	82.00	82.00
95	PINK ROSE	OP	53.00	53.00
95	PINK ROSE IN VASE	OP	41.00	41.00
95	SPRING BUTTERFLY	OP	62.00	62.00
96	SMALL ROSE BOUQUET	OP	45.00	45.00
96	WATER LILY, MEDIUM, AB	OP	210.00	210.00
I. NAKAMURA		**SPRING PARADE COLLECTION**		
90	AFRICAN VIOLET	OP	32.00	32.00
90	HYACINTH	OP	50.00	50.00
90	ROSE BASKET	CL	52.00	61.00
92	BARREL CACUS	CL	45.00	45.00
92	FLOWERING CACTUS	CL	58.00	58.00
93	SONGBIRDS	OP	90.00	90.00
T. SUZUKI		**SPRING PARADE COLLECTION**		
91	BLOSSOM BUNNY	OP	42.00	42.00
91	BUNNIES ON ICE	CL	58.00	58.00
91	BUNNY BUDDY W/CARROTT	OP	32.00	32.00
91	CHEEP CHEEP	OP	35.00	35.00
92	CUTE BUNNY	CL	38.00	38.00
92	HUMMINGBIRD	OP	58.00	58.00
92	MINI HUMMINGBIRD	OP	29.00	29.00
92	SPRING FLOWERS	OP	40.00	40.00
R. KIDO			**TEDDYLAND COLLECTION**	
91	PLAYGROUND TEDDY	CL	90.00	108.00
N. MULARGIA			**TEDDYLAND COLLECTION**	
86	MINI TEDDY	CL	15.00	18.00
87	BEACH TEDDIES	OP	60.00	60.00
87	LOVING TEDDIES	OP	75.00	75.00
87	SAILING TEDDIES	OP	100.00	100.00
87	TEETER TOTTER TEDDIES	CL	65.00	77.00
88	I LOVE YOU TEDDY	OP	50.00	50.00
88	LARGE BOUQUET TEDDY	CL	50.00	60.00
88	SMALL BOUQUET TEDDY	OP	35.00	35.00
88	TEDDIES AT EIGHT	OP	100.00	100.00
88	TEDDY FAMILY	CL	50.00	60.00
88	TOURING TEDDIES	OP	90.00	90.00
88	WINTER TEDDIES	CL	90.00	108.00
89	SHIPWRECK TEDDIES	CL	100.00	120.00
90	MOUNTAINEER TEDDY	CL	80.00	96.00
90	RAINBOW TEDDIES	CL	95.00	112.00
90	ROCKING HORSE TEDDY	CL	80.00	96.00
90	SMALL LOVING TEDDIES	OP	60.00	60.00
91	SWINGING TEDDY	OP	100.00	100.00
92	ICE CREAM TEDDIES	OP	55.00	55.00
92	PATRIOTIC TEDDY	OP	30.00	30.00
92	SMALL BEACH TEDDIES	OP	55.00	55.00
93	BLACK JACK TEDDIES	OP	97.00	97.00
94	I LOVE YOU TEDDY COUPLE	OP	95.00	95.00
95	COMPUBEAR	OP	63.00	63.00
R. NAKAI			**TEDDYLAND COLLECTION**	
83	LARGE TEDDY BEAR	CL	68.00	75.00
83	MEDIUM TEDDY BEAR	CL	44.00	53.00
83	SMALL TEDDY BEAR	CL	28.00	35.00
85	MOTHER AND CUB	CL	64.00	77.00
87	SKATEBOARD TEDDY	CL	30.00	36.00
87	SKIING TEDDY	OP	50.00	50.00
87	SURFING TEDDY	CL	45.00	54.00
87	TEDDY BEAR CHRISTMAS	OP	100.00	100.00
88	LARGE SURFING TEDDY	CL	80.00	96.00
88	TEDDIES W/HEART	OP	45.00	45.00
89	GOLFING TEDDIES	OP	100.00	100.00
89	HAPPY BIRTHDAY TEDDY	OP	50.00	50.00
89	RAINBOW MINI BEAR	CL	25.00	30.00
89	SPEEDBOAT TEDDIES	OP	90.00	90.00
89	TEDDY W/BALLOON	CL	70.00	84.00
89	VANITY TEDDU	CL	100.00	120.00
89	WINDSURFING TEDDY	CL	85.00	102.00
91	LUCK OF THE IRISH	CL	60.00	72.00
91	SMALL TEDDY W/RED HEART	OP	42.00	42.00
91	TRIM A TREE TEDDY	CL	50.00	50.00
94	TEDDY BEAR	OP	63.00	63.00
94	TEDDY BEAR W/RAINBOW BASE	OP	75.00	75.00
95	GET WELL TEDDY	CL	48.00	48.00
95	I LOVE YOU TEDDY W/LG. HEART	OP	48.00	48.00
96	CUDDLY BEAR	OP	48.00	48.00
H. SERINO			**TEDDYLAND COLLECTION**	
91	SCHOOL BEARS	CL	75.00	90.00
T. SUZUKI			**TEDDYLAND COLLECTION**	
90	BARON VON TEDDY	CL	60.00	72.00

YR	NAME	LIMIT	ISSUE	TREND
90	CHOO CHOO TEDDY	CL	100.00	120.00
90	STORYTIME TEDDIES	OP	70.00	70.00
90	TRICYCLE TEDDY	CL	40.00	48.00
91	CHRISTMAS WREATH TEDDY	CL	70.00	84.00
91	GUMBALL TEDDY	CL	63.00	63.00
91	HEART BEAR	OP	27.00	27.00
91	HIGH CHAIR TEDDY	CL	75.00	90.00
91	MERRY CHRISTMAS TEDDY	OP	55.00	55.00
91	MY FAVORITE PICTURE	OP	45.00	45.00
91	PLAY IT AGAIN TED	OP	65.00	65.00
91	SANTA BEAR CHRISTMAS	OP	70.00	70.00
91	SANTA BEAR SLEIGHRIDE	OP	70.00	70.00
91	SCUBA BEAR	CL	65.00	78.00
92	BILLARD BUDDIES	OP	70.00	70.00
92	SINGING BABY BEAR	OP	55.00	55.00
93	FLOWER TEDDY	OP	50.00	50.00
95	BABY'S BEAR'S CHRISTMAS	OP	48.00	48.00
95	FLY A KITE TEDDY	OP	41.00	41.00
95	TEDDY'S SELF PORTRAIT	OP	53.00	53.00
R. NAKAI		**THE GAMBLER COLLECTION**		
91	LUCKY 7	CL	50.00	60.00
91	MINI SLOT MACHINE	OP	30.00	30.00
91	SMALL DICE	OP	27.00	27.00
92	MINI ROLLING DICE	OP	32.00	32.00
93	LARGE ROLLING DICE	OP	60.00	60.00
93	MEDIUM ROLLING DICE	OP	48.00	48.00
93	SMALL ROLLING DICE	CL	40.00	40.00
94	LUCKY ROLL	OP	95.00	95.00
94	SUPER SLOT	OP	295.00	295.00
T. SUZUKI		**THE GAMBLER COLLECTION**		
91	LARGE SLOT MACHINE	OP	83.00	83.00
91	SMALL SLOT MACHINE	OP	70.00	70.00
N. MULARGIA		**THE VOYAGE COLLECTION**		
91	RAINBOW EXPRESS, THE	CL	125.00	150.00
91	SCHOONER	CL	95.00	95.00
92	SAILING SHIP	OP	38.00	38.00
93	EXPRESS TRAIN	CL	95.00	114.00
95	MINI CRUISE SHIP	OP	105.00	105.00
R. NAKAI		**THE VOYAGE COLLECTION**		
84	CLASSIC CAR	CL	160.00	192.00
84	LIMOUSINE	CL	46.00	55.00
84	PICKUP TRACK	CL	38.00	48.00
84	TRACTOR TRAILER	CL	40.00	48.00
90	SQUARE RIGGER	OP	250.00	250.00
93	LARGE SAN FRANCISCO CABLE CAR	OP	59.00	59.00
93	SMALL SAN FRANCISCO CABLE CAR	OP	40.00	40.00
94	BERMUDA RIG SAILBOAT	OP	105.00	105.00
94	MAINSAIL SAILBOAT	OP	230.00	230.00
94	SMALL RIVERBOAT	OP	210.00	210.00
94	SPINMAKER SAILBOAT	OP	265.00	265.00
95	AMISH BUGGY	OP	160.00	160.00
95	AMISH BUGGY W/WOOD BASE	OP	190.00	190.00
95	TALL SHIP	OP	395.00	395.00
T. SUZUKI		**THE VOYAGE COLLECTION**		
84	SPORTS CAR	CL	140.00	170.00
84	TOURING CAR	CL	140.00	170.00
90	LARGE TRAIN SET	CL	480.00	575.00
90	ORBITING SPACE SHUTTLE	OP	300.00	300.00
90	SMALL AIRPLANE	CL	200.00	240.00
90	SMALL SPACE SHUTTLE LAUNCH	CL	265.00	265.00
90	SMALL TRAIN SET	OP	100.00	100.00
91	LARGE CABLE CAR	OP	130.00	130.00
91	SMALL CABLE CAR	OP	70.00	70.00
91	SMALL ORBITING SPACE SHUTTLE	OP	90.00	90.00
92	FIRE ENGINE	OP	100.00	100.00
92	MINI BI-PLANE	OP	65.00	65.00
92	MINI CABLE CAR	CL	40.00	40.00
94	SMALL CRUISE SHIP	OP	575.00	575.00
96	SMALL CLASSIC MOTORCYCLE	OP	210.00	210.00
N. MULARGIA		**WONDERS OF THE WORLD COLLECTION**		
86	SMALL SPACE NEEDLE	CL	50.00	50.00
93	SMALL CAPITOL BLDG.	OP	100.00	100.00
94	SMALL WHITE HOUSE W/OCT. MIRROR	OP	185.00	185.00
R. NAKAI		**WONDERS OF THE WORLD COLLECTION**		
86	LARGE SPACE NEEDLE	CL	160.00	160.00
86	TAJ MAHAL	OP	1050.00	1050.00
87	US CAPITOL BLDG.	OP	250.00	250.00
93	SEARS TOWER	OP	150.00	150.00
95	LIBERTY BELL, THE	OP	160.00	160.00
95	MEDIUM TAJ MAHAL	OP	790.00	790.00
95	SMALL TAJ MAHAL	OP	215.00	215.00
T. SUZUKI		**WONDERS OF THE WORLD COLLECTION**		
90	LE PETIT EIFFEL	OP	240.00	240.00
91	CHICAGO WATER TOWER W/BASE	OP	300.00	300.00
91	CHICAGO WATER TOWER W/O BASE	CL	280.00	280.00

YR	NAME	LIMIT	ISSUE	TREND
CYBIS				
*				**ANIMAL KINGDOM**
*	BULL	100	150.00	4500.00
61	HORSE	100	150.00	2000.00
65	RACCOON, RAFFLES	CL	110.00	365.00
65	SQUIRREL, MR. FLUFFY TAIL	CL	90.00	345.00
66	THOROUGHBRED	350	425.00	1450.00
67	KITTEN, BLUE RIBBON	CL	95.00	500.00
68	BEAR	CL	85.00	400.00
68	BUFFALO	CL	115.00	180.00
68	ELEPHANT	100	600.00	5000.00
68	SNAIL, SIR ESCARGOT	CL	50.00	290.00
68	STALLION	350	475.00	845.00
69	COLTS, DARBY & JOAN	CL	295.00	475.00
70	DEER MOUSE IN CLOVER	CL	65.00	160.00
71	AMERICAN BULLFROG	CL	250.00	600.00
71	APPALOOSA COLT	CL	150.00	300.00
71	NASHUA	100	2000.00	3000.00
72	PINTO COLT	CL	175.00	250.00
75	AMERICAN WHITE BUFFALO	250	1250.00	4000.00
75	KITTEN, TABITHA	CL	90.00	150.00
75	KITTEN, TOPAZ	CL	90.00	150.00
76	BUNNY, MUFFET	CL	85.00	140.00
76	CHIPMUNK WITH BLOODROOT	225	625.00	675.00
76	PRAIRIE DOG	CL	245.00	345.00
77	BUNNY PAT-A-CAKE	CL	90.00	145.00
78	DORMOUSE MAXIMILLIAN	CL	250.00	275.00
78	DORMOUSE MAXINE	CL	195.00	225.00
78	PINKY BUNNY/CARROT	200	200.00	265.00
80	ARCTIC WHITE FOX	100	4500.00	4700.00
80	SQUIRREL, HIGHRISE	400	475.00	525.00
81	BEAVERS, EGBERT & BREWSTER	400	285.00	335.00
82	DALL SHEEP	50	*	4250.00
84	AUSTRALIAN SULPHER CRESTED COCKATOO	25	9850.00	9850.00
84	CHANTILLY, KITTEN	OP	175.00	210.00
85	BAXTER & DOYLE	400	450.00	450.00
85	BEAGLES, BRANIGAN & CLANCY	OP	375.00	600.00
85	BUNNY, SNOWFLAKE	OP	65.00	75.00
85	ELEPHANT, WILLOUGHBY	OP	195.00	245.00
85	MONDAY, RHINOCEROS	OP	85.00	145.00
86	DAPPLE GREY FOAL	OP	195.00	225.00
86	HUEY, THE HARMONIOUS HARE	OP	175.00	275.00
86	MICK, THE MELODIOUS MUTT	OP	175.00	275.00
86	WHITE-TAILED DEER	50	9500.00	11500.00
*				**BIBLICAL**
*	HOLYWATER FONT, HOLY GHOST	CL	15.00	150.00
56	HOLY CHILD OF PRAGUE	10	1500.00	75000.00
57	MADONNA, HOUSE OF GOLD	8	125.00	4025.00
60	EXODUS	50	350.00	2600.00
60	FLIGHT INTO EGYPT	50	175.00	2525.00
60	MADONNA LACE AND ROSE	OP	15.00	300.00
60	PROPHET, THE	50	250.00	3550.00
63	MOSES THE GREAT LAWGIVER	750	250.00	5550.00
64	NATIVITY, MARY	OP	*	350.00
64	ST. PETER	500	*	1275.00
76	NOAH	500	975.00	3025.00
84	CHRIST CHILD WITH LAMB	OP	*	290.00
84	NATIVITY, ANGEL, COLOR	OP	395.00	600.00
84	NATIVITY, CAMEL, COLOR	OP	625.00	850.00
84	NATIVITY, JOSEPH	OP	*	350.00
84	NATIVITY, SHEPHERD, COLOR	OP	395.00	500.00
85	NATIVITY, COW, COLOR	OP	175.00	200.00
85	NATIVITY, COW, WHITE	OP	125.00	250.00
85	NATIVITY, DONKEY, COLOR	OP	195.00	250.00
85	NATIVITY, DONKEY, WHITE	OP	130.00	175.00
85	NATIVITY, LAMB, COLOR	OP	150.00	200.00
85	NATIVITY, LAMB, WHITE	OP	115.00	150.00
*				**BIRDS & FLOWERS**
*	BIRDS & FLOWERS	250	500.00	4550.00
*	BUTTERFLY W/DOGWOOD	200	*	375.00
*	SANDPIPERS	400	700.00	1450.00
*	SKYLARKS	350	330.00	1750.00
57	TURTLE DOVES	500	350.00	4950.00
59	HUMMINGBIRD	CL	95.00	1000.00
60	BLUE-HEADED VIRIO (BUILDING NEST)	CL	60.00	1150.00
60	BLUE-HEADED VIRIO W/LILAC	275	1200.00	2250.00
60	PHEASANT	150	750.00	5050.00
61	BLUE-GREY GNATCATCHERS (PAIR)	200	400.00	2550.00
61	GOLDEN CLARION LILY	100	250.00	4550.00
62	DUCKLING (BABY BROTHER)	CL	35.00	140.00
62	SPARROW ON LOG	CL	35.00	475.00
63	IRIS	250	500.00	4550.00
63	MAGNOLIA	CL	350.00	1000.00
64	DAHLIA YELLOW	350	450.00	1850.00
64	GREAT WHITE HERON	350	850.00	3700.00
65	CHRISTMAS ROSE	500	250.00	750.00
68	CALLA LILY	500	750.00	1750.00
68	NARCISSUS	500	350.00	550.00

YR	NAME	LIMIT	ISSUE	TREND
68	WOOD DUCK	500	325.00	800.00
69	CLEMATIS W/HOUSE WREN	350	1300.00	1450.00
70	DUTCH CROCUS	350	550.00	775.00
70	MUSHROOM W/BUTTERFLY	CL	225.00	475.00
71	LITTLE BLUE HERON	500	425.00	1500.00
72	AMERICAN CRESTED IRIS	400	975.00	1200.00
72	AUTUMN DOGWOOD W/CHICKADEES	350	1100.00	1250.00
72	PANSIES W/CHINA MAID	1000	275.00	360.00
74	GOLDEN WINGED WARBLER	200	1075.00	1200.00
75	GREAT HORNED OWL (COLOR)	50	3250.00	7550.00
75	GREAT HORNED OWL (WHITE)	150	1950.00	4450.00
75	PANSIES W/CHINOLINA LADY	750	295.00	425.00
76	AMERICAN WHITE TURKEY	75	1450.00	1650.00
76	AMERICAN WILD TURKEY	75	1950.00	2250.00
76	COLONIAL BASKET	100	2750.00	5550.00
76	CONSTANCY FLOWER BASKET	CL	345.00	425.00
76	DEVOTION FLOWER BASKET	CL	345.00	450.00
76	FELICITY FLOWER BASKET	CL	325.00	350.00
76	MAJESTY FLOWER BASKET	CL	345.00	425.00
77	APPLE BLOSSOMS	400	350.00	600.00
77	CLEMATIS	CL	210.00	350.00
77	DUCKLING (BUTTERCUP & DAFFODIL)	CL	165.00	300.00
77	HERMIT THRUSH	150	1450.00	1500.00
77	KRESTREL	175	1875.00	2000.00
78	KINGLETS ON PYRACANTHA	175	900.00	1150.00
78	NESTLING BLUEBIRDS	CL	235.00	260.00
80	YELLOW CONDESA ROSE	CL	*	255.00
80	YELLOW ROSE	CL	80.00	440.00
82	SPRING BOUQUET	200	750.00	1000.00
85	AMERICAN BALD EAGLE	300	2900.00	3600.00
85	SCREECH OWL & SIBLINGS	100	3250.00	4000.00
*			**CAROUSEL-CIRCUS**	
73	CAROUSEL GOAT	325	875.00	1700.00
73	CAROUSEL HORSE	325	925.00	7550.00
74	LION	325	1025.00	1325.00
74	TIGER	325	925.00	1475.00
75	BARNABY, BEAR	CL	165.00	315.00
75	BICENTENNIAL HORSE TICONDEROGA	350	925.00	4050.00
75	BOSUN, MONKEY	CL	195.00	400.00
76	FUNNY FACE, CHILD HEAD/HOLLY	CL	325.00	750.00
76	PERFORMING PONY, POPPY	1000	325.00	1250.00
76	SEBASTIAN, SEAL	CL	195.00	225.00
77	DANDY, DANCING DOG	CL	145.00	300.00
81	BEAR, BERNHARD	325	1125.00	1175.00
81	BULL, PLUTUS	325	1125.00	2100.00
81	FROLLO	1000	750.00	850.00
81	PONY	750	975.00	1000.00
82	GIRAFFE	750	*	1800.00
84	PHINEAS, CIRCUS ELEPHANT	OP	325.00	450.00
85	CAROUSEL UNICORN	325	1275.00	2700.00
85	CIRCUS RIDER EQUESTRIENNE EXTRAORDINAIRE	150	2275.00	3550.00
85	JUMBLES AND FRIEND	750	675.00	750.00
85	VALENTINE	OP	335.00	400.00
86	PIERRE, THE PERFORMING POODLE	OP	225.00	300.00
*			**CHILDREN OF THE WORLD**	
72	ESKIMO CHILD HEAD	CL	165.00	425.00
75	INDIAN BOY HEAD	CL	425.00	925.00
75	INDIAN GIRL HEAD	CL	325.00	925.00
77	JEREMY	CL	315.00	500.00
78	JASON	CL	285.00	370.00
78	JENNIFER	CL	325.00	400.00
79	JESSICA	CL	325.00	500.00
*			**CHILDREN TO CHERISH**	
*	FIRST BOUQUET	250	150.00	325.00
57	THUMBELINA	CL	45.00	525.00
58	PETER PAN	CL	80.00	1000.00
59	TINKERBELL	CL	95.00	1500.00
60	BALLERINA, RED SHOES	CL	75.00	1250.00
62	HEIDI, COLOR	CL	165.00	575.00
62	HEIDI, WHITE	CL	165.00	575.00
63	BALLERINA ON CUE	CL	150.00	675.00
63	SPRINGTIME	CL	45.00	775.00
64	ALICE IN WONDERLAND	CL	50.00	850.00
64	REBECCA	CL	110.00	350.00
66	FIRST FLIGHT	CL	50.00	500.00
68	BABY BUST	239	375.00	1050.00
68	BALLERINA, LITTLE PRINCESS	CL	125.00	725.00
71	POLLYANNA	CL	195.00	575.00
72	RAPUNZEL, PINK	1000	425.00	1100.00
73	GOLDILOCKS	CL	145.00	500.00
73	LITTLE RED RIDING HOOD	CL	110.00	465.00
74	GRETEL	CL	260.00	420.00
74	HANSEL	CL	270.00	525.00
74	MARY, MARY	500	475.00	750.00
75	RAPUNZEL, APRICOT	1500	475.00	1200.00
75	RAPUNZEL, LILAC	1000	675.00	1000.00
75	WENDY WITH FLOWERS	*	250.00	425.00
75	YANKEE DOODLE DANDY	CL	275.00	350.00

YR	NAME	LIMIT	ISSUE	TREND
76	ELIZABETH ANN	CL	195.00	275.00
76	MELISSA	OP	285.00	425.00
77	BOYS PLAYING MARBLES	CL	285.00	400.00
78	ALICE (SEATED)	CL	350.00	540.00
78	ALLEGRA	CL	310.00	375.00
78	EDITH	CL	310.00	350.00
78	LISA AND LYNETTE	CL	395.00	470.00
78	LITTLE BOY BLUE	CL	425.00	525.00
80	LITTLE MISS MUFFET	CL	335.00	400.00
81	FLEURETTE	1000	725.00	1100.00
82	ROBIN	1000	475.00	900.00
82	SLEEPING BEAUTY	750	695.00	1500.00
84	CHOIRBOY, THE	OP	325.00	350.00
84	JACK IN THE BEANSTALK	750	575.00	600.00
84	LITTLE CHAMP	OP	325.00	400.00
84	MICHAEL	OP	235.00	375.00
85	BALLERINA, RECITAL	OP	275.00	300.00
85	BALLERINA, SWANILDA	OP	450.00	700.00
85	BETH	OP	235.00	300.00
85	CLARA	OP	395.00	400.00
85	FELECIA	OP	425.00	550.00
85	FIGURE EIGHT	750	625.00	800.00
85	JODY	OP	235.00	300.00
85	MARGUERITE	OP	425.00	550.00
85	RECITAL	OP	275.00	300.00
85	VANESSA	OP	425.00	550.00
86	CLARISSA	OP	165.00	200.00
86	ENCORE, FIGURE SKATER	750	625.00	670.00
86	KITRI	OP	450.00	575.00
86	LULLABY, BLUE	OP	125.00	175.00
86	LULLABY, IVORY	OP	125.00	175.00
86	LULLABY, PINK	OP	125.00	175.00
87	PANDORA BLUE	CL	265.00	350.00
*				**COMMEMORATIVE**
67	COLUMBIA	200	1000.00	2500.00
67	CONDUCTOR'S HANDS	250	250.00	1500.00
69	APOLLO II MOON MISSION	111	1500.00	2500.00
71	CREE INDIAN	100	2500.00	5500.00
72	CHESS SET	10	30000.00	60000.00
75	GEORGE WASHINGTON BUST	CL	275.00	350.00
77	OCEANIA	200	1250.00	1500.00
80	BRIDE, THE	100	6500.00	10500.00
81	ARION, DOLPHIN RIDER	1000	575.00	1200.00
81	KATERI TAKAKWITHA	100	2875.00	3000.00
81	PHOENIX	100	950.00	1000.00
84	1984 CYBIS HOLIDAY	OP	145.00	150.00
84	CREE INDIAN, MAGIC BOY	200	4250.00	5000.00
85	HOLIDAY ORNAMENT	OP	75.00	100.00
85	LIBERTY	100	1875.00	4000.00
86	1986 COMMEMORATIVE EGG	OP	365.00	375.00
86	LITTLE MISS LIBERTY	OP	295.00	350.00
*				**EVERYONE'S FUN TIME (LIMNETTES)**
72	COUNTRY FAIR	500	125.00	200.00
72	POND, THE	500	125.00	200.00
72	SEASHORE, THE	500	125.00	200.00
72	WINDY DAY	500	125.00	200.00
*				**FANTASIA**
69	UNICORN	500	1250.00	3800.00
74	CYBELE	500	675.00	675.00
74	FANTASIA	500	675.00	800.00
77	SEA KING'S STEED, OCEANIA	200	1250.00	1500.00
77	UNICORNS, GAMBOL AND FROLIC	1000	425.00	2300.00
78	SATIN HORSE HEAD	500	1100.00	2850.00
78	SHARMAINE, SEA NYMPH	250	1450.00	1650.00
80	PEGASUS	500	1450.00	3800.00
80	PEGASUS, FREE SPIRIT	1000	675.00	775.00
81	DESIREE, WHITE DEER	400	575.00	600.00
81	PRINCE BROCADE UNICORN	500	2200.00	2650.00
82	THERON	350	675.00	850.00
84	FLIGHT AND FANCY	1000	975.00	1175.00
85	DORE'	1000	575.00	1100.00
*				**LAND OF CHEMERIC**
77	MARIGOLD	CL	185.00	525.00
77	QUEEN TITANIA	750	725.00	2500.00
77	TIFFIN	CL	175.00	525.00
79	PIP, ELFIN PLAYER	1000	450.00	675.00
81	MELODY	1000	725.00	800.00
85	OBERON	750	825.00	850.00
*				**NORTH AMERICAN INDIAN**
69	BLACKFEET, BEAVERHEAD MEDICINE MAN	500	2000.00	2800.00
69	DAKOTA, MINNEHAHA LAUGHING WATER	500	1500.00	2500.00
69	ONONDAGA, HIAWATHA	500	1500.00	2450.00
71	SHOSHONE, SACAJAWEA	500	2250.00	2800.00
73	ESKIMO MOTHER	200	1875.00	2700.00
73	IRIQUOIS, AT THE COUNCIL FIRE	500	4250.00	5000.00
74	APACHE, CHATO	350	1950.00	3300.00
77	CROW DANCER	200	3875.00	8500.00
79	GREAT SPIRIT, WANKAN TANKA	200	3500.00	4200.00

YR	NAME	LIMIT	ISSUE	TREND
82	CHOCTAW, TASCULUSA	200	2475.00	4100.00
85	YAQUI, DEER DANCER	200	2095.00	2800.00
*			**PORTRAITS IN PORCELAIN**	
65	BEATRICE	700	225.00	1800.00
65	JULIET	800	175.00	4000.00
67	FOLK SINGER	283	300.00	900.00
67	GUINEVERE	800	250.00	2350.00
68	HAMLET	500	350.00	2000.00
68	SCARLETT	500	450.00	4000.00
69	OPHELIA	800	750.00	4400.00
71	ELEANOR OF AQUITAINE	750	875.00	4250.00
72	KWAN YIN	350	1250.00	2000.00
73	BALLET-PRINCE FLORIMOND	200	975.00	1100.00
73	BALLET-PRINCESS AURORA	200	1125.00	1500.00
73	PORTIA	750	825.00	3800.00
74	QUEEN ESTHER	750	925.00	1800.00
75	LADY MACBETH	750	850.00	1300.00
76	ABIGAIL ADAMS	600	875.00	1300.00
76	PRISCILLA	500	825.00	1500.00
78	GOOD QUEEN ANNE	350	975.00	1500.00
79	BERENGARIA	500	1450.00	3500.00
79	NEFERTITI	500	2100.00	3000.00
81	JANE EYRE	500	975.00	1500.00
82	DESDEMONA	500	1850.00	4000.00
82	LADY GODIVA	200	1875.00	3200.00
82	PERSEPHONE	200	3250.00	5200.00
84	BATHSHEBA	500	1975.00	3300.00
85	KING ARTHUR	350	2350.00	3400.00
85	KING DAVID	350	1475.00	2200.00
85	PAGLIACCI	OP	325.00	350.00
85	ROMEO AND JULIET	300	2200.00	3400.00
85	TRISTAN AND ISOLDE	200	2200.00	2200.00
86	CARMEN	500	1675.00	2000.00
*			**SPORT SCENES**	
80	JOGGER, FEMALE	CL	345.00	450.00
80	JOGGER, MALE	CL	395.00	600.00
*			**THE WONDERFUL SEASONS (LIMNETTES)**	
72	AUTUMN	500	125.00	200.00
72	SPRING	500	125.00	200.00
72	SUMMER	500	125.00	200.00
72	WINTER	500	125.00	200.00
*			**THEATRE OF PORCELAIN**	
78	COURT JESTER	250	1450.00	1800.00
80	HARLEQUIN	250	1575.00	1900.00
81	COLUMBINE	250	2250.00	2300.00
81	PUCK	250	2300.00	2500.00
*			**WHEN BELLS ARE RINGING (LIMNETTES)**	
72	EASTER EGG HUNT	500	125.00	200.00
72	INDEPENDENCE CELEBRATION	500	125.00	200.00
72	MERRY CHRISTMAS	500	125.00	200.00
72	SABBATH MORNING	500	125.00	200.00

DANBURY MINT

YR	NAME	LIMIT	ISSUE	TREND
N. ROCKWELL			**ROCKWELL FIGURINES**	
80	BOY ON STILTS	CL	55.00	60.00
80	CAUGHT IN THE ACT	CL	55.00	75.00
80	GRAMPS AT THE REINS	CL	55.00	75.00
80	GRANDPA SNOWMAN	CL	55.00	60.00
80	TRICK OR TREAT	CL	55.00	60.00
80	YOUNG LOVE	CL	55.00	125.00

DAVE GROSSMAN CREATIONS

YR	NAME	LIMIT	ISSUE	TREND
93	AFTER THE PROM	7500	75.00	85.00
93	GONE FISHING	1500	65.00	75.00
93	MISSED	7500	110.00	120.00
94	ALMOST GROWN UP	7500	75.00	85.00
94	BABY'S FIRST STEP	7500	100.00	110.00
94	BED TIME	7500	100.00	110.00
94	BRIDE & GROOM	7500	100.00	110.00
94	FOR A GOOD BOY	7500	100.00	110.00
94	LITTLE MOTHER	7500	75.00	85.00
ROCKWELL INSPIRED			**AMERICAN ROCKWELL SERIES**	
81	BREAKING HOME TIES NRV-300	RT	2000.00	2300.00
82	LINCOLN NRV-301	RT	300.00	375.00
82	THANKSGIVING NRV-302	RT	2500.00	2650.00
ROCKWELL INSPIRED			**BOY SCOUT SERIES**	
81	CAN'T WAIT BSA-01	RT	30.00	50.00
81	GOOD FRIENDS BSA-04	RT	58.00	65.00
81	GOOD FRIENDS BSA-04	RT	58.00	65.00
81	GOOD TURN BSA-05	RT	65.00	100.00
81	PHYSICALLY STRONG BSA-03	RT	56.00	60.00
81	SCOUT IS HELPFUL BSA-02	RT	38.00	45.00
81	SCOUT MEMORIES BSA-06	RT	65.00	70.00
82	GUIDING HAND BSA-07	RT	58.00	60.00
83	TOMORROW'S LEADER BSA-08	RT	45.00	55.00
B. LEIGHTON-JONES			**EMMETT KELLY CIRCUS COLLECTION**	
92	CHRISTMAS TUNES	15000	40.00	40.00
92	EMMETT AT THE ORGAN	15000	50.00	50.00

YR	NAME	LIMIT	ISSUE	TREND
92	EMMETT AT WORK	15000	45.00	45.00
92	EMMETT THE CADDY	15000	45.00	45.00
92	LOOK AT THE BIRDIE	15000	40.00	40.00
B. LEIGHTON-JONES		**EMMETT KELLY ORIGINAL CIRCUS COLLECTION**		
93	CHRISTMAS TUNES	5000	100.00	115.00
93	DEAR EMMETT	15000	45.00	140.00
93	HARD TIMES	15000	45.00	50.00
93	LION TAMER, THE	15500	55.00	65.00
93	SUNDAY DRIVER	15000	55.00	65.00
93	WALL STREET	5000	120.00	135.00
94	EMMETT THE CADDY	5000	125.00	145.00
94	HOLIDAY SKATER	15000	110.00	125.00
94	I'VE GOT IT	15000	90.00	110.00
94	PARENTHOOD	15000	110.00	125.00
94	STUCK ON BOWLING	15000	90.00	100.00
*			**GONE WITH THE WIND**	
92	SCARLETT IN GREEN DRESS	TL	70.00	70.00
93	GWW-12 RHETT	*	70.00	80.00
94	ASHLEY	OP	40.00	50.00
94	GERALD O'HARA	*	70.00	80.00
94	RHETT	OP	40.00	45.00
94	SCARLETT	OP	40.00	45.00
94	SCARLETT IN BAR B QUE DRESS	*	70.00	80.00
ROCKWELL INSPIRED			**HUCK FINN SERIES**	
79	SECRET, THE- HF-01	RT	110.00	130.00
80	LISTENING HF-02	RT	110.00	120.00
80	NO KINGS HF-03	RT	110.00	110.00
80	SNAKE ESCAPES HF-04	RT	110.00	110.00
ROCKWELL INSPIRED			**LARGE LIMITED EDITIONS**	
74	DOCTOR AND DOLL NR-100	RT	300.00	1600.00
74	SEE AMERICA FIRST NR-103	RT	100.00	300.00
75	BASEBALL NR-102	RT	125.00	450.00
75	NO SWIMMING NR-101	RT	150.00	450.00
79	LEAPFROG NR-104	RT	440.00	600.00
81	DREAMS OF LONG AGO NR-105	RT	500.00	750.00
82	CIRCUS NR-106	RT	500.00	550.00
84	MARBLE PLAYERS NR-107	RT	500.00	500.00
*			**MINIATURE BRONZE SERIES**	
93	SCENE II-TWELVE OAKS	5000	340.00	375.00
93	WIZARD OF OZ	5000	290.00	325.00
B. LEIGHTON-JONES			**MINIATURE BRONZE SERIES**	
94	ATLANTA	*	340.00	365.00
E. ROBERTS			**NATIVE AMERICAN SERIES**	
91	LONE WOLF	7500	55.00	55.00
92	TORTOISE LADY	7500	60.00	60.00
ROCKWELL INSPIRED		**NORMAN ROCKWELL COLLECTION**		
73	BACK TO SCHOOL NR-02	RT	20.00	35.00
73	CAROLLER NR-03	RT	22.50	35.00
73	DAYDREAMER NR-04	RT	22.50	50.00
73	DOCTOR & DOLL NR-12	RT	65.00	150.00
73	LAZYBONES NR-08	RT	30.00	300.00
73	LEAPFROG NR-09	RT	50.00	550.00
73	LOVE LETTER NR-06	RT	25.00	60.00
73	LOVERS NR-07	RT	45.00	66.00
73	MARBLE PLAYERS NR-11	RT	60.00	450.00
73	NO SWIMMING NR-05	RT	25.00	50.00
73	REDHEAD NR-01	RT	20.00	200.00
73	SCHOOLMASTER NR-10	RT	55.00	225.00
74	BASEBALL NR-16	RT	45.00	120.00
74	FRIENDS IN NEED NR-13	RT	45.00	96.00
74	SEE AMERICA FIRST NR-17	RT	50.00	85.00
74	SPRINGTIME '33 NR-14	RT	30.00	45.00
74	TAKE YOUR MEDICINE NR-18	RT	50.00	95.00
75	BARBERSHOP QUARTET NR-23	RT	100.00	1400.00
75	BIG MOMENT NR-21	RT	60.00	120.00
75	CIRCUS NR-22	RT	55.00	100.00
75	DISCOVERY NR-20	RT	55.00	160.00
76	DRUM FOR TOMMY NRC-24	RT	40.00	80.00
77	PALS NR-25	RT	60.00	75.00
77	SPRINGTIME '35 NR-19	RT	50.00	55.00
78	AT THE DOCTOR NR-29	RT	108.00	160.00
78	FIRST DAY OF SCHOOL NR-27	RT	100.00	135.00
78	MAGIC POTION NR-28	RT	84.00	100.00
78	YOUNG DOCTOR NRD-26	RT	100.00	100.00
79	BACK FROM CAMP NR-33	RT	96.00	110.00
79	DREAMS OF LONG AGO NR-31	RT	100.00	160.00
79	GRANDPA'S BALLERINA NR-32	RT	100.00	110.00
79	TEACHER'S PET NRA-30	RT	35.00	80.00
80	EXASPERATED NANNY NR-35	RT	96.00	96.00
80	HANKERCHIEF NR-36	RT	110.00	110.00
80	SANTA'S GOOD BOYS NR-37	RT	90.00	90.00
80	TOSS, THE- NR-34	RT	110.00	110.00
81	SPIRIT OF EDUCATION NR-38	RT	96.00	110.00
82	A VISIT WITH ROCKWELL NR-40	RT	120.00	120.00
82	AMERICAN MOTHER NRG-42	RT	100.00	110.00
82	CROQUET NR-41	RT	100.00	110.00
83	COUNTRY CRITIC NR-43	RT	75.00	75.00
83	GRADUATE NR-44	RT	30.00	35.00

YR	NAME	LIMIT	ISSUE	TREND
83	SCOTTY'S SURPRISE NRS-20	RT	25.00	25.00
84	SCOTTY'S HOME PLATE NR-46	RT	30.00	40.00
86	RED CROSS NR-47	RT	67.00	75.00
87	YOUNG LOVE NR-48	RT	70.00	70.00
88	WEDDING MARCH NR-49	RT	110.00	110.00
92	CHOOSIN UP	7500	110.00	110.00
ROCKWELL INSPIRED		**NORMAN ROCKWELL COLLECTION MINIATURES**		
79	BACK TO SCHOOL NR-202	RT	18.00	25.00
79	CAROLLER NR-203	RT	20.00	25.00
79	DAYDREAMER NR-04	RT	20.00	30.00
79	DOCTOR AND DOLL NR-212	RT	40.00	40.00
79	LAZYBONES NR-208	RT	22.00	30.00
79	LEAPFROG NR-209	RT	32.00	32.00
79	LOVE LETTER NR-206	RT	26.00	30.00
79	LOVERS NR-207	RT	28.00	30.00
79	MARBLE PLAYERS NR-211	RT	36.00	38.00
79	NO SWIMMING NR-205	RT	22.00	30.00
79	REDHEAD NR-201	RT	18.00	48.00
79	SCHOOLMASTER NR-210	RT	34.00	40.00
80	BASEBALL NR-216	RT	40.00	50.00
80	FRIENDS IN NEED NR-213	RT	30.00	40.00
80	SEE AMERICA FIRST NR-217	RT	28.00	35.00
80	SPRINGTIME '33 NR-214	RT	24.00	80.00
80	SUMMERTIME '33 NR-215	RT	22.00	25.00
80	TAKE YOUR MEDICINE NR-218	RT	36.00	40.00
82	BARBERSHOP QUARTET NR-223	RT	40.00	50.00
82	BIG MOMENT NR-221	RT	36.00	40.00
82	CIRCUS NR-222	RT	35.00	40.00
82	DISCOVERY NR-220	RT	35.00	45.00
82	DRUM FOR TOMMY NRC-224	RT	25.00	30.00
82	SPRINGTIME '35 NR-219	RT	24.00	30.00
83	SANTA ON THE TRAIN NR-245	RT	35.00	55.00
84	AT THE DOCTOR'S NR-229	RT	35.00	35.00
84	DREAMS OF LONG AGO NR-231	RT	30.00	30.00
84	FIRST DAY OF SCHOOL NR-227	RT	35.00	35.00
84	MAGIC POTION NR-228	RT	30.00	40.00
84	PALS NR-225	RT	25.00	25.00
84	YOUNG DOCTOR NRD-226	RT	30.00	50.00
ROCKWELL INSPIRED			**ROCKWELL CLUB SERIES**	
81	YOUNG ARTISTS RCC-01	RT	96.00	105.00
82	DIARY RCC-02	RT	35.00	50.00
83	RUNAWAY PANTS RCC-03	RT	65.00	75.00
84	GONE FISHING RCC-04	RT	30.00	55.00
ROCKWELL INSPIRED			**TOM SAWYER MINIATURES**	
83	FIRST SMOKE TSM-02	RT	40.00	45.00
83	LOST IN CAVE TSM-05	RT	40.00	45.00
83	TAKE YOUR MEDICINE TSM-04	RT	40.00	45.00
83	WHITEWASHING THE FENCE TSM-01	RT	40.00	50.00
ROCKWELL INSPIRED			**TOM SAWYER SERIES**	
75	WHITEWASHING THE FENCE TS-01	RT	60.00	200.00
76	FIRST SMOKE TS-02	RT	60.00	200.00
77	TAKE YOUR MEDICINE TS-03	RT	63.00	170.00
78	LOST IN CAVE TS-04	RT	70.00	145.00

DEPARTMENT 56

Price ranges may reflect various demands in the market from one geographic region to another; condition of piece; specific markings found on piece; and/or changes in production of piece.

YR	NAME	LIMIT	ISSUE	TREND
*				**ALPINE VILLAGE**
86	ALPINE VILLAGERS 6542-0, (SET OF 3)	RT	13.00	26.00
87	ALPINE VILLAGE SIGN 6571-4	RT	6.00	11.00
89	FARM ANIMALS 5945-5, (SET OF 4)	RT	15.00	45.00
90	TOY PEDDLER 5616-2, (SET OF 3)	OP	22.00	22.00
92	BUYING BAKERS BREAD 5619-7, (SET OF 2)	RT	20.00	22.00
*				**CHRISTMAS IN THE CITY**
87	CITY PEOPLE 5965-0, (SET OF 5)	RT	27.50	50.00
89	POPCORN VENDOR 5958-7, (SET OF 3)	RT	22.00	22.00
89	RIVER STREET ICE HOUSE CART 5959-5	RT	20.00	45.00
91	"CITY FIRE DEPT." 5547-6, FIRE TRUCK	RT	18.00	20.00
91	ALL AROUND THE TOWN 5545-0, (SET OF 2)	RT	18.00	17.00
91	CAROLING THRU THE CITY 5548-4, (SET OF 3	OP	27.50	28.00
91	FIRE BRIGADE, THE 5546-8, (SET OF 2)	RT	20.00	22.00
91	MARKET DAY 5641-3, (SET OF 3)	RT	35.00	30.00
91	SKATING PARTY 5523-9, (SET OF 3)	OP	27.50	28.00
92	DON'T DROP THE PRESENTS 5532-8, (SET OF	RT	25.00	25.00
92	VILLAGE EXPRESS VAN 5865-3, GREEN	OP	25.00	25.00
92	VILLAGE EXPRESS VAN 9951-1, BLACK	RT	25.00	105.00
92	WELCOME HOME, 5533-6, (SET OF 2)	RT	27.50	28.00
93	CHRISTMAS AT THE PARK 5866-1, (SET OF 3)	OP	27.50	28.00
93	PLAYING IN THE SNOW 5556-5, (SET OF 3)	OP	25.00	25.00
93	STREET MUSICIANS 5564-6, (SET OF 3)	OP	45.00	45.00
93	TOWN TREE 5565-4, (SET OF 5)	OP	45.00	45.00
93	TOWN TREE TRIMMERS 5566-2, (SET OF 4)	OP	32.50	33.00
94	HOT DOG VENDOR 5886-6, (SET OF 3)	RT	*	*
94	VILLAGE EXPRESS VAN-BACHMAN'S 729-3	RT	22.50	70.00
94	VILLAGE EXPRESS VAN-CHRISTMAS DOVE 730-7	RT	25.00	50.00
94	VILLAGE EXPRESS VAN-CHRISTMAS PLACE 732-	RT	24.98	75.00
94	VILLAGE EXPRESS VAN-FORTUNOFF'S 735-8	RT	22.50	125.00
94	VILLAGE EXPRESS VAN-LOCK,STOCK.. 731-5	RT	22.50	120.00

YR	NAME	LIMIT	ISSUE	TREND
94	VILLAGE EXPRESS VAN-LTD. ED. 733-1	RT	25.00	115.00
94	VILLAGE EXPRESS VAN-N. POLE CITY 736-6	RT	25.00	50.00
94	VILLAGE EXPRESS VAN-ROBERTS CHRISTMAS WN	RT	22.50	50.00
94	VILLAGE EXPRESS VAN-STAT'S 741-2	RT	22.50	40.00
94	VILLAGE EXPRESS VAN-THE LEMON TREE 721-8	RT	30.00	45.00
94	VILLAGE EXPRESS VAN-VAN-BRONNER'S 737-4	RT	22.50	45.00
94	VILLAGE EXPRESS VAN-VAN-EUROPEAN IMPORTS	RT	22.50	40.00
94	VILLAGE EXPRESS VAN-VAN-WILLIAM GLEN 738	RT	22.50	50.00
94	VILLAGE EXPRESS VAN-VAN-WINDSOR SHOPPE 7	RT	25.00	45.00
94	VILLAGE STREET CAR 5240-0 MOTORIZED	OP	65.00	65.00
*	**CHRISTMAS IN THE CITY - PROMOTIONAL**			
92	VILLAGE EXPRESS VAN 9977-5, GOLD	RT	*	960.00
*	**DICKENS' VILLAGE**			
84	ORIGINAL CAROLERS, SET OF THREE WHITE PO	RT	10.00	95.00
86	CHRISTMAS CAROL CHARACTERS 6501-3, SET O	RT	12.50	91.00-104.00
88	POULTERER 5926-9	RT	32.50	50.00
89	CHRISTMAS SPIRITS FIGURES 5589-1 (SET OF	OP	27.50	28.00
89	DAVID COPPERFIELD CHARACTERS 5551-4, (SE	RT	32.50	30.00
89	LAMPLIGHTER 5577-8, (SET OF 2)	OP	9.00	9.00
90	C.H. WATT PHYSICIAN 5568-9	OP	40.00	40.00
91	OLIVER TWIST CHARACTERS 554-9, (SET OF	RT	35.00	30.00
92	BIRD SELLER, THE 5803-3 (SET OF 3)	RT	25.00	30.00
92	OLD PUPPETEER, THE 5802-5 (SET OF 3)	RT	32.00	33.00
92	VILLAGE STREET PEDDLERS 5804-1, (SET OF	RT	16.00	13.00
93	CHELSEA LANE SHOPPERS 5816-5, (SET OF 4)	OP	30.00	30.00
93	CHELSEA MARKET FISH MONGERS 5814-9, (SET	OP	25.00	25.00
93	CHELSEA MARKET FLOWER MONGERS 5815-7, (S	OP	27.50	28.00
93	CHELSEA MARKET FRUIT MONGERS 5813-0, (SE	OP	25.00	25.00
94	THATCHER 5829-7, (SET OF 3)	OP	35.00	35.00
95	COBBLER AND CLOCK PEDDLER 5839-4, (SET O	OP	25.00	25.00
95	FIVE GOLDEN RINGS 5838-1, (SET OF 2)	OP	27.50	28.00
95	FOUR CALLING BIRDS 5837-9, (SET OF 2)	OP	*	*
95	SIX GEESE A LAYING 5838-2, (SET OF 2)	OP	*	*
95	THREE FRENCH HENS 5837-8, (SET OF 3)	OP	32.50	33.00
95	YE OLDE LAMP LIGHTER, DICKENS' VILLAGE S	OP	20.00	20.00
*	**NEW ENGLAND VILLAGE**			
90	'TIS THE SEASON 5539-5	RT	12.50	13.00
90	AMISH BUGGY 5949-8	RT	22.00	50.00
90	REST YE MERRY GENTLEMEN 5540-9	RT	12.50	13.00
90	SLEEPY HOLLOW CHARACTERS 5956-0 (SET OF	RT	27.50	45.00
91	CAROLING THRU THE CITY 5548-4, (SET OF 3	OP	27.50	28.00
91	MARKET DAY, 5641-3, (SET OF 3)	OP	35.00	30.00
91	SKATING PARTY 5523-9, (SET OF 3)	OP	27.50	28.00
92	HARVEST SEED CART 5645-6, (SET OF 3)	RT	27.50	28.00
92	TOWN TINKER 5646-4, (SET OF 2)	RT	24.00	30.00
92	VILLAGE PINE TREE, LG. 5218-3	OP	12.50	13.00
92	VILLAGE PINE TREE, SM. 5219-1	OP	10.00	10.00
93	BLUE STAR ICE HARVESTERS 5650-2, (SET OF	OP	27.50	28.00
93	KNIFE GRINDER 5649-9, (SET OF 2)	OP	22.50	23.00
95	J. BREWSTER 5657-0 (BREWSTER BAY COTTAGE	OP	45.00	45.00
95	T.T. JULIAN 5657-0 (BREWSTER BAY COTAGES	OP	45.00	45.00
*	**NORTH POLE COLLECTION**			
90	SANTA & MRS. CLAUS 5609-0, (SET OF 2)	OP	15.00	15.00
90	SANTA'S LITTLE HELPERS 5610-3, (SET OF 3	RT	28.00	50.00
90	SLEIGH & EIGHT TINY REINDEER 5611-1, (SE	OP	42.00	42.00
91	BAKER'S ELEVES 5603-0, (SET OF 3)	RT	27.50	28.00
91	TOYMAKER ELVES 5602-2, (SET OF 3)	RT	27.50	25.00
92	LETTERS FOR SANTA 5604-9, (SET OF 3)	RT	30.00	50.00
92	TESTING THE TOYS 5605-7, (SET OF 2)	OP	16.50	17.00
*	**RETIRED HERITAGE VILLAGE COLLECTION ACCESSORIES**			
86	PORCELAIN TREES 6537-4, (SET OF 2)	RT	14.00	30.00
87	CITY WORKERS 5967-6 (SET OF 4)	RT	15.00	30.00
88	SNOW CHILDREN 5938-2, (SET OF 3)	RT	17.00	20.00
89	VIOLET VENDOR/CAROLERS/CHESTNUT,5580-8 S	RT	23.00	30.00
*	**SNOWBABIES**			
86	BEST FRIENDS 7958-8	RT	12.00	190.00
86	CLIMBING ON SNOWBALL 7965-0	RT	15.00	65.00
86	GIVE ME A PUSH 7955-3	RT	12.00	33.00-50.00
86	HANGING PAIR 7966-9	RT	15.00	135.00
86	HOLD ON TIGHT 7956-1	OP	12.00	14.00
86	I'M MAKING SNOWBALLS 7962-6	RT	12.00	26.00
86	SNOWBABY/PICTURE FRAME 7970-7 (SET OF 2)	RT	15.00	225.00
87	CLIMBING ON TREE 7971-5 (SET OF 2)	RT	25.00	475.00
87	DON'T FALL OFF 7968-5	RT	12.50	175.00
87	DOWN THE HILL WE GO 7960-0	OP	20.00	22.00
87	TUMBLING IN THE SNOW 7957-0 (SET OF 5)	RT	35.00	50.00
87	WINTER SURPRISE 7974-0	RT	15.00	30.00
88	ARE THESE MINE? 7977-4	OP	10.00	13.00
88	FROSTY FROLIC 7981-2	4800	35.00	700.00
88	POLAR EXPRESS 7978-2	RT	22.00	49.00
88	TINY TRIO 7979-0 (SET OF 3)	RT	20.00	115.00
89	ALL FALL DOWN 7984-7 (SET OF 4)	RT	36.00	65.00
89	FINDING FALLEN STARS 7985-5	6000	32.50	175.00
89	FROSTY FUN 7983-9	RT	27.50	50.00-75.00
89	HELPFUL FRIENDS 7982-0	RT	30.00	34.00
89	ICY IGLOO 7987-1	OP	37.50	38.00
89	PENGUIN PARADE 7986-3	RT	25.00	65.00
89	WHO ARE YOU? 7949-9	12500	32.50	105.00

YR	NAME	LIMIT	ISSUE	TREND
90	A SPECIAL DELIVERY 7948-0	OP	13.50	14.00
90	I WILL PUT UP THE TREE 6800-4	RT	22.00	24.00
90	PLAYING GAMES IS FUN 7947-2	RT	30.00	30.00
90	READ ME A STORY 7945-6	OP	25.00	25.00
90	TWINKLE LITTLE STARS 7942-1 (SET OF 2)	RT	37.50	38.00
90	WE WILL MAKE IT SHINE 7946-4	RT	45.00	75.00
90	WISHING ON A STAR 7943-0	RT	20.00	20.00
91	DANCING TO A TUNE 6808-0 (SET OF 3)	RT	30.00	30.00
91	FISHING FOR DREAMS 6809-8	OP	28.00	28.00
91	I MADE THIS JUST FOR YOU 6802-0	OP	14.50	15.00
91	IS THAT FOR ME? 6803-9 (SET OF 2)	RT	30.00	45.00
91	SNOWBABY POLAR SIGN 6804-7	OP	20.00	20.00
91	THIS IS WHERE WE LIVE 6805-5	OP	55.00	70.00
91	WAITING FOR CHRISTMAS 6807-1	RT	27.50	37.00
91	WHY DON'T YOU TALK TO ME 6801-2	OP	22.00	24.00
92	CAN I HELP TOO? 6806-3	18500	48.00	100.00
92	I NEED A HUG 6813-6	OP	20.00	20.00
92	LET'S GO SKIING 6815-2	OP	15.00	16.00
92	OVER THE MILKY WAY	RT	32.00	32.00
92	STARS IN A ROW, TIC-TAC-TOE	RT	32.50	33.00
92	THIS WILL CHEER YOU UP 6816-0	RT	30.00	30.00
92	WAIT FOR ME 6812-8	OP	48.00	48.00
92	WINKEN, BLINKEN, AND NOD 6814-4	OP	60.00	65.00
93	BABY'S FIRST SMILE 6846-2	OP	30.00	30.00
93	CAN I OPEN IT NOW? 6838-1	YR	15.00	35.00
93	CROSSING STARRY SKIES 6834-9	OP	35.00	35.00
93	I FOUND YOUR MITTENS! 6836-5	OP	30.00	30.00
93	I'LL TEACH YOU A TRICK 6835-7	OP	24.00	24.00
93	I'M MAKING AN ICE SCULPTURE! 6842-0	OP	30.00	30.00
93	LET'S ALL CHIME IN! 6845-4 SET OF 2	RT	37.50	38.00
93	LOOK WHAT I FOUND 6833-0	OP	45.00	45.00
93	NOW I LAY ME DOWN TO SLEEP 6839-0	OP	13.50	14.00
93	SO MUCH WORK TO DO! 6837-3	OP	18.00	18.00
93	SOMEWHERE IN DREAMLAND 6840-3	OP	85.00	85.00
93	WE MAKE A GREAT PAIR 6843-8	OP	30.00	30.00
93	WHERE DID HE GO? 6841-1	OP	35.00	35.00
93	WILL IT SNOW TODAY? 6844-6	RT	45.00	45.00

*
SNOWBABIES MINIATURES

YR	NAME	LIMIT	ISSUE	TREND
92	JOIN THE PARADE	RT	22.50	23.00
92	WAIT FOR ME! 7641-4	RT	22.50	23.00
92	WINKEN, BLINKEN, AND NOD 7658-9	OP	27.50	28.00

*
THE ORIGINAL SNOW VILLAGE COLLECTION

YR	NAME	LIMIT	ISSUE	TREND
94	SANTA COMES TO TOWN	*	30.00	33.00

*
THE UPSTAIRS DOWNSTAIRS BEARS

YR	NAME	LIMIT	ISSUE	TREND
94	HENRIETTA'S TEA PARTY	5600	65.00	75.00

DUNCAN ROYALE

*
1990 & 1991 SPECIAL EVENT PIECE

YR	NAME	LIMIT	ISSUE	TREND
*	NAST & MUSIC	5000	79.95	90.00

D. APHESSETCHE

CALENDAR SECRETS

YR	NAME	LIMIT	ISSUE	TREND
90	APRIL	5000	350.00	370.00
90	AUGUST	5000	300.00	300.00
90	DECEMBER	5000	410.00	410.00
90	FEBRURARY	5000	370.00	370.00
90	JANUARY	5000	260.00	260.00
90	JULY	5000	280.00	280.00
90	JUNE	5000	410.00	410.00
90	MARCH	5000	280.00	350.00
90	MAY	5000	370.00	390.00
90	NOVEMBER	5000	410.00	410.00
90	OCTOBER	5000	350.00	350.00
90	SEPTEMBER	5000	300.00	300.00

*
CHRISTMAS IMAGES

YR	NAME	LIMIT	ISSUE	TREND
91	CAROLERS, THE	10000	120.00	120.00
91	CHRISTMAS PAGEANT, THE	10000	175.00	175.00
92	ARE YOU REALLY SANTA?	10000	*	*
92	CHRISTMAS ANGEL, THE	10000	*	*
92	MIDNIGHT WATCH, THE	10000	*	*
92	SNEAKING A PEEK	10000	*	*

*
COLLECTORS CLUB

YR	NAME	LIMIT	ISSUE	TREND
91	MUSICAL NAST	CL	80.00	95.00
91	TODAY'S NAST	RT	80.00	125.00
94	WINTER SANTA	RT	125.00	125.00
95	SANTA'S GIFT	YR	100.00	100.00

*
EARLY AMERICAN

YR	NAME	LIMIT	ISSUE	TREND
91	ACCOUNTANT	10000	170.00	170.00
91	BANKER	10000	150.00	150.00
91	CHIROPRACTOR	10000	150.00	150.00
91	DENTIST	10000	150.00	150.00
91	DOCTOR	10000	150.00	150.00
91	FIREMAN	10000	150.00	150.00
91	HOMEMAKER	10000	150.00	150.00
91	LAWYER	10000	170.00	170.00
91	NURSE	10000	150.00	150.00
91	PHARMACIST	10000	150.00	150.00
91	POLICEMAN	10000	150.00	150.00
91	SALESMAN	10000	150.00	150.00
91	SECRETARY	10000	150.00	150.00

YR	NAME	LIMIT	ISSUE	TREND
91	SET OF 15	10000	2290.00	2290.00
91	STOREKEEPER	10000	150.00	150.00
91	TEACHER	10000	150.00	150.00
*			**EBONY COLLECTION**	
90	BANJO MAN	5000	80.00	80.00
90	FIDDLER, THE	5000	90.00	90.00
90	HARMONICA MAN	5000	80.00	80.00
91	FEMALE GOSPEL SINGER	5000	90.00	90.00
91	JUG MAN	5000	90.00	90.00
91	MALE GOSPEL SINGER	5000	90.00	90.00
91	MALE GOSPEL SINGER	5000	90.00	90.00
91	PREACHER	5000	90.00	90.00
91	SPOONS	5000	90.00	90.00
92	A LITTLE MAGIC	5000	80.00	80.00
92	JUG TOTTER	5000	90.00	90.00
93	EBONY ANGEL	5000	170.00	170.00
*			**EBONY COLLECTION/BUCKWHEAT**	
92	BASS	5000	90.00	90.00
92	BONGO	5000	90.00	90.00
92	JAZZMAN SET	5000	500.00	500.00
92	O'TAY	5000	70.00	90.00
92	PAINTER	5000	80.00	90.00
92	PETEE & FRIEND	5000	90.00	90.00
92	PIANO	5000	130.00	130.00
92	SAX	5000	90.00	90.00
92	SMILE FOR THE CAMERA	5000	80.00	90.00
92	TRUMPET	5000	90.00	90.00
S. BUONAIUTO			**EBONY COLLECTION/FRIENDS & FAMILY**	
94	AGNES	5000	100.00	100.00
94	DADDY	5000	120.00	120.00
94	LUNCHTIME	5000	100.00	100.00
94	MILLIE	5000	100.00	100.00
94	MOMMY & ME	5000	125.00	125.00
S. BUONAIUTO			**EBONY COLLECTION/JUBILEE DANCERS**	
93	BLISS	5000	200.00	200.00
93	FALLANA	5000	100.00	100.00
93	KESHIA	5000	100.00	100.00
93	LAMAR	5000	100.00	100.00
93	LOTTIE	5000	125.00	125.00
93	WILFRED	5000	100.00	100.00
P. APSIT			**GREATEST GIFT...LOVE**	
88	ANNUNCIATION, MARBLE	5000	270.00	270.00
88	ANNUNCIATION, PAINTED PORCELAIN	5000	270.00	270.00
88	CRUCIFIXION MARBLE	5000	300.00	300.00
88	CRUCIFIXION, PAINTED PORCELAIN	5000	300.00	300.00
88	NATIVITY, MARBLE	5000	500.00	500.00
88	NATIVITY, PAINTED PORCELAIN	5000	500.00	500.00
P. APSIT			**HISTORY OF CLASSIC ENTERTAINERS**	
87	AMERICAN	RT	160.00	350.00
87	AUGUSTE	RT	220.00	350.00
87	GRECO-ROMAN	RT	180.00	350.00
87	GROTESQUE	RT	230.00	350.00
87	HARLEQUIN	RT	250.00	350.00
87	JESTER	RT	410.00	725.00
87	PANTALONE	RT	270.00	350.00
87	PIERROT	RT	180.00	270.00
87	PULCINELLA	RT	220.00	350.00
87	RUSSIAN	RT	190.00	350.00
87	SLAPSTICK	RT	250.00	350.00
87	UNCLE SAM	RT	160.00	300.00
P. APSIT			**HISTORY OF CLASSIC ENTERTAINERS II**	
88	BOB HOPE	RT	250.00	275.00
88	FESTE	RT	250.00	275.00
88	GOLIARD	RT	200.00	275.00
88	MIME	RT	200.00	275.00
88	MOUNTEBANK	RT	270.00	275.00
88	PEDROLINO	RT	200.00	275.00
88	SIGNATURE PIECE	RT	50.00	275.00
88	TARTAGLIA	RT	200.00	275.00
88	THOMASSI	RT	200.00	275.00
88	TOUCHSTONE	RT	200.00	275.00
88	TRAMP	RT	200.00	275.00
88	WHITE FACE	RT	250.00	275.00
88	ZANNI	RT	200.00	275.00
P. APSIT			**HISTORY OF CLASSIC ENTERTAINERS-SPECIAL RELEASES**	
88	SIGNATURE PIECE	RT	50.00	50.00
90	BOB HOPE, 18 IN. (SET)	RT	1500.00	1750.00
90	BOB HOPE, 6 IN. PORCELAIN	6000	130.00	130.00
90	MIME, 18 IN.	RT	1500.00	1500.00
P. APSIT			**HISTORY OF SANTA CLAUS**	
89	KRIS KRINGLE, 18 IN.	1000	1500.00	1500.00
89	MEDIEVAL, 18 IN.	1000	1500.00	1400.00
89	NAST, 18 IN.	1000	1500.00	1500.00
89	RUSSIAN, 18 IN.	1000	1500.00	1500.00
89	SODA POP, 18 IN.	1000	1500.00	1500.00
89	ST. NICHOLAS, 18 IN.	1000	1500.00	1500.00

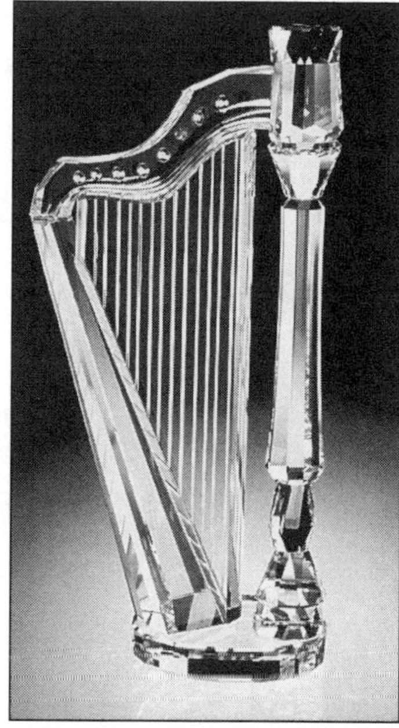

The Swarovski Silver Crystal Harp *is music to the eyes of collectors.*

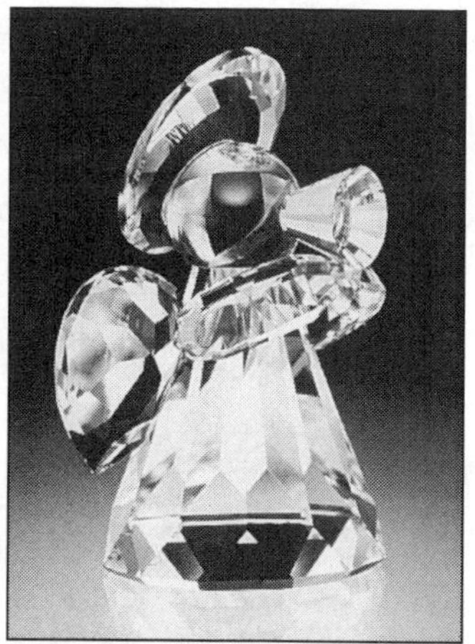

This Swarovski Silver Crystal Angel *trumpets wishes for a joyous season.*

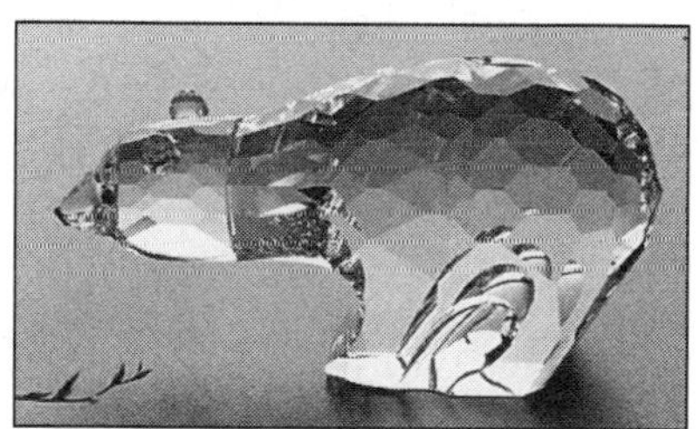

Polar Bear *is from the Swarovski Silver Crystal Collection.*

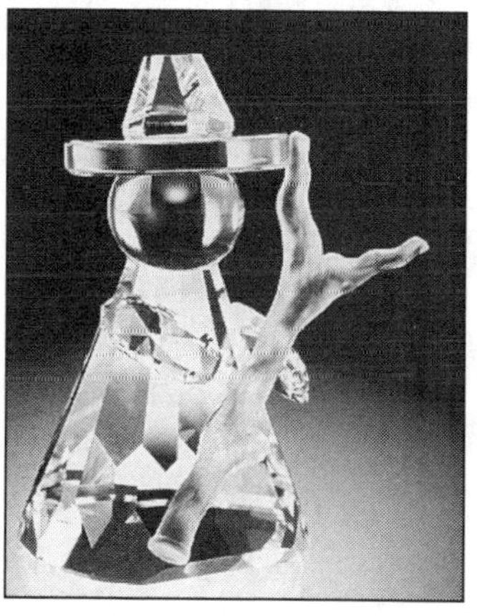

Watching over his flocks is this Swarovski Silver Crystal Shepherd.

These Swarovski Silver Crystal Wise Men *come bearing gifts for the newborn King.*

YR	NAME	LIMIT	ISSUE	TREND
P. APSIT		**HISTORY OF SANTA CLAUS I**		
83	BLACK PETER	RT	145.00	350.00
83	CIVIL WAR	10000	145.00	250.00
83	DEDT MOROZ	RT	145.00	525.00
83	KRIS KRINGLE	RT	165.00	1150.00
83	MEDIEVAL	RT	220.00	1250.00
83	NAST	RT	90.00	2350.00
83	PIONEER	RT	145.00	325.00
83	RUSSIAN	RT	145.00	600.00
83	SODA POP	RT	145.00	1350.00
83	ST. NICHOLAS	RT	175.00	1000.00
83	VICTORIAN	RT	120.00	350.00
83	WASSAIL	RT	90.00	300.00
87	BLACK PETER, 8 IN. WOOD	RT	450.00	450.00
87	CIVIL WAR, 8 IN. WOOD	500	450.00	450.00
87	DEDT MOROZ, 8 IN. WOOD	RT	450.00	450.00
87	KRIS KRINGLE, 8 IN. WOOD	500	450.00	450.00
87	MEDIEVAL, 8 IN. WOOD	500	450.00	450.00
87	NAST, 8 IN. WOOD	RT	450.00	450.00
87	PIONEER, 8 IN. WOOD	RT	450.00	450.00
87	RUSSIAN, 8 IN. WOOD	RT	450.00	450.00
87	SODA POP, 8 IN. WOOD	RT	450.00	450.00
87	ST. NICHOLAS, 8 IN. WOOD	500	450.00	450.00
87	VICTORIAN, 8 IN. WOOD	RT	450.00	450.00
87	WASSAIL, 8 IN. WOOD	RT	450.00	450.00
88	BLACK PETE, 6 IN. PORCELAIN	6000	40.00	80.00
88	CIVIL WAR, 6 IN. PORCELAIN	6000	40.00	80.00
88	DEDT MOROZ, 6 IN. PORCELAIN	6000	40.00	80.00
88	KRIS KRINGLE-6" PORCELAIN	6000	40.00	80.00
88	MEDIEVAL, 6 IN. PORCELAIN	6000	40.00	80.00
88	NAST, 6 IN. PORCELAIN	6000	40.00	80.00
88	PIONEER, 6 IN. PORCELAIN	6000	40.00	80.00
88	RUSSIAN, 6IN. PORCELAIN	6000	40.00	80.00
88	SODA POP, 6 IN. PORCELAIN	6000	40.00	80.00
88	ST. NICHOLAS, 6 IN. PORCELAIN	6000	40.00	80.00
88	VICTORIAN, 6 IN. PORCELAIN	6000	40.00	80.00
88	WASSAIL, 6 IN. PORCELAIN	6000	40.00	80.00
P. APSIT		**HISTORY OF SANTA CLAUS II**		
86	ALSACE ANGEL	10000	250.00	300.00
86	BABOUSKA	10000	170.00	200.00
86	BAVARIAN	10000	250.00	300.00
86	BEFANA	10000	200.00	250.00
86	FRAU HOLDA	10000	160.00	180.00
86	LORD OF MISRULE	10000	160.00	200.00
86	MAGI, THE	10000	350.00	400.00
86	MONGOLIAN/ASIAN	10000	240.00	300.00
86	ODIN	10000	200.00	250.00
86	PIXIE, THE	10000	140.00	175.00
86	SIR CHRISTMAS	10000	150.00	175.00
86	ST. LUCIA	10000	180.00	225.00
88	ALSACE ANGEL, 6 IN. PORCELAIN	6000	80.00	90.00
88	BABOUSKA, 6 IN. PORCELAIN	6000	70.00	80.00
88	BAVARIAN, 6 IN. PORCELAIN	6000	90.00	100.00
88	BEFANA, 6 IN. PORCELAIN	6000	70.00	80.00
88	FRAU HOLDA, 6 IN. PORCELAIN	6000	50.00	80.00
88	LORD OF MISRULE, 6 IN. PORCELAIN	6000	60.00	80.00
88	MAGI, 6 IN. PORCELAIN	6000	130.00	150.00
88	MONGOLIAN/ASIAN, 6 IN. PORCELAIN	6000	80.00	90.00
88	ODIN, 6 IN. PORCELAIN	6000	80.00	90.00
88	PIXIE, 6 IN. PORCELAIN	6000	50.00	80.00
88	SIR CHRISTMAS, 6 IN. PORCELAIN	6000	60.00	80.00
88	ST. LUCIA, 6 IN. PORCELAIN	6000	70.00	80.00
*		**HISTORY OF SANTA CLAUS III**		
90	DRUID	RT	250.00	250.00
90	JULENISSE	10000	200.00	200.00
90	ST. BASIL	10000	300.00	300.00
90	STAR MAN	10000	300.00	300.00
90	UKKO	RT	250.00	250.00
91	GRANDFATHER FROST & SNOW MAIDEN	10000	400.00	400.00
91	HOTEISHO	10000	200.00	200.00
91	JUDAH MACCACBEE	10000	250.00	250.00
91	KNICKERBOCKER	10000	300.00	300.00
91	SAMICHLAUS	10000	350.00	350.00
*		**HISTORY OF SANTA CLAUS-SPECIAL RELEASES**		
91	SIGNATURE PIECE	OP	50.00	50.00
92	NAST & SLEIGH	5000	500.00	500.00
*		**SANTA 1ST SERIES-PAINTED PEWTER**		
86	BLACK PETER	500	30.00	30.00
86	CIVIL WAR	500	30.00	30.00
86	DEDT MOROZ	500	30.00	30.00
86	KRIS KRINGLE	500	30.00	30.00
86	MEDIEVAL	500	30.00	30.00
86	NAST	500	30.00	30.00
86	PIONEER	500	30.00	30.00
86	RUSSIAN	500	30.00	30.00
86	SET OF 12	500	360.00	425.00
86	SODA POP	500	30.00	30.00
86	ST. NICHOLAS	500	30.00	30.00

YR	NAME	LIMIT	ISSUE	TREND
86	VICTORIAN	500	30.00	30.00
86	WASSAIL	500	30.00	30.00
*				**SANTA 2ND SERIES-PAINTED PEWTER**
88	ALSACE ANGEL	500	30.00	30.00
88	BABOUSKA	500	30.00	30.00
88	BAVARIAN	500	30.00	30.00
88	BEFANA	500	30.00	30.00
88	FRAU HOLDA	500	30.00	30.00
88	LORD OF MISRULE	500	30.00	30.00
88	MAGI	500	30.00	30.00
88	MONGOLIAN	500	30.00	30.00
88	ODIN	500	30.00	30.00
88	PIXIE	500	30.00	30.00
88	SET OF 12	500	360.00	425.00
88	SIR CHRISTMAS	500	30.00	30.00
88	ST. LUCIA	500	30.00	30.00
*				**WOODLAND FAIRIES**
88	ALMOND BLOSSOM	RT	70.00	70.00
88	APPLE	RT	70.00	70.00
88	CALLA LILY	RT	70.00	70.00
88	CHERRY	10000	70.00	70.00
88	CHESTNUT	10000	70.00	70.00
88	CHRISTMAS TREE	RT	70.00	70.00
88	ELM	10000	70.00	70.00
88	LIME TREE	RT	70.00	70.00
88	MULBERRY	10000	70.00	70.00
88	PEAR BLOSSOM	RT	70.00	70.00
88	PINE TREE	10000	70.00	70.00
88	POPLAR	10000	70.00	70.00
88	SYCAMORE	RT	70.00	70.00

EGGSPRESSIONS

YR	NAME	LIMIT	ISSUE	TREND
*				**EGGSHELL**
93	AMERICA'S PRIDE	OP	140.00	140.00
93	ANGELICA	OP	50.00	50.00
93	APPLE BLOSSOM BQT	OP	62.00	62.00
93	BELLS	OP	55.00	55.00
93	BILL & COO	OP	55.00	55.00
93	BIRTH DAY! DEC	OP	40.00	40.00
93	BIRTH DAY! - APR	OP	40.00	40.00
93	BIRTH DAY! - AUG	OP	40.00	40.00
93	BIRTH DAY! - FEB	OP	40.00	40.00
93	BIRTH DAY! - JAN	OP	40.00	40.00
93	BIRTH DAY! - JUL	OP	40.00	40.00
93	BIRTH DAY! - JUN	OP	40.00	40.00
93	BIRTH DAY! - MAR	OP	40.00	40.00
93	BIRTH DAY! - MAY	OP	40.00	40.00
93	BIRTH DAY! - NOV	OP	40.00	40.00
93	BIRTH DAY! - OCT	OP	40.00	40.00
93	BIRTH DAY! - SEP	OP	40.00	40.00
93	BLUE BIRDS HAPPINESS	OP	79.00	79.00
93	BLUSH	OP	105.00	105.00
93	BRR RABBIT	OP	140.00	140.00
93	BUTTERCUP	OP	85.00	85.00
93	BUTTERFLY WINGS	OP	50.00	50.00
93	CANDYLAND	OP	100.00	100.00
93	CARDINALS	OP	70.00	70.00
93	CHOO-CHOO CHRISTMAS	OP	130.00	130.00
93	CHRISTMAS CURIOSITY	OP	110.00	110.00
93	COLOURS	OP	55.00	55.00
93	DAYTIME DEN	OP	125.00	125.00
93	DEAR ONE	OP	100.00	100.00
93	DOGWOOD	OP	50.00	50.00
93	DRUMMER BOY	OP	100.00	100.00
93	EBONY	OP	105.00	105.00
93	ELEGANT CHOICE	OP	167.00	167.00
93	FAMILY OUTING	OP	100.00	100.00
93	FANTAZIA	OP	50.00	50.00
93	GABRIELA	OP	45.00	45.00
93	GOLDEN CRYSTAL	OP	125.00	125.00
93	IN TUNE	OP	130.00	130.00
93	ISADORA	OP	130.00	130.00
93	KACHINA	OP	130.00	130.00
93	KEWPIE DOLL	OP	110.00	110.00
93	KRIS KRINGLE	OP	45.00	45.00
93	LARA	OP	115.00	115.00
93	LOBO	OP	85.00	85.00
93	LOVE DUET	OP	140.00	140.00
93	LOVE IN FLIGHT	OP	100.00	100.00
93	MARCELLA	OP	45.00	45.00
93	MARIA	OP	115.00	115.00
93	MCGREGOR'S GARDEN	OP	105.00	105.00
93	MIDAS	OP	105.00	105.00
93	MINY JULEP	OP	100.00	100.00
93	MISS ELLIE	OP	45.00	45.00
93	MISTY ROSE	OP	45.00	45.00
93	OH, NUTS	OP	100.00	100.00
93	PEARL	OP	100.00	100.00
93	PETER	OP	45.00	45.00

YR	NAME	LIMIT	ISSUE	TREND
93	PETUNIA	OP	45.00	45.00
93	POINSETTIA	OP	60.00	60.00
93	ROMANTIQUE	OP	75.00	75.00
93	SANTA'S WORKSHOP	125	130.00	130.00
93	SECRET GARDEN	OP	158.00	158.00
93	SERENA	OP	140.00	140.00
93	SILVER JEWELS	OP	105.00	105.00
93	SKYE	OP	100.00	100.00
93	SLUMBERING STEGGY	OP	85.00	85.00
93	SNOWFLAKE	OP	50.00	50.00
93	STAR PRANCER	OP	140.00	140.00
93	STORYTELLER	OP	130.00	130.00
93	SUMMER ROSE	OP	45.00	45.00
93	TABITHA	OP	40.00	40.00
93	TANNENBAUM	OP	55.00	55.00
93	TINY TREASURES	OP	110.00	110.00
93	TOGETHERNESS	OP	100.00	100.00
93	TRYKE	OP	90.00	90.00
93	VELVET PRINCESS	OP	170.00	170.00
93	WAITING	OP	100.00	100.00
93	WARRIOR'S PRIDE	OP	85.00	85.00
93	WELCOME CANDLE	OP	63.00	63.00
93	WINTER COLT	OP	105.00	105.00
93	WINTER COLT (STAND)	OP	105.00	105.00
93	WINTER HAVEN	OP	105.00	105.00
93	WINTER SONG	OP	115.00	115.00
93	WINTER WONDERLAND	OP	105.00	105.00
93	YELLOW ROSE	OP	105.00	105.00
94	ABSOLUTELY AMETHYST	OP	100.00	100.00
94	ANGEL BUNNY	250	220.00	220.00
94	ANGEL OF HOPE	250	130.00	130.00
94	ANGEL OF LOVE	250	110.00	110.00
94	BEARY BLUE CHRISTMAS	250	100.00	100.00
94	BEARY PINK CHRISTMAS	250	100.00	100.00
94	CAROLING MICE	250	120.00	120.00
94	CHICK'S & BUNNIES	OP	88.00	88.00
94	CHRISTMAS JOY	250	105.00	105.00
94	ETERNITY	250	170.00	170.00
94	FROSTY'S CHEER	500	64.00	64.00
94	GOLDEN HARMONY	250	160.00	160.00
94	GRANDMA'S GOODIES	OP	99.00	99.00
94	HARVEST FAIRY	OP	95.00	95.00
94	HOIDAY MEMORIES	250	190.00	190.00
94	JESSICA	125	240.00	240.00
94	LAVENDER LOVE	250	130.00	130.00
94	LOVE BIRDS	250	120.00	120.00
94	MAKING SPIRITS BRIGHT	25	300.00	300.00
94	MOTHER'S PRIDE	250	120.00	120.00
94	OH, HOLY NIGHT	250	160.00	160.00
94	OLD ST. NICKOLAS	500	64.00	64.00
94	PASSION	25	500.00	500.00
94	PASTEL & PEARLS	OP	112.00	112.00
94	PRE-SCHOOL PLAY	OP	108.00	108.00
94	PRISTINE PEARLS	OP	90.00	90.00
94	PURR-FECT HUG	RT	150.00	150.00
94	ROSE MARIE	OP	49.00	49.00
94	SANTA'S LITTLE ELVES	250	130.00	130.00
94	SANTA'S LITTLE SWEETHEART	100	100.00	100.00
94	SERENADE	250	120.00	120.00
94	SERENITY	250	115.00	115.00
94	SKIP A LONG	250	120.00	120.00
94	SPRING MELODY	250	130.00	130.00
94	SWEET DREAMS	OP	100.00	100.00
94	TEDDY BEAR SING ALONG	250	115.00	115.00
94	WEDDING IN WHITE	250	160.00	160.00
95	ANDREA	250	80.00	80.00
95	ANGEL DIVINE	250	120.00	120.00
95	CABBAGE PATCH	250	105.00	105.00
95	COO	250	115.00	115.00
95	JAMIE	250	80.00	80.00
95	TARA	250	80.00	80.00

EMI

P. APSIT — **EMMETT KELLY JR.**

YR	NAME	LIMIT	ISSUE	TREND
94	THINKING OF YOU	2500	640.00	670.00

R. HARRIS — **MASTERWORKS**

YR	NAME	LIMIT	ISSUE	TREND
94	CATTLE DRIFTING BEFORE THE STORM	500	1300.00	1400.00
94	UNKNOWN EXPLORERS	500	1100.00	1125.00

T. KNAPP — **MASTERWORKS**

YR	NAME	LIMIT	ISSUE	TREND
94	COW-BOY	500	930.00	950.00
94	LUMBER CAMP AT NIGHT	500	590.00	620.00

ENESCO

Price ranges may reflect various demands in the market from one geographic region to another; condition of piece; specific markings found on piece; and/or changes in production of piece.

L. RIGG

YR	NAME	LIMIT	ISSUE	TREND
95	MARY LOUISE/FRANCES ANGEL W/HEARTS/STARS	2000	60.00	60.00
95	NATHAN & SHAWNIE - BOY/GIRL INDIANS	2000	60.00	60.00

YR	NAME	LIMIT	ISSUE	TREND
95	THOMAS & BETH - BOY/GIRL W/SONGBOOK	2000	60.00	60.00
*			**BALLERINA SERIES**	
91	LIFE IS ONE JOYOUS STEP 121207	YR	20.00	20.00
91	LIFE IS ONE JOYOUS STEP 121274	OP	25.00	25.00
91	YOU ARE VERY SPECIAL TO ME 121215	OP	40.00	40.00
*			**BARBIE GLAMOUR COLLECTION**	
94	SOLO IN THE SPOTLIGHT 1960	7500	100.00	100.00
94	SOME ENCHANTED EVENING 1960	7500	100.00	100.00
94	WEDDING ON THE CHURCH STEPS 1959	7500	100.00	100.00
*			**BIRTHDAY CLUB PIECES**	
85	OUR CLUB CAN'T BE BEAT B0001	OP	10.00	60.00-95.00
88	HAVE A BEARY SPECIAL BIRTHDAY B0104	OP	11.50	35.00
88	OUR CLUB IS A TOUGH ACT TO FOLLOW B0005	OP	13.50	30.00
88	OUR CLUB IS A TOUGH ACT TO FOLLOW B0105	OP	13.50	35.00
90	LOVE PACIFIES BC911	OP	15.00	26.00
90	TRUE BLUE FRIENDS BC912	OP	15.00	30.00
91	EVERY MAN'S HOUSE IS HIS CASTLE BC921	OP	16.50	26.00
91	I'VE GOT YOU UNDER MY SKIN BC911	OP	16.50	25.00
91	OWL ALWAYS BE YOUR FRIENDS BC932	OP	16.00	18.00
91	PUT A LITTLE PUNCH...BIRTHDAY BC931	OP	16.00	17.00
92	ALL ABOARD FOR BIRTHDAY CLUB FUN B0007	OP	16.00	25.00
92	ALL ABOARD FOR BIRTHDAY CLUB FUN B0107	OP	16.00	25.00
92	HAPPINESS IS BELONGING B0008	OP	16.00	18.00
92	HAPPINESS IS BELONGING B0108	OP	16.00	18.00
P. HILLMAN			**CALICO KITTENS**	
95	A STITCH IN TIME SAVES NINE129429	3000	35.00	35.00
95	ALL ABOUT ANGELS	5000	25.00	25.00
95	BUTTONED UP WITH LOVE 104094	*	13.50	14.00
95	GRANDMA'S ARE SEW FULL OF LOVE 104108	*	13.50	14.00
95	HARK - A HERALD ANGEL 144193	*	17.50	18.00
95	HATS OFF TO A PERFECT FRIENDSHIP 129437	*	20.00	20.00
95	NOTHING IS SWEETER THAN MOM 104086	*	13.50	14.00
95	YOUR PATCHWORK CHARM SHOWS THROUGH 12945	*	17.50	18.00
96	HEY DIDDLE, DIDDLE THE CAT & THE FIDDLE	7500	20.00	20.00
96	I'VE BEEN A GOOD KITTY	*	17.50	17.50
96	WE WISH YOU A MERRY CHRISTMAS 932418	*	17.50	17.50
96	YOU'RE EARNED YOUR WINGS 178454	5000	35.00	35.00
P. HILLMAN			**CALICO KITTENS APRIL SHOWERS**	
96	APRIL SHOWERS 155500	*	17.50	17.50
96	FRIENDSHIP GROWS WHEN SHARED 129321	*	15.00	15.00
96	I'M HOOKED ON YOU 129313	*	17.50	17.50
96	KITE TAILS 155497	*	17.50	17.50
P. HILLMAN			**CALICO KITTENS HALLOWEEN**	
95	GOBBLIN' UP THE FUN 144231	*	15.00	15.00
95	I'M BEWITCHED WITH FRIENDSHIP 144258	*	15.00	15.00
96	WE'VE CARVED A PERFECT FRIENDSHIP 178586	*	13.50	13.50
96	YOU'RE THE BEST IN THE FIELD 178594	*	13.50	13.50
P. HILLMAN			**CALICO KITTENS HOLIDAY HARMONY**	
95	FIRST NOEL, THE	*	17.50	18.00
95	I'LL BE HOME FOR CHRISTMAS 144614	*	17.50	18.00
95	JOLLY OLD ST. NICHOLAS 144630	*	17.50	18.00
95	OH, TANNENBAUM 144428	*	17.50	18.00
95	SILENT NIGHT 144622	*	17.50	18.00
95	SILVER BELLS 144436	*	22.50	23.00
95	WINTER WONDERLAND 144444	*	17.50	18.00
P. HILLMAN			**CALICO KITTENS ITTY BITTY KITTIES**	
*	APRIL SHOWERS 155578	*	7.00	7.00
*	I LOVE MY KITTY 14432	*	7.00	7.00
*	I LOVE SPRING 155578	*	7.00	7.00
*	TO MY KITTY 144274	*	7.00	7.00
96	CONGRATULATIONS 167312	*	7.50	7.50
96	GET WELL 167339	*	7.50	7.50
96	GRADUATION 167347	*	7.50	7.50
96	HAPPY BIRTHDAY 167320	*	7.50	7.50
96	I LOVE YOU 167304	*	7.50	7.50
96	MY LITTLE SWEET TART	*	7.00	7.00
96	NEW BABY 167355	*	7.50	8.00
96	YOU ARE MY SUNSHINE 155578	*	7.00	7.00
P. HILLMAN			**CALICO KITTENS ITTY BITTY KITTY CHRISTMAS KITTY**	
*	TITLE N/A 178462	*	7.00	7.00
*	TITLE N/A 178462	*	7.00	7.00
P. HILLMAN			**CALICO KITTENS KITTY CAPERS**	
96	HATS OFF TO THE HOLIDAYS	*	12.50	12.50
96	I'M ALL YOURS	*	12.50	12.50
96	NOT PURR-FECT, JUST PURR-FECTLY HAPPY	*	12.50	12.50
96	WRAPPED UP IN YOU	*	15.00	15.00
96	YOU BRIGHTEN MY HOLIDAYS	*	15.00	15.00
P. HILLMAN			**CALICO KITTENS MY HEART BELONGS TO KITTY**	
96	FOR THE ONE I LOVE	*	17.50	17.50
96	HOPE ALL YOUR DREAMS COME TRUE	*	20.00	20.00
96	MY FUNNY VALENTINE	*	17.50	17.50
96	SWEETS FOR THE SWEET	*	20.00	20.00
P. HILLMAN			**CALICO KITTENS PICKS OF THE LITTER**	
96	A LITTLE LITTER OF BLESSINGS 168602	*	15.00	15.00
96	HELLO, LITTLE ONE 129410	*	17.50	17.50
96	NEW KIT ON THE BLOCK 903140	*	12.50	12.50
96	OUR FRIENDSHIP IS SQUEEKY CLEAN 132713	*	15.00	15.00

YR	NAME	LIMIT	ISSUE	TREND
96	TUMMY FULL OF LOVE FOR YOU 132713	*	12.50	12.50
96	WAGON OUR TAILS FOR YOU 172693	*	17.50	17.50
P. HILLMAN		**CALICO KITTENS PURR-FECT PERSONALITIES**		
95	A PLAYFUL AFTERNOON 112429	*	14.50	15.00
95	A PURR-FECT PAIR 112445	*	14.50	15.00
95	ALWAYS THINKING OF YOU 112437	*	14.50	15.00
95	AN EXPECTED TREAT 112321	*	14.50	15.00
95	BLUE WITHOUT YOU 129615	*	17.50	18.00
95	FISHING FOR A FRIEND 112453	*	14.50	15.00
95	FRIENDSHIP HAS MANY RICHES 129755	*	17.50	18.00
95	GOOD AS NEW 113301	*	14.50	15.00
95	GREAT SCOT WE'RE THE BEST OF FRIENDS 129	*	17.50	18.00
95	I'M LOST WITHOUT YOU 112488	*	14.50	15.00
95	IT'S NO MYSTERY WE'RE FRIENDS 129585	*	17.50	18.00
95	MY FAVORITE COMPANION 112410	*	14.50	15.00
95	SWEET DREAMS 112461	*	14.50	15.00
95	WE'RE INSER-PURR-ABLE FRIENDS 129577	*	17.50	18.00
95	YOU'RE MY ALL AMERICAN FRIEND 129607	*	17.50	18.00
96	I'D NEVER DESERT YOU 903116	*	17.50	17.50
96	TRIED AND TRUE FOR THE RED, WHITE & BLUE	*	17.50	17.50
P. HILLMAN		**CALICO KITTENS SPRING & EASTER**		
*	HAPPY SPRING 102687	*	11.00	11.00
*	PURR-FECT FRIEND 102687	*	11.00	11.00
95	EGGSTRA SPECIAL 102687	*	11.00	11.00
95	FRIENDSHIP IS THE BEST BLESSING 102679	*	20.00	20.00
95	FURRY AND FEATHERED FRIENDS 102636	*	20.00	20.00
95	LOVE BLOOMS FUR-EVER 102644	*	17.50	18.00
95	YOU MAKE LIFE COLORFUL 102601	*	25.00	25.00
P. HILLMAN		**CALICO KITTENS VALENTINES**		
*	SEW IN LOVE	*	11.00	11.00
*	SEW SWEET	*	11.00	11.00
95	BE MINE	*	11.00	11.00
95	LOVE POURS FROM MY HEART 102210	*	22.50	23.00
95	MY LOVE BLOSSOMS FOR YOU 102547	*	15.00	15.00
95	PAWS-ITIVELY IN LOVE 102571	*	25.00	25.00
95	YOU MAKE IT ALL BETTER 102202	*	15.00	15.00
L. RIGG			**CHAPEAU NOELLE**	
94	BEAR W/HAND MIRROR - JOAN	2000	30.00	30.00
94	BEAR W/TEA SET - LINDA	2000	30.00	30.00
94	BRIDE BEAR - DIANE	2000	30.00	30.00
94	MRS. SANTA - BEAR W/COOKIES	2000	30.00	30.00
94	SANTA - BEAR W/LIST/PEN	2000	30.00	30.00
95	ALLISON- BEAR PAINTING	2000	30.00	30.00
95	JULIET - BEAR HOLDING DOVE	2000	30.00	30.00
95	MARY LOUISE/FRANCES - ANGEL H/O	5000	12.50	13.00
95	ROMEO - BEAR HOLDING ROSE	2000	30.00	30.00
95	SANTA/MRS. SANTA H/O/	5000	12.50	13.00
95	SUSIE- BEAR W/BASKET	2000	30.00	30.00
95	THOMAS & BETH - CAROLERS H/O	5000	12.50	13.00
P. HILLMAN			**CHERISHED TEDDIES**	
92	RICHARD	OP	55.00	55.00
93	TEDDY ROOSEVELT	OP	20.00	20.00
94	INGRID	YR	20.00	20.00
94	PRISCILLA GRETA	OP	50.00	50.00
95	ABC & 123, YOU'RE A FRIEND TO ME!/LINDA	*	15.00	15.00
95	BEST IS YET TO COME, THE/BOY - 127949	*	12.50	13.00
95	BEST IS YET TO COME, THE/GIRL-127957	*	12.50	13.00
95	CAN I BE YOUR FOOTBALL HERO?/BUTCH 15638	*	15.00	15.00
95	FRIENDSHIP KEEPS ME ON MY TOES/MINDY 156	*	15.00	15.00
95	FRIENDSHOP MAKES IT ALL BETTER/LAURA 156	*	15.00	15.00
95	KISS THE HURT AND MAKE IT WELL 127965	*	15.00	15.00
95	LET'S HEAR IT FOR FRIENDSHIP!/DEBBIE 156	*	15.00	15.00
95	NICKOLAS	YR	20.00	20.00
95	SEAL OF FRIENDSHIP 137596	*	10.00	10.00
95	TRUNK FULL OF BEAR HUGS 103977	*	22.50	23.00
96	TWO BOYS W/LANTERN 141089	*	50.00	50.00
96	WISHING YOU A COZY CHRISTMAS/CHERYL & CA	*	25.00	25.00
P. HILLMAN		**CHERISHED TEDDIES ACROSS THE SEAS**		
96	FROM RUSSIA WITH LOVE/NADIA 202320	*	17.50	17.50
96	I FOUND AN AMIGO IN YOU/CARLOS 202339	*	17.50	17.50
96	LOVE FANS A BEAUTIFUL FRIENDSHIP/MACHIKO	*	17.50	17.50
96	OUR FRIENDSHIP IS BON APPETIT/CLAUDETTE	*	17.50	17.50
96	OUR FRIENDSHIP IS FROM SEA. SHINING SEA/	*	17.50	17.50
96	OUR FRIENDSHIP KNOWS NO BOUNDARIES/FRANZ	*	17.50	17.50
96	OUR FRIENDSHIP SPANS MANY MILES/LIAN 202	*	17.50	17.50
96	OUR LOVE IS IN THE HIGHLANDS/LORNA 20245	*	17.50	17.50
96	RIDING ACROSS THE GREAT WHITE NORTH/PRES	*	17.50	17.50
96	TULIPS BLOSSOM W/FRIENDSHIP/KATRIEN 2024	*	17.50	17.50
96	YOU MAKE EVERYDAY A FIESTA/FERNANDO 2023	*	17.50	17.50
96	YOU'RE A JOLLY OL' CHAP!/WILLIAM 202878	*	17.50	17.50
96	YOU'RE THE HEWEL OF MY HEART/RAJUL 20239	*	17.50	17.50
96	YOU'RE THE SWEDISH OF THEM ALL/KERSTIN 1	*	17.50	17.50
P. HILLMAN		**CHERISHED TEDDIES ADOPTION CENTER**		
96	IN GRANDMOTHER'S ATTIC/TASHA 156353	19960	55.00	55.00
96	YOU MAKE WISHES COME TRUE 131865	YR	17.50	17.50
P. HILLMAN			**CHERISHED TEDDIES ANGELS**	
96	HARK THE HERALD ANGELS SING/STORMI 17000	*	20.00	20.00

YR	NAME	LIMIT	ISSUE	TREND
P. HILLMAN	**CHERISHED TEDDIES CHARTER SYMBOL MEMBERSHIP**			
96	R. HARRISON HARTFORD/RED PENCIL CT102	*	*	*
P. HILLMAN	**CHERISHED TEDDIES CHRISTMAS**			
92	BEAR ON ROCKING REINDEER/MUSICAL	SU	60.00	85.00
92	BEAR ON ROCKING REINDEER/MUSICAL WATERBALL	*	60.00	70.00
92	BETH ON ROCKING REINDEER	SU	22.50	43.00
92	CHARLIE	OP	45.00	45.00
92	DOUGLAS	RT	20.00	45.00
92	JACOB	OP	22.50	23.00
92	STEVEN	OP	20.00	20.00
92	THEADORE, SAMANTHA, TYLER	OP	20.00	20.00
93	ALICE	YR	17.50	50.00
93	ALICE (9 IN.)	SU	100.00	100.00
93	BEAR PLAYING WITH TRAIN MUSICAL	OP	40.00	40.00
93	CAROLYN	OP	22.50	23.00
93	FAMILY ON TOBOGGAN	*	170.00	195.00
93	GIRL WITH MUFF MUSICAL WATERBALL	*	50.00	70.00
93	HANS	SU	20.00	20.00
93	JOINTED BEAR CHRISTMAS MUSICAL	SU	60.00	75.00
93	MARY	OP	25.00	25.00
93	THEADORE, SAMANTHA, TYLER	SU	160.00	160.00
94	BEAR ON ROCKING HORSE MUSICAL	OP	165.00	165.00
94	BOY AND GIRL IN SLEIGH MUSICAL	OP	100.00	100.00
94	ERIC	OP	22.50	23.00
94	INGRID	YR	20.00	45.00
94	NILS	OP	22.50	23.00
94	SONJA	OP	20.00	20.00
95	HUGS OF LOVE & FRIENDSHIP/KRISTEN 141194	OP	20.00	20.00
P. HILLMAN	**CHERISHED TEDDIES CIRCUS**			
96	BRUNO	*	17.50	24.00
96	CIRCUS ELEPHANT WITH BEAR	*	22.50	22.5
96	CIRCUS SEAL WITH BALL	*	10.00	10.00
96	CLOWN ON BALL MUSICAL	*	40.00	40.00
P. HILLMAN	**CHERISHED TEDDIES CLUB**			
95	CUB E. BEAR CT001	YR	17.50	30.00
95	HILARY HUGABEAR CT952	YR	17.50	25.00
95	MAYOR WILSON T. BEARY CT952	YR	20.00	25.00
P. HILLMAN	**CHERISHED TEDDIES CUSTOMER APPRECIATION**			
93	CUSTOMER APPRECIATION	YR	23.00	65.00
P. HILLMAN	**CHERISHED TEDDIES DICKENS VILLAGE**			
94	BEAR CRATCHIT	OP	17.50	18.00
94	EBEARNEZER SCROOGE	OP	17.50	18.00
94	GABRIEL, GARLAND, GLORIA	*	55.00	55.00
94	JACOB BEARLY	OP	17.50	18.00
94	MRS. CRATCHIT	OP	18.50	19.00
94	TINY TED-BEAR	*	10.00	10.00
P. HILLMAN	**CHERISHED TEDDIES DOWN STRAWBERRY LANE**			
96	A DASH OF LOVE SWEETENS ANY DAY!/MATTHEW	*	15.00	15.00
96	BUNNY MINI	*	3.50	4.00
96	COZY TEA FOR TWO/THELMA 156302	*	22.50	22.50
96	LOVE GROWS IN MY HEART/ELLA 156329	*	15.00	15.00
96	YOU'RE BERRY SPECIAL TO ME/JENNA 156337	*	15.00	15.00
96	YOU'RE MY BERRY BEST FRIEND!/TARA 156310	*	15.00	15.00
P. HILLMAN	**CHERISHED TEDDIES EASTER**			
93	ABIGAIL	SU	16.00	16.00
93	CHARITY	SU	20.00	75.00
93	CHELSEA	RT	15.00	45.00
93	DAISY	SU	15.00	100.00
93	HEIDI AND DAVID	SU	25.00	25.00
93	HENRIETTA	SU	22.50	65.00
93	MOLLY	SU	30.00	30.00
94	BECKY	SU	20.00	20.00
94	BESSIE	SU	15.00	50.00
94	COURTNEY	SU	15.00	15.00
94	FAITH	SU	20.00	60.00
94	GIRL WITH BLUE BONNET AND CHICK MINI	*	7.00	7.00
94	GIRL WITH DAISY HEADBAND MINI	*	7.00	7.00
94	GIRL WITH WHITE HAT MINI	*	7.00	7.00
94	HENRY	SU	20.00	50.00
P. HILLMAN	**CHERISHED TEDDIES EASTER/SPRING**			
96	BLESSINGS BLOOM WHEN YOU ARE NEAR/VIOLET	*	15.00	20.00
96	LOVE KEEPS ME AFLOAT/ROBERT 156272	*	13.50	20.00
P. HILLMAN	**CHERISHED TEDDIES EASTER/SPRING RAINBOW LANE**			
95	BUNNY	OP	13.50	14.00
95	DONALD	OP	20.00	20.00
95	GAIL	OP	20.00	20.00
95	HOPE	OP	20.00	20.00
95	JENNIFER	OP	22.50	23.00
95	LISA	OP	20.00	20.00
95	MELISSA	OP	20.00	20.00
95	PETER	OP	17.50	18.00
P. HILLMAN	**CHERISHED TEDDIES ENGAGEMENT PARTY 1996**			
95	PARK BENCH W/2 BEARS CRT240	*	12.50	13.00
P. HILLMAN	**CHERISHED TEDDIES FALL HARVEST**			
95	FALLING GOR YOU/PAT 141313	OP	22.50	23.00
96	YOU'RE MY LITTLE PUMPKIN/DANIEL 176214	*	22.50	22.50

YR	NAME	LIMIT	ISSUE	TREND
P. HILLMAN		**CHERISHED TEDDIES FOUNDERS DAY EVENT 1995**		
95	TOWN TATTLER SIGNAGE CRT109	*	6.00	6.00
P. HILLMAN		**CHERISHED TEDDIES GCC EARLY INTRO**		
96	A MOTHER'S HEART IS FULL OF LOVE/JESSICA	*	25.00	25.00
P. HILLMAN		**CHERISHED TEDDIES GENERAL**		
92	ANNA	OP	22.50	23.00
92	BEAR IN STOCKING HAT MUSICAL WATERBALL	*	60.00	80.00
92	BENJI	RT	13.50	30.00
92	BETH	RT	17.50	40.00
92	BETH AND BLOSSOM	OP	50.00	50.00
92	CAMILLE	OP	20.00	20.00
92	CHRISTOPHER	OP	50.00	50.00
92	COUPLE IN BASKET WITH UMBRELLA MUSICAL	OP	60.00	60.00
92	JACKI	*	10.00	15.00
92	JASMINE	SU	22.50	23.00
92	JEREMY	RT	15.00	35.00
92	JOSHUA	OP	20.00	20.00
92	KAREN	*	10.00	10.00
92	KATIE	OP	20.00	20.00
92	MANDY	RT	15.00	20.00
92	NATHANIEL AND NELLIE	OP	30.00	30.00
92	SARA	OP	10.00	10.00
92	THEADORE, SAMANTHA, TYLER	OP	20.00	20.00
92	THEADORE, SAMANTHA, TYLER (9 IN.)	*	130.00	140.00
92	ZACHARY	OP	30.00	30.00
93	BABY IN CRADLE MUSICAL	OP	60.00	60.00
93	BOY PRAYING MUSICAL	OP	37.50	38.00
93	FREDA AND TINA	OP	35.00	35.00
93	GIRL PRAYING MUSICAL	OP	37.50	38.00
93	HARRISON	*	15.00	40.00
93	JONATHAN	*	15.00	40.00
93	PATRICE	OP	18.50	19.00
93	PATRICK	OP	18.50	19.00
93	PRISCILLA	OP	15.00	50.00
93	PRISCILLA ANN	YR	24.00	70.00
93	ROBBIE AND RACHEL	OP	27.50	28.00
93	TEDDY AND ROOSEVELT	YR	20.00	80.00
93	THOMAS	OP	15.00	15.00
93	TRACIE AND NICOLE	OP	35.00	35.00
94	BABY BOY JOINTED MUSICAL	OP	60.00	60.00
94	BABY GIRL JOINTED MUSICAL	OP	60.00	60.00
94	BEAR AS BUNNY MUSICAL	OP	60.00	60.00
94	BEAR HOLDING HARP MUSICAL	OP	45.00	45.00
94	BEAR WITH GOOSE MUSICAL	OP	45.00	45.00
94	BEAR WITH HORSE MUSICAL	OP	150.00	150.00
94	BEAR WITH TOY CHEST MUSICAL	OP	45.00	45.00
94	BETSEY	OP	12.50	13.00
94	BETTY	OP	18.50	19.00
94	BILLY	OP	12.50	13.00
94	BOBBIE	OP	12.50	13.00
94	BOY AND GIRL IN LAUNDRY BASKET MUSICAL	OP	60.00	60.00
94	BRIDE AND GROOM MUSICAL	OP	50.00	50.00
95	A CUP FULL OF CHEER/MADELINE 135593	OP	20.00	20.00
95	A CUP FULL OF FRIENDSHIP/MARILYN 135682	OP	20.00	20.00
95	A CUP FULL OF LOVE/MARGARET 103667	OP	20.00	22.00
95	ALLISON AND ALEXANDRIA	OP	25.00	25.00
95	GIRL BEAR ON OTTOMAN MUSICAL 128058	OP	55.00	55.00
95	HERE'S SOME CHEER TO LAST THE YEAR/AMAND	YR	17.50	18.00
95	KISS THE HURT AND MAKE IT WELL	*	15.00	15.00
95	LOVE ME TENDER/MILLIE 128023	OP	12.50	13.00
95	LOVE ME TRUE/DOROTHY 128023	OP	12.50	13.00
95	MY PRAYER IS FOR YOU/CHRISTIAN 103837	OP	18.50	19.00
95	MY PRAYER IS FOR YOU/CHRISTINE103845	OP	18.50	19.00
95	OUR HEARTS BELONG TO YOU/PRISCILLA & GRE	19950	50.00	50.00
95	PRISCILLA AND GRETA-INTERNATIONAL	*	50.00	140.00
95	TAKE ME TO YOUR HEART/CHRISTY 128023	OP	12.50	13.00
95	WE"RE BEARY GOOD PALS/SETH & SARABETH 12	OP	25.00	25.00
95	WE'RE IN THIS TOGETHER/TUCKER & TRAVIS	OP	25.00	25.00
P. HILLMAN		**CHERISHED TEDDIES GRADUATE**		
95	GIRL GRADUATE	OP	12.50	13.00
P. HILLMAN		**CHERISHED TEDDIES GRADUATION**		
95	BOY GRADUATE	OP	12.50	13.00
P. HILLMAN		**CHERISHED TEDDIES HALLOWEEN**		
93	BRENDA	SU	15.00	15.00
93	BUCKEY	SU	15.00	15.00
93	CONNIE	OP	15.00	15.00
93	GARY	OP	18.50	19.00
93	GRETEL	OP	18.50	19.00
93	MILES	OP	17.00	17.00
93	PRUDENCE	OP	17.00	17.00
94	BREANNA	OP	15.00	15.00
94	STACIE	OP	18.50	19.00
94	TAYLOR	OP	15.00	15.00
95	"BEE" MY FRIEND/BEA 141348	OP	15.00	15.00
95	BEARY SCARY HALLOWEEN HOUSE	OP	20.00	20.00
95	FUTURE "BEARETH" ALL THINGS, THE/CARRIE	OP	18.50	19.00
96	YOU HAVE A SPECIAL PLACE IN MY HEART/AND	*	18.50	18.50
96	YOU'RE THE CAT'S MEOW/TABITHA 176257	*	15.00	15.00

YR	NAME	LIMIT	ISSUE	TREND
P. HILLMAN		**CHERISHED TEDDIES HOLIDAY DANGLING**		
95	A STRING OF GOOD TIDINGS/NOLAN 176141	*	20.00	20.00
96	AN OLD FASHIONED NOEL TO YOU/NOEL 176109	*	15.00	15.00
96	CATCHIN THE HOLIDAY SPIRIT/HOLDEN 176095	*	15.00	15.00
96	DROPPING YOU A HOLIDAY GREETING/JOLENE 1	*	20.00	20.00
96	STRIKING UP ANOTHER YEAR/JEFFREY 176044	*	17.50	17.50
96	TOY SOLDIER DATED 1996 176052	YR	12.50	12.50
96	YOU ALWAYS BRING JOY/JOY 176087	*	15.00	15.00
P. HILLMAN		**CHERISHED TEDDIES LAPLANDERS**		
95	WARM HEARTED FRIENDS/EARL 131873	OP	17.50	18.00
96	FEEL THE PEACE/HOLD THE JOY/SHARE.../OLG	YR	50.00	50.00
96	FRIENDS ARE ALWAYS PULLING FOR YOU/ERICA	*	22.50	22.50
P. HILLMAN		**CHERISHED TEDDIES MEMBERS ONLY**		
96	EMILY E. CLAIRE CT962	*	17.50	17.50
96	KURTIS D. CLAW CT961	*	17.50	17.50
P. HILLMAN		**CHERISHED TEDDIES MESSENGERS OF THE HEART**		
95	BOY AND GIRL CUPID	*	25.00	40.00
95	BOY AND GIRL CUPID (1 OF 2)	*	18.50	27.00
95	BOY AND GIRL CUPID (2 OF 2)	*	18.50	27.00
95	BOY BEAR CUPID	SU	17.50	22.00
95	CUPID BABY BOY ON PILLOW	SU	13.50	20.00
95	CUPID BABY GIRL ON PILLOW	SU	13.50	20.00
95	CUPID BOY SITTING (1 OF 2)	*	13.50	27.00
95	CUPID BOY SITTING (2 OF 2)	*	13.50	27.00
95	GIRL BEAR CUPID	SU	15.00	30.00
95	GIRL CUPID (1 OF 2)/BE MINE	*	15.00	27.00
95	GIRL CUPID (1 OF 2)/LOVE	*	15.00	*
P. HILLMAN		**CHERISHED TEDDIES MISCELLANEOUS**		
96	RESIN EGG	OP	8.50	10.00
P. HILLMAN		**CHERISHED TEDDIES MONTHLY FRIENDS TO CHERISH**		
95	A DAY AT THE PARK/JULIE - JULY 914819	OP	15.00	15.00
95	A NEW YEAR W/OLD FRIENDS/JACK - JANUARY	OP	15.00	15.00
95	BE MINE/PHOEBE-FEBRUARY 914762	OP	15.00	15.00
95	FRIENDSHIP IS IN BLOOM/MAY - MAY 914797	OP	15.00	15.00
95	FRIENDSHIP IS IN THE AIR/MARK - MARCH 91	OP	15.00	15.00
95	HAPPY HOLIDAYS, FRIEND/DENISE-DECEMBER 9	OP	15.00	15.00
95	PLANTING THE SEED OF FRIENDSHIP/JUNE - J	OP	15.00	15.00
95	SCHOOL DAYS/SETH-SEPTEMBER 914835	OP	15.00	15.00
95	SHOWERS OF FRIENDSHIP/ALAN-APRIL 914789	OP	15.00	30.00
95	SMOOTH SMILING/ARTHUR-AUGUST 914827	OP	15.00	15.00
95	SWEET TREATS/OSCAR-OCTOBER 914843	OP	15.00	15.00
95	THANKS FOR FRIENDS /NICHOLE-NOVEMBER 914	OP	15.00	15.00
P. HILLMAN		**CHERISHED TEDDIES NATIVITY**		
92	ANGIE	OP	15.00	15.00
92	CRECHE WITH COVERLET	OP	50.00	50.00
92	MARIA WITH BABY JOSH	OP	35.00	35.00
92	SAMMY	OP	17.50	18.00
92	THREE KINGS/SET OF 3	*	55.00	150.00
93	MINI NATIVITY IN CRECHE	*	32.50	100.00
93	NATIVITY COLLECTOR SET	*	100.00	190.00
93	NATIVITY MUSICAL	SU	60.00	80.00
93	NATIVITY WITH CRECHE MUSICAL	*	85.00	100.00
94	RONNIE	OP	13.50	14.00
95	AN ANGEL TO WATCH OVER YOU/CELESTE 14126	OP	20.00	20.00
P. HILLMAN		**CHERISHED TEDDIES ONCE UPON A TEDDY**		
94	FATHER	OP	13.50	14.00
94	JACK AND JILL	OP	30.00	30.00
94	LITTLE BO PEEP	OP	22.50	23.00
94	LITTLE JACK HORNER	OP	20.00	20.00
94	LITTLE MISS MUFFET	OP	20.00	20.00
94	MARY, MARY QUITE CONTRARY	OP	22.50	23.00
94	TOM, TOM THE PIPER'S SON	OP	20.00	20.00
P. HILLMAN		**CHERISHED TEDDIES OUR CHERISHED FAMILY**		
94	MOTHER	*	20.00	40.00
94	OLDER DAUGHTER	OP	10.00	10.00
94	OLDER SON	OP	10.00	10.00
94	OUR CHERISHED FAMILY GIFT SET	*	85.00	140.00
94	YOUNG DAUGHTER	OP	9.00	9.00
94	YOUNG SON	OP	9.00	9.00
P. HILLMAN		**CHERISHED TEDDIES SANTA EXPRESS**		
96	A FIRST CLASS DELIVERY FOR YOU/TONY 2194	*	17.50	17.50
96	ALL ABOARD THE SANTA EXPRESS/LIONEL 2190	*	22.50	22.50
96	FRIENDSHIP IS ..PERFECT END..HOLIDAYS/CA	*	22.50	22.50
96	HE KNOWS IF YOU'RE BEEN BAD OR GD/COLIN	*	17.50	17.50
96	ROLLING ALONG W/FRIENDS & SMILES 219096	*	17.50	17.50
P. HILLMAN		**CHERISHED TEDDIES SANTA'S WORKSHOP**		
95	A CUP OF HOMEMADE LOVE/HOLLY 141119	OP	18.50	19.00
95	BUILDING A STURDY FRIENDSHIP/YULE 141143	OP	22.50	23.00
95	HANDSEWN HOLIDAYS/MERI 141135	OP	20.00	20.00
95	PAINTING YOUR HOLIDAYS W/LOVE/GINGER 141	OP	22.50	23.00
95	YOU'RE AT THE TOP OF MY LIST/NICKOLAS 14	YR	20.00	20.00
96	BEARER OF GOOD TIDINGS/KLAUS 176036	YR	20.00	20.00
P. HILLMAN		**CHERISHED TEDDIES ST. PATRICK'S DAY**		
94	KATHLEEN	OP	12.50	13.00
94	SEAN	OP	12.50	13.00
95	KEVIN	OP	12.50	20.00
95	MAUREEN	OP	12.50	20.00

YR	NAME	LIMIT	ISSUE	TREND
P. HILLMAN		**CHERISHED TEDDIES SWEETHEART BALL**		
95	JACK AND JILL	OP	35.00	35.00
96	LOVE UNVEILS A HAPPY HEART/DARREL 156450	*	17.50	17.50
96	MY HEART WISHES FOR YOU/DARLA 156469	*	20.00	20.00
96	SWEETHEARTS FOREVER/CRAIG & CHERI 156485	OP	25.00	25.00
96	WON'T YOU BE MY SWEETHEART?/JILLY 156477	*	17.50	17.50
96	YOU STEAL MY HEART AWAY/ROBIN 156434	*	17.50	17.50
96	YOU'RE THE HERO OF MY HEART/MARIAN 15644	*	20.00	20.00
P. HILLMAN		**CHERISHED TEDDIES SYMBOL OF MEMBERSHIP '96**		
96	R. HARRRISON HARTFORD/YELLOW PENCIL CT00	*	*	*
P. HILLMAN		**CHERISHED TEDDIES T IS FOR TEDDIES**		
95	BEAR W/ "A" BLOCK 158488A	*	5.00	5.00
95	BEAR W/"B" BLOCK 158488B	*	5.00	5.00
95	BEAR W/"C" BLOCK 158488C	*	5.00	5.00
95	BEAR W/"D" BLOCK 158488D	*	5.00	5.00
95	BEAR W/"E" BLOCK 158488E	*	5.00	5.00
95	BEAR W/"F" BLOCK 158488F	*	5.00	5.00
95	BEAR W/"G" BLOCK 158488G	*	5.00	5.00
95	BEAR W/"H" BLOCK 158488H	*	5.00	5.00
95	BEAR W/"I" BLOCK 158488I	*	5.00	5.00
95	BEAR W/"J" BLOCK 158488J	*	5.00	5.00
95	BEAR W/"K" BLOCK 158488K	*	5.00	5.00
95	BEAR W/"L" BLOCK 158488L	*	5.00	5.00
95	BEAR W/"M" BLOCK 158488M	*	5.00	5.00
95	BEAR W/"N" BLOCK 158488N	*	5.00	5.00
95	BEAR W/"O" BLOCK 158488O	*	5.00	5.00
95	BEAR W/"P" BLOCK 158488P	*	5.00	5.00
95	BEAR W/"Q" BLOCK 158488Q	*	5.00	5.00
95	BEAR W/"R" BLOCK 158488R	*	5.00	5.00
95	BEAR W/"S" BLOCK 158488S	*	5.00	5.00
95	BEAR W/"T" BLOCK 158488T	*	5.00	5.00
95	BEAR W/"U" BLOCK 158488U	*	5.00	5.00
95	BEAR W/"V" BLOCK 158488V	*	5.00	5.00
95	BEAR W/"W" BLOCK 158488W	*	5.00	5.00
95	BEAR W/"X" BLOCK 158488X	*	5.00	5.00
95	BEAR W/"Y" BLOCK 158488Y	*	5.00	5.00
95	BEAR W/"Z" BLOCK 158488Z	*	5.00	5.00
P. HILLMAN		**CHERISHED TEDDIES THANKSGIVING**		
94	JEDEDIAH	OP	17.50	18.00
94	PATIENCE	OP	17.50	18.00
94	PHOEBE	OP	13.50	14.00
94	THANKSGIVING QUILT	OP	12.00	12.00
94	WILLIE	OP	15.00	15.00
94	WINONA	OP	15.00	15.00
94	WYATT	OP	15.00	15.00
94	WYLIE	*	15.00	26.00
P. HILLMAN		**CHERISHED TEDDIES THROUGH THE YEARS**		
93	AGE 1	OP	13.50	14.00
93	AGE 2	OP	13.50	14.00
93	AGE 3	OP	15.00	15.00
93	AGE 4	OP	15.00	15.00
93	AGE 5	OP	15.00	15.00
93	AGE 6	OP	16.50	17.00
93	BABY	OP	16.50	17.00
P. HILLMAN		**CHERISHED TEDDIES UNDER THE BIG TOP**		
95	CLOWN ON BALL MUSICAL 111430	*	40.00	40.00
96	YOU TAKE CENTER RING W/ME/CLAUDIA 103721	*	17.50	24.00
96	YOU'RE THE TOPS W/ME/WALLY 103934	*	17.50	17.50
P. HILLMAN		**CHERISHED TEDDIES VALENTINE**		
93	AMY	OP	13.50	14.00
93	MARIE	OP	20.00	20.00
93	MICHAEL AND MICHELLE	SU	30.00	30.00
93	TIMOTHY	OP	15.00	15.00
94	ELIZABETH AND ASHLEY	SU	25.00	25.00
94	KELLY	SU	15.00	15.00
94	NANCY	SU	15.00	15.00
94	OLIVER AND OLIVIA	SU	25.00	25.00
94	VICTORIA	SU	16.50	55.00
P. HILLMAN		**CHERISHED TEDDIES VALENTINE MINI**		
94	HUGS AND KISSES	*	7.00	7.00
94	LOVE YA	*	7.00	7.00
94	YOU'RE PURR-FECT	*	7.00	7.00
P. HILLMAN		**CHERISHED TEDDIES WE BEAR THANKS**		
96	BEAR IN MIND, YOU'RE SPECIAL,JOHN 141283	*	15.00	15.00
96	BEAR IN MIND, YOU'RE SPECIAL/DINA 141275	*	15.00	15.00
96	GIVING THANKS FOR OUR FAMILY/BARBARA 141	*	12.50	12.50
96	SUITED UP FOR THE HOLIDAYS/RICK 141291	*	12.50	12.50
96	TABLE W/FOOD/DOG 141542	*	30.00	30.00
P. HILLMAN		**CHERISHED TEDDIES/ALLISON & ALEXANDRIA**		
95	TWO FRIENDS MEAN TWICE THE LOVE 127981	*	25.00	25.00
L. RIGG		**FOUR SEASONS**		
95	CAROL - WINTER ICE SKATER	2000	30.00	30.00
95	DENISE - SPRING IN APRON	2000	30.00	30.00
95	EMILY - SUMMER SAILOR SUIT	2000	30.00	30.00
95	MELISSA- FALL W/CORNUCOPIA	2000	30.00	30.00
*		**FROM BARBIE WITH LOVE**		
95	BALLERINA, 1961 PVC 113875	*	5.00	5.00

YR	NAME	LIMIT	ISSUE	TREND
95	BARBIE BUST PORTRAIT PORCELAIN 125601	*	15.00	15.00
95	BRIDE 1963 MUSICAL 113905	7500	100.00	100.00
95	ENCHANTED EVENING, 1960 PVC 133396	*	5.00	5.00
95	GRADUATION, 1963 PVC 113867	*	5.00	5.00
95	HAPPY HOLIDAYS 1988 BARBIE 154199	YR	30.00	100.00
95	MAGNIFICENCE 1965 143111	7500	100.00	100.00
95	MIDNIGHT BLUE '65 MUSICAL 113891	7500	100.00	100.00
95	ORIGINAL SWIMSUIT, 1959 RESIN 113700	*	30.00	30.00
95	PICNIC, 1959 RESIN 113727	*	30.00	30.00
95	POODLE PARADE, 1965 RESIN 113719	*	30.00	30.00
95	SENIOR PROM 1963 MUSICAL 125776	7500	100.00	100.00
95	SENIOR PROM, 1963 PORCELAIN 124370	*	100.00	100.00
95	SOPHISTICATED LADY '63 MUSICAL 113883	7500	100.00	100.00
95	SUBURBAN SHOPPER, 1959 RESIN 113751	*	30.00	30.00
95	WEDDING DAY, 1959 PVC 113859	*	5.00	5.00
96	ARABIAN NIGHTS, 1964 RESIN 171026	*	35.00	35.00
96	BARBIE/SCARLETT O'HARA-GRN VELVET/MUSICA	7500	50.00	50.00
96	CINDERELLA, 1964 RESIN 170992	*	35.00	35.00
96	ENCHANTED EVENING, 1960 MUSICAL 185787	2500	100.00	100.00
96	GUINEVERE, 1964 RESIN 171018	*	35.00	35.00
96	HAPPY HOLIDAY BARBIE, 1989 MUSICAL 18883	YR	100.00	100.00
96	HERE COMES THE BRIDE MUSICAL/PORCELAIN 1	7500	100.00	100.00
96	HOLIDAY DANCE 1965 , MUSCIAL 188786	7500	100.00	100.00
96	QUEEN OF HEARTS BARBIE PORCELAIN 157651	5000	125.00	125.00
96	RED RIDING HOOD, 1964 RESIN 171034	*	35.00	35.00
	K. WICKL			**GNOMES**
93	SIGFRIED & SOPHIA	1000	70.00	70.00
94	HUBERT & HENRIETTA	2000	80.00	80.00
94	LOTHAR	1994	100.00	100.00
95	ALBERT, RESIN 127434	*	7.50	8.00
95	ALBERT, RESIN 146129	*	7.50	8.00
95	ANDREAS AND AVA , RESIN 146099	*	50.00	50.00
95	BRINA & BORG, RESIN 127191	*	25.00	25.00
95	CATRINA AND CHARLES, RESIN 146358	*	25.00	25.00
95	ETHAN, RESIN 127450	*	5.50	5.50
95	ETHAN, RESIN 146145	*	7.50	8.00
95	FERDINAND 146072	15	300.00	300.00
95	FERDINARD, RESIN 153257	*	8.50	9.00
95	GOBBY & LOU, RESIN 127183	*	25.00	25.00
95	GUSTAV, RESIN 146064	*	20.00	20.00
95	JOHANN'S DANCE SCHOOL 127493	2000	55.00	55.00
95	JOSHUA, RESIN 127485	*	5.50	5.50
95	JULIA , RESIN 146110	*	7.50	8.00
95	JULIA, RESIN 127442	*	7.50	8.00
95	KATY, RESIN 127477	*	5.50	5.50
95	LOREN AND LINDA, RESIN 146056	*	40.00	40.00
95	LOREN, RESIN 127213	*	25.00	25.00
95	LOUIS, RESIN 146102	*	30.00	30.00
95	MAGGIE, RESIN 127469	*	5.50	5.50
95	MAGGIE, RESIN 146137	*	7.50	8.00
95	NEWBORNS, RESIN 146153	*	7.50	8.00
95	OMA, RESIN 127426	*	7.50	8.00
95	OPA, RESIN 127221	*	7.50	8.00
95	PETER, RESIN 153265	*	7.50	8.00
95	PURDY AND PIPPEN, RESIN 153281	*	7.50	8.00
95	SIDNEY, RESIN 127167	*	25.00	25.00
96	ABRAM RESIN 146080	*	*	*
96	AMADEUS, RESIN 173185	*	*	*
96	BILL AND BELLA, RESIN 173177	*	*	*
96	CATRINA AND CHARLES, RESIN 195529	*	*	*
96	FRANZ AND CHRISTOPH & KATYA, RESIN 12720	*	*	*
96	KARL, RESIN 195499	*	*	*
96	LUSCKY, RESIN 173231	*	*	*
96	MARY AND MICHAEL, RESIN 195510	*	*	*
96	NICHOLAS, RESIN 146048	*	*	*
96	OPA, RESIN 127175	*	*	*
96	STEPHIE AND STOPHIE, RESIN 195480	*	*	*
	S. BUTCHER			**GROWING IN GOD'S GARDEN OF LOVE**
96	SOME PLANT, SOME WATER, BUT GOD..INCREAS	OP	37.50	37.50
96	SOWING SEEDS OF KINDNESS 163856	OP	37.50	37.50
	S. BUTCHER			**GROWING IN GRACE**
95	AGE 1-BABY WITH CAKE 136190	OP	25.00	25.00
95	AGE 2-GIRL WITH BLOCKS 136212	OP	25.00	25.00
95	AGE 3-GIRL WITH FLOWERS 136220	OP	25.00	25.00
95	AGE 4-GIRL WITH DOLL 136239	OP	27.50	28.00
95	AGE 5-GIRL WITH LUNCH BOX 136247	OP	27.50	27.50
95	AGE 6-GIRL ON BICYCLE 136255	OP	30.00	30.00
95	IT'S A GIRL-ANGEL W/INFANT ANNOUNCEMENT	OP	22.50	23.00
95	SWEET SIXTEEN-GIRL HOLDING 16 ROSES 1362	OP	40.00	40.00
96	AGE 10-GIRL BOWLING 183873	OP	37.50	37.50
96	AGE 7-GIRL DRESSED AS NURSE 163740	OP	32.50	33.00
96	AGE 8-GIRL SHOOTING MARBLES 163759	OP	32.50	33.00
96	AGE 9-GIRL WITH CHARM BRACELET 183865	OP	30.00	30.00
	L. RIGG			**HISTORY OF HATS**
95	PETITE COLLECTION - 6 ASST. PREPACK	30000	15.00	15.00
	KINKA			**KINKA**
88	BABIES ARE DREAMS YOU CAN CUDDLE 117552	OP	37.50	40.00
88	BABIES ARE DREAMS YOU CAN CUDDLE 117560	OP	45.00	50.00

YR	NAME	LIMIT	ISSUE	TREND
88	FOR YOU...JUST BECAUSE 117781	OP	37.50	40.00
88	JUST FOR YOU ON THIS SPECIAL DAY 117501	OP	22.50	25.00
88	KEEP THE WARM GLOW OF THE SEASON 117455	OP	37.50	38.00
88	LOVE TO YOU 117757	OP	37.50	40.00
88	MAY YOUR LIFE BE FILLED WITH 117498	OP	37.50	40.00
88	THINKING OF YOU 117749	OP	37.50	38.00
88	THINKING OF YOU...NOW & ALWAYS 117528	OP	22.50	25.00
88	WISHING YOU CLOUDLESS SKIES 117471	OP	37.50	40.00
88	WISHING YOU JOY, HAPPINESS 117536	OP	40.00	45.00
88	WISHING YOU JOY, HAPPINESS 117544	OP	50.00	55.00
88	YOU ARE SPECIAL TO ME 117773	OP	37.50	40.00
88	YOUR FRIENDSHIP & THOUGHTFULNESS 117463	OP	37.50	40.00
88	YOUR FRIENDSHIP WILL BE 117765	OP	37.50	40.00
89	A BOUQUET OF FLOWERS FOR YOU 119024	OP	30.00	30.00
89	BABIES ARE CHRISTMAS DREAMS 117722	YR	15.00	16.00
89	BABIES ARE CHRISTMAS DREAMS 118540	YR	15.00	16.00
89	CHRISTMAS IS A SPECIAL GIFT 117692	OP	33.50	34.00
89	CHRISTMAS IS A TIME TO GATHER 117676	OP	55.00	55.00
89	EASTER IS A TIME FILLED WITH 116629	OP	50.00	50.00
89	GATHER YOUR CHRISTMAS DREAMS 117862	OP	55.00	55.00
89	GATHER YOUR DREAMS AND WISHES 119032	OP	30.00	30.00
89	HAPPY 25TH ANNIVERSARY 119121	OP	75.00	75.00
89	HAPPY 40TH ANNIVERSARY 119148	OP	75.00	75.00
89	HAPPY 50TH ANNIVERSARY 119156	OP	75.00	75.00
89	IT'S THE TIME FOR CHRISTMAS 117889	OP	50.00	50.00
89	IT'S TIME FOR CHRISTMAS 117846	OP	37.50	38.00
89	JUST FOR YOU 119083	OP	30.00	30.00
89	KEEP ME IN YOUR DREAMS 119695	OP	50.00	50.00
89	KEEP THE SPIRIT 119113	OP	30.00	30.00
89	KEEP THE TRUE LIGHT OF CHRISTMAS 117684	OP	25.00	25.00
89	LOVE TO YOU 120391	OP	120.00	120.00
89	LOVE TO YOU AT THIS SPECIAL TIME 118877	OP	45.00	45.00
89	LOVE TO YOU AT THIS SPECIAL TIME 118885	OP	50.00	50.00
89	MAY APRIL SHOWERS BRING 118958	OP	30.00	30.00
89	MAY GOD'S LOVE BLESS 118842	OP	45.00	45.00
89	MAY THE GLOW OF GOD'S LOVE 116661	OP	50.00	50.00
89	MAY THE GLOW OF GOD'S LOVE 116688	OP	20.00	20.00
89	MAY THE LOVE IN YOUR HEARTS 116572	OP	15.00	16.00
89	MAY THIS DAY TOUCH YOUR HEART 119105	OP	30.00	30.00
89	MAY THIS SPECIAL SEASON 118559	YR	25.00	25.00
89	MAY YOUR DAYS BE FILLED 118834	YR	45.00	45.00
89	MAY YOUR DAYS BE FILLED WITH LOVE 118915	OP	30.00	30.00
89	NATIVITY SCENE (3 WISE MEN) 118192	OP	45.00	45.00
89	NATIVITY SCENE (SET OF 9) 118214	OP	115.00	115.00
89	NATIVITY SCENE (SHEPHERD) 118206	OP	30.00	30.00
89	NATIVITY SCENE 118184	OP	40.00	40.00
89	REJOICE IN GOD'S PROMISE OF LOVE 116637	OP	37.50	38.00
89	REMEMBER THE DREAMS 118966	OP	75.00	75.00
89	THINKING OF YOU & WISHING 119016	OP	24.00	30.00
89	WILL YOU STOP & COUNT 117870	OP	50.00	50.00
89	WILL YOU STOP AND COUNT 117838	OP	37.50	38.00
89	WISH ON THE CHRISTMAS STAR 117854	OP	37.50	38.00
89	WISH ON THE CHRISTMAS STAR 117897	OP	50.00	50.00
89	WISHING YOU CLOUDLESS SKIES 408565	2500	170.00	170.00
89	WISHING YOU EVERY HAPPINESS 117730	OP	25.00	25.00
89	WISHING YOU LOVE AND HAPPINESS 116556	OP	50.00	50.00
89	WISHING YOU LOVE AND HAPPINESS 116564	OP	37.50	38.00
89	WISHING YOU PINK ROSES 119075	OP	30.00	30.00
89	WISHING YOU SPECIAL BLESSINGS 116653	OP	17.50	18.00
89	WISHING YOU SPECIAL MOMENTS 119091	OP	30.00	30.00
89	WISHING YOUR BABY 118834	OP	17.50	18.00
89	YOU BRING JOY INTO MY LIFE 119296	OP	15.00	16.00
89	YOU'RE A DOLL 118931	OP	30.00	30.00
90	CHRISTMAS FILLS YOUR HEART 119725	OP	25.00	25.00
90	CHRISTMAS IS A GIFT FROM GOD 119849	OP	20.00	20.00
90	CHRISTMAS IS A TIME OF LOVE 119822	OP	60.00	60.00
90	CHRISTMAS IS A TIME TO SHARE 119830	OP	37.50	38.00
90	CHRISTMAS IS A TIME TO SHARE 119938	OP	17.50	18.00
90	I'M WRAPPING UP ALL MY DREAMS 119717	OP	60.00	60.00
90	MAY THIS CHRISTMAS DAY 119865	OP	40.00	40.00
90	MAY YOUR HEART BE FILLED 119911	OP	65.00	65.00
90	MAY YOUR STOCKING BE FILLED 119857	OP	22.50	23.00
90	SOUND OF LOVE IS FELT, THE- 119881	OP	25.00	25.00
90	SWEET MUSIC & BEAUTIFUL MEMORIES 119873	OP	25.00	25.00
90	WISHING YOU GENTLE MOMENTS 119946	OP	17.50	118.00
91	BABIES ARE THE GREATEST GIFT/GOD 121266	OP	25.00	25.00
91	BABIES TOUCH YOUR HEART 118788	OP	55.00	55.00
91	KEEP THE SPECIAL MEMORIES 122777	OP	75.00	75.00
91	MAY GOD'S LOVE FILL YOUR HEART 120553	OP	50.00	50.00
91	MAY GOD'S LOVE FILL YOUR LIFE 120561	OP	45.00	45.00
91	MAY THE BLESSINGS OF EASTER BRING 120529	OP	25.00	25.00
91	MAY THIS SPECIAL SEASON REAWAKEN 122688	OP	60.00	60.00
91	MAY YOUR LIFE BE FILLED WITH 121312	OP	120.00	120.00
91	MAY YOUR LIFE TOGETHER BE FILLED 121398	OP	22.50	23.00
91	MEMORIES ARE MADE OF SIMPLE JOYS 122653	OP	60.00	60.00
91	MUSIC AND MEMORIES FILL THIS 119873	OP	27.00	27.00
91	PLEASE FEEL BETTER SOON 121258	OP	22.50	23.00
91	REJOICE IN GOD'S LOVE 120537	OP	22.50	23.00
91	SOUND OF LOVE IS FELT IN HEARTS 119881	OP	27.00	27.00

YR	NAME	LIMIT	ISSUE	TREND
91	SPRING IS A TIME OF LOVE 120588	OP	19.00	19.00
91	WARM WISHES TO SOMEONE SPECIAL 122726	OP	60.00	60.00
91	WISHING YOU GENTLE HUGS 120510	OP	25.00	25.00
91	WISHING YOU GOD'S BLESSINGS 120545	OP	22.50	23.00
91	WITH LOVE TO MY SPECIAL ONE 120502	OP	45.00	45.00
92	CHRISTMAS FILLS YOUR HEART 119725	OP	15.00	16.00
92	CHRISTMAS IS A GIFT FROM GOD 119849	OP	12.50	13.00
92	CHRISTMAS IS A SPECIAL GIFT 117692	OP	16.75	17.00
92	CHRISTMAS IS A TIME OF LOVE 119822	OP	30.00	30.00
92	CHRISTMAS IS A TIME OF LOVE 119962	OP	13.50	14.00
92	CHRISTMAS IS A TIME TO BELIEVE 122718	OP	13.75	13.75
92	CHRISTMAS IS A TIME TO SHARE 117676	OP	27.50	28.00
92	CHRISTMAS IS A TIME TO SHARE 119830	OP	18.75	19.00
92	CHRISTMAS IS A TIME TO SHARE 119938	OP	10.00	10.00
92	CHRISTMAS IS PEACE, LOVE 118184	OP	22.50	23.00
92	CHRISTMAS IS PEACE, LOVE 118214	OP	60.00	60.00
92	GATHER YOUR CHRISTMAS DREAMS 117862	OP	27.50	28.00
92	I'M WRAPPING UP ALL MY DREAMS 119717	OP	30.00	30.00
92	IT'S THE SEASON OF SHARING 125342	OP	16.25	17.00
92	IT'S TIME FOR CHRISTMAS 117889	OP	25.00	25.00
92	JOIN IN THE CHORUS 125318	OP	10.00	10.00
92	KEEP THE SPECIAL MEMORIES 122777	OP	37.50	38.00
92	MAY CHRISTMAS BLESS YOU W/GIFTS 118192	OP	22.50	23.00
92	MAY CHRISTMAS BRING YOU ALL/JOY 120413	OP	20.00	20.00
92	MAY GOD'S SPECIAL BLESSINGS 123145	OP	33.00	33.00
92	MAY THIS CHRISTMAS DAY TOUCH 119865	OP	20.00	20.00
92	MAY THIS SPECIAL SEASON 118559	OP	15.00	16.00
92	MAY THIS SPECIAL SEASON 122688	OP	30.00	30.00
92	MAY YOU SHARE A NEW YEAR 119733	OP	11.25	12.00
92	MAY YOUR DAYS BE FILLED WITH LOVE 123188	OP	60.00	60.00
92	MAY YOUR STOCKING BE FILLED 119857	OP	12.50	13.00
92	MEMORIES ARE MADE OF SIMPLE JOYS 122653	OP	30.00	30.00
92	MY FAVORITE THINGS 125334	OP	15.00	16.00
92	REJOICE IN GOD'S LOVE 121789	OP	37.50	38.00
92	SANTA'S LITTLE HELPER 125326	OP	16.25	17.00
92	SOUND OF LOVE IS FELT, THE- 119881	OP	13.50	14.00
92	SWEET MUSIC & BEAUTIFUL MEMORIES 119070	OP	13.50	14.00
92	THREE PIECE CHRISTMAS COLLECTION 118176	OP	56.25	57.00
92	WARM WISHES TO SOMEONE SPECIAL 122726	OP	30.00	30.00
92	WILL YOU STOP AND COUNT THE STARS 117838	OP	18.75	19.00
92	WILL YOU STOP AND COUNT THE STARS 117870	OP	25.00	25.00
92	WISH ON THE CHRISTMAS STAR 117897	OP	25.00	25.00
92	WISHING YOU EVERY HAPPINESS 117730	OP	13.50	14.00
92	WISHING YOU GENTLE MOMENTS 119946	OP	10.00	10.00
92	WISHING YOU MANY MOMENTS OF LOVE 123137	OP	30.00	30.00
92	WISHING YOU SPECIAL BLESSINGS 117609	OP	12.50	13.00
92	WONDER OF THIS SPECIAL SEASON, THE- 1182	OP	15.00	16.00
L. RIGG				**LUCY & ME**
94	DIANE	2000	30.00	33.00
94	JOAN	2000	30.00	33.00
94	LINDA	2000	30.00	33.00
95	15TH ANNIVERSARY	1993	10.00	10.00
95	ALISON	2000	30.00	30.00
95	BEAR W/COLLECTION OF LUCY & ME FIGS	2000	30.00	30.00
95	FOUR SEASONS	2000	30.00	30.00
95	MRS. SANTA CLAUS	2000	30.00	30.00
95	ROMEO & JULIET	2000	30.00	30.00
95	SANTA CLAUS	2000	30.00	30.00
95	SUSIE	2000	30.00	30.00
M. RHYNER-NADIG				**MARY'S MOO MOOS BARN UNTO US**
96	AW, STUCK! THIS IS ALL I HAVE FOR HIM	OP	16.50	16.50
96	BARN UNTO US	OP	6.00	6.00
96	HAY! WE HAVE PLENTY OF ROOM	OP	13.50	13.50
96	HERD IT FROM AN ANGEL	OP	16.50	16.50
96	I WOOD BUILD SOMETHING FOR HIM	OP	16.50	16.50
96	IS HE REALLY AKING MOO-MY?	OP	16.50	16.50
96	STACKED IN OUR FAVOR	OP	16.50	16.50
96	WEE, WEE, WEE, FOLLOWED THE STAR	OP	13.50	13.50
96	YOU BRING SUNSHINE TO OUR LIVES	OP	13.50	13.50
M. RHYNER-NADIG				**MARY'S MOO MOOS BOO MOOS**
96	I CAST MY SPELL ON MOO!	OP	13.50	13.50
96	LIFE IS A MOOSQUERADE	OP	13.50	13.50
96	MUSICAL STUMP	OP	12.50	12.50
96	PEEK-A-MOO!	OP	13.50	13.50
96	WHO-O-O ARE MOOO-O-O?	OP	13.50	13.50
M. RHYNER-NADIG				**MARY'S MOO MOOS COUNTRY WEDDING**
96	BEST BULL	OP	13.50	13.50
96	FLOUR GIRL	OP	10.00	10.00
96	GROOMS BULL	OP	13.50	13.50
96	I'LL NEVER LOVE AN UDDER	OP	15.00	15.00
96	MILK MAID	OP	13.50	13.50
96	MILK MAID OF HONOR	OP	13.50	13.50
96	RING BEARER	OP	10.00	10.00
M. RHYNER-NADIG				**MARY'S MOO MOOS COUNTRY WEDDING MUSICAL**
96	WEDDING MARCH	OP	100.00	100.00
M. RHYNER-NADIG				**MARY'S MOO MOOS MOO IN THE BOX**
96	HOOFY HOLIDAYS	OP	12.50	12.50
96	I LOVE MOO!	OP	12.50	12.50

YR	NAME	LIMIT	ISSUE	TREND
96	MOOEY CHRISTMAS	OP	12.50	12.50
M. RHYNER-NADIG		**MARY'S MOO MOOS MOOEY CHRISTMAS**		
96	WHEEE ARE MOOVIN!	OP	170.00	170.00
96	WHEEE ARE MOOVIN!/DATED	YR	12.50	12.50
M. RHYNER-NADIG		**MARY'S MOO MOOS MOOSENGERS OF LOVE**		
96	HAY! I LOVE YOU	OP	6.75	6.75
96	HOLSTEIN YOU CLOSE	OP	6.25	6.25
96	I LOVE YOU DAIRY MUCH	OP	6.25	6.25
M. RHYNER-NADIG		**MARY'S MOO MOOS SPRING IS IN THE AIR**		
96	ALL A-BUZZ OVER YOU	OP	6.75	6.75
96	I'M MOOVIN INTO SPRING	OP	10.00	10.00
96	SPRING IS IN THE AIR	OP	7.50	7.50
96	TAKE ME OUT TO THE BULL GAME	OP	6.75	6.75
M. ATTWELL		**MEMORIES OF YESTERDAY**		
88	ANYWAY, FIDO LOVES ME 114588	OP	30.00	33.00
88	CAN I KEEP HER MOMMY? 114545	OP	25.00	28.00
88	DEAR SANTA 115002	OP	50.00	75.00
88	GOOD MORNING, MR. SNOWMAN 115401	OP	75.00	85.00
88	HANG ON TO YOUR LUCK! 114510	OP	25.00	28.00
88	HE KNOWS IF YOU'VE BEEN BAD/GOOD 115355	OP	40.00	45.00
88	HOW 'BOUT A LITTLE KISS? 114987	RT	25.00	28.00
88	HOW DO YOU SPELL S-O-R-R-Y? 114529	RT	25.00	40.00
88	HUSH! 114553	RT	45.00	70.00
88	I HOPE SANTA IS HOME 115010	OP	30.00	50.00
88	I PRAY THE LORD MY SOUL TO KEEP 523259	OP	25.00	47.00
88	IF YOU CAN'T BE GOOD, BE CAREFUL 114596	OP	50.00	55.00
88	IS IT REALLY SANTA? 115347	OP	50.00	65.00
88	IT HURTS WHEN FIDO HURTS 114561	OP	30.00	33.00
88	IT'S THE THOUGHT THAT COUNTS 115029	OP	25.00	28.00
88	MOMMY, I TEARED IT 114480	OP	25.00	28.00
88	MOMMY, I TEARED IT 523488	10000	25.00	310.00
88	MOMMY, I TEARED IT, 9 IN. 115924	CL	85.00	145.00
88	NOW HE CAN BE YOUR FRIEND, TOO! 115363	OP	45.00	50.00
88	NOW I LAY ME DOWN TO SLEEP 114499	OP	20.00	45.00
88	SPECIAL DELIVERY 114979	RT	30.00	45.00
88	WAITING FOR SANTA 114995	OP	40.00	55.00
88	WE WISH YOU A MERRY CHRISTMAS 115371	OP	70.00	75.00
88	WE'S HAPPY! HOW'S YOURSELF 114502	OP	40.00	45.00
88	WELCOME SANTA 114960	OP	45.00	60.00
88	WHAT WILL I GROW UP TO BE? 114537	OP	40.00	45.00
89	AS GOOD AS HIS MOTHER EVER MADE 522392	9600	32.50	33.00
89	AS GOOD AS HIS MOTHER EVER MADE 522392	OP	32.50	150.00
89	BLOW WIND, BLOW 520012	OP	40.00	40.00
89	DADDY, I COULD NEVER FILL/SHOES 520187	OP	30.00	30.00
89	FOR FIDO AND ME 522457	OP	70.00	70.00
89	HERE COMES THE BRIDE AND GROOM 520896	OP	50.00	50.00
89	HERE COMES THE BRIDE, 9 IN. 520527	CL	95.00	95.00
89	I'SE SPOKEN FOR 520071	RT	30.00	30.00
89	JOY TO YOU AT CHRISTMAS 522449	OP	45.00	45.00
89	KNITTING YOU A WARM & COZY WINTER 522414	OP	37.50	38.00
89	LET'S BE NICE LIKE WE WAS BEFORE 520047	OP	50.00	50.00
89	LONG AND SHORT OF IT, THE- 522384	OP	32.50	33.00
89	MUST FEED THEM OVER CHRISTMAS 522406	OP	38.50	39.00
89	SHOULD I...? 520209	OP	50.00	50.00
89	THIS ONE'S FOR YOU DEAR 520195	OP	50.00	50.00
89	WE'S HAPPY! HOW'S YOURSELF? 520616	RT	70.00	70.00
90	A DASH OF SOMETHING W/SOMETHING 524727	OP	55.00	55.00
90	A LAPFUL OF LUCK 524689	OP	15.00	30.00
90	A LAPFUL OF LUCK 525014	5000	30.00	30.00
90	COLLECTION SIGN 513156	OP	7.00	7.00
90	GOT TO GET HOME FOR THE HOLIDAYS 524751	OP	100.00	100.00
90	GREATEST TREASURE THE WORLD, THE- 524808	OP	50.00	50.00
90	HE HASN'T FORGOTTEN ME 523267	OP	30.00	32.00
90	HERE COMES THE BRIDE AND GROOM 520136	OP	80.00	80.00
90	HOLD IT! YOU'RE JUST SWELL 520020	OP	50.00	50.00
90	HOPING TO SEE YOU SOON 524824	OP	30.00	55.00
90	HUSH-A-BYE BABY 524778	OP	80.00	80.00
90	I'M NOT AS BACKWARD AS I LOOKS 523240	OP	32.50	33.00
90	I'SE BEEN PAINTING 524700	OP	37.50	38.00
90	KISS THE PLACE AND MAKE IT WELL 520039	OP	50.00	50.00
90	LET ME BE YOUR GUARDIAN ANGEL 524670	OP	32.50	33.00
90	LUCK AT LAST! HE LOVES ME 520217	OP	35.00	35.00
90	NOT A CREATURE WAS STIRRIN' 524697	OP	45.00	45.00
90	TIME FOR BED, 9 IN. 523275	TL	95.00	95.00
90	WHERE'S MUVVER? 520101	OP	30.00	30.00
91	COULD YOU LOVE ME FOR MYSELF? 525618	OP	30.00	30.00
91	FRIENDSHIP HAS NO BOUNDARIES 525545	YR	30.00	30.00
91	GIVE IT YOUR BEST SHOT 525561	OP	35.00	35.00
91	GOOD MORNING, LITTLE BOO-BOO 525766	RT	40.00	40.00
91	HE LOVES ME, 9 IN. 525022	TL	100.00	100.00
91	I MUST BE SOMEBODY'S DARLING 522635	OP	30.00	30.00
91	I'M AS COMFY AS CAN BE 525480	OP	50.00	50.00
91	JUST THINKING 'BOUT YOU 523461	OP	70.00	70.00
91	OPENING PRESENTS IS MUCH FUN! 524735	OP	37.50	38.00
91	PULL YOURSELVES TOGETHER GIRLS 522783	OP	30.00	30.00
91	S'NO USE LOOKIN' BACK NOW! 527203	OP	75.00	75.00
91	SITTING PRETTY 522708	OP	40.00	40.00
91	THEM DISHES NEARLY DONE 524611	OP	50.00	50.00

YR	NAME	LIMIT	ISSUE	TREND
91	TYING THE KNOT 522678	OP	60.00	60.00
91	WE ALL LOVES A CUDDLE 524832	OP	30.00	30.00
91	WE BELONG TOGETHER S-0001	OP	30.00	40.00
91	WELCOME TO YOUR NEW HOME M4911	YR	*	40.00
91	WHEREVER I AM/I'M DREAMING OF YOU 522686	OP	40.00	40.00
91	WHO EVER TOLD MOTHER/TWINS? 520063	OP	33.50	34.00
91	WHY DON'T YOU SING ALONG? 522600	OP	55.00	55.00
91	WISHFUL THINKING 522597	OP	45.00	45.00
92	A KISS FROM FIDO 523119	OP	35.00	35.00
92	A WHOLE BUNCH OF LOVE FOR YOU 522732	RT	40.00	40.00
92	HURRY UP FOR THE LAST TRAIN 525863	OP	40.00	40.00
92	I PRAY THE LORD MY SOUL TO KEEP 525596	OP	65.00	65.00
92	I'M HOPIN' YOU'RE MISSING ME TOO 525499	OP	55.00	55.00
92	I'SE SO HAPPY YOU CALLED 526401	TL	100.00	100.00
92	I'SE SUCH A GOOD LITTLE GIRL 522759	OP	30.00	30.00
92	NOW BE A GOOD DOG FIDO 524581	OP	45.00	45.00
92	SEND ALL LIFE'S LITTLE WORRIES 527505	OP	30.00	30.00
92	TIME FOR BED 527076	OP	30.00	30.00
92	YOU'LL ALWAYS BE MY HERO 524743	OP	50.00	50.00
93	HULLO! DID YOU COME BY UNDERGROUND?	OP	40.00	40.00
93	HULLO! DID YOU COME BY UNDERGROUND?	500	*	*
93	I'M ALWAYS LOOKING OUT FOR YOU	OP	55.00	55.00
93	LITTLE MISS MUFFET	18000	50.00	50.00
93	MARY HAD A LITTLE LAMB	18000	45.00	45.00
93	MARY, MARY QUITE CONTRARY	18000	45.00	45.00
93	MOTHER GOOSE	18000	50.00	50.00
93	NOW I'M THE FAIREST OF THEM ALL	OP	35.00	35.00
93	SIMPLE SIMON	18000	35.00	35.00
93	WOT'S ALL THIS TALK ABOUT LOVE?	OP	100.00	100.00
94	A LITTLE LOVE SONG-FOR YOU!	OP	35.00	35.00
94	DAYS OF THE WEEK SET	1994	250.00	250.00
94	THANK GOD FOR FIDO	OP	30.00	30.00
94	TWEEDLE DUM & TWEEDLE DEE	10000	25.00	25.00
94	WOT'S ALL THIS TALK ABOUT LOVE?	OP	27.50	28.00
95	A LITTLE HELP FROM FAIRYLAND	1995	55.00	55.00
95	BOO-BOO'S BAND SET OF FIVE	OP	12.50	13.00
95	DEAR OLD DEAR, WHIS YOU WERE HERE	5000	37.50	38.00
95	DEAR OLD DEAR, WISH YOU WERE HERE	5000	37.50	38.00
95	I COMFORT FIDO & HE COMFORTS ME	5000	50.00	50.00
95	JOIN ME FOR A LITTLE SONG	5000	50.00	50.00
95	SHARING THE COMMON THREAD OF LOVE	OP	100.00	100.00
95	WON'T YOU SKATE WITH ME	5000	35.00	35.00
95	WRAPPED IN LOVE & HAPPINESS	OP	35.00	35.00
96	A BASKET FULL OF LOVE	OP	50.00	50.00
96	A MOO ADDITION TO OUR FAMILY	7300	60.00	60.00
96	GOD BLESS OUR FUTURE	5000	45.00	45.00
96	HOW GOOD OF GOD TO MAKE US ALL	5000	50.00	50.00
96	JUST LIKE DADDY	7500	27.50	27.50
96	JUST LONGING TO SEE YOU	7500	27.50	27.50
96	LOVING YOU ONE STITCH AT A TIME	5000	50.00	50.00
96	PUT YOUR BEST FOOT FORWARD	5000	50.00	50.00
96	WE ARE ALL HIS CHILDREN	OP	27.50	27.50
96	WE'D DO ANYTHING FOR YOU, DEAR	5000	37.50	37.50
96	WE'RE IN TROUBLE NOW!	7500	37.50	37.50
96	WHENEVER I GET A MOMENT-I THINK OF YOU	7500	37.50	37.50
96	YOU WARM MY HEART	7500	35.00	35.00
M. ATTWELL		**MEMORIES OF YESTERDAY A LOVING WISH**		
96	YOU ARE MY SHINING STAR	OP	25.00	25.00
96	YOU BRIGHTEN MY DAYS	OP	25.00	25.00
M. ATTWELL		**MEMORIES OF YESTERDAY COMFORTING THOUGHTS**		
95	YOU'RE MY SUNSHINE ON A RAINY DAY	OP	37.50	38.00
M. ATTWELL		**MEMORIES OF YESTERDAY EVENT ONLY**		
96	A SWEET TREAT FOR YOU	YR	30.00	30.00
96	HOPING TO SEE YOU SOON	YR	15.00	15.00
M. ATTWELL		**MEMORIES OF YESTERDAY FRIENDSHIP**		
96	I LOVE YOU THIS MUCH!	OP	25.00	25.00
96	I MISS YOU	OP	25.00	25.00
96	THINKING OF YOU	OP	25.00	25.00
96	YOU AND ME	OP	22.50	22.50
M. ATTWELL		**MEMORIES OF YESTERDAY HERITAGE**		
96	I DO LIKE MY HOLIDAY CREWS	1996	100.00	100.00
96	PETER PAN COLLECTOR'S SET	1000	150.00	150.00
96	TUCKING MY DEARS ALL SAFE AWAY	YR	50.00	50.00
M. ATTWELL		**MEMORIES OF YESTERDAY NATIVITY PAGEANT**		
95	INNKEEPER	OP	27.50	28.00
96	SHEPHERD	OP	27.50	27.50
M. ATTWELL		**MEMORIES OF YESTERDAY PETER PAN**		
96	JOHN	OP	30.00	30.00
96	MICHAEL	OP	30.00	30.00
96	PETER PAN	OP	25.00	25.00
96	TINKERBELL	OP	20.00	20.00
96	WENDY	OP	25.00	25.00
M. ATTWELL		**MEMORIES OF YESTERDAY SOCIETY**		
96	FORGET-ME-NOT	OP	*	*
96	PEACE HEAVENLY PEACE	OP	30.00	30.00
96	YOU'VE GOT MY VOTE	OP	40.00	40.00

YR	NAME	LIMIT	ISSUE	TREND
M. ATTWELL				**MEMORIES OF YESTERDAY WHEN I GROW UP**
96	BUSINESSMAN	OP	25.00	25.00
96	BUSNINESSWOMAN	OP	25.00	25.00
M. ATTWELL				**MEMORIES OF YESTERDAY SYMBOL OF MEMBERSHIP**
93	I'M THE GIRL FOR YOU	OP	*	*
94	BLOWING A KISS TO A DEAR I MISS	OP	*	*
95	TIME TO CELEBRATE	OP	*	*
S. BUTCHER				**NOAH'S ARK**
95	CONGRATULATIONS, YOU EARNED YOUR STRIPES	OP	15.00	15.00
96	I'D GOAT ANYWHERE WITH YOU 163694	OP	10.00	10.00
P. FAGAN				**PENNYWHISTLE LANE**
94	TRUNK OF TEDDIES	1000	60.00	60.00
S. BUTCHER				**PRECIOUS MOMENTS**
*	DOME W/KIDS ON CLOUD FIGURINE E7350	*	*	800.00
76	HE CARETH FOR YOU E1377B	SU	9.00	110.00
76	LOVE ONE ANOTHER E1376	OP	10.00	37.50-130.00
76	PRAISE THE LORD ANYHOW E1374B	RT	8.00	100.00
76	PRAYER CHANGES THINGS E1375B	SU	11.00	170.00
77	BOY & GIRL ON SEESAW E1375A	RT	11.00	125.00
77	HE LEADETH ME E1377A	SU	9.00	250.00
77	HIS BURDEN IS LIGHT E1380G	RT	8.00	125.00
77	JESUS IS THE ANSWER E1381	SU	11.50	155.00
77	JESUS IS THE ANSWER E1381R	OP	55.00	60.00
77	JESUS IS THE LIGHT E1373G	RT	7.00	90.00
77	LOVE IS KIND E1379A	SU	8.00	115.00
77	O HOW I LOVE JESUS E1380B	RT	8.00	110.00
77	SMILE, GOD LOVES YOU E1373B	RT	7.00	60.00-115.00
78	COME LET US ADORE HIM E2011	RT	10.00	250.00
78	GOD UNDERSTANDS E1379B	SU	8.00	115.00
78	JESUS IS BORN E2012	SU	12.00	115.00
78	MAKE A JOYFUL NOISE E1374G	CL	8.00	125.00
78	UNTO US A CHILD IS BORN E2013	SU	12.00	115.00
78	WE HAVE SEEN HIS STAR E2010	SU	8.00	100.00
79	BUT LOVE GOES ON FOREVER E-3115	OP	16.50	35.00-105.00
79	CHRISTMAS IS A TIME TO SHARE E-2802	SU	20.00	100.00
79	CROWN HIM LORD OF ALL E-2803	SU	20.00	85.00
79	EGGS OVER EASY E3118	RT	12.00	105.00
79	GOD UNDERSTANDS E-1379B	SU	8.00	115.00
79	HAND THAT ROCKS THE FUTUREM THE- E-3108	SU	13.00	120.00
79	HE CARETH FOR YOU E-1377B	SU	9.00	110.00
79	HE LEADETH ME E-1377A	SU	9.00	110.00
79	HE WATCHES OVER US ALL E-3105	SU	11.00	75.00
79	IT'S WHAT'S INSIDE THAT COUNTS E-3119	SU	13.00	110.00
79	JESUS IS BORN E-2012	SU	12.00	140.00
79	JESUS IS BORN E-2801	SU	37.00	285.00-350.00
79	JESUS IS THE ANSWER E-1381	SU	11.50	160.00
79	JESUS LOVES ME E-1372B	OP	7.00	100.00
79	JESUS LOVES ME E-1372G	OP	7.00	100.00
79	LORD BLESS YOU AND KEEP YOU, THE- E-3114	OP	16.00	75.00
79	LOVE IS KIND E-1379A	SU	8.00	115.00
79	LOVE LIFTED ME E-1375A	OP	11.00	58.00-160.00
79	LOVE ONE ANOTHER E-1376	OP	10.00	40.00-125.00
79	LOVING IS SHARING E-3110B	RT	13.00	100.00
79	LOVING IS SHARING E-3110G	OP	13.00	100.00
79	MAKE A JOYFUL NOISE E-1374G	OP	8.00	135.00
79	MOTHER SEW DEAR E-3106	OP	13.00	100.00
79	NATIVITY SET OF 9 PCS. E2800	OP	70.00	175.00
79	PEACE ON EARTH E-2804	SU	20.00	165.00
79	PRAYER CHANGES THINGS E-1375B	SU	11.00	175.00
79	PURR-FECT GRANDMA , THE-E-3109	OP	13.00	100.00
79	THEE I LOVE E-3116	OP	16.50	80.00
79	THOU ART MINE E-3113	OP	16.00	50.00
79	TO THEE W/LOVE E3120	SU	13.00	60.00-100.00
79	UNTO US A CHILD IS BORN E-2013	SU	12.00	115.00
79	WALKING BY FAITH E-3117	OP	35.00	100.00
79	WE HAVE SEEN HIS STAR E-2010	SU	8.00	90.00
80	BEAR YE ONE ANOTHER'S BURDENS E-5200	SU	20.00	80.00
80	BLESSED ARE THE PURE IN HEART E-3104	SU	9.00	40.00
80	COME LET US ADORE HIM 104000 (SET OF 9)	OP	70.00	130.00
80	COME LET US ADORE HIM E-5619	SU	10.00	40.00
80	COW WITH BELL FIGURINE E-5638	OP	16.00	40.00
80	DONKEY FIGURINE E-5621	OP	6.00	25.00
80	GOD IS LOVE E-5213	SU	17.00	75.00
80	HEAVENLY LIGHT, THE- E-5637	OP	15.00	60.00
80	ISN'T HE WONDERFUL E-5639	SU	12.00	60.00
80	ISN'T HE WONDERFUL E-5640	SU	12.00	67.00
80	LET NOT THE SUN GO DOWN...WRATH E-5203	SU	22.50	165.00
80	LORD BLESS YOU AND KEEP YOU, THE- E-4720	SU	14.00	40.00
80	LORD BLESS YOU AND KEEP YOU, THE- E-4721	OP	14.00	55.00
80	LOVE CANNOT BREAK/TRUE FRIENDSHIP E-4722	SU	22.50	155.00
80	LOVE LIFTED ME E-5201	SU	25.00	100.00
80	MY GUARDIAN ANGEL E5207	SU	35.00	190.00
80	NATIVITY WALL E-5644 (SET OF 2)	OP	60.00	160.00
80	PEACE AMID THE STORM E-4723	SU	22.50	100.00
80	PRAYER CHANGES THINGS E-5214	SU	35.00	130.00
80	REJOICE O EARTH E-5636	OP	15.00	45.00
80	REJOICING WITH YOU E-4724	OP	25.00	55.00
80	SILENT KNIGHT E5642	SU	55.00	215.00

YR	NAME	LIMIT	ISSUE	TREND
80	THANK YOU FOR COMING TO MY AIDE E-5202	SU	22.50	150.00
80	THEY FOLLOWED THE STAR E-5624	OP	130.00	260.00
80	THEY FOLLOWED THE STAR E-5641	SU	75.00	195.00
80	TO A SPECIAL DAD E-5212	OP	20.00	35.00-72.00
80	WEE THREE KINGS E-5635	OP	40.00	100.00
81	BLESS THIS HOUSE E-7164	SU	45.00	200.00
81	BUT LOVE GOES ON FOREVER E-0001	YR	*	175.00
81	BUT LOVES GOES ON FOREVER E6118	SU	16.00	60.00
81	FORGIVING IS FORGETTING E-9252	SU	37.50	75.00
81	GOD IS LOVE, DEAR VALENTINE E-7153	SU	16.00	45.00
81	GOD IS LOVE, DEAR VALENTINE E-7154	SU	16.00	40.00
81	GOD IS WATCHING OVER YOU E-7163	SU	27.50	95.00
81	HIS SHEEP AM I E-7161	SU	25.00	90.00
81	I BELIEVE IN MIRACLES E-7156	SU	17.00	115.00
81	LET THE WHOLE WORLD KNOW E-7165	SU	35.00	95.00
81	LORD GIVE ME PATIENCE E-7159	SU	25.00	55.00
81	LOVE BEARETH ALL THINGS E-7158	OP	25.00	40.00-75.00
81	LOVE IS SHARING E-7162	SU	25.00	165.00
81	PEACE ON EARTH E-4725	SU	25.00	80.00
81	PERFECT GRANDPA , THE-E-7160	SU	25.00	70.00
81	THANKING HIM FOR YOU E-7155	SU	16.00	53.00
82	3 MINI NATIVITY HOUSES/PALM TREE E-2387	OP	45.00	100.00
82	ANIMAL COLLECTION, BUNNY E-9267C	SU	6.50	25.00
82	ANIMAL COLLECTION, DOG E-9267B	SU	6.50	25.00
82	ANIMAL COLLECTION, KITTY W/BOW E-9267D	SU	6.50	25.00
82	ANIMAL COLLECTION, LAMB W/BIRD E-9267E	SU	6.50	25.00
82	ANIMAL COLLECTION, PIG W/PATCHES E-9267F	SU	6.50	25.00
82	ANIMAL COLLECTION, TEDDY BEAR E-9267A	SU	6.50	25.00
82	BABY'S FIRST STEP E2840	SU	25.00	75.00
82	BLESS YOU TWO E-9255	OP	21.00	42.00
82	BUNDLES OF JOY E-2374	OP	27.50	100.00
82	BUT LOVE GOES ON FOREVER PLAQUE E-0102	YR	*	100.00
82	CAMEL E2363	OP	20.00	45.00
82	CHRISTMAS JOY FROM HEAD TO TOE E2361	SU	25.00	65.00
82	COME LET US ADORE HIM E-2395 (SET OF 11)	OP	80.00	150.00
82	DROPPING IN FOR CHRISTMAS E-2350	OP	30.00	100.00
82	DROPPING OVER FOR CHRISTMAS E-2070	RT	9.00	60.00
82	END IS IN SIGHT, THE E-9253	SU	25.00	60.00-160.00
82	ESPECIALLY FOR EWE E-9282C	SU	8.00	33.00
82	FIRST NOEL, THE- E-2365	SU	16.00	70.00
82	FIRST NOEL, THE-E-2366	SU	16.00	70.00
82	GOAT FIGURINE E-2364	SU	10.00	50.00
82	HOLY SMOKES E2351	RT	27.00	110.00
82	HOW CAN 2 WALK TOGETHER...AGREE E-9263	SU	35.00	140.00
82	I'LL PLAY MY DRUM FOR HIM E-2356	SU	30.00	95.00
82	I'LL PLAY MY DRUM FOR HIM E-2360	OP	16.00	35.00
82	I'LL PLAY MY DRUM FOR HIM E2355	SU	45.00	165.00
82	IF GOD BE FOR US...AGAINST US E-9285	SU	27.50	60.00
82	JESUS LOVES ME E-9278	OP	9.00	24.00
82	JESUS LOVES ME E-9279	OP	9.00	27.00
82	JOY TO THE WORLD E2343	SU	9.00	45.00
82	JOY TO THE WORLD E2344	SU	20.00	85.00
82	LET HEAVEN AND NATURE SING E2346	SU	50.00	145.00
82	LET HEAVEN AND NATURE SING E2347	15000	40.00	45.00
82	LET LOVE REIGN E9273	RT	22.50	70.00
82	LET US CALL THE CLUB TO ORDER E-0103	YR	*	55.00
82	LOVE IS PATIENT E-9251	SU	35.00	85.00
82	MAY YOUR CHRISTMAS BE COZY E2345	SU	23.00	75.00
82	MAY YOUR CHRISTMAS BE WARM E-2348	SU	30.00	110.00
82	O COME ALL YE FAITHFUL E2352	SU	45.00	150.00
82	O COME ALL YE FAITHFUL E2353	RT	27.50	60.00-100.00
82	OUR FIRST CHRISTMAS TOGETHER E-2377	SU	35.00	85.00
82	PEACE ON EARTH E-9287	SU	37.50	125.00
82	PRAISE THE LORD ANYHOW E9254	LE	35.00	55.00-200.00
82	SEEK YE THE LORD E-9261	SU	21.00	50.00
82	SEEK YE THE LORD E-9262	SU	21.00	65.00
82	SENDING YOU A RAINBOW E-9288	SU	22.50	95.00
82	SHARING OUR JOY TOGETHER E-2834	SU	25.00	53.00
82	TELL ME THE STORY OF JESUS E-2349	SU	30.00	110.00
82	TELL ME THE STORY OF JESUS E2349	SU	30.00	110.00
82	TO SOME BUNNY SPECIAL E-9282A	SU	8.00	35.00
82	TRUST IN THE LORD E-9289	SU	20.00	70.00
82	WE ARE GOD'S WORKMANSHIP 523879	2000	500.00	650.00
82	WE ARE GOD'S WORKMANSHIP E-9258	OP	19.00	40.00
82	WE'RE IN IT TOGETHER E-9259	SU	24.00	60.00
82	YOU HAVE TOUCHED SO MANY HEARTS 527661	SU	35.00	38.00
82	YOU HAVE TOUCHED SO MANY HEARTS E-2821	OP	25.00	45.00
82	YOU HAVE TOUCHED...HEARTS 523283	2000	500.00	600.00
82	YOU'RE WORTH YOUR WEIGHT IN GOLD E-9282B	SU	8.00	35.00
83	BABY FIGURINES E-2852	OP	12.00	23.00
83	BABY'S FIRST PICTURE E2841	RT	45.00	145.00
83	BLESSINGS FROM MY HOUSE TO YOURS E-0503	SU	27.00	75.00
83	BRINGING GOD'S BLESSING TO YOU E-0509	SU	35.00	75.00
83	GOD BLESS THIS BRIDE E-2832	OP	35.00	55.00
83	GOD BLESSED OUR YEARS TOGETHER E-2853	OP	35.00	55.00
83	GOD HAS SENT HIS SON E-0507	SU	32.50	80.00
83	GOD'S PROMISES ARE SURE E-9260	SU	30.00	75.00
83	HE UPHOLDETH THOSE WHO FALL E-0526	SU	28.50	110.00
83	HIS EYE IS ON THE SPARROW E0530	RT	28.50	115.00

Simple Simon *from the "Once Upon a Fairytale" series was inspired by the artwork of Mabel Lucie Attwell. The Memories of Yesterday Collection is produced by Enesco Corp.*

With her gander standing close by, Mother Goose, *from the "Once Upon a Fairytale" series from the Memories of Yesterday line, is ready to wander.*

The price of A Dress For Cinderelly, *from the Walt Disney Classics Collection, has fluctuated on the secondary market more than the length of skirt hems.*

Jiminy Cricket *was the first gift sculpture to members of the Walt Disney Collectors Society.*

YR	NAME	LIMIT	ISSUE	TREND
83	I GET A KICK OUT OF YOU E-2827	SU	50.00	145.00
83	IT'S A PERFECT BOY E-0512	SU	18.50	47.00
83	JESUS IS THE LIGHT THAT SHINES E-0502	SU	23.00	70.00
83	JOIN IN ON THE BLESSINGS E-0104	YR	*	55.00
83	LOVE IS KIND E2847	15000	40.00	45.00
83	MAY YOUR BIRTHDAY BE A BLESSING E-2826	SU	37.50	100.00
83	ONWARD CHRISTIAN SOLDIERS E-0523	OP	24.00	35.00-115.00
83	PRAISE THE LORD ANYHOW E-9254	RT	35.00	90.00
83	PRECIOUS MEMORIES E-2828	OP	45.00	70.00
83	PREPARE YE THE WAY OF THE LORD E-0508	SU	75.00	135.00
83	PRESS ON E-9265	OP	40.00	60.00-115.00
83	SHARING OUR SEASON TOGETHER E-0501	SU	50.00	145.00
83	TO A VERY SPECIAL MOM E-2824	OP	27.50	45.00
83	TO A VERY SPECIAL SISTER E-2825	OP	37.50	65.00
83	TO GOD BE THE GLORY E-2823	SU	40.00	85.00
83	TUBBY'S FIRST CHRISTMAS E-0511	SU	12.00	35.00
84	A MONARCH IS BORN E-5380	SU	33.00	80.00
84	AUTUMN'S PRAISE 12084	LE	30.00	70.00
84	AUTUMN'S PRAISE MUSICAL 408751	LE	200.00	165.00
84	CLOWN BALANCING BALL 12238A	SU	13.50	20.00
84	CLOWN BENDING OVER BALL 12238C	SU	13.50	20.00
84	CLOWN HOLDING BALLOON 12238B	SU	13.50	20.00
84	CLOWN HOLDING FLOWER POT 12238D	SU	13.50	20.00
84	FOR GOD SO LOVED THE WORLD E-5382	SU	70.00	140.00
84	GET INTO THE HABIT OF PRAYER 12203	SU	19.00	47.00
84	GOD BLESS OUR HOME 12319	OP	40.00	70.00
84	GOD BLESS OUR YEARS TOGETHER 12440	CL	175.00	250.00
84	GOD BLESSED/LOVE & HAPPINESS E-2854	OP	35.00	55.00
84	GOD BLESSED/LOVE & HAPPINESS E-2855	OP	35.00	55.00
84	GOD BLESSED/LOVE & HAPPINESS E-2856	OP	35.00	55.00
84	GOD BLESSED/LOVE & HAPPINESS E-2857	OP	35.00	55.00
84	GOD BLESSED/LOVE & HAPPINESS E-2859	OP	35.00	55.00
84	GOD BLESSED/LOVE & HAPPINESS E-2860	OP	35.00	55.00
84	GOD SENDS THE GIFT OF HIS LOVE E-6613	SU	22.50	58.00-115.00
84	HIS NAME IS JESUS E-5381	SU	45.00	95.00
84	I'LL PLAY MY DRUM FOR HIM E-5384	OP	10.00	21.00
84	I'M SENDING YOU A WHITE CHRISTMAS E-2829	OP	37.50	65.00
84	ISN'T HE PRECIOUS? E-5379	OP	20.00	40.00
84	IT IS BETTER TO GIVE...TO RECEIVE 12297	SU	19.00	85.00
84	JOY TO THE WORLD E-5378	SU	18.00	36.00-48.00
84	LORD, KEEP MY LIFE IN TUNE 12165	SU	37.50	85.00
84	LOVE COVERS ALL 12009	SU	27.50	65.00
84	LOVE IS KIND E5377	RT	27.50	85.00
84	LOVE NEVER FAILS 12300	OP	25.00	45.00
84	MAY YOUR CHRISTMAS BE BLESSED E-5376	SU	37.50	70.00
84	OH WORSHIP THE LORD E-5385	SU	10.00	45.00
84	OH WORSHIP THE LORD E-5386	SU	10.00	55.00
84	PART OF ME WANTS TO BE GOOD 12149	SU	19.00	65.00
84	SEEK AND YE SHALL FIND E-0105	YR	*	55.00
84	SUMMER'S JOY 12076	LE	30.00	100.00
84	SUMMER'S JOY MUSICAL 408743	LE	200.00	170.00
84	VOICE OF SPRING MUSICAL, THE- 408735	LE	200.00	165.00
84	VOICE OF SPRING, THE- 12068	LE	30.00	275.00
84	WINTER'S SONG 12092	LE	30.00	88.00-175.00
84	WINTER'S SONG MUSICAL 408778	LE	200.00	165.00
84	WISHING YOU A MERRY CHRISTMAS E-5383	YR	17.00	35.00
85	ANGEL OF MERCY 102482	OP	20.00	35.00
85	BABY'S FIRST CHRISTMAS 15539	YR	13.00	30.00
85	BABY'S FIRST CHRISTMAS 15547	YR	13.00	35.00
85	BABY'S FIRST TRIP 16012	SU	32.50	225.00
85	BIRDS OF A FEATHER COLLECT E-0106	YR	*	47.00
85	BROTHERLY LOVE 100544	SU	37.00	80.00
85	FRIENDS NEVER DRIFT APART 100250	OP	35.00	60.00
85	GOD BLESS AMERICA 102938	LE	30.00	80.00
85	GOD BLESS THE DAY WE FOUND YOU 100145	SU	40.00	65.00
85	GOD BLESS THE DAY WE FOUND YOU 100153	SU	40.00	65.00
85	GOD SENT HIS LOVE 15881	YR	17.00	32.00
85	GOD SENT YOU JUST IN TIME 15504	RT	45.00	100.00
85	HALO, AND MERRY CHRISTMAS 12351	SU	40.00	150.00
85	HE CLEASNSED MY SOUL 100277	OP	24.00	45.00
85	HONK IF YOU LOVE JESUS 15490	OP	13.00	27.00
85	I BELIEVE IN THE OLD RUGGED CROSS 103632	OP	25.00	45.00
85	I'M A POSSIBILITY 100188	RT	22.00	60.00
85	ISN'T EIGHT JUST GREAT 109460	OP	18.50	28.00
85	IT'S THE BIRTHDAY OF A KING 102962	SU	19.00	35.00
85	JESUS IS COMING SOON 12343	SU	22.50	40.00
85	JOY OF THE LORD...MY STRENGTH, THE-10013	OP	35.00	75.00
85	LET'S KEEP IN TOUCH 102520	OP	65.00	115.00
85	LORD I'M COMING HOME 100110	OP	22.50	45.00
85	LOVE COVERS ALL 12009	SU	27.50	65.00
85	LOVE RESCUED ME 102393	OP	22.50	45.00
85	MAY YOUR BIRTHDAY BE GIGANTIC 15970	OP	12.50	35.00
85	MAY YOUR CHRISTMAS BE DELIGHTFUL 15482	OP	25.00	45.00
85	O WORSHIP THE LORD 100064	OP	24.00	45.00
85	O WORSHIP THE LORD 102229	OP	24.00	40.00
85	SENDING MY LOVE 100056	SU	22.50	55.00
85	SERVING THE LORD 100161	SU	19.00	65.00
85	SERVING THE LORD 100293	SU	19.00	45.00
85	SET OF 3-BUNNY,TURTLE & LAMB 102296	SU	5.50	25.00

YR	NAME	LIMIT	ISSUE	TREND
85	SHEPHERD OF LOVE 102261	OP	10.00	21.00
85	SILENT NIGHT 15814	SU	37.50	60.00-90.00
85	TO MY FAVORITE PAW 100021	SU	22.50	58.00-115.00
85	TO MY FOREVER FRIEND 100072	OP	33.00	90.00
85	WISHING YOU A COZY CHRISTMAS 102342	YR	18.00	35.00
85	WISHING YOU GRR-EATNESS 109479	OP	18.50	28.00
85	YOU CAN FLY 12335	SU	25.00	65.00
86	A TUB FULL OF LOVE 104817	OP	22.50	35.00
86	BEAR THE GOOD NEWS OF CHRISTMAS 104515	YR	12.50	19.00
86	CHEERS TO THE LEADER 104035	OP	22.50	38.00
86	COME LET US ADORE HIM 104000 (SET OF 9)	OP	95.00	135.00
86	COME LET US ADORE HIME 104523	OP	400.00	465.00
86	CONGRATULATIONS, PRINCESS 106208	OP	20.00	35.00
86	GOD BLESS YOU GRADUATE 106194	OP	20.00	35.00
86	GREATEST GIFT IS A FRIEND, THE- 109231	OP	30.00	45.00
86	HALLELUJAH COUNTRY 105821	OP	35.00	45.00-250.00
86	HAPPY DAYS ARE HERE AGAIN 104396	SU	25.00	60.00
86	HAVE I GOT NEWS FOR YOU 105635	SU	22.50	50.00
86	HE WALKS WITH ME 107999	LE	25.00	33.00
86	HE'S THE HEALER OF BROKEN HEARTS 100080	OP	33.00	55.00
86	HEAVEN BLESS YOUR TOGETHERNESS 106755	OP	65.00	100.00
86	I PICKED A VERY SPECIAL MOM 100536	LE	37.50	70.00
86	I WOULD BE SUNK WITHOUT YOU 102970	OP	15.00	24.00
86	LORD GIVETH...TAKETH AWAY, THE- 100226	RT	33.50	40.00
86	LORD. HELP US KEEP...ACT TOGETHER 101850	RT	35.00	98.00-175.00
86	LOVE IS THE BEST GIFT OF ALL 110930	YR	22.50	40.00
86	LOVE IS THE GLUE THAT MENDS 104027	SU	33.50	60.00
86	MY LOVE WILL NEVER LET YOU GO 103497	OP	25.00	45.00
86	NO TEARS PAST THE GATE 101826	OP	40.00	80.00
86	OH WHAT FUN IT IS TO RIDE 109819	OP	85.00	140.00
86	PRECIOUS MEMORIES 106763	OP	37.50	65.00
86	SCENT FROM ABOVE 100528	RT	19.00	60.00
86	SHARING OUR CHRISTMAS TOGETHER 102490	SU	40.00	75.00
86	SITTING PRETTY 104825	SU	22.50	53.00
86	SPIRIT IS WILLING...IS WEAK , THE-100196	RT	19.00	75.00
86	THEY FOLLOWED THE STAR 108243	OP	75.00	125.00
86	THIS IS THE DAY THE LORD HATH MADE 12157	SU	22.50	45.00
86	TO MY DEER FRIEND 100048	OP	33.00	75.00
86	TO TELL THE TOOTH YOU'RE SPECIAL 105813	SU	38.50	100.00
86	WE ARE ALL PRECIOUS IN HIS SIGHT 102903	OP	30.00	80.00
86	WE BELONG TO THE LORD 103004	SP	50.00	180.00
86	WE GATHER TO ASK/LORD'S BLESSING 109762	RT	130.00	150.00
86	WE'RE PULLING FOR YOU 106151	SU	40.00	70.00
86	WISHING YOU A MERRY CHRISTMAS 109754	OP	35.00	55.00
86	WITH THIS RING... 104019	OP	40.00	65.00
87	A GROWING LOVE E-0108	YR	*	46.00
87	A TUB FULL OF LOVE 112313	OP	22.50	35.00
87	BELIEVE THE IMPOSSIBLE 109487	SU	35.00	75.00
87	BLESSED ARE THEY THAT OVERCOME 115479	YR	27.50	35.00
87	FAITH TAKES THE PLUNGE 111155	OP	27.50	45.00
87	GOOD LORD HAS BLESSED US TENFOLD, THE	LE	90.00	150.00
87	HAPPY BIRTHDAY POPPY 106836	SU	27.50	60.00
87	LORD HELP ME MAKE THE GRADE 106216	SU	25.00	55.00
87	MOMMY, I LOVE YOU 109975	OP	22.50	35.00
87	MOMMY, I LOVE YOU 112143	OP	22.50	35.00
87	O COME LET US ADORE HIM 111333	SU	200.00	240.00
87	OH WHAT FUN IT IS TO RIDE 109819	OP	85.00	140.00
87	PUPPY LOVE IS FROM ABOVE 106798	RT	45.00	55.00
87	SCENT FROM ABOVE 100528	OP	19.00	60.00
87	SENDING YOU MY LOVE 109967	OP	35.00	55.00
87	SEW IN LOVE 106844	OP	45.00	65.00
87	SHARING IS UNIVERSAL E-0107	YR	*	45.00
87	THIS IS THE DAY...LORD HATH MADE E2838	SU	20.00	60.00
87	THIS TOO SHALL PASS 114014	OP	23.00	35.00
87	WISHING YOU A BASKET/BLESSINGS 109924	OP	23.00	40.00
88	A FRIEND IS SOMEONE WHO CARES 520632	RT	30.00	35.00
88	BELIEVE THE IMPOSSBILE 109487	OP	35.00	75.00
88	BON VOYAGE! 522201	SU	75.00	90.00
88	DON'T LET THE HOLIDAYS...DOWN 522112	RT	42.50	90.00
88	EGGSPECIALLY FOR YOU 520667	OP	45.00	60.00
88	FRIENDSHIP HITS THE SPOT 520748	OP	55.00	70.00
88	GREATEST OF THESE IS LOVE, THE- 521868	SU	27.50	45.00
88	HAVE A BERRY MERRY CHRISTMAS 522856	SU	15.00	27.00
88	HE IS THE STAR OF THE MORNING 522252	SU	55.00	75.00
88	HIS LOVE WILL SHINE ON YOU 522376	YR	30.00	55.00
88	I BELONG TO THE LORD 520853	SU	25.00	45.00
88	ISN'T HE PRECIOUS 522988	SU	15.00	20.00
88	JESUS IS THE ONLY WAY 520756	SU	40.00	60.00
88	JESUS IS THE SWEETEST NAME I KNOW 523097	SU	22.50	32.00
88	JESUS LOVES ME 104531	1000	500.00	1550.00
88	JESUS THE SAVIOR IS BORN 520357	OP	25.00	50.00
88	JUST A LINE TO WISH...A HAPPY DAY 520721	SU	65.00	75.00
88	LIGHT OF THE WORLD IS JESUS, THE- 521507	OP	60.00	80.00
88	LORD HAS BLESSED US TENFOLD, THE- 114022	YR	90.00	175.00
88	LORD IS YOUR LIGHT..HAPPINESS, THE- 5208	OP	50.00	70.00
88	LORD, TURN MY LIFE AROUND 520551	SU	35.00	38.00
88	MAKE A JOYFUL NOISE 520322	1500	500.00	900.00
88	MAY YOUR LIFE BE...W/TOUCHDOWNS 522023	OP	45.00	60.00
88	MEOWIE CHRISTMAS 109800	OP	30.00	45.00

YR	NAME	LIMIT	ISSUE	TREND
88	MERRY CHRISTMAS DEER 522317	OP	50.00	65.00
88	MY DAYS ARE BLUE WITHOUT YOU 520802	SU	65.00	100.00
88	MY HEART IS EXPOSED WITH LOVE 520624	OP	45.00	55.00
88	OH HOLY NIGHT 522546	YR	25.00	40.00
88	OUR FIRST CHRISTMAS TOGETHER 115290	SU	50.00	75.00
88	PEACE ON EARTH 109749	SU	100.00	145.00
88	PUPPY LOVE 520764	OP	12.50	20.00
88	REJOICE O EARTH 520268	OP	13.00	22.00
88	SOME BUNNY'S SLEEPING 115274	SU	13.50	19.00
88	SOMETHING'S MISSING...NOT AROUND 105643	SU	32.50	70.00
88	TELL IT TO JESUS 521477	OP	35.00	42.00
88	THANK YOU LORD FOR EVERYTHING 522031	SU	55.00	75.00
88	TIME TO WISH YOU/MERRY CHRISTMAS 115339	YR	24.00	32.00
88	TIS THE SEASON 111163	SU	27.50	35.00
88	TO BE WITH YOU IS UPLIFTING 522260	OP	20.00	35.00
88	WE NEED A GOOD FRIEND..RUFF TIMES 520810	SU	35.00	45.00
88	WISHING YOU A COZY CHRISTMAS 521949	SU	42.50	60.00
88	WISHING YOU A HAPPY EASTER 109886	OP	23.00	35.00
88	WISHING YOU A PERFECT CHOICE 520845	OP	55.00	70.00
88	WISHING YOU A...SUCCESSFUL SEASON 522120	OP	60.00	75.00
88	WISHING YOU ROADS OF HAPPINESS 520780	OP	60.00	80.00
88	YOU ARE MY NUMBER ONE 520829	OP	25.00	35.00
88	YOUR LOVE IS SO UPLIFTING 520675	OP	60.00	80.00
89	ALWAYS IN HIS CARE 225290	YR	8.00	15.00
89	ALWAYS IN HIS CARE 524522	YR	30.00	45.00
89	ALWAYS ROOM FOR ONE MORE C-0109	YR	*	40.00
89	BLESSINGS FROM ABOVE 523747	OP	45.00	90.00
89	CHRISTMAS FIREPLACE	SU	37.50	45.00
89	EASTER'S ON ITS WAY 521892	OP	60.00	70.00
89	FAITH IS A VICTORY 521396	RT	25.00	145.00
89	GOD IS LOVE DEAR VALENTINE 523518	OP	27.50	35.00
89	GOOD FRIENDS ARE FOREVER 521817	OP	50.00	55.00
89	GOOD FRIENDS ARE FOREVER 525049	*	*	*
89	GOOD LORD ALWAYS DELIVERS, THE- 523453	OP	27.50	35.00
89	HAPPY BIRTHDAY DEAR JESUS 524875	SU	13.50	25.00
89	HAPPY TRIP 521280	OP	35.00	65.00
89	HEAVEN BLESS YOU 520934	OP	35.00	45.00
89	HIGH HOPES 521957	SU	30.00	47.00
89	HOPE YOU'RE UP...THE TRAIL AGAIN 521205	SU	35.00	47.00
89	I'LL NEVER STOP LOVING YOU 521418	OP	37.50	42.00
89	JESUS IS THE SWEETEST NAME I KNOW 523097	OP	22.50	35.00
89	LORD, HELP ME STICK TO MY JOB 521450	OP	30.00	45.00
89	LOVE IS FROM ABOVE 521841	SU	45.00	50.00
89	MY HAPPINESS C-0110	YR	*	40.00
89	ONCE UPON A HOLY NIGHT 523836	YR	25.00	40.00
89	REJOICE O EARTH 617334	OP	125.00	125.00
89	SOME BUNNIES SLEEPING 522996	SU	12.00	30.00
89	SWEEP ALL YOUR WORRIES AWAY 521779	OP	40.00	40.00-135.00
89	THAT'S WHAT FRIENDS ARE FOR 521183	OP	45.00	55.00
89	THERE SHALL BE SHOWERS..BLESSINGS 522090	OP	60.00	80.00
89	THINKING OF YOU IS...LIKE TO DO 522287	SU	30.00	33.00
89	THIS DAY HAS BEEN MADE IN HEAVEN 523496	OP	30.00	35.00
89	TIME HEALS 523739	OP	37.50	42.00
89	WE'RE GOING TO MISS YOU 524913	OP	50.00	55.00
89	YIELD NOT TO TEMPTATION 521310	SU	27.50	46.00
90	A REFLECTION OF HIS LOVE 522279	OP	50.00	55.00
90	A SPECIAL DELIVERY 521493	OP	30.00	35.00
90	A UNIVERSAL LOVE 527173	LE	32.50	40.00
90	ANGELS WE HAVE HEARD ON HIGH 524921	OP	60.00	70.00
90	BEING 9 IS JUST DIVINE 521833	OP	25.00	30.00
90	BLESS THOSE WHO SERVE... (A.F.) 526584	SU	32.50	45.00
90	BLESS THOSE WHO SERVE... (ARMY) 526576	SU	32.50	45.00
90	BLESS THOSE WHO SERVE... (BLACK) 527297	SU	32.50	42.00
90	BLESS THOSE WHO SERVE... (GIRL) 527289	SU	32.50	45.00
90	BLESS THOSE WHO SERVE... (MARINE) 527521	SU	32.50	42.00
90	BLESS THOSE WHO SERVE... (NAVY) 526568	SU	32.50	50.00
90	BRING THE LITTLE ONES TO JESUS 527556	OP	90.00	100.00
90	CLUB IS OUT OF THIS WORLD, THE C0112	YR	*	45.00
90	FRIENDSHIP GROWS WHEN YOU PLANT 524271	OP	40.00	100.00
90	GOD BLESS THE U.S.A. 527564	LE	32.50	40.00
90	GOOD FRIENDS ARE FOR ALWAYS 524123	OP	27.50	35.00
90	GOOD NEWS IS SO UPLIFTING 523615	OP	60.00	70.00
90	HE ISMY INSPIRATION 523038	OP	60.00	65.00
90	HE LOVES ME 524263	LE	35.00	45.00
90	HOPPY EASTER, FRIEND 521906	OP	40.00	45.00
90	HUG ONE ANOTHER 521299	RT	45.00	50.00
90	I CAN'T SPELL SUCCESS W/O YOU 523763	OP	40.00	50.00
90	I WILL CHERISH ..OLD RUGGED CROSS 523534	YR	27.50	40.00
90	I WOULD BE LOST W/O YOU 526142	OP	27.50	32.00
90	IN THE SPOTLIGHT OF HIS GRACE 520543	SU	35.00	38.00
90	IT'S A PERFECT BOY 525286	OP	16.50	20.00
90	IT'S NO YOLK/I SAY I LOVE YOU 522104	OP	60.00	70.00
90	JOY ON ARRIVAL 523178	OP	50.00	55.00
90	MAY ONLY GOOD THINGS...YOUR WAY 524425	OP	30.00	40.00
90	MAY YOU HAVE AN OLD.....CHRISTMAS 417777	LE	200.00	165.00
90	MAY YOUR BIRTHDAY BE A BLESSING 524301	OP	30.00	35.00
90	MAY YOUR CHRISTMAS BE MERRY 524166	YR	27.50	35.00
90	MAY YOUR WORLD BE TRIMMED W/JOY 522082	SU	55.00	55.00
90	MY WARMEST THOUGHTS ARE YOU 524085	OP	55.00	60.00-68.00

YR	NAME	LIMIT	ISSUE	TREND
90	SHARING A GIFT OF LOVE 527114	YR	30.00	50.00
90	SHARING THE GOOD NEWS TOGETHER-C0111	YR	*	40.00
90	TAKE HEED WHEN YOU STAND 521272	OP	55.00	60.00
90	THERE'S A LIGHT....TUNNEL 521485	SU	55.00	60.00
90	THIS LAND IS OUR LAND 527777	LE	35.00	35.00
90	THUMB-BODY LOVES YOU 521698	SU	55.00	60.00
90	TO A SPECIAL MUM 521965	OP	30.00	40.00
90	TO A VERY SPECIAL MOM & DAD 521434	SU	35.00	45.00
90	WE ARE GOD'S WORKMANSHIP 525960	YR	27.50	40.00
90	WE HAVE COME FROM A FAR 526959	OP	17.50	25.00
90	WHAT THE WORLD NEEDS NOW 524352	OP	50.00	60.00
90	YOU ARE MY HAPPINESS 526185	YR	37.50	47.00
90	YOU ARE SUCH A PURR-FECT FRIEND 526010	2000	500.00	625.00
90	YOU ARE THE TYPE I LOVE 523542	OP	40.00	45.00
90	YOU DESERVE AN OVATION 520578	OP	35.00	40.00
90	YOU HAVE TOUCHED SO MANY HEARTS 523283	2000	600.00	545.00-675.00
90	YOU HAVE TOUNCHED.....HEARTS 422282	LE	175.00	175.00
91	BLESSED ARE THE MEEK.. .EARTH 523313	LE	55.00	60.00
91	BLESSED ARE THE PEACEMAKERS..523348	LE	55.00	55.00
91	BLESSED ARE THE POOR IN SPIRIT...523437	LE	55.00	70.00
91	BLESSED ARE THE PURE IN HEART...523399	LE	55.00	55.00
91	BLESSED ARE THEY THAT MOURN..523380	LE	55.00	60.00
91	BLESSED ARE THEY...BE FILLED 523321	LE	55.00	60.00
91	BLESSED ARE....SHALL OBTAIN MERCY 523291	LE	55.00	55.00
91	GOING HOME 525979	OP	60.00	65.00
91	WE ARE GOD'S WORKMANSHIP 523879	2000	*	650.00
92	15 HAPPY YEARS TOGETHER/TWEET 530786	LE	100.00	110.00
92	A SPECIAL CHIME FOR JESUS 524468	OP	32.50	33.00
92	A UNIVERSAL LOVE 527173	YR	32.50	50.00
92	AMERICA, YOU'RE BEAUTIFUL 528862	OP	35.00	40.00
92	AN EVENT FOR ALL SEASONS 530158	OP	30.00	45.00
92	BABY'S FIRST BIRTHDAY 524069	OP	25.00	30.00
92	BLESS-UM YOU 527335	OP	35.00	35.00
92	BRINGING YOU A MERRY CHRISTMAS 527599	RT	45.00	45.00
92	BUT THE GREATEST OF THESE IS LOVE 527688	YR	27.50	32.00
92	FRUIT..SPIRIT IS LOVE, THE- 521213	OP	30.00	32.00
92	GATHER YOUR DREAMS 529680	2000	550.00	550.00
92	HAPPINESS IS AT OUR FINGERTIPS 529931	LE	35.00	60.00
92	HAPPY BIRTHDAY JESUS 530492	OP	20.00	22.00
92	HIS LITTLE TREASURE PM931	OP	30.00	35.00
92	HOPE YOU'RE OVER THE HUMP 521671	SU	17.50	19.00
92	I ONLY HAVE ARMS FOR YOU 527769	OP	15.00	17.00
92	I'M LOST WITHOUT YOU 526142	YR	27.50	32.00
92	I'M SO GLAD GOD...FRIEND LIKE YOU 523623	RT	50.00	55.00
92	IT'S SO UPLIFTING/FRIEND LIKE YOU 524905	OP	40.00	45.00
92	JESUS IS THE ANSWER E-1381R	OP	55.00	60.00
92	LORD TURNED MY LIFE AROUND, THE- 520535	SU	35.00	38.00
92	LOVING PM932	OP	30.00	32.00
92	LOVING, CARING..ALONG THE WAY C0113	OP	25.00	30.00
92	LOVING,CARING...ALONG THE WAY C0013	OP	25.00	28.00
92	MAGIC STARTS W/YOU, THE- 529648	LE	16.00	24.00
92	MAKE A JOYFUL NOISE 528617	YR	27.50	30.00
92	MAY YOUR BIRTHDAY BE MAMMOTH 521825	OP	25.00	30.00
92	MAY YOUR EVERY WISH COME TRUE 524298	OP	50.00	55.00
92	MAY YOUR FUTURE BE BLESSED	OP	35.00	35.00
92	OUR FRIENDSHIP IS SODA-LICIOUS 524336	OP	65.00	70.00
92	RING OUT THE GOOD NEWS 529966	OP	17.50	20.00
92	RING THOSE CHRISTMAS BELLS 525898	OP	95.00	100.00
92	SAFE IN THE ARMS OF JESUS 521922	OP	30.00	35.00
92	SEALED W/A KISS 524441	OP	50.00	55.00
92	THERE IS NO GREATER...A FRIEND...521000	OP	30.00	32.00
92	THIS LAND IS OUR LAND 527777	YR	35.00	40.00
92	TIED UP FOR THE HOLIDAYS 527580	SU	40.00	45.00
92	TO THE APPLE OF GOD'S EYE 522015	OP	32.50	35.00
92	TUBBY'S FIRST CHRISTMAS 525278	OP	10.00	15.00
92	WISHING YOU A COMFY CHRISTMAS 527750	OP	27.50	30.00
92	WISHING YOU A HO HO HO 527629	OP	40.00	45.00
92	WISHING YOU WERE HERE 526916	OP	100.00	115.00
92	WISHING YOU/SWEETEST CHRISTMAS 530166	YR	27.50	40.00
92	YOU ARE MY FAVORITE STAR 527378	OP	60.00	60.00-65.00
92	YOU'RE MY NUMBER ONE FRIEND 530026	LE	30.00	30.00
92	YOU'RE THE END OF MY RAINBOW C0014	OP	25.00	30.00
92	YOU'RE THE END OF MY RAINBOW C0114	OP	25.00	30.00
93	A REFLECTION OF HIS LOVE 529095	YR	27.50	28.00
93	BRING THE LITTLE ONES TO JESUS 531359	LE	50.00	50.00
93	FRIENDS TO THE VERY END 526150	OP	40.00	40.00
93	HE IS NOT HERE FOR HE IS RISEN..527106	OP	60.00	60.00
93	I STILL DO 530999	OP	30.00	30.00
93	I STILL DO 531006	OP	30.00	30.00
93	I WILL ALWAYS BE THINKING OF YOU 523631	OP	45.00	45.00
93	I'M SO GLAD I PICKED YOU...FRIEND 524379	OP	40.00	40.00
93	IT IS NO SECRET WHAT GOD CAN DO 531111	LE	30.00	30.00
93	LORD BLESS...KEEP YOU, THE- 532134	OP	30.00	30.00
93	LORD BLESS..KEEP YOU, THE- 532118	OP	40.00	40.00
93	LORD BLESS..KEEP YOU, THE- 532126	OP	30.00	30.00
93	LORD IS COUNTING ON YOU, THE- 531707	OP	32.50	33.00
93	LORD TEACH US TO PRAY 524158	OP	35.00	35.00
93	LORD WILL PROVIDE, THE- 523593	LE	40.00	45.00
93	NOTHING CAN DAMPEN..CARING 603864	OP	35.00	35.00

YR	NAME	LIMIT	ISSUE	TREND
93	OINKY BIRTHDAY 524506	OP	13.50	14.50
93	SERENITY PRAYER GIRL 530697	OP	35.00	35.00
93	SHARING SWEET MEMORIES TOGETHER 526487	OP	45.00	45.00
93	SURROUNDED W/JOY 531677	OP	30.00	30.00
93	SURROUNDED W/JOY 531685	OP	17.50	18.00
93	TO A VERY SPECIAL SISTER 528633	OP	60.00	60.00
93	YOU ARE/ROSE OF HIS CREATION 531243	2000	*	500.00
93	YOU SUIT ME TO A TEE 526193	OP	35.00	35.00
94	CARING	OP	35.00	35.00
94	PRECIOUS MOMENTS LAST FOEVER E6901	SU	10.00	100.00
94	SERENITY PRAYER BOY 530700	OP	35.00	35.00
94	SHARING	OP	35.00	35.00
94	SO GLAD I PICKED YOU AS A FRIEND	OP	40.00	40.00
94	YOU'RE AS PRETTY AS A CHRISTMAS TREE	OP	27.50	28.00
95	A POPPY FOR YOU 604208	OP	35.00	35.00
95	ALWAYS TAKE TIME TO PRAY	OP	35.00	35.00
95	ANOTHER YEAR AND MORE GREY HARES 128686	OP	17.50	18.00
95	BLESS YOUR SOLE 531162	OP	25.00	25.00
95	COME LET US ADORE HIM/MINI NAT. STARTER	OP	35.00	35.00
95	COME LET US ADORE HIM/NATIVITY STARTER S	OP	50.00	50.00
95	DREAMS REALLY DO COME TRUE 128309	OP	37.50	38.00
95	GOD BLESS THE DAY WE FOUND YOU 100145R	OP	60.00	60.00
95	GOD BLESS THE DAY WE FOUND YOU 100153R	OP	60.00	60.00
95	HALLELUJAH FOR THE CROSS 532002	OP	35.00	35.00
95	HAPPY HULA DAYS 128694	OP	30.00	30.00
95	HE COVERS THE EARTH W/HIS BEAUTY	OP	30.00	30.00
95	HE COVERS THE EARTH WITH..BEAUTY 142654	YR	30.00	30.00
95	HE'S GOT THE WHOLE WORLD IN HIS HANDS	2000	*	*
95	I CAN'T BEAR TO LET YOU GO 532037	OP	50.00	50.00
95	I GIVE YOU MY LOVE FOREVER TRUE 129100	OP	70.00	70.00
95	I ONLY HAVE ICE FOR YOU 530956	OP	55.00	55.00
95	I'LL GIVE HIM MY HEART 150088	OP	40.00	40.00
95	JUST A LINE TO SAY YOU'RE SPECIAL 522864	OP	50.00	50.00
95	LORD HELP ME TO STAY ON COURSE 532096	OP	35.00	35.00
95	LOVE BLOOMS ETERNAL	OP	35.00	35.00
95	MAKING A TRAIL TO BETHLEHEM 142751	OP	30.00	00.00
95	MAKING SPIRITS BRIGHT 150118	OP	37.50	38.00
95	MONEY'S NOT THE ONLY GREEN THING..SAVING	OP	50.00	50.00
95	SENDING MY LOVE YOUR WAY 528609	OP	40.00	40.00
95	SENDING YOU OCEANS OF LOVE 532010	OP	35.00	35.00
95	TAKE TIME TO SMELL THE FLOWERS 524387	OP	30.00	30.00
95	VAYA CON DIOS (GO WITH GOD) 531146	OP	32.50	33.00
95	WALK IN THE SUNSHINE 524212	OP	35.00	35.00
95	WHAT THE WORLD NEEDS IS LOVE 531065	OP	45.00	45.00
95	YOU FILL THE PAGES OF MY LIFE	OP	67.50	68.00
95	YOU WILL ALWAYS BE OUR HERO 136271	YR	40.00	40.00
95	YOU'RE ONE IN A MILLION TO ME	OP	35.00	35.00
96	ALL SING HIS PRAISES 184012	OP	32.50	33.00
96	ANGELS ON EARTH 183776	OP	40.00	40.00
96	COLOR YOUR WORLD WITH THANKSGIVING 18385	OP	50.00	50.00
96	ENTER HIS COURT WITH THANKSGIVING 521221	OP	35.00	35.00
96	HE LOVES ME	2000	*	*
96	IT MAY BE GREENER, BUT....HARD TO CUT 16	OP	37.50	37.50
96	LORD IS WITH YOU, THE 526835	OP	27.50	27.50
96	LOVE NEVER LEAVES A MOTHER'S ARMS 523941	OP	40.00	40.00
96	MAKING A TRAIL TO BETHLEHEM 184004	OP	18.50	18.50
96	MATCHING TO THE BEAT OF FREEDOM'S DRUM 5	OP	35.00	35.00
96	MINI SET ADDITION/WEE THREE KINGS 213624	OP	55.00	55.00
96	MY TRUE LOVE GAVE TO ME 529273	OP	40.00	40.00
96	NATIVITY SET ADDITION/SHEPHERD W/LAMBS 1	OP	40.00	40.00
96	PEACH ON EARTH...ANYWAY 183342	YR	32.50	33.00
96	SING IN EXCELSIS DEO 183830	OP	125.00	125.00
96	SNOWBUNNY LOVES YOU LIKE I DO 183792	OP	18.50	18.50
96	SUN IS ALWAYS SHINING SOMEWHERE, THE 163	OP	37.50	37.50
96	SWEETER AS THE YEARS GO BY 522333	OP	60.00	60.00
96	TAKE IT TO THE LORD IN PRAYER 163767	OP	30.00	30.00
96	WHAT A DIFFERENCE...MADE IN MY LIFE 5311	OP	50.00	50.00
96	YOU DESERVE A HALO-THANK YOU 531693	OP	55.00	55.00
S. BUTCHER		**PRECIOUS MOMENTS BABY'S FIRST**		
84	BABY'S FIRST HAIRCUT 12211	SU	32.50	138.00
84	BABY'S FIRST PICTURE E-2841	RT	45.00	155.00
84	BABY'S FIRST STEP E-2840	SU	35.00	80.00
88	BABY'S FIRST PET 520705	OP	45.00	70.00
90	BABY'S FIRST MEAL 524077	OP	35.00	42.00
92	BABY'S FIRST WORD 527238	OP	25.00	30.00
S. BUTCHER		**PRECIOUS MOMENTS BIRTHDAY**		
95	WISHING YOU A HAPPY BEAR HUG 520659	OP	27.50	28.00
96	I HAVEN'T SEEN MUCH OF YOU LATELY 531057	OP	13.50	14.00
S. BUTCHER		**PRECIOUS MOMENTS BIRTHDAY CLUB**		
86	FISHING FOR FRIENDS BC-861	YR	10.00	130.00
86	OUR CLUB CAN'T BE BEAT B-0001	YR	*	75.00
87	A SMILE'S THE CYMBAL OF JOY B-0002	YR	*	55.00
87	A SMILE'S THE CYMBAL OF JOY B-0102	YR	*	70.00
87	HI SUGAR BC-871	YR	11.00	90.00
88	HAVE A BEARY SPECIAL BIRTHDAY B-0004	YR	*	30.00
88	SOMEBUNNY CARES BC-881	YR	13.50	47.00
88	SWEETEST CLUB AROUND, THE- B-0003	YR	*	45.00
88	SWEETEST CLUB AROUND, THE- B-0103	YR	*	40.00

YR	NAME	LIMIT	ISSUE	TREND
89	CAN'T BEEHIVE MYSELF WITHOUT YOU BC-891	YR	13.50	45.00
89	HAVE A BEARY SPECIAL BIRTHDAY B-0104	YR	*	35.00
90	COLLECTING MAKES GOOD SCENTS BC-901	YR	15.00	40.00
90	I'M NUTS OVER MY COLLECTION BC-902	YR	15.00	40.00
90	JEST TO LET YOU KNOW YOU'RE TOPS B-0006	YR	*	26.00
90	JEST TO LET YOU KNOW YOU'RE TOPS B-0106	YR	*	25.00
90	OUR CLUB IS A TOUGH ACT TO FOLLOW B-0005	YR	*	30.00
90	OUR CLUB IS A TOUGH ACT TO FOLLOW B-0005	YR	*	30.00
93	PUT A LITTLE PUNCH INTO YOUR BIRTHDAY	OP	15.00	15.00
94	OWL ALWAYS BE YOUR FRIEND	OP	16.00	16.00
S. BUTCHER	**PRECIOUS MOMENTS BIRTHDAY SERIES**			
86	BRIGHTEN SOMEONE'S DAY 105953	SU	12.50	35.00
86	SHOWERS OF BLESSINGS 105945	RT	16.00	50.00
88	FRIENDS TO THE END 104418	SU	15.00	40.00
88	HELLO WORLD! 521175	OP	13.50	24.00
89	NOT A CREATURE WAS STIRRING 524484	OP	17.00	30.00
89	TO MY FAVORITE FAN 521043	SU	16.00	40.00
90	CAN'T BE WITHOUT YOU 524492	OP	16.00	20.00
90	HOW CAN I EVER FORGET YOU 526924	OP	15.00	18.00
90	LET'S BE FRIENDS 527270	OP	15.00	18.00
92	HAPPY BIRDIE 527343	SU	16.00	18.00
S. BUTCHER	**PRECIOUS MOMENTS BIRTHDAY TRAIN**			
85	BLESS THE DAYS OF OUR YOUTH 16004	OP	15.00	35.00
85	GOD BLESS YOU ON YOUR BIRTHDAY 15962	OP	11.00	30.00
85	HAPPY BIRTHDAY LITTLE LAMB 15946	OP	10.00	30.00
85	HEAVEN BLESS YOUR SPECIAL DAY 15954	OP	11.00	30.00
85	KEEP LOOKING UP 15997	OP	13.50	30.00
85	MAY YOUR BIRTHDAY BE WARM 15938	OP	10.00	30.00
85	THIS DAY IS SOMETHING...ROAR ABOUT 15989	OP	13.50	30.00
88	ISN'T EIGHT JUST GREAT 109460	OP	18.50	27.00
88	WISHING YOU GRR-EATNESS 109479	OP	18.50	27.00
90	MAY YOUR BIRTHDAY BE MAMMOTH 521825	OP	25.00	30.00
92	BEING NINE IS JUST DIVINE 521833	OP	25.00	30.00
S. BUTCHER	**PRECIOUS MOMENTS BOYS & GIRLS CLUBS OF AMERICA**			
97	SHOOT FOR THE STARS..STRIKE OUT 521701	LE	60.00	60.00
S. BUTCHER	**PRECIOUS MOMENTS BRIDAL PARTY**			
83	BRIDE E-2846	OP	18.00	30.00
83	GROOMSMAN WITH FROG E-2836	OP	13.00	28.00
83	JUNIOR BRIDESMAID E-2845	OP	12.00	25.00
83	NO FLOWER IS AS SWEET AS YOU E-2831	OP	13.00	24.00
84	FLOWER GIRL E-2835	OP	11.00	24.00
84	RINGBEARER E-2833	OP	11.00	22.00
86	GOD BLESS..FAMILY (PARENTS/BRIDE) 100501	OP	35.00	60.00
86	GOD BLESS..FAMILY (PARENTS/GROOM) 100498	OP	35.00	55.00
86	GROOM E-2837	OP	13.50	38.00
87	WEDDING ARCH 102369	SU	22.50	45.00
S. BUTCHER	**PRECIOUS MOMENTS CALENDAR GIRL**			
87	APRIL 110027	OP	27.50	35.00-110.00
87	FEBRUARY 109991	OP	27.50	45.00
87	JANUARY 109983	OP	37.50	55.00
87	JUNE 110043	OP	40.00	80.00
87	MARCH 110019	OP	27.50	45.00
87	MAY 110035	OP	27.50	35.00-150.00
88	AUGUST 110078	OP	40.00	55.00
88	DECEMBER 110116	OP	27.50	45.00
88	JULY 110051	OP	35.00	50.00
88	NOVEMBER 110108	OP	32.50	42.00
88	OCTOBER 110094	OP	35.00	50.00
88	SEPTEMBER 110086	OP	27.50	45.00
S. BUTCHER	**PRECIOUS MOMENTS CLOWN**			
85	I GET A BANG OUT OF YOU 12262	OP	35.00	60.00
85	LORD KEEP ME ON THE BALL 12270	OP	35.00	60.00
85	LORD WILL CARRY YOU THROUGH, THE- 12467	RT	30.00	80.00
85	WADDLE I DO WITHOUT YOU 12459	RT	30.00	85.00
S. BUTCHER	**PRECIOUS MOMENTS COLLECTORS CLUB**			
81	HELLO, LORD, IT'S ME AGAIN PM-811	CL	25.00	450.00
81	PUT ON A HAPPY FACE PM-822	CL	25.00	200.00
82	BUT LOVE GOES ON FOREVER-PLAQUE E-0202	YR	*	65.00
82	LET US CALL THE CLUB TO ORDER E-0303	YR	*	60.00
82	SMILE, GOD LOVES YOU PM-821	CL	25.00	225.00
83	DAWN'S EARLY LIGHT PM-831	CL	27.50	90.00
83	GOD'S RAY OF MERCY PM-841	CL	25.00	60.00
83	JOIN IN ON THE BLESSINGS E-0404	YR	*	80.00
84	I LOVE TO TELL THE STORY PM-852	CL	27.50	55.00
84	LORD IS MY SHEPHERD, THE- PM-851	SU	25.00	80.00
84	SEEK AND YE SHALL FIND E-0005	YR	*	50.00
84	TRUST IN THE LORD TO THE FINISH PM-842	CL	25.00	55.00
86	BIRDS OF A FEATHER...TOGETHER E-0006	YR	*	50.00
86	FEED MY SHEEP PM-871	CL	25.00	50.00
86	GRANDMA'S PRAYER PM-861	CL	25.00	80.00
86	I'M FOLLOWING JESUS PM-862	CL	25.00	85.00
86	LOVING YOU DEAR VALENTINE PM873	OP	25.00	35.00
86	LOVING YOU DEAR VALENTINE PM874	OP	25.00	40.00
87	A GROWING LOVE E-0008	YR	*	35.00
87	IN HIS TIME PM-872	CL	25.00	48.00
87	SHARING IS UNIVERSAL E-0007	YR	*	45.00
88	ALWAYS ROOM FOR ONE MORE C-0009	YR	*	35.00
88	GOD BLESS YOU/TOUCHING MY LIFE PM-881	CL	27.50	55.00

YR	NAME	LIMIT	ISSUE	TREND
88	YOU JUST CAN'T CHUCK...FRIENDSHIP PM-882	CL	27.50	46.00
89	MOW POWER TO YOU PM-892	CL	27.50	40.00
89	MY HAPPINESS C-0010	YR	*	40.00
89	YOU WILL ALWAYS BE MY CHOICE PM-891	CL	27.50	40.00
90	AN EVENT WORTH WADING FOR 527319	YR	32.50	40.00
90	CLUB IS OUT OF THIS WORLD, THE C0012	YR	*	30.00
90	LORD, KEEP ME/TEE PEE TOP SHAPE PM-912	YR	27.50	40.00
90	ONE STEP AT A TIME PM-911	YR	33.00	40.00
90	SHARING THE GOOD NEWS TOGETHER C0011	YR	*	35.00
90	TEN YEARS AND STILL GOING STRONG PM-901	CL	30.00	50.00
90	YOU ARE A BLESSING TO ME PM-902	CL	27.50	50.00
91	THIS LAND IS OUR LAND 527386	LE	350.00	385.00
92	ONLY LOVE CAN MAKE A HOME PM-921	YR	30.00	45.00
92	SOWING THE SEEDS OF LOVE PM922	OP	30.00	35.00
93	MEMORIES ARE MADE OF THIS 529982	LE	30.00	30.00
S. BUTCHER		**PRECIOUS MOMENTS CROSS**		
95	LOVE BLOOMS ETERNAL 127019	OP	35.00	35.00
96	STANDING IN THE PRESENCE OF THE LORD 163	YR	37.50	37.50
S. BUTCHER		**PRECIOUS MOMENTS EASTER SEALS**		
96	YOU CAN ALWAYS COUNT ON ME 526827	OP	30.00	30.00
97	GIVE ABILITY A CHANCE 192368	LE	30.00	30.00
S. BUTCHER		**PRECIOUS MOMENTS EVENTS**		
87	YOU ARE MY MAIN EVENT 115231	YR	30.00	75.00
88	SHARING BEGINS IN THE HEART 520861	YR	25.00	60.00
90	I'M A PRECIOUS MOMENTS FAN 523526	YR	25.00	45.00
90	YOU CAN ALWAYS BRING A FRIEND 527122	YR	27.50	50.00
92	AN EVENT WORTH WADING FOR 527319	YR	32.50	45.00
S. BUTCHER		**PRECIOUS MOMENTS FAMILY CHRISTMAS SCENE**		
85	GOD GAVE HIS BEST 15806	SU	13.00	35.00
85	MAY YOU HAVE...SWEETEST CHRISTMAS 15776	SU	17.00	45.00
85	STORY OF GOD'S LOVE, THE- 15784	OP	22.50	55.00
85	TELL ME A STORY 15792	SU	10.00	32.00
86	SHARING OUR CHRISTMAS TOGETHER 102490	SU	37.00	70.00
89	HAVE A BEARY MERRY CHRISTMAS 522856	SU	15.00	20.00
90	CHRISTMAS FIREPLACE 524883	OP	37.50	55.00
S. BUTCHER		**PRECIOUS MOMENTS MUSICAL**		
79	COME LET US ADORE HIM E-2810	SU	60.00	150.00
79	LORD BLESS YOU AND KEEP YOU, THE- E-7180	OP	55.00	110.00
79	MOTHER SEW DEAR E-7182	OP	35.00	60.00-100.00
79	PURR-FECT GRANDMA, THE- E-7184	SU	35.00	60.00-100.00
80	CHRISTMAS IS A TIME TO SHARE E-2806	RT	45.00	165.00
80	CROWN HIM LORD OF ALL E-2807	SU	45.00	115.00
80	JESUS IS BORN E-2809	SU	45.00	145.00
80	MY GUARDIAN ANGEL E-5205	SU	27.50	90.00
80	MY GUARDIAN ANGEL E-5206	SU	27.50	100.00
80	PEACE ON EARTH E-4726	SU	29.00	145.00
80	REJOICE O EARTH E-5645	RT	40.00	110.00
80	SILENT NIGHT E-5642	SU	55.00	220.00
80	UNTO US A CHILD IS BORN E-2808	SU	45.00	110.00
81	HAND THAT ROCKS THE FUTURE, THE-E-5204	OP	37.50	60.00-105.00
81	LET THE WHOLE WORLD KNOW E-7165	SU	60.00	100.00
81	LET THE WHOLE WORLD KNOW E7186	SU	60.00	160.00
81	LOVE IS SHARING E-7185	RT	40.00	165.00
82	I'LL PLAY MY DRUM FOR HIM E-2355	SU	45.00	165.00
83	LET HEAVEN AND NATURE SING E-2345	SU	30.00	165.00
83	SHARING OUR SEASON TOGETHER E-0519	RT	70.00	150.00
83	WEE THREE KINGS E-0520	SU	60.00	135.00
84	HEAVEN BLESS YOU 100285	SU	45.00	95.00
84	WE SAW A STAR 12408	SU	50.00	100.00
84	WISHING YOU A MERRY CHRISTMAS E-5394	SU	55.00	115.00
85	OUR 1ST CHRISTMAS TOGETHER 101702	RT	50.00	128.00
87	I'M SENDING YOU A WHITE CHRISTMAS 112402	RT	55.00	145.00
88	YOU HAVE TOUCHED SO MANY HEARTS 112577	SU	40.00	65.00
90	LORD HELP KEEP ME IN BALANCE 520691	SU	60.00	75.00
90	THIS DAY HAS BEEN MADE IN HEAVEN 523682	OP	60.00	65.00
91	SLEEPING BABY BOY 429570	OP	65.00	70.00
91	SLEEPING BABY GIRL 429589	OP	65.00	70.00
92	DO NOT OPEN TILL CHRISTMAS 522244	OP	75.00	90.00
92	THIS DAY HAS BEEN MADE IN HEAVEN 523682	OP	60.00	65.00
S. BUTCHER		**PRECIOUS MOMENTS NOAH'S ARK**		
92	BUNNIES 530123	OP	9.00	9.00
92	ELEPHANTS 530131	OP	18.00	18.00
92	GIRAFFES 530115	OP	16.00	16.00
92	NOAH'S ARK 8/PC COLL. SET 530948	OP	190.00	190.00
92	PIGS 530085	OP	12.00	12.00
92	SHEEP 530077	OP	10.00	10.00
93	LLAMAS 531375	OP	15.00	15.00
S. BUTCHER		**PRECIOUS MOMENTS REJOICE IN THE LORD**		
84	HAPPINESS IS THE LORD 12378	SU	15.00	40.00
84	HE IS MY SONG 12394	SU	17.50	45.00
84	LORD GIVE ME A SONG 12386	SU	15.00	40.00
84	THERE'S A SONG IN MY HEART 12173	SU	11.00	38.00
86	LORD KEEP MY LIFE IN TUNE 12580	SU	37.50	110.00
S. BUTCHER		**PRECIOUS MOMENTS RETIRED**		
78	WISHING YOU A SEASON FILLED W/JOY E-2805	RT	20.00	100.00
79	BE NOT WEARY IN WELL DOING E-3111	RT	14.00	140.00
79	BLESSED ARE THE PEACEMAKERS E-3107	RT	13.00	100.00
79	COME LET US ADORE HIM E-2011	RT	10.00	300.00

YR	NAME	LIMIT	ISSUE	TREND
79	GOD LOVETH A CHEERFUL GIVER E-1378	RT	9.50	900.00
79	GOD'S SPEED E-3112	RT	14.00	85.00
79	HIS BURDEN IS LIGHT E-1380G	RT	17.00	125.00
79	JESUS IS THE LIGHT E-1373G	RT	15.00	40.00-130.00
79	O, HOW I LOVE JESUS E-1380B	RT	17.00	110.00
79	PRAISE THE LORD ANYHOW E-1374B	RT	17.00	100.00
79	SMILE, GOD LOVES YOU E-1373B	RT	15.00	60.00-135.00
81	THERE IS JOY IN SERVING JESUS E-7157	RT	17.00	60.00
82	DROPPING OVER FOR CHRISTMAS E-2375	RT	30.00	100.00
82	NOBODY'S PERFECT E-9268	RT	21.00	75.00
82	O COME ALL YE FAITHFUL E-2353	RT	27.50	60.00-100.00
82	TASTE & SEE THAT THE LORD IS GOOD E-9274	RT	22.50	68.00-250.00
83	CHRISTMASTIME IS FOR SHARING E-0504	RT	37.00	90.00
83	SURROUNDED WITH JOY E-0507	RT	35.00	75.00
83	THIS IS YOUR DAY TO SHINE E-2822	RT	37.50	80.00-155.00
83	YOU CAN'T RUN AWAY FROM GOD E-0525	RT	28.50	125.00
85	HELP, LORD, I'M IN A SPOT 100269	RT	18.50	65.00
85	LORD KEEP ME ON MY TOES 100129	RT	22.50	100.00
86	MAKE ME A BLESSING 100102	RT	35.00	90.00
86	SMILE ALONG THE WAY 101842	RT	30.00	155.00
87	HAPPINESS DIVINE 109584	RT	25.00	60.00
87	HIS EYE IS ON THE SPARROW E-0530	RT	28.50	125.00
87	HOLY SMOKES E-2351	RT	30.00	125.00
87	I BELIEVE IN MIRACLES E-7156R	RT	22.50	70.00
87	LET LOVE REIGN E-9273	RT	22.50	68.00-250.00
87	LORD/KEEP OUR ACT TOGETHER 101850	RT	35.00	155.00
87	LOVE IS KIND E-5377	RT	27.50	85.00
87	SCENT FROM ABOVE 100528	RT	19.00	60.00
87	SMILE ALONG THE WAY 101842	RT	35.00	170.00
87	SPIRIT IS WILLING, THE- 100196	RT	19.00	58.00-75.00
88	MANY MOONS...CANOE, BLESSUM YOU 520772	RT	50.00	225.00
88	SENDING YOU SHOWERS OF BLESSINGS 520683	RT	32.50	75.00
88	SOMEDAY MY LOVE 520799	RT	40.00	75.00
89	I'M SO GLAD YOU FLUTTERED...LIFE 520640	RT	40.00	280.00-375.00
S. BUTCHER		**PRECIOUS MOMENTS SUGAR TOWN**		
92	AUNT RUTH AND AUNT DOROTHY 529486	OP	20.00	21.00
92	CAR 529443	OP	22.50	24.00
92	CHAPEL 529621	RT	85.00	85.00
92	DUSTY 529435	OP	15.00	18.00
92	EVERGREEN TREE 528684	OP	15.00	17.00
92	FENCE 529796	OP	10.00	11.00
92	GRANDFATHER 529516	OP	15.00	17.00
92	KATYLYNNE 529524	OP	20.00	21.00
92	NATIVITY 529508	OP	20.00	21.00
92	PHILIP 529494	OP	17.00	18.00
92	SAM BUTCHER 529567	LE	22.50	32.00
92	SAM BUTCHER 529842	OP	22.50	24.00
92	SAMMY 528668	OP	17.00	150.00
95	BIRD BATH 150223	OP	8.50	9.00
95	BUS STOP 150207	OP	8.50	9.00
95	CONDUCTOR 150169	OP	20.00	20.00
95	DOG AND KITEEN ON PARK BENCH 529540	OP	13.00	13.00
95	FIRE HYDRANT 150215	OP	5.00	5.00
95	FUEL BOY 531871	OP	22.50	23.00
95	GIRLS WITH GIFTS 531812	OP	22.50	23.00
95	LUGGAGE CART WITH KITTEN 150185	OP	13.00	13.00
95	RAILROAD CROSSING SIGN 150177	OP	12.00	12.00
95	STREET SIGN 532185	OP	10.00	10.00
95	SUGAR TOWN ENHANCEMENT SET 152269	OP	45.00	45.00
95	SUGAR TOWN TRAIN STATION/COLLECTORS SET	OP	190.00	190.00
95	TRAIN STATION NIGHT LIGHT 150150	OP	100.00	100.00
95	WE HAVE COME FROM AFAR 530913	OP	12.00	12.00
96	A PRINCE OF A GUY 526037	OP	35.00	35.00
96	BONFIRE WITH BUNNIES 184152	OP	10.00	10.00
96	COCOA 184063	OP	7.50	7.50
96	FLAG POLE WITH KITTEN 184136	OP	15.00	15.00
96	HANK AND SHARON 184098	OP	25.00	25.00
96	LEROY 184071	OP	18.50	18.50
96	LIGHTED TREE 184039	OP	45.00	45.00
96	LIGHTED WARMING HUT 192341	OP	60.00	60.00
96	MAZIE 184055	OP	18.50	18.50
96	MY LOVE BLOOMS FOR YOU 521728	OP	50.00	50.00
96	PRETTY AS A PRINCESS 526053	OP	35.00	35.00
96	SKATING POND 184047	OP	40.00	40.00
96	SKATING SIGN 184020	LE	15.00	15.00
96	SUGAR TOWN ENCHANCEMENT SET 184160	OP	40.00	40.00
96	SUGAR TOWN SKATING POND SET 184128 7 PC	OP	184.50	185.00
96	WOODEN BARREL HOT COCOA STAND 184144	OP	15.00	15.00
S. BUTCHER		**PRECIOUS MOMENTS THE FOUR SEASONS**		
85	SUMMER'S JOY 12076	YR	30.00	100.00
85	VOICE OF SPRING, THE- 12068	YR	30.00	300.00
86	AUTUMN'S PRAISE 12084	YR	30.00	70.00
86	WINTER'S SONG 12092	YR	30.00	135.00
S. BUTCHER			**SAMMY'S CIRCUS**	
93	COLLIN 529214	SU	20.00	20.00
93	DUSTY 529176	SU	22.50	12.00
93	KATIE 529184	SU	17.50	17.00
93	MARKIE 528099	SU	18.50	19.00

YR	NAME	LIMIT	ISSUE	TREND
93	SAMMY 529222	OP	20.00	20.00
93	TIPPY 529192	SU	12.00	12.00
95	JORDAN 529168	SU	20.00	20.00
96	JENNIFER 163708	SU	20.00	20.00
*			**SHARING SEASON GIFTS**	
92	CLUB'S THAT'S OUT...THIS WORLD, THE PM03	OP	*	70.00
*			**SMALL WORLD OF MUSIC**	
94	1963 CHEVROLET CORVETTE STING RAY	7500	300.00	300.00
95	'53 CORVETTE/MUSICAL 341460	*	30.00	30.00
95	'55 FORD THUNDERBIRD/MUSICAL 869058	*	30.00	30.00
95	'57 CHEVROLET BEL AIR/MUSICAL 869031	*	30.00	30.00
95	'64 1/2 FORD MUSTANG/MUSICAL 341452	*	30.00	30.00
95	'65 CORVETTE STING RAY/MUSICAL 819204	*	30.00	30.00
95	A CHEESE RING CIRCUS/MUSICAL 869023	*	30.00	30.00
95	A REFRESHING PAUSE/MUSICAL 153168	*	30.00	30.00
95	A THRIST FOR FUN/MUSCIAL 128775	*	250.00	250.00
95	A-B-C- SAW/MUSICAL 868965	*	50.00	50.00
95	CALLING TO COLLECT/MUSICAL	*	250.00	250.00
95	CLARA'S DREAM/MUSICAL	*	30.00	30.00
95	FLEET SWEETS/MUSICAL	*	30.00	30.00
95	IT'S THE REAL THING/MUSICAL 128910	*	50.00	50.00
95	LITTLE LOVE BOAT/MUSICAL 551104	*	30.00	30.00
95	MAESTRO OF MISCHIEF/MUSICAL 138126	*	70.00	70.00
95	MINI MOUSEICIANS/MUSICAL 868981	*	30.00	30.00
95	MONTMARTRE/MUSICAL 869007	*	30.00	30.00
95	POP HOP SOAD SHOPPE/MUSICAL 138282	*	30.00	30.00
95	PRACTICE MAKES PERFECT/MUSICAL	*	50.00	50.00
95	PRESENTING..PINOCCHIO/MUSICAL 596302	*	350.00	350.00
95	ROCK-A-BEAR BABY/MUSICAL 868973	*	50.00	50.00
95	ROCKIN' & ROLLIN'/MUSICAL 598003	*	150.00	150.00
95	SANTA'S SECRET HELPER/MUSICAL	*	30.00	30.00
95	SIR MICKEY TO THE RESCUE/MUSICAL 123633	*	400.00	400.00
95	SPINING TAILS/MUSICAL 114944	*	200.00	200.00
95	SPINNING A YARN/MUSICAL 137006	*	30.00	30.00
95	THAT'S ALL FOLKS/MUSICAL	*	100.00	100.00
95	TO BOLDLY GO.../MUSICAL 323608	*	300.00	300.00
95	TO THE RESCUE/MUSICAL 551163	*	30.00	30.00
95	WISHES A-WEIGH/MUSICAL	*	70.00	70.00
96	'56 CORVETTE/MUSICAL	*	30.00	30.00
96	'59 CADILLAC/MUSICAL	*	30.00	30.00
96	BAKING SWEET MEMORIES/MUSICAL 184861	*	30.00	30.00
96	CHEVY BLAZER/MUSICAL 175021	*	30.00	30.00
96	COLOSSAL, THE/MUSICAL	*	600.00	600.00
96	COWARDLY LION, THE/MUSICAL 175110	*	30.00	30.00
96	DODGE RAM TRUCK/MUSICAL 174106	*	30.00	30.00
96	DOROTHY/MUSICAL 175099	*	30.00	30.00
96	F100 FORD PICK-UP/MUSICAL	*	30.00	30.00
96	FORD EXPLORER/MUSICAL 174092	*	30.00	30.00
96	HOLIDAY HORSEPLAY/MUSICAL	*	30.00	30.00
96	I'D LIKE TO BUY THE WORLD A COKE/MUSICAL	*	250.00	250.00
96	IT SEAMS LIKE CHRISTMAS/MUSICAL	*	30.00	30.00
96	JEEP GRAND CHEROKEE/MUSICAL 175013	*	30.00	30.00
96	LAST MINUTE SHOP WORK/MUSICAL	*	30.00	30.00
96	LULLABY LAND/MUSICAL	*	30.00	30.00
96	MERRY-GO-ROUND MAGIC/MUSICAL 167150	*	30.00	30.00
96	MICEST DECORATIONS, THE/MUSICAL	*	30.00	30.00
96	PERFECT HARMONY/MUSICAL 920339	*	30.00	30.00
96	SCARECROW. THE/MUSICAL 175129	*	30.00	30.00
96	SERVING UP FUN/MUSICAL 168025	*	30.00	30.00
96	SEW PETTY/MUSICAL 165360	*	30.00	30.00
96	SPOTTIN' ADVENTURE/MUSICAL 165387	*	30.00	30.00
96	TASTEFULLY TRIMMED/MUSICAL 184888	*	30.00	30.00
96	TEA FOR TWO/MUSICAL 902675	*	30.00	30.00
96	TIN MAN, THE/MUSICAL 175099	*	30.00	30.00
96	TINY TOONLAND/MUSICAL	*	30.00	30.00
96	TOGETHER W/COCA-COLA/MUSICAL 165409	*	150.00	150.00
96	WHAT CHILD IS THIS?/MUSICAL 184365	*	30.00	30.00
K. HAHN			**SMALL WORLD OF MUSIC**	
95	BAKING YOU HAPPY/MUSICAL 136999	*	30.00	30.00
95	SUPPLIES IN DEMAND/MUSICAL 136980	*	30.00	30.00
S. BUTCHER			**TO HAVE AND TO HOLD**	
96	A SILVER CELEBRATION TO SHARE 163813	OP	70.00	70.00
96	A YEAR OF BLESSINGS 163783	OP	70.00	70.00
96	EACH HOUR IS PRECIOUS WITH YOU 163791	OP	70.00	70.00
96	FIFTY YEARS AS PRECIOUS AS GOLD 163848	OP	70.00	70.00
96	FORTY YEARS OF PRECIOUS MEMORIES 163821	OP	70.00	70.00
96	LOVE VOWS TO ALWAYS BLOOM 129097	OP	70.00	70.00
96	TEN YEARS HEART TO HEART 163805	OP	70.00	70.00
S. BUTCHER			**YOU ARE ALWAYS THERE FOR ME**	
96	FATHER HELPING SON BAT 163627	OP	50.00	50.00
96	MOTHER KISSING DAUGHTER'S OWIE 163600	OP	50.00	50.00
96	SISTER CONSOLING SISTER 163635	OP	50.00	50.00

FENTON ART GLASS

YR	NAME	LIMIT	ISSUE	TREND
D. JOHNSON			**BIRDS OF WINTER ED. I**	
87	CLOCK 8600BC 6"	1500	49.50	50.00
87	FAIRY LIGHT 7300BC 4 1/2"	4500	29.50	30.00
87	LAMP 9702BC 18 1/2"	500	250.00	250.00

YR	NAME	LIMIT	ISSUE	TREND
	D. JOHNSON		**BIRDS OF WINTER ED. II**	
88	CLOCK 8600BD 6"	1500	55.00	55.00
88	FAIRY LIGHT 9300BD 4 1/2"	4500	29.50	30.00
88	LAMP 7209BD 21" STUDENT	500	274.00	274.00
	D. JOHNSON		**BIRDS OF WINTER ED. III**	
89	CLOCK 8600BL 6"	1500	59.50	60.00
89	FAIRY LIGHT 7300BL 4 1/2"	4500	29.50	30.00
89	LAMP 7204BL 16"	500	250.00	250.00
	D. JOHNSON		**BIRDS OF WINTER ED. IV**	
90	CLOCK 8600NB 6"	1500	59.50	60.00
90	FAIRY LIGHT 7300NB 4 1/2"	4500	29.50	30.00
90	LAMP 7209NB 21" STUDENT	500	275.00	275.00
	F. BURTON		**CHRISTMAS AT HOME ED. I**	
90	CLOCK 8600HD 6"	1500	75.00	75.00
90	FAIRY LIGHT 7300HD 4 1/2"	3500	39.00	39.00
90	LAMP 7204HD 16"	1000	250.00	250.00
	F. BURTON		**CHRISTMAS AT HOME ED. II**	
90	CLOCK 8600HJ 6"	1500	75.00	75.00
90	FAIRY LIGHT 7300HJ 4 1/2"	3500	39.00	39.00
90	LAMP 7204HJ 16"	1000	250.00	250.00
	F. BURTON		**CHRISTMAS AT HOME ED. III**	
92	CLOCK 8600HQ 6"	1500	75.00	75.00
92	FAIRY LIGHT 7300HQ 4 1/2"	3500	39.00	39.00
92	LAMP 9830HQ 20"	1000	250.00	250.00
	F. BURTON		**CHRISTMAS AT HOME ED. IV**	
93	CLOCK 8600HT	1500	79.00	79.00
93	FAIRY LIGHT 7300HT	3500	39.00	39.00
93	LAMP 7204HT 16"	1000	265.00	265.00
	M. DICKINSON		**CHRISTMAS CLASSICS ED. I**	
78	FAIRY LIGHT 7300CV	*	25.00	25.00
78	LAMP, 7204CV 16" COLONIAL	YR	125.00	125.00
	K. CUNNINGHAM		**CHRISTMAS CLASSICS ED. II**	
79	FAIRY LIGHT 7300NC	*	30.00	30.00
79	LAMP, 7204NC 16" COLONIAL	YR	150.00	150.00
	D. JOHNSON		**CHRISTMAS CLASSICS ED. III**	
80	FAIRY LIGHT 7300GH	*	32.50	33.00
80	LAMP, 7204GH 16" COLONIAL	YR	165.00	165.00
	D. JOHNSON		**CHRISTMAS CLASSICS ED. IV**	
81	FAIRY LIGHT 7300AC	*	35.00	35.00
81	LAMP 7204AC 16" COLONIAL	YR	175.00	175.00
81	LAMP 7510AC 20" STUDENT	*	225.00	225.00
	R. SPINDLER		**CHRISTMAS CLASSICS ED. V**	
82	FAIRY LIGHT 7300OC	*	35.00	35.00
82	LAMP 7204OC 16" COLONIAL	YR	175.00	175.00
82	LAMP 7510OC 21" STUDENT	*	225.00	225.00
	D. JOHNSON		**CHRISTMAS FANTASY ED. I**	
83	FAIRY LIGHT 7300AI	7500	35.00	35.00
	D. JOHNSON		**CHRISTMAS FANTASY ED. II**	
84	FAIRY LIGHT 7300GE	7500	37.50	38.00
84	LAMP 7512GE 10 1/2" HURRICANE	7500	75.00	75.00
	D. JOHNSON		**CHRISTMAS FANTASY ED. III**	
85	FAIRY LIGHT 7300WP	7500	37.50	38.00
	L. EVERSON		**CHRISTMAS FANTASY ED. IV**	
87	FAIRY LIGHT 7300CV	CL	37.50	38.00
*			**CHRISTMAS LIMITED EDITIONS**	
95	ANGEL, HEAVENLY BELL 5144TW 5 3/4"	1900	35.00	35.00
	M. DICKINSON		**CHRISTMAS LIMITED EDITIONS**	
86	BASKET, 9" 7436JW	5000	100.00	100.00
86	LAMP 9702JW	2500	250.00	250.00
86	VASE, 9" 7661JW	5000	95.00	95.00
	L. PIPER		**CHRISTMAS LIMITED EDITIONS**	
86	CLOCK, 6" 8600XS	5000	59.00	59.00
86	FAIRY LIGHT, 2 PC 7300XS	5000	35.00	35.00
86	LAMP, 16" 7204XS	2500	195.00	195.00
	M. REYNOLDS		**CHRISTMAS LIMITED EDITIONS**	
92	EGG, 3 1/2" 5140SD MANAGER SCENE ON RUBY	2500	30.00	30.00
92	EGG, 3 1/2" 5140SU POINSETTA ON CRYSTAL	2500	30.00	30.00
93	EGG, 3 1/2" 5140SV WOODS ON WHITE	2500	35.00	35.00
93	EGG, 3 1/2" 5140SW ANGEL ON GREEN	2500	35.00	35.00
94	EGG 5145VG 3 1/2" MAGNOLIA ON GOLD	1500	35.00	35.00
94	EGG 5145VK 3 1/2" PARTRIDGE ON RUBY	1500	35.00	35.00
95	ANGEL 5542TA RADIANT-MUSICAL BASE	900	85.00	85.00
95	EGG 5145TH 3 1/2" BOW & HOLLY ON IVORY	900	35.00	35.00
95	EGG 5145TP 3 1/2" CHICKADEE ON GOLD	900	35.00	35.00
95	PITCHER, 2996V2 GOLDEN HOLIDAY PINE CONE	900	79.00	79.00
96	ANGEL, 7 1/2" 5542QB	1000	59.50	60.00
96	EGG, 3 1/2" 5145AC	1500	37.50	37.50
96	EGG, 3 1/2" 5145CH HOLLY BERRIES ON GOLD	1500	37.50	37.50
96	EGG, 3 1/2" 5145QP PARTRIDGE ON SPRUCE	1500	35.00	35.00
96	FAIRY LIGHT, 4 1/2" 7300AC	2000	39.50	39.50
	R. SPINDLER		**CHRISTMAS LIMITED EDITIONS**	
96	EGG, 3 1/2" 5145QV MOONLIT MEADOW ON RUB	1500	39.50	39.50
96	FAIRY LIGHT 9401N7 NATIVITY SCENE	1500	49.00	49.00
	F. BURTON		**CHRISTMAS STAR "OUR HOME IS BLESSED"**	
95	EGG 5145VT 3 1/2"	1500	45.00	45.00

YR	NAME	LIMIT	ISSUE	TREND
95	FAIRY LIGHT 7300VT 4 1/2"	1500	45.00	45.00
95	LAMP 2940VT 21" STUDENT	500	275.00	275.00
	F. BURTON	**CHRISTMAS STAR "SILENT NIGHT"**		
94	EGG ON STAND 5145VS	1500	45.00	45.00
94	FAIRY LIGHT 7300VS 4 1/2"	1500	45.00	45.00
94	LAMP 7204VS 16"	500	275.00	275.00
	F. BURTON	**CHRISTMAS STAR ED. III**		
96	EGG, 5145SN 3 1/2"	1750	45.00	45.00
96	FAIRY LIGHT 7300SN 4 1/2"	1750	48.00	48.00
96	LAMP 7204SN 16"	750	275.00	275.00
	F. BURTON	**COLLECTIBLE EGGS EDITIONS**		
94	EGG 5140A7 ENAMELED FLOWERS/BLUE	2500	37.50	38.00
	S. JACKSON	**COLLECTIBLE EGGS EDITIONS**		
94	EGG 5140A2 TULIPS/SEA MIST	2500	32.50	33.00
94	EGG 5140A3 VIOLETS/MILK PEARL	2500	32.50	33.00
94	EGG 5140A4 TULIPS/SEA MIST	2500	32.50	33.00
94	EGG 5140A5 SPRING LANDSCAPE/OPAL	2500	32.50	33.00
	K. PLAUCHE	**COLLECTIBLE EGGS EDITIONS**		
93	EGG 5140D2 SCROLLING FLORAL/GRN	2500	30.00	30.00
93	EGG 5140D8 W/GOLD ON PLUM	2500	35.00	35.00
94	EGG 5140A6 METALLIC FLORAL/PLUM	2500	32.50	33.00
	M. REYNOLDS	**COLLECTIBLE EGGS EDITIONS**		
91	EGG, 5140C9 PARTRIDGE	1500	29.50	30.00
91	EGG, 5140E7 SKATER	1500	29.50	30.00
91	EGG, 5140H7 WHITE SCENE	1500	29.50	30.00
91	EGG, 5140N9 POINSETTIAS	1500	29.50	30.00
91	EGG, 5140Q9 GOLD DESIGN	1500	29.50	30.00
91	EGG, 5140X9 SHELL	1500	35.00	35.00
91	EGG, 5140Z7 SNOW SCENE	1500	29.50	30.00
92	EGG 51407Z UNICORN	2500	30.00	30.00
92	EGG, 51407U CROQUET	2500	30.00	30.00
92	EGG, 51407V FLORAL & BRONZE	2500	30.00	30.00
92	EGG, 51407W BUTTERFLIES	2500	30.00	30.00
92	EGG, 51407Y IRIS	2500	30.00	30.00
92	EGG, 51407Y PINK FLORAL	2500	30.00	30.00
93	EGG 5140D3 W/GOLD ON RUBY	2500	00.00	30.00
93	EGG 5140D4 SEA GULSS/OCEAN BLUE	2500	30.00	30.00
93	EGG 5140D5 COTTAGE/WHITE OPAL	2500	30.00	30.00
93	EGG 5140D6 PAISLEY/DUSTY ROSE	2500	30.00	30.00
93	EGG, 5140D1 FUSCHIA FLORAL/WHITE	2500	30.00	30.00
93	EGG, 5140ZN SANDCARVED/BLK	1500	35.00	35.00
94	EGG 5140A1 GOLD	2500	32.50	33.00
95	EGG 5145S2 SCROLLS/BLACK	2500	32.50	33.00
95	EGG 5145S3 SCENE/WHITE	2500	32.50	33.00
95	EGG 5145S4 FLORAL/WHITE	2500	32.50	33.00
95	EGG 5145S5 FLORAL/GREEN	2500	32.50	33.00
95	EGG 5145S6 FLORAL/BLUE	2500	32.50	33.00
95	EGG 5145S7 FLORAL/GOLD	2500	32.50	33.00
95	EGG 5145S8 HUMMINGBIRD/DUSTY ROSE	2500	35.00	35.00
96	EGG, 5145F2 HUMMINGBIRD/FRENCH OPAL	2500	37.50	37.50
96	EGG, 5145F5 LAKE SCENE	2500	37.50	37.50
96	EGG, 5145F6 JEWELED	2500	37.50	37.50
	R. SPINDLER	**COLLECTIBLE EGGS EDITIONS**		
96	EGG, 5145F1 HONEYSUCKLE/DUSTY ROSE	2500	37.50	37.50
96	EGG, 5145F3 BUTTERFLIES	2500	37.50	37.50
96	EGG, 5145F4 MORNING GLORIES	2500	37.50	37.50
96	EGG, 5145F7 FISH/SPRUCE	2500	37.50	37.50
*		**CONNOISSEUR COLLECTION**		
83	BASKET 6432IM 9"	1000	75.00	75.00
83	CRUET/STOPPER 6462IM	1000	75.00	75.00
83	EPERGNE SET, 7605BR 5 PC	500	200.00	200.00
83	VASE 7659GJ 7"	1500	50.00	50.00
84	BASKET 3134PV 10"	1250	85.00	85.00
84	CANDY BOX W/COVER 9394UE 3 PC.	1250	75.00	75.00
84	CANE 5090PV 18"	YR	35.00	35.00
84	TOP HAT 3193PV 8"	1500	65.00	65.00
84	VASE 9458AV 8" SWAN	1500	65.00	65.00
85	EPERGNE SET 809GO 4 PC.	1000	95.00	95.00
85	PUNCH SET 3712GO 14 PC.	500	250.00	250.00
86	BASKET 7438JD	1500	49.00	49.00
86	BOUDOIR LAMP 7802CZ	750	145.00	145.00
86	CRUET/STOPPER 7863CZ	1000	75.00	75.00
86	HANDLED URN 3194ZS 13"	1000	185.00	185.00
86	HANDLED VASE 3190KF 7"	1000	100.00	100.00
86	VANITY SET 3104BI 4 PC.	1000	125.00	125.00
88	BASKET 3132OT	2500	65.00	65.00
88	PITCHER 2065ZC	3500	60.00	60.00
88	VASE 2556ZI 6"	3500	50.00	50.00
89	EPERGNE SET 7605RE 5 PC.	2000	250.00	250.00
89	PITCHER 7060RE	2500	55.00	55.00
89	VASE 6453RG 8"	2000	65.00	65.00
89	VASE 8354RE	2500	45.00	45.00
91	CANDY BOX 9394FN 3 PC.	1000	90.00	90.00
91	FISH PAPERWEIGHT 5193RE	2000	30.00	30.00
93	OWL 5258FN 6"	1500	95.00	95.00
	D. BARBOUR	**CONNOISSEUR COLLECTION**		
85	VASE 8808SB 7 1/2"	950	135.00	135.00

YR	NAME	LIMIT	ISSUE	TREND
86	LAMP 7400SB 20"	500	350.00	350.00
87	VASE 1796BY 7 1/4"	950	95.00	95.00
F. BURTON			**CONNOISSEUR COLLECTION**	
91	VASE 8812G1	850	125.00	125.00
92	COVERED BOX 6080RH	1250	95.00	95.00
92	VASE 8817QZ 8"	750	150.00	150.00
93	LAMP 2780CX SPRING WOODS REVERSE	500	590.00	590.00
93	PERFUME/STOPPER 1710R5	1250	95.00	95.00
94	CLOCK 8691JV 4 1/2"	850	150.00	150.00
94	LAMP 5582JB HUMMINGBIRD REVERSE	300	590.00	590.00
94	PITCHER 2729JI 10" LATTICE	750	165.00	165.00
95	LAMP 5486VU 21" BUTTEFLY	300	595.00	595.00
96	LAMP 6805EA	400	750.00	750.00
96	PITCHER 2960WQ DRAGON FLY 8"	1250	165.00	165.00
R. DELANEY			**CONNOISSEUR COLLECTION**	
83	VASE 7542FJ 4 1/2"	2000	32.50	33.00
86	VASE 8812JY 10 1/2"	1000	95.00	95.00
L. EVERSON			**CONNOISSEUR COLLECTION**	
84	VASE 9651HD 9"	750	75.00	75.00
85	BASKET 7634EB 8 1/2"	1250	95.00	95.00
85	LAMP 7602EB 22"	350	300.00	300.00
85	VASE 8806GC 7 1/2"	1000	125.00	125.00
86	VASE 8812ET 10 1/2"	1000	95.00	95.00
87	PITCHER 9468QY 8"	950	85.00	85.00
88	CANDY 6080ZX	2000	95.00	95.00
89	BASKET 1330TE 7"	2500	85.00	85.00
89	CANDY BOX W/COVER 2085TM	2500	85.00	85.00
89	LAMP 9308TT 21"	1000	250.00	250.00
90	BASKET 7731QH 7"	YR	75.00	75.00
90	CRUET/STOPPER 7701QJ	YR	85.00	85.00
90	EPERGNE SET 7202QJ 2 PC.	YR	125.00	125.00
90	LAMP 7412QH 21"	YR	295.00	295.00
90	WATER SET 7700QH 7 PC.	YR	275.00	275.00
91	VASE 7252QH 7 1/2"	1500	65.00	65.00
92	VASE 5541QH 6 1/2"	1500	45.00	45.00
*** PIPER/BARBOUR**			**CONNOISSEUR COLLECTION**	
90	LAMP 9308RB 20"	YR	250.00	250.00
90	VASE 7790RB 6"	YR	49.50	50.00
90	VASE 7791RB 6 1/2"	YR	45.00	45.00
*** PIPER/BURTON**			**CONNOISSEUR COLLECTION**	
90	BASKET 7732QD 5 1/2"	YR	57.50	58.00
90	VASE 7792QD 9"	YR	75.00	75.00
91	LAMP 6701RB 20"	500	275.00	275.00
K. PLAUCHE			**CONNOISSEUR COLLECTION**	
96	BOX W/LID 6584CD MELON	1250	150.00	150.00
M. REYNOLDS			**CONNOISSEUR COLLECTION**	
91	BASKET 4647MD	1500	64.00	64.00
91	VASE 8812FQ	850	125.00	125.00
92	PITCHER 1211RW 9"	950	110.00	110.00
92	PITCHER 5531QP 4 1/2"	1500	65.00	65.00
92	VASE 1684RP	950	110.00	110.00
93	AMPHORA W/STAND 2748FW	850	285.00	285.00
93	BOWL 2747RX RUBY STRETCH W/GOLD SCROLLS	1250	95.00	95.00
93	VASE 7661P4 9" GOLD LEAVES	950	175.00	175.00
93	VASE 8805X3	950	125.00	125.00
94	VASE 2743JP 7"	850	185.00	185.00
94	VASE 2744JK 8" PLUM OPAL.	750	165.00	165.00
94	VASE 3161JQ 11" GOLD	750	175.00	175.00
95	AMPHORA W/STAND 2947US 10 1/4"	890	195.00	195.00
95	GINGER JAR 2950VN 8 1/2" 3 PC.	790	275.00	275.00
95	PITCHER 2796ZM 9 1/2"	490	250.00	250.00
95	VASE 7691WF 7"	890	125.00	125.00
96	VASE 2782DD 11"	1250	195.00	195.00
96	VASE 3254QJ QUEEN'S BIRD 11"	1150	250.00	250.00
96	VASE 9855EV	1150	195.00	195.00
*** REYNOLDS/DELANEY**			**CONNOISSEUR COLLECTION**	
94	BOWL 7727JC 14" BRANBERRY CAMEO	500	390.00	390.00
R. SPINDLER			**CONNOISSEUR COLLECTION**	
96	VASE 9866TR TROUT 8"	1350	135.00	135.00
M. YATES			**CONNOISSEUR COLLECTION**	
83	VASE 7661LJ 9"	850	75.00	75.00
84	VASE 7661MD 9"	750	125.00	125.00
*** YATES/RICHARDS**			**CONNOISSEUR COLLECTION**	
85	VASE 8802LY 12"	800	150.00	150.00
M. REYNOLDS			**EASTER LIMITED EDITIONS**	
95	FAIRY LIGHT 8405YZ	CL	49.00	49.00
*****			**FAMILY SIGNATURE SERIES**	
93	VASE 2752RN 9" ALPINE THISTLE/RUBY CARNI	CL	105.00	105.00
94	BASKET 1217AO 11" AUTUMN GOLD OPALESCENT	CL	70.00	70.00
94	BASKET 2779RN 8 1/2" RUBY CARNIVAL	CL	65.00	65.00
94	VASE 1216EH 10" FUCHSIA	CL	95.00	95.00
95	CANDY W/COVER 2970RN 9" RED CARNIVAL	CL	65.00	65.00
95	SHOWCASE DEALER ITEM 3558CR	CL	75.00	75.00
96	SHOWCASE DEALER ITEM 9550DC	CL	75.00	75.00
96	VASE 5357TE 8 1/2"	*	75.00	75.00
F. BURTON			**FAMILY SIGNATURE SERIES**	
93	VASE 1786PV 10" VINTAGE ON PLUM	CL	80.00	80.00

YR	NAME	LIMIT	ISSUE	TREND
94	PITCHER 1568CW 6 1/2" CRANBERRY	CL	85.00	85.00
94	VASE 1559CW 9 1/2" PANSIES ON CRANBERRY	CL	95.00	95.00
95	PITCHER 1566FS 9 1/2" THISTLE	CL	125.00	125.00
95	VASE 1567CW 7"	CL	75.00	75.00
95	VASE 1649KG 9 1/2" GOLDEN FLAX ON COBALT	CL	95.00	95.00
96	BASKET 3076KT 8"	CL	85.00	85.00
K. PLAUCHE			**FAMILY SIGNATURE SERIES**	
96	VASE 4759SE 10" MAGNOLIA & BERRY ON SPRU	OP	80.00	80.00
M. REYNOLDS			**FAMILY SIGNATURE SERIES**	
93	BASKET 6730PJ 8 1/2" LILACS	YR	65.00	65.00
93	VASE 1640C1 11" CRANBERRY	CL	110.00	110.00
93	VASE 7661Z8 9" COTTAGE SCENE	CL	90.00	90.00
94	BASKET 2738PJ 7 1/2" LILACS	CL	65.00	65.00
94	BASKET 2787ST 8" STIEGEL GREEN	CL	60.00	60.00
94	CANDY W/COVER 7380AW 9 1/2" AUTUMN LEAVE	CL	60.00	60.00
95	BASKET 1131DX 8 1/2" TRELLIS	CL	85.00	85.00
95	BASKET 1135JE 9 1/2" CORALENE FLORAL	CL	75.00	75.00
96	PITCHER 3065DP 6 1/2"	CL	70.00	70.00
96	VASE 5357TE 8 1/2"	CL	75.00	75.00
R. SPINDLER			**FAMILY SIGNATURE SERIES**	
95	VASE 1554S9 9" SUMMER GARDEN ON SPRUCE	CL	85.00	85.00
96	BASKET 3127NG 7"	OP	75.00	75.00
96	VASE 1563PD 11" FEATHER	CL	95.00	95.00
*			**HISTORICAL COLLECTION**	
88	BANANA BOWL A3720UO 12"	*	33.00	33.00
88	BASKET 9134TO BUTTERFLY & BERRY	*	25.00	25.00
88	BASKET 9435TO	*	29.50	30.00
88	BASKET 9436TO	*	32.50	33.00
88	BASKET A3830UO BASKET 10"	*	30.00	30.00
88	BASKET A3834UO 6 1/2"	*	16.50	17.00
88	BASKET W/LOOPED HANDLE A3335UO	*	22.50	23.00
88	BONBON W/HANDLES A3937UO	*	*	*
88	BOWL 8428TO FANTAIL FOOTED	*	27.50	27.50
88	BOWL 9425TO	*	22.50	23.00
88	BUTTERFLY ON STAND 5171TO	*	15.00	15.00
88	CRUET W/STOPPER A3863UO 6 1/2"	*	35.00	35.00
88	EPERGNE 4801TO 4 PC.	*	75.00	75.00
88	EPERGNE A3701UO 10" 4 PC.	*	55.00	55.00
88	EPERGNE A3801UO 4 PC. MINI	*	47.50	48.00
88	HAT, BUTTERFLY & BERRY 9495TO	*	12.50	13.00
88	KITCHEN SET 8603TO 4 PC.	*	89.50	90.00
88	LAMP 9101TO 24"	*	199.50	200.00
88	LAMP A3308UO 25" GONE W/THE WIND	*	199.50	199.50
88	NUT DISH 8442TO 3 TOED	*	17.50	17.50
88	PITCHER 52 OZ. & 12" BOWL A3000UO	*	77.50	78.00
88	PUNCH SET A3712UO 14 PC.	*	275.00	275.00
88	ROSE BOWL 8454TO FRAPERY FOOTED	*	23.50	24.00
88	ROSE BOWL A3854UO 4 1/2"	*	12.50	13.00
88	ROSE BOWL A3861UO 4 1/4"	*	12.50	13.00
88	TOOTHPICK HOLDER A3795UO 2 3/4"	*	6.50	7.00
88	VASE A3362UO 6 1/2" JACK IN THE PULPIT	*	22.50	23.00
88	WATER SET 3407TO 7 PC. CACTUS	*	139.50	140.00
88	WATER SET A3908UO 7 PC.	*	99.00	99.00
89	BASKET 1435XC 5"	*	36.50	37.00
89	BASKET 1830XC 5 1/2"	*	36.50	37.00
89	BASKET 3138XC 7"	*	39.50	40.00
89	BASKET 3334XC 7"	*	25.00	25.00
89	BASKET 3834XC 4 1/2"	*	17.50	17.50
89	BASKET 8330XC 7"	*	25.00	25.00
89	BASKET 9638XC	*	22.50	23.00
89	BOWL 2323XC 10"	*	49.50	50.00
89	BOWL 9027XC	*	29.50	30.00
89	BUTTER W/COVER 9580XC	*	28.50	29.00
89	COMPORT 8234XC	*	19.50	20.00
89	CREAMER 1461XC	*	30.00	30.00
89	CRUET W/STOPPER 1865XC	*	49.00	49.00
89	CRUET W/STOPPER 3863XC 6 1/2"	*	35.00	35.00
89	EPERGNE 4801XC 4 PC.	*	75.00	75.00
89	FAIRY LIGHT 1803XC 3 PC.	*	85.00	85.00
89	FAIRY LIGHT 3608XC	*	16.50	17.00
89	LAMP 1413XC 22"	*	250.00	250.00
89	LAMP 3313XC 21" STUDENT	*	199.50	200.00
89	PUNCH SET 3712XC 14 PC	*	275.00	275.00
89	TOP HAT 1492XC	*	25.00	25.00
89	VASE 1353XC 10"	*	37.50	38.00
89	WATER SET 1404XC 7 PC.	*	199.50	200.00
89	WATER SET 3908XC 7 PC.	*	99.50	100.00
90	BASKET 1830BX 5 1/2"	*	36.50	37.00
90	BASKET 1832BX 7"	*	39.50	40.00
90	BASKET 8437BX	*	26.50	27.00
90	BOWL 1826BX 10"	*	55.00	55.00
90	BOWL 8229BX 10"	*	32.50	33.00
90	BOWL W/BRIDE'S BASKET 1825BX 10"	*	125.00	125.00
90	CANDY W/COVER 8489BX 7"	*	28.50	29.00
90	CRUET W/STOPPER 1860BX 7 1/2"	*	49.00	49.00
90	EPERGNE 4801BX 4 PC.	*	75.00	75.00
90	FENTON LOGO 9799BX 3" X 5"	*	15.00	15.00
90	LAMP 1800BX 22"	*	250.00	250.00

YR	NAME	LIMIT	ISSUE	TREND
90	LAMP 1801BX 22"	*	250.00	250.00
90	ROSE BOWL 8453BX	*	16.50	17.00
90	TABLE SET 9700BX 4 PC. MINI	*	52.50	53.00
90	VASE 1853BX 10"	*	39.50	40.00
90	VASE 8458BX 10"	*	17.00	17.00
90	VASE 8651BX 3 1/2"	*	13.50	14.00
90	WATER SET 1802BX 7 PC.	*	199.50	200.00
91	BASKET 4617DT 7"	*	29.50	30.00
91	BASKET 4618DT 10"	*	32.50	33.00
91	BASKET 4632BO 7" WILDFLOWER	*	28.50	29.00
91	BASKET 4633BO 6"	*	25.00	25.00
91	BASKET 4646DT	*	28.50	29.00
91	BOWL 4619DT 10"	*	33.50	34.00
91	BOWL 4627BO 10 1/4"	*	35.00	35.00
91	BOX 4679DT	*	33.50	34.00
91	BUTTER W/COVER 8680DT	*	35.00	35.00
91	CANDLESTICKS 4672BO 3 1/2"	*	32.50	33.00
91	COMPORT 4693BO 6 1/2"	*	22.50	23.00
91	CUSPIDOR 4643DT	*	22.50	22.50
91	FENTON LOGO 9799DT 2 3/4" X 5"	*	20.00	20.00
91	LAMP 4603BO 15"	*	195.00	195.00
91	LAMP 4603DT 15"	*	195.00	195.00
91	LAMP 4605BO/JU 20"	*	215.00	215.00
91	OWL 5254DT	*	29.50	30.00
91	PUNCH BOWL SET 4601BO 14 PC.	*	285.00	285.00
91	PUNCH SET 4601DT 14 PC.	*	300.00	300.00
91	TOOTHPICK HOLDER 4644DT	*	10.00	10.00
91	URN W/COVER 4602BO/JU	*	65.00	65.00
91	VASE 4651BO 10"	*	25.00	25.00
91	VASE 4653BO 9"	*	25.00	25.00
91	WATER SET 4609DT 5 PC.	*	87.50	88.00
92	BASKET 2725XV 7"	*	27.50	27.50
92	BASKET 2728XV 4"	*	19.50	20.00
92	BASKET 3077XV 11"	*	49.50	50.00
92	BASKET 3335GP	*	35.00	35.00
92	BASKET 5481GF 10 1/2"	*	49.00	49.00
92	BASKET 5483GF 10 1/2"	*	89.00	89.00
92	BOWL 3983XV 12"	*	35.00	35.00
92	BOWL 5482GF 9 1/2"	*	65.00	65.00
92	BOX W/CPVER 4600GP	*	85.00	85.00
92	CANDLESTICK 5526GF 4	*	59.00	59.00
92	CANDLESTICKS 3674XV 6"	*	32.50	33.00
92	CANDY BOX 3784XV	*	37.50	38.00
92	CREAMER 2726XV 4"	*	22.50	23.00
92	CRUET W/STOPPER 3863GP	*	45.00	45.00
92	EPERGNE 3701XV 4 PC.	*	99.00	99.00
92	EPERGNE 4801GP 4PC.	*	99.00	99.00
92	FENTON LOGO 9799XV	*	20.00	20.00
92	LAMP 1801XV 21"	*	295.00	295.00
92	LAMP 3313GP 21"	*	235.00	235.00
92	OWL 5252GP 7"	*	45.00	45.00
92	PITCHER 1875XV 8 1/2"	*	75.00	75.00
92	PUNCH CUP 4642XV	*	13.00	13.00
92	PUNCH SET 4601XV 14 PC.	*	315.00	315.00
92	TUMBLER 1876XV	*	25.00	25.00
92	TUMBLER 2727XV 2" MINI	*	9.50	10.00
92	TUMBLER 3949GP	*	12.50	13.00
92	VASE 2056XV 5"	*	39.50	40.00
92	VASE 3183XV 6 1/2"	*	25.00	25.00
92	VASE 3355GP 6"	*	27.00	27.00
92	VASE 5479GF 6"	*	35.00	35.00
92	VASE 5480GF 12"	*	45.00	45.00
92	WATER SET 1870XV 5 PC.	*	175.00	175.00
92	WATER SET 2730XV 5 PC.	*	60.00	60.00
92	WATER SET 3908GP 5 PC.	*	99.00	99.00
93	BASKET 3337RV 7"	OP	29.50	30.00
93	BASKET 3834RV 4 1/2"	OP	25.00	25.00
93	BASKET, DRAPERY 9435XV	OP	45.00	45.00
93	BOWL 2754XV SWAN	OP	45.00	45.00
93	CANDLESTICKS, SWAN 5172XV	OP	45.00	45.00
93	CANDY W/COVER 3784RV FOOTED	OP	37.50	38.00
93	CRUET W/STOPPER 3863RV 6 1/2"	OP	47.50	48.00
93	EPERGNE 4 PC. 3701RV 10"	OP	99.00	99.00
93	EPERGNE, MINI HOBNAIL 3801XV	OP	49.50	49.50
93	FENTON LOGO 9799RV 2 3/4" X 5"	OP	20.00	20.00
93	LAMP 3313RV 21" STUDENT W/PRISMS	OP	250.00	250.00
93	LAMP, POPPY GONE W/THE WING 9101XV	OP	225.00	225.00
93	PITCHER 3764RV 54 OZ.	OP	59.00	59.00
93	PUNCH SET 14 PC. 3712RV	OP	275.00	275.00
93	ROSE BOWL, DRAPERY 8454XV	OP	25.00	25.00
93	SWAN 5127XV	OP	15.00	15.00
93	TUMBLER 3949RV 9 OZ.	OP	12.50	13.00
93	VASE 3356RV 7 1/2" JACK IN THE PULPIT	OP	27.50	28.00
93	VASE 3854RV 4 1/2"	OP	17.50	18.00
93	WATER SET 5 PC. 3908RV	OP	109.00	109.00
94	BASKET 5551SS 9" FOOTED	OP	39.50	40.00
94	BASKET 5555SS 7" FOOTED	OP	29.50	30.00
94	BOW W/COVER-LION 2799SS	OP	35.00	35.00
94	BOWL 2773SS 8"	OP	37.50	38.00

YR	NAME	LIMIT	ISSUE	TREND
94	BOWL 5552SS 12"	OP	45.00	45.00
94	CANDLESTICKS 5526SS 4"	OP	45.00	45.00
94	CANDY COVER 4381ST 5 1/2"	OP	55.00	55.00
94	COMPORT 5554SS 5 1/4"	OP	29.50	30.00
94	EPERGNE 2 PC. 4802SS	OP	65.00	65.00
94	EPERGNE SET 5 PC. 7601SS	OP	175.00	175.00
94	FENTON LOGO 9799SS 5"	OP	25.00	25.00
94	GOBLET 5561SS 6 1/2"	OP	22.50	23.00
94	JUG 5562SS 8"	OP	60.00	60.00
94	ROSE BOWL 2759SS 3 1/2"	OP	25.00	25.00
94	ROSE BOWL 2759ST 3 1/2"	OP	29.50	30.00
94	SPARROW 5259ST 5"	OP	29.50	30.00
94	URN W/COVER 4602SS	OP	65.00	65.00
94	VASE 5559ST 8"	*	39.50	40.00
94	VASE 7", JACK IN THE PULPIT 5553SS	OP	29.50	30.00
94	VASE HANDERCHIEF 5559ST 8"	OP	29.50	30.00
94	VASE HANDKERCHIEF 5559SS 8"	OP	29.50	30.00
94	WATER SET 5 PC. 5560SS	OP	150.00	150.00
95	BASKET 1142JE 7" FOOTED	OP	37.50	38.00
95	BASKET 2932UL 8"	*	135.00	135.00
95	BOWL 2909UK 10 1/4"	*	150.00	150.00
95	CANDLESTICKS 2911KA 3"	OP	49.50	50.00
95	CANDY BOX W/COVER 9488KA 10 1/2"	OP	49.50	49.50
95	CENTERPIECE 4 PC. 2990KA 9 1/2"	OP	95.00	95.00
95	COMPORT 1134KA 5 1/4"	OP	32.50	33.00
95	EPERGNE 5 PC. 7601KA 13"	OP	185.00	185.00
95	FENTON LOGO 9499KA 5" OVAL	OP	25.00	25.00
95	LAMP 7502UQ 33"	*	495.00	495.00
95	PITCHER 2968UN 10"	*	175.00	175.00
95	TOP HAT 1137JE 4 1/2"	OP	49.50	49.50
95	TUMBLER 9049KA 4 1/2"	OP	19.50	20.00
95	VASE 1136JE 6" FAN	OP	49.50	49.50
95	VASE 2767JE 4 1/2"	OP	32.50	33.00
95	VASE 2955UU 9"	*	150.00	150.00
95	VASE W/COLBALT BASE 1140JE	OP	59.50	60.00
95	WATER SET 5 PC. 9001KA	OP	135.00	135.00
96	BASKET 4833TG 6"	*	25.00	25.00
96	BASKET 4835TG 9 1/2"	*	49.50	50.00
96	COMPORT 4854TG 6 1/2"	*	35.00	35.00
96	COMPORT 8231XC	*	20.00	20.00
96	CRUET W/STOPPER 7701TE 7"	*	85.00	85.00
96	EPERGNE 4806TG 4 1/2" MINI	*	35.00	35.00
96	EPERGNE 4808TG 10"	*	115.00	115.00
96	LAMP 1705TE 24"	*	395.00	395.00
96	LOGO 9499TG 2 1/2"	*	25.00	25.00
96	PITCHER 5367TE 6 1/2"	*	75.00	75.00
96	VASE 1146TE 7"	*	49.50	50.00
96	VASE 1795TE 11"	*	85.00	85.00
F. & B. FENTON			**HISTORICAL COLLECTION**	
95	BASKET 1135JE	OP	75.00	75.00
M. REYNOLDS			**HISTORICAL COLLECTION**	
96	BASKET 1531MS 8"	1250	95.00	95.00
96	VASE 1689MS 9 1/2" HUMMINGBIRD	1250	95.00	95.00
96	VASE 2750MS 8" MELON	1250	85.00	85.00
R. SPINDLER			**HISTORICAL COLLECTION**	
96	LAMP 5581MD 21"	500	495.00	495.00
96	PITCHER 1671MD 7 1/2"	1250	95.00	95.00
96	SHOWCASE DEALER 7603MD	1250	125.00	125.00
*			**MARY GREGORY**	
95	BASKET 8637RG	YR	65.00	65.00
M. REYNOLDS			**MARY GREGORY**	
94	BASKET 8637RY 7 1/2" OVAL	CL	59.00	59.00
95	BASKET 8637RG 7 1/2" OVAL	CL	65.00	65.00
95	EGG ON STAND 5145RG 4" RUBY	CL	37.50	38.00
96	HAT BASKET 1532RK 6 1/2" CRANBERRY	2000	95.00	95.00
96	VASE 1554VP 9"	1500	135.00	135.00
*			**MINIATURES**	
96	EPERGNE 4806TG 4 1/2"	CL	35.00	35.00
96	PUNCH BOWL & CUPS 6800DZ 3 3/4"	CL	59.00	59.00
*			**MOUTHBLOWN EGGS**	
94	EGG 5031FU	YR	75.00	75.00
94	EGG 5031FV	YR	75.00	75.00
95	EGG 5031YW	YR	75.00	75.00
95	EGG 5031YX	YR	75.00	75.00
F. BURTON			**MOUTHBLOWN EGGS**	
92	EGG, 5" 5031Q2 PETAL PINK IRID.	CL	65.00	65.00
92	EGG, 5" 5031Q3 SEAMIST GREEN IRID.	CL	65.00	65.00
94	EGG, 5" 5031FV BLUE	CL	75.00	75.00
96	EGG, 5" 1642JM CRANBERRY-BLUE BIRD	CL	95.00	95.00
M. REYNOLDS			**MOUTHBLOWN EGGS**	
91	EGG, 3 1/2" 5030QB MOTHER OF PEARL	CL	49.00	49.00
91	EGG, 4 1/2" 5031WD MOTHER OF PEARL	CL	59.00	59.00
93	EGG 5031WE 5" PLUM	YR	69.00	69.00
93	EGG 5031WJ 5" OCEAN BLUE	YR	69.00	69.00
94	EGG, 5" 5031FU ROSE	CL	75.00	75.00
95	EGG, 5" 5031YW SPRUCE	CL	75.00	75.00
95	EGG, 5" 5031YX GOLD	CL	75.00	75.00

YR	NAME	LIMIT	ISSUE	TREND
96	EGG, 5" 1642JO FRENCH OPAL-BUTTERFLY	CL	75.00	75.00
*				**VALENTINE'S DAY**
92	BASKET 6567CR 6' CRANBERRY	CL	50.00	50.00
92	PERFUME W/OVAL STOPPER 6580CR	CL	60.00	60.00
92	VASE 6568CR 4"	CL	35.00	35.00
93	BASKET 2732CR 7" CAPRICE	CL	59.00	59.00
93	SOUTHERN GIRL 5141NX 8" ROSE PEARL IRID.	CL	45.00	45.00
93	TRINKET BOX 2740CR 5"	CL	79.00	79.00
93	VASE 2749CR 5 1/2" MELON	CL	45.00	45.00
94	BASKET 2736CR 7" CRANBERRY OPALESCENT	CL	65.00	65.00
94	PERFUME W/STOPPER 2760CR 5"	CL	75.00	75.00
94	VASE 2755CR 5 1/2" RIBBED	CL	47.50	48.00
95	BASKET 2745CR 8" MELON, CRANBERRY OPAL.	CL	69.00	69.00
95	PITCHER 2774CR 5 1/2" MELON	CL	69.00	69.00
96	BASKET 7122CR 8" MELON	CL	75.00	75.00
96	FAIRY LIGHT 2903CR CRANBERRY	CL	135.00	135.00
96	PERFUME 7100CR 5" MELON	CL	95.00	95.00
M. REYNOLDS				**VALENTINE'S DAY**
93	SOUTHERN GIRL 5141NI 8"	CL	49.00	49.00
95	PERFUME, W/HEART STOPPER 2785YB	2500	49.00	49.00

FIGI COLLECTIONS INC.

YR	NAME	LIMIT	ISSUE	TREND
S. KEHRLI				**SANTA'S CRYSTAL VALLEY**
95	A GIFT FOR SANTA CV-701	CL	250.00	250.00
95	CAPTURE THE SPIRIT CV-106	OP	50.00	50.00
95	FINISHING TOUCH, THE CV-501	CL	130.00	130.00
95	POLAR BEAR ANGLE CV-101	OP	50.00	50.00
95	ROCKING HORSE DREAMS CV-104	OP	50.00	50.00
95	SANTA EXPRESS, THE CV-502	CL	130.00	130.00
95	SANTA'S DILEMMA CV-303	OP	75.00	75.00
95	SANTA'S REFLECTION CV-102	OP	50.00	50.00
95	SLEDDING WITH SANTA CV-302	OP	75.00	75.00
95	SMILE MR. SNOWMAN CV-301	OP	75.00	75.00
95	STAR BRIGHT CV-103	RT	50.00	50.00
96	A VERY SPECIAL REQUEST CV-601	5000	190.00	190.00
96	AUDITION, THE CV-602	5000	190.00	190.00
96	DREAMS CAN COME TRUE CV-401	15000	100.00	100.00
96	FROLICKING FRIENDS CV-110	OP	70.00	70.00
96	JOURNEY TO CRYSTAL VALLEY CV-1001	975	500.00	500.00
96	MAGIC IN THE MAKING CV-801	2500	400.00	400.00
96	ROOM FOR ONE MORE? CV-402	15000	100.00	100.00
96	SECRET RECIPE CV-109	OP	70.00	70.00

FLAMBRO

Price ranges may reflect various demands in the market from one geographic region to another; condition of piece; specific markings found on piece; and/or changes in production of piece.

YR	NAME	LIMIT	ISSUE	TREND
*				**ANNUAL EMMETT KELLY JR. NUTCRACKER**
90	1990 NUTCRACKER	YR	50.00	50.00
*				**CIRCUS WORLD MUSEUM CLOWNS**
85	FELIX ADLER (GROTESQUE)	9500	80.00	95.00
85	PAUL JEROME (HOBO)	9500	80.00	125.00
85	PAUL JUNG (NEAT)	9500	80.00	120.00
87	ABE GOLDSTEIN, KEYSTONE KOP	7500	90.00	90.00
87	FELIX ADLER WITH BALLOON	7500	90.00	90.00
87	PAUL JEROME WITH DOG	7500	90.00	90.00
87	PAUL JUNG, SITTING	7500	90.00	90.00
C. PRACHT				**DADDY LOVES YOU**
91	C'MON DADDY!	2500	100.00	100.00
91	MAKE YOU...GIGGLE!	2500	100.00	100.00
91	SOO...YOU LIKE IT?	2500	100.00	100.00
91	YOU'RE SOOO...SWEET	2500	100.00	100.00
*				**EKJ JAPANESE FIGURINE**
93	VIGILANTE, THE	OP	75.00	75.00
*				**EKJ MEMBERS ONLY FIGURINES**
90	MERRY-G0-ROUND	CL	125.00	125.00
91	10 YEARS OF COLLECTING	*	100.00	100.00
93	RINGMASTER	CL	125.00	125.00
94	BIRTHDAY MAIL	CL	100.00	125.00
95	SALUTE TO OUR VETS	*	75.00	75.00
96	I LOVE YOU	*	95.00	95.00
*				**EMMETT KELLY JR. A DAY AT THE FAIR**
90	75 CENTS PLEASE	*	65.00	65.00
90	LOOK AT YOU	RT	65.00	65.00
90	RIDE THE WILD MOUSE	*	65.00	65.00
90	STEP RIGHT UP	*	65.00	65.00
90	STILT MAN, THE	RT	65.00	65.00
90	THANKS EMMETT	*	65.00	65.00
90	THREE FOR A DIME	*	65.00	65.00
90	YOU CAN DO IT, EMMETT	RT	65.00	65.00
90	YOU GO FIRST, EMMETT	RT	65.00	65.00
91	COIN TOSS	*	65.00	65.00
91	POPCORN!	*	65.00	65.00
91	TROUBLE WITH HOT DOGS, THE	*	65.00	65.00
*				**EMMETT KELLY JR. FIGURINES**
81	LOOKING OUT TO SEE	12000	75.00	1170.00-2275.00
81	SWEEPING UP	12000	75.00	585.00-780.00
82	THINKER, THE	15000	60.00	700.00-975.00

The Maud Humphrey Bogart Collection features turn-of-the-century children such as the ones in Sharing Secrets. *The line is produced by Hamilton Gifts.*

The figurine Susanna *was inspired by the art of Maud Humphrey Bogart and produced by Hamilton Gifts.*

This little girl and her puppy will be Friends for Life. *The figure is from the Maud Humphrey Bogart Collection produced by Hamilton Gifts.*

This little gal doesn't mind always being the bridesmaid. Playing Bridesmaid *is from the Maud Humphrey Bogart Collection produced by Hamilton Gifts.*

YR	NAME	LIMIT	ISSUE	TREND
82	WET PAINT	15000	80.00	455.00-806.00
82	WHY ME?	15000	65.00	350.00-462.00
83	BALANCING ACT, THE	10000	75.00	600.00-845.00
83	BALLOONS FOR SALE	10000	75.00	480.00-570.00
83	HOLE IN THE SOLE	10000	75.00	200.00-384.00
83	SPIRIT OF CHRISTMAS I	3500	125.00	1475.00-2080.00
83	WISHFUL THNKING	10000	65.00	462.00
84	BIG BUSINESS	9500	110.00	350.00-455.00
84	EATING CABBAGE	12000	75.00	375.00-488.00
84	PIANO PLAYER	9500	160.00	455.00-553.00
84	SPIRIT OF CHRISTMAS II	3500	270.00	260.00-390.00
85	EMMETT'S FAN	12000	80.00	585.00
85	IN THE SPOTLIGHT	12000	103.00	125.00-325.00
85	MAN'S BEST FRIEND	9500	98.00	350.00-481.00
85	NO STRINGS ATTACHED	9500	98.00	100.00-163.00
85	SPIRIT OF CHRISTMAS III	3500	220.00	340.00-520.00
86	BEDTIME	12000	98.00	90.00-137.00
86	COTTON CANDY	12000	98.00	180.00-260.00
86	ENTERTAINERS, THE	12000	120.00	120.00-135.00
86	FAIR GAME	2500	450.00	1500.00-1900.00
86	MAKING NEW FRIENDS	9500	140.00	250.00-325.00
86	SPIRIT OF CHRISTMAS IV	3500	150.00	400.00
87	MY FAVORITE THINGS	9500	109.00	315.00
87	ON THE ROAD AGAIN	9500	109.00	135.00
87	OVER A BARREL	9500	130.00	150.00
87	SATURDAY NIGHT	7500	153.00	265.00-620.00
87	SPIRIT OF CHRISTMAS V	2400	170.00	585.00-700.00
87	TOOTHACHE	12000	98.00	120.00
88	AMEN	12000	120.00	140.00
88	DINING OUT	12000	120.00	140.00
88	SPIRIT OF CHRISTMAS VI	2400	194.00	520.00
88	WHEELER DEALER	7500	160.00	210.00
89	65TH BIRTHDAY COMMEMORATIVE	1989	275.00	2340.00
89	HURDY-GURDY MAN	9500	150.00	175.00
89	MAKING UP	7500	200.00	275.00
89	NO LOITERING	7500	200.00	260.00-300.00
90	BALLOONS FOR SALE II	7500	250.00	250.00
90	CONVENTION BOUND	7500	225.00	230.00
90	MISFORTUNE?	3500	400.00	455.00
90	SPIRIT OF CHRISTMAS VII	3500	275.00	350.00
90	WATCH THE BIRDIE	9500	200.00	210.00
91	ARTIST AT WORK	7500	295.00	295.00
91	FINISHING TOUCH	7500	245.00	245.00
91	FOLLOW THE LEADER	7500	200.00	200.00
91	SPIRIT OF CHRISTMAS VIII	3500	250.00	250.00
92	NO USE CRYING	7500	200.00	200.00
92	PEANUT BUTTER?	7500	200.00	200.00
92	READY-SET-GO	7500	200.00	200.00
95	35 YEARS OF CLOWNING	5000	240.00	240.00
95	35 YEARS OF CLOWNING	5000	240.00	240.00
95	ALL STAR CIRCUS/20TH ANNIVERSARY	5000	240.00	240.00
95	ALL-STAR CIRCUS 20TH ANNIVERSARY	5000	240.00	240.00
95	BEDTIME	OP	35.00	35.00
95	DINING OUT	OP	35.00	35.00
95	ENTERTAINER, THE	OP	45.00	45.00
95	HURDY GURDYMAN	OP	40.00	40.00
95	NO LOITERING	OP	50.00	50.00
95	SPIRIT OF CHRISTMAS XII	3500	200.00	200.00
95	SPIRIT OF CHRISTMAS XII	3500	200.00	200.00
96	AM. CIRCUS EXTRAVAGANZAS 125TH ANNIVERSA	5000	240.00	240.00
96	AMEN	OP	35.00	35.00
96	DAREDEVIL MOTOR SHOW 35TH ANNIVERSARY	5000	240.00	240.00
96	MAKING UP	OP	55.00	55.00
96	MISFORTUNE	OP	60.00	60.00
96	SPIRIT OF CHRISTMAS VI	OP	55.00	55.00
96	SPIRIT OF CHRISTMAS XIII	3500	200.00	200.00
96	TOOTHACHE	OP	35.00	35.00
96	WHEELER DEALER	OP	65.00	65.00
M. WU		**EMMETT KELLY JR. LITTLE EMMETTS**		
94	AGE 1	OP	9.00	9.00
94	AGE 10	OP	25.00	25.00
94	AGE 2	OP	9.50	10.00
94	AGE 3	OP	12.00	12.00
94	AGE 4	OP	12.00	12.00
94	AGE 5	OP	15.00	16.00
94	AGE 6	OP	15.00	16.00
94	AGE 7	OP	17.00	15.00
94	AGE 8	OP	21.00	21.00
94	AGE 9	OP	22.00	22.00
94	LITTLE ARTIST PICTURE FRAME	OP	22.00	22.00
94	LITTLE EMMETT COUNTING LESSON-MUSICAL	OP	30.00	30.00
94	LITTLE EMMETT COUNTRY ROAD	OP	35.00	35.00
94	LITTLE EMMETT FISHING	OP	35.00	35.00
94	LITTLE EMMETT RAINDROPS	OP	35.00	35.00
94	LITTLE EMMETT SHADOW SHOW	OP	40.00	40.00
94	LITTLE EMMETT SOMEDAY	OP	50.00	50.00
94	LITTLE EMMETT WITH BLACKBOARD	OP	30.00	30.00
94	LITTLE EMMETT YOU'VE GOT A FRIEND	OP	33.00	33.00
94	PLAYFUL BOOKENDS	OP	40.00	40.00

YR	NAME	LIMIT	ISSUE	TREND
95	BIRTHDAY HAUL	OP	30.00	30.00
95	DANCE LESSIONS-MUSICAL	OP	50.00	50.00
95	LITTLE EMMETT NOEL, NOEL	OP	40.00	40.00
*		**EMMETT KELLY JR. METAL SCULPTURES**		
91	BALANCING ACT, TOO	5000	125.00	125.00
91	CAROUSEL RIDER	5000	125.00	125.00
91	EMMETT'S POOCHES	5000	125.00	125.00
91	MAGICIAN, THE	5000	125.00	125.00
*		**EMMETT KELLY JR. MINIATURES**		
86	BALANCING ACT	*	25.00	40.00-50.00
86	BALLOONS FOR SALE	*	25.00	35.00-45.00
86	HOLE IN THE SOLE	RT	25.00	40.00-55.00
86	LOOKING OUT TO SEE	RT	25.00	75.00-125.00
86	SWEEPING UP	RT	25.00	75.00-125.00
86	THINKER, THE	*	25.00	35.00-50.00
86	WET PAINT	*	25.00	35.00-45.00
86	WHY ME?	RT	25.00	40.00-55.00
86	WISHFUL THINKING	RT	25.00	50.00-70.00
87	EATING CABBAGE	*	30.00	35.00-50.00
87	EMMETT'S FAN	*	30.00	40.00-50.00
87	SPIRIT OF CHRISTMAS I	*	40.00	55.00-125.00
88	BIG BUSINESS	*	35.00	39.00
89	COTTON CANDY	*	30.00	30.00
89	MAN'S BEST FRIEND?	*	35.00	35.00
90	MY FAVORITE THINGS	*	45.00	45.00
90	SATURDAY NIGHT	*	50.00	50.00
90	SPIRIT OF CHRISTMAS III	*	50.00	50.00
91	IN THE SPOTLIGHT	*	35.00	35.00
91	NO STRINGS ATTACHED	*	35.00	35.00
95	BEDTIME	OP	35.00	35.00
95	DINING OUT	OP	35.00	35.00
95	ENTERTAINERS, THE	OP	45.00	45.00
95	HURDY GURDY MAN	OP	40.00	40.00
95	NO LOITTERING	OP	50.00	50.00
*		**EMMETT KELLY JR. PROFESSIONALS**		
93	AFTER THE PARADE	75000	190.00	190.00
93	KITTENS FOR SALE	75000	190.00	190.00
93	ON MANEUVERS	OP	50.00	50.00
93	PILOT	OP	50.00	50.00
93	REALTOR	OP	50.00	50.00
93	SPIRIT OF CHRISTMAS 1X	35000	200.00	200.00
93	SPIRIT OF CHRISTMAS X	35000	200.00	200.00
93	VETERINARIAN	OP	50.00	50.00
93	WORLD TRAVELER	75000	190.00	190.00
94	FOREST FRIENDS	75000	190.00	190.00
94	LET HIM EAT CAKE	RT	300.00	300-500
94	LION TAMER	75000	190.00	190.00
94	SPIRIT OF CHRISTMAS V	*	40.00	40.00
94	SPIRIT OF CHRISTMAS X1	35000	200.00	200.00
95	COACH	OP	55.00	55.00
95	COACH	OP	55.00	55.00
95	DOCTOR	OP	55.00	55.00
95	DOCTOR	OP	55.00	55.00
95	FIREMAN	OP	55.00	55.00
95	FIREMAN	OP	55.00	55.00
95	GOLFER	OP	55.00	55.00
95	GOLFER	OP	55.00	55.00
95	LAWYER	OP	55.00	55.00
95	LAWYER	OP	55.00	55.00
95	POLICE MAN	OP	55.00	55.00
95	POLICEMAN	OP	55.00	55.00
96	BOWLER	OP	55.00	55.00
96	DENTIST	OP	55.00	55.00
96	FARMER	OP	55.00	55.00
96	MAILMAN	OP	55.00	55.00
96	SKIER	OP	55.00	55.00
96	TEACHER	OP	55.00	55.00
*		**EMMETT KELLY JR. REAL RAGS COLLECTION**		
93	BIG BUSINESS II	OP	140.00	140.00
93	CHECKING HIS LIST	OP	100.00	100.00
93	LOOKING OUT TO SEE II	OP	100.00	100.00
93	SWEEPING UP II	OP	100.00	100.00
93	THINKER	OP	120.00	120.00
94	A GOOD LIKENESS	3000	120.00	120.00
94	EATING CABBAGE TOO	3000	100.00	100.00
94	ONE IN TWO	3000	100.00	100.00
94	RUDOLPH HAS A RED NOSE	3000	135.00	135.00
95	BALLOONS FOR SALE 2	3000	120.00	120.00
95	I'VE GOT RHYTHM	3000	140.00	140.00
95	NO STRINGS ATTACHED 2	3000	120.00	120.00
95	WATCH OUT BELOW	3000	120.00	120.00
M. WU		**LITTLE EMMETT WATERGLOBE**		
95	LOOKING BACKWARD	OP	75.00	75.00
95	LOOKING FORWARD	OP	75.00	75.00
J. BERG VICTOR		**PLEASANTVILLE 1893**		
90	1ST CHURCH OF PLEASANTVILLE	OP	35.00	35.00
90	BAND STAND, THE	OP	12.00	12.00
90	DEPARTMENT STORE	OP	25.00	25.00

YR	NAME	LIMIT	ISSUE	TREND
90	GERBER HOUSE, THE	OP	30.00	30.00
90	MASON'S HOTEL AND SALOON	OP	35.00	35.00
90	PLEASANTVILLE LIBRARY	OP	32.00	32.00
90	REVEREND LITTLEFIELD'S HOUSE	OP	34.00	34.00
90	SWEET SHOPPE & BAKERY	OP	40.00	40.00
90	TOY STORE	OP	30.00	30.00
91	COURT HOUSE	OP	36.00	36.00
91	FIRE HOUSE	OP	40.00	40.00
91	METHODIST CHURCH	OP	40.00	40.00
91	SCHOOL HOUSE	OP	36.00	36.00
92	APOTHECARY/ICE CREAM SHOP	OP	36.00	36.00
92	BANK/REAL ESTATE OFFICE	RT	36.00	36.00
92	BLACKSMITH/LIVERY	OP	40.00	40.00
92	COVERED BRIDGE	RT	36.00	36.00
92	MISS FOUNTAINS	OP	48.00	48.00
92	RAILROAD STATION	OP	40.00	40.00
92	TUBBS, JR. HOUSE	OP	40.00	40.00
93	BALCOMB'S FARM	OP	40.00	40.00
93	BALCOMB'S FARMHOUSE	OP	40.00	40.00
93	BLACKSMITH SHOP	OP	40.00	40.00
93	LIVERY STABLE AND RESIDENCE	OP	40.00	40.00
94	GAZEBO/BANDSTAND	OP	25.00	25.00
94	SACRED HEART CATHOLIC CHURCH	OP	40.00	40.00
94	SACRED HEART RECTORY	OP	40.00	40.00
R. MUSGRAVE				**POCKET DRAGONS**
*	A POCKET-SIZED TREE	*	*	65.00
*	DENNIS THE DRAGON	*	*	117.00
*	PUTTING ME ON THE TREE	*	*	78.00
*	WIZARDRY FOR FUN AND PROFIT	*	*	585.00
93	A BIG HUG	RT	35.00	30.00
93	BATH TIME	OP	90.00	90.00
93	BOOK END, THE	OP	90.00	90.00
93	FUZZY EARS	OP	16.50	17.00
93	I ATE THE WHOLE THING	OP	32.50	33.00
93	LET'S MAKE COOKIES	OP	90.00	90.00
93	LITTLE BIT	OP	16.50	17.00
93	LITTLE JEWEL-BROOCH	OP	19.50	20.00
93	OH GOODY!	OP	16.50	17.00
93	POCKET RIDER-BROOCH	OP	19.50	20.00
93	READING THE GOOD PARTS	OP	70.00	70.00
93	TREASURE	OP	90.00	90.00
93	WE'RE VERY BRAVE	OP	37.50	38.00
93	YOU CAN'T MAKE ME	OP	15.00	15.00
94	A BOOK MY SIZE	OP	30.00	30.00
94	A LITTLE SECURITY	OP	20.00	20.00
94	BUTTERFLY KISSES	OP	29.50	30.00
94	CANDY CANE	OP	55.00	55.00
94	COFFEE PLEASE	OP	24.00	24.00
94	DANCE PARTNER	OP	23.00	23.00
94	GARGOYLES JUST WANT TO HAVE FUN	OP	30.00	30.00
94	IN TROUBLE AGAIN	OP	35.00	35.00
94	IT'S DARK OUT THERE	OP	45.00	45.00
94	IT'S MAGIC	OP	31.00	31.50
94	PLAYING DRESS UP	OP	30.00	30.00
94	RAIDING THE COOKIE JAR	3500	200.00	200.00
94	SNUGGLES	OP	35.00	35.00
95	BUT I'M TOO LITTLE	OP	15.00	15.00
95	BYE...	OP	15.00	15.00
95	CLASSICAL DRAGON	OP	80.00	80.00
95	ELEMENTARY MY DEAR	OP	35.00	35.00
95	HEDGEHOG'S JOKE, THE	OP	27.00	27.00
95	HI!	OP	15.00	15.00
95	I'LL BE THE BRIDE	OP	37.00	37.00
95	I'LL BE THE GROOM	OP	37.00	37.00
95	IT'S A PRESENT	OP	21.00	21.00
95	JINGLES	OP	23.00	23.00
95	PURPLE	OP	27.00	27.00
95	SEES ALL, KNOWS ALL	OP	35.00	35.00
95	TELLING SECRETS	OP	48.00	48.00
95	TUMBLY	OP	21.00	21.00
95	WATSON	OP	22.50	23.00
96	CHRISTMAS SKATES	OP	36.00	36.00
96	D-PRESSING	OP	28.00	28.00
96	I'M SO PRETTY	OP	23.00	23.00
96	PILLOW FIGHT	3500	157.00	157.00
96	POCKET PIPER	OP	37.00	37.00
96	QUARTET	OP	80.00	80.00
96	RED RIBBON	OP	17.00	17.00
96	SWEETIE PIE	OP	28.00	28.00
96	WHATCHA DOING	OP	23.00	23.00
D. RUST				**POCKET DRAGONS**
93	SANTA'S STOWAWAY	10000	30.00	30.00
94	70 TH BIRTHDAY COMMEMORATIVE	5000	30.00	30.00
R. MUSGRAVE				**POCKET DRAGONS APPEARANCE FIGURINE**
94	PACKED AND READY	OP	47.00	47.00
R. MUSGRAVE				**POCKET DRAGONS CHRISTMAS EDITION**
93	CHRISTMAS ANGEL	RT	45.00	65.00
94	DEAR SANTA	RT	50.00	50.00

YR	NAME	LIMIT	ISSUE	TREND
95	CHASING SNOWFLAKES	YR	35.00	35.00
	R. MUSGRAVE	**POCKET DRAGONS COLLECTORS CLUB GIFT**		
93	BITSY	RT	*	15.00
93	WANT A BITE?	RT	50.00	50.00
94	BLUE RIBBON DRAGON	RT	*	75.00
94	FRIENDSHIP PIN	RT	*	N/A
	R. MUSGRAVE	**POCKET DRAGONS MEMBERS ONLY**		
93	PEN PALS	RT	90.00	135.00
94	BEST SEAT IN THE HOUSE, THE	5/95	75.00	75.00
95	MAKING TIME FOR YOU	YR	29.50	30.00
95	PARTY TIME	YR	75.00	75.00
	R. MUSGRAVE	**POCKET DRAGONS/'95 CHRISTMAS EDITION**		
95	CHASING SNOWFLAKES	OP	35.00	35.00
	C. BEYLON	**RAGGEDY ANN & ANDY**		
88	70 YEARS YOUNG	2500	95.00	110.00-130.00
88	GIDDY UP	3500	95.00	110.00-130.00
88	OOPS!	3500	80.00	95.00-110.00
88	WET PAINT	3500	70.00	85.00-100.00

FRANKLIN MINT

YR	NAME	LIMIT	ISSUE	TREND
	N. ROCKWELL	**JOYS OF CHILDHOOD**		
76	COASTING ALONG	3700	120.00	175.00
76	DRESSING UP	3700	120.00	175.00
76	FISHING HOLE, THE	3700	120.00	175.00
76	HOPSCOTCH	3700	120.00	175.00
76	MARBLE CHAMP, THE	3700	120.00	175.00
76	NURSE, THE	3700	120.00	175.00
76	RIDE 'EM COWBOY	3700	120.00	175.00
76	STILT WALKER, THE	3700	120.00	175.00
76	TIME OUT	3700	120.00	175.00
76	TRICK OR TREAT	3700	120.00	175.00

GANZ

YR	NAME	LIMIT	ISSUE	TREND
	C. THAMMAVONGSA	**CHEESERVILLE PICNIC COLLECTION MINI**		
91	BASKET OF APPLES	OP	2.25	2.25
91	BASKET OF PEACHES	OP	2.00	2.00
91	BLUEBERRY CAKE	RT	2.50	3.00
91	BREAD BASKET	OP	2.50	3.00
91	CANDY'	OP	2.00	2.00
91	CHERRY PIE	RT	2.00	2.00
91	CHOCOLATE CAKE	OP	2.50	3.00
91	CHOCOLATE CHEESECAKE	OP	2.00	2.00
91	DOUGHNUT BASKET	OP	2.50	3.00
91	EGG TART	OP	1.00	1.00
91	FOOD BKT. W/BLUE CLOTH	RT	6.50	7.00
91	FOOD BKT. W/GREEN CLOTH	OP	7.50	8.00
91	FOOD BKT. W/PINK CLOTH	RT	6.00	6.00
91	FOOD BKT. W/PURPLE CLOTH	OP	6.00	6.00
91	FOOD TROLLEY	RT	12.00	12.00
91	HAZELNUT ROLL	RT	2.00	2.00
91	HONEY JAR	RT	2.00	2.00
91	HOT DOG	OP	2.25	2.25
91	ICE CREAM GROUP	OP	2.00	2.00
91	LEMON CAKE	RT	2.00	2.00
91	NAPKIN IN CAN	RT	2.00	2.00
91	SET OF FOUR BOTTLES	RT	10.00	10.00
91	STRAWBERRY CAKE	OP	2.00	2.00
91	SUNDAE	OP	2.00	2.00
91	WINE GLASS	OP	1.25	1.25
94	MAYFLOWER MEADOW BASE	OP	50.00	50.00
	C. THAMMAVONGSA	**CHEESERVILLE PICNIC COLLECTION MUSICALS**		
91	BLOSSOM & HICKORY JEWELRY BX	RT	65.00	65.00
91	FLORAL TRINKET BOX	OP	32.00	32.00
91	MAMA & SWEET CICELY WATERGLOBE	RT	55.00	55.00
91	MEADLEY MEADOWMOUSE WATERGLOBE	OP	47.00	47.00
91	MEDLEY MEADOWMOUSE COOKIE JAR	RT	75.00	75.00
91	PICNIC BASE	OP	60.00	60.00
91	SUNFLOWER BASE	RT	65.00	65.00
91	SWEET CICELY DOLL BASKET	OP	85.00	85.00
91	TRINKET BOX	OP	30.00	30.00
91	VIOLET WOODSWORTH COOKIE JAR	RT	75.00	75.00
92	APRIL SHOWERS BRING MAY FLWRS	OP	7.50	8.00
92	DECORATED W/LOVE	OP	7.50	8.00
92	FOR SOMEBUNNY SPECIAL	OP	7.50	8.00
93	"SECRET TREASURES" TRINKET BX	OP	35.00	35.00
93	WISHING WELL	OP	50.00	50.00
94	BANDSTAND BASE, THE	OP	48.50	49.00
	C. THAMMAVONGSA	**LITTLE CHEESERS/CHRISTMAS COLLECTION**		
91	ABNER APPLETON RINGING BELL	RT	14.00	15.00
91	AUNTIE BLOSSOM W/ORNAMENTS	OP	14.00	15.00
91	CHEESER SNOWMAN	OP	7.50	8.00
91	CHRISTMAS TREE	OP	9.00	9.00
91	COUSIN WOODY PLAYING FLUTE	OP	14.00	15.00
91	FROWZY ROQUEFORT III SKATING	RT	14.00	15.00
91	GRANDMAMA & LITTLE TRUFFLE	RT	19.00	19.00
91	GRANDPAPA & SWEET CICELY	OP	19.00	19.00
91	GRANDPAPA BLOWING HORN	OP	14.00	15.00
91	GREAT AUNT ROSE W/TRAY	OP	14.00	15.00

YR	NAME	LIMIT	ISSUE	TREND
91	HARLEY & HARRIET DANCING	RT	19.00	19.00
91	HICKORY PLAYING CELLO	OP	14.00	15.00
91	JENNY ON SLEIGH	OP	16.00	16.00
91	JEREMY W/TEDDY BEAR	OP	12.00	12.00
91	LAMP POST	OP	8.50	9.00
91	LITTLE TRUFFLE W/STOCKING	OP	8.00	8.00
91	MAMA POURING TEA	RT	14.00	15.00
91	MARIGOLD & OSCAR STEALING A X-M KISS	OP	19.00	19.00
91	MEDLEY PLAYING DRUM	OP	8.00	8.00
91	MYRTLE MEADOWMOUSE W/BK	RT	14.00	15.00
91	OUTDOOR SCENE BASE	RT	35.00	35.00
91	PARLOR SCENE BASE	OP	37.50	38.00
91	SANTA CHEESER	OP	13.00	13.00
91	VIOLET W/SNOWBALL	OP	8.00	8.00
93	ALL I WANT FOR CHRISTMAS	OP	18.00	18.00
93	CANDLEHOLDER-SANTA CHEESER	OP	19.00	19.00
93	CANDY CANE	OP	2.00	2.00
93	CHRISTMAS GIFT	OP	3.00	3.00
93	CHRISTMAS GREETINGS	OP	16.50	17.00
93	CHRISTMAS STOCKING	OP	3.00	3.00
93	GENGERBREAD HOUSE	OP	3.00	3.00
93	ICE POND BASE	OP	5.50	5.50
93	SLEIGH RIDE	OP	11.00	11.00
93	TOY SOLDIER	OP	3.00	3.00
93	TOY TRAIN	OP	3.00	3.00
94	CHRISTMAS COLLECTION BASE	OP	50.00	50.00
94	SANTA'S SLEIGH	10000	22.00	22.00
	C. THAMMAVONGSA			**LITTLE CHEESERS/MUSICALS**
92	J. BUTTERFIELD CHRISTMAS WATERGLOBE	RT	55.00	55.00
92	LITTLE TRUFFLE CHRISTMAS WATERGLOBE	OP	45.00	45.00
92	SANTA CHEESER ROLY-POLY	RT	55.00	55.00
93	I'LL BE HOME FOR X'MAS	OP	30.00	30.00
93	WE WISH YOU A MERRY CHRISTMAS	OP	25.00	25.00
	C. THAMMAVONGSA			**SPRINGTIME/CHEESERVILLE COLLECTION**
92	A BASKET FULL OF JOY	OP	16.00	16.00
92	A WHEELBARROW OF SUNSHINE	OP	17.00	17.00
92	HIPPITY-HOP. IT'S EASTERTIME!	OP	16.00	16.00
92	SPRINGTIME DELIGHTS	OP	12.00	12.00
92	TULIPS & RIBBONS TRINKET BX MUSICAL	RT	28.00	28.00
93	BALLERINA SWEETHEART	OP	10.00	10.00
93	BLOSSOM HAS A LITTLE LAMB	OP	16.50	17.00
93	FIRST KISS	OP	24.00	24.00
93	FOR MY SWEETHEART	OP	22.00	22.00
93	FRIENDS FOREVER	OP	22.00	22.00
93	GENTLY DOWN THE STREAM	10000	27.00	27.00
93	GIFT FROM HEAVEN	OP	10.00	10.00
93	HIGS & KISSES	OP	11.00	11.00
93	I LOVE YOU	OP	22.00	22.00
93	PLAYING CUPID	OP	10.00	10.00
93	SUGAR & SPICE	OP	24.00	24.00
93	SUNDAY STROLL	OP	22.00	22.00
94	BIRTHDAY PARTY	OP	22.00	22.00
94	GET WELL	OP	22.00	22.00
94	HIP HIP HOORAY	OP	22.00	22.00
	C. THAMMAVONGSA			**THE CHRISTMAS COLLECTION**
94	CHRISTMAS TRIMMINGS	10000	24.00	24.00
94	JOY TO THE WORLD	OP	10.00	10.00
94	LET IT SNOW	OP	12.00	12.00
94	MISTLETOE MAGIC	OP	14.00	15.00
94	SANTA PIG	OP	11.00	11.00
94	YULETIDE CAROLS	OP	19.00	19.00
	C. THAMMAVONGSA			**THE COWTOWN COLLECTION**
93	BUFFALO BULL CODY	OP	15.00	16.00
93	BULL MASTERSON	OP	15.00	16.00
93	BULL ROGERS	OP	17.00	17.00
93	BULL RUTH	RT	13.00	13.00
93	BUTTERMILK & BUTTERCUP	OP	16.00	16.00
93	COWLAMITY JANE	OP	15.00	16.00
93	DAISY MOO	OP	11.00	11.00
93	GLORIA BOVINE & RUDOLPH BULLENTINO	OP	20.00	20.00
93	JETHRO BOVINE	RT	15.00	15.00
93	LI'L ORPHAN ANGUS	OP	11.00	11.00
93	MOO WEST	OP	15.00	16.00
93	OLD MOODONALD	OP	13.50	14.00
94	AMOOLIA STEERHEART	OP	25.00	25.00
94	COWSEY JONES & THE CANNONBULL EXPRESS	OP	26.50	27.00
94	GERONIMOO	OP	17.00	17.00
94	HEIFERELLA	OP	16.50	17.00
94	KING COWMOOAMOOA	OP	16.50	17.00
94	MA & PA CATTLE	OP	23.50	24.00
94	POCOWHANTIS	OP	16.50	17.00
94	SET OF THREE CACTI	OP	17.00	17.00
94	TCHAICOWSKY	OP	19.00	19.00
94	TEXAS LONESTEER	10000	50.00	50.00
	C. THAMMAVONGSA			**THE LITTLE HOPPERS COLLECTION**
94	BUBBLE BATH	OP	7.50	8.00
94	LET'S PLAY BALL	OP	7.00	7.00
94	SOMEBUNNY LOVES YOU	OP	7.50	8.00

YR	NAME	LIMIT	ISSUE	TREND
94	SWEET NOTHINGS	OP	15.00	15.00
94	TENDER LOVING CARE	OP	10.00	10.00
94	TRICYCLE BUILT FOR TWO	OP	16.00	16.00
C. THAMMAVONGSA		**THE PIGSVILLE COLLECTION**		
93	BAKIN' AT THE BEACH	OP	11.00	11.00
93	ICE CREAM ANYONE?	RT	9.00	9.00
93	ME & MY ICE CREAM	RT	17.00	17.00
93	MOTHER LOVE	OP	13.00	13.00
93	NAP TIME	OP	11.00	11.00
93	P.O.P DISPLAY SIGN	OP	8.00	8.00
93	PIG AT THE BEACH	OP	9.00	9.00
93	PRIMA BALLERINA	RT	11.00	11.00
93	SOAP SUDS	OP	12.00	12.00
93	SQUEAKY CLEAN	OP	11.00	11.00
93	TIPSY	OP	9.00	9.00
93	TRUE LOVE	OP	12.00	12.00
93	WEE LITTLE PIGGY	OP	8.00	8.00
94	BEDTIME	OP	9.50	10.00
94	BIRTHDAY SURPRISE	OP	9.50	10.00
94	OLE FISHING HOLD	OP	16.00	16.00
94	PLAY BALL	OP	11.50	12.00
94	PRETTY PIGLET	OP	8.00	8.00
94	SANDCASTLE	OP	12.00	12.00
94	SNACKTIME	OP	11.50	12.00
94	SPECIAL TEST	OP	11.50	12.00
94	STORYTIME	OP	13.00	13.00
94	WEDDED BLISS	OP	16.00	16.00
C. THAMMAVONGSA		**THE PIGSVILLE COLLECTION ACCESSORIES**		
94	BARN	OP	35.00	35.00
94	SILO	OP	15.00	16.00
C. THAMMAVONGSA		**THE VALENTINE COLLECTION**		
94	CHAMPAGNE & ROSES	OP	14.00	15.00
94	I LOVE YOU	OP	9.50	10.00
94	I'M ALL YOURS	OP	11.50	12.00
94	LOVESTRUCK	OP	10.00	10.00
94	SWEETHEART PIG	OP	8.00	8.00
94	TOGETHER FOREVER	OP	15.00	16.00
C. THAMMAVONGSA		**THE WEDDING COLLECTION**		
92	BLOSSOM THISTLEDOWN BRIDE	OP	16.00	16.00
92	COUSIN WOODY & LI'L TRUFFLE	OP	20.00	20.00
92	FROWZY ROQUEFORT III W/GRAMOPHONE	OP	20.00	20.00
92	GRANDMAMA & GRANDPAPA THISTLEDOWN	RT	20.00	20.00
92	GREAT AUNT ROSE BESIDE TABLE	OP	20.00	20.00
92	HARLEY & HARRIET HARVESTMOUSE	OP	20.00	20.00
92	HICKORY HARVESTMOUSE GROOM	OP	16.00	16.00
92	J. BUTTERFIELD/SWEET CICELY BRIDESMAID	OP	20.00	20.00
92	LITTLE TRUFFLE RINGBEARER	OP	10.00	10.00
92	MAMA & PAPA WOODSWORTH DANCING	OP	20.00	20.00
92	MARIGOLD THISTLEDOWN & OSCAR ROBBINS	OP	20.00	20.00
92	MYRTLE MEADOWMOUSE W/MEDLEY	RT	20.00	20.00
92	PASTOR SMALLWOOD	OP	16.00	16.00
92	WEDDING PROCESSION	OP	40.00	40.00
93	BIG DAY, THE	OP	20.00	20.00
C. THAMMAVONGSA		**THE WEDDING COLLECTION ACCESSORIES**		
93	BANQUET TABLE	OP	14.00	15.00
93	GAZEBO BASE	OP	42.00	42.00
C. THAMMAVONGSA		**THE WEDDING COLLECTION MINI**		
92	BIBLE TRINKET BOX	OP	16.50	17.00
92	BIG CHOCOLATE CAKE	RT	4.50	5.00
92	BRIDE CANDLEHOLDER	OP	20.00	20.00
92	CAKE TRINKET BOX	OP	14.00	15.00
92	CANDLES	OP	3.00	3.00
92	CHERRY JELLO	OP	3.00	3.00
92	CHOCOLATE PASTRY	RT	2.00	2.00
92	CHOCOLATE PUDDING	OP	2.50	3.00
92	FLOUR BAG	RT	2.00	2.00
92	FLOWER VASE	RT	3.00	3.00
92	FRUIT SALAD	OP	3.00	3.00
92	GRASS BASE	RT	3.50	4.00
92	GROOM CANDLEHOLDER	OP	20.00	20.00
92	HONEY POT	OP	2.00	2.00
92	RING CAKE	OP	3.00	3.00
92	SALT CAN	RT	2.00	2.00
92	SOUFFLE	RT	2.50	3.00
92	SOUP POT	OP	3.00	3.00
92	TEA POT SET	RT	3.00	3.00
92	TEDDY MOUSE	RT	2.00	2.00
93	GOOSEBERRY CHAMPAGNE	OP	3.00	3.50
93	WEDDING CAKE	OP	4.50	5.00
C. THAMMAVONGSA		**THE WEDDING COLLECTION MUSICALS**		
92	BLOSSOM & HICKORY WEDDING WATERGLOBE	OP	55.00	55.00
92	WEDDING BASE	OP	32.00	32.00
92	WOODEN BASE FOR WEDDING PROCESSIONAL	OP	25.00	25.00
93	BLOSSOM & HICKORY MUSICAL	RT	50.00	50.00
93	WHITE MUSICAL WD. BASE/GAZABO EVERGREEN	OP	25.00	25.00

GARTLAN USA

YR	NAME	LIMIT	ISSUE	TREND
*	JOE MONTANA A/P H/S	250	500.00	750.00

YR	NAME	LIMIT	ISSUE	TREND
*	JOE MONTANA (CLUB MINI)	*	75.00	135.00
*	PETE ROSE H/S	2000	125.00	1375.00
*** BARNUM**				
*	YOGI BERRA H/S A/P	250	350.00	375.00
*** HEYDA**				
*	CARL YASTREZEMSKI H/S A/P	250	150.00	495.00
*	JOE DIMAGGIO AP H/S	325	695.00	2400.00
*	JOHNNY BENCH H/S A/P	250	*	550.00
*	KAREEM ABDUL-JABBAR H/S	1989	175.00	495.00
*	KAREEM ABDUL-JABBAR PURPLE UNIFORM H/S	33	275.00	5500.00
*	KAREEN ABDUL-JABBAR A/P	100	200.00	600.00
*	WAYNE GRETZKY (CLUB MINI)	*	75.00	295.00
*	WAYNE GRETZKY H/S	1851	250.00	1000.00
*** ROGER**				
*	MAGIC JOHNSON H/S	250	175.00	3700.00
*	MAGIC JOHNSON PURPLE UNIFORM H/S	32	275.00	6900.00
*	MIKE SCHMIDT H/S	1987	150.00	950.00
*	MIKE SCHMIDT H/S	1987	150.00	975.00
*	MIKE SCHMIDT H/S A/P	20	275.00	1500.00 *
*** HEYDA**				
*	KAREEM ABDUL-JABBAR A/P	100	200.00	450.00
ROGER		**ALL-STAR GEMS MINIATURE FIGURINES**		
90	MIKE SCHMIDT	10000	75.00	75.00
F. BARNUM		**ALL-STAR GEMS MINIATURE FIGURINES**		
90	GEORGE BRETT	10000	75.00	75.00
90	PETE ROSE	10000	75.00	75.00
90	WHITEY FORD	10000	75.00	75.00
90	YOGI BERRA	10000	75.00	75.00
91	JOE MONTANA	10000	79.00	79.00
92	HANK AARON	10000	79.00	79.00
V. BOVA		**ALL-STAR GEMS MINIATURE FIGURINES**		
91	MONTE IRVIN	10000	79.00	79.00
L. HEYDA		**ALL-STAR GEMS MINIATURE FIGURINES**		
89	CARL YASTRZEMSKI	10000	75.00	75.00
89	JOHNNY BENCH	10000	75.00	75.00
89	STEVE CARLTON	10000	75.00	75.00
89	TED WILLIAMS	10000	75.00	75.00
90	DARYL STRAWBERRY	10000	75.00	75.00
90	JOHN WOODEN	10000	75.00	75.00
90	WAYNE GRETZKY	10000	75.00	75.00
91	BOBBY HULL	10000	75.00	75.00
91	BRETT HULL	10000	75.00	75.00
J. SLOCKBOWER		**ALL-STAR GEMS MINIATURE FIGURINES**		
90	LUIS APARICIO	10000	75.00	75.00
91	KEN GRIFFEY, JR.	10000	75.00	75.00
91	ROD CAREW	10000	75.00	75.00
91	WARREN SPAHN	10000	75.00	75.00
92	CARLTON FISK	10000	79.00	79.00
92	ISIAH THOMAS	10000	79.00	79.00
J. MARTIN		**BASEBALL/FOOTBALL/HOCKEY SERIES**		
86	GEORGE BRETT BASEBALL ROUNDER	OP	9.95	16.00
86	GEORGE BRETT BASEBALL ROUNDER, SIGNED	2000	29.95	30.00
86	GEORGE BRETT CERAMIC BASEBALL	OP	19.95	20.00
86	GEORGE BRETT CERAMIC BASEBALL, SIGNED	2000	49.50	50.00
T. SIZEMORE		**BASEBALL/FOOTBALL/HOCKEY SERIES**		
85	PETE ROSE CERAMIC BASEBALL	OP	9.95	16.00
85	PETE ROSE CERAMIC BASEBALL, SIGNED	4192	39.00	75.00
C. SOILEAU		**BASEBALL/FOOTBALL/HOCKEY SERIES**		
87	ROGER STAUBACH CERAMIC FOOTBALL	OP	9.95	16.00
87	ROGER STAUBACH CERAMIC FOOTBALL, SIGNED	1979	39.00	39.00
M. TAYLOR		**BASEBALL/FOOTBALL/HOCKEY SERIES**		
90	WAYNE GRETZKY CERAMIC HOCKEY	OP	18.00	18.00
91	JOE MONTANGA CERAMIC FOOTBALL	OP	18.00	18.00
92	CARLTON FISH CERAMIC BASEBALL	OP	18.00	18.00
L. HEYDA		**BOB COUSY COLLECTION**		
94	BOB COUSY	RT	225.00	300.00
94	BOB COUSY MINI	5000	40.00	40.00
R. SUN		**EDDIE MATHEWS COLLECTION**		
94	EDDIE MATHEWS	50	150.00	300.00
94	EDDIE MATHEWS MINI	RT	40.00	100.00
J. SLOCKBOWER		**FRANK THOMAS**		
95	FRANK THOMAS (AUTOGRAPHED)	SO	200.00	650.00
95	FRANK THOMAS MINI	RT	40.00	75.00
L. HEYDA		**KAREEM ABDUL-JABBAR SKY HOOK COLLECTION**		
89	KAREEM ABDUL-JABBAR, THE CAPTAIN, SIGNED	1989	175.00	49.00
K.L. SUN		**KRISTI YAMAGUCHI COLLECTION**		
93	KRISTI YAMAGUCHI	RT	195.00	300.00
93	KRISTI YAMAGUCHI MINI	RT	79.00	79.00
*****		**LEAVE IT TO BEAVER/JERRY MATHERS**		
95	LEAVE IT TO BEAVER 7 1/2" AP	234	250.00	250.00
95	LEAVE IT TO BEAVER AUTOGRAPHED	1963	195.00	195.00
95	LEAVE IT TO BEAVER MINI AUTOGRAPHED	5000	50.00	50.00
ROGER		**MAGIC JOHNSON GOLD RIM COLLECTION**		
88	MAGIC JOHNSON COMMEMORATIVE	32	275.00	2800.00
88	MAGIC JOHNSON-MAGIC IN MOTION	1737	125.00	650.00

YR	NAME	LIMIT	ISSUE	TREND
88	MAGIC JOHNSON-MAGIC IN MOTION, PROOF	250	175.00	3700.00
F. BARNUM		**MASTER'S MUSEUM COLLECTION**		
91	JOE MONTANA (SET)	500	*	*
L. HEYDA		**MASTER'S MUSEUM COLLECTION**		
91	KAREEM ABDUL-JABBAR	500	3000.00	3000.00
91	TED WILLIAMS (SET)	500	*	*
91	WAYNE GRETZKY (SET)	500	*	*
F. BARNUM		**MEMBERS ONLY FIGURINE**		
91	JOE MONTANA-ROAD UNIFORM	*	75.00	125.00
L. HEYDA		**MEMBERS ONLY FIGURINE**		
90	WAYNE GRETZKY-HOME UNIFORM	*	75.00	200.00
91	KAREEM ABDUL-JABBAR (MINI)	*	75.00	79.00
ROGER		**MIKE SCHMIDT 500TH HOME RUN EDITION**		
87	FIGURINE, SIGNED	1987	150.00	800.00
87	PLAQUE-ONLY PERFECT, SIGNED	500	150.00	340.00
V. BOVA		**NEGRO LEAGUE SERIES**		
91	BUCK LEONARD	1972	195.00	195.00
91	JAMES (COOL PAPA) BELL	1499	195.00	195.00
91	MATCHED-NUMBER SET #1-950	950	500.00	500.00
91	RAY DANDRIDGE	1987	195.00	195.00
B. FORBES		**PETE ROSE DIAMOND COLLECTION**		
88	FAREWELL CERAMIC BASEBALL CARD	OP	9.95	16.00
88	FAREWELL CERAMIC BASEBALL CARD, SIGNED	4258	39.00	65.00
H. REED		**PETE ROSE PLATINUM EDITION**		
85	PETE ROSE-FOR THE RECORD, SIGNED	4192	125.00	1375.00
J. MARTIN		**PLAQUES**		
86	GEORGE BRETT-ROYALTY IN MOTION, SIGNED	2000	85.00	195.00
86	REGGIE JACKSON-THE ROUNDTRIPPER, PROOF	SO	200.00	300.00
86	REGGIE JACKSON-THE ROUNDTRIPPER, SIGNED	500	150.00	240.00
87	ROGER STAUBACH, SIGNED	1979	85.00	195.00
T. SIZEMORE		**PLAQUES**		
85	PETE ROSE-DESIRE TO WIN, SIGNED	4192	75.00	75.00
J. MARTIN		**REGGIE JACKSON 500TH HOME RUN EDITION**		
86	CERAMIC BASEBALL CARD	OP	9.95	16.00
86	CERAMIC BASEBALL CARD, SIGNED	500	39.00	65.00
J. HOFFMAN		**RINGO STARR**		
96	BEATLES, RINGO STARR 9 1/2"	1000	350.00	350.00
96	BEATLES, RINGO STARR MINI	10000	50.00	50.00
96	RINGO STARR 9 1/2" AP	250	600.00	600.00
96	RINGO STARR/DRUMMING	5000	150.00	150.00
L. CELLA		**SAM SNEAD COLLECTION**		
94	SAM SNEAD	RT	150.00	150.00
94	SAM SNEAD MINI	RT	40.00	40.00
R. SUH		**SHAQUILLE O'NEAL**		
95	SHAQUILLE O'NEAL (AUTOGRAPHED)	SO	225.00	800.00
95	SHAQUILLE O'NEAL MINI	RT	40.00	50.00
L. CELLA		**SHAQUILLE O'NEAL CLUB FIGURINE**		
94	SHAQUILLE O'NEAL	*	40.00	80.00
F. BARNUM		**SIGNED FIGURINES**		
89	YOGI BERRA	2000	225.00	250.00
90	GEORGE BRETT	2500	225.00	225.00
90	WHITEY FORD	2360	225.00	225.00
91	JOE MONTANA H/S	2250	325.00	425.00
92	HANK AARON	1982	225.00	225.00
V. BOVA		**SIGNED FIGURINES**		
91	AL BARLICK	1989	175.00	175.00
91	MONTE IRVIN	1973	225.00	225.00
L. HEYDA		**SIGNED FIGURINES**		
89	CARL YASTRZEMSKI-YAZ	1989	150.00	350.00
89	JOE DIMAGGIO H/S	2214	275.00	1375.00
89	JOHN WOODEN-COACHING CLASSICS	1975	175.00	175.00
89	JOHNNY BENCH H/S	1989	150.00	375.00
89	STEVE CARLTON H/S	3290	175.00	235.00
89	TED WILLIAMS H/S	2654	295.00	575.00
89	WAYNE GRETZKY	1851	225.00	650.00
89	WAYNE GRETZKY, ARTIST PROOF H/S	300	695.00	1800.00
90	DARRYL STRAWBERRY	2500	225.00	225.00
90	JOE DIMAGGIO-PINSTRIPE YANKEE CLIPPER	325	695.00	2400.00
91	BOBBY HULL-THE GOLDEN JET	1983	225.00	225.00
91	BRETT HULL-THE GOLDEN BRETT	1986	225.00	225.00
91	HULL MATCHED FIGURINES	950	500.00	500.00
J. SLOCKBOWER		**SIGNED FIGURINES**		
90	LUIS APARICIO	1974	225.00	225.00
91	KEN GRIFFEY, JR.	1989	225.00	225.00
91	ROD CAREW-HITTING SPLENDOR	1991	225.00	225.00
91	WARREN SPAHN	1973	225.00	225.00
92	CARLTON FISK	1972	225.00	225.00
92	ISIAH THOMAS	1990	225.00	225.00
V. DAVIS		**TROY AIKMAN**		
95	TROY AIKMAN (AUTOGRAPHED)	SO	200.00	800.00
95	TROY AIKMAN MINI	RT	40.00	90.00

GENESIS DESIGNS

YR	NAME	LIMIT	ISSUE	TREND
M. MORRIS				
95	REX NANOOK	2500	160.00	160.00

GLASS EYE

YR	NAME	LIMIT	ISSUE	TREND
93	AQUARIUM	1000	17.50	20.00
93	CHERRY BLOSSOM	1000	17.50	20.00
94	CORAL REEF	1500	22.50	25.00
94	HEART AND VINES	1500	22.50	25.00
95	AURORA BOREALIS	150	165.00	175.00
95	GENESIS	500	50.00	55.00

GOEBEL INC.

Price ranges may reflect various demands in the market from one geographic region to another; condition of piece; specific markings found on piece; and/or changes in production of piece.

YR	NAME	LIMIT	ISSUE	TREND
*	LET'S TELL THE WORLD HUM-487	*	*	1200.00-1500.00
M.I. HUMMEL				
95	ANGLER, THE	*	320.00	320.00
95	COME BACK SOON	*	135.00	135.00
95	FESTIVAL HARMONY W/FLUTE	*	100.00	100.00
95	JUST DOZING	*	220.00	220.00
95	PIXIE	*	105.00	105.00
95	RING AROUND THE ROSIE MUSICAL	10000	675.00	675.00
95	TO KEEP YOU WARM	*	195.00	195.00
96	CHRISTMAS SONG	*	115.00	115.00
96	GOOSE GIRL	*	200.00	200.00
B. TIMBERLAKE				
96	AUTUMN AFTERNOONS	500	490.00	490.00
96	AUTUMN AFTERNOONS	500	490.00	490.00
M.I. HUMMEL		**BAVARIAN VILLAGE COLLECTION**		
96	HAPPY PASTIME	RT	175.00	175.00
G. BOCHMANN				**BETSEY CLARK**
72	BLESS YOU	CL	18.00	275.00
72	FRIENDS	CL	21.00	400.00
72	LITTLE MIRACLE	CL	24.50	350.00
72	SO MUCH BEAUTY	CL	24.50	350.00
LORE				**BLUMENKINDER**
66	A BUTTERFLY'S KISS	CL	27.50	*
66	APRONFUL OF FLOWERS	CL	25.00	*
66	BAREFOOT LAD	CL	27.50	*
66	BEARER OF GIFTS	CL	27.50	*
66	DISPLAY PLAQUE	CL	4.00	*
66	FLOWER FARMER, THE	CL	30.00	*
66	FLUTE RECITAL	CL	25.00	*
66	GARDEN ROMANCE	CL	50.00	*
66	HER FIRST BOUQUET	CL	30.00	*
66	HER KITTEN	CL	27.50	*
66	NATURE'S TREASURES	CL	25.00	*
66	ST. VALENTINE'S MESSENGER	CL	30.00	*
66	TENDER LOVING CARE	CL	30.00	*
69	FIRST JOURNEY	CL	25.00	*
69	FIRST LOVE	CL	25.00	*
69	GARDEN PRINCES	CL	50.00	*
69	SUMMER MAGIC	CL	50.00	*
71	BIRD SONG	CL	65.00	*
71	BOYFRIEND, THE	CL	65.00	*
71	CELLO RECITAL	CL	80.00	*
71	COUNTRY LAD	CL	35.00	*
71	COUNTRY MAIDEN	CL	35.00	*
71	COURTING COUNTRY STYLE	CL	80.00	*
72	FIRST DATE	CL	95.00	*
72	PARTY GUEST	CL	95.00	*
73	ACCOMPANIST, THE	CL	95.00	*
73	BY A GARDEN POND	CL	75.00	*
73	EASTER TIME	CL	80.00	240.00
73	HITCHHIKER, THE	CL	80.00	*
73	KITTENS	CL	75.00	*
73	PATIENT, THE	CL	95.00	*
75	BOTH IN HARMONY	CL	95.00	*
75	COMPANIONS	CL	85.00	*
75	FOR YOU-WITH LOVE	CL	95.00	*
75	HAPPY MINSTEL	CL	95.00	*
75	LOYAL FRIEND	CL	85.00	*
75	LUCKY ONE, THE	CL	150.00	*
75	SPRINGTIME	CL	95.00	*
75	WITH LOVE	CL	150.00	*
79	BIRTHDAY MORNING	CL	201.00	*
79	FARMHOUSE COMPANIONS	CL	175.00	*
79	GARDEN FRIENDS	CL	175.00	*
79	HARVEST TREAT	CL	175.00	*
79	LOVING TOUCH	CL	201.00	*
79	SWEET TREAT	CL	149.00	*
80	DANCING SONG	CL	175.00	*
80	DRUMMER BOY	CL	180.00	*
80	FLUTIST	CL	175.00	*
80	ROMANCE	CL	175.00	*
80	SPRING SONG	CL	180.00	*
80	VIOLINIST	CL	180.00	*
82	AUTUMN DELIGHT	CL	165.00	*
82	HAPPY SAILING	CL	150.00	*
82	LITTLE MOMMY	CL	165.00	*

YR	NAME	LIMIT	ISSUE	TREND
82	MAIL CALL	CL	165.00	*
82	PLAY BELL	CL	165.00	*
82	SPINNING TOP, THE	CL	150.00	*
P. LARSEN		**BOB TIMBERLAKE SIGNATURE**		
96	AUTUMN AFTERNOONS	500	500.00	500.00
B. TIMBERLAKE		**BOB TIMBERLAKE SIGNATURE**		
96	FEBRUARY AT RIVERWOOD	*	135.00	135.00
96	FEBRUARY AT RIVERWOOD	OP	135.00	135.00
96	FEBRUARY AT RIVERWOOD	OP	135.00	135.00
96	GATE LATCH	*	60.00	60.00
96	GATE LATCH	OP	60.00	60.00
96	GATE LATCH	OP	60.00	60.00
96	LATE SHOW AT RIVERWOOD	500	500.00	500.00
96	LATE SHOW AT RIVERWOOD 3 PCS.	500	500.00	500.00
96	LATE SNOW AT RIVERWOOD	500	500.00	500.00
96	RITUAL, THE	*	135.00	135.00
96	RITUAL, THE	OP	135.00	135.00
96	RITUAL, THE	OP	135.00	135.00
M.I. HUMMEL		**CENTURY COLLECTION**		
87	PLEASANT JOURNEY HUM-406	CL	500.00	2500.00-6000.00
95	STRIKE UP THE BAND	CL	1200.00	1200.00
96	LOVE'S BOUNTY	*	1200.00	1200.00
M.I. HUMMEL		**CLUB EXCLUSIVE**		
95	A STORY FROM GRANDMA	10000	1300.00	1300.00
95	COUNTRY SUITOR	*	195.00	195.00
95	STRUM ALONG	*	135.00	135.00
96	AT GRANDPA'S	CL	1300.00	1300.00
G. SKROBEK		**CO-BOY**		
*	BERT THE SOCCER STAR	CL	*	50.00
*	CANDY THE BAKER'S DELIGHT	CL	*	50.00
*	CONNY THE NIGHT WATCHMAN	CL	*	50.00
*	ED THE WINE CELLAR STEWARD	CL	*	50.00
*	JACK THE PHARMACIST	CL	*	50.00
*	JIM THE BOWLER	CL	*	50.00
*	JOHN THE HAWKEYE HUNTER	CL	*	50.00
*	MARK-SAFETY FIRST	CL	*	50.00
*	MAX THE BOXING CHAMP	CL	*	50.00
*	PETRL THE VILLAGE ANGLER	CL	*	50.00
*	TONI THE SKIER	CL	*	50.00
71	BIT THE BACHELOR	CL	16.00	45.00
71	FIPS THE FOXY FISHERMAN	CL	16.00	60.00
71	FRITZ THE HAPPY BOOZER	CL	16.00	50.00
71	MIKE THE JAM MAKER	CL	16.00	60.00
71	PLUM THE PASTRY CHEF	CL	16.00	60.00
71	ROBBY THE VEGETARIAN	CL	16.00	90.00
71	SAM THE GOURMET	CL	16.00	60.00
71	TOM THE HONEY LOVER	CL	16.00	75.00
71	WIM THE COURT SUPPLIER	CL	16.00	60.00
72	BOB THE BOOKWORM	CL	20.00	50.00
72	BRUM THE LAWYER	CL	20.00	50.00
72	CO-BOY PLAQUE	CL	20.00	50.00
72	KUNI THE BIG DIPPER	CL	20.00	60.00
72	PORZ THE MUSHROOM MUNCHER	CL	20.00	60.00
72	SEPP THE BEER BUDDY	CL	20.00	60.00
72	UTZ THE BANKER	CL	20.00	50.00
78	GIL THE GOALIE	CL	34.00	50.00
78	PAT THE PITCHER	CL	34.00	50.00
78	TOMMY TOUCHDOWN	CL	34.00	50.00
80	CARL THE CHEF	CL	49.00	50.00
80	DOC THE DOCTOR	CL	49.00	50.00
80	GERD THE DIVER	CL	49.00	50.00
80	HERB THE HORSEMAN	CL	49.00	50.00
80	MONTY THE MOUNTAIN CLIMBER	CL	49.00	50.00
80	TED THE TENNIS PLAYER	CL	49.00	50.00
81	AL THE TRUMPET PLAYER	CL	45.00	50.00
81	BEN THE BLACKSMITH	CL	45.00	50.00
81	GEORGE THE GOURMAND	CL	45.00	50.00
81	GREG THE GOURMET	CL	45.00	50.00
81	GRETA THE HAPPY HOUSEWIFE	CL	45.00	50.00
81	NICK THE NIGHTCLUB SINGER	CL	45.00	50.00
81	NIELS THE STRUMMER	CL	45.00	50.00
81	PETER THE ACCORDIONIST	CL	45.00	50.00
81	WALTER THE JOGGER	CL	45.00	50.00
84	BRAD THE CLOCKMASTER	CL	75.00	95.00
84	CHRIS THE SHOEMAKER	CL	45.00	50.00
84	CHUCK THE CHIMNEY SWEEP	CL	45.00	50.00
84	FELIX THE BAKER	CL	45.00	50.00
84	HERMAN THE BUTCHER	CL	45.00	50.00
84	HOMER THE DRIVER	CL	45.00	50.00
84	MARTHE THE NURSE	CL	45.00	50.00
84	PAUL THE DENTIST	CL	45.00	50.00
84	RICK THE FIREMAN	CL	45.00	50.00
84	RUDY THE WORLD TRAVELER	CL	45.00	50.00
84	SID THE VINTNER	CL	45.00	50.00
87	BANK-PETE THE PIRATE	CL	80.00	80.00
87	BANK-UTZ THE MONEY BAGS	CL	80.00	80.00
87	CHUCK ON HIS PIG	CL	75.00	75.00
87	CLOCK-CONY THE WATCHMAN	CL	125.00	125.00

YR	NAME	LIMIT	ISSUE	TREND
87	CLOCK-SEPP AND THE BEER KEG	CL	125.00	125.00
T. DEGRAZIA				**DEGRAZIA**
84	DISPLAY PLAQUE	CL	45.00	95.00
84	FLOWER BOY	OP	65.00	110.00
84	FLOWER GIRL	OP	65.00	110.00
84	MY FIRST HORSE	OP	65.00	110.00
84	SUNFLOWER BOY	CL	65.00	300.00
84	WHITE DOVE	OP	45.00	80.00
84	WONDERING	OP	85.00	135.00
85	CHILD	OP	25.00	40.00
85	JOSEPH	OP	55.00	70.00
85	LITTLE MADONNA	OP	80.00	125.00
85	MARY	OP	55.00	65.00
85	NATIVITY SET (3 PIECES)	OP	135.00	195.00
85	PIMA DRUMMER BOY	OP	65.00	110.00
86	BLUE BOY, THE	OP	70.00	95.00
86	FESTIVAL LIGHTS	OP	75.00	95.00
86	MERRY LITTLE INDIAN	12500	175.00	245.00
87	LOVE ME	OP	95.00	110.00
87	WEE THREE	OP	180.00	195.00
88	ANGEL CHRISTMAS PRAYER	OP	70.00	80.00
88	BEAUTIFUL BURDEN	OP	175.00	185.00
88	FLOWER BOY PLAQUE	OP	80.00	80.00
88	LOS NINOS	5000	595.00	645.00
88	MERRILY, MERRILY, MERRILY	OP	95.00	110.00
89	MY BEAUTIFUL ROCKING HORSE	OP	225.00	245.00
89	MY FIRST ARROW	OP	95.00	110.00
89	TWO LITTLE LAMBS	OP	70.00	80.00
90	ALONE	OP	395.00	395.00
90	BIGGEST DRUM	YR	135.00	135.00
90	CRUCIFIXION	YR	295.00	295.00
90	DESERT HARVEST	5000	155.00	155.00
90	EL BURRITO	OP	60.00	60.00
90	LITTLE PRAYER	YR	85.00	85.00
90	NAVAJO BOY	YR	135.00	135.00
90	SUNFLOWER GIRL	OP	95.00	95.00
91	NAVAJO MOTHER	YR	*	*
91	SHEPHERD BOY	OP	95.00	95.00
91	WANDERER	YR	75.00	75.00
92	NAVAJO MADONNA	OP	135.00	135.00
92	SUN SHOWERS	5000	195.00	195.00
G. BOCHMANN				**FASHIONS ON PARADE**
82	AT THE TEA DANCE	OP	30.00	50.00
82	COSMOPOLITAN, THE	OP	30.00	50.00
82	EDWARDIAN GRACE	OP	30.00	50.00
82	GARDEN FANCIER, THE	OP	30.00	50.00
82	STROLLING ON THE AVENUE	OP	30.00	50.00
82	VISITOR, THE	OP	30.00	50.00
83	BRIDE AND GROOM	OP	65.00	100.00
83	DEMURE ELEGANCE	OP	32.50	50.00
83	GENTLE THOUGHTS	OP	32.50	50.00
83	HER TREASURED DAY (BRIDE)	OP	32.50	50.00
83	IMPATIENCE	CL	32.50	50.00
83	REFLECTIONS	OP	32.50	50.00
83	WAITING FOR HIS LOVE (GROOM)	OP	32.50	50.00
84	CENTER COURT	CL	32.50	45.00
84	ON THE FAIRWAY	CL	32.50	45.00
84	SKIMMING GENTLY	CL	32.50	45.00
85	A GENTLE MOMENT	CL	22.50	35.00
85	A LAZY DAY	CL	22.50	35.00
85	AFTERNOON TEA	OP	32.50	50.00
85	GENTLE BREEZES	OP	32.50	50.00
85	RIVER OUTING	OP	32.50	50.00
85	TO THE HUNT	OP	32.50	50.00
86	EQUESTRIAN	OP	36.00	50.00
86	FASHIONS ON PARADE PLAQUE	OP	10.00	13.00
86	SOUTHERN BELLE	OP	36.00	50.00
87	PARIS IN FALL	OP	55.00	55.00
87	PROMENADE IN NICE	OP	55.00	55.00
87	SAY PLEASE	OP	55.00	55.00
87	SHEPHERDESS, THE	OP	55.00	55.00
87	SILVER LACE AND RHINESTONES	OP	55.00	55.00
87	VISCOUNTESS DIANA, THE	OP	55.00	55.00
88	BRIDE AND GROOM (2ND SET)	OP	110.00	110.00
88	FOREVER AND ALWAYS (BRIDE)	OP	55.00	55.00
88	PROMISE, THE- (GROOM)	OP	55.00	55.00
N. ROCKWELL				**GOEBEL**
63	ADVERTISING PLAQUE	CL	*	600.00
63	BOYHOOD DREAMS	CL	12.00	400.00
63	BUTTERCUP TEST (BEGUILING BUTTERCUP)	CL	10.00	400.00
63	FIRST LOVE (A SCHOLARLY PACE)	CL	30.00	400.00
63	HOME CURE	CL	16.00	400.00
63	LITTLE VETERINARIAN (MYSTERIOUS MALADY)	CL	15.00	40.00
63	MOTHER'S HELPER (PRIDE OF PARENTHOOD)	CL	15.00	400.00
63	MY FIRST SMOKE	CL	9.00	400.00
63	MY NEW PAL (A BOY MEETS HIS DOG)	CL	12.00	400.00
63	PATIENT ANGLERS (FISHERMAN'S PARADISE)	CL	18.00	400.00
63	SHE LOVES ME (DAY DREAMER)	CL	8.00	400.00

YR	NAME	LIMIT	ISSUE	TREND
63	TIMELY ASSISTANCE (LOVE AID)	CL	16.00	400.00
	M.I. HUMMEL			**GOEBEL COLLECTORS CLUB**
85	SMILING THROUGH HUM-408	CL	125.00	4000.00-5000.00
88	SURPRISE , THE-HUM-431	CL	125.00	2000.00-3000.00
	M.I. HUMMEL			**M.I. HUMMEL**
*	A FAIR MEASURE HUM-345	OP	230.00	285.00-5000.00
*	A FARM BOY & GOOSE GIRL BOOKEND HUM60A&B	TW	*	350.00-1200.00
*	ACCORDION BOY HUM-185	RT	160.00	195.00-700.00
*	ADORATION HUM-23	CL	*	1600.00-2100.00
*	ADORATION HUM-23/I	OP	300.00	345.00-1250.00
*	ADORATION HUM-23/III	OP	470.00	535.00-2000.00
*	ADORATION WITH BIRD, HUM-105	CL	*	7000.00-8000.00
*	ADVENTURE BOUND HUM-347	OP	3300.00	3600.00-6000.00
*	ANGEL DUET HUM-261	OP	180.00	215.00-800.00
*	ANGEL DUET, CANDLEHOLDER HUM-193	OP	180.00	215.00-1700.00
*	ANGEL LIGHTS, CANDLEHOLDER HUM-241	SU	*	250.00-350.00
*	ANGEL SERENADE HUM-83	OP	180.00	215.00-700.00
*	ANGEL WITH ACCORDION HUM-238 B	OP	45.00	50.00-100.00
*	ANGEL WITH LUTE HUM-238 A	OP	45.00	50.00-100.00
*	ANGEL WITH TRUMPET HUM-238 C	OP	45.00	50.00-100.00
*	ANGEL/ACCORDION, CANDLEHLDER HUM111/39/0	SU	*	50.00-175.00
*	ANGEL/ACCORDION, CANDLEHLDER HUM111/39/1	CL	*	150.00-300.00
*	ANGEL/ACCORDION, CANDLEHOLDER HUM 1/39/0	OP	*	50.00-175.00
*	ANGEL/LUTE, CANDLEHOLDER HUM 1/38/0	OP	*	50.00-175.00
*	ANGEL/LUTE, CANDLEHOLDER HUM 111/38/0	SU	*	50.00-175.00
*	ANGEL/LUTE, CANDLEHOLDER HUM 111/38/1	CL	*	150.00-300.00
*	ANGEL/TRUMPET, CANDLEHOLDER HUM 1/40/0	SU	*	50.00-175.00
*	ANGEL/TRUMPET, CANDLEHOLDER HUM 111/40/0	SU	*	50.00-175.00
*	ANGEL/TRUMPET, CANDLEHOLDER HUM 111/40/1	CL	*	150.00-300.00
*	ANGEL/TWO CHILDREN AT FEET HUM-108	CL	*	3000.00-15000.00
*	ANGELIC SLEEP, CANDLEHOLDER HUM-25	SU	*	170.00-650.00
*	ANGELIC SONG HUM-144	OP	125.00	145.00-500.00
*	APPLE TREE BOY HUM-142	CL	*	550.00-850.00
*	APPLE TREE BOY HUM-142/3/O	OP	120.00	140.00-450.00
*	APPLE TREE BOY HUM-142/I	OP	225.00	275.00-750.00
*	APPLE TREE BOY HUM-142/V	OP	1000.00	1200.00-1600.00
*	APPLE TREE BOY HUM-142/X	CL	*	12000.00-30000.00
*	APPLE TREE BOY, CANDLEHOLDER HUM-677	OP	142.50	146.00
*	APPLE TREE BOY, TABLE LAMP HUM-230	TW	*	275.00-900.00
*	APPLE TREE BOY/GIRL-BOOKENDS HUM-252 A&B	TW	*	275.00-400.00
*	APPLE TREE GIRL HUM-141	CL	*	550.00-850.00
*	APPLE TREE GIRL HUM-141/3/O	OP	120.00	140.00-450.00
*	APPLE TREE GIRL HUM-141/I	OP	225.00	275.00-750.00
*	APPLE TREE GIRL HUM-141/V	OP	1000.00	1200.00-1600.00
*	APPLE TREE GIRL HUM-141/X	SU	*	12000.00-20000.00
*	APPLE TREE GIRL, CANDLEHOLDER HUM-676	OP	142.50	146.00
*	APPLE TREE GIRL, TABLE LAMP HUM-229	TW	*	275.00-900.00
*	ARTIST HUM-304	OP	200.00	245.00-5000.00
*	AUF WIEDERSEHEN HUM-153	CL	*	600.00-1100.00
*	AUF WIEDERSEHEN HUM-153/I	OP	250.00	295.00-1000.00
*	AUF WIEDERSEHEN HUM-153/O	OP	200.00	245.00-500.00
*	AUTHORIZED RETAILER PLAQUE HUM-460	CL	*	200.00-1500.00
*	AUTUMN HARVEST HUM-355	OP	180.00	200.00-3000.00
*	BA-BEE RING 30/0 A&B	CL	*	6500.00
*	BA-BEE-RING 30/I A&B	CL	*	8000.00-9000.00
*	BA-BEE-RING 30/I A&B	CL	*	2000.00-3500.00
*	BA-BEE-RING HUM-30/O A&B	OP	160.00	190.00-675.00
*	BAKER HUM-128	OP	160.00	195.00-700.00
*	BAND LEADER HUM-129	OP	170.00	200.00-700.00
*	BAND LEADER HUM-129/4/O	OP	80.00	105.00
*	BARNYARD HERO HUM-195	CL	*	600.00-1100.00
*	BARNYARD HERO HUM-195/2/O	OP	140.00	165.00-400.00
*	BARNYARD HERO HUM-195/I	OP	265.00	300.00-650.00
*	BASHFUL HUM-377	OP	170.00	195.00-1500.00
*	BE PATIENT HUM-197	CL	*	500.00-950.00
*	BE PATIENT HUM-197/2/O	OP	160.00	195.00-450.00
*	BE PATIENT HUM-197/I	OP	230.00	295.00-600.00
*	BEGGING HIS SHARE HUM-9	OP	200.00	250.00-850.00
*	BIG HOUSECLEANING HUM-363	OP	230.00	285.00-3000.00
*	BIRD DUET HUM-169	OP	120.00	140.00-500.00
*	BIRTHDAY SERENADE HUM-218	CL	*	850.00-1000.00
*	BIRTHDAY SERENADE HUM-218/2/O	OP	150.00	170.00-625.00
*	BIRTHDAY SERENADE HUM-218/O	OP	250.00	295.00-950.00
*	BIRTHDAY SERENADE, TABLE LAMP HUM-231	TW	*	400.00-3000.00
*	BIRTHDAY SERENADE, TABLE LAMP HUM-234	TW	*	325.00-2000.00
*	BLESSED CHILD (KRUMBAD) HUM-78/I	TW	*	30.00-50.00
*	BLESSED CHILD (KRUMBAD) HUM-78/II	TW	*	35.00-60.00
*	BLESSED CHILD (KRUMBAD) HUM-78/II 1/2	OP	35.00	50.00-150.00
*	BLESSED CHILD (KRUMBAD) HUM-78/III	TW	*	45.00-400.00
*	BLESSED CHILD (KRUMBAD) HUM-78/O	CL	*	150.00-300.00
*	BLESSED CHILD (KRUMBAD) HUM-78/V	TW	*	80.00-150.00
*	BLESSED CHILD (KRUMBAD) HUM-78/VI	TW	*	150.00-850.00
*	BLESSED CHILD (KRUMBAD) HUM-78/VIII	TW	*	300.00-1000.00
*	BLESSED EVENT HUM-333	OP	280.00	320.00-5000.00
*	BOOK WORM BOOKENDS, BOY & GIRL HUM-14	CL	*	220.00-250.00
*	BOOK WORM HUM-3/I	OP	250.00	200.00-1000.00
*	BOOK WORM HUM-3/II	TW	*	1200.00-3500.00
*	BOOK WORM HUM-3/III	TW	*	1250.00-4000.00
*	BOOK WORM HUM-8	OP	180.00	215.00-750.00

YR	NAME	LIMIT	ISSUE	TREND
*	BOOK WORM, BOOKENDS, HUM-14 A&B	SU	*	200.00-1500.00
*	BOOTS HUM-143	CL	*	600.00-1000.00
*	BOOTS HUM-143/I	OP	270.00	330.00-950.00
*	BOOTS HUM-143/O	OP	160.00	200.00-675.00
*	BOY W/HORSE, CANDLESTICK HUM-117	OP	50.00	55.00-225.00
*	BOY WITH ACCORDION HUM-390	OP	70.00	85.00-200.00
*	BOY WITH BIRD, ASHTRAY HUM-166	TW	*	130.00-600.00
*	BOY WITH HORSE HUM-239 C	OP	45.00	55.00-100.00
*	BOY WITH TOOTHACHE HUM-217	OP	185.00	210.00-500.00
*	BROTHER HUM-95	OP	165.00	200.00-700.00
*	BUILDER HUM-305	OP	200.00	245.00-5000.00
*	BUSY STUDENT HUM-367	OP	140.00	160.00-1000.00
*	CANDLELIGHT, CANDLEHOLDER HUM-192	OP	190.00	230.00-1700.00
*	CARNIVAL HUM-328	OP	190.00	215.00-5000.00
*	CELESTIAL MUSICIAN HUM-188	CL	*	310.00-1500.00
*	CELESTIAL MUSICIAN HUM-188/I	TW	230.00	275.00-310.00
*	CELESTIAL MUSICIAN HUM-188/O	OP	180.00	215.00-225.00
*	CHICK GIRL HUM-57	CL	*	450.00-1000.00
*	CHICK GIRL HUM-57/2/O	OP	125.00	145.00-150.00
*	CHICK GIRL HUM-57/I	OP	220.00	275.00-950.00
*	CHICK GIRL HUM-57/O	OP	145.00	165.00-575.00
*	CHICK GIRL, BOX (NEW STYLE) HUM III-57	TW	*	150.00-200.00
*	CHICK GIRL, BOX (OLD STYLE) HUM-III-57	CL	*	425.00-750.00
*	CHICKEN-LICKEN HUM-385	OP	240.00	280.00-1500.00
*	CHILD IN BED, LOOKING LEFT HUM-137 A	CL	*	5000.00-7000.00
*	CHILD IN BED, LOOKING RIGHT HUM-137 B	CL	*	75.00-500.00
*	CHILD IN BED, PLAQUE HUM-137	OP	55.00	65.00-75.00
*	CHIMNEY SWEEP HUM-12	CL	*	375.00-800.00
*	CHIMNEY SWEEP HUM-12/2/O	OP	110.00	120.00-300.00
*	CHIMNEY SWEEP HUM-12/I	OP	180.00	215.00-775.00
*	CHRIST CHILD HUM-18	TW	*	125.00-500.00
*	CHRISTMAS SONG HUM-343	OP	180.00	215.00-5000.00
*	CINDERELLA HUM-337	OP	240.00	285.00-5000.00
*	CLOSE HARMONY HUM-336	OP	240.00	285.00-5000.00
*	CONFIDENTIALLY HUM-314	OP	230.00	285.00-5000.00
*	CONGRATULATIONS HUM-17/2	CL	*	4500.00-8000.00
*	CONGRATULATIONS HUM-17/O	OP	160.00	200.00-700.00
*	COQUETTES HUM-179	OP	230.00	285.00-1000.00
*	CROSSROADS HUM-331	OP	350.00	400.00-5000.00
*	CULPRITS HUM-56	CL	*	750.00-950.00
*	CULPRITS HUM-56 A	OP	245.00	290.00-625.00
*	CULPRITS, TABLE LAMP HUM-44	CL	*	600.00-750.00
*	CULPRITS, TABLE LAMP HUM-44 A	TW	*	300.00-600.00
*	DOCTOR HUM-127	OP	135.00	155.00-575.00
*	DOLL BATH HUM-319	OP	230.00	285.00-5000.00
*	DOLL MOTHER HUM-67	OP	190.00	210.00-750.00
*	DOLL MOTHER/PRAYER..BKENDS HUM-76 A&B	CL	*	12500.00
*	DUET (WITH "LIPS" BASE) HUM-130	CL	*	1250.00
*	DUET (WITHOUT TIES), HUM-130	CL	*	2250.00
*	DUET HUM-130	OP	225.00	280.00-950.00
*	EASTER GREETINGS! HUM-378	OP	185.00	200.00-1500.00
*	EVENTIDE (RARE) HUM-99	CL	*	3000.00-5000.00
*	EVENTIDE HUM-99	OP	290.00	325.00-1200.00
*	EVENTIDE, TABLE LAMP HUM-104	CL	*	8000.00-10000.00
*	FAREWELL HUM-65	CL	220.00	240.00-950.00
*	FAREWELL HUM-65/I	CL	*	265.00-950.00
*	FAREWELL HUM-65/O	CL	*	5000.00-8000.00
*	FAREWELL, TABLE LAMP HUM-103	CL	*	8000.00-10000.00
*	FARM BOY HUM-66	OP	190.00	225.00-800.00
*	FARM BOY/GOOSE GIRL BOOKENDS HUM-60 A&B	SU	*	350.00-1200.00
*	FAVORITE PET HUM-361	OP	230.00	285.00-1500.00
*	FEATHERED FRIENDS HUM-344	OP	220.00	275.00-5000.00
*	FEEDING TIME HUM-199	CL	*	500.00-950.00
*	FEEDING TIME HUM-199/I	OP	220.00	275.00-550.00
*	FEEDING TIME HUM-199/O	OP	160.00	195.00-450.00
*	FESTIVAL HARMONY (FLUTE) HUM-173	CL	*	1800.00
*	FESTIVAL HARMONY (FLUTE) HUM-173/II	TW	*	400.00-750.00
*	FESTIVAL HARMONY (FLUTE) HUM-173/O	OP	260.00	310.00-600.00
*	FESTIVAL HARMONY (MANDOLIN) HUM-172	CL	*	1800.00
*	FESTIVAL HARMONY (MANDOLIN) HUM-172/O	OP	260.00	310.00-600.00
*	FLITTING BUTTERFLY, PLAQUE HUM-139	OP	55.00	65.00-500.00
*	FLOWER VENDOR HUM-381	OP	200.00	245.00-1500.00
*	FLYING ANGEL HUM-366	CL	105.00	125.00-250.00
*	FOLLOW THE LEADER HUM-369	OP	1000.00	1200.00-5000.00
*	FOR FATHER HUM-87	OP	180.00	210.00-750.00
*	FOR MOTHER HUM-257	CL	*	205.00-800.00
*	FOR MOTHER HUM-257/2/O	OP	105.00	125.00
*	FOR MOTHER HUM-257/O	OP	170.00	200.00-205.00
*	FOREST SHRINE HUM-183	OP	460.00	530.00-1800.00
*	FRIENDS HUM-136	CL	*	2000.00-4000.00
*	FRIENDS HUM-136/I	OP	180.00	200.00-875.00
*	FRIENDS HUM-136/V	OP	1000.00	1200.00-4000.00
*	GAY ADVENTURE HUM-356	OP	160.00	190.00-3000.00
*	GIRL W/FIR TREE, CANDLESTICK HUM-116	OP	50.00	55.00-225.00
*	GIRL W/NOSEGAY, CANDLESTICK HUM-115	OP	50.00	55.00-225.00
*	GIRL WITH DOLL HUM-239 B	OP	45.00	55.00-100.00
*	GIRL WITH NOSEGAY HUM-239 A	OP	45.00	55.00-100.00
*	GIRL WITH SHEET OF MUSIC HUM-389	OP	70.00	85.00-200.00
*	GIRL WITH TRUMPET HUM-391	OP	70.00	85.00-200.00

YR	NAME	LIMIT	ISSUE	TREND
*	GLOBE TROTTER HUM-79	CL	170.00	190.000-725.00
*	GOING TO GRANDMA'S HUM-52	CL	*	850.00-1600.00
*	GOING TO GRANDMA'S HUM-52/I	TW	*	370.00-1500.00
*	GOING TO GRANDMA'S HUM-52/O	OP	230.00	260.00-950.00
*	GOOD FRIENDS HUM-182	OP	160.00	195.00-700.00
*	GOOD FRIENDS, BOOKENDS HUM-251 A&B	TW	*	275.00-700.00
*	GOOD FRIENDS, TABLE LAMP HUM-228	TW	*	275.00-750.00
*	GOOD HUNTING HUM-307	OP	200.00	245.00-5000.00
*	GOOD SHEPHERD HUM-42/I	CL	*	7000.00
*	GOOD SHEPHERD HUM-42/O	OP	200.00	250.00-800.00
*	GOOSE GIRL HUM-47	CL	*	850.00
*	GOOSE GIRL HUM-47/3/O	OP	145.00	165.00-600.00
*	GOOSE GIRL HUM-47/II	OP	380.00	400.00-1300.00
*	GOOSE GIRL HUM-47/O	OP	185.00	225.00-750.00
*	GUIDING ANGEL HUM-357	OP	70.00	85.00-200.00
*	HAPPINESS HUM-86	OP	110.00	130.00-450.00
*	HAPPY BIRTHDAY HUM-176	CL	*	550.00-1000.00
*	HAPPY BIRTHDAY HUM-176/I	OP	250.00	295.00-1000.00
*	HAPPY BIRTHDAY HUM-176/O	OP	180.00	210.00-475.00
*	HAPPY DAYS HUM-150	CL	*	900.00-1600.00
*	HAPPY DAYS HUM-150/2/O	OP	150.00	170.00-375.00
*	HAPPY DAYS HUM-150/I	OP	400.00	450.00-1500.00
*	HAPPY DAYS HUM-150/O	OP	250.00	300.00-600.00
*	HAPPY DAYS, TABLE LAMP HUM-232	TW	*	400.00-1500.00
*	HAPPY DAYS, TABLE LAMP HUM-235	TW	*	350.00-1000.00
*	HAPPY PASTIME HUM-69	OP	135.00	160.00-575.00
*	HAPPY PASTIME, ASHTRAY HUM-62	TW	*	130.00-600.00
*	HAPPY PASTIME, BOX (NEW STYLE)HUM III/69	TW	*	150.00-200.00
*	HAPPY PASTIME,BOX (OLD STYLE) HUM III/69	CL	*	425.00-750.00
*	HAPPY TRAVELIER, HUM-109	CL	*	1400.00
*	HAPPY TRAVELLER HUM-109	CL	*	175.00
*	HAPPY TRAVELLER HUM-109/II	CL	*	350.00-850.00
*	HAPPY TRAVELLER HUM-109/O	OP	120.00	140.00-300.00
*	HAPPY TRAVELLER, 7 3/4 IN. HUM-109	CL	*	1250.00
*	HEAR YE, HEAR YE HUM-15	CL	*	1400.00-1700.00
*	HEAR YE, HEAR YE HUM-15/2/O	OP	125.00	145.00-150.00
*	HEAR YE, HEAR YE HUM-15/I	OP	200.00	250.00-850.00
*	HEAR YE, HEAR YE HUM-15/II	TW	400.00	450.00-1500.00
*	HEAR YE, HEAR YE HUM-15/O	OP	*	200.00-700.00
*	HEAVENLY ANGEL HUM-21/I	OP	210.00	250.00-900.00
*	HEAVENLY ANGEL HUM-21/II	TW	390.00	425.00-1600.00
*	HEAVENLY ANGEL HUM-21/O	OP	100.00	120.00-425.00
*	HEAVENLY ANGEL HUM-21/O 1/2	OP	170.00	215.00-750.00
*	HEAVENLY LULLABY HUM-262	OP	155.00	185.00-800.00
*	HEAVENLY PROTECTION HUM-88	CL	*	850.00-2300.00
*	HEAVENLY PROTECTION HUM-88/I	OP	370.00	425.00-650.00
*	HEAVENLY PROTECTION HUM-88/II	TW	590.00	625.00-1200.00
*	HEAVENLY SONG, CANDLEHOLDER, HUM-113	CL	*	3000.00-10000.00
*	HELLO HUM-124	CL	*	400.00-1000.00
*	HELLO HUM-124/I	TW	*	240.00-1000.00
*	HELLO HUM-124/O	OP	180.00	215.00 400.00
*	HERALD ANGELS, CANDLEHOLDER HUM-37	TW	*	175.00 700.00
*	HOLY CHILD HUM-70	TW	*	160.00-700.00
*	HOLY WATER FONT, ANGEL CLOUD HUM-206	OP	45.00	50.00-500.00
*	HOLY WATER FONT, ANGEL DUET HUM-146	OP	45.00	50.00-200.00
*	HOLY WATER FONT, ANGEL SHRINE HUM-147	OP	45.00	50.00-250.00
*	HOLY WATER FONT, ANGEL SITTING HUM-167	OP	45.00	50.00-300.00
*	HOLY WATER FONT, ANGEL W/BIRD HUM-22	CL	*	250.00-275.00
*	HOLY WATER FONT, ANGEL W/BIRD HUM-22/I	CL	*	300.00-600.00
*	HOLY WATER FONT, ANGEL W/BIRD HUM-22/O	OP	35.00	40.00-250.00
*	HOLY WATER FONT, ANGEL/NEWS HUM-242	CL	*	1500.00
*	HOLY WATER FONT, ANGEL/PRAYER HUM-91 A&B	OP	70.00	80.00-500.00
*	HOLY WATER FONT, ANGELS AT PRAYER HUM-91	CL	*	400.00-500.00
*	HOLY WATER FONT, CHILD JESUS HUM-26	CL	*	300.00-500.00
*	HOLY WATER FONT, CHILD JESUS HUM-26/I	CL	200.00	200.00-500.00
*	HOLY WATER FONT, CHILD JESUS HUM-26/O	OP	35.00	40.00-250.00
*	HOLY WATER FONT, CHILD W/FLOWERS HUM-36	CL	*	275.00-425.00
*	HOLY WATER FONT, CHILD/FLOWERS HUM-36/I	CL	*	150.00-400.00
*	HOLY WATER FONT, CHILD/FLOWERS HUM-36/O	OP	35.00	40.00-250.00
*	HOLY WATER FONT, CROSS WITH DOVES HUM-77	CL	*	5000.00-10000.00
*	HOLY WATER FONT, GOOD SHEPHERD HUM-35	CL	*	375.00-425.00
*	HOLY WATER FONT, GOOD SHEPHERD HUM-35/I	CL	*	150.00-400.00
*	HOLY WATER FONT, GOOD SHEPHERD HUM-35/O	OP	35.00	40.00-250.00
*	HOLY WATER FONT, GUARD. ANGEL HUM-248/I	CL	*	1300.00-1500.00
*	HOLY WATER FONT, GUARD. ANGEL HUM-248/O	OP	45.00	50.00-250.00
*	HOLY WATER FONT, GUARDIAN ANGEL HUM 29/0	CL	*	950.00-1500.00
*	HOLY WATER FONT, GUARDIAN ANGEL HUM 29/I	CL	*	1500.00-2000.00
*	HOLY WATER FONT, GUARDIAN ANGEL HUM-29	CL	*	1300.00-1500.00
*	HOLY WATER FONT, HEAVENLY ANGEL HUM-207	OP	45.00	50.00-500.00
*	HOLY WATER FONT, HOLY FAMILY HUM-246	OP	45.00	50.00-275.00
*	HOLY WATER FONT, MADONNA W/CHILD HUM-243	OP	45.00	50.00-275.00
*	HOLY WATER FONT, WHITE ANGEL HUM-75	OP	35.00	40.00-250.00
*	HOLY WATER FONT, WORSHIP HUM-164	OP	45.00	50.00-300.00
*	HOLY WATER FONT,ANGEL W/BIRD HUM-354C	CL	*	*
*	HOLY WATER FONT,ANGEL W/LANTERN HUM-354A	CL	*	*
*	HOLY WATER FONT,ANGEL W/TRUMPET	CL	*	*
*	HOME FROM MARKET HUM-198	CL	*	425.00-750.00
*	HOME FROM MARKET HUM-198/2/O	OP	120.00	145.00-325.00
*	HOME FROM MARKET HUM-198/I	OP	180.00	210.00-475.00

YR	NAME	LIMIT	ISSUE	TREND
*	HOMEWARD BOUND HUM-334	OP	295.00	330.00-5000.00
*	HUM-253 GIRL W/BASKET	CL	*	*
*	HUM-254 GIRL PLAYING A MANDOLIN	CL	*	*
*	JOYFUL & LET'S SING WD BOOKENDS, HUM-120	CL	*	15000.00
*	JOYFUL HUM-53	OP	100.00	120.00-425.00
*	JOYFUL, ASHTRAY HUM-33	TW	*	140.00-600.00
*	JOYFUL, BOX (OLD STYLE) HUM III/53	CL	*	425.00-500.00
*	JOYFUL, BOX(NEW STYLE)HUM III/53	CL	*	180.00-200.00
*	JOYOUS NEWS HUM-27/3	CL	*	220.00-2000.00
*	JOYOUS NEWS HUM-27/I	CL	*	250.00-500.00
*	JOYOUS NEWS HUM-27/III	OP	180.00	215.00-220.00
*	JUST RESTING HUM-112	CL	*	650.00-800.00
*	JUST RESTING HUM-112/3/O	OP	125.00	145.00-500.00
*	JUST RESTING HUM-112/I	OP	225.00	280.00-750.00
*	JUST RESTING, TABLE LAMP HUM II/112	CL	*	350.00-700.00
*	JUST RESTING, TABLE LAMP HUM-225	CL	*	475.00-800.00
*	JUST RESTING, TABLE LAMP HUM-225/I	TW	*	290.00-550.00
*	JUST RESTING, TABLE LAMP HUM-225/II	TW	*	340.00-700.00
*	KISS ME HUM-311	OP	230.00	285.00-5000.00
*	KNITTING LESSON HUM-256	OP	440.00	500.00-1100.00
*	LATEST NEWS HUM-184	OP	240.00	290.00-1000.00
*	LET'S SING HUM-110	CL	*	400.00
*	LET'S SING HUM-110/I	OP	140.00	165.00-350.00
*	LET'S SING HUM-110/O	OP	105.00	125.00-450.00
*	LET'S SING, ASHTRAY HUM-114	TW	*	130.00-1000.00
*	LET'S SING, BOX (NEW STYLE) III/110	TW	*	150.00-200.00
*	LET'S SING, BOX (OLD STYLE) III/110	CL	*	425.00-750.00
*	LETTER TO SANTA HUM-340	OP	285.00	330.00-5000.00
*	LITTLE BAND (ON BASE) HUM-392	TW	*	220.00-350.00
*	LITTLE BAND ON MUSIC BOX	TW	*	330.00-400.00
*	LITTLE BAND, CANDLEHOLDER/BOX HUM-388	TW	*	220.00-350.00
*	LITTLE BOOKKEEPER HUM-306	OP	240.00	285.00-5000.00
*	LITTLE CELLIST HUM-89	CL	*	1500.00
*	LITTLE CELLIST HUM-89/I	OP	180.00	210.00-750.00
*	LITTLE CELLIST HUM-89/II	TW	380.00	400.00-1400.00
*	LITTLE DRUMMER HUM-240	OP	125.00	145.00-350.00
*	LITTLE FIDDLER HUM-2/4/O	OP	80.00	105.00
*	LITTLE FIDDLER HUM-2/I	TW	370.00	400.00-1500.00
*	LITTLE FIDDLER HUM-2/II	TW	*	1200.00-3500.00
*	LITTLE FIDDLER HUM-2/III	TW	*	1300.00-4000.00
*	LITTLE FIDDLER HUM-2/O	OP	190.00	215.00-750.00
*	LITTLE FIDDLER HUM-4	OP	170.00	200.00-725.00
*	LITTLE FIDDLER, PLAQUE HUM-93	TW	*	140.00-525.00
*	LITTLE FIDDLER,PLAQUE (RARE) HUM-93	CL	*	3000.00-5000.00
*	LITTLE FIDDLER/PLAQ. WD FRAME, HUM-107	CL	*	5000.00-6000.00
*	LITTLE GABRIEL HUM-32/I	CL	*	1200.00-2500.00
*	LITTLE GABRIEL HUM-32/O	CL	*	145.00-500.00
*	LITTLE GABRIEL, 5 IN. HUM-32	OP	115.00	140.00-155.00
*	LITTLE GABRIEL, HUM-32	CL	*	1500.00-2500.00
*	LITTLE GARDENER HUM-74	OP	100.00	120.00-425.00
*	LITTLE GOAT HERDER HUM-200	CL	*	475.00-825.00
*	LITTLE GOAT HERDER HUM-200/I	OP	200.00	235.00-525.00
*	LITTLE GOAT HERDER HUM-200/O	OP	160.00	195.00-450.00
*	LITTLE GOAT HERDER, BOOKENDS HUM-250 A&B	TW	*	275.00-700.00
*	LITTLE GUARDIAN HUM-145	OP	125.00	145.00-500.00
*	LITTLE HELPER HUM-73	OP	100.00	120.00-425.00
*	LITTLE HIKER HUM-16	CL	*	450.00-750.00
*	LITTLE HIKER HUM-16/2/O	OP	100.00	120.00-425.00
*	LITTLE HIKER HUM-16/I	OP	180.00	215.00-650.00
*	LITTLE PHARMACIST HUM-322	OP	200.00	240.00-5000.00
*	LITTLE SCHOLAR HUM-80	OP	180.00	210.00-750.00
*	LITTLE SHOPPER HUM-96	OP	120.00	135.00-500.00
*	LITTLE SWEEPER HUM-171/4/O	OP	80.00	105.00
*	LITTLE SWEEPER HUM-171/O	OP	110.00	135.00-140.00
*	LITTLE TAILOR HUM-308	OP	200.00	245.00-5000.00
*	LITTLE THRIFTY, BANK HUM-118	OP	130.00	145.00-650.00
*	LOST SHEEP HUM-68	CL	*	300.00-700.00
*	LOST SHEEP HUM-68/2/O	CL	125.00	135.00-325.00
*	LOST SHEEP HUM-68/O	CL	180.00	190.00-425.00
*	LOST STOCKING HUM-374	OP	120.00	140.00-4000.00
*	LULLABY, CANDLEHOLDER HUM-24/I	TW	*	170.00-650.00
*	LULLABY, CANDLEHOLDER HUM-24/III	TW	*	450.00-1800.00
*	M.I. HUMMEL (ENGLISH), PLAQUE HUM-187 A	OP	75.00	75.00-225.00
*	MADONNA PLAQUE(WHITE OVERGLAZE)HUM 48/II	CL	*	400.00-500.00
*	MAIL IS HERE, THE-PLAQUE HUM-140	TW	*	225.00-900.00
*	MAIL IS HERE, THE-HUM-226	OP	470.00	530.00-1250.00
*	MAIL IS HERE, THE-PLAQ. OVERGLAZE HUM140	CL	*	1250.00
*	MARCH WINDS HUM-43	OP	135.00	155.00-575.00
*	MAX AND MORITZ HUM-123	OP	190.00	215.00-750.00
*	MEDITATION HUM-13/2/O	OP	120.00	140.00-325.00
*	MEDITATION HUM-13/II	TW	*	350.00-5000.00
*	MEDITATION HUM-13/O	OP	190.00	215.00-800.00
*	MEDITATION HUM-13/V	TW	*	1200.00-5000.00
*	MEDITATION, HUM-13	CL	*	4000.00-5000.00
*	MERRY WANDERER HUM-11	CL	*	550.00-700.00
*	MERRY WANDERER HUM-11/2/O	OP	115.00	135.00-500.00
*	MERRY WANDERER HUM-11/O	OP	160.00	195.00-650.00
*	MERRY WANDERER HUM-7/I	TW	360.00	400.00-1600.00
*	MERRY WANDERER HUM-7/II	TW	1100.00	1200.00-3500.00

YR	NAME	LIMIT	ISSUE	TREND
*	MERRY WANDERER HUM-7/III	TW	*	1250.00-4000.00
*	MERRY WANDERER HUM-7/O	OP	220.00	275.00-950.00
*	MERRY WANDERER HUM-7/X	TW	*	12000.00-20000.00
*	MERRY WANDERER, PLAQUE HUM-92	TW	*	140.00-525.00
*	MERRY WANDERER/PLAQ. WD FRAME, HUM-106	CL	*	5000.00-6000.00
*	MISCHIEF MAKER HUM-342	OP	220.00	275.00-5000.00
*	MOTHER'S DARLING HUM-175	OP	180.00	210.00-750.00
*	MOTHER'S HELPER HUM-133	OP	160.00	195.00-650.00
*	MOUNTAINEER HUM-315	OP	180.00	210.00-5000.00
*	NOT FOR YOU! HUM-317	OP	200.00	240.00-5000.00
*	ON SECRET PATH HUM-386	OP	210.00	245.00-1500.00
*	OUT OF DANGER HUM-56 B	OP	245.00	290.00-625.00
*	OUT OF DANGER, TABLE LAMP, HUM-44 B	TW	*	300.00-600.00
*	PHOTOGRAPHER HUM-178	OP	230.00	285.00-1000.00
*	PLAYMATES HUM-58	CL	*	450.00-1000.00
*	PLAYMATES HUM-58/2/O	OP	125.00	145.00-150.00
*	PLAYMATES HUM-58/I	OP	220.00	275.00-950.00
*	PLAYMATES HUM-58/O	OP	145.00	165.00-575.00
*	PLAYMATES, BOX (NEW STYLE) HUM III/58	TW	*	150.00-200.00
*	PLAYMATES, BOX (OLD STYLE) HUM III/58	CL	*	425.00-750.00
*	PLAYMATES/CHICK GIRL BOOKENDS HUM-61 A&B	SU	*	350.00-1200.00
*	PLAYMATES/CHICK GIRL/BOOKENDS HUM 61 A&B	TW	*	350.00-1200.00
*	POSTMAN HUM-119/2/O	OP	115.00	135.00-140.00
*	POSTMAN HUM-119/O	OP	170.00	200.00-205.00
*	PRAYER BEFORE BATTLE HUM-20	OP	145.00	165.00-600.00
*	PRAYER BEFORE BATTLE, ASHTRAY HUM-19	CL	*	5000.00-10000.00
*	PUPPY LOVE & SERENADE/DOG BKENDS HUM-122	CL	*	15000.00
*	PUPPY LOVE HUM-1	RT	125.00	250.00-925.00
*	QUARTET, PLAQUE HUM-134	TW	*	240.00-950.00
*	RETEAT TO SAFETY HUM-201	CL	*	600.00-1100.00
*	RETREAT TO SAFETY HUM-201/2/O	OP	140.00	160.00-400.00
*	RETREAT TO SAFETY HUM-201/I	OP	250.00	300.00-650.00
*	RETREAT TO SAFETY, PLAQUE HUM-126	TW	*	175.00-600.00
*	RIDE INTO CHRISTMAS HUM-396	CL	*	450.00-2500.00
*	RIDE INTO CHRISTMAS HUM-396/2/O	OP	200.00	235.00-245.00
*	RIDE INTO CHRISTMAS HUM-396/I	OP	360.00	425.00-440.00
*	RING AROUND THE ROSIE HUM-348	OP	2300.00	2600.00-5000.00
*	RUN-A-WAY HUM-327	OP	210.00	250.00-5000.00
*	SAINT GEORGE HUM-55	OP	280.00	320.00-3000.00
*	SCHOOL BOY HUM-82	CL	*	550.00-700.00
*	SCHOOL BOY HUM-82/2/O	OP	120.00	140.00-525.00
*	SCHOOL BOY HUM-82/II	OP	380.00	450.00-1500.00
*	SCHOOL BOY HUM-82/O	OP	160.00	195.00-675.00
*	SCHOOL BOYS HUM-170	CL	*	2100.00-5000.00
*	SCHOOL BOYS HUM-170/I	OP	1000.00	1200.00-1500.00
*	SCHOOL BOYS HUM-170/III	CL	*	1800.00-2200.00
*	SCHOOL GIRL HUM-81	CL	*	325.00-700.00
*	SCHOOL GIRL HUM-81/2/O	OP	120.00	140.00-500.00
*	SCHOOL GIRL HUM-81/O	OP	160.00	195.00-650.00
*	SCHOOL GIRLS HUM-177	CL	*	2100.00-5000.00
*	SCHOOL GIRLS HUM-177/I	OP	1000.00	1200.00-1500.00
*	SCHOOL GIRLS HUM-177/III	CL	*	1800.00-2200.00
*	SENSITIVE HUNTER HUM-6	CL	*	700.00-900.00
*	SENSITIVE HUNTER HUM-6/2/O	OP	125.00	145.00-150.00
*	SENSITIVE HUNTER HUM-6/I	OP	210.00	250.00-900.00
*	SENSITIVE HUNTER HUM-6/II	TW	*	350.00-2000.00
*	SENSITIVE HUNTER HUM-6/O	OP	160.00	195.00-675.00
*	SERENADE HUM-85	CL	*	750.00-1500.00
*	SERENADE HUM-85/4/O	OP	80.00	105.00
*	SERENADE HUM-85/II	OP	380.00	450.00-1400.00
*	SERENADE HUM-85/O	OP	110.00	130.00-450.00
*	SHE LOVES ME, SHE LOVES ME NOT! HUM-174	OP	150.00	190.00-650.00
*	SHE LOVES ME..NOT, TABLE LAMP HUM-227	TW	*	275.00-750.00
*	SHEPHERD'S BOY HUM-64	OP	185.00	225.00-750.00
*	SHINING LIGHT HUM-358	OP	70.00	85.00-200.00
*	SHRINE, TABLE LAMP HUM-100	CL	*	8000.00-10000.00
*	SIGNS OF SPRING HUM-203	CL	*	550.00-1000.00
*	SIGNS OF SPRING HUM-203/2/O	CL	*	200.00-1200.00
*	SIGNS OF SPRING HUM-203/I	CL	*	250.00-575.00
*	SILENT NIGHT CANDLEHLDR/BLK CHILD HUM-54	CL	*	7500.00-10000.00
*	SILENT NIGHT, CANDLEHOLDER HUM-54	TW	*	270.00-1000.00
*	SILENT NIGHT/BLK CHILD/ADVENT GRP HUM-31	CL	*	20000.00-25000.00
*	SILENT NIGHT/WHT CHILD.ADVENT GRP HUM-31	CL	*	12500.00
*	SINGING LESSON (WITHOUT BASE) HUM-41	CL	*	5000.00-10000.00
*	SINGING LESSON HUM-63	OP	100.00	120.00-425.00
*	SINGING LESSON, ASHTRAY HUM-34	TW	*	140.00-600.00
*	SINGING LESSON, BOX(NEW STYLE)HUM III/63	TW	*	150.00-200.00
*	SINGING LESSON,BOX(OLD STYLE)HUM III/63	CL	*	425.00-750.00
*	SISTER HUM-98	CL	*	285.00-650.00
*	SISTER HUM-98/2/O	OP	120.00	135.00-225.00
*	SISTER HUM-98/O	OP	165.00	200.00-300.00
*	SKIER HUM-59	OP	185.00	200.00-775.00
*	SMART LITTLE SISTER HUM-346	OP	210.00	250.00-5000.00
*	SOLIDIER BOY HUM-332	OP	180.00	210.00-5000.00
*	SOLOIST HUM-135	CL	*	135.00-475.00
*	SOLOIST HUM-135/4/O	OP	80.00	105.00
*	SOLOIST HUM-135/O	OP	110.00	130.00-135.00
*	SPRING CHEER HUM-72	TW	*	175.00-600.00
*	SPRING DANCE HUM-353/I	TW	*	500.00-2000.00

Celestial Musician *plays an angelic tune. He is just one of many children captured by artist Sister Maria Innocentia Hummel.*

M.I. Hummel's Pleasant Journey *is the second issue in the Goebel "Century Collection."*

This delightful pair of Bavarian children are Going Home. *The figure is produced by Goebel from the artwork of M.I. Hummel.*

Sister Maria Innocentia Hummel's Hear Ye, Hear Ye *is hand painted in the unmistakable Goebel earthtones.*

YR	NAME	LIMIT	ISSUE	TREND
*	SPRING DANCE HUM-353/O	OP	*	310.00-4000.00
*	STANDING BOY, PLAQUE HUM-168	TW	*	175.00-1000.00
*	STAR GAZER HUM-132	OP	180.00	205.00-750.00
*	STITCH IN TIME HUM-255	CL	*	290.00-750.00
*	STITCH IN TIME HUM-255/4/O	OP	80.00	100.00
*	STITCH IN TIME HUM-255/O	OP	230.00	285.00-290.00
*	STORMY WEATHER HUM-71	CL	*	460.00-1250.00
*	STORMY WEATHER HUM-71/2/O	OP	250.00	300.00-310.00
*	STORMY WEATHER HUM-71/I	OP	380.00	450.00-460.00
*	STREET SINGER HUM-131	OP	155.00	190.00-650.00
*	STROLLING ALONG HUM-5	CL	120.00	225.00-900.00
*	SUPREME PROTECTION HUM-364	CL	*	300.00-600.00
*	SUPREME PROTECTION HUM-364 (ALTERED J)	CL	*	600.00-850.00
*	SURPRISE HUM-94	CL	*	450.00-950.00
*	SURPRISE HUM-94/3/O	OP	130.00	150.00-500.00
*	SURPRISE HUM-94/I	OP	235.00	285.00-900.00
*	SWAYING LULLABY, PLAQUE HUM-165	TW	*	175.00-1000.00
*	SWEET MUSIC HUM-186	OP	160.00	200.00-700.00
*	TELLING HER SECRET HUM-196	CL	*	725.00-1350.00
*	TELLING HER SECRET HUM-196/I	TW	*	375.00-875.00
*	TELLING HER SECRET HUM-196/O	OP	250.00	295.00-675.00
*	TINY BABY IN CRIB, WALL PLAQ., HUM-138	CL	*	3000.00-4000.00
*	TO MARKET HUM-49	CL	*	600.00-1700.00
*	TO MARKET HUM-49/3/O	OP	140.00	160.00-600.00
*	TO MARKET HUM-49/I	TW	*	425.00-1700.00
*	TO MARKET HUM-49/O	OP	225.00	285.00-950.00
*	TO MARKET, TABLE LAMP HUM-101	CL	*	500.00-1000.00
*	TO MARKET, TABLE LAMP HUM-223	TW	*	375.00-700.00
*	TO MARKET,TABLE LAMP(PL. POST) HUM-101	CL	*	6000.00-10000.00
*	TO MARKET,TBL LAMP TREE TRK POST HUM-101	CL	*	1500.00-2000.00
*	TRUMPET BOY HUM-97	OP	110.00	130.00-475.00
*	TUNEFUL ANGEL HUM-359	OP	70.00	85.00-200.00
*	TUNEFUL GOOD NIGHT, PLAQUE HUM-180	TW	*	175.00-750.00
*	UMBRELLA BOY HUM-152	CL	*	2200.00-6000.00
*	UMBRELLA BOY HUM-152 A	CL	*	1500.00-2500.00
*	UMBRELLA BOY HUM-152/II A	OP	1200.00	1450.00-1600.00
*	UMBRELLA BOY HUM-152/O A	OP	490.00	575.00-1500.00
*	UMBRELLA GIRL HUM-152 B	CL	*	1500.00-6000.00
*	UMBRELLA GIRL HUM-152/II B	OP	1200.00	1450.00-1600.00
*	UMBRELLA GIRL HUM-152/O B	OP	490.00	575.00-1500.00
*	VACATION TIME, PLAQUE HUM-125	TW	*	175.00-700.00
*	VILLAGE BOY HUM-51	CL	*	850.00-1100.00
*	VILLAGE BOY HUM-51/2/O	OP	115.00	140.00-500.00
*	VILLAGE BOY HUM-51/3/O	OP	100.00	120.00-425.00
*	VILLAGE BOY HUM-51/I	TW	*	250.00-1000.00
*	VILLAGE BOY HUM-51/O	OP	195.00	250.00-825.00
*	VISITING AN INVALID HUM-382	OP	185.00	200.00-1500.00
*	VOLUNTEER TABLE LAMP, HUM-102	CL	*	8000.00-10000.00
*	VOLUNTEERS HUM-50	CL	*	1200.00-1500.00
*	VOLUNTEERS HUM-50/2/O	OP	190.00	215.00-450.00
*	VOLUNTEERS HUM-50/I	TW	*	425.00-1400.00
*	VOLUNTEERS HUM-50/O	OP	250.00	295.00-1000.00
*	WAITER HUM-154	CL	*	550.00-1100.00
*	WAITER HUM-154/I	OP	240.00	285.00-950.00
*	WAITER HUM-154/O	OP	180.00	210.00-725.00
*	WAITER W/WHISKY HUM 154/0	CL	*	1500.00-2000.00
*	WASH DAY HUM-321/4/O	OP	80.00	105.00
*	WASH DAY HUM-321/O	OP	230.00	285.00-290.00
*	WATCHFUL ANGEL HUM-194	OP	270.00	310.00-2000.00
*	WAYSIDE DEVOTION HUM-28	CL	*	1600.00-1850.00
*	WAYSIDE DEVOTION HUM-28/II	OP	370.00	410.00-1400.00
*	WAYSIDE DEVOTION HUM-28/III	OP	480.00	540.00-1600.00
*	WAYSIDE HARMONY HUM-111	CL	*	650.00-800.00
*	WAYSIDE HARMONY HUM-111/3/O	OP	125.00	145.00-500.00
*	WAYSIDE HARMONY HUM-111/I	OP	220.00	270.00-750.00
*	WAYSIDE HARMONY, TABLE LAMP HUM II/111	CL	*	350.00-750.00
*	WAYSIDE HARMONY, TABLE LAMP HUM-224	CL	*	475.00-800.00
*	WAYSIDE HARMONY, TABLE LAMP HUM-224/I	TW	*	290.00-550.00
*	WAYSIDE HARMONY, TABLE LAMP HUM-224/II	TW	*	340.00-700.00
*	WE CONGRATULATE (WITH BASE) HUM-220	OP	135.00	150.00-375.00
*	WEARY WANDERER HUM-204	OP	200.00	250.00-800.00
*	WHICH HAND? HUM-258	OP	165.00	195.00-800.00
*	WHITSUNTIDE HUM-163	OP	270.00	300.00-1200.00
*	WORSHIP HUM-84	CL	*	450.00-1500.00
*	WORSHIP HUM-84/O	OP	135.00	160.00-525.00
*	WORSHIP HUM-84/V	TW	*	2000.00
41	HUM 148	CL	*	*
41	HUM 149	CL	*	*
43	HUM-155	CL	*	*
43	HUM-156	CL	*	*
43	HUM-158 GIRL STANDING WITH DOG IN ARMS	CL	*	*
43	HUM-159 GIRL STANDING W/FLOWERS IN ARMS	CL	*	*
43	HUM-160 GIRL STANDING TIERED DRESS/FLWRS	CL	*	*
43	HUM-161 GIRL STANDING HANDS IN POCKETS	CL	*	*
46	HUM-162 GIRL STANDING WITH HANDBAG	CL	*	*
47	FESTIVAL HARMONY (FLUTE) HUM-173	CL	95.00	1250.00
47	FESTIVAL HARMONY (FLUTE) HUM-173	CL	95.00	2500.00-3500.00
47	SWEET MUSIC W/STRIPPED SLIPPERS HUM-186	CL	*	1200.00-1600.00
48	COQUETTES HUM-179	OP	*	285.00-1000.00

YR	NAME	LIMIT	ISSUE	TREND
48	OLD MAN READING NEWSPAPER HUM-181	CL	*	15000.00-20000.00
48	OLD MAN READING NEWSPAPER/TBL LAMPHUM202	CL	*	15000.00-20000.00
48	OLD MAN WALKING TO MARKET HUM-191	CL	*	15000.00-20000.00
48	OLD WOMAN KNITTING HUM-189	CL	*	15000.00-20000.00
48	OLD WOMAN WALKING TO MARKET HUM-190	CL	*	15000.00-20000.00
48	SIGNS OF SPRING W/TWO SHOES HUM 203/2/O	CL	120.00	1200.00
50	FESTIVAL HARMONY (MANDOLIN) HUM-172	CL	95.00	1250.00
50	FESTIVAL HARMONY (MANDOLIN) HUM-172	CL	95.00	2500.00-3000.00
51	BIRTHDAY SERENADE HUM-218/1	CL	*	1250.00
51	HUM-215 JESUS STANDING W/LAMB IN ARMS	CL	*	*
51	ORCHESTRA HUM-212	CL	*	*
52	HAPPY PASTIME/CANDY JAR HUM-221	CL	*	5000.00-10000.00
52	LITTLE VELMA HUM-219	CL	*	5000.00-7000.00
52	WE CONGRATULATE W/BASE HUM-220/2/O	CL	*	450.00-550.00
54	HUM 236A & B	CL	*	12500.00
54	HUM-233 BOY FEEDING BIRDS	CL	*	*
55	HOLY WATER FONT, ANGEL JOYOUS NEWS H-241	CL	*	1250.00
55	HOLY WATER FONT, ANGEL JOYOUS NEWS H-242	CL	*	1250.00
55	HONEY LOVER HUM-312	CL	190.00	4000.00-5000.00
55	LITTLE PHARMACIST HUM-322	CL	*	2000.00-3000.00
55	MADONNA HOLDING CHILD HUM-151	CL	44.00	9000.00-12000.00
55	PROFESSOR, THE HUM-320	CL	180.00	4000.00-5000.00
55	STANDING MADONNA W/CHILD HUM-247	CL	*	12500.00
56	BIRTHDAY PRESENT HUM-341	CL	140.00	4000.00-5000.00
56	LETTER TO SANTA CLAUS HUM-340	CL	30.00	15000.00-20000.00
57	RING AROUND THE ROSIE HUM-348	CL	70.00	12500.00
62	GIRL W/ACCORDION HUM-259	CL	*	5000.00-10000.00
64	MORNING STROLL HUM-375	CL	170.00	3000.00-4000.00
72	CHICKEN-LICKEN HUM-385/4/O	OP	28.50	105.00
72	EASTER TIME HUM-384	OP	27.50	250.00-1500.00
72	RUN-A-WAY, THE HUM-327	OP	28.50	250.00-5000.00
74	POET, THE HUM-397	CL	220.00	2000.00-3000.00
78	LITTLE ARCHITECT, THE HUM-410	CL	290.00	2000.00-3000.00
79	BIRD WATCHER HUM-300	OP	80.00	215.00-5000.00
79	BOY AND GIRL, WALL VASE HUM-360 A	TW	*	140.00-650.00
79	BOY, WALL VASE HUM-360 B	TW	*	120.00-650.00
79	GIRL, WALL VASE HUM-360 C	TW	*	120.00-650.00
79	MERRY CHRISTMAS, PLAQUE HUM-323	OP	55.00	125.00-3000.00
79	SEARCHING ANGEL, PLAQUE HUM-310	OP	55.00	120.00-5000.00
80	VALENTINE JOY HUM-399	CL	95.00	5000.00-7500.00
81	DAISIES DON'T TELL HUM-380	CL	80.00	125.00
81	IN TUNE HUM-414	OP	115.00	280.00-3000.00
81	ON HOLIDAY "HOLIDAY SHOPPER" HUM-350	CL	85.00	4000.00-5000.00
81	ON HOLIDAY HUM-350	OP	85.00	170.00-3000.00
81	SWEET GREETINGS HUM-352	OP	85.00	200.00-3000.00
81	THOUGHTFUL HUM-415	OP	105.00	215.00-225.00
81	TIMID LITTLE SISTER HUM-394	OP	190.00	425.00-3000.00
82	BOTANIST HUM-351	OP	84.00	200.00-3000.00
82	LITTLE NURSE HUM-376	OP	95.00	245.00-4000.00
83	KNIT ONE, PURL ONE HUM-432	OP	52.00	120.00
83	WITH LOVING GREETINGS HUM-309	OP	80.00	190.00-5000.00
84	FESTIVAL HARMONY (MANDOLIN) HUM-172/II	CL	95.00	600.00-750.00
84	FLYING HIGH HUM-452	CL	75.00	150.00-250.00
84	JUST DOZING HUM-451	OP	220.00	220.00
85	BAKING DAY HUM-330	OP	95.00	275.00-5000.00
85	GOING HOME HUM-383	OP	125.00	310.00-4000.00
85	JUBILEE HUM-416	CL	200.00	425.00
85	JUST FISHING HUM-373	OP	85.00	225.00-4000.00
85	SING WITH ME HUM-405	OP	125.00	310.00-3000.00
87	GENTLE GLOW, CANDLEHOLDER HUM-439	OP	110.00	200.00-210.00
87	IN THE MEADOW HUM-459	OP	110.00	200.00-250.00
87	KINDERGARTNER HUM-467	OP	100.00	200.00-250.00
87	PEACE ON EARTH HUM-484	CL	80.00	135.00
87	SING ALONG HUM-433	OP	145.00	275.00-285.00
88	A BUDDING MAESTRO HUM-477	OP	45.00	130.00
88	ACCOMPANIST, THE HUM-453	OP	39.00	105.00
88	LITTLE SWEEPER HUM-171	CL	*	140.00-450.00
88	SONG OF PRAISE HUM-454	OP	39.00	105.00
88	SOUND THE TRUMPET HUM-457	OP	45.00	125.00
88	SOUNDS OF THE MANDOLIN HUM-438	OP	65.00	125.00
88	WINTER SONG HUM-476	OP	45.00	125.00
89	AN APPLE A DAY HUM-403	OP	195.00	275.00-3000.00
89	BIRTHDAY CAKE, CANDLEHOLDER HUM-338	OP	95.00	140.00-5000.00
89	BIRTHDAY PRESENT HUM-341/3/O	OP	140.00	140.00
89	CHRISTMAS ANGEL HUM-301	OP	160.00	250.00-5000.00
89	DADDY'S GIRLS HUM-371	OP	130.00	225.00-4000.00
89	FLYING ANGEL, HUM-366	OP	65.00	110.00
89	HOSANNA HUM-480	OP	68.00	125.00
89	I'LL PROTECT HIM HUM-483	OP	55.00	85.00-100.00
89	I'M HERE HUM-478	OP	50.00	125.00
89	IN D MAJOR HUM-430	OP	135.00	200.00-210.00
89	IS IT RAINING? HUM-420	OP	175.00	255.00-265.00
89	LOVE FROM ABOVE HUM-481	CL	75.00	135.00
89	MAKE A WISH HUM-475	OP	135.00	200.00-250.00
89	ONE FOR YOU, ONE FOR ME HUM-482	OP	50.00	125.00
89	POSTMAN HUM-119	CL	*	205.00-700.00
89	TUBA PLAYER HUM-437	OP	160.00	260.00-270.00
89	WASH DAY HUM-321	CL	*	285.00-5000.00
90	BATH TIME HUM-412	OP	300.00	375.00-3000.00

YR	NAME	LIMIT	ISSUE	TREND
90	GOOD FRIENDS, CANDLEHOLDER HUM-679	OP	142.50	146.00
90	GRANDMAS'S GIRL HUM-561	OP	100.00	145.00-175.00
90	GRANDPA'S BOY HUM-562	OP	100.00	145.00-175.00
90	HORSE TRAINER HUM-423	OP	155.00	215.00-225.00
90	SHE LOVES ME, CANDLEHOLDER HUM-678	OP	142.50	146.00
90	SLEEP TIGHT HUM-424	OP	155.00	215.00-225.00
90	WHAT'S NEW? HUM-418	OP	200.00	275.00-285.00
91	A NAP HUM-534	OP	95.00	150.00
91	ART CRITIC HUM-318	OP	230.00	285.00-5000.00
91	EVENING PRAYER HUM-495	OP	95.00	105.00
91	FRIEND OR FOE HUM-434	OP	190.00	215.00-225.00
91	GUARDIAN, THE- HUM-455	OP	140.00	165.00-190.00
91	LAND IN SIGHT HUM-530	CL	1600.00	1600.00-1800.00
91	PROFESSOR, THE- HUM-320/O	OP	180.00	200.00-5000.00
91	SCAMP HUM-553	OP	95.00	110.00
91	STORYBOOK TIME HUM-458	OP	330.00	380.00
91	WE WISH YOU THE BEST HUM-600	CL	1300.00	1400.00-1800.00
91	WHISTLER'S DUET HUM-413	OP	235.00	280.00-3000.00
92	A SWWET OFFERING HUM-549	OP	75.00	80.00
92	LUCKY FELLOW HUM-560	CL	75.00	100.00
92	MY WISH IS SMALL HUM-463/O	CL	170.00	200.00-250.00
93	A FREE FLIGHT HUM-569	OP	185.00	195.00
93	CELESTIAL MUSICIAN (MINI) HUM-188/4/0	OP	*	310.00-1500.00
93	LITTLE ARCHITECT HUM-410/I	OP	*	300.00-3000.00
93	ONE PLUS ONE HUM-556	CL	115.00	125.00
93	PARADE OF LIGHTS HUM-616	OP	235.00	250.00
94	CALL TO GLORY HUM-739	OP	250.00	250.00
94	FESTIVAL HARMONY (MANDOLIN) HUM-172/4/O	OP	95.00	95.00
94	HEAVENLY ANGEL TREE TOPPER HUM-755	OP	450.00	450.00
94	I'M CAREFREE HUM-633	OP	365.00	375.00-750.00
94	LITTLE VISITOR HUM-563	OP	180.00	180.00
94	MORNING STROLL HUM-375/3/O	OP	170.00	175.00
94	POET, THE HUM-397/I	OP	220.00	225.00
94	WE COME IN PEACE HUM-754	OP	350.00	350.00
95	ANGLER, THE HUM-566	OP	320.00	320.00
95	COME BACK SOON HUM-545	OP	135.00	135.00
95	FESTIVAL HARMONY (FLUTE) HUM-173/4/O	OP	95.00	95.00
95	GOOSE GIRL ANN. CLOCK HUM-750	OP	200.00	200.00
95	LUCKY BOY	15000	190.00	190.00
95	OOH, MY TOOTH HUM-533	OP	110.00	110.00
95	PIXIE HUM-768	OP	105.00	105.00
95	TO KEEP YOU WARM HUM-759	OP	195.00	195.00
96	A TUNEFUL TRIO	20000	450.00	450.00
96	BLOSSOM TIME	OP	155.00	155.00
96	CHRISTMAS SONG	OP	115.00	115.00
96	DELICIOUS	OP	155.00	155.00
96	LOVE'S BOUNTY	OP	1200.00	1200.00
96	NIMBLE FINGERS	OP	225.00	225.00
96	PEN PALS	OP	55.00	55.00
96	SHEPHARD BOY	OP	295.00	295.00
M.I. HUMMEL		**M.I. HUMMEL CENTURY COLLECTION**		
86	CHAPEL TIME, CLOCK HUM-442	CL	500.00	1500.00-3000.00
88	CALL TO WORSHIP, CLOCK HUM-441	CL	600.00	900.00-1150.00
89	HARMONY IN FOUR PARTS HUM-471	CL	850.00	1750.00-2000.00
90	LET'S TELL THE WORLD HUM-487	CL	875.00	1250.00-1500.00
92	ON OUR WAY HUM-472	CL	950.00	950.00-1200.00
93	WELCOME SPRING HUM-635	CL	1085.00	1200.00-1500.00
94	ROCK-A-BYE HUM 574	CL	1150.00	1200.00
95	STRIKE UP THE BAND HUM-668	OP	1200.00	1200.00
M.I. HUMMEL		**M.I. HUMMEL COLLECTORS CLUB ANNIVERSARY**		
90	FLOWER GIRL HUM-548	OP	105.00	165.00
90	LITTLE PAIR, THE- HUM-449	OP	170.00	275.00
91	HONEY LOVER HUM-312/I	CL	190.00	210.00-5000.00
M.I. HUMMEL		**M.I. HUMMEL COLLECTORS CLUB EXCLUSIVES**		
*	I BROUGHT YOU A GIFT HUM-479	CL	*	125.00
77	VALENTINE GIFT HUM-387	CL	45.00	600.00-3000.00
78	SMILING THROUGH, PLAQUE HUM-690	CL	50.00	200.00-250.00
80	VALENTINE JOY HUM-399	CL	95.00	250.00-7500.00
81	DAISIES DON'T TELL HUM-380	CL	80.00	350.00
82	IT'S COLD HUM-421	CL	80.00	300.00-350.00
83	WHAT NOW? HUM-422	CL	80.00	300.00-350.00
84	COFFEE BREAK HUM-409	CL	90.00	300.00-3000.00
85	SMILING THROUGH HUM-408	CL	125.00	300.00-350.00
86	BIRTHDAY CANDLE, CANDLEHOLDER HUM-440	CL	95.00	300.00-350.00
87	MORNING CONCERT HUM-447	CL	98.00	225.00-275.00
88	SURPRISE, THE- HUM-431	CL	125.00	275.00-325.00
89	HELLO WORLD HUM-429	CL	130.00	250.00-300.00
90	I WONDER HUM-486	CL	140.00	175.00-300.00
91	GIFT FROM A FRIEND HUM-485	CL	160.00	200.00-300.00
91	TWO HANDS, ONE TREAT HUM-493	CL	*	125.00
92	CHEEKY FELLOW HUM-554	CL	120.00	130.00
92	MY WISH IS SMALL HUM-463	CL	170.00	1500.00
93	I DIDN'T DO IT HUM-626	CL	175.00	175.00-200.00
93	SWEET AS CAN BE HUM-541	OP	125.00	125.00
94	AT GRANDPA'S HUM-621	10000	1300.00	1300.00
94	FOR KEEPS HUM-630	OP	*	80.00-100.00
94	LITTLE TROUBADOUR HUM-558	OP	130.00	130.00
95	A STORY FROM GRANDMA HUM 620	10000	1300.00	1300.00

YR	NAME	LIMIT	ISSUE	TREND
G. SKROBEK		**M.I. HUMMEL COLLECTORS CLUB EXCLUSIVES**		
79	BUST OF SISTER M.I. HUMMEL HU-3	CL	75.00	300.00-350.00
M.I. HUMMEL			**M.I. HUMMEL MADONNA**	
*	FLOWER MADONNA, COLOR HUM-10/I	CL	350.00	430.00-900.00
*	FLOWER MADONNA, COLOR HUM-10/III	CL	*	475.00-1250.00
*	FLOWER MADONNA, WHITE HUM-10/I	OP	165.00	165.00-600.00
*	FLOWER MADONNA, WHITE HUM-10/III	TW	*	300.00-750.00
*	MADONNA PLAQUE HUM-48	CL	*	600.00-800.00
*	MADONNA PLAQUE HUM-48/II	TW	*	120.00-750.00
*	MADONNA PLAQUE HUM-48/O	TW	*	75.00-350.00
*	MADONNA PLAQUE HUM-48/V	CL	*	1500.00
*	MADONNA W/HALO WHITE HUM-45/II	TW	150.00	150.00-350.00
*	MADONNA W/HALO, COLOR HUM-45/I	OP	105.00	125.00-350.00
*	MADONNA W/HALO, COLOR HUM-45/III	SU	*	150.00-600.00
*	MADONNA W/HALO, COLOR HUM-45/O	SU	*	60.00-275.00
*	MADONNA W/HALO, WHITE HUM-45	OP	*	32.00
*	MADONNA W/HALO, WHITE HUM-45/I	OP	70.00	70.00-200.00
*	MADONNA W/HALO, WHITE HUM-45/O	TW	*	40.00-175.00
*	MADONNA W/O HALO, COLOR HUM-46/I	TW	*	125.00-350.00
*	MADONNA W/O HALO, COLOR HUM-46/III	TW	*	150.00-600.00
*	MADONNA W/O HALO, COLOR HUM-46/O	TW	*	60.00-275.00
*	MADONNA W/O HALO, WHITE HUM-46/I	SU	*	70.00-200.00
*	MADONNA W/O HALO, WHITE HUM-46/III	SU	*	225.00
*	MADONNA W/O HALO, WHITE HUM-46/O	SU	*	40.00-175.00
77	MADONNA HOLDING CHILD, BLUE HUM-151	TW	*	850.00-3000.00
77	MADONNA HOLDING CHILD, WHITE HUM-151	TW	*	350.00-2500.00
M.I. HUMMEL			**M.I. HUMMEL NATIVITY**	
*	ANGEL KNEELING/SERENADE HUM-214D (COLOR)	OP	70.00	140.00
*	ANGEL KNEELING/SERENADE HUM-214D (WHITE)	CL	*	165.00-290.00
*	ANGEL SERENADE (LARGE) HUM-260E	SU	*	135.00-150.00
*	ANGEL SERENADE HUM-214/D	OP	*	90.00-290.00
*	ANGEL/GOOD NIGHT HUM-214C (COLOR)	OP	70.00	70.00-175.00
*	COW, LYING (LARGE) HUM-260M	SU	*	150.00-170.00
*	DONKEY HUM-214/J	OP	*	70.00-255.00
*	DONKEY HUM-214J (COLOR)	OP	60.00	70.00-155.00
*	DONKEY HUM-214J (WHITE)	CL	*	130.00-255.00
*	DONKEY, STANDING (LARGE) HUM-260L	SU	*	135.00-150.00
*	FLYING ANGEL HUM-366	OP	*	125.00-275.00
*	FLYING ANGEL HUM-366 (COLOR)	OP	105.00	125.00-250.00
*	FLYING ANGEL HUM-366 (WHITE)	OP	*	125.00-250.00
*	GOOD NIGHT (LARGE) HUM-260D	SU	*	140.00-160.00
*	GOOD NIGHT ANGEL HUM-214/C	OP	*	90.00-190.00
*	INFANT JESUS (LARGE) HUM-260C	SU	*	130.00
*	INFANT JESUS HUM-214A/K (COLOR)	OP	50.00	65.00-70.00
*	INFANT JESUS HUM-214A/K (WHITE)	CL	*	60.00-70.00
*	INFANT JESUS HUM-214A/K/1	OP	*	65.00
*	JOSEPH HUM-214/B	OP	*	175.00-420.00
*	JOSEPH HUM-214B (COLOR)	OP	150.00	175.00-390.00
*	JOSEPH HUM-214B (WHITE)	CL	*	145.00-420.00
*	KING ON ONE KNEE HUM 214/M	OP	*	175.00-475.00
*	KING ON ONE KNEE HUM-214 M/O	OP	*	140.00-145.00
*	KING ON ONE KNEE HUM-214M (COLOR)	OP	150.00	175.00-395.00
*	KING ON ONE KNEE HUM-214M (WHITE)	CL	*	225.00-475.00
*	KING ON TWO KNEES HUM-214 N/O	OP	*	135.00-140.00
*	KING STANDING HUM-214 L/O	OP	*	150.00-155.00
*	KING W/CASHBOX HUM 214/N	OP	*	160.00-475.00
*	KING, KNEE W/CASH BOX HUM-214N (COLOR)	OP	140.00	160.00-370.00
*	KING, KNEE W/CASH BOX HUM-214N (WHITE)	CL	*	225.00-475.00
*	KING, KNEELING (LARGE) HUM-260P	SU	*	470.00-500.00
*	KING, STANDING (LARGE) HUM-260O	SU	*	490.00-540.00
*	LAMB HUM-214/O	OP	*	20.00-130.00
*	LAMB HUM-214O	OP	*	55.00-130.00
*	LAMB HUM-214O (COLOR)	OP	18.00	20.00-50.00
*	LITTLE TOOTER (LARGE) HUM-260K	SU	*	170.00-195.00
*	MADONNA (LARGE) HUM-260A	SU	*	520.00-550.00
*	MOORISH KING STANDING HUM 214/L	OP	*	185.00-475.00
*	MOORISH KING, STANDING (LARGE) HUM-260N	SU	*	490.00-540.00
*	MOORISH KING, STANDING HUM-214L (COLOR)	OP	155.00	185.00-400.00
*	MOORISH KING, STANDING HUM-214L (WHITE)	CL	*	225.00-475.00
*	NATIVITY SET (LARGE) 16 PIECES HUM-260	TW	*	5000.00-5500.00
*	ONE SHEEP, LYING (LARGE) HUM-260R	SU	*	50.00-70.00
*	OX (COW) HUM-214/K	OP	*	70.00-255.00
*	OX (COW) HUM-214K (COLOR)	OP	60.00	70.00-155.00
*	OX (COW) HUM-214K (WHITE)	CL	*	130.00-255.00
*	SAINT JOSEPH (LARGE) HUM-260B	SU	*	520.00-550.00
*	SHEEP, STANDING W/LAMB (LARGE) HUM-260H	SU	*	115.00
*	SHEPHERD BOY W/FLUTE HUM-214H (COLOR)	OP	100.00	125.00-270.00
*	SHEPHERD BOY W/FLUTE HUM-214H (WHITE)	CL	*	170.00-320.00
*	SHEPHERD BOY, KNEELING (LARGE) HUM-260J	SU	*	295.00-325.00
*	SHEPHERD KNEELING HUM-214/G	OP	*	130.00-320.00
*	SHEPHERD KNEELING HUM-214G (COLOR)	OP	110.00	130.00-295.00
*	SHEPHERD KNEELING HUM-214G (WHITE)	CL	*	170.00-320.00
*	SHEPHERD W/SHEEP HUM-214/F	OP	*	175.00-470.00
*	SHEPHERD W/SHEEP HUM-214F (COLOR)	OP	155.00	175.00-395.00
*	SHEPHERD W/SHEEP HUM-214F (WHITE)	CL	*	220.00-470.00
*	SHEPHERD, STANDING (LARGE) HUM-260G	SU	*	525.00-575.00
*	SHEPHERD/LI'L TOOTER HUM-214/H	OP	*	125.00-320.00
*	STABLE HUM-260S	OP	400.00	400.00

YR	NAME	LIMIT	ISSUE	TREND
*	VIRGIN MARY HUM-214/A	OP	*	175.00
*	VIRGIN MARY HUM-214A (COLOR)	OP	150.00	175.00-2500.00
*	VIRGIN MARY HUM-214A (WHITE)	CL	*	195.00-3000.00
*	WE CONGRATULATE (LARGE) HUM-260F	SU	*	370.00-415.00
*	WE CONGRATULATE HUM-214/E	OP	*	160.00-470.00
*	WE CONGRATULATE HUM-214E (COLOR)	OP	140.00	160.00-370.00
*	WE CONGRATULATE HUM-214E (WHITE)	CL	*	270.00-470.00
51	VIRGIN MARY/INFANT JESUS H214/A	CL	*	70.00-3000.00
88	INFANT JESUS HUM-214A/K/O	OP	*	40.00
88	JOSEPH HUM-214B/O	OP	*	130.00
88	MARY HUM-214/A/M/O	OP	*	130.00-135.00
89	ANGEL, GOOD NIGHT HUM-214C (WHITE)	CL	*	265.00-415.00
89	DONKEY HUM-214J/O	OP	*	50.00
89	FLYING ANGEL HUM-366/O	OP	*	95.00
89	LAMB HUM-214O/O	OP	*	20.00
89	MARY HUM-214A/M/O	OP	*	130.00
89	OX HUM-214K/O	OP	*	50.00
90	KING ON ONE KNEE HUM-214M/O	OP	*	140.00
90	KING ON TWO KNEES HUM-214N/O	OP	*	135.00
90	KING STANDING HUM-214L/O	OP	*	130.00-135.00
91	LITTLE TOOTER HUM-214H/O	OP	*	100.00
91	SHEPHERD KNEELING HUM-214G/O	OP	*	120.00
91	SHEPHERD STANDING HUM-214F/O	OP	*	150.00
	M.I. HUMMEL			**PEN PAL SERIES**
96	FOR MOTHER	*	55.00	55.00
96	MARCH WINDS	*	55.00	55.00
96	ONE OF YOU, ONE OF ME	*	55.00	55.00
96	SISTER	*	55.00	55.00
96	SOLOIST	*	55.00	55.00
96	VILLAGE BOY	*	55.00	55.00
	*****			**PRECIOUS MOMENTS MINIATURES**
96	GOD LOVETH A CHEERFUL GIVER	OP	70.00	70.00
96	HIS BURDEN IS LIGHT	*	70.00	70.00
96	I'M SENDING YOU A WHITE CHRISTMAS	5000	100.00	100.00
96	LOVE IS KIND	OP	70.00	70.00
96	LOVE ONE ANOTHER	OP	70.00	70.00
96	MAKE A JOYFUL NOISE	OP	70.00	70.00
96	PRAISE THE LORD ANYHOW	OP	70.00	70.00
96	PRAYER CHANGES THINGS	OP	70.00	70.00
96	THIS BURDEN IS LIGHT	OP	70.00	70.00
	B. TIMBERLAKE			**PRECIOUS MOMENTS MINIATURES**
96	FRIENDS OF FRIENDSHIP	*	135.00	135.00
	P. LARSEN			**PRECIOUS PLACES**
95	FIELDS OF FRIENDSHIP	OP	625.00	625.00
	M.I. HUMMEL			**SPECIAL EVENT FIGURINE**
95	OOH, MY TOOTH	*	110.00	110.00
	M.I. HUMMEL			**TRIO COLLECTION**
96	A TUNEFUL TRIO	20000	450.00	450.00
	M.I. HUMMEL			**UNICEF COMMEMORATIVE SERIES**
94	FRIENDS TOGETHER 662/O	OP	260.00	275.00
95	GENTLE FELLOWSHIP	25000	550.00	550.00
96	WE CAME IN PEACE	*	350.00	350.00

GOEBEL MINIATURES

YR	NAME	LIMIT	ISSUE	TREND
	R. OLSZEWSKI			**AMERICANA SERIES**
81	PLAINSMAN, THE- 660-B	RT	45.00	245.00
82	AMERICAN BALD EAGLE 661-B	RT	45.00	305.00
83	SHE SOUNDS THE DEEP 662-B	RT	45.00	70.00
84	EYES ON THE HORIZON 663-B	RT	45.00	250.00
85	CENTRAL PARK SUNDAY 664-B	RT	45.00	70.00
86	AMERICANA DISPLAY 951-D	SU	80.00	105.00
86	CARROUSEL RIDE 665-B	RT	45.00	125.00
87	TO THE BANDSTAND 666-B	RT	45.00	70.00
89	BLACKSMITH 667-P	RT	55.00	165.00
	R. OLSZEWSKI			**CHILDREN'S SERIES**
80	BLUMENKINDER-COURTING 630-P	RT	55.00	275.00
81	SUMMER DAYS 631-P	RT	65.00	345.00
82	OUT AND ABOUT 632-P	RT	85.00	415.00
83	BACKYARD FROLIC 633-P	RT	65.00	100.00
84	GRANDPA 634-P	CL	75.00	110.00
85	SNOW HOLIDAY 635-P	CL	75.00	100.00
86	CLOWNING AROUND (OLD STYLE) 636-P	CL	85.00	210.00
87	CAROUSEL DAYS (PLAIN BASE) 637-P	CL	85.00	775.00
87	CARROUSEL DAYS 637-P	CL	85.00	200.00
88	CHILDREN'S DISPLAY (SMALL)	CL	45.00	60.00
88	LITTLE BALLERINA 638-P	CL	85.00	110.00
89	CLOWNING AROUND (NEW STYLE) 636-P	CL	85.00	100.00
90	BUILDING BLOCKS CASTLE (LARGE) 968-D	CL	75.00	100.00
	*** LARSEN**			**CLASSIC CLOCKS**
95	ALEXIS	2500	200.00	200.00
95	BLINKING ADMIRAL	2500	200.00	200.00
95	PLAY	2500	250.00	250.00
	R. OLSZEWSKI			**DEGRAZIA: GOEBEL MINIATURES**
89	MERRY LITTLE INDIAN (NEW STYLE0 508-P	SU	110.00	175.00
	R. OLSZEWSKI			**DISNEY-CINDERELLA**
91	ANASTASIA 172-P	SU	85.00	100.00
91	CINDERELLA 176-P	SU	85.00	125.00

YR	NAME	LIMIT	ISSUE	TREND
91	CINDERELLA'S COACH DISPLAY 978-D	SU	95.00	120.00
91	CINDERELLA'S DREAM CASTLE 976-D	SU	95.00	115.00
91	DRIZELLA 174-P	SU	85.00	100.00
91	FAIRY GODMOTHER 180-P	SU	85.00	105.00
91	FOOTMAN 181-P	SU	85.00	100.00
91	GUS 177-P	SU	75.00	80.00
91	JAQ 173-P	SU	75.00	80.00
91	LUCIFER 175-P	SU	75.00	95.00
91	PRINCE CHARMING 179-P	SU	85.00	135.00
91	STEPMOTHER 178-P	SU	85.00	100.00
*			**DISNEY-PETER PAN**	
94	CAPTAIN HOOK 188-P	SU	160.00	175.00
94	LOST BOY-FOX 191-P	SU	130.00	130.00
94	LOST BOY-RABBIT 192-P	SU	130.00	130.00
94	NEVERLAND DISPLAY 997-D	SU	150.00	160.00
94	SMEE 190-P	SU	140.00	150.00
R. OLSZEWSKI			**DISNEY-PETER PAN**	
92	JOHN 186-P	SU	90.00	130.00
92	MICHAEL 187-P	SU	90.00	110.00
92	NANA 189-P	SU	95.00	110.00
92	PETER PAN 184-P	SU	90.00	160.00
92	PETER PAN'S LONDON 986-D	SU	125.00	135.00
92	WENDY 185-P	SU	90.00	130.00
*			**DISNEY-PINOCCHIO**	
92	MONSTRO THE WHALE 985-D	SU	120.00	200.00
R. OLSZEWSKI			**DISNEY-PINOCCHIO**	
90	GEPPETTO'S TOY SHOP DISPLAY 965-D	SU	95.00	130.00
90	GEPPETTO/FIGARO 682-P	SU	90.00	110.00
90	GIDEON 683-P	SU	75.00	100.00
90	J. WORTHINGTON FOULFELLOW 684-P	SU	95.00	115.00
90	JIMINY CRICKET 685-P	SU	75.00	115.00
90	PINOCCHIO 686-P	SU	75.00	140.00
91	BLUE FAIRY 693-P	SU	95.00	120.00
91	LITTLE STREET LAMP DISPLAY 964-D	SU	65.00	100.00
91	STROMBOLI 694-P	SU	95.00	120.00
91	STROMBOLI'S STREET WAGON 979-D	SU	105.00	135.00
*			**DISNEY-SNOW WHITE**	
92	PATH IN THE WOODS 996-D	SU	140.00	170.00
92	SNOW WHITE'S QUEEN 182-P	SU	100.00	140.00
92	SNOW WHITE'S WITCH 183-P	SU	100.00	140.00
R. OLSZEWSKI			**DISNEY-SNOW WHITE**	
87	BASHFUL 165-P	SU	60.00	100.00
87	COZY COTTAGE DISPLAY 941-D	SU	35.00	260.00
87	DOC 162-P	SU	60.00	100.00
87	DOPEY 167-P	SU	60.00	160.00
87	GRUMPY 166-P	SU	60.00	100.00
87	HAPPY 164-P	SU	60.00	100.00
87	SLEEPY 163-P	SU	60.00	100.00
87	SNEEZY 161-P	SU	60.00	100.00
87	SNOW WHITE 168-P	SU	60.00	160.00
88	HOUSE IN THE WOODS DISPLAY 944-D	SU	60.00	120.00
90	SNOW WHITE'S PRINCE 170-P	SU	80.00	125.00
90	WISHING WELL DISPLAY, THE- 969-D	SU	65.00	115.00
91	CASTLE COURTYARD DISPLAY 981-D	SU	105.00	120.00
92	SNOW WHITE QUEEN 182-P	SU	100.00	140.00
R. OLSZEWSKI			**DISNEYANA CONVENTION**	
94	MICKEY'S SELF-PORTRAIT	500	295.00	850.00
R. OLSZEWSKI			**FIRST EDITION M.I. HUMMEL**	
88	DOLL BATH HUM-252P	10000	95.00	105.00
88	LITTLE FIDDLER HUM-250P	10000	90.00	115.00
88	LITTLE SWEEPER HUM-253P	10000	90.00	105.00
88	MERRY WANDERER HUM-254P	10000	95.00	170.00
88	STORMY WEATHER HUM-251P	10000	115.00	130.00
89	APPLE TREE BOY HUM-257P	10000	115.00	130.00
89	POSTMAN HUM-255P	10000	95.00	105.00
89	VISITING AN INVALID HUM-256P	10000	105.00	115.00
90	BAKER HUM-262P	10000	100.00	105.00
90	CINDERELLA HUM-264P	10000	115.00	115.00
90	WAITER HUM-263P	10000	100.00	115.00
91	ACCORDION BOY HUM-266P	10000	105.00	115.00
91	BUSY STUDENT HUM-268P	10000	105.00	115.00
91	MERRY WANDERER DEALER PLAQUE HUM-280P	10000	130.00	435.00
91	MORNING CONCERT HUM-269P	TL	175.00	175.00
91	RIDE INTO CHRISTMAS HUM-279P	OP	195.00	195.00
91	SERENADE HUM-265P	10000	105.00	115.00
91	WE CONGRATULATE HUM-267P	10000	130.00	130.00-140.00
92	GOOSE GIRL HUM-283P	OP	130.00	130.00
92	SCHOOL BOY HUM-281P	OP	120.00	120.00
92	WAYSIDE HARMONY HUM-282P	OP	140.00	180.00
R. OLSZEWSKI			**HISTORICAL SERIES**	
80	CAPODIMONTE (OLD STYLE) 600-P	CL	90.00	495.00
81	MASQUERADE-ST. PETERSBURG 601-P	CL	65.00	220.00
83	CHERRY PICKERS, THE 602-P	SU	85.00	270.00
84	MOOR WITH SPANISH HORSE 603-P	OP	85.00	110.00
85	CAPODIMONTE (NEW STYLE) 600-P	SU	90.00	170.00
85	FLORAL BOUQUET POMPADOUR 604-P	OP	85.00	115.00
87	MEISSEN PARROT 605-P	OP	85.00	110.00

YR	NAME	LIMIT	ISSUE	TREND
88	HISTORICAL DISPLAY 943-D	SU	45.00	60.00
88	MINTON ROOSTER 606-P	7500	85.00	110.00
89	FARMER W/DOVES 607-P	OP	85.00	110.00
90	ENGLISH COUNTRY GARDEN 970-D	OP	85.00	105.00
90	GENTLEMAN FOX HUNT 616-P	SU	145.00	180.00
92	POULTRY SELLER 608-G	1500	200.00	230.00
	R. OLSZEWSKI		**JACK AND THE BEANSTALK**	
94	BEANSELLER 742-P	5000	210.00	210.00
94	JACK AND THE BEANSTALK DISPLAY 999-D	5000	225.00	250.00
94	JACK AND THE COW 743-P	5000	180.00	185.00
94	JACK'S MOM 741-P	5000	145.00	160.00
*			**MICKEY MOUSE**	
90	MICKEY MOUSE SELLER	SU	165.00	430.00
	R. OLSZEWSKI		**MICKEY MOUSE**	
90	FANTASIA LIVING BROOMS 972-D	SU	85.00	215.00
90	SORCERER'S APPRENTICE , THE-171-P	SU	80.00	180.00
	R. OLSZEWSKI		**NATIVITY COLLECTION**	
91	HOLY FAMILY DISPLAY 982-D	OP	85.00	90.00
91	JOSEPH 401-P	SU	95.00	125.00
91	JOYFUL CHERUBS 403-P	SU	130.00	175.00
91	MOTHER/CHILD 400-P	SU	120.00	150.00
91	STABLE DONKEY, THE- 402-P	SU	95.00	125.00
92	3 KINGS DISPLAY 987-D	OP	85.00	100.00
92	BALTHAZAR 405-P	SU	135.00	195.00
92	CASPAR 406-P	SU	135.00	195.00
92	MELCHIOR 404-P	SU	135.00	195.00
94	CAMEL & TENDER 819292	OP	380.00	390.00
94	FINAL NATIVITY DISPLAY 991-D	OP	260.00	270.00
94	GUARDIAN ANGEL 407-P	OP	200.00	220.00
94	SHEEP & SHEPHERD 819290	OP	230.00	235.00
	*** YENAWINE**		**NATURE'S MOMENTS**	
95	BATHING BEAUTIES	OP	95.00	95.00
95	FISH PARADISE	OP	110.00	110.00
95	GATHERING GOODIES	OP	95.00	95.00
95	HIDE AND SEEK	OP	110.00	110.00
95	PENGUINS PLUNGE	OP	95.00	95.00
95	POLAR PLAYGROUND	OP	110.00	110.00
95	PREPARING FOR FLIGHT	OP	80.00	80.00
95	ROBYN REFRESHER	OP	95.00	95.00
95	SUMMER SURPRISE	OP	95.00	95.00
95	TOUCH AND GO	OP	95.00	95.00
	R. OLSZEWSKI		**NIGHT BEFORE CHRISTMAS (1ST EDITION)**	
90	EIGHT TINY REINDEER 691-P	SU	110.00	120.00
90	MAMA & PAPA 692-P	SU	110.00	125.00
90	ST. NICHOLAS 690-P	SU	95.00	115.00
90	SUGAR PLUM BOY 687-P	SU	70.00	90.00
90	SUGAR PLUM GIRL 689-P	SU	70.00	90.00
90	YULE TREE 688-P	SU	90.00	100.00
91	UP TO THE HOUSETOP 966-D	5000	95.00	105.00
	R. OLSZEWSKI		**ORIENTAL SERIES**	
80	KUAN YIN (OLD STYLE) 640-W	CL	40.00	255.00
82	GEISHA, THE- 641-P	SU	65.00	195.00
84	KUAN YIN (NEW STYLE) 640-W	SU	45.00	165.00
85	TANG HORSE 642-P	OP	65.00	95.00
86	BLIND MAN AND THE ELEPHANT, THE 643-P	SU	70.00	160.00
87	CHINESE WATER DRAGON 644-P	SU	70.00	155.00
87	ORIENTAL DISPLAY (SMALL) 945-D	SU	45.00	65.00
89	TIGER HUNT 645-P	OP	85.00	100.00
90	CHINESE TEMPLE LION 646-P	OP	90.00	110.00
90	EMPRESS GARDEN 967-D	OP	95.00	125.00
	R. OLSZEWSKI		**PENDANTS**	
85	FLOWER GIRL PENDANT 561-P	OP	125.00	150.00
86	CAMPER BIALOSKY 151-P	CL	95.00	275.00
87	FESTIVAL OF LIGHTS 562-P	OP	90.00	195.00
88	MICKEY MOUSE 169-P	5000	92.00	255.00
90	HUMMINGBIRD 697-P	OP	125.00	145.00
91	CHRYSANTHEMUM PENDANT 222-P	OP	135.00	145.00
91	DAFFODIL PENDANT 221-P	OP	135.00	145.00
91	POINSETTIA PENDANT	OP	135.00	145.00
91	ROSE PENDANT	OP	135.00	145.00
	N. ROCKWELL		**PORTRAIT OF AMERICA**	
88	BOTTOM OF THE SIXTH 365-P	SU	85.00	115.00
88	CHECK UP 363-P	SU	85.00	95.00
88	DOCTOR AND THE DOLL, THE 361-P	SU	85.00	135.00
88	MARBLES CHAMPION 362-P	CL	85.00	85.00
88	NO SWIMMING 360-P	CL	85.00	85.00
88	ROCKWELL DISPLAY 952-D	CL	80.00	93.00
88	TRIPLE SELF-PORTRAIT 364-P	SU	85.00	175.00
89	BOTTOM DRAWER 366-P	7500	85.00	85.00
	HUGHES		**SATURDAY EVENING POST**	
92	BOY WITH WAGON	OP	*	*
92	CHILDREN CROSSING	OP	*	*
92	CROSSING GUARD	OP	*	*
92	MARKET VIGNETTE	OP	*	*
92	STORE OWNER	OP	*	*
	R. OLSZEWSKI		**SATURDAY EVENING POST**	
92	CROSSING GUARD VIGNETTE	OP	*	*

YR	NAME	LIMIT	ISSUE	TREND
N. ROCKWELL		**SATURDAY EVENING POST**		
91	CITY CLERK	OP	*	*
91	HOME COMING VIGNETTE 990-D	2000	190.00	250.00
91	MARRIAGE LICENSE VIGNETTE	OP	*	*
91	MOTHER 369-P	OP	*	*
91	SOLDIER 368-P	OP	*	*
91	WEDDING COUPLE	OP	*	*
92	TRIPLE SELF PORTRAIT	OP	*	*
92	TRIPLE SELF PORTRAIT VIGNETTE	OP	*	*
R. OLSZEWSKI		**SPECIAL RELEASE-ALICE IN WONDERLAND**		
82	ALICE IN THE GARDEN 670-P	CL	60.00	675.00
83	DOWN THE RABBIT HOLE 671-P	CL	75.00	425.00
84	CHESHIRE CAT, THE 672-P	CL	75.00	480.00
R. OLSZEWSKI		**SPECIAL RELEASE-WIZARD OF OZ**		
84	SCARECROW 673-P	CL	75.00	400.00
85	TINMAN 674-P	CL	80.00	240.00
86	COWARDLY LION, THE 675-P	CL	85.00	260.00
87	OZ DISPLAY 942-D	CL	45.00	565.00
87	WICKED WITCH, THE- 676-P	CL	85.00	105.00
88	MUNCHKINS, THE- 677-P	CL	85.00	100.00
92	DOROTHY/GLINDA 695-P	CL	120.00	135.00-150.00
92	GOOD-BYE TO OZ DISPLAY 980-D	OP	110.00	160.00
R. OLSZEWSKI		**SPECIAL RELEASES**		
91	PORTRAIT OF THE ARTIST (CONVENTION) 658-	CL	195.00	450.00
91	PORTRAIT OF THE ARTIST (PROMO) 658-P	OP	195.00	205.00
92	SUMMER DAYS COLLECTOR PLAQUE 659-P	OP	130.00	145.00
94	DRESDEN TIME PIECE 450-P	750	1250.00	1300.00
REMINGTON		**THE AMERICAN FRONTIER COLLECTION**		
87	BRONCO BUSTER, THE 350-B	SU	80.00	175.00
87	EIGHT COUNT 310-B	SU	75.00	90.00
87	END OF THE TRAIL, THE340-B	SU	80.00	125.00
87	FIRST RIDE , THE-330-B	SU	85.00	100.00
87	GRIZZLY'S LAST STAND 320-B	SU	65.00	80.00
87	INDIAN SCOUT AND BUFFALO 300-B	SU	95.00	135.00
R. OLSZEWSKI		**THE AMERICAN FRONTIER COLLECTION**		
87	AMERICAN FRONTIER DISPLAY 947-D	SU	80.00	110.00
R. OLSZEWSKI		**THREE LITTLE PIGS**		
89	LITTLE STICKS PIG 678-P	7500	75.00	105.00
89	THREE LITTLE PIGS HOUSE 956-D	7500	50.00	115.00
90	LITTLE STRAW PIG 679-P	7500	75.00	105.00
91	HUNGRY WOLF, THE- 681-P	7500	80.00	105.00
91	LITTLE BRICKS PIG 680-P	7500	75.00	105.00
R. OLSZEWSKI		**WILDLIFE SERIES**		
80	CHIPPING SPARROW 620-P	OP	55.00	85.00
81	OWL-DAYLIGHT ENCOUNTER 621-P	CL	65.00	390.00
82	WESTERN BLUEBIRD 622-P	CL	65.00	150.00
83	RED-WINGED BLACKBIRD 623-P	CL	65.00	190.00
84	WINTER CARDINAL 624-P	CL	65.00	250.00
85	AMERICAN GOLDFINCH 625-P	OP	65.00	90.00
86	AUTUMN BLUE JAY 626-P	SU	65.00	175.00
87	COUNTRY DISPLAY (SMALL) 940-D	OP	45.00	65.00
87	MALLARD DUCK 627-P	OP	75.00	105.00
88	SPRING ROBIN 628-P	CL	75.00	165.00
89	HOODED ORIOLE 629-P	OP	80.00	100.00
90	COUNTRY LANDSCAPE (LG.) 957-D	OP	85.00	110.00
90	HUMMINGBIRD 696-P	CL	85.00	175.00
90	WILDLIFE DISPLAY (LARGE) 957-D	OP	85.00	95.00
92	AUTUMN BLYE JAY (ARCHIVE RELEASE) 626-P	OP	125.00	135.00
*** NORRGARD**		**WINTER LIGHTS**		
95	ONCE UPON A WINTER DAY	OP	275.00	275.00
R. OLSZEWSKI		**WOMEN'S SERIES**		
80	DRESDEN DANCER 610-P	CL	55.00	350.00
81	HUNT WITH HOUNDS, THE (OLD STYLE) - 611-	CL	75.00	400.00
82	PRECIOUS YEARS 612-P	CL	65.00	230.00
83	ON THE AVENUE 613-P	CL	65.00	115.00
84	ROSES 614-P	CL	65.00	115.00
85	HUNT WITH HOUNDS, THE (NEW STYLE0 611-P	CL	75.00	110.00
86	I DO 615-P	CL	85.00	235.00
89	WOMEN'S DISPLAY (SMALL) 950-D	CL	40.00	65.00

GORHAM

Price ranges may reflect various demands in the market from one geographic region to another; condition of piece; specific markings found on piece; and/or changes in production of piece.

YR	NAME	LIMIT	ISSUE	TREND
N. ROCKWELL		**A BOY AND HIS DOG (FOUR SEASONS)**		
72	A BOY MEETS HIS DOG	RT	200.00	1450.00
72	ADVENTURERS BETWEEN ADVENTURES (SET)	RT	*	*
72	MYSTERIOUS MALADY, THE- (SET)	RT	*	*
72	PRIDE OF PARENTHOOD (SET)	RT	*	*
N. ROCKWELL		**A HELPING HAND (FOUR SEASONS)**		
80	CLOSED FOR BUSINESS (SET)	RT	*	*
80	COAL SEASONS COMING (SET)	RT	*	*
80	SWATTER'S RIGHT (SET)	RT	*	*
80	YEAR END COURT	RT	650.00	675.00
N. ROCKWELL		**DAD'S BOY (FOUR SEASONS)**		
81	CAREFUL AIM (SET)	RT	*	*
81	IN HIS SPIRIT (SET)	RT	*	*

YR	NAME	LIMIT	ISSUE	TREND
81	SKI SKILLS	RT	750.00	775.00
81	TROUT DINNER (SET)	RT	*	*
N. ROCKWELL		**FOUR AGES OF LOVE (FOUR SEASONS)**		
74	FLOWERS IN TENDER BLOOM (SET)	RT	*	*
74	FONDLY DO WE REMEMBER (SET)	RT	*	*
74	GAILY SHARING VINTAGE TIMES	RT	300.00	950.00
74	SWEET SONG SO YOUNG (SET)	RT	*	*
N. ROCKWELL		**GOING ON SIXTEEN (FOUR SEASONS)**		
78	CHILLING CHORE	RT	400.00	660.00
78	PILGRIMAGE (SET)	RT	*	*
78	SHEAR AGONY (SET)	RT	*	*
78	SWEET SERENADE (SET)	RT	*	*
N. ROCKWELL		**GRAND PALS (FOUR SEASONS)**		
77	FISH FINDERS (SET)	RT	*	*
77	GHOSTLY GOURDS (SET)	RT	*	*
77	SNOW SCULPTURING	RT	350.00	660.00
77	SOARING SPIRITS (SET)	RT	*	*
N. ROCKWELL		**GRANDPA AND ME**		
75	DAY DREAMERS (SET)	RT	*	*
75	GAY BLADES	2500	300.00	900.00
75	GOIN' FISHING (SET)	RT	*	*
75	PENSIVE PALS (SET)	RT	*	*
J.C. LEYENDECKER		**LEYENDECKER ANNUAL CHRISTMAS FIGURINES**		
88	CHRISTMAS HUG	7500	95.00	95.00
N. ROCKWELL		**LIFE WITH FATHER (FOUR SEASONS)**		
83	A TOUGH ONE (SET)	RT	*	*
83	BIG DECISION	RT	250.00	250.00
83	BLASTING OUT (SET)	RT	*	*
83	CHEERING THE CHAMPS (SET)	RT	*	*
N. ROCKWELL		**ME AND MY PAL (FOUR SEASONS)**		
76	A LICKING GOOD BATH	RT	300.00	1050.00
76	DISASTROUS DARING (SET)	RT	*	*
76	FISHERMAN'S PARADISE (SET)	RT	*	*
76	YOUNG MAN'S FANCY (SET)	RT	*	*
T. NAST		**MINIATURE CHRISTMAS FIGURINES**		
85	CHRISTMAS SANTA	RT	20.00	20.00
86	CHRISTMAS SANTA	RT	25.00	25.00
87	ANNUAL THOMAS NAST SANTA	RT	25.00	25.00
N. ROCKWELL		**MINIATURE CHRISTMAS FIGURINES**		
79	TINY TIM	RT	15.00	20.00
80	SANTA PLANS HIS TRIP	RT	15.00	16.00
81	YULETIDE RECKONING	RT	20.00	20.00
82	CHECKING GOOD DEEDS	RT	20.00	20.00
83	SANTA'S FRIEND	RT	20.00	20.00
84	DOWNHILL DARING	RT	20.00	20.00
N. ROCKWELL		**MINIATURES**		
81	AT THE VETS	CL	27.50	35.00
81	BEGUILING BUTTERCUP	CL	45.00	45.00
81	BOY MEETS HIS DOG	CL	37.50	38.00
81	DOWNHILL DARING	CL	45.00	70.00
81	FLOWERS IN TENDER BLOOM	CL	60.00	60.00
81	GAY BLADES	CL	45.00	70.00
81	SNOW SCULPTURE	CL	45.00	60.00
81	SWEET SERENADE	CL	45.00	45.00
81	SWEET SONG SO YOUNG	CL	55.00	55.00
81	YOUNG MAN'S FANCY	CL	55.00	55.00
82	ANNUAL VISIT, THE	CL	50.00	70.00
82	MARRIAGE LICENSE	CL	60.00	70.00
82	RUNAWAY, THE	CL	50.00	50.00
82	TRIPLE SELF PORTRAIT	CL	60.00	135.00
82	VINTAGE TIMES	CL	50.00	50.00
83	TROUT DINNER	RT	60.00	60.00
84	CAREFUL AIMS	CL	55.00	55.00
84	GHOSTLY GOURDS	CL	60.00	60.00
84	GOIN' FISHING	CL	60.00	60.00
84	IN HIS SPIRIT	CL	60.00	60.00
84	PRIDE OF PARENTHOOD	CL	50.00	50.00
84	SHEAR AGONY	CL	60.00	60.00
84	YEARS END COURT	CL	60.00	60.00
85	BEST FRIENDS	CL	27.50	28.00
85	ENGINEER	CL	55.00	55.00
85	LITTLE RED TRUCK	CL	25.00	25.00
85	MUSCLE BOUND	CL	30.00	30.00
85	NEW ARRIVAL	CL	32.50	35.00
85	SPRING CHECKUP	CL	60.00	60.00
85	TO LOVE AND CHERISH	CL	32.50	35.00
86	FOOTBALL SEASON	CL	60.00	60.00
86	GRADUATE, THE	CL	30.00	40.00
86	LEMONADE STAND	CL	60.00	60.00
86	LITTLE ANGEL	CL	50.00	60.00
86	MORNING WALK	CL	60.00	60.00
86	OLD SIGN PAINTER, THE	CL	70.00	75.00
86	SHOULDER RIDE	CL	50.00	60.00
86	WELCOME MAT	CL	70.00	70.00
87	BABYSITTER	RT	75.00	75.00
87	BETWEEN THE ACTS	RT	60.00	60.00
87	CINDERELLA	RT	70.00	75.00

YR	NAME	LIMIT	ISSUE	TREND
87	MILKMAID, THE	RT	80.00	80.00
87	PROM DRESS, THE	RT	75.00	75.00
87	SPRINGTIME	RT	65.00	70.00
87	STARSTRUCK	RT	75.00	75.00
N. ROCKWELL		**OLD BUDDIES (FOUR SEASONS)**		
84	ENDLESS DEBATES (SET)	RT	*	*
84	FINAL SPEECH (SET)	RT	*	*
84	HASTY RETREAT (SET)	RT	*	*
84	SHARED SUCCESS	RT	250.00	250.00
N. ROCKWELL		**OLD TIMERS (FOUR SEASONS MINIATURES)**		
82	CANINE SOLO	RT	250.00	250.00
82	FANCY FOOTWORK (SET)	RT	*	*
82	LAZY DAYS (SET)	RT	*	*
82	SWEET SURPRISE (SET)	RT	*	*
*		**PARASOL LADY**		
91	ON THE BOARDWALK	OP	95.00	95.00
94	AT THE FAIR	OP	95.00	95.00
94	SUNDAY PRMENADE	OP	95.00	95.00
N. ROCKWELL		**ROCKWELL**		
74	AT THE VETS	CL	25.00	65.00
74	BATTER UP	CL	40.00	160.00
74	CAPTAIN	CL	45.00	95.00
74	FISHING	CL	50.00	100.00
74	MISSING TOOTH	CL	30.00	85.00
74	SKATING	CL	37.50	85.00
74	TINY TIM	CL	30.00	95.00
74	WEIGHING IN	RT	40.00	120.00
75	BOY AND HIS DOG	CL	38.00	90.00
75	NO SWIMMING	CL	35.00	150.00
75	OLD MILL POND	CL	45.00	95.00
76	GOD REST YE MERRY GENTLEMEN	CL	50.00	1200.00
76	INDEPENDENCE	CL	40.00	150.00
76	MARRIAGE LICENSE	CL	50.00	165.00
76	OCCULTIST, THE	CL	50.00	175.00
76	SAYING GRACE	CL	75.00	120.00
76	TACKLED (AD STAND)	CL	35.00	95.00
80	JOLLY COACHMAN	7500	75.00	140.00
81	CHRISTMAS DANCERS	RT	130.00	180.00
81	DAY IN THE LIFE BOY II	CL	75.00	85.00
81	WET SPORT	CL	85.00	100.00
82	A DAY IN THE LIFE BOY III	CL	85.00	90.00
82	A DAY IN THE LIFE GIRL III	CL	85.00	115.00
82	APRIL FOOL'S (AT THE CURIOSITY SHOP)	CL	55.00	110.00
82	MARRIAGE LICENSE	RT	110.00	500.00
82	MERRIE CHRISTMAS	RT	75.00	150.00
82	SAYING GRACE	RT	110.00	550.00
82	TACKLED (ROCKWELL NAME SIGNED)	CL	45.00	100.00
82	TRIPLE SELF PORTRAIT	5000	300.00	500.00
83	ANTIQUE DEALER	RT	130.00	175.00
83	CHRISTMAS GOOSE	7500	75.00	75.00
83	FACTS OF LIFE	RT	110.00	110.00
84	CARD TRICKS	RT	110.00	175.00
84	SANTA'S FRIEND	RT	75.00	150.00
84	SERENADE	RT	95.00	160.00
85	OLD SIGN PAINTER, THE	RT	130.00	200.00
85	PUPPET MAKER	RT	130.00	170.00
86	DRUM FOR TOMMY	RT	90.00	90.00
87	SANTA PLANNING HIS ANNUAL VISIT	RT	95.00	95.00
88	CONFRONTATION	RT	75.00	75.00
88	CRAMMING	RT	80.00	80.00
88	DELORES & EDDIE	RT	75.00	75.00
88	DIARY, THE	RT	75.00	80.00
88	GARY COOPER IN HOLLYWOOD	RT	90.00	90.00
88	HOME FOR THE HOLIDAYS	RT	100.00	100.00
N. ROCKWELL		**TENDER YEARS (FOUR SEASONS)**		
79	CHILLY RECEPTION (SET)	RT	*	*
79	COOL AID (SET)	RT	*	*
79	NEW YEAR LOOK	RT	500.00	600.00
79	SPRING TONIC (SET)	RT	*	*
N. ROCKWELL		**TRAVELING SALESMAN (FOUR SEASONS)**		
85	COUNTRY PEDDLER (SET)	RT	*	*
85	EXPERT SALESMAN (SET)	RT	*	*
85	HORSE TRADER	RT	275.00	275.00
85	TRAVELING SALESMAN (SET)	RT	*	*
VASARI		**VASARI FIGURINES**		
71	MERCENARY WARRIOR	250	250.00	500.00
71	MING WARRIOR	250	200.00	400.00
71	SWISS WARRIOR	250	250.00	1000.00
73	AUSTRIAN HUSSAR	250	400.00	800.00
73	CELLINI	250	400.00	800.00
73	CHRIST	250	250.00	500.00
73	COSSACK, THE	250	250.00	500.00
73	CRECHE	250	500.00	1000.00
73	D'ARTAGNAN	250	250.00	800.00
73	ENGLISH CRUSADER	250	250.00	500.00
73	FRENCH CRUSADER	250	250.00	500.00
73	GERMAN HUSSAR	250	250.00	500.00
73	GERMAN MERCENARY	250	250.00	500.00

YR	NAME	LIMIT	ISSUE	TREND
73	ITALIAN CRUSADER	250	250.00	500.00
73	LEONARDO DA VINCI	200	250.00	500.00
73	MICHELANGELO	200	250.00	500.00
73	PIRATE	250	250.00	400.00
73	PORTHOS	250	250.00	500.00
73	ROMAN CENTURION	250	250.00	400.00
73	SPANISH GRANDEE	250	250.00	400.00
73	THREE KINGS (SET OF 3)	200	750.00	1500.00
73	THREE MUSKETEERS (SET OF 3)	200	750.00	1500.00
73	VENETIAN NOBLEMAN	250	200.00	400.00
73	VIKING	250	200.00	400.00
N. ROCKWELL		**YOUNG LOVE (FOUR SEASONS)**		
73	A SCHOLARLY PACE (SET)	2500	*	*
73	BEGUILING BUTTERCUP (SET)	2500	*	*
73	DOWNHILL DARING (SET)	2500	250.00	1100.00
73	FLYING HIGH (SET)	2500	*	*

GRANGET

YR	NAME	LIMIT	ISSUE	TREND
G. GRANGET			**GRANGET PORCELAINS**	
*	BOBWHITE QUAIL, OFF SEASON	350	*	3000.00
*	CALIFORNIA SEA LIONS, SEA FROLIC	500	1375.00	4200.00
*	CANADIAN GEESE, HEADING SOUTH	150	4650.00	14200.00
*	CEDAR WAXWINGS, ANXIOUS MOMENTS	175	2675.00	2675.00
*	CROWNED CRANES, THE DANCE	25	20000.00	20000.00
*	DOLPHIN GROUP	350	*	5000.00
*	DOLPHINS, PLAY TIME, DECORATED	100	9000.00	*
*	DOLPHINS, PLAY TIME, UNDECORATED	500	3500.00	3500.00
*	GREAT BLUE HERONS, THE CHALLENGE	150	5000.00	14200.00
*	HALLA	350	*	4100.00
*	MEADOWLARK, SPRING IS HERE	175	2450.00	2450.00
*	MOURNING DOVES, ENGAGES	250	*	1200.00-1750.00
*	OPEN JUMPER, THE CHAMPION	500	1350.00	1350.00
*	PEREGRINE FALCON, WOOD, 10 IN.	2500	500.00	500.00
*	PEREGRINE FALCON, WOOD, 12.5 IN.	1500	700.00	700.00
*	PEREGRINE FALCON, WOOD, 20 IN.	250	2000.00	2000.00
*	PINTAIL DUCKS, SAFE AT HOME	350	*	9700.00
*	RED DEER STAG, THE ROYAL STAG	150	4850.00	4850.00
*	RING-NECKED PHEASANTS, TAKE COVER	125	*	5000.00
*	RUFFED GROUSE	150	2000.00	2000.00
*	SCREECH OWL WITH CHICKADEES, DISTAIN	175	2250.00	5650.00
*	SECRETARY BIRD	100	6000.00	14000.00
*	SPRINGBOK, THE SENTINEL	150	2000.00	2000.00
*	STAG	350	*	4400.00
*	WOODCOCKS, A FAMILY AFFAIR	200	*	1500.00
74	BLUE TITMOUSE, LIVELY FELLOW	750	1295.00	1295.00
74	CATFINCH, SPRING MELODY	750	1675.00	1675.00
74	GOLDEN-CRESTED WRENS, TINY ACROBATS	700	2060.00	2060.00
74	GOLDFINCH, MORNING HOUR	750	1250.00	1250.00
74	GREAT TITMOUSE ADULTS, BUSY ACTIVITY	750	2175.00	2175.00
74	KINGFISHER, DEFECTED PREY	600	1975.00	1975.00
74	ROBIN, A DAY BEGINS	750	1795.00	1795.00
76	AMERICAN BALD EAGLE, FREEDOM IN FLIGHT	200	3400.00	9500.00
76	AMERICAN ROBIN, IT'S SPRING AGAIN	150	1950.00	1950.00
76	BLUEBIRDS, RELUCTANT FLEDGLING	350	1750.00	4600.00
76	DOUBLE EAGLE, 24 KT GOLD VERMEIL/PEWTER	1200	250.00	250.00
76	SECRETARY BIRD, THE CONTEST	100	6000.00	11000.00
77	RELUCTANT FLEDGLING	350	1750.00	1750.00

GREENWICH WORKSHOP

YR	NAME	LIMIT	ISSUE	TREND
J. CHRISTENSEN				**BRONZE**
*	CANDLEMAN, THE	*	*	3100.00
J. CHRISTENSEN				**FANTASY/BRONZE**
*	SIX BIRD HUNTERS	*	*	4500.00
F. MCCARTHY				**WESTERN**
*	THUNDER OF HOOVES	*	*	10500.00

GUND INC.

YR	NAME	LIMIT	ISSUE	TREND
R. SWEDLIN-RAIFFE			**SIGNATURE COLLECTION**	
96	BEARMANI	575	150.00	150.00

HAMILTON COLLECTION

YR	NAME	LIMIT	ISSUE	TREND
*			**A CELEBRATION OF ROSES**	
89	BRANDY	OP	55.00	55.00
89	COLOR MAGIC	OP	55.00	55.00
89	HONOR	OP	55.00	55.00
89	MISS ALL-AMERICAN BEAUTY	OP	55.00	55.00
89	TIFFANY	OP	55.00	55.00
90	OREGOLD	OP	55.00	55.00
91	OLE'	OP	55.00	55.00
91	PARADISE	OP	55.00	55.00
D. FRYER		**AMERICAN GARDEN FLOWERS**		
87	AZALEA	15000	75.00	75.00
87	CAMELIA	9800	55.00	75.00
87	GARDENIA	15000	75.00	75.00
87	ROSE	15000	75.00	75.00
88	CALLA LILLY	15000	75.00	75.00
88	DAY LILY	15000	75.00	75.00
88	PETUNIA	15000	75.00	75.00

YR	NAME	LIMIT	ISSUE	TREND
89	PANSY	15000	75.00	75.00
H. DEATON		**AMERICAN WILDLIFE BRONZE COLLECTION**		
79	BOBCAT	7500	60.00	75.00
79	COUGAR	7500	60.00	125.00
79	WHITE-TAILED DEER	7500	60.00	105.00
80	BEAVER	7500	60.00	65.00
80	POLAR BEAR	7500	60.00	65.00
80	SEA OTTER	7500	60.00	65.00
J. VILLENA		**CELEBRATION OF OPERA**		
86	CARMEN	7500	95.00	95.00
86	CIO-CIO-SAN	7500	95.00	95.00
87	FIGARO	7500	95.00	95.00
88	AIDA	7500	95.00	95.00
88	CANIO	7500	95.00	95.00
88	MIMI	7500	95.00	95.00
*		**CORAL KINGDOM**		
95	ATHENA	OP	35.00	35.00
FRANCESCO		**EXOTIC BIRDS OF THE WORLD**		
84	BUDGERIGAR	7500	75.00	105.00
84	COCKATOO, THE	7500	75.00	115.00
84	DIAMOND DOVE, THE	7500	75.00	95.00
84	FISHER'S WHYDAH, THE	7500	75.00	95.00
84	PEACH-FACED LOVEBIRD, THE	7500	75.00	95.00
84	QUETZAL, THE	7500	75.00	95.00
84	RED LOG, THE	7500	75.00	95.00
84	RUBENIO PARAKEET, THE	7500	75.00	95.00
M. WALD		**FRESHWATER CHALLENGE**		
91	RAINBOW LURE	OP	75.00	75.00
91	RAINBOW LURE	OP	75.00	75.00
91	STRIKE, THE	OP	75.00	75.00
91	STRIKE, THE	OP	75.00	75.00
91	SUN CATCHER	OP	75.00	75.00
92	PRIZED CATCH	OP	75.00	75.00
H. DEATON		**GREAT ANIMALS OF THE AMERICAN WILDERNESS**		
83	BIGHORN	7500	75.00	75.00
83	ELK	7500	75.00	75.00
83	GRIZZLY BEAR	7500	75.00	75.00
83	MOUNTAIN LION	7500	75.00	75.00
83	MUSTANG	7500	75.00	75.00
83	PLAINS BISON	7500	75.00	75.00
83	PRONGHORN ANTELOPE	7500	75.00	75.00
83	TIMBER WOLF	7500	75.00	75.00
*		**HEROES OF BASEBALL-PORCELAIN BASEBALL CARDS**		
90	BROOKS ROBINSON	OP	19.50	20.00
90	DUKE SNIDER	OP	19.50	20.00
90	GIL HODGES	OP	19.50	20.00
90	ROBERTO CLEMENTE	OP	19.50	20.00
90	WHITEY FORD	OP	19.50	20.00
90	WILLIE MAYS	OP	19.50	20.00
91	CASEY STENGEL	OP	19.50	20.00
91	ERNIE BANKS	OP	19.50	20.00
91	JACKIE ROBINSON	OP	19.50	20.00
91	MICKEY MANTLE	OP	19.50	20.00
91	SATCHEL PAGE	OP	19.50	20.00
91	YOGI BERRA	OP	19.50	20.00
*		**INTERNATIONAL SANTA**		
92	FATHER CHRISTMAS	OP	55.00	55.00
92	GRANDFATHER FROST	OP	55.00	55.00
92	SANTA CLAUS	OP	55.00	55.00
93	BELSNICKEL	OP	55.00	55.00
93	JOLLY OLD ST. NICK	OP	55.00	55.00
93	KRIS KRINGLE	OP	55.00	55.00
94	PERE NOEL	OP	55.00	55.00
94	YULETIDE SANTA	OP	55.00	55.00
95	ALPINE SANTA	OP	55.00	55.00
95	DEDUSHKA MOROZ	OP	55.00	55.00
ITO		**LEGENDARY FLOWERS OF THE ORIENT**		
85	CHERRY BLOSSOM	15000	55.00	55.00
85	CHINESE PEONY	15000	55.00	55.00
85	CHRYSANTHEMUM	15000	55.00	55.00
85	GOLD BAND LILY	15000	55.00	55.00
85	IRIS	15000	55.00	55.00
85	JAPANESE ORCHID	15000	55.00	55.00
85	LOTUS	15000	55.00	55.00
85	WISTERIA	15000	55.00	55.00
*		**LITTLE FRIENDS OF THE ARCTIC**		
95	YOUNG PRINCE, THE	OP	37.50	38.00
D.T. LYTTLETON		**LITTLE NIGHT OWLS**		
90	BARN OWL	OP	45.00	45.00
90	SNOWY OWL	OP	45.00	45.00
90	TAWNY OWL	OP	45.00	45.00
91	BARRED OWL	OP	45.00	45.00
91	GREAT GREY OWL	OP	45.00	45.00
91	GREAT HORNED OWL	OP	45.00	45.00
91	SHORT-EARED OWL	OP	45.00	45.00
91	WHITE-FACED OWL	OP	45.00	45.00

YR	NAME	LIMIT	ISSUE	TREND
FRANCESCO		**MAGNIFICENT BIRDS OF PARADISE**		
85	BLACK SICKLE-BILLED BIRD OF PARADISE	12500	75.00	95.00
85	BLUE BIRD OF PARADISE	12500	75.00	95.00
85	EMPEROR OF GERMANY	12500	75.00	95.00
85	GOLDIE'S BIRD OF PARADISE	12500	75.00	95.00
85	GREATER BIRD OF PARADISE	12500	75.00	95.00
85	MAGNIFICENT BIRD OF PARADISE	12500	75.00	95.00
85	PRINCESS STEPHANIE BIRD OF PARADISE	12500	75.00	95.00
85	RAGGIANA BIRD OF PARADISE	12500	75.00	95.00
H. DEATON		**MAJESTIC WILDLIFE OF NORTH AMERICA**		
85	ALASKAN MOOSE	7500	75.00	75.00
85	BARREN GROUND CARIBOU	7500	75.00	75.00
85	BLACK BEAR	7500	75.00	75.00
85	COYOTE	7500	75.00	75.00
85	HARBOUR SEAL	7500	75.00	75.00
85	MOUNTAIN GOAT	7500	75.00	75.00
85	OCELOT	7500	75.00	75.00
85	WHITE-TAILED DEER	7500	75.00	75.00
*		**MASTERS OF THE EVENING WILDERNESS**		
94	GREAT SNOWY OWL, THE	OP	37.50	38.00
95	AUTUMN BARN OWLS	OP	37.50	38.00
95	GREAT HORNED WOL	OP	37.50	38.00
95	GRET GREY OWL	OP	37.50	38.00
S. DOUGLAS		**MYSTIC SPIRITS**		
95	SPIRIT OF THE WOLF	OP	55.00	55.00
D. GEENTZ		**NATURE'S MAJESTIC CATS**		
95	TIGRESS AND CUBS	OP	55.00	55.00
*		**NOBLE AMERICAN INDIAN WOMEN**		
93	SACAJAWEA	OP	55.00	55.00
93	WHITE ROSE	OP	55.00	55.00
94	FALLING STAR	OP	55.00	55.00
94	MINNEHAHA	OP	55.00	55.00
94	PINE LEAF	OP	55.00	55.00
95	LILY OF THE MOHAWKS	OP	55.00	55.00
95	LOZEN	OP	55.00	55.00
95	POCAHONTAS	OP	55.00	55.00
*		**NOBLE WARRIORS**		
93	DELIVERANCE	OP	135.00	135.00
94	SPIRIT OF THE PLAINS	OP	135.00	135.00
95	TOP GUN	OP	135.00	135.00
95	WINDRIDER	OP	135.00	135.00
*		**NOLAN RYAN COLLECTORS ED., THE/PORCELAIN BASEBALL**		
93	ANGELS 1972-C #595	OP	19.50	20.00
93	ASTROS 1985-C #7	OP	19.50	20.00
93	METS 1968-C #177	OP	19.50	20.00
93	METS 1969-C #533	OP	19.50	20.00
93	RANGERS 1990-C #1	OP	19.50	20.00
93	RANGERS 1992-C #1	OP	19.50	20.00
W. YOUNGSTROM		**OCEAN ODYSSEY**		
95	BREACHING THE WATERS	OP	55.00	55.00
95	RIDING THE WAVES	OP	55.00	55.00
*		**PRINCESS OF THE PLAINS**		
94	NOBLE GUARDIAN	OP	55.00	55.00
94	SNOW PRINCESS	OP	55.00	55.00
94	WILD FLOWER	OP	55.00	55.00
95	NATURE'S GUARDIAN	OP	55.00	55.00
95	WINTER'S ROSE	OP	55.00	55.00
R. MANNING		**PROTECT NATURE'S INNOCENTS**		
95	AFRICAN ELEPHANT	OP	14.95	15.00
J. LAMB		**PUPPY PLAYTIME SCULPTURE COLLECTION**		
90	DOUBLE TAKE	OP	29.50	30.00
91	A NEW LEASH ON LIFE	OP	29.50	30.00
91	CABIN FEVER	OP	29.50	30.00
91	CATCH OF THE DAY	OP	29.50	30.00
91	FUN AND GAMES	OP	29.50	30.00
91	GETTING ACQUAINTED	OP	29.50	30.00
91	HANGING OUT	OP	29.50	30.00
91	WEEKEND GARDENER	OP	29.50	30.00
P. COOPER		**PUSS IN BOOTS**		
92	CAUGHT NAPPING	OP	35.00	35.00
92	SWEET DREAMS	OP	35.00	35.00
93	ALL DRESSED UP	OP	35.00	35.00
93	HIDE'N GO SEEK	OP	35.00	35.00
93	SITTING PRETTY	OP	35.00	35.00
93	TENNIS ANYONE?	OP	35.00	35.00
94	DAYDREAMER	OP	35.00	35.00
94	TEE TIME	OP	35.00	35.00
P. COZZOLINO		**RINGLING BROS. CIRCUS ANIMALS**		
83	ACROBATIC SEAL	9800	49.50	50.00
83	BABY ELEPHANT	9800	49.50	55.00
83	MINIATURE SHOW HORSE	9800	49.50	68.00
83	MR. CHIMPANZEE	9800	49.50	50.00
83	PERFORMING POODLES	9800	49.50	50.00
83	SKATING BEAR	9800	49.50	50.00
84	PARADE CAMEL	9800	49.50	50.00
84	ROARING LION	9800	49.50	50.00

YR	NAME	LIMIT	ISSUE	TREND
N. ROCKWELL		**ROCKWELL HOME OF THE BRAVE**		
82	BACK TO HIS OLD JOB	7500	75.00	75.00
82	HERO'S WELCOME	7500	75.00	75.00
82	REMINISCING	7500	75.00	85.00
82	TAKING MOTHER OVER THE TOP	7500	75.00	75.00
82	UNCLE SAM TAKES WINGS	7500	75.00	75.00
82	WILLIE GILLIS IN CHURCH	7500	75.00	75.00
JACQUELINE B.				**SNUGGLE BABIES**
88	BABY BEARS	OP	35.00	35.00
88	BABY BUNNIES	OP	35.00	35.00
88	BABY FOXES	OP	35.00	35.00
88	BABY SKUNKS	OP	35.00	35.00
89	BABY CHIPMUNKS	OP	35.00	35.00
89	BABY FAWNS	OP	35.00	35.00
89	BABY RACCOONS	OP	35.00	35.00
89	BABY SQUIRRELS	OP	35.00	35.00
T. SULLIVAN				**SPIRIT OF THE EAGLE**
94	SPIRIT OF INDEPENDENCE	OP	55.00	55.00
95	BLAZING MAJESTIC SKIES	OP	55.00	55.00
95	NOBLE AND FREE	OP	55.00	55.00
95	PROUD SYMBOL OF FREEDOM	OP	55.00	55.00
*				**THE GIBSON GIRLS**
86	ACTRESS, THE	OP	75.00	75.00
87	BRIDE, THE	OP	75.00	75.00
87	CAREER GIRL, THE	OP	75.00	75.00
87	COLLEGE GIRL, THE	OP	75.00	75.00
87	SPORTSWOMAN, THE	OP	75.00	75.00
88	ARTIST, THE	OP	75.00	75.00
88	DEBUTANTE, THE	OP	75.00	75.00
88	SOCIETY GIRL, THE	OP	75.00	75.00
G. GRANGET				**THE NOBLE SWAN**
85	NOBLE SWAN, THE	5000	295.00	295.00
*				**THE ROMANCE OF FLOWERS**
87	SPRINGTIME BOUQUET	15000	95.00	95.00
87	SUMMER BOUQUET	15000	95.00	95.00
88	AUTUMN BOUQUET	15000	95.00	95.00
88	WINTER BOUQUET	15000	95.00	95.00
E. DAUB				**THE SPLENDOR OF BALLET**
87	GISELLE	15000	95.00	95.00
87	JULIET	15000	95.00	95.00
87	KITRI	15000	95.00	95.00
87	ODETTE	15000	95.00	95.00
88	AURORA	15000	95.00	95.00
89	CLARA	15000	95.00	95.00
89	FIREBIRD	15000	95.00	95.00
89	SWANILDA	15000	95.00	95.00
M. WALD				**TROPICAL TREASURES**
89	FLAG-TAIL SURGEONFISH	OP	37.50	38.00
89	PENNANT BUTTERFLY FISH	OP	37.50	38.00
89	SAIL-FINNED SURGEONFISH	OP	37.50	38.00
89	SEA HORSE	OP	37.50	38.00
90	BEAKED CORAL BUTTERFLY FISH	OP	37.50	38.00
90	BLUE GIRDLED ANGEL FISH	OP	37.50	38.00
90	SPOTTED ANGEL FISH	OP	37.50	38.00
90	ZEBRA TURKEY FISH	OP	37.50	38.00
C. DEHAAN				**UNBRIDLED SPIRITS**
94	WILD FURY	OP	135.00	135.00
M. GRIFFIN				**VISIONS OF CHRISTMAS**
93	SANTA'S DELIVERY	OP	135.00	135.00
93	TOYS IN PROGRESS	OP	135.00	135.00
94	MRS. CLAUS' KITCHEN	OP	135.00	135.00
95	GIFTS FROM ST. NICK	OP	135.00	135.00
C. BURGESS		**WILD DUCKS OF NORTH AMERICA**		
87	COMMON MALLARD	15000	95.00	95.00
87	GREEN WINGED TAIL	15000	95.00	95.00
87	HOODED MERGANSER	15000	95.00	95.00
87	WOOD DUCK	15000	95.00	95.00
88	AMERICAN WIDGEON	15000	95.00	95.00
88	BUFFLEHEAD	15000	95.00	95.00
88	NORTHERN PINFALL	15000	95.00	95.00
88	RUDDY DUCK DRAKE	15000	95.00	95.00
D. GEENTY				**WOLVES OF THE WILDERNESS**
95	A WOLF'S PRIDE	OP	55.00	55.00
95	MOTHER'S WATCH	OP	55.00	55.00

HAMILTON GIFTS

YR	NAME	LIMIT	ISSUE	TREND
M. HUMPHREY BOGART	**MAUD HUMPHREY BOGART COLLECTOR'S CLUB FIGURINES**			
90	A FLOWER FOR YOU H5596	OP	65.00	65.00
91	FRIENDS FOR LIFE MH911	OP	60.00	140.00
M. HUMPHREY BOGART		**MAUD HUMPHREY BOGART FIGURINES**		
88	A PLEASURE TO MEET YOU H1310	RT	65.00	80.00
88	BRIDE, THE H1313	19500	90.00	90.00
88	CLEANING HOUSE H1303	RT	60.00	70.00
88	LITTLE CHICKADEES H1306	RT	65.00	70.00
88	MAGIC KITTEN, THE- H1308	RT	66.00	85.00
88	MY FIRST DANCE H1311	RT	60.00	200.00
88	SARAH H1312	RT	60.00	275.00

YR	NAME	LIMIT	ISSUE	TREND
88	SEAMSTRESS H1309	RT	66.00	250.00
88	SUSANNA H1305	RT	60.00	250.00
88	TEA AND GOSSIP H1301	RT	65.00	110.00
89	A SUNDAY OUTING H1386	15000	135.00	140.00
89	BRIDE, THE-PORCELAIN H1388	15000	125.00	128.00
89	GIFT OF LOVE H1319	RT	65.00	65.00
89	IN THE ORCHARD H1373	24500	33.00	36.00
89	KITTY'S LUNCH H1355	19500	60.00	66.00
89	LITTLE BO PEEP H1382	24000	45.00	49.00
89	LITTLE CAPTIVE, THE- H1374	19500	55.00	58.00
89	LITTLE CHICKADEES-PORCELAIN H1389	15000	*	110.00
89	LITTLE RED RIDING HOOD H1381	24500	42.50	46.00
89	MAGIC KITTEN, THE-PORCELAIN H5543	19500	125.00	125.00
89	MY FIRST BIRTHDAY H1320	RT	47.00	50.00
89	NO MORE TEARS H1351	24500	44.00	49.00
89	PLAYING BRIDESMAID H5500	19000	125.00	100.00
89	SCHOOL DAYS H1318	RT	42.50	60.00
89	SCHOOL LESSON H1356	19500	77.00	100.00
89	SEALED WITH A KISS H1316	RT	45.00	70.00
89	SPECIAL FRIENDS H1317	RT	66.00	115.00
89	SPECIAL FRIENDS-PORCELAIN H1390	15000	125.00	120.00
89	SPRING BEAUTIES H1387	15000	135.00	131.00
89	SPRINGTIME GATHERING H1385	7500	295.00	200.00
89	WINTER FUN H1354	15000	46.00	60.00
90	A CHANCE ACQUAINTANCE H5589	19500	70.00	135.00
90	A LITTLE ROBIN H1347	19500	55.00	58.00
90	A SPECIAL GIFT H5550	19500	70.00	99.00
90	AUTUMN DAYS H1348	24500	45.00	49.00
90	HOLIDAY SURPRISE H5551	24500	50.00	55.00
90	KITTY'S BATH H1384	19500	103.00	109.00
90	LITTLE PLAYMATES H1349	19500	48.00	53.00
90	MY WINTER HAT H5554	24500	40.00	46.00
90	PLAYTIME H1383	19500	60.00	66.00
90	SARAH (WATERBALL) H5594	19500	75.00	79.00
90	SUSANNA (WATERBALL) H5595	19500	75.00	79.00
90	WINTER DAYS H5553	24500	50.00	55.00
90	WINTER FRIENDS H5552	19500	64.00	69.00
91	ALL BUNDLED UP 910015	19500	85.00	85.00
91	CLEANING HOUSE (WATERBALL) H5654	19500	75.00	75.00
91	DOUBLES 910023	19500	70.00	70.00
91	GRADUATE, THE- H5559	19500	75.00	75.00
91	HUSH A BYE BABY H5695	19500	62.00	62.00
91	LITTLE BOY BLUE H5612	19500	55.00	55.00
91	LITTLE MISS MUFFET H5621	24500	75.00	75.00
91	MELISSA (WATERBALL) 910074	19500	40.00	40.00
91	MELISSA 910031	24500	55.00	55.00
91	MY FIRST DANCE (WATERBALL) H5655	19000	75.00	75.00
91	MY FIRST DANCE-PORCELAIN H5650	15000	110.00	110.00
91	MY SNOW SHOVEL 910058	19500	70.00	70.00
91	MY WINTER HAT 921017	15000	80.00	80.00
91	PINWHEEL, THE- H5600	24500	45.00	45.00
91	SARAH-PORCELAIN H5651	15000	110.00	110.00
91	SPRING BOUQUET H5598	24500	44.00	44.00
91	SPRING FROLIC H5590	15000	170.00	170.00
91	SUSANNA-PORCELAIN H5652	15000	110.00	110.00
91	TEA AND GOSSIP-PORCELAIN H5653	15000	132.00	132.00
91	WINTER DAYS (WATERBALL) 915130	19500	75.00	75.00
91	WINTER FRIENDS (WATERBALL) 915149	19500	75.00	75.00
91	WINTER FUN 921025	15000	90.00	90.00
91	WINTER RIDE 910066	19500	60.00	60.00
M. HUMPHREY BOGART		**MAUD HUMPHREY BOGART GALLERY FIGURINES**		
91	MOTHERS TREASURES H5619	15000	118.00	118.00
91	SHARING SECRETS 910007	15000	120.00	120.00
M. HUMPHREY BOGART		**MAUD HUMPHREY BOGART PETITE FIGURINES**		
91	CLEANING HOUSE H5611	OP	24.00	24.00
91	GIFT OF LOVE H5620	OP	24.00	24.00
91	MAGIC KITTEN, THE- H5623	OP	24.00	24.00
91	MY FIRST DANCE H-5623	OP	24.00	24.00
91	SARAH H5613	OP	24.00	24.00
91	SEAMSTRESS, THE- H5627	OP	24.00	24.00
91	SPECIAL FRIENDS H5625	OP	24.00	24.00
91	SUSANNA H5626	OP	24.00	24.00

HAMILTON/BOEHM

YR	NAME	LIMIT	ISSUE	TREND
*		**FAVORITE GARDEN FLOWERS**		
85	CALIFORNIA POPPY	9800	195.00	225.00
85	CARNATION	9800	195.00	225.00
85	DAFFODIL	9800	195.00	225.00
85	HIBISCUS	9800	195.00	225.00
85	MORNING GLORY	9800	195.00	225.00
85	ROSE	9800	195.00	225.00
85	SWEET PEA	9800	195.00	225.00
85	TULIP	9800	195.00	225.00
*		**ROSES OF DISTINCTION**		
83	ANGEL FACE ROSE	9800	135.00	175.00
83	ELEGANCE ROSE	9800	135.00	175.00
83	MR. LINCOLN ROSE	9800	135.00	175.00
83	PEACE ROSE	9800	135.00	195.00

YR	NAME	LIMIT	ISSUE	TREND
83	QUEEN ELIZABETH ROSE	9800	135.00	175.00
83	ROYAL HIGHNESS ROSE	9800	135.00	175.00
83	TROPICANA ROSE	9800	135.00	175.00
83	WHITE MASTERPIECE ROSE	9800	135.00	195.00

HANFORD'S

YR	NAME	LIMIT	ISSUE	TREND
M. CRUNKLETON		**LINCOLN COUNTY GARDEN CLUB II**		
89	AUNT LENA	RT	40.00	95.00
89	BIG BEULAH	RT	40.00	40.00
89	CHARLOTTE DEAR	RT	40.00	95.00
89	GERTRUDE	RT	40.00	40.00
89	GRANDMA MATTIE	RT	40.00	125.00
89	JACKUELINE ADEL	RT	40.00	40.00
89	LADY MARGARET II	RT	40.00	40.00
89	LARRY LAVINSKI	RT	40.00	40.00
89	MISTER BOB	40	40.00	40.00
89	MOLLY BLUME	RT	40.00	95.00
89	MOZELL	RT	40.00	95.00
89	SISTER ALMA	RT	40.00	95.00
89	TRUMAN WILLARD	RT	40.00	40.00
M. CRUNKLETON		**LINCOLN COUNTY GARDEN CLUB III**		
90	AGNES	RT	40.00	40.00
90	ANNIE LEA	RT	40.00	175.00
90	BIG GUY	RT	40.00	40.00
90	DINAH JANE	RT	40.00	40.00
90	DONNA JEAN	RT	40.00	40.00
90	FLORABEL'S MOM	RT	40.00	95.00
90	LADY MARGARET III	RT	40.00	125.00
90	LEONA MILLER	RT	40.00	95.00
90	MAUDE	RT	40.00	275.00
90	MISS TILLY	RT	40.00	95.00
90	MS LILA	RT	40.00	255.00
90	REBECCA MARIE	RT	40.00	95.00

HAWTHORNE

YR	NAME	LIMIT	ISSUE	TREND
S. SMITH			**THE FAIRY TALE FOREST**	
94	GOLDILOCKS & THE THREE BEARS 78651	*	24.90	25.00
94	GOLDILOCKS & THE THREE BEARS 78653	*	24.90	25.00
94	LITTLE RED RIDING HOOD 78654	CL	49.80	50.00

HELEN SABATTE DESIGNS INC.

YR	NAME	LIMIT	ISSUE	TREND
H. SABATTE			**AMER. CHRISTMAS CAROLLERS**	
93	FATHER	5000	48.00	48.00
93	GRADE SCHOOL BOY	5000	48.00	48.00
93	GRADE SCHOOL GIRL	5000	48.00	48.00
93	MOTHER	5000	48.00	48.00
93	PRE SCHOOL BOY	5000	48.00	48.00
93	PRE SCHOOL GIRL	5000	48.00	48.00
93	TEENAGE BOY	5000	48.00	48.00
93	TEENAGE GIRL	5000	48.00	48.00
93	TRADITIONAL GRANDFATHER	5000	48.00	48.00
93	TRADITIONAL GRANDMOTHER	5000	48.00	48.00
94	TEENAGE BOY HOLDING WATER SNOWGLOBE	200	45.00	50.00
94	TEENAGER GIRL HOLDING WATER SNOWGLOBE	200	45.00	50.00
H. SABATTE			**CHILDHOOD MEMORIES**	
95	MAN WITH SNOWMAN	*	48.00	48.00
95	PRE-SCHOOL BOY WITH SNOWFLAKES	CL	45.00	45.00
95	PRE-SCHOOL BOY WITH SNOWMAN	*	45.00	45.00
95	PRE-SCHOOL GIRL WITH SNOWFLAKES	CL	45.00	45.00
95	PRE-SCHOOL GIRL WITH SNOWMAN	*	45.00	45.00
95	WOMAN WITH SNOWMAN	*	48.00	48.00
96	MOTHER WITH GINGERBREAD BOARD	*	65.00	65.00
96	PRE-SCHOOL BOY W/GINGERBREAD COOKIES	*	45.00	45.00
96	PRE-SCHOOL GIRL W/GINGERBREAD COOKIES	*	45.00	45.00
H. SABATTE				**COLLEGE**
95	TEEN BOY WITH PENNANT	*	48.00	48.00
95	TEEN GIRL WITH PENNANT	*	48.00	48.00
H. SABATTE				**GARDEN**
96	MAN W/GARDEN SUPPLIES	*	60.00	60.00
96	WOMAN W/GARDEN SUPPLIES	*	65.00	65.00
H. SABATTE			**NIGHT BEFORE CHRISTMAS**	
94	GRADE SCHOOL GIRL W/DEAR SANTA LETTER	CL	52.00	52.00
95	PRE-SCHOOL BOY WITH BEAR & BOOKS	*	50.00	50.00
96	MOTHER WITH CHRISTMAS WRAP	*	50.00	50.00
H. SABATTE				**OLDE ENGLISH**
96	MAN.BROWN	*	80.00	80.00
96	MAN/GREEN	*	80.00	80.00
96	WOMAN/RED	*	80.00	80.00
H. SABATTE			**SPECIAL ACCESSORIES**	
95	FATHER WITH SKATES	*	45.00	45.00
95	FATHER WITH SKIES	*	48.00	48.00
95	MOTHER WITH SKATES	*	45.00	45.00
95	MOTHER WITH SKIES	*	48.00	48.00
95	PRE-SCHOOL BOY WITH CAT	*	45.00	45.00
95	PRE-SCHOOL BOY WITH DOG	*	45.00	45.00
95	PRE-SCHOOL BOY WITH PHOTO ALBUM	CL	48.00	48.00
95	PRE-SCHOOL GIRL WITH CAT	*	45.00	45.00
95	PRE-SCHOOL GIRL WITH DOG	*	45.00	45.00

Lladró has a unique look all its own. Flower Song *exudes the elegance and emotion collectors of this magnificent line have come to love.*

Good Night *little darling says this Lladró mother to her young child.*

This little one is eager for the arrival of a new brother or sister. Anticipation *is produced by Lladró.*

A woman this beautiful must be a Lady of Taste. *The piece is produced by Lladró.*

YR	NAME	LIMIT	ISSUE	TREND
95	PRE-SCHOOL GIRL WITH PHOTO ALBUM	CL	48.00	48.00
95	TEENAGE BOY WITH AIRPLANES	*	45.00	45.00
95	TEENAGE BOY WITH SKATES	*	45.00	45.00
95	TEENAGE BOY WITH SKIES	*	48.00	48.00
95	TEENAGE GIRL WITH SKATES	*	45.00	45.00
95	TEENAGE GIRL WITH SKIES	*	48.00	48.00
95	WOMAN WITH APPLES	*	48.00	48.00
96	GRADE SCHOOL BOY W/RAGGEDY ANDY	*	48.00	48.00
96	GRADE SCHOOL GIRL W/RAGGEDY ANN	*	48.00	48.00
96	PRE-SCHOOL BOY WITH ADVENT CALENDAR	*	48.00	48.00
96	PRE-SCHOOL GIRL WITH ADVENT CALENDAR	*	48.00	48.00
H. SABATTE				**THE COLLECTOR**
94	BEAR COLLECTOR-MAN	5000	60.00	65.00
94	BEAR COLLECTOR-WOMAN	5000	65.00	70.00
95	GRADE SCHOOL BOY WITH TEAPOT	CL	50.00	50.00
95	PRE-SCHOOL GIRL WITH 3 BEARS & BOOKS	*	50.00	50.00
95	TEENAGE BOY WITH BEARS & BOOKS	*	50.00	50.00
95	WOMAN WITH TEAPOTS	CL	65.00	65.00
96	GRADE SCHOOL BOY W/RADDEGY ANDY	*	48.00	48.00
96	MOTHER WITH DOLLS & BOOKS	*	68.00	68.00
96	PRE-SCHOOL GIRL W/DOLL CASE, ETC.	*	50.00	50.00
H. SABATTE				**THE COLONIAL**
95	PILGRIM MAN	*	48.00	48.00
95	PILGRIM WOMAN	*	48.00	48.00
96	PILGRIM BOY	*	48.00	48.00
96	PILGRIM GIRL	*	48.00	48.00
H. SABATTE				**THE FATHER CHRISTMAS SERIES**
94	FATHER CHRISTMAS W/CHRISTMAS GREENERY	500	75.00	75.00
94	FATHER CHRISTMAS W/TRADITIONAL TREE	500	80.00	80.00
H. SABATTE				**THE NEW ENGLANDER**
95	FISHERMAN-CHILD	*	48.00	48.00
95	FISHERMAN-OLD	*	48.00	48.00
95	FISHERMAN-YOUNG	*	48.00	48.00
95	LOBSTER BOY	*	48.00	48.00
95	LOBSTERMAN	*	49.00	49.00
95	MAN W/STARFISH SNOWMAN	*	47.00	47.00
95	MAN WITH BLUEBERRY SCOPE	*	48.00	48.00
95	MAN WITH CRANBERRY SCOPE	*	48.00	48.00
95	PRE-SCHOOL BOY W/STARFISH SNOWMAN	*	45.00	45.00
95	PRE-SCHOOL GIRL W/STARFISH SNOWMAN	*	45.00	45.00
95	SAILOR BOY WITH SAILBOAT	*	45.00	45.00
95	SAILOR BOY WITH XMAS SAILBOAT	*	46.00	46.00
95	SAILOR GIRL WITH SAILBOAT	*	45.00	45.00
95	SAILOR GIRL WITH XMAS SAILBOAT	*	46.00	46.00
95	WOMAN W/STARFISH SNOWMAN	*	47.00	47.00
95	WOMAN WITH BLUEBERRIES	*	48.00	48.00
95	WOMAN WITH CRANBERRIES	*	48.00	48.00
H. SABATTE				**THE PUPPETEER**
95	MAN WITH SANTA PUPPET	*	54.00	54.00
H. SABATTE				**THE WEDDING**
95	BRIDE	*	65.00	65.00
95	GROOM	*	60.00	60.00

HOUSE OF HATTEN

D. CALLA

YR	NAME	LIMIT	ISSUE	TREND
95	FOUR SEASONS	1250	*	N/A

HUTSCHENREUTHER

YR	NAME	LIMIT	ISSUE	TREND
GRANGET		**AMERICAN LIMITED EDITION COLLECTION**		
*	A FAMILY AFFAIR	200	*	3700.00
*	ANXIOUS MOMENT	175	*	5225.00
*	ARABIAN STALLION	300	*	8525.00
*	BLUE DOLPHINS	100	*	10000.00
*	CHALLENGE, THE	150	*	14000.00
*	CHRISTMAS ROSE	375	*	3050.00
*	CONTEST, THE	100	*	14000.00
*	DANCE-CROWNCRESTED CRANE, THE	25	*	30000.00
*	DECORATED SEA LIONS	100	*	6000.00
*	DISDAIN-OWL	175	*	5200.00
*	DOLPHIN GROUP	500	*	4000.00
*	ENGAGED	250	*	1750.00
*	FIRST LESSON	175	*	3550.00
*	FISH HAWK, THE	500	*	12000.00
*	FREEDOM IN FLIGHT	200	*	9000.00
*	FRIENDLY ENEMIES-WOODPECKER	175	*	5200.00
*	HEADING SOUTH	150	*	14000.00
*	IT'S SPRING AGAIN	250	*	3475.00
*	JOE-STAG	150	*	12000.00
*	LINNET ON EAR OF RYE	250	*	1175.00
*	OFF SEASON	125	*	4125.00
*	OLYMPIC CHAMPION	500	*	3650.00
*	PROUD PARENT	250	*	13750.00
*	PYGMY OWLS	650	*	6225.00
*	QUINCE	375	*	2850.00
*	REDSTART ON QUINCE BRANCH	250	*	1300.00
*	RELUCTANT FLEDGLING	350	*	3475.00
*	SAFE AT HOME	350	*	9000.00
*	SAW WHET OWL	750	*	3575.00

YR	NAME	LIMIT	ISSUE	TREND
*	SEA FROLIC-SEA LION	500	*	3500.00
*	SENTINEL-SPRINGBOOK, THE	150	*	5200.00
*	SILVER HERON	500	*	5000.00
*	SPARROWHAWK W/KINGBIRD	500	*	8250.00
*	SPRING IS HERE	175	*	4500.00
*	TAKE COVER	125	*	14000.00
*	TO RIDE THE WIND	500	*	8650.00
*	WATER LILY	375	*	4150.00
*	WHOOPING CRANES	300	*	8000.00
*	WREN ON WILD ROSE	250	*	1675.00
D. VALENZA			**PORTRAIT FIGURINES**	
77	CATHERINE THE GREAT	500	500.00	1100.00
77	HELEN OF TORY	500	500.00	1050.00
77	ISOLDE	500	500.00	2650.00
77	JENNIE CHURCHHILL	500	500.00	925.00
77	JUDITH	500	500.00	1575.00
77	LILLIAN RUSSELL	500	500.00	1825.00
77	QUEEN ISABELLE	500	500.00	925.00

IRIS ARC

YR	NAME	LIMIT	ISSUE	TREND
M. GENOA			**CRYSTAL KINGDOM**	
93	BASKET OF VIOLETS	RT	190.00	225.00
93	BIRDBATH	RT	190.00	225.00
93	COUNTRY CHURCH	OP	590.00	590.00
94	BLUEBIRD BASKET	OP	190.00	190.00
94	HUMMINGBIRDS	OP	290.00	290.00
94	MYSTIC STAR CASTLE	OP	390.00	390.00
C. HUGHES			**CRYSTAL KINGDOM**	
93	NOB HILL VICTORIAN	OP	1000.00	1000.00
94	GARDEN COTTAGE	OP	390.00	390.00

ISPANKY

YR	NAME	LIMIT	ISSUE	TREND
L. ISPANKY			**ISPANKY PORCELAINS**	
*	EXODUS, BRONZE	100	1500.00	1500.00
*	OWL	300	750.00	825.00
*	PRINCESS OF THE NILE	500	275.00	450.00
*	ROSH HASHANA, GRAY BEARD	2	275.00	10000.00
*	ROSH HASHANA, WHITE BEARD	400	275.00	1300.00
66	ORCHIDS	250	1000.00	1500.00
67	ARTIST GIRL	500	200.00	1800.00
67	BALLERINA	500	350.00	1000.00
67	BALLET DANCERS	500	350.00	1000.00
67	BIRD OF PARADISE	250	1500.00	1500.00
67	CAVALRY SCOUT, DECORATED	200	1000.00	1200.00
67	CAVALRY SCOUT, WHITE	150	675.00	900.00
67	DRUMMER BOY, DECORATED	200	250.00	285.00
67	DRUMMER BOY, WHITE	600	150.00	185.00
67	DUTCH IRIS	250	1400.00	1500.00
67	FORTY-NINER, DECORATED	200	450.00	650.00
67	FORTY-NINER, WHITE	350	250.00	250.00
67	GREAT SPIRIT, WHITE	150	750.00	750.00
67	HORSE	300	300.00	600.00
67	HUNT, DECORATED	200	2000.00	3850.00
67	HUNT, WHITE	150	1200.00	1485.00
67	KING ARTHUR	500	300.00	750.00
67	LOVE	300	375.00	950.00
67	MEDITATION	300	350.00	1000.00
67	MORNING	500	300.00	1500.00
67	MOSES	400	400.00	1800.00
67	ON THE TRAIL, WHITE	150	750.00	1125.00
67	PACK HORSE, DECORATED	200	700.00	1250.00
67	PACK HORSE, WHITE	150	500.00	350.00
67	PILGRIM FAMILY, DECORATED	200	500.00	750.00
67	PILGRIM FAMILY, WHITE	350	350.00	350.00
67	PIONEER SCOUT, DECORATED	200	1000.00	1000.00
67	PIONEER SCOUT, WHITE	200	675.00	405.00
67	PIONEER WOMAN, DECORATED	200	350.00	550.00
67	PIONEER WOMEN, WHITE	150	225.00	350.00
67	PROMISES	100	225.00	2500.00
67	TULIPS, RED	50	1800.00	4500.00
67	TULIPS, YELLOW	50	1800.00	4500.00
68	PEGASUS, DECORATED	300	375.00	800.00
68	PEGASUS, WHITE	300	300.00	800.00
68	QUEEN OF SPRING	200	750.00	1200.00
69	AUTUMN WIND	500	300.00	1500.00
69	DAFFODILS	250	950.00	950.00
69	GREAT SPIRIT, DECORATED	200	1500.00	1850.00
69	ISAIAH	300	475.00	1100.00
69	MARIA	350	750.00	1000.00
69	MERMAID GROUP, DECORATED	200	1000.00	1800.00
69	MERMAID GROUP, WHITE	200	950.00	950.00
69	STORM	500	400.00	950.00
70	CELESTE	200	475.00	500.00
70	DAWN	300	500.00	1000.00
70	EVENING	300	375.00	650.00
70	HORSEPOWER	100	1650.00	3250.00
70	ICARUS	350	350.00	650.00
70	KING AND QUEEN, PAIR	250	750.00	1200.00
70	ON THE TRAIL, DECORATED	200	1700.00	1700.00

YR	NAME	LIMIT	ISSUE	TREND
70	PEACE, DECORATED	100	375.00	750.00
70	PEACE, WHITE	100	300.00	450.00
70	REVERIE	200	200.00	850.00
70	THRASHER	300	1000.00	1000.00
71	BEAUTY AND THE BEAST	15	4500.00	4500.00
71	BETSY ROSS	350	750.00	1325.00
71	CHRISTINE	300	350.00	800.00
71	DAVID	400	450.00	600.00
71	DEBUTANTE	500	350.00	625.00
71	ETERNAL LOVE	300	400.00	650.00
71	EXCALIBUR	15	3500.00	3500.00
71	FELICIA	15	2500.00	2500.00
71	FREEDOM	250	300.00	500.00
71	JESSAMY 1	400	450.00	600.00
71	MR. AND MRS. OTTER	500	250.00	600.00
71	PEACE RIDERS	1	35000.00	35000.00
71	QUEST	15	1500.00	1500.00
71	ROMEO AND JULIET, DECORATED	500	375.00	950.00
71	SWAN LAKE	300	1000.00	2500.00
71	TEKIEH	15	1800.00	1800.00
72	ANNABEL LEE	500	750.00	750.00
72	CINDERELLA	400	375.00	375.00
72	MADAME BUTTERFLY	300	1500.00	1500.00
72	PRINCESS AND THE FROG	500	675.00	675.00
72	SPIRIT OF THE SEA	450	500.00	500.00
72	SPRING BALLET	400	450.00	600.00
72	SPRING BOUQUET	50	3000.00	15000.00
73	AARON	350	1200.00	2400.00
73	ABRAHAM	500	600.00	1400.00
73	EMERALD DRAGON	100	2500.00	3250.00
73	LORELEI	500	550.00	650.00
73	LOVE LETTERS	450	750.00	850.00
73	MAID OF THE MIST	350	450.00	850.00
73	MESSIAH	750	450.00	500.00
73	REBEKAH	300	400.00	775.00
73	TEXAS RANGERS	400	1650.00	1650.00
74	BANBURY CROSS	350	550.00	1025.00
74	BELLE OF THE BALL	500	550.00	950.00
74	DIANNE	500	500.00	900.00
74	HAMLET AND OPHELIA	350	1250.00	1350.00
74	HOLY FAMILY, DECORATED	450	900.00	1595.00
74	HOLY FAMILY, WHITE	450	750.00	700.00
74	KING LEAR AND CORDELIA	250	1250.00	1250.00
74	SECOND BASE	500	650.00	1100.00
75	APOTHEOSIS OF THE SCULPTOR	250	495.00	1000.00
75	HEALING HAND, DECORATED	600	750.00	1250.00
75	HEALING HAND, WHITE	600	650.00	800.00
75	JOSHUA	350	750.00	1200.00
75	MADONNA WITH HALO, DECORATED	500	350.00	495.00
75	MADONNA WITH HALO, WHITE	500	250.00	250.00
75	MADONNA, THE BLESSED SAINT, DECORATED	500	295.00	350.00
75	MADONNA, THE BLESSED SAINT, WHITE	500	195.00	250.00
75	MEMORIES	500	600.00	900.00
75	SPRING FEVER	600	650.00	1050.00
76	LYDIA	400	450.00	835.00
76	PIANO GIRL	800	300.00	725.00
76	SOPHISTICATION	800	350.00	575.00
76	SWANILDA	1000	285.00	800.00
77	DAISY	1000	325.00	575.00
77	DAY DREAMS	1000	300.00	600.00
77	MORNING GLORY	1000	325.00	620.00
77	POPPY	1000	325.00	575.00
77	SERENE HIGHNESS	100	2500.00	4250.00
77	SNOW DROP	1000	325.00	430.00
77	THUNDER	500	500.00	795.00
78	LITTLE MERMAID	800	350.00	520.00
78	MY NAME IS IRIS	700	500.00	900.00
78	NARCISSUS	700	500.00	620.00
78	ROMANCE	500	800.00	1200.00
78	TEN COMMANDMENTS, DECORATED	500	950.00	1525.00
78	TEN COMMANDMENTS, WHITE	700	600.00	850.00
78	WATER LILY	1000	325.00	620.00

J.H. BOONE

N.J. ROSE — **BEAR CUB SOCIETY**

YR	NAME	LIMIT	ISSUE	TREND
95	HUCKLEBERRY BINGE	3000	80.00	80.00
96	SURPRISE	3000	80.00	80.00

N.J. ROSE — **CLASSIC**

YR	NAME	LIMIT	ISSUE	TREND
96	BUFFALO BILL	OP	125.00	125.00
96	FIRE WOLF	OP	100.00	100.00
96	FLY WITH EAGLES	OP	85.00	85.00
96	MEDICINE ROCK	OP	110.00	110.00

T. SNYDER — **EARTH MATES COLLECTION**

YR	NAME	LIMIT	ISSUE	TREND
95	WISDOM KEEPER	2500	155.00	155.00

T. SNYDER — **EARTH SONG COLLECTION**

YR	NAME	LIMIT	ISSUE	TREND
95	AMAZON	2500	135.00	135.00
95	CONGO	2500	140.00	140.00
95	EARTH MATES	2500	275.00	275.00

YR	NAME	LIMIT	ISSUE	TREND
95	EARTH SONG	1950	275.00	275.00
95	IMPALA/MASAI	2500	160.00	160.00
95	KINGS IN THE CRADLE	2500	155.00	155.00
95	LAST FRONTIER	2500	140.00	140.00
95	MOUNTAIN FORTRESS	2500	155.00	155.00
95	NORTHERN WILDERNESS	2500	135.00	135.00
95	OUTBACK	2500	135.00	135.00
95	PRIDE OF AFRICA	1500	250.00	250.00
95	RHYTHM OF LIFE	2500	135.00	135.00
95	SACRED PATHS	2500	135.00	135.00
95	SAVAGE KINSHIP	2500	140.00	140.00
95	SAVANNA TITANS	2500	155.00	155.00
95	SPRINGBOK	2500	95.00	95.00
95	THIN ICE	2500	95.00	95.00
96	EMBRACE	2500	85.00	85.00
96	SAMBURU ELDER	1500	85.00	85.00
96	SEBRINA	1500	85.00	85.00
96	ZULU WARRIOR	2500	85.00	85.00
G. ROSE		**KINDRED SPIRIT COLLECTION**		
95	BUFFALO SPIRIT	1500	250.00	250.00
96	WOLF PAWS	3000	95.00	95.00
N.J. ROSE		**NEIL J. ROSE COLLECTION**		
95	ARCTIC PHANTOMS	2500	92.00	92.00
95	BUFFALO HEART	2500	85.00	85.00
95	COUGAR ROCK	1950	275.00	275.00
95	DENIZEN OF THE NORTH	2500	92.00	92.00
95	FLAME, THE	2500	105.00	105.00
95	FREE SPIRIT	2500	180.00	180.00
95	GIFT OF THE WOLF	2500	60.00	60.00
95	LEGEND OF SPIRIT LAKE	2500	95.00	95.00
95	MISTRAL	2500	75.00	75.00
95	PIPE HOLDER	1950	260.00	260.00
95	RISING SUN	3500	135.00	135.00
95	SILENT STALKER	2500	105.00	105.00
95	TOWERING ANTLERS	2500	115.00	115.00
95	WILDERNESS MAURAUDER	1500	180.00	180.00
96	BETRAYAL	2500	275.00	275.00
96	ROCK MOUNTAIN RECLUSE	2500	100.00	100.00
96	SNOW FLOWER	2500	95.00	95.00
P. CARRICO				**TRACES**
95	MATERNAL INSTINCT	2500	240.00	240.00
95	MONARCH MOUNTAIN	1950	280.00	280.00
95	REFUGE	1950	100.00	100.00
95	SILENT LANDING	2500	105.00	105.00
96	SACRED SPIRITS	1950	250.00	250.00

JAN HAGARA COLLECTABLES

YR	NAME	LIMIT	ISSUE	TREND
J. HAGARA				
95	DANA	7500	59.50	60.00
95	JENNIFER & BASKET	7500	72.50	72.50
95	TAMMY	7500	59.50	60.00
J. HAGARA				**MINIATURES**
89	HEATHER	RT	18.00	18.00
89	MANDY	RT	18.00	25.00
89	RACHAEL	RT	18.00	18.00
89	TIPPI	RT	18.00	18.00
J. HAGARA				**SHELFSITTER**
95	ADRIANNE	7500	47.00	47.00
95	MATTHEW HAS TURNED THE PAGE	7500	38.50	39.00
96	LITTLE SHARICE & ROCKER	7500	71.50	71.50
J. HAGARA				**SIGNATURE**
85	ALICE AND ANDREA	RT	75.00	250.00
85	BECKY	RT	55.00	375.00
85	JESSICA	RT	55.00	100.00
85	MEMORIES	RT	75.00	250.00
85	STORYTIME	RT	135.00	300.00
85	THERESA	RT	55.00	260.00
87	NIKKI & SANTA	RT	135.00	260.00
J. HAGARA			**VICTORIAN CHILDREN**	
*	JAN AT AGE FOUR	*	*	75.00
*	MISSY	*	*	50.00
83	ANNE	RT	25.00	90.00
83	JENNY	RT	25.00	175.00
83	JODY	RT	25.00	60.00
83	LISA	RT	25.00	60.00
83	LYDIA	RT	25.00	100.00
83	VICTORIA	RT	25.00	65.00
84	AMANDA	RT	30.00	100.00
84	BRIAN	RT	30.00	40.00
84	CAROL	RT	30.00	200.00
84	CRISTINA	RT	30.00	75.00
85	ANGIE	RT	30.00	125.00
85	BRIAN & CINNAMON BEAR	RT	30.00	200.00
85	DAPHNE & UNICORN	RT	45.00	85.00
85	STACY	RT	30.00	125.00
85	STEPHEN	RT	30.00	125.00
86	ASHLEY	RT	25.00	60.00
86	CHRIS	RT	30.00	100.00

YR	NAME	LIMIT	ISSUE	TREND
86	DAISIES FROM JIMMY	RT	45.00	125.00
86	LARRY	RT	30.00	75.00
86	MEG	RT	30.00	75.00
86	MELANIE	RT	30.00	100.00

JAN'S ORIGINALS

J. BENSON — **GEORGIA & SOUTH CAROLINA SERIES**

YR	NAME	LIMIT	ISSUE	TREND
92	SHRIMP BOAT	500	48.00	63.00
92	SHRIMP BOAT	1000	48.00	60.00

J. BENSON — **GEORGIA SERIES**

YR	NAME	LIMIT	ISSUE	TREND
90	OLD DALLAS HIGH SCHOOL	500	48.00	48.00
90	PAULDING COURTHOUSE	500	52.00	52.00
91	LOST MOUNTAIN STORE	1000	48.00	65.00
92	1ST PRESBYTERIAN CHURCH, ST. MARY'S	500	48.00	60.00
92	BARNSLEY GARDENS RUINS	500	48.00	60.00
92	BIB CHICKEN	1000	46.00	46.00
92	CARTERSVILLE DEPOT	500	48.00	48.00
92	CLOCK TOWER	1000	46.00	55.00
92	FOX THEATRE	1000	48.00	55.00
92	GEORGIA TECH	1000	52.00	60.00
92	O'HARA HOMEPLACE	100	50.00	60.00
92	OLD ST. MARYS METHODIST CHURCH	500	48.00	60.00
92	ORANGE HALL	500	46.00	55.00
92	RIVERVIEW HOTEL	500	50.00	60.00
92	TROLLEY, THE	500	46.00	55.00
92	UNIVERSITY OF GEORGIA	1000	48.00	60.00
92	VARSITY, THE	500	50.00	50.00
92	WATERWHEEL OF BERRY COLLEGE	1000	46.00	55.00
93	1ST BAPTIST CHURCH ST. MARYS	500	48.00	48.00
93	4-WAY LUNCH	500	46.00	46.00
93	COBB CTY. COURTHOUSE	1000	50.00	50.00
93	COBB CTY. YOUTH MUSEUM	500	48.00	48.00
93	MILLER'S DOCK	500	50.00	50.00
93	ROSELAWN	500	52.00	52.00
93	SPENCER HOUSE	500	48.00	48.00
94	1902 STOCK EXCHANGE	800	48.00	48.00
94	1ST BAPTISTI CHURCH-CARTERSVILLE	500	50.00	50.00
94	1ST PRESBYTERIAN CHURCH-CARTERSVILLE	500	50.00	50.00
94	ADAITSVILLE DEPOT	500	48.00	48.00
94	BLUE GOOSE	500	48.00	48.00
94	CAMDEN CTY. HIGH SCHOOL	200	52.00	52.00
94	EPISCOPAL CHURCH OF THE ASCENIOUS	500	48.00	48.00
94	FIRST COCA COLA BOTTLING	1000	48.00	48.00
94	FLOYD CTY. COURTHOUSE	*	*	*
94	GEORGIA STATE CAPITOL	500	76.00	76.00
94	GOODBREAD HOUSE	500	48.00	48.00
94	GRAND THEATRE	500	46.00	46.00
94	JACKSON HOUSE, THE	1000	52.00	52.00
94	LOEW'S GRANT THEATRE	1000	52.00	52.00
94	MARIETTA DEPOT	1000	50.00	50.00
94	PAVILION, THE	500	48.00	48.00
94	SAM JONES MEMORIAL METHODIST	500	50.00	50.00
94	WHITE COLUMNS WSB-TV	1000	52.00	52.00
94	YOUNG BROTHERS PHARMACY	500	48.00	48.00
95	GREYFIELD PLANTATION	1000	52.00	52.00
95	OLD CAMDEN CTY. COURTHOUSE	500	52.00	52.00
95	SKYLINE OF ATLANTA, GA. 1996	*	54.00	54.00

JEFFREY SCOTT CO.

M. GORETTI — **THE BIRD SANCTUARY**

YR	NAME	LIMIT	ISSUE	TREND
93	HERITAGE EAGLE	5000	50.00	60.00
94	HARMONY IN THE WILD	2500	65.00	75.00

JOHN HINE STUDIOS LTD.

Price ranges may reflect various demands in the market from one geographic region to another; condition of piece; specific markings found on piece; and/or changes in production of piece.

D. WINTER — **DAVID WINTER SCENES**

YR	NAME	LIMIT	ISSUE	TREND
92	AT ROSE COTTAGE/VIGNETTE	5000	39.00	39.00
92	AT THE BAKEHOUSE/VIGNETTE	5000	35.00	35.00
92	AT THE BOTHY/VIGNETTE BASE	5000	39.00	39.00
92	DAUGHTER	5000	30.00	30.00
92	FARM HAND AND SPADE	5000	40.00	40.00
92	FARMER AND PLOUGH	5000	60.00	60.00
92	FARMER'S WIFE	5000	45.00	45.00
92	FATHER	5000	45.00	45.00
92	GIRL SELLING EGGS	5000	30.00	30.00
92	GOOSE GIRL	5000	45.00	45.00
92	HOT CROSS BUN SELLER	5000	60.00	60.00
92	LADY CUSTOMER	5000	45.00	45.00
92	MOTHER	5000	50.00	50.00
92	SMALL BOY & DOG	5000	45.00	45.00
92	SON	5000	30.00	30.00
92	WOMAN AT PUMP	5000	45.00	45.00
93	BOB CRATCHIT & TINY TIM	5000	50.00	50.00
93	CHRISTMAS SNOW/VIGNETTE	5000	50.00	50.00
93	EBENEZER SCROOGE	5000	45.00	45.00
93	FRED	5000	35.00	35.00
93	MISS BELLE	5000	35.00	35.00

YR	NAME	LIMIT	ISSUE	TREND
93	MRS. FEZZIWIG	5000	35.00	35.00
93	TOM THE STREET SHOVELER	5000	60.00	60.00
95	WINTERVILLE DIORAMA	OP	80.00	80.00
S. KUCK				**HEART STRINGS**
92	DAY DREAMING	15000	92.50	93.00
92	HUSH, IT'S SLEEPYTIME	15000	97.50	98.00
92	TAKING TEA	15000	92.50	93.00
92	WATCH ME WALTZ	15000	97.50	98.00

JUNE MCKENNA COLLECTIBLES INC.

YR	NAME	LIMIT	ISSUE	TREND
J. MCKENNA				**12" LIMITED EDITION**
95	PEACEFUL JOURNEY	4000	250.00	250.00
96	MAGIC OF CHRISTMAS	400	250.00	250.00
J. MCKENNA				**3-D BLACK FOLK ART**
96	ALL I WANT FOR CHRISTMAS	YR	70.00	70.00
96	I'VE GOT THE TREE	YR	70.00	70.00
96	JASMINE	YR	70.00	70.00
96	JEREMIAH	YR	70.00	70.00
96	SPLISH SPLASH	YR	70.00	70.00
96	UNCLE TOM'S CHRISTMAS	YR	160.00	160.00
J. MCKENNA				**3-D FIGURINE**
96	BRIDE & GROOM	YR	70.00	70.00
96	HELPFUL FRIENDS	YR	90.00	90.00
96	MR. SANTA W/ RAG DOLL	YR	70.00	70.00
96	MRS. SANTA W/ RAG DOLL	YR	70.00	70.00
96	SET OF THREE TREES	YR	60.00	60.00
J. MCKENNA				**6" CHRISTMAS FIGURINE**
95	FINISHING TOUCH	YR	70.00	70.00
95	JOEY'S CHRISTMAS	YR	70.00	70.00
J. MCKENNA				**7" LIMITED EDITION**
95	CHRISTMAS LULLABY/RED	RT	120.00	120.00
96	CHRISTMAS LULLABY/BLUE	7500	120.00	120.00
96	POLAR BEAR EXPRESS	2500	120.00	120.00
J. MCKENNA				**AMISH FLATBACK**
96	AMISH BROTHER	YR	30.00	30.00
96	AMISH FATHER	YR	30.00	30.00
96	AMISH GRANDMA	YR	32.00	32.00
96	AMISH GRANDPA	YR	32.00	32.00
96	AMISH MOTHER	YR	30.00	30.00
96	AMISH SISTER	YR	30.00	30.00
96	SUNDAY OUTING	YR	50.00	50.00
J. MCKENNA				**BLACK FOLK ART**
83	BLACK BOY WITH WATERMELON	CL	12.00	40.00
83	BLACK GIRL WITH WATERMELON	CL	12.00	40.00
84	BLACK MAN WITH PIG	CL	13.00	40.00
84	BLACK WOMAN WITH BROOM	CL	13.00	40.00
85	KIDS IN A TUB 3D	CL	30.00	60.00
85	KISSING COUSINS-SILL SITTER	CL	36.00	60.00
85	WATERMELON PATCH KIDS	CL	24.00	63.00
86	BLACK BUTLER	CL	13.00	40.00
87	AUNT BERTHA 3D	CL	36.00	72.00
87	LIL' WILLIE 3D	CL	36.00	72.00
87	SWEET PRISSY 3D	CL	36.00	72.00
87	UNCLE JACOB 3D	CL	36.00	72.00
88	NETTY	CL	16.00	50.00
88	RENTY	CL	16.00	40.00
89	DELIA	CL	16.00	40.00
89	JAKE	CL	16.00	40.00
90	TASHA	CL	17.00	40.00
90	TYREE	CL	17.00	40.00
J. MCKENNA				**CAROLERS**
85	BOY CAROLER	CL	36.00	75.00
85	GIRL CAROLER	CL	36.00	75.00
85	MAN CAROLER	CL	36.00	75.00
85	WOMAN CAROLER	CL	36.00	75.00
J. MCKENNA				**FLATBACK FIGURINE**
95	SANTA CAROLING	YR	60.00	60.00
95	TRAVEL PLANS	YR	70.00	70.00
96	GREETINGS/DOORWAY	YR	50.00	50.00
96	SANTA/TREE TOPPER	YR	70.00	70.00
J. MCKENNA				**ICICLE**
96	SANTA W/PIPE	YR	17.00	17.00
J. MCKENNA				**JUNE MCKENNA FIGURINES**
84	TREE TROPPER	CL	70.00	225.00
85	SOLDIER	CL	40.00	175.00
86	LITTLE ST. NICK	CL	50.00	100.00
86	MALE ANGEL	CL	44.00	400.00-2500.00
87	PATRIOTIC SANTA	CL	50.00	125.00
88	MRS. SANTA	CL	50.00	125.00
92	TAKING A BREAK	RT	60.00	70.00
93	A GOOD NIGHT'S SLEEP	RT	70.00	70.00
93	ANGEL NAME PLAQUE	OP	70.00	70.00
93	BAKING COOKIES	RT	450.00	450.00
93	BELLS OF CHRISTMAS	RT	40.00	40.00
93	CHILDREN ICE SKATERS	OP	70.00	70.00
93	CHRISTMAS CHEER	RT	120.00	120.00
93	CHRISTMAS EVE	4 YR	35.00	35.00

YR	NAME	LIMIT	ISSUE	TREND
93	MR. SNOWMAN	OP	40.00	40.00
93	NATIVITY COW	OP	30.00	30.00
93	NATIVITY DONKEY	OP	30.00	30.00
93	NATIVITY RAM WITH EWE	OP	30.00	30.00
93	PATRIOT, THE	4000	250.00	250.00
93	SANTA AND FRIENDS	OP	70.00	70.00
93	SANTA NAME PLAQUE	RT	70.00	70.00
93	SANTA'S LOVE	RT	40.00	40.00
93	SNOW FAMILY, THE	OP	40.00	40.00
93	TOMORROW'S CHRISTMAS	RT	250.00	250.00
94	ALL ABOARD NORTH POLE EXPRESS	*	500.00	500.00
94	BRINGING HOME CHRISTMAS	4 YR	35.00	35.00
94	CHILDREN CAROLERS	OP	90.00	90.00
94	CONDUCTOR	OP	70.00	70.00
94	DECORATING FOR CHRISTMAS	OP	70.00	70.00
94	MRS. CLAUS, DANCING	7500	120.00	120.00
94	NOT ONCE BUT TWICE	10000	40.00	40.00
94	POSTMARKED NORTH POLE	10000	40.00	40.00
94	SANTA'S ONE MAN BAND	7500	120.00	120.00
94	SAY CHEESE, PLEASE	OP	250.00	250.00
94	SNOWMAN AND CHILD	OP	70.00	70.00
94	ST. NICHOLAS	4000	250.00	250.00
94	STAR OF BETHLEHEM	OP	40.00	40.00
94	WELCOME TO THE WORLD	RT	400.00	400.00
J. MCKENNA				**LIMITED EDITION**
83	FATHER CHRISTMAS	RT	90.00	3500.00
84	OLD SAINT NICK	CL	100.00	1500.00
85	WOODLAND	CL	140.00	1900.00
86	VICTORIAN	CL	150.00	600.00
87	CHRISTMAS EVE	CL	170.00	575.00
87	KRIS KRINGLE	CL	350.00	500.00
88	BRINGING HOME CHRISTMAS	CL	170.00	325.00
88	REMEMBERANCE OF CHRISTMAS PAST	4000	400.00	550.00
89	COMING TO TOWN	4000	220.00	220.00
89	SANTA'S WARDROBE	1500	750.00	750.00
89	SEASONS GREETINGS	CL	200.00	325.00
90	NIGHT BEFORE CHRISTMAS	1000	750.00	750.00
90	WILDERNESS	4000	200.00	200.00
92	BEDTIME STORIES	2000	500.00	500.00
92	CHRISTMAS GATHERING	4000	220.00	220.00
92	COMING TO TOWN	4000	220.00	220.00
92	HOT AIR BALLOON	1500	800.00	800.00
J. MCKENNA				**LIMITED FLATBACK**
95	CHRISTMAS DELIVERY	10000	40.00	40.00
95	LIGHT OF CHRISTMAS	10000	40.00	40.00
96	HAPPY HOLIDAYS	3000	40.00	40.00
96	YULETIDE JOY	3000	40.00	40.00
J. MCKENNA				**NATIVITY SET**
96	NATIVITY SET	OP	150.00	150.00
J. MCKENNA				**REGISTERED EDITION**
86	COLONIAL	CL	150.00	425.00
87	WHITE CHRISTMAS	CL	170.00	1500.00
88	JOLLY OLE ST. NICK	CL	170.00	250.00
89	TRADITIONAL	OP	180.00	180.00
90	TOY MAKER	OP	200.00	200.00
91	CHECKING HIS LIST	OP	230.00	230.00
92	FORTY WINKS	OP	250.00	250.00
95	A CHRISTMAS TREAT FOR ALL	YR	260.00	260.00
95	CHRISTMAS DOWN ON THE FARM	YR	260.00	260.00
96	CHRISTMAS OVER LOAD	YR	260.00	260.00
J. MCKENNA				**SPECIAL LIMITED EDITION**
89	LAST GENTLE NUDGE	RT	280.00	280.00
89	SANTA & HIS MAGIC SLEIGH	RT	280.00	280.00
90	CHRISTMAS DREAMS	4000	280.00	280.00
90	SANTA'S REINDEER	1500	400.00	400.00
90	UP ON THE ROOFTOP	RT	280.00	280.00
95	ALL-BOARD - TOY CAR	RT	250.00	250.00
96	INTERNATIONAL SANTA	YR	160.00	160.00
96	LOGGING CAR	YR	250.00	250.00
96	SHOW ME THE WAY	YR	500.00	500.00
J. MCKENNA				**VICTORIAN LIMITED EDITION**
90	EDWARD 3D	CL	180.00	450.00
90	ELIZABETH 3D	CL	180.00	450.00

KAISER

YR	NAME	LIMIT	ISSUE	TREND
W. GAWANTKA				**ANIMALS**
69	PORPOISE GROUP (3), WHITE BISQUE	CL	85.00	400.00
75	DOLPHIN GROUP (5), 520/5, WHITE BISQUE	800	850.00	3000.00
75	GERMAN SHEPHERD 528, COLOR BISQUE	CL	250.00	675.00
75	GERMAN SHEPHERD 528, WHITE BISQUE	CL	185.00	450.00
76	IRISH SETTER 535, COLOR BISQUE	1000	290.00	675.00
76	IRISH SETTER 535, WHITE/BASE	1500	*	450.00
78	DOLPHIN GROUP (4), 596/4, WHITE BISQUE	4500	75.00	1000.00
78	KILLER WHALE 579, COLOR/BISQUE	2000	420.00	800.00
78	KILLER WHALE 579, WHITE/BISQUE	2000	85.00	425.00
78	KILLER WHALES (2), 594, COLOR	2000	925.00	2025.00
78	KILLER WHALES (2), 594, WHITE	2000	425.00	1050.00
79	BEAR & CUB 521, COLOR BISQUE	900	400.00	1100.00

YR	NAME	LIMIT	ISSUE	TREND
79	BEAR & CUB 521, WHITE BISQUE	CL	125.00	400.00
85	BROOK TROUT 739, COLOR BISQUE	OP	250.00	500.00
85	PIKE 737, COLOR BISQUE	OP	350.00	700.00
85	RAINBOW TROUT 739, COLOR BISQUE	OP	250.00	500.00
85	TROUT 739, COLOR BISQUE	OP	95.00	500.00
91	LION 701201, WHITE BISQUE	1500	650.00	650.00
91	LION 701203, COLOR BISQUE	1500	1300.00	1300.00
H. LIEDERLY				**ANIMALS**
82	TWO WILD BOARS 664, COLOR BISQUE	1000	650.00	890.00
G. TAGLIARIOL				**ANIMALS**
80	BISON 630, COLOR BISQUE	2000	620.00	1100.00
80	BISON 690, WHITE BISQUE	2000	350.00	500.00
*		**BIRDS OF AMERICA COLLECTION**		
*	BALD EAGLE II 497, COLORED	CL	*	1300.00
*	ROADRUNNER 492, COLOR/BASE	CL	350.00	900.00
*	ROBIN & WORM, COLOR/BASE	CL	60.00	90.00
*	ROBIN II 537, COLOR/BASE	1000	260.00	900.00
*	SCREECH OWL 532, WHITE/BASE	CL	175.00	200.00
*	SNOWY OWL 776, COLOR/BASE	1500	*	1200.00
*	SNOWY OWL 776, WHITE/BASE	1500	*	700.00
*	SPARROW HAWK 749, COLOR/BASE	3000	575.00	950.00
70	SCARLET TANAGER, COLOR/BASE	CL	60.00	90.00
85	PINTAILS 747, COLOR/BASE	1500	*	850.00
85	PINTAILS 747, WHITE/BASE	1500	*	375.00
W. GAWANTKA		**BIRDS OF AMERICA COLLECTION**		
*	BABY TITMICE 501, COLOR/BASE	CL	400.00	525.00
*	BABY TITMICE 501, WHITE/BASE	1200	200.00	800.00
72	BLUE BIRD 496, COLOR, BASE	2500	120.00	500.00
72	GOSHAWK 491, COLOR/BASE	1500	2400.00	4400.00
72	GOSHAWK 491, WHITE/BASE	1500	850.00	2000.00
72	SEAGULL 498, COLOR/BASE	CL	850.00	1150.00
72	SEAGULL 498, WHITE/BASE	700	550.00	1600.00
73	BLUEJAY 503, COLOR/BASE	1500	475.00	1200.00
73	CARDINAL 504, COLOR/BASE	1500	60.00	600.00
73	ROBIN 502, COLOR/BASE	1500	340.00	725.00
74	FALCON 507, COLOR/BASE	1500	820.00	2000.00
76	BALD EAGLE IV 552, COLOR/BASE	1500	450.00	1000.00
76	BALD EAGLE IV 552, WHITE/BASE	1500	210.00	575.00
80	BALD EAGLE VI 634, WHITE/BASE	3000	*	700.00
84	BALD EAGLE IX 714, COLOR/BASE	3500	500.00	850.00
84	BALD EAGLE IX 714, WHITE/BASE	4000	190.00	400.00
85	BALD EAGLE X 746, COLOR/BASE	1500	*	1200.00
85	BALD EAGLE X 746, WHITE/BASE	1500	375.00	700.00
85	BALD EAGLE XI 751, COLOR/BASE	1000	880.00	1500.00
85	BALD EAGLE XI 751, WHITE/BASE	1000	*	925.00
U. NETZSCH		**BIRDS OF AMERICA COLLECTION**		
68	PAIR OF MALLARDS 456, COLOR/BASE	CL	150.00	500.00
68	PAIR OF MALLARDS 456, WHITE/BASE	2000	75.00	525.00
68	PIDGEON GROUP 475, COLOR/BASE	1500	150.00	825.00
68	PIDGEON GROUP 475, WHITE/BASE	2000	60.00	425.00
G. TAGLIARIOL		**BIRDS OF AMERICA COLLECTION**		
*	BALD EAGLE VII 637, COLOR/BASE	200	*	20800.00
*	HORNED OWL II 524, COLOR/BASE	1000	650.00	2200.00
*	HORNED OWL II 524, WHITE/BASE	1000	*	1000.00
*	PELICAN 534, WHITE/BASE	CL	*	625.00
75	SPARROW 516, COLOR/BASE	1500	300.00	600.00
75	WOOD DUCKS 514, COLOR/BASE	800	*	2850.00
75	WOODPECKERS 515, COLOR/BASE	800	900.00	1800.00
76	BALTIMORE ORIOLE 536, COLOR/BASE	1000	280.00	750.00
76	CANADIAN GEESE 550, WHITE/BASE	1500	1500.00	3500.00
76	PELICAN 534, COLOR/BASE	1200	925.00	1800.00
76	PHEASANT 556, COLOR/BASE	1500	3200.00	6100.00
77	OWL IV 559, COLOR/BASE	1000	*	1300.00
78	BABY TITMICE 601, COLOR/BASE	2000	*	1000.00
78	BABY TITMICE 601, WHITE/BASE	2000	*	600.00
78	BALD EAGLE V 600, COLOR/BASE	1500	*	3900.00
78	PAIR OF MALLARDS II 572, COLOR/BASE	1500	*	1200.00
78	PAIR OF MALLARDS II 572, WHITE/BASE	1500	*	2400.00
79	SWAN 602, COLOR/BASE	2000	*	1400.00
81	KINGFISHER 639, COLOR/BASE	CL	45.00	60.00
81	QUAILS 640, COLOR/BASE	1500	*	2400.00
81	ROOSTER 642, COLOR/BASE	1500	860.00	1350.00
81	ROOSTER 642, WHITE/BASE	1500	380.00	700.00
82	BALD EAGLE VIII 656, COLOR/BASE	CL	800.00	900.00
82	BALD EAGLE VIII 656, WHITE/BASE	1000	400.00	925.00
82	HUMMINGBIRD GROUP 660, COLOR/BASE	3000	650.00	1300.00
84	PHEASANT 715, COLOR/BASE	1500	1000.00	2000.00
M. TANDY		**BIRDS OF AMERICA COLLECTION**		
84	PEREGRINE FALCON 723, COLOR/BASE	1500	850.00	5000.00
86	SPARROW HAWK 777, COLORED BISQUE	10000	950.00	1400.00
86	SPARROW HAWK 777, WHITE BISQUE	1000	440.00	725.00
W. GAWANTKA			**HORSE SCULPTURE**	
71	PONY GROUP 488, COLOR/BASE	CL	150.00	350.00
71	PONY GROUP 488, WHITE/BASE	2500	50.00	425.00
74	MARE & FOAL II 510, COLOR/BASE	CL	650.00	800.00
75	LIPIZZANER/MAESTOSO 517, COLOR/BASE	CL	*	1150.00
75	LIPIZZANER/MAESTOSO 517, WHITE/BASE	CL	*	750.00
76	HASSAN/ARABIAN 553, COLOR/BASE	1500	600.00	1250.00

YR	NAME	LIMIT	ISSUE	TREND
76	HASSAN/ARABIAN 553, WHITE/BASE	CL	250.00	600.00
78	CAPITANO/LIPIZZANER 597, COLOR	1500	625.00	1500.00
78	CAPITANO/LIPIZZANER 597, WHITE	CL	275.00	600.00
80	MARE & FOAL III 636, COLOR/BASE	1500	950.00	1650.00
80	MARE & FOAL III 636, WHITE/BASE	1500	300.00	675.00
80	ORION/ARABIAN 629, COLOR/BASE	2000	600.00	1050.00
80	ORION/ARABIAN 629, WHITE/BASE	2000	250.00	450.00
87	PACER 792, COLOR/BASE	1500	1217.00	1350.00
87	PACER 792, WHITE/BASE	1500	574.00	675.00
87	TROTTER 780, COLOR/BASE	1500	1217.00	1350.00
87	TROTTER 780, WHITE/BASE	1500	574.00	675.00
90	ARGOS 633101, WHITE BISQUE/BASE	1000	578.00	700.00
90	ARGOS 633103, LIGHT COLOR/BASE	1000	1194.00	1400.00
90	ARGOS 633143, COLOR/BASE	1000	1194.00	1400.00
*				**HUMAN FIGURES**
*	FATHER & DAUGHTER 752, COLOR	2500	390.00	725.00
*	FATHER & DAUGHTER 752, WHITE	2500	175.00	375.00
*	MOTHER & CHILD 757, COLOR	3500	600.00	900.00
*	MOTHER & CHILD 757, WHITE	4000	300.00	425.00
*	MOTHER & CHILD 775, COLOR	3500	600.00	900.00
*	MOTHER & CHILD 775, WHITE	4000	300.00	425.00
G. BOCHMANN				**HUMAN FIGURES**
60	MOTHER & CHILD 398, WHITE BISQUE	OP	*	325.00
W. GAWANTKA				**HUMAN FIGURES**
82	FATHER & SON 659, COLOR/BASE	2500	400.00	725.00
82	FATHER & SON 659, WHITE/BASE	2500	100.00	400.00
82	ICE PRINCESS 667, COLOR	5000	375.00	750.00
82	ICE PRINCESS 667, WHITE	5000	200.00	425.00
82	SWAN LAKE BALLET 641, COLOR	2500	650.00	1300.00
82	SWAN LAKE BALLET 641, WHITE	2500	200.00	1000.00
83	MOTHER & CHILD/BUST 696, COLOR	3500	500.00	1075.00
83	MOTHER & CHILD/BUST 696, WHITE	4000	225.00	450.00

KURT S. ADLER/SANTA'S WORLD

YR	NAME	LIMIT	ISSUE	TREND
*** KSA/STEINBACH**				**AMERICAN PRESIDENTS STEINBACH NUTCRACKER**
93	BEN FRANKLIN ES922	RT	225.00	225.00
93	TEDDY ROOSEVELT ES644	10000	225.00	225.00
96	THOMAS JEFFERSON ES866	7500	260.00	260.00
C. STEINBACH				**AMERICAN PRESIDENTS STEINBACH NUTCRACKER**
92	ABRAHAM LINCOLN ES622	RT	195.00	210.00
92	GEORGE WASHINGTON ES623	12000	195.00	210.00
N. BAILEY				**ANGEL DARLINGS**
96	BOTTOMS UP	OP	15.00	15.00
96	BUDDIES H4765/3	OP	15.00	15.00
96	CUDDLES H4765/4	OP	15.00	15.00
96	DREAM BUILDERS H4765/4	OP	15.00	15.00
96	PEEK-A-BOO H4765/2	OP	15.00	15.00
*** KSA/STEINBACH**				**BIBLICAL**
96	NOAH ES893	1000	260.00	260.00
*** KSA/STEINBACH**				**CAMELOT STEINBACH NUTCRACKER**
93	SIR LANCELOT ES638	12000	225.00	225.00
94	SIR GALAHAD ES862	12000	225.00	225.00
94	SIR LANCELOT SMOKER ES833	7500	150.00	150.00
95	QUEEN GUENEVERE ES869	10000	245.00	245.00
C. STEINBACH				**CAMELOT STEINBACH NUTCRACKER**
91	MERLIN THE MAGICIAN ES610	RT	185.00	1650.00
92	KING ARTHUR ES621	RT	195.00	285.00
*** KSA/STEINBACH**				**CAMELOT STEINBACH SMOKING FIGURINE**
93	KING ARTHUR ES832	7500	175.00	175.00
C. STEINBACH				**CAMELOT STEINBACH SMOKING FIGURINE**
92	MERLIN THE MAGICIAN ES830	7500	150.00	150.00
*				**CURRIER & IVES WATERGLOBE COLLECTION**
92	OUR FIRST CHRISTMAS J1037	OP	40.00	40.00
92	WE WISH YOU A MERRY CHRISTMAS J1048	OP	40.00	40.00
K. ADLER				**FABRICHE ANGEL SERIES**
92	HEAVENLY MESSENGER W1584	RT	41.00	41.00
K. ADLER				**FABRICHE BEAR & FRIENDS**
92	LAUGHING ALL THE WAY J1567	RT	83.00	83.00
92	NOT A CREATURE WAS STIRRING W1534	RT	67.00	67.00
93	TEDDY BEAR PARADE W1601	RT	73.00	73.00
P. MAUK				**FABRICHE CAMELOT FIGURE**
93	MERLIN THE MAGICIAN J7966	RT	120.00	120.00
93	YOUNG ARTHUR J7967	RT	120.00	120.00
94	KING ARTHUR J3372	RT	110.00	110.00
*				**FABRICHE COLLECTION**
92	JOLLY OLD NICK W1557	OP	56.00	56.00
92	MASTER TOYMAKER W1566	OP	61.00	61.00
92	OLD FATHER FROST W1559	OP	56.00	56.00
92	SPECIAL DELIVERY W1558	OP	56.00	56.00
T. RUBEL				**FABRICHE COLLECTION**
92	HE DID IT AGAIN J7944	OP	160.00	160.00
K. ADLER				**FABRICHE HOLIDAY FIGURINES**
92	BUNDLES OF JOY W1578	RT	78.00	78.00
92	CHRISTMAS IS IN THE AIR W1590	OP	110.00	110.00
92	HOMEWARD BOUND W1566	OP	61.00	61.00
92	HUGS AND KISSES W1531	RT	67.00	67.00

YR	NAME	LIMIT	ISSUE	TREND
92	ST. NICHOLAS THE BISHOP W1532	OP	78.00	78.00
93	ALL THAT JAZZ W1620	RT	67.00	67.00
93	BRINGING THE GIFTS W1605	OP	60.00	60.00
93	CHECKING IT TWICE W1604	OP	56.00	56.00
93	FOREVER GREEN W1607	RT	56.00	56.00
93	PAR FOR THE CLAUS W1603	OP	60.00	60.00
93	PLAYTIME FOR SANTA W1619	RT	67.00	67.00
93	STOCKING STUFFER W1622	OP	56.00	56.00
93	TOP BRASS W1630	OP	67.00	67.00
93	WITH ALL THE TRIMMINGS W1616	OP	76.00	76.00
94	ALL STAR SANTA W1652	OP	56.00	56.00
94	BASKET OF GOODIES W1650	OP	60.00	60.00
94	CHECKING HIS LIST W1643	OP	60.00	60.00
94	FIREFIGHTING FRIENDS W1654	OP	72.00	72.00
94	FRIENDSHIP W1642	OP	65.00	65.00
94	HO, HO, HO SANTA W1632	OP	56.00	56.00
94	HOLIDAY EXPRESS W1636	OP	100.00	100.00
94	OFFICER CLAUS W1677	OP	56.00	56.00
94	PEACE SANTA W1631	OP	60.00	60.00
94	SANTA'S FISHTALES W1640	OP	60.00	60.00
94	SCHUSSING CLAUS W1651	OP	78.00	78.00
95	ALL ABOARD FOR CHRISTMAS W1679	OP	56.00	56.00
95	ARMCHAIR QUARTERBACK W1693	OP	90.00	90.00
95	CAPTAIN CLAUS W1680	OP	56.00	56.00
95	DIET STARTS TOMORROW W1691	OP	60.00	60.00
95	FATHER CHRISTMAS W1687	OP	56.00	56.00
95	GIFT FROM HEAVEN W1694	OP	60.00	60.00
95	KRIS KINGLE W1685	OP	55.00	55.00
95	MERRY MEMORIES W1735	OP	56.00	56.00
95	PERE NOEL W1686	OP	55.00	55.00
95	STRIKE UP THE BAND W1681	OP	55.00	55.00
95	TEE TIME W1734	OP	60.00	60.00
	*** GIORDANO**	**FABRICHE HOLIDAY FIGURINES**		
94	MERRY ST. NICK W1641	OP	100.00	100.00
	W. JOYCE	**FABRICHE HOLIDAY FIGURINES**		
94	SANTA CALLS W1678	OP	55.00	55.00
	*** KSA/WRG**	**FABRICHE HOLIDAY FIGURINES**		
94	MAIL MUST GO THROUGH W1667	OP	110.00	110.00
	M. ROTHENBERG	**FABRICHE HOLIDAY FIGURINES**		
91	SANTA FIDDLER W1549	RT	100.00	100.00
92	AN APRON FULL OF LOVE W1582	OP	75.00	75.00
92	BRINGING IN THE YULE LOG W1589	RT	200.00	200.00
92	MERRY KISSMAS W1548	RT	140.00	140.00
92	SANTA STEALS A KISS & A COOKIE W1581	RT	150.00	150.00
92	SANTA'S CAT NAP W1504	RT	98.00	98.00
92	SANTA'S ICE CAPADES W1588	OP	110.00	110.00
93	HERE KITTY W1616	RT	90.00	90.00
94	STAR GAZING SANTA W1656	OP	120.00	120.00
95	MRS. SANTA CAROLLER W1690	OP	70.00	70.00
95	SANTA CAROLER W1689	OP	70.00	70.00
	T. RUBEL	**FABRICHE HOLIDAY FIGURINES**		
92	I'M LATE, I'M LATE J7947	OP	100.00	100.00
92	IT'S TIME TO GO J7943	RT	150.00	150.00
	R. VOLPI	**FABRICHE HOLIDAY FIGURINES**		
95	WOODLAND SANTA W1731	RT	67.00	67.00
	*** WD. RIVER GALL.**	**FABRICHE HOLIDAY FIGURINES**		
95	NIGHT BEFORE CHRISTMAS W1692	OP	60.00	60.00
	M. ROTHENBERG	**FABRICHE SANTA AT HOME**		
93	GRANDPA SANTA'S PIGGYBACK RIDE W1621	7500	84.00	84.00
94	CHRISTMAS WALTZ, THE W1635	RT	135.00	135.00
94	SANTA'S NEW FRIEND W1655	OP	110.00	110.00
94	SANTA'S NEW FRIENDS W1655	OP	110.00	110.00
95	BABY BURPING SANTA W1732	OP	80.00	80.00
95	FAMILY PORTRAIT W1727	OP	140.00	140.00
95	SANTA'S HORSEY RIDE W1728	OP	80.00	80.00
	M. ROTHENBERG	**FABRICHE SANTA'S HELPERS**		
92	A STITCH IN TIME W1591	5000	135.00	135.00
93	LITTLE OLDE CLOCKMAKER W1629	RT	134.00	134.00
	*** KSA/SMITHSONIAN**	**FABRICHE SMITHSONIAN MUSEUM**		
91	SANTA ON A BICYCLE W1527	RT	150.00	150.00
92	HOLIDAY DRIVE W1556	OP	156.00	156.00
92	PEACE ON EARTH ANGEL TREETOP W1585	OP	52.00	52.00
92	PEACE ON EARTH FLYING ANGEL W1585	OP	49.00	49.00
93	HOLIDAY FLIGHT W1617	OP	144.00	144.00
95	TOYS FOR GOOD BOYS AND GIRLS W1696	OP	75.00	75.00
	K. ADLER	**FABRICHE THOMAS NAST FIGURINES**		
91	HELLO! LITTLE ONE! W1552	12000	90.00	90.00
92	CAUGHT IN THE ACT W1577	RT	133.00	133.00
92	CHRISTMAS SING-A-LONG W1576	12000	110.00	110.00
93	DEAR SANTA W1602	RT	110.00	110.00
	K. ADLER	**GALLERY OF ANGELS**		
94	GUARDIAN ANGEL M1099	2000	150.00	150.00
94	UNSPOKEN WORD M1100	2000	150.00	150.00
	P.F. BOLINGER	**HALLOWEEN**		
96	DR PUMPKIN HW535	OP	50.00	50.00
96	EAT AT DRAC'S HW493	OP	22.00	22.00
96	PUMPKIN GRUMPKIN HW494	OP	18.00	18.00

YR	NAME	LIMIT	ISSUE	TREND
96	PUMPKIN PLUMPKIN HW494	OP	18.00	18.00
96	PUMPKINS ARE US HW534	OP	17.00	17.00
P.F. BOLINGER		**HELPING HAND SANTAS**		
94	ALDWYN OF THE GREENWOOD J8196	OP	145.00	145.00
94	BERWYN THE GRAND J8198	OP	175.00	190.00
94	CARADOC THE KIND J8199	OP	70.00	80.00
94	FLORIAN OF THE BERRY BUSH J8199	OP	70.00	80.00
94	GUSTAVE THE GUTSY J8199	OP	70.00	80.00
94	SILVANUS THE CHEERFUL J8197	OP	165.00	165.00
95	BOUNTIFUL J8234	OP	164.00	164.00
95	LUMINATUS J8241	OP	136.00	136.00
96	HARMONIOUS 56509	OP	115.00	115.00
96	NOAH J6487	OP	56.00	56.00
96	UNCLE SAM J6488	OP	56.00	56.00
P.F. BOLINGER		**HO HO HO GANG**		
94	CHRISTMAS GOOSE J8201	OP	25.00	25.00
94	HOLY MACKEREL J8202	OP	25.00	25.00
94	SANTA COB J8203	RT	28.00	28.00
94	SURPRISE J8201	OP	25.00	25.00
94	SURPRISE J8201	OP	25.00	25.00
94	SURPRISE J8201	OP	22.00	22.00
94	WILL HE MAKE IT? J8203	RT	28.00	28.00
95	COOKIE CLAUS J8286	OP	40.00	40.00
95	DO NOT DISTURB J8233	OP	56.00	56.00
95	LARGE NORTH POLE J8237	OP	56.00	56.00
95	NO HAIR DAY J8287	OP	50.00	50.00
95	NORTH POLE J8237	OP	60.00	60.00
95	NORTH POLE J8238	OP	48.00	48.00
95	SMALL NORTH POLE J8238	OP	45.00	45.00
95	WILL WORK FOR COOKIES J8235	OP	40.00	40.00
95	WISHFUL THINKING J8239	OP	39.00	39.00
96	BOX OF CHOCOLATE J6510	OP	33.00	33.00
96	CHRISTMAS SHOPPING SANTA J6497	OP	22.00	22.00
96	CLAU A LOUNGER J6478	OP	33.00	33.00
96	FIRE DEPARTMENT NORTH POLE J6508	OP	50.00	50.00
96	FIREMAN SANTA J6476	OP	28.00	28.00
96	JOY OF COOKING J6496	OP	28.00	28.00
96	LOVE SANTA J6493	OP	18.00	18.00
96	NOEL ROLY POLY J6489	OP	20.00	20.00
96	NORTH POLE PRO-AM J6479	OP	28.00	28.00
96	ON STRIKE FOR MORE COOKIES J6506	OP	33.00	33.00
96	POLICE DEPARTMENT NORTH POLE J6507	OP	50.00	50.00
96	POLICEMAN SANTA J6475	OP	28.00	28.00
96	SAVE THE REINDEER J6498	OP	28.00	28.00
96	SOME ASSEMBLY REQUIRED J6477	OP	53.00	53.00
H. ADLER		**HOLLY BEARIES**		
96	ANGEL BEAR J7342	OP	14.00	14.00
96	TEDDY TOWER J7221	OP	23.00	23.00
H. ADLER		**HOLLY BEARIES CALENDAR BEARS**		
96	CLAIRMONT, DEMPSEY & PETE J7215/JUL	OP	16.00	16.00
96	CLARA & CARANATON THE KITTY J7215/OCT	OP	16.00	16.00
96	FERGUS & FRITZI'S FROSTY FROLIC J7215/JA	OP	16.00	16.00
96	GRANDMA GLADYS J7215/DEC	OP	16.00	16.00
96	MOTHERS DAY DEAR J7318	OP	15.00	15.00
96	NICOLE & NICOLAS SUN BATHING J7215/AUG	OP	16.00	16.00
96	PETUNIA & NATHAN PLANT ROSES J7215/MAY	OP	16.00	16.00
96	PHILO'S POT OF GOLD J7215/MAR	OP	16.00	16.00
96	PINKY & VICTORIA ARE SWEETES J7215/FEB	OP	16.00	16.00
96	SKEETER & SIGOURNEY START SCHOOL J7215/S	OP	16.00	16.00
96	SUNSHINE CATCHING RAINDROPS J7215/APR	OP	16.00	16.00
96	TEDDY TOWER J7221	OP	23.00	23.00
96	THORNDIKE & FILBERT CATCH FISH J7215/JUN	OP	16.00	16.00
96	THORNDIKE ALL DRESSED UP J7215/NOV	OP	16.00	16.00
*** KSA/JHP**		**JIM HENSON'S MUPPET NUTCRACKERS**		
93	KERMIT THE FROG H1223	RT	90.00	90.00
*** KSA/DISNEY**		**MICKEY UNLIMITED**		
92	GOOFY H1216	OP	78.00	78.00
92	MICKEY MOUSE SOLDIER H1194	OP	72.00	72.00
92	MICKEY MOUSE SORCERER H1221	OP	100.00	100.0
93	DONALD DUCK H1235	OP	90.00	90.00
93	MICKEY MOUSE W/GIFT BOXES W1608	RT	78.00	78.00
93	PINNOCHIO H1222	OP	110.00	110.00
94	DONALD DUCK DRUMMER W1681	RT	45.00	45.00
94	MICKEY BANDLEADER W1669	RT	45.00	45.00
94	MICKEY SANTA NUTCRACKER H1237	OP	90.00	90.00
94	MINNIE MOUSE SOLDIER NUTCRACKER H1236	OP	90.00	90.00
94	MINNIE W/CYMBALS W1670	RT	45.00	45.00
*** KSA/STEINBACH**		**MINI SERIES**		
96	MERLIN MINI NUTCRACKER ES335	15000	50.00	50.00
96	ROBIN HOOD MINI NUTCRACKER ES338	10000	50.00	50.00
*** KSA/STEINBACH**		**NUTCRACKER TALES OF SHERWOOD FOREST**		
92	ROBIN HOOD ES863	7500	225.00	225.00
95	FRIAR TUCK ES890	7500	245.00	245.00
96	SHERIFF OF NOTTINGHAM ES892	7500	260.00	260.00
J. MOSTROM		**OLD WORLD SANTA SERIES**		
92	CHELSEA GARDEN SANTA W2721	RT	33.50	34.00
92	LARGE BLACK FOREST SANTA W2717	3000	110.00	110.00

YR	NAME	LIMIT	ISSUE	TREND
92	LARGE FATHER CHRISTMAS W2719	3000	106.00	106.00
92	MRS. CLAUS W2714	5000	37.00	37.00
92	PATRIOTIC SANTA W2720	3000	128.00	128.00
92	PERE NOEL W2723	5000	33.50	34.00
92	SMALL BLACK FOREST SANTA W2712	5000	40.00	40.00
92	SMALL FATHER CHRISTMAS W2712	5000	33.50	34.00
92	SMALL FATHER FROST W2716	RT	43.00	43.00
92	SMALL GRANDFATHER FROST W2716	RT	106.00	106.00
92	ST. NICHOLAS W2713	5000	30.00	30.00
92	WORKSHOP SANTA W2715	5000	43.00	43.00
93	GOOD KING WENCESLAS W2928	3000	134.00	134.00
93	MEDIEVAL KING OF CHRISTMAS W2881	3000	390.00	390.00
*	**OSCAR & BERTIE WATERGLOBE COLLECTION**			
92	BEARS ON ROCKING HORSE J1034	OP	56.00	56.00
92	SANTA BEAR WITH PACKAGES J1033	OP	41.00	41.00
*	**SATURDAY EVENING POST WATERGLOBE COLLECTION**			
92	CHRISTMAS TRIO NORMAN ROCKWELL J1035	OP	40.00	40.00
92	SANTA'S SURPRISE J.C. LEYENDECKER J1036	OP	40.00	40.00
*	**KSA/JHP — SESAME STREET SERIES**			
93	BIG BIRD FABRICHE J7928	OP	60.00	60.00
93	BIG BIRD NUTCRACKER H1199	RT	60.00	60.00
	P.F. BOLINGER — SNOW PEOPLE			
96	COOLA HULA J6430	OP	20.00	20.00
96	SNOWPOKE J6431	OP	28.00	28.00
96	SNOWY J6429	OP	28.00	28.00
	C. STEINBACH — STEINBACH MUSICAL COLLECTION			
92	SKI LIFT MUSICAL ES27	2000	150.00	150.00
*	**KSA/STEINBACH — STEINBACH NUTCRACKER CHRISTMAS LEGENDS**			
93	FATHER CHRISTMAS ES645	7500	225.00	225.00
94	ST. NICHOLAS, THE BISHOP ES865	7500	225.00	225.00
95	1930S SANTA CLAUS ES891	7500	245.00	245.00
*	**KSA/STEINBACH — STEINBACH NUTCRACKER COLLECTION**			
84	OIL SHEIK	RT	100.00	300.00
91	COLUMBUS ES697	RT	194.00	210.00
92	HAPPY SANTA ES601	RT	190.00	205.00
*	**KSA/STEINBACH — STEINBACH NUTCRACKER FAMOUS CHIEFTAINS**			
93	CHIEF SITTING BULL ES637	8500	225.00	225.00
94	CHIEF SITTING BULL SMOKER ES834	RT	150.00	150.00
94	RED CLOUD ES864	8500	225.00	225.00
95	BLACK HAWK ES889	7500	245.00	245.00
*	**KSA/STEINBACH — THREE MUSKATEERS**			
96	ARAMIS ES722	7500	130.00	130.00
	K. ADLER — VISIONS OF SANTA SERIES			
92	SANTA COMING OUT OF FIREPLACE J1023	RT	29.00	29.00
92	SANTA HOLDING CHILD J826	RT	24.50	25.00
92	SANTA SPILLING BAG OF TOYS J1022	RT	25.50	26.00
92	SANTA W/LITTLE GIRLS ON LAP J1024	7500	24.50	25.00
92	SANTA W/SACK HOLDING TOY J827	RT	24.50	25.00
92	WORKSHOP SANTA J825	RT	27.00	27.00
*	**WATERGLOBE COLLECTION**			
92	SANTA WITH TWO GIRLS J1038	OP	40.00	40.00
*	**KSA/ZUBER — ZUBER NUTCRACKER SERIES**			
92	ANNAPOLIS MIDSHIPMAN, THE EK7	RT	125.00	125.00
92	BAVARIAN, THE EK16	RT	130.00	130.00
92	BRONCO BILLY THE COWBOY EK1	RT	125.00	125.00
92	CHIMNEY SWEEP, THE EK6	RT	125.00	125.00
92	COUNTRY SINGER, THE EK19	RT	125.00	125.00
92	FISHERMAN, THE EK17	5000	125.00	125.00
92	GEPETTO, THE TOYMAKER EK9	RT	125.00	125.00
92	GOLD PROSPECTOR, THE EK18	RT	125.00	125.00
92	GOLFER, THE EK5	RT	125.00	125.00
92	INDIAN, THE EK15	RT	135.00	135.00
92	NOR'EASTER SEA CAPTAIN, THE EK3	5000	125.00	125.00
92	PAUL BUNYAN THE LUMBERJACK EK2	RT	125.00	125.00
92	PILGRIM, THE EK14	RT	125.00	125.00
92	TYROLEAN, THE EK4	RT	125.00	125.00
92	WEST POINT CADET W/CANON, THE EK6	RT	130.00	130.00
93	HERR DROSSELMEIR NUTCRACKER EK21	RT	150.00	150.00
93	ICE CREAM VENDOR, THE EK24	RT	150.00	150.00
93	NAPOLEON BONAPARTE EK23	RT	150.00	150.00
93	PIZZAMAKER, THE EK22	5000	150.00	150.00
94	GARDENER, THE EK26	RT	150.00	150.00
94	JAZZ PLAYER EK25	2500	145.00	145.00
94	KURT THE TRAVELING SALESMAN EK28	RT	155.00	155.00
94	MOUSE KING EK31	2500	150.00	150.00
94	PETER PAN EK28	2500	145.00	145.00
94	SCUBA DIVER EK27	2500	150.00	150.00
94	SOCCER PLAYER EK30	2500	145.00	145.00

LANCE CORP.

YR	NAME	LIMIT	ISSUE	TREND
	F. BARNUM — CHILMARK			
87	SAVING THE COLORS	RT	350.00	350.00
87	SURPRISE ENCOUNTER	RT	250.00	730.00
88	JOHNNY SHILOH	RT	100.00	225.00
91	STONEWALL JACKSON	RT	295.00	295.00
92	KENNESAW MOUNTAIN	*	650.00	1000.00

YR NAME	LIMIT	ISSUE	TREND
M. BOYETT			**CHILMARK**
81 PLIGHT OF THE HUNTSMAN	RT	495.00	825.00
82 BLOOD BROTHERS	RT	250.00	610.00
82 WINGS OF LIBERTY	SO	625.00	1250.00
84 FLAT OUT FOR RED RIVER STATION	RT	3000.00	6000.00
86 EAGLE CATCHER	RT	300.00	1100.00
95 RAINMAKER, THE	YR	350.00	360.00
G. DELODZIA			**CHILMARK**
81 FREEDOM EAGLE	SO	195.00	950.00
P. JACKSON			**CHILMARK**
86 CAMELOT CHESS SET	RT	2250.00	2250.00
*** KEIM/HAZEN**			**CHILMARK**
81 BUDWEISER WAGON	RT	2000.00	3025.00
D. LAROCCA			**CHILMARK**
79 CAVALRY OFFICER	RT	125.00	525.00
79 COWBOY	RT	125.00	650.00
88 DRAGON SLAYER	RT	385.00	500.00
A. MCGRORY			**CHILMARK**
88 END OF THE TRAIL (MINI)	RT	225.00	300.00
D. POLLAND			**CHILMARK**
74 CHEYENNE	RT	200.00	2850.00
76 RESCUE	RT	275.00	1200.00
77 FALL-MUSTANGS	3500	120.00	120.00
77 SPRING-MUSTANGS	3500	120.00	120.00
77 WINTER-MUSTANGS	3500	120.00	120.00
78 BUFFALO HUNT	RT	360.00	2220.00
78 COLD SADDLES, MEAN HORSES	RT	200.00	875.00
78 COUNTING COUP	RT	225.00	1800.00
78 CROW SCOUT	RT	250.00	1500.00
78 MAVERICK CALF	RT	250.00	1500.00
78 MONDAY MORNING WASH	RT	200.00	1100.00
78 OUTLAWS, THE	RT	450.00	1000.00
78 PAINTING THE TOWN	RT	300.00	1550.00
79 GETTING ACQUAINTED	RT	215.00	950.00
80 AFRICAN ELEPHANT	RT	275.00	400.00
80 BORDER RUSTLERS	RT	1295.00	1500.00
80 MANDAN HUNTER	RT	65.00	825.00
81 AMBUSHED	RT	2375.00	2725.00
81 BUFFALO ROBE	RT	200.00	315.00
81 DOG SOLDIER	2500	200.00	300.00
81 ENEMY TRACKS	RT	225.00	720.00
81 U.S. MARSHAL	RT	95.00	485.00
81 WAR PARTY	RT	550.00	1025.00
81 WHEN WAR CHIEFS MEET	RT	300.00	865.00
82 APACHE GAN DANCER	2500	95.00	110.00
82 APACHE HOSTILE	2500	95.00	110.00
82 ARAPAHO DRUMMER	2500	95.00	110.00
82 BUFFALO PRAYER	RT	95.00	300.00
82 COMANCHE PLAINES DRUMMER	2500	95.00	110.00
82 CROW MEDICINE DANCER	2500	95.00	110.00
82 FLATHEAD WAR DANCER	2500	95.00	110.00
82 HOPI KACHINA DANCER	2500	95.00	110.00
82 JEMEZ EAGLE DANCER	RT	95.00	350.00
82 LAST ARROW	RT	95.00	350.00
82 NAVAJO KACHINA DANCER	2500	95.00	110.00
82 SIOUX WAR CHIEF	RT	95.00	350.00
82 YAKIMA SALMON FISHERMAN	RT	200.00	750.00
83 BOUNTY HUNTER	RT	250.00	450.00
83 CHIEF, THE	RT	275.00	1700.00
83 LINE RIDER	RT	195.00	1000.00
83 MUSTANGER	2500	425.00	550.00
83 TOO MANY ACES	RT	400.00	500.00
83 WILD BUNCH, THE	RT	200.00	325.00
84 EYE TO EYE	2500	375.00	475.00
84 GUIDON, THE	*	*	*
84 NOW OR NEVER	RT	265.00	800.00
84 UNIT COLORS	RT	250.00	1450.00
85 BAREBACK RIDER	2500	225.00	300.00
85 BARREL RACER	2500	275.00	325.00
85 BULL RIDER	2500	265.00	335.00
85 CALF ROPER	2500	300.00	375.00
85 OH GREAT SPIRIT	RT	300.00	1270.00
85 SADDLE BRONC RIDER	2500	250.00	300.00
85 STEER WRESTLING	2500	500.00	600.00
85 TEAM ROPING	2500	500.00	625.00
86 FIGHTING STALLIONS	2500	250.00	300.00
88 I WILL FIGHT NO MORE FOREVER	RT	350.00	825.00
89 GERONIMO	RT	375.00	700.00
90 BUFFALO SPIRIT	RT	110.00	195.00
90 COCHISE	RT	400.00	550.00
90 PEQUOT WARS	RT	395.00	675.00
90 RED RIVER WARS	RT	425.00	750.00
90 TECUMSEH'S REBELLION	RT	350.00	675.00
91 CRAZY HORSE	750	295.00	650.00
91 KIOWA PRINCESS	RT	300.00	300.00
92 STRONG HEARTS TO THE FRONT	RT	425.00	615.00
93 SACRED GROUND RECLAIMED	RT	495.00	600.00
94 HORSE BREAKING	RT	395.00	400.00

YR	NAME	LIMIT	ISSUE	TREND
B. RODDEN				**CHILMARK**
79	MOSES	RT	100.00	250.00
80	CHARGE OF THE 7TH CALVARY	RT	600.00	975.00
C. ROUSELL				**CHILMARK**
84	CHEYENNE (REMINGTON)	RT	400.00	600.00
85	BRONCO BUSTER (LARGE)	RT	400.00	400.00
J. ROYCE				**CHILMARK**
84	GARDEN UNICORN	RT	160.00	200.00
J. SLOCKBOWER				**CHILMARK**
92	CHIEF JOSEPH METART	RT	975.00	1700.00
92	GERONIMO	RT	975.00	1000.00
93	CRAZY HORSE	750	975.00	1000.00
93	SITTING BULL	750	1075.00	1100.00
B. SYLVAN				**CHILMARK**
79	CAROUSEL	RT	115.00	115.00
79	PEGASUS	RT	95.00	200.00
79	UNICORN	RT	115.00	600.00
D. POLLAND				**CHILMARK AMERICAN WEST CHRISTMAS**
91	MERRY CHRISTMAS NEIGHBOR	RT	395.00	625.00
92	MERRY CHRISTMAS MY LOVE	RT	350.00	400.00
93	ALMOST HOME	RT	375.00	385.00
94	COWBOY CHRISTMAS	RT	250.00	260.00
M. BOYETT				**CHILMARK LEGACY OF COURAGE**
81	APACHE SIGNALS	RT	175.00	550.00
81	BLACKFOOT SNOW HUNTER	RT	175.00	650.00
81	BUFFALO STALKER	RT	175.00	550.00
81	COMANCHE	RT	175.00	600.00
81	IROQUOIS WARFARE	RT	175.00	575.00
81	UNCONQUERED SEMINOLE	RT	175.00	550.00
81	VICTOR CHEYENNE	RT	175.00	500.00
82	ARAPAHO SENTINEL	RT	195.00	480.00
82	DANCE OF THE EAGLES	RT	150.00	225.00
82	KIOWA SCOUT	RT	195.00	525.00
82	LISTENING FOR HOOVES	RT	150.00	460.00
82	MANDAN BUFFALO DANCER	RT	195.00	575.00
82	PLAINS TALK, PAWNEE	RT	195.00	600.00
82	SHOSHONE EAGLE CATCHER	RT	225.00	1800.00
82	TRACKER NEZ PERCE, THE	RT	150.00	575.00
83	A WARRIOR'S TRIBUTE	RT	335.00	640.00
83	ALONG THE CHEROKEE TRACE	RT	295.00	700.00
83	CIRCLING THE ENEMY	RT	295.00	400.00
83	FOREST WATCHER	RT	215.00	550.00
83	MOMENT OF TRUTH	RT	295.00	575.00
83	RITE OF THE WHITETAIL	RT	295.00	400.00
83	WINTER HUNT	RT	295.00	375.00
*** SLOCKBOWER**				**CHILMARK MICKEY & CO.**
92	CRUSING	RT	275.00	1700.00
93	SUNDAY DRIVE	RT	325.00	1200.00
94	BEACH BOUND	RT	350.00	875.00
A.T. MCGRORY				**CHILMARK OFF CANVAS**
90	SMOKE SIGNAL	RT	345.00	675.00
90	VIGIL	RT	345.00	600.00
90	WARRIOR	RT	300.00	450.00
*				**CHILMARK PEWTER CIVIL WAR**
87	SAVING THE COLORS	RT	350.00	650.00
92	KENNESAW MTN.	RT	650.00	1550.00
92	PARSON'S BATTERY	RT	495.00	525.00
F. BARNUM				**CHILMARK PEWTER CIVIL WAR**
88	A FATHER'S FAREWELL	RT	150.00	300.00
89	LEE TO THE REAR	RT	300.00	850.00
90	LEE AND JACKSON	RT	375.00	500.00
93	ABE LINCOLN BUST	RT	2000.00	2275.00
D. POLLAND				**CHILMARK PEWTER CIVIL WAR**
77	SUMMER-MUSTANGS	3500	120.00	525.00
F. BARNUM				**CHILMARK PEWTER CIVIL WAR CHRISTMAS SPECIALS**
92	MERRY CHRISTMAS YANK	RT	350.00	525.00
93	SILENT NIGHT	RT	350.00	500.00
94	CHRISTMAS TRUCE	RT	295.00	300.00
95	PEACE ON EARTH	YR	350.00	360.00
F. BARNUM				**CHILMARK PEWTER CIVIL WAR EVENT SPECIALS**
93	JOHNNY REB	RT	95.00	135.00
94	BILLY YANK	RT	95.00	100.00
95	SEAMAN, CSS ALABAMA	RT	95.00	100.00
F. BARNUM				**CHILMARK PEWTER CIVIL WAR REDEMPTION SPECIALS**
92	ZOUAVES 1ST MANASSAS	RT	375.00	525.00
93	LETTER TO SARAH	RT	3959.00	400.00
94	ANGEL OF FREDERICKSBURG	RT	275.00	300.00
95	REBEL YELL	YR	*	*
M. JOVINE				**CHILMARK PEWTER HORSES**
80	AFFIRMED	RT	850.00	1300.00
C. KEIM				**CHILMARK PEWTER HORSES**
81	CLYDESDALE WHEEL HORSE	RT	120.00	450.00
A. PETITTO				**CHILMARK PEWTER HORSES**
78	PADDOCK WALK	RT	85.00	225.00
D. POLLAND				**CHILMARK PEWTER HORSES**
86	WILD STALLION	RT	145.00	360.00

YR	NAME	LIMIT	ISSUE	TREND
B. RODDEN		**CHILMARK PEWTER HORSES**		
76	RUNNING FREE	RT	75.00	320.00
76	STALLION	RT	75.00	275.00
77	CHALLENGE, THE	RT	175.00	275.00
77	RISE AND SHINE	RT	135.00	200.00
80	BORN FREE	RT	250.00	700.00
*		**CHILMARK PEWTER MICKEY & CO.**		
86	LIGHTS, CAMERA, ACTION/BRONZE	50	3300.00	3300.00
89	GOLD EDITION HOLLYWOOD MICKEY	RT	200.00	780.00
89	HOLLYWOOD MICKEY	SU	165.00	250.00
91	MICKEY'S CAROUSEL RIDE	2500	150.00	150.00
94	LIGHTS, CAMERA, ACTION/PEWTER	500	1525.00	1525.00
94	MICKEY ON PARADE/BRONZE	RT	975.00	975.00
94	MICKEY ON PARADE/METALART	RT	525.00	525.00
94	MICKEY ON PARADE/PEWTER	750	400.00	400.00
94	MOUSE IN A MILLION/BRONZE	RT	1275.00	1275.00
94	MOUSE IN A MILLION/METALART	RT	675.00	675.00
94	MOUSE IN A MILLION/PEWTER	RT	525.00	525.00
94	PUTTIN' ON THE RITZ/BRONZE	RT	2025.00	2025.00
94	PUTTIN' ON THE RITZ/METALART	250	1025.00	1025.00
94	PUTTIN' ON THE RITZ/PEWTER	350	775.00	775.00
*	**CHILMARK PEWTER MICKEY & CO. /THE SORCERER'S APPRENTICE**			
90	DREAM, THE	TL	225.00	235.00
90	INCANTATION, THE	TL	150.00	180.00
90	REPENTANT APPRENTICE, THE	RT	19598.00	225.00
90	SORCERER'S APPRENTICE, THE	TL	225.00	235.00
90	WHIRLPOOL, THE	TL	225.00	250.00
P.W. BASTON	**CHILMARK PEWTER MICKEY & CO. TWO WHEELING**			
94	GET YOUR MOTOR RUNNIN'/BRONZE	RT	1200.00	1650.00
94	GET YOUR MOTOR RUNNIN'/METALART	RT	475.00	625.00
94	HEAD OUT ON THE HIGHWAY/METALART	950	475.00	500.00
95	LOOKING FOR ADVENTURE/BRONZE	50	1200.00	1225.00
95	LOOKING FOR ADVENTURE/METALART	950	475.00	500.00
BASTON/ SLOCKBOWER	**CHILMARK PEWTER MICKEY & CO. TWO WHEELING**			
94	HEAD OUT ON THE HIGHWAY/BRONZE	50	1200.00	1225.00
A.T. MCGRORY		**CHILMARK PEWTER OFF CANVAS**		
91	BLANKET SIGNAL	RT	750.00	875.00
F. BARNUM		**CHILMARK PEWTER THE CAVALRY GENERALS**		
92	J.E.B. STUART	RT	375.00	525.00
93	GEORGE ARMSTRONG CUSTER	950	375.00	400.00
93	NATHAN BEDFORD FORREST	950	375.00	400.00
94	PHILIP SHERIDAN	950	375.00	400.00
M. BOYETT		**CHILMARK PEWTER WILDLIFE**		
80	DUEL OF THE BIGHORNS	RT	725.00	1225.00
80	LEAD CAN'T CATCH HIM	RT	645.00	850.00
80	PRAIRIE SOVEREIGN	RT	645.00	800.00
80	VOICE OF EXPERIENCE	RT	645.00	875.00
V. HAYTON		**CHILMARK PEWTER WILDLIFE**		
80	RUBY-THROATED HUMMINGBIRD	RT	275.00	385.00
D. POLLAND		**CHILMARK PEWTER WILDLIFE**		
79	ELEPHANT	RT	315.00	500.00
79	RHINO	RT	135.00	400.00
80	GIRAFFE	RT	125.00	145.00
80	KUDU	RT	140.00	160.00
B. RODDEN		**CHILMARK PEWTER WILDLIFE**		
78	BUFFALO	RT	170.00	400.00
F. BARNUM		**CHILMARK THE ADVERSARIES**		
91	ROBERT E. LEE	RT	350.00	1750.00
92	STONEWALL JACKSON	RT	375.00	525.00
92	ULYSSES S. GRANT	RT	350.00	650.00
93	WM. TECUMSEH SHERMAN	RT	375.00	600.00
D. POLLAND		**CHILMARK THE MEDICINE MEN**		
92	FALSE FACE/METALART	1000	550.00	550.00
92	FALSE FACE/PEWTER	RT	375.00	375.00
A. MCGRORY		**CHILMARK THE SEEKERS**		
92	BUFFALO VISION	RT	1075.00	1075.00
93	BEAR VISION	500	1375.00	1375.00
93	EAGLE VISION	500	1250.00	1250.00
D. POLLAND		**CHILMARK THE WARRIORS**		
92	SPIRIT OF THE WOLF/METALART	1000	500.00	510.00
92	SPIRIT OF THE WOLF/PEWTER	RT	350.00	875.00
93	SON OF THE MORNING STAR/METALART	1000	495.00	500.00
93	SON OF THE MORNING STAR/PEWTER	RT	375.00	475.00
T. SULLIVAN		**CHILMARK TO THE GREAT SPIRIT**		
92	SHOOTING STAR	RT	775.00	775.00
93	GRAY ELK	950	775.00	775.00
93	TWO EAGLES	950	775.00	775.00
94	THUNDER CLOUD	950	775.00	775.00
D. LIBERTY		**CRYSTALS OF ZORN**		
89	BATTLE ON THE PLAINS OF XENON	950	265.00	265.00
89	CHARGING THE STONE	950	395.00	395.00
89	GUARDING THE CRYSTAL	950	460.00	460.00
89	RESPONSE OF ORNIC FORCE	950	285.00	285.00
89	RESTORATION	950	435.00	435.00
89	U.S.S. STRIKES BACK	500	675.00	675.00
90	ASMUND'S WORKSHOP	950	275.00	275.00

YR	NAME	LIMIT	ISSUE	TREND
90	STRUGGLING FOR SUPREMACY	950	400.00	400.00
90	VESTING THE GRAIL	950	200.00	200.00
*			**GENERATIONS OF MICKEY**	
87	ANTIQUE MICKEY	RT	95.00	600.00
89	MICKEY'S GALA PREMIERE	2500	150.00	150.00
89	SORCERER'S APPRENTICE	RT	150.00	400.00
89	STEAM BOAT WILLIE	RT	165.00	450.00
90	BAND CONCERT, THE	2000	185.00	200.00
90	BAND CONCERT, THE (PAINTED)	RT	215.00	390.00
90	DISNEYLAND MICKEY	2500	150.00	150.00
91	MOUSE, THE-1935	1200	185.00	185.00
91	PLANE CRAZY-1928	2500	175.00	175.00
P.W. BASTON			**HUDSON PEWTER FIGURES**	
69	BETSY ROSS	CL	30.00	110.00
69	COLONIAL BLACKSMITH	CL	30.00	110.00
69	GEORGE WASHINGTON (CANNON)	CL	35.00	90.00
69	JOHN HANCOCK	CL	15.00	110.00
72	BENJAMIN FRANKLIN	CL	15.00	90.00
72	GEORGE WASHINGTON	CL	15.00	90.00
72	JAMES MADISON	CL	15.00	65.00
72	JOHN ADAMS	CL	15.00	90.00
72	THOMAS JEFFERSON	CL	15.00	90.00
75	DECLARATION WALL PLAQUE	RT	*	400.00
75	FAVORED SCHOLAR, THE	RT	*	800.00
75	LEE'S NINTH GENERAL ORDER	CL	*	350.00
75	LINCOLN'S GETTYBURG ADDRESS	CL	*	350.00
75	NEIGHBORING PEWS	RT	*	800.00
75	SPIRIT OF '76	RT	*	1100.00
75	WASHINGTON'S LETTER OF ACCEPTANCE	CL	*	350.00
75	WEIGHING THE BABY	RT	*	800.00
H. WILSON			**HUDSON PEWTER FIGURES**	
76	BALD EAGLE	CL	100.00	113.00
76	GREAT HORNED OWL	CL	*	42.00
D. LAROCCA			**MILITARY COMMEMORATIVES**	
91	DESERT LIBERATOR (PAINTED PORCELAIN)	5000	125.00	125.00
91	DESERT LIBERATOR (PEWTER)	950	295.00	295.00
D. POLLAND			**MINIATURE SCULPTURE SOCIETY**	
92	BLACK HAWK	*	25.00	250.00
P.W. BASTON			**SEBASTIAN EXCHANGE**	
83	NEWSPAPER BOY	RT	28.50	80.00
84	FIRST THINGS FIRST	RT	30.00	40.00
P.W. BASTON, JR.			**SEBASTIAN EXCHANGE**	
85	NEWSSTAND	RT	30.00	40.00
86	NEWS WAGON	RT	35.00	50.00
87	IT'S ABOUT TIME	RT	25.00	40.00
P.W. BASTON			**SEBASTIAN MINIATURES**	
92	FIREFIGHTER	RT	28.00	55.00
92	I KNOW I LEFT IT HERE SOMEWHERE	1000	28.50	30.00
93	LAMPLIGHTER, THE	1000	28.00	30.00
93	PUMPKIN ISLAND LIGHT	3500	55.00	60.00
93	SOAP BOX DERBY	500	46.00	50.00
94	A JOB WELL DONE	1000	27.50	30.00
94	BOSTON LIGHT	3500	45.00	50.00
94	EGG ROCK LIGHT	3500	55.00	60.00
94	NUBBLE LIGHT	3500	45.00	50.00
P.W. BASTON, JR.			**SEBASTIAN MINIATURES**	
83	HARRY HOOD	RT	*	225.00
85	IT'S HOODS (WAGON)	RT	*	90.00
91	AMERICA SALUTES DESERT STORM-BRONZE	RT	26.50	100.00
91	AMERICA SALUTES DESERT STORM-PAINTED	RT	49.50	225.00
91	HAPPY HOOD HOLIDAYS	RT	32.50	75.00
P.W. BASTON			**SEBASTIAN MINIATURES AMERICA REMEMBERS**	
79	FAMILY SING	RT	29.50	90.00
80	FAMILY PICNIC	RT	29.50	80.00
81	FAMILY READS ALOUD	RT	34.50	60.00
82	FAMILY FISHING	RT	34.50	75.00
83	FAMILY FEAST	RT	37.50	75.00
P.W. BASTON			**SEBASTIAN MINIATURES CHILDREN AT PLAY**	
78	SIDEWALK DAYS BOY	RT	19.50	50.00
78	SIDEWALK DAYS GIRL	RT	19.50	50.00
79	BUILDING DAYS BOY	RT	19.50	40.00
79	BUILDING DAYS GIRL	RT	19.50	40.00
80	SNOW DAYS BOY	RT	19.50	50.00
80	SNOW DAYS GIRL	RT	19.50	50.00
81	SAILING DAYS BOY	RT	19.50	40.00
81	SAILING DAYS GIRL	RT	19.50	40.00
82	SCHOOL DAYS BOY	RT	19.50	50.00
82	SCHOOL DAYS GIRL	RT	19.50	50.00
P.W. BASTON			**SEBASTIAN MINIATURES COLLECTORS SOCIETY**	
80	S.M.C SOCIETY PLAQUE ('80 CHARTER)	RT	*	25.00
P.W. BASTON, JR.			**SEBASTIAN MINIATURES COLLECTORS SOCIETY**	
86	STATUE OF LIBERTY (AT&T)	RT	*	190.00
87	WHITE HOUSE (GOLD, OVAL BASE)	RT	17.00	50.00
P.W. BASTON, JR.			**SEBASTIAN MINIATURES HOLIDAY MEMORIES-MEMBER ONLY**	
90	LEPRECHAUN	YR	27.50	28.00
90	THANKSGIVING HELPER	YR	39.50	40.00
91	TRICK OR TREAT	YR	25.50	65.00

YR	NAME	LIMIT	ISSUE	TREND
P.W. BASTON		**SEBASTIAN MINIATURES JIMMY FUND**		
83	SCHOOLBOY	RT	24.50	30.00
84	CATCHER	RT	24.50	60.00
P.W. BASTON, JR.		**SEBASTIAN MINIATURES JIMMY FUND**		
85	HOCKEY PLAYER	RT	24.50	40.00
86	SOCCER PLAYER	RT	25.00	25.00
87	FOOTBALL PLAYER	RT	26.50	27.00
88	SANTA	RT	32.50	33.00
P.W. BASTON, JR.		**SEBASTIAN MINIATURES MEMBER ONLY**		
89	COLLECTORS, THE	YR	39.50	40.00
P.W. BASTON		**SEBASTIAN MINIATURES SHAKESPEAREAN-MEMBER ONLY**		
84	ANNE BOYELIN	RT	17.50	30.00
84	HENRY VIII	RT	19.50	30.00
85	FALSTAFF	RT	19.50	30.00
85	MISTRESS FORD	RT	17.50	30.00
86	JULIET	RT	17.50	30.00
86	ROMEO	RT	19.50	30.00
87	COUNTESS OLIVIA	RT	19.50	30.00
87	MALVOLIO	RT	21.50	30.00
88	AUDREY	RT	22.50	30.00
88	TOUCHSTONE	RT	22.50	30.00
89	CLEOPATRA	RT	27.00	30.00
89	MARK ANTHONY	RT	27.00	30.00
P.W. BASTON, JR.		**SEBASTIAN MINIATURES SHAKESPEAREAN-MEMBER ONLY**		
88	SHAKESPEARE	RT	23.50	30.00
P.W. BASTON		**WASHINGTON IRVING-MEMBER ONLY**		
80	RIP VAN WINKLE	CL	19.50	20.00
81	DAME VAN WINKLE	CL	19.50	20.00
81	ICHABOD CRANE	CL	19.50	20.00
82	BROM BONES (HEADLESS HORSEMAN)	CL	22.50	23.00
82	KATRINA VAN TASSEL	CL	19.50	20.00
83	DIEDRICH KNICKERBOCKER	CL	22.50	23.00

LAND OF LEGEND

YR	NAME	LIMIT	ISSUE	TREND
T. RAINE		**CASTLE COLLECTION**		
78	DENNIS THE DRAGON/COUNTERSIGN	CL	55.00	225.00
86	CASTLE OF THE EXILED PRINCE	CL	225.00	200.00
86	CASTLE OF THE GOLDEN CHALICE	CL	60.00	60.00
86	CASTLE OF THE RANSOMED KING	CL	250.00	200.00
86	CASTLE OF THE RED KNIGHT	CL	65.00	65.00
86	CASTLE OF THE SLEEPING PRINCESS	CL	235.00	235.00
86	SORCERERS RETREAT	CL	50.00	55.00
87	WIZARD'S TOWER	CL	215.00	208.00
H. HENRIKSEN		**DRAGONS**		
89	COUNTERSIGN FOR SERIES	*	75.00	90.00
90	DRAGON OF THE GOLDEN HOARD	*	270.00	350.00
90	GUARDIAN OF THE KEEP	*	295.00	375.00
90	HATCHED	*	295.00	395.00
90	LET SLEEPING DRAGONS LIE	3000	450.00	595.00
90	LEVIATHAN	*	325.00	424.00
90	WYVERN	*	295.00	375.00
T. RAINE		**DREAM CASTLES**		
88	CAMELOT	CL	32.50	33.00
88	FAIRYTALE	CL	32.50	33.00
88	GRAND VIZIERS	CL	32.50	33.00
88	VALKYRIES TOWER	CL	32.50	33.00
T. RAINE		**DREAM DRAGONS**		
88	BATHTIME	RT	31.50	31.50
88	BREAKOUT	RT	31.50	32.00
88	DOUBLE TROUBLE	RT	35.00	35.00
88	DREAM BABY	RT	31.50	32.00
88	HAZY DAZE	RT	31.50	32.00
88	HELP	RT	31.50	31.50
88	HI THERE	RT	31.50	32.00
88	LITTLE SISTER	RT	31.50	31.50
88	STRIKE ONE	RT	35.00	35.00
88	WILD WHEELS	RT	35.00	35.00
89	ESPECIALLY FOR YOU	RT	35.00	35.00
89	KISS, THE	RT	45.00	45.00
89	LIPSTICK AND LASHES	RT	35.00	35.00
89	LOVE LETTER	RT	35.00	35.00
89	OFF TO SCHOOL	RT	35.00	35.00
89	PARTY TIME	RT	45.00	45.00
89	SHE LOVES ME	RT	35.00	35.00
89	STAY COOL	RT	35.00	35.00
T. RAINE		**ETHELRED FLAMETAIL**		
89	BLACK KNIGHT, THE	CL	79.50	80.00
89	EARLY DAYS	CL	37.50	38.00
89	EUREKA	CL	49.50	50.00
89	FLYING LESSON, THE	CL	65.00	65.00
89	HELLO WORLD	CL	37.50	38.00
89	JEREMY THE DANDY	CL	89.50	90.00
89	LIFT OFF	CL	105.00	105.00
89	MAGIC WATER. THE	CL	65.00	65.00
89	MERCHANT, THE	CL	67.50	68.00
89	MR. BONZER	CL	62.50	63.00
89	ON THE RUNWAY	CL	49.50	50.00

YR	NAME	LIMIT	ISSUE	TREND
89	PRINCESS NYNEVE	CL	59.50	60.00
89	RANOL	CL	29.50	30.00
89	SCHOOL DAYS	CL	89.50	90.00
89	SWAMP BIRD	CL	39.50	40.00
89	TENDER LOVING CARE	CL	115.00	115.00
89	THREE CHEERS	CL	115.00	115.00
89	TREE POPPER	CL	45.00	45.00
89	TROLL, THE	CL	67.50	68.00
89	WILY WIZARD, THE	CL	79.50	80.00
89	YOUNG INVENTOR, THE	CL	45.00	45.00
T. RAINE				**FANTASY FIGURINES**
88	BEHEMOTH ON WOODEN BASE	2500	220.00	220.00
88	ELFIN KING ON WOODEN BASE	2500	275.00	275.00
88	ETERNAL HERO ON WOODEN BASE	CL	220.00	220.00
88	UNION OF OPPOSITES ON WOODEN BASE	CL	300.00	300.00
T. RAINE				**GENIES BY TOM RAINE**
89	FLIGHT TO BAGDAD	OP	170.00	170.00
89	FREE AT LAST	OP	150.00	150.00
89	KEY OF KNOWLEDGE	OP	170.00	170.00
89	YES MASTER	OP	150.00	150.00
H. HENRIKSEN				**JESTERS**
89	COUNTERSIGN FOR SERIES	OP	75.00	90.00
89	HIS MAJESTRY BALDWICK/INCREDIBLY SIMPLE	3000	295.00	375.00
89	JOCKOMO, THE DOG	RT	59.00	59.00
89	JOLLIES PITCHBELLY	OP	175.00	200.00
89	LA DI DA TOOGOODE	RT	185.00	185.00
89	MERRY ANDREW	RT	130.00	130.00
89	PUCK, BABY BEAR	RT	59.00	59.00
89	SMACK THICKWIT	OP	185.00	230.00
89	TWIT COXCOMBE	RT	140.00	140.00
89	URSULA, MOTHER BEAR	RT	95.00	95.00
H. HENRIKSEN				**LAND OF LEGEND FELLOWSHIP**
90	SELF TAUGHT	TL	100.00	100.00
R. MUSGRAVE				**LAND OF LEGEND FELLOWSHIP**
90	TAKE A CHANCE	TL	*	*
T. RAINE				**LAND OF LEGEND FELLOWSHIP**
89	HUBBLE BUBBLE	RT	95.00	130.00
89	SWORD IN THE STONE, THE	RT	*	75.00
T. RAINE				**LIMITED EDITION CASTLES**
88	SCHLOSS NEUSCHWANSTEIN	CL	750.00	910.00
D. TATE				**LIMITED EDITION CASTLES**
86	SCHLOSS RHEINIUNGFRAU	1500	335.00	335.00
R. MUSGRAVE				**POCKET DRAGONS**
89	A GOOD EGG	RT	36.50	43.00
89	ATTACK	OP	45.00	55.00
89	BABY BROTHER	OP	19.50	24.00
89	DO I HAVE TO?	OP	52.50	63.00
89	DROWSY DRAGON	OP	35.00	35.00
89	FLOWERS FOR YOU	OP	42.50	48.00
89	GALLANT DEFENDER, THE	OP	36.50	43.00
89	GARGOYLE HOPING FOR RASPBERRY TEACAKE	RT	139.50	140.00
89	LOOK AT ME	RT	42.50	43.00
89	NEW BUNNY SHOES	OP	28.50	35.00
89	NO UGLY MONSTERS ALLOWED	OP	47.50	58.00
89	OPERA GARGOYLE	RT	85.00	105.00
89	PINK 'N PRETTY	OP	23.90	30.00
89	POCKET DRAGON COUNTERSIGN	RT	50.00	63.00
89	POCKET MINSTREL, THE	RT	36.50	43.00
89	SCRIBBLES	OP	37.50	45.00
89	SEA DRAGON	RT	45.00	55.00
89	SIR NIGEL SMYTHEBE-SMOKE	OP	147.50	175.00
89	STALKING THE COOKIE JAR	OP	31.00	39.00
89	STORYTIME AT WIZARD'S HOUSE	3000	375.00	450.00
89	TEDDY MAGIC	RT	85.00	105.00
89	TOADY GOLDTRAYLER	OP	52.50	63.00
89	WALKIES	OP	65.00	79.00
89	WHAT COOKIE?	OP	42.50	50.00
89	WIZARDRY FOR FUN AND PROFIT	3000	375.00	450.00
89	YOUR PAINT IS STIRRED	RT	42.50	53.00
90	APPRENTICE, THE	OP	25.00	30.00
90	TAG-A-LONG	OP	19.50	24.00
91	A JOYFUL NOISE	OP	27.50	28.00
91	FRIENDS	OP	85.00	85.00
91	I'M A KITTY	OP	50.00	50.00
91	PICK ME UP	OP	27.50	28.00
91	PLAYING FOOTSIE	OP	27.50	28.00
91	PRACTICE MAKES PERFECT	OP	42.50	43.00
91	SLEEPY HEAD	OP	52.50	53.00
91	TICKLE	OP	35.00	35.00
91	TWINKLE TOES	OP	27.50	28.00
T. RAINE				**THE SECRET OF THE SWAN PRINCESS**
89	ALARCH SILVERBEARD	CL	79.50	80.00
89	ASPARD	CL	65.00	65.00
89	CASTLE OF THE SWAN PRINCESS	CL	99.50	100.00
89	DRAGON'S LAIR	CL	75.00	75.00
89	JUDGE'S RETREAT	CL	85.00	85.00
89	KIBOLD WALTER	CL	65.00	65.00

YR	NAME	LIMIT	ISSUE	TREND
89	MASTERS OF THE FOREST	CL	75.00	75.00
89	PALACE OF THE EMPEROR CHILD	CL	75.00	75.00
89	RONTUNDO THE TUSCAN	CL	65.00	65.00
89	SALIX THE BOLD	CL	65.00	65.00
MUSGRAVE/ HENRIKSEN				**UNDER THE HEDGE**
89	A WINTER'S FRIEND	RT	25.00	25.00
89	BASKETS OF LOVE	OP	39.50	48.00
89	CAREFULLY WRAPPED	RT	30.00	30.00
89	COUNTERSIGN	OP	39.50	48.00
89	COUSIN BERTHA'S REVENGE	OP	42.50	50.00
89	DECK THE HALLS	3000	99.50	120.00
89	FASHION PLATE, THE	RT	47.50	48.00
89	FATHER CHRISTMAS	OP	45.00	55.00
89	FAVORITE UNCLE	OP	42.50	58.00
89	KEEP YOUR TAIL WARM	OP	59.50	70.00
89	OUT OF TOWN GUEST	OP	42.50	58.00
89	SNOWBALLS AND TOP HATS	RT	39.50	40.00
89	TRAPPED ON THE SUMMIT	RT	37.50	38.00
90	ARTFUL BOWLER, THE	OP	47.50	60.00
90	ARTIST, THE	OP	62.50	75.00
90	AUNT VIOLET & PUDGY	OP	50.00	60.00
90	COUSIN REGGIE	OP	59.50	70.00
90	JELLY SANWICHES	OP	82.50	98.00
90	JUNIUS BUG	OP	42.50	50.00
90	JUST GUARDING THE HAMPER	OP	47.50	58.00
90	MIGHTY PERCY AT THE BAT	OP	49.50	60.00
90	MISS AMELIA'S TURN	OP	45.00	55.00
90	SLOW AND STEADY	OP	59.50	70.00
90	SPARKLING CLEAN	OP	95.50	115.00
90	SPOTTING STRAYS	OP	50.00	60.00
90	STEMS AND BOWLES LTD.	OP	159.00	190.00
90	SUNDAE AFTERNOON	OP	199.00	235.00
90	TEA TABLE, THE	OP	39.50	48.00
90	WAITING FOR A LIGHT	OP	82.50	98.00
90	WATCHING THE HERD	OP	45.00	55.00
90	WICKET KEEPER, THE	OP	55.00	70.00
H. HENRIKSEN				**WIZARDS**
89	COUNTERSIGN FOR WIZARDS' SERIES	OP	75.00	90.00
89	FORESHADOW THE SEER	OP	135.00	160.00
89	LACKEY	RT	95.00	95.00
89	MERLYN THE WIZARD WATCHER	RT	49.50	50.00
89	MERRYWEATHER SUNLIGHTER	3000	295.00	350.00
89	MORIAH	OP	159.00	190.00
89	MYDWYNTER	RT	135.00	135.00
89	REPOSITORY OF MAGIC	RT	130.00	130.00
89	RIMBAUGH	OP	159.00	190.00
89	THORBAULD	RT	175.00	175.00
91	BALANCE OF TRUTH	2500	270.00	270.00
91	DRAGON MASTER, THE	1500	675.00	675.00
91	FORESHADOW THE SEER (WITH CRYSTALS)	OP	190.00	190.00
91	HOWLAND THE WISE	2500	300.00	300.00
91	MORIAH (WITH CRYSTALS)	OP	225.00	225.00
91	PONDERING THE QUEST	2500	270.00	270.00
91	RIMBAUGH (WITH CRYSTALS)	OP	225.00	225.00

LEGENDS

YR	NAME	LIMIT	ISSUE	TREND
*	CHIEF JOSEPH	*	*	1650.00
*	ONE MORE COUP	*	*	1375.00
C. PARDELL				
90	LAKOTA LOVE SONG	RT	380.00	965.00
C. PARDELL				**AMERICAN WEST PREMIER EDITION**
91	FIRST COUP	SO	1150.00	1200.00
91	UNEXPECTED RESCUER	SO	990.00	2000.00
92	AMERICAN HORSE TAKES HIS NAME	950	1300.00	1300.00
C. PARDELL				**ANNUAL COLLECTORS EDITION**
*	MEDICINE GIFT OF MANHOOD	*	990.00	1900.00
*	NIGHT BEFORE, THE	*	990.00	1900.00
*	SPIRIT OF THE WOLF	*	950.00	1225.00
90	NIGHT BEFORE, THE	SO	990.00	1900.00
91	MEDICINE GIFT OF MANHOOD	SO	990.00	1900.00
92	SPIRIT OF THE WOLF	500	950.00	1225.00
93	TOMORROW'S WARRIOR	*	590.00	1400.00
K. CANTRELL				**ENDANGERED WILDLIFE COLLECTION**
90	FOREST SPIRIT	SO	290.00	1195.00
92	SPIRIT SONG	*	350.00	695.00
K. CANTRELL				**ENDANGERED WILDLIFE COLLECTION-EAGLE SERIES**
89	SENTINEL	*	280.00	585.00
C. PARDELL				**GALLERY EDITIONS**
92	RESOLUTE	*	7950.00	13,000.00
C. PARDELL				**INDIAN ARTS COLLECTION**
89	CHIEF'S BLANKET	SO	350.00	600.00
90	KACHINA CARVER	*	270.00	450.00
90	STORY TELLER	*	290.00	325.00
C. PARDELL				**THE LEGACIES OF THE WEST PREMIER EDITION**
90	MYSTIC VISION	SO	990.00	2895.00
90	VICTORIOUS	SO	1275.00	3875.00
91	DEFIANT COMANCHE	SO	1300.00	2550.00

YR	NAME	LIMIT	ISSUE	TREND
91	NO MORE, FOREVER	SO	1500.00	2900.00
92	ESTEEMED WARRIOR	SO	1750.00	2250.00
C. PARDELL		**THE LEGENDARY WEST COLLECTION**		
87	JOHNSON'S LAST FLIGHT	SO	590.00	1200.00
87	PONY EXPRESS	RT	320.00	450.00
87	WHITE FEATHER'S VISION	SO	390.00	2000.00
89	CRAZY HORSE	*	390.00	900.00
C. PARDELL		**THE LEGENDARY WEST PREMIER EDITION**		
88	RED CLOUD'S COUP	SO	480.00	6000.00
89	PURSUED	SO	750.00	6000.00
89	SONGS OF GLORY	SO	850.00	4300.00
90	CROW WARRIOR	SO	1225.00	4500.00
91	TRIUMPHANT	SO	1150.00	2000.00
92	FINAL CHARGE	*	1250.00	1600.00
92	FINAL CHARGE, THE	750	1250.00	1600.00

LENOX CHINA/CRYSTAL COLLECTION

YR	NAME	LIMIT	ISSUE	TREND
*		**AMERICAN FASHION**		
83	SPRINGTIME PROMENADE	OP	95.00	95.00
84	FIRST WALTZ	OP	95.00	95.00
84	TEA AT THE RITZ	OP	95.00	95.00
85	GOVERNOR'S GARDEN PARTY	OP	95.00	95.00
86	BELLE OF THE BALL	OP	95.00	95.00
86	GRAND TOUR	OP	95.00	95.00
87	CENTENNIAL BRIDE	OP	95.00	95.00
87	GALA AT THE WHITE HOUSE	OP	95.00	95.00
*		**BABY BEARS**		
91	POLAR BEAR	OP	45.00	45.00
*		**BABY BIRD PAIRS**		
91	ROBINS	OP	64.00	64.00
*		**BIBLICAL CHARACTERS**		
92	MOSES, THE LAWGIVER	OP	95.00	95.00
*		**CAROUSEL ANIMALS**		
87	CAROUSEL HORSE	9500	136.00	152.00
88	CAROUSEL UNICORN	9500	136.00	152.00
89	CAROUSEL CIRCUS HORSE	9500	136.00	152.00
89	CAROUSEL REINDEER	9500	136.00	152.00
90	CAROUSEL CHARGER	9500	136.00	152.00
90	CAROUSEL ELEPHANT	9500	136.00	152.00
90	CAROUSEL LION	9500	136.00	152.00
91	CAROUSEL POLAR BEAR	9500	152.00	152.00
91	PRIDE OF AMERICA	TL	152.00	152.00
91	WESTERN HORSE	OP	152.00	152.00
92	CAMELOT HORSE	OP	152.00	152.00
*		**COUNTRY KIDS**		
91	GOOSE GIRL	OP	75.00	75.00
*		**DOVES & ROSES**		
91	DOVE'S OF PEACE	OP	95.00	95.00
91	LOVE'S PROMISE	OP	95.00	95.00
92	DOVE'S OF HONOR	OP	119.00	119.00
*		**ENDANGERED BABY ANIMALS**		
90	PANDA	OP	39.00	39.00
91	BABY FLORIDA PANTHER	OP	57.00	57.00
91	BABY GREY WOLF	OP	57.00	57.00
91	ELEPHANT	OP	57.00	57.00
*		**EXOTIC BIRDS**		
91	COCKATOO	OP	49.50	50.00
*		**FLORAL SCULPTURES**		
86	RUBRUM LILY	OP	119.00	136.00
87	IRIS	OP	119.00	136.00
88	MAGNOLIA	OP	119.00	136.00
88	PEACE ROSE	OP	119.00	136.00
*		**GARDEN BIRDS**		
85	CHICKADEE	OP	39.00	45.00
86	BLUE JAY	OP	39.00	45.00
86	EASTERN BLUEBIRD	OP	39.00	45.00
86	TUFTED TITMOUSE	OP	39.00	45.00
87	AMERICAN GOLDFINCH	OP	39.00	45.00
87	CARDINAL	OP	39.00	45.00
87	RED-BREASTED NUTHATCH	OP	39.00	45.00
87	TURTLE DOVE	OP	39.00	45.00
88	CEDAR WAXWING	OP	39.00	45.00
88	HUMMINGBIRD	OP	39.00	45.00
89	DOWNY WOODPECKER	OP	39.00	45.00
89	ROBIN	OP	39.00	45.00
89	SAW WHET OWL	OP	45.00	45.00
90	BALTIMORE ORIOLE	OP	45.00	45.00
90	CHIPPING SPARROW	OP	45.00	45.00
90	WOOD DUCK	OP	45.00	45.00
90	WREN	OP	45.00	45.00
91	BROADBILLED HUMMINGBIRD	OP	45.00	45.00
91	DARK-EYED JUNCO	OP	45.00	45.00
91	GOLDEN CROWNED KINGLET	OP	45.00	45.00
91	PURPLE FINCH	OP	45.00	45.00
91	ROSE GROSBEAK	OP	45.00	45.00
92	SCARLET TANGER	OP	45.00	45.00

YR	NAME	LIMIT	ISSUE	TREND
*	**GARDEN FLOWERS**			
88	CATTLEYA ORCHID	OP	39.00	45.00
88	PARROT TULIP	OP	39.00	39.00
88	TEA ROSE	OP	39.00	45.00
89	IRIS	OP	45.00	45.00
90	CARNATION	OP	45.00	45.00
90	DAFFODIL	OP	45.00	45.00
90	DAY LILY	OP	45.00	45.00
91	CALLA LILY	OP	45.00	45.00
91	CAMELIA	OP	45.00	45.00
91	MAGNOLIA	OP	45.00	45.00
91	MORNING GLORY	OP	45.00	45.00
91	POINSETTIA	OP	39.00	39.00
*	**GENTLE MAJESTY**			
90	BEAR HUG POLAR BEAR	OP	76.00	76.00
90	PENGUINS	OP	76.00	76.00
91	KEEPING WARM (FOXES)	OP	76.00	76.00
*	**INTERNATIONAL BRIDES**			
90	RUSSIAN BRIDE	OP	136.00	136.00
*	**INTERNATIONAL HORSE SCULPTURES**			
88	ARABIAN KNIGHT	OP	136.00	136.00
89	THOROUGHBRED	OP	136.00	136.00
90	APPALOOSA	OP	136.00	136.00
90	LIPPIZAN	OP	136.00	136.00
J.W. SMITH	**JESSIE WILCOX SMITH**			
91	FEEDING KITTY	OP	60.00	60.00
91	ROSEBUDS	OP	60.00	60.00
*	**KINGS OF THE SKY**			
89	AMERICAN BALD EAGLE	OP	195.00	195.00
91	DEFENDER OF FREEDOM	TL	234.00	234.00
91	GOLDEN EAGLE	OP	234.00	234.00
*	**LEGENDARY PRINCESSES**			
85	RAPUNZEL	OP	119.00	136.00
86	SLEEPING BEAUTY	OP	119.00	136.00
87	SNOW QUEEN	OP	119.00	136.00
88	CINDERELLA	OP	136.00	136.00
89	SNOW WHITE	OP	136.00	136.00
89	SWAN PRINCESS	OP	136.00	136.00
90	CLEOPATRA	OP	136.00	136.00
90	GUINEVERE	OP	136.00	136.00
90	JULIET	OP	136.00	136.00
91	PEACOCK MAIDEN	OP	136.00	136.00
91	POCOHONTAS	9500	136.00	136.00
92	FIREBIRD	OP	156.00	156.00
*	**LENOX BABY BOOK**			
90	BABY'S FIRST SHOES	OP	57.00	57.00
91	BABY'S FIRST CHRISTMAS	OP	57.00	57.00
91	BABY'S FIRST STEPS	OP	57.00	57.00
92	BABY'S FIRST PORTRAIT	OP	57.00	57.00
*	**LENOX PUPPY COLLECTION**			
90	BEAGLE	OP	76.00	76.00
91	COCKER SPANIEL	OP	76.00	76.00
92	POODLE	OP	76.00	76.00
*	**LENOX SEA ANIMALS**			
91	DANCE OF THE DOLPHINS	OP	119.00	119.00
*	**LIFE OF CHRIST**			
90	CHILDREN'S BLESSING, THE	OP	95.00	95.00
90	GOOD SHEPHERD, THE	OP	95.00	95.00
90	MADONNA AND CHILD	OP	95.00	95.00
91	JESUS, THE TEACHER	9500	95.00	95.00
91	SAVIOR, THE	OP	95.00	95.00
92	A CHILD'S PRAYER	OP	95.00	95.00
92	CHILDREN'S DEVOTION PAINTED	OP	195.00	195.00
*	**MOTHER & CHILD**			
86	CHERISHED MOMENT	OP	119.00	119.00
86	SUNDAY IN THE PARK	OP	119.00	119.00
87	STORYTIME	OP	119.00	119.00
88	PRESENT, THE	OP	119.00	119.00
89	CHRISTENING	OP	119.00	119.00
90	BEDTIME PRAYERS	OP	119.00	119.00
91	AFTERNOON STROLL	7500	136.00	136.00
91	EVENING LULLABY	7500	136.00	136.00
92	MORNING PLAYTIME	OP	136.00	136.00
*	**NATIVITY**			
86	HOLY FAMILY	OP	119.00	136.00
87	THREE ANGELS	OP	119.00	152.00
88	ANIMALS OF THE NATIVITY	OP	119.00	152.00
88	SHEPHERDS	OP	119.00	152.00
89	ANGELS OF ADORATION	OP	136.00	152.00
90	CHILDREN OF BETHLEHEM	OP	136.00	152.00
91	STANDING CAMEL & DRIVER	9500	152.00	152.00
91	TOWNSPEOPLE OF BETHLEHEM	OP	136.00	152.00
*	**NATURE'S BEAUTIFUL BUTTERFLIES**			
89	BLUE TEMORA	OP	39.00	45.00
90	MONARCH	OP	39.00	45.00
90	PURPLE EMPEROR	OP	45.00	45.00
90	YELLOW SWALLOWTAIL	OP	39.00	45.00

YR	NAME	LIMIT	ISSUE	TREND
91	ADONIS	OP	45.00	45.00
91	MALACHITE	OP	45.00	45.00
*		**NORTH AMERICAN BIRD PAIRS**		
90	HUMMINGBIRDS	OP	119.00	119.00
91	BLUE JAY PAIRS	9500	119.00	119.00
91	CHICKADEES	9500	119.00	119.00
92	CARDINAL	OP	119.00	119.00
*		**NORTH AMERICAN WILDLIFE**		
91	WHITE-TAILED DEER	OP	195.00	195.00
*		**OWLS OF AMERICA**		
88	SNOWY OWL	OP	136.00	136.00
89	BARN OWL	OP	136.00	136.00
90	SCREECH OWL	OP	136.00	136.00
91	GREAT HORNED OWL	9500	136.00	136.00
*		**PARENT & CHILD BIRD PAIRS**		
92	BLUE JAY PAIRS	OP	119.00	119.00
*		**PORCELAIN DUCK COLLECTION**		
91	MALLARD DUCK	OP	45.00	45.00
91	WOOD DUCK	OP	45.00	45.00
92	BLUE WINGED TEAL DUCK	OP	45.00	45.00
*		**SANTA CLAUS COLLECTIONS**		
90	FATHER CHRISTMAS	OP	136.00	136.00
91	AMERICANA SANTA	OP	136.00	136.00
91	KRIS KRINGLE	OP	136.00	136.00
*		**STREET CRIER COLLECTION**		
90	FRENCH FLOWER MAIDEN	OP	136.00	136.00
91	BELGIAN LACE MAKER	OP	136.00	136.00
*		**WILDLIFE OF THE SEVEN CONTINENTS**		
84	NORTH AMERICAN BIGHORN SHEEP	OP	120.00	120.00
85	ASIAN ELEPHANT	OP	120.00	120.00
85	AUSTRAILIAN KOALA	OP	120.00	120.00
86	SOUTH AMERICAN PUMA	OP	120.00	120.00
87	ANARCTIC SEALS	OP	136.00	136.00
87	EUROPEAN RED DEER	OP	136.00	136.00
88	AFRICAN LION	OP	136.00	136.00
*		**WOODLAND ANIMALS**		
90	RACCOON	OP	39.00	39.00
90	RED SQUIRREL	OP	39.00	39.00
91	CHIPMUNK	OP	39.00	39.00

LILLIPUT LANE LTD.

Price ranges may reflect various demands in the market from one geographic region to another; condition of piece; specific markings found on piece; and/or changes in production of piece.

YR	NAME	LIMIT	ISSUE	TREND
*		**NORMAN ROCKWELL**		
*	COURT JESTER RL405	*	*	1100.00-1200.00
*	DAY DREAMER R1411	*	*	1500.00
*	LOVE LETTER R1406	*	*	900.00
*	PRACTICE MAKES PERFECT RL408	*	*	850.00-1150.00
*	SPRINGTIME '27 R1410	*	*	1500.00
*	SUMMER STOCK RL401	*	*	1100.00
*	YOUNG LOVE R1409	*	*	900.00

LLADRO

Price ranges may reflect various demands in the market from one geographic region to another; condition of piece; specific markings found on piece; and/or changes in production of piece.

YR	NAME	LIMIT	ISSUE	TREND
*	1991 TREE TOPPER L-225	*	*	225.00
*	AFGHAN L1069	*	*	375.00
*	BASHFUL GIRL L-5026	*	*	200.00
*	BASKET C1543	*	*	550.00
*	BASKET OF ROSES C1544	*	*	875.00
*	BOYS PLAYING WITH GOAT L1129	*	*	970.00
*	DOG IN BASKET	*	*	300.00
*	FLOWER POT L-5028	*	*	650.00
*	FORD FIESTA L-7017	*	*	750.00
*	GARDEN CLASSIC S7617	*	*	1150.00
*	GARDEN SONG S-7618	*	*	750.00
*	GAYLE L-5109	*	*	450.00
*	GREAT DANE L1068	*	*	438.00-485.00
*	GROUP OF EAGLE OWLS L-1223	*	*	1050.00
*	HEN L1041	*	*	275.00
*	JAPANESE VASE L-1536	*	*	1400.00
*	KARENA L-5107	*	*	425.00
*	KITAKAMI CRUISE LL1605	500	5800.00	8000.00
*	LAWYER L1090	*	*	312.50
*	LITTLE BALLET GIRL L-5104	*	*	300.00
*	MISS TERESA L-4999	*	*	350.00
*	MOTHER KISSING CHILD L-1329	*	*	1500.00
*	OLYMPIC PUPPET	*	*	800.00
*	PEACOCK FLOWER VASE L-1200	*	*	2350.00
*	RAM	*	*	250.00
*	RND. BASKET-BLUE FLOWERS C1554.1	*	*	177.00
*	RND. BRN. BASKET-PINK LACE C1553	*	*	293.00
*	RND. BRN. BASKT-BLUE LACE C1554	*	*	184.00
*	SHAKESPEARE L1338	*	*	1050.00
*	SHERUFF PUPPET	*	*	600.00
*	SOLDIER'S HEAD VASE L1105	*	*	375.00
*	SOUTHERN TEA LL1597	TL	1775.00	2250.00

YR	NAME	LIMIT	ISSUE	TREND
*	SPRINGTIME 27 RL-406	*	*	1200.00
*	SPRINGTIME OF '27 RL-410	*	*	1100.00
*	TINKERBELL L-7518	*	*	3200.00
*	TURTLE DOVE NEST LL3519	RT	3600.00	6000.00
69	BEAGLE PUPPY LYING L1072	RT	16.50	250.00
69	BIRD L1054	RT	14.00	140.00
69	DEER L1064	RT	27.50	285.00
69	FOX AND CUB L1065	RT	175.00	370.00
69	GIRL MANICURING L1082	RT	14.50	295.00-325.00
69	GIRL WITH BRUSH L1081	RT	14.50	300.00
69	GIRL WITH MOTHER'S SHOE L1084	RT	14.50	310.00
69	OLD DOG L1067	RT	40.00	450.00
69	OLD FOLKS L1033G/M	RT	140.00	1100.00-1870.00
69	PLATES SATYR (PAN RIGHT) L1006	RT	45.00	550.00
69	SHEPHERDESS WITH DOG L1034	RT	30.00	250.00
71	CLOWN L1126	RT	71.00	1350.00
71	GIRL WITH BONNET L1147	RT	20.00	300.00
71	GIRL WITH PARASOL AND GEESE L4510	RT	40.00	250.00
71	PUPPY LOVE L1127	OP	50.00	300.00
77	LITTLE RED RIDING HOOD L-4965	RT	210.00	560.00
77	TENNIS PLAYER PUPPET L-4966	RT	60.00	260.00
80	A SUCCESSFUL HUNT LL5098	RT	5200.00	5250.00
80	AFTER THE DANCE L-5092	RT	165.00	360.00
80	CANDID L-5039	RT	145.00	500.00
80	FLOWER PEDDLER L-5029	RT	675.00	1300.00
80	LITTLE FLOWER SELLER L-5082	RT	750.00	1800.00
80	SAMSON AND DELILAH L5051	RT	350.00	1500.00
80	TAKING A BOW L-L5095	RT	165.00	300.00
82	AMY SCHOOL GIRL-LETTER "A" L-5145	RT	110.00	1525.00
82	BABY WITH DUMMY L-5102	RT	58.00	280.00
82	BILLY FOOTBALL PLAYER L-5135	RT	140.00	700.00
82	GIRL SOCCER PLAYER L-5134	RT	140.00	500.00
82	KITTY L-5164	RT	125.00	500.00
82	LITTLE BOY BULLFIGHTER L-5115	RT	123.00	400.00
82	SCHOOL GIRL IVEZ L-5147	CL	123.00	600.00
82	SEWING A TROUSSEAU L5126	RT	185.00	400.00
83	ARACELY WITH PET DUCK L-5202	RT	75.00	225.00
84	GRACEFUL SWAN L-5230	OP	35.00	100.00
84	PENGUIN L-5247	RT	70.00	250.00
84	PENGUIN L-5248	RT	70.00	250.00
84	PENGUIN L-5249	RT	70.00	200.00
84	SPANISH SOLDIER L5255	RT	185.00	700.00
84	SWAN WITH WINGS SPREAD L-5231	OP	50.00	140.00
85	AEROBICS FLOOR EXERCISE L-5335	RT	110.00	300.00
85	AEROBICS PUSH-UPS L-5334	RT	110.00	300.00
85	AEROBICS SCISSOR FIGURE L-5336	*	*	350.00
85	EIGHTEENTH CENTURY COACH LL1485	500	14000.00	26000.00
85	GYMNAST BALANCING BALL L-5332	RT	95.00	400.00
85	LITTLE LEAGUER CATCHING L-5290	RT	150.00	500.00
85	LITTLE LEAGUER EXERCISING L-5289	RT	150.00	425.00
85	LITTLE LEAGUER ON BENCH L-5291	RT	150.00	510.00
85	MOTHER, CHILD AND LAMB L-5299	RT	180.00	800.00
85	PREDICTING THE FUTURE L-5191	RT	135.00	450.00
87	CHRISTOPHER COLUMBUS LL2176	RT	1000.00	1300.00
87	GREAT HORNED OWL L-5420	RT	150.00	310.00
87	ST. NICHOLAS L5427	RT	425.00	650.00
88	GARDEN PARTY LL1578	500	5500.00	7200.00
89	CIRCUS PARADE LL1609	1000	5200.00	6500.00
89	MOUNTED WARRIORS LL1608	500	2850.00	3400.00
90	A CHRISTMAS WISH L5711G	OP	350.00	400.00
90	A FAWN AND A FRIEND L5674G	OP	450.00	500.00
90	A QUIET MOMENT L5673G	OP	450.00	525.00
90	A RIDE IN THE PARK LL5718	RT	3200.00	3525.00
90	AFTER SCHOOL L5707G	RT	280.00	300.00
90	AFTERNOON STROLL L5687G	RT	275.00	300.00
90	ANGEL CARE L5727G	OP	190.00	200.00
90	ANGELIC VOICE L5724G	OP	125.00	150.00
90	ANTICIPATION L5650G	RT	300.00	355.00
90	BACK TO SCHOOL L5702G	RT	350.00	375.00
90	BARNYARD REFLECTIONS L5684G	RT	460.00	540.00
90	BARNYARD SCENE L5659G/M	OP	200.00	250.00
90	BEAUTIFUL BURRO L5683G	RT	280.00	350.00
90	BEHAVE! L5703G	RT	230.00	275.00
90	BETWEEN CLASSES L5709G	RT	280.00	320.00
90	BREEZY AFTERNOON L5682G/M	OP	180.00	190.00
90	CAN I HELP? L5689G	OP	250.00	300.00
90	CAT NAP L5640G	OP	125.00	140.00
90	CATHY L5643G	OP	200.00	225.00
90	CINDY L5646G	OP	190.00	200.00
90	CIRCUS SERENADE L5694G	RT	300.00	350.00
90	CONCERTINA L5695G	RT	300.00	350.00
90	COURTNEY L5648G	OP	200.00	225.00
90	DOG'S BEST FRIEND L5688G	OP	250.00	300.00
90	DON'T LOOK DOWN L5698G	OP	330.00	400.00
90	ELIZABETH L5645G	OP	190.00	210.00
90	FANTASY FRIEND L5710G	RT	420.00	500.00
90	FIRST BALLET L5714G	OP	370.00	425.00
90	FOLLOW ME L5722G	OP	140.00	150.00
90	GIDDY UP L5664G	RT	190.00	210.00

YR	NAME	LIMIT	ISSUE	TREND
90	HANG ON! L5665G	TL	225.00	295.00
90	HEAVENLY CHIMES L5723G	OP	100.00	110.00
90	HEAVENLY DREAMER L5728G	OP	100.00	110.00
90	HI THERE! L5672G	OP	450.00	525.00
90	I FEEL PRETTY L5678G/M	OP	190.00	225.00
90	IN NO HURRY L5679G	RT	550.00	650.00
90	INVINCIBLE LL2188	300	1100.00	1250.00
90	JUST A LITTLE KISS L5701G	OP	320.00	380.00
90	KING'S GUARD, THE- L5642G	RT	950.00	1050.00
90	LAND OF THE GIANTS L5716G	RT	275.00	300.00
90	LITTLE DUTCH GARDENER L5671G	RT	400.00	480.00
90	MAKING A WISH L5725G	OP	125.00	150.00
90	MANDOLIN SERENADE L5696G	RT	300.00	350.00
90	MARSHLAND MATES L5691G	OP	950.00	1100.00
90	MAY DANCE L5662G	OP	170.00	200.00
90	MOMMY, IT'S COLD L5715G	RT	360.00	400.00
90	MUSICAL MUSE L5651G	OP	375.00	450.00
90	MY FIRST CLASS L5708G	RT	280.00	320.00
90	NOTHING TO DO L5649G/M	OP	190.00	225.00
90	ON THE AVENUE L5686G	RT	275.00	320.00
90	ON THE ROAD L5681G	RT	320.00	525.00
90	ONCE UPON A TIME L5721G	OP	550.00	655.00
90	OVER THE CLOUDS L5697G	OP	275.00	295.00
90	PROMENADE L5685G	RT	275.00	330.00
90	ROCK A BYE BABY L5715G	RT	300.00	425.00
90	SARA L5647G	OP	200.00	225.00
90	SHARING SECRETS L5720G	OP	290.00	345.00
90	SITTING PRETTY L5699G	OP	300.00	350.00
90	SLEEPY KITTEN L5712G	OP	110.00	125.00
90	SNOW MAN, THE- L5713G	OP	300.00	360.00
90	SOUTHERN CHARM L5700G	OP	675.00	1000.00
90	SPRING DANCE L5663G	OP	170.00	200.00
90	STREET HARMONIES L5692G	RT	3200.00	3800.00
90	SUNNING IN IPANEMA L5660G	RT	370.00	500.00
90	SUSAN L5644G	OP	190.00	210.00
90	SWAN AND THE PRINCESS, THE- L5705G	RT	350.00	425.00
90	SWAN SONG L5704G	TL	350.00	400.00
90	SWEEP AWAY THE CLOUDS L5726G	OP	125.00	150.00
90	TEE TIME L5675G	RT	280.00	325.00
90	TRAVELING ARTIST L5661G	RT	250.00	300.00
90	TRAVELING IN STYLE L5680G	RT	425.00	500.00
90	TRINO AT THE BEACH L5666G	TL	390.00	450.00
90	TWILIGHT YEARS L5677G	OP	370.00	425.00
90	VALENCIAN BEAUTY L5670G	RT	175.00	200.00
90	VALENCIAN FLOWERS L5669G	RT	370.00	425.00
90	VALENCIAN HARVEST L5668G	RT	175.00	200.00
90	VENECIAN CARNIVAL L5658G	RT	500.00	590.00
90	WANDERING MINSTREL L5676G	RT	270.00	315.00
90	WE CAN'T PLAY L5706G	OP	200.00	230.00
91	A CRADLE OF KITTENS L5784G	OP	360.00	390.00
91	ACADEMY DAYS L5768G	RT	280.00	300.00
91	ALICE IN WONDERLAND L5740G	OP	440.00	500.00
91	ALLEGORY OF LIBERTY L5819G	OP	1950.00	2100.00
91	ASHLEY L5756G	RT	265.00	310.00
91	BABY JESUS L5745G	OP	170.00	180.00
91	BACKSTAGE PREPARATION L5817G/M	RT	490.00	525.00
91	BEAUTIFUL TRESSES L5757G	RT	725.00	800.00
91	BEST FOOT FORWARD L5738G	RT	280.00	300.00
91	BIG SISTER L5735G	OP	650.00	690.00
91	BRIDAL PORTRAIT L5742G	TL	480.00	550.00
91	BULL & DONKEY L5744G	OP	250.00	280.00
91	CAREFREE L5790G	OP	300.00	320.00
91	CAROUSEL CANTER L57323G	RT	1700.00	1900.00
91	CAROUSEL CHARMER L5731G	RT	1700.00	1900.00
91	CHARM LL5801	RT	650.00	700.00
91	CHARMING DUET L5766G	OP	575.00	620.00
91	CHECKING THE TIME L5762G	TL	560.00	600.00
91	CLAUDETTE L5755G	RT	265.00	325.00
91	COLUMBUS REFLECTING LL1741	RT	1850.00	2000.00
91	COLUMBUS, TWO ROUTES LL1740	TL	1500.00	1600.00
91	COME OUT AND PLAY L5797G	RT	275.00	300.00
91	CURTAIN CALL L5814G/M	RT	490.00	525.00
91	DANCE OF LOVE L5820G	RT	575.00	630.00
91	DANCING CLASS L5741G	OP	340.00	375.00
91	DON'T FORGET ME L5743G	OP	150.00	150.00
91	ELEGANT PROMENADE L5802G	OP	775.00	830.00
91	FAIRY GODMOTHER L5791G	RT	375.00	400.00
91	FAITHFUL STEED L5769G	RT	370.00	400.00
91	FIRST SAMPLER L5767G	TL	625.00	700.00
91	FLIRT, THE - L5789G	OP	185.00	185.00
91	FLORAL GETAWAY L5795G	RT	625.00	750.00
91	GIFT OF BEAUTY L5775G	TL	850.00	900.00
91	GRACEFUL OFFERING L5773G	TL	850.00	900.00
91	HATS OFF TO FUN L5765G	TL	475.00	500.00
91	HAVING A BALL L5813G	OP	225.00	250.00
91	HEAVENLY SWING LL1739	1000	1900.00	2000.00
91	HOLD HER STILL L5753G	RT	650.00	700.00
91	HOLY NIGHT L5796G	RT	330.00	375.00
91	HORTICULTURIST L5733G	RT	450.00	500.00

YR	NAME	LIMIT	ISSUE	TREND
91	I DO L5835G	OP	165.00	200.00
91	I'VE GOT IT L5827G	TL	170.00	170.00
91	IN FULL RELAVE L5815G/M	RT	490.00	530.00
91	INTERRUPTED NAP L5760G	TL	325.00	340.00
91	JAZZ BASS L5834G	OP	395.00	430.00
91	JAZZ HORN L5832G	OP	295.00	300.00
91	JAZZ SAX L5833G	OP	295.00	300.00
91	LAP FULL OF LOVE L5739G	TL	275.00	300.00
91	LIBERTY EAGLE LL1738	1500	1000.00	1050.00
91	LITTLE DREAMERS L5772G/M	OP	230.00	230.00
91	LITTLE LAMB L5750G	OP	40.00	40.00
91	LITTLE PRINCE L5737G	RT	295.00	310.00
91	LITTLE UNICORN L5826G/M	OP	275.00	300.00
91	LITTLE VIRGIN L5752G	RT	295.00	340.00
91	LITTLEST CLOWN L5811G	OP	235.00	250.00
91	LOVER'S PARADISE L5779G	OP	2250.00	2400.00
91	MAGIC OF LAUGHTER, THE- L5771G	OP	950.00	1100.00
91	MARY L5747G	OP	275.00	300.00
91	MILKMAID L5798G	RT	450.00	500.00
91	MINSTEL'S LOVE L5821G	RT	525.00	580.00
91	MUSICAL PARTNERS L5763G	TL	625.00	690.00
91	MUSICALLY INCLINED L5810G	RT	235.00	255.00
91	MY CHORES L5782G	TL	325.00	350.00
91	MY PUPPIES L5807G	RT	325.00	345.00
91	NATURE'S GIFT L5774G	RT	900.00	1000.00
91	NEW WORLD MEDALLION LL5808	RT	200.00	200.00
91	NEXT AT BAT L5828G	OP	170.00	170.00
91	NOT TOO CLOSE L5781G	RT	365.00	460.00
91	OCEAN BEAUTY L5785G	OP	625.00	650.00
91	ON HER TOES L5818G/M	RT	490.00	525.00
91	ON THE MOVE L5838G	OP	340.00	400.00
91	ONWARD! LL1742	RT	2500.00	2800.00
91	OUT FOR A ROMP L5761G	TL	375.00	400.00
91	OUT FOR A SPIN L5770G	RT	390.00	425.00
91	OUTING IN SEVILLE LL1756	500	23000.00	24000.00
91	PILGRIM COUPLE L5734G	RT	490.00	530.00
91	PLAYING TAG L5804G	RT	170.00	200.00
91	PRECIOUS BALLERINA L5793G	TL	575.00	630.00
91	PRECIOUS CARGO L5794G	RT	460.00	500.00
91	PRESTO! L5759G	RT	275.00	330.00
91	PRIMA BALLERINA L5816G/M	RT	490.00	525.00
91	PRINCESS AND THE UNICORN, THE- LL1755	RT	1750.00	2000.00
91	PUPPET SHOW L5736G	OP	280.00	300.00
91	REVERENT MOMENT L5792G	RT	295.00	310.00
91	SEEDS OF LAUGHTER L5764G	RT	525.00	585.00
91	SHALL WE DANCE? L5799G	RT	600.00	700.00
91	SHARING SWEETS L5836G	OP	220.00	250.00
91	SHEPHERD BOY L5749G	OP	225.00	250.00
91	SHEPHERD GIRL L5748G	OP	150.00	170.00
91	SING WITH ME L5837G	OP	240.00	240.00
91	SINGAPORE DANCERS L5754G	RT	950.00	1100.00
91	SOPHISTICATE L5787G	OP	185.00	200.00
91	SPECIAL DELIVERY L5783G	RT	525.00	550.00
91	ST. JOSEPH L5746G	OP	350.00	380.00
91	STORY HOUR L5786G	OP	550.00	600.00
91	SUNDAY BEST L5758G	OP	725.00	800.00
91	TALK OF THE TOWN L5788G	OP	185.00	200.00
91	TICKLING L5806G/M	RT	130.00	150.00
91	TIRED FRIEND L5812G	OP	225.00	250.00
91	TUMBLING L5805G/M	RT	130.00	150.00
91	VALENCIAN CRUISE LL1731	1000	2700.00	2900.00
91	VENICE VOWS LL1732	1000	3755.00	4000.00
91	WALK WITH FATHER L5751G	RT	375.00	400.00
91	WALKING THE FIELDS L5780G	RT	725.00	800.00
91	YOUTH LL5800	RT	650.00	700.00
92	A QUIET AFTERNOON L5843G	TL	1050.00	1150.00
92	AFTERNOON JAUNT L5855G	RT	420.00	450.00
92	AFTERNOON VERSE L2231M	OP	580.00	580.00
92	ALL DRESSED UP L5909G	OP	440.00	440.00
92	ALL TUCKERED OUT L5846G/M	OP	220.00	250.00
92	ARCTIC ALLIES L2227M	OP	585.00	600.00
92	AT THE BALL L5859G	OP	295.00	325.00
92	ATTENTIVE BUNNY L5905G	OP	75.00	75.00
92	AVIATOR, THE L5891G	OP	375.00	425.00
92	BOUQUET OF BLOSSOMS L5895G	OP	295.00	295.00
92	BOY'S BEST FRIEND L2226M	OP	390.00	400.00
92	CHERISH L2224M	OP	1750.00	1860.00
92	CIRCUS MAGIC L5892G	OP	470.00	500.00
92	CIRCUS TIME LL1758	2500	9200.00	9600.00
92	DOWN THE AISLE L5903G	OP	295.00	295.00
92	DRESSING FOR THE BALLET L5865G	RT	395.00	425.00
92	DRESSING THE BABY L5845G	OP	295.00	295.00
92	EASTER BONNETS L5852G	RT	265.00	340.00
92	EASTER BUNNIES L5902G	OP	240.00	240.00
92	FAIRY FLOWERS L5861G	TL	630.00	650.00
92	FAIRY GARLAND L5860G	TL	630.00	640.00
92	FALLAS QUEEN L5869G	TL	420.00	450.00
92	FEATHERED FANTASY L5851G	OP	1200.00	1250.00
92	FINAL TOUCHES L5866G	TL	395.00	425.00

YR	NAME	LIMIT	ISSUE	TREND
92	FLIRTATIOUS JESTER L5844G	OP	890.00	930.00
92	FLORAL ADMIRATION L5853G	RT	690.00	735.00
92	FLORAL FANTASY L5854G	TL	690.00	700.00
92	FRAGRANT BOUQUET L5862G	OP	350.00	350.00
92	FREE SPIRIT L2220M	RT	235.00	235.00
92	FRIENDLY SPARROW L2225M	OP	295.00	330.00
92	FRIENDSHIP IN BLOOM L5893G	TL	650.00	700.00
92	FROM THIS DAY FORWARD L5885G	OP	265.00	290.00
92	GARDEN SONG L7618G	OP	295.00	295.00
92	GRAND ENTRANCE L5857G	RT	265.00	265.00
92	GUESS WHAT I HAVE L2233M	OP	340.00	365.00
92	GUEST OF HONOR L5877G	OP	195.00	195.00
92	HAWAIIAN CEREMONY LL1757	1000	9800.00	10000.00
92	HIPPITY HOP L5886G	TL	95.00	95.00
92	INSPIRING MUSE L580G	OP	1200.00	1200.00
92	JAZZ CLARINET L5928G	OP	295.00	295.00
92	JAZZ DRUMS L5929G	OP	595.00	600.00
92	JAZZ DUO L5930G	OP	795.00	900.00
92	JUST A LITTLE MORE L5908G	OP	370.00	370.00
92	JUST ONE MORE L5899G	OP	450.00	450.00
92	JUSTICE EAGLE LL5863	1500	1700.00	1800.00
92	LOAVES & FISHES, THE- L5896G	OP	695.00	750.00
92	LOVING FAMILY, THE- L5848G	RT	950.00	1000.00
92	LOVING MOUSE L5883G	OP	285.00	285.00
92	LOVING VALENCIANA L5868G	TL	365.00	395.00
92	MAKING A WISH L5910G	OP	790.00	830.00
92	MARY'S CHILD L2230M	RT	525.00	525.00
92	MATERNAL JOY LL5864	1500	1600.00	1800.00
92	MISCHIEVOUS MOUSE L5881G	OP	285.00	285.00
92	MODERN MOTHER L5873G	OP	325.00	325.00
92	MOTORING IN STYLE LL5884	1500	3700.00	3800.00
92	NEW LAMB L2223M	OP	365.00	375.00
92	OFF WE GO L5874G	RT	365.00	390.00
92	PLAYFUL PUSH L2234M	OP	850.00	860.00
92	PLAYFUL UNICORN L5880G/M	OP	295.00	325.00
92	POOR LITTLE BEAR L2232M	OP	250.00	250.00
92	PREENING BUNNY L5906G	OP	75.00	75.00
92	PRESENTING CREDENTIALS LL5911	1500	19500.00	20000.00
92	READER, THE- LL3560	200	2650.00	2800.00
92	RESTFUL MOUSE L5882G	OP	285.00	285.00
92	SEASONAL GIFTS L2229M	OP	450.00	480.00
92	SERENE VALENCIANA L5867G	RT	365.00	390.00
92	SHOT ON GOAL L5879G	OP	1100.00	1100.00
92	SISTER'S PRIDE L5878G	OP	595.00	625.00
92	SITTING BUNNY L5907G	OP	75.00	75.00
92	SLEEP TIGHT L5900G	OP	450.00	500.00
92	SLEEPING BUNNY L5904G	OP	75.00	75.00
92	SNACK TIME L5889G	TL	95.00	95.00
92	SNOWY SUNDAY L2228M	OP	550.00	600.00
92	SORROWFUL MOTHER LL5849	1500	1750.00	1800.00
92	SPRING SPLENDOR L5898G	OP	440.00	440.00
92	SURPRISE L5901G	OP	325.00	325.00
92	SWAN BALLET L5920G	OP	210.00	210.00
92	SWANS TAKE FLIGHT L5912G	OP	2850.00	2940.00
92	TAKE YOUR MEDICINE L5921G	OP	360.00	360.00
92	TEA IN THE GARDEN LL1759	2000	9500.00	9700.00
92	TENDER MOMENT L2222M	OP	400.00	425.00
92	THAT TICKLES L5888G	TL	95.00	95.00
92	TRIMMING THE TREE L5897G	OP	900.00	930.00
92	UNDERFOOT L2219M	OP	360.00	400.00
92	VOYAGE OF COLUMBUS, THE- LL5847	RT	1450.00	1700.00
92	WAITING TO DANCE L5858G	TL	295.00	325.00
92	WASHING UP L5887G	TL	95.00	95.00
92	WAY OF THE CROSS, THE- LL5890	2000	975.00	1000.00
92	YOUNG MOZART LL5915	RT	500.00	1200.00
93	ANGELS MELODY	RT	145.00	170.00
93	AUGUMN GLOW	1500	750.00	900.00
93	BABY'S FIRST	RT	57.00	62.00
93	BLESSING, THE	2000	1345.00	1550.00
93	DAYS OF YORE	1000	2050.00	2200.00
93	DISCOVERY MUG	1992	90.00	100.00
93	GRACEFUL MOMENT	3000	1475.00	1575.00
93	HAND OF JUSTICE, THE	1000	1250.00	1400.00
93	HOLIDAY GLOW	1500	750.00	900.00
93	HUMBLE GRACE	2000	2150.00	2350.00
93	INDIAN BRAVE	1500	2250.00	2500.00
93	INSPIRED VOYAGE	1000	4800.00	5000.00
93	LIMITED EDITION EGG	RT	145.00	160.00
93	OUR FIRST	RT	52.00	65.00
93	OUR LADY OF ROCIO	2000	3500.00	3800.00
93	TRAIL BOSS	1500	2450.00	2700.00
93	WHERE TO STIR	1500	5250.00	5500.00
94	1994 LIMITED EDITION EGG	RT	150.00	175.00
94	A MOMENT'S PAUSE	3500	1495.00	1600.00
94	ALLEGORY OF TIME	5000	1290.00	1309.00
94	AMERICAN COWBOY	3000	950.00	1000.00
94	AT PEACE	1000	1650.00	1800.00
94	AT THE HELM	3500	1495.00	1600.00
94	CIRCUS FANFARE	1500	14240.00	15000

YR	NAME	LIMIT	ISSUE	TREND
94	CONQUERED BY LOVE	2500	2850.00	3000.00
94	ETHEREAL MUSIC	1000	2450.00	2600.00
94	FAREWELL OF THE SAMURAI	2500	3950.00	4100.00
94	FLORAL ENCHANTMENT	300	2990.00	3100.00
94	FLORAL FIGURE	300	2198.00	2300.00
94	FLOWER WAGON	3000	3290.00	3400.00
94	FLUVIAL CUP WITH BRANCH	500	1590.00	1790.00
94	FLUVIAL CUP WITH ROSES	500	1150.00	1350.00
94	FLUVIAL CUP WITH WATER LILY	500	1350.00	1550.00
94	GENTLE MOMENT	1000	1795.00	2000.00
94	HIGH SPEED	1500	3830.00	4000.00
94	INDIAN CHIEF	3000	1095.00	1200.00
94	INDIAN PRINCESS	3000	1630.00	1800.00
94	LARGE NEOCLASSIC CUP	300	2695.00	2850.00
94	NATURAL BEAUTY	500	650.00	725.00
94	NEOCLASSIC CUP (BISQUE)	500	1250.00	1400.00
94	NEOCLASSIC CUP (COLOR)	500	1370.00	1575.00
94	PEGASUS	1500	1950.00	2100.00
94	ROMANTIC VASE (BLUE)	300	2250.00	2400.00
94	ROMANTIC VASE (WHITE)	300	2598.00	2700.00
94	SAINT JAMES THE APOSTLE	1000	950.00	1100.00
94	TRAPPER	3000	950.00	1100.00
*			**ASSORTED FIGURINES**	
*	CARD PLAYERS, NUMBERED L1327	RT	3800.00	5700.00
71	GIRL WITH CALLA LILLIES L4650	OP	18.00	120.00
71	VIOLINIST AND GIRL L1039	RT	120.00	850.00
73	GIRL WITH GUITAR LL2016	RT	650.00	1800.00
73	ORIENTAL MAN LL2021	RT	500.00	1850.00
73	PEACE LL1202	RT	550.00	7500.00
73	THREE GRACES LL2028	RT	950.00	3500.00
74	FOREST, THE- LL1243	RT	1250.00	3300.00
74	PASSIONATE DANCE LL2051	RT	450.00	4000.00
74	PEASANT WOMAN LL2049	RT	400.00	1300.00
77	GIRL WITH CALLA LILLIES SITTING L4972	OP	65.00	150.00
77	MOUNTAIN COUNTRY LADY LL1330	RT	900.00	1950.00
81	RESCUE, THE- LL3506	RT	3500.00	4450.00
82	CONCERTO LL2063	RT	1000.00	1300.00
83	FEARFUL FLIGHT LL1377	750	7000.00	14000.00
84	BOY GRADUATE L5198	OP	160.00	300.00
84	CHARLIE THE TRAMP L5233	RT	150.00	700.00
84	FLOWERS OF THE SEASON L1454	OP	1460.00	2500.00
84	GIRL GRADUATE L5199	OP	160.00	290.00
85	BUST OF LADY FROM ELCHE L5269	RT	432.00	775.00
85	CONSIDERATION L5355	RT	100.00	250.00
85	LA GIACONDA L5337	RT	110.00	450.00
86	CAN CAN L5370	RT	700.00	1250.00
86	PETITE PAIR L5384	RT	225.00	450.00
86	PUPPET PAINTER, THE- L5396	OP	500.00	875.00
86	SIDEWALK SERENADE L5388	RT	750.00	1200.00
88	PETITE MAIDEN L5383	RT	110.00	375.00
*			**BRIDAL FIGURINES**	
75	WEDDING L4808	OP	50.00	150.00
83	MATRIMONY L1404	OP	320.00	600.00
84	HERE COMES THE BRIDE L1446	OP	517.50	1000.00
85	OVER THE THRESHOLD L5282	OP	150.00	300.00
85	WEDDING DAY L5274	OP	240.00	400.00
86	MY WEDDING DAY L1494	OP	800.00	1500.00
87	BRIDE, THE L5439G	TL	250.00	440.00
87	I LOVE YOU TRULY L1528	OP	375.00	600.00
89	BRIDE'S MAID L5598	OP	150.00	190.00
89	WEDDING CAKE L5587G	OP	595.00	775.00
*			**CAPRICHOS FIGURINES**	
87	IRIS BASKET C1542	RT	825.00	1400.00
87	IRIS WITH VASE C1551	RT	199.00	375.00
87	ORCHID ARRANGEMENT C1541	RT	500.00	1800.00
87	VIOLET FAN W/BASE C1546	RT	600.00	1400.00
87	WHITE FAN W/BASE C1546.3	RT	600.00	1400.00
*			**CHILDREN WITH ANIMALS**	
71	GIRL SEATED WITH FLOWERS L1088	RT	45.00	725.00
73	BOY WITH DONKEY L1181	RT	50.00	450.00
74	CARESS L1246	RT	50.00	275.00
74	FRIENDSHIP L1230	RT	68.00	300.00
74	GIRL WITH DUCKS L1267	RT	55.00	350.00
74	HONEY LICKERS L1248	RT	100.00	500.00
75	AGRESSIVE DUCK L1288	RT	170.00	450.00
75	DEVOTION L1278	RT	140.00	450.00
75	FEEDING TIME L1277G	RT	120.00	360.00
76	GIRL WITH CATS L1309	OP	120.00	300.00
76	GIRL WITH PUPPIES IN BASKET L1311	OP	120.00	325.00
77	ON THE FARM L1306	RT	130.00	240.00
78	NAUGHTY DOG L4982G	RT	130.00	260.00
79	AVOIDING THE DUCK L5033	RT	160.00	360.00
79	LITTLE FRISKIES L5032	OP	107.50	225.00
81	MY HUNGRY BROOD L5074	OP	295.00	425.00
83	STUBBORN MULE L5178	RT	250.00	510.00
84	A LITTER OF LOVE L1441	OP	385.00	600.00
85	PLAYING WITH DUCKS AT THE POND L5303	RT	425.00	900.00
86	LITTER OF FUN L5364	OP	275.00	475.00

YR	NAME	LIMIT	ISSUE	TREND
86	THIS ONE'S MINE L5376G	TL	300.00	500.00
87	I HOPE SHE DOES L5450	OP	190.00	350.00
87	SLEEPY TRIO L5443	OP	190.00	300.00
*				**CHILDREN'S THEMES**
*	AMY L5145	*	110.00	1500.00
*	ELLEN L5146	*	110.00	1500.00
*	IVY L5147	*	100.00	650.00
*	OLIVIA L5148	*	100.00	500.00
*	URSULA L5149	*	100.00	550.00
71	BEAGLE PUPPY (SITTING) L1071G/M	RT	17.50	135.00-295.00
71	SEESAW L4867	OP	55.00	290.00
73	GIRL WITH DOLL L1211G	RT	72.00	420.00
74	FEEDING THE DUCKS L4849	RT	60.00	220.00
74	SEESAW L1255	RT	110.00	500.00
80	BLOOMING ROSES L1339	RT	325.00	400.00
80	SLEIGHRIDE L5037	OP	585.00	950.00
83	A BARROW OF BLOSSOMS L1419	OP	390.00	650.00
83	AUTUMN L5218G/M	OP	90.00	200.00
83	BALLOONS FOR SALE L5141	OP	145.00	240.00
83	FLOWER HARMONY L1418	TL	130.00	250.00
83	FROM MY GARDEN L1416	OP	140.00	300.00
83	NATURE'S BOUNTY L1417G	TL	160.00	350.00
83	PONDERING L5173	OP	300.00	440.00
83	PRETTY PICKINGS L5222G/M	OP	80.00	150.00
83	ROSES FOR MY MOM L5088	RT	645.00	1100.00
83	SPRING IS HERE L5223G/M	OP	80.00	150.00
83	SPRING L5217G/M	OP	90.00	175.00
83	STORYTIME L5229	RT	245.00	850.00
83	SUMMER L5219	OP	90.00	175.00
83	SWEET SCENT L5221G/M	OP	80.00	150.00
83	WINTER L5220G/M	OP	90.00	190.00
84	BOY MEETS GIRL L1188	RT	310.00	325.00
84	COURTSHIP L5072	RT	327.00	765.00
84	DANCING THE POLKA L5252	RT	205.00	440.00
84	FOLK DANCING L5256	RT	205.00	550.00
84	NOSTALGIA L5071	RT	185.00	375.00
85	A VISIT WITH GRANNY L5305	RT	275.00	500.00
85	BOY ON CAROUSEL HORSE L1470	OP	470.00	900.00
85	CHILDREN AT PLAY L5304	RT	220.00	500.00
85	FALL CLEAN-UP L5286	OP	295.00	575.00
85	GIRL ON CAROUSEL HORSE L1469	OP	470.00	900.00
85	GLORIOUS SPRING L5284	OP	355.00	700.00
85	ICE CREAM VENDOR L5325G	TL	380.00	625.00
85	LOVE IN BLOOM L5292	OP	225.00	425.00
85	SUMMER ON THE FARM L5285	OP	235.00	450.00
85	WINTER FROST L5287	OP	270.00	525.00
85	YOUNG STREET MUSICIANS L5306	RT	300.00	1475.00
86	A NEW FRIEND L1506	RT	110.00	300.00
86	A STITCH IN TIME L5344	OP	425.00	800.00
86	BEDTIME L5347	OP	300.00	550.00
86	BOY & HIS BUNNY L1507G/M	RT	90.00	250.00
86	CHILDREN'S GAMES L5379	OP	325.00	675.00
86	FORGOTTEN L1502G	RT	125.00	340.00
86	IN THE MEADOW L1508G	RT	100.00	200.00
86	LITTLE SCULPTOR L5358	RT	160.00	390.00
86	NATURE BOY L1505G	RT	100.00	300.00
86	NEGLECTED L1503	RT	125.00	340.00
86	RAG DOLL L1501	RT	125.00	340.00
86	RAGAMUFFIN L1500	RT	125.00	340.00
86	SPRING FLOWERS L1509	RT	100.00	1125.00
86	STILL LIFE L5363	OP	180.00	400.00
86	SWEET HARVEST L5380	RT	450.00	900.00
86	TRY THIS ONE L5361	OP	225.00	400.00
87	AT ATTENTION L5407	RT	175.00	350.00
87	BUGLER, THE L5406	RT	175.00	400.00
87	CADET CAPTAIN L5404	RT	175.00	350.00
87	CIRCUS TRAIN L1517	RT	2900.00	4300.00
87	DRUMMER BOY, THE L5403	RT	225.00	410.00
87	FLAG BEARER, THE - L5405	RT	200.00	500.00
87	HAPPY BIRTHDAY L5429	OP	100.00	140.00
87	MUSIC TIME L5430	RT	500.00	700.00
87	MY BEST FRIEND L5401	OP	150.00	250.00
87	NAPTIME L5448	OP	135.00	260.00
87	ONE, TWO, THREE L5426	TL	240.00	400.00
87	TIME TO REST L5399	RT	175.00	310.00
87	WANDERER, THE- L5400	OP	150.00	200.00
89	BABY DOLL L5608	OP	150.00	175.00
89	HELLO FLOWERS L5543	RT	385.00	550.00
89	JOY IN A BASKET L5595	OP	215.00	275.00
89	LET'S MAKE UP L5555	OP	215.00	275.00
89	MY NEW PET L5549	OP	150.00	160.00
89	PLAYFUL ROMP L5594	OP	215.00	275.00
89	PRETTY POSIES L5548	RT	425.00	525.00
89	PUPPY DOG TAILS L5539	OP	1200.00	1600.00
*				**CLOWNS**
71	CLOWN L4618	OP	70.00	400.00
71	PELUSA CLOWN L1125	RT	70.00	875.00
76	SAD CLOWN L4924	RT	200.00	1550.00
81	CLOWN WITH CLOCK L5056	RT	290.00	850.00

YR	NAME	LIMIT	ISSUE	TREND
81	CLOWN WITH CONCERTINA L5058	RT	290.00	550.00
81	CLOWN WITH SAXAPHONE L5059	RT	320.00	610.00
81	CLOWN WITH VIOLIN AND TOP HAT L5057	RT	270.00	800.00
81	CLOWN WITH VIOLIN L1126	RT	71.00	1400.00
81	GIRL CLOWN WITH TRUMPET L5060	RT	290.00	550.00
82	JESTER L5129	OP	220.00	450.00
82	PENSIVE CLOWN L5130	OP	250.00	450.00
85	CLOWN WITH CONCERTINA L1027	OP	95.00	800.00
85	PIERROT WITH CONCERTINA L5279	OP	95.00	150.00
85	PIERROT WITH PUPPY & BALL L5278	OP	95.00	150.00
85	PIERROT WITH PUPPY L5277	OP	95.00	150.00
89	BLUES, THE L5600	RT	265.00	385.00
89	FINE MELODY L5585	RT	225.00	300.00
89	MELANCHOLY L5542	OP	375.00	450.00
89	REFLECTING L5612	RT	335.00	410.00
89	SAD CLOWN L5611	OP	335.00	425.00
89	SAD NOTE L5586	RT	185.00	300.00
89	STAR STRUCK L5610	OP	335.00	425.00
*			**DON QUIXOTE FIGURINES**	
71	DON QUIXOTE L1030	OP	225.00	1400.00
71	SANCHO PANZA L1031	RT	65.00	525.00
74	DON QUIXOTE L4854	OP	40.00	200.00
75	MAN FROM LAMANCHA LL1269	RT	700.00	4000.00
77	IMPOSSIBLE DREAM LL1318	RT	2400.00	4500.00
77	WRATH OF DON QUIXOTE L1343	RT	250.00	950.00
78	DON QUIXOTE & SANCHO L4998	RT	875.00	3200.00
80	LETTERS TO DULCINEA L3509	OP	1275.00	2050.00
83	A TOAST BY SANCH0 L5165	RT	100.00	420.00
83	BRAVE KNIGHT, THE L1385	RT	350.00	700.00
84	QUEST, THE- L5224	OP	125.00	300.00
85	I HAVE FOUND THEE, DUICINEA LL5341	RT	1850.00	3000.00
86	DON QUIXOTE & THE WINDMILL L1497	OP	1100.00	2000.00
86	ORATION L5357	OP	170.00	300.00
87	I AM DON QUIXOTE! L1522	OP	2600.00	3850.00
87	LISTEN TO DON QUIXOTE LL1520	750	1800.00	2750.00
88	RETURN TO LA MANCHA LL1580	500	6400.00	8200.00
*				**ELITE**
93	ORIENTAL GARDEN	750	22500.00	24500.00
93	PAELLA VALENCIANO	500	10000.00	11000.00
94	CINDERELLA'S ARRIVAL	1500	25950.00	27000.00
*			**FANTASY FIGURINES**	
*	AT THE STROKE OF TWELVE L1493	1500	4250.00	7100.00
*	FANTASIA LL1487	5000	1500.00	2700.00
*	LEPRECHAUN L1721	OP	1200.00	1400.00
*	SPRITE LL1720	OP	*	1325.00
71	CENTAUR BOY L1013	RT	45.00	375.00
71	CENTAUR GIRL L1012	RT	45.00	425.00
73	CINDERELLA L4828	OP	47.00	250.00
73	FAIRY L4595	RT	27.50	150.00
83	DAYDREAMING NYMPH L1402	RT	210.00	600.00
83	FANTASY L1414	OP	115.00	250.00
83	ILLUSION L1413	OP	115.00	250.00
83	MIRAGE L1415	OP	115.00	250.00
83	PONDERING NYMPH L1403	RT	210.00	600.00
83	SLEEPING NYMPH L1401	RT	210.00	700.00
85	CAMELOT LL1458	3000	1000.00	1550.00
85	DEMURE CENTAUR GIRL L5320	RT	157.00	400.00
85	WISTFUL CENTAUR GIRL L5319	RT	157.00	470.00
86	REY DE BASTOS LL5369	RT	325.00	575.00
86	REY DE COPAS LL5366	RT	325.00	575.00
86	REY DE ESPADAS LL5368	RT	325.00	575.00
86	REY DE OROS LL5367	RT	325.00	575.00
*				**FLOWERS**
74	FLORAL LL1184	RT	400.00	2200.00
74	FLORAL LL1185	RT	475.00	1800.00
74	FLORAL LL1186	RT	575.00	2200.00
83	BEGONIA L5186	RT	67.50	100.00
83	CALIFORNIA POPPY L5190	RT	97.50	180.00
83	CHRYSANTHEMUM L5189	RT	100.00	150.00
83	DAHLIA L5180	RT	65.00	150.00
83	JAPANESE CAMELIA L5181	RT	60.00	90.00
83	LACTIFLORA PEONY L5185	RT	65.00	100.00
83	MINIATURE BEGONIA L5188	RT	80.00	120.00
83	RHODODENDRON L5187	RT	67.50	100.00
83	THREE PINK ROSES L5181	RT	65.00	110.00
83	TWO YELLOW ROSES L5183	RT	5750.00	85.00
83	WHITE CARNATION L5184	RT	65.00	100.00
83	WHITE PEONY L5182	RT	85.00	125.00
*			**FOREIGN FIGURINES**	
71	FLAMENCO DANCERS L4519	OP	495.00	800.00
71	FLAMENCO DANCERS ON HORSEBACK L4647	RT	412.00	1100.00
74	EMBROIDERER L4865	RT	115.00	710.00
74	ESKIMO L1195G	OP	30.00	125.00
75	ORIENTAL L2056	OP	35.00	100.00
75	ORIENTAL L2057	OP	30.00	100.00
75	THAILANDIA L2058	OP	650.00	1850.00
77	THAI DANCERS L2069	OP	300.00	700.00
79	GROWING ROSES L1354	RT	485.00	635.00

YR	NAME	LIMIT	ISSUE	TREND
81	GRETEL L5064	RT	255.00	490.00
81	ILSA L5066	RT	275.00	625.00
81	INGRID L5065	RT	370.00	800.00
82	AMPARO L5125	RT	130.00	400.00
82	DRUM BEATS LL3524	1500	1875.00	3000.00
82	DUTCH WOMAN WITH TULIPS L1399	RT	750.00	750.00
82	PHILIPPINE FOLKLORE LL3522	RT	1450.00	2300.00
83	DESERT PEOPLE LL3555	750	1680.00	3000.00
83	ROAD TO MANDALAY LL3556	RT	1390.00	2450.00
84	AZTEC DANCER L2143	RT	462.50	650.00
84	AZTEC INDIAN L2139	RT	552.50	600.00
84	BLUE GOD LL3552	RT	900.00	1500.00
84	FIRE BIRD LL3553	RT	800.00	1300.00
84	LADY FROM MAJORCA L5240	RT	120.00	375.00
85	AROMA OF THE ISLANDS L1480	OP	260.00	500.00
85	HAWAIIAN DANCER L1478	OP	230.00	425.00
85	IN A TROPICAL GARDEN L1479G	TL	230.00	425.00
86	A RIDE IN THE COUNTRY L5354	RT	225.00	400.00
86	A TIME TO REST L5391	RT	170.00	410.00
86	DEEP IN THOUGHT L5389	RT	170.00	250.00-488.00
86	ESKIMO RIDERS L5353	OP	150.00	255.00
86	HAWAIIAN FESTIVAL LL1496	4000	1850.00	3100.00
86	HINDU CHILDREN L5352	OP	250.00	450.00
86	SPANISH DANCER L5390	RT	170.00	250.00-450.00
86	TAHITIAN DANCING GIRLS L1498G	TL	750.00	1300.00
87	HAWAIIAN BEAUTY L1512	RT	575.00	950.00
87	LEHUA L1532	RT	275.00	550.00
87	LEILANI L1530	RT	275.00	525.00
87	MALIA L1531	RT	275.00	525.00
87	MEXICAN DANCERS L5415	OP	800.00	1200.00
87	MOMI L1529	RT	275.00	525.00
*				
	GRES FIGURINES			
75	WIND, THE- L1279	OP	250.00	800.00
77	GRACEFUL DUO L2073	RT	775.00	1600.00
78	RAIN IN SPAIN L2077	RT	190.00	475.00
79	A NEW HAIRDO L2070	RT	1060.00	1400.00
79	PENSIVE L3514	OP	500.00	1000.00
80	A WINTRY DAY L3513	RT	525.00	700.00
82	AMERICAN HERITAGE L2127	RT	525.00	750.00
82	CONTEMPLATION L3526	OP	265.00	600.00
82	LOST IN THOUGHT L2125	RT	210.00	250.00
82	MOTHER'S LOVE L3521	RT	1000.00	1150.00
82	VENUS L2128	CL	650.00	1100.00
82	WEARY L3525	OP	360.00	650.00
84	FAIRY BALLERINA L2137	RT	500.00	1200.00
84	KING, THE- L2136	RT	510.00	700.00
84	MYSTICAL JOSEPH L2135	RT	427.50	675.00
84	SEA HARVEST L2142	RT	535.00	675.00
85	A TRIBUTE TO PEACE L2150	OP	470.00	900.00
85	YOUNG MADONNA L2149	RT	400.00	675.00
*				
	HISTORICAL FIGURINES			
82	CERVANTES L5132	RT	925.00	1175.00
83	QUEEN ELIZABETH LL1275	RT	3650.00	4950.00
84	COLUMBUS LL1432	RT	575.00	1250.00
84	HENRY VIII LL1384	RT	650.00	875.00
85	NAPOLEON BONAPARTE LL5338	RT	275.00	500.00
85	NAPOLEON PLANNING BATTLE LL1459	TL	875.00	1400.00
86	EL GRECO L5359	RT	300.00	550.00
86	NEW WORLD, THE-LL1486	4000	700.00	1300.00
88	BEETHOVEN LL5339	RT	800.00	1250.00
*				
	IN THE GARDEN FIGURINES			
71	GIRL WITH FLOWERS L1172G	RT	27.00	285.00
75	FLOWER HARVEST L1286	OP	200.00	500.00
75	LITTLE GARDENER L1283	OP	250.00	765.00
75	MY FLOWERS L1284	OP	200.00	525.00
75	MY GOODNESS L1285G	TL	190.00	395.00
75	PICKING FLOWERS L1287	OP	170.00	420.00
76	VICTORIAN GIRL ON SWING L1297	RT	520.00	1800.00
78	DAUGHTERS L5013	RT	425.00	875.00
79	FLOWER CURTSY L5027	OP	230.00	450.00
79	WATERING THE FLOWER POTS L1376	RT	400.00	1100.00
79	WILDFLOWER L5030	RT	360.00	700.00
86	AT THE BALL L5398	RT	375.00	560.00-700.00
86	SCARECROW & THE LADY L5385	OP	350.00	700.00
86	SUNDAY IN THE PARK L5365	OP	375.00	600.00
86	TIME FOR REFLECTION L5378	OP	425.00	750.00
87	COURTING TIME L5409	RT	425.00	575.00
87	FEEDING THE PIGEONS L5428	RT	490.00	700.00
87	IN THE GARDEN L5416	OP	200.00	335.00
87	INSPIRATION LL5413	RT	1200.00	2100.00
87	POETRY OF LOVE L5442	OP	500.00	875.00
87	STUDYING IN THE PARK L5425	RT	675.00	975.00
87	WILL YOU MARRY ME? L5447	RT	750.00	1200.00
*				
	LITERARY FIGURINES			
71	HAMLET LL1144	RT	250.00	3500.00
71	OTHELLO AND DESDEMONA LL1145	RT	275.00	2300.00
71	ROMEO AND JULIET L4750	OP	150.00	1200.00
74	HAMLET AND YORICK L1254	RT	325.00	1150.00

YR	NAME	LIMIT	ISSUE	TREND
84	REFLECTIONS OF HAMLET L1455	RT	1000.00	1500.00
*			**LLADRO ANGELS**	
71	ANGEL WITH CHILD L4635	OP	15.00	100.00
71	ANGEL WITH HORN L4540	OP	13.00	100.00
71	ANGEL, BLACK L4537G/M	OP	13.00	100.00
71	ANGEL, CHINESE L4536G/M	OP	45.00	100.00
71	ANGEL, PRAYING L4538G/M	OP	13.00	100.00
71	ANGEL, RECLINING L4541G/M	OP	13.00	100.00
71	ANGEL, THINKING L4539G/M	OP	13.00	100.00
71	GROUP OF ANGELS L4542G/M	OP	31.00	200.00
74	ANGEL WITH CLARINET L1232	RT	60.00	425.00
74	ANGEL WITH FLUTE L1233	RT	60.00	325.00
74	ANGEL WITH LUTE L1231	RT	60.00	425.00
77	CHERUB, DREAMING L4961	OP	40.00	100.00
77	CHERUB, PUZZLED L4959	OP	40.00	100.00
77	CHERUB, SMILING L4960	OP	40.00	100.00
77	CHERUB, WONDERING L4962G/M	OP	40.00	100.00
85	CAREFREE ANGEL WITH FLUTE L1463	RT	220.00	550.00
85	CAREFREE ANGEL WITH LYRE L1464	RT	220.00	600.00
*			**LLADRO ANIMAL FIGURINES**	
71	ELEPHANTS (2) L1151	OP	45.00	400.00
71	ELEPHANTS (3) L1150	OP	100.00	775.00
71	HORSE GROUP/ALL WHITE L1022	OP	465.00	2000.00
71	HORSES L4655	OP	110.00	650.00
71	PLAYFUL HORSES L4597	RT	240.00	1200.00
71	SHEPHERDESS WITH LAMB L2005	RT	100.00	700.00
73	ORIENTAL HORSE LL2030	RT	1100.00	4000.00
74	BEAR, WHITE L1207G	OP	16.00	70.00
74	BEAR, WHITE L1208G	OP	16.00	70.00
74	BEAR, WHITE L1209G	OP	16.00	70.00
74	HUNT, THE- LL1308	RT	4750.00	6875.00
74	HUNTING SCENE LL1238	RT	800.00	2025.00
74	RACE, THE- L1249	RT	450.00	2000.00
79	HORSE HEADS L3511	RT	260.00	675.00
79	JOCKEY WITH LASS LL5036	OP	950.00	2275.00
81	SUCCESSFUL HUNT LL5098	RT	5200.00	5150.00
83	BORN FREE L1420	OP	1520.00	3000.00
83	FLIGHT OF GAZELLES LL1352	RT	2450.00	3100.00
83	WINTER WONDERLAND L1429	OP	1025.00	2100.00
84	ELK LL3501	RT	950.00	1200.00
84	HORSE GROUP L1021	RT	950.00	1575.00
84	KITTY CONFRONTATION L1442	OP	155.00	300.00
84	PURR-FECT L1444	OP	350.00	625.00
85	ANTELOPE DRINKING L5302	RT	215.00	640.00
85	GAZELLE L5271	RT	205.00	400.00
85	PACK OF HUNTING DOGS LL5342	RT	925.00	1575.00
85	THOROUGHBRED HORSE LL5340	RT	625.00	985.00
86	FOX HUNT LL5362	RT	5200.00	8500.00
87	DESERT TOUR L5402	RT	950.00	1000.00
*			**LLADRO BIRD FIGURINES**	
71	DOVE L1015G	RT	21.00	100.00
71	DOVE L1016G	OP	36.00	170.00
73	EAGLE OWL LL1223	RT	450.00	1000.00
73	EAGLES LL1189	RT	900.00	3150.00
73	SEA BIRDS WITH NEST LL1194	RT	600.00	2775.00
73	TURKEY GROUP LL1196	RT	650.00	1800.00
74	FLYING DUCK L1263G	OP	20.00	85.00
74	FLYING DUCK L1264G	OP	20.00	85.00
74	FLYING DUCK L1265G	OP	20.00	85.00
74	KISSING DOVES L1169G	CL	32.00	140.00
74	TURTLE DOVES LL1240	RT	500.00	2500.00
77	DUCKLINGS L1307	OP	47.50	145.00
77	DUCKS AT POND LL1317	RT	4250.00	5650.00
79	SPRING BIRDS L1368	RT	1600.00	2500.00
80	IBIS L1319	OP	1550.00	2600.00
83	NEST OF EAGLES LL3523	300	6900.00	9500.00-10900.00
83	TURTLE DOVES LL3520	750	6800.00	12000.00
84	CRANES L1456	OP	1000.00	1900.00
84	DOVE GROUP L1335	RT	950.00	1650.00
84	FLYING PARTRIDGES LL2064	RT	3500.00	4300.00
84	HOW DO YOU DO! L1439	OP	185.00	265.00
85	FLOCK OF BIRDS LL1462	1500	1125.00	1700.00
87	BARN OWL L5421	RT	120.00	200.00
87	GREAT GRAY OWL L5419	RT	190.00	200.00
87	HAWK OWL L5422	RT	120.00	200.00
87	HORNED OWL L5420	RT	150.00	310.00
87	SHORT EARED OWL L5418	RT	200.00	350.00
89	BOWLING CRANE L1613	OP	385.00	475.00
89	COURTING CRANES L1611	OP	565.00	700.00
89	DANCING CRANE L1614	OP	385.00	475.00
89	FLUTTERING CRANE L1598	OP	115.00	150.00
89	FREEDOM LL5602	RT	875.00	925.00
89	LANDING CRANE L1600	OP	115.00	150.00
89	NESTING CRANE L1599	OP	95.00	110.00
89	PREENING CRANES L1612	OP	985.00	500.00
*			**LLADRO COLLECTORS SOCIETY**	
85	LITTLE PALS S7600	RT	95.00	3200.00
86	LITTLE TRAVELER S7602	RT	95.00	1350.00

YR	NAME	LIMIT	ISSUE	TREND
87	SPRING BOUQUETS S7603	RT	125.00	900.00
88	FLOWER SONG S7607	RT	175.00	675.00
88	SCHOOL DAYS S7604	RT	125.00	650.00
89	MY BUDDY S7609	RT	145.00	400.00
90	CAN I PLAY? S7610	RT	150.00	450.00
91	PICTURE PERFECT S7612	RT	350.00	500.00
91	SUMMER STROLL S7611	RT	195.00	400.00
*		**LLADRO HARLEQUINS AND DANCERS**		
71	IDYL L1017M	RT	115.00	600.00
74	BALLERINA L4855	OP	45.00	325.00
74	CARNIVAL COUPLE L4882	TL	60.00	300.00
74	SAD HARLEQUIN L4558	RT	110.00	560.00
74	WAITING BACKSTAGE L4559	RT	110.00	450.00
74	YOUNG HARLEQUIN L1229	OP	70.00	500.00
76	CLOSING SCENE L4935	OP	180.00	500.00
79	ACT II L5035	OP	700.00	1400.00
79	DANCER L5050	OP	85.00	200.00
82	LOST LOVE L5128	RT	400.00	700.00
84	BALLERINA, WHITE L4855.3	RT	110.00	250.00
84	BALLET TRIO L5235	OP	785.00	1600.00
84	CLOSING SCENE/WHITE L4935.3	RT	202.50	270.00
*			**LLADRO MINIATURES**	
86	BALANCING ACT L5392	RT	35.00	210.00
86	CURIOSITY L5393	RT	25.00	170.00
86	ON GUARD L5350	RT	50.00	210.00
86	POOR PUPPY L5394	RT	25.00	150.00
86	WOE IS ME L5351	RT	45.00	225.00
86	WOLF HOUND L5356	RT	45.00	250.00
87	COUGAR L5435	RT	65.00	310.00
87	ELEPHANT L5438	RT	50.00	165.00
87	KANGAROO L5433	RT	65.00	150.00
87	LION L5436	RT	50.00	225.00
87	MONKEY L5432	RT	60.00	150.00
87	POLAR BEAR L5434	OP	65.00	100.00
87	RHINO L5437	RT	50.00	180.00
92	CAT L5308	RT	35.00	80.00
92	COCKER SPANIEL L5310	RT	35.00	95.00
92	COCKER SPANIEL PUP L5309	RT	35.00	100.00
92	KITTEN L5307	RT	65.00	110.00
*			**LLADRO SCULPTURES**	
*	DIGNITY LL3015	150	1400.00	1850.00
81	ADORATION LL3545	RT	1050.00	1600.00
81	AFRICAN WOMAN LL3546	RT	1300.00	2000.00
81	ANXIETY LL3530	RT	1075.00	1800.00
81	BATHER LL3551	RT	975.00	1350.00
81	BOXER LL3550	RT	850.00	1400.00
81	COMPANIONSHIP LL3529	65	1000.00	1800.00
81	DANTINESS LL3539	RT	1000.00	1400.00
81	DEMURE LL3543	RT	1250.00	1700.00
81	DREAMING LL3537	RT	475.00	1400.00
81	IN THE DISTANCE LL3534	RT	525.00	1275.00
81	OBSERVER LL3533	RT	900.00	1600.00
81	PLENTITUDE LL3532	RT	1000.00	1400.00
81	POSE LL3540	RT	1250.00	1450.00
81	RECLINING NUDE LL3547	RT	650.00	875.00
81	REFLECTIONS LL3544	75	650.00	1000.00
81	RELAXATION LL3536	RT	525.00	1000.00
81	REPOSING LL3549	RT	425.00	575.00
81	SERENITY LL3548	RT	925.00	1500.00
81	SLAVE LL3535	RT	950.00	1100.00
81	TOGETHERNESS LL3527	RT	375.00	875.00
81	TRANQUILITY LL3541	RT	1000.00	1450.00
81	VICTORY LL3531	RT	1500.00	1800.00
81	WRESTLING LL3528	RT	950.00	1125.00
81	YOGA LL3542	RT	650.00	900.00
81	YOUTH LL3538	RT	525.00	1100.00
83	DAWN LL3000	300	325.00	525.00
83	INDOLENCE LL3003	150	1465.00	2075.00
83	MONKS LL3001	RT	1675.00	2500.00
83	VENUS IN THE BATH LL3005	RT	1175.00	1450.00
83	WAITING LL3002	RT	1550.00	1900.00
87	CLASSIC BEAUTY LL3012	500	1300.00	1700.00
87	NYMPH, THE- LL3014	250	1000.00	1400.00
87	YOUTHFUL INNOCENCE LL3013	500	1300.00	1775.00
88	CELLIST LL3018	RT	650.00	830.00
88	MUSE LL3017	300	650.00	650.00
88	PASSION LL3016	750	865.00	1150.00
88	TRUE AFFECTION LL3019	300	750.00	1000.00
89	DEMURENESS LL3020	RT	400.00	675.00
90	AFTER THE BATH LL3023	RT	350.00	1050.00
90	DAYDREAMING LL3022	500	550.00	730.00
90	DISCOVERIES LL3024	100	1500.00	1800.00
91	RESTING NUDE LL3025	RT	650.00	1000.00
91	UNADORNED BEAUTY LL3026	200	1700.00	1875.00
93	AWAKENING, THE	300	1200.00	1500.00
93	FLIGHT OF FANCY	300	1400.00	1600.00
94	DANAE	300	2880.00	3025.00
94	EBONY	300	1295.00	1400.00

This Raccoon *figure by Maruri aptly captures the nature of the animal.*

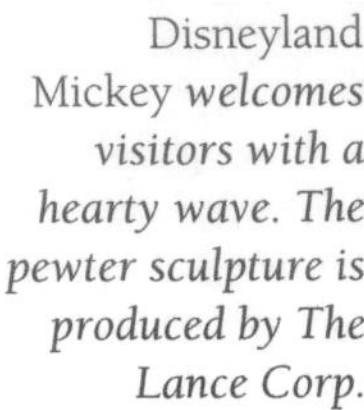

Disneyland Mickey *welcomes visitors with a hearty wave. The pewter sculpture is produced by The Lance Corp.*

What more could she want? Sitting Pretty *is from the "Beautiful Dreamers" series produced by Rhodes Studios.*

With a handle touting the Gettysburg Address, this Abraham Lincoln Character Jug *is from a Royal Doulton collection honoring Presidents of the United States.*

This beautiful Anri wood-carved Pinocchio *figure has no strings attached. The piece is available in five sizes.*

YR	NAME	LIMIT	ISSUE	TREND
94	MODESTY	300	1295.00	1495.00
*			**LLADRO SPORTS FIGURINES**	
72	FEMALE EQUESTRIAN L4516	OP	170.00	750.00
73	LADY GOLFER L4851	RT	70.00	240.00
73	MALE GOLFER L4824	OP	66.00	300.00
74	SOCCER PLAYER LL1266	RT	2000.00	7500.00
83	FEMALE TENNIS PLAYER L1427	RT	200.00	360.00
83	MALE SOCCER PLAYER L5200	RT	155.00	500.00
83	MALE TENNIS PLAYER L1426	RT	200.00	400.00
84	GOLFING COUPLE L1453	OP	248.00	500.00
84	TORCH BEARER L5251	RT	100.00	325.00
85	GENTLEMAN EQUESTRIAN L5329	RT	160.00	500.00
85	HIKER L5280	RT	195.00	400.00
85	LADY EQUESTRIAN L5328	RT	160.00	400.00
85	RACING MOTORCYCLIST L5270	RT	360.00	700.00
85	WAITING TO TEE OFF L5301	OP	145.00	300.00
*			**MOTHER & CHILD**	
*	MOTHER AND SON L2131	OP	850.00	1500.00
71	MOTHER AND CHILD L4575	OP	50.00	250.00
71	MOTHER AND CHILD L4701	OP	45.00	300.00
76	BABY'S OUTING L4938	OP	250.00	700.00
77	COMFORTING BABY LL1329	RT	350.00	1000.00
77	MY BABY LL1331	RT	275.00	950.00
86	FAMILY ROOTS L5371	OP	575.00	900.00
87	GOODNIGHT L5449	OP	225.00	350.00
87	TENDERNESS L1527	OP	260.00	425.00
89	A GIFT OF LOVE L5596	OP	400.00	500.00
89	LATEST ADDITION L1606	OP	385.00	475.00
*			**NAUTICAL FIGURINES**	
71	SEA CAPTAIN L4621G/M	RT	45.00	260.00
73	GOING FISHING L4809	OP	33.00	150.00
73	YOUNG SAILOR L4180	OP	33.00	140.00
76	HELMSMAN, THE- L1325	RT	600.00	1200.00
80	IN THE GONDOLA L1350	OP	1850.00	3100.00
83	A TALL YARN L5207	OP	260.00	525.00
83	FISHING WITH GRAMPS L5215	OP	410.00	825.00
83	ON THE LAKE L5216	RT	660.00	910.00
83	SEA FEVER L5166G	RT	130.00	380.00
83	STORMY SEA L3554	OP	675.00	1100.00
83	WHALER, THE- L2121	RT	820.00	1000.00
83	YACHTSMAN L5206	RT	110.00	200.00
84	NAUTICAL WATCH L2134	RT	450.00	750.00
84	VENETIAN SERENADE LL1433	RT	2600.00	3750.00
85	LOVE BOAT LL5343	3000	825.00	1300.00
85	SAILOR SERENADES HIS GIRL L5276	RT	315.00	1000.00
87	CARNIVAL TIME LL5423	RT	2400.00	4000.00
*			**NUDES**	
*	INNOCENCE/GREEN L3558	RT	960.00	1500.00
*	INNOCENCE/RED L3558/3	RT	960.00	1200.00
73	LYRIC MUSE LL2031	RT	750.00	2050.00
78	NATIVE L3502	OP	700.00	2400.00
79	NUDE WITH DOVE LL3503	RT	250.00	900.00
79	NUDE WITH ROSE L3517	OP	225.00	750.00
82	VENUS AND CUPID LL1392	RT	1100.00	1850.00
85	CLASSIC FALL LL1466	TL	620.00	1000.00
85	CLASSIC SPRING LL1465	TL	620.00	1000.00
85	HAWAIIAN FLOWER VENDOR L2154	OP	245.00	450.00
85	PEACE OFFERING L3559	OP	397.00	650.00
85	YOUTHFUL BEAUTY LL1461	5000	750.00	1150.00
86	NATURE GIRL L5346	RT	450.00	850.00
86	PASTORAL SCENE LL5386	TL	1100.00	2300.00
87	ARTIST'S MODEL L5417	RT	425.00	500.00
*			**ORIENTAL FIGURINES**	
73	ORIENTAL FLOWER ARRANGER L4840	OP	90.00	500.00
77	GEISHA L4807	RT	190.00	500.00
78	BUTTERFLY L4991	OP	125.00	300.00
78	CHRYSANTHEMUM L4990	OP	125.00	300.00
78	ORIENTAL SPRING L4988	OP	125.00	300.00
78	SAYONARA L4989	OP	125.00	300.00
80	A RICKSHAW RIDE L1383	OP	1500.00	2100.00
82	AUGUST MOON L5122	OP	185.00	270.00
82	MY PRECIOUS BUNDLE L5123	OP	150.00	225.00
83	FISH A'PLENTY L5172	RT	190.00	400.00
83	MARIKO L1421	TL	850.00	1500.00
84	KIYOKO L1450	OP	235.00	500.00
84	MAYUMI L1449	OP	235.00	500.00
84	MICHIKO L1447	OP	235.00	450.00
84	SPRINGTIME IN JAPAN L1445	OP	965.00	1750.00
84	TERUKO L1451	OP	235.00	500.00
84	YUKI L1448	OP	285.00	500.00
85	NIPPON LADY L5327	OP	325.00	550.00
86	LADY OF THE EAST L1488	RT	625.00	1075.00
86	ORIENTAL MUSIC LL1491	5000	1350.00	2300.00
*			**PASTORAL FIGURINES**	
71	GIRL GEESE L1036M	RT	37.50	155.00
71	GIRL WITH BASKET L1034	RT	30.00	275.00
71	GIRL WITH DUCK L1052M	RT	30.00	195.00
71	GIRL WITH GEESE L1035G	TL	37.50	170.00

YR	NAME	LIMIT	ISSUE	TREND
71	GIRL WITH GEESE L4568	RT	45.00	200.00
71	GIRL WITH LAMB L1010G	RT	26.00	250.00
71	GIRL WITH LAMB L4505	OP	20.00	115.00
71	GIRL WITH MILKPAIL L4682	RT	28.00	300.00
71	GIRL WITH PIG L1011G/M	OP	13.00	95.00
71	GIRL WITH SHEEP L4584	RT	27.00	175.00
71	GIRL WITH SWAN AND DOG L4866	RT	26.00	200.00
71	SHEPHERDESS L4660	RT	21.00	200.00
71	SHEPHERDESS W/BASKET AND ROOSTER L4591	RT	20.00	120.00
71	SHEPHERDESS WITH GOATS L1001G	RT	80.00	650.00
73	GETTING HER GOAT L4812	RT	55.00	525.00
73	GIRL WITH GEESE L4815	RT	72.00	280.00
73	GIRL WITH RABBIT L4826	RT	40.00	200.00
73	SHEPHERDESS L4835	RT	42.00	400.00
75	GIRL WITH PIGEONS L4915	RT	110.00	250.00
83	ARACELY WITH DUCKS L5202	RT	125.00	275.00
83	JOSEFA FEEDING DUCK L5201	RT	125.00	250.00
85	MOTHER AND CHILD WITH LAMB L5299	RT	180.00	725.00
86	LOVERS SERENADE L5382	RT	350.00	800.00
*			**PERIOD FIGURINES**	
71	DRESSMAKER L4700	RT	45.00	475.00
74	LADY WITH DOG L4761	RT	60.00	310.00
74	LADY WITH PARASOL L4879	OP	48.00	350.00
74	LOVERS FROM VERONA L1250	RT	330.00	1150.00
75	LADY WITH SHAWL L4914	OP	220.00	700.00
76	LOVERS IN THE PARK L1274	RT	450.00	1300.00
76	MY DOG L4893	OP	85.00	220.00
76	SCHOOL GIRL L1313	RT	200.00	650.00
76	SPRING BREEZE L4936	OP	145.00	400.00
76	WINDBLOWN GIRL L4922	OP	150.00	360.00
79	ANNIVERSARY WALTZ L1372	OP	260.00	575.00
79	SWINGING L1366	RT	825.00	1375.00
80	READING L5000	OP	150.00	250.00
80	REMINISCING L1270	RT	975.00	1375.00
80	SUNNY DAY L5003	RT	192.50	350.00
80	UNDER THE WILLOW L1346	RT	1600.00	2100.00
80	WAITING IN THE PARK L1374	RT	235.00	425.00
83	AFTERNOON TEA L1428	OP	115.00	250.00
83	DEBUTANTE, THE L1431	OP	115.00	260.00
83	FLAPPER L5175	TL	185.00	375.00
83	HIGH SOCIETY L1430	RT	305.00	650.00
83	ROARING 20'S L5174	OP	172.50	250.00
83	THOUGHTS L1272	RT	87.50	3400.00
84	ON THE TOWN L1452	RT	220.00	425.00
84	PLEASANTRIES L1440	RT	960.00	1900.00
84	VOWS L1434	RT	600.00	875.00
85	ENGLISH LADY L5324	RT	225.00	500.00
85	MEDIEVAL COURTSHIP L5300	RT	735.00	825.00
85	MILANESE LADY L5323	RT	180.00	400.00
85	PARISIAN LADY L5321G	TL	192.50	300.00
85	SOCIALITE OF THE TWENTIES L5283	OP	175.00	350.00
85	VIENNESE LADY L5322	RT	160.00	300.00
86	A LADY OF TASTE L1495	OP	575.00	1000.00
86	A NEW HAT L5345	RT	200.00	400.00
86	A TOUCH OF CLASS L5377	OP	475.00	800.00
86	RECEPTION, THE- L1504	RT	625.00	1000.00
86	SERENADE L5381	RT	450.00	600.00
86	THREE SISTERS LL1492	3000	1850.00	3200.00
87	A FLOWER FOR MY LADY L1513	RT	1150.00	1475.00
87	CAFE DE PARIS L1511	TL	1900.00	2900.00
87	INTERMEZZO L5424	RT	325.00	575.00
87	ISABEL L5412	RT	225.00	475.00
87	PILAR L5410	RT	200.00	425.00
87	STROLL IN THE PARK L1519	OP	1600.00	2500.00
87	SUNDAY STROLL L5408	RT	250.00	625.00
87	TERESA L5411	RT	225.00	330.00-475.00
*			**PROFESSIONAL FIGURINES**	
*	DENTIST L4723	RT	36.00	750.00
71	DOCTOR L4602-3	RT	33.00	200.00
71	NURSE L4603-3	RT	35.00	200.00
71	OBSTETRICIAN L4763-3	RT	40.00	290.00
73	PHARMACIST L4844	RT	70.00	2000.00
75	JUDGE LL1281	RT	325.00	1300.00
83	ARCHITECT L5214	RT	140.00	425.00
83	FEMALE PHYSICIAN L5197	OP	120.00	250.00
83	LAMPLIGHTER L5205	OP	170.00	400.00
83	LAWYER L5213	OP	250.00	550.00
83	MAESTRO, MUSIC PLEASE! L5196	RT	135.00	490.00
83	PROFESSOR L5208	RT	205.00	675.00
83	SAY CHEESE L5195	RT	170.00	500.00
83	SCHOOL MARM L5209	RT	205.00	700.00
83	SHARPENING THE CUTLERY L5204	RT	210.00	800.00
84	ARTISTIC ENDEAVOR L5234	RT	225.00	600.00
84	WINE TASTER L5239	OP	190.00	400.00
85	CONCERT VIOLINIST L5330	RT	220.00	450.00
85	TAILOR, THE- L5326	RT	335.00	1150.00
86	POET, THE L5397	RT	425.00	925.00
87	MIDWIFE L5431	RT	175.00	600.00

YR	NAME	LIMIT	ISSUE	TREND
*			**RELIGIOUS FIGURINES**	
*	BLESSED LADY LL1579	RT	1150.00	2975.00
71	KING BALTASAR L1020	OP	345.00	1795.00
71	KING GASPAR L1018M	OP	345.00	1800.00
71	KING MELCHOR L1019	OP	345.00	1795.00
71	NUNS L4611G/M	OP	37.50	150.00
73	EVE AT TREE LL2029	RT	450.00	3000.00
73	MADONNA AND CHILD LL2043	RT	400.00	1500.00
73	MADONNA WITH CHILD LL2018	RT	450.00	1700.00
77	CHOIR LESSON L4973	RT	*	1500.00
78	NUNS L2075	OP	90.00	240.00
80	HOLY MARY, NUMBERED L1394	OP	1000.00	1400.00
82	BABY JESUS L1388	OP	85.00	130.00
82	COW L1390	OP	95.00	200.00
82	DONKEY L1389	OP	95.00	200.00
82	MARY L1387	OP	240.00	375.00
82	ST. JOSEPH L1387	OP	250.00	335.00
83	JESUS IN TIBERIAS LL3557	1200	2600.00	4900.00
83	JESUS L5167	OP	130.00	275.00
83	KING BALTASAR L1425	OP	315.00	575.00
83	KING GASPAR L1424	OP	265.00	450.00
83	KING MELCHOR L1423	OP	225.00	420.00
83	MADONNA WITH FLOWERS L5171	OP	172.50	300.00
83	MONKS AT PRAYER L5155	OP	130.00	260.00
83	MOSES L5170	OP	175.00	400.00
84	FRIAR JUNIPER L2138	RT	160.00	375.00
84	MONK L2060	OP	60.00	150.00
84	MYSTICAL JOSEPH L2135	RT	427.50	675.00
84	ST. CHRISTOPHER L5246	RT	265.00	610.00
84	ST. MICHAEL LL3515	1500	2200.00	4700.00
84	ST. THERESA LL2061	RT	775.00	1575.00
85	NATIVITY SCENE, HAUTE RELIEF L5281	RT	210.00	450.00
86	BLESSED FAMILY L1499	OP	200.00	400.00
86	SEWING CIRCLE L5360	RT	600.00	1200.00
86	ST. VINCENT L5387	RT	190.00	400.00
87	BALTASAR L1516	RT	275.00	925.00
87	GASPAR'S PAGE L1514	RT	275.00	400.00
87	MELCHOR L1515	RT	290.00	600.00
87	SAINT NICHOLAS L5427	RT	425.00	650.00
89	JESUS THE ROCK LL1615	1000	1175.00	1500.00
89	PIOUS LL5541	SO	1075.00	1200.00
*			**SPORTS FIGURINES**	
85	BIKING IN THE COUNTRY L5272	RT	295.00	750.00
*			**VALENCIAN FIGURINES**	
74	GIRL FROM VALENCIA L4841	OP	35.00	200.00
76	VALENCIAN LADY WITH FLOWERS L1304	OP	200.00	610.00
83	APPRECIATION L1396	OP	420.00	800.00
83	FULL OF MISCHIEF L1395	OP	420.00	800.00
83	MS. VALENCIA L1422	OP	175.00	290.00
83	REVERIE L1398	OP	490.00	950.00
83	SECOND THOUGHTS L1397	OP	490.00	800.00
83	VALENCIAN BOY L1400	RT	297.50	420.00
84	MAKING PAELLA L5254	RT	215.00	500.00
85	FESTIVAL IN VALENCIA LL1457	RT	1400.00	2300.00
85	VALENCIAN COUPLE ON HORSE LL1472	3000	885.00	1500.00
86	CARMENCITA L5373	RT	120.00	210.00
86	FLORAL OFFERING LL1490	RT	2500.00	4475.00
86	LOLITA L5372	RT	120.00	210.00
86	PEPITA L5374	RT	120.00	340.00
86	TERESITA L5375	RT	120.00	325.00
86	VALENCIAN BOY L5395	OP	200.00	400.00
86	VALENCIAN CHILDREN L1489	OP	700.00	1200.00
87	VALENCIAN BOUQUET L1524	RT	250.00	400.00
87	VALENCIAN COUPLE ON HORSEBACK L4648	RT	900.00	1200.00
87	VALENCIAN DREAMS L1525	RT	240.00	450.00
87	VALENCIAN FLOWERS L1526	RT	375.00	550.00
87	VALENCIAN GARDEN L1518	RT	1100.00	1800.00
*			**VARIOUS**	
*	PLAYING CARDS L1327M, NUMBERED	OP	3800.00	6400.00
78	BETH L1358G	RT	75.00	210.00
78	HEATHER L1359G	RT	75.00	210.00
78	JULIA L1361	RT	75.00	200.00
78	LAURA L1360G	RT	75.00	215.00
78	PHYLLIS L1356G	RT	75.00	215.00
78	SHELLEY L1357G	RT	75.00	200.00
*			**VEHICULAR FIGURINES**	
71	ANTIQUE AUTO LL1146	RT	1000.00	6575.00
73	HANSOM CARRIAGE LL1225	RT	1450.00	1250.00
79	CAR IN TROUBLE LL1375	RT	3000.00	5000.00
82	FIRST DATE LL1393	1500	3800.00	6000.00
83	SCOOTING L5143	RT	575.00	925.00
85	COACH XVIII CENTURY LL1485	500	14000.00	25750.00
87	A HAPPY ENCOUNTER LL1523	1500	2900.00	4950.00
87	A SUNDAY DRIVE LL1510	1000	2600.00	3950.00
87	LANDAU CARRIAGE, THE L1521	OP	2500.00	3800.00
89	HER LADYSHIP, NUMBERED L5097	RT	5900.00	6700.00

YR	NAME	LIMIT	ISSUE	TREND
MAFEKING COLLECTION				
M. GREEN				**MAN'S BEST FRIEND**
95	MICKEY'S EYES	75	295.00	300.00
MARK HOPKINS SCULPTURE				
M. HOPKINS				**EARTH COLLECTION**
95	BEAR	750	400.00	400.00
95	COUGAR	750	400.00	400.00
95	WOLF	750	400.00	400.00
M. HOPKINS				**FISHING COLLECTION**
95	GOTCHA!	950	375.00	375.00
M. HOPKINS				**GOLF COLLECTION**
95	WOODS	950	395.00	395.00
96	DOWN THE MIDDLE	950	300.00	950.00
96	GREEN, THE	OP	160.00	160.00
96	LINING IT UP	950	300.00	300.00
M. HOPKINS				**GREAT CATS OF AMERICAN COLLECTION**
95	SACRED GROUND	750	1495.00	1495.00
M. HOPKINS				**GREAT MYSTERY COLLECTION**
95	WAKAN TONKA	450	1495.00	1495.00
M. HOPKINS				**KIDS ON THE MOVE**
95	RACE YA! (BOY)	950	435.00	435.00
95	RACE YA! (GIRL)	950	435.00	435.00
M. HOPKINS				**KIDS PLAY GALLERY**
93	FASTBREAK	950	315.00	315.00
93	TIRE SWING, THE	550	650.00	650.00
T. RUSH				**LIVING REEF COLLECTION**
95	LORD OF THE REEF	950	775.00	775.00
M. HOPKINS				**MARK HOPKINS PREMIERE EDITIONS**
96	SURVIVAL - LARGE	250	3500.00	3500.00
M. HOPKINS				**MHS ANNUAL SCULPTURE SERIES**
95	SURVIVAL	YR	795.00	795.00
M. HOPKINS				**NATURE'S CHILDREN COLLECTION**
95	BEAR HUG	750	825.00	825.00
M. HOPKINS				**NAUTICAL & SEA LIFE GALLERY**
93	FAIR WIND	RT	550.00	600.00
93	HEAVY WEATHER AHEAD	SU	500.00	500.00
93	TAKING A SIGHT	SU	450.00	450.00
M. HOPKINS				**NOBLESSENCE GALLERY**
93	AMONG THE ASPEN	550	1125.00	1125.00
93	BREAK OUT	250	1250.00	1250.00
93	BROKEN TREATY	450	975.00	975.00
93	EAGLE DANCE	750	700.00	700.00
93	GOLDEN EAGLE	RT	975.00	1050.00
93	MOUNTAIN OVERLOOK	550	975.00	975.00
93	PHANTOMS OF THE FOREST	SU	685.00	685.00
93	SOARING	450	975.00	975.00
93	SONS & BROTHERS	250	1250.00	1250.00
94	ANCIENT OF DAYS	750	1250.00	1250.00
94	BATTLE WORN	250	975.00	975.00
94	CATCH OF THE DAY	550	1150.00	1150.00
94	CRY OF FREEDOM	450	1100.00	1100.00
94	EARTH MOTHER	750	1250.00	1250.00
94	GATHERING WISDOM	450	875.00	875.00
94	GENERATIONS OF TIME	750	1250.00	1250.00
94	GUARDIAN OF THE PLAINS	750	975.00	975.00
94	I HAVE SEEN TOMORROW	450	1000.00	1000.00
94	LICK AND A PROMISE, A	750	850.00	850.00
94	MATERNAL PRIDE	750	975.00	975.00
94	MOTHER'S NATURE	SU	685.00	685.00
94	NIGHT HUNTER	750	875.00	875.00
94	PEACE NO MORE	450	950.00	950.00
94	POUNCING LYNX	750	650.00	650.00
94	VISION QUEST	250	1500.00	1500.00
M. HOPKINS				**ON THE RIDGE COLLECTION**
95	FISHING ROCK	550	750.00	750.00
95	SPIRIT OF THE MOUNTAIN	550	750.00	750.00
M. HOPKINS				**PORTRAITS OF THE WILD COLLECTION**
95	LONE SCOUT	650	600.00	600.00
95	NO LIMIT	650	600.00	600.00
95	SILENT APPROACH	650	600.00	600.00
M. HOPKINS				**SKY COLLECTION**
96	RED-TAILED HAWK	450	450.00	450.00
M. HOPKINS				**SPORTS & WILDLIFE GALLERY**
93	DOWNRIVER RUN	450	950.00	950.00
93	FISHING HOLE	450	650.00	650.00
93	I CAN'T LOOK	950	325.00	325.00
93	NOT AGAIN	950	325.00	325.00
93	TEACHING THE WAY	450	750.00	750.00
94	FOREVER FREE	950	625.00	625.00
M. HOPKINS				**THE ARTS GALLERY**
93	JAZZ BASS	750	550.00	550.00
93	JAZZ DRUMS	750	850.00	850.00
M. HOPKINS				**THE EAGLES COLLECTION**
95	MOUNTAIN MAJESTY	450	975.00	975.00

YR	NAME	LIMIT	ISSUE	TREND
M. HOPKINS		**THE MARK HOPKINS STUDIO**		
94	BORN TO FLY	450	925.00	925.00
T. RUSH		**THE MARK HOPKINS STUDIO**		
93	CHASE, THE	950	695.00	695.00
93	SPOOKED	950	975.00	975.00
93	TURNING POINT	950	695.00	695.00
94	ALPHA WOLF	950	225.00	225.00
94	FACES IN THE DEEP	950	600.00	600.00
94	FIRST STRIKE	950	775.00	775.00
94	HONEY	950	225.00	225.00
94	LURED AWAY	950	750.00	750.00
94	OCEAN MONARCHS	950	575.00	575.00
94	PROTECTING THE INNOCENT	950	550.00	550.00
94	RACE TO THE FLY	950	675.00	675.00
94	RETURN TO THE SKIES	950	225.00	225.00
94	RISE TO THE CHALLENGE	950	225.00	225.00
M. HOPKINS		**VOICE OF JAZZ COLLECTION**		
95	BODY AND SOUL	750	625.00	625.00
95	TRIO	750	675.00	675.00
M. HOPKINS		**WAY OF THE PEOPLE COLLECTION I**		
95	LEGEND KEEPER	450	925.00	925.00
M. HOPKINS		**WAY OF THE PEOPLE COLLECTION II**		
95	SEASON OF INNOCENCE	450	925.00	925.00
M. HOPKINS		**WAY OF THE WARRIOR COLLECTION**		
96	HOKA HAY	450	1350.00	1350.00
M. HOPKINS		**WILD WATERS COLLECTION**		
95	RELEASE, THE	450	1095.00	1095.00
T. RUSH		**WILDLIFE STUDIES COLLECTION II**		
95	CLAP OF THUNDER	950	250.00	250.00
95	CURIOSITY	950	250.00	250.00
95	SCENT OF DANGER	950	285.00	285.00
95	TERRITORIAL RIGHT	950	250.00	250.00
T. RUSH		**WILDLIFE STUDIES COLLECTION III**		
95	ELK COUNTRY	950	335.00	335.00
95	GREAT PLAINS BUFFALO	950	310.00	310.00
95	HAWK EYE	950	275.00	275.00
MARTY SCULPTURE				
M. CAREY		**THE HERD**		
95	PRIDE & JOY PORTRAIT HEAD	5000	130.00	130.00
95	RUMBLE BASE	MO	45.00	45.00
95	RUMBLE SIGHS	MO	29.00	29.00
95	RUMBLE TRIES	MO	29.00	29.00
95	THUNDER PORTRAIT HEAD	5000	150.00	150.00
MARURI USA				
W. GAITHER		**AFRICAN SAFARI ANIMALS**		
81	MYALA	300	1450.00	1450.00
83	AFRICAN ELEPHANT	150	3500.00	3500.00
83	BLACK MANED LION	300	1450.00	1450.00
83	CAPE BUFFALO	300	2200.00	2200.00
83	GRANT'S ZEBRAS, PAIR	500	1200.00	1200.00
83	SABLE	500	1200.00	1200.00
83	SOUTHERN GREATER KUDU	300	1800.00	1800.00
83	SOUTHERN IMPALA	300	1200.00	1200.00
83	SOUTHERN LEOPARD	300	1450.00	1450.00
83	SOUTHERN WHITE RHINO	150	3200.00	3200.00
*		**AMERICAN EAGLE GALLERY**		
85	E-8501	CL	45.00	45.00
85	E-8502	OP	55.00	65.00
85	E-8503	OP	60.00	60.00
85	E-8504	OP	65.00	75.00
85	E-8505	CL	65.00	65.00
85	E-8506	OP	75.00	90.00
85	E-8507	OP	75.00	90.00
85	E-8508	CL	75.00	75.00
85	E-8509	CL	85.00	85.00
85	E-8510	OP	85.00	85.00
85	E-8511	CL	85.00	85.00
85	E-8512	OP	147.50	148.00
87	E-8521	CL	40.00	50.00
87	E-8522	OP	45.00	50.00
87	E-8523	CL	55.00	55.00
87	E-8524	OP	175.00	195.00
89	E-8931	OP	55.00	60.00
89	E-8932	OP	75.00	80.00
89	E-8933	OP	95.00	95.00
89	E-8934	OP	135.00	135.00
89	E-8935	OP	175.00	185.00
89	E-8936	OP	185.00	195.00
91	E-9141 EAGLE LANDING	OP	60.00	60.00
91	E-9142 EAGLE W/TOTEM POLE	OP	75.00	75.00
91	E-9143 PAIR IN FLIGHT	OP	95.00	95.00
91	E-9144 EAGLE W/SALMON	OP	110.00	110.00
91	E-9145 EAGLE W/SNOW	OP	135.00	135.00
91	E-9146 EAGLE W/BABIES	OP	145.00	145.00
95	EAGLE	OP	65.00	65.00

YR	NAME	LIMIT	ISSUE	TREND
95	EAGLE	OP	60.00	60.00
95	EAGLE	OP	80.00	80.00
95	EAGLE	OP	75.00	75.00
95	EAGLE	OP	90.00	90.00
95	EAGLE	OP	110.00	110.00
W. GAITHER				**AMERICANA**
81	GRIZZLY BEAR AND INDIAN	CL	650.00	650.00
82	SIOUX BRAVE AND BISON	300	985.00	985.00
W. GAITHER				**BABY ANIMALS**
81	AFRICAN LION CUBS	1500	195.00	195.00
81	BLACK BEAR CUBS	1500	195.00	195.00
81	MOURNING DOVES	350	780.00	780.00
81	WOLF CUBS	1500	195.00	195.00
W. GAITHER				**BIRDS OF PREY**
81	AMERICAN BALD EAGLE I	CL	165.00	1150.00
81	SCREECH OWL	300	960.00	960.00
82	AMERICAN BALD EAGLE II	CL	245.00	850.00
83	AMERICAN BALD EAGLE III	CL	445.00	445.00
84	AMERICAN BALD EAGLE IV	CL	360.00	360.00
86	AMERICAN BALD EAGLE V	CL	325.00	325.00
*				**EYES OF THE NIGHT**
90	DOUBLE BARN OWL O-8807	OP	125.00	125.00
90	DOUBLE SNOWY OWL O-8809	OP	245.00	245.00
90	SINGLE GREAT HORNED OWL O-8803	OP	60.00	60.00
90	SINGLE GREAT HORNED OWL O-8808	OP	145.00	145.00
90	SINGLE SCREECH OWL O-8801	OP	50.00	50.00
90	SINGLE SCREECH OWL O-8806	OP	90.00	90.00
90	SINGLE SNOWY OWL O-8802	OP	50.00	50.00
90	SINGLE SNOWY OWL O-8805	OP	80.00	80.00
90	SINGLE TAWNY OWL O-8804	OP	60.00	60.00
*				**GRACEFUL REFLECTIONS**
91	MUTE SWAN WITH BABY SW-9152	OP	95.00	95.00
91	PAIR-MUTE SWAN SW-9153	OP	145.00	145.00
91	PAIR-MUTE SWAN SW-9154	OP	195.00	195.00
91	SINGLE MUTE SWAN SW-9151	OP	85.00	85.00
*				**HUMMINGBIRDS**
91	ALLEW'S WITH HIBISCUS H-8906	OP	195.00	195.00
91	ANNA'S W/LILY H-8905	OP	160.00	160.00
91	RUBY-THROATED W/AZALEA H-8911	OP	75.00	75.00
91	RUBY-THROATED W/ORCHID H-8901	OP	150.00	150.00
91	RUFOUS WITH TRUMPET CREEPER H-8901	OP	70.00	70.00
91	VIOLET-CROWNED W/GENTIAN H-8913	OP	75.00	75.00
91	WHITE-EARED W/MORNING GLORY H-8912	OP	75.00	75.00
95	ALLEN'S & BABIES W/ROSE	OP	120.00	120.00
95	ALLEN'S W/EASTER LILY	OP	95.00	95.00
95	ANNA'S W/TRUMPET CREEPER	OP	130.00	130.00
95	BROAD-BILLED W/AMARYLLIS	OP	150.00	150.00
95	VIOLET-CROWNED W/IRIS	OP	95.00	95.00
95	WHITE-EARED W/TULIP	OP	145.00	145.00
ITO				**LEGENDARY FLOWERS OF THE ORIENT**
85	CHERRY BLOSSOM	15000	45.00	55.00
85	CHINESE PEONY	15000	45.00	55.00
85	CHRYSANTHEMUM	15000	45.00	55.00
85	IRIS	15000	45.00	55.00
85	LILY	15000	45.00	55.00
85	LOTUS	15000	45.00	45.00
85	ORCHID	15000	45.00	55.00
85	WISTERIA	15000	45.00	55.00
*				**MAJESTIC OWLS OF THE NIGHT**
87	BURROWING OWL	15000	55.00	55.00
88	BARRED OWL	15000	55.00	55.00
88	ELF OWL	15000	55.00	55.00
*				**MARURI STUDIOS**
93	WILD WINGS	3500	395.00	395.00
94	WALTZ OF THE DOLPHINS	3500	300.00	300.00
W. GAITHER				**NORTH AMERICAN GAME ANIMALS**
84	WHITE TAIL DEER	950	285.00	285.00
W. GAITHER				**NORTH AMERICAN GAME BIRDS**
81	CANADIAN GEESE, PAIR	CL	2000.00	2000.00
81	EASTERN WILD TURKEY	CL	300.00	300.00
82	RUFFED GROUSE	200	1745.00	1745.00
83	BOBTAIL QUAIL, FEMALE	CL	375.00	375.00
83	BOBTAIL QUAIL, MALE	CL	375.00	375.00
83	WILD TURKEY HEN WITH CHICKS	CL	300.00	300.00
W. GAITHER				**NORTH AMERICAN SONGBIRDS**
82	BLUEBIRD	CL	95.00	95.00
82	CARDINAL, MALE	CL	95.00	95.00
82	CAROLINA WREN	CL	95.00	95.00
82	CHICKADEE	CL	95.00	95.00
82	MOCKINGBIRD	CL	95.00	95.00
83	CARDINAL, FEMALE	CL	95.00	95.00
83	ROBIN	CL	95.00	95.00
W. GAITHER				**NORTH AMERICAN WATERFOWL I**
81	BLUE WINGED TEAL	200	980.00	980.00
81	CANVASBACK DUCKS	300	780.00	780.00
81	FLYING WOOD DUCKS	CL	880.00	880.00
81	MALLARD DUCKS	CL	2380.00	2380.00

Left: The first in Enesco Corp.'s Mother's Day series, Thinking of You is What I Really Like to Do *by Sam Butcher was issued in honor of Mother's Day 1994 in the Precious Moments Collection. The detailed porcelain bisque bas relief plate originally retailed at $50.*

Rockin' in my Blue Suede Shoes *by B. Emmett was part of The Bradford Exchange Musical Tribute to the Elvis the King collection. The plate was limited to a 95-day production in 1994 and sold for $29.90.*

These Friends Forever *share more than their quilting project on this commemorative issue collector's plate by P. Buckley Moss. Originally retailing for $85, the 1993 Anna-Perenna Inc. issue was limited to 5,000.*

Part of The Bradford Exchange's Native Beauty collection, 1994's The Promise *was limited to a 95-day production and retailed for $29.90.*

The world seems so big and white to this little explorer in Donald Zolan's Snowy Adventure *from Pemberton & Oakes. Produced in 1990 for only 44 days, the plate originally retailed for $22.*

Victorian Lullaby *from the Victorian Nursery Heirloom collection by Cindy McClure was issued in 1994 by Ashton-Drake Galleries. The bassinet was also available.*

Left: Corinne Layton's Alicia *is a vision in lace. Alicia was added to Ashton-Drake's "Victorian Lace" series in 1993.*

Dressed buckaroo style and strumming his guitar, Danny *was issued in 1994 as part of Artaffect's Country Musicians Collection.*

*Issued in editions of 1,000 each in 1988, these beautifully attired Gorham Small Wonders dolls–*Marguerite, Patina *and* Madeline*–were created by Brenda Gerardi.*

Amey *by S. Stone Aikens was issued by Gorham as a 10th anniversary doll in 1990. Originally retailing for $650, she can be purchased on the secondary market for $700-$1,150.*

1987 charter members of the Hallmark Keepsake Ornament Collector's Club received Wreath of Memories *as part of their membership kits. It features miniature reproductions of favorite Hallmark Keepsake ornaments.*

The second in the "Betsey Clark: Home for Christmas" ornament series reads, "There's no place like Christmas, Noel 1987." This Hallmark Keepsake Ornament titled Home for Christmas *now commands four times its original price of $5.*

Continuing the Treasury of Christmas ornament collection, Enesco Corp. offered Dream Wheels *in 1993 for $29.50.*

Barbie is everywhere these days, including on the Christmas tree. The Holiday Barbie *ornament was the second in a series of Hallmark Keepsake Ornaments and matches Mattel's* Holiday Barbie *doll, also issued in 1994.*

Ivy House *is a 1994 ornament from Lilliput Lane.*

From Enesco Corp.'s Memories of Yesterday collection by Mabel Lucie Attwell, Let's Be Nice Like We Was Before*–a sweet rendition of two children–was issued in 1989.*

Incredible detail characterizes Star Catcher Santa *from the Memories of Christmas collection issued by Prizm in 1994.*

Right: This 1994 event-only piece from the Walt Disney Classics Collection was titled Mr. Smee "Oh Dear, Oh Dear" *and was part of the Peter Pan collection.*

In his quest to give to the poor, Robin Hood *joined the Nutcracker Tales of Sherwood Forest collection by Hans Christian Steinbach of Kurt S. Adler. Limited to 7,500, it originally sold for $225.*

The Poodle *was Swarovski's addition to its A Pet's Corner collection for 1992. The open edition piece by designer Michael Stamey orginally retailed at $125.*

Enesco Corp. added A Stitch in Time Saves Nine *by Priscilla Hillman to its Calico Kittens collection in 1995. The piece was limited to 3,000 and retailed for $35.*

The Screech Owl by W.D. Gaither clutches a snake supper. The figure joined the Birds of Prey collection from Maruri USA in 1981.

*Royal Doulton continued its "Great General" series in 1993 with the Civil War's most famous heroes–*Robert E. Lee *and* Ulysses S. Grant. *Each piece was limited to 5,000.*

The Sioux Brave and Bison *depict the cruel dance of survival in 1982's entry in the Americana Collection from Maruri USA. The sculpture by W.D. Gaither was limited to 300 and originally retailed for $985.*

Above: Rodway Cottage *by Marty Bell was limited to 2,450 in 1988. The retired lithograph from Marty Bell Fine Art originally retailed for $620 and currently commands $2,000.*

Left: Thomas Kinkade found this Victorian Christmas *so nostalgic, he couldn't resist painting Norman Rockwell in the lower left corner. Issued by Lightpost Publishing in 1992, the archival paper print was limited to 980. The original price of $225 has escalated to a secondary market value of $850.*

Sandra Kuck captured the overwhelming emotions of motherhood in God's Gift *issued by V.F. Fine Arts in 1991.*

Thomas Kinkade thought the light cascading through the windows onto the snow below created an illuminated welcome mat in this 1992 print, Olde Porterfield Gift Shop, *which he created for Lightpost Publishing.*

Limited to only 150 prints, Sandra Kuck's First Recital *from V.F. Fine Arts epitomizes a more romantic era.*

Robert Bateman remains one of the most popular artists of all time. His Downy Woodpecker on Goldenrod *was produced in a limited edition of 950 by Mill Pond Press in 1978.*

Robert Bateman's Giant Panda *sits nestled among the vegetation and mist in this 1985 Mill Pond Press release.*

Left: Spencer Collin Lighthouses celebrated 10 years by introducing its Tenth Anniversary Lighthouse *as part of the "Trademark Series" in 1994.*

Bishop's Oast *is from popular collectible maker Department 56.*

Below: Rosie's Cottage *became part of the Shoemaker's Dream collection from John Hine Studios Ltd. in 1991. The open edition by J. Herbert originally retailed for $40.*

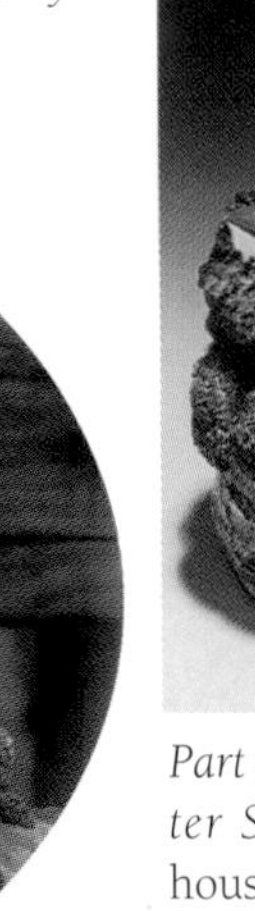

Part of the "Admiral's Lights–Flag Quarter Series," the Yerba Buena Lighthouse *sheds a friendly glow on Spencer Collin Lighthouses. It was limited to 3,000 and retailed for $90 in 1994.*

From its cheery red door to the bell in the tower, the Country School *welcomes students in this 1995 piece from Brandywine Woodcrafts. Part of the Country Lane collection, the open edition piece originally retailed for $30.*

Who wouldn't want to make themselves at home at Winnie's Place*? The piece is produced by Lilliput Lane.*

YR	NAME	LIMIT	ISSUE	TREND
81	WOOD DUCK, DECOY	950	480.00	480.00
W. GAITHER		**NORTH AMERICAN WATERFOWL II**		
81	MALLARD DUCKS, PAIR	1500	225.00	225.00
82	BUFFLEHEAD DUCKS, PAIR	1500	225.00	225.00
82	GOLDENEYE DUCKS, PAIR	1500	225.00	225.00
82	PINTAIL DUCKS, PAIR	1500	225.00	225.00
82	WIDGEON, FEMALE	CL	225.00	225.00
82	WIDGEON, MALE	CL	225.00	225.00
83	LOON	CL	245.00	245.00
*			**POLAR EXPEDITION**	
90	BABY ARCTIC FOX P-9002	OP	50.00	50.00
90	BABY EMPEROR PENGUIN P-9001	OP	45.00	45.00
90	BABY HARP SEALS P-9005	OP	65.00	65.00
90	MOTHER & BABY EMPEROR PENGUINS P-9006	OP	80.00	80.00
90	MOTHER & BABY HARP SEALS P-9007	OP	90.00	90.00
90	MOTHER & BABY POLAR SEALS P-9008	OP	125.00	125.00
90	POLAR BEAR CUB P-9003	OP	50.00	50.00
90	POLAR BEAR CUBS P-9004	OP	60.00	60.00
90	POLAR EXPEDITION SIGN P-9009	OP	18.00	18.00
92	ARCTIC FOX CUBS PLAYING P-9223	OP	65.00	65.00
92	BABY HARP SEAL P-221	OP	55.00	55.00
92	EMPEROR PENUINS P-9222	OP	60.00	60.00
92	POLAR BEAR FAMILY P-9224	OP	90.00	90.00
*			**PRECIOUS PANDA**	
92	LAZY LUNCH PP-9202	OP	60.00	60.00
92	MOTHER'S CUDDLE PP-9204	OP	120.00	120.00
92	SNACK TIME PP-9201	OP	60.00	60.00
92	TUG OF WAR PP-9203	OP	70.00	70.00
*			**SANTAS WORLD TRAVELS**	
96	SANTAS SAFARI	5000	225.00	225.00
W. GAITHER			**SIGNATURE COLLECTION**	
85	AMERICAN BALD EAGLE	CL	60.00	60.00
85	CANADA GOOSE	CL	60.00	60.00
85	HAWK	CL	60.00	60.00
85	PINTAIL DUCK	CL	60.00	60.00
85	SNOW GOOSE	CL	60.00	60.00
85	SWALLOW	CL	60.00	60.00
*			**SONGBIRDS OF BEAUTY**	
91	BLUEBIRD WITH APPLE BLOSSOM SB-9105	OP	85.00	85.00
91	CARDINAL WITH CHERRY BLOSSOM SB-9103	OP	85.00	85.00
91	CHICKADEE WITH ROSES SB-9101	OP	85.00	85.00
91	DOUBLE BLUEBIRD W/PEACH BLOSSOM SB-9107	OP	145.00	145.00
91	DOUBLE CARDINAL WITH DOGWOOD SB-9108	OP	145.00	145.00
91	GOLDFINCH WITH HAWTHORNE SB-9102	OP	85.00	85.00
91	ROBIN & BABY WITH AZALEA SB-9106	OP	115.00	115.00
91	ROBIN WITH LILLIES SB-9104	OP	85.00	85.00
W. GAITHER			**SPECIAL COMMISSIONS**	
81	WHITE BENGAL TIGER	240	340.00	340.00
82	CHEETAH	200	995.00	995.00
83	ORANGE BENGAL TIGER	240	340.00	340.00
*			**STUDIO COLLECTION**	
90	MAJESTIC EAGLES MS-100	CL	350.00	350.00
91	DELICATE MOTION MS-200	3500	325.00	325.00
92	IMPERIAL PANDA MS-300	3500	350.00	350.00
W. GAITHER			**STUMP ANIMALS**	
82	RED FOX	1200	175.00	175.00
83	OWL	1200	175.00	175.00
83	RACCOON	CL	175.00	175.00
84	BOBCAT	CL	175.00	175.00
84	CHIPMUNK	1200	175.00	175.00
84	GRAY SQUIRREL	1200	175.00	175.00
84	PELICAN	CL	260.00	260.00
84	SAND PIPER	CL	260.00	260.00
*			**WINGS OF LOVE DOVES**	
87	D-8701 SINGLE DOVE	OP	45.00	55.00
87	D-8702 DOUBLE DOVE	OP	55.00	65.00
87	D-8703 SINGLE DOVE	OP	65.00	65.00
87	D-8704 DOUBLE DOVE	OP	75.00	85.00
87	D-8705 SINGLE DOVE	OP	95.00	95.00
87	D-8706 DOUBLE DOVE	OP	175.00	175.00
90	D-9021 DOUBLE DOVE	OP	50.00	55.00
90	D-9022 DOUBLE DOVE	OP	75.00	75.00
90	D-9023 DOUBLE DOVE	OP	115.00	115.00
90	D-9024 DOUBLE DOVE	OP	150.00	150.00

MICHAEL GARMAN PRODUCTIONS

YR	NAME	LIMIT	ISSUE	TREND
M. GARMAN				**CITYSCAPES**
95	MINI POLL HALL BLUES	OP	250.00	275.00
95	MINI WEST SIDE NEWS	OP	250.00	275.00
M. GARMAN				**FIREFIGHTER**
95	ADVANCING THE LINE	OP	72.00	72.00
M. GARMAN				**PROFESSIONAL**
95	HEALING TOUCH	OP	70.00	70.00
M. GARMAN				**SPORT**
96	LONG BALL	OP	60.00	60.00
96	TEE TIME	OP	60.00	60.00

YR	NAME	LIMIT	ISSUE	TREND

MIDWEST OF CANNON FALLS

YR	NAME	LIMIT	ISSUE	TREND
L.R. SMITH				*****
93	GNOME SANTA RIDING WHITE DEER	1463	270.00	270.00
95	ANGEL WITH LION & LAMB FIGURE	1500	125.00	125.00
95	WEE WILLIE SANTA	2500	50.00	50.00
C. ULBRICHT				**A CHRISTMAS CAROL**
93	BOB CRATCHIT AND TINY TIM NUTCRACKER 095	CL	240.00	240.00
93	EBENEZER SCROOGE NUTCRACKER	6000	210.00	210.00
94	GHOST OF CHRISTMAS PRESENT NUTCRACKER 12	CL	190.00	190.00
95	SCROOGE NUTCRACKER 09584-3	CL	210.00	210.00
C. ULBRICHT				**AMERICAN FOLK HERO**
94	DAVY CROCKETT NUTCRACKER 12960-9	CL	190.00	190.00
94	JOHNNY APPLESEED NUTCRACKER 12959-3	CL	196.00	196.00
95	PAUL BUNYAN NUTCRACKER 12800-8	CL	220.00	220.00
J.P. LLOBERA				**BELENES PUIG NATIVITY COLLECTION**
85	NATIVITY, SET OF 6 00205-6	OP	250.00	250.00
85	SHEPHERD, SET OF 2 00458-6	OP	110.00	110.00
85	WISE MEN, SET OF 3 00459-3	OP	185.00	185.00
86	SHEEP, SET OF 3 00475-3	OP	28.00	28.00
87	SHEPHERD & ANGEL SCENE, SET OF 7 06084-1	OP	305.00	305.00
88	STANDING CAMEL 08792-3	OP	115.00	115.00
89	ANGEL 02087-6	OP	50.00	50.00
89	BABY JESUS 02085-2	OP	62.00	62.00
89	DONKEY 02082-1	OP	26.00	26.00
89	JOSEPH 02086-9	OP	62.00	62.00
89	MOTHER MARY 02084-5	OP	62.00	62.00
89	OX 02083-8	OP	26.00	26.00
89	SHEPHERD CARRYING LAMB 02092-0	OP	56.00	56.00
89	SHEPHERD W/STAFF 02091-3	OP	56.00	56.00
89	WISE MAN W/FRANKINCENSE 02088-3	OP	66.00	66.00
89	WISE MAN W/FRANKINCENSE ON CAMEL 02077-7	OP	155.00	155.00
89	WISE MAN W/GOLD 02075-3	OP	66.00	66.00
89	WISE MAN W/GOLD ON CAMEL 02075-3	OP	155.00	155.00
89	WISE MAN W/MYRRH 02090-6	OP	66.00	66.00
89	WISE MAN W/MYRRH ON CAMEL 02076-0	OP	155.00	155.00
90	RESTING CAMEL 04025-6	OP	115.00	115.00
*****				**CANNON VALLEY COLLECTION**
94	APPLE TREE, 2 ASSTD. 11484-1	OP	10.00	10.00
94	CANNON VALLEY SIGN 11297-7	OP	5.50	5.50
94	CHICKEN, 3 ASSTED 11299-1	OP	2.00	2.00
94	CHILDREN, 2 ASSTD. 11461-2	OP	5.50	5.50
94	COW, 3 ASSTD. 11309-7	OP	5.50	5.50
94	FAMILY FARMHOUSE/LIGHTED 11292-2	OP	43.00	43.00
94	FARM COUPLE, 2 ASSTD. 11458-2	OP	7.50	8.00
94	FARM TOWN WINDMILL 11306-6	OP	9.50	10.00
94	FARM TRACTOR 11305-9	OP	9.50	10.00
94	FLAGPOLE 11300-4	OP	5.30	5.30
94	GENERAL STORE/LIGHTED 11295-3	OP	43.00	43.00
94	HAY WAGON & HORSE SET 11303-5	OP	19.00	19.00
94	HEN HOUSE/LIGHTED 11294-6	RT	33.00	33.00
94	HORSE, 2 ASSTD. 11485-8	OP	10.00	10.00
94	LITTLE RED SCHOOLHOUSE/LIGHTED 11293-9	OP	43.00	43.00
94	MAILBOX & WATER PUMP, 2 ASSTD. 11301-1	RT	4.00	4.00
94	PICK UP TRUCK 11304-2	OP	12.00	12.00
94	RED BARN/LIGHTED 11296-0	OP	43.00	43.00
94	SPLIT RAIL FENCE 12676-9	OP	2.00	2.00
94	SUNDAY BEST COUPLE W/CHILDREN, 2 ASSTD.	OP	7.50	8.00
95	ACE'S GARAGE/LIGHTED 12665-3	OP	45.00	45.00
95	APPLE TREE, SET OF 3 12677-6	OP	7.00	7.00
95	CHICKEN, 2 ASSTD. 12657-8	OP	3.00	3.00
95	CHURCH/LIGHTED 12664-6	OP	45.00	45.00
95	COW W/CALF, 2 ASSTD. 12673-8	OP	6.50	6.50
95	DAIRY BARN/LIGHTED 12666-0	CL	49.00	49.00
95	DOG BU BOGHOUSE 12658-5	OP	5.00	5.00
95	FARM CAT 12808-4	OP	5.00	5.00
95	FARM CHILDREN, 4 ASSTD. 12671-4	OP	7.50	8.00
95	FARMER W/FEED BAG 12672-1	OP	7.50	8.00
95	FARMYARD LIGHT 12683-7	OP	5.00	5.00
95	FIRE HYDRANT 12685-1	OP	3.00	3.00
95	FOUR SQUARE FARMHOUSE/LIGHTED 12662-2	OP	49.00	49.00
95	GRAIN ELEVATOR/LIGHTED 12663-9	OP	45.00	45.00
95	GRANDPARENTS, 2 ASSTD. 12661-5	OP	6.00	6.00
95	GRAVEL ROAD 12682-0	OP	9.00	9.00
95	MECHANIC 12660-8	OP	6.00	6.00
95	MINISTER 12674-5	OP	6.00	6.00
95	OUTHOUSE 12668-4	OP	11.00	11.00
95	PARKING METER 12686-8	OP	3.00	3.00
95	PICKET FENCE 13260-9	OP	6.00	6.00
95	PIG & PIGLETS 11302-8	OP	5.30	5.30
95	PINE TREE, SET OF 2 12680-6	OP	7.50	8.00
95	SILO 12667-7	OP	16.00	16.00
95	STOREKEEPER 11459-9	OP	5.50	5.50
95	TEACHER & CHILDREN, 3 ASSTD. 11460-5	OP	5.50	5.50
95	TELEPHONE POLE 12684-4	OP	5.00	5.00
95	TURKEY, 2 ASSTD. 12659-2	OP	5.00	5.00
95	WATER TOWER 13116-9	OP	13.00	13.00
95	WOODU CAR 12669-1	OP	12.00	12.00
96	BATTERY OPERATED MINI LIGHT, SET OF 10 1	OP	9.00	9.00

YR	NAME	LIMIT	ISSUE	TREND
96	BORDER COLLIE & SHEEP, SET OF 3 16677-2	OP	10.00	10.00
96	CHRISTMAS DECORATION, SET OF 12 16964-3	OP	10.00	10.00
96	CORNSTALK 16679-6	OP	5.50	5.50
96	FIRE FIGHTERS, 2 ASSTD. 16674-1	OP	8.00	8.00
96	FIRE TRUCK 16676-5	OP	13.00	13.00
96	GARDENERS, SET OF 2 16675-8	OP	13.00	13.00
96	HAY RAKE 16759-5	OP	8.00	8.00
96	HOMETOWN CAFE/LIGHTED 16669-7	3600	45.00	45.00
96	HORSE, 2 ASSTD. 16930-8	OP	6.00	6.00
96	OLD OAK TREE 16681-9	OP	11.00	11.00
96	PLAYING CHECKERS 16680-2	OP	13.00	13.00
96	PLOW 16761-8	OP	6.50	6.50
96	PRAIRIE STYLE BARN/LIGHTED 16667-3	OP	49.00	49.00
96	SPREADER 16760-1	OP	9.00	9.00
96	TRACTOR 16678-9	OP	9.50	10.00
96	VICTORIAN FARM HOUSE/LIGHTED 16666-6	OP	45.00	45.00
96	VOLUNTEER FIRE DEPT./LIGHTED 16668-0	OP	49.00	49.00
*		**COTTONTAIL LANE COLLECTION**		
93	ARBOR W/FENCE SET 02188-0	OP	14.00	15.00
93	BIRDBATH, BENCH & MAILBOX 02184-2	RT	4.00	4.00
93	BRIDGE & GAZEBO, 2 ASSTD. 02182-9	OP	11.50	12.00
93	BUNNY COUPLE ON BICYCLE 02978-7	RT	5.30	6.00
93	LAMPPOST. BIRDHOUSE & MAILBOX, 3 ASSTD.	RT	4.50	5.00
93	STROLLING BUNNY, 2 ASSTD. 02976-3	RT	4.20	5.00
93	TREES, 3 ASSSTD. 02194-1	RT	6.20	7.00
94	BIRDHOUSE, SUNDIAL & FOUNTAIN, 3 ASSTD.	OP	4.50	5.00
94	BUNNY MARCHING BAND, 6 ASSTD. 00355-8	OP	4.20	5.00
94	BUNNY PREPARING FOR EASTER, 3 ASSTD. 029	OP	4.20	5.00
94	BUNNY SHOPPING COUPLE, 2 ASSTD. 10362-3	OP	4.20	5.00
94	COBBLESTONE ROAD 10072-1	OP	9.00	9.00
94	CONE-SHAPED TREE SET 10369-2	OP	7.50	8.00
94	COTTONTAIL LANE SIGN 10063-9	OP	5.00	5.00
94	EASTER BUNNY, 2 ASSTD. 00356-5	OP	4.20	5.00
94	EGG STAND & FLOWER CART, 2 ASSTD. 10354-	OP	6.00	6.00
94	POLICEMAN, CONDUCTOR BUNNY, 2 ASSTD. 003	OP	4.20	5.00
94	SWEEPER & FLOWER PEDDLER BUNNY COUPLE 00	OP	4.20	5.00
94	TOPIARY TREES. 3 ASSTD. 00346-6	RT	2.50	3.00
94	TRAIN STATION COUPLE, 2 ASSTD. 00357-2	OP	4.20	5.00
94	TREE & SHRUB, 2 ASSTD. 00382-4	OP	5.00	5.00
94	WEDDING BUNNY COUPLE, 2 ASSTD. 00347-3	OP	4.20	5.00
95	BUNNY CHEF, 2 ASSTD. 12433-8	OP	5.00	5.00
95	BUNNY CHILD COLLECTING EGG, 2 ASSTD. 028	RT	4.20	5.00
95	BUNNY COUPLE AT CAFE 12444-4	OP	7.00	7.00
95	BUNNY KIDS AT CARROT JUICE STAND 12437-6	OP	5.30	5.30
95	BUNNY MINISTER, SOLOLIST, 2 ASSTD. 12434	OP	5.00	5.00
95	BUNNY PLAYING PIANO 12439-0	OP	5.30	5.30
95	BUNNY PLAYING, 2 ASSTD. 12442-0	OP	6.50	6.50
95	BUNNY POPCORN, BALLOON VENDOR, 2 ASSTD.	OP	6.70	7.00
95	ELECTRIC STREET LAMPPOST, SET OF 4 12461	OP	25.00	25.00
95	MAYOR BUNNY & BUNNY W/FLAG POLE, 2 ASSTD	OP	5.50	5.50
95	OUTDOOR BUNNY, 3 ASSTD. 12435-2	OP	5.00	5.00
95	PROFESSIONAL BUNNY, 3 ASSTD. 12438-3	OP	5.00	5.00
95	STREET SIGN, 3 ASSTD. 12433-8	OP	4.50	5.00
95	STROLLING BUNNY, 2 ASSTD. 12440-6	OP	5.50	5.50
96	BUNNIES SITTING IN GAZEBO 15801-2	OP	10.00	10.00
96	BUNNY BAND QUARTET, SET OF 4 15799-2	OP	16.00	16.00
96	BUNNY CHILDREN WORKING IN GARDEN 15796-1	OP	3.50	4.00
96	BUNNY PICNICKING, SET OF 4 15798-5	OP	15.00	15.00
96	GARDEN SHOPKEEPER, SET OF 2 15800-5	OP	10.00	10.00
96	GARDEN TABLE W/POTTED PLANTS & FLOWERS 1	OP	9.00	9.00
96	GARDEN W/WATERFALL & POND 15797-8	OP	15.00	15.00
96	TREE W/PAINTED FLOWERS, SET OF 3 15924-8	OP	20.00	20.00
*		**CREEPY HOLLOW COLLECTION**		
92	HALLOWEEN SIGN, 2 ASSTD. 06709-3	RT	6.00	6.00
92	WITCH 06706-2	OP	6.00	6.00
93	HAUNTED TREE, 2 ASSTD. 05892-3	OP	7.00	7.00
93	HINGED DRACULA'S COFFIN 08545-5	RT	11.00	11.00
93	PUMPKIN HEAD GHOST 06661-4	RT	5.50	5.50
93	PUMPKIN PATCH SIGN, 2 ASSTD. 05898-5	RT	6.50	6.50
93	SKELETON 06651-5	RT	5.50	5.50
93	TRICK OR TREATER, 3 ASSTD. 08591-2	RT	5.50	5.50
94	BLACK PICKET FENCE 10685-3	OP	13.50	14.00
94	CREEPY HOLLOW SIGN 10647-1	OP	5.50	5.50
94	GHOST, 3 ASSTD. 10652-5	OP	6.00	6.00
94	MAD SCIENTIST 10646-4	OP	6.00	6.00
94	OUTHOUSE 10648-8	OP	7.00	7.00
94	PHANTOM OF THE OPERA 10645-7	OP	6.00	6.00
94	STREET SIGN, 2 ASSTD. 10644-0	OP	5.70	6.00
94	TOMBSTONE SIGN, 3 ASSTD. 10642-6	OP	3.50	4.00
94	WEREWOLF 10643-4	OP	6.00	6.00
95	CEMETERY GATE 13366-8	OP	16.00	16.00
95	FLYING WITCH, GHOST, 2 ASSTD. 13362-0	OP	11.00	11.00
95	GHOUL USHER 13515-0	OP	6.50	6.50
95	GHOULISH ORGANIST PLAYING ORGAN 13363-7	OP	13.00	13.00
95	GRAVE DIGGER, 2 ASSTD. 13360-6	OP	10.00	10.00
95	HEARSE W/MONSTERS 13364-4	OP	15.00	15.00
95	HINGED TOMB 13516-7	RT	15.00	15.00
95	HUNCHBACK 13359-0	OP	9.00	9.00
95	PUMPKIN STREET LAMP, SET OF 4 13365-1	OP	25.00	25.00

YR	NAME	LIMIT	ISSUE	TREND
95	ROAD OF BONES 13371-2	OP	9.00	9.00
95	STREET SIGN, 3 ASSTD. 13357-6	OP	5.50	5.50
95	THEATER GOER, SET OF 2 13358-3	OP	9.00	9.00
95	TICKET SELLER 13361-3	OP	10.00	10.00
96	BONE FENCE 16961-2	OP	9.50	10.00
96	COVERED BRIDGE 16664-2	OP	22.00	22.00
96	DRAGON 16936-0	OP	8.50	9.00
96	GHOSTLY KING 16659-8	OP	8.00	8.00
96	GYPSY 16656-7	OP	8.00	8.00
96	GYPSY WITCH 16655-0	OP	8.00	8.00
96	HEADLESS HORSEMAN 16658-1	OP	11.00	11.00
96	INN KEEPER 16660-4	OP	7.00	7.00
96	SCHOOL TEACHER 16657-4	OP	8.00	8.00
96	SKELETON BUTLER 16661-1	OP	7.00	7.00
L.R. SMITH		**LEO R. SMITH III COLLECTION**		
91	COSSACK SANTA 01092-1	RT	103.00	103.00
91	FISHERMAN SANTA 03311-1	RT	270.00	270.00
91	MILKMAKER 03541-2	RT	170.00	170.00
91	PILGRIM MAN 03313-5	RT	84.00	84.00
91	PILGRIM RIDING TURKEY 03312-8	RT	230.00	230.00
91	PILGRIM WOMAN 03315-9	RT	84.00	84.00
91	STARS & STRIPES SANTA 01743-2	RT	190.00	190.00
91	TIS A WITCHING TIME 03544-3	RT	140.00	140.00
91	TOYMAKER 03540-5	RT	120.00	120.00
91	WOODSMAN SANTA 03310-4	RT	230.00	230.00
92	DREAMS OFNIGHT BUFFALO 07999-7	CL	250.00	250.00
92	GREAT PLAINS SANTA 08049-8	RT	270.00	270.00
92	MS. LIBERTY 07866-2	RT	190.00	190.00
92	SANTA OF PEACE 07328-5	RT	250.00	250.00
92	WOODLAND BRAVE 07867-9	RT	87.00	87.00
93	DANCING SANTA 09042-8	RT	170.00	170.00
93	FOLK ANGEL 05444-4	RT	145.00	145.00
93	GNOME SANTA ON DEER 05206-8	CL	270.00	270.00
93	SANTA FISHERMAN 08979-8	CL	250.00	250.00
93	VOYAGEUR 09043-5	CL	170.00	170.00
94	GIFT GIVER SANTA 12056-9	CL	180.00	180.00
94	OLD WORLD SANTA 12053-8	RT	75.00	75.00
94	SANTA SKIER 12054-5	RT	190.00	190.00
94	STAR OF THE ROUNDUP COWBOY 11966-1	CL	100.00	100.00
94	WEATHERWISE ANGEL 12055-2	CL	150.00	150.00
95	ANGEL W/LION & LAMB 13990-5	RT	125.00	125.00
95	CIRCLE OF NATURE WREATH 16120-3	CL	200.00	200.00
95	GARDENING ANGEL 16118-0	CL	130.00	130.00
95	HARE LEAPING OVER THE GARDEN 16121-0	CL	100.00	100.00
95	MAIZE MAIDEN ANGEL 13992-9	CL	45.00	45.00
95	ORCHARD SANTA 13989-9	CL	125.00	125.00
95	OTTER WALL HANGING 16122-7	CL	150.00	150.00
95	OWL LADY 13988-2	RT	100.00	100.00
95	SANTA IN SLEIGH 13987-5	CL	125.00	125.00
95	SUNBRINGER SANTA 13991-2	CL	125.00	125.00
95	WEE WILLIE SANTA 13993-6	RT	50.00	50.00
C. ULBRICHT		**NUTCRACKER COLLECTION**		
86	PILGRIM 00393-0	CL	145.00	145.00
93	MR. CLAUS 09588-1	CL	180.00	180.00
93	MRS. CLAUS 09587-4	CL	180.00	180.00
94	PRINCE ON ROCKING HORSE 12964-7	CL	160.00	160.00
95	FATHER TIME 12794-0	OP	220.00	220.00
95	FEMALE HEALTH CARE PROFESSIONAL 13189-3	OP	200.00	200.00
95	FEMALE VOLLEYBALL PLAYER 13986-8	OP	200.00	200.00
95	HUCK FINN 12788-9	CL	220.00	220.00
95	KING NUTCRACKER 13190-9	OP	200.00	200.00
95	LEPRECHAUN 09110-4	CL	170.00	170.00
95	MOSES 13186-2	CL	220.00	220.00
95	MOTHER GOOSE 13182-4	OP	220.00	220.00
95	NATURE SANTA W/BIRDHOUSE 12790-2	CL	220.00	220.00
95	PINPCCHIO 13184-8	CL	200.00	200.00
95	SANTA COOKIE BAKER 13191-6	CL	220.00	220.00
95	SANTA RIDING ROCKING REINDEER 12786-5	RT	200.00	200.00
95	SANTA W/TREE 12791-9	CL	200.00	200.00
95	WITCH 13183-1	OP	220.00	220.00
96	CANDYLAND SANTA 17016-8	OP	200.00	200.00
96	CINDERELLA 17014-4	OP	200.00	200.00
96	FIREFIGHTER 17017-5	OP	200.00	200.00
96	FLY FISHERMAN 17022-9	OP	190.00	190.00
96	GARDENING SANTA 17025-0	OP	190.00	190.00
96	GHOST OF CHRISTMAS PAST 18299-4	CL	200.00	200.00
96	GHOST OF CHRISTMAS YET TO COME 17021-2	CL	190.00	190.00
96	PIED PIPER 17026-7	OP	190.00	190.00
96	ROCK & ROLL SINGER 17020-5	OP	200.00	200.00
96	SACAJAWEA 17018-2	CL	200.00	200.00
96	SCARECROW 17023-6	OP	190.00	190.00
96	WYATT EARP 17019-9	1000	200.00	200.00
C. ULBRICHT		**NUTCRACKER FANTASY**		
91	CLARA 03657-0	OP	125.00	125.00
91	HERR DROSSELMEYER 03656-3	OP	170.00	170.00
91	MOUSE KING NUTCRACKER 04510-7	OP	170.00	170.00
91	PRINCE 03665-5	OP	160.00	160.00
91	TOY SOLDIER 03666-2	OP	160.00	160.00

YR	NAME	LIMIT	ISSUE	TREND
95	BIKER NUTCRACKER 13187-9	OP	220.00	220.00
95	CLOWN NUTCRACKER 13188-6	OP	200.00	200.00
95	DRUMMER NUTCRACKER 12792-6	CL	220.00	220.00
95	KING OF CHRISTMAS NUTCRACKER 13665-2	OP	250.00	250.00
*	**ORE MOUNTAIN A CHRISTMAS CAROL**			
93	BOB CRATCHIT 09421-1	RT	120.00	120.00
93	GHOST OF CHRISTMAS PRESENT 12041-5	CL	116.00	116.00
93	SCROOGE 05522-9	RT	104.00	104.00
94	GHOST OF CHRISTMAS FUTURE 10449-1	RT	116.00	116.00
94	GHOST OF CHRISTMAS PAST10447-7	RT	116.00	116.00
94	MARLEY'S GHOST NUTCRACKER	4000	116.00	116.00
*	**ORE MOUNTAIN EASTER NUTCRACKER COLLECTION**			
84	MARCH HARE 00312-1	RT	77.00	77.00
*	**ORE MOUNTAIN NUTCRACKER COLLECTION**			
84	PINOCCHIO 00160-8	OP	60.00	60.00
88	NORDIC SANTA 08872-2	RT	84.00	84.00
88	SANTA W/TREE & TOYS 07666-8	RT	117.00	117.00
89	COUNTRY SANTA 09326-9	OP	95.00	95.00
89	FISHERMAN 09327-6	RT	90.00	90.00
89	GOLFER 09325-2	RT	85.00	85.00
90	ELF 04154-3	RT	70.00	70.00
90	MERLIN THE MAGICIAN 04207-6	RT	67.00	67.00
90	SEA CAPTAIN 04157-4	RT	108.00	108.00
90	SORCERER 10471-2	RT	100.00	100.00
90	UNCLE SAM 04206-9	RT	50.00	50.00
90	WINDSOR CLUB 04160-4	RT	85.00	85.00
90	WITCH 04159-8	RT	75.00	75.00
90	WOODLAND SANTA 04191-8	RT	105.00	105.00
91	CLOWN 03561-0	RT	115.00	115.00
91	NUTCRACKER-MAKER 03601-3	RT	62.00	62.00
92	CHRISTOPHER COLUMBUS 00152-3	RT	80.00	80.00
92	COWBOY 00298-8	RT	97.00	97.00
92	FARMER 01109-6	RT	65.00	65.00
92	INDIAN 00195-0	RT	96.00	96.00
92	PILGRIM 00188-2	RT	96.00	96.00
92	RINGMASTER 00196-7	RT	135.00	135.00
92	SANTA W/SKIS 01305-2	RT	86.00	86.00
92	VICTORIAN SANTA 00187-5	RT	130.00	130.00
93	CAT WITCH 09426-6	OP	93.00	93.00
93	FIREMAN W/DOG 06592-1	OP	134.00	134.00
93	GEPETTO SANTA 09417-4	RT	115.00	115.00
93	SANTA W/ANIMALS 09424-2	RT	80.00	80.00
93	WHITE SANTA 09533-1	RT	100.00	100.00
94	ANNIE OAKLEY 10464-4	RT	128.00	128.00
94	BASEBALL PLAYER 10459-0	RT	111.00	111.00
94	BLACK SANTA 10460-6	OP	74.00	74.00
94	CAVALIER 12952-4	OP	80.00	80.00
94	CAVALIER 12953-1	OP	65.00	65.00
94	CAVALIER 12958-6	OP	57.00	57.00
94	CONFEDERATE SOLIDER 12837-4	OP	93.00	93.00
94	ENGINEER 10454-5	RT	108.00	108.00
94	GARDENING LADY 10450-7	OP	104.00	104.00
94	MINER 10493-4	RT	110.00	110.00
94	NATURE LOVER 10446-0	RT	112.00	112.00
94	PINECONE SANTA 10461-3	RT	92.00	92.00
94	PRINCE CHARMING 10457-6	RT	125.00	125.00
94	PUMPKIN HEAD SCARECROW 10451-1	OP	127.00	127.00
94	REGAL PRINCE 10452-1	OP	140.00	140.00
94	SANTA IN NIGHTSHIRT 10462-0	RT	76.00	76.00
94	SANTA W/BASKET 10472-9	OP	100.00	100.00
94	SNOW KING 10470-5	RT	97.00	97.00
94	SOCCER PLAYER 10494-1	OP	100.00	100.00
94	SULTAN KING 104552-2	RT	130.00	130.00
94	TOY VENDOR 11987-7	OP	124.00	124.00
94	UNION SOLDIER 12836-7	OP	93.00	93.00
95	AMERICAN COUNTRY SANTA 13195-4	OP	165.00	165.00
95	AUGUST THE STRONG 13185-5	OP	190.00	190.00
95	BARBEQUE DAD 13193-0	OP	176.00	176.00
95	BASKETBALL PLAYER 12784-1	OP	135.00	135.00
95	BEEFEATER 12797-1	OP	175.00	175.00
95	CHIMNEY SWEEP 00326-8	OP	70.00	70.00
95	DOWNHILL SANTA SKIER 13197-8	OP	145.00	145.00
95	HANDYMAN 12806-0	OP	135.00	136.00
95	HOCKEY PLAYER 12783-4	OP	155.00	155.00
95	HUNTER 12785-8	OP	136.00	136.00
95	JACK FROST 12803-9	OP	150.00	150.00
95	JOLLY ST. NICK W/TOYS 13709-3	OP	135.00	135.00
95	KING RICHARD THE LIONHEARTED 12798-8	OP	165.00	165.00
95	LAW SCHOLAR 12789-6	OP	127.00	127.00
95	PEDDLER 12805-3	OP	140.00	140.00
95	PIERRE LE CHEF 12802-2	OP	147.00	147.00
95	PIZZA BAKER 13194-7	OP	170.00	170.00
95	RIVERBOAT GAMBLER 12787-2	OP	137.00	137.00
95	ROYAL LION 13985-1	OP	130.00	130.00
95	SANTA AT WORKBENCH 13335-4	OP	108.00	108.00
95	TEACHER 13196-1	OP	165.00	165.00
96	ANGEL WCANDLE 17010-6	OP	220.00	220.00
96	ATTORNEY 17012-0	OP	120.00	120.00

YR	NAME	LIMIT	ISSUE	TREND
96	CHIMNEY SWEEP 17043-4	OP	120.00	120.00
96	COUNT DRACULA 17050-2	OP	150.00	150.00
96	COW FARMER 17054-0	OP	120.00	120.00
96	DRUMMER 17044-1	OP	120.00	120.00
96	EAST COAST SANTA 17047-2	OP	200.00	200.00
96	EMERGENCY MEDICAL TECHNICIAN 17013-7	OP	140.00	140.00
96	FEMALE FARMER 17011-3	OP	145.00	145.00
96	FRANKENSTEIN 17009-0	OP	170.00	170.00
96	GUARD 17046-5	OP	120.00	120.00
96	HARLEQUIN SANTA 17174-5	OP	180.00	180.00
96	KING W/SCEPTER 17045-8	OP	120.00	120.00
96	MALE FARMER 17015-1	OP	145.00	145.00
96	NORTHWOODS SANTA 17048-9	OP	200.00	200.00
96	PRINCE 17038-0	OP	120.00	120.00
96	SANTA ONE-MAN BAND MUSICAL 17051-9	OP	170.00	170.00
96	SPORTS FAN 17173-8	OP	120.00	120.00
96	VICTORIAN SANTA 17172-1	OP	180.00	180.00
96	WESTERN 17049-6	OP	250.00	250.00
*	**ORE MOUNTAIN NUTCRACKER FANTASY COLLECTION**			
88	HERR DROSSELMEYER 14 1/2" 07506-7	OP	75.00	75.00
88	MOUSE KING, THE 10" 07509-8	OP	60.00	60.00
88	PRINCE, THE 12 3/4", 2 ASSTD. 07507-4	OP	75.00	75.00
88	TOY SOLDIER, THE 11" 07508-1	OP	70.00	70.00
91	BUNNY W/EGG 00145--5	RT	77.00	77.00
91	CLARA 8" 01254-3	RT	77.00	77.00
92	BUNNY PAINTER 06480-1	RT	77.00	77.00
93	MOUSE KING, THE 05350-8	CL	100.00	100.00
94	HERR DROSSELMEYER 10456-9	CL	110.00	110.00
94	MARLEY'S GHOST 10448-4	RT	116.00	116.00
94	NUTCRACKER PRINCE 11001-0	CL	104.00	104.00
95	CLARA 12801-5	CL	125.00	125.00
95	TOY SOLDIER 12804-6	CL	125.00	125.00
C. ULBRICHT				**SANTA SERIES**
93	MR. SANTA CLAUS NUTCRACKER	5000	180.00	180.00
93	MRS. CLAUS NUTCRACKER	5000	180.00	180.00
C. ULBRICHT				**TRADITIONAL SANTA SERIES**
92	FATHER CHRISTMAS NUTCRACKER 07094-9	RT	190.00	190.00
93	TOYMAKER NUTCRACKER 09531-7	CL	220.00	220.00
94	VICTORIAN SANTA NUTCRACKER 12961-1	CL	220.00	220.00
WENDT & KUHN				**WENDT & KUHN**
76	ANGEL W/SLED 02940-4	RT	36.50	37.00
76	SANTA W/ANGEL 00473-9	OP	50.00	50.00
78	MADONNA W/CHILD 01207-9	OP	120.00	120.00
79	ANGEL PLAYING VIOLIN 00403-6	RT	34.00	34.00
79	ANGEL TRIO 00471-5	OP	140.00	140.00
79	BAVARIAN MOVING VAN 02854-4	OP	134.00	134.00
79	GIRL W/CRADLE, SET OF 2 01203-1	RT	37.50	38.00
79	GIRL W/PORRIDGE BOWL 01198-0	OP	29.00	29.00
79	GIRL W/SCISSORS 01197-3	OP	29.00	29.00
79	MARGARITA ANGELS, SET OF 6 02938-1	OP	94.00	94.00
79	PIED PIPER & CHILDREN, SET OF 7 02843-8	RT	120.00	120.00
80	ANGEL PULLING WAGON 00553-8	RT	43.00	43.00
80	LITTLE PEOPLE NAPKIN RINGS, 6 ASSTD. 035	OP	21.50	22.00
81	ANGEL W/TREE & BASKET 01190-8	RT	24.00	24.00
81	ANGELS AT CRADLE 01193-5	OP	73.00	73.00
81	SANT W/ANGEL IN SLEIGH 01192-8	RT	52.00	52.00
83	ANGEL BRASS MUSICIANS, SET OF 6 00470-8	OP	92.00	92.00
83	ANGEL CONDUCTOR ON STAND 00469-2	OP	21.00	21.00
83	ANGEL PERCUSSION MUSICIANS, SET OF 6 004	OP	110.00	110.00
83	ANGEL STRING MUSICIANS, SET OF 6 00455-5	RT	105.00	105.00
83	ANGEL STING & WOODLAND MUSICIANS, SET OF	OP	108.00	108.00
83	GIRL W/WAGON 01196-6	RT	27.00	27.00
83	MARGARITA BIRTHDAY ANGELS, SET OF 3 0048	RT	44.00	44.00
84	ANGELS BEARING TOYS, SET OF 6 00451-7	RT	97.00	97.00
87	CHILD ON SKIS, 2 ASSTD. 06083-4	RT	28.00	28.00
87	CHILD ON SLED 06085-8	RT	25.50	26.00
88	CHILDREN CARRYING LATERNS PROCESSION, 6	OP	117.00	117.00
88	LUCIA PARADE, SET OF 3 07667-5	RT	75.00	75.00
89	ANGEL AT PIANO 09403-7	OP	31.00	31.00
90	ANGEL DUET IN CELESTIAL STARS 04158-1	RT	60.00	60.00
91	BIRDHOUSE 01209-3	RT	22.50	23.00
91	BOY ON ROCKING HORSE, 2 ASSTD/ 01202-4	RT	35.00	35.00
91	DISPLAY BASE FO WENDT & KUHN FIGURINES 0	OP	32.00	32.00
91	FLOWER CHILDREN, SET OF 6 01213-0	OP	130.00	130.00
91	GIRL W/DOLL 01200-0	OP	31.50	32.00
91	WHITE ANGELS W/VIOLIN 01205-5	RT	25.50	26.00
92	WENDT & KUHN DISPLAY SIGN W/SITTING ANGE	OP	20.00	20.00
94	BUSY ELF, 3 ASSTD. 12856-5	OP	22.00	22.00
94	CHILD W/FLOWERS SET 12947-0	OP	45.00	45.00
94	SANTA W/TREE 12942-5	OP	29.00	29.00
94	SUN, MOON, STAR SET 12943-2	OP	69.00	69.00
96	ANGELS BEARING GIFTS 17039-7	OP	120.00	120.00
96	BLUEBERRY CHILDREN 17040-3	OP	110.00	110.00

MILL POND PRESS

YR	NAME	LIMIT	ISSUE	TREND
R. BATEMAN				**BATEMAN SCULPTURES**
82	RED-TAILED HAWK STUDY	250	950.00	1750.00

Cape Buffalo *by artist F. Contreras is from wildlife art producer Creart.*

Wild American Bison, *created by F. Contreras, is produced by Creart.*

Legendary Native Americans Crazy Horse, Geronimo, Red Cloud, Sitting Bull, Cochise *and* Chief Joseph *comprise "The Great Chieftains" series by western artist Gregory Perillo. The line is produced by Artaffects.*

YR	NAME	LIMIT	ISSUE	TREND
83	MERGANSER DUCKLING	250	695.00	695.00
84	PEREGRINE IN FLIGHT	90	850.00	1500.00

MISS MARTHA ORIGINALS

Price ranges may reflect various demands in the market from one geographic region to another; condition of piece; specific markings found on piece; and/or changes in production of piece.

M. ROOT — ALL GOD'S CHILDREN

YR	NAME	LIMIT	ISSUE	TREND
85	ABE 1357	RT	24.95	660.00
85	BOOKER T 1320	RT	18.95	715.00-1500.00
85	CALLIE, 2 1/4 IN. 1362	RT	12.00	150.00-240.00
85	CALLIE, 4 1/2 IN. 1361	RT	18.95	425.00-475.00
85	EMMA 1322	RT	26.95	1300.00
85	TOM 1353	RT	15.95	225.00
85	TOM 1353	RT	16.00	360.00
86	AMY 1405W	RT	22.00	27.00
86	ANGEL 1401W	OP	20.00	26.00
86	ANNIE MAE, 6 IN. 1311	RT	18.95	145.00
86	ANNIE MAE, 8 1/2 IN. 1310	RT	26.95	150.00
86	BECKY 1402W	OP	22.00	27.00
86	GRANDMA 1323	RT	29.95	2250.00-3000.00
86	JACOB 1407W	RT	26.00	28.00
86	LI'L EMMIE, 3 1/2 IN. 1345	RT	12.99	110.00
86	LI'L EMMIE, 4 1/4 IN. 1344	RT	15.99	115.00
86	PRISSY (BEAR) 1558	OP	18.00	25.00
86	PRISSY (MOON PIE) 1557	OP	20.00	32.00
86	RACHEL 1404W	OP	20.00	28.00
86	SELINA JANE (6 STRANDS) 1338	RT	21.95	150.00
86	SELINA JANE (9 STRANDS) 1338	RT	21.95	100.00-250.00
86	SELINA JANE (9 STRANDS) 1338	RT	21.95	500.00
86	ST. NICHOLAS BLACK 1316	RT	30.00	125.00-130.00
86	ST. NICHOLAS WHITE 1315	RT	30.00	115.00-130.00
86	TOBY 4 1/2" 1331	RT	16.00	130.00
86	TOBY, 3 1/2 IN. 1332	RT	12.99	110.00
86	TOBY, 4 1/2 IN. 1331	RT	15.99	130.00
86	UNCLE BUD, 6 IN. 1304	RT	18.95	115.00
86	UNCLE BUD, 8 1/2 IN. 1303	RT	26.95	210.00
87	AUNT SARAH IN BLUE 1440	RT	45.00	165.00
87	AUNT SARAH IN RED 1440	RT	45.00	200.00-400.00
87	BECKY WITH PATCH 1402	RT	18.95	115.00-175.00
87	BEN 1504	RT	21.95	150.00-300.00
87	BLOSSOM IN BLUE 1500	RT	59.95	100.00-300.00
87	BLOSSOM IN RED 1500	RT	59.95	320.00
87	BONNIE & BUTTONS 1502	RT	24.00	80.00
87	CASSIE 1503	RT	21.95	45.00-135.00
87	CASSIE 1503	RT	22.00	130.00
87	CHARITY 1408	RT	28.00	45.00
87	GINNIE 1508	RT	22.00	250.00-375.00
87	JESSIE-NO BASE 1501	RT	18.95	195.00-450.00
87	MOSES 1506	RT	30.00	50.00-120.00
87	PADDY PAW & LUCY 1553	OP	24.00	26.00
87	PADDY PAW & LUKE 1551	OP	24.00	26.00
87	PRIMAS JONES 1377	RT	39.95	455.00
87	PRIMAS JONES W/BASE	RT	39.95	455.00-650.00
87	PRIMAS JONES W/BASE 1377	RT	40.00	775.00
87	PRIMAS JONES1377	RT	40.00	525.00-750.00
87	PRISSY W/BASKET 1346	RT	16.00	105.00
87	PRISSY W/YARN HAIR (6 STRANDS) 1343	RT	18.95	90.00
87	PRISSY W/YARN HAIR (9 STRANDS) 1343	RT	19.00	500.00
87	PUD 1550	RT	10.00	800.00-1250.00
87	TAT 1801	RT	30.00	32.00
87	TIFFANY1511	OP	32.00	32.00
87	WILLIE-NO BASE 1406	RT	18.95	30.00
88	BEAN (CLEAR WATER) 1521	RT	36.00	120.00-275.00
88	BETSY (CLEAR WATER) 1513	RT	36.00	225.00
88	BOONE 1510	RT	16.00	100.00
88	CALVIN 777	RT	200.00	943.00-1820.00
88	HANNAH 1515	OP	36.00	37.00
88	JOHN 1514	RT	30.00	125.00
88	KEZIA 1518	OP	36.00	37.00
88	LISA 1512	RT	30.00	135.00
88	MAYA 1520	RT	36.00	375.00-390.00
88	MEG (LONG HAIR) 1505	RT	21.00	350.00
88	MEG (SHORT HAIR) 1505	RT	21.00	625.00
88	MEG IN BEIGE DRESS 1505	RT	21.00	950.00
88	MICHAEL & KIM 1517	OP	36.00	38.00
88	MOE & POKEY 1552	RT	16.00	35.00-50.00
88	PEANUT 1509	RT	16.00	85.00
88	PEANUT 1509	RT	16.00	75.00-130.00
88	SALLY 1507	RT	18.95	135.00
88	TANSY & TEDDY W/GREEN SOCKS 1516	RT	30.00	260.00
88	TANSY & TEDI 1516	OP	*	37.00
89	ADAM 1525	RT	25.00	1300.00
89	BEAN (CLEAR WATER) 1521	RT	36.00	90.00-150.00
89	BEVERLY 1525	RT	50.00	300.00
89	BO 1530	RT	22.00	44.00
89	BOOTSIE 1529	RT	22.00	40.00
89	DAVID 1528	OP	28.00	30.00
89	JESSICA & JEREMY 1522-23	RT	195.00	1150.00-1398.00

YR	NAME	LIMIT	ISSUE	TREND
89	JESSIE 1501	OP	30.00	32.00
89	SASHA 1531	OP	30.00	32.00
89	TARA 1527	OP	36.00	37.00
90	JEROME 1532	OP	30.00	32.00
90	JOSEPH 1537	OP	30.00	30.00
90	KACIE 1533	OP	38.00	38.00
90	MARY 1536	OP	30.00	30.00
90	PRESHUS 1538	OP	24.00	24.00
90	SUNSHINE 1535	OP	38.00	38.00
90	TESS 1534	OP	30.00	32.00
90	THALIYAH 778	RT	150.00	1000.00
91	BESSIE & CORKIE 1547	OP	70.00	70.00
91	BILLY 1545	RT	36.00	85.00-1200.00
91	DORI IN GREEN DRESS 1544	RT	30.00	195.00-375.00
91	DORI/PEACH DRESS 1544	OP	28.00	30.00
91	FATHER CHRISTMAS BLACK 1772	RT	195.00	450.00
91	NELLIE 1546	RT	36.00	60.00-120.00
91	SAMANTHA 1542	RT	38.00	55.00
91	SAMUEL 1541	OP	30.00	32.00
92	BARNEY 1557	OP	32.00	33.00
92	BEAN (PAINTED WATER) 1521	RT	36.00	85.00-120.00
92	BETH 1558	OP	32.00	33.00
92	BETSY (PAINTED WATER) 1513	RT	36.00	75.00-120.00
92	CAITLIN 1554	RT	36.00	36.00
92	FAITH 1555	RT	32.00	65.00
92	JOY 1548	OP	30.00	30.00
92	MELISSA 1556	OP	32.00	32.00
92	MERCI 1559	OP	36.00	37.00
92	RAKIYA 1561	OP	36.00	36.00
92	STEPHEN (NATIVITY SHEPHERD) 1563	OP	36.00	36.00
92	THOMAS 1549	OP	30.00	30.00
92	VALERIE 1560	OP	36.00	37.00
93	NATHANIEL	OP	36.00	36.00
93	SIMON & ANDREW 1565	OP	45.00	45.00
93	SYLVIA 1564	OP	36.00	37.00
93	ZACK 1566	OP	34.00	34.00
94	CHANTEL 1573	OP	39.00	39.00
94	CHERI 1574	OP	38.00	38.00
94	JUSTIN 1576	OP	37.00	37.00
94	NIAMBI 1577	OP	34.00	34.00
94	TISH 1572	OP	38.00	38.00
94	URIEL 2000	YR	45.00	45.00
M. ROOT				**ANGELIC MESSENGERS**
94	CIEARA 2500	OP	38.00	38.00
94	MARIAH 2501	OP	38.00	38.00
M. ROOT				**CHRISTMAS**
86	SAINT NICHOLAS BLACK 1316	RT	29.95	90.00-130.00
86	SAINT NICHOLAS WHITE 1315	RT	29.95	70.00-100.00
87	FATHER CHRISTMAS BLACK 1751	RT	145.00	485.00
87	FATHER CHRISTMAS WHITE 1750	RT	145.00	485.00
87	FATHER CHRISTMAS WHITE 1750	RT	145.00	665.00
88	FATHER CHRISTMAS BLACK 1758	RT	195.00	390.00
88	FATHER CHRISTMAS WHITE 1757	RT	195.00	390.00
88	SANTA CLAUS BLACK 1768	RT	185.00	550.00
88	SANTA CLAUS WHITE 1767	RT	185.00	550.00
88	SANTA CLAUS WHITE 1767	RT	185.00	555.00
89	FATHER CHRISTMAS BLACK 1770	RT	195.00	300.00-600.00
89	FATHER CHRISTMAS WHITE 1769	RT	195.00	300.00-600.00
91	FATHER CHRISTMAS WHITE 1771	RT	195.00	475.00
92	FATHER CHRISTMAS BLACK 1774	RT	195.00	275.00-400.00
92	FATHER CHRISTMAS BLACK BUST 1776	RT	145.00	300.00
92	FATHER CHRISTMAS WHITE 1773	RT	195.00	275.00-400.00
92	FATHER CHRISTMAS WHITE BUST 1775	RT	145.00	300.00
M. ROOT				**COLLECTOR'S CLUB**
89	MOLLY 1524	RT	38.00	370.00
90	JOEY 1539	RT	32.00	280.00
91	MANDY 1540	RT	36.00	180.00-225.00
92	OLIVIA 1562	RT	36.00	100.00-150.00
93	GARRETT 1567	RT	36.00	72.00-85.00
93	PEEK-A-BOO	RT	*	25.00-75.00
94	ALEXANDRIA 1575	YR	36.00	36.00
94	LINDY	YR	*	*
M. ROOT				**HISTORICAL**
89	HARRIET TUBMAN 1900	RT	65.00	100.00-175.00
90	SOJOURNER TRUTH 1901	OP	65.00	65.00
91	FREDERICK DOUGLASS 1902	OP	70.00	70.00
92	DR. DANIEL WILLIAMS 1903	OP	70.00	70.00
92	FRANCES HARPER 1905	OP	70.00	70.00
92	GEORGE WASHINGTON CARVER 1907	OP	70.00	70.00
92	MARY BETHUNE 1904 (MISPELLED)	CL	70.00	135.00-200.00
94	AUGUSTUS WALLEY (BUFFALO SOLDIER) 1908	RT	95.00	95.00
94	BESSIE SMITH 1909	OP	70.00	70.00
M. ROOT				**INTERNATIONAL**
87	KAMEOK 1802	OP	26.00	28.00
87	KARL 1808	OP	26.00	28.00
87	KELLI 1805	OP	30.00	30.00
87	LITTLE CHIEF 1804	OP	32.00	32.00
87	PIKE 1806	OP	30.00	32.00

YR	NAME	LIMIT	ISSUE	TREND
88	KATRINA 1803	RT	26.00	68.00-90.00
93	MINNIE 1568	OP	36.00	36.00
M. ROOT				**SUGAR AND SPICE**
87	BLESSED ARE THE PEACEMAKERS (ELI) 1403	RT	21.95	325.00
87	FRIENDS SHOW LOVE (BECKY) 1402	RT	21.95	420.00
87	FRIENDSHIP WARMS...HEART (JACOB) 1407	RT	21.95	420.00
87	GOD IS LOVE (ANGEL) 1401	RT	21.95	420.00
87	JESUS LOVES ME (AMY) 1405	RT	21.95	425.00
87	OLD FRIENDS ARE BEST (RACHEL) 1404	RT	21.95	425.00
87	SHARING WITH FRIENDS (WILLIE) 1406	RT	21.95	425.00
88	JUAN 1807	RT	22.00	520.00

MUSEUM COLLECTIONS INC.

YR	NAME	LIMIT	ISSUE	TREND
N. ROCKWELL				**AMERICAN FAMILY I**
79	BABY'S FIRST STEP	22500	90.00	220.00
80	BIRTHDAY PARTY	22500	110.00	150.00
80	FIRST HAIRCUT	22500	90.00	140.00
80	HAPPY BIRTHDAY, DEAR MOTHER	22500	90.00	150.00
80	LITTLE MOTHER	22500	110.00	110.00
80	SWEET SIXTEEN	22500	90.00	90.00
80	WASHING OUR DOG	22500	110.00	110.00
81	BRIDE AND GROOM	22500	110.00	180.00
81	MOTHER'S LITTLE HELPERS	22500	110.00	110.00
N. ROCKWELL				**CHRISTMAS**
80	CHECKING HIS LIST	YR	65.00	85.00
81	RINGING IN GOOD CHEER	YR	95.00	95.00
82	WAITING FOR SANTA	YR	95.00	95.00
83	HIGH HOPES	YR	95.00	95.00
84	SPACE-AGE SANTA	YR	65.00	65.00
N. ROCKWELL				**CLASSIC**
80	BEDTIME	OP	65.00	95.00
80	COBBLER, THE	OP	65.00	85.00
80	FOR A GOOD BOY	OP	65.00	75.00
80	LIGHTHOUSE KEEPERS'S DAUGHTER	OP	65.00	65.00
80	MEMORIES	OP	65.00	65.00
80	TOYMAKER, THE	OP	65.00	85.00
81	A DOLLHOUSE FOR SIS	OP	65.00	65.00
81	MUSIC LESSON. THE	OP	65.00	65.00
81	MUSIC MASTER	OP	65.00	65.00
81	OFF TO SCHOOL	OP	65.00	65.00
81	PUPPY LOVE	OP	65.00	65.00
81	WHILE THE AUDIENCE WAITS	OP	65.00	65.00
82	COUNTRY DOCTOR, THE	OP	65.00	65.00
82	DREAMS IN THE ANTIQUE SHOP	OP	65.00	65.00
82	KITE MAKER, THE	OP	65.00	65.00
82	SPRING FEVER	OP	65.00	65.00
82	WORDS OF WISDOM	OP	65.00	65.00
83	A FINAL TOUCH	OP	65.00	65.00
83	A SPECIAL TREAT	OP	65.00	65.00
83	BORED OF EDUCATION	OP	65.00	65.00
83	BRAVING THE STORM	OP	65.00	65.00
83	HIGH STEPPING	OP	65.00	65.00
83	WINTER FUN	OP	65.00	65.00
84	ALL WRAPPED UP	OP	65.00	65.00
84	BIG RACE, THE	OP	65.00	65.00
84	GOIN' FISHIN'	OP	65.00	65.00
84	SATURDAY'S HERO	OP	65.00	65.00
N. ROCKWELL				**COMMEMORATIVE**
81	NORMAN ROCKWELL DISPLAY	5000	125.00	150.00
82	SPIRIT OF AMERICA	5000	125.00	125.00
83	NORMAN ROCKWELL, AMERICA'S ARTIST	5000	125.00	125.00
84	OUTWARD BOUND	5000	125.00	125.00
85	ANOTHER MASTERPIECE BY NORMAN ROCKWELL	5000	125.00	150.00
86	PAINTER AND THE PUPS, THE	5000	125.00	150.00

OLSZEWSKI STUDIOS

YR	NAME	LIMIT	ISSUE	TREND
R. OLSZEWSKI				**MINIATURES**
94	GRAND ENTRANCE, THE	1500	225.00	300.00
94	LITTLE TINKER, THE	750	235.00	400.00
94	TINKER'S TREASURE CHEST & TO BE..., THE	CL	235.00	350.00

PACIFIC RIM

YR	NAME	LIMIT	ISSUE	TREND
*				**BUNNY TOES**
94	MAZIE AT PLAY	OP	13.00	13.00
94	SWEETHEARTS	OP	50.00	50.00
94	TILLIE MAKING A WREATH	OP	13.00	13.00
94	TIMOTHY WITH FLOWER CART	OP	17.00	17.00
94	TIMOTHY WITH TULIPS	OP	13.00	13.00
94	WENDELL AT THE MAILBOX	OP	17.00	17.00
94	WENDELL WITH EGGS IN HAT	OP	13.00	13.00
94	WILLIS & SKEETER	OP	17.00	17.00
94	WINIFRED WITH BLOOMS	OP	13.00	13.00
95	BUNNY GAZEBO	OP	50.00	50.00
95	GARDEN TRELLIS	OP	30.00	30.00
95	HANNAH WITH MAXIMILIAN	OP	13.00	13.00
95	TILLIE WITH HER BIKE	OP	15.00	15.00
95	TIMOTHY WITH EGGS	OP	13.00	13.00
95	WENDELL WITH FLOWERS	OP	13.00	13.00

YR	NAME	LIMIT	ISSUE	TREND
95	WILLIS & SKEETER GARDENING	OP	15.00	15.00
95	WINIFRED PAINTS EGGS	OP	15.00	15.00
96	BETSY & JUSTIN	1440	15.00	15.00
P. SEBERN				**BUNNY TOES**
95	BUNNY TOES LOGO SIGN	OP	20.00	20.00
96	BETSY-CELEBRATE	1440	7.50	8.00
96	JUSTINE-STARS & STRIPES	1440	7.50	7.50
P. SEBERN		**BUNNY TOES BIRTHDAY BUNNIES**		
95	ANABELL GLIDING ALONG	OP	20.00	20.00
95	BETH BACK TO SCHOOL	OP	20.00	20.00
95	CALLIE BUNDLE UP	OP	20.00	20.00
95	CARLY STRIKING A POSE	OP	20.00	20.00
95	CHARLOTTE BEST OF THE BUNCH	OP	20.00	20.00
95	CHESTER SHARING WITH FRIENDS	OP	20.00	20.00
95	CHRISTOPHER & CORY THE BEST SHOT	OP	20.00	20.00
95	DINAH IRRESISTIBLE	OP	20.00	20.00
95	DOUGLAS FROSTY FRIENDS	OP	20.00	20.00
95	GOLDIE TAKING TURNS	OP	20.00	20.00
95	HARVEY GIDDY-UP AND GO	OP	20.00	20.00
95	JEREMY CLEAR SAILING	OP	20.00	20.00
95	JOEY AUTUMN CHORES	OP	20.00	20.00
95	MAGGIE JOY OF LIVING	OP	20.00	20.00
95	MOLLY SWEET WISHES	OP	20.00	20.00
95	NICHOLAS BETWEEN TIDES	OP	20.00	20.00
95	PENELOPE WISHFUL THINKING	OP	20.00	20.00
95	PHOEBE FIRST OUTING	OP	20.00	20.00
95	PIETER HIGHER EDUCATION	OP	20.00	20.00
95	RUSSEL & ROBBY SHARING THE HARVEST	OP	20.00	20.00
95	VIOLET THANK YOU NOTES	OP	20.00	20.00
95	WILBUR LAZY DAZE	OP	20.00	20.00
95	WILEY WINTER GAMES	OP	20.00	20.00
95	ZACHARY WAITIN' ON THE WIND	OP	20.00	20.00

PANTON/KRYSTONIA

YR	NAME	LIMIT	ISSUE	TREND
*			**WORLD OF KRYSTONIA**	
*	SMALL TOKKEL	*	*	50.00
87	GRUMBLYPEG GRUNCH-1081	RT	52.00	100.00
87	LARGE GRAFFYN ON GRUMBLYPEG GRUNCH-1011	RT	52.00	100.00
87	LARGE HAAPF-1901	RT	38.00	85.00
87	LARGE KRAK N'BORG-3001	RT	240.00	650.00
87	LARGE MOPLOS-1021	RT	90.00	350.00
87	LARGE MYZER-1201	RT	50.00	180.00
87	LARGE RUEGGAN-1701	RT	55.00	115.00
87	LARGE TURFEN-1601	RT	50.00	100.00
87	LARGE WODEMA-1301	RT	50.00	100.00
87	LARGE WODEMA-1301	RT	50.00	150.00
87	MEDIUM STOOPE-1101	RT	52.00	85.00
87	OWHEY-1071	RT	32.00	115.00
87	SMALL GRAFFYN/GRUNCH-1012	RT	45.00	200.00
87	SMALL GROC-1042B	RT	34.00	3700.00
87	SMALL N'BORG-1091	RT	50.00	225.00
87	SMALL SHEPF-1152	RT	40.00	100.00
88	LARGE N'GRALL-2201	RT	108.00	220.00
88	SMALL TULAN CAPTAIN-2502	RT	44.00	100.00
88	TARNHOLD - 3203	RT	60.00	280.00
88	TARNHOLD MED.-3202	RT	120.00	160.00
89	CAUGHT AT LAST - 1107	RT	150.00	325.00
89	CAUGHT AT LAST!-1107	RT	150.00	215.00
91	DRAGONS PLAY	RT	65.00	245.00
91	N'BORG 6" 609	RT	29.00	30.00
91	PULTZR - 501	RT	55.00	325.00
93	ALL MINE	OP	40.00	45.00
93	ESCUBLAR	7500	170.00	185.00
93	GILBRAN OF WENLOCK	15000	65.00	75.00
93	HAGGA-BEAST	7500	125.00	150.00
93	HIS SECRET	15000	60.00	70.00
93	HULBERT	OP	38.00	45.00
93	MUFFLER	OP	24.00	28.00
93	OOPS	OP	38.00	43.00
93	POMPON	OP	24.00	28.00
93	SHEPF	OP	23.00	28.00
93	STOOPE	OP	23.00	28.00
93	TAG THE TROLL	OP	48.00	53.00
94	BOLL	RT	52.00	57.00
94	CHECKIN IT OUT	15000	36.00	40.00
94	ELDER PHYL	OP	20.00	22.00
94	IKSHAR	OP	46.00	50.00
94	LEARNING IS GWEAT	OP	48.00	52.00
94	OH SWEET DREAMS	OP	35.00	40.00
94	OKINAWATHE	7500	99.00	120.00
94	ONE UNHAAPFY RIDE	4500	125.00	140.00
94	PHYLONEOUS POOK	OP	20.00	22.00
94	POOKBALL	OP	20.00	22.00
94	SCHNOOGLES	OP	48.00	53.00
94	SPYKE	OP	20.00	25.00
94	WELCOME TO KRYSTONIA	15000	60.00	65.00
94	WODEMA	OP	23.00	28.00
95	A DEFINITE MAYBE	15000	60.00	70.00
95	AH HAH!	OP	48.00	53.00

YR	NAME	LIMIT	ISSUE	TREND
95	DELTA	OP	70.00	75.00
95	ENOUGH IS ENOUGH	2999	250.00	280.00
95	POPOTOMPOTAN	OP	32.00	35.00
95	ROOT	15000	85.00	95.00
95	STOOPE THE STUPENDOUS	15000	65.00	70.00
95	TINCHACHUIK	7500	104.00	120.00
95	WHEY	OP	20.00	73.00
*	**WORLD OF KRYSTONIA COLLECTOR'S CLUB**			
89	KEY	RT	*	100.00
89	PULTZR	RT	55.00	150.00
89	PULTZR W/KEY	RT	55.00	150.00

PAPEL FREELANCE

C. JOHNSON — **LIFE'S ENDEARMENTS**

YR	NAME	LIMIT	ISSUE	TREND
94	COACHING	OP	30.00	32.00
94	LEARNING TO SHARE	OP	25.00	27.00
94	MY FIRST FRIEND	OP	22.50	25.00
94	MY TEDDY TALKS	OP	25.00	27.00
94	PUPPY LOVE	OP	22.50	25.00
94	SISTERS	OP	30.00	32.00

PAVILION OF T'SANG YING-HSUAN

S. FU — **THE FORBIDDEN CITY MUSIC BOX COLLECTION**

YR	NAME	LIMIT	ISSUE	TREND
91	EMPEROR'S WEDDING, THE	84-DAY	39.50	45.00

PEMBERTON & OAKES

D. ZOLAN — **ZOLAN'S CHILDREN**

YR	NAME	LIMIT	ISSUE	TREND
82	ERIK AND THE DANDELION	17000	48.00	90.00
83	SABINA IN THE GRASS	6800	48.00	130.00
84	WINTER ANGEL	8000	28.00	150.00
85	TENDER MOMENT	10000	29.00	60.00

PHILIP L. MARACCI STUDIO

P. MARCACCI

YR	NAME	LIMIT	ISSUE	TREND
93	HOTEL ARIZONA	33	2800.00	3000.00
93	KEEPER OF THE WIND	33	2800.00	3000.00
93	NOSEY NEIGHBOR	33	865.00	925.00
93	ONE LOST MITTEN	33	1200.00	1400.00
93	SEBASTIAN	33	1050.00	1200.00
93	WOULD YA LOOK AT THAT	33	925.00	1000.00
94	ALMOST	33	900.00	1000.00
94	CROWN PRINCESS	33	575.00	650.00
94	HEIRS TO THE THRONE	33	885.00	950.00
94	NOWHERE TO HIDE	33	750.00	800.00
94	SAVANNAH SOVEREIGN	33	4800.00	5000.00

POLLAND STUDIOS

D. POLLAND — **COLLECTIBLE BRONZES**

YR	NAME	LIMIT	ISSUE	TREND
67	BULL SESSION	11	200.00	1200.00
69	BLOWIN' COLD	30	375.00	1250.00
69	BREED, THE	30	350.00	975.00
69	BUFFALO HUNT	30	450.00	1250.00
69	COMANCHERO	30	350.00	750.00
69	DANCING INDIAN WITH LANCE	50	250.00	775.00
69	DANCING INDIAN WITH TOMAHAWK	50	250.00	775.00
69	DANCING MEDICINE MAN	50	250.00	775.00
69	DRAWN SABERS	50	2000.00	5650.00
69	LOOKOUTS	30	375.00	1300.00
69	TOP MONEY	30	275.00	800.00
69	TRAIL HAZZARD	30	700.00	1750.00
69	WAR CRY	30	350.00	975.00
69	WHEN ENEMIES MEET	30	700.00	2350.00
70	COFFEE TIME	50	1200.00	2900.00
70	LOST DISPATCH, THE	50	1200.00	2950.00
70	WANTED	50	500.00	1150.00
71	AMBUSH AT ROCK CANYON	5	20000.00	45000.00
71	OH SUGAR!	40	700.00	1525.00
71	SHAKIN' OUT A LOOP	40	500.00	1075.00
72	BUFFALO ROBE	50	1000.00	2350.00
73	BUNCH QUITTER	60	750.00	1975.00
73	CHALLENGE	60	750.00	1800.00
73	TRACKING	60	500.00	1500.00
73	WAR PARTY	60	1500.00	5500.00
75	CHEYENNE	6	1300.00	1800.00
75	COUNTING COUP	6	1450.00	1950.00
75	CROW SCOUT	6	1300.00	1800.00
76	BUFFALO HUNT	6	2200.00	3500.00
76	MANDAN HUNTER	12	775.00	775.00
76	MONDAY MORNING WASH	6	2800.00	2800.00
76	PAINTING THE TOWN	6	3000.00	4200.00
76	RESCUE	6	2400.00	3000.00
80	BUFFALO PRAYER	25	375.00	675.00

D. POLLAND — **COLLECTOR SOCIETY**

YR	NAME	LIMIT	ISSUE	TREND
87	I COME IN PEACE	CL	35.00	230.00
87	I COME IN PEACE, SILENT TRAIL (SET)	CL	335.00	1000.00
87	SILENT TRAIL	CL	300.00	750.00
88	DISPUTED TRAIL	CL	300.00	500.00
88	HUNTER, THE	CL	35.00	250.00
88	HUNTER, THE- DISPUTED TRAIL (SET)	CL	335.00	825.00

YR	NAME	LIMIT	ISSUE	TREND
89	APACHE BIRDMAN	CL	300.00	450.00
89	CRAZY HORSE	CL	35.00	150.00
89	CRAZY HORSE, APACHE BIRDMAN (SET)	CL	335.00	700.00
90	BUFFALO PONY	CL	300.00	350.00
90	CHIEF PONTIAC	CL	35.00	125.00
90	CHIEF PONTIAC, BUFFALO PONY (SET)	CL	335.00	625.00
91	SIGNAL, THE	YR	350.00	350.00
91	WAR DANCER	YR	35.00	35.00
91	WAR DANCER & THE SIGNAL (SET)	YR	385.00	385.00
D. POLLAND			**PEWTER COLLECTION**	
84	FEDERAL STALLION	1500	145.00	185.00
85	HUNTING COUGAR	1500	145.00	180.00
85	RUNNING FREE	1500	250.00	300.00

POSSIBLE DREAMS

YR	NAME	LIMIT	ISSUE	TREND
*	CRINKLE BASEBALL PLAYER 4 1/2"	*	19.50	20.00
*	CRINKLE DOCTOR 3 1/2"	*	19.50	20.00
*	CRINKLE FIREMAN 4 1/2"	*	19.50	20.00
*	CRINKLE FISHERMAN 4 1/2"	*	19.50	20.00
*	CRINKLE FOOTBALL PLAYER 4 1/4"	*	19.50	20.00
*	CRINKLE GOLFER 4 1/4"	*	19.50	20.00
*	CRINKLE HOCKEY PLAYER 4 1/4"	*	19.50	20.00
*	CRINKLE POLICEMAN 4 1/2"	*	19.50	20.00
*	CRINKLE POSTMAN 4 1/2"	*	19.50	20.00
*	CRINKLE SOCCER PLAYER 4"	*	19.50	20.00
*	SANTA W/CANDY CANE 6 1/2"	*	17.50	18.00
J.C. LEYENDECKER				
*	TRADITIONAL SANTA 7 1/2"	OP	66.00	66.00
91	HUGGING SANTA 8"	OP	52.50	53.00
91	TRADITIONAL SANTA 10"	RT	100.00	130.00
92	SANTA ON LADDER 8 1/2"	RT	59.00	59.00
*	**CLOTHTIQUE AMERICAN ARTIST COLLECTION**			
*	A NEW SUIT FOR SANTA 9 1/2" SET OF TWO	OP	90.00	90.00
*	AND FEATHERED FRIEND 10"	OP	79.80	80.00
*	CHRISTMAS LIGHT 10"	OP	53.50	54.00
*	CHRISTMAS STORIES 8"	OP	63.50	64.00
*	DRESSED FOR THE HOLIDAY 10 1/4"	OP	47.00	47.00
*	FRESH FROM THE OVEN 11"	OP	49.00	49.00
*	MUSICAL READY FOR CHRISTMAS 10"	OP	99.00	99.00
*	NOT A CREATURE STIRRING 8 3/4"	OP	44.00	44.00
*	REFUGE FROM THE STORM 10 1/2"	OP	49.00	49.00
*	TWELVE DAYS OF CHRISTMAS 10 3/4"	OP	48.00	48.00
*	VISIONS OF SUGARPLUMS 10"	OP	50.00	50.00
91	A FRIENDLY VISIT 11 1/2"	RT	99.50	103.00
91	A PEACEFUL EVE 10"	RT	99.50	103.00
91	ALPINE CHRISTMAS 11 1/4"	RT	129.00	133.00
91	FATHER CHRISTMAS 10 1/4"	RT	59.50	61.00
91	MAGIC OF CHRISTMAS 11 1/4"	RT	132.00	140.00
91	SANTA'S CUISINE 10 1/2"	RT	137.50	150.00
91	TRADITIONS 10 "	RT	50.00	60.00
92	AN ANGEL'S KISS 10 1/2"	RT	85.00	90.00
92	CHRISTMAS COMPANY 9"	RT	73.00	120.00
92	HERALDING THE WAY 10 1//4"	RT	72.00	76.00
92	LIGHTING THE WAY 11"	RT	85.00	85.00
92	MUSIC MAKERS 9"	RT	135.00	170.00
92	OUT OF THE FOREST 10 1/4"	RT	60.00	70.00
92	PEACE ON EARTH 10 1/4"	RT	87.50	95.00
92	SANTA IN R. CHAIR 9 1/4"	RT	85.00	103.00
93	A BEACON OF LIGHT 11"	OP	60.00	64.00
93	A BRIGHTER DAY 9 1/2"	OP	67.50	68.00
93	EASY PUTT 9"	OP	110.00	110.00
93	FATHER EARTH 10"	OP	77.00	77.00
93	ICE CAPERS 7 3/4"	OP	99.50	100.00
93	JUST SCOOTING ALONG 10"	OP	79.50	80.00
93	NATURE'S LOVE 10"	OP	75.00	80.00
93	STRUMMING THE LUTE 9"	OP	79.00	79.00
93	TREE PLANTER, THE 10"	OP	79.50	80.00
93	WORKSHOP, THE 9 3/4" MUSIC	RT	140.00	160.00
94	A TOUCH OF MAGIC 10"	OP	90.00	90.00
94	CAPTAIN CLAUS 10"	OP	74.00	74.00
94	CHRISTMAS SURPRISE 10"	OP	83.50	84.00
94	GENTLE CRAFTSMAN, THE 8 1/2"	OP	77.00	77.00
94	GIFTS FROM GARDEN 10"	RT	73.50	74.00
94	SPIRIT OF SANTA 11"	OP	65.00	65.00
94	SPIRIT/CHRISTMAS PAST 10"	OP	75.50	76.00
94	TEA TIME 10"	OP	85.50	86.00
94	TEDDY LOVE 10"	OP	85.00	85.00
95	A GOOD ROUND 11"	OP	73.00	73.00
95	CHRISTMAS CALLER 10 1/2"	OP	57.50	58.00
95	COUNTRY SOUNDS 8 1/2"	OP	74.00	74.00
95	GIVING THANKS 7 1/4"	OP	45.50	46.00
95	PATCHWORK SANTA 10"	OP	67.50	68.00
95	RIDING HIGH 10 1/2"	OP	115.00	115.00
95	SANTA AND THE ARK 10 1/2"	OP	71.50	72.00
95	SOUTHWEST SANTA 10"	OP	65.00	65.00
95	STORY TELLER, THE 8 1/4"	OP	76.00	76.00
95	SUN FLOWER SANTA 10"	OP	75.00	75.00

YR	NAME	LIMIT	ISSUE	TREND
*				**CLOTHTIQUE ELVES**
*	WORKING ELVES 6" SET OF THREE	OP	66.00	66.00
*				**CLOTHTIQUE GIRL**
*	GIRL AT MANGER 7" SET OF THREE	OP	74.00	74.00
*				**CLOTHTIQUE LI'L DRUMMER BOY**
*	LI'L DRUMMER BOY 7" SET OF TWO	OP	59.50	60.00
*				**CLOTHTIQUE LONDONSHIRE**
*	ALBERT 10"	RT	65.00	70.00
*	EARL OF HAMLETT 12"	RT	65.00	70.00
*	MAGGIE 10 1/2"	RT	57.00	57.00
*	WALTER 8"	RT	33.00	33.00
*	WENDY 8"	RT	33.00	33.00
93	NIGEL AS SANTA 10"	OP	53.50	54.00
95	ADMIRAL WALDO 11"	OP	65.00	65.00
95	BETH 7 1/4"	OP	35.00	35.00
95	CHRISTOPHER 7 1/2"	OP	35.00	35.00
95	COUNTESS OF HAMLETT 10 3/4"	OP	65.00	65.00
95	DAVID 7 1/2"	OP	37.50	38.00
95	DEBBIE 7 1/2"	OP	37.50	38.00
95	DIANNE 8"	OP	33.00	33.00
95	DR. ISAAC 11"	RT	65.00	70.00
95	EARL'S FREE TIME 11"	OP	57.00	57.00
95	JEAN CLAUDE 7 1/2"	OP	35.00	35.00
95	LORD WINSTON 12"	RT	65.00	70.00
95	MARGARET OF FOXCROFT 11"	OP	65.00	65.00
95	NICOLE 7 1/2"	OP	35.00	35.00
95	OFFICER KEVIN 11"	RT	65.00	70.00
95	PHILLIP 8"	OP	33.00	33.00
95	REBECCA 7 1/2"	OP	35.00	35.00
95	RICHARD 7 1/2"	OP	35.00	35.00
95	RODNEY 10 1/2"	OP	65.00	65.00
95	SIR RED 11"	RT	72.00	72.00
95	TIFFANY SORBET 8"	OP	65.00	65.00
96	SIR ROBERT 12"	OP	65.00	65.00
*				**CLOTHTIQUE NATIVITIES**
*	HOLY FAMILY 9" - 11 3/4" SET OF TWO	OP	150.00	150.00
*	HOLY FAMILY SET 10 1/2" 3 PC	OP	90.00	90.00
*	HOLY FAMILY SET 12" 2 PC	OP	166.00	166.00
*	WISE MEN 7 1/2-11 3/4" SET OF THREE	OP	174.00	174.00
*				**CLOTHTIQUE PEPSI SANTA COLLECTION**
94	HOLIDAY HOST 10"	OP	59.00	59.00
95	JOLLY TRAVELER 7 1/2"	OP	90.00	90.00
*				**CLOTHTIQUE PROFESSIONALS**
*	DOCTOR 9 1/2"	OP	37.50	38.00
*	FIREMAN 9 1/2"	OP	37.50	38.00
*	GOLFER 9 1/2"	OP	37.50	38.00
*	LIFESTYLES-FISHERMAN 10"	OP	37.50	38.00
*	LIFESTYLES-WOMAN GOLFER 9 3/4"	OP	29.50	30.00
*	NURSE 9 1/2"	OP	37.50	38.00
*	POLICEMAN 9 1/2"	OP	37.50	38.00
*	POSTMAN 9 1/2"	OP	37.50	38.00
*				**CLOTHTIQUE ROCKWELLS**
89	DEAR SANTA 7 3/4"	RT	70.50	71.00
89	SANTA W/GLOBE 8"	RT	73.00	73.00
90	HOBO 11 1/2"	OP	159.00	159.00
90	LOVE LETTERS 11"	OP	172.00	172.00
91	GIFT, THE 12 1/2"	OP	160.00	160.00
91	GRAMPS W/REINS 12 1/2"	OP	290.00	290.00
91	MAN W/GEESE 12 1/4"	OP	120.00	120.00
91	SANTA PLOTTING 12"	OP	160.00	160.00
91	SPRINGTIME 11 1/2"	OP	130.00	130.00
92	BALANCING BUDGET 11"	OP	120.00	120.00
92	MARRIAGE LICENSE 11 3/4"	OP	195.00	195.00
*				**CLOTHTIQUE SANTAS COLLECTION**
*	4 SOMEONE SPECIAL 9 1/2"	OP	39.00	39.00
*	FIRST NOEL MUSICAL, THE 8 1/4"	OP	62.00	62.00
*	GINGERBREAD BAKER, THE 10"	OP	35.00	35.00
*	HEAVEN SENT	OP	50.00	50.00
*	HO HO HOLE IN ONE	OP	43.00	43.00
*	JUMPIN' JACK SANTA 9 1/2"	OP	45.50	46.00
*	MASTER TOYMAKER 9 1/2"	OP	44.80	45.00
*	MODERN SKIER SANTA 10"	OP	66.50	67.00
*	SANTA W/DOLL 10 1/2"	OP	40.00	40.00
*	SANTA'S PET PROJECT 7"	OP	37.00	37.00
*	SHAMROCK SANTA 9 1/2"	OP	41.50	42.00
*	THREE ALARM SANTA 11 1/2"	OP	42.50	43.00
*	WISHES COME TRUE 9"	OP	59.00	59.00
86	CHRISTMAS MAN 10"	RT	60.00	60.00
86	SANTA W/PACK 10"	RT	60.00	60.00
86	TRADITIONAL SANTA 10"	RT	60.00	60.00
87	COLONIAL SANTA 10"	RT	32.00	32.00
87	TRADITIONAL DELUXE SANTA 10"	RT	32.00	32.00
87	UKKO 10"	RT	32.00	32.00
88	CARPENTER, SANTA 10"	RT	40.00	40.00
88	FRONTIER SANTA 10"	RT	38.00	40.00
88	RUSSIAN ST. NICHOLAS 10"	OP	38.00	38.00
88	ST. NICHOLAS 10"	RT	38.00	40.00

YR	NAME	LIMIT	ISSUE	TREND
88	WEIHNACHTSMAN 10"	RT	38.00	40.00
89	BABY'S FIRST CHRISTMAS 10"	CL	42.00	42.00
89	EXHAUSTED SANTA 7 3/4"	RT	60.00	60.00
89	MRS. CLAUS W/DOLL 10"	RT	42.00	42.00
89	PELZE NICHOL 10"	RT	40.00	45.00
89	SANTA W/EMBLEM ROBE 10"	*	40.00	40.00
89	TRADITIONAL SANTA 10"	RT	40.00	40.00
90	HARLEM SANTA 10"	RT	46.00	50.00
90	SANTA PLEASE STOP HERE 10"	RT	63.00	63.00
90	SANTA W/BLUE ROBE 10"	RT	46.00	51.00
90	SKIING SANTA 10"	RT	62.00	162.00
90	WORKBENCH SANTA 8"	RT	72.00	75.00
91	FATHER CHRISTMAS 10"	RT	43.00	49.00
91	KRIS KRINGLE 10"	RT	43.00	43.00
91	MRS. CLAUS IN COAT 10"	RT	47.00	60.00
91	SANTA DECORATING TREE 7 1/4"	RT	60.00	60.00
91	SANTA SHELF SITTER 7 1/4"	RT	55.50	60.00
91	SIBERIAN SANTA 10"	RT	49.00	50.00
91	TRUE SPIRIT OF XMAS 8"	RT	97.00	97.00
92	1940 TRADITIONAL SANTA 10 1/2"	RT	44.00	68.00
92	AFRICAN/AMERICAN SANTA 8"	RT	65.00	65.00
92	ENGINEER SANTAS MUSIC 9 3/4"	RT	130.00	130.00
92	FIREMAN SANTA 11 1/4"	OP	60.00	60.00
92	NICHOLAS 10"	RT	57.50	61.00
92	SANTA ON BED 6 3/4" H X 8 1/2" L	RT	76.00	76.00
92	SANTA ON SLED 8"	RT	75.00	75.00
92	SANTA-SLEIGH MUSIC 9 1/4"	RT	79.00	80.00
92	SANTA/MOTORBIKE 11 1/4"	RT	115.00	125.00
92	SANTA/REINDEER 12 1/2"	RT	79.00	81.00
93	EUROPEAN SANTA 10"	OP	53.00	53.00
93	FIREMAN & CHILD 10"	OP	55.00	55.00
93	HIS FAVORITE COLOR 10"	OP	48.00	48.00
93	MODERN SHOPPER, THE 10"	OP	40.00	40.00
93	SANTA W/GROCERIES 10 1/2"	OP	47.50	48.00
93	VICTORIAN SANTA 9 1/2"	OP	55.50	60.00
94	A WELCOME VISIT 10"	OP	59.50	60.00
94	CHRISTMAS CHEER 10"	OP	55.00	55.00
94	CHRISTMAS IS FOR CHILDREN 10"	OP	59.00	59.00
94	GOOD TIDINGS 10"	OP	49.00	49.00
94	HOLIDAY FRIEND 8"	OP	99.00	99.00
94	MRS. CLAUS 10"	OP	55.00	55.00
94	MRS. CLAWS 10"	OP	69.00	69.00
94	MUSICAL CHRISTMAS GUEST 10"	OP	75.00	75.00
94	OUR HERO 11"	OP	59.50	60.00
94	PLAYMATES 6 1/2"	OP	99.00	99.00
94	PUPPY LOVE 9"	OP	59.00	59.00
94	YULETIDE JOURNEY 10"	OP	55.50	56.00
95	A FRISKY FRIEND 10"	OP	45.50	46.00
95	A LONG TRIP 10 1/2"	OP	95.00	95.00
95	FINISHING TOUCH 9 3/4"	OP	54.70	55.00
95	HOME SPUN HOLIDAY 8 3/4"	OP	49.50	49.50
95	HOOK, LINE & SANTA 9 1/2"	OP	49.70	50.00
95	SOUNDS OF CHRISTMAS 9 1/2"	OP	57.50	58.00
95	SPECIAL TREAT 9 3/4"	OP	50.50	50.50
95	STOCKINGS WERE HUNG 8 1/2"	OP	65.00	65.00
95	VICTORIAN EVERGREEN SANTA 10 1/2"	OP	49.00	49.00
95	VICTORIAN PUPPETEER 10"	OP	51.30	52.00
96	AUTOGRAPH FOR A FAN 10"	OP	39.00	39.00
*		**CLOTHTIQUE SIGNATURE SERIES**		
*	#721001 & 721002 TWO PC SET	OP	198.00	198.00
*	#721004 & 721005 S/S TWO PIECE SET	OP	198.00	198.00
*	KRIS KRINGLE USA 12"	OP	99.00	99.00
*	ST. NICHOLAS 12" CIRCA 1300	OP	99.00	99.00
95	DEPT STORE SANTA USA 1940	OP	108.00	108.00
95	FATHER XMAS ENGLAND 12"	OP	90.00	90.00
*				**CRINKLE ANGEL**
*	CRINKLE ANGEL W/CANDLE 4 3/4"	*	19.80	20.00
*	CRINKLE ANGEL W/DOVE 4 1/2"	*	19.80	20.00
*	CRINKLE ANGEL W/HARP 4 1/2"	*	19.80	20.00
*	CRINKLE ANGEL W/LAMB 4 3/4"	*	19.80	20.00
*	CRINKLE ANGEL W/LANTERN 4 1/2"	*	19.80	20.00
*	CRINKLE ANGEL W/MONDOLIN 4 3/4"	*	19.80	20.00
*				**CRINKLE CLAUS**
*	AMERICAN SANTA 4"	*	15.50	16.00
*	ARTIC SANTA 3 1/2"	*	15.70	16.00
*	AUSTRIAN SANTA 3 3/4"	*	15.80	16.00
*	AUTUMN PEPPERGRASS 4 1/2"	OP	31.00	31.00
*	BELL SHAPE SANTA 5/12"	*	23.50	24.00
*	BISHOP OF MAYA 4 3/4"	*	19.90	20.00
*	BLACK FOREST GIFT GIVER 4 3/4"	*	19.90	20.00
*	BLACK FOREST SANTA 3 1/4"	*	7.80	8.00
*	BUCKETS OF FRUIT FOR....5"	*	45.00	45.00
*	C/C ROLY POLY SANTA 3 1/2"	RT	12.50	13.00
*	CANDLE STICK SANTA 5"	*	15.80	16.00
*	CELTIC SANTA 4 1/2"	*	19.90	20.00
*	CHOO-CHOOS FOUR CHILDREN 5"	*	25.00	25.00
*	CHRISTMAS TREE SANTA 5 3/4"	*	19.90	20.00
*	CRESCENT MOON SANTA 4 3/4"	*	19.00	19.00

YR	NAME	LIMIT	ISSUE	TREND
*	CRINKLE CLAUS W/DOME GERMAN SANTA 120mm	*	45.00	45.00
*	CRINKLE CLAUS W/DOME SANTA/CHIMNEY 6"	*	45.00	45.00
*	CRINKLE CLAUS W/DOME ST. NICHOLAS 120mm	*	45.00	45.00
*	DAINTY WHISKERS 4 1/2"	OP	30.00	30.00
*	DASHING THRU THE SNOW 5 3/4"	*	45.00	45.00
*	DISPLAY FIGURINE 4"	*	11.00	11.00
*	ENGLISH SANTA 3 3/4"	*	15.80	16.00
*	FEEDIN' FOREST FRIENDS 5"	*	27.50	28.00
*	FOREST SANTA 4 1/4"	*	15.50	16.00
*	FRENCH SANTA 3 1/2"	*	15.70	16.00
*	GERMAN SANTA 3 3/4"	*	15.80	16.00
*	GOODY PRINGLE 4 3/4"	OP	31.00	31.00
*	HARD BOILED SANTA 3 1/4"	*	13.70	13.70
*	HIGH HAT SANTA 6 1/4"	*	13.40	14.00
*	HOUR GLASS SANTA 5 1/2"	*	15.00	15.00
*	ICELAND VISITOR 4 1/2"	*	19.90	20.00
*	ITALIAN SANTA 3 1/2"	*	15.70	16.00
*	JOLLY ST. NICK 3 1/2"	*	15.00	15.00
*	MERRY HEART 4 1/2"	OP	30.00	30.00
*	MERRY OL'ENGLAND 4 1/4"	*	19.90	20.00
*	NETHERLANDS SANTA 4"	*	15.70	16.00
*	NORTHLAND SANTA 4 1/2"	*	19.90	20.00
*	PATIENCE FINNEY 4 1/4"	OP	31.00	31.00
*	PINE CONE SANTA 4"	*	15.50	16.00
*	RAG DOLL DELIVERY 6"	*	34.50	35.00
*	ROLY POLY SANTA 5 1/2"	*	23.00	23.00
*	RUNNING DOWN THE LIST 5 3/4"	*	33.00	33.00
*	RUSSIAN SANTA 3 1/2"	*	15.70	16.00
*	RUSSIAN SANTA 4"	RT	15.50	16.00
*	SANTA IN SLED 4 1/2"	RT	17.00	17.00
*	SANTA ON BAG 4"	RT	15.00	15.00
*	SANTA ON ROOF 5"	*	28.50	29.00
*	SANTA SITTING PRETTY 3 1/4"	*	13.90	13.90
*	SANTA W/ANIMALS 4"	RT	15.00	15.00
*	SANTA W/BOOK 4"	*	13.80	13.80
*	SANTA W/CANDY CANE 4 1/2"	RT	13.00	13.00
*	SANTA W/CANDY CANE 5"	*	27.00	27.00
*	SANTA W/CANE & BAG 3 1/4"	RT	12.00	12.00
*	SANTA W/GIFTS 5"	RT	27.00	27.00
*	SANTA W/LANTERN & BAG 4 1/2"	RT	15.50	16.00
*	SANTA W/LANTERN 5"	RT	12.50	13.00
*	SANTA W/LANTERN 5"	RT	27.00	27.00
*	SANTA W/LIST 4 1/2"	RT	15.00	15.00
*	SANTA W/NOAH'S ARK 4 1/2"	*	15.50	16.00
*	SANTA W/PATCHWORK BAG 6 1/2"	*	19.00	19.00
*	SANTA W/STAR 4 3/4"	*	14.00	15.00
*	SANTA W/TEDDY BEAR 4 1/4"	*	16.00	16.00
*	SANTA W/TREE 3 3/4"	*	14.20	15.00
*	SANTA W/WREATH 4"	RT	16.30	17.00
*	SCANDINAVIAN SANTA 3 3/4"	*	15.80	16.00
*	SLIM LINE SANTA 6 1/4"	RT	12.00	12.00
*	TICK TOCK SANTA 4 3/4"	*	15.00	15.00
*	TIP TOP SANTA 5 1/2"	*	23.50	24.00
*	VELVET WINTERBERRY 5"	OP	30.00	30.00
*				**CRINKLE COUSIN**
*	CRINKLE COUSIN W/CLOCK 3"	*	15.50	16.00
*	CRINKLE COUSIN W/CLOWN 2 3/4"	*	15.50	16.00
*	CRINKLE COUSIN W/DOLLS 2 1/2"	*	15.50	16.00
*	CRINKLE COUSIN W/LANTERN 3 1/2"	*	15.50	16.00
*	CRINKLE COUSIN W/TEDDY 3"	*	15.50	16.00
*				**CRINKLE CRACKERS**
95	CRINKLE CRACKER ADMIRAL 5 3/4"	*	18.50	19.00
95	CRINKLE CRACKER CAPTAIN 6"	*	13.00	13.00
95	CRINKLE CRACKER CORPORAL 5 3/4"	*	14.60	15.00
95	CRINKLE CRACKER FRENCH 4"	*	13.50	14.00
95	CRINKLE CRACKER FRENCH ROLY POLY 3 3/4"	*	13.90	13.90
95	CRINKLE CRACKER GENERAL 4 3/4"	*	15.50	16.00
95	CRINKLE CRACKER LIEUTENANT 8"	*	26.50	27.00
95	CRINKLE CRACKER MAJOR 5"	*	14.50	15.00
95	CRINKLE CRACKER PRIVATE 6"	*	15.00	15.00
95	CRINKLE CRACKER ROLY POLY SERGEANT 4"	*	13.50	14.00
95	CRINKLE CRACKER RUSSIAN 4"	*	13.50	14.00
95	CRINKLE CRACKER RUSSIAN ROLY POLY 3 3/4"	*	13.50	14.00
95	CRINKLE CRACKER U.S. 3 3/4"	*	13.50	14.00
95	CRINKLE CRACKER U.S. ROLY POLY 3 3/4"	*	13.90	13.90
95	FRENCH CRINKLE CRACKER 5 1/2"	*	22.00	22.00
95	RUSSIAN CRINKLE CRACKER 7 3/4"	*	29.50	30.00
95	U.S. CRINKLE CRACKER 7 1/2"	*	29.00	29.00
*				**LIMITED EDITION SANTAS**
88	FATHER CHRISTMAS 17"	RT	240.00	240.00
88	KRIS KRINGLE 17"	RT	240.00	240.00
88	PATRIOTIC SANTA 17"	RT	240.00	240.00
89	TRADITIONAL SANTA 17"	RT	240.00	240.00
*				**PEPSI**
*	PEPSI SANTA W/LIST 6"	OP	9.90	10.00
90	PEPSI COLA SANTA 10"	OP	68.00	68.00
90	PEPSI COLA SANTA 10"	*	75.00	75.00
92	PEPSI COLA SANTA SITTING 8"	*	84.00	84.00

YR	NAME	LIMIT	ISSUE	TREND
*		**SANTA CLAUS NETWORK COLLECTORS CLUB**		
*	A FROSTY FRIENDS 10"	OP	47.00	47.00
92	GIFT GIVER, THE	OP	30.00	30.00
93	SANTA'S SPECIAL FRIENDS 7 1/2"	RT	59.00	59.00
93	SPECIAL DELIVERY	RT	30.00	30.00
94	JOLLY ST. NICK PREMIUM	OP	30.00	30.00
94	ON A WINTER'S EVE 10"	RT	65.00	65.00
95	CHECKING HIS LIST	OP	30.00	30.00
95	MARIONETTE SANTA 8"	YR	50.00	50.00
96	A COOKIE FROM SANTA PREMIUM	OP	30.00	30.00
*		**SANTA GO ROUNDS**		
*	ROLY POLY CHRISTMAS TREE 4 1/4"	RT	15.80	16.00
*	SANTA ON SLED 4 1/4"	RT	15.80	16.00
J.C. LEYENDECKER		**SATURDAY EVENING POST**		
91	HUGGING SANTA 10 3/4"	RT	129.00	145.00
92	SANTA ON LADDER 11"	RT	135.00	145.00
N. ROCKWELL		**SATURDAY EVENING POST**		
*	DEAR SANTA 11 1/2"	RT	180.00	180.00
89	SANTA W/GLOBE 11 1/2"	RT	175.00	175.00
91	DOCTOR & DOLL 12 1/2"	RT	196.00	210.00
91	GONE FISHING 11 3/4"	RT	250.00	275.00
92	SANTA'S HELPERS 11"	RT	170.00	180.00
92	SELF PORTRAIT 14"	RT	230.00	255.00
*		**THICKETS**		
93	CLOVIS BUTTONS 3 1/2"	OP	23.00	23.00
93	JEWEL BLOSSOM 4 3/4"	OP	35.00	35.00
93	LILY BLOSSOM 4 3/4"	RT	35.00	35.00
93	MAUDE TWEEDY 3 1/2"	RT	25.00	26.00
93	MORNING GLORY 4"	OP	29.00	29.00
93	MR. CLAWS 5"	RT	32.00	32.00
93	MRS. CLAWS 4 3/4"	OP	32.00	32.00
93	MUSICAL - LILY BLOSSOM 6 3/4"	OP	59.50	60.00
93	OLIVER DOONE, THE GROOM 4 1/2"	RT	29.50	30.00
93	ORCHID BEASLEY 3 3/4"	RT	25.00	25.00
93	PEABLOSSOM THORNDIKE 3 1/2"	RT	25.00	25.00
93	RAINDROP 5 3/4"	OP	45.00	45.00
93	ROSE BLOSSOM 4 3/4"	OP	35.00	35.00
94	LADY SLIPPER 3 1/2"	OP	19.50	20.00
94	MORNING DEW 5"	OP	29.00	29.00
94	PRECIOUS PETALS 5"	OP	32.00	32.00
94	SUNSHINE 4 3/4"	OP	31.70	32.00
94	SWEETIE FLOWERS	OP	31.50	32.00
95	ANGEL DEAR 4"	OP	32.00	32.00
95	BUTTERCUP 4 3/4"	OP	32.00	32.00
95	CECILY PICKWICK 4 1/2"	OP	32.00	32.00
95	CLEM JINGLES 5 1/4"	OP	37.00	37.00
95	EMILY FEATHERS THE BRIDE 4 1/2"	OP	29.50	30.00
95	KATY HOLLYBERRY 5"	OP	35.00	35.00
95	MERRY TAILS 2 1/2"	OP	11.50	12.00
95	P. BLOSSOM THORNDIKE 5" MUSICAL	OP	45.50	46.00
95	PARSLEY DIVINE 5 1/4"	OP	37.00	37.00
95	PENNY PRINGLE 4 1/2"	OP	32.00	32.00
95	PITTYPAT 4 3/4"	OP	32.00	32.00
95	RAINDROP 8" MUSICAL	OP	55.50	56.00
95	RILEY PICKENS 4 1/2"	OP	32.00	32.00
95	TILLIE LILY 4 3/4"	OP	32.00	32.00
95	TIMMY EVERGREEN 4 1/4"	OP	29.00	29.00
95	VIOLET WIGGLES 4 1/2"	OP	32.00	32.00

PRINCETON GALLERY

YR	NAME	LIMIT	ISSUE	TREND
*		**PEGASUS**		
92	WINGS OF MAGIC	OP	95.00	95.00

PRIZM

YR	NAME	LIMIT	ISSUE	TREND
P. ULVILDEN		**MEMORIES OF CHRISTMAS**		
94	CZECHOSLOVAKIAN SANTA	3600	85.00	90.00
94	GINGERBREAD SANTA	3600	85.00	90.00
94	MIDNIGHT VISITOR	3600	85.00	90.00
94	SANTA'S ARK	3600	85.00	90.00
94	STAR CATCHER SANTA	3600	85.00	90.00
94	STARCOAT SANTA	3600	85.00	90.00
95	CZECH SANTA	3600	85.00	85.00
95	GINGERBREAD SANTA	3600	85.00	85.00
95	MIDNIGHT VISITOR	3600	85.00	85.00
95	SANTA'S ARK	3600	85.00	85.00
95	STAR CATCHER	3600	85.00	85.00
95	STARCOAT SANTA	3600	85.00	85.00
96	AUSSIE SANTA W/BOOMER	3600	85.00	85.00
96	GOOD NEWS SANTA	3600	85.00	85.00
96	STORYTIME SANTA	3600	85.00	85.00
96	UKRAINIAN SANTA	3600	85.00	85.00

R.J. ERNST ENTERPRISES

YR	NAME	LIMIT	ISSUE	TREND
A. MURRAY		**LITTLE MISSES YOUNG AND FAIR**		
82	HEART OF A CHILD	5000	65.00	65.00
83	WHERE WILD FLOWERS GROW	2000	65.00	65.00
85	FINAL TOUCH	2000	75.00	75.00
85	WHISPERED MOMENTS	2000	75.00	75.00

YR NAME	LIMIT	ISSUE	TREND
R. MONEY			**MY FAIR LADIES**
82 LADY SABRINA	5000	85.00	85.00
R. MONEY			**SEEMS LIKE YESTERDAY**
81 STOP AND SMELL THE ROSES	5000	24.50	25.00
82 HOME BY LUNCH	5000	24.50	25.00
82 IT'S GOT MY NAME ON IT	5000	24.50	25.00
82 LISA'S CREEK	5000	24.50	25.00
82 MY MAGIC HAT	5000	24.50	25.00
GLENICE			**YESTERDAYS**
82 AMBER	5000	24.50	25.00
84 ELMER	5000	24.50	25.00
85 KATIE	600	24.50	25.00
RAWCLIFFE CORP.			
J. DESTEFANO			**ANGEL FAIRIES OF THE SEASONS**
94 ANGEL FAIRY OF FALL	4500	95.00	95.00
94 ANGEL FAIRY OF SPRING	4500	95.00	95.00
94 ANGEL FAIRY OF SUMMER	4500	95.00	95.00
94 ANGEL FAIRY OF WINTER	4500	95.00	95.00
J. DESTEFANO			**BABY BUBBLE FAIRIES**
93 AMBER, OCTOBER FAIRY	6700	70.00	70.00
93 AZURE, AUGUST FAIRY	6700	70.00	70.00
93 BLUSH, MARCH FAIRY	6700	70.00	70.00
93 CHARTREUSE, APRIL FAIRY	6700	70.00	70.00
93 CORAL, JUNE FAIRY	6700	70.00	70.00
93 EMERALD, DECEMBER FAIRY	6700	70.00	70.00
93 LAVENDER, SETP, FAIRY	6700	70.00	70.00
93 MAGENTA, FEBRUARY FAIRY	6700	70.00	70.00
93 SAFFRON, JULY FAIRY	6700	70.00	70.00
93 TURQUOISE, JANUARY FAIRY	6700	70.00	70.00
93 VERMILLION, NOVEMBER FAIRY	6700	70.00	70.00
93 VIOLET, MAY FAIRY	6700	70.00	70.00
J. DESTEFANO			**FOUR SEASONS FAIRIES**
93 ARIA, SUMMER FAIRY	9500	95.00	95.00
93 HARVEST, FALL FAIRY	9500	95.00	95.00
93 PETAL, SPRING FAIRY	9500	95.00	95.00
93 SNOW, WINTER FAIRY	9500	95.00	95.00
J. DESTEFANO			**GARDEN FAIRIES**
93 DEW FAIRY, THE	4500	115.00	115.00
93 DREAM FAIRY, THE	4500	115.00	115.00
93 FAIRY SLIPPER, THE	4500	115.00	115.00
93 ILLUSIVE FAIRY, THE	4500	115.00	115.00
J. DESTEFANO			**STAR TREK**
93 LUKE SKYWALKER X-WING FIGHTER	15000	95.00	95.00
93 USS ENTERPRISE NCC-1701-D	4500	100.00	100.00
94 DARTH VADER TIE FIGHTER	15000	135.00	135.00
94 DEEP SPACE NINE SPACE STATION	4500	300.00	300.00
94 HAN SOLO MILLENNIUM FALCON	15000	115.00	115.00
RECO INTERNATIONAL			
J. MCCLELLAND			**CLOWN FIGURINES BY JOHN MCCLELLAND**
87 MR. CURE-ALL	9500	35.00	35.00
87 MR. LOVABLE	9500	35.00	35.00
87 MR. ONE-NOTE	9500	35.00	35.00
87 MR. TIP	9500	35.00	35.00
88 MR. COOL	9500	35.00	35.00
88 MR. HEART-THROB	9500	35.00	35.00
88 MR. MAGIC	9500	35.00	35.00
J. MCCLELLAND			**FACES OF LOVE**
88 CUDDLES	OP	29.50	33.00
88 SUNSHINE	OP	29.50	33.00
G. GRANGET			**GRANGET CRYSTAL SCULPTURE**
* RUFFED GROUSE	350	1000.00	1000.00
73 LONG EARRED OWL, ASIO OTUS	350	2250.00	2250.00
J. BERGSMA			**LAUGHABLES**
95 ANNIE, GEORGE & HARRY	OP	17.50	18.00
95 CODY & SPOT	OP	15.00	16.00
95 DAFFODIL & PRINCE	OP	13.50	14.00
95 DAISY & JEREMIAH	OP	15.00	16.00
95 JOEY & JUMPER	OP	15.00	16.00
95 MERLIN & GEMINI	OP	15.00	16.00
95 MILLIE & MITTENS	OP	15.00	16.00
95 PATCHES AND POKEY	OP	15.00	16.00
95 PATTY & PETUNIA	OP	16.50	17.00
95 SUNNY	OP	13.50	14.00
95 WHISKERS & WILLIE	OP	13.50	14.00
A. FAZIO			**SOPHISTICATED LADIES FIGURINES**
87 BIANKA	9500	29.50	33.00
87 CERISSA	9500	29.50	33.00
87 CHELSEA	9500	29.50	33.00
87 CLEO	9500	29.50	33.00
87 FELICIA	9500	29.50	33.00
87 NATASHA	9500	29.50	33.00
87 PHOEBE	9500	29.50	33.00
87 SAMANTHA	9500	29.50	33.00
J. MCCLELLAND			**THE RECO ANGEL COLLECTION**
86 ADORATION	OP	21.50	24.00

YR	NAME	LIMIT	ISSUE	TREND
86	DEVOTION	OP	14.50	15.00
86	FAITH	OP	21.50	24.00
86	GLORIA	OP	12.00	12.00
86	HARMONY	OP	12.00	12.00
86	HOPE	OP	21.50	24.00
86	INNOCENCE	OP	12.00	12.00
86	JOY	OP	14.50	15.00
86	LOVE	OP	12.00	12.00
86	PEACE	OP	18.00	24.00
86	PRAISE	OP	18.00	20.00
86	SERENITY	OP	21.50	24.00
88	MINSTRAL	OP	12.00	12.00
88	REVERENCE	OP	12.00	12.00
J. MCCLELLAND		**THE RECO CLOWN COLLECTION**		
85	ARABESQUE	OP	12.00	13.00
85	BOW JANGLES	OP	12.00	13.00
85	CURLY	OP	12.00	13.00
85	HOBO	OP	12.00	13.00
85	PROFESSOR, THE	OP	12.00	13.00
85	RUFFLES	OP	12.00	13.00
85	SAD EYES	OP	12.00	13.00
85	SCAMP	OP	12.00	13.00
85	SPARKLES	OP	12.00	13.00
85	TOP HAT	OP	12.00	13.00
85	WHOOPIE	OP	12.00	13.00
85	WINKIE	OP	12.00	13.00
87	DISCO DAN	OP	12.00	13.00
87	DOMINO	OP	12.00	13.00
87	HAPPY GEORGE	OP	12.00	13.00
87	JOKER, THE	OP	12.00	13.00
87	JOLLY JOE	OP	12.00	13.00
87	LOVE	OP	12.00	13.00
87	MR. BIG	OP	12.00	13.00
87	SMILEY	OP	12.00	13.00
87	TRAMP	OP	12.00	13.00
87	TWINKLE	OP	12.00	13.00
87	WISTFUL	OP	12.00	13.00
87	ZANY JACK	OP	12.00	13.00
J. MCCLELLAND		**THE RECO COLLECTION CLOWN BUSTS**		
88	BOW JANGLES	5000	40.00	40.00
88	DOMINO	5000	40.00	40.00
88	HOBO	5000	40.00	40.00
88	LOVE	5000	40.00	40.00
88	SPARKLES	5000	40.00	40.00

RED MILL MFG.

YR	NAME	LIMIT	ISSUE	TREND
C. BUCHER				
96	HARMONY ANGEL	2500	35.00	35.00
T. FITZGERALD				
95	NICOLE ANGEL	2500	35.00	35.00
R. WETHERBEE				
96	SANTA	2500	35.00	35.00
L. JOHNSON			**ANGEL II COLLECTION**	
94	CHRISTINA	2500	34.95	35.00
R. BENJAMIN			**FLIGHTS OF FANCY**	
93	LIBERTY	5000	37.95	38.00
R.C. SOMMERS			**FLIGHTS OF FANCY**	
93	INTEGRITY	3000	77.95	78.00
93	VALOR	2500	48.95	49.00
J. TEASDALE			**FLIGHTS OF FANCY**	
93	SENTINEL	2500	54.95	55.00
R. WETHERBEE			**FLIGHTS OF FANCY**	
93	COURAGEOUS	2500	65.95	66.00
93	MAJESTIC	3000	74.95	75.00

RHODES STUDIO

YR	NAME	LIMIT	ISSUE	TREND
ROCKWELL INSPIRED		**ROCKWELL'S AGE OF WONDER**		
91	HUSH-A-BYE	TL	34.95	35.00
91	SPLISH SPLASH	TL	34.95	35.00
91	STAND BY ME	TL	36.95	37.00
ROCKWELL INSPIRED		**ROCKWELL'S BEAUTIFUL DREAMERS**		
91	DEAR DIARY	TL	37.95	38.00
91	SECRET SONNETS	TL	39.95	40.00
91	SITTING PRETTY	TL	37.95	38.00
ROCKWELL INSPIRED		**ROCKWELL'S GEMS OF WISDOM**		
91	LOVE CURES ALL	TL	39.95	40.00
91	PRACTICE MAKES PERFECT	TL	39.95	40.00
ROCKWELL INSPIRED		**ROCKWELL'S HEIRLOOM SANTA COLLECTION**		
90	SANTA'S WORKSHOP	150-DAY	49.95	50.00
91	CHRISTMAS DREAM	150-DAY	49.95	50.00
ROCKWELL INSPIRED			**ROCKWELL'S HOMETOWN**	
91	BELL TOWER	TL	36.95	37.00
91	FIREHOUSE	TL	36.95	37.00
91	GREYSTONE CHURCH	TL	34.95	35.00
91	ROCKWELL'S RESIDENCE	TL	34.95	35.00
ROCKWELL INSPIRED			**ROCKWELL'S MAIN STREET**	
90	ANTIQUE SHOP, THE	150-DAY	28.00	28.00

YR	NAME	LIMIT	ISSUE	TREND
90	COUNTRY STORE, THE	150-DAY	32.00	32.00
90	ROCKWELL'S STUDIO	150-DAY	28.00	28.00
90	TOWN OFFICES, THE	150-DAY	32.00	32.00
91	BANK, THE	150-DAY	36.00	36.00
91	LIBRARY, THE	150-DAY	36.00	36.00
91	RED LION INN	150-DAY	39.00	39.00

RIVER SHORE

YR	NAME	LIMIT	ISSUE	TREND
	R. BROWN			**BABIES OF ENDANGERED SPECIES**
84	BAXTER (BEAR)	15000	45.00	45.00
84	CAROLINE (ANETLOPE)	15000	45.00	45.00
84	CHESTER (PRAIRIE DOG)	15000	45.00	45.00
84	DAISY (WOOD BISON)	15000	45.00	45.00
84	SIDNEY (COUGAR)	15000	45.00	45.00
84	TREVOR (FOX)	15000	45.00	45.00
84	VIOLET (OTTER)	15000	45.00	45.00
84	WEBSTER (TIMBERWOLF)	15000	45.00	45.00
	M. HAGUE			**LOVABLE TEDDY MUSICAL FIGURINE COLLECTION**
87	APRIL	OP	29.50	30.00
87	AUSTIN	OP	29.50	30.00
87	GILBERT	OP	29.50	30.00
87	WILLIAM	OP	29.50	30.00
88	ADAM	OP	29.50	30.00
88	HARVEY	OP	29.50	30.00
88	HENRY	OP	29.50	30.00
88	KATIE	OP	29.50	30.00
	R. BROWN			**LOVEABLE BABY ANIMALS**
78	AKIKU-SEAL	15000	37.50	150.00
78	ALFRED-RACCOON	15000	42.50	45.00
79	MATILDA-KOALA	15000	45.00	45.00
79	SCOOTER-CHIPMUNK	15000	45.00	55.00
	N. ROCKWELL			**ROCKWELL SINGLE ISSUES**
81	LOOKING OUT TO SEA	9500	85.00	145.00
82	GRANDPA'S GUARDIAN	9500	125.00	125.00
	R. BROWN			**WILDERNESS BABIES**
85	ABERCROMBIE (POLAR BEAR)	15000	45.00	45.00
85	ANNABEL (MOUNTAIN GOAT)	15000	45.00	45.00
85	ARIANNE (RABBIT)	15000	45.00	45.00
85	CARMEN (BURRO)	15000	45.00	45.00
85	ELROD (FOX)	15000	45.00	45.00
85	PENELOPE (DEER)	15000	45.00	45.00
85	REGGIE (RACCOON)	15000	45.00	45.00
85	ROCKY (BOBCAT)	15000	45.00	45.00
	R. BROWN			**WILDLIFE BABY ANIMALS**
78	FANNY-FAWN	15000	45.00	90.00
79	ROOSEVELT-BEAR	15000	50.00	65.00
79	ROSCOE-RED FOX	15000	50.00	50.00
80	PRISCILLA-SKUNK	15000	50.00	50.00

RJB DESIGNS

YR	NAME	LIMIT	ISSUE	TREND
	J. DESTEFANO			**BABY BUBBLE FAIRIES**
93	BABY BUBBLE FAIRIES	OP	*	20.00
	R. BRENNAN			**CINDER CLAUS**
93	SANTA (3 FT.)	75	950.00	1000.00
93	SANTA (4 FT.)	40	1300.00	1500.00
93	SANTA-SPECIAL EDITION	850	200.00	225.00
94	AMBERT	250	200.00	225.00
94	CUTHBERT	250	200.00	225.00
94	DRUSILLA	100	20.00	23.00
94	GARRICK	250	200.00	225.00
94	MONTGOMERY	250	200.00	225.00
94	SANTA (3 FT.)	60	950.00	975.00
94	SANTA (4 FT.)	20	1300.00	1400.00
94	SANTA (5 FT.)	3	3500.00	3750.00
95	CORNELIUS	250	200.00	200.00
95	CULVER	250	200.00	200.00
95	ROSCOE	250	200.00	200.00
95	STODDARD	250	200.00	200.00
95	WILHELMINA	100	200.00	200.00

ROHN

YR	NAME	LIMIT	ISSUE	TREND
	E. ROHN			**AROUND THE WORLD**
71	COOLIE	100	700.00	1300.00
72	GYPSY	125	1450.00	1850.00
73	MATADOR	90	2400.00	3100.00
73	SHERIFF	100	1500.00	2250.00
74	AUSSIE-HUNTER	90	1000.00	1300.00
	E. ROHN			**CLOWNS-BIG TOP SERIES**
79	WHITE FACE	100	1000.00	3500.00
80	TRAMP	100	1200.00	2500.00
81	AUGUSTE	100	1400.00	1700.00
83	SWEETHEART	200	925.00	1500.00
	E. ROHN			**CLOWNS-HEY RUBE**
79	AUGUSTE	300	190.00	350.00
79	TRAMP	300	190.00	350.00
79	WHITEFACE	300	190.00	350.00

YR	NAME	LIMIT	ISSUE	TREND
E. ROHN				**FAMOUS PEOPLE**
75	HARRY S. TRUMAN	75	2400.00	4000.00
79	NORMAN ROCKWELL	200	1950.00	2300.00
81	RONALD REAGAN	200	3000.00	3000.00
85	SHERLOCK HOLMES	2210	155.00	190.00
86	DR. JOHN WATSON	2210	155.00	155.00
93	SHERLOCK HOLMES & DR. WATSON	OP	185.00	200.00
E. ROHN				**FAMOUS PEOPLE-BISQUE**
79	LINCOLN	500	100.00	500.00
79	NORMAN ROCKWELL	YR	100.00	200.00
81	REAGAN	2500	140.00	200.00
83	J.F. KENNEDY	500	140.00	400.00
E. ROHN				**KINARA SERIES**
92	KENTE WOMAN	OP	40.00	45.00
E. ROHN				**PORTRAIT SERIES**
92	MARTIN LUTHER KING	OP	60.00	75.00
E. ROHN				**RELIGIOUS & BIBLICAL**
77	ZAIDE	70	1950.00	5000.00
78	SABBATH	70	1825.00	5000.00
85	MENTOR, THE	15	9500.00	9500.00
E. ROHN				**REMEMBER WHEN**
71	AMERICAN GI	100	600.00	1750.00
71	RIVERBOAT CAPTAIN	100	1000.00	2400.00
73	APPRENTICE	175	500.00	850.00
73	JAZZ MAN	150	750.00	3500.00
74	MISSY	250	250.00	500.00
74	RECRUIT (SET W/FN-5)	250	250.00	500.00
77	CASEY	300	275.00	500.00
77	FLAPPER	500	325.00	500.00
77	SOU' WESTER	450	300.00	500.00
77	WALLY	250	250.00	500.00
80	SHOWMAN (W.C. FIELDS)	300	220.00	500.00
81	CLOWN PRINCE	25	2000.00	2400.00
E. ROHN				**SMALL WORLD SERIES**
*	JOHNNIE'S	1500	90.00	90.00
74	BIG BROTHER	250	90.00	90.00
74	BURGLERS	250	120.00	120.00
74	KNEE DEEP	500	60.00	60.00
74	QUACKERS	250	75.00	75.00
75	FIELD MUSHROOMS	250	90.00	90.00
75	OYSTER MUSHROOM	250	140.00	140.00
E. ROHN				**WESTERN**
71	APACHE INDIAN	125	800.00	2000.00
71	CHOSEN ONE (INDIAN MAID)	125	850.00	2000.00
71	CROW INDIAN	100	800.00	1500.00
71	TRAIL-HAND	100	1200.00	1600.00
E. ROHN				**WILD WEST**
82	RODEO CLOWN	100	2600.00	3500.00

ROMAN INC.

YR	NAME	LIMIT	ISSUE	TREND
F. HOOK				**A CHILD'S WORLD 1ST EDITION**
80	BEACH BUDDIES, SIGNED	15000	29.00	600.00
80	BEACH BUDDIES, UNSIGNED	15000	29.00	500.00
80	HELPING HANDS	15000	45.00	75.00
80	KISS ME GOOD NIGHT	15000	29.00	50.00
80	MY BIG BROTHER	15000	39.00	200.00
80	NIGHTTIME THOUGHTS	15000	25.00	75.00
80	SOUNDS OF THE SEA	15000	45.00	150.00
F. HOOK				**A CHILD'S WORLD 2ND EDITION**
81	ALL DRESSED UP	15000	36.00	75.00
81	CAT NAP	15000	42.00	100.00
81	I'LL BE GOOD	15000	36.00	75.00
81	MAKING FRIENDS	15000	42.00	46.00
81	SEA AND ME, THE	15000	39.00	50.00
81	SUNDAY SHCOOL	15000	39.00	75.00
F. HOOK				**A CHILD'S WORLD 3RD EDITION**
81	BEAR HUG	15000	42.00	55.00
81	PATHWAY TO DREAMS	15000	47.00	80.00
81	ROAD TO ADVENTURE	15000	47.00	50.00
81	SISTERS	15000	64.00	110.00
81	SPRING BREEZE	15000	37.50	50.00
81	YOUTH	15000	37.50	50.00
F. HOOK				**A CHILD'S WORLD 4TH EDITION**
82	ALL BUNDLED UP	15000	37.50	50.00
82	BEDTIME	15000	35.00	38.00
82	BIRDIE	15000	37.50	50.00
82	FLOWER GIRL	15000	42.00	50.00
82	MY DOLLY!	15000	39.00	50.00
82	RING BEARER	15000	39.00	50.00
F. HOOK				**A CHILD'S WORLD 5TH EDITION**
83	BROTHERS	15000	64.00	75.00
83	FINISH LINE	15000	39.00	42.00
83	HANDFUL OF HAPPINESS	15000	36.00	50.00
83	HE LOVES ME...	15000	49.00	60.00
83	PUPPY'S PAL	15000	39.00	42.00
83	RING AROUND THE ROSIE	15000	99.00	105.00

YR	NAME	LIMIT	ISSUE	TREND
F. HOOK		**A CHILD'S WORLD 6TH EDITION**		
84	CAN I HELP?	15000	37.50	50.00
84	FUTURE ARTIST	15000	42.00	50.00
84	GOOD DOGGIE	15000	47.00	50.00
84	LET'S PLAY CATCH	15000	33.00	40.00
84	NATURE'S WONDERS	15000	29.00	40.00
84	SAND CASTLES	15000	37.50	50.00
F. HOOK		**A CHILD'S WORLD 7TH EDITION**		
85	ART CLASS	15000	99.00	105.00
85	DON'T TELL ANYONE	15000	49.00	50.00
85	LOOK AT ME!	15000	42.00	50.00
85	MOTHER'S HELPER	15000	45.00	50.00
85	PLEASE HEAR ME	15000	29.00	30.00
85	YUMMM!	15000	36.00	40.00
F. HOOK		**A CHILD'S WORLD 8TH EDITION**		
85	CHANCE OF SHOWERS	15000	33.00	40.00
85	DRESS REHEARSAL	15000	33.00	40.00
85	ENGINE	15000	36.00	50.00
85	JUST STOPPED BY	15000	36.00	50.00
85	PRIVATE OCEAN	15000	29.00	40.00
85	PUZZLING	15000	36.00	50.00
F. HOOK		**A CHILD'S WORLD 9TH EDITION**		
87	HOPSCOTCH	15000	67.50	75.00
87	LI'L BROTHER	15000	60.00	75.00
I. SPENCER		**CATNIPPERS**		
85	A BAFFLING YARN	15000	45.00	50.00
85	A CHRISTMAS MOURNING	15000	45.00	50.00
85	A TAIL OF TWO KITTIES	15000	45.00	50.00
85	CAN'T WE BE FRIENDS	15000	45.00	50.00
85	FLORA AND FELINA	15000	45.00	50.00
85	FLYING TIGER-RETIRED	15000	45.00	50.00
85	PAW THAT REFRESHES, THE	15000	45.00	50.00
85	SANDY CLAWS	15000	45.00	50.00
*		**CERAMICA EXCELSIS**		
77	CHRIST KNOCKING AT THE DOOR	5000	60.00	60.00
77	MADONNA AND CHILD WITH ANGELS	5000	60.00	60.00
77	MADONNA WITH CHILD	5000	65.00	75.00
77	ST. FRANCIS	5000	60.00	60.00
77	WHAT HAPPENED TO YOUR HAND?	5000	60.00	60.00
78	ASSUMPTION MADONNA	5000	56.00	56.00
78	CHRIST ENTERING JERUSALEM	5000	96.00	96.00
78	CHRIST IN THE GARDEN OF GETHSEMANE	5000	40.00	60.00
78	FLIGHT INTO EGYPT	5000	59.00	90.00
78	GUARDIAN ANGEL WITH BOY	5000	69.00	69.00
78	GUARDIAN ANGEL WITH GIRL	5000	69.00	69.00
78	HOLY FAMILY AT WORK	5000	96.00	96.00
78	INFANT OF PRAGUE	5000	37.50	60.00
79	JESUS SPEAKS IN PARABLES	5000	90.00	90.00
79	MOSES	5000	77.00	77.00
79	NOAH	5000	77.00	77.00
80	DANIEL IN THE LION'S DEN	5000	80.00	80.00
80	DAVID	5000	77.00	77.00
80	WAY TO EMMAUS	5000	155.00	155.00
81	INNOCENCE	5000	95.00	100.00
81	JOURNEY TO BETHLEHEM	5000	89.00	89.00
81	SERMON ON THE MOUNT	5000	56.00	56.00
81	WAY OF THE CROSS	5000	59.00	59.00
83	GOOD SHEPHERD	5000	49.00	49.00
83	HOLY FAMILY	5000	72.00	72.00
83	JESUS WITH CHILDREN	5000	74.00	74.00
83	KNEELING SANTA	5000	95.00	100.00
83	ST. ANNE	5000	49.00	49.00
83	ST. FRANCIS	5000	59.50	60.00
E. WILLIAMS		**CLASSIC BRIDES OF THE CENTURY**		
89	1900-FLORA	5000	175.00	175.00
89	1910-ELIZABETH GRACE	5000	175.00	175.00
89	1920-MARY CLAIRE	5000	175.00	175.00
89	1930-KATHLEEN	5000	175.00	175.00
89	1940-MARGARET	5000	175.00	175.00
89	1950-BARBARA ANN	5000	175.00	175.00
89	1960-DIANNE	5000	175.00	175.00
89	1970-HEATHER	5000	175.00	175.00
89	1980-JENNIFER	5000	175.00	175.00
92	1990-STEPHANIE HELEN	5000	175.00	175.00
L. MARTIN		**DOLFI ORIGINAL-10 IN. STONEART**		
89	A SHOULDER TO LEARN ON	OP	400.00	400.00
89	BAREFOOT IN SPRING	OP	400.00	400.00
89	BIG CHIEF SITTING DOG	OP	325.00	325.00
89	BIRDLAND CAFE	OP	300.00	300.00
89	DRESS REHERSAL	OP	495.00	495.00
89	FLOWER CHILD	OP	300.00	300.00
89	FRIENDS & FLOWERS	OP	400.00	400.00
89	GARDEN SECRETS	OP	300.00	300.00
89	HAVE I BEEN THAT GOOD	OP	495.00	495.00
89	HOLIDAY HERALD	OP	300.00	300.00
89	LITTLE SANTA	OP	325.00	325.00
89	MARY & JOEY	OP	495.00	495.00
89	MERRY LITTLE LIGHT	OP	325.00	325.00

YR	NAME	LIMIT	ISSUE	TREND
89	MOTHER HEN	OP	300.00	300.00
89	MUD PUDDLES	OP	300.00	300.00
89	MY FAVORITE THINGS	OP	400.00	400.00
89	MY FIRST CAKE	OP	300.00	300.00
89	MY FIRST KITTEN	OP	300.00	300.00
89	PAMPERED PUPPIES	OP	300.00	300.00
89	PUPPY EXPRESS	OP	300.00	300.00
89	SING A SONG OF JOY	OP	400.00	400.00
89	SLEEPYHEAD	OP	300.00	300.00
89	STUDY BREAK	OP	325.00	325.00
89	WRAPPED IN LOVE	OP	300.00	300.00
L. MARTIN		**DOLFI ORIGINAL-10 IN. WOOD**		
89	A SHOULDER TO LEAN ON	2000	1000.00	1000.00
89	BAREFOOT IN SPRINGS	2000	1000.00	1000.00
89	BIG CHIEF SITTING DOG	2000	825.00	825.00
89	BIRDLAND CAFE	2000	750.00	750.00
89	DRESS REHEARSAL	2000	1250.00	1250.00
89	FLOWER CHILD	2000	750.00	750.00
89	FRIENDS & FLOWERS	2000	1000.00	1000.00
89	GARDEN SECRETS	2000	750.00	750.00
89	HAVE I BEEN THAT GOOD	2000	1250.00	1250.00
89	HOLIDAY HERALD	2000	750.00	750.00
89	LITTLE SANTA	2000	825.00	825.00
89	MARY & JOEY	2000	1250.00	1250.00
89	MERRY LITTLE LIGHT	2000	825.00	825.00
89	MOTHER HEN	2000	750.00	750.00
89	MUD PUDDLES	2000	750.00	750.00
89	MY FAVORITE THINGS	2000	1000.00	1000.00
89	MY FIRST CAKE	2000	750.00	750.00
89	MY FIRST KITTEN	2000	750.00	750.00
89	PAMPERED PUPPIES	2000	750.00	750.00
89	PUPPY EXPRESS	2000	750.00	750.00
89	SING A SONG OF JOY	2000	1000.00	1000.00
89	SLEEPYHEAD	2000	750.00	750.00
89	STUDY BREAK	2000	825.00	825.00
89	WRAPPED IN LOVE	2000	750.00	750.00
L. MARTIN		**DOLFI ORIGINAL-5 IN. WOOD**		
89	A SHOULDER TO LEAN ON	5000	300.00	300.00
89	BAREFOOT IN SPRING	5000	300.00	300.00
89	BIG CHIEF SITTING DOG	5000	250.00	250.00
89	BIRDLAND CAFE	5000	230.00	230.00
89	DRESS REHEARSAL	5000	375.00	375.00
89	FLOWER CHILD	5000	230.00	230.00
89	FRIENDS & FLOWERS	5000	300.00	300.00
89	GARDEN SECRETS	5000	230.00	230.00
89	HAVE I BEEN THAT GOOD	5000	375.00	375.00
89	HOLIDAY HERALD	5000	230.00	230.00
89	LITTLE SANTA	5000	250.00	250.00
89	MARY & JOEY	5000	375.00	375.00
89	MERRY LITTLE LIGHT	5000	250.00	250.00
89	MOTHER HEN	5000	230.00	230.00
89	MUD PUDDLES	5000	230.00	230.00
89	MY FAVORITE THINGS	5000	300.00	300.00
89	MY FIRST CAKE	5000	230.00	230.00
89	MY FIRST KITTEN	5000	230.00	230.00
89	PAMPERED PUPPIES	5000	230.00	230.00
89	PUPPY EXPRESS	5000	230.00	230.00
89	SING A SONG OF JOY	5000	300.00	300.00
89	SLEEPYHEAD	5000	230.00	230.00
89	STUDY BREAK	5000	250.00	250.00
89	WRAPPED IN LOVE	5000	230.00	230.00
L. MARTIN		**DOLFI ORIGINAL-7 IN. STONEART**		
89	A SHOULDER TO LEAN ON	OP	150.00	150.00
89	BAREFOOT IN SPRING	OP	150.00	150.00
89	BIG CHIEF SITTING DOG	OP	120.00	120.00
89	BIRDLAND CAFE	OP	110.00	110.00
89	DRESS REHEARSAL	OP	185.00	185.00
89	FLOWER CHILD	OP	110.00	110.00
89	FRIENDS & FLOWERS	OP	150.00	150.00
89	GARDEN SECRETS	OP	110.00	110.00
89	HAVE I BEEN THAT GOOD	OP	185.00	185.00
89	HOLIDAY HERALD	OP	110.00	110.00
89	LITTLE SANTA	OP	120.00	120.00
89	MARY & JOEY	OP	185.00	185.00
89	MERRY LITTLE LIGHT	OP	120.00	120.00
89	MOTHER HEN	OP	110.00	110.00
89	MUD PUDDLES	OP	110.00	110.00
89	MY FAVORITE THINGS	OP	150.00	150.00
89	MY FIRST CAKE	OP	110.00	110.00
89	MY FIRST KITTEN	OP	110.00	110.00
89	PAMPERED PUPPIES	OP	110.00	110.00
89	PUPPY EXPRESS	OP	110.00	110.00
89	SING A SONG OF JOY	OP	150.00	150.00
89	SLEEPYHEAD	OP	110.00	110.00
89	STUDY BREAK	OP	120.00	120.00
89	WRAPPED IN LOVE	OP	110.00	110.00
E. SIMONETTI		**FONTANINI COLLECTORS CLUB MEMBERS-ONLY FIGURINES**		
91	PILGRIMAGE, THE	YR	24.95	25.00

Even the jolly old elf needs a break. For Santa *is produced by United Design.*

Artist Lowell Davis has a way of putting a humorous twist on things. Bottoms Up *was created for Schmid.*

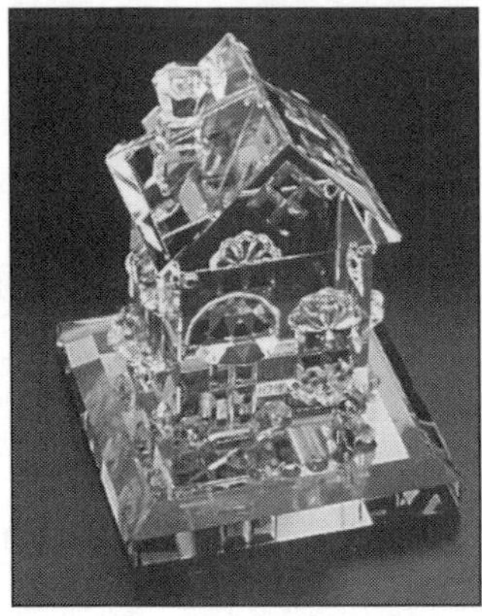

Garden Cottage *crystal figure captures all the hues of the rainbow. The piece is from Iris Arc Crystal.*

With Santa soaring high above, of course Christmas is in the Air. *The fabric maché figure is from Kurt S. Adler.*

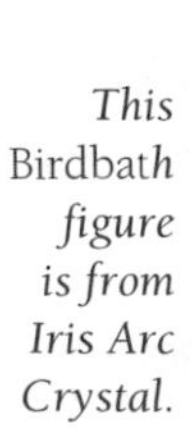

This Birdbath *figure is from Iris Arc Crystal.*

YR	NAME	LIMIT	ISSUE	TREND
92	SHE RESCUED ME	YR	23.50	25.00
E. SIMONETTI				**FONTANINI PRESEPIO COLLECTION**
92	ARIEL	TL	29.50	30.00
E. SIMONETTI				**FONTANINI, THE COLLECTIBLE CRECHE**
73	10CM., (15 PIECE SET)	OP	63.60	100.00
73	12CM., (15 PIECE SET)	OP	76.50	110.00
73	19CM., (15 PIECE SET)	OP	175.50	280.00
79	16CM., (15 PIECE SET)	OP	178.50	285.00
80	30CM., (15 PIECE SET)	OP	670.00	800.00
82	17CM., (15 PIECE SET)	OP	189.00	325.00
F. HOOK				**FRANCES HOOK'S FOUR SEASONS**
84	WINTER	12500	95.00	100.00
85	FALL	12500	95.00	100.00
85	SPRING	12500	95.00	100.00
85	SUMMER	12500	95.00	100.00
I. SPENCER				**HEARTBEATS**
86	MIRACLE	5000	145.00	150.00
87	STORYTIME	5000	145.00	150.00
F. HOOK				**HOOK**
82	SAILOR MATES	2000	290.00	325.00
82	SUN SHY	2000	290.00	325.00
86	CARPENTER BUST	YR	95.00	100.00
86	CARPENTER BUST-HEIRLOOM EDITION	YR	95.00	100.00
87	LITTLE CHILDREN, COME TO ME	15000	45.00	50.00
87	MADODNNA AND CHILD	15000	39.50	50.00
E. ROHN				**JAM SESSION**
85	BANJO PLAYER	7500	145.00	150.00
85	BASS PLAYER	7500	145.00	150.00
85	CLARINET PLAYER	7500	145.00	150.00
85	CORONET PLAYER	7500	145.00	150.00
85	DRUMMER	7500	145.00	150.00
85	TROMBONE PLAYER	7500	145.00	150.00
E. ROHN				**ROHN'S CLOWNS**
84	AUGUSTE	7500	95.00	100.00
84	HOBO	7500	95.00	100.00
84	WHITE FACE	7500	95.00	100.00
I. SPENCER				**SPENCER**
85	FLOWER PRINCESS	5000	195.00	200.00
85	MOON GODDESS	5000	195.00	200.00
G. DELLE NOTTI				**THE MASTERPIECE COLLECTION**
81	HOLY FAMILY, THE	5000	98.00	100.00
R. FERRUZZI				**THE MASTERPIECE COLLECTION**
82	MADONNA OF THE STREETS	5000	65.00	75.00
F. LIPPE				**THE MASTERPIECE COLLECTION**
79	ADORATION	5000	73.00	80.00
P. MIGNARD				**THE MASTERPIECE COLLECTION**
80	MADONNA WITH GRAPES	5000	85.00	90.00
A. TRIPI				**THE MUSEUM COLLECTION BY ANGELA TRIPI**
90	MENTOR, THE	1000	290.00	300.00
91	A GENTLEMAN'S GAME	1000	175.00	175.00
91	CADDIE, THE	1000	135.00	150.00
91	CHRISTOPHER COLUMBUS	1000	250.00	250.00
91	FIDDLER, THE	1000	175.00	175.00
91	ST. FRANCIS OF ASSISI	1000	175.00	175.00
91	TEE TIME AT ST. ANDREW'S	1000	175.00	175.00

RON LEE'S WORLD OF CLOWNS

YR	NAME	LIMIT	ISSUE	TREND
R. LEE				**THE ORIGINAL RON LEE COLLECTION**
76	ALLIGATOR BOWLING 504	CL	15.00	50.00
76	BEAR FISHING 512	CL	15.00	50.00
76	CLOWN AND DOG ACT 101	CL	48.00	125.00
76	CLOWN AND ELEPHANT ACT 107	CL	56.00	110.00
76	CLOWN TIGHTROPE WALKER 104	CL	50.00	125.00
76	DOG FISHING 512	CL	15.00	50.00
76	FROG SURFING 502	CL	15.00	50.00
76	HIPPO ON SCOOTER 505	CL	15.00	50.00
76	HOBO JOE HITCHHIKING 116	CL	55.00	65.00
76	HOBO JOE WITH BALLOONS 120	CL	66.00	90.00
76	HOBO JOE WITH PAL 115	CL	66.00	150.00
76	HOBO JOE WITH UMBRELLA 117	CL	58.00	110.00
76	KANGAROOS BOXING 508	CL	15.00	50.00
76	OWL WITH GUITAR 500	CL	15.00	50.00
76	PENGUIN ON SNOWSKIS 503	CL	15.00	50.00
76	PIG PLAYING VIOLIN 510	CL	15.00	50.00
76	PINKY LYING DOWN 112	CL	25.00	40.00
76	PINKY SITTING 119	CL	25.00	40.00
76	PINKY STANDING 118	CL	25.00	75.00
76	PINKY UPSIDE DOWN 111	CL	25.00	40.00
76	RABBIT PLAYING TENNIS 507	CL	15.00	50.00
76	TURTLE ON SKATEBOARD 501	CL	15.00	50.00
77	BEAR ON ROCK 523	CL	18.00	55.00
77	KOALA BEAR IN TREE 514	CL	15.00	50.00
77	KOALA BEAR ON LOG 516	CL	15.00	50.00
77	KOALA BEAR WITH BABY 515	CL	15.00	50.00
77	MONKEY WITH BANANA 521	CL	18.00	55.00
77	MOUSE AND CHEESE 520	CL	18.00	55.00
77	MR. PENGUIN 518	CL	18.00	60.00

YR	NAME	LIMIT	ISSUE	TREND
77	OWL GRADUATE 519	CL	22.00	60.00
77	PELICAN AND PYTHON 522	CL	18.00	55.00
78	BOBBI ON UNICYCLE 204	CL	45.00	80.00
78	BOW TIE 222	CL	67.50	150.00
78	BUTTERFLY AND FLOWER 529	CL	22.00	60.00
78	CLANCY, THE COP 210	CL	55.00	100.00
78	CLARA-BOW 205	CL	52.00	90.00
78	COCO-HANDS ON HIPS 218	CL	70.00	125.00
78	CORKY THE DRUMMER BOY 202	CL	53.00	110.00
78	CUDDLES 208	CL	37.00	75.00
78	DOLPHINS 525	CL	22.00	60.00
78	DRIVER THE GOLFER 211	CL	55.00	75.00
78	ELEPHANT ON BALL 214	CL	26.00	60.00
78	ELEPHANT ON STAND 213	CL	26.00	60.00
78	ELEPHANT SITTING 215	CL	26.00	60.00
78	FANCY PANTS 224	CL	55.00	110.00
78	FIREMAN WITH HOSE 216	CL	62.00	110.00
78	HEY RUBE 220	CL	35.00	75.00
78	HUMMINGBIRD 528	CL	22.00	60.00
78	JERI IN A BARREL 219	CL	75.00	145.00
78	JOCKO WITH LOLLIPOP 221	CL	67.50	150.00
78	OSCAR ON STILTS 223	CL	55.00	110.00
78	PIERROT PAINTING 207	CL	50.00	130.00
78	POLLY THE PARROT & CRACKERS 201	CL	63.00	135.00
78	POPPY WITH PUPPET 209	CL	60.00	100.00
78	PRINCE FROG 526	CL	22.00	60.00
78	SAD SACK 212	CL	48.00	150.00
78	SAILFISH 524	CL	18.00	75.00
78	SEA OTTER ON BACK 531	CL	22.00	60.00
78	SEA OTTER ON ROCK 532	CL	22.00	60.00
78	SEAGULL 527	CL	22.00	60.00
78	SKIPPY SWINGING 239	CL	52.00	75.00
78	SPARKY SKATING 206	CL	55.00	175.00
78	TINKER BOWING 203	CL	37.00	75.00
78	TOBI-HANDS OUTSTRETCHED 217	CL	70.00	225.00
78	TURTLE ON ROCK 530	CL	22.00	60.00
79	BUTTONS BICYCLING 229	CL	75.00	150.00
79	CAROUSEL HORSE 232	CL	119.00	165.00
79	DARBY TIPPING HAT 238	CL	35.00	100.00
79	DARBY WITH FLOWER 235	CL	35.00	100.00
79	DARBY WITH UMBRELLA 236	CL	35.00	100.00
79	DARBY WITH VIOLIN 237	CL	35.00	100.00
79	DOCTOR SAWBONES 228	CL	75.00	150.00
79	FEARLESS FRED IN CANNON 234	CL	80.00	200.00
79	HARRY AND THE HARE 233	CL	69.00	175.00
79	KELLY AT THE PIANO 241	CL	185.00	400.00
79	KELLY IN KAR 230	CL	164.00	300.00
79	KELLY'S KAR 231	CL	75.00	150.00
79	LILI 227	CL	75.00	145.00
79	TIMMY TOOTING 225	CL	35.00	65.00
79	TUBBY TUBA 226	CL	35.00	60.00
80	BANJO WILLIE 258	CL	68.00	150.00
80	CAROUSEL HORSE 248	CL	88.00	200.00
80	CAROUSEL HORSE 249	CL	88.00	200.00
80	CHUCKLES JUGGLING 244	CL	98.00	150.00
80	CUBBY HOLDING BALLOON 240	CL	50.00	70.00
80	DENNIS PLAYING TENNIS 252	CL	74.00	140.00
80	DOCTOR JAWBONES 260	CL	85.00	200.00
80	DONKEY WHAT? 243	CL	60.00	175.00
80	EMILE 257	CL	43.00	140.00
80	HAPPY WAVING 255	CL	43.00	140.00
80	HOBO JOE IN TUB 259	CL	96.00	125.00
80	JAQUE DOWNHILL RACER 253	CL	74.00	150.00
80	JINGLES TELLING TIME 242	CL	75.00	140.00
80	JO-JO AT MAKE-UP MIRROR 250	CL	86.00	150.00
80	MONKEY 251	CL	60.00	150.00
80	P.T. DINGHY 245	CL	65.00	135.00
80	PEANUTS PLAYING CONCERTINA 247	CL	65.00	225.00
80	RONI RIDING HORSE 246	CL	115.00	230.00
80	RUFORD 254	CL	43.00	140.00
80	ZACH 256	CL	43.00	140.00
81	AL AT THE BASS 284	CL	48.00	75.00
81	BOSOM BUDDIES 299	CL	135.00	150.00
81	BOZO ON UNICYCLE 279	CL	28.00	110.00
81	BOZO PLAYING CYMBOLS 277	CL	28.00	110.00
81	BOZO RIDING CAR 278	CL	28.00	110.00
81	CARNEY AND SEAL ACT 300	CL	63.00	100.00
81	CAROUSEL HORSE 280	CL	88.00	180.00
81	CAROUSEL HORSE 281	CL	88.00	175.00
81	EXECUTIVE HITCHHIKING 267	CL	23.00	80.00
81	EXECUTIVE READING 264	CL	23.00	80.00
81	EXECUTIVE RESTING 266	CL	23.00	80.00
81	EXECUTIVE WITH UMBRELLA 265	CL	23.00	80.00
81	HARPO 296	CL	120.00	270.00
81	HOBO JOE PRAYING 298	CL	57.00	75.00
81	KEVIN AT THE DRUMS 283	CL	50.00	125.00
81	LARRY AND HIS HOTDOGS 274	CL	76.00	150.00
81	LOUIE HITCHING A RIDE 269	CL	47.00	90.00
81	LOUIE ON PARK BENCH 268	CL	56.00	75.00

YR	NAME	LIMIT	ISSUE	TREND
81	LOUIE ON RAILROAD CAR 270	CL	77.00	140.00
81	MICKEY TIGHTROPE WALKER 292	CL	50.00	100.00
81	MICKEY UPSIDE DOWN 293	CL	50.00	100.00
81	MICKEY WITH UMBRELLA 291	CL	50.00	100.00
81	MY SON DARREN 295	CL	57.00	100.00
81	NICKY SITTING ON BALL 289	CL	39.00	65.00
81	NICKY STANDING ON BALL 290	CL	39.00	65.00
81	PERRY SITTING WITH BALLOON 287	CL	37.00	70.00
81	PERRY STANDING WITH BALLOON 288	CL	37.00	70.00
81	PICKLES AND POOCH 297	CL	90.00	190.00
81	PISTOL PETE 272	CL	76.00	150.00
81	ROCKETMAN 294	CL	77.00	140.00
81	RON AT THE PIANO 285	CL	46.00	75.00
81	RON LEE TRIO 282	CL	144.00	375.00
81	TIMOTHY IN BIG SHOE 286	CL	37.00	70.00
82	ALI ON HIS MAGIC CARPET 335	CL	105.00	180.00
82	BARNUM FEEDING BACON 315	CL	120.00	210.00
82	BEAVER PLAYING ACCORDIAN 807	CL	23.00	60.00
82	BENNY PULLING CAR 310	CL	190.00	300.00
82	BURRITO BANDITO 334	CL	150.00	225.00
82	BUSTER IN BARREL 308	CL	85.00	110.00
82	CAMEL 818	CL	57.00	125.00
82	CAPTAIN CRANBERRY 320	CL	115.00	165.00
82	CAPTAIN MIS-ADVENTURE 703	CL	250.00	400.00
82	CARNEY AND DOG ACT 301	CL	63.00	125.00
82	CHARLIE CHAPLAIN 701	CL	230.00	450.00
82	CHARLIE IN THE RAIN 321	CL	80.00	140.00
82	CHICO PLAYING GUITAR 336	CL	70.00	140.00
82	CLANCY, THE COP AND DOG 333	CL	115.00	190.00
82	CLARENCE, THE LAWYER 331	CL	100.00	170.00
82	DENNY EATING ICE CREAM 305	CL	39.00	110.00
82	DENNY HOLDING GIFT BOX 306	CL	39.00	110.00
82	DENNY JUGGLING BALL 307	CL	39.00	110.00
82	DOG PLAYING GUITAR 805	CL	23.00	60.00
82	DR. PAINLESS AND PATIENT 311	CL	195.00	310.00
82	FIREMAN WATERING HOUSE 303	CL	99.00	140.00
82	FISH WITH SHOE 803	CL	23.00	60.00
82	FOX IN AN AIRPLANE 806	CL	23.00	60.00
82	GEORGIE GOING ANYWHERE 302	CL	95.00	125.00
82	GIRAFFE 816	CL	57.00	125.00
82	HERBIE BALANCING HAT 327	CL	26.00	75.00
82	HERBIE DANCING 325	CL	26.00	75.00
82	HERBIE HANDS OUTSTRETCHED 326	CL	26.00	75.00
82	HERBIE LEGS IN AIR 329	CL	26.00	75.00
82	HERBIE LYING DOWN 328	CL	26.00	75.00
82	HERBIE TOUCHING GROUND 330	CL	26.00	75.00
82	HOBO JOE ON CYCLE 322	CL	125.00	225.00
82	HORSE 819	CL	57.00	125.00
82	KUKLA AND FRIEND 316	CL	100.00	175.00
82	LAUREL & HARDY 700	CL	225.00	400.00
82	LIMOUSINE SERVICE 705	CL	330.00	575.00
82	LION 817	CL	57.00	125.00
82	LITTLE HORSE-HEAD UP 341	CL	29.00	72.00
82	MARION WITH MARRIONETTE 317	CL	105.00	180.00
82	MURPHY ON UNICYCLE 337	CL	115.00	225.00
82	NAPPY SNOOZING 346	CL	110.00	170.00
82	NORMAN PAINTING DUMBO 314	CL	126.00	180.00
82	OSTRICH 813	CL	57.00	125.00
82	PARROT ROLLERSKATING 809	CL	23.00	60.00
82	PIG BRICK LAYER 800	CL	23.00	60.00
82	PINBALL PAL 332	CL	150.00	250.00
82	QUINCY LYING DOWN 304	CL	80.00	150.00
82	RABBIT WITH EGG 801	CL	23.00	60.00
82	REINDEER 812	CL	57.00	125.00
82	ROBIN RESTING 338	CL	110.00	170.00
82	RON LEE CAROUSEL	CL	10000.00	12500.00
82	ROOSTER 815	CL	57.00	125.00
82	ROOSTER WITH BARBELL 808	CL	23.00	60.00
82	SAMMY RIDING ELEPHANT 309	CL	90.00	140.00
82	SEAL BLOWING HIS HORNS 804	CL	23.00	60.00
82	SELF PORTRAIT 702	CL	355.00	700.00
82	SELF PORTRAIT 702	CL	1000.00	2000.00
82	SLIM CHARGING BULL 313	CL	195.00	350.00
82	SMOKEY, THE BEAR 802	CL	23.00	60.00
82	STEPPIN' OUT 704	CL	325.00	550.00
82	THREE MAN VALENTINOS 319	CL	55.00	90.00
82	TIGER 814	CL	57.00	125.00
82	TOO LOOSE-L'ARTISTE 312	CL	150.00	230.00
82	TOU TOU 323	CL	70.00	140.00
82	TOY SOLDIER 324	CL	95.00	200.00
82	TURTLE WITH GUN 811	CL	57.00	125.00
82	TWO MAN VALENTINOS 318	CL	45.00	90.00
82	WALRUS WITH UMBRELLA 810	CL	23.00	60.00
83	BANDWAGON, THE 707	CL	900.00	1800.00
83	BEETHOVEN'S FOURTH PAWS 358	CL	59.00	80.00
83	BLACK CAROUSEL HORSE 1001	CL	450.00	640.00
83	BUMBLES SELLING BALLOONS 353	CL	80.00	140.00
83	BUSTER AND HIS BALLOONS 363	CL	47.00	60.00
83	CAPTAIN FREDDY 375	CL	85.00	310.00

YR	NAME	LIMIT	ISSUE	TREND
83	CASEY CRUSING 351	CL	57.00	80.00
83	CATCH THE BRASS RING 708	CL	510.00	1250.00
83	CECIL AND SAUSAGE 354	CL	90.00	150.00
83	CHEF'S CUISINE 361	CL	57.00	80.00
83	CHESTNUT CAROUSEL HORSE 1002	CL	450.00	640.00
83	CIMBA THE ELEPHANT 706	CL	225.00	375.00
83	CLYDE JUGGLING 339	CL	39.00	45.00
83	CLYDE UPSIDE DOWN 340	CL	39.00	45.00
83	COCO AND HIS COMPACT 369	CL	55.00	100.00
83	COTTON CANDY 377	CL	150.00	245.00
83	DARING DUDLEY 367	CL	65.00	125.00
83	DOOR TO DOOR DABNEY 373	CL	100.00	175.00
83	ENGINEER BILLIE 356	CL	190.00	350.00
83	FLIPPER DIVING 345	CL	115.00	175.00
83	GAZEBO 1004	CL	450.00	640.00
83	GILBERT TEE'D OFF 376	CL	60.00	95.00
83	HOBI IN HIS HAMMOCK 344	CL	85.00	140.00
83	I LOVE YOU FROM MY HEART 360	CL	35.00	50.00
83	JOGGER, THE- 372	CL	75.00	95.00
83	JOSEPHINE 370	CL	55.00	100.00
83	KNICKERS BALANCING FEATHER 366	CL	47.00	75.00
83	LAST SCOOP, THE- 379	CL	175.00	275.00
83	LAST SCOOP, THE- 379	CL	175.00	275.00
83	LAST SCOOP, THE900	CL	325.00	325.00
83	LITTLE HORSE-HEAD DOWN 342	CL	29.00	72.00
83	LITTLE SATURDAY NIGHT 348	CL	53.00	80.00
83	LOU PROPOSING 365	CL	57.00	70.00
83	MATINEE JITTERS 378	CL	175.00	200.00
83	MATINEE JITTERS 901	CL	325.00	400.00
83	MY DAUGHTER DEBORAH 357	CL	63.00	90.00
83	NO CAMPING OR FISHING 902	CL	325.00	375.00
83	ON THE ROAD AGAIN 355	CL	220.00	400.00
83	RICHES TO RAGS 374	CL	55.00	175.00
83	RIDE 'EM RONI 347	CL	125.00	175.00
83	RUFUS AND HIS REFUSE 343	CL	65.00	160.00
83	SAY IT WITH FLOWERS 359	CL	35.00	70.00
83	SINGIN' IN THE RAIN 362	CL	105.00	180.00
83	TATTERS AND BALLOONS 352	CL	65.00	75.00
83	TEETER TOTTIE SCOTTIE 350	CL	55.00	85.00
83	TOTTIE SCOTTIE 349	CL	39.00	60.00
83	UP, UP AND AWAY 364	CL	50.00	80.00
83	WHITE CAROUSEL HORSE 1003	CL	450.00	640.00
83	WILT THE STILT 368	CL	49.00	75.00
84	A BOZO LUNCH 390	CL	148.00	225.00
84	BAGGY PANTS 387	CL	98.00	180.00
84	BLACK CIRCUS HORSE 711A	CL	305.00	440.00
84	CHESTNUT CIRCUS HORSE 710A	CL	305.00	440.00
84	GIVE A DOG A BONE 383	CL	95.00	140.00
84	JUST FOR YOU 386	CL	110.00	225.00
84	LOOK AT THE BIRDY 388	CL	138.00	200.00
84	MY FELLOW AMERICAN 391	CL	138.00	275.00
84	NO CAMPING OR FISHING 380	CL	175.00	318.00
84	NO LOITERING 392	CL	113.00	160.00
84	PEPPERMINTS, THE- 384	CL	150.00	210.00
84	RUDY HOLDING BALLOONS 713	CL	230.00	230.00
84	RUDY HOLDING BALLOONS 713	CL	230.00	350.00
84	SATURDAY NIGHT 714	CL	250.00	500.00
84	T.K. AND OH!! 385	CL	85.00	150.00
84	TISKET AND TASKET 393	CL	93.00	190.00
84	WHEELER SHEILA 381	CL	75.00	140.00
84	WHITE CIRCUS HORSE 709	CL	305.00	440.00
85	CLOWNS OF THE CARIBBEAN PS101	CL	1250.00	2000.00
85	GIRAFFE GETTING A BATH 428	CL	160.00	340.00
85	WHISKERS BATHING 749	CL	305.00	305.00
85	WHISKERS HITCHHIKING 745	CL	240.00	750.00
85	WHISKERS HOLDING BALLOON 746	CL	265.00	600.00
85	WHISKERS HOLDING UMBRELLA 747	CL	265.00	600.00
85	WHISKERS ON THE BEACH 750	CL	230.00	650.00
85	WHISKERS SWEEPING 744	CL	240.00	875.00
86	BATHING BUDDIES 450	CL	145.00	200.00
86	CAPTAIN CRANBERRY 469	CL	140.00	165.00
86	GETTING EVEN 485	CL	85.00	110.00
86	HARI AND HARE 454	CL	57.00	75.00
86	RIDE 'EM PEANUTS 463	CL	55.00	68.00
86	WET PAINT 436	CL	80.00	125.00
87	FIRST & MAIN L110	CL	368.00	525.00
87	HEARTBROKEN HARRY L101	CL	63.00	125.00
87	LOVABLE LUKE L102	8500	70.00	70.00
87	PUPPY LOVE L103	8500	71.00	145.00
87	SUGARLAND EXPRESS L109	CL	342.00	375.00
87	WOULD YOU LIKE TO RIDE? L104	CL	246.00	325.00
88	FIFTH WHEEL, THE L117	CL	250.00	295.00
88	NEW RON LEE CAROUSEL	CL	7000.00	9500.00
88	TO THE RESCUE L127	CL	130.00	350.00
88	TUNNEL OF LOVE L123	CL	490.00	550.00
88	WHEN YOU'RE HOT, YOU'RE HOT! L128	CL	221.00	525.00
89	BE IT EVER SO HUMBLE L111	CL	900.00	1100.00
89	CATCH A FALLING STAR L148	CL	57.00	57.00
89	CIRCUS LITTLE L143	CL	990.00	1265.00

YR	NAME	LIMIT	ISSUE	TREND
89	FIREMAN, THE L169	CL	68.00	85.00
89	FISHERMAN, THE - L194	7500	72.00	72.00
89	GOLFER, THE- L188	CL	72.00	90.00
89	GREATEST LITTLE SHOE ON EARTH, THE- L210	CL	165.00	210.00
89	HUGHIE MUNGUS L144	CL	250.00	325.00
89	I PLEDGE ALLEGIANCE L134	3750	131.00	131.00
89	IF I WERE A RICH MAN L133	CL	315.00	425.00
89	IN OVER MY HEAD L135	CL	95.00	125.00
89	LAWYER, THE- L171	CL	68.00	75.00
89	O' SOLO MIA L139	CL	85.00	150.00
89	POLICEMAN, THE- L165	CL	68.00	80.00
89	SH-H-H-H! L146	CL	210.00	700.00
89	SNOWDRIFTER L163	CL	230.00	350.00
89	TEE FOR TWO L141	CL	125.00	150.00
89	TODAY'S CATCH L147	CL	230.00	300.00
89	WISHFUL THINKING L114	CL	230.00	375.00
90	BIG WHEEL, THE L236	2750	240.00	240.00
90	CANDY MAN L217	2750	350.00	350.00
90	FILL'ER UP L248	2250	280.00	280.00
90	HEARTBROKEN HOBO L233	CL	116.00	145.00
90	HENRY 8-3/4 L260	2750	37.00	37.00
90	HORSIN' AROUND L262	2750	37.00	37.00
90	KISS! KISS! L251	2750	37.00	37.00
90	ME TOO! L231	3500	70.00	70.00
90	NA! NA! L252	2750	33.00	33.00
90	NEW SELF PORTRAIT, THE- L218	CL	800.00	950.00
90	PUSH AND PULL L249	2250	260.00	260.00
90	SCOOTER L234	2750	240.00	240.00
90	SNOWDRIFTER II L250	1250	340.00	340.00
90	TANDEM MANIA L235	2750	360.00	360.00
90	UNI-CYCLE L237	2750	240.00	240.00
91	ANYWHERE? L269	1500	125.00	125.00
91	BUSINESS IS BUSINESS L266	1500	110.00	110.00
91	CRUISING L265	1500	170.00	170.00
91	FALL L282	1500	120.00	120.00
91	GILBERT'S DILEMMA L270	1750	90.00	90.00
91	GIVE ME LIBERTY L313	1776	155.00	155.00
91	HAPPY BIRTHDAY PUPPY LOVE L278	1750	73.00	73.00
91	I'M SINGIN' IN THE RAIN L208	1500	135.00	135.00
91	LIT'L SNOWDRIFTER L298	1750	70.00	70.00
91	OUR NATION'S PRIDE L312	1776	150.00	150.00
91	PUPPY LOVE SCOOTIN' L275	1750	73.00	73.00
91	PUPPY LOVE'S FREE RIDE L276	1750	73.00	73.00
91	PUPPY LOVE'S TREAT L277	1750	73.00	73.00
91	SPRING L280	1500	95.00	95.00
91	SUMMER L281	1500	95.00	95.00
91	TA DA! L294	1500	120.00	120.00
91	UNITED WE STAND L314	1776	150.00	150.00
91	WINTER L279	1500	115.00	115.00
R. LEE		**THE RON LEE COLLECTOR'S CLUB RENEWAL SCULPTURES**		
87	DOGGIN' ALONG CC1	YR	75.00	120.00
88	MIDSUMMER'S DREAM CC2	YR	97.00	145.00
89	PEEK-A-BOO CHARLIE CC3	YR	65.00	95.00
R. LEE		**THE RON LEE LOONEY TUNE COLLECTION**		
91	1940 BUG BUNNY LT165	2750	85.00	85.00
91	BUGS BUNNY LT150	2750	123.00	123.00
91	DAFFY DUCK LT140	2750	80.00	85.00
91	ELMER FUDD LT125	2750	87.00	90.00
91	FOGHORN LEGHORN & HENRY HAWK LT160	2750	115.00	115.00
91	MARVIN THE MARTIAN LT170	2750	75.00	75.00
91	MICHIGAN J. FROG LT110	2750	115.00	115.00
91	MT. YOSEMITE LT180	850	160.00	225.00
91	PEPE LEPEW & PENELOPE LT145	2750	115.00	115.00
91	PORKY PIG LT115	2750	97.00	100.00
91	SYLVESTER & TWEETY LT135	2750	110.00	115.00
91	TASMANIAN DEVIL LT120	2750	105.00	105.00
91	TWEETY LT155	2750	110.00	115.00
91	WESTERN DAFFY DUCK LT105	2750	87.00	90.00
91	WILE E. COYOTE & ROADRUNNER LT175	2750	165.00	175.00
91	YOSEMITE SAM LT130	2750	110.00	110.00

ROYAL DOULTON

YR	NAME	LIMIT	ISSUE	TREND
N. PEDLEY		**AGE OF INNOCENCE**		
91	FEEDING TIME	9500	245.00	245.00
91	MAKING FRIENDS	9500	270.00	270.00
91	PUPPY LOVE	9500	270.00	270.00
M. ABBERLEY		**ANTAGONISTS CHARACTER JUGS**		
86	GEORGE III & GEORGE WASHINGTON	9500	195.00	195.00
M. ALCOCK		**BEATRIX POTTER**		
93	BENJAMIN BUNNY	OP	65.00	65.00
93	JEMIMA PUDDLEDUCK	OP	65.00	65.00
93	JEREMY FISHER	OP	65.00	65.00
93	MRS. RABBIT	OP	65.00	65.00
93	PETER RABBIT	OP	65.00	65.00
93	TOM KITTEN	OP	65.00	65.00
95	PETER IN BED	OP	39.95	40.00
A. HUGHES		**BEATRIX POTTER**		
95	FOXY WHISKERED GENTLEMAN	OP	65.00	65.00

YR	NAME	LIMIT	ISSUE	TREND
	W. PLATT			**BEATRIX POTTER**
95	TAILOR OF GLOUCESTER	O	65.00	65.00
	W. PLATT			**BRAMBLY HEDGE FIGURES**
93	MR. SALTAPPLE	OP	40.00	40.00
93	MRS. SALTAPPLE	OP	40.00	40.00
	V. ANNAND			**BRITISH SPORTING HERITAGE**
93	HENLEY	5000	475.00	475.00
94	ASCOT	5000	450.00	450.00
95	WIMBLEDON	5000	475.00	475.00
	M. ALCOCK			**CHARACTER JUG OF THE YEAR**
94	CAPTAIN HOOK	OP	235.00	235.00
	S. TAYLOR			**CHARACTER JUG OF THE YEAR**
93	VICE-ADMIRAL LORD NELSON	OP	225.00	225.00
95	CAPTAIN BLIGH	OP	200.00	200.00
	*			**CHARACTER JUGS**
91	FORTUNE TELLER	YR	130.00	130.00
91	SANTA CLAUS MINIATURE	5000	50.00	50.00
92	WINSTON CHURCHILL	YR	195.00	195.00
	W. HARPER			**CHARACTER JUGS**
91	HENRY VIII	1991	395.00	395.00
	D. BIGGS			**CHARACTER SCULPTURES**
95	GULLIVER	OP	285.00	285.00
	A. MASLANKOWSKI			**CHARACTER SCULPTURES**
93	LONG JOHN SILVER	OP	250.00	250.00
93	ROBINHOOD	OP	250.00	250.00
94	PIED PIPER	OP	260.00	260.00
94	WIZARD	OP	340.00	340.00
	R. TABBENOR			**CHARACTER SCULPTURES**
93	CAPTAIN HOOK	OP	250.00	250.00
93	DICK TURPIN	OP	250.00	250.00
94	D'ARTAGNAN	OP	260.00	260.00
	P. GEE			**CHARACTER STUDIES**
94	PIPER, THE	OP	295.00	295.00
	P. PARSONS			**CHARACTER STUDIES**
94	GRANDPA'S STORY	OP	275.00	275.00
94	WHEN I WAS YOUNG	OP	275.00	275.00
95	RICHARD THE LIONHEART	OP	500.00	500.00
	R. TABBENOR			**CHARACTER STUDIES**
93	FATHER CHRISTMAS	OP	195.00	195.00
	A. MASLANKOWSKI			**CHILD FIGURES**
93	BALLET SHOES	OP	73.50	74.00
93	DADDY'S GIRL	OP	75.00	75.00
	P. PARSONS			**CHILD FIGURES**
94	FLOWERS FOR MOTHER	OP	98.00	98.00
	N. PEDLEY			**CHILD FIGURES**
93	ALMOST GROWN	OP	65.00	65.00
93	BEST WISHES	OP	165.00	165.00
93	BIRTHDAY GIRL	OP	130.00	130.00
93	FLOWERGIRL	OP	99.00	99.00
93	MY FIRST FIGURINE	OP	110.00	110.00
94	A POSY FOR YOU	OP	98.00	98.00
94	FIRST RECITAL	OP	98.00	98.00
94	HELLO DADDY	OP	125.00	125.00
94	MOTHER'S HELPER	OP	98.00	98.00
94	SPECIAL FRIEND	OP	98.00	98.00
94	YOUNG MELODY	OP	98.00	98.00
95	HOMETIME	OP	135.00	135.00
95	SPECIAL TREAT	OP	135.00	135.00
95	WHAT'S THAT MATTER	OP	135.00	135.00
	M. ALCOCK			**CHRISTMAS MINI JUGS**
94	SNOWMAN MINI	2500	62.00	62.00
	W. HARPER			**CHRISTMAS MINI JUGS**
93	ELE MINI	2500	55.00	55.00
	M. DAVIES			**DANCERS OF THE WORLD**
77	DANCERS, FLAMENCO	750	400.00	1300.00
77	DANCERS, INDIAN TEMPLE	750	400.00	1300.00
78	DANCERS, PHILIPPINE	750	450.00	675.00
78	DANCERS, SCOTTISH	750	450.00	1050.00
79	DANCERS, KURDISH	750	550.00	550.00
79	DANCERS, MEXICAN	750	550.00	550.00
80	DANCERS, CHINESE	750	750.00	625.00
80	DANCERS, NORTH AMERICAN INDIAN	750	950.00	575.00
80	DANCERS, POLISH	750	750.00	675.00
81	DANCERS, BRETON	750	850.00	575.00
81	DANCERS, WEST INDIAN	750	850.00	625.00
82	DANCERS, BALINESE	750	950.00	575.00
	M. DAVIES			**FEMMES FATALES**
79	CLEOPATRA	750	750.00	1300.00
81	HELEN OF TROY	750	1250.00	1100.00
82	QUEEN OF SHEBA	750	1250.00	1100.00
83	TZ'U-HSI	750	1250.00	1100.00
84	EVE	750	1250.00	1100.00
85	LUCREZIA BORGIA	750	1250.00	1300.00
	V. ANNAND			**FIGURE OF THE YEAR**
93	PATRICIA	RT	250.00	275.00

YR	NAME	LIMIT	ISSUE	TREND
	P. GEE		**FIGURE OF THE YEAR**	
91	AMY	YR	245.00	245.00
92	MARY	YR	225.00	225.00
94	JENNIFER	OP	250.00	260.00
	N. PEDLEY		**FIGURE OF THE YEAR**	
95	DEBORAH	OP	225.00	225.00
	V. ANNAND		**FLOWERS OF LOVE**	
95	CAMELLIAS	OP	325.00	325.00
95	FORGET ME NOTS	OP	325.00	325.00
	V. ANNAND		**FOUR SEASONS**	
93	SPRINGTIME	OP	325.00	325.00
94	AUTUMNTIME	OP	325.00	325.00
94	SUMMERTIME	OP	325.00	325.00
95	WINTERTIME	OP	325.00	325.00
	P. GEE		**GAINSBOROUGH LADIES**	
*	MARY, COUNTESS HOWE	5000	650.00	650.00
91	COUNTESS OF SEFTON	5000	650.00	650.00
91	HON FRANCES DUNCOMBE	5000	650.00	650.00
91	LADY SHEFFIELD	5000	650.00	650.00
*			**GENTLE ARTS**	
*	ADORNMENT	750	1350.00	1350.00
*	FLOWER ARRANGING	750	1350.00	1350.00
	M. DAVIES		**GENTLE ARTS**	
84	SPINNING	750	1250.00	1400.00
	P. PARSONS		**GENTLE ARTS**	
85	TAPESTRY WEAVING	750	1250.00	1250.00
86	WRITING	750	1350.00	1350.00
87	PAINTING	750	1350.00	1350.00
	R. JEFFERSON		**GREAT LOVERS**	
93	ROMEO & JULIET	150	5250.00	5250.00
94	ROBINHOOD & MAID MARIAN	150	5250.00	5250.00
	V. ANNAND		**HN FIGURES**	
94	ANNIVERSARY	OP	575.00	575.00
	P. GEE		**IMAGES**	
93	GIFT OF FREEEDOM	OP	85.00	85.00
	A. HUGHES		**IMAGES**	
93	BROTHER & SISTER	OP	50.00	50.00
	P. PARSONS		**IMAGES**	
93	OUR FIRST CHRISTMAS	OP	475.00	175.00
	A. HUGHES		**IMAGES OF NATURE**	
93	ALWAYS AND FOREVER	OP	55.00	55.00
	A. MASLANKOWSKI		**IMAGES OF NATURE**	
94	NEW ARRIVAL	OP	50.00	50.00
	M. DAVIES		**LADY MUSICIANS**	
70	CELLO	750	250.00	1100.00
71	VIRGINALS	750	250.00	1250.00
72	LUTE	750	250.00	800.00
72	VIOLIN	750	250.00	1000.00
73	FLUTE	750	250.00	900.00
73	HARP	750	275.00	1300.00
74	CHITARRONE	750	250.00	625.00
74	CYMBALS	750	325.00	600.00
75	DULCIMER	750	375.00	575.00
75	HURDY GURDY	750	375.00	550.00
76	FRENCH HORN	750	400.00	500.00
76	VIOLA D'AMORE	750	400.00	500.00
	D. BIGGS		**LARGE SIZE JUGS**	
95	ALFRED HITCHCOCK	OP	200.00	200.00
	W. HARPER		**LARGE SIZE JUGS**	
94	GLENN MILLER	OP	270.00	270.00
	R. JEFFERSON		**LES SAISONS**	
*	L'ETE	300	850.00	895.00
*	L'HIVER	300	850.00	795.00
86	AUTOMNE	300	850.00	875.00-1000.00
87	PRINTEMPS	300	850.00	825.00
	A. MASLANKOWSKI		**LIMITED EDITION FIGURES**	
93	WINSTON S. CHURCHILL	5000	595.00	595.00
	R. TABBENOR		**LIMITED EDITION FIGURES**	
93	ROBERT E. LEE	5000	1175.00	1175.00
93	ULYSSES S. GRANT	5000	1175.00	1175.00
94	FIELD MARSHAL MONTGOMERY	1994	1100.00	1100.00
	D. BIGGS		**LIMITED EDITION JUGS**	
94	ALADDIN'S GENIE	1500	335.00	335.00
	W. HARPER		**LIMITED EDITION JUGS**	
93	WILLIAM SHAKESPHERE	2500	625.00	625.00
94	OLIVER CROMWELL	2500	475.00	475.00
95	CHARLES DICKENS	2500	500.00	500.00
	*** NOKE/FENTON**		**LIMITED EDITION JUGS**	
94	DIAMOND ANNIVERSARY TINIES	2500	325.00	325.00
	S. TAYLOR		**LIMITED EDITION JUGS**	
93	NAPOLEON	2000	225.00	225.00
	W. HARPER		**LIMITED EDITION TOBY JUGS**	
93	FATHER CHRISTMAS TOBY	3500	125.00	125.00
	S. TAYLOR		**LIMITED EDITION TOBY JUGS**	
93	CLOWN TOBY	3000	175.00	175.00

YR	NAME	LIMIT	ISSUE	TREND
94	KING & QUEEN OF DIAMONDS TOBY	2500	260.00	260.00
94	LEPRECHAUN TOBY	2500	150.00	150.00
95	JUDGE AND THIEF TOBY	OP	185.00	185.00
P. GEE				**MINIATURES**
93	TOP O' THE HILL	OP	120.00	120.00
N. PEDLEY				**MINIATURES**
94	HANNAH	OP	142.00	142.00
R. JEFFERSON				**MYTHS & MAIDENS**
82	LADY & UNICORN	300	2500.00	3000.00
83	LEDA & SWAN	300	2500.00	2950.00
84	JUNO & PEACOCK	300	2500.00	2950.00
85	EUROPA & BULL	300	2500.00	2950.00
86	DIANA THE HUNTRESS	300	2500.00	2950.00
A MASLANKOWSKI				**NATIVITY**
93	HOLY FAMILY (JESUS, MARY & JOSEPH)	RT	250.00	275.00
S. TAYLOR				**PRESIDENTIAL SERIES**
93	ABRAHAM LINCOLN	25000	190.00	190.00
94	THOMAS JEFFERSON	2500	200.00	200.00
95	GEORGE WASHINGTON	2500	200.00	200.00
*				**PRESTIGE FIGURES**
91	COLUMBINE	*	1250.00	1250.00
91	FIGHTER ELEPHANT	*	2500.00	2500.00
91	FOX	*	1550.00	1550.00
91	HARLEQUIN	*	1250.00	1250.00
91	JACK POINT	*	2900.00	2900.00
91	KING CHARLES	*	2500.00	2500.00
91	LEOPARD ON ROCK	*	3000.00	3000.00
91	LION ON ROCK	*	3000.00	3000.00
91	MATADOR AND BULL	*	21500.00	21500.00
91	MOOR, THE	*	2500.00	2500.00
91	PRINCESS BADOURA	*	28000.00	28000.00
91	ST. GEORGE AND DRAGON	*	13600.00	13600.00
91	TIGER	*	1950.00	1950.00
91	TIGER ON ROCK	*	3000.00	3000.00
A. MASLANKOWSKI				**PRESTIGE FIGURES**
93	DUKE OF WELLINGTON	1500	1750.00	1750.00
93	VICE-ADMIRAL LORD NELSON	950	1750.00	1750.00
95	CHARGE OF THE LIGHT BRIDGADE	SP	16000.00	16,000.00
P. GEE				**PRETTY LADIES**
93	AMY'S SITER	OP	225.00	225.00
N. PEDLEY				**PRETTY LADIES**
93	HELEN	OP	225.00	225.00
93	JOANNE	OP	185.00	185.00
93	NICOLE	OP	155.00	155.00
94	HOLLY	OP	195.00	195.00
95	GEMMA	OP	195.00	195.00
95	HANNAH	OP	250.00	250.00
95	HAPPY BIRTHDAY	OP	250.00	250.00
D. TOTTLE				**PRETTY LADIES**
94	ALEXANDRA	OP	250.00	250.00
*				**QUEENS OF REALM**
*	MARY, QUEEN OF SCOTS	SO	550.00	750.00
*	QUEEN ANNE	5000	525.00	550.00
P. PARSONS				**QUEENS OF REALM**
*	QUEEN ELIZABETH I	SO	495.00	550.00
*	QUEEN VICTORIA	SO	495.00	950.00
P. GEE				**REYNOLDS COLLECTION**
91	LADY WORSLEY HN3318	5000	550.00	575.00
P. GEE				**REYNOLDS LADIES**
93	COUNTLESS SPENCER	5000	595.00	595.00
*				**ROYAL DOULTON COLLECTORS' CLUB**
80	JOHN DOULTON JUG (8 O'CLOCK)	YR	70.00	125.00
81	SLEEPY DARLING FIGURE	YR	100.00	195.00
82	DOG OF FO	YR	50.00	150.00
82	PRIZED POSSESSIONS FIGURE	YR	125.00	475.00
83	LOVING CUP	YR	75.00	275.00
83	SPRINGTIME	YR	125.00	350.00
84	PRIDE & JOY FIGURE	YR	125.00	225.00
84	SIR HENRY DOULTON JUG	YR	50.00	125.00
85	TOP OF THE HILL PLATE	YR	34.95	75.00
85	WINTERTIME FIGURE	YR	125.00	195.00
86	ALBERT SAGGER TOBY JUG	YR	34.95	70.00
86	AUCTIONEER FIGURE	YR	150.00	195.00
87	COLLECTOR BUNNYKINS	YR	40.00	295.00
87	SUMMERTIME FIGURE	YR	140.00	150.00
88	BEEFEATER TINY JUG	YR	25.00	125.00
88	OLD SALT TEA POT	YR	135.00	250.00
88	TOP OF THE HILL MINIATURE FIGURINE	YR	95.00	125.00
M. DAVIES				**ROYAL DOULTON FIGURINES**
67	INDIAN BRAVE	500	2500.00	7000.00
71	PALIO, THE	500	2500.00	6550.00
R. GARBE				**ROYAL DOULTON FIGURINES**
33	BEETHOVEN	25	*	6250.00
M. DAVIES				**ROYALTY**
73	QUEEN ELIZABETH II	750	200.00	1900.00
80	QUEEN MOTHER	1500	650.00	1300.00

YR	NAME	LIMIT	ISSUE	TREND
81	DUKE OF EDINBURGH	750	395.00	400.00
E. GRIFFITHS				**ROYALTY**
82	LADY DIANA SPENCER HN2885	1500	395.00	800.00
82	PRINCE OF WALES HN2883	1500	395.00	525.00
82	PRINCE OF WALES HN2884	1500	750.00	800.00
82	PRINCESS OF WALES HN2887	1500	750.00	1000.00
86	DUCHESS OF YORK	1500	495.00	500.00
*				**SEASONAL FIGURES**
94	CHRISTMAS SURPRISE BUNNYKINS	OP	50.00	50.00
M. ALCOCK				**SEASONAL FIGURES**
93	HALLOWEEN BUNNYKINS	OP	50.00	50.00
W. PLATT				**SEASONAL FIGURES**
95	EASTER GREETINGS BUNNYKINS	OP	50.00	50.00
A. MASLANKOWSKI				**SENTIMENTS**
93	CHRISTMAS DAY	OP	65.00	65.00
94	CHRISTMAS PARCELS	OP	60.00	60.00
S. KEENAN				**SHIP FIGUREHEADS**
*	AJAX	950	*	550.00
*	BENMORE	950	*	550.00
*	CHIEFTAIN	950	*	650.00
*	HIBERNIA	950	*	850.00
*	LALLA ROOKH	950	*	750.00
*	LORD NELSON	950	*	750.00
*	MARY, QUEEN OF SCOTS	950	*	1200.00
*	POCAHONTAS	950	*	950.00
W. HARPER				**SMALL SIZE JUGS**
93	SHAKESPHERE	OP	95.00	95.00
S. TAYLOR				**SMALL SIZE JUGS**
93	WINSTON CHURCHILL	OP	99.00	99.00
E. GRIFFITHS				**SOLDIERS OF THE REVOLUTION**
75	SOLDIERS, CONNECTICUT	350	750.00	800.00
75	SOLDIERS, DELAWARE	350	750.00	800.00
75	SOLDIERS, GEORGIA	350	750.00	875.00
75	SOLDIERS, MARYLAND	350	750.00	800.00
75	SOLDIERS, MASSACHUSETTS	350	750.00	800.00
75	SOLDIERS, NEW HAMPSHIRE	350	750.00	825.00
75	SOLDIERS, NEW JERSEY	350	750.00	1500.00
75	SOLDIERS, NEW YORK	350	750.00	800.00
75	SOLDIERS, NORTH CAROLINA	350	750.00	800.00
75	SOLDIERS, PENNSYLVANIA	350	750.00	800.00
75	SOLDIERS, RHODE ISLAND	350	750.00	800.00
75	SOLDIERS, SOUTH CAROLINA	350	750.00	800.00
75	SOLDIERS, VIRGINIA	350	1500.00	2800.00
L. ISPANKY				**SOLDIERS OF THE REVOLUTION**
77	SOLDIERS, WASHINGTON	750	*	2250.00
M. ABBERLEY				**STAR CROSSED LOVERS CHARACTER JUGS**
*	ANTHONY & CLEOPATRA	SO	195.00	195.00
86	NAPOLEON & JOSEPHINE	9500	195.00	195.00
S. TAYLOR				**STAR CROSSED LOVERS CHARACTER JUGS**
88	SAMSON & DELILAH	9500	195.00	195.00
89	KING ARTHUR & GUINEVERE	9500	195.00	195.00
N. PEDLEY				**VANITY FAIR**
93	DAWN	OP	125.00	125.00
93	GIFT OF LOVE	OP	125.00	125.00
94	GOOD COMPANION	OP	185.00	185.00
94	LINDSAY	OP	142.00	142.00
95	TAKE ME HOME	OP	195.00	195.00
T. POTTS				**VANITY FAIR**
93	MARIA	OP	125.00	125.00

ROYAL WORCESTER

Price ranges may reflect various demands in the market from one geographic region to another; condition of piece; specific markings found on piece; and/or changes in production of piece.

YR	NAME	LIMIT	ISSUE	TREND
*				**200TH ANNIVERSARY COLLECTION**
89	AUGUSTA VASE	200	4500.00	4500.00
89	CHAMBERLAIN CROCUS POT	200	4000.00	4000.00
89	CLARENCE VASE	200	1500.00	1500.00
89	ELIZABETH VASE	200	1500.00	1500.00
89	FLIGHT BOWL	200	1200.00	1200.00
89	GLOUCESTER ICE PAIL	200	4000.00	4000.00
89	HANCOCK VASE	200	2500.00	2500.00
89	KING GEORGE III VASE	200	4000.00	4000.00
89	QUEEN CHARLOTTE VASE	200	4000.00	4000.00
89	REGENT POT POURRI	200	3500.00	3500.00
P.W. BASTON				**BICENTENNIAL LIMITED EDITION COMMEMORATIVES**
74	BLACKSMITH	500	200.00	400.00
74	CABINETMAKER	500	200.00	400.00
74	CLOCKMAKER	500	200.00	500.00
74	POTTER	500	200.00	400.00
D. FRIAR				**BIRDS AND FLOWERS OF AMERICA SCULPTURES**
84	BLUEBIRD AND FIR, THE	9800	135.00	135.00
84	CARDINAL AND DOWNY HAWTHORNE, THE	9800	135.00	135.00
84	CHICKADEE AND DAISY, THE	9800	135.00	135.00
84	GOLDFINCH AND DOGWOOD, THE	9800	135.00	135.00
84	KINGFISHER AND WATER LILY, THE	9800	135.00	135.00
84	ROBIN AND NARCISSUS, THE	9800	135.00	135.00

YR	NAME	LIMIT	ISSUE	TREND
84	SWALLOW AND WILD ROSE, THE	9800	135.00	135.00
84	WREN AND BLACKBERRY, THE	9800	135.00	135.00
D. LINDER			**DORIS LINDER PORCELAINS**	
47	QUEEN ELIZABETH ON TOMMY	100	275.00	13200.00
59	HEREFORD BULL	1000	350.00	650.00-775.00
60	FOX HUNTER	500	500.00	*
61	ANGUS BULL	500	350.00	*
61	JERSEY COW	500	300.00	550.00-600.00
61	OFFICER OF ROYAL HORSE GUARDS	150	500.00	*
61	OFFICER OF THE LIFE GUARDS	150	500.00	*
61	SANTA GERTRUDIS BULL	500	350.00	700.00
62	QUARTER HORSE	500	400.00	*
63	ARAB STALLION	500	450.00	*
63	MERANO	500	500.00	1375.00
64	BRITISH FRIESIAN BULL	500	400.00	800.00-900.00
64	JERSEY BULL	500	400.00	900.00-975.00
64	SHIRE STALLION	500	700.00	1350.00
65	HYPERION	500	525.00	850.00
66	DAIRY SHORTHORN BULL	500	475.00	875.00-900.00
66	PERCHERON STALLION	500	725.00	*
66	ROYAL CANADIAN MOUNTY	500	875.00	1500.00
66	WELSH MOUNTAIN PONY	500	3000.00	2750.00
67	ARKLE	500	525.00	825.00
68	BRAHMA BULL	500	400.00	*
68	BULLDOG	500	*	*
68	CHAROLAIS BULL	500	400.00	800.00-875.00
68	DUKE OF EDINBURGH	750	100.00	*
69	APPALOOSA	750	550.00	1200.00-1500.00
69	SULFOLK PUNCH	500	650.00	975.00
70	MARION COAKES-MOULD	750	750.00	1500.00
71	PALOMINO	750	975.00	*
71	PRINCESS GRACE & FOAL, COLOR	750	1500.00	1600.00
71	PRINCESS GRACE & FOAL, WHITE	250	1400.00	1500.00
72	NIJINSKY	500	2000.00	2000.00
73	AMERICAN SADDLE HORSE	750	1450.00	*
73	PRINCESS ANNE ON DOUBLET	750	4250.00	4250.00
75	GALLOPING PONIES, COLORED	500	3300.00	*
75	GALLOPING, CLASSIC	250	2500.00	*
76	DUKE OF MARLBOROUGH	350	5200.00	5200.00
76	GALLOPING IN WINTER	250	3500.00	*
76	HACKNEY	500	1500.00	1500.00
76	MILL REEF	500	2000.00	2000.00
76	NEW BORN, COLOR	500	1800.00	1800.00
76	NEW BORN, WHITE	150	1250.00	1250.00
76	RED RUM	250	2000.00	2000.00
76	RICHARD MEADE	500	2450.00	2450.00
77	CLYDESDALE	500	1250.00	1250.00
77	GRUNDY	500	1800.00	1800.00
77	HIGHLAND BULL	500	900.00	900.00
D. DOUGHTY			**DOROTHY DOUGHTY PORCELAINS**	
35	AMERICAN REDSTARTS AND HEMLOCK	66	*	5500.00
36	BLUEBIRDS	350	500.00	8550.00
36	GOLDFINCHES & THISTLE	250	350.00	4500.00
37	CARDINALS	500	500.00	6000.00
38	BALTIMORE ORIOLES	250	350.00	*
38	CHICKADEES & LARCH	300	350.00	8700.00
40	BOBWHITE QUAIL	22	275.00	11000.00
40	CRABAPPLES	250	400.00	4000.00
40	MOCKINGBIRDS	500	450.00	7500.00
41	APPLE BLOSSOMS	250	400.00	2500.00
42	CRABAPPLE BLOSSOM SPRAYS AND A BUTTERFLY	250	*	800.00
42	INDIGO BUNTING AND PLUM TWIG	5000	*	*
42	INDIGO BUNTINGS, BLACKBERRY SPRAYS	500	375.00	2700.00
42	MOCKINGBIRDS AND PEACH BLOSSOM	500	*	*
47	ORANGE BLOSSOMS & BUTTERFLY	250	500.00	4400.00
50	HUMMINGBIRDS AND FUSCHSIA	500	*	2800.00
50	MAGNOLIA WARBLER	150	1100.00	2700.00
50	MEXICAN FEIJOA	250	600.00	3500.00
52	KINGLETS & NOBLE PINE	500	450.00	2500.00
52	RED-EYED VIREOS	500	450.00	2000.00
52	YELLOW-HEADED BLACKBIRDS	350	650.00	2200.00
55	GNATCATCHERS	500	600.00	3750.00
55	MYRTLE WARBLERS	500	550.00	2500.00
56	BEWICK'S WRENS & YELLOW JASMINE	500	600.00	3000.00
56	SCARLET TANAGERS	500	675.00	3600.00
57	OVENBIRDS	250	650.00	4500.00
57	PARULA WARBLERS	500	600.00	2700.00
58	PHOEBES ON FLAME VINE	500	750.00	4000.00
58	YELLOWTHROATS ON WATER HYACINTH	350	750.00	3000.00
59	CACTUS WRENS	500	1250.00	3500.00
59	ELF OWL	500	875.00	*
60	CANYON WRENS	500	750.00	3000.00
61	HOODED WARBLERS	500	950.00	4300.00
62	LAZULI BUNTING & CHOKECHERRIES, COLOR	500	1350.00	3700.00
62	LAZULI BUNTING & CHOKECHERRIES, WHITE	100	1350.00	2800.00
62	SCISSOR-TAILED FLYCATCHER, COLOR	250	950.00	*
62	SCISSOR-TAILED FLYCATCHER, WHITE	75	950.00	1450.00
63	AUDUBON WARBLERS	500	1350.00	3100.00
63	VERMILLION FLYCATCHERS	500	250.00	1700.00

YR	NAME	LIMIT	ISSUE	TREND
64	BLUE TITS & PUSSY WILLOW	500	250.00	3000.00
64	LESSER WHITETHROATS	500	350.00	2600.00
64	MOORHEN CHICK	500	1000.00	*
64	MOUNTAIN BLUEBIRDS	500	950.00	2000.00
64	ROBIN	500	750.00	*
64	WRENS & BURNET ROSE	500	650.00	1000.00
65	CERULEAN WARBLERS & RED MAPLE	500	1350.00	2400.00
65	CHUFFCHAFF	500	1500.00	2400.00
65	KINGFISHER COCK & AUTUMN BEECH	500	1250.00	2100.00
66	LARK SPARROW	500	750.00	*
67	DOWNY WOODPECKER & PECAN, COLOR	400	1500.00	1700.00
67	DOWNY WOODPECKER & PECAN, WHITE	75	1000.00	1900.00
68	CAROLINA PAROQUET, COLOR	350	1200.00	2000.00
68	CAROLINA PAROQUET, WHITE	75	600.00	*
68	GRAY WAGTAIL	500	600.00	*
68	REDSTARTS & GORSE	500	1900.00	2300.00
71	NIGHTINGALE & HONEYSUCKLE	500	2500.00	2000.00
72	GOLDCRESTS, PAIR	500	4200.00	*
77	MEADOW PIPIT	500	1800.00	1800.00
N. ROESSLER		**NORBERT E.J. ROESSLER BRONZES**		
76	HUMMER, WITH FUSHSIA	500	225.00	225.00
76	MARLIN	500	250.00	250.00
R. VAN RUYCKEVELT		**RONALD VAN RUYCKEVELT PORCELAINS**		
*	ALICE	500	1875.00	1875.00
*	CECILIA	500	1875.00	1875.00
56	HOGFISH & SERGEANT MAJOR	500	375.00	650.00
58	RED HIND	500	375.00	900.00
61	PASSIONFLOWER	500	300.00	400.00
61	SQUIRRELFISH	500	400.00	9000.00
62	FLYING FISH	300	400.00	450.00
62	HIBISCUS	500	300.00	350.00
62	SAILFISH	500	400.00	550.00
64	ROCK BEAUTY	500	425.00	850.00
64	TARPON	500	500.00	975.00
65	BLUE MARLIN	500	500.00	1000.00
66	SWORDFISH	500	575.00	650.00
67	BLUEFIN TUNA	500	500.00	*
67	BUTTERFLY FISH	500	375.00	1600.00
68	BLUE ANGEL FISH	500	375.00	900.00
68	DOLPHIN	500	500.00	900.00
68	HONFLEUR A-105	290	*	600.00
68	HONFLEUR A-106	290	*	600.00
68	MALLARDS	500	*	2000.00
68	MENNECY A-101	338	*	725.00
68	MENNECY A-102	334	*	725.00
68	RAINBOW PARROT FISH	500	1500.00	1500.00
68	RING-NECKED PHEASANTS	500	*	3300.00
69	ARGENTEUIL A-108	338	*	*
69	BOBWHITE QUAIL, PAIR	500	*	2000.00
69	CASTELNEAU PINK	429	*	850.00
69	CASTELNEAU YELLOW	163	*	850.00
69	SAINT DENIS A-109	500	*	950.00
70	AMERICAN PINTAIL, PAIR	500	*	3000.00
71	ELAINE	750	600.00	625.00
71	GREEN-WINGED TEAL	500	1450.00	1450.00
71	LANGUEDOC	216	*	1150.00
72	WHITE DOVES	25	3600.00	28000.00
76	PICNIC	250	2850.00	2850.00
76	QUEEN ELIZABETH I	250	3850.00	3850.00
76	QUEEN MARY I	250	4850.00	4850.00
77	QUEEN ELIZABETH II	250	*	*
D. FRIAR		**ROYAL WORCESTER GREAT AMERICAN BIRDS OF PREY**		
85	AMERICAN KESTREL	9800	195.00	195.00
85	BALD EAGLE	9800	195.00	195.00
85	COOPERS HAWK	9800	195.00	195.00
85	GREAT HORNED OWL	9800	195.00	195.00
85	GYRFALCON	9800	195.00	195.00
85	PEREGRINE FALCON	9800	195.00	195.00
85	RED TAIL HAWK	9800	195.00	195.00
85	SCREECH OWL	9800	195.00	195.00
R. VAN RUYCKEVELT		**RUTH VAN RUYCKEVELT PORCELAINS**		
59	LISETTE	500	100.00	*
59	PENELOPE	500	100.00	*
60	BEATRICE	500	125.00	*
60	CAROLINE	500	125.00	*
62	LOUISA	500	400.00	975.00
63	SISTER OF LONDON HOSPITAL	500	*	500.00
63	SISTER OF ST. THOMAS HOSPITAL	500	*	500.00
64	MELANIE	500	150.00	*
64	ROSALIND	500	150.00	*
64	TEA PARTY	250	400.00	7000.00
66	SISTER OF UNIVERSITY COLLEGE HOSPITAL	500	*	500.00
67	ELIZABETH	750	300.00	800.00
68	CHARLOTTE AND JANE	500	1000.00	1600.00
68	MADELINE	500	300.00	800.00
68	MARION	500	275.00	600.00
69	BRIDGET	500	300.00	650.00
69	EMILY	500	300.00	600.00

YR	NAME	LIMIT	ISSUE	TREND
70	SISTER OF THE RED CROSS	750	*	500.00
71	FELICITY	750	600.00	600.00
78	ESTHER	500	*	*
	K. POTTS			**SPECIAL ISSUE**
88	QUEEN ELIZABETH I	100	15000.00	15000.00

SAMSONS STUDIOS

YR	NAME	LIMIT	ISSUE	TREND
	S. BUTCHER			**MCCOONS COUNTY**
*	BOX SOCIAL	RT	80.00	100.00
*	CHECKERBOARD SQUARE	RT	85.00	125.00
*	GOOD-BYE MARY LOU - ARMY	RT	60.00	70.00
*	GOOD-BYE MARY LOU - NAVY	RT	60.00	80.00
*	MAMA SANG TENOR	RT	70.00	90.00
*	MCCOON COUNTY FAIR	RT	80.00	100.00
*	WISHING YOU A TWO TON CHRISTMAS	RT	70.00	100.00
	S. BUTCHER			**MCCOONS STUDIOS**
*	SATURDAY NIGHT HO-DOWN	RT	150.00	175.00
	S. BUTCHER			**SNUGGLE BUGS**
*	BON VOYAGE	RT	15.00	75.00
*	HAPPY BIRTHDAY TO YOU	RT	15.00	45.00
*	I'M SENDING YOU MY BERRY VEST	RT	15.00	80.00
*	LET LOVE BLOOM	RT	15.00	70.00
*	LET'S POOL OUR RESOURCES	RT	15.00	75.00
*	YOU ARE MY FAVORITE PAIL	RT	15.00	80.00
*	YOU ARE MY NO. 1	RT	15.00	45.00
*	YOU ARE OUT OF THIS WORLD	RT	15.00	45.00
*	YOU ARE THE END OF MY RAINBOW	RT	15.00	300.00
*	YOU TAKE THE CAKE	RT	15.00	45.00
	T. CLARK			**TOM CLARK CREATIONS**
*	DAISY AND ERIC	*	*	750.00

SANDICAST

YR	NAME	LIMIT	ISSUE	TREND
	S. BRUE			**BARKITECTURE**
93	BEACON HILL TOWNHOUSE & BOSTON TERRIER	RT	12.50	15.00
93	EIFFEL TOWER & POODLE	RT	12.50	15.00
93	ENGLISH THATCHED COTTAGE & LABRADOR	RT	12.50	15.00
93	GERMAN CASTLE & ROTTWEILER	RT	12.50	15.00
93	IGLOO & HUSKY	RT	12.50	15.00
93	IRISH COTTAGE & SETTER	RT	12.50	15.00
93	JAPANESE PAGODA & AKITA	RT	12.50	15.00
93	LOG CABIN & BLOODHOUND	RT	12.50	15.00
93	MAYAN TEMPLE & CHIHUAHUA	RT	12.50	15.00
93	SCOTTISH CASTLE & WESTIE	RT	12.50	15.00
93	SWISS CHALET & ST. BERNARD	RT	12.50	15.00
93	TIBETAN TEMPLE & LHASA	RT	12.50	15.00
	S. BRUE			**COLLECTOR'S GUILD**
94	COLLECTOR'S GUILD MEMBERSHIP KIT	YR	20.00	25.00
	S. BRUE			**FOREVER FRIENDS**
93	BASSET & PUP	*	34.00	45.00
93	BEAGEL & PUP	*	34.00	45.00
93	BOXER PUP, BRINDLE	RT	34.00	45.00
93	BOXER PUP, FAWN	*	34.00	45.00
93	CAT & KITTEN, BLACK	*	34.00	45.00
93	CAT & KITTEN, BLACK AND WHITE	*	34.00	45.00
93	CAT & KITTEN, CALICO	*	34.00	45.00
93	CAT & KITTEN, ORANGE AND WHITE	*	34.00	45.00
93	CAT, GRAY AND WHITE	*	34.00	45.00
93	CAT, WHITE	*	34.00	45.00
93	COCKER & PUP, BLACK	RT	34.00	45.00
93	COCKER & PUP, BUFF	RT	34.00	45.00
93	COCKER & PUP, PARTI BLACK	RT	34.00	45.00
93	COCKER & PUP, PARTI BUFF	RT	34.00	45.00
93	GOLDEN RETRIEVER & PUP	*	34.00	45.00
93	HARP SEAL & PUP	*	34.00	45.00
93	LION & CUB	*	34.00	45.00
93	PENGUIN & CHICK	*	34.00	45.00
93	SCHNAUZER & PUP	*	34.00	45.00
94	LAB & PUP, BLACK	*	34.00	40.00
94	LAB & PUP, CHOCOLATE	*	34.00	40.00
94	LAB & PUP, YELLOW	*	34.00	40.00
94	POLAR BEAR & CUB	*	31.00	37.00
	S. BRUE			**LIFE SIZE**
93	CAT, BLACK AND WHITE	*	54.00	45.00
93	CAVALIER KING CHARLES SPANIEL	*	54.00	65.00
93	PANDA CUB	*	69.00	80.00
94	COLLIE PUP, SABLE	*	54.00	60.00
94	JACK RUSSELL TERRIER	*	54.00	60.00
94	JACK RUSSELL TERRIER, BLACK AND WHITE	*	54.00	60.00
94	ST. BERNARD PUP	*	54.00	60.00
	S. BRUE			**LIL' SNOOZERS**
94	KITTEN, MIDNIGHT	*	4.50	6.00
94	NODDER, MIDNIGHT	*	4.50	6.00
94	YAWNER, BLACK	*	4.50	6.00
	S. BRUE			**LION KING**
94	ADULT SIMBA	RT	34.00	40.00
94	MUFASA & SIMBA	RT	34.00	40.00
94	PRIDE ROCK DISPLAY	RT	30.00	35.00

YR	NAME	LIMIT	ISSUE	TREND
94	SIMBA & NALA	RT	34.00	40.00
94	YOUNG NALA	RT	9.00	12.00
94	YOUNG SIMBA	RT	9.00	12.00
S. BRUE				**NATURE'S HABITAT**
94	BISON	5000	40.00	50.00
94	GRIZZLY BEAR	5000	40.00	50.00
94	HABITAT	5000	50.00	60.00
94	MOOSE	5000	40.00	50.00
94	TIMBER WOLF	RT	20.00	25.00
S. BRUE				**ORIGINALS**
93	DOBIE, RED (II), UNCROPPED	*	20.00	25.00
94	AUSTRALIAN SHEPHERD	*	20.00	25.00
94	GREYHOUND	*	20.00	25.00
94	GREYHOUND, FAWN	*	20.00	25.00
94	GREYHOUND, WHITE & BRINDLE	*	20.00	25.00
S. BRUE				**PESKY PEEPERS**
94	CHOW, BLACK	*	5.50	7.00
94	CHOW, RED	*	5.50	7.00
94	COCKER, BLACK	*	5.50	7.00
94	JACK RUSSELL TERRIER	*	5.50	7.00
94	KITTY, BLACK	*	5.50	7.00
94	ROTTWEILER	*	5.50	7.00
94	SHIH TZU, BLACK/WHITE	*	5.50	7.00
94	SHIH TZU, GOLD/WHITE	*	5.50	7.00
94	ST. BERNARD	*	5.50	7.00
S. BRUE				**WILD CREATURES**
94	FERRET	*	24.00	30.00
94	WOLF	*	24.00	30.00

SARAH'S ATTIC

YR	NAME	LIMIT	ISSUE	TREND
S. SCHULTZ				
*	BEVERLY JANE SUNDAY BEST	500	160.00	300.00
88	SUNSHINE DOLL	RT	118.00	700.00
88	SUNSHINE DOLL	RT	118.00	700.00
89	BEVERLY JANE AMERICAN (RED DRESS)	500	160.00	300.00
89	LONG JOURNEY	RT	19.00	35.00
90	SLEEPY RABBIT	RT	15.50	25.00
90	TESSY RABBIT	RT	17.00	20.00
90	TESSY RABBIT	RT	15.00	20.00
90	THELMA RABBIT	RT	33.00	40.00
90	THOMAS RABBIT	RT	33.00	40.00
90	WOODLAND SANTA	RT	100.00	125.00
91	SILENT NIGHT	RT	33.00	44.00
S. SCHULTZ				**AMERICANA COLLECTION**
88	AMERICANA BEAR	CL	17.50	18.00
88	AMERICANA BEAR	CL	70.00	70.00
88	AMERICANA BUNNY	CL	70.00	70.00
88	AMERICANA CLOWN	OP	80.00	80.00
88	BETSY BEAR W/FLAG	CL	22.50	23.00
88	BETSY ROSS	OP	34.00	40.00
88	COLONIAL BEAR W/HAT	CL	22.50	23.00
88	INDIAN BRAVE	OP	10.00	10.00
88	INDIAN GIRL	OP	10.00	10.00
88	PILGRIM BOY	OP	12.50	13.00
88	PILGRIM GIRL	OP	12.50	13.00
88	TURKEY	OP	10.00	12.00
90	BRIGHT SKY	TL	70.00	70.00
90	IRON HAWK	TL	70.00	70.00
90	LITTLE DOVE	TL	40.00	40.00
90	SPOTTED EAGLE	TL	30.00	30.00
S. SCHULTZ				**ANGELS IN THE ATTIC**
89	ANGEL ABBEE	CL	9.50	18.00
89	ANGEL ALEX	CL	10.00	15.00
89	ANGEL AMELIA	CL	10.00	15.00
89	ANGEL ASHBEE	CL	9.50	18.00
89	ANGEL ASHLEE	CL	14.00	25.00
89	ANGEL BEVIE	CL	10.00	10.00
89	ANGEL BONNIE	CL	17.00	21.00
89	ANGEL CLYDE	CL	17.00	20.00
89	ANGEL DAISY	CL	14.00	15.00
89	ANGEL DUSTY	CL	12.00	85.00
89	ANGEL EDDIE	CL	10.00	10.00
89	ANGEL EMMY LOU	CL	12.00	12.00
89	ANGEL FLOPPY	CL	10.00	10.00
89	ANGEL GRAMPS	CL	17.00	90.00
89	ANGEL GRAMS	CL	17.00	90.00
89	ANGEL JEFFREY	CL	14.00	15.00
89	ANGEL JESSICA	CL	14.00	15.00
89	ANGEL PATSY	CL	13.00	15.00
89	ANGEL RAYBURN	CL	12.00	20.00
89	ANGEL REBA	CL	12.00	15.00
89	ANGEL REGGIE	CL	12.00	14.00
89	ANGEL RUTHIE	CL	12.00	13.00
89	ANGEL SHOOTER	CL	12.50	18.00
89	ANGEL WENDALL	CL	10.00	15.00
89	ANGEL WENDY	CL	10.00	15.00
89	ANGEL WILBUR	CL	9.50	14.00
89	ANGEL WINNIE	CL	10.00	14.00

YR	NAME	LIMIT	ISSUE	TREND
89	SAINT WILLIE BILL	CL	30.00	40.00
89	ST. ANNE	CL	29.00	32.00
89	ST. GABBE	CL	30.00	33.00
89	ST. GEORGE	CL	60.00	65.00
90	ANGEL BEAR IN BASKET	CL	23.00	23.00
90	ANGEL BILLI	CL	18.00	21.00
90	ANGEL BUSTER	CL	15.00	16.00
90	ANGEL CINDI	CL	18.00	20.00
90	ANGEL FLOSSY	CL	15.00	25.00
90	ANGEL LENA	CL	36.00	38.00
90	ANGEL LOUISE	CL	17.00	21.00
90	ANGEL RABBIT IN BASKET	CL	25.00	25.00
90	ANGEL TRAPPER	CL	17.00	21.00
90	ANGEL TRUDY	CL	36.00	36.00
91	ANGEL BERT GOLFING	1000	60.00	60.00
91	ANGEL DONALD WITH DOG	1000	50.00	50.00
91	CONTENTMENT	RT	100.00	180.00
92	LOVE	RT	80.00	180.00
95	DIGNITY ANGEL/4330	OP	55.00	55.00
95	LOUISE ANGEL/4472	2500	34.00	34.00
95	LOVE ANGEL/4328	OP	40.00	40.00
95	PRAYER OF LOVE/4437	SO	85.00	170.00
95	RESPECT ANGEL/4329	OP	32.00	32.00
95	WILLIE BILL ANGEL/4471	2500	34.00	34.00
96	APRIL ANGEL/4514	4000	40.00	40.00
96	MAY ANGEL/4515	4000	40.00	40.00
S. SCHULTZ		**BEARY ADORABLES COLLECTION**		
87	ABBEE BEAR	CL	10.00	10.00
87	ALEX BEAR	CL	11.50	12.00
87	AMELIA BEAR	CL	11.50	12.00
87	ASHBEE BEAR	CL	10.00	10.00
87	BEAR ON TRUNK	CL	20.00	20.00
87	COLLECTIBLE BEAR	CL	16.00	16.00
88	ARCTIC PICNIC BEAR	CL	7.00	7.00
88	BEAR IN BASKET	CL	48.00	48.00
88	BENNI BEAR	CL	7.00	7.00
88	EINSTEIN BEAR	CL	8.50	9.00
88	GHOST BEAR	CL	12.00	12.00
88	HONEY PICNIC BEAR	CL	16.50	17.00
88	JESTER CLOWN BEAR	CL	12.50	13.00
88	LEFTY BEAR	CL	80.00	80.00
88	MARTI PICNIC BEAR	CL	12.50	13.00
88	RUFUS PICNIC BEAR	CL	15.00	16.00
89	ANGEL BEAR	CL	24.50	25.00
89	DAISY BEAR	CL	48.00	55.00
89	GRISWALD BEAR	CL	48.00	55.00
89	MIKEY BEAR	CL	26.00	26.00
89	MINI TEDDY BEAR	CL	5.00	5.00
89	MISSY BEAR	CL	26.00	26.00
89	SAMMY BEAR	CL	12.00	15.00
89	SID BEAR	CL	18.00	25.00
89	SOPHIE BEAR	CL	18.00	25.00
89	SPICE BEAR	CL	12.00	15.00
89	SUGAR BEAR	CL	12.00	12.00
90	BAILEY 50'S BEAR	RT	30.00	30.00
90	BELINDA 50'S BEAR	RT	25.00	25.00
90	BEULAH 50'S BEAR	RT	30.00	30.00
90	BIRKEY 50'S BEAR	RT	25.00	25.00
90	DUDLEY BROWN BEAR	RT	32.00	32.00
90	FRANNY BROWN BEAR	RT	32.00	32.00
90	JOEY BROWN BEAR	RT	32.00	32.00
90	MARGIE BROWN BEAR	RT	32.00	32.00
90	MISS LOVE BROWN BEAR	RT	42.00	42.00
90	OLIVER BLACK BEAR	RT	32.00	32.00
91	DUDLEY BEAR	CL	32.00	32.00
91	FRANNY BEAR	RT	32.00	32.00
91	JOEY BEAR	RT	32.00	32.00
91	MISS LOVE BEAR	RT	42.00	42.00
91	NARGI BEAR	RT	32.00	32.00
91	OLIVER BEAR	RT	32.00	32.00
92	ANDY-FATHER BEAR	RT	20.00	21.00
92	AUNT EUNICE BEAR	OP	24.00	24.00
92	BELLHOP & SECOND HAND ROSE	OP	40.00	40.00
92	BELLHOP BEAR	OP	24.00	24.00
92	BRANDY BABY BEAR	CL	14.00	15.00
92	DOWAGER TWINS BEAR	OP	24.00	24.00
92	EDDIE BEAR WITH TRUNK	OP	40.00	40.00
92	IRISH BEAR	OP	24.00	24.00
92	IRISH BEAR AT PUB	OP	40.00	40.00
92	JUST TED BEAR	OP	24.00	24.00
92	JUST TED WITH MIRROR	OP	40.00	40.00
92	LIBRARIAN WITH DESK	OP	40.00	40.00
92	MANDY MOTHER BEAR	RT	20.00	20.00
92	ME AND MY SHADOW	OP	26.00	26.00
92	MICHAUD BEAR	OP	35.00	35.00
92	PROFESSOR WITH BOARD	OP	40.00	40.00
92	SECOND HAND ROSE BEAR	OP	24.00	24.00
92	TOMMY WITH DOG	OP	40.00	40.00
92	TOMMY'S BEAR	OP	24.00	24.00

YR	NAME	LIMIT	ISSUE	TREND
93	ANGEL FAITH BLACK	1994	40.00	40.00
93	ANGEL GRACE WHITE	1994	40.00	40.00
93	BEARY HAPPY HALLOWEEN	CL	18.00	18.00
93	BEARY HUGGABLE BEAR	CL	18.00	18.00
93	BEARY MERRY CHRISTMAS	CL	20.00	20.00
93	BEARY SPECIAL BROTHER BEAR	CL	18.00	18.00
93	BEARY SPECIAL FATHER BEAR	CL	22.00	22.00
93	BEARY SPECIAL MOTHER BEAR	CL	18.00	18.00
93	BEARY SPECIAL SISTER BEAR	CL	18.00	18.00
93	BLESSED IS HE	CL	48.00	150.00
93	DOWAGER TWINS ON COUCH	CL	60.00	60.00
93	EDDIE BEAR	CL	24.00	24.00
93	HEAVENLY PEACE	RT	47.00	47.00
93	HEAVENLY UNITING	RT	45.00	45.00
93	I LOVE YOU BEARS	CL	22.00	22.00
93	I'M BEARY SORRY BEAR	CL	18.00	18.00
93	LIBRARIAN BEAR	CL	24.00	24.00
93	ME AND MY SHADOW WITH CHAIR	CL	45.00	45.00
93	MISS YOU BEARY MUCH BEAR	CL	18.00	18.00
93	MR. WARD	RT	40.00	40.00
93	PROFESSOR BEAR	OP	24.00	24.00
93	RISEN CHRIST	1994	48.00	48.00
93	WITCHIE BEAR	CL	24.00	24.00
93	WITCHIE WITH POT	CL	40.00	40.00
93	YOU'RE BEARY SPECIAL BEAR	CL	18.00	18.00
94	ADORA WITH HARP	4000	26.00	26.00
94	ANGEL BEAR WITH HORSE	2050	26.00	26.00
94	ANGEL BUNNY WITH CAGE	2050	20.00	20.00
94	ANGEL CASEY	2050	32.00	32.00
94	ANGEL JONATHON	2050	32.00	32.00
94	ANGEL LACY	2050	32.00	32.00
94	ANGEL PUP WITH VICTROLA	2050	20.00	20.00
94	BEARY SPECIAL BIRTHDAY BEAR	CL	20.00	20.00
94	BEARY SPECIAL FRIEND BEAR	CL	20.00	20.00
94	BLESSED IS HE II	2500	66.00	66.00
94	ENOS WITH HORN	4000	26.00	26.00
94	GET WELL SOON BEAR	CL	20.00	20.00
94	WINGS OF LOVE BLACK BOY	RT	36.00	36.00
94	WINGS OF LOVE BLACK GIRL	RT	36.00	36.00
95	BAY CITY BEAUTY	CL	26.00	27.00
95	BAY CITY BEAUTY W/TRUNK	OP	40.00	40.00
S. SCHULTZ		**BLACK HERITAGE COLLECTION**		
87	GRAMPS	CL	16.00	16.00
87	GRAMS	CL	16.00	16.00
89	PAPPY JAKE	CL	40.00	95.00
89	QUILTING LADIES	CL	90.00	285.00
90	BROTHERLY LOVE	RT	80.00	160.00
90	CALEB	CL	23.00	30.00
90	HARPSTER W/BANJO	RT	60.00	250.00
90	HATTIE	RT	40.00	85.00
90	LIBBY W/BIBS	RT	36.00	145.00
90	LUCAS W/BIBS	CL	36.00	145.00
90	PEARL, TAP DANCER	RT	45.00	65.00
90	PERCY, TAP DANCER	RT	45.00	65.00
90	PORTIA	CL	30.00	30.00
90	PREACHER I	RT	55.00	150.00
90	SUSIE MAE	CL	22.00	22.00
90	WHOOPIE & WOOSTER	RT	50.00	250.00
91	BLACK BABY TANSY	CL	40.00	45.00
91	BRAIDED RUG	*	35.00	35.00
91	CALEB W/VEGETABLES	RT	50.00	50.00
91	CALEB WITH FOOTBALL	6000	40.00	40.00
91	CHIPS, BLACK BOY GRADUATE	6000	46.00	46.00
91	CORPORAL PERVIS	RT	60.00	110.00
91	CRICKET, BLACK GIRL GRADUATE	6000	46.00	46.00
91	GENERAL OF LOVE, COOKSTOVE	*	100.00	100.00
91	HARPSTER W/HARMONICA	RT	60.00	110.00
91	HATTIE QUILTING	RT	60.00	115.00
91	KETTLES	*	13.00	13.00
91	LIBBY W/PUPPY	RT	50.00	75.00
91	LUCAS W/DOG	RT	50.00	75.00
91	NIGHTTIME PEARL	CL	50.00	60.00
91	NIGHTTIME PERCY	CL	50.00	60.00
91	PAPPY JAKE & SUSIE MAE	RT	60.00	60.00
91	PIE	*	7.00	7.00
91	PORTIA QUILTING	RT	40.00	40.00
91	PRAISE THE LORD II	RT	100.00	100.00
91	SADIE & OSIE MAE	RT	70.00	70.00
91	UNCLE REUBEN	RT	70.00	120.00
91	VICTORIAN PORTIA	RT	35.00	35.00
91	VICTORIAN WEBSTER	RT	35.00	35.00
91	WHOOPIE & WOOSTER II	RT	70.00	70.00
92	BLACK TEACHER MISS LETTIE	RT	50.00	50.00
92	BUFFALO SOLDIER	RT	80.00	115.00
92	CLARENCE, PORTER	RT	80.00	120.00
92	ESTHER WITH BUTTER CHURN	CL	70.00	70.00
92	GRANNY WYNNE & OLIVIA	RT	85.00	85.00
92	MUSIC MASTERS	CL	300.00	350.00
95	AHMAD/4453	7500	23.00	23.00

YR	NAME	LIMIT	ISSUE	TREND
95	ALICIA/YVETTE/4410	5000	50.00	50.00
95	ANGELIKA/4456	7500	25.00	25.00
95	BESSIE COLEMAN/4313	2500	50.00	50.00
95	BILL PICKET/4281	2500	56.00	56.00
95	BLESSED FAMILY NATIVITY/4364	5000	70.00	70.00
95	BLESSED IS HE III/4387	YR	60.00	60.00
95	BLESSED IS SHE/4312	5000	50.00	50.00
95	BOOK OF WISDOM/4315	4000	52.00	52.00
95	BUFFALO BILL/4311	RT	60.00	60.00
95	BUFFALO SOLDIER/4285	5000	165.00	165.00
95	CALF & CHICKS/4459	OP	25.00	25.00
95	CALVIN/4319	4000	28.00	28.00
95	CHAIRTY/4318	4000	28.00	28.00
95	CHIEF JOSEPH/4282	RT	56.00	56.00
95	ELROY/4411	5000	25.00	25.00
95	F. DOUGLASS/4402	2500	55.00	55.00
95	H.O. FLIPPER/4403	2500	55.00	55.00
95	HUGS/4185	OP	36.00	36.00
95	IDA B. WELLS/4400	2500	65.00	65.00
95	ISHAMAEL/4454	7500	23.00	23.00
95	JABARI/4455	7500	23.00	23.00
95	JARRELL/4452	7500	23.00	23.00
95	JOAH/4451	7500	*	23.00
95	KISSES/4186	OP	30.00	30.00
95	LAKEISHA/4450	7500	25.00	25.00
95	LAMB & DUCKS/4458	OP	25.00	25.00
95	LEAN ON ME/4369	5000	55.00	55.00
95	LIBBY W/CANDLE/4396	4000	26.00	26.00
95	LIFT YOUR HEARTS/4413	5000	50.00	50.00
95	LOVE/4187	OP	50.00	50.00
95	LOVING TOUCH/4314	4000	66.00	66.00
95	LUCAS W/BEAR/4397	4000	26.00	26.00
95	O.A.D. WASH./4404	2500	51.00	51.00
95	OLD TIME TUNE/4317	4000	54.00	54.00
95	PIGLET/4457	OP	11.00	11.00
95	ROSA PARKS/4401	YR	65.00	65.00
95	STITCH OR LOVE/4316	4000	60.00	60.00
95	TUSKEGEE AIR./4405	2500	60.00	60.00
95	WAGS/4412	OP	9.00	9.00
96	BELIEVE IN YOUR/4522	3000	70.00	70.00
96	BLESSED IS HE IV/4520	2000	70.00	70.00
96	BREEZE/4537	2000	24.00	24.00
96	CARTER/4536	2500	30.00	30.00
96	CAYLA/4535	2500	36.00	36.00
96	CLOWN HICKORY/4485	10000	29.00	29.00
96	CLOWN SASSAFRAS/4484	10000	29.00	29.00
96	JAZZ MAN/4499	2000	150.00	150.00
96	LOVE OF MY LIFE II/4534	2500	75.00	75.00
96	MA RAINEY/4500	2000	50.00	50.00
96	MARY MAHONEY/4501	1000	50.00	50.00
96	MISTY/4539	2000	50.00	24.00
96	NOAH'S ARK/4529	SO	130.00	130.00
96	SPECIAL BEAR/4476	5000	23.00	23.00
96	SPECIAL BLACK GIRL/4477	5000	29.00	29.00
96	SPECIAL WHITE GIRL/4478	5000	29.00	29.00
96	SUMMER-4538	2000	24.00	24.00
96	SUNDAY TILLIE/BW/4530	2500	75.00	75.00
96	SUNDAY TILLIE/YG/4532	2500	75.00	75.00
96	SUNDAY WILLIE/BW/4531	2500	75.00	75.00
96	SUNDAY WILLIE/YG/4533	2500	75.00	75.00
96	TRUSE IN EACH OTHER/4523	3000	70.00	70.00
S. SCHULTZ			**CHERISHED MEMORIES**	
91	BLACK BABY BOY (1-2 YRS.)	*	50.00	50.00
91	BLACK BABY BOY (BIRTH-1 YR.)	*	50.00	50.00
91	BLACK BABY GIRL (1-2 YRS.)	*	50.00	50.00
91	BLACK BABY GIRL (BIRTH-1 YR.)	*	50.00	50.00
91	WHITE BABY BOY (1-2 YRS.)	*	60.00	60.00
91	WHITE BABY BOY (BIRTH-1 YR.)	*	60.00	60.00
91	WHITE BABY GIRL (1-2 YRS.)	*	60.00	60.00
91	WHITE BABY GIRL (BIRTH-1 YR.)	*	60.00	60.00
S. SCHULTZ			**CHILDREN OF LOVE**	
91	BENJAMIN WITH DRUMS	10000	46.00	46.00
91	CHARITY SEWING FLAGS	10000	46.00	46.00
91	SKIP BUILDING HOUSE	10000	50.00	50.00
91	SUSIE PAINTING TRAIN	10000	46.00	46.00
S. SCHULTZ			**CLASSROOM MEMORIES**	
88	MISS PRITCHETT	CL	28.00	38.00
91	ACHIEVING OUR GOALS	RT	80.00	83.00
91	CLASSROOM MEMORIES	6000	80.00	80.00
S. SCHULTZ			**COLLECTOR'S CLUB**	
95	FRIENDS FOREVER/4444	YR	65.00	65.00
95	HORSIN' AROUND/4445	YR	65.00	65.00
95	PLAYTIME PALS/4446	YR	65.00	65.00
S. SCHULTZ			**COOKIE KIDS & FRIENDS**	
95	CHIP/C004	OP	29.50	30.00
95	COOKIE KIDS SIGN/C001	OP	39.00	39.00
95	HONEY/C007	OP	29.50	30.00
95	OATIE/C002	OP	29.50	30.00

YR	NAME	LIMIT	ISSUE	TREND
95	PEANUT/C005	OP	29.50	30.00
95	SPRINKLES/C006	OP	29.50	30.00
95	SUGAR/C003	OP	29.50	30.00
S. SCHULTZ		**COTTON TALE COLLECTION**		
86	WINNIE MOM RABBIT	CL	14.00	17.00
87	BONNIE	CL	30.00	100.00
87	CLYDE	CL	30.00	100.00
87	FLOPPY	CL	19.00	21.00
87	WENDALL BOY RABBIT	CL	14.00	27.00
87	WENDALL PA RABBIT	CL	17.00	25.00
87	WENDY GIRL RABBIT	CL	15.00	27.00
88	AMOS HARE	CL	11.00	12.00
88	BILLI RABBIT	CL	27.00	36.00
88	BOY RABBIT RES. CANDLE	CL	9.00	10.00
88	CINDI RABBIT	CL	27.00	36.00
88	GIRL RABBIT RES. CANDLE	CL	9.00	10.00
88	IZZY HARE	CL	8.00	10.00
88	LIZZY HARE	CL	8.00	10.00
88	MADDY HARE	CL	11.00	11.00
88	RABBIT IN BASKET	CL	48.00	48.00
88	WENDALL MINI BOY RABBIT	CL	7.50	10.00
88	WENDY MINI GIRL RABBIT	CL	7.50	10.00
88	WILBUR MINI PAPA RABBIT	CL	8.50	10.00
88	WINNIE MINI MAMA RABBIT	CL	8.50	10.00
89	COOKIE RABBIT	CL	29.00	110.00
89	CRUMB RABBIT	CL	29.00	40.00
89	NANA RABBIT	RT	50.00	65.00
89	PAPA RABBIT	RT	50.00	65.00
89	SLEEPING BABY BUNNY	CL	15.50	16.00
89	TESSY RABBIT	CL	15.00	21.00
89	THELMA RABBIT	CL	33.00	41.00
89	THOMAS RABBIT	CL	33.00	41.00
89	TOBY RABBIT	CL	17.00	21.00
90	CHUCKLES FARM RABBIT	TL	53.00	54.00
90	COOKIE FARM RABBIT	TL	47.00	48.00
90	CRUMB FARM RABBIT	TL	53.00	54.00
90	HANNAH RABBIT QUILTING	CL	32.00	32.00
90	HEATHER RABBIT W/DOLL	OP	20.00	22.00
90	HENRY RABBIT W/PIPE	CL	32.00	32.00
90	HERBIE RABBIT W/BOOK	CL	22.00	22.00
90	MOLLY RABBIT W/VEST	CL	75.00	75.00
90	NANA FARM RABBIT	CL	100.00	100.00
90	OLLY RABBIT W/VEST	CL	65.00	100.00
90	PAPA FARM RABBIT	CL	80.00	80.00
90	SLEEPY FARM RABBIT	CL	35.00	35.00
90	ZEB SAILOR DAD	CL	26.00	28.00
90	ZEB W/CARROTS	RT	18.00	35.00
90	ZEKE SAILOR BOY	CL	26.00	26.00
90	ZEKE W/CARROTS	CL	17.00	35.00
90	ZELDA SAILOR MOM	CL	28.00	28.00
90	ZELDA W/CARROTS	RT	18.00	35.00
90	ZOE SAILOR GIRL	CL	26.00	26.00
90	ZOE W/CARROTS	RT	17.00	35.00
91	VICTORIAN TABITHA	CL	30.00	48.00
91	VICTORIAN TESSY	CL	20.00	38.00
91	VICTORIAN THELMA	CL	60.00	60.00
91	VICTORIAN THOMAS	CL	60.00	60.00
91	VICTORIAN TOBY	TL	40.00	60.00
91	VICTORIAN TUCKER	CL	37.00	37.00
93	X-MAS TOBY	RT	20.00	20.00
95	GLIMMER/4362	RT	50.00	50.00
95	GLITZ/4363	RT	50.00	50.00
S. SCHULTZ		**CUDDLY CRITTERS COLLECTION**		
87	SPARKY	OP	9.00	10.00
88	BUSTER BOY CAT	CL	14.00	15.00
88	CAROUSEL HORSE	CL	31.00	31.00
88	COW W/BELL	CL	35.00	35.00
88	FLOSSY GIRL CAT	CL	9.50	10.00
88	KITTY CAT W/BONNET	CL	12.00	12.00
88	LAZY-CAT ON BACK	CL	13.00	13.00
88	LILA MRS. MOUSE	CL	17.50	18.00
88	LOUISE MAMA CAT	CL	20.00	20.00
88	LUCKY BOY MOUSE	CL	13.00	13.00
88	LUCKY GIRL MOUSE	CL	12.00	12.00
88	MYRTLE THE PIG	CL	38.00	45.00
88	PAPA MOUSE	CL	17.50	18.00
88	ROCKING HORSE	CL	56.00	56.00
88	SLEEPING CAT	CL	6.00	6.00
88	TRAPPER PAPA CAT	CL	20.00	20.00
89	MADAM DONNA	CL	35.50	45.00
89	MESSIEUR PIERRE	CL	35.50	45.00
89	OTIS PAPA CAT	CL	13.00	13.00
89	PUDDIN GIRL CAT	CL	10.00	10.00
89	WHISKERS BOY CAT	CL	10.00	10.00
89	WIGGLY PIG	CL	17.00	25.00
90	BOY SQUIRREL SONNY	CL	18.00	18.00
90	GIRL SQUIRREL SIS	CL	18.00	18.00
90	HORACE & SISSY DOGS	OP	50.00	50.00
90	JASPER DAD CAT	OP	36.00	36.00

YR	NAME	LIMIT	ISSUE	TREND
90	LULU GIRL CAT	OP	26.00	26.00
90	MA SQUIRREL SASHA	CL	19.00	19.00
90	PA SQUIRREL SHERMAN	CL	19.00	19.00
90	PENNY GIRL DOG	OP	35.00	35.00
90	REBECCA MOM DOG	OP	40.00	40.00
90	SCOOTER BOY DOG	OP	30.00	30.00
90	SCUFFY BOY CAT	OP	26.00	26.00
90	WINNIE MOM CAT	OP	36.00	36.00
91	JIGGS, SLEEPING CAT	*	10.00	10.00
95	GIDDY-UP/4180	RT	38.00	38.00
S. SCHULTZ			**DAISY COLLECTION**	
89	SALLY BOOBA	CL	40.00	65.00
90	BOMBER	CL	52.00	60.00
90	JACK BOY BALL & GLOVE	CL	40.00	45.00
90	JEWEL	CL	62.00	70.00
90	SPARKY	CL	55.00	60.00
90	SPIKE	CL	46.00	50.00
90	STRETCH	CL	52.00	60.00
S. SCHULTZ			**DREAMS OF TOMORROW**	
96	NURSE TILLIE II/4502	5000	29.00	29.00
S. SCHULTZ			**GINGER BABIES COLLECTION**	
89	GINGER	CL	17.00	17.00
89	MOLASSES	CL	17.00	17.00
90	GINGER BOY NUTMEG	CL	15.50	20.00
90	GINGER GIRL CINNAMON	CL	15.50	20.00
S. SCHULTZ			**HAPPY COLLECTION**	
87	HAPPY W/BALLOONS	CL	22.00	22.00
87	LARGE HAPPY CLOWN	CL	22.00	22.00
87	SITTING HAPPY	CL	26.00	26.00
88	LADY CLOWN	CL	20.00	20.00
90	ENCORE CLOWN W/DOG	2000	100.00	100.00
S. SCHULTZ			**HEAVENLY WINGS COLLECTION**	
89	ANGELICA ANGEL	6000	21.00	25.00
89	HEAVENLY GUARDIAN	CL	40.00	40.00
89	REGINA	CL	24.00	30.00
90	ADORA W/BUNNY	10000	50.00	50.00
90	ADORA W/PINK GOWN	CL	35.00	75.00
90	BOY ANGEL INST. ADAIR	CL	29.00	29.00
90	ENOS W/BLUE GOWN	CL	33.00	75.00
90	ENOS W/FROG	10000	50.00	50.00
S. SCHULTZ			**LABOR OF LOVE**	
95	BABY/4288	OP	25.00	25.00
95	BEACH/4302	RT	29.00	29.00
95	BIRTHDAY/4290	OP	29.00	29.00
95	BIRTHDAY/4299	OP	29.00	29.00
95	BIRTHDAY/4301	OP	29.00	29.00
95	BIRTHDAY/4303	OP	29.00	29.00
95	BOTTLE/4306	RT	29.00	29.00
95	BOY STOCKING/4436	OP	18.00	18.00
95	BOY TRUMPET/4432	OP	18.00	18.00
95	BOY WREATH/4434	OP	18.00	18.00
95	CAMPFIRE/4293	RT	29.00	29.00
95	CANNING/4297	RT	29.00	29.00
95	COMPUTER/4304	OP	29.00	29.00
95	FISHING/4300	OP	29.00	29.00
95	GIRL PRAYING/4431	OP	18.00	18.00
95	GIRL WREATH/4435	OP	18.00	18.00
95	GOLFING/4308	OP	29.00	29.00
95	GROWING/4305	OP	29.00	29.00
95	HAPPINESS/4291	OP	29.00	29.00
95	HEALING/4292	OP	29.00	29.00
95	IRONING/4289	OP	29.00	29.00
95	MECHANIC/4298	RT	29.00	29.00
95	MOWING/4296	RT	29.00	29.00
95	PLANTING/4287	OP	29.00	29.00
95	PROTECT. BLUE/4383	OP	12.00	12.00
95	PROTECT. BLUE/4385	OP	12.00	12.00
95	PROTECT. GOLD/4378	OP	12.00	12.00
95	PROTECT. GOLD/4380	OP	12.00	12.00
95	PROTECT. GOLD/4382	OP	12.00	12.00
95	PROTECT. GOLD/4384	OP	12.00	12.00
95	PROTECT. PINK/4379	OP	12.00	12.00
95	PROTECT. PINK/4381	OP	12.00	12.00
95	ROLLER BLADING/4309	OP	29.00	29.00
95	SENDING SMILES/4307	OP	29.00	29.00
95	SEWING/4296	OP	29.00	29.00
95	STUDYING/4294	OP	25.00	25.00
95	TOOLS/4310	RT	29.00	29.00
96	COMPTR. BOY/4487	OP	29.00	29.00
96	COMPTR. GIRL/4486	OP	29.00	29.00
96	COMPTR. GIRL/4488	OP	29.00	29.00
96	COMPTR. SEWING/4489	OP	29.00	29.00
96	GOLFER/4490	OP	29.00	26.00
S. SCHULTZ			**LITTLE CHARMERS COLLECTION**	
87	AMBER-SMALL GIRL STANDING	CL	15.00	18.00
87	ARCHIE-SMALL BOY STANDING	CL	15.00	16.00
87	ASHLEE	CL	60.00	65.00
87	BARE BOTTOM BABY	CL	9.50	15.00

YR	NAME	LIMIT	ISSUE	TREND
87	BASEBALL PLAYER	CL	24.00	30.00
87	BEAU-CUPIE BOY	CL	20.00	22.00
87	BEVIE	CL	18.00	20.00
87	BLONDIE-GIRL DOLL SITTING	CL	16.00	18.00
87	BUTCH-BOY BOOK SITTING	CL	16.00	18.00
87	BUTTONS-CUPIE GIRL	CL	20.00	22.00
87	CHEERLEADER	CL	16.00	18.00
87	CLEMENTINE-GIRL SAILOR SUIT	CL	14.50	17.00
87	CORKY-BOY SAILOR SUIT	CL	14.50	17.00
87	CUPCAKE W/ROPE	CL	19.00	21.00
87	DAISY	CL	36.00	40.00
87	DUSTY	CL	19.00	21.00
87	EDDIE	CL	18.00	20.00
87	EMMY LOU	CL	14.00	16.00
87	FOOTBALL PLAYER	CL	24.00	26.00
87	MAN GOLFER	CL	24.00	26.00
87	SHOOTER	CL	19.00	21.00
87	TWINKLE W/POLE	CL	19.00	21.00
87	WILLIE BILL	CL	20.00	22.00
87	WOMAN GOLFER	CL	24.00	26.00
88	BASKETBALL PLAYER	CL	24.00	26.00
88	BOWLER	CL	24.00	26.00
88	BOY W/CLOWN DOLL	CL	40.00	45.00
88	GIRL W/DOG	CL	43.00	47.00
88	GIRL W/TEACUP	CL	37.00	40.00
88	JESSICA	CL	44.00	45.00
89	JENNIFER & DOG	CL	57.00	60.00
89	MOOSE BOY SITTING	OP	18.00	20.00
90	WHITE BABY TANSY	10000	40.00	40.00
S. SCHULTZ			**MARTIN LUTHER KING, JR.**	
95	BIRMINGHAM JAIL/4407	YR	65.00	65.00
95	WEDDING DAY/4406	YR	85.00	85.00
96	I HAVE A DREAM/4540	10000	50.00	65.00
96	RACIAL HARMONY/4541	5000	114.00	114.00
S. SCHULTZ			**MATT & MAGGIE**	
86	MAGGIE	RT	14.00	25.00
86	MAGGIE CANDLEHOLDER	CL	12.00	12.00
86	MATT	CL	14.00	25.00
86	MATT CANDLEHOLDER	CL	12.00	12.00
87	MAGGIE ON HEART	CL	9.00	13.00
87	MATT & MAGGIE W/BEAR	RT	100.00	155.00
87	MATT ON HEART	CL	9.00	13.00
87	STANDING MAGGIE	CL	11.00	13.00
87	STANDING MATT	CL	11.00	13.00
88	LARGE MAGGIE	RT	48.00	60.00
88	LARGE MATT	RT	48.00	60.00
88	SMALL SITTING MAGGIE	CL	11.50	37.00
88	SMALL SITTING MATT	CL	11.50	37.00
89	MAGGIE BENCH SITTER	CL	32.00	40.00
89	MATT BENCH SITTER	CL	32.00	40.00
89	MINI MAGGIE	CL	6.00	10.00
89	MINI MATT	CL	6.00	10.00
S. SCHULTZ			**MEMORY LANE COLLECTION**	
87	BARBER SHOP	CL	13.00	15.00
87	BARN	CL	16.50	18.00
87	CHURCH	CL	19.00	20.00
87	COTTAGE	CL	13.00	15.00
87	DRUG STORE	CL	13.00	15.00
87	GENERAL STORE	CL	13.00	15.00
87	GRANDMA'S HOUSE	CL	13.00	15.00
87	HOUSE W/DORMERS	CL	15.00	16.00
87	MILL	CL	16.50	18.00
87	SCHOOL	CL	14.00	15.00
88	BANK	CL	13.00	15.00
88	MINI BARBER SHOP	CL	6.50	10.00
88	MINI BARN	CL	6.00	8.00
88	MINI CHURCH	CL	6.50	10.00
88	MINI DRUG STORE	CL	6.00	8.00
88	MINI GENERAL STORE	CL	6.00	8.00
88	MINI GRANDMA'S HOUSE	CL	7.00	8.00
88	MINI MILL	CL	6.50	7.00
88	MINI SALT BOX	CL	6.00	6.00
88	MINI SCHOOL	CL	6.50	7.00
88	TRAIN DEPOT	CL	13.50	14.00
89	BRITON CHURCH	CL	25.00	25.00
89	FIRE STATION	CL	20.00	20.00
89	MINI BANK	CL	6.00	6.00
89	MINI DEPOT	CL	7.00	7.00
89	POST OFFICE	CL	25.00	25.00
S. SCHULTZ			**MICHAUD BEARS**	
95	BAY CITY BEAUTY/4334	RT	26.00	26.00
95	BEAU. W/TRUNK/4335	RT	40.00	40.00
95	LOVE HEALS ALL/4438	OP	28.00	28.00
95	PROXY BEAR/4332	RT	20.00	20.00
95	PROXY W/JEWELRY/4333	RT	33.00	33.00
S. SCHULTZ		**PREMIER EDITION FOR CLUB CONTEST WINNERS**		
96	ANGELS ON ASSIGN/4544	YR	65.00	65.00

YR	NAME	LIMIT	ISSUE	TREND
	S. SCHULTZ			**PROMOTION FIGURINES**
95	FLAGS IN HEAV./4386	YR	45.00	45.00
96	ABIGAIL/4543	YR	36.00	36.00
96	ARETHA/4542	YR	36.00	36.00
	S. SCHULTZ			**ROSE COLLECTION**
89	SWEET ROSE	CL	50.00	50.00
90	TIFFANY VICTORIAN GIRL	TL	40.00	40.00
90	TYLER VICTORIAN BOY	TL	40.00	40.00
90	VICTORIAN BOY CODY	CL	46.00	46.00
	S. SCHULTZ			**SANTAS OF THE MONTH**
88	APRIL SANTA BLACK	CL	50.00	250.00
88	APRIL SANTA WHITE	CL	50.00	125.00
88	AUGUST SANTA WHITE	CL	50.00	125.00
88	DECEMBER SANTA BLACK	TL	50.00	250.00
88	DECEMBER SANTA WHITE	CL	50.00	125.00
88	FEBRUARY SANTA BLACK	TL	50.00	250.00
88	FEBRUARY SANTA WHTIE	CL	50.00	125.00
88	JANUARY SANTA BLACK	TL	50.00	250.00
88	JANUARY SANTA WHITE	CL	50.00	125.00
88	JULY SANTA BLACK	TL	50.00	250.00
88	JULY SANTA WHITE	CL	50.00	125.00
88	JUNE SANTA	TL	50.00	250.00
88	JUNE SANTA WHITE	CL	50.00	125.00
88	MARCH SANTA BLACK	TL	50.00	250.00
88	MARCH SANTA WHITE	CL	50.00	125.00
88	MAY SANTA BLACK	CL	50.00	250.00
88	MAY SANTA WHITE	CL	50.00	125.00
88	MINI APRIL SANTA	CL	14.00	30.00
88	MINI AUGUST SANTA	CL	14.00	30.00
88	MINI DECEMBER SANTA	CL	14.00	30.00
88	MINI FEBRUARY SANTA	CL	14.00	30.00
88	MINI JANUARY SANTA	CL	14.00	30.00
88	MINI JULY SANTA	CL	14.00	30.00
88	MINI JUNE SANTA	CL	14.00	30.00
88	MINI MARCH SANTA	CL	14.00	30.00
88	MINI MAY SANTA	CL	14.00	30.00
88	MINI NOVEMBER SANTA	CL	14.00	30.00
88	MINI OCTOBER SANTA	CL	14.00	30.00
88	MINI SEPTEMBER SANTA	CL	14.00	30.00
88	NOVEMBER SANTA BLACK	TL	50.00	250.00
88	NOVEMBER SANTA WHITE	CL	50.00	125.00
88	OCTOBER SANTA BLACK	TL	50.00	250.00
88	OCTOBER SANTA WHITE	CL	50.00	125.00
88	SEPTEMBER SANTA BLACK	TL	50.00	250.00
88	SEPTEMBER SANTA WHITE	CL	50.00	125.00
90	APR. SANTA SPRING/JOY	CL	150.00	150.00
90	APR. SPRING TIME	CL	90.00	100.00
90	APRIL, MRS.	CL	110.00	110.00
90	AUG. FUN IN THE SUN	CL	90.00	100.00
90	AUGUST SANTA BLACK	CL	50.00	250.00
90	AUGUST SANTA SUMMERS TRN.	CL	110.00	125.00
90	AUGUST, MRS.	CL	90.00	100.00
90	DEC. A GIFT OF PEACE	CL	90.00	90.00
90	DEC. SANTA PEACE	CL	120.00	125.00
90	DECEMBER, MRS.	CL	110.00	130.00
90	FEB. FROM THE HEART	CL	90.00	90.00
90	FEB. SANTA CUPIDS HELP	CL	120.00	120.00
90	FEBRUARY, MRS.	CL	110.00	110.00
90	JAN. FRUITS OF LOVE	CL	90.00	90.00
90	JAN. SANTA WINTER FUN	CL	80.00	85.00
90	JANUARY, MRS.	CL	80.00	105.00
90	JULY CELEBRATE AMERICA	CL	90.00	95.00
90	JULY SANTA GOD BLESS	CL	100.00	110.00
90	JULY, MRS.	CL	100.00	120.00
90	JUNE HOMERUN	CL	90.00	95.00
90	JUNE SANTA GRADUATION	CL	70.00	70.00
90	JUNE, MRS.	CL	70.00	95.00
90	MAR. IRISH LOVE	CL	100.00	100.00
90	MAR. SANTA IRISH DELIGHT	CL	120.00	145.00
90	MARCH, MRS.	CL	80.00	95.00
90	MASQUERADE TILLIE	TL	45.00	45.00
90	MAY CADDY CHATTER	CL	100.00	100.00
90	MAY SANTA PAR FOR COURSE	CL	100.00	100.00
90	MAY, MRS.	CL	80.00	110.00
90	NOV. HARVEST OF LOVE	TL	120.00	120.00
90	NOV. SANTA GIVE THANKS	CL	100.00	120.00
90	NOVEMBER, MRS.	CL	90.00	110.00
90	OCT. MASQUERADE	CL	120.00	120.00
90	OCT. SANTA SEASONS PLENTY	CL	120.00	120.00
90	OCTOBER, MRS.	CL	90.00	110.00
90	SEP. SANTA TOUCHDOWN	CL	90.00	90.00
90	SEPT. LESSONS IN LOVE	TL	90.00	90.00
90	SEPTEMBER, MRS.	CL	90.00	95.00
	S. SCHULTZ			**SARAH'S GANG**
86	ORIGINAL KATIE	CL	14.00	20.00
86	ORIGINAL TILLIE	CL	14.00	25.00
86	ORIGINAL TWINKIE	CL	14.00	20.00
86	ORIGINAL WHIMPY	CL	14.00	20.00

YR	NAME	LIMIT	ISSUE	TREND
86	ORIGINAL WILLIE	CL	14.00	28.00
86	TILLIE CANDLE HOLDER	CL	12.00	13.00
87	CUPCAKE ON HEART	CL	12.00	21.00
87	KATIE ON HEART	CL	12.00	21.00
87	ORIGINAL CUPCAKE	CL	16.00	20.00
87	SITTING KATIE	CL	14.00	21.00
87	SITTING WHIMPY	CL	14.00	21.00
87	TILLIE ON HEART	CL	9.00	21.00
87	TWINKIE ON HEART	CL	9.00	21.00
87	WHIMPY ON HEART	CL	9.00	19.00
87	WILLIE CANDLE HOLDER	CL	12.00	13.00
87	WILLIE ON HEART	CL	9.00	21.00
88	CUPCAKE	CL	20.00	21.00
88	KATIE	CL	20.00	21.00
88	TILLIE	CL	20.00	21.00
88	TWINKIE	CL	20.00	21.00
88	WHIMPY	CL	20.00	21.00
88	WILLIE	CL	20.00	21.00
89	AMERICANA CUPCAKE	CL	21.00	24.00
89	AMERICANA KATIE	CL	21.00	24.00
89	AMERICANA TILLIE	CL	21.00	24.00
89	AMERICANA TWINKIE	CL	21.00	24.00
89	AMERICANA WHIMPY	CL	21.00	24.00
89	AMERICANA WILLIE	CL	21.00	24.00
89	BABY RACHEL	CL	20.00	20.00
89	SMALL COUNTRY TILLIE	CL	16.00	25.00
89	SMALL COUNTRY WILLIE	CL	18.00	25.00
89	SMALL SAILOR KATIE	CL	14.00	18.00
89	SMALL SAILOR WHIMPY	CL	14.00	18.00
89	SMALL SCHOOL CUPCAKE	CL	11.00	18.00
89	SMALL SCHOOL TWINKIE	CL	11.00	18.00
90	AMERICANA RACHEL	CL	30.00	30.00
90	BEACHTIME BABY RACHEL	CL	35.00	50.00
90	BEACHTIME CUPCAKE	CL	35.00	50.00
90	BEACHTIME KATIE & WHIMPY	CL	60.00	70.00
90	BEACHTIME TILLIE	CL	35.00	50.00
90	BEACHTIME TWINKIE	CL	35.00	50.00
90	BEACHTIME WILLIE	CL	35.00	50.00
90	CLOWN TILLIE	CL	40.00	45.00
90	CLOWN WILLIE	CL	40.00	45.00
90	DEVIL CUPCAKE	CL	40.00	40.00
90	DEVIL TWINKIE	CL	40.00	45.00
90	PUMPKIN RACHEL	CL	40.00	45.00
90	SCARECROW WHIMPY	CL	40.00	40.00
90	WITCH KATIE	CL	40.00	45.00
91	CRACKER, COCKER SPANIAL	TL	9.00	9.00
91	DOCTOR TWINKIE	6000	50.00	50.00
91	EXECUTIVE WHIMP	6000	46.00	46.00
91	KATIE, WHITE BRIDE	TL	47.00	47.00
91	NURSE CUPCAKE	6000	46.00	46.00
91	PEACHES, BLACK FLOWER GIRL	CL	40.00	40.00
91	PERCY, BLACK MINISTER	CL	50.00	50.00
91	PUG, BLACK RING BEARER	CL	40.00	40.00
91	RACHEL, WHITE FLOWER GIRL	CL	40.00	40.00
91	TEACHER TILLIE	6000	50.00	50.00
91	THANKSGIVING KATIE	RT	32.00	32.00
91	THANKSGIVING RACHEL	RT	32.00	32.00
91	THANKSGIVING TILLIE	RT	32.00	32.00
91	THANKSGIVING WHIMPY	RT	32.00	32.00
91	THANKSGIVING WILLIE	10000	32.00	32.00
91	TILLIE, BLACK BRIDE	CL	47.00	50.00
91	TWINKIE, WHITE MINISTER	CL	50.00	52.00
91	TYLER, WHITE RING BEARER	CL	40.00	40.00
91	WHIMPY, WHITE GROOM	CL	47.00	50.00
91	WILLIE, BLACK GROOM	CL	47.00	47.00
95	CUPCAKE/4346	OP	28.00	28.00
95	KATIE/4344	OP	28.00	28.00
95	LARGE FLOWER POT84355	OP	6.00	6.00
95	PORCE SET 5 PC./4353	OP	250.00	250.00
95	RACHEL/4348	OP	28.00	28.00
95	ROLLER BLADES/4356	OP	8.00	8.00
95	SMALL FLOWER POT/4354	OP	5.00	5.00
95	SPARKY/4357	OP	10.00	10.00
95	TILLIE/4342	OP	28.00	28.00
95	TRAP/4360	OP	6.50	6.50
95	TWINKIE/4347	OP	28.00	28.00
95	WAGON OF FUN/4361	OP	25.00	25.00
95	WHIMPY/4345	OP	28.00	28.00
95	WICKER CHAIR/4358	OP	20.00	20.00
95	WICKER SETTEE/4359	OP	25.00	25.00
95	WILLIE/4343	OP	28.00	28.00

S. SCHULTZ **SARAH'S NEIGHBORHOOD FRIENDS**

YR	NAME	LIMIT	ISSUE	TREND
90	ANNIE W/FLOWER BASKET	CL	56.00	56.00
90	ANNIE W/VIOLIN	CL	40.00	40.00
90	BUBBA W/LANTERN	CL	40.00	40.00
90	BUBBA W/LEMONADE	CL	54.00	100.00
90	BUD W/BOOK	CL	40.00	40.00
90	BUD W/NEWSPAPER	CL	40.00	40.00
90	HEWETT W/APPLES	CL	40.00	40.00

YR	NAME	LIMIT	ISSUE	TREND
90	HEWETT W/DRUM	CL	40.00	40.00
90	PANSY W/BUGGY	CL	50.00	50.00
90	PANSY W/SLED	CL	35.00	35.00
90	WALDO DOG	CL	10.00	10.00
90	WALDO W/FLOWERS	CL	14.00	15.00
90	WEASEL W/CAP	CL	40.00	40.00
90	WEASEL W/PAPER	CL	40.00	40.00
91	ANNIE, WHITE MARY	CL	30.00	30.00
91	BABES, BLACK BABY JESUS	CL	20.00	20.00
91	BUBBA, BLACK KING	CL	40.00	40.00
91	BUD, WHITE JOSEPH	CL	34.00	34.00
91	CRATE OF LOVE, BLACK	CL	40.00	40.00
91	CRATE OF LOVE, WHITE	CL	40.00	40.00
91	DOLLY, WHITE BABY JESUS	CL	20.00	20.00
91	EXECUTIVE NOAH	CL	46.00	46.00
91	HEWITT, WHITE KING W/DRUM	CL	40.00	40.00
91	KITTEN IN BASKET	TL	15.00	16.00
91	NOAH, BLACK JOSEPH	TL	36.00	36.00
91	NURSE PANSY	6000	46.00	46.00
91	PANSY, BLACK ANGEL	TL	30.00	30.00
91	SHELBY, BLACK MARY	CL	30.00	30.00
91	TEACHER ANNIE	6000	55.00	55.00
91	WALDO, DOG W/SHOE	TL	15.00	16.00
91	WEASEL, WHITE KING W/KITTEN	CL	40.00	40.00
S. SCHULTZ			**SNOWFLAKE COLLECTION**	
89	BOO MINI SNOWMAN	CL	6.00	10.00
89	FLURRY	CL	12.00	18.00
89	WINTER FROLIC	CL	60.00	72.00
90	AMERICAN SNOW OLD GLORY	RT	24.00	25.00
95	CHILLY/4418	1000	44.00	44.00
95	CHILLY/JINGLES/4417	SO	80.00	80.00
95	FLURRY & BOO/4414	1000	30.00	30.00
95	SNOWY/4416	1000	30.00	30.00
96	CHILLY/SNOWFLAKE/4482	5000	32.00	32.00
96	FILLY/SNOWCRYSTAL/4483	5000	36.00	36.00
96	TOPPER/TABBY/4481	5000	32.00	32.00
S. SCHULTZ			**SPIRIT OF AMERICA**	
96	BETSY/4491	2500	40.00	40.00
96	GOD BLESS AMERICA/4497	1776	30.00	30.00
96	GOD BLESS AMERICA/4498	1776	30.00	30.00
96	I'M PROUD BEAR/4495	2500	10.00	10.00
96	PEACHES/4493	2500	26.00	26.00
96	PUG/4494	2500	26.00	26.00
96	ROSS/4492	2500	36.00	36.00
96	USA SANTA/4496	1775	100.00	100.00
S. SCHULTZ			**SPIRIT OF CHRISTMAS COLLECTION**	
87	COLONEL SANTA	CL	30.00	30.00
87	FATHER SNOW	CL	42.00	46.00
87	JINGLE BELLS	CL	20.00	28.00
87	KRIS KRINGLE	CL	100.00	120.00
87	LARGE SANTA W/CANE	CL	27.00	33.00
87	LONG JOURNEY	CL	19.00	36.00
87	MINI SANTA W/CANE	CL	8.00	10.00
87	MRS. CLAUS	CL	26.00	28.00
87	NAUGHTY OR NICE SANTA AT D	CL	100.00	100.00
87	SANTA SITTING	CL	18.00	20.00
87	SANTA W/POCKETS	CL	34.00	34.00
87	SANTA'S WORKSHOP	CL	50.00	90.00
87	SMALL SANTA W/TREE	CL	14.00	17.00
88	BLESSED CHRISTMAS	RT	100.00	100.00
88	CHRISTMAS CLOWN	CL	88.00	88.00
88	CHRISTMAS W/CHILDREN	4000	80.00	80.00
88	COW/OX	CL	16.50	17.00
88	ELF GRABBING HAT	CL	8.00	10.00
88	ELF W/GIFT	CL	8.00	9.00
88	JESUS-NATURAL	CL	11.00	11.00
88	JOSEPH-NATURAL	CL	11.00	11.00
88	LARGE MRS. CLAUS RES. CANDLE	CL	11.00	12.00
88	LARGE SANTA RES. CANDLE	CL	11.00	12.00
88	MARY-NATURAL	CL	12.00	12.00
88	MINI JESUS	CL	4.00	5.00
88	MINI JESUS-NATURAL	CL	4.00	5.00
88	MINI JOSEPH	CL	6.00	6.00
88	MINI JOSEPH-NATURAL	CL	5.00	5.00
88	MINI LONG JOURNEY	CL	11.00	11.00
88	MINI MARY	CL	8.00	8.00
88	MINI MARY-NATURAL	CL	5.00	5.00
88	MINI SANTA RES. CANDLE	CL	7.00	7.00
88	SANTA IN CHIMNEY	CL	110.00	140.00
88	SANTA KNEELING	CL	22.00	22.00
88	SANTA W/ELF	CL	90.00	90.00
88	SHEEP	CL	8.00	8.00
88	SITTING ELF	CL	7.00	15.00
88	SMALL ANGEL RES. CANDLE	CL	9.50	10.00
88	SMALL MRS. CLAUS	CL	8.50	9.00
88	SMALL MRS. CLAUS RES. CANDLE	CL	10.00	10.00
88	SMALL SANTA RES. CANDLE	CL	10.00	10.00
88	SMALL SITTING SANTA	CL	11.00	11.00

YR	NAME	LIMIT	ISSUE	TREND
89	BLINKEY ELF BALL	CL	16.00	20.00
89	CHRISTMAS JOY	RT	32.00	33.00
89	COLONEL SANTA 2	CL	35.00	36.00
89	FATHER SNOW 2	RT	32.00	40.00
89	JINGLE BELLS 2	RT	25.00	25.00
89	JOLLY 2	RT	17.00	18.00
89	LONG JOURNEY 2	RT	35.00	45.00
89	MAMA SANTA SITTING	CL	30.00	42.00
89	MAMA SANTA STOCKING	CL	50.00	51.00
89	MINI COLONEL SANTA	CL	14.00	20.00
89	MINI FATHER SNOW	CL	16.00	17.00
89	MINI JINGLE BELLS	CL	16.00	17.00
89	MINI JOLLY	CL	10.00	11.00
89	MINI NAUGHTY OR NICE	CL	20.00	21.00
89	MINI ST. NICK	CL	14.00	15.00
89	PAPA SANTA SITTING	CL	30.00	41.00
89	PAPA SANTA STOCKING	CL	50.00	62.00
89	SILENT NIGHT	RT	33.00	45.00
89	ST. NICK 2	CL	43.00	45.00
89	STINKY ELF SITTING	CL	16.00	18.00
89	WINKY ELF LETTER	CL	16.00	21.00
89	WOODLAND SANTA	RT	100.00	140.00
89	YULE TIDINGS 2	RT	23.00	31.00
90	BELLS OF X-MAS	RT	35.00	38.00
90	CHRISTMAS MUSIC	RT	60.00	65.00
90	CHRISTMAS WISHES	RT	50.00	51.00
90	CHRISTMAS WONDER SANTA	RT	50.00	55.00
90	LOVE THE CHILDREN	RT	75.00	78.00
90	SANTA CLAUS EXPRESS	RT	150.00	155.00
91	SHARING LOVE SANTA	RT	120.00	130.00
91	TREASURES OF LOVE SANTA	RT	140.00	145.00
95	AMERICAN SANTA/4467	1776	100.00	100.00
95	CARE BASKET/4424	5000	26.00	26.00
95	CARING/4423	5000	29.00	29.00
95	CHERISH THE CHILDREN/4466	7500	70.00	70.00
95	CHRISTINE/4420	5000	26.00	26.00
95	CHRISTMAS DREAMS/4463	1000	64.00	64.00
95	CHRISTMAS JOY/4331	2000	60.00	60.00
95	CHRISTMAS WARM./4421	OP	90.00	90.00
95	COFFEE POT/4422	OP	5.00	5.00
95	COUNTRY TREE/4419	OP	33.00	33.00
95	HAPPINESS/4426	5000	34.00	34.00
95	HELPFULNESS/4425	5000	37.00	37.00
95	JOY TO THE WORLD/4462	1000	64.00	64.00
95	JOYFULNESS/4428	5000	28.00	28.00
95	KINDNESS/4427	5000	30.00	30.00
95	MRS. SANTA/4430	5000	42.00	42.00
95	PEACE ON EARTH/4464	7500	80.00	80.00
95	SANTA'S LOVE/4465	7500	98.00	98.00
95	SANTA/4429	5000	45.00	45.00
95	TILLIE CAROLING/4461	5000	26.00	26.00
95	WILLIE CAROLING/4460	5000	26.00	26.00
S. SCHULTZ			**SPRINGTIME TREASURES**	
96	AMEN BIBLE/4524	OP	20.00	20.00
96	BUNNY BUN/4510	1500	18.00	18.00
96	BUNNY LOVE/4513	1500	18.00	18.00
96	HERBIE RABBIT/4509	1500	33.00	33.00
96	HETHER RABBIT/4508	1500	33.00	33.00
96	JANGLES RABBIT/4511	1500	24.00	24.00
96	JINGLES RABBIT/4512	1500	24.00	24.00
96	SANTA & FRIENDS/4517	1000	100.00	100.00
96	SPIRITUAL GUID-B 4518	2000	65.00	65.00
96	SPIRITUAL GUID-G 4519	2000	65.00	65.00
96	SPRING TREASURES/4516	1000	100.00	100.00
S. SCHULTZ			**TATTERED N' TORN COLLECTION**	
90	BLACK MUFFIN & PUFFIN	10000	55.00	55.00
90	BLACK PRISSY & PEANUT	2000	120.00	120.00
90	BOY RAG DOLL OPIE	4000	50.00	50.00
90	GIRL RAG DOLL POLLY	4000	50.00	50.00
90	MUFFIN BLACK RAG DOLL	500	90.00	200.00
90	PUFFIN BLACK RAG DOLL	OP	90.00	200.00
90	WHITE MUFFIN & PUFFIN	10000	55.00	55.00
90	WHITE PRISSY & PEANUT	2000	120.00	120.00
S. SCHULTZ			**TENDER MOMENTS**	
95	ALL DONE/4395	3000	29.00	29.00
95	BUNDLE OF JOY/4392	3000	20.00	20.00
95	BUNDLE OF LOVE/4393	3000	29.00	29.00
95	FAMILY IS LOVE/4320	RT	60.00	60.00
95	HAVING FUN/4322	RT	44.00	44.00
95	LITTLE ENGINEER/4389	3000	25.00	25.00
95	LULLABY/4390	3000	29.00	29.00
95	ME BIG GIRL/4394	3000	29.00	29.00
95	PRECIOUS DREAMS/4391	3000	28.00	28.00
95	REFRESHMENTS/4326	RT	16.00	16.00
95	REMEMBRANCE/4470	2000	100.00	100.00
95	SQUEAKS/4327	RT	5.00	5.00
95	STUDY TIME/4325	RT	32.00	32.00
95	SWEET DREAMS/4388	3000	29.00	29.00

YR	NAME	LIMIT	ISSUE	TREND
95	TIME. KNOWL./4323	RT	47.00	47.00
95	TREASURE MOMENTS/4321	RT	70.00	70.00
95	WOW/4324	RT	36.00	36.00
96	BUBBLES/4503	3000	35.00	35.00
96	DINNER TIME/4507	3000	32.00	32.00
96	MIKEY BEAR II/BW/4528	2500	60.00	60.00
96	MIKEY BEARII-VG/4526	2500	60.00	60.00
96	MISSY BEAR II-VG-4525	2500	60.00	60.00
96	MISSY BEAR II/BW/4527	2500	60.00	60.00
96	TA DA/4506	3000	32.00	32.00
96	YACKY JACKIE/4504	3000	32.00	32.00
S. SCHULTZ		**UNITED HEARTS COLLECTION**		
91	BARNEY THE GREAT BEAR	CL	40.00	50.00
91	BEACH ANNIE & WALDO	CL	40.00	41.00
91	BEACH BUBBA W/INNERTUBE	CL	34.00	40.00
91	BEACH PANSY WITH KITTEN	CL	34.00	40.00
91	BIBI-MISS LIBERTY BEAR	CL	30.00	35.00
91	CHILLY SNOWMAN	CL	33.00	41.00
91	CHRISTMAS ADORA	CL	36.00	42.00
91	CHRISTMAS ENOS	CL	36.00	37.00
91	CHRISTMAS TREE WITH HEARTS	CL	40.00	40.00
91	CLOWN BIBI & BIFF BEARS	CL	35.00	40.00
91	EMILY W/BUGGY	CL	53.00	58.00
91	GIDEON WITH BEAR & ROSE	CL	40.00	42.00
91	HEWITT W/LEPRECHAUN	CL	56.00	65.00
91	JACK BOY GRADUATION	CL	40.00	41.00
91	LIBERTY PAPA BARNEY & BIFF	CL	64.00	75.00
91	NOAH W/POT OF GOLD	CL	36.00	45.00
91	SALLY BOOBA GRADUATION	CL	45.00	48.00
91	SCHOOL CHUCKLES RABBIT	CL	26.00	27.00
91	SCHOOL COOKIE RABBIT W/KIT	CL	28.00	29.00
91	SCHOOL CRUMB RABBIT-DUNCE	CL	32.00	40.00
91	SCHOOL DESK WITH BOOK	TL	15.00	16.00
91	SHELBY W/SHAMROCK	CL	36.00	40.00
91	THANKSGIVING CORNSTALK	TL	30.00	30.00
91	THANKSGIVING CUPCAKE	CL	36.00	37.00
91	THANKSGIVING TWINKIE	CL	32.00	33.00
91	TILLIE WITH SKATES	CL	32.00	38.00
91	TOBY & TESSIE W/WHEELBARROW	CL	44.00	45.00
91	VALENTINE PEANUT W/CANDY	CL	32.00	33.00
91	VALENTINE PRISSY WITH DOG	CL	36.00	37.00
91	WILLIE ON SLED	CL	32.00	41.00
91	WOOLY LAMB	CL	16.00	16.00
92	SPARKY DOG GRADUATION	TL	16.00	16.00
92	TABITHA RABBIT W/BUNNY	TL	32.00	33.00

SCHMID

Price ranges may reflect various demands in the market from one geographic region to another; condition of piece; specific markings found on piece; and/or changes in production of piece.

YR	NAME	LIMIT	ISSUE	TREND
L. DAVIS		**COUNTRY PRIDE**		
81	BUSTIN' WITH PRIDE	RT	100.00	225.00
81	DUKE'S MIXTURE	RT	100.00	225.00
81	PLUM TUCKERED OUT	RT	100.00	900.00
81	SURPRISE IN THE CELLAR	RT	100.00	965.00
L. DAVIS		**DAVIS CAT TALES**		
82	COMPANY'S COMING	RT	60.00	250.00
82	FLEW THE COOP	RT	60.00	350.00
82	ON THE MOVE	RT	70.00	600.00
82	RIGHT CHURCH, WRONG PEW	RT	70.00	350.00
L. DAVIS		**DAVIS CHRISTMAS FIGURINES**		
83	HOOKER AT MAILBOX/PRESENTS	CL	80.00	750.00
84	COUNTRY CHRISTMAS	RT	80.00	465.00
84	KITTENS WITH PRESENTS	2500	80.00	450.00-475.00
85	CHRISTMAS AT FOXFIRE FARM	CL	80.00	260.00
86	CHRISTMAS AT RED OAK	CL	80.00	200.00
87	BLOSSOM'S GIFT	CL	150.00	325.00
88	CUTTING THE FAMILY CHRISTMAS TREE	CL	220.00	325.00
89	PETER AND THE WREN	2250	165.00	375.00
90	WINTERING DEER	2500	165.00	275.00
91	CHRISTMAS AT RED OAK II	CL	250.00	250.00
92	BORN ON A STARRY NIGHT	2500	225.00	225.00
94	VISIONS OF SUGAR PLUMS	2500	250.00	250.00
95	BAH HUMBUG	2500	200.00	200.00
L. DAVIS		**DAVIS SPECIAL EDITION FIGURINES**		
83	CRITICS, THE	RT	400.00	1100.00
85	HOME FROM MARKET	RT	400.00	1400.00
89	FROM A FRIEND TO A FRIEND	RT	750.00	1650.00
90	WHAT RAT RACE?	RT	800.00	1000.00
92	LAST LAFF	1200	900.00	975.00
L. DAVIS		**DEALER COUNTER SIGNS**		
80	RFD AMERICA	CL	40.00	175.00-275.00
81	UNCLE REMUS	CL	30.00	300.00
85	FOX FIRE FARM	CL	30.00	150.00-275.00
90	MR. LOWELL'S FARM	OP	50.00	60.00
92	LITTLE CRITTERS	OP	50.00	50.00
D. POLLAND		**DON POLLAND FIGURINES I**		
83	A SECOND CHANCE	RT	350.00	650.00

YR	NAME	LIMIT	ISSUE	TREND
83	CHALLENGE	RT	275.00	600.00
83	DANGEROUS MOMENT	RT	250.00	350.00
83	DOWNED	RT	250.00	600.00
83	ESCAPE	RT	175.00	650.00
83	FIGHTING BULLS	RT	200.00	600.00
83	GREAT HUNT, THE	RT	3750.00	3775.00
83	HOT PURSUIT	RT	225.00	550.00
83	HUNTER, THE	RT	225.00	500.00
83	YOUNG BULL	RT	125.00	250.00
86	DOWN FROM THE HIGH COUNTRY	RT	225.00	300.00
86	EAGLE DANCER	RT	170.00	300.00
86	PLAINS WARRIOR	RT	350.00	550.00
86	RUNNING WOLF-WAR CHIEF	RT	170.00	300.00
86	SECOND CHANCE	RT	125.00	650.00
86	SHOOTING THE RAPIDS	RT	195.00	500.00
86	WAR TROPHY	RT	225.00	500.00
L. DAVIS				**FARM SET**
85	BARN	RT	47.50	250.00-425.00
85	CHICKEN HOUSE	RT	19.00	55.00
85	CORN CRIB AND SHEEP PEN	RT	25.00	75.00
85	GARDEN AND WOOD SHED	RT	25.00	60.00
85	GOAT YARD AND STUDIO	RT	32.50	80.00
85	HEN HOUSE	RT	32.50	75.00
85	HOG HOUSE	RT	27.50	80.00
85	MAIN HOUSE	RT	42.50	105.00
85	PRIVY	OP	12.50	40.00
85	REMUS' CABIN	RT	42.50	100.00
85	SMOKE HOUSE	RT	12.50	70.00
85	WINDMILL	OP	25.00	45.00
L. DAVIS				**FRIENDS OF MINE**
89	SUN WORSHIPPERS	RT	120.00	140.00
89	SUN WORSHIPPERS MINI	RT	32.50	40.00
91	WARM MILK	RT	120.00	135.00-150.00
91	WARM MILK MINI	RT	32.50	38.00
92	CAT AND JENNY WREN	5000	170.00	170.00
92	CAT AND JENNY WREN MINI	OP	35.00	35.00
92	SUNDAY AFTERNOON TREAT	RT	130.00	175.00
92	SUNDAY AFTERNOON TREAT MINI	RT	37.50	38.00
L. DAVIS				**LITTLE CRITTERS**
89	GITTIN' A NIBBLE	RT	50.00	60.00
90	GREAT AMERICAN CHICKEN RACE	2500	225.00	250.00
90	HOME SQUEEZINS	RT	90.00	90.00
90	MILK MOUSE	2500	175.00	230.00
90	OUTING WITH GRANDPA	RT	200.00	250.00
90	PRIVATE TIME	RT	18.00	45.00
90	PUNKIN PIG	RT	250.00	375.00
90	PUNKIN WINE	CL	100.00	145.00
91	HITTIN THE SACK	CL	70.00	70.00
91	ITISKIT, ITASKET	OP	45.00	45.00
91	TOAD STRANGLER	CL	57.00	60.00
91	WHEN COFFEE NEVER TASTED SO GOOD	1250	800.00	800.00
92	A WOLF IN SHEEP'S CLOTHING	YR	110.00	110.00
92	A WOLF IN SHEEP'S CLOTHING	YR	110.00	110.00
92	CHARIVARI	950	250.00	250.00
92	CHRISTOPHER CRITTER	RT	150.00	100.00-150.00
92	DOUBLE YOLKER	YR	70.00	70.00
92	MISS PRIVATE TIME	YR	35.00	35.00
L. DAVIS				**LOWELL DAVIS FARM CLUB**
85	BRIDE, THE	RT	45.00	425.00
86	THIRSTY ?	YR	*	45.00
87	CACKLE BERRIES	RT	*	*
87	PARTY'S OVER, THE	RT	55.00	140.00
88	CHOW TIME	RT	65.00	95.00
88	ICE CREAM CHURN	RT	*	55.00
89	CAN'T WAIT	RT	75.00	110.00
90	NOT A SHARING SOUL	RT	*	40.00
90	PIT STOP	RT	75.00	130.00
91	ARRIVAL OF STANLEY	RT	100.00	100.00
91	DON'T PICK THE FLOWERS	RT	100.00	150.00
91	NEW ARRIVAL	RT	*	35.00
92	CHECK'S IN THE MAIL	RT	100.00	100.00
92	GARDEN TOAD	RT	*	*
92	HOG WILD	RT	100.00	100.00
93	LUKE 12:6	RT	*	*
93	SUMMER DAYS	YR	100.00	100.00
93	SURVIVOR, THE	RT	45.00	75.00
94	DUTCH TREAT	YR	100.00	100.00
95	FREE KITTENS	YR	40.00	40.00
L. DAVIS				**PROMOTIONAL FIGURINE**
91	LEAVIN THE RAT RACE	*	125.00	145.00
92	HEN SCRATCH	*	90.00	100.00
L. DAVIS				**QUILTIN' BEE**
92	BIG LIKE DADDY	OP	80.00	80.00
92	BIRDS OF A FEATHER	OP	80.00	80.00
92	CORN FLABIN	OP	80.00	80.00
92	GOLDIE AND HER PEEPS	OP	80.00	80.00
92	LUNCH BREAK	OP	80.00	80.00
92	WHAT'S FOR DESSERT	OP	80.00	80.00

YR	NAME	LIMIT	ISSUE	TREND
L. DAVIS				**RFD AMERICA**
79	BLOSSOM	RT	180.00	1700.00
79	BROKEN DREAMS	RT	185.00	1150.00
79	COUNTRY ROAD	RT	120.00	875.00
79	FOWL PLAY	RT	100.00	300.00
79	IGNORANCE IS BLISS	RT	165.00	1250.00
79	SLIM PICKINS	RT	185.00	650.00
80	CREEK BANK BANDIT	RT	37.50	385.00
80	FORBIDDEN FRUIT	RT	32.50	170.00
80	GOOD, CLEAN FUN	RT	40.00	105.00
80	ITCHING POST	RT	30.00	100.00
80	MILKING TIME	RT	32.50	250.00
80	NEW DAY	RT	20.00	175.00
80	STRAWBERRY PATCH	RT	25.00	100.00
80	SUNDAY AFTERNOON	RT	32.50	235.00
80	WILBUR	RT	110.00	600.00
81	COUNTRY BOY	RT	45.00	325.00
81	DOUBLE TROUBLE	RT	42.50	500.00
81	DRY AS A BONE	RT	45.00	300.00
81	HIGHTAILING IT	RT	50.00	425.00
81	PUNKIN SEEDS	RT	250.00	1600.00
81	ROOTED OUT	RT	45.00	100.00
81	SCALLAWAGS	RT	65.00	165.00
81	SPLIT DECISION	RT	45.00	255.00
81	STUDIO MOUSE	RT	60.00	325.00
81	UNDER THE WEATHER	RT	25.00	90.00
81	UP TO NO GOOD	RT	200.00	875.00-900.00
82	A SHOE TO FILL	RT	37.50	175.00
82	BABY BLOSSOM	RT	40.00	300.00
82	BABY BOBS	RT	47.50	225.00
82	BLOSSOM & CALF	RT	250.00	850.00
82	BRAND NEW DAY	RT	23.50	155.00
82	COUNTRY CROOK	RT	37.50	375.00
82	IDLE HOURS	RT	37.50	275.00
82	MOON RAIDERS	RT	180.00	300.00
82	MOVING DAY	RT	43.50	300.00
82	STRAY DOG	RT	35.00	70.00
82	THINKING BIG	RT	35.00	90.00
82	TREED	RT	155.00	300.00
82	TWO'S COMPANY	RT	43.50	225.00
82	WAITING FOR HIS MASTER	RT	50.00	150.00-300
82	WHEN MAMA GETS MAD	RT	37.50	340.00
83	CITY SLICKER	RT	150.00	275.00
83	COUNTING THE DAYS	RT	40.00	65.00
83	FAIR WEATHER FRIEND	RT	25.00	90.00
83	FALSE ALARM	RT	65.00	170.00
83	HAPPY HUNTING GROUND	RT	160.00	240.00
83	HI GIRLS, THE NAME'S BIG JACK	RT	200.00	380.00
83	HIS EYES ARE BIGGER THAN STOMACH	CL	235.00	330.00-365.00
83	LICKIN' GOOD	RT	35.00	250.00
83	MAKIN' TRACKS	RT	70.00	115.00
83	MAMA'S PRIZE LEGHORN	RT	55.00	120.00
83	STIRRING UP TROUBLE	RT	160.00	245.00
83	WOMEN'S WORK	RT	35.00	85.00
84	ANYBODY HOME	CL	35.00	125.00
84	CATNAPPING TOO	RT	70.00	140.00
84	COUNTRY KITTY	CL	52.00	110.00
84	COURTIN'	RT	45.00	125.00
84	GONNA PAY FOR HIS SINS	OP	27.50	50.00
84	GOSSIPS	RT	110.00	225.00
84	HEADED HOME	RT	253.00	53.00
84	HIS MASTER'S DOG	RT	45.00	100.00-200.00
84	HUH?	RT	40.00	125.00
84	MAD AS A WET HEN	RT	185.00	750.00
84	ONE FOR THE ROAD	OP	37.50	65.00
84	PASTURE PALS	RT	52.00	125.00
84	PRAIRIE CHORUS	RT	135.00	1100.00-1300.00
85	BARN CATS	*	39.50	65.00
85	COUNTRY COUSINS	OP	42.50	75.00
85	COUNTRY CROONER	OP	25.00	50.00
85	DON'T PLAY WITH YOUR FOOD	RT	28.50	105.00
85	FURS GONNA FLY	950	145.00	350.00
85	HOG HEAVEN	RT	165.00	350.00
85	LOVE AT FIRST SIGHT	RT	70.00	120.00
85	OUT OF STEP	*	45.00	95.00
85	OZARK BELLE	RT	35.00	75.00
85	RENOIR	RT	45.00	75.00
85	TOO GOOD TO WASTE ON KIDS	OP	70.00	125.00
85	WILL YOU/RESPECT ME IN THE MORNING	*	35.00	80.00
86	BIT OFF MORE THAN HE COULD CHEW	OP	39.50	55.00-65.00
86	COMFY?	OP	39.00	75.00
86	FEELIN' HIS OATS	1500	150.00	250.00
86	MAMA?	RT	15.00	48.00
87	BOTTOMS UP	RT	80.00	100.00
87	CHICKEN THIEF	RT	200.00	360.00
87	EASY PICKINS	RT	45.00	85.00
87	GLUTTON FOR PUNISHMENT	RT	95.00	155.00
87	MAIL ORDER BRIDE	RT	150.00	175.00-300.00
87	ORPHANS, THE	OP	50.00	55.00-125.00

YR	NAME	LIMIT	ISSUE	TREND
87	TWO IN THE BUSH	RT	150.00	325.00
87	WHEN THE CAT'S AWAY	OP	40.00	60.00
88	BROTHERS	RT	55.00	85.00
88	FLEAS	OP	20.00	25.00
88	GOLDIE AND HER PEEPS	OP	25.00	35.00
88	HAPPY HOUR	OP	57.50	90.00
88	IN A PICKLE	OP	40.00	50.00
88	MAKING A BEE LINE	RT	75.00	130.00
88	MISSOURI SPRING	RT	115.00	185.00
88	NO PRIVATE TIME	RT	200.00	350.00
88	PERFECT TEN	RT	95.00	175.00
88	SAWIN' LOGS	OP	85.00	100.00
88	WHEN THREE FOOT'S A MILE	RT	230.00	270.00
88	WINTERING LAMB	RT	200.00	260.00
88	WISHFUL THINKING	*	55.00	75.00
89	A TRIBUTE TO HOOKER	RT	180.00	250.00
89	BOY'S NIGHT OUT, THE	1500	190.00	225.00
89	COON CAPERS	OP	67.50	85.00
89	FAMILY OUTING	OP	45.00	65.00
89	GITTIN' A NIBBLE	OP	50.00	50.00
89	LEFTOVERS	OP	90.00	95.00
89	MEETING OF SHELDON	RT	120.00	150.00
89	MOTHER HEN	OP	37.50	55.00
89	NEW FRIEND	OP	45.00	65.00
89	SUN WORSHIPPERS	5000	120.00	140.00
89	SUN WORSHIPPERS MINI FIGURINE	OP	32.50	43.00
89	WOODSCOLT	RT	300.00	375.00
90	CORN CRIB MOUSE	RT	35.00	40.00
90	DEALER COUNTER SIGN	OP	50.00	70.00
90	FINDERS KEEPERS	OP	39.50	50.00
90	FOREPLAY	RT	59.50	75.00
90	HANKY PANKY	RT	65.00	100.00
90	HOME SQUEEZINS	OP	90.00	90.00
90	LAST STRAW, THE	OP	125.00	175.00
90	LITTLE BLACK LAMB (BABA)	RT	30.00	40.00
90	LONG DAYS, COLD NIGHTS	RT	175.00	200.00
90	OUTING WITH GRANDPA	2500	200.00	185.00
90	PIGGIN OUT	CL	250.00	245.00
90	PRIVATE TIME	OP	18.00	18.00
90	SEEIN' RED	RT	35.00	50.00
90	SUNDAY AFTERNOON TREAT	5000	120.00	130.00
90	SUNDAY AFTERNOON TREAT MINI	5000	32.50	30.00
90	TRICKS OF THE TRADE	RT	300.00	330.00
91	COCK OF THE WALK	2500	300.00	250.00-300.00
91	FIRST OFFENSE	RT	70.00	75.00
91	GUN SHY	RT	70.00	70.00
91	HEADING FOR THE PERSIMMON GROVE	RT	80.00	80.00
91	KISSIN COUSINS	RT	80.00	80.00
91	LONG HOT SUMMER	1950	250.00	250.00
91	SOOIEEE	RT	350.00	350.00
91	WARM MILK	5000	200.00	135.00-150.00
91	WARM MILK MINI FIGURINE	OP	37.50	38.00
91	WASHED ASHORE	RT	70.00	70.00
92	DON'T PLAY WITH FIRE	OP	120.00	120.00
92	FREE LUNCH	OP	85.00	85.00
92	GRASS IS ALWAYS GREENER, THE	OP	195.00	195.00
92	HEADED SOUTH	OP	45.00	45.00
92	HONEYMOON'S OVER, THE	1950	300.00	300.00
92	LOWELL DAVIS PROFILE	OP	65.00	65.00
92	MY FAVORITE CHORES	1500	750.00	750.00
92	MY FAVORITE CHORES	1500	750.00	750.00
92	OH SHEEEEIT	OP	120.00	120.00
92	OZARK'S VITTLES	OP	60.00	60.00
92	SAFE HAVEN	OP	95.00	95.00
92	SCHOOL YARD DOGS	OP	100.00	100.00
92	SHE LAY LOW	OP	120.00	120.00
92	SNAKE DOCTOR	OP	70.00	70.00
93	BE MY VALENTINE	OP	35.00	35.00
93	DON'T OPEN TILL CHRISTMAS	OP	35.00	35.00
93	DRY HOLE	OP	30.00	30.00
93	FREELOADERS, THE	1250	230.00	230.00
93	HAPPY BIRTHDAY MY SWEET	OP	35.00	35.00
93	HOME FOR CHRISTMAS	OP	80.00	80.00
93	I'M THANKFUL FOR YOU	OP	35.00	35.00
93	IF YOU CAN'T BEAT 'EM JOIN 'EM	1750	250.00	250.00
93	KICKIN' HIMSELF	OP	80.00	80.00
93	KING OF THE MOUNTAIN	750	500.00	500.00
93	NO HUNTING	1000	95.00	95.00
93	OH WHERE IS HE NOW?	1250	250.00	250.00
93	PEEP SHOW	OP	35.00	35.00
93	SHEEP SHEERIN' TIME	1200	500.00	500.00
93	SUMMER DAYS	YR	100.00	100.00
93	SWEET TOOTH	OP	60.00	60.00
93	TRICK OR TREAT	OP	35.00	35.00
94	ATTIC ANTICS	OP	100.00	100.00
94	FIRST OUTING	OP	65.00	65.00
94	HELPIN' HIMSELF	OP	65.00	65.00
94	HITTIN' THE TRAIL	1250	250.00	250.00
94	MAMA CAN WILLIE STAY FOR SUPPER?	1250	200.00	200.00

YR	NAME	LIMIT	ISSUE	TREND
94	NOT A HAPPY CAMPER	OP	75.00	75.00
94	OH MOTHER WHAT IS IT?	1000	250.00	250.00
94	PECKING ORDER	OP	200.00	200.00
94	QU'EST-CEQUE CEST?	OP	200.00	200.00
94	TWO TIMER	OP	95.00	95.00
94	WARMIN'	1250	270.00	270.00
95	BLOSSOM'S BEST	750	300.00	300.00
95	CUSSIN' UP A STORM	OP	45.00	45.00
95	STICKS & STONES	OP	30.00	30.00
95	UNINVITED CALLER	OP	35.00	35.00
L. DAVIS				**ROUTE 66**
91	JUST CHECK THE AIR	RT	700.00	1450.00
91	JUST CHECK THE AIR	2500	550.00	550.00
91	LITTLE BIT OF SHADE	OP	100.00	100.00
91	NEL'S DINER	RT	700.00	1550.00
91	NEL'S DINER	2500	550.00	550.00
92	FRESH SQUEEZED	350	600.00	700.00
92	FRESH SQUEEZED	2500	550.00	425.00
92	GOING TO GRANDMA	OP	80.00	80.00
92	QUIET DAY AT MAPLE GROVE	OP	130.00	130.00
92	RELIEF	OP	80.00	80.00
92	WELCOME MAT	1500	400.00	400.00
92	WHAT ARE PALS FOR?	OP	100.00	100.00
L. DAVIS				**UNCLE REMUS**
81	BRER BEAR	RT	80.00	1050.00
81	BRER COYOTE	RT	80.00	500.00
81	BRER FOX	RT	70.00	900.00
81	BRER RABBIT	RT	85.00	1900.00
81	BRER WEASEL	RT	80.00	675.00
81	BRER WOLF	RT	85.00	595.00

SCULPTURE BY SHALAH

YR	NAME	LIMIT	ISSUE	TREND
S. PERKINS				**BRONZE**
93	FARMER, THE	20	*	1800.00
93	MISS DOLLIE	20	*	1500.00
94	CALL OF THE LAND	20	*	1800.00
94	CELEBRATION OF A COWGIRL	10	*	9000.00
94	NEIGHBOR	20	*	1050.00
94	REMEMBERING	20	*	950.00
S. PERKINS				**BRONZE FOUNTAIN**
94	JOY IN THE MORNING	13	*	5500.00
95	WISHFUL THINKIN	20	*	7500.00

SEBASTIAN STUDIOS

YR	NAME	LIMIT	ISSUE	TREND
P.W. BASTON		**LARGE CERAMASTONE FIGURES**		
*	SANTA FE...ALL THE WAY	CL	*	800.00
*	ST. FRANCIS PLAQUE	CL	*	800.00
39	PAUL REVERE PLAQUE	CL	*	425.00
40	BASKET	CL	*	350.00
40	BRETON MAN	CL	*	800.00
40	BRETON WOMAN	CL	*	800.00
40	CANDLE HOLDER	CL	*	350.00
40	CAROLER	CL	*	350.00
40	HORN OF PLENTY	CL	*	350.00
40	JESUS	CL	*	350.00
40	LAMB	CL	*	350.00
40	MARY	CL	*	800.00
47	LARGE VICTORIAN COUPLE	CL	*	800.00
48	WOODY AT THREE	CL	*	800.00
56	JELL-O COW MILK PITCHER	CL	*	200.00
58	SWIFT INSTRUMENT GIRL	CL	*	600.00
59	WASP PLAQUE	CL	*	600.00
63	ABRAHAM LINCOLN TOBY JUG	CL	*	800.00
63	ANNE BOLEYN	CL	*	800.00
63	DAVID COPPERFIELD	CL	*	800.00
63	DORA	CL	*	800.00
63	GEORGE WASHINGTON TOBY JUG	CL	*	800.00
63	HENRY VIII	CL	*	800.00
63	JOHN F. KENNEDY TOBY JUG	CL	*	800.00
63	MENDING TIME	CL	*	800.00
63	TOM SAWYER	CL	*	800.00
64	COLONIAL BOY	CL	*	800.00
64	COLONIAL GIRL	CL	*	800.00
64	COLONIAL MAN	CL	*	800.00
64	COLONIAL WOMAN	CL	*	800.00
64	IBM FATHER	CL	*	800.00
64	IBM MOTHER	CL	*	800.00
64	IBM PHOTOGRAPHER	CL	*	800.00
64	IBM SON	CL	*	800.00
64	IBM WOMAN	CL	*	800.00
65	DENTIST, THE	CL	*	800.00
65	N.E. HOME FOR LITTLE WANDERERS	CL	*	800.00
65	STANLEY MUSIC BOX	CL	*	400.00
66	GUITARIST	CL	*	800.00
67	INFANT OF PRAGUE	CL	*	800.00
73	BLACKSMITH	CL	*	350.00
73	CABINETMAKER	CL	*	350.00
73	CLOCKMAKER	CL	*	800.00

YR	NAME	LIMIT	ISSUE	TREND
73	POTTER	CL	*	350.00
75	MINUTEMAN	CL	*	800.00
78	MT. RUSHMORE	CL	*	425.00

P.W. BASTON

SEBASTIAN MINIATURES

YR	NAME	LIMIT	ISSUE	TREND
*	BABE RUTH	CL	*	800.00
*	BOB HOPE	CL	*	800.00
*	CORONATION CROWN	CL	*	800.00
*	EAGLE PLAQUE	CL	*	1500.00
*	KING, THE	CL	*	800.00
*	ORTHO GYNECIC	CL	*	800.00
*	SYLVANIA ELECTRIC-BULB DISPLAY	CL	*	800.00
38	SHAKER LADY	CL	*	100.00
38	SHAKER MAN	CL	*	100.00
39	BENJAMIN FRANKLIN	CL	*	100.00
39	CORONADO	CL	*	100.00
39	CORONADO'S SENORA	CL	*	100.00
39	DEBORAH FRANKLIN	CL	*	100.00
39	EVANGELINE	CL	*	125.00
39	GABRIEL	CL	*	125.00
39	GEORGE WASHINGTON	CL	*	55.00
39	INDIAN MAIDEN	CL	*	125.00
39	INDIAN WARRIOR	CL	*	125.00
39	JOHN ALDEN	CL	*	45.00
39	MARGARET HOUSTON	CL	*	100.00
39	MARTHA WASHINGTON	CL	*	55.00
39	PRISCILLA	CL	*	45.00
39	SAM HOUSTON	CL	*	100.00
39	WILLIAMSBURG GOVERNOR	CL	*	100.00
39	WILLIAMSBURG LADY	CL	*	100.00
40	ANN STVYVESANT	CL	*	100.00
40	ANNIE OAKLEY	CL	*	100.00
40	BUFFALO BILL	CL	*	100.00
40	CATHERINE LAFITTE	CL	*	100.00
40	DAN'L BOONE	CL	*	100.00
40	ELIZABETH MONROE	CL	*	165.00
40	HANNAH PENN	CL	*	125.00
40	JAMES MONROE	CL	*	165.00
40	JEAN LAFITTE	CL	*	100.00
40	JOHN HARVARD	CL	*	135.00
40	JOHN SMITH	CL	*	135.00
40	MRS. DAN'L BOONE	CL	*	100.00
40	MRS. HARVARD	CL	*	135.00
40	PETER STVYVESANT	CL	*	100.00
40	POCOHONTAS	CL	*	135.00
40	WILLIAM PENN	CL	*	125.00
41	DOVES	CL	*	800.00
41	DUCKLINGS	CL	*	800.00
41	KITTEN (SITTING)	CL	*	800.00
41	KITTEN (SLEEPING)	CL	*	800.00
41	PEACOCK	CL	*	800.00
41	PHEASANT	CL	*	800.00
41	ROOSTER	CL	*	800.00
41	SECRETS	CL	*	800.00
41	SWAN	CL	*	800.00
42	ACCORDION	CL	*	350.00
42	CYMBALS	CL	*	350.00
42	DRUM	CL	*	350.00
42	HORN	CL	*	350.00
42	MAJORETTE	CL	*	350.00
42	TUBA	CL	*	350.00
46	PURITAN SPINNER	CL	*	800.00
46	SATCHEL-EYE DYER	CL	*	135.00
47	DAHL'S FISHERMAN	CL	*	165.00
47	DILEMMA	CL	*	300.00
47	DOWN EAST	CL	*	135.00
47	FIRST COOKBOOK AUTHOR	CL	*	135.00
47	FISHER PAIR PS	CL	*	800.00
47	HOWARD JOHNSON PIEMAN	CL	*	425.00
47	MR. BEACON HILL	CL	*	125.00
47	MRS. BEACON HILL	CL	*	125.00
47	PRINCE PHILIP	CL	*	250.00
47	PRINCESS ELIZABETH	CL	*	250.00
47	TOLLHOUSE TOWN CRIER	CL	*	150.00
48	A HARVEY GIRL	CL	*	275.00
48	DEMOCRATIC VICTORY	CL	*	425.00
48	JORDAN MARSH OBSERVER	CL	*	165.00
48	MARY LYON	CL	*	275.00
48	MR. RITTENHOUSE SQUARE	CL	*	165.00
48	MR. SHERATON	CL	*	375.00
48	MRS. RITTENHOUSE SQUARE	CL	*	165.00
48	NATHANIEL HAWTHORNE	CL	*	185.00
48	REPUBLICAN VICTORY	CL	*	800.00
48	SITZMARK	CL	*	185.00
48	SLALOM	CL	*	185.00
48	SWEDISH BOY	CL	*	400.00
48	SWEDISH GIRL	CL	*	400.00
49	BOY SCOUT PLAQUE	CL	*	325.00
49	DUTCHMAN'S PIPE	CL	*	200.00
49	EMMETT KELLY	CL	*	275.00

YR	NAME	LIMIT	ISSUE	TREND
49	EUSTACE TILLY	CL	*	1250.00
49	GATHERING TULIPS	CL	*	250.00
49	GIANT ROYAL BENGAL TIGER	CL	*	1500.00
49	MARK TWAIN HOME IN HANNIBAL, MO, THE	CL	*	800.00
49	MENOTOMY INDIAN	CL	*	220.00
49	PATRICK HENRY	CL	*	125.00
49	PAUL BUNYAN	CL	*	250.00
49	SARAH HENRY	CL	*	125.00
49	THINKER, THE	CL	*	220.00
49	UNCLE MISTLETOE	CL	*	250.00
50	MR. OBOCELL	CL	*	100.00
50	NATIONAL DIAPER SERVICE	CL	*	275.00
50	PHOEBE, HOUSE OF 7 GABLES	CL	*	165.00
51	CARL MOORE (WEEI)	CL	*	250.00
51	CAROLINE CABOT (WEEI)	CL	*	275.00
51	CHARLES ASHLEY (WEEI)	CL	*	275.00
51	CHIEF PONTIAC	CL	*	550.00
51	CHIQUITA BANANA	CL	*	375.00
51	CHRISTOPHER COLUMBUS	CL	*	275.00
51	E.B. RIDEOUT (WEEI)	CL	*	275.00
51	GREAT STONE FACE	CL	*	800.00
51	IRON MASTER'S HOUSE, THE	CL	*	425.00
51	JESSE BUFFMAN (WEEI)	CL	*	275.00
51	JORDON MARSH/RIDES THE A.W. HORSE	CL	*	325.00
51	JUDGE PYNCHEON	CL	*	200.00
51	MIT SEAL	CL	*	400.00
51	MOTHER PARKER (WEEI)	CL	*	275.00
51	OBSERVER & DAME NEW ENGLAND, THE	CL	*	350.00
51	PRISCILLA FORTESUE (WEEI)	CL	*	275.00
51	SEB. DEALER PLAQUE (MARBLEHEAD)	CL	*	325.00
51	SIR FRANCES DRAKE	CL	*	275.00
52	AERIAL TRAMWAY	CL	*	450.00
52	BABY (JELL-O)	CL	*	575.00
52	FAT MAN, THE (JELL-O)	CL	*	575.00
52	FAVORED SCHOLAR	CL	*	250.00
52	FIRST HOUSE, THE - PLYMOUTH PLANTATION	CL	*	175.00
52	LOST IN THE KITCHEN (JELL-O)	CL	*	475.00
52	MARBLEHEAD HIGH SCHOOL PLAQUE	CL	*	250.00
52	NEIGHBORING PEWS	CL	*	250.00
52	OLD POWDER HOUSE	CL	*	275.00
52	OUR LADY OF GOOD VOYAGE	CL	*	225.00
52	SCOTTISH GIRL (JELL-O)	CL	*	375.00
52	ST. JOAN D'ARC	CL	*	325.00
52	ST. SEBASTIAN	CL	*	325.00
52	STORK (JELL-O)	CL	*	475.00
52	TABASCO SAUCE	CL	*	425.00
52	WEIGHING THE BABY	CL	*	250.00
53	BLESSED JULIE BILLART	CL	*	425.00
53	BOY JESUS IN THE TEMPLE	CL	*	375.00
53	DARNED WELL HE CAN	CL	*	325.00
53	HOLGRAVE THE DAGUERROTYPIST	CL	*	225.00
53	LION (JELL-O)	CL	*	375.00
53	OLD PUT ENJOYS A LICKING	CL	*	325.00
53	R.H. STEARNS CHESTNUT HILL MALL	CL	*	250.00
53	SCHOOLBOY OF 1850, THE	CL	*	375.00
53	ST. TERESA OF LISIEUX	CL	*	250.00
54	BLUEBIRD GIRL	CL	*	425.00
54	CAMPFIRE GIRL	CL	*	425.00
54	DACHSHUND (AUDIOVOX)	CL	*	325.00
54	HORIZON GIRL	CL	*	425.00
54	KERNEL-FRESH ASHTRAY	CL	*	425.00
54	MOOSE (JELL-O)	CL	*	375.00
54	OUR LADY OF LALECHE	CL	*	325.00
54	RABBIT (JELL-O)	CL	*	375.00
54	RESOLUTE INS. CO. CLIPPER PS	CL	*	325.00
54	SCUBA DIVER	CL	*	425.00
54	ST. PIUS X	CL	*	440.00
54	STIMALOSE (MEN)	CL	*	800.00
54	STIMALOSE (WOMAN)	CL	*	185.00
54	SWAN BOAT BROOCH-EMPTY SEATS	CL	*	800.00
54	SWAN BOAT BROOCH-FULL SEATS	CL	*	800.00
54	WHALE (JELL-O)	CL	*	375.00
54	WILLIAM PENN	CL	*	200.00
55	CAPTAIN DOLIBER	CL	*	325.00
55	DAVY CROCKETT	CL	*	250.00
55	GIRAFFE (JELL-O)	CL	*	375.00
55	HORSE HEAD PS	CL	*	375.00
55	OLD WOMAN IN THE SHOE (JELL-O)	CL	*	550.00
55	SANTA (JELL-O)	CL	*	550.00
55	SECOND BANK-STATE ST. TRUST PS	CL	*	325.00
56	77TH BENGAL LANCER (JELL-O)	CL	*	800.00
56	ALIKE, BUT OH SO DIFFERENT	CL	*	325.00
56	ARTHRITIC HANDS (J&J)	CL	*	800.00
56	EASTERN PAPER PLAQUE	CL	*	375.00
56	ELSIE THE COW BILLBOARD	CL	*	800.00
56	GIRL ON DIVING BOARD	CL	*	425.00
56	GREEN GIANT, THE	CL	*	425.00
56	MICHIGAN MILLERS PS	CL	*	240.00
56	MRS. OBOCELL	CL	*	425.00

YR	NAME	LIMIT	ISSUE	TREND
56	NYU GRAD SCHOOL OF BUS. ADMIN. BLDG.	CL	*	325.00
56	PERMACEL TOWER OF TAPE ASHTRAY	CL	*	800.00
56	PRAYING HANDS	CL	*	275.00
56	RARICAL BLACKSMITH	CL	*	400.00
56	ROBIN HOOD & FRIAR TUCK	CL	*	425.00
56	ROBIN HOOD & LITTLE JOHN	CL	*	425.00
56	TEXCEL TAPE BOY	CL	*	400.00
56	THREE LITTLE KITTENS (JELL-O)	CL	*	400.00
57	ALONG THE ALBANY ROAD PS	CL	*	800.00
57	BORDEN'S CENTENNIAL (ELSIE THE COW)	CL	*	800.00
57	COLONIAL FUND DOORWAY PS	CL	*	800.00
57	IBM 305 RAMAC	CL	*	425.00
57	JAMESTOWN CHURCH	CL	*	425.00
57	JAMESTOWN SHIPS	CL	*	400.00
57	MAYFLOWER PS	CL	*	325.00
57	NABISCO BUFFALO BEE	CL	*	800.00
57	NABISCO SPOONMAN	CL	*	800.00
57	OLDE JAMES FORT	CL	*	275.00
57	SPEEDY ALKA SELTZER	CL	*	800.00
58	CBS MISS COLUMBIA PS	CL	*	800.00
58	CLIQUOT CLUB ESKIMO PS	CL	*	1600.00
58	COMMODORE STEPHEN DECATUR	CL	*	150.00
58	CONNECTICUT BANK & TRUST	CL	*	250.00
58	HANNAH DUSTON PS	CL	*	285.00
58	HARVARD TRUST COLONIAL MAN	CL	*	300.00
58	JACKIE GLEASON	CL	*	800.00
58	JORDAN MARSH OBSERVER	CL	*	225.00
58	MT. VERNON	CL	*	425.00
58	ROMEO & JULIET	CL	*	425.00
58	SALEM SAVINGS BANK	CL	*	275.00
59	ALCOA WRAP PS	CL	*	375.00
59	ALEXANDER SMITH WEAVER	CL	*	400.00
59	FIORELLO LAGUARDIA	CL	*	150.00
59	FLEISCHMAN'S MARGARINE PS	CL	*	275.00
59	GIOVANNI VERRAZZANO	CL	*	150.00
59	H.P. HOOD CO. CIGAR STORE INDIAN	CL	*	800.00
59	HARVARD TRUST CO. TOWN CRIER	CL	*	375.00
59	HENRY HUDSON	CL	*	150.00
59	MRS. S.O.S.	CL	*	325.00
59	SIESTA COFFEE PS	CL	*	800.00
60	INFANTRYMAN, THE	CL	*	800.00
60	MARINE MEMORIAL	CL	*	350.00
60	MASONIC BIBLE	CL	*	350.00
60	METROPOLITAN LIFE TOWER PS	CL	*	375.00
60	PETER STVYVESANT	CL	*	150.00
60	SON OF THE DESERT	CL	*	240.00
60	SUPP-HOSE LADY	CL	*	325.00
60	TONY PIET	CL	*	800.00
61	BUNKY KNUDSEN	CL	*	800.00
61	MERCHANT'S WARREN SEA CAPTAIN	CL	*	225.00
61	POPE JOHN 23RD	CL	*	425.00
61	ST. JUDE THADDEUS	CL	*	425.00
62	BIG BROTHER BOB EMERY	CL	*	800.00
62	BLUE BELLE HIGHLANDER	CL	*	225.00
62	SEAMAN'S BANK FOR SAVINGS	CL	*	350.00
62	YANKEE CLIPPER SULFIDE	CL	*	800.00
63	DIA-MEL FAT MAN	CL	*	400.00
63	JACKIE KENNEDY TOBY JUG	CL	*	800.00
63	JOHN F. KENNEDY TOBY JUG	CL	*	800.00
63	NAUMKEAG INDIAN	CL	*	250.00
65	HENRY WADSWORTH LONGFELLOW	CL	*	300.00
65	PANTI-LEGS GIRL PS	CL	*	275.00
65	POPE PAUL VI	CL	*	425.00
65	STATE STREET BANK GLOBE	CL	*	275.00
66	GARDENER MAN	CL	*	275.00
66	GARDENER WOMEN	CL	*	275.00
66	GARDENERS (THERMOMETER)	CL	*	350.00
66	LITTLE GEORGE	CL	*	400.00
66	MASSACHUSETTS SPCA	CL	*	300.00
66	PAUL REVERE PLAQUE (W.T. GRANT)	CL	*	325.00
66	TOWN LYNE INDIAN	CL	*	800.00
67	DOC BERRY OF BERWICK (YELLOW SHIRT)	CL	*	325.00
67	ORTHO-NOVUM	CL	*	800.00
68	CAPTAIN JOHN PARKER	CL	*	325.00
68	WATERMILL CANDY PLAQUE	CL	*	800.00
70	UNCLE SAM IN ORBIT	CL	*	375.00
71	BOSTON GAS TANK	CL	*	400.00
71	TOWN MEETING PLAQUE	CL	*	375.00
72	GEORGE & HATCHET	CL	*	425.00
72	MARTHA & THE CHERRY PIE	CL	*	375.00

SEYMOUR MANN

KENJI — **BUNNY MUSICAL**

YR	NAME	LIMIT	ISSUE	TREND
91	BUNNY IN TEACUP MH-781	OP	25.00	25.00
91	BUNNY IN TEAPOT MH-780	OP	25.00	25.00

KENJI — **CAT MUSICAL FIGURINES**

YR	NAME	LIMIT	ISSUE	TREND
85	CATS BALL SHAPE	CL	25.00	25.00
86	CATS W/RIBBON MH-481 A/C	RT	30.00	30.00
87	BROWN CAT IN BAG	CL	30.00	30.00

YR	NAME	LIMIT	ISSUE	TREND
87	BROWN CAT IN TEACUP	RT	30.00	30.00
87	CAT IN BAG MH-614	RT	30.00	30.00
87	CAT IN BAG MH-617	RT	30.00	30.00
87	CAT IN GARBAGE CAN MH-190	RT	35.00	35.00
87	CAT IN ROSE TEACUP MH-600VG	RT	30.00	30.00
87	CAT IN TEACUP MH-600VGG	RT	30.00	30.00
87	CAT IN TEACUP MH-600VGG	RT	30.00	30.00
87	CAT ON TIPPED GARBAGE CAN MH-498	RT	35.00	35.00
87	KITTENDS W/BALLS OF YARN MH-612	RT	30.00	30.00
87	MUSICAL BEAR MH-602	RT	27.50	28.00
87	TEAPOT CAT MH-631	RT	30.00	30.00
87	VALENTINE CAT IN BAG MUSICAL MH-600	RT	33.50	34.00
87	VALENTINE CAT IN TEACUP MH-600VLT	RT	33.50	34.00
88	BROWN CAT IN HAT MH-634B/6	RT	35.00	35.00
88	CAT IN HAT BOX MH-634	RT	35.00	35.00
88	CAT IN HAT MH-634B	RT	35.00	35.00
89	CAT IN BASINET MH-714	RT	35.00	35.00
89	CAT IN BASKET MH-713B	RT	35.00	35.00
89	CAT IN FLOWER MH-709	RT	35.00	35.00
89	CAT IN GIFT BOX MUSICAL MH-732	RT	40.00	40.00
89	CAT IN SHOE MH-718	RT	30.00	30.00
89	CAT IN WATER CAN MUSICAL MH-712	RT	35.00	35.00
89	CAT ON BASKET MH-713	RT	35.00	35.00
89	CAT W/COFFEE CUP MUSICAL MH-706	RT	35.00	35.00
89	CAT W/SWING MUSICAL MH-710	RT	35.00	35.00
90	BRIDE/GROOM CAT MH-738	RT	37.50	38.00
90	CAT ASLEEP MH-735	RT	17.50	18.00
90	CAT CALICO IN EASY CHAIR MH-743VG	RT	27.50	28.00
90	CAT IN BOOTIE MH-728	RT	35.00	35.00
90	CAT IN DRESS MH-751VG	RT	37.50	38.00
90	CAT ON GIFT BOX MUSIC MH-740	RT	40.00	40.00
90	CAT ON PILLOW MH-731	RT	17.50	18.00
90	CAT SAILOR IN ROCKING BOAT MH-734	RT	45.00	45.00
90	CAT W/BOW ON PINK PILLOW MH-741P	RT	33.50	36.00
90	CAT W/PARROT MH-730	RT	37.50	38.00
90	CATS GRADUATION MH-745	RT	27.50	28.00
90	GREY CAT IN BOOTIE MH-728G/6	CL	35.00	35.00
90	KITTEN TRIO IN CARRIAGE MH-742	CL	37.50	38.00
91	BROWN CAT IN BAG	RT	30.00	30.00
91	BROWN CAT IN HAT	RT	35.00	35.00
91	BROWN CAT IN TEACUP	CL	30.00	30.00
91	CAT IN BAG	CL	30.00	30.00
91	CAT IN BASKET MH-768	RT	35.00	35.00
91	CAT IN BOOTIE	CL	35.00	35.00
91	CAT IN GARBAGE CAN	CL	35.00	35.00
91	CAT IN GARBAGE CAN	RT	35.00	35.00
91	CAT IN HAT	CL	35.00	35.00
91	CAT IN HAT BOX	CL	35.00	35.00
91	CAT IN ROSE TEACUP	CL	30.00	30.00
91	CAT IN ROSE TEACUP	RT	30.00	30.00
91	CAT IN TEACUP	CL	30.00	30.00
91	CAT MOMMA MH-758	RT	35.00	35.00
91	CAT ON TIPPED GARBAGE CAN	CL	35.00	35.00
91	CAT W/BOW ON PINK PILLOW MH-741P	RT	33.50	34.00
91	CAT WATCHING BUTTERFLY MH-784	RT	17.50	18.00
91	CAT WATCHING CANARY MH-783	RT	25.00	25.00
91	CATS BALL SHAPE	CL	25.00	25.00
91	CATS W/RIBBON	CL	30.00	30.00
91	FAMILY CAT MH-770	RT	35.00	35.00
91	GREY CAT IN BOOTIE	CL	35.00	35.00
91	KITTENS W/BALLS OF YARN	CL	30.00	30.00
91	LITTEN PICKING TULIPS MH-756	RT	40.00	40.00
91	MUSICAL BEAR	CL	27.50	28.00
91	REVOLVING CAT W/BUTTERFLY MH-759	RT	40.00	40.00
91	TEAPOT CAT	CL	30.00	30.00
JAIMY			**CHRISTMAS COLLECTION**	
89	SANTA IN SLED W/REINDEER CJ-3	RT	25.00	25.00
89	SANTA MUSICALS CJ-1/4	RT	27.50	28.00
89	SANTA ON HORSE CJ-33A	RT	33.50	34.00
89	SANTA W/LIST CJ-23	RT	27.50	28.00
90	MR. & MRS. SANTA MUSICAL	CL	37.50	38.00
90	SANTA ON CHIMNEY MUSICAL	CL	33.50	34.00
90	SANTA PACKING BAG CJ-210	CL	33.50	34.00
91	REINDEER BARN LITE UP HOUSE	CL	55.00	55.00
JAIMY			**CHRISTMAS COLLECTION**	
90	ROLY POLY SANTA 3 ASST. CJ-263/4/7	RT	17.50	18.00
90	SANTA W/LIST CJ-23	RT	27.50	28.00
91	APOTHECARY LITE UP CJ-128	RT	33.50	34.00
91	BEIGE CHURCH LITE UP HOUSE MER-360A	RT	35.00	35.00
91	BOY & GIRL ON BELL CJ-132	RT	13.50	14.00
91	BOY ON HORSE CJ-457	RT	6.00	6.00
91	CAROLERS UNDER LAMPPOST CJ-114A	RT	7.50	8.00
91	CHURCH LITE UP MER-410	RT	17.50	18.00
91	COVERED BRIDGE CJ-101	RT	27.50	28.00
91	EMILY'S TOYS CJ-127	RT	35.00	35.00
91	FATHER & MOTERH W/DAUGHTER CJ-133	RT	13.50	14.00
91	FATHER CHRISTMAS CJ-233	RT	33.50	34.00
91	FATHER CHRISTMAS W/HOLLY CJ-239	RT	35.00	35.00
91	FIRE STATION CJ-129	RT	50.00	50.00

YR	NAME	LIMIT	ISSUE	TREND
91	FOUR MEN TALKING CJ-138	RT	27.50	28.00
91	GIFT SHOP LITE UP CJ-125	RT	33.50	34.00
91	GIRLS W/INSTRUMENTS CJ-131	RT	13.50	14.00
91	HORSE & COACH CJ-207	RT	25.00	25.00
91	KIDS BUILDING IGLOO CJ-137	RT	13.50	14.00
91	LADY W/DOGS CJ-208	RT	13.50	14.00
91	MAN W/WHEELBARROW CJ-134	RT	13.50	14.00
91	NEWSBOY UNDER LAMPPOST CJ-144B	RT	15.00	15.00
91	OLD CURIOSITY LITE UP CJ-201	RT	37.50	38.00
91	PLAYHOUSE LITE UP CJ-122	RT	50.00	50.00
91	SANTA CAT ROLY POLY CJ-252	RT	17.50	18.00
91	SANTA FIXING SLED CJ-237	RT	35.00	35.00
91	SANTA IN BARREL WATERBALL CJ-243	RT	33.50	34.00
91	SANTA IN TOY SHOP CJ-441	RT	33.50	34.00
91	SANTA ON TRAIN CJ-458	RT	6.00	6.00
91	SANTA PACKING BAG CJ-210	RT	33.50	34.00
91	SANTA PACKING BAG CJ-236	RT	35.00	35.00
91	SANTA SLEEPING MUSICAL CJ-214	RT	30.00	30.00
91	SANTA W/BAG & LIST CJ-431	RT	33.50	34.00
91	SANTA W/DEER MUSCIAL	RT	33.50	34.00
91	SANTA W/GIRL WATERBALL	RT	33.50	34.00
91	SANTA W/LANTERN MUSICAL CJ-211	RT	33.50	34.00
91	SANTA W/LIST CJ-23R	RT	27.50	28.00
91	SKATER, THE CJ-205	RT	25.00	25.00
91	SNOWBALL FIGHT CJ-124B	RT	25.00	25.00
91	SOUP SELLER WATERBALL CJ-209	RT	25.00	25.00
91	STONE COTTAGE LITE UP CJ-100	RT	37.50	38.00
91	STONE HOUSE LITE UP CJ-102	RT	45.00	45.00
91	TE OLDE TOWN TAVERN CJ-130	RT	45.00	45.00
91	THREE LADDIES W/FOOD CJ-136	RT	13.50	14.00
91	TOY SELLER, THE CJ-206	RT	13.50	14.00
91	TRADER SANTA MUSICAL CJ-442	RT	30.00	30.00
91	TWO OLD MEN TALKING CJ-107	RT	13.50	14.00
91	VILLAGE MILL LIT EUP CJ-104	RT	30.00	30.00
91	VILLAGE PEOPLE CJ-116A	RT	60.00	60.00
91	WOMAN W/COW CJ-135	RT	15.00	15.00
E. MANN			**CHRISTMAS COLLECTION**	
89	CATS IN BASKET XMAS-664	RT	7.50	8.00
90	FIRE STATION LITE UP HOUSE	CL	25.00	25.00
90	SANTA ON SEE SAW TR-14	RT	30.00	30.00
91	ELF W/DOLL HOUSE CB-14	RT	30.00	30.00
91	ELF W/HAMMER CB-11	RT	30.00	30.00
91	ELF W/ROCKING HORSE CB-10	RT	30.00	30.00
91	ELF W/TEDDY BEAR CB-12	RT	30.00	30.00
91	SANTA ON WHITE HORSE CJ 338	RT	33.50	34.00
91	TEDDY BEAR ON WHEELS CB-42	RT	25.00	25.00
J. WHITE			**CHRISTMAS COLLECTION**	
85	TRUMPETING ANGEL W/JESUS XMAS-627	RT	40.00	40.00
85	VIRGIN W/CHRIST MUSICAL XMAS-528	RT	33.50	34.00
86	ANTIQUE SANTA MUSICAL XMAS-364	RT	20.00	20.00
86	JUMBO SANTA/TOYS XMAS-38	RT	45.00	45.00
89	CAT IN TEACUP MUSICAL XMAS-600	RT	30.00	30.00
90	ANTIQUE SHOP LITE UP HOUSE MER-373	RT	27.50	28.00
90	BAKERY LITE UP HOUSE MER-376	RT	27.50	28.00
90	BETHLEHEM LITE UP SET 3 CP-59893	RT	120.00	120.00
90	BRICK CHURCH LITE UP HOUSE MER-360C	RT	35.00	35.00
90	CATHEDRAL LITE UP HOUSE MER-362	RT	37.50	38.00
90	CHURCH LITE UP HOUSE MER-310	RT	27.50	28.00
90	DEEP GOLD CHURCH LITE UP HSE MER-360D	RT	35.00	35.00
90	DOUBLE STORE LITE UP HOUSE MER-311	RT	27.50	28.00
90	GRIST MILL LITE UP HOUSE MER-372	CL	27.50	28.00
90	INN LITE UP HOUSE MER-316	CL	27.50	28.00
90	LEATHERWORKS LITE UP HOUSE	CL	27.50	28.00
90	LIBRARY LITE UP HOUSES	CL	27.50	28.00
90	LIGHT HOUSE LITE UP HOUSE	CL	27.50	28.00
90	MANSION LITE UP HOUSE	CL	27.50	28.00
90	N. ENG. CHURCH LITE UP HOUSE MER-375	CL	27.50	28.00
90	N. ENG. GEN. STORE LITE UP HSE MER-377	CL	27.50	28.00
90	RAILROAD STATION LITE UP HOUSE	CL	27.50	28.00
90	SCHOOL LITE UP HOUSE	CL	27.50	28.00
90	TOWN HALL LITE UP HOUSE	CL	27.50	28.00
91	2 TONE CSTONE CHURCH MER-360B	RT	35.00	35.00
91	CHURCH W/BLU ROOF LITE UP HSE MER-360E	RT	35.00	35.00
91	FLORAL PLAQUE XMAS-911	OP	10.00	10.00
91	FLOWER BASKET XMAS-912	OP	10.00	10.00
91	RESTAURANT LITE UP HOUSE	CL	27.50	28.00
91	TOY STORE LITE UP HOUSE	CL	27.50	28.00
91	TRAIN SET MER-378	RT	25.00	25.00
E. MANN			**CHRISTMAS IN AMERICA**	
88	CAPITOL, WHITE HOUSE, MT. VERNON	RT	75.00	150.00
88	DOCTOR'S OFFICE LITE UP	RT	27.50	28.00
89	SANTA IN SLEIGH	CL	25.00	45.00
90	CART WITH PEOPLE	RT	25.00	35.00
J. WHITE			**CHRISTMAS IN AMERICA**	
91	NEW ENGLAND CHURCH LITE UP MER-375	RT	27.50	28.00
91	NEW ENGLAND GEN'L STORE LITE UP MER-377	RT	27.50	28.00
L. SCIOLA			**CHRISTMAS VILLAGE**	
91	AWAY, AWAY	CL	30.00	30.00

YR	NAME	LIMIT	ISSUE	TREND
91	COUNSEL HOUSE	CL	60.00	60.00
91	CURIOSITY SHOP	CL	45.00	45.00
91	EMILY'S TOYS	CL	45.00	45.00
91	FIRE STATION, THE	CL	60.00	60.00
91	ON THIN ICE	CL	30.00	30.00
91	PLAYHOUSE, THE	CL	60.00	60.00
91	PUBLIC LIBRARY	CL	50.00	50.00
91	SCROOGE/MARLEY'S COUNTING HOUSE	CL	45.00	45.00
91	STORY TELLER, THE CJ-204	CL	20.00	20.00
91	YE OLD GIFT SHOPPE	CL	50.00	50.00
JAIMY			**DICKENS COLLECTION**	
91	CRATCHIT'S LITE UP HOUSE CJ-200	RT	37.50	38.00
91	CRATCHIT/TINY TIM MUSICAL CJ-117	RT	33.50	34.00
91	SCROOGE MUSICAL	RT	30.00	30.00
91	SCROOGE/MARLEY COUNTING HOUSE CJ-202	RT	37.50	38.00
J. WHITE			**DICKENS COLLECTION**	
89	CRATCHIT'S LITE UP XMS-7000A	RT	30.00	30.00
89	FEZZIWIG'S LITE UP XMS-7000C	RT	30.00	30.00
89	GIFT SHOPPE LITE UP XMS-7000H	RT	30.00	30.00
89	SCROOGE/MARLEY LITE UP XMS-7000B	RT	30.00	30.00
90	BLACK SWAN INN LITE UP XMS-7000E	RT	30.00	30.00
90	CRATCHIT FAMILY MER-121	RT	37.50	38.00
90	CRATCHIT/TINY TIM MUSICAL MER-105	RT	33.50	34.00
90	HEN POULTRY LITE UP	CL	30.00	30.00
90	TEA AND SPICE LITE UP	CL	30.00	30.00
90	WAITE FISH STORE LITE UP	CL	30.00	30.00
J. SAUERBREY			**GINGERBREAD CHRISTMAS COLLECTION**	
91	GINGERBREAD CHURCH LITE UP HSE CJ-403	CL	65.00	65.00
91	GINGERBREAD HOUSE LITE UP CJ-404	CL	65.00	65.00
91	GINGERBREAD MANSION LITE UP	CL	70.00	70.00
91	GINGERBREAD ROCKING HORSE MUSIC	CL	33.50	34.00
91	GINGERBREAD SWAN MUSICAL	CL	33.50	34.00
91	GINGERBREAD SWEET SHOP LITE UP HOUSE	CL	60.00	60.00
91	GINGERBREAD TEDDY BEAR MUSIC	CL	33.50	34.00
91	GINGERBREAD TOY SHOP LITE UP HOUSE	CL	60.00	60.00
91	GINGERBREAD VILLAGE LITE UP HOUSE	CL	60.00	60.00
JAIMY			**VICTORIAN CHRISTMAS COLLECTION**	
90	TWO BOYS WITH SNOWMAN	CL	12.00	12.00
91	LITTLE MATCH GIRL	CL	9.00	9.00
J. WHITE			**VICTORIAN CHRISTMAS COLLECTION**	
90	TOY/DOLL HOUSE LITE UP	CL	27.50	28.00
90	VICTORIAN HOUSE LITE UP HOUSE	CL	27.50	28.00
90	YARN SHOP LITE UP HOUSE	CL	27.50	28.00
91	ANTIQUE SHOP LITE UP HOUSE	CL	27.50	28.00
91	BEIGE CHURCH LITE UP HOUSE	CL	35.00	35.00
91	BOOK STORE LITE UP HOUSE	CL	27.50	28.00
91	CHURCH LITE UP HOUSE	CL	37.50	38.00
91	COUNTRY STORE LITE UP HOUSE	CL	27.50	28.00
91	INN LITE UP HOUSE MER-352	CL	27.50	28.00
E. MANN			**WIZARD OF OZ-40TH ANNIVERSARY**	
79	DOROTHY, SCARECROW, LION, TINMAN	RT	7.50	45.00
79	DOROTHY, SCARECROW, LION, TINMAN-MUSICAL	RT	12.50	75.00

SHADE TREE CREATIONS INC.

YR	NAME	LIMIT	ISSUE	TREND
B. VERNON				**COWBOYS**
80	BEER DRINKER	RT	20.00	100.00
80	CARD SHARK	RT	20.00	80.00
80	EARLY RISER	RT	20.00	125.00
81	GUNFIGHTER (1ST RELEASE)	RT	20.00	100.00
81	REDNECK (1ST RELEASE)	RT	20.00	150.00
81	URBAN COWBOY (PAINTED)	RT	20.00	950.00
83	URBAN COWBOY (BROWN)	RT	15.00	550.00
87	GOLFER	RT	30.00	30.00
88	COMPUTER WIZARD	RT	25.00	45.00
89	EXECUTIVE	RT	30.00	65.00
89	HAPPY HOUR	RT	30.00	30.00
89	HENPECKED & HOGTIED	RT	30.00	80.00
89	YEE HAW	RT	25.00	70.00
90	CAMERA CRAZY	RT	30.00	40.00
90	SMOKIN'-STURGIS RALLY	RT	35.00	400.00
90	THIS JOB	RT	30.00	30.00
90	TOURIST	RT	30.00	40.00
91	BOWLER	RT	30.00	30.00
91	GUNFIGHTER (2ND RELEASE)	RT	30.00	65.00
91	MECHANIC	RT	30.00	30.00
91	REDNECK (2ND RELEASE)	RT	30.00	125.00
91	SKIER	RT	30.00	30.00
95	DRAGGIN BUTT	OP	35.00	35.00
95	SEX MACHINE	OP	40.00	40.00
95	WOAH DERNIT	OP	40.00	40.00

SILVER DEER LTD.

YR	NAME	LIMIT	ISSUE	TREND
*	CRYSTAL STARSHIP	*	*	410.00
G. TRUEX			**CRYSTAL COLLECTIBLES**	
84	PINOCCHIO, 120MM	CL	195.00	250.00
90	JOE COOL CRUISIN	CL	165.00	165.00

YR	NAME	LIMIT	ISSUE	TREND
SO!				
K. GRAVES				**ANIMAL LOVE**
95	BROWN BEAR LOVE	1000	85.00	85.00
95	FERRET LOVE	1000	85.00	85.00
95	HAMADRYAD BABOON	1000	85.00	85.00
95	LEOPARD LOVE	1000	85.00	85.00
95	MANDRILL BABOON LOVE	1000	85.00	85.00
95	PANDA LOVE	1000	85.00	85.00
K. GRAVES				**CHESS SET**
93	KATALIN'S ADV. IN ALICE'S WONDERLAND	500	1100.00	1100.00
93	TOURNAMENT OF THE TREE FROGS	500	750.00	750.00
94	A WEE MAC CHESS TOURNAMENT	500	850.00	850.00
94	IMAGES OF THE SOUTHWEST	500	2500.00	2500.00
K. GRAVES				**IMAGINALS**
93	BILLY THE KITTY (KITTEN)	5000	50.00	50.00
93	BLACK BARK (STAFFORDSHIRE TERRIER)	5000	50.00	50.00
93	CHIEF SITTING BULLDOG	5000	50.00	50.00
93	CHOW MEIN	5000	50.00	50.00
93	DACHS HOLIDAY (DACHSHUND)	5000	50.00	50.00
93	DOLLY POODLE	5000	50.00	50.00
93	FLUIGATOR, THE (SKUNK)	5000	50.00	50.00
93	KAT FLOOSIE (CAT)	5000	50.00	50.00
93	MA BARKER (BEAGLE)	5000	50.00	50.00
93	MISS KITTY (CAT)	5000	50.00	50.00
93	ONE NOTE E. COYOTE	5000	50.00	50.00
93	PANCHO GATO (CAT)	5000	50.00	50.00
93	WILD NANOOK/NORTH (ALASKAN MALAMUTE)	5000	50.00	50.00
93	WYATT MOUSETRAP (CAT)	5000	50.00	50.00
94	BIG NOST KAT (WILD CAT)	5000	50.00	50.00
94	BLACK FOOTED FERRET, THE	5000	50.00	50.00
94	BOSTON BEENE (BOSTON TERRIER)	5000	50.00	50.00
94	CALAMITY CAIRN (CAIRN TERRIER)	5000	50.00	50.00
94	DANIEL SPANIEL (ENG. SPRINGER SPANIEL)	5000	50.00	50.00
94	DAVY COCKER (COCKER SPANIEL PUPPY)	5000	50.00	50.00
94	GERONIMEOW (CAT)	5000	50.00	50.00
94	GOLD N. TREEVER	5000	50.00	50.00
94	HERR MAX VON SCHAFFRHUND (GERMAN SHPRD.)	5000	50.00	50.00
94	JUDGE ROY MEAN (BULL TERRIER)	5000	50.00	50.00
94	MALTESE FALCONIER, THE	5000	50.00	50.00
94	MELANIE COLLIE ROSE	5000	50.00	50.00
94	PUGLIACCI (PUG)	5000	50.00	50.00
94	RED EYED AL (ALBINO FERRET)	5000	50.00	50.00
94	REV. LUTHER ST. BERNARD	5000	50.00	50.00
94	RITA RAT	5000	50.00	50.00
94	ROUGH RIDER ROTTIE (ROTTWEILER)	5000	50.00	50.00
94	RUDOLPHO RAT	5000	50.00	50.00
94	SIAM SAM (SIAMESE CAT)	5000	50.00	50.00
94	SIAM SUE (SIAMESE CAT)	5000	50.00	50.00
94	TY-PHOON SHAR-PEI	5000	50.00	50.00
94	WILD SPOTS DOOLIN (DALMATIAN)	5000	50.00	50.00
94	WILD, WILD WESTIE (W. HIGHLAND TERRIER)	5000	50.00	50.00
94	YORKIE YORKIER PUDDIN' (YORKSHIRE TERR.)	5000	50.00	50.00
95	CATS DOMINO	5000	50.00	50.00
95	CHEF BRIARD DEE	5000	50.00	50.00
95	COUNT BORZOI	5000	45.00	45.00
95	GOLD N. TRRVER	5000	50.00	50.00
95	LABRACADABRA	5000	50.00	50.00
95	MADAMA PAPILLION	5000	45.00	45.00
95	PUGLIACCI	5000	45.00	45.00
96	DOGGIE SCHNAUZER MD	5000	50.00	50.00
96	SHAGGY BOB TALE	5000	55.00	55.00
96	ZANE GREYHOUND	5000	50.00	50.00
SPORTS IMPRESSIONS				
*	DON MATTINGLY ERROR	500	125.00	850.00
*				**500 HOME RUN CLUB**
90	EDDIE MATTHEWS	5512	100.00	125.00
90	FRANK ROBINSON	5586	150.00	150.00
90	HARMON KILLEBREW	5573	150.00	150.00
90	JIMMY FOX	5534	150.00	150.00
90	MEL OTT	5511	150.00	150.00
90	TED WILLIAMS	5251	150.00	150.00
90	WILLIE MCCOVEY	5521	150.00	150.00
*				**BASEBALL SUPERSTAR FIGURINE SERIES**
88	ABBOTT & COSTELLO	5000	145.00	145.00
88	BABE RUTH	5000	125.00	125.00
88	LOU GEHRIG	5000	125.00	125.00
88	ROBERTO CLEMENTE	5000	125.00	125.00
88	TY COBB	5000	125.00	125.00
89	CY YOUNG	5000	125.00	125.00
89	HONUS WAGNER	5000	125.00	125.00
89	THURMAN MUNSON	5000	125.00	125.00
*				**BASEBALL SUPERSTAR FIGURINES**
87	DON MATTINGLY	CL	125.00	400.00
87	KEITH HERNANDEZ	2500	125.00	185.00
87	MICKEY MANTLE	CL	125.00	300.00
87	TED WILLIAMS F/S	CL	125.00	150.00
87	WADE BOGGS F/S	CL	125.00	150.00

YR	NAME	LIMIT	ISSUE	TREND
88	AL KALINE G/E	2500	125.00	150.00
88	ANDRE DAWSON G/E	2500	125.00	150.00
88	BOB FELLER	2500	125.00	185.00
88	JOSE CANSECO	CL	125.00	250.00
88	PAUL MOLITOR	2500	125.00	125.00
88	REGGIE JACKSON (YANKEES)	CL	125.00	275.00
89	ALAN TRAMMELL	2500	125.00	125.00
89	DUKE SNIDER	2500	125.00	125.00
89	FRANK VIOLA	2500	125.00	125.00
89	KIRK GIBSON	CL	125.00	185.00
89	REGGIE JACKSON (ANGELS)	CL	125.00	165.00
89	WILL CLARK f/s	CL	125.00	225.00
*	**BASEBALL'S 3000 HIT CLUB**			
89	ROD CAREW	3053	150.00	150.00
*	**BASEBALL'S 3000 HIT WINNERS PITCHERS SERIES**			
89	TOM SEAVER	CL	150.00	150.00
*	**BASEBALL'S 500 HOME RUN HITTERS**			
89	ERNIE BANKS	5512	150.00	150.00
89	HANK AARON	5755	150.00	150.00
89	WILLIE MAYS	5660	150.00	150.00
*	**BASEBALL'S CY YOUNG AWARD WINNERS**			
89	OREL HERSHISER	5055	125.00	165.00
*	**COLLECTORS' CLUB FIGURINE**			
89	MICK-MICKEY MANTLE, THE- H/S	TL	125.00	375.00
*	**KINGS OF K**			
90	NOLAN RYAN	500	195.00	195.00
90	STEVE CARLTON	500	195.00	195.00
90	TOM SEAVER	500	195.00	195.00
*	**NEW YORK METS SUPERSTAR FIGURINES**			
89	DARRYL STRAWBERRY	5018	125.00	125.00
89	DWIGHT GOODEN	5016	125.00	125.00
89	GARY CARTER	5008	125.00	125.00
89	GREGG JEFFERIES	5009	125.00	125.00
89	HOWARD JOHNSON	5020	125.00	125.00
89	KEVIN MCREYNOLDS	5022	125.00	125.00
*	**NFL LIMITED EDITION FIGURINES**			
90	BOOMER ESIASON-AWAY	995	195.00	195.00
90	BOOMER ESIASON-HOME	995	195.00	195.00
90	DAN MARINO-AWAY	995	195.00	195.00
90	DAN MARINO-HOME	995	195.00	195.00
90	JOE MONTANA-AWAY	995	195.00	195.00
90	JOE MONTANA-HOME	995	195.00	195.00
90	JOHN ELWAY-AWAY	995	195.00	195.00
90	JOHN ELWAY-HOME	995	195.00	195.00
90	LAWRENCE TAYLOR-AWAY	995	195.00	195.00
90	LAWRENCE TAYLOR-HOME	995	195.00	195.00
90	RANDALL CUNNINGHAM-AWAY	995	195.00	195.00
90	RANDALL CUNNINGHAM-HOME	995	195.00	195.00
*	**RENAISSANCE 13 IN. SCULPTURES**			
90	DON MATTINGLY	2950	395.00	395.00
*	**SPECIAL INDIVIDUAL RELEASES**			
89	MANTLE-SWITCH HITTER	CL	295.00	345.00
90	JOE MORGAN-NEWEST HALL OF FAMER	1990	195.00	195.00
91	RICKEY HENDERSON	939	150.00	150.00
91	ROCKWELL-YER OUT	2500	195.00	195.00
*	**SUPER SIZE FIGURINES**			
89	JOSE CANSECO	CL	250.00	275.00
89	TED WILLIAMS	CL	250.00	275.00
90	MICKEY MANTLE	CL	250.00	275.00
90	REGGIE JACKSON	CL	250.00	250.00
90	THURMAN MUNSON	995	250.00	250.00
90	TOM SEAVER	CL	250.00	250.00
*	**TEAM OF DREAMS**			
90	CAL RIPKEN, JR.	1990	150.00	150.00
90	DON MATTINGLY	1990	150.00	150.00
90	ERIC DAVIS	1990	150.00	150.00
90	KEN GRIFFEY, JR.	1990	150.00	150.00
90	KEVIN MITCHELL	1990	150.00	150.00
90	KIRBEY PUCKETT	1990	150.00	150.00
90	LENNY DYKSTRA	1990	150.00	150.00
90	MARK LANGSTON	1990	150.00	150.00
*	**TODAY'S STAR SERIES**			
90	DON MATTINGLY	2950	65.00	65.00
90	DWIGHT GOODEN	2950	65.00	65.00
90	KEN GRIFFEY, JR.	2950	65.00	65.00
90	LENNY DYKSTRA	2950	65.00	65.00
90	NOLAN RYAN	2950	65.00	65.00

STUDIO COLLECTION

T. RUBEL — **SANTA'S ANIMAL KINGDOM**

YR	NAME	LIMIT	ISSUE	TREND
94	SANTA'S ANIMAL KINGDOM-STIFFENED	2500	125.00	135.00

STUDIOS OF HARRY SMITH

H. SMITH

YR	NAME	LIMIT	ISSUE	TREND
91	CAT ON PILLOW	150	145.00	300.00
91	MYSTICAL DRAGON	SO	175.00	350.00

YR	NAME	LIMIT	ISSUE	TREND

SUMMERHILL CRYSTAL

YR	NAME	LIMIT	ISSUE	TREND
*			**SUMMERHILL CRYSTAL**	
92	BICYCLE	500	64.00	64.00
92	L'ARC DU TRIOMPHE	5000	220.00	220.00
92	LARGE DRAGON	1500	320.00	320.00
92	PRINCESS COACH	1500	700.00	700.00
92	SACRE COEUR	5000	190.00	190.00
92	VENUS	500	96.00	96.00

SWAROVSKI AMERICA

YR	NAME	LIMIT	ISSUE	TREND
E. MEIR			**A PET'S CORNER**	
96	ST. BERNARD	OP	*	*
M. STAMEY			**A PET'S CORNER**	
91	KITTEN 7634NR028000	RT	47.50	49.50
91	SITTING CAT	OP	75.00	85.00
A. STOCKER			**A PET'S CORNER**	
87	DACHSHUND, MINI	OP	20.00	225.00
90	BEAGLE, PUPPY	OP	40.00	50.00
90	TERRIER, SCOTCH	OP	60.00	75.00
92	POODLE	OP	125.00	140.00
A. STOCKER			**AFRICAN WILDLIFE**	
88	ELEPHANT, LARGE 7640NR60	RT	70.00	100.00
88	HIPPOPOTAMUS 7626NR65	RT	70.00	125.00
88	RHINOCEROS, SMALL	OP	70.00	75.00
89	ELEPHANT, SMALL	OP	50.00	65.00
89	HIPPOPOTAMUS, SMALL 7626NR055000	RT	70.00	90.00
90	RHINOCEROS, SMALL 7622NR60	RT	70.00	90.00
C. SCHNEIDERBAUER		**AMONG FLOWERS AND FOLIAGE**		
92	BUMBLEBEE	OP	85.00	85.00
92	HUMMINGBIRD	RT	195.00	210.00
94	BUTTERFLY ON LEAF	OP	75.00	75.00
95	DRAGONFLY	OP	85.00	85.00
*				**ANIMALS**
*	BEAR, GIANT 7637NR112	RT	125.00	1900.00
*	HUMMINGBIRD RHODIUM 7552NR200	RT	*	1800.00
*	HUMMINGBIRD-GOLD 7552NR100	RT	200.00	1250.00
*	SPARROW, LARGE 7650NR32	RT	38.00	150.00
*	TURTLE, KING SIZE 7632NR75	RT	58.00	225.00
84	BLOWFISH, LARGE 7644NR41	RT	40.00	90.00
85	BEE-GOLD 7553NR100	RT	200.00	1250.00
85	BEE-RHODUIM 7553NR200	RT	200.00	1800.00
85	BUTTERFLY-GOLD 7551NR100	RT	*	1250.00
85	BUTTERFLY-RHODIUM 7551NR200	RT	*	1800.00
88	DUMBO NO TUSKS 7640NR35-3	RT	*	4500.00
88	DUMBO W/SM. TUSKS 7640NR35-2	RT	*	5500.00
88	ORLANDO DUMBO W/LG. TUSKS 7640NB35-1	RT	*	5500.00
89	DUMBO W/LG. EARS & TUSKS 7640NR35-4	RT	*	5000.00
89	DUMBO W/LG. EARS, NO TUSKS	RT	*	4500.00
90	DUMBO W/FLYING EARS	RT	*	1500.00
M. SCHRECK				**ANIMALS**
*	BEAR, KING SIZE 7637NR92	RT	95.00	1500.00
*	BEAR, SMALL	RT	*	95.00
*	CAT, MEDIUM 7634NR52	RT	38.00	300.00
*	CHICKEN, MINI 7651NR20	RT	16.00	100.00
*	DACHSHUND, MINI 7672NR42	RT	*	75.00
*	DUCK, LARGE 7653NR75	RT	44.00	250.00
*	DUCK, MEDIUM 7653NR55	RT	*	125.00
*	DUCK, MINI 7653NR45	RT	16.00	100.00
*	ELEPHANT, LARGE 7640NR55	RT	*	250.00
*	FALCON HEAD, SMALL	RT	*	110.00
*	FROG W/CLEAR EYES	RT	*	175.00
*	HEDGEHOG, KING SIZE 7630NR60	RT	98.00	600.00
*	MOUSE, KING SIZE 7631NR60	RT	95.00	650.00
*	MOUSE, LARGE 7631NR50	RT	69.00	250.00
*	MOUSE, MINI 7655NR23	RT	16.00	125.00
*	MOUSE, SMALL 2 TAIL STYLES	RT	*	60.00
*	MOUSE, SMALL 7631NR30	RT	35.00	60.00
*	PIG, LARGE 7638NR65	RT	50.00	200.00
*	RABBIT, LARGE	RT	*	200.00
*	RABBIT, MINI 7652NR20	RT	16.00	100.00
*	SEAL, LARGE	RT	*	120.00
*	SWAN, MINI 7658NR27	RT	16.00	125.00
77	CAT, LARGE 7634NR70	RT	44.00	90.00
79	SPARROW, MINI 7650NR20	RT	16.00	75.00
82	CAT, MINI 7659NR31	RT	16.00	85.00
84	BEAR, MINI 7670NR32	RT	16.00	125.00
84	DACHSHUND 7641NR75	RT	48.00	70.00
84	FALCON HEAD. LARGE 7645NR100	RT	600.00	1200.00
84	FROG 7642NR48	RT	30.00	125.00
86	FALCON HEAD, SMALL 7645NR45	RT	60.00	125.00
M. STAMEY				**ANIMALS**
*	OWL 7621NR000003	RT	*	150.00
*	SNAIL 7648NR30	RT	*	55.00
*	SOUTH SEA SHELL	RT	*	135.00
*	WALRUS	RT	*	200.00
88	WHALE 7628NR80	RT	70.00	125.00
89	TOUCAN 7621NR000002	RT	70.00	130.00

YR	NAME	LIMIT	ISSUE	TREND
89	WALRUS 7620NR100000	RT	120.00	200.00
A. STOCKER				**ANIMALS**
*	DACHSHUND, MINI 7672NR042	RT	20.00	55.00
*	RABBIT, MINI LYING	RT	*	100.00
*	RHINOCEROS 7622NR70	RT	*	125.00
87	PARTRIDGE 7625NR50	RT	85.00	200.00
M. SCHRECK				**BARNYARD FRIENDS**
82	PIG, MINI	OP	16.00	30.00
84	PIG, MEDIUM	OP	35.00	47.50
G. STAMEY				**BARNYARD FRIENDS**
87	HEN, MINI	OP	35.00	45.00
87	ROOSTER, MINI	OP	35.00	55.00
88	CHICKS (SET OF 3) MINI	RT	35.00	45.00
A. STOCKER				**BARNYARD FRIENDS**
93	DICK GOSLING	OP	38.00	38.00
93	HARRY GOSLING	OP	38.00	38.00
93	MOTHER GOOSE	OP	75.00	75.00
93	TOM GOSLING	OP	38.00	38.00
A. HIRZINGER				**BEAUTIES OF THE LAKE**
95	SWAN, MINI	OP	4500.00	4500.00
M. SCHRECK				**BEAUTIES OF THE LAKE**
77	SWAN, LARGE	OP	55.00	95.00
77	SWAN, MEDIUM	OP	44.00	85.00
83	DRAKE, MINI	OP	20.00	45.00
86	MALLARD 7647NR80	RT	80.00	150.00
89	SWAN, SMALL	OP	35.00	50.00
M. STAMEY				**BEAUTIES OF THE LAKE**
89	MALLARD, GIANT	OP	2000.00	4500.00
94	FROG	OP	50.00	50.00
96	GOLDFISH, MINI	OP	*	*
A. STOCKER				**BEAUTIES OF THE LAKE**
86	DUCK - STANDING, MINI	OP	22.00	38.00
86	DUCK - SWIMMING, MINI	OP	16.00	38.00
A. HIRZINGER				**CENTENARY EDITION**
95	CENTENARY SWAN	YR	150.00	150.00
M. SCHRECK				**COLLECTORS SOCIETY ANNUAL EDITIONS**
87	LOVE BIRDS, THE DO1X861/TOGETHERNESS	RT	150.00	4500.00
M. STAMEY				**COLLECTORS SOCIETY ANNUAL EDITIONS**
90	DOLPHINS, THE DO1X901/LEAD ME	RT	225.00	1500.00
91	SEALS, THE DO1X911/SAVE ME	RT	225.00	600.00
92	BIRTHDAY CAKE, THE 003-0169678	RT	85.00	225.00
92	WHALES, THE DO1X921/CARE FOR ME	RT	265.00	650.00
A. STOCKER				**COLLECTORS SOCIETY ANNUAL EDITIONS**
88	WOODPECKERS, THE DO1X881/SHARING	RT	165.00	1900.00
89	TURTLEDOVES, THE DO1X891/AMOUR	RT	195.00	1100.00
M. ZENDRON				**COLLECTORS SOCIETY ANNUAL EDITIONS**
*	ELEPHANT, THE DO1X931/INSPIRATION AFRIC	RT	325.00	1250.00
*				**COLLECTORS SOCIETY MEMBER EDITIONS**
91	DOLPHINS BROOCH 003-8901707	RT	*	150.00
93	ELEPHANT BROOCH 003-8902448	RT	*	125.00
95	CENTENARY SWAN BROOCH	YR	125.00	125.00
A. STAMEY				**COLLECTORS SOCIETY MEMBER EDITIONS**
94	KUDU, THE DO1X941/INSPIRATION AFRICA	RT	*	450.00
A. STOCKER				**COLLECTORS SOCIETY MEMBER EDITIONS**
95	LION, THE DO1X951/INSPIRATION AFRICA	RT	*	325.00
*				**COMMEMORATIVE SINGLE ISSUE**
90	ELEPHANT-COMMEMORATIVE ITEM/WALT DISNEY	CL	125.00	1250.00
93	ELEPHANT	OP	150.00	150.00
M. STAMEY				**CRYSTAL MELODIES**
96	VIOLIN	OP	*	*
M. ZENDRON				**CRYSTAL MELODIES**
92	HARP	OP	175.00	210.00
92	LUTE	OP	125.00	140.00
M. SCHRECK				**ENDANGERED SPECIES**
77	TURTLE, LARGE	OP	48.00	75.00
77	TURTLE, SMALL	OP	35.00	50.00
81	TURTLE, GIANT	OP	2500.00	4500.00
M. STAMEY				**ENDANGERED SPECIES**
91	KIWI	OP	37.50	45.00
93	MOTHER KANGAROO WITH BABY	OP	95.00	95.00
A. STOCKER				**ENDANGERED SPECIES**
87	KOALA	OP	50.00	65.00
89	KOALA, MINI	OP	35.00	45.00
92	LYING BABY BEAVER	RT	47.50	50.00
92	MOTHER BEAVER	OP	110.00	125.00
92	SITTING BABY BEAVER	OP	47.50	50.00
93	BABY PANDA	OP	25.00	25.00
93	MOTHER PANDA	OP	120.00	120.00
*				**EXQUISITE ACCENTS**
87	BIRD'S NEST	OP	90.00	125.00
M. SCHRECK				**EXQUISITE ACCENTS**
80	BIRDBATH	OP	150.00	210.00
87	DINNER BELL, MEDIUM	OP	80.00	95.00
87	DINNER BELL, SMALL	OP	60.00	65.00

One of Lladro's additions to their Children's Themes collection for 1985 was Boy on Carousel Horse, *which is currently valued at $750.*

This Sand Piper *finds rest on a piece of washed up driftwood. The sculpture, produced by Maruri, is from the "Shore Birds" series by W.D. Gaither.*

This little one wants to make sure her doll isn't sick. Love Cures All *is produced by Rhodes Studios.*

The 1991 Santa Claus *motion musical plays "Have Yourself a Merry Little Christmas." The figure is by S. Nahene for WACO Products Corp.*

YR	NAME	LIMIT	ISSUE	TREND
M. STAMEY			**EXQUISITE ACCENTS**	
92	ROSE, THE	OP	150.00	150.00
95	ORCHID, THE/PINK	OP	140.00	140.00
95	ORCHID, THE/YELLOW	OP	140.00	140.00
A. STOCKER			**EXQUISITE ACCENTS**	
95	ANGEL	OP	210.00	210.00
M. ZENDRON			**FABULOUS CREATURES**	
96	FABULOUS CREATURES "THE UNICORN"	OP	325.00	325.00
A. HIRZINGER			**FEATHERED FRIENDS**	
93	PELICAN	OP	38.00	38.00
E. MEIR			**FEATHERED FRIENDS**	
95	DOVE	OP	55.00	55.00
*			**FRUIT**	
*	GRAPES, LARGE 7550NR30015	RT	250.00	1250.00
M. SCHRECK			**FRUIT**	
*	GIANT PINEAPPLE-RHODIUM 7507NR260002	RT	1750.00	3500.00
*	LARGE APPLE PHOTO STAND/RHODIUM	RT	80.00	375.00
*	LARGE PINEAPPLE-RHODIUM 7507NR105002	RT	*	450.00
*	SMALL APPLE PHOTO STAND-RHODIUM	RT	40.00	275.00
87	SMALL PINEAPPLE-RHODIUM 7507NR060002	RT	55.00	200.00
*			**IN A SUMMER MEADOW**	
82	BUTTERFLY	OP	44.00	85.00
86	BUTTERFLY, MINI 7671NR30	RT	16.00	130.00
E. MEIR			**IN A SUMMER MEADOW**	
95	LADYBUG	OP	29.50	30.00
C. SCHNEIDERBAUER			**IN A SUMMER MEADOW**	
92	SPARROW	OP	29.50	30.00
M. SCHRECK			**IN A SUMMER MEADOW**	
76	MOUSE, MEDIUM 7631NR40	RT	48.00	85.00
85	HEDGEHOG, LARGE 7630NR50	RT	120.00	300.00
85	HEDGEHOG, MEDIUM 7630NR40	RT	70.00	250.00
87	HEDGEHOG, SMALL 7630NR30	RT	50.00	450.00
M. STAMEY			**IN A SUMMER MEADOW**	
86	SNAIL	RT	35.00	55.00
A. STOCKER			**IN A SUMMER MEADOW**	
88	MOTHER RABBIT	OP	60.00	75.00
88	RABBIT - SITTING, MINI	OP	35.00	45.00
88	RABBIT, LYING MINI 7678NR030	RT	35.00	55.00
91	FIELD MOUSE	OP	47.50	50.00
94	FIELD MICE	OP	43.00	43.00
M. ZENDRON			**INSPIRATION AFRICA**	
95	BABY ELEPHANT	OP	155.00	155.00
*			**JULIA'S WORLD**	
90	JULIA W/MANDOLIN	OP	29.50	30.00
90	LENA & PEPI/BENCH	OP	55.00	55.00
90	LENA W/LUTE	OP	29.50	30.00
90	MARIAN	OP	29.50	30.00
90	PEPI & MOPSY	OP	55.00	55.00
90	PEPI W/DRUM	OP	29.50	30.00
90	SALI	OP	29.50	30.00
90	SALI W/ACCORDION	OP	29.50	30.00
M. SCHRECK			**KINGDOM OF ICE AND SNOW**	
84	PENGUIN, LARGE 7643NR85	RT	44.00	110.00
84	PENGUIN, MINI	OP	16.00	38.00
85	SEAL, LARGE 7645NR85	OP	44.00	95.00
A. STOCKER			**KINGDOM OF ICE AND SNOW**	
86	BABY SEAL, MINI	OP	30.00	45.00
86	POLAR BEAR, LARGE	OP	140.00	210.00
*			**NATIVITY**	
91	HOLY FAMILY WITH ARCH 7475NR001	RT	250.00	300.00
92	ANGEL 7475NR000009	RT	65.00	100.00
92	SHEPHERD 7475NR000007	RT	65.00	100.00
92	WISE MEN (SET OF 3)	RT	175.00	225.00
*			**OUR CANDLEHOLDERS**	
87	STAR, LARGE	OP	250.00	375.00
89	STAR, MEDIUM	OP	200.00	260.00
M. SCHRECK			**OUR CANDLEHOLDERS**	
83	WATER LILIY, MEDIUM	OP	150.00	250.00
83	WATER LILY, MEDIUM	OP	150.00	260.00
85	WATER LILY, LARGE	OP	200.00	375.00
85	WATER LILY, SMALL	OP	100.00	175.00
A. STOCKER			**OUR CANDLEHOLDERS**	
90	NEO-CLASSIC, LARGE	RT	220.00	250.00
90	NEO-CLASSIC, MEDIUM	RT	190.00	225.00
90	NEO-CLASSIC, SMALL	RT	170.00	200.00
A. HIRZINGER			**OUR WOODLAND FRIENDS**	
95	OUTLET	OP	45.00	45.00
E. MEIR			**OUR WOODLAND FRIENDS**	
94	ROE DEER FAWN	OP	75.00	75.00
M. SCHRECK			**OUR WOODLAND FRIENDS**	
79	OWL, MINI	OP	16.00	30.00
79	OWL, SMALL 7636NR46	RT	59.00	85.00
79	OWL. LARGE	OP	90.00	125.00
81	BEAR, LARGE	OP	75.00	95.00
82	BEAR, SMALL 7637NR54	RT	44.00	85.00

YR	NAME	LIMIT	ISSUE	TREND
83	OWL, GIANT	OP	1200.00	2000.00
85	BEAR, MINI	OP	16.00	55.00
85	SQUIRREL	OP	35.00	65.00
A. STOCKER			**OUR WOODLAND FRIENDS**	
87	FOX	OP	50.00	125.00
88	FOX - RUNNING, MINI	OP	35.00	45.00
88	FOX - SITTING, MINI	OP	35.00	45.00
89	MUSHROOMS	OP	35.00	45.00
M. SCHRECK			**PAPERWEIGHTS**	
82	CONE	RT	80.00	225.00
87	CHATON, LARGE	OP	190.00	260.00
87	CHATON, SMALL	OP	50.00	65.00
87	PYRAMID, LARGE	OP	90.00	250.00
87	PYRAMID, SMALL	OP	100.00	125.00
90	CHATON, GIANT	OP	3900.00	4500.00
*			**RETIRED**	
*	BUTTERFLY, MINI	RT	16.00	85.00
*	ELEPHANT	RT	90.00	1500.00
*	RABBIT, LARGE 7652NR45	RT	38.00	175.00
85	BUTTERFLY	RT	200.00	1100.00
85	HUMMINGBIRD	RT	200.00	1100.00
M. SCHRECK			**RETIRED**	
*	BEAR, GIANT SIZE	RT	125.00	1020.00
*	DOG 7635NR70	RT	44.00	85.00
*	DUCK, MEDIUM	RT	38.00	125.00
*	KING SIZE APPLE PHOTO STAND-RHODIUM	RT	120.00	500.00
81	DINNER BELL, LARGE	RT	80.00	150.00
81	EGG	RT	60.00	150.00
G. STAMEY			**SILVER CRYSTAL CITY**	
*	TOWN HALL 7474NR000027	RT	*	150.00
90	SILVER CRYSTAL CITY-CATHEDRAL	RT	95.00	130.00
90	SILVER CRYSTAL CITY-HOUSES I & II	RT	75.00	85.00
90	SILVER CRYSTAL CITY-HOUSES III & IV	RT	75.00	85.00
90	SILVER CRYSTAL CITY-POPLARS	RT	40.00	60.00
91	CITY GATES 7474NR000023	RT	95.00	110.00
91	CITY TOWER 7474NR000022	RT	37.50	55.00
A. STOCKER			**SILVER CRYSTAL WORLDWIDE LIMITED EDITION**	
95	EAGLE	RT	1750.00	5000.00
*			**SOUTH SEA**	
86	BLOWFISH, SMALL	OP	35.00	55.00
87	BLOWFISH, MINI	OP	22.00	30.00
M. STAMEY			**SOUTH SEA**	
88	OPEN SHELL WITH PEARL	OP	120.00	175.00
91	BUTTERFLY FISH	OP	150.00	175.00
91	SOUTH SEA SHELL 7624NR072000	RT	110.00	135.00
93	SEA HORSE	OP	85.00	85.00
95	CONCH	OP	29.50	30.00
95	DOLPHIN	OP	210.00	210.00
95	MARITIME TRIO	OP	104.00	104.00
95	SHELL	OP	29.50	30.00
95	STARFISH	OP	29.50	30.00
*			**SPARKLING FRUIT**	
85	GRAPES, MEDIUM 7550NR20029	RT	300.00	450.00
85	GRAPES, SMALL 7550NR20015	RT	200.00	300.00
M. SCHRECK			**SPARKLING FRUIT**	
*	KING SIZE APPLE PHOTO STAND-GOLD	RT	*	475.00
*	LARGE APPLE PHOTO STAND - GOLD	RT	*	375.00
*	SMALL APPLE PHOTO STAND - GOLD	RT	*	250.00
81	PINEAPPLE, GIANT	OP	1750.00	3250.00
81	PINEAPPLE, LARGE	RT	150.00	450.00
86	PINEAPPLE, SMALL	RT	55.00	85.00
M. STAMEY			**SPARKLING FRUIT**	
91	APPLE	OP	175.00	185.00
91	PEAR	OP	175.00	185.00
M. SCHRECK			**THE GAME OF KINGS**	
84	CHESS SET	OP	950.00	1375.00
M. STAMEY			**UP IN THE TREES**	
89	OWL	RT	70.00	120.00
89	PARROT 7621NR000004	RT	70.00	130.00
90	KINGFISHER 7621NR000001	RT	75.00	130.00
*			**WHEN WE WERE YOUNG**	
94	REPLICA HEDGEHOG	OP	38.00	38.00
94	REPLICA CAT	OP	38.00	38.00
94	REPLICA MOUSE	OP	38.00	38.00
94	STARTER SET	OP	113.00	113.00
G. STAMEY			**WHEN WE WERE YOUNG**	
88	LOCOMOTIVE	OP	150.00	155.00
88	TENDER	OP	55.00	55.00
88	WAGON	OP	85.00	95.00
89	OLD TIMER AUTOMOBILE	RT	130.00	155.00
90	PETROL WAGON	OP	75.00	95.00
91	SANTA MARIA	OP	375.00	375.00
93	TIPPING WAGON	OP	95.00	95.00
94	SAILBOAT	OP	195.00	195.00
95	TRAIN, MINI	OP	125.00	125.00

YR	NAME	LIMIT	ISSUE	TREND
A. STOCKER			**WHEN WE WERE YOUNG**	
90	AIRPLANE	OP	135.00	155.00
M. ZENDRON			**WHEN WE WERE YOUNG**	
93	KRIS BEAR	OP	75.00	75.00
95	KRIS BEAR ON SKATES	OP	75.00	75.00

TAY PORCELAINS

YR	NAME	LIMIT	ISSUE	TREND
*			**TAY PORCELAINS**	
*	TURTLEDOVES, GROUP OF TWO, 10 IN.	500	*	500.00
70	BLUE JAY, 13 IN.	500	375.00	675.00
70	EAGLE, 12 X 15 IN.	500	1000.00	1650.00
70	EUROPEAN WOODCOCK, 10.5 IN.	500	325.00	550.00
70	LIMPKIN, 20 IN.	500	600.00	1100.00
71	FALCON, 13 IN.	500	500.00	925.00
71	PHEASANT, 30 IN.	500	1500.00	2400.00
71	QUAIL GROUP, 10 IN.	500	400.00	725.00
71	ROADRUNNER, 10 X 19 IN.	500	800.00	*
72	GRAY PARTRIDGE, 11.5 IN.	500	800.00	1400.00
73	AUSTRIAN OFFICER ON HORSEBACK	100	1200.00	1350.00
74	AMERICAN WOODCOCK, 10.5 IN.	500	625.00	700.00
74	BOREAL CHICKADEE, 7 IN.	5000	275.00	360.00
74	GREAT CRESTED FLYCATCHER, 9 IN.	1000	300.00	360.00
74	GYRAFALCON, 18 IN.	300	1250.00	1500.00
74	MALLARD DUCK, 13.5 IN.	500	900.00	1050.00
74	MALLARD DUCK, FLYING, 15 IN.	500	550.00	675.00
74	OWL, 10.5 IN.	500	350.00	450.00
74	TURTLEDOVES ON ROOF TILE, 9.5 IN.	500	335.00	375.00
75	CAROLINA DUCKS, GROUP OF TWO, 13 IN.	500	1350.00	1500.00
75	ORIOLE, 9.5 IN.	1000	300.00	325.00
75	SMERGOS DUCKS, GROUP OF TWO, 10 IN.	500	1000.00	1100.00
75	WHITE-THROATED SPARROW, 5.5 IN.	500	360.00	400.00
76	BLUEBIRDS, GROUP OF TWO, 9.5 IN.	500	500.00	550.00
76	CUSTER ON HORSE, 13 X 14.5 IN.	500	1500.00	1500.00
76	INDIAN ON HORSE, 13 X 14.5 IN.	500	1500.00	1500.00
76	ROBIN, 8 IN.	500	400.00	450.00

THE GLASS BARON

YR	NAME	LIMIT	ISSUE	TREND
J. BECHAM			**WILDLIFE SERIES**	
94	LEADER OF THE PACK	250	*	*

THOMAS F. CLARK CO.

YR	NAME	LIMIT	ISSUE	TREND
T. CLARK			**TOM CLARK CREATIONS**	
*	ABEDNEGO	*	*	75.00
*	ABRAHAM	*	*	180.00
*	ADAM	*	*	125.00
*	AHAB	*	*	350.00
*	ALPHA	*	*	150.00
*	BELLE KRINGLE	*	*	200.00
*	BLACKSMITH	*	*	280.00
*	CALEB	*	*	200.00
*	COWBOY	*	*	150.00
*	DAFFY	*	*	225.00
*	ERNEST	*	*	270.00
*	GERBER	*	*	400.00

TUDOR MINT

YR	NAME	LIMIT	ISSUE	TREND
J. WATSON				
91	POWER OF THE CRYSTAL, THE	3500	478.00	525.00
S. RILEY			**EXHIBITION ONLY STUDIES**	
93	DACTRIUS	*	63.92	70.00
J. WATSON			**EXHIBITION ONLY STUDIES**	
94	VEXIUS	*	66.40	70.00
S. RILEY			**EXTRAVAGANZA STUDIES**	
92	SAURIA	403	31.90	40.00
94	LITHIA	*	31.90	33.00
J. WATSON			**EXTRAVAGANZA STUDIES**	
93	DEINOS	463	31.90	35.00
S. RILEY			**MYTH & MAGIC CLUB**	
90	QUEST FOR THE TRUTH, THE	1282	79.90	83.00
92	FRIENDS	*	30.30	32.00
92	PLAYMATES	3778	27.10	30.00
93	MYSTICAL ENCOUNTER, THE	*	31.60	35.00
94	CRYSTAL SHIELD, THE	OP	44.00	48.00
94	KEEPER OF THE DRAGONS, THE	*	79.90	85.00
95	BATTLE FOR THE CRYSTAL, THE	OP	108.00	108.00
J. WATSON			**MYTH & MAGIC CLUB**	
91	GAME OF STRAX, THE	2533	23.90	25.00
91	WELL OF ASPIRATIONS, THE	2973	79.90	85.00
92	ENCHANTED POOL, THE	*	79.90	85.00
S. RILEY			**MYTH & MAGIC-LARGE STUDIES**	
90	DANCE OF THE DOLPHINS, THE	1537	280.00	300.00
90	DRAGON MASTER, THE	1500	280.00	300.00
90	VII SEEKERS OF KNOWLEDGE, THE	7500	280.00	300.00
J. WATSON			**MYTH & MAGIC-LARGE STUDIES**	
92	GATHERING OF THE UNICORNS, THE	5000	296.00	325.00
S. RILEY			**ONE YEAR ONLY STUDIES**	
94	DRAGON OF THE UNDERWORLD, THE	YR	66.40	70.00

YR	NAME	LIMIT	ISSUE	TREND
95	GUARDIAN OF THE CRYSTAL, THE	YR	108.00	108.00
	J. WATSON			**ONE YEAR ONLY STUDIES**
93	FLYING DRAGON, THE	YR	63.90	70.00

UNITED DESIGN CORP.

YR	NAME	LIMIT	ISSUE	TREND
	S. BRADFORD			**ANGELS COLLECTION**
91	CHRISTMAS ANGEL AA-003	10000	125.00	125.00
91	CLASSICAL ANGEL AA-005	10000	79.00	79.00
91	GIFT, THE- AA-009	3500	140.00	500.00
91	HEAVENLY SHEPHERDESS AA-008	10000	99.00	99.00
91	MESSENGER OF PEACE AA-006	10000	75.00	75.00
91	TRUMPETER ANGEL AA-004	10000	99.00	99.00
91	WINTER ROSE ANGEL AA-007	10000	65.00	65.00
93	GIFT, THE- '93	RT	120.00	140.00
94	EARTH ANGEL	10000	84.00	84.00
94	HARVEST ANGEL	10000	84.00	84.00
	P. JONAS			**ANGELS COLLECTION**
91	ANGEL WAIF AA-012	OP	15.00	16.00
91	PEACE DESCENDING ANGEL AA-013	OP	20.00	20.00
91	ROSETTI ANGEL AA-011	OP	20.00	20.00
91	VICTORIAN CUPID ANGEL AA-010	OP	15.00	16.00
	K. MEMOLI			**ANGELS COLLECTION**
93	ANGEL OF FLIGHT	10000	100.00	100.00
93	MADONNA	10000	100.00	100.00
94	ANGEL WITH CHRIST CHILD	10000	84.00	84.00
94	DREAMING OF ANGELS	10000	120.00	120.00
	D. NEWBURN			**ANGELS COLLECTION**
93	ANGEL WITH BIRDS	10000	75.00	75.00
93	ANGEL WITH LEAVES	10000	70.00	70.00
93	ANGEL WITH LEAVES, EMERALD	RT	70.00	90.00
93	ANGEL WITH LILIES	10000	80.00	80.00
93	ANGELS WITH LILIES, CRIMSON	RT	80.00	100.00
94	ANGEL WITH BOOK	10000	84.00	84.00
94	ANGEL, ROSES & BLUEBIRDS	10000	65.00	65.00
94	GIFT, THE- '94	RT	140.00	150.00
	S. BRADFORD			**BACKYARD BIRDS**
88	BABY ROBIN, SMALL BB-006	OP	10.00	10.00
88	BABY ROBINS BB-008	OP	15.00	18.00
88	BLUEBIRD BB-009	OP	15.00	20.00
88	BLUEBIRD, SMALL BB-001	OP	10.00	10.00
88	CARDINAL, SMALL BB-002	OP	10.00	10.00
88	CHICKADEE BB-010	OP	15.00	17.00
88	CHICKADEE, SMALL BB-003	OP	10.00	10.00
88	FEMALE CARDINAL BB-011	OP	15.00	17.00
88	FEMALE HUMMINGBIRD, SMALL BB-005	RT	10.00	10.00
88	FLYING HUMMINGBIRD, SMALL BB-004	OP	10.00	10.00
88	HANGING BLUEBIRD BB-017	RT	11.00	17.00
88	HANGING CARDINAL BB-018	RT	11.00	11.00
88	HANGING CHICKADEE BB-019	RT	11.00	11.00
88	HANGING HUMMINGBIRD, LARGE BB-023	RT	15.00	16.00
88	HANGING HUMMINGBIRD, SMALL BB-022	RT	11.00	11.00
88	HANGING ROBIN BB-020	RT	11.00	11.00
88	HANGING SPARROW BB-021	RT	11.00	11.00
88	HUMMINGBIRD BB-012	OP	15.00	17.00
88	MALE CARDIDNAL BB-013	OP	15.00	17.00
88	RED-WINGED BLACKBIRD BB-014	RT	15.00	17.00
88	ROBIN BB-015	OP	15.00	20.00
88	SPARROW BB-016	OP	15.00	17.00
88	SPARROW, SMALL BB-007	OP	10.00	10.00
89	BABY BLUE JAY BB-027	OP	15.00	16.00
89	BALTIMORE ORIOLE BB-024	OP	19.50	22.00
89	BLUE JAY BB-026	OP	19.50	22.00
89	GOLDFINCH BB-028	OP	16.50	20.00
89	HOOT OWL BB-025	OP	15.00	20.00
89	SAW-WHET OWL BB-029	OP	15.00	18.00
89	WOODPECKER BB-030	OP	16.50	20.00
90	BABY CEDAR WAXWINGS BB-033	OP	22.00	22.00
90	BLUEBIRD (UPRIGHT) BB-031	OP	20.00	20.00
90	CEDAR WAXWING BB-032	OP	20.00	20.00
90	EVENING GROSBEAK BB-034	OP	22.00	22.00
90	FEMALE INDIGO BUNTING BB-039	OP	20.00	20.00
90	INDIGO BUNTING BB-036	OP	20.00	20.00
90	NUTHATCH, WHITE-THROATED BB-037	OP	20.00	20.00
90	PAINTED BUNTING BB-040	OP	20.00	20.00
90	PAINTED BUNTING, FEMALE BB-041	OP	20.00	20.00
90	PURPLE FINCH BB-038	OP	20.00	20.00
90	ROSE BREASTED GROSBEAK BB-042	OP	20.00	20.00
	D. KENNICUTT			**EASTER BUNNY FAMILY**
88	BUNNIES, BASKET OF SEC-001	RT	13.00	18.00
88	BUNNY BOY W/DUCK SEC-002	RT	13.00	18.00
88	BUNNY GIRL W/HEN SEC-004	RT	13.00	18.00
88	BUNNY, EASTER SEC-003	RT	13.00	18.00
88	RABBIT, GRANDMA SEC-005	RT	15.00	18.00
88	RABBIT, GRANPA SEC-006	RT	15.00	18.00
88	RABBIT, MOMMA W/BONNET SEC-007	RT	15.00	18.00
89	AUNTIE BUNNY SEC-008	RT	20.00	23.00
89	BUNNY W/PRIZE EGG SEC-010	OP	19.50	20.00
89	DUCKY W/BONNET, BLUE SEC-015	OP	10.00	12.00

YR	NAME	LIMIT	ISSUE	TREND
89	DUCKY W/BONNET, PINK SEC-014	OP	10.00	12.00
89	EASTER EGG HUNT SEC-012	OP	16.50	20.00
89	LITTLE SIS W/LOLLY SEC-009	OP	14.50	18.00
89	ROCK-A-BYE BUNNY SEC-013	OP	20.00	23.00
89	SIS & BUBBA SHARING SEC-011	OP	22.50	23.00
90	BUBBA W/WAGON SEC-016	OP	16.50	18.00
90	EASTER BUNNY W/CRYSTAL SEC-017	OP	23.00	23.00
90	HEN W/CHICK SEC-018	OP	23.00	23.00
90	MOMMA MAKING BASKET SEC-019	OP	23.00	23.00
90	MOTHER GOOSE SEC-020	OP	16.50	20.00
91	BABY IN BUGGY, BOY SEC-027	RT	20.00	20.00
91	BABY IN BUGGY, GIRL SEC-029	RT	20.00	20.00
91	BUBBA IN WHEELBARROW SEC-021	OP	20.00	20.00
91	BUNNY BOY W/ BASKET SEC-025	OP	20.00	20.00
91	FANCY FIND SEC-028	OP	20.00	20.00
91	LOP-EAR W/CRYSTAL SEC-022	OP	23.00	23.00
91	NEST OF BUNNY EGGS SEC-023	OP	17.50	18.00
91	VICTORIAN AUNTIE BUNNY SEC-026	OP	20.00	20.00
91	VICTORIAN MOMMA SEC-024	OP	20.00	20.00
K. MEMOLI				**FAERIE TALES**
90	FAERIE FLIGHT	7500	39.00	39.00
90	SLEEPING FAERIE	7500	39.00	39.00
90	WATER SPRITE	7500	39.00	39.00
90	WIND SPRITE	7500	39.00	39.00
90	WINTER FAERIE	7500	39.00	39.00
90	WOOD SPRITE	7500	39.00	39.00
MEMOLI/JONAS				**LEGEND OF SANTA CLAUS**
90	SAFE ARRIVAL CF-027	7500	150.00	150.00
S. BRADFORD				**LEGEND OF SANTA CLAUS**
86	ROOFTOP SANTA CF-004	RT	65.00	79.00
86	SANTA WITH PUPS CF-003	RT	65.00	250.00
87	DREAMING OF SANTA CF-008	RT	65.00	250.00
87	MRS. SANTA CF-006	RT	60.00	75.00
87	ON SANTA'S KNEE CF-007	15000	65.00	79.00
87	SANTA ON HORSEBACK CF-011	RT	75.00	250.00
88	FATHER CHRISTMAS CF-018	7500	75.00	85.00
88	LOAD 'EM UP CF-016	RT	79.00	250.00
89	A PURRR-FECT CHRISTMAS CF-019	7500	95.00	95.00
89	CHRISTMAS HARMONY CF-020	7500	85.00	85.00
90	VICTORIAN SANTA CF-028	7500	125.00	125.00
90	WAITING FOR SANTA CF-026	7500	100.00	100.00
91	VICTORIAN SANTA W/TEDDY CF-033	7500	150.00	150.00
K. MEMOLI				**LEGEND OF SANTA CLAUS**
91	BLESSED FLIGHT CF-032	7500	159.00	159.00
91	REINDEER WALK CF-031	7500	150.00	150.00
L. MILLER				**LEGEND OF SANTA CLAUS**
86	ELF PAIR CF-005	10000	60.00	75.00
86	KRIS KRINGLE CF-002	RT	60.00	75.00
86	SANTA AT REST CF-001	RT	70.00	250.00
87	CHECKING HIS LIST CF-009	15000	75.00	85.00
87	LOADING SANTA'S SLEIGH CF-010	15000	100.00	100.00
88	ASSEMBLY REQUIRED CF-017	7500	79.00	95.00
88	ST. NICHOLAS CF-015	7500	75.00	85.00
89	HITCHING UP CF-021	7500	90.00	90.00
90	FOREST FRIENDS CF-025	7500	90.00	90.00
90	PUPPY LOVE CF-024	7500	100.00	100.00
91	FOR SANTA CF-029	7500	99.00	99.00
91	SANTA AT WORK CF-030	7500	99.00	99.00
L. MILLER				**LEGEND OF THE LITTLE PEOPLE**
89	A FRIENDLY TOAST LL-003	RT	35.00	45.00
89	ADVENTURE BOUND LL-002	RT	35.00	45.00
89	CADDY'S HELPER LL-007	RT	35.00	45.00
89	MAGICAL DISCOVERY LL-005	RT	45.00	45.00
89	SPRING WATER SCRUB LL-006	RT	35.00	45.00
89	TREASURE HUNT LL-004	RT	45.00	45.00
89	WOODLAND CACHE LL-001	RT	35.00	45.00
90	A LITTLE JIG LL-018	RT	45.00	45.00
90	A LOOK THROUGH THE SPYGLASS LL-015	RT	40.00	45.00
90	A PROCLAMATION LL-013	RT	45.00	50.00
90	FISHIN' HOLE LL-012	RT	35.00	45.00
90	GATHERING ACORNS LL-014	RT	100.00	100.00
90	HEDGEHOG IN HARNESS LL-010	RT	45.00	45.00
90	HUSKING ACORNS LL-008	RT	60.00	60.00
90	MINSTRAL MAGIC LL-017	RT	45.00	45.00
90	TRAVELING FAST LL-009	RT	45.00	45.00
90	WOODLAND SCOUT LL-011	RT	40.00	45.00
90	WRITING THE LEGEND LL-016	RT	65.00	65.00
91	EASTER BUNNY'S CART, THE LL-020	RT	45.00	45.00
91	FIRE IT UP LL-023	RT	50.00	50.00
91	GOT IT LL-021	RT	45.00	45.00
91	IT'S ABOUT TIME LL-022	RT	55.00	55.00
91	VIKING LL-019	RT	45.00	45.00
P. JONAS				**LIL' DOLLS**
91	ANGELA BEAR LD-010	10000	35.00	35.00
91	ARCHIBALD BEAR LD-009	10000	35.00	35.00
91	BETTY BUTTON'S SURPRISE LD-008	10000	35.00	35.00
91	GEORGIE BEAR LD-001	10000	35.00	35.00
91	JENNY BEAR LD-002	10000	35.00	35.00

YR	NAME	LIMIT	ISSUE	TREND
91	NUTCRACKER LD-006	RT	35.00	35.00
	D. NEWBURN			**LIL' DOLLS**
91	ADDIE LD-013	10000	35.00	35.00
91	AMY LD-003	10000	35.00	35.00
91	BECKY BUNNY LD-005	10000	35.00	35.00
91	KRISTA LD-014	10000	35.00	35.00
91	MARCHING IN TIME LD-007	10000	35.00	35.00
91	SAM LD-004	10000	35.00	35.00
91	SARA LD-011	10000	35.00	35.00
91	TESS LD-015	10000	35.00	35.00
91	TOM LD-012	10000	35.00	35.00
	S. BRADFORD			**MUSICMAKERS**
89	HERALD ANGEL MM-011	12000	79.00	79.00
89	TEDDY BEAR BAND MM-012	12000	99.00	99.00
	D. KENNICUTT			**MUSICMAKERS**
89	CHRISTMAS TREE MM-008	OP	69.00	69.00
89	EVENING CAROLERS MM-005	OP	69.00	69.00
89	SNOWSHOE SLED RIDE MM-007	OP	69.00	69.00
89	TEDDIES AND FROSTY MM-010	OP	69.00	69.00
89	TEDDY DRUMMERS MM-009	OP	69.00	69.00
89	WINTER FUN MM-006	OP	69.00	69.00
91	A CHRISTMAS GIFT MM-015	OP	59.00	59.00
91	CRYSTAL ANGEL MM-017	OP	59.00	59.00
91	DASHING THROUGH THE SNOW MM-013	OP	59.00	59.00
91	TEDDY SOLDIERS MM-018	OP	69.00	69.00
91	TWO FAERIES MM-014	OP	59.00	59.00
	L. MILLER			**MUSICMAKERS**
89	COMING TO TOWN MM-001	OP	69.00	69.00
89	MERRY LITTLE CHRISTMAS MM-002	OP	69.00	69.00
89	MERRY MAKING MM-003	RT	69.00	90.00
89	SANTA'S SLEIGH MM-004	OP	69.00	69.00
	D. KENNICUTT			**PARTY ANIMALS**
84	DEMOCRATIC DONKEY ('84)	RT	14.50	16.00
90	DEMOCRATIC DONKEY ('90)	RT	16.00	16.00
90	GOP ELEPHANT ('90)	RT	16.00	16.00
	L. MILLER			**PARTY ANIMALS**
84	GOP ELEPHANT ('84)	RT	14.50	16.00
86	DEMOCRATIC DONKEY ('86)	RT	14.50	15.00
86	GOP ELEPHANT ('86)	RT	14.50	15.00
88	DEMOCRATIC DONKEY ('88)	RT	14.50	16.00
88	GOP ELEPHANT ('88)	RT	14.50	16.00
	P. JONAS			**PENNIBEARS**
90	ATTIC FUN PB-019	RT	20.00	22.00
90	BABY HUGS PB-007	RT	20.00	22.00
90	BATHTIME BUDDIES PB-023	RT	20.00	22.00
90	BEAUTIFUL BRIDE PB-004	RT	20.00	24.00
90	BIRTHDAY BEAR PB-018	RT	20.00	24.00
90	BOOOO BEAR PB-025	RT	20.00	22.00
90	BOUQUET BOY PB-003	RT	20.00	20.00
90	BOUQUET GIRL PB-001	RT	20.00	22.00
90	BUTTERFLY BEAR PB-005	RT	20.00	22.00
90	BUTTONS & BOWS PB-012	RT	20.00	22.00
90	COOKIE BANDIT PB-006	RT	20.00	22.00
90	COUNT BEARACULA PB-027	RT	22.00	24.00
90	COUNTRY QUILTER PB-030	RT	22.00	26.00
90	COUNTRY SPRING PB-013	RT	20.00	22.00
90	DOCTOR BEAR PB-008	RT	20.00	22.00
90	DRESS UP FUN PB-028	RT	22.00	24.00
90	GARDEN PATH PB-014	RT	20.00	22.00
90	GIDDIAP TEDDY PB-011	RT	20.00	24.00
90	HANDSOME GROOM PB-015	RT	20.00	22.00
90	HONEY BEAR PB-002	RT	20.00	20.00
90	LAZY DAYS PB-009	RT	20.00	22.00
90	NAP TIME PB-016	RT	20.00	22.00
90	NURSE BEAR PB-017	RT	20.00	22.00
90	PETITE MADEMOISELLE PB-010	RT	20.00	22.00
90	PUPPY BATH PB-020	RT	20.00	22.00
90	PUPPY LOVE PB-021	RT	20.00	22.00
90	SANTA BEAR-ING GIFTS PB-031	RT	24.00	26.00
90	SCARECROW TEDDY PB-029	RT	24.00	24.00
90	SNEAKY SNOWBALL PB-026	RT	20.00	22.00
90	SOUTHERN BELLE PB-024	RT	20.00	22.00
90	STOCKING SURPRISE PB-032	RT	22.00	26.00
90	TUBBY TEDDY PB-022	RT	20.00	22.00
91	A WILD RIDE PB-052	RT	26.00	26.00
91	BAKING GOODIES PB-043	RT	26.00	26.00
91	BEAR FOOTIN' IT PB-037	RT	24.00	24.00
91	BEARLY AWAKE PB-033	RT	22.00	22.00
91	BOO HOO BEAR PB-050	RT	22.00	22.00
91	BOUNTIFUL HARVEST PB-045	RT	24.00	24.00
91	BUMP-BEAR CROP PB-035	RT	26.00	26.00
91	BUNNY BUDDIES PB-042	RT	22.00	22.00
91	CHRISTMAS REINBEAR PB-046	RT	28.00	28.00
91	COUNTRY LULLABYE PB-036	RT	24.00	24.00
91	CURTAIN CALL PB-049	RT	24.00	24.00
91	GOODNIGHT LITTLE PRINCE PB-041	RT	26.00	26.00
91	GOODNIGHT SWEET PRINCESS PB-040	RT	26.00	26.00
91	HAPPY HOBO PB-051	RT	26.00	26.00

YR	NAME	LIMIT	ISSUE	TREND
91	LIL' MER-TEDDY PB-034	RT	24.00	24.00
91	PILGRIM PROVIDER PB-047	RT	32.00	32.00
91	SUMMER SAILING PB-039	RT	26.00	26.00
91	SWEET LIL 'SIS PB-048	RT	22.00	22.00
91	SWEETHEART BEARS PB-044	RT	28.00	28.00
91	WINDY DAY PB-038	RT	24.00	24.00
P. JONAS	**PENNIBEARS COLLECTOR'S CLUB MEMBERS ONLY EDITIONS**			
90	FIRST COLLECTION PB-C90	RT	26.00	26.00
91	COLLECTING MAKES CENTS PB-C91	RT	26.00	26.00
H. HENRIKSEN	**STORYTIME RHYMES & TALES**			
91	HUMPTY DUMPTY 008	RT	64.00	64.00
91	LITTLE JACK HORNER 007	RT	50.00	50.00
91	LITTLE MISS MUFFET 006	RT	64.00	64.00
91	MISTRESS MARY 002	RT	64.00	64.00
91	MOTHER GOOSE 001	RT	64.00	64.00
91	OWL & PUSSY CAT 004	RT	100.00	100.00
91	SIMPLE SIMON 003	RT	90.00	90.00
91	THREE LITTLE PIGS 005	RT	100.00	100.00
S. BRADFORD	**SUZY'S ZOO**			
90	BABY QUACKER	OP	20.00	20.00
90	BUNNY BABY	OP	20.00	20.00
90	BUNNY BRIDE & GROOM	OP	25.00	25.00
90	CORKY PILGRIM	OP	25.00	25.00
90	CORKY TURTLE & HAT	OP	22.50	23.00
90	CORKY, HEART FELT	OP	22.50	23.00
90	JACK & FLOWERS	OP	22.50	23.00
90	MARMOT BABY, RAINY DAY	OP	20.00	20.00
90	MARMOT CAROLERS	OP	25.00	25.00
90	MARMOT SISTERS/PALS	OP	25.00	25.00
90	MARMOTS DANCING	OP	25.00	25.00
90	MARTHA MARMOT	OP	22.50	23.00
90	OLLIE MARMOT	OP	22.50	23.00
90	POLLY QUACKER	OP	22.50	23.00
90	RITZ, SIGNING-I LOVE YOU	OP	22.50	23.00
90	RITZ-HAY THERE	OP	20.00	20.00
90	SUZY & FAVORITE PILLOW	OP	22.50	23.00
90	SUZY & TEDDY	OP	22.50	23.00
90	SUZY, ARTIST	OP	22.50	23.00
90	SUZY, BEAUTY QUEEN	OP	25.00	25.00
90	TEDDY	OP	20.00	20.00
90	TILLIAMOOK & FLOWERS	OP	22.50	23.00
90	TILLIAMOOK, BALLERINA	OP	22.50	23.00
S. BRADFORD	**THE LEGEND OF SANTA CLAUS**			
93	NORTHWOODS SANTA	7500	100.00	110.00
93	VICT., LION AND LAMB SANTA	7500	100.00	110.00
94	STAR SANTA WITH POLAR BEAR	7500	130.00	130.00
K. MEMOLI	**THE LEGEND OF SANTA CLAUS**			
93	DEAR SANTA	7500	170.00	185.00
93	JOLLY ST. NICK	7500	130.00	140.00
93	JOLLY ST. NICK, VICT.	7500	120.00	130.00
94	LONGSTOCKING DILEMMA	7500	170.00	170.00
94	LONGSTOCKING DILEMMA, VICT.	7500	170.00	170.00
94	STORY OF CHRISTMAS, THE	10000	180.00	180.00
L. MILLER	**THE LEGEND OF SANTA CLAUS**			
93	NIGHT BEFORE CHRISTMAS	7500	100.00	110.00
93	SANTA'S FRIENDS	7500	100.00	110.00
94	SANTA RIDING DOVE	7500	120.00	120.00

VAILLANCOURT FOLK ART

YR	NAME	LIMIT	ISSUE	TREND
N. BAILEY	**ANGEL DARLINGS**			
96	ALMOST FITS H4765/1	OP	15.00	15.00
J. VAILLANCOURT	**COLLECTIBLE RABBIT**			
95	CHALKWARE PEDDLAR, 9513	OP	130.00	130.00
95	LTD. LADY RABBIT, 9502	250	190.00	190.00
95	RABBIT AND CHICKS, 9505	OP	90.00	90.00
95	RABBIT AND LAMB, 9504	OP	150.00	150.00
95	RABBIT LEANING ON EGG, 9508	OP	130.00	130.00
95	RABBIT ON DUCK, 9506	OP	60.00	60.00
95	RABBIT ON MALLARD, 9507	OP	80.00	80.00
95	RABBIT W/APRON, 9511	OP	65.00	65.00
95	RABBIT/BARREL, 9512	OP	110.00	110.00
95	RABBIT/UMBRELLA, 9514	OP	140.00	140.00
95	ROCKER RABBIT, 9503	OP	130.00	130.00
95	SMALL BUNNY, 9509	OP	50.00	50.00
95	SMALL RABBIT, 9510	OP	40.00	40.00
95	TWO RABBITS, 9501	OP	190.00	190.00
96	CAT, 9602	OP	150.00	150.00
96	LARGE RABBIT, 9601	OP	180.00	180.00
96	LTD BOY/CHICK, 9603	OP	190.00	190.00
96	RABBIT, 9604	OP	100.00	100.00
96	RABBIT, 9605	OP	90.00	90.00
96	RUNNING RABBIT, 9606	OP	150.00	150.00
96	TINY RABBIT, 9607	OP	40.00	40.00
J. VAILLANCOURT	**COLLECTIBLE SANTA**			
95	ANGEL, 9539	OP	40.00	40.00
95	BELSNICKLE, 95129	OP	70.00	70.00
95	BELSNICKLE, 9533	OP	90.00	90.00
95	BELSNICKLE, 9534	OP	80.00	80.00

YR	NAME	LIMIT	ISSUE	TREND
95	BELSNICKLE, 9538	OP	50.00	50.00
95	BLUE FATHER CHRISTMAS, 9537	OP	110.00	110.00
95	F.C. ON DONKEY, 9541	250	300.00	300.00
95	F.C. PULLING SLED, 9543	250	300.00	300.00
95	LARGE F.C. ON DONKEY, 9542	OP	250.00	250.00
95	LARGE WALKING, 9531	OP	1900.00	1900.00
95	SANTA HOLDING LARGE BAG, 9532	OP	250.00	250.00
95	SANTA, 9535	OP	130.00	130.00
95	SNOW ANGEL, 9540	OP	70.00	70.00
95	STOCKING, 9536	OP	190.00	190.00
96	ANGEL	OP	90.00	90.00
96	BELSNICKLE, 9637	OP	70.00	70.00
96	BELSNICKLE, 9643	OP	140.00	140.00
96	CHILDREN ON SLED, 9636	OP	350.00	350.00
96	F.C. ON MOTORCYCLE	OP	130.00	130.00
96	F.C., 9644	OP	130.00	130.00
96	FATHER CHRISTMAS, 9633	OP	90.00	90.00
96	FATHER CHRISTMAS, 9635	OP	350.00	350.00
96	GERMAN TREE, 9638	OP	30.00	30.00
96	LTD. F.C., 9641	250	300.00	300.00
96	SANTA, 9631	OP	150.00	150.00
96	SANTA, 9632	OP	90.00	90.00
96	SNOWMAN ARTIST, 9640	OP	120.00	120.00
96	SNOWMAN, 9639	OP	50.00	50.00
96	STARLIGHT SANTA, 9630	OP	100.00	100.00

VICKILANE

YR	NAME	LIMIT	ISSUE	TREND
V. ANDERSON				
94	BUNNY ANGEL #1610	OP	13.00	13.00
94	BUNNY ANGEL #1611	OP	13.00	13.00
94	BUNNY ANGEL #1612	OP	13.00	13.00
94	BUNNY ANGEL #1613	OP	13.00	13.00
94	BUNNY ANGEL #1614	OP	13.00	13.00
94	BUNNY ANGEL #1615	OP	13.00	13.00
94	CHILD ANGEL #6011	OP	20.00	20.00
V. ANDERSON				**ACCESSORIES**
93	FIREPLACE	OP	20.00	20.00
V. ANDERSON				**AMISH/COUNTRY KIDS**
94	BROTHERLY LOVE	OP	*	*
94	PATIENCE	OP	20.00	20.00
V. ANDERSON				**BLESSINGS FROM ABOVE**
94	CHILD ANGEL #6009	OP	18.00	18.00
94	CHILD ANGEL #0010	OP	25.00	25.00
V. ANDERSON				**CHARACTER CAPERS**
94	DILIGENCE	OP	20.00	20.00
94	FAITH	OP	*	*
V. ANDERSON				**CHRISTMAS**
93	FUZZY	OP	22.50	23.00
93	GRANDMA & GRANDPA	OP	25.00	25.00
93	ROSEBERRY	OP	22.00	22.00
93	SPARKY	OP	18.00	18.00
93	SUGAR PLUM	OP	22.00	22.00
V. ANDERSON				**CLUB PIECE**
94	MISS APRIL	OP	28.00	28.00
94	SWEET SECRETS	RT	*	*
V. ANDERSON				**COW-LLECTOR**
94	COW WITH BAG OF OATS	OP	*	*
94	COW WITH SUNGLASSES	OP	*	*
V. ANDERSON				**LIL BLESSINGS**
94	BUNNY ANGEL CLOUD	OP	12.00	12.00
V. ANDERSON				**NITE BEAR-FORE**
93	PAPA BEARS	OP	22.00	22.00
V. ANDERSON				**PURRFECTLY PRECIOUS KITTY**
94	KITTIES BEHIND FENCE	OP	*	*
V. ANDERSON				**SCHOOL HOUSE BUNNIES**
94	BOY WITH BASKETBALL	OP	18.00	18.00
94	BOYS WITH BOOKS	OP	20.00	20.00
94	GIRL READING	OP	20.00	20.00
94	SCHOOL TEACHER	OP	20.00	20.00
V. ANDERSON				**SKIN TONE**
94	CHILD ANGEL #6013	OP	20.00	20.00
94	CHILD ANGEL #6014	OP	22.00	22.00
V. ANDERSON				**SWEET THUMPINS**
94	BUNNY THROWING SNOW	RT	31.00	31.00
94	HAPPY EARS	OP	31.00	31.00
94	NEW BORN EXCITEMENT	OP	31.00	31.00
94	NURSE BUNNY	OP	31.00	31.00
94	SWEETHEART BUNNIES	OP	31.00	31.00
94	UNJURED BUNNY	OP	31.00	31.00
V. ANDERSON				**THE LORD IS MY SHEPHERD**
94	LAMB ANGEL	OP	*	*
94	LAMB AT DOOR	OP	*	*
94	LAMB BUILD ALTAR	OP	*	*
94	LAMB READING	OP	*	*
94	LAMB WORSHIPPING	OP	*	*
V. ANDERSON				**THIS LITTLE PIGGY**
94	PIG EATING APPLES	OP	22.00	22.00

YR	NAME	LIMIT	ISSUE	TREND
V. ANDERSON				**TIME FOR TEDDY**
93	NEWLYWED BEAR	OP	20.00	20.00
93	SNOWMEN BEARS	OP	*	*
93	TEDDY BEAR	OP	10.00	10.00
V. ANDERSON				**WHITE OR BLACK**
94	CHILD ANGEL #6012	OP	20.00	20.00

WACO PRODUCTS CORP.

YR	NAME	LIMIT	ISSUE	TREND
S. NAKANE				**MELODY IN MOTION**
94	CAROLER BOY, THE	10000	172.00	180.00
94	CAROLER GIRL, THE	10000	172.00	180.00
95	'95 SANTA CLAUS	6000	190.00	190.00
95	COCA-COLA NORMAN ROCKWELL GONE FISHIN'	YR	194.00	200.00
95	COCA-COLA POLAR BEAR	6000	180.00	180.00
96	WILLIE THE FIREMAN	1500	200.00	200.00
96	WILLIE THE ORGAN GRINDER	3000	200.00	200.00
S. NAKANE				**MELODY IN MOTION/10TH ANNIVERSARY ED.**
95	WILLIE THE CONDUCTOR	10000	220.00	220.00
S. NAKANE				**MELODY IN MOTION/CAROUSEL COLLECTION**
94	BLUE DANUBE CAROUSEL	OP	180.00	190.00
S. NAKANE				**MELODY IN MOTION/CLOCK**
93	ARTIST, THE	OP	240.00	250.00
S. NAKANE				**MELODY IN MOTION/HERITAGE COLLECTION**
93	SOUTH OF THE BORDER	OP	180.00	190.00
94	CAMPFIRE COWBOY	OP	180.00	190.00
94	CHRISTMAS CAROLER BOY	10000	172.00	180.00
94	CHRISTMAS CAROLER GIRL	10000	172.00	180.00
94	WHEN I GROW UP	OP	200.00	210.00
S. NAKANE				**MELODY IN MOTION/MADAME**
88	MADAME CELLO PLAYER	OP	130.00	130.00
88	MADAME FLUTE PLAYER	OP	130.00	130.00
88	MADAME HARP PLAYER	OP	130.00	130.00
88	MADAME HARPSICHORD PLAYER	OP	130.00	130.00
88	MADAME LYRE PLAYER	OP	130.00	130.00
88	MADAME MANDOLIN PLAYER	OP	130.00	130.00
88	MADAME VIOLIN PLAYER	OP	130.00	130.00
S. NAKANE				**MELODY IN MOTION/SANTA**
86	SANTA CLAUS-1986	RT	100.00	225.00
87	SANTA CLAUS-1987	RT	104.00	175.00
88	SANTA CLAUS-1988	RT	130.00	165.00
89	WILLIE THE SANTA	RT	130.00	150.00
90	SANTA CLAUS-1990	RT	150.00	150.00
91	SANTA CLAUS-1991	12000	150.00	150.00
93	1993 COCA-COLA SANTA	6000	180.00	190.00
94	1994 COCA-COLA SANTA	9000	190.00	*
S. NAKANE				**MELODY IN MOTION/SPOTLIGHT CLOWN**
89	SPOTLIGHT CLOWN BANJO	RT	120.00	120.00
89	SPOTLIGHT CLOWN CORNET	RT	120.00	120.00
89	SPOTLIGHT CLOWN TROMBONE	RT	120.00	120.00
89	SPOTLIGHT CLOWN TUBA	RT	120.00	120.00
89	SPOTLIGHT CLOWN WITH BINGO THE DOG	RT	130.00	130.00
89	SPOTLIGHT CLOWN WITH UPRIGHT BASS	RT	130.00	130.00
S. NAKANE				**MELODY IN MOTION/TIMEPIECE**
89	CLOCKPOST WILLIE	OP	150.00	150.00
89	LULL'ABY WILLIE	OP	170.00	170.00
90	GRANDFATHER'S CLOCK	OP	200.00	200.00
91	HUNTER TIMEPIECE	OP	250.00	250.00
91	ROBIN HOOD TIMEPIECE	OP	300.00	300.00
C. JOHNSON				**MELODY IN MOTION/VARIOUS**
91	LITTLE JOHN	7000	180.00	180.00
91	ROBIN HOOD	OP	180.00	180.00
S. NAKANE				**MELODY IN MOTION/VARIOUS**
85	SALTY N' PEPPER	RT	130.00	130.00
86	CELLIST, THE	OP	130.00	130.00
86	FIDDLER, THE	OP	130.00	130.00
86	GUITARIST, THE	OP	130.00	130.00
87	ACCORDION CLOWN	RT	84.00	84.00
87	BALLOON CLOWN	OP	110.00	110.00
87	CAROUSEL, THE	OP	240.00	240.00
87	CLARINET CLOWN	RT	84.00	84.00
87	SAXOPHONE CLOWN	RT	84.00	84.00
87	VIOLIN CLOWN	RT	84.00	84.00
89	GRAND CAROUSEL, THE	OP	3000.00	3000.00
90	ACCORDION BOY	8000	120.00	120.00
90	BLACKSMITH	5000	110.00	110.00
90	HUNTER	OP	110.00	110.00
90	SHOEMAKER	5000	110.00	110.00
90	WOODCHOPPER	5000	110.00	110.00
91	VICTORIA PARK CAROUSEL	OP	300.00	300.00
S. NAKANE				**MELODY IN MOTION/VENDOR**
87	ORGAN GRINDER	OP	130.00	130.00
89	ICE CREAM VENDOR	OP	140.00	140.00
89	PEANUT VENDOR	OP	140.00	140.00
S. NAKANE				**MELODY IN MOTION/WILLIE**
85	WILLIE THE HOBO	OP	96.00	130.00
85	WILLIE THE TRUMPETER	OP	96.00	130.00
85	WILLIE THE WHISTLER	OP	96.00	130.00

YR	NAME	LIMIT	ISSUE	TREND
87	LAMPPOST WILLIE	OP	84.00	110.00
91	WILLIE THE FISHERMAN	OP	150.00	150.00
93	HEARTBREAK WILLIE	OP	180.00	190.00
93	LAMPLIGHT WILLIE	OP	240.00	250.00
93	WILLIE THE GOLFER	OP	240.00	250.00
94	CHATTANOOGA CHOO-CHOO	OP	180.00	190.00
94	DAY'S END	OP	240.00	250.00
94	JACKPOT WILLIE	OP	180.00	190.00
94	LONGEST DRIVE	OP	150.00	160.00
94	LOW PRESSURE JOB	OP	240.00	250.00
94	SMOOTH SAILING	OP	200.00	210.00
94	WILLIE THE GOLFER	OP	240.00	250.00
J. UNGER			**THE HERMAN COLLECTION**	
90	BIRTHDAY/CAKE	OP	36.00	36.00
90	BOWLING/WIFE	OP	32.00	32.00
90	DOCTOR/FAT MAN	OP	36.00	36.00
90	DOCTOR/HIGH COST	OP	32.00	32.00
90	FRY PAN	OP	40.00	40.00
90	GOLF/CAMEL	OP	44.00	44.00
90	HUSBAND/CHECK	OP	36.00	36.00
90	HUSBAND/NEWSPAPER	OP	41.00	41.00
90	LAWYER/CABINET	OP	44.00	44.00
90	STOP SMOKING	OP	40.00	40.00
90	TENNIS/WIFE	OP	32.00	32.00
90	WEDDING RING	OP	41.00	41.00
WALT DISNEY CLASSICS COLLECTION				
*				**BAMBI**
92	BAMBI	OP	195.00	290.00
92	BAMBI & FLOWER	RT	298.00	485.00
92	BAMBI SERIES, COMPLETE SET	*	*	2940.00
92	FIELD MOUSE	RT	195.00	1300.00
92	FIELD MOUSE-LITTLE APRIL SHOWER	7500	195.00	1550.00
92	FLOWER	RT	78.00	175.00
92	FRIEND OWL	RT	195.00	245.00
92	SCROLL "BIG OPENING TITLE"	RT	29.00	45.00
92	THUMPER	CL	55.00	85.00
92	THUMPER'S SISTERS	RT	69.00	100.00
*				**CINDERELLA**
92	A DRESS FOR CINDERELLY	RT	800.00	2000.00
92	BIRDS WITH SASH	RT	149.00	165.00
92	BRUNO-JUST LEARN TO LIKE CATS	RT	69.00	95.00
92	CHALK MOUSE	RT	65.00	95.00
92	CINDERELLA	RT	195.00	325.00
92	CINDERELLA (WHEEL)	RT	195.00	340.00
92	CINDERELLA'S SEWING BOOK (NO MARK)	RT	69.00	100.00
92	CINDERELLA, LUCIFER, BRUNO (SET OF 3)	RT	*	500.00
92	GUS	RT	65.00	95.00
92	JAQ	RT	65.00	90.00
92	LUCIFER	RT	69.00	110.00
92	NEEDLE MOUSE	RT	69.00	95.00
92	SCROLL "CINDERELLA OPENING TITLE"	RT	29.00	45.00
93	LUCIFER	RT	69.00	100.00
95	BASHFUL	OP	95.00	95.00
95	DOC	OP	95.00	95.00
95	DOPEY	OP	95.00	95.00
95	GRUMPY	OP	180.00	180.00
95	HAPPY	OP	125.00	125.00
95	SCROLL-SNOW WHITE OPENING TITLE	OP	29.00	29.00
95	SLEEPY	OP	95.00	95.00
95	SNEEZY	OP	90.00	90.00
*			**COLLECTOR'S SOCIETY**	
92	JIMINY CRICKET (CLEF)	RT	*	150.00
93	MICKEY MOUSE "BRAVE LITTLE TAILOR"	RT	160.00	300.00
94	CHESHIRE CAT "TWAS BRILLIG" (CLEF)	RT	*	115.00
94	DONALD DUCK "ADMIRAL DUCK"	RT	165.00	165.00
94	DUMBO "SIMPLY ADORABLE"	RT	*	55.00
94	PECOS BILL & WIDOWMAKER	RT	650.00	700.00
95	CRUELLA DE VIL "101 DALMATIONS"	RT	250.00	250.00
*				**DELIVERY BOY**
92	MICKEY	RT	125.00	225.00
92	MINNIE	RT	125.00	210.00
92	PLUTO (WHEEL-INCISED)	RT	125.00	200.00
92	SCROLL "THE DELIVERY BOY"	RT	29.00	45.00
*			**ENCHANTED PLACES**	
95	DWARF'S COTTAGE	OP	180.00	180.00
95	WHITE RABBIT'S COTTAGE	OP	175.00	175.00
95	WOODCUTTER'S COTTAGE	OP	170.00	170.00
*				**EVENT PIECES**
93	"FLIGHT OF FANCY"	RT	35.00	50.00
94	MR. SMEE "OH DEAR, OH DEAR" EVENT	RT	90.00	100.00
95	LUCKY	RT	40.00	40.00
95	WICKED WITCH	*	130.00	130.00
*				**FANTASIA**
92	BROOMS--BUCKET BRIGADE	RT	75.00	150.00
92	SORCERER MICKEY "MISCHIEVOUS APPRENTICE"	RT	195.00	250.00
93	BLUE CENTAURETTE "BEAUTY IN BLOOM"	RT	195.00	335.00
93	PINK CENTAURETTE "ROMANTIC REFLECTIONS"	RT	175.00	225.00

YR	NAME	LIMIT	ISSUE	TREND
93	SCROLL "FANTASIA OPENING TITLE"	RT	29.00	60.00
94	CUPIDS "LOVE'S LITTLE HELPERS"	RT	290.00	290.00
94	LG. MUSHROOM "MUSHROOM DANCER"	RT	60.00	75.00
94	MED. MUSHROOM "MUSHROOM DANCER"	RT	50.00	75.00
94	SM. MUSHROOM HOP LOW	OP	35.00	35.00
*				**HOLIDAY SERIES**
95	PRESENTS FOR MY PALS	YR	150.00	150.00
*				**MR. DUCK STEPS OUT**
93	DEWEY "I GOT SOMETHING' FOR YA"	RT	65.00	75.00
93	DONALD & DAISY "OH BOY,WHAT A JITTERBUG"	RT	295.00	750.00
93	DONALD AND DAISY	RT	298.00	600.00
93	HUEY "TAG-ALONG TROUBLE"	RT	65.00	75.00
93	LOUIE "TAG-ALONG TROUBLE"	RT	65.00	75.00
93	SCROLL "MR. DUCK STEPS OUT"	RT	29.00	50.00
94	DONALD "WITH LOVE FROM DAISY"	OP	180.00	180.00
*				**PETER PAN**
93	CAPT. HOOK "I'VE GOT YOU THIS TIME!"	RT	275.00	925.00
93	CROCODILE "TICK-TOCK, TICK TOCK"	OP	315.00	315.00
93	PETER PAN "NOBODY CALLS PAN A COWARD!"	RT	165.00	225.00
93	SCROLL "PETER PAN"	RT	29.00	50.00
93	TINKERBELL "A FIREFLY! A PIXIE AMAZING"	RT	215.00	750.00
*				**SNOW WHITE**
94	SNOW WHITE "THE FAIREST ONE OF ALL"	RT	165.00	200.00
*				**SYMPHONY HOUR**
93	CLARABELLE	RT	198.00	260.00
93	GOOFY (WHEEL)	RT	198.00	1200.00
93	HORACE	RT	198.00	205.00
93	MAESTRO MICHEL MOUSE	RT	185.00	230.00
93	SCROLL "SYMPHONY HOUR"	RT	29.00	45.00
94	CLARA CLUCK "BRAVO BRAVISSIMO"	OP	185.00	185.00
*				**THREE CABALLEROS**
95	AMIGO DONALD	RT	180.00	180.00
95	AMIGO JOSE	RT	180.00	180.00
95	AMIGO PANCHITO	RT	180.00	180.00
*				**THREE LITTLE PIGS**
93	BIG BAD WOLF "WHO'S AFRAID...?"	RT	295.00	750.00
93	FIDDLER PIG "HEY DIDDLE,...FIDDLE"	RT	75.00	100.00
93	FIFER PIG "I TOOT MY FLUTE,..HOOT"	RT	75.00	100.00
93	PRACTICAL PIG "WORK & PLAY DON'T MIX"	RT	75.00	100.00
93	SCROLL "THREE LITTLE PIGS"	RT	29.00	33.00
*				**TRIBUTE SERIES**
95	PALS FOREVER	CL	180.00	180.00
95	SLUE FOOT SUE	CL	695.00	695.00

WEE FOREST FOLK

A. PETERSEN

YR	NAME	LIMIT	ISSUE	TREND
72	MISS MOUSEY W/BOW HAT M-2B	CL	4.25	300.00
72	MISS MOUSEY W/STRAW HAT M-2A	CL	4.25	300.00
76	MRS. MOUSEY W/HAT M-15A	CL	4.25	*
82	OFFICE MOUSEY M-68	CL	23.00	550.00
83	RUNNING DOE/LITTLE DEER B-107B	OP	35.00	42.00
92	GRETA M-169A	CL	35.00	90.00
92	HANS M-169A	CL	35.00	90.00
92	TUCKERED OUT! M-136A	CL	46.00	160.00
93	CHRISTMAS EVE M-191	OP	145.00	155.00
93	FIRST KISS! M-192	OP	65.00	65.00
93	LITTLE MICE WHO LIVED IN A SHOE M-189	OP	395.00	420.00
93	LORD & LADY MOUSEBATTEN M-195	OP	85.00	90.00
93	MUMMY, THE M-194	OP	34.00	37.00
93	ONE-MOUSE BAND M-196	OP	95.00	100.00
93	PETER PUMPKIN EATER M-190	CL	98.00	140.00
93	WELCOME CHICK! M-193	OP	64.00	68.00
94	CHIEF MOUSE-ASOIT M-197	OP	90.00	90.00
94	MIDNIGHT SNACK M-201	OP	230.00	230.00
94	PILGRIM'S WELCOME M-198	OP	55.00	55.00
94	WE GATHER TOGETHER M-199	OP	90.00	90.00
94	WEDDING PAIR, THE M-200	OP	98.00	98.00
94	YARD SALE, THE M-202	OP	325.00	325.00
95	BROOM SERVICE M-205	OP	62.00	60.00
95	CAUGHT IN THE ACT M-209	OP	49.00	49.00
95	CHRISTMAS WISH M-203	OP	156.00	156.00
95	CLEMENTINE M-204	OP	86.00	86.00
95	HEAVENLY SLUMBER M-210	OP	49.00	45.00
95	HIGH FLYER M-207	OP	88.00	85.00
95	JACK IN THE SANDBOX M-206	OP	108.00	100.00
95	STRUGGLING ARTIST M-208	OP	49.00	49.00
95	WANDERLUST M-211	OP	68.00	68.00

A. PETERSEN — ANIMALS

YR	NAME	LIMIT	ISSUE	TREND
73	MISS DUCKY	CL	6.00	*
74	BABY HIPPO	CL	7.00	*
74	MISS AND BABY HIPPO	CL	15.00	900.00
74	MISS HIPPO	CL	8.00	*
75	"DOC" RAT	CL	12.00	250.00
75	SPEEDY RAT	CL	11.50	250.00
77	NUTSY SQUIRREL	CL	3.00	450.00
78	BEAVER WOOD CUTTER	CL	8.00	350.00
78	MOLE SCOUT	CL	9.00	175.00

YR	NAME	LIMIT	ISSUE	TREND
79	TURTLE JOGGER	CL	4.00	350.00
A. PETERSEN				**BEARS**
77	BLUEBERRY BEARS	CL	8.75	525.00
77	BOY BLUEBERRY BEAR	CL	4.50	475.00
77	GIRL BLUEBERRY BEAR	CL	4.25	450.00
78	BIG LADY BEAR	CL	7.50	*
78	TRAVELING BEAR	CL	8.00	320.00
95	DON'T BE SHY BB-1	OP	76.00	75.00
95	FATHER'S NIGHT BB-5	OP	159.00	155.00
95	GOOD PICKIN'S BB-4	OP	64.00	60.00
95	JUST A PEEK BB-6	OP	159.00	155.00
95	LUNCH ON A LOG BB-3	OP	89.00	85.00
95	WELCOME HOME BB-2	OP	108.00	100.00
W. PETERSEN				**BOOK/FIGURINE**
88	TOM & EON BK-1	SU	45.00	22.00
A. PETERSEN				**BUNNIES**
72	DOUBLE BUNNIES	CL	4.25	350.00
72	HOUSEKEEPING BUNNY	CL	4.50	350.00
73	BROOM BUNNY	CL	9.50	*
73	MARKET BUNNY	CL	9.00	*
73	MUFF BUNNY	CL	9.00	*
73	PROFESSOR, THE	CL	4.75	360.00
73	SIR RABBIT	CL	4.50	350.00
73	SUNDAY BUNNY	CL	4.75	*
77	BATTER BUNNY	CL	4.50	375.00
77	TENNIS BUNNY	CL	3.75	300.00
78	WEDDING BUNNIES	CL	12.50	450.00
80	PROFESSOR RABBIT	CL	14.00	450.00
85	TINY EASTER BUNNY	CL	25.00	85.00
92	WINDY DAY! B-13	OP	37.00	40.00
A. PETERSEN				**CHRISTMAS CAROL**
87	BOB CRATCHIT AND TINY TIM CC-2	OP	36.00	43.00
87	GHOST OF CHRISTMAS PAST CC-4	OP	24.00	30.00
87	GHOST OF CHRISTMAS PRESENT CC-5	OP	54.00	57.00
87	GHOST OF CHRISTMAS YET TO COME CC-6	OP	24.00	28.00
87	MARLEY'S GHOST CC-3	OP	24.00	28.00
87	SCROOGE CC-1	OP	23.00	28.00
88	FEZZIWIGS, THE CC-7	OP	65.00	80.00
A. PETERSEN				**CINDERELLA**
88	CINDERELLA'S SLIPPER W/PRINCE C-1	CL	62.00	170.00
88	CINDERELLA'S WEDDING C-5	CL	62.00	150.00
88	FLOWER GIRL C-6	CL	22.00	80.00
88	FLOWER GIRLS, THE C-4	CL	42.00	105.00
88	MEAN STEPMOTHER, THE C-3	CL	32.00	125.00
88	UGLY STEPSISTERS, THE C-2	CL	62.00	145.00
89	CINDERELLA'S SLIPPER C-1A	CL	32.00	110.00
89	FAIRY GODMOTHER, THE C-7	CL	69.00	170.00
A. PETERSEN				**FAIRY TALE SERIES**
80	RED RIDING HOOD	CL	13.00	500.00
80	RED RIDING HOOD & WOLF	CL	29.00	1150.00
W. PETERSEN				**FOREST SCENE**
88	WOODLAND SERENADE	RT	125.00	325.00
89	HEARTS AND FLOWERS	OP	110.00	112.00
90	MOUSIE COMES A CALLING	OP	128.00	145.00
91	MOUNTAIN STREAM	OP	128.00	140.00
92	LOVE LETTER	OP	98.00	108.00
93	PICNIC ON THE RIVERBANK FS-6	OP	150.00	175.00
94	WAYSIDE CHAT FS-7	OP	170.00	165.00
A. PETERSEN				**FOXES**
77	DANDY FOX	CL	6.00	475.00
77	FANCY FOX	CL	4.75	475.00
78	BARRISTER FOX	CL	7.50	675.00
A. PETERSEN				**FROGS**
74	FROG ON ROCK	CL	6.00	*
74	PRINCE CHARMING	CL	7.50	450.00
77	FROG FRIENDS	CL	5.95	400.00
77	GRAMPA FROG	CL	6.00	450.00
77	SPRING PEEPERS	CL	3.50	*
78	SINGING FROG	CL	5.50	275.00
W. PETERSEN				**LIMITED EDITION**
81	BEAUTY AND THE BEAST	CL	89.00	1750.00
84	POSTMOUSTER	CL	46.00	725.00
85	HELPING HAND	RT	62.00	700.00
87	STATUE IN THE PARK	CL	93.00	900.00
88	UNCLE SAMMY	CL	85.00	275.00
A. PETERSEN				**MICE**
72	MARKET MOUSE	CL	4.25	250.00
72	MISS MOUSE	CL	4.25	325.00
72	MISS MOUSEY	CL	4.00	300.00
73	MISS NURSEY MOUSE	CL	4.00	550.00
74	FARMER MOUSE	CL	3.75	400.00
74	GOOD KNIGHT MOUSE	CL	7.50	425.00
74	WOOD SPRITE	CL	4.00	425.00
75	BRIDE MOUSE	CL	4.00	500.00
75	TWO MICE WITH CANDLE	CL	4.50	400.00
75	TWO TINY MICE	CL	4.50	425.00
76	FAN MOUSE	CL	5.75	470.00

YR	NAME	LIMIT	ISSUE	TREND
76	JUNE BELLE	CL	4.25	375.00
76	MAMA MOUSE WITH BABY	CL	6.00	400.00
76	MAY BELLE	CL	4.25	300.00
76	MOUSE WITH MUFF	CL	9.00	*
76	MRS. MOUSEY	CL	4.00	*
76	NIGHTIE MOUSE	CL	4.75	425.00
76	SHAWL MOUSE	CL	9.00	*
76	TEA MOUSE	CL	5.75	475.00
77	BABY SITTER	CL	5.75	375.00
77	KING "TUT" MOUSE	CL	4.50	*
77	QUEEN "TUT" MOUSE	CL	4.50	*
78	BRIDGE CLUB MOUSE	CL	6.00	275.00
78	BRIDGE CLUB MOUSE PARTNER	CL	6.00	275.00
78	CHIEF NIP-A-WAY MOUSE	CL	7.00	450.00
78	COWBOY MOUSE	CL	6.00	450.00
78	PICNIC MICE	CL	14.50	425.00
78	PIRATE MOUSE	CL	6.50	375.00
78	SECRETARY, MISS SPELL/MISS PELL	CL	4.50	425.00
78	TOWN CRIER MOUSE	CL	10.50	475.00
78	WEDDING MICE	CL	7.50	550.00
79	CHRIS-MISS	CL	9.00	375.00
79	CHRIS-MOUSE	CL	9.00	175.00
79	GARDENER MOUSE	CL	12.00	400.00
79	MOUSE ARTISTE	CL	12.50	500.00
79	MOUSE BABY, HEART BOOK	CL	9.50	350.00
79	MOUSE BALLERINA	CL	12.50	425.00
79	MOUSE DUET	CL	25.00	625.00
79	MOUSE PIANIST	CL	17.00	550.00
79	MOUSE VIOLINIST	CL	9.00	275.00
79	RAGGEDY AND MOUSE	CL	12.00	375.00
79	ROCK-A-BYE BABY MOUSE	CL	17.00	400.00
80	CARPENTER MOUSE	CL	15.00	375.00
80	COMMO-DOORMOUSE	CL	14.00	700.00
80	FISHERMOUSE	CL	16.00	600.00
80	MISS BOBBIN	OP	22.00	60.00
80	MISS POLLY MOUSE	CL	23.00	350.00
80	MISS TEACH	CL	18.00	450.00
80	MRS. TIDY AND HELPER	CL	24.00	525.00
80	PHOTOGRAPHER MOUSE	CL	23.00	550.00
80	PIRATE MOUSE	CL	16.00	1400.00
80	SANTA MOUSE	CL	12.00	315.00
80	WITCH MOUSE	CL	12.00	225.00
81	BARRISTER MOUSE	CL	16.00	475.00
81	BLUE DEVIL	CL	12.50	100.00
81	CAROLERS, THE	CL	29.00	500.00
81	DOC MOUSE & PATIENT	CL	14.00	425.00
81	FLOWER GIRL	CL	15.00	300.00
81	GRADUATE MOUSE	CL	15.00	110.00
81	LITTLE DEVIL	CL	12.50	30.00
81	LITTLE GHOST	CL	8.50	20.00
81	LONE CAROLER	CL	15.50	475.00
81	MOM AND SQUEAKY CLEAN	CL	27.00	55.00
81	MOTHER'S HELPER	CL	11.00	450.00
81	MOUSEY EXPRESS	CL	22.00	125.00
81	NURSE MOUSEY	CL	14.00	400.00
81	PEARL KNIT MOUSE	CL	20.00	225.00
81	SCHOOL MARM MOUSE	CL	19.50	475.00
82	ARTY MOUSE	CL	19.00	110.00
82	BABY SITTER	CL	23.50	85.00
82	BEACH MOUSEY	CL	19.00	100.00
82	BEDDY-BYE MOUSEY	CL	29.00	50.00
82	BOY SWEETHEART	CL	13.50	450.00
82	EASTER BUNNY MOUSE	CL	18.00	35.00
82	GIRL SWEETHEART	CL	13.50	25.00
82	HAPPY BIRTHDAY!	CL	17.50	30.00
82	HOLLY MOUSE	CL	13.50	30.00
82	LAMPLIGHT CAROLERS	CL	35.00	300.00
82	LITTLE FIRE CHIEF	CL	29.00	550.00
82	LITTLE SLEDDERS	CL	24.00	325.00
82	LITTLEST ANGEL	CL	15.00	80.00
82	ME AND RAGGEDY ANN	CL	18.50	35.00
82	MISS TEACH & PUPIL	CL	29.50	425.00
82	MOON MOUSE	CL	15.50	650.00
82	MOUSEY'S TEDDY	CL	29.00	425.00
82	POOREST ANGEL	CL	15.00	125.00
82	SAY "CHEESE"	CL	15.50	525.00
82	SNOWMOUSE & FRIEND	CL	23.50	400.00
82	SWEETHEARTS	CL	26.00	425.00
82	TEA FOR TWO	CL	26.00	350.00
82	WEDDING MICE	CL	29.50	135.00
83	BIRTHDAY GIRL	CL	18.50	30.00
83	CHIEF GERONIMOUSE	CL	21.00	90.00
83	CHRISTMAS MORNING	CL	35.00	275.00
83	CLOWN MOUSE	CL	22.00	400.00
83	CUPID MOUSE	CL	22.00	40.00
83	FIRST CHRISTMAS	CL	16.00	325.00
83	GET WELL SOON!	CL	15.00	375.00
83	HARVEST MOUSE	CL	23.00	425.00
83	MERRY CHRIS-MISS	CL	17.00	370.00

YR	NAME	LIMIT	ISSUE	TREND
83	MERRY CHRIS-MOUSE	CL	16.00	370.00
83	MOUSE CALL	CL	24.00	750.00
83	MOUSEY NURSE	CL	15.00	30.00
83	MOUSEY'S CONE	*	22.00	70.00
83	MOUSEY'S DOLLHOUSE	CL	30.00	450.00
83	MOUSEY'S TRICYCLE	OP	24.00	45.00
83	PACK MOUSE	CL	19.00	325.00
83	ROCKING TOT	CL	19.00	75.00
83	ROPE 'EM MOUSEY	CL	19.00	375.00
83	WASH DAY	CL	23.00	500.00
84	CAMPFIRE MOUSE	CL	26.00	375.00
84	CHRIS-MOUSE PAGEANT	OP	38.00	55.00
84	FIRST DAY OF SCHOOL	CL	27.00	175.00
84	MOM & GINGER BAKER	*	38.00	65.00
84	PEN PAL MOUSEY	CL	26.00	350.00
84	PETER'S PUMPKIN	CL	19.00	105.00
84	PRUDENCE PIE MAKER	CL	18.50	115.00
84	SANTA'S TRAINEE	CL	36.50	500.00
84	SPRING GARDENER	CL	26.00	40.00
84	TIDY MOUSE	CL	38.00	400.00
84	TRAVELING MOUSE	CL	28.00	275.00
84	WITCHY BOO!	RT	21.00	35.00
85	ATTIC TREASURE	RT	42.00	140.00
85	CHRIS-MOUSE TREE	OP	28.00	45.00
85	COME PLAY!	CL	18.00	85.00
85	FAMILY PORTRAIT	CL	54.00	300.00
85	FIELD MOUSE	OP	46.00	90.00
85	MOUSE TALK	CL	44.00	125.00
85	PAGEANT SHEPHERDS	CL	35.00	250.00
85	PAGEANT WISEMAN	CL	58.00	250.00
85	PIGGY-BACK MOUSEY	CL	28.00	425.00
85	QUILTING BEE	OP	30.00	40.00
85	SHEPHERD KNEELING	OP	20.00	25.00
85	SHEPHERD STANDING	OP	20.00	25.00
85	STROLLING WITH BABY	OP	42.00	60.00
85	SUNDAY DRIVERS	CL	58.00	275.00
85	UNDER THE CHRIS-MOUSE TREE	OP	48.00	80.00
85	WISEMAN IN ROBE	OP	26.00	35.00
85	WISEMAN KNEELING	OP	29.00	35.00
85	WISEMAN WITH TURBAN	OP	28.00	35.00
86	CHRIST-MOUSE STOCKING	OP	34.00	40.00
86	COME & GET IT!	CL	34.00	120.00
86	DOWN THE CHIMNEY	CL	48.00	250.00
86	FIRST DATE	OP	60.00	65.00
86	FIRST HAIRCUT	CL	58.00	200.00
86	FUN FLOAT	OP	34.00	40.00
86	JUST CHECKING	OP	34.00	40.00
86	MOUSE ON CAMPUS	CL	25.00	115.00
86	SWEET DREAMS	CL	58.00	175.00
86	WALTZING MATILDA	CL	48.00	160.00
87	BAT MOUSE	CL	25.00	75.00
87	CHOIR MOUSE	CL	23.00	110.00
87	DON'T CRY!	CL	33.00	110.00
87	DRUMMER MOUSE	CL	29.00	60.00
87	LITTLEST WITCH	CL	24.00	85.00
87	LITTLEST WITCH AND SKELETON	OP	49.00	60.00
87	MARKET MOUSE	CL	49.00	135.00
87	MISS NOEL	OP	32.00	40.00
87	PAGEANT ANGEL	OP	19.00	25.00
87	PAGEANT STABLE	OP	56.00	70.00
87	RED WAGON, THE	CL	54.00	200.00
87	SCOOTER MOUSE	OP	34.00	40.00
87	SKELETON MOUSEY	CL	27.00	90.00
87	TOOTH FAIRY	OP	32.00	40.00
87	TRUMPETER	CL	29.00	65.00
87	TUBA PLAYER	CL	29.00	65.00
88	ALOHA!	CL	32.00	80.00
88	FORTY WINKS	OP	36.00	45.00
88	MOUSEY'S EASTER BASKET	CL	32.00	120.00
89	COMMENCEMENT DAY	OP	28.00	35.00
89	ELF TALES	RT	48.00	85.00
89	FATHER CHRIS-MOUSE	OP	34.00	40.00
89	HAUNTED MOUSE HOUSE	OP	125.00	180.00
89	PRIMA BALLERINA	OP	35.00	40.00
90	CHRIS-MOUSE SLIPPER	OP	35.00	40.00
90	COLLEEN O'GREEN	OP	40.00	45.00
90	HANS & GRETA	CL	64.00	160.00
90	POLLY'S PARASOL	CL	39.00	115.00
90	STARS & STRIPES	OP	34.00	40.00
90	ZELDA	OP	37.00	45.00
91	APRIL SHOWERS	OP	27.00	35.00
91	GRAMMY-PHONE	OP	75.00	85.00
91	LITTLE SQUIRT	OP	49.00	55.00
91	MOUSIE'S EGG FACTORY	OP	73.00	90.00
91	NIGHT PRAYER	OP	52.00	60.00
91	NUTCRACKER, THE	OP	49.00	60.00
91	RED RIDING HOOD/GRANDMOTHER'S HOUSE	OP	295.00	295.00
91	SEA SOUNDS	OP	34.00	40.00
91	SILENT NIGHT	OP	64.00	75.00

YR	NAME	LIMIT	ISSUE	TREND
91	TEA FOR THREE	OP	135.00	160.00
92	ADAM'S APPLES	OP	148.00	148.00
92	HIGH ON THE HOG	CL	52.00	130.00
92	MISS DAISY	OP	42.00	48.00
92	MRS. MOUSEY'S STUDIO	OP	150.00	160.00
92	OLD BLACK STOVE, THE	OP	130.00	140.00
92	PEEKABOO!	OP	52.00	55.00
92	SNOW BUDDIES	OP	58.00	65.00
A. PETERSEN				**MINUTEMICE**
74	CONCORDIAN ON DRUM W/GLASSES MM-4	CL	9.00	*
74	CONCORDIAN WOOD BASE W/HAT MM-4B	CL	8.00	*
74	CONCORDIAN WOOD BASE W/TAN COAT MM-4A	CL	8.00	*
74	LITTLE FIFER ON DRUM MM-5B	CL	8.00	*
74	LITTLE FIFER ON DRUM W/FOFE MM-5	CL	8.00	*
74	LITTLE FIFER ON WOOD BASE MM-5A	CL	8.00	*
74	MOUSE CARRYING LARGE DRUM BB-3	CL	8.00	*
74	MOUSE ON DRUM W/BLACK HAT MM-2	CL	9.00	*
74	MOUSE ON DRUM W/FIFE MM-1	CL	9.00	*
74	MOUSE ON DRUM W/FIFE WOOD BASE MM-1A	CL	9.00	*
79	CONCORD MINUTE MOUSE MM-10	OP	14.00	15.00
79	MINUTE MOUSE AND RED COAT MM-9	OP	28.00	28.00
79	RED COAT MOUSE MM-11	OP	14.00	15.00
A. PETERSEN				**MOLES**
78	MOLE SCOUT MO-1	CL	4.25	325.00
94	BELL FINGER MOLE MO-2	OP	44.00	44.00
95	MOLE'S BED SLED MO-3	OP	59.00	59.00
A. PETERSEN				**MOUSE SPORTS**
75	BOBSLED THREE	CL	12.00	450.00
75	SKATER MOUSE	CL	4.50	350.00
76	MOUSE SKIER	CL	4.25	350.00
76	TENNIS STAR	CL	3.75	225.00
77	GOLFER MOUSE	CL	5.25	275.00
77	SKATING STAR MOUSE	CL	3.75	325.00
80	SKATER MOUSE	CL	16.50	375.00
80	SKIER MOUSE (RED/YELLOW, RED/GREEN)	CL	13.00	300.00
80	SKIER MOUSE MS-9	OP	13.00	40.00
81	GOLFER MOUSE	CL	15.50	510.00
82	TWO IN A CANOE	OP	29.00	60.00
84	LAND HO!	CL	36.50	240.00
84	TENNIS ANYONE?	CL	18.00	130.00
85	FISHIN' CHIP	CL	46.00	215.00
89	JOE DI'MOUSIO	OP	39.00	45.00
94	CAMPING OUT MS-16	OP	75.00	75.00
A. PETERSEN				**OWLS**
74	MR. AND MRS. OWL	CL	6.00	475.00
74	MR. OWL	CL	3.25	225.00
74	MRS. OWL	CL	3.00	225.00
75	COLONIAL OWLS	CL	11.50	425.00
79	"GRAD" OWL	CL	4.25	450.00
80	GRADUATE OWL	CL	12.00	425.00
A. PETERSEN				**PIGGIES**
78	BOY PIGLET/PICNIC PIGGY	CL	4.00	675.00
78	GIRL PIGLET/PICNIC PIGGY	CL	4.00	675.00
78	JOLLY TAR PIGGY	CL	4.50	225.00
78	MISS PIGGY SCHOOL MARM	CL	4.50	275.00
78	PICNIC PIGGIES	CL	7.75	250.00
78	PIGGY BAKER	CL	4.50	325.00
78	PIGGY JOGGER	CL	4.50	160.00
80	NURSE PIGGY	CL	15.50	21.00
80	PIG O' MY HEART	CL	12.00	235.00
80	PIGGY BALLERINA	CL	15.50	235.00
80	PIGGY POLICEMAN	CL	17.50	275.00
81	HOLLY HOG	CL	25.00	390.00
A. PETERSEN				**RACCOONS**
77	HIKER RACCOON	CL	4.50	650.00
77	MOTHER RACCOON	CL	4.50	335.00
78	BIRD WATCHER RACCOON	CL	6.50	550.00
78	RACCOON SKATER	CL	4.75	325.00
78	RACCOON SKIER	CL	6.00	400.00
A. PETERSEN				**ROBIN HOOD SERIES**
90	FRIAR TUCK	CL	32.00	85.00
90	MAID MARION	CL	32.00	85.00
90	ROBIN HOOD	CL	37.00	85.00
D. PETERSEN				**TINY TEDDIES**
83	TINY TEDDY	CL	16.00	165.00
84	BOO BEAR	SU	20.00	75.00
84	DRUMMER BEAR	SU	22.00	70.00
84	HUGGY BEAR	SU	26.00	80.00
84	LITTLE TEDDY	CL	20.00	120.00
84	RIDE 'EM TEDDY!	SU	32.00	90.00
84	SAILOR TEDDY	SU	20.00	75.00
84	SANTA BEAR	SU	27.00	110.00
84	SEASIDE TEDDY	SU	28.00	90.00
87	CHRISTMAS TEDDY	SU	26.00	75.00
87	WEDDING BEARS	SU	54.00	130.00
88	HANSEL & GRETEL/WITCH'S HOUSE	SU	175.00	240.00
89	MOMMA BEAR	SU	27.00	135.000

YR	NAME	LIMIT	ISSUE	TREND
A. PETERSEN			**WIND IN THE WILLOWS**	
82	BADGER	CL	18.00	480.00
82	MOLE	CL	18.00	575.00
82	RATTY	CL	18.00	475.00
82	TOAD	CL	18.00	575.00

WHITLEY BAY

YR	NAME	LIMIT	ISSUE	TREND
L. HEYDA			**SANTA SERIES**	
87	GLOBE	10000	225.00	225.00
87	SANTA	10000	150.00	150.00
89	ELF	10000	225.00	225.00
89	ENTRY	10000	275.00	275.00
89	HUG	10000	225.00	225.00
89	LETTERS	10000	375.00	375.00
89	LISTS	10000	275.00	275.00
89	SLEIGH	10000	375.00	375.00

WILLITTS DESIGNS

YR	NAME	LIMIT	ISSUE	TREND
A. DEZENDORF		**AMISH HERITAGE COLLECTION**		
96	CAROLING	3500	300.00	300.00
96	DOLL QUILT, THE	RT	60.00	60.00
96	FIRST KISS	RT	110.00	110.00
96	SPECIAL PLAYMATES	RT	95.00	95.00
96	TUCKERED OUT	RT	60.00	60.00
T. BLACKSHEAR		**EBONY VISIONS COLLECTION**		
95	A WINTER HOLIDAY	RT	120.00	120.00
95	AUTUMN LEAVE	RT	120.00	120.00
95	CAROLINE'S BEDTIME PRAYER	RT	75.00	75.00
95	KATIE AND BETH	RT	95.00	95.00
95	MADONNA, THE	RT	160.00	160.00
95	MIRACLE OF SPRING, THE	RT	120.00	120.00
95	NURTURER, THE	RT	160.00	160.00
95	PREMIER COMMUNION SERVICE	1500	300.00	300.00
95	PROTECTOR, THE	YR	195.00	195.00
95	SADIE MAE'S HUNGRY GEESE	RT	85.00	85.00
95	SIBLINGS, THE	YR	120.00	120.00
95	STORY TELLER PREMIER, THE	SO	410.00	410.00
95	SUMMERTIME FUN	RT	120.00	120.00
95	TENDER TOUCH, THE	RT	185.00	185.00
96	A CHANCE TO DREAM	RT	135.00	135.00
96	BATH TIME	RT	110.00	110.00
96	DREAMER, THE	RT	135.00	135.00
96	GUARDIAN, THE	RT	300.00	300.00
96	MUSIC MAKER, THE	RT	300.00	300.00
C. PYLE	**HISTORY OF ANGELS COLLECTION BY BILL DALE**			
95	ANGEL GABRIEL, THE	9500	120.00	120.00
95	MUSICAL ANGELS	9500	160.00	160.00
96	ANGELIC DOUBLE/STRUGGLE OF THE SOUL, THE	9500	200.00	200.00

Ornaments

Clara Johnson Scroggins

Who would have guessed that one day ornament manufacturers would sponsor collector's clubs, offer special "member's only issues" and host gatherings at which "event-only" ornaments could be purchased on a limited basis?

Who could have predicted that one day collectors would be insuring their collections, carefully ascertaining reliable secondary market values for the appraisal of their ornaments? Or cataloging their collections with the aid of sourcebooks and storing their collections, carefully logged and labeled, in climate controlled quarters?

Who could have known that "first in a series" would be a phrase that sent shivers down the spines of collectors and into a buying frenzy or that one day ornaments would sell on the secondary market for up to 10 times their original retail value?

That's the point to which ornament collecting has evolved today. And did you notice that these once holiday-only items are rarely referred to as "Christmas" ornaments in today's marketplace? Ornament makers have broadened their scope to include more than just Yuletide treasures, thus making ornaments a year-round collectible. Easter, Independence Day and Thanksgiving are just some of the holidays which are often commemorated in the form of ornaments. Producers are also personalizing ornaments, making them wonderful gifts for friends and loved ones.

But more importantly, and perhaps more than any other collectible, ornaments reflect the changes in our life and times. From the early beginnings of elegant European blown glass, to the lively and often humorous artplas ornaments of today, this is a collectible that transcends all areas of passions and interests. Ornaments offer something for everyone. The themes are so varied and the media so diverse, this is a collectible with an affinity for the unique. Children thrill in owning an ornament depicting their favorite sports figure and delight in the ornaments featuring licensed characters from their favorite movies or products. Hallmark, Enesco and Carlton are just a few of the makers leading the way in this ever-changing industry rapidly aligning itself with the era of pop culture.

Timeless themes also abound in this diverse class of collecting as well. Generations-old themes, mediums and traditions are even more prevalent, and perhaps just as popular, as the "here today, gone tomorrow" themes of the '90s. Nostalgic collectors entranced by the magical look of blown glass can revel in the designs brought back by today's importers and makers such as Old World Christmas, Christopher Radko and Kurt S. Adler. Crystal, sterling silver and porcelain offered by Reed and Barton, Anna-Perenna, Swarovski and many more offer a variety of appealing themes in media just as alluring.

What drives the secondary market of this somewhat new arena? Perhaps its diversity is its greatest thrust. In an industry producing for the masses, it's only logical that the laws of supply and demand would dictate the growth of the secondary market. Sports collectors, car enthusiasts, train aficionados, bear lovers, angel adorers and animation zealots frequently "cross over" to the realm of ornament collecting when the subject matter lends itself to their particular area of interest—which it often does. The competition to attain an ornament aligned with that area of interest often makes buying it at the retail level somewhat difficult. That's where the secondary market begins. And so too does our chapter on the prices and trends of perhaps the world's most popular collectible.

CLARA JOHNSON SCROGGINS, who has authored six books on Hallmark ornaments, is a consultant and speaker who appears at collectibles events around the country. Her ornament collection is recognized as the largest in the country.

ORNAMENTS

AMERICAN GREETINGS

*

AMERICAN GREETINGS CHRISTMAS ORNAMENTS

YR	NAME	LIMIT	ISSUE	TREND
80	ACRYLIC DISC-HOLLY HOBBIE C-23	YR	1.75	5.00
80	ACRYLIC DISC-MOTHER C-22	YR	1.75	4.00
80	STRAWBERRY SHORTCAKE/XMAS SUGARPLUM C-27	CL	3.50	4.00
81	ACRYLIC DISC-FIRST XMAS TOGETHER WXX-240	YR	4.00	4.00
81	ACRYLIC DISC-HOLLY HOBBIE WXX-239	YR	4.00	5.00
81	ACRYLIC DISC-MOTHER WXX-237	YR	4.00	5.00
81	ACRYLIC DISC-ZIGGY & FRIENDS WXX-236	YR	4.00	5.00
81	PORCELAIN HOLLY HOBBIE WXX-56	CL	3.00	4.00
82	ACRYLIC DISC-FRIENDSHIP/DESIGN WXO-32	YR	5.00	6.00
82	HOLLY HOB. PLUM PUDD PORCLN BELL WXO-45	CL	5.25	6.00
82	HOLLY HOBBIE FIG. PORCLN BELL WXO-48	YR	12.00	14.00
83	ACRYLIC DISC-FIRST XMAS TOGETHER CO-1901	YR	5.75	7.00
83	ACRYLIC DISC-FRIENDSHIP CO-1902	YR	5.75	7.00
83	ACRYLIC DISC-LOVE CO-1903	YR	5.75	7.00
83	HIMSELF THE ELF/PORC. BELL CO-1403	CL	12.00	12.00
83	RELIGIOUS ACRYLIC DISC CO-1904	YR	5.75	7.00
83	STRAWBERRY SHORTCAKE/PORC. BELL CO-1401	CL	12.00	12.00
83	STRWBRRY SHORTCAKE..SPECIAL GIFT CO-1225	CL	9.00	12.00
83	ZIGGY PORCELAIN FIGURINE BELL CO-1402	CL	12.00	12.00
84	CAREBEARS DECORATING THE TREE AO-1102	CL	15.00	20.00
84	HIMSELF THE ELF SCULPTED ORN. AO-407	CL	7.50	8.00
84	HOLLY HOBBIE CERAMIC FIGURE BELL AO-701	CL	10.00	10.00
84	HOLLY HOBBIE SCULPTED ORNAMENT AO-403	CL	7.50	15.00
84	MUSICAL-BABY'S FIRST CHRISTMAS AO-1001	YR	17.50	22.00
84	STRAWBERRY SHORTCAKE & FRIENDS AO-1101	CL	15.00	30.00
84	STRWBRRY SHORTCAKE SCULPTED ORN. AO-402	CL	9.00	12.00
84	TENDERHEART BEAR SCULPTED ORN. AO-406	CL	6.50	10.00
85	BABY'S FIRST CHRISTMAS BX-302	YR	7.00	10.00
85	HOLLY HOBBIE PORCELAIN/BELL BX-901	YR	10.00	10.00
85	MOUSE ON WATCH BX-303	CL	7.00	7.00
85	ZIGGY & FRIENDS ADMIRING TREE BX-1102	CL	13.00	13.00
86	ACRYLIC DISC A WREATH OF LOVE DX-503	CL	3.75	5.00
86	ACRYLIC DISC BABY'S FIRST XMAS DX-504	YR	3.75	5.00
86	ACRYLIC DISC FIRST XMAS TOGETHER DX-502	YR	3.75	5.00
86	ACRYLIC DISC SPECIAL FRIEND DX-501	YR	3.75	5.00
86	BABY'S FIRST CHRISTMAS DX-1609	CL	7.50	10.00
86	CERAMIC BELL BABY'S FIRST XMAS DX-1002	YR	6.50	8.00
86	CERAMIC BELL CHRISTMAS IS LOVE DX-1003	CL	6.50	7.00
86	CERAMIC BELL FIRST XMAS TOGETHER DX-1001	YR	6.50	13.00
86	GONE FISHIN' DX-1605	CL	8.00	8.00
86	OUT W/OLD IN W/NEW - ZIGGY DX-1501	YR	6.50	7.00
87	BRASS SAILBOAT CX-702	YR	6.50	7.00
87	CERAMIC OLD-FASHIONED TEDDY CX-402	CL	5.00	5.00
87	IRIDESCENT UNICORN CX-203	CL	4.00	4.00
87	PORCELAIN BELLS 1ST XMAS TOGETHER CX-302	YR	6.50	7.00
87	PORCELAIN BELLS BABY'S FIRST XMAS CX-301	YR	6.50	7.00
87	SCULPTED DIMEN. 1ST XMAS TOGETHER CX-104	YR	7.00	9.00
87	SCULPTED DIMEN./BOY FIRST XMAS CX-403	YR	7.50	9.00
87	SCULPTED DIMEN./CAROUSEL HORSE CX-801	CL	8.50	9.00
87	SCULPTED DIMEN./GIRL FIRST XMAS CX-404	YR	7.50	9.00
87	SCULPTED DIMEN./SANTA REF CX-112	YR	7.00	7.00
87	WOODEN ORNAMENT ROCKING HORSE CX-1104	YR	3.25	5.00
87	WOODEN ORNAMENT ZIGGY & FUZZ CX-1003	CL	4.50	5.00
88	ACRYLIC DISC FIRST XMAS TOGETHER AX-1007	YR	4.00	5.00
88	ACRYLIC DISC MADONNA & CHILD AX-1039	UD	4.25	5.00
88	BABY BOY'S FIRST XMAS AX-1004	YR	7.50	8.00
88	BABY GIRL'S FIRST XMAS AX-1005	YR	7.50	8.00
88	BABY'S FIRST XMAS PHOTO FRAME AX-1001	YR	5.00	5.00
88	BOWLING MOUSE AX-1017	UD	7.00	7.00
88	BRASS OUR HOME TO YOUR HOME AX-1010	YR	5.50	6.00
88	CAROUSEL HORSE AX-1040	UD	8.50	9.00
88	CERAMIC COW BELL AX-1034	UD	6.50	7.00
88	COPPER REINDEER WEATHERVANE	YR	4.50	5.00
88	LOVEBIRDS FIRST XMAS TOGETHER AX-1006	YR	7.00	7.00
88	MUSICAL ZIGGY & FUZZ FRIENDSHIP AX-1013	YR	7.00	7.00
88	NEW YEAR ZIGGY AX-1049	YR	6.50	7.00
88	ROCKING HORSE BABY'S FIRST XMAS AX-1003	YR	3.50	4.00
89	ACRYLIC DISC REWORK DX-1012	YR	4.24	5.00
89	BEAR ON ROCKING HORSE DX-1001	YR	7.95	8.00
89	BEAR ON ROCKING HORSE DX-1002	YR	7.95	8.00
89	BEAR ON ROCKING HORSE DX-1030	YR	7.50	8.00
89	BRASS SAILBOAT DX-1022	YR	6.50	7.00
89	BUNNIES IN SWING DX-1005	YR	8.50	9.00
89	CAMEO-LOOK DOVE DISK DX-1016	YR	5.95	6.00
89	COOKING BEAR DX-1029	YR	7.50	8.00
89	DEER LEAPING OVER LANDSCAPE DX-1004	YR	4.95	5.00
89	DINOSAUR DRIVING TRAIN DX-1010	YR	7.95	8.00
89	HEART PHOTO FRAME-CANDY CANE DX-1023	YR	5.95	6.00
89	HEART SHAPE W/HOLLY DX-1007	YR	5.95	6.00
89	KITTEN IN STOCKING DX-1011	YR	4.50	5.00
89	LACE-LOOK BEAR EMBROID HOOP DX-1003	YR	5.50	6.00
89	NAUTICAL-LIFE RING W/HOLLY DX-1028	YR	5.95	6.00
89	PAPER DOLL CHAIN ON CERAMIC BELL DX-1009	YR	6.95	7.00

YR	NAME	LIMIT	ISSUE	TREND
89	POLAR BEARS HOLDING HANDS DX-1035	YR	6.95	7.00
89	VICTORIAN EMBROIDERY HOOP DX-1008	YR	6.50	7.00
89	VICTORIAN HOUSE DX-1013	YR	4.50	5.00
89	WOOD DISC W/TREE DX-1033	YR	4.50	5.00
89	WOOD HEART W/SILK MISTLETOE DX-1015	YR	4.50	5.00
89	ZIGGY ELF W/JINGLE BELLS DX-1014	YR	6.95	7.00
90	2 BEARS W/GIFT ON SLED DX-1010	YR	4.50	5.00
90	ANGEL HOLDING HEART DX-1012	YR	4.50	5.00
90	BEAR ON BLOCK DX-1001	YR	7.95	8.00
90	BEAR ON BLOCK DX-1002	YR	7.95	8.00
90	BEAR ON ROCKING HORSE DX-1003	YR	4.50	5.00
90	BEARS PUTTING STAR ON XMAS TREE DX-1007	YR	5.95	6.00
90	BI-PLANE WITH SANTA DX-1015	YR	7.95	8.00
90	BIRDS IN MAILBOX DX-1008	YR	6.95	7.00
90	CAROUSEL REINDEER DX-1033	YR	7.95	8.00
90	CONV. HEART SHAPED DISC W/LTG. DX-1006	YR	5.50	6.00
90	FATHER CHRISTMAS DX-1035	YR	7.50	8.00
90	NATIVITY..CHRIST CHILD DX-1019	YR	5.50	6.00
90	SLEIGH & HOUSE DX-1009	YR	5.95	6.00
90	TOY SOLDIER W/DRUM DX-1034	YR	5.95	6.00
90	VICKY BELL DX-1014	YR	7.50	8.00

ANHEUSER-BUSCH INC.

YR	NAME	LIMIT	ISSUE	TREND
*****	**A & EAGLE COLLECTOR ORNAMENT SERIES**			
91	BUDWEISER GIRL N3178	OP	15.00	15.00
92	1893 COLUMBIAN EXPOSITION N3649	OP	15.00	15.00
93	GREATEST TRIUMPH N4089	OP	15.00	15.00
S. SAMPSON	**CHRISTMAS ORNAMENT SERIES**			
92	CLYDESDALES MINI PLATE ORNAMENTS N3650	OP	23.00	23.00
M. URDAHL	**CHRISTMAS ORNAMENT SERIES**			
93	BUDWEISER 6-PK MINI PLATE ORN. N4220	OP	10.00	10.00

ANNA-PERENNA

YR	NAME	LIMIT	ISSUE	TREND
P. BUCKLEY MOSS				
93	SECOND ANGEL	YR	27.50	50.00
94	CHRISTMAS SKATERS	YR	27.50	28.00
94	THIRD ANGEL	YR	27.50	50.00
95	CHRISTMAS NIGHT	OP	27.50	28.00
P. BUCKLEY MOSS	**ANNUAL CHRISTMAS ORNAMENTS**			
91	NOEL	*	25.00	120.00
92	SLEIGHRIDE	*	27.50	60.00
P. BUCKLEY MOSS	**HOLLY SERIES**			
93	SNOWMAN, THE	YR	27.50	70.00

ANNALEE MOBILITEE

YR	NAME	LIMIT	ISSUE	TREND
82	ELF HEAD	1908	2.95	25.00
83	GINGERBREAD BOY	11835	10.95	35.00
84	SNOWMAN HEAD	13677	7.95	30.00
84	STAR	3275	5.95	25.00
85	3 IN. ANGEL ON CLOUD	*	6.50	30.00
85	SUN	1692	6.50	25.00
86	ANGEL HEAD	*	7.95	30.00
86	BABY ANGEL	YR	11.95	35.00
86	CLOWN HEAD	5701	7.95	25.00
93	3 IN. BEAR ORNAMENT W/ STAND	OP	12.95	13.00
93	5 IN. GINGERBREAD BOY ORNAMENT	OP	16.95	17.00
93	DEER HEAD ORNAMENT	OP	34.50	750.00
93	SANTA HEAD ORNAMENT	OP	8.95	9.00
93	SNOWMAN HEAD ORNAMENT	OP	11.45	12.00
94	3 IN. SUN W/SANTA HAT ORNAMENT	12881	7.95	8.00
94	5 IN. GINGERBREAD BOY ORNAMENT	RT	17.50	18.00
94	5 IN. OLD WORLD SANTA ORN.	7540	23.50	24.00
94	7 IN. SANTA HEAD ORNAMENT	12616	9.50	10.00
94	7 IN. SNOWMAN HEAD ORNAMENT	10062	11.95	12.00
94	DEER HEAD ORNAMENT	RT	10.50	11.00
94	PEPI HERRMAN CRYSTAL ORNAMENT	OP	29.95	30.00
95	3 IN. ANGEL W/INSTRUMENT	OP	14.50	15.00
95	3 IN. BABY IN BLUE PJ'S	OP	11.95	12.00
95	3 IN. BABY IN PINK PJ'S	OP	11.95	12.00
95	3 IN. GREEN ELF W/STAR	OP	11.95	12.00
95	3 IN. HONEY BEAR	OP	12.95	13.00
95	3 IN. RED ELF W/STAR	OP	11.95	12.00
95	3 IN. SUN W/SANTA HAT	OP	8.50	9.00
95	3 IN. WINTER ELF	OP	11.95	12.00
95	5 IN. GINGERBREAD BOY	OP	17.95	18.00
95	5 IN. OLD WORLD SANTA	OP	23.50	24.00
95	DEER HEAD	OP	10.95	11.00
95	SANTA HEAD	OP	9.95	10.00
95	SNOWMAN HEAD	OP	11.95	12.00
96	18 IN. SANTA HANGING GINGERGREAD	OP	77.00	77.00
96	3 IN. ANGEL W/INSTRUMENT	OP	16.00	16.00
96	3 IN. GINGERBREAD BOY	OP	15.00	15.00
96	3 IN. HOLLY BERRY ANGEL	OP	17.00	17.00
96	3 IN. HONEY BEAR	OP	14.00	14.00
96	3 IN. JSUT-A-JESTER	OP	20.50	20.50
96	3 IN. MIDNIGHT SNACK MOUSE	OP	18.00	18.00
96	3 IN. MOUSE IN SANTA'S HAT	OP	18.00	18.00
96	3 IN. MRS. SANTA	OP	16.50	16.50

YR	NAME	LIMIT	ISSUE	TREND
96	3 IN. RED ELF W/STAR	OP	13.00	13.00
96	3 IN. SANTA	OP	16.50	16.50
96	3 IN. SKI BUNNY	OP	20.00	20.00
96	3 IN. SNOWMAN	OP	16.50	16.50
96	3 IN. WINTER ELF	OP	14.00	14.00
96	5 IN. OLD WORLD SANTA	OP	23.50	23.50
96	ELF HEAD/GREEN	OP	10.00	10.00
96	ELF HEAD/RED	OP	10.00	10.00
96	SANTA HEAD	OP	10.00	10.00
96	SNOWMAN HEAD	OP	12.50	13.00
96	TRIM-A-TREE PUPPY	OP	18.00	18.00

ANRI

YR	NAME	LIMIT	ISSUE	TREND
L. GAITHER		**CHRISTMAS EVE**		
95	HITCHING PRANCER	500	140.00	140.00
96	GETTING READY	500	140.00	140.00
*		**DISNEY FOUR STAR COLLECTION**		
89	MAESTRO MICKEY	YR	25.00	25.00
90	MINNIE MOUSE	YR	25.00	25.00
J. FERRANDIZ		**FERRANDIZ MESSAGE COLLECTION**		
89	LET THE HEAVENS RING	1000	215.00	215.00
90	HEAR THE ANGELS SING	1000	225.00	225.00
J. FERRANDIZ		**FERRANDIZ WOODCARVINGS**		
88	HEAVENLY DRUMMER	1000	175.00	225.00
89	HEAVENLY STRINGS	1000	190.00	190.00
S. KAY		**SARAH KAY'S FIRST CHRISTMAS**		
95	FIRST XMAS STOCKING	500	99.00	99.00
96	ALL I WANT FOR CHRISTMAS	500	198.00	195.00

ARMANI

Price ranges may reflect various demands in the market from one geographic region to another; condition of piece; specific markings found on piece; and/or changes in production of piece.

YR	NAME	LIMIT	ISSUE	TREND
G. ARMANI		**CHRISTMAS**		
91	1991 CHRISTMAS ORNAMENT 799A	RT	11.50	12.00
92	1992 CHRISTMAS ORNAMENT 788F	YR	23.50	24.00
G. ARMANI		**COMMEMORATIVE**		
95	1995 CHRISTMAS ORNAMENT	RT	300.00	30.00
96	1996 CHRISTMAS ORNAMENT	YR	30.00	30.00

ARTAFFECTS

YR	NAME	LIMIT	ISSUE	TREND
G. PERILLO		**ANNUAL BELL ORNAMENT**		
85	HOME SWEET WIGWAM	OP	14.00	14.00
86	PEEK-A-BOO	OP	15.00	33.00
87	ANNUAL BELL ORNAMENT	YR	15.00	33.00
88	ANNUAL BELL ORNAMENT	YR	17.50	18.00
89	ANNUAL BELL ORNAMENT	YR	17.50	18.00
90	ANNUAL BELL ORNAMENT	YR	17.50	18.00
91	ANNUAL BELL ORNAMENT	YR	19.50	20.00
G. PERILLO		**ANNUAL CHRISTMAS ORNAMENTS**		
85	PAPOOSE ORNAMENT	YR	14.00	40.00
86	CHRISTMAS CACTUS	YR	15.00	50.00
87	ANNUAL ORNAMENT	YR	15.00	35.00
88	ANNUAL ORNAMENT	YR	17.50	25.00
89	ANNUAL ORNAMENT	YR	17.50	25.00
90	ANNUAL ORNAMENT	YR	17.50	18.00
91	ANNUAL ORNAMENT	YR	19.50	19.50
G. PERILLO		**KACHINA ORNAMENTS**		
91	DAWN KACHINA	OP	17.50	18.00
91	KACHINA MOTHER	OP	17.50	18.00
91	OLD KACHINA	OP	17.50	18.00
91	SNOW KACHINA	OP	17.50	18.00
91	SUN KACHINA	OP	17.50	18.00
91	TOTEM KACHINA	OP	17.50	18.00
G. PERILLO		**SAGEBRUSH KIDS BELL ORNAMENTS**		
87	CAROLERS, THE	OP	9.00	9.00
87	CHRISTMAS CANDLE	OP	9.00	9.00
87	CHRISTMAS HORN	OP	9.00	9.00
87	FIDDLER, THE	OP	9.00	9.00
87	GIFT, THE	OP	9.00	9.00
87	HARPIST, THE	OP	9.00	9.00
G. PERILLO		**SAGEBRUSH KIDS COLLECTION**		
91	MOCCASIN ORNAMENT	OP	15.00	16.00
91	SHIELD ORNAMENT	OP	15.00	16.00
91	TEE-PEE ORNAMENT	OP	15.00	16.00
C. ROEDA		**SIMPLE WONDERS**		
91	ASHLEY	OP	22.50	23.00
91	BRITTANY	OP	22.50	23.00
91	KIM	OP	22.50	23.00
91	LITTLE FEATHER	OP	22.50	23.00
91	MEGAN	OP	22.50	23.00
91	NICOLE	OP	22.50	23.00
92	SWEET SURPRISE	YR	15.00	16.00

ARTHUR COURT DESIGNS

YR	NAME	LIMIT	ISSUE	TREND
A. COURT		**CHRISTMAS ORNAMENT SERIES**		
94	BUNNIES ON A SLEIGH	8200	22.00	24.00

YR	NAME	LIMIT	ISSUE	TREND

ARTISTS OF THE WORLD

Price ranges may reflect various demands in the market from one geographic region to another; condition of piece; specific markings found on piece; and/or changes in production of piece.

YR	NAME	LIMIT	ISSUE	TREND
T. DEGRAZIA				**ANNUAL ORNAMENT**
93	WARM WISHES	YR	65.00	75.00
94	LITTLE PRAYER	YR	49.50	52.00
T. DEGRAZIA				**DEGRAZIA**
95	HEAVENLY FLOWERS	*	62.50	63.00
95	MY BEAUTIFUL ROCKING HORSE	1995	125.00	125.00
T. DEGRAZIA				**DEGRAZIA ANNUAL ORNAMENTS**
86	PIMA, INDIAN DRUMMER BOY	YR	27.50	300.00-450.00
87	WHITE DOVE	YR	29.50	75.00
88	FLOWER GIRL	YR	32.50	45.00-50.00
89	FLOWER BOY	YR	35.00	45.00-50.00
90	MERRY LITTLE INDIAN	10000	87.50	95.00-100.00
90	PINK PAPOOSE	YR	35.00	45.00-50.00
91	CHRISTMAS PRAYER	YR	49.50	50.00
92	BEARING GIFT	YR	55.00	55.00
93	LIGHTING THE WAY	YR	57.50	58.00

BAND CREATIONS

YR	NAME	LIMIT	ISSUE	TREND
*** RICHARDS/PENFIELD**				**AMERICA'S FARMLAND COLL. - AMERICA'S COUNTRY BARN**
96	DOUBLE-CRIB BARN	OP	29.95	30.00
96	DUTCH BARN	OP	29.95	30.00
96	ENGLISH BARN	OP	29.95	30.00
96	GAMBREL ROOF BARN	OP	29.95	30.00
96	LOG BARN	OP	29.95	30.00
96	POLYGONAL BARN	OP	29.95	30.00
96	ROUND BARN	OP	29.95	30.00
*** RICHARDS/PENFIELD**				**BEST FRIENDS**
94	ANGEL ORNAMENTS-4 ASSORTED	OP	5.00	5.00
95	DOUBLE ANGELS	OP	8.00	8.00
*** RICHARDS/PENFIELD**				**BEST FRIENDS - ANGELS OF THE MONTH**
93	APRIL ANGEL	OP	10.00	10.00
93	AUGUST ANGEL	OP	10.00	10.00
93	DECEMBER ANGEL	OP	10.00	10.00
93	FEBRUARY ANGEL	OP	10.00	10.00
93	JANUARY ANGEL	OP	10.00	10.00
93	JULY ANGEL	OP	10.00	10.00
93	JUNE ANGEL	OP	10.00	10.00
93	MARCH ANGEL	OP	10.00	10.00
93	MAY ANGEL	OP	10.00	10.00
93	NOVEMBER ANGEL	OP	10.00	10.00
93	OCTOBER ANGEL	OP	10.00	10.00
93	SEPTEMBER ANGEL	OP	10.00	10.00
96	APRIL ANGEL	OP	10.00	10.00
96	AUGUST ANGEL	OP	10.00	10.00
96	DECEMBER ANGEL	OP	10.00	10.00
96	FEBRUARY ANGEL	OP	10.00	10.00
96	JANUARY ANGEL	OP	10.00	10.00
96	JULY ANGEL	OP	10.00	10.00
96	JUNE ANGEL	OP	10.00	10.00
96	MARCH ANGEL	OP	10.00	10.00
96	MAY ANGEL	OP	10.00	10.00
96	NOVEMBER ANGEL	OP	10.00	10.00
96	OCTOBER ANGEL	OP	10.00	10.00
96	SEPTEMBER ANGEL	OP	10.00	10.00
*** RICHARDS/PENFIELD**				**BEST FRIENDS - KRINGLE TOPPERS**
96	AMERICA, SANTA CLAUS	OP	10.00	10.00
96	AUSTRIA, CHRISTKIND	OP	10.00	10.00
96	ENGLAND, FATHER CHRISTMAS	OP	10.00	10.00
96	GERMANY, PELSNICKEL	OP	10.00	10.00
96	NETHERLANDS, ST. NICKOLAS	OP	10.00	10.00
96	PERE NOEL, FRANCE	OP	10.00	10.00
96	RUSSIAN, FATHER FROST	OP	10.00	10.00
96	SCANDINAVIA, JULNISSE	OP	10.00	10.00

BIEDERMANN & SONS

YR	NAME	LIMIT	ISSUE	TREND
93	BABY'S FIRST CHRISTMAS	400	12.00	14.00
93	FOUR CALLING BIRDS (BRASS)	RT	12.50	19.00
93	FOUR CALLING BIRDS (SILVER)	500	18.00	55.00
94	BABY'S FIRST CHRISTMAS	400	12.00	13.00
94	DRUMMER BOY (BRASS)	14500	12.50	18.00
94	DRUMMER BOY (SILVER)	500	18.00	140.00

BING & GRONDAHL

YR	NAME	LIMIT	ISSUE	TREND
J. WOODSON				**CHRISTMAS IN AMERICA**
86	CHRISTMAS EVE IN WILLIAMSBURG	CL	12.50	90.00
87	CHRISTMAS EVE AT THE WHITE HOUSE	CL	15.00	16.00
88	CHRISTMAS EVE AT ROCKEFELLER CENTER	CL	18.50	19.00
89	CHRISTMAS IN NEW ENGLAND	YR	20.00	20.00
90	CHRISTMAS EVE AT THE CAPITOL	YR	20.00	20.00
91	INDEPENDENCE HALL	YR	23.50	24.00
92	CHRISTMAS IN SAN FRANCISCO	YR	25.00	25.00
93	COMING HOME FOR CHRISTMAS	YR	25.00	25.00
H. HANSEN				**SANTA CLAUS**
89	SANTA'S WORKSHOP	YR	20.00	20.00

YR	NAME	LIMIT	ISSUE	TREND
90	SANTA'S SLEIGH	YR	20.00	20.00
91	JOURNEY, THE	YR	23.50	24.00
92	SANTA'S ARRIVAL	YR	25.00	25.00
93	SANTA'S GIFTS	YR	25.00	25.00

BRANDYWINE WOODCRAFTS

M. WHITING — **WILLIAMSBURG ORNAMENTS**

YR	NAME	LIMIT	ISSUE	TREND
94	GUNSMITH	350	9.50	10.00

BRIERCROFT

B. FARLOW

YR	NAME	LIMIT	ISSUE	TREND
94	BELL ANGEL	5000	6.00	10.00

BUCCELLATI

***** — **CHRISTMAS ORNAMENTS**

YR	NAME	LIMIT	ISSUE	TREND
86	SNOWY VILLAGE SCENE-2464	500	195.00	400.00
87	SHOOTING STAR-2469	500	240.00	350.00
88	SANTA CLAUS-2470	500	225.00	300.00
89	CHRISTMAS TREE-2471	750	230.00	230.00
90	ZENITH-2479	750	250.00	250.00
91	WREATH-3561	750	300.00	300.00
92	CHERUBS 3562	500	300.00	300.00

G. BUCCELLATI — **CHRISTMAS ORNAMENTS**

YR	NAME	LIMIT	ISSUE	TREND
93	CHRISTMAS CANDLE	500	300.00	320.00
94	CHRISTMAS FIREPLACE	500	300.00	320.00

CARRIAGE HOUSE STUDIO INC.

M. FURLONG — **GIFTS FROM GOD**

YR	NAME	LIMIT	ISSUE	TREND
85	CHARIS ANGEL, THE	3000	45.00	100.00
86	ANGEL OF LIGHT, THE	3000	45.00	100.00
86	HALLELUJAH ANGEL, THE	3000	45.00	125.00
88	CELESTIAL ANGEL, THE	3000	45.00	100.00
89	CORONATION ANGEL	3000	45.00	60.00

M. FURLONG — **JOYEUX NOEL**

YR	NAME	LIMIT	ISSUE	TREND
90	CELEBRATION ANGEL	10000	45.00	45.00
91	THANKSGIVING ANGEL	10000	45.00	45.00
92	JOYEUX NOEL ANGEL	10000	45.00	45.00

M. FURLONG — **MUSICAL SERIES**

YR	NAME	LIMIT	ISSUE	TREND
80	CAROLER, THE	3000	50.00	100.00
81	LYRIST, THE	3000	45.00	60.00
82	LUTIST, THE	3000	45.00	75.00
83	CONCERTINIST, THE	3000	45.00	75.00
84	HERALD ANGEL, THE	3000	45.00	75.00

CAVANAGH GROUP

***** — **COCA-COLA BRAND HISTORICAL BUILDING**

YR	NAME	LIMIT	ISSUE	TREND
91	1930's SERVICE STATION	CL	9.99	12.00
91	EARLY COCA-COLA BOTTLING COMPANY	CL	9.99	12.00
91	JACOB'S PHARMACY	CL	9.99	12.00
91	PEMBERTON HOUSE, THE	CL	9.99	12.00

***** — **COCA-COLA BRAND NORTH POLE BOTTLING WORKS**

YR	NAME	LIMIT	ISSUE	TREND
93	BLAST OFF	OP	8.99	9.00
93	DELIVERY FOR SANTA	OP	8.99	9.00
93	FILL'ER UP	CL	8.99	10.00
93	ICE SCULPTING	OP	8.99	9.00
93	LONG WINTER'S NAP	OP	8.99	9.00
93	NORTH POLE EXPRESS	CL	8.99	10.00
93	THIRSTING FOR ADVENTURE	CL	8.99	10.00
93	TOPS ON REFRESHMENT	OP	8.99	9.00
94	POWER DRIVE	OP	8.99	9.00
94	SANTA'S RESTAURANT	OP	8.99	9.00
94	SELTZER SURPRISE	OP	8.99	9.00
94	TOPS OFF REFRESHMENT	OP	8.99	9.00
95	BARREL OF BEARS	OP	9.00	9.00
95	FOUNTAIN GLASS FOLLIES	OP	9.00	9.00
95	NORTH POLE FLYING SCHOOL	OP	9.00	9.00
96	REFRESHING SURPRISE	OP	9.00	9.00
96	RUSH DELIVERY	OP	9.00	9.00
96	TO: MRS. CLAUS	OP	9.00	9.00

***** — **COCA-COLA BRAND POLAR BEAR COLLECTION**

YR	NAME	LIMIT	ISSUE	TREND
94	DOWNHILL SLEDDER	OP	8.99	9.00
94	NORTH POLE DELIVERY	OP	8.99	9.00
94	SKATING COCA-COLA POLAR BEAR	OP	8.99	9.00
94	VENDING MACHINE MISCHIEF	OP	8.99	9.00
95	POLAR BEAR ON BOTTLE OPENER	OP	9.00	9.00
95	SNOWBOARDIN' BEAR	OP	9.00	9.00
96	CHRISTMAS STAR, THE	OP	9.00	9.00
96	HOLLYWOOD	OP	9.00	9.00

***** — **COCA-COLA BRAND TRIM A TREE COLLECTION**

YR	NAME	LIMIT	ISSUE	TREND
90	AWAY WITH A TIRED & THIRSTY FACE	CL	9.99	13.00
90	HOSPITALITY	CL	9.99	13.00
90	MERRY CHRISTMAS AND A HAPPY NEW YEAR	CL	9.99	53.00
90	SEASON'S GREETINGS	CL	9.99	13.00
91	A TIME TO SHARE	CL	9.99	12.00
91	CHRISTMAS IS LOVE	CL	9.99	12.00
92	HAPPY HOLIDAYS	CL	9.99	12.00
92	SSSHHH!	CL	9.99	12.00
93	DECORATING THE TREE	CL	9.99	11.00

YR	NAME	LIMIT	ISSUE	TREND
93	EXTRA BRIGHT REFRESHMENT	CL	9.99	11.00
93	TRAVEL REFRESHED	CL	9.99	11.00
94	BUSY MAN'S PAUSE	OP	9.99	10.00
94	FOR SPARKLING HOLIDAYS	OP	9.99	10.00
94	THINGS GO BETTER WITH COKE	OP	9.99	10.00
95	IT WILL REFRESH YOU TOO	OP	10.00	10.00
95	PLEASE PAUSE HERE	OP	10.00	10.00
96	PAUSE THAT REFRESHES, THE	OP	10.00	10.00
96	THEY REMEMBERED ME	OP	10.00	10.00
*			**MEMBER ORNAMENT**	
93	HO HO HO - SANTA	YR	*	*
94	FISHING BEAR	YR	*	*
95	HOSPITALITY - SANTA	YR	*	*
*			**THE COCA-COLA SANTA**	
95	CHRISTMAS IS LOVE	OP	10.00	10.00
95	SANTA AT THE MANTLE	OP	10.00	10.00
95	SSSHHH!	OP	10.00	10.00

CAZENOVIA ABROAD

YR	NAME	LIMIT	ISSUE	TREND
*			**CHRISTMAS ORNAMENTS**	
68	BUNNY P104B	*	9.00	40.00
68	CAT P105C	*	9.00	40.00
68	DUCK P103D	*	9.00	40.00
68	ELEPHANT P102E	*	9.00	40.00
68	ROOSTER P106R	*	10.00	40.00
68	STANDING ANGEL P107SA	*	9.00	45.00
68	TEDDY BEAR P101TB	*	9.00	40.00
68	TIPTOE ANGEL P108TTA	*	10.00	40.00
69	FAWN P109F	*	12.00	45.00
70	PEACE P111P	*	12.00	45.00
70	PORKY P112PK	*	15.00	45.00
70	SNOW MAN P110SM	*	12.00	45.00
71	KNEELING ANGEL P113KA	*	15.00	55.00
72	ROCKING HORSE P114RH	*	15.00	55.00
73	TREETOP ANGEL P115TOP	*	10.00	42.00
74	OWL P116O	*	15.00	45.00
75	STAR P117ST	*	15.00	45.00
76	HATCHING CHICK P118CH	*	15.00	45.00
77	RAGGEDY ANN P119RA	*	17.50	45.00
78	SHELL P120SH	*	20.00	40.00
79	TOY SOLDIER P121TS	*	20.00	40.00
80	BURRO P122BU	*	20.00	40.00
81	CLOWN P123CL	*	25.00	40.00
82	REBECCA P124RE	*	25.00	40.00
83	MOUSE P126MO	*	27.50	45.00
83	RAGGEDY ANDY P125AND	*	27.50	45.00
84	CHERUB P127CB	*	30.00	45.00
84	REINDEER & SLEIGH H100	*	1250.00	1500.00
85	SHAGGY DOG P132SD	*	45.00	50.00
86	BIG SISTER P134BS	*	60.00	60.00
86	LITTLE BROTHER P135LB	*	55.00	55.00
86	PETER RABBIT P133PR	*	50.00	50.00
87	LAMB P136LA	*	60.00	60.00
87	SEA HORSE P137SE	*	35.00	30.00
88	PARTRIDGE P138PA	*	70.00	70.00
88	SQUIRREL P139SQ	*	70.00	70.00
89	SWAN P140SW	OP	45.00	45.00
90	MORAVIAN STAR P141PS	OP	65.00	65.00
91	ANGEL P144A	OP	63.00	63.00
91	BUNNY RABBIT P143BR	OP	65.00	65.00
91	HEDGEHOG P142HH	OP	65.00	65.00
92	HUMPTY DUMPTY P145HD	OP	70.00	70.00

CHRISTINA'S WORLD

YR	NAME	LIMIT	ISSUE	TREND
*	**CHRISTINA**		**ABSTRACTS**	
94	OP ART 80 MM ART970	48	9.00	9.00
*	**CHRISTINA**		**HUNDERTWASSER**	
94	BLUE SEA & GOLDEN SHIPS HUN 853	48	13.00	13.00
94	GOLDEN ONION DOMES HUN852	48	13.00	13.00
94	RED ONION DOMES HUN854	48	13.00	13.00
*	**CHRISTINA**		**KIMONO PRINTS**	
94	MANDARIN GLITTER FANS ART995	48	13.00	13.00
94	SILVER GREY GLITTER MOUNTAINS ART95	48	13.00	13.00
*	**CHRISTINA**		**MARDI GRAS**	
94	RED GLACIER 115MM MAR662	48	18.00	18.00
*	**CHRISTINA**		**MATISSE REMEMBERED**	
94	MATISSE UMBRELLA	200	18.00	18.00
*	**CHRISTINA**		**SECRET GARDEN**	
95	90 MM ETCHED FEATHER GAR916	96	9.00	9.00

CYBIS

YR	NAME	LIMIT	ISSUE	TREND
*			**CHRISTMAS COLLECTION**	
83	1983 HOLIDAY BELL	YR	145.00	1000.00
84	1984 HOLIDAY BELL	YR	145.00	700.00
85	1985 HOLIDAY ANGEL	YR	75.00	500.00
86	1986 HOLIDAY CHERUB ORNAMENT	YR	75.00	500.00
87	1987 HEAVENLY ANGELS	YR	95.00	400.00

YR	NAME	LIMIT	ISSUE	TREND
88	1988 HOLIDAY ORNAMENT	YR	95.00	375.00

DAVE GROSSMAN CREATIONS

YR	NAME	LIMIT	ISSUE	TREND
*		**ANNUAL ROCKWELL BALL ORNAMENTS**		
75	SANTA WITH FEATHER QUILL	RT	3.50	25.00
76	SANTA AT GLOBE	RT	4.00	20.00
77	GRANDPA ON ROCKING HORSE	RT	4.00	15.00
78	SANTA WITH MAP	RT	4.50	15.00
79	SANTA AT DESK WITH MAIL BAG	RT	5.00	15.00
80	SANTA ASLEEP WITH TOYS	RT	5.00	12.00
81	SANTA WITH BOY ON FINGER	RT	5.00	10.00
82	SANTA FACE ON WINTER SCENE	RT	5.00	10.00
83	COACHMAN WITH WHIP	RT	5.00	10.00
84	CHRISTMAS BOUNTY MAN	RT	5.00	10.00
85	OLD ENGLISH TRIO	RT	5.00	10.00
86	TINY TIM ON SHOULDER	RT	5.00	5.00
87	SKATING LESSON	RT	5.00	5.00
88	BIG MOMENT	RT	5.50	5.50
89	DISCOVERY	RT	6.00	6.00
90	BRINGING HOME THE TREE	RT	6.00	6.00
91	DOWNHILL DARING	RT	6.00	6.00
92	ON THE ICE	YR	6.00	6.00
93	GRANPS	YR	24.00	28.00
94	COMMEMORATIVE	YR	6.00	8.00
94	TRIPLE SELF PORTRAIT	OP	30.00	35.00
*		**ANNUAL ROCKWELL FIGURINE ORNAMENTS**		
78	CAROLER	RT	15.00	75.00
79	DRUM FOR TOMMY	RT	20.00	50.00
80	SANTA'S GOOD BOYS	RT	20.00	40.00
81	LETTERS TO SANTA	RT	20.00	40.00
82	CORNETTIST	RT	20.00	30.00
83	FIDDLER	RT	20.00	30.00
84	CHRISTMAS BOUNTY	RT	20.00	30.00
85	JOLLY COACHMAN	RT	20.00	30.00
86	GRANDPA AND ROCKING HORSE	RT	20.00	35.00
87	SKATING LESSON	RT	20.00	30.00
88	BIG MOMENT	RT	20.00	30.00
89	DISCOVERY	RT	20.00	25.00
90	BRINGING HOME THE TREE	RT	20.00	20.00
91	DOWNHILL DARING	RT	20.00	20.00
92	ON THE ICE	YR	20.00	20.00
93	GRANPS	YR	6.00	8.00
94	MERRY CHRISTMAS	*	24.00	28.00
ROCKWELL INSPIRED		**CHARACTER DOLL ORNAMENTS**		
83	DOCTOR AND DOLL	RT	20.00	30.00
83	LOVERS	RT	20.00	30.00
83	SAMPLERS	RT	20.00	30.00
*		**EMMETT KELLY ANNUAL FIGURINE ORNAMENT**		
92	CHRISTMAS TUNES	YR	15.00	16.00
B. LEIGHTON JONES		**EMMETT KELLY ANNUAL FIGURINE ORNAMENT**		
86	A CHRISTMAS CAROL	CL	12.00	12.00
87	CHRISTMAS WREATH	CL	14.00	14.00
88	CHRISTMAS DINNER	CL	15.00	16.00
89	CHRISTMAS FEAST	YR	15.00	16.00
90	JUST WHAT I NEEDED	YR	15.00	16.00
91	EMMETT THE SNOWMAN	YR	15.00	16.00
B. LEIGHTON-JONES		**EMMETT KELLY ANNUAL ORNAMENT**		
93	DOWNHILL ORNAMENT	YR	20.00	24.00
B. LEIGHTON-JONES		**EMMETT KELLY ORIGINAL CIRCUS COLLECTION**		
94	HOLIDAY SKATER	*	20.00	24.00
*		**GONE WITH THE WIND ORNAMENT**		
92	SCARLETT-GREEN DRESS	YR	20.00	20.00
93	GWO-93 ORNAMENT	*	20.00	24.00
94	GOLD PLATED DISC ORNAMENT	OP	13.00	15.00
94	LIMITED EDITION ORNAMENT	*	25.00	28.00
94	LIMITED EDITION ORNAMENT	*	20.00	24.00
R. BROWN		**GONE WITH THE WIND ORNAMENT**		
91	PRISSY	YR	20.00	20.00
91	PRISSY	CL	20.00	20.00
D. GEENTY		**GONE WITH THE WIND ORNAMENT**		
87	ASHLEY	CL	15.00	45.00
87	RHETT	CL	15.00	45.00
87	SCARLETT	CL	15.00	45.00
87	TARA	CL	15.00	45.00
88	RHETT AND SCARLETT	CL	20.00	40.00
89	MAMMY	CL	20.00	20.00
90	SCARLETT-RED DRESS	CL	20.00	20.00

DEPARTMENT 56

Price ranges may reflect various demands in the market from one geographic region to another; condition of piece; specific markings found on piece; and/or changes in production of piece.

YR	NAME	LIMIT	ISSUE	TREND
*		**CCP ORNAMENTS**		
86	APOTHECARY SHOP	CL	3.50	20.00
86	CHRISTMAS CAROL VILLAGE (SET OF 3)	CL	13.00	35.00
86	GENERAL STORE	CL	3.50	20.00
86	LIVERY STABLE & BOOT SHOP	CL	3.50	20.00
86	NATHANIEL BINGHAM FABRICS	CL	3.50	20.00

YR	NAME	LIMIT	ISSUE	TREND
86	NEW ENGLAND VILLAGE (SET OF 7)	CL	25.00	*
86	RED SCHOOLHOUSE	CL	3.50	20.00
86	SCROOGE	CL	4.35	16.00
86	STEEPLE CHURCH	CL	3.50	20.00
*		**CHRISTMAS CAROL CHARACTER ORNAMENTS**		
86	BOB CRATCHIT & TINY TIM	CL	4.35	16.00
86	CHRISTMAS CAROL CHARACTERS (SET OF 3)	CL	13.00	35.00
86	POULTERER	CL	4.35	16.00
*		**DICKENS' VILLAGE**		
94	DEDLOCK ARMS INN 9872-8	RT	12.50	10.00
95	SIR JOHN FALSTAFF INN 9870-1	RT	15.00	10.00
*		**MISCELLANEOUS ORNAMENTS**		
84	DICKENS TIN ORNAMENTS (SET OF 6)	CL	12.00	165.00
88	BALSAM BELL BRASS DICKENS' CANDLESTICK	CL	3.00	10.00
88	BOB & MRS. CRATCHIT	CL	18.00	33.00-38.00
88	SCROOGE'S HEAD	CL	12.95	24.00
88	TINY TIM'S HEAD	CL	10.00	24.00
*		**SNOWBABIES ORNAMENTS**		
86	CRAWLING, LITE-UP, CLIP-ON 7953-7	OP	7.00	8.00
86	ORNAMENT ON BRASS RIBBON 7961-8	RT	8.00	50.00
86	SITTING, LITE-UP, CLIP-ON 7952-9	RT	7.00	32.00
86	WINGED, LITE-UP, CLIP-ON 7954-5	RT	7.00	35.00
87	ADRIFT, LITE-UP, CLIP-ON	RT	8.50	100.00
87	MINI, LITE-UP, CLIP-ON 7976-6	OP	9.00	12.00
87	MOON BEAMS 7951-0	OP	7.50	9.00
88	TWINKLE LITTLE STAR 7980-4	RT	7.00	25.00
89	NOEL 7988-0	OP	7.50	8.00
89	STAR BRIGHT 7990-1	OP	7.50	8.00
89	SURPRISE 7989-8	OP	12.00	12.00
90	PENGUIN, LITE-UP, CLIP ON 7940-5	OP	5.00	5.00
90	POLAR BEAR, LITE-UP, CLIP-ON 7941-3	OP	5.00	5.00
90	ROCK-A-BYE BABY 7939-1	RT	7.00	7.00
91	MY FIRST STAR 6811-0	OP	7.00	7.00
91	MY FIRST STAR 6811-0	OP	7.00	7.00
91	SWINGING ON A STAR 6810-1	OP	9.50	10.00
91	SWINGING ON A STAR 6810-1	OP	9.50	10.00
93	SPRINKLING STARS IN THE SKY 6848-9	OP	13.50	14.00
93	WEE... THIS IS FUN! 6847-9	OP	13.50	14.00
*		**VILLAGE LIGHT-UP ORNAMENTS**		
85	ABEL BEASLEY BUTCHER	CL	6.00	20.00
85	BEAN AND SON SMITHY SHOP	CL	6.00	20.00
85	CANDLE SHOP	CL	6.00	16.00
85	CROWNTREE INN	CL	6.00	16.00
85	DICKENS' VILLAGE (SET OF 8)	CL	48.00	150.00
85	DICKENS' VILLAGE CHURCH	CL	6.00	26.00
85	GOLDEN SWAN BAKER	CL	6.00	20.00
85	GREEN GROCER	CL	6.00	20.00
85	JONES & CO. BRUSH & BASKET SHOP	CL	6.00	20.00
86	APOTHECARY SHOP	CL	6.00	16.00
86	BRICK TOWN HALL	CL	6.00	19.00
86	GENERAL STORE	CL	6.00	22.00
86	LIVERY STABLE & BOOT SHOP	CL	6.00	18.00
86	NATHANIEL BINGHAM FABRICS	CL	6.00	18.00
86	NEW ENGLAND VILLAGE (SET OF 7)	CL	42.00	200.00
86	RED SCHOOLHOUSE	CL	6.00	60.00-75.00
86	STEEPLE CHURCH	CL	6.00	75.00-130.00
87	BARLEY BREE FARMHOUSE	CL	6.00	20.00
87	BLYTHE POND MILL HOUSE	CL	6.00	18.00
87	BRICK ABBEY	CL	6.00	35.00-75.00
87	CHESTERTON MANOR HOUSE	CL	6.00	20.00
87	CHRISTMAS CAROL COTTAGES (SET OF 3)	CL	16.95	45.00
87	COTTAGE OF BOB CRATCHIT & TINY TIM, THE	CL	6.00	15.00
87	CRAGGY COVE LIGHTHOUSE	CL	6.00	100.00
87	DICKENS' VILLAGE (SET OF 6)	CL	36.00	130.00
87	FEZZIWIG'S WAREHOUSE	CL	6.00	15.00
87	JACOB ADAMS BARN	CL	6.00	22.00
87	JACOB ADAMS FARMHOUSE	CL	6.00	25.00
87	KENILWORTH CASTLE	CL	6.00	22.00
87	NEW ENGLAND VILLAGE (SET OF 6)	CL	36.00	200.00
87	OLD CURIOSITY SHOP, THE	CL	6.00	18.00
87	SCROOGE & MARLEY COUNTINGHOUSE	CL	6.00	15.00
87	SMYTHE WOOLEN MILL	CL	6.00	25.00
87	TIMBER KNOLL LOG CABIN	CL	6.00	27.00
87	WESTON TRAIN STATION	CL	6.00	22.00

ENESCO

Price ranges may reflect various demands in the market from one geographic region to another; condition of piece; specific markings found on piece; and/or changes in production of piece.

YR	NAME	LIMIT	ISSUE	TREND
*		**ANGEL SERIES-DATED**		
89	WARM WISHES AND HAPPINESS-117706	YR	12.00	12.00
90	CHRISTMAS IS A TIME OF LOVE-119970	YR	17.00	17.00
90	XMAS BRING JOY OF BEAUT. SEASON-120413	YR	35.00	35.00
*		**BABY'S FIRST CHRISTMAS-DATED SERIES**		
89	SOMEWHERE IN THE EVENING SKY-117587	YR	12.00	15.00
90	MAY BABY'S FIRST XMAS BE FILLED-119741	YR	17.00	17.00
P. HILLMAN		**CALICO KITTENS FOR YOU WITH MESSAGES**		
96	TITLE N/A 178497	*	12.50	12.50

YR	NAME	LIMIT	ISSUE	TREND
P. HILLMAN		**CALICO KITTENS I LOVE MY KITTY**		
95	BIRD SEED FROM KITTY 144355	*	13.50	14.00
95	I LOVE MY CAT 144320	*	11.00	11.00
95	MERRY CHRISTMAS KITTY 144266	*	11.00	11.00
95	TITLE N/A	*	11.00	11.00
95	TITLE N/A	*	11.00	11.00
95	TO MY CAT 144398	*	11.00	11.00
95	TO MY KITTY 144274	*	11.00	11.00
P. HILLMAN		**CALICO KITTENS ITTY BITTY KITTY CHRISTMAS KITTY**		
96	TITLE N/A 178462	*	7.00	7.00
96	TITLE N/A 178489	*	12.50	12.50
96	TITLE N/A 178500	*	12.50	12.50
96	TITLE N/A 178519	*	12.50	12.50
96	TITLE N/A 178551	*	10.00	10.00
P. HILLMAN		**CHERISHED TEDDIES**		
95	BABY ANGEL ON CLOUD 141240	OP	13.50	14.00
95	BOY AND GIRL WITH BANNER 141259	*	13.50	20.00
95	YOU'RE SKATED INTO MY HEART 141232	YR	12.50	13.00
96	BEAR W/DANGLING MITTENS 177768	*	12.50	12.50
P. HILLMAN		**CHERISHED TEDDIES CHRISTMAS**		
92	ANGEL BEAR	*	12.50	55.00
92	BEAR IN STOCKING	*	16.00	50.00
92	BEAR ON ROCKING REINDEER	*	20.00	45.00
92	SISTER WITH BLUE HAT	*	12.50	21.00
92	SISTER WITH RED HAT	*	12.50	21.00
92	SISTER WITH SANTA'S CAP	*	12.50	21.00
93	ANGEL WITH BELLS	OP	12.50	13.00
93	ANGEL WITH HARP	OP	12.50	13.00
93	ANGEL WITH HORN	OP	12.50	13.00
93	BABY BOY'S FIRST CHRISTMAS	*	12.50	32.00
93	BABY GIRL'S FIRST CHRISTMAS	*	12.50	36.00
93	BEAR IN SANTA CAP	*	12.50	20.00
93	GIRL WITH MUFF	*	13.50	50.00
94	BABY IN BASKET	*	15.00	40.00
94	BEARS IN SLED	*	15.00	37.00
94	DRUMMER BOY	*	10.00	30.00
95	BEAR WITH ICE SKATES	*	12.50	20.00
P. HILLMAN		**CHERISHED TEDDIES HOLIDAY DANGLING**		
96	JOY AND HO HO	*	12.50	12.50
P. HILLMAN		**CHERISHED TEDDIES MESSENGERS OF THE HEART**		
95	BOY BEAR FLYING CUPID	*	13.00	20.00
95	GIRL BEAR FLYING CUPID	*	13.00	20.00
P. HILLMAN		**CHERISHED TEDDIES SANTA'S WORKSHOP**		
95	ELF BEAR WITH CANDY CANE 651389	*	12.50	15.00
95	ELF BEAR WITH DOLL 625434	*	12.50	15.00
95	ELF BEAR WITH REINDEER TOY 625442	*	12.50	15.00
95	MRS. CLAUS HOLDING TRAY OF COOKIES 62542	*	12.50	21.00
95	SANTA BEAR 651370	*	12.50	15.00
*		**FROM BARBIE WITH LOVE**		
96	BARBIE AS S. O'HARA IN GRN VELVET 182028	YR	12.50	12.50
96	DECOUPAGE HEART 189103	*	9.00	9.00
96	DECOUPAGE ROUND 189030	*	7.50	8.00
96	HAPPY HOLIDAY BARBIE, 1989 188867	YR	12.50	12.50
96	HAPPY HOLIDAY BARBIE, 1996 188824	YR	12.50	12.50
96	HOLIDAY DANCE 1965 188808	*	12.50	12.50
96	QUEEN OF HEARTS BARBIE 157724	*	9.00	9.00
K. WICKL		**GNOMES**		
96	KARL, RESIN 195502	*	*	*
96	WILLIE. RESIN 153273	*	*	*
S. BUTCHER		**JOY TO THE WORLD**		
95	JOY TO THE WORLD 1ST ISSUE 150320	OP	20.00	20.00
96	JOY TO THE WORLD 2ND ISSUE 153338	OP	20.00	20.00
KINKA		**KINKA**		
89	BABIES ARE CHRISTMAS DREAMS-117722	OP	15.00	16.00
89	MAY THE CHRISTMAS STAR TOUCH-117595	OP	13.50	14.00
89	MAY THIS SEASON BE FILLED WITH-117714	OP	13.50	14.00
89	MAY YOU SHARE A NEW YEAR FILLED-119733	OP	22.50	23.00
89	SOMEWHERE IN THE EVENING SKY-117587	YR	12.00	15.00
89	WARM WISHES AND EVERY HAPPINESS-117706	YR	12.00	12.00
90	LOVE TO YOU-119954	YR	13.50	*
90	MAY CHRISTMAS BRING YOU-120413	YR	35.00	*
91	CHRISTMAS IS A TIME WHEN GOD-122742	YR	22.50	23.00
91	MAY THE TRUE SPIRIT-122750 (DATED)	YR	40.00	40.00
91	MAY THIS SPECIAL SEASON-122696	OP	22.50	23.00
91	MEMORIES ARE MADE OF-122661	OP	22.50	23.00
91	WISHING YOU SPECIAL BLESSINGS-122785	YR	17.50	18.00
92	CHRISTMAS IS LOVE-125369	OP	10.00	10.00
92	HEAVEN'S BUNDLE OF JOY-122734	OP	10.00	10.00
92	LIFE IS ONE JOYOUS STEP-125350	OP	10.00	10.00
92	LOVE TO YOU/THIS WONDROUS TIME-119954	OP	7.50	8.00
92	MAY THE CHRISTMAS STAR TOUCH-117595	OP	7.50	8.00
92	MAY THIS SEASON BE FILLED W/JOY-117714	OP	7.50	8.00
92	MAY THIS SPECIAL SEASON-122688	OP	11.25	12.00
92	MEMORIES ARE MADE OF SIMPLE JOYS-122661	OP	11.25	12.00
92	SOUND OF LOVE IS FELT, THE-120693	OP	10.00	10.00
92	SWEET MUSIC & BEAUTIFUL MEMORIES-120707	OP	10.00	10.00

Angelic Guide *lights the way as* Hear Ye, Hear Ye *proclaims his joy for the season. Each was based on artwork by M.I. Hummel and introduced in 1991 by Goebel.*

Inspired by Walt Disney's animation classic "Fantasia," Flight of Fancy *was available only at 1994 Walt Disney Classics Collection dealer events.*

Ladies and gentlemen, start your engines. This Hallmark Keepsake Ornament titled 1957 Corvette *is one fine dream machine.*

Hamilton Gifts released these six ornaments in 1991. Artist Maud Humphrey Bogart's open edition pieces, including Cleaning House *and* My First Dance, *sold for $24 each.*

YR	NAME	LIMIT	ISSUE	TREND
*** RHYNER-NADIG**		**MARY'S MOO MOOS COWABUNGAS**		
96	I LOVE MOO	OP	7.50	7.50
96	SHUCK'S YOU'RE SWEET	OP	7.50	7.50
96	UDDERLY WONDERFUL	OP	7.50	7.50
*** RHYNER-NADIG**		**MARY'S MOO MOOS MOO SENGERS OF LOVE**		
96	CUPID H/O W/STAND	OP	6.75	6.75
96	GIRL/HEART H/O	OP	6.75	6.75
*** RHYNER-NADIG**		**MARY'S MOO MOOS MOOEY CHRISTMAS**		
96	BABY'S 1ST CHRISTMAS	OP	12.50	12.50
96	BOY/GIRL ON SLED	OP	12.50	12.50
96	COWBOY	OP	12.50	12.50
96	GIRL SKATER	OP	12.50	12.50
96	SANTA/DATED	OP	6.25	6.25
96	WHEEE ARE MOOVIN!	YR	25.00	25.00
M. ATTWELL		**MEMORIES OF YESTERDAY**		
88	BABY'S FIRST CHRISTMAS 1988-520373	YR	13.50	22.00
88	BABY'S FIRST CHRISTMAS-520373	YR	13.50	30.00
88	SPECIAL DELIVERY! 1988-520381	YR	13.50	28.00
88	SPECIAL DELIVERY!-520381	YR	13.50	35.00
89	A SURPRISE FOR SANTA-522473	YR	13.50	22.00
89	A SURPRISE FOR SANTA-522473 (1989)	YR	13.50	20.00
89	BABY'S FIRST CHRISTMAS-522465	OP	15.00	22.00
89	BABY'S FIRST CHRISTMAS-522465	OP	15.00	20.00
89	CHRISTMAS TOGETHER-522562	OP	15.00	34.00
89	CHRISTMAS TOGETHER-522562	OP	15.00	25.00
90	MOONSTRUCK-524794	OP	15.00	16.00
90	MOONSTRUCK-524794	RT	15.00	20.00
90	NEW MOON-524646	OP	15.00	16.00
90	NEW MOON-524646	OP	15.00	25.00
90	TIME FOR BED-524638	YR	15.00	16.00
90	TIME FOR BED-524638	YR	15.00	25.00
91	JUST WATCHIN' OVER YOU-525421	OP	17.50	18.00
91	JUST WATCHIN' OVER YOU-525421	OP	17.50	18.00
91	LUCKY ME-525448	OP	16.00	16.00
91	LUCKY ME-525448	OP	16.00	16.00
91	LUCKY YOU-525847	OP	16.00	16.00
91	LUCKY YOU-525847	OP	16.00	16.00
91	S'NO USE LOOKIN' BACK NOW!-52718	YR	17.50	18.00
91	S'NO USE LOOKIN' BACK NOW!-527181	YR	17.50	18.00
91	STAR FISHIN'-525820	OP	16.00	16.00
91	STAR FISHIN-525820	OP	16.00	16.00
92	I'LL FLY ALONG TO SEE YOU SOON-525804	YR	16.00	16.00
92	MERRY CHRISTMAS, LITTLE BOO-BOO-528803	OP	37.50	38.00
92	MOMMY, I TEARED IT-527041	YR	15.00	16.00
92	SAILIN' WITH MY FRIENDS-587575	OP	25.00	25.00
92	STAR LIGHT, STAR BRIGHT-528838	OP	16.00	16.00
92	SWINGING TOGETHER-580481	YR	17.50	18.00
93	HOW 'BOUT A LITTLE KISS?	OP	16.50	17.00
93	WISH I COULD FLY TO YOU?	OP	16.00	16.00
94	GIVE YOURSELF A HUG FROM ME	OP	17.50	18.00
95	HAPPY LANDINGS	YR	16.00	16.00
95	I PRAY THE LORD MY SOUL TO KEEP	OP	15.00	15.00
95	NOW I LAY ME DOWN TO SLEEP	OP	15.00	15.00
96	CAN I KEEP HER, MOMMY?	OP	13.50	13.50
M. ATTWELL		**MEMORIES OF YESTERDAY FRIENDSHIP**		
96	I LOVE YOU THIS MUCH!	OP	13.50	13.50
M. ATTWELL		**MEMORIES OF YESTERDAY SOCIETY MEMBERS ONLY**		
92	WITH LUCK/I'S IN HEAVEN-MY922	YR	16.00	16.00
93	I'M BRINGING GOOD LUCK-WHEREVER YOU ARE	OP	16.00	16.00
M. ATTWELL		**MEMORIES OF YESTERDAY-WINTER MEMORIES SERIES**		
89	I'SE SWINGIN'-564923 (DATED)	YR	15.00	30.00
90	MAY EVERYTHING GO WITH A SWING-569550	YR	16.00	16.00
91	SWING WITH ME-580473 (DATED	YR	16.00	16.00
S. BUTCHER		**PRECIOUS MOMENTS**		
80	BABY'S FIRST CHRISTMAS E-5631	SU	6.00	40.00-80.00
80	BABY'S FIRST CHRISTMAS E-5632	SU	6.00	40.00-80.00
80	WE HAVE SEEN HIS STAR E-6120	RT	9.00	60.00
80	WEE THREE KINGS (3PC SET) E-5634	SU	25.00	150.00
81	BUT LOVE GOES ON FOREVER E-5627	SU	6.00	115.00
81	BUT LOVE GOES ON FOREVER E-5628	SU	6.00	110.00
81	COME LET US ADORE HIM (4PC SET) E-5633	SU	20.00	135.00
81	LET THE HEAVENS REJOICE E-5629	YR	6.00	260.00
81	UNTO US A CHILD IS BORN E-5630	SU	6.00	65.00
82	BABY'S FIRST CHRISTMAS E-2362	SU	9.00	40.00
82	BABY'S FIRST CHRISTMAS E-2372	SU	9.00	45.00
82	BABY'S FIRST CHRISTMAS E2362	SU	9.00	40.00
82	CAMEL, DONKEY & COW (3 PC SET) E-2386	SU	25.00	100.00
82	DROPPING IN FOR CHRISTMAS E-2369	RT	9.00	40.00-75.00
82	DROPPING OVER FOR CHRISTMAS E-2376	RT	9.00	65.00
82	FIRST NOEL , THE-E-2367	SU	9.00	55.00
82	FIRST NOEL, THE- E-2368	RT	9.00	35.00-75.00
82	I'LL PLAY MY DRUM FOR HIM E-2359	YR	9.00	85.00
82	I'LL PLAY MY DRUM FOR HIM E2359	OP	9.00	85.00
82	JOY TO THE WORLD E-2343	SU	9.00	45.00
82	MOUSE WITH CHEESE E-2381	SU	9.00	135.00
82	OUR FIRST CHRISTMAS TOGETHER E-2385	OP	9.00	35.00
82	OUR FIRST CHRISTMAS TOGETHER E2385	SU	9.00	45.00
82	SET OF 3-CAMEL, DONKEY & COW E2386	SU	25.00	100.00

YR	NAME	LIMIT	ISSUE	TREND
82	UNICORN E-2371	RT	9.00	60.00
83	BLESSED ARE THE PURE IN HEART E-0518	YR	9.00	45.00
83	JESUS IS THE LIGHT THAT SHINES E-0537	SU	9.00	65.00
83	LET HEAVEN AND NATURE SING E-0532	RT	9.00	45.00
83	LOVE IS PATIENT E-0535	SU	9.00	55.00
83	LOVE IS PATIENT E-0536	SU	9.00	60.00
83	MOTHER SEW DEAR E-0514	OP	9.00	24.00
83	O COME ALL YE FAITHFUL E-0531	SU	10.00	55.00
83	PERFECT GRANDPA, THE- E-0517	SU	9.00	40.00
83	PURR-FECT GRANDMA, THE- E-0516	OP	9.00	27.00
83	SURROUND US WITH JOY E-0513	YR	9.00	55.00
83	TELL ME THE STORY OF JESUS E-0533	SU	9.00	50.00
83	TO A SPECIAL DAD E-0515	SU	9.00	45.00
83	TO THEE WITH LOVE E-0534	RT	9.00	45.00
84	BLESSED ARE THE PURE IN HEART E-5392	YR	10.00	32.00
84	HAVE A HEAVENLY CHRISTMAS 12416	OP	12.00	30.00
84	JOY TO THE WORLD E-5388	RT	10.00	45.00
84	LOVE IS KIND E-5391	SU	10.00	35.00
84	MAY GOD BLESS YOU/PERFECT SEASON E-5390	SU	10.00	35.00
84	PEACE ON EARTH E-5389	SU	10.00	35.00
84	WISHING YOU A MERRY CHRISTMAS E-5387	YR	10.00	30.00
85	ANGEL OF MERCY 102407	OP	10.00	20.00
85	BABY'S FIRST CHRISTMAS 102504	YR	10.00	32.00
85	BABY'S FIRST CHRISTMAS 102512	YR	10.00	30.00
85	BABY'S FIRST CHRISTMAS 15903	YR	10.00	45.00
85	BABY'S FIRST CHRISTMAS 15911	YR	10.00	35.00
85	GOD SENT HIS LOVE 15768	YR	10.00	30.00
85	HAPPINESS IS THE LORD 15830	SU	10.00	32.00
85	HONK IF YOU LOVE JESUS 15857	SU	10.00	25.00
85	IT'S A PERFECT BOY 102415	SU	10.00	25.00
85	LORD KEEP ME ON MY TOES 102423	RT	10.00	45.00
85	LOVE RESCUE ME 102385	OP	10.00	22.00
85	MAY YOUR CHRISTMAS BE DELIGHTFUL 15849	SU	10.00	25.00
85	MAY YOUR CHRISTMAS BE HAPPY 15822	SU	10.00	35.00
85	OUR FIRST CHRISTMAS TOGETHER 102350	YR	10.00	30.00
85	ROCKING HORSE 102474	SU	10.00	25.00
85	SERVE WITH A SMILE 102431	SU	10.00	30.00
85	SERVE WITH A SMILE 102458	SU	10.00	30.00
85	SHEPHERD OF LOVE 102288	SU	10.00	25.00
85	TRUST AND OBEY 102377	OP	10.00	22.00
85	WISHING YOU A COZY CHRISTMAS 102326	YR	10.00	32.00
86	BABY'S FIRST CHRISTMAS 109401	YR	12.00	45.00
86	BABY'S FIRST CHRISTMAS 109428	YR	12.00	45.00
86	HE CLEANSED MY SOUL 112380	OP	12.00	24.00
86	I'M A POSSIBILITY 111120	SU	10.00	27.00
86	I'M SENDING YOU A WHITE CHRISTMAS 112372	SU	11.00	27.00
86	LOVE IS THE BEST GIFT OF ALL 109770	YR	11.00	30.00
86	OUR FIRST CHRISTMAS TOGETHER 112399	YR	11.00	30.00
86	REINDEER 102466	YR	11.00	175.00
86	WADDLE I DO WITHOUT YOU 112364	OP	10.00	20.00
86	YOU HAVE TOUCHED SO MANY HEARTS 112356	OP	10.00	20.00
87	BABY'S FIRST CHRISTMAS 109401	YR	12.00	45.00
87	BABY'S FIRST CHRISTMAS 109428	YR	12.00	45.00
87	BEAR THE GOOD NEWS IF CHRISTMAS 104515	YR	11.00	30.00
87	DASHING THROUGH THE SNOW 521574	OP	15.00	20.00
87	I'M A POSSIBILITY 111120	OP	10.00	25.00
88	A GROWING LOVE 520349	*	*	85.00
88	ALWAYS ROOM FOR ONE MORE 522961	OP	*	100.00
88	BABY'S FIRST CHRISTMAS 115282	YR	15.00	30.00
88	BABY'S FIRST CHRISTMAS 520241	YR	13.00	30.00
88	BABY'S FIRST CHRISTMAS 523194	YR	15.00	25.00
88	BABY'S FIRST CHRISTMAS 523208	YR	15.00	25.00
88	CHEERS TO THE LEADER 113999	SU	13.50	35.00
88	CHRISTMAS IS RUFF WITHOUT YOU 520462	YR	13.00	32.00
88	DON'T LET THE HOLIDAYS..DOWN 521590	OP	15.00	20.00
88	GLIDE THROUGH THE HOLIDAYS 521566	RT	13.50	35.00
88	GOD SENT YOU JUST IN TIME 113972	SU	13.50	35.00
88	HANG ON FOR THE HOLLY DAYS 520292	YR	13.00	25.00
88	I BELIEVE IN THE OLD RUGGED CROSS 522953	OP	15.00	20.00
88	MAKE A JOYFUL NOISE 522910	SU	15.00	19.00
88	MAY ALL YOUR CHRISTMASES..521302	OP	13.50	20.00
88	MY LOVE WILL NEVER LET YOU GO 114006	SU	13.50	33.00
88	OH HOLY NIGHT 522848	YR	13.50	32.00
88	OUR FIRST CHRISTMAS TOGETHER 520233	YR	13.00	21.00
88	OUR FIRST CHRISTMAS TOGETHER 521558	YR	17.50	35.00
88	PEACE ON EARTH 523062	YR	25.00	75.00
88	REJOICE O EARTH 113980	RT	13.50	40.00
88	SMILE ALONG THE WAY 113964	SU	15.00	26.00
88	TIME TO WISH YOU/MERRY CHRISTMAS 115320	YR	13.00	45.00
88	TO MY FOREVER FRIEND 113956	OP	16.00	25.00
88	YOU ARE MY GIFT COME TRUE 520276	YR	12.50	19.00
89	BABY'S FIRST CHRISTMAS 523771	YR	15.00	22.00
89	BABY'S FIRST CHRISTMAS 523798	YR	15.00	22.00
89	BUNDLES OF JOY 525057	LE	17.50	32.00
89	CELEBRATING...SHARING & CARING 227986	YR	7.00	10.00
89	FRIENDS NEVER DRIFT APART 522937	RT	17.50	19.00
89	HAPPY TRAILS IS TRUSTING JESUS 523224	OP	15.00	20.00
89	LOVE ONE ANOTHER 522929	OP	17.50	20.00
89	MAY YOUR CHRISTMAS BE/HAPPY HOME 523704	YR	27.50	50.00

YR	NAME	LIMIT	ISSUE	TREND
89	OH HOLY NIGHT 522848	YR	13.50	40.00
89	ONCE UPON A HOLY NIGHT 523852	YR	15.00	30.00
89	OUR FIRST CHRISTMAS TOGETHER 522945	YR	17.50	27.00
89	OUR FIRST CHRISTMAS TOGETHER 525324	YR	17.50	30.00
89	WISHING YOU A PURR-FECT HOLIDAY 520497	YR	15.00	30.00
90	A UNIVERSAL LOVE 238899	YR	8.00	12.00
90	BABY'S FIRST CHIRSTMAS (BOY) 527084	YR	15.00	22.00
90	BABY'S FIRST CHIRSTMAS (GIRL) 527092	YR	15.00	25.00
90	GOOD LORD ALWAYS DELIVERS, THE- 527165	SU	15.00	20.00
90	MAY YOUR CHRISTMAS BE MERRY 524174	YR	15.00	30.00
90	MAY YOUR CHRISTMAS BE MERRY 526940	YR	30.00	35.00
90	SHARING A GIFT OF LOVE 233196	YR	8.00	8.00
90	SNO-BUNNY FALLS FOR YOU LIKE I DO 520438	YR	15.00	28.00
91	MAY YOUR CHRISTMAS BE MERRY 526940	YR	30.00	40.00
92	15 YEARS-TWEET MUSIC TOGETHER 530840	LE	15.00	20.00
92	BABY'S FIRST CHRISTMAS 527475	YR	15.00	19.00
92	BABY'S FIRST CHRISTMAS 527483	YR	15.00	19.00
92	BABY'S FIRST CHRISTMAS 530859	YR	15.00	19.00
92	BABY'S FIRST CHRISTMAS 530867	YR	15.00	19.00
92	BUT THE GREATEST OF THESE IS LOVE 527696	YR	15.00	24.00
92	BUT THE GREATEST OF THESE IS LOVE 527734	YR	30.00	32.00
92	GOOD FRIENDS ARE FOR ALWAYS 524131	OP	15.00	18.00
92	I'M NUTS ABOUT YOU 520411	YR	16.00	27.00
92	IT'S SO UPLIFTING...FRIEND...YOU 528846	OP	16.00	17.00
92	LORD KEEP ME ON MY TOES 525332	OP	15.00	17.00
92	OUR FIRST CHRISTMAS TOGETHER 528870	YR	17.50	21.00
92	OUR FIRST CHRISTMAS TOGETHER 530506	OP	17.50	19.00
92	SHARE IN THE WARMTH OF CHRISTMAS	OP	15.00	18.00
92	SLOW DOWN & ENJOY THE HOLIDAYS 520489	YR	16.00	19.00
92	THERE'S A CHRISTIAN WELCOME HERE 528021	YR	22.50	30.00
92	WISHING YOU/SWEETEST CHRISTMAS530190	YR	30.00	35.00
92	WISHING YOU/SWEETEST CHRISTMAS530212	OP	15.00	30.00
93	AN EVENT FOR ALL SEASONS 529974	LE	15.00	15.00
93	AN EVENT FOR ALL SEASONS 530158	OP	30.00	30.00
93	WISHING YOU/SWEETEST CHRISTMAS530182	OP	8.00	8.00
94	BABY'S FIRST CHRISTMAS 530255	OP	16.00	16.00
94	BABY'S FIRST CHRISTMAS 530263	OP	16.00	16.00
94	MEMORIES ARE MADE OF THIS 529982	OP	30.00	30.00
94	OUR FIRST CHRISTMAS TOGETHER 529206	OP	18.50	19.00
94	TAKE A BOW CUZ YOU'RE MY CHRISTMAS STAR	OP	16.00	16.00
94	YER A PEL-I-CAN COUNT ON	OP	16.00	16.00
94	YOU ARE ALWAYS IN MY HEART 530972	OP	16.00	16.00
94	YOU'RE AS PRETTY AS A CHRISTMAS TREE	OP	27.50	28.00
94	YOU'RE PRETTY AS A CHRISTMAS TREE 529206	OP	16.00	16.00
94	YOU'RE PRETTY AS A CHRISTMAS TREE 530395	OP	30.00	30.00
95	BABY'S FIRST CHRISTMAS 142719	OP	17.50	18.00
95	BABY'S FIRST CHRISTMAS 142727	OP	17.50	18.00
95	FOLLOW YOUR HEART 528080	OP	30.00	30.00
95	HE COVERS THE EARTH W/HIS BEAUTY 142662	OP	17.00	17.00
95	HE COVERS THE EARTH W/HIS BEAUTY 142689	OP	30.00	30.00
95	HIPPO HOLIDAYS	OP	17.00	17.00
95	JOY FROM HEAD TO MISTLETOE 150126	OP	17.00	17.00
95	MERRY CHRISMOOSE 150134	OP	17.00	17.00
95	OUR FIRST CHRISTMAS TOGETHER 142700	OP	18.50	19.00
95	YOU'RE "A" NUMBER ONE IN MY BOOK, TEACHE	OP	17.00	17.00
96	BABY'S FIRST CHRISTMAS-BOY 183946	YR	17.50	17.50
96	BABY'S FIRST CHRISTMAS-GIRL 183938	YR	17.50	17.50
96	GOD'S PRECIOUS GIFT 183881	OP	20.00	20.00
96	OUR FIRST CHRISTMAS TOGETHER 183911	YR	22.50	22.50
96	PEACH ON EARTH...ANYWAY 183350	YR	30.00	30.00
96	PEACH ON EARTH...ANYWAY 183369	YR	18.50	18.50
96	WHEN THE SKATING'S RUFF, TRY PRAYER 1839	OP	18.50	18.50
S. BUTCHER	**PRECIOUS MOMENTS BIRTHDAY**			
95	HIPPO HOLIDAYS 520403	OP	17.00	17.00
96	OWL BE HOME FOR CHRISTMAS 128708	YR	18.50	18.50
S. BUTCHER	**PRECIOUS MOMENTS COLLECTORS' CLUB PIECES**			
84	CELEBRATING A DECADE..SHARING 227986	YR	7.00	10.00
90	7 CHAPEL WINDOWS ORNAMENT SET PM890	OP	105.00	105.00
90	BLESSED ARE THE MEEK...PM390	OP	15.00	15.00
90	BLESSED ARE THE MERCIFUL..PM590	OP	15.00	15.00
90	BLESSED ARE THE PEACEMAKERS...PM790	OP	15.00	15.00
90	BLESSED ARE THE POOR...PM190	OP	15.00	15.00
90	BLESSED ARE THE PURE... PM690	OP	15.00	15.00
90	BLESSED ARE THEY THAT HUNGER...PM490	OP	15.00	15.00
90	BLESSED ARE THEY THAT MOURN..PM290	OP	15.00	15.00
92	LOVING...SHARING ALONG THE WAY PM040	OP	12.50	30.00
S. BUTCHER	**PRECIOUS MOMENTS COMMEMORATIVE EASTER SEALS ORNAMENT**			
93	YOU'RE MY NUMBER ONE FRIEND 250112	OP	8.00	8.00
94	IT IS NO SECRET WHAT GOD CAN DO	OP	6.50	7.00
95	TAKE TIME TO SMELL THE FLOWERS	OP	7.50	8.00
96	YOU CAN ALWAYS COUNT ON ME	OP	6.50	6.50
S. BUTCHER	**PRECIOUS MOMENTS SPECIAL EDITION MEMBERS ONLY**			
93	LOVING,CARING & SHARING ALONG THE WAY	OP	15.00	15.00
94	YOU ARE THE END OF MY RAINBOW	OP	15.00	15.00
S. BUTCHER	**PRECIOUS MOMENTS SUGAR TOWN**			
92	BOY STANDING BY CHAPEL 530484	LE	17.50	20.00
95	SUGAR TOWN DOCTOR'S OFFICE 530441	LE	17.50	18.00
96	TRAIN STATION 184101	LE	18.50	18.50

YR	NAME	LIMIT	ISSUE	TREND
*			**SHARING SEASON GIFTS**	
86	BIRDS OF A FEATHER COLLECT... PM864	OP	*	160.00
87	BRASS FILIGREE BELL SHAPED PM009	OP	*	45.00
88	A GROWING LOVE 520349	OP	*	85.00
89	ALWAYS ROOM FOR ONE MORE 522961	OP	*	100.00
90	MY HAPPINESS PM904	OP	*	95.00
91	SHARING THE GOOD NEWS TOGETHER PM037	OP	*	80.00
*			**TREASURY OF CHRISTMAS**	
81	BABY'S FIRST CHRISTMAS 1981-E-6145	YR	6.00	22.00
81	FLYIN' SANTA CHRISTMAS SPECIAL-E6136	YR	9.00	110.00
81	LOOK OUT BELOW-E-6135	TL	6.00	60.00
81	NOT A CREATURE WAS STIRRING-E-6149	TL	4.00	45.00
81	OUR HERO-E-6146	TL	4.00	55.00
81	SAWIN' ELF HELPER-E-6138	TL	6.00	45.00
81	SNOW SHOE-IN SANTA-E-6139	TL	6.00	50.00
81	WHOOPS, IT'S 1981-E-6148	YR	7.50	75.00
81	WHOOPS-E-6147	TL	3.50	95.00
82	A SAVIOR IS BORN THIS DAY-E-6949	TL	4.00	18.00
82	BABY'S FIRST CHRISTMAS 1982-E-6952	YR	4.00	10.00
82	BABY'S FIRST CHRISTMAS 1982-E-6979	YR	10.00	35.00
82	BUNNY WINTER PLAYGROUND 1982-E-6978	YR	10.00	55.00
82	CAROUSEL HORSES-E-6958	TL	8.00	65.00
82	FLYIN' SANTA CHRISTMAS SPECIAL-E6136	YR	9.00	105.00
82	GRANDCHILD'S FIRST CHRISTMAS 1982-E-6983	YR	5.00	15.00
82	MERRY CHRISTMAS GRANDMA-E-6975	TL	5.00	5.00
82	MERRY CHRISTMAS TEACHER-E-6984	TL	7.00	7.00
82	PENGUIN POWER-E-6977	TL	6.00	18.00
82	POLAR BEAR FUN WHOOPS IT'S 1982-E-6953	YR	10.00	85.00
82	TOY SOLDIER 1982-E-6957	YR	6.50	65.00
82	VICTORIAN SLEIGH-E-6946	TL	9.00	9.00
83	ARCTIC CHARMER-E-6945	TL	7.00	35.00
83	BABY'S FIRST CHRISTMAS-E-0271	YR	6.00	6.00
83	BABY'S FIRST CHRISTMAS-E-0273	TL	9.00	9.00
83	CAROUSEL HORSE-E-0278	TL	9.00	50.00
83	CAROUSEL HORSES-E-6980	TL	8.00	65.00
83	GRANDCHILD'S FIRST CHRISTMAS-E0272	YR	5.00	5.00
83	TO A SPECIAL TEACHER-E-0276	TL	5.00	15.00
83	TOY DRUM TEDDY-E-0274	TL	9.00	9.00
83	TOY SHOP-E-0277	TL	8.00	32.00
83	WATCHING AT THE WINDOW-E-0275	TL	13.00	40.00
83	WIDE OPEN THROTTLE-E-0242	TL	12.00	35.00
83	WING-A-DING ANGEL-E-6948	TL	7.00	40.00
84	BABY'S FIRST CHRISTMAS 1984-E-6215	YR	6.00	6.00
84	BUNNY'S CHRISTMAS STOCKING-E-6251	YR	2.00	28.00
84	CAROUSEL HORSE-E-6913	TL	1.50	20.00
84	CHRISTMAS NEST-E-6249	TL	3.00	3.00
84	CUCKOO CLOCK-E-6217	TL	8.00	40.00
84	FERRIS WHEEL MICE-E-6216	TL	9.00	9.00
84	GODCHILD'S FIRST CHRISTMAS-E-6287	TL	7.00	7.00
84	GRANDCHILD'S FIRST CHRISTMAS 1984-E-6286	YR	5.00	5.00
84	HAPPY HOLIDAYS-E-6248	TL	2.00	2.00
84	HOLIDAY PENGUIN-E-6240	TL	1.50	20.00
84	JOY TO THE WORLD-E-6209	TL	9.00	48.00
84	LETTER TO SANTA-E-6210	TL	5.00	35.00
84	LITTLE DRUMMER-E-6241	TL	2.00	2.00
84	LUCY & ME PHOTO FRAMES-E-6211	TL	5.00	5.00
84	MERRY CHRISTMAS MOTHER-E-6213	TL	10.00	35.00
84	OWL BE HOME FOR CHRISTMAS-E-6230	TL	10.00	10.00
84	PEEK-A-BEAR BABY'S/CHRISTMAS-E-6228	TL	10.00	10.00
84	PEEK-A-BEAR BABY'S/CHRISTMAS-E-6229	TL	9.00	9.00
84	PENGUINS ON ICE-E-6280	TL	7.50	30.00
84	SANTA IN THE BOX-E-6292	TL	6.00	35.00
84	SANTA ON ICE-E-6252	TL	2.50	25.00
84	SANTA'S TROLLEY-E-6231	TL	11.00	55.00
84	TREASURED MEMORIES THE NEW SLED-E-6256	TL	7.00	70.00
84	UP ON THE HOUSE TOP-E-6280	TL	9.00	30.00
85	A STOCKING FULL FOR 1985-56464	YR	6.00	6.00
85	ANGEL IN FLIGHT-55816	TL	8.00	25.00
85	BABY BLOCKS-55883	TL	12.00	12.00
85	BABY RATTLE PHOTO FRAME-56006	TL	5.00	5.00
85	BABY'S FIRST CHRISTMAS-55840	TL	15.00	16.00
85	CAROUSEL REINDEER-55808	TL	12.00	50.00
85	CHILD'S SECOND CHRISTMAS-55867	TL	11.00	20.00
85	CHRISTMAS LIGHTS-56200	TL	8.00	40.00
85	CHRISTMAS PENGUIN-55824	TL	7.50	40.00
85	CHRISTMAS TOY CHEST-55891	TL	10.00	25.00
85	CHRISTMAS TREE PHOTOFRAME-56871	TL	10.00	10.00
85	FISHING FOR STARS-55875	TL	9.00	15.00
85	FLYING SANTA CHRISTMAS SPECIAL-56383	TL	8.00	45.00
85	GRANDCHILD'S FIRST ORNAMENT-55921	TL	7.00	12.00
85	JOY PHOTO FRAME-55956	YR	6.00	22.00
85	LOOK OUT BELOW-56375	TL	6.00	50.00
85	MERRY CHRISTMAS GRANDMA-56197	YR	7.00	7.00
85	MERRY CHRISTMAS TEACHER-56448	YR	9.00	9.00
85	NIGHT BEFORE CHRISTMAS, THE-55972	TL	5.00	5.00
85	NORTH POLE EXPRESS-56073	TL	9.00	50.00
85	NOT A CREATURE WAS STIRRING-56421	YR	5.50	45.00
85	OLD FASHIONED ROCKING HORSE-55859	TL	10.00	10.00
85	OUR HERO-56413	YR	5.50	55.00

YR	NAME	LIMIT	ISSUE	TREND
85	SANTA CLAUS BALLOON-55794	YR	8.50	40.00
85	SAWIN ELF HELPER-56391	YR	8.00	45.00
85	SCOTTIE CELEBRATING CHRISTMAS-56065	TL	10.00	15.00
85	SKATING WALRUS-56081	TL	9.00	45.00
85	SNOW SHOE-IN SANTA-56405	YR	8.00	50.00
85	ST. NICHOLAS CIRCA 1910-56359	TL	6.00	15.00
85	TOBOGGAN RIDE-56286	TL	6.00	12.00
85	VICTORIAN DOLL HOUSE-56251	YR	13.00	30.00
85	WE THREE KINGS-55964	YR	4.50	15.00
86	1ST CHRISTMAS TOGETHER 1986-551171	YR	9.00	22.00
86	ANTIQUE TOY-551317	TL	9.00	25.00
86	BABY BEAR SLEIGH, THE-551651	TL	9.00	25.00
86	BABY'S FIRST CHRISTMAS 1986-551724	YR	6.50	7.00
86	BABY'S FIRST CHRISTMAS-551716	TL	5.50	10.00
86	BAH, HUMBUG!-553387	TL	9.00	20.00
86	CHRISTMAS ANGEL, THE-551244	10000	22.50	55.00
86	CHRISTMAS CALENDAR-551333	TL	7.00	20.00
86	CHRISTMAS RATTLE-553379	TL	8.00	25.00
86	CHRISTMAS SCOTTIE-551201	TL	7.00	15.00
86	CHRISTMAS WISHES FROM PANDA-552623	TL	6.00	10.00
86	COUNTRY COUSINS MERRY XMAS, DAD-552704	TL	7.00	10.00
86	COUNTRY COUSINS MERRY XMAS, DAD-552712	TL	7.00	15.00
86	COUNTRY COUSINS MERRY XMAS, MOM-552704	TL	7.00	10.00
86	COUNTRY COUSINS MERRY XMAS, MOM-552712	TL	7.00	15.00
86	ELF STRINGING POPCORN-551198	TL	10.00	18.00
86	FIRST CHRISTMAS TOGETHER-551708	TL	6.00	23.00
86	FROM OUR HOUSE TO YOUR HOUSE-553360	TL	15.00	20.00
86	GOD BLESS US EVERYONE-553395	TL	10.00	22.00
86	GRANDMOTHER'S LITTLE ANGEL-552747	TL	8.00	15.00
86	HAVE A HEAVENLY HOLIDAY-551260	TL	9.00	1.00
86	HOLIDAY FISHERMAN-551309	TL	8.00	35.00
86	HOLIDAY TRAIN-553417	TL	10.00	24.00
86	I LOVE MY GRANDPARENTS-553263	YR	6.00	6.00
86	M.V.B. (MOST VALUABLE BEAR)-554219	TL	3.00	3.00
86	MERRY CHRISTMAS MOM & DAD-553271	YR	6.00	6.00
86	MERRY CHRISTMAS TEACHER-552666	TL	6.50	12.00
86	MERRY CHRISTMAS-553646	TL	8.00	14.00
86	MY SPECIAL FRIEND-552615	TL	2.50	18.00
86	OLD FASHIONED DOLL HOUSE-551287	TL	15.00	25.00
86	PEEK-A-BEAR GRANDCHILD'S/XMAS-552070	YR	6.00	6.00
86	PEEK-A-BEAR PRESENT-552089	TL	2.50	3.00
86	S. CLAUS HOLLYCOPTER-553344	TL	13.50	30.00
86	SANTA AND CHILD-551236	TL	13.50	25.00
86	SANTA'S HELPERS-552607	TL	2.50	3.00
86	SIAMESE KITTEN-551279	TL	9.00	20.00
87	1ST CHRISTMAS TOGETHER 1987-556335	YR	9.00	25.00
87	BABY'S FIRST CHRISTMAS 1987-556254	YR	7.00	25.00
87	BABY'S FIRST CHRISTMAS 1987-556297	YR	2.00	5.00
87	BABY'S FIRST CHRISTMAS-555061	TL	12.00	15.00
87	BABY'S FIRST CHRISTMAS-555088	TL	7.50	12.00
87	BABY'S FIRST CHRISTMAS-555118	TL	6.00	10.00
87	BABY'S FIRST CHRISTMAS-556041	TL	10.00	10.00
87	BEARY CHRISTMAS FAMILY-556300	TL	2.00	5.00
87	BOY ON A ROCKING HORSE-555983	TL	12.00	20.00
87	BUCKET O'LOVE-556491	TL	2.50	3.00
87	CAROUSEL GOOSE-556076	TL	17.00	40.00
87	CAROUSEL MOBILE-553409	TL	15.00	60.00
87	CHRISTMAS TRAIN-557196	TL	10.00	18.00
87	COUNTRY COUSINS KATIE/ICE SKATING-556378	TL	8.00	30.00
87	COUNTRY COUSINS SCOOTER SNOWMAN-556386	TL	8.00	35.00
87	GRANDCHILD'S FIRST CHRISTMAS-556416	TL	10.00	25.00
87	I'M DREAMING OF/BRIGHT CHRISTMAS-556602	TL	2.50	3.00
87	KITTY'S 1ST CHRISTMAS-552917	TL	4.00	5.00
87	KITTY'S BED-556408	TL	12.00	50.00
87	KITTY'S JACK-IN-THE-BOX-555959	TL	11.00	15.00
87	LITTLE SAILOR ELF-556068	TL	10.00	20.00
87	MERRY CHRISTMAS KITTY-552933	TL	3.50	5.00
87	MERRY CHRISTMAS PUPPY-552925	TL	3.50	5.00
87	MERRY CHRISTMAS TEACHER-555967	TL	7.50	10.00
87	MERRY CHRISTMAS TEACHER-556319	TL	2.00	5.00
87	MOUSE IN A MITTEN-555975	TL	7.50	30.00
87	NIGHT CAPS-556084	TL	5.50	8.00
87	OUR FIRST CHRISTMAS TOGETHER-556548	TL	13.00	18.00
87	PEAK-A-BEAR MY SPECIAL FRIEND-556513	TL	6.00	20.00
87	PEEK-A-BEAR LETTER TO SANTA-555991	TL	8.00	15.00
87	PUPPY LOVE-556505	TL	6.00	15.00
87	PUPPY'S 1ST CHRISTMAS-552909	TL	4.00	5.00
87	ROCKING HORSE PAST JOYS-556157	TL	10.00	10.00
87	SANTA'S LIST-556394	TL	7.00	25.00
87	SKATING SANTA 1987-556211	YR	13.50	80.00
87	SLEIGH AWAY-555401	TL	12.00	20.00
87	SUGAR PLUM BEARIES-555193	TL	4.50	5.00
87	TEDDY TAKES A SPIN-556467	TL	13.00	18.00
87	TEDDY'S SUSPENDERS-556262	TL	8.50	16.00
87	THREE LITTLE BEARS-556556	TL	7.50	12.00
87	TINY TOY THIMBLE MOBILE-556475	TL	12.00	15.00
88	1ST CHRISTMAS TOGETHER 1988-554596	YR	17.50	18.00
88	BABY'S FIRST CHRISTMAS 1988-554928	YR	7.50	10.00
88	CHRISTMAS IS COMING-554901	TL	12.00	18.00

YR	NAME	LIMIT	ISSUE	TREND
88	CHRISTMAS PIN-UP 489409	TL	11.00	25.00
88	CHRISTMAS THIM-BELL-558389	YR	4.00	6.00
88	CHRISTMAS TRAIN, THE-554944	TL	15.00	20.00
88	GRAMOPHONE KEEPSAKE-558818	TL	13.00	22.00
88	HAPPY HOWLADAYS-558605	YR	7.00	12.00
88	MERRY CHRISTMAS ENGINE-554561	TL	22.50	35.00
88	MERRY CHRISTMAS GRANDPA-560065	TL	8.00	10.00
88	NORTH POLE DEADLINE-489387	TL	13.50	18.00
88	SANTA TURTLE-558559	TL	10.00	20.00
88	SANTA'S SURVEY-554642	TL	35.00	70.00
88	TEDDY BEAR BALL, THE-558567	TL	10.00	12.00
88	TURTLE GREETINGS-558583	TL	8.50	22.00
89	89 CAUGHT IN THE ACT-830046	TL	12.50	13.00
89	BABY'S FIRST CHRISTMAS 1989-562807	YR	8.00	12.00
89	BOTTOM'S UP 1989-830003	TL	11.00	20.00
89	CLARA-568406	YR	12.50	22.00
89	COWARDLY LION, THE-567787	YR	12.00	22.00
89	DOROTHY-567760	YR	12.00	25.00
89	FIRST CHRISTMAS TOGETHER 1989-562823	TL	11.00	12.00
89	GONE WITH THE WIND-567698	YR	13.50	25.00
89	HOE! HOE! HOE!-564761	YR	20.00	31.00
89	PAUSE THAT REFRESHES, THE-563226	TL	15.00	20.00
89	PURR-FECT FIT!, THE-566462	TL	15.00	16.00
89	SANTA'S LITTLE REINDEAR-568430	TL	15.00	16.00
89	SCARECROW, THE-567795	YR	12.00	20.00
89	STATIC IN THE ATTIC-562947	TL	13.00	15.00
89	TIN MAN, THE-567779	YR	12.00	20.00
89	VICTORIAN SLEIGH RIDE-562890	TL	22.50	23.00
89	YE OLDE PUPPET SHOW-562939	TL	17.50	20.00
90	'TWAS THE NIGHT BEFORE CHRISTMAS-577545	TL	17.50	18.00
90	A CALLING HOME AT CHRISTMAS-568457	TL	15.00	16.00
90	BREWING WARM WISHES-564974	TL	10.00	12.00
90	CLARA'S PRINCE-568422	YR	12.50	18.00
90	FESTIVE FLIGHT-566101	TL	11.00	14.00
90	HANG IN THERE-566055	TL	13.50	14.00
90	HAPPY HOLIDAY READINGS-568104	TL	8.00	10.00
90	HAVE A COKE AND A SMILE-571512	TL	15.00	16.00
90	HEADING FOR HAPPY HOLIDAYS 577537	TL	17.50	18.00
90	MCHAPPY HOLIDAYS-577529	TL	17.50	18.00
90	MERRY CHRISTMAS TEACHER-566098	TL	11.00	11.00
90	MOUSE HOUSE-575186	TL	16.00	16.00
90	NUTCRACKER, THE-568422	YR	12.50	18.00
90	OVER ONE MILLION HOLIDAY WISHES!-577553	YR	17.50	20.00
90	PURR-FECT PALS-563218	TL	8.00	12.00
90	SANTA'S SUITCASE-566462	TL	25.00	25.00
90	SEAMAN'S GREETINGS-566047	TL	11.00	11.00
90	TEN LORDS A-LEAPING-573949	TL	15.00	16.00
90	TONS OF TOYS-577510	TL	13.00	18.00
90	YOU MALT MY HEART-577596	TL	25.00	25.00
91	A REAL CLASSIC-831603	YR	10.00	10.00
91	ALL CAUGHT UP IN CHRISTMAS-583537	TL	10.00	10.00
91	ALL I WANT FOR CHRISTMAS-577596	TL	25.00	25.00
91	BABY'S FIRST CHRISTMAS 1991-586935	YR	12.50	13.00
91	CHECKING IT TWICE-583936	TL	25.00	25.00
91	CHRISTMAS CHEER-585769	TL	13.50	14.00
91	CHRISTMAS COUNTDOWN-568376	TL	20.00	20.00
91	CHRISTMAS CUTIE-576182	TL	13.50	14.00
91	CHRISTMAS IS IN THE AIR-581453	YR	15.00	16.00
91	CHRISTMAS IS MY GOAL-581550	TL	17.50	18.00
91	CHRISTMAS KAYAK-583723	TL	13.50	15.00
91	DREAM A LITTLE DREAM-575593	TL	17.50	18.00
91	FROSTY THE SNOWMAN-576425	TL	15.00	16.00
91	GLOW OF CHRISTMAS, THE-581801	TL	20.00	20.00
91	HAPPY MEAL ON WHEELS-583715	TL	22.50	23.00
91	HERE'S THE SCOOP-583693	TL	13.50	14.00
91	HOLIDAY AHOY-568368	TL	12.50	13.00
91	HOLIDAY TREATS-581542	YR	17.50	18.00
91	HOLIDAY WING DING-574333	TL	22.50	23.00
91	IT'S TEA-LIGHTFUL-694789	TL	13.50	15.00
91	JUGGLIN' THE HOLIDAYS-587028	TL	13.00	13.00
91	LIGHTING THE WAY-588776	TL	20.00	20.00
91	MARILYN MONROE-583774	YR	20.00	20.00
91	MEOW MATES-576220	TL	12.00	12.00
91	NORTH POLE HERE I COME-574333	TL	22.50	23.00
91	OUR MOST PRECIOUS GIFT-585726	YR	17.50	18.00
91	PEDAL PUSHIN' SANTA-566098	TL	20.00	20.00
91	RUDOLPH-588784	TL	17.50	18.00
91	SANTA'S STEED-587044	YR	15.00	18.00
91	STARRY EYED SANTA-587176	TL	15.00	16.00
91	THINGS GO BETTER WITH COKE-580597	TL	17.00	18.00
91	TUBA TOTIN' TEDDY-568449	TL	15.00	16.00
91	WARMEST WISHES-573825	YR	17.50	25.00
92	A CHILD'S CHRISTMAS-586358	TL	25.00	25.00
92	A CHRISTMAS TOAST-588261	TL	20.00	20.00
92	A POUND OF GOOD CHEERS-582034	TL	17.50	18.00
92	A SURE SIGN OF CHRISTMAS-588857	TL	22.50	23.00
92	A WATCHFUL EYE-595713	YR	15.00	16.00
92	A-B-C-SON'S GREETINGS-588806	TL	16.50	17.00
92	BABY'S FIRST CHRISTMAS-586943	YR	12.50	13.00

YR	NAME	LIMIT	ISSUE	TREND
92	BEGINNING TO LOOK/CHRISTMAS-588253	TL	15.00	16.00
92	BLESS OUR HOME-595772	YR	12.00	12.00
92	CARTIN' HOME HOLIDAY TREATS-832790	TL	13.50	14.00
92	CHECKIN' HIS LIST-595756	YR	12.50	13.00
92	CHRISTMAS BIZ-593168	TL	22.50	23.00
92	CHRISTMAS CAT NAPPIN'-595764	YR	12.00	12.00
92	CHRISTMAS CURE-ALLS-588938	TL	20.00	20.00
92	CHRISTMAS EVE-MERGENCY-588849	TL	27.00	27.00
92	CHRISTMAS IS IN THE AIR-831174	TL	25.00	25.00
92	CHRISTMAS LIFTS THE SPIRITS-582018	TL	25.00	25.00
92	CHRISTMAS TRIMMIN'-590932	TL	17.00	17.00
92	COLD, CRISP TASTE OF COKE, THE-583766	TL	17.00	17.00
92	DIAL 'S' FOR SANTA-589373	TL	25.00	25.00
92	FESTIVE FIDDLERS-586501	YR	20.00	20.00
92	FESTIVE NEWFLASH-588792	TL	17.50	18.00
92	FIRED UP FOR CHRISTMAS-595799	YR	12.00	12.00
92	FIRESIDE FRIENDS-588830	TL	20.00	20.00
92	GOOD CATCH-595721	YR	12.50	13.00
92	GUTEN CHEERS-587192	YR	22.50	23.00
92	HAVE A SOUP-ER CHRISTMAS-588911	TL	17.50	18.00
92	HOLIDAY TAKE-OUT-593508	YR	17.50	18.00
92	HOLIDAYS ARE A HIT, THE-581577	TL	17.50	18.00
92	HOLIDAYS GIVE ME A LIFT-588865	TL	30.00	30.00
92	HOPPY HOLIDAYS-588814	YR	13.50	14.00
92	LIGHTS...CAMERA...CHRISTMAS!-594369	TL	20.00	20.00
92	MC HO HO HO-585181	TL	22.50	23.00
92	MERRY KISSES-831166	TL	17.50	18.00
92	MERRY MISTLE TOAD-588288	TL	15.00	16.00
92	MOON WATCH-587184	TL	20.00	20.00
92	MUSIC MICE-TRO!-575143	TL	12.00	12.00
92	ON TARGET TWO-GETHER-575623	YR	17.00	17.00
92	PUT ON A HAPPY FACE-588237	TL	15.00	16.00
92	SMALL FRY'S FIRST CHRISTMAS-586749	TL	17.00	17.00
92	SPECIAL DELIVERY-832812	TL	12.00	12.00
92	SPECIAL DELIVERY-840440	YR	22.50	23.00
92	SPIRITED STALLION-594407	YR	15.00	16.00
92	SPREADING SWEET JOY-580465	YR	13.50	14.00
92	SUNDAE RIDE-583707	TL	20.00	20.00
92	SWINGIN' CHRISTMAS-584096	TL	15.00	16.00
92	TAKE A CHANCE ON THE HOLIDAYS-594075	TL	20.00	20.00
92	TEE-RIFIC HOLIDAYS-590827	TL	25.00	25.00
92	TIC-TAC-MISTLE-TOE-588296	YR	23.00	23.00
92	TIP TOP TIDINGS-581828	TL	13.00	13.00
92	TO A DEAR BABY-587168	YR	18.50	19.00
92	TOYFUL' RUDOLPH-593982	TL	22.50	23.00
92	TRUNK OF TREASURES-588636	YR	20.00	20.00
92	WARMTH OF THE SEASON, THE-586994	TL	20.00	20.00
92	WATCHING FOR SANTA-840432	TL	25.00	25.00
92	WEAR THE SEASON WITH A SMILE-595829	YR	10.00	10.00
92	WRAPPIN' UP WARM WISHES-593141	YR	17.50	18.00
92	YULE TIDE TOGETHER-588903	TL	20.00	20.00
93	25 POINTS FOR CHRISTMAS	OP	25.00	25.00
93	A KICK OUT OF CHRISTMAS	OP	10.00	10.00
93	A PAUSE FOR CLAUS	OP	22.50	23.00
93	ALL YOU ADD IS LOVE	OP	18.50	19.00
93	ARIEL'S UNDER-THE-SEA TREE	OP	22.50	23.00
93	BABY'S FIRST CHRISTMAS DINNER	OP	12.00	12.00
93	BEARLY BALANCED	OP	15.00	15.00
93	BORN TO SHOP	OP	26.50	27.00
93	CELEBRATING W/A SPLASH	OP	17.00	17.00
93	CHRISTMAS DANCER	OP	15.00	15.00
93	CHRISTMAS IN THE MAKING	OP	20.00	20.00
93	CHRISTMAS IS IN THE AIR	OP	25.00	25.00
93	CHRISTMAS KICKS	OP	17.50	18.00
93	CHRISTMAS MAIL CALL	OP	20.00	20.00
93	CHRISTMAS-TO-GO	OP	25.50	26.00
93	CLOWNIN' AROUND	OP	10.00	10.00
93	COOL YULE	OP	12.00	12.00
93	COUNTIN' ON A MERRY CHRISTMAS	OP	22.50	23.00
93	DESIGNED W/YOU IN MIND	OP	16.00	16.00
93	DREAM WHEELS	OP	29.50	30.00
93	DUCKING THE SEASON'S RUSH	OP	17.50	18.00
93	DUNK THE HALLS	OP	18.50	19.00
93	FAIREST ONE OF ALL, THE	OP	20.00	20.00
93	FOCUSING ON CHRISTMAS	OP	27.50	28.00
93	FOR A SHARP UNCLE	OP	10.00	10.00
93	FRIENDS THROUGH THICK & THIN	OP	10.00	10.00
93	GOOFY ABOUT SKIING	OP	22.50	23.00
93	HANGINING OUT FOR THE HOLIDAYS	OP	15.00	15.00
93	HAPPILY EVER AFTER	OP	25.00	25.00
93	HAPPY HAUL-IDAYS	OP	30.00	30.00
93	HAVE A CHERRY CHRISTMAS, SISTER	OP	13.50	14.00
93	HAVE A HOLLY JELL-O CHRISTMAS	OP	19.50	20.00
93	HEART FILLED DREAMS	OP	10.00	10.00
93	HEARTS AGLOW	OP	18.50	19.00
93	HERE COMES RUDOLPH	OP	17.50	18.00
93	HERE COMES SANTA CLAWS	OP	22.50	23.00
93	HOLIDAY MEW-SIC	OP	20.00	20.00
93	HOLIDAY ORDERS	OP	20.00	20.00

YR	NAME	LIMIT	ISSUE	TREND
93	HOLIDAY TREASURES	OP	18.50	19.00
93	HOLIDAY WISHES	OP	17.50	18.00
93	HOME TWEET HOME	OP	10.00	10.00
93	HOT OFF THE PRESS	OP	27.50	28.00
93	I'M DREAMING OF A WHITE-OUT CHRISTMAS	OP	22.50	23.00
93	IT'S BEGINNING TO LOOK A LOT LIKE...	OP	22.50	23.00
93	JOYEUX NOEL	OP	24.50	25.00
93	LIGHT UP YOUR HOLIDAYS W/COKE	OP	27.50	28.00
93	LIGHTS..CAMERA..CHRISTMAS	OP	20.00	20.00
93	LOVE'S SWEET DANCE	OP	29.50	30.00
93	MAGIC CARPET RIDE	OP	25.00	25.00
93	MERRY CHRISTMAS, BABY	OP	10.00	10.00
93	MERRY CHRISTMAS, DAUGHTER	OP	20.00	20.00
93	MERRY MC-CHOO-CHOO	OP	30.00	30.00
93	MICKEY'S HOLIDAY TREASURE	OP	12.00	12.00
93	ON YOUR MARK,GET SET,IS THAT TO GO?	OP	13.50	14.00
93	PITTER-PATTER POST OFFICE	OP	20.00	20.00
93	PLANE O' HOLIDAY FUN	OP	27.50	28.00
93	POOL HALL-IDAYS	OP	19.00	19.00
93	ROCKIN' W/SANTA	OP	13.50	14.00
93	ROUNDIN' UP CHRISTMAS TOGETHER	OP	25.00	25.00
93	SANTA'S MAGIC RIDE	OP	24.00	24.00
93	SEE-SAW SWEETHEARTS	OP	10.00	10.00
93	SLEDDIN' MR. SNOWMAN	OP	13.00	13.00
93	SLIMMIN' SANTA	OP	18.50	19.00
93	SMOOTH MOVE, MOM	OP	20.00	20.00
93	SPECIAL DELIVERY FOR SANTA	OP	10.00	10.00
93	SPOT OF LOVE	OP	20.00	20.00
93	SPREADING JOY	OP	27.50	28.00
93	SWEET SEASONS EATINGS	OP	22.50	23.00
93	SWEET WHISKERED WISHES	OP	17.00	17.00
93	T'WAY THE NIGHT BEFORE CHRISTMAS	OP	22.50	23.00
93	TANGLED UP FOR CHRISTMAS	OP	14.50	15.00
93	TERRIFIC TOYS	OP	20.00	20.00
93	TO MY GEM	OP	27.50	28.00
93	TOASTY TIDINGS	OP	20.00	20.00
93	TOOL TIME, YULE TIME	OP	18.50	19.00
93	TOP MARKS FOR TEACHER	OP	10.00	10.00
93	TOY TO THE WORLD	OP	25.00	25.00
93	TREASURE THE HOLIDAYS, MAN'	OP	25.00	25.00
93	WARM & HEARTY WISHES	OP	17.50	18.00
93	WATCHING FOR SANTA	OP	25.00	25.00
94	'A' FOR SANTA	OP	17.50	18.00
94	A BOUGH FOR BELLE!	OP	18.50	19.00
94	A CHRISTMAS TAIL	OP	20.00	20.00
94	A HOLIDAY OPPORTUNITY	OP	20.00	20.00
94	A REAL BOY FOR CHRISTMAS	OP	15.00	15.00
94	A SIGN OF PEACE	OP	18.50	19.00
94	AHOY JOY!	OP	20.00	20.00
94	ANSWERING CHRISTMAS WISHES	OP	17.50	18.00
94	ARIEL'S CHRISTMAS SURPRISE!	OP	20.00	20.00
94	BUBBLIN' W/JOY	OP	12.50	13.00
94	BULDING A SEW-MAN	OP	18.50	19.00
94	BUNDLE OF JOY	OP	10.00	10.00
94	CHRISTMAS CROSSROADS	OP	20.00	20.00
94	CHRISTMAS CRUSIN'	OP	22.50	23.00
94	CHRISTMAS FISHES FROM SANTA PAWS	OP	18.50	19.00
94	CHRISTMAS FLY-BY	OP	15.00	15.00
94	CHRISTMAS SWISHES	OP	17.50	18.00
94	CHRISTMAS TEE TIME	OP	25.00	25.00
94	CHRISTMAS TWO-GETHER	OP	12.50	13.00
94	COCOA 'N' KISSES FOR SANTA	OP	22.50	23.00
94	COOL CRUISE	19640	20.00	20.00
94	EXERCISING GOOD TASTE	OP	17.50	18.00
94	FEATURED PRESENTATION	OP	20.00	20.00
94	GALIANT GREETING	OP	20.00	20.00
94	GOOD FORTUNE TO YOU	OP	25.00	25.00
94	GOOD THINGS CROP UP AT CHRISTMAS	OP	25.00	25.00
94	GOOD TIDINGS,TIDINGS,TIDINGS..	OP	20.00	20.00
94	GOOFY DELIVERY	OP	22.50	23.00
94	GRANDMAS ARE SEW SPECIAL	OP	12.50	13.00
94	HAND-TOSSED TIDINGS	OP	17.50	18.00
94	HANDLE W/CARE	OP	20.00	20.00
94	HAPPY HOWL-IDAYS	OP	22.50	23.00
94	HAVE A BALL AT CHRISTMAS	OP	15.00	15.00
94	HAVE A MERRY DAIRY CHRISTMAS	OP	22.50	23.00
94	HAVE A TOTEM-LY TERRIFIC CHRISTMAS	OP	30.00	30.00
94	HOLIDAY HONEYS	OP	20.00	20.00
94	HOLIDAY SHOW-STOPPER	OP	15.00	15.00
94	HOLIDAY STARS	OP	20.00	20.00
94	I CAN BEAR-LY WAIT FOR A COKE	OP	18.50	19.00
94	L'IL STOCKING STUFFER	OP	17.50	18.00
94	LATEST MEWS FROM HOME, THE	OP	16.00	16.00
94	MERRY CHRISTMAS TOOL YOU, DAD	OP	22.50	23.00
94	MERRY LITTLE TWO-STEP	OP	12.50	13.00
94	MERRY MEMO-RIES	OP	22.50	23.00
94	MERRY MENAGE	OP	20.00	20.00
94	MERRY MISCHIEF	OP	15.00	15.00
94	MERRY REINDEER RIDE	OP	20.00	20.00

YR	NAME	LIMIT	ISSUE	TREND
94	MINNIE'S HOLIDAY TREASURE	OP	12.00	12.00
94	NUTCRACKER SWEETHEART	OP	15.00	15.00
94	ON THE ROAD W/COKE	OP	25.00	25.00
94	ONCE UPON A TIME	OP	15.00	15.00
94	PEACE ON EARTH 132942	OP	12.50	13.00
94	PEACE ON EARTHWORM	OP	20.00	20.00
94	PICTURE PERFECT CHRISTMAS	OP	15.00	15.00
94	PURDY PACKAGES, PARDNER!	OP	20.00	20.00
94	PURE CHRISTMAS PLEASURE	OP	20.00	20.00
94	ROCKIN' RANGER	OP	25.00	25.00
94	SANTA CLAUS IS COMIN'	OP	20.00	20.00
94	SANTA DELIVERS	OP	12.00	12.00
94	SANTA'S L'IL HELPER	OP	12.50	13.00
94	SANTA...PHONE HOME	OP	25.00	25.00
94	SANTA..YOU'RE THE POPS!	OP	22.50	23.00
94	SEASONED W/LOVE	OP	22.50	23.00
94	SKI-SON'S GREETINGS	OP	20.00	20.00
94	SPECIAL DELIVERY	OP	20.00	20.00
94	SWEET DREAMS	OP	12.50	13.00
94	SWEET GREETINGS	OP	12.50	13.00
94	SWEETS FOR MY SWEETIE	OP	15.00	15.00
94	TEED-OFF DONALD	OP	15.00	15.00
94	TO COIN A PHRASE, MERRY CHRISTMAS	OP	20.00	20.00
94	TO MY FAVORITE V.I.P.	OP	20.00	20.00
94	WAY TO A MOUSE'S HEART, THE	OP	15.00	15.00
94	WHAT'S SHAKIN' FOR CHRISTMAS	OP	18.50	19.00
94	WISHING UPON A STAR	OP	18.50	19.00
94	WISHING YOU WELL AT CHRISTMAS	OP	25.00	25.00
94	YULE FUEL	OP	20.00	20.00
94	YULETIDE YUMMIES	OP	20.00	20.00
95	1955 BLACK FORD THUNDERBIRD 146838	OP	20.00	20.00
95	1955 RED FORD THUNDERBIRD 128821	19550	20.00	20.00
95	1956 FORD F-100 TRUCK 128813	*	*	25.00
95	1957 CHEVY BEL AIR 128848	*	*	20.00
95	1959 CADILLAC ELDORADO 132705	*	*	20.00
95	1965 CHEVROLET CORVETTE STINGRAY 128856	*	*	20.00
95	57 HVN	OP	20.00	20.00
95	A CAROUSEL FOR ARIEL 142212	OP	17.50	18.00
95	A LITTLE SOMETHING EXTRA..EXTRA 137251	10000	25.00	25.00
95	A SIP OF GOOD MEASURE 139610	OP	17.50	18.00
95	ABOVE THE CROWD-R.MCDONALD HOUSE 129089	OP	20.00	20.00
95	ALL TUCKED IN 139734	OP	15.00	15.00
95	BUBBLIN' W/JOY 136581	OP	15.00	15.00
95	CADDY	OP	20.00	20.00
95	CHOC FULL OF WISHES 128945	OP	20.00	20.00
95	CHRISTMAS BELLE 142182	OP	20.00	20.00
95	CHRISTMAS EVE MISCHIEF 139726	*	*	18.00
95	CHRISTMAS IN THE BAG 139645	*	*	18.00
95	CHRISTMAS VACATION 142158	OP	20.00	20.00
95	CORVETTE	OP	20.00	20.00
95	CRACKIN' A SMILE 129046	OP	17.50	18.00
95	DASHING THROUGH THE SNOW 128996	OP	20.00	20.00
95	DREAMIN OF THE ONE I LOVE 139696	OP	25.00	25.00
95	FRIENDS FUR-EVER	OP	20.00	20.00
95	FUN IN HAND 139661	OP	17.50	18.00
95	GOOFED-UP! 136697	OP	20.00	20.00
95	GOTTA HAVE A CLUE 139653	OP	20.00	20.00
95	HAPPY YULEGLIDE 129003	OP	17.50	18.00
95	HAVE A COKE & A SMILE 128953	OP	22.50	23.00
95	HO, HO, HOLE IN ONE! 111953	OP	20.00	20.00
95	HOLIDAY BIKE HIKE 111937	OP	20.00	20.00
95	HOLIDAY BOUND 136689	OP	20.00	20.00
95	HOLIDAY RIDE 14224	OP	17.50	18.00
95	HOME FOR THE HOWL-I-DAYS 111732	OP	20.00	20.00
95	HUSTLING UP SOME CHEER 112038	OP	20.00	20.00
95	JUST FORE CHRISTMAS 142174	OP	15.00	15.00
95	LOOKING OUR HOLIDAY BEST 139750	OP	25.00	25.00
95	MAKIN' TRACKS W/MICKEY 136662	OP	20.00	20.00
95	MAZE OF OUR LIVES, THE 139599	OP	17.50	18.00
95	MERRY CHRISTMAS TO ME 139742	OP	20.00	20.00
95	MERRY MONOPOLY 132969	OP	22.50	23.00
95	MICKEY AT THE HELM 132063	OP	17.50	18.00
95	MICKEY'S AIRMAIL 136670	OP	20.00	20.00
95	MINNIE'S MERRY CHRISTMAS 136611	OP	20.00	20.00
95	MOM'S TAXI/DODGE CARAVAN 128872	OP	25.00	25.00
95	NO TIME TO SPARE AT CHRISTMAS 111961	OP	20.00	20.00
95	NUTTY ABOUT CHRISTMAS 137030	OP	22.50	23.00
95	ON THE BALL AT CHRISTMAS	OP	15.00	15.00
95	ON THE BALL AT CHRISTMAS 136700	*	*	15.00
95	PLANELY DELICIOUS 109665	OP	20.00	20.00
95	PUPPY LOVE	OP	17.50	18.00
95	RX:MAS GREETINGS 129054	OP	17.50	18.00
95	SANTA'S SPEEDWAY 129011	OP	20.00	20.00
95	SCORING BIG AT CHRISTMAS 112046	OP	20.00	20.00
95	SERVING UP THE BEST 3RD & FINAL 112054	OP	17.50	18.00
95	SNACK THAT HITS THE SPOT	OP	15.00	15.00
95	SNEAKING A PEEK 139718	OP	22.50	23.00
95	STARRING ROLL AT CHRISTMAS 137057	OP	17.50	18.00
95	SWEET ON YOU 136719	OP	22.50	23.00

YR	NAME	LIMIT	ISSUE	TREND
95	SWISHING YOU SWEET GREETINGS 105201	OP	20.00	20.00
95	TAIL WAGGIN' WISHES 142190	OP	17.50	18.00
95	THINGS GO BETTER WITH COKE TR951	*	*	15.00
95	TIME FOR REFRESHMENTS 111872	OP	20.00	20.00
95	TINKERTOY JOY 137049	OP	20.00	20.00
95	TRUCKIN'	OP	25.00	25.00
95	TRUNK FULL FO TREASURES 128961	20000	25.00	25.00
95	WISHING YOU A PERFECT HOLIDAY	OP	5.00	5.00
95	YOU'RE MY CUP OF TEA 129038	OP	20.00	20.00
95	YULE LOGON FOR CHRISTMAS CHEER 122513	OP	20.00	20.00
96	#1 COACH 168440	*	*	9.00
96	'TIS THE SEASON TO BE NUTTY 175234	*	*	17.50
96	100 YEARS..AND STILL ON A ROLL 173770	19960	*	17.50
96	1956 CHEVROLET CORVETTE 175269	19560	*	22.50
96	1965 FORD MUSTANG 173800	*	*	22.50
96	A BOOT FULL OF CHEER 166952	*	20.00	20.00
96	A CENTURY OF GOOD TASTE 8TH & FINAL 1667	*	20.00	20.00
96	A MAGIC MOMENT 172197	*	*	17.50
96	A SPALSH OF COOL YULE 213713	*	*	20.00
96	A WORLD OF GOOD TASTE 175420	20000	*	20.00
96	A-JOY MATIE, THROW ME A LIFESAVERS 16667	*	20.00	20.00
96	ALL FIRED UP FOR CHRISTMAS 168475	*	*	25.00
96	AN APPOINTMENT WITH SANTA 166979	*	20.00	20.00
96	BABY'S FIRST CHRISTMAS 166944	*	9.00	9.00
96	CAMPAIGN FOR CHRISTMAS 176818	19960	*	17.50
96	CHEVY BLAZER 167223	*	*	22.50
96	DELIVERING HOLIDAY CHEERS 177318	*	*	25.00
96	DODGE RAM TRUCK 167258	*	*	22.50
96	DOWNHILL DELIVERY 167053	*	25.00	25.00
96	FORD EXPLORER 167231	*	*	22.50
96	FRIENDS ARE TEA-RIFFIC TR962	*	*	25.00
96	GIFTS FROM MICKEY 168467	*	*	20.00
96	GOIN' FISHIN' 168459	*	*	22.50
96	HAPPY HOLIDAY 172200	*	*	17.50
96	HAVE A CRACKER JACK CHRISTMAS 172979	*	*	25.00
96	HOLIDAY IN BLOOM 172669	*	*	25.00
96	HOLIDAY TINKERTOY TREE 166995	*	17.50	17.50
96	I LOVE DAD 166901	*	9.00	9.00
96	I LOVE GRANDMA 166898	*	9.00	9.00
96	I LOVE MOM 166928	*	9.00	9.00
96	I LOVE MY DAUGHTER 166863	*	9.00	9.00
96	I LOVE MY GODCHILD 166944	*	9.00	9.00
96	I LOVE MY SON 168432	*	*	9.00
96	IN STORE FOR MORE 167134	*	*	25.00
96	IN-LINE TO HELP SANTA 166855	*	20.00	20.00
96	IT'S PLANE TO SEE..COKE IS IT 166723	*	25.00	25.00
96	JEEP GRAND CHEROKEE 167215	*	*	22.50
96	LIFE'S SWEET CHOICES 172634	*	*	25.00
96	MINNIE'S MALL HAUL 168491	*	*	25.00
96	MOTORCYCLE MICKEY 136654	*	25.00	25.00
96	ON A ROLL WITH DIET COKE 167061	*	20.00	20.00
96	PLANE CRAZY 168386	*	*	22.50
96	PLAY IT AGAIN, NICK 166987	*	17.50	17.50
96	SANTA'S ON THE LINE 167037	*	25.00	25.00
96	SERVIN' UP JOY 166847	*	20.00	20.00
96	SITTING PRETTY 172219	*	*	17.50
96	SPECIAL BEAR-LIVERY 129062	*	15.00	15.00
96	STEPPIN' WITH MINNIE 136603	*	13.50	13.50
96	SUMMONS FOR A MERRY CHRISTMAS 166960	*	22.50	22.50
96	SWINGING ON A STAR 166642	*	20.00	20.00
96	TAILS A'WAGON 167126	*	*	20.00
96	THOU ART MY LAMP, O LORD 173894	*	*	25.00
96	TREES TO PLEASE 168386	*	*	25.00
96	YO HO HOLIDAYS T0003	*	*	*
G. ARMGARDT			**TREASURY OF CHRISTMAS**	
90	JINGLE BELL ROCK 1990-563390	YR	13.50	18.00
C. BAKER			**TREASURY OF CHRISTMAS**	
89	HOLLY-FAIRY-565199	YR	15.00	35.00
90	CHRISTMAS TREE FAIRY, THE-565202	YR	15.00	25.00
S. BUTCHER			**TREASURY OF CHRISTMAS**	
94	'TIS THE SEASON TO GO SHOPPING	OP	22.50	23.00
94	A CHILD IS BORN	OP	25.00	25.00
94	BABY'S FIRST CHRISTMAS	OP	20.00	20.00
94	BABY'S FIRST CHRISTMAS	OP	20.00	20.00
94	DROPPING IN FOR THE HOLIDAYS	OP	20.00	20.00
94	DRUMMING UP A SEASON OF JOY	OP	18.50	19.00
94	FRIENDSHIPS WARM THE HOLIDAYS	OP	20.00	20.00
94	MAY ALL YOUR WISHES COME TRUE	OP	20.00	20.00
94	MAY YOUR HOLIDAY BE BRIGHTENED W/LOVE	OP	15.00	15.00
94	OUR FIRST CHRISTMAS TOGETHER	OP	25.00	25.00
94	RINGING UP HOLIDAY WISHES	OP	18.50	19.00
94	SENDING YOU A SEASON'S GREETING	OP	25.00	25.00
94	SWEET HOLIDAYS	OP	11.00	11.00
95	BABY'S FIRST CHRISTMAS 125946	OP	15.00	15.00
95	BABY'S FIRST CHRISTMAS125954	OP	15.00	15.00
95	BRINGING HOLIDAY WISHES TO YOU 125911	OP	22.50	23.00
95	FRIENDS ARE THE GREATEST TREASURE 125962	20000	25.00	25.00
95	HAPPY BIRTHDAY JESUS 125857	OP	15.00	15.00

YR	NAME	LIMIT	ISSUE	TREND
95	HAPPY BIRTHDAY JESUS 125857	*	*	15.00
95	I'M IN A SPIN OVER YOU 125873	OP	15.00	15.00
95	LETS SNUGGLE TOGETHER FOR CHRISTMAS 1258	OP	15.00	15.00
95	OUR FIRST CHRISTMAS TOGETHER 125881	OP	22.50	23.00
95	PRETTY UP FOR THE HOLIDAYS 125830	OP	20.00	20.00
95	TWINKLE, TWINKLE CHRISTMAS STAR 125903	OP	17.50	18.00
95	YOU BRING THE LOVE TO CHRISTMAS 125849	OP	15.00	15.00
95	YOU PULL THE STRINGS TO MY HEART 125938	OP	20.00	20.00
M. COOK			**TREASURY OF CHRISTMAS**	
88	DAIRY CHRISTMAS-557501	TL	10.00	15.00
89	CHRISTMAS COOK-OUT-561045	TL	9.00	12.00
89	DECK THE HOGS-565490	TL	12.00	16.00
89	FELIZ NAVIDAD! 1989-564842	YR	11.00	20.00
89	PINATA RIDIN'-565504	TL	11.00	18.00
89	SCRUB-A-DUB CHIPMUNK-561037	TL	8.00	10.00
89	SPREADING CHRISTMAS JOY-564850	TL	10.00	10.00
89	TOP OF THE CLASS-565237	TL	11.00	11.00
90	CHRISTMAS IS MAGIC-564826	TL	10.00	10.00
90	FLEECE NAVIDAD-571903	TL	13.50	14.00
90	HAVE A NAVAHO-HO-HO 1990-571970	YR	15.00	18.00
90	LIGHTING UP CHRISTMAS-564834	TL	10.00	14.00
90	MERRY MOUSTRONAUTS-573558	TL	20.00	20.00
90	REELING IN THE HOLIDAYS-560405	TL	8.00	10.00
91	CHRISTMAS TO GO-580600	YR	22.50	23.00
91	DOUBLE SCOOP SNOWMOUSE-564796	TL	13.50	14.00
91	HAVE A MARIACHI CHRISTMAS-580619	TL	13.50	14.00
91	WALKIN'WITH MY BABY-561029	TL	10.00	10.00
92	LA LUMINARIA-586579	TL	13.50	14.00
J. DAVIS			**TREASURY OF CHRISTMAS**	
82	HOLIDAY SKIER-E-6954	TL	7.00	30.00
83	GARFIELD CUTS THE ICE-E-8771	TL	6.00	45.00
83	STOCKING FULL FOR 1983-E-8773	YR	8.00	45.00
84	DEER! ODIE-E6226	TL	6.00	40.00
84	FUN IN SANTA'S SLEIGH-E-6225	TL	12.00	35.00
84	GARFIELD HARK! THE HERALD ANGEL-E-6224	TL	7.50	45.00
84	GARFIELD THE SNOW CAT-E-6227	TL	12.00	12.00
84	STOCKING FULL FOR 1984-E-8773	YR	6.00	35.00
85	GARFIELD-IN-THE-BOX-56189	YR	6.50	7.00
85	HOPPY CHRISTMAS-56154	YR	8.50	30.00
85	MERRY CHRISTMAS MOTHER-56146	YR	8.50	9.00
85	MERRY CHRISTMAS TEACHER-56170	YR	6.00	6.00
85	NORTH POLE EXPRESS-56138	YR	12.00	35.00
85	SKI TIME-56111	YR	13.00	40.00
86	GIFT WRAP OLDIE-553611	YR	7.00	7.00
86	LIGHTEN UP!-553603	TL	10.00	22.00
87	GARFIELD MERRY KISSMAS-555215	TL	8.50	20.00
87	GARFIELD SUGAR PLUM FAIRY-556009	TL	8.50	25.00
87	GARFIELD THE NUTCRACKER-556017	TL	8.50	15.00
88	DEER GARFIELD-558702	TL	12.00	18.00
88	GARFIELD BAGS O'FUN-558761	YR	3.30	5.00
88	NIGHT-WATCH CAT-558362	TL	13.00	20.00
88	SPECIAL DELIVERY-558699	TL	9.00	16.00
89	A CHAINS OF PACE FOR ODIE-563269	TL	12.00	12.00
89	GOD BLESS US EVERYONE-563242	TL	13.50	14.00
89	HO-HO HOLIDAY SCROOGE-563234	TL	13.50	14.00
89	JOY RIDIN'-563463	TL	15.00	18.00
89	MINE, ALL MINE!-564079	YR	15.00	25.00
89	SCROOGE WITH THE SPIRIT-563250	TL	13.50	15.00
90	AN APPLE A DAY-572594	TL	12.00	15.00
90	DEAR SANTA-572608	TL	17.00	17.00
90	FROSTY GARFIELD 1990-572551	YR	13.50	20.00
90	GARFIELD NFL ATLANTA FALCONS-573159	TL	12.50	13.00
90	GARFIELD NFL BUFFALO BILLS-573108	TL	12.50	13.00
90	GARFIELD NFL CHICAGO BEARS-573248	TL	12.50	13.00
90	GARFIELD NFL CINCINNATI BENGALS-573000	TL	15.50	13.00
90	GARFIELD NFL CLEVELAND BROWNS-573019	TL	12.50	13.00
90	GARFIELD NFL DALLAS COWBOYS-573183	TL	12.50	13.00
90	GARFIELD NFL DENVER BRONCOS-573043	TL	12.50	13.00
90	GARFIELD NFL DETROIT LIONS-573256	TL	12.50	13.00
90	GARFIELD NFL GREEN BAY PACKERS-573264	TL	12.50	13.00
90	GARFIELD NFL HOUSTON OILERS-573027	TL	12.50	13.00
90	GARFIELD NFL INDIANAPOLIS COLTS-573116	TL	12.50	13.00
90	GARFIELD NFL KANSAS CITY CHIEFS-573051	TL	12.50	13.00
90	GARFIELD NFL LOS ANGELES RAIDERS-573078	TL	12.50	13.00
90	GARFIELD NFL LOS ANGELES RAMS-572764	TL	12.50	13.00
90	GARFIELD NFL MIAMI DOLPHINS-573124	TL	12.50	13.00
90	GARFIELD NFL NEW ENGLAND PATRIOTS-573132	TL	12.50	13.00
90	GARFIELD NFL NEW ORLEANS SAINTS-573167	TL	12.50	13.00
90	GARFIELD NFL NEW YORK GIANTS-573191	TL	12.50	13.00
90	GARFIELD NFL NEW YORK JETS-573140	TL	12.50	13.00
90	GARFIELD NFL PHILADELPHIA EAGLES-573205	TL	12.50	13.00
90	GARFIELD NFL PHOENIX CARDINALS-573213	TL	12.50	13.00
90	GARFIELD NFL PITTSBURG STEELERS-573035	TL	12.50	13.00
90	GARFIELD NFL SAN DIEGO CHARGERS-573086	TL	12.50	13.00
90	GARFIELD NFL SAN FRANCISCO 49ERS-573175	TL	12.50	13.00
90	GARFIELD NFL SEATTLE SEAHAWKS-573094	TL	12.50	13.00
90	GARFIELD NFL TAMPA BAY BUCCANEERS-573280	TL	12.50	13.00
90	GARFIELD NFL WASHINGTON REDSKINS-573221	TL	12.50	13.00
90	LITTLE RED RIDING CAT-572632	YR	13.50	18.00

YR	NAME	LIMIT	ISSUE	TREND
90	MINNESOTA VIKINGS-573272	TL	12.50	13.00
90	OH SHOOSH!-572624	TL	17.00	17.00
90	OVER THE ROOFTOPS-572721	TL	17.50	18.00
90	POP GOES THE ODIE-572578	TL	15.00	16.00
90	TROUBLE ON WHEELS-564052	TL	20.00	20.00
91	ALL DECKED OUT-572659	TL	13.50	14.00
91	HAVE A BALL THIS CHRISTMAS-572616	YR	15.00	20.00
91	HERE COMES SANTA PAWS-572535	TL	20.00	20.00
91	HOLIDAY HIDEOUT-585270	TL	15.00	16.00
91	HOT STUFF SANTA-573523	TL	25.00	30.00
91	MERRY CHRISTMAS GO-ROUND-585203	TL	20.00	20.00
91	PINOCCHIO-577391	TL	15.00	16.00
91	STRAIGHT TO SANTA-830534	TL	13.50	14.00
91	SWEET BEAMS-572586	TL	13.50	14.00
92	4 X 4 HOLIDAY FUN-580783	TL	20.00	20.00
92	A ROCKIN' GARFIELD CHRISTMAS-572527	TL	17.50	18.00
92	FAST TRACK CAT-585289	TL	17.50	18.00
92	HOLIDAY CAT NAPPING-585319	TL	20.00	20.00
92	HOLIDAY ON ICE-585254	TL	17.50	17.00
92	RING MY BELL-580740	YR	13.50	14.00
93	BAH HUMBUG	OP	15.00	15.00
93	GRADE A WISHES FROM GARFIELD	OP	20.00	20.00
94	MINE, MINE, MINE	OP	20.00	20.00
M. GILMORE			**TREASURY OF CHRISTMAS**	
82	CRESCENT SANTA-E-6950	TL	10.00	65.00
82	DEAR SANTA-E-6959	TL	10.00	15.00
84	BABY'S FIRST CHRISTMAS 1984-E-6212	YR	10.00	10.00
85	BABY'S FIRST CHRISTMAS 1985-56014	YR	6.00	6.00
85	MERRY CHRISTMAS GODCHILD-55832	TL	8.00	30.00
86	BABY BEAR SLEIGH-551651	TL	9.00	30.00
86	BABY'S FIRST CHRISTMAS 1986-551678	YR	10.00	15.00
86	CAROUSEL UNICORN-551252	TL	12.00	75.00
86	MERRY CHRISTMAS-551341	TL	8.00	75.00
86	TIME FOR CHRISTMAS-551325	TL	13.00	25.00
87	BABY'S FIRST CHRISTMAS 1987-556238	YR	10.00	25.00
87	CAROUSEL LION-556025	TL	12.00	25.00
87	HOME SWEET HOME-556033	TL	15.00	55.00
87	PARTRIDGE IN A PEAR TREE-556173	TL	9.00	33.00
87	TEDDY'S STOCKING-555940	TL	10.00	20.00
87	THREE FRENCH HENS-556440	TL	9.00	25.00
87	TWINKLE BEAR-556572	TL	8.00	15.00
87	TWO TURTLEDOVES-556432	TL	9.00	33.00
88	1ST CHRISTMAS TOGETHER-554537	TL	15.00	16.00
88	A CHIPMUNK HOLIDAY-554898	TL	11.00	18.00
88	A MOUSE CHECK-554553	TL	13.50	18.00
88	AIRMAIL FOR TEACHER-489425	TL	13.50	25.00
88	AN EYE ON CHRISTMAS-554545	TL	22.50	35.00
88	BABY'S FIRST CHRISTMAS 1988-554936	YR	10.00	16.00
88	CHRISTMAS TRADITION-558400	TL	10.00	18.00
88	FIVE GOLDEN RINGS-559121	TL	11.00	30.00
88	FOREVER FRIENDS-554626	TL	12.00	27.00
88	FOUR CALLING BIRDS-556459	TL	11.00	30.00
88	LI'L DRUMMER BEAR-554952	TL	12.00	20.00
88	NORTH POLE LINEMAN-558834	TL	10.00	20.00
88	SIX GEESE A-LAYING-559148	TL	11.00	30.00
88	TWO FOR TEA-559776	TL	20.00	30.00
89	ALL SET FOR SANTA-563080	TL	17.50	18.00
89	BABY'S FIRST CHRISTMAS 1989-562815	YR	10.00	13.00
89	BY THE LIGHT OF THE MOON-563005	TL	12.00	15.00
89	CAUGHT IN THE ACT-830046	TL	12.50	13.00
89	CHESTNUTS ROASTIN'-562912	TL	13.00	28.00
89	CHRISTMAS COOKIN'-563048	TL	22.50	25.00
89	EIGHT MAIDS A-MILKING-562750	TL	12.00	18.00
89	MERRY CHRISTMAS POPS-562971	TL	12.00	24.00
89	MISTLE-TOAST-1989-562963	YR	15.00	21.00
89	NINE DANCERS DANCING-562769	TL	15.00	18.00
89	OLD TOWN'S CHURCH-554871	TL	17.50	18.00
89	READIN' & RIDIN'-830054	TL	13.50	14.00
89	SARDINE EXPRESS-554588	TL	17.50	20.00
89	SEVEN SWANS A-SWIMMING-562742	TL	12.00	12.00
89	STICKIN' TO IT-563013	TL	10.00	16.00
89	TRAVELIN' TRIKE-562882	TL	15.00	16.00
90	A CAROLING WEE GO-573671	TL	12.00	12.00
90	ALL ABOARD-567671	TL	17.50	18.00
90	ALL EYE WANT FOR CHRISTMAS-573647	TL	27.50	28.00
90	BABY'S FIRST CHRISTMAS 1990-573973	YR	10.00	10.00
90	BABY'S FIRST CHRISTMAS 1990-573981	YR	12.00	14.00
90	DECK THE HALLS-573701	TL	22.50	23.00
90	ELEVEN DRUMMERS DRUMMING-573957	TL	15.00	16.00
90	FIRST CLASS CHRISTMAS-830038	TL	10.00	10.00
90	HAVE A COOL YULE-830496	TL	12.00	12.00
90	HERE'S LOOKING AT YOU-830259	TL	17.50	18.00
90	LITTLE JACK HORNER-574058	TL	17.50	18.00
90	MERRY MAILMAN-573698	TL	15.00	16.00
90	NORTH POLE OR BUST-562998	TL	25.00	25.00
90	OLD KING COLE-575682	TL	20.00	20.00
90	OLD MOTHER MOUSE-573922	TL	17.50	18.00
90	PROF. MICHAEL BEAR/ONE BEAR BAND-573663	TL	22.50	23.00
90	RAILROAD REPAIRS-573930	TL	12.50	13.00

YR	NAME	LIMIT	ISSUE	TREND
90	SANTA'S SWEETS-563196	TL	20.00	20.00
90	STUCK ON YOU-573655	TL	12.50	13.00
90	SWEETEST GREETINGS 1990-830011	YR	10.00	15.00
90	TH-INK-IN' OF YOU-562920	TL	20.00	20.00
90	TWELVE PIPERS PIPING-573965	TL	15.00	16.00
90	WARMEST WISHES-573825	YR	17.50	25.00
90	YOU'RE WHEEL SPECIAL-573728	TL	15.00	16.00
90	YULETIDE RIDE 1990-577502	YR	13.50	22.00
91	A CHRISTMAS CAROL-583928	TL	22.50	23.00
91	A DECADE OF TREASURES-587052	YR	37.50	38.00
91	A QUARTER POUNDER WITH CHEER-581569	TL	20.00	20.00
91	A SONG FOR SANTA-573779	TL	25.00	25.00
91	AIMING FOR THE HOLIDAYS-830941	TL	12.00	12.00
91	CHRISTMAS CABBOSE-574856	TL	25.00	25.00
91	CHRISTMAS FILLS THE AIR-831921	TL	12.00	12.00
91	CHRISTMAS TRIMMINGS-575631	TL	17.00	17.00
91	COME LET US ADORE HIM-573736	TL	9.00	9.00
91	CRYSTAL BALL CHRISTMAS-575666	TL	22.50	23.00
91	DREAMIN' OF A WHITE CHRISTMAS-583669	TL	15.00	16.00
91	FINISHING TOUCH, THE-831530	YR	10.00	12.00
91	FIRED UP FOR CHRISTMAS-586587	TL	32.50	33.00
91	FITTIN' MITTENS-830976	TL	12.00	12.00
91	FOR A DOG-GONE GREAT UNCLE-586706	YR	12.00	12.00
91	FOR A PURR-FECT AUNT-586692	YR	12.00	12.00
91	FOR A PURR-FECT MOM-586641	YR	12.00	12.00
91	FOR A SPECIAL DAD-586668	YR	17.50	18.00
91	FROM THE SAME MOLD-581798	TL	17.00	17.00
91	GUMBALL WIZARD-575658	TL	13.00	13.00
91	KURIOUS KITTY-573868	TL	17.50	19.00
91	LETTERS TO SANTA-830925	TL	15.00	16.00
91	LIGHTS..CAMERA..KISSMAS!-583626	YR	15.00	18.00
91	MARY, MARY QUITE CONTRARY-574066	TL	22.50	23.00
91	MERRY MILLIMETERS-583677	TL	17.00	17.00
91	MOON BEAM DREAMS-573760	TL	12.00	12.00
91	MR. MAILMOUSE-587109	TL	17.00	17.00
91	ODE TO JOY-830968	TL	10.00	10.00
91	ONE FOGGY CHRISTMAS EVE-586625	TL	30.00	30.00
91	PEDDLING FUN-586714	YR	16.00	16.00
91	PETER, PETER PUMPKIN EATER-574015	TL	20.00	20.00
91	SANTA DELIVERS LOVE-562904	TL	17.50	18.00
91	SANTA'S KEY MAN-830461	TL	11.00	11.00
91	SNEAKING SANTA'S SNACK-830933	TL	13.00	13.00
91	SPECIAL KEEPSAKES-586722	YR	13.50	14.00
91	SWEET STEED-583634	TL	15.00	16.00
91	THROUGH THE YEARS-574252	YR	17.50	18.00
91	TIE-DINGS OF JOY-830488	YR	12.00	12.00
91	TOM, TOM THE PIPER'S SON-575690	TL	15.00	16.00
91	WITH LOVE-586676	YR	13.00	13.00
92	A BOOT-IFUL CHRISTMAS-840165	YR	20.00	20.00
92	A CHRISTMAS YARN-593516	YR	20.00	20.00
92	A GOLD STAR FOR TEACHER-831948	TL	15.00	16.00
92	A MUG FULL OF LOVE-832928	YR	13.50	14.00
92	A TALL ORDER-832758	TL	12.00	12.00
92	BEARLY SLEEPY-578029	YR	17.50	18.00
92	BUBBLE BUDDY-586978	TL	13.50	14.00
92	CANDLELIGHT SERENADE-832766	TL	12.00	12.00
92	CATCH A FALLING STAR-583944	TL	15.00	16.00
92	CATCH A FALLING STAR-583944	TL	15.00	16.00
92	CHRISTMAS NITE CAP-834424	TL	13.50	14.00
92	CHRISTOPHER COLUMOUSE-832782	YR	12.00	12.00
92	COZY CHRISTMAS CARRIAGE-586730	TL	22.50	23.00
92	FIREHOUSE FRIENDS-586951	YR	22.50	23.00
92	FUR-EVER FRIENDS-590797	TL	13.50	14.00
92	GINGER-BRED GREETING-831581	YR	12.00	12.00
92	HAVE A COOL CHRISTMAS-832944	YR	13.50	14.00
92	HOLIDAY GLOW PUPPET SHOW-832774	TL	15.00	16.00
92	HOLIDAY HAPPENINGS-588555	TL	30.00	30.00
92	HOLIDAY HONORS-833029	YR	15.00	16.00
92	HUMPTY DUMPTY-574244	TL	25.00	25.00
92	IT'S A GO FOR CHRISTMAS-587095	TL	15.00	16.00
92	KNITTEN' KITTENS-832952	YR	17.50	18.00
92	MAKING TRACKS TO SANTA-832804	TL	15.00	16.00
92	NORTH POLE PEPPERMINT PATROL-840157	TL	25.00	25.00
92	NUTCRACKER, THE-574023	TL	25.00	25.00
92	POPPIN' HOPPIN' HOLIDAYS-831263	YR	25.00	25.00
92	POST-MOUSTER GENERAL-587117	TL	20.00	20.00
92	QUEEN OF HEARTS-575712	TL	17.50	18.00
92	ROCK-A-BYE BABY-575704	TL	13.50	14.00
92	SANTA'S MIDNIGHT SNACK-588598	TL	20.00	20.00
92	SEED-SON'S GREETINGS-588571	TL	27.00	27.00
92	SEW CHRISTMASY-583820	TL	25.00	25.00
92	SWEET AS CANEBE-583642	TL	15.00	16.00
92	TANKFUL TIDINGS-831271	TL	30.00	30.00
92	THROUGH THE YEARS-586862	YR	17.50	18.00
92	TO THE POINT-831182	TL	13.50	14.00
92	WINDOW WISH LIST-586854	TL	30.00	30.00
95	4-ALARM CHRISTMAS 6TH & FINAL ISSUE 1287	OP	17.50	18.00
95	BUTTONING UP OUR HOLIDAY BEST TR952	*	*	23.00
95	FIRST CLASS CHRISTMAS TR954	*	*	23.00

YR	NAME	LIMIT	ISSUE	TREND
95	HOLIDAY HIGH-LIGHT TR953	*	*	15.00
95	SEA-SON'S GREETINGS, TEACHER 112070	OP	17.50	18.00
95	TO SANTA, POST HASTE 112151	OP	15.00	15.00
*** GILMORE STUDIOS**			**TREASURY OF CHRISTMAS**	
93	A BRIGHT IDEA	OP	22.50	23.00
93	A MISTLE-TOW	OP	15.00	15.00
93	BABY'S FIRST CHRISTMAS	OP	17.50	18.00
93	CARVING CHRISTMAS WISHES	OP	25.00	25.00
93	DELIVERED TO THE NICK IN TIME	OP	13.50	14.00
93	FESTIVE FIREMAN	OP	17.00	17.00
93	FOR A STAR AUNT	OP	12.00	12.00
93	GRANDMA'S LIDDLE GRIDDLE	OP	10.00	10.00
93	HAVE A COOL CHRISTMAS	OP	10.00	10.00
93	HAVE A DARN GOOD CHRISTMAS	OP	21.00	21.00
93	MY SPECIAL CHRISTMAS	OP	17.50	18.00
93	NOT A CREATURE WAS STIRRING...	OP	27.50	28.00
93	SAY CHEESE	OP	13.50	14.00
93	SEEING IS BELIEVING	OP	20.00	20.00
93	SNEAKING A PEEK	OP	10.00	10.00
93	SUGAR CHEF SHOPPE	OP	23.50	24.00
93	SWEETEST RIDE, THE	OP	18.50	19.00
93	TIME FOR SANTA	OP	17.50	18.00
93	TO A GRADE A TEACHER	OP	10.00	10.00
93	TREE FOR TWO	OP	17.50	18.00
94	'TWAS THE NITE BEFORE CHRISTMAS	OP	18.50	19.00
94	ALMOST TIME FOR SANTA	OP	25.00	25.00
94	BUTTONS 'N' BOW BOUTIQUE	OP	22.50	23.00
94	CHIMINY CHEER	OP	22.50	23.00
94	CHRISTMAS CUSTOMS	10000	17.50	18.00
94	COZY CANDLELIGHT DINNER	OP	25.00	25.00
94	ESPECIALLY FOR YOU	OP	27.50	28.00
94	FINE FEATHERED FESTIVITIES	OP	22.50	23.00
94	FINISHING FIRST	OP	20.00	20.00
94	FROM OUR HOUSE TO YOURS	OP	25.00	25.00
94	GOOD FRIENDS ARE FOREVER	OP	13.50	14.00
94	HOLIDAY CHEW-CHEW	OP	22.50	23.00
94	HOLIDAY FREEZER TEASER	OP	25.00	25.00
94	JOY FROM HEAR TO HOSE	OP	15.00	15.00
94	LATEST SCOOP FROM SANTA, THE	OP	18.50	19.00
94	MELTED MY HEART	OP	15.00	15.00
94	SANTA' S SING-A-LONG	OP	20.00	20.00
94	SANTA' SECRET TEST DRIVE	OP	20.00	20.00
94	SANTA'S GINGER-BRED DOE	OP	15.00	1500
94	SUGAR 'N SPICE FOR SOMEONE NICE	OP	30.00	30.00
94	TO THE SWEETEST BABY	OP	18.50	19.00
94	TOY TINKER TOPPER	OP	20.00	20.00
94	YOU'RE A WHEEL COOL BROTHER	OP	22.50	23.00
94	YOU'RE A WINNER SON!	OP	18.50	19.00
J. GROSSMAN			**TREASURY OF CHRISTMAS**	
86	SANTA CALUS SHOPPE, THE- CIRCA 1905-5515	TL	8.00	18.00
K. HAHN			**TREASURY OF CHRISTMAS**	
89	FULL HOUSE MOUSE-565016	TL	13.50	22.00
89	I FEEL PRETTY-565024	TL	20.00	25.00
90	BABY'S CHRISTMAS FEAST-565040	TL	13.50	22.00
90	BUBBLE TROUBLE-575038	TL	20.00	20.00
90	CATCH OF THE DAY-575070	TL	25.00	25.00
90	COFFEE BREAK-564990	TL	15.00	16.00
90	DON'T OPEN 'TIL CHRISTMAS-575089	TL	16.50	17.00
90	I CAN'T WEIGHT TIL CHRISTMAS-575119	TL	17.50	18.00
90	SLOTS O LUCK-830518	TL	13.50	22.00
90	WARMEST WISHES-565032	TL	15.00	16.00
90	YIPPIE-I-YULETIDE-564982	TL	15.00	24.00
90	YOU'RE SEW SPECIAL-565008	YR	20.00	25.00
91	A HOLIDAY SCENT STATION-575054	TL	15.00	16.00
91	BATHING BEAUTY-860581	TL	13.50	14.00
91	DECK THE HALLS-575127	TL	15.00	15.00
91	HATS OFF TO CHRISTMAS-586757	YR	22.50	23.00
91	MERRY MOTHER-TO-BE-575046	TL	13.50	14.00
91	TEA FOR TWO-573299	TL	30.00	30.00
92	CAMPIN' COMPANIONS-590282	TL	20.00	20.00
92	FRIENDSHIPS PRESERVED-586749	YR	22.50	23.00
92	JESUS LOVES ME-595837	YR	10.00	10.00
92	JOY TO THE WHIRLED-589551	TL	20.00	20.00
92	MERRY CHRISTMAS MOTHER EARTH-595810	YR	11.00	11.00
92	MERRY MAKE-OVER-589586	TL	20.00	20.00
92	SALUTE THE SEASON-595780	YR	12.00	12.00
92	SPINNING CHRISTMAS DREAMS-590908	TL	22.50	23.00
92	SQUIRRELIN' IT WAY-595748	YR	12.00	12.00
92	TREASURE THE EARTH-593826	TL	25.00	25.00
93	A TOAST LADLED W/LOVE	OP	15.00	15.00
93	DECEMBER 25..DEAR DIARY	OP	10.00	10.00
93	DO NOT OPEN 'TIL CHRISTMAS	OP	15.00	15.00
93	GOOD GROUNDS FOR FRIENDSHIP	OP	24.50	25.00
93	GREETINGS IN STEREO	OP	19.50	20.00
93	JEWEL BOX BALLET	OP	20.00	20.00
93	MICE CAPADES	OP	26.50	27.00
93	PAINT YOUR HOLIDAYS BRIGHT	OP	10.00	10.00
93	WHEEL MERRY WISHES	OP	15.00	15.00

YR	NAME	LIMIT	ISSUE	TREND
93	YOU'RE A HIT W/ME, BROTHER	OP	10.00	10.00
94	BUILDING MEMORIES	OP	25.00	25.00
94	EXPECTING JOY	OP	12.50	13.00
94	FRIENDS ARE THE SPICE OF LIFE	OP	20.00	20.00
94	HAPPY HOLI-DATE	OP	22.50	23.00
94	HAVE A DINO-MITE CHRISTMAS	OP	18.50	19.00
94	HOLIDAY CATCH	OP	12.50	13.00
94	MERRY MISS MERRY	OP	12.00	12.00
94	O' COME ALL YE FAITHFUL	OP	15.00	15.00
94	ONE SMALL STEP...	19690	30.00	30.00
94	OPEN FOR BUSINESS	OP	17.50	18.00
94	RING IN THE HOLIDAYS	OP	12.50	13.00
95	..GOOD WILL TOWARD MEN 132942	19450	25.00	25.00
95	CHRISTMAS FISHES, DAD 139629	OP	17.50	18.00
95	FRIENDSHIPS BLOOM THROUGH ALL SEASONS 6T	OP	22.50	23.00
95	GET IN THE SPIRIT..RECYCLE 3RD ISSUE 132	OP	17.50	18.00
95	JACKPOT JOY! 7TH ISSUE 132896	OP	17.50	18.00
95	MISS MERRY'S SECRET 7TH ISSUE 132934	OP	20.00	20.00
95	NIGHT B 4 CHRISTMAS, THE 134848	OP	20.00	20.00
95	ON THE MOVE AT CHRISTMAS 142220	OP	17.50	18.00
95	YOU'RE THE PERFECT FIT TO002	*	*	*
96	15 YEARS OF HITS 175463	10000	*	25.00
96	CATCH OF THE HOLIDAY 132888	*	20.00	20.00
96	DECKED OUT FOR CHRISTMAS 176796	*	*	25.00
96	HAIR'S THE PLACE 173029	*	*	25.00
96	HOLIDAY DREAMS OF GREEN 173797	*	*	15.00
96	RIDING HIGH 1ST ISSUE TR964	*	*	20.00
96	SANTA'S SACKS 111945	*	15.00	15.00
96	TRACKING REINDEER PAUSE 173789	*	*	25.00
J. HENSON			**TREASURY OF CHRISTMAS**	
84	MUPPET BABIES BABY'S/CHRISTMAS-E-6222	YR	10.00	60.00
84	MUPPET BABIES BABY'S/CHRISTMAS-E-6223	YR	10.00	60.00
J. JONIK			**TREASURY OF CHRISTMAS**	
89	STAR OF STARS-564389	TL	9.00	10.00
89	YULETIDE TREE HOUSE-564915	TL	20.00	22.00
90	HANG ONTO YOUR HAT-564397	TL	8.00	9.00
91	SANTA WINGS IT-573612	TL	13.00	13.00
92	JOLLY OL' GENT-585645	TL	13.50	14.00
R. MOREHEAD			**TREASURY OF CHRISTMAS**	
88	OLD FASHIONED ANGEL-559164	TL	12.50	15.00
88	PRETTY BABY-559156	TL	12.50	13.00
D. OLSEN			**TREASURY OF CHRISTMAS**	
94	FORMULA FOR LOVE	OP	10.00	10.00
D. PARKER			**TREASURY OF CHRISTMAS**	
88	BABY'S FIRST CHRISTMAS-558397	TL	16.00	25.00
J. PENCHOFF			**TREASURY OF CHRISTMAS**	
92	HEAVEN SENT-588423	TL	12.50	13.00
M. PETERS			**TREASURY OF CHRISTMAS**	
89	JUST WHAT I WANTED-563668	TL	13.50	14.00
90	FLEAS NAVIDAD-563978	TL	13.50	14.00
90	PUCKER UP!-563676	TL	11.00	11.00
90	TWEET GREETINGS-564044	TL	15.00	16.00
90	WHAT'S THE BRIGHT IDEA-563684	TL	13.50	14.00
91	DECK THE HALLS-860573	TL	12.00	12.00
M. RHYNER			**TREASURY OF CHRISTMAS**	
92	SPEEDIN' MR. SNOWMAN-595802	YR	12.00	12.00
L. RIGG			**TREASURY OF CHRISTMAS**	
85	CHRISTMAS PLANE RIDE-56049	TL	10.00	20.00
86	LUCY & ME CHRISTMAS TREE-552542	TL	7.00	25.00
86	LUCY & ME SKI TIME-552658	TL	6.50	7.00
86	MERRY CHRISTMAS 1986-552186	YR	8.00	8.00
86	MERRY CHRISTMAS 1986-552534	YR	8.00	20.00
87	LUCY & ME ANGEL ON A CLOUD-555452	TL	12.00	20.00
87	LUCY & ME MAILBOX BEAR-556564	TL	3.00	5.00
87	LUCY & ME STORYBOOK BEAR-555444	TL	6.50	14.00
87	MERRY CHRISTMAS 1987-555428	TL	8.00	8.00
87	MERRY CHRISTMAS 1987-555436	YR	8.00	8.00
87	TIME FOR CHRISTMAS-555452	TL	12.00	20.00
88	JESTER BEAR-558222	TL	8.00	20.00
88	MERRY CHRISTMAS 1988-557595	YR	10.00	12.00
88	MERRY CHRISTMAS 1988-557609	YR	10.00	12.00
88	TEDDY BEAR GREETINGS-558214	TL	8.00	12.00
88	TOY CHEST KEEPSAKE-558206	TL	12.50	15.00
89	CHRISTMAS 1989-565210	YR	12.00	12.00
89	CHRISTMAS 1989-568325	YR	12.00	12.00
90	A SPOONFUL OF LOVE-568570	TL	10.00	10.00
90	BABY BEAR CHRISTMAS 1990-575860	YR	12.00	13.00
90	BEARING HOLIDAY WISHES-568619	TL	22.50	23.00
90	BEARY CHRISTMAS 1990-576158	YR	12.00	15.00
90	CHRISTMAS SWINGTIME 1990-568597	TL	13.00	13.00
90	CHRISTMAS SWINGTIME 1990-568600	YR	13.00	13.00
91	BEARY MERRY MAILMAN-830151	TL	13.50	14.00
91	CHRISTMAS SWINGTIME 1991-576166	YR	13.00	15.00
91	CHRISTMAS SWINGTIME 1991-5761714	YR	13.00	15.00
91	CHRISTMAS TWO-GETHER-575615	TL	22.50	23.00
91	CRANK UP THE CAROLS-575887	TL	17.50	18.00
91	LOVE IS THE SECRET INGREDIENT-568562	TL	15.00	16.00

From Enesco Corp.'s Memories of Yesterday, A Surprise for Santa–1989 *by Mabel Lucie Attwell was limited to one year of production and sold for $13.50.*

"Sharing is caring" the members of the Salvation Army Band *seem to proclaim. The musical ornament, which plays "Joy to the World," is produced by Hallmark.*

Starship Enterprise *from the Hallmark Keepsake Ornament line realized secondary market prices out of this world.*

Is somebody posing as the Jolly Old Elf? *Santa is produced by Lladró.*

YR	NAME	LIMIT	ISSUE	TREND
91	TIRE-D LITTLE BEAR-575852	YR	12.50	13.00
92	MOONLIGHT SWING-568627	TL	15.00	16.00
92	TASTY TIDINGS-575836	YR	13.50	14.00
G.G. SANTIAGO		**TREASURY OF CHRISTMAS**		
88	CHRISTMAS VACATION-558451	TL	8.00	15.00
88	CHRISTMAS WATCH-558443	TL	11.00	15.00
88	ICE FAIRY, THE-558516	TL	23.00	30.00
88	MOUSE UPON A PIPE-489220	TL	10.00	24.00
88	PARTY MOUSE-558435	TL	12.00	15.00
88	SANTA CLAUS BALLOON-489212	TL	10.00	16.00
88	STOCKING STORY-558419	TL	10.00	16.00
88	SWEET CHERUB-558478	TL	7.00	9.00
88	TIME OUT-558486	TL	11.00	27.00
88	WINTER TALE-558427	TL	6.00	19.00
89	HO! HO! YO-YO!-565105	YR	12.00	12.00
89	SPECIAL DELIVERY-565091	YR	12.00	20.00
89	WEIGHTIN' FOR SANTA-565148	TL	7.50	8.00
90	BUMPER CAR SANTA-565083	YR	20.00	25.00
N. TEIBER		**TREASURY OF CHRISTMAS**		
89	TEA FOR TWO-693758	TL	12.50	14.00
89	TEA TIME-694797	TL	12.50	14.00
90	FIREPLACE FROLIC-564435	TL	25.00	25.00
90	HOLIDAY TEA TOAST-694770	TL	13.50	14.00
T. WILSON		**TREASURY OF CHRISTMAS**		
90	A NIGHT BEFORE CHRISTMAS-572438	TL	17.50	18.00
90	CHEERS 1990-572411	YR	13.50	15.00
90	MERRY KISSMAS-572446	TL	10.00	10.00
91	RIS-SKI BUSINESS-576719	TL	10.00	10.00
92	FINISHING TOUCHES, THE-585610	TL	17.50	18.00
K. WISE		**TREASURY OF CHRISTMAS**		
89	HANGIN' IN THERE 1989-565598	YR	10.00	15.00
90	MEOW-Y CHRISTMAS 1990-565601	YR	10.00	12.00
S. ZIMNICKI		**TREASURY OF CHRISTMAS**		
89	BUNKIE-561835	TL	22.50	25.00
89	POPPER-561878	TL	12.00	15.00
89	SPARKLES-561843	TL	17.50	20.00
90	BLINKIE-570214	TL	15.00	16.00
90	SMITCH-570184	TL	22.50	23.00
90	TUMBLES 1990-566519	YR	16.00	22.00
90	TWIDDLES-566551	TL	15.00	16.00
90	TWINKLE & SPRINKLE-570206	TL	22.50	23.00
91	SNUFFY-566578	TL	17.50	19.00
91	STAMPER-830267	YR	13.50	15.00
92	CARVER-570192	YR	17.50	18.00
92	SPARKY & BUFFER-561851	TL	25.00	25.00
93	CHIMIER	OP	25.00	25.00
93	SPEEDY	OP	25.00	25.00
94	TOODLES	OP	25.00	25.00
*		**TREASURY OF CHRISTMAS COLLECTORS CLUB**		
93	CAN'T WEIGHT FOR THE HOLIDAYS-MOO	OP	18.50	18.50
94	SPRY FRY - MOO	OP	15.00	15.00
95	THINGS GO BETTER W/COKE - MOO	OP	15.00	15.00
GILMORE STUDIOS		**TREASURY OF CHRISTMAS COLLECTORS CLUB**		
93	TREASURE CARD, THE - SOM	OP	20.00	20.00
95	BUTTONING UP OUR HOLIDAY BEST-MOO	OP	22.50	22.50
95	FIRST CLASS CHRISTMAS - MOO	OP	22.50	22.50
95	HOLIDAY HIGH-LIGH- MOO	OP	15.00	15.00
K. HAHN		**TREASURY OF CHRISTMAS COLLECTORS CLUB**		
93	TOGETHER WE CAN SHOOT FOR THE STARS-MOO	OP	17.50	18.00
94	SEEDLINGS GREETINGS-MOO	OP	22.50	22.50
95	YOU'RE THE PERFECT FIT - SOM	OP	17.50	17.50
95	YOU'RE THE PERFECT FIT-SOM (CHARTER MEM)	OP	17.50	17.50
M. GILMORE		**TREASURY OF CHRISTMAS BABY'S FIRST CHRISTMAS**		
95	BABY'S SWEET FEAST 3RD & FINAL 588733	OP	17.50	18.00
K. HAHN		**TREASURY OF CHRISTMAS BEST FRIENDS**		
96	THERE'S A FRIENDSHIP BREWING 7TH ISSUE 1	*	25.00	25.00
*		**TREASURY OF CHRISTMAS CAMPBELL'S SOUP**		
95	A WELL BALANCED MEAL FOR SANTA 4TH & FIN	OP	17.50	18.00
96	SPICE UP THE SEASON 1ST ISSUE 111724	*	20.00	20.00
*		**TREASURY OF CHRISTMAS CARNIVAL**		
96	HOLD ON, SANTA! 1ST ISSUE 167088	*	25.00	25.00
K. HAHN		**TREASURY OF CHRISTMAS CASINO CHRISTMAS**		
95	GET IN THE SPIRIT...RECYCLE 7TH & FINAL	*	*	18.00
*		**TREASURY OF CHRISTMAS CHARTER MEMBERS ONLY**		
96	YO HO HOLIDAYS TO103	*	*	*
K. HAHN		**TREASURY OF CHRISTMAS CHARTER MEMBERS ONLY**		
95	YOU'RE THE PERFECT FIT TO102	*	*	*
*		**TREASURY OF CHRISTMAS CLOCK**		
96	IT'S TIME FOR CHRISTMAS 1ST ISSUE 175455	*	*	25.00
*		**TREASURY OF CHRISTMAS COCA-COLA**		
95	MAKE MINE A COKE 7TH ISSUE 128988	OP	25.00	25.00
*		**TREASURY OF CHRISTMAS COKE TRAIN**		
96	COCA-COLA CHOO CHOO 1ST ISSUE TR961	*	*	35.00
96	ON TRACK WITH COKE 2ND ISSUE TR963	*	*	25.00
M. GILMORE		**TREASURY OF CHRISTMAS COOKIE CUTTER CUTIES**		
95	SWEET HARMONY 3RD & FINAL 586773	OP	17.50	18.00

YR	NAME	LIMIT	ISSUE	TREND
M. GILMORE		**TREASURY OF CHRISTMAS COZY CUP**		
95	WE'VE SHARED SEW MUCH 9TH ISSUE 112097	OP	25.00	25.00
96	A CUP OF CHEER 10TH & FINAL 135070	*	25.00	25.00
*		**TREASURY OF CHRISTMAS HOLIDAY CHEERS**		
95	SALUTE' 3RD & FINAL 593133	OP	22.50	23.00
M. GILMORE		**TREASURY OF CHRISTMAS HOLIDAY HAT SHOPPE**		
95	FILLED TO THE BRIM 3RD & FINAL 595039	OP	25.00	25.00
*		**TREASURY OF CHRISTMAS MCDONALD'S**		
95	MERRY MCMEAL 6TH & FINAL 129070	OP	17.50	18.00
K. HAHN		**TREASURY OF CHRISTMAS MISS MERRY MOUSE**		
96	MERRY MANICURE 8TH ISSUE 173339	*	*	25.00
M. GILMORE		**TREASURY OF CHRISTMAS TAILOR MADE CHRISTMAS**		
95	A THIMBLE OF THE SEASON 2ND ISSUE 137243	OP	22.50	23.00
K. HAHN		**TREASURY OF CHRISTMAS TAILOR MADE CHRISTMAS**		
96	SEW DARN CUTE 3RD ISSUE 176761	*	*	25.00
*		**TREASURY OF CHRISTMAS TOBIN FRALEY CAROUSEL HORSE**		
96	TOBIN'S DEBUT DANCER 1ST ISSUE 173886	20000	*	20.00
*		**TREASURY OF CHRISTMAS TOY CHEST TREASURES**		
95	TOYS TO TREASURE 6TH ISSUE 112119	OP	20.00	20.00
96	TOYLAND, TOYLAND 7TH ISSUE 173878	*	*	20.00
*		**TREASURY OF CHRISTMAS/CHRISTMAS CAROUSEL**		
95	YULE TIDE PRANCER 6TH & FINAL 588660	OP	15.00	15.00
M. GILMORE		**TREASURY OF CHRISTMAS/CHRISTMAS SPECTACLES**		
95	SIESTA SANTA 5TH & FINAL 112089	OP	25.00	25.00
*		**TREASURY OF CHRISTMAS/CHRISTMAS TOGETHER**		
95	HOW..DO I LOVE THEE 7TH ISSUE 104949	OP	22.50	23.00
96	A PICTURE PERFECT PAIR 8TH ISSUE 167002	*	25.00	25.00

FENTON ART GLASS

YR	NAME	LIMIT	ISSUE	TREND
M. REYNOLDS		**CHRISTMAS LIMITED EDITIONS**		
96	ORNAMENT, 1714AC	2000	27.50	27.50

FLAMBRO

Price ranges may reflect various demands in the market from one geographic region to another; condition of piece; specific markings found on piece; and/or changes in production of piece.

YR	NAME	LIMIT	ISSUE	TREND
*		**EMMETT KELLY JR.**		
89	65TH BIRTHDAY CHRISTMAS ORNAMENT	CL	24.00	30.00-65.00
90	30 YEARS OF CLOWNING	YR	30.00	40.00-65.00
91	EKJ WITH STOCKING AND TOYS	YR	30.00	30.00
92	HOME FOR CHRISTMAS	YR	24.00	24.00
93	CHRISTMAS MAIL	YR	25.00	50.00
94	70TH BIRTHDAY COMMEMORATIVE	YR	24.00	24.00
95	ALL-STAR CIRCUS 20TH ANNIVERSARY	YR	25.00	25.00
M. WU		**LITTLE EMMETT**		
95	CHRISTMAS WRAP	OP	11.50	12.00
95	DECK THE NECK	OP	11.50	12.00
*		**RAGGEDY ANN & ANDY**		
89	RAGGEDY ANDY W/CANDY CANE	YR	13.50	18.00
89	RAGGEDY ANN W/GIFT STOCKING	YR	13.50	18.00

GANZ

YR	NAME	LIMIT	ISSUE	TREND
C. THAMMAVONGSA		**CHEESERVILLE PICNIC COLLECTION**		
91	AUNTIE MARIGOLD EATING COOKIE	OP	13.00	13.00
91	BABY CICELY	OP	8.00	8.00
91	BABY TRUFFLE	OP	8.00	8.00
91	BLOSSOM & HICKORY IN LOVE	OP	19.00	19.00
91	COUSIN WOODY WITH BEAD & FRUIT	OP	14.00	15.00
91	FELLOW W/PICNIC HAMPER	RT	13.00	13.00
91	FELLOW W/PLATE OF COOKIES	RT	13.00	13.00
91	GRANDMAMAM THISTLEDOWN HOLDING BREAD	OP	14.00	15.00
91	GRANDPAPA THISTLEDOWN CARRYING BKT	OP	13.00	13.00
91	HARLEY HARVESTMOUSE WAVING	OP	13.00	13.00
91	HARRIET HARVESTMOUSE	RT	13.00	13.00
91	JENNY BUTTERFIELD KNEELING	OP	13.00	13.00
91	JEREMY BUTTERFIELD	OP	13.00	13.00
91	LADY W/GRAPES	RT	14.00	15.00
91	LI'L TRUFFLE EATING GRAPES	OP	8.00	8.00
91	LI'L TRUFFLE SMWLLING FLOWERS	OP	16.50	17.00
91	MAMA FIXING SWEET CICELY'S HAIR	RT	16.50	17.00
91	MAMA WITH ROLLING PIN	OP	13.00	13.00
91	MAMA WOODSWORTH W/CAFE	RT	14.00	15.00
91	MARIGOLD THISTLEDOWN PICKING UP JAR	OP	14.00	15.00
91	MEDLEY MEADOWMOUSE/BOUQUET	OP	13.00	13.00
91	PAPA WOODSWORTH	OP	13.00	13.00
91	PICNIC BUDDIES	OP	19.00	19.00
91	VIOLET WITH PEACHES	OP	13.00	13.00
92	SWEET CICELY MUSICAL DOLL IN BKT	OP	85.00	85.00
93	CHUCKLES THE CLOWN	OP	16.00	16.00
93	CLOWNIN' AROUND	OP	10.50	11.00
93	FOR SOMEONE SPECIAL	OP	13.50	14.00
93	LI'L CHEESERS DISPLAY PLAQUE	OP	25.00	25.00
93	STORYTELLER, THE	10000	25.00	25.00
93	STRUMMIN' AWAY	OP	13.00	13.00
93	SUNDAY DRIVE	OP	40.00	40.00
93	SWEET DREAMS	OP	27.50	28.00
93	WILLY'S TOE-TAPPIN' TUNES	OP	15.00	15.00

YR	NAME	LIMIT	ISSUE	TREND
93	WORDS OF WISDOM	OP	14.00	15.00
94	FIDDLE-DEE-DEE	OP	13.00	13.00
94	MELODY MAKER	OP	17.00	17.00
94	OOM-PAH-PAH	OP	13.00	13.00
94	SWINGIN' SAX	OP	13.00	13.00
94	WASHBOARD BLUES	OP	13.00	13.00
94	WHAT A HOOT!	OP	13.00	13.00
C. THAMMAVONGSA		**COWTOWN/CHRISTMAS COLLECTION**		
94	BILLY THE CALF	OP	14.00	15.00
94	BRONCO BULLY	OP	13.00	13.00
94	CALF-IN-THE-BOX	OP	12.50	13.00
94	CHRISTMAS CACTUS	OP	13.50	14.00
94	CHRISTMOOS EVE	OP	12.00	12.00
94	DOWNHILL DAR DEBULL	OP	12.00	12.00
94	HALLEMOOAH	OP	12.00	12.00
94	JINGLE BELL	OP	15.50	16.00
94	LI'L RED GLIDING HOOF	OP	12.00	12.00
94	LITTLE DRUMMER CALF	OP	12.00	12.00
94	SAINT NICOWLAS	OP	16.00	16.00
94	SANTA COWS	OP	18.00	18.00
94	SANTA'S LITTLE HEIFER	OP	12.50	13.00
C. THAMMAVONGSA		**COWTOWN/VALENTINE COLLECTION**		
94	I LOVE MOO	OP	15.00	16.00
94	ROBIN HOOF & MAID MOOIAN	OP	23.00	23.00
94	ROMECOW & MOOLIET	OP	22.00	22.00
94	WANTED: A SWEETHEART	OP	16.00	16.00
C. THAMMAVONGSA		**LITTLE CHEESERS/CHRISTMAS COLLECTION**		
92	ABNER APPLETON ORNAMENT	OP	15.00	15.00
92	JENNY BUTTERFIELD ORNAMENT	OP	17.00	17.00
92	JEREMY/ TEDDY BEAR ORNAMENT	OP	13.00	13.00
92	LITTLE TRUFFLE ORNAMENT	OP	9.50	10.00
92	MYRTLE MEADOWMOUSE ORNAMENT	OP	15.00	15.00
92	SANTA CHEESER ORNAMENT	OP	14.00	15.00
93	BABY'S FIRST X'MAS ORNAMENT	OP	12.50	13.00
93	DASHING THROUGH THE SNOW ORN.	OP	11.00	11.00
93	LITTLE STOCKING STUFFER ORNAMENT	OP	10.50	11.00
93	MEADLEY MEADOWMOUSE X'MAS BELL	OP	17.00	17.00
93	OUR 1ST CHRISTMAS TOGETHER ORN.	OP	18.50	19.00
93	SANTA'S LITTLE HELPER ORN.	OP	11.00	11.00
93	SKATING INTO YOUR HEART ORN.	OP	10.00	10.00
94	ALL I WANT FOR CHRISTMAS	RT	13.50	14.00
94	ANGEL	OP	8.00	8.00
94	CANDY CANE CAPER	OP	9.00	9.00
94	CHEESER SHOWMAN	RT	5.00	5.00
94	CHELSEA'S STOCKING BELL	OP	15.50	16.00
94	COUSIN WOODY PLAYING FLUTE	RT	10.00	10.00
94	GRANDPA BLOWING HORN	RT	10.00	10.00
94	HICKORY PLAYING CELLO	RT	10.00	10.00
94	MEDLEY PLAYING DRUM	RT	5.50	5.50
94	MRS. CLAUS	OP	9.00	9.00
94	PEACE ON EARTH	OP	8.00	8.00
94	SANTA SILVERWOOD	OP	9.00	9.00
94	SANTA'S WORKSHOP	OP	10.00	10.00
94	SLEIGH RIDE	RT	9.00	9.00
94	SWINGING INTO THE SEASON	OP	11.00	11.00
94	VIOLET WITH SNOWBALL	RT	5.50	5.50
C. THAMMAVONGSA		**LITTLE CHEESERS/THE SILVERWOODS**		
94	CHRISTMAS SURPRISE	OP	8.50	9.00
94	COMFORT AND JOY	OP	6.00	6.00
94	DECK THE HALLS	OP	9.50	10.00
94	GIDDY UP!	OP	8.50	9.00
94	HICKORY DICKORY DOCK	OP	9.50	10.00
94	XMAS EXPRESS	OP	8.50	9.00
C. THAMMAVONGSA		**PIGSVILLE/CHRISTMAS COLLECTION**		
94	CAROLER	OP	10.00	10.00
94	CHRISTMAS TREATS	OP	9.00	9.00
94	DRUMMER PIG	OP	10.00	10.00
94	JOY TO THE WORLD	OP	10.00	10.00
94	SANTA PIG	OP	11.00	11.00
94	WHEEEEEE! PIGGY	OP	9.00	9.00
C. THAMMAVONGSA		**PIGSVILLE/THE VALENTINE COLLECTION**		
94	LOVESTRUCK	OP	10.50	11.00

GLASS EYE

YR	NAME	LIMIT	ISSUE	TREND
93	COBALT WAVE	2000	19.00	22.00
94	CRANBERRY OPALESCENT LACE	2000	19.00	22.00

GOEBEL INC.

Price ranges may reflect various demands in the market from one geographic region to another; condition of piece; specific markings found on piece; and/or changes in production of piece.

YR	NAME	LIMIT	ISSUE	TREND
M.I. HUMMEL				
90	LIGHT UP THE NIGHT HUM-622	CL	95.00	125.00
91	ANGELIC GUIDE HUM-571	CL	95.00	165.00
93	HERALD ON HIGH HUM-623	CL	155.00	155.00-160.00
96	CHRISTMAS SONG	*	115.00	115.00
96	CHRISTMAS SONG	OP	115.00	115.00

YR	NAME	LIMIT	ISSUE	TREND
B. TIMBERLAKE				
96	CHRISTMAS CARDINAL	OP	35.00	35.00
*		**ANGEL BELLS ANNUAL ORNAMENT**		
76	ANGEL WITH FLUTE-BLUE	YR	9.00	100.00
76	ANGEL WITH FLUTE-PINK	YR	9.00	100.00
76	ANGEL WITH FLUTE-RED	YR	9.00	100.00
76	ANGEL WITH FLUTE-WHITE	YR	7.00	70.00
77	ANGEL WITH BANJO-GREEN	YR	9.00	35.00
77	ANGEL WITH BANJO-PURPLE	YR	9.00	35.00
77	ANGEL WITH BANJO-WHITE	YR	7.00	30.00
77	ANGEL WITH BANJO-YELLOW	YR	9.00	35.00
78	ANGEL WITH HARP-BLUE	YR	11.00	35.00
78	ANGEL WITH HARP-PINK	YR	11.00	35.00
78	ANGEL WITH HARP-RUST	YR	11.00	35.00
78	ANGEL WITH HARP-WHITE	YR	9.00	30.00
79	ANGEL WITH ACCORDION-GREEN	YR	11.00	35.00
79	ANGEL WITH ACCORDION-PURPLE	YR	11.00	35.00
79	ANGEL WITH ACCORDION-WHITE	YR	9.00	30.00
79	ANGEL WITH ACCORDION-YELLOW	YR	11.00	35.00
80	ANGEL WITH SAXAPHONE-BLUE	YR	13.50	35.00
80	ANGEL WITH SAXAPHONE-PINK	YR	13.50	35.00
80	ANGEL WITH SAXAPHONE-RUST	YR	13.50	35.00
80	ANGEL WITH SAXAPHONE-WHITE	YR	11.50	30.00
81	ANGEL WITH SONG SHEET-GREEN	YR	14.00	35.00
81	ANGEL WITH SONG SHEET-PURPLE	YR	14.00	35.00
81	ANGEL WITH SONG SHEET-WHITE	YR	12.00	30.00
81	ANGEL WITH SONG SHEET-YELLOW	YR	14.00	35.00
82	ANGEL WITH FRENCH HORN-GREEN	YR	14.00	35.00
82	ANGEL WITH FRENCH HORN-RED	YR	14.00	35.00
82	ANGEL WITH FRENCH HORN-RUST	YR	14.00	35.00
82	ANGEL WITH FRENCH HORN-WHITE	YR	12.00	30.00
83	ANGEL WITH REED PIPE-BROWN	YR	14.00	35.00
83	ANGEL WITH REED PIPE-ORANGE	YR	14.00	35.00
83	ANGEL WITH REED PIPE-PURPLE	YR	14.00	35.00
83	ANGEL WITH REED PIPE-WHITE	YR	12.00	30.00
84	ANGEL WITH DRUM-GREEN	YR	14.00	35.00
84	ANGEL WITH DRUM-RED	YR	14.00	35.00
84	ANGEL WITH DRUM-WHITE	YR	12.00	30.00
85	ANGEL WITH TRUMPET-BLUE	YR	14.00	35.00
85	ANGEL WITH TRUMPET-GREEN	YR	14.00	35.00
85	ANGEL WITH TRUMPET-RED	YR	14.00	35.00
85	ANGEL WITH TRUMPET-WHITE	YR	12.00	30.00
86	ANGEL WITH BELLS-GREEN	YR	15.00	35.00
86	ANGEL WITH BELLS-RED	YR	15.00	35.00
86	ANGEL WITH BELLS-WHITE	YR	12.50	30.00
86	ANGEL WITH BELLS-YELLOW	YR	15.00	35.00
87	ANGEL CONDUCTOR-BLUE	YR	17.25	35.00
87	ANGEL CONDUCTOR-GREEN	YR	17.25	35.00
87	ANGEL CONDUCTOR-RED	YR	17.25	35.00
87	ANGEL CONDUCTOR-WHITE	YR	15.00	30.00
88	ANGEL WITH STAR-GREEN	YR	20.00	20.00
88	ANGEL WITH STAR-RED	YR	20.00	20.00
88	ANGEL WITH STAR-WHITE	YR	17.00	17.00
88	ANGEL WITH STAR-YELLOW	YR	20.00	20.00
*		**ANNUAL CHRISTMAS BELL ORNAMENT**		
84	CHRISTMAS TREE	YR	14.00	25.00
85	SANTA	YR	14.00	15.00
86	WREATH	YR	15.00	16.00
87	TEDDY BEAR	YR	17.25	18.00
88	CRYSTAL BELL	YR	7.50	15.00
*			**ANNUAL ORNAMENT**	
78	SANTA-COLOR	YR	15.00	17.00
78	SANTA-WHITE	YR	7.50	12.00
79	ANGEL/TREE-COLOR	YR	16.00	18.00
79	ANGEL/TREE-WHITE	YR	8.00	13.00
80	MRS. SANTA-COLOR	YR	17.00	17.00
80	MRS. SANTA-WHITE	YR	9.00	14.00
81	NUTCRACKER, THE-COLOR	YR	18.00	18.00
81	NUTCRACKER, THE-WHITE	YR	10.00	10.00
82	SANTA IN CHIMNEY-COLOR	YR	18.00	18.00
82	SANTA IN CHIMNEY-WHITE	YR	10.00	10.00
83	CLOWN-COLOR	YR	18.00	18.00
83	CLOWN-WHITE	YR	10.00	10.00
84	SNOWMAN-COLOR	YR	18.00	18.00
84	SNOWMAN-WHITE	YR	10.00	10.00
85	ANGEL-COLOR	YR	18.00	18.00
85	ANGEL-WHITE	YR	9.00	9.00
86	DRUMMER BOY-COLOR	YR	18.00	18.00
86	DRUMMER BOY-WHITE	YR	9.00	9.00
87	ROCKING HORSE-COLOR	YR	20.00	20.00
87	ROCKING HORSE-WHITE	YR	10.00	10.00
88	DOLL-COLOR	YR	22.50	23.00
88	DOLL-WHITE	YR	12.50	13.00
89	DOVE-COLOR	YR	20.00	20.00
89	DOVE-WHITE	YR	12.50	13.00
90	GIRL IN SLEIGH	YR	30.00	30.00
91	BABY ON MOON	YR	35.00	35.00

YR	NAME	LIMIT	ISSUE	TREND
*				**ANNUAL ORNAMENT-GLASS**
79	SANTA	15000	12.00	12.00
80	ANGEL WITH TREE	15000	12.00	12.00
81	MRS. SANTA	15000	12.00	12.00
82	NUTCRACKER, THE	15000	4.00	4.00
B. TIMBERLAKE				**BOB TIMBERLAKE SIGNATURE**
96	CHRISTMAS CARDINAL	YR	35.00	35.00
C. BYJ				**CHARLOT BYJ ANNUAL ORNAMENT**
86	SANTA LUCIA ANGEL	CL	18.00	25.00
87	CHRISTMAS PAGEANT	CL	20.00	20.00
88	ANGEL WITH SHEET MUSIC	CL	22.00	22.00
C. BYJ				**CHARLOT BYJ BABY ORNAMENT**
86	BABY ORNAMENT	CL	18.00	18.00
87	BABY SNOW	CL	20.00	20.00
88	BABY'S 1ST STOCKING	CL	27.50	28.00
*				**CHRISTMAS ORNAMENTS**
86	ANGEL WITH HORN-COLOR	OP	8.00	8.00
86	ANGEL WITH HORN-WHITE	OP	6.00	6.00
86	ANGEL WITH LANTERN-COLOR	OP	8.00	8.00
86	ANGEL WITH LANTERN-WHITE	OP	6.00	6.00
86	ANGEL WITH LUTE-COLOR	OP	8.00	8.00
86	ANGEL WITH LUTE-WHITE	OP	6.00	6.00
86	ANGEL-RED WITH BELL	OP	6.00	6.00
86	ANGEL-RED WITH BOOK	OP	6.00	6.00
86	ANGEL-RED WITH SONG	OP	6.00	6.00
86	TEDDY BEAR-RED BOOTS	OP	5.00	5.00
86	TEDDY BEAR-RED HAT	OP	5.00	5.00
86	TEDDY BEAR-RED SCARF	OP	5.00	5.00
87	THREE ANGELS WITH INSTRUMENTS (SET)	OP	30.00	30.00
87	THREE ANGELS WITH TOYS (SET)	OP	30.00	30.00
88	ANGEL WITH ACCORDIAN	OP	10.00	10.00
88	ANGEL WITH BANJO	OP	10.00	10.00
88	ANGEL WITH MUSIC (SET)	OP	30.00	30.00
88	ANGEL WITH TOY ROCKING HORSE	OP	10.00	10.00
88	ANGEL WITH TOY TEDDY BEAR	OP	10.00	10.00
88	ANGEL WITH TOY TRAIN	OP	10.00	10.00
88	ANGEL WITH TOYS (SET OF 3)	OP	30.00	30.00
88	ANGEL WITH VIOLIN	OP	10.00	10.00
88	NUTCRACKER	OP	15.00	16.00
88	SAINT NICK	OP	15.00	16.00
88	SANTA'S BOOT	OP	7.50	8.00
88	SNOWMAN	OP	10.00	10.00
G. SKROBEK				**CO-BOY ANNUAL ORNAMENT**
86	COBOY WITH WREATH	CL	18.00	25.00
87	COBOY WITH CANDY CANE	CL	25.00	25.00
88	COBOY WITH TREE	CL	30.00	30.00
M.I. HUMMEL				
96	CHRISTMAS SONG	*	115.00	115.00
M.I. HUMMEL				
95	FESTIVAL HARMONY W/FLUTE	*	100.00	100.00
M.I. HUMMEL				**M.I. HUMMEL ANNUAL FIGURINE ORNAMENTS**
88	FLYING HIGH HUM-452	CL	75.00	165.00
89	LOVE FROM ABOVE HUM-481	CL	75.00	125.00
90	PEACE ON EARTH HUM-484	CL	80.00	125.00
91	ANGELIC GUIDE HUM-571	CL	95.00	125.00
92	LIGHT UP THE NIGHT HUM-622	OP	95.00	100.00
93	HERALD ON HIGH HUM-623	YR	155.00	185.00
M.I. HUMMEL				**M.I. HUMMEL ANNUAL ORNAMENT**
93	CELESTIAL MUSICIAN HUM-646	CL	90.00	110.00
94	FESTIVAL HARMONY W/MANDOLIN OR. HUM-647	CL	95.00	110.00
95	FESTIVAL HARMONY W/FLUTE OR. HUM-648	OP	100.00	100.00
M.I. HUMMEL				**M.I. HUMMEL CHRISTMAS BELL ORNAMENTS**
89	RIDE INTO CHRISTMAS HUM-775	CL	35.00	50.00-60.00
90	LETTER TO SANTA CLAUS HUM-776	CL	37.50	50.00-60.00
91	HEAR YE, HEAR YE HUM-777	CL	39.50	50.00-60.00
92	HARMONY IN FOUR PARTS HUM-778	OP	45.00	50.00
93	CELESTIAL MUSICIAN HUM-779	YR	50.00	50.00
M.I. HUMMEL				**M.I. HUMMEL CHRISTMAS ORNAMENT**
*	FESTIVAL HARMONY W/FLUTE HUM-693	OP	125.00	125.00
M.I. HUMMEL				**UNICEF**
93	FRIENDS FOREVER HUM-662	25000	260.00	275.00-500.00

GORHAM

Price ranges may reflect various demands in the market from one geographic region to another; condition of piece; specific markings found on piece; and/or changes in production of piece.

YR	NAME	LIMIT	ISSUE	TREND
*				**ANNUAL CRYSTAL ORNAMENTS**
85	CRYSTAL ORNAMENT	CL	22.00	22.00
86	CRYSTAL ORNAMENT	CL	25.00	25.00
87	CRYSTAL ORNAMENT	CL	25.00	25.00
88	CRYSTAL ORNAMENT	CL	28.00	28.00
89	CRYSTAL ORNAMENT	CL	28.00	28.00
90	CRYSTAL ORNAMENT	CL	30.00	30.00
91	CRYSTAL ORNAMENT	CL	35.00	35.00
92	CRYSTAL ORNAMENT	YR	32.50	33.00
*				**ANNUAL SNOWFLAKE ORNAMENTS**
70	STERLING SNOWFLAKE	CL	10.00	250.00-325.00

YR	NAME	LIMIT	ISSUE	TREND
71	STERLING SNOWFLAKE	CL	10.00	90.00-125.00
72	STERLING SNOWFLAKE	CL	10.00	75.00-125.00
73	STERLING SNOWFLAKE	CL	10.95	65.00-110.00
74	STERLING SNOWFLAKE	CL	17.50	45.00-75.00
75	STERLING SNOWFLAKE	CL	17.50	45.00-75.00
76	STERLING SNOWFLAKE	CL	20.00	45.00-75.00
77	STERLING SNOWFLAKE	CL	22.50	45.00-70.00
78	STERLING SNOWFLAKE	CL	22.50	45.00-70.00
79	STERLING SNOWFLAKE	CL	32.80	70.00
80	SILVERPLATED SNOWFLAKE	CL	15.00	75.00
81	STERLING SNOWFLAKE	CL	50.00	65.00
82	STERLING SNOWFLAKE	CL	37.50	75.00
83	STERLING SNOWFLAKE	CL	45.00	45.00-80.00
84	STERLING SNOWFLAKE	CL	45.00	45.00-75.00
85	STERLING SNOWFLAKE	CL	45.00	45.00-75.00
86	STERLING SNOWFLAKE	CL	45.00	45.00-60.00
87	STERLING SNOWFLAKE	CL	50.00	60.00
88	STERLING SNOWFLAKE	CL	50.00	50.00
89	STERLING SNOWFLAKE	CL	50.00	50.00
90	STERLING SNOWFLAKE	CL	50.00	50.00
91	STERLING SNOWFLAKE	CL	55.00	55.00
92	STERLING SNOWFLAKE	YR	50.00	50.00
*			**ARCHIVE COLLECTIBLE**	
88	VICTORIAN HEART	OP	50.00	50.00
89	VICTORIAN WREATH	OP	50.00	50.00
90	ELIZABETHAN CUPID	OP	60.00	60.00
91	STERLING BAROQUE ANGELS	OP	55.00	55.00
92	MADONNA AND CHILD	YR	50.00	50.00
*			**BABY'S FIRST CHRISTMAS CRYSTAL**	
91	BABY'S FIRST ROCKING HORSE	OP	35.00	35.00

HADLEY COMPANIES

YR	NAME	LIMIT	ISSUE	TREND
	A. AGNEW		**HADLEY COLLECTION**	
95	ARCTIC WOLVES	45 DAYS	20.00	30.00
	D. BARNHOUSE		**HADLEY COLLECTION**	
95	REPAIRS	45 DAYS	20.00	30.00
	D. BRESH		**HADLEY COLLECTION**	
95	WARMTH OF WINTER II	45 DAYS	20.00	30.00
	T. REDLIN		**HADLEY COLLECTION**	
95	SHARING THE EVENING	45 DAYS	20.00	30.00

HALLMARK KEEPSAKE ORNAMENTS

YR	NAME	LIMIT	ISSUE	TREND
*				
76	BABY'S FIRST CHRISTMAS 250QX211-1	YR	2.50	112.00
76	HAPPY HOLIDAYS KISSING BALLS QX225-1	YR	5.00	225.00
77	HOLLY & POINSETTIA TABLE DECOR. OHD320-2	YR	8.00	132.00
77	MR. & MRS. SNOWMAN KISSING BALL QX 225-2	YR	5.00	107.00
77	OLD FASHION CUSTOMS KISSING BALL QX225-5	YR	5.00	147.00
78	CHRISTMAS STAR TREE TOPPERS QX 702-3	YR	7.50	40.00
78	HEAVENLY MINSTREL TABLETOP QHD 921-9	YR	35.00	375.00
78	HOLIDAY MEMORIES KISSING BALL QHD 900-3	YR	5.00	120.00
78	LITTLE TRIMMER COLLECTION QX 132-3	YR	9.00	280.00
79	LITTLE TRIMMER SET QX 159-9	YR	9.00	270.00
80	BELLRINGER-2ND EDITION 1500QX157-4	YR	15.00	66.00
80	BRASS STAR TREE TOPPERS QX 705-4	YR	25.00	52.00
80	CHRISTMAS KITTEN TEST ORNAMENT QX353-4	YR	4.00	260.00
80	ROCKING HORSE, THE QX 340-7	YR	2.00	23.00
81	FROSTY FRIENDS QX 433-5	YR	8.00	352.00
81	YARN & FABRIC ORNAMENT ANGEL QX 162-1	YR	3.00	11.00
81	YARN & FABRIC ORNAMENT SANTA QX 161-4	YR	3.00	11.00
81	YARN & FABRIC ORNAMENT SNOWMAN QX 163-4	YR	3.00	11.00
81	YARN & FABRIC ORNAMENT SOLDIER QX 164-1	YR	3.00	11.00
82	BRASS PROMOTIONAL ORNAMENT NO NUMBER	YR	3.50	42.00
83	SILVER BELL QX 110-9	YR	12.00	31.00
84	BABY'S FIRST CHRISTMAS-GIRL QX 240-1	YR	4.50	19.00
84	CHRISTMAS MEMORIES PHOTOHOLDER QX 300-4	YR	6.50	21.00
85	DISNEY CHRISTMAS QX 271-2	YR	4.75	24.00
85	HEAVENLY TRUMPETER 2750QX405-2	YR	27.50	82.00
87	ELVES-EMIL PAINTER ELF-FIGURINE QSP930-9	YR	10.00	30.00
87	ELVES-HANS CARPENTER ELF-FIGURE QSP930-7	YR	10.00	30.00
87	ELVES-KURT BLUE PRINT ELF FIGUREQSP931-7	YR	10.00	30.00
87	HALLIS STAR-TREE TOPPER EPCA	YR	*	32.00
89	CANDY CANE 450QXM560-2	YR	4.50	19.00
90	FESTIVE ANGEL TREE TOPPER 975QXM578-3	YR	9.75	29.00
90	PENGUIN PAL 450QXM574-6	YR	4.50	19.00
90	PORCELAIN BEAR 8TH ED. QX 442-6	YR	8.75	21.00
93	HOLIDAY EXPRESS QXM 545-2	YR	50.00	50.00
94	BETSEY'S COUNTRY CHRISTMAS 3RD ED. 500QX	YR	5.00	9.00
94	FEELIN' GROOVY 795QX595-3	YR	7.95	11.00
94	GARFIELD 1295QX575-3	YR	12.95	16.00
94	GODPARENT 500QX242-3	YR	5.00	6.00
94	GRANDPARENTS 500QX242-6	YR	5.00	6.00
94	MARY ENGELBREIT 500QX241-6	YR	5.00	6.00
94	U.S. CHRISTMAS STAMPS 1095QX520-6	YR	10.95	20.00
95	BABY'S FIRST CHRISTMAS-BABY BOY QX 231-9	YR	5.00	6.00
95	BABY'S FIRST CHRISTMAS-BABY GIRL QX231-7	YR	5.00	6.00
95	GARFIELD QX500-7	YR	10.95	13.00
95	MAGIC SCHOOL BUS, THE QX584-9	YR	10.95	13.00

YR	NAME	LIMIT	ISSUE	TREND
95	MARY ENGELBRIET QX240-9	YR	5.00	7.00
95	NUMBER ONE TEACHER QX594-9	YR	7.95	12.00
95	U.S. CHRISTMAS STAMPS 3RD & FINAL QX506-	YR	10.95	12.00
P. ANDREWS				
94	CANDY CAPER 895QX577-6	YR	8.95	15.00
94	DAUGHTER 695QX562-3	YR	6.95	11.00
94	GRANDMOTHER 695QX567-3	YR	7.95	9.00
94	HEARTS IN HARMONY 1095QX440-6	YR	10.95	11.00
94	ICE SHOW 795QX594-6	YR	7.95	12.00
94	IN THE PINK 995QX576-3	YR	9.95	13.00
94	JOYOUS SONG 895QX447-3	YR	8.95	10.00
94	NEW HOME 895QX566-3	YR	8.95	12.00
94	OUR FIRST CHRISTMAS TOGETHER 1895QX570-6	YR	18.95	22.00
94	SON 695QX562-6	YR	6.95	9.00
94	TIME OF PEACE 795QX581-3	YR	7.95	12.00
95	BABY'S FIRST CHRISTMAS QX 554-7	YR	18.95	25.00
95	BABY'S FIRST CHRISTMAS QX 555-7	YR	9.95	13.00
95	BARBIE: SOLO IN THE SPOTLIGHT 2ND SERIES	YR	14.95	31.00
95	CELEBRATION OF ANGELS FIRST SERIES QX507	YR	12.95	22.00
95	CHRISTMAS PATROL QX595-9	YR	7.95	10.00
95	COWS OF BALI QX599-9	YR	8.95	11.00
95	GRANDMOTHER QX576-7	YR	7.95	11.00
95	HEAVEN'S GIFT QX605-7	YR	20.00	26.00
95	HOLIDAY BARBIE 3RD SERIES QX1505-7	YR	14.95	25.00
95	IN A HEARTBEAT QX581-7	YR	8.95	11.00
95	JOY TO THE WORLD QX586-7	YR	8.95	12.00
95	MERRY OLDE SANTA 6TH SERIES QX513-9	YR	14.95	20.00
95	NEW HOME QX583-9	YR	8.95	13.00
95	THREE WISHES QX597-9	YR	7.95	10.00
N. AUBE				
95	CHRISTMAS FEVER QX596-7	YR	7.95	12.00
95	TENNIS, ANYONE? QX590-7	YR	7.95	9.00
M. BASTIN				
95	VERA THE MOUSE QX553-7	YR	8.95	10.00
R. BISHOP				
94	LOU RANKIN SEAL 995QX545-6	YR	9.95	14.00
94	OUR FIRST CHRISTMAS TOGETHER 995QX564-3	YR	9.95	15.00
T. BLACKSHEAR				
80	CHECKING IT TWICE 2000QX158-4	YR	20.00	177.00
A. BROWNSWORD				
95	FOREVER FRIENDS BEAR QX525-8	YR	8.95	16.00
R. CHAD				
94	BATMAN 1295QX585-3	YR	12.95	20.00
94	HELPFUL SHEPHERD 895QX553-6	YR	8.95	11.00
94	MERRY OLDE SANTA 5TH ED. 1495QX525-6	YR	14.95	25.00
95	MULETIDE GREETINGS QX600-9	YR	7.95	11.00
95	OUR FAMILY QX570-9	YR	7.95	11.00
95	POPEYE QX525-7	YR	10.95	17.00
95	SPECIAL CAT QX571-7	YR	7.95	9.00
95	SPECIAL DOG QX571-9	YR	7.95	9.00
95	SUPERMAN QLX730-9	YR	28.00	31.00
K. CROW				
87	NORTH POLE POWER & LIGHT 627XPR933-3	YR	2.95	16.00
88	CHRISTMAS MORNING 2450QLX701-3	YR	24.50	34.00
88	MISTLETOAD 700QX468-7	YR	7.00	24.00
88	NIGHT BEFORE CHRISTMAS QX 451-7	YR	6.50	16.00
91	WOODLAND BABIES 600QXM566-7	YR	6.00	24.00
93	PEEK-A-BOO TREE QX524-4	YR	10.75	18.00
94	CHEERS TO YOU! 1095QX579-6	YR	10.95	20.00
94	CHEERY CYCLISTS 1295QX578-6	YR	12.95	26.00
94	DEAR SANTA MOUSE 1495QX580-6	YR	14.95	21.00
94	EXTRA-SPECIAL DELIVERY 795QX583-3	YR	7.95	12.00
94	FOLLOW THE SUN 895QX584-6	YR	8.95	12.00
94	JINGLE BELL BAND 1095QX578-3	YR	10.95	17.00
94	SANTA'S LEGO SLEIGH 1095QX545-3	YR	10.95	16.00
95	BOBBIN' ALONG QX587-9	YR	8.95	16.00
95	GRANDPA QX576-9	YR	8.95	14.00
95	HAPPY WRAPPERS QX603-7	YR	10.95	15.00
95	HOCKEY PUP QX591-7	YR	9.95	11.00
95	IN TIME WITH CHRISTMAS QX604-9	YR	12.95	16.00
95	LEGO FIREPLACE WITH SANTA QX476-9	YR	10.95	14.00
95	MY FIRST HOT WHEELS QLX727-9	YR	28.00	36.00
95	ON THE ICE QX604-7	YR	7.95	12.00
95	OUR LITTLE BLESSINGS QX520-9	YR	12.95	16.00
95	POCAHONTAS AND CAPT. JOHN SMITH QX1619-7	YR	14.95	18.00
95	POLAR COASTER QX611-7	YR	8.95	11.00
95	SANTA'S SERENADE QX601-7	YR	8.95	13.00
95	SPACE SHUTTLE QLX739-	YR	24.50	31.00
95	SURFIN' SANTA QX601-9	YR	9.95	11.00
95	WEE LITTLE CHRISTMAS QLX732-9	YR	22.00	24.00
P. DUTKIN				
87	FAVORITE SANTA 2250QX445-7	YR	22.50	25.00
88	ST. LOUIE NICK QX 453-9	YR	7.75	21.00
T. FRALEY				
94	TOBIN FRALEY CAROUSEL 3RD ED. 2800QX522-	YR	28.00	39.00
95	TOBIN FRALEY CAROUSEL 4TH AND FINAL QX50	YR	28.00	29.00
95	TOBIN FRALEY HOLIDAY CAROUSEL 2ND SERIES	YR	32.00	36.00

YR	NAME	LIMIT	ISSUE	TREND
J. FRANCIS				
93	A CHILD'S CHRISTMAS QX588-2	YR	9.75	12.00
94	JUMP-ALONG JACKALOPE 895QX575-6	YR	8.95	11.00
94	NEPHEW 795QX554-6	YR	7.95	11.00
94	NIECE 795QX554-3	YR	7.95	12.00
94	RELAXING MOMENT 1495QX535-6	YR	14.95	21.00
95	ACROSS THE MILES QX 584-7	YR	8.95	11.00
95	BARREL-BACK RIDER QX518-9	YR	9.95	11.00
95	CHRISTMAS MORNING QX599-7	YR	10.95	13.00
95	DREAM ON QX600-7	YR	10.95	14.00
95	GRANDCHILD'S FIRST CHRISTMAS QX577-7	YR	7.95	11.00
95	JUMPING FOR JOY QLX734-7	YR	28.00	35.00
95	PEZ SANTA QX526-7	YR	7.95	12.00
95	TAKIN' A HIKE QX602-9	YR	7.95	13.00
D. LEE				
80	HEAVENLY MINSTREL 15QX156-7	YR	15.00	320.00
81	ANGEL QX 139-6	YR	5.50	82.00
83	DIANA DOLL QX 423-7	YR	9.00	23.00
84	CLASSICAL ANGEL 2750QX459-1	YR	27.50	75.00
90	GOLF'S MY BAG 775QX496-3	YR	7.75	17.00
93	FROSTY FRIENDS 14TH ED. 975QX414-2	YR	9.75	25.00
94	FOR MY GRANDMA,PHOTOHOLDER 695QX561-3	YR	6.95	9.00
95	HEADIN' HOME QLX732-7	YR	22.00	28.00
95	TWO FOR TEA QX582-9	YR	9.95	11.00
J. LYLE				
89	BROTHER 725QX445-2	YR	7.25	15.00
93	OUR FIRST CHRISTMAS TOGETHER 975QX564-2	YR	9.75	13.00
94	GENTLE NURSE 695QX597-3	YR	6.95	10.00
94	HAPPY BIRTHDAY, JESUS 1295QX542-3	YR	12.95	18.00
94	NORMAN ROCKWELL ART 500QX241-3	YR	5.00	7.00
95	BROTHER QX567-9	YR	6.95	10.00
95	GRANDPARENTS QX241-9	YR	5.00	6.00
95	OUR CHRISTMAS TOGETHER QX580-9	YR	9.95	13.00
95	OUR FIRST CHRISTMAS TOGETHER QX317-7	YR	6.95	9.00
95	OUR FIRST CHRISTMAS TOGETHER QX579-7	YR	16.95	20.00
95	REJOICE! QX598-7	YR	10.95	14.00
95	SISTER QX568-7	YR	6.95	9.00
L. NORTON				
95	ROMULAN WARBIRD QX1726-7	YR	24.00	30.00
D. PALMITER				
94	MERRY FISHMAS 895QX591-3	YR	8.95	15.00
94	OUR FIRST CHRISTMAS..PHOTOHOLDER QX565-3	YR	8.95	13.00
94	PRACTICE MAKES PERFECT 895QX586-3	YR	8.95	11.00
94	SWEET GREETING 1095QX580-3	YR	10.95	19.00
95	COMING TO SEE SANTA QLX736-9	YR	32.00	37.00
95	DAUGHTER QX567-7	YR	6.95	8.00
95	FOR MY GRANDMA: PHOTOHOLDER QX572-9	YR	8.95	9.00
95	FRIENDLY BOOST QX582-7	YR	8.95	11.00
95	GODCHILD QX570-7	YR	7.95	10.00
95	MERRY RV QX602-7	YR	12.95	19.00
95	PEANUTS FIFTH AND FINAL QLX727-7	YR	24.50	30.00
95	SON QX566-9	YR	6.95	9.00
95	WAITING UP FOR SANTA QX610-6	YR	8.95	12.00
S. PIKE				
85	BETSEY CLARK 13TH & FINAL 500QX263-2	YR	5.00	23.00
88	"OWLIDAY" WISH 650QX455-9	YR	6.50	16.00
90	SPENCER SPARROW, ESQ. 675QX431-2	YR	6.75	17.00
90	STOCKING KITTEN 675QX456-5	YR	6.75	13.00
94	BROTHER 695QX551-6	YR	6.95	11.00
94	DAD-TO-BE 795QX547-3	YR	7.95	14.00
94	GRANDDAUGHTER 695QX552-3	YR	6.95	10.00
94	GRANDSON 695QX552-6	YR	6.95	9.00
94	MOM-TO-BE 795QX550-6	YR	7.95	13.00
94	SISTER 695QX551-3	YR	6.95	9.00
95	DUDLEY THE DRAGON QX620-9	YR	10.95	13.00
95	FOREST FROLICS 7TH & FINAL QLX729-9	YR	28.00	36.00
M. PYDA-SEVCIK				
90	FIRST CHRISTMAS TOGETHER QX 488-3	YR	9.75	17.00
D. RHODUS				
94	CAT NAPS 1ST ED. 795QX531-3	YR	7.75	21.00
94	HOLIDAY PATROL 895QX582-6	YR	8.95	11.00
94	MAKING IT BRIGHT 895QX540-3	YR	8.95	12.00
94	REINDEER PRO 795QX592-6	YR	7.95	11.00
94	SISTER TO SISTER 995QX553-3	YR	9.95	15.00
94	SPECIAL CAT, PHOTOHOLDER 795QX560-6	YR	7.95	9.00
94	SPECIAL DOG, PHOTOHOLDER 795QX560-3	YR	7.95	12.00
95	CAT NAPS 2ND SERIES QX509-7	YR	7.95	13.00
95	DAD-TO-BE QX566-7	YR	7.95	9.00
95	FELIZ NAVIDAD QX586-9	YR	7.95	10.00
95	MOM-TO-BE QX565-9	YR	7.95	11.00
95	SKI HOUND QX590-9	YR	8.95	11.00
95	THOMAS THE TANK ENGINE NO. 1 QX585-7	YR	9.95	12.00
N. ROCKWELL				
95	SANTA'S VISITOR: NORMAN ROCKWELL QX240-7	YR	5.00	11.00
A. ROGERS				
90	NUTSHELL HOLIDAY 575QX465-2	YR	5.75	21.00
92	KRINGLES, THE- 600QXM538-1	YR	6.00	22.00

YR	NAME	LIMIT	ISSUE	TREND
93	MERRY OLDE SANTA 4TH ED. 1475QX484-2	YR	14.75	27.00
93	PUPPY LOVE 775QX504-5	YR	7.75	15.00
94	BEATLES GIFT SET QX 537-3	YR	48.00	92.00
94	CARING DOCTOR 895QX582-3	YR	8.95	15.00
94	DAD 795QX546-3	YR	7.95	11.00
94	FELIZ NAVIDAD 895QX579-3	YR	8.95	16.00
94	GODCHILD 895QX445-3	YR	8.95	9.00
94	MOM 795QX546-6	YR	7.95	12.00
94	OUR CHRISTMAS TOGETHER 995QX481-6	YR	9.95	14.00
94	PUPPY LOVE 4TH ED. 795QX525-3	YR	7.95	11.00
94	RED HOT HOLIDAY 795QX584-3	YR	7.95	12.00
94	THICK 'N THIN 1095QX569-3	YR	10.95	14.00
94	TOU CAN LOVE 895QX564-6	YR	8.95	14.00
95	CHRIS MOUSE TREE 11TH SERIES QLX730-7	YR	12.50	16.00
95	FRIENDS SHARE FUN QLX734-9	YR	16.50	25.00
95	GRANDDAUGHTER QX577-9	YR	6.95	11.00
95	GRANDSON QX578-7	YR	6.95	9.00
95	HOLIDAY SWIM QLX731-9	YR	18.50	21.00
95	MOM AND DAD QX565-7	YR	9.95	13.00
95	PUPPY LOVE FIFTH SERIES QX513-7	YR	7.95	12.00
E. SEALE				
87	CHRISTMAS IS GENTLE 1750QX444-9	YR	17.50	57.00
88	TREETOP DREAMS QX 459-7	YR	6.75	22.00
88	WONDERFUL SANTACYCLE, THE- 225QX411-4	YR	22.50	33.00
93	YOU'RE ALWAYS WELCOME QXC569-2	YR	9.75	37.00
94	COLORS OF JOY 795QX589-3	YR	7.95	12.00
94	FABULOUS DECADE 5TH ED. 795QX526-3	YR	7.95	14.00
94	FROSTY FRIENDS 995QX529-3	YR	9.95	17.00
94	KITTY'S CATAMARAN 1095QX541-6	YR	10.95	13.00
94	KRINGLE'S KAYAK 795QX588-6	YR	7.95	14.00
94	MAGIC CARPET RIDE 795QX588-3	YR	7.95	17.00
94	MISTLETOE SURPRISE 1295QX599-6	YR	12.95	25.00
95	AIR EXPRESS	YR	7.95	10.00
95	FABULOUS DECADE 6TH SERIES QX514-7	YR	7.95	12.00
95	FROSTY FRIENDS 16TH SERIES QX516-9	YR	10.95	14.00
95	NORTH POLE 911 QX595-7	YR	10.95	13.00
95	OUR FIRST CHRISTMAS TOGETHER:PHOTOHOLDER	YR	8.95	11.00
95	PACKED WITH MEMORIES:PHOTOHOLDER QX563-9	YR	7.95	11.00
95	ROLLER WHIZ QX593-7	YR	7.95	11.00
95	SANTA IN PARIS QX587-7	YR	8.95	11.00
L. SICKMAN				
85	TUFTED TITMOUSE QX 479-5	YR	6.50	26.00
86	OPEN HOUSE ORNAMENT QX0440-3	YR	12.75	47.00
89	ORNAMENT EXPRESS, THE- 2200QX580-5	YR	22.00	39.00
90	DOVE OF PEACE 2475QXC447-6	25400	24.75	50.00
94	FRIENDSHIP SUNDAE 1095QX476-6	YR	10.95	18.00
94	ROCKING HORSE 14TH ED. 1095QX501-6	YR	10.95	17.00
94	STAMP OF APPROVAL 795QX570-3	YR	7.95	11.00
95	DELIVERING KISSES QX410-7	YR	10.95	16.00
95	IMPORTANT MEMO QX584-7	YR	8.95	11.00
95	ROCKING HORSE 15TH SERIES QX516-7	YR	10.95	15.00
95	YULETIDE CENTRAL 2ND SERIES QX507-9	YR	18.95	23.00
B. SIEDLER				
88	CHRIS MOUSE STAR QLX 715-4	YR	8.75	50.00
88	HAPPY HOLIDATA QX 471-4	YR	6.50	24.00
88	REINDOGGY QX 452-7	YR	5.75	26.00
93	MESSAGES OF CHRISTMAS QLX747-2	YR	35.00	31.00
94	BIG SHOT 795QX587-3	YR	7.95	13.00
94	BUSY BATTER 795QX587-6	YR	7.95	12.00
94	CHAMPION TEACHER 695QX583-6	YR	6.95	11.00
94	FRIENDLY PUSH 895QX568-6	YR	8.95	13.00
94	IT'S A STRIKE 895QX585-6	YR	8.95	11.00
94	KEEP ON MOWIN' 895QX541-3	YR	8.95	11.00
94	KICKIN' ROO 795QX591-6	YR	7.95	10.00
94	MOM AND DAD 995QX566-6	YR	9.95	13.00
94	OPEN-AND-SHUT HOLIDAY 995QX569-6	YR	9.95	15.00
94	OWLIVER 795QX522-6	YR	7.95	12.00
94	THRILL A MINUTE 895QX586-6	YR	8.95	12.00
94	WINNIE THE POOH AND TIGGER 1295QX574-6	YR	12.95	25.00
95	ACORN 500 QX 592-9	YR	10.95	11.00
95	CATCH THE SPIRIT QX589-9	YR	7.95	12.00
95	DAD QX564-9	YR	7.95	11.00
95	FAITHFUL FAN QX589-7	YR	8.95	10.00
95	GOODY GUMBALLS! QLX736-7	YR	12.50	21.00
95	GOPHER FUN QX588-7	YR	9.95	13.00
95	LOU RANKIN BEAR QX406-9	YR	9.95	13.00
95	MOM QX564-7	YR	7.95	11.00
95	OUR FIRST CHRISTMAS TOGETHER QX579-9	YR	8.95	11.00
95	PEANUTS GANG 3RD SERIES QX505-9	YR	9.95	13.00
95	PERFECT BALANCE QX592-7	YR	7.95	9.00
95	WATER SPORTS QX603-9	YR	14.95	19.00
95	WINNIE THE POOH -TOO MUCH HUNNY QLX729-7	YR	24.50	47.00
95	WINNIE THE POOH AND TIGGER QX500-9	YR	12.95	20.00
95	WINNING PLAY, THE QX588-9	YR	7.95	13.00
D. UNRUH				
86	JOLLY ST. NICK 2250QX429-6	YR	22.50	58.00
86	MAGICAL UNICORN 2750QX429-3	YR	27.50	82.00
87	CHRISTMAS TIME MIME 2750QX442-9	YR	27.50	40.00

YR	NAME	LIMIT	ISSUE	TREND
88	IN A NUTSHELL 550QX469-7	YR	5.50	19.00
93	GLOWING PEWTER WREATH 1875QX530-2	YR	18.75	39.00
94	COACH 795QX593-3	YR	7.95	11.00
94	GRANDCHILD'S FIRST CHRISTMAS 795QX567-6	YR	7.95	10.00
94	GRANDPA 795QX561-6	YR	7.95	11.00
94	LUCINDA AND TEDDY 2175QX481-3	SPEC. ED	21.75	29.00
94	OUT OF THIS WORLD TEACHER 795QX576-6	YR	7.95	16.00
94	SECRET SANTA 795QX573-6	YR	7.95	9.00
95	ANNIVERSARY YEAR: PHOTOHOLDER QX 581-9	YR	8.95	11.00
95	REFRESHING GIFT QX406-7	YR	14.95	19.00
	L. VOTRUBA			
90	FIRST CHRISTMAS TOGETHER QX 213-6	YR	4.75	15.00
90	FIRST CHRISTMAS TOGETHER QX 314-6	YR	6.75	16.00
90	FIRST XMAS TOGETHER PHOTOHOLDER QX488-6	YR	7.75	15.00
93	BABY'S FIRST CHRISTMAS-GIRL 475QX209-2	YR	4.75	8.00
94	CHILD CARE GIVER 795QX590-6	YR	7.95	13.00
94	COCK-A-DOODLE CHRISTMAS QX 539-6	YR	8.95	12.00
94	OUR FIRST CHRISTMAS TOGETHER 695QX318-6	YR	6.95	16.00
95	BABY'S FIRST CHRISTMAS: PHOTOHOLDER QX55	YR	7.95	11.00
95	BINGO BEAR QX591-9	YR	7.95	16.00
95	GODPARENT QX241-7	YR	5.00	6.00
95	HAPPY HOLIDAYS: PHOTOHOLDER QX630-7	YR	2.95	9.00
95	SANTA'S DINER QLX733-7	YR	24.50	29.00
95	SISTER TO SISTER QX568-9	YR	8.00	12.00
	D. LEE		**20TH ANNIVERSARY**	
93	TANNENBAUM'S DEPT. STORE 2600QX561-2	YR	26.00	47.00
	E. SEALE		**20TH ANNIVERSARY**	
93	FROSTY FRIENDS 2000QX568-2	YR	20.00	45.00
	L. SICKMAN		**20TH ANNIVERSARY**	
93	SHOPPING WITH SANTA QX567-5	YR	24.00	36.00
	D. UNRUH		**20TH ANNIVERSARY**	
93	GLOWING PEWTER WREATH QX530-2	YR	18.75	30.00
	D. UNRUH		**A CHRISTMAS CAROL COLLECTION**	
91	BOB CRATCHIT 1375QX499-7	YR	13.75	23.00
91	EBENEZER SCROOGE 1375QX498-9	YR	13.75	27.00
91	MERRY CAROLERS 2975QX479-9	YR	29.75	60.00
91	MRS. CRATCHIT 1375QX499-7	YR	13.75	20.00
91	TINY TIM 1075QX503-7	YR	10.75	26.00
	J. LEE		**ACCESSORIES FOR COLLECTOR'S SERIES**	
95	NOSTALGIC HOUSES AND SHOPS QX508-9	YR	8.95	11.00
	P. ANDREWS		**ALL IS BRIGHT**	
95	ANGEL OF LIGTH QK115-9	YR	11.95	14.00
95	GENTLE LULLABY QK115-7	YR	11.95	14.00
	D. PALMITER		**ALL-AMERICAN TRUCKS**	
95	1956 FORD TRUCK FIRST SERIES QX 552-7	YR	13.95	37.00
	*		**AMERICAN COUNTRY COLLECTION**	
86	MARY EMMERLING 795QX275-2	YR	7.95	19.00
	*		**ANGEL BELLS**	
95	CAROLE QX114-7	YR	12.95	19.00
	L. VOTRUBA		**ANGEL BELLS**	
95	JOY QK113-7	YR	12.95	27.00
95	NOELLE QK113-9	YR	12.95	19.00
	L. SICKMAN		**ANNIVERSARY EDITION**	
95	PEWTER ROCKING HORSE QX616-7	YR	20.00	29.00
	B. SIEDLER		**ANNIVERSARY EDITION**	
95	WHEEL OF FORTUNE QX588-9	YR	12.95	25.00
	*		**ANNIVERSARY ORNAMENTS**	
92	25 YEARS TOGETHER 1000AGA711-3	YR	10.00	22.00
92	25 YEARS TOGETHER ANN. BELL 800AGA713-4	YR	10.00	16.00
92	40 YEARS TOGETHER 1000AGA731-6	YR	10.00	27.00
92	50 YEARS TOGETHER 1000AGA721-4	YR	10.00	27.00
92	50 YEARS TOGETHER ANN. BELL 800AGA723-5	YR	10.00	17.00
92	OUR FIFTH ANNIVERSARY 1000AGA731-9	YR	10.00	20.00
92	OUR FIRST ANNIVERSARY 1000AGA731-8	YR	10.00	22.00
92	OUR TENTH ANNIVERSARY 1000AGA731-7	YR	10.00	20.00
93	25 YEARS TOGETHER 1000AGA768-6	YR	10.00	24.00
93	25 YEARS TOGETHER ANN. BELL 800AGA768-7	YR	10.00	24.00
93	40 YEARS TOGETHER 1000AGA786-8	YR	10.00	24.00
93	50 YEARS TOGETHER 1000AGA778-7	YR	10.00	22.00
93	50 YEARS TOGETHER ANN. BELL 800AGA778-8	YR	10.00	22.00
93	OUR FIFTH ANNIVERSARY 1000AGA786-6	YR	10.00	22.00
93	OUR FIRST ANNIVERSARY 1000AGA786-5	YR	10.00	22.00
93	OUR TENTH ANNIVERSARY 1000AGA786-7	YR	10.00	22.00
	D. MCGEHEE		**ART MASTERPIECE**	
86	MADONNA & CHILD 3RD & FINAL QX 350-6	YR	6.75	21.00
	R. CHAD		**ARTISTS' FAVORITES**	
88	BABY REDBIRD 500QX410-1	YR	5.00	12.00
92	ELFIN MARIONETTE 1175QX593-1	YR	11.75	21.00
	K. CROW		**ARTISTS' FAVORITES**	
90	WELCOME, SANTA 1175QX477-3	YR	11.75	24.00
91	NOAH'S ARK 1375QX486-7	YR	13.75	32.00
92	MOTHER GOOSE 1375QX498-4	YR	13.75	25.00
	P. DUTKIN		**ARTISTS' FAVORITES**	
88	VERY STRAWBERRY 475QX409-1	YR	4.75	13.00
	J. FRANCIS		**ARTISTS' FAVORITES**	
89	BABY PARTRIDGE 675QX452-5	YR	6.75	13.00

YR	NAME	LIMIT	ISSUE	TREND
90	GENTLE DREAMERS 875QX475-6	YR	8.75	20.00
91	TRAMP AND LADDIE 775QX439-7	YR	7.75	21.00
	D. LEE			**ARTISTS' FAVORITES**
87	DECEMBER SHOWERS 550QX448-7	YR	5.50	19.00
87	THREE MEN IN A TUB 800QX454-7	YR	8.00	20.00
88	CYMBALS OF CHRISTMAS 550QX411-1	YR	5.50	22.00
89	PLAYFUL ANGEL 675QX453-5	YR	6.75	21.00
90	DONDER'S DINER 1375QX482-3	YR	13.75	17.00
90	HAPPY WOODCUTTER 975QX476-3	YR	9.75	20.00
91	HOOKED ON SANTA 775QX410-9	YR	7.75	18.00
92	TURTLE DREAMS 875QX499-1	YR	8.75	20.00
	M. PYDA-SEVCIK			**ARTISTS' FAVORITES**
90	ANGEL KITTY 875QX474-6	YR	8.75	21.00
	A. ROGERS			**ARTISTS' FAVORITES**
88	MERRY MINT UNICORN 850QX423-4	YR	8.50	17.00
89	MERRY-GO-ROUND UNICORN 1075QX447-2	YR	10.75	16.00
	E. SEALE			**ARTISTS' FAVORITES**
87	WEE CHIMNEY SWEEP 625QX451-9	YR	6.25	18.00
89	MAIL CALL 875QX452-2	YR	8.75	15.00
90	MOUSEBOAT 775QX475-3	YR	7.75	12.00
91	SANTA SAILOR 975QX438-9	YR	9.75	18.00
92	POLAR POST 875QX491-4	YR	8.75	15.00
	L. SICKMAN			**ARTISTS' FAVORITES**
89	CAROUSEL ZEBRA 925QX451-5	YR	9.25	18.00
89	CHERRY JUBILEE 500QX453-2	YR	5.00	20.00
91	POLAR CIRCUS WAGON 1375QX439-9	YR	13.75	23.00
92	STOCKED WITH JOY 775QX593-4	YR	7.75	16.00
	B. SIEDLER			**ARTISTS' FAVORITES**
87	BEARY SPECIAL 475QX455-7	YR	4.75	15.00
88	LITTLE JACK HORNER 800QX408-1	YR	8.00	18.00
88	MIDNIGHT SNACK 600QX410-4	YR	6.00	18.00
89	BEAR-I-TONE 475QX454-2	YR	4.75	15.00
92	UNCLE ART'S ICE CREAM 875QX500-1	YR	8.75	20.00
	L. VOTRUBA			**ARTISTS' FAVORITES**
91	FIDDLIN' AROUND 775QX438-7	YR	7.75	16.00
*				**BABY CELEBRATIONS**
89	BABY'S CHRISTENING KEEPSAKE 700BBY132-5	YR	7.00	30.00
89	BABY'S FIRST BIRTHDAY 5500BBY172-9	YR	5.50	31.00
89	BABY'S FIRST CHRISTMAS-BOY 475BB145-3	YR	4.75	13.00
89	BABY'S FIRST CHRISTMAS-GIRL 475BBY155-3	YR	4.75	11.00
90	BABY'S CHRISTENING 1000BBY132-6	YR	10.00	22.00
90	BABY'S FIRST CHRISTMAS-BOY PONY BBY145-4	YR	10.00	22.00
90	BABY'S FIRST CHRISTMAS-GIRL BUNNY BBY155	YR	10.00	35.00
91	BABY'S CHRISTENING LAMB 1000BBY131-7	YR	10.00	14.00
91	BABY'S FIRST CHRISTMAS-BOY PONY BBY141-6	YR	10.00	14.00
91	BABY'S FIRST CHRISTMAS-GIRL BUNNY BBY151	YR	10.00	25.00
92	BABY'S CHRISTENING-WHITE HEART BBY133-1	YR	8.50	11.00
92	BABY'S FIRST CHRISTMAS-BLUE PONYBBY145-6	YR	8.50	11.00
92	BABY'S FIRST CHRISTMAS-BUNNY 850BBY155-7	YR	8.50	10.00
93	BABY'S 1ST CHRISTMAS PHOTOHOLDERBBY147-0	YR	10.00	29.00
93	BABY'S CHRISTENING 1200BBY291-7	YR	12.00	15.00
93	BABY'S CHRISTENING PHOTOHOLDER BBY 133-5	YR	10.00	13.00
93	BABY'S FIRST CHRISTMAS MOON 1400BBY291-9	YR	14.00	17.00
93	BABY'S FIRST CHRISTMAS RABBIT BBY291-8	YR	12.00	29.00
93	GRANDDAUGHTER FIRST CHRISTMAS BBY 280-2	YR	14.00	28.00
93	GRANDSON'S FIRST CHRISTMAS BBY 280-1	YR	14.00	28.00
*				**BABY'S FIRST CHRISTMAS**
94	BABY'S FIRST CHRISTMAS-BOY 500QX243-6	YR	5.00	6.00
94	BABY'S FIRST CHRISTMAS-GIRL 500QX243-3	YR	5.00	6.00
	K. CROW			**BABY'S FIRST CHRISTMAS**
94	BABY'S FIRST CHRISTMAS 795QX571-3	YR	7.95	13.00
95	BABY'S FIRST CHRISTMAS MUSICAL QLX 731-7	YR	22.00	25.00
	D. RHODUS			**BASEBALL HEROES**
94	BABE RUTH 1ST ED. 1295QX532-3	YR	12.95	47.00
95	LOU GEHRIG QX502-9	YR	12.95	19.00
	D. PALMITER			**BATMAN**
95	BATMOBILE QX573-9	YR	14.95	18.00
*				**BEARINGERS OF VICTORIA CIRCLE**
93	ABEARNATHY/SON 495XPR974-7	YR	4.95	7.00
93	BEARNADETTE/DAUGHTER 495XPR974-8	YR	4.95	7.00
93	FIREPLACE HEARTH XPR974-9	YR	4.95	8.00
93	MAMA BEARINGER 495XPR974-5	YR	4.95	8.00
93	PAPA BEARINGER 495XPR974-6	YR	4.95	7.00
*				**BEAUTY OF AMERICA COLLECTION**
77	DESERT 250QX159-5	YR	2.50	30.00
77	MOUNTAINS 250QX158-2	YR	2.50	27.00
77	SEASHORE 250QX160-2	YR	2.50	47.00
77	WHARF 250QX161-5	YR	2.50	36.00
*				**BELLRINGER SERIES**
81	SWINGIN' BELLRINGER QX 441-5	YR	15.00	92.00
84	ELFIN ARTIST QX 438-4	YR	15.00	35.00
	D. LEE			**BELLRINGER SERIES**
82	ANGEL QX 455-6	YR	15.00	90.00
*				**BETSEY CLARK**
89	HOME FOR XMAS, 4TH ED. 500QX230-2	YR	5.00	22.00
93	BETSEY'S COUNTRY CHRISTMAS 2ND ED. 500QX	YR	5.00	10.00

YR	NAME	LIMIT	ISSUE	TREND
	S. PIKE			**BETSEY CLARK**
87	HOME FOR CHRISTMAS 500QX272-7	YR	5.00	20.00
*				**BICENTENNIAL COMMEMORATIVES**
76	BICENTENNIAL '76 COMMEMORATIVE QX 203-1	YR	2.50	60.00
76	BICENTENNIAL CHARMERS 300QX198-1	YR	3.00	43.00
76	COLONIAL CHILDREN (2) 400QX208-1	YR	4.00	42.00
	D. LEE			**BRASS ORNAMENTS**
82	BRASS BELL 1200QX460-6	YR	12.00	17.00
	E. SEALE			**BRASS ORNAMENTS**
82	SANTA'S SLEIGH 900QX478-6	YR	9.00	26.00
	L. SICKMAN			**BRASS ORNAMENTS**
82	SANTA AND REINDEER 900QX467-6	YR	9.00	43.00
*				**CAROUSEL SERIES**
79	CARROUSEL-2ND EDITION 650QX146-7	YR	6.50	172.00
80	MERRY CARROUSEL 750QX141-4	YR	7.50	140.00
81	CARROUSEL-4TH EDITION 900QX427-5	YR	9.00	85.00
	L. SICKMAN			**CAROUSEL SERIES**
83	SANTA & FRIENDS 1100QX401-9	YR	11.00	46.00
	P. DUTKIN			**CHRIS MOUSE**
86	CHRIS MOUSE DREAMS 1300QLX705-6	YR	13.00	65.00
*				**CHRISTMAS CAROUSEL HORSE COLLECTION**
89	CAROUSEL DISPLAY STAND 629XPR972-3	YR	1.00	11.00
	J. LEE			**CHRISTMAS CAROUSEL HORSE COLLECTION**
89	GINGER 629XPR972-1	YR	3.95	18.00
89	HOLLY 629XPR972-2	YR	3.95	18.00
89	SNOW 929XPR971-9	YR	3.95	28.00
89	STAR 629XPR972-0	YR	3.95	18.00
*				**CHRISTMAS CLASSICS**
86	NUTCRACKER BALLET 1750QLX704-3	YR	17.50	72.00
87	A CHRISTMAS CAROL 1600QLX702-9	YR	16.00	45.00
	J. FRANCIS			**CHRISTMAS CLASSICS**
90	LITTLEST ANGEL , THE-1400QLX730-3	YR	14.00	36.00
	D. LEE			**CHRISTMAS CLASSICS**
88	NIGHT BEFORE CHRISTMAS-3RD ED. 1500QLX71	YR	15.00	27.00
89	LITTLE DRUMMER BOY 1350QLX724-2	YR	13.50	35.00
*				**CHRISTMAS EXPRESSIONS COLLECTION**
77	BELL 350QX154-2	YR	3.50	40.00
77	MANDOLIN 350QX157-5	YR	3.50	42.00
77	ORNAMENTS 350QX155-5	YR	3.50	42.00
77	WREATH 350QX156-2	YR	3.50	37.00
	L. SICKMAN			**CHRISTMAS MEDLEY COLLECTION**
86	FAVORITE TIN DRUM 850QX514-3	YR	8.50	21.00
86	JOYFUL CAROLERS 975QX513-6	YR	9.75	29.00
	B. SIEDLER			**CHRISTMAS MEDLEY COLLECTION**
86	FESTIVE TREBLE CLEF 875QX513-3	YR	8.75	20.00
	D. UNRUH			**CHRISTMAS MEDLEY COLLECTION**
86	CHRISTMAS GUITAR 700QX512-6	YR	7.00	18.00
86	HOLIDAY HORN 800QX514-6	YR	8.00	26.00
	K. CROW			**CHRISTMAS PIZZAZZ COLLECTION**
87	JOLLY FOLLIES 850QX466-9	YR	8.50	23.00
87	MISTLETOAD 700QX468-7	YR	7.00	24.00
	P. DUTKIN			**CHRISTMAS PIZZAZZ COLLECTION**
87	ST. LOUIE NICK 775QX453-9	YR	7.75	21.00
	D. LEE			**CHRISTMAS PIZZAZZ COLLECTION**
87	CHRISTMAS FUN PUZZLE 800QX467-9	YR	8.00	18.00
	E. SEALE			**CHRISTMAS PIZZAZZ COLLECTION**
87	DOC HOLIDAY 800QX467-7	YR	8.00	31.00
	B. SIEDLER			**CHRISTMAS PIZZAZZ COLLECTION**
87	HAPPY HOLIDATA 650QX471-7	YR	6.50	24.00
	D. UNRUH			**CHRISTMAS PIZZAZZ COLLECTION**
87	HOLIDAY HOURGLASS 800QX470-7	YR	8.00	17.00
	L. SICKMAN			**CHRISTMAS SKY LINE COLLECTION**
92	CABOOSE 975QX532-1	YR	9.75	23.00
92	COAL CAR 975QX540-1	YR	9.75	18.00
92	LOCOMOTIVE 975QX531-1	YR	9.75	37.00
92	STOCK CAR 975QX531-4	YR	9.75	18.00
	A. ROGERS			**CHRISTMAS VISITORS**
95	ST. NICHOLAS FIRST SERIES QX508-7	YR	14.95	32.00
	D. PALMITER			**CLASSIC AMERICAN CARS**
91	1957 CORVETTE-1ST EDITION 1275QX431-9	YR	12.75	180.00
92	1966 MUSTANG 1275QX428-4	YR	12.75	42.00
93	1956 FORD THUNDERBIRD 1275QX527-5	YR	12.75	30.00
94	1957 CHEVROLET BEL AIRE 4TH ED. 1275QX5	YR	12.95	33.00
95	1969 CHEVROLET CAMARO QX523-9	YR	12.95	19.00
	D. PALMITER			**CLAUS & CO. R.R. ORNAMENTS**
91	CABOOSE 395XPR973-3	YR	3.95	11.00
91	GIFT CAR 395XPR973-1	YR	3.95	11.00
91	PASSENGER CAR 395XPR973-2	YR	3.95	11.00
91	TRESTLE TRACK FOR TRAIN 295XPR973-4	YR	2.95	8.00
*				**CLOTH DOLL ORNAMENTS**
77	ANGEL 175QX220-2	YR	1.75	52.00
77	SANTA 175QX221-5	YR	1.75	82.00
	L. SICKMAN			**CLOTHESPIN SOLDIER**
84	CANADIAN MOUNTIE QX447-1	YR	5.00	22.00

YR	NAME	LIMIT	ISSUE	TREND
85	SCOTTISH-4TH EDITION 550QX471-5	YR	5.50	22.00
86	CLOTHESPIN SOLDIER-5TH ED. 550QX406-3	YR	5.50	22.00
87	SAILOR 550QX480-7	YR	5.50	20.00
*			**COLLECTIBLE SERIES**	
79	BELLRINGER-1ST EDITION 10QX147-9	YR	10.00	350.00
79	SNOOPY AND FRIENDS 800QX141-9	YR	8.00	107.00
80	BELLRINGERS, THE-2ND EDITION 15QX157-4	YR	15.00	75.00
80	THIMBLE-3RD EDITION 400QX132-1	YR	4.00	152.00
81	NORMAN ROCKWELL-2ND EDITION 850QX511-5	YR	8.50	37.00
83	BELLRINGER, THE-5TH EDITION 1500QX403-9	YR	15.00	119.00
84	BETSEY CLARK-12TH EDITION 500QX249-4	YR	5.00	25.00
84	PORCELAIN BEAR-2ND EDITION 700QX454-1	YR	7.00	33.00
84	ROCKING HORSE-4TH EDITION 1000QX435-4	YR	10.00	65.00
84	TWELVE DAYS OF CHRISTMAS 600QX348-4	YR	6.00	265.00
84	WOOD CHILDHOOD ORNAMENTS 650QX439-4	YR	6.50	36.00
86	CINNAMON BEAR-4TH EDITION 775QX405-6	YR	7.75	44.00
87	CINNAMON BEAR-5TH EDITION 775QX442-7	YR	7.75	37.00
89	WINTER SURPRISE-1ST EDITION 1075QX427-2	YR	10.75	20.00
90	BETSEY CLARK: HOME FOR XMAS 5TH ED. 500Q	YR	5.00	16.00
90	CINNAMON BEAR-8TH EDITION 875QX442-6	YR	8.75	32.00
91	BETSEY CLARK: HOME FOR XMAS 6TH ED. 500Q	YR	5.00	16.00
92	BETSEY'S COUNTRY CHRISTMAS 1ST ED. 500QX	YR	5.00	20.00
K. CROW			**COLLECTIBLE SERIES**	
89	HARK! IT'S HERALD-1ST EDITION 675QX455-5	YR	6.75	21.00
90	HARK! IT'S HERALD-2ND EDITION 675QX446-3	YR	6.75	19.00
P. DUTKIN			**COLLECTIBLE SERIES**	
83	CINNAMON BEAR-1ST EDITION 700QX428-9	YR	7.00	54.00
85	CINNAMON BEAR-3RD EDITION 750QX479-2	YR	7.50	50.00
T. FRALEY			**COLLECTIBLE SERIES**	
92	TOBIN FRALEY CAROUSEL 2800QX489-1	YR	28.00	32.00
J. FRANCIS			**COLLECTIBLE SERIES**	
80	SNOOPY & FRIENDS-2ND EDITION 900QX154-1	YR	9.00	97.00
81	SNOOPY & FRIENDS-3RD EDITION 1200QX436-2	YR	12.00	82.00
90	WINTER SURPRISE-2ND EDITION 1075QX444-3	YR	10.75	18.00
92	WINTER SURPRISE 4TH ED. 1175QX427-1	YR	11.75	17.00
D. LEE			**COLLECTIBLE SERIES**	
85	NOSTALGIC HOUSES & SHOPS 1375QX497-5	YR	13.75	97.00
91	MERRY OLDE SANTA-2ND EDITION 1475QX435-9	YR	14.75	71.00
92	FROSTY FRIENDS 975QX429-1	YR	9.75	24.00
92	HARK! IT'S HERALD 4TH ED. 775QX446-4	YR	7.75	18.00
J. LYLE			**COLLECTIBLE SERIES**	
91	HEAVENLY ANGELS-1ST EDITION 775QX436-7	YR	7.75	26.00
91	WINTER SURPRISE-3RD EDITION 1075QX427-7	YR	10.75	20.00
92	HEAVENLY ANGELS 2ND ED. 775QX445-4	YR	7.75	24.00
93	HEAVENLY ANGELS 3RD ED. 775QX494-5	YR	7.75	15.00
D. MCGEHEE			**COLLECTIBLE SERIES**	
84	ART MASTERPIECE-1ST EDITION 650QX349-4	YR	6.50	13.00
85	ART MASTERPIECE-2ND EDITION 675QX377-2	YR	6.75	14.00
85	NORMAN ROCKWELL-6TH EDITION 750QX374-5	YR	7.50	21.00
D. PALMITER			**COLLECTIBLE SERIES**	
87	NORMAN ROCKWELL-8TH EDITION 775QX370-7	YR	7.75	15.00
J. PATTEE			**COLLECTIBLE SERIES**	
87	CONSTITUTION, THE 600QZ377-7	YR	6.50	14.00
S. PIKE			**COLLECTIBLE SERIES**	
85	12 DAYS OF CHRISTMAS-2ND ED. 650QX371-2	YR	6.50	45.00
86	BETSEY CLARK: HOME FOR XMAS 500QX277-6	YR	5.00	21.00
88	BEAR-PORCELAIN 800QX404-4	YR	8.00	30.00
88	BETSEY CLARK: HOME FOR XMAS 500QX271-4	YR	5.00	18.00
88	FIVE GOLDEN RINGS-5TH EDITION 650QX371-4	YR	6.50	20.00
91	FROSTY FRIENDS-12TH EDITION 975QX432-7	YR	9.75	30.00
A. ROGERS			**COLLECTIBLE SERIES**	
89	CHRISTMAS KITTY-1ST EDITION 1475QX544-5	YR	14.75	23.00
89	MINIATURE CRECHE-5TH EDITION 925QX459-2	YR	9.25	18.00
90	CHRISTMAS KITTY-2ND EDITION 1475QX450-6	YR	14.75	26.00
91	CHRISTMAS KITTY-3RD EDITION 1475QX437-7	YR	14.75	21.00
91	HARK! IT'S HERALD-3RD ED. 675QX437-9	YR	6.75	17.00
91	PUPPY LOVE-1ST EDITION 775QX537-9	YR	7.75	35.00
92	PUPPY LOVE 2ND ED. 775QX448-4	YR	7.75	32.00
E. SEALE			**COLLECTIBLE SERIES**	
82	CAROUSEL SERIES-5TH EDITION 1000QX478-3	YR	10.00	95.00
82	FROSTY FRIENDS-3RD EDITION 800QX452-3	YR	8.00	190.00
82	SNOOPY & FRIENDS-4TH EDITION 1300QX480-3	YR	13.00	105.00
83	FROSTY FRIENDS-4TH EDITION 800QX400-7	YR	8.00	255.00
84	FROSTY FRIENDS-5TH EDITION 800QX437-1	YR	8.00	70.00
85	FROSTY FRIENDS-6TH EDITION 850QX482-2	YR	8.50	60.00
85	MINIATURE CRECHE-1ST EDITION 875QX482-5	YR	8.75	29.00
86	MINIATURE CRECHE-2ND EDITION 900QX407-6	YR	9.00	55.00
87	FROSTY FRIENDS-8TH EDITION 850QX440-9	YR	8.50	50.00
87	MINIATURE CRECHE-3RD EDITION 900QX481-9	YR	9.00	23.00
88	FROSTY FRIENDS-9TH EDITION 875QX403-1	YR	8.75	52.00
89	FROSTY FRIENDS-10TH EDITION 925QX457-2	YR	9.25	38.00
90	CLAUS CONSTRUCTION 775QX488-5	YR	7.75	23.00
90	FABULOUS DECADE-1ST EDITION 775QX446-6	YR	7.75	35.00
90	FROSTY FRIENDS-11TH EDITION 975QX439-6	YR	9.75	23.00
90	HEART OF CHRISTMAS-1ST ED. 1375QX472-6	YR	13.75	60.00
90	MERRY OLDE SANTA-1ST EDITION 1475QX473-6	YR	14.75	62.00
91	FABULOUS DECADE-2ND EDITION 775QX411-9	YR	7.75	31.00

YR	NAME	LIMIT	ISSUE	TREND
91	HEART OF CHRISTMAS-2ND ED. 1375QX435-7	YR	13.75	30.00
92	FABULOUS DECADE 3RD ED. 775QX424-4	YR	7.75	30.00
92	HEART OF CHRISTMAS 3RD ED. 1375QX441-1	YR	13.75	24.00
93	HEART OF CHRISTMAS 4TH ED. 1475QX448-2	YR	14.75	23.00
94	HEART OF CHRISTMAS 5TH ED. 1495QX526-6	YR	14.95	20.00
L. SICKMAN			**COLLECTIBLE SERIES**	
81	ROCKING HORSE-1ST EDITION 900QX422-2	YR	9.00	600.00
82	CLOTHESPIN SOLDIER-1ST ED. 500QX458-3	YR	5.00	115.00
82	ROCKING HORSE-2ND EDITION 1000QX502-3	YR	10.00	357.00
82	TIN LOCOMOTIVE-1ST EDITION 1300QX460-3	YR	13.00	525.00
83	CLOTHESPIN SOLDIER-2ND ED. 500QX402-9	YR	5.00	52.00
83	ROCKING HORSE-3RD EDITION 1000QX417-7	YR	10.00	237.00
83	SNOOPY & FRIENDS-5TH EDITION 1300QX416-9	YR	13.00	75.00
83	TIN LOCOMOTIVE-2ND EDITION 1300QX404-9	YR	13.00	260.00
84	TIN LOCOMOTIVE-3RD EDITION 1400QX440-4	YR	14.00	75.00
85	ROCKING HORSE-5TH EDITION 1075QX493-2	YR	10.75	55.00
85	TIN LOCOMOTIVE-4TH EDITION 1475QX497-2	YR	14.75	71.00
86	ROCKING HORSE-6TH EDITION 1075QX401-6	YR	10.75	52.00
86	TIN LOCOMOTIVE-5TH EDITION 1475QX403-6	YR	14.75	66.00
87	ROCKING HORSE-7TH EDITION 1075QX482-9	YR	10.75	52.00
87	TIN LOCOMOTIVE-6TH EDITION 1475QX484-9	YR	14.75	57.00
88	ROCKING HORSE-8TH EDITION 1075QX402-4	YR	10.75	41.00
88	TIN LOCOMOTIVE-7TH EDITION 1475QX400-4	YR	14.75	41.00
89	ROCKING HORSE-9TH EDITION 1075QX462-2	YR	10.75	35.00
89	TIN LOCOMOTIVE-8TH EDITION 1475QX460-2	YR	14.75	47.00
90	ROCKING HORSE-10TH EDITION 1075QX464-6	YR	10.75	47.00
91	ROCKING HORSE-11TH EDITION 1075QX414-7	YR	10.75	29.00
92	ROCKING HORSE 12TH ED. 1075QX426-1	YR	10.75	26.00
B. SIEDLER			**COLLECTIBLE SERIES**	
86	FROSTY FRIENDS-7TH EDITION 850QX405-3	YR	8.50	57.00
88	THIMBLE SNOWMAN 575QX405-4	YR	5.75	17.00
92	OWLIVER 1ST ED. 775QX454-4	YR	7.75	17.00
D. UNRUH			**COLLECTIBLE SERIES**	
87	HOLIDAY HEIRLOOM QX 485-7	34600	25.00	29.00
88	MINIATURE CRECHE-4TH EDITION 850QX403-4	YR	8.50	17.00
92	MERRY OLDE SANTA 3RD ED. 1475QX441-4	YR	14.75	30.00
L. VOTRUBA			**COLLECTIBLE SERIES**	
90	GIFT BRINGERS-ST. LUCIA 500QX280-3	YR	5.00	24.00
90	GREATEST STORY-1ST EDITION 1275QX465-6	YR	12.75	22.00
91	GREATEST STORY-2ND EDITION 1275QX412-9	YR	12.75	24.00
92	GIFT BRINGERS, THE/KOLYADA 4TH ED. 500QX	YR	5.00	14.00
92	GREATEST STORY 3RD ED. 1275QX425-1	YR	12.75	20.00
K. CROW			**COLORFUL WORLD**	
95	CRAYOLA QX551-9	YR	10.95	18.00
*			**COLORS OF CHRISTMAS**	
77	CANDLE 350QX203-5	YR	3.50	59.00
77	JOY 350QX201-5	YR	3.50	59.00
77	WREATH 350QX202-2	YR	3.50	59.00
78	ANGEL 350QX354-3	YR	3.50	45.00
78	CANDLE 350QX357-6	YR	3.50	85.00
78	LOCOMOTIVE 350QX356-3	YR	3.50	45.00
79	HOLIDAY WREATH 350QX353-9	YR	3.50	40.00
79	PARTRIDGE IN A PEAR TREE 350QX351-9	YR	3.50	37.00
79	WORDS OF CHRISTMAS 350QX350-7	YR	3.50	75.00
80	JOY 400QX350-1	YR	4.00	20.00
82	NATIVITY 450QX308-3	YR	4.50	45.00
82	SANTA'S FLIGHT 450QX308-6	YR	4.50	35.00
D. PALMITER			**COLORS OF CHRISTMAS**	
78	MERRY CHRISTMAS 350QX355-6	YR	3.50	47.00
L. SICKMAN			**COLORS OF CHRISTMAS**	
77	BELL 350QX200-2	YR	3.50	52.00
79	STAR OVER BETHLEHEM 350QX352-7	YR	3.50	62.00
*			**COMMEMORATIVES**	
77	BABY'S FIRST CHRISTMAS 350QX131-5	YR	3.50	125.00
77	FIRST CHRISTMAS TOGETHER 350QX132-2	YR	3.50	64.00
77	FOR YOUR NEW HOME 350QX263-5	YR	3.50	37.00
77	GRANDDAUGHTER 350QX208-2	YR	3.50	27.00
77	GRANDMOTHER 350QX260-2	YR	3.50	42.00
77	GRANDSON 350QX209-5	YR	3.50	27.00
77	LOVE 350QX262-2	YR	3.50	27.00
77	MOTHER 350QX261-5	YR	3.50	22.00
78	25TH CHRISTMAS TOGETHER 350QX269-3	YR	3.50	20.00
78	BABY'S FIRST CHRISTMAS 350QX200-3	YR	3.50	65.00
78	FIRST CHRISTMAS TOGETHER 350QX218-3	YR	3.50	38.00
78	FOR YOUR NEW HOME 350QX217-6	YR	3.50	27.00
78	GRANDDAUGHTER 350QX216-3	YR	3.50	35.00
78	GRANDMOTHER 350QX267-6	YR	3.50	39.00
78	GRANDSON 350QX215-6	YR	3.50	37.00
78	LOVE 350QX268-3	YR	3.50	35.00
78	MOTHER 350QX266-3	YR	3.50	35.00
79	BABY'S FIRST CHRISTMAS 350QX208-7	YR	3.50	25.00
79	BABY'S FIRST CHRISTMAS 800QX154-7	YR	8.00	110.00
79	FRIENDSHIP 350QX203-9	YR	3.50	25.00
79	GRANDDAUGHTER 350QX211-9	YR	3.50	27.00
79	GRANDMOTHER 350QX252-7	YR	3.50	24.00
79	GRANDSON 350QX210-7	YR	3.50	27.00
79	LOVE 350QX258-7	YR	3.50	26.00

YR	NAME	LIMIT	ISSUE	TREND
79	MOTHER 350QX251-9	YR	3.50	20.00
79	NEW HOME 350QX212-7	YR	3.50	27.00
79	OUR FIRST CHRISTMAS TOGETHER 350QX209-9	YR	3.50	47.00
79	OUR TWENTY-FIFTH ANNIVERSARY 350QX250-7	YR	3.50	22.00
79	TEACHER 350QX213-9	YR	3.50	13.00
80	25TH CHRISTMAS TOGETHER 400QX206-1	YR	4.00	15.00
80	BABY'S FIRST CHRISTMAS 400QX200-1	YR	4.00	23.00
80	BEAUTY OF FRIENDSHIP 400QX303-4	YR	4.00	47.00
80	BLACK BABY'S FIRST CHRISTMAS 400QX229-4	YR	4.00	20.00
80	CHRISTMAS AT HOME 400QX210-1	YR	4.00	14.00
80	CHRISTMAS LOVE 400QX207-4	YR	4.00	29.00
80	DAD 400QX214-1	YR	4.00	15.00
80	DAUGHTER 400QX212-1	YR	4.00	27.00
80	FIRST CHRISTMAS TOGETHER 400QX205-4	YR	4.00	24.00
80	FIRST CHRISTMAS TOGETHER 400QX305-4	YR	4.00	47.00
80	FRIENDSHIP 400QX208-1	YR	4.00	15.00
80	GRANDDAUGHTER 400QX202-1	YR	4.00	25.00
80	GRANDFATHER 400QX231-4	YR	4.00	17.00
80	GRANDMOTHER 400QX204-1	YR	4.00	14.00
80	GRANDPARENTS 400QX213-4	YR	4.00	22.00
80	GRANDSON 400QX201-4	YR	4.00	22.00
80	LOVE 400QX302-1	YR	4.00	57.00
80	MOTHER 400QX203-4	YR	4.00	15.00
80	MOTHER 400QX304-1	YR	4.00	31.00
80	MOTHER AND DAD 400QX230-1	YR	4.00	16.00
80	SON 400QX211-4	YR	4.00	29.00
80	TEACHER 400QX209-4	YR	4.00	14.00
81	25TH CHRISTMAS TOGETHER 450QX707-5	YR	4.50	16.00
81	25TH CHRISTMAS TOGETHER 550QX504-2	YR	5.50	21.00
81	50TH CHRISTMAS TOGETHER QX 708-2	YR	4.50	15.00
81	BABY'S FIRST CHRISTMAS 1300QX440-2	YR	13.00	47.00
81	BABY'S FIRST CHRISTMAS 550QX516-2	YR	5.50	26.00
81	BABY'S FIRST CHRISTMAS 850QX513-5	YR	8.50	13.00
81	BABY'S FIRST CHRISTMAS-BLACK 450QX602-2	YR	4.50	17.00
81	BABY'S FIRST CHRISTMAS-BOY 450QX601-5	YR	4.50	17.00
81	BABY'S FIRST CHRISTMAS-GIRL 450QX600-2	YR	4.50	18.00
81	DAUGHTER 450QX607-5	YR	4.50	28.00
81	FATHER 450QX609-5	YR	4.50	13.00
81	FIRST CHRISTMAS TOGETHER 450QX706-2	YR	4.50	20.00
81	FIRST CHRISTMAS TOGETHER 550QX505-5	YR	5.50	15.00
81	FRIENDSHIP 450QX704-2	YR	4.50	14.00
81	FRIENDSHIP 550QX503-5	YR	5.50	26.00
81	GIFT OF LOVE, THE- 450QX705-5	YR	4.50	17.00
81	GODCHILD 450QX603-5	YR	4.50	13.00
81	GRANDDAUGHTER 450QX605-5	YR	4.50	21.00
81	GRANDFATHER 450QX701-5	YR	4.50	14.00
81	GRANDMOTHER 450QX702-2	YR	4.50	15.00
81	GRANDPARENTS 450QX703-5	YR	4.50	14.00
81	GRANDSON 450QX604-2	YR	4.50	20.00
81	HOME 450QX709-5	YR	4.50	17.00
81	LOVE 550QX502-2	YR	5.50	45.00
81	MOTHER 450QX608-2	YR	4.50	15.00
81	MOTHER AND DAD 450QX700-2	YR	4.50	11.00
81	SON 450QX606-2	YR	4.50	22.00
81	TEACHER 450QX800-2	YR	4.50	12.00
82	25TH CHRISTMAS TOGETHER 450QX211-6	YR	4.50	13.00
82	50TH CHRISTMAS TOGETHER 450QX212-3	YR	4.50	16.00
82	BABY'S FIRST CHRISTMAS (BOY) 450QX216-3	YR	4.50	18.00
82	BABY'S FIRST CHRISTMAS (GIRL) 450QX207-3	YR	4.50	21.00
82	BABY'S FIRST XMAS-PHOTOHOLDER 650QX312-6	YR	6.50	25.00
82	DAUGHTER 450QX204-6	YR	4.50	25.00
82	FIRST CHRISTMAS TOGETHER 450QX211-3	YR	4.50	25.00
82	FIRST CHRISTMAS TOGETHER 550QX302-6	YR	5.50	14.00
82	FIRST CHRISTMAS TOGETHER 850QX306-6	YR	8.50	22.00
82	FRIENDSHIP 450QX208-6	YR	4.50	17.00
82	FRIENDSHIP 550QX304-6	YR	5.50	24.00
82	GODCHILD 450QX222-6	YR	4.50	15.00
82	GRANDDAUGHTER 450QX224-3	YR	4.50	15.00
82	GRANDFATHER 450QX207-6	YR	4.50	11.00
82	GRANDMOTHER 450QX200-3	YR	4.50	14.00
82	GRANDPARENTS 450QX214-6	YR	4.50	13.00
82	GRANDSON 450QX224-6	YR	4.50	21.00
82	LOVE 450QX209-6	YR	4.50	16.00
82	LOVE 550QX304-3	YR	5.50	25.00
82	MOMENTS OF LOVE 450QX209-3	YR	4.50	15.00
82	MOTHER 450QX205-3	YR	4.50	14.00
82	MOTHER AND DAD 450QX222-3	YR	4.50	13.00
82	NEW HOME 450QX212-6	YR	4.50	16.00
82	SISTER 450QX208-3	YR	4.50	22.00
82	SON 450QX204-3	YR	4.50	21.00
82	TEACHER 450QX214-3	YR	4.50	9.00
83	10TH CHRISTMAS TOGETHER 650QX430-7	YR	6.50	17.00
83	25TH CHRISTMAS TOGETHER 450QX224-7	YR	4.50	18.00
83	BABY'S 1ST XMAS PHOTOHOLDER QX 302-9	YR	7.00	20.00
83	BABY'S FIRST CHRISTMAS 450QX200-7	YR	4.50	21.00
83	BABY'S FIRST CHRISTMAS 450QX200-9	YR	4.50	21.00
83	BABY'S SECOND CHRISTMAS 450QX226-7	YR	4.50	24.00
83	CHILD'S THIRD CHRISTMAS 450QX226-9	YR	4.50	19.00
83	DAUGHTER 450QX203-7	YR	4.50	27.00

YR	NAME	LIMIT	ISSUE	TREND
83	FIRST CHRISTMAS TOGETHER 600QX306-9	YR	6.00	19.00
83	FIRST CHRISTMAS TOGETHER 600QX310-7	YR	6.00	29.00
83	FIRST CHRISTMAS TOGETHER 750QX301-7	YR	7.50	17.00
83	FRIENDSHIP 450QX207-7	YR	4.50	16.00
83	FRIENDSHIP 600QX305-9	YR	6.00	16.00
83	GODCHILD 450QX201-7	YR	4.50	13.00
83	GRANDCHILD'S FIRST CHRISTMAS 400Q430-9	YR	14.00	30.00
83	GRANDCHILD'S FIRST CHRISTMAS 600QX312-9	YR	6.00	22.00
83	GRANDDAUGHTER 450QX202-7	YR	4.50	29.00
83	GRANDMOTHER 450QX205-7	YR	4.50	19.00
83	GRANDPARENTS 650QX429-9	YR	6.50	19.00
83	GRANDSON 450QX201-9	YR	4.50	29.00
83	LOVE 450QX207-9	YR	4.50	18.00
83	LOVE 600QX305-7	YR	6.00	17.00
83	LOVE 600QX310-9	YR	6.00	30.00
83	LOVE IS A SONG 450QX223-9	YR	4.50	24.00
83	MOTHER 600QX306-7	YR	6.00	16.00
83	NEW HOME 450QX210-7	YR	4.50	20.00
83	SISTER 450QX206-9	YR	4.50	17.00
83	SON 450QX202-9	YR	4.50	24.00
83	TEACHER 450QX224-9	YR	4.50	16.00
83	TEACHER 600QX304-9	YR	6.00	11.00
84	A GIFT OF FRIENDSHIP 450QX260-4	YR	4.50	18.00
84	BABY BOY FIRST CHRISTMAS 450QX240-4	YR	4.50	19.00
84	BABY GIRL FIRST CHRISTMAS 450QX340-1	YR	4.50	35.00
84	BABY'S 1ST XMAS PHOTOHOLDER QX 300-1	YR	7.00	18.00
84	BABY'S FIRST CHRISTMAS 1400QX438-1	YR	14.00	41.00
84	BABY'S FIRST CHRISTMAS 600QX340-1	YR	6.00	35.00
84	BABY'S SECOND CHRISTMAS 450QX241-1	YR	4.50	11.00
84	BABYSITTER 450QX253-1	YR	4.50	12.00
84	CHILD'S THIRD CHRISTMAS 450QX261-1	YR	4.50	17.00
84	DAUGHTER 450QX244-4	YR	4.50	24.00
84	FATHER 600QX257-1	YR	6.00	16.00
84	FIRST CHRISTMAS TOGETHER 450QX245-1	YR	4.50	18.00
84	FIRST CHRISTMAS TOGETHER 600QX342-1	YR	6.00	16.00
84	FRIENDSHIP 450QX248-1	YR	4.50	13.00
84	FROM OUR HOME TO YOURS 450QX248-4	YR	4.50	21.00
84	FUN OF FRIENDSHIP, THE- 600QX343-1	YR	6.00	30.00
84	GODCHILD 450QX242-1	YR	4.50	16.00
84	GRANDCHILD'S FIRST CHRISTMAS 110QX460-1	YR	11.00	21.00
84	GRANDCHILD'S FIRST CHRISTMAS 450QX257-4	YR	4.50	13.00
84	GRANDDAUGHTER 450QX243-1	YR	4.50	20.00
84	GRANDMOTHER 450QX244-1	YR	4.50	15.00
84	GRANDPARENTS 450QX256-1	YR	4.50	13.00
84	GRANDSON 450QX242-4	YR	4.50	20.00
84	GRATITUDE 600QX344-4	YR	6.00	10.00
84	HEARTFUL OF LOVE 1000QX443-4	YR	10.00	39.00
84	LOVE 450QX255-4	YR	4.50	19.00
84	LOVE-THE SPIRIT OF CHRISTMAS 450QX247-4	YR	4.50	22.00
84	MIRACLE OF LOVE, THE- 600QX342-4	YR	6.00	26.00
84	MOTHER 600QX343-4	YR	6.00	13.00
84	MOTHER AND DAD 650QX258-1	YR	6.50	20.00
84	NEW HOME 450QX245-4	YR	4.50	42.00
84	SISTER 650QX259-4	YR	6.50	20.00
84	SON 450QX243-4	YR	4.50	21.00
84	TEACHER 450QX249-1	YR	4.50	11.00
84	TEN YEARS TOGETHER 650QX258-4	YR	6.50	16.00
84	TWENTY-FIVE YEARS TOGETHER 650QX259-1	YR	6.50	18.00
85	BABY'S FIRST CHRISTMAS 1500QX499-2	YR	15.00	45.00
85	BABY'S FIRST CHRISTMAS 1600QX499-5	YR	16.00	37.00
85	BABY'S FIRST CHRISTMAS 500QX260-2	YR	5.00	18.00
85	BABY'S SECOND CHRISTMAS 600QX478-5	YR	6.00	27.00
85	DAUGHTER 550QX503-2	YR	5.50	11.00
85	FIRST CHRISTMAS TOGETHER 475QX261-2	YR	4.75	15.00
85	FIRST CHRISTMAS TOGETHER 675QX370-5	YR	6.75	11.00
85	FIRST CHRISTMAS TOGETHER 800QX507-2	YR	8.00	9.00
85	GOOD FRIENDS 475QX265-2	YR	4.75	17.00
85	GRANDCHILD'S FIRST CHRISTMAS 500QX260-5	YR	5.00	11.00
85	GRANDDAUGHTER 475QX263-5	YR	4.75	18.00
85	HEART FULL OF LOVE 675QX378-2	YR	6.75	11.00
85	HOLIDAY HEART 800QX498-2	YR	8.00	15.00
85	NIECE 575QX520-5	YR	5.75	8.00
85	TEACHER,OWL 600QX505-2	YR	6.00	12.00
85	TWENTY-FIVE YEARS TOGETHER 800QX500-5	YR	8.00	15.00
85	WITH APPRECIATION 675QX375-2	YR	6.75	7.00
86	BABY'S FIRST CHRISTMAS 550QX271-3	YR	5.50	20.00
86	BABY-SITTER 475QX275-6	YR	4.75	7.00
86	FIFTY YEARS TOGETHER 1000QX400-6	YR	10.00	18.00
86	FIRST CHRISTMAS TOGETHER 1600QX400-3	YR	16.00	17.00
86	FIRST CHRISTMAS TOGETHER 475QX270-3	YR	4.75	16.00
86	FIRST CHRISTMAS TOGETHER 7000QX379-3	YR	7.00	14.00
86	FRIENDSHIP GREETING 800QX427-3	YR	8.00	10.00
86	FRIENDSHIP'S GIFT 600QX381-6	YR	6.00	9.00
86	FROM OUR HOME TO YOURS 600QX383-3	YR	6.00	12.00
86	GODCHILD 475QX271-6	YR	4.75	12.00
86	GRANDCHILD'S FIRST CHRISTMAS 1000QX411-6	YR	10.00	13.00
86	GRANDPARENTS 750QX432-3	YR	7.50	16.00
86	MOTHER 700QX382-6	YR	7.00	17.00
86	NEPHEW 675QX381-3	YR	6.25	10.00

YR	NAME	LIMIT	ISSUE	TREND
86	NIECE 600QX426-6	YR	6.00	8.00
86	SEASON OF THE HEART 475QX270-6	YR	4.75	11.00
86	TEACHER 475QX275-3	YR	4.75	11.00
86	TEN YEARS TOGETHER 750QX401-3	YR	7.50	17.00
87	BABY LOCKET 1500QX461-7	YR	15.00	21.00
87	BABY'S 1ST XMAS PHOTOHOLDER 750QX461-9	YR	7.50	25.00
87	BABY'S FIRST CHRISTMAS 600QX372-9	YR	6.00	15.00
87	FIRST CHRISTMAS TOGETHER 1500QX446-9	YR	15.00	22.00
87	FIRST CHRISTMAS TOGETHER 650QX371-9	YR	6.50	14.00
87	FIRST CHRISTMAS TOGETHER 800QX445-9	YR	8.00	25.00
87	GRANDMOTHER 475QX277-9	YR	4.75	11.00
87	HOLIDAY GREETINGS 600QX375-7	YR	6.00	11.00
87	NIECE 475QX275-9	YR	4.75	10.00
87	TWENTY-FIVE YEARS TOGETHER 750QX443-9	YR	7.50	23.00
87	WARMTH OF FRIENDSHIP 600QX375-9	YR	6.00	11.00
87	WORD OF LOVE 800QX447-7	YR	8.00	15.00
88	BABY BOY'S FIRST CHRISTMAS 475QX272-1	YR	4.75	15.00
88	BABY GIRL'S FIRST CHRISTMAS 475QX272-4	YR	4.75	14.00
88	BABY'S FIRST CHRISTMAS PHOTOHLDR 750QX47	YR	7.50	21.00
88	FIFTY YEARS TOGETHER 675QX374-1	YR	6.75	16.00
88	FIRST CHRISTMAS TOGETHER 475QX274-1	YR	4.75	17.00
88	GODCHILD 475QX278-4	YR	4.75	16.00
88	GRANDMOTHER 475QX276-4	YR	4.75	14.00
88	LOVE GROWS 475QX275-4	YR	4.75	19.00
88	MOTHER 650QX375-1	YR	6.50	15.00
88	TEN YEARS TOGETHER 475QX275-1	YR	4.75	14.00
88	YEAR TO REMEMBER 700QX416-4	YR	7.00	16.00
89	FIRST CHRISTMAS TOGETHER 475QX273-2	YR	4.75	17.00
89	FIVE YEARS TOGETHER 475QX273-5	YR	4.75	17.00
89	FROM OUR HOME TO YOURS 625QX384-5	YR	6.25	12.00
89	GRANDDAUGHTER 475QX278-2	YR	4.75	14.00
89	GRANDSON 475QX278-5	YR	4.75	13.00
89	LANGUAGE OF LOVE 625QX383-5	YR	6.25	16.00
89	MOTHER 975QX440-5	YR	9.75	21.00
89	SISTER 475QX279-2	YR	4.75	13.00
89	TEACHER 575QX412-5	YR	5.75	21.00
89	WORLD OF LOVE 475QX274-5	YR	4.75	21.00
90	BABY'S FIRST CHRISTMAS:BABY BOY QX 206-3	YR	4.75	17.00
90	BABY'S FIRST CHRISTMAS:BABY GIRL QX 206-	YR	4.75	17.00
90	BABY'S FIRST XMAS PHOTOHOLDER 775QX484-3	YR	7.75	22.00
90	CHILD CARE GIVER 675QX316-6	YR	6.75	11.00
90	FROM OUR HOME TO YOURS 475QX216-6	YR	4.75	10.00
90	GRANDPARENTS 475QX225-3	YR	4.75	10.00
90	OUR FIRST CHRISTMAS TOGETHER 475QX213-6	YR	4.75	16.00
90	OUR FIRST CHRISTMAS TOGETHER 675QX314-6	YR	6.75	17.00
90	OUR FIRST CHRISTMAS TOGETHER 975QX488-3	YR	9.75	19.00
90	OUR FIRST XMAS/PHOTOHOLDER 775QX488-6	YR	7.75	17.00
90	PEACEFUL KINGDOM 475QX210-6	YR	4.75	16.00
90	SISTER 475QX227-3	YR	4.75	11.00
91	EXTRA-SPECIAL FRIENDS 475QX227--9	YR	4.75	11.00
91	FIRST CHRISTMAS TOGETHER QX 222-9	YR	4.75	12.00
91	FIVE YEARS TOGETHER 775QX492-7	YR	7.75	14.00
91	FORTY YEARS TOGETHER 775QX493-9	YR	7.75	12.00
91	GRANDMOTHER 475QX230-7	YR	4.75	11.00
91	MOM AND DAD 975QX546-7	YR	9.75	17.00
91	MOTHER 975QX545-7	YR	9.75	20.00
91	SWEETHEART 975QX495-7	YR	9.75	19.00
91	TEN YEARS TOGETHER 775QX492-9	YR	7.75	15.00
92	FOR MY GRANDMA PHOTOHOLDER QX 518-4	YR	7.75	12.00
92	GRANDMOTHER 475QX201-1	YR	4.75	10.00
92	GRANDPARENTS 475QX200-4	YR	4.75	10.00
92	TEACHER 475QX226-4	YR	4.75	11.00
P. ANDREWS			**COMMEMORATIVES**	
92	BABY'S FIRST CHRISTMAS 1875QX458-1	YR	18.75	31.00
R. BISHOP			**COMMEMORATIVES**	
91	GODCHILD 675QX548-9	YR	6.75	13.00
91	NEW HOME 675QX544-9	YR	6.75	19.00
R. CHAD			**COMMEMORATIVES**	
88	CHILD'S THIRD CHRISTMAS 600QX471-4	YR	6.00	21.00
89	BABY'S FIRST CHRISTMAS 725QX449-2	YR	7.25	50.00
90	MOM AND DAD 875QX459-3	YR	8.75	18.00
91	GRANDDAUGHTER'S 1ST CHRISTMAS 675QX511-9	YR	6.75	11.00
91	GRANDSON'S FIRST CHRISTMAS 675QX511-7	YR	6.75	15.00
92	FRIENDLY GREETINGS 775QX504-1	YR	7.75	13.00
92	SPECIAL CAT PHOTOHOLDER QX 541-4	YR	7.75	13.00
92	SPECIAL DOG PHOTOHOLDER QX 542-1	YR	7.75	21.00
K. CROW			**COMMEMORATIVES**	
86	FRIENDS ARE FUN 475QX272-3	YR	4.75	26.00
86	NEW HOME 475QX274-6	YR	4.75	25.00
87	CHILD'S THIRD CHRISTMAS 575QX459-9	YR	5.75	22.00
88	BABY'S FIRST CHRISTMAS 975QX470-1	YR	9.75	31.00
91	FRIENDS ARE FUN 975QX528-9	YR	9.75	17.00
92	BROTHER 675QX468-4	YR	6.75	12.00
92	SISTER 675QX468-1	YR	6.75	12.00
J. FRANCIS			**COMMEMORATIVES**	
89	BABY'S FIRST CHRISTMAS 675QX381-5	YR	6.75	13.00
89	BABY'S SECOND CHRISTMAS 675QX449-5	YR	6.75	25.00
89	CHILD'S FOURTH CHRISTMAS 675QX543-2	YR	6.75	16.00

Holy Shepherds, *which sold as a set, is the final issue in the miniature series by Lladró.*

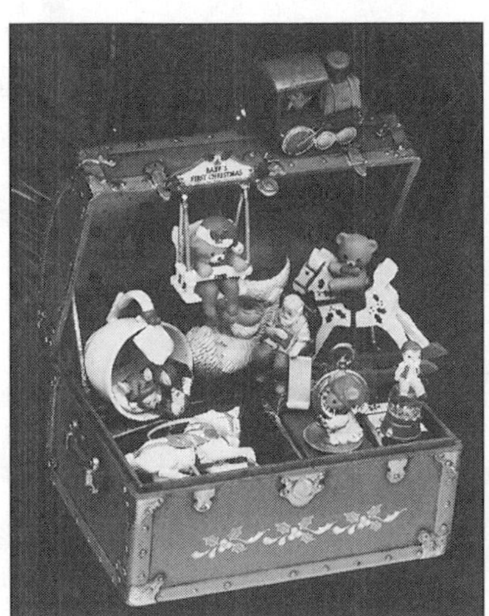

To commemorate Enesco Corp.'s 10th anniversary, the Treasury of Christmas Ornaments collection offered A Decade of Treasures *featuring a toy chest filled with miniature replicas of the most popular Treasury ornaments from the past decade. Production was limited to 1,991.*

To aid the cause of the World Wildlife Fund in 1991, Enesco Corp. produced Our Most Precious Gift, *limited to a year, as part of the Treasury of Christmas collection.*

This sterling ornament speaks for itself. I Love Santa *is produced by Hand & Hammer.*

YR	NAME	LIMIT	ISSUE	TREND
89	CHILD'S THIRD CHRISTMAS 675QX469-5	YR	6.75	19.00
89	GODCHILD 625QX311-2	YR	6.25	9.00
89	GRANDDAUGHTER'S FIRST XMAS 675QX382-2	YR	6.75	15.00
89	GRANDSON'S FIRST CHRISTMAS 675QX382-5	YR	6.75	15.00
90	BABY'S FIRST CHRISTMAS 775QX485-6	YR	7.75	27.00
90	BABY'S FIRST CHRISTMAS 975QX485-3	YR	9.75	18.00
90	BABY'S SECOND CHRISTMAS 675QX486-3	YR	6.75	25.00
90	CHILD'S FOURTH CHRISTMAS 675QX487-3	YR	6.75	16.00
90	CHILD'S THIRD CHRISTMAS 675QX486-6	YR	6.75	19.00
90	GODCHILD 675QX317-6	YR	6.75	11.00
90	GRANDDAUGHTER'S FIRST XMAS 675QX310-6	YR	6.75	13.00
90	GRANDSON'S FIRST CHRISTMAS 675QX306-3	YR	6.75	12.00
91	A CHILD'S CHRISTMAS 975QX488-7	YR	9.75	13.00
91	BABY'S FIRST CHRISTMAS 1775QX510-7	YR	17.75	19.00
91	BABY'S FIRST CHRISTMAS 775QX488-9	YR	7.75	27.00
91	BABY'S SECOND CHRISTMAS 675QX489-7	YR	6.75	25.00
91	CHILD'S FOURTH CHRISTMAS 675QX490-7	YR	6.75	16.00
91	CHILD'S THIRD CHRISTMAS 675QX489-9	YR	6.75	19.00
92	A CHILD'S CHRISTMAS 975QX457-4	YR	9.75	17.00
92	BABY'S FIRST CHRISTMAS 775QX464-4	YR	7.75	24.00
92	BABY'S SECOND CHRISTMAS 675QX465-1	YR	6.75	12.00
92	CHILD'S FOURTH CHRISTMAS 675QX466-1	YR	6.75	16.00
92	CHILD'S THIRD CHRISTMAS 675QX465-4	YR	6.75	15.00
92	DAUGHTER 675QX503-1	YR	6.75	17.00
92	SON 675QX502-4	YR	6.75	15.00
M. HAMILTON			**COMMEMORATIVES**	
91	BABY'S FIRST CHRISTMAS-BOY 475QX221-7	YR	4.75	17.00
91	BABY'S FIRST CHRISTMAS-GIRL 475QX222-7	YR	4.75	14.00
D. LEE			**COMMEMORATIVES**	
83	BABY'S FIRST CHRISTMAS 1400QX402-7	YR	14.00	35.00
84	BABY'S FIRST CHRISTMAS 1600QX904-1	YR	16.00	32.00
85	BABY'S FIRST CHRISTMAS 575QX370-2	YR	5.75	16.00
87	BABY'S FIRST CHRISTMAS 975QX411-3	YR	9.75	27.00
87	BABY'S SECOND CHRISTMAS 575QX460-7	YR	5.75	24.00
87	FIRST CHRISTMAS TOGETHER 950QX446-7	YR	9.50	22.00
89	DAD 725QX441-2	YR	7.25	12.00
89	FRIENDSHIP TIME 975QX413-2	YR	9.75	26.00
90	DAD 675QX453-3	YR	6.75	13.00
91	DAD 775QX512-7	YR	7.75	15.00
91	DAD-TO-BE 575QX487-9	YR	5.75	13.00
91	FLAG OF LIBERTY 675QX524-9	YR	6.75	7.00
91	MOM-TO-BE 575QX487-7	YR	5.75	15.00
92	DAD-TO-BE 675QX461-1	YR	6.75	16.00
92	MOM-TO-BE 675QX461-4	YR	6.75	16.00
92	OUR FIRST CHRISTMAS TOGETHER 975QX506-1	YR	9.75	16.00
J. LYLE			**COMMEMORATIVES**	
86	GRANDDAUGHTER 475QX273-6	YR	4.75	17.00
87	FIRST CHRISTMAS TOGETHER 450QX272-9	YR	4.75	18.00
87	LOVE IS EVERYWHERE 475QX278-7	YR	4.75	26.00
88	MOTHER AND DAD 800QX414-4	YR	8.00	17.00
88	SPIRIT OF CHRISTMAS 475QX276-1	YR	4.75	15.00
89	GRANDMOTHER 475QX277-5	YR	4.75	12.00
89	GRANDPARENTS 475QX277-2	YR	4.75	11.00
89	TEN YEARS TOGETHER 475QX274-2	YR	4.75	16.00
90	GRANDDAUGHTER 475QX228-6	YR	4.75	11.00
90	TEN YEARS TOGETHER 475QX215-3	YR	4.75	10.00
91	ACROSS THE MILES 675QX315-7	YR	6.75	11.00
91	SISTER 675QX548-7	YR	6.75	17.00
92	FOR THE ONE I LOVE 975QX484-4	YR	9.75	17.00
D. MCGEHEE			**COMMEMORATIVES**	
84	FIRST CHRISTMAS TOGETHER 1600QX904-4	YR	16.00	26.00
84	FIRST CHRISTMAS TOGETHER 750QX340-4	YR	7.50	17.00
85	BABY LOCKET 1600QX401-2	YR	16.00	19.00
85	GODCHILD 675QX380-2	YR	6.75	8.00
85	LOVE AT CHRISTMAS 575QX371-5	YR	5.75	32.00
86	BABY LOCKET 1600QX412-3	YR	16.00	20.00
88	FIVE YEARS TOGETHER 475QX274-4	YR	4.75	16.00
91	GIFT OF JOY 875QX531-9	YR	8.75	18.00
D. PALMITER			**COMMEMORATIVES**	
85	SPECIAL FRIENDS 575QX372-5	YR	5.75	7.00
86	BABY'S FIRST CHRISTMAS 600QX380-3	YR	6.00	15.00
J. PATTEE			**COMMEMORATIVES**	
85	FRIENDSHIP 775QX506-2	YR	7.75	9.00
85	FROM OUR HOUSE TO YOURS 775QX520-2	YR	7.75	6.00
85	GRANDMOTHER 475QX262-5	YR	4.75	10.00
85	SISTER 725QX506-5	YR	7.25	14.00
86	BABY'S FIRST XMAS PHOTOHOLDER 800QX379-2	YR	8.00	24.00
86	CHILD'S THIRD CHRISTMAS 650QX413-6	YR	6.50	17.00
86	GRANDMOTHER 475QX274-3	YR	4.75	12.00
86	JOY OF FRIENDS 675QX382-3	YR	6.75	14.00
86	SWEETHEART 1100QX408-6	YR	11.00	37.00
87	BABY'S FIRST CHRISTMAS-BOY 475QX274-9	YR	4.75	20.00
87	BABY'S FIRST CHRISTMAS-GIRL 475QX274-7	YR	4.75	14.00
87	NEW HOME 600QX376-7	YR	6.00	22.00
88	DAUGHTER 575QX415-1	YR	5.75	47.00
88	FROM OUR HOME TO YOURS 475QX279-4	YR	4.75	14.00
88	GRANDPARENTS 475QX277-1	YR	4.75	13.00
88	GRATITUDE 600QX375-4	YR	6.00	10.00

YR	NAME	LIMIT	ISSUE	TREND
88	SON 575QX415-4	YR	5.75	36.00
88	TWENTY-FIVE YEARS TOGETHER 675QX373-4	YR	6.75	16.00
90	FIFTY YEARS TOGETHER 975QX490-6	YR	9.75	16.00
90	FORTY YEARS TOGETHER 975QX490-3	YR	9.75	12.00
90	JESUS LOVES ME 675QX315-6	YR	6.75	13.00
90	TWENTY-FIVE YEARS TOGETHER 975QX489-6	YR	9.75	13.00
S. PIKE			**COMMEMORATIVES**	
83	MOM AND DAD 650QX429-7	YR	6.50	20.00
85	GRANDPARENTS 700QX380-5	YR	7.00	7.00
85	MOTHER 675QX372-2	YR	6.75	12.00
86	GRATITUDE 600QX432-6	YR	6.00	10.00
86	HUSBAND 800QX383-6	YR	8.00	12.00
87	BABYSITTER 475QX279-7	YR	4.75	11.00
87	GRANDPARENTS 475QX277-7	YR	4.75	13.00
87	MOTHER 650QX373-7	YR	6.50	13.00
87	MOTHER AND DAD 700QX462-7	YR	7.00	18.00
88	BABY'S FIRST CHRISTMAS 600QX372-1	YR	6.00	17.00
88	BABY'S SECOND CHRISTMAS 600QX471-1	YR	6.00	27.00
88	FIRST CHRISTMAS TOGETHER 900QX489-4	YR	9.00	19.00
88	TEACHER 625QX417-1	YR	6.25	15.00
89	MOM AND DAD 975QX442-5	YR	9.75	18.00
91	FIRST CHRISTMAS TOGETHER QX 313-9	YR	6.75	17.00
91	UNDER THE MISTLETOE 875QX494-9	YR	8.75	18.00
92	NEW HOME 875QX519-1	YR	8.75	16.00
M. PYDA-SEVCIK			**COMMEMORATIVES**	
85	BABY-SITTER 475QX264-2	YR	4.75	13.00
85	FRIENDSHIP 675QX378-5	YR	6.75	13.00
85	NEW HOME 475QX269-5	YR	4.75	19.00
86	MOTHER AND DAD 750QX431-6	YR	7.50	17.00
87	FROM OUR HOME TO YOURS 475QX279-9	YR	4.75	15.00
87	GODCHILD 475QX276-7	YR	4.75	16.00
90	NEW HOME 675QX434-3	YR	6.75	18.00
91	GRANDDAUGHTER 475QX229-9	YR	4.75	16.00
91	GRANDPARENTS 475QX230-9	YR	4.75	9.00
91	GRANDSON 475QX229-7	YR	4.75	11.00
D. RHODUS			**COMMEMORATIVES**	
89	CHILD'S FIFTH CHRISTMAS 675QX543-5	YR	6.75	16.00
89	FIRST CHRISTMAS TOGETHER 675QX383-2	YR	6.75	20.00
90	CHILD'S FIFTH CHRISTMAS 675QX487-6	YR	6.75	16.00
90	FRIENDSHIP KITTEN 675QX414-3	YR	6.75	14.00
90	SWEETHEART 1175QX489-3	YR	11.75	22.00
91	CHILD'S FIFTH CHRISTMAS 675QX490-9	YR	6.75	16.00
91	JESUS LOVES ME 775QX314-7	YR	7.75	12.00
92	ACROSS THE MILES 675QX304-4	YR	6.75	11.00
92	CHILD'S FIFTH CHRISTMAS 675QX466-4	YR	6.75	16.00
A. ROGERS			**COMMEMORATIVES**	
89	25 YEARS TOGETHER PHOTOHOLDER 875QX485-5	YR	8.75	12.00
89	40 YEARS TOGETHER PHOTOHOLDER 875QX545-2	YR	8.75	15.00
89	50 YEARS TOGETHER PHOTOHOLDER 875QX486-2	YR	8.75	15.00
89	FIRST CHRISTMAS TOGETHER 675QX485-2	YR	9.75	21.00
90	BABY'S FIRST CHRISTMAS 675QX303-6	YR	6.75	18.00
91	TEACHER 475QX228-9	YR	4.75	9.00
92	HOLIDAY MEMO 775QX504-4	YR	7.75	14.00
92	LOVE TO SKATE 875QX484-1	YR	8.75	17.00
92	MOM 775QX516-4	YR	7.75	15.00
92	SECRET PAL 775QX542-4	YR	7.75	12.00
E. SEALE			**COMMEMORATIVES**	
82	BABY'S FIRST CHRISTMAS 1300QX455-3	YR	13.00	37.00
82	BABY'S FIRST CHRISTMAS 550QX302-3	YR	5.50	30.00
82	FIRST XMAS TOGETHER-LOCKET 1500QX456-3	YR	15.00	22.00
82	TEACHER-APPLE 550QX301-6	YR	5.50	11.00
83	FIRST XMAS TOGETHER-LOCKET 1500QX432-9	YR	15.00	31.00
84	FIRST CHRISTMAS TOGETHER 1500QX436-4	YR	15.00	20.00
85	CHILD'S THIRD CHRISTMAS 600QX475-5	YR	6.00	23.00
85	FIRST CHRISTMAS TOGETHER 1675QX400-5	YR	16.75	19.00
86	DAUGHTER 575QX430-6	YR	5.75	27.00
86	LOVING MEMORIES 900QX409-3	YR	9.00	25.00
86	SON 575QX430-3	YR	5.75	26.00
87	FIFTY YEARS TOGETHER 800QX443-7	YR	8.00	17.00
87	GRANDCHILD'S FIRST CHRISTMAS 900QX460-9	YR	9.00	18.00
90	TEACHER 775QX448-3	YR	7.75	10.00
92	1ST CHRISTMAS TOGETHER PHOTO. QX 469-4	YR	8.75	18.00
92	FRIENDSHIP LINE 975QX503-4	YR	9.75	21.00
92	GRANDDAUGHTER 675QX560-4	YR	6.75	15.00
92	GRANDSON 675QX561-1	YR	6.75	17.00
L. SICKMAN			**COMMEMORATIVES**	
80	BABY'S FIRST CHRISTMAS 1200QX156-1	YR	12.00	45.00
82	CHRISTMAS MEMORIES 650QX311-6	YR	6.50	16.00
82	FATHER 450QX205-6	YR	4.50	13.00
82	TEACHER 650QX312-3	YR	6.50	13.00
83	BABY'S FIRST CHRISTMAS 750QX301-9	YR	7.50	14.00
83	FIRST CHRISTMAS TOGETHER 450QX208-9	YR	4.50	23.00
83	LOVE 1300QX422-7	YR	13.00	27.00
85	FIRST CHRISTMAS TOGETHER 1300QX493-5	YR	13.00	21.00
86	BABY'S FIRST CHRISTMAS 900QX412-6	YR	9.00	32.00
86	FIRST CHRISTMAS TOGETHER 1200QX409-6	YR	12.00	19.00
87	DAUGHTER 575QX463-7	YR	5.75	20.00
87	SISTER 600QX474-7	YR	6.00	10.00

YR	NAME	LIMIT	ISSUE	TREND
87	SON 575QX463-9	YR	5.75	30.00
87	SWEETHEART 1100QX447-9	YR	11.00	22.00
88	BABYSITTER 475QX279-1	YR	4.75	9.00
89	DAUGHTER 625QX443-2	YR	6.25	15.00
89	SON 625QX444-5	YR	6.25	15.00
89	SWEETHEART 975QX486-5	YR	9.75	28.00
91	FIRST CHRISTMAS TOGETHER QX 491-9	YR	8.75	20.00
91	TERRIFIC TEACHER 675QX530-9	YR	6.75	12.00
B. SIEDLER			**COMMEMORATIVES**	
85	SON 550QX502-5	YR	5.50	28.00
86	BABY'S SECOND CHRISTMAS 650QX413-3	YR	6.50	22.00
87	DAD 600QX462-9	YR	6.00	31.00
87	TEACHER 575QX466-7	YR	5.75	16.00
88	DAD 700QX414-1	YR	7.00	18.00
90	BROTHER 575QX449-3	YR	5.75	14.00
90	COPY OF CHEER 775QX448-6	YR	7.75	14.00
90	DAD-TO-BE 575QX491-3	YR	5.75	18.00
90	DAUGHTER 575QX449-6	YR	5.75	15.00
90	MOM-TO-BE 575QX491-6	YR	5.75	27.00
90	SON 575QX451-6	YR	5.75	13.00
91	BIG CHEESE, THE 675QX532-7	YR	6.75	15.00
91	BROTHER 675QX547-9	YR	6.75	13.00
91	DAUGHTER 575QX547-7	YR	5.75	20.00
91	SON 575QX546-9	YR	5.75	14.00
92	DAD 775QX467-4	YR	7.75	17.00
92	GRANDDAUGHTER'S 1ST CHRISTMAS 675QX463-4	YR	6.75	14.00
92	GRANDSON'S 1ST CHRISTMAS 675QX462-1	YR	6.75	16.00
92	MOM AND DAD 975QX467-1	YR	9.75	32.00
92	V.P. OF IMPORTANT STUFF 675QX505-1	YR	6.75	12.00
92	WORLD-CLASS TEACHER 775QX505-4	YR	7.75	15.00
D. UNRUH			**COMMEMORATIVES**	
88	SWEETHEART 975QX490-1	YR	9.75	14.00
92	ANNIVERSARY YEAR, PHOTOHOLDER 975QX485-1	YR	9.75	20.00
92	GODCHILD 675QX594-1	YR	6.75	15.00
L. VOTRUBA			**COMMEMORATIVES**	
85	BABY'S FIRST CHRISTMAS 700QX478-2	YR	7.00	14.00
85	FATHER 650QX376-2	YR	6.50	7.00
85	GRANDCHILD'S FIRST CHRISTMAS 1100QX495-5	YR	11.00	16.00
85	GRANDSON 475QX262-2	YR	4.75	20.00
85	MOTHER AND DAD 775QX509-2	YR	7.75	18.00
86	FATHER 650QX431-3	YR	6.50	13.00
86	GRANDSON 475QX273-3	YR	4.75	17.00
86	SISTER 675QX380-6	YR	6.75	14.00
86	TIMELESS LOVE 600QX379-6	YR	6.00	16.00
86	TWENTY-FIVE YEARS TOGETHER 800QX410-3	YR	8.00	19.00
87	GRANDDAUGHTER 600QX374-7	YR	6.00	12.00
87	GRANDSON 475QX276-9	YR	4.75	16.00
87	HEART IN BLOSSOM 600QX372-7	YR	6.00	18.00
87	HUSBAND 700QX373-9	YR	7.00	9.00
87	TEN YEARS TOGETHER 700QX444-7	YR	7.00	20.00
87	TIME FOR FRIENDS 475QX280-7	YR	4.75	15.00
88	FIRST CHRISTMAS TOGETHER 675QX373-1	YR	6.75	24.00
88	GRANDDAUGHTER 475QX277-4	YR	4.75	17.00
88	GRANDSON 475QX278-1	YR	4.75	15.00
88	LOVE FILLS THE HEART 600QX374-4	YR	6.00	17.00
88	NEW HOME 600QX376-1	YR	6.00	17.00
88	SISTER 800QX499-4	YR	8.00	19.00
89	BABY'S 1ST XMAS PHOTOHOLDER 625QX468-2	YR	6.25	32.00
89	BABY'S FIRST CHRISTMAS-BOY 475QX272-5	YR	4.75	12.00
89	BABY'S FIRST CHRISTMAS-GIRL 475QX272-2	YR	4.75	11.00
89	FESTIVE YEAR 775QX384-2	YR	7.75	15.00
89	GRATITUDE 675QX385-2	YR	6.75	11.00
89	NEW HOME 475QX275-5	YR	4.75	16.00
90	ACROSS THE MILES 675QX317-3	YR	6.75	13.00
90	FIVE YEARS TOGETHER 475QX210-3	YR	4.75	15.00
90	GRANDMOTHER 475QX223-6	YR	4.75	11.00
90	GRANDSON 475QX229-3	YR	4.75	10.00
90	MOTHER 875QX453-6	YR	8.75	17.00
91	25 YEARS TOGETHER PHOTOHOLDER QX493-7	YR	8.75	16.00
91	BABY'S FIRST XMAS-PHOTOHOLDER 775QX486-9	YR	7.75	17.00
91	FIFTY YEARS TOGETHER-PHOTOHOLDER 875QX49	YR	8.75	15.00
91	FIRST CHRISTMAS TOGETHER QX 491-7	YR	8.75	15.00
91	FROM OUR HOME TO YOURS 475QX228-7	YR	4.75	14.00
92	BABY'S 1ST CHRISTMAS PHOTOHOLDER QX464-1	YR	7.75	17.00
92	BABY'S FIRST CHRISTMAS-BOY 475QX219-1	YR	4.75	10.00
92	BABY'S FIRST CHRISTMAS-GIRL 475QX220-4	YR	4.75	10.00
92	FROM OUR HOME TO YOURS 475QX213-1	YR	4.75	10.00
92	OUR FIRST CHRISTMAS TOGETHER 675QX301-1	YR	6.75	14.00
*		**COUNTRY CHRISTMAS COLLECTION**		
85	OLD-FASHIONED DOLL 1450QX519-5	YR	14.50	26.00
85	WHIRLIGIG SANTA 1250QX519-2	YR	12.50	19.00
M. PYDA-SEVCIK		**COUNTRY CHRISTMAS COLLECTION**		
85	COUNTRY GOOSE 775QX518-5	YR	7.75	11.00
L. SICKMAN		**COUNTRY CHRISTMAS COLLECTION**		
85	SHEEP AT CHRISTMAS 825QX517-5	YR	8.25	20.00
L. VOTRUBA		**COUNTRY CHRISTMAS COLLECTION**		
85	ROCKING HORSE MEMORIES 1000QX518-2	YR	10.00	11.00

YR	NAME	LIMIT	ISSUE	TREND
*		**COUNTRY TREASURES COLLECTION**		
86	REMEMBERING CHRISTMAS 865QX510-6	YR	8.75	20.00
K. CROW		**COUNTRY TREASURES COLLECTION**		
86	LITTLE DRUMMERS 1250QX511-6	YR	12.50	22.00
86	WELCOME CHRISTMAS 825QX510-3	YR	8.25	21.00
L. SICKMAN		**COUNTRY TREASURES COLLECTION**		
86	COUNTRY SLEIGH 1000QX511-3	YR	10.00	18.00
D. UNRUH		**COUNTRY TREASURES COLLECTION**		
86	NUTCRACKER SANTA 1000QX512-3	YR	10.00	45.00
K. CROW		**CRAYOLA CRAYON**		
90	BRIGHT MOVING COLORS 875QX458-6	YR	8.75	37.00
91	BRIGHT VIBRANT CAROLS 975QX421-9	YR	9.75	30.00
92	BRIGHT BLAZING COLORS 4TH ED. 975QX426-4	YR	9.75	28.00
93	BRIGHT SHINING CASTLE 5TH ED. 1075QX442-	YR	10.75	22.00
94	BRIGHT PLAYFUL COLORS 1095QX527-3	YR	10.95	19.00
95	BRIGHT N'SUNNY TEPEE 7TH SERIES QX524-7	YR	10.95	13.00
L. SICKMAN		**CRAYOLA CRAYON**		
89	BRIGHT JOURNEY 875QX-435-2	YR	8.75	41.00
*		**CROWN CLASSICS COLLECTION**		
81	ANGEL 450QX507-5	YR	4.50	24.00
81	TREE PHOTOHOLDER 550QX515-5	YR	5.50	20.00
81	UNICORN 850QX516-5	YR	8.50	20.00
83	ENAMELED CHRISTMAS WREATH 900QX311-9	YR	9.00	11.00
83	MEMORIES TO TREASURE 700QX303-7	YR	7.00	18.00
83	MOTHER AND CHILD 750QX302-7	YR	7.50	31.00
*		**DECORATIVE BALL ORNAMENTS**		
76	CARDINALS 225QX205-1	YR	2.25	45.00
76	CHICKADEES 225QX204-1	YR	2.25	43.00
77	CHRISTMAS MOUSE 350QX134-2	YR	3.50	67.00
77	RABBIT 250QX139-5	YR	2.50	99.00
77	SQUIRREL 250QX138-2	YR	2.50	95.00
77	STAINED GLASS 350QX152-2	YR	3.50	42.00
78	DRUMMER BOY 350QX252-3	YR	3.50	25.00
78	HALLMARK'S ANTIQUE CARD COLL. 350QX220-3	YR	3.50	40.00
78	JOY 350QX254-3	YR	3.50	29.00
78	MERRY CHRISTMAS (SANTA) 350QX202-3	YR	3.50	47.00
78	NATIVITY 350QX253-6	YR	3.50	43.00
78	QUAIL, THE- 350QX251-6	YR	3.50	32.00
78	YESTERDAY'S TOYS 350QX250-3	YR	3.50	25.00
79	BEHOLD THE STAR 350QX255-9	YR	3.50	30.00
79	BLACK ANGEL 350QX207-9	YR	3.50	19.00
79	CHRISTMAS CHICKADEES 350QX204-7	YR	3.50	25.00
79	CHRISTMAS COLLAGE 350QX257-9	YR	3.50	21.00
79	LIGHT OF CHRISTMAS, THE- 350QX256-7	YR	3.50	21.00
79	NIGHT BEFORE CHRISTMAS 350QX214-7	YR	3.50	37.00
80	CHRISTMAS CARDINALS 400QX224-1	YR	4.00	23.00
80	CHRISTMAS CHOIR 400QX228-1	YR	4.00	58.00
80	CHRISTMAS TIME 400QX226-1	YR	4.00	23.00
80	HAPPY CHRISTMAS 400QX222-1	YR	4.00	25.00
80	JOLLY SANTA 400QX227-4	YR	4.00	22.00
80	NATIVITY 400QX225-4	YR	4.00	26.00
80	SANTA'S WORKSHOP 400QX223-4	YR	4.00	20.00
81	CHRISTMAS 1981-SCHNEEBERG 450QX809-5	YR	4.50	17.00
81	CHRISTMAS IN THE FOREST 450QX813-5	YR	4.50	115.00
81	CHRISTMAS MAGIC 450QX810-2	YR	4.50	18.00
81	LET US ADORE HIM 450QX811-5	YR	4.50	47.00
81	MERRY CHRISTMAS 450QX814-2	YR	4.50	15.00
81	SANTA'S COMING 450QX812-2	YR	4.50	22.00
81	SANTA'S SURPRISE 450QX815-5	YR	4.50	19.00
81	TRADITIONAL (BLACK SANTA) 450QX801-5	YR	4.50	76.00
82	CHRISTMAS ANGEL 450QX220-6	YR	4.50	17.00
82	CURRIER & IVES 450QX201-3	YR	4.50	16.00
82	SEASON FOR CARING 450QX221-3	YR	4.50	18.00
83	1983 450QX220-9	YR	4.50	22.00
83	AN OLD FASHIONED CHRISTMAS 450QX217-9	YR	4.50	20.00
83	ANGELS 500QX219-7	YR	5.00	19.00
83	ANNUNCIATION, THE 450QX216-7	YR	4.50	21.00
83	CHRISTMAS JOY 450QX216-9	YR	4.50	24.00
83	CHRISTMAS WONDERLAND 450QX221-9	YR	4.50	85.00
83	CURRIER & IVES 450QX215-9	YR	4.50	15.00
83	HERE COMES SANTA 450QX217-7	YR	4.50	34.00
83	ORIENTAL BUTTERFLIES 450QX218-7	YR	4.50	23.00
83	SEASON'S GREETING 450QX219-9	YR	4.50	18.00
83	WISE MEN, THE- 450QX220-7	YR	4.50	33.00
T. BLACKSHEAR		**DECORATIVE BALL ORNAMENTS**		
82	SANTA 450QX221-6	YR	4.50	15.00
L. SICKMAN		**DECORATIVE BALL ORNAMENTS**		
79	CHRISTMAS TRADITIONS 350QX253-9	YR	3.50	30.00
*		**DESIGNER KEEPSAKES**		
82	MERRY CHRISTMAS 450QX225-6	YR	4.50	16.00
82	OLD FASHIONED CHRISTMAS 450QX227-6	YR	4.50	33.00
82	OLD WORLD ANGELS 450QX226-3	YR	4.50	20.00
82	PATTERNS OF CHRISTMAS 450QX226-6	YR	4.50	19.00
82	STAINED GLASS 450QX228-3	YR	4.50	17.00
82	TWELVE DAYS OF CHRISTMAS 450QX203-6	YR	4.50	22.00
*		**EASTER ORNAMENTS**		
91	BABY'S FIRST EASTER 875QEO518-9	YR	8.75	27.00

YR	NAME	LIMIT	ISSUE	TREND
91	DAUGHTER 575QEO517-9	YR	5.75	29.00
91	EASTER MEMORIES PHOTOHOLDER QEO 513-7	YR	7.75	19.00
91	FULL OF LOVE 775QEO514-9	YR	7.75	39.00
91	GENTLE LAMB 675QEO515-9	YR	6.75	19.00
91	GRANDCHILD 675QEO517-7	YR	6.75	22.00
91	LI'L DIPPER 675QEO514-7	YR	6.75	22.00
91	LILY EGG 975QEO513-9	YR	9.75	24.00
91	SON 575QEO518-7	YR	5.75	24.00
91	SPIRIT OF EASTER 775QEO516-9	YR	7.75	34.00
91	SPRINGTIME STROLL 675QEO516-7	YR	6.75	24.00
94	SPRINGTIME BONNETS 775QEO809-6	YR	7.75	23.00
94	SWEET EASTER WISHES 875QEO819-6	YR	8.75	24.00
95	APRIL SHOWERS QEO 826-3	YR	6.95	7.00
95	BABY'S FIRST EASTER QEO 823-7	YR	7.95	13.00
95	BUGS BUNNY QEO 827-9	YR	8.95	12.00
95	BUNNY WITH CRAYONS QEO 824-9	YR	7.95	14.00
95	BUNNY WITH SEED PACKETS QEO 825-9	YR	8.95	16.00
95	DAUGHTER QEO 823-9	YR	5.95	13.00
95	EASTER BEAGLE QEO 825-7	YR	7.95	17.00
95	EASTER EGG COTTAGES QEO 820-7	YR	8.95	15.00
95	GARDEN CLUB QEO 820-9	YR	7.95	15.00
95	HAM 'N EGGS QEO 827-7	YR	7.95	11.00
95	HERE COMES EASTER QEO 821-7	YR	7.95	14.00
95	LILY QEO 826-7	YR	6.95	8.00
95	MINIATURE TRAIN QEO 826-9	YR	4.95	10.00
95	SON QEO 824-7	YR	5.95	12.00
95	SPRINGTIME BARBIE, FIRST SERIES QEO 806-	YR	12.95	32.00
95	SPRINGTIME BONNETS, THIRD SERIES QEO 822	YR	7.95	13.00
95	THREE FLOWERPOT FRIENDS QEO 822-9	YR	14.95	20.00
P. ANDREWS			**EASTER ORNAMENTS**	
93	BARRIOW OF GIGGLES 875QEO840-2	YR	8.75	24.00
93	DAUGHTER 575QEO834-2	YR	5.75	22.00
93	SON 575QEO833-5	YR	5.75	22.00
94	DAUGHTER 575QEO815-6	YR	5.75	15.00
94	SON 575QEO816-3	YR	5.75	15.00
R. CHAD			**EASTER ORNAMENTS**	
93	TIME FOR EASTER 875QEO838-5	YR	8.75	24.00
96	PORK N' BEANS QEO817-4	YR	7.95	8.00
K. CROW			**EASTER ORNAMENTS**	
92	EASTER PARADE 675QEO930-1	YR	6.75	36.00
92	GRANDCHILD 675QEO927-4	YR	6.75	24.00
94	COLORFUL SPRING 775QEO816-6	YR	7.75	27.00
94	HERE COMES EASTER 775QEO809-3	YR	7.75	24.00
96	HIPPITY HOP DELIVERY QEO814-4	YR	7.95	8.00
96	LOCOMOTIVE QEO807-4	YR	7.95	8.00
J. FRANCIS			**EASTER ORNAMENTS**	
92	BABY'S FIRST EASTER 675QEO927-1	YR	6.75	22.00
92	BLESS YOU 675QEO929-1	YR	6.75	24.00
92	SOMEBUNNY LOVES YOU 675QEO929-4	YR	6.75	27.00
93	MAYPOLE STROLL 2800QEO839-5 SET OF THREE	YR	28.00	60.00
94	BABY'S FIRST EASTER 675QEO815-3	YR	6.75	19.00
96	APPLE BLOSSOM LANE QEO808-4	YR	8.95	9.00
96	LOOK WHAT I FOUND! QEO818-1	YR	7.95	8.00
J. LEE			**EASTER ORNAMENTS**	
92	SPRINGTIME EGG 875QEO932-1	YR	8.75	23.00
93	BEST-DRESSED TURTLE 575QEO839-2	YR	5.75	22.00
93	EASTER PARADE 675QEO832-5	YR	6.75	29.00
93	LI'L PEPPER 775QEO831-2	YR	7.75	24.00
93	NUTTY EGGS 675QEO838-2	YR	6.75	22.00
93	SPRINGTIME BONNETS 775QEO832-2	YR	7.75	25.00
J. LYLE			**EASTER ORNAMENTS**	
92	PROMISE OF EASTER 875QEO931-4	YR	8.75	22.00
93	CHICKS-ON-A-TWIRL 775QEO837-5	YR	7.75	22.00
96	JOYFUL ANGELS FIRST SERIES QEO818-4	YR	9.95	10.00
D. PALMITER			**EASTER ORNAMENTS**	
92	JOY BEARER 875QEO933-4	YR	8.75	32.00
93	BABY'S FIRST EASTER 675QEO834-5	YR	6.75	19.00
94	RIDING A BREEZE 575QEO821-3	YR	5.75	15.00
96	GARDEN CLUB QEO809-1	YR	7.95	8.00
96	HERE COMES EASTER 3RD SERIES QEO809-4	YR	7.95	8.00
S. PIKE			**EASTER ORNAMENTS**	
92	EVERYTHING'S DUCKY! 675QEO933-1	YR	6.75	22.00
92	SUNNY WISHER 575QEO934-4	YR	5.75	22.00
D. RHODUS			**EASTER ORNAMENTS**	
94	EASTER PARADE 675QEO813-6	YR	6.75	19.00
96	PARADE PALS QEO815-1	YR	7.95	8.00
A. ROGERS			**EASTER ORNAMENTS**	
92	CRAYOLA BUNNY 775QEO930-4	YR	7.75	34.00
92	DAUGHTER 575QEO928-4	YR	5.75	22.00
92	SON 575QEO928-1	YR	5.75	22.00
94	SWEET AS SUGAR 875QEO808-6	YR	8.75	17.00
94	YUMMY RECIPE 775QEO814-3	YR	7.75	20.00
96	DAFFY DUCK QEO815-4	YR	8.95	9.00
E. SEALE			**EASTER ORNAMENTS**	
94	SUNNY BUNNY GARDEN 1500QEO814-6 SET OF 3	YR	15.00	30.00
96	EGGSTRA SPECIAL SURPRISE QEO816-1	YR	8.95	9.00
96	STRAWBERRY PATCH QEO817-1	YR	6.95	7.00

YR	NAME	LIMIT	ISSUE	TREND
L. SICKMAN			**EASTER ORNAMENTS**	
93	BACKYARD BUNNY 675QEO840-5	YR	6.75	22.00
93	LOP-EARED BUNNY 575QEO831-5	YR	5.75	19.00
94	TREETOP COTTAGE 975QEO818-6	YR	9.75	20.00
B. SIEDLER			**EASTER ORNAMENTS**	
92	COSMIC RABBIT 775QEO936-4	YR	7.75	23.00
92	CULTIVATED GARDENER 575QEO935-1	YR	5.75	19.00
92	EGGS IN SPORTS 675QEO934-1	YR	6.75	37.00
92	EGGSPERT PAINTER 675QEO936-1	YR	6.75	24.00
93	EGGS IN SPORTS 675QEO833-2	YR	6.75	30.00
93	GRANDCHILD 675QEO835-2	YR	6.75	22.00
94	EGGS IN SPORTS 675QEO813-3	YR	6.75	19.00
D. UNRUH			**EASTER ORNAMENTS**	
93	BEAUTIFUL MEMORIES,PHOTOHLDR 675QEO836-2	YR	6.75	18.00
93	RADIANT WINDOW 775QEO836-5	YR	7.75	24.00
94	JOYFUL LAMB 575QEO820-6	YR	5.75	15.00
94	PEANUTS 775QEO817-6	YR	7.75	27.00
94	PEEPING OUT 675QEO820-3	YR	6.75	15.00
96	EASTER MORNING QEO816-4	YR	7.95	8.00
96	STRIKE UP THE BAND! QEO814-1	YR	14.95	15.00
L. VOTRUBA			**EASTER ORNAMENTS**	
92	BELLE BUNNY 975QEO935-4	YR	9.75	24.00
92	ROCKING BUNNY 975QEO932-4	YR	9.75	24.00
92	WARM MEMORIES 775QEO931-1	YR	7.75	19.00
93	LOVELY LAMB 975QEO837-2	YR	9.75	22.00
94	COLLECTOR'S PLATE 775QEO823-3	YR	7.75	25.00
94	DIVINE DUET 675QEO818-3	YR	6.75	16.00
94	EASTER ART SHOW 775QEO819-3	YR	7.75	17.00
96	PETER RABBIT FIRST SERIES QEO807-1	YR	8.95	9.00
*			**FABRIC ORNAMENTS**	
81	CALICO KITTY 300QX403-5	YR	3.00	20.00
81	CARDINAL CUTIE 300QX400-2	YR	3.00	23.00
81	GINGHAM DOG 300QX402-2	YR	3.00	19.00
81	PEPPERMINT MOUSE 300QX401-5	YR	3.00	25.00
*			**FOLK ART AMERICANA**	
95	FETCHING THE FIREWOOD QKL105-7	YR	16.95	26.00
95	FISHING PARTY QK103-9	YR	15.95	25.00
95	GUIDING SANTA QK103-7	YR	18.95	27.00
95	LEARNING TO SKATE QK104-7	YR	14.95	25.00
L. SICKMAN			**FOLK ART AMERICANA**	
93	ANGEL IN FLIGHT 1575QK105-2	YR	15.75	30.00
93	POLAR BEAR ADV. 1500QK105-5	YR	15.00	42.00
93	RIDING IN THE WOODS 1575QK106-5	YR	15.75	45.00
93	RIDING THE WIND 1575QK104-5	YR	15.75	36.00
93	SANTA CLAUS 1675QK107-2	YR	16.75	155.00
94	CATCHING 40 WINKS 1675QK118-3	YR	16.75	20.00
94	GOING TO TOWN 1575QK116-6	YR	15.75	21.00
94	RACING THROUGH THE SNOW 1575QK117-3	YR	15.75	22.00
94	RARIN' TO GO 1575QK119-3	YR	15.75	27.00
94	ROUNDUP TIME 1675QK117-6	YR	16.75	19.00
*			**FOOTBALL HELMET COLLECTION**	
96	CHICAGO BEARS FOOTBALL HELMET	YR	9.95	10.00
96	DALLAS COWBOYS FOOTBALL HELMET	YR	9.95	10.00
96	EAGLES FOOTBALL HELMET	YR	9.95	10.00
96	KANSAS CITY CHEIFTS FOOTBALL HELMET	YR	9.95	10.00
96	PANTHERS FOOTBALL HELMET	YR	9.95	10.00
96	PATRIOTS FOOTBALL HELMET	YR	9.95	10.00
96	RAIDERS FOOTBALL HELMET	YR	9.95	10.00
96	REDSKINS FOOTBALL HELMET	YR	9.95	10.00
96	SAN FRANCISCO 49ERS FOOTBALL HELMET	YR	9.95	10.00
96	VIKINGS FOOTBALL HELMET	YR	9.95	10.00
D. RHODUS			**FOOTBALL LEGENDS**	
95	JOE MONTANA/KANSAS CITY QXI620-7	YR	14.95	62.00
95	JOE MONTANA/SAN FRANCISCO FIRST SERIES Q	YR	14.95	27.00
*			**FROSTED IMAGES**	
80	DOVE 400QX308-1	YR	4.00	35.00
80	DRUMMER BOY 400QX309-4	YR	4.00	21.00
80	SANTA 400QX310-1	YR	4.00	20.00
81	ANGEL 400QX509-5	YR	4.00	47.00
81	MOUSE 400QX508-2	YR	4.00	19.00
81	SNOWMAN 400QX510-2	YR	4.00	20.00
R. CHAD			**GARDEN ELVES COLLECTION**	
94	DAISY DAYS 995QX598-6	YR	9.95	10.00
94	HARVEST JOY 995QX599-3	YR	9.95	10.00
94	TULIP TIME 995QX598-3	YR	9.95	10.00
94	YULETIDE CHEER 995QX597-6	YR	9.95	10.00
L. VOTRUBA			**GIFT BRINGERS**	
89	ST. NICHOLAS 1ST EDITION 550QX279-5	YR	5.00	13.00
91	CHRISTKINDL 500QX211-7	YR	5.00	16.00
93	MAGI, THE 5TH ED. 500QX206-5	YR	5.00	12.00
*			**GOLD CROWN ORNAMENTS**	
91	SANTA'S PREMIERE 1075QX523-7	YR	10.75	33.00
P. DUTKIN			**GOLD CROWN ORNAMENTS**	
86	ON THE RIGHT TRACK QSP 420-1	YR	15.00	37.00
E. SEALE			**GOLD CROWN ORNAMENTS**	
94	EAGER FOR...TENDER TOUCHES 1500QX533-6	YR	15.00	23.00

YR	NAME	LIMIT	ISSUE	TREND
L. VOTRUBA		**GOLD CROWN ORNAMENTS**		
92	O CHRISTMAS TREE 1075QX541-1	YR	10.75	21.00
*		**HALLMARK EXPO ORNAMENTS**		
93	GOLD DOVE OF PEACE	SO	10.00	10.00
93	GOLD SANTA	SO	10.00	10.00
93	GOLD SLEIGH	SO	10.00	10.00
93	GOLD STAR AND HOLLY	SO	10.00	10.00
94	GOLD BOWS	SO	10.00	10.00
94	GOLD POINSETTIA	SO	10.00	10.00
94	MRS. CLAUS' CUPBOARD QXC484-3	YR	55.00	225.00
*		**HALLMARK KEEPSAKE ORNAMENTS**		
89	FESTIVE ANGEL 975QXM578-3	YR	9.75	12.00
93	MARY ENGELBREIT 500QX207-5	YR	5.00	11.00
93	TOBIN FRALEY CAROUSEL 2ND ED. 2800QX550-	YR	28.00	30.00
94	BARNEY 995QX596-6	YR	9.95	15.00
P. ANDREWS		**HALLMARK KEEPSAKE ORNAMENTS**		
93	BABY'S FIRST CHRISTMAS 1075QX551-5	YR	10.75	17.00
93	GRANDMOTHER 675QX566-5	YR	6.75	10.00
93	ON HER TOES 875QX526-5	YR	8.75	16.00
93	OUR FIRST CHRISTMAS TOGETHER 675QX301-5	YR	6.75	12.00
93	STAR TEACHER PHOTOHOLDER QX564-5	YR	5.75	8.00
93	SWAT TEAM, THE 1275QX539-5	YR	12.75	21.00
94	A FELINE OF CHRISTMAS 895QX581-6	YR	8.95	23.00
R. BISHOP		**HALLMARK KEEPSAKE ORNAMENTS**		
94	ANNIVERSARY YR. PHOTOHOLDER 1095QX568-3	YR	10.95	15.00
R. CHAD		**HALLMARK KEEPSAKE ORNAMENTS**		
93	GODCHILD 875QX587-5	YR	8.75	12.00
93	GRANDDAUGHTER 675QX563-5	YR	6.75	10.00
93	GRANDSON 675QX563-2	YR	6.75	10.00
93	ONE-ELF MARCHING BAND 1275QX534-2	YR	12.75	22.00
93	POPPING GOOD TIMES 1475QX539-2	YR	14.75	24.00
93	SUPERMAN 1275QX575-2	YR	12.75	32.00
K. CROW		**HALLMARK KEEPSAKE ORNAMENTS**		
93	BABY'S FIRST CHRISTMAS 775QX552-5	YR	7.75	29.00
93	BEARY GIFTED 775QX576-2	YR	7.75	13.00
93	CURLY 'N' KINGLY 1075QX528-5	YR	10.75	18.00
93	QUICK AS A FOX 875QX579-2	YR	8.75	13.00
93	ROOM FOR ONE MORE 875QX538-2	YR	8.75	37.00
94	A SHARP FLAT 1095QX577-3	YR	8.95	15.00
J. FRANCIS		**HALLMARK KEEPSAKE ORNAMENTS**		
93	ACROSS THE MILES 875QX591-2	YR	8.75	13.00
93	BABY'S SECOND CHRISTMAS 675QX599-2	YR	6.75	19.00
93	BOWLING FOR ZZZS 775QX556-5	YR	7.75	13.00
93	CARING NURSE 675QX578-5	YR	6.75	15.00
93	CHILD'S FOURTH CHRISTMAS 675QX521-5	YR	6.75	13.00
93	CHILD'S THIRD CHRISTMAS 675QX599-5	YR	6.75	14.00
93	GRANDCHILD'S FIRST CHRISTMAS QX 555-2	YR	6.75	11.00
93	SNOWY HIDEWAWAY 975QX531-2	YR	9.75	16.00
J. LEE		**HALLMARK KEEPSAKE ORNAMENTS**		
93	BIRD WATCHER 975QX525-2	YR	9.75	18.00
93	DAD 775QX585-5	YR	7.75	14.00
93	DAD-TO-BE 675QX553-2	YR	6.75	13.00
93	FELIZ NAVIDAD 875QX536-5	YR	8.75	14.00
93	ICICLE BICYCLE 975QX583-5	YR	9.75	15.00
93	LOOK FOR THE WONDER 1275QX568-5	YR	12.75	23.00
93	MOM 775QX585-2	YR	7.75	15.00
93	MOM-TO-BE 675QX553-5	YR	6.75	11.00
93	OUR CHRISTMAS TOGETHER 1075QX594-2	YR	10.75	17.00
93	PEEP INSIDE 1375QX532-2	YR	13.75	20.00
93	PUTT-PUTT PENGUIN 975QX579-5	YR	9.75	15.00
93	SNOW BEAR ANGEL 775QX535-5	YR	7.75	14.00
93	SNOWBIRD 775QX576-5	YR	7.75	13.00
93	TO MY GRANDMA 775QX555-5	YR	7.75	11.00
93	WATER BED SNOOZE 975QX537-5	YR	9.75	17.00
J. LYLE		**HALLMARK KEEPSAKE ORNAMENTS**		
93	ANNIVERSARY YEAR PHOTOHOLDER QX597-2	YR	9.75	14.00
93	HE IS BORN 975QX536-2	YR	9.75	22.00
93	READY FOR FUN 775QX512-4	YR	7.75	13.00
93	SILVERY NOEL 1275QX530-5	YR	12.75	19.00
93	STAR OF WONDER 675QX598-2	YR	6.75	20.00
D. PALMITER		**HALLMARK KEEPSAKE ORNAMENTS**		
93	BABY'S FIRST CHRISTMAS 1875QX551-2	YR	18.75	23.00
93	COACH 675QX593-5	YR	6.75	12.00
93	LITTLE DRUMMER BOY 875QX537-2	YR	8.75	15.00
93	MAKING WAVES 975QX577-5	YR	9.75	21.00
93	MOM AND DAD 975QX584-5	YR	9.75	14.00
93	NEW HOME 775QX590-5	YR	7.75	27.00
93	PINK PANTHER, THE 1275QX575-5	YR	12.75	19.00
S. PIKE		**HALLMARK KEEPSAKE ORNAMENTS**		
93	FABULOUS DECADE 775QX447-5	YR	7.75	14.00
D. RHODUS		**HALLMARK KEEPSAKE ORNAMENTS**		
93	CHILD'S FIFTH CHRISTMAS 675QX522-2	YR	6.75	13.00
93	LOU RANKIN POLAR BEAR 975QX574-5	YR	9.75	22.00
94	ALL PUMPED UP 895QX592-3	YR	8.95	17.00
A. ROGERS		**HALLMARK KEEPSAKE ORNAMENTS**		
93	BABY'S FIRST CHRISTMAS PHOTOHOLDER QX 55	YR	7.75	19.00
93	BROTHER 675QX554-2	YR	6.75	7.00

YR	NAME	LIMIT	ISSUE	TREND
93	GREAT CONNECTIONS 1075QX540-2	YR	10.75	21.00
93	HOWLING GOOD TIME 975QX525-5	YR	9.75	15.00
93	NEPHEW 675QX573-5	YR	6.75	8.00
93	NIECE 675QX573-2	YR	6.75	8.00
93	OUR FIRST CHRISTMAS TOGETHER 1875QX595-5	YR	18.75	29.00
93	SISTER 675QX554-5	YR	6.75	13.00
93	TOP BANANA 775QX592-5	YR	7.75	15.00
E. SEALE		**HALLMARK KEEPSAKE ORNAMENTS**		
93	APPLE FOR TEACHER 775QX590-2	YR	7.75	11.00
93	CHRISTMAS BREAK 775QX582-5	YR	7.75	14.00
93	HIGH TOP-PURR 875QX533-2	YR	8.75	20.00
93	MAKIN' MUSIC 975QX532-5	YR	9.75	16.00
93	PEOPLE FRIENDLY 875QX593-2	YR	8.75	12.00
93	SISTER TO SISTER 975QX588-5	YR	9.75	40.00
93	SMILE! IT'S CHRISTMAS PHOTOHOLDERQX533-5	YR	9.75	17.00
94	BABY'S FIRST CHRISTMAS 1295QX574-3	YR	12.95	18.00
L. SICKMAN		**HALLMARK KEEPSAKE ORNAMENTS**		
87	VILLAGE EXPRESS 2450QLX707-2	YR	24.50	90.00
93	CLEVER COOKIE 775QX566-2	YR	7.75	16.00
93	MAXINE 875QX538-5	YR	8.75	16.00
93	STRANGE AND WONDERFUL LOVE QX596-5	YR	8.75	14.00
93	U.S. CHRISTMAS STAMPS 1ST ED. 1075QX529-	YR	10.75	18.00
93	WARM AND SPECIAL FRIENDS QX589-5	YR	10.75	18.00
94	ANGEL HARE 895QX589-6	YR	8.95	19.00
B. SIEDLER		**HALLMARK KEEPSAKE ORNAMENTS**		
93	BIG ROLLER 875QX535-2	YR	8.75	13.00
93	DUNKIN' ROO 775QX557-5	YR	7.75	14.00
93	FILLS THE BILL 875QX557-2	YR	8.75	13.00
93	HOME FOR CHRISTMAS 775QX556-2	YR	7.75	13.00
93	OWLIVER 2ND ED. 775QX542-5	YR	7.75	13.00
93	PERFECT MATCH 875QX577-2	YR	8.75	15.00
93	THAT'S ENTERTAINMENT 875QX534-5	YR	8.75	12.00
D. UNRUH		**HALLMARK KEEPSAKE ORNAMENTS**		
93	JULIANNE AND TEDDY 2175QX529-5	YR	21.75	30.00
93	OUR 1ST CHRISTMAS TOGETHER PHOTO.QX595-2	YR	8.75	12.00
93	OUR FAMILY PHOTOHOLDER 775QX589-2	YR	7.75	12.00
93	WAKE-UP CALL 875QX526-2	YR	8.75	13.00
94	BABY'S FIRST CHRISTMAS 1895QX563-3	YR	18.95	27.00
L. VOTRUBA		**HALLMARK KEEPSAKE ORNAMENTS**		
93	BABY'S FIRST CHRISTMAS-BOY QX 210-5	YR	4.75	10.00
93	BIG ON GARDENING 975QX584-2	YR	9.75	14.00
93	DAUGHTER 675QX587-2	YR	6.75	10.00
93	FAITHFUL FIRE FIGHTER 775QX578-2	YR	8.00	15.00
93	GRANDPARENTS 475QX208-5	YR	4.75	9.00
93	SON 675QX586-5	YR	6.75	10.00
93	SPECIAL CAT PHOTOHOLDER QX523-5	YR	7.75	12.00
93	SPECIAL DOG PHOTOHOLDER QX596-2	YR	7.75	11.00
*	**HALLMARK KEEPSAKE ORNAMENTS COLLECTOR'S CLUB**			
91	FIVE YEARS TOGETHER QXC315-9	YR	*	40.00
94	SWEET BOUQUET QXC480-6	YR	*	15.00
P. ANDREWS	**HALLMARK KEEPSAKE ORNAMENTS COLLECTOR'S CLUB**			
90	SUGAR PLUM FAIRY 2775QXC447-3	25400	27.75	42.00
93	GENTLE TIDINGS 2500QXC544-2	YR	25.00	32.00
R. CHAD	**HALLMARK KEEPSAKE ORNAMENTS COLLECTOR'S CLUB**			
92	CHRISTMAS TREASURES 2200QXC546-4	YR	22.00	142.00
K. CROW	**HALLMARK KEEPSAKE ORNAMENTS COLLECTOR'S CLUB**			
89	VISIT FROM SANTA QXC580-2	YR	*	30.00
90	CLUB HOLLOW QXC445-6	YR	*	27.00
91	HIDDEN TREASURE/LI'L KEEPER 1500QXC476-9	YR	*	35.00
P. DUTKIN	**HALLMARK KEEPSAKE ORNAMENTS COLLECTOR'S CLUB**			
89	SITTING PURRTY QXC581-2	YR	*	45.00
J. FRANCIS	**HALLMARK KEEPSAKE ORNAMENTS COLLECTOR'S CLUB**			
90	ARMFUL OF JOY 975QXC445-3	YR	9.75	30.00
93	FORTY WINKS QXC 529-4	YR	*	18.00
94	HOLIDAY PURSUIT QXC 482-3	YR	*	19.00
D. LEE	**HALLMARK KEEPSAKE ORNAMENTS COLLECTOR'S CLUB**			
88	ANGELIC MINSTREL 2950QX408-4	YR	29.50	30.00
92	RODNEY TAKES FLIGHT QXC508-1	YR	*	21.00
94	ON CLOUD NINE 1200QXC485-3	YR	12.00	15.00
J. LYLE	**HALLMARK KEEPSAKE ORNAMENTS COLLECTOR'S CLUB**			
93	SHARING CHRISTMAS 2000QXC543-5	YR	20.00	26.00
94	JOLLY HOLLY SANTA QXC 483-3	*	22.00	37.00
S. PIKE	**HALLMARK KEEPSAKE ORNAMENTS COLLECTOR'S CLUB**			
89	COLLECT A DREAM 900QXC428-5	YR	9.00	32.00
A. ROGERS	**HALLMARK KEEPSAKE ORNAMENTS COLLECTOR'S CLUB**			
90	CROWN PRINCE QXC560-3	YR	*	40.00
91	SECRETS FOR SANTA 2375QXC479-7	28700	23.75	42.00
E. SEALE	**HALLMARK KEEPSAKE ORNAMENTS COLLECTOR'S CLUB**			
88	CHRISTMAS IS SHARING 1750QX407-1	YR	17.50	31.00
89	CHRISTMAS IS PEACEFUL 1850QXC451-2	YR	18.50	30.00
92	CHIPMUNK PARCEL SERVICE QXC519-4	YR	*	22.00
92	SANTA'S CLUB LIST 1500QXC729-1	YR	15.00	29.00
93	IT'S IN THE MAIL QXC527-2	YR	*	20.00
L. SICKMAN	**HALLMARK KEEPSAKE ORNAMENTS COLLECTOR'S CLUB**			
87	CAROUSEL REINDEER QXC 581-7	YR	8.00	60.00
88	SLEIGHFUL OF DREAMS 800QXC580-1	YR	8.00	53.00

YR	NAME	LIMIT	ISSUE	TREND
90	CHRISTMAS LIMITED 1975QXC476-6	38700	19.75	92.00
91	GALLOPING INTO CHRISTMAS 1975QXC477-9	28400	19.75	57.00
93	TRIMMED W/MEMORIES 1200QXC543-2	YR	12.00	19.00
B. SIEDLER		**HALLMARK KEEPSAKE ORNAMENTS COLLECTOR'S CLUB**		
88	HOLD ON TIGHT QXC570-4	YR	*	75.00
88	OUR CLUBHOUSE QXC580-4	YR	*	39.00
91	BEARY ARTISTIC 1000QXC725-9	YR	10.00	35.00
D. UNRUH		**HALLMARK KEEPSAKE ORNAMENTS COLLECTOR'S CLUB**		
88	HOLIDAY HEIRLOOM-2ND EDITION 2500QX406-4	34600	25.00	25.00
89	HOLIDAY HEIRLOOM-3RD ED. 2500QXC460-5	YR	25.00	26.00
89	NOELLE 1975QXC448-3	YR	19.75	29.00
92	VICTORIAN SKATER 2500QXC406-7	14700	25.00	45.00
94	MAJESTIC DEER 2500QXC483-6	*	25.00	29.00
D. UNRUH		**HALLMARK KEEPSAKE ORNAMENTS COLLECTORS' CLUB**		
87	WREATH OF MEMORIES QXC580-9	YR	*	47.00
*		**HANDCRAFTED ORNAMENTS**		
78	ANGELS 800QX150-3	YR	8.00	347.00
78	CALICO MOUSE 450QX137-6	YR	4.50	174.00
78	CAROUSEL SERIES-1ST EDITION 600QX146-3	YR	6.00	350.00
78	JOY 450QX138-3	YR	4.50	75.00
78	PANORAMA BALL 600QX145-6	YR	6.00	130.00
78	RED CARDINAL 450QX144-3	YR	4.50	157.00
78	ROCKING HORSE 600QX148-3	YR	6.00	87.00
78	SCHNEEBERG BELL 800QX152-3	YR	8.00	182.00
78	SKATING RACCOON 600QX142-3	YR	6.00	77.00
79	A CHRISTMAS TREAT 500QX134-7	YR	5.00	65.00
79	CHRISTMAS EVE SURPRISE 650QX157-9	YR	6.50	55.00
79	CHRISTMAS HEART 650QX140-7	YR	6.50	110.00
79	CHRISTMAS IS FOR CHILDREN 500QX135-9	YR	5.00	80.00
79	DRUMMER BOY, THE 800QX143-9	YR	8.00	112.00
79	HOLIDAY SCRIMSHAW 400QX152-7	YR	4.00	200.00
79	SANTA'S HERE 500QX138-7	YR	5.00	62.00
79	SKATING SNOWMAN, THE- 500QX139-9	YR	5.00	72.00
80	A CHRISTMAS TREAT 550QX134-7	YR	5.50	65.00
80	CHRISTMAS IS FOR CHILDREN 550QX135-9	YR	5.50	80.00
80	ELFIN ANTICS 900QX142-1	YR	9.00	207.00
80	HEAVENLY SOUNDS 750QX152-1	YR	7.50	77.00
80	SANTA 1980 550QX146-1	YR	5.50	87.00
80	SKATING SNOWMAN 550QX139-9	YR	5.50	72.00
80	SNOWFLAKE SWING, THE- 400QX133-4	YR	4.00	42.00
81	A HEAVENLY NAP 650QX139-4	YR	6.50	42.00
81	A WELL-STOCKED STOCKING 900QX154-7	YR	9.00	60.00
81	CANDYVILLE EXPRESS 750QX418-2	YR	7.50	87.00
81	CHRISTMAS FANTASY 1300QX155-4	YR	13.00	74.00
81	DOUGH ANGEL 550QX139-6	YR	5.50	90.00
81	DRUMMER BOY 250QX148-1	YR	2.50	35.00
81	LOVE AND JOY 900QX425-2	YR	9.00	87.00
81	MR. & MRS. CLAUS SET 1200QX448-5	YR	12.00	347.00
81	SAILING SANTA 1300QX439-5	YR	13.00	215.00
81	SPACE SANTA 650QX430-2	YR	6.50	97.00
82	CHRISTMAS FANTASY 1300QX155-4	YR	13.00	74.00
82	CLOISONNE ANGEL 1200QX145-4	YR	12.00	82.00
82	COWBOY SNOWMAN 800QX480-6	YR	8.00	52.00
82	CYCLING SANTA 2000QX435-5	YR	20.00	140.00
82	EMBROIDERED TREE 650QX494-6	YR	6.50	33.00
82	JOGGING SANTA 800QX457-6	YR	8.00	45.00
82	JOLLY CHRISTMAS TREE 650QX465-3	YR	6.50	72.00
82	PEEKING ELF 650QX419-5	YR	6.50	33.00
82	SANTA BELL 1500QX148-7	YR	15.00	57.00
82	TIN SOLDIER 650QX483-6	YR	6.50	45.00
83	CHRISTMAS KITTEN 400QX454-3	YR	4.00	31.00
83	CYCLING SANTA 2000QX435-6	YR	20.00	140.00
83	EMBROIDERED HEART 650QX421-7	YR	6.50	19.00
83	HOLIDAY PUPPY 350QX412-7	YR	3.50	29.00
83	JACK FROST 900QX407-9	YR	9.00	52.00
83	JOLLY SANTA 350QX425-9	YR	3.50	27.00
83	MADONNA AND CHILD 1200QX428-7	YR	12.00	40.00
83	MAILBOX KITTEN 650QX415-7	YR	6.50	51.00
83	MOUSE IN BELL 1000QX419-7	YR	10.00	59.00
83	PEPPERMINT PENGUIN 650QX408-9	YR	6.50	37.00
83	PORCELAIN DOLL-DIANA 900QX423-7	YR	9.00	32.00
83	SANTA'S MANY FACES 600QX311-7	YR	6.00	27.00
83	SANTA'S ON HIS WAY 1000QX426-9	YR	10.00	27.00
83	SKATING RABBIT 800QX409-7	YR	8.00	45.00
83	SKI LIFT SANTA 800QX418-7	YR	8.00	60.00
83	UNICORN 1000QX426-7	YR	10.00	60.00
88	JINGLE BELL CLOWN 1500QX477-4	YR	15.00	19.00
88	KRINGLE PORTRAIT 750QX421-4	YR	7.50	23.00
88	KRINGLE TREE 650QX495-4	YR	6.50	36.00
88	PEANUTS 475QX280-1	YR	4.75	24.00
T. BLACKSHEAR		**HANDCRAFTED ORNAMENTS**		
81	CHECKING IT TWICE 2250QX158-4	YR	22.50	182.00
82	THREE KINGS 850QX307-3	YR	8.50	18.00
R. CHAD		**HANDCRAFTED ORNAMENTS**		
88	SOFT LANDING 700QX475-1	YR	7.00	18.00
88	WINTER FUN 850QX478-1	YR	8.50	20.00
K. CROW		**HANDCRAFTED ORNAMENTS**		
88	CHRISTMAS CUCKOO 800QX480-1	YR	8.00	22.00

YR	NAME	LIMIT	ISSUE	TREND
88	COOL JUGGLER 650QX487-4	YR	6.50	17.00
88	PEEK-A-BOO KITTENS 750QX487-1	YR	7.50	19.00
88	SLIPPER SPANIEL 450QX472-4	YR	4.50	12.00
D. LEE		**HANDCRAFTED ORNAMENTS**		
78	ANGEL 400QX139-6	YR	4.50	92.00
78	ANIMAL HOME 600QX149-6	YR	6.00	175.00
79	DOWNHILL RUN, THE 650QX145-9	YR	6.50	140.00
79	READY FOR CHRISTMAS 650QX133-9	YR	6.50	120.00
79	SKATING RACCOON 650QX142-3	YR	6.50	77.00
80	A CHRISTMAS VIGIL 900QX144-1	YR	9.00	100.00
80	A HEAVENLY NAP 650QX139-4	YR	6.50	42.00
80	A SPOT OF CHRISTMAS CHEER 800QX153-4	YR	8.00	132.00
80	ANIMAL'S CHRISTMAS, THE 800QX150-1	YR	8.00	55.00
80	CAROLING BEAR 750QX140-1	YR	7.50	125.00
80	DRUMMER BOY 550QX147-4	YR	5.50	87.00
81	CHRISTMAS DREAMS 1200QX437-5	YR	12.00	210.00
81	FRIENDLY FIDDLER, THE- 800QX434-2	YR	8.00	67.00
81	ICE FAIRY 650QX431-5	YR	6.50	70.00
81	ICE SCULPTOR, THE- 800QX432-2	YR	8.00	89.00
81	TOPSY-TURVY TUNES 750QX429-5	YR	7.50	72.00
82	BAROQUE ANGEL 1500QX456-6	YR	15.00	137.00
82	ICE SCULPTOR, THE- 800QX432-2	YR	8.00	89.00
82	PINECONE HOME 800QX461-3	YR	8.00	160.00
82	RACCOON SURPRISES 900QX479-3	YR	9.00	142.00
82	SANTA'S WORKSHOP 1000QX450-3	YR	10.00	80.00
83	BAROQUE ANGELS 1300QX422-9	YR	13.00	67.00
83	RAINBOW ANGEL 550QX416-7	YR	5.50	97.00
83	SANTA'S WORKSHOP 1000QX450-3	YR	10.00	80.00
83	SKIING FOX 800QX420-7	YR	8.00	37.00
88	TRAVELS WITH SANTA 1000QX477-1	YR	10.00	28.00
88	UNCLE SAM NUTCRACKER 700QX488-4	YR	7.00	23.00
J. LYLE		**HANDCRAFTED ORNAMENTS**		
88	CHRISTMAS SCENES 475QX273-1	YR	4.75	18.00
J. PATTEE		**HANDCRAFTED ORNAMENTS**		
88	CHRISTMAS MEMORIES PHOTOHOLDER QX 372-4	YR	6.50	17.00
88	GLOWING WREATH 600QX492-1	YR	6.00	13.00
88	SHINY SLEIGH 575QX492-4	YR	5.75	16.00
88	SPARKLING TREE 600QX483-1	YR	6.00	16.00
S. PIKE		**HANDCRAFTED ORNAMENTS**		
88	PARTY LINE 875QX476-1	YR	8.75	24.00
88	SQUEAKY CLEAN 675QX475-4	YR	6.75	19.00
M. PYDA-SEVCIK		**HANDCRAFTED ORNAMENTS**		
88	SANTA FLAMINGO 475QX483-4	YR	4.75	21.00
A. ROGERS		**HANDCRAFTED ORNAMENTS**		
88	CHRISTMAS CARDINAL 475QX494-1	YR	4.75	13.00
88	JOLLY WALRUS 450QX473-1	YR	4.50	16.00
88	KRINGLE MOON 550QX495-1	YR	5.50	28.00
88	LOVING BEAR 475QX493-4	YR	4.75	12.00
88	PURRFECT SNUGGLE 625QX474-4	YR	6.25	21.00
88	STARRY ANGEL 475QX494-4	YR	4.75	15.00
E. SEALE		**HANDCRAFTED ORNAMENTS**		
83	ANGEL MESSENGER 650QX408-7	YR	6.50	90.00
83	BRASS SANTA 900QX423-9	YR	9.00	19.00
83	CAROLING OWL 450QX411-7	YR	4.50	37.00
83	CHRISTMAS KOALA 400QX419-9	YR	4.00	27.00
83	HITCHHIKING SANTA 800QX424-7	YR	8.00	39.00
83	MOUNTAIN CLIMBING SANTA 650QX407-7	YR	6.50	30.00
83	SCRIMSHAW REINDEER 800QX424-9	YR	8.00	28.00
83	SNEAKER MOUSE 450QX400-9	YR	4.50	32.00
88	FILLED WITH FUDGE 475QX419-1	YR	4.75	21.00
88	SWEET STAR 500QX418-4	YR	5.00	20.00
88	TEENY TASTER 475QX418-1	YR	4.75	16.00
88	TOWN CRIER, THE- 550QX473-4	YR	5.50	16.00
L. SICKMAN		**HANDCRAFTED ORNAMENTS**		
78	DOVE 450QX190-3	YR	4.50	80.00
78	HOLLY & POINSETTIA BALL 600QX147-6	YR	6.00	80.00
79	OUTDOOR FUN 800QX150-7	YR	8.00	107.00
80	SANTA'S FLIGHT 550QX138-1	YR	5.50	110.00
81	ST. NICHOLAS 550QX446-2	YR	5.50	45.00
81	STAR SWING 550QX421-5	YR	5.50	28.00
82	ELFIN ARTIST 900QX457-3	YR	9.00	47.00
82	SPIRIT OF CHRISTMAS, THE- 1000QX452-6	YR	10.00	105.00
83	BELL WREATH 650QX420-9	YR	6.50	27.00
83	EMBROIDERED STOCKING 650QX479-6	YR	6.50	16.00
83	MOUSE ON CHEESE 650QX413-7	YR	6.50	45.00
83	OLD-FASHIONED SANTA 1100QX409-9	YR	11.00	62.00
83	TIN ROCKING HORSE 650QX414-9	YR	6.50	41.00
88	AMERICANA DRUM 775QX488-1	YR	7.75	19.00
88	GOIN' CROSS COUNTRY 850QX476-4	YR	8.50	19.00
88	NOAH'S ARK 850QX490-4	YR	8.50	31.00
88	OLD-FASHIONED CHURCH 400QX498-1	YR	4.00	15.00
88	OLD-FASHIONED SCHOOL HOUSE 400QX497-1	YR	4.00	15.00
88	SAILING! SAILING! 850QX491-1	YR	8.50	22.00
B. SIEDLER		**HANDCRAFTED ORNAMENTS**		
88	ARCTIC TENOR 400QX472-1	YR	4.00	14.00
88	GO FOR THE GOLD 800QX417-4	YR	8.00	21.00
88	GONE FISHING 500QX479-4	YR	5.00	16.00

YR	NAME	LIMIT	ISSUE	TREND
88	HOE-HOE-HOE 500QX422-1	YR	5.00	14.00
88	HOLIDAY HERO 500QX423-1	YR	5.00	14.00
88	LOVE SANTA 500QX486-4	YR	5.00	15.00
88	NICK THE KICK 500QX422-4	YR	5.00	16.00
88	PAR FOR SANTA 500QX479-1	YR	5.00	15.00
88	POLAR BOWLER 500QX478-1	YR	5.00	14.00
D. UNRUH				**HANDCRAFTED ORNAMENTS**
88	A KISS FROM SANTA 450QX482-1	YR	4.50	21.00
88	FELIZ NAVIDAD 675QX416-1	YR	6.75	21.00
88	KISS THE CLAUS 500QX486-1	YR	5.00	12.00
88	OREO 400QX481-4	YR	4.00	13.00
88	SNOOPY & WOODSTOCK 600QX474-1	YR	6.00	27.00
D. LEE				**HANDCRAFTED ORNAMENTS: ADORABLE ADORNMENTS**
75	BETSEY CLARK 250QX157-1	YR	2.50	230.00
75	DRUMMER BOY 250QX161-1	YR	2.50	200.00
75	MRS. SANTA 250QX156-1	YR	2.50	260.00
75	RAGGEDY ANDY 250QX160-1	YR	2.50	360.00
75	RAGGEDY ANN 250QX159-1	YR	2.50	310.00
75	SANTA 250QX155-1	YR	2.50	270.00
*				**HANDCRAFTED ORNAMENTS: NOSTALGIA**
77	NATIVITY 500QX181-5	YR	5.00	172.00
D. LEE				**HANDCRAFTED ORNAMENTS: NOSTALGIA**
77	ANGEL 500QX182-2	YR	5.00	127.00
L. SICKMAN				**HANDCRAFTED ORNAMENTS: NOSTALGIA**
75	DRUMMER BOY 350QX130-1	YR	3.50	170.00
75	JOY 350QX132-1	YR	3.50	230.00
75	LOCOMOTIVE (DATED) 350QX127-1	YR	3.50	165.00
75	PEACE ON EARTH (DATED) 350QX131-1	YR	3.50	165.00
75	ROCKING HORSE 350QX128-1	YR	3.50	160.00
75	SANTA & SLEIGH 350QX129-1	YR	3.50	250.00
76	DRUMMER BOY 400QX130-1	YR	4.00	170.00
76	LOCOMOTIVE 400QX222-1	YR	4.00	172.00
76	PEACE ON EARTH 400QX223-1	YR	4.00	142.00
76	ROCKING HORSE 400QX128-1	YR	4.00	163.00
77	ANTIQUE CAR 500QX180-2	YR	5.00	67.00
77	TOYS 500QX183-5	YR	5.00	152.00
*				**HANDCRAFTED ORNAMENTS: TREE TREATS**
76	ANGEL 300QX176-1	YR	3.00	200.00
76	REINDEER 300QX178-1	YR	3.00	117.00
76	SANTA 300QX177-1	YR	3.00	197.00
76	SHEPHERD 300QX175-1	YR	3.00	117.00
*				**HANDCRAFTED ORNAMENTS: TWIRL-ABOUTS**
77	BELLRINGER 600QX192-2	YR	6.00	62.00
77	WEATHER HOUSE 600QX191-5	YR	6.00	101.00
D. LEE				**HANDCRAFTED ORNAMENTS: TWIRL-ABOUTS**
77	DELLA ROBIA WREATH 450QX193-5	YR	4.50	117.00
L. SICKMAN				**HANDCRAFTED ORNAMENTS: TWIRL-ABOUTS**
76	ANGEL 450QX171-1	YR	4.50	167.00
76	PARTRIDGE 450QX174-1	YR	4.50	197.00
76	SANTA 450QX172-1	YR	4.50	120.00
76	SOLDIER 450QX173-1	YR	4.50	102.00
77	SNOWMAN 450QX190-2	YR	4.50	74.00
*				**HANDCRAFTED ORNAMENTS: YESTERYEARS**
76	DRUMMER BOY 500QX184-1	YR	5.00	157.00
76	PARTRIDGE 500QX183-1	YR	5.00	117.00
76	SANTA 500QX182-1	YR	5.00	172.00
76	TRAIN 500QX181-1	YR	5.00	172.00
*				**HEIRLOOM CHRISTMAS COLLECTION**
85	LACY HEART 875QX511-2	YR	8.75	16.00
85	VICTORIAN LADY 950QX513-2	YR	9.50	21.00
J. PATTEE				**HEIRLOOM CHRISTMAS COLLECTION**
85	SNOWFLAKE 650QX510-5	YR	6.50	12.00
S. PIKE				**HEIRLOOM CHRISTMAS COLLECTION**
85	KEEPSAKE BASKET 1500QX514-5	YR	15.00	16.00
M. PYDA-SEVCIK				**HEIRLOOM CHRISTMAS COLLECTION**
85	CHARMING ANGEL 975QX512-5	YR	9.75	19.00
*				**HERE COMES SANTA**
79	SANTA'S MOTORCAR 1ST SERIES 900QX155-9	YR	9.00	575.00
80	SANTA'S EXPRESS 1200QX143-4	YR	12.00	137.00
81	ROOFTOP DELIVERIES 1300QX438-2	YR	13.00	265.00
K. CROW				**HERE COMES SANTA**
87	SANTA'S WOODY 1400QX484-7	YR	14.00	45.00
88	KRINGLE KOACH 1400QX400-1	YR	14.00	38.00
89	CHRISTMAS CABOOSE 11TH ED. 1475QX458-5	YR	14.75	37.00
L. SICKMAN				**HERE COMES SANTA**
82	JOLLY TROLLEY QX 464-3	YR	15.00	107.00
83	SANTA'S EXPRESS 1300QX403-7	YR	13.00	295.00
84	SANTA'S DELIVERIES 1300QX432-4	YR	13.00	82.00
85	SANTA'S FIRE ENGINE 1400QX496-5	YR	14.00	52.00
90	FESTIVE SURREY 12TH ED. 1475QX492-3	YR	14.75	36.00
91	SANTA'S ANTIQUE CAR-13TH ED. 1475QX434-9	YR	14.75	40.00
92	KRINGLE TOURS 14TH ED. 1475QX434-1	YR	14.75	31.00
93	HAPPY HAULI-DAYS 15TH ED. 1475QX410-2	YR	14.75	28.00
94	MAKIN' TRACTOR TRACKS 16TH ED. 1495QX529	YR	14.95	35.00
95	SANTA'S ROADSTER 17TH SERIES QX517-9	YR	14.95	20.00

YR	NAME	LIMIT	ISSUE	TREND
B. SIEDLER		**HERE COMES SANTA**		
86	KRINGLES KOOL TREATS 1400QX404-3	YR	14.00	55.00
P. ANDREWS		**HOLIDAY BARBIE COLLECTION**		
93	HOLIDAY BARBIE 1ST ED. 1495QX572-2	YR	14.75	107.00
94	HOLIDAY BARBIE 2ND ED. 1495QX521-6	YR	14.95	33.00
95	HOLIDAY BARBIE 1495QX500-6	YR	14.95	35.00
*		**HOLIDAY CHIMES**		
80	SANTA MOBILE 550QX136-1	YR	5.50	41.00
81	SANTA MOBILE 550QX136-1	YR	5.50	41.00
81	SNOWMAN CHIMES 550QX445-5	YR	5.50	26.00
82	ANGEL CHIMES 550QX502-6	YR	5.50	25.00
E. SEALE		**HOLIDAY CHIMES**		
82	TREE CHIMES 550QX484-6	YR	5.50	51.00
L. SICKMAN		**HOLIDAY CHIMES**		
78	REINDEER CHIMES 450QX320-3	YR	4.50	39.00
79	REINDEER CHIMES 450QX320-3	YR	4.50	40.00
79	STAR CHIMES 450QX137-9	YR	4.50	60.00
80	REINDEER CHIMES 550QX320-3	YR	5.50	39.00
80	SNOWFLAKE CHIMES 550QX165-4	YR	5.50	21.00
81	SNOWFLAKE CHIMES 550QX165-4	YR	5.50	21.00
82	BELL CHIMES 550QX494-3	YR	5.50	21.00
*		**HOLIDAY ENCHANTMENT**		
93	JOURNEY TO THE FOREST 1375QK101-2	YR	13.75	25.00
93	MAGI, THE 1375QK102-5	YR	13.75	30.00
R. CHAD		**HOLIDAY ENCHANTMENT**		
93	BRINGING HOME THE TREE 1375QK104-2	YR	13.75	27.00
L. VOTRUBA		**HOLIDAY ENCHANTMENT**		
93	ANGELIC MESSENGER 1375QK103-2	YR	13.75	29.00
93	VISION OF SUGARPLUMS 1375QK100-5	YR	13.75	27.00
95	AWAY IN A MANAGER QK109-7	YR	13.95	16.00
95	FOLLOWING THE STAR QK109-9	YR	13.95	16.00
L. VOTRUBA		**HOLIDAY FAVORITES**		
94	DAPPER SNOWMAN 1375QK105-3	YR	13.75	16.00
94	GRACEFUL FAWN 1175QK103-3	YR	11.75	14.00
94	JOLLY SANTA 1375QK104-6	YR	13.75	19.00
94	JOYFUL LAMB 1175QK103-6	YR	11.75	16.00
94	PEACEFUL DOVE 1175QK104-3	YR	11.75	17.00
L. SICKMAN		**HOLIDAY FLIERS**		
93	TIN AIRPLANE 775QX562-2	YR	7.75	19.00
93	TIN BLIMP 775QX562-5	YR	7.75	19.00
93	TIN HOT AIR BALLOON 775QX561-5	YR	7.75	15.00
*		**HOLIDAY HIGHLIGHTS**		
77	DRUMMER BOY 350QX312-2	YR	3.50	69.00
77	JOY 350QX310-2	YR	3.50	46.00
77	PEACE ON EARTH 350QX311-5	YR	3.50	69.00
77	STAR 350QX313-5	YR	3.50	52.00
78	DOVE 350QX310-3	YR	3.50	110.00
78	SANTA 350QX307-6	YR	3.50	72.00
78	SNOWFLAKE 350QX308-3	YR	3.50	52.00
79	CHRISTMAS ANGEL 350QX300-7	YR	3.50	80.00
79	CHRISTMAS CHEER 350QX303-9	YR	3.50	60.00
79	CHRISTMAS TREE 350QX302-7	YR	3.50	60.00
79	LOVE 350QX304-7	YR	3.50	90.00
79	SNOWFLAKE 350QX301-9	YR	3.50	37.00
80	THREE WISE MEN 400QX300-1	YR	4.00	21.00
80	WREATH 400QX301-4	YR	4.00	72.00
81	CHRISTMAS STAR 550QX501-5	YR	5.50	20.00
81	SHEPHERD SCENE 550QX500-2	YR	5.50	21.00
82	ANGEL 550QX309-6	YR	5.50	27.00
82	CHRISTMAS MAGIC 550QX311-3	YR	5.50	26.00
82	CHRISTMAS SLEIGH 550QX309-3	YR	5.50	70.00
83	CHRISTMAS STOCKING 600QX303-9	YR	6.00	39.00
83	TIME FOR SHARING 600QX307-7	YR	6.00	39.00
D. PALMITER		**HOLIDAY HIGHLIGHTS**		
78	NATIVITY 350QX309-6	YR	3.50	72.00
E. SEALE		**HOLIDAY HIGHLIGHTS**		
83	STAR OF PEACE 600QX304-7	YR	6.00	19.00
*		**HOLIDAY HUMOR**		
84	A CHRISTMAS PRAYER 450QX246-1	YR	4.50	20.00
84	FLIGHTS OF FANTASY 450QX256-4	YR	4.50	13.00
84	FRISBEE PUPPY 500QX444-4	YR	5.00	40.00
84	NAPPING MOUSE 550QX435-1	YR	5.50	49.00
84	REINDEER RACETRACK 450QX254-4	YR	4.50	15.00
84	SANTA STAR 550QX450-4	YR	5.50	37.00
84	SNOWMOBILE SANTA 650QX431-4	YR	6.50	26.00
85	DOGGY IN A STOCKING 550QX474-2	YR	5.50	29.00
85	LAMB IN LEGWARMERS 700QX480-2	YR	7.00	18.00
85	MOUSE WAGON 575QX476-2	YR	5.75	52.00
85	NATIVITY SCENE 475QX264-5	YR	4.75	21.00
86	OPEN ME FIRST 725QX422-6	YR	7.25	24.00
87	CHRISTMAS CUDDLE 575QX453-7	YR	5.75	24.00
87	DR SEUSS: GRINCH'S CHRISTMAS 475QX278-3	YR	4.75	34.00
87	JAMMIE PIES 475QX283-9	YR	4.75	10.00
87	JOY RIDE 1150QX440-7	YR	11.50	47.00
87	LET IT SNOW 650QX458-9	YR	6.50	18.00
87	PEANUTS 475QX281-9	YR	4.75	25.00
87	SANTA AT THE BAT 775QX457-9	YR	7.75	17.00

YR	NAME	LIMIT	ISSUE	TREND
87	SPOTS 'N STRIPES 550QX452-9	YR	5.50	16.00
K. CROW			**HOLIDAY HUMOR**	
86	CHATTY PENGUIN 575QX417-6	YR	5.75	17.00
86	PLAYFUL POSSUM 1100QX425-3	YR	11.00	24.00
86	RAH RAH RABBIT 700QX421-6	YR	7.00	25.00
87	HAPPY SANTA 475QX456-9	YR	4.75	22.00
87	NIGHT BEFORE CHRISTMAS 650QX451-7	YR	6.50	16.00
87	PRETTY KITTEN 1100QX448-9	YR	11.00	18.00
87	SLEEPY SANTA 625QX450-7	YR	6.25	30.00
P. DUTKIN			**HOLIDAY HUMOR**	
85	KITTY MISCHIEF 500QX474-5	YR	5.00	19.00
85	MERRY MOUSE 450QX403-2	YR	4.50	22.00
85	SKATEBOARD RACCOON 650QX473-2	YR	6.50	25.00
85	SOCCER BEAVER 650QX477-5	YR	6.50	16.00
86	KITTY MISCHIEF 500QX474-5	YR	5.00	19.00
86	MERRY MOUSE 450QX403-2	YR	4.50	22.00
86	SKATEBOARD RACCOON 650QX473-2	YR	6.50	25.00
86	SNOW BUDDIES 800QX423-6	YR	8.00	29.00
86	SOCCER BEAVER 650QX477-5	YR	6.50	16.00
86	TIPPING THE SCALES 675QX418-6	YR	6.75	21.00
86	TOUCHDOWN SANTA 800QX423-3	YR	8.00	29.00
87	FUDGE FOREVER 500QX449-7	YR	5.00	29.00
87	JOGGING THROUGH THE SNOW 725QX457-7	YR	7.25	16.00
D. LEE			**HOLIDAY HUMOR**	
84	MUSICAL ANGEL 550QX434-4	YR	5.50	57.00
84	PEPPERMINT 1984 450QX456-1	YR	4.50	47.00
84	THREE KITTENS IN A MITTEN 800QX431-1	YR	8.00	37.00
85	SNOW-PITCHING SNOWMAN 450QX470-2	YR	4.50	19.00
85	STARDUST ANGEL 575QX475-2	YR	5.75	30.00
85	THREE KITTENS IN A MITTEN 800QX431-1	YR	8.00	37.00
86	HEAVENLY DREAMER 575QX 417-3	YR	5.75	18.00
86	SNOW-PITCHING SNOWMAN 450QX470-2	YR	4.50	19.00
86	TREETOP TRIO 975QX424-6	YR	11.00	25.00
86	WYNKEN, BLYNKEN AND NOD 975QX424-6	YR	9.75	40.00
87	TREETOP TRIO 1100QX425-6	YR	11.00	25.00
D. MCGEHEE			**HOLIDAY HUMOR**	
86	COOKIES FOR SANTA 450QX414-6	YR	4.50	18.00
S. PIKE			**HOLIDAY HUMOR**	
87	OWLIDAY WISH 650QX455-9	YR	6.50	16.00
87	PADDINGTON BEAR 550QX472-7	YR	5.50	21.00
E. SEALE			**HOLIDAY HUMOR**	
84	BELL RINGER SQUIRREL 1000QX443-1	YR	10.00	30.00
84	CHRISTMAS OWL 600QX444-1	YR	6.00	26.00
84	MARATHON SANTA 800QX456-4	YR	8.00	32.00
84	MOUNTAIN CLIMBING SANTA 650QX407-7	YR	6.50	30.00
84	POLAR BEAR DRUMMER 450QX430-1	YR	4.50	20.00
84	RACCOON'S CHRISTMAS 900QX-447-4	YR	9.00	49.00
84	ROLLER SKATING RABBIT 500QX457-1	YR	5.00	26.00
84	SNOWY SEAL 400QX450-1	YR	4.00	17.00
85	BAKER ELF 575QX491-2	YR	5.75	26.00
85	CHILDREN IN THE SHOE 950QX490-5	YR	9.50	41.00
85	DAPPER PENGUIN 500QX477-2	YR	5.00	22.00
85	DO NOT DISTURB BEAR 775QX481-2	YR	7.75	29.00
85	NIGHT BEFORE CHRISTMAS 1300QX449-4	YR	13.00	37.00
85	ROLLER SKATING RABBIT 500QX457-1	YR	5.00	26.00
85	SANTA'S SKI TRIP 1200QX496-2	YR	12.00	56.00
85	SNOWY SEAL 400QX450-1	YR	4.00	17.00
85	TRUMPET PANDA 450QX471-2	YR	4.50	17.00
86	DO NOT DISTURB BEAR 775QX481-2	YR	7.75	24.00
86	LI'L JINGLER 675QX419-3	YR	6.75	35.00
86	MOUSE IN THE MOON 550QX416-6	YR	5.50	18.00
86	SANTA'S HOT TUB 1200QX426-3	YR	12.00	43.00
86	WALNUT SHELL RIDER 600QX419-6	YR	6.00	18.00
87	CHOCOLATE CHIPMUNK 600QX456-7	YR	6.00	34.00
87	JACK FROSTING 700QX449-9	YR	7.00	41.00
87	LI'L JINGLER 675QX419-3	YR	6.75	33.00
87	MOUSE IN THE MOON 550QX416-6	YR	5.50	18.00
87	SEASONED GREETINGS 625QX454-9	YR	6.25	16.00
87	TREETOP DREAMS 675QX459-7	YR	6.75	22.00
87	WALNUT SHELL RIDER 600QX419-6	YR	6.00	18.00
L. SICKMAN			**HOLIDAY HUMOR**	
84	FORTUNE COOKIE ELF 450QX452-4	YR	4.50	35.00
84	SNOWSHOE PENGUIN 650QX453-1	YR	6.50	42.00
85	BEARY SMOOTH RIDE 650QX480-5	YR	6.50	17.00
85	CANDY APPLE MOUSE 750QX470-5	YR	6.50	51.00
86	BEARY SMOOTH RIDE 650QX480-5	YR	6.50	17.00
86	MERRY KOALA 500QX415-3	YR	5.00	16.00
86	POPCORN MOUSE 675QX421-3	YR	6.75	40.00
87	MERRY KOALA 500QX415-3	YR	5.00	16.00
B. SIEDLER			**HOLIDAY HUMOR**	
84	SANTA MOUSE 450QX433-4	YR	4.50	45.00
85	BOTTLECAP FUN BUNNIES 775QX481-5	YR	7.75	29.00
85	ENGINEERING MOUSE 550QX473-5	YR	5.50	18.00
85	ICE-SKATING OWL 500QX476-5	YR	5.00	16.00
85	SUN AND FUN SANTA 775QX492-2	YR	7.75	32.00
85	SWINGING ANGEL BELL 1100QX492-5	YR	11.00	31.00
86	JOLLY HIKER 500QX483-2	YR	5.00	17.00
86	SKI TRIPPER 675QX420-6	YR	6.75	17.00

YR	NAME	LIMIT	ISSUE	TREND
86	SPECIAL DELIVERY 500QX415-6	YR	5.00	18.00
87	BRIGHT CHRISTMAS DREAMS QX 473-7	YR	7.25	92.00
87	ICY TREAT 450QX450-9	YR	4.50	16.00
87	JOLLY HIKER 500QX483-2	YR	5.00	17.00
87	RACCOON BIKER 700QX458-7	YR	7.00	20.00
87	REINDOGGY 575QX452-7	YR	5.75	26.00
87	SNOOPY AND WOODSTOCK 725QX472-9	YR	7.25	28.00
D. UNRUH				**HOLIDAY HUMOR**
86	ACORN INN 850QX424-3	YR	8.50	26.00
86	HAPPY CHRISTMAS TO OWL 600QX418-3	YR	6.00	15.00
86	PUPPY'S BEST FRIEND 650QX420-3	YR	6.50	20.00
87	HOT DOGGER 650QX471-9	YR	6.50	17.00
L. VOTRUBA				**HOLIDAY HUMOR**
87	NATURE'S DECORATIONS 475QX273-9	YR	4.75	19.00
*				**HOLIDAY SCULPTURE**
83	SANTA 400QX308-7	YR	4.00	26.00
L. SICKMAN				**HOLIDAY SCULPTURE**
83	HEART 400QX307-9	YR	4.00	39.00
*				**HOLIDAY TRADITIONS**
89	FIRST CHRISTMAS, THE- 775QX547-5	YR	7.75	12.00
89	GENTLE FAWN 775QX548-5	YR	7.75	14.00
89	GEORGE WASHINGTON BICENTEN. 625QX386-2	YR	6.25	12.00
89	OLD-WORLD GNOME 775QX434-5	YR	7.75	23.00
89	SWEET MEMORIES PHOTOHOLDER 675QX438-5	YR	6.75	16.00
K. CROW				**HOLIDAY TRADITIONS**
89	HANG IN THERE 525QX430-5	YR	5.25	30.00
89	PEEK-A-BOO KITTIES 750QX487-1	YR	7.50	19.00
J. FRANCIS				**HOLIDAY TRADITIONS**
89	JOYFUL TRIO 975QX437-2	YR	9.75	14.00
89	PADDINGTON BEAR 575QX429-2	YR	5.75	17.00
J. LYLE				**HOLIDAY TRADITIONS**
89	NORMAN ROCKWELL 475QX276-2	YR	4.75	15.00
S. PIKE				**HOLIDAY TRADITIONS**
89	OWLIDAY GREETINGS 400QX436-5	YR	4.00	14.00
89	PARTY LINE 875QX476-1	YR	8.75	24.00
89	SPENCER SPARROW, ESQ. 675QX431-2	YR	6.75	17.00
89	STOCKING KITTEN 675QX456-5	YR	6.75	13.00
M. PYDA-SEVCIK				**HOLIDAY TRADITIONS**
89	FELIZ NAVIDAD 675QX439-2	YR	6.75	23.00
D. RHODUS				**HOLIDAY TRADITIONS**
89	SNOOPY & WOODSTOCK 675QX433-2	YR	6.75	21.00
A. ROGERS				**HOLIDAY TRADITIONS**
89	CRANBERRY BUNNY 575QX426-2	YR	5.75	14.00
89	SPECIAL DELIVERY 525QX432-5	YR	5.75	16.00
E. SEALE				**HOLIDAY TRADITIONS**
89	TEENY TASTER 475QX418-1	YR	4.75	16.00
B. SIEDLER				**HOLIDAY TRADITIONS**
89	CAMERA CLAUS 575QX546-5	YR	5.75	16.00
89	DEER DISGUISE 575QX426-5	YR	5.75	18.00
89	GONE FISHING 575QX479-4	YR	5.75	16.00
89	GYM DANDY 575QX418-5	YR	5.75	14.00
89	HERE'S THE PITCH 575QX545-5	YR	5.75	16.00
89	HOPPY HOLIDAYS 775QX469-2	YR	7.75	17.00
89	KRISTY CLAUS 575QX424-5	YR	5.75	12.00
89	NORTH POLE JOGGER 575QX546-2	YR	5.75	16.00
89	ON THE LINKS 575QX419-2	YR	5.75	17.00
89	POLAR BOWLER 575QX478-4	YR	5.75	14.00
89	SEA SANTA 575QX415-2	YR	5.75	17.00
89	SNOWPLOW SANTA 575QX420-5	YR	5.75	16.00
D. UNRUH				**HOLIDAY TRADITIONS**
89	A KISS FROM SANTA 450QX482-1	YR	4.50	21.00
89	OREO COOKIE 400QX481-4	YR	4.00	13.00
*				**HOLIDAY WILDLIFE**
82	CARDINALIS QX 313-3	YR	7.00	337.00
83	CHICKADEE 700QX309-9	YR	7.00	67.00
84	PHEASANTS 725QX347-4	YR	7.25	25.00
85	PARTRIDGE 750QX376-5	YR	7.50	22.00
86	CEDAR WAXWING 750QX321-6	YR	7.50	23.00
88	PURPLE FINCH 775QX371-1	YR	7.75	16.00
L. VOTRUBA				**HOLIDAY WILDLIFE**
87	SNOW GOOSE 750QX371-7	YR	7.50	15.00
*				**HOOP STARS**
95	SHAQUILLE O'NEAL FIRST SERIES QX1551-7	YR	14.95	31.00
*				**ICE SCULPTURES**
82	ARCTIC PENGUIN 400QX300-3	YR	4.00	15.00
82	SNOWY SEAL 400QX300-6	YR	4.00	18.00
P. ANDREWS				**INVITATION TO TEA**
95	COZY COTTAGE TEAPOT QK112-7	YR	15.95	19.00
95	EUROPEAN CASTLE QK112-9	YR	15.95	19.00
95	VICTORIAN HOME TEAPOT QX111-9	YR	15.95	19.00
P. ANDREWS				**KEEPSAKE CLUB**
95	BARBIE: BRUNETTE DEBUT 1959 QXC539-7	YR	14.95	35.00
D. PALMITER				**KEEPSAKE CLUB**
95	1958 FORD EDSEL CITATION CONVERTIBLE QXC	YR	12.95	62.00

YR	NAME	LIMIT	ISSUE	TREND
	E. SEALE			**KEEPSAKE CLUB**
95	FISHING FOR FUN QXC520-7	YR	*	14.00
	L. SICKMAN			**KEEPSAKE CLUB**
95	HOME FROM THE WOODS QXC105-9	YR	15.95	23.00
	B. SIEDLER			**KEEPSAKE CLUB**
95	COLLECTING MEMORIES QXC411-7	YR	20.00	19.00
*				**KEEPSAKE COLLECTION**
73	BETSEY CLARK 250XHD100-2	YR	2.50	85.00
73	BETSEY CLARK-FIRST EDITION 250XHD110-2	YR	2.50	125.00
73	CHRISTMAS IS LOVE 250XHD106-2	YR	2.50	65.00
73	ELVES 250XHD103-5	YR	2.50	60.00
73	MANGER SCENE 250XHD102-2	YR	2.50	70.00
73	SANTA WITH ELVES 250XHD101-5	YR	2.50	70.00
74	ANGEL 250QX110-1	YR	2.50	70.00
74	BETSEY CLARK-SECOND EDITION 250QX108-1	YR	2.50	70.00
74	BUTTONS & BO (2) 350QX113-1	YR	3.50	47.00
74	CHARMERS 250QX109-1	YR	2.50	37.00
74	CURRIER & IVES (2) 350QX112-1	YR	3.50	50.00
74	LITTLE MIRACLES (4) 450QX115-1	YR	4.50	55.00
74	NORMAN ROCKWELL 250QX106-1	YR	2.50	80.00
74	NORMAN ROCKWELL 250QX111-1	YR	2.50	70.00
74	RAGGEDY ANN & RAGGEDY ANDY(4) 450QX114-1	YR	4.50	80.00
74	SNOWGOOSE 250QX107-1	YR	2.50	75.00
*				**KEEPSAKE MAGIC COLLECTION**
89	HOLIDAY BELL 1750QLX722-2	YR	17.50	28.00
	R. CHAD			**KEEPSAKE MAGIC COLLECTION**
89	MOONLIT NAP 875QLX713-4	YR	8.75	22.00
89	RUDOLPH RED-NOSED REINDEER 1950QLX725-2	YR	19.50	61.00
	K. CROW			**KEEPSAKE MAGIC COLLECTION**
89	TINY TINKER 1950QLX717-4	YR	19.50	42.00
	J. FRANCIS			**KEEPSAKE MAGIC COLLECTION**
89	ANIMALS SPEAK , THE1350QLX723-2	YR	13.50	105.00
	D. LEE			**KEEPSAKE MAGIC COLLECTION**
89	BUSY BEAVER 1750QLX724-5	YR	17.50	47.00
89	FIRST CHRISTMAS TOGETHER 1750QLX734-2	YR	17.50	33.00
	S. PIKE			**KEEPSAKE MAGIC COLLECTION**
89	FOREST FROLICS-1ST EDITION 2450QLX728-2	YR	24.50	75.00
	D. RHODUS			**KEEPSAKE MAGIC COLLECTION**
89	UNICORN FANTASY 950QLX723-5	YR	9.50	18.00
	E. SEALE			**KEEPSAKE MAGIC COLLECTION**
89	BABY'S FIRST CHRISTMAS 3000QLX727-2	YR	30.00	57.00
89	KRINGLE'S TOY SHOP 2450QLX701-7	YR	24.50	52.00
89	SPIRIT OF ST. NICK 2450QLX728-5	YR	24.50	65.00
	L. SICKMAN			**KEEPSAKE MAGIC COLLECTION**
89	METRO EXPRESS 2800QLX727-5	YR	28.00	67.00
	B. SIEDLER			**KEEPSAKE MAGIC COLLECTION**
89	BACKSTAGE BEAR 1350QLX721-5	YR	13.50	25.00
89	LOVING SPOONFUL 1950QLX726-2	YR	19.50	32.00
	D. UNRUH			**KEEPSAKE MAGIC COLLECTION**
89	JOYOUS CAROLERS 3000QLX729-5	YR	30.00	57.00
	L. VOTRUBA			**KEEPSAKE MAGIC COLLECTION**
89	ANGEL MELODY 950QLX720-2	YR	9.50	19.00
	D. PALMITER			**KIDDIE CAR CLASSICS**
94	MURRAY CHAMPION 1ST ED. 1395QX542-6	RT	13.95	40.00
95	MURRAY FIRE TRUCK 2ND SERIES QX502-7	YR	13.95	31.00
	E. WEIRICK			**KIDDIE CAR CLASSICS**
93	'55 MURRAY FIRE CHIEF	19500	45.00	100.00
93	'68 MURRAY BOAT JOLLY ROGER	19500	50.00	50.00
94	'39 LINCOLN ZEPHYR	24500	50.00	50.00
94	'41 SPITFIRE AIRPLANE	19500	50.00	50.00
94	'55 DUMP TRUCK	19500	48.00	90.00
94	'55 RANCH WAGON	19500	48.00	48.00
94	'55 RED CHAMPION	19500	45.00	45.00
94	'56 DRAGNET POLICE CAR	24500	50.00	50.00
94	'56 KIDILLAC PREMIUM	OP	50.00	100.00
94	'56 MARK V	24500	45.00	45.00
94	'56 SPEEDWAY PACE CAR	24500	45.00	45.00
94	'58 ATOMIC MISSILE	24500	55.00	55.00
94	'61 CIRCUS CAR	24500	48.00	48.00
	K. CROW			**KITTENS IN TOYLAND**
88	KITTENS IN TOYALND/TRAIN 500QXM562-1	YR	5.00	29.00
89	SCOOTER 450QXM561-2	YR	4.50	19.00
90	SAILBOAT 450QXM573-6	YR	4.50	22.00
91	AIRPLANE 450QXM563-9	YR	4.50	19.00
92	POGO STICK 450QXM5391	YR	4.50	17.00
*				**LIGHTED ORNAMENTS COLLECTION**
86	MR. & MRS. SANTA 1450QLX705-2	YR	14.50	75.00
86	SANTA AND SPARKY-1ST ED. 2200QLX703-3	YR	22.00	80.00
86	SUGARPLUM COTTAGE 1100QLX701-1	YR	11.00	36.00
	K. CROW			**LIGHTED ORNAMENTS COLLECTION**
86	BABY'S FIRST CHRISTMAS 1950QLX710-3	YR	19.50	41.00
86	KEEP ON GLOWIN' 1000QLX707-6	YR	10.00	42.00
86	SANTA'S SNACK 1000QLX706-6	YR	10.00	52.00
	D. LEE			**LIGHTED ORNAMENTS COLLECTION**
86	GENERAL STORE 1575QLX705-3	YR	15.75	57.00

Barbie's popularity never seems to wane. Holiday Barbie, *second in a series of Hallmark Keepsake Ornaments, matches a doll offered by Mattel.*

This little fellow helps Santa make dreams come true for boys and girls around the world. The Lladró Elf *was introduced in 1992.*

The first subject in Enesco Corp.'s Precious Moments Collection, Love One Another, *became an ornament in 1989. This adorable couple sharing the stump is one of the collection's most beloved pieces.*

The 1991 Christmas Ball *is the first in a series by Lladró. The 3-1/2" bas relief porcelain ornament features pink and blue trim in a matte finish.*

YR	NAME	LIMIT	ISSUE	TREND
	E. SEALE			**LIGHTED ORNAMENTS COLLECTION**
86	CHRISTMAS SLEIGH RIDE 2450QLX701-2	YR	24.50	125.00
86	FIRST CHRISTMAS TOGETHER 2200QLX707-3	YR	14.00	30.00
	L. SICKMAN			**LIGHTED ORNAMENTS COLLECTION**
86	GENTLE BLESSINGS 1500QLX708-3	YR	15.00	137.00
86	VILLAGE EXPRESS 2450QLX707-2	YR	24.50	90.00
	D. UNRUH			**LIGHTED ORNAMENTS COLLECTION**
86	SANTA'S ON HIS WAY 1500QLX711-5	YR	15.00	62.00
	L. VOTRUBA			**LIGHTED ORNAMENTS COLLECTION**
86	MERRY CHRISTMAS BELL 850QLX709-3	YR	8.50	20.00
86	SHARING FRIENDSHIP 850QLX706-3	YR	8.50	21.00
*				**LION KING**
94	MUFASA AND SIMBA 1495QX540-6	YR	14.95	25.00
94	SIMBA AND NALSA 1295QX530-3	YR	12.95	31.00
94	TIMON & PUMBAA 895QX536-6	YR	8.95	17.00
	K. CROW			**LION KING**
94	SIMBA, SARABI AND MUFASA QLX 551-3	YR	32.00	65.00
95	SIMBA, PUMBAA & TIMON QX615-9	YR	12.95	18.00
*				**LITTLE FROSTY FRIENDS**
80	A COOL YULE 650QX137-4	YR	6.50	525.00
	J. LEE			**LITTLE FROSTY FRIENDS**
90	LITTLE SEAL 620XPR972-1	YR	2.95	10.00
90	MEMORY WREATH 620XPR972-4	YR	2.95	10.00
	E. SEALE			**LITTLE FROSTY FRIENDS**
90	LITTLE HUSKY 620XPR972-2	YR	2.95	15.00
	B. SIEDLER			**LITTLE FROSTY FRIENDS**
90	LITTLE BEAR 620XPR972-3	YR	2.95	10.00
90	LITTLE FROSTY 620XPR972-0	YR	2.95	12.00
*				**LITTLE TRIMMERS**
78	DRUMMER BOY 250QX136-3	YR	2.50	57.00
78	SANTA 250QX135-6	YR	2.50	55.00
78	THIMBLE MOUSE-1ST EDITION 250QX133-6	YR	2.50	265.00
79	A MATCHLESS CHRISTMAS 400QX132-7	YR	4.00	55.00
79	ANGEL DELIGHT 300QX130-7	YR	3.00	90.00
79	SANTA 300QX135-6	YR	3.00	57.00
79	THIMBLE SERIES-MOUSE 300QX133-6	YR	3.00	265.00
80	CHRISTMAS OWL 400QX131-4	YR	4.00	40.00
80	CHRISTMAS TEDDY 250QX135-4	YR	2.50	110.00
80	CLOTHESPIN SOLDIER 350QX134-4	YR	3.50	35.00
80	MERRY REDBIRD 350QX160-1	YR	3.50	57.00
80	SWINGIN' ON A STAR 400QX130-1	YR	4.00	75.00
80	THIMBLE SERIES-A XMAS SALUTE 400QX131-9	YR	4.00	155.00
81	CLOTHESPIN DRUMMER BOY 450QX408-2	YR	4.50	42.00
81	JOLLY SNOWMAN 350QX407-5	YR	3.50	44.00
81	PERKY PENGUIN 350QX409-5	YR	3.50	56.00
81	PUPPY LOVE 350QX406-2	YR	3.50	34.00
81	STOCKING MOUSE, THE- 450QX412-2	YR	4.50	97.00
82	CHRISTMAS KITTEN 400QX454-3	YR	4.00	31.00
82	CHRISTMAS OWL 450QX131-4	YR	4.50	40.00
82	MERRY MOOSE 550QX415-5	YR	5.50	47.00
82	PERKY PENGUIN 400QX409-5	YR	4.00	56.00
	D. LEE			**LITTLE TRIMMERS**
78	PRAYING ANGEL 250QX134-3	YR	2.50	75.00
82	MUSICAL ANGEL 550QX459-6	YR	5.50	77.00
	E. SEALE			**LITTLE TRIMMERS**
82	JINGLING TEDDY 400QX477-6	YR	4.00	33.00
	L. SICKMAN			**LITTLE TRIMMERS**
82	COOKIE MOUSE 450QX454-6	YR	4.50	52.00
82	DOVE LOVE 450QX462-3	YR	4.50	51.00
	P. ANDREWS			**LOONEY TUNES COLLECTION**
93	PORKY PIG 875QX565-2	YR	8.75	16.00
	R. CHAD			**LOONEY TUNES COLLECTION**
94	ROAD RUNNER AND WILE E. COYOTE QX 560-2	YR	12.95	19.00
95	BUGS BUNNY QX501-9	YR	8.95	14.00
95	SYLVESTER AND TWEETY QX501-7	YR	13.95	19.00
	J. LYLE			**LOONEY TUNES COLLECTION**
93	ELMER FUDD 875QX549-5	YR	8.75	17.00
	D. PALMITER			**LOONEY TUNES COLLECTION**
93	SYLVESTER & TWEETY 975QX540-5	YR	9.75	26.00
94	DAFFY DUCK 895QX541-6	YR	8.95	14.00
94	SPEEDY GONZALES 895QX534-3	YR	8.95	14.00
94	TASMANIAN DEVIL 895QX560-5	YR	8.95	42.00
94	YOSEMITE SAM 895QX534-6	YR	8.95	13.00
	L. SICKMAN			**LOONEY TUNES COLLECTION**
93	BUGS BUNNY 875QX541-2	YR	9.75	19.00
*				**MAGIC ORNAMENTS**
84	ALL ARE PRECIOUS 800QLX704-1	YR	8.00	22.00
84	BRASS CAROUSEL 900QLX707-1	YR	9.00	82.00
84	CHRISTMAS IN THE FOREST 800QLX703-4	YR	8.00	17.00
84	SANTA'S WORKSHOP 1300QLX700-4	YR	13.00	55.00
84	STAINED GLASS 800QLX703-1	YR	8.00	17.00
84	SUGARPLUM COTTAGE 1100QLX701-1	YR	11.00	36.00
85	ALL ARE PRECIOUS 800QLX704-4	YR	8.00	22.00
85	CHRISTMAS EVE VISIT 1200QLX710-5	YR	12.00	24.00
85	KATYBETH 1075QLX710-2	YR	10.75	36.00
85	MR. AND MRS. SANTA 1450QLX705-2	YR	14.50	75.00

YR	NAME	LIMIT	ISSUE	TREND
85	SANTA'S WORKSHOP 1300QLX700-4	YR	13.00	55.00
85	SUGARPLUM COTTAGE 1100QLX701-1	YR	11.00	36.00
85	SWISS CHEESE LANE 1300QLX706-5	YR	13.00	43.00
87	BABY'S FIRST CHRISTMAS 1350QLX704-9	YR	13.50	31.00
87	FIRST CHRISTMAS TOGETHER 1150QLX708-7	YR	11.50	40.00
87	LACY BRASS SNOWFLAKE 1150QLX709-7	YR	11.50	18.00
87	SEASON FOR FRIENDSHIP 850QLX706-9	YR	8.50	16.00
88	FIRST CHRISTMAS TOGETHER 1200QLX702-7	YR	12.00	31.00
88	SONG OF CHRISTMAS 850QLX711-1	YR	8.50	20.00
88	TREE OF FRIENDSHIP 850QLX710-4	YR	8.50	18.00
90	BLESSINGS OF LOVE 1400QLX736-3	YR	14.00	37.00
90	OUR FIRST CHRISTMAS TOGETHER1800QLX725-5	YR	18.00	45.00
91	ANGEL OF LIGHT 3000QLT723-9	YR	30.00	60.00
92	ANGEL OF LIGHT 3000QLX723-9	YR	30.00	37.00
94	BARNEY 2400QLX750-6	YR	24.00	34.00
	P. ANDREWS		**MAGIC ORNAMENTS**	
90	ELF OF THE YEAR 1000QLX735-6	YR	10.00	22.00
91	KITTY IN A MITTY 450QXM587-9	YR	4.50	12.00
92	LIGHTING THE WAY 1800QLX723-1	YR	18.00	37.00
93	SONG OF THE CHIMES 2500QLX740-5	YR	25.00	45.00
	R. CHAD		**MAGIC ORNAMENTS**	
88	MOONLIT NAP 875QLX713-4	YR	8.75	22.00
90	HOLIDAY FLASH 1800QLX733-3	YR	18.00	32.00
91	ELFIN ENGINEER 1000QLX720-9	YR	10.00	20.00
91	SPARKLING ANGEL 1800QLX715-7	YR	18.00	28.00
92	OUR FIRST CHRISTMAS TOGETHER2000QLX722-1	YR	20.00	33.00
93	OUR FIRST CHRISTMAS TOGETHER QLX735-5	YR	20.00	31.00
93	ROAD RUNNER AND WILE E. COYOTE QLX741-5	YR	30.00	57.00
	K. CROW		**MAGIC ORNAMENTS**	
87	CHRISTMAS MORNING 2450QLX701-3	YR	24.50	34.00
87	KEEP ON GLOWIN! 1000QLX707-6	YR	10.00	42.00
87	KEEPING COZY 1175QLX704-7	YR	11.75	27.00
88	CHRISTMAS IS MAGIC 1200QLX717-1	YR	12.00	45.00
88	CIRCLING THE GLOBE 1050QLX712-4	YR	10.50	33.00
90	ELFIN WHITTLER 2000QLX726-5	YR	20.00	45.00
90	SANTA'S HO-HO-HOEDOWN 2500QLX725-6	YR	25.00	80.00
91	ARCTIC DOME 2500QLX711-7	YR	25.00	46.00
91	SANTA'S HOT LINE 1800QLX715-9	YR	18.00	35.00
91	TOYLAND TOWER 2000QLX712-9	YR	20.00	34.00
92	BABY'S FIRST CHRISTMAS 2200QLX728-1	YR	22.00	72.00
92	ENCHANTED CLOCK 3000QLX727-4	YR	30.00	48.00
92	NUT SWEET NUT 1000QLX708-1	YR	10.00	20.00
92	SANTA SUB 1800QLX732-1	YR	18.00	36.00
93	BELLS ARE RINGING 2800QLX740-2	YR	28.00	46.00
93	DOLLHOUSE DREAMS 2200QLX737-2	YR	22.00	40.00
93	SANTA'S SNOW-GETTER 1800QLX735-2	YR	18.00	32.00
94	FELIZ NAVIDAD 2800QLX743-3	YR	28.00	40.00
94	KRINGLE TROLLEY 2000QLX741-3	YR	20.00	23.00
94	SANTA'S SING-ALONG 2400QLX747-3	YR	24.00	28.00
94	WINNIE THE POOH PARADE 3200QLX749-3	YR	32.00	50.00
	P. DUTKIN		**MAGIC ORNAMENTS**	
91	FRIENDSHIP TREE 1000QLX716-9	YR	10.00	18.00
	J. FRANCIS		**MAGIC ORNAMENTS**	
92	WATCH OWLS 1200QLX708-4	YR	12.00	21.00
93	BABY'S FIRST CHRISTMAS 2200QLX736-5	YR	22.00	36.00
94	BABY'S FIRST CHRISTMAS 2000QLX746-6	YR	20.00	31.00
94	CANDY CANE LOOKOUT 1800QLX737-6	YR	18.00	29.00
	D. LEE		**MAGIC ORNAMENTS**	
84	SANTA'S ARRIVAL 1300QLX702-4	YR	13.00	60.00
84	VILLAGE CHURCH 1500QLX702-1	YR	15.00	40.00
85	LITTLE RED SCHOOLHOUSE 1575QLX711-2	YR	15.75	85.00
85	VILLAGE CHURCH 1500QLX702-1	YR	15.00	40.00
87	TRAIN STATION 1275QLX703-9	YR	12.75	36.00
90	FIRST CHRISTMAS TOGETHER QLX 725-5	YR	18.00	39.00
91	IT'S A WONDERFUL LIFE 2000QLX723-7	YR	20.00	60.00
91	JINGLE BEARS 2500QLX732-3	YR	25.00	40.00
91	MOLE FAMILY HOME 2000QLX714-9	YR	20.00	32.00
92	LOOK! IT'S SANTA 1400QLX709-4	YR	14.00	32.00
92	SANTA'S ANSWERING MACHINE 2200QLX724-1	YR	22.00	14.00
93	DOG'S BEST FRIEND 1200QLX717-2	YR	12.00	21.00
93	RADIO NEWS FLASH 2200QLX736-2	YR	22.00	39.00
94	WHITE CHRISTMAS 2800QLX746-3	YR	28.00	50.00
	J. LYLE		**MAGIC ORNAMENTS**	
85	SEASON OF BEAUTY 800QLX712-2	YR	8.00	20.00
88	RADIANT TREE 1175QLX712-1	YR	11.75	17.00
90	PARTRIDGES IN A PEAR 1400QLX721-2	YR	14.00	26.00
94	AWAY IN A MANGER 1600QLX738-3	YR	16.00	26.00
	D. MCGEHEE		**MAGIC ORNAMENTS**	
91	FESTIVE BRASS CHURCH 1400QLX717-9	YR	14.00	22.00
	L. NORTON		**MAGIC ORNAMENTS**	
91	STARSHIP ENTERPRISE 2000QLX719-9	YR	20.00	302.00
93	U.S.S ENTERPRISE QLX741-2	YR	24.00	42.00
	D. PALMITER		**MAGIC ORNAMENTS**	
90	BABY'S FIRST CHRISTMAS 2800QLX724-6	YR	28.00	51.00
92	GOOD SLEDDING AHEAD 2800QLX724-4	YR	28.00	40.00
92	UNDER CONSTRUCTION 1800QLX732-4	YR	18.00	31.00
93	LAMPLIGHTER, THE 1800QLX719-2	YR	18.00	30.00

YR	NAME	LIMIT	ISSUE	TREND
94	GINGERBREAD FANTASY 4400QLX738-2	YR	44.00	90.00
	S. PIKE		**MAGIC ORNAMENTS**	
87	MEOWY CHRISTMAS 1000QLX708-9	YR	10.00	51.00
88	KITTY CAPERS 1300QLX716-4	YR	13.00	33.00
90	FOREST FROLICS 2500QLX723-6	YR	25.00	60.00
91	FOREST FROLICS 2500QLX721-9	YR	25.00	55.00
91	HOLIDAY GLOW 1400QLX717-7	YR	14.00	25.00
92	FOREST FROLICS 4TH ED. 2800QLX725-4	YR	28.00	49.00
93	FOREST FROLICS 5TH ED. 2500QLX716-5	YR	25.00	42.00
94	FOREST FROLICS 6TH ED. 2800QLX743-6	YR	28.00	36.00
	M. PYDA-SEVCIK		**MAGIC ORNAMENTS**	
88	HEAVENLY GLOW 1175QLX711-4	YR	11.75	20.00
	D. RHODUS		**MAGIC ORNAMENTS**	
90	MRS. SANTA'S KITCHEN 2500QLX726-3	YR	25.00	67.00
91	PEANUTS 1800QLX722-9	YR	18.00	52.00
92	PEANUTS 1800QLX721-4	YR	18.00	42.00
92	SHUTTLECRAFT "GALILEO" 2400QLX133-1	YR	21.00	33.00
93	PEANUTS 3RD ED. 1800QLX715-5	YR	18.00	32.00
94	PEANUTS 4TH ED. 2000QLX740-6	YR	20.00	28.00
	A. ROGERS		**MAGIC ORNAMENTS**	
89	CHRIS MOUSE COOKOUT 950QLX722-5	YR	9.50	53.00
90	CHRIS MOUSE WREATH 1000QLX729-6	YR	10.00	33.00
90	LETTER TO SANTA 1400QLX722-6	YR	14.00	23.00
90	SONG AND DANCE 2000QLX725-3	YR	20.00	77.00
90	STARLIGHT ANGEL 1400QLX730-6	YR	14.00	29.00
92	CHRIS MOUSE TALES 1200QLX707-4	YR	12.00	27.00
93	BEARYMORES, THE 575QXM512-5	YR	5.75	18.00
93	CHRIS MOUSE FLIGHT 9TH ED. 1200QLX715-2	YR	12.00	23.00
93	RAIDING THE FRIDGE 1600QLX718-5	YR	16.00	28.00
94	CHRIS MOUSE JELLY 10TH ED. 1200QLX739-3	YR	12.00	22.00
94	PEEKABOO PUP 2000QLX742-3	YR	20.00	22.00
	E. SEALE		**MAGIC ORNAMENTS**	
84	NATIVITY 1200QLX700-1	YR	12.00	27.00
85	BABY'S FIRST CHRISTMAS 1650QLX700-5	YR	16.50	37.00
85	NATIVITY 1200QLX700-1	YR	12.00	27.00
87	LOVING HOLIDAY 2200QLX701-6	YR	22.00	37.00
87	MEMORIES ARE FOREVER-PHOTO 850QLX706-7	YR	8.50	23.00
88	BABY'S FIRST CHRISTMAS 2400QLX718-4	YR	24.00	38.00
88	KRINGLE'S TOY SHOP 2450QLX701-7	YR	24.50	52.00
91	BABY'S FIRST CHRISTMAS 3000QLX724-7	YR	30.00	55.00
91	SANTA SPECIAL 4000QLX716-7	YR	40.00	70.00
91	SKI TRIP 2800QLX726-6	YR	28.00	54.00
92	SANTA SPECIAL 4000QLX716-7	YR	40.00	70.00
92	YULETIDE RIDER 2800QLX731-4	YR	28.00	42.00
93	NORTH POLE MERRYTHON QLX739-2	YR	25.00	45.00
94	CONVERSATION W/SANTA 2800QLX742-6	YR	28.00	30.00
94	EAGLE HAS LANDED, THE 2400QLX748-6	YR	24.00	37.00
	L. SICKMAN		**MAGIC ORNAMENTS**	
87	GOOD CHEER BLIMP 1600QLX704-6	YR	16.00	41.00
88	BEARLY REACHING 950QLX715-1	YR	9.50	27.00
88	COUNTRY EXPRESS 2450QLX721-1	YR	24.50	60.00
88	FESTIVE FEEDER 1150QLX720-4	YR	11.50	41.00
88	PARADE OF THE TOYS 2200QLX719-4	YR	24.50	37.00
90	CHILDREN'S EXPRESS 2800QLX724-3	YR	28.00	60.00
91	FIRST CHRISTMAS TOGETHER QX 713-7	YR	25.00	47.00
91	KRINGLES'S BUMPER CARS 2500QLX711-9	YR	25.00	45.00
92	CHRISTMAS PARADE 3000QLX727-1	YR	30.00	56.00
92	CONTINENTAL EXPRESS 3200QLX726-4	YR	32.00	62.00
92	FEATHERED FRIENDS 1400QLX709-1	YR	14.00	27.00
93	HOME ON THE RANGE 3200QLX739-5	YR	32.00	55.00
94	COUNTRY SHOWTIME 2200QLX741-6	YR	22.00	30.00
94	MAXINE 2000QLX750-3	YR	20.00	32.00
	B. SIEDLER		**MAGIC ORNAMENTS**	
84	CITY LIGHTS 1000QLX701-4	YR	10.00	42.00
85	CHRIS MOUSE-FIRST EDITION 1250QLX703-2	YR	12.50	70.00
87	CHRIS MOUSE-3RD EDITION 100QLX705-7	YR	11.00	52.00
90	BEARY SHORT NAP 1000QLX732-6	YR	10.00	24.00
90	DEER CROSSING 1800QLX721-3	YR	18.00	40.00
90	HOP 'N POP POPPER 2000QLX735-3	YR	20.00	87.00
90	STARSHIP CHRISTMAS 1800QLX733-6	YR	18.00	45.00
91	CHRIS MOUSE MAIL 1000QLX720-7	YR	10.00	30.00
93	SANT'A WORKSHOP 2800QLX737-5	YR	28.00	44.00
93	WINNIE THE POOH 2400QLX742-2	YR	24.00	34.00
94	ROCK CANDY MINER 2000QLX740-3	YR	20.00	28.00
	D. UNRUH		**MAGIC ORNAMENTS**	
87	ANGELIC MESSENGERS 1875QLX711-3	YR	18.75	55.00
88	LAST-MINUTE HUG 1950QLX718-1	YR	22.00	44.00
88	SKATER'S WALTZ 2450QLX720-1	YR	24.50	46.00
90	CHRISTMAS MEMORIES 2500QLX727-6	YR	25.00	47.00
91	BRINGING HOME THE TREE 2800QLX724-9	YR	28.00	47.00
91	FATHER CHRISTMAS 1400QLX714-7	YR	14.00	35.00
91	SALVATION ARMY BAND 3000QLX727-3	YR	30.00	67.00
94	TOBIN FRALEY HOL. CAROUSEL 1ST ED. 3200Q	YR	32.00	50.00
	L. VOTRUBA		**MAGIC ORNAMENTS**	
85	LOVE WREATH 850QLX702-5	YR	8.50	26.00
87	BRIGHT NOEL 700QLX705-9	YR	7.00	27.00
92	DANCING NUTCRACKER, THE 3000QLX726-1	YR	30.00	45.00

YR	NAME	LIMIT	ISSUE	TREND
93	LAST MINUTE SHOPPING 2800QLX738-5	YR	28.00	45.00
94	VERY MERRY MINUTES 2400QLX744-3	YR	24.00	40.00
	R. CHAD		**MARY'S ANGELS**	
88	BUTTERCUP 500QX407-4	YR	5.00	35.00
89	BLUEBELL 2ND ED. 575QX454-5	YR	5.75	43.00
90	ROSEBUD 575QX442-3	YR	5.75	42.00
91	IRIS 675QX427-9	YR	6.75	25.00
92	LILY 5TH ED. 675QX427-4	YR	6.75	45.00
93	IVY 6TH ED. 675QX428-2	YR	6.75	19.00
94	JASMINE 7TH ED. 695QX527-6	YR	6.95	16.00
95	CAMELLIA 8TH SERIES QX514-9	YR	6.95	12.00
	E. SEALE		**MATCHBOX MEMORIES**	
91	EVERGREEN INN 875QX538-9	YR	8.75	17.00
91	HOLIDAY CAFE 875QX539-9	YR	8.75	14.00
91	SANTA'S STUDIO 875QX539-7	YR	8.75	15.00
	L. SICKMAN		**METAL ORNAMENTS**	
77	SNOWFLAKE COLLECTION (4) 500QX210-2	YR	5.00	92.00
	*		**MINIATURE ORNAMENTS**	
88	SNEAKER MOUSE 400QXM571-1	YR	4.00	19.00
88	SWEET DREAMS 700QXM560-4	YR	7.00	22.00
89	HEAVENLY GLOW TREE TOPPER QXM 566-1	YR	9.75	14.00
89	KITTENS IN TOYLAND-2ND ED. 450QXM561-2	YR	4.50	19.00
89	KRINGLES, THE-1ST EDITION 600QXM562-2	YR	6.00	33.00
89	MOTHER 600QXM564-5	YR	6.00	14.00
89	ROLY-POLY RAM 300QXM570-5	YR	3.00	13.00
89	SPECIAL FRIEND 450QXM565-2	YR	4.50	14.00
90	AIR SANTA 450QXM565-6	YR	4.50	12.00
90	BRASS HORN 300QXM579-3	YR	3.00	7.00
90	BRASS PEACE 300QXM579-6	YR	3.00	7.00
90	BRASS YEAR 300QXM583-3	YR	3.00	8.00
90	LOVING HEARTS 300QXM552-3	YR	3.00	12.00
91	BRASS CHURCH 300QXM597-9	YR	3.00	9.00
91	BRASS SOLDIER 300QXM598-7	YR	3.00	9.00
91	INN-4TH EDITION 850QXM562-7	YR	8.50	19.00
91	OUR 1ST CHRISTMAS TOGETHER 600QXM581-9	YR	6.00	17.00
92	DANCING ANGELS TREE TOPPER QXM 589-1	YR	9.75	12.00
92	HOLIDAY HOLLY 975QXM536-4	YR	9.75	21.00
93	DANCING ANGELS TREE-TOPPER QXM 589-1	YR	9.75	13.00
94	DANCING ANGELS TREE-TOPPER QXM 589-1	YR	9.75	13.00
94	GRACEFUL CAROUSEL HORSE 775QXM405-6	YR	7.75	17.00
	P. ANDREWS		**MINIATURE ORNAMENTS**	
90	FIRST CHRISTMAS TOGETHER 600QXM553-6	YR	6.00	14.00
91	BRASS BELLS 300QXM597-7	YR	3.00	9.00
92	GOING PLACES 375QXM587-1	YR	3.75	10.00
92	MOM 450QXM550-4	YR	4.50	14.00
92	SKI FOR TWO 450QXM582-1	YR	4.50	13.00
92	VISIONS OF ACORNS 450QXM585-1	YR	4.50	14.00
93	EARS TO PALS 375QXM407-5	YR	3.75	9.00
93	MOM 450QXM515-5	YR	4.50	13.00
93	NATURE'S ANGELS 450QXM512-2	YR	4.50	14.00
93	SNUGGLE BIRDS 575QXM518-2	YR	5.75	14.00
	R. BISHOP		**MINIATURE ORNAMENTS**	
91	WEE TOYMAKER 850QXM596-7	YR	8.50	15.00
94	BEARY PERFECT TREE 475QXM407-6	YR	4.75	10.00
94	HEARTS A-SAIL 575QXM400-6	YR	5.75	12.00
94	JUST MY SIZE 375QXM408-6	YR	3.75	9.00
	R. CHAD		**MINIATURE ORNAMENTS**	
90	PERFECT FIT 450QXM551-6	YR	4.50	12.00
90	TYPE OF JOY 450QXM564-6	YR	4.50	9.00
91	ALL ABOARD 450QXM586-9	YR	4.50	17.00
91	RING-A-DING ELF 850QXM566-9	YR	8.50	19.00
91	TREELAND TRIO 850QXM589-9	YR	8.50	18.00
91	VISION OF SANTA 450QXM593-7	YR	4.50	15.00
92	HICKORY, DICKORY, DOCK 375QXM586-1	YR	3.75	12.00
92	SPUNKY MONKEY 300QXM592-1	YR	3.00	14.00
93	LEARNING TO SKATE 300QXM412-2	YR	3.00	9.00
93	LIGHTING A PATH 300QXM411-5	YR	3.00	9.00
93	REFRESHING FLIGHT 575QXM411-2	YR	5.75	14.00
94	POUR SOME MORE 575QXM515-6	YR	5.75	12.00
	K. CROW		**MINIATURE ORNAMENTS**	
89	SANTA'S ROADSTER 600QXM566-5	YR	6.00	19.00
90	ACORN WREATH 600QXM568-6	YR	6.00	12.00
90	BUSY CARVER 450QXM567-3	YR	4.50	12.00
90	STAMP COLLECTOR 450QXM562-3	YR	4.50	10.00
91	FLY BY 450QXM585-9	YR	4.50	17.00
91	KEY TO LOVE 450QXM568-9	YR	4.50	16.00
92	BUCK-A-ROO 450QXM581-4	YR	4.50	15.00
92	FEEDING TIME 575QXM548-1	YR	5.75	15.00
92	FRIENDS ARE TOPS 450QXM552-1	YR	4.50	11.00
92	HOOP IT UP 450QXM583-1	YR	4.50	12.00
93	'ROUND THE MOUNTAIN QXM 402-5	YR	7.25	14.00
94	A MERRY FLIGHT 575QX407-3	YR	5.75	12.00
94	CUTE AS A BUTTON 375QXM410-3	YR	3.75	9.00
94	SWEET DREAMS 300QXM409-6	YR	3.00	11.00
	P. DUTKIN		**MINIATURE ORNAMENTS**	
89	SHARING A RIDE 850QXM576-5	YR	8.50	15.00

YR	NAME	LIMIT	ISSUE	TREND
	J. FRANCIS		**MINIATURE ORNAMENTS**	
89	MERRY SEAL 600QXM575-5	YR	6.00	15.00
90	BABY'S FIRST CHRISTMAS 850QXM570-3	YR	8.50	17.00
90	HOLIDAY CARDINAL 300QXM552-6	YR	3.00	12.00
90	PANDA'S SURPRISE 450QXM561-6	YR	4.50	13.00
91	BABY'S FIRST CHRISTMAS 600QXM579-9	YR	6.00	22.00
91	UPBEAT BEAR 600QXM590-7	YR	6.00	16.00
92	BLACK-CAPPED CHICKADEE 300QXM548-4	YR	3.00	19.00
92	CHRISTMAS COPTER 575QXM584-4	YR	5.75	15.00
92	GRANDCHILD'S FIRST CHRISTMAS 575QXM550-1	YR	5.75	14.00
92	HOLIDAY SPLASH 575QXM583-4	YR	5.75	12.00
93	COUNTRY FIDDLING 375QXM406-2	YR	3.75	10.00
93	PULL OUT A PLUM 575QXM409-5	YR	5.75	12.00
93	SPECIAL FRIENDS 450QXM516-5	YR	4.50	10.00
93	WOODLAND BABIES 575QXM510-2	YR	5.75	14.00
94	SCOOTING ALONG 675QXM517-3	YR	6.75	15.00
	D. LEE		**MINIATURE ORNAMENTS**	
88	BABY'S FIRST CHRISTMAS 600QXM574-4	YR	5.00	12.00
89	STOCKING PAL 450QXM567-2	YR	4.50	12.00
90	GOING SLEDDING 450QXM568-3	YR	4.50	15.00
90	SANTA'S STREETCAR 850QXM576-6	YR	8.50	19.00
90	SNOW ANGEL 600QXM577-3	YR	6.00	14.00
90	STOCKING PAL 450QXM567-2	YR	4.50	12.00
91	FRIENDLY FAWN 600QXM594-7	YR	6.00	16.00
91	HEAVENLY MINSTREL 975QXM568-7	YR	9.75	24.00
91	OLD ENGLISH VILLAGE 850QXM562-7	YR	8.50	29.00
91	SILVERY SANTA 975QXM567-9	YR	9.75	24.00
91	SPECIAL FRIENDS 850QXM579-7	YR	8.50	19.00
92	COOL UNCLE SAM 300QXM556-1	YR	3.00	15.00
92	COZY KAYAK 375QXM555-1	YR	3.75	12.00
94	HAVE A COOKIE 575QXM516-6	YR	5.75	14.00
	J. LYLE		**MINIATURE ORNAMENTS**	
88	BRASS ANGEL 150QXM567-1	YR	1.50	19.00
88	BRASS STAR 150QXM566-4	YR	1.50	19.00
88	BRASS TREE 150QXM567-4	YR	1.50	19.00
89	BRASS PARTRIDGE 300QXM572-5	YR	3.00	12.00
89	BRASS SNOWFLAKE 450QXM570-2	YR	4.50	14.00
89	COZY SKATER 450QXM573-5	YR	4.50	12.00
89	LITTLE STAR BRINGER 600QXM562-2	YR	6.00	19.00
90	BRASS BOUQUET 600QMX577-6	YR	6.00	6.00
90	COZY SKATER 450QXM573-5	YR	4.50	12.00
90	MOTHER 450QXM571-6	YR	4.50	17.00
91	CARDINAL CAMEO 600QXM595-7	YR	6.00	17.00
91	CARING SHEPHERD 600QXM594-9	YR	6.00	17.00
91	FANCY WREATH 450QXM591-7	YR	4.50	14.00
92	ANGELIC HARPIST 450QXM552-4	YR	4.50	13.00
92	BABY'S FIRST CHRISTMAS 450QXM5494	YR	4.50	19.00
92	THIMBLE BELLS 600QXM546-1	YR	6.00	22.00
93	PEAR-SHAPED TONES 375QXM405-2	YR	3.75	8.00
94	BABY'S FIRST CHRISTMAS 575QXM400-3	YR	5.75	13.00
94	FRIENDS NEED HUGS 450QXM401-6	YR	4.50	12.00
94	JOURNEY TO BETHLEHEM 575QXM403-6	YR	5.75	12.00
	D. MCGEHEE		**MINIATURE ORNAMENTS**	
88	FIRST CHRISTMAS TOGETHER 400QXM574-1	YR	4.00	12.00
88	JOYOUS HEART 350QXM569-1	YR	3.50	29.00
	D. PALMITER		**MINIATURE ORNAMENTS**	
90	BEAR HUG 600QXM563-3	YR	6.00	13.00
90	PUPPY LOVE 600QXM566-6	YR	6.00	14.00
91	N. POLE BUDDY 450QXM592-7	YR	4.50	19.00
92	CHRISTMAS BONUS 300QXM581-1	YR	3.00	8.00
92	WEE THREE KINGS 575QXM553-1	YR	5.75	17.00
92	WOODLAND BABIES 600QXM544-4	YR	6.00	16.00
93	CRYSTAL ANGEL 975QXM401-5	YR	9.75	75.00
93	NORTH POLK FIRE TRUCK 475QXM410-5	YR	4.75	13.00
93	VISIONS OF SUGARPLUMS 725QXM402-2	YR	7.25	16.00
	J. PATTEE		**MINIATURE ORNAMENTS**	
88	FOLK ART LAMB 250QXM568-1	YR	2.75	22.00
88	FOLK ART REINDEER 250QXM568-4	YR	3.00	19.00
88	FRIENDS SHARE JOY 200QXM576-4	YR	2.00	15.00
88	HAPPY SANTA 450QXM561-4	YR	4.50	20.00
88	LOVE IS FOREVER 200QXM577-4	YR	2.00	15.00
89	FOLK ART BUNNY 450QXM569-2	YR	4.50	11.00
89	KITTY CART 300QXM572-2	YR	3.00	9.00
90	BRASS SANTA 300QXM578-6	YR	3.00	7.00
90	RUBY REINDEER 600QXM581-6	YR	6.00	12.00
	S. PIKE		**MINIATURE ORNAMENTS**	
88	MOTHER 300QXM572-4	YR	3.00	12.00
88	THREE LITTLE KITTENS 600QXM569-4	YR	6.00	18.00
89	ACORN SQUIRREL 450QXM568-2	YR	4.50	9.00
89	BABY'S FIRST CHRISTMAS 600QXM573-2	YR	6.00	14.00
89	LOVEBIRDS 600QXM563-5	YR	6.00	14.00
89	ROLY-POLY PIG 300QXM571-2	YR	3.00	17.00
89	THREE LITTLE KITTENS 600QXM569-4	YR	6.00	18.00
90	ACORN SQUIRREL 450QXM568-2	YR	4.50	9.00
90	ROLY-POLY PIG 300QXM571-2	YR	3.00	17.00
90	SPECIAL FRIENDS 600QXM572-6	YR	6.00	13.00
90	TEACHER 450QXM565-3	YR	4.50	9.00
91	COOL 'N' SWEET 450QXM586-7	YR	4.50	19.00

YR	NAME	LIMIT	ISSUE	TREND
91	COURIER TURTLE 450QXM585-7	YR	4.50	14.00
92	NATURE'S ANGELS 450QXM545-1	YR	4.50	19.00
92	SNUG KITTY 375QXM555-4	YR	3.75	12.00
M. PYDA-SEVCIK			**MINIATURE ORNAMENTS**	
90	THIMBLE BELLS 600QXM554-3	YR	6.00	27.00
91	THIMBLE BELLS-2ND EDITION 600QXM565-9	YR	6.00	22.00
D. RHODUS			**MINIATURE ORNAMENTS**	
89	LOAD OF CHEER 600QXM574-5	YR	6.00	19.00
89	PINECONE BASKET 450QXM573-4	YR	4.50	9.00
89	STARLIT MOUSE 450QXM565-5	YR	4.50	16.00
91	BRIGHT BOXERS 450QXM587-7	YR	4.50	17.00
91	BUSY BEAR 450QXM593-9	YR	4.50	12.00
91	HOLIDAY SNOWFLAKE 300QXM599-7	YR	3.00	12.00
92	FAST FINISH 375QXM530-1	YR	3.75	12.00
94	CORNY ELF 450QXM406-3	YR	4.50	10.00
A. ROGERS			**MINIATURE ORNAMENTS**	
88	COUNTRY WREATH 400QXM573-1	YR	4.00	12.00
89	COUNTRY WREATH 450QXM573-1	YR	4.50	12.00
89	HAPPY BLUEBIRD 450QXM566-2	YR	4.50	14.00
89	KRINGLES, THE QXM 562-5	YR	6.00	30.00
89	SANTA'S MAGIC RIDE 850QXM563-2	YR	8.50	19.00
90	BASKET BUDDY 600QXM569-6	YR	6.00	12.00
90	COUNTRY HEART 450QXM569-3	YR	4.50	9.00
90	HAPPY BLUEBIRD 450QXM566-2	YR	4.50	12.00
90	KRINGLES, THE- 600QXM575-3	YR	6.00	24.00
90	MADONNA AND CHILD 600QXM564-3	YR	6.00	12.00
91	FELIZ NAVIDAD 600QXM588-7	YR	6.00	16.00
91	GRANDCHILD'S 1ST CHRISTMAS 450QXM569-7	YR	4.50	14.00
91	KRINGLES, THE-3RD EDITION 6000QXM564-7	YR	6.00	24.00
91	LULU & FAMILY 600QXM567-7	YR	6.00	18.00
92	BEARYMORES, THE 575QXM554-4	YR	5.75	22.00
92	PERFECT BALANCE 300QXM557-1	YR	3.00	12.00
93	SECRET PAL 375QXM517-2	YR	3.75	8.00
94	BEARYMORES, THE 575QXM513-3	YR	5.75	14.00
94	MELODIC CHERUB 375QXM406-6	YR	3.75	10.00
94	MOM 450QXM401-3	YR	4.50	10.00
94	TEA W/TEDDY 725QXM404-6	YR	7.25	16.00
E. SEALE			**MINIATURE ORNAMENTS**	
90	STRINGING ALONG 850QXM560-6	YR	8.50	17.00
90	WARM MEMORIES 450QXM571-3	YR	4.50	12.00
91	TINY TEA PARTY 2900QXM582-7	YR	29.00	150.00
91	TOP HATTER 600QXM588-9	YR	6.00	17.00
92	BRIGHT STRINGERS 375QXM584-1	YR	3.75	14.00
92	INSIDE STORY 725QXM588-1	YR	7.25	19.00
92	POLAR POLKA 450QXM553-4	YR	4.50	14.00
92	SEW, SEW TINY 2900QXM579-4	YR	29.00	60.00
93	CHRISTMAS CASTLE 575QXM408-5	YR	5.75	13.00
93	GRANDMA 450QXM516-2	YR	4.50	12.00
93	INTO THE WOODS 375QXM404-5	YR	3.75	8.00
93	TINY GREEN THUMBS QXM 403-2 SET OF SIX	YR	29.00	45.00
94	BAKING TINY TREATS QXM 403-3 SET OF SIX	YR	29.00	59.00
L. SICKMAN			**MINIATURE ORNAMENTS**	
89	LITTLE SOLDIER 450QXM567-5	YR	4.50	10.00
89	PUPPY CART 300QXM571-5	YR	3.00	9.00
90	LION AND LAMB 450QXM567-6	YR	4.50	10.00
90	LITTLE SOLDIER 450QXM567-5	YR	4.50	10.00
90	SANTA'S JOURNEY 850QXM582-6	YR	8.50	19.00
91	LI'L POPPER 450QXM589-7	YR	4.50	17.00
91	NOEL 300QXM598-9	YR	3.00	12.00
92	FRIENDLY TIN SOLDIER 450QXM587-4	YR	4.50	17.00
92	LITTLE TOWN OF BETHLEHEM 300QXM586-4	YR	3.00	22.00
93	I DREAM OF SANTA 375QXM405-5	YR	3.75	12.00
93	MONKEY MELODY 575QXM409-2	YR	5.75	14.00
93	ON THE ROAD 575QXM400-2	YR	5.75	16.00
94	CENTURIES OF SANTA 600QXM515-3	YR	6.00	22.00
94	JOLLY VISITOR 575QXM405-3	YR	5.75	14.00
94	LOVE WAS BORN 450QXM404-3	YR	4.50	12.00
94	NOAH'S ARK 2450QXM410-6 SET OF THREE	YR	24.50	49.00
94	NUTCRACKER GUILD 575QXM514-6	YR	5.75	15.00
94	ON THE ROAD 575QXM510-3	YR	5.75	12.00
B. SIEDLER			**MINIATURE ORNAMENTS**	
88	CANDY CANE ELF 300QXM570-1	YR	3.00	19.00
88	LITTLE DRUMMER BOY 450QXM578-4	YR	4.50	26.00
88	PENGUIN PAL-1ST EDITION 375QXM563-1	YR	3.75	29.00
88	SNUGGLY SKATER 450QXM571-4	YR	4.50	27.00
89	OLD-WORLD SANTA 300QXM569-5	YR	3.00	9.00
89	SLOW MOTION 600QXM575-2	YR	6.00	16.00
89	STROLLIN' SNOWMAN 450QXM574-2	YR	4.50	15.00
90	CHRISTMAS DOVE 450QXM563-6	YR	4.50	12.00
90	GRANDCHILD'S FIRST XMAS 600QXM572-3	YR	6.00	12.00
90	OLD-WORLD SANTA 300QXM569-5	YR	3.00	9.00
90	SWEET SLUMBER 450QXM566-3	YR	4.50	12.00
90	WEE NUTCRACKER 850QXM584-3	YR	8.50	17.00
91	MOM 600QXM569-9	YR	6.00	17.00
91	PENGUIN PAL-4TH EDITION 450QXM562-9	YR	4.50	17.00
91	SEASIDE OTTER 450QXM590-9	YR	4.50	12.00
92	GERBIL INC. 375QXM592-4	YR	3.75	11.00
92	PUPPET SHOW 300QXM557-4	YR	3.00	12.00

YR	NAME	LIMIT	ISSUE	TREND
93	CHEESE PLEASE 375QXM407-2	YR	3.75	8.00
93	MERRY MASCOT 375QXM404-2	YR	3.75	10.00
	D. UNRUH			**MINIATURE ORNAMENTS**
88	HOLY FAMILY 850QXM561-1	YR	8.50	15.00
88	JOLLY ST. NICK 800QXM572-1	YR	8.00	36.00
88	SKATER'S WALTZ 700QXM560-1	YR	7.00	22.00
89	HOLY FAMILY 850QXM561-1	YR	8.50	15.00
90	NATIVITY 450QXM570-6	YR	4.50	14.00
91	FIRST CHRISTMAS TOGETHER QXM 581-9	YR	6.00	19.00
92	A+ TEACHER 375QXM551-1	YR	3.75	8.00
92	COCA-COLA SANTA 575QXM588-4	YR	5.75	19.00
92	GRANDMA 450QXM551-4	YR	4.50	14.00
92	MINTED FOR SANTA 375QXM585-4	YR	3.75	15.00
93	MARCH OF THE TEDDY BEARS 450QXM400-5	YR	4.50	17.00
94	MARCH OF THE TEDDY BEARS 450QXM510-6	YR	4.50	12.00
	L. VOTRUBA			**MINIATURE ORNAMENTS**
88	GENTLE ANGEL 200QXM577-1	YR	2.00	19.00
89	BUNNY HUG 300QXM577-5	YR	3.00	12.00
89	FIRST CHRISTMAS TOGETHER 850QXM564-2	YR	8.50	12.00
89	HOLIDAY DEER 300QXM577-2	YR	3.00	12.00
89	REJOICE 300QXM578-2	YR	3.00	10.00
89	SCRIMSHAW REINDEER 450QXM568-5	YR	4.50	9.00
90	CLOISONNE POINSETTIA 1050QMX553-3	YR	10.50	24.00
91	COUNTRY SLEIGH 450QXM599-9	YR	4.50	14.00
91	LOVE IS BORN 600QXM595-9	YR	6.00	18.00
92	HARMONY TRIO 1175QXM547-1	YR	11.75	24.00
92	SNOWSHOE BUNNY 375QXM556-4	YR	3.75	12.00
93	BABY'S FIRST CHRISTMAS 575QXM514-5	YR	5.75	14.00
93	CLOISONNE SNOWFLAKE 975QXM401-2	YR	9.75	20.00
93	THIMBLE BELLS 575QXM514-2	YR	5.75	15.00
94	DAZZLING REINDEER 975QXM402-6	YR	9.75	20.00
94	JOLLY WOLLY SNOWMAN 375QXM409-3	YR	3.75	10.00
94	NATURE'S ANGELS 450QXM512-6	YR	4.50	12.00
	E. SEALE			**MOTHER GOOSE**
93	HUMPTY DUMPTY 1ST ED. 1375QX528-2	YR	13.75	30.00
94	HEY DIDDLE, DIDDLE 2ND ED. 1395QX521-3	YR	13.95	27.00
	*** SEALE/VOTRUBA**			**MOTHER GOOSE**
95	JACK AND JILL 3RD SERIES QX509-9	YR	13.95	20.00
	J. FRANCIS			**MR. AND MRS. CLAUS**
93	A FITTING MOMENT 8TH ED. 1475QX420-2	YR	14.75	28.00
	D. UNRUH			**MR. AND MRS. CLAUS**
86	MERRY MISTLETOE TIME 1300QX402-6	YR	13.00	87.00
87	HOME COOKING 1325QX483-7	YR	13.25	50.00
88	SHALL WE DANCE? 1300QX401-1	YR	13.00	42.00
89	HOLIDAY DUET 1325QX457-5	YR	13.25	42.00
90	POPCORN PARTY 5TH ED. 1375QX439-3	YR	13.75	45.00
91	CHECKING HIS LIST 6TH ED. 1375QX433-9	YR	13.75	30.00
92	GIFT EXCHANGE 7TH ED. 1475QX429-4	YR	14.75	27.00
94	A HANDWARMING PRESENT 9TH ED. 1495QX528-	YR	14.95	21.00
95	CHRISTMAS EVE KISS 10TH & FINAL SERIES Q	YR	14.95	19.00
	*			**MUSICAL**
82	BABY'S FIRST CHRISTMAS 1600QMB900-7	YR	16.00	67.00
82	FIRST CHRISTMAS TOGETHER 1600QMB901-9	YR	16.00	75.00
82	LOVE 1600QMB900-9	YR	16.00	70.00
83	BABY'S FIRST CHRISTMAS 1600QMB903-9	YR	16.00	70.00
83	FRIENDSHIP 1600QMB904-7	YR	16.00	102.00
83	MOTHER'S DAY-A MOTHER'S LOVE MDQ 340-7	YR	14.00	75.00
83	NATIVITY 1600QMB904-9	YR	16.00	150.00
	E. SEALE			**MUSICAL**
83	TWELVE DAYS OF CHRISTMAS 1500QMB415-9	YR	15.00	77.00
	S. PIKE			**NATURE'S ANGELS**
91	PUPPY 450QXM565-7	YR	4.50	22.00
	E. SEALE			**NATURE'S ANGELS**
90	BUNNY 450QXM573-3	YR	4.50	24.00
	*** BASTIN/FRANCIS**			**NATURE'S SKETCHBOOK**
95	BACKYARD ORCHARD QK106-9	YR	18.95	22.00
95	CHRISTMAS CARDINAL QK107-7	YR	18.95	22.00
	*** BASTIN/LYLE**			**NATURE'S SKETCHBOOK**
95	RAISING A FAMILY QK106-7	YR	18.95	22.00
95	VIOLETS AND BUTTERFLIES QK107-9	YR	16.95	22.00
	*			**NEW ATTRACTIONS**
89	FESTIVE ANGEL 675QX463-5	YR	6.75	18.00
89	GRACEFUL SWAN 675QX464-2	YR	6.75	17.00
89	ROOSTER WEATHERVANE 575QX467-5	YR	5.75	11.00
90	COUNTRY ANGEL 675QX504-6	YR	6.75	112.00
90	FELIZ NAVIDAD 675QX517-3	YR	6.75	20.00
90	GARFIELD 475QX230-3	YR	4.75	14.00
90	GINGERBREAD ELF 575QX503-3	YR	5.75	13.00
90	GOOSE CART 775QX523-6	YR	7.75	11.00
90	HOME FOR THE OWLIDAYS 675QX518-3	YR	6.75	13.00
90	MOOY CHRISTMAS 675QX493-3	YR	6.75	17.00
90	NUTSHELL CHAT 675QX519-3	YR	6.75	19.00
90	PEANUTS 475QX223-3	YR	4.75	18.00
91	MARY ENGELBREIT 475QX223-7	YR	4.75	18.00
91	PEANUTS 500QX225-7	YR	5.00	17.00
92	EGG NOG NEST 775QX512-1	YR	7.75	14.00
92	PEANUTS 500QX224-4	YR	5.00	16.00

YR	NAME	LIMIT	ISSUE	TREND
92	SANTA JOLLY WOLLY 775QX537-4	YR	7.75	7.00
	P. ANDREWS		**NEW ATTRACTIONS**	
90	SPOON RIDER 975QX549-6	YR	9.75	16.00
90	TWO PEAS IN A POD 475QX492-6	YR	4.75	27.00
92	FELIZ NAVIDAD 675QX518-1	YR	6.75	15.00
92	JESUS LOVES ME 775QX302-4	YR	7.75	11.00
92	LOVING SHEPHERD 775QX515-1	YR	7.75	14.00
92	MEMORIES TO CHERISH 1075QX516-1	YR	10.75	16.00
92	TOBOGGAN TAIL 775QX545-9	YR	7.75	16.00
	R. CHAD		**NEW ATTRACTIONS**	
89	BALANCING ELF 675QX489-5	YR	6.75	20.00
89	NUTSHELL DREAMS 575QX465-5	YR	5.75	18.00
89	NUTSHELL WORKSHOP 575QX487-2	YR	5.75	18.00
91	DINOCLAUS 775QX527-7	YR	7.75	17.00
92	SPIRIT OF CHRISTMAS STRESS 875QX523-1	YR	8.75	19.00
	K. CROW		**NEW ATTRACTIONS**	
89	COOL SWING 625QX487-5	YR	6.25	31.00
89	GOIN' SOUTH 425QX410-5	YR	4.25	20.00
89	LET'S PLAY 725QX488-2	YR	7.25	17.00
90	BEARBACK RIDER 975QX548-3	YR	9.75	20.00
90	HOT DOGGER 775QX497-6	YR	7.75	16.00
90	JOY IS IN THE AIR 775QX550-3	YR	7.75	20.00
90	SANTA SCHNOZ 675QX498-3	YR	6.75	18.00
90	THREE LITTLE PIGGIES 775QX499-6	YR	7.75	15.00
91	ON A ROLL 675QX534-7	YR	6.75	16.00
91	UP 'N' DOWN JOURNEY 975QX504-7	YR	9.75	24.00
92	DOWN-UNDER HOLIDAY 775QX514-4	YR	7.75	18.00
92	FUN ON A BIG SCALE 1075QX513-4	YR	10.75	18.00
92	GENIUS AT WORK 1075QX537-1	YR	10.75	18.00
92	HELLO-HO-HO 975QX514-1	YR	9.75	18.00
92	SANTA MARIA 1275QX507-4	YR	12.75	13.00
	P. DUTKIN		**NEW ATTRACTIONS**	
89	CACTUS COWBOY 675QX411-2	YR	6.75	37.00
89	PEPPERMINT CLOWN 2475QX450-5	YR	24.75	25.00
90	S. CLAUS TAXI 1175QX468-6	YR	11.75	25.00
	J. FRANCIS		**NEW ATTRACTIONS**	
90	KITTY'S BEST PAL 675QX471-6	YR	6.75	16.00
92	DECK THE HOGS 875QX520-4	YR	8.75	16.00
	D. LEE		**NEW ATTRACTIONS**	
89	TV BREAK 625QX409-2	YR	6.25	16.00
90	BILLBOARD BUNNY 775QX519-6	YR	7.75	15.00
90	COYOTE CAROLS 875QX499-3	YR	8.75	19.00
90	POOLSIDE WALRUS 775QX498-6	YR	7.75	15.00
90	STITCHES OF JOY 775QX518-6	YR	7.75	20.00
91	CHILLY CHAP 675QX533-9	YR	6.75	15.00
91	FELIZ NAVIDAD 675QX527-9	YR	6.75	20.00
91	SKI LIFT BUNNY 675QX544-7	YR	6.75	16.00
92	A SANTA-FULL 975QX599-1	YR	9.75	28.00
92	COOL FLIERS 1075QX547-4	YR	10.75	20.00
92	GONE WISHIN' 875QX517-1	YR	8.75	13.00
92	HONEST GEORGE 775QX506-4	YR	7.75	15.00
92	PLEASE PAUSE HERE 1475QX529-1	YR	14.75	32.00
92	SANTA'S ROUNDUP 875QX508-4	YR	8.75	19.00
92	SKIING 'ROUND 875QX521-4	YR	8.75	17.00
92	TASTY CHRISTMAS 975QX599-4	YR	9.75	17.00
	J. LYLE		**NEW ATTRACTIONS**	
89	SPARKLING SNOWFLAKE 775QX547-2	YR	7.75	17.00
90	HOLIDAY CARDINALS 775QX524-3	YR	7.75	16.00
90	NORMAN ROCKWELL ART 475QX229-6	YR	4.75	14.00
91	NORMAN ROCKWELL ART 500QX225-9	YR	5.00	16.00
92	NORMAN ROCKWELL ART 500QX222-4	YR	5.00	13.00
	D. PALMITER		**NEW ATTRACTIONS**	
92	GARFIELD 775QX537-4	YR	7.75	16.00
92	GREEN THUMB SANTA 775QX510-1	YR	7.75	14.00
92	RAPID DELIVERY 875QX509-4	YR	8.75	17.00
	S. PIKE		**NEW ATTRACTIONS**	
90	BORN TO DANCE 775QX504-3	YR	7.75	17.00
90	CHIMING IN 975QX436-6	YR	9.75	18.00
90	COZY GOOSE 575QX496-6	YR	5.75	12.00
90	MEOW MART 775QX444-6	YR	7.75	15.00
91	NUTTY SQUIRREL 575QX483-3	YR	5.75	13.00
92	HOLIDAY WISHES 775QX513-1	YR	7.75	14.00
	M. PYDA-SEVCIK		**NEW ATTRACTIONS**	
89	COUNTRY CAT 625QX467-2	YR	6.25	16.00
89	NOSTALGIC LAMB 675QX466-5	YR	6.75	13.00
90	CHRISTMAS CROC 775QX437-3	YR	7.75	16.00
	D. RHODUS		**NEW ATTRACTIONS**	
89	WIGGLY SNOWMAN 675QX489-2	YR	6.75	20.00
90	SNOOPY & WOODSTOCK 675QX472-3	YR	6.75	20.00
91	GARFIELD 775QX517-7	YR	7.75	21.00
91	SNOOPY AND WOODSTOCK 675QX519-7	YR	6.75	22.00
	A. ROGERS		**NEW ATTRACTIONS**	
89	NUTSHELL HOLIDAY 575QX465-2	YR	5.75	21.00
90	BABY UNICORN 975QX548-6	YR	9.75	17.00
90	JOLLY DOLPHIN 675QX468-3	YR	6.75	17.00
90	LONG WINTER'S NAP 675QX470-3	YR	6.75	15.00
91	CUDDLY LAMB 675QX519-9	YR	6.75	13.00

YR	NAME	LIMIT	ISSUE	TREND
91	NUTSHELL NATIVITY 675QX517-6	YR	6.75	21.00
92	HOLIDAY TEATIME 1475QX543-1	YR	14.75	25.00
92	SNOOPY & WOODSTOCK 875QX595-4	YR	8.75	22.00
L. SCHULER				**NEW ATTRACTIONS**
92	GOLF'S A BALL 675QX598-4	YR	6.75	16.00
E. SEALE				**NEW ATTRACTIONS**
89	CLAUS CONSTRUCTION 775QX488-5	YR	7.75	23.00
90	HANG IN THERE 675QX471-3	YR	6.75	17.00
90	KING KLAUS 775QX410-6	YR	7.75	12.00
90	STOCKING PALS 1075QX549-3	YR	10.75	18.00
91	BASKET BELL PLAYERS 775QX537-7	YR	7.75	18.00
91	YULE LOGGER 875QX496-7	YR	8.75	23.00
92	BEAR BELL CHAMP 775QX507-1	YR	7.75	14.00
92	MERRY "SWISS" MOUSE 775QX511-4	YR	7.75	13.00
92	NORTH POLE FIRE FIGHTER 975QX510-4	YR	9.75	18.00
92	SANTA'S HOOK SHOT 1275QX543-4	YR	12.75	25.00
92	TREAD BEAR 875QX509-1	YR	8.75	16.00
L. SICKMAN				**NEW ATTRACTIONS**
89	HORSE WEATHERVANE 575QX463-2	YR	5.75	14.00
90	CHRISTMAS PARTRIDGE 775QX524-6	YR	7.75	15.00
91	CHRISTMAS WELCOME 975QX529-9	YR	9.75	16.00
91	JOLLY WOLLY SANTA 775QX541-9	YR	7.75	19.00
91	JOLLY WOLLY SNOWMAN 775QX542-7	YR	7.75	16.00
91	JOLLY WOLLY SOLDIER 775QX542-9	YR	7.75	15.00
91	NIGHT BEFORE CHRISTMAS 975QX530-7	YR	9.75	19.00
91	OLD-FASHIONED SLED 875QX431-7	YR	8.75	13.00
91	PARTRIDGE IN A PEAR TREE 975QX529-7	YR	9.75	17.00
91	SNOWY OWL 775QX526-9	YR	7.75	16.00
92	SILVER STAR 2800QX532-4	YR	28.00	40.00
B. SIEDLER				**NEW ATTRACTIONS**
89	RODNEY REINDEER 675QX407-2	YR	6.75	11.00
90	BEARY GOOD DEAL 675QX473-3	YR	6.75	13.00
90	PEPPERONI MOUSE 675QX497-3	YR	6.75	14.00
90	PERFECT CATCH 775QX469-3	YR	7.75	15.00
90	POLAR JOGGER 575QX466-6	YR	5.75	14.00
90	POLAR PAIR 575QX462-6	YR	5.75	13.00
90	POLAR SPORT 775QX515-6	YR	7.75	15.00
90	POLAR TV 775QX516-6	YR	7.75	13.00
90	POLAR V.I.P. 575QX466-3	YR	5.75	12.00
90	POLAR VIDEO 575QX463-3	YR	5.75	12.00
91	ALL STAR 675QX532-9	YR	6.75	16.00
91	NOTES OF CHEER 575QX535-7	YR	5.75	13.00
91	POLAR CLASSIC 675QX528-7	YR	6.75	16.00
92	PARTRIDGE IN PEAR TREE 875QX523-4	YR	8.75	16.00
D. UNRUH				**NEW ATTRACTIONS**
90	LITTLE DRUMMER BOY 775QX523-3	YR	7.75	14.00
90	LOVABLE DEARS 875QX547-6	YR	8.75	14.00
91	SWEET TALK 875QX536-7	YR	8.75	15.00
92	CHEERFUL SANTA 975QX515-4	YR	9.75	26.00
L. VOTRUBA				**NEW ATTRACTIONS**
90	HAPPY VOICES 675QX464-5	YR	6.75	11.00
91	FOLK ART REINDEER 875QX535-9	YR	8.75	15.00
91	JOYOUS MEMORIES-PHOTOHOLDER 675QX536-9	YR	6.75	16.00
*				**NFL ORNAMENTS**
96	NFL BALL ORNAMENTS	YR	5.95	6.00
D. UNRUH				**NIGHT BEFORE CHRISTMAS**
94	FATHER 450QXM512-3	YR	4.50	12.00
L. VOTRUBA				**NIGHT BEFORE CHRISTMAS**
92	HOUSE 1375QXM5541	YR	13.75	35.00
93	BED 450QXM511-5	YR	4.50	18.00
L. SICKMAN				**NOEL RAILROAD**
89	LOCOMOTIVE 850QXM576-2	YR	8.50	44.00
90	COAL CAR 850QXM575-6	YR	8.50	29.00
91	PASSENGER CAR-3RD EDITION 850QXM564-9	YR	8.50	26.00
92	BOX CAR 700QXM5441	YR	7.00	22.00
93	FLATBED CAR 700QXM510-5	YR	7.00	19.00
94	STOCK CAR 700QXM511-3	YR	7.00	16.00
*				**NORMAN ROCKWELL**
80	SANTA'S VISITORS 650QX306-1	YR	6.50	195.00
88	AND TO ALL A GOOD NIGHT 775QX340-4	YR	7.75	16.00
P. DUTKIN				**NORMAN ROCKWELL**
93	FILLING THE STOCKINGS 1575QK115-5	YR	15.75	28.00
93	JOLLY POSTMAN 1575QK116-2	YR	15.75	28.00
J. LYLE				**NORMAN ROCKWELL**
88	CHRISTMAS SCENES 475QX273-1	YR	4.75	24.00
D. MCGEHEE				**NORMAN ROCKWELL**
84	CAUGHT NAPPING 750QX341-1	YR	7.50	27.00
S. PIKE				**NORMAN ROCKWELL**
86	CHECKING UP 775QX321-3	YR	7.75	18.00
L. SICKMAN				**NORTH POLE NUTCRACKERS**
92	ERIC THE BAKER 875QX524-4	YR	8.75	15.00
92	FRANZ THE ARTIST 875QX526-1	YR	8.75	20.00
92	FRIEDA THE ANIMALS' FRIEND 875QX526-4	YR	8.75	19.00
92	LUDWIG THE MUSICIAN 875QX528-1	YR	8.75	17.00
92	MAX THE TAILOR 875QX525-1	YR	8.75	17.00
92	OTTO THE CARPENTER 875QX525-4	YR	8.75	17.00

YR	NAME	LIMIT	ISSUE	TREND
	D. LEE			**NOSTALGIC HOUSES & SHOPS**
84	VICTORIAN DOLLHOUSE 1300QX448-1	YR	13.00	205.00
86	CHRISTMAS CANDY SHOPPE 1375QX403-3	YR	13.75	227.00
87	HOUSE ON MAIN ST. 1400QX483-9	YR	14.00	67.00
88	HALL BROS CARD SHOP 1450QX401-4	YR	14.50	45.00
89	U.S. POST OFFICE 1425QX458-2	YR	14.25	48.00
90	HOLIDAY HOME 7TH ED.1475QX469-6	YR	14.75	51.00
91	FIRE STATION-8TH EDITION 1475QX413-9	YR	14.75	47.00
92	FIVE-AND-TEN-CENT STORE 9TH ED. 1475QX42	YR	14.75	32.00
93	COZY HOME 10TH ED. 1475QX417-5	YR	14.75	32.00
94	NEIGHBORHOOD DRUGSTORE 11TH ED. 1495QX52	YR	14.95	20.00
	D. PALMITER			**NOSTALGIC HOUSES & SHOPS**
95	TOWN CHURCH 12TH SERIES QX515-9	YR	14.95	22.00
	P. ANDREWS			**OLD ENGLISH VILLAGE**
94	HAT SHOP 700QXM514-3	YR	7.00	16.00
	D. LEE			**OLD ENGLISH VILLAGE**
88	FAMILY HOME-1ST EDITION 850QXM563-4	YR	8.50	44.00
89	SWEET SHOP 850QXM561-5	YR	8.50	34.00
90	SCHOOL 850QXM576-3	YR	8.50	24.00
91	COUNTRY INN QXM 562-7	YR	8.50	19.00
92	CHURCH 700QXM5384	YR	7.00	29.00
93	TOY SHOP 700QXM513-2	YR	7.00	17.00
	D. PALMITER			**OLD WORLD SILVER**
93	SILVER DOVE OF PEACH 2475QK107-5	YR	24.75	34.00
93	SILVER SLEIGH 2475QK108-2	YR	24.75	34.00
93	SILVER STAR AND HOLLY 2475QK108-5	YR	24.75	34.00
94	SILVER BOWS 2475QK102-3	YR	24.75	28.00
	D. UNRUH			**OLD WORLD SILVER**
93	SILVER SANTA 2475QK109-2	YR	24.75	47.00
94	SILVER BELLS 2475QK102-6	YR	24.75	26.00
94	SILVER POINSETTIA 2475QK100-6	YR	24.75	30.00
94	SILVER SNOWFLAKES 2475QK101-6	YR	24.75	28.00
	P. DUTKIN			**OLD-FASHIONED CHRISTMAS COLLECTION**
87	LITTLE WHITTLER 600QX469-9	YR	6.00	25.00
	M. PYDA-SEVCIK			**OLD-FASHIONED CHRISTMAS COLLECTION**
87	COUNTRY WREATH 575QX470-9	YR	5.75	18.00
	L. SICKMAN			**OLD-FASHIONED CHRISTMAS COLLECTION**
87	FOLK ART SANTA 525QX474-9	YR	5.25	27.00
87	NOSTALGIC ROCKER 650QX468-9	YR	6.50	20.00
	D. UNRUH			**OLD-FASHIONED CHRISTMAS COLLECTION**
87	IN A NUTSHELL 550QX469-7	YR	5.50	19.00
*				**OLYMPIC ORNAMENTS**
96	IZZY - THE MASCOT QXE572-4	YR	9.95	10.00
96	PARADE OF NATIONS QXE574-1	YR	10.95	11.00
	D. MCGEHEE			**OLYMPIC ORNAMENTS**
96	CLOISONNE MEDALLION QXE404-1	YR	9.75	10.00
96	INVITATION TO THE GAMES QXE551-1	YR	14.95	15.00
	E. SEALE			**OLYMPIC ORNAMENTS**
96	OLYMPIC TRIUMPH QXE573-1	YR	10.95	11.00
	D. UNRUH			**OLYMPIC ORNAMENTS**
96	LIGHTING THE FLAME QXE744-4	YR	28.00	28.00
*				**OPEN HOUSE ORNAMENTS**
86	SANTA & HIS REINDEER 975QX0440-6	YR	9.75	28.00
86	SANTA'S PANDA PAL 550QX0441-3	YR	5.00	17.00
	E. SEALE			**ORNAMENT PREMIERE**
95	WISH LIST QX585-9	YR	15.00	18.00
	L. SICKMAN			**PEACE ON EARTH**
91	ITALY FIRST EDITION 1175QX512-9	YR	11.75	27.00
92	SPAIN 2ND ED. 1175QX517-4	YR	11.75	21.00
93	POLAND 3RD ED. 1175QX524-2	YR	11.75	19.00
*				**PEANUTS COLLECTION**
77	PEANUTS (2) 400QX163-5	YR	4.00	72.00
77	PEANUTS 250QX162-2	YR	2.50	57.00
77	PEANUTS 350QX135-5	YR	3.50	61.00
78	PEANUTS 250QX203-6	YR	2.50	52.00
78	PEANUTS 250QX204-3	YR	2.50	52.00
78	PEANUTS 350QX205-6	YR	3.50	55.00
78	PEANUTS 350QX206-3	YR	3.50	50.00
89	A CHARLIE BROWN CHRISTMAS 475QX276-5	YR	4.75	35.00
	R. BISHOP			**PEANUTS COLLECTION**
94	LUCY QX 520-3	YR	9.95	16.00
	D. RHODUS			**PEANUTS COLLECTION**
93	PEANUTS GANG 1ST ED. 975QX531-5	YR	9.75	36.00
*				**PERSONALIZED ORNAMENTS**
93	COOL SNOWMAN 875QP605-2	YR	8.75	9.00
93	PEANUTS 900QP604-5	YR	9.00	9.00
93	REINDEER IN THE SKY 875QP605-5	YR	8.75	6.00
	P. ANDREWS			**PERSONALIZED ORNAMENTS**
95	BABY BEAR QP615-7	YR	12.95	14.00
	K. CROW			**PERSONALIZED ORNAMENTS**
93	MAILBOX DELIVERY 1475QP601-5	YR	14.75	11.00
93	ON THE BILLBOARD 1275QP602-2	YR	12.75	11.00
94	ETCH-A-SKETCH 1295QP600-6	YR	12.95	10.00
94	MAILBOX DELIVERY 1495QP601-5	YR	14.95	11.00
94	ON THE BILLBOARD 1295QP602-2	YR	12.95	11.00

YR NAME	LIMIT	ISSUE	TREND
94 REINDEER ROOTERS 1295QP605-6	YR	12.95	13.00
95 ETCH-A-SKETCH QP601-5	YR	12.95	14.00
95 MAILBOX DELIVERY QP601-5	YR	14.95	15.00
95 ON THE BILLBOARD QP602-2	YR	12.95	14.00
95 REINDEER ROOTERS QP605-6	YR	12.95	14.00
J. FRANCIS	**PERSONALIZED ORNAMENTS**		
93 BABY BLOCK PHOTOHOLDER QP603-5	YR	14.75	16.00
93 PLAYING BALL 1275QP603-2	YR	12.75	11.00
94 BABY BLOCK PHOTOHOLDER 1495QP603-5	YR	14.95	16.00
94 PLAYING BALL 1295QP603-2	YR	12.95	11.00
95 PLAYING BALL 603-2	YR	12.95	14.00
D. PALMITER	**PERSONALIZED ORNAMENTS**		
93 GOING GOLFIN' 1275QP601-2	YR	12.75	11.00
94 GOIN' FISHIN' 1495QP602-3	YR	14.95	15.00
94 GOIN' GOLFIN' 1295QP601-2	YR	12.75	11.00
D. RHODUS	**PERSONALIZED ORNAMENTS**		
94 FROM THE HEART 1495QP603-6	YR	24.95	25.00
95 FROM THE HEART QP603-6	YR	14.95	15.00
A. ROGERS	**PERSONALIZED ORNAMENTS**		
93 FILLED W/COOKIES 1275QP604-2	YR	12.75	11.00
E. SEALE	**PERSONALIZED ORNAMENTS**		
93 HERE'S YOUR FORTUNE 1075QP600-2	YR	10.75	9.00
93 SANTA SAYS 1475QP600-5	YR	12.75	13.00
94 COMPUTER CAT 'N' MOUSE 1295QP604-6	YR	12.95	10.00
94 SANTA SAYS 1495QP600-5	YR	14.95	13.00
95 CHAMP. THE QP604-6	YR	12.95	14.00
95 KEY NOTE QP614-9	YR	12.95	15.00
B. SIEDLER	**PERSONALIZED ORNAMENTS**		
94 HOLIDAY HELLO 2495QXR611-6	YR	24.95	25.00
L. VOTRUBA	**PERSONALIZED ORNAMENTS**		
93 FESTIVE ALBUM PHOTOHOLDER QP602-5	YR	12.75	13.00
94 COOKIE TIME 1295QP607-3	YR	12.95	10.00
94 FESTIVE ALBUM PHOTOHOLDER 1295QP602-5	YR	12.95	13.00
94 NOVEL IDEA 1295QP606-6	YR	12.95	13.00
95 COOKIE TIME QP607-3	YR	12.95	14.00
95 NOVEL IDEA QP606-6	YR	12.95	14.00
A. ROGERS			**PLAYFUL PALS**
93 COCA-COLA SANTA 1475QX574-2	YR	14.75	24.00
*			**PLUSH ANIMALS**
81 CHRISTMAS TEDDY 500QX404-2	YR	5.50	17.00
81 RACCOON TUNES 550QX405-5	YR	5.50	18.00
K. CROW			**POCAHONTAS**
95 CAPTAIN JOHN SMITH AND MEEKO QX1617-9	YR	12.95	16.00
95 PERCY, FLIT AND MEEKO QX1617-9	YR	9.95	20.00
95 POCAHONTAS QX1617-7	YR	12.95	20.00
S. PIKE			**PORCELAIN BEAR**
89 CINNAMON TEDDY-7TH EDITION 875QX461-5	YR	8.75	17.00
*			**PORTRAITS IN BISQUE**
93 JOY OF SHARING 1575QK114-2	YR	15.75	27.00
S. PIKE			**PORTRAITS IN BISQUE**
93 CHRISTMAS FEAST 1575QK115-2	YR	15.75	29.00
93 MISTLETOE KISS 1575QK114-5	YR	15.75	26.00
*			**PROPERTY ORNAMENTS**
75 BETSEY CLARK (2) 350QX167-1	YR	3.50	45.00
75 BETSEY CLARK (4) 450QX168-1	YR	4.50	50.00
75 BETSEY CLARK-3RD EDITION 300QX133-1	YR	3.00	55.00
75 BUTTONS & BO (4) 500QX139-1	YR	5.00	45.00
75 CHARMERS 300QX135-1	YR	3.00	40.00
75 LITTLE MIRACLES (4) 500QX140-1	YR	5.00	40.00
75 MARTY LINKS 300QX136-1	YR	3.00	35.00
75 NORMAN ROCKWELL 250QX166-1	YR	2.50	55.00
75 NORMAN ROCKWELL 300QX134-1	YR	3.00	55.00
76 BETSEY CLARK (3) 450QX218-1	YR	4.50	52.00
76 BETSEY CLARK 250QX210-1	YR	2.50	43.00
76 BETSEY CLARK-FOURTH EDITION 300QX195-1	YR	3.00	100.00
76 CHARMERS (2) 350QX215-1	YR	3.50	52.00
76 CURRIER & IVES 250QX209-1	YR	2.50	47.00
76 CURRIER & IVES 300QX197-1	YR	3.00	47.00
76 HAPPY THE SNOWMAN (2) QX216-1	YR	3.50	47.00
76 MARTY LINKS (2) 400QX207-1	YR	4.00	40.00
76 NORMAN ROCKWELL 300QX196-1	YR	3.00	72.00
76 RAGGEDY ANN 250QX212-1	YR	2.50	62.00
76 RUDOLPH AND SANTA 250QX213-1	YR	2.50	77.00
77 BETSEY CLARK-FIFTH EDITION 350QX264-2	YR	3.50	415.00
77 CHARMERS 350QX153-5	YR	3.50	51.00
77 CURRIER & IVES 350QX130-2	YR	3.50	57.00
77 DISNEY (2) 400QX137-5	YR	4.00	42.00
77 DISNEY 350QX133-5	YR	3.50	47.00
77 GRANDMA MOSES 350QX150-2	YR	3.50	57.00
77 NORMAN ROCKWELL 350QX151-5	YR	3.50	67.00
78 BETSEY CLARK-SIXTH EDITION 350QX201-6	YR	3.50	60.00
78 DISNEY 350QX207-6	YR	3.50	70.00
78 JOAN WALSH ANGLUND 350QX221-6	YR	3.50	62.00
78 SPENCER SPARROW 350QX219-6	YR	3.50	50.00
79 BETSEY CLARK-SEVENTH EDITION 350QX201-9	YR	3.50	31.00
79 JOAN WALSH ANGLUND 350QX205-9	YR	3.50	32.00
79 MARY HAMILTON 350QX254-7	YR	3.50	21.00

YR	NAME	LIMIT	ISSUE	TREND
79	PEANUTS-TIME TO TRIM 350QX202-7	YR	3.50	33.00
79	SPENCER SPARROW 350QX200-7	YR	3.50	24.00
79	WINNIE-THE-POOH 350QX206-7	YR	3.50	29.00
80	BETSEY CLARK 650QX307-4	YR	6.50	51.00
80	BETSEY CLARK'S CHRISTMAS 750QX149-4	YR	7.50	32.00
80	BETSEY CLARK-EIGHTH EDITION 400QX215-4	YR	4.00	28.00
80	DISNEY 400QX218-1	YR	4.00	26.00
80	JOAN WALSH ANGLUND 400QX217-4	YR	4.00	24.00
80	MARTY LINKS 400QX221-4	YR	4.00	14.00
80	MARY HAMILTON 400QX219-4	YR	4.00	17.00
80	MUPPETS 400QX220-1	YR	4.00	31.00
80	PEANUTS 400QX216-1	YR	4.00	25.00
81	BETSEY CLARK 900QX423-5	YR	9.00	61.00
81	BETSEY CLARK BLUE CAMEO QX 512-2	YR	8.50	25.00
81	BETSEY CLARK-9TH EDITION 450QX802-2	YR	4.50	26.00
81	DISNEY 450QX805-5	YR	4.50	22.00
81	JOAN WALSH ANGLUND 450QX804-2	YR	4.50	20.00
81	MARTY LINKS 450QX808-2	YR	4.50	16.00
81	MARY HAMILTON 450QX806-2	YR	4.50	17.00
81	MUPPETS 450QX807-5	YR	4.50	31.00
81	PEANUTS 450QX803-5	YR	4.50	25.00
82	BETSEY CLARK 850QX305-6	YR	8.50	24.00
82	BETSEY CLARK SERIES QX 215-6	YR	4.50	26.00
82	DISNEY 450QX217-3	YR	4.50	28.00
82	JOAN WALSH ANGLUND 450QX219-3	YR	4.50	17.00
82	MARY HAMILTON 450QX217-6	YR	4.50	18.00
82	MISS PIGGY & KERMIT 450QX218-3	YR	4.50	33.00
82	MUPPETS PARTY 450QX218-6	YR	4.50	37.00
82	NORMAN ROCKWELL 450QX202-3	YR	4.50	21.00
82	NORMAN ROCKWELL-3RD EDITION 850QX305-3	YR	8.50	20.00
82	PEANUTS 450QX200-6	YR	4.50	30.00
83	BETSEY CLARK 900QX440-1	YR	9.00	28.00
83	BETSEY CLARK-11TH EDITION 450QX211-9	YR	4.50	26.00
83	DISNEY 450QX212-9	YR	4.50	42.00
83	MARY HAMILTON 450QX213-7	YR	4.50	26.00
83	MISS PIGGY 1300QX405-7	YR	13.00	205.00
83	MUPPETS, THE- 450QX214-7	YR	4.50	47.00
83	NORMAN ROCKWELL 450QX215-7	YR	4.50	42.00
83	NORMAN ROCKWELL 4TH EDITION 750QX300-7	YR	7.50	28.00
83	PEANUTS 450QX212-7	YR	4.50	24.00
83	SHIRT TALES 450QX214-9	YR	4.50	19.00
84	BETSEY CLARK ANGEL 900QX462-4	YR	9.00	30.00
84	CURRIER & IVES 450QX250-1	YR	4.50	20.00
84	DISNEY 450QX250-4	YR	4.50	28.00
84	KATYBETH 900QX463-1	YR	9.00	18.00
84	KIT 550QX453-4	YR	5.50	22.00
84	MUPPETS, THE- 450QX251-4	YR	4.50	27.00
84	PEANUTS 450QX252-1	YR	4.50	28.00
84	SHIRT TALES 450QX252-4	YR	4.50	15.00
85	A DISNEY CHRISTMAS 475QX271-2	YR	4.75	29.00
85	BETSEY CLARK 850QX508-5	YR	8.50	20.00
85	FRAGGLE ROCK HOLIDAY 475QX265-5	YR	4.75	16.00
85	HUGGA BUNCH 500QX271-5	YR	5.00	17.00
85	MERRY SHIRT TALES 475QX267-2	YR	4.75	17.00
85	PEANUTS 475QX266-5	YR	4.75	21.00
85	RAINBOW BRITE AND FRIENDS 475QX268-2	YR	4.75	18.00
86	KATYBETH W/STAR 700QX435-3	YR	7.00	18.00
86	NORMAN ROCKWELL 475QX276-3	YR	4.75	21.00
86	PEANUTS 475QX276-6	YR	4.75	27.00
86	SHIRT TALES PARADE 475QX277-3	YR	4.75	13.00
J. FRANCIS			**PROPERTY ORNAMENTS**	
81	DIVINE MISS PIGGY, THE 120QX425-5	YR	12.00	85.00
81	KERMIT THE FROG 900QX424-2	YR	9.00	97.00
82	DIVINE MISS PIGGY, THE 1200QX425-5	YR	12.00	85.00
D. LEE			**PROPERTY ORNAMENTS**	
82	KERMIT THE FROG 1100QX495-6	YR	11.00	90.00
83	KERMIT THE FROG 1100QX495-6	YR	11.00	90.00
84	MUFFIN 550QX442-1	YR	5.50	26.00
D. MCGEHEE			**PROPERTY ORNAMENTS**	
84	NORMAN ROCKWELL QX 251-1	YR	4.50	17.00
85	NORMAN ROCKWELL 475QX266-2	YR	4.75	25.00
M. PYDA-SEVCIK			**PROPERTY ORNAMENTS**	
86	STATUE OF LIBERTY, THE 600QX384-3	YR	6.00	19.00
E. SEALE			**PROPERTY ORNAMENTS**	
83	BETSEY CLARK 650QX404-7	YR	6.50	35.00
84	SNOOPY & WOODSTOCK 750QX439-1	YR	7.50	80.00
86	HEATHCLIFF 750QX436-3	YR	7.50	18.00
L. SICKMAN			**PROPERTY ORNAMENTS**	
75	BETSEY CLARK 250QX163-1	YR	2.50	38.00
75	CURRIER & IVES (2) 250QX164-1	YR	2.50	40.00
75	CURRIER & IVES (2) 400QX137-1	YR	4.00	45.00
75	RAGGEDY ANN & RAGGEDY ANDY 400QX138-1	YR	4.00	65.00
75	RAGGEDY ANN 250QX165-1	YR	2.50	45.00
B. SIEDLER			**PROPERTY ORNAMENTS**	
85	KIT THE SHEPHERD 575QX484-5	YR	5.75	20.00
85	MUFFIN THE ANGEL 575QX483-5	YR	5.75	23.00
85	SNOOPY AND WOODSTOCK 750QX491-5	YR	7.50	47.00
86	PADDINGTON BEAR 600QX435-6	YR	6.00	33.00

YR	NAME	LIMIT	ISSUE	TREND
86	SNOOPY AND WOODSTOCK 800QX438-3	YR	8.00	38.00
	B. SIEDLER	**REINDEER CHAMPS**		
86	DASHER 1ST EDITION 750QX422-3	YR	7.50	122.00
87	DANCER 750QX480-9	YR	7.50	45.00
88	PRANCER 750QX405-1	YR	7.50	30.00
89	VIXEN 4TH EDITION 775QX456-2	YR	7.75	19.00
90	COMET 5TH ED. 775QX443-3	YR	7.75	21.00
91	CUPID 6TH EDITION775QX434-7	YR	7.75	25.00
92	DONNER 7TH ED. 875QX528-4	YR	8.75	23.00
93	BLITZEN 8TH ED. 875QX433-1	YR	8.75	18.00
	L. SICKMAN	**ROCKING HORSE**		
88	DAPPLED 450QXM562-4	YR	4.50	42.00
89	PALOMINO 450QXM560-5	YR	4.50	27.00
90	PINTO 450QXM574-3	YR	4.50	22.00
91	GREY ARABIAN 450QXM563-7	YR	4.50	22.00
92	BROWN HORSE 450QXM5454	YR	4.50	17.00
93	APPALOOSA 450QXM511-2	YR	4.50	12.00
93	ROCKING HORSE 13TH ED. 1075QX416-2	YR	10.75	25.00
94	WHITE 450QXM511-6	YR	4.50	11.00
	K. CROW	**SANTA & HIS REINDEER COLLECTION**		
92	COMET & CUPID 495XPR973-7	YR	4.95	11.00
92	DASHER & DANCER 495XPR973-5	YR	4.95	16.00
92	DONDER & BLITZEN 495XPR973-8	YR	4.95	16.00
92	PRANCER & VIXEN 495XPR973-6	YR	4.95	11.00
92	SANTA & SLEIGH 495XPR973-9	YR	4.95	13.00
*		**SANTA & SPARKY**		
87	PERFECT PORTRAIT 1950QLX701-9	YR	19.50	55.00
88	ON WITH THE SNOW 1950QLX719-1	YR	19.50	35.00
*		**SANTA CLAUS-THE MOVIE**		
85	SANTA CLAUS 675QX300-5	YR	6.75	5.00
85	SANTA'S VILLLAGE 675QX300-2	YR	6.75	5.00
*		**SARAH, PLAIN AND TALL COLLECTION**		
94	COUNTRY CHURCH, THE 795XPR945-0	YR	7.95	19.00
94	HAYS TRAIN STATION, THE-795XPR945-2	YR	7.95	17.00
94	MRS. PARKLEY'S GENERAL STORE 795XPR945-1	YR	7.95	16.00
94	SARAH'S MAINE HOME 795XPR945-4	YR	7.95	22.00
94	SARAH'S PARIRIE HOME 795XPR945-3	YR	7.95	20.00
*		**SEWN TRIMMERS**		
79	ANGEL MUSIC 200QX343-9	YR	2.00	21.00
79	MERRY SANTA 200QX342-7	YR	2.00	21.00
79	ROCKING HORSE, THE- 200QX340-7	YR	2.00	23.00
79	STUFFED FULL STOCKING 200QX341-9	YR	2.00	24.00
	P. ANDREWS	**SHOWCASE ORNAMENTS/CHRISTMAS LIGHTS**		
94	MOONBEAMS 1575QK111-6	YR	15.75	21.00
	R. CHAD	**SHOWCASE ORNAMENTS/CHRISTMAS LIGHTS**		
94	PEACEFUL VILLAGE 1575QK110-6	YR	15.75	23.00
	D. PALMITER	**SHOWCASE ORNAMENTS/CHRISTMAS LIGHTS**		
94	HOME FOR THE HOLIDAYS 1575QK112-3	YR	15.75	21.00
	A. ROGERS	**SHOWCASE ORNAMENTS/CHRISTMAS LIGHTS**		
94	MOTHER AND CHILD 1575QK112-6	YR	15.75	27.00
	J. LYLE	**SPECIAL EDITION**		
95	VICTORIAN TOY BOX QLX735-7	YR	42.00	47.00
	D. UNRUH	**SPECIAL EDITION**		
95	BEVERLY AND TEDDY QX525-9	YR	21.75	24.00
	A. ROGERS	**STAR TREK**		
95	CAPTAIN JAMES T. KIRK QX1553-9	YR	13.95	31.00
95	CAPTAIN JEAN-LUC PICARD QX1573-7	YR	13.95	27.00
	L. NORTON	**STAR TREK: THE NEXT GENERATION**		
94	KLINGON BIRD OF PREY 2400QLX738-6	YR	24.00	42.00
*		**SYMBOLS OF CHRISTMAS**		
95	JOLLY SANTA QX108-7	YR	15.95	20.00
95	SWEET SONG QX108-9	YR	15.95	20.00
*		**TALE OF PETER RABBIT**		
94	BEATRIX POTTER 500QX244-3	YR	5.00	9.00
	K. CROW	**TEDDY BEAR YEARS COLLECTION**		
94	BABY'S SECOND CHRISTMAS 795QX571-6	YR	7.95	10.00
95	BABY'S FIRST CHRISTMAS QX 555-9	YR	7.95	18.00
95	BABY'S SECOND CHRISTMAS QX556-7	YR	7.95	13.00
95	CHILD'S THIRD CHRISTMAS QX562-7	YR	7.95	10.00
	J. FRANCIS	**TEDDY BEAR YEARS COLLECTION**		
94	CHILD'S FOURTH CHRISTMAS 695QX572-6	YR	6.95	11.00
94	CHILD'S THIRD CHRISTMAS 695QX572-3	YR	6.95	11.00
95	CHILD'S FOURTH CHRISTMAS QX562-9	YR	6.95	9.00
	D. RHODUS	**TEDDY BEAR YEARS COLLECTION**		
94	CHILD'S FIFTH CHRISTMAS 695QX573-3	YR	6.95	11.00
95	CHILD'S FIFTH CHRISTMAS QX563-7	YR	6.95	9.00
	E. SEALE	**TENDER TOUCHES**		
91	FANFARE BEAR 875QX533-7	YR	8.75	17.00
91	GLEE CLUB BEARS 875QX496-9	YR	8.75	18.00
91	LOOK OUT BELOW 875QX495-9	YR	8.75	18.00
91	LOVING STITCHES 875QX498-7	YR	8.75	28.00
91	PLUM DELIGHTFUL 875QX497-7	YR	8.75	16.00
91	SNOW TWINS 875QX497-9	YR	8.75	16.00
93	DOWNHILL DASH	OP	23.00	23.00
93	GARDEN CAPERS	OP	20.00	20.00
93	HANDLING BIG THIRST	OP	21.00	21.00

YR	NAME	LIMIT	ISSUE	TREND
93	LIBERTY MOUSE	OP	21.00	21.00
93	MR. REPAIR BEAR	OP	18.00	18.00
93	PATRIOT GEORGE	OP	25.00	25.00
93	SCULPTING SANTA	OP	20.00	20.00
93	STITCHING STARS	OP	21.00	21.00
93	TEETER FOR TWO	OP	23.00	23.00
94	"TENTS" SITUATIONS	OP	25.00	25.00
94	CHIPMUNK KETTLEDRUM	RT	18.00	21.00
94	CHRISTMAS PLAYERS	OP	25.00	25.00
94	EASTER STROLL	OP	21.00	21.00
94	LOVE AT FIRST SIGHT	OP	23.00	23.00
94	MAKING A SPLASH	OP	20.00	20.00
94	OLD SWIMMING HOLE, THE	9500	60.00	60.00
94	PLAYGROUND GO ROUND	OP	23.00	23.00
94	SOMETHING'S BREWING	OP	23.00	23.00
94	TEE FOR TWO	OP	23.00	23.00
94	WHERE'S THE FIRE	OP	25.00	25.00
D. RHODUS				**THE FLINTSTONES**
94	FRED & BARNEY 1495QX500-3	YR	14.95	21.00
95	BETTY AND WILMA QX541-7	YR	14.95	17.00
95	FRED AND DINO QLX728-9	YR	28.00	35.00
A. ROGERS				**THE KRINGLES**
93	WREATH QXM 513-5	YR	5.75	12.00
*				**THE OLYMPIC SPIRIT**
95	CENTENNIAL GAMES ATLANTA 1996 QX316-9	YR	7.95	16.00
*				**THIMBLE SERIES**
79	A CHRISTMAS SALUTE 300QX131-9	YR	3.00	155.00
81	ANGEL 450QX413-5	YR	4.50	120.00
82	THIMBLE-5TH EDITION 500QX451-3	YR	5.00	62.00
83	THIMBLE ELF - 6TH EDITION 500QX401-7	YR	5.00	26.00
86	PARTRIDGE-THIMBLE 9TH ED. 575QX406-6	YR	5.75	19.00
A. ROGERS				**THIMBLE SERIES**
89	PUPPY 12TH ED. 575QX455-2	YR	5.75	18.00
B. SIEDLER				**THIMBLE SERIES**
84	ANGEL 500QX430-4	YR	5.00	46.00
85	SANTA QX 472-5	YR	5.50	27.00
87	DRUMMER 575QX441-9	YR	5.75	24.00
J. LYLE				**TIME FOR LOVE**
90	CARDINALS 475QX213-3	YR	4.75	11.00
D. PALMITER				**TINY TOON ADVENTURE**
94	BABS BUNNY 575QXM411-6	YR	5.75	12.00
94	BUSTER BUNNY 575QXM516-3	YR	5.75	12.00
94	DIZZY DEVIL 575QXM413-3	YR	5.75	14.00
94	HAMTON 575QXM412-6	YR	5.75	12.00
94	PLUCKY DUCK 575QXM412-3	YR	5.75	12.00
*				**TRADITIONAL ORNAMENTS**
84	A SAVIOR IS BORN 450QX254-1	YR	4.50	25.00
84	AMANDA DOLL 900QX432-1	YR	9.00	24.00
84	EMBROIDERED HEART 650QX421-7	YR	6.50	19.00
84	HOLIDAY FRIENDSHIP 1300QX445-1	YR	13.00	26.00
84	HOLIDAY STARBURST 500QX253-4	YR	5.00	16.00
84	OLD FASHIONED ROCKING HORSE 750QX346-4	YR	7.50	16.00
84	PEACE ON EARTH 750QX341-4	YR	7.50	20.00
84	SANTA 750QX458-4	YR	7.50	15.00
84	SANTA SULKY DRIVER 900QX436-1	YR	9.00	27.00
84	WHITE CHRISTMAS 1600QX905-1	YR	16.00	67.00
84	XMAS MEMORIES PHOTOHOLDER 650QX300-4	YR	6.50	24.00
85	CHRISTMAS TREATS 550QX507-5	YR	5.50	15.00
85	OLD-FASHIONED WREATH 750QX373-5	YR	7.50	15.00
86	HOLIDAY JINGLE BELL 1600QX404-6	YR	16.00	37.00
86	MEMORIES TO CHERISH PHOTO. QX 427-6	YR	7.50	21.00
87	SPECIAL MEMORIES PHOTOHOLDER 675QX464-7	YR	6.75	17.00
K. CROW				**TRADITIONAL ORNAMENTS**
87	HEAVENLY HARMONY 1500QX465-9	YR	15.00	31.00
87	PROMISE OF PEACE 650QX374-9	YR	11.00	16.00
P. DUTKIN				**TRADITIONAL ORNAMENTS**
85	SANTA PIPE 950QX494-2	YR	9.50	19.00
D. LEE				**TRADITIONAL ORNAMENTS**
84	CUCKOO CLOCK 1000QX455-1	YR	10.00	43.00
85	SPIRIT OF SANTA CLAUS, THE- 2250QX498-5	YR	22.50	90.00
J. LYLE				**TRADITIONAL ORNAMENTS**
87	CURRIER & IVES: AMERICAN FARM 475QX282-9	YR	4.75	17.00
87	I REMEMBER SANTA 475QX278-9	YR	4.75	18.00
87	NORMAN ROCKWELL: XMAS SCENES 475QX282-7	YR	4.75	18.00
D. PALMITER				**TRADITIONAL ORNAMENTS**
84	MADONNA AND CHILD 600QX344-1	YR	6.00	27.00
J. PATTEE				**TRADITIONAL ORNAMENTS**
86	CHRISTMAS BEAUTY 600QX322-3	YR	6.00	7.00
86	GLOWING CHRISTMAS TREE 700QX428-6	YR	7.00	12.00
86	HEIRLOOM SNOWFLAKE 675QX515-3	YR	6.75	16.00
S. PIKE				**TRADITIONAL ORNAMENTS**
84	NEEDLEPOINT WREATH 650QX459-4	YR	6.50	12.00
85	CANDLE CAMEO 675QX374-2	YR	6.75	14.00
85	PEACEFUL KINGDOM 575QX373-2	YR	5.75	16.00
85	SEWN PHOTOHOLDER 700QX379-5	YR	7.00	19.00
86	MAGI, THE- 475QX272-6	YR	4.75	14.00

YR	NAME	LIMIT	ISSUE	TREND
	E. SEALE		**TRADITIONAL ORNAMENTS**	
84	ALPINE ELF 600QX452-1	YR	6.00	33.00
84	GIFT OF MUSIC 1500QX451-1	YR	15.00	87.00
84	TWELVE DAYS OF CHRISTMAS 1500QX415-9	YR	15.00	77.00
87	JOYOUS ANGEL 775QX465-7	YR	7.75	17.00
	L. SICKMAN		**TRADITIONAL ORNAMENTS**	
84	CHICKADEE 600QX451-4	YR	6.00	33.00
84	EMBROIDERED STOCKING 650QX479-6	YR	6.50	16.00
84	HOLIDAY JESTER 1100QX437-4	YR	11.00	31.00
84	NOSTALGIC SLED 600QX442-4	YR	6.00	20.00
84	UNCLE SAM 600QX449-1	YR	6.00	37.00
85	NOSTALGIC SLED 600QX442-4	YR	6.00	20.00
86	BLUEBIRD 725QX428-3	YR	7.25	42.00
87	GOLDFINCH 700QX464-9	YR	7.00	49.00
	D. UNRUH		**TRADITIONAL ORNAMENTS**	
87	CHRISTMAS KEYS 575QX473-9	YR	5.75	22.00
	L. VOTRUBA		**TRADITIONAL ORNAMENTS**	
86	STAR BRIGHTENERS 600QX322-6	YR	6.00	10.00
	*		**TREE TOPPER**	
77	ANGEL TREE TOPPER 900HD230-2	YR	9.00	425.00
79	TIFFANY ANGEL TREE TOPPER 1000QX703-7	YR	10.00	31.00
84	ANGEL TREE TOPPER 2450QTT710-1	YR	24.50	36.00
86	A SHINING STAR 1750QLT709-6	YR	17.50	60.00
86	SANTA TREE TOPPER 1800QTO700-6	YR	18.00	35.00
	K. CROW		**TURN OF THE CENTURY PARADE**	
95	FIREMAN, THE/FIRST SERIES QK102-7	YR	16.95	26.00
	*		**TWELVE DAYS OF CHRISTMAS**	
89	SIX GEESE A-LAYING 6TH ED. 675QX381-2	YR	6.75	16.00
90	SEVEN SWANS-A-SWIMMING 7TH ED. 675QX303-	YR	6.75	18.00
91	EIGHT MAIDS-A-MILKING 8TH ED. 675QX308-9	YR	6.75	18.00
94	ELEVEN PIPERS PIPING 11TH ED. 695QX318-3	YR	6.95	8.00
95	TWELVE DRUMMERS DRUMMING 12TH & FINAL QX	YR	6.95	9.00
	S. PIKE		**TWELVE DAYS OF CHRISTMAS**	
87	FOUR COLLY BIRDS 650QX370-9	YR	6.50	29.00
88	FIVE GOLDEN RINGS 650QX371-4	YR	6.50	29.00
	M. PYDA-SEVCIK		**TWELVE DAYS OF CHRISTMAS**	
92	NINE LADIES DANCING 9TH ED. 675QX303-1	YR	6.75	16.00
	L. VOTRUBA		**TWELVE DAYS OF CHRISTMAS**	
86	THREE FRENCH HENS 650QX378-6	YR	6.50	30.00
	D. LEE		**WINDOWS OF THE WORLD**	
85	MEXICAN QX 490-2	YR	9.75	95.00
87	HAWAIIAN 1000QX482-7	YR	10.00	20.00
88	FRENCH 1000QX402-1	YR	10.00	34.00
89	GERMAN 5TH ED. 1075QX462-5	YR	10.75	25.00
90	IRISH 6TH ED. 1075QX463-6	YR	10.75	16.00
	B. SIEDLER		**WINDOWS OF THE WORLD**	
86	DUTCH 1000QX408-3	YR	10.00	45.00
	B. SIEDLER		**WINNIE THE POOH COLLECTION**	
91	CHRISTOPHER ROBIN 975QX557-9	YR	9.75	30.00
91	KANGA AND ROO 975QX561-7	YR	9.75	43.00
91	PIGLET AND EEYORE 975QX557-7	YR	9.75	42.00
91	RABBIT 975QX560-7	YR	9.75	27.00
91	TIGGER 975QX560-9	YR	9.75	97.00
91	WINNIE-THE POOH 975QX556-9	YR	9.75	46.00
92	OWL 975QX561-4	YR	9.75	24.00
93	EEYORE 975-QX571-2	YR	9.75	16.00
93	KANGA AND ROO 975QX567-2	YR	9.75	17.00
93	OWL 975QX569-5	YR	9.75	16.00
93	RABBIT 975QX570-2	YR	9.75	16.00
93	TIGGER AND PIGLET 975QX570-5	YR	9.75	32.00
93	WINNIE THE POOH 975QX571-5	YR	9.75	29.00
	P. ANDREWS		**WIZARD OF OZ COLLECTION**	
94	COWARDLY LION, THE 995QX544-6	YR	9.95	20.00
	J. LYLE		**WIZARD OF OZ COLLECTION**	
94	DOROTHY AND TOTO 1095QX543-3	YR	10.95	34.00
95	GELINDA, WITCH OF THE NORTH QX574-9	YR	13.95	23.00
	D. UNRUH		**WIZARD OF OZ COLLECTION**	
94	SCARECROW 995QX543-6	YR	9.95	22.00
94	TIN MAN 995QX544-3	YR	9.95	23.00
	*		**WOOD CHILDHOOD**	
89	TRUCK 6TH ED. 775QX459-5	YR	7.75	18.00
	K. CROW		**WOOD CHILDHOOD**	
86	REINDEER 750QX407-3	YR	7.50	22.00
	P. DUTKIN		**WOOD CHILDHOOD**	
85	TRAIN-2ND IN SERIES 700QX472-2	YR	7.00	36.00
88	AIRPLANE, 5TH ED. 750QX404-1	YR	7.50	24.00
	B. SIEDLER		**WOOD CHILDHOOD**	
87	HORSE 750QX441-7	YR	7.50	17.00
	*		**YARN ORNAMENTS**	
73	ANGEL 125XHD78-5	YR	1.25	29.00
73	BLUE GIRL 125XHD85-2	YR	1.25	25.00
73	BOY CAROLER 125XHD83-2	YR	1.25	26.00
73	CHOIR BOY 125XHD80-5	YR	1.25	27.00
73	ELF 125XHD79-2	YR	1.25	26.00
73	GREEN GIRL 125XHD84-5	YR	1.25	26.00
73	LITTLE GIRL 125XHD82-5	YR	1.25	23.00

YR	NAME	LIMIT	ISSUE	TREND
73	MR. SANTA 125XHD74-5	YR	1.25	27.00
73	MR. SNOWMAN 125XHD76-5	YR	1.25	23.00
73	MRS. SANTA 125XHD75-2	YR	1.25	25.00
73	MRS. SNOWMAN 125XHD77-2	YR	1.25	23.00
73	SOLDIER 100XHD81-2	YR	1.00	23.00
74	ANGEL 150QX103-1	YR	1.50	27.00
74	ELF 150QX101-1	YR	1.50	23.00
74	MRS. SANTA 150QX100-1	YR	1.50	27.00
74	SANTA 150QX105-1	YR	1.50	27.00
74	SNOWMAN 150QX104-1	YR	1.50	23.00
74	SOLDIER 150QX102-1	YR	1.50	23.00
75	DRUMMER BOY 175QX123-1	YR	1.75	26.00
75	LITTLE GIRL 175QX126-1	YR	1.75	22.00
75	MRS. SANTA 175QX125-1	YR	1.75	24.00
75	RAGGEDY ANDY 175QX122-1	YR	1.75	42.00
75	RAGGEDY ANN 175QX121-1	YR	1.75	37.00
75	SANTA 175QX124-1	YR	1.75	23.00
76	CAROLER 175QX126-1	YR	1.75	22.00
76	DRUMMER BOY 175QX123-1	YR	1.75	27.00
76	MRS. SANTA 175QX125-1	YR	1.75	24.00
76	RAGGEDY ANDY 175QX122-1	YR	1.75	42.00
76	RAGGEDY ANN 175QX121-1	YR	1.75	37.00
76	SANTA 175QX124-1	YR	1.75	23.00
78	GREEN BOY 200QX123-1	YR	2.00	23.00
78	GREEN GIRL 200QX126-1	YR	2.00	19.00
78	MR. CLAUS 200QX340-3	YR	2.00	23.00
78	MRS. CLAUS 200QX125-1	YR	2.00	24.00
80	ANGEL 300QX162-1	YR	3.00	11.00
80	SANTA 300QX161-4	YR	3.00	11.00
80	SNOWMAN 300QX163-4	YR	3.00	11.00
80	SOLDIER 300QX164-1	YR	3.00	11.00
*		**YESTERYEARS COLLECTION**		
77	ANGEL 600QX172-2	YR	6.00	90.00
77	HOUSE 600QX170-2	YR	6.00	122.00
77	JACK-IN-THE-BOX 600QX171-5	YR	6.00	122.00
77	REINDEER 600QX173-5	YR	6.00	127.00
L. SICKMAN		**YULETIDE CENTRAL**		
94	LOCOMOTIVE 1ST ED. 1895QX531-6	YR	18.95	46.00
HAMILTON GIFTS				
M. HUMPHREY BOGART		**MAUD HUMPHREY BOGART ORNAMENTS**		
89	SARAH H1367	19500	35.00	38.00
90	CATHERINE H1366	19500	35.00	38.00
90	GRETCHEN H1369	19500	35.00	38.00
90	MICHELLE H1370	19500	35.00	38.00
90	REBECCA H5513	19500	35.00	38.00
90	VICTORIA H1365	19500	35.00	38.00
91	CLEANING HOUSE 915084	OP	24.00	24.00
91	GIFT OF LOVE 915092	OP	24.00	24.00
91	MY FIRST DANCE 915106	OP	24.00	24.00
91	SARAH 915165	OP	24.00	24.00
91	SPECIAL FRIENDS 915114	OP	24.00	24.00
91	SUSANNA 915122	OP	24.00	24.00
92	HOLLIES FOR YOU 915726	YR	24.00	24.00
HAND & HAMMER				
C. DEMATTEO		**HAND & HAMMER ANNUAL ORNAMENTS**		
87	SILVER BELLS-737	YR	38.00	50.00
88	SILVER BELLS-792	YR	39.50	40.00
89	SILVER BELLS-843	YR	39.50	40.00
90	SILVER BELLS REV.-964	YR	39.00	39.00
90	SILVER BELLS-1080	YR	39.50	40.00
90	SILVER BELLS-865	YR	39.00	39.00
91	SILVER BELLS-1080	OP	39.50	40.00
92	SILVER BELLS-1148	4100	39.50	40.00
C. DEMATTEO		**HAND & HAMMER ORNAMENTS**		
80	ICICLE-009	490	25.00	30.00
81	GABRIEL WITH LIBERTY CAP-301	275	25.00	50.00
81	GABRIEL-320	SU	25.00	32.00
81	ROUNDEL-109	220	25.00	45.00
82	CARVED HEART-425	SU	29.00	48.00
82	FLEUR DE LYS ANGEL-343	320	28.00	35.00
82	MADONNA & CHILD-388	175	28.00	50.00
82	STRAW STAR-448	590	25.00	40.00
83	CALLIGRAPHIC DEER-511	SU	25.00	29.00
83	CHERUB-528	295	29.00	50.00
83	DOVE-522	*	13.00	13.00
83	EGYPTIAN CAT-521	*	13.00	13.00
83	FIRE ANGEL-473	315	25.00	30.00
83	INDIAN-494	190	29.00	50.00
83	JAPANESE SNOWFLAKE-534	350	29.00	35.00
83	POLLOCK ANGEL-502	SU	35.00	50.00
83	SARGENT ANGEL-523	690	29.00	34.00
83	SUNBURST-543	*	13.00	50.00
83	WISE MAN-549	SU	29.00	36.00
84	BEARDSLEY ANGEL-398	OP	28.00	48.00
84	BIRD & CHERUB-588	*	13.00	30.00
84	BUNNY-582	*	13.00	30.00

YR	NAME	LIMIT	ISSUE	TREND
84	CRESCENT ANGEL-559	SU	30.00	32.00
84	FREER STAR-553	*	13.00	30.00
84	IBEX-584	400	29.00	50.00
84	MANGER-601	SU	29.00	32.00
84	MORAVIAN STAR-595	OP	38.00	50.00
84	MT. VERNON WEATHERVANE-602	SU	32.00	39.00
84	NINE HEARTS-572	275	34.00	50.00
84	PINEAPPLE-558	SU	30.00	38.00
84	PRAYING ANGEL-576	SU	29.00	30.00
84	ROCKING HORSE-581	*	13.00	13.00
84	ROSETTE-571	220	32.00	50.00
84	USHS 1984 ANGEL-574	SU	35.00	50.00
84	WILD SWAN-592	SU	35.00	50.00
84	WREATH-575	*	13.00	30.00
85	ABIGAIL-613	500	32.00	50.00
85	ANGEL-607	225	36.00	50.00
85	ANGEL-612	217	32.00	50.00
85	ART DECO DEER-620	SU	34.00	38.00
85	AUDUBON BLUEBIRD-615	SU	48.00	60.00
85	AUDUBON SWALLOW-614	SU	48.00	60.00
85	BICYCLE-669	*	13.00	30.00
85	BUTTERFLY-646	SU	39.00	39.00
85	CAMEL-655	*	13.00	30.00
85	CAROUSEL PONY-618	*	13.00	13.00
85	CHERUB-642	815	37.00	37.00
85	CRANE-606	150	39.00	50.00
85	EAGLE-652	375	30.00	50.00
85	FAMILY-659	915	32.00	40.00
85	FRENCH QUARTER HEART-647	OP	37.00	36.00
85	GEORGE WASHINGTON-629	SU	35.00	39.00
85	GRASSHOPPER-634	OP	32.00	39.00
85	GUARDIAN ANGEL-616	1340	35.00	39.00
85	HALLEY'S COMET-621	432	35.00	50.00
85	HERALD ANGEL-641	SU	36.00	40.00
85	HOSANNA-635	715	32.00	50.00
85	LAFARGE ANGEL-658	SU	32.00	50.00
85	LIBERTY BELL-611	SU	32.00	40.00
85	MADONNA-666	227	35.00	50.00
85	MERMAID-622	SU	35.00	75.00
85	MILITIAMAN-608	460	25.00	30.00
85	MODEL A FORD-604	*	13.00	30.00
85	NUTCRACKER-609	510	30.00	50.00
85	OLD NORTH CHURCH-661	OP	35.00	39.00
85	PEACOCK-603	470	34.00	37.00
85	PIAZZA-653	SU	32.00	50.00
85	REINDEER-656	*	13.00	30.00
85	SAMANTHA-648	SU	35.00	36.00
85	SHEPHERD-617	1770	35.00	39.00
85	ST. NICHOLAS-670	*	13.00	30.00
85	TEDDY-637	SU	37.00	40.00
85	UNICORN-660	SU	37.00	37.00
85	USHS BLUEBIRD-631	SU	29.00	50.00
85	USHS MADONNA-630	SU	35.00	50.00
85	USHS SWALLOW-632	SU	29.00	50.00
86	ARCHANGEL-684	SU	29.00	65.00
86	BEAR CLAUS-692	*	13.00	13.00
86	CHRISTMAS TREE-708	*	13.00	13.00
86	HALLELUJAH-686	*	38.00	38.00
86	KRINGLE BEAR-723	*	13.00	30.00
86	LAFARGE ANGEL-710	SU	31.00	50.00
86	MOTHER GOOSE-719	OP	34.00	40.00
86	NATIVITY-679	SU	36.00	38.00
86	NIGHTINGALE-716	SU	35.00	50.00
86	NUTCRACKER-681	1356	37.00	37.00
86	PHAETON-683	*	13.00	13.00
86	PRANCER-698	OP	38.00	38.00
86	SALEM LAMB-712	SU	32.00	40.00
86	SANTA SKATES-715	SU	36.00	36.00
86	SNOWFLAKE-713	SU	36.00	40.00
86	TEDDY BEAR-685	SU	38.00	40.00
86	TEDDY-707	*	13.00	30.00
86	USHS ANGEL-703	SU	35.00	50.00
86	VICTORIAN SANTA-724	250	32.00	35.00
86	WINGED DOVE-680	SU	35.00	36.00
86	WREATH-714	SU	36.00	38.00
87	ANGEL WITH LYRE-750	SU	32.00	40.00
87	ART DECO ANGEL-765	SU	38.00	40.00
87	BUFFALO-777	SU	36.00	36.00
87	CAT-754	OP	37.00	37.00
87	CLIPPER SHIP-756	SU	35.00	35.00
87	DOVE-747	*	13.00	13.00
87	FIRST CHRISTMAS-771	*	13.00	13.00
87	HUNTING HORN-738	OP	37.00	37.00
87	MINUTEMAN-776	SU	35.00	40.00
87	NOEL-731	OP	38.00	38.00
87	OLD IRONSIDES-767	OP	35.00	39.00
87	PEGASUS-745	*	13.00	13.00
87	REINDEER-752	OP	38.00	38.00
87	RIDE A COCK HORSE-757	SU	34.00	39.00

YR	NAME	LIMIT	ISSUE	TREND
87	SANTA AND SLEIGH-751	SU	32.00	40.00
87	SANTA-741	*	13.00	13.00
87	SNOW QUEEN-746	SU	35.00	39.00
87	SNOWMAN-753	825	38.00	38.00
87	STOCKING-772	*	13.00	13.00
87	SWEETHEART STAR-740	SU	39.50	40.00
87	USHS GLORIA ANGEL-748	SU	39.00	50.00
88	ANGEL-797	*	13.00	13.00
88	ANGEL-818	SU	32.00	40.00
88	BANK-812	400	40.00	115.00
88	BOSTON STATE HOUSE	OP	34.00	40.00
88	BUGGY-817	*	13.00	13.00
88	CABLE CAR-848	OP	38.00	38.00
88	CAROUSEL HORSE-811	2150	34.00	34.00
88	CHRISTMAS TREE-798	*	13.00	13.00
88	CONN. STATE HOUSE-833	OP	38.00	38.00
88	CORONADO-864	OP	38.00	38.00
88	DOVE-786	112	36.00	50.00
88	DRUMMER BEAR-773	*	13.00	13.00
88	EIFFEL TOWER-861	225	38.00	100.00
88	FIRST CHRISTMAS-842	*	13.00	13.00
88	JACK IN THE BOX-789	SU	39.50	40.00
88	LOCKET BEAR-844	*	25.00	25.00
88	MADONNA-787	600	35.00	35.00
88	MADONNA-809	15	39.00	50.00
88	MADONNA-815	SU	39.00	50.00
88	MAGI-788	SU	39.50	40.00
88	NATIVITY-821	SU	32.00	39.00
88	NIGHT BEFORE CHRISTMAS COL.-841	10000	160.00	160.00
88	OLD KING COLE-824	SU	34.00	39.00
88	RABBIT-816	*	13.00	13.00
88	SANTA WITH SCROLL-814	250	34.00	37.00
88	SKATERS-790	SU	39.50	40.00
88	SLEIGH-834	OP	34.00	38.00
88	STAR OF THE EAST-785	SU	35.00	35.00
88	STAR-806	311	13.00	150.00
88	STAR-854	275	32.00	35.00
88	STOCKING BEAR-835	*	13.00	13.00
88	STOCKING-774	*	13.00	13.00
88	STOCKING-827	*	13.00	13.00
88	THUMBELINA-803	SU	35.00	40.00
88	US CAPITOL-820	OP	38.00	40.00
89	1989 BARNESVILLE BUGGY-950	*	13.00	13.00
89	1989 NUTCRACKER-872	1790	38.00	38.00
89	1989 SANTA-856	1715	35.00	35.00
89	1989 USHS ANGEL-901	SU	38.00	38.00
89	BUGLE BEAR-935	*	12.00	12.00
89	GOOSE-857	650	37.00	37.00
89	INDEPENDENCE HALL-908	OP	38.00	38.00
89	JACK IN THE BOX BEAR-936	*	12.00	12.00
89	L&T UGLY DUCKLING-917	SU	38.00	38.00
89	MFA ANGEL WITH TREE-906	SU	36.00	42.00
89	MFA DURER SNOWFLAKE-907	2000	36.00	42.00
89	MFA LAFARGE ANGEL SET-937	SU	98.00	98.00
89	MFA NOEL-905	SU	36.00	42.00
89	PRESIDENTIAL SEAL-858	500	39.00	39.00
89	STOCKING BEAR-95	*	12.00	12.00
89	STOCKING WITH TOYS-956	*	12.00	12.00
89	SWAN BOAT-904	OP	38.00	38.00
89	VICTORIAN HEART-954	*	13.00	13.00
90	1990 PETER RABBIT-1018	4315	39.50	40.00
90	1990 SANTA-869	2250	38.00	38.00
90	1990 SNOWFLAKE-1033	1415	36.00	38.00
90	1990 USHS ANGEL-1061	SU	39.00	39.00
90	ANGEL WITH HORN-939	*	*	*
90	ANGEL WITH STAR-871	OP	38.00	38.00
90	ANGEL WITH VIOLIN-1024	SU	39.00	39.00
90	ANGELS-1039	SU	36.00	36.00
90	BEARDSLEY ANGEL-1040	SU	34.00	34.00
90	BLAKE ANGEL-961	*	36.00	36.00
90	BOSTON LIGHT, THE-1032	OP	39.50	40.00
90	CARDINALS-870	OP	39.00	39.00
90	CAROUSEL HORSE-866	1915	38.00	38.00
90	CARRIAGE-960	*	13.00	13.00
90	CAT ON PILLOW-915	*	13.00	13.00
90	CHRISTMAS SEAL-931	*	25.00	25.00
90	CHURCH-921	OP	37.00	37.00
90	CLOWN WITH DOG-958	*	13.00	13.00
90	COCKATOO-969	*	13.00	13.00
90	COLONIAL CAPITOL-965	OP	39.00	39.00
90	CONESTOGA WAGON-1027	OP	38.00	38.00
90	COVERED BRIDGE-920	OP	37.00	37.00
90	CURRIER & IVES VICTORIAN VILLAGE-923	2000	140.00	140.00
90	DUCKLINGS-1114	OP	38.00	38.00
90	ELK-1023	*	13.00	13.00
90	EMBER-1124	120	*	*
90	FARMHOUSE-919	OP	37.00	37.00
90	FATHER CHRISTMAS-970	SU	36.00	36.00
90	FERREL'S ANGEL 1990-1084	*	15.00	16.00

YR	NAME	LIMIT	ISSUE	TREND
90	FIRST BAPTIST ANGEL-997	200	35.00	35.00
90	FIRST CHRISTMAS BEAR-940	SU	35.00	35.00
90	FLOPSY BUNNIES-995	SU	39.50	40.00
90	FLORIDA STATE CAPITOL-1044	2000	39.50	40.00
90	GEORGIA STATE CAPITOL-1042	2000	39.50	40.00
90	GOOSE & WREATH-868	OP	37.00	37.00
90	GOVERNOR'S PALACE-966	OP	39.00	39.00
90	HEART ANGEL-959	SU	39.00	39.00
90	JEMIMA PUDDLEDUCK-1020	*	30.00	30.00
90	JEREMY FISHER-992	OP	39.50	40.00
90	JOY-1047	SU	39.00	39.00
90	JOY-867	1140	36.00	36.00
90	K. GREENAWAY WINDOW-924	*	*	*
90	KOALA SAN DIEGO ZOO-1095	OP	36.00	36.00
90	LANDING DUCK-1021	*	13.00	13.00
90	LIBERTY BELL-1028	OP	38.00	38.00
90	LOCOMOTIVE-1100	SU	39.00	39.00
90	MADONNA & CHILD-930	*	*	*
90	MERRY CHRISTMAS LOCKET-948	*	25.00	25.00
90	MILL-922	OP	37.00	37.00
90	MOLE & RAT WIND IN WILLOWS-944	OP	36.00	36.00
90	MONTPELIER-1113	OP	36.00	36.00
90	MOUSE WITH CANDY CANE-916	*	13.00	13.00
90	MRS. RABBIT-991	OP	39.50	40.00
90	NORTH CAROLINA STATE CAPITOL-1043	2000	39.50	40.00
90	OLD FASHIONED SANTA-971	SU	36.00	36.00
90	PATRIOTIC SANTA-972	SU	36.00	36.00
90	PEGASUS-1037	SU	35.00	35.00
90	PETER RABBIT LOCKET ORNAMENT-1019	*	30.00	30.00
90	PETER RABBIT-993	OP	39.50	40.00
90	PETER'S FIRST CHRISTMAS-994	SU	39.50	40.00
90	PRESIDENTIAL HOMES-990	OP	350.00	350.00
90	SAN FRANCISCO ROW HOUSE-1071	OP	39.50	40.00
90	SAN FRANCISCO STREET-933	*	*	*
90	SANTA & REINDEER-929	395	39.00	43.00
90	SANTA IN BALLOON-973	SU	36.00	36.00
90	SANTA IN THE MOON-941	SU	38.00	38.00
90	SANTA ON REINDEER-974	SU	36.00	36.00
90	SANTA UP TO DATE-975	SU	36.00	36.00
90	SOUTH CAROLINA STATE CAPITOL-1045	2000	39.50	40.00
90	STEADFAST TIN SOLDIER-1050	SU	36.00	36.00
90	TEDDY BEAR LOCKET-949	*	25.00	25.00
90	TEDDY BEAR WITH HEART-957	*	13.00	13.00
90	TOAD WIND IN WILLOWS-945	OP	38.00	38.00
90	WHITE TAIL DEER-1022	*	13.00	13.00
91	1991 SANTA-1056	OP	38.00	38.00
91	ALICE IN WONDERLAND-1159	OP	140.00	140.00
91	ALICE-1119	OP	39.00	39.00
91	ANGEL WITH HORN-1026	OP	32.00	32.00
91	APPLEY DAPPLY-1091	OP	39.50	40.00
91	CAROUSEL HORSE-1025	OP	38.00	38.00
91	COLUMBUS-1140	1500	39.00	39.00
91	COW JUMPED OVER THE MOON-1055	SU	38.00	38.00
91	FIR TREE-1145	OP	39.00	39.00
91	I LOVE SANTA-998	OP	36.00	36.00
91	LARGE JEMIMA PUDDLEDUCK-1083	OP	49.50	50.00
91	LARGE PETER RABBIT-1116	OP	49.50	50.00
91	LARGE TAILOR OF GLOUCESTER-1117	OP	49.50	50.00
91	MAD TEA PARTY-1120	OP	39.00	39.00
91	MFA SNOWFLAKE 1991-1143	OP	36.00	36.00
91	MOMMY & BABY KANGAROO-1078	OP	36.00	36.00
91	MOMMY & BABY KOALA BEAR-1077	OP	36.00	36.00
91	MOMMY & BABY PANDA BEAR-1079	OP	36.00	36.00
91	MOMMY & BABY SEAL-1075	OP	36.00	36.00
91	MOMMY & BABY WOLVES-1076	OP	36.00	36.00
91	MRS. RABBIT 1991-1086	OP	39.50	40.00
91	NATIVITY-1118	OP	38.00	38.00
91	NUTCRACKER-1151	OP	49.50	50.00
91	OLIVERS ROCKING HORSE-1085	OP	37.00	37.00
91	PAUL REVERE-1158	OP	39.00	39.00
91	PETER RABBIT WITH BOOK-1093	OP	39.50	40.00
91	PIG ROBINSON-1090	OP	39.50	40.00
91	PRECIOUS PLANET-1142	2000	120.00	120.00
91	QUEEN OF HEARTS-1122	OP	39.00	39.00
91	TAILOR OF GLOUCESTER-1087	OP	39.50	40.00
91	USHS ANGEL 1991-1139	OP	38.00	38.00
91	VOYAGES OF COLUMBUS, THE-1141	1500	39.00	39.00
91	WAITING FOR SANTA-1123	OP	38.00	38.00
91	WHITE RABBIT-1121	OP	39.00	39.00
92	AMERICA AT PEACE-1245	2000	85.00	85.00
92	ANDREA-1163	OP	36.00	36.00
92	ANGEL W/DOUBLE HORN-1212	2000	49.50	50.00
92	ANGEL-1213	2000	39.00	39.00
92	BOB & TINY TIM-1242	OP	36.00	36.00
92	CHOCOLATE POT-1209	OP	49.50	50.00
92	CHRISTMAS TREE & HEART-1162	OP	36.00	36.00
92	COWARDLY LION-1287	OP	36.00	36.00
92	DELLA ROBBIA ORNAMENT-1219	OP	39.00	39.00
92	DOROTHY-1284	OP	36.00	36.00

YR	NAME	LIMIT	ISSUE	TREND
92	FAIRY TALE ANGEL-1222	OP	36.00	36.00
92	HEART OF CHRISTMAS-1301	OP	*	*
92	JEMIMA PUDDLEDUCK 1992-1167	OP	39.50	40.00
92	JESSOPS CLOCK-1308	OP	*	*
92	JOY-1164	OP	39.50	40.00
92	MARLEY'S GHOST-1243	OP	36.00	36.00
92	MFA SNOWFLAKE-1246	OP	39.00	39.00
92	MRS. CRATCHIT-1244	OP	36.00	36.00
92	MRS. RABBIT-1181	OP	39.50	40.00
92	NOAH'S ARK-1166	OP	36.00	36.00
92	PARROT-1233	OP	37.00	37.00
92	PRINCESS & THE PEA-1247	OP	39.00	39.00
92	REVERE TEAPOT-1207	OP	49.50	50.00
92	ROUND TEAPOT-1206	OP	49.50	50.00
92	SCARECROW-1286	OP	36.00	36.00
92	SCROOGE-1241	OP	36.00	36.00
92	ST. JOHN ANGEL-1236	10000	39.00	39.00
92	ST. JOHN LION-1235	10000	39.00	39.00
92	TIN MAN-1285	OP	36.00	36.00
92	UNICORN-1165	OP	36.00	36.00

J. WALPOLE — **HAND & HAMMER ORNAMENTS**

YR	NAME	LIMIT	ISSUE	TREND
87	NAPTIME-732	SU	32.00	32.00
87	SANTA STAR-739	SU	32.00	32.00

HAWTHORNE

* — **GONE WITH THE WIND ORNAMENTS**

YR	NAME	LIMIT	ISSUE	TREND
95	RED HORSE SALOON/BUTLER MANSION 79043	*	29.90	30.00
95	TARA/ATLANTA CHURCH 79041	*	29.90	30.00
95	TWELVE OAKS/KENNEDY STORE 79042	*	29.90	30.00

* — **ROCKWELL'S MAIN STREET/ILLUMINATED**

YR	NAME	LIMIT	ISSUE	TREND
94	ANTIQUE SHOP & TOWN OFFICES 79902	*	29.90	30.00
94	BANK & LIBRARY 79903	*	29.90	30.00
94	RED LION INN & ROCKWELL RESIDENCE 79904	*	29.90	30.00
94	STUDIO & COUNTRY STORE 79901	*	29.90	30.00

* — **THOMAS KINKADE'S CANDLELIGHT COTTAGES**

YR	NAME	LIMIT	ISSUE	TREND
95	CEDAR NOOKE/CANDLELIT 79964	*	29.90	30.00
95	OLD PORTERFIELD TEA ROOM/MERRITT'S 79962	*	29.90	30.00
95	SEASIDE/SWEETHEART 79963	*	29.90	30.00
95	SWANBROOKE/CHANDLER'S 79961	*	29.90	30.00

HELEN SABATTE DESIGNS INC.

E. WEIRICK — **KIDDIE CAR CLASSICS**

YR	NAME	LIMIT	ISSUE	TREND
95	'37 STEELCRAFT AUBURN LUXURY	24500	65.00	65.00
95	'50 TORPEDO	OP	50.00	50.00
95	'59 DELUXE KIDILLAC	OP	55.00	55.00
95	'61 CASEY JONES LOCOMOTIVE	OP	55.00	55.00

JAN HAGARA COLLECTABLES

J. HAGARA — **ORNAMENTS**

YR	NAME	LIMIT	ISSUE	TREND
84	ANNE	TL	10.00	100.00
84	JENNY	TL	10.00	70.00
84	JIMMY	TL	10.00	175.00
84	LISA	TL	10.00	40.00

J. HAGARA — **VICTORIAN CHILDREN**

YR	NAME	LIMIT	ISSUE	TREND
84	ANNE	RT	10.00	125.00
84	BETSY	RT	10.00	50.00
84	JENNY	RT	10.00	125.00
84	JIMMY	RT	10.00	150.00
84	JODY	RT	10.00	45.00
84	LISA	RT	10.00	50.00
84	LYDIA	RT	10.00	45.00
84	VICTORIA	RT	10.00	125.00
85	CHRIS	RT	7.00	50.00
86	JILL	RT	15.00	30.00
86	NOEL	RT	10.00	50.00
87	AMANDA	RT	14.00	45.00
87	BRIAN	RT	14.00	45.00
87	CRISTINA	RT	14.00	30.00
87	HOLLY	RT	15.00	18.00
87	LAURIE	RT	14.00	30.00
87	MARC	RT	14.00	35.00
87	NIKKI	RT	10.00	50.00
87	STACY	RT	14.00	45.00
87	STEPHEN	RT	14.00	45.00

JOHN HINE STUDIOS LTD.

Price ranges may reflect various demands in the market from one geographic region to another; condition of piece; specific markings found on piece; and/or changes in production of piece.

D. WINTER — **CHRISTMAS ORNAMENTS**

YR	NAME	LIMIT	ISSUE	TREND
91	A CHRISTMAS CAROL	CL	15.00	25.00
91	HOGMANAY	RT	15.00	25.00
91	MR. FEZZIWIG'S EMPORIUM	RT	15.00	25.00
91	SCROOGE'S COUNTING HOUSE	RT	15.00	25.00
92	FAIRYTALE CASTLE	RT	15.00	17.00
92	FRED'S HOME	RT	15.00	17.00
92	SUFFOLK HOUSE	RT	15.00	17.00
92	TUDOR MANOR HOUSE	RT	15.00	17.00
93	GRANGE, THE	RT	15.00	8.00

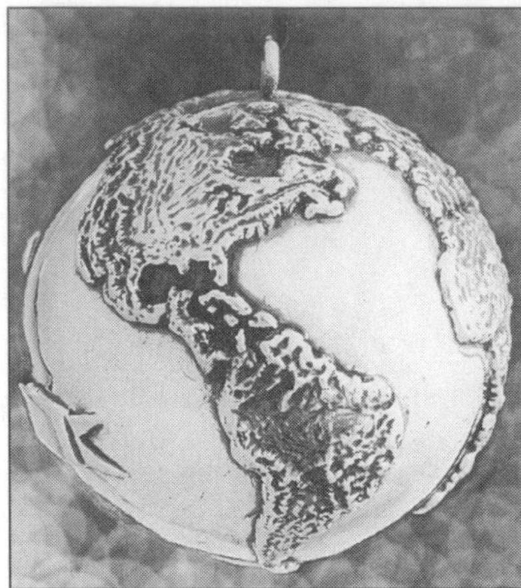

Hand & Hammer's Precious Planet *reminds us that we all have a responsibility to treat our earth as an invaluable treasure.*

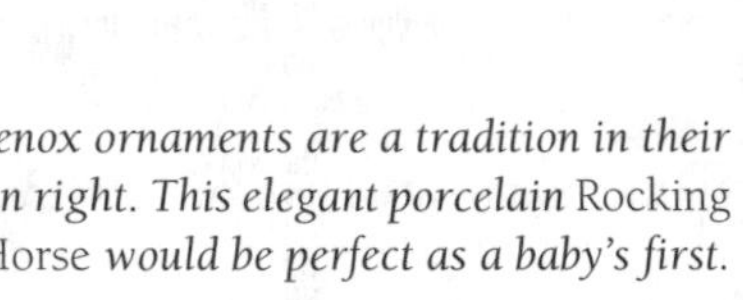

Lenox ornaments are a tradition in their own right. This elegant porcelain Rocking Horse *would be perfect as a baby's first.*

With his bagful of goodies bulging at the seams, Cheerful Santa *gives a hearty wave to collectors of Hallmark Keepsake Ornaments.*

Add a Victorian touch to any Christmas tree with Susanna *from the Maud Humphrey Bogart collection produced in 1991 by Hamilton Gifts Ltd.*

YR	NAME	LIMIT	ISSUE	TREND
93	SCROOGE'S SCHOOL	RT	15.00	8.00
93	TOMFOOL'S COTTAGE	RT	15.00	8.00
93	WILL-'O-THE-WISP	RT	15.00	8.00
94	OLD JOE'S BEETLING SHOP	OP	17.50	18.00
94	SCROOGES' FAMILY HOME	OP	17.50	18.00
94	WHAT COTTAGE?	OP	17.50	18.00
95	BUTTERCUP COTTAGE	OP	17.50	18.00
95	FLOWER SHOP, THE	OP	17.50	18.00
95	LOOKING FOR SANTA	OP	17.50	18.00
95	MISS BELLES COTTAGE	OP	17.50	18.00
95	ROBIN HOOD MOUSE	OP	17.50	18.00
95	SEASON'S GREETINGS	OP	17.50	18.00
D. WINTER			**DAVID WINTER ORNAMENTS**	
92	SET	YR	60.00	100.00

JUNE MCKENNA COLLECTIBLES INC.

YR	NAME	LIMIT	ISSUE	TREND
JUNE MCKENNA				
93	ANGEL OF PEACE-PINK	OP	30.00	30.00
93	ANGEL OF PEACE-WHITE	OP	30.00	30.00
93	CHRISTMAS TREAT	OP	30.00	30.00
93	ELF BERNIE	OP	30.00	30.00
93	FINAL NOTES	OP	30.00	30.00
93	OLD LAMPLIGHTER	OP	30.00	30.00
94	ELF RICKEY	OP	30.00	30.00
94	ELF TAMMY	OP	30.00	30.00
94	GUIDING LIGHT ANGEL-GREEN	OP	30.00	30.00
94	GUIDING LIGHT ANGEL-PINK	OP	30.00	30.00
94	GUIDING LIGHT ANGEL-WHITE	OP	30.00	30.00
94	NUTCRACKER	OP	30.00	30.00
94	PRIMITIVE	OP	16.00	17.00
94	QUICK AS A WINK	OP	16.00	17.00
94	RINGING IN CHRISTMAS	OP	30.00	30.00
94	SANTA WITH PIPE	OP	30.00	30.00
94	SANTA WITH SKIS	OP	30.00	30.00
94	SNOW SHOWERS	OP	30.00	30.00
94	WHISPERING	OP	16.00	17.00
J. MCKENNA			**3-D BLACK FOLK ART**	
96	FUN AT THE BEACH/SANTA	YR	70.00	70.00
J. MCKENNA			**FLATBACK ORNAMENTS**	
82	ANGEL WITH TOYS	CL	14.00	85.00
82	BABY BEAR, TEESHIRT	CL	11.00	60.00
82	CANDY CANE	CL	10.00	45.00
82	COLONIAL MAN	CL	12.00	150.00
82	COLONIAL WOMAN	CL	12.00	150.00
82	KATE GREENAWAY BOY	CL	12.00	275.00
82	KATE GREENAWAY GIRL	CL	12.00	300.00
82	MAMA BEAR, BLUE CAP	CL	12.00	90.00
82	PAPA BEAR, RED CAPE	CL	12.00	90.00
82	SANTA WITH TOYS	CL	14.00	80.00
83	BABY	CL	11.00	60.00
83	BABY BEAR IN VEST	CL	11.00	50.00
83	FATHER BEAR IN SUIT	CL	12.00	75.00
83	GLORIA ANGEL	CL	14.00	475.00
83	GRANDMA	CL	12.00	65.00
83	GRANDPA	CL	12.00	65.00
83	MOTHER BEAR IN DRESS	CL	12.00	75.00
83	RAGGEDY ANDY	CL	12.00	75.00
83	RAGGEDY ANN	CL	12.00	75.00
83	ST. NICK WITH LANTERN	CL	14.00	75.00
84	ANGEL WITH HORN	CL	14.00	75.00
84	COUNTRY BOY	CL	12.00	70.00
84	COUNTRY GIRL	CL	12.00	70.00
84	MR. CLAUS	CL	14.00	65.00
84	MRS. CLAUS	CL	14.00	60.00
84	OLD WORLD SANTA	CL	14.00	65.00
85	AMISH MAN	CL	13.00	50.00
85	AMISH WOMAN	CL	13.00	50.00
85	BABY PIG	CL	11.00	60.00
85	BRIDE	CL	25.00	125.00
85	FATHER PIG	CL	12.00	75.00
85	GROOM	CL	25.00	125.00
85	MOTHER PIG	CL	12.00	75.00
85	PRIMITIVE SANTA	CL	17.00	85.00
86	AMISH BOY	CL	13.00	65.00
86	SANTA WITH BAG	CL	16.00	65.00
86	SANTA WITH BEAR	CL	14.00	40.00
86	SANTA WITH BELLS (BLUE)	CL	14.00	65.00
86	SANTA WITH BELLS (GREEN)	CL	14.00	375.00
88	1776 SANTA	CL	17.00	40.00
88	ELIZABETH, SILL SITTER	CL	20.00	150.00
88	GUARDIAN ANGEL	CL	16.00	40.00
88	SANTA WITH BOOK (BLUE & RED)	CL	17.00	75.00
88	SANTA WITH TOYS	CL	17.00	40.00
88	SANTA WITH WREATH	CL	17.00	40.00
89	GLORIOUS ANGEL	OP	17.00	17.00
89	SANTA WITH TREE	CL	17.00	40.00
89	WINKING SANTA	CL	17.00	40.00
90	ELF JEFFREY	CL	17.00	40.00

YR	NAME	LIMIT	ISSUE	TREND
90	HARVEST SANTA	CL	17.00	40.00
90	HO HO HO	CL	17.00	40.00
91	BOY ANGEL	CL	20.00	20.00
91	ELF JOEY	OP	20.00	20.00
91	GIRL ANGEL	OP	20.00	20.00
91	SANTA WITH BANNER	OP	20.00	20.00
91	SANTA WITH LIGHTS, BLACK	OP	20.00	20.00
92	ELF SCOTTY	OP	25.00	25.00
92	NORTH POLE NEWS	OP	25.00	25.00
92	PRAYING ANGEL	OP	25.00	25.00
92	SANTA WITH BASKET	OP	25.00	25.00
92	SANTA WITH SACK	OP	25.00	25.00
95	ANGEL W/TEDDY	YR	30.00	30.00
95	ANGEL W/WREATH	YR	30.00	30.00
95	COUNTRY SANTA	YR	30.00	30.00
95	ELF/DANNY	YR	30.00	30.00
95	SANTA & HELPER/BROWN	YR	30.00	30.00
95	SANTA NUTCRACKER	YR	30.00	30.00
95	SANTA TEACHER	YR	30.00	30.00
95	WHO'S THIS FROSTY	YR	30.00	30.00
96	ANGEL W/HARPE - ELIZABETH	YR	30.00	30.00
96	ANGEL W/HORN - MARY	YR	30.00	30.00
96	ANGEL W/LYRE - KATHLEEN	YR	30.00	30.00
96	CHRISTMAS TREAT/RED	YR	30.00	30.00
96	ELF CADDIE	YR	30.00	30.00
96	FIREMAN SANTA	YR	30.00	30.00
96	FISHING SANTA	YR	30.00	30.00
96	GOLFING SANTA	YR	30.00	30.00
96	MR. GOODBY KISS	YR	30.00	30.00
96	MRS. GOODBY KISS	YR	30.00	30.00
96	NUTCRACKER	YR	30.00	30.00
96	SANTA & HELPER/WHITE	YR	30.00	30.00
96	SANTA W/TEDDY	YR	30.00	30.00
96	SNOWMAN	YR	30.00	30.00
J. MCKENNA			**HEAD ORNAMENTS**	
95	CHRISTMAS KISS	YR	17.00	17.00
95	HELPING HAND	YR	17.00	17.00
95	I LOVE YOU	YR	17.00	17.00
95	MOON SHAPE SANTA	YR	17.00	17.00
95	PRIMITIVE SANTA	YR	17.00	17.00
95	QUICK AS A WINK	YR	17.00	17.00
95	SANTA W/HOLLY	YR	17.00	17.00
95	SANTA W/PIPE	YR	17.00	17.00
95	WHISPERING SANTA	YR	17.00	17.00
96	PATRIOTIC SANTA	YR	17.00	17.00
96	SANTA W/TASSEL	YR	17.00	17.00
96	SNOWMAN	YR	17.00	17.00
J. MCKENNA				**ICICLE**
96	ANGEL/LONG RED HAIR	YR	17.00	17.00
96	ANGEL/SHORT BLONDE HAIR	YR	17.00	17.00
96	ANGEL/SHORT BROWN HAIR	YR	17.00	17.00
96	BLACK ANGEL	YR	17.00	17.00
96	SANTA W/HAT	YR	17.00	17.00
96	SNOWMAN	YR	17.00	17.00

KIRK STIEFF

YR	NAME	LIMIT	ISSUE	TREND
D. BACORN			**COLONIAL WILLIAMSBURG**	
83	SILVERPLATE TREETOP STAR	YR	29.50	30.00
87	SILVERPLATE ROCKING HORSE	OP	19.95	30.00
87	SILVERPLATE TIN DRUM	OP	19.95	30.00
88	SILVERPLATE LAMB	OP	19.95	22.00
88	SILVERPLATE UNICORN	YR	22.00	22.00
89	SILVERPLATE DOLL ORNAMENT	YR	22.00	22.00
D. BACORN			**KIRK STIEFF ORNAMENTS**	
83	CHARLESTON LOCOMOTIVE	CL	17.50	20.00
84	UNICORN	CL	17.50	20.00
86	STERLING SILVER ICICLE	OP	35.00	50.00
K. STIEFF			**KIRK STIEFF ORNAMENTS**	
89	SMITHSONIAN CAROUSEL HORSE	YR	50.00	50.00
89	SMITHSONIAN CAROUSEL SEAHORSE	YR	50.00	50.00
90	TOY SHIP	YR	23.00	23.00
K. STIEFF		**THE NUTCRACKER STAINED GLASS ORNAMENT**		
86	BATTLE, THE	CL	17.50	18.00
86	CLARA'S GIFT	CL	17.50	18.00
86	NUTCRACKER PRINCE, THE	CL	17.50	18.00
86	SET OF FOUR	CL	69.95	40.00
86	SUGAR PLUM FAIRY, THE	CL	17.50	18.00
J. BARATA			**TWELVE DAYS OF CHRISTMAS**	
85	PARTRIDGE IN A PEAR TREE	YR	9.95	11.00
85	TWO TURTLE DOVES	YR	9.95	11.00
86	FOUR CALLING BIRDS	YR	9.95	11.00
86	THREE FRENCH HENS	YR	9.95	11.00
87	FIVE GOLDEN RINGS	YR	9.95	11.00
87	SIX GEESE A-LAYING	YR	9.95	11.00
88	EIGHT MAIDS A-MILKING	YR	9.95	11.00
88	SEVEN SWANS A-SWIMMING	YR	9.95	11.00
89	NINE LADIES DANCING	YR	10.95	11.00
89	TEN LORDS A-LEAPING	YR	10.95	11.00

KURT S. ADLER/SANTA'S WORLD

YR	NAME	LIMIT	ISSUE	TREND
	J. MOSTROM			**CHILDREN'S HOUR**
95	ALICE IN WONDERLAND J5751	RT	22.50	23.00
95	BOW PEEP J5753	OP	27.00	27.00
95	CINDERELLA J5762	OP	28.00	28.00
95	LITTLE BOY BLUE J5755	RT	18.00	18.00
95	MISS MUFFET J5753	OP	27.00	27.00
95	MOTHER GOOSE J5754	OP	27.00	27.00
95	RED RIDING HOOD J5751	OP	22.50	23.00
	J. MOSTROM			**CHRISTMAS IN CHELSEA**
92	ALLISON SITTING IN CHAIR W2812	RT	25.50	26.00
92	ALLISON W2729	RT	21.00	21.00
92	AMANDA W2709	RT	21.00	21.00
92	AMY W2729	RT	21.00	21.00
92	CHRISTINA W2812	RT	25.50	26.00
92	CHRISTOPHER W2709	RT	21.00	21.00
92	DELPHINIUM W2728	OP	20.00	20.00
92	HOLLY HOCK W2728	OP	20.00	20.00
92	HOLLY W2709	RT	21.00	21.00
92	PEONY W2728	OP	20.00	20.00
92	ROSE W2728	OP	20.00	20.00
94	ALICE,MARGUERITE W2973	OP	28.00	28.00
94	GUARDIAN ANGEL W/BABY W2974	RT	31.00	31.00
95	EDMOND W/VIOLIN W3078	OP	32.00	32.00
95	JOSE W/VIOLIN W3078	OP	32.00	32.00
95	PAULINE W/VIOLIN W3078	OP	32.00	32.00
	M. ROTHENBERG			**CORNHUSK MICE**
93	BALLERINA CORNHUSK MICE W2700	RT	13.50	14.00
93	NUTCRACKER STE. FANTASY CORNHUSK MOUSE	RT	15.50	16.00
94	CLARA, PRINCE W2948	OP	16.00	16.00
94	COWBOY W2951	OP	18.00	18.00
94	DROSSELMEIR FAIRY, MOUSE KING W2949	OP	16.00	16.00
94	FATHER CHRISTMAS W2979	OP	18.00	18.00
94	FATHER CHRISTMAS W2982	OP	25.00	25.00
94	LITTLE POCAHONTAS, INDIAN BRAVE W2950	OP	18.00	18.00
95	ANGEL MICE W3088	OP	10.00	10.00
95	BABY'S FIRST MOUSE W3087	OP	10.00	10.00
95	MISS TAMMIE MOUSE W3086	OP	17.00	17.00
95	MR. JAMIE MOUSE W3086	OP	17.00	17.00
95	MRS. MOLLY MOUSE W3086	OP	17.00	17.00
	*			**FABRICHE COLLECTION**
92	HELLO LITTLE ONE! W1561	OP	22.00	22.00
92	HUGS AND KISSES W1560	OP	22.00	22.00
92	MERRY CHRISMOUSE W1565	RT	10.00	10.00
92	NOT A CREATURE WAS STIRRING W1563	OP	22.00	22.00
94	HOIDAY FLIGHT W1637	OP	40.00	40.00
	K. ADLER			**FABRICHE COLLECTION**
92	CHRISTMAS IN THE AIR W1593	RT	35.50	36.00
93	HOMEWARD BOUND W1596	OP	27.00	27.00
93	MASTER TOYMAKER W1595	OP	27.00	27.00
93	PAR FOR THE CLAUS W1625	OP	27.00	27.00
93	SANTA W/LIST W1510	OP	20.00	20.00
94	ALL STAR SANTA W1665	OP	27.00	27.00
94	CHECKING HIS LIST W1634	OP	23.50	24.00
94	COOKIES FOR SANTA W1639	OP	28.00	28.00
94	FIREFIGHTING FRIENDS W1668	OP	28.00	28.00
94	SANTA'S FISHTALES W1666	OP	29.00	29.00
95	CAPTAIN CLAUS W1711	OP	25.00	25.00
95	STRIKE UP THE BAND W1710	OP	25.00	25.00
	M. ROTHENBERG			**FABRICHE COLLECTION**
92	AN APRON FULL OF LOVE W1594	OP	27.00	27.00
	H. ADLER			**HOLLY BEARIES**
96	ANGEL STARCATCHER 57222	OP	20.00	20.00
	J. MOSTROM			**INTERNATIONAL CHRISTMAS**
94	CATHY, JOHNNY W2945	RT	24.00	24.00
94	ESKIMO-ATOM UKPIK W2967	RT	28.00	28.00
94	GERMANY-KATERINA,HANS W2969	OP	27.00	27.00
94	NATIVE AMERICAN-WHITE DOVE,LITTLE WOLF	RT	28.00	28.00
94	POLAND-MARISSA,HEDWIG W2965	OP	27.00	27.00
94	SCOTLAND-BONNIE, DOUGLAS W2966	OP	27.00	27.00
94	SPAIN-MARIA. MIGUEL W2968	OP	27.00	27.00
	J. MOSTROM			**LITTLE DICKENS**
94	LITTLE BOB CRACHIT W2961	OP	30.00	30.00
94	LITTLE MARLEY'S GHOST W2964	OP	33.50	34.00
94	LITTLE MRS. CRACHIT W2962	OP	27.00	27.00
94	LITTLE SCROOGE IN BATHROBE W2959	OP	30.00	30.00
94	LITTLE SCROOGE IN OVERCOAT W2960	OP	30.00	30.00
94	LITTLE TINY TIM W2963	OP	22.50	23.00
	*			**POLONAISE COLLECTION**
94	GOLDEN CHERUB HEAD GP372	RT	18.00	70.00
94	GOLDEN ROCKING HORSE GP355	RT	22.50	24.00
95	WIZARD OF OZ 4 PC. BOXED SET GP505	5000	124.00	124.00
96	COCA COLA BEAR GP630	OP	37.00	37.00
96	COCA COLA BOTTLE GP631	OP	33.00	33.00
96	COCA COLA BOTTLE TOP GP633	OP	27.00	27.00
96	COCA COLA DISK GP632	OP	26.00	26.00
96	COCA COLA VENDING MACHINE GP634	OP	37.00	37.00

YR	NAME	LIMIT	ISSUE	TREND
96	POLONAISE MEDIEVAL HORSE GP640	OP	35.00	35.00
KING FEATURES			**POLONAISE COLLECTION**	
96	BETTY BOOP GP624	OP	32.00	32.00
KSA/KOMOZJA			**POLONAISE COLLECTION**	
94	ANGEL HEAD GP372	RT	18.00	18.00
94	ANGEL W/BELL GP396	RT	20.20	20.20
94	BEER GLASS GP366	OP	18.00	18.00
94	CARDINAL GP420	OP	18.00	18.00
94	CAT W/BALL GP390	RT	23.00	23.00
94	DINOSAURS GP397	OP	22.50	23.00
94	EGYPTIANS 12 PC. GP500	RT	200.00	200.00
94	GLASS ACORN GP342	OP	11.00	11.00
94	GLASS ANGEL GP309	OP	18.00	18.00
94	GLASS APPLE GP339	OP	11.00	11.00
94	GLASS CHURCH GP369	OP	18.00	18.00
94	GLASS CLOWN GP301	OP	13.50	14.00
94	GLASS CLOWN GP302	RT	22.50	23.00
94	GLASS CLOWN GP303	RT	22.50	23.00
94	GLASS DICE GP363	OP	18.00	18.00
94	GLASS DOLL GP377	RT	13.50	14.00
94	GLASS GNOME GP347	OP	18.00	18.00
94	GLASS KNIGHT GP304	OP	18.00	18.00
94	GLASS OWL GP328	OP	20.00	20.00
94	GLASS TOP GP359	OP	9.00	9.00
94	GLASS TURKEY GP326	OP	20.00	20.00
94	GUARDMAN GP407	OP	15.50	16.00
94	HOLY FAMILY GP371	OP	28.00	28.00
94	LOCOMOTIVE GP353	OP	22.50	23.00
94	MADONNA W/CHILD GP370	OP	22.50	23.00
94	MERLIN GP373	RT	20.00	20.00
94	MOOSE KING GP406	OP	20.00	20.00
94	NEFERTITI GP349	OP	25.00	25.00
94	NIGHT & DAY GP307	OP	22.50	23.00
94	NUTCRACKER GP404	OP	20.00	20.00
94	OLD FASHIONED CAR GP380	RT	13.50	14.00
94	PARROTT GP332	RT	15.50	16.00
94	PEACOCK GP323	OP	28.00	28.00
94	PEACOCK GP324	OP	18.00	18.00
94	PIERROT THE CLOWN GP405	RT	18.00	18.00
94	PUPPY GP333	OP	15.50	16.00
94	PYRAMID GP352	OP	22.50	23.00
94	ROCKING HORSE GP355	OP	22.50	23.00
94	ROCKING HORSE GP356	OP	22.50	23.00
94	SAINT NICK GP316	OP	28.00	28.00
94	SANTA BOOT GP375	OP	20.00	20.00
94	SANTA GP317	OP	22.50	23.00
94	SANTA HEAD GP315	OP	13.50	14.00
94	SANTA HEAD GP374	OP	18.00	18.00
94	SNOWMAN W/PARCEL GP313	OP	22.50	23.00
94	SNOWMAN W/SPECS GP312	RT	20.00	20.00
94	SPARROW GP329	OP	15.50	16.00
94	SPHINX GP350	RT	22.50	23.00
94	SWAN GP325	OP	20.00	20.00
94	TEDDY BEAR GP338	OP	15.50	16.00
94	TRAIN COACHES GP354	OP	15.50	16.00
94	TRAIN SET GP501	OP	90.00	90.00
94	TROPICAL FISH GP409	OP	22.50	23.00
94	TUTENKHAMEN GP348	OP	25.00	25.00
94	ZODIAC SUN GP381	OP	22.50	23.00
95	ALARM CLOCK GP452	OP	25.00	25.00
95	BLESSED MOTHER GP413	OP	22.50	23.00
95	CAT IN BOOT GP478	OP	28.00	28.00
95	CAT W/BOW GP446	OP	22.50	23.00
95	CEASAR GP422	OP	25.00	25.00
95	CHRIST CHILD GP414	OP	20.00	20.00
95	CHRISTMAS TREE GP461	OP	22.50	23.00
95	CLARA GP408	OP	20.00	20.00
95	CLOWN HEAD GP460	OP	25.00	25.00
95	COWBOY HEAD GP462	OP	30.00	30.00
95	CROCODILE GP468	OP	28.00	28.00
95	EAGLE GP453	OP	28.00	28.00
95	EGYPTIAN SET 4 PC. GP500/4	OP	110.00	110.00
95	ELEPHANT GP	OP	28.00	28.00
95	FISH 4 PC. GP506	OP	110.00	110.00
95	HERR DROSSELMEIR GP465	OP	30.00	30.00
95	HOLY FAMILY 3 PC. GP504	OP	84.00	84.00
95	INDIAN GP463	OP	30.00	30.00
95	LOCOMOTIVE GP447	OP	28.00	28.00
95	NOAH'S ARK GP469	OP	25.00	25.00
95	NUTCRACKER SUITE 4 PC. GP507	OP	110.00	110.00
95	PETER PAN GP419	OP	22.50	23.00
95	PETER PAN SET 4 PC. GP503	OP	124.00	124.00
95	POLONAISE AFRO-AM. SANTA GP389/1	OP	25.00	25.00
95	POLONAISE CARDINAL GP473	OP	25.00	25.00
95	POLONAISE HOUSE GP455	OP	25.00	25.00
95	POLONAISE SANTA GP389	OP	25.00	25.00
95	ROMAN CENTURIAN GP427	OP	22.50	23.00
95	ROMAN SET 7 PC. GP402	OP	164.00	164.00
95	SAILING SHIP GP415	OP	30.00	30.00

YR	NAME	LIMIT	ISSUE	TREND
95	SANTA GP442	OP	25.00	25.00
95	SANTA ON GOOSE ON SLED GP479	OP	30.00	30.00
95	SHARK GP417	OP	18.00	18.00
95	ST. JOSEPH GP412	OP	22.50	23.00
95	TELEPHONE GP448	OP	25.00	25.00
95	TREASURE CHEST GP416	OP	20.00	20.00
95	WIZARD OF OZ 6 PC. GP508	RT	170.00	170.00
95	WIZARD OF OZ DOROTHY GP434	OP	25.00	25.00
95	WIZARD OF OZ LION GP433	OP	22.50	23.00
95	WIZARD OF OZ SCARECROW GP435	OP	25.00	25.00
95	WIZARD OF OZ TINMAN GP436	OP	25.00	25.00
96	ANTIQUE CARS BOXED SET GP522	OP	124.00	124.00
96	BOXED SET OF DICE GP509	OP	60.00	60.00
96	CANDLEHOLDER GP450	OP	20.00	20.00
96	CINDERELLA 4 BOXED SET GP512	OP	134.00	134.00
96	CINDERELLA BOXED SET GP511	7500	190.00	190.00
96	CINDERELLA COACH GP487	OP	33.00	33.00
96	CINDERELLA GP488	OP	28.00	28.00
96	COCA COLA 4 PC BOXED SET GP517	OP	135.00	135.00
96	COSSACK GP604	OP	35.00	35.00
96	EGYPTIAN CAT GP351	OP	30.00	30.00
96	EGYPTIAN II BOXED SET GP510	OP	170.00	170.00
96	EGYPTIAN PRINCESS GP482	OP	33.00	33.00
96	ELVES GP611/23	OP	30.00	30.00
96	EMERALD CITY GP623	OP	32.00	32.00
96	FIRE ENGINE GP605	OP	30.00	30.00
96	GIFT BOXES GP614	OP	25.00	25.00
96	GLASS SLIPPER GP490	OP	20.00	20.00
96	GLINDA THE GOOD WITCH GP621	OP	32.00	32.00
96	GRAMPHONE GP446	OP	22.50	22.50
96	HORUS GP484	OP	33.00	33.00
96	KING BALTHAZAR GP607	OP	30.00	30.00
96	KING KEPTUNE GP496	OP	35.00	35.00
96	LIGHT BULB GP449	OP	20.00	20.00
96	LITTLE MERMAID GP492	OP	28.00	28.00
96	MEDIEVAL BOXED SET GP519	OP	160.00	160.00
96	MEDIEVAL DRAGON GP642	OP	35.00	35.00
96	MEDIEVAL KNIGHT GP641	OP	35.00	35.00
96	MEDIEVAL LADY GP643	OP	35.00	35.00
96	MUMMY GP483	OP	33.00	33.00
96	NEFERTITI 96 GP485	OP	33.00	33.00
96	PHARAOH GP481	OP	35.00	35.00
96	PRINCE CHARMING GP489	OP	28.00	28.00
96	RAGGEDY ANN GP321	OP	28.00	28.00
96	RUSSIAN 5 BOXED SET GP514	OP	190.00	190.00
96	RUSSIAN BISHOP GP603	OP	35.00	35.00
96	RUSSIAN WOMEN GP602	OP	35.00	35.00
96	SANTA CAR GP367	OP	*	*
96	SANTA PILOT GP365	OP	33.00	33.00
96	SEA HORSE GP494	OP	25.00	25.00
96	SPINX GP480	OP	33.00	33.00
96	ST. BASILS CATHEDRAL GP600	OP	35.00	35.00
96	STING RAY GP495	OP	28.00	28.00
96	THREE KINGS BOXED SET GP516	OP	144.00	144.00
96	TSAR IVAN GP601	OP	35.00	35.00
96	TUTENKHANIEN #2 GP476	OP	35.00	35.00
96	WICKED WITCH GP606	OP	32.00	32.00
96	WINTER BOY GP615	OP	22.50	22.50
96	WINTER GIRL GP615	OP	22.50	22.50
96	WIZARD IN BALLOON GP622	OP	32.00	32.00
96	WIZARD OF OZ II BOXED SET GP518	RT	164.00	164.00
STEFAN			**POLONAISE COLLECTION**	
95	CRECHE GP358	OP	28.00	28.00
95	DOVE ON BALL GP472	OP	25.00	25.00
95	GOOSE W/WREATH GP475	OP	25.00	25.00
95	HUMPTY DUMPTY GP477	OP	25.00	25.00
95	ICICLE SANTA GP474	OP	25.00	25.00
95	PARTIDGE GP467	OP	33.50	34.00
95	SANTA MOON GP454	OP	28.00	28.00
95	STAR SANTA GP470	OP	25.00	25.00
95	TURTLE DOVES GP471	OP	25.00	25.00
96	FRENCH HEN GP626	OP	33.00	33.00
96	STAR SNOWMAN GP625	OP	32.00	32.00
J. MOSTROM			**ROYAL HERITAGE**	
93	ANASTASIA W2922	RT	28.00	28.00
93	CAROLINE W2924	OP	25.50	26.00
93	CHARLES W2924	OP	25.50	26.00
93	ELIZABETH W2924	OP	25.50	26.00
93	JOELLA W2979	RT	27.00	27.00
93	KELLY W2979	RT	27.00	27.00
93	NICHOLAS W2923	RT	25.50	26.00
93	PATINA W2923	RT	25.50	26.00
93	SASHA W2923	RT	25.50	26.00
94	ICE FAIRY/WINTER FAIRY W2972	RT	25.50	26.00
94	SNOW PRINCESS W2971	OP	28.00	28.00
95	BENJAMIN J5756	OP	24.50	25.00
95	BLYTHE J5756	OP	24.50	25.00
96	ANGELIQUE ANGEL BABY W3278	OP	25.00	25.00
96	BRIANNA IVORY W7663	OP	25.00	25.00

YR	NAME	LIMIT	ISSUE	TREND
96	BRIANNA PINK W7663	OP	25.00	25.00
96	ETOILE ANGEL BABY W3278	OP	25.00	25.00
96	FRANCIS WINTER BOY W 3279	OP	28.00	28.00
96	GABRIELLE IN PINK COAT W3276	OP	28.00	28.00
96	GISELLE W/BOW W3277	OP	28.00	28.00
96	GISELLE WINTER GIRL W/PACKAGE W3279	OP	28.00	28.00
96	LADY COLETTE IN SLIP W3301	OP	32.00	32.00
96	LAURIELLE LADY SKATER W3281	OP	36.00	36.00
96	MINIOTTE W/MUFF W3279	OP	28.00	28.00
96	MONIQUE W/HAT BOX W3217	OP	28.00	28.00
96	NICOLE W/BALLOON W3277	OP	28.00	28.00
96	RENE VICTORIAN LADY W3280	OP	36.00	36.00
*		**SMITHSONIAN FABRICHE COLLECTION**		
92	FABRICHE SANTA BEAR W1563	OP	22.00	22.00
KSA/SMITHSONIAN		**SMITHSONIAN MUSEUM CAROUSEL**		
87	ANTIQUE CAROUSEL BUNNY, THE S3027/12	RT	14.50	15.00
87	ANTIQUE CAROUSEL GOAT, THE S3027/1	RT	14.50	15.00
88	ANTIQUE CAROUSEL GIRAFFE, THE S3027/4	RT	14.50	15.00
88	ANTIQUE CAROUSEL HORSE, THE S3027/3	RT	14.50	15.00
89	ANTIQUE CAROUSEL CAT, THE S3027/6	RT	14.50	15.00
89	ANTIQUE CAROUSEL LION, THE S3027/5	RT	14.50	15.00
90	ANTIQUE CAROUSEL SEAHORSE, THE S3027/8	RT	14.50	15.00
90	ANTIQUE CAROUSEL ZEBRA, THE S3027/17	RT	14.50	15.00
91	ANTIQUE CAROUSEL HORSE, THE S3027/10	OP	14.50	15.00
91	ANTIQUE CAROUSEL ROOSTER, THE S3027/9	RT	14.50	15.00
92	ANTIQUE CAROUSEL ELEPHANT, THE S3027/11	OP	14.50	15.00
93	ANTIQUE CAROUSEL HORSE, THE S3027/14	OP	15.00	15.00
93	ANTIQUE CAROUSEL TIGER, THE S3027/13	OP	15.00	15.00
94	ANTIQUE CAROUSEL PIG, THE S3027/15	OP	15.50	16.00
94	ANTIQUE CAROUSEL REINDEER, THE S3027/15	OP	15.50	16.00
95	ANTIQUE CAROUSEL CAMEL, THE S3027/14	OP	15.00	15.00
95	ANTIQUE FROG S32027/18	OP	15.50	16.00
95	ARMORED HORSE S3027/17	OP	15.50	16.00
KSA/SMITHSONIAN		**SMITHSONIAN MUSEUM FABRICHE**		
92	HOLIDAY DRIVE W1580	OP	38.00	38.00
92	SANTA ON A BICYCLE W1547	OP	31.00	31.00
K. ADLER		**STEINBACH ORNAMENT SERIES**		
92	KING'S GUARD, THE ES300	OP	27.00	27.00
*		**VATICAN LIBRARY**		
96	CHERUBUM BOXED SET GP521	OP	*	*
96	DANCING CHERUBS ON BALL GP652	OP	*	*
96	FULL BODY CHERUB GP650	OP	*	*
96	GARDEN OF MAY BOXED SET GP520	OP	*	*
96	LILY GLASS GP655	OP	*	*
96	MADONNA & CHILD GP653	OP	*	*
96	ROSE GLASS GP654	OP	*	*

LANCE CORP.

YR	NAME	LIMIT	ISSUE	TREND
P.W. BASTON		**SEBASTIAN CHRISTMAS ORNAMENTS**		
43	MADONNA OF THE CHAIR	CL	2.00	175.00
81	SANTA CLAUS	CL	28.50	30.00
82	MADONNA OF THE CHAIR (REISSUE)	CL	15.00	35.00
P.W. BASTON, JR.		**SEBASTIAN CHRISTMAS ORNAMENTS**		
85	HOME FOR THE HOLIDAYS	CL	10.00	17.00
86	HOLIDAY SLEIGH RIDE	CL	10.00	14.00
87	SANTA	CL	10.00	13.00
88	DECORATING THE TREE	CL	12.50	14.00
89	FINAL PREPARATIONS FOR CHRISTMAS	CL	13.90	13.90
90	STUFFING THE STOCKINGS	CL	14.00	15.00
91	MERRY CHRISTMAS	OP	14.50	15.00
92	FINAL CHECK	OP	14.50	15.00

LAND OF LEGEND

YR	NAME	LIMIT	ISSUE	TREND
R. MUSGRAVE		**POCKET DRAGONS**		
90	ONE SIZE FITS ALL	OP	19.50	20.00
90	PUTTING ME ON THE TREE	5000	47.50	48.00

LENOX CHINA/CRYSTAL COLLECTION

YR	NAME	LIMIT	ISSUE	TREND
*		**ANNUAL BELL SERIES**		
87	PARTRIDGE BELL	YR	45.00	45.00
88	ANGEL BELL	OP	45.00	45.00
89	ST. NICHOLAS BELL	OP	45.00	45.00
90	CHRISTMAS TREE BELL	OP	49.00	49.00
91	TEDDY BEAR BELL	YR	49.00	49.00
92	SNOWMAN BELL	YR	49.00	49.00
*		**ANNUAL ORNAMENT**		
82	1982 ORNAMENT	YR	30.00	70.00
83	1983 ORNAMENT	YR	35.00	75.00
84	1984 ORNAMENT	YR	38.00	65.00
85	1985 ORNAMENT	YR	37.50	60.00
86	1986 ORNAMENT	YR	38.50	50.00
87	1987 ORNAMENT	YR	39.00	45.00
88	1988 ORNAMENT	YR	39.00	45.00
89	1989 ORNAMENT	YR	39.00	39.00
90	1990 ORNAMENT	YR	42.00	42.00
91	1991 ORNAMENT	YR	39.00	39.00
92	1992 ORNAMENT	YR	39.00	39.00

YR	NAME	LIMIT	ISSUE	TREND
BOTTICELLI				**CATHEDRAL PORTRAITS**
91	15TH CENTURY MADONNA & CHILD	OP	29.00	29.00
91	16TH CENTURY MADONNA & CHILD	OP	29.00	29.00
*				**CHRISTMAS CAROUSEL**
89	BLACK HORSE	OP	19.50	20.00
89	CAT	OP	19.50	20.00
89	CHRISTMAS CAROUSEL SET	OP	470.00	470.00
89	ELEPHANT	OP	19.50	20.00
89	GOAT	OP	19.50	20.00
89	HARE	OP	19.50	20.00
89	LION	OP	19.50	20.00
89	PALOMINO	OP	19.50	20.00
89	PINTO	OP	19.50	20.00
89	POLAR BEAR	OP	19.50	20.00
89	REINDEER	OP	19.50	20.00
89	SEA HORSE	OP	19.50	20.00
89	SWAN	OP	19.50	20.00
89	TIGER	OP	19.50	20.00
89	UNICORN	OP	19.50	20.00
89	WHITE HORSE	OP	19.50	20.00
89	ZEBRA	OP	19.50	20.00
90	CAMEL	OP	19.50	20.00
90	FROG	OP	19.50	20.00
90	GIRAFFE	OP	19.50	20.00
90	MEDIEVAL HORSE	OP	19.50	20.00
90	PANDA	OP	19.50	20.00
90	PIG	OP	19.50	20.00
90	ROOSTER	OP	19.50	20.00
90	SET OF 24	OP	468.00	468.00
90	ST. BERNARD	OP	19.50	20.00
*				**COMMEMORATIVES**
89	BABY'S FIRST CHRISTMAS (DATED)	YR	22.50	25.00
89	FIRST CHRISTMAS TOGETHER (DATED)	YR	22.50	25.00
*				**CRYSTAL BALL ORNAMENTS**
91	CRYSTAL ABBEY BALL	OP	45.00	45.00
91	CRYSTAL STARLIGHT BALL-BLUE	OP	45.00	45.00
91	CRYSTAL STARLIGHT BALL-GREEN	OP	45.00	45.00
91	CRYSTAL STARLIGHT BALL-RED	OP	45.00	45.00
92	CRYSTAL OPTIKA	OP	37.00	37.00
*				**DAYS OF CHRISTMAS**
87	PARTRIDGE	OP	22.50	23.00
88	TWO TURTLE DOVES	OP	22.50	23.00
89	THREE FRENCH HENS	OP	22.50	23.00
90	FOUR CALLING BIRDS	OP	25.00	25.00
91	FIVE GOLDEN RINGS	OP	25.00	25.00
92	SIX GEESE A-LAYING	OP	25.00	25.00
*				**GOLDEN RENAISSANCE ANGELS**
91	ANGEL WITH MANDOLIN	OP	25.00	25.00
91	ANGEL WITH TRUMPET	OP	25.00	25.00
91	ANGEL WITH VIOLIN	OP	25.00	25.00
*				**HOLIDAY HOMECOMING**
88	HEARTH	CL	22.50	23.00
89	DOOR-DATED	OP	22.50	23.00
90	HUTCH-DATED	YR	25.00	25.00
91	WINDOW (DATED)	YR	25.00	25.00
92	STOVE (DATED)	YR	25.00	25.00
*				**LENOX CARVED ORNAMENTS**
87	PORTRAIT WREATH	CL	21.00	21.00
89	GEORGIAN FRAME	OP	21.00	25.00
*				**LENOX CHINA ANNUAL ORNAMENTS**
82	1982 ORNAMENT	YR	30.00	90.00
83	1983 ORNAMENT	YR	35.00	75.00
84	1984 ORNAMENT	YR	38.00	65.00
85	1985 ORNAMENT	YR	37.50	60.00
86	1986 ORNAMENT	YR	38.50	50.00
87	1987 ORNAMENT	YR	39.00	45.00
88	1988 ORNAMENT	YR	39.00	45.00
89	1989 ORNAMENT	YR	39.00	39.00
90	1990 ORNAMENT	YR	42.00	42.00
*				**LENOX CHRISTMAS KEEPSAKES**
90	ROCKING HORSE	OP	42.00	42.00
90	SWAN	OP	42.00	42.00
91	SLEIGH	OP	42.00	42.00
92	FIRE ENGINE	OP	42.00	42.00
*				**LENOX CHRISTMAS VILLAGE**
89	VILLAGE CHURCH-DATED	OP	39.00	39.00
90	VILLAGE INN-DATED	YR	39.00	39.00
91	VILLAGE TOWN HALL (DATED)	YR	39.00	39.00
92	SWEET SHOP (DATED)	YR	39.00	39.00
*				**LENOX CRYSTAL BALL ORNAMENTS**
84	DEEP CUT BALL	YR	35.00	50.00
85	CUT BALL	YR	35.00	50.00
86	CUT BALL	YR	35.00	45.00
87	CUT BALL	YR	29.00	29.00
88	CHRISTMAS LIGHTS BALL	YR	30.00	30.00
89	CRYSTAL LIGHTS ORNAMENT	OP	30.00	30.00
89	STARLIGHT ORNAMENT	OP	34.00	34.00

YR	NAME	LIMIT	ISSUE	TREND
*		**LENOX CRYSTAL ORNAMENTS**		
89	ANNUAL CHRISTMAS TREE	YR	26.00	26.00
89	BABY'S FIRST CHRISTMAS	YR	26.00	26.00
89	CANDLELIGHT BELL	OP	38.00	38.00
89	CHRISTMAS LIGHTS TREE TOP ORNAMENT	OP	55.00	55.00
89	CRYSTAL ICICLE	OP	30.00	30.00
89	NATIVITY	OP	26.00	26.00
89	OUR FIRST CHRISTMAS	YR	26.00	26.00
89	SNOWFLAKE	OP	26.00	32.00
90	1990 CHRISTMAS TREE	YR	30.00	30.00
90	BABY'S FIRST CHRISTMAS-1990	YR	30.00	30.00
90	CANDY CANE	OP	30.00	30.00
90	CHRISTMAS GOOSE	OP	30.00	29.00
90	OUR FIRST CHRISTMAS-1990	YR	32.00	32.00
91	ABBEY TREETOPPER	OP	54.00	54.00
91	ANGEL PENDENT	OP	29.00	29.00
91	BABY'S FIRST CHRISTMAS-1991	YR	29.00	29.00
91	BIRD-BLUE	OP	29.00	29.00
91	BIRD-CLEAR	OP	29.00	29.00
91	BIRD-GREEN	OP	29.00	29.00
91	BIRD-RED	OP	29.00	29.00
91	CHRISTMAS STOCKING	OP	29.00	29.00
91	CHRISTMAS TREE-1991	YR	29.00	29.00
91	DOVE	OP	32.00	32.00
91	HERALD ANGEL-BLUE	OP	29.00	29.00
91	HERALD ANGEL-CLEAR	OP	29.00	29.00
91	HERALD ANGEL-GREEN	OP	29.00	29.00
91	HERALD ANGEL-RED	OP	29.00	29.00
91	OUR FIRST CHRISTMAS-1991	YR	29.00	29.00
91	SNOWMAN	OP	32.00	32.00
*				**NATIVITY**
89	JOSEPH	OP	21.00	21.00
89	MARY & CHILD	OP	21.00	21.00
90	BALTHAZAR	OP	22.00	22.00
90	GASPAR	OP	22.00	22.00
90	MELCHIOR	OP	22.00	22.00
*			**RENAISSANCE ANGELS**	
87	ANGEL WITH MANDOLIN	CL	21.00	21.00
87	ANGEL WITH TRUMPET	OP	21.00	21.00
87	ANGEL WITH VIOLIN	CL	21.00	21.00
89	ANGEL TREETOPPER	OP	100.00	100.00
*			**SANTA'S PORTRAITS**	
89	SANTA'S VISIT	OP	27.00	27.00
90	SANTA WITH GARLAND	OP	29.00	29.00
90	SANTA'S RIDE	OP	29.00	29.00
91	SANTA AND CHILD	OP	29.00	29.00
92	SANTA IN CHIMNEY	OP	29.00	29.00
*			**VICTORIAN HOMES**	
90	SHEFFIELD MANOR	OP	25.00	25.00
91	CAMBRIDGE MANOR	OP	25.00	25.00
*			**VICTORIAN LACE**	
91	CHRISTMAS TREE	OP	25.00	25.00
91	FAN	OP	25.00	25.00
*				**YULETIDE**
85	CHRISTMAS TREE	OP	18.00	18.00
85	TEDDY BEAR	CL	18.00	18.00
89	ANGEL WITH HORN	OP	18.00	18.00
89	SANTA WITH TREE	OP	18.00	18.00
90	DOVE	OP	19.50	20.00
91	SNOWMAN	OP	19.50	20.00
92	GOOSE	OP	20.00	20.00
*			**YULETIDE EXPRESS**	
88	LOCOMOTIVE	OP	39.00	39.00
89	CABOOSE-DATED	OP	39.00	90.00
90	PASSENGER-DATED	OP	39.00	39.00
91	DINING CAR (DATED)	YR	39.00	39.00
92	TENDER CAR (DATED)	YR	39.00	39.00

LILLIPUT LANE LTD.

YR	NAME	LIMIT	ISSUE	TREND
*		**ANNUAL CHRISTMAS ORNAMENT**		
96	FIR TREE COTTAGE	OP	30.00	30.00
*		**CHRISTMAS ORNAMENT SERIES**		
92	MISTLETOE COTTAGE	RT	27.50	28.00
93	ROBIN COTTAGE	RT	35.00	100.00
94	IVY HOUSE	RT	37.50	50.00
95	PLUM COTTAGE	RT	40.00	40.00

LLADRO

Price ranges may reflect various demands in the market from one geographic region to another; condition of piece; specific markings found on piece; and/or changes in production of piece.

YR	NAME	LIMIT	ISSUE	TREND
88	ANGEL TREE ORNAMENTS L-1604	TL	75.00	175.00
90	ANGEL TREE TOPPER L-5719	TL	115.00	250.00
91	HOLY SHEPHERDS ORNAMENTS L-5809	TL	97.50	175.00
92	BABY'S FIRST L5922G	YR	55.00	55.00
92	CHRISTMAS MORNING L5940G	YR	97.50	98.00
92	ELF L5938G	YR	50.00	50.00
92	MRS. CLAUS L5939G	YR	55.00	55.00

YR	NAME	LIMIT	ISSUE	TREND
92	OUR FIRST L5923G	YR	50.00	50.00
92	SANTA L5842G	YR	55.00	55.00
92	SNOWMAN L5841G	YR	50.00	50.00
93	1993 CHRISTMAS BALL	RT	54.00	60.00
93	1993 CHRISTMAS BELL	RT	39.50	45.00
93	1993 TREE TOPPER--BLUE	RT	125.00	145.00
94	1994 CHRISTMAS BALL	RT	55.00	65.00
94	1994 CHRISTMAS BELL	RT	39.50	45.00
94	ANGELIS VIOLINIST	RT	150.00	175.00
94	JOYFUL OFFERING	RT	245.00	275.00
*				**ANGEL ORCHESTRA**
91	HEAVENLY HARPIST	YR	135.00	135.00
92	ANGELIC CYMBALIST	YR	140.00	140.00
*				**ANNUAL ORNAMENT**
88	CHRISTMAS BALL L1603M	YR	60.00	100.00
88	CHRISTMAS BALL L5656M	YR	65.00	75.00-125.00
90	CHRISTMAS BALL L5730M	YR	70.00	70.00
91	CHRISTMAS BALL L5829M	YR	52.00	59.00-85.00
92	CHRISTMAS BALL L5914M	YR	52.00	52.00
*				**MINIATURE ORNAMENTS**
88	MINIATURE ANGELS L1604 (SET OF 3)	YR	75.00	150.00-250.00
89	HOLY FAMILY L5657G (SET OF 3)	YR	79.50	90.00-150.00
90	THREE KINGS L5729G (SET OF 3)	YR	87.50	125.00
91	HOLY SHEPHERDS L5809G	YR	97.50	100.00
*				**TREE TOPPER ORNAMENTS**
90	ANGEL TREE TOPPER (BLUE)	YR	115.00	115.00
91	ANGEL TREE TOPPER L5831G (PINK)	YR	115.00	160.00
92	ANGEL TREE TOPPER L5875G (GREEN)	YR	120.00	120.00

MARGARET FURLONG DESIGNS

YR	NAME	LIMIT	ISSUE	TREND
M. FURLONG				
94	VICTORIA HEART ANGEL	RT	24.95	25.00
95	VICTORIA LILY OF THE VALLEY ANGEL	30000	24.95	25.00
96	SUNFLOWER ANGEL	YR	21.00	21.00
M. FURLONG				**FLORA ANGELICA**
95	FAITH ANGEL	RT	45.00	45.00
96	HOPE ANGEL	CL	45.00	45.00

MIDWEST OF CANNON FALLS

YR	NAME	LIMIT	ISSUE	TREND
*** WENDT & KUHN**				
78	ANGEL CLIP-ON 00729-7	OP	20.00	20.00
89	TRUMPETING ANGEL, 2 ASSTD. 09402-0	RT	14.00	15.00
91	ANGEL IN RING 01208-6	OP	12.00	12.00
94	ANGEL ON MOON, STAR, 12 AASTED 12945-6	OP	20.00	20.00
L.R. SMITH				**LEO R. SMITH III COLLECTION**
94	FLYING WOODSMAN SANTA 11921-1	RT	35.00	35.00
95	ANGEL OF LOVE 16123-4	CL	32.00	32.00
95	ANGEL OF PEACE 16199-9	CL	32.00	32.00
95	ANGEL OF YOUR DREAMS 16130-2	CL	32.00	32.00
95	PARTRIDGE ANGEL 13994-3	CL	30.00	30.00
95	SANTA ON REINDEER 13780-2	CL	35.00	35.00
96	ANGEL OF HEAVEN & EARTH 18396-0	CL	33.00	33.00
96	ANGEL OF LIGHT 18076-1	CL	33.00	33.00
96	ANGEL OF MUSIC 18073-4	CL	33.00	33.00
96	BELSNICKLE SANTA 18074-7	CL	39.00	39.00
*				**MOUSEKINS**
94	HEATHCLIFF GREY "TIME TO CELEBRATE"	YR	10.00	10.00

MISS MARTHA ORIGINALS

Price ranges may reflect various demands in the market from one geographic region to another; condition of piece; specific markings found on piece; and/or changes in production of piece.

YR	NAME	LIMIT	ISSUE	TREND
M. ROOT				**ALL GOD'S CHILDREN**
87	CAMEO D-1912	ST	24.00	100.00
87	DOLL D-1924 (SET OF 24)	ST	28.00	2080.00

OLD WORLD CHRISTMAS

YR	NAME	LIMIT	ISSUE	TREND
E.M. MERCK				**ANGELS AND FEMALE FIGURES**
85	RED GIRL WITH TREE 1010309	RT	4.25	10.00
85	SMALL GIRL WITH TREE 101029	RT	3.00	6.00
92	ANGEL ON FORM 1044	RT	9.00	11.00
92	GUARDIAN ANGEL 1043	RT	8.00	10.00
92	HONEY CHILD 1042	RT	7.50	8.00
E.M. MERCK				**ANIMALS**
88	JUMBO ELEPHANT 1213	RT	7.00	10.00
93	PASTEL BUTTERFLY 1268	RT	8.45	10.00
94	WOODLAND SQUIRREL 1291	RT	20.00	21.00
E.M. MERCK				**BIRDS FOR HANGING**
84	COCK ROBIN 161012	RT	3.50	8.00
88	SWANS ON LAKE 1612	RT	5.50	10.00
90	DUCK 1613	RT	5.00	7.00
91	LARGE PARROT ON BALL 1617	RT	10.00	12.00
93	ROOSTER AT HEN HOUSE 1629	RT	6.50	12.00
E.M. MERCK				**BIRDS WITH CLIP**
85	BLUE BIRD 181078	RT	3.30	8.00
85	MED. PEACOCK WITH TINSEL TAIL 187215	RT	4.80	10.00
85	NUTHATCH 181076	RT	3.60	8.00
86	BIRD IN NEST 1801	RT	6.75	12.00

YR	NAME	LIMIT	ISSUE	TREND
87	FAT BURGUNDY BIRD 1813	RT	5.00	10.00
87	LILAC BIRD 1811	RT	5.70	10.00
87	RED-BREASTED SONGBIRD 1812	RT	6.25	7.00
87	SHINY GOLD BIRD 1807	RT	3.50	6.00
90	SMALL RED-HEADED SONGBIRD 1823	RT	6.25	7.00
91	FESTIVE BIRD 1832	RT	6.25	8.00
E.M. MERCK			**CHURCHES AND HOUSES**	
85	SQUARE HOUSE 201040	RT	4.00	10.00
90	CHRISTMAS CHALET 2014	RT	6.75	10.00
91	THATCHED COTTAGE 2019	RT	6.30	8.00
E.M. MERCK			**CLOWNS AND MALE FIGURES**	
86	CLOWN WITH ACCORDION 2409	RT	5.60	12.00
86	CLOWN WITH BANJO 2407	RT	3.75	8.00
86	CLOWN WITH DRUM 2408	RT	5.60	12.00
86	JESTER 2419	RT	4.00	8.00
E.M. MERCK			**COLLECTOR'S EDITIONS**	
92	FLYING PEACOCK WITH WINGS 1550	RT	22.50	24.00
92	FLYING SONGBIRD WITH WINGS 1551	RT	21.75	24.00
E.M. MERCK			**FRUITS AND VEGETABLES**	
85	LARGE BASKET OF GRAPES 281053	RT	6.00	12.00
86	PEAR WITH FACE 2805	RT	3.75	8.00
90	STRAWBERRY CLUSTER 2836	RT	4.20	7.00
E.M. MERCK				**HEARTS**
87	BURGUNDY HEART W/GLITTER 3004	RT	4.30	8.00
88	VALENTINE 3005	RT	4.20	7.00
E.M. MERCK			**MISCELLANEOUS FORMS**	
88	CLIP-ON TULIP 3605	RT	6.30	7.00
89	MORNING GLORIES 3608	RT	8.90	10.00
90	ASSORTED CHRISTMAS STARS 3620	RT	5.70	8.00
90	LARGE SNOWFLAKE 3622	RT	11.25	14.00
92	ASSORTED NORTHERN STARS 3640	RT	6.20	7.00
92	ASSORTED SPIRALS 3636	RT	8.25	9.00
94	VICTORIAN FLORAL DROP 3659	RT	21.25	25.00
E.M. MERCK			**MUSICAL INSTRUMENTS**	
86	CELLO 3801	RT	3.60	8.00
88	LARGE BELL WITH ACORNS 3804	RT	7.00	8.00
E.M. MERCK				**NUTCRACKERS**
87	AUSTRIAN MUSKETEER NUTCRACKER 72048	RT	31.75	75.00
87	BRITISH GUARD NUTCRACKER 72041	RT	35.00	65.00
87	PURSSIAN SERGEANT NUTCRACKTER 72045	RT	35.50	75.00
92	LG. BAVARIAN DUKE NUTCRACKER 72242	RT	99.00	150.00
E.M. MERCK				**REFLECTORS**
86	PINK REFLECTOR 4202	RT	5.98	10.00
90	ASSORTED 6 CM. REFLECTORS 4207	RT	5.80	8.00
90	ASSORTED REFLECTORS W/DIAMONDS 4206	RT	8.00	11.00
E.M. MERCK				**SANTAS**
84	LARGE SANTA IN BASKET 401001	RT	7.00	15.00
85	BLUE FATHER CHRISTMAS 4010498	RT	4.20	10.00
85	JOLLY FATHER CHRISTMAS 401043	RT	3.50	8.00
85	PINK FATHER CHRISTMAS 4010499	RT	4.20	10.00
85	SANTA WITH TREE ON FORM 401026	RT	4.80	10.00
85	SMALL SANTA IN BASKET 401105	RT	4.95	10.00
85	SMALL SANTA WITH PACK 401065	RT	2.90	6.00
86	SANTA IN CHIMNEY 4005	RT	5.25	10.00
86	SANTA WITH GLUED ON TREE 4009	RT	4.80	10.00
86	SMALL BLUE SANTA 4010	RT	3.00	6.00
86	ST. NICHOLAS HEAD 4008	RT	3.55	8.00
89	ST. NICHOLAS 4020	RT	10.00	10.00
90	FESTIVE SANTA HEAD 4039	RT	9.75	12.00
90	WHITE CLIP-ON SANTA 4026	RT	6.00	11.00
93	LG. FATHER CHRISTMAS HEAD 4066	RT	22.50	25.00
E.M. MERCK			**STORYBOOK SANTAS**	
94	POLAR EXPRESS 9701	RT	9.00	12.00
E.M. MERCK				**TRANSPORTATION**
90	LARGE ZEPPELIN 4605	RT	6.75	10.00
92	RACE CAR 4609	RT	5.50	8.00
E.M. MERCK				**TREE TOPS**
89	ANGEL IN INDENT TREE TOP 5009	RT	27.00	27.00
ORREFORS				
O. ALBERIUS			**CHRISTMAS ORNAMENTS**	
84	DOVE	YR	30.00	45.00
85	ANGEL	YR	30.00	40.00
86	REINDEER	YR	30.00	35.00
87	SNOWMAN	YR	30.00	35.00
88	SLEIGH	YR	30.00	35.00
89	CHRISTMAS TREE 1989	YR	35.00	35.00
90	HOLLY LEAVES AND BERRIES	YR	35.00	35.00
91	STOCKING	YR	40.00	40.00
92	STAR	YR	35.00	35.00
93	BELL	OP	35.00	35.00
PACIFIC RIM				
P. SEBERN			**BRISTOL WATERFRONT**	
95	PORTSHEAD LIGHTHOUSE LIGHT COVER ORN.	OP	10.00	10.00

YR	NAME	LIMIT	ISSUE	TREND
PANTON/KRYSTONIA				
*		**WORLD OF KRYSTONIA**		
94	GRAFYNSSORPRISE	RT	19.00	23.00
94	WHAT KRYSTAL	RT	19.00	23.00
PFALTZGRAFF				
B.B. RICHARDS				
93	LITTLEST ANGEL	5000	12.50	15.00
POSSIBLE DREAMS				
* *		**CLOTHTIQUE ANGEL TREE TOPPER**		
*	ANGEL 12 IN.	OP	54.00	54.00
*	ANGEL 12 IN.	OP	54.00	54.00
*	ANGEL 14 1/2 IN.	OP	59.00	59.00
*	ANGEL 14 1/4 IN.	OP	59.00	59.00
*	ANGEL 7 IN.	OP	25.20	26.00
*	ANGEL 7 IN. SET OF THREE	OP	73.00	73.00
*	ANGEL 8 IN. SET OF THREE	OP	70.00	70.00
*	ANGEL 9 1/2 IN.	OP	35.00	35.00
*	ANGEL 9 1/2 IN.	OP	35.00	35.00
*	ANGEL 9 1/2 IN. SET OF THREE	OP	96.00	96.00
*	ANGEL 9 IN.	OP	32.50	33.00
*	ANGEL 9 IN.	OP	32.50	33.00
*	ANGEL GOLD 10 IN.	OP	33.00	33.00
*	ANGEL GOLD 14 IN.	OP	57.50	58.00
*	ANGEL GOLD/BEIGE 13 IN.	OP	65.00	65.00
*	ANGEL GREEN/WHITE 13 IN.	OP	65.00	65.00
*	ANGEL MAUVE/LILAC 7 IN.	OP	24.00	24.00
*	ANGEL MAUVE/LILAC 9 IN.	OP	31.50	32.00
*	ANGEL PEACH/TEAL 12 IN.	OP	53.00	53.00
*	ANGEL PEACH/TEAL 7 IN.	OP	24.00	24.00
*	ANGEL PEACH/TEAL 9 IN.	OP	31.50	32.00
*	ANGEL PURPLE/TEAL 7 IN.	OP	24.00	24.00
*	ANGEL PURPLE/TEAL 9 IN.	OP	31.50	32.00
*	ANGEL RED/CREAM 7 IN.	OP	24.00	24.00
*	ANGEL RED/CREAM 9 IN.	OP	31.50	32.00
*	ANGEL W/SCROLL 10 IN.	OP	40.00	40.00
*	ANGELS 10 IN. SET OF THREE	OP	78.00	78.00
*	CLOTHTIQUE & LACE ANGEL 10 1/2 IN.	OP	37.00	37.00
* *			**CLOTHTIQUE ELVES**	
*	ELVES 7 IN. SET OF THREE	OP	56.50	57.00
* *			**CLOTHTIQUE ORNAMENTS**	
*	1040s SANTA 5 1/2 IN.	OP	19.50	20.00
*	1940s SANTA 7 IN.	OP	24.00	24.00
*	ANGEL 10 IN.	OP	44.00	44.00
*	ANGEL 9 1/2 IN.	OP	36.50	37.00
*	ANGEL 9 1/2 IN. SET OF THREE	OP	108.00	108.00
*	ANGEL GOLD 7 IN.	OP	26.00	26.00
*	ANGEL GOLD 9 IN.	OP	33.90	34.00
*	ANGEL MAUVE/LILAC 7 IN.	OP	24.00	24.00
*	ANGEL MAUVE/LILAC 9 IN.	OP	31.50	32.00
*	ANGEL PEACH/TEAL 7 IN.	OP	24.00	24.00
*	ANGEL PEACH/TEAL 9 IN.	OP	31.50	32.00
*	ANGEL PURPLE/TEAL 7 IN.	OP	24.00	24.00
*	ANGEL PURPLE/TEAL 9 IN.	OP	31.50	32.00
*	ANGEL RED/CREAM 7 IN.	OP	24.00	24.00
*	ANGEL RED/CREAM 9 IN.	OP	31.50	32.00
*	ANGEL/BLUE 9 IN.	OP	44.00	44.00
*	ANGEL/GOLD 9 IN.	OP	44.00	44.00
*	ANGEL/RED 9 IN.	OP	44.00	44.00
*	ANGELS 6 IN. SET OF THREE	OP	57.00	57.00
*	ANGELS 7 1/4 IN. SET OF THREE	OP	79.00	79.00
*	ANGELS 7 IN. SET OF THREE	OP	79.00	79.00
*	AWNGEL 9 1/2 IN.	OP	36.50	37.00
*	BEIGE SANTA 7 IN.	OP	22.50	23.00
*	CHERUB 5 1/3 IN. SET OF THREE	OP	43.00	43.00
*	CHERUBS 5 1/2 IN. SET OF THREE	OP	45.00	45.00
*	CHERUBS 5 IN. SET OF THREE	OP	45.00	45.00
*	CHERUBS GOLD 5 1/2 IN. SET OF THREE	OP	39.50	40.00
*	COLONIAL SANTA 7 IN.	OP	23.00	23.00
*	FATHER CHRISTMAS 7 1/4 IN.	OP	20.00	20.00
*	FIREMAN SANTA 6 IN.	OP	17.50	18.00
*	FIREMAN SANTA 7 3/4 IN.	OP	23.50	24.00
*	FIRST CHRISTMAS 7 IN.	OP	22.50	23.00
*	KRIS KRINGLE 7 IN.	OP	20.00	20.00
*	MRS. CLAUS 5 1/2 IN.	OP	16.00	16.00
*	MRS. CLAUS 6 1/2 IN.	OP	22.00	22.00
*	MRS. CLAUS 6 1/2 IN.	OP	22.00	22.00
*	NICHOLAS 5 1/2 IN.	OP	19.50	20.00
*	NICHOLAS 7 IN.	OP	24.00	24.00
*	PATRIOTIC SANTA 7 1/4 IN.	OP	20.00	20.00
*	SANTA 5 1/2 IN.	OP	16.00	16.00
*	SANTA GREEN COAT 5 1/2 IN.	OP	13.50	14.00
*	SANTA GREEN COAT 7 IN.	OP	15.00	15.00
*	SANTA IN BED 6 3/4 IN.	OP	35.50	36.00
*	SANTA IN RED 7 IN.	OP	23.00	23.00
*	SANTA RED COAT 5 1/2 IN.	OP	13.50	14.00
*	SANTA RED COAT 7 IN.	OP	15.00	15.00

YR	NAME	LIMIT	ISSUE	TREND
*	SANTA W/BLUE CAPE 7 IN.	OP	22.00	22.00
*	SANTA W/LIST 7 IN.	OP	22.00	22.00
*	SANTA W/STAFF 7 IN.	OP	22.00	22.00
*	SANTA WHITE COAT 5 1/2 IN.	OP	13.50	14.00
*	SANTA WHITE COAT 7 IN.	OP	15.00	15.00
*	SKIING SANTA 7 1/2 IN.	OP	25.50	26.00
*	STOP HERE PLEASE 6 1/4 IN.	OP	30.00	30.00
*	TRADITIONAL SANTA 5 1/2 IN.	OP	16.00	16.00
*	TRADITIONAL SANTA 7 IN.	OP	22.00	22.00
*	WORKING SANTA 7 IN.	OP	22.00	22.00
* *				**CLOTHTIQUE SANTAS**
*	SANTA CLAWS 9 3/4 IN.	OP	69.00	69.00
* *				**CRINKLE CLAUS**
*	BISHOP OF MAYA	*	7.80	8.00
*	FATHER CHRISTMAS 3 IN.	*	7.80	8.00
*	GERMAN SANTA 3 IN.	*	7.80	8.00
*	NIBBLY DO 2 3/4 IN.	OP	10.50	11.00
*	PERE NOEL SANTA 3 1/4 IN.	*	7.80	8.00
*	SNUGGLES 3 1/4 IN.	OP	11.70	12.00
*	ST. NICHOLAS 3 IN.	*	7.80	8.00
* *				**PEPSI**
*	PEPSI BOTTLE CAP 2 1/2 IN.	OP	2.90	3.00
*	PEPSI BOTTLE IN WREATH 4 IN.	OP	7.90	8.00
*	PEPSI SANTA 7 IN.	OP	27.00	27.00
*	PEPSI SANTA IN WREATH 3 1/2 IN.	OP	7.40	8.00
*	PEPSI SANTA ON BOTTLE 3 1/2 IN.	OP	13.50	14.00
*	PEPSI SANTA W/BARREL 4 IN.	OP	12.20	12.20
*	PEPSI SANTA/BALLOON 4 1/2 IN.	OP	14.00	15.00
*	PEPSI SANTA/PEPSI CAN 2 1/2 IN.	OP	13.00	13.00
*	PEPSI SANTA/XMAS BALL 3 1/2 IN.	OP	13.50	14.00
*	PEPSI SIGN/WREATH 3 1/2 IN.	OP	7.40	8.00
* *				**THICKETS**
*	BEAU PEEK 3 IN.	OP	14.00	15.00
*	CANDY TAILS 2 1/4 IN.	RT	11.50	12.00
*	CHRISTMAS WHISKERS 3 IN.	RT	11.50	12.00
*	FICKLE TAILS 2 3/4 IN.	OP	11.50	12.00
*	HARMONY HOLIDAY 2 1/4 IN.	OP	12.00	12.00
*	JINGLE BELLS 3 1/4 IN.	RT	12.00	12.00
*	KRIS KRINKLE 3 IN.	OP	12.50	13.00
*	MELODY TWINKLE PAWS 2 3/4 IN.	OP	13.00	13.00
*	RASCAL DOODLE 3 IN.	OP	20.00	20.00
*	TINSEL TUNE 2 1/2 IN.	OP	11.50	12.00
*	TRICKY TAILS 2 3/4 IN.	OP	11.50	12.00
*	TWINKLE TAILS 2 3/4 IN.	OP	11.50	12.00
95	HOLLY TAILS 2 1/4 IN.	OP	11.50	12.00
RECO INTERNATIONAL				
J. MCCLELLAND				**THE RECO ANGEL COLLECTION HANG-UPS**
87	ADORATION	OP	10.00	10.00
87	DEVOTION	OP	7.50	8.00
87	GLORIA	OP	7.50	8.00
87	HARMONY	OP	7.50	8.00
87	HOPE	OP	10.00	10.00
87	INNOCENCE	OP	7.50	8.00
87	JOY	OP	7.50	8.00
87	LOVE	OP	7.50	8.00
87	PEACE	OP	10.00	10.00
87	SERENITY	OP	10.00	10.00
J. MCCLELLAND				**THE RECO CLOWN COLLECTION HANG-UPS**
87	ARABESQUE	OP	8.00	8.00
87	BOW JANGLES	OP	8.00	8.00
87	CURLY	OP	8.00	8.00
87	HOBO	OP	8.00	8.00
87	PROFESSOR, THE	OP	8.00	8.00
87	RUFFLES	OP	8.00	8.00
87	SAD EYES	OP	8.00	8.00
87	SCAMP	OP	8.00	8.00
87	SPARKLES	OP	8.00	8.00
87	TOP HAT	OP	8.00	8.00
87	WHOOPIE	OP	8.00	8.00
87	WINKIE	OP	8.00	8.00
S. KUCK				**THE RECO ORNAMENT COLLECTION**
88	BILLY	YR	15.00	16.00
88	LISA	YR	15.00	16.00
89	HEATHER	YR	15.00	16.00
89	TIMOTHY	YR	15.00	16.00
90	AMY	YR	15.00	16.00
90	JOHNNY	YR	15.00	16.00
90	PEACE ON EARTH	17500	17.50	18.00
REED & BARTON				
*				**12 DAYS OF CHRISTMAS**
83	PARTRIDGE IN A PEAR TREE	YR	16.50	20.00
83	TURTLE DOVES	YR	16.50	20.00
84	CALLING BIRDS	YR	18.50	20.00
84	FRENCH HENS	YR	18.50	20.00
85	GEESE A'LAYING	YR	20.00	20.00
85	GOLD RINGS	YR	20.00	20.00

Angelic Symbolist *is an elegant tree topper produced by Lladró.*

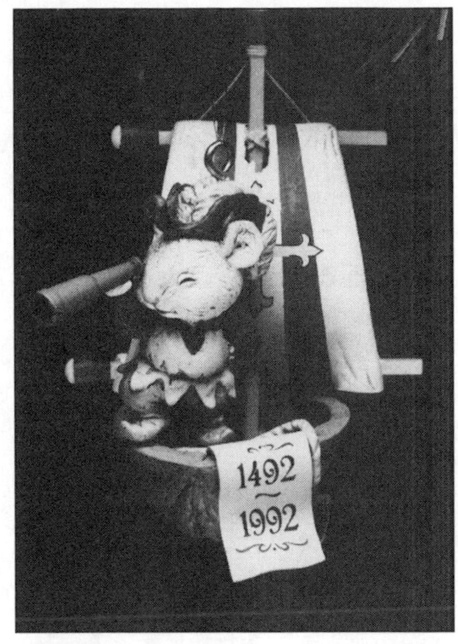

The 500 year anniversary of Christopher Columbus' famous voyage was commemorated by 1992's Christopher Columumouse *from Enesco Corp. in their Treasury of Christmas collection.*

The Treasury of Christmas collection from Enesco Corp. offered this 1992 time limited piece, Merry Makeover.

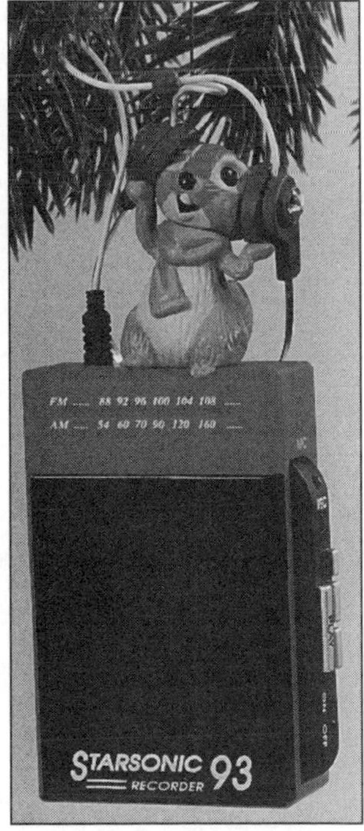

Hallmark was the first to introduce a voice-recordable ornament. Messages of Christmas *enables a collector to record a special message in his own voice.*

YR	NAME	LIMIT	ISSUE	TREND
86	MAIDS A'MILKING	YR	20.00	20.00
86	SWANS A'SWIMMING	YR	20.00	20.00
87	LADIES DANCING	YR	20.00	20.00
87	LORDS A'LEAPING	YR	20.00	20.00
88	DRUMMERS DRUMMING	YR	20.00	20.00
88	PIPERS PIPING	YR	20.00	20.00
*	**12 DAYS OF CHRISTMAS STERLING & LEAD CRYSTAL**			
88	PARTRIDGE IN A PEAR TREE	YR	25.00	28.00
89	TWO TURTLE DOVES	YR	25.00	28.00
90	FRENCH HENS	YR	27.50	28.00
91	CALLING BIRDS	YR	27.50	28.00
92	FIVE GOLDEN RINGS	YR	27.50	28.00
*	**CAROUSEL HORSE**			
88	GOLD COVERED-1988	YR	15.00	16.00
88	SILVERPLATE-1988	YR	13.50	14.00
89	GOLD COVERED-1989	YR	15.00	16.00
89	SILVERPLATE-1989	YR	13.50	14.00
90	GOLD COVERED-1990	YR	14.50	15.00
90	SILVERPLATE-1990	YR	13.50	14.00
91	GOLD COVERED-1991	YR	15.00	16.00
91	SILVERPLATE-1991	YR	13.50	14.00
92	GOLD COVERED-1992	YR	15.00	16.00
92	SILVERPLATE-1992	YR	13.50	14.00
*	**CATHEDRALS**			
90	GOTHIC	YR	12.50	13.00
90	MOORISH	YR	12.50	13.00
*	**CHRISTMAS CROSS**			
71	24KT. GOLD OVER STERLING-V1971	YR	17.50	225.00
71	STERLING SILVER-1971	YR	10.00	300.00
72	24KT. GOLD OVER STERLING-V1972	YR	17.50	80.00
72	STERLING SILVER-1972	YR	10.00	125.00
73	24KT. GOLD OVER STERLING-V1973	YR	17.50	60.00
73	STERLING SILVER-1973	YR	10.00	70.00
74	24KT. GOLD OVER STERLING-V1974	YR	20.00	55.00
74	STERLING SILVER-1974	YR	12.95	45.00
75	24KT. GOLD OVER STERLING-V1975	YR	20.00	50.00
75	STERLING SILVER-1975	YR	12.95	45.00
76	24KT. GOLD OVER STERLING-V1976	YR	19.95	50.00
76	STERLING SILVER-1976	YR	13.95	55.00
77	24KT. GOLD OVER STERLING-V1977	YR	18.50	50.00
77	STERLING SILVER-1977	YR	15.00	45.00
78	24KT. GOLD OVER STERLING-V1978	YR	20.00	50.00
78	STERLING SILVER-1978	YR	16.00	60.00
79	24KT. GOLD OVER STERLING-V1979	YR	24.00	45.00
79	STERLING SILVER-1979	YR	20.00	60.00
80	24KT. GOLD OVER STERLING-V1980	YR	40.00	50.00
80	STERLING SILVER-1980	YR	35.00	60.00
81	24KT. GOLD OVER STERLING-V1981	YR	40.00	45.00
81	STERLING SILVER-1981	YR	35.00	45.00
82	24KT. GOLD OVER STERLING-V1982	YR	40.00	45.00
82	STERLING SILVER-1982	YR	35.00	53.00
83	24KT. GOLD OVER STERLING-V1983	YR	40.00	45.00
83	STERLING SILVER-1983	YR	35.00	50.00
84	24KT. GOLD OVER STERLING-V1984	YR	45.00	45.00
84	STERLING SILVER-1984	YR	35.00	45.00
85	24KT. GOLD OVER STERLING-V1985	YR	40.00	40.00
85	STERLING SILVER-1985	YR	35.00	40.00
86	24KT. GOLD OVER STERLING-V1986	YR	40.00	40.00
86	STERLING SILVER-1986	YR	38.50	39.00
87	24KT. GOLD OVER STERLING-V1987	YR	40.00	40.00
87	STERLING SILVER-1987	YR	35.00	35.00
88	24KT. GOLD OVER STERLING-V1988	YR	40.00	40.00
88	STERLING SILVER-1988	YR	35.00	35.00
89	24KT. GOLD OVER STERLING-V1989	YR	40.00	40.00
89	STERLING SILVER-1989	YR	35.00	35.00
90	24KT. GOLD OVER STERLING-V1990	YR	45.00	45.00
90	STERLING SILVER-1990	YR	40.00	40.00
91	24KT. GOLD OVER STERLING-V1991	YR	45.00	45.00
91	STERLING SILVER-1991	YR	40.00	40.00
92	24KT GOLD OVER STERLING-1992	YR	45.00	45.00
92	STERLING SILVER-1992	YR	40.00	40.00
*	**COLORS OF CHRISTMAS**			
90	VICTORIAN HOUSE	YR	12.50	13.00
90	WREATH	YR	12.50	13.00
*	**DISNEY CHRISTMAS ORNAMENTS**			
87	MICKEY	YR	25.00	40.00
88	MINNIE	YR	25.00	25.00
*	**FLORA OF CHRISTMAS**			
90	POINSETTIA/SNOWDROP (PAIR)	YR	25.00	25.00
91	MISTLETOE & CHRISTMAS IVY	YR	25.00	25.00
*	**HOLLY BALL**			
76	1976 SILVER PLATED	YR	13.95	50.00
77	1977 SILVER PLATED	YR	15.00	35.00
78	1978 SILVER PLATED	YR	15.00	35.00
79	1979 SILVER PLATED	YR	15.00	35.00
*	**HOLLY BELL**			
80	1980 BELL	YR	22.50	40.00

YR	NAME	LIMIT	ISSUE	TREND
80	GOLD PLATE BELL-V1980	YR	25.00	45.00
81	1981 BELL	YR	22.50	35.00
81	GOLD PLATE BELL-V1981	YR	27.50	35.00
82	1982 BELL	YR	22.50	35.00
82	GOLD PLATE BELL-V1982	YR	27.50	35.00
83	1983 BELL	YR	23.50	40.00
83	GOLD PLATE BELL-V1983	YR	30.00	35.00
84	1984 BELL	YR	25.00	30.00
84	GOLD PLATE BELL-V1984	YR	28.50	35.00
85	1985 BELL	YR	25.00	35.00
85	GOLD PLATE BELL-V1985	YR	28.50	29.00
86	1986 BELL	YR	25.00	35.00
86	GOLD PLATE BELL-V1986	YR	28.50	33.00
87	1987 BELL	YR	27.50	30.00
87	GOLD PLATE BELL-V1987	YR	30.00	30.00
88	1988 BELL	YR	27.50	30.00
88	GOLD PLATE BELL-V1988	YR	30.00	30.00
89	1989 BELL	YR	27.50	28.00
89	GOLD PLATE BELL-V1989	YR	30.00	30.00
90	1990 BELL	YR	27.50	28.00
90	GOLD PLATE BELL-V1990	YR	30.00	30.00
91	1991 BELL	YR	27.50	28.00
91	GOLD PLATE BELL-V1991	YR	30.00	30.00
92	GOLD PLATE BELL-V1992	YR	30.00	30.00
92	SILVER PLATE BELL-1992	YR	27.50	28.00
RJB DESIGNS				
R. BRENNAN				**CINDER CLAUS**
93	'93 CINDER CLAUS	1000	42.00	45.00
94	'94 CINDER CLAUS	1000	42.00	45.00
96	CINDER CLAUS	1000	38.00	38.00
ROMAN INC.				
I. SPENCER				**CATNIPPERS**
88	CHRISTMAS MOURNING	OP	15.00	16.00
88	PUSS IN BERRIES	OP	15.00	16.00
88	RING A DING-DING	OP	15.00	16.00
89	BOW BRUMMEL	OP	15.00	16.00
89	HAPPY HOLIDAZE	OP	15.00	16.00
89	SANDY CLAWS	OP	15.00	16.00
90	FELIX NAVIDAD	OP	15.00	16.00
90	SOCK IT TO ME SANTA	OP	15.00	16.00
90	STUCK ON CHRISTMAS	OP	15.00	16.00
91	CHRISTMAS KNIGHT	OP	15.00	16.00
91	FAUX PAW	OP	15.00	16.00
91	MEOWY CHRISTMAS	OP	15.00	16.00
92	HOLLY DAYS ARE HAPPY DAYS	OP	15.00	16.00
92	PAWTRIDGE IN A PURR TREE	OP	15.00	16.00
92	SNOW BIZ	OP	15.00	16.00
E. SIMONETTI		**FONTANINI ANNUAL CHRISTMAS ORNAMENT**		
91	1991 ANNUAL (BOY)	YR	8.50	9.00
91	1991 ANNUAL (GIRL)	YR	8.50	9.00
92	1992 ANNUAL (BOY)	YR	8.50	9.00
92	1992 ANNUAL (GIRL)	YR	8.50	9.00
I. SPENCER			**THE DISCOVERY OF AMERICA**	
91	KITSTOPHER KOLUMBUS	1992	15.00	16.00
91	QUEEN KITSABELLA	1992	15.00	16.00
ROYAL COPENHAGEN				
C. MAGADINE				**BING & GRONDAHL**
96	CHRISTMAS EVE AT THE STATUE OF LIBERTY	YR	25.00	25.00
SAMSONS STUDIOS				
S. BUTCHER				**MCCOONS COUNTY**
87	HERE COMES SANTA CLAUS	CL	15.00	40.00
SARAH'S ATTIC				
S. SCHULTZ			**GOLD PLATED ORNAMENTS**	
95	ADORA/X001	1000	20.00	20.00
95	BLESSED FAMILY/X003	1000	24.00	24.00
95	BLESSED IS HE III/X002	1000	24.00	24.00
95	CLAUDIA/BREWSTER/X006	1000	23.00	23.00
95	OH MY!/X005	1000	23.00	23.00
95	TILLIE/X004	1000	23.00	23.00
S. SCHULTZ		**SANTAS OF THE MONTH ORNAMENTS**		
88	APRIL MINI SANTA	CL	14.00	17.00
88	AUG. MINI SANTA	CL	14.00	17.00
88	DEC. MINI SANTA	CL	14.00	17.00
88	FEB. MINI SANTA	CL	14.00	17.00
88	JAN. MINI SANTA	CL	14.00	17.00
88	JULY MINI SANTA	CL	14.00	17.00
88	JUNE MINI SANTA	CL	14.00	17.00
88	MARCH MINI SANTA	CL	14.00	17.00
88	MAY MINI SANTA	CL	14.00	17.00
88	NOV. MINI SANTA	CL	14.00	17.00
88	OCT. MINI SANTA	CL	14.00	17.00
88	SEPT. MINI SANTA	CL	14.00	17.00

YR	NAME	LIMIT	ISSUE	TREND

SCHMID

Price ranges may reflect various demands in the market from one geographic region to another; condition of piece; specific markings found on piece; and/or changes in production of piece.

YR	NAME	LIMIT	ISSUE	TREND
*				**DISNEY ANNUAL**
85	SNOW BIZ	YR	8.50	20.00
86	TREE FOR TWO	YR	8.50	15.00
87	MERRY MOUSE MEDLEY	YR	8.50	10.00
88	WARM WINTER RIDE	YR	11.00	45.00
89	MERRY MICKEY CLAUS	YR	11.00	11.00
90	HOLLY JOLLY CHRISTMAS	YR	13.50	30.00
91	MICKEY & MINNIE'S ROCKIN' CHRISTMAS	YR	13.50	14.00
L. DAVIS				**FRIENDS OF MINE**
89	SUN WORSHIPPERS	YR	32.50	35.00
90	SUNDAY AFTERNOON TREAT	YR	37.50	35.00
91	WARM MILK	YR	37.50	38.00
92	CAT AND JENNY WREN	YR	35.00	35.00
M. LILLEMOE				**KITTY CUCUMBER ANNUAL**
89	RING AROUND THE ROSIE	YR	25.00	25.00
90	SWAN LAKE	YR	12.00	12.00
91	TEA PARTY	YR	12.00	24.00
L. DAVIS				**LOWELL DAVIS COUNTRY CHRISTMAS**
83	MAILBOX & GIFTS	YR	17.50	55.00-60.00
84	CAT IN BOOT	YR	17.50	28.00-44.00
85	WILBUR IN TROUGH	YR	17.50	60.00
86	CHURCH	YR	17.50	33.00-44.00
87	BLOSSOM IN WREATH	YR	19.50	46.00-59.00
88	WISTERIA IN WREATH	YR	19.50	33.00
89	WREN	YR	19.50	44.00
90	BARN	YR	19.50	20.00
91	CHURCH AT RED OAK II	YR	25.00	27.00
92	BORN ON A STARRY NIGHT	YR	25.00	25.00
L. DAVIS				**LOWELL DAVIS GLASS ORNAMENTS**
86	CHRISTMAS AT RED OAK	YR	5.00	20.00
87	BLOSSOM'S GIFT	YR	5.50	10.00
88	HOPE MOM LIKES IT	YR	6.00	18.00
89	PETER AND THE WREN	YR	6.50	10.00
90	WINTERING DEER	YR	6.50	10.00
91	CHURCH AT RED OAK II	YR	7.50	28.00
92	BORN ON A STARRY NIGHT BALL	YR	7.50	8.00

SCULPTURE WORKSHOP DESIGNS

YR	NAME	LIMIT	ISSUE	TREND
F. KREITCHET				**ANNUAL**
85	RETURN OF THE CHRISTMAS COMET, THE	7500	39.00	100.00
86	LIBERTY/PEACE	7500	49.00	150.00
87	CHRISTMAS AT HOME	2500	57.00	90.00
88	CHRISTMAS DOVES	2500	57.00	80.00
89	SANTA'S REINDEER	2500	60.00	75.00
90	JOYFUL ANGELS	2500	75.00	75.00
91	ANGEL & SHEPHERDS	2500	75.00	75.00
F. KREITCHET				**ANNUAL-SPECIAL COMMEMORATIVE**
87	BICENTENNIAL OF/U.S. CONSTITUTION, THE	200	95.00	250.00
89	PRESIDENTIAL SIGNATURES, THE	200	95.00	125.00
91	U.S. BILL OF RIGHTS, THE	200	150.00	150.00
F. KREITCHET				**SANTA SERIES**
92	FOREVER SANTA	2500	68.00	68.00

SEYMOUR MANN

YR	NAME	LIMIT	ISSUE	TREND
JAIMY				**CHRISTMAS COLLECTION**
89	FLAT RED SANTA ORNAMENT CJ-115R	OP	2.88	3.00
89	FLAT SANTA ORNAMENT CJ-115	OP	7.50	8.00
91	ELF WITH REINDEER CJ-422	CL	9.00	9.00
J. WHITE				**CHRISTMAS COLLECTION**
85	ANGEL WALL ORNAMENT CHRISTMAS-523	CL	12.00	12.00
86	CUPID HEAD ORNAMENT CHRISTMAS-53	OP	25.00	25.00
86	SANTA ORNAMENT CHRISTMAS-384	CL	7.50	8.00
89	CHRISTMAS CAT IN TEACUP CHRISTMAS-660	OP	13.50	14.00
J. SAUERBREY				**GINGERBREAD CHRISTMAS COLLECTION**
91	GINGERBREAD ANGEL CJ-411	CL	7.50	8.00
91	GINGERBREAD HOUSE CJ-416	CL	7.50	8.00
91	GINGERBREAD MAN CJ-415	CL	7.50	8.00
91	GINGERBREAD MOUSE/BOOT CJ-409	CL	7.50	8.00
91	GINGERBREAD MRS. CLAUS CJ-414	CL	7.50	8.00
91	GINGERBREAD REINDEER CJ-410	CL	7.50	8.00
91	GINGERBREAD SANTA CJ-408	CL	7.50	8.00
91	GINGERBREAD SLEIGH CJ-406	CL	7.50	8.00
91	GINGERBREAD SNOWMAN CJ-412	CL	7.50	8.00
91	GINGERBREAD TREE CJ-407	CL	7.50	8.00
JAIMY				**VICTORIAN CHRISTMAS COLLECTION**
93	COUPLE AGAINST WIND CJ-420	CL	15.00	16.00

SHELIA'S COLLECTIBLES

YR	NAME	LIMIT	ISSUE	TREND
S. THOMPSON				
95	CHESTNUT HOUSE	TL	19.00	19.00
95	DRAYTON HOUSE	TL	19.00	19.00
95	GOELLER HOUSE	TL	19.00	19.00
95	STOCKTON PLACE ROW	TL	19.00	19.00

YR	NAME	LIMIT	ISSUE	TREND
96	ARTIST HOUSE	OP	19.00	19.00
96	DRAGON HOUSE	OP	19.00	19.00
96	E.B. HALL	OP	19.00	19.00
96	MAIL POUCH BARN	OP	19.00	19.00
96	MARKET	OP	19.00	19.00
96	RUTLEDGE	OP	19.00	19.00
96	VICTORIA	OP	19.00	19.00
S. THOMPSON			**GOLDEN TOUCH ORIGINALS**	
96	CAPITOL	OP	19.00	19.00
96	PINK HOUSE	OP	19.00	19.00
96	ST. PHILIPS CHURCH	OP	19.00	19.00
96	THOMAS POINT LIGHT	OP	19.00	19.00
96	TITMAN HOUSE	OP	19.00	19.00
96	WHITE COTTAGE	OP	19.00	19.00
S. THOMPSON			**GOLDEN TOUCH ORIGINALS OUR STARS**	
96	BANTA HOUSE	*	21.00	21.00
96	GREENMAN HOUSE	*	21.00	21.00
96	RILEY-CUTTER HOUSE	*	21.00	19.00
96	WELLER HOUSE	*	21.00	21.00
S. THOMPSON			**WEST COAST LIGHTHOUSES**	
95	POINT FERMIN	*	19.00	19.00

STUDIOS OF HARRY SMITH

YR	NAME	LIMIT	ISSUE	TREND
H. SMITH			**CHRISTMAS TREE ORNAMENTS**	
95	ANGEL	150	350.00	350.00
95	HUMMINGBIRD	150	250.00	250.00

SWAROVSKI AMERICA

YR	NAME	LIMIT	ISSUE	TREND
*			**HOLIDAY ORNAMENTS**	
86	ANGEL/NOEL, LARGE	YR	35.00	75.00
86	DOVE/PEACE, SMALL	YR	18.00	60.00
86	HOLLY/MERRY CHRISTMAS, SMALL	YR	18.00	60.00
86	LARGE PARTRIDGE/MERRY CHRISTMAS	YR	35.00	75.00
86	MEDIUM ANGEL/JOYEUX NOEL	YR	22.50	75.00
86	MEDIUM BELL/MERRY CHRISTMAS	YR	22.50	75.00
86	SMALL ANGEL/NOEL	YR	18.00	60.00
86	SMALL BELL/MERRY CHRISTMAS	YR	18.00	60.00
86	SNOWFLAKE, MEDIUM	YR	22.50	75.00
86	SNOWFLAKE, SMALL	YR	18.00	70.00
87	1987 HOLIDAY ETCHING-CANDLE	YR	20.00	175.00
88	1988 HOLIDAY ETCHING-WREATH	YR	25.00	60.00
89	1989 HOLIDAY ETCHING-DOVE	YR	35.00	175.00
90	1990 HOLIDAY ETCHING-MERRY CHRISTMAS	YR	25.00	125.00
91	1991 HOLIDAY ORNAMENT	YR	35.00	80.00
M. ZENDRON			**HOLIDAY ORNAMENTS**	
95	SWAROVSKI '95 HOLIDAY ORNAMENT	CL	40.00	40.00
96	SWAROVSKI '96 HOLIDAY ORNAMENT	OP	45.00	45.00

TOWLE SILVERSMITHS

YR	NAME	LIMIT	ISSUE	TREND
*			**CHRISTMAS ANGEL**	
91	1991 ANGEL	CL	45.00	55.00
*			**GRANDE BAROQUE 12 DAYS SERIES**	
91	FOUR COLLY BIRDS	CL	40.00	95.00
92	FIVE GOLDEN RINGS	CL	40.00	50.00
93	SIX GEESE A LAYING	CL	40.00	43.00
94	SEVEN SWANS A SWIMMING	OP	40.00	40.00
95	EIGHT MAIDS A MILKING	OP	40.00	40.00
*			**REMEMBRANCE COLLECTION**	
90	OLD MASTER SNOWFLAKE-1990	CL	45.00	60.00
91	OLD MASTER SNOWFLAKE-1991	CL	45.00	60.00
92	OLD MASTER SNOWFLAKE-1992	CL	45.00	60.00
*			**SONGS OF CHRISTMAS MEDALLIONS**	
78	SILENT NIGHT MEDALLION	CL	35.00	60.00
79	DECK THE HALLS	CL	35.00	50.00
80	JINGLE BELLS	CL	52.50	60.00
81	HARK THE HEARLD ANGELS SING	CL	52.50	60.00
82	O CHRISTMAS TREE	CL	35.00	50.00
83	SILVER BELLS	CL	40.00	60.00
84	LET IT SNOW	CL	30.00	50.00
85	CHESTNUTS ROASTING ON OPEN FIRE	CL	35.00	50.00
86	IT CAME UPON A MIDNIGHT CLEAR	CL	35.00	45.00
87	WHITE CHRISTMAS	CL	35.00	45.00
*			**STERLING CHRISTMAS ORNAMENTS**	
89	FACETED BALL	OP	38.00	38.00
89	FLUTED BALL	OP	38.00	38.00
89	PLAIN BALL	OP	38.00	38.00
89	POMANDER BALL	OP	33.00	33.00
*			**STERLING FLORAL MEDALLIONS**	
83	CHRISTMAS ROSE	CL	40.00	50.00
84	HAWTHORNE/GLASTONBURY THORN	CL	40.00	50.00
85	POINSETTIA	CL	35.00	60.00
86	LAUREL BAY	CL	35.00	70.00
87	MISTLETOE	CL	35.00	75.00
88	HOLLY	CL	40.00	60.00
89	IVY	CL	35.00	50.00
90	CHRISTMAS CACTUS	CL	40.00	50.00
91	CHRYSANTHEMUM	CL	40.00	50.00

YR	NAME	LIMIT	ISSUE	TREND
92	STAR OF BETHLEHEM	CL	40.00	45.00
*	**STERLING NATIVITY MEDALLION**			
88	ANGEL GABRIEL	CL	40.00	100.00
89	JOURNEY, THE	CL	40.00	70.00
90	NO ROOM AT THE INN	CL	40.00	60.00
91	TIDINGS OF JOY	CL	40.00	60.00
92	STAR OF BETHLEHEM	CL	40.00	60.00
*	**STERLING TWELVE DAYS OF CHRISTMAS MEDALLIONS**			
71	PARTRIDGE IN PEAR TREE	CL	20.00	700.00
72	TWO TURTLE DOVES	CL	20.00	250.00
73	THREE FRENCH HENS	CL	20.00	150.00
74	FOUR MOCKINGBIRDS	CL	30.00	100.00
75	FIVE GOLDEN RINGS	CL	30.00	100.00
76	SIX GEESE-A-LAYING	CL	30.00	125.00
77	SEVEN SWANS-A-SWIMMING	CL	35.00	75.00
78	EIGHT MAIDS-A-MILKING	CL	37.00	90.00
79	NINE LADIES DANCING	CL	37.00	75.00
80	TEN LORDS-A-LEAPING	CL	76.00	80.00
81	ELEVEN PIPERS PIPING	CL	50.00	80.00
82	TWELVE DRUMMERS DRUMMING	CL	35.00	80.00
*	**TWELVE DAYS OF CHRISTMAS**			
79	SILVERPLATE ETCHED	1000	3.60	10.00
79	SILVERPLATE ETCHED	1000	3.60	10.00
79	SILVERPLATE ETCHED	1000	3.60	10.00
79	SILVERPLATE ETCHED	1000	3.60	10.00
79	SILVERPLATE ETCHED	1000	3.60	10.00
79	SILVERPLATE ETCHED	1000	3.60	10.00
79	SILVERPLATE ETCHED	1000	3.60	10.00
79	SILVERPLATE ETCHED	1000	3.60	10.00
79	SILVERPLATE ETCHED	1000	3.60	10.00
79	SILVERPLATE ETCHED	1000	3.60	10.00
79	SILVERPLATE ETCHED	1000	3.60	10.00
79	SILVERPLATE ETCHED	1000	3.60	10.00
88	GOLDPLATE ETCHED	2500	7.00	7.00
88	GOLDPLATE ETCHED	2500	7.00	7.00
88	GOLDPLATE ETCHED	2500	7.00	7.00
88	GOLDPLATE ETCHED	2500	7.00	7.00
88	GOLDPLATE ETCHED	2500	7.00	7.00
88	GOLDPLATE ETCHED	2500	7.00	7.00
88	GOLDPLATE ETCHED	2500	7.00	7.00
88	GOLDPLATE ETCHED	2500	7.00	7.00
88	GOLDPLATE ETCHED	2500	7.00	7.00
88	GOLDPLATE ETCHED	2500	7.00	7.00
88	GOLDPLATE ETCHED	2500	7.00	7.00
88	GOLDPLATE ETCHED	2500	7.00	7.00
91	PARTRIDGE IN PEAR TREE	CL	45.00	45.00
92	TWO TURTLEDOVES IN WREATH	CL	45.00	45.00

UNITED DESIGN CORP.

YR	NAME	LIMIT	ISSUE	TREND
S. BRADFORD	**ANGELS COLLECTION**			
91	FRA ANGELICO DRUMMER, BLUE IBO-414	OP	20.00	20.00
91	FRA ANGELICO DRUMMER, IVORY IBO-420	OP	20.00	20.00
91	FRA ANGELICO DRUMMER, IVORY IBO-420	OP	20.00	20.00
91	GIRL CUPID W/ROSE, IVORY IBO-413	OP	15.00	16.00
91	VICTORIAN CUPID IBO-415	OP	15.00	16.00
92	ANGEL AND TAMBOURINE IBO-422	OP	20.00	20.00
92	ANGEL AND TAMBOURINE, IVORY IBO-425	OP	20.00	20.00
92	MARY AND DOVE IBO-424	OP	20.00	20.00
92	ST. FRANCIS AND CRITTERS IBO-423	OP	20.00	20.00
P. JONAS	**ANGELS COLLECTION**			
90	CRYSTAL ANGEL IBO-401	OP	20.00	20.00
90	CRYSTAL ANGEL, IVORY IBO-405	OP	20.00	20.00
90	ROSE OF SHARON IBO-402	OP	20.00	20.00
90	ROSE OF SHARON, IVORY IBO-406	OP	20.00	20.00
90	STAR GLORY IBO-403	OP	15.00	16.00
90	STAR GLORY, IVORY IBO-407	OP	15.00	16.00
90	VICTORIAN ANGEL IBO-404	OP	15.00	16.00
90	VICTORIAN ANGEL, IVORY IBO-408	OP	15.00	16.00
91	ANGEL WAIF, IVORY IBO-411	OP	15.00	16.00
91	PEACE DESCENDING IBO-418	OP	20.00	20.00
91	PEACE DESCENDING, IVORY IBO-412	OP	20.00	20.00
91	ROSETTI ANGEL IBO-416	OP	20.00	20.00
91	ROSETTI ANGEL, IVORY IBO-410	OP	20.00	20.00
91	VICTORIAN CUPID, IVORY IBO-409	OP	15.00	16.00

VICKILANE

YR	NAME	LIMIT	ISSUE	TREND
V. ANDERSON	**LIL BLESSINGS**			
94	BUNNY ANGEL #1610	OP	13.00	13.00
94	BUNNY ANGEL #1611	OP	13.00	13.00
94	BUNNY ANGEL #1612	OP	13.00	13.00
94	BUNNY ANGEL #1613	OP	13.00	13.00
94	BUNNY ANGEL #1614	OP	13.00	13.00
94	BUNNY ANGEL #1615	OP	13.00	13.00

WALLACE SILVERSMITHS

YR	NAME	LIMIT	ISSUE	TREND
*	**24K GOLDPLATE SCULPTURES**			
88	ANGEL	CL	15.99	16.00
88	CANDY CANE	CL	15.99	16.00

YR	NAME	LIMIT	ISSUE	TREND
88	CHRISTMAS TREE	CL	15.99	16.00
88	DOVE	CL	15.99	16.00
88	NATIVITY SCENE	CL	15.99	16.00
88	SNOWFLAKE	CL	15.99	16.00
*		**ANNUAL SILVERPLATED BELLS**		
71	1ST EDITION SLEIGH BELL	CL	12.95	1000.00
72	2ND EDITION SLEIGH BELL	CL	12.95	400.00
73	3RD EDITION SLEIGH BELL	CL	12.95	400.00
74	4TH EDITION SLEIGH BELL	CL	13.95	150.00
75	5TH EDITION SLEIGH BELL	CL	13.95	250.00
76	6TH EDITION SLEIGH BELL	CL	13.95	300.00
77	7TH EDITION SLEIGH BELL	CL	14.95	75.00
78	8TH EDITION SLEIGH BELL	CL	14.95	75.00
79	9TH EDITION SLEIGH BELL	CL	15.95	125.00
80	10TH EDITION SLEIGH BELL	CL	18.95	50.00
81	11TH EDITION SLEIGH BELL	CL	18.95	60.00
82	12TH EDITION SLEIGH BELL	CL	19.95	90.00
83	13TH EDITION SLEIGH BELL	CL	19.95	80.00
84	14TH EDITION SLEIGH BELL	CL	21.95	75.00
85	15TH EDITION SLEIGH BELL	CL	21.95	90.00
86	16TH EDITION SLEIGH BELL	CL	21.95	35.00
87	17TH EDITION SLEIGH BELL	CL	21.99	25.00
88	18TH EDITION SLEIGH BELL	CL	21.99	25.00
89	19TH EDITION SLEIGH BELL	CL	24.99	25.00
90	20TH EDITION SLEIGH BELL	CL	25.00	25.00
90	SPECIAL EDITION SLEIGH BELL, GOLD	CL	35.00	75.00
91	21ST EDITION SLEIGH BELL	CL	25.00	25.00
92	22ND EDITION SLEIGH BELL	CL	25.00	40.00
93	23RD EDITION SLEIGH BELL	CL	25.00	25.00
94	24TH EDITION SLEIGH BELL	CL	25.00	25.00
95	25TH EDITION SLEIGH BELL	CL	30.00	30.00
*		**ANTIQUE PEWTER BELLS**		
89	REINDEER	CL	15.99	16.00
89	TEDDY BEAR	CL	15.99	16.00
89	TOY SOLDIER	CL	15.99	16.00
90	CAROUSEL HORSE	CL	16.00	16.00
90	SANTA CLAUS	CL	16.00	16.00
*		**ANTIQUE PEWTER ORNAMENTS**		
*	CANDY CANE	CL	9.99	10.00
*	DOVE	CL	9.99	10.00
*	GINGERBREAD HOUSE	CL	9.99	10.00
*	ROCKING HORSE	CL	9.99	10.00
*	TEDDY BEAR	CL	9.99	10.00
*	TOY SOLDIER	CL	9.99	10.00
89	ANGEL WITH CANDLES	CL	9.99	10.00
89	CHERUB WITH HORN	CL	9.99	10.00
89	SANTA	CL	9.99	10.00
89	TEDDY BEAR	CL	9.99	10.00
89	WREATH	CL	9.99	10.00
*		**CAMEO FRAME ORNAMENTS**		
89	ANGEL	OP	14.99	15.00
89	CHRISTMAS BALL	OP	14.99	15.00
89	DINO	OP	14.99	15.00
89	ELEPHANT	OP	14.99	15.00
89	KITTEN	OP	14.99	15.00
89	SANTA	OP	14.99	15.00
89	SNOWMAN	OP	14.99	15.00
89	SOLDIER	OP	14.99	15.00
89	WREATH	OP	14.99	15.00
*		**CANDY CANES**		
81	PEPPERMINT	CL	8.95	225.00
82	WINTERGREEN	CL	9.95	60.00
83	CINNAMON	CL	10.95	50.00
84	CLOVE	CL	10.95	50.00
85	DOVE MOTIF	CL	11.95	50.00
86	BELL MOTIF	CL	11.95	80.00
87	TEDDY BEAR	CL	12.95	50.00
88	CHRISTMAS ROSE	CL	13.99	40.00
89	CHRISTMAS CANDLE	CL	14.99	35.00
90	REINDEER	CL	16.00	20.00
*		**CATHEDRAL ORNAMENT**		
88	1988-1ST EDITION	CL	24.99	25.00
89	1989-2ND EDITION	CL	24.99	25.00
90	1990-3RD EDITION	CL	25.00	25.00
*		**CHRISTMAS COOKIE ORNAMENT**		
80	ANGEL	CL	5.95	20.00
80	SANTA	CL	5.95	10.00
80	SNOWMAN	CL	5.95	15.00
80	TREE	CL	5.95	15.00
81	BELL	CL	5.95	15.00
81	DRUM	CL	5.95	15.00
81	REINDEER	CL	5.95	15.00
82	DOVE	CL	5.95	20.00
82	MOUSE	CL	5.95	15.00
82	TRAIN	CL	5.95	15.00
83	BOY CAROLER	CL	5.95	15.00
83	GINGERBREAD HOUSE	CL	5.95	10.00
83	HUSKY	CL	5.95	20.00

YR	NAME	LIMIT	ISSUE	TREND
83	JACK-IN-THE-BOX	CL	5.95	10.00
83	MRS. CLAUS	CL	5.95	10.00
83	ROCKING HORSE	CL	5.95	10.00
83	TOY SOLDIER	CL	5.95	10.00
84	CAROL SINGER	CL	6.95	15.00
84	HORN	CL	6.95	10.00
84	MOTHER AND CHILD	CL	6.95	15.00
84	PUPPY IN BOOT	CL	6.95	10.00
85	BOY SKATER	CL	10.95	10.00
85	CLOWN	CL	6.95	10.00
85	HOT-AIR BALLOON	CL	10.95	10.00
85	TEDDY BEAR	OP	6.95	10.00
85	UNICORN	CL	6.95	10.00
86	CARROUSEL HORSE	CL	6.95	20.00
86	DOG ON SLED	CL	6.95	20.00
86	DRESSED KITTEN	CL	6.95	15.00
86	GIRL HONEY BEAR	CL	6.95	10.00
86	GOOSE	CL	6.95	15.00
86	NEW DESIGN SNOWMAN	CL	6.95	20.00
86	PANDA	CL	5.95	10.00
86	PENGUIN	CL	6.95	10.00
86	SANTA HEAD	CL	6.95	10.00
86	TUGBOAT	CL	6.95	10.00
87	ANGEL WITH HEART	OP	7.95	10.00
87	GIRAFFE	CL	7.95	10.00
87	POLAR BEAR	OP	7.95	10.00
87	SKI CABIN	CL	7.95	10.00
87	SNOWBIRD	CL	7.95	10.00
88	ANGEL	OP	8.99	10.00
88	BABY BEAR	OP	8.99	10.00
88	CHRISTMAS VILLAGE	OP	8.99	10.00
88	DRAGON	OP	8.99	10.00
88	ELEPHANT	OP	8.99	10.00
88	GOOSE	OP	8.99	10.00
88	NIGHT BEFORE, THE	OP	8.99	10.00
88	POLAR BEAR	OP	8.99	10.00
88	TEDDY BEAR	OP	8.99	10.00
89	ROCKING HORSE	OP	9.99	10.00
89	SANTA	OP	9.99	10.00
89	SNOWBIRD	OP	9.99	10.00
*		**GRANDE BAROQUE 12 DAY SERIES**		
88	PARTRIDGE	CL	39.99	80.00
89	TWO TURTLE DOVES	CL	39.99	100.00
90	THREE FRENCH HENS	CL	40.00	75.00
*		**STERLING MEMORIES**		
89	BEAR WITH BLOCKS	OP	34.99	35.00
89	CAROLERS	OP	34.99	35.00
89	CHURCH	OP	34.99	35.00
89	DOVE	OP	34.99	35.00
89	DRUMMER BOY	OP	34.99	35.00
89	MOTHER & CHILD	OP	34.99	35.00
89	NATIVITY ANGEL	OP	34.99	35.00
89	REINDEER	OP	34.99	35.00
89	ROCKING HORSE	OP	34.99	35.00
89	SLEIGH	OP	34.99	35.00
89	SNOWFLAKE	OP	34.99	35.00
89	SNOWMAN	OP	34.99	35.00
*		**STERLING MEMORIES-HAND ENAMELED WITH COLOR**		
89	CANDY CANE	OP	34.99	35.00
89	CHURCH	OP	34.99	35.00
89	ELF WITH GIFT	OP	34.99	35.00
89	FIREPLACE	OP	34.99	35.00
89	KNEELING ANGEL	OP	34.99	35.00
89	SANTA	OP	34.99	35.00
89	SINGLE CANDLE	OP	34.99	35.00
89	TOY SOLDIER	OP	34.99	35.00
89	TRAIN	OP	34.99	35.00

WALT DISNEY CLASSICS COLLECTION

YR	NAME	LIMIT	ISSUE	TREND
*		**COLLECTOR'S SOCIETY**		
93	FLIGHT OF FANCY	*	35.00	50.00

WATERFORD WEDGWOOD USA

YR	NAME	LIMIT	ISSUE	TREND
*		**WATERFORD CRYSTAL CHRISTMAS ORNAMENTS**		
78	1978 ORNAMENT	YR	25.00	100.00
79	1979 ORNAMENT	YR	28.00	75.00
80	1980 ORNAMENT	YR	28.00	65.00
81	1981 ORNAMENT	YR	28.00	45.00
82	1982 ORNAMENT	YR	28.00	45.00
83	1983 ORNAMENT	YR	28.00	50.00
84	1984 ORNAMENT	YR	28.00	50.00
85	1985 ORNAMENT	YR	28.00	75.00
86	1986 ORNAMENT	YR	28.00	50.00
87	1987 ORNAMENT	YR	29.00	40.00
88	1988 ORNAMENT	YR	30.00	35.00
89	1989 ORNAMENT	YR	32.00	35.00
*		**WEDGWOOD CHRISTMAS ORNAMENTS**		
88	JASPER CHRISTMAS TREE ORNAMENT	OP	20.00	28.00

YR	NAME	LIMIT	ISSUE	TREND
89	JASPER ANGEL ORNAMENT	OP	25.00	28.00
90	JASPER SANTA CLAUS ORNAMENT	OP	28.00	28.00
91	JASPER WREATH ORNAMENT	OP	28.00	28.00
92	JASPER STOCKING ORNAMENT	OP	25.00	25.00

WENDALL AUGUST FORGE

L. YOUNGO — **COLLECTORS GUILD MEMBER'S ONLY**

YR	NAME	LIMIT	ISSUE	TREND
95	HEAVENLY HARPIST	10000	*	*

D. BRUCK — **RELIGIOUS SERIES**

YR	NAME	LIMIT	ISSUE	TREND
95	STAR OF BETHLEHEM	YR	*	*

WILLITTS DESIGNS

A. DEZENDORF — **AMISH HERITAGE COLLECTION**

YR	NAME	LIMIT	ISSUE	TREND
96	POCKET QUILT 3RD OF 4	YR	20.00	20.00

C. SCHULTZ — **CERAMIC PEANUTS ORNAMENTS**

YR	NAME	LIMIT	ISSUE	TREND
88	CHARLIE BROWN	SO	7.50	8.00
88	FLYING ACE	SO	7.50	8.00
88	JOE COOL	SO	7.50	8.00
88	LUCY	SO	7.50	8.00
88	SKATING SNOOPY	SO	7.50	8.00
88	SLEDDING SNOOPY	SO	7.50	8.00
88	WOODSTOCK (BELL)	SO	7.50	8.00

* — **COCA-COLA SANTA**

YR	NAME	LIMIT	ISSUE	TREND
90	COCA-COLA SIX PACK ORNAMENT	OP	20.00	20.00
90	HAPPY HOLIDAYS COKE BOTTLE	OP	10.00	10.00

T. BLACKSHEAR — **EBONY VISIONS COLLECTION**

YR	NAME	LIMIT	ISSUE	TREND
95	POCKET QUILT 2ND OF 4	YR	20.00	20.00

C. PYLE — **HISTORY OF ANGELS COLLECTION BY BILL DALE**

YR	NAME	LIMIT	ISSUE	TREND
95	ASCENSION OF THE SOUL	RT	25.00	25.00
95	CHERUB ORNAMENT W/FLUTE	RT	17.50	17.50
95	CHERUB ORNAMENT W/HARP	RT	17.50	17.50

C. SCHULTZ — **PEANUTS**

YR	NAME	LIMIT	ISSUE	TREND
90	CHARLIE BROWN SHEPERD ORNAMENT	SO	10.00	10.00
90	SNOOPY SHEPERD ORNAMENT	SO	10.00	10.00

C. SCHULTZ — **PEANUTS BASEBALL ORNAMENTS**

YR	NAME	LIMIT	ISSUE	TREND
88	CHARLIE BROWN	SO	10.00	10.00
88	LINUS	SO	10.00	10.00
88	LUCY	SO	10.00	10.00
88	PEPPERMINT PATTY	SO	10.00	10.00
88	SCHROEDER	SO	10.00	10.00
88	SNOOPY	SO	10.00	10.00

C. SCHULTZ — **WOODEN SNOOPY ORNAMENTS**

YR	NAME	LIMIT	ISSUE	TREND
88	SNOOPY-8438	SO	5.50	5.50
88	SNOOPY-8439	OP	5.50	5.50
88	SNOOPY-8440	SO	5.50	5.50

Plates

Susan K. Elliott

If the circle can be considered a form of perfection, then plate collectors enjoy a perfect form of art.

Since the first dated annual Christmas plates appeared in 1895 in Denmark, collectors have been happily anticipating the "next" edition to be released. Bing & Grondahl issued that first blue and white collector's plate, *Behind the Frozen Window*, at approximately 50 cents. Today, as the series enjoys over 100 years of continuous production, that rare first edition sells for about $5,000.

Of course, these days not all plates are round, made of porcelain, or colored blue and white. New shapes include ovals, rounded squares, and even hearts. Today's plates may be sculpted in bas relief, incised, lighted or able to play a tune. They're made of wood, molded resin, pewter, crystal or porcelain. Subjects range from cute to elegant, with every possibility in between, and in a full range of colors and accent borders.

Until the 1960s, collector's plates continued to be made in Europe and produced only for Christmas. Royal Copenhagen introduced a second Danish Christmas series in 1908, and Rosenthal began a dated Christmas series in Germany in 1907.

Other key events in plate collecting history include:

- 1965: Lalique introduces a crystal plate, *Deux Oiseeaux* (*Two Birds*)
- 1969: Bing & Grondahl releases the first Mother's Day plate, *Dog and Puppies*, in blue and white
- 1969: Wedgwood issues *Windsor Castle* as first in a new Christmas series, produced in its famous blue and white jasperware
- 1970: Franklin Mint introduces original art by Norman Rockwell on a sterling silver plate, *Bringing Home the Tree*
- 1971: two Christmas series featuring art by Sister Maria Innocentia Hummel begin, with the Goebel Hummel issue, *Heavenly Angel*, later becoming one of the most valuable plates in the market.

The 1970s saw a boom in collecting of all types, spurred by the celebration of the U.S. Bicentennial in 1976. Historical subject plates abounded, and more and more makers, both American and European, focused on plates as a collectible. New artists entered the field, elevating the art and generating more attention to the artists themselves.

The development of the First International Plate Collectors Convention in 1975 provided a platform for the limited edition hobby to grow, and grow it has, expanding into many related types of art forms such as figurines, cottages, ornaments, dolls and graphics. The number of platemakers peaked in the 1980s, with production shifting to fewer, major producers such as The Bradford Exchange by the 1990s.

Plate collectors of the '90s are likely to collect other genre besides plates, searching for graphics by favorite artists such as Thomas Kinkade, Sandra Kuck, Terry Redlin and Lena Liu to round out their collections.

As plate collecting enters its second hundred years, the art form remains an ever-changing and always growing collectible.

SUSAN K. ELLIOTT began enjoying plates just before attending the first International Plate Collectors Convention in 1975. She writes extensively about collectibles and is the executive director of the National Association of Limited Edition Dealers (NALED).

PLATES

AMERICAN ARTISTS

YR	NAME	LIMIT	ISSUE	TREND
	F. STONE			
*	CIGAR/SIGNED	*	95.00	95.00
*	CIGAR/UNSIGNED	*	75.00	75.00
	D. ZOLAN			**FAMILY TREASURES**
81	CORA'S RECITAL	18500	39.50	40.00
82	CORA'S TEA PARTY	18500	39.50	40.00
83	CORA'S GARDEN PARTY	18500	39.50	40.00
	F. STONE			**FAMOUS FILLIES**
87	LADY'S SECRET	9500	65.00	85.00
88	GENUINE RISK	9500	65.00	85.00
88	RUFFIAN	9500	65.00	85.00
92	GO FOR THE WAND	9500	65.00	85.00
	F. STONE			**FRED STONE CLASSIC SERIES**
86	ETERNAL LEGACY, THE	950	75.00	95.00
86	SHOE-8,000 WINS, THE	9500	75.00	95.00
88	FOREVER FRIENDS	9500	75.00	95.00
89	ALYSHEBA	9500	75.00	85.00
	F. STONE			**GOLD SIGNATURE SERIES**
90	SECRETARIAT FINAL TRIBUTE, SIGNED	4500	150.00	395.00
90	SECRETARIAT FINAL TRIBUTE, UNSIGNED	7500	75.00	75.00
91	OLD WARRIORS, SIGNED	4500	150.00	525.00
91	OLD WARRIORS, UNSIGNED	7500	75.00	75.00
	F. STONE			**GOLD SIGNATURE SERIES II**
91	KELSO, DBL. SIGNATURES	1500	175.00	175.00
91	KELSO, SGL. SIGNATURE	3000	150.00	150.00
91	KELSO, UNSIGNED	7500	75.00	75.00
91	NORTHERN DANCER, DBL. SIGNATURES	1500	175.00	225.00
91	NORTHERN DANCER, SGL. SIGNATURE	3000	150.00	150.00
91	NORTHERN DANCER, UNSIGNED	7500	75.00	75.00
	F. STONE			**GOLD SIGNATURE SERIES III**
92	DANCE SMARTLY-P. DAY, DBL. SIGNATURES	1500	175.00	175.00
92	DANCE SMARTLY-P. DAY, SGL. SIGNATURE	3000	150.00	150.00
92	DANCE SMARTLY-P. DAY, UNSIGNED	7500	75.00	75.00
93	AMERICAN TRIPLE CROWN, SIGNED 1937-46	2500	195.00	195.00
93	AMERICAN TRIPLE CROWN, SIGNED 1948-78	2500	195.00	200.00
93	AMERICAN TRIPLE CROWN, UNSIGNED 1937-46	7500	75.00	75.00
93	AMERICAN TRIPLE CROWN, UNSIGNED 1948-78	7500	75.00	75.00
94	AMERICAN TRIPLE CROWN, SIGNED 1919-35	2500	95.00	100.00
94	AMERICAN TRIPLE CROWN, UNSIGNED 1919-35	7500	75.00	75.00
	F. STONE			**GOLD SIGNATURE SERIES IV**
95	JULIE KRONA/DBL. SIGNATURE	2500	150.00	150.00
95	JULIE KRONA/UNSIGNED	7500	75.00	75.00
	F. STONE			**MARES & FOALS 6 1/2 IN. SERIES**
91	PATIENCE	19500	25.00	25.00
92	KIDNAPPED MARE	19500	25.00	25.00
92	PASTURE PEST	19500	25.00	25.00
92	WATER TROUGH	19500	25.00	25.00
93	ARABIAN MARE & FOAL	19500	25.00	25.00
93	CONTENTMENT	19500	25.00	25.00
	F. STONE			**MARES & FOALS SERIES**
86	PASTURE PEST	12500	49.50	130.00
86	TRANQUILITY	12500	49.50	95.00
86	TRANQUILITY 6 1/2"	12500	25.00	25.00
86	WATER TROUGH	12500	49.50	160.00
87	ARABIANS, THE	12500	49.50	50.00
89	DIAMOND IN THE ROUGH 6 1/2"	RT	25.00	25.00
	F. STONE			**MARES & FOALS SERIES II**
89	DIAMOND IN THE ROUGH	RT	35.00	65.00
89	FIRST DAY, THE	OP	35.00	35.00
	M. SEELEY			**OLD FRENCH DOLL COLLECTION**
79	A.T., THE	5000	39.00	55.00
79	BRU, THE	5000	39.00	200.00
79	E.J., THE	5000	39.00	75.00
80	ALEZANDRE	5000	39.00	45.00
81	MARQUE, THE	5000	39.00	43.00
81	SCHMITT, THE	5000	39.00	43.00
	F. STONE			**RACING LEGENDS**
89	PHAR LAP	9500	75.00	75.00
89	SUNDAY SILENCE	9500	75.00	80.00
90	JOHN HENRY-SHOEMAKER	9500	75.00	75.00
	F. STONE			**SPORT OF KINGS SERIES**
84	MAN O'WAR	9500	65.00	250.00
84	SECRETARIAT	9500	65.00	325.00
85	JOHN HENRY-MCCARRON	9500	65.00	200.00
86	SEATTLE SLEW	9500	65.00	65.00
	F. STONE			**THE HORSES OF FRED STONE**
82	ARABIAN MARE AND FOAL	9500	55.00	130.00
82	PATIENCE	9500	55.00	150.00
82	SAFE AND SOUND	9500	55.00	100.00
83	CONTENTMENT	9500	55.00	95.00

YR	NAME	LIMIT	ISSUE	TREND
F. STONE			**THE STALLION SERIES**	
83	ANDALUSIAN	12500	49.50	140.00
83	BLACK STALLION	12500	49.50	140.00

AMERICAN ROSE SOCIETY

YR	NAME	LIMIT	ISSUE	TREND
*			**ALL-AMERICAN ROSE**	
75	ARIZONA	9800	39.00	142.00
75	OREGOLD	9800	39.00	142.00
75	ROSE PARADE	9800	39.00	137.00
76	AMERICA	9800	39.00	140.00
76	CATHEDRAL	9800	39.00	140.00
76	SEASHELL	9800	39.00	140.00
76	YANKEE DOODLE	9800	39.00	140.00
77	DOUBLE DELIGHT	9800	39.00	115.00
77	FIRST EDITION	9800	39.00	115.00
77	PROMINENT	9800	39.00	115.00
78	CHARISMA	9800	39.00	89.00
78	COLOR MAGIC	9800	39.00	107.00
79	FRIENDSHIP	9800	39.00	79.00
79	PARADISE	9800	39.00	39.00
79	SUNDOWNER	9800	39.00	75.00
80	CHERISH	9800	49.00	80.00
80	HONOR	9800	49.00	55.00
80	LOVE	9800	49.00	80.00
81	BING CROSBY	9800	49.00	49.00
81	MARINA	9800	49.00	69.00
81	WHITE LIGHTNIN'	9800	49.00	69.00
82	BRANDY	9800	49.00	69.00
82	FRENCH LACE	9800	49.00	54.00
82	MON CHERI	9800	49.00	49.00
82	SHREVEPORT	9800	49.00	54.00
83	SUN FLARE	9800	49.00	69.00
83	SWEET SURRENDER	9800	49.00	55.00
84	IMPATIENT	9800	49.00	55.00
84	INTRIGUE	9800	49.00	58.00
84	OLYMPIAD	9800	49.00	55.00
85	PEACE	9800	49.50	50.00
85	QUEEN ELIZABETH	0000	49.50	50.00
85	SHOWBIZ	9800	49.50	50.00

ANHEUSER-BUSCH INC.

YR	NAME	LIMIT	ISSUE	TREND
D. LANGENECKERT			**ARCHIVES PLATE SERIES**	
92	1893 COLUMBIAN EXPOSITION N3477	CL	27.50	28.00
92	GANYMEDE N4004	CL	27.50	45.00
D. LANGENECKERT			**CIVIL WAR SERIES**	
92	GENERAL GRANT N3478	CL	45.00	45.00
93	GENERAL ROBERT E. LEE N3590	CL	45.00	45.00
93	PRESIDENT ABRAHAM LINCOLN N3591	CL	45.00	45.00
B. KEMPER			**HOLIDAY PLATE SERIES**	
89	WINTERS DAY N2295	RT	30.00	80.00
89	WINTERS EVENING N2295	RT	30.00	75.00
94	HOMETOWN HOLIDAY N4572	CL	27.50	28.00
N. KOERBER			**HOLIDAY PLATE SERIES**	
93	SPECIAL DELIVERY N4002	RT	27.50	28.00
S. SAMPSON			**HOLIDAY PLATE SERIES**	
90	AN AMERICAN TRADITION N2767	RT	30.00	50.00
91	SEASON'S BEST, THE- N3034	CL	30.00	30.00
92	A PERFECT CHRISTMAS N3440	CL	27.50	28.00
M. URDAHL			**MAN'S BEST FRIEND SERIES**	
90	BUDDIES N2615	RT	30.00	75.00
90	SIX PACK N3005	RT	30.00	40.00
92	SOMETHING'S BREWING N3147	CL	30.00	30.00
93	OUTSTANDING IN THEIR FIELD N4003	CL	27.50	28.00
95	THIS BUD'S FOR YOU N4945	25-DAY	27.50	28.00
*			**OLYMPIC TEAM SERIES**	
91	'92 OLYMPIC TEAM WINTER PLATE N3180	CL	35.00	35.00
92	'92 OLYMPIC TEAM SUMMER PLATE N3122	CL	35.00	35.00

ANNA-PERENNA

YR	NAME	LIMIT	ISSUE	TREND
P. BUCKLEY MOSS				
*	HELLO GRANDPA	OP	75.00	75.00
89	HELLO GRANDMA	CL	75.00	110.00
93	FRIENDS FOREVER	5000	85.00	85.00
93	STORYTELLER, THE	5000	100.00	100.00
94	SCHOOL DAYS	5000	85.00	85.00
94	VISITNG NURSE	5000	85.00	85.00
95	FRIENDS FOREVER	5000	85.00	85.00
P. BUCKLEY MOSS			**AMERICAN SILHOUETTES FAMILY SERIES**	
81	FAMILY OUTING	5000	75.00	100.00
82	HOMEMAKERS QUILTING	5000	75.00	140.00
82	JOHN AND MARY	5000	75.00	100.00
84	LEISURE TIME	5000	75.00	90.00
P. BUCKLEY MOSS			**AMERICAN SILHOUETTES VALLEY SERIES**	
81	FROSTY FROLIC	5000	75.00	90.00
82	HAY RIDE	5000	75.00	90.00
83	SUNDAY RIDE	5000	75.00	90.00
84	MARKET DAY	5000	75.00	120.00

YR	NAME	LIMIT	ISSUE	TREND
	P. BUCKLEY MOSS	**AMERICAN SILHOUETTES-CHILDREN'S SERIES**		
81	FIDDLERS TWO	5000	75.00	100.00
83	MARY WITH THE LAMBS	5000	75.00	90.00
84	RING-AROUND-THE-ROSIE	5000	75.00	195.00
84	WAITING FOR TOM	5000	75.00	180.00
	P. BUCKLEY MOSS	**ANNUAL CHRISTMAS PLATE**		
84	NOEL, NOEL	5000	67.50	330.00
85	HELPING HANDS	5000	67.50	230.00
86	NIGHT BEFORE CHRISTMAS	5000	67.50	145.00
87	CHRISTMAS SLEIGH	5000	75.00	100.00
88	CHRISTMAS JOY	7500	75.00	75.00
89	CHRISTMAS CAROL	7500	80.00	95.00
90	CHRISTMAS EVE	7500	80.00	80.00
91	SNOWMAN, THE	7500	80.00	80.00
92	CHRISTMAS WARMTH	7500	85.00	85.00
93	JOY TO THE WORLD	7500	85.00	85.00
94	CHRISTMAS NIGHT	7500	85.00	85.00
95	CHRISTMAS AT HOME	5000	42.50	43.00
96	UNDER THE MISTLETOE	7500	42.50	43.00
	P. BUCKLEY MOSS	**HEARTLAND SERIES**		
*	BLACKSMITH, THE	OP	90.00	90.00
*	PRAIRIE WINTER	OP	90.00	90.00
*	SUNDAY OUTING	OP	90.00	90.00
93	SCHOOLHOUSE, THE	5000	90.00	90.00
	P. BUCKLEY MOSS	**JOYFUL CHILDREN COLLECTION**		
93	DANCE OF THE BUTTERFLIES	5000	70.00	70.00
93	PURPLE UMBRELLA	5000	70.00	70.00
94	DOLL'S HOUSE, THE	5000	70.00	70.00
94	MEDICS, THE	5000	70.00	70.00
	P. BUCKLEY MOSS	**MOTHER'S LOVE SERIES**		
91	TENDER HANDS	CL	85.00	135.00
92	MOTHER'S LOVE	OP	85.00	85.00
93	MOTHER'S WORLD	5000	80.00	80.00
94	MOTHER'S JOY	5000	80.00	80.00
95	NEWBORN, THE	5000	40.00	40.00
96	TREASURED BABE	5000	40.00	40.00
	P. BUCKLEY MOSS	**SINGLE ISSUE ART PLATE**		
93	SUMMER WEDDING	5000	100.00	100.00
95	MUSEUM PLATE, THE	5000	40.00	40.00
95	SKATING JOY	5000	40.00	40.00
96	WEDDING DAY	5000	45.00	45.00
	P. BUCKLEY MOSS	**THE CELEBRATION SERIES**		
86	WEDDING JOY	5000	100.00	275.00
87	CHRISTENING, THE	5000	100.00	180.00
88	ANNIVERSARY, THE	5000	100.00	155.00
89	FAMILY REUNION	5000	100.00	150.00
	P. BUCKLEY MOSS	**TREASURED FRIENDS COLLECTION**		
95	LEARNED PAIR	5000	42.50	43.00
95	LORDS OF THE REALM	5000	42.50	43.00
96	NOBLE FILLY	5000	42.50	42.50
	T. KRUMEICH	**UNCLE TAD'S CATS**		
79	OLIVER'S BIRTHDAY	5000	75.00	230.00
80	PEACHES & CREAM	5000	75.00	100.00
81	PRINCESS AURORA	5000	80.00	100.00
81	WALTER'S WINDOW	5000	80.00	120.00

ANRI

YR	NAME	LIMIT	ISSUE	TREND
*		**ANRI FATHER'S DAY**		
72	ALPINE FATHER & CHILDREN	CL	35.00	100.00
73	ALPINE FATHER & CHILDREN	CL	40.00	100.00
74	CLIFF GAZING	CL	50.00	100.00
76	SAILING	CL	60.00	100.00
*		**ANRI MOTHER'S DAY**		
72	ALPINE MOTHER & CHILDREN	CL	35.00	50.00
73	ALPINE MOTHER & CHILDREN	CL	40.00	50.00
74	ALPINE MOTHER & CHILDREN	CL	50.00	60.00
75	ALPINE STROLL	CL	60.00	70.00
76	KNITTING	CL	60.00	70.00
*		**CHRISTMAS**		
79	MOSS GATHERERS	RT	135.00	180.00
80	WINTRY CHURCHGOING	RT	165.00	150.00
81	SANTA CLAUS IN TYROL	RT	165.00	200.00
82	STAR SINGERS, THE	RT	165.00	170.00
83	UNTO US A CHILD IS BORN	RT	165.00	325.00
84	YULETIDE IN THE VALLEY	RT	165.00	175.00
	J. MALFERTHEINER	**CHRISTMAS**		
71	ST. JAKOB IN GARDEN	RT	37.50	70.00
72	PIPERS AT ALBEROBELLO	RT	45.00	80.00
73	ALPINE HORN	RT	45.00	400.00
74	YOUNG MAN AND GIRL	RT	50.00	100.00
75	CHRISTMAS IN IRELAND	RT	60.00	60.00
76	ALPINE CHRISTMAS	RT	65.00	185.00
77	LEGEND OF HELIGENBLUT	RT	65.00	90.00
78	KLOCKLER SINGERS	RT	80.00	80.00
85	GOOD MORNING, GOOD CHEER	RT	165.00	165.00
86	A GRODEN CHRISTMAS	RT	165.00	200.00
87	DOWN FROM THE ALPS	RT	195.00	250.00

YR	NAME	LIMIT	ISSUE	TREND
88	CHRISTKINDL MARKT	RT	220.00	240.00
88	FLIGHT INTO EGYPT	RT	275.00	280.00
90	HOLY NIGHT	RT	300.00	310.00

* — **DISNEY FOUR STAR COLLECTION**

YR	NAME	LIMIT	ISSUE	TREND
89	MICKEY MINI PLATE	RT	40.00	50.00
90	MINNIE MINI PLATE	RT	40.00	50.00
91	DONALD MINI PLATE	RT	50.00	50.00

J. FERRANDIZ — **FERRANDIZ CHRISTMAS**

YR	NAME	LIMIT	ISSUE	TREND
72	CHRIST IN THE MANGER	RT	35.00	250.00
73	CHRISTMAS	RT	40.00	225.00
74	HOLY NIGHT	RT	50.00	100.00
75	FLIGHT INTO EGYPT	RT	60.00	100.00
76	GIRL WITH FLOWERS	RT	65.00	200.00
76	TREE OF LIFE	RT	60.00	100.00
78	LEADING THE WAY	RT	77.50	180.00
79	DRUMMER, THE	RT	120.00	200.00
80	REJOICE	RT	150.00	160.00
81	SPREADING THE WORD	RT	150.00	150.00
82	SHEPHERD FAMILY, THE	RT	150.00	150.00
83	PEACE ATTEND THEE	RT	150.00	150.00

J. FERRANDIZ — **FERRANDIZ MOTHER'S DAY SERIES**

YR	NAME	LIMIT	ISSUE	TREND
72	MOTHER SEWING	RT	35.00	200.00
73	ALPINE MOTHER & CHILD	RT	40.00	150.00
74	MOTHER HOLDING CHILD	RT	50.00	150.00
75	DOVE GIRL	RT	60.00	150.00
76	MOTHER KNITTING	RT	60.00	200.00
77	ALPINE STROLL	RT	65.00	150.00
78	BEGINNING, THE	RT	75.00	150.00
79	ALL HEARTS	RT	120.00	175.00
80	SPRING ARRIVALS	RT	150.00	175.00
81	HARMONY	RT	150.00	150.00
82	WITH LOVE	RT	150.00	150.00

J. FERRANDIZ — **FERRANDIZ WOODEN WEDDING PLATES**

YR	NAME	LIMIT	ISSUE	TREND
72	BOY AND GIRL EMBRACING	CL	40.00	150.00
73	WEDDING SCENE	CL	40.00	150.00
74	WEDDING	CL	48.00	150.00
75	WEDDING	CL	60.00	150.00
76	WEDDING	CL	60.00	125.00

ARABIA ANNUAL

R. UOSIKKINEN — **KALEVALA**

YR	NAME	LIMIT	ISSUE	TREND
76	VAINAMOINEN'S SOWING	*	30.00	250.00
77	AINO'S FATE	*	30.00	35.00
78	LEMMINKAINEN'S CHASE	2500	39.00	44.00
79	KULLERVO'S REVENGE	YR	39.50	47.00
80	VAINAMOINEN'S RESCUE	YR	45.00	65.00
81	VAINAMOINEN'S MAGIC	YR	49.50	50.00
82	JOUKAHAINEN SHOOTS THE HORSE	YR	55.50	68.00
83	LEMMINKAINEN'S ESCAPE	YR	60.00	90.00
84	LEMMINKAINEN'S MAGIC FEATHERS	YR	49.50	93.00
85	LEMMINKAINEN'S GRIEF	YR	60.00	80.00
86	OSMATAR CREATING ALE	YR	60.00	80.00
87	VAINAMOINEN TRICKS ILMARINEN	YR	65.00	85.00
88	HEAR VAINAMOINEN WEEP	YR	69.00	115.00
89	FOUR MAIDENS	YR	75.00	87.00
90	ANNIKKA	YR	85.00	105.00
91	LEMMINKAIN'S MOTHER SAYS DON'T/WAR	YR	85.00	89.00

ARMSTRONG'S

R. SKELTON — **COMMEMORATIVE ISSUES**

YR	NAME	LIMIT	ISSUE	TREND
83	70 YEARS YOUNG	15000	85.00	90.00
84	FREDDIE THE TORCHBEARER	15000	62.50	90.00

L. DEWINNE — **FACES OF THE WORLD**

YR	NAME	LIMIT	ISSUE	TREND
88	CLARA (BELGIUM)	14-DAY	24.50	25.00
88	COLLETTE (FRANCE)	14-DAY	24.50	25.00
88	ERIN (IRELAND)	14-DAY	24.50	25.00
88	GRETA (AUSTRIA)	14-DAY	24.50	25.00
88	HEATHER (ENGLAND)	14-DAY	24.50	25.00
88	LUISA (SPAIN)	14-DAY	24.50	25.00
88	MARIA (ITALY)	14-DAY	24.50	25.00
88	TAMIKO (JAPAN)	14-DAY	24.50	25.00

R. SKELTON — **FREDDIE THE FREELOADER**

YR	NAME	LIMIT	ISSUE	TREND
79	FREDDIE IN THE BATHTUB	10000	60.00	210.00
80	FREDDIE'S SHACK	10000	60.00	90.00
81	FREDDIE ON THE GREEN	10000	60.00	70.00
82	LOVE THAT FREDDIE	10000	60.00	65.00

R. SKELTON — **FREDDIE'S ADVENTURES**

YR	NAME	LIMIT	ISSUE	TREND
82	BRONCO FREDDIE	15000	60.00	35.00
82	CAPTAIN FREDDIE	15000	60.00	90.00
83	SIR FREDDIE	15000	62.50	70.00
84	GERTRUDE AND HEATHCLIFFE	15000	62.50	70.00

R. SKELTON — **FREEDOM COLLECTION**

YR	NAME	LIMIT	ISSUE	TREND
90	ALL-AMERICAN, THE	9000	62.50	90.00
90	ALL-AMERICAN, THE-SIGNED	1000	195.00	380.00
91	INDEPENDENCE DAY	9000	62.50	63.00
91	INDEPENDENCE DAY-SIGNED	1000	195.00	250.00
92	LET FREEDOM RING	9000	62.50	63.00
92	LET FREEDOM RING-SIGNED	1000	195.00	280.00

YR	NAME	LIMIT	ISSUE	TREND
93	FREDDIE'S GIFT OF LIFE	9000	62.50	63.00
93	FREDDIE'S GIFT OF LIFE-SIGNED	1000	195.00	280.00
W. LANTZ				**HAPPY ART SERIES**
81	WOODY'S TRIPLE SELF-PORTRAIT	9000	39.50	40.00
81	WOODY'S TRIPLE SELF-PORTRAIT-SIGNED	1000	100.00	100.00
83	GOTHIC WOODY	9000	39.50	40.00
83	GOTHIC WOODY-SIGNED	1000	100.00	100.00
84	BLUE BOY WOODY	9000	39.50	40.00
84	BLUE BOY WOODY-SIGNED	1000	100.00	100.00
S. ETEM				**INFINITE LOVE**
87	A PAIR OF DREAMS	CL	24.50	25.00
87	EYES SAY I LOVE YOU, THE	14-DAY	24.50	25.00
87	KISS A LITTLE GIGGLE	14-DAY	24.50	25.00
87	ONCE UPON A SMILE	14-DAY	24.50	25.00
88	BUNDLE OF JOY	14-DAY	24.50	25.00
88	GRINS FOR GRANDMA	14-DAY	24.50	25.00
88	LOVE GOES FORTH IN LITTLE FEET	14-DAY	24.50	25.00
89	A MOMENT TO CHERISH	CL	24.50	25.00
R. SKELTON				**SIGNATURE COLLECTION**
88	HOOKED ON FREDDIE	9000	62.50	63.00
88	HOOKED ON FREDDIE-SIGNED	1000	175.00	180.00
SCHENKEN				**SPORTS**
*	PETE ROSE- UNSIGNED	10000	45.00	60.00
*	PETE ROSE-HANDSIGNED	1000	100.00	600.00
A. D'ESTREHAN				**STATUE OF LIBERTY**
86	DEDICATION	10000	39.50	50.00
86	IMMIGRANTS, THE	10000	39.50	50.00
86	INDEPENDENCE	10000	39.50	50.00
86	RE-DEDICATION	10000	39.50	50.00
A. D'ESTREHAN				**THE CONSTITUTION SERIES**
87	GREAT CHASE, THE	10000	39.50	40.00
87	U.S. CONSTITUTION VS. GUERRIERE	10000	39.50	40.00
87	U.S. CONSTITUTION VS. JAVA	10000	39.50	40.00
87	U.S. CONSTITUTION VS. TRIPOLI	10000	39.50	40.00
S. ETEM				**THE MISCHIEF MAKERS**
86	BUCKLES	10000	39.95	40.00
86	PUDDLES	10000	39.95	40.00
87	TRIX	10000	39.95	40.00
88	NAP	10000	39.95	40.00
R. SKELTON				**THE SIGNATURE COLLECTION**
86	ANYONE FOR TENNIS?	9000	62.50	63.00
86	ANYONE FOR TENNIS?-SIGNED	1000	125.00	300.00
87	IRONING THE WAVES	9000	62.50	80.00
87	IRONING THE WAVES-SIGNED	1000	125.00	270.00
88	CLIFFHANGER, THE	9000	62.50	70.00
88	CLIFFHANGER, THE-SIGNED	1000	150.00	280.00

ART WORLD OF BOURGEAULT

YR	NAME	LIMIT	ISSUE	TREND
R. BOURGEAULT				**THE ENGLISH COUNTRYSIDE**
80	COUNTRY SQUIRE, THE	1500	70.00	370.00
81	WILLOWS, THE	1500	85.00	370.00
82	ROSE COTTAGE	1500	90.00	370.00
83	THATCHED BEAUTY	1500	95.00	370.00
R. BOURGEAULT				**THE ENGLISH COUNTRYSIDE SINGLE ISSUES**
84	ANNE HATHAWAY COTTAGE, THE	500	150.00	640.00
85	LILAC COTTAGE	500	125.00	350.00
87	SUFFOLK PINK	50	220.00	427.00
88	STUART HOUSE	50	325.00	571.00
89	LARK RISE	50	450.00	603.00
R. BOURGEAULT				**THE ROYAL GAINSBOROUGH SERIES**
90	LISA-CAROLINE, THE	*	65.00	65.00
91	A GAINSBOROUGH LADY	*	*	*
R. BOURGEAULT				**THE ROYAL LITERARY SERIES**
85	JOHN BUNYAN COTTAGE, THE	4500	60.00	90.00
87	THOMAS HARTY COTTAGE, THE	4500	65.00	90.00
88	JOHN MILTON COTTAGE, THE	4500	65.00	90.00
89	ANNE HATHAWAY COTTAGE, THE	4500	65.00	90.00
R. BOURGEAULT				**WHERE IS ENGLAND**
90	FORGET-ME-NOT	50	525.00	705.00
91	FLEECE INN, THE	50	525.00	705.00
92	MILLBROOK HOUSE	50	525.00	525.00
93	COTSWOLD BEAUTY	50	525.00	525.00

ARTAFFECTS

YR	NAME	LIMIT	ISSUE	TREND
G. PERILLO				**AMERICA'S INDIAN HERITAGE**
87	CHEYENNE NATION	CL	24.50	65.00
88	ARAPAHO NATION	CL	24.50	50.00
88	BLACKFOOT NATION	CL	24.50	100.00
88	CHIPPEWA NATION	CL	24.50	50.00
88	CROW NATION	CL	24.50	60.00
88	KIOWA NATION	CL	24.50	50.00
88	NEZ PERCE NATION	CL	24.50	60.00
88	SIOUX NATION	CL	24.50	70.00
G. PERILLO				**AMERICAN BLUES SPECIAL OCCASION**
92	HAPPILY EVER AFTER - WEDDING	*	35.00	40.00
92	MY SUNSHINE - MOTHERHOOD	*	35.00	40.00
92	PERFECT TREE, THE - CHRISTMAS	*	35.00	40.00

YR	NAME	LIMIT	ISSUE	TREND
	K. SOLDWEDEL	**AMERICAN MARITIME HERITAGE**		
87	U.S.S. CONSTITUTION	CL	35.00	40.00
	G. PERILLO	**AN OLD FASHIONED CHRISTMAS**		
93	UP ON THE ROOF TOP	*	29.50	30.00
94	CHRISTMAS DELIGHT	*	29.50	30.00
94	CHRISTMAS EVE	*	29.50	30.00
94	TOY SHOPPE, THE	*	29.50	30.00
	J. EGGERT	**ANGLER'S DREAM**		
83	BROOK TROUT	9800	55.00	75.00
83	CHINOOK SALMON	9800	55.00	75.00
83	LARGEMOUTH BASS	9800	55.00	75.00
83	STRIPED BASS	9800	55.00	75.00
	G. PERILLO	**ARCTIC FRIENDS**		
82	SIBERIAN LOVE	7500	100.00	105.00
82	SNOW PALS	7500	*	*
	R. SAUBER	**BABY'S FIRSTS**		
89	BABY'S FIRST STEP	CL	21.50	23.00
89	CHRISTMAS MORN	CL	21.50	23.00
89	FIRST BIRTHDAY	CL	21.50	23.00
89	PICTURE PERFECT	CL	21.50	23.00
89	VISITING THE DOCTOR	CL	21.50	23.00
	B. LEIGHTON-JONES	**BACKSTAGE**		
90	BUBBLING OVER	CL	29.50	30.00
90	LETTER, THE	CL	29.50	30.00
90	RUNAWAY, THE	CL	29.50	30.00
	M. HOOKS	**BAKER STREET**		
83	SHERLOCK HOLMES	CL	55.00	75.00
83	WATSON	9800	55.00	65.00
	C. BECKER	**BECKER BABIES**		
83	SNOW PUFF	CL	29.95	60.00
84	PALS	CL	29.95	60.00
84	SMILING THROUGH	CL	29.95	60.00
	B.P. GUTMANN	**BESSIE'S BEST**		
84	LOOKING FOR TROUBLE	CL	29.95	65.00
84	MY BABY	CL	29.95	65.00
84	NEW LOVE, THE	CL	29.95	65.00
84	OH! OH! A BUNNY	CL	29.95	65.00
84	TAPS	CL	29.95	65.00
	G. PERILLO	**BRING UNTO ME THE CHILDREN**		
94	A LITTLE LOVE SONG	CL	29.50	30.00
94	BAPTISM, THE	CL	29.50	30.00
94	COMMUNION	CL	29.50	30.00
94	HEAVENLY EMBRACE	CL	29.50	30.00
94	LORD'S PRAYER, THE	CL	29.50	30.00
94	LOVE'S BLESSING	CL	29.50	30.00
94	SWEET DREAMS	CL	29.50	30.00
94	SWEET SERENITY	CL	29.50	30.00
	G. PERILLO	**CHIEFTAINS I**		
79	CHIEF JOSEPH	7500	65.00	115.00
79	CHIEF SITTING BULL	7500	65.00	405.00
80	CHIEF GERONIMO	7500	65.00	90.00
80	CHIEF RED CLOUD	7500	65.00	125.00
81	CHIEF CRAZY HORSE	7500	65.00	155.00
	G. PERILLO	**CHIEFTANS 2**		
83	CHIEF PONTIAC	7500	70.00	90.00
83	CHIEF VICTORIO	7500	70.00	90.00
84	CHIEF BLACK KETTLE	7500	70.00	115.00
84	CHIEF COCHISE	7500	70.00	90.00
84	CHIEF TECUMSEH	7500	70.00	90.00
	G. PERILLO	**CHILD LIFE**		
83	SIESTA	10000	45.00	55.00
84	SWEET DREAMS	10000	45.00	55.00
	R. SAUBER	**CHILDHOOD DELIGHTS**		
83	AMANDA	7500	45.00	75.00
	G. PERILLO	**CHILDREN OF THE PRAIRIE**		
93	BEACH COMBER	*	29.50	30.00
93	DAYDREAMERS	*	29.50	30.00
93	PATIENCE	*	29.50	30.00
93	PLAY TIME	*	29.50	30.00
93	SENTINAL, THE	*	29.50	30.00
93	SISTERS	*	29.50	30.00
93	TENDER LOVING CARE	*	29.50	30.00
93	WATCHFUL WAITING	*	29.50	30.00
	A. TOBEY	**CHRISTIAN COLLECTION**		
87	BRING TO ME THE CHILDREN	*	35.00	40.00
87	HEALER, THE	*	35.00	40.00
87	WEDDING FEAST AT CANA	*	35.00	40.00
	M. LEONE	**CHRISTMAS CELEBRATIONS OF YESTERDAY**		
93	CHRISTMAS BLESSINGS	*	27.00	30.00
93	CHRISTMAS EVE	*	27.00	30.00
93	CHRISTMAS ON MAIN STREET	*	27.00	30.00
93	CHRISTMAS ON THE FARM	*	27.00	30.00
93	CHRISTMAS PARTY	*	27.00	30.00
93	HOME FOR CHRISTMAS	*	27.00	30.00
93	TRIMMING THE TREE	*	27.00	30.00
93	WREATH MAKER	*	27.00	30.00

YR	NAME	LIMIT	ISSUE	TREND
	J. DENEEN		**CLASSIC AMERICAN CARS**	
89	CADILLAC	CL	35.00	40.00
89	CORD	CL	35.00	35.00
89	DUESENBERG	CL	35.00	40.00
89	RUXTON	CL	35.00	40.00
90	HUDSON	CL	35.00	40.00
90	LINCOLN	CL	35.00	40.00
90	PACKARD	CL	35.00	40.00
90	PIERCE-ARROW	CL	35.00	40.00
	J. DENEEN		**CLASSIC AMERICAN TRAINS**	
88	A RACE AGAINST TIME	CL	35.00	60.00
88	COMPETITION	CL	35.00	50.00
88	HOMEWARD BOUND	CL	35.00	50.00
88	MIDDAY STOP	CL	35.00	60.00
88	ROUND THE BEND	CL	35.00	60.00
88	SILVER BULLET, THE	CL	35.00	70.00
88	TAKING THE HIGH ROAD	CL	35.00	50.00
88	TRAVELING IN STYLE	CL	35.00	60.00
	G. PERILLO		**CLUB MEMBER LIMITED EDITION**	
92	PENCIL, THE	YR	35.00	80.00
92	STUDIES IN B/W SET OF FOUR	YR	75.00	80.00
93	WATCHER OF THE WILDERNESS	YR	60.00	65.00
	G. PERILLO		**COUNCIL OF NATIONS**	
92	BOLDNESS OF THE SENECA	CL	29.50	30.00
92	COURAGE OF THE ARAPAHO	CL	29.50	30.00
92	DIGNITY OF THE NEZ PERCE	CL	29.50	30.00
92	NOBILITY OF THE ALGONQUIN	CL	29.50	30.00
92	POWER OF THE BLACKFOOT	CL	29.50	30.00
92	PRIDE OF THE CHEYENNE	CL	29.50	30.00
92	STRENGTH OF THE SIOUX	CL	29.50	50.00
92	WISDOM OF THE CHEROKEE	CL	29.50	30.00
	S. MILLER-MAXWELL		**GOOD SPORTS**	
89	ALLEY CATS	CL	22.50	30.00
89	PURRFECT GAME	CL	22.50	30.00
89	QUARTERBACK SNEAK	CL	22.50	30.00
89	TEE TIME	CL	22.50	30.00
89	TWO/LOVE	CL	22.50	30.00
89	WHAT'S THE CATCH?	CL	22.50	30.00
	J. DENEEN		**GREAT AMERICAN TRAINS**	
92	ALTON LIMITED, THE	CL	27.00	30.00
92	BLACKHAWK LIMITED, THE	CL	27.00	30.00
92	BROADWAY LIMITED, THE	CL	27.00	30.00
92	CAPITOL LIMITED, THE	CL	27.00	30.00
92	MERCHANTS LIMITED, THE	CL	27.00	30.00
92	PANAMA SPECIAL LIMITED, THE	CL	27.00	30.00
92	SOUTHWESTERN LIMITED, THE	CL	27.00	30.00
92	SUNSHINE SPECIAL LIMITED, THE	CL	27.00	30.00
	MAGO		**HEAVENLY ANGELS**	
92	ANGEL CAKE	CL	27.00	30.00
92	ANGEL'S KISS, THE	CL	27.00	30.00
92	CAUGHT IN THE ACT	CL	27.00	30.00
92	HEAVENLY HELPER	CL	27.00	30.00
92	HEAVENLY LIGHT	CL	27.00	30.00
92	HUSH-A-BYE	CL	27.00	30.00
92	MY ANGEL	CL	27.00	30.00
92	SLEEPY SENTINEL	CL	27.00	30.00
	R. SAUBER		**HOW DO I LOVE THEE?**	
82	ALAINA	19500	39.95	60.00
82	TAYLOR	19500	39.95	60.00
83	EMBRACE	19500	39.95	60.00
83	RENDEZVOUS	19500	39.95	60.00
	G. PERILLO		**INDIAN BRIDAL**	
90	AUTUMN BLOSSOM	CL	25.00	30.00
90	MISTY WATERS	CL	25.00	30.00
90	SUNNY SKIES	CL	25.00	30.00
90	YELLOW BIRD	CL	25.00	30.00
	G. PERILLO		**INDIAN NATIONS**	
83	APACHE (SET)	7500	*	*
83	BLACKFOOT	7500	140.00	425.00
83	CHEYENNE (SET)	7500	*	*
83	SIOUX (SET)	7500	*	*
	A. CHESTERMAN		**LANDS BEFORE TIME**	
94	IMPERIAL DYNASTY	CL	29.50	30.00
94	KNIGHTS IN SHINING ARMOUR	CL	29.50	30.00
94	PHAROAH'S RETURN	CL	29.50	30.00
94	ROMAN HOLIDAY	CL	29.50	30.00
	G. PERILLO		**LEGENDS OF THE WEST**	
82	DANIEL BOONE	10000	65.00	85.00
83	BUFFALO BILL	10000	65.00	85.00
83	DAVY CROCKETT	10000	65.00	85.00
83	KIT CARSON	10000	65.00	85.00
	G. PERILLO		**LIVING IN HARMONY**	
91	PEACEABLE KINGDOM	CL	29.50	30.00
	B.P. GUTMANN		**MAGICAL MOMENT**	
81	HAPPY DREAMS	OP	29.95	100.00
81	HARMONY	OP	29.95	90.00
82	HIS MAJESTY	OP	29.95	60.00

YR	NAME	LIMIT	ISSUE	TREND
82	THANK YOU GOD	OP	29.95	50.00
82	WAITING FOR DADDY	OP	29.95	50.00
83	LULLABY, THE	OP	29.95	50.00
	MAGO	**MAGO'S MOTHERHOOD**		
90	SERENITY	CL	50.00	55.00
	G. PERILLO	**MARCH OF DIMES: OUR CHILDREN, OUR FUTURE**		
89	A TIME TO BE BORN	CL	29.00	35.00
	MONET/CASSAT	**MASTERPIECES OF IMPRESSIONISM**		
80	WOMAN WITH PARASOL	17500	35.00	75.00
81	YOUNG MOTHER SEWING	17500	35.00	60.00
82	SARA IN GREEN BONNET	17500	35.00	60.00
83	MARGOT IN BLUE	17500	35.00	50.00
	N. ROCKWELL	**MASTERPIECES OF ROCKWELL**		
80	AFTER THE PROM	17500	42.50	150.00
80	CHALLENGER, THE	17500	50.00	75.00
82	GIRL AT THE MIRROR	17500	50.00	100.00
82	MISSING TOOTH	17500	50.00	75.00
	B. JOHNSON	**MASTERPIECES OF THE WEST**		
80	TEXAS NIGHT HERDER	17500	35.00	75.00
	LEIGH	**MASTERPIECES OF THE WEST**		
82	COWBOY STYLE	17500	35.00	75.00
	G. PERILLO	**MASTERPIECES OF THE WEST**		
82	INDIAN STYLE	17500	35.00	150.00
	REMINGTON	**MASTERPIECES OF THE WEST**		
80	INDIAN TRAPPER	17500	35.00	100.00
	H. GARRIDO	**MELODIES OF CHILDHOOD**		
83	MARY HAD A LITTLE LAMB	19500	35.00	50.00
83	ROW, ROW, ROW YOUR BOAT	19500	35.00	50.00
83	TWINKLE, TWINKLE, LITTLE STAR	19500	35.00	50.00
	B.P. GUTMANN	**MOTHER'S LOVE**		
84	DADDY'S HERE	OP	29.95	60.00
	G. PERILLO	**MOTHER'S LOVE**		
88	FEELINGS	YR	35.00	95.00
89	MOONLIGHT	YR	35.00	70.00
90	PRIDE & JOY	YR	39.50	55.00
91	LITTLE SHADOW	YR	39.50	50.00
	G. PERILLO	**MOTHERHOOD SERIES**		
83	MADRE	10000	50.00	80.00
84	MADONNA OF THE PLAINS	3500	50.00	90.00
85	ABUELA	3500	50.00	80.00
86	NAP TIME	3500	50.00	80.00
	G. PERILLO	**NATIVE AMERICAN CHRISTMAS**		
93	LITTLE SHEPHERD, THE	YR	35.00	40.00
94	JOY TO THE WORLD	YR	45.00	50.00
	G. PERILLO	**NATURE'S HARMONY**		
82	BENGAL TIGER	12500	50.00	65.00
82	PEACEABLE KINGDOM, THE	12500	100.00	225.00
82	ZEBRA	12500	50.00	65.00
83	BLACK PANTHER	12500	50.00	75.00
83	ELEPHANT	12500	50.00	85.00
	G. PERILLO	**NORTH AMERICAN WILDLIFE**		
89	MOUNTAIN LION	CL	29.50	50.00
89	MUSTANG	CL	29.50	50.00
89	WHITE-TAILED DEER	CL	29.50	40.00
90	AMERICAN BALD EAGLE	CL	29.50	30.00
90	BIGHORN SHEEP	CL	29.50	40.00
90	BUFFALO	CL	29.50	40.00
90	POLAR BEAR	CL	29.50	40.00
90	TIMBER WOLF	CL	29.50	40.00
	C. BECKER	**NURSERY PAIR**		
83	AWAKENING, THE	OP	25.00	60.00
83	IN SLUMBERLAND	OP	25.00	60.00
	N. ROCKWELL	**ON THE ROAD SERIES**		
84	CITY PRIDE	OP	35.00	75.00
84	COUNTRY PRIDE	OP	35.00	75.00
84	PRIDE OF STOCKBRIDGE	OP	35.00	75.00
	G. PERILLO	**PERILLO CHRISTMAS**		
87	SHINING STAR	YR	29.50	210.00
88	SILENT LIGHT	YR	35.00	125.00
89	SNOW FLAKE	YR	35.00	55.00
90	BUNDLE UP	YR	39.50	80.00
91	CHRISTMAS JOURNEY	YR	39.50	55.00
	G. PERILLO	**PERILLO SANTAS**		
80	SANTA'S JOY	OP	29.95	55.00
81	SANTA'S BUNDLE	OP	29.95	50.00
	G. PERILLO	**PERILLO'S FAVORITES**		
94	BUFFALO AND THE BRAVE	CL	45.00	50.00
94	HOME OF THE BRAVE AND FREE	CL	35.00	40.00
	G. PERILLO	**PERILLO'S FOUR SEASONS**		
91	AUTUMN	CL	25.00	30.00
91	SPRING	CL	25.00	30.00
91	SUMMER	CL	25.00	30.00
91	WINTER	CL	25.00	30.00
	J.H. DOLPH	**PLAYFUL PETS**		
82	CURIOSITY	7500	45.00	75.00

YR	NAME	LIMIT	ISSUE	TREND
82	MASTER'S HAT	7500	45.00	75.00
	J. EGGERT			**PORTRAIT SERIES**
86	CHANTILLY	CL	24.50	40.00
86	DYNASTY	CL	24.50	40.00
86	JAMBALAYA	CL	24.50	40.00
86	VELVET	CL	24.50	40.00
	G. PERILLO			**PORTRAITS BY PERILLO-MINI PLATES**
89	BRIGHT SKY	9500	19.50	20.00
89	LITTLE FEATHER	9500	19.50	20.00
89	RUNNING BEAR	9500	19.50	20.00
89	SMILING EYES	9500	19.50	20.00
90	BLUE BIRD	9500	19.50	20.00
90	PROUD EAGLE	9500	19.50	20.00
90	SPRING BREEZE	9500	19.50	20.00
90	WILDFLOWER	9500	19.50	20.00
	R. SAUBER			**PORTRAITS OF AMERICAN BRIDES**
86	CAROLINE	CL	29.50	80.00
86	JACQUELINE	CL	29.50	40.00
87	ELIZABETH	CL	29.50	40.00
87	EMILY	CL	29.50	50.00
87	LAURA	CL	29.50	50.00
87	MEREDITH	CL	29.50	50.00
87	REBECCA	CL	29.50	65.00
87	SARAH	CL	29.50	50.00
	G. PERILLO			**PRIDE OF AMERICA'S INDIANS**
86	BRAVE AND FREE	CL	24.50	60.00
86	DARK-EYED FRIENDS	CL	24.50	35.00
86	NOBLE COMPANIONS	CL	24.50	35.00
87	KINDRED SPIRITS	CL	24.50	40.00
87	LOYAL ALLIANCE	CL	24.50	70.00
87	PEACEFUL COMRADES	CL	24.50	40.00
87	SMALL AND WISE	CL	24.50	40.00
87	WINTER SCOUTS	CL	24.50	30.00
	G. PERILLO			**PROUD YOUNG SPIRITS**
90	BIRDS OF A FEATHER	CL	29.50	40.00
90	FAST FRIENDS	CL	29.50	40.00
90	FREEDOMS WATCH	CL	29.50	40.00
90	LOYAL GUARDIAN	CL	29.50	40.00
90	PRAIRIE PALS	CL	29.50	40.00
90	PROTECTOR OF THE PLAINS	CL	29.50	55.00
90	WATCHFUL EYES	CL	29.50	60.00
90	WOODLAND SCOUTS	CL	29.50	40.00
	MAGO			**REFLECTIONS OF YOUTH**
88	AMY	CL	29.50	40.00
88	ANDREW	CL	29.50	40.00
88	BETH	CL	29.50	40.00
88	JESSICA	CL	29.50	40.00
88	JULIA	CL	29.50	50.00
88	LAUREN	CL	29.50	40.00
88	MICHELLE	CL	29.50	60.00
88	SEBASTIAN	CL	29.50	40.00
	N. ROCKWELL			**ROCKWELL AMERICANA**
81	SHUFFLETON'S BARBERSHOP	17500	75.00	150.00
82	BREAKING HOME TIES	17500	75.00	125.00
83	WALKING TO CHURCH	17500	75.00	125.00
	N. ROCKWELL			**ROCKWELL TRILOGY**
81	STOCKBRIDGE IN WINTER 1	OP	35.00	60.00
82	STOCKBRIDGE IN WINTER 2	OP	35.00	60.00
82	STOCKBRIDGE IN WINTER 3	OP	35.00	60.00
	L. MARCHETTI			**ROMANTIC CITIES OF EUROPE**
89	PARIS	CL	35.00	55.00
89	VENICE	CL	35.00	70.00
90	LONDON	CL	35.00	55.00
90	MOSCOW	CL	35.00	40.00
	KNOX/ROBERTSON			**ROSE WREATHS**
93	GENTLE PERSUASION	*	27.00	30.00
93	SUMMER'S BOUNTY	*	27.00	30.00
93	SUNSET SPLENDOR	*	27.00	30.00
93	VICTORIAN FANTASY	*	27.00	30.00
94	FLORAL FASCINATION	*	27.00	30.00
94	LOVE'S EMBRACE	*	27.00	30.00
94	SWEET SUNSHINE	*	27.00	30.00
94	SWEETHEARTS DELIGHT	*	27.00	30.00
	K. SOLDWEDEL			**SAILING THROUGH HISTORY**
86	FLYING CLOUD	CL	29.50	65.00
86	MAYFLOWER	CL	29.50	65.00
86	SANTA MARIA	CL	29.50	65.00
	N. ROCKWELL			**SIMPLER TIMES SERIES**
84	LAZY DAZE	7500	35.00	75.00
84	ONE FOR THE ROAD	7500	35.00	75.00
	R. SAUBER			**SONGS OF STEPHEN FOSTER**
84	BEAUTIFUL DREAMER	3500	60.00	80.00
84	JEANIE WITH THE LIGHT BROWN HAIR	3500	60.00	80.00
84	OH! SUSANNAH	3500	60.00	80.00
	MAGO			**SPECIAL ISSUE**
94	DIVINE INTERVENTION	CL	35.00	40.00

YR	NAME	LIMIT	ISSUE	TREND
	H.C. CHRISTY			**SPECIAL ISSUE**
87	WE THE PEOPLE	OP	35.00	40.00
	G. PERILLO			**SPECIAL ISSUE**
81	APACHE BOY	5000	95.00	180.00
83	PAPOOSE	3000	100.00	130.00
84	LOVERS, THE	OP	50.00	105.00
84	NAVAJO GIRL	3500	95.00	355.00
86	NAVAJO BOY	3500	95.00	175.00
	F. TIPTON HUNTER			**SPECIAL OCCASIONS**
82	BUBBLES	OP	29.95	50.00
82	BUTTERFLIES	OP	29.95	50.00
	G. PERILLO			**SPIRITS OF NATURE**
93	DEFENDER OF THE MOUNTAIN	3500	60.00	65.00
93	GUARDIAN OF SAFE PASSAGE	3500	60.00	65.00
93	KEEPER OF THE FOREST	3500	60.00	65.00
93	PROTECTOR OF THE NATIONS	3500	60.00	65.00
93	SPIRIT OF THE PLAINS	3500	60.00	65.00
	G. PERILLO			**STUDIES IN BLACK & WHITE COLLECTOR'S CLUB ONLY**
92	DETERMINATION	YR	*	*
92	DEVOTION	YR	*	*
92	DIGNITY	YR	75.00	80.00
92	DILIGENCE	YR	*	*
	MAGO			**STUDIES OF EARLY CHILDHOOD**
90	ANYBODY HOME?	CL	34.90	37.00
90	CHRISTOPHER & KATE	CL	34.90	46.00
90	PEEK-A-BOO	CL	34.90	37.00
90	THREE-PART HARMONY	OP	34.90	58.00
	G. PERILLO			**TENDER MOMENTS**
85	SUNSET	2000	150.00	255.00
85	WINTER ROMANCE	2000	*	*
	T. NEWSOM			**THE ADVENTURES OF PETER PAN**
90	ENCOUNTER, THE	CL	29.50	40.00
90	FLYING OVER LONDON	CL	29.50	40.00
90	LOOK AT ME	CL	29.50	40.00
90	NEVER LAND	CL	29.50	40.00
	G. PERILLO			**THE ARABIANS**
86	SILVER STREAK	3500	95.00	155.00
	T. NEWSOM			**THE CARNIVAL SERIES**
82	CAROUSEL	19500	35.00	50.00
82	KNOCK EM' DOWN	19500	35.00	50.00
	G. PERILLO			**THE COLTS**
85	APPALOOSA	5000	40.00	105.00
85	ARABIAN	5000	40.00	105.00
85	PINTO	5000	40.00	115.00
85	THOROUGHBRED	5000	40.00	105.00
	J. DENEEN			**THE GREAT TRAINS**
85	SANTA FE	7500	35.00	105.00
85	TWENTIETH CENTURY LTD.	7500	35.00	105.00
86	EMPIRE BUILDER	7500	35.00	105.00
	L. MARCHETTI			**THE LIFE OF JESUS**
92	AGONY IN THE GARDEN, THE	CL	27.00	30.00
92	BLESSING OF THE CHILDREN, THE	CL	27.00	30.00
92	DESCENT FROM THE CROSS, THE	CL	27.00	30.00
92	ENTRY INTO JERUSALEM, THE	CL	27.00	30.00
92	HEALING OF THE SICK, THE	CL	27.00	30.00
92	LAST SUPPER, THE	CL	27.00	30.00
92	RESURRECTION, THE	CL	27.00	30.00
92	SERMON ON THE MOUNT, THE	CL	27.00	30.00
	G. PERILLO			**THE MAIDENS**
85	SHIMMERING WATERS	5000	60.00	155.00
85	SNOW BLANKET	5000	60.00	155.00
85	SONG BIRD	5000	60.00	155.00
	G. PERILLO			**THE PLAINSMEN**
78	BUFFALO HUNT (BRONZE)	2500	300.00	505.00
79	PROUD ONE, THE (BRONZE)	2500	300.00	805.00
	G. PERILLO			**THE PRINCESSES**
82	LILY OF THE MOHAWKS	7500	50.00	90.00
82	MINNEHAHA	7500	50.00	70.00
82	POCAHONTAS	7500	50.00	60.00
82	SACAJAWEA	7500	50.00	90.00
	G. PERILLO			**THE PROFESSIONALS**
79	BIG LEAGUER, THE	15000	29.95	40.00
80	BALLERINA'S DILEMMA	15000	32.50	40.00
81	QUARTERBACK	15000	32.50	50.00
81	RODEO JOE	15000	35.00	45.00
82	MAJOR LEAGUER	15000	35.00	50.00
83	HOCKEY PLAYER, THE	15000	35.00	50.00
	G. PERILLO			**THE STORYBOOK COLLECTION**
80	LITTLE RED RIDING HOOD	CL	29.95	40.00
81	CINDERELLA	CL	29.95	45.00
81	HANSEL & GRETEL	CL	29.95	35.00
82	GOLDILOCKS & THE 3 BEARS	CL	29.95	45.00
	G. PERILLO			**THE THOROUGHBREDS**
84	MAN O' WAR	9500	50.00	155.00
84	SEABISCUIT	9500	50.00	155.00
84	SECRETARIAT	9500	50.00	355.00

YR	NAME	LIMIT	ISSUE	TREND
84	WHIRLAWAY	9500	50.00	255.00
G. PERILLO				**THE TRIBAL PONIES**
84	ARAPAHO TRIBAL PONY	3500	65.00	155.00
84	COMANCHE TRIBAL PONY	3500	65.00	155.00
84	CROW TRIBAL PONY	3500	65.00	205.00
H.C. CHRISTY				**THE TRIBUTE SERIES**
82	GEE, I WISH	OP	29.95	50.00
J.M. FLAGG				**THE TRIBUTE SERIES**
82	I WANT YOU	OP	29.95	50.00
N. ROCKWELL				**THE TRIBUTE SERIES**
83	SOLDIER'S FAREWELL	OP	29.95	50.00
G. PERILLO				**THE WAR PONIES**
83	APACHE WAR PONY	7500	60.00	110.00
83	NEZ PERCE WAR PONY	7500	60.00	120.00
83	SIOUX WAR PONY	7500	60.00	110.00
G. PERILLO				**THE YOUNG CHIEFTAINS**
85	YOUNG JOSEPH	5000	50.00	105.00
85	YOUNG SITTING BULL	5000	50.00	110.00
86	YOUNG CRAZY HORSE	5000	50.00	105.00
86	YOUNG GERONIMO	5000	50.00	105.00
86	YOUNG RED CLOUD	5000	50.00	105.00
R. SAUBER				**TIMELESS LOVE**
89	PROPOSAL, THE	CL	35.00	40.00
89	SWEET EMBRACE	CL	35.00	35.00
90	AFTERNOON LIGHT	CL	35.00	35.00
90	QUIET MOMENTS	CL	35.00	35.00
R. SAUBER				**TIMES OF OUR LIVES COLLECTION**
82	WEDDING, THE 10 1/4 IN.	OP	37.50	40.00
84	HAPPY BIRTHDAY 10 1/4 IN.	OP	37.50	40.00
85	ALL ADORE HIM 10 1/4 IN.	OP	37.50	40.00
85	HOME SWEET HOME 10 1/4 IN.	OP	37.50	40.00
86	ANNIVERSARY, THE 10 1/4 IN.	OP	37.50	40.00
86	CHRISTENING, THE 10 1/4 IN.	OP	37.50	40.00
86	SWEETHEARTS 10 1/4 IN.	OP	37.50	50.00
87	FATHERHOOD 10 1/4 IN.	OP	37.50	40.00
87	MOTHERHOOD 10 1/4 IN.	OP	37.50	40.00
87	SWEET SIXTEEN	OP	37.50	40.00
88	ALL ADORE HIM 6 1/2 IN.	OP	19.50	23.00
88	ANNIVERSARY, THE 6 1/2 IN.	OP	19.50	23.00
88	CHRISTENING, THE 6 1/2 IN.	OP	19.50	23.00
88	FATHERHOOD 6 1/2 IN.	OP	19.50	23.00
88	HAPPY BIRTHDAY 6 1/2 IN.	OP	19.50	23.00
88	HOME SWEET HOME 6 1/2 IN.	OP	19.50	23.00
88	MOTHERHOOD 6 1/2 IN.	OP	19.50	23.00
88	SWEETHEARTS 6 1/2 IN.	OP	19.50	23.00
88	WEDDING, THE 6 1/2 IN..	OP	19.50	23.00
89	GOD BLESS AMERICA 10 1/4 IN.	CL	39.50	40.00
89	GOD BLESS AMERICA 6 1/4 IN.	CL	21.50	23.00
89	VISITING THE DOCTOR	CL	39.50	40.00
90	MOTHER'S JOY 10 1/4 IN.	OP	39.50	40.00
90	MOTHER'S JOY 6 1/2 IN.	OP	22.50	23.00
G. PERILLO				**TRIBAL IMAGES**
94	BLACKFOOT CHIEFTANS	CL	35.00	40.00
94	CHEYENNE CHIEFTANS	CL	35.00	40.00
94	CROW CHIEFTANS	CL	35.00	40.00
94	SIOUX CHEIFTANS	CL	35.00	40.00
J. TERRESON				**UNICORN MAGIC**
83	AFTERNOON OFFERING	7500	50.00	60.00
83	MORNING ENCOUNTER	7500	50.00	60.00
G. PERILLO				**WAR PONIES OF THE PLAINS**
92	FREE SPIRIT	CL	27.00	30.00
92	GENTLE WARRIOR	CL	27.00	30.00
92	NIGHTSHADOW	CL	27.00	30.00
92	PRAIRIE PRANCER	CL	27.00	30.00
92	PROUND COMPANION	CL	27.00	30.00
92	SUN DANCER	CL	27.00	30.00
92	THUNDERFOOT	CL	27.00	30.00
92	WINDCATCHER	CL	27.00	30.00
R. SAUBER				**WINTER MINDSCAPE**
89	PEACEFUL VILLAGE	CL	29.50	65.00
89	SNOWBOUND	CL	29.50	40.00
90	COUNTRY MORNING	CL	29.50	40.00
90	FIRST FREEZE	CL	29.50	40.00
90	JANUARY THAW	CL	29.50	40.00
90	PAPA'S SURPRISE	CL	29.50	40.00
90	SLEIGH RIDE	CL	29.50	40.00
90	WELL TRAVELED ROAD	CL	29.50	40.00
G. PERILLO				**YOUNG EMOTIONS**
86	SMILES	5000	*	*
86	TEARS	5000	75.00	255.00

ARTISTS OF THE WORLD

Price ranges may reflect various demands in the market from one geographic region to another; condition of piece; specific markings found on piece; and/or changes in production of piece.

YR	NAME	LIMIT	ISSUE	TREND
T. DEGRAZIA				**CELEBRATION**
93	CAROLING	5000	39.50	40.00

YR	NAME	LIMIT	ISSUE	TREND
93	HOLIDAY LULLABY	5000	39.50	40.00
93	LORD'S CANDLE, THE	5000	39.50	40.00
93	PINATA PARTY	5000	39.50	40.00
T. DEGRAZIA				**CHILDREN**
76	LOS NINOS	5000	35.00	785.00
77	WHITE DOVE	5000	40.00	90.00
78	FLOWER GIRL	9500	45.00	70.00
78	FLOWER GIRL-SIGNED	500	100.00	455.00
78	LOS NINOS-SIGNED	500	100.00	905.00
78	WHITE DOVE-SIGNED	500	100.00	455.00
79	FLOWER BOY	9500	45.00	55.00
79	FLOWER BOY-SIGNED	500	100.00	455.00
80	LITTLE COCOPAH	9500	50.00	70.00
80	LITTLE COCOPAH GIRL-SIGNED	500	100.00	325.00
81	BEAUTIFUL BURDEN	9500	50.00	55.00
81	BEAUTIFUL BURDEN-SIGNED	500	100.00	325.00
81	MERRY LITTLE INDIAN-SIGNED	500	100.00	455.00
82	MERRY LITTLE INDIAN	9500	55.00	55.00
83	WONDERING	10000	60.00	50.00
84	PINK PAPOOSE	10000	65.00	45.00
85	SUNFLOWER BOY	10000	65.00	65.00
T. DEGRAZIA				**CHILDREN AT PLAY**
85	MY FIRST HORSE	15000	65.00	70.00
86	GIRL WITH SEWING MACHINE	15000	65.00	70.00
87	LOVES ME	15000	65.00	70.00
88	MERRILY, MERRILY, MERRILY	15000	65.00	70.00
89	MY FIRST ARROW	15000	65.00	90.00
90	AWAY WITH MY KITE	15000	65.00	80.00
T. DEGRAZIA				**CHILDREN MINI-PLATES**
80	LOS NINOS	5000	15.00	305.00
81	WHITE DOVE	5000	15.00	40.00
82	FLOWER BOY	5000	15.00	40.00
82	FLOWER GIRL	5000	15.00	40.00
83	BEAUTIFUL BURDEN	5000	20.00	55.00
83	LITTLE COCOPAH INDIAN GIRL	5000	15.00	30.00
84	MERRY LITTLE INDIAN	5000	20.00	30.00
84	WONDERING	5000	20.00	30.00
85	PINK PAPOOSE	5000	20.00	30.00
85	SUNFLOWER BOY	5000	20.00	30.00
K. FUNG NG				**CHILDREN OF ABERDEEN**
79	GIRL WITH LITTLE BROTHER	*	50.00	50.00
80	SAMPAN GIRL	*	50.00	50.00
81	GIRL WITH LITTLE SISTER	*	55.00	55.00
82	GIRL WITH SEASHELLS	*	60.00	60.00
83	GIRL WITH SEABIRDS	*	60.00	60.00
84	BROTHER AND SISTER	*	60.00	60.00
T. DEGRAZIA				**CHILDREN OF THE SUN**
87	BRIGHT FLOWERS OF THE DESERT	150-DAY	37.90	50.00
87	MY LITTLE PINK BIRD	150-DAY	34.50	50.00
87	SPRING BLOSSOMS	150-DAY	34.50	50.00
88	GENTLE WHITE DOVE, THE	150-DAY	37.90	50.00
88	GIFTS FROM THE SUN	150-DAY	37.90	50.00
88	GROWING GLORY	150-DAY	37.90	50.00
88	SUNFLOWER MAIDEN	150-DAY	39.90	50.00
89	SUN SHOWERS	150-DAY	39.90	50.00
T. DEGRAZIA				**FIESTA OF THE CHILDREN**
90	CASTANETS IN BLOOM	150-DAY	34.50	50.00
90	WELCOME TO THE FIESTA	150-DAY	34.50	40.00
91	FIESTA FLOWERS	150-DAY	34.50	50.00
92	FIESTA ANGELS	150-DAY	34.50	45.00
T. DEGRAZIA				**FLORAL FIESTA**
94	FLOWERS FOR MOTHER	5000	39.50	42.00
94	LITTLE FLOWER VENDOR	5000	39.50	42.00
T. DEGRAZIA				**HOLIDAY**
76	FESTIVAL OF LIGHTS	9500	45.00	90.00
76	FESTIVAL OF LIGHTS-SIGNED	500	100.00	325.00
77	BELL OF HOPE	9500	45.00	60.00
77	BELL OF HOPE-SIGNED	500	100.00	190.00
78	LITTLE MADONNA	9500	45.00	55.00
78	LITTLE MADONNA-SIGNED	500	100.00	340.00
79	NATIVITY, THE	9500	50.00	80.00
79	NATIVITY, THE-SIGNED	500	100.00	185.00
80	LITTLE PIMA DRUMMER	9500	50.00	60.00
80	LITTLE PIMA DRUMMER-SIGNED	500	100.00	190.00
81	A LITTLE PRAYER	9500	55.00	50.00
81	A LITTLE PRAYER-SIGNED	500	100.00	195.00
82	BLUE BOY	10000	60.00	50.00
82	BLUE BOY-SIGNED	96	100.00	200.00
83	HEAVENLY BLESSINGS	10000	65.00	30.00
84	NAVAJO MADONNA	10000	65.00	50.00
85	SAGUARO DANCE	10000	65.00	50.00
T. DEGRAZIA				**HOLIDAY-MINI PLATES**
80	FESTIVAL OF LIGHTS	5000	15.00	255.00
81	BELL OF HOPE	5000	15.00	55.00
82	LITTLE MADONNA	5000	15.00	100.00
82	NATIVITY, THE	5000	15.00	100.00
83	LITTLE PIMA DRUMMER	5000	15.00	30.00

Valentine sweethearts make the best kind. Be Mine *was created by Sandra Kuck as part of "A Childhood Almanac" series for Reco.*

Times Remembered *by Sandra Kuck was the 1986 annual Mother's Day plate from Reco International. Limited to one year of production, the plate is currently valued at $40 - $75.*

The 1983 addition to Incolay Studios' Romantic Poets Collection was I Stood Tiptoe, *second in the Nature Quartet Series.*

Corinne Layton captures the pastime of playing dress-up in Olivia, *fourth issue in the "Heirlooms and Lace" series produced by Edwin M. Knowles.*

YR	NAME	LIMIT	ISSUE	TREND
83	LITTLE PRAYER	5000	20.00	30.00
84	BLUE BOY	5000	20.00	30.00
84	HEAVENLY BLESSINGS	5000	20.00	30.00
85	NAVAJO MADONNA	5000	20.00	30.00
85	SAGUARO DANCE	5000	20.00	30.00
T. DEGRAZIA				**WESTERN**
86	MORNING RIDE	5000	65.00	90.00
87	BRONCO	5000	65.00	90.00
88	APPACHE SCOUT	5000	65.00	90.00
89	ALONE	5000	65.00	90.00

BAREUTHER

YR	NAME	LIMIT	ISSUE	TREND
H. MUELLER				**CHRISTMAS**
67	STIFTSKIRCHE	10000	12.00	90.00
68	KAPPLKIRCHE	10000	12.00	30.00
69	CHRISTKINDLESMARKT	10000	12.00	20.00
70	CHAPEL IN OBERNDORF	10000	12.50	25.00
72	CHRISTMAS IN MUNICH	10000	14.50	30.00
73	SLEIGH RIDE	10000	15.00	40.00
74	BLACK FOREST CHURCH	10000	19.00	20.00
75	SNOWMAN	10000	21.50	35.00
76	CHAPEL IN THE HILLS	10000	23.50	30.00
77	STORY TIME	10000	24.50	45.00
78	MITTENWALD	10000	27.50	35.00
79	WINTER DAY	10000	35.00	40.00
80	MITTENBERG	10000	37.50	40.00
81	WALK IN THE FOREST	10000	39.50	40.00
82	BAD WIMPFEN	10000	39.50	45.00
83	NIGHT BEFORE CHRISTMAS, THE	10000	39.50	40.00
84	ZEIL ON THE RIVER MAIN	10000	42.50	50.00
85	WINTER WONDERLAND	10000	42.50	60.00
86	CHRISTMAS IN FORCHHEIM	10000	42.50	75.00
87	DECORATING THE TREE	10000	42.50	90.00
88	ST. COLOMAN CHURCH	10000	52.50	70.00
89	SLEIGH RIDE	10000	52.50	85.00
90	OLD FORGE IN ROTHENBURG, THE	10000	52.50	55.00
91	CHRISTMAS JOY	10000	56.50	60.00
92	MARKET PLACE IN HEPPENHEIM	10000	59.50	60.00
93	WINTER FUN	10000	59.50	60.00
94	COMING HOME FOR CHRISTMAS	10000	59.50	60.00
L. RICHTER				**CHRISTMAS**
71	TOYS FOR SALE	10000	12.75	30.00

BELLEEK

YR	NAME	LIMIT	ISSUE	TREND
*				**CHRISTMAS**
70	CASTLE CALDWELL	7500	25.00	80.00
71	CELTIC CROSS	7500	25.00	65.00
72	FLIGHT OF THE EARLS	7500	30.00	40.00
73	TRIBUTE TO YEATS	7500	38.50	45.00
74	DEVENISH ISLAND	7500	45.00	195.00
75	CELTIC CROSS, THE	7500	48.00	85.00
76	DOVE OF PEACE	7500	55.00	60.00
77	WREN	7500	55.00	60.00

BERLIN DESIGN

YR	NAME	LIMIT	ISSUE	TREND
*				**CHRISTMAS**
70	CHRISTMAS IN BERNKASTEL	4000	14.50	130.00
71	CHRISTMAS IN ROTHENBURG	20000	14.50	50.00
72	CHRISTMAS IN MICHELSTADT	20000	15.00	60.00
73	CHRISTMAS IN WENDLESTEIN	20000	20.00	60.00
74	CHRISTMAS IN BREMEN	20000	25.00	55.00
75	CHRISTMAS IN DORTLAND	20000	30.00	40.00
76	CHRISTMAS IN AUGSBURG	20000	32.00	80.00
77	CHRISTMAS IN HAMBURG	20000	32.00	35.00
78	CHRISTMAS IN BERLIN	20000	36.00	90.00
79	CHRISTMAS IN GREETSIEL	20000	47.50	65.00
80	CHRISTMAS IN MITTENBERG	20000	50.00	60.00
81	CHRISTMAS EVE IN HAHNENKLEE	20000	55.00	60.00
82	CHRISTMAS EVE IN WASSERBERG	20000	55.00	55.00
83	CHRISTMAS IN OBERNDORF	20000	55.00	70.00
84	CHRISTMAS IN RAMSAU	20000	55.00	60.00
85	CHRISTMAS IN BAD WIMPFEN	20000	55.00	60.00
86	CHRISTMAS EVE IN GELNHAUS	20000	65.00	70.00
87	CHRISTMAS EVE IN GOSLAR	20000	65.00	70.00
88	CHRISTMAS EVE IN RUHPOLDING	20000	65.00	95.00
89	CHRISTMAS EVE IN FRIEDECHSDADT	20000	80.00	85.00
90	CHRISTMAS EVE IN PARTENKIRCHEN	20000	80.00	85.00
91	CHRISTMAS EE IN ALLENDORF	20000	80.00	85.00
*				**HISTORICAL**
75	WASHINGTON CROSSING THE DELAWARE	YR	30.00	40.00
76	TOM THUMB	YR	32.00	35.00
77	ZEPPELIN	YR	32.00	35.00
78	BENZ MOTOR CAR MUNICH	10000	36.00	36.00
79	JOHANNES GUTENBERG	10000	47.50	48.00
*		**HOLIDAY WEEK OF THE FAMILY KAPPELMANN**		
84	MONDAY	*	33.00	33.00
84	TUESDAY	*	33.00	37.00
85	FRIDAY	*	35.00	40.00

YR	NAME	LIMIT	ISSUE	TREND
85	THURSDAY	*	35.00	38.00
85	WEDNESDAY	*	33.00	37.00
86	SATURDAY	*	35.00	40.00
86	SUNDAY	*	35.00	40.00

BIEDERMANN & SONS

*

YR	NAME	LIMIT	ISSUE	TREND
93	FOUR CALLING BIRDS	250	17.50	20.00
94	DRUMMER BOY	250	20.00	50.00

BING & GRONDAHL

YR	NAME	LIMIT	ISSUE	TREND
A. HALLIN			**CENTENNIAL COLLECTION**	
95	BEHIND THE FROZEN WINDOW	YR	59.50	69.00
D. JENSEN			**CENTENNIAL COLLECTION**	
92	CROWS ENJOYING CHRISTMAS	YR	59.50	63.00
H. THELANDER			**CENTENNIAL COLLECTION**	
93	CHRISTMAS ELF	YR	59.50	60.00
94	CHRISTMAS IN CHURCH	YR	59.50	60.00
H. VLUGENRING			**CENTENNIAL COLLECTION**	
92	COPENHAGEN CHRISTMAS	YR	59.50	60.00
C. ROLLER			**CHILDREN'S DAY PLATE**	
85	MAGICAL TEA PARTY, THE	YR	24.50	30.00
86	A JOYFUL FLIGHT	YR	26.50	35.00
86	LITTLE GARDENERS, THE	YR	29.50	42.00
86	LITTLE GARDENERS, THE	YR	29.50	45.00
88	WASH DAY	YR	34.50	45.00
89	BEDTIME	YR	37.00	30.00
S. VESTERGAARD			**CHILDREN'S DAY PLATE**	
90	MY FAVORITE DRESS	YR	37.00	45.00
91	FUN ON THE BEACH	YR	45.00	60.00
92	A SUMMER DAY IN THE MEADOW	YR	45.00	69.00
93	CAROUSEL, THE	YR	45.00	60.00
94	LITTLE FISHERMAN, THE	YR	45.00	60.00
AARESTRUP				**CHRISTMAS**
30	YULE TREE	YR	1.50	99.00
K. BONFILS				**CHRISTMAS**
54	ROYAL BOAT	YR	7.00	89.00
55	KAULUNDORG CHURCH	YR	8.00	123.00
56	CHRISTMAS IN COPENHAGEN	YR	8.50	123.00
57	CHRISTMAS CANDLES	YR	9.00	139.00
58	SANTA CLAUS	YR	9.50	115.00
59	CHRISTMAS EVE	YR	10.00	129.00
60	VILLAGE CHURCH	YR	10.00	170.00
61	WINTER HARMONY	YR	10.50	80.00
62	WINTER NIGHT	YR	11.00	79.00
C. ERSGAARD				**CHRISTMAS**
10	OLD ORGANIST, THE	YR	1.50	110.00
H. FLUGENRING				**CHRISTMAS**
31	TOWN HALL SQUARE	YR	2.50	90.00
32	LIFE BOAT	YR	2.50	95.00
33	KORSOR-NYBORG FERRY	YR	3.00	77.00
34	CHURCH BELL IN TOWER	YR	3.00	77.00
A. FRIIS				**CHRISTMAS**
17	CHRISTMAS BOAT	YR	1.50	90.00
18	FISHING BOAT	YR	1.50	90.00
19	OUTSIDE LIGHTED WINDOW	YR	2.00	89.00
20	HARE IN THE SNOW	YR	2.00	82.00
21	PIGEONS	YR	2.00	82.00
22	STAR OF BETHLEHEM	YR	2.00	55.00
23	ERMITAGE, THE	YR	2.00	79.00
24	LIGHTHOUSE	YR	2.50	79.00
25	CHILD'S CHRISTMAS	YR	2.50	79.00
26	CHURCHGOERS	YR	2.50	79.00
27	SKATING COUPLE	YR	2.50	95.00
28	ESKIMOS	YR	2.50	69.00
29	FOX OUTSIDE FARM	YR	2.50	89.00
31	CHRISTMAS TRAIN	YR	2.50	87.00
F. GARDE				**CHRISTMAS**
00	CHURCH BELLS	YR	0.75	1600.00
98	ROSES AND STAR	YR	0.75	978.00
99	CROWS	YR	0.75	2000.00
F. HALLIN				**CHRISTMAS**
95	BEHIND THE FROZEN WINDOW	YR	0.50	7000.00
96	NEW MOON	YR	0.50	2400.00
97	SPARROWS	YR	0.75	1400.00
E. HANSEN				**CHRISTMAS**
02	GOING TO CHURCH	YR	1.50	99.00
M. HYLDAHL				**CHRISTMAS**
00	EXPECTANT CHILDREN	YR	1.00	290.00
46	COMMEMORATION CROSS	YR	5.00	79.00
47	DYBBOL MILL	YR	5.00	99.00
48	WATCHMAN	YR	5.50	65.00
49	LANDSOLDATEN	YR	5.50	73.00
50	KRONBORG CASTLE	YR	5.50	109.00
51	JENS BANG	YR	6.00	95.00
D. JENSEN				**CHRISTMAS**
02	GOTHIC CHURCH INTERIOR	YR	1.00	437.00

YR	NAME	LIMIT	ISSUE	TREND
05	CHRISTMAS NIGHT	YR	1.00	179.00
06	SLEIGHING TO CHURCH	YR	1.00	110.00
15	DOG OUTSIDE WINDOW	YR	1.50	139.00
84	CHRISTMAS LETTER, THE	YR	54.50	75.00
85	CHRISTMAS EVE AT THE FARMHOUSE	YR	54.50	77.00
86	SILENT NIGHT, HOLY NIGHT	YR	54.50	75.00
87	SNOWMAN'S CHRISTMAS EVE, THE	YR	59.50	77.00
88	IN THE KINGS GARDEN	YR	64.50	77.00
89	CHRISTMAS ANCHORAGE	YR	59.50	71.00
90	CHANGING OF THE GUARDS	YR	64.50	71.00
91	COPENHAGEN STOCK EXCHANGE	YR	69.50	55.00
P. JORGENSEN				**CHRISTMAS**
00	ST. PETRI CHURCH	YR	1.00	80.00
16	SPARROWS AT CHRISTMAS	YR	1.50	65.00
T. LARSEN				**CHRISTMAS**
13	BRINGING HOME THE TREE	YR	1.50	49.00
14	AMALIENBORG CASTLE	YR	1.50	25.00
O. LARSON				**CHRISTMAS**
35	LILLEBELT BRIDGE	YR	3.00	77.00
36	ROYAL GUARD	YR	3.00	77.00
37	ARRIVAL OF CHRISTMAS GUESTS	YR	3.00	80.00
40	CHRISTMAS LETTERS	YR	4.00	149.00
41	HORSES ENJOYING MEAL	YR	4.00	243.00
42	DANISH FARM	YR	4.00	174.00
43	RIBE CATHEDRAL	YR	5.00	174.00
44	SORGENFRI CASTLE	YR	5.00	99.00
45	OLD WATER MILL, THE	YR	5.00	119.00
H. MOLTKE				**CHRISTMAS**
00	ANGELS AND SHEPHERDS	YR	1.50	79.00
C. OLSEN				**CHRISTMAS**
04	FREDERICKSBERG HILL	YR	1.00	179.00
F. PLOCKROSS				**CHRISTMAS**
07	LITTLE MATCH GIRL	YR	1.00	133.00
B. PRAMVIG				**CHRISTMAS**
52	THORSVALDSEN MUSEUM	YR	6.00	70.00
53	SNOWMAN	YR	7.50	79.00
S. SABRA				**CHRISTMAS**
00	THREE WISE MEN	YR	1.00	450.00
J. STEENSEN				**CHRISTMAS**
92	CHRISTMAS AT THE RECTORY	YR	69.50	79.00
93	FATHER CHRISTMAS IN COPENHAGEN	YR	69.50	72.00
H. THELANDER				**CHRISTMAS**
63	CHRISTMAS ELF	YR	11.00	127.00
64	FIR TREE AND HARE, THE	YR	11.50	47.00
65	BRINGING HOME THE TREE	YR	12.00	49.00
66	HOME FOR CHRISTMAS	YR	12.00	47.00
67	SHARING THE JOY	YR	13.00	65.00
68	CHRISTMAS IN CHURCH	YR	14.00	39.00
69	ARRIVAL OF GUESTS	YR	14.00	30.00
70	PHEASANTS IN SNOW	YR	14.50	25.00
71	CHRISTMAS AT HOME	YR	15.00	25.00
72	CHRISTMAS IN GREENLAND	YR	16.50	25.00
73	COUNTRY CHRISTMAS	YR	19.50	25.00
74	CHRISTMAS IN THE VILLAGE	YR	22.00	25.00
75	OLD WATER MILL	YR	27.50	39.00
76	CHRISTMAS WELCOME	YR	27.50	39.00
77	COPENHAGEN CHRISTMAS	YR	29.50	39.00
78	CHRISTMAS TALE	YR	32.00	49.00
79	WHITE CHRISTMAS	YR	36.50	20.00
80	CHRISTMAS IN WOODS	YR	42.50	49.00
81	CHRISTMAS PEACE	YR	49.50	49.00
82	CHRISTMAS TREE	YR	54.50	83.00
83	CHRISTMAS IN OLD TOWN	YR	54.50	75.00
I. TJERNE				**CHRISTMAS**
38	LIGHTING THE CANDLES	YR	3.00	109.00
39	OLD LOCK-EYE, THE SANDMAN	YR	3.00	149.00
J. WOODSON				**CHRISTMAS IN AMERICA**
86	CHRISTMAS EVE IN WILLIAMSBURG	YR	29.50	155.00
87	CHRISTMAS EVE AT THE WHITE HOUSE	YR	34.50	40.00
88	CHRISTMAS EVE AT ROCKEFELLER CENTER	YR	34.50	50.00
89	CHRISTMAS IN NEW ENGLAND	YR	37.00	50.00
90	CHRISTMAS EVE AT THE CAPITOL	YR	39.50	50.00
91	CHRISTMAS EVE AT INDEPENDENCE HALL	YR	45.00	50.00
92	CHRISTMAS IN SAN FRANCISCO	YR	47.50	50.00
93	COMING HOME FOR CHRISTMAS	YR	47.50	50.00
94	CHRISTMAS EVE IN ALASKA	YR	47.50	50.00
J. WOODSON				**CHRISTMAS IN AMERICA ANNIVERSARY PLATE**
91	CHRISTMAS EVE IN WILLIAMSBURG	YR	69.50	74.00
AARESTRUP				**JUBILEE-5 YEAR CYCLE**
80	YULE TREE	YR	60.00	75.00
J. BONFILS				**JUBILEE-5 YEAR CYCLE**
90	ROYAL YACHT DANNEBROG, THE	YR	95.00	79.00
C. ERSGAARD				**JUBILEE-5 YEAR CYCLE**
30	OLD ORGANIST, THE	YR	*	199.00
H. FLUGENRING				**JUBILEE-5 YEAR CYCLE**
85	LIFEBOAT AT WORK	YR	65.00	90.00

YR	NAME	LIMIT	ISSUE	TREND
A. FRIIS				**JUBILEE-5 YEAR CYCLE**
50	ESKIMOS	YR	*	239.00
65	CHURCHGOERS	YR	25.00	105.00
F. GARDE				**JUBILEE-5 YEAR CYCLE**
20	CHURCH BELLS	YR	*	75.00
F. HALLIN				**JUBILEE-5 YEAR CYCLE**
15	FROZEN WINDOW	YR	*	189.00
M. HYLDAHL				**JUBILEE-5 YEAR CYCLE**
55	DYBBOL MILL	YR	*	239.00
60	KRONBORG CASTLE	YR	25.00	159.00
D. JENSEN				**JUBILEE-5 YEAR CYCLE**
25	DOG OUTSIDE WINDOW	YR	*	159.00
T. LARSEN				**JUBILEE-5 YEAR CYCLE**
45	AMALIENBORG CASTLE	YR	*	219.00
70	AMALIENBORG CASTLE	YR	30.00	25.00
O. LARSON				**JUBILEE-5 YEAR CYCLE**
75	HORSES ENJOYING MEAL	YR	40.00	59.00
E. PLOCKROSS				**JUBILEE-5 YEAR CYCLE**
35	LITTLE MATCH GIRL	YR	*	759.00
S. SABRA				**JUBILEE-5 YEAR CYCLE**
40	THREE WISE MEN	YR	*	1839.00
L. JENSEN				**MOTHER'S DAY**
90	HEN WITH CHICKS	YR	52.50	60.00
91	NANNY GOAT AND HER TWO FRISKY KIDS, THE	YR	54.50	75.00
92	PANDA WITH CUBS	YR	59.50	75.00
H. THELANDER				**MOTHER'S DAY**
69	DOGS AND PUPPIES	YR	9.75	31.50
70	BIRD AND CHICKS	YR	10.00	30.00
71	CAT AND KITTEN	YR	11.00	14.00
72	MARE AND FOAL	YR	12.00	13.00
73	DUCK AND DUCKLINGS	YR	13.00	14.00
74	BEAR AND CUBS	YR	16.50	17.00
75	DOE AND FAWNS	YR	19.50	20.00
76	SWAN FAMILY	YR	22.50	20.00
77	SQUIRREL AND YOUNG	YR	23.50	20.00
78	HERON	YR	24.50	20.00
79	FOX AND CUBS	YR	27.50	30.00
80	WOODPECKER AND YOUNG	YR	29.50	29.00
81	HARE AND YOUNG	YR	36.50	30.00
82	LIONESS AND CUBS	YR	39.50	50.00
83	RACCOON AND YOUNG	YR	39.50	50.00
84	STORK AND NESTLINGS	YR	39.50	50.00
85	BEAR AND CUBS	YR	39.50	39.00
86	ELEPHANT WITH CALF	YR	39.50	39.00
87	SHEEP WITH LAMBS	YR	42.50	89.00
88	CRESTED PLOYER & YOUNG	YR	47.50	70.00
88	LAPWING MOTHER WITH CHICKS	YR	49.50	60.00
89	COW WITH CALF	YR	49.50	70.00
A. THERKELSEN				**MOTHER'S DAY**
93	ST. BERNARD DOG AND PUPPIES	YR	59.50	75.00
*				**OLYMPIC**
72	MUNICH, GERMANY	CL	20.00	20.00
76	MONTREAL, CANADA	CL	29.50	59.00
80	MOSCOW, RUSSIA	CL	43.00	89.00
84	LOS ANGELES, USA	CL	45.00	260.00
88	SEOUL, KOREA	CL	60.00	95.00
92	BARCELONA, SPAIN	CL	74.50	90.00
H. HANSEN				**SANTA CLAUS COLLECTION**
89	SANTA'S WORKSHOP	YR	59.50	70.00
90	SANTA'S SLEIGH	YR	59.50	85.00
91	SANTA'S JOURNEY	YR	69.50	75.00
92	SANTA'S ARRIVAL	YR	74.50	78.00
93	SANTA'S GIFTS	YR	74.50	78.00
94	CHRISTMAS STORIES	YR	74.50	75.00
*				**STATUE OF LIBERTY**
85	STATUE OF LIBERTY	10000	60.00	90.00
S. VESTERGAARD				**YOUNG ADVENTURER PLATE**
90	LITTLE VIKING, THE	YR	52.50	70.00

BOEHM STUDIOS

YR	NAME	LIMIT	ISSUE	TREND
*				**EGYPTIAN COMMEMORATIVE**
78	TUTANKHAMUN	5000	125.00	170.00
78	TUTANKHAMUN, HANDPAINTED	225	975.00	975.00
*				**PANDA**
82	PANDA, HARMONY	5000	65.00	70.00
82	PANDA, PEACE	5000	65.00	70.00

BRADFORD EXCHANGE

YR	NAME	LIMIT	ISSUE	TREND
*				**101 DALMATIONS**
93	WATCH DOGS	CL	29.90	30.00
94	A HAPPY REUNION	CL	29.90	30.00
94	HELLO DARLING	CL	32.90	33.00
95	A MESSY GOOD TIME	95-DAY	29.90	30.00
A. WHITE				**101 DALMATIONS**
94	HALFWAY HOME	CL	32.90	37.00

YR	NAME	LIMIT	ISSUE	TREND
	L. GARRISON			**A CHRISTMAS CAROL**
93	GHOST OF CHRISTMAS PRESENT	CL	29.90	30.00
93	GOD BLESS US EVERYONE	CL	29.90	30.00
94	A MERRY CHRISTMAS TO ALL	CL	29.90	30.00
94	A SPIRIT'S WARNING	CL	29.90	30.00
94	A VISIT FROM MARLEY'S GHOST	CL	29.90	30.00
94	REMEMBERING CHRISTMAS PAST	CL	29.90	30.00
94	TRUE SPIRIT OF CHRISTMAS, THE	CL	29.90	30.00
	W. GOEBEL			**A COUNTRY WONDERLAND**
95	THE QUIET HOUR	95-DAY	29.90	30.00
	R. RUST			**A HIDDEN WORLD**
93	HUNTER GROWLS, SPIRITS PROWL	CL	32.90	33.00
93	IN MOONGLOW ONE DRINKS	CL	32.90	33.00
93	SINGS AT THE MOON, SPIRITS SING IN TUNE	CL	34.90	35.00
93	TWO BY NIGHT, TWO BY LIGHT	CL	29.90	30.00
93	TWO BY STEAM, TWO IN DREAM	CL	32.90	33.00
	J. ANDERSON			**A MOTHER'S LOVE**
95	REMEMBRANCE	95-DAY	29.90	30.00
	M. SARNAT			**A SEASON OF LOVE**
96	A CHERISHED MOMENT	*	29.95	30.00
	C. JACKSON			**A VISIT FROM ST. NICK**
95	TWAS THE NIGHT BEFORE CHRISTMAS	CL	49.00	49.00
95	UP TO THE HOUSETOP	CL	49.00	49.00
96	TO MY WONDERING EYES	*	59.00	59.00
	J. BARKLEM			**A VISIT TO BRAMBLY HEDGE**
94	SUMMER STORY	*	39.90	40.00
	*			**ALADDIN**
93	A FRIEND LIKE ME	CL	29.90	30.00
93	MAGIC CARPET RIDE	CL	29.90	30.00
94	ALADDIN IN LOVE	CL	29.90	30.00
94	TRAVELING COMPANIONS	CL	29.90	30.00
95	BEE YOURSELF	95-DAY	29.90	30.00
95	GROUP HUG	95-DAY	29.90	30.00
	S. GUSTAFSON			**ALICE IN WONDERLAND**
93	ADVICE FROM A CATERPILLAR	CL	29.90	30.00
93	CHESHIRE CAT, THE	CL	29.90	30.00
93	MAD TEA PARTY, THE	CL	29.90	30.00
94	CROQUET WITH THE QUEEN	CL	29.90	30.00
	L.K. MARTIN			**AMERICA THE BEAUTIFUL**
96	OH BEAUTIFUL/SPACIOUS SKIES	*	*	*
	D. EVERHART			**AMERICA'S FAVORITE CLASSIC CARS**
93	CORVETTE 1957	*	54.00	54.00
93	THUNDERBIRD 1956	*	54.00	54.00
94	BEL AIR 1957	*	54.00	54.00
94	MUSTANG 1965	-	54.00	54.00
	*			**AMERICA'S TRIUMPH IN SPACE**
94	NEW EXPLORERS, THE	CL	34.90	35.00
94	RENDEVOUS W/VICTORY	CL	34.90	35.00
	R. SCHAAR			**AMERICA'S TRIUMPH IN SPACE**
93	BEYOND THE BOUNDS OF EARTH	CL	32.90	33.00
93	CONQUERING THE NEW FRONTIER	CL	32.90	33.00
93	EAGLE HAS LANDED, THE	CL	29.90	30.00
93	FLIGHT OF GLORY	CL	32.90	35.00
93	MARCH TOWARDS DESTINY, THE	CL	29.90	30.00
94	CONQUERING THE NEW FRONTIER	CL	32.90	32.90
94	TRIUMPHANT FINALE, THE	CL	34.90	35.00
	C. WYSOCKI			**AMERICAN FRONTIER**
93	TIMBERLINE JACK'S TRADING POST	CL	29.90	30.00
94	BUSTLING BOOMTOWN	CL	29.90	30.00
94	DR. LIVINGWELL'S MEDICINE SHOW	CL	29.90	30.00
94	HEARTY HOMESTEADERS	CL	29.90	30.00
94	KIRBYVILLE	CL	29.90	30.00
94	OKLAHOMA OR BUST	CL	29.90	30.00
	T. KINKADE			**AN OLD-FASHIONED CHRISTMAS**
93	ALL FRIENDS ARE WELCOME	CL	29.90	30.00
	M. SILVERSMITH			**ANCIENT SEASONS**
95	EDGE OF NIGHT	95-DAY	29.90	30.00
	P. HEFFERNAN			**BABE RUTH CENTENNIAL**
95	THE 60TH HOMER	95-DAY	29.90	30.00
	A. ISAKOV			**BASKETS OF LOVE**
93	ANDREW AND ABBEY	CL	29.90	30.00
93	CODY AND COURTNEY	CL	29.90	30.00
93	EMILY AND ELLIOTT	CL	32.90	35.00
93	HEATHER AND HANNAH	CL	32.90	33.00
93	JUSTIN AND JESSICA	CL	32.90	33.00
93	KATIE AND KELLY	CL	34.90	35.00
	J. GRIFFIN			**BATTLES OF THE AMERICAN CIVIL WAR**
95	GETTYSBURG	95 DAY	29.90	30.00
95	VICKSBURG	95-DAY	29.90	30.00
	D. KINGSTON BAKER			**BEAR ESSENTIALS OF LIFE**
96	LOVE	*	*	*
	S. SHERWOOD			**BEARY MERRY CHRISTMAS**
96	A MOMENT TO TREASURE	*	29.95	30.00
96	A ROMANTIC RIDE	*	29.95	30.00

YR	NAME	LIMIT	ISSUE	TREND
*				**BEATITUDES**
96	BLESSED/THE PURE IN HEART	*	*	*
L. LIU				**BEAUTIFUL GARDENS**
94	IRIS GARDEN	*	34.00	35.00
94	PEONY GARDEN	*	34.00	39.00
95	LILY GARDEN	95-DAY	39.00	39.00
96	HIBISCUS GARDEN	*	47.00	47.00
96	MORNING GLORY GARDEN	*	44.00	44.00
*				**BEAUTY & THE BEAST**
94	A SPOT OF TEA	CL	34.90	40.00
D. TERBUSH				**BENEATH THE WAVES**
95	ALL GOD'S CHILDREN	95-DAY	29.90	30.00
95	HUMPBACK WHALES	95-DAY	29.90	30.00
95	SEA OF LIGHT	95-DAY	29.90	30.00
J. MADAY				**BUNNY WORKSHOP**
95	MAKE TODAY EGGSTRA SPECIAL	95-DAY	19.95	20.00
L. DUBIN				**BYGONE DAYS**
95	MAIN STREET SPLENDOR	95-DAY	29.90	30.00
95	SAM'S GROCERY STORE	95-DAY	29.90	30.00
95	SATURDAY MATINEE	95-DAY	29.90	30.00
95	THE BARBER SHOP	95-DAY	29.90	30.00
95	THE CORNER NEWSSTAND	95-DAY	29.90	30.00
L. BURNS				**CABBAGE ROSE CORNERS**
96	ROSE PETAL GIFT SHOPPE	*	*	*
F. BUCHWITZ				**CABINS OF COMFORT RIVER**
95	COMFORT BY CAMPLIGHTS FIRE	95-DAY	29.90	30.00
TSENG				**CAROUSEL DAYDREAMS**
95	SWEPT AWAY	CL	39.90	40.00
95	SWEPT AWAY	CL	39.90	40.00
96	DREAMS OF DESTINY	*	49.90	50.00
96	WISHFUL THINKING	OP	49.90	50.00
C. WYSOCKI				**CHARLES WYSOCKI'S PEPPERCRICKET GROVE**
93	PEPPERCRICKET FARMS	CL	24.90	30.00
M.A. LASHER				**CHERISHED TRADITIONS**
96	GOOSE IN THE POND	OP	29.90	30.00
M. LESHER				**CHERISHED TRADITIONS**
95	THE WEDDING RING	95-DAY	29.90	30.00
*				**CHERUBS OF INNOCENCE**
95	FIRST KISS, THE	95 DAY	29.00	29.00
W. BOUGUEREAU				**CHERUBS OF INNOCENCE**
94	FIRST KISS, THE	CL	29.90	35.00
95	LOVE AT REST	95-DAY	29.90	30
95	THOUGHTS OF LOVE	95-DAY	29.90	30.00
P.L. TOOLE				**CHOIR OF ANGELS**
96	SONG OF PEACE	*	34.95	35.00
G. RUNNING WOLF				**CHOSEN MESSENGERS**
94	OVERSEERS, THE	CL	29.90	30.00
94	PATHFINDERS, THE	CL	29.90	30.00
94	PROVIDERS, THE	CL	32.90	33.00
94	SURVEYORS, THE	CL	32.90	37.00
R. AKERS				**CHRISTMAS CAMEOS**
94	PROPOSAL UNDER THE STARS	*	65.00	70.00
R. MCGINNIS				**CHRISTMAS IN THE VILLAGE**
95	VILLAGE TOY SHOP, THE	95 DAY	29.95	30.00
96	VILLAGE CONFECTIONARY	*	29.95	30.00
J. TANTON				**CHRISTMAS MEMORIES**
93	A WINTER'S TALE	CL	29.90	30.00
93	CHRISTMAS CELEBRATION	CL	29.90	30.00
93	FINISHING TOUCHES	CL	29.90	30.00
93	WELCOME TO OUR HOME	CL	29.90	30.00
T. TAYLOR				**CIVIL WAR: 1861-1865**
96	GETTYSBURG: TRIUMPH & TRAGEDY	*	*	*
M. HAMPSHIRE				**CLASSIC MELODIES FROM "THE SOUND OF MUSIC"**
95	SING ALONG WITH MARIA	95-DAY	29.90	30.00
L. MOSER				**CLASSIC ROSES**
96	BEAUTY IN BLOOM	OP	34.95	35.00
96	PRETTY IN PINK	*	34.95	35.00
M. STUTZMAN				**COMMEMORATING THE KING**
93	ROCK AND ROLL LEGEND	CL	29.75	35.00
94	TIGER, THE: FAITH, SPIRIT, DISCIPLINE	CL	29.75	35.00
*				**CORINTHIAN ANGELS**
96	LOVE IS PATIENT	*	*	*
D. KLAUBA				**COSTUMING OF A LEGEND: DRESSING GONE WITH THE WIND**
93	RED DRESS, THE	CL	29.90	35.00
D. CASEY				**COW-HIDE**
96	COWMOOFLAGE	*	34.95	35.00
96	COWPANSIONS	OP	34.95	35.00
*				**CURRIER & IVES CHRISTMAS**
96	WINTER MOON-FEEDING CHICKENS	*	34.95	35.00
J. THORNBRUGH				**DEER FRIENDS AT CHRISTMAS**
94	A GLISTENING SEASON	CL	29.90	35.00
94	ALL A GLOW	CL	29.90	35.00
94	ALL AGLOW	CL	29.90	35.00
95	WOODLAND SPLENDOR	95-DAY	29.90	30.00

YR	NAME	LIMIT	ISSUE	TREND
	D. LOCHER	**DICK TRACY: AMERICA'S FAVORITE DETECTIVE**		
96	CRIME STOPPER, THE	*	*	*
*		**DISNEY TREASURED MOMENTS PLATE COLLECTION**		
94	CINDERELLA	CL	29.90	35.00
*		**DISNEY'S MUSICAL MEMORIES**		
96	ALADDIN'S MAGICAL NEW WORLD	OP	32.90	33.00
*		**DISNEYLAND'S 40TH ANNIVERSARY**		
96	IT'S A SMALL WORLD	OP	32.95	33.00
	R. MCCAUSLAND	**DIVINE LIGHT**		
96	BLESSED IS THE CHILD	OP	34.95	35.00
	J. GADAMUS	**DOG DAYS**		
93	FIRST FLUSH	CL	32.90	35.00
93	LITTLE RASCALS	CL	32.90	33.00
93	PIER GROUP	CL	29.90	30.00
93	SWEET DREAMS	CL	29.90	30.00
93	WAGON TRAIN	CL	32.90	33.00
93	WHERE'D HE GO	CL	32.90	33.00
	M. DUDASH	**ENCHANTED CHARMS OF OZ**		
96	THERE'S NO PLACE LIKE HOME	OP	*	*
	D. HENDERSON	**ESCAPE TO THE COUNTRY**		
96	COUNTY LINE FARMER'S MARKET	*	29.95	30.00
	D.R. PIERCE	**EYES OF THE WILD**		
93	EYES IN THE MIST	CL	29.50	35.00
	G. ANGELINI	**FABULOUS CARS OF THE FIFTIES**		
94	'59 RED FORD FAIRLANE	CL	27.75	32.00
	D. PARKER	**FACES OF THE WILD**		
95	THE WOLF	95-DAY	39.90	40.00
95	WOLF, THE	CL	39.90	40.00
96	BOBCAT, THE	*	44.90	45.00
	M. JOBE	**FAIRYLAND**		
95	FAREWELL TO THE NIGHT	95-DAY	34.90	35.00
95	MAGICAL MISCHIEF	95-DAY	32.90	33.00
96	DAZZLING BEGINNINGS	OP	34.90	35.00
	C. BRENDERS	**FAMILY AFFAIR**		
95	DEN MOTHER	95 DAY	29.90	30.00
	R. RUST	**FAMILY CIRCLES**		
93	GREAT GRAY OWL FAMILY	CL	29.90	30.00
94	BARRED OWL FAMILY	CL	29.90	30.00
94	GREAT HORNED OWL FAMILY	CL	29.90	30.00
94	SPOTTED OWL FAMILY	CL	29.90	30.00
	S. WHEELER	**FAMILY'S LOVE**		
96	GIVING THANKS	*	29.95	30.00
	L. KAATZ	**FIELD PUP FOLLIES**		
94	FOWL PLAY	*	29.90	35.00
94	HAT CHECK	*	29.90	35.00
94	SLEEPING ON THE JOB	*	29.90	30.00
	G. BEECHAM	**FIERCE & FREE: THE BIG CATS**		
96	TIGER, THE	*	39.90	40.00
	M. BUDDEN	**FLEETING ENCOUNTERS**		
95	AUTUMN RETREAT	95-DAY	29.90	30.00
	G. KURZ	**FLORAL FROLICS**		
94	SPRING SURPRISES	CL	29.90	35.00
95	FUZZY FUN	95-DAY	32.90	33.00
95	SUNNY HIDEOUT	95-DAY	32.90	33.00
	L. LIU	**FLORAL GREETINGS**		
95	CIRCLE OF INSPIRATION	95-DAY	34.90	35.00
	L. LIU	**FLOWER FAIRIES**		
93	MAGIC MAKERS	CL	29.50	35.00
	D. SIVAVEC	**FOOTSTEPS OF KING**		
94	FLYING CIRCLE G RANCH: WALLS, MS	CL	32.75	35.00
	H. SCHAARE	**FOOTSTEPS OF THE BRAVE**		
93	AT JOURNEY'S END	CL	29.90	30.00
93	AT STORM'S PASSAGE	CL	24.90	25.00
93	HORIZONS OF DESTINY	CL	27.90	30.00
93	NOBLE QUEST	CL	24.90	25.00
93	PATH OF HIS FOREFATHERS	CL	27.90	30.00
93	REVERENT TRAIL, THE	CL	29.90	30.00
93	SOULFUL REFLECTION	CL	29.90	30.00
93	WITH BOUNDLESS VISION	CL	27.90	30.00
	C. FALBERG	**FOREVER GLAMOROUS BARBIE**		
95	ENCHANTED EVENING	CL	49.90	50.00
96	MIDNIGHT BLUE	*	49.90	50.00
	E. TOTTEN	**FRESHWATER GAME FISH OF NORTH AMERICA**		
95	BROWN TROUT	95-DAY	29.90	30.00
95	NORTHERN PIKE	95-DAY	29.90	30.00
	L. CHANG	**FRIENDSHIP IN BLOOM**		
94	PAWS IN THE POSIES	CL	29.90	35.00
95	PATIENCE & IMPATIENCE	95-DAY	34.90	35.00
	J. STRAIN	**GALLANT MEN OF THE CIVIL WAR**		
95	JOHN HUNT MORGAN	95-DAY	29.90	30.00
95	ROBERT E. LEE	95 DAY	29.90	30.00
	D. RICHARDSON	**GARDENS OF INNOCENCE**		
94	HOPE	CL	29.90	35.00
95	PATIENCE	95-DAY	34.90	35.00

YR	NAME	LIMIT	ISSUE	TREND
95	PEACE	95-DAY	34.90	35.00
95	SERENITY	95-DAY	34.90	35.00
96	LOVE	OP	36.90	37.00
L. CHANG		**GARDENS OF PARADISE**		
93	TRANQUILITY	CL	29.50	35.00
D. RUST		**GETTING AWAY FROM IT ALL**		
95	MOUNTAIN HIDEAWAY	95-DAY	29.90	30.00
B. BARRETT		**GLORY OF CHRIST**		
96	WEDDING AT CANA	OP	29.90	30.00
M. PHALEN		**GONE WITH THE WIND**		
95	RHETT'S BRIGHT PROMISE	95-DAY	39.90	40.00
95	SCARLETT RADIANCE	95-DAY	39.90	40.00
A. JENKS		**GONE WITH THE WIND MUSICAL TREASURES**		
95	CHARITY BAZAAR	95-DAY	32.90	33.00
95	THE PROPOSAL	95-DAY	32.90	33.00
S. GARDNER		**GREAT MOMENTS IN BASEBALL**		
93	JOE DIMAGGIO: THE STREAK	CL	29.90	35.00
94	SATCHEL PAIGE	CL	34.90	40.00
95	CARL HUBBELL: THE 1934 ALL STATE	95-DAY	36.90	37.00
R. BROWN		**GREAT SUPER BOWL QUARTERBACKS**		
95	JOE MONTANA: KING OF THE COMEBACKS	95DAY	29.90	30.00
R. BROWN		**GREAT SUPERBOWL QUARTERBACKS**		
95	JOE MONTANA: KING OF COMEBACK	95-DAY	29.90	30.00
96	BOB GRIESE	*	32.90	33.00
B. JAXON		**GUIDANCE FROM ABOVE**		
95	APPEAL TO THUNDER	95-DAY	29.90	30.00
95	BLESSING THE FUTURE	95-DAY	29.90	30.00
J. DALY		**HAPPY HEARTS**		
95	CHILDHOOD FRIENDS	95-DAY	29.90	30.00
95	CONTENTMENT	95-DAY	29.90	30.00
95	FAVORITE GIFT	95-DAY	29.90	30.00
95	PLAYMATES	95-DAY	29.90	30.00
R. NANINI		**HEART OF CAT COUNTRY**		
96	ALL ABOARD	*	29.95	30.00
J. GIBSON		**HEART STRINGS**		
96	FAMILY TIES	*	29.95	30.00
RAPHAEL INSPIRED		**HEART TO HEART**		
95	THINKING OF YOU	95-DAY	29.90	30.00
E. STEINBRUCK		**HEART TO HEART**		
96	FEELINGS OF ENDEARMENT	OP	29.90	30.00
T. KINKADE		**HEAVEN ON EARTH**		
95	BUT THE PATHOF JUST	95-DAY	29.90	30.00
95	FOR THOU ART MY LAMP	95-DAY	29.90	30.00
95	I AM THE WAY	95-DAY	29.90	30.00
95	IN HIM WAS LIFE	95-DAY	29.90	30.00
95	THY WORD IS A LAMP	95-DAY	29.90	30.
L. BOGLE		**HEAVEN SENT**		
94	SWEET DREAMS	CL	29.90	30.00
95	PRECIOUS GIFT	95-DAY	32.90	33.00
D. BROOKS		**HEAVEN'S LITTLE SWEETHEARTS**		
96	AN ANGEL'S KINDNESS	*	29.95	30.00
R. AKERS		**HEAVENLY CHORUS**		
95	HARK THE HERALD ANGELS SING	CL	39.90	40.00
96	O COME ALL YE FAITHFUL	*	39.90	40.00
A. PECH		**HEIRLOOM MEMORIES**		
94	PINK LEMONADE ROSES	CL	29.90	30.00
94	PORCELAIN TREASURE	CL	29.90	30.00
94	RHYTHMS IN LACE	CL	29.90	30.00
94	TEATIME TULIPS	CL	29.90	30.00
94	VICTORIAN ROMANCE	CL	29.90	30.00
R. RUST		**HIDEAWAY LAKE**		
93	ECHOES OF MORNING	CL	34.90	35.00
93	FISHING FOR DREAMS	CL	34.90	35.00
93	RUSTY'S RETREAT	CL	34.90	35.00
93	SUNSET CABIN	CL	34.90	35.00
M. LEONE		**HOME IN THE HEARTLAND**		
96	APPLE BLOSSOM FESTIVAL, THE	OP	34.95	35.00
T. KINKADE		**HOME IS WHERE THE HEART IS**		
92	HOME SWEET HOME	CL	29.90	35.00
C. WYSOCKI		**HOMETOWN MEMORIES**		
95	A FAREWELL KISS	95-DAY	29.90	30.00
95	CAPTURING THE MOMENT	95-DAY	29.90	30.00
95	JASON SPARKLING THE LIGHTHOUSE	95-DAY	29.90	30.00
95	SUMMER DELIGHTS	95-DAY	29.90	30.00
95	TRANQUIL DAYS/RAVENSWHIP COVER	95-DAY	29.90	30.00
R. DOCKEN		**HUNTERS OF THE SPIRIT**		
95	PROVIDER	95-DAY	29.90	30.00
96	HUNTER, THE	OP	29.90	30.00
M. BIERLINSKI		**ILLUSIONS OF NATURE**		
95	A TRIO OF WOLVES	95-DAY	29.90	30.00
J. GRENDE		**ILLUSIVE WINGS**		
96	NUTMEG IMPRESSIONS	*	29.95	30.00
C. JACKSON		**IMMORTALS OF THE DIAMOND**		
95	PRIDE OF THE YANKEES	95-DAY	39.90	40.00

YR	NAME	LIMIT	ISSUE	TREND
	T. CLAUSNITZER		**IN A HIDDEN GARDEN**	
93	CURIOUS KTTENS	CL	29.90	30.00
94	AMBER GAZE	CL	29.90	30.00
94	FASCINATING FIND	CL	29.90	30.00
94	THORUGH EYES OF BLUE	CL	29.90	30.00
	D. SIVAVEC		**IT'S A WONDERFUL LIFE**	
96	BY THE LIGHT OF THE MOON	OP	34.95	35.00
96	I'M THE ANSWER TO YOUR PRAYER	*	34.95	35.00
	C. LAYTON		**KEEPSAKES OF THE HEART**	
93	AFTERNOON TEA	CL	29.90	30.00
93	FOREVER FRIENDS	CL	29.90	30.00
93	RIDING COMPANIONS	CL	29.90	30.00
93	SENTIMENTAL SWEETHEARTS	CL	29.90	30.00
	C. POULIN		**KINDRED MOMENTS**	
95	SISTERS ARE BLOSSOMS	95 DAY	19.95	20.00
96	FOREVER FRIENDS	*	22.95	23.00
	D, CASEY		**KINDRED SPIRITS**	
96	SPIRIT OF THE WOLF	OP	29.95	30.00
	C. PUOLIN		**KINDRED THOUGHTS**	
95	SISTERS	95-DAY	29.90	30.00
	M. JOBE		**KINGDOM OF ENCHANTMENT**	
96	MOONBEAM TRAILS	*	29.95	30.00
	C. FRACE		**KINGDOM OF GREAT CATS: SIGNATURE COLLECTION**	
94	MYSTIC REALM	CL	39.90	40.00
	M. FERRARO		**KINGDOM OF THE UNICORN**	
93	CHASING A DREAM	CL	29.90	30.00
93	FOUNTAIN OF YOUTH, THE	CL	29.90	30.00
93	IN CRYSTAL WATERS	CL	29.90	30.00
93	MAGIC BEGINS, THE	CL	29.90	30.00
	T. KINKADE		**KINKADE'S ILLUMINATED COTTAGES**	
94	FLAGSTONE PATH, THE	CL	*	*
95	CHERRY BLOSSOM HIDEAWAY	CL	34.90	35.00
95	THE GARDEN WALK	CL	34.90	35.00
	T. KINKADE		**LAMPLIGHT VILLAGE**	
95	LAMPLIGHT BROOKE	95 DAY	29.90	30.00
95	LAMPLIGHT BROOKE	95-DAY	29.90	30.00
95	LAMPLIGHT INN	95-DAY	29.90	30.00
95	LAMPLIGHT LANE	95-DAY	29.90	30.00
	D. CHERRY		**LAND OF OZ: NEW DIMENSION**	
95	STEP INTO THE EMERALD CITY	95-DAY	34.90	35.00
	D. STANLEY		**LEGEND OF THE WHITE BUFFALO**	
95	MYSTIC SPIRIT	95-DAY	29.90	30.00
96	SPIRIT OF THE BUFFALO SHAMAN	*	29.90	30.00
	J. BARSON		**LEGENDS OF BASEBALL**	
94	LEFTY GROVE	CL	31.75	36.00
	B. BENGER		**LEGENDS OF BASEBALL**	
92	BABE RUTH: THE CALLED SHOT	CL	24.75	28.00
	W. TERRY		**LEGENDS OF THE MOON**	
96	MOON OF RUNNING WOLVES	*	34.95	35.00
	*		**LEGENDS: WORLD RECORD WHITETAILS**	
96	JORDAN BUCK, THE	*	*	*
	R. BARRETT		**LIFE OF CHRIST**	
94	JESUS CALMS THE WATERS	CL	32.90	33.00
94	JESUS ENTERS JERUSALEM	CL	29.90	30.00
94	PASSION IN THE GARDEN, THE	CL	29.90	30.00
95	THE CRUCIFIXION	95-DAY	34.90	35.00
	C. NICK		**LIGHT OF THE WORLD**	
96	PRAYER IN THE GARDEN	*	29.90	30.00
	*		**LION KING**	
95	A CRUNCHY FEAST	95-DAY	32.90	33.00
95	LIKE FATHER, LIKE SON	95-DAY	29.90	30.00
	*		**LION KING**	
95	CIRCLE OF LIFE, THE	95 DAY	29.90	30.00
	C. JAGODITS		**LITTER RASCAL**	
96	SNEAKING SECONDS	*	29.95	30.00
	C. JAGODITS		**LITTLE BANDITS**	
93	ALL TIED UP	CL	29.90	30.00
93	EVERYTHING'S COMING UP DAISIES	CL	32.90	33.00
93	HANDLE WITH CARE	CL	29.90	30.00
93	OUT OF HAND	CL	32.90	33.00
93	PUPSICLES	CL	32.90	33.00
93	UNEXPECTED GUESTS	CL	32.90	33.00
	*		**LITTLE MERMAID**	
94	FIREWORKS AT FIRST SIGHT	CL	34.90	40.00
94	FOREVER LOVE	CL	34.90	40.00
	G. BEECHAM		**LORD OF FOREST & CANYON**	
95	FOREST EMPEROR	95-DAY	29.90	30.00
95	GOLDEN MONARCH	95-DAY	29.90	30.00
95	PROUD LEGACY	95-DAY	29.90	30.00
	R. MCGINNIS		**LOVING HEARTS**	
96	BEAUTY & SPLENDOR	*	29.95	30.00
96	PATIENT & KIND	*	29.95	30.00
	C. NOTARILE		**MAGIC OF MARILYN**	
93	FOR OUR BOYS IN KOREA, 1954	CL	24.75	30.00

YR	NAME	LIMIT	ISSUE	TREND
G. DIECKHONER				**MAJESTIC PATRIOTS**
95	MY COUNTRY TIS OF THEE	95-DAY	29.90	30.00
G. WILMOTT				**MAJESTIC TRAINS OF YESTERYEAR**
96	INYO V&T, THE	*	*	*
*				**MASTERS OF LAND & SKY**
96	SUPREME SUMMONS	*	29.90	30.00
*				**MICKEY & MINNIE THROUGH THE YEARS**
95	BRAVE LITTLE TAILOR	95-DAY	29.90	30.00
95	MICKEY'S BIRTHDAY PARTY 1942	95-DAY	29.90	30.00
*				**MICKEY & MINNIE THROUGH THE YEARS**
95	MICKEY'S BIRTHDAY PARTY	95 DAY	29.90	30.00
S. GARDNER				**MICKEY MANTLE COLLECTION**
96	BRONX BOMER	*	39.95	40.00
J. WELTY				**MIRACLE OF CHRISTMAS**
96	ONCE UPON A HOLY NIGHT	OP	34.95	35.00
S. KUCK				**MOMENTS AT HOME**
95	MOMENTS OF CARING	95-DAY	29.90	30.00
C. FISHER				**MOMENTS IN THE GARDEN**
96	LUMINOUS JEWELS	*	29.95	30.00
96	RADIANT GEMS	OP	29.95	30.00
96	SHIMMERING SPLENDOR	OP	29.95	30.00
B. LANGTON				**MOMENTS OF SERENITY**
94	MORNING REFLECTIONS	CL	*	*
R. AKERS				**MUSICAL CAROUSEL TREASURES**
93	SWEET STANDER	CL	49.00	55.00
K. MILNAZIK				**MUSICAL MOMENTS FROM THE WIZARD OF OZ**
93	OVER THE RAINBOW	CL	29.90	35.00
B. EMMETT				**MUSICAL TRIBUTE TO ELVIS THE KING**
94	ROCKIN' BLUE SUEDE SHOES	CL	29.90	35.00
95	AMERICAN DREAM	95-DAY	32.90	33.00
96	LOVE: THE GREATEST GIFT	OP	34.90	35.00
B.H. BOND				**MYSTERIOUS CASE OF FOWL PLAY**
94	GLAMOURPUSS	CL	29.90	30.00
94	INSPECTOR CLAWSEAU	CL	29.90	30.00
94	SOPHISICAT	CL	29.90	30.00
95	TUXEDO	95-DAY	29.90	30.00
S. HILL				**MYSTIC GARDENS**
93	COMPANION SPIRITS	CL	32.90	35.00
93	FAITHFUL FELLOWSHIP	CL	32.90	35.00
93	MAJESTIC MESSENGER	CL	29.90	30.00
93	ROYAL UNITY	CL	34.90	35.00
93	SOUL MATES	CL	29.90	30.00
93	SPIRITUAL HARMONY	CL	32.90	33.00
V. CRANDELL				**MYSTIC SPIRITS**
95	ARCTIC NIGHTS	95-DAY	32.90	33.00
95	MOON SHADOWS	95-DAY	29.90	30.00
C. JACKSON				**NATIVE AMERICAN LEGENDS: CHIEFS OF DESTINY**
94	SITTING BULL	TL	39.90	40.00
95	RED CLOUD	CL	44.90	45.00
95	SITTING BULL	CL	39.90	40.00
96	TECUMSEH	*	44.90	45.00
L. BOGLE				**NATIVE BEAUTY**
94	PROMISE, THE	CL	29.90	35.00
95	FIRST GLANCE	95-DAY	29.90	30.00
95	MORNING STAR	95-DAY	29.90	30.00
95	PROMISE, THE	95 DAY	29.90	30.00
95	QUIET TIME	95-DAY	29.90	30.00
95	WARM THOUGHTS	95-DAY	29.90	30.00
J. COLE				**NATIVE VISIONS**
95	BRINGERS OF THE STORM	95-DAY	29.90	30.00
95	WATER VISION	95-DAY	29.90	30.00
J. KRAMER-COLE				**NATIVE VISIONS**
96	LISTENING	OP	29.90	30.00
96	MAN WHO SEES FAR	OP	29.90	30.00
L. MARTIN				**NATURE'S LITTLE TREASURES**
93	GARDEN WHISPERS	CL	29.90	35.00
94	DELICATE SPLENDOR	CL	32.90	33.00
94	MINIATURE GLORY	CL	32.90	33.00
94	MINUTE ENCHANTMENT	CL	34.90	40.00
94	PERFECT JEWELS	CL	32.90	33.00
94	WINGS OF GRACE	CL	32.90	33.00
95	MISTY MORNING	95-DAY	36.90	37.00
D. PARKER				**NATURE'S NOBILITY**
96	BUCK, THE	OP	39.95	40.00
R. COPPLE				**NEW HORIZONS**
93	BLDG. FOR A NEW GENERATION	CL	29.90	30.00
93	POWER OF GOD, THE	CL	29.90	30.00
93	WINGS OF SNOWY GRANDEUR	CL	32.90	33.00
94	MASTER OF THE CHASE	CL	32.90	33.00
95	COASTAL DOMAIN	95-DAY	32.90	33.00
M. CORNING				**NFL 75TH ANNIV. ALL-TIME TEAM**
96	GALE SAYERS/JACK LAMBERT	*	34.95	35.00
96	JOHNNY UNITAS/BOB LILY	*	34.95	35.00
M. JOBE				**NIGHT FAIRIES**
94	TRAILS OF STARLIGHT	CL	29.90	30.00

YR	NAME	LIMIT	ISSUE	TREND
	J. HANSEL	**NIGHTSONG: THE LOON**		
94	EVENING MIST	CL	29.90	30.00
94	MOONLIGHT ECHOES	CL	29.90	30.00
94	NOCTURNAL GLOW	CL	32.90	33.00
94	TRANQUIL REFLECTIONS	CL	32.90	33.00
95	LOONS BY THE LILY PAD	95-DAY	34.90	35.00
95	PEACEFUL HOMESTEAD	95-DAY	34.90	35.00
	D. NINGEWANCE	**NIGHTWATCH: THE WOLF**		
94	MIDNIGHT GUARD	CL	29.90	30.00
94	MOONLIGHT SERENADE	CL	29.90	30.00
94	SNOWY LOOKOUT	CL	29.90	30.00
	D. WENZEL	**NORTHWOODS SPIRIT**		
94	TIMELESS WATCH	CL	29.90	35.00
95	EVENING RESPITE	95-DAY	29.90	30.00
95	FOREST ECHO	95-DAY	29.90	30.00
95	TIMBERLAND GAZE	95-DAY	29.90	30.00
	P. WEIRS	**NOSY NEIGHBORS**		
95	HOUSE SITTING	95-DAY	29.90	30.00
95	OBSERVATION DECK	95-DAY	32.90	33.00
95	SURPRISE VISIT	95-DAY	32.90	33.00
96	LIFEGUARD ON DUTY	*	34.90	35.00
	K. WEISBERG	**NOTHERN CHAMPIONS**		
95	MIDNIGHT HARMONY	95-DAY	29.90	30.00
	*	**NOTORIOUS DISNEY VILLAINS**		
93	WICKED QUEEN, THE	CL	29.90	30.00
94	CRUELLA DE VIL	CL	29.90	30.00
94	MALEFICENT	CL	29.90	30.00
94	URSELLA	CL	29.90	30.00
	T. KINKADE	**OLD FASHIONED CHRISTMAS**		
93	A HOLIDAY GATHERING	CL	32.90	35.00
93	ALL FRIENDS ARE WELCOME	CL	29.90	30.00
93	CHRISTMAS TREE COTTAGE	CL	32.90	33.00
93	WINTER'S MEMORIES	CL	29.90	30.00
95	THE BEST TRADITION	95-DAY	32.90	33.00
	H. GARRIDO	**OUR HEAVENLY MOTHER**		
96	CONSTANCY	*	34.90	35.00
	W. NELSON	**PANDA BEAR HUGS**		
93	ROCK-A-BYE	*	39.00	40.00
94	A PLAYFUL INTERLUDE	*	39.00	40.00
94	A TASTE OF LIFE	*	39.00	40.00
94	LOVING A DVICE	*	39.00	40.00
	J. BARNES	**PATHWAYS OF THE HEART**		
93	DAYBREAK	CL	29.90	30.00
93	OCTOBER RADIANCE	CL	29.90	30.00
94	A NIGHT TO REMEMBER	CL	29.90	30.00
94	DISTANT LIGHTS	CL	29.90	30.00
94	HARMONY WITH NATURE	CL	29.90	30.00
94	PEACEFUL EVENING	CL	29.90	30.00
	M. RIEN	**PAWS IN PLAY**		
96	BREAK TIME	*	34.95	35.00
	D. GEISNESS	**PEACE ON EARTH**		
93	WINTER LULLABY	CL	29.90	30.00
94	HEAVENLY SLUMBER	CL	29.90	30.00
94	SNOWY SILENCE	CL	32.90	37.00
94	SWEET EMBRACE	CL	32.90	33.00
	M. HARVEY	**PEACEABLE KINGDOM**		
94	NOAH'S ARK	CL	29.90	35.00
	W. VON SCHWARZBEK	**PICKED FROM AN ENGLISH GARDEN**		
95	LASTING TREASURES	95-DAY	29.90	30.00
95	NATURE'S WONDERS	95-DAY	29.90	30.00
	E.C SEGAR	**POPEYE: THE ONE & ONLY**		
96	POPEYE THE SAILORMAN	*	*	*
	D. BRAUD	**PORTRAITS OF MAJESTY**		
95	EMPEROR OF HIS REALM	95-DAY	29.90	30.00
95	REFLECTIONS OF KINGS	95-DAY	29.90	30.00
95	SOLEMN SOVEREIGN	95-DAY	29.90	30.00
	*	**PORTRAITS OF VALOR**		
93	EMANCIPATION PROCLAMATION	CL	29.90	30.00
	*	**PORTRAITS OF VALOR**		
93	GETTYSBURG ADDRESS, THE	CL	29.90	30.00
93	LINCOLN-DOUGLAS DEBATE, THE	CL	29.90	30.00
	T. KINKADE	**POSTCARDS FROM THOMAS KINKADE**		
95	NEW YORK CITY	95-DAY	34.90	35.00
95	PARIS	95-DAY	34.90	35.00
95	SAN FRANCISCO	95-DAY	34.90	35.00
	L. KAATZ	**PRACTICE MAKES PERFECT**		
94	ONES THAT GOT AWAY, THE	CL	29.90	30.00
94	WHAT'S A MOTHER TO DO?	CL	29.90	30.00
95	MORE THAN A MOUTHFUL	95-DAY	34.90	35.00
95	ON THE RIGHT TRACK	95-DAY	34.90	35.00
	S. KUCK	**PRECIOUS ANGELS**		
95	ANGEL OF GRACE	95-DAY	29.90	30.00
95	ANGEL OF HOPE	95-DAY	29.90	30.00
95	ANGEL OF LAUGHTER	95-DAY	29.90	30.00
95	ANGEL OF SHARING	95 DAY	29.90	30.00
95	ANGEL OF SUNSHINE	95-DAY	29.90	30.00

YR	NAME	LIMIT	ISSUE	TREND
J. GRANDE				**PRECIOUS VISIONS**
95	BRIEF INTERLUDE	95-DAY	29.90	30.00
95	BRILLIANT MOMENT	95 DAY	29.90	30.00
95	ENDURING ELEGANCE	95-DAY	32.90	33.00
95	TIMELESS RADIANCE	95-DAY	29.90	30.00
J. SPURLOCK				**PRIDE OF AMERICA**
95	WINGS OF GLORY	95-DAY	29.90	30.00
*				**PROMISE OF A SAVIOR**
93	A CHILD IS BORN	CL	29.90	30.00
93	AN ANGEL'S MESSAGE	CL	29.90	30.00
93	ANGELS WERE WATCHING	CL	29.90	30.00
93	GIFTS TO JESUS	CL	29.90	30.00
93	HEAVENLY KING, THE	CL	29.90	30.00
93	HOLY MOTHER AND CHILD	CL	29.90	30.00
M. AMERMAN				**PROUD HERITAGE**
95	PEACEFUL DEFENDER	*	34.90	35.00
M. RODERICK				**PURRFECTLY AT HOME**
96	HOME SWEET HOME	*	39.95	40.00
96	KITTY CORNER	*	39.95	40.00
K. DANIEL				**QUIET MOMENTS**
95	A LOVING HAND	95-DAY	29.90	30.00
95	KEPT WITH CARE	95-DAY	29.90	30.00
95	PUPPY LOVE	95-DAY	29.90	30.00
L. MARTIN				**RADIANT MESSENGERS**
94	BEAUTY	CL	29.90	35.00
94	PEACE	CL	29.90	30.00
95	INSPIRATION	95-DAY	29.90	30.00
C. NOTARILE				**REFLECTIONS OF MARILYN**
94	ALL THAT GLITTERS	CL	29.90	30.00
94	SHIMMERING HEAT	CL	29.90	35.00
95	A TWINKLE IN HER EYE	95-DAY	29.90	30.00
N. GIORGIO				**REMEMBERING ELVIS**
95	THE LEGEND	95-DAY	29.90	30.00
96	DREAM, THE	*	29.90	30.00
N. ROCKWELL				**ROCKWELL COMMEMORATIVE STAMPS**
94	FREEDOM FROM FEAR	CL	29.90	35.00
94	FREEDOM FROM WANT	CL	29.90	35.00
95	FREEDOM OF SPEECH	95-DAY	29.90	30.00
95	FREEDOM OF WORSHIP	95-DAY	29.90	30.00
N. ROCKWELL				**ROCKWELL SOCIETY CHRISTMAS**
94	CHRISTMAS MARVEL	*	32.90	37.00
N. ROCKWELL				**ROCKWELL SOCIETY HERITAGE**
94	APPRENTICE, THE	*	29.90	35.00
*				**ROYAL ENCHANTMENTS**
95	GIFT, THE	CL	39.90	40.00
J. PENCHOFF				**ROYAL ENCHANTMENTS**
95	THE COURTSHIP	95-DAY	39.90	40.00
95	THE GIFT	CL	39.90	40.00
K. RANDLE				**SACRED CIRCLE**
93	BEFORE THE HUNT	CL	29.90	30.00
93	GHOST DANCE	CL	32.90	33.00
93	SPIRITUAL GUARDIAN	CL	29.90	30.00
94	DEER DANCE	CL	32.90	33.00
94	PAINTED HORSE, THE	CL	34.90	35.00
94	WOLF DANCE, THE	CL	32.90	33.00
S. KUCK				**SANDRA KUCK'S MOTHER'S DAY COLLECTION**
95	HOME IS WHERE THE HEART IS	95-DAY	35.00	35.00
H. BOND				**SANTA'S LITTLE HELPERS**
94	STOCKING STUFFERS	CL	29.90	35.00
94	WRAPPING UP THE HOLIDAYS	CL	24.90	30.00
B. HIGGINS BOND				**SANTA'S LITTLE HELPERS**
95	COZY KITTENS	95-DAY	24.90	25.00
95	HOLIDAY MISCHIEF	95-DAY	24.90	25.00
S. GUSTAFSON				**SANTA'S ON HIS WAY**
94	CHECKING IT TWICE	CL	29.90	35.00
95	GIFTS FOR ONE AND ALL	95-DAY	29.90	30.00
95	SANTA'S FIRST STOP	95-DAY	29.90	30.00
L. GARRISON				**SCENES OF CHRISTMAS PAST**
94	A GATHERING OF FAITH	CL	32.50	37.00
L. ZABEL				**SEASONS ON THE OPEN RANGE**
96	SEASON OF GOLD	OP	29.95	30.00
*				**SERAPHIM CLASSICS: ANGELS OF INSPIRATION**
96	ISABEL "GENTLE SPIRIT"	*	*	*
J. THORNBRUGH				**SIGNS OF SPRING**
94	A FAMILY FEAST	CL	*	*
95	AWAITING NEW ARRIVALS	95-DAY	29.90	30.00
95	HOW FAST THEY GROWN	95-DAY	29.90	30.00
95	OUR FIRST HOME	95-DAY	29.90	30.00
D. CASEY				**SILENT JOURNEY**
95	JOURNEY OF THE WILD	95-DAY	29.90	30.00
95	UNBRIDLED MAJESTY	95-DAY	29.90	30.00
95	WHERE PATHS CROSS	95 DAY	29.90	30.00
95	WHERE THE BUFFALO ROAM	95-DAY	29.90	30.00
95	WISDOM SEEKER	95-DAY	29.90	30.00

Shuffleton's Barbershop, *the first issue in the "Rockwell Annual" series, recaptures the days when a trip to the barber resulted in more than a haircut. Produced by Artaffects.*

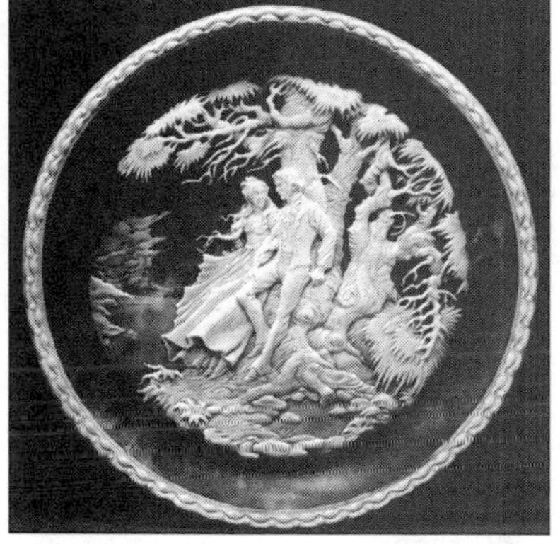

Incolay Studios released the ninth issue in the Romantic Poets Collection in 1985. The Recollection *was limited to one year of production and retailed for $70.*

Guess who's been sleeping in their bed? Goldilocks *is the first issue in the "Classic Fairy Tales" series produced by Edwin M. Knowles.*

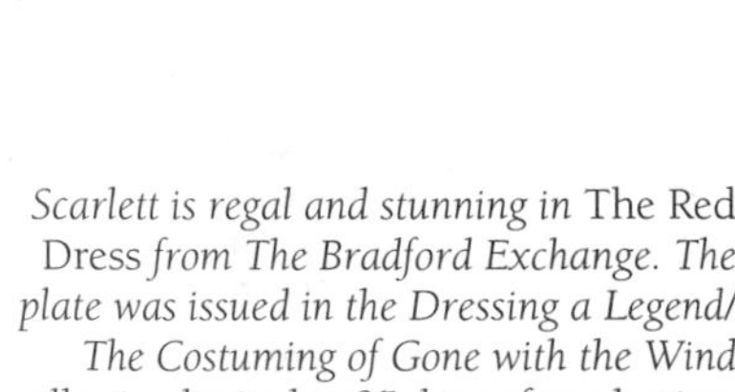

Scarlett is regal and stunning in The Red Dress *from The Bradford Exchange. The plate was issued in the Dressing a Legend/ The Costuming of Gone with the Wind collection limited to 95 days of production.*

YR	NAME	LIMIT	ISSUE	TREND
R. IVERSON				**SOFT ELEGANCE**
95	ALEXANDRA IN AMETHYSTS	95-DAY	29.90	30.00
95	EMILY IN EMERALDS	95-DAY	29.90	30.00
95	TABITHA ON TAFFETA	95-DAY	29.90	30.00
J. TANTON				**SOME BEARY NICE PLACES**
94	WELCOME TO THE LIBEARY	CL	29.90	35.00
95	BEARENIAL GARDEN	95-DAY	32.90	33.00
95	WELCOME TO OUR MUSIC	95-DAY	32.90	33.00
*				**SOMEONE TO WATCH OVER ME**
96	BY MY SIDE	*	29.90	30.00
L. BOGLE				**SOUL MATES**
95	LOVERS, THE	95 DAY	29.90	30.00
95	THE AWAKENING	95-DAY	29.90	30.00
95	THE LOVERS	95-DAY	29.90	30.00
96	PERFET HARMONY	OP	29.90	30.00
96	STIRRING, THE	OP	29.90	30.00
96	WARM INTERLUDE	OP	29.90	30.00
B. PARRISH				**SOUL OF THE WILDERNESS**
96	WINTER SOLSTICE	*	34.95	35.00
G. DIECKHONER				**SOVEREIGNS OF THE SKY**
94	SPIRIT OF FREEDOM	CL	39.00	40.00
94	SPIRIT OF PRIDE	CL	39.00	40.00
95	SPIRIT OF GLORY	95-DAY	44.00	44.00
D. GRANT				**SOVEREIGNS OF THE WILD**
93	SNOW QUEEN, THE	CL	29.90	30.00
94	AFRICAN EVENING	CL	29.90	30.00
94	COOL CATS	CL	29.90	30.00
94	LET US SURVIVE	CL	29.90	30.00
94	SIBERIAN SNOW TIGERS	CL	29.90	30.00
E. LEPAGE				**SPIRITS OF THE WILDERNESS**
96	EBONY CHIEF	OP	34.90	35.00
B. LANGTON				**STUDY OF A CHAMPION**
96	FAITHFUL BUDDY	OP	29.90	30.00
S. KUCK				**SUGAR AND SPICE**
93	BEST FRIENDS	CL	29.90	35.00
94	MORNING PRAYERS	CL	32.90	37.00
Y. LANTZ				**SUNFLOWER SERENADE**
96	GOLDEN SUNSHINE	*	*	*
T. SIZEMORE				**SUPERSTARS OF BASEBALL**
94	WILLIE 'SAY HEY' MAYS	CL	29.90	35.00
95	BOB GIBSON	95-DAY	29.90	30.00
95	CARL "YAZ" YASTRZEMSKI	95-DAY	29.90	30.00
95	FRANK "ROBBY" ROBINSON	95-DAY	29.90	30.00
N. GIORGIO				**SUPERSTARS OF COUNTRY MUSIC**
93	BARBARA MANDRELL	CL	32.90	33.00
93	DOLLY PARTON: I WILL ALWAYS LOVE YOU	CL	29.90	30.00
93	GLEN CAMPBELL: RHINESTONE COWBOY	CL	32.90	33.00
93	KENNY ROGERS: SWEET MUSIC MAN	CL	29.90	30.00
D. HENDERSON				**TAKE ME OUT TO THE BALLGAME**
94	COUNTY STADIUM	CL	34.75	40.00
R. AKERS				**TALE OF PETER RABBIT & BENJAMIN BUNNY**
94	A POCKET FULL OF ONIONS	*	39.00	44.00
94	A POCKET FULL OF ONIONS	*	39.00	40.00
95	SAFELY HOME	95-DAY	44.00	44.00
96	OPON THE SCARECROW	*	44.00	44.00
J. MONTE				**TEA FOR TWO**
96	SPRING ROSE TEAPOT	*	34.95	35.00
A. ISAKOV				**THAT'S WHAT FRIENDS ARE FOR**
94	FRIENDS ARE FOREVER	CL	29.90	35.00
95	FRIENDS ARE FUN	95-DAY	29.90	30.00
C. NICK				**THE LIGHT OF THE WORLD**
95	THE LAST SUPPER	95-DAY	29.90	30.00
H. GARRIDO				**THOSE WHO GUIDE US**
96	ST. ANTHONY	*	29.90	30.00
96	ST. JUDE	OP	29.90	30.00
K. NOLES				**THROUGH A CHILD'S EYES**
94	LITTLE BUTTERFLY	CL	29.90	35.00
95	PRAIRIE SONG	95-DAY	32.90	33.00
95	TREETOP WONDER	95-DAY	29.90	30.00
95	WATER LILY	95-DAY	32.90	33.00
95	WOODLAND ROSE	95-DAY	29.90	30.00
R. TAYLOR				**THUNDER IN THE SKY**
96	MIGHTY 8TH, THE- COMING HOME	*	29.95	30.00
F. MILLER				**THUNDERING WATERS**
94	NIAGARA FALLS	CL	34.90	35.00
95	HAVASU FALLS	95-DAY	29.90	30.00
95	LOWER FALLS, YELLOWSTONE	95 DAY	34.90	35.00
L. DANIELS				**TIMBERLAND SECRETS**
96	A MOMENT'S PAUSE	OP	29.90	30.00
96	WINTRY WATCH	OP	29.90	30.00
P.C. WEIRS				**TO SOAR WITH EAGLES**
96	ABOVE THE TURBULENT TIDE	*	32.95	33.00
J.K. COLE				**TOUCHING THE SPIRIT**
93	RUNNING WITH THE WIND	CL	29.50	35.00

YR	NAME	LIMIT	ISSUE	TREND
	K. RANDLE		**TRAINS OF THE GREAT WEST**	
93	EARLY MORNING ARRIVAL	CL	29.90	30.00
93	MOONLIT JOURNEY	CL	29.90	30.00
93	MOUNTAIN HIDEAWAY	CL	29.90	30.00
93	SNOWY PASS, THE	CL	29.90	30.00
	I. MAKAROVA		**TREASURES OF RUSSIAN TRADITION**	
96	COLBALT MAJESTY	*	*	*
	H. KREBS		**TRIUMPH IN THE AIR**	
95	STRUCK BY THUNDER	95-DAY	34.90	35.00
	J. BARNES		**TWILIGHT MEMORIES**	
95	WINTER'S TWILIGHT	95-DAY	29.90	30.00
	S. EIDE		**TWO'S COMPANY**	
95	BROTHERLY LOVE	95-DAY	29.90	30.00
95	GOLDEN HARVEST	95-DAY	29.90	30.00
95	SEEING DOUBLE	95-DAY	29.90	30.00
95	SPRING SPANIELS	95-DAY	29.90	30.00
	K. MCELROY		**UNBRIDLED MYSTERY**	
96	DARK SPLENDOR	OP	29.95	30.00
	C. SAMS		**UNDER A SNOWY VEIL**	
95	FIRST SNOW	95-DAY	29.90	30.00
95	SNOW MATES	95-DAY	29.90	30.00
95	WINTER'S DAWN	95-DAY	29.90	30.00
95	WINTER'S WARMTH	95-DAY	29.90	30.00
	D. MCCAFFREY		**UNDER THE NORTHERN LIGHTS**	
96	CATCHING THE ELUSIVE LIGHT	*	29.90	30.00
	P. WEIRS		**UNTAMED SPIRITS**	
93	WILD HEARTS	CL	29.90	30.00
94	BREAKAWAY	CL	29.90	30.00
94	DISTANT THUNDER	CL	29.90	30.00
94	FOREVER FREE	CL	29.90	30.00
	P. WEIRS		**UNTAMED WILDERNESS**	
95	UNEXPECTED ENCOUNTER	95-DAY	29.90	30.00
96	FLEETING SPLENDOR	OP	29.90	30.00
	G. DIECKHONER		**VANISHING PARADISES**	
93	AN AFRICAN SAFARI	CL	29.90	30.00
93	PANDA'S WORLD, THE	CL	29.90	30.00
93	RAINFOREST, THE	CL	29.90	30.00
93	SPLENDORS OF INDIA	CL	29.90	30.00
	S. KUCK		**VICTORIAN CHRISTMAS**	
95	DEAR SANTA	72 DAY	35.00	35.00
96	NIGHT BEFORE CHRISTMAS	*	35.00	35.00
	C. LASSEN		**VISIONS BENEATH THE SEA**	
96	MIRACLE IN LIFE	*	*	*
	D. CASEY		**VISIONS FROM EAGLE RIDGE**	
95	ASSEMBLY OF PRIDE	95-DAY	29.90	30.00
96	LEGACY OF LIBERTY	*	29.90	30.00
	D. COOK		**VISIONS OF GLORY**	
95	IWO JIMA	95-DAY	29.90	30.00
	H. GARRIDO		**VISIONS OF OUR LADY**	
94	OUR LADY OF GRACE	CL	29.90	35.00
94	OUR LADY OF LOURDES	CL	29.90	30.00
94	OUR LADY OF MEDJUGORJE	CL	29.90	30.00
	L. MEDARIS		**VISIONS OF THE SACRED**	
94	SNOW RIDER	CL	29.90	30.00
	D. STANLEY		**VISIONS OF THE SACRED**	
95	BUFFALO CALLER	95-DAY	32.90	33.00
95	JOURNEY OF HARMONY	95-DAY	32.90	33.00
96	GATHERER, THE	OP	36.90	37.00
	M.A. LASHER		**WARM COUNTRY MOMENTS**	
94	MABEL'S SUNNY RETREAT	CL	29.90	30.00
95	HANNA'S SECRET GARDEN	95-DAY	29.90	30.00
	B. MOCK		**WELCOME TO THE NEIGHBORHOOD**	
95	LILAC LANE	95-DAY	34.90	35.00
95	TULIP TERRACE	95-DAY	34.90	35.00
	J. BARNES		**WHEN ALL HEARTS COME HOME**	
93	CHRISTMAS WISH	CL	29.90	30.00
93	COMFORT AND JOY	CL	29.90	30.00
93	GRANDPA'S FARM	CL	29.90	30.00
93	NIGHT BEFORE CHRISTMAS	CL	29.90	30.00
93	NIGHT DEPARTURE	CL	29.90	30.00
93	OH CHRISTMAS TREE	CL	29.90	30.00
93	OH CHRISTMAS TREE	CL	29.90	30.00
93	PEACE ON EARTH	CL	29.90	30.00
93	SUPPER AND SMALL TALK	CL	29.90	30.00
	R. MCGINNIS		**WHEN DREAMS BLOSSOM**	
94	DREAMS TO GATHER	CL	29.90	30.00
94	DREAMS TO GATHER	CL	29.90	30.00
95	A PLACE TO DREAM	95-DAY	32.90	33.00
95	DREAMING OF YOU	95-DAY	32.90	33.00
	F. MITTELSTADT		**WHERE EAGLES SOAR**	
95	LAKESIDE EAGLES	95-DAY	29.90	30.00
95	LIGHTHOUSE EAGLES	95-DAY	29.90	30.00
95	NOBLE LEGACY	95-DAY	29.90	30.00
	K. O'MALLEY		**WHISPERS ON THE WIND**	
96	ALLEN'S HUMMINGBIRD	*	44.95	45.00

YR	NAME	LIMIT	ISSUE	TREND
	T. HIRATA			**WILD SPIRITS**
93	SOLITARY WATCH	CL	29.50	35.00
	J. WELTY			**WINDOWS OF GLORY**
93	KING OF KINGS	CL	29.90	35.00
	K. DANIEL			**WINDOWS ON A WORLD OF SONG**
93	BEDROOM, THE: BLUEBIRDS	CL	34.90	35.00
93	DEN, THE: BLACK-CAPPED CHICKADEES	CL	34.90	35.00
93	LIBRARY, THE: CARDINALS	CL	34.90	35.00
94	KITCHEN, THE: GOLDFINCHES	CL	34.90	35.00
	D.L. RUST			**WINGS OF WINTER**
93	MOONLIGHT RETREAT	CL	29.50	35.00
	C. JACKSON			**WINNIE THE POOH & FRIENDS**
94	TIME FOR A LITTLE SOMETHING	CL	39.90	40.00
96	RUMBLY IN MY TUMBLY	*	44.90	45.00
	C. JACKSON			**WINNIE THE POOH: 3D**
95	BOUNCING TIGGERS DO BEST	CL	39.90	40.00
	S. KOZAR			**WINTER EVENING REFLECTIONS**
96	AS TWILIGHT FALLS	*	39.95	40.00
	S. TIMM			**WINTER GARLANDS**
96	LEWELS IN THE SNOW	OP	34.95	35.00
	N. GLAZIER			**WINTER SHADOWS**
95	CANYON MOON	95-DAY	29.90	30.00
95	SHADOWS OF GRAY	95-DAY	29.90	30.00
	P. WEIRS			**WINTER SHADOWS**
96	ICY SHADOWS	OP	29.90	30.00
	L. DANIELS			**WOLF PUPS: YOUNG FACES OF THE WILDERNESS**
96	CALL OF THE FUTURE	OP	29.95	30.00
	G. ALEXANDER			**WOODLAND TRANQUILITY**
94	WINTER'S CALM	CL	29.90	35.00
95	CROSSING BOUNDARIES	95-DAY	29.90	30.00
95	FROSTY MOON	95-DAY	29.90	30.00
95	WINTER'S CALM	95 DAY	29.90	30.00
96	SUNSET AT CORNUCOPIA	OP	34.90	35.00
	J. HANSEL			**WOODLAND WINGS**
94	TWILIGHT FLIGHT	CL	34.90	35.00
95	PEACEFUL JOURNEY	95-DAY	34.90	35.00
	D. TERBUSH			**WORLD BENEATH THE WAVES**
96	ALL THE MIRACLES TO SEA	OP	29.90	30.00
	J. HANSEL			**WORLD OF THE EAGLE**
94	SENTINEL OF THE NIGHT	CL	29.90	30.00
95	MIDNIGHT DUTY	95-DAY	32.90	33.00
	T. CALUSNITZER			**WORLD OF WILDLIFE: CELEBRATING EARTH DAY**
95	A DELICATE BALANCE	95-DAY	29.90	30.00
	J. GRIFFIN			**WORLD WAR II: A REMEMBRANCE**
94	D-DAY	CL	29.90	30.00
95	BATTLE OF THE PHILIPPINES	95-DAY	32.90	33.00
95	DOOLITTLE'S RAID OVER TOKYO	95-DAY	32.90	*
	C. WYSOCKI			**WYSOCKI'S PEPPERCRICKET GROVE**
93	BLACK CROW ANTIQUE SHOPPE	CL	24.90	25.00
93	BUDZEN'S FRUITS AND VEGETABLES	CL	24.90	25.00
93	GINGERNUT VALLEY INN	CL	24.90	25.00
93	LIBERTY STAR FARMS	CL	24.90	25.00
93	OVERFLOW ANTIQUE MARKET	CL	24.90	25.00
93	PUMPKIN HOLLOW EMPORIUM	CL	24.90	25.00
93	VIRGINIA'S MARKET	CL	24.90	25.00

BRIERCROFT

YR	NAME	LIMIT	ISSUE	TREND
	D. WINDBERG			**AMERICAN SNOWSCAPE**
95	JOYOUS EVENSONG	1500	65.00	65.00

BYLINY'S PORCELAIN

YR	NAME	LIMIT	ISSUE	TREND
	U.L. DUBOVIKOV			**JEWELS OF THE GOLDEN RING**
91	ST. BASIL'S, MOSCOW	195-DAY	29.87	35.00

C.U.I./CAROLINA COLLECTION

YR	NAME	LIMIT	ISSUE	TREND
	*			**CHRISTMAS**
91	CHECKIN' IT TWICE FIRST ED.	RT	39.50	40.00
	G. GEIVETTE			**CLASSIC CAR**
92	CHEVY 1957	RT	40.00	45.00
	*			**COORS FACTORY**
92	COORS FACTORY FIRST ED.	CL	29.50	30.00
93	COORS FACTORY SECOND ED.	CL	29.50	30.00
	T. STORTZ			**COORS WINTERFEST**
92	SKATING PARTY	RT	29.50	30.00
	G. GEIVETTE			**CORVETTE**
92	CORVETTE 1953	CL	40.00	45.00
	C.L. BRAGG			**ENVIRONMENTAL**
91	REINFOREST MAGIC FIRST ED.	RT	39.50	40.00
	M. HOFFMAN			**ENVIRONMENTAL**
92	FIRST BREATH	RT	40.00	45.00
	R. CRUWYS			**FIRST ENCOUNTER**
93	STAND OFF	CL	29.50	30.00
94	CLASS CLOWN	CL	29.50	30.00
	*			**GIRL IN THE MOON**
91	MILLER GIRL IN THE MOON FIRST ED.	9950	39.50	40.00

YR	NAME	LIMIT	ISSUE	TREND
	J. KILLEN			**GREAT AMERICAN SPORTING DOGS**
92	BLACK LAB FIRST ED.	20000	40.00	45.00
93	BRITTANY SPANIEL SIXTH ED.	CL	40.00	45.00
93	ENGLISH SETTER FIFTH ED.	CL	40.00	45.00
93	GOLDEN RETRIEVER SECOND ED.	CL	40.00	45.00
93	SPRINGER SPANIEL THIRD ED.	CL	40.00	45.00
93	YELLOW LABRADOR FOURTH ED.	CL	40.00	45.00
	P. KETHLEY			**NATIVE AMERICAN**
91	HUNT FOR THE BUFFALO FIRST ED.	RT	39.50	40.00

CAVANAGH GROUP

YR	NAME	LIMIT	ISSUE	TREND
	*			**AMERICAN LIFE**
95	BOY FISHING	5000	60.00	60.00
95	HILDA CLARK WITH ROSES	2500	60.00	60.00
	*			**COCA-COLA BRAND HERITAGE COLLECTION**
94	SANTA AT THIS DESK	5000	60.00	65.00
	*			**THE COCA-COLA SANTA**
95	GOOD BOYS AND GIRLS	2500	60.00	60.00
96	TRAVEL REFRESHED	2500	60.00	60.00

CLARISSA'S CREATIONS

YR	NAME	LIMIT	ISSUE	TREND
	C. JOHNSON			
90	LITTLE BALLERINA	14-DAY	48.00	55.00
94	MEMORIES	25000	48.00	50.00

CRESTLEY COLLECTION

YR	NAME	LIMIT	ISSUE	TREND
	*			**A TRIBUTE TO ROY ROGERS**
94	HAPPY TRAILS TO YOU	*	19.95	22.00
	S. WOODS			**BACKYARD BUDDIES**
94	OCTOBER HARVEST	*	19.95	22.00
	S. WHEELER			**CHRISTMAS/PRIMROSE HILL**
94	BE IT EVER SO HUMBLE	*	19.95	22.00
	T. CATHEY			**HEAVENLY HEARTS**
94	PRUDENCE	*	19.95	22.00
	T. DUBOIS			**MONDAY'S TROLL FAIR OF FACE**
94	SUNDAY'S TROLL	*	19.95	22.00
	*			**PICTURE PURRFECT**
94	EVERYONE NEEDS A TEDDY	*	19.95	22.00
	*			**PICTURE PURRFECT CATS**
95	KITTEN ON THE KEYS	OP	19.95	20.00
	S. EVANS			**PROFILES OF BRAVERY**
94	FIERCE & THE MIGHTY, THE	*	19.95	22.00
	T. DUBOIS			**TEDDY BEAR FAIR**
94	POWER OF LOVE, THE	*	19.95	22.00
	L. KENDRICK			**VISION QUEST**
94	VALLEY OF THE SPIRIT	*	19.95	22.00

CROWN PARIAN

YR	NAME	LIMIT	ISSUE	TREND
	PARIAN			**FREDDIE THE FREELOADER**
79	FREDDIE IN THE BATHTUB	OP	55.00	174.00
80	FREDDIE'S SHACK	OP	55.00	78.00
81	FREDDIE ON THE GREEN	OP	60.00	51.00
82	LOVE THAT FREDDIE	OP	60.00	34.00
	PARIAN			**FREDDIE'S ADVENTURE**
82	BRONCO FREDDIE	OP	60.00	27.00
82	CAPTAIN FREDDIE	OP	60.00	29.00
83	SIR FREDDIE	OP	62.50	25.00
84	GERTRUDE AND HEATHCLIFFE	OP	62.50	75.00

D'ARCEAU LIMOGES

YR	NAME	LIMIT	ISSUE	TREND
	A. RESTIEAU			**CHRISTMAS**
75	LA FRUITE EN EGYPTE	*	24.32	30.00
76	DANS LA CRECHE	*	24.32	29.00
77	REFUS D'HEBERGEMENT	*	24.32	29.00
78	LA PURIFICATION	YR	26.81	29.00
79	L'ADORATION DES ROIS	YR	26.81	31.00
80	JOYEUSE NOUVELLE	YR	28.74	32.00
81	GUIDES PAR L'ETOILE	YR	28.74	30.00
82	L'ANNUCIATION	YR	30.74	35.00
	A. RESTIEAU			**LAFAYETTE**
73	NORTH ISLAND LANDING	*	19.82	22.00
73	SECRET CONTRACT, THE	*	14.82	22.00
74	BATTLE OF BRANDYWINE	*	19.82	22.00
74	CITY TAVERN MEETING	*	19.82	22.00
75	MESSAGES TO FRANKLIN	*	19.82	22.00
75	SIEGE AT YORKTOWN	*	19.82	22.00

DAVE GROSSMAN CREATIONS

YR	NAME	LIMIT	ISSUE	TREND
	ROCKWELL INSPIRED			**BOY SCOUT**
81	CAN'T WAIT	RT	30.00	50.00
82	GUIDING HAND	RT	30.00	40.00
83	TOMORROW'S LEADER	RT	30.00	45.00
	B. LEIGHTON-JONES			**EMMETT KELLY CHRISTMAS PLATE**
93	DOWNHILL PLATE	YR	30.00	35.00
	B. LEIGHTON-JONES			**EMMETT KELLY ORIGINAL CIRCUS COLLECTION**
94	HOLIDAY SKATER	YR	30.00	35.00

YR	NAME	LIMIT	ISSUE	TREND
B. LEIGHTON-JONES			**EMMETT KELLY PLATES**	
86	CHRISTMAS CAROL	CL	20.00	25.00
87	CHRISTMAS WREATH	YR	20.00	25.00
88	CHRISTMAS DINNER	YR	20.00	50.00
89	CHRISTMAS FEAST	YR	20.00	40.00
90	JUST WHAT I NEEDED	YR	24.00	40.00
91	EMMETT THE SNOWMAN	YR	25.00	50.00
92	CHRISTMAS TUNES	YR	25.00	30.00
ROCKWELL INSPIRED			**HUCK FINN**	
79	SECRET	RT	40.00	45.00
80	LISTENING	RT	40.00	45.00
80	NO KINGS	RT	40.00	45.00
81	SNAKE ESCAPES	RT	40.00	45.00
E. ROBERTS			**NATIVE AMERICAN SERIES**	
91	LONE WOLF	10000	45.00	48.00
92	TORTOISE LADY	10000	45.00	48.00
ROCKWELL INSPIRED			**NORMAN ROCKWELL COLLECTION**	
78	YOUNG DOCTOR	RT	50.00	70.00
79	BUTTERBOY	RT	40.00	45.00
79	LEAPFROG	RT	50.00	55.00
80	BACK TO SCHOOL	RT	24.00	30.00
80	CHRISTMAS TRIO	RT	75.00	80.00
80	LOVERS	RT	60.00	65.00
81	DREAMS OF LONG AGO	RT	60.00	65.00
81	NO SWIMMING	RT	25.00	30.00
81	SANTA'S GOOD BOYS	RT	75.00	80.00
82	AMERICAN MOTHER	RT	45.00	50.00
82	DOCTOR AND DOLL	RT	65.00	100.00
82	FACES OF CHRISTMAS	RT	75.00	80.00
82	LOVE LETTER	RT	27.00	35.00
83	CHRISTMAS CHORES	RT	75.00	80.00
83	CIRCUS	RT	65.00	70.00
83	DOCTOR AND DOLL	RT	27.00	30.00
83	DREAMBOAT	RT	24.00	35.00
84	BIG MOMENT	RT	27.00	30.00
84	TINY TIM	RT	75.00	80.00
84	VISIT WITH ROCKWELL	RT	65.00	70.00
ROCKWELL INSPIRED			**SATURDAY EVENING POST**	
91	DOWNHILL DARING	YR	25.00	30.00
91	MISSED	YR	25.00	30.00
92	CHOOSIN UP	YR	25.00	30.00
ROCKWELL INSPIRED			**TOM SAWYER**	
75	WHITEWASHING THE FENCE	RT	26.00	40.00
76	FIRST SMOKE	RT	26.00	40.00
77	TAKE YOUR MEDICINE	RT	26.00	45.00
78	LOST IN CAVE	RT	26.00	45.00

DELPHI

YR	NAME	LIMIT	ISSUE	TREND
D. SIVAVEC			**BEATLES '67-70, THE**	
92	ALL YOU NEED IS LOVE	CL	27.75	30.00
92	SGT. PEPPER, THE 25TH ANNIVERSARY	CL	27.75	30.00
93	ABBEY ROAD	CL	30.75	32.00
93	HEY JUDE	CL	30.75	32.00
93	LET IT BE	CL	30.75	32.00
93	MAGICAL MYSTERY TOUR	CL	30.75	32.00
M. STUTZMAN			**COMMEMORATING THE KING**	
93	BLUES AND BLACK LEATHER	CL	29.75	30.00
93	GOLDEN BOY	CL	29.75	30.00
93	LAS VEGAS, LIVE	CL	29.75	60.00
93	OUTSTANDING YOUNG MAN	OP	29.75	30.00
93	PRIVATE PRESLEY	CL	29.75	30.00
93	ROCK AND ROLL LEGEND, THE	CL	29.75	59.00
93	SCREEN IDOL	CL	29.75	30.00
93	TIGER'S FAITH, SPIRIT & DISCIPLINE, THE	OP	29.75	30.00
P. PALMA			**DREAM MACHINES**	
88	'56 T-BIRD	CL	24.75	45.00
88	'57 'VETTE	CL	24.75	30.00
89	'56 CONTINENTAL	CL	27.75	30.00
89	'57 BEL AIR	CL	27.75	39.00
89	'57 CHRYSLER 300C	CL	27.75	30.00
89	'58 BIARRITZ	CL	27.75	30.00
B. EMMETT			**ELVIS ON THE BIG SCREEN**	
92	G.I. BLUES	CL	29.75	50.00
92	LOVING YOU	CL	29.75	45.00
92	VIVA LAS VEGAS	CL	32.75	70.00
93	BLUE HAWAII	CL	32.75	35.00
93	HARUM SCARUM	CL	34.75	35.00
93	JAILHOUSE ROCK	CL	32.75	35.00
93	SPEEDWAY	CL	34.75	35.00
93	SPINOUT	CL	34.75	35.00
N. GIORGIO			**ELVIS PRESLEY HIT PARADE**	
92	BLUE CHRISTMAS	CL	32.75	35.00
92	BLUE SUEDE SHOES	CL	29.75	30.00
92	HEARTBREAK HOTEL	CL	29.75	30.00
92	HOUND DOG	CL	32.75	35.00
92	RETURN TO SENDER	CL	32.75	35.00
93	ALWAYS ON MY MIND	CL	34.75	35.00

YR	NAME	LIMIT	ISSUE	TREND
93	BLUE MOON OF KENTUCKY	CL	34.75	35.00
93	MYSTERY TRAIN	CL	34.75	35.00
93	PEACE IN THE VALLEY	CL	36.75	40.00
93	SUSPICIOUS MINDS	CL	36.75	40.00
93	TEDDY BEAR	CL	34.75	35.00
93	WEAR MY RING ROUND YOUR NECK	CL	36.75	40.00
B. EMMETT		**ELVIS PRESLEY: IN PERFORMANCE**		
90	'68 COMEBACK SPECIAL	CL	24.75	79.00
91	ALOHA FROM HAWAII	CL	27.75	70.00
91	BACK IN TUPELO, 1956	CL	27.75	55.00
91	BENEFIT FOR THE USS ARIZONA	CL	29.75	50.00
91	CONCERT IN BATON ROUGE, 1974	CL	29.75	40.00
91	IF I CAN DREAM	CL	27.75	55.00
91	KING OF LAS VEGAS	CL	24.75	70.00
91	MADISON SQUARE GARDEN, 1972	CL	29.75	45.00
91	TAMPA, 1955	CL	29.75	38.00
92	IN THE SPOTLIGHT:HAWAII '72	CL	31.75	33.00
92	ON STAGE IN WICHITA, 1974	CL	31.75	50.00
92	TOUR FINALE: INDIANAPOLIS '77	CL	31.75	33.00
B. EMMETT		**ELVIS PRESLEY: LOOKING AT A LEGEND**		
88	ELVIS AT/GATES OF GRACELAND	RT	24.75	110.00
89	HOMECOMING	CL	27.75	55.00
89	JAILHOUSE ROCK	CL	24.75	125.00
89	MEMPHIS FLASH, THE	CL	27.75	70.00
90	A STUDIO SESSION	CL	27.75	42.00
90	ELVIS AND GLADYS	CL	27.75	60.00
90	ELVIS IN HOLLYWOOD	CL	29.75	50.00
90	ELVIS ON HIS HARLEY	CL	29.75	50.00
90	STAGE DOOR AUTOGRAPHS	CL	29.75	55.00
91	CHRISTMAS AT GRACELAND	CL	32.75	95.00
91	CLOSING THE DEAL	CL	34.75	45.00
91	ENTERING SUN STUDIO	CL	32.75	45.00
91	GOING FOR THE BLACK BELT	CL	32.75	62.00
91	HIS HAND IN MINE	CL	32.75	55.00
91	LETTERS FROM FANS	CL	32.75	60.00
92	ELVIS RETURNS TO THE STAGE	CL	34.75	55.00
G. ANGELINI		**FABULOUS CARS OF THE FIFTIES**		
93	'57 BLUE BELAIR	CL	27.75	30.00
93	'57 RED CORVETTE	CL	24.75	30.00
93	'57 WHITE T-BIRD	CL	24.75	30.00
93	'59 PINK CADILLAC	CL	27.75	30.00
94	'56 LINCOLN PREMIER	CL	27.75	30.00
94	'59 RED FORD FAIRLANE	CL	27.75	30.00
D. SIVAVEC		**IN THE FOOTSTEPS OF THE KING**		
93	GRACELAND: MEMPHIS, TN	CL	27.75	30.00
V. GADINO		**INDIANA JONES**		
89	INDIANA JONES	CL	24.75	30.00
89	INDIANA JONES AND HIS DAD	CL	24.75	50.00
90	A FAMILY DISCUSSION	CL	27.75	60.00
90	INDIANA JONES/DR. SCHNEIDER	CL	27.75	40.00
90	YOUNG INDIANA JONES	CL	27.75	60.00
91	INDIANA JONES/THE HOLY GRAIL	CL	27.75	60.00
J. BARSON		**LEGENDS OF BASEBALL**		
92	LOU GEHRIG: THE LUCKIEST MAN	CL	24.75	25.00
93	CY YOUNG: THE PERFECT GAME	CL	27.75	30.00
93	HONUS WAGNER: FLYING DUTCHMAN	CL	29.75	30.00
93	JIMMIE FOX: THE BEAST	CL	29.75	30.00
93	ROGER HOMSBY: 424 SEASON	CL	27.75	30.00
93	TRIS SPEAKER: THE GRAY EAGLE	CL	29.75	30.00
93	TY COBB: THE GEORGIA PEACH	CL	27.95	30.00
93	WALTER JOHNSON: THE SHUTOUT	CL	29.75	30.00
B. BENGER		**LEGENDS OF BASEBALL**		
92	BABE RUTH: THE CALLED SHOT	CL	24.95	25.00
C. NOTARILE		**MARILYN MONROE**		
89	MARILYN MONROE/7 YEAR ITCH	CL	24.75	90.00
90	DIAMONDS/GIRL'S BEST FRIEND	CL	24.75	95.00
91	MARILYN MONROE/RIVER OF NO RETURN	CL	27.75	65.00
92	ALL ABOUT EVE	CL	29.75	49.00
92	DON'T BOTHER TO KNOCK	CL	31.75	50.00
92	HOW TO MARRY A MILLIONAIRE	CL	27.75	60.00
92	MARILYN MONROE AS CHERIE IN BUS STOP	CL	29.75	60.00
92	MARILYN MONROE IN NIAGARA	CL	29.75	70.00
92	MONKEY BUSINESS	CL	31.75	55.00
92	MY HEART BELONGS TO DADDY	CL	29.75	55.00
92	THERE'S NO BUSINESS/SHOW BUSINESS	CL	27.75	95.00
92	WE'RE NOT MARRIED	CL	31.75	70.00
D. ZWIERZ		**PORTRAITS OF THE KING**		
91	ARE YOU LONESOME TONIGHT?	CL	27.75	50.00
91	I'M YOURS	CL	30.75	50.00
91	LOVE ME TENDER	CL	27.75	45.00
91	TREAT ME NICE	CL	30.75	35.00
92	FOLLOW THAT DREAM	CL	32.75	35.00
92	JUST BECAUSE	CL	32.75	35.00
92	WONDER OF YOU, THE	CL	30.75	32.00
92	YOU'RE A HEARTBREAKER	CL	32.75	35.00
D. HENDERSON		**TAKE ME OUT TO THE BALLGAME**		
93	BRIGGS STADIUM:HOME OF THE TIGERS	CL	32.75	35.00

YR	NAME	LIMIT	ISSUE	TREND
93	CLEVELAND STADIUM:HOME OF THE INDIANS	CL	34.75	35.00
93	COMISKEY PARK:HOME OF THE WHITE SOX	CL	32.75	35.00
93	COUNTY STADIUM:HOME OF THE CHAMPS	CL	34.75	35.00
93	FENWAY PARK:HOME OF THE GREEN MONSTER	CL	32.75	35.00
93	WRIGLEY FIELD:THE FRIENDLY CONFINES	CL	29.75	30.00
93	YANKEE STADIUM:HOUSE THAT RUTH BUILT	CL	29.75	30.00
94	EBBETS FIELD:HOME OF THE DODGERS	CL	34.75	35.00
D. HNEDERSON		**TAKE ME OUT TO THE BALLGAME**		
93	MEMORIAL STADIUM:HOME OF THE ORIOLES	CL	34.75	35.00
N. GIORGIO			**THE BEATLES COLLECTION**	
91	A HARD DAY'S NIGHT	CL	27.75	50.00
91	BEATLES, THE - LIVE IN CONCERT	CL	24.75	60.00
91	HELLO AMERICA	CL	24.75	50.00
92	BEATLES '65	CL	27.75	30.00
92	BEATLES, THE - AT SHEA STADIUM	CL	29.75	30.00
92	HELP	CL	27.75	30.00
92	RUBBER SOUL	CL	29.75	30.00
92	YESTERDAY AND TODAY	CL	29.75	30.00
C. NOTARILE			**THE MAGIC OF MARILYN**	
92	FOR OUR BOYS IN KOREA, 1954	CL	24.75	25.00
92	OPENING NIGHT	CL	24.75	30.00
92	STRASBERG'S CLASS	CL	29.75	30.00
93	CURTAIN CALL	CL	29.75	30.00
93	PHOTO OPPORTUNITY	CL	29.75	30.00
93	RISING STAR	CL	27.75	30.00
93	SHINING STAR	CL	29.75	30.00
93	STOPPING TRAFFIC	CL	27.75	30.00

DEPARTMENT 56

Price ranges may reflect various demands in the market from one geographic region to another; condition of piece; specific markings found on piece; and/or changes in production of piece.

YR	NAME	LIMIT	ISSUE	TREND
R. INNOCENTI			**A CHRISTMAS CAROL**	
91	CRATCHIT'S CHRISTMAS PUDDING, THE	18000	60.00	75.00
92	MARLEY'S GHOST APPEARS TO SCROOGE	18000	60.00	65.00
92	SPIRIT OF CHRISTMAS PRESENT, THE	18000	60.00	65.00
94	VISIONS OF CHRISTMAS PAST	18000	60.00	65.00
*			**DICKENS' VILLAGE**	
87	DICKENS' VILLAGE 5917-0 (SET OF 4)	CL	140.00	225.00

DUNCAN ROYALE

YR	NAME	LIMIT	ISSUE	TREND
S. MORTON			**HISTORY OF SANTA CLAUS I**	
*	COLLECTION OF 12 PLATES	RT	480.00	485.00
85	KRIS KRINGLE	RT	40.00	70.00
85	MEDIEVAL	RT	40.00	55.00
85	PIONEER	10000	40.00	45.00
86	CIVIL WAR	10000	40.00	45.00
86	NAST	RT	40.00	80.00
86	RUSSIAN	RT	40.00	45.00
86	SODA POP	RT	40.00	70.00
87	BLACK PETER	10000	40.00	45.00
87	DEDT MOROZ	10000	40.00	45.00
87	ST. NICHOLAS	RT	40.00	80.00
87	VICTORIAN	RT	40.00	45.00
87	WASSAIL	RT	40.00	45.00

EDNA HIBEL STUDIOS

YR	NAME	LIMIT	ISSUE	TREND
E. HIBEL				**ALLEGRO**
78	PLATE & BOOK	7500	120.00	140.00
E. HIBEL				**ARTE OVALE**
80	TAKARA, BLANCO	700	450.00	1150.00
80	TAKARA, COBALT BLUE	1000	595.00	2325.00
80	TAKARA, GOLD	300	1000.00	4150.00
84	TARO-KUN, BLANCO	700	450.00	830.00
84	TARO-KUN, COBALT BLUE	1000	995.00	1100.00
84	TARO-KUN, GOLD	300	1000.00	2650.00
E. HIBEL			**CHRISTMAS ANNUAL**	
85	ANGELS' MESSAGE, THE	YR	45.00	230.00
86	GIFT OF THE MAGI	YR	45.00	280.00
87	FLIGHT INTO EGYPT	YR	49.00	255.00
88	ADORATION OF THE SHEPHERDS	YR	49.00	180.00
89	PEACEFUL KINGDOM	YR	49.00	170.00
90	NATIVITY, THE	YR	49.00	155.00
E. HIBEL				**DAVID SERIES**
79	WEDDING OF DAVID & BATHSHEBA	5000	250.00	625.00
80	DAVID, BATHSHEBA & SOLOMON	5000	275.00	400.00
82	DAVID THE KING	5000	275.00	300.00
82	DAVID THE KING, COBALT A/P	25	275.00	1150.00
84	BATHSHEBA	5000	275.00	300.00
84	BATHSHEBA, COBALT A/P	100	275.00	1150.00
E. HIBEL			**EDNA HIBEL HOLIDAY**	
91	FIRST HOLIDAY, THE	YR	49.00	85.00
91	FIRST HOLIDAY, THE - GOLD	1000	99.00	145.00
92	CHRISTMAS ROSE, THE	YR	49.00	50.00
92	CHRISTMAS ROSE, THE - GOLD	1000	99.00	100.00
E. HIBEL				**EROICA**
90	COMPASSION	10000	49.50	70.00
92	DARYA	10000	49.50	50.00

YR	NAME	LIMIT	ISSUE	TREND
E. HIBEL		**FAMOUS WOMEN & CHILDREN**		
80	PHARAOH'S DAUGHTER & MOSES, GOLD	2500	350.00	630.00
80	PHARAOH'S DAUGHTER & MOSES, COBALT BLUE	500	350.00	1400.00
82	ANNA & THE CHILDREN OF THE KING OF SIAM	2500	350.00	500.00
82	ANNA & THE CHILDREN OF THE KING OF SIAM-	500	350.00	1400.00
82	CORNELIA & HER JEWELS, COBALT BLUE	500	350.00	1400.00
82	CORNELIA & HER JEWELS, GOLD	2500	350.00	500.00
84	MOZART & THE EMPRESS MARIE THERESA-COBAL	500	350.00	950.00
84	MOZART & THE EMPRESS MARIE THERESA-GOLD	2500	350.00	400.00
E. HIBEL		**FLOWER GIRL ANNUAL**		
85	LILY	15000	79.00	295.00
86	IRIS	15000	79.00	230.00
87	ROSE	15000	79.00	180.00
88	CAMELLIA	15000	79.00	170.00
89	PEONY	15000	79.00	100.00
92	WISTERIA	15000	79.00	80.00
E. HIBEL		**INTERNATIONAL MOTHER LOVE FRENCH**		
85	YVETTE AVEC SES ENFANTS	5000	125.00	230.00
91	LIBERTE, EGALITE, FRATERNITE	5000	95.00	100.00
E. HIBEL		**INTERNATIONAL MOTHER LOVE GERMAN**		
82	GESA UND KINDER	5000	195.00	200.00
83	ALEXANDER UND KINDER	5000	195.00	200.00
E. HIBEL		**MARCH OF DIMES: OUR CHILDREN, OUR FUTURE**		
90	A TIME TO EMBRACE	CL	29.00	35.00
E. HIBEL		**MOTHER AND CHILD**		
73	COLETTE & CHILD	15000	40.00	730.00
74	SAYURI & CHILD	15000	40.00	430.00
75	KRISTINA & CHILD	15000	50.00	395.00
76	MARILYN & CHILD	15000	55.00	395.00
77	LUCIA & CHILD	15000	60.00	345.00
81	KATHLEEN & CHILD	15000	85.00	280.00
E. HIBEL		**MOTHER'S DAY**		
92	MOLLY & ANNIE	YR	39.00	75.00
92	MOLLY & ANNIE - PLATINUM	500	275.00	280.00
92	MOLLY & ANNIE, GOLD	2500	95.00	155.00
E. HIBEL		**MOTHER'S DAY ANNUAL**		
84	ABBY & LISA	YR	29.50	395.00
85	ERICA & JAMIE	YR	29.50	245.00
86	EMILY & JENNIFER	YR	29.50	330.00
87	CATHERINE & HEATHER	YR	34.50	280.00
88	SARAH & TESS	YR	34.90	200.00
89	JESSICA & KATE	YR	34.90	130.00
90	ELIZABETH, JORDAY & JANIE	YR	36.90	100.00
91	MICHELE & ANNA	YR	36.90	60.00
92	OLIVIA & HILDY	YR	39.90	60.00
E. HIBEL		**MUSEUM COMMEMORATIVE**		
77	FLOWER GIRL OF PROVENCE	12750	175.00	430.00
80	DIANA	3000	350.00	400.00
E. HIBEL		**NOBILITY OF CHILDREN**		
76	LA CONTESSA ISABELLA	12750	120.00	430.00
77	LE MARQUIS MAURICE PIERRE	12750	120.00	230.00
78	BARONESSE JOHANNA	12750	130.00	230.00
79	CHIEF RED FEATHER	12750	140.00	195.00
E. HIBEL		**NORDIC FAMILIES**		
87	A TENDER MOMENT	7500	79.00	100.00
E. HIBEL		**ORIENTAL GOLD**		
75	YASUKO	2000	275.00	2975.00
76	MR. OBATA	2000	275.00	2000.00
78	SAKURA	2000	295.00	1750.00
79	MICHIO	2000	325.00	1450.00
E. HIBEL		**SCANDINAVIAN MOTHER & CHILD**		
87	PEARLS & FLOWERS	7500	55.00	230.00
89	ANEMONE & VIOLET	7500	75.00	95.00
90	HOLLY & TALIA	7500	75.00	90.00
E. HIBEL		**THE WORLD I LOVE**		
81	LEAH'S FAMILY	17500	85.00	230.00
82	KAYLIN	17500	85.00	380.00
83	EDNA'S MUSIC	17500	85.00	200.00
83	O'HANA	17500	85.00	200.00
E. HIBEL		**TO LIFE ANNUAL**		
86	GOLDEN'S CHILD	5000	99.00	280.00
87	TRIUMPH! EVERYONE A WINNER	19500	55.00	65.00
88	WHOLE EARTH BLOOMED AS A SACRED PLACE	15000	85.00	95.00
89	LOVERS OF THE SUMMER PALACE	5000	65.00	80.00
92	PEOPLE OF THE FIELDS	5000	49.00	50.00
E. HIBEL		**TRIBUTE TO ALL CHILDREN**		
84	GERARD	19500	55.00	100.00
84	GISELLE	19500	55.00	100.00
85	WENDY	19500	55.00	130.00
86	TODD	19500	55.00	130.00

EDWIN M. KNOWLES

YR	NAME	LIMIT	ISSUE	TREND
B. LANGTON		**A LOVING LOOK: DUCK FAMILIES**		
91	FAMILY OUTING	150-DAY	34.50	40.00
L. ROBERTS		**A SWAN IS BORN**		
87	AT THE BARRE	CL	24.50	25.00

YR	NAME	LIMIT	ISSUE	TREND
87	HOPES AND DREAMS	CL	24.50	25.00
87	IN POSITION	CL	24.50	30.00
88	JUST FOR SIZE	CL	24.50	45.00
M. HAMPSHIRE				**AESOP'S FABLES**
88	GOOSE THAT LAID THE GOLDEN EGG, THE	CL	27.90	30.00
88	HARE & THE TORTOISE, THE	CL	27.90	30.00
89	FOX & THE GRAPES, THE	CL	30.90	31.00
89	JAY AND THE PEACOCK, THE	CL	30.90	35.00
89	LION & THE MOUSE, THE	CL	30.90	45.00
89	MILK MAID AND HER PAIL, THE	CL	30.90	50.00
MARSTEN/ MANDRAJJI				**AMERICAN INNOCENTS**
86	ABIGAIL IN THE ROSE GARDEN	CL	19.50	25.00
86	ANN BY THE TERRACE	CL	19.50	20.00
86	ELLEN AND JOHN IN THE PARLOR	CL	19.50	20.00
86	WILLIAM ON THE ROCKING HORSE	CL	19.50	50.00
D. SPAULDING				**AMERICANA HOLIDAYS**
78	FOURTH OF JULY	YR	26.00	30.00
79	THANKSGIVING	YR	26.00	30.00
80	EASTER	YR	26.00	30.00
81	VALENTINE'S DAY	YR	26.00	30.00
82	FATHER'S DAY	YR	26.00	30.00
83	CHRISTMAS	YR	26.00	30.00
84	MOTHER'S DAY	YR	26.00	30.00
A. BRACKENBURY				**AMY BRACKENBURY'S CAT TALES**
87	A CHANCE MEETING: WHITE AM. SHORTHAIRS	CL	21.50	45.00
87	GONE FISHING: MAINE COONS	CL	21.50	78.00
88	ALL WRAPPED UP: HIMALAYANS	CL	24.90	45.00
88	FLOWER BED: BRITISH SHORTHAIRS	CL	24.90	25.00
88	KITTENS AND MITTENS: SILVER TABBIES	CL	24.90	25.00
88	STRAWBERRIES AND CREAM: CREAM PERSIANS	CL	24.90	65.00
W. CHAMBERS				**ANNIE**
83	ANNIE AND GRACE	CL	19.00	20.00
83	ANNIE AND SANDY	CL	19.00	20.00
83	DADDY WARBUCKS	CL	19.00	20.00
84	ANNIE AND THE ORPHANS	CL	21.00	25.00
85	TOMORROW	CL	21.00	25.00
86	ANNIE AND MISS HANNIGAN	CL	21.00	25.00
86	ANNIE, LILY AND ROOSTER	CL	24.00	44.00
86	GRAND FINALE	CL	24.00	25.00
J. THORNBRUGH				**BABY OWLS OF NORTH AMERICA**
91	BEGINNING TO EXPLORE: BOREAL OWLS	CL	32.90	35.00
91	FORTY WINKS:SAW-WHET OWLS	CL	27.90	45.00
91	OUT ON A LIMB: GREAT GRAY OWLS	CL	30.90	45.00
91	OUT ON A LIMB:GREAT GRAY OWL	CL	30.90	50.00
91	PEEK-A-WHOO:SCREECH OWLS	CL	27.90	40.00
91	THREE OF A KIND: GREAT HORNED OWLS	CL	30.90	45.00
91	TREE HOUSE, THE: NORTHERN PYGMY OWLS	CL	30.90	45.00
92	THREE'S COMPANY: LONG EARED OWLS	CL	32.90	33.00
92	WHOO'S THERE: BARRED OWLS	CL	32.90	33.00
J. THORNBRUGH				**BACKYARD HARMONY**
91	ANNOUNCING SPRING	CL	30.90	58.00
91	SINGING LESSON, THE	CL	27.90	39.00
91	WELCOMING A NEW DAY	CL	27.90	30.00
92	AT THE PEEP OF DAY	CL	32.90	40.00
92	MORNING HARVEST, THE	CL	30.90	48.00
92	SPRING TIME PRIDE	CL	30.90	50.00
92	TODAY'S DISCOVERIES	CL	32.90	33.00
92	TREETOP SERENADE	CL	32.90	59.00
*				**BAMBI**
91	BASHFUL BAMBI	CL	34.90	35.00
92	BAMBI'S MORNING GREETINGS	CL	37.90	38.00
92	BAMBI'S NEW FRIENDS	CL	34.90	35.00
92	BAMBI'S SKATING LESSON	CL	37.90	38.00
92	HELLO LITTLE PRINCE	CL	37.90	38.00
93	WHAT'S UP POSSUMS?	CL	37.90	38.00
*				**BEAUTY AND THE BEAST**
93	A BLOSSOMING ROMANCE	CL	29.90	30.00
93	A MISMATCH	CL	34.90	35.00
93	BE OUR GUEST	CL	34.90	35.00
93	BELLE'S FAVORITE STORY	CL	34.90	35.00
93	LEARNING TO LOVE	CL	32.90	33.00
93	LOVE'S FIRST DANCE	CL	29.90	30.00
93	PAPA'S WORKSHOP	CL	32.90	33.00
93	WARMING UP	CL	32.90	33.00
94	A GIFT FOR BELLE	CL	36.90	37.00
94	A SPOT OF TEA	CL	34.90	35.00
94	ENCHANTE'S CHERIE	CL	36.90	37.00
E. LICEA				**BIBLICAL MOTHERS**
83	BATHSHEBA AND SOLOMON	YR	39.50	45.00
84	JUDGMENT OF SOLOMON	YR	39.50	35.00
84	PHARAOH'S DAUGHTER AND MOSES	YR	39.50	45.00
85	MARY AND JESUS	YR	39.50	45.00
85	SARAH AND ISAAC	YR	44.50	50.00
86	REBEKAH, JACOB AND ESAU	YR	44.50	45.00
S. TIMM				**BIRDS OF THE SEASONS**
90	BLUEBIRDS IN SPRING	CL	24.90	30.00
90	CARDINALS IN WINTER	CL	24.90	45.00

YR	NAME	LIMIT	ISSUE	TREND
91	BALTIMORE ORIOLES IN SUMMER	CL	27.90	30.00
91	BLUE JAYS IN EARLY FALL	CL	27.90	40.00
91	CEDAR WAXWINGS IN FALL	CL	29.90	50.00
91	CHICKADEES IN WINTER	CL	29.90	43.00
91	NUTHATCHES IN FALL	CL	27.90	30.00
91	ROBINS IN EARLY SPRING	CL	27.90	35.00
K. DANIEL		**BRITANNICA'S BIRDS OF YOUR GARDEN**		
85	BALTIMORE ORIOLE, THE	CL	22.50	35.00
85	BLUE JAY, THE	CL	19.50	30.00
85	CARDINAL, THE	CL	19.50	40.00
86	BLUEBIRD, THE	CL	22.50	35.00
86	CHICKADEES, THE	CL	22.50	40.00
86	HUMMINGBIRD, THE	CL	24.50	32.00
86	ROBIN, THE	CL	22.50	35.00
87	CEDAR WAXWING, THE	CL	24.90	35.00
87	DOWNY WOODPECKER, THE	CL	24.50	40.00
87	GOLDFINCH, THE	CL	24.50	35.00
K. DANIEL			**CALL OF THE WILDERNESS**	
91	FIRST OUTING	CL	29.90	53.00
91	HOWLING LESSON	CL	29.90	60.00
91	SILENT WATCH	CL	32.90	50.00
91	WINTER TRAVELERS	CL	32.90	33.00
92	A NEW FUTURE	CL	34.90	35.00
92	AHEAD OF THE PACK	CL	32.90	33.00
92	MORNING MIST	CL	36.90	37.00
92	NORTHERN SPIRITS	CL	34.90	35.00
92	SILENT ONE, THE	CL	36.90	37.00
92	TWILIGHT FRIENDS	CL	34.90	35.00
D. BROWN				**CAROUSEL**
87	IF I LOVED YOU	CL	24.90	30.00
88	CAROUSEL WALTZ, THE	CL	24.90	30.00
88	MR. SNOW	CL	24.90	25.00
88	YOU'LL NEVER WALK ALONG	CL	24.90	35.00
J. GRIFFIN				**CASABLANCA**
90	HERE'S LOOKING AT YOU, KID	CL	34.90	36.00
90	WE'LL ALWAYS HAVE PARIS	CL	34.90	41.00
91	A FRANC FOR YOUR THOUGHTS	CL	37.90	58.00
91	PLAY IT AGAIN SAM	CL	37.90	55.00
91	RICK'S CAFE AMERICCAIN	CL	37.90	40.00
91	WE LOVED EACH OTHER ONCE	CL	37.90	40.00
J.W. SMITH			**CHILDHOOD HOLIDAYS**	
86	THANKSGIVING	CL	19.50	20.00
86	VALENTINE'S DAY	CL	22.50	23.00
T.C. CHIU		**CHINA'S NATURAL TREASURES**		
91	GIANT PANDA, THE	CL	32.90	35.00
91	SIBERIAN TIGER, THE	CL	29.90	44.00
91	SNOW LEOPARD, THE	CL	29.90	30.00
92	ASIAN ELEPHANT, THE	CL	32.90	45.00
92	GOLDEN MONKEY, THE	CL	34.90	50.00
92	TIBETAN BROWN BEAR, THE	CL	32.90	40.00
A. LEIMANIS			**CHRISTMAS IN THE CITY**	
92	A CHRISTMAS SNOWFALL	CL	34.90	44.00
92	YULETIDE CELEBRATION	CL	34.90	54.00
93	HOLIDAY CHEER	CL	34.90	35.00
93	MAGIC OF CHRISTMAS, THE	CL	34.90	35.00
*				**CINDERELLA**
88	A DREAM IS A WISH YOUR HEART MAKES	CL	29.90	70.00
88	BIBBIDI-BOBBIDI-BOO	CL	29.90	67.00
89	A DRESS OF CINDERELLY	CL	32.90	80.00
89	OH SING SWEET NIGHTENGALE	CL	32.90	40.00
89	SO THIS IS LOVE	CL	32.90	70.00
90	AT THE STROKE OF MIDNIGHT	CL	32.90	50.00
90	HAPPILY EVER AFTER	CL	34.90	40.00
90	IF THE SHOE FITS	CL	34.90	50.00
S. GUSTAFSON			**CLASSIC FAIRY TALES**	
91	FROG PRINCE, THE	CL	32.90	60.00
91	GOLDILOCKS AND THE 3 BEARS	CL	29.90	53.00
91	LITTLE RED RIDING HOOD	CL	29.90	54.00
91	THREE LITTLE PIGS, THE	CL	32.90	55.00
92	HANSEL AND GRETEL	CL	34.90	66.00
92	JACK AND THE BEANSTALK	CL	32.90	56.00
92	PUSS IN BOOTS	CL	34.90	35.00
92	TOM THUMB	CL	34.90	35.00
S. GUSTAFSON			**CLASSIC MOTHER GOOSE**	
92	LITTLE BO PEEP	CL	29.90	55.00
92	LITTLE MISS MUFFET	CL	29.90	45.00
92	MARY HAD A LITTLE LAMB	CL	29.90	49.00
92	MARY, MARY, QUITE CONTRARY	CL	29.90	55.00
H.H. INGMIRE			**COZY COUNTRY CORNERS**	
90	LAZY MORNING	CL	24.90	50.00
90	WARM RETREAT	CL	24.90	50.00
91	A SUNNY SPOT	CL	27.90	40.00
91	APPLE ANTICS	CL	29.90	55.00
91	ATTIC AFTERNOON	CL	27.90	50.00
91	HIDE AND SEEK	CL	29.90	45.00
91	MIRROR MISCHIEF	CL	27.90	58.00
91	TABLE TROUBLE	CL	29.90	55.00

YR	NAME	LIMIT	ISSUE	TREND
J. CSATARI				**CSATARI GRANDPARENT**
80	BEDTIME STORY	CL	18.00	20.00
81	SKATING LESSON, THE	CL	20.00	23.00
82	COOKIE TASTING, THE	CL	20.00	20.00
83	SWINGER, THE	CL	20.00	20.00
84	SKATING QUEEN, THE	CL	22.00	25.00
85	PATRIOT'S PARADE, THE	CL	22.00	22.00
86	HOME RUN, THE	CL	22.00	25.00
87	SNEAK PREVIEW, THE	CL	22.00	23.00
T. KINKADE				**ENCHANTED COTTAGES**
93	FALLBROOKE COTTAGE	CL	29.90	30.00
93	JULIANNE'S COTTAGE	CL	29.90	30.00
93	ROSE GARDEN COTTAGE	CL	29.90	30.00
93	SEASIDE COTTAGE	CL	29.90	30.00
93	SWEETHEART COTTAGE	CL	29.90	30.00
93	WEATHERVANE COTTAGE	CL	29.90	30.00
*				**FANTASIA: (THE SORCERER'S APPRENTICE) GOLDEN ANNIVERSARY**
90	APPRENTICE'S DREAM, THE	CL	29.90	65.00
90	MISCHIEVOUS APPRENTICE	CL	29.90	65.00
91	DREAMS OF POWER	CL	32.90	65.00
91	MICKEY MAKES MAGIC	CL	34.90	40.00
91	MICKEY'S MAGICAL WHIRLPOOL	CL	32.90	50.00
91	PENITENT APPRENTICE, THE	CL	34.90	40.00
91	WIZARDRY GONE WILD	CL	32.90	60.00
92	AN APPRENTICE AGAIN	CL	34.90	40.00
B. BRADLEY				**FATHER'S LOVE**
84	BATTER UP	CL	19.50	20.00
84	OPEN WIDE	CL	19.50	20.00
85	LITTLE SHAVER	CL	19.50	20.00
85	SWING TIME	CL	22.50	25.00
L. KAATZ				**FIELD PUPPIES**
87	CAUGHT IN THE ACT-THE GOLDEN RETRIEVER	CL	24.90	55.00
87	DOG TIRED-THE SPRINGER SPANIEL	CL	24.90	50.00
88	A PERFECT SET-LABRADOR	CL	27.90	45.00
88	FRITZ'S FOLLY-GERMAN SHORTHAIRED POINTER	CL	27.90	40.00
88	MISSING/POINT/IRISH SETTER	CL	27.90	30.00
88	SHIRT TALES-COCKER SPANIEL	CL	27.90	60.00
89	COMMAND PERFORMANCE-WIEMARANER	CL	29.90	40.00
89	FINE FEATHERED FRIENDS-ENGLISH SETTER	CL	29.90	30.00
L. KAATZ				**FIELD TRIPS**
90	GONE FISHING	CL	24.90	25.00
91	BOXED IN	CL	27.90	30.00
91	CHESAPEAKE BAY RETRIEVERS	CL	29.90	30.00
91	DUCKING DUTY	CL	24.90	25.00
91	HAT TRICK	CL	29.90	30.00
91	PAIL PALS	CL	29.90	34.00
91	PUPPY TALES	CL	27.90	40.00
91	PUPS 'N BOOTS	CL	27.90	30.00
J. GIORDANO				**FIRST IMPRESSIONS**
91	ALL EARS	CL	32.90	65.00
91	FINE FEATHERED FRIEND	CL	32.90	44.00
91	TAKING A GANDER	CL	29.90	40.00
91	TWOS' COMPANY	CL	29.90	35.00
91	WHAT'S UP?	CL	32.90	35.00
92	BETWEEN FRIENDS	CL	32.90	35.00
F. HOOK				**FRANCES HOOK LEGACY**
85	DAYDREAMING	CL	19.50	20.00
85	FASCINATION	CL	19.50	20.00
86	DISAPPOINTMENT	CL	22.50	23.00
86	DISCOVERY	CL	22.50	23.00
86	WONDERMENT	CL	22.50	23.00
87	EXPECTATION	CL	22.50	23.00
M. BUDDEN				**FREE AS THE WIND**
92	AIRBORNE	CL	32.90	33.00
92	ALOFT	CL	29.90	50.00
92	SKYWARD	CL	29.90	52.00
93	ASCENT	CL	32.90	33.00
93	FLIGHT	CL	32.90	33.00
93	HEAVENWARD	CL	32.90	33.00
J. DOWN				**FRIENDS I REMEMBER**
83	FISH STORY	CL	17.50	18.00
84	OFFICE HOURS	CL	17.50	18.00
85	A COAT OF PAINT	CL	17.50	18.00
85	FRINGE BENEFITS	CL	19.50	20.00
85	HERE COMES THE BRIDE	CL	19.50	20.00
86	FLOWER ARRANGEMENT	CL	21.50	22.00
86	HIGH SOCIETY	CL	19.50	20.00
86	TASTE TEST	CL	21.50	22.00
K. DANIEL				**FRIENDS OF THE FOREST**
87	RABBIT, THE	CL	24.50	30.00
87	RACCOON, THE	CL	24.50	35.00
87	SQUIRREL, THE	CL	27.90	28.00
88	CHIPMUNK, THE	CL	27.90	28.00
88	FOX, THE	CL	27.90	28.00
88	OTTER, THE	CL	27.90	28.00
T. KINKADE				**GARDEN COTTAGES OF ENGLAND**
91	CANDLELIT COTTAGE	CL	30.90	45.00

Norman Rockwell's The Young Scholar *was the 15th issue in the Rockwell Heritage collection by Edwin M. Knowles. Production was limited to the year 1991 for the Rockwell Society of America.*

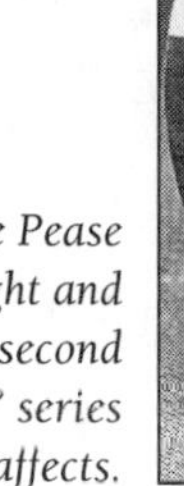

Like a soft lullaby, Bessie Pease Gutmann captures the sweet sight and sound of Harmony. *The plate is second in the "Magical Moments" series produced by Artaffects.*

Reco International released Ortwin the Deer *in 1987. From the Vanishing Animal Kingdoms collection, it was limited to 21,500.*

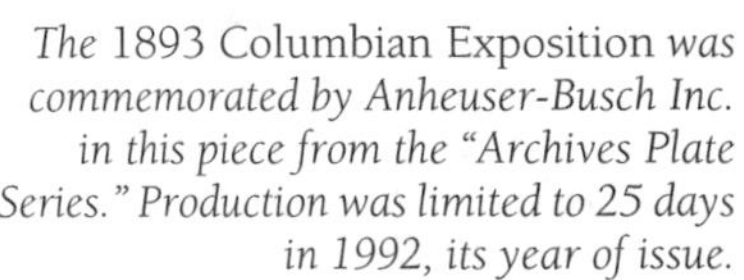

The 1893 Columbian Exposition *was commemorated by Anheuser-Busch Inc. in this piece from the "Archives Plate Series." Production was limited to 25 days in 1992, its year of issue.*

YR	NAME	LIMIT	ISSUE	TREND
91	CEDAR NOOK COTTAGE	CL	27.90	34.00
91	CHANDLER'S COTTAGE	CL	27.90	59.00
91	MCKENNA'S COTTAGE	CL	30.90	57.00
91	OPEN GATE COTTAGE	CL	30.90	50.00
91	WOODSMAN'S THATCH COTTAGE	CL	32.90	58.00
92	MERRITT'S COTTAGE	CL	32.90	55.00
92	STONEGATE COTTAGE	CL	32.90	60.00
B. HIGGINS BOND				**GARDEN SECRETS**
93	BLOOMIN' KITTIES	CL	24.90	25.00
93	FLORAL PURR-FUME	CL	24.90	25.00
93	FLOWER FANCIERS	CL	24.90	25.00
93	FRISKY BUSINESS	CL	24.90	25.00
93	KITTY CORNER	CL	24.90	25.00
93	MEADOW MISCHIEF	CL	24.90	25.00
93	NINE LIVES	CL	24.90	25.00
93	PUSSYCAT POTPOURRI	CL	24.90	25.00
R. KURSAR				**GONE WITH THE WIND**
78	SCARLETT	CL	21.50	230.00
79	ASHLEY	CL	21.50	120.00
80	MELANIE	CL	21.50	55.00
81	RHETT	CL	23.50	45.00
82	MAMMY LACING SCARLETT	CL	23.50	70.00
83	MELANIE GIVES BIRTH	CL	23.50	80.00
84	SCARLET'S GREEN DRESS	CL	25.50	70.00
85	RHETT AND BONNIE	CL	25.50	80.00
85	SCARLETT AND RHETT: THE FINALE	CL	29.50	70.00
J. CASTARI				**GRANDPARENTS**
81	SKATING LESSON, THE	CL	20.00	20.00
84	SKATING QUEEN, THE	CL	22.00	22.00
85	PATRIOT'S PARADE, THE	CL	22.00	22.00
87	SNEAK PREVIEW, THE	CL	22.00	22.00
L. CABLE				**GREAT CATS OF THE AMERICAS**
89	COUGAR, THE	CL	29.90	45.00
89	JAGUAR, THE	CL	29.90	60.00
89	LYNX, THE	CL	32.90	35.00
90	BOBCAT, THE	CL	32.90	35.00
90	JAGUARUNDI, THE	CL	32.90	35.00
90	MARGAY, THE	CL	34.90	40.00
90	OCELOT, THE	CL	32.90	35.00
91	PAMPAS CAT, THE	CL	34.90	35.00
C. LAYTON				**HEIRLOOMS AND LACE**
89	ANNA	CL	34.90	60.00
89	VICTORIA	CL	34.90	55.00
90	OLIVIA	CL	37.90	115.00
90	TESS	CL	37.90	85.00
91	BRIDGET	CL	37.90	115.00
91	REBECCA	CL	37.90	75.00
E. HIBEL				**HIBEL CHRISTMAS**
85	ANGEL'S MESSAGE, THE	YR	45.00	50.00
86	GIFTS OF THE MAGI, THE	YR	45.00	45.00
87	FLIGHT INTO EGYPT, THE	YR	49.00	55.00
88	ADORATION OF THE SHEPHERD	YR	49.00	77.00
89	PEACEFUL KINGDOM	YR	49.00	49.00
90	NATIVITY	YR	49.00	65.00
E. HIBEL				**HIBEL MOTHER'S DAY**
84	ABBY AND LISA	YR	29.50	30.00
85	ERICA AND JAMIE	YR	29.50	30.00
86	EMILY AND JENNIFER	YR	29.50	45.00
87	CATHERINE AND HEATHER	YR	34.50	49.00
88	SARAH AND TESS	YR	34.90	35.00
89	JESSICA AND KATE	YR	34.90	40.00
90	ELIZABETH, JORDAN & JANIE	YR	36.90	46.00
91	MICHELE AND ANNA	YR	36.90	37.00
T. KINKADE				**HOME FOR THE HOLIDAYS**
91	HOME BEFORE CHRISTMAS	CL	32.90	50.00
91	HOME TO GRANDMA'S	CL	29.90	40.00
91	SLEIGH RIDE HOME	CL	29.90	49.00
92	HOME AWAY FROM HOME	CL	34.90	52.00
92	HOMESPUN HOLIDAY	CL	32.90	45.00
92	HOMETIME YULETIDE	CL	34.90	65.00
92	JOURNEY HOME, THE	CL	34.90	35.00
92	WARMTH OF HOME, THE	CL	32.90	59.00
T. KINKADE				**HOME IS WHERE THE HEART IS**
92	A CARRIAGE RIDE HOME	CL	32.90	33.00
92	A WARM WELCOME HOME	CL	29.90	30.00
92	HOME SWEET HOME	CL	29.90	65.00
93	AMBER AFTERNOON	CL	32.90	33.00
93	COUNTRY MEMORIES	CL	32.90	33.00
93	HOMETOWN HOSPITALITY	CL	34.90	35.00
93	OUR SUMMER HOME	CL	34.90	35.00
93	TWILIGHT CAFE, THE	CL	34.90	35.00
R. MCGINNIS				**HOME SWEET HOME**
89	GEORGIAN, THE	CL	39.90	40.00
89	GREEK REVIVAL, THE	CL	39.90	35.00
89	VICTORIAN, THE	CL	39.90	40.00
90	MISSION, THE	CL	39.90	40.00

YR	NAME	LIMIT	ISSUE	TREND
L. KAATZ				**IT'S A DOG'S LIFE**
92	LITERARY LABS	CL	29.90	30.00
92	WE'VE BEEN SPOTTED	CL	29.90	30.00
93	BARRELING ALONG	CL	32.90	33.00
93	DOGS AND SUDS	CL	34.90	35.00
93	LODGING A COMPLAINT	CL	32.90	33.00
93	PAWS FOR A PICNIC	CL	34.90	35.00
93	PLAY BALL	CL	34.90	35.00
93	RETRIEVING OUR DIGNITY	CL	32.90	33.00
J.W. SMITH				**J.W. SMITH CHILDHOOD HOLIDAYS**
86	CHRISTMAS	CL	19.50	20.00
86	EASTER	CL	19.50	25.00
86	THANKSGIVING	CL	19.50	30.00
86	VALENTINE'S DAY	CL	22.50	25.00
87	FOURTH OF JULY	CL	22.50	23.00
87	MOTHER'S DAY	CL	22.50	23.00
B. JERNER				**JERNER'S LESS TRAVELED ROAD**
88	COVERED BRIDGE, THE	CL	32.90	35.00
88	MURMURING STREAM, THE	CL	29.90	35.00
88	WEATHERED BARN, THE	CL	29.90	35.00
89	FLOWERING MEADOW, THE	CL	32.90	30.00
89	HIDDEN WATERFALL, THE	CL	32.90	35.00
89	WINTER'S PEACE	CL	32.90	35.00
T.C. CHIU				**JEWELS OF THE FLOWERS**
91	AMETHYST FLIGHT	CL	32.90	40.00
91	EMERALD PAIR	CL	32.90	50.00
91	OPAL SPLENDOR	CL	34.90	40.00
91	RUBY ELEGANCE	CL	32.90	55.00
91	SAPPHIRE WINGS	CL	29.90	30.00
91	TOPAZ BEAUTIES	CL	29.90	35.00
92	AQUAMARINE GLIMMER	CL	34.90	35.00
92	PEARL LUSTER	CL	34.90	55.00
S. GUSTAFSON				**KEEPSAKE RHYMES**
92	HUMPTY DUMPTY	CL	29.90	43.00
93	OLD KING COLE	CL	29.90	30.00
93	PAT-A-CAKE	CL	29.90	90.00
93	PETER PUMPKIN EATER	CL	29.90	60.00
*				**LADY AND THE TRAMP**
92	DOG POUND BLUES	CL	37.90	38.00
92	FIRST DATE	CL	34.90	35.00
92	MERRY CHRISTMAS TO ALL	CL	37.90	38.00
92	PUPPY LOVE	CL	34.90	35.00
93	DOUBLE SIAMESE TROUBLE	CL	37.90	38.00
93	MOONLIGHT ROMANCE	CL	39.90	40.00
93	RUFF HOUSE	CL	39.90	40.00
93	TELLING TAILS	CL	39.90	40.00
M. KUNSTLER				**LINCOLN, MAN OF AMERICA**
86	GETTYSBURG ADDRESS, THE	CL	24.50	30.00
87	BEGINNINGS IN NEW SALEM	CL	27.90	35.00
87	INAUGURATION, THE	CL	24.50	25.00
87	LINCOLN-DOUGLAS DEBATES, THE	CL	27.50	30.00
88	EMANCIPATION PROCLAMATION	CL	27.90	35.00
88	FAMILY MAN, THE	CL	27.90	30.00
B. JERNER				**LIVING WITH NATURE-JERNER'S DUCKS**
86	MALLARD, THE	CL	19.50	33.00
86	PINTAIL, THE	CL	19.50	30.00
87	AMERICAN WIDGEON, THE	CL	22.90	45.00
87	GADWALL, THE	CL	24.90	45.00
87	GREEN WINGED TEAL, THE	CL	22.50	40.00
87	NORTHERN SHOVELER, THE	CL	22.90	40.00
87	WOOD DUCK, THE	CL	22.50	36.00
88	BLUE-WINGED TEAL, THE	CL	24.90	40.00
D. SMITH				**MAJESTIC BIRDS OF NORTH AMERICA**
88	BALD EAGLE, THE	CL	29.90	30.00
88	GREAT HORNED OWL, THE	CL	32.90	33.00
88	PEREGRINE FLACON, THE	CL	29.90	30.00
89	AMERICAN KESTRAL, THE	CL	32.90	33.00
89	RED-TAILED HAWK, THE	CL	32.90	33.00
89	WHITE GYRFALCON, THE	CL	32.90	35.00
90	GOLDEN EAGLE, THE	CL	34.90	35.00
90	OSPREY, THE	CL	34.90	35.00
M. HAMPSHIRE				**MARY POPPINS**
89	A SPOONFUL OF SUGAR	CL	29.90	30.00
89	MARY POPPINS	CL	29.90	30.00
90	A JOLLY HOLIDAY WITH MARY	CL	32.90	35.00
90	WE LOVE TO LAUGH	CL	32.90	50.00
91	CHIM CHIM CHER-EE	CL	32.90	40.00
91	TUPPENCE A BAG	CL	32.90	55.00
*				**MICKEY'S CHRISTMAS CAROL**
92	BAH HUMBUG!	CL	29.90	30.00
92	WHAT'S SO MERRY ABOUT CHRISTMAS?	CL	29.90	30.00
93	A CHRISTMAS FEAST	CL	34.90	35.00
93	A CHRISTMAS SURPRISE	CL	32.90	33.00
93	A COZY CHRISTMAS	CL	34.90	35.00
93	GOD BLESS US EVERY ONE	CL	32.90	33.00
93	MARLEY'S WARNING	CL	34.90	35.00
93	YULETIDE GREETINGS	CL	32.90	33.00

YR	NAME	LIMIT	ISSUE	TREND
K. MILNAZIK		**MUSICAL MOMENTS FROM THE WIZARD OF OZ**		
93	DING DONG THE WITCH IS DEAD	CL	29.90	30.00
93	IF I ONLY HAVE A BRAIN	CL	29.90	30.00
93	LULLABYE LEAGUE, THE	CL	29.90	30.00
93	MUNCHKIN LAND	CL	29.90	30.00
93	OVER THE RAINBOW	CL	29.90	30.00
93	WE'RE OFF THE SEE THE WIZARD	CL	29.90	30.00
W. CHAMBERS				**MY FAIR LADY**
89	I COULD HAVE DANCED ALL NIGHT	CL	24.90	25.00
89	OPENING DAY AT ASCOT	CL	24.90	25.00
89	RAIN IN SPAIN, THE	CL	27.90	28.00
89	SHOW ME	CL	27.90	28.00
90	GET ME TO THE CHURCH ON TIME	CL	27.90	28.00
90	I'VE GROWN ACCUSTOMED TO YOUR FACE	CL	27.90	40.00
M. JOBE				**NATURE'S CHILD**
90	FAITHFUL FRIENDS	CL	32.90	33.00
90	LOST LAMB, THE	CL	29.90	30.00
90	SEEMS LIKE YESTERDAY	CL	32.90	35.00
90	SHARING	CL	29.90	30.00
90	TRUSTED COMPANION	CL	32.90	47.00
91	HAND IN HAND	CL	32.90	44.00
C. DECKER				**NATURE'S GARDEN**
93	A MORNING SPLASH	CL	29.90	30.00
93	FLURY OF ACTIVITY	CL	32.90	33.00
93	HANGING AROUND	CL	32.90	33.00
93	SPRINGTIME FRIENDS	CL	29.90	30.00
93	TINY TWIRLING TREASURES	CL	32.90	33.00
J. THORNBRUGH				**NATURE'S NURSERY**
92	TESTING THE WATERS	CL	29.90	30.00
93	HIDE AND SEEK	CL	29.90	30.00
93	PIGGYBACK RIDE	CL	29.90	30.00
93	RACE YA MOM	CL	29.90	30.00
93	TAKING THE PLUNGE	CL	29.90	30.00
93	TIME TO WAKE UP	CL	29.90	30.00
J.W. SMITH				**NOT SO LONG AGO**
88	MOTHER'S LITTLE HELPER	CL	24.90	28.00
88	STORY TIME	CL	24.90	25.00
88	SUPPERTIME FOR KITTY	CL	24.90	30.00
88	WASH DAY FOR DOLLY	CL	24.90	30.00
M. KUNSTLER				**OKLAHOMA!**
85	OH, WHAT A BEAUTIFUL MORNIN'	CL	19.50	20.00
86	I CAIN'T SAY NO	CL	19.50	20.00
86	OKLAHOMA!	CL	19.50	20.00
86	SURREY W/THE FRINGE ON TOP	CL	19.50	20.00
M. WEBER				**OLD FASHIONED FAVORITES**
91	APPLE CRISP	CL	29.90	73.00
91	BLUEBERRY MUFFINS	CL	29.90	60.00
91	CHOCOLATE CHIP OATMEAL COOKIES	CL	29.90	110.00
91	PEACH COBBLER	CL	29.90	75.00
K. PRITCHETT				**ONCE UPON A TIME**
88	LITTLE RED RIDING HOOD	CL	24.90	30.00
88	RAPUNZEL	CL	24.90	30.00
88	THREE LITTLE PIGS	CL	27.90	35.00
89	BEAUTY AND THE BEAST	CL	27.90	55.00
89	GOLDILOCKS AND THE THREE BEARS	CL	27.90	35.00
89	PRINCESS AND THE PEA, THE	CL	27.90	30.00
*				**PINOCCHIO**
89	GEPETTO CREATES PINOCCHIO	CL	29.90	65.00
90	I'VE GOT NO STRINGS ON ME	CL	32.90	50.00
90	IT'A AN ACTOR' S LIFE FOR ME	CL	32.90	50.00
90	PINOCCHIO AND THE BLUE FAIRY	CL	29.90	67.00
91	A REAL BOY	CL	32.90	70.00
91	PLEASURE ISLAND	CL	32.90	50.00
W. CHAMBERS				**PORTRAITS OF MOTHERHOOD**
87	MOTHER'S HERE	CL	29.50	35.00
88	FIRST TOUCH	CL	29.50	35.00
M.T. FANGEL				**PRECIOUS LITTLE ONES**
88	LITTLE FLEDGLINGS	CL	29.90	35.00
88	LITTLE RED ROBINS	CL	29.90	35.00
88	PEEK-A-BOO	CL	29.90	40.00
88	SATURDAY NIGHT BATH	CL	29.90	35.00
N. GLAZIER		**PROUD SENTINELS OF THE AMERICAN WEST**		
93	CAT NAP	CL	29.90	30.00
93	CROWN PRINCE	CL	32.90	33.00
93	DESERT BIGHORN-MORMON RIDGE	CL	32.90	33.00
93	YOUNGBLOOD	CL	29.90	45.00
J. GIORDANO				**PURRFECT POINT OF VIEW**
91	UNEXPECTED VISITORS	CL	29.90	30.00
92	AFTERNOON CATNAP	CL	29.90	30.00
92	COZY COMPANY	CL	29.90	30.00
92	WISTFUL MORNING	CL	29.90	40.00
C. WILSON				**PUSSYFOOTING AROUND**
91	FISH TALES	CL	24.90	30.00
91	TEATIME TABBIES	CL	24.90	30.00
91	TWO MAESTROS	CL	24.90	27.00
91	YARN SPINNERS	CL	24.90	30.00

YR	NAME	LIMIT	ISSUE	TREND
R.B. PIERCE		**ROMANTIC AGE OF STEAM**		
92	BROADWAY LIMITED, THE	CL	29.90	30.00
92	CHIEF, THE	CL	32.90	33.00
92	CRESCENT LIMITED, THE	CL	32.90	33.00
92	EMPIRE BUILDER, THE	CL	29.90	30.00
92	TWENTIETH CENTURY LIMITED	CL	32.90	33.00
93	DAYLIGHT, THE	CL	34.90	35.00
93	JUPITER, THE	CL	34.90	35.00
93	OVERLAND LIMITED, THE	CL	34.90	35.00
T. BROWNING		**SANTA'S CHRISTMAS**		
91	SANTA'S CHEER	CL	29.90	44.00
91	SANTA'S GIFT	CL	32.90	50.00
91	SANTA'S LOVE	CL	29.90	40.00
91	SANTA'S PROMISE	CL	32.90	65.00
92	SANTA'S MAGIC	CL	32.90	69.00
92	SANTA'S SURPRISE	CL	32.90	60.00
M. JOBE		**SEASON FOR SONG**		
91	FROSTY CHORUS	CL	34.90	40.00
91	SILVER SERENADE	CL	34.90	40.00
91	SNOWY SYMPHONY	CL	34.90	60.00
91	WINTER CONCERT	CL	34.90	50.00
K. RANDLE		**SEASON OF SPLENDOR**		
92	A COUNTRY WEEKEND	CL	32.90	45.00
92	AUTUMN GRANDEUR	CL	29.90	43.00
92	HARVEST MEMORIES	CL	32.90	54.00
92	SCHOOL DAYS	CL	29.90	38.00
92	WOODLAND MILL STREAM	CL	32.90	64.00
93	INDIAN SUMMER	CL	32.90	59.00
N. GLAZIER		**SHADOWS & LIGHT: WINTER'S WILDLIFE**		
92	WINTER'S CHILDREN	CL	29.90	50.00
93	CUB SCOUTS	CL	29.90	59.00
93	LITTLE SNOWMAN	CL	29.90	47.00
93	SNOW CAVE, THE	CL	29.90	40.00
M. SKOLSKY		**SINGIN' IN THE RAIN**		
90	GOOD MORNING	CL	32.90	35.00
90	SINGIN' IN THE RAIN	CL	32.90	35.00
91	BROADWAY MELODY	CL	32.90	40.00
91	WE'RE HAPPY AGAIN	CL	32.90	40.00
*		**SLEEPING BEAUTY**		
91	AWAKENED BY A KISS	CL	39.90	83.00
91	HAPPY BIRTHDAY BRIAR ROSE	CL	42.90	58.00
91	ONCE UPON A DREAM	CL	39.90	43.00
92	TOGETHER AT LAST	CL	42.90	60.00
C. LAYTON		**SMALL BLESSINGS**		
92	BLESS US O LORD FOR THESE, THY GIFTS	CL	29.90	62.00
92	BLESSED ARE THE PURE IN HEART	CL	32.90	33.00
92	JESUS LOVES ME, THIS I KNOW	CL	32.90	33.00
92	NOW I LAY ME DOWN TO SLEEP	CL	29.90	59.00
92	THIS LITTLE LIGHT OF MINE	CL	32.90	33.00
93	BLESS OUR HOME	CL	32.90	33.00
*		**SNOW WHITE AND THE SEVEN DWARFS**		
91	A SPECIAL TREAT	CL	32.90	49.00
91	DANCE OF SNOW WHITE/SEVEN DWARFS, THE	CL	29.90	55.00
91	WITH A SMLE AND A SONG	CL	29.90	30.00
92	A KISS FOR DOPEY	CL	32.90	35.00
92	A WISH COME TRUE	CL	34.90	35.00
92	FIRESIDE LOVE STORY	CL	34.90	68.00
92	POISON APPLE, THE	CL	32.90	66.00
92	STUBBORN GRUMPY	CL	34.90	35.00
92	TIME TO TIDY UP	CL	34.90	35.00
93	A SURPRISE IN THE CLEARING	CL	36.90	37.00
93	HAPPY ENDING	CL	36.90	37.00
93	MAY I HAVE THIS DANCE?	CL	36.90	37.00
H. BOND		**SONGS OF THE AMERICAN SPIRIT**		
91	AMERICA THE BEAUTIFUL	CL	29.90	45.00
91	BATTLE HYMN OF THE REPLUBLIC	CL	29.90	49.00
91	MY COUNTRY 'TIS OF THEE	CL	29.90	44.00
91	STAR SPANGLED BANNER, THE	CL	29.90	30.00
T. CRNKOVICH		**SOUND OF MUSIC**		
86	DO-RE-MI	CL	19.50	20.00
86	MY FAVORITE THINGS	CL	22.50	23.00
86	SOUND OF MUSIC	CL	19.50	20.00
87	CLIMB EV'RY MOUNTAIN	CL	24.90	40.00
87	EDELWEISS	CL	22.50	40.00
87	I HAVE CONFIDENCE	CL	22.50	40.00
87	LAENDLER WALTZ	CL	22.50	30.00
87	MARIA-WEDDING SCENE	CL	24.90	40.00
E. GIGNILLIAT		**SOUTH PACIFIC**		
87	DITES MOI	CL	24.90	25.00
87	HAPPY TALK	CL	24.50	25.00
87	SOME ENCHANTED EVENING	CL	24.50	25.00
88	HONEY BUN	CL	24.90	25.00
J. BEAUDOIN		**STATELY OWLS**		
89	GREAT HORNED OWL, THE	CL	29.90	30.00
89	SNOWY OWL, THE	CL	29.90	35.00
90	BARN OWL, THE	CL	32.90	33.00
90	BARRED OWL, THE	CL	32.90	40.00

YR	NAME	LIMIT	ISSUE	TREND
90	GREAT GREY OWL, THE	CL	34.90	36.00
90	SCREECH OWL, THE	CL	32.90	33.00
90	SHORT-EARED OWL, THE	CL	32.90	35.00
91	SAW-WHET OWL, THE	CL	34.90	35.00
H. SUNDBLOM			**SUNDBLOM SANTAS**	
89	SANTA BY THE FIRE	CL	27.90	40.00
90	CHRISTMAS VIGIL	CL	27.90	45.00
91	TO ALL A GOOD NIGHT	CL	32.90	40.00
92	SANTA'S ON HIS WAY	CL	32.90	65.00
J. WELTY			**SWEETNESS AND GRACE**	
92	FAVORITE BUDDY	CL	34.90	35.00
92	GOD BLESS TEDDY	CL	34.90	40.00
92	SUNSHINE AND SMILES	CL	34.90	59.00
92	SWEET DREAMS	CL	34.90	35.00
M. KUNSTLER			**THE AMERICAN JOURNEY**	
87	WESTWARD HO	CL	29.90	35.00
88	CHRISTMAS AT THE NEW CABIN	CL	29.90	35.00
88	CROSSING THE RIVER	CL	29.90	35.00
88	KITCHEN WITH A VIEW	CL	29.90	35.00
H. INGMIRE			**THE COMFORTS OF HOME**	
92	CURIOUS PAIR	CL	24.90	25.00
92	SLEEPYHEADS	CL	24.90	25.00
93	A COZY FIRESIDE	CL	29.90	30.00
93	FELINE FROLIC	CL	29.90	30.00
93	MOTHER'S RETREAT	CL	27.90	28.00
93	PLAYTIME	CL	27.90	28.00
93	WASHDAY HELPERS	CL	29.90	30.00
93	WELCOME FRIENDS	CL	27.90	28.00
*			**THE DISNEY TREASURED MOMENTS COLLECTION**	
92	CINDERELLA	CL	29.90	30.00
92	SNOW WHITE & THE SEVEN DWARFS	CL	29.90	30.00
93	ALICE IN WONDERLAND	CL	32.90	33.00
93	BEAUTY AND THE BEAST	CL	34.90	35.00
93	JUNGLE BOOK, THE	CL	34.90	35.00
93	PETER PAN	CL	32.90	33.00
93	PINOCCHIO	CL	34.90	35.00
93	SLEEPING BEAUTY	CL	32.90	33.00
G. LAMBERT			**THE FOUR ANCIENT ELEMENTS**	
84	EARTH	CL	27.50	28.00
84	WATER	CL	27.50	28.00
85	AIR	CL	29.50	30.00
85	FIRE	CL	29.50	44.00
W. CHAMBERS			**THE KING AND I**	
84	A PUZZLEMENT	CL	19.50	30.00
85	GETTING TO KNOW YOU	CL	19.50	20.00
85	SHALL WE DANCE?	CL	19.50	35.00
85	WE KISS IN A SHADOW	CL	19.50	20.00
*			**THE LITTLE MERMAID**	
93	A SONG FROM THE SEA	CL	29.90	30.00
93	A VISIT TO THE SURFACE	CL	29.90	30.00
93	ARIEL'S TREASURED COLLECTION	CL	32.90	33.00
93	DADDY'S GIRL	CL	32.90	33.00
93	KISS THE GIRL	CL	32.90	33.00
93	UNDERWATER BUDDIES	CL	32.90	33.00
C. TENNANT			**THE OLD MILL STREAM**	
90	NEW LONDON GRIST MILL	CL	39.90	40.00
91	GLADE CREEK GRIST MILL	CL	39.90	45.00
91	OLD RED MILL	CL	39.90	45.00
91	WAYSIDE INN GRIST MILL	CL	39.90	45.00
E. LICEA			**THE STORY OF CHRISTMAS BY EVE LICEA**	
87	ANNUNCIATION, THE	YR	44.90	50.00
88	NATIVITY, THE	YR	44.90	50.00
89	ADORATION OF THE SHEPHERDS	YR	49.90	50.00
90	JOURNEY OF THE MAGI	YR	49.90	56.00
91	GIFTS OF THE MAGI	YR	49.90	52.00
92	REST ON THE FLIGHT INTO EQYPT	YR	49.90	51.00
T. KINKADE			**THOMASHIRE**	
92	OLD THOMASHIRE MILL	CL	29.90	30.00
92	OLDE PORTERFIELD TEA ROOM	CL	29.90	30.00
92	PYE CORNER COTTAGE	CL	32.90	33.00
92	SWANBROOK COTTAGE	CL	32.90	33.00
93	BLOSSOM HILL CHURCH	CL	32.90	33.00
93	OLDE GARDEN COTTAGE	CL	32.90	33.00
W. CHAMBERS			**TOM SAWYER**	
87	TOM AND BECKY	CL	27.90	30.00
87	TOM SAWYER THE PIRATE	CL	27.90	28.00
87	WHITEWASHING THE FENCE	CL	27.50	28.00
88	FIRST PIPES	CL	27.90	30.00
J. BEAUDOIN			**UNDER MOTHER'S WING**	
92	ARCTIC SPRING:SNOWY OWLS	CL	29.90	44.00
92	FOREST EDGE:GREAT GRAY OWLS	CL	29.90	35.00
92	LOFTY-LIMB:GREAT HORNED OWLS	CL	34.90	40.00
92	TREETOP TRIO:LONG EARED OWLS	CL	32.90	40.00
92	VAST VIEW:SAW WHET OWLS	CL	32.90	50.00
92	WOODLAND WATCH:SPOTTED OWLS	CL	32.90	60.00
93	HAPPY HOME:SHORT EARED OWL	CL	34.90	35.00
93	PERFECT PERCH:BARRED OWL	CL	34.90	35.00

YR	NAME	LIMIT	ISSUE	TREND
W. ANDERSON		**UPLAND BIRDS OF NORTH AMERICA**		
86	GROUSE, THE	CL	24.50	30.00
86	PHEASANT, THE	CL	24.50	25.00
87	GRAY PARTRIDGE, THE	CL	27.50	30.00
87	QUAIL, THE	CL	27.50	30.00
87	WILD TURKEY, THE	CL	27.50	28.00
87	WOODCOCK, THE	CL	27.90	28.00
J. WELTY		**WINDOWS OF GLORY**		
93	EVERLASTING FATHER, THE	CL	32.90	33.00
93	GOOD SHEPHERD, THE	CL	32.90	33.00
93	KING OF KINGS	CL	29.90	30.00
93	LIGHT OF THE WORLD, THE	CL	32.90	33.00
93	MESSIAH, THE	CL	32.90	33.00
93	PRINCE OF PEACE	CL	29.90	30.00
J. AUCKLAND		**WIZARD OF OZ**		
77	OVER THE RAINBOW	CL	19.00	43.00
78	IF I ONLY HAD A BRAIN	CL	19.00	70.00
78	IF I ONLY HAD A HEART	CL	19.00	40.00
78	IF I WERE KING OF THE FOREST	CL	19.00	45.00
79	FOLLOW THE YELLOW BRICK ROAD	CL	19.00	45.00
79	WICKED WITCH OF THE WEST	CL	19.00	45.00
79	WONDERFUL WIZARD OF OZ	CL	19.00	45.00
80	GRAND FINALE, THE	CL	24.00	50.00
R. LASLO		**WIZARD OF OZ: A NATIONAL TREASURE**		
91	YELLOW BRICK RD.	CL	29.90	57.00
92	I EVEN SCARE MYSELF	CL	32.90	33.00
92	I HAVEN'T GOT A BRAIN	CL	29.90	30.00
92	I'LL NEVER GET HOME	CL	34.90	35.00
92	I'M A LITTLE RUSTY YET	CL	32.90	33.00
92	I'M MELTING	CL	34.90	35.00
92	THERE'S NO PLACE LIKE HOME	CL	34.90	35.00
92	WE'RE OFF TO SEE THE WIZARD	CL	32.90	33.00
J. WILCOX SMITH		**YESTERDAY'S INNOCENTS**		
92	MY FIRST BOOK	CL	29.90	30.00
92	TIME TO SMELL THE ROSES	CL	29.90	53.00
93	HUSH, BABY'S SLEEPING	CL	32.90	45.00
93	READY AND WAITING	CL	32.90	49.00
T. KINKADE		**YULETIDE MEMORIES**		
92	A BEACON OF FAITH	CL	29.90	30.00
92	MAGIC OF CHRISTMAS, THE	CL	29.90	84.00
93	A WINTER'S TALK	CL	29.90	30.00
93	MOONLIT SLEIGHRIDE	CL	29.90	30.00
93	OLDE PORTERFIELD GIFT SHOPPE	CL	29.90	30.00
93	SILENT NIGHT	CL	29.90	30.00
93	SKATER'S DELIGHT	CL	29.90	30.00
93	WONDER OF THE SEASON, THE	CL	29.90	30.00

ENCHANTICA

YR	NAME	LIMIT	ISSUE	TREND
J. WOODWARD		**DRAGON COLLECTION**		
92	SPRING DRAGON-GORGOYLE	RT	50.00	65.00
92	WINTER DRAGON-GRAWLFANG	RT	50.00	65.00
93	AUTUMN DRAGON-SNARLGARD	RT	50.00	65.00
93	SUMMER DRAGON-ARANGAST	RT	50.00	65.00

ENESCO

YR	NAME	LIMIT	ISSUE	TREND
*		**BARBIE**		
94	35TH ANNIVERSARY	5000	30.00	30.00
94	HOLIDAY 1994	5000	30.00	30.00
P. HILLMAN		**CHERISHED TEDDIES**		
95	SANTA COOKIE 141585	*	25.00	25.00
95	SEASON OF JOY, THE 141550	YR	35.00	35.00
96	BEAR IN BUNNY OUTFIT DATED 1996 156590	YR	35.00	35.00
96	MOTHER'S DAY 156493	YR	35.00	35.00
96	SEASON OF PEACE, THE DATED 1996 176060	*	35.00	35.00
P. HILLMAN		**CHERISHED TEDDIES NURSERY RHYME PLATES**		
95	JACK AND JILL 114901	OP	35.00	35.00
95	LITTLE BO PEEP 164658	*	35.00	35.00
95	MARY HAD A LITTLE LAMB 128902	OP	35.00	35.00
95	MOTHER GOOSE/FRIENDS 170968	*	35.00	35.00
95	OLD KING COLE 135437	OP	35.00	35.00
95	WEE WILLIE WINKIE 170941	*	35.00	35.00
96	LITTLE JACK HORNER 151998	OP	35.00	35.00
96	LITTLE MISS MUFFET 145033	OP	35.00	35.00
P. HILLMAN		**CHERISHED TEDDIES ONCE UPON A TEDDY**		
95	GIRL IN GREEN DRESS	OP	35.00	35.00
96	EASTER	OP	35.00	35.00
P. HILLMAN		**CHERISHED TEDDIES VILLAGE**		
96	A PICNIC FOR TWO	*	45.00	45.00
*		**FROM BARBIE WITH LOVE**		
95	HAPPY HOLIDAYS BARBIE 1988 154180	YR	30.00	30.00
95	HAPPY HOLIDAYS BARBIE 1995 143154	YR	30.00	30.00
95	SOLO IN SPOTLIGHT. 1960 114383	5000	30.00	30.00
95	SOLO IN THE SPOTLIGHT 1960 173533	2500	100.00	100.00
96	1920'S FLAPPER BARBIE 174777	YR	30.00	30.00
96	A ROYAL SURPRISE, 1964 MINI 171050	*	12.50	12.50

YR	NAME	LIMIT	ISSUE	TREND
96	ARABIAN NIGHTS, 1964 MINI 171069	*	12.50	12.50
96	BARBIE AS SCARLETT O'HARA IN GREEN VELVE	10000	35.00	35.00
96	CINDERELLA, 1964 MINI 171042	*	12.50	12.50
96	ENCHANTED EVENING, 1960 185787	10000	100.00	100.00
96	GIBSON GIRL BARBIE 174769	10000	30.00	30.00
96	HAPPY HOLIDAY BARBIE 1996 188816	YR	30.00	30.00
96	HAPPY HOLIDAY BARBIE, 1989 188859	YR	30.00	30.00
96	HERE COMES THE BRIDE 170984	*	30.00	30.00
96	HOLIDAY DANCE 1965 188786	10000	100.00	100.00
96	QUEENS OF HEARTS BARBIE 157678	*	25.00	25.00
96	RED RIDING HOOD, 1964 MINI 171077	*	12.50	12.50
KINKA	**KINKA COLLECTOR PLAQUE**			
89	KINKA 119601	OP	10.00	10.00
M. RHYNER-NADIG	**MARY'S MOO MOOS MOOEY CHRISTMAS**			
96	WHEEE ARE MOVIN!	YR	17.50	17.50
M. ATTWELL	**MEMORIES OF YESTERDAY**			
93	LOOK OUT-SOMETHING GOOD..YOUR WAY!	YR	50.00	55.00
94	PLEASANT DREAMS & SWEET REPOSE	OP	50.00	55.00
95	JOIN ME FOR A LITTLE SONG	OP	50.00	50.00
M. ATTWELL	**MEMORIES OF YESTERDAY MEMBERS ONLY**			
95	5TH ANNIVERSAY SOCIETY PIN	OP	*	*
S. BUTCHER	**PRECIOUS MOMENTS**			
96	PEACH ON EARTH...ANYWAY 183377	YR	50.00	50.00
S. BUTCHER	**PRECIOUS MOMENTS -JOY OF CHRISTMAS**			
82	I'LL PLAY MY DRUM FOR HIM E2357	YR	40.00	75.00
S. BUTCHER	**PRECIOUS MOMENTS CHRISTMAS BLESSINGS**			
90	WISHING YOU A YUMMY CHRISTMAS 523801	YR	50.00	75.00
91	BLESSING FROM ME TO THEE 523860	YR	50.00	65.00
92	BUT THE GREATEST/LOVE 527742	YR	50.00	55.00
S. BUTCHER	**PRECIOUS MOMENTS CHRISTMAS COLLECTION**			
81	COME LET US ADORE HIM E-5646	15000	40.00	55.00
82	LET HEAVEN AND NATURE SING E-2347	15000	40.00	45.00
83	WEE THREE KINGS E-0538	15000	40.00	45.00
84	UNTO US A CHILD IS BORN E-5395	15000	40.00	45.00
S. BUTCHER	**PRECIOUS MOMENTS CHRISTMAS LOVE**			
86	I'M SENDING YOU A WHITE CHRISTMAS 101834	YR	45.00	60.00
87	MY PEACE I GIVE TO THEE 102954	YR	45.00	95.00
88	MERRY CHRISTMAS DEER 520284	YR	50.00	85.00
89	MAY YOUR CHRISTMAS BE/HAPPY HOME 523003	YR	50.00	60.00
S. BUTCHER	**PRECIOUS MOMENTS COLLECTION**			
92	WISHING YOU/SWEETEST CHRISTMAS 530204	YR	50.00	60.00
94	YOU'RE AS PRETTY AS A CHRISTMAS TREE	OP	50.00	50.00
95	HE COVERS THE EARTH W/HIS BEAUTY 142670	OP	50.00	50.00
S. BUTCHER	**PRECIOUS MOMENTS INSPIRED THOUGHTS**			
82	MAKE A JOYFUL NOISE E-7174	15000	40.00	50.00
83	I BELIEVE IN MIRACLES E-9257	15000	40.00	50.00
84	LOVE IS KIND E-2847	15000	40.00	50.00
85	LOVE ONE ANOTHER E-5215	15000	40.00	70.00
S. BUTCHER	**PRECIOUS MOMENTS JOY OF CHRISTMAS**			
82	I'LL PLAY MY DRUM FOR HIM E-2357	YR	40.00	90.00
83	CHRISTMASTIME IS FOR SHARING E-0505	YR	40.00	100.00
84	TELL ME THE STORY OF JESUS 15237	YR	40.00	100.00
84	WONDER OF CHRISTMAS, THE E-5396	YR	40.00	85.00
S. BUTCHER	**PRECIOUS MOMENTS MOTHER'S DAY**			
66	OF ALL THE MOTHERS....AS PRECIOUS AS MY	LE	50.00	50.00
93	THINKING OU YOU...REALLY..TO DO 531766	YR	50.00	55.00
95	HE HATH MADE EVERYTHING...TIME 2ND ED. 1	YR	50.00	50.00
S. BUTCHER	**PRECIOUS MOMENTS MOTHER'S LOVE**			
80	MOTHER SEW DEAR E-5217	15000	40.00	55.00
82	PURR-FECT GRANDMA, THE E-7173	15000	40.00	50.00
83	HAND THAT ROCKS THE FUTURE, THE E-9256	15000	40.00	50.00
84	LOVING THEY NEIGHBOR E2848	15000	40.00	45.00
84	LOVING THY NEIGHBOR E-2848	15000	40.00	50.00
S. BUTCHER	**PRECIOUS MOMENTS OPEN EDITIONS**			
81	LORD BLESS YOU AND KEEP YOU, THE E-5216	SU	30.00	40.00
82	JESUS LOVES ME E-9275	SU	30.00	45.00
82	JESUS LOVES ME E-9276	SU	30.00	45.00
82	OUR FIRST CHRISTMAS TOGETHER E-2378	SU	30.00	50.00
82	REJOICING WITH YOU E-7172	SU	30.00	45.00
94	BRING THE LITTLE ONES TO JESUS 531359	YR	50.00	55.00
S. BUTCHER	**PRECIOUS MOMENTS THE FOUR SEASONS SERIES**			
85	SUMMER'S JOY 12114	YR	40.00	60.00
85	VOICE OF SPRING, THE 12106	YR	40.00	75.00
86	AUTUMN'S PRAISE 12122	YR	40.00	50.00
86	WINTER'S SONG 12130	YR	40.00	60.00

FAIRMONT

YR	NAME	LIMIT	ISSUE	TREND
T. DEGRAZIA	**ARTISTS OF THE WORLD**			
76	FESTIVAL OF LIGHTS	OP	45.00	120.00
77	BELL OF HOPE	OP	45.00	43.00
78	LITTLE MADONNA	OP	45.00	50.00
79	NAVTITY, THE	OP	50.00	63.00
80	PRIME INDIAN DRUMMER	OP	50.00	61.00
81	LITTLE PRAYER ANGEL	OP	55.00	33.00
82	BLUE BOY	OP	60.00	34.00
83	HEAVENLY BLESSINGS	OP	65.00	24.00

YR	NAME	LIMIT	ISSUE	TREND
84	NAVAJO MADONNA	OP	65.00	27.00
85	SAGUARO DANCE	OP	65.00	40.00
T. DEGRAZIA		**ARTISTS OF THE WORLD/CHILDREN**		
78	FLOWER GIRL	OP	45.00	50.00
79	FLOWER BOY	OP	45.00	59.00
80	LITTLE COCOPAH INDIAN GIRL	OP	50.00	65.00
81	BEAUTIFUL BURDEN	OP	50.00	59.00
82	MERRY LITTLE INDIAN	OP	55.00	85.00
83	WONDERING	OP	60.00	27.00
84	PINK PAPOOSE	OP	65.00	24.00
84	SUNFLOWER BOY	OP	65.00	32.00
85	MY FIRST HORSE	OP	65.00	65.00
86	GIRL AT SEWING MACHINE	OP	65.00	65.00
87	LOVE ME	OP	65.00	60.00
88	MERRILY, MERRILY, MERRILY	OP	65.00	65.00
89	MY FIRST ARROWN	OP	65.00	83.00
90	AWAY WITH MY KITE	OP	65.00	80.00
R. SKELTON			**FAMOUS CLOWNS**	
76	FREDDIE THE FREELOADER	10000	55.00	500.00
77	W.C. FIELDS	10000	55.00	90.00
78	HAPPY	10000	55.00	80.00
79	PLEDGE, THE	10000	55.00	70.00
79	PLEDGE, THE	OP	55.00	62.00
I. SPENCER			**SPENCER SPECIAL**	
78	HUG ME	10000	55.00	155.00
78	SLEEP LITTLE BABY	10000	65.00	130.00

FENTON ART GLASS

YR	NAME	LIMIT	ISSUE	TREND
*		**AMERICAN CRAFTSMAN CARNIVAL**		
70	GLASSMAKER	200	10.00	225.00
70	GLASSMAKER	600	10.00	145.00
70	GLASSMAKER	YR	10.00	70.00
71	PRINTER	YR	10.00	85.00
72	BLACKSMITH	YR	10.00	155.00
73	SHOEMAKER	YR	12.50	75.00
74	COOPER	YR	12.50	60.00
75	SILVERSMITH REVERE	YR	12.50	65.00
76	GUNSMITH	YR	15.00	50.00
77	POTTER	YR	15.00	40.00
78	WHEELWRIGHT	YR	15.00	30.00
79	CABINETMAKER	YR	15.00	25.00
80	TANNER	YR	16.50	25.00
81	HOUSEWRIGHT	YR	17.50	20.00
D. JOHNSON			**BIRDS OF WINTER ED. I**	
87	PLATE W/STAND 7418BC 8"	4500	39.50	40.00
D. JOHNSON			**BIRDS OF WINTER ED. II**	
88	PLATE W/STAND 7418BD 8"	4500	39.50	40.00
D. JOHNSON			**BIRDS OF WINTER ED. III**	
89	PLATE W/STAND 7418BL 8"	4500	39.50	40.00
D. JOHNSON			**BIRDS OF WINTER ED. IV**	
90	PLATE W/STAND 7418NB 8"	4500	39.50	40.00
F. BURTON			**CHRISTMAS AT HOME ED. I**	
90	PLATE W/STAND 7418HD 8"	3500	45.00	45.00
F. BURTON			**CHRISTMAS AT HOME ED. II**	
90	PLATE W/ STAND 7418HJ 8"	3500	45.00	45.00
F. BURTON			**CHRISTMAS AT HOME ED. III**	
92	PLATE W/STAND 7418HQ 8"	3500	49.00	49.00
F. BURTON			**CHRISTMAS AT HOME ED. IV**	
93	PLATE W/STAND 7418HT	3500	49.00	49.00
K. CUNNINGHAM			**CHRISTMAS CLASSICS ED. II**	
79	PLATE, 7418NC 8"	*	35.00	35.00
D. JOHNSON			**CHRISTMAS CLASSICS ED. III**	
80	PLATE 7418GH 8"	*	38.50	39.00
D. JOHNSON			**CHRISTMAS CLASSICS ED. IV**	
81	PLATE 7418AC 8"	*	42.50	43.00
R. SPINDLER			**CHRISTMAS CLASSICS ED. V**	
82	PLATE 7418OC 8"	*	42.50	43.00
D. JOHNSON			**CHRISTMAS FANTASY ED. I**	
83	PLATE 7418AI 8"	7500	45.00	45.00
D. JOHNSON			**CHRISTMAS FANTASY ED. II**	
84	PLATE 7418GE 8"	7500	50.00	50.00
D. JOHNSON			**CHRISTMAS FANTASY ED. III**	
85	PLATE 7418WP 8"	7500	50.00	50.00
L. EVERSON			**CHRISTMAS FANTASY ED. IV**	
87	PLATE 7418CV 8"	CL	50.00	50.00
F. BURTON			**CHRISTMAS STAR**	
94	SILENT NIGHT	1500	65.00	70.00
95	OUR HOME IS BLESSED W/STAND 7418VT 8"	1500	65.00	65.00
F. BURTON			**CHRISTMAS STAR ED. III**	
96	PLATE 7418SN 8"	1750	65.00	65.00
M. REYNOLDS			**EASTER LIMITED EDITIONS**	
95	COVERED HEND & EGG 5188YZ	950	95.00	95.00
M. REYNOLDS			**HANDPAINTED MOTHER'S DAY**	
80	NEW BORN	CL	28.50	30.00
81	GENTLE FAWN	CL	32.50	35.00

YR	NAME	LIMIT	ISSUE	TREND
82	NATURES AWAKENING	CL	35.00	40.00
83	WHERE'S MOM	CL	35.00	40.00
84	PRECIOUS PANDA	CL	35.00	40.00
85	MOTHER'S LITTLE LAMB	CL	35.00	40.00
90	WHITE SWAN	CL	45.00	50.00
91	MOTHER'S WATCHFUL EYE	CL	45.00	50.00
92	LET'S PLAY WITH MOM	CL	49.50	50.00
93	MOTHER DEER	CL	49.50	50.00
94	LOVING PUPPY	CL	49.50	50.00
*			**HISTORICAL COLLECTION**	
91	CAKEPLATE 4671BO 11 1/4"	*	39.50	40.00
91	PLATE 4611DT 12"	*	35.00	35.00
M. REYNOLDS			**MARY GREGORY**	
94	PLATE W/STAND 8319RY	CL	65.00	65.00
95	PLATE W/STAND 8319RG 9"	CL	65.00	65.00

FITZ & FLOYD

YR	NAME	LIMIT	ISSUE	TREND
R. HAVINS			**ANNUAL CHRISTMAS PLATE**	
92	THE MAGIC OF THE NUTCRACKER	CL	65.00	70.00
T. KERR			**ANNUAL CHRISTMAS PLATE**	
93	A DICKENS CHRISTMAS	5000	75.00	80.00
94	NIGHT BEFORE CHRISTMAS	7500	75.00	80.00
R. HAVINS			**THE MYTH OF SANTA CLAUS**	
93	FATHER FROST	5000	70.00	75.00
94	CANDYLAND SANTA	5000	75.00	80.00
R. HAVINS			**THE TWELVE DAYS OF CHRISTMAS**	
93	TWELVE DAYS OF CHRISTMAS	5000	75.00	80.00
R. HAVINS			**WONDERLAND**	
93	A MAD TEA PARTY	5000	70.00	75.00

FLAMBRO

YR	NAME	LIMIT	ISSUE	TREND
*			**EMMETT KELLY JR.**	
95	ALL WRAPPED UP IN CHRISTMAS	5000	30.00	30.00
C. KELLY			**EMMETT KELLY JR.**	
83	WHY ME?-PLATE I	10000	40.00	455.00
84	BALLOONS FOR SALE-PLATE II	10000	40.00	355.00
85	BIG BUSINESS-PLATE III	10000	40.00	355.00
86	AND GOD BLESS AMERICA-PLATE IV	10000	40.00	330.00
D. RUST			**EMMETT KELLY JR.**	
88	TIS THE SEASON	10000	50.00	80.00
89	LOOKING BACK-65TH BIRTHDAY	6500	50.00	130.00
91	WINTER	10000	60.00	50.00
92	AUTUMN	10000	60.00	50.00
92	SPRING	10000	60.00	50.00
92	SUMMER	10000	60.00	50.00
93	SANTA'S STOWAWAY	10000	30.00	35.00
94	70TH BIRTHDAY COMMEMORATIVE	5000	30.00	35.00
C. BEYLON			**RAGGEDY ANN & ANDY**	
88	70 YEARS YOUNG	10000	35.00	35.00

FOUNTAINHEAD

YR	NAME	LIMIT	ISSUE	TREND
M. FERNANDEZ			**AS FREE AS THE WIND**	
89	AS FREE AS THE WIND	*	295.00	450.00
M. FERNANDEZ			**THE SEASONS**	
86	FALL CARDINALS	5000	85.00	85.00
87	SPRING ROBINS	5000	85.00	85.00
87	SUMMER GOLDFINCHES	5000	85.00	85.00
87	WINTER CHICKADEES	5000	85.00	85.00
M. FERNANDEZ			**THE TWELVE DAYS OF CHRISTMAS**	
88	A PARTRIDGE IN A PEAR TREE	7500	155.00	155.00
88	TWO TURTLE DOVES	7500	*	*
89	FOUR CALLING BIRDS	7500	*	*
89	THREE FRENCH HENS	7500	155.00	155.00
M. FERNANDEZ			**THE WINGS OF FREEDOM**	
85	COURTSHIP FLIGHT	2500	250.00	1650.00
86	WINGS OF FREEDOM	2500	250.00	1100.00

FRANKLIN MINT

YR	NAME	LIMIT	ISSUE	TREND
N. MATTHEWS				
95	KITTEN COMPANIONS	45 DAYS	55.00	55.00
T. POLITOWICZ				
95	IMPERIAL HUMMINGBIRD, THE	45 DAYS	29.95	30.00

GARTLAN USA

YR	NAME	LIMIT	ISSUE	TREND
M./J. TAYLOR			**AL BARLICK**	
91	PLATE	15	*	20.00
M./J. TAYLOR			**BOB COUSY COLLECTION**	
93	PLATE 3 1/4"	OP	15.00	20.00
93	PLATE 8 1/2"	5000	30.00	40.00
93	SIGNED PLATE 10 1/4"	950	100.00	130.00
94	BOB COUSY 10 1/4"	RT	175.00	200.00
94	BOB COUSY 3 1/4"	OP	15.00	15.00
94	BOB COUSY 8 1/4"	5000	30.00	30.00

YR	NAME	LIMIT	ISSUE	TREND
M. TAYLOR				**BRETT & BOBBY HULL**
91	HOCKEY'S GOLDEN BOYS 3 1/4"	OP	15.00	25.00
91	HOCKEY'S GOLDEN BOYS 8 1/2"	10000	30.00	40.00
91	HOCKEY'S GOLDEN BOYS SIGNED 10 1/4"	950	250.00	255.00
92	PLATE A/P	300	350.00	355.00
M. TAYLOR				**CARL YASTRZEMSKI-THE IMPOSSIBLE DREAM**
93	PLATE 3 1/4"	OP	15.00	20.00
93	PLATE 8 1/2"	10000	30.00	40.00
93	SIGNED PLATE 10 1/4"	950	150.00	165.00
M. TAYLOR				**CARLTON FISK**
92	PLATE 3 1/4"	OP	15.00	20.00
92	PLATE 8 1/2"	10000	30.00	35.00
92	SIGNED PLATE 10 1/4"	950	70.00	110.00
92	SIGNED PLATE, A/P 10 1/4"	300	175.00	230.00
M. TAYLOR				**COACHING CLASSICS-JOHN WOODEN**
89	COLLECTOR PLATE 3 1/4"	OP	15.00	20.00
89	COLLECTOR PLATE 8 1/2"	10000	30.00	35.00
89	COLLECTOR PLATE, SIGNED 10 1/4"	1975	100.00	105.00
M. TAYLOR				**DALE EARNHARDT**
95	PLATE 3 1/4"	OP	14.95	15.00
95	PLATE 8 1/2"	10000	29.95	30.00
95	SIGNED PLATE 10 1/4"	1994	150.00	155.00
M. TAYLOR				**DARRYL STRAWBERRY**
90	PLATE 3 1/4"	OP	15.00	20.00
90	PLATE 8 1/2"	10000	30.00	50.00
90	SIGNED PLATE 10 1/4"	2500	70.00	130.00
M. TAYLOR				**FRANK THOMAS**
94	PLATE 3 1/4"	OP	14.95	15.00
94	PLATE 8 1/2"	10000	29.95	30.00
94	SIGNED PLATE 10 1/4"	1994	150.00	155.00
J. MARTIN				**GEORGE BRETT GOLD CROWN COLLECTION**
86	GEORGE BRETT, BASEBALL ALL STAR 3 1/4"	OP	12.95	25.00
86	GEORGE BRETT, SIGNED 10 1/4"	2000	100.00	205.00
M. TAYLOR				**GORDIE HOWE**
92	SIGNED PLATE 10 1/4"	2358	90.00	120.00
92	SIGNED PLATE 3 1/4"	OP	15.00	20.00
92	SIGNED PLATE 8 1/2"	10000	30.00	40.00
92	SIGNED PLATE, A/P 10 1/4"	250	150.00	175.00
M. TAYLOR				**JOE MONTANA**
91	PLATE 3 1/4"	OP	15.00	20.00
91	PLATE 8 1/2"	10000	30.00	40.00
91	SIGNED PLATE 10 1/4"	2250	125.00	130.00
91	SIGNED PLATE, A/P 10 1/4"	250	195.00	200.00
94	PLATE, K.C. CHIEFS 3 1/4"	OP	14.95	15.00
94	PLATE, K.C. CHIEFS 8 1/2"	10000	29.95	30.00
M. TAYLOR				**JOHNNY BENCH**
89	COLLECTOR PLATE 3 1/4"	OP	15.00	20.00
89	COLLECTOR PLATE, SIGNED 10 1/4"	1989	100.00	205.00
M. TAYLOR				**KAREEM ABDUL-JABBAR SKY-HOOK COLLECTION**
89	COLLECTOR PLATE 3 1/4"	CL	16.00	35.00
89	KAREEM ABDUL-JABBAR, SIGNED 10 1/4"	1989	100.00	210.00
M. TAYLOR				**KEN GRIFFEY JR.**
92	PLATE 3 1/4"	OP	15.00	20.00
92	PLATE 8 1/2"	10000	30.00	40.00
92	SIGNED PLATE 10 1/4"	1989	100.00	115.00
92	SIGNED PLATE, A/P 10 1/2"	300	195.00	200.00
M./J. TAYLOR				**KRISTI YAMAGUCHI COLLECTION**
93	KRISTI YAMAGUCHI 8 1/4"	5000	30.00	30.00
93	KRISTI YAMAGUCHI 10 1/4"	50	150.00	200.00
93	KRISTI YAMAGUCHI 3 1/4"	OP	15.00	15.00
93	PLATE 3 1/4"	OP	15.00	20.00
93	PLATE 8 1/2"	5000	30.00	40.00
93	SIGNED PLATE 10 1/4"	950	100.00	130.00
M. TAYLOR				**LEAVE IT TO BEAVER/JERRY MATHERS**
95	LEAVE IT TO BEAVER 10 1/4"	1963	125.00	125.00
95	LEAVE IT TO BEAVER 10 1/4" AP	234	175.00	175.00
95	LEAVE IT TO BEAVER 3 1/4"	OP	15.00	15.00
95	LEAVE IT TO BEAVER 8 1/4"	10000	40.00	40.00
M. TAYLOR				**LUIS APARICIO**
90	PLATE 3 1/4"	OP	15.00	25.00
90	PLATE 8 1/2"	10000	30.00	50.00
90	SIGNED PLATE 10 1/4"	1984	70.00	130.00
90	SIGNED PLATE, A/P 10 1/4"	250	150.00	155.00
R. WINSLOW				**MAGIC JOHNSON GOLD RIM COLLECTION**
87	MAGIC JOHNSON-THE MAGIC SHOW	CL	14.50	30.00
87	MAGIC JOHNSON-THE MAGIC SHOW SIGNED	1987	100.00	450.00
C. PALUSO				**MIKE SCHMIDT 500TH HOME RUN EDITION**
87	MIKE SCHMIDT (A/P)	56	150.00	155.00
87	MIKE SCHMIDT H/S DATED	50	100.00	600.00
87	MIKE SCHMIDT-POWER AT THE PLATE	OP	14.50	20.00
87	MIKE SCHMIDT-POWER AT THE PLATE SIGNED	1987	100.00	400.00
M. TAYLOR				**PATRICK EWING**
95	PLATE 3 1/4"	OP	14.95	15.00
95	PLATE 8 1/2"	10000	29.95	30.00
95	SIGNED PLATE 10 1/4"	950	150.00	155.00

YR	NAME	LIMIT	ISSUE	TREND
B. FORBES		**PETE ROSE DIAMOND COLLECTION**		
88	PETE ROSE SIGNED A/P 10 1/4"	50	300.00	400.00
88	PETE ROSE-THE REIGNING LEGEND 3 1/4"	OP	14.50	20.00
88	PETE ROSE-THE REIGNING LEGEND SIGNED	950	195.00	285.00
T. SIZEMORE		**PETE ROSE PLATINUM EDITION**		
85	PETE ROSE "THE BEST OF BASEBALL"	4192	100.00	400.00
85	PETE ROSE H/S DATED	50	100.00	680.00
85	PETE ROSE-THE BEST OF BASEBALL 3 1/4"	OP	12.95	25.00
M. TAYLOR				**PHIL ESPOSITO**
92	PLATE 3 1/4"	OP	15.00	20.00
92	PLATE 8 1/2"	10000	30.00	40.00
92	SIGNED PLATE 10 1/4"	1984	150.00	155.00
92	SIGNED PLATE, A/P 10 1/2"	300	195.00	200.00
M. TAYLOR				**RINGO STARR**
96	RINGO STARR 10 1/4" AP	250	400.00	400.00
96	RINGO STARR 10"	1000	225.00	225.00
96	RINGO STARR 3 3/4" MINI	OP	15.00	15.00
96	RINGO STARR 8 1/4"	10000	30.00	30.00
M. TAYLOR				**ROD CAREW**
91	HITTING FOR THE HALL 3 1/4"	OP	15.00	25.00
91	HITTING FOR THE HALL 8 1/2"	10000	30.00	50.00
91	HITTING FOR THE HALL, SIGNED	950	70.00	155.00
C. SOILEAU		**ROGER STAUBACH STERLING COLLECTION**		
87	ROGER STAUBACH 3 1/4"	OP	12.95	25.00
87	ROGER STAUBACH, SIGNED 10 1/4"	1979	100.00	160.00
M./J. TAYLOR			**SAM SNEAD COLLECTION**	
93	PLATE 3 1/2"	OP	15.00	20.00
93	PLATE 8 1/2"	5000	30.00	40.00
93	SIGNED PLATE 10 1/4"	950	100.00	140.00
94	SAM SNEAD 10 1/4"	50	100.00	200.00
94	SAM SNEAD 3 1/4"	OP	15.00	15.00
94	SAM SNEAD 8 1/4"	5000	30.00	30.00
M. TAYLOR			**SHAQUILLE O'NEAL**	
94	PLATE 3 1/4"	OP	14.95	15.00
94	PLATE 8 1/2"	10000	30.00	40.00
94	SIGNED PLATE 10 1/4"	1993	195.00	200.00
M. TAYLOR		**SHAQUILLE O'NEAL CLUB PLATE**		
94	SHAQUILLE O'NEAL	*	30.00	50.00
J. MARTIN			**THE ROUND TRIPPER**	
86	REGGIE JACKSON 3 1/4"	OP	12.95	25.00
M. TAYLOR				**TOM SEAVER**
92	SIGNED PLATE 10 1/4"	1992	90.00	120.00
92	SIGNED PLATE 3 1/4"	OP	15.00	20.00
92	SIGNED PLATE 8 1/2"	10000	30.00	40.00
92	SIGNED PLATE, A/P 10 1/4"	250	195.00	200.00
M. TAYLOR				**TROY AIKMAN**
94	PLATE 3 1/2"	OP	14.95	15.00
94	PLATE 8 1/2"	10000	30.00	40.00
94	SIGNED PLATE 10 1/4"	1993	150.00	155.00
95	TROY AIKMAN 10 1/4" AUTOGRAPHED	SO	125.00	200.00
95	TROY AIKMAN 8 1/4"	10000	30.00	30.00
95	TROY AIKMAN MINI 3 1/4"	OP	15.00	15.00
M. TAYLOR				**WAYNE GRETZKY**
89	COLLECTOR PLATE	300	300.00	430.00
89	COLLECTOR PLATE 3 1/4"	OP	15.00	25.00
89	COLLECTOR PLATE 8 1/2"	10000	45.00	55.00
89	COLLECTOR PLATE, H/S BY GRETZKY & HOWE	1851	225.00	290.00
M. TAYLOR				**WHITEY FORD**
90	PLATE 3 1/4"	OP	15.00	20.00
90	PLATE 8 1/2"	10000	30.00	40.00
90	SIGNED PLATE 10 1/4"	2360	70.00	110.00
90	SIGNED PLATE, A/P 10 1/4"	250	175.00	180.00
M. TAYLOR				**YOGI BERRA**
89	COLLECTOR PLATE 3 1/4"	OP	15.00	25.00
89	COLLECTOR PLATE 8 1/2"	10000	30.00	40.00
89	COLLECTOR PLATE, SIGNED 10 1/4"	2150	100.00	125.00
89	COLLECTOR PLATE,SIGNED A/P 10 1/4"	250	175.00	180.00

GEORGETOWN COLLECTION INC.

YR	NAME	LIMIT	ISSUE	TREND
C. THEROUX		**CHILDREN OF THE GREAT SPIRIT**		
93	BUFFALO CHILD	CL	29.95	35.00
93	WINTER BABY	CL	29.95	35.00

GHENT COLLECTION

YR	NAME	LIMIT	ISSUE	TREND
E. BIERLY		**AMERICAN BICENTENNIAL WILDLIFE**		
76	AMERICAN WHITETAIL DEER	2500	95.00	95.00
C. FRACE		**AMERICAN BICENTENNIAL WILDLIFE**		
76	AMERICAN BISON	2500	95.00	95.00
A. GILBERT		**AMERICAN BICENTENNIAL WILDLIFE**		
76	AMERICAN WILD TURKEY	2500	95.00	95.00
H. MOELLER		**AMERICAN BICENTENNIAL WILDLIFE**		
76	AMERICAN BALD EAGLE	2500	95.00	95.00
N. ROCKWELL			**APRIL FOOL ANNUAL**	
78	APRIL FOOL	10000	35.00	60.00
79	APRIL FOOL	10000	35.00	35.00
80	APRIL FOOL	10000	37.50	45.00

GOEBEL INC.

Price ranges may reflect various demands in the market from one geographic region to another; condition of piece; specific markings found on piece; and/or changes in production of piece.

YR	NAME	LIMIT	ISSUE	TREND
*	GUIDING ANGEL	*	47.50	59.00
*	TENDER WATCH	*	47.50	59.00
75	ANNIVERSARY PLATE 1975	*	100.00	125.00
80	ANNIVERSARY PLATE 1980	*	225.00	50.00
85	ANNIVERSARY PLATE 1985	*	225.00	250.00
	M.I. HUMMEL			
95	FESTIVAL HARMONY WITH FLUTE 1995	YR	127.00	129.00
95	FRIENDS FOREVER	OP	210.00	215.00
96	CHRISTMAS SONG	*	130.00	130.00
96	WINTER MELODY	*	195.00	195.00
	M.I. HUMMEL			**ANNUAL PLATE**
95	COME BACK SOON	CL	250.00	250.00
	M.I. HUMMEL			**FIGURAL CHRISTMAS PLATES**
95	FESTIVAL HARMONY W/FLUTE	*	125.00	125.00
96	CHRISTMAS SONG	*	130.00	139.00
	M.I. HUMMEL			**FOUR SEASONS ANNUAL PLATE**
96	WINTER MELODY	*	195.00	195.00
	M.I. HUMMEL			**FRIENDS FOREVER**
92	MEDITATION HUM-292	CL	180.00	190.00
93	FOR FATHER HUM-293	CL	195.00	200.00
94	SWEET GREETINGS PLATE HUM-294	CL	205.00	210.00
95	SURPRISE	YR	210.00	225.00
95	SURPRISE PLATE HUM-295	OP	210.00	210.00
	M.I. HUMMEL			**LITTLE MUSIC MAKER**
84	LITTLE FIDDLER HUM-744	CL	30.00	60.00
85	SERENADE HUM-741	CL	30.00	60.00
86	SOLOIST HUM-743	CL	35.00	60.00
87	BAND LEADER HUM-742	CL	40.00	100.00
	M.I. HUMMEL			
96	CHRISTMAS SONG	OP	130.00	130.00
96	WINTER MELODY	OP	195.00	195.00
	M.I. HUMMEL			**M.I. HUMMEL ANNIVERSARY PLATES**
75	STORMY WEATHER HUM-280	CL	100.00	100.00
80	RING AROUND THE ROSIE HUM-281	CL	225.00	225.00
85	AUF WIEDERSEHEN HUM-282	CL	225.00	250.00
	M.I. HUMMEL			**M.I. HUMMEL ANNUAL COLLECTIBLE PLATES**
71	HEAVENLY ANGEL HUM-264	CL	25.00	600.00
72	HEAR YE, HEAR YE HUM-265	CL	30.00	40.00
73	GLOBE TROTTER HUM-266	CL	32.50	75.00
74	GOOSE GIRL HUM-267	CL	40.00	50.00
75	RIDE INTO CHRISTMAS HUM-268	CL	50.00	40.00
76	APPLE TREE GIRL HUM-269	CL	50.00	50.00
77	APPLE TREE BOY HUM-270	CL	52.50	80.00
78	HAPPY PASTIME HUM-271	CL	65.00	40.00
79	SINGING LESSON HUM-272	CL	90.00	30.00
80	SCHOOL GIRL HUM-273	CL	100.00	44.00
81	UMBRELLA BOY HUM-274	CL	100.00	45.00
82	UMBRELLA GIRL HUM-275	CL	100.00	125.00
83	ANNUAL PLATE, 1995 COME BK SOON HUM-291	OP	250.00	250.00
83	POSTMAN HUM-276	CL	108.00	193.00
84	LITTLE HELPER HUM-277	CL	108.00	83.00
85	CHICK GIRL HUM-278	CL	110.00	94.00
86	PLAYMATES HUM-279	CL	125.00	165.00
87	FEEDING TIME HUM-283	CL	135.00	400.00
88	LITTLE GOAT HERDER HUM-284	CL	145.00	100.00
89	FARM BOY HUM-285	CL	160.00	130.00
90	SHEPHERD'S BOY HUM-286	CL	170.00	250.00
91	JUST RESTING HUM-287	CL	196.00	149.00
92	WAYSIDE HARMONY HUM-288	CL	210.00	268.00
93	DOLL BATH HUM-289	CL	210.00	320.00
94	DOCTOR HUM-290	CL	225.00	250.00
95	COME BACK SOON	YR	250.00	250.00
	M.I. HUMMEL			**M.I. HUMMEL CHRISTMAS PLATES**
87	CELESTIAL MUSICIAN	20000	35.00	69.00
88	ANGEL DUET	20000	40.00	50.00
89	GUIDING LIGHT	20000	*	75.00
90	TENDER WATCH	20000	*	75.00
	M.I. HUMMEL			**M.I. HUMMEL CLUB EXCLUSIVE-CELEBRATION**
86	VALENTINE GIFT HUM-738	CL	90.00	125.00
87	VALENTINE JOY HUM-737	CL	98.00	149.00
88	DAISIES DON'T TELL HUM-736	CL	115.00	140.00
89	IT'S COLD HUM-735	CL	120.00	140.00
	M.I. HUMMEL			**M.I. HUMMEL PLAQUES**
47	M.I. HUMMEL PLAQUES (IN ENGLISH) HUM-187	CL	*	175.00-1500.00
49	M.I. HUMMEL DEALER'S PLAQ FRENCH HUM-208	CL	*	5000.00-7000.00
54	STAR GLAZER, WALL PLAQUE HUM-237	CL	*	12500.00
68	MERRY WANDERER WALL PLAQUE HUM-263	CL	*	12500.00
93	ARTIST PLAQUE HUM-756	CL	260.00	325.00
95	PUPPY LOVE, DISPLAY PLAQUE HUM-767	OP	240.00	240.00
	M.I. HUMMEL			**M.I. HUMMEL PLAQUES - SPANISH VERSION**
86	GOEBEL AUTHORIZED RETAILER PLAQ. HUM-460	OP	*	300.00-1500.00
	M.I. HUMMEL			**M.I. HUMMEL PLAQUES - SWEDISH VERSION**
86	GOEBEL AUTHORIZED RETAILER PLAQ. HUM-460	OP	*	300.00-1000.00

Andalusian *by Fred Stone from "The Stallion Series" by American Artists was issued in 1983. Limited to 12,500, it is currently valued at $125.*

Issued in 1986, Lesley *was the third release in the "Country Series" by Jan Hagara, an artist known for her elegantly dressed Victorian-era children.*

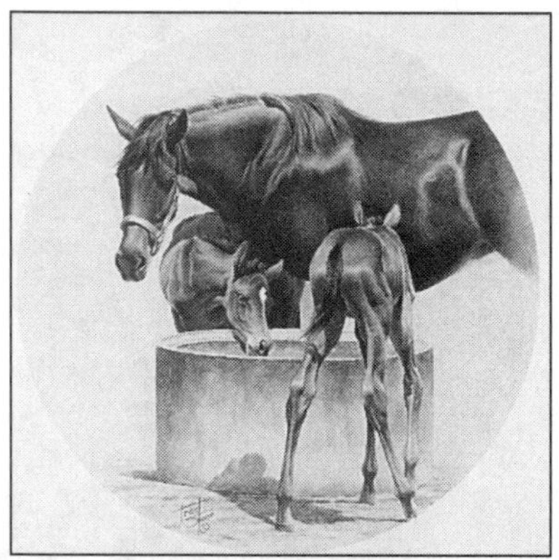

Equine artist Fred Stone is capable of capturing perfectly the sinewy stance of a horse from any angle. In The Water Trough, *first in the "Mare & Foal" series, Stone also captures the special bond between a mother and her young foal. Produced by Artaffects.*

First in the "Sport of Kings" series from American Artists is Man O' War *by Fred Stone. The 1984 plate depicts the famous race horse and the groom Will Harbut, Man O'War's constant companion for 17 years, until the two died within two weeks of each other.*

Early Riser *by P.D. Jackson is produced by Reco.*

YR	NAME	LIMIT	ISSUE	TREND
	M.I. HUMMEL			**M.I. HUMMEL PLAQUES IN SPANISH**
51	M.I. HUMMEL DEALER'S PLAQ SPAN. HUM-213	CL	*	8000.00-12000.00
	M.I. HUMMEL			**M.I. HUMMEL PLAQUES MADE IN GERMANY**
49	M.I. HUMMEL DEALER'S PLAQ GERMAN HUM-205	CL	*	850.00-1700.00
	M.I. HUMMEL			**M.I. HUMMEL PLAQUES MADE IN SWEDISH**
49	M.I. HUMMEL DEALER'S PLAQ SWED. HUM-209	CL	*	5000.00-7000.00
	M.I. HUMMEL			**M.I. HUMMEL PLAQUES SCHMID BROS.**
35	M.I. HUMMEL DEALER'S PLAQ/SCHMID HUM-210	CL	*	20000.00-25000.00
	M.I. HUMMRL			**M.I. HUMMEL PLAQUES- BRITISH VERSION**
86	GOEBEL AUTHORIZED RETAILER PLAQ. HUM-460	OP	*	300.00-750.00
	M.I. HUMMEL			**M.I. HUMMEL PLAQUES- DUTCH VERSION**
86	GOEBEL AUTHORIZED RETAILER PLAQ. HUM-460	OP	*	300.00-1500.00
	M.I. HUMMEL			**M.I. HUMMEL PLAQUES- FRENCH VERISON**
86	GOEBEL AUTHORIZED RETAILER PLAQ. HUM-460	OP	*	300.00-1000.00
	M.I. HUMMEL			**M.I. HUMMEL PLAQUES- GERMAN VERSION**
86	GOEBEL AUTHORIZED RETAILER PLAQ. HUM-460	OP	*	300.00-1000.00
	M.I. HUMMEL			**M.I. HUMMEL PLAQUES- ITALIAN VERSION**
86	GOEBEL AUTHORIZED RETAILER PLAQ. HUM-460	OP	*	300.00-1500.00
	M.I. HUMMEL			**M.I. HUMMEL PLAQUES- U.S. VERSION**
86	GOEBEL AUTHORIZED RETAILER PLAQ. HUM-460	CL	*	225.00
	M.I. HUMMEL			**MAIL ORDER**
91	KITCHEN MOULD COLLECTION HUM-669	CL	99.00	150.00
91	KITCHEN MOULD COLLECTION HUM-671	CL	99.00	150.00
91	KITCHEN MOULD COLLECTION HUM-672	CL	99.00	150.00
91	KITCHEN MOULD COLLECTON HUM-670	CL	99.00	150.00
	M.I. HUMMEL			**THE LITTLE HOMEMAKERS**
88	LITTLE SWEEPER HUM-745	CL	45.00	60.00
89	WASH DAY HUM-746	CL	50.00	60.00
90	A STITCH IN TIME HUM-747	CL	50.00	60.00
91	CHICKEN LICKEN HUM-748	CL	70.00	60.00

GORHAM

Price ranges may reflect various demands in the market from one geographic region to another; condition of piece; specific markings found on piece; and/or changes in production of piece.

YR	NAME	LIMIT	ISSUE	TREND
	N. ROCKWELL			**A BOY AND HIS DOG FOUR SEASONS PLATES**
71	ADVENTURES BETWEEN ADVENTURES (SET)	YR	*	*
71	BOY MEETS HIS DOG	YR	50.00	145.00
71	MYSTERIOUS MALADY, THE (SET)	YR	*	*
71	PRIDE OF PARENTHOOD (SET)	YR	*	*
	N. ROCKWELL			**A HELPING HAND FOUR SEASONS PLATES**
79	CLOSED FOR BUSINESS (SET)	YR	*	*
79	COAL SEASON'S COMING (SET)	YR	*	*
79	SWATTER'S RIGHTS (SET)	YR	*	*
79	YEAR END COURT	YR	100.00	50.00
	R. DONNELLY			**AMERICAN ARTIST COLLECTION**
76	APACHE MOTHER & CHILD	9800	25.00	60.00
	BARRYMORE			**BARRYMORE**
71	QUIET WATERS	15000	25.00	30.00
72	LITTLE BOATYARD, STERLING	1000	100.00	150.00
72	NANTUCKET, STERLING	1000	100.00	105.00
72	SAN PEDRO HARBOR	15000	25.00	30.00
	N. ROCKWELL			**BAS RELIEF**
81	BEGUILING BUTTERCUP	UD	62.50	75.00
81	SWEET SONG SO YOUNG	UD	100.00	105.00
82	FLOWERS IN TENDER BLOOM	UD	100.00	105.00
82	FLYING HIGH	UD	62.50	70.00
	N. ROCKWELL			**BOY SCOUT PLATES**
75	OUR HERITAGE	18500	19.50	45.00
76	A SCOUT IS LOYAL	18500	19.50	60.00
77	A GOOD SIGN	18500	19.50	55.00
77	SCOUTMASTER, THE	18500	19.50	65.00
78	CAMPFIRE STORY	18500	19.50	30.00
78	POINTING THE WAY	18500	19.50	55.00
80	BEYOND THE EASEL	18500	45.00	50.00
	C. RUSSELL			**CHARLES RUSSELL**
80	IN WITHOUT KNOCKING	9800	38.00	80.00
81	BRONC TO BREAKFAST	9800	38.00	95.00
82	WHEN IGNORANCE IS BLISS	9800	45.00	95.00
83	COWBOY LIFE	9800	45.00	105.00
	GORHAM			**CHINA BICENTENNIAL**
72	1776 PLATE	18500	17.50	40.00
76	1776 BICENTENNIAL	8000	17.50	40.00
	N. ROCKWELL			**CHRISTMAS**
74	TINY TIM	YR	12.50	40.00
75	GOOD DEEDS	YR	17.50	40.00
76	CHRISTMAS TRIO	YR	19.50	25.00
77	YULETIDE RECKONING	YR	19.50	35.00
78	PLANNING CHRISTMAS VISIT	YR	24.50	30.00
79	SANTA'S HELPERS	YR	24.50	30.00
80	LETTER TO SANTA	YR	27.50	35.00
81	SANTA PLANS HIS VISIT	YR	29.50	55.00
82	JOLLY COACHMAN	YR	29.50	35.00
83	CHRISTMAS DANCERS	YR	29.50	40.00
84	CHRISTMAS MEDLEY	17500	29.95	35.00
85	HOME FOR THE HOLIDAYS	17500	29.95	35.00

YR	NAME	LIMIT	ISSUE	TREND
86	MERRY CHRISTMAS GRANDMA	17500	29.95	70.00
87	HOMECOMING, THE	17500	35.00	55.00
88	DISCOVERY	17500	37.50	40.00
*		**CHRISTMAS/CHILDREN'S TELEVISION WORKSHOP**		
81	SESAME STREET CHRISTMAS	YR	17.50	20.00
82	SESAME STREET CHRISTMAS	YR	17.50	20.00
83	SESAME STREET CHRISTMAS	YR	19.50	25.00
N. ROCKWELL		**DAD'S BOYS FOUR SEASONS PLATES**		
80	CAREFUL AIM (SET)	YR	*	*
80	IN HIS SPIRITS (SET)	YR	*	*
80	SKI SKILLS	YR	135.00	105.00
80	TROUT DINNER (SET)	YR	*	*
T. DEGRAZIA		**DEGRAZIACHILDREN**		
76	LOS NINOS	OP	35.00	675.00
77	WHITE DOVE, THE	OP	40.00	40.00-75.00
J. CLYMER		**ENCOUNTERS, SURVIVAL AND CELEBRATIONS**		
82	A FINE WELCOME	7500	50.00	80.00
83	ALOUETTE	7500	62.50	70.00
83	TRADER, THE	7500	62.50	70.00
83	TRAPPER TAKES A WIFE, THE	7500	62.50	70.00
83	WINTER CAMP	7500	62.50	80.00
83	WINTER TRAIL	7500	50.00	130.00
N. ROCKWELL		**FOUR AGES OF LOVE**		
73	FLOWERS IN TENDER BLOOM (SET)	YR	*	*
73	FONDLY WE DO REMEMBER (SET)	YR	*	*
73	GAILY SHARING VINTAGE TIME	YR	60.00	170.00
73	SWEET SONG SO YOUNG (SET)	YR	*	*
*		**FOUR SEASONS**		
71	BOY AND HIS DOG	OP	50.00	50.00-224.00
72	YOUNG LOVE	OP	60.00	60.00-100.00
73	AGES OF LOVE	OP	60.00	60.00-165.00
74	GRANDPA AND ME	OP	60.00	70.00
75	ME AND MY PAL	OP	70.00	85.00
76	GRAND PALS	OP	70.00	85.00
77	GOING ON SIXTEEN	OP	75.00	85.00
78	TENDER YEARS	OP	100.00	100.00
79	A HELPING HAND	OP	100.00	100.00
80	DAD'S BOY	OP	135.00	89.00
N. ROCKWELL		**FOUR SEASONS LANDSCAPES**		
80	SUMMER RESPITE	YR	45.00	85.00
81	AUTUMN REFLECTION	YR	45.00	70.00
82	WINTER DELIGHT	YR	50.00	70.00
83	SPRING RECESS	YR	60.00	65.00
REMBRANDT INSPIRED		**GALLERY OF MASTERS**		
71	MAN WITH A GILT HELMET	10000	50.00	55.00
72	SELF PORTRAIT WITH SASKIA	10000	50.00	55.00
73	HONORABLE MRS. GRAHAM, THE	7500	50.00	55.00
N. ROCKWELL		**GOING ON SIXTEEN FOUR SEASONS PLATES**		
77	CHILLING CHORE	YR	75.00	100.00
77	PILGRIMAGE (SET)	YR	*	*
77	SHEAR AGONY (SET)	YR	*	*
77	SWEET SERENADE (SET)	YR	*	*
GORHAM		**GORHAM MUSEUM DOLL PLATES**		
84	BELTON BEBE	5000	29.00	60.00
84	CHRISTMAS LADY	7500	32.50	40.00
84	LYDIA	5000	29.00	130.00
85	JUMEAU	5000	29.00	40.00
85	LUCILLE	5000	29.00	40.00
N. ROCKWELL		**GRAND PALS FOUR SEASONS PLATES**		
76	FISH FINDERS (SET)	YR	*	*
76	GHOSTLY GOURDS (SET)	YR	*	*
76	SNOW SCULPTURING	YR	70.00	125.00
76	SOARING SPIRITS (SET)	YR	*	*
N. ROCKWELL		**GRANDPA AND ME FOUR SEASONS PLATES**		
74	DAY DREAMERS (SET)	YR	*	*
74	GAY BLADES	YR	60.00	95.00
74	GOIN' FISHING (SET)	YR	*	*
74	PENSIVE PALS (SET)	YR	*	*
J. RITTER		**JULIAN RITTER**		
77	CHRISTMAS VISIT	9800	24.50	35.00
78	VALENTINE, FLUTTERING HEART	7500	45.00	50.00
J. RITTER		**JULIAN RITTER, FALL IN LOVE**		
77	ENCHANTMENT	5000	100.00	105.00
77	FROLIC (SET)	5000	*	*
77	GUTSY GAL (SET)	5000	*	*
77	LONELY CHILL (SET)	5000	*	*
J. RITTER		**JULIAN RITTER, TO LOVE A CLOWN**		
78	AWAITED REUNION	5000	120.00	125.00
78	SHOWTIME BECKONS	5000	120.00	125.00
78	TOGETHER IN MEMORIES	5000	120.00	125.00
78	TWOSOME TIME	5000	120.00	125.00
J.C. LEYENDECKER		**LEYENDECKER ANNUAL CHRISTMAS PLATES**		
88	CHRISTMAS HUG	10000	37.50	55.00
N. ROCKWELL		**LIFE WITH FATHER FOUR SEASONS PLATES**		
82	A TOUGH ONE (SET)	YR	*	*
82	BIG DECISION	YR	100.00	250.00

YR	NAME	LIMIT	ISSUE	TREND
82	BLASTING OUT (SET)	YR	*	*
82	CHEERING THE CHAMPS (SET)	YR	*	*
N. ROCKWELL		**ME AND MY PALS FOUR SEASONS PLATES**		
75	A LICKIN' GOOD BATH	YR	70.00	120.00
75	DISASTROUS DARING (SET)	YR	*	*
75	FISHERMAN'S PARADISE (SET)	YR	*	*
75	YOUNG MAN'S FANCY (SET)	YR	*	*
*		**MOPPET PLATES-ANNIVERSARY**		
76	MOPPET PLATE ANNIVERSARY	20000	13.00	20.00
*		**MOPPET PLATES-CHRISTMAS**		
73	MOPPET PLATE CHRISTMAS	YR	10.00	40.00
74	MOPPET PLATE CHRISTMAS	YR	12.00	20.00
75	MOPPET PLATE CHRISTMAS	YR	13.00	20.00
76	MOPPET PLATE CHRISTMAS	YR	13.00	20.00
77	MOPPET PLATE CHRISTMAS	YR	13.00	20.00
78	MOPPET PLATE CHRISTMAS	YR	10.00	15.00
79	MOPPET PLATE CHRISTMAS	YR	12.00	15.00
80	MOPPET PLATE CHRISTMAS	YR	12.00	20.00
81	MOPPET PLATE CHRISTMAS	YR	12.00	20.00
82	MOPPET PLATE CHRISTMAS	YR	12.00	15.00
83	MOPPET PLATE CHRISTMAS	YR	12.00	15.00
*		**MOPPET PLATES-MOTHER'S DAY**		
73	MOPPET PLATE MOTHER'S DAY	YR	10.00	35.00
74	MOPPET PLATE MOTHER'S DAY	YR	12.00	25.00
75	MOPPET PLATE MOTHER'S DAY	YR	13.00	20.00
76	MOPPET PLATE MOTHER'S DAY	YR	13.00	20.00
77	MOPPET PLATE MOTHER'S DAY	YR	13.00	20.00
78	MOPPET PLATE MOTHER'S DAY	YR	10.00	15.00
N. ROCKWELL		**OLD BUDDIES FOUR SEASONS PLATES**		
83	ENDLESS DEBATE (SET)	YR	*	*
83	FINAL SPEECH (SET)	YR	*	*
83	HASTY RETREAT (SET)	YR	*	*
83	SHARED SUCCESS	YR	115.00	120.00
N. ROCKWELL		**OLD TIMERS FOUR SEASONS PLATES**		
81	CANINE SOLO	YR	100.00	105.00
81	FANCY FOOTWORK (SET)	YR	*	*
81	LAZY DAYS (SET)	YR	*	*
81	SWEET SURPRISE (SET)	YR	*	*
B. FELDER		**PASTORAL SYMPHONY**		
*	HE LOVES ME	7500	42.50	55.00
82	GATHER THE CHILDREN	7500	42.50	55.00
82	WHEN I WAS A CHILD	7500	42.50	55.00
84	SUGAR AND SPICE	7500	42.50	55.00
R. PAILTHORPE		**PEWTER BICENTENNIAL**		
71	BURNING OF THE GASPEE	5000	35.00	40.00
72	BOSTON TEA PARTY	5000	35.00	40.00
N. ROCKWELL		**PRESIDENTIAL**		
76	DWIGHT D. EISENHOWER	9800	30.00	40.00
76	JOHN F. KENNEDY	9800	30.00	70.00
F. REMINGTON		**REMINGTON WESTERN**		
73	A NEW YEAR ON THE CIMARRON	YR	25.00	40.00
73	AIDING A COMRADE	YR	25.00	80.00
73	FIGHT FOR THE WATER HOLE, THE	YR	25.00	80.00
73	FLIGHT, THE	YR	25.00	70.00
75	A BREED	YR	20.00	50.00
75	OLD RAMOND	YR	20.00	50.00
76	A TRAPPER	5000	37.50	70.00
76	CAVALRY OFFICER	5000	37.50	70.00
GORHAM		**SILVER BICENTENNIAL**		
72	1776 PLATE	500	500.00	500.00
R. PAILTHORPE		**SILVER BICENTENNIAL**		
72	BURNING OF THE GASPEE	750	500.00	500.00
73	BOSTON TEA PARTY	750	550.00	580.00
F. QUAGON		**SINGLE RELEASE**		
76	BLACK REGIMENT, THE 1778	7500	25.00	60.00
N. ROCKWELL		**SINGLE RELEASE**		
74	GOLDEN RULE, THE	YR	12.50	35.00
74	WEIGHING IN	YR	12.50	90.00
75	BEN FRANKLIN	YR	19.50	40.00
76	MARRIAGE LICENSE, THE	*	37.50	60.00
78	TRIPLE SELF PORTRAIT MEMORIAL PLATE	YR	37.50	65.00
80	ANNUAL VISIT, THE	YR	32.50	75.00
81	DAY IN LIFE OF BOY	YR	50.00	85.00
81	DAY IN LIFE OF GIRL	YR	50.00	105.00
N. ROCKWELL		**TENDER YEARS FOUR SEASONS PLATES**		
78	CHILLY RECEPTION (SET)	YR	*	*
78	COOL AID (SET)	YR	*	*
78	NEW YEAR LOOK	YR	100.00	75.00
78	SPRING TONIC (SET)	YR	*	*
B. PORT		**TIME MACHINE TEDDIES PLATES**		
86	MISS EMILY, BEARING UP	5000	32.50	40.00
87	BIG BEAR, THE TOY COLLECTOR	5000	32.50	50.00
88	HUNNY MUNNY	5000	37.50	40.00
GORHAM		**VERMEIL BICENTENNIAL**		
72	1776 PLATE	250	750.00	800.00

YR	NAME	LIMIT	ISSUE	TREND
	N. ROCKWELL	**YOUNG LOVE FOUR SEASONS PLATES**		
72	A SCHOLARLY PACE (SET)	YR	*	*
72	BEGUILING BUTTERCUP (SET)	YR	*	*
72	DOWNHILL DARING	YR	60.00	130.00
72	FLYING HIGH (SET)	YR	*	*

GRANDE COPENHAGEN

YR	NAME	LIMIT	ISSUE	TREND
*		**CHRISTMAS**		
75	ALONE TOGETHER	UD	24.50	25.00
76	CHRISTMAS WREATH	UD	24.50	30.00
77	FISHWIVES AT GAMMELSTRAND	UD	26.50	30.00
78	HANS CHRISTIAN ANDERSON	UD	32.50	38.00
79	PHEASANTS	UD	34.50	53.00
80	SNOW QUEEN IN THE TIVOLI	UD	39.50	40.00
81	LITTLE MATCH GIRL IN NYHAVN	UD	42.50	43.00
82	SHEPHERDESS/CHIMNEY SWEEP	UD	45.00	55.00
83	LITTLE MERMAID NEAR KRONBORG	UD	45.00	115.00
84	SANDMAN AT AMALIENBORG	UD	45.00	60.00

H & G STUDIOS

YR	NAME	LIMIT	ISSUE	TREND
	B. BURKE	**ANNUAL MOTHER'S DAY PLATE**		
96	A MOTHER'S JOY	7500	39.00	39.00
	B. BURKE	**CHRISTMAS MEMORIES**		
95	CHRISTMAS PRESENTS	7500	39.00	39.00
	D. PATRICK LEWAN	**CITY OF BEARS**		
95	BEARY PATCH PARK	7500	35.00	35.00
	A. MURRAY	**GENTLE HEARTS**		
95	A PROMISE KEPT	5000	35.00	35.00
	D. PATRICK LEWAN	**OVAL PLATE**		
95	VICTORIAN COUNTRY HOME	5000	39.00	39.00
	D. PATRICK LEWAN	**VICTORIAN TREASURES**		
95	VICTORIAN DREAMS	7500	35.00	35.00
96	VICTORIAN ROMANCE	7500	35.00	35.00
	S. CEPELLO	**WOLVES & WARRIORS**		
95	SPIRIT TRAIL	7500	35.00	35.00

HACKETT AMERICAN

YR	NAME	LIMIT	ISSUE	TREND
	ALEXANDER	**SPORTS**		
*	ARNOLD PALMER H/S	RT	125.00	230.00
*	GARY PLAYER H/S	RT	125.00	400.00
*	REGGIE JACKSON, PROOF	RT	250.00	*
86	JOE MONTANA D/S	RT	125.00	800.00
	PALUSO	**SPORTS**		
81	REGGIE JACKSON H/S	RT	100.00	900.00
82	STEVE GARVEY H/S	RT	100.00	160.00
83	NOLAN RYAN H/S	RT	100.00	800.00
83	TOM SEAVER H/S	RT	100.00	330.00
84	STEVE CARLTON H/S	RT	100.00	270.00
85	E. MATHEWS D/S	RT	125.00	230.00
85	H. KILLEBREW D/S	RT	125.00	330.00
85	HANK AARON H/S	RT	125.00	300.00
85	SANDY KOUFAX H/S	RT	125.00	385.00
85	WHITEY FORD H/S	RT	125.00	300.00
85	WILLIE MAYS H/S	RT	125.00	335.00
86	DON SUTTON D/S	RT	125.00	330.00
86	REGGIE JACKSON D/S	RT	125.00	400.00
86	ROGER CLEMENS D/S	RT	125.00	600.00
86	TOM SEAVER 300 D/S	RT	125.00	255.00
86	WALLY JOYNER D/S	RT	125.00	300.00
	SIMON	**SPORTS**		
*	DWIGHT GOODEN U/S	RT	55.00	105.00
*	GARY CARTON D/S	RT	125.00	180.00

HADLEY COMPANIES

YR	NAME	LIMIT	ISSUE	TREND
	T. REDLIN	**AMERICAN MEMORIES**		
87	COMING HOME	9500	85.00	90.00
88	LIGHTS OF HOME	9500	85.00	90.00
89	HOMEWARD BOUND	9500	85.00	90.00
91	FAMILY TRADITIONS	9500	85.00	90.00
	T. REDLIN	**ANNUAL CHRISTMAS**		
91	HEADING HOME	9500	65.00	70.00
92	PLEASURES OF WINTER	19500	65.00	70.00
93	WINTER WONDERLAND	19500	65.00	70.00
95	SHARING THE EVENING	45 DAYS	29.95	30.00
	T. REDLIN	**COUNTRY DOCTOR COLLECTION**		
95	HOUSE CALLS	45 DAYS	29.95	30.00
95	MORNING ROUNDS	45 DAYS	30.00	30.00
95	OFFICE HOURS	45 DAYS	29.95	30.00
95	WEDNESDAY AFTERNOON	45 DAYS	29.95	30.00
	S. HANKS	**DAYS OF INNOCENCE**		
95	DUET	45 DAYS	29.95	30.00
	T. REDLIN	**GLOW SERIES**		
85	EVENING GLOW	5000	55.00	475.00
85	MORNING GLOW	5000	55.00	225.00
85	TWILIGHT GLOW	5000	55.00	105.00
88	AFTERNOON GLOW	5000	55.00	60.00

YR	NAME	LIMIT	ISSUE	TREND
	D. BARNHOUSE			**HEARTLAND COLLECTION**
95	REPAIRS	45 DAYS	29.95	30.00
	M. CAPSER			**HEARTLAND COLLECTION**
95	PICKETS AND VINES	45 DAYS	29.95	30.00
	S. HAMRICK			**HEARTLAND COLLECTION**
95	BIRD'S EYE VIEW	45 DAYS	29.95	30.00
	T. REDLIN			**LOVERS COLLECTION**
92	LOVERS	9500	50.00	55.00
	T. REDLIN			**NAVAJO VISIONS SUITE**
93	NAVAJO FANTASY	5000	50.00	55.00
93	YOUNG WARRIOR	5000	50.00	55.00
	T. REDLIN			**NAVAJO WOMAN**
90	FEATHERED HAIR TIES	5000	50.00	55.00
91	NAVAJO SUMMER	5000	50.00	55.00
92	TURQUOISE NECKLACE	5000	50.00	55.00
93	PINK NAVAJO	5000	50.00	55.00
	T. REDLIN			**RETREAT**
87	EVENING RETREAT	9500	65.00	70.00
87	MORNING RETREAT	9500	65.00	105.00
88	GOLDEN RETREAT	9500	65.00	100.00
89	MOONLIGHT RETREAT	9500	65.00	70.00
	T. REDLIN			**SEASONS**
95	SPRING FEVER	45 DAYS	30.00	30.00
95	SUMMERTIME	45 DAYS	30.00	30.00
95	WINTERTIME	45 DAYS	29.95	30.00
	T. REDLIN			**THAT SPECIAL TIME**
91	EVENING SOLITUDE	9500	65.00	70.00
92	AROMA OF ALL	9500	65.00	70.00
93	WELCOME TO PARADISE	9500	65.00	70.00
	O. FRANCA			**TRANQUILITY SUITE**
95	NAVAJO MEDITATING	9500	50.00	50.00
	T. REDLIN			**WINDOWS TO THE WILD**
90	MASTER'S DOMAIN	9500	65.00	70.00
91	WINTER WINDBREAK	9500	65.00	70.00
92	EVENING COMPANY	9500	65.00	70.00
94	NIGHT MAPLING	9500	65.00	70.00

HALLMARK GALLERIES

YR	NAME	LIMIT	ISSUE	TREND
	L. VOTRUBA			
87	LIGHT SHINES AT CHRISTMAS 800QX481-7	YR	8.00	63.00
88	WAITING FOR SANTA 800QX406-1	YR	8.00	43.00
89	MORNING OF WONDER 825QX461-2	YR	8.25	27.00
91	LET IT SNOW!-5TH EDITION 875QX436-9	YR	8.75	23.00
	L. VOTRUBA			**COLLECTOR'S PLATE**
90	COOKIES FOR SANTA 875QX443-6	YR	8.75	25.00
92	SWEET HOLIDAY HARMONY 6TH ED. 875QX446-1	YR	8.75	24.00
	*			**EASTER COLLECTION**
95	COLLECTOR'S PLATE QEO 821-9	YR	7.95	15.00
	L. VOTRUBA			**EASTER COLLECTION**
96	KEEPING A SECRET QEO822-1	YR	7.95	8.00

HAMILTON COLLECTION

YR	NAME	LIMIT	ISSUE	TREND
	B.P. GUTMANN			**A CHILD'S BEST FRIEND**
85	GOING TO TOWN	CL	24.50	80.00
85	GOOD MORNING	CL	24.50	80.00
85	IN DISGRACE	CL	24.50	95.00
85	MINE	CL	24.50	95.00
85	ON THE UP AND UP	CL	24.50	90.00
85	REWARD, THE	CL	24.50	65.00
85	SYMPATHY	CL	24.50	60.00
85	WHO'S SLEEPY	CL	24.50	95.00
	J.M. VASS			**A COUNTRY SEASON OF HORSES**
90	A WINTER'S WALK	CL	29.50	30.00
90	AUTUMN GRANDEUR	CL	29.50	35.00
90	CLIFFSIDE BEAUTY	CL	29.50	30.00
90	CRISP COUNTRY MORNING	CL	29.50	30.00
90	FIRST DAY OF SPRING	CL	29.50	40.00
90	FROSTY MORNING	CL	29.50	30.00
90	RIVER RETREAT	CL	29.50	30.00
90	SUMMER SPLENDOR	CL	29.50	30.00
	N. NOEL			**A COUNTRY SUMMER**
85	BUTTERFLY BEAUTY	CL	29.50	40.00
85	GOLDEN PUPPY, THE	CL	29.50	35.00
86	MY BUNNY	CL	29.50	40.00
86	ROCKING CHAIR, THE	CL	29.50	40.00
88	PIGLET, THE	CL	29.50	35.00
88	TEAMMATES	CL	29.50	35.00
	M. HANSON			**A GARDEN SONG**
94	GOLDEN GLORIES	CL	29.50	30.00
94	IN FULL BLOOM	CL	29.50	30.00
94	WINTER'S SPLENDOR	CL	29.50	30.00
	L. MARTIN			**A LISI MARTIN CHRISTMAS**
92	SANTA'S LITTLES REINDEER	CL	29.50	30.00
93	A TASTE OF THE HOLIDAYS	CL	29.50	30.00
93	CHRISTMAS DREAMS	CL	29.50	30.00
93	CHRISTMAS STORY, THE	CL	29.50	30.00

YR	NAME	LIMIT	ISSUE	TREND
93	CHRISTMAS WATCH	CL	29.50	30.00
93	NIGHT BEFORE CHRISTMAS, THE	CL	29.50	30.00
93	NOT A CREATURE WAS STIRRING	CL	29.50	30.00
93	TRIMMING THE TREE	CL	29.50	30.00
P. HILLMAN		**A TREASURY OF CHERISHED TEDDIES**		
95	A NEW YEAR WITH OLD FRIENDS	CL	29.50	30.00
95	VALENTINES FOR YOU	CL	29.50	30.00
J. LAMB		**ALL IN A DAY'S WORK**		
94	DECOY DELIVERY	CL	29.50	30.00
94	LUNCH BREAK	CL	29.50	30.00
94	PUPPY PATROL	CL	29.50	30.00
94	WHERE'S THE FIRE?	CL	29.50	30.00
T. FREEMAN		**AMERICA'S GREATEST SAILING SHIPS**		
88	AMERICA	CL	29.50	50.00
88	BONHOMME RICHARD	CL	29.50	40.00
88	CHARLES W. MORGAN	CL	29.50	40.00
88	EAGLE	CL	29.50	50.00
88	ENTERPRISE	CL	29.50	40.00
88	GERTRUDE L. THEBAUD	CL	29.50	50.00
88	GREAT REPUBLIC	CL	29.50	40.00
88	U.S.S. CONSTITUTION	CL	29.50	40.00
D. PRECHTEL		**AMERICAN CIVIL WAR**		
90	ABRAHAM LINCOLN	CL	37.50	65.00
90	GENERAL ROBERT E. LEE	CL	37.50	80.00
90	GENERAL THOMAS "STONEWALL" JACKSON	CL	37.50	55.00
90	GENERALS GRANT AND LEE AT APPOMATTOX	CL	37.50	50.00
91	A LETTER FORM HOME	CL	37.50	65.00
91	GENERAL J.E.B. STUART	CL	37.50	50.00
91	GENERAL PHILIP SHERIDAN	CL	37.50	65.00
91	GOING HOME	CL	37.50	50.00
92	ASSEMBLING THE TROOP	CL	37.50	80.00
92	STANDING WATCH	CL	37.50	80.00
P.J. SWEANY		**AMERICAN ROSE GARDEN**		
88	AMERICAN SPIRIT	CL	29.50	30.00
88	PEACE ROSE	CL	29.50	30.00
89	AMERICAN HERITAGE	CL	29.50	40.00
89	BLUE MOON	CL	29.50	40.00
89	CORAL CLUSTER	CL	29.50	30.00
89	ECLIPSE	CL	29.50	30.00
89	PRESIDENT HERBERT HOOVER	CL	29.50	30.00
89	WHITE KNIGHT	CL	29.50	40.00
R. TANENBAUM		**ANDY GRIFFITH**		
92	A STARTING CONCLUSION	CL	29.50	30.00
92	SHERIFF ANDY TAYLOR	CL	29.50	30.00
93	AN EXPLOSIVE SITUATION	CL	29.50	30.00
93	AUNT BEE'S KITCHEN	CL	29.50	30.00
93	MAYBERRY SING-ALONG	CL	29.50	30.00
93	MEETING AUNT BEE	CL	29.50	30.00
93	OPIE'S BIG CATCH	CL	29.50	30.00
93	SURPRISE! SURPRISE!	CL	29.50	30.00
M. SUSINNO		**ANGLER'S PRIZE**		
91	AUTUMN BEAUTY	CL	29.50	40.00
91	BLUE RIBBON TROUT	CL	29.50	30.00
91	BRONZEBACK FIGHTER	CL	29.50	40.00
91	FRESHWATER BARRACUDA	CL	29.50	40.00
91	SUN DANCERS	CL	29.50	40.00
91	TROPHY BASS	CL	29.50	40.00
92	OLD MOONEYES	CL	29.50	40.00
92	SILVER KING	CL	29.50	30.00
*		**BEAUTY OF WINTER**		
92	SILENT NIGHT	CL	29.50	30.00
93	MOONLIGHT SLEIGHRIDE	CL	29.50	30.00
R. TANENBAUM		**BEST OF BASEBALL**		
93	EXCEPTIONAL BROOKS ROBINSON, THE	CL	29.50	30.00
93	EXTRAORDINARY LOU GEHRIG, THE	CL	29.50	30.00
93	GREAT WILLIE MAYS, THE	CL	29.50	30.00
93	IMMORTAL BABE RUTH, THE	CL	29.50	30.00
93	INCREDIBLE NOLAN RYAN, THE	CL	29.50	30.00
93	LEGENDARY MICKLE MANTLE, THE	CL	29.50	30.00
93	PHENOMENAL ROBERTO CLEMENTE, THE	CL	29.50	30.00
93	REMARKABLE JOHNNY BENCH, THE	CL	29.50	30.00
93	UNBEATABLE DUKE SNIDER, THE	CL	29.50	30.00
93	UNFORGETTABLE PHIL RIZZUTO, THE	CL	29.50	30.00
P./A. BIALOSKY		**BIALOSKY & FRIENDS**		
92	FAMILY ADDITION	CL	29.50	30.00
93	BREAKFAST IN BED	CL	29.50	30.00
93	HONEY FOR SALE	CL	29.50	30.00
93	LET'S GO FISHING	CL	29.50	30.00
93	MY FIRST TWO-WHEELER	CL	29.50	30.00
93	SLEIGH RIDE	CL	29.50	30.00
93	SWEETHEART	CL	29.50	30.00
93	U.S. MAIL	CL	29.50	30.00
D. MANNING		**BIG CATS OF THE WORLD**		
89	AFRICAN SHADE	CL	29.50	35.00
89	VIEW FROM ABOVE	CL	29.50	35.00
90	ABOVE THE TREETOPS	CL	29.50	35.00
90	DEEP IN THE JUNGLE	CL	29.50	35.00

YR	NAME	LIMIT	ISSUE	TREND
90	MOUNTAIN DWELLER	CL	29.50	35.00
90	ON THE PROWL	CL	29.50	35.00
90	SPIRIT OF THE MOUNTAIN	CL	29.50	35.00
90	SPOTTED SENTINEL	CL	29.50	35.00
J. CHENG		**BIRDS OF THE TEMPLE GARDENS**		
89	CRANES OF ETERNAL LIFE	CL	29.50	35.00
89	DOVES OF FIDELITY	CL	29.50	35.00
89	GOLDFINCHES OF VIRTUE	CL	29.50	35.00
89	HONORABLE SWALLOWS	CL	29.50	35.00
89	IMPERIAL GOLDCREST	CL	29.50	35.00
89	MAGPIES: BIRDS OF GOOD OMEN	CL	29.50	35.00
89	ORIENTAL WHITE EYES OF BEAUTY	CL	29.50	35.00
89	PHEASANTS OF GOOD FORTUNE	CL	29.50	35.00
B.P. GUTMANN		**BUNDLES OF JOY**		
88	A LITTLE BIT OF HEAVEN	CL	24.50	80.00
88	AWAKENING	CL	24.50	80.00
88	BILLY	CL	24.50	30.00
88	HAPPY DREAMS	CL	24.50	80.00
88	SUN KISSED	CL	24.50	30.00
88	SWEET INNOCENCE	CL	24.50	35.00
88	TASTING	CL	24.50	50.00
88	TOMMY	CL	24.50	35.00
P. SWEANY		**BUTTERFLY GARDEN**		
87	COMMON BLUE	CL	29.50	40.00
87	CRIMSON PATCHED LONGWING	CL	29.50	40.00
87	MONARCH	CL	29.50	40.00
87	ORANGE SULPHUR	CL	29.50	35.00
87	SPICEBUSH SWALLOWTAIL	CL	29.50	50.00
87	TIGER SWALLOWTAIL	CL	29.50	35.00
88	MORNING CLOAK	CL	29.50	35.00
88	RED ADMIRAL	CL	29.50	40.00
J. TIFT		**CALL OF THE NORTH**		
93	WINTER'S DAWN	CL	29.50	30.00
94	ARCTIC SECLUSION	CL	29.50	30.00
94	EVENING SILENCE	CL	29.50	30.00
94	FOREST TWILIGHT	CL	29.50	30.00
94	MOONLIT WILDERNESS	CL	29.50	30.00
94	SENTINELS OF THE SUMMIT	CL	29.50	30.00
94	SILENT SNOWFALL	CL	29.50	30.00
94	SNOWY WATCH	CL	29.50	30.00
R. CROSS		**CALL TO ADVENTURE**		
93	BOUNTY, THE	CL	29.50	30.00
93	USS CONSTITUTION	CL	29.50	30.00
94	BONHOMME RICHARD	CL	29.50	30.00
94	BOSTON	CL	29.50	30.00
94	GOLDEN WEST	CL	29.50	30.00
94	HANNAH	CL	29.50	30.00
94	IMPROVEMENT	CL	29.50	30.00
94	OLD NANTUCKET	CL	29.50	30.00
Q. LEMONDS		**CAMEO KITTENS**		
93	BLOSSOM	CL	29.50	30.00
93	CAT TAILS	CL	29.50	30.00
93	GINGER SNAP	CL	29.50	30.00
93	LADY BLUE	CL	29.50	30.00
93	TINY HEART STEALER	CL	29.50	30.00
94	SCOUT	CL	29.50	30.00
94	TIGER'S TEMPTATION	CL	29.50	30.00
94	WHISKER ANTICS	CL	29.50	30.00
*		**CAPTAIN JEAN-LUC PICARD WALL PLAQUE**		
94	CAPTAIN JEAN-LUC PICARD (AUTOGRAPHED)	5000	195.00	200.00
T. UTZ		**CAREFREE DAYS**		
82	AUTUMN WANDERER	CL	24.50	25.00
82	BATHTIME VISITOR	CL	24.50	35.00
82	BEST FRIENDS	CL	24.50	35.00
82	FEEDING TIME	CL	24.50	30.00
82	FIRST CATCH	CL	24.50	35.00
82	MONKEY BUSINESS	CL	24.50	30.00
82	NATURE HUNT	CL	24.50	30.00
82	TOUCHDOWN	CL	24.50	30.00
B.P. GUTMANN		**CHILDHOOD REFLECTIONS**		
91	FRIENDLY ENEMIES	CL	29.50	40.00
91	HARMONY	CL	29.50	80.00
91	KITTY'S BREAKFAST	CL	29.50	40.00
91	LITTLE MOTHER	CL	29.50	30.00
91	LULLABY	CL	29.50	40.00
91	OH! OH! A BUNNY	CL	29.50	30.00
91	SMILE, SMILE, SMILE	CL	29.50	40.00
91	THANK YOU, GOD	CL	29.50	40.00
D. CROOK		**CHILDREN OF THE AMERICAN FRONTIER**		
86	A LADY NEEDS A LITTLE PRIVACY	CL	24.50	45.00
86	DESPERADOES, THE	CL	24.50	30.00
86	IN TROUBLE AGAIN	CL	24.50	40.00
86	RIDERS WANTED	CL	24.50	35.00
86	TUBS AND SUDS	CL	24.50	30.00
87	A COWBOY'S DOWNFALL	CL	24.50	30.00
87	A SPECIAL PATIENT	CL	24.50	45.00
87	RUNAWAY BLUES	CL	24.50	30.00

YR	NAME	LIMIT	ISSUE	TREND
	M. GNATEK			**CIVIL WAR GENERALS**
94	GEORGE ARMSTRONG CUSTER	CL	29.50	30.00
94	J.E.B. STEWART	CL	29.50	30.00
94	JAMES LONGSTREET	CL	29.50	30.00
94	JOSHUA L. CHAMBERLAIN	CL	29.50	30.00
94	NATHAN BEDFORD FORREST	CL	29.50	30.00
94	ROBERT E. LEE	CL	29.50	30.00
	G. HINKE			**CLASSIC AMERICAN SANTAS**
93	A CHRISTMAS EVE VISITOR	CL	29.50	30.00
94	A CHRISTMAS CHORUS	CL	29.50	30.00
94	AN EXCITING CHRISTMAS EVE	CL	29.50	30.00
94	PREPARING THE SLEIGH	CL	29.50	30.00
94	REINDEER'S STABLE, THE	CL	29.50	30.00
94	REST YE MERRY GENTLEMEN	CL	29.50	30.00
94	SANTA'S CANDY KITCHEN	CL	29.50	30.00
94	UP ON THE ROOFTOP	CL	29.50	30.00
	M. LACOURCIERE			**CLASSIC CORVETTES**
94	1957 CORVETTE	CL	29.50	30.00
94	1963 CORVETTE	CL	29.50	30.00
94	1968 CORVETTE	CL	29.50	30.00
94	1986 CORVETTE	CL	29.50	30.00
	B. CHRISTIE			**CLASSIC SPORTING DOGS**
89	BEAGLES	CL	24.50	40.00
89	GOLDEN RETRIEVERS	CL	24.50	60.00
89	LABRADOR RETRIEVERS	CL	24.50	65.00
89	POINTERS	CL	24.50	35.00
89	SPRINGER SPANIELS	CL	24.50	45.00
90	BRITTANY SPANIELS	CL	24.50	50.00
90	GERMAN SHORT-HAIRED POINTERS	CL	24.50	60.00
90	IRISH SETTERS	CL	24.50	40.00
	K. MILNAZIK			**CLASSIC TV WESTERNS**
90	BONANZA	CL	29.50	60.00
90	LONE RANGER AND TONTO, THE	CL	29.50	70.00
90	ROY ROGERS AND DALE EVANS	CL	29.50	65.00
91	HAVE GUN, WILL TRAVEL	CL	29.50	50.00
91	HOPALONG CASSIDY	CL	29.50	65.00
91	RAWHIDE	CL	29.50	50.00
91	VIRGINIAN, THE	CL	29.50	70.00
91	WILD WILD WEST	CL	29.50	65.00
	H. BOND			**CORAL PARADISE**
89	LIVING OASIS, THE	CL	29.50	30.00
90	CARIBBEAN SPECTACLE	CL	29.50	30.00
90	FOREST BENEATH THE SEA	CL	29.50	30.00
90	MYSTERIES OF THE GALAPAGOS	CL	29.50	30.00
90	RICHES OF THE CORAL SEA	CL	29.50	30.00
90	SHIMMERING REEF DWELLERS	CL	29.50	40.00
90	TROPICAL PAGEANTRY	CL	29.50	40.00
90	UNDERSEA VILLAGE	CL	29.50	40.00
	K. GEORGE			**COTTAGE PUPPIES**
93	ENDEARING INNOCENCE	CL	29.50	30.00
93	LITTLE GARDENERS	CL	29.50	30.00
93	SPRINGTIME FANCY	CL	29.50	30.00
94	A GARDENING TRIO	CL	29.50	30.00
94	LAZY AFTERNOON	CL	29.50	30.00
94	PICNIC PLAYTIME	CL	29.50	30.00
94	SUMMERTIME PALS	CL	29.50	30.00
94	TAKING A BREAK	CL	29.50	30.00
	G. PERRILLO			**COUNCIL OF NATIONS**
91	STRENGTH OF THE SIOUX	CL	29.50	30.00
92	BOLDNESS OF THE SENECA	CL	29.50	30.00
92	COURAGE OF THE ARAPAHO	CL	29.50	30.00
92	DIGNITY OF THE NEZ PARCE	CL	29.50	30.00
92	NOBILITY OF THE ALGONQUI	CL	29.50	30.00
92	POWER OF THE BLACKFOOT	CL	29.50	30.00
92	PRIDE OF THE CHEYENNE	CL	29.50	30.00
92	WISDOM OF THE CHEROKEE	CL	29.50	30.00
	E. DERTNER			**COUNTRY GARDEN COTTAGES**
92	RIVERBANK COTTAGE	CL	29.50	30.00
92	SHEPHERD'S COTTAGE	CL	29.50	30.00
92	SUNDAY OUTING	CL	29.50	30.00
93	APRIL COTTAGE	CL	29.50	30.00
93	DAYDREAM COTTAGE	CL	29.50	30.00
93	GARDEN GLORIOUS	CL	29.50	30.00
93	SUMMER SYMPHONY	CL	29.50	30.00
93	THIS SIDE OF HEAVEN	CL	29.50	30.00
	G. GERARDI			**COUNTRY KITTIES**
89	ALL WASHED UP	CL	24.50	40.00
89	ATTIC ATTACK	CL	24.50	50.00
89	CAPTIVE AUDIENCE	CL	24.50	40.00
89	JUST FOR THE FERN OF IT	CL	24.50	35.00
89	MISCHIEF MAKERS	CL	24.50	50.00
89	ROCK AND ROLLERS	CL	24.50	35.00
89	STROLLER DERBY	CL	24.50	40.00
89	TABLE MANNERS	CL	24.50	40.00
	B. HARRISON			**CURIOUS KITTENS**
90	KEEPING IN STEP	CL	29.50	40.00
90	RAINY DAY FRIENDS	CL	29.50	40.00

YR	NAME	LIMIT	ISSUE	TREND
91	A PAW'S IN THE ACTION	CL	29.50	40.00
91	ALL WOUND UP	CL	29.50	40.00
91	CHANCE MEETING	CL	29.50	40.00
91	DELIGHTFUL DISCOVERY	CL	29.50	40.00
91	MAKING TRACKS	CL	29.50	40.00
91	PLAYING CAT AND MOUSE	CL	29.50	40.00
92	CAT BURGLAR	CL	29.50	40.00
92	LITTLE SCHOLAR	CL	29.50	40.00
K. THAYER				**DAUGHTERS OF THE SUN**
93	A SECRET GLANCE	CL	29.50	30.00
93	CHIPPEWA CHARMER	CL	29.50	30.00
93	DELIGHTED DANCER	CL	29.50	30.00
93	EVENING DANCER	CL	29.50	30.00
93	SHINING FEATHER	CL	29.50	30.00
93	SUN DANCER	CL	29.50	30.00
94	PRIDE OF YAKIMA	CL	29.50	30.00
94	RADIANT BEAUTY	CL	29.50	30.00
J. HAGARA				**DEAR TO MY HEART**
90	ADDIE	CL	29.50	30.00
90	CATHY	CL	29.50	30.00
90	DACY	CL	29.50	30.00
90	JIMMY	CL	29.50	30.00
90	PAUL	CL	29.50	30.00
91	JENNY	CL	29.50	30.00
91	JOY	CL	29.50	30.00
91	SHELLY	CL	29.50	30.00
J. LAMB				**DELIGHTS OF CHILDHOOD**
89	CRAYON CREATIONS	CL	29.50	35.00
89	LITTLE MOTHER	CL	29.50	35.00
90	BATHING BEAUTY	CL	29.50	35.00
90	IS THAT YOU, GRANNY?	CL	29.50	40.00
90	NATURE'S LITTLE HELPER	CL	29.50	35.00
90	SHOWER TIME	CL	29.50	40.00
90	SO SORRY	CL	29.50	40.00
90	STORYTIME FRIENDS	CL	29.50	35.00
K. HAYNES				**DREAMSICLES**
94	FLYING LESSON, THE	CL	19.50	20.00
R. TANENBAUM				**DRIVERS OF VICTORY LANE**
94	BILL ELLIOTT	CL	29.50	30.00
94	JEFF GORDON	CL	29.50	30.00
S. MORTON				**ELVIS REMEMBERED**
89	EARLY YEARS	CL	37.50	90.00
89	ELVIS PRESLEY	CL	37.50	125.00
89	FOREVER YOURS	CL	37.50	90.00
89	KING, THE	CL	37.50	100.00
89	LOVING YOU	CL	37.50	90.00
89	MOODY BLUES	CL	37.50	90.00
89	ROCKIN' IN THE MOONLIGHT	CL	37.50	90.00
89	TENDERLY	CL	37.50	90.00
J. ENRIGHT				**ENCHANTED SEASCAPES**
93	BLUE PARADISE	CL	29.50	30.00
93	SANCTUARY OF THE DOLPHIN	CL	29.50	30.00
94	EDGE OF TIME	CL	29.50	30.00
94	LOST BENEATH THE BLUE	CL	29.50	30.00
94	OASIS OF THE GODS	CL	29.50	30.00
94	RHAPSODY OF HOPE	CL	29.50	30.00
94	SEA OF LIGHT	CL	29.50	30.00
94	SPHERE OF LIFE	CL	29.50	30.00
M. BELL				**ENGLISH COUNTRY COTTAGES**
90	PERIWINKLE TEA ROOM	CL	29.50	50.00
91	CHAPLAIN'S GARDEN, THE	CL	29.50	40.00
91	GAMEKEEPER'S COTTAGE	CL	29.50	80.00
91	GINGER COTTAGE	CL	29.50	65.00
91	LARKSPUR COTTAGE	CL	29.50	50.00
91	LORNA DOONE COTTAGE	CL	29.50	50.00
91	LULLABYE COTTAGE	CL	29.50	40.00
91	MURRLE COTTAGE	CL	29.50	40.00
J. LAMB				**FARMYARD FRIENDS**
92	LITTLE COWHANDS	CL	29.50	30.00
92	MISTAKEN IDENTITY	CL	29.50	30.00
93	AN APPLE A DAY	CL	29.50	30.00
93	FOLLOW THE LEADER	CL	29.50	30.00
93	FOWL PLAY	CL	29.50	30.00
93	PARTNERS IN CRIME	CL	29.50	30.00
93	PONY TALES	CL	29.50	30.00
93	SHREADING THE EVIDENCE	CL	29.50	30.00
D. O'DRISCOLL				**FAVORITE AMERICAN SONGBIRDS**
89	BLUE JAYS OF SPRING	CL	29.50	40.00
89	GOLDFINCHES OF SUMMER	CL	29.50	40.00
89	RED CARDINALS OF WINTER	CL	29.50	40.00
89	ROBINS & APPLE BLOSSOMS	CL	29.50	40.00
90	AUTUMN CHICKADEES	CL	29.50	40.00
90	BLUEBIRDS AND MORNING GLORIES	CL	29.50	40.00
90	TUFTED TITMOUSE AND HOLLY	CL	29.50	30.00
91	CAROLINA WRENS OF SPRING	CL	29.50	30.00
T. BLACKSHEAR				**FIFTY YEARS OF OZ**
89	FIFTY YEARS OF OZ	CL	37.50	70.00

YR	NAME	LIMIT	ISSUE	TREND
*		**FIRST OFFICER SPORK WALL PLAQUE**		
94	FIRST OFFICER SPOCK (AUTOGRAPHED)	2500	195.00	200.00
J. DENEEN		**FORGING NEW FRONTIERS**		
94	BIG BOY	CL	29.50	30.00
94	CRESTING THE SUMMIT	CL	29.50	30.00
94	HIGH COUNTRY LOGGING	CL	29.50	30.00
94	RACE IS ON, THE	CL	29.50	30.00
94	SPRING ROUNDUP	CL	29.50	30.00
94	WINTER IN THE ROCKIES	CL	29.50	30.00
C. MICARELLI		**GLORY OF CHRIST**		
92	ASCENSION, THE	CL	29.50	30.00
92	JESUS TEACHING	CL	29.50	30.00
93	BAPTISM OF CHRIST, THE	CL	29.50	30.00
93	JESUS HEALS THE SICK	CL	29.50	30.00
93	LAST SUPPER	CL	29.50	30.00
93	NATIVITY, THE	CL	29.50	30.00
94	DESCENT FROM THE CROSS	CL	29.50	30.00
94	JESUS WALKS ON WATER	CL	29.50	30.00
T. FOGARTY		**GLORY OF THE GAME**		
94	B. THOMPSON'S SHOT HEARD ROUND THE WORLD	CL	29.50	30.00
94	HANK AARON'S RECORD-BREAKING HOME RUN	CL	29.50	30.00
T. XARAS		**GOLDEN AGE OF AMERICAN RAILROADS**		
91	ABOVE THE CANYON	CL	29.50	95.00
91	BIG BOY, THE	CL	29.50	65.00
91	BLUE COMET, THE	CL	29.50	50.00
91	EMPIRE BUILDER, THE	CL	29.50	65.00
91	MORNING LOCAL, THE	CL	29.50	65.00
91	PENNSYLVANIA K-4, THE	CL	29.50	95.00
91	PORTRAIT IN STEAM	CL	29.50	80.00
91	SANTA FE SUPER CHIEF, THE	CL	29.50	110.00
92	AN AMERICAN CLASSIC	CL	29.50	35.00
92	FINAL DESTINATION	CL	29.50	40.00
C. LAWSON		**GOLDEN CLASSICS**		
87	HANSEL AND GRETEL	CL	37.50	40.00
87	JACK AND THE BEANSTALK	CL	37.50	40.00
87	RUMPELSTILTSKIN	CL	37.50	40.00
87	SLEEPING BEAUTY	CL	37.50	40.00
87	SNOW WHITE AND ROSE RED	CL	37.50	40.00
88	CINDERELLA	CL	37.50	40.00
88	GOLDEN GOOSE, THE	CL	37.50	40.00
88	SNOW QUEEN, THE	CL	37.50	40.00
J. LAMB		**GOOD SPORTS**		
90	BASS MASTERS, THE	CL	29.50	40.00
90	DOUBLE PLAY	CL	29.50	40.00
90	HOLE IN ONE	CL	29.50	65.00
90	SLAP SHOT	CL	29.50	50.00
90	SPOTTED ON THE SIDELINE	CL	29.50	40.00
90	WIDE RETRIEVER	CL	29.50	50.00
91	BASSETBALL	CL	29.50	40.00
91	NET PLAY	CL	29.50	50.00
92	BOXER REBELLION	CL	29.50	30.00
92	GREAT TRY	CL	29.50	40.00
R. WADDEY		**GREAT FIGHTER PLANES OF WW II**		
92	BIG HOG	CL	29.50	30.00
92	F4F WILDCAT	CL	29.50	30.00
92	OLD CROW	CL	29.50	30.00
92	P-38F LIGHTNING	CL	29.50	30.00
92	P-40 FLYING TIGER	CL	29.50	30.00
92	P-47 THUNDERBOLT	CL	29.50	30.00
93	F6F HELLCAT	CL	29.50	30.00
93	P-39M AIRACOBRA	CL	29.50	30.00
WYLAND		**GREAT MAMMALS OF THE SEA**		
91	CHILDREN OF THE SEA	CL	35.00	65.00
91	DOLPHIN PARADISE	CL	35.00	50.00
91	HAWAII DOLPHINS	CL	35.00	40.00
91	ISLANDS	CL	35.00	65.00
91	KISSING DOLPHINS	CL	35.00	40.00
91	ORCA JOURNEY	CL	35.00	40.00
91	ORCA TRIO	CL	35.00	50.00
91	ORCAS	CL	35.00	50.00
F. MOODY		**GREATEST SHOW ON EARTH**		
81	AERIALISTS	CL	30.00	35.00
81	CLOWNS	CL	30.00	50.00
81	ELEPHANTS	CL	30.00	35.00
81	EQUESTRIANS	CL	30.00	35.00
81	GREAT PARADE	CL	30.00	35.00
81	MIDWAY	CL	30.00	35.00
82	GRANDE FINALE	CL	30.00	35.00
82	LION TAMER	CL	30.00	35.00
P. BROOKS		**GROWING UP TOGETHER**		
90	MY VERY BEST FRIENDS	CL	29.50	40.00
90	PICNIC PALS	CL	29.50	30.00
90	TEA FOR TWO	CL	29.50	30.00
90	TENDER LOVING CARE	CL	29.50	30.00
91	BEDTIME BLESSINGS	CL	29.50	30.00
91	FISHING BUDDIES	CL	29.50	30.00
91	KITTEN CABOODLE	CL	29.50	30.00

YR	NAME	LIMIT	ISSUE	TREND
91	NEWFOUND FRIENDS	CL	29.50	30.00
S. KUCK		**HEARTS AND FLOWERS**		
92	CAROUSEL OF DREAMS	120-DAY	32.50	33.00
J. KRITZ		**I LOVE LUCY PLATE COLLECTION**		
89	CALIFORNIA, HERE WE COME	CL	29.50	120.00
89	IT'S JUST LIKE CANDY	CL	29.50	100.00
90	BIG SQUEEZE, THE	CL	29.50	105.00
90	EATING THE EVIDENCE	CL	29.50	110.00
90	TWO OF A KIND	CL	29.50	70.00
91	QUEEN OF THE GYPSIES	CL	29.50	70.00
92	A RISING PROBLEM	CL	29.50	110.00
92	NIGHT AT THE COPA	CL	29.50	90.00
KOSEKI/EBIHARA		**JAPANESE BLOSSOMS OF AUTUMN**		
85	ARROWROOT	CL	45.00	50.00
85	BELLFLOWER	CL	45.00	50.00
85	BUSH CLOVER	CL	45.00	50.00
85	MAIDEN FLOWER	CL	45.00	50.00
85	PAMPAS GRASS	CL	45.00	50.00
85	PURPLE TROUSERS	CL	45.00	50.00
85	WILD CARNATION	CL	45.00	50.00
SHUHO/KAGE		**JAPANESE FLORAL CALENDAR**		
81	NEW YEAR'S DAY	CL	32.50	35.00
82	AUTUMN	CL	32.50	35.00
82	BOY'S DOLL DAY FESTIVAL	CL	32.50	35.00
82	BUDDHA'S BIRTHDAY	CL	32.50	35.00
82	EARLY SPRING	CL	32.50	35.00
82	EARLY SUMMER	CL	32.50	35.00
82	GIRL'S DOLL DAY FESTIVAL	CL	32.50	35.00
82	SPRING	CL	32.50	35.00
82	SUMMER	CL	32.50	35.00
83	FESTIVAL OF THE FULL MOON	CL	32.50	35.00
83	LATE AUTUMN	CL	32.50	35.00
83	WINTER	CL	32.50	35.00
J. LANDENBERGER		**JEWELED HUMMINGBIRDS PLATE COLLECTION**		
89	AMETHYST-THROATED HUMMINGBIRDS	CL	37.50	40.00
89	ANDEAN EMERALD HUMMINGBIRDS	CL	37.50	40.00
89	BLUE-HEADED SAPPHIRE HUMMINGBIRDS	CL	37.50	40.00
89	GARNET-THROATED HUMMINGBIRDS	CL	37.50	40.00
89	GREAT SAPPHIRE WING HUMMINGBIRDS	CL	37.50	40.00
89	PEARL CORONET HUMMINGBIRDS	CL	37.50	40.00
89	RUBY-THROATED HUMMINGBIRDS	CL	37.50	40.00
89	RUBY-TOPAZ HUMMINGBIRDS	CL	37.50	40.00
P. COOPER		**KITTEN CLASSICS**		
85	BIRDWATCHER	CL	29.50	30.00
85	CAT NAP	CL	29.50	40.00
85	COUNTRY KITTY	CL	29.50	30.00
85	FIRST PRIZE	CL	29.50	30.00
85	LITTLE RASCAL	CL	29.50	30.00
85	PURRFECT TREASURE	CL	29.50	30.00
85	TIGER'S FANCY	CL	29.50	30.00
85	WILD FLOWER	CL	29.50	30.00
C. REN		**LAST WARRIORS**		
93	LONE WINTER JOURNEY	CL	29.50	30.00
93	MORNING OF RECKONING	CL	29.50	30.00
93	TWILIGHTS LAST GLEAMING	CL	29.50	30.00
93	WINTER 'OF '41	CL	29.50	30.00
94	CONFRONTING DANGER	CL	29.50	30.00
94	SOLEMN REFLECTION	CL	29.50	30.00
94	SOLITARY HUNTER	CL	29.50	30.00
94	VICTORY'S REWARD	CL	29.50	30.00
V. DEZERIN		**LEGEND OF FATHER CHRISTMAS**		
94	FEAST OF THE HOLIDAY, THE	CL	29.50	30.00
94	GIFTS FROM FATHER CHRISTMAS	CL	29.50	30.00
94	RETURN OF FATHER CHRISTMAS, THE	CL	29.50	30.00
M. HUMPHREY BOGART		**LITTLE LADIES**		
89	PLAYING BRIDESMAID	CL	29.50	90.00
90	A DAY IN THE COUNTRY	CL	29.50	50.00
90	KITTY'S BATH	CL	29.50	60.00
90	LITTLE CAPTIVE	CL	29.50	50.00
90	PLAYING MAMA	CL	29.50	65.00
90	SEAMSTRESS, THE	CL	29.50	65.00
90	SUSANNA	CL	29.50	50.00
91	FIRST PARTY	CL	29.50	30.00
91	MAGIC KITTEN, THE	CL	29.50	30.00
91	SARAH	CL	29.50	50.00
*		**LITTLE RASCALS**		
85	BUTCH'S CHALLENGE	CL	24.50	30.00
85	DARLA'S DEBUT	CL	24.50	30.00
85	MY GAL	CL	24.50	50.00
85	PETE'S PAL	CL	24.50	30.00
85	ROUGHIN' IT	CL	24.50	50.00
85	SKELETON CREW	CL	24.50	30.00
85	SPANKY'S PRANKS	CL	24.50	30.00
85	THREE FOR THE SHOW	CL	24.50	40.00
G. GERARDI		**LITTLE SHOPKEEPERS**		
90	SEW TIRED	CL	29.50	30.00
91	BREAK TIME	CL	29.50	30.00

YR	NAME	LIMIT	ISSUE	TREND
91	CANDY CAPERS	CL	29.50	40.00
91	CHAIN REACTION	CL	29.50	50.00
91	INFERIOR DECORATORS	CL	29.50	40.00
91	PURRFECT FIT	CL	29.50	30.00
91	TOYING AROUND	CL	29.50	40.00
91	TULIP TAG	CL	29.50	40.00
L. DANIELLE				**LORE OF THE WEST**
93	A CHIEF'S PRIDE	CL	29.50	30.00
93	A MILE IN HIS MOCASSINS	CL	29.50	30.00
93	PATH OF HONOR	CL	29.50	30.00
94	GROWING UP BRAVE	CL	29.50	30.00
94	IN HER SEPS	CL	29.50	30.00
94	NOMADS OF THE SOUTHWEST	CL	29.50	30.00
94	PATHWAYS OF THE PUEBLO	CL	29.50	30.00
94	SACRED SPIRIT OF THE PLAINS	CL	29.50	30.00
M. WEISTLING				**LUCY COLLAGE**
93	LUCY	CL	37.50	80.00
S. BOTTICELLI				**MADONNA AND CHILD**
93	MADONNA COL BAMBINO	CL	37.50	40.00
93	MADONNA DEL MAGNIFICAT	CL	37.50	40.00
A. CORREGGIO				**MADONNA AND CHILD**
93	VIRGIN ADORING CHRIST CHILD	CL	37.50	40.00
L. DAVINCI				**MADONNA AND CHILD**
92	VIRGIN OF THE ROCKS	CL	37.50	40.00
P. MIGNARD				**MADONNA AND CHILD**
93	VIRGIN OF THE GRAPE	CL	37.50	40.00
B.E. MURILLO				**MADONNA AND CHILD**
93	MADONNA OF ROSARY	CL	37.50	40.00
R. SANZIO				**MADONNA AND CHILD**
92	MADONNA DELLA SEDIA	CL	37.50	40.00
93	SISTINE MADONNA	CL	37.50	40.00
T. HIRATA				**MAJESTY OF FLIGHT**
89	COASTAL JOURNEY	CL	37.50	50.00
89	COMMANDING THE MARSH	CL	37.50	40.00
89	EAGLE SOARS, THE	CL	37.50	50.00
89	REALM OF THE RED-TAIL	CL	37.50	45.00
89	SENTRY OF THE NORTH	CL	37.50	50.00
90	FIERCE AND FREE	CL	29.50	50.00
90	SILENT WATCH	CL	29.50	50.00
90	VANTAGE POINT, THE	CL	29.50	50.00
L. PICKEN				**MAN'S BEST FRIEND**
92	GOOD CATCH	CL	29.50	30.00
92	MAKING WAVES	CL	29.50	30.00
92	SPECIAL DELIVERY	CL	29.50	30.00
93	BEDTIME STORY	CL	29.50	30.00
93	FAITHFUL FRIEND	CL	29.50	30.00
93	LET'S PLAY BALL	CL	29.50	30.00
93	SITTING PRETTY	CL	29.50	30.00
93	TIME FOR A WALK	CL	29.50	30.00
93	TRUSTED COMPANION	CL	29.50	30.00
R. TANENBAUM				**MIKE SCHMIDT**
94	ULTIMATE COMPETITOR: MIKE SCHMIDT, THE	CL	29.50	30.00
P. COOPER				**MIXED COMPANY**
90	A STICKY SITUATION	CL	29.50	40.00
90	ALL WRAPPED UP	CL	29.50	40.00
90	PICTURE PERFECT	CL	29.50	35.00
90	TWO AGAINST ONE	CL	29.50	40.00
90	WHAT'S UP	CL	29.50	35.00
91	A MOMENT TO UNWIND	CL	29.50	40.00
91	OLE	CL	29.50	40.00
91	PICNIC PROWLERS	CL	29.50	35.00
C. REN				**MYSTIC WARRIORS**
92	DELIVERANCE	CL	29.50	30.00
92	MAN WHO WALKS ALONE	CL	29.50	30.00
92	MYSTIC WARRIOR	CL	29.50	30.00
92	SPIRIT OF THE PLAINS	CL	29.50	30.00
92	SUN SEEKER	CL	29.50	30.00
92	TOP GUN	CL	29.50	30.00
92	WINDRIDER	CL	29.50	30.00
93	BLUE THUNDER	CL	29.50	30.00
93	PEACE MAKER	CL	29.50	30.00
93	SUN GLOW	CL	29.50	30.00
M. RICHTER				**NATURE'S MAJESTIC CATS**
93	AFRICAN LION	CL	29.50	30.00
93	HIMALAYAN SNOW LEOPARD	CL	29.50	30.00
93	SIBERIAN TIGER	CL	29.50	30.00
94	AFRICAN CHEETAH	CL	29.50	30.00
94	AMERICAN COUGAR	CL	29.50	30.00
94	ASIAN CLOUDED LEOPARD	CL	29.50	30.00
94	CANADIAN LYNX	CL	29.50	30.00
94	EAST AFRICAN LEOPARD	CL	29.50	30.00
G. MURRAY				**NATURE'S NIGHTTIME REALM**
92	BOBCAT	CL	29.50	30.00
92	COUGAR	CL	29.50	30.00
93	CHEETAH	CL	29.50	30.00
93	JAGUAR	CL	29.50	30.00

YR	NAME	LIMIT	ISSUE	TREND
93	LION	CL	29.50	30.00
93	LYNX	CL	29.50	30.00
93	SNOW LEOPARD	CL	29.50	30.00
93	WHITE TIGER	CL	29.50	30.00
	R. PARKER			**NATURE'S QUIET MOMENTS**
88	A CURIOUS PAIR	CL	37.50	40.00
88	JUST RESTING	CL	37.50	40.00
88	NORTHERN MORNINGS	CL	37.50	40.00
89	AUTUMN FORAGING	CL	37.50	40.00
89	CREEKSIDE	CL	37.50	40.00
89	MOUNTAIN BLOOMS	CL	37.50	40.00
89	OLD MAN OF THE MOUNTAIN	CL	37.50	40.00
89	WAITING OUT THE STORM	CL	37.50	40.00
	D. WRIGHT			**NOBLE AMERICAN INDIAN WOMEN**
89	SACAJAWEA	CL	29.50	50.00
90	LILY OF THE MOHAWK	CL	29.50	40.00
90	MINNEHAHA	CL	29.50	40.00
90	PINE LEAF	CL	29.50	50.00
90	POCAHONTAS	CL	29.50	50.00
90	WHITE ROSE	CL	29.50	50.00
91	FALLING STAR	CL	29.50	50.00
91	LOZEN	CL	29.50	30.00
	J. SEEREY-LESTER			**NOBLE OWLS OF AMERICA**
86	MORNING MIST	15000	55.00	60.00
87	AUTUMN MIST	15000	55.00	60.00
87	DAWN IN THE WILLOWS	15000	55.00	60.00
87	PRAIRIE SUNDOWN	15000	55.00	60.00
87	SNOWY WATCH	15000	55.00	60.00
87	WINTER VIGIL	15000	55.00	60.00
88	HIDING PLACE	15000	55.00	60.00
88	WAITING FOR DUSK	15000	55.00	60.00
	R. TANENBAUM			**NOLAN RYAN**
94	27 SEASONS	CL	29.50	30.00
94	BIRTH OF A LEGEND	CL	29.50	30.00
94	FAREWELL	CL	29.50	30.00
94	MILLION-DOLLAR PLAYER	CL	29.50	30.00
94	MR. FASTBALL	CL	29.50	30.00
94	STRIKEOUT EXPRESS, THE	CL	29.50	30.00
	R. LAWRENCE			**NORTH AMERICAN DUCKS**
91	AUTUMN FLIGHT	CL	29.50	40.00
91	RESTING PLACE, THE	CL	29.50	30.00
91	TWIN FLIGHT	CL	29.50	30.00
92	MISTY MORNING	CL	29.50	30.00
92	OVERCAST	CL	29.50	30.00
92	PERFECT PINTAILS	CL	29.50	30.00
92	SPRINGTIME THAW	CL	29.50	30.00
92	SUMMER RETREAT	CL	29.50	30.00
	J. KILLEN			**NORTH AMERICAN GAMEBIRDS**
90	BOBWHITE QUAIL	CL	37.50	50.00
90	GAMBEL QUAIL	CL	37.50	40.00
90	MOURNING DOVE	CL	37.50	50.00
90	RING-NECKED PHEASANT	CL	37.50	40.00
90	RUFFED GROUSE	CL	37.50	40.00
90	WOODCOCK	CL	37.50	50.00
91	CHUKAR PARTRIDGE	CL	37.50	50.00
91	WILD TURKEY	CL	37.50	50.00
	R. LAWRENCE			**NORTH AMERICAN WATERBIRDS**
88	CANADA GEESE	CL	37.50	50.00
88	HOODED MERGANSERS	CL	37.50	60.00
88	PINTAILS	CL	37.50	50.00
88	WOOD DUCKS	CL	37.50	60.00
89	AMERICAN WIDGEONS	CL	37.50	60.00
89	CANVASBACKS	CL	37.50	60.00
89	MALLARD PAIR	CL	37.50	65.00
89	SNOW GEESE	CL	37.50	50.00
	S. FISHER			**NUTCRACKER BALLET**
78	CLARA	CL	19.50	40.00
79	GODFATHER	CL	19.50	20.00
79	SNOW QUEEN AND KING	CL	19.50	45.00
79	SUGAR PLUM FAIRY	CL	19.50	50.00
80	CLARA AND THE PRINCE	CL	19.50	50.00
80	WALTZ OF THE FLOWERS	CL	19.50	25.00
	D. BOBNICK			**OFFICIAL HONEYMOONER'S COMMEMORATIVE PLATE**
93	OFFICAL HONEYMOONER'S COMM. PLATE, THE	CL	37.50	95.00
	D. KILMER			**OFFICIAL HONEYMOONERS PLATE COLLECTION**
87	BABY, YOU'RE THE GREATEST	CL	24.50	145.00
87	HONEYMOONERS, THE	CL	24.50	135.00
87	HUCKLEBUCK, THE	CL	24.50	135.00
88	BANG! ZOOM!	CL	24.50	135.00
88	GOLFER, THE	CL	24.50	135.00
88	HONEYMOON EXPRESS, THE	CL	24.50	275.00
88	ONLY WAY TO TRAVEL, THE	CL	24.50	140.00
88	TV CHEFS, THE	CL	24.50	140.00
	J. PITCHER			**ON WINGS OF EAGLES**
94	BY DAWN'S EARLY LIGHT	CL	29.50	30.00
	S. BARLOWE			**OUR CHERISHED SEAS**
92	FLIGHT OF THE DOLPHINS	CL	37.50	40.00

The Bradford Exchange released Time for a Little Something *as part of the Winnie the Pooh and Friends collection in 1994.*

This playful pair is twice as nice. Produced as both a plate and an ornament, Irene Spencer's Happy Holidaze *captures the capriciousness of kittens celebrating Christmas in their own special way. Produced by Roman Inc.*

Mary, Mary *doesn't look at all "quite contrary" in this 1979 plate by John McClelland. Part of Reco International's Mother Goose collection, it was limited to one year of production.*

Thy Kingdom Come *by Abbie Williams is the second issue in "The Lord's Prayer" series produced by Roman. The piece was limited to just a 10-day firing period.*

YR	NAME	LIMIT	ISSUE	TREND
92	LIONS OF THE SEA	CL	37.50	40.00
92	PALACE OF THE SEALS	CL	37.50	40.00
92	WHALE SONG	CL	37.50	40.00
93	EMPORERS OF THE ICE	CL	37.50	40.00
93	ORCA BALLET	CL	37.50	40.00
93	SEA TURTLES	CL	37.50	40.00
93	SPLENDOR OF THE SEA	CL	37.50	40.00
R. MASSEY				**PASSAGE TO CHINA**
83	ALLIANCE	15000	55.00	60.00
83	EMPRESS OF CHINA	15000	55.00	60.00
85	CHALLENGE	15000	55.00	60.00
85	FLYING CLOUD	15000	55.00	60.00
85	GRAND TURK	15000	55.00	60.00
85	ROMANCE OF THE SEAS	15000	55.00	60.00
85	SEA SERPENT	15000	55.00	60.00
85	SEA WITCH	15000	55.00	60.00
B. HARRISON				**PETALS AND PURRS**
88	BLUSHING BEAUTIES	CL	24.50	60.00
88	FORGET-ME-NOT	CL	24.50	40.00
88	MORNING GLORIES	CL	24.50	40.00
88	SPRING FEVER	CL	24.50	40.00
89	GOLDEN FANCY	CL	24.50	35.00
89	PINK LILLIES	CL	24.50	35.00
89	SIAMESE SUMMER	CL	24.50	35.00
89	SUMMER SUNSHINE	CL	24.50	35.00
T. BLACKSHEAR				**PORTRAITS FROM OZ**
89	DOROTHY	CL	29.50	160.00
89	SCARECROW	CL	29.50	120.00
89	TIN MAN	CL	29.50	130.00
90	COWARDLY LION	CL	29.50	135.00
90	GLINDA	CL	29.50	105.00
90	TOTO	CL	29.50	225.00
90	WICKED WITCH	CL	29.50	200.00
90	WIZARD	CL	29.50	110.00
T. UTZ				**PORTRAITS OF CHILDHOOD**
81	BUTTERFLY MAGIC	CL	24.95	30.00
82	SWEET DREAMS	CL	24.95	30.00
83	TURTLE TALK	CL	24.95	30.00
84	FRIENDS FOREVER	CL	24.95	30.00
J. PITCHER				**PORTRAITS OF THE BALD EAGLE**
93	IN BOLD DEFIANCE	CL	37.50	40.00
93	MASTER OF THE SUMMER SKIES	CL	37.50	40.00
93	RULER OF THE SKY	CL	37.50	40.00
93	SPRING'S SENTINEL	CL	37.50	40.00
J. MEGER				**PORTRAITS OF THE WILD**
94	CALL OF AUTUMN	CL	29.50	30.00
94	DEVOTED PROTECTOR	CL	29.50	30.00
94	INTERLUDE	CL	29.50	30.00
94	WATCHFUL EYES	CL	29.50	30.00
94	WINTER SOLITUDE	CL	29.50	30.00
S. BUTCHER				**PRECIOUS MOMENTS BIBLE STORY**
90	COME LET US ADORE HIM	CL	29.50	30.00
92	CARPENTER SHOP, THE	CL	29.50	30.00
92	CRUCIFIXION, THE	CL	29.50	30.00
92	FLIGHT INTO EGYPT, THE	CL	29.50	30.00
92	JESUS IN THE TEMPLE	CL	29.50	30.00
92	THEY FOLLOWED THE STAR	CL	29.50	30.00
93	HE IS NOT HERE	CL	29.50	30.00
S. BUTCHER				**PRECIOUS MOMENTS CLASSICS**
93	GOD LOVETH A CHEERFUL GIVER	CL	35.00	40.00
93	MAKE A JOYFUL NOISE	CL	35.00	40.00
T. UTZ				**PRECIOUS MOMENTS PLATES**
79	FRIEND IN THE SKY	CL	21.50	55.00
80	SAND IN HER SHOE	CL	21.50	30.00
80	SEASHELLS	CL	21.50	35.00
80	SNOW BUNNY	CL	21.50	25.00
81	DAWN	CL	21.50	30.00
82	MY KITTY	CL	21.50	40.00
B.P. GUTMANN				**PRECIOUS PORTRAITS**
87	BUNNY	CL	24.50	35.00
87	FAIRY GOLD	CL	24.50	40.00
87	GOLDILOCKS	CL	24.50	35.00
87	MISCHIEF	CL	24.50	35.00
87	PEACH BLOSSOM	CL	24.50	40.00
87	SUNBEAM	CL	24.50	40.00
D. WRIGHT				**PRINCESSES OF THE PLAINS**
93	GENTLE BEAUTY	CL	29.50	30.00
93	NOBLE BEAUTY	CL	29.50	30.00
93	PRAIRIE FLOWER	CL	29.50	30.00
93	SNOW PRINCESS	CL	29.50	30.00
93	WILD FLOWER	CL	29.50	30.00
93	WINTER'S ROSE	CL	29.50	30.00
94	MOUNTAIN PRINCESS	CL	29.50	30.00
94	NATURE'S GUARDIAN	CL	29.50	30.00
K. FREEMAN				**PROUD INDIAN FAMILIES**
91	NAMING CEREMONY, THE	CL	29.50	30.00
91	PLAYING WITH TRADITION	CL	29.50	30.00

YR	NAME	LIMIT	ISSUE	TREND
91	POWER OF THE BASKET, THE	CL	29.50	30.00
91	STORYTELLER, THE	CL	29.50	30.00
92	CEREMONIAL DRESS	CL	29.50	30.00
92	MARRIAGE CEREMONY, THE	CL	29.50	30.00
92	PREPARING THE BERRY HARVEST	CL	29.50	30.00
92	SOUNDS OF THE FOREST	CL	29.50	30.00
93	BEAUTIFUL CREATIONS	CL	29.50	30.00
93	JEWELRY MAKER, THE	CL	29.50	30.00
J. SCHMIDT				**PROUD INNOCENCE**
94	DESERT BLOOM	CL	29.50	30.00
R. SWANSON				**PROUD NATION**
89	AUTUMN TREAT	CL	24.50	35.00
89	DRESSED UP FOR THE POW WOW	CL	24.50	35.00
89	IN A BIG LAND	CL	24.50	30.00
89	JUST A FEW DAYS OLD	CL	24.50	35.00
89	NAVAJO LITTLE ONE	CL	24.50	50.00
89	NEWEST LITTLE SHEEPHERDER	CL	24.50	35.00
89	OUT WITH MAMA'S FLOCK	CL	24.50	30.00
89	UP THE RED ROCKS	CL	24.50	30.00
J. LAMB				**PUPPY PLAYTIME**
87	CABIN FEVER-BLACK LABRADORS	CL	24.50	50.00
87	CATCH OF THE DAY-GOLDEN RETRIEVERS	CL	24.50	50.00
87	DOUBLE TAKE-COCKER SPANIELS	CL	24.50	80.00
87	FUN AND GAMES-POODLE	CL	24.50	40.00
87	GETTING ACQUAINTED-BEAGLES	CL	24.50	40.00
87	HANGING OUT-GERMAN SHEPHERD	CL	24.50	50.00
87	NEW LEASH ON LIFE-MINI SCHNAUZER	CL	24.50	40.00
87	WEEKEND GARDENER-LHASA APSOS	CL	24.50	40.00
D. GREEN				**QUIET MOMENTS OF CHILDHOOD**
91	CHRISTINA'S SECRET GARDEN	CL	29.50	40.00
91	ELIZABETH'S AFTERNOON TEA	CL	29.50	50.00
91	ERIC & ERIN'S STORYTIME	CL	29.50	30.00
92	CHILDREN'S DAY BY THE SEA	CL	29.50	30.00
92	DANIELS' MORNING PLAYTIME	CL	29.50	30.00
92	JESSICA'S TEA PARTY	CL	29.50	35.00
92	JORDAN'S PLAYFUL PUPS	CL	29.50	35.00
92	MEGAN & MONIQUE'S BAKERY	CL	29.50	40.00
M. STEELE				**QUILTED COUNTRYSIDE**
91	COUNTRY MERCHANT, THE	CL	29.50	40.00
91	OLD COUNTRY STORE, THE	CL	29.50	55.00
91	QUILTER'S CABIN, THE	CL	29.50	50.00
91	SPRING CLEANING	CL	29.50	40.00
91	SUMMER HARVEST	CL	29.50	30.00
91	WINTER'S END	CL	29.50	30.00
92	ANTIQUES STORE, THE	CL	29.50	30.00
92	WASH DAY	CL	29.50	30.00
L. BYWATERS				**RENAISSANCE ANGELS**
94	ANGELIC INNOCENCE	CL	29.50	30.00
94	DOVES OF PEACE	CL	29.50	30.00
S. MORTON				**REPUBLIC PICTURES FILM LIBRARY COLLECTION**
92	ATTACK AT TARAWA	CL	37.50	40.00
92	FIGHTING SEABEES, THE	CL	37.50	40.00
92	QUIET MAN, THE	CL	37.50	40.00
92	RIDE HOME, THE	CL	37.50	40.00
92	SHOWDOWN W/LAREDO	CL	37.50	40.00
92	THOUGHTS OF ANGELIQUE	CL	37.50	40.00
92	WAR OF THE WILDCATS	CL	37.50	40.00
93	ANGEL & THE BADMAN	CL	37.50	40.00
93	FLYING TIGERS	CL	39.50	40.00
93	SANDS OF IWO JIMA	CL	37.50	40.00
N. ROCKWELL				**ROCKWELL HOME OF THE BRAVE**
81	BACK TO HIS OLD JOB	18000	35.00	60.00
81	HERO'S WELCOME	18000	35.00	60.00
81	REMINISCING	18000	35.00	60.00
81	WAR HERO	18000	35.00	40.00
82	TAKING MOTHER OVER THE TOP	18000	35.00	40.00
82	UNCLE SAM TAKES WINGS	18000	35.00	80.00
82	WAR BOND	18000	35.00	40.00
82	WILLIE GILLIS IN CHURCH	18000	35.00	60.00
D. TUTWILER				**ROMANCE OF THE RAILS**
94	CRESCENT LIMITED	CL	29.50	30.00
94	MORNING STAR	CL	29.50	30.00
94	ORANGE BLOSSOM SPECIAL	CL	29.50	30.00
94	PORTLAND ROSE	CL	29.50	30.00
94	STARLIGHT LIMITED	CL	29.50	30.00
94	SUNRISE LIMITED	CL	29.50	30.00
94	SUNSET LIMITED	CL	29.50	30.00
94	WESTERN STAR	CL	29.50	30.00
D. SWEET				**ROMANTIC CASTLES OF EUROPE**
90	LUDWIG'S CASTLE	19500	55.00	60.00
91	DAVINCI'S CHAMBORD	19500	55.00	60.00
91	EILEAN DONAN	19500	55.00	60.00
91	LEGENDARY CASTLE OF LEEDS, THE	19500	55.00	60.00
91	PALACE OF THE MOORS	19500	55.00	60.00
91	SWISS ISLE FORTRESS	19500	55.00	60.00
92	ELTZ CASTLE	19500	55.00	60.00
92	KYLEMORE ABBEY	19500	55.00	60.00

YR	NAME	LIMIT	ISSUE	TREND
	Q. LEMONDS	**ROMANTIC FLIGHTS OF FANCY**		
94	MORNING MINUET	CL	29.50	30.00
94	SUNLIT WALTZ	CL	29.50	30.00
	J. GROSSMAN	**ROMANTIC VICTORIAN KEEPSAKE**		
92	AS FAIR AS A ROSE	CL	35.00	40.00
92	BONNIE BLUE EYES	CL	35.00	40.00
92	DEAREST KISS	CL	35.00	40.00
92	FIRST LOVE	CL	35.00	40.00
92	PRECIOUS FRIENDS	CL	35.00	40.00
92	SPRINGTIME BEAUTY	CL	35.00	40.00
92	SUMMERTIME FANCY	CL	35.00	40.00
94	BONNETS AND BOUQUETS	CL	35.00	40.00
	N. ROCKWELL	**SATURDAY EVENING POST BASEBALL COLLECTION**		
92	100TH YEAR OF BASEBALL	CL	19.50	25.00
93	BOTTOM OF THE SIXTH	CL	19.50	25.00
93	DUGOUT, THE	CL	19.50	25.00
93	ROOKIE, THE	CL	19.50	25.00
	N. ROCKWELL	**SATURDAY EVENING POST PLATE COLLECTION**		
89	EASTER MORNING	CL	35.00	65.00
89	FACTS OF LIFE, THE	CL	35.00	40.00
89	WONDERS OF RADIO, THE	CL	35.00	40.00
90	FIRST FLIGHT	CL	35.00	55.00
90	FURLOUGH	CL	35.00	40.00
90	JURY ROOM	CL	35.00	40.00
90	TRAVELING COMPANION	CL	35.00	40.00
90	WINDOW WASHER, THE	CL	35.00	50.00
	B. PERRY	**SCENES OF AN AMERICAN CHRISTMAS**		
94	CHRISTMAS EVE WORKSHIP	CL	29.50	30.00
94	I'LL BE HOME FOR CHRISTMAS	CL	29.50	30.00
	J. PITCHER	**SEASONS OF THE BALD EAGLE**		
91	AUTUMN IN THE MOUNTAINS	CL	37.50	40.00
91	SPRING ON THE RIVER	CL	37.50	40.00
91	SUMMER ON THE SEACOAST	CL	37.50	40.00
91	WINTER IN THE VALLEY	CL	37.50	40.00
	T. UTZ	**SINGLE ISSUE**		
83	PRINCESS GRACE	CL	39.50	65.00
	C. FRACE	**SMALL WONDERS OF THE WILD**		
89	HIDEAWAY	CL	29.50	50.00
90	EXPLORING A NEW WORLD	CL	29.50	30.00
90	EYES OF WONDER	CL	29.50	30.00
90	QUIET MORNING	CL	29.50	30.00
90	READY FOR ADVENTURE	CL	29.50	30.00
90	THREE OF A KIND	CL	29.50	80.00
90	UNO	CL	29.50	30.00
90	YOUNG EXPLORERS	CL	29.50	40.00
	*	**SPOCK COMMEMORATIVE WALL PLAQUE**		
93	SPOCK/STAR TREK VI THE UNDISCOVERED CTY	2500	195.00	200.00
	J. LAMB	**SPORTING GENERATION**		
91	GOLDEN MOMENTS	CL	29.50	30.00
91	LIKE FATHER, LIKE SON	CL	29.50	40.00
91	LOOKOUT, THE	CL	29.50	30.00
92	FIRST TIME OUT	CL	29.50	30.00
92	PICKING UP THE SCENT	CL	29.50	30.00
92	POINT OF INTEREST	CL	29.50	30.00
92	SPRINGING INTO ACTION	CL	29.50	30.00
92	WHO'S TRACKING WHO	CL	29.50	30.00
	T. UTZ	**SPRINGTIME OF LIFE**		
85	AMONG THE DAFFODILS	CL	29.50	35.00
85	AUNT TILLIE'S HATS	CL	29.50	35.00
85	GRANNY'S BOOTS	CL	29.50	35.00
85	JUST LIKE MOMMY	CL	29.50	35.00
85	LITTLE EMILY	CL	29.50	35.00
85	MY FAVORITE DOLLS	CL	29.50	35.00
85	MY MASTERPIECE	CL	29.50	35.00
85	TEDDY'S BATHTIME	CL	29.50	35.00
	*	**STAINED GLASS GARDENS**		
89	COCKATOO'S GARDEN, THE	15000	55.00	60.00
89	GARDEN SUNSET	15000	55.00	60.00
89	PEACOCK AND WISTERIA	15000	55.00	60.00
89	WATERFALL AND IRIS	15000	55.00	60.00
90	A HOLLYHOCK SUNRISE	15000	55.00	60.00
90	PEACEFUL WATERS	15000	55.00	60.00
90	ROSES AND MAGNOLIAS	15000	55.00	60.00
90	SPRINGTIME IN THE VALLEY	15000	55.00	60.00
	T. BLACKSHEAR	**STAR TREK 25TH ANNIVERSARY COMMEMORATIVE COLLECTION**		
91	KIRK	CL	35.00	100.00
91	SPOCK	CL	35.00	115.00
91	STAR TREK 25TH ANNIVERSARY PLATE	CL	37.50	135.00
92	MCCOY	CL	35.00	40.00
92	SCOTTY	CL	35.00	40.00
92	UHURA	CL	35.00	40.00
93	CHEKOV	CL	35.00	40.00
93	SULU	CL	35.00	40.00
94	U.S.S. ENTERPRISE NCC-1701	CL	35.00	40.00
	M. WEISTLING	**STAR TREK THE MOVIES**		
94	STAR TREK II: THE WRATH OF KHAN	CL	35.00	40.00
94	STAR TREK IV: THE VOYAGE HOME	CL	35.00	40.00

YR	NAME	LIMIT	ISSUE	TREND
K. BIRDSONG		**STAR TREK THE VOYAGERS**		
94	KLINGON BATTLECRUISER	CL	35.00	40.00
94	ROMULAN WARBIRD	CL	35.00	40.00
94	U.S.S. ENTERPRISE NCC-1701	CL	35.00	40.00
94	U.S.S. ENTERPRISE NCC-1701-D	CL	35.00	40.00
T. BLACKSHEAR		**STAR TREK: THE NEXT GENERATION**		
93	CAPTAIN JEAN-LUC PICARD	CL	35.00	135.00
93	COMMANDER WILLIAM T. RIKER	CL	35.00	40.00
94	LIEUTENANT COMMANDER DATA	CL	35.00	95.00
94	LIEUTENANT WORF	CL	35.00	40.00
K. BIRDSONG		**STAR TREK: THE NEXT GENERATION-THE EPISODES**		
94	BEST OF BOTH WORLDS, THE	CL	35.00	40.00
94	ENCOUNTER AT FAR POINT	CL	35.00	40.00
T. BLACKSHEAR		**STAR WARS 10TH ANNIVERSARY COMMEMORATIVE PLATE**		
90	STAR WARS 10TH ANNIVERSARY PLATE	CL	39.50	90.00
T. BLACKSHEAR		**STAR WARS PLATE COLLECTION**		
87	HANS SOLO	CL	29.50	85.00
87	IMPERIAL WALKERS, THE	CL	29.50	105.00
87	LUKE AND YODA	CL	29.50	70.00
87	LUKE SKYWALKER AND DARTH VADER	CL	29.50	70.00
87	PRINCESS LEIA	CL	29.50	105.00
87	R2-D2 AND WICKET	CL	29.50	60.00
88	CREW IN THE COCKPIT	CL	29.50	175.00
88	SPACE BATTLE	CL	29.50	325.00
M. WEISTLING		**STAR WARS TRILOGY**		
93	EMPIRE STRIKES BACK, THE	CL	37.50	40.00
93	RETURN OF THE JEDI	CL	37.50	40.00
93	STAR WARS	CL	37.50	40.00
T. UTZ		**SUMMER DAYS OF CHILDHOOD**		
83	A JUMPING CONTEST	CL	29.50	35.00
83	A STOLEN KISS	CL	29.50	35.00
83	BALLOON CARNIVAL	CL	29.50	35.00
83	BIRTHDAY PARTY, THE	CL	29.50	35.00
83	BLOWING BUBBLES	CL	29.50	35.00
83	COOLING OFF	CL	29.50	35.00
83	FIRST CUSTOMER	CL	29.50	35.00
83	GARDEN MAGIC	CL	29.50	35.00
83	KITTY'S BATHTIME	CL	29.50	35.00
83	LITTLE BEACHCOMBER	CL	29.50	35.00
83	MOUNTAIN FRIENDS	CL	29.50	35.00
83	PLAYING DOCTOR	CL	29.50	35.00
F. MCCARTHY		**THE FIERCE AND THE FREE**		
92	BIG MEDICINE	CL	29.50	30.00
93	LAND OF THE WINTER HAWK	CL	29.50	30.00
93	WARRIOR OF SAVAGE SPLENDOR	CL	29.50	30.00
94	CHALLENGE, THE	CL	29.50	30.00
94	WAR PARTY	CL	29.50	30.00
F. MCCARTHY		**THE WEST OF FRANK MCCARTHY**		
91	ATTACKING THE IRON HORSE	CL	37.50	65.00
91	ATTEMPT ON THE STAGE	CL	37.50	50.00
91	BRINGING OUT THE FURS	CL	37.50	50.00
91	HEADED NORTH	CL	37.50	40.00
91	HOSTILE THREAT, THE	CL	37.50	50.00
91	KIOWA RAIDER	CL	37.50	50.00
91	ON THE OLD NORTH TRAIL	CL	37.50	50.00
91	PRAYER, THE	CL	37.50	55.00
J. MCCLELLAND		**THE WONDER OF CHRISTMAS**		
91	MY FAVORITE ORNAMENT	CL	29.50	30.00
91	SANTA'S SECRET	CL	29.50	30.00
91	WAITING FOR SANTA	CL	29.50	30.00
93	CAROLER, THE	CL	29.50	30.00
D. ZOLAN		**THE WORLD OF ZOLAN**		
92	FIRST KISS	CL	29.50	30.00
92	MORNING DISCOVERY	CL	29.50	30.00
93	FLOWERS FOR MOTHER	CL	29.50	30.00
93	LETTER TO GRANDMA	CL	29.50	30.00
93	LITTLE FISHERMAN, THE	CL	29.50	30.00
93	TWILIGHT PRAYER	CL	29.50	30.00
T. UTZ		**THORNTON UTZ 10TH ANNIVERSARY PLATE COLLECTION**		
89	AMONG THE DAFFODILS	CL	29.50	45.00
89	BEST FRIENDS	CL	29.50	35.00
89	DAWN	CL	29.50	35.00
89	FRIENDS IN THE SKY	CL	29.50	35.00
89	JUST LIKE MOMMY	CL	29.50	35.00
89	LITTLE EMILY	CL	29.50	35.00
89	MY KITTY	CL	29.50	35.00
89	PLAYING DOCTOR	CL	29.50	35.00
89	TEDDY'S BATHTIME	CL	29.50	35.00
89	TURTLE TALK	CL	29.50	35.00
M. TSANG		**TIMELESS EXPRESSIONS OF THE ORIENT**		
90	FIDELITY	15000	75.00	100.00
91	BEAUTY	15000	55.00	60.00
91	FEMININITY	15000	75.00	80.00
91	LONGEVITY	15000	75.00	80.00
92	COURAGE	15000	55.00	60.00
H. BOND		**TREASURED DAYS**		
87	AMANDA	CL	24.50	50.00

YR	NAME	LIMIT	ISSUE	TREND
87	ASHLEY	CL	29.50	65.00
87	CHRISTOPHER	CL	24.50	50.00
87	JEREMY	CL	24.50	50.00
87	SARA	CL	24.50	35.00
88	JUSTIN	CL	24.50	50.00
88	LINDSAY	CL	24.50	50.00
88	NICHOLAS	CL	24.50	50.00
C. DEHAAN		**UNBRIDLED SPIRIT**		
92	DESERT SHADOWS	CL	29.50	30.00
92	SURF DANCER	CL	29.50	30.00
92	WINTER RENEGADE	CL	29.50	30.00
93	AUTUMN REVERIE	CL	29.50	30.00
93	BLIZZARD'S PERIL	CL	29.50	30.00
93	DESERT DUEL	CL	29.50	30.00
93	MIDNIGHT RUN	CL	29.50	30.00
93	MOONLIGHT MAJESTY	CL	29.50	30.00
93	PAINTED SUNRISE	CL	29.50	30.00
93	SUNRISE SURPRISE	CL	29.50	30.00
T. UTZ		**UTZ MOTHER'S DAY**		
83	A GIFT OF LOVE	TL	27.50	40.00
83	MOTHER'S ANGEL	TL	27.50	30.00
83	MOTHER'S HELPING HAND	TL	27.50	30.00
J. HARRISON		**VANISHING RURAL AMERICA**		
91	AMERICA'S HEARTLAND	CL	29.50	30.00
91	AUTUMN'S PASSAGE	CL	29.50	50.00
91	COUNTRY PATH	CL	29.50	40.00
91	COVERED IN FALL	CL	29.50	50.00
91	QUIET REFLECTIONS	CL	29.50	50.00
91	RURAL DELIVERY	CL	29.50	30.00
91	STOREFRONT MEMORIES	CL	29.50	50.00
91	WHEN THE CIRCUS CAME TO TOWN	CL	29.50	40.00
J. GROSSMAN		**VICTORIAN CHRISTMAS MEMORIES**		
92	A VISIT FROM ST. NICHOLAS	CL	29.50	30.00
92	WITH VISIONS OF SUGAR PLUMS	CL	29.50	30.00
93	CHRISTMAS ANGELS	CL	29.50	30.00
93	CHRISTMAS DELIVERY	CL	29.50	30.00
93	CHRISTMAS INNOCENCE	CL	29.50	30.00
93	GRANDFATHER FROST	CL	29.50	30.00
93	JOYOUS NOEL	CL	29.50	30.00
93	MERRY OLDE KRIS KRINGLE	CL	29.50	30.00
M. HUMPHREY BOGART		**VICTORIAN PLAYTIME**		
91	A BUSY DAY	CL	29.50	30.00
92	A LITTLE PERSUASION	CL	29.50	30.00
92	CLEANING HOUSE	CL	29.50	30.00
92	LITTLE MASTERPIECE	CL	29.50	30.00
92	PEEK-A-BOO	CL	29.50	30.00
92	PLAYING BRIDE	CL	29.50	30.00
92	TEA AND GOSSIP	CL	29.50	30.00
92	WAITING FOR A NIBBLE	CL	29.50	30.00
C. DEHAAN		**WARRIOR'S PRIDE**		
94	BLACKFOOT WAR PONY	CL	29.50	30.00
94	CROW WAR PONY	CL	29.50	30.00
94	RUNNING FREE	CL	29.50	30.00
94	SOUTHERN CHEYENNE	CL	29.50	30.00
R. PARKER		**WINGED REFLECTIONS**		
89	ABOVE THE BREAKERS	CL	37.50	40.00
89	AMONG THE REEDS	CL	37.50	40.00
89	FOLLOWING MAMA	CL	37.50	40.00
89	FREEZE UP	CL	37.50	40.00
89	WINGS ABOVE THE WATER	CL	37.50	40.00
90	AT THE WATER'S EDGE	CL	29.50	30.00
90	EARLY SPRING	CL	29.50	30.00
90	SUMMER LOON	CL	29.50	30.00
T. XARAS		**WINTER RAILS**		
92	WINTER CLOSING	CL	29.50	30.00
93	BY SEA OR RAIL	CL	29.50	30.00
93	COAL COUNTRY	CL	29.50	30.00
93	COUNTRY CROSSROADS	CL	29.50	30.00
93	DARBY CROSSING	CL	29.50	30.00
93	DAYLIGHT RUN	CL	29.50	30.00
93	LONG HAUL, THE	CL	29.50	30.00
93	TIMBER LINE	CL	29.50	30.00
J. SEEREY-LESTER		**WINTER WILDLIFE**		
89	AMONG THE CATTAILS	15000	55.00	60.00
89	CLOSE ENCOUNTERS	15000	55.00	60.00
89	EARLY SNOW	15000	55.00	60.00
89	FIRST SNOW	15000	55.00	60.00
89	LYING IN WAIT	15000	55.00	60.00
89	OUT OF THE BLIZZARD	15000	55.00	60.00
89	REFUGE, THE	15000	55.00	60.00
89	WINTER HIDING	15000	55.00	60.00
T. BLACKSHEAR		**WIZARD OF OZ COMMEMORATIVE**		
88	DOROTHY MEETS THE SCARECROW	CL	24.50	115.00
88	WE'RE OFF TO SEE THE WIZARD	CL	24.50	215.00
89	A GLIMPSE OF THE MUNCHKINS	CL	24.50	120.00
89	GREAT AND POWERFUL OZ, THE	CL	24.50	150.00
89	IF I WERE KING OF THE FOREST	CL	24.50	150.00

YR	NAME	LIMIT	ISSUE	TREND
89	THERE'S NO PLACE LIKE HOME	CL	24.50	155.00
89	TIN MAN SPEAKS, THE	CL	24.50	130.00
89	WITCH CASTS A SPELL, THE	CL	24.50	145.00
G. GIORDANO				**WOODLAND ENCOUNTERS**
91	ANYONE FOR A SWIM?	CL	29.50	40.00
91	HI NEIGHBOR	CL	29.50	30.00
91	LUNCHTIME VISITOR	CL	29.50	30.00
91	MEADOW MEETING	CL	29.50	30.00
91	NATURE SCOUTS	CL	29.50	40.00
91	PEEK-A-BOO!	CL	29.50	30.00
91	WANT TO PLAY?	CL	29.50	30.00
92	FIELD DAY	CL	29.50	40.00
A. AGNEW				**YEAR OF THE WOLF**
93	BROKEN SILENCE	CL	29.50	30.00
93	LEADER OF THE PACK	CL	29.50	30.00
93	SOLITUDE	CL	29.50	30.00
94	A SECOND GLANCE	CL	29.50	30.00
94	FREE AS THE WIND	CL	29.50	30.00
94	GUARDIANS OF THE HIGH COUNTRY	CL	29.50	30.00
94	SONG OF THE WOLF	CL	29.50	30.00
94	TUNDRA LIGHT	CL	29.50	30.00

HAMILTON/BOEHM

YR	NAME	LIMIT	ISSUE	TREND
BOEHM				**AWARD WINNING ROSES**
79	ANGEL FACE ROSE	15000	45.00	65.00
79	ELEGANCE ROSE	15000	45.00	65.00
79	MR. LINCOLN ROSE	15000	45.00	65.00
79	PEACE ROSE	15000	45.00	65.00
79	QUEEN ELIZABETH ROSE	15000	45.00	65.00
79	ROYAL HIGHNESS ROSE	15000	45.00	65.00
79	TROPICANA ROSE	15000	45.00	65.00
79	WHITE MASTERPIECE ROSE	15000	45.00	65.00
BOEHM				**GAMEBIRDS OF NORTH AMERICA**
84	AMERICAN WOODCOCK	15000	62.50	65.00
84	BOB WHITE QUAIL	15000	62.50	65.00
84	CALIFORNIA QUAIL	15000	62.50	65.00
84	PRAIRIE GROUSE	15000	62.50	65.00
84	RING-NECKED PHEASANT	15000	62.50	65.00
84	RUFFED GROUSE	15000	62.50	65.00
84	WILD TURKEY	15000	62.50	65.00
84	WILLOW PARTRIDGE	15000	62.50	65.00
BOEHM				**HUMMINGBIRD COLLECTION**
80	BLUE THROATED	15000	62.50	85.00
80	BRAZILIAN RUBY	15000	62.50	85.00
80	BROADBILLED	15000	62.50	65.00
80	BROADTAIL	15000	62.50	65.00
80	CALLIOPE	15000	62.50	85.00
80	CRIMSON TOPAZ	15000	62.50	65.00
80	RUFOUS FLAME BEARER	15000	62.50	85.00
80	STREAMERTAIL	15000	62.50	85.00
BOEHM				**OWL COLLECTION**
80	BARN OWL	15000	45.00	65.00
80	BARRED OWL	15000	45.00	65.00
80	BOREAL OWL	15000	45.00	80.00
80	GREAT HORNED OWL	15000	45.00	65.00
80	SAW WHET OWL	15000	45.00	65.00
80	SCREECH OWL	15000	45.00	65.00
80	SHORT EARED OWL	15000	45.00	65.00
80	SNOWY OWL	15000	45.00	65.00
BOEHM				**WATER BIRDS**
81	AMERICAN PINTAIL	15000	62.50	65.00
81	CANADA GEESE	15000	62.50	80.00
81	CANVAS BACK	15000	62.50	65.00
81	COMMON MALLARD	15000	62.50	65.00
81	GREEN WINGED TEAL	15000	62.50	65.00
81	HOODED MERGANSER	15000	62.50	90.00
81	ROSS'S GEESE	15000	62.50	65.00
81	WOOD DUCKS	15000	62.50	65.00

HAVILAND

YR	NAME	LIMIT	ISSUE	TREND
R. HETREAU				**TWELVE DAYS OF CHRISTMAS**
70	PARTRIDGE	30000	25.00	60.00
71	TWO TURTLE DOVES	30000	25.00	30.00
72	THREE FRENCH HENS	30000	27.50	30.00
73	FOUR CALLING BIRDS	30000	28.50	35.00
74	FIVE GOLDEN RINGS	30000	30.00	35.00
75	SIX GEESE A'LAYING	30000	32.50	35.00
76	SEVEN SWANS	30000	38.00	40.00
77	EIGHT MAIDS	30000	40.00	45.00
78	NINE LADIES DANCING	30000	45.00	70.00
79	TEN LORDS A'LEAPING	30000	50.00	55.00
80	ELEVEN PIPERS PIPING	30000	55.00	70.00
81	TWELVE DRUMMERS	30000	60.00	65.00

HAVILAND & PARLON

YR	NAME	LIMIT	ISSUE	TREND
*				**CHRISTMAS MADONNAS**
72	BY RAPHAEL	5000	35.00	45.00
73	BY FERUZZI	5000	40.00	80.00

YR	NAME	LIMIT	ISSUE	TREND
74	BY RAPHAEL	5000	42.50	45.00
75	BY MURILLO	7500	42.50	45.00
76	BY BOTTICELLI	7500	45.00	50.00
77	BY BELLINI	7500	48.00	50.00
78	BY LIPPI	7500	48.00	55.00
79	MADONNA OF THE EUCHARIST	7500	49.50	115.00
*				**TAPESTRY I**
71	UNICORN IN CAPTIVITY	10000	35.00	70.00
72	START OF THE HUNT	10000	35.00	35.00
73	CHASE OF THE UNICORN	10000	35.00	76.00
74	END OF THE HUNT	10000	37.50	74.00
75	UNICORN SURROUNDED	10000	40.00	40.00
76	BROUGHT TO THE CASTLE	10000	42.50	43.00
*		**THE LADY AND THE UNICORN**		
77	TO MY ONLY DESIRE	20000	45.00	45.00
78	SIGHT	20000	45.00	45.00
79	SOUND	20000	47.50	48.00
80	TOUCH	15000	52.50	110.00
81	SCENT	10000	59.00	59.00
82	TASTE	10000	59.00	65.00

HUTSCHENREUTHER

YR	NAME	LIMIT	ISSUE	TREND
	G. GRANGET		**GUNTHER GRANGET**	
72	AMERICAN SPARROWS	5000	50.00	155.00
72	EUROPEAN SPARROWS	5000	30.00	70.00
73	AMERICAN KILDEER	2250	75.00	95.00
73	AMERICAN SQUIRREL	2500	75.00	80.00
73	EUROPEAN SQUIRREL	2500	35.00	55.00
74	AMERICAN PARTRIDGE	2500	75.00	95.00
75	AMERICAN RABBITS	2500	90.00	95.00
76	FREEDOM IN FLIGHT	5000	100.00	105.00
76	FREEDOM IN FLIGHT, GOLD	200	200.00	195.00
76	WRENS	5000	100.00	105.00
77	BEARS	2500	100.00	105.00
78	FOXES' SPRING JOURNEY	1000	125.00	205.00
	W.C. HALLETT		**THE GLORY OF CHRISTMAS**	
82	NATIVITY, THE	25000	80.00	130.00
83	ANNUNCIATION, THE	25000	80.00	120.00
84	SHEPHERDS, THE	25000	80.00	105.00
85	WISEMAN, THE	25000	80.00	105.00

IMPERIAL CHING-TE CHEN

YR	NAME	LIMIT	ISSUE	TREND
	Z. HUIMIN	**BEAUTIES OF THE RED MANSION**		
86	PAO-CHAI	CL	27.92	35.00
86	YUAN-CHUN	CL	27.92	35.00
87	HSI-CHUN	CL	30.92	40.00
87	HSI-FENG	CL	30.92	35.00
88	HSIANG-YUN	CL	34.92	45.00
88	KO-CHING	CL	32.92	45.00
88	LI-WAN	CL	32.92	40.00
88	MIAO-YU	CL	30.92	35.00
88	TAI-YU	CL	32.92	40.00
88	YING-CHUN	CL	30.92	40.00
89	CHIAO-CHIEH	CL	34.92	40.00
89	TAN-CHUN	CL	34.92	50.00
	Z. SONG MAO	**BLESSINGS FROM A CHINESE GARDEN**		
88	GIFT OF PURITY, THE	CL	39.92	45.00
89	GIFT OF BEAUTY, THE	CL	42.92	50.00
89	GIFT OF GRACE, THE	CL	39.92	45.00
89	GIFT OF HAPPINESS, THE	CL	42.92	45.00
90	GIFT OF JOY, THE	CL	42.92	50.00
90	GIFT OF TRUTH, THE	CL	42.92	50.00
	Z. HUIMIN	**FLOWER GODDESSES OF CHINA**		
91	CAMELLIA GODDESS, THE	CL	37.92	55.00
91	CHRYSANTHEMUM GODDESS, THE	CL	34.92	40.00
91	LOTUS GODDESS, THE	CL	34.92	40.00
91	NARCISSUS GODDESS, THE	CL	37.92	65.00
91	PEONY GODDESS, THE	CL	37.92	45.00
91	PLUM BLOSSOM GODDESS, THE	CL	37.92	45.00
	J. XUE-BING		**GARDEN OF SATIN WINGS**	
92	A MORNING DREAM	CL	29.92	35.00
93	A GARDEN WHISPER	CL	29.92	35.00
93	AN EVENING MIST	CL	29.92	35.00
	J. XUE-BING		**LEGENDS OF WEST LAKE**	
89	LADY WHITE	CL	29.92	40.00
90	APRICOT FAIRY, THE	CL	32.92	35.00
90	BRIGHT PEARL	CL	32.92	35.00
90	LADY SILKWORM	CL	29.92	30.00
90	LAUREL PEAK	CL	29.92	35.00
90	RISING SUN TERRACE	CL	32.92	35.00
90	THREAD OF SKY	CL	34.92	40.00
91	ANCESTORS OF TEA	CL	34.92	60.00
91	CASE OF THE FOLDING FANS, THE	CL	36.92	45.00
91	FLY-IN PEAK	CL	36.92	45.00
91	PHOENIX MOUNTAIN	CL	34.92	35.00
91	THREE POOLS MIRRORING/MOON	CL	36.92	70.00
	J. XUE-BING	**MAIDENS OF THE FOLDING SKY**		
92	BRIDE YEN CHUN	CL	32.92	35.00

YR	NAME	LIMIT	ISSUE	TREND
92	LADY LU	CL	29.92	35.00
92	MISTRESS YANG	CL	29.92	35.00
93	PARROT MAIDEN	CL	32.92	35.00
Z. SONG MAO		**SCENES FROM THE SUMMER PALACE**		
88	JADE BELT BRIDGE	CL	29.92	35.00
88	MARBLE BOAT, THE	CL	29.92	35.00
89	BOATERS ON KUMMING LAKE	CL	34.92	40.00
89	GARDEN/HARMONIOUS PLEASURE	CL	32.92	35.00
89	GREAT STAGE, THE	CL	32.92	35.00
89	HALL THAT DISPELS THE CLOUDS	CL	32.92	35.00
89	LONG PROMENADE, THE	CL	32.92	35.00
89	SEVENTEEN ARCH BRIDGE	CL	34.92	40.00
S. FU		**THE FORBIDDEN CITY**		
90	FLYING KITES/SPRING DAY	CL	39.92	45.00
90	PAVILION OF 10,000 SPRINGS	CL	39.92	45.00
90	PAVILION/FLOATING JADE GREEN	CL	42.92	45.00
91	DRESSING THE EMPRESS	CL	45.92	45.00
91	HALL OF THE CULTIVATING MIND, THE	CL	42.92	50.00
91	LATERN FESTIVAL, THE	CL	42.92	50.00
91	NINE DRAGON SCREEN	CL	42.92	65.00
91	PAVILION OF FLOATING CUPS	CL	45.92	48.00

INCOLAY

YR	NAME	LIMIT	ISSUE	TREND
*		**'TWAS THE NIGHT BEFORE CHRISTMAS**		
92	HAPPY CHRISTMAS TO ALL	OP	69.00	90.00
92	IT MUST BE ST. NICK	OP	74.00	150.00
92	UP ON THE ROOFTOP	OP	69.00	130.00
92	WITH VISIONS OF SUGAR PLUMS	OP	74.00	125.00
93	I SPRANG FROM MY BED	OP	74.00	148.00
93	UP THE CHIMNEY HE ROSE	OP	74.00	145.00
*		**CHRISTMAS CAMEO COLLECTION**		
92	EVENING CAROLERS	OP	65.00	84.00
R. AKERS		**CHRISTMAS CAMEO COLLECTION**		
90	HOME WITH THE TREE	*	60.00	73.00
91	SKATERS AT TWILIGHT	YR	60.00	76.00
93	SLEDING BY STARLIGHT	YR	65.00	99.00
94	PROPOSAL UNDER THE STARS	YR	65.00	65.00
*		**LOVE SONNETS OF SHAKESPEARE**		
87	LOVE ALTERS NOT	OP	60.00	65.00
87	SHALL I COMPARE THEE	OP	55.00	55.00
87	SINCE I FIRST SAW YOU	OP	60.00	65.00
87	THOU ART TOO DEAR	OP	55.00	55.00
88	YOU SHALL SHINE MORE BRIGHT	OP	60.00	65.00
88	YOUR FAIR EYES	OP	60.00	65.00
*		**LOVE THEMES FROM GRAND OPERA**		
90	MADAME BUTTERFLY	OP	65.00	65.00
90	MARRIAGE OF FIGARO, THE	OP	70.00	89.00
91	AIDA	OP	70.00	100.00
91	LA TRAVIATA	OP	70.00	80.00
91	TRISTAN AND ISOIDE	OP	70.00	77.00
R. AKERS		**LOVE THEMES FROM GRAND OPERA**		
90	CARMEN	*	65.00	65.00
*		**MAJESTIC SAILING SHIPS**		
92	BREDNOUGHT, THE	OP	65.00	80.00
92	CHARLES W. MORGAN, THE	OP	65.00	75.00
92	FLYING CLOUD	OP	65.00	80.00
92	SEA WITCH, THE	OP	65.00	70.00
D. STAPLEFORD		**MAJESTIC SAILING SHIPS**		
93	CHARLES W. MORGAN	YR	65.00	65.00
93	FLYING CLOUD, THE	YR	65.00	65.00
94	DREADNOUGHT, THE	YR	65.00	65.00
94	SEA WITCH, THE	YR	65.00	65.00
R. AKERS		**NIGHT BEFORE CHRISTMAS**		
93	HAPPY CHRISTMAS	YR	69.00	69.00
94	I SPRANG FROM MY BED	YR	74.00	74.00
94	IT MUST BE ST. NICK	YR	74.00	74.00
94	UP ON THE ROOFTOP	YR	69.00	69.00
94	UP THE CHIMNEY	YR	74.00	74.00
94	VISIONS OF SUGAR PLUMS	YR	74.00	74.00
*		**NORTH AMERICA'S WILDLIFE HERITAGE**		
91	AT STREAM'S EDGE	OP	65.00	68.00
91	IN THE POND'S SHALLOWS	OP	65.00	65.00
92	BENEATH THE OPEN SKY	OP	70.00	70.00
92	BESIDE THE SHELTERING KNOLL	OP	75.00	75.00
92	ON THE RIVERBANK	OP	70.00	100.00
92	THROUGH THE GRASSY CLEARING	OP	75.00	75.00
92	UPON THE ROCKY LEDGE	OP	70.00	100.00
93	NEAR THE RUNNING BROOK	OP	75.00	75.00
D. CLIFF		**NORTH AMERICAN WILDLIFE HERITAGE**		
93	AT STREAMS EDGE (DEER)	YR	65.00	65.00
93	IN PONDS SHALLOW (MOOSE)	YR	65.00	65.00
94	BENEATH THE OPEN SKY (RAM)	YR	70.00	70.00
94	BESIDE THE SHELTERING KNOLL (WOLF)	YR	70.00	70.00
94	GRASSY CLEARING, THE (ELK)	YR	75.00	75.00
94	NEAR THE RUNNIN BROOK (BISON)	YR	75.00	75.00
94	ON THE RIVERBANK	YR	70.00	70.00
94	UPON THE ROCKY LEDGE (MTN. LION)	YR	70.00	70.00

YR	NAME	LIMIT	ISSUE	TREND
	R. AKERS		**ROMANTIC POET SERIES**	
81	KISS, THE	YR	65.00	70.00
82	MY HEART LEAPS UP	YR	70.00	75.00
83	I STOOD TIPTOE	YR	70.00	75.00
84	DREAM, THE	YR	70.00	75.00
85	RECOLLECTION, THE	YR	70.00	75.00
	G. APPLEBY		**ROMANTIC POET SERIES**	
77	SHE WALKS IN BEAUTY	YR	60.00	60.00
78	A THING OF BEAUTY	YR	60.00	65.00
79	ODE TO A SKYLARK	YR	65.00	70.00
80	PHANTOM OF DELIGHT	YR	65.00	70.00
*			**SHAKESPEARE LOVERS**	
88	ROMEO AND JULIET	OP	65.00	70.00
89	HAMLET AND OPHELIA	OP	65.00	80.00
89	MACBETH AND LADY MACBETH	OP	70.00	85.00
89	PETRUCHIO AND KATHARINA	OP	70.00	75.00
90	BENEDICK AND BEATRICE	OP	70.00	85.00
90	FERDINAND AND MIRANDA	OP	75.00	100.00
90	LYSANDER AND HERMIA	OP	70.00	85.00
90	OTHELLO AND DESDEMONA	OP	75.00	100.00
	R. AKERS		**SHAKESPEARE LOVERS**	
90	ROMEO & JULIET	*	65.00	105.00
*			**THE FALL OF TROY**	
87	JUDGMENT OF PARIS, THE	OP	55.00	55.00
88	HECTOR AND ANDROMACHE	OP	55.00	55.00
88	HELEN AND PARIS	OP	55.00	55.00
88	TROJAN HORSE, THE	OP	55.00	55.00
*			**VICTORIAN DREAM HOMES**	
92	125 MAIN STREET	OP	55.00	90.00
92	212 THIRD AVENUE	OP	55.00	79.00
92	367 RIVERSIDE DRIVE	OP	60.00	85.00
92	432 FAIRVIEW LANE	OP	60.00	78.00
	C. WORKMASTER		**VICTORIAN DREAM HOMES**	
93	125 MAIN STREET	YR	55.00	55.00
94	212 THIRD AVENUE	YR	55.00	55.00
94	367 RIVERSIDE DRIVE	YR	60.00	60.00
94	432 FAIRVIEW LANE	YR	60.00	60.00

INTERNATIONAL SILVER

YR	NAME	LIMIT	ISSUE	TREND
	M. DEOLIVEIRA		**BICENTENNIAL**	
72	SIGNING DECLARATION	7500	40.00	300.00
73	PAUL REVERE	7500	40.00	165.00
74	CONCORD BRIDGE	7500	40.00	120.00
75	CROSSING DELAWARE	7500	50.00	85.00
76	VALLEY FORGE	7500	50.00	70.00
77	SURRENDER AT YORKTOWN	7500	50.00	65.00

JAN HAGARA COLLECTABLES

YR	NAME	LIMIT	ISSUE	TREND
	J. HAGARA		**FALL IN LOVE AGAIN**	
95	TAMMY	7500	39.00	39.00
	J. HAGARA		**VICTORIAN CHILDREN**	
79	DAISIES FROM MARYBETH	*	37.50	150.00
79	LISA	5000	60.00	90.00
80	ADRIANNE	5000	60.00	250.00
80	CARA	*	24.50	250.00
80	DAISIES FROM JIMMY	*	37.50	300.00
81	HEARTS & FLOWERS	*	24.50	250.00
81	LYDIA	5000	60.00	175.00
82	DAISIES FOR MOMMY	*	37.50	120.00
82	MELANEE	5000	60.00	125.00
83	CAROL	15000	45.00	210.00
84	CHRIS	15000	45.00	150.00
85	NOEL	15000	45.00	100.00
86	LESLEY	RT	42.50	120.00
86	NIKKI	15000	45.00	100.00
88	HANNAH	15000	50.00	125.00

JOHN HINE STUDIOS LTD.

Price ranges may reflect various demands in the market from one geographic region to another; condition of piece; specific markings found on piece; and/or changes in production of piece.

YR	NAME	LIMIT	ISSUE	TREND
	D. WINTER		**ANNUAL CHRISTMAS PIECES**	
94	SCROOGE FAMILY HOME, THE (PLAQUE)	3500	125.00	135.00
95	MISS BELLE'S COTTAGE (PLAQUE)	4000	120.00	125.00
	D. WINTER		**COLLECTORS GUILD EXCLUSIVE**	
89	STREET SCENE(BAS RELIEF PLAQUE)	RT	*	100.00-200.00
	D. WINTER		**DAVID WINTER CAMEOS**	
92	OXFORDSHIRE GOAT YARD	RT	*	*
	M. FISHER		**DAVID WINTER PLATE COLLECTION**	
91	A CHRISTMAS CAROL	10000	30.00	50.00
91	COTSWOLD VILLAGE	10000	30.00	50.00
92	CHICHESTER CROSS	10000	30.00	50.00
92	LITTLE MILL	10000	30.00	50.00
92	OLD CURIOSTY SHOP, THE	10000	30.00	50.00
92	SCROOGE'S COUNTING HOUSE	10000	30.00	50.00
93	LITTLE FORGE	10000	30.00	35.00
	D. WINTER		**DAVID WINTER PLATE COLLECTION**	
93	DOVE COTTAGE	10000	30.00	30.00

YR	NAME	LIMIT	ISSUE	TREND
93	FORGE, THE	10000	30.00	22.00
*				**SPECIAL EVENTS**
90	CARTWRIGHT'S COTTAGE	RT	40.00	50.00-125.00

KAISER

YR	NAME	LIMIT	ISSUE	TREND
G. NEUBACHER				**AMERICA, THE BEAUTIFUL**
88	CALIFORNIA QUAIL	9500	49.50	59.00
88	SNOWY EGRET	9500	49.50	50.00
90	BROWSING FOR DELICACIES	9500	49.50	59.00
90	SCANNING THE TERRITORY	9500	49.50	59.00
G. WILLIAMS				**AMERICAN CATS**
91	KITS IN A CRADLE, SIAMESE	7500	49.50	50.00
91	LAZY RIVER DAYS, SHORTHAIRS	7500	49.50	50.00
91	TAKING IT EASY, PERSIANS	7500	49.50	50.00
91	TREE VIEW, SHORTHAIRS	7500	49.50	50.00
K. BAUER				**ANNIVERSARY**
75	TENDER MOMENT	CL	25.00	28.00
82	BETROTHAL	CL	40.00	40.00
H. BLUM				**ANNIVERSARY**
79	ROMANTIC INTERLUDE	CL	32.00	32.00
80	LOVE AT PLAY	CL	40.00	40.00
81	RENDEZVOUS	CL	40.00	40.00
T. SCHOENER				**ANNIVERSARY**
72	LOVE BIRDS	CL	16.50	30.00
73	IN THE PARK	CL	16.50	25.00
74	CANOEING	CL	20.00	30.00
76	SERENADE	CL	25.00	25.00
77	SIMPLE GIFT	CL	25.00	25.00
78	VIKING TOAST	CL	30.00	30.00
83	SUNDAY AFTERNOON	CL	40.00	40.00
R. HERSEY				**ARABIAN NIGHTS**
89	SCHEHERAZADE	9500	75.00	75.00
J. TRUMBALL				**BICENTENNIAL PLATE**
76	SIGNING DECLARATION	CL	75.00	175.00
J. FRANCIS				**BIRD DOG SERIES**
*	BEAGLE	19500	39.50	50.00
*	BLACK LABRADOR	19500	39.50	50.00
*	COCKER SPANIEL	19500	39.50	50.00
*	ENGLISH POINTER	19500	39.50	50.00
*	ENGLISH SETTER	19500	39.50	50.00
*	GERMAN SHORT HAIR POINTER	19500	39.50	50.00
*	GOLDEN LABRADOR	19500	39.50	50.00
*	IRISH SETTER	19500	39.50	50.00
A. SCHLESINGER				**CHILDHOOD MEMORIES**
85	WAIT A LITTLE	CL	29.00	29.00
W. ZEUNER				**CHILDREN'S PRAYER**
82	NOW I LAY ME DOWN TO SLEEP	CL	29.50	30.00
82	SAYING GRACE	CL	29.50	30.00
K. BAUER				**CHRISTMAS PLATES**
71	SILENT NIGHT	CL	13.50	25.00
72	WELCOME HOME	CL	16.50	45.00
74	CHRISTMAS CAROLERS	CL	25.00	35.00
81	ADORATION BY THREE KINGS	CL	40.00	45.00
82	BRINGING HOME THE TREE	CL	40.00	50.00
H. BLUM				**CHRISTMAS PLATES**
79	CHRISTMAS EVE	CL	32.00	50.00
80	JOYS OF WINTER	CL	40.00	45.00
C. MARATTI				**CHRISTMAS PLATES**
76	CHRIST/SAVIOUR BORN	CL	25.00	40.00
J. NORTHCOTT				**CHRISTMAS PLATES**
75	BRINGING HOME THE TREE	CL	25.00	35.00
T. SCHOENER				**CHRISTMAS PLATES**
70	WAITING FOR SANTA CLAUS	CL	12.50	30.00
73	HOLY NIGHT	CL	18.00	45.00
77	THREE KINGS, THE	CL	25.00	30.00
78	SHEPHERDS IN THE FIELD	CL	30.00	35.00
G. NEUBACHER				**CLASSIC FAIRY TALES COLLECTION**
82	FROG KING	*	39.50	40.00
83	LITTLE RED RIDING HOOD	*	39.50	40.00
83	PUSS IN BOOTS	*	39.50	40.00
84	CINDERELLA	*	39.50	40.00
84	HANSEL AND GRETEL	*	39.50	40.00
84	SLEEPING BEAUTY	*	39.50	40.00
R. CLARKE				**DANCE, BALLERINA, DANCE**
*	OPENING NIGHT	CL	47.50	48.00
*	PIROUETTE	CL	47.50	48.00
*	RECITAL, THE	CL	47.50	48.00
*	SWAN LAKE	CL	47.50	48.00
82	FIRST SLIPPERS	CL	47.50	48.00
83	AT THE BARRE	CL	47.50	48.00
*				**EGYPTIAN**
80	NEFERTITI	10000	275.00	475.00
80	TUTANKHAMEN	10000	275.00	475.00
R.J. MAY				**FAITHFUL COMPANIONS**
90	BEAGLE	9500	49.50	50.00
90	COCKER SPANIEL	9500	49.50	50.00

YR	NAME	LIMIT	ISSUE	TREND
90	DASHCHUND	9500	49.50	50.00
90	DOBERMAN	9500	49.50	50.00
90	ENGLISH SPRINGER SPANIEL	9500	49.50	50.00
90	GERMAN SHEPHERD	9500	49.50	50.00
90	GOLDEN RETRIEVER	9500	49.50	50.00
90	ROTTWEILER	9500	49.50	50.00
	A. LOHMANN	**FAMOUS HORSES**		
83	SNOW KNIGHT	CL	95.00	95.00
84	NORTHERN DANCER	CL	95.00	95.00
	G. NEUBACHER	**FAMOUS LULLABIES**		
85	SLEEP BABY SLEEP	*	39.50	40.00
86	A MOCKINGBIRD	*	39.50	46.00
86	AU CLAIR DE LUNE	*	39.50	44.00
86	ROCKABYE BABY	*	39.50	41.00
87	WELSH LULLABYE	*	39.50	57.00
88	BRAHMS' LULLABYE	*	39.50	45.00
	G. LOATES	**FEATHERED FRIENDS**		
78	BLUE JAYS	CL	70.00	100.00
79	CARDINALS	CL	80.00	90.00
80	WAXWINGS	CL	80.00	85.00
81	GOLDFINCH	CL	80.00	85.00
	I. CENKOVCAN	**FOUR SEASONS**		
81	AUTUMN	*	50.00	64.00
81	SPRING	*	50.00	64.00
81	SUMMER	*	50.00	64.00
81	WINTER	*	50.00	64.00
	W. GAWANTKA	**GARDEN AND SONG BIRDS**		
73	CARDINALS	CL	200.00	250.00
73	TITMOUSE	CL	200.00	250.00
	K. BAUER	**GREAT YACHTS**		
72	CETONIA	CL	50.00	50.00
72	WESTWARD	CL	50.00	50.00
	G. NEUBACHER	**HAPPY DAYS**		
79	AEROPLANE, THE	CL	75.00	75.00
80	JULIE	CL	75.00	76.00
81	WINTER FUN	CL	75.00	75.00
82	LOOKOUT, THE	CL	75.00	75.00
	J. LITTLEJOHN	**HARMONY AND NATURE**		
85	SPRING ENCORE	CL	39.50	40.00
	*	**KING TUT**		
78	KING TUT	CL	65.00	110.00
	G. NEUBACHER	**MEMORIES OF CHRISTMAS**		
83	WONDER OF CHRISTMAS, THE	CL	42.50	43.00
84	A CHRISTMAS DREAM	CL	39.50	43.00
85	CHRISTMAS EVE	CL	39.50	40.00
86	A VISIT WITH SANTA	CL	39.50	40.00
	K. BAUER	**MOTHER'S DAY**		
82	PHEASANT FAMILY	CL	40.00	45.00
83	TENDER CARE	CL	40.00	70.00
	H. BLUM	**MOTHER'S DAY**		
81	SAFE NEAR MOTHER	CL	40.00	45.00
	J. NORTHCOTT	**MOTHER'S DAY**		
80	RACCOON FAMILY	CL	40.00	50.00
	N. PETERNER	**MOTHER'S DAY**		
79	A MOTHER'S DEVOTION	CL	32.00	45.00
	T. SCHOENER	**MOTHER'S DAY**		
71	MARE AND FOAL	CL	13.00	30.00
72	FLOWERS FOR MOTHER	CL	16.50	25.00
73	CATS	CL	17.00	45.00
74	FOX	CL	20.00	45.00
75	GERMAN SHEPHERD	CL	25.00	95.00
76	SWAN AND CYGNETS	CL	25.00	30.00
77	MOTHER RABBIT AND YOUNG	CL	25.00	35.00
78	HEN AND CHICKS	CL	30.00	55.00
	*	**OBERAMMERGAU PASSION PLAY**		
91	OBERAMMERGAU, COBALT	400	64.00	64.00
91	OBERAMMERGAU, SEPIA	700	38.00	38.00
	K. BAUER	**OBERAMMERGAU PASSION PLAY**		
70	OBERAMMERGAU	CL	40.00	40.00
	T. SCHOENER	**OBERAMMERGAU PASSION PLAY**		
70	OBERAMMERGAU	CL	25.00	30.00
	A. LOHMANN	**ON THE FARM**		
*	DUCKS ON THE POND	*	50.00	108.00
*	GIRL FEEDING ANIMALS	*	50.00	108.00
*	GIRL WITH GOATS	*	50.00	108.00
*	WHITE HORSE	*	50.00	108.00
81	DUCK, THE	*	50.00	108.00
82	ROOSTER, THE	*	50.00	108.00
83	HORSES, THE	*	50.00	108.00
83	POND, THE	*	50.00	108.00
	R. HORTON	**RACING FOR PRIDE AND PROFIT**		
*	PROFIT OR PRISON	9500	*	60.00
84	AGING VICTOR, THE	9500	50.00	50.00
85	SECOND GOES HUNGRY	9500	50.00	50.00
86	NO TIME TO BOAST	9500	50.00	50.00
87	FIRST FISH TO MARKET	9500	50.00	60.00

YR	NAME	LIMIT	ISSUE	TREND
88	GYPSY TRADERS	9500	60.00	60.00
	G. NEUBACHER			**ROMANTIC PORTRAITS**
81	LILIE	CL	200.00	210.00
82	CAMELIA	CL	175.00	180.00
83	ROSE	CL	175.00	185.00
84	DAISY	CL	175.00	180.00
	J. MCKERNAN			**THE GRADUATE**
86	BOY	7500	39.50	40.00
86	GIRL	7500	39.50	40.00
	D. KING			**TRADITIONAL FAIRY TALES**
83	CINDERELLA	*	39.50	40.00
83	JACK AND THE BEANSTALK	*	39.50	40.00
84	THREE LITTLE PIGS	*	39.50	40.00
84	TOM THUMB	*	39.50	40.00
85	DICK WITTINGTON	*	39.50	40.00
85	GOLDILOCKS	*	39.50	40.00
	T. BOYER			**WALLPLATES: #837 WATER FOWL COLLECTION**
89	PAIR OF CANVASBACKS	15000	49.50	50.00
89	PAIR OF CAROLINA WOOD DUCKS	15000	49.50	50.00
89	PAIR OF GREENWINGED TEALS	15000	49.50	50.00
89	PAIR OF MALLARD	15000	49.50	50.00
89	PAIR OF PINTAILS	15000	49.50	50.00
89	PAIR OF REDHEADS	15000	49.50	50.00
	G. NEUBACHER			**WALLPLATES: FOREST SURPRISES**
89	DEERHEAD ORCHID	9500	49.50	59.00
89	MARSH MARIGOLD	9500	49.50	59.00
90	VIOLETS	9500	49.50	59.00
90	WILD IRIS	9500	49.50	59.00
	L. TURNER			**WALLPLATES: NOBLE HORSE COLLECTION**
88	ARABIAN	OP	49.50	50.00
88	GELDERLANDER	OP	49.50	50.00
88	HOLSTEIN	OP	49.50	50.00
88	QUARTER HORSE	OP	49.50	50.00
88	THOROUGHBRED	OP	49.50	50.00
88	TRAKEHNER	OP	49.50	50.00
	D. TWINNEY			**WALLPLATES: STABLE DOOR COLLECTION**
88	FIRST STEPS	OP	29.50	30.00
88	IMPUDENCE	OP	29.50	30.00
88	PRIDE	OP	29.50	30.00
88	VISITOR, THE	OP	29.50	30.00
	E. BIERLY			**WATER FOWL**
85	CANVASBACK DUCKS	19500	55.00	89.00
85	MALLARD DUCKS	19500	55.00	89.00
85	PINTAIL DUCKS	19500	55.00	89.00
85	WOOD DUCKS	19500	55.00	89.00
	G. NEUBACHER			**WILDFLOWERS**
86	TRILLIUM	9500	39.50	65.00
87	SPRING BEAUTY	9500	45.00	64.00
87	WILD ASTERS	9500	49.50	59.00
87	WILD ROSES	9500	49.50	59.00
	R. ORR			**WOODLAND CREATURES**
85	FIRST ADVENTURE	10-DAY	37.50	38.00
85	FISHING TRIP	10-DAY	37.50	38.00
85	HIDING PLACE, THE	10-DAY	37.50	38.00
85	MEADOWLAND VIGIL	10-DAY	37.50	38.00
85	MORNING LESSON	10-DAY	37.50	38.00
85	RESTING IN THE GLEN	10-DAY	37.50	38.00
85	SPRINGTIME FROLIC	10-DAY	37.50	38.00
85	STARTLED SENTRY	10-DAY	37.50	38.00

KONIGSZELT BAYERN

YR	NAME	LIMIT	ISSUE	TREND
	H. KELLER			**HEDI KELLER CHRISTMAS**
79	ADORATION, THE	*	29.50	33.00
80	FLIGHT INTO EGYPT	*	29.50	33.00
81	RETURN INTO GALILEE	*	29.50	31.00
82	FOLLOWING THE STAR	*	29.50	32.00
83	REST ON THE FLIGHT	*	29.50	35.00
84	NATIVITY, THE	*	29.50	35.00
85	GIFT OF THE MAGI	*	34.50	40.00
86	ANNUNCIATION	*	34.50	40.00

KPM-ROYAL CORPORATION

YR	NAME	LIMIT	ISSUE	TREND
	*			**CHRISTMAS**
69	CHRISTMAS STAR	5000	28.00	400.00
70	THREE KINGS	5000	28.00	300.00
71	CHRISTMAS TREE	5000	28.00	300.00
72	CHRISTMAS ANGEL	5000	31.00	320.00
73	CHRIST CHILD ON SLED	5000	33.00	300.00
74	ANGEL AND HORN	5000	35.00	200.00
75	SHEPHERDS	5000	40.00	175.00
76	STAR OF BETHLEHEM	5000	43.00	150.00
77	MARY AT CRIB	5000	46.00	100.00
78	THREE WISE MEN	5000	49.00	60.00
79	MANGER, THE	5000	55.00	60.00
80	SHEPHERDS IN FIELDS	5000	55.00	60.00

Curiosity: Asian Elephants *from the "Tomorrow's Promise" series, is one of many wildlife plates produced by The Bradford Exchange.*

Gorham's first doll plate, Lydia, *from the Gorham Museum Doll Plates collection, debuted in 1984 with an edition of 5,000. The gold-banded 8-1/2-inch plate retailed for $29 and is currently valued at $125.*

Share the sweet melody of Morning Song *by Jody Bergsma. Issued in 1985 as part of the Days Gone By collection by Reco International, production was limited to 14 days.*

Portraying a bond that will last forever is Sue Etem's A Pair of Dreams *from the "Infinite Love" series produced by Armstrong's.*

YR	NAME	LIMIT	ISSUE	TREND
L.L. KNICKERBOCKER CO. INC.				
R.T. GORDON				
94	VARSITY BEAR PHOTO C15001	2500	31.25	32.00
LALIQUE				
M. LALIQUE				**ANNUAL**
65	DEUX OISEAUX (TWO BIRDS)	2000	25.00	1200.00
66	ROSE DE SONGERIE (DREAM ROSE)	5000	25.00	125.00
67	BALLET DE POISSON (FISH BALLET)	5000	25.00	100.00
68	GAZELLE FANTAISIE (GAZELLE FANTASY)	5000	25.00	65.00
69	PAPILLON (BUTTERFLY)	5000	30.00	40.00
70	PAON (PEACOCK)	5000	30.00	60.00
71	HIBOU (OWL)	5000	35.00	70.00
72	COQUILLAGE (SHELL)	5000	40.00	65.00
73	PETIT GEAI (JAYLING)	5000	42.50	100.00
74	SOUS D'ARGENT (SILVER PENNIES)	5000	47.50	100.00
75	DUO DE POISSON (FISH DUET)	5000	50.00	140.00
76	AIGLE (EAGLE)	5000	60.00	75.00
LANCE CORP.				
*	**12 DAYS OF CHRISTMAS (CHILLMARK PEWTER/STAINED GLASS)**			
79	PARTRIDGE IN A PEAR TREE 8 IN.	RT	99.50	100.00
80	TWO TURTLE DOVES 8 IN.	RT	99.50	100.00
A. PETITTO	**A CHILD'S CHRISTMAS (HUDSON PEWTER)**			
78	BEDTIME STORY	10000	35.00	60.00
78	BEDTIME STORY	SU	35.00	60.00
79	LITTLEST ANGELS	10000	35.00	60.00
79	LITTLEST ANGELS	SU	35.00	60.00
80	HEAVEN'S CHRISTMAS TREE	10000	42.50	60.00
80	HEAVEN'S CHRISTMAS TREE	SU	42.50	60.00
81	FILLING THE SKY	10000	47.50	60.00
81	FILLING THE SKY	SU	47.50	60.00
C. TERRIS	**AMERICA'S FAVORITE BIRDS (HUDSON PEWTER/CRYSTAL)**			
78	CRYSTAL WREN 8 IN.	RT	79.50	80.00
R. LAMB	**AMERICAN COMM. (HUDSON PEWTER)**			
75	HYDE PARK 6 IN.	RT	*	55.00
75	LOG CABIN 6 IN.	RT	*	55.00
75	MONTICELLO 6 IN.	RT	*	55.00
75	MT. VERNON 6 IN.	RT	*	55.00
75	SPIRIT OF '76 6 IN.	RT	*	55.00
P.W. BASTON	**AMERICAN EXPANSION (HUDSON PEWTER)**			
75	AMERICAN EXPANSION	CL	*	60.00
75	AMERICAN INDEPENDENCE	CL	*	110.00
75	AMERICAN WAR BETWEEN THE STATES, THE	CL	*	175.00
75	SPIRIT OF '76 (6 IN. PLATE)	CL	27.50	110.00
*	**CHRISTMAS (CHILMARK PEWTER)**			
77	CURRIER & IVES CHRISTMAS 8 IN.	RT	60.00	75.00
78	TRIMMING THE TREE 8 IN.	RT	65.00	75.00
79	THREE WISEMEN 8 IN.	RT	65.00	75.00
A. MCGRORY	**CHRISTMAS (HUDSON PEWTER)**			
93	CRACK THE WHIP	950	55.00	55.00
94	HOME FOR CHRISTMAS	950	50.00	50.00
A. PETITTO	**CHRISTMAS (HUDSON PEWTER)**			
87	CAROLING ANGELS, THE	SU	47.50	60.00
J. WANAT	**CHRISTMAS (HUDSON PEWTER)**			
86	BRINGING HOME THE TREE	SU	47.50	60.00
86	BRINGING HOME THE TREE	SU	47.50	60.00
D. EVERHART	**MICKEY'S CHRISTMAS (HUDSON PEWTER)**			
86	GOD BLESS US, EVERY ONE	SU	47.50	60.00
87	JOLLY OLD SAINT NICK	SU	55.00	60.00
88	HE'S CHECKING IT TWICE	SU	50.00	60.00
*	**MOTHER'S DAY (CHILMARK PEWTER)**			
74	FLOWERS OF THE FIELD 8 IN.	RT	60.00	75.00
80	1980 MOTHER'S DAY	RT	90.00	90.00
A. PETITTO	**MOTHER'S DAY (HUDSON PEWTER)**			
79	CHERISHED 6 IN.	RT	42.50	55.00
80	1980 MOTHER'S DAY 6 IN.	RT	42.50	55.00
A. PETITTO	**SAILING SHIPS (HUDSON PEWTER)**			
78	AMERICA 6 IN.	RT	35.00	55.00
78	CONSTITUTION 6 IN.	RT	35.00	55.00
78	FLYING CLOUD 6 IN.	RT	35.00	55.00
78	MORGAN 6 IN.	RT	35.00	55.00
P.W. BASTON	**SEBASTIAN PLATES**			
74	SPIRIT OF '76 (9 IN.)	RT	27.50	75.00
76	DECLARATION OF INDEPENDENCE (8 1/2 IN.)	RT	25.00	50.00
78	MOTIF NO. 1	CL	75.00	60.00
78	ZODIAC (8 IN.)	RT	60.00	75.00
79	GRAND CANYON	CL	75.00	60.00
80	IN THE CANDY STORE	CL	39.50	45.00
80	LONE CYPRESS	CL	75.00	160.00
81	DOCTOR, THE	CL	39.50	45.00
83	LITTLE MOTHER	CL	39.50	45.00
84	SWITCHING THE FREIGHT	CL	42.50	90.00
HOLLIS/YOURDON	**SONG BIRDS OF THE FOUR SEASONS (HUDSON PEWTER)**			
78	CARDINAL (WINTER 6 IN.)	RT	35.00	55.00

YR	NAME	LIMIT	ISSUE	TREND
78	HUMMINGBIRD (SUMMER 6 IN.)	RT	35.00	55.00
78	SPARROW (AUTUMN 6 IN.)	RT	35.00	55.00
78	WOOD THRUSH (SPRING 6 IN.)	RT	35.00	55.00
A. MCGRORY		**SONGS OF CHRISTMAS (HUDSON PEWTER)**		
88	SILENT NIGHT	SU	55.00	60.00
89	HARK! THE HERALD ANGELS SING	SU	60.00	60.00
90	FIRST NOEL, THE	SU	60.00	60.00
91	WE THREE KINGS	SU	60.00	60.00
A. HOLLIS		**TWAS THE NIGHT BEFORE CHRISTMAS (HUDSON PEWTER)**		
82	NOT A CREATURE WAS STIRRING	SU	47.50	60.00
83	VISIONS OF SUGAR PLUMS	SU	47.50	60.00
84	HIS EYES HOW THEY TWINKLED	SU	47.50	60.00
85	HAPPY CHRISTMAS TO ALL	SU	47.50	60.00

LENOX CHINA/CRYSTAL COLLECTION

YR	NAME	LIMIT	ISSUE	TREND
N. ADAMS		**AMERICAN WILDLIFE**		
82	BLACK BEARS	9500	65.00	70.00
82	BUFFALO	9500	65.00	70.00
82	DALL SHEEP	9500	65.00	70.00
82	JACK RABBITS	9500	65.00	70.00
82	MOUNTAIN LIONS	9500	65.00	70.00
82	OCELOTS	9500	65.00	70.00
82	OTTERS	9500	65.00	70.00
82	POLAR BEARS	9500	65.00	70.00
82	RACCOONS	9500	65.00	70.00
82	RED FOXES	9500	65.00	70.00
82	SEA LIONS	9500	65.00	70.00
82	WHITE TAILED DEER	9500	65.00	70.00
*		**ANNUAL CHRISTMAS PLATES**		
92	SLEIGH	YR	75.00	75.00
L. BYWATER		**ANNUAL CHRISTMAS PLATES**		
93	MIDNIGHT SLEIGH RIDE	CL	119.00	125.00
*		**ANNUAL HOLIDAY**		
91	SLEIGH	YR	75.00	78.00
J. VAN ZYLE		**ARCTIC WOLVES**		
93	CRY OF THE WILD	CL	29.90	30.00
93	FAR COUNTRY CROSSING	CL	29.90	30.00
93	MIDNIGHT RENEGADE	CL	29.90	30.00
93	NIGHTWATCH	CL	29.90	30.00
93	ON THE EDGE	CL	29.90	30.00
93	PICKING UP THE TRAIL	CL	29.90	30.00
Q. LEMONDS		**BIG CATS OF THE WORLD**		
93	BLACK PANTHER	OP	39.50	40.00
93	BOBCAT	OP	39.50	40.00
93	CHINESE LEOPARD	OP	39.50	40.00
93	COUGAR	OP	39.50	40.00
93	LION	OP	39.50	40.00
93	SNOW LEOPARD	OP	39.50	40.00
93	TIGER	OP	39.50	40.00
93	WHITE TIGER	OP	39.50	40.00
W. MUMM		**BIRDS OF THE GARDEN**		
92	SPRING GLORY, CARDINALS	OP	39.50	40.00
93	BLOSSOMING BOUGH, CHICKADEES	OP	39.50	40.00
93	BLUEBIRDS HAVEN, BLUEBIRDS	OP	39.50	40.00
93	INDIGO MEADOW, INDIGO BUNTINGS	OP	39.50	40.00
93	JEWELS OF THE GARDEN, HUMMINGBIRDS	OP	39.50	40.00
93	SCARLET TANAGERS	OP	39.50	40.00
93	SUNBRIGHT SONGBIRDS, GOLDFINCH	OP	39.50	40.00
E. BOEHM		**BOEHM BIRDS**		
70	WOOD THRUSH	YR	35.00	98.00
71	GOLDFINCH	YR	35.00	49.00
72	MOUNTAIN BLUEBIRD	YR	37.50	48.00
73	MEADOWLARK	YR	41.00	30.00
74	RUFOUS HUMMINGBIRD	YR	45.00	50.00
75	AMERICAN REDSTART	YR	50.00	60.00
76	CARDINALS	YR	53.00	80.00
77	ROBINS	YR	55.00	44.00
78	MOCKINGBIRDS	YR	58.00	60.00
79	GOLDEN-CROWNED KINGLETS	YR	65.00	94.00
80	BLACK-THROATED BLUE WARBLERS	YR	80.00	110.00
81	EASTERN PHOEBES	YR	90.00	100.00
E. BOEHM		**BOEHM WOODLAND WILDLIFE**		
73	RACCOONS	YR	50.00	55.00
74	RED FOXES	YR	52.50	57.00
75	COTTONTAIL RABBITS	YR	58.50	63.00
76	EASTERN CHIPMUNKS	YR	62.50	65.00
77	BEAVER	YR	67.50	72.00
78	WHITETAIL DEER	YR	70.00	75.00
79	SQUIRRELS	YR	76.00	76.00
80	BOBCATS	YR	82.50	87.00
81	MARTENS	YR	100.00	150.00
82	RIVER OTTERS	YR	100.00	175.00
D. CROWLEY		**CHILDREN OF THE SUN & MOON**		
93	DESERT BLOSSOM	OP	39.50	40.00
93	FEATHERS & FURS	OP	39.50	40.00
93	SHY ONE	OP	39.50	40.00
94	DAUGHTER OF THE SUN	OP	39.90	40.00

YR	NAME	LIMIT	ISSUE	TREND
94	INDIGO GIRL	OP	39.90	40.00
94	LITTLE FLOWER	OP	39.90	40.00
94	RED FEATHERS	OP	39.90	40.00
94	STARS IN HER EYES	OP	39.90	40.00
*		**CHRISTMAS TREES AROUND THE WORLD**		
91	GERMANY	YR	75.00	78.00
92	FRANCE	YR	75.00	80.00
*		**COLONIAL CHRISTMAS WREATH**		
81	COLONIAL VIRGINIA	YR	65.00	80.00
82	MASSACHUSETTS	YR	70.00	95.00
83	MARYLAND	YR	70.00	80.00
84	RHODE ISLAND	YR	70.00	80.00
85	CONNECTICUT	YR	70.00	80.00
86	NEW HAMPSHIRE	YR	70.00	75.00
87	PENNSYLVANIA	YR	70.00	78.00
88	DELAWARE	YR	70.00	68.00
89	NEW YORK	YR	75.00	80.00
90	NEW JERSEY	YR	75.00	80.00
91	SOUTH CAROLINA	YR	75.00	78.00
92	NORTH CAROLINA	YR	75.00	80.00
Q. LEMONDS		**CUBS OF THE BIG CATS**		
93	JAGUAR CUB	CL	29.90	30.00
L. PICKEN		**DARLING DALMATIONS**		
93	ALL FIRED UP	CL	29.90	30.00
93	CAUGHT IN THE ACT	CL	29.90	30.00
93	FIRE BRIGADE	CL	29.90	30.00
93	PLEASE DON'T PICK THE FLOWERS	CL	29.90	30.00
93	PUPS IN BOOTS	CL	29.90	30.00
93	THREE ALARM FIRE	CL	29.90	30.00
J. HOLDERBY		**DOLPHINS OF THE SEVEN SEAS**		
93	BOTTLENOSE DOLPHINS	OP	39.50	40.00
R. KELLY		**EAGLE CONSERVATION**		
93	DAYBREAK ON RIVER'S EDGE	OP	39.50	40.00
93	EAGLES ON MT. MCKINLEY	OP	39.50	40.00
93	LONE SENTINEL	OP	39.50	40.00
93	NORTHERN HERITAGE	OP	39.50	40.00
93	NORTHWOOD'S LEGEND	OP	39.50	40.00
93	RIVER SCOUT	OP	39.50	40.00
93	SOARING THE PEAKS	OP	39.50	40.00
93	SOLO FLIGHT	OP	39.50	40.00
R. SANDERSON		**ENCHANTED WORLD OF THE UNICORN**		
92	HIDDEN GLADE OF UNICORN	CL	29.90	30.00
92	JOYFUL MEADOW OF UNICORN	CL	29.90	30.00
92	MISTY HILLS OF UNICORN	CL	29.90	30.00
92	SECRET GARDEN OF UNICORN	CL	29.90	30.00
92	SPRINGTIME PASTURE OF UNICORN	CL	29.90	30.00
92	TROPICAL PARADISE OF UNICORN	CL	29.90	30.00
*		**GARDEN BIRD PLATE COLLECTION**		
88	BLUEJAY	OP	48.00	53.00
88	CHICKADEE	OP	48.00	53.00
89	HUMMINGBIRD	OP	48.00	53.00
91	CARDINAL	OP	48.00	53.00
91	DOVE	OP	48.00	53.00
92	GOLDFINCH	OP	48.00	53.00
G. COHELEACH		**GREAT CATS OF THE WORLD**		
93	CHINESE LEOPARD	OP	39.50	40.00
93	COUGAR	OP	39.50	40.00
93	JAGUAR	OP	39.50	40.00
93	LION	OP	39.50	40.00
93	LIONESS	OP	39.50	40.00
93	SIBERIAN TIGER	OP	39.50	40.00
93	SNOW LEOPARD	OP	39.50	40.00
93	WHITE TIGER	OP	39.50	40.00
R. HOOVER		**INTERNATIONAL VICTORIAN SANTAS**		
92	KRIS KRINGLE	CL	39.50	40.00
93	FATHER CHRISTMAS	CL	39.50	40.00
94	GRANDFATHER FROST	CL	39.50	40.00
95	AMERICAN SANTA CLAUS	CL	39.50	40.00
S. COMBES		**KING OF THE PLAINS**		
94	AFRICAN ANCIENTS	OP	39.90	40.00
94	END OF THE LINE	OP	39.90	40.00
94	GUARDIAN	OP	39.90	40.00
94	LAST ELEPHANT, THE	OP	39.90	40.00
94	PROTECTING THE FLANKS	OP	39.90	40.00
94	RAINBOW TRAIL	OP	39.90	40.00
94	SPARRING BULLS	OP	39.90	40.00
94	TSAVA ELEPHANT	OP	39.90	40.00
L. BYWATERS		**MAGIC OF CHRISTMAS**		
93	GIFTS FOR ALL	OP	39.50	40.00
93	SANTA OF THE NORTHERN FOREST	OP	39.50	40.00
93	SANTA'S GIFT OF PEACE	OP	39.50	40.00
94	A BERRY MERRY CHRISTMAS	OP	39.50	40.00
94	COMING HOME	OP	39.50	40.00
94	SANTA'S SENTINELS	OP	39.50	40.00
94	WONDER OF WONDERS	OP	39.50	40.00
C. MCCLUNG		**NATURE'S COLLAGE**		
92	CEDAR WAXWING, AMONG THE BERRIES	OP	34.50	35.00

YR	NAME	LIMIT	ISSUE	TREND
92	GOLD FINCHES, GOLDEN SPLENDOR	OP	34.50	35.00
93	BLUEBIRDS, SUMMER INTERLUDE	CL	39.50	40.00
93	BLUEJAYS, WINTER SONG	CL	39.50	40.00
93	CARDINALS, SPRING COURTSHIP	CL	39.50	40.00
93	CHICKADEES, ROSE MORNING	CL	39.50	40.00
93	HUMMINGBIRDS, JEWELED GLORY	CL	39.50	40.00
93	INDIGO BUNTINGS, INDIGO EVENING	CL	39.50	40.00
L. LAFFIN		**OWLS OF NORTH AMERICA**		
93	SPIRIT OF THE ARCTIC, SNOWY OWL	OP	39.50	40.00
*		**PIERCED NATIVITY**		
93	HOLY FAMILY	OP	45.00	45.00
94	HERALDING ANGELS	OP	45.00	45.00
94	SHEPHERDS	OP	45.00	45.00
94	THREE KINGS	OP	45.00	45.00
G. COHELEACH		**ROYAL CATS OF GUY COHELEACH**		
94	AFTERNOON SHADE	OP	39.50	40.00
94	AMBUSH IN THE SNOW	OP	39.50	40.00
94	CAT NAP	OP	39.50	40.00
94	JUNGLE JAQUAR	OP	39.50	40.00
94	LION IN WAIT	OP	39.50	40.00
94	ROCKY MOUNTAIN PUMA	OP	39.50	40.00
94	ROCKY REFUGE	OP	39.50	40.00
94	SIESTA	OP	39.50	40.00
J. HOLDERBY		**WHALE CONSERVATION**		
93	ORCA	OP	39.50	40.00

LIGHTPOST PUBLISHING

Price ranges may reflect various demands in the market from one geographic region to another; condition of piece; specific markings found on piece; and/or changes in production of piece.

YR	NAME	LIMIT	ISSUE	TREND
T. KINKADE		**T. KINKADE SIGNATURE COLLECTION**		
91	CEDAR NOOK	2500	49.95	50.00
91	CHANDLER'S COTTAGE	2500	49.95	50.00
91	HOME TO GRANDMA'S	2500	49.95	50.00
91	SLEIGH RIDE HOME	2500	49.95	50.00

LILLIPUT LANE LTD.

YR	NAME	LIMIT	ISSUE	TREND
R. DAY		**AMERICAN LANDMARKS COLLECTION**		
90	COUNTRY CHURCH	RT	35.00	35.00
90	MAIL BARN	5000	35.00	125.00
90	RIVERSIDE CHAPEL	RT	35.00	35.00

LLADRO

Price ranges may reflect various demands in the market from one geographic region to another; condition of piece; specific markings found on piece; and/or changes in production of piece.

YR	NAME	LIMIT	ISSUE	TREND
LLADRO		**LLADRO PLATE COLLECTION**		
72	MOTHERS DAY PLATE L-7007	*	*	150.00
93	DUCK PLATE L-6000G	OP	38.00	40.00
93	GREAT VOYAGE, THE L-5964G	OP	50.00	50.00
93	LOOKING OUT L-5998G	OP	38.00	40.00
93	SWINGING L-5999G	OP	38.00	40.00
94	APPLE PICKING L-6159M	OP	32.00	33.00
94	FLAMINGO L-6161M	OP	32.00	33.00
94	FRIENDS L-6158	OP	32.00	33.00
94	RESTING L-6162M	OP	32.00	33.00
94	TURTLEDOVE L-6160	OP	32.00	33.00

MAFEKING COLLECTION

YR	NAME	LIMIT	ISSUE	TREND
M. GREEN		**FOREVER FRIENDS**		
93	HIDE AWAY, THE	500	85.00	100.00
94	RUFOUS (THE HUMMINGBIRD)	500	34.75	85.00
M. GREEN		**MAN'S BEST FRIEND**		
93	DEREK (THE LABRADOR RETRIEVER)	500	65.00	85.00
93	DIVOT (THE GERMAN SHEPHERD)	500	85.00	100.00
94	MICKEY (SPANIEL CROSS)	500	39.95	45.00
94	PEPPER (THE AIREDALE)	500	39.95	85.00
M. GREEN		**MY LITTLE BEAR**		
93	BEAR WITH ME	500	85.00	100.00
93	SHIZAM (THE MAGICIAN)	500	85.00	100.00
M. GREEN		**THE LORD'S CHILDREN**		
93	A FRAGRANCE IN TIME	500	85.00	100.00
93	HEAR MY PRAYERS	500	75.00	85.00
94	TRADITIONS	500	39.95	85.00

MARCH OF DIMES

YR	NAME	LIMIT	ISSUE	TREND
E. HIBEL		**OUR CHILDREN, OUR FUTURE**		
90	A TIME TO EMBRACE	CL	29.00	29.00
S. KUCK		**OUR CHILDREN, OUR FUTURE**		
89	A TIME TO LOVE	CL	29.00	46.00
J. MCCLELLAND		**OUR CHILDREN, OUR FUTURE**		
89	A TIME TO PLANT	CL	29.00	29.00
G. PERILLO		**OUR CHILDREN, OUR FUTURE**		
89	A TIME TO BE BORN	CL	29.00	30.00
A. WILLIAMS		**OUR CHILDREN, OUR FUTURE**		
90	A TIME TO LAUGH	CL	29.00	29.00
D. ZOLAN		**OUR CHILDREN, OUR FUTURE**		
89	A TIME FOR PEACE	CL	29.00	29.00

YR	NAME	LIMIT	ISSUE	TREND
	MARIGOLD			
	CARRENO			**SPORT**
89	JOE DIMAGGIO F/BLUE SIGNATURE	RT	60.00	110.00
89	JOE DIMAGGIO H/S	RT	100.00	1200.00
89	MICKEY MANTLE H/S	RT	100.00	645.00
89	MICKEY MANTLE U/S	RT	60.00	95.00
90	JOE DIMAGGIO AP H/S	RT	*	2200.00
	MARURI USA			
	W. GAITHER			**EAGLE PLATE SERIES**
84	FREE FLIGHT	CL	150.00	175.00
	MORGANTOWN			
	C. YATES			**YATE'S COUNTRY LADIES**
81	ANGELICA	OP	75.00	75.00
82	VIOLET	OP	75.00	75.00
83	HEATHER	OP	75.00	75.00
84	LAUREL	OP	75.00	90.00
	C. YATES			**HEAVENS ABOVE**
89	CASSIOPEIA	OP	64.50	65.00
90	ORION	OP	64.50	120.00
90	PEGASUS	OP	64.50	200.00
91	CYGNUS	OP	64.50	150.00
	C. YATES			**STAR OF BETHLEHEM**
88	HOLY FAMILY, THE	OP	34.50	35.00
89	SHEPHERDS IN THE FIELD	OP	34.50	54.00
90	LED BY THE STAR	OP	37.50	50.00
91	TIDINGS OF GREAT JOY	OP	37.50	200.00
	MUSEUM COLLECTIONS INC.			
	N. ROCKWELL			**AMERICAN FAMILY I**
79	BABY'S FIRST STEP	9900	28.50	61.00
79	BIRTHDAY PARTY	9900	28.50	38.00
79	BRIDE AND GROOM	9900	28.50	38.00
79	FIRST HAIRCUT	9900	28.50	38.00
79	FIRST PROM	9900	28.50	38.00
79	HAPPY BIRTHDAY DEAR MOTHER	9900	28.50	45.00
79	LITTLE MOTHER	9900	28.50	38.00
79	MOTHER'S LITTLE HELPERS	9900	28.50	38.00
79	STUDENT, THE	9900	28.50	38.00
79	SWEET SIXTEEN	9900	28.50	38.00
79	WASHING OUR DOG	9900	28.50	38.00
79	WRAPPING CHRISTMAS PRESENTS	9900	28.50	38.00
	N. ROCKWELL			**AMERICAN FAMILY II**
80	ALMOST GROWN UP	22500	35.00	40.00
80	COURAGEOUS HERO	22500	35.00	40.00
80	GIVING THANKS	22500	35.00	40.00
80	HOME RUN SLUGGER	22500	35.00	40.00
80	LITTLE SALESMAN	22500	35.00	40.00
80	LITTLE SHAVER	22500	35.00	40.00
80	NEW ARRIVAL	22500	35.00	55.00
80	SPACE PIONEERS	22500	35.00	40.00
80	SPACE PIONEERS	22500	35.00	40.00
80	SWEET DREAMS	22500	35.00	40.00
80	WE MISSED YOU DADDY	22500	35.00	40.00
81	AT THE CIRCUS	22500	35.00	40.00
81	GOOD FOOD, GOOD FRIENDS	22500	35.00	40.00
	N. ROCKWELL			**CHRISTMAS**
79	DAY AFTER CHRISTMAS	YR	75.00	85.00
80	CHECKING HIS LIST	YR	75.00	85.00
81	RINGING IN GOOD CHEER	YR	75.00	85.00
82	WAITING FOR SANTA	YR	75.00	85.00
83	HIGH HOPES	YR	75.00	85.00
84	SPACE AGE SANTA	YR	55.00	65.00
	N. ROCKWELL GALLERY			
	*			**N. ROCKWELL CENTENNIAL**
93	COBBLER, THE	CL	39.90	40.00
93	TOYMAKER, THE	CL	39.90	40.00
	*			**ROCKWELL'S CHRISTMAS LEGACY**
92	SANTA'S WORKSHOP	CL	49.90	50.00
93	MAKING A LIST	CL	49.90	50.00
93	VISIONS OF SANTA	CL	54.90	55.00
93	WHILE SANTA SLUMBERS	CL	54.90	55.00
	NEWELL			
	S. STILWELL			**WEBER'S CALENDAR**
84	JULY	OP	19.00	19.00
84	JUNE	OP	19.00	19.00
85	AUGUST	OP	19.00	19.00
85	NOVEMBER	OP	19.00	19.00
85	OCTOBER	OP	19.00	19.00
85	SEPTEMBER	OP	19.00	19.00
86	APRIL	OP	19.00	25.00
86	DECEMBER	OP	19.00	20.00
86	FEBRUARY	OP	19.00	19.00
86	JANUARY	OP	19.00	19.00
86	MARCH	OP	19.00	22.00

YR	NAME	LIMIT	ISSUE	TREND
86	MAY	OP	19.00	55.00

NOSTALGIA

YR	NAME	LIMIT	ISSUE	TREND
L. CASIGA				**HISPANIC COLLECTORS**
95	RINCONCITO CRIOLLO	12000	30.00	30.00
E. DIUZ				**HISPANIC COLLECTORS**
95	LA GARITA	9000	30.00	30.00
J. FELLIN				**HISPANIC COLLECTORS**
95	A LA LUZ DE MI BALCON	12000	30.00	30.00

OSIRIS PORCELAIN

YR	NAME	LIMIT	ISSUE	TREND
N.N. BICHAY				**LEGEND OF TUTANKHAMEN**
91	TUTANKHAMEN AND HIS PRINCESS	195-DAY	39.84	45.00

PEMBERTON & OAKES

YR	NAME	LIMIT	ISSUE	TREND
D. ZOLAN				**ADVENTURES OF CHILDHOOD**
89	ALMOST HOME	RT	19.60	55.00
89	CRYSTAL'S CREEK	RT	19.60	35.00
89	SUMMER SUDS	RT	22.00	30.00
90	SNOWY ADVENTURE	RT	22.00	30.00
91	FORESTS & FAIRY TALES	RT	24.40	25.00
D. ZOLAN				**ANNIVERSARY (10TH)**
88	RIBBONS AND ROSES	RT	24.40	45.00
D. ZOLAN				**CHILDHOOD DISCOVERIES (MINIATURE)**
90	AUTUMN LEAVES	RT	14.40	35.00
90	COLORS OF SPRING	RT	14.40	40.00
90	FIRST KISS	RT	14.40	55.00
91	ENCHANTED FOREST	RT	16.60	35.00
91	JUST DUCKY	RT	16.60	30.00
91	RAINY DAY PALS	RT	16.60	35.00
92	DOUBLE TROUBLE	RT	16.60	35.00
93	PEPPERMINT KISS	RT	16.60	30.00
95	TENDER HEARTS	RT	16.60	17.00
D. ZOLAN				**CHILDHOOD FRIENDSHIP**
86	BEACH BREAK	RT	19.00	50.00
87	LITTLE ENGINEERS	RT	19.00	60.00
88	DOZENS OF DAISIES	RT	19.00	35.00
88	SHARING SECRETS	RT	19.00	50.00
89	TINY TREASURES	RT	19.00	50.00
90	COUNTRY WALK	RT	19.00	25.00
D. ZOLAN				**CHILDREN AND PETS**
84	GOLDEN MOMENT	RT	19.00	23.00
84	TENDER MOMENT	RT	19.00	37.00
85	MAKING FRIENDS	RT	19.00	22.00
85	TENDER BEGINNING	RT	19.00	32.00
86	BACKYARD DISCOVERY	RT	19.00	23.00
86	WAITING TO PLAY	RT	19.00	27.00
D. ZOLAN				**CHILDREN AT CHRISTMAS**
81	A GIFT FOR LAURIE	RT	48.00	50.00
82	CHRISTMAS PRAYER	RT	48.00	70.00
83	ERIK'S DELIGHT	RT	48.00	65.00
84	CHRISTMAS SECRET	RT	48.00	50.00
85	CHRISTMAS KITTEN	RT	48.00	59.00
86	LAURIE AND THE CRECHE	RT	48.00	64.00
D. ZOLAN				**CHRISTMAS**
91	CANDLELIGHT MAGIC	RT	24.80	55.00
D. ZOLAN				**CHRISTMAS (MINIATURE)**
93	SNOWY ADVENTURE	RT	16.60	25.00
94	CANDLELIGHT MAGIC	CL	16.60	17.00
D. ZOLAN				**COMPANION TO BROTHERLY LOVE**
89	SISTERLY LOVE	RT	22.00	35.00
D. ZOLAN				**EASTER (MINIATURE)**
91	EASTER MORNING (EASTER)	RT	16.60	35.00
D. ZOLAN				**FATHER'S DAY**
86	DADDY'S HOME	RT	19.00	100.00
D. ZOLAN				**FATHER'S DAY (MINIATURE)**
94	TWO OF A KIND	RT	16.60	25.00
D. ZOLAN				**GRANDPARENT'S DAY**
90	IT'S GRANDMA & GRANDPA	RT	24.40	35.00
93	GRANDPA'S FENCE	RT	24.40	35.00
D. ZOLAN				**HEIRLOOM OVALS**
92	MY KITTY	RT	18.80	40.00
*				**LOCKHART WILDLIFE**
70	WOODCOCK-GROUSE	OP	150.00	209.00
71	TEAL-MALLARD	OP	150.00	170.00
72	MOCKINGBIRD-CARDINAL	OP	162.50	140.00
73	TURKEY-PHEASANT	OP	162.50	225.00
74	AMERICAN BOLD EAGLE	OP	150.00	675.00
75	WHITE-TAILED DEER	OP	100.00	109.00
76	AMERICAN BUFFALO	OP	165.00	124.00
77	GREAT HORNED OWL	OP	100.00	100.00
78	AMERICAN PANTHER	OP	175.00	75.00
79	RED FOXES	OP	120.00	65.00
80	TRUMPETER SWAN	OP	200.00	220.00
D. ZOLAN				**MARCH OF DIMES: OUR CHILDREN, OUR FUTURE**
89	A TIME FOR PEACE (1ST IN SERIES)	RT	29.00	45.00

YR	NAME	LIMIT	ISSUE	TREND
D. ZOLAN		**MEMBERS ONLY SINGLE ISSUE (MINIATURE)**		
90	BY MYSELF	RT	14.40	60.00
93	SUMMER'S CHILD	RT	16.60	30.00
94	LITTLE SLUGGER	CL	16.60	17.00
D. ZOLAN		**MEMBERSHIP (MINIATURE)**		
87	FOR YOU	RT	12.50	75.00
88	MAKING FRIENDS	RT	12.50	65.00
89	GRANDMA'S GARDEN	RT	12.50	65.00
90	A CHRISTMAS PRAYER	RT	14.40	45.00
91	GOLDEN MOMENT	RT	15.00	35.00
92	BROTHERLY LOVE	RT	15.00	50.00
93	NEW SHOES	RT	17.00	35.00
94	MY KITTY	CL	*	30.00
D. ZOLAN		**MOMENTS TO REMEMBER (MINIATURE)**		
92	ALMOST HOME	RT	16.60	25.00
92	JUST WE TWO	RT	16.60	35.00
93	FOREST FRIENDS	RT	16.60	25.00
93	TINY TREASURES	RT	16.60	25.00
D. ZOLAN		**MOTHER'S DAY**		
88	MOTHER'S ANGELS	RT	19.00	65.00
D. ZOLAN		**MOTHER'S DAY (MINIATURE)**		
90	FLOWERS FOR MOTHER (MOTHER'S DAY)	RT	14.40	45.00
92	TWILIGHT PRAYER (MOTHER'S DAY)	RT	16.60	35.00
93	JESSICA'S FIELD	RT	16.60	35.00
94	ONE SUMMER DAY	RT	16.60	25.00
R. ANDERSON		**NUTCRACKER II**		
88	ROYAL WELCOME, THE	RT	24.40	30.00
S. FISHER		**NUTCRACKER II**		
81	GRAND FINALE	RT	24.40	35.00
82	ARABIAN DANCERS	RT	24.40	65.00
83	DEW DROP FAIRY	RT	24.40	55.00
84	CLARA'S DELIGHT	RT	24.40	40.00
85	BEDTIME FOR NUTCRACKER	RT	24.40	45.00
86	CROWNING OF CLARA, THE	RT	24.40	40.00
M. VICKERS		**NUTCRACKER II**		
89	SPANISH DANCER, THE	RT	24.40	26.00
D. ZOLAN		**NUTCRACKER II**		
87	DANCE OF THE SNOWFLAKES	RT	24.40	45.00
D. ZOLAN		**PLAQUES**		
91	NEW SHOES	RT	18.80	30.00
92	EASTER MORNING	RT	18.80	25.00
92	GRANDMA'S GARDEN	RT	18.80	25.00
92	SMALL WONDER	RT	18.80	25.00
D. ZOLAN		**PLAQUES-SINGLE ISSUE**		
91	FLOWERS FOR MOTHER	RT	16.80	25.00
D. ZOLAN		**SINGLE ISSUE**		
93	WINTER FRIENDS	RT	18.80	35.00
D. ZOLAN		**SINGLE ISSUE (MINIATURE)**		
86	BACKYARD DISCOVERY	RT	12.50	95.00
86	DADDY'S HOME	RT	12.50	800.00
89	MY PUMPKIN	RT	14.40	60.00
89	SUNNY SURPRISE	RT	12.50	60.00
91	BACKYARD BUDDIES	RT	16.60	35.00
91	THINKER, THE	RT	16.60	35.00
93	QUIET TIME	RT	16.60	40.00
94	LITTLE FISHERMAN	RT	16.60	17.00
D. ZOLAN		**SINGLE ISSUE BONE CHINA (MINIATURE)**		
92	WINDOWS OF DREAMS	RT	18.80	25.00
D. ZOLAN		**SINGLE ISSUE DAY TO DAY SPODE**		
91	DAISY DAYS	RT	48.00	50.00
*		**SPECIAL MOMENTS**		
89	MEADOW MAGIC	OP	22.00	24.00
D. ZOLAN		**SPECIAL MOMENTS OF CHILDHOOD**		
88	BROTHERLY LOVE	RT	19.00	45.00
88	SUNNY SURPRISE	RT	19.00	27.00
89	SUMMER'S CHILD	RT	22.00	26.00
90	CONE FOR TWO	RT	24.60	25.00
90	MEADOW MAGIC	RT	22.00	30.00
90	RODEO GIRL	RT	24.60	25.00
D. ZOLAN		**THANKSGIVING**		
81	I'M THANKFUL TOO	RT	19.00	85.00
D. ZOLAN		**THANKSGIVING (MINIATURE)**		
93	I'M THANKFUL TOO	RT	16.60	25.00
D. ZOLAN		**THE BEST OF ZOLAN IN MINIATURE**		
85	SABINA	RT	12.50	110.00
86	ERIK AND DANDELION	RT	12.50	115.00
86	TENDER MOMENT	RT	12.50	85.00
86	TOUCHING THE SKY	RT	12.50	75.00
87	A GIFT FOR LAURIE	RT	12.50	75.00
87	SMALL WONDER	RT	12.50	75.00
D. ZOLAN		**TIMES TO TREASURE BONE CHINA (MINIATURE)**		
93	GARDEN SWING	RT	16.60	17.00
93	LITTLE TRAVELER	RT	16.60	25.00
94	SEPTEMBER GIRL	CL	16.60	17.00
94	SUMMER GARDEN	CL	16.60	17.00

YR	NAME	LIMIT	ISSUE	TREND
D. ZOLAN			**WONDER OF CHILDHOOD**	
82	TOUCHING THE SKY	RT	19.00	25.00
83	SPRING INNOCENCE	RT	19.00	24.00
84	WINTER ANGEL	RT	22.00	30.00
85	SMALL WONDER	RT	22.00	30.00
86	GRANDMA'S GARDEN	RT	22.00	39.00
87	DAY DREAMER	RT	22.00	35.00
D. ZOLAN			**YESTERDAY'S CHILDREN (MINIATURE)**	
94	LITTLE FRIENDS	CL	16.60	17.00
94	SEASIDE TREASURES	CL	16.60	17.00
D. ZOLAN			**ZOLAN'S CHILDREN**	
78	ERIK AND DANDELION	RT	19.00	270.00
79	SABINA IN THE GRASS	RT	22.00	210.00

PFALTZGRAFF

YR	NAME	LIMIT	ISSUE	TREND
B.B. RICHARDS				
93	LITTLEST ANGEL	5000	18.50	23.00
94	CHRISTMAS TRADITION	10000	15.00	18.00
94	HARVEST MEMORIES	10000	15.00	18.00

PICKARD

YR	NAME	LIMIT	ISSUE	TREND
RAPHAEL			**ANNUAL CHRISTMAS**	
76	ALBA MADONNA	7500	60.00	100.00
79	ADORATION OF THE MAGI	10000	70.00	75.00
80	MADONNA AND CHILD	10000	80.00	85.00
81	MADONNA AND CHILD WITH ANGELS	10000	90.00	100.00
G. DAVID			**ANNUAL CHRISTMAS**	
78	REST ON FLIGHT INTO EGYPT	10000	65.00	85.00
L. LOTTO			**ANNUAL CHRISTMAS**	
77	NATIVITY, THE	7500	65.00	90.00
J. SANCHEZ			**CHILDREN OF MEXICO**	
81	MARIA	5000	85.00	95.00
81	MIGUEL	5000	85.00	95.00
82	REGINA	5000	90.00	100.00
83	RAPHAEL	5000	90.00	100.00
*			**GEMS OF NATURE: HUMMINGBIRDS**	
89	RUBY-THROATED HUMMINGBIRD	CL	29.00	29.00
90	BLACK CHINNED HUMMINGBIRD	CL	32.00	35.00
90	BROAD-BILLED HUMMINGBIRD	CL	32.00	32.00
90	CALLIOPE HUMMINGBIRD	CL	32.00	45.00
90	RUFOUS HUMMINGBIRD	CL	29.00	38.00
91	ANNA'S HUMMINGBIRD/PETUNIAS	CL	34.00	38.00
91	COSTA'S HUMMINGBIRD & HOLLYHOCKS	CL	34.00	44.00
91	WHITE-EARED HUMMINGBIRD	CL	32.00	44.00
*			**HAWAIIAN SPLENDOR**	
92	AN EVENING IN THE ISLANDS	CL	34.00	50.00
92	COASTAL HARMONY	CL	34.00	52.00
92	TROPICAL ENCHANTMENT	CL	34.00	37.00
92	TWILIGHT PARADISE	CL	34.00	55.00
*			**HOLIDAY TRADITIONS**	
92	CHRISTMAS HOMECOMING	CL	29.00	45.00
92	QUIET UNDER THE EAVES	CL	29.00	65.00
93	HEART OF CHRISTMAS, THE	CL	29.00	29.00
93	SNOWS OF YESTERYEAR	CL	29.00	30.00
*			**INNOCENT ENCOUNTERS**	
88	JUST PASSING BY	CL	34.00	29.00
88	MAKING FRIENDS	CL	34.00	37.00
89	EYE TO EYE	CL	34.00	25.00
89	LET'S PLAY	CL	34.00	30.00
J. LOCKHART			**LOCKHART WILDLIFE**	
70	WOODCOCK/RUFFED GROUSE, PAIR	2000	150.00	264.00
71	TEAL/MALLARD, PAIR	2000	150.00	170.00
72	MOCKINGBIRD/CARDINAL, PAIR	2000	162.50	180.00
73	TURKEY/PHEASANT, PAIR	2000	162.50	264.00
74	AMERICAN BALD EAGLE	2000	150.00	700.00
75	WHITE TAILED DEER	2500	100.00	140.00
76	AMERICAN BUFFALO	2500	165.00	180.00
77	GREAT HORN OWL	2500	100.00	115.00
78	AMERICAN PANTHER	2000	175.00	200.00
79	RED FOXES	2500	120.00	130.00
80	TRUMPETER SWAN	2000	200.00	220.00
I. SPENCER			**MOTHER'S LOVE**	
80	MIRACLE	7500	95.00	100.00
81	STORY TIME	7500	110.00	110.00
82	FIRST EDITION	7500	115.00	120.00
83	PRECIOUS MOMENT	7500	120.00	150.00
I. SPENCER			**SYMPHONY OF ROSES**	
82	WILD IRISH ROSE	10000	85.00	95.00
83	YELLOW ROSE OF TEXAS	10000	90.00	100.00
84	HONEYSUCKLE ROSE	10000	95.00	125.00
85	ROSE OF WASHINGTON SQUARE	10000	100.00	170.00

PORSGRUND

YR	NAME	LIMIT	ISSUE	TREND
G. BRATILE			**CHRISTMAS (ANNUAL)**	
68	CHURCH SCENE	UD	12.00	125.00
69	THREE KINGS	UD	12.00	12.00

YR	NAME	LIMIT	ISSUE	TREND
70	ROAD TO BETHLEHEM	UD	12.00	12.00
71	A CHILD IS BORN	UD	12.00	12.00
72	HARK THE HERALD ANGELS	UD	12.00	12.00
73	PROMISE OF THE SAVIOR	UD	12.00	12.00
74	SHEPHERDS, THE	UD	15.00	36.00
75	ROAD TO TEMPLE	UD	19.50	20.00
76	JESUS AND THE ELDERS	UD	22.00	26.00
77	DRAUGHT OF THE FISH	UD	24.00	28.00

PRINCETON GALLERY

YR	NAME	LIMIT	ISSUE	TREND
K. MCELROY				
95	UNICORN BY THE SEA, THE	95 DAYS	29.90	30.00
J. VAN ZYLE				**ARCTIC WOLVES**
91	SONG OF THE WILDERNESS	CL	29.50	30.00
92	IN THE EYE OF THE MOON	CL	29.50	30.00
R. SANDERSON				**CIRCUS FRIENDS COLLECTION**
89	DON'T BE SHY	*	29.50	30.00
90	CHEER UP MR. CLOWN	*	29.50	30.00
90	LOOKS LIKE RAIN	*	29.50	30.00
90	MAKE ME A CLOWN	*	29.50	30.00
Q. LEMOND				**CUBS OF THE BIG CATS**
90	COUGAR CUB	*	29.50	30.00
91	CHEETAH	CL	29.50	30.00
91	LION CUB	CL	29.50	30.00
91	SNOW LEOPARD	CL	29.50	30.00
91	TIGER	CL	29.50	30.00
92	LYNX CUB	CL	29.50	30.00
92	WHITE TIGER CUB	CL	29.50	30.00
L. PICKEN				**DARLING DALMATIONS**
91	DALMATION	CL	29.50	30.00
92	FIREHOUSE FROLIC	CL	29.50	30.00
R. SANDERSON				**ENCHANTED WORLD OF THE UNICORN**
91	RAINBOW VALLEY	CL	29.50	30.00
92	GOLDEN SHORE	CL	29.50	30.00

R.J. ERNST ENTERPRISES

YR	NAME	LIMIT	ISSUE	TREND
S. MORTON				**A BEAUTIFUL WORLD**
81	TAHITIAN DREAMER	RT	27.50	35.00
82	FLIRTATION	RT	27.50	35.00
84	ELKE OF OSLO	RT	27.50	30.00
S. KUHNLY				**CLASSY CARS**
82	26T, THE	RT	24.50	32.00
82	31A, THE	RT	24.50	35.00
83	PICKUP, THE	RT	24.50	30.00
84	PANEL VAN	RT	24.50	40.00
S. MORTON				**COMMEMORATIVES**
81	JOHN LENNON	RT	39.50	160.00
82	ELVIS PRESLEY	RT	39.50	145.00
82	MARILYN MONROE	RT	39.50	80.00
83	JUDY GARLAND	RT	39.50	100.00
84	JOHN WAYNE	RT	39.50	80.00
S. MORTON				**ELVIRA**
88	MISTRESS OF THE DARK	RT	29.50	30.00
88	NIGHT ROSE	CL	29.50	30.00
88	RED VELVET	RT	29.50	30.00
S. MORTON				**ELVIS PRESLEY**
87	EARLY YEARS	RT	39.50	40.00
87	KING, THE	RT	39.50	40.00
87	LOVING YOU	RT	39.50	40.00
87	TENDERLY	RT	39.50	40.00
88	ELVIS PRESLEY	RT	39.50	40.00
88	FOREVER YOURS	RT	39.50	40.00
88	MOODY BLUES	RT	39.50	40.00
88	ROCKIN' IN THE MOONLIGHT	RT	39.50	40.00
89	ELVIS PRESLEY- SPECIAL REQUEST	RT	150.00	155.00
S. MORTON				**HOLLYWOOD GREATS**
81	GARY COOPER	RT	29.95	35.00
81	JOHN WAYNE	RT	29.95	110.00
82	CLARK GABLE	RT	29.95	75.00
84	ALAN LADD	RT	29.95	100.00
S. MORTON				**HOLLYWOOD, WALK OF FAME**
89	ELIZABETH TAYLOR	RT	39.50	40.00
89	JIMMY STEWART	RT	39.50	40.00
89	JOAN COLLINS	RT	39.50	40.00
89	TOM SELLECK	RT	39.50	40.00
90	BURT REYNOLDS	RT	39.50	40.00
90	SYLVESTER STALLONE	RT	39.50	40.00
S. MORTON				**REPUBLIC PICTURES LIBRARY**
91	ATTACK AT TARAWA	RT	37.50	40.00
91	RID EHOME, THE	RT	37.50	40.00
91	SHOWDOWN WITH LAREDO	RT	37.50	40.00
91	THOUGHTS OF ANGELIQUE	RT	37.50	40.00
92	ANGEL AND THE BADMAN	RT	37.50	40.00
92	FLIGHTING SEABEES, THE	RT	37.50	40.00
92	WAR OF THE WILDCATS	RT	37.50	40.00
93	FLYING TIGERS	RT	37.90	40.00
93	SANDS OF IWO JIMA	RT	37.50	40.00

YR	NAME	LIMIT	ISSUE	TREND
93	TRIBUTE, THE 12 IN.	RT	97.50	100.00
94	TRIBUTE, THE 8 1/4 IN.	9500	29.50	30.00
R. MONEY				**SEEMS LIKE YESTERDAY**
81	STOP & SMELL THE ROSES	RT	24.50	30.00
82	HOME BY LUNCH	RT	24.50	30.00
82	LISA'S CREEK	RT	24.50	30.00
83	IT'S GOT MY NAME ON IT	RT	24.50	30.00
83	MY MAGIC HAT	RT	24.50	30.00
84	LITTLE PRINCE	RT	24.50	30.00
S. MORTON				**STAR TREK**
84	MR. SPOCK	RT	29.50	175.00
85	BEAM US DOWN SCOTTY	RT	29.50	90.00
85	CAPTAIN KIRK	RT	29.50	100.00
85	CHEKOV	RT	29.50	55.00
85	DR. MCCOY	RT	29.50	80.00
85	ENTERPRISE, THE	RT	39.50	105.00
85	SCOTTY	RT	29.50	70.00
85	SULU	RT	29.50	70.00
85	UHURA	RT	29.50	55.00
S. MORTON				**STAR TREK: COMMEMORATIVE COLLECTION**
87	A PIECE OF THE ACTION	RT	29.50	110.00
87	AMOK TIME	RT	29.50	105.00
87	CITY ON THE EDGE OF FOREVER, THE	RT	29.50	210.00
87	DEVIL IN THE DARK, THE	RT	29.50	105.00
87	JOURNEY TO BABEL	RT	29.50	145.00
87	MENAGERIE, THE	RT	29.50	130.00
87	MIRROR, MIRROR	RT	29.50	180.00
87	TROUBLE WITH TRIBBLES, THE	RT	29.50	110.00
R. MONEY				**TURN OF THE CENTURY**
81	RIVERBOAT HONEYMOON	RT	35.00	40.00
82	CHILDREN'S CAROUSEL	RT	35.00	40.00
84	FLOWER MARKET	RT	35.00	40.00
85	BALLOON RACE	RT	35.00	40.00
D. PUTNAM				**WOMEN OF THE WEST**
79	EXPECTATIONS	RT	39.50	40.00
81	SILVER DOLLAR SAL	RT	39.50	50.00
82	SCHOOL MARM	RT	30.50	40.00
83	DOLLY	RT	39.50	40.00

RAYMON TROUP STUDIO

YR	NAME	LIMIT	ISSUE	TREND
W. RAYMON				**AMERICAN LANDMARKS COLLECTION**
95	IVY GREEN	1500	39.95	40.00
95	OLD MILL, THE	1500	40.00	40.00

RECO INTERNATIONAL

YR	NAME	LIMIT	ISSUE	TREND
S. KUCK				**A CHILDHOOD ALMANAC**
85	BE MINE-FEBRUARY	RT	29.50	40.00
85	CHRISTMAS MAGIC-DECEMBER	CL	35.00	50.00
85	EASTER MORNING-APRIL	RT	29.50	50.00
85	FIRESIDE DREAMS-JANUARY	RT	29.50	50.00
85	FOR MOM-MAY	RT	29.50	40.00
85	GIVING THANKS-NOVEMBER	CL	29.50	40.00
85	INDIAN SUMMER-OCTOBER	RT	29.50	40.00
85	JUST DREAMING-JUNE	RT	29.50	50.00
85	SCHOOL DAYS-SEPTEMBER	RT	29.50	50.00
85	STAR SPANGLED SKY-JULY	CL	29.50	40.00
85	SUMMER SECRETS-AUGUST	RT	29.50	50.00
85	WINDS OF MARCH-MARCH	RT	29.50	40.00
S. KUCK				**A CHILDREN'S CHRISTMAS PAGEANT**
86	SILENT NIGHT	RT	32.50	50.00
87	HARK THE HERALD ANGELS SING	RT	32.50	40.00
88	WHILE SHEPHERDS WATCHED...	RT	32.50	40.00
89	WE THREE KINGS	YR	32.50	40.00
S. DEVLIN				**AMERICANA**
72	GASPEE INCIDENT	RT	200.00	350.00
B. FARNSWORTH				**AMISH TRADITIONS**
94	FAMILY OUTING	CL	29.50	30.00
94	GOLDEN HARVEST	CL	29.50	30.00
94	QUILTING BEE, THE	CL	29.50	30.00
95	LAST DAY OF SCHOOL	95 DAY	29.50	30.00
S. KUCK				**BAREFOOT CHILDREN**
87	GOLDEN AFTERNOON	CL	29.50	40.00
87	NIGHT-TIME STORY	RT	29.50	40.00
88	CAROUSEL MAGIC	CL	29.50	50.00
88	GRANDMA'S TRUNK	RT	29.50	40.00
88	LITTLE SWEETHEARTS	CL	29.50	40.00
88	PRETTY AS A PICTURE	RT	29.50	40.00
88	REHEARSAL, THE	CL	29.50	40.00
88	UNDER THE APPLE TREE	CL	29.50	40.00
J. MCCLELLAND				**BECKY'S DAY**
85	AWAKENING	CL	24.50	30.00
85	GETTING DRESSED	RT	24.50	30.00
86	BREAKFAST	RT	27.50	30.00
86	EVENING PRAYER	RT	27.50	30.00
86	LEARNING IS FUN	RT	27.50	30.00
86	MUFFIN MAKING	RT	27.50	35.00
86	TUB TIME	CL	27.50	40.00

YR	NAME	LIMIT	ISSUE	TREND
G. RATNAVIRA		**BIRDS OF THE HIDDEN FOREST**		
94	MACAW WATERFALL	CL	29.50	30.00
94	PARADISE VALLEY	CL	29.50	30.00
95	TOUCAN TREASURE	96-DAY	29.50	30.00
*		**BOHEMIAN ANNUALS**		
74	1974	RT	130.00	160.00
75	1975	RT	140.00	160.00
76	1976	RT	150.00	160.00
J. BERGSMA		**CASTLES & DREAMS**		
92	BIRTH OF A DREAM, THE	CL	29.50	30.00
92	DREMAS COME TRUE	CL	29.50	30.00
93	BELIEVE IN YOUR DREAMS	CL	29.50	30.00
94	FOLLOW YOUR DREAMS	CL	29.50	30.00
J. HALL		**CELEBRATION OF LOVE**		
92	10TH ANNIVERSARY (6 1/2 IN.)	OP	25.00	30.00
92	10TH ANNIVERSARY (9 1/4 IN.)	OP	35.00	40.00
92	25TH ANNIVERSARY (6 1/2 IN.)	OP	25.00	30.00
92	25TH ANNIVERSARY (9 1/4 IN.)	OP	35.00	40.00
92	50TH ANNIVERSARY (6 1/2 IN.)	OP	25.00	30.00
92	50TH ANNIVERSARY (9 1/4 IN.)	OP	35.00	40.00
92	HAPPY ANNIVERSARY (6 1/2 IN.)	OP	25.00	30.00
92	HAPPY ANNIVERSARY (9 1/4 IN.)	OP	35.00	40.00
J. MCCLELLAND		**CHILDREN'S GARDEN**		
93	GARDEN FRIENDS	CL	29.50	30.00
93	PUPPY LOVE	CL	29.50	30.00
93	TEA FOR THREE	CL	29.50	30.00
S. KUCK		**CHRISTENING GIFT**		
95	GOD'S GIFT	OP	29.90	30.00
J. BERGSMA		**CHRISTMAS SERIES**		
90	DOWN THE GLISTENING LANE	CL	35.00	40.00
91	A CHILD IS BORN	CL	35.00	40.00
92	CHRISTMAS DAY	CL	35.00	40.00
93	I WISH YOU AN ANGEL	CL	35.00	40.00
J. BERGSMA		**CHRISTMAS WISHES**		
94	I WISH YOU LOVE	CL	29.50	30.00
S. KUCK		**DAYS GONE BY**		
83	AMY'S MAGIC HORSE	RT	29.50	30.00
83	SUNDAY BEST	RT	29.50	40.00
84	AFTERNOON RECITAL	CL	29.50	55.00
84	EASTER AT GRANDMA'S	RT	29.50	30.00
84	LITTLE ANGLERS	RT	29.50	30.00
84	LITTLE TUTOR	RT	29.50	34.00
85	MORNING SONG	RT	29.50	31.00
85	SURREY RIDE, THE	RT	29.50	31.00
*		**DRESDEN CHRISTMAS**		
71	SHEPHERD SCENE	RT	15.00	50.00
72	NIKLAS CHURCH	RT	15.00	30.00
73	SCHWANSTEIN CHURCH	RT	18.00	40.00
74	VILLAGE SCENE	RT	20.00	30.00
75	ROTHENBURG SCENE	RT	24.00	30.00
76	VILLAGE CHURCH	RT	26.00	40.00
77	OLD MILL (ISSUE CLOSED)	RT	28.00	30.00
*		**DRESDEN MOTHER'S DAY**		
72	DOE AND FAWN	RT	15.00	20.00
73	MARE AND COLT	RT	16.00	30.00
74	TIGER AND CUB	RT	20.00	25.00
75	DACHSHUNDS	RT	24.00	30.00
76	OWL AND OFFSPRING	RT	26.00	30.00
77	CHAMOIS (ISSUE CLOSED)	RT	28.00	30.00
C. HOPKINS		**ENCHANTED NORFIN TROLLS**		
93	TROLL AND HIS DRAGON, THE	CL	19.50	20.00
93	TROLL MAIDEN	CL	19.50	20.00
93	WIZARD TROLL, THE	CL	19.50	20.00
94	CHEF LE TROLL	CL	19.50	21.00
94	IF TROLLS COULD FLY	CL	19.50	20.00
94	MINSTREL TROLL	CL	19.50	20.00
94	QUEEN OF THE TROLLS	CL	19.50	21.00
94	TROLL IN SHINNING ARMOR	CL	19.50	20.00
C.M. BARKER		**FLOWER FAIRIES YEAR COLLECTION**		
90	PINE TREE FAIRY, THE	CL	29.50	30.00
90	RED CLOVER FAIRY, THE	CL	29.50	30.00
90	ROSE HIP FAIRY, THE	CL	29.50	30.00
90	WILD CHERRY BLOSSOM FAIRY, THE	CL	29.50	30.00
J. POLUSZYNSKI		**FOUR SEASONS**		
73	FALL	RT	50.00	75.00
73	SPRING	RT	50.00	75.00
73	SUMMER	RT	50.00	75.00
73	WINTER	RT	50.00	75.00
*		**FURSTENBERG CHRISTMAS**		
71	RABBITS	RT	15.00	30.00
72	SNOWY VILLAGE	RT	15.00	20.00
73	CHRISTMAS EVE	RT	18.00	40.00
74	SPARROWS	RT	20.00	30.00
75	DEER FAMILY	RT	22.00	30.00
76	WINTER BIRDS	RT	25.00	30.00

YR	NAME	LIMIT	ISSUE	TREND
E. GROSSBERG		**FURSTENBERG DELUXE CHRISTMAS**		
71	WISE MEN	RT	45.00	50.00
72	HOLY FAMILY	RT	45.00	50.00
73	CHRISTMAS EVE	RT	60.00	65.00
*		**FURSTENBERG EASTER**		
71	SHEEP	RT	15.00	160.00
72	CHICKS	RT	15.00	65.00
73	BUNNIES	RT	16.00	85.00
74	PUSSYWILLOW	RT	20.00	40.00
75	EASTER WINDOW	RT	22.00	30.00
76	FLOWER COLLECTING	RT	25.00	30.00
*		**FURSTENBERG MOTHER'S DAY**		
72	HUMMINGBIRDS, FE	RT	15.00	50.00
73	HEDGEHOGS	RT	16.00	40.00
74	DOE AND FAWN	RT	20.00	30.00
75	SWANS	RT	22.00	30.00
76	KOALA BEARS	RT	25.00	30.00
J. POLUSZYNSKI		**FURSTENBERG OLYMPIC**		
72	MUNICH	RT	20.00	75.00
76	MONTREAL	RT	37.50	40.00
S. KUCK		**GAMES CHILDREN PLAY**		
79	ME FIRST	RT	45.00	50.00
80	FOREVER BUBBLES	RT	45.00	50.00
81	SKATING PALS	RT	45.00	50.00
82	JOIN ME	10000	45.00	50.00
D. BARLOWE		**GARDENS OF AMERICA**		
92	COLONIAL SPLENDOR	CL	29.50	30.00
D. BARLOWE		**GARDENS OF BEAUTY**		
88	DUTCH COUNTRY GARDEN	CL	29.50	30.00
88	ENGLISH COUNTRY GARDEN	CL	29.50	30.00
88	JAPANESE GARDEN	CL	29.50	30.00
88	NEW ENGLAND GARDEN	CL	29.50	30.00
89	GERMAN COUNTRY GARDEN	CL	29.50	30.00
89	HAWAIIAN GARDEN	CL	29.50	30.00
89	ITALIAN GARDEN	CL	29.50	30.00
89	MEXICAN GARDEN	CL	29.50	30.00
S. KUCK		**GIFT OF LOVE MOTHER'S DAY COLLECTION**		
93	MORNING GLORY	RT	65.00	65.00
94	MEMORIES FROM THE HEART	RT	65.00	65.00
I. DRECHSLER		**GOD'S OWN COUNTRY**		
90	COMING HOME	CL	30.00	30.00
90	DAYBREAK	CL	30.00	30.00
90	PEACEFUL GATHERING	CL	30.00	30.00
90	QUIET WATERS	CL	30.00	30.00
J. BERGSMA		**GLORY OF CHRIST**		
94	FOREVER IN MY HEART	CL	35.00	40.00
C. MICARELLI		**GLORY OF CHRIST**		
92	ASCENSION, THE	CL	29.50	30.00
93	BAPTISM OF CHRIST, THE	CL	29.50	30.00
93	JESUS HEALS THE SICK	CL	29.50	30.00
93	JESUS TEACHING	CL	29.50	30.00
93	LAST SUPPER, THE	CL	29.50	30.00
93	NATIVITY, THE	CL	29.50	30.00
94	DESCENT FROM THE CROSS	CL	29.50	30.00
94	JESUS WALKS ON WATER	CL	29.50	30.00
J. MCCLELLAND		**GOLF COLLECTION**		
92	PAR EXCELLENCE	CL	35.00	40.00
*		**GRAFBURG CHRISTMAS**		
75	BLACK-CAPPED CHICKADEE	RT	20.00	60.00
76	SQUIRRELS	RT	22.00	30.00
S. KUCK		**GRANDPARENT COLLECTOR'S PLATES**		
81	GRANDMA'S COOKIE JAR	YR	37.50	40.00
81	GRANDPA AND THE DOLLHOUSE	YR	37.50	40.00
G. KATZ		**GREAT STORIES FROM THE BIBLE**		
87	JOSEPH'S COAT OF MANY COLORS	CL	29.50	40.00
87	KING SAUL & DAVID	CL	29.50	40.00
87	MOSES AND THE TEN COMMANDMENTS	CL	29.50	40.00
87	MOSES IN THE BULRUSHES	CL	29.50	40.00
88	DANIEL READS THE WRITING ON THE WALL	CL	29.50	40.00
88	KING SOLOMON	CL	29.50	40.00
88	REBEKAH AT THE WELL	CL	29.50	40.00
88	STORY OF RUTH, THE	CL	29.50	40.00
J. BERGSMA		**GUARDIANS OF THE KINGDOM**		
90	GUARDIANS OF THE INNOCENT CHILDREN	17500	35.00	40.00
90	MIRACLE OF LOVE, THE	17500	35.00	40.00
90	RAINBOW TO RIDE ON	RT	35.00	40.00
90	SPECIAL FRIENDS ARE FEW	17500	35.00	40.00
91	IN FAITH I AM FREE	17500	35.00	40.00
91	MAGIC OF LOVE, THE	17500	35.00	40.00
91	ONLY WITH THE HEART	17500	35.00	40.00
91	TO FLY WITHOUT WINGS	17500	35.00	40.00
H. ROE		**HAVEN OF THE HUNTERS**		
94	EAGLE'S CASTLE	CL	29.50	30.00
94	SANCTUARY OF THE HAWK	CL	29.50	30.00
J. YORK		**HEART OF THE FAMILY**		
92	SHARING SECRETS	CL	29.50	30.00

YR	NAME	LIMIT	ISSUE	TREND
93	SPINNING DREAMS	CL	29.50	30.00
S. KUCK		**HEARTS & FLOWERS**		
91	CATS IN THE CRADLE	CL	32.50	40.00
91	PATIENCE	CL	29.50	44.00
91	TEA PARTY	CL	29.50	60.00
92	CAROUSEL OF DREAMS	CL	32.50	35.00
92	DELIGHTFUL BUNDLE	CL	34.50	40.00
92	STORYBOOK MEMORIES	CL	32.50	35.00
93	EASTER MORNING VISITOR	CL	34.50	40.00
93	ME AND MY PONY	CL	34.50	40.00
W. LOWE		**IN THE EYE OF THE STORM**		
91	FIRST STRIKE	CL	29.50	30.00
92	NIGHT FORCE	CL	29.50	30.00
92	TRACKS ACROSS THE SAND	CL	29.50	30.00
J. BERGSMA		**J. BERGSMA MOTHER'S DAY SERIES**		
90	BEAUTY OF LIFE, THE	CL	35.00	40.00
92	LIFE'S BLESSING	CL	35.00	40.00
P. JEPSON		**KINGDOM OF THE GREAT CATS**		
94	SUMMIT SANCTUARY	CL	29.50	30.00
95	OUT OF THE MIST	36 DAY	29.50	30.00
MERLI		**KING'S CHRISTMAS**		
73	ADORATION	RT	100.00	275.00
74	MADONNA	RT	150.00	250.00
75	HEAVENLY CHOIR	RT	160.00	240.00
76	SIBLINGS	RT	200.00	230.00
A. FALCHI		**KING'S FLOWERS**		
73	CARNATION	RT	85.00	130.00
74	RED ROSE	RT	100.00	150.00
75	YELLOW DAHLIA	RT	110.00	165.00
76	BLUEBELLS	RT	130.00	175.00
77	ANEMONES	RT	130.00	175.00
MERLI		**KING'S MOTHER'S DAY**		
73	DANCING GIRL	RT	100.00	230.00
74	DANCING BOY	RT	115.00	250.00
75	MOTHERLY LOVE	RT	140.00	230.00
76	MAIDEN	RT	180.00	200.00
S. SOMERVILLE		**KITTENS 'N HATS**		
94	OPENING NIGHT	CL	29.50	30.00
94	SITTING PRETTY	CL	29.50	30.00
95	LITTLE LEAGUE	48 DAY	29.50	30.00
J. BERGSMA		**LAND OF OUR DREAMS**		
89	LAND OF NOD	19000	35.00	40.00
89	SECRET DOOR, THE	19000	35.00	40.00
89	STARS, THE	19500	35.00	40.00
89	SWING, THE	19000	35.00	40.00
S. KUCK		**LITTLE ANGEL PLATE COLLECTION**		
94	ANGEL OF CHARITY	CL	29.50	30.00
94	ANGEL OF GRACE	CL	29.50	30.00
94	ANGEL OF HOPE	CL	29.50	30.00
94	ANGEL OF JOY	CL	29.50	30.00
S. KUCK		**LITTLE PROFESSIONALS**		
82	ALL IS WELL	RT	39.50	60.00
83	TENDER LOVING CARE	RT	39.50	60.00
84	LOST AND FOUND	10000	39.50	50.00
85	READING, WRITING AND...	RT	39.50	50.00
J. BERGSMA		**MAGIC COMPANIONS**		
94	BELIEVE IN LOVE	CL	29.50	30.00
94	IMAGINE PEACE	CL	29.50	30.00
S. KUCK		**MARCH OF DIMES: OUR CHILDREN, OUR FUTURE**		
89	A TIME TO LOVE (2ND IN SERIES)	RT	29.00	50.00
J. MCCLELLAND		**MARCH OF DIMES: OUR CHILDREN, OUR FUTURE**		
89	A TIME TO PLANT (3RD IN SERIES)	CL	29.00	50.00
*		**MARMOT CHRISTMAS**		
70	POLAR BEAR, FE	RT	13.00	60.00
71	AMERICAN BUFFALO	RT	14.50	40.00
71	BUFFALO BILL	RT	16.00	60.00
72	BOY AND GRANDFATHER	RT	20.00	50.00
73	SNOWMAN	RT	22.00	50.00
74	DANCING	RT	24.00	30.00
75	QUAIL	RT	30.00	40.00
76	WINDMILL	RT	40.00	50.00
*		**MARMOT FATHER'S DAY**		
70	STAG	RT	12.00	100.00
71	HORSE	RT	12.50	40.00
*		**MARMOT MOTHER'S DAY**		
72	SEAL	RT	16.00	65.00
73	BEAR WITH CUB	RT	20.00	150.00
74	PENGUINS	RT	24.00	50.00
75	RACCOONS	RT	30.00	50.00
76	DUCKS	RT	40.00	50.00
J. MCCLELLAND		**MCCLELLAND CHILDREN'S CIRCUS COLLECTION**		
82	KATIE THE TIGHTROPE WALKER	RT	29.50	50.00
82	TOMMY THE CLOWN	RT	29.50	50.00
83	JOHNNY THE STRONGMAN	RT	29.50	40.00
84	MAGGIE THE ANIMAL TRAINER	CL	29.50	30.00

YR	NAME	LIMIT	ISSUE	TREND
M. ATTWELL			**MEMORIES OF YESTERDAY**	
93	HUSH	OP	29.50	30.00
93	I'VE BEEN PAINTING	OP	29.50	30.00
93	JUST LOOKING PRETTY	OP	29.50	30.00
93	TIME FOR BED	OP	29.50	30.00
94	GIVE IT YOUR BEST SHOT	OP	29.50	30.00
94	I PRAY THE LORD MY SOUL TO KEEP	OP	29.50	30.00
94	JUST THINKING ABOUT YOU	OP	29.50	30.00
94	WHAT WILL I GROW UP TO BE	OP	29.50	30.00
*			**MOSER CHRISTMAS**	
70	HARDCANY CASTLE	RT	75.00	175.00
71	KARLSTEIN CASTLE	RT	75.00	85.00
72	OLD TOWN HALL	RT	85.00	95.00
73	KARLOVY VARY CASTLE	RT	90.00	100.00
*			**MOSER MOTHER'S DAY**	
71	PEACOCKS	RT	75.00	100.00
72	BUTTERFLIES	RT	85.00	95.00
73	SQUIRRELS	RT	90.00	100.00
J. MCCLELLAND			**MOTHER GOOSE**	
79	MARY, MARY	YR	22.50	75.00
80	LITTLE BOY BLUE	YR	22.50	25.00
81	LITTLE MISS MUFFET	YR	24.50	30.00
82	LITTLE JACK HORNER	YR	24.50	30.00
83	LITTLE BO PEEP	YR	24.50	30.00
84	DIDDLE, DIDDLE DUMPLING	YR	24.50	30.00
85	MARY HAD A LITTLE LAMB	YR	27.50	30.00
86	JACK AND JILL	YR	27.50	30.00
S. KUCK			**MOTHER'S DAY COLLECTION**	
85	ONCE UPON A TIME	RT	29.50	65.00
86	TIMES REMEMBERED	YR	29.50	65.00
87	A CHERISHED TIME	YR	29.50	50.00
88	A TIME TOGETHER	YR	29.50	60.00
J. BERGSMA			**MOTHER'S DAY SERIES**	
93	MY GREATEST TREASURES	CL	35.00	40.00
KELLY			**NOBLE AND FREE**	
94	GATHERING STORM	CL	29.50	30.00
94	MOONLIGHT RUN	CL	29.50	35.00
94	PROTECTED JOURNEY	CL	29.50	35.00
C. MICARELLI			**NUTCRACKER BALLET**	
89	CHRISTMAS EVE PARTY	CL	35.00	40.00
90	CLARA AND HER PRINCE	CL	35.00	40.00
90	DREAM BEGINS, THE	CL	35.00	40.00
91	DANCE OF THE SNOW FAIRIES	CL	35.00	40.00
92	LAND OF SWEETS, THE	CL	35.00	40.00
92	SUGAR PLUM FAIRY, THE	CL	35.00	40.00
P.D. JACKSON			**OSCAR & BERTIE'S EDWARDIAN HOLIDAY**	
91	SNAPSHOT	CL	29.50	30.00
92	EARLY RISE	CL	29.50	30.00
S. BARLOWE			**OUR CHERISHED SEAS**	
91	FLIGHT OF THE DOLPHINS	CL	37.50	40.00
91	LIONS OF THE SEA	CL	37.50	40.00
91	WHALE SONG	CL	37.50	40.00
92	PALACE OF THE SEALS	CL	37.50	40.00
S. KUCK			**PLATE OF THE MONTH COLLECTION**	
90	APRIL	CL	25.00	30.00
90	AUGUST	CL	25.00	30.00
90	DECEMBER	CL	25.00	30.00
90	FEBRUARY	CL	25.00	30.00
90	JANUARY	CL	25.00	30.00
90	JULY	CL	25.00	30.00
90	JUNE	CL	25.00	30.00
90	MARCH	CL	25.00	30.00
90	MAY	CL	25.00	30.00
90	NOVEMBER	CL	25.00	30.00
90	OCTOBER	CL	25.00	30.00
90	SEPTEMBER	CL	25.00	30.00
J. MEGER			**PORTRAITS OF THE WILD**	
95	BABIES OF SPRING	28 DAY	29.50	30.00
95	CALL OF AUTUMN	28 DAY	29.50	30.00
S. KUCK			**PRECIOUS ANGELS**	
94	ANGEL OF SHARING	CL	29.90	30.00
95	ANGEL OF GRACE	95 DAY	29.90	30.00
95	ANGEL OF HOPE	95 DAY	29.90	30.00
95	ANGEL OF LAUGHTER	95 DAY	29.90	30.00
95	ANGEL OF SUNSHINE	95 DAY	29.90	32.00
S. KUCK			**PREMIER COLLECTION**	
91	KITTEN	RT	95.00	175.00
91	PUPPY	RT	95.00	140.00
J. MCCLELLAND			**PREMIER COLLECTION**	
91	LOVE	7500	75.00	75.00
*			**ROYALE**	
69	APOLLO MOON LANDING	RT	30.00	85.00
*			**ROYALE CHRISTMAS**	
69	CHRISTMAS FAIR	RT	12.00	130.00
70	VIGIL MASS	RT	13.00	110.00
71	CHRISTMAS NIGHT	RT	16.00	50.00

YR	NAME	LIMIT	ISSUE	TREND
72	ELKS	RT	16.00	50.00
73	CHRISTMAS DOWN	RT	20.00	40.00
74	VILLAGE CHRISTMAS	RT	22.00	65.00
75	FEEDING TIME	RT	26.00	40.00
76	SEAPORT CHRISTMAS	RT	27.50	30.00
77	SLEDDING	RT	30.00	40.00
*			**ROYALE FATHER'S DAY**	
70	FRIGATE CONSTITUTION	RT	13.00	85.00
71	MAN FISHING	RT	13.00	40.00
72	MOUNTAINEER	RT	16.00	60.00
73	CAMPING	RT	18.00	50.00
74	EAGLE	RT	22.00	40.00
75	REGATTA	RT	26.00	40.00
76	HUNTING	RT	27.50	40.00
77	FISHING	RT	30.00	40.00
J. POLUSZYNSKI			**ROYALE GAME PLATES**	
72	SETTERS	RT	180.00	200.00
73	FOX	RT	200.00	250.00
W. SCHIENER			**ROYALE GAME PLATES**	
74	OSPREY	RT	250.00	250.00
75	CALIFORNIA QUAIL	RT	265.00	270.00
*			**ROYALE GERMANIA CHRISTMAS ANNUAL**	
70	ORCHID	RT	200.00	675.00
71	CYCLAMEN	RT	200.00	330.00
72	SILVER THISTLE	RT	250.00	300.00
73	TULIPS	RT	275.00	325.00
74	SUNFLOWERS	RT	300.00	350.00
75	SNOWDROPS	RT	450.00	500.00
76	FLAMING HEART	RT	450.00	500.00
*			**ROYALE GERMANIA CRYSTAL MOTHER'S DAY**	
71	ROSES	RT	135.00	675.00
72	ELEPHANT AND YOUNGSTER	RT	180.00	250.00
73	KOALA BEAR AND CUB	RT	200.00	230.00
74	SQUIRRELS	RT	240.00	250.00
75	SWAN AND YOUNG	RT	350.00	375.00
*			**ROYALE MOTHER'S DAY**	
70	SWAN AND YOUNG	RT	12.00	85.00
71	DOE AND FAWN	RT	13.00	60.00
72	RABBITS	RT	16.00	40.00
73	OWL FAMILY	RT	18.00	40.00
74	DUCK AND YOUNG	RT	22.00	40.00
75	LYNX AND CUBS	RT	26.00	40.00
76	WOODCOCK AND YOUNG	RT	27.50	35.00
77	KOALA BEAR	RT	30.00	40.00
S. KUCK			**SANDRA KUCK MOTHER'S DAY**	
95	HOME IS WHERE THE HEART IS	48 DAY	35.00	40.00
A. FAZIO			**SOPHISTICATED LADIES COLLECTION**	
85	CLEO	CL	29.50	35.00
85	FELICIA	CL	29.50	35.00
85	PHOEBE	CL	29.50	35.00
85	SAMANTHA	CL	29.50	35.00
86	BIANKA	CL	29.50	35.00
86	CERISSA	CL	29.50	35.00
86	CHELSEA	CL	29.50	35.00
86	NATASHA	CL	29.50	35.00
S. KUCK			**SPECIAL OCCASIONS BY RECO**	
88	WEDDING, THE	OP	35.00	40.00
89	WEDDING DAY (6 1/2 IN.)	OP	25.00	30.00
90	SPECIAL DAY, THE	OP	25.00	30.00
C. MICARELLI			**SPECIAL OCCASIONS-WEDDING**	
91	FROM THIS DAY FORWARD (6 1/2 IN.)	OP	25.00	30.00
91	FROM THIS DAY FORWARD (9 1/2 IN.)	OP	35.00	40.00
91	TO HAVE AND TO HOLD (6 1/2 IN.)	OP	25.00	30.00
91	TO HAVE AND TO HOLD (9 1/2 IN.)	OP	35.00	40.00
T. UTZ			**SPRINGTIME OF LIFE**	
85	TEDDY'S BATHTIME	CL	29.50	35.00
86	AMONG THE DAFFODILS	CL	29.50	35.00
86	AUNT TILLIE'S HATS	CL	29.50	35.00
86	GRANNY'S BOOTS	CL	29.50	35.00
86	JUST LIKE MOMMY	CL	29.50	35.00
86	LITTLE EMILY	CL	29.50	35.00
86	MY FAVORITE DOLLS	CL	29.50	35.00
86	MY MASTERPIECE	CL	29.50	40.00
S. KUCK			**SUGAR & SPICE**	
93	BEST FRIENDS	CL	29.90	30.00
93	SISTERS	CL	29.90	30.00
94	GARDEN OF SUNSHINE	CL	34.90	40.00
94	LITTLE ONE	CL	32.90	35.00
94	MORNING PRAYERS	CL	32.90	40.00
94	TEDDY BEAR TALES	CL	32.90	40.00
95	A SPECIAL DAY	95 DAY	34.90	40.00
95	FIRST SNOW	95 DAY	34.90	40.00
S. KUCK			**TIDINGS OF JOY**	
92	PEACE ON EARTH	OP	35.00	50.00
93	REJOICE	OP	35.00	50.00
94	NOEL	CL	35.00	40.00

YR	NAME	LIMIT	ISSUE	TREND
	J. BERGSMA			**TOTEMS OF THE WEST**
94	PEACE AT LAST	CL	29.50	30.00
94	WATCHMEN, THE	CL	29.50	30.00
	S. BARLOWE			**TOWN AND COUNTRY DOGS**
90	FOX HUNT	CL	35.00	40.00
91	GOLDEN FIELDS (GOLDEN RETRIEVER)	CL	35.00	40.00
91	RETRIEVAL, THE	CL	35.00	40.00
	R. JOHNSON			**TRAINS OF THE ORIENT**
93	GOLDEN ARROW-ENGLAND, THE	*	29.50	30.00
94	AUSTRIA	*	29.50	30.00
94	BAVAROA	*	29.50	30.00
94	FRANCE	*	29.50	30.00
94	FRANKONIA	*	29.50	30.00
94	GREECE	*	29.50	30.00
94	RUMANIA	*	29.50	30.00
94	TURKEY	*	29.50	30.00
	J. MCCLELLAND			**TREASURED SONGS OF CHILDHOOD**
88	A TISKET, A TASKET	CL	29.50	35.00
88	BAA, BAA, BLACK SHEEP	RT	32.90	35.00
88	TWINKLE, TWINKLE, LITTLE STAR	RT	29.50	30.00
89	I'M A LITTLE TEAPOT	CL	32.90	40.00
89	PAT-A-CAKE	CL	34.90	40.00
89	RAIN, RAIN GO AWAY	RT	32.90	35.00
89	ROUND THE MULBERRY BUSH	CL	32.90	40.00
90	HUSH LITTLE BABY	CL	34.90	40.00
	S. BARLOWE			**VANISHING ANIMAL KINGDOMS**
86	OLEPI THE BUFFALO	21500	35.00	40.00
86	RAMA THE TIGER	21500	35.00	40.00
87	COOLIBAH THE KOALA	21500	35.00	45.00
87	ORTWIN THE DEER	21500	35.00	40.00
87	YEN-POH THE PANDA	21500	35.00	40.00
88	MAMAKUU THE ELEPHANT	21500	35.00	60.00
	S. KUCK			**VICTORIAN CHRISTMAS**
95	DEAR SANTA	72 DAY	35.00	40.00
	S. KUCK			**VICTORIAN MOTHER'S DAY**
89	MOTHER'S SUNSHINE	RT	35.00	65.00
90	REFLECTION OF LOVE	RT	35.00	65.00
91	A PRECIOUS TIME	RT	35.00	60.00
91	BOUQUETS OF LOVE	YR	35.00	40.00
92	LOVING TOUCH	RT	35.00	40.00
92	TO BE ANNOUNCED	YR	35.00	40.00
	E. BERKE			**WESTERN**
74	MOUNTAIN MAN	RT	165.00	170.00
	C. CORCILIUS			**WOMEN OF THE PLAINS**
94	NO BOURDENES	CL	29.50	30.00
94	PRIDE OF A MAIDEN	CL	29.50	30.00
	J. MCCLELLAND			**WONDER OF CHRISTMAS**
91	SANTA'S SECRET	CL	29.50	30.00
92	MY FAVORITE ORNAMENT	CL	29.50	30.00
92	WAITING FOR SANTA	CL	29.50	30.00
93	CANDLELIGHT CHRISTMAS	CL	29.50	30.00
	J. MCCLELLAND			**WORLD OF CHILDREN**
77	RAINY DAY FUN	10000	50.00	60.00
78	WHEN I GROW UP	15000	50.00	60.00
79	YOU'RE INVITED	15000	50.00	60.00
80	KITTENS FOR SALE	15000	50.00	60.00

REECE

YR	NAME	LIMIT	ISSUE	TREND
	*			**WATERFOWL**
73	MALLARDS & WOOD DUCKS (PAIR)	900	250.00	375.00
74	CANVASBACK & CANADIAN GEESE (PAIR)	900	250.00	375.00
75	PINTAILS & TEAL (PAIR)	900	250.00	425.00

REED & BARTON

YR	NAME	LIMIT	ISSUE	TREND
	*			**'TWAS THE NIGHT BEFORE CHRISTMAS**
89	'TWAS THE NIGHT BEFORE CHRISTMAS	4000	75.00	85.00
	J. DOWNING			**'TWAS THE NIGHT BEFORE CHRISTMAS**
90	VISIONS OF SUGARPLUMS	3500	75.00	85.00
91	AWAY TO THE WINDOW	3500	74.00	79.00
	*			**AUDUBON**
70	PINE SISKIN	5000	60.00	175.00
71	RED-SHOULDERED HAWK	5000	60.00	75.00
72	STILT SANDPIPER	5000	60.00	70.00
73	RED CARDINAL	5000	60.00	65.00
74	BOREAL CHICKADEE	5000	65.00	75.00
75	YELLOW-BREASTED CHAT	5000	65.00	75.00
76	BAY-BREASTED WARBLER	5000	65.00	75.00
77	PURPLE FINCH	5000	65.00	75.00

RHODES STUDIO

YR	NAME	LIMIT	ISSUE	TREND
	*			**BOUNTIFUL HARVEST**
92	BASKET FULL OF APPLES	OP	39.00	120.00
92	BUSHEL OF PEACHES	OP	39.00	65.00
93	FRESH OFF THE PLUM TREE	OP	39.00	50.00
93	PEARS FROM THE GROVE	OP	39.00	65.00
	*			**LEGENDARY STEAM TRAINS**
89	AMERICAN STANDARD 4-4-0	OP	65.00	89.00

YR	NAME	LIMIT	ISSUE	TREND
90	BEST FRIEND/CHARLESTON 0-4-OT	OP	70.00	110.00
90	CHALLENGER CLASS, THE 4-6-6-4	OP	70.00	110.00
90	HUDSON J3 STREAMLINER 4-6-4	OP	65.00	92.00
91	K-28, THE- 2-8-2	OP	70.00	100.00
91	K4 CLASS, THE- 4-6-2	OP	70.00	125.00
*			**MIRACLES OF LIGHT**	
92	NATIVITY OF HOPE	OP	90.00	90.00
92	NATIVITY OF JOY	OP	90.00	90.00
92	NATIVITY OF LOVE	OP	85.00	90.00
92	NATIVITY OF PEACE	OP	85.00	90.00
93	NATIVITY OF FAITH	OP	90.00	90.00
93	NATIVITY OF PRAISE	OP	90.00	90.00
*			**TREASURES OF THE DORE BIBLE**	
86	MOSES/TEN COMMANDMENTS	OP	59.00	59.00
87	JACOB AND THE ANGEL	OP	59.00	59.00
87	REBEKAH AT THE WELL	OP	64.00	70.00
88	DANIEL IN THE LION'S DEN	OP	64.00	65.00
88	ELIJAH AND/CHARIOT OF FIRE	OP	64.00	75.00
88	JUDGMENT OF SOLOMON	OP	64.00	64.00
*			**VILLAGE LIGHTS**	
93	CHURCH AT THE BEND	OP	54.00	54.00
93	EVERGREEN BOOKS	OP	54.00	54.00
93	HOLLY STREET BAKERY	OP	49.00	49.00
93	KRINGLE'S GENERAL STORE	OP	54.00	54.00
93	MISTLETOE TOY SHOP	OP	49.00	49.00
93	MRS. SUGARPLUM'S CHOCOLATES	OP	54.00	54.00
*			**WATERFOWL LEGACY**	
91	MALLARD'S DESCENT	OP	69.00	120.00
92	IN FLIGHT	OP	69.00	100.00
92	TAKING OFF	OP	74.00	135.00
92	WIND RIDERS	OP	74.00	150.00
93	FLYING IN	OP	74.00	125.00
93	RISING UP	OP	74.00	74.00

RICHARD DI SILVIO STUDIO

YR	NAME	LIMIT	ISSUE	TREND
	R. DISILVIO			
92	COLUMBUS DISCOVERY OF AMERICA	2000	29.95	30.00
	R. DISILVIO		**PANTHEON OF COMPOSERS**	
92	GIACOMO PUCCINI	YR	29.95	30.00
92	GIOACCHINO ROSSINI	YR	29.95	30.00
92	LUDWIG VAN BEETHOVEN	YR	29.95	30.00
92	WOLFGANG A. MOZART	YR	29.95	30.00
93	FRANZ LISZT	YR	29.95	30.00
93	GIUSEPPE VERDI	YR	29.95	30.00
93	PETER TEHACKOVSKY	YR	29.95	30.00
93	RICHARD WAGNER	YR	29.95	30.00
	R. DISILVIO		**WEDDING COLLECTION**	
93	KISS OF ETERNAL LOVE	10000	29.95	30.00

RIVER SHORE

YR	NAME	LIMIT	ISSUE	TREND
	R. BROWN		**BABY ANIMALS**	
79	AKIKU	20000	50.00	75.00
80	ROOSEVELT	20000	50.00	90.00
81	CLOVER	20000	50.00	70.00
82	ZUELA	20000	50.00	70.00
	ROCKWELL/ BROWN		**FAMOUS AMERICANS**	
76	BROWN'S LINCOLN	9500	40.00	40.00
77	ROCKWELL'S TRIPLE SELF-PORTRAIT	9500	45.00	50.00
78	PEACE CORPS	9500	45.00	50.00
79	SPIRIT OF LINDBERGH	9500	50.00	50.00
	E. CHRISTOPHERSON		**LITTLE HOUSE ON THE PRAIRIE**	
85	A BELL FOR WALNUT GROVE	10-DAY	29.50	48.00
85	CAROLINE'S EGGS	10-DAY	29.50	48.00
85	FOUNDER'S DAY PICNIC	10-DAY	29.50	50.00
85	INGALL'S FAMILY	10-DAY	29.50	48.00
85	MARY'S GIFT	10-DAY	29.50	48.00
85	MEDICINE SHOW	10-DAY	29.50	48.00
85	SWEETHEART TREE, THE	10-DAY	29.50	48.00
85	WOMEN'S HARVEST	10-DAY	29.50	48.00
	M. HAGUE		**LOVABLE TEDDIES**	
85	BEARLY FRIGHTFUL	10-DAY	21.50	22.00
85	BEDTIME BLUES	10-DAY	21.50	22.00
85	CAUGHT IN THE ACT	10-DAY	21.50	22.00
85	FIRESIDE FRIENDS	10-DAY	21.50	22.00
85	HARVEST TIME	10-DAY	21.50	22.00
85	MISSED A BUTTON	10-DAY	21.50	22.00
85	SUNDAY STROLL	10-DAY	21.50	22.00
85	TENDER LOVING BEAR	10-DAY	21.50	22.00
	N. ROCKWELL		**NORMAN ROCKWELL SINGLE ISSUE**	
79	SPRING FLOWERS	17000	75.00	150.00
80	LOOKING OUT TO SEA	17000	75.00	140.00
82	GRANDPA'S GUARDIAN	17000	80.00	75.00
82	GRANDPA'S TREASURES	17000	80.00	75.00
	J. LAMB		**PUPPY PLAYTIME**	
87	DOUBLE TAKE	14-DAY	24.50	30.00
87	FUN AND GAMES	14-DAY	24.50	30.00
88	A NEW LEASH ON LIFE	14-DAY	24.50	30.00

YR	NAME	LIMIT	ISSUE	TREND
88	CABIN FEVER	14-DAY	24.50	28.00
88	CATCH OF THE DAY	14-DAY	24.50	28.00
88	GETTING ACQUAINTED	14-DAY	24.50	28.00
88	HANGING OUT	14-DAY	24.50	28.00
88	WEEKEND GARDENER	14-DAY	24.50	28.00
N. ROCKWELL		**ROCKWELL FOUR FREEDOMS**		
81	FREEDOM OF SPEECH	17000	65.00	85.00
82	FREEDOM FROM FEAR	17000	65.00	65.00
82	FREEDOM FROM WANT	17000	65.00	65.00
82	FREEDOM OF WORSHIP	17000	65.00	75.00
*				**SIGNS OF LOVE**
81	A KISS FOR MOTHER	OP	18.50	8.00
81	A WATCHFUL EYE	OP	21.50	6.00
82	A GENTLE PERSUASION	OP	23.50	5.00
83	A PROTECTIVE EMBRACE	OP	23.50	8.00
83	A TENDER COAXING	OP	23.50	8.00
84	A REASSURING TOUCH	OP	23.50	8.00
85	A LOVING GUIDANCE	OP	26.50	27.00
85	A TRUSTING HUG	OP	26.50	34.00
D. CROOK			**WE THE CHILDREN**	
87	FREEDOM OF SPEECH, THE	14-DAY	24.50	24.50
88	CRUEL AND UNUSUAL PUNISHMENT	14-DAY	24.50	25.00
88	QUARTERING OF SOLDIERS	14-DAY	24.50	25.00
88	RIGHT TO BEAR ARMS	14-DAY	24.50	25.00
88	RIGHT TO VOTE	14-DAY	24.50	25.00
88	SELF INCRIMINATION	14-DAY	24.50	25.00
88	TRIAL BY JURY	14-DAY	24.50	25.00
88	UNREASONABLE SEARCH AND SEIZURE	14-DAY	24.50	25.00

ROCKWELL SOCIETY

YR	NAME	LIMIT	ISSUE	TREND
N. ROCKWELL			**A MIND OF HER OWN**	
86	SITTING PRETTY	CL	24.90	25.00
87	BREAKING THE RULES	CL	27.90	30.00
87	GOOD INTENTIONS	CL	27.90	25.00
87	SERIOUS BUSINESS	CL	24.90	25.00
88	KISS AND TELL	CL	29.90	30.00
88	ON MY HONOR	CL	29.90	30.00
88	SECOND THOUGHTS	CL	27.90	28.00
88	WORLD'S AWAY	CL	27.90	28.00
N. ROCKWELL			**AMERICAN DREAM**	
86	YOUNG MAN'S DREAM	OP	22.90	20.00
N. ROCKWELL				**CHRISTMAS**
74	SCOTTY GETS HIS TREE	YR	24.50	90.00
75	ANGEL WITH BLACK EYE	YR	24.50	34.00
76	GOLDEN CHRISTMAS	YR	24.50	35.00
77	TOY SHOP WINDOW	YR	24.50	25.00
78	CHRISTMAS DREAM	YR	24.50	30.00
79	SOMEBODY'S UP THERE	YR	24.50	30.00
80	SCOTTY PLAYS SANTA	YR	24.50	28.00
81	WRAPPED UP IN CHRISTMAS	YR	25.50	26.00
82	CHRISTMAS COURTSHIP	YR	25.50	26.00
83	SANTA IN THE SUBWAY	YR	25.50	26.00
84	SANTA IN THE WORKSHOP	YR	27.50	28.00
85	GRANDPA PLAYS SANTA	YR	27.50	28.00
86	DEAR SANTY CLAUS	YR	27.90	27.00
87	SANTA'S GOLDEN GIFT	YR	29.90	30.00
88	SANTA CLAUS	YR	29.90	30.00
89	JOLLY OLD ST. NICK	YR	29.90	30.00
90	A CHRISTMAS PRAYER	YR	29.90	30.00
91	SANTA'S HELPERS	YR	32.90	33.00
92	CHRISTMAS SURPRISE, THE	YR	32.90	44.00
93	TREE BRIGADE, THE	YR	32.90	39.00
94	CHRISTMAS MARVEL	YR	32.90	33.00
*			**CHRISTMAS LEGACY**	
93	FILLING EVERY STOCKING	OP	54.90	55.00
93	SANTA'S MAGICAL VIEW	OP	54.90	55.00
N. ROCKWELL		**COLONIALS-THE RAREST ROCKWELLS**		
85	UNEXPECTED PROPOSAL	CL	27.90	28.00
86	LIGHT FOR THE WINTER	CL	30.90	38.00
86	WORDS OF COMFORT	CL	27.90	28.00
87	CLINCHING THE DEAL	CL	30.90	31.00
87	JOURNEY HOME, THE	CL	30.90	31.00
87	PORTRAIT FOR A BRIDEGROOM	CL	30.90	31.00
88	SIGN OF THE TIMES	CL	32.90	33.00
88	YE GLUTTON	CL	32.90	33.00
N. ROCKWELL				**COMING OF AGE**
90	A NEW LOOK	CL	32.90	35.00
90	BACK TO SCHOOL	CL	29.90	30.00
90	HER FIRST FORMAL	CL	32.90	40.00
90	HOME FROM CAMP	CL	29.90	30.00
90	MUSCLEMAN, THE	CL	32.90	33.00
91	A BALCONY SEAT	CL	32.90	33.00
91	DOORWAY TO THE PAST	CL	34.90	49.00
91	MEN ABOUT TOWN	CL	34.90	35.00
91	PATHS OF GLORY	CL	34.90	35.00
91	SCHOOL'S OUT!	CL	34.90	60.00

YR	NAME	LIMIT	ISSUE	TREND
N. ROCKWELL				**GOLDEN MOMENTS**
88	GRANDMA'S LOVE	OP	19.90	30.00
N. ROCKWELL				**HERITAGE**
77	TOY MAKER	YR	14.50	90.00
78	COBBLER	YR	19.50	50.00
79	LIGHTHOUSE KEEPER'S DAUGHTER	YR	19.50	25.00
80	SHIP BUILDER	YR	19.50	21.00
81	MUSIC MAKER	YR	19.50	21.00
82	TYCOON	YR	19.50	21.00
83	PAINTER	YR	19.50	21.00
84	STORYTELLER	YR	19.50	21.00
85	GOURMET	YR	19.50	21.00
86	PROFESSOR	YR	22.90	23.00
87	SHADOW ARTIST	YR	22.90	30.00
88	BANJO PLAYER, THE	YR	22.90	25.00
88	VETERAN, THE	YR	22.90	25.00
90	OLD SCOUT, THE	YR	24.90	28.00
91	FAMILY DOCTOR, THE	YR	27.90	50.00
91	YOUNG SCHOLAR, THE	YR	24.90	30.00
N. ROCKWELL				**INNOCENCE & EXPERIENCE**
91	AMERICAN HEROES, THE	OP	32.90	35.00
91	MAGICIAN, THE	OP	32.90	36.00
91	RADIO OPERATOR, THE	OP	29.90	28.00
91	SEA CAPTAIN, THE	OP	29.90	30.00
N. ROCKWELL				**LIGHT CAMPAIGN**
83	ROOM THAT LIGHT MADE, THE	OP	19.50	20.00
N. ROCKWELL				**MOTHER'S DAY**
76	A MOTHER'S LOVE	YR	24.50	75.00
77	FAITH	YR	24.50	35.00
78	BEDTIME	YR	24.50	28.00
79	REFLECTIONS	YR	24.50	25.00
80	A MOTHER'S PRIDE	YR	24.50	25.00
81	AFTER THE PARTY	YR	24.50	25.00
82	COOKING LESSON, THE	YR	25.50	26.00
83	ADD TWO CUPS AND LOVE	YR	25.50	26.00
84	GRANDMA'S COURTING DRESS	YR	25.50	26.00
85	MENDING TIME	YR	27.50	28.00
86	PANTRY RAID	YR	27.90	28.00
87	GRANDMA'S SURPRISE	YR	29.90	30.00
88	MY MOTHER	YR	29.90	30.00
89	SUNDAY DINNER	YR	29.90	30.00
90	EVENING PRAYERS	YR	29.90	30.00
91	BUILDING OUR FUTURE	YR	32.90	33.00
91	GENTLE REASSURANCE	YR	32.90	33.00
92	A SPECIAL DELIVERY	YR	32.90	34.00
N. ROCKWELL				**REDISCOVERED WOMEN**
81	DREAMING IN THE ATTIC	OP	19.50	20.00
82	WAITING ON THE SHORE	OP	22.50	23.00
83	FLIRTING IN THE PARLOR	OP	22.50	23.00
83	GOSSIPING IN THE ALCOVE	OP	22.50	23.00
83	MAKING BELIEVE AT THE MIRROR	OP	22.50	23.00
83	PONDERING ON THE PORCH	OP	22.50	23.00
83	STANDING IN THE DOORWAY	OP	22.50	23.00
83	WALKING AT THE DANCE	OP	22.50	23.00
N. ROCKWELL				**ROCKWELL HERITAGE**
92	FAMILY DOCTOR, THE	OP	27.90	43.00
93	JEWELER, THE	OP	27.90	46.00
94	HALLOWEEN FROLIC	OP	27.90	28.00
95	APPRENTICE, THE	OP	29.90	30.00
N. ROCKWELL				**ROCKWELL ON TOUR**
83	PROMENADE A PARIS	CL	16.00	16.00
83	WALKING THROUGH MERRIE ENGLANDE	CL	16.00	16.00
83	WHEN IN ROME	CL	16.00	16.00
84	DIE WALK AM RHEIN	CL	16.00	16.00
N. ROCKWELL				**ROCKWELL'S AMERICAN DREAM**
85	A COUPLE'S COMMITMENT	CL	19.90	30.00
85	A FAMILY'S FULL MEASURE	CL	22.90	34.00
85	A YOUNG GIRL'S DREAM	CL	19.90	19.00
86	A MOTHER'S WELCOME	CL	22.90	23.00
86	A YOUNG MAN'S DREAM	CL	22.90	39.00
86	MUSICIAN'S MAGIC, THE	CL	22.90	23.00
87	AN ORPHAN'S HOPE	CL	24.90	27.00
87	LOVE'S REWARD	CL	24.90	35.00
N. ROCKWELL				**ROCKWELL'S GOLDEN MOMENTS**
87	GRANDMA'S LOVE	CL	19.90	44.00
87	GRANDPA'S GIFT	CL	19.90	30.00
88	BEST FRIENDS	CL	22.90	23.00
88	END OF DAY	CL	22.90	25.00
89	EVENING'S REPOSE	CL	24.90	25.00
89	KEEPING COMPANY	CL	24.90	25.00
89	LOVE LETTERS	CL	22.90	23.00
89	NEWFOUND WORLDS	CL	22.90	23.00
N. ROCKWELL				**ROCKWELL'S LIGHT CAMPAIGN**
83	THIS IS THE ROOM THAT LIGHT MADE	CL	19.50	20.00
84	BIRTHDAY WISH, THE	CL	21.50	22.00
84	CLOSE HARMONY	CL	21.50	22.00
84	EVENING'S EASE	CL	19.50	20.00

YR	NAME	LIMIT	ISSUE	TREND
84	FATHER'S HELP	CL	19.50	20.00
84	GRANDPA'S TREASURE CHEST	CL	19.50	20.00
N. ROCKWELL		**ROCKWELL'S REDISCOVERED WOMEN**		
*	COMPLETE COLLECTION	100-DAY	267.00	267.00
84	CONFIDING IN THE DEN	CL	22.50	23.00
84	DREAMING IN THE ATTIC	CL	19.50	20.00
84	FLIRTING IN THE PARLOR	CL	22.50	30.00
84	GOSSIPING IN THE ALCOVE	CL	22.50	23.00
84	MAKING BELIEVE AT THE MIRROR	CL	22.50	25.00
84	MEETING ON THE PATH	CL	22.50	23.00
84	PONDERING ON THE PORCH	CL	22.50	23.00
84	REMINISCING IN THE QUIET	CL	22.50	23.00
84	STANDING IN THE DOORWAY	CL	22.50	25.00
84	WAITING AT THE DANCE	CL	22.50	25.00
84	WAITING ON THE SHORE	CL	22.50	23.00
84	WORKING IN THE KITCHEN	CL	22.50	23.00
N. ROCKWELL		**ROCKWELL'S THE ONES WE LOVE**		
88	TENDER LOVING CARE	CL	19.90	35.00
89	A TIME TO KEEP	CL	19.90	27.00
89	GROWING STRONG	CL	22.90	23.00
89	INVENTOR AND THE JUDGE, THE	CL	22.90	30.00
89	READY FOR THE WORLD	CL	22.90	23.00
90	COUNTRY DOCTOR, THE	CL	24.90	25.00
90	HOMECOMING, THE	CL	24.90	22.00
90	OUR LOVE OF COUNTRY	CL	24.90	25.00
90	STORY HOUR, THE	CL	22.90	24.00
91	A HELPING HAND	CL	24.90	25.00
N. ROCKWELL		**ROCKWELL'S TREASURED MEMORIES**		
91	EVENING PASSAGE	CL	32.90	33.00
91	HEAVENLY DREAMS	OP	32.90	33.00
91	QUIET REFLECTIONS	CL	29.90	15.00
91	ROMANTIC REVERIE	CL	29.90	30.00
91	SENTIMENTAL SHORES	OP	32.90	35.00
91	TENDER ROMANCE	CL	32.90	33.00

ROMAN INC.

YR	NAME	LIMIT	ISSUE	TREND
R.J. ZOLAN				
95	CHILDHOOD DREAMS	OP	7.50	8.00
A. WILLIAMS		**ABBIE WILLIAMS COLLECTION**		
91	BLESS THE CHILD	OP	29.50	30.00
91	LEGACY OF LOVE	OP	29.50	30.00
F. HOOK		**A CHILD'S PLAY**		
82	BREEZY DAY	CL	29.95	35.00
82	KITE FLYING	CL	29.95	35.00
84	BATHTUB SAILOR	CL	29.95	35.00
84	FIRST SNOW, THE	CL	29.95	35.00
F. HOOK		**A CHILD'S WORLD**		
80	LITTLE CHILDREN, COME TO ME	15000	45.00	65.00
I. SPENCER		**CATNIPPERS**		
86	CHRISTMAS MOURNING	9500	34.50	35.00
92	HAPPY HOLIDAZE	9500	34.50	35.00
E. SIMONETTI		**FONTANINI ANNUAL CHRISTMAS PLATE**		
86	A KING IS BORN	YR	60.00	60.00
87	O COME, LET US ADORE HIM	YR	60.00	65.00
88	ADORATION OF THE MAGI	YR	70.00	75.00
89	FLIGHT INTO EGYPT	YR	75.00	85.00
F. HOOK		**FRANCES HOOK COLLECTION-SET I**		
82	BABY BLOSSOMS	15000	24.95	75.00
82	DAISY DREAMER	15000	24.95	75.00
82	I WISH, I WISH	15000	24.95	75.00
82	TREES SO TALL	15000	24.95	75.00
F. HOOK		**FRANCES HOOK COLLECTION-SET II**		
83	CAN I KEEP HIM	15000	24.95	50.00
83	CAUGHT IT MYSELF	15000	24.95	50.00
83	SO CUDDLY	15000	24.95	50.00
83	WINTER WRAPPINGS	15000	24.95	50.00
F. HOOK		**FRANCES HOOK LEGACY**		
85	DAYDREAMING	CL	19.50	26.00
85	DISAPPOINTMENT	CL	22.50	26.00
85	DISCOVERY	CL	22.50	26.00
85	EXPECTATION	CL	22.50	26.00
85	FASCINATION	CL	19.50	26.00
85	WONDERMENT	CL	22.50	26.00
A. WILLIAMS		**GOD BLESS YOU, LITTLE ONE**		
91	BABY'S FIRST BIRTHDAY (BOY)	OP	29.50	30.00
91	BABY'S FIRST BIRTHDAY (GIRL)	OP	29.50	30.00
91	BABY'S FIRST SMILE	OP	19.50	20.00
91	BABY'S FIRST STEP	OP	19.50	20.00
91	BABY'S FIRST TOOTH	OP	19.50	20.00
91	BABY'S FIRST WORD	OP	19.50	20.00
A. WILLIAMS		**LORD'S PRAYER**		
86	AS WE FORGIVE	CL	24.50	30.00
86	DELIVER US FROM EVIL	CL	24.50	30.00
86	FORGIVE OUR TRESPASSES	CL	24.50	30.00
86	GIVE US THIS DAY	CL	24.50	30.00
86	LEAD US NOT	CL	24.50	30.00
86	OUR FATHER	CL	24.50	30.00

YR	NAME	LIMIT	ISSUE	TREND
86	THINE IS THE KINGDOM	CL	24.50	30.00
86	THY KINGDOM COME	CL	24.50	30.00
	A. WILLIAMS			**LOVE'S PRAYER**
88	LOVE BELIEVES ALL THINGS	CL	29.50	35.00
88	LOVE DOES NOT INSIST ON ITS OWN WAY	CL	29.50	35.00
88	LOVE IS NEVER ARROGANT OR RUDE	CL	29.50	35.00
88	LOVE IS NEVER IRRITABLE OR RESENTFUL	CL	29.50	35.00
88	LOVE IS NEVER JEALOUS OR BOASTFUL	CL	29.50	35.00
88	LOVE IS PATIENT AND KIND	CL	29.50	35.00
88	LOVE NEVER ENDS	CL	29.50	35.00
88	LOVE REJOICES IN THE RIGHT	CL	29.50	35.00
	A. WILLIAMS			**MAGIC OF CHILDHOOD**
85	BEST BUDDIES	CL	24.50	35.00
85	FEEDING TIME	CL	24.50	30.00
85	GETTING ACQUAINTED	CL	24.50	30.00
85	SPECIAL FRIENDS	CL	24.50	30.00
86	A HANDFUL OF LOVE	CL	24.50	30.00
86	LAST ONE IN	CL	24.50	30.00
86	LOOK ALIKES	CL	24.50	30.00
86	NO FAIR PEEKING	CL	24.50	30.00
	A. WILLIAMS			**MARCH OF DIMES: OUR CHILDREN, OUR FUTURE**
90	A TIME TO LAUGH	CL	29.00	35.00
	G. DELLE NOTTI			**MASTERPIECE COLLECTION**
81	HOLY FAMILY, THE	5000	95.00	115.00
	R. FERRUZZI			**MASTERPIECE COLLECTION**
82	MADONNA OF THE STREETS	5000	85.00	100.00
	F. LIPPE			**MASTERPIECE COLLECTION**
79	ADORATION	5000	65.00	75.00
	P. MIGNARD			**MASTERPIECE COLLECTION**
80	MADONNA WITH GRAPES	5000	87.50	100.00
	MORCALDO/ LUCCHESI			**MILLENIUM SERIES**
92	SILENT NIGHT	CL	49.50	49.50
93	ANNUNCIATION, THE	5000	49.50	50.00
94	PEACE ON EARTH	5000	49.50	49.50
95	CAUSE OF OUR JOY	5000	49.50	49.50
	A. WILLIAMS			**PRECIOUS CHILDREN**
93	BLESS BABY BROTHER	*	29.50	30.00
93	BLOWING BUBBLES	*	29.50	30.00
93	DON'T WORRY, MOTHER DUCK	*	29.50	30.00
93	LET'S SAY GRACE	*	29.50	30.00
93	MOTHER'S LITTLE ANGEL	*	29.50	30.00
93	PICKING DAISIES	*	29.50	30.00
93	TEA PARTY, THE	*	29.50	30.00
93	TREETOP DISCOVERY	*	29.50	30.00
	G. PETTY			**PRETTY GIRLS OF THE ICE CAPADES**
83	ICE PRINCESS	CL	24.50	35.00
*				**PROMISE OF A SAVIOR**
93	A CHILD IS BORN	CL	29.90	30.00
93	AN ANGEL'S MESSAGE	CL	29.90	30.00
93	ANGELS WERE WATCHING	CL	29.90	30.00
93	GIFTS TO JESUS	CL	29.90	30.00
93	HEAVENLY KING, THE	CL	29.90	30.00
93	HOLY MOTHER & CHILD	CL	29.90	30.00
*				**ROMAN CATS**
84	GRIZABELLA	CL	29.50	35.00
84	MR. MISTOFFELEES	CL	29.50	35.00
84	RUM RUM TUGGER	CL	29.50	35.00
	F. HOOK			**ROMAN MEMORIAL**
84	CARPENTER, THE	YR	100.00	140.00
	E. MORCALDO			**SERAPHIM COLLECTION**
95	HELENA-HEAVEN'S HERALD	7200	49.50	50.00
	A. WILLIAMS			**SINGLE RELEASES**
87	CHRISTENING, THE	OP	29.50	30.00
90	DEDICATION, THE	OP	29.50	30.00
	I. SPENCER			**SWEETEST SONGS**
86	A BABY'S PRAYER	CL	39.50	45.00
86	THIS LITTLE PIGGIE	CL	39.50	45.00
88	LONG, LONG AGO	CL	39.50	45.00
89	ROCKABYE	CL	39.50	45.00
	B. SARGENT			**TENDER EXPRESSIONS**
92	THOUGHTS OF YOU ARE IN MY HEART	CL	29.50	30.00
	G. PETTY			**THE ICE CAPADES CLOWN**
83	PRESENTING FREDDIE TRENKLER	CL	24.50	35.00
	R.J. ZOLAN			**RICHARD JUDSON ZOLAN COLLECTION**
92	BUTTERFLY NET, THE	CL	29.50	30.00
94	RING, THE	CL	29.50	30.00
94	TERRACE DANCING	CL	29.50	30.00
95	VISIT, THE	OP	7.50	8.00

RORSTRAND

YR	NAME	LIMIT	ISSUE	TREND
	G. NYLUND			**CHRISTMAS**
68	BRINGING HOME THE TREE	YR	12.00	510.00
69	FISHERMAN SAILING HOME	YR	13.50	50.00
70	NILS WITH HIS GEESE	YR	13.50	50.00
71	NILS IN LAPLAND	YR	15.00	20.00
72	DALECARLIAN FIDDLER	YR	15.00	20.00

YR	NAME	LIMIT	ISSUE	TREND
73	FARM IN SMALAND	YR	16.00	60.00
74	VADSLENA	YR	19.00	40.00
75	NILS IN VASTMANLAND	YR	20.00	35.00
76	NILS IN UAPLAND	YR	20.00	40.00
77	NILS IN VARMLAND	YR	29.50	30.00
78	NILS IN FJALLBACKA	YR	32.50	50.00
79	NILS IN VAESTERGOETLAND	YR	38.50	39.00
80	NILS IN HALLAND	YR	55.00	65.00
81	NILS IN GOTLAND	YR	55.00	45.00
82	NILS AT SKANSEN	YR	47.50	40.00
83	NILS IN OLAND	YR	42.50	55.00
84	ANGERMAN LAND	YR	42.50	35.00
85	NILS IN JAMTLAND	YR	42.50	65.00
86	NILS IN KARLSKR	YR	42.50	50.00
87	DALSLAND, FORGET-ME-NOT	YR	47.50	150.00
88	NILS IN HALSINGLAND	YR	55.00	60.00
89	NILS VISITS GOTHENBORG	YR	60.00	60.00
A. WILLIAMS				**CHRISTMAS**
90	NILS IN KVIKKJOKK	YR	75.00	75.00
91	NILS IN MEDELPAD	YR	85.00	85.00
92	GASTRIKLAND, LILY OF THE VALLEY	YR	92.50	93.00
93	NARKE'S CASTLE	YR	92.50	93.00

ROSENTHAL

YR	NAME	LIMIT	ISSUE	TREND
*				**CHRISTMAS**
10	WINTER PEACE	YR	*	575.00
11	THREE WISE MEN	YR	*	350.00
12	STARDUST	YR	*	265.00
13	CHRISTMAS LIGHTS	YR	*	250.00
14	CHRISTMAS SONG	YR	*	350.00
15	WALKING TO CHURCH	YR	*	190.00
16	CHRISTMAS DURING WAR	YR	*	240.00
17	ANGEL OF PEACE	YR	*	210.00
18	PEACE ON EARTH	YR	*	210.00
19	ST. CHRISTOPHER WITH CHRIST CHILD	YR	*	225.00
20	MANGER IN BETHLEHEM	YR	*	350.00
21	CHRISTMAS IN MOUNTAINS	YR	*	210.00
22	ADVENT BRANCH	YR	*	210.00
23	CHILDREN IN WINTER WOODS	YR	*	210.00
24	DEER IN THE WOODS	YR	*	210.00
25	THREE WISE MEN	YR	*	210.00
26	CHRISTMAS IN MOUNTAINS	YR	*	200.00
27	STATION ON THE WAY	YR	*	210.00
28	CHALET CHRISTMAS	YR	*	200.00
29	CHRISTMAS IN ALPS	YR	*	225.00
30	GROUP OF DEER UNDER PINES	YR	*	225.00
31	PATH OF THE MAGI	YR	*	225.00
32	CHRIST CHILD	YR	*	200.00
33	THRU THE NIGHT TO LIGHT	YR	*	200.00
34	CHRISTMAS PEACE	YR	*	200.00
35	CHRISTMAS BY THE SEA	YR	*	200.00
36	NURNBERG ANGELS	YR	*	200.00
37	BERCHTESGADEN	YR	*	200.00
38	CHRISTMAS IN THE ALPS	YR	*	200.00
39	SCHNEEKOPPE MOUNTAIN	YR	*	200.00
40	MARIEN CHURCH IN DANZIG	YR	*	250.00
41	STRASSBURG CATHEDRAL	YR	*	250.00
42	MARIANBURG CASTLE	YR	*	300.00
43	WINTER IDYL	YR	*	300.00
44	WOOD SCAPE	YR	*	300.00
45	CHRISTMAS PEACE	YR	*	400.00
46	CHRISTMAS IN AN ALPINE VALLEY	YR	*	240.00
47	DILLINGEN MADONNA	YR	*	985.00
48	MESSAGE TO THE SHEPHERDS	YR	*	875.00
49	HOLY FAMILY, THE	YR	*	200.00
50	CHRISTMAS IN THE FOREST	YR	*	200.00
51	STAR OF BETHLEHEM	YR	*	450.00
52	CHRISTMAS IN THE ALPS	YR	*	200.00
53	HOLY LIGHT, THE	YR	*	200.00
54	CHRISTMAS EVE	YR	*	200.00
55	CHRISTMAS IN A VILLAGE	YR	*	200.00
56	CHRISTMAS IN THE ALPS	YR	*	200.00
57	CHRISTMAS BY THE SEA	YR	*	200.00
58	CHRISTMAS EVE	YR	*	200.00
59	MIDNIGHT MASS	YR	*	200.00
60	CHRISTMAS IN A SMALL VILLAGE	YR	*	200.00
61	SOLITARY CHRISTMAS	YR	*	225.00
62	CHRISTMAS EVE	YR	*	200.00
63	SILENT NIGHT	YR	*	200.00
64	CHRISTMAS MARKET IN NUREMBERG	YR	*	225.00
65	CHRISTMAS MUNICH	YR	*	200.00
66	CHRISTMAS IN ULM	YR	*	275.00
67	CHRISTMAS IN REGINBURG	YR	*	200.00
68	CHRISTMAS IN BREMEN	YR	*	200.00
69	CHRISTMAS IN ROTHENBURG	YR	*	220.00
70	CHRISTMAS IN COLOGNE	YR	*	175.00
71	CHRISTMAS IN GARMISCH	YR	42.00	100.00
72	CHRISTMAS IN FRANCONIA	YR	50.00	100.00
73	LUBECK-HOLSTEIN	YR	77.00	110.00

YR	NAME	LIMIT	ISSUE	TREND
74	CHRISTMAS IN WURZBURG	YR	85.00	100.00
	E. HIBEL		**NOBILITY OF CHILDREN**	
76	LA CONTESSA ISABELLA	12750	120.00	120.00
77	LA MARQUIS MAURICE-PIERRE	12750	120.00	120.00
78	BARONESSE JOHANNA	12750	130.00	140.00
79	CHIEF RED FEATHER	12750	140.00	180.00
	E. HIBEL			**ORIENTAL GOLD**
76	YASUKO	2000	275.00	650.00
77	MR. OBATA	2000	275.00	500.00
78	SAKURA	2000	295.00	400.00
79	MICHIO	2000	325.00	375.00
	B. WIINBLAD		**WIINBLAD CHRISTMAS**	
71	MARIA & CHILD	UD	100.00	700.00
72	CASPAR	UD	100.00	290.00
73	MELCHIOR	UD	125.00	335.00
74	BALTHAZAR	UD	125.00	300.00
75	ANNUNCIATION, THE	UD	195.00	200.00
76	ANGEL WITH TRUMPET	UD	195.00	200.00
77	ADORATION OF SHEPHERDS	UD	225.00	225.00
78	ANGEL WITH HARP	UD	275.00	295.00
79	EXODUS FROM EGYPT	UD	310.00	310.00
80	ANGEL WITH GLOCKENSPIEL	UD	360.00	360.00
81	CHRIST CHILD VISITS TEMPLE	UD	375.00	375.00
82	CHRISTENING OF CHRIST	UD	375.00	375.00

ROYAL BAYREUTH

YR	NAME	LIMIT	ISSUE	TREND
*				**CHRISTMAS**
72	CARRIAGE IN THE VILLAGE	4000	15.00	80.00
73	SNOW SCENE	4000	16.50	20.00
74	OLD MILL, THE	4000	24.00	24.00
75	FOREST CHALET 'SERENITY'	4000	27.50	28.00
76	CHRISTMAS IN THE COUNTRY	5000	40.00	40.00
77	PEACE ON EARTH	5000	40.00	40.00
78	PEACEFUL INTERLUDE	5000	45.00	45.00
79	HOMEWARD BOUND	5000	50.00	50.00

ROYAL COPENHAGEN

YR	NAME	LIMIT	ISSUE	TREND
	S. VESTERGAARD		**AMERICA'S MOTHER'S DAY**	
88	WESTERN TRAIL	YR	34.50	35.00
89	INDIAN LOVE CALL	YR	37.00	35.00
90	SOUTHERN BELLE	YR	39.50	39.00
91	MOTHER'S DAY AT THE MISSION	YR	42.50	39.00
92	TURN OF THE CENTURY BOSTON	YR	45.00	40.00
*				**CHRISTMAS**
62	LITTLE MERMAID, THE	YR	11.00	309.00
	R. BOCHER			**CHRISTMAS**
16	SHEPHERD AT CHRISTMAS	YR	1.50	129.00
26	CHRISTIANSHAVN CANAL	YR	2.00	145.00
36	ROSKILDE CATHEDRAL	YR	2.50	243.00
45	A PEACEFUL MOTIF	YR	4.00	599.00
51	CHRISTMAS ANGEL	YR	5.00	439.00
	A. BOESEN			**CHRISTMAS**
13	FREDERIK CHURCH SPIRE	YR	1.50	163.00
14	HOLY SPIRIT CHURCH	YR	1.50	210.00
	H. HANSEN			**CHRISTMAS**
49	OUR LADY'S CATHEDRAL	YR	5.00	339.00
57	GOOD SHEPHERD, THE	YR	8.00	163.00
58	SUNSHINE OVER GREENLAND	YR	9.00	163.00
59	CHRISTMAS NIGHT	YR	9.00	163.00
60	STAG, THE	YR	10.00	185.00
	O. JENSEN			**CHRISTMAS**
11	DANISH LANDSCAPE	YR	1.00	210.00
17	OUR SAVIOR CHURCH	YR	2.00	129.00
18	SHEEP AND SHEPHERDS	YR	2.00	129.00
19	IN THE PARK	YR	2.00	115.00
21	AABENRAA MARKETPLACE	YR	2.00	115.00
23	DANISH LANDSCAPE	YR	2.00	97.00
25	CHRISTIANSHAVN	YR	2.00	115.00
29	GRUNDTVIG CHURCH	YR	2.00	113.00
32	FREDERIKSBERG GARDENS	YR	2.50	129.00
34	HERMITAGE CASTLE, THE	YR	2.50	210.00
	T. KJOLNER			**CHRISTMAS**
41	DANISH VILLAGE CHURCH	YR	3.00	499.00
48	NODEBO CHURCH	YR	4.50	309.00
53	FREDERIKSBERG CASTLE	YR	6.00	163.00
	A. KROG			**CHRISTMAS**
15	DANISH LANDSCAPE	YR	1.50	210.00
	K. LANGE			**CHRISTMAS**
40	GOOD SHEPHERD, THE	YR	3.00	597.00
47	GOOD SHEPHERD, THE	YR	4.50	339.00
52	CHRISTMAS IN THE FOREST	YR	5.00	163.00
54	AMALIENBORG PALACE	YR	6.00	195.00
55	FANO GIRL	YR	7.00	243.00
56	ROSENBORG CASTLE	YR	7.00	210.00
61	TRAINING SHIP	YR	10.00	195.00
63	HOJSAGER MILL	YR	11.00	109.00
64	FETCHING THE TREE	YR	11.00	69.00

Sports Impressions says Farewell *to 27-year baseball veteran Nolan Ryan.*

Marry Me, Scarlett *from 1991 was the first issue in the Critic's Choice: Gone with the Wind collection from W.S. George.*

Famous for capturing the graceful beauty of his subjects, artist Fred Stone sets the pace in the area of equine art. Patience *is the first issue in his series "The Horses of Fred Stone" issued by Artaffects.*

YR	NAME	LIMIT	ISSUE	TREND
65	LITTLE SKATERS	YR	12.00	74.00
66	BLACKBIRD	YR	12.00	38.00
67	ROYAL OAK, THE	YR	13.00	38.00
68	LAST UMIAK, THE	YR	13.00	38.00
69	OLD FARMYARD, THE	YR	14.00	38.00
70	CHRISTMAS ROSE AND CAT	YR	14.00	38.00
71	HARE IN WINTER	YR	15.00	25.00
72	IN THE DESERT	YR	16.00	27.00
73	TRAIN HOMEWARD BOUND	YR	22.00	27.00
74	WINTER TWILIGHT	YR	22.00	30.00
75	QUEEN'S PALACE	YR	27.50	25.00
77	IMMERVAD BRIDGE	YR	32.00	27.00
78	GREENLAND SCENERY	YR	35.00	27.00
79	CHOOSING CHRISTMAS TREE	YR	42.50	82.00
80	BRINGING HOME THE TREE	YR	49.50	35.00
81	ADMIRING CHRISTMAS TREE	YR	52.50	82.00
82	WAITING FOR CHRISTMAS	YR	54.50	82.00
83	MERRY CHRISTMAS	YR	54.50	82.00
84	JINGLE BELLS	YR	54.50	82.00
85	SNOWMAN	YR	54.50	95.00
86	CHRISTMAS VACATION	YR	54.50	83.00
H. NIELSEN				**CHRISTMAS**
38	ROUND CHURCH IN OSTERLARS	YR	3.00	439.00
39	GREENLAND PACK-ICE	YR	3.00	597.00
B. OLSEN				**CHRISTMAS**
24	SAILING SHIP	YR	2.00	129.00
27	SHIP'S BOY AT TILLER	YR	2.00	173.00
30	FISHING BOATS	YR	2.50	145.00
33	FERRY AND THE GREAT BELT	YR	2.50	195.00
35	KRONBORG CASTLE	YR	2.50	309.00
V. OLSON				**CHRISTMAS**
44	DANISH VILLAGE SCENE	YR	4.00	405.00
50	BOESLUNDE CHURCH	YR	5.00	399.00
G. RODE				**CHRISTMAS**
20	MARY AND CHILD JESUS	YR	2.00	115.00
28	VICAR'S FAMILY	YR	2.00	145.00
31	MOTHER AND CHILD	YR	2.50	145.00
E. SELSCHAU				**CHRISTMAS**
22	THREE SINGING ANGELS	YR	2.00	97.00
C. THOMSEN				**CHRISTMAS**
08	MADONNA AND CHILD	YR	1.00	4900.00
10	MAGI, THE	YR	1.00	179.00
12	CHRISTMAS TREE	YR	1.00	210.00
N. THORSSON				**CHRISTMAS**
37	MAIN STREET COPENHAGEN	YR	2.50	339.00
42	BELL TOWER	YR	4.00	565.00
43	FLIGHT INTO EGYPT	YR	4.00	759.00
46	ZEALAND VILLAGE CHURCH	YR	4.00	275.00
S. USSING				**CHRISTMAS**
09	DANISH LANDSCAPE	YR	1.00	243.00
S. VESTERGAARD				**CHRISTMAS**
76	DANISH WATERMILL	YR	27.50	27.00
87	WINTER BIRDS	YR	59.50	98.00
88	CHRISTMAS EVE IN COPENHAGEN	YR	59.50	98.00
89	OLD SKATING POND, THE	YR	59.50	113.00
90	CHRISTMAS AT TIVOLI	YR	69.50	210.00
91	FESTIVAL OF SANTA LUCIA, THE	YR	69.50	113.00
92	QUEEN'S CARRIAGE	YR	69.50	83.00
93	CHRISTMAS GUESTS	YR	69.50	113.00
94	CHRISTMAS SHOPPING	YR	72.50	83.00
95	CHRISTMAS AT THE MANOR HOUSE	YR	72.50	75.00
H. HANSEN			**CHRISTMAS IN DENMARK**	
91	BRINGING HOME THE TREE	YR	72.50	113.00
92	CHRISTMAS SHOPPING	YR	72.50	83.00
93	SKATING PARTY, THE	YR	74.50	113.00
94	SLEIGH RIDE, THE	YR	74.50	83.00
C. MAGADINE			**FIRST/BING & GRONDAHL**	
96	CHRISTMAS EVE AT THE STATUE OF LIBERTY	YR	47.50	48.00
J. NIELSEN				**NATURE'S CHILDREN**
93	ROBINS, THE	YR	39.50	40.00
94	FAWN, THE	YR	39.50	40.00

ROYAL CORNWALL

YR	NAME	LIMIT	ISSUE	TREND
Y. KOUTSIS				**CREATION**
77	IN HIS IMAGE	10000	45.00	130.00
77	IN THE BEGINNING	10000	37.50	90.00
78	ADAM'S RIB	10000	45.00	125.00
78	BANISHED FROM EDEN	10000	45.00	125.00
78	NOAH AND THE ARK	10000	45.00	120.00
80	JACOB'S LADDER	10000	45.00	75.00
80	JACOB'S WEDDING	10000	45.00	75.00
80	JOSEPH INTERPRETS PHARAOH'S DREAM	10000	45.00	75.00
80	JOSEPH'S COAT OF MANY COLORS	10000	45.00	75.00
80	REBEKAH AT THE WELL	10000	45.00	75.00
80	SODOM AND GOMORRAH	10000	45.00	75.00
80	TOWER OF BABEL	10000	45.00	75.00

YR	NAME	LIMIT	ISSUE	TREND
Y. KOUTSIS		**CREATION CALHOUN CHARTER RELEASE**		
77	ADAM'S RIB	19500	29.50	100.00
77	IN HIS IMAGE	19500	29.50	120.00
77	IN THE BEGINNING	19500	29.50	152.00
77	NOAH AND THE ARK	19500	29.50	90.00
78	JACOB'S LADDER	19500	29.50	80.00
78	JACOB'S WEDDING	19500	29.50	80.00
78	JOSEPH INTERPRETS PHARAOH'S DREAM	19500	29.50	80.00
78	JOSEPH'S COAT OF MANY COLORS	19500	29.50	80.00
78	REBEKAH AT THE WELL	19500	29.50	80.00
78	SODOM AND GOMORRAH	19500	29.50	80.00
78	TOWER OF BABEL	19500	29.50	80.00

ROYAL DEVON

YR	NAME	LIMIT	ISSUE	TREND
N. ROCKWELL			**ROCKWELL CHRISTMAS**	
75	DOWNHILL DARING	YR	24.50	30.00
76	CHRISTMAS GIFT, THE	YR	24.50	35.00
77	BIG MOMENT, THE	YR	27.50	50.00
78	PUPPETS FOR CHRISTMAS	YR	27.50	30.00
79	ONE PRESENT TOO MANY	YR	31.50	30.00
80	GRAMPS MEETS GRAMPS	YR	33.00	35.00
N. ROCKWELL			**ROCKWELL MOTHER'S DAY**	
75	DOCTOR AND DOLL	YR	23.50	45.00
76	PUPPY LOVE	YR	24.50	100.00
77	FAMILY, THE	YR	24.50	80.00
78	MOTHER'S DAY OFF	YR	27.00	35.00
79	MOTHER'S EVENING OUT	YR	30.00	35.00
80	MOTHER'S TREAT	YR	32.50	35.00

ROYAL DOULTON

YR	NAME	LIMIT	ISSUE	TREND
*			**CHRISTMAS PLATES**	
93	SLEIGH RIDE	*	45.00	45.00
93	TOGETHER FOR CHRISTMAS	*	45.00	50.00
*			**FAMILY CHRISTMAS PLATES**	
91	DAD PLAYS SANTA	YR	60.00	60.00

ROYAL GRAFTON/THE COLLECTOR'S TREASURY

YR	NAME	LIMIT	ISSUE	TREND
M. JACKSON		**THE BEAUTY OF POLAR WILDLIFE**		
91	BABY SEALS	150-DAY	27.50	35.00

ROYAL WICKFORD PORCELAIN

YR	NAME	LIMIT	ISSUE	TREND
G. TERP			**ALICE IN WONDERLAND**	
87	CATERPILLAR, THE	45-DAY	29.50	48.00
87	DUCHESS AND COOK, THE	45-DAY	29.50	48.00
87	TEA PARTY, THE	45-DAY	29.50	43.00
87	TWEEDLEDEE-TWEEDLEDUM	45-DAY	29.50	30.00
87	WHITE KNIGHT, THE	45-DAY	29.50	48.00
88	HUMPTY DUMPTY	45-DAY	29.50	30.00
88	LION AND THE UNICORN, THE	45-DAY	29.50	30.00
88	OFF WITH THEIR HEADS	45-DAY	29.50	30.00
88	RED AND WHITE QUEENS	45-DAY	29.50	30.00
88	TALKING FLOWERS	45-DAY	29.50	30.00
88	WALRUS AND CARPENTER	45-DAY	29.50	30.00
88	WHITE RABBIT, THE	45-DAY	29.50	30.00
L. DUBIN			**THE LIL' PEDDLERS**	
87	APPLE A DAY	YR	29.50	48.00
87	BALLOONS N' THINGS	YR	29.50	30.00
87	CHIMNEY SWEEP	YR	29.50	30.00
87	COBBLESTONE DELI	YR	29.50	30.00
87	COOLIN' OFF	YR	29.50	50.00
87	EXTRA, EXTRA	YR	29.50	50.00
87	FORGET ME NOTS	YR	29.50	50.00
87	JUST PICKED	YR	29.50	30.00
87	OVEN FRESH	YR	29.50	30.00
87	PENNY CANDY	YR	29.50	30.00
87	POPPIN' CORN	YR	29.50	30.00
87	TODAY'S CATCH	YR	29.50	30.00

ROYAL WORCESTER

YR	NAME	LIMIT	ISSUE	TREND
P.W. BASTON			**BIRTH OF A NATION**	
72	BOSTON TEA PARTY	10000	45.00	210.00
73	PAUL REVERE	10000	45.00	195.00
74	CONCORD BRIDGE	10000	50.00	135.00
75	SIGNING DECLARATION	10000	65.00	135.00
76	CROSSING DELAWARE	10000	65.00	135.00
77	WASHINGTON'S INAUGURATION	1250	65.00	135.00
P.W. BASTON			**CURRIER AND IVES PLATES**	
74	ROAD IN WINTER	5570	59.50	100.00
75	OLD GRIST MILL	3200	59.50	100.00
76	WINTER PASTIME	1500	59.50	90.00
77	HOME TO THANKSGIVING	546	59.50	225.00
P. COOPER			**KITTEN CLASSICS**	
85	BIRDWATCHER	CL	29.50	30.00
85	CAT NAP	CL	29.50	35.00
85	COUNTRY KITTY	CL	29.50	35.00
85	LITTLE RASCAL	CL	29.50	30.00
85	PURRFECT TREASURE	CL	29.50	30.00
85	TIGER'S FANCY	CL	29.50	35.00

YR	NAME	LIMIT	ISSUE	TREND
85	WILD FLOWER	CL	29.50	30.00
86	FIRST PRIZE	CL	29.50	30.00
	P. COOPER			**KITTEN ENCOUNTERS**
87	BEDTIME BUDDIES	CL	29.50	30.00
87	BUNNY CHASE	CL	29.50	30.00
87	FISHFUL THINKING	CL	29.50	42.00
87	FLUTTER BY	CL	29.50	30.00
87	JUST DUCKY	CL	29.50	35.00
87	PUPPY PAL	CL	29.50	35.00
88	CAT AND MOUSE	CL	29.50	35.00
88	STABLEMATES	CL	29.50	50.00
	*			**SPODE MARITIME PLATES**
80	CONSTITUTION & GUERRIRE	2000	150.00	150.00
80	CONSTITUTION & JAVA	2000	150.00	150.00
80	PELICAN & ARGUS	2000	150.00	150.00
80	PRESIDENT & LITTLE BELT	2000	150.00	150.00
80	SHANNON & CHESAPEAKE	2000	150.00	150.00
80	UNITED STATES/MACEDONIAN	2000	150.00	150.00
	J. COOKE			**WATER BIRDS OF NORTH AMERICA**
85	AMERICAN PINTAILS	15000	55.00	55.00
85	CANADA GEESE	15000	55.00	55.00
85	CANVASBACKS	15000	55.00	55.00
85	GREEN WINGED TEALS	15000	55.00	55.00
85	HOODED MERGANSERS	15000	55.00	55.00
85	MALLARDS	15000	55.00	55.00
85	SNOW GEESE	15000	55.00	55.00
85	WOOD DUCKS	15000	55.00	55.00

SARAH'S ATTIC

YR	NAME	LIMIT	ISSUE	TREND
	S. SCHULTZ			**CLASSROOM MEMORIES**
91	CLASSROOM MEMORIES	CL	80.00	80.00

SCHMID

YR	NAME	LIMIT	ISSUE	TREND
	*			**A YEAR WITH PADDINGTON BEAR PLATES**
79	PYRAMID OF PRESENTS	25000	12.50	28.00
80	SPRINGTIME	25000	12.50	25.00
81	SANDCASTLES	25000	12.50	25.00
82	SCHOOL DAYS	25000	12.50	13.00
	B. HUMMEL			**CHRISTMAS**
71	ANGEL	YR	15.00	29.00
72	ANGEL WITH FLUTE	YR	15.00	20.00
73	NATIVITY, THE	YR	15.00	70.00
74	GUARDIAN ANGEL, THE	YR	18.50	20.00
75	CHRISTMAS CHILD	YR	25.00	30.00
76	SACRED JOURNEY	YR	27.50	30.00
77	HERALD ANGEL	YR	27.50	30.00
78	HEAVENLY TRIO	YR	32.50	33.00
79	STARLIGHT ANGEL	YR	38.00	40.00
80	PARADE INTO TOYLAND	YR	45.00	50.00
81	A TIME TO REMEMBER	YR	45.00	50.00
82	ANGELIC PROCESSION	YR	45.00	50.00
83	ANGELIC MESSENGER	YR	45.00	50.00
84	A GIFT FROM HEAVEN	YR	45.00	50.00
85	HEAVENLY LIGHT	YR	45.00	47.00
86	TELL THE HEAVENS	YR	45.00	50.00
87	ANGELIC GIFTS	YR	47.50	50.00
88	CHEERFUL CHERUBS	YR	53.00	75.00
89	ANGELIC MUSICIAN	YR	53.00	75.00
90	ANGEL'S LIGHT	YR	53.00	75.00
91	MESSAGE FROM ABOVE	YR	60.00	75.00
92	SWEET BLESSINGS	YR	65.00	75.00
	L. DAVIS			**DAVIS CAT TALES PLATES**
83	COMPANY'S COMING	12500	37.50	175.00
83	FLEW THE COOP	12500	37.50	140.00
83	ON THE MOVE	12500	37.50	140.00
83	RIGHT CHURCH, WRONG PEW	12500	37.50	185.00
	L. DAVIS			**DAVIS CHRISTMAS PLATES**
83	HOOKER AT MAILBOX WITH PRESENT	7500	45.00	120.00
84	COUNTRY CHRISTMAS	7500	45.00	120.00
85	CHRISTMAS AT FOXFIRE FARM	7500	45.00	130.00
86	CHRISTMAS AT RED OAK	7500	45.00	120.00
87	BLOSSOM'S GIFT	7500	47.50	100.00
89	PETER AND THE WREN	7500	47.50	80.00
90	WINTERING DEER	7500	47.50	50.00
91	CHRISTMAS AT RED OAK II	7500	55.00	75.00
92	BORN ON A STARRY NIGHT	7500	55.00	75.00
	L. DAVIS			**DAVIS COUNTRY PRIDE PLATES**
81	DUKE'S MIXTURE	7500	35.00	185.00
81	PLUM TUCKERED OUT	7500	35.00	200.00
81	SURPRISE IN THE CELLAR	7500	35.00	140.00
82	BUSTIN' WITH PRIDE	7500	35.00	120.00
	L. DAVIS			**DAVIS RED OAK SAMPLER**
85	GENERAL STORE	5000	45.00	110.00
87	COUNTRY WEDDING	5000	45.00	120.00
89	COUNTRY SCHOOL	5000	45.00	75.00

YR	NAME	LIMIT	ISSUE	TREND
90	BLACKSMITH SHOP	5000	52.50	75.00
L. DAVIS		**DAVIS SPECIAL EDITION PLATES**		
84	CRITICS, THE	12500	45.00	100.00
84	GOOD OLE DAYS PRIVY SET 2	5000	60.00	175.00
85	HOME FROM MARKET	7500	55.00	150.00
*			**DISNEY ANNUAL**	
83	SNEAK PREVIEW	20000	22.50	25.00
84	COMMAND PERFORMANCE	20000	22.50	25.00
85	SHOW BIZ	20000	22.50	25.00
86	TREE FOR TWO	20000	22.50	25.00
87	MERRY MOUSE MEDLEY	20000	25.00	25.00
88	WARM WINTER RIDE	20000	25.00	25.00
89	MERRY MICKEY CLAUS	20000	32.50	75.00
90	HOLLY JOLLY CHRISTMAS	20000	32.50	35.00
91	MICKEY AND MINNIE'S ROCKIN' CHRISTMAS	20000	37.00	40.00
*			**DISNEY CHRISTMAS**	
73	SLEIGH RIDE	YR	10.00	275.00
74	DECORATING THE TREE	YR	10.00	75.00
75	CAROLING	YR	12.50	15.00
76	BUILDING A SNOWMAN	YR	13.00	15.00
77	DOWN THE CHIMNEY	YR	13.00	15.00
78	NIGHT BEFORE CHRISTMAS	YR	15.00	30.00
79	SANTA'S SURPRISE	15000	17.50	30.00
80	SLEIGH RIDE	15000	17.50	35.00
81	HAPPY HOLIDAYS	15000	17.50	22.00
82	WINTER GAMES	15000	18.50	30.00
*			**DISNEY MOTHER'S DAY**	
74	FLOWERS FOR MOTHER	YR	10.00	50.00
75	SNOW WHITE & DWARFS	YR	12.50	50.00
76	MINNIE MOUSE	YR	13.00	25.00
77	PLUTO'S PALS	YR	13.00	25.00
78	FLOWERS FOR BAMBI	YR	15.00	35.00
79	HAPPY FEET	10000	17.50	20.00
80	MINNIE'S SURPRISE	10000	17.50	30.00
81	PLAYMATES	10000	17.50	35.00
82	A DREAM COME TRUE	10000	18.50	40.00
J. FERRANDIZ		**FERRANDIZ BEAUTIFUL BOUNTY PORCELAIN PLATES**		
82	A MID-WINTER'S DREAM	10000	40.00	50.00
82	AUTUMN'S BLESSING	10000	40.00	50.00
82	SPRING BLOSSOMS	10000	40.00	40.00
82	SUMMER'S GOLDEN HARVEST	10000	40.00	40.00
J. FERRANDIZ		**FERRANDIZ MUSIC MAKERS PORCELAIN PLATES**		
81	ENTERTAINER, THE	10000	25.00	30.00
81	FLUTIST, THE	10000	25.00	30.00
82	MAGICAL MEDLEY	10000	25.00	30.00
82	SWEET SERENADE	10000	25.00	30.00
J. FERRANDIZ		**FERRANDIZ PORCELAIN CHRISTMAS PLATES**		
72	CHRIST IN THE MANAGER	*	30.00	175.00
73	CHRISTMAS	*	30.00	230.00
J. FERRANDIZ		**FERRANDIZ WOODEN BIRTHDAY PLATES**		
72	BOY	*	15.00	150.00
72	GIRL	*	15.00	175.00
73	BOY	*	20.00	200.00
73	GIRL	*	20.00	150.00
74	BOY	*	22.00	175.00
74	GIRL	*	22.00	175.00
L. DAVIS			**FRIENDS OF MINE**	
89	SUNDAY WORSHIPPERS	7500	53.00	75.00
90	SUNDAY AFTERNOON TREAT	7500	53.00	75.00
91	WARM MILK	7500	55.00	75.00
92	CAT AND JENNY WREN	7500	55.00	75.00
M. LILLEMOE			**KITTY CUCUMBER ANNUAL**	
89	RING AROUND THE ROSIE	20000	25.00	25.00
90	SWAN LAKE	20000	25.00	25.00
91	TEA PARTY	2500	25.00	25.00
92	DANCE ROUND THE MAYPOLE	2500	25.00	50.00
B. HUMMEL			**MOTHER'S DAY**	
72	PLAYING HOOKY	YR	15.00	16.00
73	LITTLE FISHERMAN	YR	15.00	35.00
74	BUMBLEBEE	YR	18.50	20.00
75	MESSAGE OF LOVE	YR	25.00	30.00
76	DEVOTION FOR MOTHER	YR	27.50	30.00
77	MOONLIGHT RETURN	YR	27.50	30.00
78	AFTERNOON STROLL	YR	32.50	33.00
79	CHERUB'S GIFT	YR	38.00	38.00
80	MOTHER'S LITTLE HELPERS	YR	45.00	50.00
81	PLAYTIME	YR	45.00	52.00
82	FLOWER BASKET, THE	YR	45.00	50.00
83	SPRING BOUQUET	YR	45.00	75.00
84	A JOY TO SHARE	YR	45.00	50.00
85	A MOTHER'S JOURNEY	YR	45.00	50.00
86	HOME FROM SCHOOL	YR	45.00	75.00
88	YOUNG READER	YR	52.50	80.00
89	PRETTY AS A PICTURE	YR	53.00	80.00
90	MOTHER'S LITTLE ATHLETE	YR	53.00	75.00
91	SOFT & GENTLE	YR	55.00	75.00

YR	NAME	LIMIT	ISSUE	TREND
*		PADDINGTON BEAR/MUSICIAN'S DREAM PLATES		
83	BEAT GOES ON, THE	10000	17.50	25.00
83	KNOWING THE SCORE	10000	17.50	20.00
83	PERFECT HARMONY	10000	17.50	25.00
83	TICKLING THE IVORY	10000	17.50	25.00
C. SCHULZ		**PEANUTS CHRISTMAS**		
72	SNOOPY GUIDES THE SLEIGH	YR	10.00	35.00
73	CHRISTMAS EVE AT DOGHOUSE	YR	10.00	90.00
74	CHRISTMAS AT FIREPLACE	YR	10.00	50.00
75	WOODSTOCK AND SANTA CLAUS	YR	12.50	20.00
76	WOODSTOCK'S CHRISTMAS	YR	13.00	20.00
77	DECK THE DOGHOUSE	YR	13.00	20.00
78	FILLING THE STOCKING	YR	15.00	40.00
79	CHRISTMAS AT HAND	15000	17.50	25.00
80	WAITING FOR SANTA	15000	17.50	25.00
81	A CHRISTMAS WISH	15000	17.50	30.00
82	PERFECT PERFORMANCE	15000	18.50	50.00
C. SCHULZ		**PEANUTS MOTHER'S DAY PLATES**		
72	LINUS	*	10.00	10.00
73	MOM?	*	10.00	10.00
74	SNOOPY/WOODSTOCK/PARADE	*	10.00	15.00
75	A KISS FOR LUCY	*	12.50	15.00
76	LINUS AND SNOOPY	*	13.00	35.00
77	DEAR MOM	*	13.00	30.00
78	THOUGHTS THAT COUNT	*	15.00	25.00
79	A SPECIAL LETTER	*	17.50	25.00
80	A TRIBUTE TO MOM	*	17.50	25.00
81	MISSION FOR MOM	*	17.50	20.00
82	WHICH WAY TO MOTHER	*	18.50	20.00
C. SCHULZ		**PEANUTS SPECIAL EDITION PLATE**		
76	BICENTENNIAL	*	13.00	30.00
C. SCHULZ		**PEANUTS VALENTINE'S DAY PLATES**		
77	HOME IS WHERE THE HEART IS	*	13.00	35.00
78	HEAVENLY BLISS	*	13.00	30.00
79	LOVE MATCH	*	17.50	30.00
80	FROM SNOOPY, WITH LOVE	*	17.50	25.00
81	HEARTS-A-FLUTTER	*	17.50	20.00
82	LOVE PATCH	*	17.50	25.00
C. SCHULZ		**PEANUTS WORLD'S GREATEST ATHLETE**		
82	CROWD WENT WILD, THE	10000	17.50	25.00
82	GO DEEP	10000	17.50	25.00
82	PUCK STOPS HERE, THE	10000	17.50	25.00
82	WAY YOU PLAY THE GAME, THE	10000	17.50	20.00
*		**RAGGEDY ANN ANNUAL PLATES**		
80	SUNSHINE WAGON, THE	10000	17.50	90.00
81	RAGGEDY SHUFFLE, THE	10000	17.50	50.00
82	FLYING HIGH	10000	18.50	20.00
83	WINNING STREAK	10000	22.50	25.00
84	ROCKING RODEO	10000	22.50	25.00
*		**RAGGEDY ANN BICENTENNIAL PLATE**		
76	BICENTENNIAL PLATE	*	13.00	50.00
*		**RAGGEDY ANN CHRISTMAS PLATES**		
75	GIFTS OF LOVE	*	12.50	50.00
76	MERRY BLADES	*	13.00	40.00
77	CHRISTMAS MORNING	*	13.00	25.00
78	CHECKING THE LIST	*	15.00	20.00
79	LITTLE HELPER	*	17.50	20.00
*		**RAGGEDY ANN VALENTINE'S DAY PLATES**		
78	AS TIME GOES BY	*	13.00	25.00
79	DAISIES DO TELL	*	17.50	20.00
*		**WALT DISNEY SPECIAL EDITION PLATES**		
78	MICKEY MOUSE AT FIFTY	15000	25.00	90.00
80	HAPPY BIRTHDAY PINOCCHIO	7500	17.50	50.00
81	ALICE IN WONDERLAND	7500	17.50	25.00
82	GOOFY'S GOLDEN JUBILEE	7500	18.50	30.00
82	HAPPY BIRTHDAY PLUTO	7500	17.50	40.00
87	SNOW WHITE GOLDEN ANNIVERSARY	5000	47.50	50.00
88	MICKEY MOUSE & MINNIE MOUSE-60TH ANNIV.	10000	50.00	110.00
89	SLEEPING BEAUTY-30TH ANNIVERSARY	5000	80.00	95.00
90	FANTASIA RELIEF PLATE	20000	25.00	40.00
90	FANTASIA-SORCERER'S APPRENTICE	5000	59.00	80.00
90	PINOCCHIO'S FRIEND	YR	25.00	25.00

SILVER DEER LTD.

YR	NAME	LIMIT	ISSUE	TREND
E. ERIKSEN				**CHRISTMAS**
72	MAID OF COPENHAGEN	YR	16.50	37.00
S. OTTO				**CHRISTMAS**
73	FIR TREE, THE	YR	22.00	25.00
74	CHIMNEY SWEEP, THE	YR	25.00	25.00
75	UGLY DUCKLING, THE	YR	27.50	28.00
77	SNOWMAN	YR	29.50	30.00
78	LAST DREAM OF THE OLD OAK TREE	YR	32.00	32.00
79	OLD STREET LAMP, THE	YR	36.50	37.00
80	WILLIE WINKIE	YR	42.50	43.00
81	UTTERMOST PARTS OF THE SEA	YR	49.50	50.00
82	TWELVE BY THE MAILCOACH	YR	54.50	55.00
83	STORY OF THE YEAR, THE	YR	54.50	55.00

YR	NAME	LIMIT	ISSUE	TREND
84	NIGHTINGALE, THE	YR	54.50	55.00
85	KRONBERG CASTLE	YR	60.00	60.00
86	BELL, THE	YR	60.00	75.00
87	THUMBELINA	YR	60.00	60.00
88	BELL DEEP, THE	YR	60.00	60.00
89	OLD HOUSE, THE	YR	60.00	60.00
90	GRANDFATHER'S PICTURE BOOK	YR	64.50	72.00
91	WINDMILL, THE	YR	64.50	75.00
G. SAUSMARK				**CHRISTMAS**
70	H.C. ANDERSON HOUSE	YR	14.50	39.00
M. STAGE				**CHRISTMAS**
71	LITTLE MATCH GIRL	YR	15.00	38.00
76	SNOW QUEEN, THE	YR	27.50	28.00
*				**MOTHER'S DAY**
70	BOUQUET FOR MOTHER	*	14.50	75.00
71	MOTHER'S LOVE	*	15.00	40.00
72	GOOD NIGHT	*	16.50	35.00
73	FLOWERS FOR MOTHER	*	20.00	35.00
74	DAISIES FOR MOTHER	*	25.00	35.00
75	SURPRISE FOR MOTHER	*	27.50	28.00
76	COMPLETE GARDENER, THE	*	27.50	28.00
77	LITTLE FRIENDS	*	29.50	30.00
78	DREAMS	*	32.00	32.00
79	PROMENADE	*	36.50	37.00
80	NURSERY SCENE	*	42.50	43.00
81	DAILY DUTIES	*	49.50	50.00
82	MY BEST FRIEND	*	54.50	55.00
83	AN UNEXPECTED MEETING	*	54.50	55.00
S. OTTO				**MOTHER'S DAY**
87	COMPLETE ANGLER, THE	YR	60.00	60.00
88	LITTLE BAKERY, THE	YR	60.00	60.00
89	SPRINGTIME	YR	60.00	60.00
90	SPRING EXCURSION, THE	YR	64.50	65.00
91	WALKING AT THE BEACH	YR	64.50	65.00
M. STAGE				**MOTHER'S DAY**
84	WHO ARE YOU?	YR	54.50	55.00
86	MEETING ON THE MEADOW	YR	60.00	60.00

SPODE

YR	NAME	LIMIT	ISSUE	TREND
R. HARM				**AMERICAN SONG BIRDS**
72	SET OF TWELVE	UD	350.00	765.00
G. WEST				**CHRISTMAS**
70	PARTRIDGE	UD	35.00	35.00
71	ANGEL'S SINGING	UD	35.00	35.00
72	THREE SHIPS A'SAILING	UD	35.00	38.00
73	WE THREE KINGS OF ORIENT	UD	35.00	55.00
74	DECK THE HALLS	UD	35.00	55.00
75	CHRISTBAUM	UD	45.00	45.00
76	GOOD KING WENCESLAS	UD	45.00	55.00
77	HOLLY & IVY	UD	45.00	45.00
78	WHILE SHEPHERDS WATCHED	UD	45.00	45.00
79	AWAY IN A MANGER	UD	50.00	50.00
80	BRINGING IN THE BOAR'S HEAD	UD	60.00	60.00
81	MAKE WE MERRY	UD	65.00	65.00

SPORTS IMPRESSIONS

YR	NAME	LIMIT	ISSUE	TREND
*				
95	CHARLES BARKLEY	2500	150.00	150.00
C. HAYES				
95	DREAM TEAM II	1994	150.00	150.00
GLENICE				**CELEBRITY IMPRESSIONS**
*	HULK HOGAN	5000	39.50	40.00
*	MIKE TYSON	5000	39.50	40.00
J. CATALANO				**COLLECTOVAL PLATES**
90	KINGS OF K	*	195.00	195.00
T. FOGARTY				**COLLECTOVAL PLATES**
90	LIFE OF A LEGEND	1968	195.00	195.00
B. JOHNSON				**COLLECTOVAL PLATES**
90	FENWAY TRADITION	1000	195.00	195.00
M. PETRONELLA				**COLLECTOVAL PLATES**
90	GOLDEN YEARS	1000	195.00	195.00
*				**GOLD EDITION PLATES**
89	KIRK GIBSON	2500	125.00	125.00
*				**GOLD EDITION PLATES**
*	JACKIE ROBINSON	1956	150.00	150.00
J. CATALANO				**GOLD EDITION PLATES**
88	JOSE CANSECO	2500	125.00	125.00
88	YANKEE TRADITION	CL	150.00	155.00
89	MANTLE SWITCH HITTER	CL	150.00	300.00
89	OREL HERSHISER	2500	125.00	125.00
89	WILL CLARK	CL	125.00	150.00
91	MICHAEL JORDAN	CL	150.00	200.00
T. FOGARTY				**GOLD EDITION PLATES**
88	PAUL MOLITOR	1000	125.00	125.00
89	DARRYL STRAWBERRY #2	CL	125.00	130.00
89	DWIGHT GOODEN	5000	125.00	125.00

YR	NAME	LIMIT	ISSUE	TREND
89	FRANK VIOLA	2500	125.00	125.00
	B. JOHNSON		**GOLD EDITION PLATES**	
86	DON MATTINGLY	CL	125.00	180.00
86	WADE BOGGS	CL	125.00	145.00
88	DUKE SNIDER	1500	125.00	125.00
	E. LAPERE		**GOLD EDITION PLATES**	
87	AL KALINE	1000	125.00	125.00
88	BOB FELLER	2500	125.00	125.00
89	ALAN TRAMMELL	1000	125.00	125.00
	R. LEWIS		**GOLD EDITION PLATES**	
89	GREATEST CENTERFIELDERS	5000	150.00	150.00
90	ANDRE DAWSON	CL	150.00	150.00
90	LIVING TRIPLE CROWN WINNERS	CL	150.00	190.00
90	TOM SEAVER	CL	150.00	150.00
	MUNDY		**GOLD EDITION PLATES**	
91	MAGIC JOHNSON	CL	150.00	200.00
	SALK		**GOLD EDITION PLATES**	
92	TEAM USA BASKETBALL	CL	150.00	250.00
	R. SIMON		**GOLD EDITION PLATES**	
86	KEITH HERNANDEZ	CL	125.00	170.00
86	LARRY BIRD	CL	125.00	200.00
86	MICKEY MANTLE AT NIGHT	CL	95.00	275.00
87	CARL YASTRZEMSKI	CL	125.00	170.00
87	DARRYL STRAWBERRY #1	CL	125.00	130.00
87	GARY CARTER	CL	125.00	150.00
87	LENNY DYKSTRA	1000	125.00	125.00
87	MICKEY, WILLIE, & DUKE	CL	150.00	525.00
87	TED WILLIAMS U/S	CL	95.00	335.00
88	BROOKS ROBINSON	CL	125.00	200.00
	J. CATALANO		**NFL GOLD EDITION PLATES**	
90	BOOMER ESIASON	1990	150.00	150.00
90	DAN MARINO	*	150.00	150.00
90	JOE MONTANA 49ERS	CL	150.00	150.00
90	JOHN ELWAY	*	150.00	150.00
90	LAWRENCE TAYLOR	*	150.00	150.00
90	RANDALL CUNNINGHAM	*	150.00	150.00
	M. PETRONELLA		**NFL PLATINUM EDITION PLATES**	
90	BOOMER ESIASON	*	49.95	50.00
90	DAN MARINO	5000	49.95	50.00
90	JOE MONTANA	5000	49.95	50.00
90	JOHN ELWAY	5000	49.95	50.00
90	LAWRENCE TAYLOR	5000	49.95	50.00
90	RANDALL CUNNINGHAM	5000	49.95	50.00
	J. CATALANO		**REGULAR EDITION PLATES**	
*	JOSE CANSECO	10000	49.50	65.00
*	WHO'S ON FIRST	10000	49.50	75.00
*	WILL CLARK	10000	49.50	65.00
*	YANKEE TRADITION	10000	49.50	65.00
	T. FOGARTY		**REGULAR EDITION PLATES**	
*	FRANK VIOLA	10000	49.50	65.00
*	KIRK GIBSON	10000	49.50	65.00
*	PAUL MOLITOR	10000	49.50	65.00
	B. JOHNSON		**REGULAR EDITION PLATES**	
*	BABE RUTH	10000	49.50	75.00
*	DON MATTINGLY R/E	5000	49.50	75.00
*	DUKE SNIDER	5000	49.50	75.00
*	LOU GEHRIG	10000	49.50	75.00
*	WADE BOGGS	2000	49.50	65.00
	E. LAPERE		**REGULAR EDITION PLATES**	
*	AL KALINE	10000	49.50	65.00
*	ALAN TRAMMEL	10000	49.50	65.00
*	BOB FELLER	10000	49.50	65.00
	R. LEWIS		**REGULAR EDITION PLATES**	
*	ANDRE DAWSON	10000	49.50	65.00
*	CY YOUNG	10000	49.50	75.00
*	HONUS WAGNER	10000	49.50	75.00
*	LIVING TRIPLE CROWN	10000	49.50	75.00
*	NOLAN RYAN	5000	150.00	150.00
*	R. CLEMENTE	10000	49.50	75.00
*	TY COBB	10000	49.50	75.00
	R. SIMON		**REGULAR EDITION PLATES**	
*	B. ROBINSON	2000	49.50	75.00
*	CARL YASTRZEMSKI	3000	49.50	65.00
*	CARY CARTER	2000	49.50	65.00
*	DARRYL STRAWBERRY R/E	2000	49.50	75.00
*	DEM BUMS	10000	49.50	75.00
*	K. HERNANDEZ	2000	49.50	65.00
*	LARRY BIRD	2000	49.50	65.00
*	LENNY DYKSTRA	2000	49.50	65.00
*	MICKEY MANTLE R/E	3500	49.50	75.00
*	MICKEY, WILLIE, DUKE F/S	3500	49.50	175.00
*	TED WILLIAMS	3000	49.50	65.00
*	THURMAN MUNSON	10000	49.50	75.00
	M. PETRONELLA		**THE GOLDEN YEARS**	
90	DUKE SNIDER	5000	60.00	60.00
90	MICKEY MANTLE	5000	60.00	60.00

YR	NAME	LIMIT	ISSUE	TREND
90	WILLIE MAYS	5000	60.00	60.00

STUDIO COLLECTION

YR	NAME	LIMIT	ISSUE	TREND
T. RUBEL				**SANTA'S ANIMAL KINGDOM**
94	SANTA'S ANIMAL KINGDOM COLLECTORS PLATE	5000	30.00	32.00

U.S. HISTORICAL SOCIETY

YR	NAME	LIMIT	ISSUE	TREND
W. HOMER				**YOUNG AMERICA**
73	YOUNG AMERICA OF WINSLOW HOMER-6 PLATES	2500	425.00	1100.00

VAGUE SHADOWS

YR	NAME	LIMIT	ISSUE	TREND
*				**PRIDE OF AMERICA'S INDIAN**
86	DARK-EYED FRIENDS	OP	24.50	20.00
86	NOBLE COMPANIONS	OP	24.50	19.00
87	KINDRED SPIRITS	OP	24.50	26.00
87	LOYAL ALLIANCE	OP	24.50	50.00
87	PEACEFUL COMMRADES	OP	24.50	36.00
87	SMALL AND WISE	OP	24.50	35.00
87	WINTER SCOUTS	OP	24.50	28.00
*				**THE CHIEFTAINS**
79	CHIEF JOSEPH	OP	65.00	105.00
79	CHIEF SITTING BULL	OP	65.00	400.00
80	CHIEF RED CLOUD	OP	65.00	119.00
80	GERONIMO	OP	65.00	82.00
81	CHIEF CRAZY HORSE	OP	65.00	140.00

V. PALEKH ART STUDIOS

YR	NAME	LIMIT	ISSUE	TREND
A. KOVALEV				**RUSSIAN LEGENDS**
88	PRINCESS/SEVEN BOGATYRS, THE	195	29.87	60.00
G. LUBIMOV				**RUSSIAN LEGENDS**
88	RUSSIAN AND LUDMILLA	195	29.87	55.00
V. VLESHKO				**RUSSIAN LEGENDS**
88	GOLDEN COCKEREL, THE	195	32.87	33.00
88	LUKOMORYA	195	32.87	33.00
89	FISHERMAN AND THE MAGIC FISH	195	32.87	33.00
89	PRIEST AND HIS SERVANT, THE	195	34.87	35.00
89	TSAR SALTAN	195	32.87	33.00
90	MOROZKO	195	36.87	37.00
90	SADKO	195	34.87	35.00
90	SILVER HOOF	195	36.87	37.00
90	STONE FLOWER	195	34.87	35.00
90	TWELVE MONTHS, THE	195	36.87	37.00

VENETO FLAIR

YR	NAME	LIMIT	ISSUE	TREND
V. TIZIANO				**BELLINI**
71	MADONNA	500	45.00	400.00
*				**BIRDS**
72	FALCON	2000	37.50	38.00
72	OWL	2000	37.50	100.00
73	MALLARD	2000	45.00	45.00
V. TIZIANO				**CHRISTMAS**
71	THREE KINGS	1500	55.00	160.00
72	SHEPHERDS	2000	55.00	90.00
73	CHRIST CHILD	2000	55.00	55.00
74	ANGEL	*	55.00	55.00
V. TIZIANO				**DOGS**
72	GERMAN SHEPHERD	2000	37.50	75.00
73	COLLIE	2000	40.00	45.00
73	DACHSHUND	2000	45.00	43.00
73	DOBERMAN	2000	37.50	35.00
73	POODLE	2000	37.50	45.00
*				**EASTER**
73	RABBITS	2000	50.00	90.00
74	CHICKS	2000	50.00	55.00
75	LAMB	2000	50.00	55.00
76	COMPOSITE	2000	55.00	55.00
*				**ST. MARK'S OF VENICE**
84	NOAH AND THE DOVE	UD	60.00	65.00
85	MOSES AND THE BURNING BUSH	UD	60.00	65.00
86	ABRAHAM AND THE JOURNEY	UD	60.00	66.00
86	JOSEPH AND THE COAT	UD	63.00	65.00
V. TIZIANO				**WILDLIFE**
71	DEER	500	37.50	450.00
72	ELEPHANT	1000	37.50	275.00
73	PUMA	2000	37.50	65.00
74	TIGER	2000	40.00	50.00

VILETTA

YR	NAME	LIMIT	ISSUE	TREND
*				**DISNEYLAND**
76	BETSY ROSS	3000	15.00	100.00
76	CROSSING THE DELAWARE	3000	15.00	100.00
76	SIGNING THE DECLARATION	3000	15.00	100.00
76	SPIRIT OF '76	3000	15.00	100.00
79	MICKEY'S 50TH ANNIVERSARY	5000	37.00	50.00
*				**NUTCRACKER BALLET**
78	CLARA AND NUTCRACKER	OP	19.50	10.00
79	GIFT FROM GODFATHER	OP	19.50	9.00

YR	NAME	LIMIT	ISSUE	TREND
79	SNOW KING AND QUEEN	OP	19.50	24.00
79	SUGARPLUM FAIRY, THE	OP	19.50	10.00
80	WALTZ OF THE FLOWERS	OP	19.50	11.00
*				**NUTCRACKER BALLET**
80	CARLA AND THE PRINCE	OP	19.50	15.00
D. ZOLAN				**ZOLAN'S CHILDREN**
78	ERIK AND DANDELION	OP	19.00	240.00
79	SABRINA IN THE GRASS	OP	22.00	150.00
80	BY MYSELF	OP	24.00	24.00
81	FOR YOU	OP	24.00	24.00

VILLEROY & BOCH

YR	NAME	LIMIT	ISSUE	TREND
C. BARKER				**FLOWER FAIRY**
79	LAVENDER	CL	35.00	130.00
80	CANDYTUFT	CL	35.00	90.00
80	SWEET PEA	CL	35.00	130.00
81	APPLEBLOSSOM	CL	35.00	100.00
81	BLACKTHORN	CL	35.00	80.00
81	HELIOTROPE	CL	35.00	80.00
B. ZVORYKIN				**RUSSIAN FAIRY TALES MARIA MOREVNA**
82	KOSHCHEY CARRIES OFF MARIA MOREVNA	27500	70.00	75.00
82	MARIA MOREVNA AND TSAREVICH IVAN	27500	70.00	85.00
82	TSAREVICH IVAN AND THE BEAUTIFUL CASTLE	27500	70.00	105.00
B. ZVORYKIN				**RUSSIAN FAIRY TALES SNOW MAIDEN**
80	SNOW MAIDEN, THE	27500	70.00	120.00
81	SNEGUROCHKA AND LEI, THE SHEPHERD BOY	27500	70.00	70.00
81	SNEGUROCHKA AT THE COURT/TSAR BERENDEI	27500	70.00	70.00
B. ZVORYKIN				**RUSSIAN FAIRY TALES THE FIREBIRD**
81	IN SEARCH OF THE FIREBIRD	27500	70.00	105.00
81	IVAN AND TSAREVNA ON THE GREY WOLF	27500	70.00	75.00
81	WEDDING OF TSAREVNA ELENA THE FAIR, THE	27500	70.00	109.00
B. ZVORYKIN				**RUSSIAN FAIRY TALES THE RED KNIGHT**
81	RED KNIGHT, THE	27500	70.00	55.00
81	VASSILISSA AND HER STEPSISTERS	27500	70.00	55.00
81	VASSILISSA IS PRESENTED TO THE TSAR	27500	70.00	65.00

W.S. GEORGE

YR	NAME	LIMIT	ISSUE	TREND
*				**A BLACK TIE AFFAIR: THE PENGUIN**
92	BABY-SITTERS	OP	29.50	30.00
92	LITTLE EXPLORER	OP	29.50	30.00
92	PENGUIN PARADE	OP	29.50	30.00
93	BELLY FLOPPING	OP	29.50	30.00
C. JAGODITS				**A BLACK TIE AFFAIR: THE PENGUIN**
92	BABY-SITTERS	CL	29.50	35.00
92	LITTLE EXPLORER	CL	29.50	35.00
92	PENGUIN PARADE	CL	29.50	35.00
93	BELLY FLOPPING	CL	29.50	35.00
G. BEECHAM				**A DELICATE BALANCE: VANISHING WILDLIFE**
92	TOMORROW'S HOPE	CL	29.50	35.00
93	EYES ON THE NEW DAY	CL	32.50	40.00
93	PRESENT DREAMS	CL	32.50	40.00
93	TODAY'S FUTURE	CL	29.50	35.00
*				**A DELICATE BALANCE: VANISHING WILDLIFE**
92	TOMORROW'S HOPE	OP	29.50	30.00
93	EYES ON THE NEW DAY	OP	32.50	33.00
93	PRESENT DREAMS	OP	32.50	33.00
93	TODAY'S FUTURE	OP	29.50	30.00
B. LANGTON				**A LOVING LOOK: DUCK FAMILIES**
90	FAMILY OUTING	CL	34.50	40.00
91	FAMILY TREE, THE	CL	37.50	55.00
91	QUIET MOMENT	CL	37.50	40.00
91	SAFE AND SOUND	CL	37.50	40.00
91	SLEEPY START	CL	34.50	40.00
91	SPRING ARRIVALS	CL	37.50	75.00
R. STINE				**A TREASURY OF SONGBIRDS**
92	AFTERNOON CALM	CL	32.50	40.00
92	DAWN'S RADIANCE	CL	32.50	40.00
92	GOLDEN DAYBREAK	CL	32.50	40.00
92	MORNING GLORY	CL	29.50	35.00
92	SPRINGTIME SPLENDOR	CL	29.50	35.00
93	ALLURING DAYLIGHT	CL	34.50	40.00
93	SAPPHIRE DAWN	CL	34.50	40.00
93	SCARLET SUNRISE	CL	34.50	40.00
H. LAMBSON				**ALASKA: THE LAST FRONTIER**
91	AUTUMN GRANDEUR	CL	34.50	40.00
91	ICY MAJESTY	CL	34.50	40.00
92	ARCTIC JOURNEY	CL	39.50	45.00
92	DOWN THE TRAIL	CL	37.50	45.00
92	GRACEFUL PASSAGE	CL	39.50	45.00
92	MOONLIGHT LOOKOUT	CL	37.50	45.00
92	MOUNTAIN MONARCH	CL	37.50	40.00
92	SUMMIT DOMAIN	CL	39.50	45.00
*				**ALONG AN ENGLISH LANE**
93	COTTAGE AROUND THE BEND	OP	29.50	30.00
93	FRIENDS AND FLOWERS	OP	29.50	30.00
93	GREETING THE DAY	OP	29.50	30.00
93	SUMMER'S BRIGHT WELCOME	OP	29.50	30.00

YR	NAME	LIMIT	ISSUE	TREND
	M. HARVEY			**ALONG AN ENGLISH LANE**
93	COTTAGE AROUND THE BEND	CL	29.50	35.00
93	FRIENDS AND FLOWERS	CL	29.50	35.00
93	GREETING THE DAY	CL	29.50	35.00
93	SUMMER'S BRIGHT WELCOME	CL	29.50	35.00
	H. JOHNSON			**AMERICA THE BEAUTIFUL**
88	GRAND CANYON, THE	CL	34.50	40.00
88	YOSEMITE FALLS	CL	34.50	40.00
89	GREAT SMOKEY MOUNTAINS, THE	CL	37.50	40.00
89	YELLOWSTONE RIVER	CL	37.50	40.00
90	ACADIA	CL	37.50	45.00
90	CRATER LAKE	CL	39.50	45.00
90	EVERGLADES, THE	CL	37.50	40.00
90	GRAND TETONS, THE	CL	39.50	45.00
*				**AMERICA'S PRIDE**
92	MISTY FJORDS	OP	29.50	62.00
	R. RICHERT			**AMERICA'S PRIDE**
92	MISTY FJORDS	CL	29.50	70.00
92	RUGGED SHORES	CL	29.50	55.00
93	CANYON CLIMB	CL	34.50	40.00
93	GOLDEN VISTA	CL	34.50	40.00
93	LOFTY REFLECTIONS	CL	32.50	40.00
93	MIGHTY SUMMIT	CL	32.50	70.00
93	MOUNTAIN MAJESTY	CL	34.50	40.00
93	TRANQUIL QATERS	CL	32.50	40.00
	M. MCDONALD			**ART DECO**
89	A FLAPPER WITH GREYHOUNDS	CL	39.50	55.00
90	ARRIVING IN STYLE	CL	39.50	80.00
90	ON THE TOWN	CL	39.50	80.00
90	TANGO DANCERS	CL	39.50	65.00
*				**BABY CATS OF THE WILD**
92	MORNING MISCHIEF	OP	29.50	30.00
93	BUDDY SYSTEM, THE	OP	32.90	33.00
93	NAP TIME	OP	32.50	33.00
93	TOGETHERNESS	OP	29.50	30.00
*				**BEAR TRACKS**
92	DENAIL FAMILY	OP	29.50	30.00
93	ALONG THE ICE FLOW	OP	29.50	30.00
93	BREAKING COVER	OP	29.50	30.00
93	HEAVY GOING	OP	29.50	30.00
93	HIGH COUNTRY CHAMPION	OP	29.50	30.00
93	THEIR FIRST SEASON	OP	29.50	30.00
	J. SEEREY-LESTER			**BEAR TRACKS**
92	DENALI FAMILY	CL	29.50	35.00
93	ALONG THE ICE FLOW	CL	29.50	35.00
93	BREAKING COVER	CL	29.50	35.00
93	HEAVY GOING	CL	29.50	35.00
93	HIGH COUNTRY CHAMPION	CL	29.50	35.00
93	THEIR FIRST SEASON	CL	29.50	35.00
	C. BARKER			**BELOVED HYMNS OF CHILDHOOD**
88	AWAY IN A MANGER	CL	29.50	35.00
88	LORD'S MY SHEPHERD, THE	CL	29.50	50.00
89	ALL GLORY, LAUD AND HONOUR	CL	32.50	35.00
89	I LOVE TO HEAR THE STORY	CL	32.50	35.00
89	LOVE DIVINE	CL	32.50	35.00
89	NOW THANK WE ALL OUR GOD	CL	32.50	35.00
90	ALL PEOPLE ON EARTH DO DWELL	CL	34.50	40.00
90	LOVING SHEPHERD OF THY SHEEP	OP	34.50	40.00
	W. RANE			**BLESSED ARE THE CHILDREN**
90	I AM THE GOOD SHEPHERD	CL	29.50	55.00
91	BLESSED ARE THE PEACEMAKERS	CL	34.50	50.00
91	HOSANNA IN THE HIGHEST	CL	32.50	45.00
91	I AM THE VINE, YOU ARE THE BRANCHES	CL	34.50	65.00
91	JESUS HAD COMPASSION ON THEM	CL	32.50	40.00
91	LET THE LITTLE CHILDREN COME TO ME	CL	29.50	40.00
91	SEEK AND YOU WILL FIND	CL	34.50	45.00
91	WHOEVER WELCOMES THIS LITTLE CHILD	CL	32.50	45.00
	B. BURKE			**BONDS OF LOVE**
89	PRECIOUS EMBRACE	CL	29.50	40.00
90	CHERISHED MOMENT	CL	29.50	35.00
91	TENDER CARESS	CL	32.50	40.00
92	LOVING TOUCH	CL	32.50	45.00
92	TREASURED KISSES	CL	32.50	50.00
94	ENDEARING WHISPERS	CL	32.50	35.00
	H. GARRIDO			**CHRISTMAS STORY**
92	GIFTS OF THE MAGI	CL	29.50	35.00
93	ADORATION OF THE SHEPHERDS	CL	29.50	35.00
93	ANNUNCIATION, THE	CL	29.50	35.00
93	JOURNEY OF THE MAGI	CL	29.50	35.00
93	NATIVITY, THE	CL	29.50	35.00
93	REST ON THE FLIGHT INTO EGYPT	CL	29.50	35.00
	L. KAATZ			**CLASSIC WATERFOWL: THE DUCKS UNLIMITED**
88	GEESE IN THE AUTUMN FIELDS	CL	36.50	40.00
88	MALLARDS AT SUNRISE	CL	36.50	45.00
89	CANVASBACKS, BREAKING AWAY	CL	39.50	45.00
89	GREEN WINGS/MORNING MARSH	CL	39.50	45.00
89	PINTAILS IN INDIAN SUMMER	CL	39.50	45.00

YR	NAME	LIMIT	ISSUE	TREND
90	BLUEBILLS COMING IN	CL	41.50	45.00
90	SNOW GEESE AGAINST NOVEMBER SKIES	CL	41.50	45.00
90	WOOD DUCKS TAKING FLIGHT	CL	39.50	45.00
J. PENALVA		**COLUMBUS DISCOVERS AMERICA: THE 500TH ANNIVERSARY**		
92	ASHORE AT DAWN	CL	29.50	50.00
92	BRINGING TOGETHER TWO CULTURES	CL	32.50	65.00
92	COLUMBUS RAISES THE FLAG	CL	32.50	60.00
92	QUEEN'S APPROVAL, THE	CL	32.50	60.00
92	TREASURES FROM THE NEW WORLD	CL	32.50	55.00
92	UNDER FULL SAIL	CL	29.50	35.00
G. KURZ			**COUNTRY BOUQUETS**	
91	GARDEN'S BOUNTY	CL	32.50	40.00
91	MORNING SUNSHINE	CL	29.50	45.00
91	SUMMER PERFUME	CL	29.50	55.00
91	WARM WELCOME	CL	32.50	55.00
M. HARVEY			**COUNTRY NOSTALGIA**	
89	APPLE CIDER PRESS,THE	CL	29.50	45.00
89	OLD HAND PUMP, THE	CL	32.50	45.00
89	SPRING BUGGY, THE	CL	29.50	35.00
89	VINTAGE SEED PLANTER, THE	CL	29.50	45.00
90	ANTIQUE SPINNING WHEEL, THE	CL	34.50	40.00
90	DAIRY CANS, THE	CL	32.50	40.00
90	FORGOTTEN PLOW, THE	CL	34.50	40.00
90	WOODEN BUTTER CHURN, THE	CL	32.50	50.00
P. JENNIS		**CRITIC'S CHOICE: GONE WITH THE WIND**		
91	"MARRY ME, SCARLETT!"	CL	27.50	50.00
91	A DECLARATION OF LOVE	CL	30.50	60.00
91	PARIS HAT, THE	CL	30.50	50.00
91	SCARLETT ASKS A FAVOR	CL	30.50	50.00
91	WAITING FOR RHETT	CL	27.50	50.00
92	BUGGY RIDE, THE	CL	32.50	35.00
92	SCARLETT GETS HER WAY	CL	32.50	55.00
92	SCARLETT'S GETS DOWN TO BUSINESS	CL	34.50	40.00
92	SCARLETT'S SHOPPING SPREE	CL	32.50	35.00
92	SMITTEN SUITOR, THE	CL	32.50	50.00
93	AT CROSS PURPOSES	CL	34.50	35.00
93	SCARLETT'S HEART IS W/TARA	CL	34.50	35.00
G. BUSH				**DR. ZHIVAGO**
91	LARA'S LOVE	CL	39.50	50.00
91	LOVE POEMS FOR LARA	CL	39.50	45.00
91	ZHIVAGO AND LARA	CL	39.50	45.00
91	ZHIVAGO SAYS FAREWELL	CL	39.50	45.00
*			**DUCKS UNLIMITED**	
88	CANADA GEESE/AUTUMN FIELDS	OP	36.50	37.00
90	PINTAILS IN INDIAN SUMMER	OP	39.50	40.00
J. FAULKNER				**ELEGANT BIRDS**
88	GREAT BLUE HERON	CL	32.50	35.00
88	SWAN, THE	CL	32.50	35.00
89	ANHINGA, THE	CL	35.50	40.00
89	FLAMINGO, THE	CL	35.50	40.00
89	SNOWY EGRET	CL	32.50	40.00
90	SANDHILL AND WHOOPING CRANE	CL	35.50	40.00
E. ANTONACCIO			**ENCHANTED GARDENS**	
93	A PEACEFUL RETREAT	CL	24.50	30.00
93	A PLACE TO DREAM	CL	24.50	30.00
93	PLEASANT PATHWAYS	CL	24.50	30.00
93	TRANQUIL HIDEAWAY	CL	24.50	30.00
*			**ENCHANTED GARDENS**	
93	A PEACEFUL RETREAT	OP	24.50	25.00
93	A PLACE TO DREAM	OP	24.50	25.00
93	PLEASANT PATHWAYS	OP	24.50	25.00
93	TRANQUIL HIDEAWAY	OP	24.50	25.00
*			**ENDANGERED SPECIES**	
89	RED WOLF, THE	OP	30.50	31.00
91	VICUNA, THE	OP	33.50	34.00
*			**EYES OF THE WILD**	
93	EYES IN THE MIST	OP	29.50	30.00
93	EYES IN THE PINES	OP	29.50	30.00
93	EYES IN THE SNOW	OP	29.50	30.00
93	EYES OF GOLD	OP	29.50	30.00
93	EYES OF SILENCE	OP	29.50	30.00
93	EYES OF STRENGTH	OP	29.50	30.00
93	EYES OF WONDER	OP	29.50	30.00
93	EYES ON THE SLY	OP	29.50	30.00
D. PIERCE			**EYES OF THE WILD**	
93	EYES IN THE MIST	CL	29.50	35.00
93	EYES IN THE PINES	CL	29.50	35.00
93	EYES IN THE SNOW	CL	29.50	35.00
93	EYES OF GOLD	CL	29.50	35.00
93	EYES OF SILENCE	CL	29.50	35.00
93	EYES OF WONDER	CL	29.50	35.00
93	EYES ON THE SLY	CL	29.50	35.00
94	EYES OF STRENGTH	CL	29.50	35.00
*			**FACES OF NATURE**	
92	CANYON OF THE CAT	RT	29.50	50.00
92	WOLFE RIDGE	OP	29.50	30.00
93	TRAIL OF THE TALISMAN	OP	29.50	30.00

YR	NAME	LIMIT	ISSUE	TREND
93	TWO BEARS CAMP	OP	29.50	30.00
93	WAMBLI OKIYE	OP	29.50	30.00
93	WINTERING WITH THE WAPITI	OP	29.50	30.00
93	WITHIN SUNRISE	OP	29.50	30.00
93	WOLFPACK OF THE ANCIENTS	OP	29.50	30.00
	J. KRAMER-COLE			**FACES OF NATURE**
92	CANYON OF THE CAT	CL	29.50	35.00
92	WOLF RIDGE	CL	29.50	35.00
93	TRAIL OF THE TALISMAN	CL	29.50	35.00
93	TWO BEARS CAMP	CL	29.50	35.00
93	WAMBLI OKIYE	CL	29.50	35.00
93	WINTERING WITH THE WAPITI	CL	29.50	35.00
93	WITHIN SUNRISE	CL	29.50	35.00
93	WOLFPACK OF THE ANCIENTS	CL	29.50	35.00
	N. ANDERSON			**FEDERAL DUCK STAMP PLATE COLLECTION**
90	CANVASBACKS	CL	30.50	40.00
90	LESSER SCAUP, THE	CL	27.50	45.00
90	MALLARD	CL	27.50	60.00
90	RUDDY DUCKS, THE	CL	30.50	30.00
91	CINNAMON TEAL	CL	32.50	35.00
91	FULVOUS WISTLING DUCK	CL	32.50	50.00
91	PINTAILS	CL	30.50	32.00
91	REDHEADS, THE	CL	32.50	50.00
91	SNOW GOOSE	CL	32.50	35.00
91	WIGEONS	CL	30.50	40.00
*				**FELINE FANCY**
93	GEOGRAPHERS, THE	OP	34.50	35.00
93	GLOBETROTTERS	OP	34.50	39.00
93	LITTLE ATHLETES	OP	34.50	35.00
93	YOUNG ADVENTURERS	OP	34.50	35.00
	H. RONNER			**FELINE FANCY**
93	GEOGRAPHERS, THE	CL	34.50	40.00
93	GLOBETROTTERS	CL	34.50	40.00
93	LITTLE ATHLETES	CL	34.50	40.00
93	YOUNG ADVENTURERS	CL	34.50	40.00
	D. BUSH			**FIELD BIRDS OF NORTH AMERICA**
91	AUTUMN MOMENT: AMERICAN WOODCOCK	CL	42.50	75.00
91	IN DISPLAY: RUFFED GOOSE	CL	39.50	50.00
91	MISTY CLEARING: WILD TURKEY	CL	42.50	60.00
91	MORNING LIGHT: BOBWHITE QUAIL	CL	42.50	65.00
91	WINTER COLORS: RING-NECKED PHEASANT	CL	39.50	55.00
92	SEASON'S END:WILLOW PTARMIGAN	CL	42.50	50.00
*				**FLORAL FANCIES**
93	SITTING PINK	OP	34.50	35.00
93	SITTING PRETTY	OP	34.50	35.00
93	SITTING SOFTLY	OP	34.50	35.00
93	SITTING SUNNY	OP	34.50	35.00
	C. CALLOG			**FLORAL FANCIES**
93	SITTING PINK	CL	34.50	40.00
93	SITTING PRETTY	CL	34.50	40.00
93	SITTING SOFTLY	CL	34.50	40.00
93	SITTING SUNNY	CL	34.50	40.00
	L. LIU			**FLOWER FAIRIES**
93	ARMOROUS ANGELS	OP	32.50	33.00
93	DELICATE DANCERS	OP	32.50	33.00
93	FANCIFUL FAIRIES	OP	34.50	35.00
93	MAGIC MAKERS	OP	29.50	30.00
93	MINIATURE MERMAIDS	OP	34.50	35.00
93	MISCHIEF MASTERS	OP	32.50	33.00
93	PETAL PLAYMATES	OP	29.50	30.00
93	WINGED WONDERS	OP	34.50	35.00
	G. KURZ			**FLOWERS FROM GRANDMA'S GARDEN**
90	COUNTRY CUTTINGS	CL	24.50	50.00
90	MORNING BOUQUET, THE	CL	24.50	45.00
91	A COUNTRY WELCOME	CL	29.50	60.00
91	GARDENER'S DELIGHT	CL	27.50	65.00
91	HARVEST IN THE MEADOW	CL	27.50	35.00
91	HOMESPUN BEAUTY	CL	27.50	40.00
91	NATURE'S BOUNTY	CL	27.50	55.00
91	SPRINGTIME ARRANGEMENT, THE	CL	29.50	55.00
	V. MORLEY			**FLOWERS OF YOUR GARDEN**
88	CHRYSANTHEMUMS	CL	27.50	30.00
88	DAISIES	CL	27.50	45.00
88	LILACS	CL	24.50	50.00
88	PEONIES	CL	27.50	30.00
88	ROSES	CL	24.50	70.00
89	DAFFODILS	CL	27.50	30.00
89	IRISES	CL	29.50	35.00
89	TULIPS	CL	29.50	35.00
	C. GILLIES			**GARDEN OF THE LORD**
92	ASK IN PRAYER	CL	34.50	40.00
92	LORD BLESS YOU, THE	CL	32.50	40.00
92	LORD'S LOVE, THE	CL	32.50	40.00
92	LOVE ONE ANOTHER	CL	29.50	35.00
92	PERFECT PEACE	CL	29.50	35.00
92	TRUST IN THE LORD	CL	32.50	40.00
93	GIVE THANKS TO THE LORD	CL	34.50	40.00

YR	NAME	LIMIT	ISSUE	TREND
93	PEACE BE WITH YOU	CL	34.50	40.00
*			**GARDENS OF PARADISE**	
92	SERENITY	OP	29.50	30.00
92	TRANQUILITY	OP	29.50	30.00
93	BEAUTY	OP	32.50	33.00
93	ELEGANCE	OP	32.50	33.00
93	GRANDEUR	OP	32.50	33.00
93	HARMONY	OP	32.50	33.00
93	MAJESTY	OP	32.50	33.00
93	SPLENDOR	OP	32.50	33.00
L. CHANG			**GARDENS OF PARADISE**	
92	SPLENDOR	CL	32.50	40.00
92	TRANQUILITY	CL	29.50	35.00
93	BEAUTY	CL	32.50	40.00
93	ELEGANCE	CL	32.50	40.00
93	GRANDEUR	CL	32.50	40.00
93	HARMONY	CL	32.50	40.00
93	MAJESTY	CL	32.50	40.00
93	SERENITY	CL	29.50	35.00
W. NELSON			**GENTLE BEGINNINGS**	
91	A TOUCH OF LOVE	CL	34.50	70.00
91	LAP OF LOVE	CL	37.50	45.00
91	TENDER LOVING CARE	CL	34.50	60.00
91	UNDER WATCHFUL EYES	CL	37.50	65.00
92	FIRST STEPS	CL	37.50	50.00
92	HAPPY TOGETHER	CL	37.50	50.00
R. COBANE			**GLORIOUS SONGBIRDS**	
91	BALTIMORE ORIOLES/AUTUMN LEAVES	CL	34.50	40.00
91	BLUEBIRDS IN A BLUEBERRY BUSH	CL	34.50	40.00
91	CARDINALS ON A SNOWY BRANCH	CL	29.50	40.00
91	CEDAR WAXWING/WINTER BERRIES	CL	32.50	35.00
91	CHICKADEES AMONG THE LILACS	CL	32.50	35.00
91	GOLDFINCHES IN/THISTLE	CL	32.50	35.00
91	INDIGO BUNTINGS AND/BLOSSOMS	CL	29.50	35.00
91	ROBINS WITH DOGWOOD IN BLOOM	CL	34.50	40.00
*			**GOLDEN AGE OF THE CLIPPER SHIP**	
89	TWILIGHT UNDER FULL SAIL	OP	29.50	30.00
C. VICKERY			**GOLDEN AGE OF THE CLIPPER SHIP**	
89	BLUE JACKET AT SUNSET, THE	CL	29.50	35.00
89	TWILIGHT UNDER FULL SAIL, THE	CL	29.50	35.00
89	YOUNG AMERICA, HOMEWARD	CL	32.50	35.00
90	DAVY CROCKET AT DAYBREAK	CL	32.50	40.00
90	FLYING CLOUD	CL	32.50	50.00
90	GOLDEN EAGLE CONQUERS WIND	CL	32.50	40.00
90	LIGHTNING IN LIFTING FOG, THE	CL	34.50	40.00
90	SEA WITCH, MISTRESS/OCEANS	CL	34.50	50.00
H. ROGERS			**GONE WITH THE WIND: GOLDEN ANNIVERSARY**	
88	BURNING OF ATLANTA, THE	CL	24.50	70.00
88	PROPOSAL, THE	CL	27.50	110.00
88	SCARLETT AND ASHLEY AFTER THE WAR	CL	27.50	75.00
88	SCARLETT AND HER SUITORS	CL	24.50	75.00
89	A QUESTION OF HONOR	CL	29.50	45.00
89	FRANKLY MY DEAR	CL	29.50	65.00
89	HOME TO TARA	CL	27.50	50.00
89	MELANIE AND ASHLEY	CL	32.50	50.00
89	SCARLETT'S RESOLVE	CL	29.50	50.00
89	STROLLING IN ATLANTA	CL	27.50	55.00
90	A TOAST TO BONNIE BLUE	CL	32.50	55.00
90	SCARLETT & RHETT'S HONEYMOON	CL	32.50	60.00
C. FRACE			**GRAND SAFARI: IMAGES OF AFRICA**	
92	A MOMENT'S REST	CL	34.50	40.00
92	ELEPHANT'S OF KILIMANJARO	CL	34.50	40.00
92	GREATER KUDO, THE	CL	37.50	45.00
92	LONE HUNTER	CL	37.50	45.00
92	QUIET TIME IN SAMBURU	CL	37.50	45.00
92	UNDIVIDED ATTENTION	CL	37.50	45.00
G. BEECHAM			**HEART OF THE WILD**	
91	A GENTLE TOUCH	CL	29.50	55.00
92	AN AFTERNOON TOGETHER	CL	32.50	50.00
92	MOTHER'S PRIDE	CL	29.50	105.00
92	QUIET TIME?	CL	32.50	35.00
E. DZENIS			**HOLLYWOOD'S GLAMOUR GIRLS**	
89	JEAN HARLOW-DINNER AT EIGHT	CL	24.50	45.00
90	CAROL LOMBAR/THE GAY BRIDE	CL	29.50	35.00
90	GRETA GARBO-IN GRAND HOTEL	CL	29.50	35.00
90	LANA TURNER-POSTMAN RINGS TWICE	CL	29.50	35.00
H.T. BECKER			**HOMETOWN MEMORIES**	
93	A WINTER RIDE	OP	29.50	30.00
93	A WINTER RIDE	CL	29.50	35.00
93	HEADING HOME	OP	29.50	30.00
93	HEADING HOME	CL	29.50	35.00
93	MOONLIGHT SKATERS	OP	29.50	30.00
93	MOONLIGHT SKATERS	CL	29.50	35.00
93	MOUNTAIN SLEIGH RIDE	OP	29.50	30.00
93	MOUNTAIN SLEIGH RIDE	CL	29.50	35.00
L. LIU			**HUMMINGBIRD TREASURY**	
92	RUBY-THROATED HUMMINGBIRD, THE	OP	29.50	30.00

YR	NAME	LIMIT	ISSUE	TREND
92	RUFOUS HUMMINGBIRD, THE	OP	32.50	33.00
	W. NELSON	**LAST OF THEIR KIND: THE ENDANGERED SPECIES**		
88	PANDA, THE	CL	27.50	50.00
88	SNOW LEOPARD, THE	CL	27.50	50.00
89	ASIAN ELEPHANT, THE	CL	30.50	30.00
89	RED WOLF, THE	CL	30.50	30.00
90	BLACK-FOOTED FERRET, THE	CL	33.50	35.00
90	BRIDLED WALLABY, THE	CL	30.50	30.00
90	SIBERIAN TIGER, THE	CL	33.50	40.00
90	SLENDER-HORNED GAZELLE, THE	CL	30.50	30.00
91	PRZEWALSKI'S HORSE	CL	33.50	35.00
91	VICUNA, THE	CL	33.50	35.00
	L. LIU	**LENA LIU'S BASKET BOUQUETS**		
92	IRISES	CL	32.50	55.00
92	LILIES	CL	32.50	65.00
92	PANSIES	CL	29.50	50.00
92	PARROT TULIPS	CL	32.50	50.00
92	PEONIES	CL	32.50	50.00
92	ROSES	CL	29.50	35.00
92	TULIPS AND LILACS	CL	32.50	40.00
93	BEGONIAS	CL	32.50	32.50
93	CALLA LILLIES	CL	32.50	40.00
93	HYDRANGEAS	CL	32.50	40.00
93	MAGNOLIAS	CL	32.50	40.00
93	ORCHIDS	CL	32.50	40.00
	L. LIU	**LENA LIU'S FLOWER FAIRIES**		
93	AMOROUS ANGELS	CL	32.50	35.00
93	DELICATE DANCERS	CL	32.50	35.00
93	MAGIC MAKERS	CL	29.50	35.00
93	MISCHIEF MASTERS	CL	32.50	35.00
93	PETAL PLAYMATES	CL	29.50	35.00
93	WINGED WONDERS	CL	34.50	40.00
	L. LIU	**LENA LIU'S HUMMINGBIRD TREASURY**		
92	ANNA'S HUMMINGBIRD	CL	29.50	35.00
92	RUBY-THROATED HUMMINGBIRD, THE	CL	29.50	35.00
92	RUFOUS HIUMMINGBIRD, THE	CL	32.50	40.00
92	VIOLET-CROWNED HUMMINGBIRD	CL	32.50	40.00
93	ALLEN'S HUMMINGBIRD, THE	CL	34.50	40.00
93	BOARD-BILLED HUMMINGBIRD	CL	34.50	40.00
93	CALLIOPE HUMMINGBIRD	CL	34.50	40.00
93	WHITE-EARED HUMMINGBIRD	CL	32.50	40.00
	B. BURKE	**LITTLE ANGELS**		
92	ANGELS WE HAVE HEARD ON HIGH	OP	29.50	48.00
92	ANGELS WE HAVE HEARD ON HIGH	CL	29.50	35.00
92	O TANNEMBAUM	CL	29.50	35.00
92	O TANNENBAUM	OP	29.50	60.00
93	FIRST NOEL, THE	OP	32.50	33.00
93	FIRST NOEL, THE	CL	32.50	40.00
93	HARK THE HEARLD ANGELS SING	CL	32.50	40.00
93	HARK THE HERALD ANGELS SING	OP	32.50	33.00
93	IT CAME UPON A MIDNIGHT CLEAR	OP	32.50	33.00
93	IT CAME UPON A MIGNIGHT CLEAR	CL	32.50	40.00
93	JOY TO THE WORLD	OP	32.50	33.00
93	JOY TO THE WORLD	CL	32.50	40.00
	P. WILDERMUTH	**MAJESTIC HORSE**		
92	AMERICAN GOLD: THE QUARTERHORSE	CL	34.50	45.00
92	CLASSIC BEAUTY: THOROUGHBRED	CL	34.50	50.00
92	REGAL SPIRIT:THE ARABIAN	CL	34.50	55.00
92	WESTERN FAVORITE: AM. PAINT HORSE	CL	34.50	60.00
	A. SAKHAVARZ	**MELODIES IN THE MIST**		
93	AMONG THE DEWDROPS	OP	34.50	35.00
93	AMONG THE DEWDROPS	CL	34.50	40.00
93	EARLY MORNING RAIN	OP	34.50	35.00
93	EARLY MORNING RAIN	CL	34.50	40.00
93	FEEDING TIME	OP	37.50	38.00
93	FEEDING TIME	CL	37.50	45.00
93	GARDEN PARTY, THE	OP	37.50	38.00
93	GARDEN PARTY, THE	CL	37.50	45.00
93	SPRING RAIN	OP	37.50	38.00
93	SPRING RAIN	CL	37.50	45.00
93	UNPLEASANT SURPRISE	OP	37.50	38.00
93	UNPLEASANT SURPRISE	CL	37.50	45.00
	*	**MEMORIES OF A VICTORIAN CHILDHOOD**		
92	AN ARMFUL OF TREASURES	CL	32.50	50.00
92	SWEET SLUMBER	CL	29.50	60.00
92	THROUGH THICK AND THIN	CL	32.50	55.00
92	YOU'D BETTER NOT POUT	CL	29.50	30.00
93	A TRIO OF BOOKWORMS	CL	32.50	65.00
93	PUGNACIOUS PLAYMATE	CL	32.50	65.00
	J. SIAS	**NATURE'S LEGACY**		
90	BLUE SNOW AT HALF DOME	CL	24.50	35.00
91	AUTUMN SPLENDOR IN THE SMOKEY MTNS.	CL	27.50	30.00
91	GOLDEN MAJESTY/ROCKY MOUNTAINS	CL	29.50	35.00
91	HAVASU CANYON	CL	27.50	30.00
91	MISTY MORNING/MT. MCKINLEY	CL	24.50	40.00
91	MOUNT RANIER	CL	27.50	28.00
91	MT. RANIER/TWILIGHT REFLECTIONS	CL	27.50	40.00

Artist P. Buckley Moss captures the simplistic pleasures of Amish life in Family Outing, *the first issue in The Family Collection produced by Anna-Perenna.*

This merry duo strikes a chord with collectors. Fiddlers Two, *by artist P. Buckley Moss, is the first issue in "The Children Collection" series.*

Valentine Joy *was produced as an M.I. Hummel Club exclusive available to members only.*

Chick Girl, *from the art of Sister Maria Innocentia Hummel, was the 1985 issue in a legendary plate series that spanned 25 years.*

YR	NAME	LIMIT	ISSUE	TREND
91	RADIANT SUNSET OVER THE EVERGLADES	CL	29.50	35.00
91	WINTER PEACE IN YELLOWSTONE PARK	CL	29.50	35.00
C. FRACE			**NATURE'S LOVABLES**	
90	KOALA, THR	CL	27.50	45.00
91	BABY HARP SEAL	CL	30.50	65.00
91	BANDIT	CL	32.50	45.00
91	BOBCAT: NATURE'S DAWN	CL	30.50	35.00
91	CHINESE TREASURE	CL	27.50	30.00
91	CLOUDED LEOPARD	CL	32.50	40.00
91	NEW ARRIVAL	CL	27.50	50.00
91	ZEBRA FOAL	CL	32.50	65.00
C. FRACE			**NATURE'S PLAYMATES**	
91	DOUBLE TROUBLE	CL	32.50	50.00
91	PALS	CL	32.50	50.00
91	PARTNERS	CL	29.50	50.00
91	RECESS	CL	32.50	50.00
91	SECRET HEIGHTS	CL	29.50	40.00
92	AMBASSADORS	CL	36.50	40.00
92	CURIOUS TRIO	CL	34.50	40.00
92	PEACE ON ICE	CL	36.50	40.00
92	PLAYMATES	CL	34.50	40.00
92	SURPRISE	CL	34.50	40.00
L. LIU			**NATURE'S POETRY**	
89	MORNING SERENADE	CL	24.50	40.00
89	SONG OF PROMISE	CL	24.50	45.00
90	GENTLE REFRAIN	CL	27.50	35.00
90	MELODY AT DAYBREAK	CL	29.50	35.00
90	MORNING CHORUS	CL	27.50	40.00
90	NATURE'S HARMONY	CL	27.50	55.00
90	TENDER LULLABY	CL	27.50	30.00
91	CHERUB CHORALE	CL	32.50	55.00
91	DELICATE ACCORD	CL	29.50	40.00
91	LYRICAL BEGINNINGS	CL	29.50	40.00
91	MOTHER'S MELODY	CL	32.50	45.00
91	SONG OF SPRING	CL	32.50	45.00
W. GOEBEL			**ON GOLDEN WINGS**	
93	AS DAY BREAKS	OP	32.50	33.00
93	AS DAY BREAKS	CL	32.50	40.00
93	DAYLIGHT FLIGHT	OP	32.50	33.00
93	DAYLIGHT FLIGHT	CL	32.50	40.00
93	EARLY RISERS	OP	29.50	30.00
93	EARLY RISERS	CL	29.50	35.00
93	FIRST LIGHT	OP	32.90	33.00
93	MORNING LIGHT	OP	29.50	30.00
93	MORNING LIGHT	CL	29.50	35.00
93	WINTER DAWN	OP	32.50	33.00
93	WINTER DAWN	CL	32.50	40.00
94	FIRST LIGHT	CL	34.50	40.00
L. LIU			**ON GOSSAMER WINGS**	
88	MALACHITES	CL	27.50	30.00
88	MONARCH BUTTERFLIES	CL	24.50	40.00
88	RED-SPOTTED PURPLE	CL	27.50	35.00
88	WESTERN TIGER SWALLOWTAILS	CL	24.50	40.00
88	WHITE PEACOCKS	CL	27.50	50.00
89	EASTERN TAILED BLUES	CL	27.50	30.00
89	RED ADMIRALS	CL	29.50	40.00
89	ZEBRA SWALLOWTAILS	CL	29.50	35.00
*			**ON THE WING**	
93	ON THE WING	OP	34.50	35.00
93	SPRINGING FORTH	OP	34.50	35.00
T. HUMPHREY			**ON THE WING**	
92	GLORIOUS ASCENT	CL	32.50	40.00
92	RISING MALLARD	CL	29.50	35.00
92	TAKING WING	CL	32.50	40.00
92	UPWARD BOUND	CL	32.50	40.00
92	WINGED SPLENDOR	CL	29.50	35.00
93	ON THE WING	CL	34.50	40.00
93	SPRINGING FORTH	CL	24.50	40.00
93	WONDROUS MOTION	CL	34.50	40.00
L. LIU			**ON WINGS OF SNOW**	
91	COCKATOOS, THE	CL	37.50	45.00
91	DOVES, THE	CL	34.50	40.00
91	EGRETS, THE	CL	37.50	40.00
91	PEACOCKS, THE	CL	37.50	40.00
91	SWANS, THE	CL	34.50	40.00
92	HERONS, THE	CL	37.50	45.00
C. BRENDERS			**OUR WOODLAND FRIENDS**	
89	FASCINATION	CL	29.50	30.00
90	BENEATH THE PINES	CL	29.50	30.00
90	HIGH ADVENTURE	CL	32.50	35.00
90	SHY EXPLORERS	CL	32.50	40.00
91	A JUMP INTO LIFE: SPRING FAWN	CL	34.50	45.00
91	FOREST SENTINEL: BOBCAT	CL	34.50	45.00
91	FULL HOUSE FOX FAMILY	CL	32.50	65.00
91	GOLDEN SEASON: GRAY SQUIRREL	CL	32.50	40.00
*			**PASSIONS OF SCARLETT O'HARA**	
92	AS GOD IS MY WITNESS	OP	34.50	55.00

YR	NAME	LIMIT	ISSUE	TREND
92	DREAMS OF ASHLEY	OP	32.50	64.00
92	FOND FAREWELL, THE	OP	32.50	44.00
92	WALTZ, THE	OP	32.50	60.00
93	BRAVE SCARLETT	OP	34.50	35.00
93	DANGEROUS ATTRACTION	OP	36.50	37.00
93	END OF AN ERA, THE	OP	36.50	37.00
93	EVENING PRAYERS	OP	34.50	35.00
93	NAPTIME	OP	36.50	37.00
93	NIGHTMARE	OP	34.50	35.00
P. JENNIS		**PASSIONS OF SCARLETT O'HARA**		
92	AS GOD IS MY WITNESS	CL	34.50	40.00
92	DREAMS OF ASHLEY	CL	32.50	75.00
92	FIERY EMBRACE	CL	29.50	70.00
92	FOND FAREWELL, THE	CL	32.50	55.00
92	PRIDE AND PASSION	CL	29.50	70.00
92	WALTZ, THE	CL	32.50	80.00
93	BRAVE SCARLETT	CL	34.50	40.00
93	DANGEROUS ATTRACTION	CL	36.50	40.00
93	EVENING PRAYERS	CL	34.50	40.00
93	NAPTIME	CL	36.50	40.00
93	NIGHTMARE	CL	34.50	40.00
94	END OF AN ERA, THE	CL	36.50	40.00
C. FRACE		**PAW PRINTS: BABY CATS OF THE WILD**		
92	MORNING MISCHIEF	CL	29.50	35.00
93	BUDDY SYSTEM, THE	CL	32.50	40.00
93	NAP TIME	CL	32.50	40.00
93	TOGETHERNESS	CL	29.50	35.00
L. CHANG				**PETAL PALS**
92	FLOWERING FASCINATION	CL	24.50	30.00
92	GARDEN DISCOVERY	CL	24.50	30.00
93	ALLURING LILLIES	CL	24.50	30.00
93	BLOSSOMING ADVENTURE	CL	24.50	30.00
93	DANCING DAFFODILS	CL	24.50	30.00
93	MORNING MELODY	CL	24.50	30.00
93	SPRINGTIME OASIS	CL	24.50	30.00
93	SUMMER SURPRISE	CL	24.50	30.00
C. VALENTE			**POETIC COTTAGES**	
92	BEDFORDSHIRE EVENING SKY	CL	32.50	40.00
92	GARDEN PATHS OF OXFORDSHIRE	CL	29.50	35.00
92	STONEWALL BROOK BLOSSOMS	CL	32.50	40.00
92	TWILIGHT AT WOODGREEN POND	CL	29.50	35.00
93	ALDERBURY GARDENS	CL	32.50	40.00
93	HAMPSHIRE SPRING SPLENDOR	CL	32.50	40.00
93	WILTSHIRE ROSE ARBOR	OP	32.50	40.00
93	WISTERIA SUMMER	CL	32.50	40.00
J. SALAMANCA			**PORTRAITS OF CHRIST**	
91	BECOME AS LITTLE CHILDREN	CL	32.50	65.00
91	FATHER, FORGIVE THEM	CL	29.50	95.00
91	LO, I AM WITH YOU	CL	32.50	65.00
91	PEACE I LEAVE WITH YOU	CL	34.50	70.00
91	THIS IS MY BELOVED SON	CL	32.50	55.00
91	THY WILL BE DONE	CL	29.50	55.00
92	FOLLOW ME	CL	34.50	40.00
92	FOR GOD SO LOVED THE WORLD	CL	34.50	70.00
92	I AM THE WAY, THE TRUTH & THE LIFE	CL	34.50	85.00
92	WEEP NOT FOR ME	CL	34.50	55.00
C. BRENDERS		**PORTRAITS OF EXQUISITE BIRDS**		
90	BACKYARD TREASURE-CHICKADEE	CL	29.50	40.00
90	BEAUTIFUL BLUEBIRD, THE	CL	29.50	40.00
91	IVORY-BILLED WOODPECKER	CL	32.50	35.00
91	MEADOWLARK'S SONG, THE	CL	32.50	35.00
91	RED-WINGED BLACKBIRD	CL	32.50	35.00
91	SUMMER GOLD: THE ROBIN	CL	32.50	40.00
D. SCHWARTZ		**PUREBRED HORSES OF THE AMERICAS**		
89	APPALOOSA, THE	CL	34.50	40.00
89	TENNESSEE WALKER, THE	CL	34.50	40.00
90	MUSTANG, THE	CL	37.50	40.00
90	MORGAN, THE	CL	37.50	75.00
90	QUARTERHORSE, THE	CL	37.50	40.00
90	SADDLEBRED, THE	CL	37.50	50.00
*			**RARE ENCOUNTERS**	
93	BLACK MAGIC	OP	29.50	30.00
93	FUTURE SONG	OP	32.50	33.00
93	HIGH AND MIGHTY	OP	32.50	33.00
93	LAST SANCTUARY	OP	32.50	33.00
93	SOFTLY, SOFTLY	OP	29.50	30.00
93	SOMETHING STIRRED	OP	34.50	35.00
J. SEEREY-LESTER			**RARE ENCOUNTERS**	
93	BLACK MAGIC	CL	29.50	35.00
93	FUTURE SONG	CL	32.50	40.00
93	HIGH AND MIGHTY	CL	32.50	40.00
93	LAST SANCTUARY	CL	32.50	40.00
93	SOFTLY, SOFTLY	CL	29.50	35.00
93	SOMETHING STIRRED	CL	34.50	40.00
C. SMITH			**ROMANTIC GARDENS**	
89	PLANTATION GARDEN, THE	CL	29.50	35.00
89	WOODLAND GARDEN, THE	CL	29.50	35.00

YR	NAME	LIMIT	ISSUE	TREND
90	COLONIAL GARDEN, THE	CL	32.50	35.00
90	COTTAGE GARDEN, THE	CL	32.50	45.00
C. VICKERY				**ROMANTIC HARBORS**
93	ADVENT OF THE GOLDEN BOUGH	OP	34.50	35.00
93	ADVENT OF THE GOLDEN BOUGH	CL	34.50	40.00
93	CHRISTMAS TREE SCHOONER	OP	34.50	35.00
93	CHRISTMAS TREE SCHOONER	CL	34.50	40.00
93	PRELUDE TO THE JOURNEY	OP	34.50	35.00
93	PRELUDE TO THE JOURNEY	CL	37.50	45.00
93	SHIMMERING LIGHT OF DUSK	OP	34.50	35.00
93	SHIMMERING LIGHT OF DUSK	CL	37.50	45.00
V. MORLEY				**ROMANTIC ROSES**
93	COUNTRY CHARM	CL	32.50	40.00
93	OLD-FASHIONED GRACE	CL	29.50	35.00
93	PASTORAL DELIGHT	CL	32.50	40.00
93	SPRINGTIME ELEGANCE	CL	34.50	40.00
93	SUMMER ROMANCE	CL	32.50	40.00
93	VICTORIAN BEAUTY	CL	29.50	35.00
93	VINTAGE SPLENDOR	CL	34.50	40.00
94	HEAVENLY PERFECTION	CL	34.50	40.00
L. GARRISON				**SCENES OF CHRISTMAS PAST**
87	HOLIDAY SKATERS	CL	27.50	55.00
88	CHRISTMAS EVE	CL	27.50	40.00
89	HOMECOMING, THE	CL	30.50	35.00
90	TOY STORE, THE	CL	30.50	35.00
91	CAROLLERS, THE	CL	30.50	31.00
92	FAMILY TRADITIONS	CL	32.50	45.00
93	HOLIDAY PAST	OP	32.50	45.00
94	A GATHERING OF FAITH	OP	32.50	33.00
J. BRIDGETT				**SECRET WORLD OF THE PANDA**
90	A MOTHER'S CARE	CL	27.50	35.00
91	A BAMBOO FEAST	CL	32.50	80.00
91	A DAY OF EXPLORING	CL	30.50	35.00
91	A FROLIC IN THE SNOW	CL	27.50	30.00
91	A GENTLE HUG	CL	32.50	35.00
91	LAZY AFTERNOON	CL	30.50	35.00
C. FRACE				**SOARING MAJESTY**
91	FREEDOM	CL	29.50	50.00
91	GOLDEN EAGLE, THE	CL	34.50	65.00
91	GYRFALCON, THE	CL	34.50	50.00
91	NORTHERN GOSHHAWK, THE	CL	29.50	45.00
91	OSPREY, THE	CL	32.50	40.00
91	PEREGRINE FALCON	CL	32.50	35.00
91	RED-TAILED HAWK	CL	32.50	35.00
92	RED-SHOULDERED HAWK	CL	34.50	40.00
G. KURZ				**SONNETS IN FLOWERS**
92	SONNET OF BEAUTY	CL	34.50	45.00
92	SONNET OF HAPPINESS	CL	34.50	40.00
92	SONNET OF LOVE	CL	34.50	40.00
92	SONNET OF PEACE	CL	34.50	40.00
V. GADINO				**SOUND OF MUSIC: SILVER ANNIVERSARY**
91	HILLS ARE ALIVE, THE	CL	29.50	35.00
92	LET'S START AT THE VERY BEGINNING	CL	29.50	35.00
92	MARIA'S WEDDING DAY	CL	32.50	40.00
92	SOMETHING GOOD	CL	32.50	40.00
J. SIAS				**SPIRIT OF CHIRSTMAS**
90	SILENT NIGHT	CL	29.50	45.00
91	DECK THE HALLS	CL	32.50	50.00
91	I'LL BE HOME FOR CHRISTMAS	CL	32.50	55.00
91	JINGLE BELLS	CL	29.50	30.00
91	O CHRISTMAS TREE	CL	32.50	40.00
91	WINTER WONDERLAND	CL	32.50	45.00
C. FISHER				**SPIRITS OF THE SKY**
92	EVENING GLIMMER	CL	32.50	40.00
92	FIRST LIGHT	CL	29.50	35.00
92	GOLDEN DUSK	CL	32.50	40.00
92	TWILIGHT GLOW	CL	29.50	35.00
93	AMBER FIGHT	CL	34.50	40.00
93	DAY'S END	CL	34.50	40.00
93	SUNSET SPLENDOR	CL	32.50	40.00
93	WINGED RADIANCE	CL	34.50	40.00
L. LIU				**SYMPHONY OF SHIMMERING BEAUTIES**
91	HIBISCUS MEDLEY	CL	34.50	40.00
91	IRIS QUARTET	CL	29.50	55.00
91	LILY CONCERTO	CL	32.50	55.00
91	PEONY PRELUDE	CL	32.50	35.00
91	POPPY PASTORALE	CL	32.50	40.00
91	ROSE FANTASY	CL	34.50	40.00
91	TULIP ENSEMBLE	CL	29.50	40.00
92	CARNATION SERENADE	CL	36.50	40.00
92	DAHLIA MELODY	CL	34.50	40.00
92	GLADIOLUS ROMANCE	CL	36.50	40.00
92	HOLLYHOCK MARCH	CL	34.50	40.00
92	ZINNIA FINALE	CL	36.50	40.00
*				**'TIS THE SEASON**
93	A TIME FOR TRADITION	OP	29.50	30.00
93	A WORLD DRESSED IN SNOW	OP	29.50	30.00

YR	NAME	LIMIT	ISSUE	TREND
93	WE SHALL COME REJOICING	OP	29.50	30.00
J. SIAS				**'TIS THE SEASON**
93	A TIME FOR TRADITION	CL	29.50	35.00
93	A WORLD DRESSED IN SNOW	CL	29.50	35.00
93	OUR FAMILY TREE	CL	29.50	35.00
93	WE SHALL COME REJOINING	CL	29.50	35.00
W. NELSON				**TOMORROW'S PROMISE**
92	CURIOSITY: ASIAN ELEPHANTS	CL	29.50	55.00
92	FRISKINESS: KIT FOXES	CL	32.50	50.00
92	INNOCENCE: RHINOS	CL	32.50	65.00
92	PLAYTIME PANDAS	CL	29.50	35.00
*				**TOUCHING THE SPIRIT**
93	CAMP OF THE SACRED DOGS	OP	29.50	30.00
93	HE WHO WATCHES	OP	29.50	30.00
93	KEEPER OF THE SECRET	OP	29.50	30.00
93	KINDRED SPIRITS	OP	29.50	30.00
93	MARKING TREE, THE	OP	29.50	30.00
93	RUNNING WITH THE WIND	OP	29.50	30.00
93	TWICE TRAVELED TRAIL	OP	29.50	30.00
93	WAKAN TANKA	OP	29.50	30.00
J. KRAMER-COLE				**TOUCHING THE SPIRIT**
93	CAMP OF THE SACRED DOGS	CL	29.50	35.00
93	HE WHO WATCHES	CL	29.50	35.00
93	KEEPER OF THE SECRET	CL	29.50	35.00
93	KINDRED SPIRITS	CL	29.50	35.00
93	MARKING TREE, THE	CL	29.50	35.00
93	RUNNING WITH THE WIND	CL	29.50	35.00
93	TWICE TRAVELED TRAIL	CL	29.50	35.00
93	WAKAN TANKA	CL	29.50	35.00
R. STINE				**TREASURY OF SONGBIRDS**
92	MORNING'S GLORY	150-DAY	29.50	30.00
A. CASAY				**VANISHING GENTLE GIANTS**
91	JUMPING FOR JOY	CL	32.50	40.00
91	MONARCH OF THE DEEP	CL	35.50	50.00
91	SONG OF THE HUMPBACK	CL	32.50	40.00
91	TRAVELERS OF THE SEA	CL	35.50	55.00
91	UNICORN OF THE SEA	CL	35.50	60.00
91	WHITE WHALE OF THE NORTH	CL	35.50	55.00
H. BONNER				**VICTORIAN CAT**
90	MISCHIEF WITH THE HATBOX	CL	24.50	50.00
91	DAYDREAMS	CL	27.50	50.00
91	FRISKY FELINES	CL	27.50	55.00
91	KITTENS AT PLAY	CL	27.50	50.00
91	PERFECTLY POISED	CL	29.50	50.00
91	PLAYING IN THE PARLOR	CL	29.50	60.00
91	STRING QUARTET	CL	24.50	60.00
92	MIDDAY REPOSE	CL	29.50	35.00
*				**VICTORIAN CAT CAPERS**
92	A CURIOUS KITTY	OP	27.50	55.00
92	FORBIDDEN FRUIT	OP	29.50	30.00
92	MY BOWL IS EMPTY	OP	27.50	36.00
92	PUSS IN BOOT	OP	24.50	62.00
92	VANITY FAIR	OP	27.50	28.00
92	WHO'S THE FAIREST OF THEM ALL?	OP	24.50	68.00
93	KITTEN EXPRESS, THE	OP	29.50	30.00
93	PURR-FECT PEN PAL, THE	OP	29.50	30.00
F. PATRON				**VICTORIAN CAT CAPERS**
92	A CURIOUS KITTY	CL	27.50	30.00
92	FORBIDDEN FRUIT	CL	29.50	35.00
92	MY BOWL IS EMPTY	CL	27.50	30.00
92	PUSS 'N BOOTS	CL	24.50	30.00
92	VANITY FAIR	CL	27.50	30.00
92	WHO'S THE FAIREST ON THEM ALL?	CL	24.50	30.00
93	KITTEN EXPRESS, THE	CL	29.50	35.00
93	PURRFECT PEN PAL, THE	CL	29.50	35.00
*				**WILD INNOCENTS**
93	LION CLUB	OP	29.50	30.00
93	REFLECTIONS	OP	29.50	30.00
93	SPIRITUAL HEIR	OP	29.50	30.00
93	SUNNY SPOT	OP	29.50	30.00
C. FRACE				**WILD INNOCENTS**
93	LION CUB	CL	29.50	35.00
93	REFLECTIONS	CL	29.50	35.00
93	SPIRITUAL HEIR	CL	29.50	35.00
93	SUNNY SPOT	CL	29.50	35.00
*				**WILD SPIRITS**
92	MOUNTAIN MAGIC	OP	32.50	33.00
92	SOLITARY WATCH	OP	29.50	30.00
92	TIMBER GHOST	OP	29.50	30.00
93	LONE VANGUARD	OP	34.50	35.00
93	MIGHTY PRESENCE	OP	34.50	35.00
93	QUIET VIGIL	OP	34.50	35.00
93	SILENT GUARD	OP	32.50	33.00
93	SLY EYES	OP	32.50	33.00
T. HIRATA				**WILD SPIRITS**
92	MOUNTAIN MAGIC	CL	32.50	40.00
92	SOLITARY WATCH	CL	29.50	35.00

YR	NAME	LIMIT	ISSUE	TREND
92	TIMBER GHOST	CL	29.50	35.00
93	LONG VANGUARD	CL	34.50	40.00
93	MIGHTY PRESENCE	CL	34.50	40.00
93	QUIET VIGIL	CL	34.50	40.00
93	SILENT GUARD	CL	32.50	40.00
93	SLY EYES	CL	32.50	40.00
*				**WINGS OF WINTER**
92	MOONLIGHT RETREAT	OP	29.50	30.00
93	FULL MOON COMPANIONS	OP	29.50	30.00
93	NIGHT LIGHTS	OP	29.50	30.00
93	SILENT SUNSET	OP	29.50	30.00
93	TWILIGHT SERENADE	OP	29.50	30.00
93	WHITE NIGHT	OP	29.50	30.00
93	WINTER HAVEN	OP	29.50	30.00
93	WINTER REFLECTIONS	OP	29.50	30.00
D. RUST				**WINGS OF WINTER**
92	MOONLIGHT RETREAT	CL	29.50	35.00
93	FULL MOON COMPANIONS	CL	29.50	35.00
93	NIGHT LIGHTS	CL	29.50	35.00
93	SILENT SUNSET	CL	29.50	35.00
93	TWILIGHT SERENADE	CL	29.50	35.00
93	WHITE NIGHT	CL	29.50	35.00
93	WINTER HAVEN	CL	29.50	35.00
93	WINTER REFLECTIONS	CL	29.50	35.00
C. FRACE				**WINTER'S MAJESTY**
92	CHASE, THE	CL	34.50	40.00
92	QUEST, THE	CL	34.50	40.00
93	ALASKAN FRIEND	CL	34.50	40.00
93	AMERICAN COUGAR	CL	34.50	40.00
93	ON WATCH	CL	34.50	40.00
93	SOLITUDE	CL	34.50	40.00
R. HARM				**WONDERS OF THE SEA**
91	A FAMILY AFFAIR	CL	34.50	35.00
91	HEART TO HEART	CL	34.50	40.00
91	STAND BY ME	CL	34.50	40.00
91	WARM EMBRACE	CL	34.50	45.00
C. FRACE				**WORLD'S MOST MAGNIFICENT CATS**
91	AFRICAN LEOPARD, THE	CL	29.50	60.00
91	CLOUDED LEOPARD, THE	CL	29.50	110.00
91	COUGAR	CL	24.50	80.00
91	FLEETING ENCOUNTER	CL	24.50	70.00
91	JAGUAR	CL	27.50	80.00
91	MIGHTY WARRIOR	CL	29.50	75.00
91	POWERFUL PRESENCE	CL	27.50	65.00
91	ROYAL BENGAL	CL	27.50	45.00
92	CHEETAH, THE	CL	31.50	70.00
92	SIBERIAN TIGER	CL	31.50	70.00

WATERFORD WEDGWOOD USA

YR	NAME	LIMIT	ISSUE	TREND
*				**BICENTENNIAL**
72	BOSTON TEA PARTY	YR	40.00	45.00
73	PAUL REVERE'S RIDE	YR	40.00	120.00
74	BATTLE OF CONCORD	YR	40.00	60.00
75	ACROSS THE DELAWARE	YR	40.00	110.00
75	VICTORY AT YORKTOWN	YR	45.00	55.00
76	DECLARATION SIGNED	YR	45.00	50.00
*				**MOTHER'S DAY**
71	SPORTIVE LOVE	*	20.00	20.00
72	SEWING LESSON, THE	*	20.00	20.00
73	BAPTISM OF ACHILLES, THE	*	20.00	25.00
74	DOMESTIC EMPLOYMENT	*	30.00	33.00
75	MOTHER AND CHILD	*	35.00	37.00
76	SPINNER, THE	*	35.00	35.00
77	LEISURE TIME	*	35.00	35.00
78	SWAN AND CYGNETS	*	40.00	40.00
79	DEER AND FAWN	*	45.00	45.00
80	BIRDS	*	47.50	48.00
81	MARE AND FOAL	*	50.00	60.00
82	CHERUBS WITH SWING	*	55.00	60.00
83	CUPID AND BUTTERFLY	*	55.00	55.00
84	MUSICAL CUPIDS	*	55.00	59.00
85	CUPIDS AND DOVES	YR	55.00	80.00
86	CUPIDS FISHING	YR	55.00	55.00
87	SPRING FLOWERS	YR	55.00	80.00
88	TIGER LILY	YR	55.00	59.00
89	IRISES	YR	65.00	65.00
91	PEONIES	YR	65.00	65.00
*				**WEDGWOOD CHRISTMAS**
79	BUCKINGHAM PALACE	YR	65.00	70.00
80	ST. JAMES PALACE	YR	70.00	75.00
81	MARBLE ARCH	YR	75.00	80.00
82	LAMBETH PALACE	YR	80.00	85.00
83	ALL SOULS, LANGHAM PALACE	YR	80.00	85.00
84	CONSTITUTION HILL	YR	80.00	85.00
85	TATE GALLERY, THE	YR	80.00	85.00
86	ALBERT MEMORIAL, THE	YR	80.00	145.00
87	GUILDHALL	YR	80.00	90.00
88	OBSERVATORY/GREENWICH, THE	YR	80.00	95.00

YR	NAME	LIMIT	ISSUE	TREND
89	WINCHESTER CATHEDRAL	YR	88.00	90.00
	T. HARPER			**WEDGWOOD CHRISTMAS**
69	WINDSOR CASTLE	YR	25.00	185.00
70	TRAFALGAR SQUARE	YR	30.00	55.00
71	PICADILLY CIRCUS	YR	30.00	40.00
72	ST. PAUL'S CATHEDRAL	YR	35.00	45.00
73	TOWER OF LONDON	YR	40.00	85.00
74	HOUSES OF PARLIAMENT	YR	40.00	45.00
75	TOWER BRIDGE	YR	45.00	50.00
76	HAMPTON COURT	YR	50.00	55.00
77	WESTMINISTER ABBEY	YR	55.00	60.00
78	HORSE GUARDS	YR	60.00	65.00

WENDALL AUGUST FORGE

YR	NAME	LIMIT	ISSUE	TREND
	L. YOUNGO			**COLLECTORS GUILD MEMBER'S ONLY**
95	HOLIDAY EXPRESS	YR	*	*
96	FIRST LOVE	5000	39.00	39.00

WILDLIFE INTERNATIONALE

YR	NAME	LIMIT	ISSUE	TREND
	J. RUTHVEN			**SPORTING DOGS**
85	DECOY (LABORADOR RETRIEVER)	5000	55.00	150.00
85	DUSTY (GOLDEN RETRIEVER)	5000	55.00	80.00
85	RUMMY (ENGLISH SETTER)	5000	55.00	55.00
85	SCARLETT (IRISH SETTER)	5000	55.00	150.00

WILLITTS DESIGNS

YR	NAME	LIMIT	ISSUE	TREND
	T. BLACKSHEAR			**EBONY VISIONS COLLECTION**
95	KATIE'S FIRST QUILT	RT	30.00	30.00

WINDBERG ENTERPRISES

YR	NAME	LIMIT	ISSUE	TREND
	D. WINDBERG			
75	AUTUMN'S WAY	*	650.00	650.00
75	MOUNTAIN'S MAJESTY, THE	*	*	650.00
85	JOYOUS EVENSONG	*	65.00	65.00

Prints

Jay Brown

Selling a print can be as emotional as losing a favorite pet. But often with art, the financial reward can be the perfect compensation. Perhaps you need a few quick bucks or want to clear a little wall space for a new masterpiece. What do you do?

The first thing is to determine the value of the work you wish to sell. There are magazines such as *Collector's mart* on the market that can give you some idea of the current trend. The gallery where the print was purchased or the publisher of the print should also be able to give you an idea of the current market price.

Remember that a framed or unframed print in mint condition is easier to sell and will bring you more dollars than the same print in average condition. Hopefully, you will find that the current market price is in line with what is personally acceptable to you. If you are lucky, the gallery or publisher you're dealing with may make a good offer or direct you to a collector or gallery who is looking for the work you wish to sell.

If not, you have two main options: sell at retail to a private collector, perhaps someone you know; or sell (usually on consignment) at wholesale through a dealer. In either case, it often helps to show a would-be buyer evidence that the print was purchased from (and was framed, if applicable) by a gallery with a good reputation.

One way to locate a retail buyer is to place a classified advertisement in a local newspaper and/or check to see if your friends are interested in buying the print. If the artist is in high demand, your chances for making a sale will be increased tremendously.

If your ad doesn't result in a buyer, don't fret. Selling your print through a reputable gallery is often the preferred way to go. Look for a gallery with experience in dealing with the artist whose work you wish to sell. That gallery should have a marketing plan and a clientele interested in the print. The sales commission the gallery receives will vary from 10-50 percent of the selling price. The most common commission is 33-40 percent.

Occasionally, a print will be difficult to sell due to the timing of the attempted resale. Perhaps the economy is in a decline or the artist is not in demand due to a change in collecting trends. Remember, as with any investment, there are peak times to sell. For example, you'll have better luck with an artist who is in his prime as opposed to one whose art is not as popular.

There are companies that specialize in matching buyers with sellers on the secondary market. These companies provide dealers and collectors with listings of clients interested in selling works of art. Such listings are based on information provided by the sellers. Using such a list, galleries are able to see what it costs to obtain a work of art.

Even though these listing companies make locating works on the secondary market easy for art dealers, many reputable galleries prefer to use their own client base whenever possible. By using their own collector base, galleries can normally avoid shipping costs and be assured that the condition of the work of art is as represented. But most important, by using their own client base, galleries are able to reward clients who exhibit loyalty to them.

Art is a fabulous investment, not because of the amount of potential profit that can be made upon its sale, but because of the amount of enjoyment it can give. Even though many prints turn out to be great monetary investments, it is highly recommended that buyers follow the golden rule of collecting: "Buy what you like, and all your purchases are guaranteed to be good investments."

JAY BROWN owns and operates Gallery One with locations in Mentor and Akron, Ohio, where he specializes in the retail sales of limited edition prints and original paintings and sculptures by the industry's most popular artists. He also deals extensively in the secondary market sale of these collectibles.

PRINTS

3-DIMENSIONAL EDITIONS

F. MILLER

YR	NAME	LIMIT	ISSUE	TREND
95	ELUSIVE PRIZE, THE	500	95.00	95.00
95	KEEPER OF THE FALLS	1000	145.00	145.00
95	RETURN, THE	1000	165.00	165.00
95	YOSEMITES MESSENGER TO THE GODS	1000	145.00	145.00

AMCAL FINE ARTS

C. WYSOCKI

FRAMED CANVAS

YR	NAME	LIMIT	ISSUE	TREND
95	MABEL THE STOWAWAY	CL	750.00	1500.00
96	BLACK BIRDS ROOST AT MILL CREEK	CL	795.00	1200.00
96	MAGGIE THE MESSMAKER	500	795.00	795.00

S. ROSS

PRINT

YR	NAME	LIMIT	ISSUE	TREND
95	FLORA AND FIONA	500	75.00	75.00

M. STACK

PRINT

YR	NAME	LIMIT	ISSUE	TREND
95	UNDER A SUMMER SKY	750	150.00	150.00

C. WYSOCKI

PRINT

YR	NAME	LIMIT	ISSUE	TREND
95	MABEL THE STOWAWAY	CL	175.00	300.00
95	OLDE CAPE COD	2500	195.00	320.00
95	ROOT BEER BREAK AT THE BUTTERFIELD'S	2500	165.00	260.00
96	MAGGIE THE MESSMAKER	6500	175.00	175.00
96	UNCLE JACK'S TOPIARY TENDENCIES	1000	185.00	350.00

C. WYSOCKI

UNFRAMED CANVAS

YR	NAME	LIMIT	ISSUE	TREND
95	MABLE THE STOWAWAY	500	495.00	495.00

AMERICAN ARTISTS

F. STONE

YR	NAME	LIMIT	ISSUE	TREND
*	CIGAR	*	150.00	200.00
*	SUNDAY SILENCE	950	195.00	425.00
78	AFFIRMED, STEVE CAUTHEN UP	750	100.00	625.00
78	MARE AND FOAL	500	90.00	600.00
78	MOMENT AFTER, THE	500	90.00	350.00
79	ONE, TWO, THREE	500	100.00	1000.00
79	PATIENCE	1000	90.00	1550.00
79	RIVALS, THE: AFFIRMED & ALYDAR	500	90.00	500.00
80	BELMONT, THE: BOLD FORBES	500	100.00	600.00
80	EXCELLER: BILL SHOEMAKER	500	90.00	800.00
80	GENUINE RISK	500	100.00	875.00
80	KENTUCKY DERBY, THE	750	100.00	825.00
80	KIDNAPPED MARE: FRANFRELUCHE	750	115.00	615.00
80	PASTURE PEST, THE	500	100.00	950.00
80	SPECTACULAR BID	500	65.00	350.00
81	ARABIANS, THE	750	115.00	530.00
81	CONTENTMENT	750	115.00	525.00
81	SHOE, THE: 8,000 WINS	395	200.00	7000.00
81	THOROUGHBREDS, THE	750	115.00	425.00
82	JOHN HENRY: BILL SHOEMAKER UP	595	160.00	1500.00
82	MAN O' WAR: FINAL THUNDER	750	175.00	3100.00
82	OFF AND RUNNING	750	125.00	400.00
82	POWER HORSES, THE	750	125.00	250.00
82	WATER TROUGH, THE	750	125.00	600.00
83	ANDALUSIAN, THE	750	150.00	350.00
83	DUEL, THE	750	150.00	405.00
83	FOR ONLY A MOMENT: RUFFIAN	750	175.00	1200.00
83	TRANQUILITY	750	150.00	600.00
84	NORTHERN DANCER	950	175.00	1000.00
84	NORTHERN DANCER	950	175.00	750.00
84	SECRETARIAT	950	175.00	1450.00
84	TURNING FOR HOME	750	150.00	450.00
85	ETERNAL LEGACY	950	175.00	950.00
85	FRED STONE PAINTS THE SPORT OF KINGS	750	265.00	750.00
85	JOHN HENRY: MCCARRON UP	750	175.00	750.00
85	KELSO	950	175.00	775.00
85	LEGACY, THE	950	175.00	950.00
86	FOREVER FRIENDS	950	175.00	850.00
86	NIJINSKI II	950	175.00	275.00
86	RUFFIAN & FOOLISH PLEASURE	950	175.00	1270.00
87	FIRST DAY, THE	950	175.00	275.00
87	LADY'S SECRET	950	175.00	425.00
87	RIVALRY, THE: ALYSHEBA AND BET TWICE	950	195.00	550.00
88	ALYSHEBA	950	195.00	650.00
88	CAM-FELIA	950	175.00	360.00
88	CAM-FELLA	950	175.00	350.00
88	SHOE & BALD EAGLE	950	195.00	675.00
89	BATTLE FOR THE TRIPLE CROWN	950	225.00	640.00
89	BATTLE FOR THE TRIPLE CROWN	950	225.00	650.00
89	PHAR LAP	950	195.00	275.00
90	FINAL TRIBUTE: SECRETARIAT	1150	265.00	1500.00
90	OLD WARRIORS SHOEMAKER: JOHN HENRY	1950	265.00	625.00
91	BLACK STALLION	1500	225.00	225.00
91	FOREGO	1150	225.00	250.00
91	GO FOR WAND: A CANDLE IN THE WIND	1150	225.00	225.00
92	AMERICAN TRIPLE CROWN I (1948-1978)	1500	325.00	725.00
92	DANCE SMARTLY	950	225.00	425.00

YR	NAME	LIMIT	ISSUE	TREND
93	AMERICAN TRIPLE CROWN II (1937-1946)	1500	325.00	485.00
93	AMERICAN TRIPLE CROWN III (1919-1935)	1500	225.00	250.00
95	HOLY BULL	1150	225.00	225.00
95	HOLY BULL (CANVAS)	350	375.00	375.00
95	JULIE KRONE - COLONIAL AFFAIR	1150	225.00	225.00
95	SUMMER DAYS	1150	225.00	225.00

AMERICAN LEGACY

S. ETEM

YR	NAME	LIMIT	ISSUE	TREND
*	FOUNTAIN, THE	CL	150.00	150.00
*	INDIANA SUMMER	CL	150.00	150.00
*	LITTLE BANDIT	CL	150.00	150.00

AMERICAN MASTERS

P. CROWE

YR	NAME	LIMIT	ISSUE	TREND
85	FOGGY MORNING MALLARDS	950	90.00	170.00
86	OUTLAWS II, THE	1950	60.00	340.00
87	MASTERS OF DISASTER, THE	950	90.00	100.00
87	WILD BUNCH, THE	950	90.00	150.00
87	WINTER RETREAT	950	90.00	125.00

L. DYKE

YR	NAME	LIMIT	ISSUE	TREND
78	ISAIAH 40:3 S/N	1000	40.00	450.00
78	ISAIAH 40:3 S/O	1500	30.00	70.00
78	ISAIAH 58:8 S/N	1000	35.00	390.00
78	JOHN 3:8 S/N	1000	30.00	900.00
78	PSALM 27:4 S/N	1000	40.00	675.00
79	COLLECTOR'S SUITE S/N	1000	48.00	150.00
79	JOHN 9:4 S/N	1000	45.00	150.00
79	JOHN 9:4 S/O	2000	30.00	90.00
79	PROVERBS 8:25 S/N	1000	45.00	120.00
79	PROVERBS 8:25 S/O	1800	30.00	80.00
79	PSALM 113:3 S/N	1000	40.00	120.00
79	PSALM 113:3 S/O	1500	30.00	100.00
79	PSALM 147:16 S/N	1000	45.00	155.00
79	PSALM 147:16 S/O	1200	30.00	100.00
79	SONG OF SOLOMON 2:17 S/N	1000	45.00	140.00
79	SONG OF SOLOMON 2:17 S/O	1800	30.00	95.00
80	COLLECTOR'S SUITE S/O	1800	35.00	100.00
80	DEUTERONOMY 28:8 S/N	1000	55.00	355.00
80	DEUTERONOMY 28:8 S/O	1800	37.50	200.00
80	EZEKIEL 34:15 S/N	1000	55.00	100.00
80	EZEKIEL 34:15 S/O	1800	37.50	80.00
80	PSALM 42:1 S/N	1000	55.00	280.00
80	PSALM 42:1 S/O	1200	37.50	175.00
80	PSALM 91:1 S/N	1000	45.00	80.00
80	PSALM 91:1 S/O	2200	30.00	50.00
80	QUIET ENCOUNTER (PSALM 104:13) S/N	1600	85.00	105.00
80	REVELATIONS 21:6 S/N	1000	55.00	1150.00
80	REVELATIONS 21:6 S/O	1800	35.00	900.00
80	ROMANS 15:32 S/N	1000	57.50	100.00
80	ROMANS 15:32 S/O	2200	37.50	60.00
81	EZEKIEL 32:14 S/N	1500	65.00	130.00
81	EZEKIEL 32:14 S/O	2500	40.00	70.00
81	JOHN 10:27 S/N	1000	60.00	190.00
81	JOHN 10:27 S/O	2700	37.50	100.00
81	LAMENTATIONS 3:28 S/N	1500	68.00	310.00
81	LAMENTATIONS 3:28 S/O	2500	45.00	200.00
81	MATTHEW 6:30 S/N	1000	40.00	95.00
81	MATTHEW 9:37 S/N	1000	65.00	120.00
81	MATTHEW 9:37 S/O	2200	38.00	50.00
81	PROVERBS 23:10 S/N	1000	60.00	230.00
81	PROVERBS 23:10 S/O	2200	37.50	130.00
81	PSALM 90:2 S/N	1500	67.50	120.00
81	PSALM 90:2 S/O	2500	45.00	90.00
82	DANIEL 2:21 S/N	1500	70.00	100.00
82	DANIEL 2:21 S/O	2500	45.00	60.00
82	ECCLESIASTES 3:1 S/N	1500	70.00	130.00
82	ISAIAH 45:3 S/N	1950	80.00	150.00
82	JOB 39:8 S/N	1500	70.00	175.00
82	JOB 39:8 S/O	2500	45.00	45.00
82	JOHN 8:32 S/N	1500	85.00	130.00
82	JOSHUA 2:22 S/N	1500	70.00	100.00
82	JOSHUA 2:22 S/O	2500	45.00	60.00
83	EARLY ARRIVAL (EPHESIANS 5:8) S/N	1600	75.00	250.00
83	ISAIAH 58:11 S/N	1600	85.00	350.00
83	MATTHEW 18:12 S/N	1500	75.00	180.00
83	ZACHARIAH 14:7 S/N	1600	85.00	100.00
84	MAJESTIC MORNING (AMOS 4:13) S/N	1600	85.00	150.00
84	MORGAN'S CLEARING S/N	1600	80.00	120.00
84	SHARING THE FAITH (PSALM 23) S/N	5000	85.00	350.00
84	TRANQUIL REFUGE (JEREMIAH 48:40) S/N	1600	80.00	90.00
85	A NEW PROMISE (GENESIS 9:16) S/N	1600	85.00	200.00
85	OFFERING, THE (MARK 12:41-44) S/N	3000	125.00	130.00
85	SHADY CREEK MILL (JOB 40:22) S/N	1600	85.00	250.00
87	MISSION, THE (ISAIAH 40:8) S/N	1503	85.00	460.00
88	AFTER THE STORM (LAMENTATIONS 3:26) S/N	1000	110.00	160.00

C. FRACE

YR	NAME	LIMIT	ISSUE	TREND
73	GIANT PANDA	5000	45.00	215.00
73	GOLDEN EAGLE	1000	75.00	275.00

YR	NAME	LIMIT	ISSUE	TREND
73	PRONGHORN	5000	50.00	75.00
73	TIGER	3000	35.00	200.00
74	CHEETAH KITTEN	5000	40.00	600.00
74	HARP SEAL	2000	75.00	1100.00
74	HERRING GULL	5000	45.00	300.00
74	LIONS, THE	5000	40.00	175.00
74	RACCOON	5000	50.00	300.00
74	ZEBRA	4000	60.00	160.00
75	BIGHORN COUNTRY	2500	75.00	250.00
75	LION CUB	3500	35.00	175.00
75	NORTHERN GOSHAWK	4000	50.00	1500.00
75	SAFE RETURN	3000	140.00	140.00
75	SIBERIAN TIGER	2000	80.00	150.00
75	TIGER CUB	3500	35.00	200.00
75	ZEBRA FOAL	4000	35.00	220.00
76	DOUBLE TROUBLE	2500	90.00	360.00
76	ELEPHANTS AT KILIMANJARO	1000	75.00	500.00
76	FLEETING ENCOUNTER	3000	150.00	950.00
76	FLORIDA BOBCAT	3000	40.00	200.00
76	GREATER KUDU	3000	50.00	100.00
76	MASAI GIRAFFES	3000	40.00	400.00
76	OCELOTS	5000	35.00	325.00
76	WHITE TIGER	1500	75.00	300.00
76	WHITE TIGER (REMARQUE)	1000	125.00	350.00
77	CANADA LYNX	3000	50.00	200.00
77	CAVALIER SPANIELS	1500	35.00	325.00
77	CHEETAH	3000	50.00	125.00
77	COUGAR	1000	90.00	1200.00
77	GYRFALCON	3000	40.00	90.00
78	AFRICAN LEOPARD	1500	75.00	500.00
78	AFRICAN LEOPARD (REMARQUE)	1000	125.00	600.00
78	BISON	2000	50.00	250.00
78	CHINESE TREASURE	3000	140.00	240.00
78	CLOUDED LEOPARD	2000	65.00	125.00
78	CLOUDED LEOPARD CUB	2000	75.00	150.00
78	HIMALAYAN PRINCE	2000	75.00	525.00
78	RACCOONS (3)	5000	100.00	700.00
78	RED SHOULDERED HAWK	2000	00.00	100.00
79	KOALA	2000	65.00	725.00
79	SNOW LEOPARD	1500	75.00	1800.00
79	SNOW LEOPARD (REMARQUE)	1000	125.00	2200.00
79	SNOW LEOPARD HEAD	15000	20.00	290.00
79	SNOWY OWLS	2000	65.00	120.00
80	IMPALA	2000	60.00	85.00
80	POLAR BEAR	2000	100.00	110.00
80	SCREECH OWLS	3500	20.00	155.00
80	SIBERIAN LYNX CUB	2000	75.00	150.00
80	WHITE TIGER HEAD	20000	25.00	100.00
81	AFRICAN LEOPARD CUB	2000	65.00	375.00
81	AFRICAN LEOPARD HEAD	12500	25.00	115.00
81	HIGH MOUNTAIN PATH	3000	140.00	200.00
81	LOFTY VIEW	2500	75.00	250.00
81	ROYAL PRIDE	2500	100.00	150.00
82	HARLAN'S HAWK	1500	60.00	140.00
82	JAGUAR	2000	75.00	800.00
82	JAGUAR HEAD	12500	25.00	115.00
82	LONE HUNTER	2500	100.00	220.00
82	MAJESTY	2500	80.00	100.00
82	ON WATCH	2500	80.00	1100.00
82	RACCOON (TENNESSEE CONSERVATION STAMP)	2000	50.00	200.00
82	UNO	2500	75.00	75.00
83	A MOMENT'S REST	2500	100.00	350.00
83	AFRICAN LION	3000	35.00	200.00
83	ALASKAN AUTUMN	2500	80.00	560.00
83	BLACK LEOPARD	3000	50.00	775.00
83	BOBCAT (MS WILDLIFE FED. STAMP)	5000	90.00	175.00
83	LABRADOR RETRIEVER (NTL. RETR. CLUB)	2192	125.00	175.00
83	LABRADOR RETRIEVER (NTL. RETR. CLUB/REM)	190	250.00	400.00
83	MY FRIEND	7500	35.00	65.00
83	RED RASCAL	2500	80.00	730.00
83	YOUNG EXPLORER	2500	80.00	100.00
84	AMERICAN EAGLE	2000	75.00	155.00
84	AMERICAN MONARCH	3750	120.00	400.00
84	BANDIT	2500	90.00	120.00
84	COUGAR CUB	3000	50.00	200.00
84	NEW ARRIVAL	7500	35.00	150.00
84	SOLITUDE	2500	100.00	300.00
85	A RADIANT MOMENT	3000	155.00	150.00
85	A SUNNY SPOT	2500	100.00	125.00
85	KING'S FAVORITE	2500	110.00	130.00
85	PALS	2500	70.00	150.00
85	QUIET TIME IN SAMBURU	2500	100.00	125.00
85	ROYAL BENGAL	3950	125.00	160.00
86	FIRST LIGHT	3950	125.00	135.00
86	FREEDOM	2500	120.00	750.00
86	HIDEAWAY	3950	85.00	225.00
86	THREE OF A KIND	3950	110.00	200.00
86	TREASURES OF THE SEA (FRIEND/SEA OTTER)	500	150.00	150.00
87	CHALLENGER, THE	3000	140.00	150.00

YR	NAME	LIMIT	ISSUE	TREND
87	MIGHTY WARRIOR	3000	140.00	130.00
87	MORRIS THE CAT	5000	30.00	550.00
87	PLAYMATES	2500	120.00	250.00
87	READY FOR ADVENTURE	3950	115.00	125.00
87	TAKING A BREAK	3950	100.00	110.00
88	OUT ON A LIMB	3000	140.00	150.00
88	RECESS	2500	140.00	150.00
88	WANDERER, THE	3000	140.00	410.00
89	NATURE'S DAWN	3000	140.00	140.00
89	POWERFUL PRESENCE	5619	155.00	200.00
89	SURPRISE	3000	140.00	165.00
90	AMBASSADORS	3000	155.00	130.00
90	PARTNERS	3000	55.00	500.00
C. FRAZIER				
87	BURST OF SPRING	950	65.00	90.00
87	PARADISAL SETTING	950	65.00	90.00
87	PASSING THROUGH	950	65.00	200.00
87	ROSE GARDENS	950	65.00	200.00
L. GORDON				
88	EVENING RIDE	950	75.00	250.00
88	FLOWER MARKET, THE	950	70.00	200.00
88	PLEASANT PROMENADE	950	70.00	110.00
88	SUMMER CAROUSEL	950	70.00	225.00
R. SUMMERS				
78	BOSQUE TERRITORY	1500	35.00	200.00
78	FORBIDDING WILDERNESS	1500	35.00	175.00
78	WHITE BUFFALO	1500	35.00	350.00
79	COLTER'S QUEST	1500	50.00	300.00
79	COMANCHE MOON	1500	36.00	120.00
79	FOOTPRINTS IN THE SNOW	1500	40.00	950.00
79	MIGHTY OAK ENDURETH, THE	1500	25.00	125.00
80	ANOTHER DAY	1500	52.00	325.00
80	NATURE'S CLASSROOM	1500	52.00	90.00
80	RECEDING STORM	1500	50.00	300.00
80	SLICKER TIME	1500	52.00	1350.00
81	CAMP COFFEE	1500	75.00	250.00
81	COMMUNE WITH GOD	1500	75.00	550.00
81	FIRST VISIT	1500	62.00	260.00
81	HEADIN' HOME	1500	57.00	60.00
81	LEADIN' LOOSE	1500	60.00	100.00
81	RENDEZVOUS	1500	55.00	120.00
82	BOOM TOWN	1950	75.00	275.00
82	COOLING OFF	1500	80.00	100.00
82	FAMILY TREE	1500	80.00	120.00
82	I'D LIKE TO BE THERE	1500	80.00	100.00
82	PEACEFUL VALLEY	1500	80.00	115.00
82	TEXAS GOLD	1950	90.00	150.00
83	AGAINST THE WIND	1500	90.00	155.00
83	ALL IS CALM	1500	90.00	135.00
83	PERFECT DAY, THE	1500	90.00	100.00
83	RANGE FARE	1500	95.00	125.00
84	CHANGING TIMES	1500	85.00	225.00
84	COWTOWN	1500	90.00	100.00
86	LEGEND OF THE WEST	1500	85.00	120.00
87	BARON'S DAUGHTER	750	100.00	280.00
87	COUNTRY SLICKERS	750	100.00	325.00

ANNA-PERENNA

	T. KRUMEICH	**KRUMEICH HECTOR'S WINDOW**		
*	13-COLOR LITHO, FRAMED	995	95.00	95.00
*	GENUINE STONE LITHO	325	175.00	225.00

ARMSTRONG'S

A. D'ESTREHAN				
87	SAN PEDRO	500	95.00	95.00
87	SAN PEDRO A/P	CL	95.00	95.00
87	U.S.S. CONSTITUTION	500	95.00	95.00
87	U.S.S. CONSTITUTION A/P	CL	95.00	95.00
L. DEWINNE				
87	WINDSWEPT	500	95.00	95.00
87	WINDSWEPT A/P	CL	95.00	95.00
S. ETEM				
87	BOYS, THE	500	70.00	70.00
87	BOYS, THE A/P	CL	70.00	70.00
87	SISSY AND MISSY	500	70.00	70.00
87	SISSY AND MISSY A/P	CL	70.00	70.00
G. LAMBERT				
87	LADY CUNNINGHAM	500	95.00	95.00
87	LADY CUNNINGHAM A/P	CL	95.00	95.00

ART IMPRESSIONS WEST

R. VAN BEEK				
87	COMPANIONS	450	48.00	900.00
87	DAYS OF AUTUMN	450	28.00	50.00
87	PALLET OF SPRING	450	28.00	575.00
87	SUMMER MEMORIES	450	28.00	575.00
88	END OF DAY	450	28.00	325.00
88	FOUR SEASONS SET	450	112.00	3250.00

YR	NAME	LIMIT	ISSUE	TREND
90	MT. BAKER TWIN SISTER SET	250	74.00	2000.00
94	SPRING BREEZE	950	75.00	120.00
	R. VAN BEEK			**CANVAS**
93	MORNING LIGHT ON SKAGIT FIELDS	750	195.00	475.00
94	CASCADE FAMILY TREE	450	195.00	575.00
94	SATURDAY IN OCTOBER	450	195.00	575.00
94	SPRING BREEZE	450	195.00	575.00
94	WINTER MEMORIES	450	195.00	575.00
	R. VAN BEEK			**FOUR SEASONS COLLECTIONS**
95	DAYS OF AUTUMN	450	28.00	75.00
95	END OF DAY	450	28.00	325.00
95	PALLET OF SPRING	450	28.00	575.00
95	SUMMER MEMORIES	450	28.00	575.00
	R. VAN BEEK			**LIMITED EDITION**
95	COMPANIONS	450	45.00	825.00
95	MT. BAKER TWIN SISTER SET	450	74.00	2000.00
95	SPRING BREEZE	450	75.00	430.00
	R. VAN BEEK			**LIMITED EDITION/CANVAS**
95	CASCADE FAMILY TREE	450	195.00	430.00
95	MORNING LIGHT ON SKAGIT FIELDS	450	195.00	430.00
95	SATURDAY IN OCTOBER	450	195.00	430.00
95	SPRING BREEZE	450	195.00	430.00
95	WINTER MEMORIES	450	195.00	430.00

ART WORLD OF BOURGEAULT

YR	NAME	LIMIT	ISSUE	TREND
	R. BOURGEAULT			**ROYAL LITERARY SERIES**
89	ANNE HATHAWAY COTTAGE	OP	75.00	115.00
89	JOHN BUNYAN COTTAGE	OP	75.00	115.00
89	JOHN MILTON COTTAGE	OP	75.00	115.00
89	THOMAS HARDY COTTAGE	OP	75.00	115.00
	R. BOURGEAULT			**THE ENGLISH COUNTRYSIDE**
89	COUNTRY SQUIRE, THE	550	130.00	500.00

ARTAFFECTS

YR	NAME	LIMIT	ISSUE	TREND
	MAGO			
88	BETH	950	95.00	200.00
88	JESSICA AND SEBASTIAN (PR.)	550	225.00	325.00
88	SERENITY	950	95.00	200.00
	J. DENEEN			
88	EMPIRE BUILDER	950	75.00	75.00
88	SANTA FE	950	75.00	75.00
88	TWENTIETH CENTURY LIMITED	950	75.00	75.00
	G. PERILLO			
77	MADRE	500	125.00	410.00
78	MADONNA OF THE PLAINS	500	125.00	500.00
78	SNOW PALS	500	125.00	260.00
79	SIOUX SCOUT/BUFFALO HUNT (PR.)	500	150.00	750.00
80	BABYSITTER	3000	60.00	120.00
80	PUPPIES	3000	45.00	260.00
81	PEACEABLE KINGDOM	950	100.00	104.00
82	CHIEF PONTIAC	950	75.00	100.00
82	HOOFBEATS	950	100.00	150.00
82	INDIAN STYLE	950	75.00	325.00
82	LONESONE COWBOY	950	75.00	390.00
82	MARIA	550	150.00	350.00
82	TENDER LOVE	950	75.00	104.00
82	TINKER	3000	45.00	100.00
83	MOMENT, THE (POSTER)	OP	20.00	60.00
84	NAVAJO LOVE	300	125.00	550.00
84	OUT OF THE FOREST	*	*	450.00
85	CHIEF CRAZY HORSE	950	125.00	450.00
85	CHIEF SITTING BULL	500	125.00	350.00
85	MARIGOLD	500	125.00	350.00
85	SECRETARIAT	950	125.00	125.00
85	WHIRLAWAY	950	125.00	125.00
86	LEARNING HIS WAYS	325	150.00	150.00
86	POUT	325	150.00	350.00
86	RESCUE, THE	325	150.00	450.00
86	WAR PONY	325	150.00	250.00
88	BY THE STREAM	950	100.00	100.00
88	MAGNIFICENT SEVEN	950	125.00	125.00
90	PACK, THE	950	150.00	150.00
	R. SAUBER			
82	BUTTERFLY	3000	45.00	100.00
	MAGO			**GRAND GALLERY COLLECTION**
88	AMY	2500	75.00	90.00
88	LAUREN	2500	75.00	90.00
88	MISCHIEF	2500	75.00	90.00
88	TOMORROWS	2500	75.00	90.00
	L. MARCHETTI			**GRAND GALLERY COLLECTION**
88	PARIS	2500	75.00	90.00
88	VENICE	2500	75.00	90.00
	G. PERILLO			**GRAND GALLERY COLLECTION**
88	BLACKFOOT HUNTER	2500	75.00	90.00
88	BRAVE & FREE	2500	75.00	200.00
88	CHEYENNE NATION, THE	2500	75.00	90.00
88	CHIEF CRAZY HORSE	2500	75.00	90.00

YR	NAME	LIMIT	ISSUE	TREND
88	CHIEF RED CLOUD	2500	75.00	98.00
88	LAST FRONTIER, THE	2500	75.00	90.00
88	LATE MAIL	2500	75.00	98.00
88	LILY OF THE MOHAWKS	2500	75.00	90.00
88	NATIVE AMERICAN	2500	75.00	220.00
88	NOBLE HERITAGE	2500	75.00	220.00
88	PEACEABLE KINGDOM, THE	2500	75.00	90.00
88	TENDER LOVE	2500	75.00	130.00
R. SAUBER		**GRAND GALLERY COLLECTION**		
88	GOD BLESS AMERICA	2500	75.00	90.00
88	HOME SWEET HOME	2500	75.00	90.00
88	MOTHERHOOD	2500	75.00	90.00
88	VISITING THE DOCTOR	2500	75.00	90.00
88	WEDDING, THE	2500	75.00	90.00

ARTISTS OF THE WORLD

Price ranges may reflect various demands in the market from one geographic region to another; condition of piece; specific markings found on piece; and/or changes in production of piece.

YR	NAME	LIMIT	ISSUE	TREND
T. DEGRAZIA				
94	ADORATION	950	79.50	83.00
94	BEAUTIFUL HARVEST	950	79.50	83.00
94	SPRING BLOSSOMS	950	79.50	83.00
94	YOUNG MADONNA	950	79.50	83.00

B. BOURGEAU RICHARDS COLLECTION

YR	NAME	LIMIT	ISSUE	TREND
B.B. RICHARDS				
93	ALWAYS	1000	25.00	30.00
93	BARNEY	1000	20.00	23.00
93	DAPHNEY DUBUNNY	1000	20.00	23.00
93	FOR THE CHILDREN	1000	45.00	55.00
93	GRANDMA'S TEAPOT	1000	20.00	23.00
93	MARY & PETE NEWEST ARRIVAL	1000	20.00	23.00
93	MEDORE'S PRIZE PIG	1000	40.00	45.00
93	RED ROSES FOR CONSTANCE	1000	30.00	35.00
93	SUNFLOWER FOR FLORENCE	1000	20.00	23.00
94	BIRD WATCHING	1000	15.00	18.00
94	CYNTHIA'S TEAPOT	1000	15.00	18.00
94	FISHERMAN, THE	1000	15.00	18.00
94	FRIENDSHIP GARDEN, THE	1000	37.00	42.00
94	FROM THE HEART	1000	15.00	18.00
94	INDIAN SUMMER	1000	37.00	42.00
94	INNOCENCE	1000	40.00	45.00
94	JOSEPHINE WEDS CHARLES	1000	15.00	18.00
94	JUST THREE ANGELS	1000	15.00	18.00
94	MA	1000	35.00	40.00
94	PEARL LOVES HELEN	1000	15.00	18.00
94	SARAH ON WASH DAY	1000	15.00	18.00
94	WAITING FOR PAPA	1000	25.00	30.00
B.B. RICHARDS			**AMANDA MOORE SERIES**	
93	APPLE FOR MISS AMANDA	1000	40.00	45.00
93	HOUSE ON HOLLISTER	1000	30.00	35.00
B.B. RICHARDS			**CHRISTMAS SERIES**	
93	PEACE, LOVE AND JOY	1050	32.00	40.00
94	WHERE MY HEART FINDS CHRISTMAS	1452	32.00	40.00
B.B. RICHARDS				**FLORAL SERIES**
93	WILD ROSES	1000	40.00	45.00
94	PURPLE IRIS	1000	40.00	45.00
B.B. RICHARDS		**FOUR SEASONS WEDDING SERIES**		
93	WINTER WEDDING BELLS	1000	34.00	40.00
94	WEDDING IN SPRING	1000	35.00	40.00

BRIERCROFT

YR	NAME	LIMIT	ISSUE	TREND
D. WINDBERG	**WINDBERG COLLECTORS SOCIETY MEMBERS ONLY**			
95	PERFECT SERENITY	*	150.00	150.00

BRIGHTER IMAGE PUBLISHING

YR	NAME	LIMIT	ISSUE	TREND
K. AUNCHMAN				
95	18TH HOLE HARBOURTOWN	1000	90.00	90.00

CANEY CREEK PUBLISHING

YR	NAME	LIMIT	ISSUE	TREND
P. MURRAY				**APPALACHIA**
95	AUNTY EMILY	CL	205.00	480.00
95	DENIM	680	35.00	35.00
95	LID'L FANNIE	680	30.00	30.00
95	MAUDE	680	35.00	35.00
95	MILT	680	30.00	30.00
P. MURRAY			**LAST OF THE LEGEND**	
93	DANIEL	CL	385.00	1200.00
95	WASHBOARD COMPLAINT	680	285.00	285.00

CAVANAGH GROUP

YR	NAME	LIMIT	ISSUE	TREND
SUNDBLOM		**COCA-COLA BRAND SANTA ANIMATION**		
91	SSSHH!	CL	99.99	125.00
92	SANTA'S PAUSE FOR REFRESHMENT	CL	99.99	125.00
93	TRIMMING THE TREE	CL	99.99	120.00
95	SANTA AT THE LAMPPOST	OP	110.00	115.00

YR	NAME	LIMIT	ISSUE	TREND

CHRISTOPHER PALUSO ART WORKS

C. PALUSO

YR	NAME	LIMIT	ISSUE	TREND
*	AL KALINE	750	5.00	30.00
*	ALAN TRAMMELL	750	5.00	30.00
*	ANDY HAWKINS	750	5.00	30.00
*	BABE RUTH	500	85.00	125.00
*	BASEBALL'S IRON MAN	10000	15.00	35.00
*	CHUCK CONNORS	750	5.00	50.00
*	DARRYL STRAWBERRY	1000	10.00	30.00
*	DAVE DRAVECKY	750	5.00	30.00
*	DON MATTINGLY	1000	10.00	30.00
*	DUKE SNIDER	500	5.00	30.00
*	DWIGHT GOODEN	1000	10.00	30.00
*	K. MCREYNOLDS	500	5.00	30.00
*	NOLAN RYAN	1000	50.00	300.00
*	OREL HERSHISER	750	5.00	30.00
*	RICKY HENDERSON	1000	10.00	30.00
*	RON CEY	250	5.00	30.00
*	RUPPERT JONES	750	5.00	30.00
*	RYNE SANDBERG	500	5.00	30.00
*	SPARKY ANDERSON	250	5.00	30.00
*	STEVE GARVEY	1000	10.00	30.00
*	TED WILLIAMS	500	5.00	35.00
*	TERRY KENNEDY	750	5.00	30.00
*	TONY GWYNN	351	85.00	150.00
*	WILLIE MAYS	500	5.00	35.00
*	WILLIE McCOVEY	500	5.00	30.00

CHUST COUNTRY

T. NEIFFER

YR	NAME	LIMIT	ISSUE	TREND
93	AND THE ANIMALS CAME	450	98.00	98.00
94	ADVENTURES OF COLE THE CAT, THE	850	98.00	98.00

CIRCLE FINE ART

L. NEIMAN

YR	NAME	LIMIT	ISSUE	TREND (NEIMAN)
*	12 METER YACHT RACE	250	*	1800.00
*	AL CAPONE	300	*	2000.00
*	BACKHAND	300	*	1450.00
*	CASINO	300	*	4100.00
*	CHIPPING ON	275	*	1500.00
*	DEUCE	275	*	2500.00
*	DOUBLES	300	*	3150.00
*	DOWNHILL	600	*	1800.00
*	END AROUND	300	2800.00	2800.00
*	FOUR ACES	300	*	1500.00
*	FOX HUNT	300	*	1500.00
*	GOAL	300	*	1500.00
*	HARLEQUIN	200	3600.00	3600.00
*	HARLEQUIN W/SWORD	250	*	1150.00
*	HARLEQUIN W/TEXT	200	*	1150.00
*	HOCKEY PLAYER	300	*	2800.00
*	HOMMAGE TO BOUCHER	250	*	1700.00
*	IN THE STRETCH	250	*	1400.00
*	INNSBRUCK	300	*	3000.00
*	JOCKEY	300	3200.00	3200.00
*	LEOPARD	300	*	5500.00
*	LION PRIDE	300	*	4000.00
*	MARATHON	300	*	1800.00
*	OCELOT	250	*	2000.00
*	PADDOCK	300	*	3900.00
*	PIERROT	250	*	1150.00
*	PIERROT THE JUGGLER	200	*	1150.00
*	POOL ROOM	350	*	6500.00
*	PUNCHINELLO	250	*	2200.00
*	PUNCHINELLO W/TEXT	200	*	1600.00
*	RACE, THE	300	*	700.00
*	ROULETTE	40	*	11000.00
*	SAILING	275	*	1700.00
*	SCRAMBLE	300	*	1800.00
*	SKIER	300	*	1500.00
*	SLALOM	300	*	2500.00
*	SLAPSHOT	300	*	1600.00
*	SLIDING HOME	300	*	2450.00
*	SMASH	300	*	1700.00
*	STOCK MARKET	300	*	7500.00
*	SUDDEN DEATH	250	*	3000.00
*	TEE SHOT	300	*	1850.00
*	TENNIS PLAYER	300	*	1500.00
*	TIGER	300	*	5100.00
*	TROTTERS	300	*	1850.00

N. ROCKWELL

YR	NAME	LIMIT	ISSUE	TREND (ROCKWELL)
*	AMERICAN FAMILY FOLIO	200	*	17550.00
*	ARTIST AT WORK, THE	130	*	3550.00
*	AT THE BARBER	200	*	5000.00
*	AUTUMN	200	*	3550.00
*	AUTUMN/JAPON	25	*	3700.00
*	AVIARY	200	*	4250.00
*	BARBERSHOP QUARTET	200	*	3900.00

YR	NAME	LIMIT	ISSUE	TREND
*	BASEBALL	200	*	3650.00
*	BEN FRANKLIN'S PHILADELPHIA	200	*	3675.00
*	BEN'S BELLES	200	*	3675.00
*	BIG DAY, THE	200	*	3500.00
*	BIG TOP, THE	148	*	3400.00
*	BLACKSMITH SHOP	200	*	5000.00
*	BOOKSELLER	200	*	2775.00
*	BOOKSELLER/JAPON	25	*	2800.00
*	BRIDGE, THE	200	*	3150.00
*	CAT	200	*	3500.00
*	CAT/COLLOTYPE	200	*	4050.00
*	CHEERING	200	*	3650.00
*	CHILDREN AT WINDOW	200	*	3650.00
*	CHURCH	200	*	3450.00
*	CHURCH/COLLOTYPE	200	*	4075.00
*	CIRCUS	200	*	2700.00
*	COUNTY AGRICULTURAL	200	*	3950.00
*	CRITIC, THE	200	*	4700.00
*	DAY IN THE LIFE OF A BOY	25	*	6550.00
*	DEBUT	200	*	3650.00
*	DISCOVERY	200	*	3000.00
*	DOCTOR AND BOY	200	*	9500.00
*	DOCTOR AND DOLL	200	*	12000.00
*	DRESSING UP/INK	60	*	4500.00
*	DRESSING UP/PENCIL	200	*	3775.00
*	DRUNKARD, THE	200	*	3675.00
*	EXPECTED AND UNEXPECTED, THE	200	*	3750.00
*	FAMILY TREE	200	*	6000.00
*	FIDO'S HOUSE	200	*	3600.00
*	FOOTBALL MASCOT	200	*	3700.00
*	FOUR SEASONS FOLIO	25	*	14000.00
*	FOUR SEASONS FOLIO	200	*	5500.00
*	FREEDOM FROM FEAR	200	*	6500.00
*	FREEDOM FROM WANT	200	*	6500.00
*	FREEDOM OF RELIGION	200	*	6500.00
*	FREEDOM OF SPEECH	200	*	6500.00
*	GAIETY DANCE TEAM	200	*	3000.00
*	GIRL AT MIRROR	200	*	8500.00
*	GOLDEN AGE, THE	200	*	3500.00
*	GOLDEN RULE	200	*	4500.00
*	GOLF	200	*	3700.00
*	GOSSIPS	200	*	5000.00
*	GOSSIPS/JAPON	25	*	5200.00
*	GROTTO	200	*	3500.00
*	GROTTO/COLLOTYPE	200	*	4000.00
*	HIGH DIVE	200	*	2500.00
*	HOMECOMING, THE	200	*	3700.00
*	HOUSE, THE	200	*	3700.00
*	HUCK FINN FOLIO	200	*	16000.00
*	ICHABOD CRANE	200	*	6800.00
*	INVENTOR, THE	200	*	3600.00
*	JERRY	200	*	4800.00
*	JIM GOT DOWN ON HIS KNEES	200	*	4500.00
*	LINCOLN	200	*	11500.00
*	LOBSTERMAN	200	*	5500.00
*	LOBSTERMAN/JAPON	25	*	5600.00
*	MARRIAGE LICENSE	200	*	7000.00
*	MEDICINE	200	*	3500.00
*	MEDICINE/COLOR LITHO	200	*	6000.00
*	MISS MARY JANE	200	*	4500.00
*	MOVING DAY	200	*	4000.00
*	MUSIC HATH CHARMS	200	*	4200.00
*	MY HAND SHOOK	200	*	4500.00
*	OUT THE WINDOW	200	*	3400.00
*	OUT THE WINDOW/COLLOTYPE	200	*	4000.00
*	OUTWARD BOUND	200	*	8000.00
*	POOR RICHARD'S ALMANAC	200	*	11500.00
*	PRESCRIPTION	200	*	5000.00
*	PRESCRIPTION/JAPON	25	*	5000.00
*	PROBLEM WE ALL LIVE WITH, THE	200	*	6000.00
*	PUPPIES	200	*	3700.00
*	RALEIGH THE DOG	200	*	4000.00
*	ROCKET SHIP	200	*	4000.00
*	ROYAL CROWN, THE	200	*	3500.00
*	RUNAWAY	200	*	4600.00
*	SAFE AND SOUND	200	*	3800.00
*	SATURDAY PEOPLE	200	*	3300.00
*	SAVE ME	200	*	3600.00
*	SAVING GRACE	200	*	7500.00
*	SCHOOL DAYS FOLIO	200	*	18000.00
*	SCHOOLHOUSE, THE	200	*	4500.00
*	SCHOOLHOUSE/JAPON	25	*	4700.00
*	SEE AMERICA FIRST	200	*	5700.00
*	SEE AMERICA FIRST/JAPON	25	*	5700.00
*	SETTING IN	200	*	3600.00
*	SHUFFELTON'S BARBERS	200	*	7500.00
*	SMOKING	200	*	4000.00
*	SMOKING/COLLOTYPE	200	*	4000.00
*	SPANKING	200	*	3500.00

YR	NAME	LIMIT	ISSUE	TREND
*	SPANKING/COLLOTYPE	200	*	3600.00
*	SPELLING BEE	200	*	5000.00
*	SPRING	200	*	2500.00
*	SPRING FLOWERS	200	*	5200.00
*	SPRING/JAPON	25	*	3650.00
*	STUDY FOR THE DOCTOR	200	*	6000.00
*	STUDYING	200	*	3600.00
*	SUMMER	200	*	3600.00
*	SUMMER STOCK	200	*	5000.00
*	SUMMER/JAPON	25	*	3600.00
*	SUMMERSTOCK/JAPON	25	*	5000.00
*	TEACHER'S PET	200	*	3600.00
*	TEACHER, THE	200	*	3400.00
*	TEACHER, THE/JAPON	25	*	3500.00
*	TEXAN THE	200	*	3775.00
*	THEN FOR THREE MINUTES	200	*	4500.00
*	THEN MISS WATSON	200	*	4500.00
*	THERE WARN'T NO HARM	200	*	4500.00
*	THREE FARMERS	200	*	3600.00
*	TICKETSELLER	200	*	2700.00
*	TOM SAWYER COLOR SUITE	200	*	30500.00
*	TOM SAWYER FOLIO	200	*	11000.00
*	TOP OF THE WORLD	200	*	4300.00
*	TRUMPETER	200	*	4000.00
*	TRUMPETER/JAPON	25	*	4100.00
*	TWO O'CLOCK FEEDING	200	*	3600.00
*	VILLAGE SMITHY, THE	200	*	3500.00
*	WELCOME	200	*	3500.00
*	WET PAINT	200	*	3800.00
*	WHEN I LIT MY CANDLE	200	*	4500.00
*	WHITEWASHING	200	*	3450.00
*	WHITEWASHING THE FENCE	200	*	4000.00
*	WINDOW WASHER	200	*	6500.00
*	WINTER	200	*	2300.00
*	WINTER/JAPON	25	*	3600.00
*	YE OLD PRINT SHOPPE	200	*	3500.00
*	YOUR EYES IS LOOKIN'	200	*	4600.00

COMPETITIVE IMAGES

RUSH

YR	NAME	LIMIT	ISSUE	TREND
76	GUARANTEED WINNER (SUPER BOWL III)	900	100.00	1150.00
78	SUGAR BOWL 1987: ALABAMA VS OHIO STATE	275	200.00	3000.00
79	TURN, THE (THOROUGHBRED)	275	300.00	900.00
79	YOU BETTER PASS (SUGAR BOWL)	130	300.00	4500.00
80	SPINNAKER RUN (12 M. YACHTS)	325	400.00	1000.00
80	SPIRIT OF VICTORY (USA OLYM. HOCKEY)	325	400.00	3500.00
81	CHAMPIONSHIP SEASON (U. OF GEORGIA)	325	400.00	500.00
81	HAPPY BIRTHDAY AMERICA (MCENROE)	325	400.00	1500.00
81	JACK NICKLAUS: THE GOLDEN BEAR	325	400.00	800.00
81	SLALOM	325	400.00	2500.00
81	SUPER BOWL GIANTS	410	500.00	550.00
82	COACH PAUL BEAR BRYANT	200	425.00	2500.00
82	HILTON HEAD: THE HERITAGE CLASSIC	325	425.00	2500.00
82	LAST CHUKKER, THE (POLO)	500	400.00	500.00
82	NATIONAL CHAMPION CLEMSON UNIV.	500	450.00	450.00
82	NORTH CAROLINA NATIONAL CHAMPION	500	450.00	500.00
82	PEBBLE BEACH	500	500.00	1200.00
83	DINNER WHITE NIGHT (PENN STATE)	350	450.00	500.00
83	GREENTRACK (GREYHOUND RACING)	225	425.00	500.00
83	UCLA	500	450.00	500.00
84	A DREAM OF GOLD (XXIII OLYMPIAD)	500	500.00	600.00
84	FAIRBANKS, THE (XXXIII OLYM. EQUES.)	200	500.00	550.00
84	ONE AND ONLY, THE (NEBRASKA)	225	450.00	500.00
84	WIMBLEDON WOMEN (100TH ANNIVERSARY)	500	450.00	800.00
85	A CENTURY OF EXCELLENCE (GA TECH)	225	500.00	550.00
85	CHRIS EVERT LLOYD	275	500.00	500.00
85	MIAMI ON THE MOVE (DOLPHINS)	225	500.00	600.00
85	TWENTY SIX & GLORY (OK STATE)	100	450.00	450.00
86	GLORY YEARS, THE (ICE BOWL)	135	500.00	2000.00
86	INDY 500, THE	175	500.00	600.00
86	KENTUCKY DERBY, THE	500	450.00	550.00
86	MARTINA NAVRATILOVA	275	500.00	550.00
86	OKLAHOMA NATIONAL CHAMPION (B. SWITZER)	100	500.00	800.00
86	ROYAL FINISH (KANSAS CITY)	300	522.00	600.00
86	SHOW ME SERIES, THE (K.C. WORLD SERIES)	375	450.00	550.00
86	WON FOR PAPA (SUPER BOWL)	200	500.00	4000.00
87	AMAZIN AGAIN: N.Y. METS	320	525.00	550.00
87	AMERICA'S COWBOYS (DALLAS)	310	500.00	550.00
87	BURGANDY IN GOLD (REDSKINS)	165	500.00	550.00
87	MILE HIGH DENVER BRONCOS	425	500.00	500.00
88	CUMMINGS AGAIN: BUCKS	175	500.00	550.00
88	LED BY THE SPIRIT (COTTON BOWL 88)	150	525.00	1500.00
88	NATIONAL CHAMPION HOOSIERS	250	525.00	525.00
88	NATIONAL CHAMPION JAYHAWKS	275	450.00	450.00
88	ON WISCONSIN	185	500.00	500.00
88	REACHING THE MARK (AMERICA'S CUP)	*	525.00	700.00
89	A TRADITION OF GOLD (NOTRE DAME)	275	550.00	550.00
89	HIGH FLYING CARDINALS (BASEBALL)	190	525.00	525.00
89	HIT & RUN BREWERS 1987	190	525.00	550.00

A Gaggle of Geese *focuses its attention on something we can only imagine in this image by P. Buckley Moss issued by the Moss Portfolio in 1982 at $125.*

How many hidden images can you find in Bev Doolittle's Eagle Heart? *Produced by The Greenwich Workshop.*

YR	NAME	LIMIT	ISSUE	TREND
89	SECOND AND GOLD: 1987 ROSE BOWL	150	525.00	525.00
90	ABOVE THE CROWD (M. JORDAN)	200	525.00	600.00

CROSS GALLERY

P. CROSS — **HALF BREED SERIES**

YR	NAME	LIMIT	ISSUE	TREND
89	ACH-HUA DLUBH: HALF BREED	475	190.00	1400.00
90	ACH-HUA DLUBH: HALF BREED II	475	225.00	900.00
90	ACH-HUA DLUBH: HALF BREED III	475	225.00	800.00
95	HALF-BREED IV	865	225.00	225.00
96	BANDITS, THE	865	225.00	225.00
96	HEALER, THE	250	795.00	225.00
96	WOLVES	865	225.00	225.00

P. CROSS — **LIMITED EDITION ORIGINAL GRAPHICS**

YR	NAME	LIMIT	ISSUE	TREND
85	CAROLINE (STONE LITHO)	47	300.00	600.00
88	MAIDENHOOD HOPI (STONE LITHO)	74	950.00	1100.00
89	RED CAPOTE, THE (SERIGRAPH)	275	750.00	500.00
89	ROSAPINA (ETCHING)	74	1200.00	1400.00
90	NIGHTEYES I (SERIGRAPH)	275	225.00	175.00

P. CROSS — **LIMITED EDITION PRINTS**

YR	NAME	LIMIT	ISSUE	TREND
83	AYLA-SA-XUH-XAH (PRETTY COLOURS)	475	150.00	150.00
83	ISBAALOO EETSCHIILEEHCHEE (SORTING BEAD)	475	150.00	1800.00
84	BLUE BEADED HAIR TIES	475	85.00	400.00
84	DII-TAH-SHTEH EE-WIHZA-AHOOK (COAT)	475	90.00	2000.00
84	PROFILE OF CAROLINE	475	85.00	125.00
84	THICK LODGE CLAN BOY: CROW	475	85.00	180.00
84	WHISTLING WATER CLAN GIRL: CROW	475	85.00	100.00
85	CAROLINE	475	45.00	150.00
85	WATER VISION, THE	475	150.00	225.00
86	GRAND ENTRY	475	85.00	125.00
86	RED CAPOTE, THE	475	150.00	300.00
86	WINTER MORNING	475	185.00	1400.00
86	WINTER SHAWL, THE	475	150.00	2600.00
87	ELKSKIN ROBE, THE	475	190.00	300.00
87	RED NECKLACE, THE	475	90.00	150.00
87	TINA	475	45.00	125.00
88	DANCE APACHE	475	190.00	300.00
88	MA-A-LUPPIS-SHE-LA-DUS (SHE IS ABOVE)	475	190.00	450.00
89	B'ACHUA DLUBH-BIA BII NOSKIIYAHI, II	475	225.00	415.00
89	BIAACHEE-ITAH BAH-ACHBEH	475	225.00	250.00
89	CHEY-AYJEH: PREY	475	190.00	300.00
89	DREAMER, THE	475	190.00	300.00
89	TEESA WAITS TO DANCE	475	135.00	135.00
90	BAAPE OCHIA (NIGHT WIND, TURQUOISE)	475	185.00	225.00
90	ESHTE	475	185.00	185.00
90	ISHIA-KAHDA #1 (QUIET ONE)	475	185.00	150.00

P. CROSS — **MINIATURE LINE**

YR	NAME	LIMIT	ISSUE	TREND
91	BJ	447	80.00	150.00
91	FLORAL SHAWL, THE	447	80.00	175.00
91	KENDRA	447	80.00	100.00
91	WATERCOLOR STUDY #32 FOR HALF BREED	447	80.00	80.00

P. CROSS — **STAR QUILT**

YR	NAME	LIMIT	ISSUE	TREND
85	WINTER WARMTH	475	150.00	1600.00
86	REFLECTIONS	475	185.00	850.00
88	QUILT MAKERS, THE	475	190.00	450.00

P. CROSS — **THE PAINTED LADIES' SUITE**

YR	NAME	LIMIT	ISSUE	TREND
92	ACORIA (CROW: SEAT OF HONOR)	447	185.00	175.00
92	AVISOLA	475	185.00	185.00
92	DAH-SAY (CROW HEART)	475	185.00	185.00
92	ITZA-CHU (APACHE: THE EAGLE)	475	185.00	185.00
92	KEL'HOYA (HOPI: LITTLE SPARROW HAWK)	475	185.00	185.00
92	PAINTED LADIES, THE	475	225.00	1200.00
92	SUS(H)GAH-DAYDUS(H) (CROW: QUICK)	447	185.00	185.00
92	TZE-GO-JUNI (CHIRICAHUA APACHE)	447	80.00	80.00

P. CROSS — **WOLF SERIES**

YR	NAME	LIMIT	ISSUE	TREND
85	DII-TAH-SHTEH BII-WIK; CHEDAH-BAH LIIDAH	475	185.00	2200.00
87	MORNING STAR GIVES LONG OTTER HIS HOOP	475	190.00	1850.00
89	BIAGOHT EECUEBEH HEHSHEESH-CHEDAH	475	225.00	175.00
90	AGNJNAUG AMAGUUT; INUPIAG (WOMEN/WOLVES)	1050	325.00	175.00

DEBORAH ROBINSON

D. ROBINSON

YR	NAME	LIMIT	ISSUE	TREND
84	JEWELS IN THE SUNSET	CL	*	*
84	TO GOD GIVE THE GLORY	CL	*	*
85	ME TOO	CL	*	*
87	BEAR YOUR HEART	CL	*	*
87	EVERYTHING'S COMING UP ROSES	CL	*	*
89	HIBISCUS	500	125.00	125.00
89	TIDEPOOL	CL	*	*
90	GIVE IT A WHIRL	500	125.00	125.00
91	SECRETS	CL	*	*
92	FRIENDS	500	50.00	50.00
92	SAND CASTLE	500	85.00	85.00
92	SAND TIME	500	85.00	85.00
92	WHEN WE WERE YOUNG	500	225.00	225.00
92	YESTERDAY	500	85.00	85.00

DELGADO STUDIO

YR	NAME	LIMIT	ISSUE	TREND
*	MICKEY AT NIGHT H/S	750	125.00	450.00

YR	NAME	LIMIT	ISSUE	TREND
	DELGADO			
*	CAMACHO VS MACINI S/N	500	25.00	100.00
*	CATCH, THE A/P	49	149.00	275.00
*	CATCH, THE S/N H/S	750	100.00	200.00
*	HEAD TO HEAD EASY GOER & SUNDAY SILENCE	500	100.00	250.00
*	JOHN HENRY	750	75.00	275.00
*	MONTANA TO RICE A/P	49	300.00	400.00
*	MONTANTA TO RICE H/S S/N	500	250.00	300.00
*	PAEZ VS LOPEZ S/N	500	25.00	100.00
*	RONNIE LOTT H/S S/N	1049	149.00	225.00
*	SHOES ROSES A/P, THE	25	150.00	300.00
*	SHOES ROSES S/N, THE	500	50.00	200.00
*	WITAKER, TAYLER, CAMACHO AT CAESARS S/N	500	25.00	125.00

DENNIS P. LEWAN FINE ART STUDIOS

YR	NAME	LIMIT	ISSUE	TREND
	D. PATRICK LEWAN		**A/P CANVAS FRAMED**	
*	BEAR COTTAGE	30	505.00	1600.00
*	BEAR HAUS INN, THE	45	230.00	300.00
*	BEARLY EVE	40	410.00	975.00
*	GATE TO THE COURTYARD	30	230.00	245.00
*	GRANDMANOR	40	850.00	1250.00
*	KINGSBERRY COTTAGE	40	175.00	225.00
*	LITTLE BEAR COTTAGE	40	300.00	875.00
*	MANOR HOUSE, THE	40	500.00	2400.00
*	MEAGAN'S FRIENDS	30	230.00	250.00
*	MILL CREEK MANOR	40	525.00	725.00
*	OLDE AMSTERDAM	30	495.00	550.00
*	SEACLIFF COTTAGE	40	175.00	225.00
*	SPRING IN BAVARIA	30	155.00	285.00
*	VICTORIAN FANTASY	40	410.00	975.00
*	WENTWORTH COTTAGE	30	155.00	285.00
	D. PATRICK LEWAN		**A/P CANVAS UNFRAMED**	
*	BEAR COTTAGE	30	380.00	1475.00
*	BEAR HAUS INN, THE	45	190.00	260.00
*	BEARLY EVE	40	315.00	880.00
*	GATE TO THE COURTYARD	30	185.00	200.00
*	GRAND MANOR	40	725.00	1125.00
*	KINGSBERRY COTTAGE	40	145.00	195.00
*	LITTLE BEAR COTTAGE	40	250.00	825.00
*	MANOR HOUSE, THE	40	356.00	2256.00
*	MEAGAN'S FRIENDS	30	185.00	215.00
*	MILL CREEK MANOR	40	425.00	625.00
*	OLDE AMSTERDAM	30	270.00	320.00
*	SEACLIFF COTTAGE	40	145.00	195.00
*	SPRING IN BAVARIA	30	125.00	255.00
*	VICTORIAN FANTASY	40	315.00	880.00
*	WENTWORTH COTTAGE	30	125.00	255.00
	D. PATRICK LEWAN		**A/P PAPER FRAMED**	
*	BEAR COTTAGE	50	495.00	600.00
*	MANOR HOUSE, THE	55	430.00	500.00
	D. PATRICK LEWAN		**A/P PAPER UNFRAMED**	
*	BEAR COTTAGE	50	225.00	330.00
*	MANOR HOUSE, THE	55	175.00	245.00
	D. PATRICK LEWAN		**REMARQUES, PAPER FRAMED**	
*	BEAR COTTAGE	10	595.00	670.00
	D. PATRICK LEWAN		**REMARQUES, PAPER UNFRAMED**	
*	BEAR COTTAGE	10	325.00	400.00
	D. PATRICK LEWAN		**S/N CANVAS FRAMED**	
*	BEAR COTTAGE	300	430.00	1300.00
*	BEAR HAUS INN, THE	450	190.00	250.00
*	BEARLY EVE	375	260.00	900.00
*	GATE TO THE COURTYARD	300	200.00	220.00
*	GRAND MANOR	400	700.00	1100.00
*	KINGSBERRY COTTAGE	400	150.00	200.00
*	LITTLE BEAR COTTAGE	400	250.00	800.00
*	MANOR HOUSE, THE	400	440.00	1250.00
*	MEAGAN'S FRIENDS	300	200.00	250.00
*	MILL CREEK MANOR	375	450.00	650.00
*	OLDE AMSTERDAM	300	390.00	440.00
*	SEACLIFF COTTAGE	400	150.00	200.00
*	SPRING IN BAVARIA	300	130.00	260.00
*	VICTORIAN FANTASY	375	360.00	900.00
*	WENTWORTH COTTAGE	300	130.00	260.00
	D. PATRICK LEWAN		**S/N CANVAS UNFRAMED**	
*	BEAR COTTAGE	300	305.00	1175.00
*	BEAR HAUS INN, THE	450	150.00	220.00
*	BEARLY EVE	375	265.00	805.00
*	GATE TO THE COURTYARD	300	155.00	175.00
*	GRAND MANOR	400	575.00	975.00
*	KINGSBERRY COTTAGE	400	120.00	170.00
*	LITTLE BEAR COTTAGE	400	200.00	750.00
*	MANOR HOUSE, THE	400	296.00	1106.00
*	MEAGAN'S FRIENDS	300	155.00	180.00
*	MILL CREEK MANOR	375	350.00	550.00
*	SEACLIFF COTTAGE	400	120.00	170.00
*	SPRING IN BAVARIA	300	100.00	230.00
*	VICTORIAN FANTASY	375	265.00	805.00
*	WENTWORTH COTTAGE	300	100.00	230.00

YR	NAME	LIMIT	ISSUE	TREND
D. PATRICK LEWAN			**S/N PAPER FRAMED**	
*	BEAR COTTAGE	500	420.00	500.00
*	MANOR HOUSE, THE	550	380.00	425.00
D. PATRICK LEWAN			**S/N PAPER UNFRAMED**	
*	BEAR COTTAGE	500	150.00	230.00
*	MANOR HOUSE, THE	550	125.00	170.00
*	VICTORIAN FANTASY	500	150.00	175.00

DEPARTMENT 56

YR	NAME	LIMIT	ISSUE	TREND
J. KRAMER-COLE			**COLE CONCEPT**	
95	MAHTOLA	5000	125.00	125.00
J. KRAMER-COLE			**COLLECTORS**	
95	RED SHIELD, THE	950	235.00	235.00
J. KRAMER-COLE			**EMERGING IMAGE**	
95	TOPONAS	3850	185.00	185.00
96	FEATHER, THE	2850	185.00	185.00

DIMENSIONAL AESTHETICS

YR	NAME	LIMIT	ISSUE	TREND
B. HAILS				
85	GAZEBO, THE	*	40.00	65.00
86	BRIGHT NEW DAY	*	40.00	60.00
86	RIVER VISTA (THE GAP)	*	40.00	60.00
86	SOLITUDE	*	40.00	60.00
86	TAVERN, THE	*	40.00	65.00
87	CITY BREEZES	*	80.00	250.00
87	INDIAN SUMMER	*	40.00	60.00
87	LOCK, THE	*	95.00	95.00
87	QUIET LIGHT	*	40.00	60.00
88	AZALEA BANK A/P	*	90.00	130.00
89	AZALEA GLOW	*	40.00	40.00
89	TRACERY	*	40.00	50.00

EAGLE EDITIONS LTD.

YR	NAME	LIMIT	ISSUE	TREND
J. CRANDALL				
77	SMOKE UP AHEAD	450	60.00	750.00
79	I FOUND THE PASS	500	60.00	700.00
79	PURSUED	525	60.00	1000.00
80	ON TO TAOS	560	65.00	300.00
80	SHRINE TO THE BUFFALO	525	65.00	750.00
81	CAUTION	650	40.00	250.00
81	NOT ALONE	650	55.00	350.00
82	COUREURS DES BOIS	1000	85.00	300.00
83	AN EARLY SNOW	750	85.00	100.00
J. CRANDALL			**WINGS OF VALOR**	
85	MOUSE AND THE FLEA, THE: B-17	950	85.00	300.00
87	TOMCATS 2-FITTERS 0: F-14	950	85.00	800.00
89	BLOND KNIGHT, THE: ME 109	950	145.00	1500.00

EDNA HIBEL STUDIOS

YR	NAME	LIMIT	ISSUE	TREND
E. HIBEL			**HIBEL LITHOGRAPHY ON PORCELAIN**	
78	LENORE AND CHILD (ON PORCELAIN)	395	600.00	2100.00
80	CHERYLL AND WENDY (ON PORCELAIN)	100	3900.00	11500.00
E. HIBEL			**HIBEL STONE LITHOGRAPHY**	
*	BEGGAR	70	250.00	4700.00
74	MOTHER AND FOUR CHILDREN	60	150.00	1550.00
75	SANDY (STONE LITHO)	140	75.00	1550.00
76	ELSA & BABY	300	150.00	4200.00
76	JAPANESE DOLL	28	160.00	2600.00
76	KIKUE (SILK)	145	195.00	2700.00
76	MOTHER & FOUR CHILDREN (HORIZONTAL)	300	250.00	2000.00
76	SOPHIA & CHILDREN	296	325.00	4300.00
76	SWITZERLAND	270	350.00	2300.00
77	COLETTE & CHILD	275	195.00	1750.00
77	MAYAN MAN	295	350.00	4300.00
77	MUSEUM SUITE	375	1900.00	9700.00
78	FELICIA	148	900.00	3850.00
79	AKIKO & CHILDREN	335	450.00	2800.00
79	INTERNATIONAL YEAR OF THE CHILD SUITE	420	900.00	4200.00
79	JOSEPH	335	495.00	1325.00
79	NORA	394	175.00	850.00
79	PETRA MIT KINDER	320	345.00	4000.00
79	THAI PRINCESS	335	495.00	1450.00
80	CHERYLL & WENDY	100	3900.00	11500.00
80	CHO CHO SAN	396	500.00	1050.00
80	HOPE	396	400.00	1100.00
80	SPIRIT OF MAINAU SUITE, THE	385	1200.00	3150.00
80	TINA	200	750.00	1625.00
81	JACKLIN & CHILD	197	110.00	400.00
81	LITTLE EMPEROR, THE	275	1000.00	2250.00
81	LITTLE EMPRESS	319	1000.00	2100.00
82	BETTINA AND CHILDREN	300	310.00	1400.00
82	FAMILY OF THE MOUNTAIN LAKE	305	395.00	2900.00
82	JOELLE	348	295.00	1800.00
82	KELLY	347	320.00	1700.00
82	LYDIA	298	295.00	650.00

YR	NAME	LIMIT	ISSUE	TREND
82	NARO-SAN	322	310.00	675.00
82	RENA & RACHEL	329	345.00	1025.00
83	VALERIE & CHILDREN	400	295.00	625.00
84	ARIELLE & AMY	275	295.00	675.00
84	BEVERLY & CHILD	216	160.00	425.00
84	CARESS, THE	430	325.00	700.00
84	CELESTE	256	175.00	400.00
84	CLAIRE	206	335.00	975.00
84	DES FLEURS ROUGES	298	245.00	750.00
84	DORENE & CHILD	331	250.00	525.00
84	DREAM SKETCHBOOK	298	175.00	475.00
84	GERARD	200	250.00	725.00
84	JENNIFER & CHILDREN	318	445.00	775.00
84	NATASHA & CHILDREN	308	195.00	500.00
84	NAVA & CHILDREN	385	385.00	750.00
84	SANDY & CHILDREN	419	365.00	750.00
84	SARAH & JOSHUA	343	475.00	850.00
84	WENDY WITH HAT	308	395.00	725.00
85	LA TOSCA	355	595.00	725.00
86	BELINDA & NINA	320	295.00	625.00
86	DUCHESS	320	325.00	525.00
86	NANCY WITH MEGAN	367	450.00	900.00
87	FINNISH MOTHER & CHILD	343	185.00	325.00
87	FLOWERS OF KASHMIR	297	275.00	525.00
87	MONICA MATTEAO & VANESSA	300	350.00	650.00
87	ONCE UPON A TIME	287	365.00	550.00
88	AMELIA & CHILDREN	268	675.00	825.00
88	FLOWERS OF THE ADRIATIC	286	300.00	500.00
88	JOHN M	308	185.00	325.00
88	LINDA T	302	185.00	325.00
88	NEW HAT, THE	298	310.00	550.00
88	XIN-XIN OF THE HIGH MOUNTAINS	325	1300.00	2000.00
89	HELENE & CHILDREN	280	365.00	495.00
90	TAMARA	254	360.00	500.00

FANTASTIC ART

R. SPANGLER

YR	NAME	LIMIT	ISSUE	TREND
95	ALWAYS HAVE FRESH COOKIES FOR YOUR GUEST	950	20.00	20.00
95	CHERISH THE SMALL WONDERS OF LIFE	1100	20.00	20.00
95	DRAGONS' DREAM	1100	65.00	65.00
95	FANTAIL	950	20.00	20.00
95	FIREFLY FANTASY	1100	45.00	45.00
95	HEAVENLY COMPANION	950	36.00	36.00
95	HIDDEN TREASURE	950	30.00	30.00
95	HOME IS WHERE THE MAGIC IS	950	125.00	125.00
95	HOW MUCH WOULD I WEIGH?	950	36.00	36.00
95	I'M FOREVER BLOWING BUBBLES	950	24.00	24.00
95	MAKING TIME FOR SOMEONE SPECIAL	950	24.00	24.00
95	MILK MOUSTACHE	950	24.00	24.00
95	MONDAY MORNING	1100	40.00	40.00
95	MOUNTAIN DWARF	950	15.00	15.00
95	MYSTERY SHELF, THE	950	36.00	36.00
95	NO SMOKING IV	950	34.00	34.00
95	NOT ME!	950	36.00	36.00
95	ONCE AROUNT THE CASTLE	950	36.00	36.00
95	ROYAL GUARD	950	15.00	15.00
95	SANTA'S SURPRISE	950	30.00	30.00
95	SWORDSMAN, THE	950	15.00	15.00
95	TIMELY TASK	950	28.00	28.00
95	WINTER WARRIOR	950	15.00	15.00
95	YOU SCRUB MY BACK & I'LL SCRUB YOURS	950	36.00	36.00
96	WISHFUL THINKING	950	38.00	38.00

R. SPANGLER — **FAERIEL I**

YR	NAME	LIMIT	ISSUE	TREND
95	GUIDE, THE	950	25.00	25.00

R. SPANGLER — **FAERIEL II**

YR	NAME	LIMIT	ISSUE	TREND
95	GIFT, THE	950	25.00	25.00

FLAMBRO

B. LEIGHTON-JONES — **EMMETT KELLY JR. LITHOGRAPHS**

YR	NAME	LIMIT	ISSUE	TREND
94	70TH BIRTHDAY COMMEMORATIVE	YR	150.00	150.00
94	A PICTURE IS WORTH 1,000 WORDS	YR	90.00	95.00
94	I LOVE YOU	YR	90.00	95.00
94	JOYFUL NOISE	YR	90.00	95.00
95	ALL STAR CIRCUS	2 YR	150.00	150.00

FOR ARTS SAKE

B. ABBOTT

YR	NAME	LIMIT	ISSUE	TREND
95	BLUE JAY/FALL COLOR	900	25.00	25.00
95	CARDINAL/WINTER BERRIES	900	25.00	25.00
95	GOLD FINCH/SPRING GOLD	900	25.00	25.00
95	HUMMINGBIRDS/TRUMPET NECTAR	900	25.00	25.00

FOUNTAINHEAD

M. FERNANDEZ

YR	NAME	LIMIT	ISSUE	TREND
*	HEART OF SEVEN COLORS	*	*	950.00
*	MOST PRECIOUS GIFT	*	*	950.00
*	OH, SMALL CHILD	*	*	245.00
*	SPREADING THE WORD	*	*	100.00

FRAME HOUSE

C. HARPER

YR	NAME	LIMIT	ISSUE	TREND
*	ARCTIC CIRCLE-MUSKOX	*	*	175.00
*	BARK EYES-OWL	*	90.00	90.00
*	BIG RAC' ATTACK-RACCOON	*	*	125.00
*	BLACKBERRY JAM	*	90.00	90.00
*	CARDINAL COURTSHIP	*	175.00	300.00
*	CARDINAL CRADLE	*	175.00	175.00
*	CHRISTMAS CAPER	*	25.00	35.00
*	CLAIR DE LOON	*	175.00	200.00
*	CONFISKATION-ROBIN	*	90.00	100.00
*	CONVIVIAL PURSUIT	*	125.00	125.00
*	COTTONTAIL IN A COTTONFIELD-RABBIT	*	125.00	125.00
*	CRABITAT	*	125.00	125.00
*	DREAM TEAM	*	20.00	20.00
*	EVERGLADE KITE	*	*	250.00
*	FEARLESS FEATHERS	*	125.00	125.00
*	FLAMINGO A GO GO	*	150.00	185.00
*	FROG IN GRASS	*	*	250.00
*	GIFT RAPT-RACCOON	*	175.00	175.00
*	KOALA, KOALA-KOALA BEAR	*	*	20.00
*	LOVE ON A LIMB-MONKEY	*	125.00	200.00
*	LUCKY LADYBUG	*	8.00	25.00
*	MANATEE IN THE MANGROVE	*	195.00	195.00
*	MYSTERY OF THE MISSING MIGRANT-BIRD	*	*	30.00
*	OWLTERCATION	*	175.00	185.00
*	PACK PACT-MILL	*	175.00	175.00
*	PELICAN PANTRY	*	60.00	100.00
*	PISCINE QUEUES	*	125.00	200.00
*	QUAILSAFE	*	90.00	110.00
*	RACCROBAT	*	*	10.00
*	RACCSNACK-RACCOON	*	90.00	100.00
*	SQUIRREL IN A SQUALL	*	90.00	125.00
*	SUGAR FREE	*	125.00	155.00
*	TAILGATOR	*	125.00	170.00
*	UPSIDE DOWNY	*	125.00	145.00
*	WINGDING	*	90.00	90.00
68	HOUSE WRENS	500	20.00	175.00
68	LADYBUG	500	20.00	300.00
68	LADYBUG (LITHO)	10000	6.00	50.00
68	PORTFOLIO OF FOUR PRINTS	500	60.00	375.00
69	ANHINGA (LITHO ON CANVAS)	500	50.00	225.00
69	HUNGRY EYES	500	20.00	600.00
69	WATER STRIDER	500	40.00	475.00
70	BOBWHITE FAMILY	750	30.00	150.00
70	BURROWING OWL	500	30.00	100.00
70	CARDINAL (ON CORN)	500	30.00	400.00
70	CRAYFISH MOLTING	750	30.00	125.00
70	PILEATED WOODPECKER	750	30.00	150.00
71	BEETLE BATTLE	750	30.00	125.00
71	BLUE JAY BATHING	1500	30.00	110.00
71	LADYBUG LOVERS	1500	30.00	75.00
71	PUFFIN	750	30.00	140.00
71	RED-BELLIED WOODPECKER	1500	30.00	100.00
72	BEAR IN THE BIRCHES	1500	35.00	525.00
72	BOX TURTLE	1500	30.00	125.00
72	CHIPMUNK	1500	30.00	100.00
72	FAMILY OWLBUM	1500	30.00	125.00
72	PELICAN IN A DOWNPOUR	1500	30.00	400.00
72	YELLOW BELLIED SAPSUCKER	1500	30.00	110.00
73	LAST SUNFLOWER SEED, THE	1500	30.00	300.00
73	ROUND ROBIN	1500	30.00	75.00
73	WATERMELON MOON	1500	30.00	375.00
73	WEDDING FEAST	1500	30.00	115.00
73	WOOD DUCK	1500	30.00	350.00
74	BIRDS OF A FEATHER	2000	50.00	100.00
74	COOL CARDINAL	2000	30.00	435.00
74	CROW IN THE SNOW	1500	35.00	300.00
74	FINE FEATHER	1500	30.00	120.00
74	PAINTED BUNTING	1500	30.00	125.00
74	TALL TAIL	2000	30.00	100.00
75	BIRDWATCHER	2000	40.00	325.00
75	BLUEBIRDS IN THE BLUEGRASS	2000	45.00	80.00
75	PFWHOOOO	*	*	145.00
75	RACCPACK	2000	35.00	160.00
75	WHITECOAT	2000	30.00	200.00
76	CLAWS	2000	40.00	190.00
76	CORNPONE	2500	40.00	150.00
76	DEVOTION IN THE OCEAN	2000	40.00	100.00
76	LOVE FROM ABOVE	2000	40.00	375.00
76	SKIMMERSCAPE	2000	40.00	140.00
77	BRRRTHDAY	2500	40.00	90.00
77	CATNIP	2500	50.00	125.00
77	DOLFUN	2500	50.00	90.00
77	DOWN UNDER, DOWN UNDER	2500	40.00	80.00
77	PHANCY PHEATHERS	2500	50.00	175.00

YR	NAME	LIMIT	ISSUE	TREND
77	SEEING RED	2500	40.00	150.00
77	SKIPPING SCHOOL	2500	50.00	100.00
78	BITTERN SUITE	2500	50.00	100.00
78	CRAWLING TALL	3500	50.00	90.00
78	FROG EAT FROG	2500	50.00	75.00
78	HARE'S BREADTH	2500	50.00	100.00
78	LOVEY DOVEY	2500	50.00	150.00
79	BUZZ OFF YOU TURKEY	2500	55.00	100.00
79	COOL CARNIVORE	2500	50.00	80.00
79	FURRED FEEDER	2500	50.00	75.00
79	SERENGETI SPAGHETTI	2500	55.00	110.00
80	HEXIT	1500	60.00	90.00
80	JUMBRELLA	1500	60.00	100.00
80	POTLUCK	1500	60.00	120.00
80	REDBIRDS AND REDBUDS	1500	60.00	120.00
81	FOXSIMILES	1500	60.00	100.00
81	LAST APHID	1500	60.00	135.00
81	RACC & RUIN	1500	60.00	125.00
81	ROMANCE ON THE RICHTER SCALE-WHALE	1500	60.00	140.00
82	ARMADITTO	1500	60.00	90.00
82	PRICKLEY PAIR	1500	60.00	300.00
82	TERN, STONES, AND TURNSTONES	1500	60.00	85.00
84	GREEN CUISINE	1000	90.00	110.00
84	PIER GROUP	1000	90.00	380.00
84	RACCOONNAISSANCE	1000	90.00	120.00
85	HERONDIPITY	500	175.00	300.00
85	VOWLENTINE	1000	45.00	140.00
86	B-R-R-R-R-R-DBATH	1000	125.00	170.00
86	BRRRRRDBATH	*	125.00	175.00
86	LOONRISE-LOON DUCK	500	175.00	200.00
J. HARRISON				
74	RURAL AMERICANA	1500	40.00	350.00
75	AMERICAN BYWAYS	1500	40.00	330.00
75	COUNTRY SEASONIN'	1500	40.00	300.00
75	DISAPPEARING AMERICA	1500	40.00	1400.00
76	RURAL DELIVERY	1500	40.00	400.00
76	YESTERYEAR	1500	50.00	210.00
77	BURMA SHAVE	1500	50.00	300.00
77	COMMUNITY CHURCH	1500	50.00	230.00
77	DR. PEPPER	1500	50.00	300.00
77	FALLOW AND FORGOTTON	1500	50.00	200.00
78	666 COLD TABLETS	1500	50.00	270.00
78	PHILIP MORRIS	1500	50.00	280.00
78	RC COLA	975	135.00	135.00
78	RED COVERED BRIDGE	1500	50.00	300.00
78	TOOLS	300	275.00	450.00
78	WOODPILE	1500	75.00	175.00
79	CLABBER GIRL	1500	75.00	350.00
79	GOLD DUST TWINS	1500	55.00	180.00
79	GOODY'S	1500	50.00	180.00
79	LUCKY STRIKE	1500	50.00	300.00
80	PEANUTS AND PEPSI	1500	60.00	270.00
80	TONIC AND LINIMENT	1500	85.00	225.00
80	TUBE ROSE SNUFF	1500	60.00	180.00
80	UNPAINTED COVERED BRIDGE	1500	60.00	200.00
81	7-UP AND BLACK EYED SUSANS	1500	75.00	200.00
81	BRUSH AND BUCKET	300	300.00	350.00
81	HOUSE AND BARN	1500	50.00	235.00
81	OLD DUTCH CLEANSER	1500	75.00	200.00
82	BULL OF THE WOODS	1500	75.00	115.00
82	RAILROAD CROSSING	1500	75.00	300.00
82	WINDMILL	1500	75.00	140.00
83	FILLIN' STATION	1500	80.00	200.00
83	FRESH GRITS	1500	80.00	860.00
83	LEE OVERALLS	OP	7.50	20.00
83	LIGHTHOUSE	975	135.00	315.00
83	MOUNTAIN BRIDGE	1500	80.00	300.00
83	SHRINE CIRCUS	1500	80.00	80.00
84	MEMORIES	408	90.00	200.00
84	MORTON SALT AND ROCK CITY	1500	135.00	240.00
84	RED GOOSE SHOES	1500	90.00	90.00
85	MEMORIES II	431	90.00	200.00
85	OLD STONE BARN	1500	90.00	150.00
85	SPRING CLOUDS	1500	90.00	180.00
86	FISHING VILLAGE	975	135.00	280.00
87	COCA-COLA BRIDGE	975	135.00	468.00
87	JEFFERSON ISLAND SALT	975	135.00	160.00
87	UNCLE JOHN'S SYRUP	975	135.00	200.00
88	HERSHEY BAR	975	135.00	200.00
88	RED BOAT	975	135.00	200.00
A. HUNT				
84	LAZY AFTERNOON	1500	75.00	250.00
85	FOX IN REEDS	1500	75.00	320.00
86	SNOW LEOPARD	1000	150.00	380.00
88	DAWN ALERT	TL	160.00	430.00

GARTLAN USA

J. MARTIN				**LITHOGRAPH**
86	GEORGE BRETT: THE SWING	2000	85.00	85.00

YR	NAME	LIMIT	ISSUE	TREND
C. SOILEAU				**LITHOGRAPH**
87	ROGER STAUBACH	1979	85.00	85.00
M. TAYLOR				**LITHOGRAPH**
89	KAREEM ABDUL-JABBAR: THE RECORD SETTER	1989	85.00	300.00
90	DARRYL STRAWBERRY	500	295.00	295.00
91	JOE MONTANA, SIGNED, H/S	500	495.00	545.00

GOEBEL INC.

YR	NAME	LIMIT	ISSUE	TREND
M.I. HUMMEL		**BAVARIAN VILLAGE COLLECTION**		
96	DUET	RT	280.00	280.00

GREENWICH WORKSHOP

YR	NAME	LIMIT	ISSUE	TREND
J. CHRISTENSEN				**CHRISTENSEN**
*	ANGEL WITH FISH	*	*	275.00
*	BIRDS HUNTERS FULL CAMO.	*	*	165.00
*	COLLEGE MAGIC	*	*	650.00
*	FISH WATER	*	*	3200.00
85	GIFT FOR MRS. CLAUS, THE	3500	80.00	675.00
86	JONAH	850	95.00	300.00
86	OLDE WORLD SANTA	3500	80.00	575.00
86	YOUR PLACE, OR MINE?	850	125.00	200.00
87	OLD MAN WITH ALOT ON HIS MIND	850	85.00	675.00
87	VOYAGE OF THE BASSET	850	225.00	1900.00
88	MAN WHO MINDS THE MOON, THE	850	145.00	700.00
88	WIDOW'S MITE, THE	850	145.00	2500.00
89	ANNUNCIATION, THE	850	175.00	175.00
90	BURDEN OF THE RESPONSIBLE MAN, THE	850	145.00	1600.00
90	RHYMES & REASONS	OP	150.00	675.00
90	TWO SISTERS	650	325.00	300.00
91	CANDLEMAN, THE	850	160.00	225.00
91	LAWRENCE AND A BEAR	850	145.00	400.00
91	ONCE UPON A TIME	1500	175.00	1900.00
91	ONCE UPON A TIME (REMARQUE)	500	375.00	2100.00
91	PELICAN KING	850	115.00	450.00
92	OLDEST ANGEL, THE	850	125.00	715.00
92	RESPONSIBLE WOMAN, THE	2500	175.00	280.00
92	ROYAL PROCESSIONAL, THE	1500	185.00	550.00
92	ROYAL PROCESSIONAL, THE, REMARQUE	1500	185.00	850.00
93	COLLEGE OF MAGICAL KNOWLEDGE	4500	250.00	450.00
93	GETTING IT RIGHT	4000	185.00	200.00
93	ROYAL MUSIC BARQUE, THE	2750	375.00	375.00
93	SCHOLAR, THE	3250	125.00	125.00
93	WAITING FOR THE TIDE	2250	150.00	150.00
B. DOOLITTLE				**DOOLITTLE**
*	GHOST OF THE GRIZZLY	*	*	3500.00
*	GRIZZLY TREE	*	*	3500.00
79	PINTOS	1000	65.00	11500.00
80	BUGGED BEAR	1000	85.00	3500.00
80	GOOD OMEN, THE	1000	85.00	4250.00
80	WHOO!?	1000	75.00	1800.00
81	SPIRIT OF THE GRIZZLY	1500	150.00	4600.00
81	UNKNOWN PRESENCE	1500	135.00	3400.00
81	WOODLAND ENCOUNTER	1500	145.00	11000.00
82	EAGLE'S FLIGHT	1500	185.00	3900.00
83	CHRISTMAS DAY, GIVE OR TAKE A WEEK	4800	80.00	2300.00
83	ESCAPE BY A HARE	1500	80.00	950.00
83	RUNS WITH THUNDER	1500	150.00	2100.00
83	RUSHING WAR EAGLE	1500	150.00	1850.00
84	LET MY SPIRIT SOAR	1500	195.00	7650.00
85	TWO INDIAN HORSES	12253	225.00	3650.00
85	WOLVES OF THE CROW	2650	225.00	2450.00
86	TWO BEARS OF THE BLACKFEET	2650	225.00	1600.00
86	WHERE SILENCE SPEAKS, ART OF DOOLITTLE	3500	650.00	3500.00
87	CALLING THE BUFFALO	8500	245.00	1550.00
87	GUARDIAN SPIRITS	13238	295.00	1400.00
87	SEASON OF THE EAGLE	36548	245.00	1000.00
88	DOUBLED BACK	15000	285.00	1850.00
89	SACRED GROUND	70000	265.00	925.00
90	HIDE AND SEEK SUITE	25000	900.00	1980.00
90	HIDE AND SEEK-7 PC. COMP SET	RT	1200.00	1200.00
90	HIDE AND SEEK-LG	RT	300.00	300.00
90	HIDE AND SEEK-MINI	*	*	250.00
91	SACRED CIRCLE	*	265.00	450.00
91	SACRED CIRCLE (PC)	40192	325.00	1540.00
91	SENTINEL, THE	35000	275.00	825.00
92	EAGLE HEART	48000	285.00	345.00
92	EAGLE HEART	*	285.00	285.00
93	PRAYER FOR THE WILD THINGS	*	325.00	450.00
93	WILDERNESS...WILDERNESS!	RT	65.00	65.00
94	WHEN THE WIND HAD WINGS	*	325.00	325.00
95	TWO MORE INDIAN HORSES	48000	225.00	345.00
J. CHRISTENSEN				**ETCHING**
*	ARTIST, THE	*	*	450.00
*	GIFT, THE	*	*	350.00
*	OLD ANGEL	*	*	350.00
*	WIZARD	*	*	50.00

YR	NAME	LIMIT	ISSUE	TREND
J. CHRISTENSEN				**FANTASY**
94	EVENING ANGELS	4000	195.00	195.00
94	SOMETIMES THE SPIRIT..W/BOOK	3600	195.00	195.00
94	TWO ANGEL DISCUSS BOTTICELI	2950	145.00	145.00
95	PISCATORIAL PERCUSSIONIST	3000	125.00	125.00
95	SERENADE FOR AN ORANGE CAT	3000	125.00	125.00
95	SISTERS OF THE SEA	2000	195.00	195.00
J. CHRISTENSEN				**FANTASY/ETCHING**
*	FISH WATER	*	*	300.00
*	FISHE	*	*	325.00
*	MECHANICAL FISH	*	*	300.00
*	MIDNIGHT SCHOLAR	*	*	350.00
*	MUSICIAN	*	*	300.00
J. CHRISTENSEN				**FANTASY/LITHO**
*	ANGEL IN PURSUIT FISH KNOW.	*	*	300.00
*	CONVERSATION AROUND FISH	*	*	600.00
*	FISH ANGEL	*	*	400.00
B. DOOLITTLE				**HORSE**
*	HIDE AND SEEK-NUM MINI-1C	*	*	150.00
*	HIDE AND SEEK-NUM MINI-2A	*	*	150.00
*	HIDE AND SEEK-NUM MINI-2C	*	*	150.00
*	HIDE AND SEEK-NUM MINI-3B	*	*	150.00
*	HIDE AND SEEK-NUM MINI-3D	*	*	150.00
B. DOOLITTLE				**INDIAN**
84	FOREST HAS EYES, THE	RT	175.00	5250.00
F. MCCARTHY				**INDIAN**
92	NAVAJO PONIES FOR COMANCHE	1000	225.00	310.00
92	WHEN THE LAND WAS THEIRS	1000	225.00	225.00
92	WHERE OTHERS HAD PASSED	1000	245.00	380.00
93	IN THE LAND OF ANCIENT ONES	1250	245.00	350.00
93	SIGHTING THE INTRUDERS	1000	225.00	350.00
94	SHOW OF DEFIANCE	1000	195.00	195.00
94	WAY OF ANCIENT MIGRATION	1250	245.00	245.00
S. LYMAN				**LANDSCAPE**
93	LAKE OF THE SHINING ROCKS-LANDSCAPE	*	235.00	350.00
94	NORTH COUNTRY SHORES-LANDSCAPE	*	225.00	225.00
95	CATHEDRAL SNOW-LANDSCAPE	4000	245.00	245.00
J. CHRISTENSEN				**LITHO**
*	COPADEORA	*	*	350.00
S. LYMAN				**LYMAN**
*	BIG COUNTRY, THE-GRIZZLY	*	*	20.00
83	EARLY WINTER IN THE MOUNTAINS	850	95.00	400.00
83	END OF THE RIDGE	850	95.00	800.00
83	PASS, THE	850	95.00	850.00
84	FREE FLIGHT	850	70.00	130.00
84	NOISY NEIGHBORS (R)	25	95.00	900.00
85	AUTUMN GATHERING-LANDSCAPE	850	115.00	250.00
85	BEAR & BLOSSOMS-BLACK BEAR	850	75.00	550.00
86	COLORS OF TWILIGHT	850	75.00	460.00
86	HIGH TRAIL AT SUNSET-MOUNTAIN GOAT	1000	125.00	600.00
86	MORNING SOLITUDE-GREY BLUE HERON	850	115.00	1000.00
86	SNOWY THRONE (C)	850	85.00	400.00
87	AN ELEGANT COUPLE	1000	125.00	250.00
87	CANADIAN AUTUMN-MOOSE	1500	165.00	200.00
87	ELEGANT COUPLE-WOOD DUCK	1000	125.00	150.00
87	HIGH CREEK CROSSING-BISON	1000	165.00	950.00
87	MOON SHADOWS-CANADA GOOSE	1500	135.00	150.00
87	NEW TERRITORY-GRIZZLY BEAR	*	135.00	225.00
87	TWILIGHT SNOW-BLUE JAY	950	85.00	250.00
88	INTRUDER, THE	1500	150.00	150.00
88	RAPTOR'S WATCH, THE-EAGLE	1500	150.00	300.00
88	RETURN OF THE FALCON	1500	150.00	150.00
88	SNOW HUNTER-BOBCAT	1500	135.00	135.00
88	UZUMATI: GREAT BEAR OF YOSEMITE	1750	150.00	150.00
89	COLOR IN THE SNOW-PHEASANT	1500	165.00	165.00
89	HIGH LIGHT	1250	165.00	480.00
89	LAST LIGHT OF WINTER-CANADA GOOSE	1500	175.00	1200.00
89	QUIET RAIN-CANADA GOOSE	1500	165.00	525.00
90	A MOUNTAIN CAMPFIRE	1500	195.00	2850.00
90	AMONG THE WILD BRAMBLES-KESTREL	1750	185.00	225.00
90	EVENING LIGHT	2500	225.00	1800.00
90	SILENT SNOWS-WOLF	1750	210.00	325.00
91	DANCE OF CLOUD AND CLIFF-LANDSCAPE	1500	225.00	375.00
91	DANCE OF WATER AND LIGHT	*	225.00	200.00
91	EMBERS AT DAWN	3500	225.00	1600.00
91	RIVER OF LIGHT	*	225.00	225.00
91	SECRET WATCH-LYNX	2250	150.00	150.00
92	WARMED BY THE VIEW-CAMPFIRE	8500	235.00	325.00
92	WILDERNESS WELCOME	*	235.00	595.00
92	WILDFLOWER SUITE	*	175.00	175.00
92	WOODLAND HAVEN-ELK	2500	195.00	195.00
93	FIRE DANCE-CAMPFIRE	*	235.00	350.00
93	RIPARIAN RICHES-G/B HERON	*	235.00	235.00
93	SPIRIT OF CHRISTMAS-SANTA	RT	165.00	300.00
94	MOONFIRE	*	245.00	750.00
94	MOONLIT FLIGHT,CHRISTMAS	*	165.00	290.00
94	NEW KID ON THE ROCK-OTTER	*	185.00	185.00

YR	NAME	LIMIT	ISSUE	TREND
95	MIDNIGHT FIRE	8500	245.00	245.00
95	THUNDERBOLT	7000	235.00	235.00
F. MCCARTHY				**MCCARTHY**
74	HUNT, THE	1000	75.00	1000.00
74	LONE SENTINEL	1000	55.00	1500.00
74	LONG COLUMN	1000	75.00	1300.00
74	NIGHT THEY NEEDED A GOOD RIBBON MAN, THE	1000	65.00	300.00
75	RETURNING RAIDERS	1000	75.00	460.00
75	SMOKE WAS THEIR ALLY	1000	75.00	510.00
75	SURVIVOR, THE	1000	65.00	450.00
75	WAITING FOR THE ESCORT	1000	75.00	275.00
76	HOSTILES, THE	1000	55.00	700.00
76	PACKING IN	1000	65.00	700.00
76	SIOUX WARRIORS	650	55.00	550.00
76	WARRIOR, THE	650	55.00	500.00
77	AN OLD TIME MOUNTAIN MAN	1000	65.00	3000.00
77	BEAVER MEN, THE	1000	75.00	590.00
77	COMANCHE MOON	1000	75.00	340.00
77	DISTANT THUNDER	1500	75.00	1000.00
77	DUST STAINED POSSE	1000	75.00	900.00
77	ROBE SIGNAL	850	60.00	550.00
78	AMBUSH, THE	1000	125.00	375.00
78	BEFORE THE NORTHER	1000	90.00	550.00
78	FORDING, THE	1000	75.00	350.00
78	IN THE PASS	1500	90.00	190.00
78	NIGHT CROSSING	1000	75.00	450.00
78	SINGLE FILE	1000	75.00	600.00
78	TO BATTLE	1000	75.00	650.00
79	LONER, THE	1000	75.00	500.00
79	ON THE WARPATH	1000	75.00	300.00
79	PRAYER, THE	1500	90.00	650.00
79	RETREAT TO HIGHER GROUND	2000	90.00	830.00
80	A TIME OF DECISION	1150	125.00	310.00
80	BEFORE THE CHARGE	1000	115.00	300.00
80	BURNING THE WAY STATION	1000	125.00	450.00
80	FORBIDDEN LAND	1000	125.00	300.00
80	ROAR OF THE NORTHER	1000	90.00	350.00
80	SNOW MOON	1000	115.00	475.00
80	TROOPER, THE	1000	90.00	300.00
81	COUP, THE	1000	125.00	440.00
81	CROSSING THE DIVIDE/THE OLD WEST	1500	850.00	1900.00
81	HEADED NORTH	1000	150.00	370.00
81	RACE WITH THE HOSTILES	1000	135.00	150.00
81	SURROUNDED	1000	150.00	300.00
81	UNDER HOSTILE FIRE	1000	150.00	240.00
82	ALERT	1000	135.00	175.00
82	APACHE SCOUT	1000	165.00	225.00
82	ATTACK ON THE WAGON TRAIN	1400	150.00	400.00
82	CHALLENGE, THE	1000	175.00	500.00
82	WARRIORS, THE	1000	150.00	200.00
83	BLACKFEET RAIDERS	1000	90.00	340.00
83	IN THE LAND OF THE SPARROW HAWK PEOPLE	1000	165.00	250.00
83	MOONLIT TRAIL	1000	90.00	270.00
83	OUT OF THE MIST THEY CAME	1000	165.00	300.00
83	UNDER ATTACK	5076	125.00	920.00
84	AFTER THE DUST STORM	1000	145.00	275.00
84	ALONG THE WEST FORK	1000	175.00	320.00
84	DECOYS, THE	450	325.00	690.00
84	SAVAGE TAUNT, THE	1000	225.00	400.00
84	WATCHING THE WAGONS	1400	175.00	750.00
84	WHIRLING HE RACED TO MEET THE CHALLENGE	1000	175.00	790.00
85	CHARGING THE CHALLENGER	1000	150.00	875.00
85	FIREBOAT, THE	1000	175.00	175.00
85	LAST CROSSING, THE	550	350.00	550.00
85	LONG KNIVES, THE	1000	175.00	1290.00
85	SCOUTING THE LONG KNIVES	1400	195.00	390.00
85	TRADERS, THE	1000	195.00	195.00
86	CHILDREN OF THE RAVEN	1000	185.00	980.00
86	COMANCHE WAR TRAIL	1000	165.00	165.00
86	DRIVE, THE	1000	95.00	190.00
86	RED BULL'S WAR PARTY	1000	165.00	160.00
86	SPOOKED	1400	195.00	300.00
86	WHERE TRACKS WILL BE LOST	550	350.00	500.00
87	CHIRICAHUA RAIDERS	1000	165.00	300.00
87	FOLLOWING THE HERDS	1000	195.00	670.00
87	FROM THE RIM	1000	225.00	250.00
87	IN THE LAND OF THE WINTER HAWK	1000	225.00	550.00
87	WHEN OMENS TURN BAD	1000	165.00	770.00
88	APACHE TRACKERS	1000	95.00	150.00
88	BUFFALO RUNNERS, THE	1000	195.00	300.00
88	HOSTILE LAND, THE	1000	225.00	225.00
88	IN PURSUIT OF THE WHITE BUFFALO	1500	225.00	950.00
88	LAST STAND, THE: LITTLE BIG HORN	2250	225.00	225.00
88	SABER CHARGE	2250	225.00	275.00
88	TURNING THE LEADERS	1500	225.00	275.00
89	BIG MEDICINE	1000	225.00	580.00
89	CANYON LANDS	1250	225.00	250.00
89	COMING OF THE IRON HORSE, THE	1500	225.00	300.00
89	COMING OF/IRON HORSE, THE (PRINT/PEWTER)	100	1500.00	3600.00

YR	NAME	LIMIT	ISSUE	TREND
89	DOWN FROM THE MOUNTAINS	1500	245.00	240.00
89	LOS DIABLOS	1250	225.00	275.00
90	BELOW THE BREAKING DAWN	1250	225.00	225.00
90	HOKA HEY: SIOUX WAR CRY	1250	225.00	225.00
90	ON THE OLD NORTH TRAIL	*	550.00	1000.00
90	OUT OF THE WINDSWEPT RAMPARTS	1250	225.00	225.00
90	WINTER TRAIL	1500	235.00	235.00
91	PONY EXPRESS	1000	225.00	225.00
91	PURSUIT, THE	650	550.00	550.00
91	WILD ONES, THE	1000	225.00	225.00
93	SHADOWS OF THE WARRIORS	*	225.00	350.00
F. MCCARTHY				**WESTERN**
*	CHARGE OF BUFFALO SOLDIERS	*	*	195.00
*	SPLITTING THE HERD	*	*	465.00
91	CHASE, THE	1000	225.00	225.00
92	BREAK'G THE MOONLIT SILENCE	650	375.00	400.00
92	HEADING BACK	1000	225.00	225.00
92	WHERE ANCIENT ONES HUNTED	1000	245.00	350.00
93	BY ANICENT TRAILS THEY PASS	1000	245.00	245.00
93	WITH PISTOLS DRAWN	1000	195.00	350.00
94	BENEATH THE CLIFF OF SPIRIT	1500	295.00	295.00
94	FLASHES OF LIGHTNING	550	435.00	435.00
C. WYSOCKI				**WYSOCKI**
*	HOME SWEET HOME	*	*	25.00
*	LOST IN THE WOODIES	*	*	195.00
*	MABEL THE STOWAWAY	*	*	175.00
*	MABEL THE STOWAWAY/CANVAS	*	*	495.00
*	MABEL THE STOWAWAY/FRAMED	*	*	*
*	OLD BUCKS COUNTY	*	*	275.00
*	REMINGTON THE HORTICULTWIST	*	*	400.00
*	ROOT BEAR BREAK/BUTTERFIELD	*	*	160.00
*	SMALL TOWN CHRISTMAS	*	*	145.00
79	BUTTERNUT FARMS	1000	75.00	1500.00
79	FAIRHAVEN BY THE SEA	1000	75.00	1300.00
79	FOX RUN	1000	75.00	1500.00
79	SHALL WE?	1000	75.00	500.00
80	CALEB'S BUGGY BARN	1000	80.00	500.00
80	DERBY SQUARE	1000	90.00	1200.00
80	JOLLY HILL FARMS	1000	75.00	950.00
81	CARVER COGGINS	1000	145.00	1100.00
81	OLDE AMERICA	1500	125.00	850.00
81	PAGE'S BAKE SHOPPE	1000	115.00	550.00
81	PRAIRIE WIND FLOWERS	1000	125.00	2000.00
82	CARNIVAL CAPERS	620	200.00	200.00
82	CHRISTMAS PRINT, 1982	2000	80.00	900.00
82	NANTUCKET, THE	1000	145.00	400.00
82	SLEEPY TOWN WEST	1500	150.00	490.00
82	SUNSET HILLS, TEXAS WILDCATTERS	1000	125.00	200.00
83	AMISH NEIGHBORS	1000	150.00	750.00
83	APPLE BUTTER MAKERS	1000	135.00	800.00
83	COMMEMORATIVE PRINT	2000	55.00	100.00
83	COUNTRY RACE	1000	150.00	300.00
83	PLUM ISLAND SOUND POSTER	OP	40.00	40.00
83	TEA BY THE SEA	1000	145.00	1500.00
84	A WARM CHRISTMAS LOVE	3951	80.00	400.00
84	BIRD HOUSE	1000	85.00	380.00
84	CAPE COD COLD FISH PARTY	1000	150.00	225.00
84	CHUMBUDDIES SIGNED	1000	55.00	80.00
84	COMMEMORATIVE PRINT	2000	55.00	65.00
84	COTTON COUNTRY	1000	150.00	250.00
84	FOXY FOX OUTFOXES THE FOX HUNTERS, THE	1500	150.00	500.00
84	GANG'S ALL HERE, THE W/REM	250	90.00	90.00
84	GANG'S ALL HERE, THE/TEDDY BEAR	OP	65.00	65.00
84	STORIN' UP	450	325.00	1400.00
84	SWEETHEART CHESSMATE	1000	95.00	350.00
84	WARM CHRISTMAS LOVE	3950	80.00	450.00
84	YANKEE WINK HOLLOW	1000	95.00	1400.00
85	BIRDS OF A FEATHER	1250	145.00	350.00
85	CLAMMERS AT HODGE'S HORN	1000	150.00	1300.00
85	COMMEMORATIVE PRINT	2000	55.00	60.00
85	DEVILSTONE HARBOR/AN AMERICAN CELEB.	3500	195.00	500.00
85	I LOVE AMERICA	2000	20.00	20.00
85	MERRYMAKERS SERENADE	1250	135.00	135.00
85	SALTY WITCH BAY	475	350.00	2500.00
86	COMMEMORATIVE PRINT	*	55.00	80.00
86	DADDY'S COMING HOME	1250	150.00	1400.00
86	DANCING PHEASANT FARMS	1750	165.00	450.00
86	DEVILBELLY BAY	1000	145.00	375.00
86	HICKORY HAVEN CANAL	1500	165.00	950.00
86	LADY LIBERTY INDEPENDENCE DAY	1500	140.00	300.00
86	MR. SWALLOBARK	2000	145.00	550.00
87	BACH'S MAGNIFICAT IN D MINOR	2250	150.00	1200.00
87	DAHALIA DINALHAVEN MAKES A DORY DEAL	2250	150.00	250.00
87	TWAS THE TWILIGHT BEFORE CHRISTMAS	7500	95.00	165.00
87	YEARNING FOR MY CAPTAIN	2000	150.00	350.00
87	YOU'VE BEEN SO LONG AT SEA, HORATIO	2500	150.00	225.00
88	AMERICANA BOWL, THE	3500	295.00	350.00
88	FEATHERED CRITICS	2500	150.00	150.00
88	HOME IS MY SAILOR	2500	150.00	150.00

YR	NAME	LIMIT	ISSUE	TREND
89	ANOTHER YEAR AT SEA	2500	175.00	800.00
89	BOSTONIANS AND BEANS	6711	225.00	700.00
89	CHRISTMAS GREETING	11000	125.00	150.00
89	DREAMERS	3000	175.00	325.00
89	FUN LOVIN' SILLY FOLKS	3000	185.00	360.00
89	MEMORY MAKER, THE	2500	165.00	165.00
90	BELLY WARMERS	2500	150.00	180.00
90	JINGLE BELL TEDDY AND FRIENDS	5000	125.00	125.00
90	ROBIN HOOD	2000	165.00	165.00
90	WEDNESDAY NIGHT CHECKERS	2500	175.00	175.00
90	WHERE THE BOUYS ARE	2750	175.00	175.00
91	BEAUTY AND THE BEAST	2000	125.00	125.00
91	ROCKLAND BREAKWATER LIGHT	2500	165.00	300.00
91	SEA CAPTAIN'S WIFE ABIDING	1500	150.00	150.00
91	WEST QUODDY HEAD LIGHT	2500	165.00	165.00
91	WHISTLE STOP CHRISTMAS	5000	125.00	125.00
92	ETHEL THE GOURMET-CAT	10180	150.00	385.00
92	FREDERICK THE LITERATE-CAT	6500	150.00	2550.00
92	GAY HEAD LIGHT/LIGHTHOUSE	2500	165.00	165.00
92	LOVE LETTER FROM LARAMIE	1500	150.00	150.00
92	PROUD LITTLE ANGLER	2750	150.00	190.00
93	THREE SISTERS OF NAUSET/LIGHTHOUSE	2500	165.00	165.00

GUILDHALL INC.

W. BAIZE

YR	NAME	LIMIT	ISSUE	TREND
88	BEST OF FRIENDS	575	85.00	175.00
88	WINTER ARRIVAL	575	85.00	95.00

C. DEHAAN

YR	NAME	LIMIT	ISSUE	TREND
75	THREE OF A KIND	1000	30.00	140.00
79	FOGGY MORNIN' WAIT	650	75.00	2000.00
80	CIRCLE, THE	1000	30.00	140.00
80	TEXAS PANHANDLE	650	75.00	1250.00
81	FORGIN' THE KEECHI	85	650.00	380.00
81	MAC TAVISH	650	65.00	1480.00
81	SURPRISE ENCOUNTER	750	85.00	199.00
82	O' THAT STRAWBERRY ROAN	750	85.00	384.00
83	CROSSIN' HORSE CREEK	650	100.00	320.00
83	KEEP A MOVIN' DAN	750	85.00	200.00
83	RIDIN' OL' PAINT	750	85.00	1000.00
83	TWO OLD RENEGADES	150	150.00	3600.00
84	JAKE	650	100.00	450.00
84	SPOOKED	650	95.00	1400.00
85	HORSEMEN OF THE WEST (SUITE OF 3)	650	145.00	750.00
85	KEECHI COUNTRY	750	100.00	180.00
85	OKLAHOMA PAINTS	750	100.00	420.00
85	UP THE CHISHOLM	750	85.00	200.00
86	LONER, THE (W/BELT BUCKLE)	750	145.00	640.00
86	MOON DANCERS	750	100.00	220.00
86	MUSTANGERS, THE	750	100.00	440.00
86	SEARCHERS, THE	650	100.00	270.00
87	CROW CEREMONIAL DRESS	750	100.00	220.00
87	MURPHY'S LAW	750	100.00	350.00
87	SNOW BIRDS	750	100.00	350.00
87	SUPREMECY	750	100.00	250.00
87	WINTER SONGSINGER	750	95.00	190.00
88	MORNIN' GATHER	750	100.00	350.00
88	STAGE TO DEADWOOD	750	100.00	300.00
88	WATER BREAKIN'	750	125.00	675.00
89	CROWS	800	135.00	550.00
89	KENTUCKY BLUE	750	125.00	650.00
89	QUARTER HORSE, THE	800	125.00	300.00
89	VILLAGE MARKERS	750	125.00	500.00
90	CROW AUTUMN	925	135.00	260.00
90	ESCAPE	925	135.00	200.00
90	HIGH PLAINS DRIFTERS	925	140.00	200.00
90	WAR CRY	750	125.00	300.00
91	ENCOUNTER, THE	925	140.00	300.00
91	PIPE CARRIER, THE	925	140.00	260.00
91	PRIDEFUL ONES, THE	925	150.00	200.00
91	SUNDANCE	925	140.00	180.00
92	73 DEGREES IN AMARILLO...YESTERDAY	925	140.00	195.00
92	CROSSING AT THE BIG TREES	925	140.00	200.00
92	SILENT TRAIL TALK	925	140.00	175.00

B. MOLINE

YR	NAME	LIMIT	ISSUE	TREND
88	COMPANIONS	575	85.00	185.00
88	PROTRAYING HIS HERITAGE	575	85.00	185.00

GUND INC.

H.D. MICHAEL — FLIGHTS OF FANTASY

YR	NAME	LIMIT	ISSUE	TREND
95	A NEW DAY	1500	89.00	89.00
95	KAPUT!	1500	89.00	89.00
95	TALLY HO!	1500	89.00	89.00

HADLEY COMPANIES

A. AGNEW

YR	NAME	LIMIT	ISSUE	TREND
95	BOY'S CLUB, THE	999	125.00	125.00
95	CHILD'S PLAY	999	100.00	100.00

The canvas edition of Cedar Nook Cottage *by Thomas Kinkade beckons the weary traveler. Limited to 1,960, it was released by Lightpost Publishing in 1991 for $315.*

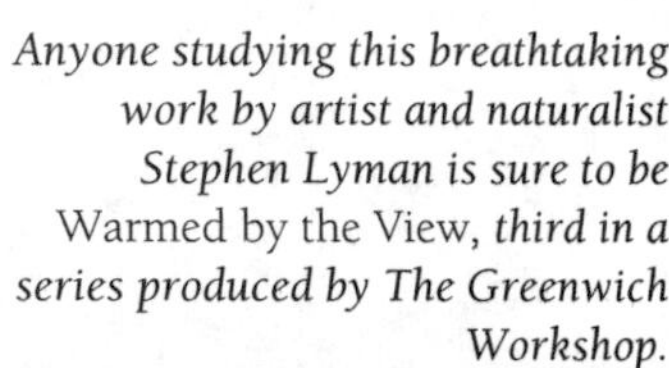

Anyone studying this breathtaking work by artist and naturalist Stephen Lyman is sure to be Warmed by the View, *third in a series produced by The Greenwich Workshop.*

Ozz França masterfully paints the beauty of a Native American couple locked in a warm embrace. The Lovers *is part of a series produced by Hadley House.*

YR	NAME	LIMIT	ISSUE	TREND
	J. BANOVICH			
95	FOLLOWING THE TRACKS	999	125.00	125.00
95	PATRIARCH, THE	750	125.00	125.00
95	RETURN, THE	999	125.00	125.00
	D. BARNHOUSE			
95	AMERICAN MADE	1250	125.00	125.00
95	BRAGGING RIGHTS	1250	125.00	125.00
95	FRIDAY EVENING	999	100.00	100.00
95	LAST CHORE OF THE DAY	1250	150.00	150.00
95	PERFECT TREE, THE	1250	150.00	150.00
95	SHOP TALK	*	30.00	30.00
95	SMALL TOWN SERVICE	1250	150.00	150.00
95	WINTER CAN BE FUN	999	125.00	125.00
96	TALES OF THE DAY	1500	150.00	150.00
	B. BENGER			
96	BEDTIME STORY, THE	999	125.00	125.00
	D. BUSH			
95	CRESCENT MOON BAY	999	125.00	125.00
95	MOONDANCE	999	125.00	125.00
95	WARMTH OF WINTER III	*	30.00	30.00
95	WINTER TRACKS	999	100.00	100.00
96	MOON SHADOWS	999	125.00	125.00
	M. CAPSER			
95	A MOMENT IN TIME	999	120.00	120.00
95	ENCHANTED WATERS	999	100.00	100.00
95	GRAPEVINE ESTATES	999	100.00	100.00
95	MARINER'S POINT	999	100.00	100.00
95	ON GENTLE WINDS	999	100.00	100.00
95	SPRING CREEK FEVER	999	100.00	100.00
95	WINTER HAVEN	999	100.00	100.00
96	ACROSS THE CALM	999	100.00	100.00
	L. DIDIER			
95	EARLY SNOW	999	125.00	125.00
95	ON SILENT WINGS	999	45.00	45.00
	H. EDWARDS			
95	A BREATH OF SPRING	*	30.00	30.00
95	ART OF WINE, THE	750	40.00	40.00
95	CIRCA 1850	*	60.00	60.00
95	HOMESPUN	*	60.00	60.00
95	SUMMER'S RETREAT	*	30.00	30.00
95	YESTERYEAR	*	60.00	60.00
96	HEART OF SPRING	*	30.00	30.00
	O. FRANCA			
90	WINDSONG	RT	100.00	300.00
91	LOVERS, THE	RT	125.00	1250.00
	S. HAMRICK			
95	A FRIEND IN THE FIELDS	999	75.00	75.00
95	ALWAYS ALERT	999	75.00	75.00
95	COLD WATER, WARM HEART	1500	75.00	75.00
95	FIELD COMPANIONS: BLACK LAB	4000	35.00	35.00
95	FIELD COMPANIONS: GOLDEN RETRIEVER	4000	35.00	35.00
95	FIELD COMPANIONS: SPRINGER SPANIEL	4000	35.00	35.00
95	FIELD COMPANIONS: YELLOW LAB	4000	35.00	35.00
95	GETTING WARM	999	75.00	75.00
	S. HANKS			
95	A CAPTIVE AUDIENCE	1500	150.00	150.00
95	COUNTRY COMFORT	999	100.00	100.00
95	DRIP CASTLE	4000	30.00	30.00
95	PACIFIC SANCTUARY	1500	150.00	150.00
95	ROOM TO THINK	999	125.00	125.00
95	SMALL MIRACLE	1500	125.00	125.00
95	STANDING ON THEIR OWN TWO FEET	1500	150.00	150.00
96	BIG SHOES TO FILL	1500	150.00	150.00
	L. HARRISON			
95	INTRIGUED	*	30.00	30.00
95	MAKING WAVES	999	75.00	75.00
95	RURAL ROUTE #2	*	30.00	30.00
95	SEA SPIRIT	999	125.00	125.00
95	WINTER NAP	999	100.00	100.00
	G. HOFF			
95	GOLDEN TREASURES	999	100.00	100.00
	N. HOWE			
95	CYGNATURE	750	125.00	125.00
95	LITTLE MELODY POSTER	*	30.00	30.00
95	SUN DANCE	750	100.00	100.00
	L. KAATZ			
95	LEFT BEHIND	*	30.00	30.00
	T. LIESS			
95	WINTER SILENCE	*	30.00	30.00
	T. MANGELSON			
96	BAD BOYS OF THE ARCTIC POSTER	*	25.00	25.00
96	CATCH OF THE DAY POSTER	*	25.00	25.00
	B. MOON			
95	SIGNING OF THE PEACE TREATY	*	30.00	30.00
	D. PLASSCHAERT			
95	OUR LEGACY	999	75.00	75.00

YR	NAME	LIMIT	ISSUE	TREND
	T. REDLIN			
77	APPLE RIVER MALLARDS	RT	100.00	200.00
77	OVER THE BLOWDOWN	RT	20.00	100.00
77	WINTER SNOWS	RT	20.00	500.00
78	BACK FROM THE FIELDS	720	40.00	450.00
78	BACKWATER MALLARDS	720	40.00	1200.00
78	OLD LOGGERS TRAIL	720	40.00	1250.00
78	OVER THE RUSHES	720	40.00	425.00
78	QUIET AFTERNOON	720	40.00	750.00
78	STARTLED	720	30.00	1200.00
79	AGING SHORELINE	960	40.00	400.00
79	COLORFUL TRIO	960	40.00	580.00
79	FIGHTING A HEADWIND	960	30.00	440.00
79	LONER, THE	960	40.00	350.00
79	MORNING CHORES	960	40.00	1650.00
79	WHITECAPS	960	40.00	590.00
80	AUTUMN RUN	960	60.00	500.00
80	BREAKING AWAY	960	60.00	450.00
80	CLEARING THE RAIL	960	60.00	900.00
80	COUNTRY ROAD	960	60.00	800.00
80	DRIFTING	960	60.00	400.00
80	HOMESTEAD, THE	960	60.00	825.00
80	INTRUDERS	960	60.00	385.00
80	NIGHT WATCH	2400	60.00	800.00
80	RUSTY REFUGE	960	60.00	525.00
80	SECLUDED POND	960	60.00	350.00
80	SILENT SUNSET	960	60.00	1000.00
80	SPRING THAW	960	60.00	600.00
80	SQUALL LINE	960	60.00	600.00
81	1981 MINNESOTA DUCK STAMP	7800	125.00	185.00
81	ALL CLEAR	960	150.00	400.00
81	APRIL SNOW	960	100.00	700.00
81	BROKEN COVEY	960	100.00	700.00
81	HIGH COUNTRY	960	100.00	525.00
81	HIGHTAILING	960	75.00	400.00
81	LANDMARK, THE	960	100.00	400.00
81	MORNING RETREAT	240	400.00	3000.00
81	PASSING THROUGH	960	100.00	400.00
81	RUSTY REFUGE II	960	100.00	780.00
81	SHARING THE BOUNTY	960	100.00	2800.00
81	SOFT SHADOWS	960	100.00	400.00
81	SPRING RUN-OFF	1700	100.00	650.00
82	1982 MINNESOTA TROUT STAMP	960	125.00	650.00
82	BIRCH LINE, THE	960	100.00	1350.00
82	EVENING RETREAT A/P	300	400.00	2300.00
82	LANDING, THE	RT	30.00	85.00
82	OCTOBER EVENING	960	100.00	1000.00
82	REFLECTIONS	960	100.00	600.00
82	SEED HUNTERS	960	100.00	800.00
82	SPRING MAPLING	960	100.00	1300.00
82	WHITEWATER	960	100.00	500.00
82	WINTER HAVEN	500	85.00	1400.00
83	1983 NORTH DAKOTA DUCK STAMP	3438	135.00	190.00
83	AUTUMN SHORELINE	RT	50.00	800.00
83	BACKWOODS CABIN	960	100.00	1350.00
83	EVENING GLOW	960	150.00	2400.00
83	EVENING SURPRISE	960	150.00	2600.00
83	HIDDEN POINT	960	150.00	850.00
83	ON THE ALERT	960	125.00	400.00
83	PEACEFUL EVENING	960	100.00	1400.00
83	PRAIRIE SPRINGS	960	150.00	600.00
83	RUSHING RAPIDS	960	125.00	1000.00
84	1984 QUAIL CONSERVATION	1500	135.00	135.00
84	BLUEBILL POINT A/P	240	300.00	900.00
84	CHANGING SEASONS-SUMMER	960	150.00	1800.00
84	CLOSED FOR THE SEASON	960	150.00	525.00
84	LEAVING THE SANCTUARY	960	150.00	2000.00
84	MORNING GLOW	960	150.00	2000.00
84	NIGHT HARVEST	960	150.00	2300.00
84	NIGHTFLIGHT	360	600.00	2800.00
84	PRAIRIE SKYLINE	960	150.00	1900.00
84	RURAL ROUTE	960	150.00	540.00
84	RUSTY REFUGE III	960	150.00	700.00
84	SILENT WINGS SUITE (SET OF 4)	960	200.00	1150.00
84	SUNDOWN	960	300.00	850.00
84	SUNNY AFTERNOON	960	150.00	850.00
84	WINTER WINDBREAK	960	150.00	800.00
85	1985 MINNESOTA DUCK STAMP	4385	135.00	175.00
85	AFTERNOON GLOW	960	150.00	1800.00
85	BREAKING COVER	960	150.00	725.00
85	BROWSING	960	150.00	1100.00
85	CLEAR VIEW	1500	300.00	850.00
85	DELAYED DEPARTURE	1500	150.00	1400.00
85	EVENING COMPANY	960	150.00	950.00
85	NIGHT LIGHT	1500	300.00	1650.00
85	RIVERSIDE POND	960	150.00	1000.00
85	RUSTY REFUGE IV	960	150.00	700.00
85	SHARING SEASON, THE	RT	60.00	250.00
85	WHISTLE STOP	960	150.00	900.00

YR	NAME	LIMIT	ISSUE	TREND
86	BACK TO THE SANTUARY	960	150.00	600.00
86	CHANGING SEASONS-AUTUMN	960	150.00	600.00
86	CHANGING SEASONS-WINTER	960	200.00	925.00
86	COMING HOME	2400	100.00	1350.00
86	HAZY AFTERNOON	2560	200.00	1100.00
86	NIGHT MAPLING	2560	200.00	775.00
86	PRAIRIE MONUMENTS	2560	200.00	850.00
86	SHARING SEASON II, THE	RT	60.00	190.00
86	SILENT FLIGHT	960	150.00	420.00
86	STORMY WEATHER	1500	200.00	700.00
86	SUNLIT TRAIL	960	150.00	440.00
86	TWILIGHT GLOW	960	200.00	1600.00
87	AUTUMN AFTERNOON	4800	100.00	900.00
87	CHANGING SEASONS-SPRING	960	200.00	850.00
87	DEER CROSSING	2400	200.00	1500.00
87	EVENING CHORES (PRINT/BOOK)	2400	400.00	1000.00
87	EVENING HARVEST	960	200.00	1600.00
87	GOLDEN RETREAT	500	800.00	2350.00
87	PREPARED FOR THE SEASON	RT	70.00	250.00
87	SHARING THE SOLITUDE	2400	125.00	900.00
87	THAT SPECIAL TIME	2400	125.00	1600.00
87	TOGETHER FOR THE SEASON	CL	70.00	170.00
88	BOULDER RIDGE	4800	150.00	200.00
88	CATCHING THE SCENT	2400	200.00	200.00
88	COUNTRY NEIGHBORS	4800	150.00	575.00
88	HOUSE CALL	6800	175.00	1450.00
88	LIGHTS OF HOME	9500	125.00	1000.00
88	MASTER'S DOMAIN, THE	2400	225.00	1150.00
88	MOONLIGHT RETREAT	530	1000.00	1390.00
88	PRAIRIE MORNING	4800	150.00	620.00
88	QUIET OF THE EVENING	4800	150.00	760.00
88	WEDNESDAY AFTERNOON	6800	175.00	1200.00
89	AROMA OF FALL	6800	200.00	1250.00
89	HOMEWARD BOUND	RT	80.00	375.00
89	INDIAN SUMMER	4800	200.00	1000.00
89	MORNING ROUNDS	6800	175.00	600.00
89	OFFICE HOURS	6800	175.00	1000.00
89	SPECIAL MEMORIES	570	1000.00	1400.00
90	BEST FRIENDS	570	1000.00	2200.00
90	EVENING SOLITUDE	RT	200.00	900.00
90	EVENING WITH FRIENDS	19500	225.00	1800.00
90	FAMILY TRADITIONS	RT	80.00	200.00
90	HEADING HOME	CL	80.00	400.00
90	MASTER OF THE VALLEY	RT	200.00	250.00
90	PURE CONTENTMENT	9500	150.00	690.00
90	WELCOME TO PARADISE	14500	150.00	800.00
91	COMFORTS OF HOME, THE	22900	175.00	570.00
91	FLYING FREE	14500	200.00	325.00
91	HUNTER'S HAVEN	*	1000.00	1150.00
91	MORNING SOLITUDE	12107	250.00	800.00
91	PLEASURES OF WINTER, THE	24500	150.00	375.00
92	SUMMERTIME	24900	225.00	300.00
95	FROM SEA TO SHINING SEA	29500	250.00	250.00
95	HARVEST MOON BALL	9500	275.00	275.00
95	NIGHT ON THE TOWN	29500	150.00	150.00
95	TOTAL COMFORT	9500	275.00	275.00
96	EVENING REHEARSALS	9500	275.00	275.00
J. VAN ZYLE				
95	CAT PUCCINO	1250	50.00	50.00
95	LAST NIGHT, LONG NIGHT	580	125.00	125.00
95	SUSHI BAR	999	100.00	100.00
96	CATCH ME IF YOU CAN	580	125.00	125.00
O. WIEGHORST				
*	BEEF HERD	*	500.00	550.00
*	HIS SPOTTED PONY	*	500.00	500.00
*	LONESOME TRAIL W/ COMPANION PRINT	*	500.00	500.00
*	NOMADS OF THE PLAINS	*	500.00	650.00
73	CORRALLING THE CAVVY	1000	200.00	500.00
74	BUFFALO SCOUT	1000	150.00	800.00
74	CALIFORNIA WRANGLER	1000	150.00	450.00
74	MISSING IN THE ROUNDUP	1000	100.00	440.00
74	NAVAJO PORTRAIT	1000	75.00	360.00
74	PACKING IN	1000	150.00	325.00
77	BOYS IN THE BUNKHOUSE	1000	150.00	350.00

HAROLD RIGSBY

				RIGSBY
H. RIGSBY				
78	AFRICAN LION I	500	20.00	200.00
78	CHEETAH	500	20.00	150.00
78	RACCOON	500	15.00	75.00
78	SIBERIAN TIGER	500	20.00	400.00
79	BOBCAT	500	15.00	75.00
79	SNOW LEOPARD	500	25.00	125.00
79	SNOW TIGER	500	25.00	250.00
80	AFRICAN LION II	200	50.00	250.00
80	BENGAL TIGER II	200	50.00	200.00
80	GIRAFFE	500	25.00	125.00
80	KOALA	500	25.00	100.00
80	RED FOX I	950	30.00	200.00

YR	NAME	LIMIT	ISSUE	TREND
80	RED FOX II	950	30.00	200.00
80	TIGER CUB	500	20.00	400.00
80	WHITE TIGER CUB	500	20.00	400.00
81	AFRICAN LION CUB	950	30.00	100.00
81	COTTONTAIL RABBIT	950	15.00	75.00
81	ZEBRA FOAL	500	50.00	400.00
82	COUGAR	500	50.00	425.00
82	GREY SQUIRREL	950	15.00	50.00
82	TIGER IV	950	20.00	75.00
83	BABY HARP SEAL	950	25.00	275.00
83	BALD EAGLE	950	15.00	100.00
83	BENGAL TIGER CUB	500	50.00	125.00
83	PANDA	950	35.00	200.00
83	WHITE BENGAL TIGER	950	20.00	125.00
84	BENGAL TIGER V	975	40.00	275.00
85	BLACK LEOPARD	975	50.00	350.00
85	GRAY WOLF	975	35.00	225.00

HELEN PAUL WATERCOLORS

H. PAUL

YR	NAME	LIMIT	ISSUE	TREND
95	GREEN PLANTER BOX	350	55.00	55.00
95	SPECIAL OCCASION	350	50.00	50.00
95	SUNFLOWER PATCH	350	75.00	75.00
96	CORNER OF THE GARDEN	350	75.00	75.00
96	SUNFLOWER BASKET	350	75.00	75.00

HISTORICAL ART PRINTS LTD.

D. TROIANI

YR	NAME	LIMIT	ISSUE	TREND
82	CONFEDERATE STANDARD BEARER	600	75.00	2300.00
82	CPL. WHEAT'S FIRST SPEC. BAT.	600	40.00	260.00
83	BEFORE THE STORM (T.J. JACKSON)	600	75.00	2300.00
83	FORWARD THE COLORS	750	85.00	1300.00
83	UNION STANDARD BEARER	600	75.00	1600.00
84	CONFEDERATE DRUMMER	625	75.00	850.00
84	J.E.B. STUART	850	95.00	1400.00
84	LEE'S TEXANS	950	95.00	1200.00
84	UNION DRUMMER	625	75.00	600.00
85	FIGHT FOR THE COLORS, THE	950	95.00	1900.00
85	GRAY WALL, THE	950	95.00	1500.00
85	REBEL YELL	950	95.00	1250.00
85	SOUTHERN STEEL (N.B. FOREST)	950	95.00	1700.00
86	BRONZE GUNS & IRON MEN	950	95.00	1200.00
86	LAST ROUNDS, THE	950	95.00	1300.00
86	MEN MUST SEE US TODAY, THE	950	95.00	800.00
86	OLD JACK	950	95.00	700.00
87	114TH PA/COLLIS ZOUAVES	750	65.00	350.00
87	2ND MD INFANTRY	750	65.00	150.00
87	8TH TEXAS CAVALRY	750	65.00	450.00
87	CLEAR THE WAY	950	125.00	2600.00
87	CO.D 2ND U.S. SHARP SHOOTER	750	65.00	400.00
87	GIVE THEM COLD STEEL...	950	95.00	2250.00
87	STARS & BARS	950	125.00	450.00
88	BAYONET	1000	100.00	500.00
88	BOY COLONEL, THE	1000	125.00	550.00
88	EAGLE OF THE 8TH	1000	125.00	650.00
88	GENERAL ROBERT E. LEE	950	125.00	425.00
88	LAST SALUTE, THE	1000	125.00	1650.00
88	SAVING THE FLAG	1000	125.00	785.00
89	12TH VIRGINIA CAVALRY, 1864	750	75.00	195.00
89	2ND U.S. CAVALRY, 1861	750	75.00	175.00
89	EMBLEMS OF VALOR	1000	125.00	625.00
89	FORLORN HOPE, THE	1000	150.00	340.00
89	THUNDER ON LITTLE KENNESAW	1000	150.00	1100.00
89	UNITED STATES MARINES 1861-1865	750	65.00	500.00
90	BONNIE BLUE FLAG, THE	1000	150.00	375.00
90	CHARGE	1000	200.00	550.00
90	GRAY COMANCHES, THE	1000	175.00	825.00
90	OPDYCKE'S TIGERS	1000	200.00	375.00
91	1ST S.C. RIFLES, 1861	950	75.00	175.00
91	DIEHARDS, THE	1000	200.00	800.00
91	MEN OF ARKANSAS	1000	200.00	450.00
91	RED DEVILS, THE	1000	200.00	650.00
91	WASHINGTON ARTILLERY OF NEW ORLEANS	950	75.00	300.00
92	RANGER MOSBY	1000	250.00	350.00
92	RETREAT BY RECOIL	1000	250.00	470.00
92	UNTIL SUNDOWN	1000	200.00	750.00

IMPERIAL GRAPHICS LTD.

L. LIU

YR	NAME	LIMIT	ISSUE	TREND
95	BURGUNDY IRISES W/FOXGLOVES	*	60.00	60.00
95	BUTTERFLY GARDEN I	*	50.00	50.00
95	BUTTERFLY GARDEN II	*	50.00	50.00
95	MAGNOLIAS & DAY LILIES	*	80.00	80.00
95	MAGNOLIAS & HYDRANGEA	*	80.00	80.00
95	PURPLE IRISES W/FOXGLOVES	*	60.00	60.00
95	RUBY THROATED HUMMINGBORD W/HIBISCUS	*	40.00	40.00
95	WHITE EARED HUMMINGBIRD W/HYDRANGEA	*	40.00	40.00
95	WREATH OF LILLIES	*	55.00	55.00
95	WREATH OF PANSIES	*	55.00	55.00

YR	NAME	LIMIT	ISSUE	TREND
96	ANGEL W/HARP	5500	40.00	40.00
96	ANGEL W/TRUMPET	5500	40.00	40.00
96	GUARDIAN ANGEL	5500	125.00	125.00
96	MESSENGERS OF LOVE	5500	60.00	60.00
96	PROTECTORS OF PEACE	5500	60.00	60.00
L. LIU				**CANVAS**
96	ANGEL W/HARP	300	145.00	145.00
96	ANGEL W/TRUMPET	300	145.00	145.00
96	GUARDIAN ANGEL	300	395.00	395.00
L. LIU				**CANVAS EDITION**
95	LILAC BREEZES	*	295.00	295.00
95	MAGNOLIA PATH	*	395.00	395.00
95	NATURE'S RETREAT	*	395.00	395.00
95	SPRING GARDEN	*	395.00	395.00
95	SWEET BOUNTY	*	295.00	295.00
96	ANGEL W/HARP	*	145.00	145.00
96	ANGEL W/TRUMPET	*	145.00	145.00
96	GUARDIAN ANGEL	*	395.00	395.00
L. LIU				**CELESTRIAL SYMPHONY - CANVAS EDITION**
95	FLUTE INTERLUDE	*	145.00	145.00
95	FRENCH HORN MELODY	*	145.00	145.00
95	PIANO SONATA	*	145.00	145.00
95	VIOLIN CONCERTO	*	145.00	145.00
L. LIU				**CELESTRIAL SYMPHONY - PAPER EDITION**
95	FLUTE INTERLUDE	*	40.00	40.00
95	FRENCH HORN MELODY	*	40.00	40.00
95	PIANO SONATA	*	40.00	40.00
95	VIOLIN CONCERTO	*	40.00	40.00
L. LIU				**LENA Y. LIU LIMITED EDITION IMAGES**
*	BASKET OF PANSIES	2500	40.00	100.00
*	FLORAL SYMPHONY	1950	95.00	100.00
*	HUMMINGBIRDS & IRIS	1950	40.00	50.00
*	IRIS GARDEN	1950	45.00	200.00
*	MIXED IRISES I	2500	50.00	65.00
*	MIXED IRISES II	2500	50.00	65.00
*	MOONLIGHT SPLENDOR	1950	60.00	75.00
*	MORNING GLORIES & HUMMER	1050	45.00	55.00
*	MORNING ROOM, THE	2500	95.00	375.00
*	ORIENTAL SCREEN	2500	95.00	375.00
*	PARENTHOOD	1950	45.00	100.00
*	PEONIES & AZALEAS	1950	35.00	70.00
*	PEONIES & FORSYTHIA	1950	35.00	70.00
*	PEONIES & WATERFALL	1950	65.00	100.00
*	ROMANTIC ABUNDANCE	1950	95.00	200.00
*	SOLITUDE	1950	60.00	300.00
*	SPRING DUET	1950	60.00	150.00
*	TWO WHITE IRISES	2500	40.00	60.00
88	CHICKADEES	950	35.00	50.00
89	SWANS & CALLAS	1950	65.00	100.00
89	WATERFALL W/BLOSSOMS	1950	65.00	225.00
L. LIU				**MUSIC ROOM IV - CANVAS EDITION**
95	SWAN MELODY	*	425.00	425.00
L. LIU				**MUSIC ROOM IV - PAPER EDITION**
95	SWAN MELODY	*	150.00	150.00
L. LIU				**PAPER EDITION**
95	LILAC BREEZES	*	80.00	80.00
95	MAGNOLIA PATH	*	135.00	135.00
95	NATURE'S RETREAT	*	145.00	145.00
95	SPRING GARDEN	*	125.00	125.00
95	SWEET BOUNTY	*	80.00	80.00
96	ANGEL W/HARP	*	40.00	40.00
96	ANGEL W/TRUMPET	*	40.00	40.00
96	GUARDIAN ANGEL	*	125.00	125.00

J.S. PERRY ORIGINALS

YR	NAME	LIMIT	ISSUE	TREND
J.S. PERRY				
84	MEW'S MIX	SO	38.00	500.00
84	PUSSYWILLOWS	800	38.00	72.00
84	STILL LIFE WITH CUPCATS	800	38.00	96.00
85	CALL OF THE WILD	800	95.00	220.00
85	CATTAILS	SO	38.00	500.00
85	FRIENDS IN HIGH PLACES	800	95.00	165.00
85	PAPA WAS A ROLLING STONE	800	38.00	96.00
85	THREE SCOOPS	800	38.00	48.00
86	HOME SWEET HOME	800	48.00	96.00
86	SUMMER TALES	800	48.00	72.00
87	BACKYARD JUNGLE GYM, THE	800	48.00	96.00
87	BOXING MATCH, THE	800	65.00	100.00
87	PEEKABOO	800	65.00	120.00
87	YOGA YOU CAN DO AT HOME	800	35.00	70.00
88	HOT PINK BIKINI, THE	800	35.00	53.00
90	GIRL'S NIGHT OUT	800	48.00	50.00
J.S. PERRY				**PUSSONALITES**
90	THE OFFICAL FELINERS TEAM PORTRAIT AP	80	48.00	48.00
94	STAR BRIGHT AP	80	35.00	35.00
96	ASPARAGUS TIPSY! AP	80	105.00	105.00
96	FORE? AP	80	105.00	105.00

YR	NAME	LIMIT	ISSUE	TREND
96	GILDA LOVES GARLIC! AP	80	168.00	168.00
96	HIGHLAND FLING AP	80	105.00	105.00
96	POWDER PUFFS AP	80	195.00	195.00
96	RAINY DAY AP	80	195.00	195.00

J.S. PERRY — **PUSSONALITIES**

YR	NAME	LIMIT	ISSUE	TREND
90	THE OFFICAL FELINERS TEAM PORTRAIT	800	48.00	72.00
92	HEY, KID!	800	65.00	98.00
92	HEY, KID! AP	80	65.00	65.00
93	STILL IFE WITH CUPCATS	800	38.00	500.00
94	STAR BRIGHT	800	35.00	53.00
96	ASPARAGUS TIPSY!	800	35.00	35.00
96	FORE?	800	35.00	35.00
96	GILDA LOVES GARLIC!	800	56.00	56.00
96	HIGHLAND FLING	800	35.00	35.00
96	POWERPUFFS	800	65.00	65.00
96	RAINY DAY	800	65.00	65.00

JACK TERRY FINE ART

J. TERRY — **FRAMED CANVAS EDITION**

YR	NAME	LIMIT	ISSUE	TREND
90	HOME FROM THE FAIR	250	495.00	515.00
91	AFTER THE CENTENNIAL PARADE	*	595.00	615.00
91	IF IT WEREN'T FOR BAD LUCK	SO	595.00	1200.00
91	PAY'S THE SAME, RAIN OR SHINE	SO	595.00	1200.00
91	SLOW AND EASY	SO	595.00	3000.00
91	TOO COLD TO SIT AND WAIT	SO	595.00	900.00
92	BIG NIGHT IN A SMALL TOWN	250	595.00	615.00
92	LADY IN RED	*	395.00	415.00
93	CHASE, THE	SO	295.00	900.00
93	CROSSING THE NUECES	SO	295.00	700.00
93	FAITHFUL EVENING	250	595.00	900.00
94	A SEASON TO REMEMBER	500	615.00	615.00
94	CLEARWATER CROSSING	500	615.00	715.00
94	HEADING HOME	500	595.00	715.00
95	A COWBOY'S TIME TO REFLECT	750	350.00	350.00
95	BAGGAGE, BULLION, AND BRAVE MEN	750	615.00	615.00
95	FAST AND FURIOUS	750	350.00	350.00
95	MISERY LOVES COMPANY	750	615.00	615.00
95	MORNING ON THE MERCED	250	615.00	615.00
95	PADRE'S GARDEN, THE	750	350.00	350.00
95	RUSTLING MUSTANGS	750	615.00	615.00
95	SAN FRANCISCO--THE 1880S	750	615.00	615.00
95	SEASONS OF CHANGE	750	350.00	350.00
95	SLEIGHBELLS AND MOONLIGHT	750	515.00	515.00
95	SOUTHERN CHARM	700	615.00	615.00
95	WHISPER VALLEY ROUNDUP	750	775.00	775.00

J. TERRY — **PAPER EDITION**

YR	NAME	LIMIT	ISSUE	TREND
90	HOME FROM THE FAIR	*	35.00	35.00
91	AFTER THE CENTENNIAL PARADE	SO	150.00	350.00
91	FRENCH REVOLUTION/PALETTE OF PARIS	*	125.00	125.00
91	IF IT WEREN'T FOR BAD LUCK	SO	150.00	450.00
91	PAY'S THE SAME, RAIN OR SHINE	*	150.00	350.00
91	SLOW AND EASY	SO	150.00	690.00
91	TOO COLD TO SIT AND WAIT	SO	150.00	475.00
92	BIG NIGHT IN A SMALL TOWN	*	125.00	125.00
92	LADY IN RED	*	125.00	125.00
93	CHASE, THE	SO	65.00	300.00
93	CROSSING THE NUECES	SO	65.00	350.00
93	FAITHFUL EVENING	950	125.00	150.00
94	A SEASON TO REMEMBER	500	150.00	150.00
94	CLEARWATER CROSSING	500	150.00	150.00
94	HEADING HOME	500	150.00	150.00
95	A COWBOY'S TIME TO REFLECT	250	75.00	75.00
95	BAGGAGE, BULLION, AND BRAVE MEN	250	150.00	150.00
95	FAST AND FURIOUS	250	75.00	75.00
95	MISERY LOVES COMPANY	250	150.00	150.00
95	MORNING ON THE MERCED	750	150.00	150.00
95	PADRE'S GARDEN, THE	250	75.00	75.00
95	RUSTLING MUSTANGS	*	150.00	150.00
95	SAN FRANCISCO--THE 1880S	*	150.00	150.00
95	SEASONS OF CHANGE	250	75.00	75.00
95	SLEIGHBELLS AND MOONLIGHT	250	150.00	150.00
95	SOUTHERN CHARM	250	150.00	150.00
95	WHISPER VALLEY ROUNDUP	250	200.00	200.00

JAN HAGARA COLLECTABLES

J. HAGARA — **VICTORIAN CHILDREN**

YR	NAME	LIMIT	ISSUE	TREND
*	BONNIE	*	*	65.00
*	HANNAH	*	*	150.00
75	TRINA	600	7.00	500.00
76	CHRIS	2000	5.00	75.00
77	SPRING & LANCE	2000	12.00	175.00
78	JUMEAU DOLL	1200	20.00	50.00
78	OLIVIA	600	55.00	800.00
79	DAISIES FROM MARYBETH	900	20.00	100.00
80	BETSY	750	45.00	400.00
80	JIMMY	750	45.00	300.00
80	LYDIA	650	65.00	350.00
81	JENNY	2000	45.00	300.00
81	STORYTIME	450	125.00	600.00

YR	NAME	LIMIT	ISSUE	TREND
82	CAROL	2000	25.00	175.00
82	IN LINE	1000	65.00	1200.00
82	MANDY	500	60.00	400.00
83	JENNIFER	700	60.00	250.00
83	PAIGE	2000	47.50	200.00
85	CYNTHIA	600	50.00	175.00
85	GOLDIE	1200	47.50	125.00
85	NOEL	2000	30.00	95.00
86	PHILLIP'S COUSINS	1000	60.00	1050.00
86	SOPHIE	1200	50.00	125.00
87	CATHY	2000	30.00	150.00
87	NIKKI	2000	30.00	95.00
87	RENNY & BLUEBEARY	950	125.00	550.00
88	ADDIE	2000	65.00	200.00
88	MATTIE-FIRST COLLECTOR'S CLUB PRINT	YR	55.00	250.00

JIM HARRISON

J. HARRISON

YR	NAME	LIMIT	ISSUE	TREND
*	C&S BANK	OP	45.00	45.00
*	CHURCH	OP	30.00	30.00
*	COKE BOTTLE THERMOMETER	OP	30.00	30.00
*	FISH HOUSE	OP	45.00	45.00
*	GEESE OVER MARSH	OP	45.00	45.00
*	GROCERY STORE	OP	30.00	30.00
*	HAMMER GALLERIES I	OP	45.00	45.00
*	HAMMER GALLERIES II	OP	*	*
*	HIS WORLD REMEMBERED	OP	45.00	45.00
*	J.J. CORN- 4TH	OP	45.00	45.00
*	LEE OVERALLS	OP	30.00	30.00
*	MAYTAG	OP	45.00	45.00
*	NICKEL COCA-COLA	OP	45.00	45.00
*	OAK TREE	OP	45.00	45.00
*	ROUND COCA-COLA	OP	30.00	30.00
*	SAND DUNES	OP	45.00	45.00
*	SOUTH CAROLINA POSTER	OP	45.00	45.00
*	SWEET SNUFF	OP	45.00	45.00
*	VINTAGE HOUSE	OP	45.00	45.00
73	COASTAL DUNES	1500	30.00	460.00
73	COASTAL MARSHES	1500	30.00	450.00
74	ABANDONED BOAT	1800	25.00	200.00
74	HOUSE IN COUNTRY	1500	25.00	200.00
74	RURAL AMERICANA/MAIL POUCH	1500	40.00	360.00
75	AMERICAN BYWAYS	1500	40.00	325.00
75	COUNTRY SEASONIN' - MORTON SALT	1500	40.00	300.00
75	DISAPPEARING AMERICA	1500	40.00	1400.00
76	RURAL DELIVER/MAIL BOX	1500	40.00	425.00
76	YESTERYEAR/WAGON	1500	50.00	200.00
77	BURMAN SHAVE	1500	50.00	300.00
77	COMMUNITY CHURCH	1500	50.00	225.00
77	DR. PEPPER	1500	50.00	300.00
77	FALLOW & FORGOTTEN/PLOW	1500	50.00	200.00
78	666 COLA TABLETS	1500	50.00	275.00
78	PHILIP MORRIS	1500	50.00	275.00
78	RED COVERED BRIDGE	1500	50.00	275.00
78	WOOD PILE	1500	75.00	175.00
79	CLABBER GIRL	1500	75.00	325.00
79	GOLD DUST TWINS	1500	55.00	175.00
79	GOODY'S	1500	50.00	175.00
79	LUCKY STRIKE	1500	50.00	300.00
80	PEPSI & PLANTERS PEANUTS/PAIR	1500	60.00	250.00
80	TONIC & LINIMENT	1500	85.00	225.00
80	TUBE ROSE SNUFF	1500	60.00	175.00
80	UNPAINTED COVERED BRIDGE	1500	60.00	200.00
81	7-UP & BLACK EYES SUSANS	1500	75.00	225.00
81	HOUSE & BARN/PAIR	1500	50.00	225.00
81	OLD DUTCH CLEANSER	1500	75.00	200.00
82	BULL OF THE WOODS	1500	75.00	200.00
82	RAILROAD CROSSING	1500	75.00	300.00
82	WINDMILL	1500	75.00	150.00
83	FILLIN' STATION	1500	80.00	200.00
83	FRESH GRITS	1500	80.00	850.00
83	MOUNTAIN BRIDGE	1500	80.00	275.00
83	SHRINE CIRCUS	1500	80.00	160.00
84	MEMORIES I	750	90.00	200.00
84	MORTON SALT	1500	135.00	250.00
84	RED GOOSE SHOES	1500	90.00	160.00
84	SIGN OF THE TIMES	3000	45.00	45.00
85	MEMORIES II	750	90.00	200.00
85	OLD STONE BARN	1500	90.00	165.00
85	SAND DUNES/INLET MARSH/PAIR	1500	75.00	200.00
85	SPRING CLOUDS	1500	90.00	175.00
85	SPRING CLOUDS	1500	90.00	175.00
85	WIRE	500	45.00	175.00
86	FISHING VILLAGE	975	135.00	275.00
86	LIGHTHOUSE	975	135.00	325.00
86	LIGHTHOUSE	1	195.00	385.00
86	ROAD, THE	2	500.00	500.00
87	COCA-COLA BRIDGE	975	135.00	475.00
87	JEFFERSON ISLAND SALT	975	135.00	200.00

YR	NAME	LIMIT	ISSUE	TREND
87	ROYAL CROWN COLA	975	315.00	200.00
87	UNCLE JOHN'S SYRUP	975	135.00	200.00
88	COCA-COLA BARN	500	275.00	325.00
88	COCA-COLA BARN	2	150.00	150.00
88	GULLS OVER BEACH	1500	75.00	175.00
88	HERSHEY BAR	975	135.00	200.00
88	RED BOAT	975	135.00	200.00
89	BABY RUTH	1000	45.00	45.00
89	BROWN'S MULE	975	135.00	135.00
89	FALL - RC COLA	975	95.00	95.00
89	VICKS VAPORUB	975	135.00	135.00
90	SANDPIPER	500	185.00	185.00
90	SANDPIPER	1	245.00	245.00
90	SODA POP SERIES	975	380.00	380.00
90	SPRING - 7-UP	975	95.00	95.00
90	SUMMER - COCA-COLA	975	95.00	95.00
90	WINTER - PEPSI	975	95.00	95.00
91	SINCLAIR STATION	500	135.00	550.00
91	TWELVE CENT GAS	975	200.00	200.00
92	CHURCH IN THE WOODS	975	185.00	185.00
93	TREES	975	185.00	185.00
94	WIND IN THE MARSH	975	185.00	185.00
95	RED BRIDGE IN SNOW	975	65.00	65.00
95	SUMMER COCA-COLA BRIDGE	975	185.00	185.00
J. HARRISON				**ARTIST PROOF**
78	TOOLS	50	325.00	500.00
80	BRUSH AND BUCKET	50	350.00	400.00
91	TWELVE CENT GAS	50	250.00	250.00
92	CHURCH IN THE WOODS	50	235.00	235.00
J. HARRISON				**REMARQUE**
91	TWELVE CENT GAS	25	350.00	350.00
J. HARRISON				**SERIGRAPH**
78	TOOLS	300	275.00	450.00
80	BRUSH AND BUCKET	300	300.00	350.00

JOHN M. BARBER ART LTD.

YR	NAME	LIMIT	ISSUE	TREND
J. BARBER				
*	BOAT SHED	750	40.00	350.00
*	RACING FOR THE OYSTERS	950	175.00	400.00
78	NELLIE CROCKETT OYSTER BOAT	750	40.00	1700.00
79	BUTLER'S BOAT YARD	500	40.00	350.00
79	HAMPTON CREEK DERELICT	500	40.00	400.00
79	SPRING PAINTING	500	40.00	125.00
82	BUYBOATS WM. B. TENNISON	950	55.00	325.00
82	SIGSBEE (B/W)	500	25.00	105.00
83	DISTANT THUNDER	950	75.00	300.00
83	SKIPJACK MAGGIE LEE, THE	950	55.00	500.00
84	BUYING OYSTERS AT DRUM POINT	950	100.00	400.00
84	COMING SQUALL	950	50.00	500.00
84	GUARDIAN OF DIAMOND SHOALS	950	65.00	150.00
84	MORNING AT COVE POINT	950	75.00	700.00
84	TRADEWINDS	950	65.00	450.00
85	BUYBOATS JACKSON CREEK	950	65.00	400.00
85	CHESAPEAKE MORNING	1450	130.00	500.00
85	GLOUCESTER PT. WATERMEN	950	75.00	750.00
85	SPINNAKER REACH	950	85.00	350.00
85	WINDWARD START	950	85.00	300.00
86	DAWN ON THE CHOPTANK	950	95.00	245.00
86	ON THE RAILWAY	950	75.00	175.00
86	TWILIGHT HARBOR	950	125.00	1250.00
86	VANISHING FLEET, THE	1650	145.00	1200.00
87	BAY COUNTRY MILL	950	135.00	250.00
87	MOONLIGHT HARBOR	950	175.00	1100.00
87	RETURNING HOME	950	145.00	1350.00
88	BREEZING UP	950	140.00	400.00
88	NIGHT PASSAGE	950	225.00	625.00
88	UNCERTAIN WEATHER	950	125.00	250.00
89	FOG OVER BLOODY POINT BAR	950	165.00	325.00
89	TOWN DOCK	950	95.00	200.00
89	UP FOR REPAIR	950	95.00	100.00
90	DAWN'S EARLY LIGHT	950	85.00	300.00
90	SUNRISE OVER MOBJACK BAY	950	185.00	350.00

KRAPF IMAGES

YR	NAME	LIMIT	ISSUE	TREND
P. KRAPF			**KRAPF IMAGES PRINTS**	
89	ANOTHER SEASON	*	90.00	90.00
89	CLOSE TO COVER	*	60.00	60.00
89	GRIZZLY COUNTRY	*	85.00	85.00
89	HUNTER'S REST	*	95.00	95.00
89	SURPRISED	*	55.00	55.00
90	AMERICAN ORIGINAL	*	80.00	80.00
90	CHIPPY ON THE ROCKS	*	50.00	50.00
90	DISTANT BUGLE	*	95.00	95.00
90	EDGE OF THE BURN	*	80.00	80.00
90	OCTOBER MORNING, CANYON DE CHELLY	*	85.00	85.00
90	ON HIS WAY	*	75.00	75.00
90	ON THE EDGE	*	90.00	90.00
90	READY	*	95.00	95.00

YR	NAME	LIMIT	ISSUE	TREND
90	YELLOWSTONE CANYON	*	80.00	80.00
91	ABOVE AND BEYOND	*	95.00	95.00
91	CAUGHT NAPPING	*	65.00	65.00

LIGHTPOST PUBLISHING

Price ranges may reflect various demands in the market from one geographic region to another; condition of piece; specific markings found on piece; and/or changes in production of piece.

YR	NAME	LIMIT	ISSUE	TREND
T. KINKADE				
*	NATIONAL PARK STAMP PRINT-1	*	*	200.00
T. KINKADE				**ARCHIVAL PAPER**
84	DAWSON	CL	150.00	200.00-750.00
84	PLACERVILLE, 1916	CL	90.00	1500.00-3000.00
85	BIRTH OF A CITY	CL	150.00	200.00-950.00
85	EVENING SERVICE	CL	90.00	200.00-475.00
85	MOONLIGHT ON THE WATERFRONT	CL	150.00	200.00-475.00
86	NEW YORK, 6TH AVENUE	CL	150.00	2000.00
86	ROOM WITH A VIEW	CL	150.00	300.00-550.00
89	CARMEL, OCEAN AVENUE	CL	225.00	450.00-750.00
89	ENTRANCE TO THE MANOR HOUSE	CL	125.00	300.00-675.00
89	EVENING AT MERRITT'S COTTAGE	CL	125.00	675.00
90	CHANDLER'S COTTAGE	CL	125.00	500.00
90	ROSE ARBOR	CL	125.00	300.00
91	AUTUMN GATE, THE	OP	225.00	1100.00
91	BOSTON	550	175.00	765.00
91	CARMEL, TUCK BOX TEA ROOM	980	235.00	750.00
91	HOME FOR THE EVENING	980	100.00	225.00
91	HOME FOR THE HOLIDAYS	980	225.00	375.00
91	VICTORIAN EVENING	RT	150.00	250.00
92	AFTERNOON LIGHT, DOGWOODS	980	185.00	500.00
92	COTTAGE-BY-THE-SEA	980	235.00	425.00
92	FALL COLORS VICTORIAN	980	*	175.00
92	HOME IS WHERE THE HEART IS	980	225.00	350.00
92	JULIANNE'S COTTAGE	980	185.00	750.00
92	MILLER' COTTAGE	980	175.00	195.00
92	SAN FRANCISCO, CALIFORNIA STREET	980	235.00	1800.00
92	SILENT NIGHT	980	185.00	500.00
92	SUNDAY AT APPLE HILL	980	175.00	600.00
92	SWANBROOKE COTTAGE	980	225.00	900.00
92	VICTORIAN CHRISTMAS	980	225.00	850.00
92	VICTORIAN GARDEN	980	275.00	1250.00
93	LAMPLIGHT BROOKE	1650	235.00	385.00
T. KINKADE				**ARCHIVAL PAPER/CANVAS**
90	BLUE COTTAGE	RT	125.00	255.00
90	NEW YORK, 1932	935	225.00	1100.00-3200.00
90	SKATING IN THE PARK	750	275.00	2000.00
T. KINKADE				**ARCHIVAL PAPER/CANVAS/COUNTRY CHURCH**
91	MOONLIT VILLAGE	935	225.00	1100.00-3100.00
T. KINKADE				**ARCHIVAL PAPER/CHRISTMAS COTTAGE**
90	CHRISTMAS COTTAGE	OP	95.00	150.00
T. KINKADE				**ARCHIVAL PAPER/HIDDEN COTTAGE**
90	HIDDEN COTTAGE	CL	125.00	500.00
T. KINKADE				**ARCHIVAL PAPER/SAN FRANCISCO**
90	SAN FRANCISCO, 1909	OP	150.00	3500.00
91	SAN FRANCISCO, UNION SQUARE	CL	225.00	450.00-750.00
T. KINKADE				**ARCHIVAL PAPER/SWEETHEART COTTAGE**
92	SWEETHEART COTTAGE	CL	150.00	325.00
T. KINKADE				**ARCHIVAL PAPER/THOMASHIRE**
92	BROADWATER BRIDGE	CL	225.00	500.00
T. KINKADE				**CANVAS EDITION**
85	MOONLIGHT ON THE WATERFRONT	260	795.00	995.00
86	ROOM WITH A VIEW	260	710.00	850.00
89	CARMEL, OCEAN AVENUE	CL	595.00	5500.00
89	ENTRANCE TO THE MANOR HOUSE	CL	565.00	3000.00
89	EVENING AT MERRITT'S COTTAGE	CL	595.00	850.00
90	CHANDLER'S COTTAGE	CL	495.00	2000.00
90	CHRISTMAS COTTAGE	CL	295.00	1600.00
90	HIDDEN COTTAGE	CL	495.00	1750.00
90	MORNING LIGHT A/P	CL	695.00	800.00
90	ROSE ARBOR	CL	495.00	900.00
90	SPRING AT STONEGATE	550	345.00	365.00
91	AUTUMN GATE, THE	980	595.00	2200.00
91	BOSTON	550	435.00	765.00
91	CARMEL, TUCK BOX TEA ROOM	980	595.00	2000.00
91	CEDAR NOOK COTTAGE	1960	315.00	415.00
91	CHRISTMAS EVE	980	395.00	495.00
91	FLAGS OVER THE CAPITOL	980	565.00	690.00
91	HOME FOR THE EVENING	980	215.00	300.00
91	HOME FOR THE HOLIDAYS	CL	595.00	1500.00
91	LIT PATH, THE	1960	215.00	315.00
91	MCKENNA'S COTTAGE	980	495.00	850.00
91	OLD P'FIELD TEA ROOM	980	495.00	950.00
91	OPEN GATE, SUSSEX	980	195.00	215.00
91	PYE CORNER COTTAGE	1960	165.00	200.00
91	VICTORIAN EVENING	RT	595.00	500.00
91	WOODMAN'S THATCH	1960	215.00	415.00
92	AMBER AFTERNOON	980	615.00	950.00
92	BESIDE STILL WATERS	1250	515.00	915.00

YR	NAME	LIMIT	ISSUE	TREND
92	BLOSSOM HILL CHURCH	980	495.00	850.00
92	BROADWATER BRIDGE	980	495.00	2000.00
92	CHRISTMAS AT AHWAHNEE	980	495.00	580.00
92	COTTAGE-BY-THE-SEA	980	615.00	1300.00
92	COUNTRY MEMORIES	980	395.00	750.00
92	EVENING CAROLERS	1960	315.00	355.00
92	FALL COLORS VICTORIAN	980	*	435.00
92	GARDEN PARTY	980	515.00	650.00
92	HOME IS WHERE THE HEART IS	980	615.00	1700.00
92	JULIANNE'S COTTAGE	980	345.00	1700.00
92	MOONLIT SLEIGHRIDE	1960	315.00	315.00
92	OLD P'FIELD GIFT SHOPPE	980	515.00	580.00
92	SAN FRANCISCO CALIFORNIA STREET	980	645.00	4200.00
92	SUNDAY AT APPLE HILL	980	515.00	1015.00
92	SWANBROOKE COTTAGE	980	595.00	2300.00
92	SWEETHEART COTTAGE	980	495.00	1000.00
92	VICTORIAN GARDEN	980	695.00	2000.00
92	WEATHERVANE HUTCH	1960	315.00	450.00
92	YOSEMITE	980	615.00	690.00
93	BEYOND AUTUMN GATE	1650	815.00	2800.00
93	BLESSING OF AUTUMN	1250	615.00	915.00
93	END OF A PERFECT DAY	1250	515.00	2000.00
93	FISHERMAN'S WHARF SAN FRANCISCO	2750	965.00	1200.00
93	HEATHER'S HUTCH	1250	395.00	515.00
93	HIDDEN COTTAGE II	1980	515.00	715.00
93	HIDDEN GAZEBO	2400	515.00	715.00
93	HOMESTEAD HOUSE	1250	615.00	690.00
93	LAMPLIGHT BROOKE	1650	615.00	1650.00
93	LAMPLIGHT LANE	980	595.00	3100.00
93	ST. NICHOLAS CIRCLE	1750	615.00	815.00
93	STONEHEARTH HUTCH	1650	415.00	575.00
93	STUDIO IN THE GARDEN	1480	415.00	465.00
93	SWEETHEART COTTAGE II	980	495.00	1650.00
93	VICTORIAN CHRISTMAS II	1650	615.00	1495.00
93	VILLAGE INN, THE	1200	515.00	900.00
93	WINTER'S END	1450	615.00	650.00
94	BEACON OF HOPE	2750	615.00	915.00
94	BLESSINGS OF SPRING	2750	515.00	615.00
94	CHRISTMAS MEMORIES	3450	515.00	580.00
94	CHRISTMAS TREE COTTAGE	2950	440.00	440.00
94	EMERALD ISLE COTTAGE	2750	515.00	580.00
94	END OF A PERFECT DAY II	2750	815.00	1400.00
94	GARDENS BEYOND AUTUMN GATE	CL	875.00	875.00
94	GUARDIAN CASTLE	4750	865.00	865.00
94	LAMPLIGHT INN	2750	615.00	815.00
94	PARIS, EIFFEL TOWER	2750	795.00	1195.00
94	POWER & THE MAJESTY, THE	2750	650.00	690.00
94	SWEETHEART COTTAGE III	1650	615.00	715.00
94	VICTORIAN CHRISTMAS IV	CL	695.00	695.00
94	WARMTH OF HOME, THE	3450	440.00	440.00
95	A LIGHT IN THE STORM	3950	650.00	690.00
95	AUTUMN LANE	2950	650.00	690.00
95	BLESSINGS OF SUMMER	4950	865.00	920.00
95	END OF A PERFECT DAY III	4950	995.00	1065.00
95	GOLDEN GATE BRIDGE, SAN FRANCISCO	3950	1090.00	1150.00
95	HOMETOWN MEMORIES I	4950	865.00	920.00
95	MAIN STREET TROLLEY	1250	650.00	690.00
95	MORNING DOGWOOD	4950	495.00	525.00
95	MORNING GLORY COTTAGE	4950	545.00	580.00
95	PETALS OF HOPE	3950	580.00	580.00
T. KINKADE		**CANVAS EDITION/BEAUTY OF THE FOREST**		
95	EVENING IN THE FOREST	OP	580.00	580.00
T. KINKADE		**CANVAS EDITION/BLOSSOM LANE**		
95	BLOSSOM BRIDGE	2950	580.00	580.00
T. KINKADE		**CANVAS EDITION/CHRISTMAS COTTAGE**		
92	SILENT NIGHT	980	395.00	995.00
95	DEER CREEK COTTAGE	OP	390.00	465.00
T. KINKADE		**CANVAS EDITION/DOGWOOD GARDENS**		
91	AFTERNOON LIGHT, DOGWOOD	OP	435.00	1700.00
T. KINKADE		**CANVAS EDITION/HOMETOWN MEMORIES**		
95	HOMETOWN CHAPEL	4950	895.00	950.00
T. KINKADE		**CANVAS EDITION/LAMPLIGHT LANE**		
95	LAMPLIGHT VILLAGE	4950	650.00	750.00
T. KINKADE		**CANVAS EDITION/MAIN STREET MEMORIES**		
95	MAIN STREET CELEBRATION	1250	650.00	690.00
95	MAIN STREET MATINEE	1250	650.00	690.00
T. KINKADE		**CANVAS EDITION/MOMENTS OF GLORY**		
93	GLORY OF WINTER	1250	615.00	615.00
T. KINKADE		**CANVAS EDITION/MOONLIGHT LANE**		
94	MOONLIGHT LANE I	2400	515.00	580.00
T. KINKADE		**CANVAS EDITION/PARIS, CITY OF LIGHTS**		
93	PARIS, CITY OF LIGHTS	1980	695.00	1400.00
T. KINKADE		**CANVAS EDITION/SAN FRANCISCO**		
91	SAN FRANCISCO, UNION SQUARE	CL	695.00	3000.00
94	SAN FRANCISCO, MARKET ST.	750	795.00	795.00
T. KINKADE		**CANVAS EDITION/SECRET GARDEN PLACES**		
94	HIDDEN ARBOR	3750	515.00	515.00

YR	NAME	LIMIT	ISSUE	TREND
T. KINKADE		**CANVAS EDITION/SIMPLER TIMES**		
95	SIMPLER TIMES I	OP	550.00	550.00
T. KINKADE		**CANVAS EDITION/SUGAR & SPICE COTTAGES**		
94	AUTUMN AT ASHLEY'S COTTAGE	OP	415.00	440.00
T. KINKADE		**CANVAS EDITION/SWEETHEART COTTAGE**		
92	MILLER'S COTTAGE	CL	495.00	1095.00
T. KINKADE		**CANVAS EDITION/SWEETHEART HIDEAWAYS**		
95	BROOKSIDE HIDEAWAY	OP	545.00	580.00
95	STEPPING STONE COTTAGE	2950	650.00	690.00
T. KINKADE		**CANVAS EDITION/VICTORIAN CHRISTMAS**		
92	VICTORIAN CHRISTMAS	CL	595.00	2200.00
94	VICTORIAN CHRISTMAS III	CL	615.00	650.00
T. KINKADE		**PAPER EDITION**		
*	MORNING LIGHT	*	*	800.00
*	SWEETHEART COTTAGE II	980	185.00	500.00
90	SPRING AT STONEGATE	550	185.00	185.00
91	CHRISTMAS EVE	980	185.00	185.00
91	FLAGS OVER THE CAPITOL	980	235.00	250.00
91	MCKENNA'S COTTGE	980	205.00	205.00
91	OLD P'FIELD TEA ROOM	980	205.00	205.00
91	OPEN GATE, SUSSEX	980	110.00	110.00
92	AMBER AFTERNOON	980	235.00	275.00
92	CHRISTMAS AT AHWAHNEE	980	205.00	205.00
92	GARDEN PARTY	980	185.00	205.00
92	OLD P'FIELD GIFT SHOPPE	980	195.00	205.00
92	YOSEMITE	980	235.00	250.00
93	LAMPLIGHT LANE	980	235.00	975.00
93	ST. NICHOLAS CIRCLE	1750	250.00	250.00
93	STUDIO IN THE GARDEN	980	175.00	175.00
93	VILLAGE INN, THE	1200	195.00	205.00
93	WINTER'S END	875	250.00	250.00
94	CHRISTMAS MEMORIES	2450	205.00	205.00
94	EMERALD ISLE COTTAGE	2750	205.00	205.00
94	GUARDIAN CASTLE	2750	300.00	300.00
94	HIDDEN ARBOR	2750	195.00	195.00
94	POWER & THE MAJESTY, THE	2750	250.00	250.00
94	WARMTH OF HOME, THE	2450	185.00	185.00
95	AUTUMN LANE	2850	235.00	250.00
95	BLOSSOM BRIDGE	2850	205.00	205.00
95	DEER CREEK COTTAGE	2850	185.00	185.00
95	END OF A PERFECT DAY III	4850	325.00	325.00
95	GOLDEN GATE BRIDGE, SAN FRANCISCO	3850	325.00	325.00
95	LIGHTS OF HOME, THE	250	225.00	225.00
95	SIMPLER TIMES I	3350	250.00	250.00
95	STEPPING STONE COTTAGE	2850	250.00	250.00
T. KINKADE		**PAPER EDITION/AUTUMN GATE**		
93	BEYOND AUTUMN GATE	1650	250.00	825.00
94	GARDENS BEYOND AUTUMN GATE	CL	325.00	325.00
T. KINKADE		**PAPER EDITION/BEAUTY OF THE FOREST**		
95	EVENING IN THE FOREST	OP	205.00	205.00
T. KINKADE		**PAPER EDITION/BLESSINGS OF THE SEASON**		
93	BLESSINGS OF AUTUMN, THE	OP	250.00	250.00
94	BLESSINGS OF SPRING, THE	OP	205.00	205.00
95	BLESSINGS OF SUMMER	4850	300.00	300.00
T. KINKADE		**PAPER EDITION/CHRISTMAS COTTAGE**		
93	STONEHEARTH HUTCH	OP	185.00	185.00
94	CHRISTMAS TREE COTTAGE	OP	185.00	185.00
T. KINKADE		**PAPER EDITION/COUNTRY CHURCH**		
92	BLOSSOM HILL CHURCH	OP	250.00	250.00
T. KINKADE		**PAPER EDITION/COUNTRY MEMORIES**		
92	COUNTRY MEMORIES	OP	185.00	185.00
T. KINKADE		**PAPER EDITION/DOGWOOD GARDENS**		
95	MORNING DOGWOOD	4850	195.00	195.00
T. KINKADE		**PAPER EDITION/END OF A PERFECT DAY**		
93	END OF A PERFECT DAY	CL	185.00	800.00
94	END OF A PERFECT DAY II	CL	300.00	300.00
T. KINKADE		**PAPER EDITION/FAMILY TRADITIONS**		
93	SUNDAY OUTING	OP	205.00	205.00
T. KINKADE		**PAPER EDITION/FLOWER COTTAGES OF CARMEL**		
95	MORNING GLORY COTTAGE	OP	205.00	205.00
T. KINKADE		**PAPER EDITION/GARDEN OF PROMISE**		
95	PETALS OF HOPE	3850	205.00	205.00
T. KINKADE		**PAPER EDITION/GREAT MANSIONS OF AMERICA**		
93	HOMESTEAD HOUSE	1250	235.00	250.00
T. KINKADE		**PAPER EDITION/HIDDEN COTTAGE**		
93	HIDDEN COTTAGE II	OP	205.00	205.00
T. KINKADE		**PAPER EDITION/HOMETOWN MEMORIES**		
95	HOMETOWN CHAPEL	OP	75.00	75.00
95	HOMETOWN MEMORIES I	OP	300.00	300.00
T. KINKADE		**PAPER EDITION/LAMPLIGHT LANE**		
94	LAMPLIGHT INN	2750	235.00	250.00
95	LAMPLIGHT VILLAGE	4850	235.00	250.00
T. KINKADE		**PAPER EDITION/MAIN STREET MEMORIES**		
95	MAIN STREET CELEBRATION	1950	250.00	250.00
95	MAIN STREET MATINEE	OP	250.00	250.00

Offering a glimpse into the life of a traveling photographer is The Memory Maker *by Charles Wysocki. Issued in 1989 in a limited edition of 2,500 by The Greenwich Workshop, the original sold for $165.*

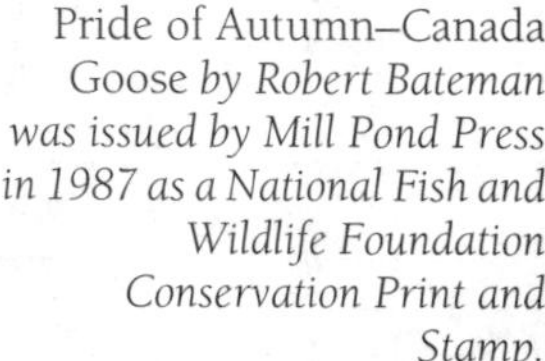

Pride of Autumn–Canada Goose *by Robert Bateman was issued by Mill Pond Press in 1987 as a National Fish and Wildlife Foundation Conservation Print and Stamp.*

Jim Daly's charming subjects show signs of Spring Fever *in this Mill Pond Press limited edition of 950. It was originally issued at $85 in 1982.*

In Harmony, *by the late artist Alan Maley, captures the quiet feeling of comfort felt by this family. Published by Past Impressions.*

YR	NAME	LIMIT	ISSUE	TREND
95	MAIN STREET TROLLEY	OP	250.00	250.00
T. KINKADE		**PAPER EDITION/MOMENTS OF GLORY**		
93	GLORY OF WINTER	1250	235.00	250.00
T. KINKADE		**PAPER EDITION/MOONLIGHT LANE**		
94	MOONLIGHT LANE I	2400	205.00	205.00
T. KINKADE		**PAPER EDITION/PARIS, CITY OF LIGHTS**		
93	PARIS, CITY OF LIGHTS	1980	285.00	285.00
94	PARIS, EIFFEL TOWER	OP	295.00	295.00
T. KINKADE		**PAPER EDITION/PLEIN-AIR COLLECTION**		
95	BIARRITZ	1200	95.00	95.00
95	BLOOMSBURY CAFE	1200	145.00	145.00
95	LUXEMBOURG GARDENS	1200	95.00	95.00
95	PACIFIC GROVE	1200	125.00	125.00
95	PARIS, ST. MICHEL	1200	125.00	125.00
95	PUERTA VALLARTA BEACH	1200	125.00	125.00
95	SAN FRANCISCO, ALCATRAZ	1200	145.00	145.00
95	VENICE CANAL	1200	95.00	95.00
95	WISTERIA ARBOR	1200	125.00	125.00
96	CHINATOWN, SAN FRANCISCO	950	95.00	95.00
96	CHINATOWN, SAN FRANCISCO	950	210.00	210.00
T. KINKADE		**PAPER EDITION/SAN FRANCISCO**		
93	FISHERMAN'S WHARF, SAN FRANCISCO	2750	300.00	325.00
94	SAN FRANCISCO, MARKET ST.	750	375.00	375.00
T. KINKADE		**PAPER EDITION/SEASIDE MEMORIES**		
94	BEACON OF HOPE	OP	235.00	250.00
95	A LIGHT IN THE STORM	OP	235.00	250.00
T. KINKADE		**PAPER EDITION/SECRET GARDEN PLACES**		
94	HIDDEN GAZEBO	2400	185.00	205.00
T. KINKADE		**PAPER EDITION/STREAMS OF LIVING WATERS**		
92	BESIDE STILL WATERS	1250	195.00	300.00
T. KINKADE		**PAPER EDITION/SUGAR & SPICE COTTAGES**		
93	HEATHER'S HUTCH	OP	185.00	185.00
94	AUTUMN AT ASHLEY'S COTTAGE	OP	185.00	185.00
T. KINKADE		**PAPER EDITION/SWEETHEART COTTAGE**		
94	SWEETHEART COTTAGE III, HAVENCREST	CL	250.00	250.00
T. KINKADE		**PAPER EDITION/SWEETHEART HIDEAWAYS**		
95	BROOKSIDE HIDEAWAY	OP	205.00	205.00
T. KINKADE		**PAPER EDITION/VICTORIAN CHRISTMAS**		
93	VICTORIAN CHRISTMAS II	CL	235.00	250.00
94	VICTORIAN CHRISTMAS III	CL	250.00	250.00
T. KINKADE		**SOCIETY MEMBER'S ONLY PIECE**		
95	LOCHAVEN COTTAGE, COLLECTOR COTTAGE II	CL	95.00	95.00
95	LOCHAVEN COTTAGE, COLLECTOR COTTAGE II	CL	315.00	450.00
T. KINKADE		**TENTH ANNIVERSARY ARCHIVE COLLECTION**		
94	CREEKSIDE TRAIL	CL	690.00	690.00
94	CREEKSIDE TRAIL	1980	275.00	275.00
94	DAYS OF PEACE	1984	275.00	275.00
94	DAYS OF PEACE	CL	690.00	690.00
94	DUSK IN THE VALLEY	1984	275.00	275.00
94	DUSK IN THE VALLEY	CL	590.00	690.00
94	SPRING IN THE ALPS	CL	225.00	225.00
94	SPRING IN THE ALPS	1984	575.00	575.00

LITTLE ANGEL PUBLISHING

YR	NAME	LIMIT	ISSUE	TREND
D. GELSINGER				
94	A FLOWER FOR BABY A/P	25	585.00	585.00
94	A FLOWER FOR BABY S/N	250	510.00	510.00
94	TOY BOX, THE A/P	25	525.00	525.00
94	TOY BOX, THE S/N	250	450.00	450.00
95	ALEXANDRIA'S TEDDY A/P	25	352.50	353.00
95	ALEXANDRIA'S TEDDY S/N	250	295.00	295.00
95	FIRELIGHT A/P	SO	595.00	595.00
95	FIRELIGHT S/N	300	520.00	520.00
95	GOLDEN GATE A/P	20	795.00	795.00
95	GOLDEN GATE S/N	200	695.00	695.00
95	LIFE'S LITTLE TANGELS A/P	SO	595.00	595.00
95	LIFE'S LITTLE TANGLES S/N	350	520.00	520.00
95	MOTHERLY LOVE A/P	30	525.00	525.00
95	MOTHERLY LOVE S/N	300	450.00	450.00
95	PERFECT TREE, THE A/P	25	352.50	353.00
95	PERFECT TREE, THE S/N	250	295.00	295.00
96	SUGAR & SPICE A/P	20	352.50	353.00
96	SUGAR & SPICE S/N	200	295.00	295.00
D. GELSINGER				**PAPER PRINT**
94	A FLOWER FOR BABY A/P	15	190.00	190.00
94	A FLOWER FOR BABY S/N	150	140.00	140.00
94	TOY BOX, THE A/P	15	170.00	170.00
94	TOY BOX, THE S/N	150	120.00	120.00
95	ALEXANDRIA'S TEDDY A/P	15	120.00	120.00
95	ALEXANDRIA'S TEDDY S/N	150	80.00	80.00
95	FIRE LIGHT A/P	15	200.00	200.00
95	FIRE LIGHT S/N	150	150.00	150.00
95	GOLDEN GATE A/P	10	230.00	230.00
95	GOLDEN GATE S/N	100	180.00	180.00
95	LIFE'S LITTLE TANGLES A/P	15	200.00	200.00
95	LIFE'S LITTLE TANGLES S/N	150	150.00	150.00
95	MOTHERLY LOVE A/P	15	170.00	170.00

YR	NAME	LIMIT	ISSUE	TREND
95	MOTHERLY LOVE S/N	150	120.00	120.00
95	PERFECT TREE, THE A/P	15	120.00	120.00
95	PERFECT TREE, THE S/N	150	80.00	80.00
96	SUGAR & SPICE A/P	5	120.00	120.00
96	SUGAR & SPICE S/N	50	80.00	80.00
D. GELSINGER				**THE SEASONS OF ANGELS**
96	SPRING ANGEL A/P	12	234.00	234.00
96	SPRING ANGEL S/N	125	184.00	184.00
96	WINTER ANGEL A/P	12	234.00	234.00
96	WINTER ANGEL S/N	125	184.00	184.00
D. GELSINGER				**THE SEASONS OF ANGELS PAPER PRINT**
96	SPRING ANGEL A/P	12	87.00	87.00
96	SPRING ANGEL S/N	125	57.00	57.00
96	WINTER ANGEL S/N	125	57.00	57.00
96	WINTER ANGLE A/P	12	87.00	87.00

LYNN'S PRINTS

YR	NAME	LIMIT	ISSUE	TREND
L. GRAEBNER				**THE AMISH**
87	BACKFIRE	750	40.00	160.00
87	BREAD AND MILK	*	40.00	40.00
87	FIRST LOVE	*	40.00	40.00
87	HORSEY'S TREAT	750	40.00	135.00
87	LITTLE APPLE PICKER	*	40.00	100.00
87	SUNDAY MEETING	750	25.00	65.00
88	AUCTION, THE	*	25.00	25.00
88	BACK PORCH QUILT FIXIN	750	25.00	95.00
88	BARN RAISING LUNCH	*	25.00	25.00
88	BARNYARD FRIENDS	*	25.00	25.00
88	CART FULL OF APPLES	750	25.00	100.00
88	MOTHERS SPECIAL DAY '88	750	20.00	100.00
88	ROADSIDE BERRY PICKIN	750	25.00	75.00
88	SHARING	*	15.00	45.00
88	SHARING THE LOAD	750	25.00	85.00
88	SWEET SMELLS	750	15.00	65.00
88	TALKING WITH DOLLY	750	15.00	45.00
89	AUTUMN PLAYTIME	*	85.00	85.00
89	CART FOR DOLLIES	*	25.00	25.00
89	COME A COURTIN	*	20.00	20.00
89	FALL AFTERNOON	*	30.00	30.00
89	FEEDING TIME BEFORE SCHOOL	*	30.00	30.00
89	FISHERMAN'S HELPER	*	30.00	30.00
89	IN TOWN CHRISTMAS	*	100.00	200.00
89	WILD GOOSE CHASE	*	30.00	30.00
89	YOU CAN'T HAVE MY DOLLY	*	20.00	20.00
90	AFTERNOON AT THE POND	*	65.00	65.00
90	AIRING THE QUILTS	*	30.00	30.00
90	BE GOOD TO EACH OTHER	50	100.00	250.00
90	CHRISTMASTIME IN THE COUNTRY	*	65.00	65.00
90	DOLLY'S QUILT	*	20.00	20.00
90	FETCH	*	20.00	20.00
90	FIRST QUILT	*	20.00	20.00
90	FIRST ROSE OF SUMMER	*	30.00	30.00
90	FOREVER YOURS DAD	*	20.00	20.00
90	FRIENDS	*	30.00	30.00
90	FRONT PORCH TEA PARTY	*	30.00	30.00
90	GRAPE PICKIN	*	30.00	30.00
90	LET'S BE FRIENDS	*	30.00	30.00
90	MMM GOOD	*	20.00	20.00
90	SUMMER SCENTS	*	20.00	20.00
90	SUNDAY MEETING HOOKY	*	65.00	65.00
91	CLOAK ROOM	*	150.00	150.00
91	COME DOWN AND HAVE A TREAT	*	25.00	25.00
91	HITCHIN A RIDE	*	25.00	25.00
91	KNIT PICKIN	*	25.00	25.00
91	MOTHER'S DAY SPECIAL 1991	*	25.00	25.00
91	ROUNDING UP THE PIGS	*	25.00	25.00
91	SEEDS FOR YOU MR. CARDINAL	*	25.00	50.00

MAFEKING COLLECTION

YR	NAME	LIMIT	ISSUE	TREND
M. GREEN				**MAN'S BEST FRIEND**
94	DEREK (THE LABRADOR RETRIEVER)	1500	17.39	25.00
94	MICKEY (SPANIEL CROSS)	1500	17.39	25.00
94	PEPPER (THE AIREDALE)	1500	17.39	25.00

MARTY BELL FINE ART

YR	NAME	LIMIT	ISSUE	TREND
M. BELL				**AMERICA THE BEAUTIFUL**
95	BLUEBIRD VICTORIAN, THE	YR	320.00	340.00
95	GRETEL'S COTTAGE	750	225.00	225.00
95	HANSEL'S HOUSE	750	225.00	225.00
95	MENDOCINO TWILIGHT	750	400.00	425.00
95	MORNING GLORY/TRIPLE	500	650.00	650.00
95	TELEGRAPH HILL	750	150.00	150.00
95	TUCK BOX CHRISTMAS	750	250.00	*
95	TUCK BOX, THE-TEA ROOM, CARMEL	500	456.00	1200.00
95	TUCK BOX, THE-TEA ROOM, CARMEL	OP	200.00	200.00
M. BELL				**AMERICA THE BEAUTIFUL/GIFT**
95	BLUEBIRD, THE	YR	*	*

YR	NAME	LIMIT	ISSUE	TREND
M. BELL				**ENGLAND**
95	BLYTON COTTAGE	750	100.00	100.00
95	BURTON COTTAGE	750	100.00	100.00
95	HOLLY COTTAGE	750	100.00	100.00
95	HONEYCOMB COTTAGE	750	100.00	1000.00
95	MILL HAY MANOR	750	850.00	850.00
95	MRS. BROWNS FOR TEA	750	100.00	100.00
95	ROSE BOWER COTTAGE/TRIPLE	500	520.00	520.00
95	SISSINGHURST GARDEN	750	488.00	488.00
95	TULIP TIME	500	456.00	456.00
M. BELL				**GARDENS OF THE HEART**
95	CLOISTER GARDEN	250	488.00	488.00
95	MAJESTY	500	700.00	742.00
95	SWEETHEART'S GATE	750	225.00	225.00
M. BELL				**HUGGA BELLS**
95	LUV BOAT, THE	350	110.00	116.00
95	MOTHERLOVE	350	116.00	116.00
95	STORYTIME	350	110.00	115.00
95	WEDDED BLISS	350	116.00	116.00
M. BELL				**LIMITED EDITION LITHOGRAPHS**
82	BIBURY COTTAGE	550	290.00	1400.00
82	BIG DADDY'S SHOE	950	64.00	300.00
82	CASTLE COMBE COTTAGE	550	264.00	1200.00
82	CROSSROADS COTTAGE	950	38.00	200.00
83	NESTLEWOOD	550	300.00	4900.00
84	PENHURST TEA ROOMS (ARCHIVAL)	1000	335.00	2750.00
84	PENHURST TEA ROOMS (CANVAS)	550	335.00	3600.00
84	WEST KINGTON DELL	550	240.00	1000.00
85	LITTLE BOXFORD	550	78.00	900.00
85	MEADOWLARK COTTAGE	550	78.00	700.00
85	SUMMER'S GLOW	550	98.00	1000.00
85	SURREY GARDEN HOUSE	550	98.00	1500.00
85	SWEET PINE COTTAGE	550	78.00	1500.00
85	WINDSONG COTTAGE	550	78.00	800.00
86	BURFORD VILLAGE STORE	550	120.00	1000.00
86	COTSWOLD PARISH CHURCH	1850	98.00	2000.00
86	HOUSEWIVES CHOICE	550	98.00	1000.00
86	LORNA DOONE COTTAGE	550	380.00	9000.00
86	YORK GARDEN SHOP	550	110.00	1000.00
87	ALDERTON VILLAGE	550	264.00	900.00
87	BROUGHTON VILLAGE	950	128.00	500.00
87	CHAPLAIN'S GARDEN, THE	550	264.00	2250.00
87	CHIPPENHAM FARM	550	120.00	900.00
87	DOVE COTTAGE GARDEN	950	272.00	500.00
87	DRIFTSONE MANOR	550	440.00	4000.00
87	DUCKSBRIDGE COTTAGE	550	430.00	2500.00
87	EASHING COTTAGE	950	128.00	350.00
87	FIDDLEFORD COTTAGE	550	78.00	1950.00
87	HALFWAY COTTAGE	950	272.00	800.00
87	LITTLE TULIP THATCH	550	120.00	600.00
87	MAY COTTAGE	950	128.00	700.00
87	MILLPOND STOCKBRIDGE, THE	550	120.00	1800.00
87	MORNING GLORY COTTAGE	550	120.00	600.00
87	SUNRISE THATCH	950	128.00	350.00
87	VICAR'S GATE, THE	550	110.00	900.00
87	WAKEHURST PLACE	950	520.00	2700.00
87	WELL COTTAGE, SANDY LANE	550	440.00	1600.00
87	WHITE LILAC THATCH	950	272.00	700.00
88	BISHOP'S ROSES, THE	2450	220.00	500.00
88	CLOVE COTTAGE	950	128.00	800.00
88	CLOVER LANE COTTAGE	1850	272.00	1400.00
88	COTSWOLD TWILIGHT	950	128.00	500.00
88	GINGER COTTAGE	1850	320.00	800.00
88	ICOMB VILLAGE GARDEN	RT	620.00	1800.00
88	JASMINE THATCH	950	272.00	700.00
88	LULLABYE COTTAGE	RT	220.00	525.00
88	MORNING'S GLOW	1850	280.00	650.00
88	MURRLE COTTAGE	1850	320.00	1000.00
88	RODWAY COTTAGE	RT	620.00	2000.00
88	SHERE VILLAGE ANTIQUES	950	272.00	825.00
88	SWEET TWILIGHT	RT	220.00	600.00
89	BLUSH OF SPRING	1250	96.00	225.00
89	FIRESIDE CHRISTMAS	550	136.00	800.00
89	GAMEKEEPER'S COTTAGE, THE	950	560.00	2000.00
89	LARKSPUR COTTAGE	2450	220.00	450.00
89	OLD BEAMS COTTAGE	950	368.00	700.00
89	PRIDE OF SPRING	1250	96.00	225.00
89	PRIMROSE COTTAGE	2450	88.00	88.00
90	ARBOR COTTAGE	950	130.00	250.00
90	BRYANTS PUDDLE THATCH	950	130.00	250.00
90	GOMSHALL FLOWER SHOP	950	396.00	2050.00
90	LITTLE WELL THATCH	950	130.00	250.00
90	LONGSTOCK LANE	950	130.00	250.00
90	LOWER BROCKHAMPTON MANOR	950	730.00	1825.00
90	OLD HERTFORDSHIRE COTTAGE	950	396.00	1500.00
90	READY FOR CHRISTMAS	550	148.00	1050.00
91	DEVON ROSES	*	96.00	200.00
91	DORSET ROSES	*	96.00	200.00

YR	NAME	LIMIT	ISSUE	TREND
91	TEA TIME	*	130.00	200.00
91	WINDWARD COTTAGE, RYE	*	228.00	625.00
M. BELL		**MEMBERS ONLY COLLECTORS CLUB**		
91	LITTLE THATCH TWILIGHT	YR	288.00	380.00
92	BLOSSOM LANE	YR	288.00	288.00
92	CANDLE AT EVENTIDE	YR	*	*

MILITARY GALLERY

YR	NAME	LIMIT	ISSUE	TREND
N. TRUDGIAN			**AIR COMBAT LEGEND**	
95	BLACK CAT RESCUE	800	65.00	65.00
95	MYNARSKI'S LANC	800	65.00	65.00
95	TRAINBUSTERS	800	65.00	65.00
N. TRUDGIAN			**NICOLAS TRUDGIAN**	
95	BOMBER FORCE	500	150.00	150.00
95	COMBAT OVER BEACHY HEAD	800	65.00	65.00
95	COMBAT OVER NEW GUINEA	800	65.00	65.00
95	INVASION FORCE	800	65.00	65.00
95	KIWI STRIKE	800	65.00	65.00
95	LAST MAN HOME	1000	150.00	150.00
95	LIGHTNING ENCOUNTER	1000	150.00	150.00
95	RETURN OF THE HUNTERS	1000	150.00	150.00
95	SQUADRON SCRAMBLE	800	65.00	65.00
95	TWILIGHT CONQUEST	600	150.00	150.00
R. TAYLOR			**ROBERT TAYLOR**	
95	AIR APACHES ON THE WARPATH	600	295.00	295.00
95	EAGLES OVER THE RHINE	1250	295.00	295.00
95	OUT OF FUEL AND SAFELY HOME	1250	295.00	295.00
95	RANGERS ON THE RAMPAGE	850	295.00	295.00
95	SIGNED BY ONE PILOT VICTORY FLYOVER	500	75.00	75.00
95	STEINHOFF TRIBUTE	1250	350.00	350.00
95	VALOR IN THE PACIFIC	1250	295.00	295.00
95	VICTORY FLYOVER	1200	295.00	450.00
95	WIDE HORIZONS	1250	100.00	100.00
R. TAYLOR			**ROBERT TAYLOR POSTER**	
95	VICTORY FLYOVER	OP	35.00	35.00
N. TRUDGIAN			**WORLD WAR II INSIGNIA**	
95	ALPINE MUSTANG	OP	65.00	65.00
95	FLYING FORTRESS	OP	65.00	65.00
95	FLYING TIGER	OP	65.00	65.00
95	KLINGS CLIFFE LIGHTNING	OP	65.00	65.00
95	MITCHELL OVER THE RIVIERA	OP	65.00	65.00
95	PACIFIC PIRATE	OP	65.00	65.00

MILL POND PRESS

YR	NAME	LIMIT	ISSUE	TREND
R. BATEMAN				
*	AFRICAN FISH EAGLE	*	265.00	265.00
*	ARKANSAS DUCK STAMP 1987-WOOD DUCK	*	200.00	200.00
*	BUFFALO AT AMBOSELI-CAPE BUFFALO	*	400.00	400.00
*	CANADA DUCK PRINT W/S 1988-PINTAILS	*	175.00	175.00
*	CANADA DUCK STAMP-1985 W/2 MALLARD DUCKS	*	200.00	200.00
*	CANADA GEESE	*	450.00	450.00
*	CANADA GEESE IN WINTER	*	*	2500.00
*	CHEETAH SIESTA	*	*	2500.00
*	CHICKADEE ON PINECONE-ETCHING	*	*	2000.00
*	COUGAR AND KIT	*	*	495.00
*	COUGAR IN THE SNOW	*	*	450.00
*	DESCENDING SHADOWS-WOLVES	*	*	295.00
*	DIK-DIKS	*	*	600.00
*	ENDANGERED SPACES-ROYAL-BEAR	*	*	925.00
*	FIRST ARRIVAL-KILLDEER BIRD	*	265.00	265.00
*	FOX-ETCHING	*	*	2200.00
*	GIANT PANDA	*	*	750.00
*	GIANT PANDA IN THE WILD	*	*	295.00
*	GOLDEN-HEADED LION TAMARIN	*	*	350.00
*	GOLDFINCH WITH MULLEIN	*	*	225.00
*	GRIZZLY BEAR-ETCHING	*	*	2200.00
*	HOODED MERGANSER-DUCK	*	*	700.00
*	LION CUBS B/W	*	*	1000.00
*	LION-ETCHING	*	*	2200.00
*	LIONESS-ETCHING	*	*	2200.00
*	LOON PAIR AND YOUNG	*	*	425.00
*	MERGANSER DUCK-BRONZE	*	*	695.00
*	MEXICAN WOLF	*	*	285.00
*	MOOSE	*	*	1200.00
*	NEW YORK DUCK STAMP W/2 S	*	175.00	175.00
*	NO. AMERICAN WILD SHEEP STAMP	*	300.00	300.00
*	PEACEFUL FLOCK-AMERICAN WIGEON	*	225.00	225.00
*	PEREGRINE AND YOUNG	*	*	395.00
*	PEREGRINE IN FLIGHT-BRONZE	*	*	1500.00
*	PICNIC TABLE	*	250.00	250.00
*	PREDATOR PORTFOLIO-WOLVERINE	*	275.00	275.00
*	RED-TAILED HAWK STUDY-BRONZE	*	*	1750.00
*	SAP BUCKET-MYRTLE WARBLER	*	195.00	195.00
*	SHADOW OF RAINFOREST-JAGUAR	*	*	1200.00
*	SIBERIAN TIGER - PRESTIGE	*	625.00	625.00
*	SIERRA EVENING-MEXICAN WOLF	*	285.00	285.00
*	SPARRING ELEPHANTS	*	325.00	325.00
*	SUMMER GARDEN - YOUNG ROBIN	*	235.00	235.00

YR	NAME	LIMIT	ISSUE	TREND
*	SYMBOL OF RAINFOREST - JAGUAR	*	235.00	235.00
*	TEXAS DUCK STAMP 1990-AMERICAN WIGEON	*	135.00	135.00
*	VERMILION FLYCATCHER	*	95.00	95.00
*	VIGILANCE - PREMIER	*	650.00	650.00
*	WASHINGTON DUCK STAMP	*	150.00	150.00
*	WILDEBEEST AT SUNSET	*	400.00	400.00
*	WINGED SPIRIT - 2 PC. SNOWY OWL	*	*	1100.00
*	WINTER PINE- G/H OWL	*	265.00	265.00
*	WINTER RUN-BULL MOOSE	*	295.00	295.00
*	WINTER TRACKS-COYOTE	*	335.00	335.00
*	WOLF SKETCH	*	250.00	250.00
78	BY THE TRACKS-KILLDEER	950	75.00	1200.00
78	CHEETAH WITH CUBS	950	95.00	450.00
78	DOWNY WOODPECKER ON GOLDENROD	950	50.00	1425.00
78	LION CUBS	950	125.00	750.00
78	MAJESTY ON THE WING-BALD EAGLE	950	150.00	4000.00
78	YOUNG BARN SWALLOW	950	75.00	700.00
79	AFTERNOON GLOW-SNOWY OWL	950	125.00	625.00
79	AMONG THE LEAVES-COTTONTAIL RABBIT	950	75.00	1400.00
79	BULL MOOSE	950	125.00	1250.00
79	COUNTRY LANE-PHEASANTS	950	85.00	300.00
79	EVENING SNOWFALL-AMERICAN ELK	950	150.00	1900.00
79	GOLDEN EAGLE	950	150.00	250.00
79	GREAT BLUE HERON	950	125.00	1300.00
79	HIGH COUNTRY-STONE SHEEP	950	125.00	325.00
79	KING OF THE REALM-LION	950	125.00	675.00
79	MASTER OF THE HERD-AMERICAN BUFFALO	950	150.00	2250.00
79	SURF AND SANDERLINGS	950	65.00	600.00
79	UP IN THE PINE-GREAT HORNED OWL	950	150.00	730.00
79	WILY AND WARY-RED FOX	950	125.00	1500.00
79	WINTER CARDINAL	950	75.00	3550.00
79	WINTER-SNOWSHOE HARE	950	95.00	1200.00
79	WOLF PACK IN MOONLIGHT	950	95.00	3000.00
79	YELLOW-RUMPED WARBLER	950	50.00	575.00
80	AFRICAN AMBER-LIONESS PAIR	950	175.00	525.00
80	ANTARCTIC ELEMENTS-SEA GULL	950	125.00	150.00
80	ARCTIC FAMILY-POLAR BEARS	950	150.00	2250.00
80	ASLEEP ON THE HEMLOCK-SCREECH OWL	950	125.00	1150.00
80	AUTUMN OVERTURE-MOOSE	950	245.00	1450.00
80	AWESOME LAND-AMERICAN ELK	950	245.00	1785.00
80	BARN OWL IN THE CHURCHYARD	950	125.00	775.00
80	BLUFFING BULL-AFRICAN ELEPHANT	950	135.00	1125.00
80	BROWN PELICAN AND PILINGS	950	165.00	950.00
80	CHAPEL DOORS	950	135.00	375.00
80	COYOTE IN WINTER SAGE	950	245.00	3600.00
80	CURIOUS GLANCE-RED FOX	950	135.00	1200.00
80	EVENING GROSBEAK	950	125.00	1175.00
80	FALLEN WILLOW-SNOWY OWL	950	200.00	950.00
80	FLYING HIGH-GOLDEN EAGLE	950	150.00	1500.00
80	HERON ON THE ROCKS	950	75.00	300.00
80	KINGFISHER IN WINTER	950	175.00	825.00
80	KITTIWAKES GREETING	950	75.00	550.00
80	LEOPARD IN A SAUSAGE TREE	950	150.00	1250.00
80	LION AT TSAVO	950	150.00	275.00
80	MISCHIEF ON THE PROWL-RACCOON	950	85.00	350.00
80	MISTY COAST-GULLS	950	135.00	600.00
80	ON THE ALERT-CHIPMUNK	950	60.00	500.00
80	PRAIRIE EVENING-SHORT-EARED OWL	950	150.00	200.00
80	ROCKY WILDERNESS-COUGAR	950	175.00	1425.00
80	SPRING CARDINAL	950	125.00	600.00
80	SPRING THAW-KILLDEER	950	85.00	150.00
80	VANTAGE POINT-BALD EAGLE	950	245.00	2100.00
80	WHITE ENCOUNTER-POLAR BEAR	950	245.00	4250.00
80	WHITE FOOTED MOUSE IN WINTERGREEN	RT	60.00	675.00
80	WHITE-FOOTED MOUSE IN WINTERGREEN	950	60.00	650.00
80	WINTER ELM-AMERICAN KESTREL	950	135.00	600.00
80	WINTER SONG-CHICKADEES	950	95.00	900.00
81	ARTIST AND HIS DOG	950	150.00	550.00
81	BRIGHT DAY-ATLANTIC PUFFINS	950	175.00	875.00
81	CANADA GEESE-NESTING	950	295.00	3500.00
81	CLEAR NIGHT-WOLVES	950	245.00	6500.00
81	COURTING PAIR-WHISTLING SWAN	950	245.00	550.00
81	COURTSHIP DISPLAY-WILD TURKEY	950	175.00	175.00
81	EDGE OF THE ICE-ERMINE	950	175.00	475.00
81	EVENING LIGHT-WHITE GYRFALCON	950	245.00	1100.00
81	GALLOPING HERD-GIRAFFES	950	175.00	1200.00
81	GRAY SQUIRREL	950	180.00	1250.00
81	HIGH CAMP AT DUSK-HORSE	950	245.00	300.00
81	IN FOR THE EVENING-SHEEP	950	150.00	1500.00
81	KINGFISHER AND ASPENS	950	225.00	720.00
81	LAST LOOK-BIGHORN SHEEP	950	195.00	225.00
81	LAUGHING GULL AND HORSESHOE CRAB	950	125.00	125.00
81	LITTLE BLUE HERON	950	95.00	275.00
81	MISTY MORNING-LOONS	950	150.00	3600.00
81	OSPREY FAMILY	950	245.00	325.00
81	PAIR OF SKIMMERS	950	150.00	200.00
81	RED-TAILED HAWK BY THE CLIFF	950	245.00	550.00
81	RED-WINGED BLACKBIRD AND RAIL FENCE	950	195.00	225.00
81	ROUGH-LEGGED HAWK IN THE ELM	950	175.00	250.00

YR	NAME	LIMIT	ISSUE	TREND
81	ROYAL FAMILY-MUTE SWANS	950	245.00	1100.00
81	SARAH E. WITH GULLS	950	245.00	3650.00
81	SHEER DROP-MOUNTAIN GOATS	950	245.00	2800.00
81	SWIFT FOX	950	175.00	350.00
81	WATCHFUL REPOSE-BLACK BEAR	950	245.00	700.00
81	WINTER MIST-GREAT HORNED OWL	950	245.00	900.00
81	WINTER WREN	950	135.00	250.00
81	WRANGLER'S CAMPSITE-GRAY JAY	950	195.00	550.00
82	ABOVE THE RIVER-TRUMPETER SWANS	950	200.00	1050.00
82	ARCTIC EVENING-WHITE WOLF	950	185.00	1750.00
82	ARCTIC PORTRAIT-WHITE GYRFALCON	950	175.00	250.00
82	AT THE ROADSIDE-RED TAILED HAWK	950	185.00	550.00
82	BAOBAB TREE AND IMPALA	950	245.00	350.00
82	BARN SWALLOWS IN AUGUST	950	245.00	425.00
82	CHEETAH PROFILE	950	245.00	500.00
82	DIPPER BY THE WATERFALL	950	165.00	200.00
82	EDGE OF THE WOODS-WHITETAIL DEER/BOOK	950	745.00	1400.00
82	FOX AT THE GRANARY	950	165.00	225.00
82	FROSTY MORNING-BLUE JAY	950	185.00	1000.00
82	GALLINULE FAMILY	950	135.00	135.00
82	GENTOO PENGUINS AND WHALE BONES	950	205.00	525.00
82	GOLDEN CROWNED KINGLET W/RHODODENDRON	950	150.00	2575.00
82	LEOPARD AMBUSH	950	150.00	600.00
82	LIVELY PAIR-CHICKADEES	950	160.00	450.00
82	MEADOW'S EDGE-MALLARD	950	175.00	1000.00
82	MERGANSER FAMILY IN HIDING	950	200.00	525.00
82	PILEATED WOODPECKER ON BEECH TREE	950	175.00	850.00
82	PIONEER MEMORIES-MAGPIE PAIR	950	175.00	250.00
82	POLAR BEAR PROFILE	950	210.00	2350.00
82	POLAR BEARS AT BAFFIN ISLAND	950	245.00	875.00
82	QUEEN ANNE'S LACE/AMERICAN GOLDFINCH	950	150.00	1000.00
82	READY FOR THE HUNT-SNOWY OWL	950	245.00	775.00
82	RED SQUIRREL	950	245.00	700.00
82	RED WOLF	950	175.00	525.00
82	SPRING MARSH-PINTAIL PAIR	950	200.00	275.00
82	STILL MORNING-HERRING GULLS	950	200.00	250.00
82	WHITE WORLD-DALL SHEEP	950	200.00	450.00
82	WHITE-FOOTED MOUSE ON ASPEN	950	90.00	225.00
82	WILLET ON THE SHORE	950	125.00	225.00
83	BALD EAGLE PORTRAIT	950	185.00	350.00
83	CALL OF THE WILD-BALD EAGLE	950	200.00	250.00
83	EARLY SNOWFALL-RUFFED GROUSE	950	195.00	225.00
83	EARLY SPRING-BLUEBIRD	950	185.00	975.00
83	EVENING IDYLL-MUTE SWANS	950	245.00	525.00
83	GHOST OF THE NORTH-GREAT GREY OWL	950	200.00	2675.00
83	GOSHAWK AND RUFFED GROUSE	950	185.00	700.00
83	GREAT HORNED OWL IN THE WHITE PINE	950	225.00	575.00
83	LOON FAMILY	950	200.00	750.00
83	MORNING ON THE FLATS-BISON	950	200.00	350.00
83	MULE DEER IN WINTER	950	200.00	350.00
83	NEW SEASON-AMERICAN ROBIN	950	200.00	450.00
83	OSPREY IN THE RAIN	950	110.00	650.00
83	PHEASANT IN CORNFIELD	950	200.00	375.00
83	RUBY-THROAT AND COLUMBINE-HUMMINGBIRD	950	150.00	3400.00
83	SNOWY OWL ON DRIFTWOOD	950	170.00	1450.00
83	SPIRITS OF THE FOREST-WOODTHRUSH	950	170.00	1750.00
83	TIGER PORTRAIT	950	130.00	400.00
83	WINTER BARN-SHEEP	950	170.00	400.00
83	WINTER LADY-CARDINAL	950	200.00	1500.00
83	WOLVES ON THE TRAIL	950	225.00	700.00
83	WOODLAND DRUMMER-RUFFED GROUSE	950	185.00	250.00
83	YOUNG ELF OWL-OLD SAGUARO	950	95.00	250.00
84	ACROSS THE SKY-SNOW GOOSE	950	220.00	675.00
84	ALONG THE RIDGE-GRIZZLY BEARS	950	200.00	950.00
84	AMERICAN GOLDFINCH-WINTER DRESS	950	75.00	225.00
84	BIG COUNTRY-PRONGHORN ANTELOPE	RT	185.00	200.00
84	COUGAR PORTRAIT	950	95.00	200.00
84	DOWN FOR A DRINK-MOURNING DOVE	950	135.00	230.00
84	HOODED MERGANSERS IN WINTER	950	210.00	650.00
84	HOUSE FINCH AND YUCCA	950	95.00	175.00
84	IN THE BRIER PATCH-COTTONTAIL	950	165.00	350.00
84	LILY PADS AND LOON	950	200.00	1875.00
84	MAY MAPLE-SCARLET TANAGER	950	175.00	750.00
84	MISTY LAKE-OSPREY	950	95.00	300.00
84	MORNING ON THE RIVER-TRUMPETER SWANS	950	185.00	300.00
84	PEREGRINE AND RUDDY TURNSTONES	950	200.00	350.00
84	READY FOR FLIGHT-PEREGRINE FALCON	950	185.00	500.00
84	RED FOX ON THE PROWL	RT	245.00	1500.00
84	REEDS- STILLIFE	950	185.00	575.00
84	SMALLWOOD-LABRADOR DOG	950	200.00	500.00
84	STRETCHING-CANADA GOOSE	950	225.00	3600.00
84	SUMMER MORNING-LOON	950	185.00	1250.00
84	TADPOLE TIME	950	135.00	475.00
84	TIGER AT DAWN	950	225.00	2500.00
84	WHITE-THROATED SPARROW AND PUSSY WILLOW	950	150.00	580.00
84	WINDOW INTO ONTARIO	950	265.00	1500.00
84	WINTER SUNSET-MOOSE	950	245.00	2700.00
85	ARCTIC TERN PAIR	950	175.00	200.00
85	BEAVER POND REFLECTIONS	RT	185.00	225.00

YR	NAME	LIMIT	ISSUE	TREND
85	CANADA GEESE FAMILY (STONE LITHO)	260	350.00	1000.00
85	CANADA GEESE OVER THE ESCARPMENT	950	135.00	275.00
85	ENTERING THE WATER-COMMON GULLS	950	195.00	200.00
85	GAMBEL'S QUAIL PAIR	950	95.00	350.00
85	GOLDEN EAGLE PORTRAIT	950	115.00	175.00
85	IN THE HIGHLANDS-GOLDEN EAGLE	950	235.00	425.00
85	IN THE MOUNTAINS-OSPREY	950	95.00	200.00
85	IRISH COTTAGE AND WAGTAIL	950	175.00	325.00
85	LEOPARD AT SERONERA	950	175.00	300.00
85	LIONS IN THE GRASS	950	265.00	1250.00
85	MORNING DEW-ROE DEER	950	175.00	175.00
85	OLD WHALING BASE AND FUR SEALS	950	195.00	550.00
85	ON THE GARDEN WALL-CHAFFINCH	950	115.00	300.00
85	ORCA PROCESSION	950	245.00	2525.00
85	PEREGRINE FALCON & WHITE-THROATED SWIFTS	950	245.00	725.00
85	SNOWY HEMLOCK-BARRED OWL	950	245.00	400.00
85	STREAM BANK-JUNE-BIRD	950	160.00	175.00
85	STRUTTING-RING-NECKED PHEASANT	950	225.00	325.00
85	SUDDEN BLIZZARD-RED-TAILED HAWK	950	245.00	600.00
85	TRUMPETER SWANS AND ASPEN	950	245.00	550.00
85	WEATHERED BRANCH-BALD EAGLE	950	115.00	300.00
85	WHITE-BREASTED NUTHATCH ON A BEECH TREE	950	175.00	300.00
85	WINTER COMPANION-YELLOW LAB. DOG	950	175.00	500.00
85	WOOD BISON PORTRAIT	950	165.00	200.00
86	A RESTING PLACE-CAPE BUFFALO	950	265.00	265.00
86	BLACK EAGLE	RT	200.00	200.00
86	BLACK-TAILED DEER IN THE OLYMPICS	RT	245.00	300.00
86	BLACKSMITH PLOVER	RT	185.00	185.00
86	CANADA GEESE WITH YOUNG	950	195.00	325.00
86	CHARGING RHINO	950	325.00	500.00
86	DARK GYRFALCON	950	225.00	325.00
86	DRIFTWOOD PERCH-STRIPED SWALLOWS	950	195.00	250.00
86	ELEPHANT HERD AND SANDGROUSE	950	235.00	235.00
86	EUROPEAN ROBIN AND HYDRANGEAS	950	130.00	245.00
86	FENCE POST AND BURDOCK	950	130.00	160.00
86	HOUSE SPARROW	950	125.00	150.00
86	HUMMINGBIRD PAIR (DIPTYCH)	950	330.00	475.00
86	IN THE GRASS-LIONESS	950	245.00	245.00
86	MALLARD FAMILY-MISTY MARSH	950	130.00	175.00
86	MALLARD PAIR-EARLY WINTER	41740	135.00	200.00
86	MALLARD PAIR-EARLY WINTER (24K GOLD)	950	1650.00	2000.00
86	MALLARD PAIR-EARLY WINTER (GOLD)	7691	250.00	375.00
86	MARGINAL MEADOW-LANDSCAPE	950	220.00	350.00
86	MOOSE AT WATER'S EDGE	950	130.00	225.00
86	MULE DEER IN ASPEN	950	175.00	175.00
86	NORTHERN REFLECTIONS-LOON FAMILY	8631	255.00	2100.00
86	PROUD SWIMMER-SNOW GOOSE	950	185.00	185.00
86	RESTING PLACE-CAPE BUFFALO	950	265.00	265.00
86	ROBINS AT THE NEST	950	185.00	225.00
86	SPLIT RAILS-SNOW BUNTINGS	950	220.00	220.00
86	SUMMERTIME-POLAR BEARS	950	225.00	475.00
86	SWIFT FOX STUDY	950	115.00	150.00
86	WILDEBEEST	950	185.00	185.00
86	WINTER IN THE MOUNTAINS-RAVEN	950	200.00	200.00
87	AT THE NEST-SECRETARY BIRDS	950	290.00	290.00
87	CONTINUING GENERATIONS-SPOTTED OWLS	950	525.00	1150.00
87	END OF SEASON-GRIZZLY	950	325.00	500.00
87	EVERGLADES-EGRET	950	360.00	360.00
87	FARM LANE AND BLUE JAYS	950	225.00	500.00
87	GREAT BLUE HERON IN FLIGHT	950	295.00	550.00
87	GREAT EGRET PREENING	950	315.00	500.00
87	GREATER KUDU BULL	950	145.00	145.00
87	HIGH KINGDOM-SNOW LEOPARD	950	325.00	875.00
87	HOUSE SPARROWS AND BITTERSWEET	950	220.00	400.00
87	HURRICAN LAKE-WOOD DUCKS	950	135.00	200.00
87	KING PENGUINS	950	130.00	135.00
87	LATE WINTER-BLACK SQUIRREL	950	165.00	175.00
87	LION AND WILDEBEEST	950	265.00	265.00
87	LIONESS AT SERENGETI	950	325.00	325.00
87	OLD WILLOW AND MALLARDS	950	325.00	390.00
87	OTTER STUDY	950	235.00	375.00
87	PEREGRINE FALCON/CLIFF (STONE LITHO)	525	350.00	625.00
87	PLOWED FIELD-SNOWY OWL	290	145.00	400.00
87	PRIDE OF AUTUMN	RT	135.00	250.00
87	PRIDE OF AUTUMN-CANADA GOOSE	950	135.00	200.00
87	RHINO AT NGORO NGORO	950	325.00	325.00
87	ROCKY POINT-OCTOBER-BOAT	950	195.00	275.00
87	RUDDY TURNSTONES	950	175.00	175.00
87	SNOWY OWL AND MILKWEED	950	235.00	950.00
87	STONE SHEEP RAM	950	175.00	175.00
87	SYLVAN STREAM-MUTE SWANS	950	125.00	125.00
87	WISE ONE, THE-ELEPHANT	950	325.00	800.00
88	CARDINAL AND WILD APPLES	950	235.00	255.00
88	CATTAILS, FIREWEED,YELLOWTHROAT WARBLER	950	235.00	275.00
88	CHALLENGE, THE-BULL MOOSE	10671	325.00	325.00
88	CHERRYWOOD WITH JUNCOS	950	245.00	300.00
88	COLONIAL GARDEN-LANDSCAPE	950	245.00	300.00
88	DOZING LYNX	950	335.00	1750.00
88	GRASSY BANK-GREAT BLUE HERON	950	285.00	285.00

YR	NAME	LIMIT	ISSUE	TREND
88	GREAT CRESTED GREBE	950	135.00	135.00
88	HARDWOOD FOREST-WHITE TAILED BUCK	950	345.00	2100.00
88	HARLEQUIN DUCK-BULL KELP (EXEC.)	950	550.00	550.00
88	HARLEQUIN DUCK-BULL KELP (GOLD)	950	300.00	300.00
88	LEOPARD AND THOMSON GAZELLE KILL	950	275.00	275.00
88	MALLARD FAMILY AT SUNSET	950	235.00	235.00
88	MUSKOKA LAKE-COMMON LOONS	950	265.00	450.00
88	PANDAS AT PLAY (STONE LITHO)	160	400.00	2500.00
88	PHEASANTS AT DUSK	950	325.00	675.00
88	PREENING PAIR-CANADA GEESE	950	235.00	300.00
88	RED CROSSBILLS	950	125.00	150.00
88	SHELTER-RURAL LANDSCAPE	950	325.00	1150.00
88	TAWNY OWL IN BEECH	950	325.00	600.00
88	TREE SWALLOW OVER POND	950	290.00	290.00
88	YOUNG SANDHILL CRANES	950	325.00	325.00
89	BACKLIGHT-MUTE SWAN	950	275.00	600.00
89	BARN SWALLOW AND HORSE COLLAR	950	225.00	225.00
89	BROAD-TAILED HUMMINGBIRD PAIR	950	225.00	225.00
89	CATCHING THE LIGHT-BARN OWL	RT	295.00	295.00
89	CENTENNIAL FARM	950	295.00	450.00
89	DISPUTE OVER PREY	950	325.00	325.00
89	DISTANT DANGER-RACCOON	1600	225.00	225.00
89	EVENING CALL-COMMON LOON	950	235.00	525.00
89	GOLDFINCH IN THE MEADOW	1600	150.00	200.00
89	MANGROVE MORNING-ROSEATE SPOONBILLS	2000	325.00	325.00
89	MIDNIGHT-BLACK WOLF	25352	325.00	1850.00
89	NEAR GLENBURNIE-ROCK	950	265.00	265.00
89	PUMPKIN TIME	950	195.00	195.00
89	VULTURE AND WILDEBEEST	550	295.00	295.00
89	YOUNG KITTIWAKE-BIRD	950	195.00	195.00
89	YOUNG SNOWY OWL	950	195.00	195.00
90	AIR, THE FOREST & THE WATCH	42,500	325.00	1200.00
90	CHINSTRAP PENGUIN	810	150.00	150.00
90	HOMAGE TO AHMED-ELEPHANT	290	3300.00	3300.00
90	IRELAND HOUSE-LANDSCAPE	950	265.00	265.00
90	KEEPER OF THE LAND-GRIZZLY	290	3300.00	3300.00
90	LUNGING HERON	1250	225.00	225.00
90	MORNING COVE-COMMON LOON	950	165.00	165.00
90	MOSSY BRANCHES-SPOTTED OWL	4500	300.00	525.00
90	MOWED MEADOW	950	190.00	190.00
90	PINTAILS IN SPRING	9651	135.00	360.00
90	POLAR BEAR	290	3300.00	3300.00
90	POWERPLAY-RHINOCEROS	950	320.00	320.00
90	ROLLING WAVES-LESSER SCAUP	3330	125.00	125.00
90	SNOW LEOPARD	290	2500.00	3500.00
90	SUMMER MORNING PASTURE-COWS	290	*	175.00
90	WHITE ON WHITE-SNOWSHOE HARE	290	195.00	590.00
91	ARCTIC CLIFF-WHITE WOLVES	13000	325.00	525.00
91	ARCTIC CLIFF-WHITE WOLVES (CONSERV.)	*	325.00	525.00
91	ARCTIC CLIFF-WHITE WOLVES (PREMIER ED.)	*	625.00	950.00
91	AT THE CLIFF-BOBCAT	RT	325.00	325.00
91	AT THE CLIFF-BOBCAT (SIGNATURE ED.)	*	*	400.00
91	BLUEBIRD AND BLOSSOMS	4500	235.00	235.00
91	BLUEBIRD AND BLOSSOMS (PRESTIGE ED.)	450	625.00	625.00
91	CEREMONIAL POSE-JAPANESE CRANE	*	*	3300.00
91	COTTAGE LANE-RED FOX	950	285.00	285.00
91	ELEPHANT COW AND CALF	950	300.00	300.00
91	ENCOUNTER IN THE BUSH-AFRICAN LIONS	950	295.00	295.00
91	ENDANGERED SPACES-GRIZZLY	4008	325.00	400.00
91	FLUID POWER-ORCA	290	2500.00	2500.00
91	GULLS ON PILINGS	1950	265.00	265.00
91	MANGROVE SHADOW-COMMON EGRET	1250	285.00	285.00
91	SCOLDING, THE-CHICKADEES AND SCREECH OWL	*	235.00	425.00
91	SEA OTTER STUDY	*	150.00	250.00
91	TRUMPETER SWAN FAMILY	290	2500.00	2500.00
91	WHISTLING SWAN-LAKE ERIE	1950	325.00	325.00
91	WIDE HORIZON-TUNDRA SWANS	2862	325.00	385.00
91	WIDE HORIZON-TUNDRA SWANS COMPANION	2862	325.00	400.00
91	YOUNG GIRAFFE	290	850.00	850.00
92	ARCTIC LANDSCAPE-POLAR BEAR	5000	345.00	725.00
92	ARCTIC LANDSCAPE-POLAR BEAR, PREM. ED.	450	800.00	800.00
92	AT THE FEEDER-CARDINAL	950	125.00	125.00
92	BEACH GRASS & TREE FROG	1250	345.00	345.00
92	CLAN OF THE RAVEN	950	235.00	850.00
92	CRIES OF COURTSHIP-CRANE	950	350.00	675.00
92	INTRUSION-MOUNTAIN GORILLA	2250	325.00	325.00
92	JUNCO IN WINTER	1250	185.00	210.00
92	PREDATOR PORTFOLIO-COUGAR	950	465.00	465.00
92	SIBERIAN TIGER	4500	325.00	325.00
92	TEMBO-ELEPHANT	1550	350.00	350.00
92	WHITE TAILED DEER THROUGH BIRCH	10000	335.00	335.00
92	WINTER COAT-LANDSCAPE	1250	245.00	245.00
93	CARDINAL & SUMAC	2500	235.00	1500.00
93	DAY LILIES AND DRAGONFLIES	1250	345.00	345.00
93	GRIZZLY AND CUBS	2250	335.00	400.00
93	KESTREL AND GRASSHOPPER	1250	335.00	335.00
93	MARBLED MURRELET-DUCK	55	1200.00	1200.00
93	ON THE BRINK-RIVER OTTERS	1250	345.00	345.00
93	PREDATOR PORTFOLIO-GRIZZLY	950	475.00	475.00

YR	NAME	LIMIT	ISSUE	TREND
93	PREDATOR PORTFOLIO-POLAR BEAR	950	485.00	485.00
93	PREDATOR PORTFOLIO-WOLF	950	475.00	475.00
93	RECLINING SNOW LEOPARD	1250	335.00	335.00
93	RIVER OTTER	290	1500.00	1500.00
93	ROSE-BREASTED GROSBEAK	290	450.00	450.00
93	SAW WHET OWL & WILD GRAPES	950	185.00	185.00
93	SHADOWS OF THE RAINFOREST	RT	345.00	510.00
93	VIGILANCE	9500	330.00	330.00
94	IN HIS PRIME-MALLARD DUCK	950	195.00	295.00
94	MERU DUCK - LESSER KUDUS	950	135.00	135.00
94	PATH OF THE PANTHER	1950	295.00	295.00
94	PREDATOR PORTFOLIO-BLACK BEAR	950	475.00	475.00
94	SALT SPRING SHEEP	1250	235.00	235.00
94	SNOWY NAP-TIGER	RT	185.00	525.00
94	SNOWY OWL	150	265.00	1275.00
94	WOLF PAIR IN THE SNOW	290	795.00	795.00
A. BRACKENBURY				
*	COTTONTAIL FAMILY-RABBIT	*	120.00	120.00
*	CRAB APPLE CRAVING-SQUIRREL	*	60.00	60.00
83	GREAT EXPECTATIONS	950	40.00	80.00
83	UNDER THE RED TWIGS-COTTONTAIL	950	40.00	80.00
84	CATTAILS	950	60.00	225.00
84	FIRST EXCURSION-CHICKEN	*	*	40.00
84	GRIZZLY IN CHOKEBERRIES	*	*	60.00
85	PROWLING BANDITS-RACCOONS	*	*	50.00
85	SLED DOGS	950	*	50.00
85	TOADALLY CAPTIVATED-DOG	950	60.00	72.00
86	CHILLY DOG-YELLOW LAB	*	*	75.00
87	STONE LYIN'-CAT	*	*	85.00
88	CAT IN THE MAIZE	*	*	80.00
88	CHOCOLATE CLUSTER-CHOCOLATE LAB	*	*	80.00
88	CORN DOGS-LAB. DOG	*	*	85.00
88	FEATHERBRAIN-LAB. DOG	*	80.00	150.00
88	POLE CAT	*	*	85.00
89	BASKET CASE-PUPPIES	950	*	95.00
89	BUREAUCATS-KITTENS	*	*	95.00
89	RED TAPE-LAB. DOG	950	*	95.00
89	WINTER COAT-GOLDEN RETRIEVER	*	*	85.00
90	PUPULATION EXPLOSION-BLK VARI.-COCKER	950	*	95.00
90	PUPULATION EXPLOSION-GLD VARI.-COCKER	950	*	95.00
90	WAGGIN' TAILS-PUPPIES	950	*	95.00
91	DAWN ON THE BEACH-SNOWY EGRET	*	*	95.00
C. BRENDERS				
*	BROKEN SILENCE-FAWNS	*	195.00	195.00
*	BUTTERFLY COLLECTION - 2ND	*	375.00	375.00
*	BUTTERFLY COLLECTION - 3RD	*	375.00	375.00
*	BUTTERFLY COLLECTION, THE	*	375.00	375.00
*	CLOSE-UP, JAGUAR	*	110.00	110.00
*	DEN MOTHER - MOTHER WOLF	*	135.00	135.00
*	DEN MOTHER-PREMIER-WOLF	*	700.00	700.00
*	FAMILY TREE, THE-OWLS	*	225.00	225.00
*	FOREST CARPENTER-PILEATED-WOODPECKER	*	195.00	195.00
*	FULL HOUSE-PREMIER ED.- FOXES	*	900.00	900.00
*	GOSLING STUDY	*	35.00	35.00
*	HUNTER'S DREAM-ELK	*	950.00	950.00
*	MONARCH IS ALIVE-PREMIER-EAGLE	*	900.00	900.00
*	ONE TO ONE - GRAY WOLF STUDY	*	220.00	220.00
*	POLAR BEAR CUB STUDY	*	35.00	35.00
*	POWER AND GRACE-DEER	*	525.00	525.00
*	RIVERBANK KESTREL	*	325.00	325.00
*	ROCKY CAMP - COUGAR (GICLEE)	*	500.00	500.00
*	SILENT PASSAGE-LION	*	400.00	400.00
*	SUMMER ROSES - WINTER WREN	*	425.00	425.00
*	TAKE FIVE - CANADA LYNX	*	340.00	340.00
*	TUNDRA SUMMIT-ARCTIC WOLVES	*	340.00	340.00
*	WREN STUDY	*	35.00	35.00
84	ON THE ALERT-RED FOX	950	95.00	475.00
84	PLAYFUL PAIR-CHIPMUNKS	950	40.00	400.00
84	SILENT HUNTER-GREAT HORNED OWL	950	95.00	600.00
84	SILENT PASSAGE-COUGAR	950	150.00	455.00
84	WATERSIDE ENCOUNTER-RACCOON	950	95.00	1000.00
85	MIGHTY INTRUDER-BLACK BEAR	950	95.00	275.00
86	ACROBATS MEAL, THE-RED SQUIRREL	950	65.00	275.00
86	BLACK-CAPPED CHICKADEES	950	40.00	525.00
86	BLUEBIRDS	950	40.00	200.00
86	COLORFUL PLAYGROUND-COTTONTAILS	950	75.00	500.00
86	DISTRIBUTED DAYDREAMS	950	95.00	370.00
86	GOLDEN SEASON-GRAY SQUIRREL	950	85.00	525.00
86	HARVEST TIME-CHIPMUNK	950	65.00	250.00
86	LATE SNOW-GREAT BLUE HERON	*	90.00	175.00
86	MEADOWLARK	1250	165.00	275.00
86	ROBINS	950	40.00	125.00
87	AUTUMN LADY-DEER	950	150.00	375.00
87	CLOSE TO MOM-BEAR	950	150.00	1500.00
87	DOUBLE TROUBLE-RACCOONS	950	120.00	650.00
87	IVORY BILLED WOODPECKER	RT	95.00	500.00
87	IVORY-BILLED WOODPECKER	950	95.00	515.00
87	MIGRATION FEVER-BARN SWALLOWS	950	150.00	350.00
87	MYSTERIOUS VISITOR-BARN OWL	950	150.00	375.00

YR	NAME	LIMIT	ISSUE	TREND
87	UNDER THE PINE TREES-CHIPMUNKS	*	65.00	225.00
87	WHITE ELEGANCE-TRUMPETER SWANS	950	115.00	390.00
87	YELLOW-BELLIED MARMOT	950	95.00	425.00
88	A HUNTER'S DREAM	950	165.00	950.00
88	APPLE HARVEST	950	115.00	290.00
88	CALIFORNIA QUAIL	*	95.00	375.00
88	FOREST SENTINEL-BOBCAT	950	135.00	500.00
88	HIDDEN IN THE PINES-GREAT HORNED OWL	950	175.00	1500.00
88	HIGH ADVENTURE-BLACK BEAR CUBS	950	105.00	425.00
88	LONG DISTANCE HUNTERS-WOLF	1250	175.00	2250.00
88	ROAMING THE PLAINS-PRONGHORNS	*	150.00	250.00
88	TALK ON THE OLD FENCE	950	165.00	775.00
88	WITNESS OF A PAST-BISON	*	110.00	175.00
89	A YOUNG GENERATION-RABBIT	1250	165.00	375.00
89	APPLE LOVER, THE-ROBIN	1500	125.00	275.00
89	COMPANIONS, THE-WOLF	18036	200.00	675.00
89	FORAGER'S REWARD-RED SQUIRREL	*	135.00	250.00
89	LORD OF THE MARSHES-BLUE HERON	950	40.00	175.00
89	MERLINS AT THE NEST	1250	165.00	375.00
89	NORTHERN COUSINS-BLACK SQUIRREL	950	95.00	250.00
89	PREDATORS WALK, THE-COUGAR	*	150.00	375.00
89	RED-WINGED BLACKBIRDS	*	40.00	100.00
89	STELLER'S JAY	1250	135.00	175.00
89	SURVIVORS, THE-CANADA GEESE	*	225.00	850.00
90	A THREATENED SYMBOL-BALD EAGLE	1950	145.00	300.00
90	BLOND BEAUTY-HORSE	RT	185.00	185.00
90	FULL HOUSE-FOX FAMILY	20106	235.00	275.00
90	GHOSTLY QUIET-SPANISH LYNX	RT	200.00	200.00
90	MONARCH IS ALIVE,THE-EAGLE	RT	265.00	325.00
90	MOUNTAIN BABY-BIGHORN SHEEP	1950	165.00	165.00
90	ON THE OLD FARM DOOR-BLUEBIRD	1500	225.00	450.00
90	SHORELINE QUARTET-WHITE IBIS	1950	265.00	265.00
90	SMALL TALK	1500	125.00	250.00
90	SPRING FAWN	1500	125.00	300.00
90	SQUIRREL'S DISH	1950	110.00	110.00
91	BALANCE OF NATURE, THE-HAWK & RABBIT	1950	225.00	225.00
91	CALM BEFORE THE CHALLENGE-MOOSE	RT	225.00	225.00
91	NESTING SEASON, THE-HOUSE SPARROW	1950	195.00	250.00
91	ONE TO ONE-GRAY WOLF	10000	245.00	510.00
91	SHADOWS IN THE GRASS (PRESTIGE ED.)	*	*	450.00
91	SHADOWS IN THE GRASS-YOUNG COUGARS	*	*	235.00
91	STUDY FOR ONE TO ONE	1950	120.00	285.00
91	WOLF STUDY	RT	125.00	125.00
92	DEN MOTHER - WOLF FAMILY	2500	250.00	400.00
92	ISLAND SHORES - SNOWY EGRET	2500	250.00	250.00
92	PATHFINDER - RED FOX	5000	245.00	370.00
92	RED FOX STUDY	1250	125.00	125.00
92	ROCKY KINGDOM - BIGHORN SHEEP	1750	255.00	255.00
92	SNOW LEOPARD PORTRAIT	1750	150.00	150.00
92	WOLF SCOUT #1-WOLF CUB	2500	105.00	105.00
92	WOLF SCOUT #2-WOLF CUB	2500	105.00	105.00
93	BLACK SPHINX	950	235.00	235.00
93	IN THE NORTHERN HUNTING GROUNDS	1750	375.00	375.00
93	MOTHER OF PEARLS-POLAR BEAR	5000	275.00	275.00
93	NARROW ESCAPE - CHIPMUNK	1750	150.00	150.00
93	ROCKY CAMP - COUGAR FAMILY	5000	275.00	275.00
93	ROCKY CAMP CUBS	950	225.00	225.00
94	DALL SHEEP PORTRAIT	950	115.00	115.00
P. CALLE				
*	EARLY ARRIVALS	*	245.00	245.00
*	LONELY WATCH	*	100.00	100.00
*	PAUSE FOR A DRINK	*	100.00	100.00
*	THEY CALL ME WILLIAM	*	265.00	265.00
*	TRAIL BOSS	*	100.00	100.00
80	CARING FOR THE HERD	RT	110.00	110.00
80	CHIEF HIGH PIPE (PENCIL)	950	75.00	165.00
80	CHIEF JOSEPH-MAN OF PEACE	950	135.00	150.00
80	LANDMARK TREE	950	125.00	225.00
80	PRAYER TO THE GREAT MYSTERY	950	245.00	450.00
80	SIOUX CHIEF	RT	85.00	85.00
80	SOMETHING FOR THE POT	950	175.00	1700.00
80	VIEW FROM THE HEIGHTS	950	245.00	350.00
80	WHEN SNOW CAME EARLY	950	85.00	250.00
80	WINTER HUNTER, THE (PENCIL)	950	65.00	450.00
81	ALMOST HOME	950	150.00	150.00
81	AND STILL MILES TO GO	950	245.00	300.00
81	ANDREW AT THE FALLS	950	150.00	175.00
81	CHIEF HIGH PIPE (COLOR)	950	265.00	275.00
81	END OF A LONG DAY	RT	150.00	150.00
81	FRESH TRACKS	RT	150.00	165.00
81	FRIENDS	RT	150.00	150.00
81	JUST OVER THE RIDGE	950	245.00	320.00
81	ONE WITH THE LAND	950	245.00	320.00
81	PAUSE AT THE LOWER FALLS	950	110.00	350.00
81	TETON FRIENDS	950	150.00	200.00
81	WINTER HUNTER, THE (COLOR)	950	245.00	725.00
82	BREATH OF FRIENDSHIP, THE	950	225.00	295.00
82	EMERGING FROM THE WOODS	RT	110.00	110.00
82	GENERATIONS IN THE VALLEY	RT	245.00	245.00

YR	NAME	LIMIT	ISSUE	TREND
82	RETURN TO CAMP	950	245.00	400.00
82	TWO FROM THE FLOCK	950	245.00	425.00
83	A WINTER'S SURPRISE	950	195.00	800.00
83	COMPANIONS	*	*	150.00
83	FREE SPIRITS	950	195.00	325.00
83	IN SEARCH OF BEAVER	950	225.00	950.00
83	STRAYS FROM THE FLYWAY	950	195.00	250.00
84	A BRACE FOR THE SPIT	950	110.00	275.00
84	CHANCE ENCOUNTER	950	225.00	300.00
84	FATE OF THE LATE MIGRANT	950	110.00	300.00
84	HEAR ME O' GREAT SPIRIT	*	175.00	275.00
84	MOUNTAIN MAN, THE	950	95.00	135.00
84	TRAPPER, THE	*	*	95.00
84	WHEN TRAILS CROSS	950	245.00	750.00
85	CARRYING PLACE, THE	RT	195.00	195.00
85	GRANDMOTHER, THE	950	*	150.00
85	STORYTELLER OF THE MOUNTAINS	950	225.00	575.00
86	FREE TRAPPER, THE	*	*	200.00
86	SNOW HUNTER, THE	950	150.00	250.00
87	IN THE LAND OF THE GIANTS	950	245.00	780.00
87	INTO THE GREAT ALONE	950	245.00	600.00
88	NEW DAY, A	950	150.00	150.00
88	VOYAGEURS & WATERFOWL	RT	265.00	300.00
89	AND A GOOD BOOK FOR COMPANY	950	135.00	190.00
89	BEAVER MEN, THE	950	125.00	125.00
89	FUR TRAPPER, THE	550	75.00	75.00
89	GREAT MOMENT, THE	950	350.00	350.00
89	MOUNTAIN MEN, THE (LITHO)	RT	400.00	400.00
89	NAVAJO MADONNA	650	95.00	95.00
89	WHERE EAGLES FLY	*	265.00	350.00
89	WINTER FEAST	1250	265.00	430.00
90	CHILDREN OF WALPI	350	160.00	160.00
90	DOLL MAKER, THE	950	95.00	95.00
90	INTERRUPTED JOURNEY	1750	265.00	300.00
90	INTERRUPTED JOURNEY (PRESTIGE ED.)	RT	465.00	465.00
90	SON OF SITTING BULL	950	95.00	95.00
91	ALMOST THERE	RT	165.00	240.00
91	IN THE BEGINNING...FRIENDS	RT	250.00	250.00
91	MAN OF THE FUR TRADE	550	110.00	110.00
91	SILENCED HONKERS, THE	1250	250.00	250.00
91	THEY CALL ME MATTHEW	950	125.00	125.00
91	WHEN TRAILS GROW COLD	2500	265.00	265.00
91	WHEN TRAILS GROW COLD (PRESTIGE ED.)	RT	465.00	465.00
94	WHEN TRAPPERS MEET (PENCIL)	750	165.00	165.00
J. DALY				
*	A GIFT OF TIME	*	395.00	395.00
*	A GIFT OF TIME-SCHOOL TEACHER	*	145.00	145.00
*	ANNIE'S RAGGEDY	*	175.00	175.00
*	CATCH OF MY DREAMS	*	45.00	45.00
*	MARSHALL, THE	*	150.00	150.00
*	MY BEST FRIENDS	*	140.00	140.00
*	SATURDAY MORNING	*	150.00	150.00
*	SUNDAY MORNING	*	350.00	350.00
82	SPRING FEVER	950	85.00	1450.00
83	SATURDAY NIGHT	950	85.00	1500.00
86	FLYING HIGH-CHILDREN	950	50.00	750.00
87	FAVORITE READER-BOY	RT	85.00	425.00
87	ODD MAN OUT-BOY	RT	85.00	675.00
88	ON THIN ICE-BOY ICE SKATING	RT	95.00	150.00
88	TERRITORIAL RIGHTS-BOY	*	85.00	350.00
88	TIE BREAKER-CHECKERS	*	95.00	275.00
88	WIPED OUT-MARBLES	*	125.00	500.00
89	IN THE DOGHOUSE-BOY/DOG	1500	75.00	300.00
89	LET'S PLAY BALL-BOY/DOG	1500	75.00	200.00
89	THIEF, THE-BOY/DOG	1500	95.00	450.00
89	THORN, THE	*	125.00	675.00
90	BIG MOMENT, THE-CLOWN W/CHILD	1500	125.00	125.00
90	CONFRONTATION	1500	85.00	145.00
90	CONTENTMENT	1500	95.00	550.00
90	HONOR AND ALLEGIANCE	1500	110.00	160.00
90	ICE MAN, THE-BOY	1500	125.00	200.00
90	IT'S THAT TIME AGAIN	1500	120.00	120.00
90	MAKE BELIEVE-LITTLE GIRLS	RT	75.00	425.00
90	RADIO DAZE	1500	150.00	150.00
90	SCHOLAR, THE	1500	110.00	110.00
91	A NEW BEGINNING	5000	125.00	125.00
91	CAT'S CRADLE	950	450.00	450.00
91	HOME TEAM: ZERO-BASEBALL	1500	150.00	150.00
91	HOMEMADE	1500	125.00	175.00
91	PILLARS OF A NATION-ELLIS ISLAND	20000	175.00	175.00
91	TIME-OUT-CHILDREN	RT	125.00	125.00
92	WALKING THE RAILS	1500	175.00	175.00
93	TO ALL A GOOD NIGHT	1500	160.00	160.00
94	MUD MATES	950	150.00	150.00
94	SLUGGER	950	75.00	75.00
94	WIND-UP, THE	950	75.00	75.00
N. ENGLE				
81	HOUSE BY THE SEA	950	75.00	1005.00
81	WILDERNESS MARSH	950	75.00	815.00

These young Dreamers *contemplate the possibilities in Charles Wysocki's 1989 offering from The Greenwich Workshop. The* Dreamers *was limited to 3,000 and originally sold for $175.*

The setting sun reflected in the water, the warm light of a cozy room and the smoke from the chimney represent the Comforts of Home *by Terry Redlin. The 1991 Hadley House release was issued at $175 and is currently valued at $570.*

Released in 1981 by Jan Hagara Collectables, Storytime *by Jan Hagara is a lithograph produced on 100% cotton rag paper. The limited edition of 450 was issued at $125 and currently lists for $600.*

There's no room at this inn. Full House—Fox Family, *by wildlife artist Carl Brenders, reveals a mother tending to the needs of her young pups. Published by Mill Pond Press.*

YR	NAME	LIMIT	ISSUE	TREND
83	MORNING ON THE YELLOWDOG RIVER	950	75.00	170.00
83	QUIET WATERS	950	75.00	275.00
83	SUMMER RIVER	950	75.00	240.00
83	WILD OCTOBER	*	75.00	125.00
83	WINTER BROOK	*	*	75.00
84	APRIL LIGHT	*	*	95.00
84	AUTUMN BLUEBERRIES	950	75.00	125.00
84	EVENING HARBOR	950	75.00	135.00
84	ISLAND HOME	*	75.00	135.00
84	ISLAND LAKE	950	95.00	160.00
84	LOST CREEK	*	15.00	135.00
84	MARCH THAW	*	95.00	175.00
84	MELTING INTO SPRING	*	95.00	175.00
84	MIDDLE ISLAND POINT	*	115.00	165.00
84	PEACEFUL MORNING-CANADAS	*	*	50.00
85	AUTUMN GOLD	*	85.00	160.00
85	AUTUMN RIVER	*	50.00	120.00
85	GREAT PASSAGE	*	175.00	215.00
85	GROUSE COUNTRY	950	85.00	300.00
85	HEMLOCK MARSH	*	115.00	160.00
85	MISTY ISLE	*	150.00	180.00
85	MOUNTAIN COVE	*	125.00	180.00
85	SALTY DOG	*	95.00	170.00
85	WILD ROSE MARSH	950	95.00	760.00
86	SUNSET SWAMP	*	*	75.00
87	FISHERMAN AT DAWN	*	95.00	245.00
87	MOUNTAIN MEADOW	*	95.00	290.00
87	SAFE HARBOR	*	95.00	130.00
88	DEEP WOODS WINTER	*	95.00	160.00
88	EDGE OF WINTER-LAKE SUPERIOR	*	150.00	255.00
88	FOREST POOL	*	110.00	180.00
88	LIGHT IN THE WILLOWS-GREAT WHITE HERON	*	*	145.00
88	VICTORIAN SPRING-GRAND HOTEL	*	150.00	170.00
89	BRIGHT RIVER	950	150.00	165.00
89	CARRIAGE WAITING	950	75.00	110.00
89	DAISY BAY	*	150.00	205.00
89	FIRST COLOR	*	135.00	180.00
89	GOLDEN BEACH	*	110.00	180.00
90	AFTERNOON VISITOR	950	*	75.00
90	FEEDER STREAM	950	150.00	195.00
90	WILD ROSES BY THE SEA	*	150.00	265.00

F. MACHETANZ

YR	NAME	LIMIT	ISSUE	TREND
*	CHANGE OF DIRECTION W/MEDAL-ESKIMO	*	320.00	320.00
*	FIRST DAY IN HARNESS	*	225.00	225.00
*	FISHING RIGHTS-BROWN BEAR	*	195.00	195.00
*	RARIN' TO GO DOG SLED	*	225.00	225.00
*	SEARCH ON THE PRESSURE ICE	*	245.00	245.00
78	FACE TO FACE	950	150.00	1890.00
78	HUNTER'S DAWN	950	125.00	525.00
78	INTO THE HOME STRETCH	950	175.00	700.00
79	BEGINNINGS	950	175.00	575.00
79	DECISIONS ON THE ICE FIELD	950	150.00	465.00
79	PICK OF THE LITTER	950	165.00	250.00
79	REACHING THE CAMPSITE	950	200.00	400.00
80	KING OF THE MOUNTAIN	950	200.00	250.00
80	NELCHINA TRAIL	950	245.00	1015.00
80	SOURDOUGH	950	245.00	1085.00
80	WHEN THREE'S A CROWD	950	225.00	850.00
81	GOLDEN YEARS	950	245.00	615.00
81	MIDDAY MOONLIGHT	950	265.00	425.00
81	WHAT EVERY HUNTER FEARS	950	245.00	850.00
81	WHERE MEN AND DOGS SEEM SMALL	950	245.00	1500.00
81	WINTER HARVEST	950	265.00	280.00
82	MIGHTY HUNTER	950	265.00	775.00
82	MOONLIGHT STAKEOUT	950	265.00	540.00
82	MOOSE TRACKS	950	265.00	465.00
82	TENDER ARCTIC, THE	950	295.00	775.00
83	NANOOK	950	*	295.00
83	THEY OPENED THE NORTH COUNTRY	950	245.00	275.00
84	END OF A LONG DAY-POLAR BEAR	950	*	200.00
84	MANY MILES TOGETHER-ESKIMO	950	245.00	245.00
84	MIDNIGHT WATCH	950	*	250.00
84	SMOKE DREAMS	950	250.00	400.00
84	STORY OF THE BEADS	950	245.00	300.00
85	END OF THE HUNT-ESKIMO	950	*	245.00
85	LAND OF THE MIDNIGHT SUN-POLAR BEAR	950	*	245.00
85	LANGUAGE OF THE SNOW-ESKIMO	950	*	195.00
85	REACHING THE PASS-DOG SLED	950	265.00	1050.00
86	KYROK-ESKIMO SEAMSTRESS	950	*	225.00
86	LEAVING THE NEST-POLAR BEAR	950	*	245.00
86	LONE MUSHER-ALASKA	950	*	245.00
86	MT. BLACKBURN-SOVEREIGN OF THE WRANGELLS	950	*	245.00
86	SON OF THE NORTH-ESKIMO	*	*	175.00
87	SPRING FEVER-POLAR BEAR	950	*	225.00
87	START OF THE DAY-ALASKA	*	*	200.00
87	TRAIL THROUGH THE PRESSURE ICE-ALASKA	*	*	225.00
88	CHANGE OF DIRECTION W/MEDAL	950	*	320.00
88	TENSE MOMENT-POLAR BEAR	*	*	200.00
88	VETERAN OF THE TRAIL-DOG SLED	*	*	175.00

YR	NAME	LIMIT	ISSUE	TREND
88	WHALING LOOKOUT-ESKIMO WHALING	*	*	195.00
89	CHIEF DANCES, THE-ESKIMO	950	*	235.00
89	INVADERS, THE-POLAR BEAR	*	*	235.00
89	TWO OF MY FAVORITE SUBJECTS	*	*	225.00
90	GLORY OF THE TRAIL-DOG MUSHING	950	*	225.00
90	GRASS IS ALWAYS GREENER, THE-DOG	950	*	200.00
90	QUALITY TIME-POLAR BEAR	950	*	200.00
91	KAYAK MAN	950	*	215.00
91	SEARCH FOR GOLD, THE	*	*	225.00
91	TUNDRA FLOWER	950	*	235.00
B. MOORE, JR.				
79	HARRY SHOURDES REDHEAD	950	65.00	135.00
79	LEE DUDLEY-CANVASBACK	950	65.00	250.00
79	WARD BROTHERS-CANADAS	950	85.00	135.00
80	WARD BROTHERS-CANVASBACKS	*	85.00	135.00
81	JOSEPH LINCOLN PINTAIL ON THE SANTEE	*	85.00	135.00
81	WAITING, THE	950	85.00	330.00
81	WIND CALLED HIS NAME, THE	950	85.00	500.00
82	GOLDEN DAWN	950	85.00	110.00
82	POINT AND HONOR	*	115.00	195.00
83	BECKY	*	75.00	225.00
86	THIS PLACE NOT FOR SALE	*	85.00	160.00
R. PARKER				
*	BLUE SHADOWS-ARCTIC FOX	*	175.00	175.00
*	BREAK IN THE ICE-CANADA GOOSE	*	*	175.00
*	COASTAL MORNING-GRIZZLY	*	195.00	195.00
*	CROSSING THE RIDGE-WOLVES	*	*	265.00
*	EVENING SILHOUETTE-COYOTES	*	225.00	225.00
*	EVENING SOLITUDE-WOLF	*	195.00	195.00
*	FALLEN TOTEM-EAGLE	*	300.00	300.00
*	FOREST FLIGHT-EAGLE	*	195.00	195.00
*	FROSTY ALDER-EVENING GROSBEAK	*	125.00	125.00
*	GRIZZLES AT THE FALLS	*	225.00	225.00
*	ICY CREEK-MINK	*	105.00	105.00
*	LAST LIGHT-COUGAR	*	235.00	235.00
*	MOUNTAIN BLOOMS-GROUND SQUIRREL	*	50.00	50.00
*	OLD MAN OF THE MOUNTAIN-BLACK BEAR	*	185.00	185.00
*	RAIDING THE CACHE	*	95.00	95.00
*	RAMPARTS-MOUNTAIN GOATS	*	200.00	200.00
*	RED-BREASTED NUTHATCH ON PI	*	95.00	95.00
*	RED-COCKADED WOODPECKER	*	120.00	120.00
*	REFLECTIONS-MALLARD DUCK	*	175.00	175.00
*	SEA OTTER WITH URCHIN	*	150.00	150.00
*	STILL WATER - MALLARD DUCK	*	105.00	105.00
*	THROUGH THE FIRS-EAGLE	*	500.00	500.00
*	WAPITI PORTRAIT-AMERICAN ELK	*	105.00	105.00
*	WARY GLANCE - CHIPMUNK	*	70.00	70.00
*	WHITE-TAILED TROPICBIRDS	*	130.00	130.00
*	WINTER'S FURY-MOUNTAIN GOATS	*	195.00	195.00
82	RACCOON PAIR	950	95.00	400.00
82	SNOW ON THE PINE-CHICKADEES	950	95.00	100.00
82	SPRING MIST-GRAY WOLF	950	155.00	375.00
82	WEATHERED WOOD-BLUEBIRDS	950	75.00	175.00
83	MALLARD FAMILY	950	95.00	175.00
83	RED SQUIRREL	*	*	65.00
83	RIVERSIDE PAUSE-RIVER OTTER	950	95.00	150.00
83	YELLOW DAWN-AMERICAN ELK	950	130.00	200.00
84	CHICKADEES IN AUTUMN	950	*	75.00
84	FACE OF THE NORTH-WOLF	950	95.00	250.00
84	FAT AND SASSY-ROBIN	*	*	95.00
84	GRAY WOLF PORTRAIT	950	115.00	175.00
84	SILENT STEPS-LYNX	950	145.00	325.00
84	WHEN PATHS CROSS	950	185.00	400.00
84	WINTER JAY-BLUE JAY	950	95.00	150.00
85	AFTERNOON SHADOWS-MULE DEER	*	*	105.00
85	MISTY DAWN-LOON	950	120.00	525.00
85	SPRING ARRIVALS-CANADA GEESE	950	120.00	200.00
85	WAITING OUT THE STORM-WOLF	950	105.00	400.00
85	WINGS OVER WINTER-BALD EAGLE	950	135.00	350.00
85	WINTER CLOAK-ERMINE	*	*	105.00
86	ABOVE THE BREAKERS-OSPREY	950	150.00	175.00
86	AT END OF DAY-WOLVES	950	235.00	325.00
86	AUTUMN FIELDS-RED FOX	*	*	220.00
86	AUTUMN FORAGING-MOOSE	950	175.00	425.00
86	AUTUMN LEAVES-RED FOX	950	95.00	100.00
86	AUTUMN MEADOW-ELK	950	195.00	200.00
86	BEHIND THE HEMLOCK-LYNX	*	*	105.00
86	CARDINAL IN BLUE SPRUCE	950	125.00	150.00
86	CARDINAL IN BRAMBLES	950	125.00	150.00
86	CREEKSIDE-COUGAR	950	225.00	350.00
86	FOLLOWING MAMA-MUTE SWANS	950	165.00	475.00
86	JUST RESTING-SEA OTTER	950	85.00	250.00
86	MORNING ON THE LAGOON-MUTE SWAN	950	95.00	100.00
86	NORTHERN MORNING-ARCTIC FOX	950	125.00	175.00
86	RIMROCK-COUGAR	950	200.00	900.00
86	WHITETAIL AND WOLVES	950	180.00	300.00
86	WINTER CREEK-COYOTE	950	130.00	275.00
87	A BREAK IN THE ICE-CANADA GEESE	*	150.00	175.00
87	ABOVE THE WAVES-COMMON TERNS	*	*	95.00

YR	NAME	LIMIT	ISSUE	TREND
87	ARCTIC SPRING-WHITE GYRFALCON	*	*	185.00
87	ARCTIC WOLF PORTRAIT	*	*	105.00
87	AUTUMN MORNING-GRIZZLY	*	*	200.00
87	BARN SWALLOWS ON FENCE POST	*	*	105.00
87	DESERT RESPITE-KIT FOX	*	*	125.00
87	EVENING GLOW-WOLF PACK	950	245.00	275.00
87	EVENING REFLECTIONS-TRUMPETER SWAN	*	*	115.00
87	FREEZE UP-CANADA GEESE	950	85.00	100.00
87	GOLDEN GRASSES-CALIFORNIA QUAIL	*	*	95.00
87	LOW WATER-RACCOON	*	*	125.00
87	ON THE RUN-WOLF PACK	950	*	245.00
87	RAIL FENCE-BLUEBIRDS	950	105.00	125.00
87	SHELTERED SPOT-LYNX	*	*	150.00
87	WALKING THE RIDGE-PRONGHORN	*	*	185.00
87	WHITE-CROWNED SPARROW ON DRIFTWOOD	*	*	125.00
87	WINTER CREEK AND WHITETAILS	950	*	185.00
87	WINTER ENCOUNTER-WOLF	950	235.00	350.00
87	WINTER PINE-DOWNY WOODPECKER	*	*	110.00
87	WINTER SAGE-COYOTE	950	225.00	350.00
87	WINTER STORM-COYOTES	950	245.00	325.00
88	EAGLES IN THE PINES	*	*	200.00
88	FIRST SNOW-ARCTIC WOLVES	*	*	175.00
88	FOX PUP AT THE DEN ENTRANCE	*	*	115.00
88	SEARCHING THE STREAM-RACCOON	*	*	125.00
88	SILENT PASSAGE-ORCAS WHALE	950	*	175.00
88	SNOW PALACE-MULE DEER	*	*	225.00
88	SUMMER-LOON	*	*	125.00
88	WINTER VALLEY-ELK	*	*	150.00
88	WINTER WREN ON IVY	*	*	95.00
89	AUTUMN ASPEN-WHITE-TAILED DEER	*	*	175.00
89	AUTUMN CORNFIELD-CARDINAL	*	*	115.00
89	AUTUMN MAPLES-WOLVES	950	*	195.00
89	DEEP WATER-ORCAS WHALE	1250	*	195.00
89	EARLY SNOWFALL-ELK	950	*	185.00
89	EARLY SPRING-GREAT BLUE HERON	*	*	135.00
89	EUCALYPTUS CLIMBER-KOALA BEAR	*	*	110.00
89	EVENING AMBER-TRUMPETER SWAN	*	*	125.00
89	FLYING REDTAIL HAWK-ORIGINAL	200	*	295.00
90	BREAKING THE SILENCE WOLVES	1250	195.00	300.00
90	ICE MORNING-RED FOX	950	*	150.00
90	INSIDE PASSAGE-ORCAS WHALE	1500	*	195.00
90	LIONESS AND CUBS	150	*	295.00
90	MOOSE IN THE BRUSH	950	*	195.00
90	WINTER LOOKOUT-COUGAR	950	*	175.00
91	DEEP SNOW-WHITETAIL DEER	950	*	175.00
91	FOREST TREK-GRAY WOLF	950	*	185.00
91	GILA WOODPECKER	950	*	135.00
91	MOONLIT TRACKS-WOLF	1500	200.00	225.00
91	MOTHER AND SON-ORCAS	950	*	185.00
R. PETERSON				
*	VOLUNTEERS	*	255.00	255.00
73	BALTIMORE ORIOLE	450	150.00	300.00
73	CARDINAL	450	150.00	580.00
73	FLICKER	450	150.00	275.00
73	WOOD THRUSH	450	150.00	370.00
74	BALD EAGLE	950	150.00	500.00
74	BARN SWALLOW	750	150.00	350.00
74	BLUE JAYS	950	150.00	350.00
74	BOBOLINK	750	150.00	275.00
74	GREAT HORNED OWL	950	150.00	525.00
75	BOBWHITES	950	150.00	320.00
75	FUR SEALS	*	25.00	25.00
75	JAYS-COLOR PLATE #30-BLUE JAY	*	150.00	150.00
75	OWLS-COLOR PLATE #16	*	150.00	150.00
75	RUFFED GROUSE	950	150.00	350.00
75	SEA OTTERS	*	25.00	150.00
76	ADELIE PENQUINS	950	*	35.00
76	BARN OWL	950	225.00	300.00
76	GOLDEN EAGLE	950	*	200.00
76	QUAILS-COLOR PLATE #9	*	*	150.00
76	ROADRUNNER	*	25.00	175.00
76	SNOWY OWL	950	175.00	525.00
77	BLUEBIRD	950	75.00	225.00
77	PEREGRINE FALCON	950	175.00	300.00
77	SCARLET TANAGER	950	125.00	200.00
77	SOOTY TERNS	450	50.00	85.00
77	WILD ORCHIDS AND TRILLIUMS	*	*	75.00
77	WILLETS	450	50.00	75.00
78	MOCKINGBIRD	950	125.00	250.00
78	RING-NECKED PHEASANT	950	200.00	250.00
78	ROBIN	950	125.00	420.00
78	ROSE-BREASTED GROSBEAK	950	*	125.00
78	SHOWY WAYSIDE FLOWERS	*	*	75.00
79	GYRFALCON	950	225.00	360.00
79	PUFFIN	*	*	175.00
81	WILD TURKEYS	*	*	195.00
83	ARCTIC GLOW-SNOWY OWL	*	*	200.00
86	LORD OF THE AIR-PEREGRINE FALCON	*	*	120.00

YR	NAME	LIMIT	ISSUE	TREND
M. REECE				
*	BERRY FOOD-CEDAR WAXWINGS	*	85.00	85.00
*	BURST OF COLOR-RING NECKED PHEASANT	*	*	200.00
*	COASTING DOWN-CANADA GEESE	*	40.00	40.00
*	COLD MORNING-MALLARDS	*	175.00	175.00
*	DARK SKY-PINTAILS	*	125.00	125.00
*	DARK SKY-SNOW GEESE	*	175.00	350.00
*	FAMILY, THE - CANADA GEESE	*	95.00	95.00
*	FLARING-MALLARDS	*	175.00	175.00
*	FLIGHT- CANADA GEESE - BRONZE	*	4000.00	4000.00
*	HEAVY SNOW-RUFFED GROUSE	*	150.00	150.00
*	HIGH COUNTRY SKIER	*	125.00	125.00
*	MADISON COUNTY BRIDGE-PHEASANTS	*	135.00	135.00
*	MISTY FLIGHT-CANADA GEESE	*	150.00	150.00
*	PAIR-TRUMPETER SWAN, THE	*	*	95.00
*	PREENING-BLUE WINGED TEAL	*	115.00	115.00
*	QUAIL COVEY-BOBWHITES	*	*	245.00
*	QUAIL RIDGE-BOBWHITES	*	175.00	175.00
*	QUIET LANDING-MALLARD-BRONZE	*	3000.00	3000.00
*	ROSEMAN BRIDGE-MADISON CITY	*	135.00	135.00
*	SHALLOW RIVER-AMERICAN WIGEON	*	195.00	195.00
*	SUNSET-CANADA GEESE	*	195.00	195.00
*	TWIN FAWNS-WHITE-TAILED DEER	*	235.00	235.00
*	WASHINGTON DUCK 1989 - AMERICAN WIGEON	*	135.00	135.00
*	WATERFOWL ART OF MAYNARD	*	650.00	650.00
*	WHITE PINE- BLUE JAY	*	85.00	85.00
48	FEDERAL DUCK STAMP-BUFFLEHEADS	200	15.00	1200.00
51	FEDERAL DUCK STAMP-GADWALLS	250	15.00	1200.00
59	FEDERAL DUCK STAMP-RETRIEVER	400	15.00	4000.00
64	BOBWHITES (STONE LITHO)	950	20.00	650.00
64	MALLARDS (STONE LITHO)	950	20.00	650.00
69	FEDERAL DUCK STAMP-WHITE-WINGED SCOTERS	750	50.00	1000.00
69	MALLARDS-PITCHING IN	500	40.00	600.00
70	EDGE OF THE HEDGEROW-BOBWHITES	950	60.00	700.00
71	FEDERAL DUCK STAMP-CINNAMON TEAL	950	75.00	5000.00
72	AGAINST THE WIND-CANVASBACKS	950	60.00	400.00
73	FEEDING TIME-CANADA GEESE	550	75.00	350.00
73	LATE AFTERNOON-MALLARD	450	150.00	245.00
73	MARSHLANDER MALLARDS	600	60.00	275.00
73	PHEASANT COUNTRY	550	60.00	275.00
73	WOOD DUCKS	550	125.00	200.00
74	A BURST OF COLOR-RING-NECKED PHESANTS	950	75.00	200.00
74	COURTSHIP FLIGHT-PINTAILS	950	75.00	190.00
74	EARLY ARRIVALS-MALLARDS	950	50.00	125.00
74	FLOODED OAKS-MALLARDS	850	150.00	300.00
74	MALLARDS-DROPPING IN	950	75.00	225.00
74	PASSING STORM, THE-CANVASBACKS	950	50.00	145.00
74	QUAIL COVER	750	150.00	300.00
74	SANDBAR, THE-CANADA GEESE	950	50.00	75.00
74	SNOW GEESE-BLUE GEESE	750	150.00	150.00
74	SNOWY CREEK-MALLARDS	950	75.00	200.00
74	SOLITUDE-WHITETAIL DEER	950	85.00	125.00
74	WINGING SOUTH-CANADA GEESE	750	150.00	245.00
74	WOODED SECLUSION-TURKEY	950	75.00	110.00
75	AFTERNOON SHADOWS-BOBWHITES	950	100.00	350.00
76	AUTUMN TRIO-RING-NECKED PHEASANTS	950	85.00	250.00
76	CANADA GEESE-COMING IN	950	85.00	200.00
76	DARK SKY-MALLARDS	950	85.00	600.00
76	FLIGHT-CANADA GEESE	950	50.00	125.00
76	GENTOO-PENGUINS	260	125.00	150.00
76	GOOD FETCH-LABRADOR RETRIEVER	950	150.00	200.00
76	RAIL FENCE, THE-BOBWHITES	950	85.00	200.00
76	SHALLOW POND-MALLARDS	950	125.00	225.00
76	THUNDERHEAD-CANADA GEESE	260	125.00	1160.00
76	WEATHERED WOOD-BOBWHITES	950	50.00	150.00
77	COVEY RISE-BOBWHITES	950	150.00	850.00
77	DARK SHADOWS-WHITETAIL DEER	950	85.00	102.00
77	EASY LANDING-PINTAILS	950	95.00	175.00
77	GRACEFUL PAIR-RING-NECKED PHEASANTS	950	50.00	100.00
77	JUMPING GREENWINGS-GREEN-WINGED TEAL	950	85.00	150.00
77	NINE TRAVELERS-CANADA GEESE	950	95.00	150.00
77	QUIET POND-MALLARDS	950	95.00	150.00
77	RESTING-WOOD DUCKS	950	50.00	100.00
77	SENTINEL, THE-WHITETAIL DEER	950	150.00	180.00
77	STICK POND-MALLARDS	950	125.00	200.00
77	THROUGH THE TREES-WOOD DUCKS	950	95.00	375.00
78	CHINSTRAP PENQUINS	*	50.00	60.00
78	CRESCENT LAKE-MALLARDS	950	125.00	225.00
78	DARK SKY-CANADA GEESE	950	175.00	350.00
78	NEW SNOW-WHITE TAIL DEER	950	95.00	114.00
78	OAK FOREST-TURKEY	950	124.00	200.00
78	OUT OF THE PINES-BOBWHITES	950	245.00	300.00
78	OVER THE POINT-LESSER SCAUPS	950	125.00	150.00
78	ROUGH WATER-CANVASBACKS	950	150.00	235.00
78	WINTER COVEY-BOBWHITES	950	225.00	575.00
79	DARK SKY-BOBWHITES	950	225.00	375.00
79	MARSH, THE	950	75.00	90.00
79	PHEASANT COVER	950	175.00	250.00
79	REGAL FLIGHT-WHISTLING SWANS	950	125.00	150.00

YR	NAME	LIMIT	ISSUE	TREND
79	RENDEZVOUS-WHITE-FRONTED GEESE	950	*	85.00
79	SUNRISE-GREEN WINGED TEAL	950	150.00	300.00
79	VALLEY, THE-PINTAILS	950	150.00	180.00
79	WINDY DAY-MALLARDS	950	150.00	180.00
79	WINTER-RING-NECKED PHEASANTS	950	125.00	150.00
80	ALONG THE SHORE-REDHEADS	950	160.00	160.00
80	DARK SKY-CANVASBACKS	950	195.00	235.00
80	DIAMOND ISLAND-MALLARDS	950	195.00	350.00
80	LANDING-CANADA GEESE	950	125.00	150.00
80	MOUNTAIN SNOW	950	95.00	225.00
80	POINTERS AND BOBWHITES	950	245.00	300.00
80	QUAIL COUNTRY	950	250.00	300.00
80	QUIET PLACE, THE-CANADA GEESE	950	175.00	380.00
80	TIMBER-WOOD DUCKS	950	160.00	300.00
80	TUNDRA-BLACK BRANT	950	85.00	102.00
80	TWILIGHT-AMERICAN WIDGEON	950	75.00	190.00
80	WILLOW, THE-GREEN-WINGED TEAL	950	*	160.00
81	DARK SKY-RUFFED GROUSE	950	245.00	350.00
81	EARLY SPRING-WILD TURKEYS	950	*	220.00
81	ESCAPE-RING-NECKED PHEASANTS	950	*	195.00
81	FROSTY MORNING-CANADA GEESE	950	175.00	350.00
82	BREAKING AWAY-PINTAILS	*	*	150.00
82	FLOODED TIMBER-MALLARDS	950	150.00	250.00
82	MINIATURE SERIES I-MALLARDS	950	*	75.00
82	MINIATURE SERIES II-WOOD DUCKS	950	*	75.00
82	QUAIL CONVEY-BOBWHITES	950	*	245.00
82	SPLASH, THE-SMALLMOUTH BASS	950	95.00	150.00
82	STONY LAKE-MALLARDS	*	*	100.00
83	ALONG THE RIVER-TRUMPETER SWANS	*	*	50.00
83	DARK SKY-PHEASANTS	950	*	125.00
83	PASSING THROUGH-LESSER SCAUP	*	*	100.00
83	RUNNING BLUES-SCALED QUAILS	*	*	100.00
83	TRANQUIL MARSH MALLARDS	*	*	60.00
84	MINIATURE SERIES III-BOBWHITES	950	*	75.00
84	MINIATURE SERIES IV-PHEASANTS	*	*	75.00
84	SECLUSION-WOOD DUCKS	*	*	150.00
85	HAZY DAY-BOBWHITES	950	150.00	350.00
85	MUSKRAT HOUSE, THE-CANVASBACKS	*	*	95.00
85	SNOWSTORM, THE-MALLARDS	950	*	95.00
85	STORM CLOUDS-CANADA GOOSE	950	125.00	250.00
85	WATER'S EDGE-CANADA GEESE	950	95.00	200.00
86	AUTUMN MARSH-MALLARDS	950	120.00	250.00
86	NORTHERN LAKE-COMMON LOONS	*	*	125.00
86	SNOW COVER-CARDINAL	*	*	95.00
87	BIRCH, THE-RUFFED GROUSE	*	*	85.00
87	CAREFUL LANDING-CANADA GEESE	*	*	175.00
87	OLD TREE-BOBWHITE QUAIL	*	*	195.00
87	RED PINE-BLACK-CAPPED CHICKADEES	*	*	95.00
87	WINTER SOLITUDE-MALLARDS	*	*	125.00
88	AUTUMN WINGS-MALLARDS	950	135.00	230.00
88	LEAPING-RAINBOW TROUT	*	*	110.00
88	OAK TIMBER-MALLARDS	*	*	165.00
88	SONORAN DESERT-GAMBEL'S QUAIL	*	*	150.00
89	FLYING LOW-CANADA GEESE	*	*	225.00
89	ICY WATER-MALLARDS	*	*	175.00
89	OVER THE MARSH-CANADA GEESE	*	*	165.00
89	UPLAND SERIES I-BOBWHITES	950	*	125.00
89	WEEDY DRAW-RING-NECKED PHEASANTS	*	*	150.00
90	AMERICAN WIGEON-WASHINGTON CENNTENIAL	1058	*	135.00
90	GREENHEAD-MALLARD	150	*	245.00
90	UPLAND SERIES II-WILD TURKEYS & REDBUD	950	*	125.00
90	UPLAND SERIES III-RING-NECKED PHEASANT	*	*	125.00
91	CHASE, THE-WOLF PACK	550	*	150.00
91	OFFSHORE LUNCH-COMMON LOONS	550	*	195.00
91	UPLAND SERIES IV-RUFFED GOOSE	950	*	125.00
92	ALERT-WHITETAILED DEER	*	175.00	175.00
J. SEEREY-LESTER				
*	BLACK JADE-WOLVES	*	550.00	550.00
*	BLACK MAGIC-PANTHER	*	475.00	475.00
*	CANADA D.U. DUCK STAMP PRIN	*	135.00	135.00
*	CANADA D.U. DUCK STAMP-EXEC.	*	375.00	375.00
*	EARLY SNOW-RED FOX	*	200.00	200.00
*	FOREST GLOW-JAGUAR	*	225.00	225.00
*	ICE COMPANIONS-HARP SEAL-SEAL PUPS	*	175.00	175.00
*	ICE FISHING-POLAR BEAR	*	225.00	225.00
*	IMPRESS, OF INDIA/NEPAL-W/C WILDLIFE	*	550.00	550.00
*	KEEPING PACE-GRIZZLY W/CUBS	*	200.00	200.00
*	LEAVING THE NEST-WOOD DUCK	*	150.00	150.00
*	N.Y. DUCK STAMP - 1990 W/	*	300.00	300.00
*	N.Y. DUCK STAMP -1990 W/MEDAL	*	550.00	550.00
*	NEW YORK DUCK STAMP 1990 RE	*	*	135.00
*	NIGHT PROWLER-WOLF	*	225.00	225.00
*	QINLING PANDA	*	225.00	225.00
*	RED FOX KIT STUDY	*	60.00	60.00
*	RETURN TO YELLOWSTONE-WOLVES	*	235.00	235.00
*	SILENT WATERS-MOOSE	*	175.00	175.00
*	SNOWBOUNDING-GRIZZLY	*	225.00	225.00
*	SQUIRREL MONKEY STUDY	*	145.00	145.00
*	YOUNG PREDATOR-LEOPARD CUB	*	200.00	200.00

YR	NAME	LIMIT	ISSUE	TREND
83	COOL RETREAT-LYNX	950	85.00	100.00
83	EARLY WINDFALL-GRAY SQUIRRELS	950	85.00	85.00
83	FIRST SNOW-GRIZZLY BEARS	950	95.00	250.00
83	LONE FISHERMAN-GREAT BLUE HERON	950	85.00	300.00
83	REFUGE, THE-RACCOONS	950	85.00	300.00
83	RIVER WATCH-PEREGRINE FALCON	950	85.00	85.00
83	WINTER LOOKOUT-COUGAR	950	85.00	500.00
84	AMONG THE CATTAILS-CANADA GEESE	950	130.00	425.00
84	ARCTIC PROCESSION-WILLOW PTARMIGAN	950	220.00	600.00
84	BASKING-BROWN PELICANS	950	115.00	125.00
84	BREAKING COVER-BLACK BEAR	950	130.00	130.00
84	CLOSE ENCOUNTER-BOBCAT	950	130.00	190.00
84	HIGH GROUND-WOLVES	950	130.00	325.00
84	ICY OUTCROP-WHITE GYRFALCON	950	115.00	200.00
84	LYING LOW-COUGAR	950	85.00	450.00
84	MORNING MIST-SNOWY OWL	RT	95.00	95.00
84	PLAINS HUNTER-PRAIRIE FALCON	950	95.00	95.00
84	SPIRIT OF THE NORTH-WHITE WOLF	950	130.00	185.00
85	AWAKENING MEADOW-COTTONTAIL	950	50.00	50.00
85	CHILDREN OF THE FOREST-RED FOX KITS	950	110.00	150.00
85	CHILDREN OF THE TUNDRA-ARCTIC WOLF PUP	950	110.00	225.00
85	COUGAR HEAD STUDY	950	60.00	60.00
85	DAYBREAK-MOOSE	950	135.00	135.00
85	FALLEN BIRCH-CHIPMUNK	950	60.00	250.00
85	FIRST LIGHT-GRAY JAYS	950	130.00	200.00
85	GATHERING, THE-GRAY WOLVES	950	165.00	350.00
85	ISLAND SANCTUARY-MALLARDS	950	95.00	175.00
85	RETURN TO WINTER-PINTAILS	RT	135.00	135.00
85	SUNDOWN REFLECTIONS-WOOD DUCK	950	85.00	85.00
85	UNDER THE PINES-BOBCAT	950	95.00	275.00
85	WINTER RENDEZVOUS-COYOTES	950	140.00	225.00
86	ABOVE THE TREELINE-COUGAR	950	139.00	130.00
86	AFTER THE FIRE-GRIZZLY BEAR	RT	95.00	95.00
86	ALONG THE ICE FLOW-POLAR BEARS	950	200.00	200.00
86	CONFLICT AT DAWN-HERON AND OSPREY	950	130.00	175.00
86	COTTONWOOD GOLD-BALTIMORE ORIOLE	950	85.00	85.00
86	EARLY ARRIVALS-SNOW BUNTINGS	950	75.00	75.00
86	HIDDEN ADMIRER-MOOSE	950	165.00	275.00
86	HIGH COUNTRY CHAMPION-GRIZZLY	950	175.00	250.00
86	KENYAN FAMILY-CHEETAHS	950	130.00	130.00
86	LAKESIDE FAMILY-CANADA GEESE	950	75.00	75.00
86	LOW TIDE-BALD EAGLES	950	130.00	130.00
86	MORNING FORAGE-GROUND SQUIRREL	RT	75.00	75.00
86	RACING THE STORM-ARCTIC WOLVES	950	200.00	350.00
86	SNOWY EXCURSION-RED SQUIRREL	950	75.00	75.00
86	SPRING MIST-CHICKADEES	950	105.00	150.00
86	TREADING THIN ICE-CHIPMUNK	950	75.00	75.00
86	WINTER HIDING-COTTONTAIL	950	75.00	75.00
86	WINTER PERCH-CARDINAL	950	85.00	175.00
86	YOUNG EXPLORER, THE-RED FOX KIT	950	75.00	75.00
87	ALPENGLOW-ARCTIC WOLF	950	200.00	275.00
87	AMBOSELI CHILD-AF/ELEPHANT	*	160.00	180.00
87	AUTUMN MIST-BARRED OWL	950	160.00	225.00
87	AUTUMN THUNDER-MUSK OXEN	950	150.00	150.00
87	BATHING-MUTE SWAN	RT	175.00	175.00
87	CANYON CREEK-COUGAR	950	195.00	450.00
87	DAWN ON THE MARSH-COYOTE	950	200.00	200.00
87	FIRST TRACKS-COUGAR	950	150.00	150.00
87	HIGH REFUGE-RED SQUIRREL	950	120.00	120.00
87	IN DEEP-BLACK BEAR CUB	950	135.00	135.00
87	LYING IN WAIT-ARCTIC FOX	950	175.00	175.00
87	OUT OF THE BLIZZARD-TIMBER WOLVES	950	215.00	500.00
87	OUT OF THE MIST-GRIZZLY	*	200.00	325.00
87	RAIN WATCH-BELTED KINGFISHER	*	125.00	200.00
87	SUNDOWN ALERT-BOBCAT	950	150.00	150.00
87	WINTER VIGIL-GREAT HORNED OWL	RT	175.00	175.00
88	BATHING-BLUE JAY	950	95.00	95.00
88	CLIFF HANGER-BOBCAT	950	200.00	200.00
88	COASTAL CLIQUE-HARBOR SEALS	950	160.00	160.00
88	EDGE OF THE FOREST-TIMBER WOLVES	950	500.00	700.00
88	EVENING MEADOW-AMERICAN GOLDFINCH	950	150.00	150.00
88	HIDING PLACE-SAW-WHET OWL	950	95.00	95.00
88	LAST SANCTUARY-FLORIDA PANTHER	RT	175.00	175.00
88	MOONLIGHT FISHERMAN-RACCOON	RT	175.00	175.00
88	MOOSE HAIR	950	165.00	230.00
88	MORNING DISPLAY-COMMON LOONS	950	135.00	330.00
88	NIGHT MOVES-AFRICAN ELEPHANTS	950	150.00	150.00
88	NORTHWOODS FAMILY-MOOSE	950	75.00	75.00
88	SAVANNA SIESTA-AFRICAN LIONS	950	165.00	165.00
88	SNOWY WATCH-GREAT GRAY OWL	950	175.00	175.00
88	SPANISH MIST-YOUNG BARRED OWL	950	175.00	175.00
88	TUNDRA FAMILY-ARCTIC WOLVES	950	200.00	200.00
88	WINTER GRAZING-BISON	950	185.00	185.00
88	WINTER SPIRIT-GRAY WOLF	950	200.00	200.00
89	BEFORE THE FREEZE-BEAVER	950	165.00	195.00
89	COUGAR RUN	950	185.00	450.00
89	EVENING DUET-SNOWY EGRETS	1250	185.00	185.00
89	FLUKE SIGHTING-HUMPBACK WHALES	RT	185.00	185.00
89	GORILLA	290	400.00	600.00

YR	NAME	LIMIT	ISSUE	TREND
89	HEAVY GOING-GRIZZLY	RT	175.00	175.00
89	HIGH AND MIGHTY-GORILLA	950	185.00	225.00
89	SNEAK PEAK-CHICKEN	950	950.00	185.00
89	SOFTLY, SOFTLY-WHITE TIGER	950	220.00	500.00
89	SPRING FLURRY-ADELIE PENGUINS	950	185.00	185.00
89	WATER SPORT-BOBCAT	RT	185.00	185.00
90	ARCTIC WOLF PUPS	290	500.00	500.00
90	BITTERSWEET WINTER-CARDINAL	1250	150.00	275.00
90	DAWN MAJESTY-WHITE TIGER	RT	185.00	185.00
90	GRIZZLY-ORIGINAL	290	*	400.00
90	IN THEIR PRESENCE-ORCAS	1250	200.00	200.00
90	MARKER 221-CANVASBACKS NEW YORK	*	*	135.00
90	MOUNTAIN CRADLE-GORILLA	1250	200.00	200.00
90	NIGHT RUN-ARCTIC WOLVES	1250	200.00	250.00
90	NORTHERN PLUNGE, THE-SEA LIONS	1250	*	200.00
90	PLUNGE-NORTHERN SEA LIONS	1250	200.00	200.00
90	SEASONAL GREETING-CARDINAL	1250	150.00	200.00
90	SPOUT-WHALES	290	500.00	500.00
90	SUITORS, THE-WOOD DUCKS	3313	135.00	185.00
90	SUMMER RAIN-COMMON LOONS	RT	200.00	200.00
90	SUMMER RAIN-COMMON LOONS (SPECIAL)	450	425.00	425.00
90	THEIR FIRST SEASON-GRIZZLY BEAR	RT	200.00	200.00
90	TOGETHERNESS-LION	1250	125.00	125.00
90	WHITETAIL SPRING-WHITETAIL DEER	RT	185.00	185.00
91	DENALI FAMILY-GRIZZLY BEAR	*	195.00	225.00
91	EVENING ENCOUNTER-GRIZZLY & WOLF	1250	185.00	185.00
91	FACE TO FACE	1250	200.00	200.00
91	MONSOON-WHITE TIGER	RT	195.00	195.00
91	MOONLIGHT CHASE-COUGAR	250	195.00	195.00
91	OUT ON A LIMB-YOUNG BARRED OWL	950	185.00	185.00
91	PANDA TRILOGY	950	375.00	375.00
91	SISTERS-ARCTIC WOLVES	1250	185.00	185.00
91	SOMETHING STIRRED-BENGAL TIGER	950	195.00	195.00
92	BANYAN AMBUSH-BLACK PANTHER	RT	235.00	235.00
92	CHASE-SNOW LEOPARD, THE	950	200.00	200.00
92	OUT OF THE DARKNESS-BLACK PANTHER	290	200.00	200.00
92	RANTHAMBHORE RUSH-TIGER	950	225.00	225.00
92	REGAL MAJESTY-BLACK PANTHER	290	200.00	200.00
93	DARK ENCOUNTER-BLACK WOLF	*	200.00	200.00
93	FREEDOM I-HARPY EAGLE	350	500.00	500.00
93	FROZEN MOONLIGHT-ARCTIC WOLVES	2500	225.00	225.00
93	GRIZZLY IMPACT	950	225.00	225.00
93	LOONLIGHT-LOON	1500	225.00	225.00
93	MORNING GLORY-BALD EAGLE	1250	225.00	225.00
93	NIGHT SPECTER- BLACK JAGUAR	1250	195.00	195.00
93	PHANTOMS OF THE TUNDRA-WOLVES	950	235.00	235.00
93	RAINS-TIGER, THE	950	225.00	225.00
93	SEEKING ATTENTION-GRIZZLY	950	200.00	200.00
93	WOLONG WHITEOUT-PANDA	950	225.00	225.00
94	ABANDONED-WOLF PUPS	*	175.00	200.00
94	CHILD OF THE OUTBACK-KOALA	950	175.00	175.00
94	COURTSHIP, THE-EGERTS	950	175.00	175.00

M. SOLBERG

YR	NAME	LIMIT	ISSUE	TREND
*	ANTELOPE RIDGE	*	150.00	150.00
*	BUFFALO BROTHERS	*	175.00	175.00
*	CHALLENGE OF THE WILD	*	225.00	225.00
*	DARK WATERS-HERON	*	70.00	70.00
*	FEMALE TIMBER WOLF	*	100.00	100.00
*	GARDEN VISITOR-RED FOX	*	210.00	210.00
*	ICE BEAR	*	210.00	210.00
*	MALE TIMBER WOLF	*	100.00	100.00
*	MCNEIL RIVER FISHERMAN-BROWN BEAR	*	175.00	175.00
*	TIMBER WOLF STUDY	*	75.00	75.00
*	TIMBER WOLF STUDY COMPANION	*	185.00	185.00
*	TOMORROW MAY BE COOLER-LION	*	135.00	135.00
*	WHITE WOLF STUDY	*	75.00	75.00
79	BENGAL TIGER	*	65.00	110.00
82	ACCEPT MY FATHERS SPIRIT	*	95.00	210.00
83	BANDITS, THE	*	125.00	145.00
85	ACROSS THE TUNDRA	*	135.00	240.00
86	CHECKING FOR STRAYS	*	*	85.00
86	EARLY MORNING CHALLENGE-ELK	*	*	150.00
86	EDGE OF NIGHT-BARN OWL	*	150.00	245.00
86	LONG CAST, THE-FISHERMAN	*	*	95.00
86	MORNING MIST-CANADA GEESE	*	95.00	125.00
86	MOUNTAIN VISTA-LANDSCAPE	950	95.00	1175.00
86	ON SCENT-GERMAN SHORTHAIRS	*	*	95.00
86	SUNLIT MIST-ELK	*	*	85.00
86	VIRGIN WATERS-LANDSCAPE	*	*	150.00
86	WHERE THE TRAIL ENDS-SNOW LEOPARD	*	*	150.00
86	WINGS OF WONDER-BALD EAGLE	950	150.00	400.00
86	WINTER REFLECTION-BEAR	*	*	150.00
87	ALERT-DOE AND FAWN	*	*	125.00
87	BAD WATER BEAR	*	*	150.00
87	FROM NORTH THEY CAME-WOLF	*	*	85.00
87	GRAND DUCK, THE-OWL	*	*	150.00
87	HANDSOME HUNTER-AMERICAN KESTREL	950	115.00	375.00
87	HIGH COUNTRY MORNING-BIGHORN SHEEP	*	*	125.00
87	MONARCH OF THE SKY-GOLDEN EAGLE	950	200.00	275.00

YR	NAME	LIMIT	ISSUE	TREND
87	MOUNTAIN SENTINEL-LION	*	*	125.00
87	ON THE HIGH SIDE-MOUNTAIN GOAT	*	*	95.00
87	SOMETHING MOVED-BOBCAT	*	*	125.00
87	YELLOWSTONE OSPREY	*	*	75.00
88	ARCTIC NOMADS	950	*	150.00
88	BLACK-CAPPED CHICKADEE	*	*	95.00
88	GATEFUL MOMENT-EAGLE	*	*	150.00
88	INTO THE STORM-CARIBOU	*	*	140.00
88	MORNING MEMORIES	*	*	135.00
88	ON SILENT WINGS-BALD EAGLE	*	150.00	275.00
88	RIVER OF DREAMS-FISHING	*	*	150.00
89	DECEPTIVE CALM-GOSHAWK	950	95.00	195.00
89	REFLECTION-WOLF	950	*	150.00
89	WHEN WINTER WARMS-POLAR BEAR	950	*	115.00
89	WHISPERING WINGS-TRUMPETER SWAN	*	*	135.00
89	WINTER WHITE-SNOWY OWL	*	*	95.00
90	BY FIRELIGHT-MOUNTAIN LION	*	160.00	150.00
90	NOMAD OF THE ICE-POLAR BEAR	1250	165.00	225.00
90	ON WATCH	950	*	150.00
90	OUT OF THE FOG-GRIZZLY BEAR	*	*	150.00
90	SERENE SETTING-AMERICAN KESTRELS	1250	150.00	250.00
90	SIGNS OF SPRING-HORSE	*	*	150.00
90	SMALL WONDER-CHIPMUNK	*	*	110.00
90	THISTLEDOWN-KESTREL	*	*	150.00
91	AFTERNOON SHADOWS-MULE DEER	*	145.00	145.00
91	AUTUMN CHALLENGE-ELK	*	*	150.00
91	KORBEL GARDENS-FLORAL	*	*	150.00
91	MOUSE TRACKS-COYOTE	*	*	150.00
F. MACHETANZ				**ALASKA**
*	HARPOONER'S MOMENT-ALASKA	*	225.00	225.00
*	TRAIL OF GREAT WHITE BEAR-ALASKA	*	225.00	225.00
J. DALY				**BOY**
*	FAVORITE READER	*	425.00	425.00
J. CHRISTENSEN				**BRONZE**
*	SIX BIRD HUNTERS	*	4500.00	4500.00
R. PARKER				**BRONZE**
*	COYOTE	*	950.00	950.00
*	RIMROCK - BRONZE	*	1450.00	1450.00
P. CALLE				**INDIAN**
*	BUFFALO SKULL BUCKLE - BRONZE	*	95.00	95.00
*	BUFFALO SKULL BUCKLE - SILVER	*	750.00	750.00
*	ONE STAR	*	125.00	125.00
P. CALLE				**MOUNTAIN MAN**
*	FIRESIDE COMPANIONS	*	150.00	150.00
*	FREE TRAPPER STUDY	*	125.00	125.00
*	FREE TRAPPER, THE - BRONZE	*	*	*
*	I CALL HIM FRIEND - PRESTIGE	*	375.00	375.00
*	MOUNTAIN MAN, THE (COLOR)	*	150.00	150.00
*	MOUNTAIN MAN, THE (PENCIL)	*	250.00	250.00
*	NEAR JOURNEY'S END	*	245.00	245.00
81	FRIEND OR FOE	950	125.00	125.00
85	FRONTIER BLACKSMITH	950	245.00	245.00
88	TRAPPER AT REST	550	95.00	95.00
89	WINTER FEAST, A PREMIER ED.	290	465.00	465.00
92	HUNTER OF GEESE	950	125.00	125.00
92	OUT OF THE SILENCE	2500	265.00	265.00
92	OUT OF THE SILENCE - PRESTIGE	290	465.00	465.00
92	THROUGH THE TALL GRASS	950	175.00	175.00
93	AND A GRIZZLY CLAW NECKLACE	750	150.00	150.00
93	I CALL HIM FRIEND	950	235.00	235.00
P. CALLE				**PORTRAIT**
92	JIMMY DOOLITTLE PORTRAIT	*	425.00	425.00
J. DALY				**PORTRAIT**
*	ALL ABOARD	*	145.00	145.00
*	EYE TO EYE	*	95.00	95.00
*	HER SECRET PLACE	*	275.00	275.00
*	PLAYMATES	*	355.00	355.00
*	SLIDING HOME	*	75.00	75.00
*	SUNDAY AFTERNOON	*	185.00	185.00
*	WINNING COACH	*	75.00	75.00
92	DOMINOES	1500	155.00	155.00
92	FAVORITE GIFT	RT	175.00	175.00
92	FLYING HORSES, THE	950	325.00	325.00
92	IMMIGRANT SPIRIT, THE	5000	125.00	125.00
93	GOOD COMPANY	1500	155.00	155.00
93	LEFT OUT	1500	110.00	110.00
93	NEW CITIZEN, THE	5000	125.00	125.00
93	SECRET ADMIRER	1500	150.00	150.00
93	WHEN I GROW UP	1500	175.00	175.00
94	CHILDHOOD FRIENDS	950	110.00	110.00
T. UTZ				**UTZ**
81	GREENHOUSE NUDE, THE	550	95.00	135.00
81	LAVENDER LACE	950	75.00	145.00
81	MELANIE	450	85.00	150.00
81	PICNIC	550	110.00	115.00
81	PINK LADY	450	85.00	175.00
81	SOFT WIND, THE	950	*	75.00

YR	NAME	LIMIT	ISSUE	TREND
83	INTERLUDE	*	*	40.00
86	MORNING MELODY	*	*	90.00
86	STRAND OF PEARLS	*	*	90.00
87	ANGELICA	*	*	85.00
87	GABRIELLA	*	*	85.00
88	GRANNY'S BOOTS	*	*	95.00
88	SOLITUDE	*	*	95.00
90	CONTEMPLATION	*	*	150.00
90	DRAGON SLAYER, THE	*	*	95.00
90	EARLY LIGHT	*	*	110.00
90	END OF THE RAINBOW	*	*	95.00
90	GOSSAMER	*	150.00	250.00
M. WARREN				**WARREN**
74	TOP HAND OF THE CONCHO	950	150.00	260.00
81	A COLD DAY	950	245.00	775.00
81	APPROACHING STORM	*	*	195.00
81	WHEN COWBOYS GET EDGY	*	*	245.00
82	NIGHT IN CHIMAYO	*	125.00	225.00
J. ZEMSKY				**ZEMSKY**
79	COME AND SEE THE NEW COLT	950	65.00	70.00
79	JORDAN AT THE WEDDING	950	65.00	160.00
79	JORDAN'S DOLLY	950	65.00	400.00
79	LOVE AT FIRST SIGHT	950	75.00	175.00
79	WHEN THE THEN AND THE NOW HOLD HANDS	950	65.00	200.00
80	JORDAN'S SPRING	*	65.00	350.00
84	JENNY IN THE ATTIC	*	75.00	175.00
84	THEY'LL BE SORRY WHEN WE'RE GONE	*	75.00	85.00

MOSS PORTFOLIO

P. BUCKLEY MOSS

YR	NAME	LIMIT	ISSUE	TREND
*	APPLE PICKER	1000	30.00	125.00
*	BARELIMBED REFLECTIONS	1000	25.00	70.00
*	BLUE BOUQUET	1000	16.00	32.00
*	CENTRAL PARK	1000	80.00	200.00
*	EMILY	1000	30.00	100.00
*	FLAG BOY	1000	16.00	40.00
*	GINNY	1000	16.00	45.00
*	GRANDMOTHER	1000	60.00	120.00
*	JOHN	1000	10.00	45.00
*	LANDSCAPE W/GEESE (GOLD)	1000	500.00	1000.00
*	LESSON IN PATIENCE	1000	150.00	300.00
*	LITTLE GIRL IN BLUE	1000	16.00	40.00
*	LORDS OF THE REALM	1000	80.00	210.00
*	MARY AND MAGNOLIA	1000	15.00	42.00
*	SHENANDOAH SILHOUETTE	1000	25.00	60.00
*	STACK OF GIRLS	1000	25.00	125.00
*	STONE HOUSE	99	600.00	1250.00
78	BECKY AND TOM	1000	10.00	100.00
78	CANADA GEESE	1000	60.00	140.00
78	DAILY CHORES	1000	16.00	100.00
78	EVENING RUN	1000	55.00	155.00
78	FAMILY OUTING	1000	65.00	300.00
78	FOUR LITTLE GIRLS	1000	30.00	150.00
78	FRESH BOUQUET	1000	15.00	160.00
78	FRIENDLY STEED	1000	50.00	150.00
78	FRIENDS	1000	35.00	160.00
78	FROSTY FROLIC	1000	75.00	400.00
78	GINNY AND CHRIS WITH LAMBS	1000	35.00	150.00
78	GOLDEN WINTER	1000	150.00	430.00
78	GOSSIP	1000	45.00	130.00
78	HELPERS	1000	35.00	125.00
78	HUNGRY BABY BIRD	1000	15.00	100.00
78	LITTLE APPLES IN A ROW	1000	100.00	310.00
78	LITTLE FELLOW	1000	57.00	150.00
78	MILK LAD	1000	15.00	125.00
78	MILK MAID	1000	15.00	125.00
78	MOMMA APPLE (BLUE)	1000	10.00	125.00
78	MOMMA APPLE (GOLD)	1000	16.00	125.00
78	MOONLIT SKATERS I (LARGE)	1000	75.00	300.00
78	MOONLIT SKATERS II (SMALL)	1000	40.00	140.00
78	MUFFET BOY I	1000	10.00	75.00
78	MUFFET GIRL I	1000	10.00	75.00
78	NINE MENNONITES GIRLS	1000	40.00	180.00
78	PERFECT PET	1000	15.00	90.00
78	POPPA APPLE (BLUE)	1000	10.00	100.00
78	POPPA APPLE (GOLD)	1000	15.00	100.00
78	QUILTING BEE	1000	55.00	200.00
78	QUILTING LADIES	1000	40.00	200.00
78	RACHEL & JACOB	1000	150.00	610.00
78	RELUCTANT BALLERINA	1000	16.00	100.00
78	SEASON'S OVER	1000	35.00	150.00
78	SERENITY IN BLACK AND WHITE	1000	120.00	360.00
78	SHOWALTER'S FARM	1000	100.00	310.00
78	SKATING AWAY I	1000	70.00	200.00
78	SKATING LESSON	1000	150.00	500.00
78	SNOW GOOSE	1000	50.00	200.00
78	SNOWY BIRCHES	1000	60.00	200.00
78	SOLITARY SKATER	1000	35.00	200.00
78	SPIRIT OF EQUUS	1000	100.00	300.00

YR	NAME	LIMIT	ISSUE	TREND
78	TENDING HER FLOCK	1000	80.00	250.00
78	WINTER CAMEO	1000	30.00	150.00
78	WINTER VISITOR	1000	80.00	180.00
78	WORKDAY'S O'ER	1000	110.00	410.00
79	A WELCOME	1000	45.00	155.00
79	APPLE HARVEST	1000	75.00	225.00
79	AWAKE, O EARTH	1000	50.00	150.00
79	BEHOLD	1000	35.00	100.00
79	DEAR LORD (LONG)	1000	30.00	100.00
79	EVERY BLESSING	1000	50.00	150.00
79	FANEUIL HALL	1000	40.00	100.00
79	GRANNY'S FAVORITE	1000	40.00	160.00
79	HAIL THE DAY, SOLACE	1000	75.00	215.00
79	HARK	1000	40.00	160.00
79	HE LIVES	1000	25.00	95.00
79	HOW CALM THE MORN	1000	75.00	245.00
79	JOY	1000	16.00	80.00
79	LOVE	1000	10.00	105.00
79	MARY'S LAMB (LARGE)	1000	75.00	180.00
79	MARY'S LAMBS (SMALL)	1000	40.00	100.00
79	MY HANDS TO THEE	1000	75.00	300.00
79	NEVER ALONE	1000	35.00	130.00
79	O GENTLE FRIEND	1000	40.00	175.00
79	OH LIFE	1000	40.00	150.00
79	PAVILION AT WOLFEBORO	1000	40.00	100.00
79	PROMISED	1000	40.00	150.00
79	PUBLIC GARDENS AND BEACON STREET	1000	50.00	260.00
79	TARRY NOT	1000	35.00	160.00
79	TIS GRACE	1000	20.00	120.00
79	TWO LITTLE HANDS	1000	35.00	150.00
79	WOMAN TALK	1000	35.00	150.00
80	CAPITOL SKATERS	1000	80.00	200.00
80	ON THE CANAL	1000	60.00	200.00
80	PEACH HARVEST	1000	150.00	500.00
80	RING AROUND A ROSIE	1000	40.00	200.00
80	STREET BY THE PARK	1000	200.00	600.00
80	WAYSIDE INN	1000	65.00	500.00
80	WAYSIDE INN (ETCHING)	99	1800.00	3250.00
80	WINTER'S HOUSE	1000	350.00	750.00
81	BLACK CAT	1000	50.00	100.00
81	BLACK CAT ON PINK CUSHION	1000	40.00	130.00
81	QUILTING DREAMS	1000	40.00	150.00
81	SAM	1000	16.00	95.00
81	SARAH	1000	16.00	155.00
81	SKATING JOY	1000	200.00	610.00
81	SOLITARY SKATER II	1000	35.00	160.00
81	SOLO	1000	15.00	150.00
81	SPRING LOVE	1000	25.00	140.00
81	STREET BY THE PARK II	1000	125.00	290.00
81	SUNDAY MORNING	1000	60.00	270.00
81	SUNDAY'S RIDE	1000	60.00	200.00
81	TOGETHER	99	450.00	2000.00
81	WAITING FOR TOM	1000	40.00	525.00
81	WINTER AT THE MILL	1000	80.00	290.00
82	APPLE DAY	1000	80.00	210.00
82	APPLE GIRL	1000	30.00	145.00
82	AUTUMN RIDE	1000	80.00	200.00
82	BALLOON RIDE	1000	100.00	220.00
82	BLUE WINTER	1000	100.00	310.00
82	CAMEO GEESE	1000	40.00	180.00
82	CHRIS	1000	25.00	100.00
82	DANIEL	1000	20.00	120.00
82	DASHING AWAY	1000	100.00	325.00
82	DONKEY BOY	1000	40.00	105.00
82	EBONY'S JET	1000	150.00	340.00
82	FLAG GIRL	1000	10.00	75.00
82	FLOWER GIRL	1000	20.00	75.00
82	FRUIT OF THE VALLEY	1000	80.00	300.00
82	GAGGLE OF GEESE	1000	125.00	290.00
82	GRANDPA'S HOUSE	1000	40.00	110.00
82	HAND IN HAND	1000	40.00	130.00
82	HAYRIDE	1000	50.00	175.00
82	HURRAH!	1000	20.00	80.00
82	LISA AND TIGER	1000	30.00	120.00
82	LITTLE GIRL'S PRAYER	1000	35.00	140.00
82	MY PLACE	1000	30.00	150.00
82	MY SISTERS	1000	40.00	150.00
82	ON THE SWING	1000	40.00	190.00
82	OUR LITTLE BROTHER	1000	50.00	180.00
82	OUR LITTLE SISTER	1000	50.00	180.00
82	PALS	1000	25.00	100.00
82	PINK BALLERINA	1000	25.00	105.00
82	PLEASE GOD	1000	50.00	190.00
82	PLEASE!	1000	35.00	130.00
82	ROCKING	1000	40.00	130.00
82	SHENANDOAH HARVEST	1000	60.00	200.00
82	SKATING DUET	1000	40.00	155.00
82	SLEIGH RIDE	1000	50.00	170.00
82	STACK OF BOYS	1000	30.00	125.00

Beginning Friends *by Paul Calle reflects upon the days when the white man and the Indian were at peace with one another. Mill Pond Press is the publisher.*

Hadley House released Terry Redlin's Morning Solitude *in 1991 for $250. It's currently valued at $745.*

Go For Wand–A Candle in the Wind *by Fred Stone, distributed by American Artists, was limited to 1,150 and originally sold for $225 in 1991.*

Robert Bateman's Shadow of the Rainforest–Jaguar *stealthily stalks its prey in this 1992 issue from Mill Pond Press. The print originally retailed for $1,200.*

YR	NAME	LIMIT	ISSUE	TREND
82	TAKING TURNS	1000	50.00	180.00
82	TOGETHER IN THE PARK	1000	80.00	190.00
82	TWO ON A BARREL	1000	25.00	130.00
82	TWO ON A SWING	1000	50.00	150.00
82	WEDDING	1000	80.00	300.00
82	WEDDING DAY	1000	160.00	380.00
82	WEDDING II	1000	90.00	220.00
82	WINTER DUET	1000	90.00	260.00
82	WINTER'S GLIMPSE	1000	40.00	145.00
83	ADAM	1000	20.00	150.00
83	AMY	1000	20.00	160.00
83	BECKY	1000	20.00	160.00
83	BROTHERS	1000	35.00	150.00
83	CARRIE	1000	30.00	100.00
83	CHERISHED	1000	35.00	150.00
83	CHICKEN FARMERS	1000	40.00	140.00
83	CHRISTMAS CAROL	1000	60.00	580.00
83	COLONIAL SLEIGH RIDE	1000	125.00	310.00
83	COUNTRY CHURCH	1000	80.00	200.00
83	EVENING GUESTS	1000	60.00	145.00
83	EVENING WELCOME	1000	60.00	210.00
83	FAMILY, THE	1000	125.00	300.00
83	FINISHING TOUCHES	1000	60.00	130.00
83	FIRST LOVE	1000	60.00	150.00
83	GAGGLE OF GEESE (SILKSCREEN)	99	600.00	2000.00
83	GINGER	1000	40.00	125.00
83	GIRLS IN GREEN	1000	40.00	125.00
83	GOLDEN AUTUMN	1000	110.00	250.00
83	GOVERNOR'S PALACE	1000	50.00	240.00
83	GRANNY'S GIRL	1000	50.00	180.00
83	JOSHUA	1000	25.00	150.00
83	KATIE	1000	25.00	150.00
83	LONG GROVE CHURCH	1000	100.00	275.00
83	LORDS OF THE VALLEY	1000	175.00	390.00
83	MARY ANN	1000	20.00	110.00
83	MONARCH	1000	35.00	120.00
83	MY GIRLS	1000	60.00	300.00
83	NOTRE DAME	1000	90.00	180.00
83	OLD MILL HOUSE	1000	125.00	280.00
83	ORCHARD GIRL	1000	40.00	200.00
83	ORCHARD HELPERS	1000	75.00	310.00
83	OUR BIG BROTHER	1000	35.00	120.00
83	QUILT, THE	1000	90.00	260.00
83	RED BIKE	1000	35.00	120.00
83	RED HOUSE	1000	100.00	300.00
83	ROTHENBURG	1000	40.00	135.00
83	SISTERS FOUR	1000	60.00	240.00
83	SPRING BOUQUET	1000	40.00	150.00
83	SPRING SHEPHERDS	1000	40.00	145.00
83	SUMMER LOVE	1000	50.00	200.00
83	SUNDAY'S APPLES	1000	50.00	210.00
83	TENDER SHEPHERD	1000	50.00	180.00
83	TERRACE HILL	1000	110.00	250.00
83	TIMOTHY	1000	30.00	125.00
83	TOGETHER ON SUNDAY (SILKSCREEN)	99	600.00	2050.00
83	WEDDING III	1000	90.00	180.00
83	WHITE CHURCH, THE	1000	80.00	250.00
83	WINTER RIDE	1000	60.00	145.00
83	WINTER SKATER	1000	40.00	145.00
83	WINTER'S DAY	1000	50.00	200.00
83	WINTER'S JOY (SILKSCREEN)	99	500.00	1150.00
84	AUTUMN TRIPTYCH	1000	150.00	340.00
84	BALLOON GIRL	1000	20.00	65.00
84	BLESSING, THE	1000	60.00	260.00
84	BROWER HOMESTEAD	1000	100.00	240.00
84	CRAZY QUILT	1000	50.00	155.00
84	ENGAGEMENT, THE	1000	40.00	125.00
84	EVENING HOUR, THE	1000	70.00	145.00
84	FIRST BORN	1000	50.00	140.00
84	FROSTY RIDE	1000	70.00	265.00
84	GRANDMA'S BED	1000	60.00	235.00
84	HITCHING A RIDE	1000	60.00	150.00
84	HOMEWARD BOUND	1000	90.00	250.00
84	LOUDMOUTHS	1000	125.00	310.00
84	MAGGIE	1000	30.00	115.00
84	MARY JEN	1000	20.00	115.00
84	MIKE AND JESSIE	1000	60.00	180.00
84	MOLLY	1000	30.00	120.00
84	NEWBORN, THE	1000	55.00	200.00
84	OHIO STAR	1000	60.00	180.00
84	PRINCELY PAIR	1000	60.00	180.00
84	RED WAGON	1000	50.00	180.00
84	SCHOOL YARD, THE	1000	60.00	180.00
84	SECRET, THE	1000	50.00	150.00
84	SUNDAY'S PRAYER	1000	50.00	210.00
84	SWAN HOUSE	1000	80.00	170.00
84	TO GRANDMOTHER'S HOUSE WE GO	1000	80.00	210.00
84	VICTORIAN LEGACY	1000	150.00	390.00
84	WEDDING RIDE, THE	1000	130.00	350.00

YR	NAME	LIMIT	ISSUE	TREND
84	WEDDING RING	1000	75.00	200.00
84	WINTER'S GLORY	1000	200.00	425.00
85	A VISIT TO THE CAPITOL	1000	30.00	120.00
85	BILLY	1000	25.00	100.00
85	CATHY	1000	20.00	150.00
85	CHILDREN'S MUSEUM CAROUSEL, THE	1000	80.00	175.00
85	CINDY	1000	40.00	125.00
85	COUNTRY ROAD	1000	160.00	400.00
85	DANIEL HARRISON HOUSE, THE	1000	100.00	240.00
85	DAREDEVIL SKATERS	1000	100.00	220.00
85	ERIN	1000	25.00	100.00
85	EVENING HOUR IN LONG GROVE	1000	70.00	200.00
85	EVERYTHING NICE	1000	65.00	140.00
85	FAMILY HEIRLOOM	1000	80.00	190.00
85	HEARTLAND, THE	1000	80.00	200.00
85	HEATHER	1000	25.00	200.00
85	IMPERIAL MAJESTY (SILKSCREEN)	99	600.00	1450.00
85	JAKE	1000	25.00	100.00
85	KENTUCKY	1000	70.00	170.00
85	LANCASTER MORN	1000	275.00	565.00
85	LITTLE SISTER	1000	35.00	100.00
85	MARY'S WEDDING	1000	65.00	250.00
85	MIKE	1000	25.00	125.00
85	MINNESOTA	1000	70.00	195.00
85	MY LITTLE BROTHERS	1000	50.00	195.00
85	NANCY	1000	40.00	145.00
85	NIGHT BEFORE CHRISTMAS, THE	1000	65.00	260.00
85	NURSES, THE	1000	70.00	190.00
85	NURSING TEAM	1000	70.00	180.00
85	OUR GIRLS	1000	60.00	175.00
85	PAT	1000	25.00	100.00
85	PICKET FENCE	1000	60.00	180.00
85	PIE MAKERS, THE	1000	80.00	200.00
85	PLAYMATES	1000	70.00	180.00
85	PLEASE MA'AM	1000	50.00	150.00
85	RED CARRIAGE	1000	65.00	190.00
85	ROBBIE	1000	20.00	100.00
85	SCREECH OWL TWINS	1000	75.00	200.00
85	SENATORS, THE	1000	275.00	600.00
85	SENTINELS, THE	1000	65.00	140.00
85	SUMMER'S BLESSING	1000	65.00	210.00
85	THREE SISTERS	1000	70.00	190.00
85	TO EACH OTHER	1000	40.00	125.00
85	TWILIGHT RIDE	1000	80.00	160.00
85	WATCH, THE	1000	30.00	180.00
85	WEDDING BOUQUET	1000	75.00	210.00
85	WEDDING JOY	5000	200.00	625.00
85	WEDDING MORN	1000	70.00	300.00
85	WINTER'S TRAVELERS	1000	60.00	180.00
86	ALLELUIA!	1000	70.00	210.00
86	ALLISON	1000	20.00	150.00
86	AMY'S FLOWERS	1000	50.00	150.00
86	ANDREW	1000	20.00	150.00
86	ANNIE & TEDDY	1000	20.00	100.00
86	BRANDON	1000	20.00	100.00
86	BRIAN	1000	20.00	150.00
86	CANADA GEESE (ETCHING)	99	600.00	1500.00
86	CAROLINE	1000	30.00	95.00
86	DEAR LORD (SHORT)	1000	30.00	75.00
86	DIANA	1000	25.00	100.00
86	EVELYN	1000	40.00	115.00
86	FIRST PROMISE	1000	70.00	175.00
86	GENTLE SWING	1000	50.00	140.00
86	HOMESTEADERS	99	1200.00	2300.00
86	JACK	1000	25.00	120.00
86	KIM	1000	20.00	150.00
86	MAID MARION	1000	50.00	145.00
86	PROFESSOR, THE	1000	40.00	150.00
86	SCHOOL DAYS	1000	70.00	195.00
86	SKATING WALTZ	1000	60.00	150.00
86	SPRING WEDDING	1000	70.00	200.00
86	STEPHANIE	1000	35.00	140.00
86	SUNDAY STROLL	1000	50.00	175.00
86	WINTER WEDDING	1000	80.00	195.00
86	WINTER'S EVE	1000	100.00	240.00
86	WINTER'S MATES	1000	50.00	180.00
87	BETTY	1000	20.00	80.00
87	BILL	1000	20.00	80.00
87	CHAMPIONS	1000	80.00	160.00
87	CHRISTMAS DANCE	1000	70.00	155.00
87	CONTEMPLATION	1000	75.00	155.00
87	SITTING PRETTY	1000	60.00	145.00
87	THREE LITTLE SISTERS	1000	70.00	180.00
87	YOUNG MAESTRO	1000	60.00	135.00
88	ANGEL'S PRAYER	1000	70.00	130.00
88	ANGELS TWO	1000	40.00	100.00
88	CAROL	1000	25.00	100.00
88	CHELSEA	1000	30.00	100.00
88	GEORGETOWN (ETCHING)	1000	1000.00	2000.00

YR	NAME	LIMIT	ISSUE	TREND
88	GRANDAD'S BUDDY	1000	45.00	105.00
88	LITTLE BROWN CHURCH	1000	100.00	250.00
89	A MOTHER'S LOVE	1000	45.00	120.00
89	FOREVER YOURS	1000	125.00	350.00
89	KATIE'S FLOWERS	1000	30.00	150.00
89	MY BIG SISTER	1000	50.00	125.00
89	OUR BEDROOM	1000	70.00	160.00
89	PARTNERS	1000	40.00	110.00
89	WINTER GEESE (ETCHING)	99	400.00	1550.00
90	BABY BOY	1000	25.00	75.00
90	BABY GIRL	1000	25.00	75.00
90	CALLING ON FRIENDS	1000	110.00	200.00
90	SHADOWS OF ETERNITY	1000	50.00	125.00
90	SISTER LOVE	1000	40.00	155.00
90	SISTERS	1000	20.00	120.00
90	SPRING MORN	1000	125.00	250.00
90	TAMMY	1000	30.00	100.00
95	ACROSS THE SILENT SNOW	226	200.00	200.00
95	AMERICAN APPLES	1000	65.00	65.00
95	APPLE BARN	1000	80.00	80.00
95	APPLE BLOSSOM TIME	1000	75.00	75.00
95	ASHLEY'S DELIGHT	1000	45.00	45.00
95	AUSTIN	1000	45.00	45.00
95	BARN DANCE AT THE WHITE BARN	1000	95.00	95.00
95	BEAUTIES IN BLUE	1000	160.00	160.00
95	BEAUTY AT THE STAR BARN	1000	75.00	75.00
95	BIRDS OF PEACE	1000	60.00	60.00
95	BOO!	1000	60.00	60.00
95	BROTHERS TOGETHER	1000	55.00	55.00
95	CAROUSEL QUEEN	1000	80.00	80.00
95	CARRIE'S TREE	1200	75.00	75.00
95	CAT DREAMS	1000	75.00	75.00
95	COLLEGE MEMORIES	1000	100.00	100.00
95	CONTENTMENT	1000	70.00	70.00
95	COOL KRIS KRINGLE	1989	45.00	45.00
95	DANNY'S BEAR	1000	45.00	45.00
95	DASHING THROUGH THE SNOW	1000	130.00	130.00
95	DAVID'S CAT	1000	35.00	35.00
95	DIANE'S CAT	1000	35.00	35.00
95	DID YOU KNOW?	1000	45.00	45.00
95	DON'T LET GO!	1000	45.00	45.00
95	DOWN TOWN	1000	75.00	75.00
95	DUTCH DREAMS	1000	70.00	70.00
95	EARLY MORNING RIDE	1000	55.00	55.00
95	EASTER FRIENDS	1000	50.00	50.00
95	ELEMENTARY SCHOOL	1000	75.00	75.00
95	EMORY & HENRY	1000	100.00	100.00
95	EVENING LIGHT	1000	65.00	65.00
95	EVENING SURPRISE	1000	50.00	50.00
95	EXCHANGE PLACE	1000	145.00	145.00
95	FEED ME	1000	25.00	25.00
95	FIDDLE DANCE	1000	50.00	50.00
95	FISHING AT HUMPBACK BRIDGE	1000	100.00	100.00
95	FREE AS THE WIND	1000	175.00	175.00
95	FT. MYER MARRIAGE CARRIAGE	1000	100.00	100.00
95	GENTLE GIANT	1000	35.00	35.00
95	GIRLS IN A ROW	1000	60.00	60.00
95	GOLDEN LOVE	1000	75.00	75.00
95	GRANDMA'S BUREAU	1000	50.00	50.00
95	GRANDMA'S REDHEAD	1000	50.00	50.00
95	GREENBRIER, THE	1000	125.00	125.00
95	HEAVENLY BABE	2000	60.00	60.00
95	HEAVENLY GRACE	1000	75.00	75.00
95	HER FLOCK	1000	55.00	55.00
95	HOTEL ROANOKE	1000	225.00	225.00
95	IOWA HAY RIDE	1000	150.00	150.00
95	IOWA MORN	1000	100.00	100.00
95	IT'S A BOY	1000	45.00	45.00
95	IT'S A GIRL	1000	45.00	45.00
95	JEFFERSON'S GENTLEMEN	1000	50.00	50.00
95	JOHN DEERE GIRL, THE	1000	75.00	75.00
95	JOHNNY SHILOH	2000	115.00	115.00
95	JUST FOR NANA	1000	45.00	45.00
95	LAKE RIDE	1000	110.00	110.00
95	LET IT RAIN	1000	50.00	50.00
95	LET'S BE PALS	1000	45.00	45.00
95	LITTLE BROWN CHRUCH REVISITED	1000	125.00	125.00
95	LITTLE RASCALS	1000	45.00	45.00
95	LOTS OF LOVE	1000	45.00	45.00
95	LOVE IN BLOOM	1000	65.00	65.00
95	LOVE'S WINTER RIDE	3000	45.00	45.00
95	MAGIC MOMENT	1000	45.00	45.00
95	MANSION, THE	1000	70.00	70.00
95	MARCHING W/OUR PIG	1000	55.00	55.00
95	MARK'S TRAIN	1000	40.00	40.00
95	MATTHEW'S TRAIN	1000	40.00	40.00
95	MEGHAN'S LAMB	1000	50.00	50.00
95	MILL HOUSE, THE	1000	60.00	60.00
95	MIRROR MIRROR ON THE WALL	1000	50.00	50.00

YR	NAME	LIMIT	ISSUE	TREND
95	MONTICELLO	1000	125.00	125.00
95	MORNING GLORY	1000	35.00	35.00
95	MOTHER IS LOVE	1000	45.00	45.00
95	MOTHER'S DAY	2000	50.00	50.00
95	MOVING IN	1000	75.00	75.00
95	MT. ZION	1000	75.00	75.00
95	MY TWO GIRLS	1000	50.00	50.00
95	NEVER ENDING LOVE	1000	60.00	60.00
95	OLD SLED, THE	1000	75.00	75.00
95	ONE MORE STAR	1500	100.00	100.00
95	OUR AMERICAN GOTHICS	1000	150.00	150.00
95	OUR FAMILY HERITAGE	1000	225.00	225.00
95	OUR GIRL SCOUT	1000	55.00	55.00
95	OUR WINTER DAY	1000	45.00	45.00
95	OUT ON A LIMB	1000	40.00	40.00
95	PAT'S PEACHES	1000	55.00	55.00
95	PEACE	1000	175.00	175.00
95	PRECIOUS FRIENDS	1000	65.00	65.00
95	PRECIOUS SISTERS	1000	50.00	50.00
95	READING, 'RITING & 'RITHMETIC	1000	100.00	100.00
95	RED BARN, THE	1000	45.00	45.00
95	ROYAL PAIR	1000	80.00	80.00
95	SALES BARN, THE	1000	135.00	135.00
95	SERVING OUR NEEDS	1000	100.00	100.00
95	SHADOWY RIDE	1000	175.00	175.00
95	SING ALONG, THE	1000	70.00	70.00
95	SNOWY MORNING ON THE FARM	1000	100.00	100.00
95	SOCIETY QUILT, THE	8933	50.00	50.00
95	SPIRIT OF THE MIDWEST	585	200.00	200.00
95	ST. JOHN'S CEMETARY	1000	225.00	225.00
95	STATE FAIR	1000	90.00	90.00
95	STAY TOGETHER	1000	50.00	50.00
95	STITCHED WITH LOVE	1000	275.00	275.00
95	STITCHING NURSE	1000	65.00	65.00
95	STITCHING SISTERS	1000	80.00	80.00
95	SUNDAY AT GRANDMA'S	1000	75.00	75.00
95	TEXAS STAR	1000	75.00	75.00
95	THREE YOUNG MEN	1000	60.00	00.00
95	TRACTORS ON PARADE	1000	135.00	135.00
95	TRAIN MAN	1000	65.00	65.00
95	TREES IN HARMONY	1000	120.00	120.00
95	TRICK OR TREAT	1000	40.00	40.00
95	TRIO, THE	1000	250.00	250.00
95	TULLIE SMITH HOUSE	1000	60.00	60.00
95	TWILIGHT FISHERMAN	1000	40.00	40.00
95	TWIN BOUQUETS	1000	45.00	45.00
95	UNDER THE MISTLETOE	7532	70.00	70.00
95	UNITED WE STAND	1000	70.00	70.00
95	VIOLET BANK	1000	75.00	75.00
95	VISIT TO THE RED SCHOOLHOUSE	1000	70.00	70.00
95	VISIT TO THE VILLAGE, A	1000	100.00	100.00
95	WATER TOWER, THE	1000	80.00	80.00
95	WATERLOO COUNTY HOMESTEAD	1000	100.00	100.00
95	WE THREE	1000	90.00	90.00
95	WEDDING IN WHITE	1000	75.00	75.00
95	WEDDING IN WINTER	1000	50.00	50.00
95	WELCOME	1000	60.00	60.00
95	WHICH ONE?	1000	60.00	60.00
95	WHITE BARN, THE	1000	55.00	55.00
95	WINFREE MEMORIAL, THE	1000	100.00	100.00
95	WINTER HARMONY	500	750.00	750.00
95	WINTER PRINCE	1000	75.00	75.00
95	WINTER'S GENTLE EVE	1000	115.00	115.00
95	WREN'S NEST REVISITED	1000	100.00	100.00
95	YATES CIDER MILL	1000	100.00	100.00
96	ALL DRESSED UP	1000	60.00	60.00
96	APPLE BLOSSOM LOVE	1000	80.00	80.00
96	DANCING JOY	1000	50.00	50.00
96	DELIVERY TEAM, THE	1000	75.00	75.00
96	FARM LIFE	1000	85.00	85.00
96	FISHERMAN, THE	1000	70.00	70.00
96	FOR THE GIRLS	1000	80.00	80.00
96	GIRL SERIES IV	1000	40.00	40.00
96	GUARDIAN ANGELS	1000	80.00	80.00
96	HAIRCUT, THE	1000	65.00	65.00
96	HERE I GO!	1000	35.00	35.00
96	JUST PURRFECT	1000	50.00	50.00
96	LIBERTY	1000	115.00	115.00
96	MOTHER'S HEART	1000	75.00	75.00
96	QUILTED CATS	1000	75.00	75.00
96	WE'RE ALWAYS TOGETHER	1000	70.00	70.00
P. BUCKLEY MOSS		**MIXED MEDIA: ETCHING/SILKSCREEN**		
95	NURSES THREE	250	250.00	250.00
P. BUCKLEY MOSS				**SILKSCREEN**
95	HORSES FOUR	500	115.00	115.00

NAME THAT TOON

YR	NAME	LIMIT	ISSUE	TREND
*				**ANHEUSER-BUSCH**
96	CLYDESDALE-FOOTBALL	2000	198.00	198.00

YR	NAME	LIMIT	ISSUE	TREND
R. LAZZARINI				**ANHEUSER-BUSCH**
96	BUD FROGS/ALLIGATOR	2000	198.00	198.00
R. LAZZARINI				**ANHEUSER-BUSCH/BUD**
95	BUD FROGS II	2000	198.00	198.00
S. WINSTON				**ANHEUSER-BUSCH/BUD**
95	BUD FROGS	2000	198.00	250.00
*				**COCA-COLA**
93	ALWAYS COOL	2000	198.00	250.00
93	ENCHANTED EVENING	2000	198.00	250.00
93	REFRESHMENT	2000	198.00	198.00
94	ALWAYS JAMMIN'	2000	198.00	198.00
94	CUBS DAY OUT	2000	198.00	250.00
95	SUNDAY AT BEACH	2000	198.00	198.00
96	LUGE	2000	198.00	198.00
A. CLOBEY				**COCA-COLA**
95	ALWAYS FRIENDS	2000	198.00	198.00
S. WINSTON				**COCA-COLA**
96	CHOICE. THE	2000	198.00	198.00
*				**COLA-COLA**
93	PAUSE THAT REFRESHES	2000	198.00	250.00
*				**HERSHEYS KISSES**
95	BUNNY HOP	2000	198.00	198.00
W. VINTON				**M&M'S**
96	M&M/T.V.	2000	198.00	198.00
*				**PILLSBURY DOUGH BOY**
95	PILLSBURY POPPIN' FRESH	2000	198.00	198.00

NEW MASTERS PUBLISHING

YR	NAME	LIMIT	ISSUE	TREND
P. BANNISTER				
78	BANDSTAND	250	75.00	550.00
80	DUST OF AUTUMN	200	200.00	1200.00
80	FADED GLORY	200	200.00	1200.00
80	GIFT OF HAPPINESS	200	200.00	2000.00
80	GIRL ON THE BEACH	200	200.00	1300.00
80	SEA HAVEN	SO	285.00	1140.00
80	SILVER BELL, THE	200	200.00	2000.00
80	TITANIA	SO	300.00	1200.00
81	CRYSTAL	300	300.00	400.00
81	EASTER	SO	300.00	1600.00
81	JULIET	SO	300.00	800.00
81	MY SPECIAL PLACE	SO	300.00	2000.00
81	PORCELAIN ROSE	SO	300.00	2000.00
81	REHEARSAL	SO	300.00	1600.00
82	AMARYLLIS	SO	285.00	1950.00
82	APRIL	SO	200.00	1300.00
82	CINDERELLA	500	285.00	300.00
82	EMILY	SO	285.00	1100.00
82	IVY	SO	285.00	700.00
82	JASMINE	SO	235.00	750.00
82	LILY	500	235.00	250.00
82	MAIL ORDER BRIDES	SO	325.00	2350.00
82	MEMORIES	SO	235.00	500.00
82	NUANCE	SO	235.00	525.00
82	PARASOLS	500	235.00	250.00
82	PRESENT, THE	SO	285.00	1000.00
83	DUCHESS, THE	SO	250.00	2500.00
83	MEMENTOS	SO	150.00	1350.00
83	OPHELIA	SO	150.00	850.00
83	WINDOW SEAT	SO	150.00	700.00
84	APRIL LIGHT	SO	150.00	600.00
84	FAN WINDOW, THE	SO	195.00	580.00
84	MAKE BELIEVE	SO	150.00	750.00
84	SCARLET RIBBONS	SO	150.00	350.00
86	PRIDE & JOY	SO	150.00	290.00
86	SOIREE	950	150.00	200.00
87	AUTUMN FIELDS	950	150.00	380.00
87	FIRST PRIZE	950	115.00	225.00
87	QUIET CORNER	SO	115.00	800.00
87	SEPTEMBER HARVEST	SO	150.00	375.00
88	APPLES AND ORANGES	SO	265.00	700.00
88	FLORIBUNDA	SO	265.00	650.00
88	GUINEVERE	485	265.00	1450.00
88	LOVE SEAT	SO	230.00	475.00
88	SUMMER CHOICES	300	250.00	900.00
89	CHAPTER ONE	SO	265.00	1600.00
89	DAYDREAMS	SO	265.00	590.00
89	LOW TIDE	SO	265.00	600.00
89	MARCH WINDS	SO	265.00	540.00
89	PEACE	SO	265.00	1100.00
89	QUILT, THE	SO	265.00	1400.00
90	GOOD FRIENDS	SO	265.00	760.00
90	LAVENDER HILL	SO	265.00	725.00
90	RENDEZVOUS	SO	265.00	650.00
90	SEASCAPES	SO	265.00	450.00
90	SISTERS	SO	265.00	1200.00
90	SONGBIRD	SO	265.00	500.00
90	STRING OF PEARLS	SO	265.00	790.00

YR	NAME	LIMIT	ISSUE	TREND
91	CELEBRATION	SO	350.00	900.00
91	CROSSROADS	SO	295.00	575.00
91	PUDDINGS & PIES	SO	265.00	550.00
91	TEATIME	SO	295.00	750.00
91	WILDFLOWERS	SO	295.00	700.00
92	BED OF ROSES	*	265.00	265.00
92	CRYSTAL BOWL	485	265.00	265.00
92	HEIRLOOM, THE	*	265.00	265.00
92	LOVE LETTERS	485	265.00	500.00
92	MORNING MIST	485	265.00	525.00
92	PERFECTION	*	85.00	85.00
93	CROWNING GLORY	485	265.00	550.00
93	DEJA VU	663	265.00	1300.00
93	IN THE WINGS	*	265.00	265.00
93	INTO THE WOODS	485	265.00	500.00
93	LILIES IN THE FIELD	*	265.00	265.00
93	RAMBLING ROSE	485	265.00	500.00
94	ANGELS	*	265.00	265.00
94	CUCKOO CLOCK	*	265.00	265.00
94	FOUNTAIN	*	265.00	265.00
94	FROM RUSSIA W/LOVE	950	165.00	500.00
94	ONCE UPON A TIME	950	265.00	700.00
95	MAGNOLIAS	*	265.00	265.00
95	NOW AND THEN	*	265.00	265.00

NEWMARK PUBLISHING USA

P. VAUGHAN

YR	NAME	LIMIT	ISSUE	TREND
95	AWAY IN A MANGER	570	95.00	120.00
95	BEAUTIFUL DREAMER	750	95.00	95.00
95	FAMILY TREE	1200	95.00	95.00
95	FOREVER FRIENDS	1200	95.00	95.00
95	HEIRLOOMS	2500	95.00	95.00
95	HER LITTLE RED SHOES	1200	95.00	95.00
95	OLE TIME RELIGION	1200	95.00	120.00
95	PEACEFUL AFTERNOON	1200	95.00	95.00

NORTHWOODS CRAFTSMAN

J. GADAMUS

YR	NAME	LIMIT	ISSUE	TREND
95	ANGEL OF LIGHT	850	110.00	110.00
95	ANGEL OF PEACE	850	110.00	110.00
95	CHANGING THE THE GUARD	750	135.00	135.00
96	ABE	850	135.00	135.00
96	SPRING ROSE	850	50.00	50.00

G. KOVACH

YR	NAME	LIMIT	ISSUE	TREND
95	BOYS OF SUMMER	950	150.00	150.00
95	EVENING AT HOLY HILL	2000	150.00	150.00
95	SANTA'S TREAT	1995	90.00	90.00
95	STAR SPANGLED NIGHT	950	150.00	150.00
96	HOME TOWN HEROES	1000	150.00	150.00
96	THOUGHTS OF HOME	950	150.00	150.00

T. SCHULTZ

YR	NAME	LIMIT	ISSUE	TREND
96	AUTUMN CRIMSON	600	50.00	50.00
96	HOMECOMING	600	90.00	90.00
96	SUMMERTIME GOLD	600	50.00	50.00

M. SINGLETON

YR	NAME	LIMIT	ISSUE	TREND
95	CIRCUS PARADE	600	50.00	50.00
95	COTTAGE BY THE SHORE	600	75.00	75.00
95	SPRING CLEANING	600	50.00	50.00
96	NOAH'S ARK	600	80.00	80.00
96	SATURDAY NIGHT DOWNTOWN	600	75.00	75.00

M. SOLBERG

YR	NAME	LIMIT	ISSUE	TREND
95	TO TOUCH THE SKY	950	150.00	150.00

J. GADAMUS — CANVAS

YR	NAME	LIMIT	ISSUE	TREND
95	ANGEL OF LIGHT	100	300.00	300.00
95	ANGEL OF PEACE	100	300.00	300.00

G. KOVACH — CANVAS

YR	NAME	LIMIT	ISSUE	TREND
95	BOYS OF SUMMER	200	350.00	350.00
95	EVENING AT HOLY HILL	200	400.00	400.00
95	SANTA'S TREAT	200	300.00	300.00
95	STAR SPANGLED NIGHT	200	350.00	350.00
96	HOME TOWN HEROES	200	375.00	375.00
96	THOUGHTS OF HOME	200	375.00	375.00

M. SINGLETON — CANVAS

YR	NAME	LIMIT	ISSUE	TREND
95	CIRCUS PARADE	50	150.00	150.00
95	COTTAGE BY THE SHORE	50	250.00	250.00
95	SPRING CLEANING	50	150.00	150.00
96	NOAH'S ARK	50	275.00	250.00
96	SATURDAY NIGHT DOWNTOWN	50	250.00	250.00

M. SOLBERG — CANVAS

YR	NAME	LIMIT	ISSUE	TREND
95	TO TOUCH THE SKY	100	350.00	350.00

ON THE WILD SIDE

J. MEGER — MEGER

YR	NAME	LIMIT	ISSUE	TREND
*	SILHOUETTE-TIMBER WOLF	*	95.00	275.00
79	WILDSIDE I-CANVASBACKS	*	100.00	800.00
80	MANITOBA MEMORIES-CANVASBACKS	*	100.00	140.00
80	SPLIT DECISION-CANVASBACKS	*	100.00	350.00
81	STACK OF BILLS-LESSER SCAUP	*	75.00	200.00

YR	NAME	LIMIT	ISSUE	TREND
81	WINGS IN THE WILLOWS	*	100.00	150.00
82	PRAIRIE POTHOLES-CANVASBACKS	*	60.00	150.00
82	STOP ON RED-REDHEADS	100	100.00	190.00
83	RISKY BUSINESS	75	75.00	175.00
84	BLUE BANDITS	60	60.00	120.00
84	GOOD MORNING	45	45.00	70.00
84	LEADING LADY	*	60.00	70.00
84	LEGACY-LOON	60	85.00	750.00
85	BURNING THROUGH	*	100.00	250.00
85	FIELDSTONES-PHEASANTS	125	125.00	400.00
85	LEGACY-EAGLE	85	85.00	400.00
85	LEGACY-MOOSE	85	85.00	115.00
85	WINDSONG-CANADA GEESE	225	225.00	425.00
86	FIRST LIGHT-LOONS	95	95.00	150.00
86	SUNDANCE-SNOWY OWL	125	125.00	950.00
86	UNINVITED GUESTS	60	75.00	80.00
87	COMING HOME	125	125.00	185.00
87	HEARTLAND-PHEASANTS	100	100.00	400.00
87	INTERLUDE	75	75.00	160.00
87	ONE MORE PASS	60	75.00	160.00
87	OUTBACK-PHEASANTS	*	75.00	225.00
87	UP AT THE LAKE	95	95.00	125.00
88	FAST MOVING GAME	60	60.00	150.00
88	HERITAGE CARDINAL	*	85.00	145.00
88	LEGACY-TIMBERWOLVES (AP)	125	85.00	500.00
88	SEPTEMBER PASSAGE	*	125.00	190.00
88	SNOWY COURTSHIP-SNOWY OWLS	125	125.00	280.00
89	EDGE OF TOWN	95	95.00	125.00
89	HOMESTEAD-PHEASANTS (AP)	125	125.00	270.00
89	MOONRIDE-LOONS	95	95.00	850.00
89	PRAIRIE DANCEHALL-PHEASANTS	95	75.00	135.00
89	THREE'S A CROWD	60	60.00	140.00
90	ALPHA-TIMBER WOLF	*	150.00	320.00
90	ALPHA-TIMBER WOLF (AP)	225	225.00	380.00
90	ALPHA-TIMBER WOLF (COLLECTOR'S EDITION)	225	275.00	550.00
90	BREEZING UP-WOOD DUCKS (AP)	*	145.00	195.00
90	FANFARE-TRUMPETER SWANS	150	150.00	250.00
90	FIRST OUTING	60	60.00	275.00
90	HIDDEN GAME-TIMBER WOLF (AP)	75	75.00	100.00
90	MOON SHADOWS-WHITE-TAILED DEER	95	95.00	300.00
90	STORM WARNING-PHEASANTS	95	95.00	410.00
91	PROMISE, THE	*	150.00	175.00
91	PROMISE, THE (COLLECTOR'S EDITION)	295	295.00	300.00
91	SNOWY PURSUIT	*	125.00	225.00

PAST IMPRESSIONS

A. MALEY				**CANVAS**
87	LOVE LETTER	CL	445.00	445.00
87	PROMISE, THE	500	625.00	625.00
89	WINTER IMPRESSIONS	CL	595.00	595.00
90	CAFE ROYALE	CL	665.00	665.00
90	FESTIVE OCCASION	CL	595.00	595.00
90	GRACIOUS ERA	CL	645.00	645.00
90	ROMANTIC ENGAGEMENT	CL	445.00	445.00
91	SUMMER CAROUSEL	CL	345.00	345.00
92	CIRCLE OF LOVE	CL	445.00	445.00
92	ELEGANT AFFAIR	CL	595.00	595.00
92	EVENING PERFORMANCE	CL	295.00	295.00
92	WALK IN THE PARK	CL	595.00	595.00
93	RAGS AND RICHES	CL	445.00	445.00
93	RECITAL, THE	CL	595.00	595.00
93	SLEIGH BELLS	CL	595.00	595.00
93	VISITING THE NURSERY	CL	445.00	445.00
94	NEW YEAR'S EVE	CL	445.00	445.00
94	PARISIAN BEAUTIES	CL	645.00	645.00
94	SUMMER ELEGANCE	CL	595.00	595.00
95	GRAND ENTRANCE	250	615.00	615.00
95	LETTER, THE	CL	465.00	465.00
95	NEW CARRIAGE	250	265.00	265.00
95	SLEIGH RACE	250	615.00	615.00
95	SOUTHERN BELLES	250	615.00	615.00
95	SUMMER ROMANCE	CL	465.00	465.00
96	BOATING PARTY, THE	350	665.00	665.00
96	PRIVATE CONVERSATION	350	615.00	615.00
A. MALEY				**PAPER PRINT**
84	GLORIOUS SUMMER	CL	150.00	800.00
84	SECLUDED GARDEN	CL	150.00	950.00
85	PASSING ELEGANCE	CL	150.00	700.00
85	SECRET THOUGHTS	CL	150.00	850.00
86	TELL ME	CL	150.00	800.00
86	WINTER ROMANCE	CL	150.00	750.00
87	DAY DREAMS	CL	200.00	400.00
87	LOVE LETTER	CL	200.00	500.00
87	LOVE LETTER A/P	450	300.00	600.00
87	PROMISE, THE	CL	200.00	450.00
88	BOARDWALK, THE	CL	250.00	400.00
88	JOYS OF CHILDHOOD	CL	250.00	350.00
88	OPENING NIGHT	CL	250.00	1950.00
88	TRANQUIL MOMENT	CL	250.00	375.00

YR	NAME	LIMIT	ISSUE	TREND
88	VICTORIAN TRIO	CL	250.00	400.00
89	ENGLISH ROSE	CL	250.00	425.00
89	IN HARMONY	CL	250.00	350.00
89	WINTER IMPRESSIONS	750	250.00	350.00
90	CAFE ROYALE	750	275.00	400.00
90	FESTIVE OCCASION	CL	250.00	250.00
90	GRACIOUS ERA	750	275.00	375.00
90	ROMANTIC ENGAGEMENT	750	275.00	300.00
90	SUMMER PASTIME	CL	250.00	400.00
91	BETWEEN FRIENDS	750	275.00	275.00
91	EVENING PERFORMANCE	750	150.00	200.00
91	SUMMER CAROUSEL	750	200.00	200.00
91	SUNDAY AFTERNOON	750	275.00	300.00
91	WINTER CAROUSEL	750	200.00	200.00
92	AN ELEGANT AFFAIR	500	260.00	300.00
92	CIRCLE OF LOVE	500	250.00	250.00
92	INTIMATE MOMENT	750	250.00	300.00
92	WALK IN THE PARK	500	260.00	260.00
92	WALK IN THE PARK	500	260.00	260.00
93	RAGS AND RICHES	500	250.00	250.00
93	RECITAL, THE	500	275.00	275.00
93	SLEIGH BELLS	500	260.00	260.00
93	VISTING THE NURSERY	500	250.00	250.00
94	NEW YEAR'S EVE	500	250.00	250.00
94	PARISIAN BEAUTIES	500	275.00	275.00
94	SUMMER ELEGANCE	500	275.00	275.00
95	GRAND ENTRANCE	500	250.00	250.00
95	LETTER, THE	500	250.00	250.00
95	NEW CARRIAGE	500	100.00	100.00
95	SLEIGH RACE	500	260.00	260.00
95	SOUTHERN BELLES	500	260.00	260.00
95	SUMMER ROMANCE	500	250.00	250.00
96	BOATING PARTY	400	275.00	275.00
96	PRIVATE CONVERSATION	400	260.00	260.00

A. MALEY — **WOMEN OF ELEGANCE/PAPER PRINT**

YR	NAME	LIMIT	ISSUE	TREND
89	ALEXANDRA	CL	125.00	200.00
89	BETH	CL	125.00	200.00
89	CATHERINE	CL	125.00	125.00
89	VICTORIA	CL	125.00	125.00

PEMBERTON & OAKES

D. ZOLAN

YR	NAME	LIMIT	ISSUE	TREND
82	ERIK AND DANDELION	880	98.00	400.00
83	BY MYSELF	880	98.00	300.00
84	SABINA IN THE GRASS	880	98.00	600.00
86	TENDER MOMENT	880	98.00	330.00
87	TOUCHING THE SKY	880	98.00	275.00
88	DAY DREAMER	1000	35.00	150.00
88	SMALL WONDER	880	98.00	300.00
88	TINY TREASURES	450	150.00	230.00
88	WAITING TO PLAY	1000	35.00	150.00
88	WINTER ANGEL	880	98.00	270.00
89	ALMOST HOME	880	98.00	300.00
89	BROTHERLY LOVE	880	98.00	360.00
89	DADDY'S HOME	880	98.00	300.00
89	GRANDMA'S MIRROR	RT	98.00	200.00
89	MOTHER'S ANGELS	880	98.00	300.00
89	RODEO GIRL	RT	98.00	180.00
89	SNOWY ADVENTURE	880	98.00	260.00
89	SUMMER'S CHILD	RT	98.00	230.00
90	CHRISTMAS PRAYER	880	98.00	245.00
90	COLORS OF SPRING	880	98.00	200.00
90	CRYSTAL'S CREEK	880	98.00	200.00
90	LAURIE AND THE CRECHE	RT	98.00	150.00
91	FLOWERS FOR MOTHER	RT	98.00	175.00

RECO INTERNATIONAL

J. MCCLELLAND — **FINE ART CANVAS REPRODUCTION**

YR	NAME	LIMIT	ISSUE	TREND
90	BEACH PLAY	350	80.00	80.00
91	FLOWER SWING	350	100.00	100.00
91	SUMMER CONVERSATION	350	80.00	80.00

S. KUCK — **LIMITED EDITION PRINT**

YR	NAME	LIMIT	ISSUE	TREND
84	JESSICA	500	60.00	400.00
85	HEATHER	500	75.00	145.00
86	ASHLEY	500	85.00	155.00

J. MCCLELLAND — **MCCLELLAND**

YR	NAME	LIMIT	ISSUE	TREND
*	I LOVE TAMMY	500	75.00	100.00
*	JUST FOR YOU	300	155.00	160.00
*	OLIVIA	300	175.00	175.00
*	REVERIE	300	110.00	100.00
*	SWEET DREAMS	300	145.00	150.00

RIE MUNOZ LTD.

R. MUNOZ

YR	NAME	LIMIT	ISSUE	TREND
71	DANCE IN KASHIM	100	8.00	450.00
73	ESKIMO STORY TELLER	300	30.00	825.00
74	KING ISLAND	300	30.00	1600.00
74	SCARY SEA	500	30.00	1500.00

YR	NAME	LIMIT	ISSUE	TREND
75	CREATION OF MAN	500	30.00	2000.00
75	CROW IN A MOUNTAIN ASH	950	30.00	845.00
77	CANNERY WORKERS, NAKNEK	500	30.00	820.00
77	CRABBING	100	30.00	350.00
77	CRANE LEGEND	500	40.00	1900.00
77	GATHERING EGGS	500	30.00	1250.00
77	GOSSIPING WOMEN	500	27.00	200.00
77	KOTZEBU BREAKUP	500	36.00	990.00
77	WINTER SUN, GAMBELL	500	30.00	550.00
78	BERRY PICKERS	500	36.00	415.00
78	RAFT OF DUCKS	950	30.00	715.00
78	RIBBON SEALS	950	20.00	480.00
79	BUTCHERING CRABS, TENAKEE	500	36.00	775.00
79	FISHING FOR KING CRAB, UKIVOK	500	36.00	875.00
79	LADIES IN THE BATH	500	36.00	500.00
80	BLUEBERRIES, BLUEBIRDS	500	30.00	295.00
80	CATS CRADLE	500	27.00	760.00
80	DOUGLAS CRAB BOAT	500	60.00	895.00
80	HAPPY HOUR, NOME	500	40.00	795.00
80	KETCHIKAN ALASKA	500	12.00	365.00
80	LAST CARIBOU	500	35.00	860.00
80	LOOSE DOGS	500	32.00	490.00
80	MIDDLETON	500	36.00	645.00
80	OFF TO SUMMER CAMP	500	40.00	590.00
80	RECESS AUKE BAY SCHOOL	500	42.00	870.00
80	STRING GAME	250	75.00	895.00
80	TUNDRA	500	32.00	440.00
81	BERRY PICKERS	550	40.00	450.00
81	BOOM BOAT	750	45.00	980.00
81	CRAB BUTCHERING PARTY	500	40.00	645.00
81	DANCER IN MOTION	500	36.00	365.00
81	FISHERMAN, KETCHIKAN	500	40.00	645.00
81	FRIENDS, GAMBELL	500	30.00	390.00
81	GATHERING GRASS	500	30.00	265.00
81	GOING BERRY PICKING, HOONAH	500	40.00	750.00
81	HOPKINS ALLEY	750	45.00	595.00
81	INTERVIEWING THE WINNER	500	40.00	650.00
81	MONKEY TREE	500	40.00	665.00
81	REINDEER ROUNDUP	200	200.00	1000.00
81	SEALIONS AT UNALASKA	750	50.00	685.00
81	STARRING	500	36.00	595.00
82	DRYING LAUNDRY & FISH	750	40.00	415.00
82	EVERGREEN BOWL	750	45.00	850.00
82	HAULING IN CRABS	750	40.00	540.00
82	ICE FISHING	750	32.00	720.00
82	IDITAROD RACE HEADQUARTERS	750	40.00	610.00
82	NOAH	750	36.00	685.00
82	RIE MUNOZ IN TAPESTRY	OP	20.00	40.00
82	SIGNS OF SPRING	750	30.00	465.00
82	SOME ALASKA BIRDS	175	45.00	565.00
82	SUMMER CAMP	750	45.00	490.00
82	SUMMER STORM, BUCKLAND	750	45.00	425.00
82	TESTING A SEAL SKIN FLOAT	750	28.00	325.00
83	CHASING MOULTING GEESE	750	32.00	645.00
83	ELFIN COVE	750	32.00	495.00
83	FISH BUYER, ELFIN COVE	750	40.00	440.00
83	IN THE PARK, FRANCE	500	15.00	550.00
83	PACKING FISH	500	28.00	220.00
83	POKER GAME	750	20.00	590.00
83	PRIEST, UNALASKA	750	36.00	595.00
83	ROOSTING BIRDS	200	85.00	530.00
83	SEAGULL STORY	750	32.00	355.00
83	SNOW BUNTINGS, GAMBELL	750	45.00	730.00
83	WHISTLING AT NORTHERN LIGHTS	500	36.00	670.00
83	WRANGELL WATER FRONT	750	40.00	465.00
84	BERRY PICKER	750	28.00	480.00
84	CHAPEL, ROCHE HARBOR	750	35.00	525.00
84	COMING HOME	750	45.00	695.00
84	CRABBER, UNALASKA	750	60.00	1175.00
84	DANCERS IN SEALGUT PARKAS	OP	20.00	20.00
84	FISH CAMP	750	48.00	395.00
84	GROCERIES NOME	750	38.00	475.00
84	IDITAROD, SHATOOLOK	750	64.00	600.00
84	ISTKA SUMMER FESTIVAL	OP	20.00	40.00
84	PACKING FISH	750	40.00	400.00
84	PAINT JOB THOMAS BASIN	750	36.00	335.00
84	POTLATCH BAR, KETCHIKAN	750	30.00	395.00
84	SANDHILL CRANES	750	50.00	695.00
84	ST. NICHOLAS, JUNEAU	750	38.00	695.00
84	STEAMBATH LAKE, ILIAMNA	750	30.00	900.00
84	STORY KNIFE	750	20.00	445.00
84	SWING, THE	750	20.00	430.00
84	TANGLED TRACES	750	20.00	385.00
84	WAITING FOR FERRY, TENAKEE	750	40.00	525.00
85	CLEANING FISH	750	40.00	245.00
85	CRAB POTS, SITKA	750	36.00	455.00
85	HALIBUT $1	750	60.00	1100.00
85	JUNEAU CANNERY	750	45.00	525.00
85	NORTH STAR COMING	750	50.00	400.00

YR	NAME	LIMIT	ISSUE	TREND
85	SPRING SUNDAY	750	38.00	395.00
85	WOMAN BEAR LEGEND	750	60.00	1000.00
86	BLUEBERRIES	750	45.00	435.00
86	CACHE	750	36.00	230.00
86	CATHEDRAL, SITKA	750	48.00	500.00
86	CLEANING SALMON	750	48.00	235.00
86	DINNER, NOME	750	40.00	355.00
86	FALL MIGRATION	750	65.00	565.00
86	GREY POUPON	750	20.00	465.00
86	INNER HARBOR	750	45.00	390.00
86	JESSIE'S FLOWERS	750	45.00	450.00
86	LATE BOAT	750	48.00	425.00
86	LOOKING FOR HALLEY'S COMET	750	30.00	600.00
86	PACKING DUNGENESS	750	25.00	375.00
86	RASPBERRY PATCH	750	20.00	255.00
86	STORM AT FISH CAMP	750	50.00	190.00
86	UNLOADING WALRUS MEAT	750	50.00	295.00
86	WHALE	750	50.00	375.00
87	ABANDONED CABIN	950	35.00	120.00
87	CASH BUYER, KOTZEBUE	750	40.00	165.00
87	DOWNHILL SKIERS, EAGLECREST	750	60.00	795.00
87	FIRST SNOW, STARR HILL	750	30.00	600.00
87	FIRST SNOW, TENAKEE	750	48.00	240.00
87	FISHERMAN'S FAMILY, EAGEGIK	750	35.00	165.00
87	GREENHOUSE	750	45.00	400.00
87	HAULING WATER, TENAKEE	750	28.00	28.00
87	MUG UP, METLAKATLA	750	45.00	105.00
87	PUNTING OVER TO THE MIDNIGHT SUN	750	42.00	220.00
87	RUSSIAN CHURCH, UNALASKA	750	30.00	180.00
87	SPRING FLOWERS	750	25.00	145.00
87	TEKAKEE CABIN	750	55.00	295.00
87	UNLOADING FREIGHT, GAMBRELL	750	65.00	950.00
88	CANNERY COOK, CRAIG	750	30.00	180.00
88	COMING INTO TENAKEE INLET	750	55.00	295.00
88	FEEDING THE SWANS CORNWALL	750	55.00	475.00
88	FOLLOWING THE LEADER	750	45.00	370.00
88	GOING FISHING	750	32.00	380.00
88	LONDON PUB	750	25.00	225.00
88	NOATAK	750	48.00	320.00
88	RUNAWAY MITTENS	750	50.00	485.00
88	SELF PORTRAIT, 4TH ST. STAIRS	750	50.00	340.00
88	WINTER VILLAGE, NOATAK	750	55.00	315.00
89	BLUE MOON CAFE	750	55.00	300.00
89	EDDIE BAUER'S IDITAROD RACER	950	60.00	525.00
89	FALL COLORS	750	55.00	370.00
89	HOLY ASSUMPTION CHURCH	750	60.00	295.00
89	MUSHER	750	40.00	185.00
89	NIGHT SLEDDING, JUNEAU	750	60.00	395.00
89	PTARMIGAN LIFT	750	60.00	700.00
89	SEABIRDS OF ALEUTIANS	750	65.00	215.00
89	WINTER, JUNEAU	750	65.00	440.00
90	ARK IN ALASKA	750	70.00	810.00
90	CREEK STREET, KETCHIKAN	750	72.00	700.00
90	EMBRACE, THE	750	35.00	750.00
90	LAUNDRY, EGEGIK	750	45.00	45.00
90	LOADING CRAB POTS	750	65.00	285.00
90	OFF TO THE BATH, TENAKEE	750	48.00	185.00
90	RUSSIAN CHURCH, JUNEAU	750	68.00	400.00
91	ANDY	950	45.00	190.00
91	MARRY ME, MY DEAR	950	40.00	85.00
91	NUMBER #27	950	45.00	95.00
91	SHADE TREE	950	65.00	65.00
91	SHARPENING AN ULU	950	68.00	68.00
91	SLIDING AT UNALAKLEET	950	90.00	250.00
91	SPRING MIGRATION	950	60.00	375.00
91	STAR PRINCESS	950	75.00	275.00
91	SWING, TENAKEE	750	55.00	215.00
91	TULIPS $2	950	50.00	125.00
91	WHALE LEGEND	950	60.00	60.00
91	WHALE WATCH	750	60.00	100.00
91	WINTER CABIN, TENAKEE	950	55.00	215.00
91	WINTER GAMES	950	65.00	195.00
92	MOLLY-O	950	100.00	225.00
92	NORTHERN LIGHTS, JUNEAU	950	125.00	825.00
R. MUNOZ				**SERIGRAPH**
74	CATS CRADLE	105	27.00	760.00
75	BELUGA WHALE & CALF	950	25.00	845.00
75	HONKERS	100	21.00	300.00
75	REINDEER HERD	*	27.00	325.00
75	SPLITTING WALRUS HIDE	100	27.00	215.00
76	CRESTED AUKLET	95	21.00	450.00
76	ICE FISHING	120	30.00	395.00
77	CANNERY WORKER	105	36.00	425.00
77	COMMERCIAL CRABBER	95	30.00	400.00
78	SEINER	350	25.00	1400.00
79	CARIBOU HUNTER	190	36.00	850.00
79	DANCER	250	50.00	795.00
79	NORTHERN LIGHTS, JUNEAU	250	75.00	775.00
79	RAVEN HAD TWO WIVES	90	50.00	1325.00

YR	NAME	LIMIT	ISSUE	TREND
80	ADRIFT	250	60.00	1130.00
80	DRUMMER & DANCER	350	36.00	475.00
80	FISH GRADER	250	50.00	1500.00
80	SUMMER VOYAGE	250	75.00	900.00
81	INVITATION	250	65.00	856.00
81	RAVEN LEGEND	77	60.00	1295.00
82	SPRING ICE FISHING	200	85.00	1300.00
83	ESKIMO GAME	200	124.00	1200.000
84	ARK IN ALASKA	200	125.00	1635.00
84	MERMAID	220	45.00	410.00
85	WOMAN BEAR LEGEND	183	60.00	1100.00
86	THROAT CHANTERS	750	110.00	1325.00
R. MUNOZ				**STONE LITHO**
74	BUTCHERING AT GAMBELL	125	85.00	690.00
75	SEATED DANCER	125	50.00	175.00
81	WHALE DANCE	100	225.00	450.00
82	ESKIMO MOTHER	100	185.00	1700.00

ROMAN INC.

YR	NAME	LIMIT	ISSUE	TREND
A. WILLIAMS				**ABBIE WILLIAMS**
88	MARY, MOTHER OF THE CARPENTER	TL	100.00	100.00
F. HOOK				**HOOK**
81	CARPENTER, THE	YR	100.00	1000.00
81	CARPENTER, THE (REMARQUE)	YR	100.00	3000.00
82	BOUQUET	1200	70.00	375.00
82	FROLICKING	1200	60.00	375.00
82	GATHERING	1200	60.00	350.00
82	LITTLE CHILDREN, COME TO ME	1950	50.00	525.00
82	LITTLE CHILDREN, COME TO ME (REMARQUE)	50	100.00	525.00
82	POSING	1200	70.00	375.00
82	POULETS	1200	60.00	375.00
82	SURPRISE	1200	50.00	375.00
F. HOOK				**PORTRAITS OF LOVE**
88	EXPECTATION	2500	25.00	25.00
88	IN MOTHER'S ARMS	2500	25.00	25.00
88	MY KITTY	2500	25.00	25.00
88	REMEMBER WHEN...	2500	25.00	25.00
88	SHARING	2500	25.00	25.00
88	SUNKISSED AFTERNOON	2500	25.00	25.00

ROYALHAUS PUBLISHING

YR	NAME	LIMIT	ISSUE	TREND
D. ROTTINGHAUS				
95	IDES OF AUTUMN, THE	950	125.00	125.00
95	SAINT NICHOLAS CHRISTMAS BREAK	550	65.00	65.00
95	SUMMER DAYS	999	125.00	125.00
96	SANCTUARY	950	125.00	125.00

SAN MARTIN FINE ART

YR	NAME	LIMIT	ISSUE	TREND
ANNE-LAN				
88	LA NAISSANCE DU PRINTEMPS	175	250.00	1350.00
88	MATERNITE	225	250.00	1150.00
88	PERSEPHONE	385	600.00	800.00
88	SETTING SUN	495	950.00	1250.00
89	EYES OF THE NIGHT	385	350.00	750.00
89	FEMME FLEUR	385	250.00	500.00
89	REVE DE CHAT	262	250.00	800.00
90	HEURE BLEUE	262	500.00	500.00
90	L'AURORE	262	500.00	500.00
90	LA GRANDE CASCADE	230	200.00	240.00
90	PLUME	385	500.00	550.00
90	PUPUCE	230	200.00	240.00
91	EGLANTINE	450	60.00	60.00
91	INVITATION AU VOYAGE	262	500.00	500.00
91	LE CHATEAU FLEURI	300	450.00	450.00
91	LOVE STORY	450	60.00	60.00

SANDY CLOUGH STUDIO

YR	NAME	LIMIT	ISSUE	TREND
S. CLOUGH				
95	GOD BLESS OUR HOME	1500	70.00	80.00
95	IN THE GARDEN	2500	75.00	75.00
95	TEA PARTY II	3500	55.00	55.00
96	SERENITY	3500	50.00	50.00
96	SUNDAY STROLL	3500	40.00	40.00

SCHMID

Price ranges may reflect various demands in the market from one geographic region to another; condition of piece; specific markings found on piece; and/or changes in production of piece.

YR	NAME	LIMIT	ISSUE	TREND
J. FERRANDIZ				**FERRANDIZ LITHOGRAPHS**
80	MOST PRECIOUS GIFT	425	125.00	1300.00
80	MOST PRECIOUS GIFT (REMARQUE)	50	225.00	2900.00
80	MY STAR	675	100.00	700.00
80	MY STAR (REMARQUE)	75	175.00	1900.00
81	HEART OF SEVEN COLORS	600	100.00	400.00
81	HEART OF SEVEN COLORS (REMARQUE)	75	175.00	1400.00
82	HE SEEMS TO SLEEP	450	150.00	800.00
82	HE SEEMS TO SLEEP (REMARQUE)	25	300.00	3250.00
82	MIRROR OF THE SOUL	225	150.00	500.00
82	MIRROR OF THE SOUL (REMARQUE)	35	250.00	2450.00

The Carpenter *by Frances Hook was released by Roman Inc. in 1981. Limited to one year of production, the original issue price was $100. Current secondary market value is $1,000.*

Jim Daly's Contentment *from Mill Pond Press shows relaxation as only a cat can express it. The 1990 limited edition of 1,500 was originally priced at $95 and is currently valued at $550.*

YR	NAME	LIMIT	ISSUE	TREND
82	OH SMALL CHILD	450	125.00	500.00
82	OH SMALL CHILD (REMARQUE)	50	225.00	1500.00
82	ON THE THRESHOLD OF LIFE	425	150.00	500.00
82	ON THE THRESHOLD OF LIFE (REMARQUE)	50	275.00	1400.00
82	RIDING THROUGH THE RAIN	900	165.00	400.00
82	RIDING THROUGH THE RAIN (REMARQUE)	100	300.00	1000.00
82	SPREADING THE WORD	675	125.00	300.00
82	SPREADING THE WORD (REMARQUE)	75	225.00	1100.00
83	FRIENDSHIP	460	165.00	500.00
83	FRIENDSHIP (REMARQUE)	15	1200.00	2350.00
84	STAR IN THE TEAPOT	410	165.00	175.00
84	STAR IN THE TEAPOT (REMARQUE)	15	1200.00	2100.00
L. DAVIS		**LOWELL DAVIS LITHOGRAPHS**		
81	DUKE'S MIXTURE	899	75.00	130.00
81	DUKE'S MIXTURE (REMARQUE)	101	150.00	375.00
81	PLUM TUCKERED OUT	899	75.00	390.00
81	PLUM TUCKERED OUT (REMARQUE)	101	100.00	350.00
81	SURPRISE IN THE CELLAR	899	75.00	553.00
81	SURPRISE IN THE CELLAR (REMARQUE)	101	100.00	400.00
82	BIRTH OF A BLOSSOM	400	125.00	325.00-520.00
82	BIRTH OF A BLOSSOM (REMARQUE)	50	200.00	450.00
82	BUSTIN' WITH PRIDE	899	75.00	125.00
82	BUSTIN' WITH PRIDE (REMARQUE)	101	150.00	250.00
82	FOXFIRE FARM	800	125.00	125.00
82	FOXFIRE FARM (REMARQUE)	100	200.00	250.00
82	SUPPERTIME	400	125.00	300.00
82	SUPPERTIME (REMARQUE)	50	200.00	450.00
85	SELF PORTRAIT	450	75.00	130.00-195.00
87	BLOSSOM'S GIFT	450	75.00	195.00
89	SUN WORSHIPPERS	750	100.00	100.00
90	SUNDAY AFTERNOON TREAT	750	100.00	100.00
91	WARM MILK	750	100.00	100.00
91	WARM MILK	750	100.00	100.00
92	CAT AND JENNY WREN	750	100.00	100.00
M.I. HUMMEL		**M.I. HUMMEL LITHOGRAPHS**		
80	MOONLIGHT RETURN	900	150.00	850.00
81	A TIME TO REMEMBER	720	150.00	300.00
82	POPPIES	450	150.00	650.00
83	ANGELIC MESSENGER (75TH ANNIV. ED.)	195	375.00	700.00
83	ANGELIC MESSENGER, CHRISTMAS MESSENGER	400	275.00	450.00
85	BIRTHDAY BOUQUET I	195	450.00	550.00
85	BIRTHDAY BOUQUET II	225	375.00	375.00
85	BIRTHDAY BOUQUET III	100	195.00	395.00

SERENDIPITY TRADING CO.

YR	NAME	LIMIT	ISSUE	TREND
B. RABBIT				
87	ELDERS, THE	950	45.00	200.00
87	FROM EARTH MAN CAME	950	65.00	200.00
88	FAITHFUL, THE	350	90.00	275.00
88	YESTERDAY, TODAY AND TOMORROW	1500	35.00	500.00
89	AFTER THE RAINS	650	65.00	200.00
89	PROMISES, DREAMS AND HOPE	650	65.00	175.00
90	ANCESTORS	350	125.00	375.00
90	COMING OF WINTER	200	250.00	750.00
90	FEAST DAY	350	125.00	375.00
90	PRICE OF PEPPERS, THE	650	75.00	75.00
90	PROPOSAL, THE	350	125.00	375.00
90	STRENGTH TOGETHER	350	125.00	375.00
90	WARMTH OF YOUR TOUCH	350	125.00	375.00

SIMON ART

YR	NAME	LIMIT	ISSUE	TREND
C. BLACK				
84	BLUE LADY	290	85.00	100.00
85	SUMMER DAY/CHARLES STREET	350	60.00	75.00
86	CHRISTMAS MORNING	225	125.00	1200.00
86	HALTON HOMESTEAD	125	100.00	850.00
86	MAITLAND HALL	125	85.00	500.00
86	NANA'S BACK DOOR	125	85.00	650.00
86	SILENT VISITOR	125	50.00	130.00
86	SNOW & THUNDER	125	125.00	275.00
86	WELCOME HOME	125	100.00	150.00
87	CENTURY FARM	395	125.00	450.00
87	FIRST CHRISTMAS	395	125.00	175.00
87	HOME FOR CHRISTMAS	395	125.00	650.00
87	JOURNEY'S END	395	125.00	700.00
87	OLD APPLE TREE, THE	395	125.00	175.00
87	SNOWED IN	395	125.00	500.00
88	CAROLE'S GARDEN	395	170.00	200.00
88	DADDY'S GIRL	395	170.00	350.00
88	MORNING ON MAIN STREET	395	200.00	500.00
89	AUNT MARTHA'S	390	170.00	175.00
89	HIGH HOUSE	390	170.00	175.00
89	SILENT NIGHT	390	170.00	170.00
90	A NIGHT'S LODGING	390	210.00	210.00
90	HOME FOR THE HOLIDAYS	450	170.00	170.00
90	MARY'S KITCHEN	490	170.00	170.00
91	SATURDAY MORNING	*	130.00	130.00
91	SPRING PLANTING	*	130.00	130.00

YR	NAME	LIMIT	ISSUE	TREND
A. KINGSLAND				
86	BROKEN FENCE	390	50.00	50.00
86	LONER, THE	560	30.00	40.00
86	MAIL BOX, THE	450	120.00	200.00
86	OLD GOLD	560	30.00	60.00
86	OLD RED	390	50.00	50.00
86	ROUNDHOUSE, THE	200	120.00	150.00
86	SEA SCAVENGERS	450	120.00	120.00
86	SILENT MIST	390	80.00	80.00
86	SNOW TRACKS	450	120.00	120.00
86	WAITING OUT WINTER	560	30.00	30.00
86	WINTER BIRCH	560	30.00	60.00
87	CALM WATERS	450	150.00	150.00
87	COUNTRY FOLK	450	150.00	150.00
87	FISHING BOATS	450	150.00	150.00
87	GIANT, THE	200	180.00	225.00
87	HOMESTEAD & RURAL ROUTE, THE (SET OF 2)	450	250.00	250.00
87	OCTOBER	450	150.00	150.00
87	WINTER DRESS	450	150.00	150.00
88	BOYS OF SUMMER	450	90.00	90.00
88	COUNTRY AUTUMN	450	150.00	150.00
88	HOME TEAM, THE	450	90.00	90.00
88	JUST A GAME	450	90.00	90.00
88	LASER FUN	450	150.00	150.00
88	SHINNY	450	150.00	400.00
88	SNOWBALLS	450	150.00	150.00
88	TADPOLES	450	150.00	150.00
89	CROSSING THE 16TH	200	180.00	180.00
89	MILL POND, THE	490	110.00	110.00
89	PLAYOFF, THE	450	180.00	270.00
89	SKATERS, THE	490	180.00	180.00
89	SNOWMAN, THE	450	180.00	180.00
89	TEMPESTUOUS SKY	450	180.00	180.00
90	A WINTER VISIT	490	200.00	200.00
90	COLLECTIBLES	490	110.00	110.00
90	MY HOME TOWN	490	180.00	180.00
90	SHADY LADY	490	190.00	190.00
90	SKI TRAIN	390	200.00	200.00
90	WHERE DREAMS BEGIN	490	190.00	250.00
91	CLEAR THE TRACK	*	180.00	180.00
91	DEDICATED	790	216.00	216.00
91	WINTER VIGIL	790	140.00	140.00
L. LESPERANCE				
83	WATERS EDGE	350	115.00	230.00
85	COOL INTERLUDE	390	115.00	250.00
85	WATCHFUL GUARDIAN	390	115.00	170.00
86	AMBUSH!	690	140.00	900.00
86	MAY BRINGS FLOWERS	690	90.00	110.00
86	SILENT REFLECTIONS	350	115.00	800.00
87	MYSTICAL SHADOWS	790	190.00	300.00
87	SUMMER'S END-COYOTES	*	150.00	150.00
87	WINGING WESTWARD	790	160.00	800.00
88	MARCH FLURRIES	790	190.00	325.00
88	MORNING PATROL	790	190.00	300.00
89	GREAT ESCAPE, THE	590	225.00	425.00
89	THOSE EYES	590	150.00	150.00
90	DELICATE BALANCE	790	200.00	200.00
90	OLD TIRE SWING, THE	790	200.00	200.00
90	PHANTOM OF THE MARSH	950	225.00	225.00
90	SILENT WINGS	790	225.00	225.00
90	SPOOKING THE HERD	590	225.00	225.00
91	PLAYTIME	790	225.00	225.00
91	SIBLINGS	*	200.00	200.00
J. LUMBERS				
85	MR. EMMET'S FISHIN' HOLE	200	200.00	5250.00
85	SATURDAY MORNING	200	250.00	4000.00
86	ADRIFT	390	200.00	2550.00
86	BEYOND THE SHORE	390	200.00	1250.00
86	CHANGING SEASONS	390	200.00	380.00
86	COUNTRY KITCHEN	390	200.00	975.00
86	DEJA VU	390	200.00	580.00
86	DUNROWAN	450	160.00	2025.00
86	GONE FISHIN'	390	200.00	4500.00
86	JOY RIDE	390	200.00	400.00
86	KITE, THE	390	200.00	980.00
86	SECRET OF THE WELL	450	160.00	770.00
87	BIG CATCH, THE	390	250.00	1200.00
87	CATS	390	250.00	2775.00
87	INHERITANCE, THE	390	250.00	1210.00
87	MEMORIES FOR SALE	390	250.00	400.00
87	SUNSET MEMORIES	390	250.00	490.00
88	BILLY NINE FINGERS	590	250.00	375.00
88	CHERRY HILL ROAD COLLECTION (SET OF 4)	490	500.00	1210.00
88	DOUBLE TROUBLE	490	250.00	1000.00
88	FIRESIDE SHADOWS	590	250.00	1000.00
88	JUST FOR YOU	590	250.00	400.00
88	LUCKY STRIKE	790	250.00	650.00
88	MISCHIEF	590	250.00	625.00

YR	NAME	LIMIT	ISSUE	TREND
88	OUT ON A LIMB	490	250.00	1000.00
89	A WINTER'S GLOW	790	250.00	475.00
89	ABANDONED HERITAGE	790	280.00	1000.00
89	LONE PINE	950	280.00	1200.00
89	MORNING REFLECTIONS	950	280.00	355.00
89	SHADES OF SUMMER	790	280.00	600.00
89	SIDE BY SIDE	2183	350.00	1000.00
89	STIRRING MEMORIES	790	280.00	750.00
89	SUMMERS PAST	790	280.00	360.00
90	AN ENCHANTED EVENING	1500	280.00	375.00
90	CAT NAPPING	1500	280.00	450.00
90	DAYS GONE BY	950	280.00	500.00
90	DIFFERENT TIMES	1500	280.00	350.00
90	PLAYING THROUGH	950	280.00	500.00
90	SHOPPING	1500	280.00	300.00
91	A BOY AND HIS DREAM	*	275.00	500.00
91	A BOY AND HIS DREAM (CS)	*	1250.00	2750.00
91	MR. HOCKEY	*	275.00	275.00
91	MR. HOCKEY (CS)	*	1250.00	600.00
91	SUN NEVER SETS, THE	*	280.00	290.00
J. REID				
*	AT BAT	650	200.00	300.00
*	O.K., BLUE JAYS!	390	150.00	200.00
*	QUEEN & SPADINA	390	150.00	950.00
*	WHERE THE WORLD COMES TO PLAY	521	300.00	350.00
85	CAT TAILS	450	125.00	125.00
85	FLOWER HOUSE	450	125.00	600.00
85	NEAR ELORA	450	125.00	200.00
85	SNOW PODS	450	125.00	125.00
86	GEORGIAN BAY SKY	450	125.00	125.00
86	NORTHERN STREAM	450	125.00	125.00
87	RAIL FENCE	450	150.00	150.00
87	SNOW BANKS	450	180.00	180.00
87	SUGAR SHACK	450	150.00	150.00
88	BEDFORD MILLS	450	170.00	170.00
88	MORNING MAIL	450	125.00	125.00
88	MURPHY'S PLACE	450	125.00	125.00
88	SILENT STREAM AND STANDING BY (SET OF 2)	450	210.00	210.00
89	CHRISTMAS HOUSE	450	170.00	170.00
89	HURON COUNTRY	450	170.00	170.00
90	DAYBREAK	450	170.00	170.00
90	SHORELINE TRILOGY (SET OF 3)	450	125.00	125.00
J. TRINIDAD				
88	A COUNTRY SCENE	590	210.00	210.00
88	A SUMMER PLACE	590	210.00	210.00
88	BACKYARD SETTING	590	210.00	210.00
88	FLOWER GIRL	590	210.00	210.00
88	LITTLE GARDENERS	450	210.00	650.00
89	CATHERINE	450	170.00	170.00
89	COUNTRY WALK	450	125.00	400.00
89	MARKET, THE	450	170.00	170.00
89	PLAYTIME	450	125.00	125.00
89	SUMMER RESORT	450	170.00	170.00
89	TEA TIME	450	210.00	210.00
90	FLOWER LOVER	590	145.00	145.00
90	GUARDIAN OF THE ROSES	590	210.00	210.00
90	SHARING	450	170.00	170.00
90	WINTER WARMTH	450	170.00	170.00

SMITH & SCHOEN

YR	NAME	LIMIT	ISSUE	TREND
R. TEJADA				**M.I. HUMMEL**
89	CHILD WITH BLUE BELLS	5000	125.00	125.00
89	SIEGLINDE'S FIRST TREE	5000	125.00	125.00

SOMERSET HOUSE PUBLISHING

YR	NAME	LIMIT	ISSUE	TREND
G. HARVEY				
74	POKER PALS	500	50.00	150.00
76	BOSS' NEW RIG	1500	60.00	160.00
76	CAREFREE COWHANDS	500	50.00	150.00
78	CROSSING THE CANYON	2000	50.00	600.00
78	DRIFTING COWHANDS	2000	60.00	500.00
78	LEAVIN' THE LINE SHACK	2000	50.00	350.00
79	CHANGING OF THE RANGELAND	250	150.00	2650.00
79	WHEN BANKERS WORE BOOTS	1000	75.00	1000.00
80	COMING HOME, THE	1000	75.00	140.00
80	EARLY RUN	1000	75.00	350.00
80	GOOD LORD WILLIN/CREEK DON'T RISE	1000	90.00	190.00
80	IN THE LAND OF THE ROCKIES	1000	90.00	200.00
80	IN THE LAND OF THE WALKIN' RAIN	1000	75.00	190.00
80	RANCHING-PUMP JACK STYLE	1000	90.00	900.00
80	RIDING THE SALT RIVER CANYON	1000	75.00	300.00
80	RIDING WITH GRANDPA	1000	90.00	190.00
80	SATURDAY NIGHT POKER PALACE	1000	75.00	175.00
80	SILENT HUNTER, THE	1000	75.00	180.00
80	SPRING PALETTE	1000	90.00	200.00
80	TEXAS FROM HIDE AND HORN	1000	90.00	275.00
80	TIMES REMEMBERED	2250	100.00	150.00
81	BOOMTOWN DRIFTERS	2250	150.00	500.00
81	OIL PATCH	1000	150.00	820.00

YR	NAME	LIMIT	ISSUE	TREND
81	ON THE STREETS OF NEW ORLEANS	1000	150.00	400.00
81	WALL STREET	SO	150.00	1100.00
81	WITH NO INTENTION OF CHARGING	1000	150.00	700.00
82	BOOT TOP DEEP	1000	150.00	1500.00
82	COWBOYS' CHRISTMAS BALL	1000	150.00	200.00
82	COWTOWN 1880	1000	150.00	1750.00
82	DALLAS 1908	1200	150.00	1150.00
82	INDEPENDENT OILMEN	1000	150.00	650.00
82	LEAVING THE OIL PATCH	1000	150.00	480.00
82	PLAZA, NEW YORK, THE	1000	150.00	450.00
82	SUPPLIES FOR THE MISSION	1000	150.00	200.00
83	COUNTRY POST OFFICE	1000	150.00	320.00
83	FAMILY CHRISTMAS	1250	150.00	450.00
83	FRESH SNOW FIRST LIGHT	1250	150.00	230.00
83	STREETCARS ALONG THE AVENUE	2500	90.00	700.00
84	AMERICAN WEST	1250	150.00	300.00
84	EARLY DOWNTOWN HOUSTON	1250	150.00	310.00
84	GRAND OPENING	1250	150.00	170.00
84	ME, GRANDPA, AND LITTLE SIS	1250	150.00	180.00
84	TOO WET TO PLOW	1000	*	700.00
84	TRADING AT THE GENERAL STORE	1250	150.00	160.00
85	A NEW LEASE	1250	150.00	390.00
85	CHESTNUT VENDOR	1250	150.00	165.00
85	DALLAS REMEMBERED	1250	150.00	400.00
85	ONLY WORKING HORSEBACK	1250	150.00	375.00
85	SANTA FE PLAZA	1250	150.00	280.00
86	INDEPENDENT TEXANS	1250	150.00	470.00
86	REFLECTIONS OF YESTERDAY (W/BOOK)	1250	275.00	1500.00
86	ROYAL STREET	1250	160.00	225.00
86	TEXAS RANCHER	1250	150.00	175.00
86	TIES OF HOME, THE	1250	150.00	180.00
87	EVENING ALONG THE AVENUE	1250	150.00	300.00
87	FIFTH AVENUE	1250	150.00	300.00
88	FLOWER CART, THE	1250	150.00	450.00
88	MEN OF THE AMERICAN WEST	1250	150.00	60.00
88	PENNSYLVANIA AVENUE	2575	150.00	1350.00
88	SATURDAY NIGHT CONTRACT	1250	150.00	650.00
89	COWBOY'S PAYDAY	1250	105.00	500.00
89	EARLY RIDERS	*	150.00	230.00
89	JEB STUART'S RETURN	1800	165.00	700.00
89	WALL STREET-NEW YORK	4378	165.00	400.00
90	AN EVENING WITH THE PRESIDENT	*	165.00	900.00
90	CITY BY THE BAY	*	165.00	800.00
90	HORSE TROLLEY ON PARK ROW	*	165.00	175.00
90	PICKET'S REPORT	1800	165.00	450.00
90	REMEMBERING THE GOOD TIMES	*	165.00	190.00
90	THINKING OF SPRING	*	165.00	240.00
90	THOUGHTS OF HOME	*	165.00	185.00
91	CATHEDRAL OF ST. BASIL, THE-RED SQUARE	*	165.00	330.00
91	GENTEEL NATION	*	165.00	200.00
91	WIND RIVER RANGE	*	165.00	185.00
	V. HOLLAN SWAIN			
86	BRIDGES AND BLOSSOMS	950	80.00	400.00
86	WHISPERING LIGHT	950	80.00	180.00
87	CASCADE OF COLOR	950	80.00	180.00
87	COURTYARD, THE	950	80.00	250.00
87	ENCHANTED POND, THE	950	80.00	155.00
87	QUIET VILLAGE, THE	950	80.00	800.00
88	MORNING LIGHT-DEVON	950	80.00	175.00
88	RIVERWALK	950	80.00	160.00
	P. VAUGHAN			
84	REFLECTIONS OF THE PAST	1000	40.00	225.00
84	TIMELESS ELEGANCE	1000	40.00	150.00
85	AUNT VERDI'S PORCH	1000	45.00	250.00
85	FRIENDSHIP QUILTS	1000	50.00	200.00
85	PRESERVED IN TIME	1000	50.00	75.00
85	SISTERS THREE	1000	50.00	150.00
85	SUMMERS REMEMBERED (PAIR)	5000	50.00	150.00
85	UPSTAIRS SEWING ROOM, THE	1000	45.00	185.00
85	YESTERDAY'S DREAMS	1000	45.00	160.00
86	A BOUQUET FOR ELIZABETH	1000	50.00	300.00
86	A CAMEO OF THE PAST	1000	50.00	90.00
86	FABRIC OF DREAMS, THE	1000	50.00	75.00
86	FOREVER YOURS (SET OF 3)	1500	90.00	110.00
86	IN THE GARRET	1000	50.00	70.00
86	VICTORIAN BOUQUET	1000	50.00	100.00
87	A BREATH OF SPRING	1000	50.00	60.00
87	COTILLION	1000	50.00	90.00
87	FIDDLER AND THE QUILT MAKER	1000	50.00	90.00
87	LITTLE WOMEN	1000	50.00	125.00
87	TEA, ROSES AND ROMANCE	1675	60.00	160.00
88	CHERISHED MOMENTS	1000	55.00	95.00
88	LOVE SONGS	1000	55.00	150.00
88	ROSE OF SHARON	1000	55.00	125.00
88	SOMETHING OLD, SOMETHING NEW	1000	55.00	700.00

SPORTS COLLECTORS WAREHOUSE

C. PALUSO

YR	NAME	LIMIT	ISSUE	TREND
86	CARL YASTRZEMSKI	452	95.00	275.00

YR	NAME	LIMIT	ISSUE	TREND
86	DON DRYSDALE	465	95.00	240.00
86	DON SUTTON	310	95.00	200.00
86	MICKEY MANTLE	250	175.00	2250.00
86	SPARKY ANDERSON	574	75.00	140.00
87	CARL HUBBELL	800	75.00	185.00
87	SANDY KOUFAX	950	100.00	325.00
88	BILL DICKEY	800	75.00	425.00
88	CHARLES GEHRINGER	800	75.00	185.00
88	LEFTY GOMEZ	800	75.00	185.00
88	MUHAMMAD ALI	300	250.00	1395.00
88	NOLAN RYAN	383	125.00	1795.00
88	TED WILLIAMS	406	185.00	950.00
89	BILLY HERMAN	800	110.00	140.00
89	BOB FELLER	500	125.00	140.00
89	JOE SEWELL	800	110.00	200.00
89	JOHNNY MIZE	500	125.00	140.00
89	LOU BOUDREAU	500	125.00	145.00
89	MONTE IRVIN	500	125.00	140.00
89	RALPH KINER	500	125.00	145.00
89	RICK FERRELL	800	110.00	145.00
89	ROY CAMPANELLA	250	600.00	1490.00
89	STAN MUSIAL	475	185.00	625.00
89	WILLIE MAYS	500	185.00	325.00
90	GORDIE HOWE	500	125.00	350.00
90	JOE MONTANA	400	400.00	790.00
90	JOHNNY UNITAS	500	150.00	280.00
90	MAURICE RICHARD	500	125.00	200.00
90	PEE WEE REESE	500	175.00	185.00
90	YOGI BERRA	500	185.00	225.00
D. SMITH				
*	ROGER CRAIG	1060	65.00	120.00
86	HUDDLE, THE	1000	60.00	3500.00
88	SWEETNESS: WALTER PAYTON	1000	200.00	460.00
89	JERRY RICE	1060	60.00	350.00
89	JOE MONTANA	1060	120.00	875.00
89	NATURAL, THE: WILL CLARK	1060	65.00	500.00
90	BO JACKSON	*	80.00	175.00
90	MONEY: M. JORDAN	1990	80.00	180.00
90	MVP: JOE MONTANA	950	325.00	975.00
90	SPECIAL TEAMS	1000	80.00	170.00
90	STEVE LARGENT	1060	120.00	425.00
90	TOP GUN: DAN MARINO	950	240.00	280.00

SPORTS IMPRESSIONS

YR	NAME	LIMIT	ISSUE	TREND
*	ARTFUL DODGERS, THE	1000	95.00	395.00
J. CATALANO				
*	MICK, THE: MANTLE	750	125.00	295.00
*	YANKEE GREATS	750	95.00	245.00
B. JOHNSON				
*	DON MATTINGLY H/S	950	125.00	200.00
*	DON MATTINGLY PLAYER OF THE YEAR H/S	950	125.00	350.00
*	DON MATTINGLY PLAYER OF THE YEAR U/S	950	95.00	200.00
R. SIMON				
*	DON MATTINGLY ROOKIE H/S	950	125.00	295.00
*	LIVING TRIPLE CROWN	950	195.00	450.00
*	MANTLE ALL STAR	750	125.00	375.00
*	MANTLE HALL OF FAME	750	125.00	375.00
*	MANTLE ROOKIE H/S	750	125.00	375.00
*	MANTLE TRIPLE CROWN	750	125.00	375.00
*	MICKEY AT NIGHT	750	125.00	450.00
*	STARS AND STRIPES	500	125.00	225.00
*	TED WILLIAMS G/E	950	125.00	250.00
91	BOYS OF SUMMER	500	335.00	350.00

STEINER PRINTS

YR	NAME	LIMIT	ISSUE	TREND
R. STEINER				
81	1981 CALIFORNIA DUCK STAMP	1150	115.00	400.00
82	UNEXPECTED SPRIG	200	45.00	80.00
83	BULL SPRIG AT BUTTE SINK	450	85.00	300.00
83	FLUSHED WOODIES	450	45.00	80.00
83	STORMY MORNING MALLARDS	450	85.00	300.00
84	1984 NEVADA DUCK STAMP	1990	135.00	250.00
84	BLACK LAB WITH PINTAIL	950	25.00	150.00
85	1985 MICHIGAN DUCK STAMP	980	135.00	200.00
85	EARLY LIGHT A/P	175	135.00	275.00
85	HONKERS AT DAWN	350	85.00	350.00
86	1986 FLORIDA DUCK STAMP	1000	135.00	250.00
86	CALIFORNIA PHEASANT (CIRCLE)	100	99.00	100.00
86	REFLECTIVE SPRIG	350	45.00	99.00
86	SILENT PARTNER	780	65.00	295.00
87	1987 CALIFORNIA DUCK STAMP	750	135.00	400.00
87	1987 CALIFORNIA DUCK STAMP (MED.)	50	300.00	900.00
87	1987 NEW HAMPSHIRE DUCK STAMP	5507	135.00	500.00
87	1987 NEW HAMPSHIRE DUCK STAMP (GOV.)	50	850.00	3500.00
87	1987 NEW HAMPSHIRE DUCK STAMP (MED.)	50	300.00	1000.00
87	CALIFORNIA QUAIL W/POPPIES	450	65.00	100.00
87	EMPERORS OVER THE ALEUTIANS	350	85.00	100.00
87	OPENING DAY	350	65.00	100.00

YR	NAME	LIMIT	ISSUE	TREND
87	PINTAILS AT THE COLORADO	450	85.00	100.00
88	1988 CALIFORNIA DUCK STAMP	750	135.00	300.00
88	1988 CALIFORNIA DUCK STAMP (MED.)	300	300.00	700.00
88	1988 NEW HAMPSHIRE DUCK STAMP	5507	135.00	300.00
88	1988 NEW HAMPSHIRE DUCK STAMP (GOV.)	100	500.00	300.00
88	1988 NEW HAMPSHIRE DUCK STAMP (MED.)	50	300.00	600.00
89	1989 ARIZONA DUCK STAMP	900	135.00	200.00
89	1989 ARIZONA DUCK STAMP (GOV.)	200	500.00	1200.00
89	1989 ARIZONA DUCK STAMP (MED.)	100	300.00	400.00
89	1989 CALIFORNIA DUCK STAMP	750	145.00	200.00
89	1989 CALIFORNIA DUCK STAMP (MED.)	300	300.00	500.00
89	1989 NEW HAMPSHIRE DUCK STAMP	5507	135.00	300.00
89	LATE SNOW WOOD DUCKS	100	65.00	85.00
90	1990 COLORADO GOVERNOR'S ED STAMP	4980	58.00	65.00
90	1990 COLORADO PRINT	14500	169.00	250.00
90	1990 COLORADO PRINT (GOV)	400	619.00	1500.00
90	1990 COLORADO PRINT (MED)	2000	319.00	500.00
90	1990 NEW HAMPSHIRE GOVERNOR'S ED STAMP	1380	54.00	65.00
90	1990 NEW HAMPSHIRE PRINT	5507	140.00	300.00
90	1990 NEW HAMPSHIRE PRINT (GOV)	135	505.00	2000.00
90	1990 NEW HAMPSHIRE PRINT (MED)	50	305.00	600.00
90	1990 RHODE ISLAND GOVERNOR'S ED STAMP	1800	57.50	65.00
90	1990 RHODE ISLAND PRINT	3000	153.50	250.00
90	1990 RHODE ISLAND PRINT (GOV)	200	558.00	1500.00
90	1990 RHODE ISLAND PRINT (MED)	300	308.50	500.00
90	GRACEFUL ASCENT	1850	45.00	80.00
91	1991 COLORADO GOVERNOR'S ED STAMP	1380	55.00	65.00
91	1991 COLORADO PRINT	8000	169.00	200.00
91	1991 COLORADO PRINT (GOV)	200	619.00	1200.00
91	1991 COLORADO PRINT (MED)	1000	319.00	400.00
91	1991 NEW HAMPSHIRE GOVERNOR'S ED STAMP	990	54.00	65.00
91	1991 NEW HAMPSHIRE PRINT	5507	154.00	200.00
91	1991 NEW HAMPSHIRE PRINT (GOV)	130	519.00	1200.00
91	1991 NEW HAMPSHIRE PRINT (MED)	50	319.00	400.00
91	1991 NEW MEXICO GOVERNOR'S ED STAMP	3990	57.50	65.00
91	1991 NEW MEXICO PRINT	12000	179.00	250.00
91	1991 NEW MEXICO PRINT (GOV)	500	649.00	1200.00
91	1991 NEW MEXICO PRINT (MED)	1000	339.00	500.00
91	1991 RHODE ISLAND GOVERNOR'S ED STAMP	1200	57.50	65.00
91	1991 RHODE ISLAND PRINT	8000	169.00	200.00
91	1991 RHODE ISLAND PRINT (GOV)	130	574.00	1200.00
91	1991 RHODE ISLAND PRINT (MED)	200	319.00	400.00
91	1991 UTAH PRINT	14028	163.00	200.00
91	1991 UTAH PRINT (GOV)	75	618.00	1800.00
91	1991 UTAH PRINT (MED)	1600	318.00	400.00
92	1992 NEW MEXICO PRINT (GOV)	95	505.00	649.00
92	1992 NEW MEXICO PRINT (MED)	600	305.00	339.00

T.S.M. & COMPANY

A. MANOCCHIA

YR	NAME	LIMIT	ISSUE	MANOCCHIA
84	COYOTE	150	45.00	85.00
84	SKIRMISH IN THE TALL GRASS	500	65.00	150.00
85	ROOM FOR ONLY ONE	600	60.00	120.00
85	SOARING	600	65.00	150.00
87	ALONE AT HOME	500	85.00	250.00
87	EVENING HUNT	500	70.00	200.00
87	SAVE THE SOUND	OP	20.00	75.00
88	HARRIS HAWK	350	60.00	75.00
89	EARLY MORNING AUSABLE	350	45.00	100.00
89	FALL FISHING	350	40.00	70.00
89	FALL FISHING	*	40.00	80.00
89	FALL WHITETAIL COUNTRY	*	35.00	80.00
89	FIRST CATCH	150	60.00	60.00
89	FISHING THE EAST BRANCH	350	40.00	80.00
89	FISHING THE EAST BRANCH	*	40.00	80.00
89	FROM HIGH ABOVE	OP	25.00	80.00
89	FROM HIGH ABOVE	*	25.00	80.00
89	MOUNT KATAHDIN-MOOSE	*	135.00	135.00
89	SPARROW	*	50.00	65.00
89	SPARROW	350	50.00	50.00
90	A WAITING GAME	*	85.00	85.00
90	BAY BRANT	*	200.00	300.00
90	IT DOESN'T GET BETTER THAN THIS...	*	75.00	75.00
90	JUSTIES SET	*	75.00	125.00
90	MOUNT KATAHDIN-WHITETAIL	*	135.00	135.00
90	TEAMWORK	*	80.00	80.00
91	AFTER THE LIMIT	*	200.00	250.00
91	EARLY MORNING WORKOUT	*	10.00	25.00
91	HONORS COURSE-9TH HOLE USGA	*	195.00	195.00
91	MOUNT KATAHDIN-BLACK BEAR	*	135.00	135.00
91	ROCK HOLE, THE	*	90.00	150.00
91	TODAY'S WATER TEMPERATURE IS...	*	45.00	45.00
91	TOO LATE FOR LUNCH	*	60.00	60.00
91	YELLOWSTONE MAGIC	*	75.00	75.00

THE ART OF GLYNDA TURLEY

G. TURLEY

YR	NAME	LIMIT	ISSUE	ARTIST PROOF
95	ABUNDANCE III	50	109.50	110.00
95	ALMOST AN ANGEL	50	84.00	84.00

YR	NAME	LIMIT	ISSUE	TREND
95	GLYNDA'S GARDEN	50	109.50	110.00
95	GRAND GLORY III	50	97.50	98.00
95	GRAND GLORY IV	50	97.50	98.00
95	HOLLYHOCKS III	50	103.50	104.00
95	IN FULL BLOOM III	50	96.00	96.00
95	LITTLE RED RIVER	50	109.50	110.00
95	MABRY IN SPRING	50	97.50	98.00
95	REMEMBER WHEN	50	109.50	110.00
95	SOUTHERN SUNDAY II	50	109.50	110.00
95	SUMMER IN VICTORIA	50	79.50	80.00
96	A SOUTHERN TRADITION I	50	109.50	110.00
96	SECRET GARDEN III	50	97.50	98.00
G. TURLEY			**CANVAS REPLICA**	
95	ABUNDANCE III	350	380.00	380.00
95	ALMOST AN ANGEL	350	260.00	260.00
95	GLYNDA'S GARDEN	350	380.00	380.00
95	GRAND GLORY III	350	320.00	320.00
95	GRAND GLORY IV	350	320.00	320.00
95	HOLLYHOCKS III	350	320.00	320.00
95	IN FULL BLOOM III	350	280.00	280.00
95	LITTLE RED RIVER	350	380.00	380.00
95	MOBRY IN SPRING	350	320.00	320.00
95	REMBER WHEN	350	380.00	380.00
95	SOUTHERN SUNDAY II	350	380.00	380.00
95	SUMMER IN VICTORIA	350	260.00	260.00
96	A SOUTHERN TRADTION V	350	380.00	380.00
96	SECRET GARDEN III	350	320.00	320.00
G. TURLEY			**PAPER EDITION**	
95	ABUNDANCE III	7500	73.00	73.00
95	ALMOST AN ANGEL	7500	56.00	56.00
95	GLYNDA'S GARDEN	7500	73.00	73.00
95	GRAND GLORY III	7500	65.00	65.00
95	GRAND GLORY IV	7500	65.00	65.00
95	HOLLYHOCKS III	7500	69.00	69.00
95	IN FULL BLOOM III	7500	64.00	64.00
95	LITTLE RED RIVER	7500	73.00	73.00
95	MABRY IN SPRING	7500	65.00	65.00
95	REMEMBER WHEN	7500	73.00	73.00
95	SOUTHERN SUNDAY II	7500	73.00	73.00
95	SUMMER IN VICTORIA	7500	53.00	53.00
96	A SOUTHERN TRADITION V	7500	73.00	73.00
96	SECRET GARDEN III	7500	65.00	65.00
G. TURLEY			**THE GLYNDA TURLEY COLLECTION**	
95	CIRCLE OF FRIENDS	4800	67.00	67.00
95	COURTYARD II	4800	99.00	99.00
95	FLOWERS FOR MONNY	4800	85.00	85.00
95	PAST TIMES	4800	78.00	78.00
95	PLAYING HOOKIE AGAIN	4800	83.00	83.00
95	SECRET GARDEN II	RT	95.00	95.00

V.F. FINE ARTS

S. KUCK

YR	NAME	LIMIT	ISSUE	TREND
86	SILHOUETTE	250	60.00	245.00
86	SUMMER REFLECTIONS	900	60.00	250.00
86	TENDER MOMENTS	500	70.00	250.00
87	A QUIET TIME	900	40.00	170.00
87	DAISY, THE	900	30.00	125.00
87	FLOWER GIRL, THE	900	40.00	125.00
87	LE PAPILLION	350	90.00	150.00
87	LOVESEAT, THE	900	30.00	235.00
87	MOTHER'S LOVE	150	195.00	825.00
87	READING LESSON, THE	900	60.00	215.00
88	FIRST RECITAL	150	200.00	800.00
88	KITTEN, THE	350	120.00	1200.00
88	LITTLE BALLERINA	150	110.00	300.00
88	MY DEAREST	350	160.00	775.00
88	WILD FLOWERS	350	160.00	255.00
89	BUNDLE OF JOY	1000	125.00	250.00
89	DAY DREAMING	900	150.00	250.00
89	INNOCENCE	900	150.00	200.00
89	PUPPY	500	120.00	600.00
89	ROSE GARDEN	500	95.00	275.00
89	SISTERS	900	95.00	275.00
89	SONATINA	900	150.00	250.00
90	CHOPSTICKS	1500	80.00	80.00
90	FIRST SNOW	500	95.00	225.00
90	LE BEAU	1500	80.00	125.00
90	LE BELLE	1500	80.00	125.00
90	LILLY POND	750	150.00	275.00
91	GOD'S GIFT	1500	95.00	170.00
91	MEMORIES	5000	195.00	235.00
92	DUET	950	125.00	185.00
92	JOYOUS DAY	1200	125.00	165.00
92	YESTERDAY	950	95.00	150.00
93	BEST FRIENDS	2500	145.00	160.00
93	GOOD MORNING	2500	145.00	160.00
93	THINKING OF YOU	2500	145.00	175.00
94	GARDEN MEMORIES	2500	145.00	175.00

YR	NAME	LIMIT	ISSUE	TREND
94	DEAR SANTA	*	495.00	495.00
94	READING TO THEODORE	*	145.00	160.00

VISUAL DELITES

YR	NAME	LIMIT	ISSUE	TREND
P. RASHFORD		**HAND PAINTED PHOTO PRINT**		
93	CASTLES MADE OF SAND	1000	375.00	375.00
P. RASHFORD				**PRINT**
91	PASSAGEWAY	500	72.00	72.00
92	TWO TREES ON A HILL	850	72.00	72.00
93	MOMENT OF SECLUSION	*	30.00	30.00
94	PATHS NOT TAKEN	500	30.00	30.00
94	PLACID AFTERNOON	500	30.00	30.00
94	PUPPY	500	22.00	22.00
P. RASHFORD				**SERIGRAPH**
89	MOUNTAIN LAKE	CL	850.00	850.00
89	NO BLUE HORIZONS	CL	285.00	285.00
90	CARAVANSERAI	465	90.00	90.00
90	WISE LIKENESS	RT	30.00	30.00

VOYAGEUR ART

YR	NAME	LIMIT	ISSUE	TREND
K. DANIEL				
*	ADORNMENT OF WINTER	*	85.00	100.00
*	CONSEQUENCE OF FIRE	*	225.00	260.00
*	FIRST RECITAL	*	125.00	175.00
*	LOST DECOY II	*	85.00	150.00
*	SEARCH FOR SURVIVAL	*	145.00	200.00
*	WINTER SILENCE	*	155.00	155.00
80	WETLAND AND WIKIS	*	120.00	175.00
81	BARNYARD TUSSLE	*	85.00	85.00
81	OUT ON A LIMB	*	85.00	125.00
81	PINE RIDGE	*	85.00	200.00
82	A TOUCH OF ORANGE	*	85.00	150.00
82	BEWILDERED	*	85.00	150.00
82	BLUE HERONS	*	85.00	150.00
82	CHICKADEE	*	50.00	50.00
82	SAFE AND SOUND	*	50.00	100.00
82	SILENT SENTINEL	*	85.00	210.00
83	PRIDE OF THE LAKES	*	85.00	400.00
84	BREAK IN THE STORM	*	85.00	125.00
84	LOST DECOY	*	85.00	150.00
85	ON THE RUN	*	85.00	110.00
85	RUFFED GROUSE SPRING CREEK	*	85.00	150.00
85	SUMMER BLUE JAY	*	85.00	100.00
85	WINGS OF THE NORTH	*	85.00	150.00
86	BOUNDARY WATER SOLITUDE	*	85.00	100.00
86	MAJESTIC VIEW	*	85.00	150.00
90	CONSEQUENCE OF TIME	*	225.00	300.00
90	MISTY WATERS	*	155.00	230.00
90	STALKING THE BLUFFS	*	150.00	200.00
90	SWEET DREAMS	*	185.00	200.00
91	RHAPSODY IN BLOOM	*	185.00	185.00

WHITE DOOR PUBLISHING

YR	NAME	LIMIT	ISSUE	TREND
G. ALEXANDER				
95	A PLACE IN THE SUN	380	125.00	125.00
D.E. KUCERA				
95	SHADOW OF A DREAM	680	150.00	150.00
96	RENEZVOUS AT TRAILS END	680	125.00	125.00
D. MIEDUCH				
95	LORD HELPS THOSE...., THE	750	150.00	150.00
J. SLOANE				
95	CHRISTMAS MAGIC	650	65.00	65.00
B.J. PARRISH			**CANVAS EDITION**	
95	NORTH POLE EXPRESS	250	395.00	395.00
C.L. PETERSON			**MEMORIES COLLECTION**	
95	..AND APPLE PIE	SO	195.00	375.00
95	GRANDMA'S QUILT	SO	185.00	485.00
95	HAYRIDE COLLECTOR EDITION	SO	185.00	345.00
95	HAYRIDE ENCORE EDITION	2000	85.00	85.00
95	HOME GROWN	SO	185.00	385.00
95	SUGAR TIME	SO	195.00	195.00
R. SALTER			**MEMORIES COLLECTION**	
95	WALKING IN A WINTER WONDERLAND	680	115.00	115.00
B.J. PARRISH			**PAPER EDITION**	
95	NORTH POLE EXPRESS	1500	175.00	175.00

WILD WINGS INC.

YR	NAME	LIMIT	ISSUE	TREND
*	WORLD RECORD -CHADWICK RAM	*	*	*
R. ABBETT				
96	ON THE WILLOWEMOC	850	145.00	145.00
S. BOURDET				
96	SEPTEMBER MORNING-CARDINAL	750	125.00	125.00
J. BRANDENBURG				
96	AUTUMN WOLF	9500	85.00	85.00
R. BURNS				
96	STODDARD'S LANE	850	125.00	125.00

YR	NAME	LIMIT	ISSUE	TREND
	C. CUMMINGS			
96	EVENING IN SPRING	750	125.00	125.00
	M. HANSON			
96	GOLDEN GLORIES-GOLDFINCHES	*	50.00	50.00
	J. HAUTMAN			
96	1996 MN DSP	2000	145.00	145.00
96	ROCKY SHALLOWS-LOONS	950	125.00	125.00
	J. KASPER			
96	SPRING FEVER-EASTERN WILD TURKEYS	950	145.00	145.00
	J. KILLEN			
96	GREAT HUNTING DOGS-LABRADORS	980	125.00	125.00
	S. KOZAR			
96	LATE SUMMER REFLECTIONS	850	145.00	145.00
	L. KROMSCHROEDER			
96	FLANK SPEED-ORCAS	950	175.00	175.00
	D. MAASS			
96	BREAKING SKIES-CANVASBACKS	850	175.00	175.00
96	THREE BIRDS UP-RUFFED GROUSE	950	175.00	175.00
	R. MILLETTE			
96	BACKWATER PASSAGE-WHITETAIL DEER	950	145.00	145.00
96	BACKWATER PASSAGE-WILD TURKEYS	950	145.00	145.00
	R. SCOTT			
96	SILENT GUNS	850	145.00	145.00
	M. SIEVE			
96	A DAY IN THE SUN-DALL SHEEP	950	145.00	145.00
96	MISTY FOREST-BALD EAGLE	1500	145.00	145.00
96	SCRAPELINE BUCK	1500	145.00	145.00
	M. SUSINNO			
96	DUPED-BROWN TROLT	850	125.00	125.00
	S. TIMM			
96	1996 WI DSP	1500	145.00	145.00
96	STARLIGHT NIGHT	950	125.00	125.00
	R. VAN GILDER			
96	PINNACLE BOONE & CROCKETT, THE	1200	175.00	175.00
	P.C. WEIRS			
96	DREAM TEAM-WHITETAIL DEER	1900	145.00	145.00
96	FROSTY MORNING	950	145.00	145.00
96	LONESOME BULL-ELK	950	145.00	145.00
	N. YOUNG			
96	BENEATH SPRING BLOSSOMS	750	125.00	125.00

WILDLIFE INTERNATIONALE

YR	NAME	LIMIT	ISSUE	TREND
	J. RUTHVEN			**RUTHVEN**
*	ALGONQUIN	750	75.00	200.00
*	ALLEN'S HUMMINGBIRD	750	75.00	125.00
*	AMERICAN WIDGEON	950	65.00	100.00
*	ANNA'S HUMMINGBIRD	750	75.00	125.00
*	BALD EAGLE-INITIAL	1000	30.00	900.00
*	BATELEUR EAGLE	750	110.00	250.00
*	BENGAL TIGER-COMMISSION, IDAHO	1000	100.00	675.00
*	BENGAL TIGER-REGAL	1000	80.00	2000.00
*	BENGAL TIGER-SAFARI	5000	65.00	1000.00
*	BLACK MANED LION	5000	65.00	120.00
*	BLUE WINGED TEAL	500	75.00	190.00
*	BLUEBIRDS-INITIAL	1000	30.00	700.00
*	BLUEBIRDS-SPRING, COMMISSION	200	*	250.00
*	BOBWHITE QUAIL-AMERICANA	1000	80.00	500.00
*	BOBWHITE QUAIL-INITIAL	1000	360.00	400.00
*	BOBWHITE QUAIL-KNOB CREEK	750	75.00	425.00
*	BROADBILLED HUMMINGBIRD	500	75.00	125.00
*	BROWN PELICAN	500	125.00	400.00
*	CALIFORNIA VALLEY QUAIL	950	50.00	100.00
*	CANADA GOOSE	1000	95.00	500.00
*	CANVASBACKS-DU COMMISSION	150	425.00	750.00
*	CANVASBACKS-NORTH AMERICAN	1000	50.00	650.00
*	CARDINAL-INITIAL	1000	30.00	900.00
*	CARDINAL-MARIEMONT	500	75.00	225.00
*	CARDINAL-SONGBIRD	950	75.00	650.00
*	CAROLINA PARAQUET	500	300.00	1200.00
*	CAROLINA WREN	950	50.00	100.00
*	CEDAR WAXWING	950	50.00	225.00
*	CHICKADEES	950	50.00	150.00
*	CHIPMUNK	750	50.00	450.00
*	CHIPPEWA BRAVE	950	50.00	125.00
*	CINNAMON TEAL	2000	30.00	285.00
*	COMMON ELDERS-DU CANADA COMMISSION	100	125.00	200.00
*	DECOY	750	125.00	1100.00
*	DOUBLE TIME	750	85.00	200.00
*	DOWNY WOODPECKER	600	55.00	425.00
*	DUSTY	950	150.00	900.00
*	EAGLE TO THE MOON	500	150.00	1590.00
*	EASTERN WILD TURKEY-INITIAL	1000	30.00	600.00
*	EASTERN WILD TURKEY-KNOB CREEK	750	75.00	500.00
*	ELEPHANTS	5000	65.00	200.00
*	FLICKERS	950	65.00	275.00
*	FLYING SNOWY OWL	950	125.00	300.00

YR	NAME	LIMIT	ISSUE	TREND
*	FOX MASQUE I	1000	30.00	175.00
*	FOX MASQUE II	1000	30.00	165.00
*	FRIENDS-INDIAN CHILDREN	500	75.00	150.00
*	GIANT PANDA	5000	65.00	700.00
*	GOLDFINCH-COMMISSION	600	55.00	375.00
*	GRANT'S ZEBRA	3500	75.00	100.00
*	GRAY FOX FAMILY	950	150.00	1300.00
*	GRAY FOX-MASTERPIECE	950	125.00	1300.00
*	GRAY FOX-WOODLAND	1500	200.00	275.00
*	GREAT HORNED OWL	1000	90.00	200.00
*	GREEN WINGED TEAL	500	75.00	200.00
*	GREY SQUIRREL	600	55.00	325.00
*	HERRING GULLS	1000	50.00	210.00
*	HOODED MERGANSER	750	75.00	190.00
*	HOODED MERGANSER (SM.)	1000	50.00	100.00
*	INDIGO BUNTING	950	50.00	125.00
*	IVORY BILLED WOODPECKERS	5000	350.00	500.00
*	JAGUAR	950	65.00	550.00
*	KIRTLAND WARBLER	1000	100.00	175.00
*	KIT FOX	500	100.00	225.00
*	LABRADOR DUCK	500	350.00	850.00
*	LEOPARD	3500	75.00	200.00
*	MALLARD-INITIAL	1000	50.00	500.00
*	MALLARD/WOOD DUCK (PR.)	99	750.00	1850.00
*	MISTY-REDHEAD DUCKS	100	125.00	300.00
*	N.Y. STATE BLUEBIRD	1000	50.00	300.00
*	NATURE CENTER CARDINAL	1000	50.00	225.00
*	OAKGROVE PINTAIL (SM.)	3000	50.00	100.00
*	ON THE HUNT	1000	90.00	120.00
*	PASSENGER PIGEON-AQUATINT	500	350.00	500.00
*	PASSENGER PIGEON-MARTHA	500	100.00	400.00
*	PEREGINE FALCON	600	65.00	65.00
*	PHEASANT (PAIR)	99	850.00	1750.00
*	PHEASANT-INITIAL	1000	30.00	100.00
*	RED FOX FAMILY	1000	90.00	1200.00
*	RED FOX-COMMISSION	1000	100.00	600.00
*	RED FOX-REGAL	1000	90.00	1700.00
*	RED FOX-WOODLAND	950	150.00	330.00
*	REDHEAD DUCKS	450	350.00	550.00
*	REDHEADED WOODPECKERS	1000	50.00	230.00
*	RIVOLI'S HUMMINGBIRD	750	75.00	125.00
*	ROADRUNNER	1000	50.00	175.00
*	ROBIN FAMILY	600	55.00	350.00
*	ROBINS	1000	50.00	360.00
*	RUBY-THROATED HUMMINGBIRD	750	75.00	125.00
*	RUDDY DUCKS-COMMISSION	650	55.00	500.00
*	RUDDY DUCKS-GEORGETOWN	1000	50.00	100.00
*	RUDDY DUCKS-NORTH AMERICAN	1000	50.00	650.00
*	RUFFED GROUSE (PAIR)	99	750.00	1200.00
*	RUFFED GROUSE-INITIAL	1000	40.00	450.00
*	RUFOUS HUMMINGBIRD	750	75.00	125.00
*	RUMMY	950	150.00	700.00
*	SAND HILL CRANE	950	150.00	150.00
*	SAW WHET OWLS	950	50.00	100.00
*	SCARLET IRISH SETTER	950	150.00	150.00
*	SCREECH OWL-HOMESTEAD	950	50.00	400.00
*	SCREECH OWLS-INITIAL	1000	30.00	600.00
*	SNOWY OWL	1000	50.00	135.00
*	TERNS	750	150.00	425.00
*	TIMBER WOLF	950	150.00	150.00
*	TOWHEES	950	75.00	250.00
*	WANDERING BRAVE	1000	90.00	900.00
*	WHITE TIGERS	1000	150.00	600.00
*	WHITE-TAILED DEER-KNOB CREEK	750	150.00	700.00
*	WHITE-TAILED DEER-OHIO DIV. WILDLIFE	500	125.00	300.00
*	WILD BOAR	200	100.00	200.00
*	WILSON'S PLOVER	500	75.00	175.00
*	WINSTON-SPRINGER SPANIEL	950	150.00	300.00
*	WOOD DUCKS-INITIAL	1000	40.00	215.00
*	WOOD DUCKS-NORTH AMERICAN	1000	90.00	650.00
*	WOOD DUCKS-OHIO DUCK STAMP (PRINT ONLY)	10000	125.00	450.00
*	WOOD DUCKS-OHIO DUCK STAMP (STAMP ONLY)	10000	5.75	60.00
76	BALD EAGLE-BICENTENNIAL	776	350.00	765.00
76	EASTERN WILD TURKEY-BICENTENNIAL	776	350.00	500.00
80	WINGS IN THE WIND	750	200.00	400.00
81	BLUEBIRDS-1981	950	75.00	500.00
81	CARDINAL-1981	950	75.00	500.00
81	MALLARD-1981	500	75.00	175.00
81	OSPREY	750	175.00	175.00
81	PHEASANT-1981	950	75.00	175.00
81	SWALLOW-TAILED KITES	500	100.00	175.00
82	KESTREL AND MOUSE	950	150.00	175.00
82	KINGLET	950	75.00	150.00
82	NUTHATCH	950	75.00	150.00
83	ARCTIC FOX	350	350.00	380.00
83	GOLDFINCH-1983	950	75.00	175.00
83	PAPAW BANDIT	600	125.00	175.00
83	PILEATED WOODPECKER	350	350.00	550.00
83	QUAIL WITH YOUNG	950	50.00	100.00

YR	NAME	LIMIT	ISSUE	TREND
84	BENGAL TIGER	950	200.00	845.00
84	RIVER OTTERS	500	125.00	300.00
84	SPRING FLOWERS	600	125.00	250.00
85	BLACK DUCK FAMILY	600	125.00	225.00
85	EASTERN FOX SQUIRREL	600	75.00	150.00
85	RACCOONS (FAMILY)	1000	125.00	250.00
85	WINTER REFLECTION	500	225.00	270.00
86	BLUEBIRDS-EASTERN	500	30.00	275.00
86	FROSTY MORNING	400	75.00	250.00
86	STONY RUN-RED FOX	750	225.00	400.00
87	WINTER QUARTET	400	75.00	200.00

WILLITTS DESIGNS

C. PYLE — **HISTORY OF ANGELS COLLECTION BY BILL DALE**

YR	NAME	LIMIT	ISSUE	TREND
95	ANGEL GABRIEL, THE	2500	30.00	30.00
95	ARCHANGEL MICHAEL, THE	2500	30.00	30.00
95	ASCENSION OF THE SOUL, THE	2500	30.00	30.00
95	GARDEN OF GETHSEMANE, THE	2500	30.00	30.00

WINDBERG ENTERPRISES

D. WINDBERG

YR	NAME	LIMIT	ISSUE	TREND
68	PELICAN	OP	*	1000.00
70	ONE SUMMER DAY 12X16	OP	10.00	100.00
70	ONE SUMMER DAY 18X24	OP	20.00	150.00
70	ONE SUMMER DAY 8X10	OP	5.00	50.00
71	BIG TREE 12X16 AMERICAN MASTERS	OP	100.00	100.00
71	BIG TREE 24X36 NEW YORK GRAPHICS	OP	200.00	200.00
71	BIG TREE 8X10 AMERICAN MASTERS	OP	50.00	50.00
71	LBJ LIBRARY & SCHOOL OF PUBLIC AFFAIRS,	OP	3.00	270.00
71	MOONGLOW	OP	1200.00	1200.00
71	SAND DUNES 12X16 W.E.I.	OP	10.00	100.00
71	SAND DUNES 18X24 W.E.I.	OP	20.00	150.00
71	SAND DUNES 24X36 NEW YORK GRAPHICS	OP	*	175.00
71	SAND DUNES 8X10 W.E.I.	OP	*	50.00
71	TRANQUILTY 12X16	OP	10.00	75.00
71	TRANQUILTY 8X10	OP	5.00	45.00
71	WOODLAND REFLECTIONS 12X16 AM. MASTERS	OP	10.00	100.00
71	WOODLAND REFLECTIONS 18X24 AM. MASTERS	OP	*	200.00
71	WOODLAND REFLECTIONS 8X10 AM. MASTERS	OP	5.00	50.00
71	YESTERYEAR 12X16	OP	10.00	100.00
71	YESTERYEAR 18X24	OP	20.00	150.00
71	YESTERYEAR 8X10	OP	5.00	50.00
72	AUTUMN MEMORIES	*	40.00	600.00
73	BLUE SPRINGTIME	*	50.00	450.00
73	COUNTRY HUES 12X16	OP	10.00	40.00
73	COUNTRY HUES 18X24	*	20.00	100.00
73	CYPRESS MIST 12X16	OP	100.00	100.00
73	CYPRESS MIST 18X24	OP	200.00	200.00
73	CYPRESS MIST 8X10	OP	50.00	50.00
73	HIDDEN COVE 12X16	OP	10.00	125.00
73	HIDDEN COVE 8X10	OP	5.00	40.00
73	OBSCURITY 12X16	OP	10.00	75.00
73	OBSCURITY 18X27	OP	20.00	150.00
73	OBSCURITY 8X10	OP	5.00	50.00
73	WINTER'S REPOSE	OP	*	250.00
74	AUTUMN'S GOLD	*	40.00	175.00
74	GLOW OF LOVE	*	50.00	1000.00
74	GOIN' COURTIN'	*	35.00	1450.00
74	HILL COUNTRY	*	50.00	500.00
74	LOVE'S REFLECTION	*	50.00	1250.00
74	MORNING MIST	*	*	350.00
74	OLD HOME PLACE	*	50.00	450.00
74	SAFE PASSAGE	*	50.00	225.00
74	SECLUSION	*	50.00	750.00
74	SUNDAY OUTING	*	30.00	1100.00
74	WINTRY PASTORAL	*	40.00	200.00
75	AUTUMN'S WAY 1 OF SET OF 4	*	325.00	325.00
75	BAYOU COUNTRY	*	220.00	220.00
75	FROM SEA TO SEA 1 OF 4	*	300.00	300.00
75	MOUNTAIN'S MAJESTY, THE 1 OF 4	*	*	300.00
75	OUR DESERT'S BOUNTY 1 OF 4	*	*	300.00
75	SECLUDED FALLS	*	60.00	375.00
75	SPRING'S WAY	*	50.00	375.00
75	SUMMER'S WAY	*	50.00	350.00
75	TRANQUIL TIMES	*	80.00	1400.00
75	UNDISTURBED	*	50.00	400.00
75	WINTER'S WAY	*	50.00	250.00
76	CONTENTMENT	*	80.00	2500.00
76	DAWN'S SERENITY 12X16	OP	100.00	100.00
76	DAWN'S SERENITY 18X24	OP	150.00	150.00
76	DAWN'S SERENITY 8X10	OP	40.00	40.00
76	FLEETING SPLENDOR	*	60.00	350.00
76	NATURE'S INNER GLOW	*	50.00	650.00
76	PELICAN'S WHARF	*	40.00	725.00
76	SNOW-CLAD RELICS	*	45.00	1450.00
77	EVENING RADIANCE	*	65.00	150.00
77	GLADSOM SOLITUDE	*	60.00	180.00
77	HARMONY IN THE HIGHLANDS	*	55.00	175.00
77	LAST STAND	*	70.00	4800.00

Jessica, *Sandra Kuck's exquisite example of innocence, was issued in 1984 by Reco International in a limited edition of only 500. The print originally retailed at $60 and now fetches $400.*

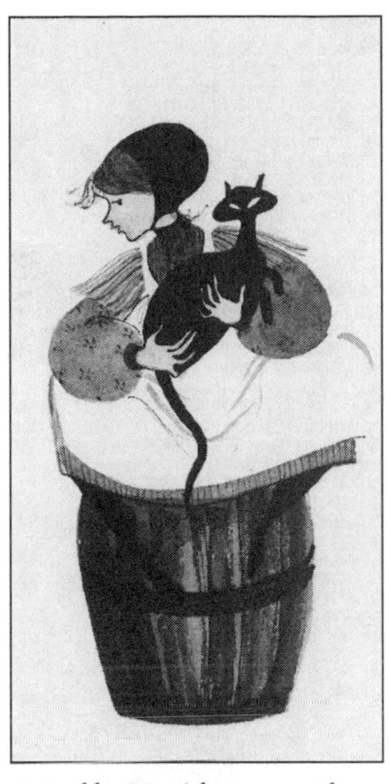

P. Buckley Moss' distinctive style is apparent in Two on a Barrel *from 1982. The Moss Portfolio issued this 1,000-print edition at $25.*

For some, the highlight of the week is Saturday Night. *This 1983 print by Jim Daly was released by Mill Pond Press for $85. Limited to 950, it's currently valued at an impressive $1,500.*

YR	NAME	LIMIT	ISSUE	TREND
77	MEMORABLE SPRINGTIDE 12X16 AM. MASTERS	OP	100.00	100.00
77	MEMORABLE SPRINGTIDE 18X24 AM. MASTERS	OP	150.00	150.00
77	MEMORABLE SPRINGTIDE 8X10 AM. MASTERS	OP	50.00	50.00
77	NIGHTLONG SENTINELS	*	375.00	375.00
78	BLACKSMITH SHOP, THE	OP	10.00	220.00
78	IN SEASONAL ATTIRE	*	70.00	275.00
78	PERPETUAL HAVEN	*	60.00	150.00
78	REFLECTIVE ELEGANCE	OP	80.00	450.00
78	ROSEATE SHORELINE	*	65.00	100.00
78	SPANNING THE STREAM OF TIME	*	70.00	375.00
79	NOCTURNAL HARMONY	*	80.00	260.00
79	SEASON OF RENEWAL	*	80.00	750.00
79	SNOW-CROWNED SILENCE	*	70.00	300.00
79	THUNDERING SPLENDOR 16X12, THE	OP	24.00	75.00
80	EMBRACED BY MOONLIGHT 12X16	OP	24.00	24.00
80	EMBRACED BY MOONLIGHT 18X24	OP	35.00	35.00
80	FLOURISH OF NATURE'S HUES 12X16, THE	OP	20.00	75.00
80	GIFT OF LOVE	*	120.00	350.00
80	MELODY OF THE MAROON BELLS 12X16	OP	24.00	24.00
80	MELODY OF THE MAROON BELLS 18X24	OP	35.00	35.00
80	MEMORABLE SPRINGTIDE 12X16 W.E.I.	OP	24.00	24.00
80	MEMORABLE SPRINGTIDE 18X24 W.E.I.	OP	35.00	35.00
80	MOTHER EARTH-FATHER SKY	*	90.00	450.00
80	OPALESCENT IMAGES 12X16	OP	24.00	24.00
80	TIMEWORN SHELFERS	*	90.00	200.00
80	WOODLAND REFLECTIONS 12X16 W.E.I.	OP	24.00	24.00
81	A MISTY COUNTRY MORN 12X16	OP	24.00	24.00
81	A MISTY COUNTRY MORN 18X24	OP	35.00	35.00
81	COMPANIONS IN NATURE 12X16	OP	24.00	24.00
81	COMPANIONS IN NATURE 18X24	OP	24.00	24.00
81	DELIGHTFUL RETREAT	*	80.00	125.00
81	ENDURING REFUGE	*	120.00	250.00
81	MOONLIT COVE 12X16	OP	24.00	24.00
81	QUIET GRANDEUR 16X12	OP	24.00	24.00
81	SLUMBEROUSE INTERLUDE	*	120.00	350.00
82	A REFRESHING PAUSE	*	120.00	1000.00
82	COMPANIONS IN NATURE 8X10	OP	12.00	12.00
82	HEARTFELT MEMORIES 12X16	OP	24.00	24.00
82	TRANQUIL CROSSING	*	120.00	120.00
82	WINTER'S VELVET MANTLE	*	150.00	350.00
83	1983 DEER UNLIMITED STAMP & PRINT	*	125.00	450.00
83	BLOOMS AMID THORNS	OP	25.00	70.00
83	DAWNLIGHT	*	160.00	260.00
83	OLD FRIENDS	*	90.00	150.00
83	SPRING VELVET	*	150.00	200.00
83	TIMELESS SENTINELS 12X16	OP	24.00	75.00
84	A TIME OF MEMORIES	*	175.00	175.00
84	CANYON GOLD 10X20	OP	24.00	24.00
84	NIGHTIME REPOSE	*	150.00	230.00
84	SUMMER LIGHT 16X12	OP	24.00	75.00
84	SUMMER OF INNOCENCE	*	300.00	500.00
85	A MISTY COUNTRY MORN 8X10	OP	12.00	12.00
85	CLASSIC ELEGANCE	*	300.00	300.00
85	COUNTRY MORN	*	90.00	125.00
85	EMBRACED BY MOONLIGHT 8X10	OP	12.00	12.00
85	ENCHANTING DOMAIN 12X16	OP	24.00	24.00
85	ENCHANTING DOMAN 8X10	OP	12.00	12.00
85	HARMONY OF NATURE, THE	*	150.00	225.00
85	HEARTFELT MEMORIES 8X10	OP	12.00	12.00
85	MELODY OF THE MAROON BELLS 8X10	OP	12.00	12.00
85	MEMORABLE SPRINGTIDE 8X10 W.E.I.	OP	12.00	12.00
85	MOONLIT COVE 8X10	OP	12.00	12.00
85	NEW DAY BREAKING	*	150.00	175.00
85	OPALESCENT IMATES 8X10	OP	12.00	12.00
85	ROUNTINE MAINTENANCE	*	225.00	440.00
85	SUMMER LIGHT 8X10	OP	12.00	40.00
85	TIMELESS SENTINELS 8X10	OP	12.00	40.00
86	EQUINE PARADISE	*	150.00	150.00
86	EVENING QUIESCENCE	OP	24.00	24.00
86	EVERLASTING SANCTUARY 12X16	OP	24.00	24.00
86	FROSTY HOMECOMING	*	195.00	550.00
86	NEPTUNE'S LACE	*	95.00	275.00
86	PASTORAL COLOURS	OP	35.00	35.00
86	PRESIDIO LA BAHIA 8X10	OP	12.00	50.00
87	A MOMENT FOR MEMORIES	*	125.00	275.00
87	ENLIGHTENED PATHWAY	*	125.00	150.00
87	MISSION ESPIRITU SANTO 8X10	OP	12.00	50.00
87	NATURE'S WINTER BLANKET	*	195.00	250.00
87	SEASIDE TREASURY 18X24	OP	35.00	100.00
88	A LAZY DAY IN THE MEADOW	*	150.00	220.00
88	AGELESS MONARCH	*	195.00	325.00
88	COACH TO EL PASO	OP	24.00	24.00
88	ONE SERENE AND MOONLIT NIBHT	*	195.00	475.00
88	SYMPHONY OF THE WILDERNESS	*	195.00	250.00
89	A CUSTOM OF GENERATIONS	OP	24.00	24.00
89	A FAMILY EARTHLY TASK	*	150.00	225.00
89	A JAUNT ACROSS THE DIVIDE	*	195.00	400.00
89	PEACE BE UNTO YOU	*	225.00	750.00
89	SEASONABLE RETURN	*	150.00	750.00

YR	NAME	LIMIT	ISSUE	TREND
90	CELEBRATION OF THE WOODLANDS	*	125.00	200.00
90	CELESTIAL GLORY	*	225.00	350.00
90	MOONLIGHTIN'	OP	225.00	425.00
90	ROARING ONWARD	*	225.00	450.00
90	SLUMBERING HOMEPLACE	OP	35.00	35.00
90	SPRINGTIME TRILOGY - TRIPTYCH	*	150.00	200.00
91	A COZY MOUNTAIN RETREAT	*	225.00	250.00
91	AMBIANCE OF AUTUMN	OP	45.00	45.00
91	BENEVOLENT PROVIDER, THE	*	225.00	350.00
91	HILL COUNTRY FLORESCENCE	OP	45.00	45.00
91	SILENT PINNACLES	OP	45.00	45.00
91	STROLLING WITH AN OLD FRIEND	*	225.00	375.00
91	TEXAS OAK	*	*	400.00
92	AFTERGLOWN OF SPRING SHOWERS	*	225.00	350.00
92	AMID TRANQUILITY OF THE MORNING	*	250.00	250.00
92	FORAGING ON A WINTER EVENING	*	250.00	350.00
93	ANTICIPATION	*	250.00	300.00
93	ROMANTIC TRADITIONS	*	150.00	950.00
93	TAKING A BREAK	*	260.00	260.00
93	TEA TIME REFLECTIONS	*	150.00	150.00
94	COURT'N BY MOONLIGHT	*	150.00	1950.00
94	FIRST LIGHT ON A WINTRY DAY	*	250.00	350.00
94	HOME AT LAST	*	250.00	300.00
94	INNOCENCE OF SPRING	*	150.00	400.00
94	LAKESIDE HIDEAWAY	OP	24.00	24.00
94	MAKING OF A MEMORY	*	250.00	300.00
94	NIGHTWATCH	OP	24.00	24.00
94	ONE SUMMER NIGHT	OP	24.00	24.00
94	RETIRED	OP	24.00	24.00
95	JOYOUS EVENSONG	*	250.00	250.00
95	MORNING DELIGHT/EVENING TREAT	*	150.00	250.00
95	PERFECT SERENITY	*	150.00	150.00
96	OUR SPECTACULAR SURROUNDINGS	*	195.00	195.00
D. WINDBERG				**CANVAS EDITION**
72	ANTICIPATION	*	350.00	350.00
93	AMID TRANQUILITY OF THE MORNING	*	350.00	350.00
93	TAKING A BREAK	*	350.00	350.00
94	FIRST LIGHT ON A WINTRY DAY	*	350.00	350.00
94	HOME AT LAST	*	350.00	350.00
94	INNOCENCE OF SPRING	*	350.00	350.00
94	MAKING OF A MEMORY	*	350.00	350.00
95	A GLIMPSE OF UPLAND GRANDEUR	250	350.00	350.00
95	AN ENCHANTING VIEW OF THE NIGHT	250	350.00	350.00
95	HILLTOP GARDENS	250	350.00	350.00
95	JOYOUS EVENSONG	*	350.00	350.00
95	MORNING DELIGHT/EVENING TREAT	*	350.00	350.00
D. WINDBERG				**FIESTA POSTER**
91	REFLECTIONS OF THE NIGHT	OP	45.00	45.00
D. WINDBERG				**NATIONAL PARK**
79	THUNDERING SPLENDOR	SO	50.00	250.00
80	FLOURISH OF NATURE'S HUES, THE	*	50.00	175.00
81	QUIET GRANDEUR	SO	50.00	150.00
86	EVERLASTING SANCTUARY	*	140.00	300.00
D. WINDBERG				**NATURAL PARK**
84	CANYON GOLD	SO	50.00	200.00
D. WINDBERG				**PAPER EDITION**
95	A GLIMPSE OF UPLAND GRANDEUR	1000	250.00	250.00
95	AN ENCHANTING VIEW OF THE NIGHT	1000	250.00	350.00
95	HILLTOP GARDENS	1000	250.00	250.00
D. WINDBERG				**POSTER**
88	AMERICAN IMPRESSIONS	OP	35.00	35.00
88	GALLERY AMERICANA	*	35.00	35.00
88	VISIONS OF AMERICA	OP	35.00	35.00
88	WIDLERNESS	OP	35.00	75.00
D. WINDBERG				**SPECIAL EDITION**
86	PRESIDIO LA BAHIA	*	80.00	400.00
87	MISSION ESPIRITU SANTO	*	80.00	125.00

WORLD ART EDITIONS

YR	NAME	LIMIT	ISSUE	TREND
MAGO				**MAGO**
82	DEPOSITION	300	325.00	325.00
82	SIPARIO	300	325.00	325.00
F. MASSERIA				**MASSERIA**
80	EDUARDO	300	275.00	2700.00
80	FIRST KISS	300	375.00	2200.00
80	NINA	300	325.00	1950.00
80	ROSANNA	300	257.00	3200.00
81	ELEANOR	300	375.00	1900.00
81	ELISA WITH FLOWER	300	325.00	2200.00
81	FIRST FLOWER	300	325.00	2200.00
81	JESSICA	300	375.00	2300.00
81	JULIE	300	375.00	950.00
81	SELENE	300	325.00	2200.00
81	SOLANGE	300	325.00	2200.00
81	SUSAN SEWING	300	375.00	2500.00
82	AMY	300	425.00	720.00
82	JAMIE	300	425.00	750.00
82	JILL	300	425.00	750.00

YR	NAME	LIMIT	ISSUE	TREND
82	JODIE	300	425.00	950.00
82	JUDITH	300	425.00	750.00
82	ROBIN	300	425.00	975.00
82	YASMIN	300	425.00	720.00
82	YVETTE	300	425.00	620.00
83	ANTONIO	300	450.00	1100.00
83	TARA	300	450.00	1100.00
84	BETTINA	250	550.00	700.00
84	CHRISTOPHER	300	450.00	700.00
84	MEMOIRS	300	450.00	700.00
84	PETER	950	395.00	495.00
84	REGINA	950	395.00	495.00
84	VINCENTE	360	550.00	1000.00
85	CHRISTINA	300	500.00	700.00
85	JORGITO	300	500.00	700.00
85	MARQUERITA	950	495.00	495.00
85	TO CATCH A BUTTERFLY	950	495.00	495.00

WREN'S NEST GALLERY INC.

L. MARTIN

YR	NAME	LIMIT	ISSUE	TREND
95	MAGNOLIAS & GREEK REVIVAL	950	65.00	65.00
95	ROYAL FLUSH	950	85.00	85.00
95	SPRING GARDEN	950	75.00	75.00
95	TREDAWAY HOME, THE	950	28.00	28.00
96	MOLTEN GOLD	950	65.00	65.00
96	NEW GEMS	950	38.00	38.00
96	TRAIL BOSS	950	110.00	110.00

L. MARTIN **AMERICA THE BEAUTIFUL**

YR	NAME	LIMIT	ISSUE	TREND
95	SPACIOUS SKIES I	500	100.00	100.00
95	SPACIOUS SKIES II	500	28.00	28.00
96	AMERICA, AMERICA I	500	85.00	85.00
96	AMERICA, AMERICA II	500	65.00	65.00
96	GOD SHED HIS GRACE ON THEE	950	100.00	100.00
96	PURPLE MOUNTAIN MAJESTIES	950	100.00	100.00

Steins

Ken Armke

Beer steins, more than nearly any other component of today's collectibles market, bridge the gap between authentic antiques and contemporary limited editions.

After all, some of the most popular lines of today's collectibles, such as Precious Moments figurines and Department 56 cottages, are not yet 20 years old. Even M.I. Hummel figurines have been around for just over 60 years.

Steins, on the other hand, have been going strong for more than 400 years. Even if one discounts the early utilitarian steins that were used for centuries, these drinking vessels emerged as an artistic collectible popular in the United States during the late 1800s.

It's no wonder then that steins are often thought of as a "traditional" aspect of the collectibles secondary market. With the exception of some of the Anheuser-Busch issues, they tend to perform with less volatility—few wondrous jumps in value and correspondingly few diastrous plunges—than do most other collectibles.

For this reason, steins—for those who enjoy them and the artwork they represent—should be looked upon with favor by those collectors seeking a longer-term commitment to their collectibles. Traditional art has always shown a strong tendency to grow in value over time to at least match inflation.

KEN ARMKE SR. is president of Opa's Haus Inc. (OHI), a leading importer and producer of collectible steins. As a nationally recognized authority on beer steins, Armke oversees OHI retail and wholesale operations including secondary market sales.

YR	NAME	LIMIT	ISSUE	TREND

STEINS

ANHEUSER-BUSCH INC.

J.C. LEYENDECKER

YR	NAME	LIMIT	ISSUE	TREND
96	SATURDAY EVENING POST FOURTH OF JULY	5000	180.00	180.00
*				**A&EAGLE**
76	A&EAGLE CS2	RT	*	125.00
76	A&EAGLE CS26	RT	*	125.00
76	A&EAGLE CS28	RT	*	220.00
75	A&EAGLE CSL2	RT	*	220.00
94	A&EAGLE TRADEMARK II CS219	RT	24.00	45.00
95	A&EAGLE TRADEMARK III CS240	OP	25.00	22.00
96	A&EAGLE TRADEMARK IV CS271	OP	*	25.00
96	TRADEMARK IV STEIN	30000	27.00	27.00
*				**ANIMAL/WILDLIFE**
88	BUDWEISER FIELD & STREAM SET CS95	RT	70.00	*
89	BALD EAGLE CS106	RT	25.00	400.00
90	ASIAN TIGER CS126	RT	27.50	100.00
91	AFRICAN ELEPHANT CS135	RT	29.00	45.00
91	AMERICAN BALD EAGLE CS164	RT	125.00	125.00
92	DOLPHIN CS187	RT	90.00	70.00
92	GIANT PANDA CS173	RT	29.00	45.00
92	KILLER WHALE CS186	RT	100.00	70.00
92	PEREGRINE FALCON CS183	OP	125.00	137.00
93	GRIZZLY BEAR CS199	OP	29.50	30.00
93	LABRADOR CS195	RT	32.50	45.00
94	GRAY WOLF CS226	OP	29.50	30.00
94	MANATEE CS203	OP	33.50	35.00
94	OSPREY STEIN CS212	RT	135.00	350.00
94	SETTER CS205	OP	32.50	30.00
95	COUGAR CS253	OP	*	30.00
95	GOLDEN RETRIEVER CS248	OP	*	30.00
95	GREAT HORNED OWL CS264	OP	137.00	130.00
95	GREAT WHITE SHARK STEIN CS247	OP	*	35.00
96	BEAGLE CS272	OP	*	30.00
*				**BREWERY SPECIFIC**
*	ADOLPHUS BUSCH	RT	*	*
85	LIMITED EDITION I CS64	RT	30.00	150.00
86	BREW HOUSE CS67	RT	20.00	24.00
86	LIMITED EDITION II CS65	RT	30.00	40.00-80.00
87	BUDWEISER STABLES CS73	RT	20.00	30.00
87	LIMITED EDITION III CS71	RT	30.00	45.00
88	CLASSIC I CS93	RT	35.00	125.00
88	GRANT'S CABIN CS83	RT	*	30.00
88	LIMITED EDITION IV CS75	RT	30.00	35.00
88	OLD SCHOOL HOUSE CS84	RT	20.00	30.00
89	CLASSIC II CS104	RT	55.00	80.00
89	LIMITED EDITION V CS98	RT	35.00	35.00
90	CLASSIC III CS113	RT	65.00	65.00
91	AFTER THE HUNT CS155	RT	100.00	70.00
91	CLASSIC IV CS130	RT	75.00	65.00
92	BERNINGHAUS CS105	RT	75.00	55.00
92	CHERUB CS182	RT	100.00	85.00
92	COLUMBIAN EXPOSITION CS169	RT	35.00	30.00
93	A&EAGLE TRADEMARK I CS191	RT	22.00	45.00
93	A&EAGLE TRADEMARK I CS201	RT	31.00	55.00
93	ADOLPHUS BUSCH CS216	OP	180.00	200.00
93	GANYMEDE CS190	RT	35.00	35.00
94	A&EAGLE TM III CS238	RT	28.00	45.00
94	AUGUST A. BUSCH ST. CS229	RT	220.00	200.00
94	BUDWEISER GREATEST TRIUMPH CS222	RT	35.00	30.00
94	SIX-PACK II MINI STEINS N4571	OP	*	19.00
95	ADOLPHUS BUSCH III CS265	OP	*	200.00
95	BUD-WEIS-ER FROG MUG N5402-5	*	*	22.00
95	MIRROR OF TRUCH CS252	OP	*	30.00
96	BUDWEISER LABEL CS282	OP	*	19.00
*				**CLYDESDALES**
76	CLYDESDALE DECANTER CS33	RT	*	*
76	CLYDESDALES CS15	RT	*	175.00
76	CLYDESDALES CS15/II	RT	*	450.00
76	CLYDESDALES CSL15	RT	*	*
76	CLYDESDALES CSL29	RT	*	*
76	CLYDESDALES CSL9	RT	*	200.00
83	BUD LIGHT BARON CS61	RT	*	40.00
86	HORSESHOE CS68	RT	15.00	40.00
87	HORSEHEAD CS76	RT	16.00	40.00
87	HORSEHEAD CS78	RT	15.00	40.00
87	HORSESHOE CS77	RT	16.00	40.00
87	WORLD FAMOUS CLYDESDALE CS74	RT	9.95	22.00
88	CLYDESDALE MARE & FOAL CS90	RT	*	24.00
88	HORSE HARNESS CS94	RT	16.00	65.00
89	PARADE DRESS CS99	RT	11.50	24.00
91	CLYDESDALES TRAINING HITCH CS131	RT	13.00	24.00
94	PROUD AND FREE CS223	OP	17.00	17.00
*				**COLLECTOR CLUB**
95	BREWHOUSE CLOCK TOWER CB2	RT	*	175.00

YR	NAME	LIMIT	ISSUE	TREND
95	CLYDESDALES AT BAUERNHF CB1	RT	*	55.00
*				**EARLY YEARS**
*	SENIOR GRANDE CS6	RT	*	625.00
75	GERMAN PILIQUE CS5	RT	*	450.00
75	GERMAN TAVERN SCENE CSL6	RT	*	250.00
75	SENIOR GRANDE CSL4	RT	*	*
76	BUDWEISER CENT. HOFBRAU ST. CS22	RT	*	350.00
76	BUDWEISER CENTENNIAL CS13	RT	*	350.00
76	BUDWEISER CENTENNIAL CSL7	RT	*	350.00
76	CORACAO DECANTER SET 5 PC SET CS31	RT	*	700.00
76	GERMAN PILIQUE CSL5	RT	*	*
76	GERMAN TAVERN SCENE CS4	RT	*	55.00
76	KATAKOMBE CS3	RT	*	250.00
76	KATAKOMBE CSL3	RT	*	325.00
76	ST. LOUIS DECANTER SET CS37	RT	*	480.00
76	ST. LOUIS DECANTER SET CS38	RT	*	1250.00
76	U.S. BICENTENNIAL CS14	RT	*	400.00
76	U.S. BICENTENNIAL CSL8	RT	*	400.00
76	WURZBURGER CS39	RT	*	350.00
P. FORD				**FIRST HUNT**
96	LABRADOR STEIN	10000	190.00	190.00
*				**GERZ MEISTERWERKE**
*	WINCHESTER GL2	RT	*	125.00
92	SANTA'S MAILBAG GM1	RT	*	190.00
93	GOLDEN RETRIEVER GM2	OP	*	170.00
93	JOHN F. KENNEDY GM4	OP	*	180.00
94	MALLARD GM7	OP	*	190.00
94	ROSIE THE RIVERTER GM9	OP	*	150.00
94	SPRINGER SPANIEL GM5	OP	*	170.00
94	WINCHESTER MODEL 94 GM10	OP	*	150.00
95	GIANT PANDA GM8	OP	*	190.00
95	POINTER GM16	OP	*	170.00
96	FOURTH OF JULY GM15	OP	*	165.00
N. ROCKWELL				**GERZ MEISTERWERKE**
93	DUGOUT, THE GL1	RT	*	95.00
93	SANTA'S HELPER GM3	OP	*	180.00
94	ALL I WANT FOR CHRISTMAS GM13	OP	*	190.00
94	TRIPLE SELF-PORTRAIT GM6	OP	*	225.00
*				**HOLIDAY**
76	BUDWEISER CHAM. CLYDESDALE CS19	RT	9.95	90.00
80	BUDWEISER CHAM. CLYDESDALES CS19/II	RT	*	165.00
81	SNOWY WOODLAND CS50	RT	9.95	240.00
82	50TH ANNIV. CELEBRATION CS57	RT	9.95	80.00
83	CAMEO WHEATLAND CS58	RT	9.95	30.00
84	COVERED BRIDGE CS62	RT	9.95	15.00
85	SNOW CAPED MTNS. CS63	RT	9.95	15.00
86	TRADITIONAL HOUSES CS66	RT	9.95	35.00
87	GRANT'S FARM GATES CS70	RT	9.95	15.00
88	COBBLESTONE PASSAGE CS88	RT	9.95	15.00
89	WINTER EVENING CS89	RT	13.00	15.00
90	AN AMERICAN TRADITION CS112	RT	13.50	10.00
90	AN AMERICAN TRADITION GOLD CS112	RT	*	150.00
90	AN AMERICAN TRADITION SIG. ED. CS112SE	RT	50.00	45.00
91	SEASON'S BEST CS133	RT	14.50	10.00
91	SEASON'S BEST, GOLD CS133	RT	*	150.00
91	SEASON'S BEST, SIG. ED. CS133SE	RT	50.00	45.00
92	A PERFECT CHRISTMAS CS167	RT	14.50	10.00
92	A PERFECT CHRISTMAS, GOLD CS167	RT	*	150.00
92	A PERFECT CHRISTMAS, SIG. ED. CS167SE	RT	50.00	65.00
93	SPECIAL DELIVERY CS192	RT	15.00	20.00
93	SPECIAL DELIVERY, GOLD CS192	RT	60.00	135.00
93	SPECIAL DELIVERY, SIG. ED. CS192	RT	*	125.00
94	'94 HOLIDAY SIG. ED. CS211SE	RT	65.00	100.00
94	1994 HOLIDAY CS211	OP	14.00	20.00
95	'95 HOLIDAY, SIG. ED. CS263SE	OP	*	70.00
95	CHRISTMAS-SATURDAY EVENING POST GL5	OP	*	95.00
S. RYAN				**HUNTER'S COMPANION**
96	BEAGLE STEIN	50000	35.00	35.00
*				**RARITIES**
*	AMERICANA CS17	RT	*	465.00
*	CLYDESDALE HOFBRAU CS29	RT	*	180.00
*	DAS FESTHAUS CS41	RT	*	250.00
*	HAMBURG CS16	RT	*	425.00
*	MINI MUGS SET OF 4 CS8	RT	*	1250.00
75	MINIATURE BAVARIAN MUG CS7	RT	*	650.00
76	CANTEEN DECANTER SET 7 PC FLORAL CS036	RT	*	*
76	CLYDESDALES CS012/VERSION OF CSL9	RT	*	300.00
76	DELFT, ASST. DESIGNS CS11	RT	*	425.00
76	GERMAN WINE SET 7 PC CS32	RT	*	700.00
76	HOLANDA DECANTER SET 7 PC BRN CS34	RT	*	*
76	HOLANDA DECANTER SET 7 PC CO. BLU CS35	RT	*	*
77	A&EAGLE, BAVARIAN SHAPE CS24	RT	*	900.00
80	BUSCH HOFBRAU STYLE CS44	RT	*	250.00
80	MICHELOB HOFBRAU ST. CS45	RT	*	80.00
80	NATURAL LIGHT HOFBRAU CS43	RT	*	250.00
81	BUDWEISER HOFBRAU ST. CS46	RT	*	90.00
*				**SPECIAL EVENT**
80	BUDWEISER CHICAGO SKYLINE CS040	RT	*	90.00

YR	NAME	LIMIT	ISSUE	TREND
81	BUDWEISER CALIFORNIA CS56	RT	*	50.00
81	BUDWEISER CHICAGOLAND CS51	RT	*	45.00
81	BUDWEISER TEXAS CS52	RT	*	55.00
83	BUDWEISER SAN FRANCISCO CS29	RT	*	200.00
89	NORTH/SOUTH DAKOTA SO42268	*	*	25.00
90	DAYTONA BUD BIKE WK. N/A-2	*	*	*
90	DAYTONA BUD SPEED W N/A-3	*	*	*
90	IDAHO: CENTENNIAL SO49804	*	*	25.00
90	INTRO. TO WI WILDLIFE DUCK N/A-4	*	*	*
90	MICHIGAN DUCKS UNLIMITED SO42208	*	*	25.00
90	SEATTLE: GOOD WILL GMS. SO47627	*	*	25.00
90	WISCONSIN WILDLIFE: DEER SO49700	*	*	25.00
90	WISCONSIN WILDLIFE: DUCK SO48249	*	*	25.00
90	WYOMING: CENTENNIAL N SP50138	*	*	25.00
91	ARKANSAS: RICE/DUCK SO51582	*	*	25.00
91	CA: BIG BEAR OKTOBERFEST SO53954	*	*	25.00
91	COLORADO: AND NO... SP52848	*	*	25.00
91	DODGE CITY DAYS SO53465	*	*	100.00
91	FORT LEWIS, WASHINGTON SO54147	*	*	25.00
91	GEORGIA FISHING: ON... SO53834	*	*	25.00
91	GEORGIA HUNTING: ON... SO54141	*	*	25.00
91	HOUSTON RODEO N/A-5	*	*	*
91	ILLINOIS STATE SO54808	*	*	25.00
91	KANSAS: GOOD TO KNOW. SO53618	*	*	25.00
91	KENTUCKY: THE CELEB. SO54022	*	*	25.00
91	MARDI GRAS: NOTHING... SO50500	*	*	45.00
91	MICHIGAN DU, LOON SO54807	*	*	25.00
91	MINNESOTA WILDLIFE: LOON SO53143	*	*	25.00
91	MISSISSIPPI BASS: ALWAY SO54822	*	*	25.00
91	MISSISSIPPI DEER: ALWAY SO54806	*	*	25.00
91	MISSOURI WAKE UP... SO54149	*	*	25.00
91	NEBRASKA: TRADITIONS SO50512	*	*	25.00
91	NEW YORK: A STATE OF... SO54214	*	*	25.00
91	OHIO: THE HEAR OF... SO55446	*	*	25.00
91	OKLAHOMA: BETTER SOON SO53689	*	*	25.00
91	OKLAHOMA: FESTIVAL OF... SO55447	*	*	25.00
91	OKTOBERFEST SO54077	*	*	25.00
91	PENNSYLVANIA: A STATE... SO54215	*	*	25.00
91	REDLANDS: CHILI COOK-OFF SO53757	*	*	25.00
91	SAN ANTONIO: FIESTA SO52190	*	*	25.00
91	SAVE LAKE PONTC'TRAIN SO54240	*	*	25.00
91	SAVE THE BAY I SO52286	*	*	25.00
91	TEMECULA: TRACTOR RACE SO53847	*	*	25.00
91	UTAH: NATURALLY SO52847	*	*	25.00
91	VERMONT: BICENTENNIAL SO53758	*	*	25.00
91	WISCONSIN WILDLIFE: BEST S055713	*	*	150.00
92	ADVERTISING THROUGH... N3989	*	*	85.00
92	ALABAMA STATE SO64282	*	*	25.00
92	ATHENS, NY FIREFIGHTERS SO64209	*	*	25.00
92	BUDWEISER BURNS COAL SO64374	*	*	25.00
92	BUDWEISER RACING N3553	*	*	*
92	CARDINALS: 100TH ANNIV. N3767	*	*	*
92	CINCINNATI: TALLSTACKS N3942	*	*	*
92	DU QUOIN: STATE FAIR N3941	*	*	*
92	GEORGIA: BASS SO63840	*	*	25.00
92	GEORGIA: DEER SO64054	*	*	25.00
92	INDIANA: CROSSROADS... SO68206	*	*	25.00
92	IOWA: THE TIME IS... SO67816	*	*	25.00
92	IT'S A BUD THING N3645	*	*	*
92	LOUISIANA: WE'RE REALLY SO67814	*	*	25.00
92	MARDI GRAS 1992: BUD SO56219	*	*	*
92	MICHIGAN DU SO64169	*	*	25.00
92	MICHIGAN DUCKS UNLIMITED N3828	*	*	*
92	MINNESOTA WILDLIFE: MALLARD SO67817	*	*	25.00
92	NC: CAROLINA ON MY... SO64215	*	*	25.00
92	NEW YORK STATE II SO67691	*	*	25.00
92	O'DOUL'S: WHAT BEER..N3522	*	*	35.00
92	PUERTO RICO: QUINTO... SO65691	*	*	*
92	TENNESSEE: WE'RE PLAY SO63887	*	*	25.00
92	TEXAS: LIVING FREE... N3648	*	*	*
92	WEST TEXAS: CENTENNIAL N3943	*	*	*
93	ARKANSAS: BREWED.. N3940	*	*	*
93	MARDI GRAS 1993 N4073	*	*	*
93	MISSOURI: ALWAYS IN... N4118	*	*	*
93	NEBRASKA WILDLIFE N4117	*	*	*
93	OHIO JAYCEES: PARTNES N4119	*	*	*
93	PHOENIX: ONE MILLION... N4105	*	*	*
93	SAVE THE BAY II N4120	*	*	*
96	1996 ST. PATRICK'S DAY CS269	OP	*	19.00
*				**SPECIALTY**
75	BUD MAN CS1	RT	*	425.00
75	BUD MAN CS1/II	RT	*	460.00
76	BUDWEISER LABEL CS18	RT	*	625.00
76	MICHELOB CS27	RT	*	175.00
77	NATURAL LIGHT CS9	RT	*	300.00
80	OKTOBERFEST BUSCH GAR. CS42	RT	*	175.00
82	POST CONV.-OLYMPIC CS53	RT	*	190.00
82	POST CONV.-OLYMPIC CS54	RT	*	190.00
82	POST CONV.-OLYMPIC CS55	RT	*	250.00
87	KING COBRA CS80	RT	*	220.00

YR	NAME	LIMIT	ISSUE	TREND
87	ST. NICK CS79	RT	*	75.00
88	ADOLPHUS BUSCH CS87	RT	*	150.00
88	AUGUST BUSCH ST. CS102	RT	*	125.00
89	ADOLPHUS BUSCH III CS114	RT	*	65.00
89	BUD MAN, 1989 STYLE CS100	RT	30.00	45.00
89	BUDWEISER LABEL CS101	RT	14.00	20.00
89	ST. LOUIS CARDINALS CS125	RT	30.00	45.00
90	A&EAGLE LOGO CS148	RT	16.00	20.00
90	AUGUST BUSCH JR. CS141	RT	*	50.00
90	BUD LIGHT LOGO CS144	RT	16.00	20.00
90	BUDWEISER ANTIQUE LABEL CS127	RT	14.00	20.00
90	BUDWEISER LOGO CS143	RT	16.00	20.00
90	BUSCH LOGO CS147	RT	16.00	20.00
90	MICHELOB DRY LOGO CS146	RT	16.00	20.00
90	MICHELOB LOGO CS145	RT	16.00	20.00
90	NINA CS107	RT	40.00	65.00
91	BEVO FOX CS160	RT	250.00	250.00
91	BEVO FOX GERZ/CS160	RT	*	225.00
91	BOTTLED BEER W/TIN N3292	*	*	*
91	BUD DRY LOGO CS156	RT	16.00	20.00
91	BUDWEISER BOTTLED BEER CS136	RT	15.00	20.00
91	BUDWEISER PEWTER N2755	*	*	125.00
91	ERIN GO BUD CS109	RT	15.00	50.00
91	GEN. ULYSSES S. GRANT CS181	RT	150.00	125.00
91	MICHELOB DRY PEWTER N2371	*	*	125.00
91	MICHELOB PEWTER CS158	RT	*	125.00
91	PINTA CS129	RT	40.00	65.00
92	1993 BUDWEISER OKTOBERFEST CS202	RT	18.00	20.00
92	BUDWEISER OKTOBERFEST CS185	OP	16.00	16.00
92	BUDWEISER RODEO CS184	RT	18.00	24.00
92	CLYDESDALES ON PARADE CS161	RT	16.00	20.00
92	GEN. ROBERT E. LEE CS188	RT	150.00	125.00
92	MINI STEINS SET OF 6 N3289	*	*	*
92	POT OF GOLD CS166	OP	15.00	15.00
92	SANTA MARIA CS138	RT	40.00	65.00
93	ABRAHAM LINCOLN CS189	RT	*	125.00
93	BOTTLED TREASURE CS193	RT	15.30	36.00
93	BUD MAN, 1993 STYLE CS213	RT	45.00	45.00
94	AIR FORCE CS228	OP	19.00	20.00
94	BUDWEISER SALUTES THE ARMY CS224	OP	19.00	18.00
94	LUCK O' THE IRISH CS210	OP	18.00	18.00
94	WALKING TALL BOOT CS251	OP	17.50	18.00
95	1995 ST. PATRICK'S DAY CS242	OP	19.00	17.00
95	BUDWEISER SALUTES THE NAVY CS243	OP	19.50	20.00
95	MARINES CS256	OP	*	20.00
96	A&EAGLE LOGO IV CS255	OP	*	27.00
*				**SPORTS**
84	1984 BUDWEISER OLYMPIC GAMES CS60	RT	*	30.00
87	1988 WINTER OLYMPICS CS81	RT	50.00	65.00
87	BUDWEISER WINTER OLYMPICS CS85	RT	25.00	30.00
88	BUDWEISER SUIMMER OLYMPICS CS91	RT	55.00	50.00
88	BUDWEISER SUMMER OLYMPICS CS92	RT	55.00	30.00
90	AM. FAVORITE PASTIME CS124	RT	20.00	35.00
91	1992 WINTER OLYMPICS CS162	RT	85.00	55.00
91	BABE RUTH CS142	RT	85.00	80.00
91	BUS. 1992 OLMPICS CS168	RT	16.00	20.00
91	CHASING CHECKERED FLAG CS132	RT	22.00	30.00
91	GRIDIRON LEGACY CS128	RT	20.00	30.00
91	HEROES OF HARDWOOD CS134	OP	*	20.00
92	1992 SUMMER OLYMPICS CS163	RT	85.00	55.00
92	JIM THORPE CS171	RT	85.00	45.00
92	PAR FOR THE COURSE CS165	RT	*	20.00
93	BILL ELLIOTT CS196	RT	150.00	125.00
93	BILL ELLIOTT, SIG. ED. CS196SE	RT	295.00	275.00
93	CENTER ICE CS209	OP	22.00	20.00
93	JOU LOUIS CS206	RT	85.00	80.00
93	RACING TEAM CS194	RT	19.00	30.00
94	1994 WORLD CUP COMMN CS230	RT	40.00	45.00
94	FORE! GOLF BAG CS225	OP	16.00	16.00
95	'96 OLYMPICS, CENTENNIAL CS259	OP	*	45.00
95	'96 OLYMPICS, CENTENNIAL CS266	OP	*	22.00
95	'96 OLYMPICS, GYMNASTICS CS262	OP	*	75.00
95	'96 OLYMPICS, TRACK CS246	OP	*	75.00
95	BASEBALL MIT STEIN CS244	OP	*	18.00
95	CHIP MANAUER MUG N5511	OP	*	22.00
95	KEN SCHRADER MUG B5510	OP	*	22.00
95	KENNY BERNSTEIN MUG N5512	*	*	22.00
96	BILLIARDS CS278	OP	*	22.00
*		**ST. PATRICK'S DAY 6TH EDITION**		
96	HORSESHOE ST. PATRICK' S DAY	OP	19.50	19.50

FENTON ART GLASS

YR	NAME	LIMIT	ISSUE	TREND
*		**CONNOISSEUR COLLECTION**		
83	CRAFTSMEN STEIN 9640WI	1500	35.00	35.00

HADLEY COMPANIES

T. REDLIN

YR	NAME	LIMIT	ISSUE	TREND
95	WINTER WONDERLAND	45 DAYS	40.00	40.00
96	PLEASURES OF WINTER	2000	59.95	60.00

The 1992 U.S. Olympic Team *is honored in this stein by Anheuser-Busch.*

The thrill of victory is celebrated in this 1992 Summer Olympics *stein by Anheuser-Busch.*

Anheuser-Busch reminds collectors that the Giant Panda *is one of many endangered species.*

Anheuser-Busch commemorates the 1893 Columbian Exposition.

YR	NAME	LIMIT	ISSUE	TREND
LONGTON CROWN				
*				**ALL-STAR SLUGGERS**
96	MICKEY MANTLE	*	39.95	40.00
L. MARTIN				**AMERICA THE BEAUTIFUL**
96	GOD'S GRACE ON THEE	OP	32.95	33.00
L. KAATZ				**CLASSIC WATERFOWL**
96	MALLARDS AT SUNRISE	*	39.95	40.00
K. DANIELS				**CRY OF THE WOLFPACK**
96	SCOUTING THE BLUFFS	*	40.00	40.00
*				**LEGENDS OF BASEBALL SIGNATURE**
96	JIMMIE FOXX: THE BEAST	OP	34.95	35.00
96	WALTER JOHNSON: BIG TRAIN	OP	34.95	35.00
K. DANIELS				**TIMBERWOLF: LORD OF THE WILDERNESS**
96	FIRST OUTING	OP	42.95	43.00
M. CORNELL IMPORTERS				
*				**CORNELL STEINS**
86	JOIN US! GEMUETLICHKEIT 3766	10000	30.00	40.00
87	A TOAST 3963	10000	87.50	113.00
87	ALPINE FLOWER 4047	5000	90.00	100.00
87	BEERWAGON 6280	4000	110.00	133.00
87	BERLIN CITY 3788	5000	130.00	159.00
87	BERLIN CITY 3789	5000	87.50	113.00
87	CLUB HUNT 4402	8000	87.00	106.00
87	ELK 6340	5000	99.50	120.00
87	ELK UNLIDDED 6342	5000	30.00	38.00
87	FARMER & PLOW 3423	10000	87.50	113.00
87	FARMER & PLOW UNLIDDED 3424	10000	35.00	49.00
87	GOLDEN HOPS & MALT 6279	4000	159.00	219.00
87	GRIZZLY BEAR 6331	5000	99.50	120.00
87	GRIZZLY BEAR UNLIDDED 6333	5000	30.00	38.00
87	HAPPY DWARF 6282	4000	106.00	137.00
87	HEIDELBERG 6278	4000	100.00	125.00
87	HOT AIR BALLOON	5000	100.00	130.00
87	JOIN US! GEMUETLICHKEIT 3767	10000	78.00	100.00
87	JOIN US! GEMUETLICHKEIT 3768	10000	125.00	150.00
87	MAY STROLL 3770	10000	79.00	100.00
87	MAY STROLL UNLIDDED 3769	10000	30.00	40.00
87	MOOSE 6337	5000	99.50	120.00
87	MOOSE UNLIDDED 6339	5000	99.50	120.00
87	WEDDING PARADE 3776	10000	85.00	104.00
87	WEDDING PARADE UNLIDDED 3775	10000	35.00	48.00
87	WHITE TAIL DEER 6343	5000	99.50	120.00
87	WHITE TAIL DEER UNLIDDED 6345	5000	30.00	38.00
87	ZITHER PLAYER 3773	10000	85.00	106.00
87	ZITHER PLAYER UNLIDDED 3772	10000	35.00	48.00
88	BEER BARREL 6285	4000	130.00	137.00
88	FATHER & SON 6291	4000	115.00	135.00
88	PROLETARIAN 3970	5000	100.00	118.00
88	ROYAL KING LUDWIG 6287	4000	194.00	200.00
88	SUMMER 6286	4000	80.00	89.00
88	TYROLEAN 4413	9000	80.00	84.00
89	AHRENS-FOX FIRE ENGINE 3719	10000	119.00	157.50
89	AHRENS-FOX FIRE ENGINE UNLIDDED 3720	10000	35.00	44.00
89	APOSTLE 6298	2000	239.00	290.00
89	BICYCLIST 4723	5000	68.00	86.00
89	CAROUSEL 6467	5000	159.00	190.00
89	CAROUSEL MUSICAL 6468	5000	184.00	220.00
89	COOPER (BARREL MAKER)	2000	110.00	135.00
89	FIREFIGHTER 4765	5000	68.00	86.00
89	GAMBRINUS 3792	10000	125.00	130.00
89	GAMBRINUS UNLIDDED 3793	10000	40.00	50.00
89	MUNICH 3790	10000	115.00	190.00
89	PROLETARIAN UNLIDDED 3972	5000	45.00	60.00
89	RED BARON 6295	4000	100.00	130.00
89	SINGER 4768	5000	68.00	86.00
89	SINGER UNLIDDED 4767	5000	38.00	45.00
89	ST. GEORGE 4409	6000	150.00	165.00
89	VILLAGE BLACKSMITH 6308	2000	110.00	135.00
89	WEDDING DANCE JUG 4048	1500	239.00	299.00
89	WEIHNACHTEN 3716	10000	150.00	185.00
89	WEIHNACHTEN 3717	10000	110.00	139.00
90	BERLIN WALL 6320	2000	100.00	110.00
90	BICYCLIST 6325	4000	120.00	130.00
90	CLIPPER 3814	10000	168.00	185.00
90	CLIPPER UNLIDDED 3811	10000	47.00	50.00
90	FIREFIGHTER 6327	4000	120.00	135.00
90	FRIEDOLIN 3785	10000	99.00	110.00
90	FRIEDOLIN UNLIDDED 3784	10000	47.00	50.00
90	GOLFER 3820	10000	168.00	185.00
90	GOLFER UNLIDDED 3816	10000	47.00	50.00
90	GRENZAU CASTLE 4590	12000	119.50	132.00
90	LORELEY 3782	10000	95.00	104.00
90	LORELEY UNLIDDED 3781	10000	42.50	47.00
90	MUNICH BIER-WAGON 6326	4000	150.00	165.00
90	NAS GRIZZLY BEAR 4451	20000	175.00	193.00
90	NAS HUMPBACK WHALE	20000	175.00	193.00

YR	NAME	LIMIT	ISSUE	TREND
90	NAS PEREGRINE FALCON 4452	20000	175.00	193.00
90	NAS WOOD DUCK 4453	20000	175.00	193.00
90	NOAH'S ARK 6469	5000	129.00	150.00
90	SEPPL 3779	10000	95.00	104.00
90	SEPPL UNLIDDED 3778	10000	42.50	47.00
90	STONEWARE NUTCRACKER 6473	5000	139.00	150.00
90	TURNVATER JAHN 3797	10000	137.50	150.00
90	TURNVATER JAHN UNLIDDED 3796	10000	95.00	104.00
90	WIESBADEN 3794	2000	125.00	140.00
90	WIESBADEN 3795	2000	100.00	115.00
E. BREIDEN			**CORNELL STEINS**	
87	MALLARD 4041	4000	100.00	130.00
87	WILD BOAR 4044	4000	100.00	130.00
P. DUEMLER			**CORNELL STEINS**	
87	BIBLE 3870	10000	80.00	99.00
87	BIBLE UNLIDDED 3869	10000	30.00	42.00
87	BICYCLISTS UNLIDDED, THE 3857	10000	30.00	42.00
87	BICYCLISTS, THE 3858	10000	80.00	100.00
87	CARDPLAYER UNLIDDED, THE 3868	10000	35.00	47.00
87	CARDPLAYER, THE 3867	10000	190.00	220.00
87	CENTURIO 3861	10000	73.50	88.00
87	CENTURIO UNLIDDED 3860	10000	30.00	42.00
87	CHERUSKAN 3873	10000	109.00	148.00
87	CHERUSKAN UNLIDDED 3872	10000	40.00	55.00
87	DR. FAUST 3851	10000	80.00	98.00
87	DR. FAUST 3852	10000	30.00	40.00
87	MINUET 3876	10000	79.00	108.00
87	MINUET UNLIDDED 3875	10000	30.00	42.00
87	PATRIZIER 3864	10000	75.00	88.00
87	PATRIZIER UNLIDDED 3863	10000	30.00	42.00
88	DRAGON SLAYER 3980	10000	165.00	200.00
88	DRAGON SLAYER BEER CHALICE 3982	10000	79.00	105.00
88	ROYALTY 3878	10000	79.50	88.00
88	ROYALTY 3880	10000	110.00	130.00
89	CRUSADER 3883	10000	145.00	179.50
89	GENERAL TILLY TANKARD 3715	5000	379.50	440.00
89	ROYALTY 3887	10000	65.00	75.00
89	ROYALTY UNLIDDED 3888	10000	35.00	47.00
W. GOSSEL			**CORNELL STEINS**	
90	BABA YAGA 4993	5000	238.00	249.00
J. LIM			**CORNELL STEINS**	
89	BALD EAGLE 3721	10000	150.00	175.00
89	BALD EAGLE 3722	10000	110.00	139.00
89	BALD EAGLE UNLIDDED 3723	10000	40.00	48.00
89	DRAGON REGIMENTAL 4992	5000	199.00	249.00

CATEGORY INDEX

BELLS

COTTAGES

DOLLS

FIGURINES

ORNAMENTS

PLATES

PRINTS

STEINS

COMPANY INDEX

H

I

J

K

L

M

N

O

P

R

S

T

U

V

W